BOOKS
KIDS WILL
SIT STILL FOR 3

Companion books from Libraries Unlimited
Books Kids Will Sit Still For
More Books Kids Will Sit Still For

Recent Titles in the
Children's and Young Adult Literature Reference Series
Catherine Barr, Series Editor

Best Books for Children: Preschool Through Grade 6
Catherine Barr and John T. Gillespie

A to Zoo: Subject Access to Children's Picture Books
Carolyn W. Lima and John A. Lima

Best Books for Middle School and Junior High Readers, Grades 6–9
John T. Gillespie and Catherine Barr

Best Books for High School Readers, Grades 9–12
John T. Gillespie and Catherine Barr

Popular Series Fiction for K–6 Readers: A Reading and Selection Guide
Rebecca L. Thomas and Catherine Barr

Popular Series Fiction for Middle School and Teen Readers: A Reading and Selection Guide
Rebecca L. Thomas and Catherine Barr

Fantasy Literature for Children and Young Adults: A Comprehensive Guide, Fifth Edition
Ruth Nadelman Lynn

The Children's and Young Adult Literature Handbook: A Research and Reference Guide
John T. Gillespie

BOOKS KIDS WILL SIT STILL FOR 3

A Read-Aloud Guide

Judy Freeman

Children's and Young Adult Literature
Reference Series

Catherine Barr, Series Editor

LIBRARIES
U N L I M I T E D
A Member of the Greenwood Publishing Group

Westport, Connecticut • London

Library of Congress Cataloging-in-Publication Data

Freeman, Judy
  Books kids will sit still for 3 : a read-aloud guide / by Judy Freeman.
      p. cm. — (Children's and young adult literature reference series)
  Includes bibliographical references (p. 733) and indexes.
  ISBN 1-59158-163-X (alk. paper) — ISBN 1-59158-164-8 (pbk. : alk. paper)
  1. Children—Books and reading—United States. 2. Children's literature—Bibliography. 3. Oral
reading. 4. School libraries—Activity programs—United States. I. Freeman, Judy. Books kids will sit
still for. II. Title. III. Series.
Z1037.F847 2006
[PN1009.A1]
011.62—dc22   2006007469

British Library Cataloguing in Publication Data is available.

Library of Congress Catalog Card Number: 2006007469
ISBN: 1-59158-163-X
        1-59158-164-8 (pbk.)

First published in 2006

Libraries Unlimited, 88 Post Road West, Westport, CT 06881
A Member of the Greenwood Publishing Group, Inc.
www.lu.com

Printed in the United States of America

The paper used in this book complies with the
Permanent Paper Standard issued by the National
Information Standards Organization (Z39.48–1984).

10 9 8 7 6 5 4 3 2 1

To Izzy,
my perpetual deus ex machina and best friend

CONTENTS

THE ANNOTATED READ-ALOUD LISTS

BIBLIOGRAPHY AND INDEXES

LIST OF ILLUSTRATIONS

ACKNOWLEDGMENTS

THE AWFUL BOOK, AS I'VE BEEN CALLING IT FOR THE TWO YEARS AND three summers it took to write, has finally been transformed into a swan, thanks to the many amazing friends, relatives, colleagues, and editors who worked with the "Attic Girl" to get it done. These include:

Izzy Feldman, my patient and understanding husband, who kept my life running on target and on schedule as I wrote and he did everything else.

My parents, Gladys and Bob Freeman, for giving me book sense.

Jane Scherer, my great friend, mentor for life, and author of the hit song "Hi Ho, Librario," who got this whole project rolling, working with me on all the typing, cataloguing, organizing, and evaluating all these books and Web sites.

My brother Richard Freeman, sister-in-law Ann Guthrie, and niece Caitlin Freeman, for selflessly giving up hours and days and weeks of their time to proofread, provide counsel, and keep me on track.

Lois and Mort Farrah, who not only proofread with dead-on accuracy, but provided countless meals and tennis games.

My sister Sharron Freeman, cousin Joan Barasovska, and friends Peggy Beck, Jill Schneider, and Carol Shields, for diversions, calls, dinners, advice, visits, and unconditional friendship.

Sam and Margaret Feldman, Charlie and Marie, and Myra and Sheru, for all those memorable working weekends with a view at Lake George.

Art Feldman, tech genius and poet, who set up my whole network and guided me through every Mac meltdown.

Pete and Jeannie Fand, Beth and Jim Incollingo (and all the little kids—Minka, Shaiah, Noah, Christopher, and Kevin), for hours of music, videos, fondue pots, and general mayhem.

The rest of the Whole Femiluh: Farrell and Anna Fand; all the Stillmans—Mira and Yank, Sandy and Josh (and Inna), Ezra and Laura (and their kids Sarah, Emma, and Jonah); and Bob Taube and Sharon McCarrell (and their kids Hannah and Abbie).

The rest of the Freeman Side: Steve, Josh, and Amy Alloy, and opera fan Beverly.

Sharon and Bruce Kalter for making the Web site so darn cute and keeping it humming.

Jillian Ingram for cat duty and always knowing who to call when the house broke.

Susan Faust for Newbery consultations and book talk.

Caroline Feller Bauer, Cathy Baxter, Esmé Raji Codell, Cathy Darby, Sharron McElmeel, Louise Sherman, and Lisa Von Drasek for e-mail and phone support at any and every hour.

Angus Killick for believing in my ideas and music.

Doug Johnson, Technology Guru, for making me laugh out loud with every e-mail and for making sure I found the camels in Istanbul's Grand Bazaar.

Leslie Fass and Jon Peters at the Donnell Children's Room of the New York Public Library for being such gracious hosts to me and my Pratt students every summer.

Ken Young for years of BER coaching and the best dinners anywhere.

David Rothrock at Follett Library Resources, who lent me hundreds of books each year and helped make each of my *Winners!* Conferences such a success, and to Karen Novick, director of PDS, SCILS, Rutgers, for making *Winners!* work for ten great years.

Follett's <www.Titlewave.com>, without which I could not have connected so many of the dots.

Mimi Boyd and Doreen Bacchetti for years of fabulous puppets and props from <mimismotifs.com>.

The Garden State Writers, a most excellent and supportive group of children's book writers, who have been together forever. Long may they write.

The students, staff, principal Ernie Shuba, and librarians Jen Maldonato and Kathy Marceski at Van Holten School in Bridgewater, New Jersey, for giving me 23 wonderful years and continuing to welcome me back every time I arrived with new books to try out.

Maren Vitali, now the librarian at Adamsville School in Bridgewater, New Jersey; Janet Steinhouse, librarian at Joyce Kilmer School in Milltown, New Jersey; and Cindy Williams, reading specialist, Matt Barbosa, former principal, and librarian Jennifer Nelson at Irving School in Highland Park, New Jersey, for working so closely with me and setting up all those school visits.

All the master teachers and eager students at all four schools for cheerfully trying out so many books and thinking up some of the best responses to literature I've ever seen.

The following teachers generously gave of their time and expertise:

    Van Holten Elementary School, Bridgewater, NJ
    Kindergarten: Lori Foley, Susan Harwick, Carolyn Richardson, Danielle Amodeo
    Grade 1: Dorothy Filep, Mary Lynn Friar, Helen Kyritsis, Gina Wright
    Grade 2: Laura Currie, Lisa D'Ascensio, LouAnn Parrino, Maren Vitali
    Grade 3: Lindsay Bezak, Laura Coughlin, Nancy Havran, Roni Sawin, Missy Tannen

    Adamsville Elementary School, Bridgewater, NJ
    Kindergarten: Kate Tricarico
    Grade 1: Amy Keppel, Lynn Moran, Kirstie Nafey, Cindy Sahns
    Grade 2: Janice Hassett, Erin Hughes, Juyon Kang, Christine Pacifico
    Grade 3: Nancy Fischer, Maridy Gamoso, Carol Horvath, Judye Judge, Kelly Mumber, Jim Pawikoski, Kelly Raszka, Maria Terroni, Denise Trabichino

    Irving Primary School, Highland Park, NJ
    Kindergarten: Christine Gappa, Barbara Holzhauser, Mary Kress
    Grade 1: Judy Arshan, Jen Lugo, Sara Masluk
    Grade 2: Sheila Bell, Carol Dobrowolski, Marsha Friedman, Amy O'Sullivan

    Joyce Kilmer Middle School, Milltown, NJ
    Grade 4: Laura Carasso, Matt Eckert, Jill Maiorano, Marge May
    Grade 5: Vicki Fisher, Joanne Perry, Eric Siegel, Rob Wrate,
    Grade 6: Jennifer Dunn, Krys Herko, Eileen Jung, Paul Mruczinski, Evie Mullane

All the teachers and librarians across the United States who attended my BER and *Winners!* conferences in Spring 2005 and cheerfully volunteered to proofread pages during lunch and offer their two cents.

Barbara Ittner, LU Acquisitions Editor, for talking me into all this.

Debby LaBoon, LU Wonderwoman and dispenser of sage advice, for organizing the *Winners!* workshops and being so much fun on the road.

My amazing editor Catherine Barr for coping with a late manuscript and whipping it into shape and Christine Weisel McNaull for her scrupulous copyediting.

PREFACE

IN THE DECADE SINCE *MORE BOOKS KIDS WILL SIT STILL FOR* WAS PUB-lished, the children's literature field has mushroomed. I read about 3,000 children's books each year, looking for treasures to tout in magazine reviews, workshops, and speeches. And for more than ten years, I've been collecting books to feature in this third volume in the Books Kids Will Sit Still For series, the biggest one yet.

My friends call me the "Attic Girl." I'm up in my study, my little garret, for weeks at a time, often until the wee hours, panning for book gold, mining for diamonds and rubies, diving for literary pearls. Every 30 books or so, Eureka! I find a gem. I've spent the past decade reading like a maniac, like a grizzled old prospector, desperately seeking fabulous books that no teacher or librarian or child could resist.

In this volume are my favorites—1,705 of them. If you can mine just 25 great new books every year to use with the children in your life, your teaching, your professional persona, your whole physical and emotional being will be better for it. It is my hope that this book will help you do just that.

What am I looking for when I compile my read-aloud lists? I consider the following:

- Books that appeal to a wide age range, including picture books for all ages
- A balanced range of stories that speak to both boys and girls
- Titles with a multicultural outlook on the world
- An even and eclectic mixture of picture books, fiction, informational nonfiction, poetry, folk-lore, and biography
- A broad spectrum of books that lend themselves to challenging and engaging follow-up activities for all learning styles, from creative drama to expository writing
- Titles that spark a practical mix of quick-and-dirty, hear-it-today, do-it-tomorrow ideas, and long-range research and writing projects
- Read-aloud books to satisfy teachers and public and school librarians
- Books that cover many curricular and interest levels and speak to real children, not just grownups
- Books that sing to me and won't let me forget them

My life has been a love affair with libraries, books, and the kids who read them. After 26 years as an elementary school librarian, 23 of them at Van Holten School in Bridgewater, New Jersey, I finally gave up my day job in 2000, declared myself Librarian Emeritus, and went off to see the world and spread the word about children's books and the power of reading. I now spend about 150 days a year on the road, giving children's literature-based workshops, seminars for BER (Bureau of Education & Research), speeches at conferences, and school assembly programs for librarians, teachers, parents, and children.

My mission is to stay current with children and their literature. Each season, I go back to my old school in Bridgewater and do what I always did as a school librarian—introduce children and teachers to new books and initiate meaningful and fun follow-up activities in language arts and across the curriculum. I also visit Irving Primary School in my hometown, Highland Park, New Jersey; Joyce Kilmer Middle School in Milltown, New Jersey; and Adamsville Elementary School, also in Bridgewater. I field-test batches of new books with groups of two to four classes per grade level, grades K to 6, to ascertain which titles and related activities bring the most benefit and joy to teachers and their students. It's not sufficient to evaluate children's books solely from an adult perspective, and it's so much fun to compare my reactions to a book with those of children and their teachers and librarians, and to try out my ideas with them.

I have field-tested hundreds of these books with eager children and their innovative and creative teachers and librarians, and have included thousands of useful strategies, ideas, activities, lessons, read-aloud techniques, writing prompts, and ways that you can incorporate literature into every aspect of your day and, yes, your life. Many of my ideas are what I call "quick and dirty," as my mom used to call it: you hear it today and take it back to inflict on your kids tomorrow.

Many of the children's books that get published are more dreadful than you could imagine. Think *The Barbie Swan Lake*. Madonna's *The English Roses*. Don't we all feel a sharp pain when we hear celebrities say, "Well, there weren't any decent children's books out there, so I just had to write one!"? (It's only partly fair to make a blanket statement condemning celebrities and their undying compulsion to write for children. Indeed, I can think of two wonderfully witty children's book writers with staying power who just happen to be actors too: Jamie Lee Curtis and John Lithgow.)

Some books are brilliant, some books bomb. And until you read a book aloud, you'll never know which way it will go. If I had listened to the book reviewer who wrote that children would not understand the "Dragnet" references in Margie Palatini's *The Web Files*, I might not have tried it out. When I read it aloud to teacher Maren Vitali's second graders at Van Holten School, I wore a gumshoe outfit, complete with trenchcoat and magnifying glass. We sang the "Dum de dum dum" part together, and I mentioned the "Dragnet" connection. The kids said, "Oh, yeah! Dragnet! We know that. It's on Nick at Night."

They got further into the mood of the book by writing and illustrating "Wanted" posters for other nefarious nursery rhyme characters such as Humpty Dumpty and the Muffin Man.

Illustration of Muffin Man Wanted Poster, follow-up to Margie Palatini's *The Web Files*, by student in Maren Vitali's class, Van Holten School, Bridgewater, NJ, 2001 or 2002.

And when I first read Jules Feiffer's *Bark, George* to myself, I though it was cute but no big deal. When I mentioned that to my fellow librarian and friend Peggy Beck, she hollered at me. "Read that book aloud to kindergarten!" she ordered, and I did. It was magical, one of the best picture books ever.

When I visit schools to test out new books, the teachers use the germs or ideas I provide for follow-ups, or come up with their own, to initiate meaningful and fun activities in language arts and across the curriculum. Together, we seek to employ higher-level thinking skills for discussion, writing, illustrating, and other creative responses.

In *Books Kids Will Sit Still For* (1990), I talked about *how* to read aloud, booktalk, use creative drama, and tell stories. I listed "101 Ways to Celebrate Books." The text is filled with practical how-to instructions. In *More Books Kids Will Sit Still For* (1995), I addressed *what* to do with books, including a chapter called "50 Ways to Recognize a Read-Aloud." A large portion of the text in that book deals with the importance of a strong School Library/Media Center program and what librarians and teachers can do to make books come alive.

When it came time to write the text for *Books Kids Will Sit Still For 3*, I thought about everything I had learned in the past decade. There was one area I hadn't specifically covered in the last two books: the *why*. Why do we need to read aloud to children and expose them to real books? Why do we need to be the reading role models for our children? Why do books make a difference in our education and daily lives? I've sought to answer those questions this time.

There are three major sections in this book. First is the text, with six new chapters under the heading, "About Children's Books and Ways to Use Them," which I hope you will find loaded with practical ideas you can read today and use with your children tomorrow. "One Librarian to Another" is a tribute to my mother, Gladys Freeman, and to librarians everywhere. "Seventeen Things You Need to Know to Be a Great School Librarian" also applies to public librarians and teachers. "The Bluebery Medal" reveals the inside story on what it was like to serve on the Newbery Committee. In "On Reading Aloud and Reading Alone" you'll find "Ten Reasons to Befriend a Great Book." "Books Across the Curriculum" contains an updated list of memorable authors and illustrators, and hands-on strategies to get children reading and writing and talking about books. I decided to revisit storytelling, creative drama, and Reader's Theater, with some new techniques and tips, in "Performance Art."

The next major section contains the extensive Annotated Read-Aloud Lists, broken into chapters, each arranged alphabetically by author. They are:

Easy Fiction / Picture Books
Fiction
Folk & Fairy Tales, Myths & Legends
Poetry, Nonsense, and Language-Oriented Nonfiction
Biography
Nonfiction

The final section includes the Professional Bibliography, plus comprehensive indexes: author and illustrator, title, and, biggest of all, the subject index, with more than 1,800 subjects, plus hundreds of see and see also cross references, so you can locate books easily.

As a former school librarian, I approached *Books Kids Will Sit Still For 3* with a predisposition toward my chosen profession. However, as a teacher working in a library, I have always worked closely with classroom and special area teachers, and my emphasis on using children's literature across the curriculum reflects that. And as a librarian, I have great respect, admiration, and affection for public librarians and the many excellent children's programs and services they provide. As the Book Aunt to dozens of nieces, nephews, cousins, and friends' children, I am ever awed by the parents and other adults who raise their children with a daily infusion of great books.

Will every book or idea apply to your particular situation or appeal to your literary tastes? Of course not. It's always up to you to pick and choose those books and ideas you can use and develop, ones that you feel will work best with *your* kids, whether you're a teacher looking for classroom read-alouds, writing prompts, and curriculum tie-ins; a school librarian looking for library lesson ideas and books to recommend for your staff, parents, and students; a public librarian, who needs to be a reader's advisory expert in every aspect of children's literature, from pre-birth to post-teen; or a parent looking for titles to share with your children to kindle their imaginations, whether as read-alouds or read-alones.

For whom did I write this book and compile my list of 1,705 favorite read-aloud titles? For all book lovers, including teachers, librarians, administrators, paraprofessionals, professors, parents, grandparents, scout leaders, booksellers, college and graduate students preparing to go into the field of education or libraries, children's book authors and illustrators, and all other adults who work with children or simply enjoy reading children's books.

Each book I recommend will, I hope, be special indeed, one that teachers and librarians and parents will welcome into their reading repertoires as well worth their precious classroom or library or read-aloud time. I've tried to focus on what I've found really works with real kids.

You are the reading role model for your children. The books you choose to use with them could resonate in their heads for years to come.

Judy Freeman
Winter, 2006

ABOUT CHILDREN'S BOOKS AND WAYS TO USE THEM

Joseph
Had a Little
Overcoat
Simms
Taback
THE CALDECOTT
MEDAL

ONE LIBRARIAN TO ANOTHER

AS LIBRARIANS AND LITERATURE CHEERLEADERS, WE CHAMPION THE notion that reading is necessary, pleasurable, and something that can help our students throughout their lives. Sometimes it helps to look back to our roots. Who inspired you to be Keeper of the Books, Literary Miracle Worker, and Language Nurturer? We mustn't be shy about passing the lessons we've learned to our students. Children need read-aloud role models now if we expect them to grow up and raise a new generation of readers.

My role models were my parents, both passionate readers, who took me, plus my older brother, Richard, and sister, Sharron, to the Haverford Public Library in Havertown, Pennsylvania, every Tuesday night when I was a child. There we each selected an armload of reading for the week and, after signing our names on each book card, piled back into the car and headed out for ice cream cones. This was a major treat for me, as my healthy-food-obsessed mother was fervently anti-sugar. My passion for books and for ice cream, often satisfied simultaneously, has never waned over the years.

My mother was always my inspiration, going back to college to finish her bachelor's degree at Temple University when I was six, persevering through one class a week until she finished four years later. She had originally attended the two-year Philadelphia Normal School, similar to a junior college today, to get her teaching certification in the late 1930s, after a malicious high school guidance counselor told her, "Oh no, dear, Penn State doesn't accept Jews."

"Kids today would never put up with a statement like that," my mother used to fume when she told the story. "How could I have been such an innocent? But we accepted what we were told back then."

Next, she enrolled at Villanova to get her Masters of Library Science when I was ten. This was not particularly typical "mom" behavior in the early 1960s, and aside from the fact that I now had to make my own breakfast and lunch, I found it admirable. I remember how excited she was to be in a black cap and gown the day she finally graduated, a real librarian, after yet another four years of raising kids, keeping a household going, and writing papers. After years of reading stories to us—and I remember that my brother was terrified of the teacher, Miss Clavell, in Ludwig Bemelman's Madeline series, and that I always considered myself Ramona to my sister Sharron's Beezus—now she set out as a school librarian to bring books to a whole schoolful of children.

One day back in 2000, I was scrolling through my messages on LM_NET, the listserv that connects more than 17,000 school librarians worldwide. (LM_NET is one of the greatest advances in school librarianship since the computerization of the card catalog. Go to <www.eduref.org/lm_net> for information on subscribing to this free listserv and to access the archived messages. One of the posts contained advice to look up an article on the state of school libraries, "Libraries on Life Support," in the February 2000 issue of *Teacher Magazine. Teacher* has always been one of my very favorite magazines for educators because of its frank, thorough, intelligent, and insightful discussions of educational issues. The article on school libraries was posted on the Web, so I logged on, read the first sentence, and sat back in my rolling chair, stunned at a long-ago coincidence.

It began: "Even the best books in the library at T. M. Peirce Elementary School in Philadelphia are dated, tattered, and discolored. The worst—many in a late stage of disintegration—are dirty and

3

fetid and leave a moldy residue on hands and clothing. Chairs and tables are old, mismatched, or broken. There isn't a computer in sight.

"There isn't a student in sight, either. Three years ago, principal Shively Willingham made the controversial decision to lock the doors and block his school's 640 students from the facility. The neglected library is as unappealing as the blighted urban neighborhood outside Peirce, Willingham argues, and perhaps just as dangerous."

My mother was the school librarian at the W. S. Peirce School (same name, different part of the city) from about 1969 to 1973. In those days, her elementary school library was a very nice, large, bright room—very attractive, with huge windows all along one wall, a back office with a glass window overlooking the rest of the library, and an up-to-date, decent collection.

The library was a safe haven for the kids, grades K to 6, and they loved to come for classes with Mrs. Freeman. It was one place they never got yelled at or hassled.

Peirce School was in a tough neighborhood, though it looked perfectly nice to me, with blocks of row houses. Every day at three o'clock, both students and staff were required to leave the building together, after which the school was locked.

During my senior year of high school, I would come in to help her whenever I had time. I remember visiting her library and reading Bernard Waber's *Lyle, Lyle, Crocodile* (Houghton Mifflin, 1965) to her classes, as well as my mother's favorite picture book, Marjorie Weinman Sharmat's *Gladys Told Me to Meet Her Here*. (My mom's name was Gladys.) I thought her being a librarian was an awful lot of fun. You got to read to kids all the time. What could be better than that? When I went off to college and decided to get my teaching certification, I came home periodically to visit Peirce and sit in on different teachers' classes to observe and write about them for my education courses.

Still, my sister and I were so mean. I remember coming home late after school, and there my mom would be, curled up in her bentwood rocking chair, legs tucked under her dress, snoozing. We'd sneer and say, "Boy, Mom, I don't know what *you're* so tired about. You only have to work from 8:30 to 3. What's the *big deal*? How hard can *that* be?" Wish I could take that back, especially since I know now from long experience exactly how exhausted she was!

Mom was a careful weeder, always bringing home from the library books that she found inappropriate, outdated, or shocking to show me before she tossed them. I remember when she came across a book called *In Ole Virginny*, which she found appalling, written in dialect, about the happy slaves on the plantation. This was in the late 1960s, and she was astonished that a book like that could still be on the shelves. Into the garbage it went, along with others equally dreadful.

She also brought home piles of books she thought I should read. I discovered *Harriet the Spy* just that way. "You *must* read this one," she told me, even though I was in high school already and obviously way too old for it. I adored it. Still do.

Isn't it amazing the effects a good librarian can have, whether she's at your school or she's your mom? How astonishing that places like the Philadelphia School District—an inner-city district that desperately needs librarians to give the gift of a love of reading to kids—should have cut librarians and, by logical extension, libraries and books, out of their kids' lives. In 1975, Philadelphia got rid of lots of their school librarians and stopped funding their libraries. Now, decades later, the administrators stammer and stumble and look for someone to blame for their students who can't or won't read. It's hard enough to hook kids on books. Without librarians, the chances get so much dimmer.

After my mother left the field in 1973, I followed in her footsteps and went to Rutgers for my MLS. My mom suffered from dementia in her 80s, and didn't recall much about what she used to do or much about anything from her past, so it was bittersweet to connect her to the *Teacher Magazine* article.

I asked her if she remembered being a librarian at Peirce School, and she said, "Yes, I do!" Surprised, I asked, "What do you remember?" You can probably relate to her still feisty and indignant answer: "I worked very hard there. They never appreciated me!"

I still have dreams about her the way she was back in the Sixties, all fired up over the latest kids' books. In her last years, she could no longer understand text or make sense of the sequence of a joke or even a slightly complicated story.

In 2000, I was in Philly to visit my folks, and brought with me the latest Newbery books to show her. I explained that I had been on the year 2000 Newbery Committee, but she couldn't connect with that. Then I pulled out the new Caldecott winner, Simms Taback's picture book *Joseph Had a Little Overcoat*. She was entranced, delighting in the clever die-cut illustrations, and able to follow the simple storyline as I read it aloud to her, one librarian to another.

SEVENTEEN THINGS YOU NEED TO KNOW TO BE A GREAT SCHOOL LIBRARIAN

LIBRARIANS ARE THE INFORMATION AND LITERARY GODDESSES AND Gods of their schools and communities. We need to celebrate librarians as the ones who help to unlock that world of reading. My personal hero of the past decade, aside from the fictional title character in Suzanne Williams's picture book *Library Lil*, is Nancy Pearl, Seattle librarian and author of *Book Lust* (Sasquatch Books, 2003), which is a book for adults, not children, of course. Not only is Nancy a prolific reader and writer, but she, unlike most of us mere mortals, was the model for the librarian action figure, the Shushing Librarian.

You can get your own plastic Librarian Action Figure from Archie McPhee, Outfitters of Popular Culture at <www.mcphee.com> (along with Ben Franklin and Li'l William Shakespeare). Note that when you push the button on her back, her arm snaps up, finger to her lips in a shushing position.

My husband, Izzy, lifted my new little doll to his ear. "Honey, what are you doing?" I asked him. "I'm trying to hear her shush."

"Iz, she's an *action* figure. You have to make your own noises with an action figure."

"I knew that!" he said, though he most definitely did not.

When the action figure came out, newspapers wrote articles and editorials about it and the library listservs hummed with discussions. Do we shush? Should we shush? Is shushing bad?

Some folks said, "But her outfit is so *dowdy!*" Nancy replied, "Dowdy! I paid a lot of money for that outfit! It's an *Eileen Fisher!*"

Archie McPhee recently released a new and improved version. The ad says:

DELUXE LIBRARIAN ACTION FIGURE!
Our Nancy Pearl Librarian Action Figure is not only one of our best selling items, it is also, surprisingly, one of our most controversial. A few complained that the figure presented a stereotype of the librarian as dowdy and stern, so we are using our new DELUXE version to address some of the concerns. Her outfit is now a rich burgundy color and she comes with a diverse selection of books and a reference computer. She does, however, still shush.

As Nancy Pearl says, "The role of a librarian is to make sense of the world of information." If that's not a qualification for superhero-dom, what is?

Librarians may not know the answer to every question, but they do know how to look it up and find it. Here are some real questions asked of school librarians, as reported on LM_NET, the school librarians' listserv.

1. Who wrote the *Diary of Anne Frank*?
2. Do you have any books with photographs of real live dinosaurs?
3. Do you have that book, *How To Kill a Mockingbird*?
4. One student asked how to spell tequila. After telling her the spelling the librarian asked what she was looking up. She was trying to find the book *Tequila Mockingbird*.
5. Do you have *Little Richard's Almanac*?

6. Librarian Alice Yucht recalls the "... serious 8-year-old who came in the library looking for information on the Dead Sea Squirrels. Boy, was he disappointed."

And then, of course, there's the question every librarian hears almost every day: "Do you have that book I read last year? It was pink?" (And often it's a teacher or parent who asks that question, not just the kids.) The wild thing is, librarians so often know exactly which book it is. Call it Book Karma.

I was speaking with my friend Deborah Schochet, a gifted and innovative third-grade teacher in Seattle. I asked her what were the latest educational buzzwords in her district, since I try to stay current and Deborah keeps abreast of every trend. There were the usual ones: guided reading, literature circles, flexible grouping, and 6+1 Trait Writing.

One I hadn't heard before was "pair share." What new concept was this? Deborah explained: "Say a teacher is reading aloud and stops to ask a pithy question. She then says, 'Turn to your neighbor and discuss the question and then we'll share your responses.'" Oh. Pair share. Of course. Well, you all know there's nothing new in education. The jargon flows fast and furious, of course, but the terminology is what changes every year, not so much the techniques themselves.

As a matter of fact, the origin of pair sharing might have come from Groucho Marx, who, as a few of you may recall, had a TV show in the 1950s called "You Bet Your Life." To each pair of contestants, he'd ask a question.

"Talk it over with your partner and come up with one answer and one answer only," he'd say. "Say the magic word, and a duck will come down and you'll win 50 bucks."

The fake duck would come down on a string with the word in its mouth. In education, no one has much in the way of discretionary funds, so we've omitted the $50. You may want to reinstitute the duck, however. It's a nice touch.

I was thinking about this as I began planning my syllabus for a "Materials for Children" class I was scheduled to teach for the School of Information and Library Science at Pratt Institute in New York City.

How could I teach 18 graduate students everything they'd need to know about children's books in 37 ½ hours? I recalled how, when I started my first job in Plainfield, New Jersey, back in—well, never mind when—I walked into my new elementary school library that first day, looked around, and, feeling greener than celery, despaired of ever knowing it all.

What practical knowledge would I have wished to possess back then? Over 26 years, as I worked in school libraries, I developed and expanded my bag-o'-teaching-tricks one new skill at a time. Here, then, are 17 of the concepts, rules, truisms, and bits of general advice that I have learned along the way.

While the following list is geared to school librarians, its salient points certainly apply to public librarians, to teachers, and to parents as well. What do we really need to know in our profession, and why do we need to know it?

1. ALWAYS READ WITH EXPRESSION

We are the reading role models for our children. They hear our voices resonating in their heads every time they pick up a book we've read aloud to them. The way we read and the literary choices we make can stay with them forever.

My favorite of my mother's memorable aphorisms came when I was in first grade and had just moved up from the soft cover pre-primer to the hard cover basal about those saccharine little white kids Dick, Jane, and Sally, and their swell dog, Spot. I had just learned to read the word "said," which opened up a whole new world of dialogue for me. From simple declarative sentences—"Run, Spot, Run! Run! Run! Run!"—we moved to dialogue and introspection: "Look, Jane," said Dick. "See Spot run. Spot can run fast."

My librarian mother took me aside and gave me the best piece of professional advice I ever received, one that I use daily in my job and life. She said, "Judy, always read with expression!" And I have. It has made my chosen profession endlessly fun and fulfilling. Thanks, Mom.

Each time you discover a new book, listen for the rhythm in it. Let it talk to you. Experiment with it. Kids ask me all the time, "How did you know how to read that story out loud? How do you make it sound like that?" One boy said, "Did that book come with directions?" We want to let kids in on those reading secrets so they'll be able to watch their own books come alive as they read.

Let your listeners discover there are wonderful voices in books. If we let ourselves listen, the characters will talk to us and sometimes be us. I call it the "Sybil Syndrome." (Remember the 1973 book *Sibyl* by Flora Rheta Schreiber and the 1976 movie, with the title character played by Sally Fields? She had 16 personalities, all bursting to get out.) When you first discover a perfect new book, you must decide which personality is most yearning to emerge for each character.

Do we really need to read aloud like Laurence Olivier? Yes, of course we do. I think it's something to keep in mind as we work on finding each book's voice. Doing 6+1 Trait Writing? How can we expect our kids to write with Voice, one of the traits, until they've experienced voices in children's books? You are the one who decides on the voice of your characters.

I heard Janet Stevens read aloud from her delightful book *And the Dish Ran Away with the Spoon*, and I still hear her voice in my head when I read the cat's dialogue aloud. When I read the dog's part, however, I hear sarcastic comedian Paul Lynde. I'm still working on finding the voices of all the characters, but each time I read the book aloud to children, I add a little more energy and inflection into my reading.

When I first read aloud Lauren Child's *I Am Too Absolutely Small for School*, I heard Lily Tomlin's Edith Ann voice as that of the little girl, Lola, explaining to her big brother, Charlie, why she wasn't ready for kindergarten. Now, I know that Lauren Child is British, and that by all rights Lola should have an English accent, but that's not how she sounded in my head when I first read the book.

I loved Margie Palatini's *The Sweet Tooth* the first time I read it to myself, but only understood how brazenly funny it is when I read it to second graders. As I pondered the voice of that tooth, at first I thought Don Rickles, but that wasn't quite right. Then it hit me. It's Nathan Lane playing Max Bialystock in the Broadway show "The Producers." The whining, the bullying, the temper tantrums. And the kid narrator is Matthew Broderick as the wimpy, cringing Leo Bloom. If you channel the voice as you read a book, you will always read with expression and attitude. It feels great to sink your teeth into a good story. For further inspiration, listen to Jim Dale's mesmerizing tour-de-force readings of the Harry Potter books, with more than 100 voices.

Harvest voices everywhere: from actors, relatives, neighbors, friends, and even politicians. Especially politicians. The books you read will be all the more spectacular for the attention you pay to your performance. Children will clamor to hear you read aloud because they know they'll be in for a special experience, one that can bond together a whole class.

2. READ EVERYTHING

How could you possibly read everything? Well, of course, you can't. Not with more than 10,000 new children's books rolling out every year. Still, if you read widely and skim like mad the stuff you can't finish, you'll find yourself getting an entirely new education. I try to learn one new fact every single day. When your job is reading children's books, it isn't hard to do.

"Have you read every book in this library?" children ask every day. "I'm working on it," you can reply.

Make yourself learn to love subjects you scorned in your pre-librarian days. Hate baseball? Read *Gold Dust* by Chris Lynch and *Satchel Paige* by Lesa Cline-Ransome. You'll change your mind.

Not a fantasy fan? You don't have to love Harry Potter, but you need to read him and understand his tremendous appeal. You can't afford to be selective based solely on your personal preferences. There are book fans who clamor for every possible subject, and you need to be able to appreciate their needs and help them stretch their reading muscles along with your own.

Now that you can easily find full-text book reviews online at <www.amazon.com> or <www.barnesandnoble.com>, it's easier to familiarize yourself with each year's new books and get a handle on the books you want to read or order for your collection, as well as the ones you can afford to skip. If you buy books from Follett Library Resources, you can access reviews and order books from their fabulous Web site at <www.TitleWave.com>. Baker & Taylor's customer site is at <www. btol.com>.

Too many teachers and librarians rely on tried-and-true titles. We all need to refresh ourselves. My rule of thumb for teachers is to find 25 fabulous new-to-you books each year—that's my benchmark number, to use a bit of jargon. If every teacher found 25 inspirational, beautiful, hilarious, touching, or eye-opening books to share with his or her children each year—a glad jumble of picture books, fiction, poetry, biography, nonfiction, jokes, and folktales—burnout rates would plummet.

For librarians, you need to find your top 100 new titles each year, since you'll be recommending them to people with such a wide range of ages, interests, and needs. Your agenda as a children's book troubadour is to provide the literary tools children need to become writers, speakers, and purveyors of the vast and rich English language, and to become informed citizens of the world.

3. READ OFF YOUR GRADE LEVEL

Teaching fifth grade? Working as a young adult librarian? Picture books are brilliant for teaching story structure to children—character, setting, plot, theme—and will make your lessons soar. Children's literature is your field. Every children's book you read, no matter the level, prepares you for the work you do: changing kids' lives. And each book helps you understand children a little bit more.

Keep up on each year's award winners, too. Since the advent of Harry Potter, adults are looking at children's books as a new source of viable literature, and it's about time. Newbery Honor winner *Al Capone Does My Shirts* by Gennifer Choldenko can stand up to any adult book on the *New York Times* bestseller list.

If you teach in the primary grades, you are still permitted to read the Newbery Medal winners. I promise you, if you read any five upper-level books on the fiction list in this book, you'll like them better than most of the bestsellers on the adult charts. They'll probably be better written, as well.

4. DON'T UNDERESTIMATE THE QUICK AND DIRTY

My mother used to love home or work activities that could be implemented with no fuss, no muss. "Quick and dirty," she'd say gleefully when she threw together a fast dinner of broiled fish, baked potatoes, and salad.

In the library or classroom setting, "quick and dirty" means no hot glue gun, no trips to the art supply store, no laminating and cutting out hundreds of little pieces for the game you want to play. Sure, we all put together long-term projects that we can use each year, but it's so satisfying when something simple turns out great.

You've just read aloud *The Frog Principal* by Stephanie Calmenson as a follow-up to telling the Grimm fairy tale "The Frog Prince." In this parody, school principal Mr. Bundy is turned into a frog by an incompetent magician and promises his students to fetch their ball from the pond if they make him their principal.

Always on the lookout for ways you can develop your students' higher-level thinking skills, you might have them make a compare-and-contrast chart or a Venn diagram. Or, quick and dirty, after you finish both stories, you can put up two fists and say to your group, "Let's see if you can tell me five ways these stories are the same and five ways they're different." Every time a child volunteers an answer, extend one finger, until they've come up with five for each hand. In a few minutes, they've run through plots, characters, settings, and themes of both stories and compared them effectively.

5. START BUNDLING

Never wanting to waste a literary minute, I came to the concept of Bundling. When reading a story to children, it's not sufficient to introduce them solely to the one book you plan to read aloud. You need to put multiple books into their hot little hands.

Why read just one book when you can introduce or follow up your reading with five to ten exciting, intriguing related titles on the same subject or theme, or by the same author—a rousing array of fiction and nonfiction, poetry and folklore, jokes and biography. "Are you going to read us *all* those books?" the kids ask, and you say, "We're going to at least get acquainted."

After you finish reading aloud Stephanie Calmenson's *The Frog Principal*, have at your side other books by that author, such as *The Principal's New Clothes*, which is also about Mr. Bundy; a version of the original Grimm fairy tale, "The Frog Prince"; another parody of the story, *The Frog Prince Continued* by Jon Scieszka; other parodies such as Ellen Jackson's *Cinder Edna*; other books on schools and principals, such as *Double Trouble in Walla Walla* by Andrew Clements; and other books that extend the children's knowledge base, such as Wendy Pfeffer's *From Tadpole to Frog*.

Introduce each title with a brief, pithy, punchy, one-or-two-sentence, 10-second show-and-tell wow of a booktalk to get them overexcited and when they cry, "Can I have that!?" you hand them out. Bundling gets more books into the lives of children with very little extra effort on your part. These may be books they have never noticed or wanted before, books that have been languishing on the shelves, unread and unloved.

6. NEVER THROW ANYTHING OUT

The minute you finally throw out or give away that cracked teapot, the dried flowers, the tacky hat, you will be sorry. Someone will publish a book employing just that prop and you'll kick yourself for attempting to be compulsively neat, a habit not typically exhibited by teachers and librarians. Organized, possibly. Neat? Maybe in your next life.

There's something so irresistible to children about a hidden surprise. Collect an assortment of boxes, bags, baskets, and other interesting containers. When you pull out a box that contains an object that corresponds to the story you are reading, the booktalk you are giving, or the poem you are reciting, watch your kids' eyes get big. "What's in the box?" they'll gasp, and when you open up the box to reveal the wind-up chattering teeth or the stuffed snake or the Sacajawea dollar, they will "ooh" and "aah" appreciatively.

Garage sale aficionados and flea market mavens are always looking for treasures, but once you start searching for literary tie-ins, the fun really begins.

My multicolored corn necklace from Santa Fe was perfect for James Stevenson's poetry books *Sweet Corn*, *Popcorn*, *Candy Corn*, and *Corn Flakes*.

A simple pencil made a perfect prop for Christopher Paul Curtis's *Bud, Not Buddy*, in which Bud awakens and realizes that Todd, the son of his new foster parents, has just inserted a pencil in Bud's nose. It also worked great for *Baloney (Henry P.)* by Jon Scieszka, in which little green alien Henry P. is late for school (again) because he misplaced his trusty *zimulis*, which we learn is Latvian for pencil.

I don't remember where I got the huge burlap mailbag that says Aeropostale on it, but I stashed it in my office, sure that I'd find something to do with it. Six months later, Sonia Levitin's *Nine for California* came out, in which Ma packs up her five children and a huge sack full of everything they will need to take a rollicking, adventure-packed, 21-day stagecoach ride to find Pa, who's been in the gold fields of Californ-y. All I needed was to pack in the burlap bag Ma's supplies—including a rope, some licorice, a little plastic bag of sugar cubes, and a slide whistle—each of which my then-student teacher Cynthia Cassidy and I lifted out of the bag as we got to that part of the story, which held a double class of second graders enthralled. The licorice treat at the end was appreciated as well.

You'll find more about using props and Magic Boxes on page 20 of *Books Kids Will Sit Still For*.

And, of course, if you never throw anything out, you will always find it a cinch to decorate your shelves and room with unusual objects, stuffed animals, puppets, and beautiful things for children to ponder, examine, admire, and enjoy. The library should be an aesthetic experience.

7. DON'T BE AFRAID TO WEED

You might think this is a contradiction of Rule No. 6, but it's not really. Freshly weeded shelves, no matter how sparse, look far more appealing than shelves stuffed with old, dry, dowdy volumes. When you come across outdated, unappealing, falling-apart, or dreadfully written and illustrated books, get rid of them.

Starting out, in my first school library, the first thing I did was to read and weed my way through the collection. I parked myself on the floor in the picture book section and relentlessly plowed through each shelf. Every time I found another turkey, I'd toss it on the floor behind me onto a huge, growing mound of books, which I then didn't know what to do with. Some I put in "Up for Grabs" boxes for teachers to take for their classrooms. Others were too awful to give away to any living soul. "Throw away perfectly good books?" I could hear the principal reprimand. But keeping them was unthinkable. So I ripped up a few each day and buried them deep in the garbage, hoping the custodian wouldn't rat on me.

Some librarians suggest getting rid of any book that hasn't circulated in five years. Use your best judgment here. Before chucking something wonderful that's been a shelf-sitter forever, ask yourself, "Is there a reason this book doesn't move? Is the cover bad? Is there a way I could interest children in the book, through a booktalk or read-aloud sampling of a chapter or page?"

As you read your way through your collection, think of yourself as the heroic book-mad title character in Suzanne Williams's *Library Lil*.

8. LAUGH EVERY DAY

A friend recited a statistic that knocked me over: Kids laugh more than 300 times a day; adults only 17. Is this true? I Googled it and found numerous references, though the numbers were different in each one. According to all the articles, the benefits to your health are legion. Laughing can help you to relax, reduce stress, lower your blood pressure, protect your heart, improve your mood and your mental health, and get along better with people. And, in the one that really hit home for me, laughter is a great workout for your abdominal muscles, just like using a rowing machine or an exercise bike. So who needs the gym? We can just laugh our way to perfect bodies. I'll buy it.

After watching my young cousins Sarah, Emma, Jonah, Minka, Shaiah, and Noah laughing themselves silly one day, I thought, yeah, it would be a good goal to start laughing more. In our jobs, if we don't allow ourselves to get overrun by crankiness, pessimism, burnout from not trying anything new, or exhaustion from trying everything new all at once, we get to laugh every single day if we choose to. If you've forgotten how, surely your children will be happy to give you lessons on loosening up.

Don't be afraid to do something silly. Teaching is performance art. Make the most of it. Wear crazy hats, sing, act, do the tango with your students. Embrace the Ms. Frizzle style of useful attire, wearing jewelry and clothing to reflect the stories you're reading and telling to your fashion-conscious students, who will exclaim over every insect pin and rainbow tie. Using literature gives you license to be an actor, to sizzle your children with books they'll never forget, and to get them to join in the mayhem.

When my students said something inadvertently hilarious, as they did all the time, I'd say, "I'll be right back," and then dash into my office, grab a scrap of paper, and write it down. If you don't keep track of these gems, you won't remember them later.

And, of course, many of the books you read will send you and your students into gales of helpless laughter. If you're looking for these books, check the subject index under Humorous Fiction, Humorous Folklore, and Humorous Poetry.

What are the funniest books I have read in the past decade? What made me laugh out loud? Here are ten of my favorite funny picture books, all of which you'll find listed alphabetically by author in the "Easy Fiction/Picture Books" chapter:

Click, Clack, Moo: Cows That Type by Doreen Cronin

Diary of a Worm by Doreen Cronin

Bark, George by Jules Feiffer

Sunny Boy! The Life and Times of a Tortoise by Candace Fleming

I Stink by Kate McMullan

Piggie Pie by Margie Palatini

No, David! by David Shannon

Raising Sweetness by Diane Stanley

Dear Mrs. LaRue: Letters from Obedience School by Mark Teague

Don't Let the Pigeon Drive the Bus! by Mo Willems

And here are ten of my favorite funny fiction books, which are all listed in the "Fiction" chapter:

Whales on Stilts by M. T. Anderson

Mercy Watson to the Rescue by Kate DiCamillo

Hey, New Kid! by Betsy Duffey

Hoot by Carl Hiaasen

Goose Chase by Patrice Kindl

Gooney Bird Greene by Lois Lowry,

Molly McGinty Has a Really Good Day by Gary Paulsen

A Long Way from Chicago by Richard Peck

The Scarecrow and His Servant by Philip Pullman

The Austere Academy by Lemony Snicket

Make a list with your children of the books that make them and you laugh out loud.

9. BE UNPREDICTABLE AND INDISPENSABLE

The library is a place for exploration and discovery. One aspect I always loved was that we librarians can spend years getting to know our students, helping them to develop their reading tastes and interests as they grow up. It's our pleasure, then, to be ever-surprising to our students as they get to know us personally as well.

Use your talents when you teach. If you love tap dancing, baseball, and cooking, first bring in your tap shoes, lead the children in some steps, and read Lynne Barasch's dumbfounding picture-book biography *Knockin' on Wood: Starring Peg Leg Bates*, about the legendary African American tap dancer who found a way to dance even though he lost a leg below the thigh in an accident when he was 12. Then, after sharing Christopher Bing's brilliant Caldecott Honor-winning rendition of Ernest Lawrence Thayer's *Casey at the Bat*, take your sports fans outside to do a choral reading of it on the playground in team format. Still hungry for books? Bring in your toque, your chef's hat, and cooking implements and introduce your hungry readers to the 641.5s.

Your children should always marvel at what happens in the library. On one day, you might ask a real, live author to visit; on another, you might ask a herpetologist to show his real live snakes. Just like a good book, you want the library to surprise, startle, and satisfy.

Our libraries aspire to be Nordstroms, a department store where people actually come up to you and say, "Can I help you? Can I get you another size in that? I'll call you when that comes in." A library is like Nordstroms, but without the price tags. A candy store without calories. A Taj Mahal of literary wonders. When teachers clamor for materials on alligators or alliteration or the Aztecs, my policy has always been "give them more than they ask for, more than they think they needed, more than they ever knew existed."

Librarians are the book wizards who can come up with brilliant poetry books, folktales, fiction and picture books, plus the regular nonfiction books, to accompany a request for books to go along with that fourth-grade unit on electricity.

No teacher can possibly read all the books in a library's collection. The librarian is the fairy god-mother who knows all the books—including that green one with the rabbit on the cover that you read last year on the first day and forgot to write down the name of . . . it was Kathryn Laskey's *Lunch Bunnies*, wasn't it?—and can pluck the perfect match for every possible lesson. Librarians have thousands of titles stashed in their heads, waiting to help children and parents and teachers make just the right connections.

Librarians love dispensing useful advice. I have always seen myself as The Tester, trying out wonderful new books on classes to figure out what activities and ideas would make each book shine even brighter. Then I pass those ideas on to others.

I'm a firm believer in the use and efficacy of neon Post-It notes. I have them in every size and color. There's something so satisfying and vivid about neon Post-It notes, one of the great inventions of the 20th century along with Stain Stick and clumping kitty litter.

When a teacher asks, "Do you have anything good for my third graders to do some experiential writing?" write a personal but pithy message on a lovely neon Post-It note, slap it on the cover of *David Goes to School* by David Shannon, and send it down to her. Your note can offer an idea or two on how to use the book.

You might write, "This is the world's quickest read and looks like it's for little kids, but don't be fooled. If you want to spark some great experiential writing about how your children have gotten in and out of trouble at school, David's your man. Other possibles: Have children write their stories from two points of view—theirs and their teacher's. Write sequels like 'David Goes to Camp,' or 'David Sleeps Over.' And it's also perfect for turning declarative sentences into dialogue, if you're reviewing punctuation."

Teachers don't have to take your advice, but they appreciate knowing that you've given them a germ of an idea to grow as they see fit.

When your brand-new book order is processed and ready to circulate, invite your teachers and staff for a Book Breakfast. Keep it simple, with juice, coffee, bagels and/or doughnuts. Sure, you could bake, and that's nice, but it's not necessary. Display the new books on your tables, arranged by subject area—science, social studies, math, poetry, fiction, picture books, etc. As teachers browse, they can tag the books they'd like to read right away with those ever-useful Post-Its.

Afterward, you can check the books out to those teachers, putting them on reserve for the requested books other teachers tagged first. Deliver the books personally to their rooms. "Book mail!" you announce when you enter. Such a simple service, but so appreciated by busy teachers. Do this several times a year. If you feed them, they will browse. Leave the remaining new books up for your students to peruse and check out.

Schools without libraries operate under a terrible handicap, often without realizing it. You don't miss what you don't have. A teacher once said to me, "Judy, you think the library is the most important room in the school." You bet. That's my job, so I'd better think so. And teachers should think it's the most important resource in the school, the first place they go when they're about to embark on a new unit of study.

The librarian is the goddess (or god) of the library. She knows where everything is and what goes with what, and she can bless a teacher's every lesson with treasures and literary good fortune. Bring her chocolates and she will shower you with books.

If librarians don't work at making themselves indispensable, they run a higher risk of being declared "a frill" and being replaced by someone without the training, skills, and expertise that a real librarian brings to the job.

10.   LET THE KIDS DO IT, TOO

We get used to being In Charge as teachers, reading aloud, presenting stimulating lessons, booktalking, dispensing essential information. It's important to step back and encourage our children to take charge, too. Raising readers calls for an all-out immersion in all aspects of literature.

When presenting a booktalk or a reading on, say, dynamic main characters who make you laugh, bounce it back to your listeners. Tell them, "Today we've met some characters who cracked me up. Next week, I want each of you to introduce us to one of your favorite funny books, which you'll need to check out of the library this week so you can prepare and practice."

Have them either find a hilarious paragraph or two that they can read aloud, or do a quick booktalk describing a humorous episode. Children love the power of handing out their books, as you did the week before, to the first person who cries, "May I have that?"

I was reading an article that talked about how children's facility with spoken language worsens when they go to school. Why? Because teachers do so much of the talking, and children are expected to be quiet and listen. We need to get them talking in purposeful ways about books, discussing in pairs and small groups their reactions to stories read or told, and presenting their observations to others in the class.

11.   ASK FOR HELP

Too many school librarians are asked to perform gargantuan tasks—teaching scores of weekly classes while serving as the teacher's prep period or operating an automated library with no additional help. This is madness. We know it's madness, and we do it anyway.

If you somehow manage to keep the library humming, even though you're working day and night and all summer to keep yourself from drowning in orders and mail and books, your administrators will chuckle patronizingly and say, "Well, isn't she just the most organized thing!" and they'll continue to pile on even more responsibilities.

While we'd all be thrilled if we could put together a raft of assistants, such as the Personal Letter Writer, Room Crew, and Homework Helper in Patricia Marx's giddy picture book *Meet My Staff*, real life is more do-it-yourself.

At some point, you need to take stock and say, "I need help!" The alternative is that you'll never get it because you never ask for it. In my district, we had almost-full-time library aides, and then the Board of Ed decided they would cut the aide time back by 40 percent because they needed to save money. The librarians got together, contacted library-loving and vocal parents, attended a board meeting, and presented our case. Voilà! Money magically reappeared and they backed off. This happens every couple of years, so one must stay vigilant. When you're backed into a corner with too much on your plate, go first to the school librarians' listserv LM_NET <www.eduref.org/lm_net> to ask for advice, and then talk to your administrators to present your problem and some plausible solutions. Don't sit and stew—make a plan.

Tap parents as a resource, and retirees, too. Along with a yearly assortment of dedicated moms, I was fortunate to snare Pauline Adamides, a grandmother of two of my former students, and Rich Federici—"Mr. Fed"—a retired high school English teacher, both of whom saved my bacon two days a week, shelving, helping kids, and assisting with whatever needed to be done.

12. FIND A MENTOR

During my first three years, as I was flailing daily, trying to be a good librarian, fellow librarian Jane Scherer became my friend and mentor. She was never too busy to listen to me hyperventilate on the phone at night and to offer practical advice. After she retired from her own library, she came over to mine and worked with me several days a week on the computer, setting up our new AV catalog. Because of Jane's unselfish devotion to making the library a better place for all, I began taking in a student teacher from Rutgers each year so I could "pay it forward."

Most likely, you are the only librarian in your building. Find another librarian with whom you can vent and brainstorm, and restore yourself. Go to library conferences. Get involved with ALA and AASL and LM_NET, the listserv for 17,000 school librarians worldwide. And when you have some experience under your belt, pass it along to another newbie. Think of yourself as the old Siamese cat called Simon in Judith Byron Schachner's picture book *The Grannyman*, teaching the new kitten the ropes.

13. EAT LUNCH IN THE TEACHERS' ROOM

"Oh, I had so much to do, I just ate at my desk," I hear librarians and teachers say wearily or defiantly or righteously. You are not a monk.

Just as your eyes go buggy if you spend too many hours staring at the computer screen without a break, your brain will fry if you spend too much time in the library staring at all the work that won't get done unless and until hell freezes over.

So get out of the room. Go to the Teachers' Room for a bit. (Remember when you were a kid and you wondered just what went on in that room? For your curious students, read them the first chapter or two of *Apple Island, or The Truth About Teachers* by Douglas Evans, in which rebellious 9-year-old Bradley, hiding out in the Teachers' Room, overhears a nefarious plot hatched by crabby teachers aiming to take over the world's schools.)

Talk to your compadres. Warm up your chocolate chip cookie in the microwave, throw yourself into a chair, and network, gossip, nosh, complain, tell jokes, and breathe deeply. It'll all be there when you get back. Staying in from lunch never changes anything. See No. 17 if you don't believe me.

14. MAKE LISTS

I don't think you're allowed in the field if you're not an inveterate list maker. Like Toad in *Frog and Toad Together* by Arnold Lobel, who couldn't function after he lost his list of things to do, I would scratch a list on an anemic scrap of paper and lose it in the compost heap I called my desk.

It took 20 years to figure out this neat little tip, but I finally mastered it. I got a medium-sized notebook for my desk and wrote down everything in it—phone calls, things to do, ideas for lessons, deadlines. If I can't find a phone number right away, I know it's in the book and I can find it instead of rummaging through piles in a panic.

As for desk detritus, I tried to follow the rule of only handling mail once and then filing it or tossing it, but I never conquered that one. I've found that if you leave the imponderable mail in a very large pile and go through it every six months, most of it will be obsolete and you can throw it out, leading to great satisfaction. Never fear, though. There's always some stuff left that acts as starter dough, allowing a whole new pile to burgeon overnight, the way issues of *National Geographic* and wire clothes hangers procreate in your house when you're not looking.

15. LEARN SOMETHING NEW EVERY YEAR

It's not so difficult to be a school librarian. The teaching and administrative skills and techniques you need to master include, simply: reading aloud; storytelling; booktalking; creative drama; Reader's Theater; integrating library skills and literature; being the school authority on poetry, folklore, fiction, picture books, nonfiction, and biography; book questioning skills; discipline; creating new lesson plans and the library's curriculum; an encyclopedic knowledge of authors and illustrators; developing book tie-in activities; teaching and maintaining the online catalog (ours was named Einstein because it knew so much); book selection, ordering, cataloging, and processing skills; motivating kids to read; developing efficient library operation systems; maintaining a stimulating reading environment; becoming a Dewey expert and child psychologist; learning to love reference; working with teachers, parents, and administrators; creating Web pages; and mastering the Internet. Loving books and kids is essential, too, but that's the easiest part.

After a typically frantic day in the library, you'll identify with the understated text and hyperbolic illustrations in Rod Clement's *Just Another Ordinary Day*, in which schoolgirl Amanda's day is anything but ordinary.

Give yourself a learning curve. It takes a minimum of three years just to begin to get familiar with your job. Don't think you need to know everything the first year, though if you *act* like you know everything, it can't hurt. After five years, it starts to get easier, though you'll still find yourself working nights and weekends trying to catch up. (See No. 17 if you think you're getting close.) If you pick a few areas to work on each year instead of trying to learn everything at once, you might be a happier, more well-rounded person in the long run.

16.   DEVELOP YOURSELF PROFESSIONALLY

We must—we must—keep up on our field, the teaching of everything. This means not only that we read children's books incessantly, but also that we read professional books written by the experts to hone our skills and attend professional development workshops to see what's new.

"Don't you ever read any books for adults?" people ask me. Oh, how I long to. In the summer and on vacations, I indulge in a little Anne Tyler for empathy, a little Janet Evanovich for hilarity. I keep a pile of grown-up books on my bed table, but I never get to them all.

At the back of this book is a list of professional books I've read and found valuable, to help you beef up your professional collection and keep pace with the latest trends and jargon.

17.   RECOGNIZE THAT YOU WILL NEVER CATCH UP: THE TWO-MINUTE RULE

Teaching can kill you. For proof, read the first chapter of Richard Peck's uproariously funny historical fiction book *The Teacher's Funeral*, set in a one-room schoolhouse in turn-of-the-century Indiana, which begins with the fabulous first line, "If your teacher has to die, August isn't a bad time of year for it."

Every year as the June calendar screeched to a close, as I cleaned, sorted, inventoried, ordered, and planned for the next year, I desperately wanted to slow down the clock, just a little, so I could finish everything—just once. In 26 years, I never did, and often repeated to myself the old chestnut: "'Time flies.' 'I can't. They go too fast.'" (Don't understand the wordplay? When you say the word *time*, think of a stopwatch.)

There will never be enough time to read all the books you want, teach all the lessons you love, turn every kid into a book hound, and make your classroom or library paradise on earth. I've come to realize that all teaching and librarianing fits into the "Two-Minute Rule": You will never have more than two minutes to do *anything* in this profession.

Consider these true-life examples:

1. There's a class due in two minutes and you forgot to pull the books you needed for your lesson. (I still have school anxiety dreams in which I can't find my lesson plans.) You rush about, whipping titles from the shelves, thanking your stars you work in a library where everything's at your fingertips—everything, that is, except for the books you needed the most, which are checked out, of course, except for the one with the suspicious-looking ooze all over the dust jacket.

2. It's two minutes before lunch and your browsers are meticulously picking out their armloads of library books while their teacher is tapping her wristwatch impatiently. You always try valiantly to get to every child, but someone always slips by you—a first grader who has just checked out a novel better suited to fifth graders; a fifth grader who says, "I don't need any library books. I have a book of my own at home." In those two minutes, you strive to change children's minds and lives.

3. It's two minutes before the end of your so-called thirty-minute lunch period and you ate your school-lunch swill in a seven-minute stupor. Whoa! You haven't been to the loo yet! Off you run. (Ours is the Profession of the Iron Bladder—once a day, whether you need it or not. Scientists should do a study.)

Relax, and do what you can. The rest will be there when you get back. I worked with a library aide at my school, Joan Grace, who would leave each day saying, "Good night. We'll try again tomorrow." That's a sensible attitude. Remember, teaching can kill you.

Once you accept the fact that there are only two minutes to do everything, you stop feeling guilty for what you didn't finish and become wonderfully efficient at using all those two minutes wisely. While fielding a call from an irate parent or from your book jobber about a messed-up order, you can do a hundred aerobic leg lifts, thus raising and lowering your blood pressure simultaneously. Like magic, you can shelve and straighten fiction books while you pull materials for a teacher and whip twenty fabulous titles into fourth graders' willing arms.

Schools and libraries are so much more fun to work in than, say, a large corporation, where they expect you to dress sedately and keep your desk clean. My friend Jill Schneider used to work for Johnson & Johnson, where she earned at least twice what I made. At the time, she told me, "I never get to laugh at my job. And they expect you to have your desk cleaned off every single night. Down to the bare wood."

Are you picturing your disaster of a desk right now? Yes, we always intend to shovel out our own Aegean stables and excavate our Seven Cities of Troy, AKA our closets and desks. Someday, real soon.

In the library, you can always clean your desk next year. Or when you retire. If you want to see how bad it can get, read Kelly DiPucchio's *Mrs. McBloom, Clean Up Your Classroom*, about a teacher who is retiring after 50 years of accumulating stuff.

I left my school librarian job after 26 years to go on the road as a children's books troubadour, spreading the word to teachers and librarians all over the United States. It's fun and fulfilling and exhausting. Just like teaching always was.

As I cleaned up my school library office, packing boxes of my book props, puppets, lesson plan books, and memories, I kept saying, "Wait! I never got to use the little wooden shoes! Wait! I never got to read these books aloud! Wait! I wanted to learn that story to tell! Wait! I wanted to finish everything. If I just had more time, I could get *organized!*"

You'll find yourself rooting for trickster Anansi when he steals Hyena's hardworking stick to get all his work done in Eric A. Kimmel's boisterous West African folktale *Anansi and the Magic Stick*. Keep dreaming. No magic wand will ever be powerful enough to do your job.

You will never finish everything. You will never have enough time. There are always more books to read, lessons to plan, ideas to hatch, teachers to win over. At the end of the day, the month, the year, the career, there's always so much more you could have done, should have done.

Never mind. Celebrate instead the good things you do finish, and know that each year you are reaching hundreds of children and teachers with your books, your ideas, and your indomitable reading spirit.

Faced with educational budget cuts, testing scares, and society's woes, we could throw up our hands and give up, or get resentful and burn out. Or we can persevere. Inspire our kids. Love what we do. Laugh every day.

Every year we must strive to learn something new, try something we never did before, take risks, and experiment. Your dedication and love of children will stay with them all their lives. Years hence, they will remember the little things—the encouragement you gave, the special book you read aloud, the time you opened yourself up to them. Children will read what they're used to unless you give them reasons to expand their bases. You're out there every day, lighting your own little candles against ignorance, ready to save, if not the whole world, then at least a small but precious corner of it.

Here's a perfect mantra for all of us librarians, teachers, and parents working together to raise literate children. I heard it from author Vicki Cobb, but its source is novelist Robert Anderson, author of *Tea and Sympathy*. He said, "Expect nothing. Blame nobody. Do something."

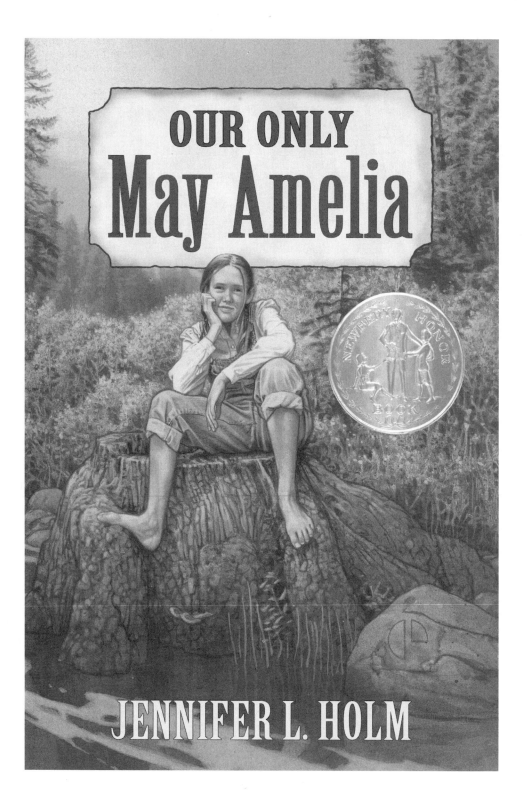

OUR ONLY
May Amelia

JENNIFER L. HOLM

THE BLUEBERY MEDAL

MOVIE STARS DON'T DO MUCH FOR ME. CHILDREN'S BOOK WRITERS
and illustrators—now there's something that makes me weak in the knees. That's why I was so dazzled in June 2005 when I spent three glorious days at the American Library Association's Annual
Conference in Chicago. Everywhere I turned—on the exhibits floor, at the Convention Center, at the
publishers' cocktail parties, and especially at the posh Newbery-Caldecott awards dinner—I met
more authors than a rock groupie does musicians. Turn this way and there's Kevin Henkes, author of
the 2005 Caldecott winner, *Kitten's First New Moon*. Turn that way and there's Mordicai Gerstein,
author of the 2004 Caldecott, *The Man Who Walked Between the Towers*. Turn all the way around and,
omigod, there's Judy Blume and Candace Fleming and Chris Raschka and Esmé Raji Codell and
Robert Sabuda and Gail Carson Levine, and more people whose pictures you've seen on dust jackets,
people you know you should recognize, people whose nametags you try unobtrusively to read before
they catch you reading them.

Many years back, at an ALA Conference in Philadelphia, my hometown, I was browsing at the
book exhibits when who should came ambling down the aisle, large as life, but Daniel Pinkwater.
And what a coincidence. Just an hour before, I had entered a contest at a publisher's booth. "Write, in
100 words or less, why you deserve to win this life-sized statue of Daniel Pinkwater," the sign said. I
had just composed and submitted an entry, written, I hoped, in the author's laconic and ironic style.

"Mr. Pinkwater, I presume," I greeted him, awestruck.

"How did you know who I was?" he asked, looking startled. As if anyone could forget his face
after looking at his jacket mug shots and his own outrageous self portraits that turn up in his book
illustrations.

"I recognized you from the illustrations in *Fat Men From Space*."

"That wasn't me," he protested. "That was Henry Kissinger."

Okay. He had a point. That picture of the rotund man in tasteless plaid sports jacket and bow
tie did also look an awful lot like Henry Kissinger. We reparteed for 20 minutes. Daniel was Gracie
Allen, I was George Burns. I tried hard to keep a straight face and do my part,

Back at Van Holten School one day that fall, I was summoned to the office by my principal,
Ernie Shuba. "This came for you," he said.

It was a huge wooden crate. We pried it open. Inside was a 6-foot-high black-and-white photo,
mounted on foam board, with a base so it could stand up. I had won Daniel Pinkwater. It was the first
time my writing had won me a prize. My last, too, now that I think about it.

I stood the statue in my library. It scared people sometimes. "Oh! I thought there was someone
standing in the corner!" they would yelp. The day custodians used to hide it behind the door of the
supply closet so when the night guy came on duty, he'd open the door and, "AAAUUGGGHH!"
They did that a lot for a while. Daniel kept me company in the library every day for years. Made me
weak in the knees.

I've always been especially bowled over by the Newbery and Caldecott books. When I was a
child, I raced to the library to check out those gold medal winners the minute they were announced. I
couldn't wait to read them.

I'll never forget when Madeleine L'Engle's *A Wrinkle in Time* won the Newbery Medal. I was in seventh grade and my mother promised to take me to the bookstore to buy it but reneged, saying—get this!—she had *other* stuff she had to do first. I wrote an impassioned letter to my heartless mother and slid it under her bedroom door in a fit of pique. This letter was my first real attempt at putting argument to paper, what teachers would now call a Persuasive Letter.

"All *right*," my mother said. "I'll get the blasted book!"

I read my hard-won copy of *A Wrinkle in Time* over and over, wondering if I would have had Meg's stamina to go to Camazotz to rescue her little brother, Charles Wallace. I still can't believe the book is more than 40 years old.

Did you know Madeleine L'Engle received something like 27 rejection letters for that book? Twenty-seven letters saying, "Not right for our list." Twenty-seven editors left saying "Whoops" when Farrar finally published it and it won that beautiful little gold medal in 1963 (along with the groundbreaking Caldecott winner, *The Snowy Day*, by Ezra Jack Keats).

I've been a reader forever, but I didn't know that mere mortals could be part of the committee that decided which books would wear those gold and silver medals. I received the call of a lifetime in the spring of 1997. The phone rang in my school library office. A guy's voice said the magic words. "Judy, on behalf of the Association for Library Services to Children (ALSC), I'd like to ask you if you'd be interested in running for the Newbery Committee for the year 2000."

"Run?" I said.

"Yes," he said,

"You have to get elected?"

"There are 14 candidates we've chosen from all the nominations. You'll be on the spring ballot, and the top seven vote getters will be on the committee. The other seven will be appointed. And two people will run for Chair. There will be 15 altogether."

So I said, "I would be delighted," and I thought, "Good lord. How will I ever read all those books?" And I thought, "Shut up. Everyone manages somehow. You will, too. Don't argue! Accept gracefully! Don't look a gift horse in the mouth!" I could almost hear my mother pelting me with aphorisms.

"Look," my husband, Izzy, said tactfully, "Maybe you shouldn't tell anyone about this. Think of how disappointed you'll be if you don't make it."

Too late. I had already told everyone I knew. It was such thrilling news to me. "I'm honored just to be nominated." Isn't that what the Academy Awards people always say? And I was.

THE NEWBERY COMMITTEE

My name and detailed resume were on the ballot that spring, and thankfully, I won one of those coveted seven elected spots. Carolyn Brodie, professor in the School of Library and Information Science at Kent State, was elected chair. Serving on the 2000 Newbery Committee was the highlight of my 30-plus-year career as a school librarian and children's literature cheerleader. Seven additional people from various parts of the country, experienced and seasoned professionals, some of whom had served on other committees, were appointed to balance out the group.

I was one of four school librarians on the committee. The others included one university professor (our chair, Carolyn Brodie), one school administrator, and nine public librarians. We hailed from all over the United States—two from Texas, two from California, one from Alaska, three from Ohio, one from New York City, one from Pittsburgh, one from Kansas, one from Georgia. Two of us were from Middlesex County, New Jersey—Carol Phillips, head of children's services at East Brunswick PL, and yours truly—and one from Roswell, New Mexico.

What was it like to be on the Newbery Committee? You know how it goes with award books—people look at the latest list and they say, "Jeez, why did *that* book win? Aren't those committees all political? How do they pick those books, anyway? Do they get a list to choose from?"

Let me tell you some of my own experiences and related musings about my extraordinary year-long experience.

First of all, each year there are 15 people on the Newbery Committee. The members are told that everything leading up to final decision must be kept secret.

My husband laughed. "You? Keep a secret? Oh sure!" but I have. I'm allowed to tell people what *I* thought of the books I read that year, but I can't reveal what the committee thought or said in any of our meetings. That's fair. Our decision represented a consensus of the entire group and was made with utmost seriousness and focus.

Did you know that the Newbery Committees until 1958 included only children's librarians from public libraries? Nowadays, you need to be a member of ALSC, a division of ALA (the American Library Association), but you can be a public librarian, school librarian, teacher, professor, reviewer, bookseller, writer, or just someone who is crazy about children's literature. Volunteer your services, and you may find yourself serving on a committee that will change your life. (Go to <www.ala.org/alsc> and join!)

The Newbery Medal, founded by Frederick Melcher and named after 18th-century British children's book publisher John Newbery, was the world's first children's book award. Melcher's original agreement with ALA was, "To encourage original creative work in the field of books for children. To emphasize to the public that contributions to the literature for children deserve similar recognition to poetry, plays, or novels. To give those librarians who make it their life work to serve children's reading interests, an opportunity to encourage good writing in this field."

The first winner was *The Story of Mankind* by Hendrik Willem van Loon, in 1922. In those days, the annual average number of children's titles published in the United States was around 700. The number has since exploded more than tenfold, though of course not all are eligible for the Newbery, "the most distinguished contribution to American literature for children published in the U.S. during the preceding year" or the Caldecott, a picture book selected for its distinguished illustrations.

To be eligible for the Newbery, books we could consider had to be originally published in the United States, in 1999, by a U.S. citizen or by a resident. (That's why the Harry Potter books can't win a Newbery. Jo Rowling is English and lives in Britain.)

One librarian sent me an e-mail congratulating me on my getting onto the Newbery Committee. She wrote, "It's great to know we'll have a school librarian on the committee who will be committed to choosing a book real kids will love to read."

Well. That's easy to assume, but I was just one of 15 well-read colleagues. The notion that I could persuade 14 people to do anything was interesting but was not what these awards are about. Each committee comes to its own conclusion, based on the Newbery criteria of selecting the most distinguished book. It is not a book popularity contest.

After my election to the committee, I immediately went into Newbery training. Hunkered down over my steaming Macintosh, typing up book reviews, my thighs grew doughy. Unpacking four new boxes of children's books daily and hoisting them up to my study in the attic, my biceps grew taut.

I had already undergone a lifetime of preparation for my reading marathon, starting when I learned to read those marvelously tacky little Dick and Jane basals in first grade. (Did you know that one of the coauthors of that series was revered children's literature professor and author of the original textbook *Children and Books*, May Hill Arbuthnot?)

Mostly I had been doing mental aerobics, reading and writing reviews of hundreds of children's books over the years for a variety of magazines. I remember, early on in my librarian career, when my husband and I moved into our new house in Highland Park, New Jersey, I spent hours that first summer, swaying blissfully in the rope hammock we set up on the front porch, plowing through books from my library's collection and raiding the public library for new stuff to read.

My neighbor, a gruff and supercilious elderly gentleman, sneered, "This is how you waste your time in the summer? You oughta be working."

"I am working. I'm a librarian and I have to read for my job," I said defensively.

"Some job," he sniffed, sure I was shirking.

That was then, when I could pick and choose whatever I felt like reading. Now, as a member of the 2000 Newbery, we were expected to read all the hundreds and hundreds of books eligible for the medal. Nobody gave us a list. We compiled the list. We read books from large and small presses, books that got stars in review journals, books that were overlooked by review journals, books publishers sent for consideration, and books we discovered in bookstores and libraries.

Each month, we sent Carolyn Brodie, our chair, a list of suggested titles, books we thought everyone on the committee needed to read. We read everything on that list, whether a title was submitted by lots of us or just one. Many were wonderful. Some were not. We read hundreds of books, including fiction, nonfiction, poetry, biography, and even picture books. I would have loved to find a picture book with a strong enough text to win the award for distinguished writing alone, not illustration. The Caldecott Medal goes to the illustrator of the most distinguished picture book, though the text is considered as part of that package.

Do you know the names of the five picture books that won Newbery Honors?

Millions of Cats by Wanda Gag (1929)

The ABC Bunny by Wanda Gag (1934)
Frog and Toad Together by Arnold Lobel (1973)
Dr. DeSoto by William Steig (1983)
Show Way by Jacqueline Woodson (2006)

A LOOK BACK AT PAST NEWBERY MEDAL WINNERS

Many Newbery and Caldecott Medal winners become fast favorites with children. I remember how some people sniffed when Peggy Rathmann's *Officer Buckle and Gloria* won the Caldecott. It was one of my students' favorite stories and I read it over and over, always finding some new nuance in the text and illustrations. It was one of my two favorite books of that year (along with Jon Scieszka and Lane Smith's *Math Curse*, which didn't win any medals). People said, "But it's not beautiful! It's funny!" The Caldecott is not a beauty contest.

When *Shiloh* by Phyllis Reynolds Naylor won the Newbery in 1992, I was elated. I never expected it to win—it had not gotten the most glowing of reviews—but one fifth-grade class in my school adored it when their teacher read it aloud in December; when the gold medal was announced in January, the class cheered.

One reviewer gave it a snide, look-down-her-nose review in the *New York Times Sunday Book Review* after it had won, and called it a good book, not a great book. Gauging the response of kids to *Shiloh* over the years, in my opinion, the 1992 Newbery Committee got that one just right.

Looking back over the list of Newberys and Honor Books—part of my getting-in-shape regimen that year—I was struck by many things. Let me share some with you.

First off were the honor books that didn't win the gold. Some of the choices were awfully tough; others seem ludicrous in retrospect. The most memorable of those, of course, is *Charlotte's Web*, which lost out to *Secret of the Andes* in 1953.

Laura Ingalls Wilder never won the gold, but she won honors for *On the Banks of Plum Creek* (1938), *By the Shores of Silver Lake* (1940), *The Long Winter* (1941), *Little Town on the Prairie* (1942), and *Those Happy Golden Years* (1944). Reminded me of that poor Susan Lucci—always the bridesmaid. Wilder gets the last laugh, though. Her books are still selling like mad, and there is now an award in her name. The Laura Ingalls Wilder Award is given every two years "to recognize an author or illustrator whose books, published in the United States, have over a period of years made a substantial and lasting contribution to literature for children." (See the Web site <www.ala.org/ala/alsc/awards scholarships/literaryawds> for more information.)

Here are some of my own particular favorites, which never won anything at all:

1939   *Ben and Me* by Robert Lawson
1943   *Homer Price* by Robert McCloskey
1945   *Stuart Little* by E. B. White
1962   *The Phantom Tollbooth* by Norton Juster
1964   *The Pushcart War* by Jean Merrill
1964   *Harriet the Spy* by Louise Fitzhugh
1964   *The Book of Three* by Lloyd Alexander
1965   *Gentle Ben* by Walt Morey
1967   *The Great Brain* by John D. Fitzgerald
1979   *What Happened in Hamelin* by Gloria Skurzynski
1993   *The Prince of the Pond* by Donna Jo Napoli
1997   *The Music of Dolphins* by Karen Hesse

Some Newberys seem outdated now and are tough to find, such as *Smoky the Cow Horse* by Will James (1927), *The Cat Who Went to Heaven* by Elizabeth Coatsworth (1931), and *Carry on, Mr. Bowditch* by Jean Lee Latham (1956), which I remember astonished me because almost every character dies in the course of the book. I know Newberys often deal with serious themes like death, and this is a biography, mind you, but I remember plowing through it and saying, "Whoops! There goes another one!"

It wasn't until 1930 that a woman won the Newbery Medal—Rachel Field for *Hitty*, but among the runners-up, between 1922 and 1930, 16 women won Honors as opposed to only 6 men. The women took over from 1973 to 1986, winning every gold medal over that 14-year span.

Not until 1936 was the Newbery given to a book with a strong female heroine—*Caddie Wood-lawn*—and up until the early 1970s, the ratio of Newbery books about boys to those about girls was about three to one. In the past 20 years, the ratio has pretty much been 50-50.

I love making lists. Most teachers do. So I compiled my list of the Newbery and Caldecott books I find work best with kids, their intended audience. It's fascinating to go back and read some of the oldies to see how they've held up. We can mine the past Newberys and find treasures there. Others suffer from outdatedness, such as an oldie I adored in eighth grade, wandering minstrel at heart as I was—Elizabeth Vining Grey's *Adam of the Road* (1943)—which was described to me by an eighth grader as the worst book she'd ever been forced to read. Ouch.

Here are my 12 personal favorite Newberys and Caldecotts. In Caldecotts, with all the amazing advancements in illustration reproduction for books, the quality of the illustrations gets more astonishing with each decade. For the complete list of Caldecott Medal winners and Honor books, go to <www.ala.org/alsc/caldecott.html>.

A DOZEN CALDECOTT MEDAL FAVORITES

1940s

Make Way for Ducklings by Robert McCloskey (Viking, 1941)
The sight of the almost life-sized, sepia-toned ducklings crossing a busy Boston intersection is still enthralling, even for kids accustomed to Technicolor. Children marvel now at those oversized old cars. Policemen aren't as hefty anymore, either.

1950s

The Biggest Bear by Lynd Ward (Houghton Mifflin, 1952)
This book contains one of my favorite memorable lines, which I encourage all readers to collect as part of their mental literary scrapbooks. Johnny Orchard's grandfather, after sidestepping a bear among the apple trees on their farm says, "Better a bear in the orchard than an Orchard in the bear."

Madeline's Rescue by Ludwig Bemelmans (Viking, 1953)
"In the middle of the night, Miss Clavell turned on the light . . . " These are words that have stayed with me since childhood, and it's because of this book (and its companion, *Madeline*), that I couldn't wait to see Paris when I grew up. It was just as beautiful as Bemelmans's magical paintings. When I saw the Seine for the first time, I could picture fearless Madeline toppling off a bridge, into the water, only to be rescued by the heroic dog, Genevieve.

1960s

The Snowy Day by Ezra Jack Keats (Viking, 1962)
Showing a little boy of color in everyday life was revolutionary back then, when virtually all books were lily white. How children's books have progressed. The story continues to shine though, year after year. Children are always tickled that they know exactly why Peter's snowball has disappeared from his pocket.

Where the Wild Things Are by Maurice Sendak (HarperCollins, 1963)
This is the favorite picture book of my whole life, one that I bought as a teenager and still have. A first edition, even. It caused an uproar when it was published, among all the grownups who were sure children would be traumatized by all those monsters, gnashing their terrible teeth and roaring their terrible roars.

Sylvester and the Magic Pebble by William Steig (Windmill, 1969)
Steig's depiction of police officers as pigs in this all-animal story was considered shocking and controversial back in 1969, when tensions ran high between youth and the authorities. And, in some exciting news, the publisher, now Simon & Schuster, has just redone the plates on this book, and the watercolors look as fresh and vibrant as the original printing.

1970s

The Funny Little Woman by Arlene Mosel, illustrated by Blair Lent (Dutton, 1972)
There's something about having a magic doubling spoon that is so appealing to all of us, and the wicked oni, three-eyed monsters, don't hurt, either.

1980s

Jumanji by Chris Van Allsburg (Houghton Mifflin, 1981)
Van Allsburg is such a chilly, antiseptic illustrator. When I first got this book, I put it in fiction, thinking young children would be too scared of it. It's so sophisticated and technically impressive. Teachers love all the follow-up possibilities—making up a new game, writing new game moves and playing Jumanji with a whole class, or writing the sequel. And, of course, children aren't afraid of the book at all.

1990s

Black and White by David Macaulay (Houghton Mifflin, 1990)
How I hated this book the first 20 times I read it. Then it won the Caldecott. In disgust, I tried it out with first- through third-grade classes and rediscovered a basic truth about children's books—adults can't always predict how children will react to any one book. This one was a howling, roaring success with kids, who were captivated by all the connections among the four intersecting stories about cows, a robber, a boy, a train, and lots of newspapers. They caught everything I had missed. And I finally fell madly in love with it.

Tuesday by David Wiesner (Clarion, 1991)
I relish showing a book that makes children spontaneously open their mouths and scream real loud, as they do when they see the frogs zooming on lilypads through the nighttime air and chasing a bewildered German shepherd. I also love that it's practically wordless, so the youngest children can "read" this Caldecott all on their own and make up their own narration.

Officer Buckle and Gloria by Peggy Rathmann (Putnam, 1995)
I've never reached my threshold on this book. The threshold is when I say, "If I have to read this book one more time, I will have to throw it against the wall." The story of a trusting, unsuspecting, well-meaning but hopelessly dull policeman and his talented dog is endlessly fun, with wonderful facial expressions that take you through every emotion.

2000s

The Man Who Walked Between the Towers by Mordicai Gerstein (Roaring Brook Press, 2003)
A love story to the Twin Towers, this true, bittersweet, life-affirming tribute inspires gasps of disbelief. Gerstein's detailed paintings from the perspectives of tightrope walker Philippe Petit up high and astonished spectators in the streets way down below are masterful and breathtaking, with two fold-out, three-panel views that will give you vertigo.

Here are three of my all-time favorite honor books that I still wanted to win the gold, although I also loved all three of the gold medal winners:

Mufaro's Beautiful Daughters by John Steptoe (Lothrop, 1987)
The Caldecott went to Jane Yolen's *Owl Moon*, illustrated by John Schoenherr.

The Stinky Cheese Man by Jon Scieszka, illustrated by Lane Smith. Viking, 1992.
The Caldecott went to Emily Arnold McCully's *Mirette on the High Wire*.

Swamp Angel by Anne Isaacs, illustrated by Paul O. Zelinsky. Dutton, 1994.
The Caldecott went to Eve Bunting's *Smoky Night*, illustrated by David Diaz. (Of course, Zelinsky finally won his gold with his glorious version of the fairy tale *Rapunzel* in 1998.)

Just in case you're telling your students that the best books are the ones with medals on them, here's a list of fabulous illustrators who have not yet won a Caldecott: Jose Aruego, Jan Brett, Marc Brown, Janell Cannon, Lynne Cherry, Henry Cole, Demi, Lisa Campbell Ernst, Loreen Leedy, Thomas Locker, David McPhail, Mercer Mayer, Susan Meddaugh, Barry Moser, Patricia Polacco, S. D. Schindler, Diane Stanley, James Stevenson, Marc Teague, Bernard Waber, and Rosemary Wells.

A DOZEN NEWBERY MEDAL BOOKS THAT CHILDREN STILL READ AND LOVE

Here's my top 12 list for Newberys, arranged chronologically. All of these remain relevant for read-alouds, read-alones, guided reading, novel studies, literature circles, book discussion groups, or whatever you want to do with them. These are books that will give readers respect for the institution of the Newbery Medal, and kids will love to read them in spite of that gold medal, not because of it. For the complete list of Newbery Medal winners and Honor books, go to: <www.ala.org/alsc/newbery.html>.

A Wrinkle in Time by **Madeleine L'Engle** (Farrar, 1962)
This look at a totalitarian society may not resonate in the same way as it did in the paranoid, Cold War, watch-out-for-Communists-in-your-soup era, but it's still a fabulous piece of science fiction.

Julie of the Wolves by **Jean Craighead George** (HarperCollins, 1972)
How exciting it felt to live out on the tundra with the wolves and brave Julie, who continues to be a much admired heroine.

Roll of Thunder, Hear My Cry by **Mildred Taylor** (Dial, 1976)
Children may read about the civil rights movement of the 1950s and 1960s as history, but experiencing segregation vicariously down South with Cassie Logan and her family, as they struggle to keep their dignity, sure hits home.

Bridge to Terabithia by **Katherine Paterson** (Crowell, 1977)
Readers grieve along with Jess Aarons when his best friend dies.

Lincoln: A Photobiography by **Russell Freedman** (Clarion, 1987)
Freedman's revolutionary book, filled with photographs and anecdotes about Lincoln, warts and all, gave the then generally dull genre of children's biography a much-needed kick in the pants, and sparked a renaissance.

Number the Stars by **Lois Lowry** (Houghton Mifflin, 1989)
A heart-stopper, this is still the best introduction to the Holocaust, one that even fourth graders can fathom.

Maniac Magee by **Jerry Spinelli** (Little, Brown, 1990)
The title character is just a runaway boy, but he's also a tall-tale, larger-than-life kind of hero who brings together the two sides of divided Two Mills, Pennsylvania, black and white. This book continues to spark a much-needed dialogue on race.

Shiloh by **Phyllis Reynolds Naylor** (Atheneum, 1991)
The sequels, *Shiloh Season* and *Saving Shiloh*, are both well worth reading in a series that ponders personal responsibility and features a dog worth risking everything for.

The Giver by **Lois Lowry** (Houghton Mifflin, 1993)
Like *A Wrinkle in Time*, this Newbery also focuses on conformist society. The open ending infuriates some kids, but it's fine for them not to have happy endings handed to them on a plate every time.

Holes by **Louis Sachar** (Farrar, 1998)
The saga of overweight, unlucky, but innocent Stanley Yelnats, sentenced to hot, desolate Camp Green Lake in Texas, where teen inmates must dig a daily hole, 5 feet around and 5 feet deep, is bursting with subplots. Unusual characters abound: there's the famous 19th-century outlaw Kissing Kate Barlow and her connection with Stanley's "no-good-dirty-rotten-pig-stealing-great-great-grandfather," cursed for eternity for breaking a promise to Madame Zeroni; the warden who lacquers her fingernails with rattlesnake venom, which is only dangerous when wet; and the tragic, searing story of Sam the onion man, which is why you must read the book yourself before attempting to read it aloud to kids below sixth grade, as there's a horrifying lynching scene that may render the book too mature for your kids and their parents to handle. Everything does tie together in unlikely but satisfying ways in this innovative and intricately plotted trifecta-winner of the Newbery, the National Book Award, and the Boston Globe-Horn Book Award for fiction.

Bud, Not Buddy by **Christopher Paul Curtis** (Delacorte, 1999)
Nancy Havran's third-grade class was so enamored of Bud's Rules and Things, they wrote some of their own, including Rule #1: "Eat dessert before you eat dinner, in case there are

peas." We may not have lived through the Great Depression as orphans looking for our real fathers. But all readers get to know Bud and root for him. White kids who've never met a black kid in their lives will respect Bud's grit and admire his drive. Mrs. Havran's third graders were scared for him every step of his adventure, wondering if they would have the courage to go on the road the way he did and stay alive. "Hitchhiking! In the middle of the night? Oh, no!" they moaned.

The Tale of Despereaux by Kate diCamillo (Candlewick, 2003)
"Such the disappointment," says the mouse mother, Antoinette, upon learning that all of her latest litter of babies have died, save one. He's a small mouse, ridiculously small, born within the walls of the castle. Despereaux, his mother names him, for all the sadness and despairs in the castle. As Despereaux falls madly, passionately in love with the Princess Pea, so I fell madly, desperately in love with Despereaux, the Princess Pea, Miggery Sow, and even Roscuro, the rat, in a brilliantly plotted book that takes four characters and weaves their stories together seamlessly. You will never look at a bowl of soup the same way.

Who are some prodigious and beloved writers who have not yet won a Newbery? Jennifer Armstrong, Joseph Bruchac, Andrew Clements, James Howe, Ben Mikaelsen, Donna Jo Napoli, Barbara Park, Jack Prelutsky, Pam Muñoz Ryan, Jon Scieszka, and Jane Yolen.

NEWBERY CRITERIA

Reading for the Newbery Committee throughout 1999, I was thoroughly intimidated by *Holes* and the Harry Potter books. Both exemplified to me the best in literature for children: exciting, innovative plots; characters out of the mainstream; settings we can dream about; and endings that make us want to turn back to page one and start all over again. How would we ever pick a new book for Newbery that came up to those standards?

Each committee member receives an official Newbery manual that lays out the specific criteria. While we might have had our own book agendas, we needed to check them at the door and follow the official guidelines.

Here is a brief description that you can find on the ALSC Web site: <www.ala.org/ala/alsc/awardsscholarships/literaryawds/newberymedal/newberyterms/newberyterms.htm>.

Newbery Criteria

1. In identifying "Distinguished Writing" in a book for children,
   a. Committee members need to consider the following:
      - Interpretation of the theme or concept
      - Presentation of information including accuracy, clarity, and organization
      - Development of a plot
      - Delineation of characters
      - Delineation of setting
      - Appropriateness of style

   Note: Because the literary qualities to be considered will vary depending on content, the committee need not expect to find excellence in each of the named elements. The book should, however, have distinguished qualities in all of the elements pertinent to it.

   b. Committee members must consider excellence of presentation for a child audience.
2. Each book is to be considered as a contribution to literature. The committee is to make its decision primarily on the text. Other aspects of a book are to be considered only if they distract from the text. Such other aspects might include illustrations, overall design of the book, etc.
3. The book must be a self-contained entity, not dependent on other media (i.e., sound or film equipment) for its enjoyment.

Note: The committee should keep in mind that the award is for literary quality and quality presentation for children. The award is not for didactic intent or for popularity.

We read like maniacs all year, trying to stay ahead. In October and again in December, we each submitted ballots of our top three books, along with short, written justifications for each. That's six nominations times 15 people, which means we could have nominated 90 books, if every book was only nominated by one person. But of course there are always bound to be duplications. Every eligible book from 1999 was considered, but as the year went on, the stronger contenders emerged. You will never see a list of the titles we discussed—it's kept secret always.

For each book I read, I wrote up copious notes, noting problems, good parts, and memorable passages to read aloud. I read all of the books on the list a minimum of two times, and often many more. When it came time to give my opinions at our two sets of book discussion meetings, at the Annual ALA Conference in New Orleans and at the Midwinter ALA Conference in San Antonio, I wanted to be sure I could remember more about each book than, "It was good. I liked it. I liked it a lot." Just like our students do.

Of course I was optimistic that the books that best fit the Newbery criteria would also be ones that readers wouldn't be able to put down. Books that would stir their emotions, from tears to laughter. Yes, books kids would sit still for. That's been my lifelong quest. Newberys are the books our students are assigned to read year after year. I hoped we'd pick a winner that reluctant readers would want to read despite a gold medal on the cover, and, as it turned out, I think we did.

THINGS TO CONSIDER WHEN READING AND DISCUSSING BOOKS

In addition to the Newbery guidelines, here is my personal list of evaluative guideposts that I use when pondering the strengths and weaknesses of a new book. Many, but not all, of the considerations coincide with the Newbery criteria.

Plot—Plan of action; holds story together; how the story is arranged. Encompasses exposition, problem, rising action, conflict, climax, falling action (dénouement), resolution.

Setting—Past, present, or future. Specific place, generic or universal setting; vital to the story (integral setting) or an unimportant backdrop.

Characterization—What types of protagonists and antagonists? (Flat, stereotyped, fully developed, round, etc.) How presented? (Through narration, character's conversations with self or others, character's thoughts, character's actions, physical description.) Major and minor; static (unchanging) or dynamic (changing).

Point of View—How the reader learns of the events, character motivation, and climax. Told in first person, second person (rare), third person; omniscient, limited omniscient, objective.

Theme—Author's purpose in writing the story, going beyond the general plot; the underlying truths or lessons to be learned about life, stated explicitly or implicitly.

Style—What makes writing memorable. Smooth, fast-paced, full of vivid description of action; or stilted, moralistic, sentimental, didactic, and patronizing to the child reader. How is the story arranged: chronological, with flashbacks, episodic.

Format—Shape, size, design of book; special features (pop-up, gatefold or die-cut pages, unusual cover or dust jacket design)

Illustrations—How do they complement/extend text? What style/medium is used?

Comparisons—With other books of same topic, theme, genre, style, author, etc.

TWENTY BASIC QUESTIONS TO ASK YOURSELF WHEN EVALUATING A NEW BOOK

1. Is the plot original or groundbreaking or surprising? Or was it predictable or preachy or overdone?

2. How is the plot presented? (Flashback, chronological, episodic, etc.) Could you follow the thread of the story throughout?

3. Do all of the events and supporting details make sense and work, within the context of the story? Are the facts accurate, even in a fantasy?

4. Does the author have a recognizable narrative style? What is distinctive about it? Does it flow naturally with interesting language, varied sentence structure, and appeal to the reader, or does it feel clunky or choppy or soporific? What tone does the author use?

5. Point of view: Who narrates the book? Is the narration believable? Were you able to lose yourself in the story and experience a willing suspension of disbelief?

6. Are the main characters worth getting to know? Can you visualize them? Do you feel you got to know them well?

7. Does the setting play an important part? If so, is it visually vivid, as in sci fi and fantasy, which may take place in an unfamiliar world?

8. Are there any parts that you feel are very well or very poorly written? Did you want to keep reading without stopping, or did you keep putting the book down?

9. Is the ending satisfying, or does the story fall apart midway? Is it an open or closed ending?

10. What is the theme? Is it intuitive to the reader or thought-provoking, or didactic or moralistic? Will children grasp what the author wanted to say?

11. Do the illustrations fit the story? Do they extend the story or just restate it?

12. Is there anything remarkable about the format?

13. Does the cover work? Will it turn kids on, off, or leave them cold?

14. When you think of the book, which scene or character first comes to mind? Will you think about this book in a week? A month? A year? Forever?

15. What did you enjoy most/least about the book?

16. What grades/age levels does this book best fit?

17. What types of children will want to read this book and why?

18. Do you agree with the published reviews (*Booklist, Horn Book, School Library Journal, Publishers Weekly, Kirkus,* the *New York Times,* etc.)? Do the published reviews agree with each other?

19. How can you use/present this book with children?

20. What other books do you have on this topic or theme, or in this style, to which you can link this title for readers? How will this book strengthen your collection?

BOOKS THAT BOMB

What were we looking for as we read widely through the hundreds of books the publishers sent us to peruse? I knew what I didn't want.

In *More Books Kids Will Sit Still For*, on page 25, I wrote about "Books That Bomb," with criteria for the types of books I reject: stories with overly worldly-wise children; manipulative tear-jerkers; stories written for adults, not kids; preachy books that hit us over the head with values; plots that fizzle; or stories with long-winded descriptions.

Finally, I rejected "Books that put you to sleep every night, even though you read just a few pages. I keep one of these on my bedside table at all times, and when I'm too keyed up to close my eyes, one or two new pages are all I need to render me unconscious. My friend Alice Yucht keeps a certain less-than-riveting Newbery Medal book next to her bed and claims she never gets past page 11 before conking out." I concur.

Flashback. My library assistant, Sharon Kalter, came in to work one day looking grim. Seems her sixth-grade daughter, Mish, had been assigned to read a certain Newbery book and was not finding it to her liking. Mish was crying and wailing, "This book is so boring. I can't stand it. I can't read it!"

Sharon told me the title of the book that was causing her daughter such anguish. I cracked up. Grabbing *More Books Kids Will Sit Still For*, I opened to the "Books That Bomb" page and read her the passage quoted.

"That's the book? Mish's book that she hates? That's the one you were describing?"

"The very one."

"That's great! I can't wait to tell Mish she's not alone!"

I won't divulge the title—you probably have your own contender for Most Boring Newbery. I'll be glad to tell you mine if you share yours.

THE 2000 NEWBERY WINNERS

Imagine 15 people sitting around a big square table, discussing books all day. Sounds like nirvana, doesn't it? At our final group meetings at ALA's Midwinter Meeting in San Antonio in January 2000, our discussions were lively, fair, and thoroughly absorbing. We plumbed the strengths and weaknesses of each book. It was like running in a 5K race. My stomach was clenched and I was sweating and cold and hyperventilating at the same time. It was exhilarating and exhausting.

After all of our discussions, it was time for balloting. We each voted for our three top books—with three points given for first choice, two points for second choice, and one point for third. The book that wins the Newbery must receive eight first-place votes, a simple majority, plus be eight points ahead of any other titles. This formula represents a consensus. Not every one of us had to love every one of the books that won.

After deliberating all day Friday, Saturday, and Sunday, these were our winners:

Getting Near to Baby by **Audrey Couloumbus. Putnam, 1999. Gr. 5–7.**
Twelve-year-old Willa Jo and 7-year-old Little Sister climb onto the roof of their overbearing Aunt Patty's house to watch the sun rise and refuse to come back inside. Instead, they spend the day on the roof as Willa Jo works out in her mind the sequence of events that brought them there, starting with the tragic death of their baby sister. Filled with humor and grit, Willa Jo's narration is straightforward and unforgettable.

26 Fairmount Avenue by **Tomie dePaola, illustrated by the author. Putnam, 1999. Gr. 1–4.**
Tomie dePaola, beloved author and illustrator, who won a Caldecott Honor for his wonderful picture book *Strega Nona* in 1976, has written many warm and humorous autobiographical picture books about growing up in his Irish and Italian family. In this slim chapter-book memoir, he recalls 1938, when his family built a new house and he started kindergarten.

Our Only May Amelia by **Jennifer L. Holm. HarperCollins, 1999. Gr. 4–7.**
"I do not think being a proper Young Lady sounds like any fun at all," confides 12-year-old tomboy May Amelia, the only girl in a family with seven older brothers, growing up in a Finnish farming community along the Nasel River in Oregon in 1899. Throughout May Amelia's impetuous narration, inspired by the diary of the author's grand-aunt, she capitalizes the first letter of Important Words and uses no quotations marks to set off her cascading monologue. Once you get used to reading this way, and it doesn't take long, it feels as if May Amelia is personally regaling you with her adventures and antics, though the book takes a more serious turn with the birth and then death of her baby sister.

And this was our gold medal winner:

Bud, Not Buddy by **Christopher Paul Curtis (Delacorte, 1999) Gr. 5–7.**
With a first line that pulls you instantly into Bud's saga—"Here we go again."—we meet Bud Caldwell as he's about to be shipped off from his orphanage to yet another foster home. Bud wakes up in the middle of the night feeling as if something is stuck in his nose. Opening his eyes, he sees Todd Amos, the son of his new foster parents, holding a #2 Ticonderoga pencil and exclaiming, "I've never gotten it in as deep as the N on any of you other little street urchins." After losing his ensuing fight with Todd, being padlocked in a shed, and stung by hornets, Bud decides to hit the road; to leave Flint, Michigan, and find his real father across the state in Grand Rapids.

He has a few clues. In the suitcase he always carries with him are his late mother's posters of a jazz band—The Dusky Devastators of the Depression!!!!!!—and the guy playing the giant fiddle, Bud figures, must be his real father. In the depths of the Great Depression, no one has much, as he discovers upon making his way to a breadline for oatmeal. He visits a Hooverville on the outskirts of Flint, where a loose-knit community of homeless folk waits to ride the rails in search of jobs. From there, he sets out to hitchhike, in the middle of the night, to Grand Rapids, where he does indeed meet up with legendary bandleader Herman E. Calloway.

Bud reveals his own secrets for survival in his list of "Bud Caldwell's Rules and Things to Have a Funner Life and Make a Better Liar Out of Yourself," which includes Number 3: "If You Got to Tell a Lie, Make Sure It's Simple and Easy to Remember." And then there's Number 83: "If an Adult Tells You Not to Worry, and You Weren't Worried Before, You Better Hurry Up and Start 'Cause You're Already Running Late."

While there is wild and uninhibited humor throughout (as when Bud is given a lift by a doctor who has bottles of blood in the car and Bud is terrified because he is convinced the man is a vampire), he deals with serious personal and social issues, including racism, homelessness, poverty, the search for family, the loss of a mother, and the effects of the Great Depression. A natural for book discussion groups, I believe *Bud, Not Buddy* is also one of the top read-alouds ever.

Note that Jennifer Holm and Audrey Couloumbis were both first-time authors, so no, it doesn't matter how well known a writer or illustrator is or who published their works. It's the book that matters. Each book must stand up to a committee's intense and appreciative scrutiny. The Newbery Manual does not permit discussion of any book not published in that year, or comparison to an author's previous work. For instance, we would never have tried to bring up Christopher Paul Curtis's *The Watsons Go to Birmingham, 1963*, his first novel, for which he won a Newbery Honor five years earlier. Our mission, our singular focus, was to find the most distinguished contributions to American children's literature published in 1999, pure and not so simple.

At 7 A.M. on Monday, January 17, 2000, on Martin Luther King Day, after a whopping five hours of sleep, I met up with the rest of the committee for the Big Phone Calls, our final bit of top secret work, prior to the Big Press Conference at 9. We huddled around a speaker phone in the ALA press office while Carolyn Brodie called each author, one by one, to share the good news. Christopher Paul Curtis was first, of course. He was warm and gracious, saying, "I wish I had something more eloquent to say!" We all had tears in our eyes, listening to him. We were ecstatic to learn the book had also just won the Coretta Scott King Award for fiction.

Tomie dePaola's secretary (well, we found out later it was really his sister Maureen) wouldn't put Carolyn through to him, as he was in his studio, working. She kept asking Carolyn who she was and where she was calling from. Carolyn finally said, very firmly, "Ma'am, I can assure you he will want to take this call!" When he came on the line, he was elated. As he said at a reception in New York City a month later, "When that Newbery Committee called me to tell me I'd won a silver, I almost wet my pants!"

Calling Jennifer Holm, author of *My Only May Amelia*, and Audrey Couloumbis, author of *Getting Near to Baby*, was not so simple. They weren't home! After many tries, Carolyn left voice mail for them, with all of us cheering in the background.

The press conference was exhilarating and packed with hundreds of people. We got to sit in reserved seats in the second row, behind the Caldecott people. When the president of ALSC announced *Bud, Not Buddy*, it was obvious that ours was a well-received choice. One of the committee members had arranged with Christopher Paul Curtis to call him on her cell phone so he could hear his name announced.

"It's a standing O!" she shouted into the phone, as we cheerfully and tearfully rose to our feet. Since the winners don't find out they have won until that morning, they are not likely to be at the ALA conference. Nowadays, as soon as the announcements are made, the Newbery and Caldecott winners are flown to New York City so they can be interviewed as celebrities on the *Today Show* the following day.

Several days later, Curtis was interviewed by Terry Gross, the host of National Public Radio's "Fresh Air." One of the things he said, which I just loved, was that he does all his writing in the children's room of his local public library. "It's the only place I can write," he said. He talked about the 11 years he spent working on the line at a GM auto factory in Flint, Michigan, and the year he took off from work to see if he could write a book. The result was *The Watsons Go to Birmingham, 1963*, which he submitted to two young adult writing contests, winning the one sponsored by Delacorte, which gave him a contract and his start.

All of us on the 2000 Newbery Committee undertook our work with the utmost seriousness, professionalism, and verve. I'll never forget the care with which we discussed every book. In the end, we were spent, but so proud of the process and the results. And sad that the Newbery Experience was over. (Or Blueberry—as one of my third-grade students had written me a Christmas card that year, saying, "I hope the book you like wins the Blueberry Award." One of the committee members, Carla Kozak, decided the girl must have meant to spell it "Bluebery.")

After the press conference, feeling mournful at the prospect of leaving our newfound friends, and ravenous, as none of us had eaten anything yet, Susan Faust, Cynthia Richey, and I headed over to San Antonio's lovely River Walk to our favorite restaurant there, Boudros. We had planes to catch, but there was just enough time for an early lunch. We sat down and ordered, and then noticed two women sitting at the next table. It was 11 A.M. and they were sipping pretty blue and fuchsia-colored drinks. Cynthia said, "Hmm. I want what they're having." Meaning the flutes of champagne that had just been placed on their table.

I noticed the one woman was wearing a saxophone pin of silver and amber, which I remembered admiring at the press conference, so I leaned over to her and said, "What are you two celebrating?"

The other one said, "We're friends, and the books we edited just won the Newbery!" I said, "Really? Well, the three of us just helped you win!" And we applauded and cheered them: Ginee So, the editor of *Our Only May Amelia*, and Wendy Lamb, editor of *Bud, Not Buddy*.

So there we were, sitting next to both editors, and I thought of my own Rule No. 37 for Having a Better Lunch and a Funner Day: "When the person next to you is drinking champagne, look thirsty." We all started laughing and jawing about the books, finding out Inside Stories about the editing, such as the fact that the cover photograph for *Our Only May Amelia* was shot in New York's Central Park, and the next thing we knew, Ginee and Wendy had ordered a bottle of champagne for the rest of us.

Tuesday, Jan. 18, 2000. I was home, slowly deflating from all the excitement, when the phone rang. It was Jennifer Holm, author of *Our Only May Amelia*. Wow! I had given Ginee So my card before leaving and when she was finally able to get in touch with the elusive Jennifer, she told her about meeting us at lunch and gave her my number. So Jenni called me at home to thank me and the committee for the Newbery Honor. It turns out she had gone to visit her father in the hospital the day before; she didn't find out about it until mid-afternoon when she called home to listen to her messages, and there we were, cheering. She reported that her father was thrilled, and so were all the nurses on his floor.

We talked about this and that, and she asked where I lived. "Highland Park!" she yelped when I told her. "My grandmother, Mildred Hearn, used to live in Highland Park. She was the secretary and nurse at Irving School!" I must have met her, because I student taught and then subbed at Irving School back then, and she lived a whole four blocks away from me. Talk about your Six Degrees of Separation—the Irving School/Highland Park/New Jersey/Newbery Medal connection.

There you have it. The almost inside story. I am always eager to hear people's opinions, both pro and con, of our final choices. It's humbling to think that over the next century, our gold medal winner, *Bud, Not Buddy*, will be assigned for reports by teachers, read aloud and purchased by parents, read under the covers by kids, given shelf space in bookstores, and honored by librarians, who might or might not agree with the choices we made.

I hope you and your students will find the book as stimulating, memorable, and downright funny as we did. And if not, there are plenty of other Newberys that might sing to you, and a new one on the way. "Here we go again."

By Doreen Cronin • Pictures by Harry Bliss

DIARY OF A WORM

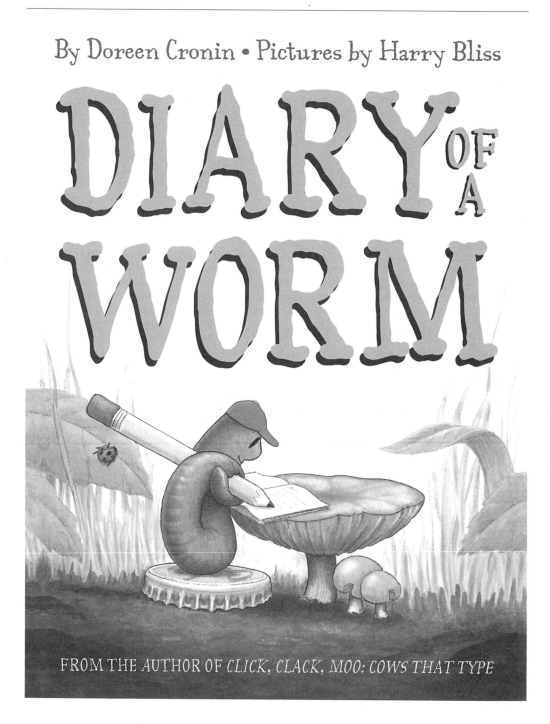

FROM THE AUTHOR OF *CLICK, CLACK, MOO: COWS THAT TYPE*

ON READING ALOUD AND READING ALONE

WHEN I READ

by Michael Harwick

> When I read,
> I get so involved,
> I feel as if I am there.
>
> When I read,
> the binding in the book falls apart.
>
> When I read, I will not do anything until I finish my book.
>
> When I read,
> the pages fall apart. They are no longer written,
> they are reality.
>
> When I read, the characters parade out of my book
> and come forth into the room.
>
> When I read, my domain's walls unfold and become an endless,
> infinite land of wonder.
>
> When I read, the words jump off the page and form shapes,
> people and animals that are my good friends (and evil foes).
>
> When I read,
> I can be on a deserted island where I got shipwrecked,
> or in a strange land where playing cards rule the kingdom.
>
> When I read,
> I go to places I have never been to before.
>
> Or I could still be in a house.
>
> When you read,
> only you can control what happens.

Michael Harwick
Eisenhower Intermediate School
Grade 4, Age 9 years
October 1998

Printed with permission of the author.

SOME CHILDREN DIVE INTO BOOKS. OTHERS ARE MORE RELUCTANT.

You are their reading role model, and the way you read and the literary choices you make can stay with them forever.

Remember that scowling boy in the back of your room last week? He was fooling around with his sneaker or something while you were reading aloud, and you thought to yourself, "Doggone it, he's not listening to or understanding a *word* of this." You felt either annoyed or disappointed, or sorrowful. But, later, he made a comment, something he either meant or didn't mean to let drop, and you realized with a start that he had taken in every word of the story and was in some way affected by it. We don't know how any one story will affect any one child, but we do know that stories affect children in ways both small and profound. Stories and books enhance our understanding of ourselves, of other people, and of the world.

Back in the old days, in the Beginning, there was the Basal Reader. And endless worksheets, cranked by hand on the ditto machine (which some of you may remember, before photocopiers and computers and the Internet). Paper hot off the ditto machine smelled sweet and spicy; students would take a page off the pile, sniff the purple print, and pass the rest down the row. We thought that was what purple smelled like.

When I started out as a school librarian in the 1970s, it seemed logical to me that if you inundated children with wonderful books, read aloud to them on a regular basis, booktalked, told them stories, acted out stories, and fooled around with words, then kids would want to read. It was sheer intuition on my part, bestowing the passion for books that my parents and teachers and librarians had bestowed upon me.

I would pass my favorite books along to teachers, many of whom lamented, "I don't have time to read to my kids. I have to teach reading." They were expected to administer lots of dittos, watch children read punchy little excerpts in their basal readers, and then ask them a lot of ponderous questions.

The dirty little secret was that if the story was excerpted in their basal, children would recoil in horror if you offered them the whole book to read. "Eeeuwww. No, I already read that," they'd say, offended you were trying to foist off something unsavory on them.

Linda Williams was a fourth-grade teacher at my school. Each classroom door had a large glass window in it, and Linda would carefully tape construction paper over the window so no one could peer in her room and see what she was up to.

She'd gather her kids to a far corner, and she'd read books to them. Lots of books. Every day. All kinds of books. Fiction books. Picture books. Joke books. Poetry. I fed her a never-ending supply from the library. She was fearless. And her reading test scores were always at the top of the list.

Then Whole Language came in, and the administration announced to the teachers, "From now on, you must READ to your children every day." Linda took down the paper. "I've become legal!" she crowed, liberated.

Here we are, 20 years later. The basals are creeping back. The phrase "Whole Language" was rejected by some as too radical and controversial for the back-to-basics movement, as if integrating real books across the curriculum was somehow a bad thing for children. Now we talk of the Balanced Literacy Approach, combining phonics and real literature and even that's considered suspicious in some quarters.

The tests have mushroomed. Science and social studies get short shrift in the elementary curriculum of too many school districts across the United States. Cutting back on science and social studies is not a viable response to the testing conundrum. For instance, in an August 30, 2005, article in the *New York Times* titled "Scientific Savvy? In U.S., Not Much" (<www. .com/2005/08/30/science/30profile.html>), Dr. Jon D. Miller, a political scientist who directs the Center for Biomedical Communications at Northwestern University Medical School in Chicago, says that only 20 percent to 25 percent of Americans are "scientifically savvy and alert." Through his many surveys, he has found disturbing failings in common scientific knowledge, including the scandalous statistic that 20 percent of American adults think the sun revolves around the earth. Certainly, basic scientific fact is taught in elementary school, but it's not getting through.

In addition, art, music, phys ed, and library are often declared unessential or frills. Make room for the tests! The experts tell us they know what's best for kids, including ever-growing canned reading programs, and teachers are teaching to the test more than ever. When I give children's literature workshops around the United States, teachers once again are telling me, "I don't have time to read books to my kids. I have to teach reading." And for some teachers, advocates of the book, the construction paper is going back up on the door.

THE WORLD'S BEST READERS

As the great Charlotte Huck, author of the classic textbook *Children's Literature in the Elementary School*, said, "We don't achieve literacy and then give children literature; we achieve literacy through literature" (Huck, Charlotte. "No Wider Than the Heart Is Wide." In J. Hickman and B. E. Cullinan [eds.], *Children's Literature in the Classroom: Weaving Charlotte's Web* [pp. 252–262]. Christopher-Gordon, 1989.)

According to an international survey by the Organisation for Economic Cooperation and Development, out of 32 industrialized nations, what country is ranked the world's best in literacy? Did you guess the United States? No, the United States was in the middle of the pack. Australia or New Zealand? No, though they were right up near the top. Where, then?

It's Finland, where children don't even start school until they're 7. According to an April 9, 2004 *New York Times* article titled "Educators Flocking to Finland, Land of Literate Children" <www.puppetools.com/nyt.html>, Finnish schools came in first in children's literacy. They only spend $5,000 per child per year. Well, sure, their society is more homogeneous and middle class than most—with no gangs, no real poverty, no racial strife, no violence, and the obvious problems those things engender. They have a great respect for education in Finland and it's so darn cold there, what else do you do in winter but read?

What's their recipe for success in Finland?

1. Teaching is a highly respected and sought-after profession there. All teachers must have at least a master's degree.
2. "Reading to children, telling folktales, and going to the library are activities cherished" in Finland.
3. Children grow up watching TV with subtitles, so they are reading, subliminally, while they watch. My gosh. Isn't that just the simplest, most sensible thing? We could do that! Send a note home to parents advising them to turn on the captioning on their TVs. When their kids grow up, they will never complain about undubbed foreign films.
4. All students must learn at least two foreign languages, and most take English. Also mandated are art, music, phys ed, woodwork, and textiles—sewing and knitting. All the stuff we call "frills" here and slash out of our budgets, the Finns see as essential to learning to love learning through play.

Finns *read* to their kids, and *tell them stories*, and *libraries* are very important in their lives. Everything librarians have always advocated. What did we learn from Steven Krashen's *The Power of Reading: Insights from the Research* (Libraries Unlimited, 2004)? His scientific studies and statistical analysis conclude: Want kids to read? Give them access to great books, read to them, and give them time and opportunity for what he calls FVR, or free voluntary reading! Voilà—everything we've done intuitively with our children turns out to be scientifically wise.

And here's the kicker, especially in the United States, where teachers are told they're too dumb to teach on their own and are given canned step-by-step reading programs to follow: in Finland, "So long as schools stick to the core national curriculum, which lays out goals and subject areas, they are free to teach the way they want."

And what will the pundits, the gasbags, the Sunday sermonizers, the Departments of Education, and the school administrators learn from this? Nothing much. They'll keep on touting phonics and drill-and-kill worksheets and canned reading programs here, and cutting funds for libraries and librarians there, and dumping our arts programs, and stating that constant testing is the only way to fix our schools. Just a little food for thought for those of us caught up in the national frenzy of testing, testing, testing, and No Child Left Undone.

Here's some more bad news: A study released in July 2004 by the National Endowment for the Arts, titled "Reading at Risk," reports that the number of non-reading adults increased by more than 17 million between 1992 and 2002. In 2002, only 47 percent of American adults are reading any "literature," which includes poems, plays, and narrative fiction. A decade before that, the figure was 54 percent. The percentage of people reading any book at all fell from 61 percent in 1992 to 57 percent in 2002.

NEA Chairman Dana Gioia said in an interview with the Associated Press, "We have a lot of functionally literate people who are no longer engaged readers. . . . This isn't a case of 'Johnny Can't Read,' but 'Johnny Won't Read.'"

What's causing this? The usual suspects: television, movies, and the Internet. Borders and Barnes & Noble may be booming, but in 1992, 72.6 million adults in the United States did not read a book. By 2002, that figure had increased to 89.9 million.

The worst news? In 2002, the newly minted adults, ages 18 to 24, were the most reluctant readers. Only 43 percent had read any literature at all, down from 53 percent a decade earlier.

We've got our work cut out for us. Do we throw our hands up in despair and give up? Certainly not. Reading statistics like these should make us even more determined to make a difference in the lives of our children. (Download a copy of the NEA survey at <www.nea.gov/news/news04/Reading AtRisk.html>.)

THANK YOU, J. K. ROWLING

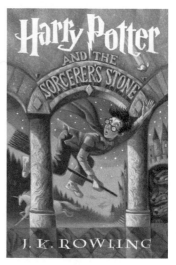

Let us now celebrate the good news. What's happened in children's literature over the past decade? Two words. Harry Potter. That miraculous boy wizard has changed adult reactions to children's literature from bemusement and condescension to one of respect and interest, and has jump-started an obsession for reading worldwide. Third graders are teaching themselves to read so they can go to Hogwarts; grown men carry Harry through the airports, not to give to their kids as gifts, but to read on the plane; teachers and parents and librarians who think children nowadays will only read short, undemanding books are watching with awe as the kids tuck into each massive tome.

The release of each Harry Potter book has been a cause for celebration all over the world, with bookstores and libraries throwing parties, and children and adults dressing up in costume. They have become the fastest-selling books in publishing history, with a quarter of a billion books between 1998 and 2005, in more than 200 countries and more than 60 languages, from Gujarati to Ancient Greek.

According to Diane Roback, children's book editor at *Publishers Weekly*, and statistics cited on Bloomburg.com, *Harry Potter and the Half-Blood Prince* may become the top-selling children's title in history. The record is now held by *The Poky Little Puppy*, which has sold more than 14.9 million copies since it was published in 1942. Scholastic printed a record 10.8 million books to prepare for the demand when the sixth Harry Potter book went on sale on July 16, 2005, and in the first 24 hours it sold nearly 7 million copies.

Maybe you were one of the jubilant readers who waited in long lines at midnight so you could get your copy and start reading. There were 2,300 midnight parties listed worldwide at <www.potter parties.com> the night the book went on sale. Who could have predicted such an extraordinary frenzy around a mere children's book?

At parties, children have pinned the piggy nose on Dudley Dursley, affixed lightning bolt decals to their foreheads, guessed how many Bertie Botts jelly beans are in the jar, and gotten sorted by the Sorting Hat into the four houses at Hogwarts. They've held birthday parties for Harry, staged readings and Reader's Theater dramatizations, and constructed their own wands. Children worldwide continue to hold endless and intricate discussions comparing the books to the movies, predicting what will happen in the final volume.

On the terrific and extensive Harry Potter Web site, <www.scholastic.com/harrypotter>, you can take the wizard challenge, consult the pronunciation guide and glossary, answer multiple-choice questions that test your recall of minute plot details, submit answers to questions in the Discussion Chamber, read some crackling interviews with J. K. Rowling, and view a video of her being greeted by thousands of cheering children at Edinburgh Castle and reading from *Harry Potter and the Half-Blood Prince*. J. K. Rowling's Web site, <www.jkrowling.com> is also top-notch.

The past few years have been banner ones for fantasy. I assume it's the Harry Potter effect; that fantastical boy wizard has cast his dazzling spell over us all as he simultaneously grows up and tries to save the world. Harry is the catalyst who has brought the power of reading to us all, both to children who were afraid of long books and now demand them—note the since-Harry spate of 500-plus-page children's books—and to grownups, who thought children's books were only for children. In an increasingly anti-literary society that prefers its news and entertainment in short, simple sound bites, Harry Potter has had an impact.

Harry is our hero. *The New York Times Sunday Book Review* revamped its weekly top ten lists to make children's books ineligible because Harry was dominating all those grownup books on the fiction lists. Nevertheless, publishers are now regularly advertising actual children's books in the *Times*, which is prohibitively expensive. Before Harry, this was rarely done. And children have been empowered to read worldwide. Not a bad record for Jo Rowling, who set out to write a good story kids would enjoy.

J. K. Rowling is now the richest woman in England, but her fame transcends mere wealth. She is the Miss Rumphius of our whole profession. (If you recall the classic picture book by Barbara Cooney, *Miss Rumphius* is an inspiring tale of a woman who finds a way to make the world more beautiful by scattering lupine flower seeds along the coastlines of Maine.) Rowling has done something profound and far-reaching for society and, through her creative and dedicated talents, has made the world far more beautiful, even in these ugly and fractured times when we have whole new sets of definitions for the word "evil."

What happens to readers AFHP (After Finishing Harry Potter), who are now suffering withdrawal symptoms? We can build on the tremendous gift J. K. Rowling has bestowed upon our children, that rekindling of a passion for reading, with an ever-diverse immersion into other great books. Is there life after Harry Potter? Of course, and it's up to us to let kids know about it. There's a world of books out there we can recommend. Here is just a sampling of some of my favorites, broken down into some of the themes and motifs found in the Harry Potter books.

Children who discover their magical powers when they go to wizard school:
> *So You Want to Be a Wizard* by Diane Duane (Delacorte, 1983)
> *Wizard's Hall* by Jane Yolen (Harcourt, 1991)

Children facing dark, evil adversaries:
> *Airborn* by Kenneth Oppel (HarperCollins, 2004)
> *Gregor the Overlander* by Suzanne Collins (Scholastic, 2003) and sequels
> *Holes* by Louis Sachar (Farrar, 1998)
> *Redwall* by Brian Jacques (Philomel, 1987) and the many others in the Redwall series
> *The Witches* by Roald Dahl (Farrar, 1983)

An alternate fantastical London or England *and* children who save the world:
> *The Amulet of Samarkand* by Jonathan Stroud (Hyperion, 2003)
> *The Golden Compass* by Philip Pullman (Knopf, 1996) and the two sequels in the His Dark Material series, *The Subtle Knife* (1997) and *The Amber Spyglass* (2000)
> *The Wee Free Men* by Terry Pratchett (HarperCollins, 2003)

A portal to another world:
> *Alice in Wonderland* and *Through the Looking Glass* by Lewis Carroll (Grosset & Dunlap, 1946)
> *The Lion, the Witch and the Wardrobe* by C. S. Lewis (Macmillan, 1950) and the other six books in the Chronicles of Narnia
> *The Phantom Tollbooth* by Norton Juster (Knopf, 1961)
> *The Same Place But Different* by Perry Nodelman (Simon & Schuster, 1995)
> *The Secret of Platform 13* by Eva Ibbotson (Dutton, 1998)

High fantasy with roots in mythology or folklore:
> *The Book of Three* and four others in the Chronicles of Prydain series by Lloyd Alexander (Henry Holt, 1964)
> *The Conch Bearer* by Chitra Banerjee Divakaruni (Roaring Brook, 2003) and its sequel, *The Mirror of Fire and Dreaming* (Roaring Brook, 2005)
> *Ella Enchanted* by Gail Carson Levine (HarperCollins, 1997)
> *The Folk Keeper* by Franny Billingsley (Simon & Schuster, 1999)
> *The Lightning Thief* (Percy Jackson & the Olympians, Book 1) by Rick Riordan (Miramax/Hyperion, 2005)
> *The Sea of Trolls* by Nancy Farmer (Atheneum, 2004)
> *Troll Fell* by Katherine Langrish (HarperCollins, 2004)

Children who are different:
> *Matilda* by Roald Dahl (Viking, 1988)
> *The Moorchild* by Eloise McGraw (McElderry, 1996)

Orphans with problems:

The Austere Academy by Lemony Snicket (HarperCollins, 2000) and others in the A Series of Unfortunate Events series

Bud, Not Buddy by Christopher Paul Curtis (Delacorte, 1999)

Dave at Night by Gail Carson Levine (HarperCollins, 1999)

James and the Giant Peach by Roald Dahl (Knopf, 2002)

Dragons and fantastical creatures:

Dealing with Dragons by Patricia Wrede (Harcourt, 1990)

Dragon's Plunder by Brad Strickland (Atheneum, 1992)

Dragonsong by Anne McCaffrey (Atheneum, 1976)

Jeremy Thatcher, Dragon Hatcher by Bruce Coville (Harcourt, 1991)

The Spiderwick Chronicles, Book 1: The Field Guide by Holly Black and Tony DiTerlizzi (Simon & Schuster, 2003) and the four others in The Spiderwick Chronicles.

If you haven't read the Harry Potter books, you're missing one of the best parts of your job. (You'll also be blown away by the recorded book version from Listening Library with the brilliant Jim Dale performing all the voices.) As librarians, teachers, and parents, it is our ongoing mission to stay as current as we can in ways to teach and raise children. This ranges from the latest professional research to the books our children are reading. At the very least, we all need to read the award winners each year, including the Newberys and Caldecotts. Reading through the best in children's fiction books is almost as good as a weekend away.

Between Harry Potter and the National Education Association's fabulous national "Read Across America" celebrations for Dr. Seuss's birthday on March 2, children have become aware of the power of reading as never before.

As it says on the NEA Web site, <www.nea.org/readacross>:

In cities and towns across the nation, teachers, teenagers, librarians, politicians, actors, athletes, parents, grandparents, and others develop NEA's Read Across America activities to bring reading excitement to children of all ages. Governors, mayors, and other elected officials recognize the role reading plays in their communities with proclamations and floor statements. Athletes and actors issue reading challenges to young readers. And teachers and principals seem to be more than happy to dye their hair green or be duct-taped to a wall if it boosts their students' reading.

In May 1997, a small reading task force at NEA came up with a big idea. 'Let's create a day to celebrate reading,' the group decided. 'We hold pep rallies to get kids excited about football. We assemble to remember that Character Counts. Why don't we do something to get kids excited about reading? We'll call it 'NEA's Read Across America' and we'll celebrate it on Dr. Seuss's birthday.' And so was born on March 2, 1998, the largest celebration of reading this country has ever seen.

Go to the NEA's site for extensive suggestions, organizational tips, links, booklists, and resources. You don't have to reinvent every wheel.

LIBRARY LILS, UNITE

What else can we do to get our kids into books? How many children say, "I don't want to" when you want them to read? "It's too much work. It's no fun. You can't make me!" Do we give up? Never. Being a teacher or librarian or parent is not for sissies.

First, go to the books themselves for a bit of personal inspiration. Take a few cues from the title character in the picture book *Library Lil* by Suzanne Williams, for example. By the time the book-toting tyke was 8, Lil had read all the books in the children's room and started in on the encyclopedias, checking out a set at a time. Balancing the stack on the palm of one hand, she'd walk down the street with the "A" volume in the other hand, while turning the pages with her teeth. When she grew up, she became a real hero—a public librarian in a town that cared more for TV than mere books. After the big storm, when the power was out in Chesterville for two weeks, Lil pushed the town's old bookmobile all over Chesterville, delivering books to all. When a motorcycle gang, led by pool-hustling, TV wrestling-addicted Bust-'em-'up Bill, rode into the now book-loving town, Lil took them on, too, and found true love along the way.

Also look at librarian Molly McGrew in Judy Sierra's *Wild About Books*:

> It started the summer of 2002,
> When the Springfield librarian, Molly McGrew,
> By mistake drove her bookmobile into the zoo.
> Molly opened the door and let down the stair
> Turned on the computer and sat in her chair.
> At first, all the animals watched from a distance,
> But Molly could conquer the strongest resistance.

Molly reads to the zoo animals. Pretty soon, all the animals are themselves reading books, picking out books that fit their interests and personalities. The otter is reading Harry Potter, for instance. At the new Insect Zoo, they even write their own haiku.

What about children? How are they affected by books and stories? Read them *Beatrice Doesn't Want To* by Laura Joffe Numeroff and see if they've had a Beatrice-like experience with a book. Floppy-eared dog Beatrice doesn't like to read. She hates books. And she hates going to the library, where her big brother Henry has to drag her for three days in a row while he works on his dinosaur report. He tries to get her to read a book. "I don't want to," she replies to each entreaty. You're driving me crazy!" he barks in exasperation. What does he do? He parks her in story hour.

The librarian reads a great book to the puppies. She reads with expression. She reads with enthusiasm. She reads with joy. And before Beatrice knows it, she's smiling. She's laughing. She's listening. She's living that story. She's loving that story.

"May I see that book, please?" she asks the librarian. "Of course," she says. Beatrice sits down and looks at each picture over and over. She relives the story. She reloves the story. "Come on, Bea," her brother, Henry, pleads. "We have to go home now." What does she say? "I don't want to!"

BEATING A BOOK TO DEATH

The universe is stuffed into every library, and we are the tour guides who can help make every destination a thrill. In our zeal to provide children with memorable literary experiences every day, we teachers and librarians and parents go all-out. We booktalk. We tell stories. We read stories. We sing stories. Sometimes we even dress as book characters and impersonate them. We lead children in creative drama and Reader's Theater productions and book group discussions to plumb the depths of a book and get to know its characters like family. We create art projects, put on puppet shows, run lap-sit programs for toddlers, and tie read-alouds into science or social studies or math. We celebrate the fictional life of a character and bask in talented writing and illustrating. We are true believers in The Word.

There are endless creative and invigorating ways to dig into a book with your children. However, some books you read aloud just because you can't resist them and you need to share. There's no flashy follow-up, no curriculum tie-ins, no pithy questions. It's liberating. You read it aloud and everyone is entranced. Bam. That's it. No guilt.

Between state standards and all those goals and objectives we must connect everything to, many teachers are expected or feel duty-bound to cover every possible teaching base, and turn every book they read into a Meaningful Learning Experience. That's when we beat the book to death.

"What did you learn from this story?" we ask children. "What is the theme of this story? What was the author trying to tell us?" I confess that I too have asked bludgeoning questions like this when discussing a book. We're always looking for the lesson, the moral, the meaning, the quick-fix answers. It's not a bad thing so long as we don't go overboard—as too many of those probing comprehension questions can be inelegant, ill-considered, and intrusive. That's the way it works in education. We make a mental checklist. Did we teach all the skills? Will they ace the test? Did we uncover all possible emotional truths in this book? Good. Next!

If you ask every question on your Bloom's Taxonomy or Guided Reading lists, I can assure you, you will make your students hate the book you just read. Pester them with one too many questions and they cry, exasperated, "Could you just *read* the *story*!" Cut to the chase. Pick one or two vital questions or activities per book. Three, tops. That's it. That's plenty. Ask yourself if you are intruding on the story in your understandable zeal to make sure that everyone "gets it."

In "A Message About Messages," a pointed and insightful article that children's book author Ursula K. Le Guin wrote for *CBC Magazine* on the Children's Book Council's Web site <www.cbc

books.org/cbcmagazine/meet/leguin_ursula_k.html>, Le Guin talks about fiction as a work of art, not simply an efficient way to disperse candy-coated messages to readers. She says that, as works of art, fiction books are not "mere vehicles for ideas," but a way to make emotional connections to stories. The whole essay is also accessible from her Web site, <www.ursulakleguin.com>, but here's a bit of it, to get you thinking about your own book connections. Le Guin writes:

> I made a note to myself a while ago: "Whenever they tell me *children want this sort of book and children need this sort of writing*, I am going to smile politely and shut my earlids. I am a writer, not a caterer. There are plenty of caterers. But what children most want and need is what we and they don't know they want and don't think they need, and only writers can offer it to them."
>
> . . . My fiction, especially for kids and young adults, is often reviewed as if it existed in order to deliver a useful little sermon ("Growing up is tough but you can make it," that sort of thing). Does it ever occur to such reviewers that the meaning of the story might lie in the language itself, in the movement of the story as read, in an inexpressible sense of discovery, rather than a tidy bit of advice?
>
> . . . Reading is a passionate act. If you read a story not just with your head, but also with your body and feelings and soul, the way you dance or listen to music, then it becomes your story. And it can mean infinitely more than any message. It can offer beauty. It can take you through pain. It can signify freedom. And it can mean something different every time you reread it.
>
> . . . I wish, instead of looking for a message when we read a story, we could think, "Here's a door opening on a new world: what will I find there?"

This made me think about children having the freedom to choose the books they check out of a library. Should we monitor their choices to make sure they're always reading books on their level?

Barbara Braxton, teacher-librarian at Palmerston District Primary School in Palmerston, ACT, Australia, wrote in a post on LM_NET, "The reason that kids who can't read want to choose the biggest, fattest books is because it is their way of showing the world they can. They know they have problems, but they don't need it broadcast to the world by being seen with a book with a low reading age or lexile written on it, or, worse still, being sent back, in front of their peers, to get something they 'can' read. Even if they come back with the simplest lift-the-flap book, you can bet your boots it won't be read—it will just help to cement their negative attitudes towards reading and the library. So instead of telling themselves 'I can't read' they will be saying 'I WON'T read.'

"And that attitude leads to more problems than you would believe, well beyond reading and the library. I would rather my kids take the biggest fattest books in the library, so that they can browse and look at the pictures and maybe even be intrigued enough to get another reader to help them (and possibly even spur their desire to become readers themselves) than take the skinniest, easiest book that will not see the light of day once it is in the library bag. We need to look at reading behavior, not just reading performance."

Some years back, a new young teacher at my school decided to keep strict tabs on what her third graders were selecting so she could be sure they didn't pick inappropriate materials that were not on their own reading levels. At book selection time, she'd stand by the circ desk and the children would present her with their choices. "Nope, too hard," she'd announce. "Go find something easier." The children would sigh and head back to the shelves. They liked it a lot, though, when she'd smile and say, "Just right! Good choice."

I appreciated her hands-on approach, as there are always students who take books that are far too simple and ones who take out the same drawing books again and again, but I worried about her students becoming too dependent on her as their "Book Maestro." I told her, "The reason I let students check out four books at a time is to make sure they have some freedom in their reading choices. How about if you stay strict with one or two titles and see what they come up with for the other two? Drawing books, joke books, and sports books have a reason for being. They let kids see that books are a source of easy pleasure and information."

She agreed to give it a try, and started sending students to the library whenever they finished their books and needed more. I watched her group turn into real readers, including those hard-to-reach boys who started taking chances on longer fiction and nonfiction.

KEY BOOKS

"Help me find a book," the kids whine or demand or whisper when they come to the library. Or they don't ask, and maybe they do fine on their own, but maybe they have never found a single book that spoke to them.

"What's your favorite book," I ask kids, to gauge their reading level, their taste, their interests. When a child says, "I don't have one. I've never read a book I really liked," this is always a shock to me. My antennas go up. I say, "Well, it could be that you've not found the right books yet, the ones that are waiting for you to discover them." And I try my hardest to help him—it's so often a him—over that very tough hurdle of finding the book that will launch him as a reader.

Kids' book prejudices can run as deep as those of the adults they learn from. Put a wide variety of children's books on display and keep tabs on them over the course of a week. You're likely to notice white kids shy away from books with a black child on the cover, boys won't read books about girls, and Asian kids, searching in vain for characters like them, often eschew fiction completely for nonfiction titles.

So many kids are wary about reading a book with a character from another time, another race, another place. The library is a bias-free oasis, where seekers are actively encouraged to take a chance on books about other groups, other lands, other lifestyles. The trick lies in our expanding children's interests and horizons to encompass the odd, the outcast, the other, and see that we are more alike than different in the long run.

Think about this. What is *your* favorite book? Do you have one? Ten? A hundred? A different one for every mood, day of the week, or location? Do you always pick the same kind of books to read? Share your tastes with the kids whose reading futures could be changed by you tomorrow.

"What is your favorite book, Miss Freeman?" kids asked me every day of my 26-year school library career. It's Norton Juster's *The Phantom Tollbooth* for fiction, and Maurice Sendak's *Where the Wild Things Are* or Jon Scieszka's *The Stinky Cheese Man* for picture books, depending on my mood of the day. But I have favorites up and down the stacks.

I would tell them, "Well, that depends. Do you want my favorite funny book, sad book, animal book, mystery, fantasy, school story, true book, biography, cookbook, joke book, poetry book, fairy tale? Or maybe my favorite science fiction book, adventure book, historical fiction book, picture book, scary book, volcano book, song book, science experiment book, or cat book?

Children often don't realize the vast choices available within a good library or bookstore. They just want a good book—whatever that means to them. They need strategies for selection, ways they can evaluate a book to see if it might be the right one for them. It's a skill we adults can help them develop.

As book recommenders, we look for the "hook" or "key" book that will draw a single child into the world of the book and unlock the pleasures of reading. Sometimes, it just takes one. We librarians have been there, in the place where a great book allows you to go, but so many younger readers never have.

I got a phone call one day from my young cousin Hannah, who was in fourth grade. "Thanks for that book you gave me," she said.

"Which book was that?" I give the kids in my life a lot of books.

"*The Music of Dolphins*," she said. "It's amazing."

"You're reading that? I thought I gave that one to Abbie," I told her, and indeed I had, thinking that Hannah's older sister, then a seventh grader, would love Karen Hesse's book. Fourth grade is pretty young to understand the nuances in the story of Mila, a human child found living at sea with the dolphin family that has cared for her, and brought to a Boston research lab, where scientists attempt to make her normal. Mila, who is now about 12, has lived with the dolphins since her parent's plane from Cuba to the United States crashed into the ocean when she was 4. She narrates the beginning of the book using her still-primitive command of English, and the print is huge, making the text look like an easy-reader. As she acquires language, the print gradually becomes smaller, reflecting her adjustment to being a human child.

Hannah said, "Well, yeah, you did give it to Abbie, but I picked it up and looked at the big print. I thought, I can read *this*, and I started it. And then I got hooked, even though the print got smaller and smaller. And now I can't stop. I just want to read this book. It's the first book I've ever read that I couldn't put down. I'm almost finished."

This key book brought Hannah into the world of reading; the book she couldn't put down; the book that made pictures in her head and wouldn't let her forget it. Some children experience this whenever they read. Others never do. "What do you think is going to happen to Mila?" I asked her.

Showing keen insight, she said, "I think she's got to go back to the dolphins. The print is getting bigger again."

Ask your students to put into words why reading is important to them and to describe their most memorable reading experiences. Ask them, "What are the best parts about knowing how to read? What was the first book you ever read that you couldn't put down?"

Make a class tape or have them write down their reading stories and share them with the rest of the class. When kids are challenged to look at reading as more than a school activity, they begin to appreciate its value. Share with them the books you couldn't put down and ask them to share with the class the books they've read that have changed their lives.

"UNSUITABLE" BOOKS

Along the way, we worry about censorship and book banning and people who want to scour the library shelves for "unsuitable" materials that might damage impressionable and fragile young minds.

A kindergarten parent sent me a note expressing shock and dismay at the language in a library book her son had brought home. The book—Selina Hastings's *Sir Gawain and the Loathly Lady* (Lothrop, 1985), about King Arthur's encounter with the Black Knight, who offers the king the chance to save his skin by answering the question, "What is it that women most desire?"—was never intended for 5-year-olds. The subject matter is sophisticated, though the plot and illustrations appeal to young children who love knights and intricate paintings. Unfortunately for the unsuspecting parent reading the story aloud, when King Arthur comes up with the correct response, the Black Knight bellows, "God damn you, Arthur! May you roast in Hell! You have tricked me of my prize!"

Out of context, the language *is* shocking to see in print. After all, even Rumpelstiltskin never let loose with obscenities; he just stamped his feet and tore himself in two. In context, the Black Knight's words are fitting and not gratuitous. If they offend you, change them when you read the tale aloud, but note that the recommended reading level for this picture book for older readers is grades 3 to 6.

For the most part, I don't like to restrict what children read, though I let them know if I think a book is too hard, too easy, or won't suit their tastes. If a child selects an overly difficult book one week and then can't fathom it, next time he will tend to search out something more suitable. Of course, when you have a class of 25 children checking out books, you won't catch every inappropriate title.

Once, an extraordinarily bright first-grade girl was insistent in her desire to check out Judy Blume's *Are You There, God? It's Me, Margaret*. Only the month before, the mother of a fourth-grade girl had raised Cain when her daughter came home with the same book, which tends to generate a fair amount of heat. The mother was concerned that her daughter was not emotionally mature enough for Margaret's descent into rampant puberty.

With that encounter fresh in mind, I was stricken to see the same book in the clutches of a 7-year-old girl who was adamant when I cheerfully suggested that she might not care for it so much, that it was really best for older girls to read. What could I do? Wrestle it out of her hands? Make it seem even more attractive by insisting she not take it? She wanted it, and no other book would do. After she left, book in tow, with sinking heart I phoned her mother to warn her of the time bomb her little girl was bringing home.

"Judy, it's OK," she told me cheerfully. "We're Swedish! I don't mind at all if she reads it. While she can read all the words, she won't understand it anyway, so why worry?" Would that all parents were so relaxed and unthreatened. Europeans tend not to be shocked at references to sex. American don't seem to notice violence sometimes, especially in movies, though Grimms' fairy tales can get them up in arms.

The following week when the child returned the book, I asked her how she had liked it. "It was boring," she said, and I introduced her to Beverly Cleary instead.

I was a little nervous about reading Paul Zelinsky's lush and dramatic Caldecott winner *Rapunzel* to second graders, but I wanted to see if the story was viable for that age. Zelinsky's retelling of the old fairy tale pulls no punches after the handsome prince discovers Rapunzel in her tower. There's that startling exchange Rapunzel has with the sorceress, "'If you please, Stepmother, help me with my dress. It is growing so tight around my waist, it doesn't want to fit me anymore.' Instantly the sorceress understood what Rapunzel did not. 'Oh, you wicked child,' she shrieked. 'What do I hear you say? I thought I had kept you safe, away from the whole world, but you have betrayed me!'"

Was I going to get flack reading this aloud? I would normally use this book for grades 3 to 6. How would second graders react? Would it go over their heads? I decided to take a chance on it, but also to jot down the children's comments. And indeed, their reactions were unexpected and intriguing.

The book's illustrations, reflecting Florentine Renaissance paintings and architecture, are spectacular, though the children were surprised that Rapunzel was not beautiful, at least not in their eyes. They loved finding the Siamese cat in the pictures, and were tickled when I told them that Zelinsky used his own cat, Skimby, as a model.

One boy winced and said, "Boy. Didn't that hurt when the sorceress climbed her hair like that?"

As I read the part about the dress, there was instant reaction from the girls in the group.

"I know. She's pregnant," one girl declared, nodding firmly. She'd obviously seen this at home.

"You mean . . . ?" another girl said, and then paused, looking shocked.

"Well, they *did* get married," a third girl joined in.

"Yeah, that's right," said the second girl.

"You mean she didn't even *know* she was pregnant?" a fourth said, incredulously.

Don't underestimate worldly wise second graders. On the other hand, sometimes they think they understand far more than they actually do. One teacher in Maine told me about one second-grade boy's reaction when she read the book aloud to her class. At the part where Rapunzel tells the sorceress that her dress is getting tight, he leaned over to the little girl next to him and said, knowingly, "It's the Fig Newtons."

"Fig Newtons?" she asked.

"Yes," he said authoritatively. "My mother says if you eat too many Fig Newtons, it'll make your clothes tight."

Both boys and girls had the same reaction at the end of the story, when Rapunzel and her prince find each other again and embrace: "EEEEEUUUUWWWWWW." That's exactly what you'd expect of second graders.

A FEW FACTS AND STUDIES ABOUT BOOKS AND READING

To become a reader, it helps to be surrounded by good books. Often, I am hired to give a series of inspirational book and storytelling assemblies for children in inner-city schools in New Jersey. Invariably, I am appalled by the dearth of available books for the children. When there is a school library, it tends to be small, inadequate, and filled with old, dusty, musty, outdated titles, and there isn't a trained librarian in sight. The worst was a so-called library with several shelves devoted to children's books. These consisted of a series of tattered Walt Disney books, and that was about it. I have never seen anything so paltry and sad.

There are often no local bookstores, and the public library may not be close enough for children to get to easily. There is simply no source for new books for these kids. I find myself mulling over how easy it is for politicians and the press to blame children and teachers for a lack of facilities that wealthier suburban schools so often take for granted.

In a May 2000 article in *School Library Journal*, "An Unequal Education," Jonathan Kozol, author of education-related classics including *Savage Inequalities: Children in America's Schools* (HarperPerennial, 1992), *Death at an Early Age* (New American Library, 1985), and *Ordinary Resurrection: Children in the Years of Hope* (HarperPerennial, 2000), writes about the importance of well-endowed school libraries in poor children's lives and the paucity of that resource in urban areas:

> Few forms of theft are quite so damaging to inner-city children as the theft of stimulation, cognitive excitement, and aesthetic provocation by municipal denial of those literary treasures known to white and middle-class Americans for generations. . . .
>
> Books . . . in short, in beautiful school libraries developed with the artfulness of skilled librarians—remain the clearest window to a world of noncommercial satisfactions and enticements that most children in poor neighborhoods will ever know.

School systems such as those in New York City, Philadelphia, and much of California got rid of their elementary librarians long ago. Now many places are trying to make amends for the years of neglect. If you let the infrastructure crumble, it becomes so much more agonizing to start from scratch again. It's kind of like rebuilding after a war.

Keith Curry Lance is the director of the Library Research Service <www.lrs.org/impact.asp>, which generates library statistics and research for library and education professionals, public officials, and the media. Lance and his colleagues have conducted numerous state studies on the impact of public school libraries and librarians on student performance and achievement.

He has found that the predictors of strong school library media programs include those that are "adequately staffed, stocked, and funded[,] . . . whose staff are actively involved leaders in their school's teaching and learning enterprise[,] . . . whose staff have collegial, collaborative relationships with classroom teachers[, and] . . . that embrace networked information technology."

Specifically, he has studied the difference in standardized test scores between schools with strong library programs and those without. His conclusions are stunning. In an article for *Threshhold* (Winter 2004), he writes,

"How much will a school's test scores improve with specific improvements in its library media program? The answer depends on the program's current status, what it improves, and how much it is improved. When library media predictors are maximized, reading scores tend to run 10 to 18 percent higher."

He concludes, "At this point, there is a clear consensus in the results now available for about a dozen states: School libraries are a powerful force in the lives of America's children. The school library is one of the few factors whose contribution to academic achievement has been documented empirically, and it is a contribution that cannot be explained away by other powerful influences on student performance. If school decision-makers want to be sure that they leave no child behind, the best insurance is a strong school library program."

There's no shortage of statistics on what we need to do to raise readers. If you are looking for hard data to present, say, at a board meeting to persuade people to fund their libraries, or at a PTA meeting to emphasize the need to read aloud to children at home and in school, check out the America Reads Challenge document, "Start Early, Finish Strong: How to Help Every Child Become a Reader," from July 1999, sponsored by the U.S. Department of Education and available on its Web site: <www.ed.gov/pubs/startearly/index.html>. The statistics and suggestions run from eye-opening to practical.

The article cites many surveys and studies, all well-documented, and the facts are startling but not surprising. One study found that only 48 percent of parents said they read to their young children, ages 1 to 3, every day, while 16 percent never read to them. A child in a family on welfare will know about 3,000 words by age 6, while a child from a high-income family typically knows 20,000 words. Children spend as much time watching TV in a day as they spend on independent reading in a whole week. Only 37 percent of 3- to 5-year-olds go to the public library once a month. The more hours of TV children watch, the lower their test scores, while the more hours they spend reading, the higher their scores. The statistics are alternately encouraging and demoralizing, but they might help spur people to action.

WHY READ ALONE OR ALOUD?

Every adult needs to be a book advocate, a booktalker, a Reader's Advisory person for children. If you're in a school or library or bookstore or even on the beach and you see a child holding a book you love, speak up. "Ohhh. That's such a wonderful book! I read that one. You're going to have the best time with it!"

What you think of as an unremarkable encounter or conversation could change a child's life. Readers are made in mysterious ways, and you never know the impact you can make when you show an interest, pass along a friendly word, or make a new recommendation.

The school classroom landscape is populated by literal readers—children and teachers who read to answer the questions, who read because they need to practice the mechanics, finish the assignment, pass the test. The school and public library landscapes encourage dreamers and browsers, take-a-chance borrowers who are only too thrilled to get lost in a story for its own sake. But too many children remain skeptical about spending their free time with a book.

"Why should I read?" too many children wonder. Why indeed? The companion books in this series, *Books Kids Will Sit Still For* (Libraries Unlimited, 1990) and *More Books Kids Will Sit Still For* (1995), focused on *how* to read aloud and *what* to read aloud, but never really discussed, point blank, *why* we should read aloud. Why should we invest time reading aloud to children? Why, too, is it so vital for them to want to read on their own?

What are some of the benefits for children of listening to read-alouds and reading books? Here is a baker's dozen.

Thirteen Reasons to Read Aloud and Read Alone

1. To bond together, either one on one, as parent and child, or together as part of a larger group.
2. To figure out how to handle new or difficult or challenging life situations.
3. To open up a global window and see how people do things in other parts of the world.
4. To visualize text and stories and exercise the mind's eye or imagination.
5. To develop empathy, tolerance, and understanding.
6. To grow language skills, exploring narrative, dialogue, the use of language, vocabulary, and the relationship between the written and spoken word.
7. To better recall and comprehend the narrative structure, plot elements, and sequence of events in a story.
8. To be exposed to eloquent, elegant, interesting, or unusual examples of language, writing styles, and words, and to hear the author's "voice" out loud, spoken with expression and fluency.
9. To share emotions, from laughter to tears.
10. To develop critical thinking skills: making inferences, drawing conclusions, identifying key words and ideas, comparing and contrasting, recognizing cause and effect, sequencing, and defining problems versus solutions.
11. To experience sheer enjoyment and the love of stories, both old favorites and brand-new ones, for their own sake.
12. To hone writing skills. As children's author Richard Peck writes in *Past, Perfect, Present Tense: New and Collected Stories* (Dial, 2004), "Nobody but a reader ever became a writer." And "You have to read a thousand stories before you can write one." And, "We write by the light of every story we ever read. Reading other people's stories shows you the way to your own."
13. To grow from an avid listener into an avid reader, learner, and thinker.

Australian teacher-librarian Barbara Braxton was working with her year three students on a unit called BookLook, focusing on picture books. She writes, "So I asked them why they should be able to still read picture books even though most of them can now manage novels."

Their responses:

"Because picture books are for everyone, not just preschoolers."

"Because sometimes you just want to read something short and simple."

"Because there are some great stories like *Possum Magic* that are not long enough to be a chapter book."

"Because reading is for entertainment as well as education."

"Because you get great ideas for your own drawings by looking at the pictures."

"Because sometimes you want to read aloud or read along with someone."

"Because the pictures make it fun."

"Because the pictures help you understand the story better."

"Because looking at the pictures saves you reading lots of words."

"Because sometimes your imagination can't make the right pictures to go with the words yet."

As Barbara says, "Sometimes the best research in the world is asking the audience."

TEN REASONS TO BEFRIEND A GREAT BOOK

What about some more personal reasons for reading alone and reading aloud? I went through lists of my favorite books to see if I could discern any patterns in my own choices. What kinds of books do I love and why? I think of myself as a *verbivore*—one who is smitten with the study of words. (Indeed, when I opened my chocolate fortune cookie at Meemah, my favorite Chinese-Malaysian restaurant in Edison, New Jersey, I wasn't a bit surprised to read, "You are a lover of words. Someday you will write a book.") What has reading done for me and for the children I have taught over the years? How has it made a difference in our lives? Could I identify for children and their librarians, teachers, and parents some concrete reasons to read?

Here, then, are ten of my own reasons to become a reader, along with examples of children's books that have lingered with me, books that make brilliant read-alouds or booktalks, and books that might turn your kids into readers. This list is for both children and adults. You can compare my ten reasons with your own, use these ten reasons as part of a booktalk with your children, or ask your kids to think up their own reasons and examples of why they should read and why they love being read to.

1.   BOOKS CAN MAKE YOU LAUGH OUT LOUD AS YOU FOOL AROUND WITH WORDS

What does a mother buffalo say to her child every day as he heads off for school? Bi-son!

Children love to laugh. The first thing that struck me, looking over my list, was how many books are on there that make me laugh out loud. There are books that make me smile or guffaw just thinking about them, not even reading them, but thinking about how I felt as I was reading them. Humor goes a long way in bringing children to books, and adults too.

When an accepted part of modern language consists of "So I'm like, no way gonna go there and she's like, Why not and I'm like y'know, I don't want to . . ." and that's *adults* talking, not just the kids, it's time to get involved in improving language. Humor is one key to nurturing readers. When children are just learning to read, the humor often flies right over their heads. Reading aloud a very funny book helps children develop a more sophisticated sense of humor and, with it, a host of comprehension and word skills unteachable in workbooks. They need to hear the language read aloud to understand what's so funny and tricky and clever about English.

The role of nonsense is to allow us to play with language. Wordplay is a first step in developing facility with language, and, most important, a sense of humor.

"Spaghetti," I said to second grader Erin, pointing to her perpetually untied sneakers, laces lapping the ground. Somehow, saying "spaghetti" entices children into tying their shoes quicker than regular nagging.

She looked down, shrugged, and grinned. "But Miss Freeman," she said, "I'm not allowed to play with my food!" Touché!

Look for books that make children laugh out loud. In *Diary of a Worm* by Doreen Cronin, the day-to-day experiences of a large, genial worm wearing a red baseball cap make listeners laugh like crazy.

"Last night, I went to the school dance," he writes, and there's a blissfully funny double-page illustration of the worms doing the Hokey Pokey. "You put your head in. You put your head out. You do the hokey pokey and you turn yourself about . . . That's all we could do."

When I read this book aloud, I always stop and have children and adults act it out, leaning their whole bodies forward, back, and in a circle, as if they were worms. With one class of fifth graders, one of the boys said, "Wait. He could use his tail, or his foot, or his rear end, or whatever you call his other end!"

Apropos of that, the whole class cracked up when we got to the page where Worm writes, "My older sister thinks she's so pretty. I told her that no matter how much time she spends looking in the mirror, her face will always look just like her rear end. Spider thought that was really funny. Mom did not."

Understanding political humor requires a certain level of background knowledge and sophistication. Like many of you, I was exhausted after the 2004 election season that ran for nine hideous months, like a bad pregnancy. I had had it with the name calling—you're a "girly man"—the "who is more macho Mr. America" posturing. Well, folks, if you're looking for a new candidate you can take under your wing, one who really fills the bill, and wouldn't dream of instituting policies just to feather his own nest, then don't miss another Doreen Cronin classic, *Duck for President*. He's the same audacious duck you know and admire from *Click, Clack, Moo, Cows That Type* and *Giggle Giggle Quack* (for which the hilarious Weston Woods video won the Carnegie Medal in 2003). He's tired of working for Farmer Brown. He wants to take *over* for Farmer Brown. So he runs first for farmer—"Vote Duck for a kindler, gentler farm"—and wins.

Running a farm is very hard work. He runs for Governor—and wins. "Running a state is very hard work." So he throws his hat in the ring and runs for the highest office in the land. And he wins again. For grades 2 through adult, the political in-jokes in the text and watercolor illustrations are great fun to pick out and discuss. (During his campaign, "He even played the saxophone on late night television.")

But running a country is no fun at all, and we see Duck, silhouetted against his desk in the Oval Office, in an illustration that harks back to a famous Kennedy photo. Checking the Help Wanted ads, he sees: "Duck Needed. No experience necessary." Back to the farm he goes. To work on the farm? No, to work on his autobiography! Note that the typewriter from *Click, Clack, Moo* is in the trash and he's now using a computer.

I asked second graders: What are the qualifications for becoming president? One boy said, "You have to be 35." Correct. "You have to be very political," said one obviously politically savvy girl. "You have to have been born in the United States of America," said another boy. One girl looked alarmed. "Oh, no. Miss Freeman, I was born in Jersey City. Does that count?" I assured her that any part of New Jersey was more or less part of the U.S.A.

Right after the 2004 elections, I was in Oklahoma City, where I met up with some teachers from the Mid-Del Schools. Kristy Hazelrig, a first-grade teacher, told me, "I said to my kids, 'Something very important is happening in our country next week. What is it?' and they shouted, 'Halloween!' And I said, 'No, it's after Halloween.' One boy, T. J., raised his hand. 'I know, I know!' 'Yes, T. J.?' He announced, proudly, 'We're gonna have an erection!'"

Mary Boren, a second-grade teacher, said, "Well, I asked my kids, 'Who can tell me what a Campaign is?' One boy raised his hand. He said, 'I know! It's something you drink, like beer.'"

Out of the mouths of babes.

2. WITH BOOKS, YOU GET TO MAKE NEW FRIENDS WHO WILL ALWAYS BE THERE FOR YOU

Notice that the best books often have larger-than-life characters. Seek out books in which the main character is someone readers get to know and love. Sometimes we dream about these characters and feel as if we know them. We see them in our mind's eye. Have your children draw portraits of the characters they are reading about, list their interesting traits and quirks, decide what they would order in a restaurant, and what their favorite clothes and games and even books would be.

In Katherine Hannigan's *Ida B: And Her Plans to Maximize Fun, Avoid Disaster, and (Possibly) Save the World*, Ida B Applewood talks to the trees in her family's orchard. She's named them all. She has a pretty perfect life, with her loving parents and her floppy-eared dog, Rufus. She's been home-schooled ever since the disastrous two weeks and three days she lasted in Ms. Myers's kindergarten class, where her teacher wouldn't call her Ida B, but only Ida. But then her Mama gets cancer and they have to sell off part of the orchard, and her parents decide there's just no way around it—Ida B will have to go back to Ernest B. Lawson Elementary School as a fourth grader, and there's not a thing she can do about it. Her heart turns rock hard, and she decides she won't like anybody: not the teacher, not the kids in her class, not even her own parents. In this character-driven novel, Ida B is someone you get to know like a treasured friend; she's spirited, funny, eccentric, complicated, and unforgettable.

When Ian Falconer's book *Olivia* first burst on the scene, I introduced the saucy pig to a second-grade class.

They were madly in love with her effervescent personality. When I asked them to make a chart of 20 adjectives that best described her, they had no trouble coming up with the following words, which I've alphabetized here: adorable, amazing, clever, copypig, creative, cute, dramatic, energetic, fabulous, funny, intelligent, lively, magnifique, obnoxious, original, outrageous, quirky, spoiled, talented, and terrific. True, copypig is not an adjective. But it was such a good invented word, they decided it belonged on the list anyway. Ask your readers, "What words would *you* use to describe your favorite book character?"

Hearing that Falconer based his character on his own niece, the children then decided what animal they would be in a story, and listed 20 words that defined their own personalities.

3. BOOKS LET YOU HEAR ANOTHER PERSON'S VOICE IN YOUR HEAD

We want our students to recognize that every good book has its own sound, sometimes in the author's voice in a third-person narrative, and sometimes in the voice of the main character who narrates in the first person.

Sometimes that voice isn't even human. Look at the New York City garbage truck in Jim McMullan's *I Stink* as he describes his day digesting all your garbage. That truck's got a mug on him, by turns grinning, scowling, and looking indestructible. "See those bags?" he asks. "I smell BREAKFAST." When I read this book aloud to three classes of kindergartners at Van Holten School, the boys fell off their chairs laughing. I blew out my vocal cords with my gravelly tough guy voice, but it was worth it.

And who would think children could empathize with a long-tailed rat? But they do in Lauren Child's *That Pesky Rat*. Hear the word rat, and we humans shudder: You dirty rat! Rat race. To rat on a friend. Rats can swim a half mile, tread water for three days, and at the end of their one-year lifespan, a rat will have 15,000 descendants. Nope, the word rat does not make us think warm and fuzzy thoughts.

Until now, that is. If we could learn to love bats with Janell Cannon's *Stellaluna*, and snakes with her *Verdi*, well, anything is possible. Really, all the narrator, a meticulous brown rat, wants is to be someone's pet, and when old, near-sighted Mr. Fortesque admires him—"My, what a pointy nose you have, and goodness me, what a long tail, and such unusual beady eyes . . ."—we cheer for the endearing rat who has worked his way into our hearts, and our heads.

Taking a cue from the personals ad the rat hangs in the pet store window, Lisa D'Ascenzio's second graders at Van Holten School composed and illustrated ads from the point of view of other lesser-loved creatures, first researching their habits and then writing about them in the best possible light.

And then, of course, there's the irrepressible Pigeon. I read Mo Willems's *Don't Let the Pigeon Drive the Bus* to my sister-in-law Ann Guthrie's preschool class of 4-year-olds at the Antioch School in Yellow Springs, Ohio. "Hey, can I drive the bus?" the gimlet-eyed blue pigeon asked them straight out. "No!!!" the children chimed spontaneously. They decided there was *no way* they were going to let that pigeon drive that bus. No how. And aren't these same kids begging and pleading with their own parents to let them stay up late and do forbidden stuff? You might think they would empathize with the poor pigeon, but it didn't happen. They loved answering him back, though, turning his monologue into a lively dialogue and watching him in full melt-down mode as he careened through every emotion. (You can read and download my teacher's guide to the Pigeon books at <www.hyperion booksforchildren.com/board/displayBook.asp?id=175>).

4. BOOKS LET US KNOW HOW OTHER PEOPLE FEEL

Reading lets us identify with others in the same boat, or with those who are in a whole different boat than we are. Being introduced to a great variety of stories helps children develop empathy, compassion, and acceptance for all types of people.

In many of Jerry Spinelli's books, the main character is a social isolate who survives out of the mainstream. There's Donald Zinkoff, the school outcast in *Loser*; the orphan title character in *Maniac Magee*; and Palmer, the boy who doesn't want to kill pigeons on Pigeon Day in *Wringer*. Readers get to reassess their capacity for empathy, figure out what they would have done in each character's shoes, and even develop a moral compass that should spill over into everyday relationships.

Sometimes we meet characters from other cultures and countries, and discover they are not so different from us, which is what happened when I read *Ruler of the Courtyard* by Rukhsana Khan to Missy Tannen's third-grade class at Van Holten School. Chickens have been the very terror of Saba's life. Every time she has to cross the courtyard to go to the bathhouse, there they are: "Bony beaks, razor claws, with GLITTERY eyes that wonder, wonder as they watch me, how easy it would be to make me scream."

One day, Saba makes it safely past the horrible chickens to the bathhouse. Once inside, she fills the bucket, finds the soap, washes her hair, and dries off. She is sitting upon the bench, combing her damp hair, and it's peaceful and cool in there. The third graders said, "Bathhouse! What's that? Where is she?" Saba lives in Pakistan.

Saba spies a curled-up brownish black something in the corner. What is it? (The students guessed correctly—a snake! They gasped.) It's within easy striking distance of the door. She knows if she screams, Nani, her grandmother, will come bursting through the door. The snake could bite. Nani could die. Saba may be terrified, but terror makes her resourceful. She throws the water bucket over the snake. She misses. (Her personal narrative caught each listener in the throat. I asked them, "What should she do? What would you do?")

And then, unbearably, after another attempt, Saba lifts up the bucket to see if the snake is alive . . . and it's not a snake at all. It's a *nala*, the drawstring that holds up Nani's baggy pants. Saba throws back her head and laughs and laughs. When she emerges from the bathhouse, is she scared of those squawking screeching chickens? No. She chases them, shouting, "I am Mighty Saba! Ruler of the Courtyard!"

Afterward, Missy Tannen's class wrote experiential stories about things that frightened them that turned out to be nothing at all, or times they dealt with something challenging all on their own. One boy described The Shot he got at the doctor's. One girl wrote about the scary time she heard a chainsaw in her house when no one else was home. Like Saba, she solved the mystery by herself.

A few years back, on the LM_NET listserv, librarians were writing in about their least-favorite children's book. One librarian from North Carolina wrote, "I don't like Eve Bunting's *Smoky Night*. My students wouldn't understand it because it's not like that around here."

Isn't that all the more reason to expose children, through books, to what life is like for other people in all walks of life, from all corners of the world, so they can come to the realization that we all share the same emotions? Caldecott winner *Smoky Night* (Harcourt, 1994) takes place during the Los Angeles riots of 1992. Daniel, a young boy, looks down from his apartment window to see looters breaking into Kim's Market. Yes, it is a tough subject, but a good picture book can often explain a tough subject to children in ways they can grasp. If we expose our children only to what they already know or have experienced, we are short-changing them about the world and their responsibility to learn about others.

5. BOOKS ALLOW YOU TO GO PLACES YOU MIGHT NEVER GET TO VISIT ON YOUR OWN

To learn about the world, it behooves us all to read widely. Vicarious travel through books may help us to get off our duffs and explore. Giving kids wanderlust and helping them satisfy their curiosity are favors they'll appreciate. Too many people in my state, New Jersey, never go to nearby meccas such as New York, Boston, Philadelphia, and Washington, not to mention Europe or Asia. Books can help children get a feel for the world, and that vicarious travel will make them want to see those places themselves when they get a bit older.

In Jane Wattenberg's hilarious rendition of *Henny-Penny*, when an acorn smacks the hen on top of her fine red comb, she squawks, "CHICKABUNGA! The sky is falling!" As she rushes to warn the king, you'll notice, integrated into each wild, photo-based collage illustration, background photos of world monuments including the Taj Mahal, the Great Pyramid of Egypt, and the Leaning Tower of Pisa. Some years hence, some of your students may be struck by an overwhelming compulsion to travel the world. Why? It could be the subliminal effects of this very book.

Closer to home is *The Hatmaker's Sign*, Candace Fleming's charming fictionalized picture-book version of the story Ben Franklin told Thomas Jefferson during a Continental Congress meeting in 1776. Jefferson was seething over the committee's call for changes to his draft of the Declaration of Independence. There were more than 80 changes, from words to full paragraphs, and Jefferson did not appreciate anyone tampering with his text. Franklin's parable, which he whispered to Jefferson, was about a hatmaker whose original shop sign was "improved upon" and edited by everyone until there was nothing left but a picture of a hat.

"How many of you have been to my hometown, Philadelphia, where part of this story takes place?" I asked the third graders after we finished the story. Only a handful raised their hands. How shocking; Philadelphia is only about an hour away. I launched into a spiel. "If you've never been to Philadelphia, it's time to start bugging your parents and making them feel guilty until they take you there to see the sights. You can see the Liberty Bell and everything. I remember whining to my parents, when I was your age, that we never went anywhere, so they took me to tour Betsy Ross's house. And not long ago, I went back and toured it again. It's such a tiny house, in the oldest part of Philadelphia. You'd love it."

One of the children asked, brightly, "Who's Betsy Ross? Was she one of the Supremes?"

6. BOOKS LET YOU TRAVEL BACK OR FORWARD IN TIME, AND LET YOU EXPERIENCE ADVENTURES VICARIOUSLY, BOTH REALISTIC AND FANTASY

Moose Flanagan starts his narrative, "Today I moved to a twelve-acre rock covered with cement, topped with bird turd and surrounded by water." Alcatraz Island, known as "The Rock," is in the middle of San Francisco Bay. While the former prison is now run as a museum, Gennifer Choldenko's Newbery Honor winner *Al Capone Does My Shirts* takes us back to the days of the Great Depression in 1935, when Alcatraz was the end-of-the-line place for the nation's worst gangsters, including Machine Gun Kelly and the nation's number one criminal, Al Capone.

Moose may be only 12, but he's already 5' 11 ½" tall. His sister Natalie is 10. She's always 10. Every year, their mom has a party for her and she turns 10 again. People always know there's something terribly wrong with Natalie. She's not stupid. If you tell her your birthday, she can tell you what day of the week you were born. She can multiply 487 times 6,421 in her head. But Natalie lives in her own world with what we now, 70 years later, recognize as severe autism.

That's why their dad has just taken a job as electrician and guard on Alcatraz Island with, as Moose says, " . . . a ton of murderers, rapists, hit men, con men, stickup men, embezzlers, connivers, burglars, kidnappers, and maybe even an innocent man or two, though I doubt it." So Natalie can go to a new school for kids with special problems. Maybe this will be the school that can help her.

Moose meets tough as nails Warden Williams and his headstrong, heartless daughter, Piper, with whom Moose will go to school on the mainland. The warden lists his rules: "There's no contact with the convicts. 2. Do not enter an area that is fenced off. Do not speak to any outsiders about what goes on here. Don't go shooting your mouth off about Al Capone."

Thanks to Piper's new moneymaking scheme at school, those rules are about to be broken. Wouldn't you pay Piper 5 cents to get one of your shirts laundered by the country's biggest con, Al Capone, aka Scarface, and the other inmates working in the prison laundry?

Utterly original, with an appealing, complex plot, alternating uproarious humor with pathos and high drama, this historical fiction book incorporates meticulous details about the time period.

I also loved Avi's *Don't You Know There's a War On?* the first time I read it, but lately it has taken on a whole new significance. Now, our children, scared about the latest wars and terrorist attacks, have more of an interest in finding out what the United States was like during the wars of the 20th century. In this case, Avi's World War II homefront novel, narrated by Howie Crispers, a Brooklyn boy who sets out to save his peach of a fifth-grade teacher, Miss Gossim, from getting fired, allows readers to relate 1943 to now. Howie's Pop is in the merchant marine in the North Atlantic, who knows where, and Mom works in the Navy Yard, and maybe it's none of Howie's beeswax, but who else can come to his teacher's rescue? Kids will understand better what life was like for some of their grandparents growing up during WWII.

The Wee Free Men by Terry Pratchett is fantasy of the finest sort. Here's the booktalk I use with children grades 5 and up, to evoke interest in a pandemonious adventure:

Tiffany lives in the country in England, a place called the Chalk. She's 9, and a dairymaid on her family's farm. Since her adored Granny Aching died two years ago, strange things have been happening on the Chalk and Tiffany has no choice but to deal with them herself. What would *you* do if a monster with eyes the size of soup plates and huge sharp teeth and claws rose out of the stream and threatened your sticky, yowling little 2-year-old brother Wentworth? "I wanna go-a *toy-lut*!" is Wentworth's usual rallying cry.

What Tiffany does is to grab her brother, race home, and look in *The Goode Childe's Book of Faerie Tales* that once belonged to Granny Aching, and find a picture of the creature—it's called Jenny Green-Teeth, by the way—after which she takes a huge frying pan from the kitchen and heads back to the stream, Wentworth in tow.

Hearing sticky Wentworth howl once again, "I wanna go-a *toy-lut*!" the monster Jenny Green-Teeth rises, screaming, out of the water, aiming straight for Wentworth. But clang!, Tiffany hits it with her frying pan. The sound the frying pan makes is more "*oiyoiyoioioioioioinnnnnggggggg*," which is the sound of a clang well done.

Down in the reeds, two tiny, red-headed, blue-skinned men in a boat whisper: "Crivens, Wee Bobby, did yer no' see that?" "Aye. We'd better offski an' tell the Big Man we've found the hag."

Hag is the Wee Free Men's word for witch. You might be thinking all witches are bad. Well, there's nothing bad about our Tiffany. She's clearly got First Sight *and* Second Thoughts, a powerful combination, especially in one so young. When you read this book to yourself or even aloud, I mean aloud, ye'll need to be thinking aboot how the Wee Free Men should sound. They're pictsies—no, not pixies, pictsies—those fierce little blue men, the Nac Mac Feegles, as the talking toad informs Tiffany, and they're there to help her. You see, another world is about to collide with this one. All the monsters are coming back. There's no one to stop them. Except Tiffany.

7. BOOKS HELP YOU COPE WITH PROBLEMS YOU HAVE IN YOUR OWN LIFE

Illness, accidents, and death are not unfamiliar to many children. Reading about someone in the same boat can help make your own sorrows or trials seem more bearable.

In Barbara Park's novel *The Graduation of Jake Moon*, Jake's grandfather Skelley raises Jake, along with Jake's mother, a single parent. Skelley was always a great guy, but when Jake was in third grade, Skelley began to change. Now, on the eve of Jake's eighth-grade graduation, Skelley no longer recognizes new faces, he has a nonstop sweet tooth, repeats questions endlessly, and has a tendency to wander if he's not watched over carefully. He was such a companion to Jake before and now he's drifting away. Jake still loves his grandfather, but no longer has friends over to the house, since the time he had a new kid spend the night and Skelley showed up at Jake's bedroom door with no pants—and no underpants, either—and the new kid ran off laughing. Jake has grown to hate his life.

On the first day of summer 2000—June 20—my 83-year-old mom, a former school librarian, Gladys Freeman, who had been ravaged by dementia, died. I laughed and cried all through Parks's on-target novel that summer, marveling at the skillful way in which she handled the many aspects of dementia. The details are right: the tremendous wear on the family, the feelings of anger and helplessness, but also the little flashes of humor.

Kids need to know about uncomfortable issues, and not just the kids with Alzheimer's in their families. The first chapter, "The Twist," describes three boys who watch an old man climb into a garbage dumpster. Two of the boys shout insults to the old guy—"Hey Pops, you go to P.U. University?" The third boy says nothing. Is he a better person than the other two? Not really. The third boy, of course, is Jake; the old man is his own grandfather and Jake can't bring himself to help or defend him. What a great discussion starter for kids.

8. BOOKS LET US FIND OUT FACTS WE NEVER KNEW BEFORE

I've become a great fan of nonfiction over the years, and each day I look for my latest Fact for the Day. Every day, I stumble upon pithy facts in the newspaper. Often, though, I find my facts in books—children's books, since that's what I read 90 percent of the time. I sneak in an adult book now and again, but I get so many children's books to read, evaluate, and review each month, I feel guilty if I get off track by too much.

It's astonishing how much of what I read comes up on "Jeopardy." My husband will say, "How did you know that a group of whales is called a pod or that the smallest snake is the thread snake, no bigger than a worm?" I read children's books. If you read children's nonfiction, you, too, will know all. Don't assume that factual or expository writing is the only way to learn new facts, however. Even poetry can yield surprising amounts of information.

I've always planted red flowers in my garden in hopes of luring ruby-throated hummingbirds there. One February, a hummingbird dive-bombed children's poet Kristine O'Connell George and her two daughters, as they were having breakfast outside on their patio in Claremont, California. (Note to self: Move to California!) She kept a written journal over the next two months, as they watched that Anna's hummingbird, which they named Anna, build a 2-inch nest in a branch of their ficus plant. Her journal became the basis of *Hummingbird Nest: A Journal of Poems*, a lovely volume of 26 observational poems and accompanying watercolors. George and her family, including their dog and cat, watched the two newly hatched babies as they grew and left the nest. George admits to suffering from empty-nest syndrome after they were gone, though new hummingbirds have continued to arrive at their feeder.

You'll find two great pages of hummingbird facts at the back of the book: Did you know they are the smallest birds in the world, with the smallest eggs. That there are 330 species native to the Western Hemisphere? That they can fly backward, sideway, and upside down, and that in flight, the hummingbird's wings beat up to 200 beats a second? After you share these poems and facts with children, they'll want to set up a feeder.

Here's an easy question everybody knows: What were George Washington's false teeth made of? Wood? Wrong, as anyone who has read the rhyming picture-book biography *George Washington's Teeth* by Deborah Chandra and Madeleine Comora can tell you. George's life was a misery of rotting teeth and infected gums. Here's how the authors describe Washington crossing the Delaware to catch the Hessian soldiers unawares on Christmas Eve 1776:

> George crossed the icy Delaware
> With nine teeth in his mouth.
> In that cold and pitchy dark,
> Two more teeth came out!

When he was elected president in 1789 at the age of 57, he had only two of his own teeth left in his mouth. According to the informative timeline at the back of the book, George's first full set of false teeth were made that year "out of hippopotamus ivory and eight human teeth held in place with gold screw rivets. The base is coated with flesh-tinted sealing wax to give a natural appearance."

Some of George's other dentures were fashioned out of walrus and elephant ivory, along with cow and elk cow teeth. He never had any wooden teeth, however.

I read this book to Missy Tannen's third graders at Van Holten School. They were astounded by the facts and loved comparing the timeline facts with the information integrated in each verse. They then each picked a famous person to research, drew a portrait, and incorporated facts about the person's life into a rhyming biographical sketch.

Rhyming biography and portrait, inspired by *George Washington's Teeth* by Deborah Chandra and Madeleine Comora, by a Grade 3 student at Van Holten School, Bridgewater, NJ (Missy Tannen's class, 2003).

One student wrote one on Jackie Robinson that read, in part:

Jackie Robinson lived from 1919–1972
When he got up to bat the baseball flew.

His father deserted his family when he was young.
His mom was probably mad so she stuck out her tongue.

In the fall of 1942, Jackie joined the Honolulu Bears pro football team.
After the games he might have gone out for ice cream.

9. BOOKS ARE BEAUTIFUL

What saves me every time is the books. The miraculous, inspirational, gorgeous books. Pleasure in a 32-page package. Bliss for the eyes and brain, if we can but appreciate it. What we try to do over the course of our careers is to get our kids to see the glory and sheer satisfaction in books, the thrill of uncovering a perfect cluster of words or a radiant illustration, and the tactile pleasure of turning a page and having something exciting and new spring into view.

I remember reading and singing Paul O. Zelinsky's jaunty pop-up book *The Wheels on the Bus* (Dutton, 1990) with a preschool class of communication-handicapped 3- and 4-year-olds. They were practically drooling as I showed them the book, licking their lips, moving their hands. They wanted to feel the pages, and if I had let them, they would have licked those pages. I know how they felt.

I wrote a teacher's guide for that book for its tenth anniversary for Penguin Putnam in 2000. The guide came in a white 9″ x 12″ envelope and on the front was a reproduction, done in blue, of a picture from the book of the storytelling guy playing his guitar. I showed it to my friends Patricia and Bert and their verbal, funny, 2-year-old son David. He looked at the picture on the envelope and said, "Wah wah wah!"

If you know the book and song, one verse goes: "The babies on the bus go wah wah wah." David had made an instant connection from an isolated picture—not even in full color—to a book he knows and loves. Never underestimate the power of pictures and observant children, even 2-year-olds.

When David was a baby and his parents read him Margaret Wise Brown's classic bedtime story, *Goodnight Moon*, he wanted to go outside every night and see the moon. The first time I met them, they were standing outside, Bert holding David in his arms, and the three of them were admiring the full moon together.

Giving a workshop in Ohio one summer, as I was talking about a writing and illustrating follow-up activity for a picture book, a teacher said, "In our school, they're so focused on the reading and the writing, they don't want the kids to draw. Actually, we're not allowed to have them write a story and draw a picture to go with it. They don't get tested on drawing." Other teachers nodded; their schools had no art teachers, either; art was considered a frill that did not translate into better test scores. The mind reels at such ignorance, but I'm hearing more stories like this as the testing frenzy intensifies.

If the art is so unimportant, why do we award the Caldecott Medal to the artist of the most distinguished American picture book for children every year? And if art isn't vital, than why do we publish 4,000 picture books each year in this country, books in which the art and words are equal partners. I owe my satisfaction in my chosen career to the authors and illustrators whose books I find so endlessly satisfying and gripping. I can't say which I appreciate more—words or art. To deny children the pleasures of art seems needlessly destructive.

For so many of our children, especially those right-brained ones who often don't like to read and write but who love to draw, art is their saving grace. As famed portrait artist Chuck Close, who struggled with dyslexia as a student in the 1940s, said about his childhood, "Art saved my life." Jan Greenberg and Sandra Jordan's splendid biography, *Chuck Close Up Close*, is filled with color reproductions of his astonishing 20-foot portraits.

Sometimes I despair at the counterproductive, ill-considered, and sometimes downright ignorant actions taken in the name of improving education. We can't change the world, maybe, but we can make our own little corner of it a pretty nice, friendly, and stimulating place for our kids, starting with books that soothe, startle, and enliven the senses.

Each year I fall madly in love with a new crop of books. In 2005, I was dazzled by Sy Montgomery's expressive and iridescent color photographs of a panther chameleon from Madagascar in Joy Cowley's *Chameleon, Chameleon*; swept away by the fall leaf constructions in Lois Ehlert's *Leaf Man*; jazzed by the bright and scribbly yellows, greens, and blues in Norton Juster's *The Hello, Goodbye Window*; enchanted by the alternating gentle watercolors and bold inks of Jon J. Muth's *Zen Shorts*; rendered breathless by the romp through the nighttime sky with a dark-haired girl and her amiable whale-sized blue fish in Eric Rohmann's *Clara and Asha*; and mystified by the handsome handmade paper collages in Ed Young's *Beyond the Great Mountains: A Visual Poem About China* that embodies Chinese calligraphy.

10. BOOKS INSPIRE US TO TELL OUR OWN STORIES

Too many children have never asked their parents or grandparents to share stories of when they were young. To collect those family stories, either in writing or on tape, is to preserve a part of ourselves before it's too late.

To demonstrate the power of family stories, read *Esperanza Rising*, Pam Muñoz Ryan's novel about a poor little rich girl, 14-year-old Esperanza, who lives with her parents on their ranch in Mexico. In 1924, after Esperanza's Pa is murdered by bandits, her mother is faced with the prospect of being forced into marriage to her husband's older stepbrother, Tío Luis, a corrupt banker with political ambitions. Mama gratefully accepts the help of former servants Hortensia and Alfonso to cross the border into California and work on a farm.

They escape by wagon and train, with only the clothes on their backs, though proper Esperanza is horrified at traveling among poor, dirty peasants. She is even more appalled at her new home, a company camp of cabins that remind her of horse stalls, and a new life picking crops in the San Joaquin Valley. In one noteworthy scene, she is instructed to sweep a platform; she's never handled a broom before and is frustrated and embarrassed when she can't figure out how to make it work. Esperanza was the author's own grandmother, and the novel, though fictionalized, is true.

Share with your children an insightful and personal review of *Esperanza Rising*, written in 2002 by then 10-year-old Luisa V. Lopez, that can be found on the Stone Soup Web site at <www.stonesoup.com/br2/2002/EsperanzaRising.html>. *Stone Soup* is a wonderful magazine, published six times a year, that consists solely of stories, poems, book reviews, and artwork by children ages 8 to 13. Some of your students will be interested in submitting their own work for possible publication.

When children are exposed to the stories of others, it's only natural that some of them will grow up to be authors themselves. From hearing stories shared, children appreciate the roles that authors and illustrators play in our society. What does an author do? New Jersey librarian Beth Lommel asked a first-grade class that question. One little boy raised his hand. "He pokes people," he said. "He pokes people?" she asked, taken aback. "Yes. He pokes people a lot," he said authoritatively. Well, actually, that answer is not so far fetched. Authors can reflect our conscience, our society, and the way we live. They can agitate, cogitate, and sometimes infuriate. Authors poke people.

So who can be an author? We all can. I remember starting my brand-new journal after midnight, on a blustery January 1, when I was 12. "What a neurotic wind," I wrote. I wish I still had that journal. I was inspired to start one upon finding my own mother's journal, which she wrote when she was 14, back in 1931. She wrote about movies. They went to the movies a lot back then, in the years before TV, and her journal was filled with commentary about movie plots and actors. Even when my mom was stricken with dementia, she could still tell you what was going on in the movie world. I wish I still had her journal, but it, too, disappeared.

Some diaries survive. *Anne Elizabeth's Diary: A Young Artist's True Story* is one that did. It was written by Anne Elizabeth Rector the year she was 12, back in 1912. She lived in Manhattan at 414 West 118th Street, near Columbia University. Her daughter, Sara Anne, found the diary in the attic after her mother's death. The original diary was brought to the attention of book publisher Little, Brown by Anne Elizabeth's granddaughter, and Kathleen Krull undertook to edit it, adding sidebars of information about life in 1912, including facts about New York City, Anne Elizabeth's school, clothing, and what it was like being a girl back then, along with photos of Anne Elizabeth and her family. Not only did Anne Elizabeth write in her diary, but she painted tiny, delicate, pen-and-ink pictures to accompany her words. ("I shall draw here, too," she wrote in her first entry. "Mother need not know.")

When you read her diary, you'll be struck by the changes girls and women have seen in the past century. On February 18, she wrote, "Went for a walk with Daddy. He said the oddest thing, that ladies should not go to school too much, that men do not approve." Mother said, ". . . all ladies should be artistic and they do not need special classes." Anne Elizabeth wrote, "Mother never praises me. She believes giving praise is bad manners." Her art teacher, Miss Pratt, though, encouraged her to develop her skills as an artist.

At the back of the book are tips from Krull on keeping a diary, which will certainly inspire readers to start theirs. Remind diarists that if they keep their writings forever, it's a meaningful way of connecting to their past and their future.

We have all known many fads and buzz words in education. Whole language, phonics (both still doing battle, but maybe finally calling a truce with the Balanced Literacy Approach), big books, fluency, phonemic awareness, Literature Circles, Guided Reading, Reading Recovery, Reading Counts, and Accelerated Reader, are some of the concepts, tools, and instructional techniques in our reading arsenals. All have one thing in common: people tout them as the one thing that's going to revolutionize education, get kids learning, or make them test better.

That one thing is always awaiting us, on the horizon, ready to save us all. Charter schools? School choice? Ritalin? The truth, as we have mostly figured out, is that education is not pure science. There is no infallible prescription, no magic one-shot method to get kids of all abilities and interests reading and learning. It's killer hard work that we parents, teachers, librarians, writers, and illustrators do, raising readers one at a time, and it never gets any easier. But we keep plugging, looking for those books and stories that can change children's lives.

Every year we must strive to learn something new, try something we never did before, take some risks, experiment. Our readers are depending on us. And those kids we encourage to love their books and libraries today will be out voting to fund our school budgets in a mere dozen years or so. We can all make a difference in how children become book people, lifelong learners, and library users.

THE STORY OF
PAPER

BY **Ying Chang Compestine**

ILLUSTRATED BY

YongSheng Xuan

BOOKS ACROSS THE CURRICULUM

WE WANT OUR LIBRARIES AND CLASSROOMS TO LOOK WARM AND inviting to all visitors. I was in a library some time back, and looking around, knew something was wrong but couldn't immediately put my finger on it. Then it struck me. There were hardly any books on display, and there were no knickknacks either. Bookstores know how to make their wares look irresistible, with tantalizing titles on display everywhere. We need to do that too. It's easy enough to make our rooms look appealing, even without the decorating budget bookstores have. "Books Everywhere," that's my motto.

One year, I brought from home a large oval rug that I had crocheted in college when I was too poor or too cheap to buy one. It was hideously garish, but sitting on the carpet in our Story Rug section, it looked downright festive. My first graders thought it was perfect, especially when I told them it was a magic flying carpet that could take us to Paris, which they all agreed was a pretty good idea.

Children notice everything. As the class settled in for its weekly dose of mayhem and literature, one girl said, "You look nice, Miss Freeman. I like your dress." Another chimed in, "I like your necklace." This was great. How many adults in your life take the time to deconstruct you and compliment you on every element they see? They admired my shoes, my hair, the new rug, and then Natalie said, "You just look magical today. I think we're going to have some magic."

It's true, there is a magical feeling to being in the library. It's called Book Magic.

I rummaged through some of the many reading and writing projects I've used with children over the past decade, and offer here a tip-of-the-iceberg sampling of some of the most interesting, provocative, practical, useful, stimulating, or just plain fun tie-ins, writing prompts, games, lists, lessons, and teaching ideas that will take you through the library and across the school curriculum. You'll find more information about all of the books described in this chapter in the second section of this book, the Annotated Read-Aloud Lists, which contain hundreds of additional suggestions for using literature.

HISTORY OF BOOKS LESSON

Share books about books themselves. For example, where does paper come from? In Ying Chang Compestine's *The Story of Paper*, a literary pourquoi tale (a how and why story explaining how something came to be), we learn how paper may have been invented.

It seems that before paper was invented, people in China wrote on their hands, on the ground with sticks, or, if they were wealthy, on silk. In trouble for never finishing their work and for their inattentiveness in class, the three enterprising Kang brothers—Ting, Pan, and Kùai—must take home notes from their teacher, written on their hands, for their parents to see. It's embarrassing. They wish their teacher had something else to write on, but silk is too extravagant.

While pounding the day's rice to make rice cakes, Kùai gets an idea and explains his plan to his brothers. They pour water, twigs, bark, leaves, and tiny scraps of cloth and silk from their mother's rag bag into a big bucket, and let it all soak for three days. Then they mash it all up into a pulp and press it into the bamboo strainers they use to make rice cakes. The result? Thin sheets, perfect to write on. Their teacher loves them, as does the emperor, who names the sheets *zhi*—paper in Chinese.

Yes, the story is fictionalized, but it's a perfect lead-in to a lesson on the history of alphabets, writing, paper, the printing press, Chinese calligraphy, and the development of libraries. You can collaborate with the art teacher to make homemade paper, and also tie this into your science unit on inventions or study of China. Pull out Ed Young's books showcasing ancient Chinese calligraphy: *Beyond the Great Mountains: A Visual Poem About China* and *Mouse Match: A Chinese Folktale*.

I loved to do a History of Books lesson with fourth graders every year. I collected pictures and objects for a show-and-tell session. I had a replica of the Dead Sea Scrolls, a sample of Egyptian hieroglyphics written on papyrus, a photograph of the Rosetta Stone, a postcard of a jewel-encrusted cover of an illuminated manuscript and a color poster of one decorated page, a reproduction of an engraving of Gutenberg's printing press, a photograph of the stern-faced Melvil Dewey, a biography of Ben Franklin, a writing slate and stylus, and a quill pen. As I told the story, starting with cuneiform writing and working up to computers, I would pass around each corresponding item for all to examine. An old-fashioned typewriter, a codex or accordion book (Ed Young's *Mouse Match* is perfect for this), a catalog card, a copy of a Dick and Jane book, and an old floppy disk would be good additions. Children take libraries for granted; this lesson lets them see how far we have come, and maybe think about what could be coming in the future. You might want to construct a timeline with them to give them a feel for the time span.

CARE OF BOOKS LESSON

Herb deals with a series of book problems in *Who's Afraid of the Big Bad Book?* by Lauren Child. Though Herb isn't all that great a reader, he loves storybooks because he can tell so much from the pictures. He's not what you'd call a neat reader either; he eats when he reads, leaving "bits of banana, cookie, and the odd pea squashed between the pages." On the night his friend Ezzie sleeps over, Herb, looking at a book of fairy tales, falls asleep with his head on the page. He awakens to a high-pitched shrieking noise: "What are you doing here? How DARE you be on this page? I am the star and I say you are not allowed in this story!" It's Goldilocks. And it dawns on Herb that he has somehow fallen into the book.

He runs through the forest and coming to a big door, he opens it. Inside there seems to be a party going on. He can't help noticing that the queen has a mustache drawn on her in ballpoint pen! Herb recalls that it's all his fault. Last year, when he was much, much younger, and going through a scribbling stage, he drew in and cut out pictures from many of his own books. He drew telephones on all the pages, and he tore out pages and put them back upside down, and now some of the characters in the book are upside down, and they're jolly cross with our friend Herb.

"Come back here, you little horror," screeches Cinderella's wickedly mean stepmother. Oh yes, Herb also cut Prince Charming out of the book to make a birthday card for his mother. Herb appeals to Cinderella's fairy godmother to help him get out of the book. She's not exactly sympathetic: "What do you expect when you go about scribbling and snippering and generally causing mayhem? This is NO WAY to treat a book, you know!"

Listeners can review each of Herb's problems along the way and come up with solutions for what he should do next. For instance, once Herb gets home, what can he do to set the book to rights? (Herb and Ezzie erase stray marks and do what they can to restore the book, though Herb does stick a brown wig on Goldilocks and a lock on the three bears' door to keep her from getting in. Serves her right for being such a meany.)

Have you been looking for a fresh and original and wildly funny way to bring up the problem of slapdash book care without feeling preachy or naggy? This one will jumpstart your yearly book care lessons, no matter how old your readers are.

Look at any well-read book, and you'll see the same thing: tiny little tears along the bottom edges of the pages. How do they get there? As children read the book, they turn the page from the bottom, which gradually weakens the paper and creates larger and larger rips. Watch your children turn the pages of their library books, and you'll realize that many of them have never been taught how to do it correctly. It's a real problem.

In kindergarten, I taught a page-turning mantra, reciting, with expression, "Squeeze, Slide, Push," as the children gently squeezed the corner of the page, slid their hands under the whole page, and carefully pushed it over. It works.

Describe what happens to a book's pages when readers are not careful, and show them some egregious examples of page damage. Express your horror, shock, dismay, and outrage that such a friend to all has been so cruelly treated. Be melodramatic and over the top. Hug the book to your chest. Rock it like a baby. Clutch your heart, thrust your arms out to the heavens, and moan, "Why? Why? Why did this have to happen? And to my favorite book! My poor, poor, pitiful book. What did this book *do* to deserve such a fate? Ripped and torn, bent and broken. Alas and alack!" Guilt works well, too.

On my *Hi Ho, Librario* CD (available from <www.rockhillworks.com>), I recorded my care-of-books song, "Alas and Alack: The Wounded Book's Lament," which has a good chorus children can join in on.

Have children been turning the book over face down or dog-earing the corners instead of using a bookmark? Vocalize your horror at that kind of treatment and you'll hear from parents who say, "My son yelled at me when I put my book down. He ran and got me a bookmark!"

Why is this important? Children who learn from adults to respect books and handle them with deference will be more likely to value reading and will pass that love on to their own children. (For more ideas, see the section called "Book Care Lessons" on page 78 of *More Books Kids Will Sit Still For*.)

SEEDING THE TABLES

Want a quick and dirty way to connect kids with more books? Seed your tables. Toronto high school librarian Lisa J. Dempster wrote about this fiendishly simple idea on LM_NET, the school librarians' listserv. She says, "Just thought I'd share a fun and subtle literacy initiative I've been enjoying lately in our library in between classes. We all know about weeding, but I've taken to seeding.

"I strategically seed the empty study tables with deliberately interesting books . . . It puts these books right in front of students, as would a visual display, or a 'face-out' display shelf, but with even more direct access and visibility: they are just sitting there on their table itching to be opened . . . It is so much fun watching students dive into books they otherwise wouldn't pick up (poetry, dance, sports, history timelines, classics, medieval art, etc.) . . . I watch the item "travel" across the room, and find it on another table at the end of the day. Most days I just use large visually appealing reference books. Other days, I'll pick a topic (poetry books, mysteries, magazines, etc.). Just leave them out all day to browse. It does add to the daily prepping, displaying and shelving factor, but is so rewarding and fun, it is positively gleeful mischief, a highlight of my day."

Now, apply that concept to the elementary and middle school. Tell the students that every day, you're going to pick a subject or theme you think they'll love and put books on that subject on display on the library tables. They are free to check out anything interesting they see. One day, do poetry; another day, do volcanoes or Gingerbread Man variants or riddles or cat stories or mysteries. See if they can tell you what the theme is for the day. Watch those books fly out of the library.

PUT YOURSELF IN ANOTHER READER'S SHOES

Pair up your students and tell them that today they are going to become mind readers. For five minutes, they are to converse together about the kinds of books they love to read and their interests in general. Then have them go to the shelves and pick a book they think their partners would love, taking into account what their partners have just revealed about their reading tastes and interests. Back at their seats, books in hand, they are to describe to each other the books they selected and why they think their partners would love them. Children can then opt to read the books hand-selected and recommended to them, or not.

Another week, ask children to model and share personal favorites with the rest of the group. For instance, do a booktalk on Books That Make You Fall Off Your Bed Laughing and read aloud uproarious examples. Then say, "For next week, I want you to find and read a book that makes you laugh out loud. Pick a passage of no more than half a page to read aloud to all of us—something that will show us all just how funny the book is." On Laughing Day, push all the desks together or make a huge circle of chairs to make a Reader's Roundtable so you can all see each other, King Arthur style, and connect via humor.

Or you could ask them to pick a favorite science or history book, or folktale, or biography, or poetry book. The object is to get students talking books with each other, to give everyone a chance to share, and get them enthused about reading each other's choices. If your group is large, break them into teams for the sharing part.

COUNTING THE MINUTES

Patricia Jeanig, library teacher at Squannacook Elementary School in Townsend, Massachusetts, came up with a simple but galactic idea to implement her school-wide reading incentive program, called "Reach for the Stars." She challenged students to keep track, not of the number of books they read or the pages they read, but of the minutes they spent reading. They noted their times on log sheets that were collected and tallied every Friday for four weeks. The school goal was set for 240,000 minutes. (Note that the Moon is 240,000 miles from the Earth. If they traveled a mile for each minute read, they could read their way to the Moon.)

She writes, "Upon reaching our goal, the PTO purchased a star through <starregistry.com> which was named after our school. The student who read the most was Principal for a Day. The class who read the most was treated to a pizza party. Results were posted each week on a bar graph in the cafeteria. It was an easy contest and a lot of fun. By keeping track of time rather than the number of pages or books read, it created a fair playing field for all students regardless of reading ability.

"The log sheets we used were very simple in design. They were collected each Friday and parent volunteers came in to do the tallying so that logs could be returned to students before the end of the day. Every reading incentive program I have been involved in we kept track of "time spent reading." It truly is a great equalizer. I've witnessed first hand as a public librarian what happens when kids start counting number of books read—they 'dummy down.' Not what we want!

"Here's an interesting side note regarding our program. Initially some parents as well as teachers were concerned that it would not be a fair contest because older kids can read longer. We are a grades 3–5 school—a third grader won! A fifth-grade class was well into first place and they slacked off a bit the final week only to be beat by a third-grade class.

"We chose a star in Ursa Major so even though it can't actually be seen, kids can find its approximate location in the sky."

MY KINDERGARTEN

When Angus Killick, director of marketing at Hyperion, asked me to do a teacher's guide and CD to go with Rosemary Wells's *My Kindergarten*—a glorious 96-page picture book that takes children through the nine months of the kindergarten year, subject by subject, with Miss Cribbage and her animal students on Cranberry Island in the state of Maine—I dropped everything and started writing songs and lesson plans. I wrote a 24-page teacher's guide. I set seven of Rosemary's poems to music, wrote eight new songs of my own, and rounded out the mix with seven traditional songs and stories.

My cousin Pete Fand is a musician who has his own little recording studio. Together, Pete and I spent a week in the studio. His then one-year-old twin boys,

one strapped to his back, kept us company, as did then 3-year-old Minka, who sang on some of the songs, along with her cousin Jonah Stillman and her friend Lena Zinner. Pete played bass, percussion, harmonica, and lots of other instruments. I played guitar. Cousin Jim Incollingo played electric guitar on several songs. It was a blast.

This is a book and CD you can use across the kindergarten curriculum. On the CD, there's "Geography Feast," which teaches directions. "This Old Man" can be used for counting and "A Song of Seasons" describes the yearly cycle. Play "Who Took the Cookies from the Cookie Jar" for recalling names, "In a Dark Dark Wood" for Halloween, "Dona Nobis Pacem" for December holidays, "Be My Valentine" for February, "Animal, Vegetable, Mineral" for science, "Punctuation" for using question marks and exclamation points, "Measurement" for math, and "Wash 'Em Up" for keeping the universe clean.

The whole CD can be downloaded without charge—save it to your computer or burn a CD—from the Hyperion Web site. Go to <www.hyperionbooksforchildren.com/board/displayBook. asp?id=1296> and click on "Teacher's Guide" or "Download songs from the My Kindergarten CD!" Sure, Hyperion would love you to buy the Rosemary Wells book too, and this is the kindergarten teacher present of the decade. I can't imagine any preschool, kindergarten, or first-grade class without a copy. But you can use the teacher's guide and the CD independently if you like. The book got a rave review in the *New York Times,* and starred reviews everywhere. And I got to pretend I was a rock star. Not a bad deal.

BOOK ACTIVITIES AND QUIZZES

In the book activities and quizzes that follow, the object is to expose readers to many titles in a short amount of time. These games are all lead-ins to simple booktalks in which you hold up the corresponding book after children have had a chance to guess the answer, and then describe the plot in one or two short sentences. Hand the book out to the child who says, "I want that one!" Your group can then collect new memorable lines, make up book award categories, write new "In What Book" questions and come up with five fiction clues to try out on each other.

When selecting books to use for these activities, pick some books the children know or have seen before and some that are new to them or books you think they'd love. It doesn't matter if they know any of the answers or not; it's the process of guessing, looking at the cover, and hearing a few enticing sentences about the book that is important. All of these activities work with children of all ages, and with picture books or fiction.

Memorable Lines

Make a chart of memorable lines from books. We want readers to look at language not just as a way to convey information, but also as a source of profound and sometimes whimsical quotes they can use in their lives. If they start looking at language now, they'll feel much more at home when they are introduced to that master of language, William Shakespeare, in a few years. See how many of the fiction and picture books, authors, and characters you can identify from the quotes below. All are from books included in the annotated lists at the back of this book.

1. "Cats go meow. Dogs go arf."
2. "Here we go again."
3. "She went boneless."
4. "I dreamed I was being chased by a giant head of lettuce. WHOA! Those vegetarian nightmares are the worst. Speaking of food, here's a tongue twister: How much chow could a chow chow chew if a chow chow could chew chow?"
5. "Everybody up! They didn't come back!"
6. "No problem at all. I always enjoy having a wolf for lunch."
7. "If your teacher has to die, August isn't a bad time of year for it."
8. "A twain twavels on twain twacks."
9. "What's the big deal? It's just a bus."
10. "I disappeared on the night before my twelfth birthday, July 28, 1988."
11. "Know what I do at night while you're asleep? Eat your TRASH, that's what. See those bags? I smell BREAKFAST!"
12. "I do not want to be a teacher when I grow up."
13. "Even though I'm small and green and slimy, I can still be a good principal, can't I?"
14. "Just make a mark and see where it takes you."
15. "If people are gonna start sendin' us these letters what got letters on 'em, we better learn how to read 'em."

ANSWER KEY: Memorable Lines

TITLE AND AUTHOR	(CHARACTERS QUOTED)
1. *Bark, George* by Jules Feiffer	(George's mother)
2. *Bud, Not Buddy* by Christopher Paul Curtis	(Bud Caldwell, in the book's first line)
3. *Knuffle Bunny* by Mo Willems	(Narrator, referring to toddler Trixie, when her stuffed rabbit is missing)
4. *Martha Walks the Dog* by Meddaugh, Susan	(Martha, the talking dog)
5. *And the Dish Ran Away with the Spoon* by Janet Stevens and Susan Stevens Crummel	(The cat)
6. *Piggie Pie* by Margie Palatini	(Gritch the Witch)
7. *The Teacher's Funeral* by Richard Peck	(Russell Culver)
8. *Hooway for Wodney Wat* by Helen Lester	(Wodney Wat)
9. *Don't Let the Pigeon Drive the Bus!* by Mo Willems	(Pigeon)
10. *Kensuke's Kingdom* by Michael Morpurgo	(Michael, in the book's first line)
11. *I Stink!* by Kate McMullan	(New York City garbage truck)
12. *Lilly's Purple Plastic Purse by* Kevin Henkes	(Lilly the mouse, angry when her adored teacher, Mr. Slinger, confiscates her purse until the end of the day)
13. *The Frog Principal* by Stephanie Calmenson	(Mr. Bundy, the principal, after being turned into a frog)
14. *The Dot* by Peter H. Reynolds	(Vashti's art teacher, after Vashti tells her, "I just can't draw.")
15. *Raising Sweetness* by Diane Stanley	(The Sheriff of Possum Trot, new Pa to the eight orphans he adopted, who does not know how to read)

Personal Favorites

Not every book can win a gold medal. What are the best books of the past decade, 1995–2005? My choices are all in this book, all 1,705 of them. When showing books to children, you can, however, identify your personal favorites, which, for children, is as much incentive to check them out as any medal.

Here is a quick and dirty booktalk technique—thinking up award categories for your favorite books and announcing the winners—along with a brief plot statement. When you write up your categories, make them sparky, arresting, and intriguing, so your children will be desperate to read them. Construct a big shiny gold medal that you can hold up to the cover of each book as you announce it. (Mine would say "Freeman's Favorite.") Then show the cover and a picture or two from the book, and hand it out to eager readers. And, yes, of course students can follow up with their own categories and booktalk their favorites. That's the whole idea.

A handful of examples:

Best Story to Read While Holding a Paintbrush

Art Dog by Thacher Hurd

Art Dog is accused of stealing the famous painting Mona Woofa, but he's innocent! What's a dog to do? He's going to hop into his brushmobile and track down the real thieves, of course. As Art Dog says, "I can smell art a mile away."

Most Talented Talking Pet

Martha Walks the Dog by Susan Meddaugh

Martha, the adorable, loudmouth, nonstop-talking dog—thanks to the alphabet soup that went up to her brain instead of down to her stomach—takes on a neighborhood bully, the snarling, vicious Bad Dog Bob.

Best Arithmetic Book for Those with Severe Math Anxiety

Math Curse by Jon Scieszka

Are you good in math? "On Monday in math class, Mrs. Fibonacci says, 'You know, you can think of almost anything as a math problem.' On Tuesday I start having problems." And now everything becomes a math problem for a kid whose whole day lurches from one mathematical situation to another, including the dreaded *fractions*. My favorite math problem:

> "If mail+box=mailbox
> 1) Does lipstick−stick=lip?
> 2) Does tunafish+tunafish=fournafish?"

Most Dangerous Book for Kids Who've Gotten in Trouble Writing on the Walls

Meanwhile . . . by Jules Feiffer

Raymond writes "Meanwhile . . ." on his wall with red marker and all of a sudden he finds himself in the midst of a swordfight on a pirate ship, and forced to walk the plank. And that's just the first four pages!

Best Geography Book for Kids Who Don't Know Where They Are

The Scrambled States of America by Laurie Keller

All 50 states decide to switch places on the map to spice up their lives a little, and boy, do they have fun!

"In What Book": Children's Books About School

Here are 18 of my favorite read-alouds dealing with teachers, librarians, and the school experience. How many can you and your readers identify?

IN WHAT BOOK . . .

1. Does a substitute teacher, Miss Viola Swamp, take over for a nice, sweet teacher when her students refuse to pay attention in class?

2. Does teacher Miss Jewls push a computer out of the classroom window to show her students how gravity works?

3. Does a young mouse become so enraged when her adored teacher, Mr. Slinger, confiscates her belongings, that she declares, "I do not want to be a teacher when I grow up!" and slips a mean picture into his bookbag?

4. Does the Springfield librarian, Molly McGrew, by mistake drive her bookmobile into the zoo, and get all of the animals reading?

5. Did Gloria Houston's relative teach for 57 years in a one-room schoolhouse?

6. Are 10-year-old Fred and all the other students in the one-room schoolhouse in a remote Alaskan village astonished by their new lady teacher, who wears pants, plays opera records, and reads Robin Hood stories aloud to the class?

7. Does a book-loving lady come to the rescue of her TV-loving town after a big storm knocks out the power for two weeks, and capture the heart of biker and non-reader Bust-'em-'up Bill?

8. Does Flora, a mouse who learns to read from watching the children from a hole above the kindergarten teacher's desk, find that reading can save your life?

9. Does Lucas Cott's teacher send a note home telling his parents he is obstreperous, which he thinks means he's going to become a baby doctor?

10. Does Mrs. Pigeon's new student, just moved to town from China, tell her second-grade class five outrageous stories about herself, one each day for a week, and claim they are all absolutely true?

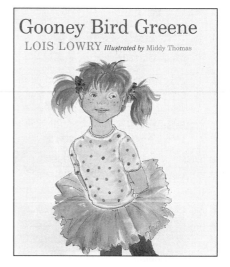

Gooney Bird Greene
LOIS LOWRY *Illustrated by* Middy Thomas

11. Does the school's headmistress, the wicked Miss Trunchbull, make life tough for a little girl with extraordinary powers of telekinesis?

12. Does Trisha suffer in reading class until fifth grade, when she encounters a patient and dedicated teacher who finally teaches her to read?

13. Are the three ill-fated Baudelaire orphans sent to Prufrock Prep, a dreadful boarding school whose motto is "Memento Mori" (Latin for "remember you will die")?

14. Does a teacher, preparing to retire after 50 years at Knickerbocker Elementary in the town of Up Yonder, ask her students to help her clear out all of her accumulated plants, books, papers, and even a full-grown Ruby Red apple tree so that sweet, young Miss Bumblesprout can take over in the fall?

15. Is a born troublemaker and orphan sent to the Hebrew Home for Boys in Harlem, from which he sneaks outside after dark and is befriended by Solly, an elderly fortune teller?

16. Does a sixth grader lose her notebook—Her Notebook that Contained Everything She Needed to Live—on the same day that her flaky grandmother Irene comes to spend Senior Citizen's Day at Our Lady of Mercy Middle School?

17. Is a little sister determined to go along with her five brothers to attend a school for former slaves run by Quakers, even though the children have to walk seven miles to get there?

18. Does Nick Allen defy his fifth-grade teacher, Mrs. Granger, who reveres the dictionary, when he insists on using the word he invented as a synonym for "pen."

ANSWER KEY: "In What Book": Children's Books About School

1. *Miss Nelson Is Missing* by Harry Allard
2. *Wayside School Is Falling Down* by Louis Sachar
3. *Lilly's Purple Plastic Purse* by Kevin Henkes
4. *Wild About Books* by Judy Sierra
5. *My Great Aunt Arizona* by Gloria Houston
6. *The Year of Miss Agnes* by Kirkpatrick Hill
7. *Library Lil* by Suzanne Williams
8. *The School Mouse* by Dick King-Smith
9. *Class Clown* by Johanna Hurwitz
10. *Gooney Bird Greene* by Lois Lowry
11. *Matilda* by Roald Dahl
12. *Thank You, Mr. Falker* by Patricia Polacco
13. *The Austere Academy* by Lemony Snicket
14. *Mrs. McBloom, Clean Up Your Classroom* by Kelly DiPucchio
15. *Dave at Night* by Gail Carson Levine
16. *Molly McGinty Has a Really Good Day* by Gary Paulsen
17. *Virgie Goes to School with Us Boys* by Elizabeth Fitzgerald Howard
18. *Frindle* by Andrew Clements

Have your students write their own questions, using the same format, about books they have read and loved, for others to guess and then read. Or get fancy and use it to introduce them to the In What Book Game I described on page 110 of *Books Kids Will Sit Still For*. For this game, children make up two or three of their own questions for fiction books they have read and loved, and then compete against each other or another class to identify the answers.

When children write "In What Book" questions, they either summarize the plot, describe a character, or pick an episode or incident to describe, without giving away any key words of the title. It wouldn't do to say, "In what book was a dog so smart he could talk." Rather, they might say, "In what book does fifth grader Amy Prochenko help to hide an ultra-intelligent talking pet, F-32, who has just escaped from the college research department lab where scientists plan to dissect his brain." (*Smart Dog* by Vivian Vande Velde)

Now try an exercise in narrowing down a book's plot elements into five key words or phrases. Be sure you don't give away the title in any of the clues. This is another easy way to booktalk. Whether or not children can identify the book, follow up each one with a short description of the book that incorporates and weaves in all five clues. You can, of course, use picture books in lieu of fiction titles.

Five Fiction Clues: What Book Is This?

The five key words or phrases are your clues; identify each of the fiction books described below.

A. TITLE & AUTHOR

1. Orphan
2. Pencil
3. Depression
4. Suitcase
5. Rocks

B. TITLE & AUTHOR

1. Castle
2. Soup
3. Rat
4. Miggery Sow
5. Red thread

C. TITLE & AUTHOR

1. Flat
2. Tea leaves
3. Bricks
4. Buttons
5. Snow globe

D. TITLE & AUTHOR

1. Aurora
2. Oxford
3. Armored bear
4. Dust
5. Daemon

E. TITLE & AUTHOR

1. Sword
2. Metropolitan Museum of Art
3. Half-blood
4. Empire State Building
5. Satyr

F. TITLE & AUTHOR

1. The Builders
2. 241
3. Messenger
4. Generator
5. Blackouts

ANSWER KEY: Five Fiction Clues: What Book Is This?

A. *The Tale of Despereaux* by Kate DiCamillo

B. *Bud, Not Buddy* by Christopher Paul Curtis

C. *Coraline* by Neil Gaiman

D. *The Golden Compass* by Philip Pullman

E. *The Lightning Thief* by Rick Riordan

F. *The City of Ember* by Jeanne DuPrau

A LIST OF MEMORABLE AUTHORS AND ILLUSTRATORS

In *Books Kids Will Sit Still For*, I drew up a list of authors and illustrators who had made a lasting contribution to children's literature and had produced a significant body of work. I broke the lists into suggested grade levels to assist teachers and librarians looking to institute monthly or weekly author/illustrator studies, either for reading aloud or having students familiarize themselves with an author's books.

I update this list every year and, while it is in no way comprehensive, I hope you can use it as a way to familiarize yourself with some of the best in the children's literature field and to introduce new and worthy writers and artists to your media-dazed students. For additional suggestions, be sure to look at the lists one grade level above and below your students', depending on their reading and maturity levels.

(Author = A, Illustrator = I, Author/Illustrator = A/I)

Preschool, Kindergarten, and Grade 1

Aliki (A/I)
Tedd Arnold (A/I)
Jose Aruego (A/I)
Frank Asch (A/I)
Jim Aylesworth (A)
Molly Bang (A/I)
Byron Barton (A/I)
Robert J. Blake (A/I)
Harry Bliss (I)
Barbara Bottner (A)
Jan Brett (A/I)
Norman Bridwell (A/I)
Marc Brown (A/I)
Anthony Browne (A/I)
Denise Brunkus (I)
Janell Cannon (A/I)
Nancy Carlson (A/I)
Eric Carle (A/I)
Judith Caseley (A/I)
Denys Cazet (A/I)
Victoria Chess (I)
Lauren Child (A/I)
Eileen Christelow (A/I)
Henry Cole (I)
Joy Cowley (A)
Judy Cox (A)
Donald Crews (A/I)
Doreen Cronin (A)
Susan Stevens Crummel (A)
Katie Davis (A/I)
Demi (A/I)
Ariane Dewey (A/I)
Kelly DiPuccio (A)
Arthur Dorros (A/I)
Olivier Dunrea (A/I)
Pamela Duncan Edwards (A)

Tim Egan (A/I)
Richard Egielski (A/I)
Lois Ehlert (A/I)
Ian Falconer (A/I)
Cathryn Falwell (A/I)
Jules Feiffer (A/I)
Denise Fleming (A/I)
Mem Fox (A)
Marla Frazee (A/I)
Don Freeman (A/I)
Saxton Freymann (A/I)
Dick Gackenbach (A/I)
Bob Graham (A/I)
Kevin Henkes (A/I)
Amy Hest (A)
Mary Ann Hoberman (A)
Syd Hoff (A/I)
Arthur Howard (A/I)
Shirley Hughes (A/I)
Pat Hutchins (A/I)
Satomi Ichikawa (A/I)
Simon James (A/I)
Steve Jenkins (A/I)
Dolores Johnson (A)
Ann Jonas (A/I)
G. Brian Karas (A/I)
Keiko Kasza (A/I)
Ezra Jack Keats (A/I)
Holly Keller (A/I)
Eric A. Kimmel (A)
Kathryn Lasky (A)
Loreen Leedy (A/I)
Helen Lester (A)
Betsy Lewin (A/I)
Leo Lionni (A/I)
Jean Little (A)
Anita Lobel (A/I)

Arnold Lobel (A/I)
Jonathan London (A)
Barbara McClintock (A/I)
Gerald McDermott (A/I)
Suse MacDonald (A/I)
Patricia C. McKissack (A)
Bruce McMillan (A/I)
Kate McMullan (A) and James McMullan (I)
David McPhail (A/I)
James Marshall (A/I)
Bill Martin, Jr. (A)
Petra Mathers (A/I)
Mercer Mayer (A/I)
Holly Meade (A/I)
Claudia Mills (A)
Barry Moser (A/I)
Bernard Most (A/I)
Mother Goose (A)
Robert Munsch (A)
Lynn Munsinger (I)
Laura Numeroff (A)
Helen Oxenbury (A/I)
Margie Palatini (A)
Dav Pilkey (A/I)
Daniel Pinkwater (A/I)
Beatrix Potter (A/I)
Giselle Potter (A/I)
Marjorie Priceman (A/I)
Robin Pulver (A)
Chris Raschka (A/I)
Peggy Rathmann (A/I)
Eric Rohmann (A/I)
Barry Root (I)

Marisabina Russo (A/I)
Cynthia Rylant (A)
Carole Lexa Schaefer (A/I)
Amy Schwartz (A/I)
Laura Vaccaro Seeger (A/I)
Maurice Sendak (A/I)
David Shannon (A/I)
George Shannon (A)
Nancy Shaw (A/I)
Erica Silverman (A)
Marc Simont (A/I)
Peter Sis (A/I)
Joseph Slate (A)
Gary Soto (A)
Alexander Stadler (A/I)
Janet Stevens (A/I)
Simms Taback (A/I)
Jean Van Leeuwen (A)
Martin Waddell (A/I)
Eileen Stoll Walsh (A/I)
Nicki Weiss (A/I)
Rosemary Wells (A/I)
Nadine Bernard Westcott (A/I)
David Wiesner (A/I)
Mo Willems (A/I)
Vera B. Williams (A/I)
Kay Winters (A)
Audrey Wood (A/I) and Don Wood (A/I)
Jane Yolen (A)
Ed Young (A/I)
Harriet Ziefert (A)

Grade 2

Verna Aardema (A)
Aesop (A)
Mary Jane Auch (A/I)
Mary Azarian (I)
Durga Bernhard (I) and Emery Bernhard (A)
Caralyn Buehner (A) and Mark Buehner (I)
Eve Bunting (A)
Stephanie Calmenson (A)
Peter Catalanotto (A/I)
David Catron (I)
Lynne Cherry (A/I)
R. Gregory Christie (I)
Brock Cole (A/I)
Joanna Cole (A)
Barbara Cooney (A/I)
Pat Cummings (A/I)
Bruce Degen (I)
Demi (A/I)
Tomie dePaola (A/I)
David Diaz (I)
Henrik Drescher (A/I)
Tim Egan (A/I)

Susan Middleton Elya (A)
Lisa Campbell Ernst (A/I)
Candace Fleming (A)
Debra Frasier (A/I)
Stephen Gammell (I)
Gail Gibbons (A/I)
Patricia Reilly Giff (A)
Kevin Hawkes (I)
Ruth Heller (A/I)
James Howe (A)
Tony Johnston (A)
William Joyce (A/I)
Steven Kellogg (A/I)
Loreen Leedy (A/I)
Elizabeth Levy (A)
Ted Lewin (A/I)
E. B. Lewis (I)
Thomas Locker (A/I)
Emily Arnold McCully (A/I)
Betsy Maestro (A/I)
Giulio Maestro (A/I)
Margaret Mahy (A)

Rafe Martin (A)
Susan Meddaugh (A/I)
Eve Merriam (A)
Tololwa M. Mollel (A)
Lilian Moore (A)
Pat Mora (A)
Kevin O'Malley (A/I)
Jon J. Muth (A/I)
Kadir Nelson (I)
Jerdine Nolan (A)
Mary Pope Osborne (A)
Peggy Parish (A)
Barbara Park (A)
Bill Peet (A/I)
Brian Pinkney (I)
Jerry Pinkney (I)
Patricia Polacco (A/I)
Gloria Rand (A) and Ted Rand (I)
Mary Rayner (A/I)
Joanne Ryder (A)
Robert Sabuda (A/I)
Allen Say (A/I)
April Pulley Sayre (A)

S. D. Schindler (I)
Jon Scieszka (A)
Dr. Seuss (A/I)
Marjorie Weinman Sharmat (A)
Carol Diggory Shields (A)
Judy Sierra (A)
David Small (I)
Lane Smith (A/I)
Meilo So (A/I)
Chris K. Soenpiet (I)
Gennady Spirin (I)
William Steig (A/I)
James Stevenson (A/I)
Sarah Stewart (A)
Marc Teague (A/I)
Chris Van Allsburg (A/I)
Judith Viorst (A)
Bernard Waber (A/I)
James Warhola (A/I)
Jeanette Winter (A/I)
Jane Yolen (A)
Paul O. Zelinsky (A/I)

Grades 3 and 4 (all authors unless noted)

David A. Adler
Jon Agee
Hans Christian Andersen
Francisco Alarcón
Caroline Arnold
Lynne Barasch
Barbara Bash (A/I)
Michael Bond
Franklyn M. Branley
Don Brown (A/I)
Joseph Bruchac
Robert Burleigh
Ann Cameron
Beverly Cleary
Brian P. Cleary
Brian Collier (I)
Raúl Colón (I)
Ellen Conford
Roald Dahl
Paula Danziger
Leo and Diane Dillon (A/I)
Betsy Duffey
Barbara Juster Esbensen

Leonard Everett Fisher (A/I)
Douglas Florian (A/I)
Jean Fritz
Kristine O'Connell George
Mordicai Gerstein (A/I)
Paul Goble (A/I)
Mary Grandpré (I)
Stephanie Greene
Nikki Grimes
Jacob and Wilhelm Grimm
Brenda Guiberson (A/I)
Cheryl Harness (A/I)
Kevin Hawkes (I)
Lee Bennett Hopkins
Deborah Hopkinson
James Howe
Johanna Hurwitz
Trina Schart Hyman (I)
Bagram Ibatoulline (I)
Eva Ibbotson
Maira Kalman (A/I)
X. J. Kennedy

Eric A. Kimmel
Dick King-Smith
Rudyard Kipling
Suzy Kline
Kathryn Lasky
Patricia Lauber
Julius Lester
J. Patrick Lewis
Myra Cohn Livingston
David Macaulay (A/I)
Megan McDonald
Ann M. Martin
Jacqueline Briggs Martin
Marianna Mayer (A/I)
A. A. Milne
Marissa Moss (A/I)
Christopher Myers (A/I)
Barbara Park
Robert Newton Peck
P. J. Petersen
Andrea Davis Pinkney
Brian Pinkney (I)
Daniel Pinkwater (A/I)
Jack Prelutsky

James Ransome (I)
Peter H. Reynolds (A/I)
Pam Muñoz Ryan
Louis Sachar
Judith St. George
Robert D. San Souci
Alvin Schwartz
Jon Scieszka
Brian Selznick (A/I)
Aaron Shepard
Diane Siebert
Shel Silverstein
Seymour Simon
Peter Sis (A/I)
Robert Kimmel Smith
Donald J. Sobol
Diane Stanley (A/I)
Hudson Talbott (A/I)
Marvin Terban
Jean Van Leeuwen
E. B. White
Laura Ingalls Wilder
David Wisniewski (A/I)
Elvira Woodruff

Grades 5 and 6 (all authors unless noted)

Arnold Adoff
Lloyd Alexander
David Almond
Jennifer Armstrong
Avi
Natalie Babbitt
Lynne Reid Banks
Susan Campbell
  Bartoletti
Joan Bauer
Marion Dane Bauer
Quentin Blake (I)
Rhoda Blumberg
Bill Brittain
Joseph Bruchac
Eve Bunting
Betsy Byars
Gennifer Choldenko
Andrew Clements
Suzanne Collins
Jane Leslie Conley
Bruce Coville

Sharon Creech
Lynn Curlee (A/I)
Christopher Paul
  Curtis
Karen Cushman
Cynthia deFelice
Kate DiCamillo
Nancy Farmer
John D. Fitzgerald
Paul Fleischman
Sid Fleischman
Russell Freedman
Jack Gantos
Jean Craighead George
Patricia Reilly Giff
Dan Gutman
Mary Downing Hahn
Virginia Hamilton
Kevin Henkes
Karen Hesse
Carl Hiaasen
Michael Hoeye

Paul B. Janeczko
Diana Wynne Jones
E. L. Konigsburg
Gordon Korman
Kathleen Krull
Janet Taylor Lisle
Lois Lowry
Geraldine
  McCaughrean
Michael Morpurgo
Jim Murphy
Donna Jo Napoli
Phyllis Reynolds
  Naylor
Kenneth Oppel
Linda Sue Park
Katherine Paterson
Gary Paulsen
Richard Peck
Philip Pullman
Rick Riordan
J. K. Rowling

Pam Muñoz Ryan
Cynthia Rylant
Louis Sachar
Marilyn Sachs
Carol Diggory Shields
Marilyn Singer
Jan Slepian
Lemony Snicket
Zilpha Keatley Snyder
Jerry Spinelli
Mary Stolz
Mildred Taylor
Wendelin Van Draanen
Vivian Vande Velde
Cynthia Voigt
Gloria Whelan
Jacqueline Woodson
Valerie Worth
Betty Ren Wright
Laurence Yep
Jane Yolen

FREEMAN'S FAVORITES

Every year, as I finish compiling my list of best books, I apply my own 50-item selection criteria (see the "50 Ways to Recognize a Read-Aloud" chapter in *More Books Kids Will Sit Still For*, page 7) and select my very favorite picture book, fiction, and nonfiction read-alouds for that year. Looking to single out the books that I found most successful, provocative, fresh, child-friendly, beloved, and pleasurable to read aloud to children, I deem it an instructive and amusing exercise.

Coming up with just one book per category can be agonizing (and sometimes impossible—see my fiction choices for 1998). You can tell a lot about a person by the books he or she loves. Your own list would most likely be vastly different; I urge you to try it for yourself, and then ask your students to come up with lists of their favorite books. (Check page 23 of *More Books Kids Will Sit Still For* for the "Freeman's Favorites" from 1984 to 1994.)

My choices from the past decade are as follows:

1995

Picture Book	*Officer Buckle and Gloria* by Peggy Rathmann (Putnam) Gr. K–2
Fiction	*Poppy* by Avi (Orchard) Gr. 4–7
Nonfiction	*Biggest, Strongest, Fastest* by Steve Jenkins (Ticknor & Fields) Gr. PreK–3

1996

Picture Book	*Lilly's Purple Plastic Purse* by Kevin Henkes (Greenwillow) Gr. PreK–2
Fiction	*The Music of Dolphins* by Karen Hesse (Scholastic) Gr. 4–8
Nonfiction	*Wilma Unlimited: How Wilma Rudolph Became the World's Fastest Woman* by Kathleen Krull, illus. by David Diaz (Harcourt) Gr. 2–5

1997

Picture Book	*Rapunzel* by Paul O. Zelinsky (Dutton) Gr. 2–6
Fiction	*Ella Enchanted* by Gail Carson Levine (HarperCollins) Gr. 4–8
Nonfiction	*A Drop of Water* by Walter Wick (Scholastic) Gr. 3–6

1998

Picture Book   *I Lost My Bear* by Jules Feiffer (Morrow) Gr. PreK–5

Fiction   *Harry Potter and the Sorcerer's Stone* by J. K. Rowling (Scholastic) Gr. 4–7

   Holes by Louis Sachar (Farrar) Gr. 5–8

Nonfiction   *Snowflake Bentley* by Jacqueline Briggs Martin, illus. by Mary Azarian (Houghton) Gr. 1–4

1999

Picture Book   *Joseph Had a Little Overcoat* by Simms Taback (Viking) Gr. PreK–1

Fiction   *Bud, Not Buddy* by Christopher Paul Curtis (Delacorte) Gr. 4–7

Nonfiction   *William Shakespeare and the Globe* by Aliki (HarperCollins) Gr. 1–6

2000

Picture Book   *Olivia* by Ian Falconer (Simon & Schuster) All Ages

Fiction   *A Year Down Yonder* by Richard Peck (Dial) Gr. 5–8

Nonfiction   *So You Want to Be President?* by Judith St. George, illus. by David Small (Philomel) Gr. 2–Adult

2001

Picture Book   *And the Dish Ran Away with the Spoon* by Janet Stevens and Susan Stevens Crummel (Harcourt) Gr. PreK–1

Fiction   *Goose Chase* by Patrice Kindl (Houghton Mifflin) Gr. 5–8

Nonfiction   *The Dinosaurs of Waterhouse Hawkins* by Barbara Kerley, illus. by Brian Selznick (Scholastic) Gr. 2–6

2002

Picture Book   *I Stink* by Kate McMullan (HarperCollins) Gr. PreK–1

Fiction   *Time Stops for No Mouse* by Michael Hoeye (Putnam) Gr. 4–8

Nonfiction   *Fireboat: The Heroic Adventures of the John J. Harvey* by Maira Kalman (Putnam) Gr. 1–12

2003

Picture Book   *Diary of a Worm* by Doreen Cronin, illus. by Betsy Lewin (HarperCollins) Gr. K–3

Fiction   *The Tale of Despereaux* by Kate DiCamillo, illus. by Timothy Basil Ering (Candlewick) Gr. 4–8

Nonfiction   *The Man Who Walked Between the Towers* by Mordicai Gerstein (Roaring Brook) Gr. K–12

2004

Picture Book   *Knuffle Bunny* by Mo Willems (Hyperion) Gr. PreK–1

Fiction   *Al Capone Does My Shirts* by Gennifer Choldenko (Putnam) Gr. 5–8

Nonfiction   *Actual Size* by Steve Jenkins (Houghton Mifflin) Gr. PreK–6

As of this writing, in the summer of 2005, I have not finished reading all of the 2005 books or testing them out on children. My favorites so far, though, at least of the 2005 titles included in this book, are as follows:

2005

Picture Book   *Sunny Boy! The Life and Times of a Tortoise* by Candace Fleming, illus. by Anne Wilsdorf (Farrar) Gr. 1–4

Fiction   *The Lightning Thief* by Rick Riordan (Miramax/Hyperion) Gr. 5–8

Nonfiction   *A Kick in the Head: An Everyday Guide to Poetic Forms* by Paul B. Janeczko, illus. by Chris Raschka (Candlewick) Gr. 5–8

Best of the Decade

If I had to pick my favorite picture book of the decade, it would have to be Peggy Rathmann's hilarious and life-affirming Caldecott winner, *Officer Buckle and Gloria*, which makes you think about safety tips, dogs, and police officers in a whole new way. (Second-grade students at Van Holten School loved coming up with new safety tips for us all to follow, including "Never tie two shoelaces together and walk" and "Never ride a bike with your eyes closed.")

For fiction, my top pick is still *Harry Potter and the Sorcerer's Stone*, the first in the series that started a reading revolution. For nonfiction, *The Man Who Walked Between the Towers* is such a poignant look at a simpler time; a healing book that lets us look beyond September 11, 2001, and dream again.

"Never ride a bike with your eyes closed." Safety tip inspired by Peggy Rathmann's *Officer Buckle and Gloria*, by a Grade 2 student at Van Holten School, Bridgewater, NJ (Loretta Ark's class, 1995).

READING AND WRITING IDEAS IN LANGUAGE ARTS

For discussing and analyzing literature and assessing and developing children's reading and writing skills, many schools are now using the 6+1 Trait Writing Model developed by the Northwest Regional Educational Laboratory <www.nwrel.org/assessment/department.php?d=1>. The seven components are:

Ideas and Content
   (which includes selecting, narrowing, and developing a topic, and adding details)
Word Choice
Conventions
   (which includes punctuation, grammar, spelling, capitalization, and paragraph structure)
Voice
Sentence Fluency
Organization
Presentation

In addition, we teachers and librarians look for good books that present a range of fiction and nonfiction genres (including realistic, fantasy, historical, hysterical, mystery, and sci fi), elements of fiction (including character, setting, plot, point of view, and theme), and styles of writing (including descriptive, dialogue, experiential, evaluative, expository, imaginative, narrative, persuasive, and technical).

We're also looking to explore all aspects of comprehension to foster higher-level thinking skills (including activating schema, comparing and contrasting, describing, determining importance, drawing conclusions, identifying the main idea and supporting details, making inferences, identifying a problem and its solution, predicting outcomes, questioning, self-monitoring, sequencing, summarizing, understanding cause and effect, using prior knowledge, and visualizing). We also worry about phonemic awareness and phonics with the younger grades and about fluency for all.

If you're involved in teaching reading using Balanced Literacy, then you're also thinking about: reading aloud, shared reading, guided reading, sustained silent reading and independent reading, book club and literature circle discussions, booktalks, and the six levels of Bloom's Taxonomy (knowledge, comprehension, application, analysis, synthesis, and evaluation), and word work (phonics, spelling, grammar, and vocabulary). Modeled, shared, interactive, guided, and independent writing also keep you hopping.

Whew. Who knew there were so many things to consider every time you select a book to read aloud or use with children? No wonder it's so challenging to teach children to read. No wonder we're so exhausted all the time.

I rummaged through some of the many reading and writing projects I've used with children over the past decade, and offer here a tip-of-the-iceberg sampling of some of the most interesting, provocative, useful, stimulating, or just plain fun ideas. You'll find more information about all of the books mentioned in the second section of this book, the Annotated Read-Aloud Lists, with hundreds of additional suggestions for using literature across the curriculum.

Word Choice

From the letters of the alphabet on up to Shakespeare, we are constantly on the lookout for ways to use the English language with our children so they will understand how stretching and satisfying it is to fiddle with words.

In *No More Nasty* by Amy MacDonald, Simon's new fifth-grade teacher is his 74-year-old Great-Aunt Matilda, whose daily badinage incorporates such prodigious words as *jackanape, pecksniffian,* and *quisling.* Give your students a matching quiz of words and their definitions (which you'll find conveniently listed at the back of MacDonald's book) before and after you read the book to see how many new words they've acquired from Aunt Mattie. Then set them loose in their dictionaries to locate other interesting words to use in a sentence, defining them in context. After they read their sentences aloud, listeners can try to define the words, and then look them up in the dictionary for confirmation.

Frindle by Andrew Clements, about Nick Allen who makes up a new word, a synonym for *pen,* will encourage children to invent their own new words.

The Word Eater by Mary Amato, about Lerner Chanse's pet worm, Fip, who can eat a word right off the printed page, is grand for talking about words and their meanings, but also for examining cause and effect. When Fip eats the words "Mack's Thumbtacks," that brand disappears from the world for good. Ask your children to consider what word they would make disappear, and what would happen globally if they did?

In Jerry Spinelli's *Loser,* the title character, Donald Zinkoff, falls over laughing every time he hears a funny word. When his teacher uses the word "jabip," he collapses to the floor, alarming her until she realizes he's having a fit of hysterical laughter. Ask your wordsmiths what words make them laugh. Compile a class list. Then have each child write an essay about one funny word, explaining its choice or a personal connection or related story about the word.

Mondegreens, Malaprops, and Mistakes with Words

Sometimes we make mistakes with words. Look at Sage in *Miss Alaineus: A Vocabulary Disaster* by Debra Frasier. Poor Sage. She prides herself on being able to define any word—"Wise girl with words," her father calls her. When she's home sick one day, she calls a classmate to get the week's vocabulary list over the phone. Her teacher, Mrs. Page, gives out a list of 15 curriculum-related words each week. Kids have to define them, learn to spell them, and use them in a sentence.

Every Friday, there's a Vocabulary Bee. Sage *thinks* she already knows the last word on the list: Miss Alaineus. She's heard that word lots of times. Her mom has a Miss Alaineus drawer in the kitchen. She used to wonder who Miss Alaineus was, but when she went with her mom to the store, her mom said, "You get the bread and I'll get Miss Alaineus things. Meet me at the register." She showed up with a green spaghetti box, with a picture of a lady whose hair looks like the spaghetti strands on the box. There she was: Miss Alaineus.

At the Vocabulary Bee, Sage's word is miscellaneous, of course, and she feels bewildered and then horribly embarrassed when her class laughs at her definition of the word.

We can all identify with her mortification. We've all had language misconceptions. Think back. What words and expressions have you or your students misheard, misinterpreted, or misstated over the years? For instance, adults often say "for all intensive purposes" instead of "for all intents and purposes." The band Creedence Clearwater Revival sang, "There's a bad moon on the rise," but many of us heard, instead, "There's a bathroom on the right."

Children recite, "And to the republic for Richard Stands," wondering who Richard Stands is. Remember Ramona Quimby, in *Ramona the Pest*, who loved that song about the "dawnzer"? You must know the song. "Oh, say can you see by the dawnzer lee light." Some kids think it's "Jose, can you see."

I love Shirley Temple Wong's evocative version of the Pledge of Allegiance in Bette Bao Lord's *In the Year of the Boar and Jackie Robinson* (HarperCollins, 1984). Recently arrived in the United States from China, Shirley's learning English, and she hears the pledge like this:

> I pledge a lesson to the frog of the United States of America
> And to the wee puppet for witches' hands,
> One Asian, in the vestibule,
> With little tea and just rice and for all."

And then there's "Mairzy Doats." When I mention the nonsense song at my workshops, more than half of the adults don't know the hidden inner meaning of this seemingly innocuous little ditty, a 1944 World War II hit by Milton Drake, AI Hoffman, and Jerry Livingston:

> Mairzy doats and dozy doats and little lamzy divey
> A kiddlely divey too, wouldn't you?
> Mairzy doats and dozy doats and little lamzy divey
> A kiddlely divey too, wouldn't you?

The song has a bridge, which most folks have never heard, but which explains everything:

> If the words sound queer and funny to your ear,
> A little bit jumbled and jivey,
> Sing "mares eat oats and does eat oats,
> And little lambs eat ivy."
> And don't forget, "A kid'll eat ivy, too, wouldn't you?"

There's a word for inadvertent misinterpretation of a word or phrase in song lyrics and such. On his Web site, <www.sfgate.com/columnists/carroll/mondegreens.shtml>, Jon Carroll, a columnist for the *San Francisco Chronicle*, describes how it came about:

> As a child, the writer Sylvia Wright heard a plaintive Scottish ballad titled "The Bonny Earl of Murray." One stanza, she believed, went like this:
>
> Ye Highlands and Ye Lowlands/Oh Where hae you been?
> They hae slay the Earl of Murray/And Lady Mondegreen.
>
> How romantic, she thought, Lady Mondegreen perishing with her lord in the fierce, romantic wars of medieval Scotland. It was only much later that she realized that they had actually slain the Earl of Murray and 'laid him on the green.'
> She began to collect similar mishearings of song lyrics, poems, patriotic utterances and the like, and in 1954 published a small article about them, coining the word "mondegreen." Then she died and 30 years passed and, voila, a columnist in San Francisco discovered the term and founded a small cottage industry—the collection and dissemination of mondegreens.

Jon Carroll was that columnist and, since his discovery, he has written a yearly column in the *San Francisco Chronicle*, sharing his collected "Mondegreens."

I started collecting Mondegreens and other misheard gems from teachers all over the United States. These are all true, or so they told me.

A kindergartner told his teacher, "I wanna sing that Disco song." "I don't recall a disco song? Could you sing it for me?" she asked. "Sure!" he said, and belted out, "Disco Man, he played one."

Another kindergartner told his teacher, "My mom's going in the hospital for an operation. She must've hurt her hand real bad—she has to have a wristerectomy."

The second grader who thought her teacher was psychic, telling her, "Wow! You must have PMS!"

One teacher's father read her Shakespeare when she was young, and she thought the words were, "Double Double, Toilet Trouble."

A first grader named Erica came home and declared to her mother, "Mom! We learned a new song!" and proceeded to belt out her version of "I'm Erica the Beautiful."

Jan Cole, a librarian at Horace Mann Elementary in Duncan, Oklahoma, wrote on LM_NET, "I met with classes today preparing them for next week's Book Fair. Even though I doubted that the four-year-olds would comprehend what I was telling them, I thought I did a good job carefully explaining that our media center would look different next week and that they would buy books (with parent help) instead of bringing them back. I used the term "Book Fair" several times. I overheard a little one comment to the child in front of her, "I can't wait until next week because the 'Book Fairy' will be here!"

On the book fair theme, librarian Wanda Nall from Hereford, Texas, wrote, "We had book fair this week in my primary school. Students shop at a designated time and of course many forget their money at that time so I tell each class "Do not worry if you forgot your money. We will have makeup day tomorrow and your teacher will let you come then." One morning at 7:30, just as I was setting up, my phone rang and it was a parent of a first-grade girl. She said, "Mrs. Nall, my daughter said she needed to wear makeup today!"

In *Junie B. Jones Is a Graduation Girl* by Barbara Park, all the kids in Junie B.'s kindergarten are so excited about getting their cats and gowns. "Cats and gowns, cats and gowns!" they chant, ecstatically, and are crushed to find there will be no cats at their graduation ceremony. Junie B. is the queen of Mondegreens and malapropisms.

When reading aloud *Miss Alaineus*, challenge your listeners to recall if they have made a verbal faux pas that they can then describe and write about to share with the rest of the class. Have them poll their parents and family. Make a class vocabulary book of Mondegreen stories, along with the correct interpretation of each misquoted line, and have fun celebrating some of the more hilarious aspects of the English language.

Punctuation

In *Granny Torrelli Makes Soup*, the dialogue in the book does not employ quotation marks. Instead, each line of dialogue is written in italics, which looks perfectly normal after a page or two. In fact, the italics stand out and it becomes easier to see how dialogue works in a narrative. *Our Only May Amelia* by Jennifer L. Holm is another fiction book that uses nonstandard punctuation, but since it doesn't use italics, it's a bit trickier to follow If you're teaching your students how to punctuate dialogue, a skill introduced in first grade and often never completely mastered, photocopy a page from the book and have children add in the proper quotation marks and commas.

Go on a wild rumpus with *Food Fight!* by Carol Diggory Shields. The food in the fridge starts to runs amok when partying one night. The rice gets steamed and pops the corn. "Chill out, you guys," the ice cubes warn. Too late. The ensuing free-for-all is described in rhyme with line after line of food puns and "Tom Swifties," in which puns are incorporated into the dialogue. The commotion wakes up the cops—ten Idaho spuds—and they restore order, proclaiming, "Put everything away and do it fast, or come tomorrow morning, you'll all be trashed!"

The delectable three-dimensional fruit and vegetable-filled illustrations were created with colorful sculpy clay. What a scrumptious source of inspiration for introducing or reinforcing punctuation skills. Maren Vitali's second graders came up with their own food-based dialogue and illustrations, employing multiple word meanings, and, of course, humor. These included:

"Leave me alone, you crazy beans," yelled the lemon sourly.

"Stop rolling on me," said the kaiser.

"I can't find a date," the prune said.

And one girl wrote hers in rhyme, just like the book. She was still having a hard time with the punctuation marks, however. Punctuation is not something you learn once. Children often put those quotation marks all over the place. She wrote:

"Wait cried" the molasses! "Don't close the door. "I'm still down here stuck on the floor"!

The content was perfect. The mechanics will improve with practice. How? Next read aloud *Punctuation Takes a Vacation* by Robin Pulver.

PUNCTUATION TAKES A VACATION

If you're teaching 6+1 Trait Writing, you know that one of the traits is conventions. (We used to call it mechanics.) Robin Pulver's *Punctuation Takes a Vacation* is one of those picture books for all ages, grades K–6, that is anything but conventional or mechanical.

"Let's give punctuation a vacation," Mr. Wright says to his students one hot day, and off they rush to the playground. All the punctuation marks—the periods, commas, exclamation points, and question marks, not to mention the apostrophes—decide to take a break too and, with a whoosh, they rush out the door.

Upon returning to the classroom, Mr. Wright begins chapter four of their class read-aloud, *Ace Scooper, Dog Detective*, but something is weird. All the punctuation in Mr. Wright's book is gone, and nothing makes sense.

Postcards arrive from Take-a-Break Lake. When you read each one aloud, your kids will love to infer from the message which punctuation mark sent it. Mr. Wright's students want to write back, but writing doesn't work well without punctuation. So they borrow some from Mr. Rongo's class next door, where punctuation seems to be running wild. They send a wonderful letter, jam-packed with odd and erroneous punctuation. Make photocopies of the letter so your children, working in small groups, can correct it. Or enlarge the page on the overhead or write it by hand onto chart paper or a whiteboard so you can all fix it together.

Once Mr. Wright's class sends the corrected letter, the punctuation, feeling appreciated, returns. Hooray! On the last page are Punctuation Rules. Your kids will be inspired to punctuate with more attention to those rules. Or, even better, get them personally involved with each punctuation mark by using punctuation puppets. I bought an adorable, practical, and now indispensable set of colorful, oversized, felt punctuation puppets from Mimi's Motifs at <www.mimismotifs.com>. For each punctuation mark, I designated a hand motion and a vocal declaration. Children practicing sentence punctuation can use the motions and sounds to act out the mechanics. When children become friends with the punctuation mark book characters, they will undoubtedly treat their own punctuation with more attention, affection, and respect.

I wrote up a formal lesson plan for the book and the creative drama possibilities as follows:

PUNCTUATION LESSON
GRADE LEVEL: GRADES 1–6

OBJECTIVE:

Children will integrate movement, drama, humor, writing, and mnemonic devices to recall, define, and use the names and functions of five basic punctuation marks: period, comma, apostrophe, question mark, and exclamation point.

MATERIALS:

1. *Punctuation Takes a Vacation* by Robin Pulver. Holiday House, 2003.
2. Punctuation puppets from Mimi's Motifs (<www.mimismotifs.com>; 877-367-6464) or make your own. Children can make and use their own miniature personal sets of punctuation puppets created with felt and popsicle sticks (see "Evaluation and Follow-up" below).

PROCEDURE:

1. Introduction

Discuss: What is your favorite punctuation mark and why? Why do we need to use punctuation? What difference does a simple comma make? Show the title (or cover) of the adult book about punctuation by Lynne Truss: *Eats, Shoots & Leaves: The Zero Tolerance Approach to Punctuation* (Gotham Books, 2004). It shows a panda holding a revolver. What does the title mean? How does the meaning change if you remove the comma from the title?

2. Development Ideas

Read aloud *Punctuation Takes a Vacation* with lots of expression. Have children identify each of the punctuation marks by its statements ("Is this the thanks we get?" asked the _____.) and postcards ("Why couldn't we take a vacation sooner? GUESS WHO.") (Question Mark)

Write the signatures of each of the postcard signers on the board and have children pair them with their real names. (The Yackety Yaks=Quotation Marks)

3. Culmination Activities

On a whiteboard, reproduce the letter that Mr. Wright's class sends to the class's missing punctuation mark, and have your students correct the punctuation, erasing and replacing all the incorrect punctuation marks.

Using the punctuation puppets from Mimi's Motifs (or ones you've made yourselves), hand out the period, comma, apostrophe, question mark, and exclamation point to volunteers. Teach the class the motions and exclamations each punctuation mark will make as follows:

PUNCTUATION MARK		EXCLAMATION	MOTION
(.)	Period	"STOP"	Punch fist straight up in the air.
(,)	Comma	"DUH"	Right arm curved, hand on head.
(')	Apostrophe	"GULP!"	Right arm curved, hand on head.
(?)	Question mark	"HUH?"	Right arm in air, curved, left fist underneath right elbow as dot.
(!)	Exclamation point	"A-HA!"	Right arm bent at elbow, finger and forearm pointing up, left fist underneath right elbow as dot

Read aloud Mr. Wright's speech to his class, varying your inflection. Say to your group: "There are many ways we could read aloud and punctuate Mr. Wright's speech. Listen to my inflection as I read it, and let's add the proper punctuation wherever we need it."

Your puppeteers, standing and facing the rest of the group, will act as the cheerleaders for their punctuation marks, holding them up at the appropriate times as the audience joins them to punctuate each sentence with sound effects and motions. You can read each sentence more than once, and in different ways. Here's one way:

> "This is weird. " (STOP)
> "The punctuation is missing? " (HUH?)
> "Uh, (DUH) oh." (STOP)
> "Where could it be?" ("HUH?")
> "Yikes! " (A-HA!)
> "Maybe punctuation took a vacation." (STOP)
> "We are—or we're (GULP!)—in big trouble now!" (A-HA!)

If you have a chalkboard or whiteboard stretching across one wall of your room, write a long, unpunctuated sentence across it. Or write it on a great long piece of dot matrix computer paper, if you still have a box of that yellowing in your closet. Have your puppeteers come up and punctuate the sentence correctly, holding up their puppets over the appropriate parts of the sentence.

SAMPLE UNPUNCTUATED SENTENCE:
Dont let the pigeon drive the bus cried the driver.

4. Evaluation and Follow-Up
Children can make and use their own miniature sets of punctuation puppets out of felt glued onto popsicle sticks, drawing faces on each with markers or fabric paint tubes. They can work in pairs to write their own unpunctuated sentences on 36-inch-long strips for the rest of the class to punctuate with their popsicle-stick puppets. Write further adventures of the punctuation marks in your own classroom.

Voice
For children to use their own voices in their writing, they need to hear the varied and singular voices of many memorable book characters and narrators in their heads.

JUNIE B. JONES
Some teachers and parents raise a ruckus over exuberant kindergartner Junie B., claiming she will somehow inculcate their children with Bad Grammar and Insouciant Behavior. It's not that way at all—in fact, she actually has the opposite effect on kids, who delight in explaining her misunderstood adult expressions and correcting her grammar.

As with all the more than two dozen books in this laugh-out-loud series that appeals every bit as much to fifth graders as first graders, it's feisty Junie B.'s slightly skewed, always kid-like takes on the world that endear her to us and remind ourselves of the times when we were littler. Children in all grades will enjoy getting under Junie B.'s skin and writing new chapters in the first person, using her unmistakable voice and point of view. We love this little scamp who parrots whatever the grownups say—usually wrongly—and the way she makes new mistakes every time you think she's learned something. Don't you all have students who fit her profile?

THE OTHER DOG
Not all voices come from humans. Narrated by the personable main character, a poodle, *The Other Dog* is Touché's dismayed account of what happened when her humans brought home a new baby. At the end of this charming narrative, author Madeleine L'Engle reveals her inspiration for the story. When she was a young, struggling actress in New York City in the 1950s, she took in a small gray poodle that was appearing with her off Broadway.

Sometimes we think we have all the best ideas for teaching at our fingertips. My follow-up idea was for the kids to write animal stories from their own pets' points of view, a la Touché. "What if I don't have a pet?" they asked. "No problem—borrow a pet you know and love from your friends, relatives, or neighbors." They were to write and illustrate a true episode, but with the spin of being narrated by the pet, who might see the entire experience from a different perspective than the humans.

However, when I read this book aloud to Lisa D'Ascenzio's second graders at Van Holten School, it was a child who gave me the simplest and best idea imaginable. One of the students came into the library and told me, "Hayley hasn't finished hers yet. She wants to add an author's note. Her pet that she wrote about died and she wants to write about him." Ahhhhh! Hayley helped me make a good idea perfect. Once the children had written their stories, we asked them to include an author's note, a tribute to a departed pet or further info on a surviving one. It gave depth and balance to the writing and illustrating project, and I greatly appreciated Hayley's insight.

My favorite story appears below, typed exactly as it was written. The student's teacher told me: "I just know she's going to be a writer. I'm sure of it."

> Hey! Chick! My name is Bubba. People call me Bub Man. Every cool sunny morning, after I shed on my master's perfect hair, I walk slickly and silently to my cool spot in the kitchen. There I do my famous business. Then I walk casually to my bed where I take my squeeky toy mouse and causually rip it apart. Then I annoy my master by silently jumping onto the counter and lightly pushing the glass vase over and pretending to lose control casually I faint. Then I get up and push the cabinet door open and slyly rip up the kibble cat food bag. Then I dicide I'm not hungry anymore, so I just leave it there and purr until I'n tired. Then I go to my bed and before going to sleep I cough up a big hair ball. Then I fall casually asleep. The End.

Personal narrative and illustration, inspired by Madeleine L'Engle's *The Other Dog*, by a Grade 2 student at Van Holten School, Bridgewater, NJ (Lisa D'Ascenzio's class, 2001).

AUTHOR'S NOTE:
Bubba the cat died in the summer of 1991 in the vet's waiting room. Bubba was 15 years old and was sick for about 3 years before he died. He was about 2 feet long and 18 inches in height. He had long silky black hair. Bubba was a truly cool cat.

Organization

Paul Mruczinski's sixth graders at Joyce Kilmer School in Milltown, New Jersey, worked in groups or four and five to draw huge, detailed storyboards of the plots of *The Case of the Cat with the Missing Ear (The Adventures of Samuel Blackthorne, Book One)* by Scott Emerson and *Al Capone Does My Shirts* by Gennifer Choldenko. Making a storyboard from a book allows readers to review the sequence and to illustrate key points of each chapter. Analyzing how a story is structured will carry over to their own writing.

Storyboard panels of *The Case of the Cat with the Missing Ear* (*The Adventures of Samuel Blackthorne*, Book One) by Scott Emerson, by students in Grade 6, Joyce Kilmer School in Milltown, NJ (Paul Mruczinski's class, 2003).

STYLES OF WRITING

We are forever searching for writing ideas that will give children meaningful experience in all kinds of writing. Using children's books as our kickoff point, let's take a look at some styles of writing and children's books that exemplify them.

Experiential Writing

One common type of writing is experiential. "Write what you know" is wise advice for the writers in all of us, and all of us have stories to tell from our own lives.

Third graders at Van Holten School scanned in photos of themselves in kindergarten and wrote about their earliest reading memories.

After I shared Mo Willem's *Knuffle Bunny* with kindergartners, Van Holten kindergarten teacher Susan Harwick had her kids "Activate Their Schema" by writing and illustrating "I Remembers," with their first words or memories of things they lost and found. I couldn't help but notice the inadvertent but pointed commentary on modern life that runs through these papers—kindergartners as sociologists. Since the advent of invented spelling, kindergarten children get to write, too, and then to read their papers aloud to the whole group, and they revel in it. They wrote:

"I remember when I lost my shoe in the garbage. I was very sad."

"I remember when I lost my Game Boy. I was sad. And I cried. Then my dad bought me a new one."

"I remember my first word was coke."

(For lots of other ideas, go to the Hyperion Web site, <www.hyperionbooksforchildren.com> and download the teacher's guide I did to go with *Knuffle Bunny*.)

Patterned Writing

At Van Holten School, librarian Jen Maldonato came up with this great idea to follow up Janet Stevens and Susan Steven Crummel's *And the Dish Ran Away with the Spoon*, and the kindergartners had a blast doing it:

Mimicking the Dog and Cow, who, in the story, suggest new rhyming endings to the original "Hey Diddle Diddle" rhyme, children worked in small groups to come up with new verses. To replace the original rhymes, they came up with wonderful doggerel, which they illustrated, including:

> Hey Diddle Diddle, the cat and the fiddle, the cow ran after the sun
> The little dog laughed to see such sport,
> And the hot dog ran away with the bun.

Kindergartners at Van Holten also had fun working in pairs to write and illustrate new verses to the song "I Know an Old Lady Who Swallowed a Fly." We looked at different versions, including Simms Taback's *There Was an Old Lady Who Swallowed a Fly*, and sang the song together. Children wrote:

> I know an old lady who swallowed a cricket.
> She got a ticket when she swallowed that cricket.
>
> I know an old lady who swallowed a bee.
> She was singing to me when she swallowed that bee.
>
> I know an old lady who swallowed a bear.
> She did not care that she swallowed that bear.
>
> I know an old lady who swallowed a goose.
> It made her tooth loose when she swallowed that goose.

For their presentations, each pair had to show the illustration and sing the words to the rest of the group. It was adorable.

Persuasive Writing

Persuasive writing, in which you use the powers of persuasion to entreat someone to rethink an idea, or to do something, or to act differently, can take the form of essays, letters, and speeches. When the third graders at Van Holten School read Judith St. George's Caldecott winner *So You Want to Be President?*, they made their own campaign posters, which is certainly another form of persuasion. They had to come up with a campaign slogan, a self portrait, and a platform.

One wrote, "If you vote for me, there will be no guns or other sharp objects."

Campaign poster, inspired by Judith St. George's *So You Want to Be President?*, by a Grade 3 student at Van Holten School, Bridgewater, NJ (Nancy Havran's or Roni Sawin's class, 2001).

Imaginative Writing

In Kevin O'Malley's easy-to-read picture book *Straight to the Pole*, a child, so overdressed in cold-weather gear only his eyes are showing, presses on through the raging snow, slipping, falling, trudging upward. "Won't somebody save me," the child cries plaintively when a wolf—really his dog—bounds up to him. Is he in the wilds of the Arctic? No, he's walking to the bus stop, and when his friends appear, similarly bundled, he is elated to learn that it's a snow day! Leaving his backpack at the bus stop, he runs off with them to go sledding. The story starts and ends on the endpapers, and the blue, purple, and white watercolors will make you shiver.

Before you start the story, ask your audience to list all the synonyms they can dredge up for the word "cold." Afterward, have them do the same for the word "hot." Now they're ready to write and illustrate a story in a similar style, about what happened during a heat wave.

Evaluative Writing

Even young children can do some evaluative writing. Read aloud the emergent readers about that lovable scamp David in David Shannon's *No, David*, *David Goes to School*, and *David Gets in Trouble*. After you finish laughing at his outrageous behavior, ask your listeners to suggest reasons why David might be a good friend to have, and reasons why he might not. Ask them to write a paragraph describing what kind of person David is, good and bad. You will see some stick up for his antics, and others be appalled by them. It's important to consider all sides in a book, and in life, too. What would David be like if he was in your class? Second graders wrote their own sequels, including "David Buys a Car," "David Goes to the Library," and "David Goes to the Doctor."

Quick Writes

With a Quick Write, there's no fuss or muss, and no major planning to worry about. Children write for a prescribed amount of time (usually from 5 to 15 minutes) in response to a question, and then share their efforts. They are writing to get their ideas down on paper, so it's not a time to focus on punctuation, grammar, or spelling. I particularly love the Quick Write for the quieter, shyer children, whose hands are not always waving in the air when you ask a question. They are often thinking deeply, even though they may keep their thoughts to themselves. When you allow them time to write down and then read aloud their thoughts, you and the other students will often be surprised at the insights in their responses.

As a source of Quick Write ideas, I love moral dilemma books in which listeners or readers put themselves in a character's place. While reading *Fanny's Dream* by Caralyn Buehner to a class of third graders, I stopped at the point where the fairy godmother shows up years after Fanny has wished for her to come and offers Fanny a choice. Does she want to go to the mayor's big ball or not? Mind you, Fanny is now married to a nice guy, farmer Heber Jensen, and has two little boys. I stopped reading right there and handed out pencil and paper to my third graders. "Think deeply about what she should do, and write down: 'Should she or shouldn't she go, and why or why not?'"

Their answers, which they read aloud, were thoughtful and heartfelt. Most, but not all, thought she shouldn't go. Some of their comments:

"I think that her family is more important than going to a ball. . ."

"Maybe she should ask Heber to go to the ball with her."

"I would not go because she has waited her hole life for this and she already married Heber and to her, he is a prince."

"No, because Fanny's MARRIED and because she has 3 children, a wonderful house, crops. She doesn't need thousands of dollars or fancy dresses— she has everything she needs."

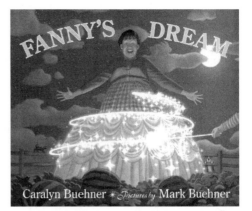

Van Holten School third-grade teacher Roni Sawin read *The Gold-Threaded Dress* by Carolyn Marsden to her class. The new kid at school, Oy, wants to be accepted by her classmates, including alpha girl Liliandra, who holds secret clubhouse meetings for her "in" group of girls. Liliandra offers Oy a chance, but the price is high. Oy will need to bring to school her beautiful pink silk traditional Thai dress and let each of the girls try it on. If she brings it, it will be ruined. If she doesn't, she'll remain an outsider.

At that point in the story, Roni Sawin asked her third graders to do a Quick Write and give Oy their best advice, based on their own experience. Should she bring the dress or not? Why? She asked them to weigh Oy's options to figure out what she should do and to predict what would happen if she did or didn't bring the dress. Then they shared their responses aloud. Christina Phillipou's letter to Oy hit the mark.

Dear Oy,

I think you shouldn't bring your dress in. Because it's your dress and if you don't want other girls to try on your dress then you don't have to! I think the girls don't deserve to try on the dress. Because it's a Thai dress. And they think your from Tiwan so how are they going to know it's an important Thai dress. And if it's only for ceremonies then don't bring it to school. I think Liliandra is useing you so she can look prettyer then you in the picture. Besides, you always have Marisa to play with. You never know. She might not let you in. Well I hope you use my advise!

Christina

P.S. She probaly dosen't even have a secret about Frankie.

Expository Writing

Do you love tarantulas? No? You may find yourself changing your mind after reading *An Interview with Harry the Tarantula* by Leigh Ann Tyson. "Good day to you. You are listening to Up Close and Personal and I am Katy Did on KBUG radio, bringing you the latest chirp." Katy's guest is Harry Spyder, a tarantula from California, and what a story he has to share, an experience so frightening that he lost hair on his back.

A little girl named Laura Weber scooped him into an empty glass bottle. In defense, Harry did what any tarantula would do. He opened his fangs in horror and, with his front legs, rubbed some hair off his back and tried to fling them at her. As Harry explains it, his hairs have little barbs that are not pleasant to touch or ingest.

I read this to Matt Eckert's fourth-grade class at Joyce Kilmer School, and we laughed like crazy at the idea of Harry flinging his hairs. So we stopped right there and acted out the sequence. Now we knew firsthand how tarantulas felt when threatened.

Katy asks him good meaty questions, including why he sheds his skin, what he eats ("Burp. Excuse me. I just ate a cricket a little while ago."), and even one about spider sex—very tastefully handled, of course. At the back is a fascinating assortment of tarantula facts. Did you know tarantulas are the biggest spiders in the world? There are about 850 kinds, on every continent except Antarctica, and their bite can be painful to humans, but their venom is not deadly to us.

Use this book to introduce spiders, but also to integrate research, expository or factual writing, and the interview process. Have students pair up to research a lesser-known or unloved animal.

Incorporating the facts they've discovered, they can then write a lively, entertaining, and information-al interview, as modeled in Tyson's book. (Matt Eckert said, "Boy, my kids usually hate doing research, but they loved doing this.") Finally, they present their interviews as a bit of factual theater for the rest of the group. Sure beats the regular animal reports. Bring out your video camera or tape recorder, or even just a simple microphone, so children can pretend they're on the air.

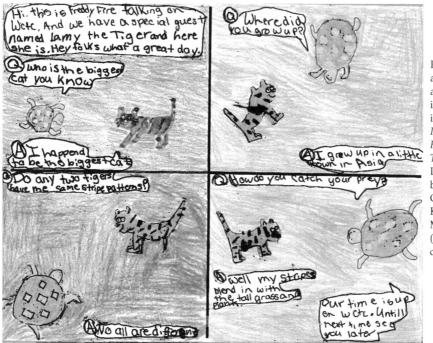

Research, writing, and book of animal interviews, inspired by *An Interview with Harry the Tarantula* by Leigh Ann Tyson, by students in Grade 4, Joyce Kilmer School, Milltown, NJ (Matt Eckert's class, 2003).

COMPREHENSION SKILLS

Making Predictions

When I was a girl, my best friend Bonnee Zabell and I used to love to tell each other jump stories—scary stories that turned out funny in the end. One that we loved and that I still tell is "The Viper," in which the phone rings and the voice at the other end says, "Hello. This is the Viper. I am coming to your house in one year," and then hangs up. He calls back in 11 months ("I'm coming to your house in one month"), then in three weeks, then six days, then in 23 hours, and finally, in 59 minutes. Finally, the doorbell rings.

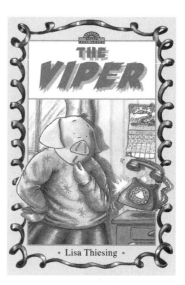

• Lisa Thiesing •

I end the story, which I tell in the first person, as if it happened to me, like this: "I didn't want to answer the door. But I couldn't help it. With trembling hands I turned the doorknob and slowly opened the door. (creeaaakkk). And there he stood. 'Hello,' he said. 'I am the Viper. The vindow viper. I've come to vash and vipe your vindows!'"

Now, in *The Viper*, Lisa Thiesing has done a colorful and funny easy-reader version of the story, with a panicked pig named Peggy answering the phone. In the story, she looks up *viper* in a book. I don't know that Bonnee or I made the connection of what a viper really was. But, of course, you can have your listeners do a bit of snake research here. There are good sound effects at the climax—you could have the kids make those noises and predict who or what will be at the door.

Here's a joke I adapted that you can use with the story, good for recalling units of time. You ask the questions; your listeners answer each question in response. Then have them try to tell it aloud to each other.

WILL YOU REMEMBER ME?

Q: Will you remember me in a thousand years? A: A millennium? YES.
Q: Will you remember me in a hundred years? A: A century? YES.
Q: Will you remember me in ten years? A: A decade? YES.
Q: Will you remember me in 365 days or 12 months? A: One year? YES.
Q: Will you remember me in 30 days or 4 weeks? A: A month? YES.
Q: Will you remember me in 7 days? A: A week? YES.
Q: Will you remember me in 24 hours? A: A day? YES.
Q: Will you remember me in 60 minutes? A: An hour? YES.
Q: Will you remember me in 60 seconds? A: A minute? YES.
Q: Will you remember me in one second? A: YES.

Q: KNOCK, KNOCK.
A: WHO'S THERE?
Q: YOU FORGOT ME ALREADY???!!!

Comparing and Contrasting

It's always interesting to have your readers take two books and compare and contrast their plots, characters, settings, story elements, and styles. You can use, as an over-the-top graphic organizer, a Venn diagram of two hula hoops that you hang on a bulletin board, or have them make a chart.

Take, for example, the two fantasy books *Gregor the Overlander* by Suzanne Collins and *The Wee Free Men* by Terry Pratchett. If you're using *Gregor* for Literature Circles, then use Pratchett's book as a read-aloud. Or use them, one after the other, for your Book Club discussions. Both Gregor and Tiffany (heroine of *The Wee Free Men*) must rescue captives from underground worlds. In *Gregor*, a boy rescues a grownup. In *The Wee Free Men*, a girl—Tiffany—rescues a boy. Gregor and Tiffany both have to make sense of a strange dialect of English. Both have to use their wits to avoid capture. And both have 2-year-old siblings whom they must care for and keep safe from evil enemies. Readers will think of other parallels you never considered.

Bloom's Taxonomy

Whether you are reading a book aloud to children or using it for Guided Reading, Literature Circles, Book Clubs, or whatever you call your book discussion groups, there are many strategies, activities, and discussion points you can employ to ensure that the children respond to what they are reading or hearing. Running a book through the six-level hierarchy of Bloom's Taxonomy helps you see if you have covered different learning styles and levels of comprehension. (For more detail, see *A Taxonomy for Learning, Teaching and Assessing: A Revision of Bloom's Taxonomy of Educational Objectives* by Lorin W. Anderson, David R. Krathwohl, and others. Longman, 2000.)

Below are questions I developed using Bloom's Taxonomy for two books, one a picture book, and the other a longer, more complex fiction book. Both are wonderful read-alouds, read-alones, and suitable for small group or whole class discussions. You can't possibly ask every question, of course, but note how the questions take children into more contemplation of their reading.

VERDI BY JANELL CANNON (GR. 1–6)

Expository or factual writing is all the rage in the schools right now. Children need to know how to write reports and manage information. But then there's that intriguing quote from Albert Einstein: "Imagination is more important than knowledge. Knowledge is limited; imagination encircles the world." There are so many outstanding books that combine imagination and knowledge and integrate fact with fiction.

Children and adults bring different life experiences to a book. The fifth graders to whom I read *Verdi* understood completely why the cocky yellow python did what he could to keep from turning green like the other old fogey snakes. Verdi is in all of us, learning to accept getting older, trying to hang on to the best parts of our youth. It's an apt book to use if you want to talk about theme, or the point the author is trying to make and what a story is all about from the inside out. I got to meet Janell Cannon, which was a thrill, and I told her that for me, personally, this was my midlife-crisis book. "Me, too," she said emphatically. "I wrote this book as I was turning 40."

Here are Bloom's Taxonomy-based comprehension questions I used with the fifth graders in our ensuing discussion, which was lively and full of enthusiastic insights about getting older and changing. This is a picture book for all ages that the children loved discussing. Questions 5 and 6 are good writing prompts as well, for making text-to-life connections; questions 7 and 8 might please Einstein. Children can work in pairs to complete the project for No. 8.

Using Bloom's Taxonomy with *Verdi*: Questions

1. How did Verdi try to stop himself from turning green? (knowledge)
2. Why didn't he want to turn green? (comprehension)
3. Once he did, how and why was he different from the other green pythons. (knowledge, comprehension)
4. In the book's last line, Verdi says, "I may be big and green, but I'm still green!" What did he mean by this? (analysis)
5. How have you changed as you have gotten older? (application)
6. What things would you like to see change in your life? What would you like to see stay the same? (evaluation)
7. This book is fiction, but the author used more than just her imagination to write Verdi's story. What kinds of facts and information did she need to find out before she could write it? Was she successful in both her use of information and in telling a good story? (analysis, evaluation)
8. Select an animal that interests you that most people either don't like or know little about. In the library, look up your animal in a book or an encyclopedia article and read about it. List 10 interesting facts you found out. Then write and illustrate a fiction story about that animal, working into it the information you found. (synthesis)

THE TALE OF DESPEREAUX BY KATE DiCAMILLO (GR. 4–8)

First, the booktalk:

"Such the disappointment," says the mouse mother, Antoinette, upon learning that all of her latest litter of babies has died, save one. He's a small mouse—ridiculously small, born within the walls of the castle. Despereaux, his mother names him, for all the sadness and despairs in the castle.

"Those are the biggest ears I've ever seen," says his older sister, Merlot. And why are his eyes open? No mouse is ever born with its eyes open.

"He'll be dead soon," says his practical father. "He can't live. Not with his eyes wide open like that."

"But, reader, he did live. This is his story."

Despereaux is sickly. He faints at loud noises. He can not learn to scurry. And on the day his sister Merlot brings him to the castle library to chew on the book pages there, something remarkable happens. Those squiggles on the pages? Despereaux can read them. They say, "Once upon a time."

And then Despereaux encounters the Princess Pea. She is beautiful. She is human. He falls in love with her. "Is it ridiculous for a very small, sickly, big-eared mouse to fall in love with a beautiful princess named Pea? . . . The answer is yes. Of course it's ridiculous. But also wonderful. And powerful."

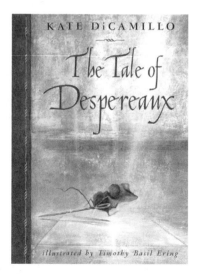

He breaks one of the most basic and elemental mouse rules: Do not ever, under any circumstances, reveal yourself to humans. He lets Princess Pea see him. Unfortunately, his brother Furlough witnesses what Despereaux is doing. "Cripes! Oh, cripes! He's nuts! He's a goner." He runs off to tell his father the terrible, unbelievable news of what he has seen.

And having broken that first rule, Despereaux breaks another. He lets the Princess Pea lift him up. In her hand. And then, worst of all, he breaks the last of the great ancient rules of mice. He speaks. To a human. To her. He says to the Princess Pea, "My name is Despereaux. I honor you." And that, dear reader, leads to his downfall.

At his trial the Mouse Council sentences him—to death. Down to the castle dungeon he is led, with the red thread of death tied around his neck. Down to the dark, fearsome dungeon to be eaten by the rats. Will he die? Oh, no, dear reader, our hero cannot die. The subtitle says it all: *Being the Story of a Mouse, a Princess, Some Soup, and a Spool of Thread.*

Using Bloom's Taxonomy with *The Tale of Despereaux*: Questions, Discussion Points, and Follow-Ups

KNOWLEDGE (Literal questions, including the 5 Ws; recalling and retelling the sequence of a story)

Verbs: Describe, name, list, define, tell, recall

1. Describe the ways in which Despereaux differs from other mice in both appearance and personality.
2. Read a book or encyclopedia article on mice. Write a description of their appearance, habits, and habitats.
3. How did the queen, Princess Pea's mother, die?
4. Why was soup outlawed in the Kingdom of Dor?

COMPREHENSION (Understanding the main idea and the characters' stated reasons for their behavior; describing, summarizing, or explaining parts of the story)

Verbs: Describe, discuss, explain, identify

1. What is "perfidy"? Why is that word used in relation to Despereaux's brother Furlough?
2. Summarize the meaning of life for the rats Botticelli Remorso and Roscuro, and for Despereaux.
3. How is Miggery Sow caught in a vicious cycle, described in chapter 25. What is a vicious cycle?
4. What is empathy and why does the Princess Pea feel empathy for Miggery Sow?
5. What is Despereaux's quest? How does it relate to his nightmare about an empty suit of armor?

APPLICATION (Relating or applying events from a story to children's own experiences or to a new situation; predicting outcomes; using clues to figure out possible plot twists)

Verbs: Show, illustrate, demonstrate, dramatize, use, solve, interview, apply, predict

1. How did Despereaux learn how to read? How did you?
2. "Do not ever, under any circumstances, reveal yourself to humans," is one of the most basic of all mouse rules. Why is this rule so vital? And why does Despereaux break it?
3. Discuss the author's statement: "Every action, reader, has a consequence." What are the consequences of the different characters' actions in the story? Think of an important action you have taken and describe its consequences.

ANALYSIS (Drawing conclusions about, analyzing and examining characters' motives using supporting evidence; comparing and contrasting similar stories)

Verbs: Interpret, analyze, criticize, examine, compare, contrast, categorize, infer

1. The narrator states, "Reader, you must know that an interesting fate . . . awaits almost everyone, mouse or man, who does not conform." What do you think this means? Do you think it is true? Give an example from your own experience.
2. The Mouse Council holds a trial for Despereaux and sentences him to death when he will not repent or renounce his actions. Why won't he repent? Is this decision just? How was his trial different from what one would encounter for humans here in the United States?

SYNTHESIS (Creating new ideas by writing, drawing, debating, or discussing; coming up with a sequel; telling the story from another character's point of view; acting out a scene, hypothesizing how a story's outcome could have been different)

Verbs: Design, compose, construct, write, develop, invent, plan, arrange

1. Interview all the characters in the story—including mice, rats, and humans, with students playing all the parts—and ask them to describe the situation in the castle between rodents and humans.
2. Have your students write up a Reader's Theater script dramatizing chapters 10 and 11—Despereaux's trial—and stage a reading.
3. Draw a map of each character's heart (Despereaux, Roscuro, the Princess Pea, Miggery Sow, the king), and label the different parts.

EVALUATION (Discussing opinions and judgments, with reasons supporting each; assessing and critiquing similar stories)

Verbs: Evaluate, compare, criticize, assess, research

1. How are the experiences of Despereaux similar to or different from those of the mouse characters in Dick King-Smith's *The School Mouse*, Avi's *Poppy*, Michael Hoeye's *Time Stops for No Mouse*, and Brian Jacques's *Redwall*?
2. What animals play the villains in these books and why? Compare and analyze the characters of villains and heroes in these and similar animal fantasies.
3. What makes mouse characters memorable and mouse books so popular with readers? Do these novels speak to you? Why or why not?

DIGGING THROUGH NONFICTION WITH DEWEY

Subject Specialists

I was reading Judy Sierra's *Wild About Books* to first graders, and they were entranced. I concluded one page, ". . . eight elephant calves and a family of skinks," and one boy's hand shot up. "Miss Freeman! I know what a skink is!"

"Ah," I said, delighted, "a subject specialist." I love subject specialists. These are the kids who know absolutely everything about one certain subject: bats, volcanoes, tornadoes, telling riddles, or baking cookies. And, of course, every class has at least one dinosaur subject specialist. Nurture these children. Refer to them as your Subject Specialists, ask them to regale the class with information every so often, and you'll soon see your other students rummaging through the nonfiction section of the library to select an area of expertise and reading every available book to soak up more facts.

Expository is just another word for informative or factual. Boys, especially, tend to gravitate to nonfiction at an early age, clamoring for books on dinosaurs and disasters, sports and science. If we want children to be able to produce expository writing, composing well-organized and interesting factual essays, then they need experience with many thrilling examples of groundbreaking nonfiction books.

Dewey Tales

In the library, as you explain to children, starting in first grade, about the division of nonfiction books into ten main categories, pull out of your shelves one or two masterful examples from each major Dewey category to booktalk and/or read aloud.

If you want your students to get personal hands-on experience delving into nonfiction, try one of the following very practical but fun Dewey activities below. The first one, "A Dewey Tale" is easy enough to do with children in grades 1 to 4. The second one, "Mrs. Dewey's Difficult Child," is more appropriate for grades 3 to 8, as the language and wordplay are a bit more sophisticated.

Many years ago, I wrote four different Dewey Tales so that I could divide a class into four groups, with each group getting its own story to translate from Dewey into English. (Otherwise, you end up with everyone trying to crowd into one area, looking for the same numbers.) Each child picks one Dewey number from the group's story, locates the corresponding number on the shelves, eyeballs all of the books with that number, and by skimming the titles of each book, determines what subject the number represents.

When you read the Dewey Tale below, you'll see that it refers to a song most children know, "I Know an Old Lady Who Swallowed a Fly." After that group translates all the numbers into words and fills in the blanks, the children should then read aloud and act out the story for the rest of the class and then sing the song.

A DEWEY TALE

Do you like _____ ? I know one about a child who's being eaten by a _____ .
     (784.6)   (597.96)

It started out as a _____ , but you can sing it, too. There's another good one about
                  (811)

an old lady who swallows a _____ , a _____ , a _____ , and even a
                          (595.44)   (636.8)   (636.7)

_____ ! If this sounds like a _____ to you, then laugh. All kinds of crazy
(636.1)   (818)

things happen in _____ .
         (686)

ANSWER KEY: **(Call number, subject, correct word to use)**

784.6 = Songs (songs)	597.96 = Snakes (snake)	811 = Poetry (poems)
595.4 = Spiders (spider)	636.8 = Cats (cat)	636.7 = Dogs (dog)
636.1 = Horses (horse)	818 = Jokes and Riddles (joke)	686 = Books (books)

Mrs. Dewey's Difficult Child

The witty story "Mrs. Dewey's Difficult Child" was written by Janet Hofstetter, now a retired high school librarian, who worked for many years in California, Missouri. Janet developed this activity to get her seventh graders up and moving around the nonfiction section of the library. I've revised it some and updated the Dewey numbers. You'll need to check your library shelves to make sure all of your Deweys correspond, and edit it according to the subjects you have available.

To complete "Mrs. Dewey's Difficult Child," first divide your class into four teams, with each team responsible for filling in blanks for one or two of the paragraphs. Provide them with scrap paper and pencils so that each person can write down one or more Dewey numbers before going to the shelves to find and identify each one.

Next, the student will go back to his or her group's table and write the correct word on the line above the number, making sure the word fits the context of the sentence. In filling in the part about the main character "listening to (552) music," a look on the shelf tells you that 552 is rocks, but "listening to rocks music" makes no sense. The astute linguist will quickly figure to use the singular "rock music," which fits perfectly.

If you like, you can also ask each group to pull one book from the shelf for each number. When all four groups have finished their paragraphs, give them a few minutes to practice reading them aloud, deciding who will read which sentence and who will hold up the corresponding book for each number they've translated from Dewey back to English.

The first time children read the story aloud, they should include each number and its translation. Students can follow along on their own copies. So one child will read, "700–799, Art; Art's real name was Arthur after the king in the 398.2's, the fairy tales."

Others from the group will hold up the art book and the fairy tale book to correspond with each number as it is read aloud.

Not only will your students learn where books are located in nonfiction, but they'll find areas they never realized existed for further exploration and reading.

After the first show-and-tell reading, have them read the story aloud again, this time in an even more dramatic reading without using the numbers at all, so they can get a better sense of the humor and flow of the story itself.

MRS. DEWEY'S DIFFICULT CHILD

by Janet Hofstetter, and revised by Judy Freeman
(reprinted with permission of the author)

_____ 's real name was Arthur, after the king in the _____ , but they called
   (700-709)   (398.2)

him _____ for short.
       (700-799)

He wasn't a bad boy when left to his own devices. He didn't steal _____ . He never
                                                                    (332.4)

dirtied his _____ because he was too lazy to climb _____ . Experimenting
              (391)   (582.16)

with _____ , playing with the _____ , watching _____ , or listening to
       (540)   (636.7)   (791.45)

_____ music were his ideas of a good _____ .
   (552)   (529)

   But school was not his favorite indoor _____. He hated _____ the worst of
                                            (796)   (510)

all, trying to avoid it in every possible way. Once he found a _____ and used it to
                                                                (737.4)

short-circuit all the _____ in the room on a dark day. Class was dismissed because
                      (537)

the _____ went off, too. And in _____ 's _____ class, he usually acted
      (536)   (700-709)   (460-469)

like a real _____ , showing off and sailing paper _____ around the room. He
             (599.8)   (629.13)

drove his teachers crazy and that's no _____!
                                        (818)

   One day, his mother said, "Come, _____ , I don't want to _____ , but
                                      (700-709)   (947)

shouldn't you practice your _____ today? You can't spend all day making model
                             (786.2)

_____ and day _____."
   (629.22)   (154.6)

   "Oh, Mom," he said. "Stop acting like a _____ all the _____. I'm not a
                                            (363.2)   (529)

_____ anymore, you know. Even an _____ has more fun than I do. John's
   (305.232)   (595.79)

mother never makes him do anything. She doesn't care how much he _____."
                                                                   (812)

   His _____ said, "Never mind, young man. Come in here right now. Don't slam
        (393)

that door! One would think you were raised in a barn with the _____! Don't bump
                                                               (636.1)

that table! Oh, dear! Those dishes were my very best _____. And you've broken
                                                      (951)

them again. Oh, you dreadful boy! You have the worst _____. A _____ in the
                                                      (395)   (573.2)

house couldn't be any worse. If anyone ever writes my _____ , they'll say I died
                                                       (B)

young all on account of my dreadful _____."
                                     (523.7)

   But she didn't, and _____ finally grew up, and now the whole thing is _____.
                        (700-799)   (973-999)

ANSWER KEY: (Call number, subject, correct word to use)

700-709	=	Art (art)	818	=	Jokes and Riddles (joke)
398.2	=	Fairy Tales (fairy tales)	947	=	Russia (Russia or "rush ya")
332.4	=	Money (money)	786.2	=	Pianos (piano)
391	=	Clothing and Dress/Fashion (clothes)	629.22	=	Automobiles (cars)
			154.6	=	Dreams (dreaming)
582.16	=	Trees (trees)	363.2	=	Police (police officer or cop)
540	=	Chemistry (chemistry)	529	=	Time (time)
636.7	=	Dogs (dog)	305.232	=	Babies (baby)
791.45	=	Television (TV)	595.79	=	Ants (ant)
552	=	Rocks (rock)	812	=	Plays (plays)
529	=	Time (time)	393	=	Mummies (Mummy or mommy)
796	=	Sports (sport)	636.1	=	Horses (horses)
510	=	Mathematics (math)	951	=	China (china)
737.4	=	Coins (coin)	395	=	Manners (manners)
537	=	Electricity (electricity or lights)	573.2	=	Prehistoric Man (caveman)
536	=	Heat (heat)	B	=	Biography (biography)
460–469	=	Spanish Language (Spanish)	523.7	=	Sun (son)
599.8	=	Monkeys/Apes (monkey or ape)	973–999	=	History (history)
629.13	=	Airplanes (airplanes)			

Melvil Dewey puppet and handpuppets of the 10 categories of the Dewey Decimal System, available from Mimi's Motifs at www.mimismotifs.com.

More About Melvil

What about this Dewey Decimal System? How did Mr. Melvil Dewey decide on his system of numbers for organizing information into like subject areas? Kate Stirk, now a college librarian at North Metro Technical College in Acworth, Georgia, was a media specialist in Central Florida for 17 years. She took an old explanation of the Dewey categories that linked each to cavemen, and rewrote it as her own story: "How Melvil Dewey Invented the Dewey Decimal System in Just One Day". I've tweaked it here and there into a story you can tell to children, with body motions and actions that help them recall, mnemonically, each of the ten Dewey subject designations.

As you describe each section of nonfiction, show where it is in the library. It is even more fun to pull a prop from a "Magic Box" to accompany each category. As children mimic each motion, reach into the box and pull out: an encyclopedia, a light bulb, a doll, a puppet, a leaf, frying pan, a fish, a scroll with Melvil's poem on it, and a magnifying glass.

The second time you tell or talk about or have your children retell the story, go over each action, and show one or two accompanying books for each section. Make sure these are books your kids will be itching to take, and hand them out as you show each one.

HOW MELVIL DEWEY INVENTED THE DEWEY DECIMAL SYSTEM IN JUST ONE DAY

Retold and adapted by Kate Stirk and fiddled with some more by Judy Freeman

Melville Dewey was a great shortener. He loved taking shortcuts, cutting corners, and shortchanging Father Time. He even shortened his own name to Melvil Dui. And then, in 1876, when he was just 21 and a student at Amherst College in Massachusetts, he created the famous Dewey Decimal System for libraries in one day! Here's how he decided what numbers went with each subject or category.

Melvil had lots of books: books by his chair, books in the kitchen, books in the bedroom and living room, books in the attic and basement, and even in the bathroom. His friends said "Mel, look at this mess. How do you ever find the books you want?"

Well, Melvil pondered this. He went to bed thinking about how he could arrange his books so he could find them.

"Oh, oh, oh" he said as he went to bed. "I have books on every subject. My biggest books are my encyclopedias, and they're filled with everything: people, places, and things. I know. I'll put them and all my books of general knowledge in the 000's!" And he fell fast asleep with his arms above his head, dreaming of books. (What else?)

(000—Raise hands above head like a big sun or a zero)

Early the next morning, Melvil woke up still thinking and worrying about his problem, and a light bulb lit up in his head. "I've got it! I'll put the thinking books in the 100's." And that's where he put the books about thinking and great thought (the philosophy books), and books about feelings and emotions (the psychology books).

(100—Point right index finger straight up, next to head, make an "O" with mouth, and make an "O" with left thumb and index finger next to left ear)

He was so excited that he had begun to figure out how to sort his books that he hollered, "Praise God" and raised both his hands into the air, which led him to put all the religion books in the 200's.

(200—Raise both hands in the air)

Melvil was so delighted, he ran down the block, past houses, the library, the school, the police station, and the firehouse. He told all his friends and neighbors his tale of book sorting. They all said, "Melvil, are you making that up?" He said, "No. This is no fairy tale. This is a story for all people to hear!" And then he decided to put all the folk and fairy tales and all the books about people and the way they live—what we call the social sciences—in the 300's.

(300—Fingers walking across hand, like the yellow pages ad)

Melvil thought about his collection of books. What was in them? What did they have in common? Words, words, words, and more words. He said: "All those words are just fine by me! People are talking in the north, south, east, and west—in all four corners of the earth! I'll put all the language books in the 400's." And that's where you'll find all those books that help us talk: the dictionaries, thesauruses, and books on other languages: French, Spanish, Chinese, Arabic, Russian, and even sign language!

(400—One hand opening and closing like a hand puppet mouth)

Melvil began to sort his books. There were hundreds of books, thousands of books, millions and billions and trillions of books! After getting half of his books put away, he took a walk to stretch his legs and clear the cobwebs from his brain. As he strolled down the street, it started to rain. The thunder rumbled, louder and louder, once, twice, three, four, five times. Kaboom!!! A flash of lightning struck a tree right in front of him and it caught on fire. Pure science! He caught one of the tree's leaves as it fluttered to earth, and then watched the sun come out from behind the clouds. He raced home, dried himself off, and counted his fingers and toes. There were still five on each hand, and five on each foot. So he made 500 the number for all books about pure science: outer space; the planet Earth

and everything on it, both living and nonliving; wild plants and animals; mountains and oceans and deserts; and weather, too, of course.
(500—clap hands five times in a sliding motion with loud verbal Kabooms)

Watching that tree catch fire reminded him he was hungry. Danger does give you an appetite! "I need to fix some lunch!" he exclaimed. So he threw six hot dogs in a frying pan over a hot flame, and then he put all his Applied Science books—that is, all the sciences that people have developed—in the 600's: books about inventions and machinery and technology, about medicine and gardening, pets and domestic animals, and that most delicious of all applied sciences, cooking. (How Melvil would have loved to have a computer to help him sort out his books. But computers hadn't been invented yet.) He gave the one hot dog to each of his six six-toed cats, and then made himself a nice healthy salad with six kinds of lettuce he grew in his own garden. (If cars and trucks had been invented back then, he might have gone for a drive, but they hadn't and he didn't.)
(600—Make OK sign with hand to look like the number 6)

After lunch, he was still hungry. He looked in the cupboards, but they were empty. He said, "Hmm. What I'd really like to do is relax and go fishing. He got out his rod and reel, jogged down to the pond, and sang a song while he tried to catch a fish. He had no luck, so he drew a nice picture of a fish instead. He said, "Hmm. This is so much fun. I wish I could relax like this every day of the week." So he decided it would be sporting to put all the fine arts and recreation books, including art, music, and dance, and all sports and games— including baseball, tennis, kite flying, tiddlywinks, and fishing, of course—in the 700's for each of the seven days in a week.
(700—Pretend to use a fishing rod to cast a hook into a pond)

Melvil sat down on the bank of the pond and rhymed

> "Oh, how I want
> And how I wish
> I could catch
> A giant fish.
> I'd catch four,
> No I'd catch eight;
> For I think that
> Fish are great!"

Poetry! Eight lines of it. All the poetry books went into the 800's, along with plays and other literature.
(800—Hands open in a book shape—thoughtful look on face)

As he trudged home, he said, "I think I've made history. I'll travel around the world from now until I'm ninety-nine from Albania to Zanzibar and tell people in every country how to arrange their libraries." He put all the history, geography, and travel books in the 900's!
(900—Hold magnifying glass and peer into the past)

And from that day to this, people have used Mr. Melvil Dewey's classification system of ten hundreds, from zero hundred to nine-ninety-nine, with one hundred set aside for each subject, to arrange their libraries. Go into any library, from Florida to Maine, from California to Kansas, from Alaska to Hawaii, and you'll see that 031 means encyclopedias, 152.4 stands for feelings, 200 is about all the world's religions, 398.2 means fairy tales, 419 means sign language, 551.5 is for weather, 641.5 is for cooking, 799.1 is fishing, 811 stands for poetry, and if you look for 973, you'll find books about the history of the United States. Is this story true? Did Mr. Dewey really think up ten categories to arrange his books? Did he invent his system in one day? Well, parts of the story are definitely true. And the other parts? We just call them *fiction*. But that's a story for another day.

Dewey Jars

Here's another way to reinforce Dewey Decimal arrangement. Librarian Barbara Jinkins from Fielder Elementary School in Katy, Texas, uses Dewey jars. She says, "I have ten large wide-mouthed glass jars labeled 100, 200, 300, and so on. I place items that represent books from each section in the jars and pull the items out as I discuss each section. A chart listing the ten sections by name should also be displayed. The kids love this!

"My favorite is the 700 section. I have all sorts of great miniatures for that one. I pull out the little football, fishing rod, soccer ball, and ski, and line them up on the table. I ask the students what these have in common. Of course, they say 'Sports.' I do the same with pictures, a paint palette, a ballerina, etc. (the Arts). I follow this group with a tiny drum as well as other musical instruments (Music). I ask the students to name the groups again and then give me the first letter of each group: **S A M**. We then refer to the 700's as the **SAM** section. They love it and never forget it.

"The students love to bring miniatures for the jars. I even had one bring in a penny once. We had a lively discussion as whether to place it in the 300 or 700 jar. Both groups defended their positions quite well. The 500 jar will have a lot of items also. The 000's and 100's are pretty tricky, but I do have several items in each.

"After you have introduced several sections, take the items out of the jars, mix them together, and let teams sort them back into the correct jars."

INVESTIGATING BIOGRAPHIES

The biography section is the weakest link in most elementary school libraries. Brilliant, compelling, fascinating biographies are still in short supply, though there are increasingly more notable exceptions, including those by David A. Adler, Don Brown, Russell Freedman, Jean Fritz, Kathleen Krull, Andrea Davis Pinkney, Judith St. George, and Diane Stanley. After weeding the outdated, inaccurate, unattractive, and downright dull biographies out of your school library collection, the shelves can look pitifully sparse. Bit by bit, we strive to build them up again, adding a handful of treasures each year with which we hope to lure our students to the genre. The Biography chapter in this book provides a list of unforgettable life stories that you can use to introduce students to the genre or to demonstrate the components of a good biography.

Got Any Biography Ideas?

Third-grade teacher Julie Kotcho mentioned to me that her class was about to start a biography unit. "Can you give us a biography intro in the library?" Sure. No problem. I figured I'd do my regular three-lesson biography unit that can be used with grades 2 to 6.

For the first lesson, I booktalk a variety of biographies to get kids interested, discuss what makes a person famous, and review how to find the books on the shelves. We break down the word into its roots: "bio" means life, "graphy" means writing, and "auto" means self, so children readily put together the meaning for the word "autobiography."

Next we go over our biography chant. Mnemonic devices always help us remember which section of the library is which, and if you add motions, it's a snappy way to get children involved physically as well as vocally.

BIOGRAPHY CHANT (by Judy Freeman)

BIO-GRA-PHY **(swing arms back and snap fingers after each syllable)**
They're IN ALPHABETICAL ORDER **(clap clap)**
By the *FAMOUS PERSON'S* last name **(hands on hips)**
NOT THE AUTHOR! **(point and shake both index fingers at each other)**
They're IN ALPHABETICAL ORDER **(clap clap)**
By the *FAMOUS PERSON'S* last name **(hands on hips)**
NOT THE AUTHOR! **(point and shake both index fingers at each other)**

Finally, I hand out handmade, laminated task cards, each with a famous person's name on it. Students work in pairs to locate one biography on the shelf, figuring out the call letters from the famous person's last name. Back at their seats, they then thumb through, skimming the book jacket and the text looking for written and/or visual clues to find out what the person did to become famous. Each duo reports back to the class, holding up the book for all to see and delivering a simple sentence:

"Amelia Earhart was the first woman pilot to try to fly around the world."

"Harry Houdini was a great magician and escape artist."

It's a good one-shot lesson, quick and dirty.

Who Am I?

For the second lesson, I booktalk several more biographies of fascinating famous folk, reading aloud compelling excerpts and anecdotes. We talk about how information is collected for a biography, through people's journals and letters, newspaper articles, and interviews.

I created a set of 25 different biography brains labeled "Who Am I?" (see sample below) about famous people whose biographies grace the library's shelves. For each class, I duplicate a set and hand them out.

Children work solo or in pairs to read the "brain" of the famous person (a brief one- or two-sentence summary of his or her life) and using the "hint" of the call letters, go to the shelves to locate one or more books that identify their mystery famous person. Skimming the books, they look for a few pertinent facts: birth and death dates, where the person lived, and reasons for fame.

"Who Am I"
worksheet developed
by Judy Freeman

WHO AM I?

When I graduated from high school in Poland, I received a medal for excellence in studies. With my husband, Pierre, I discovered a new element called radium. Our experiments were very dangerous, since we were exposed to radioactive rays. After Pierre died, I continued my work and was awarded two Nobel prizes.

WHO AM I? _____

HINT: MY BIOGRAPHIES HAVE THE CALL LETTERS: [B CUR]

FILL IN THE FOLLOWING BLANKS:

The TITLE of a biography about me is

_____

The AUTHOR is _____

The PUBLISHER is _____

The COPYRIGHT DATE is _____

This book has (circle one): a. ILLUSTRATIONS   b. PHOTOGRAPHS

There are _____ (number) other books in the biography section about my life.

BONUS When was I born and when did I die?

_____

YOUR NAME _____   ROOM NUMBER _____

In the third session, children present their mystery person, first reading the "brain" and the call letter hint from their papers, from which the rest of the class attempts to deduce each identity. In this way, the class is introduced to a slew of personalities, some familiar, some new and intriguing.

Biography Hash

Several days before my first scheduled lesson for Julie Kotcho's class, I logged on to my e-mail. I subscribe to LM_NET, the indispensable and free school librarians' listserv, and every day I read scores of posts about every possible issue a school librarian can face: censorship, cuts in funding, requests for booklists, computer problems, you name it.

There was an intriguing and lively post about a biography lesson called "Bio Stew" by librarian Patty Melville from Pittsfield, Massachusetts. Patty described how she brought in a big pot, apron, hat, and spoon. Inside the pot, she placed colored strips of paper that said "Name," Where lived," "Family members," and so on. The kids pulled out the strips and read them. Then, after she read aloud a book about Martin Luther King, Jr., the children recalled a component of the biography and returned that strip to the pot.

What a great follow-up idea, I thought. But what if . . . (As teachers, we always need to ask "what if"; when we hear a good idea, we try to put our own spin on it.) What if we were to put together a recipe the kids could actually eat? Then we could say we *ate* a biography. Hmm. Why not? I was ready for something new, ever on the lookout for innovative and irresistible ways to bombard my students with books.

A trip to the grocery store helped me put together my "recipe" as follows:

BIOGRAPHY HASH INGREDIENTS

LABEL	INGREDIENT	EXPLANATION
Birth date and place	Yellow raisins	We come out wrinkled and see the sun.
Family members	Peanuts, unsalted*	Some family members can be a bit nutty sometimes.
Childhood and school life	Goldfish crackers	Fish gather in schools, too.
Hobbies, interests, and activities	Bugles	Sometimes we like to blow our own horns.
Anecdotes	Pretzels	All people have interesting stories in their lives, with twists and turns, ups and downs, just like pretzels.
Career	Chocolate chips	When a person makes a lot of money or has good fortune, we say he or she is "in the chips."
Reasons for fame	Cheerios	We cheer a famous person's successes.
Later life/old age	M&Ms	This stands for More Mature.
Death	Black raisins	We become shriveled and the lights go out.
Photos and likenesses	Sunflower seeds	Good biographies let us see how the person looked or looks. Sunflower seeds remind me of sunflowers, which remind me of Vincent Van Gogh's paintings of sunflowers, which remind me of his self portraits . . . OK, it's a stretch, but the kids bought it.

*Check carefully to see if you have any children with peanut or other food allergies. If so, substitute other foods. For instance, instead of peanuts, you could use little cornchips, because family members are all "chips" off the old block, or little jellybeans, because family members are "human beans" or, sometimes, full of beans.

So I gathered together all the ingredients. Using the computer, I designed, then printed out and laminated, a simple new label for each category of the ten bags, boxes, and jars of snack foods. After affixing each new label to its product, I packed all the ingredients into a large picnic basket and a giant soup pot.

YOU ARE WHAT YOU EAT

Wearing my white toque and apron, I greeted the class at the door. "Perhaps you've heard of the great chef Julia Child? She couldn't make it here this week, so today, welcome to Cooking with Freeman. Last week we found out a bit about biographies. This week, let's really sink our teeth into them."

I had set up the library with 24 chairs in rows, audience-style, and two long tables across the front of the room. Children love props. Bring out a magic box or bag with a mysterious object within and they're hooked. With great flourish I lifted the soup pot and the picnic basket and placed them on the table. Dramatically, I unpacked a series of measuring cups, a wooden spoon, and a huge mixing bowl.

"Today we prove that old saying, 'You are what you eat.' I need volunteers to help me unpack our ten special ingredients." Every hand went up.

Each child selected to come up to the Cook's Table extracted from the pot or basket one ingredient and read the laminated label aloud to the class. I then explained the connections of each ingredient to a famous person's life. As we lined up the food items in chronological order on our long table, the class began to salivate audibly. When one child drew out the big brown bag of M&Ms, the class let out a collective moan.

"Are there really M&Ms in there? Could we eat them?" they asked. "Hmmm. That's an interesting thought," I replied mysteriously. "We'll have to see about that."

We talked about the ways a biography can be put together. Some are chronological, starting with the subject's birth, and ending with his or her death. Others start in adulthood and flash back to childhood. Others leave out key ingredients that may be unknown or irrelevant to the subject. We discussed the fact that biographies do not necessarily use all ten ingredients (the person may still be alive, for example, or information about the person's early life may not be known), and that the order of ingredients can vary depending on how the biographer chooses to tell the story.

GETTING TO KNOW YOU

Next I read aloud a picture-book biography. Picture-book biographies can be finished in one sitting and give a brief and visually appealing overview of a person's life. (They work well with older readers, too, who still love to view a great story.) One objective was to introduce the class to a biography about a person who had overcome or coped with adversity or dedicated his or her life to a selfless purpose. Children tend to gravitate to the rich and flamboyant as heroes, not realizing that there are often other, more worthy reasons for fame.

"Listen carefully as I read the book aloud. Try to commit to memory the most interesting facts, dates, and anecdotes. Those of you who remember the best details and can connect them to the ingredients we have assembled here may be asked to come up and assist with the mixing of our Biography Hash."

All eyes and ears were riveted to *Snowflake Bentley* by Jacqueline Briggs Martin, the visually stunning 1999 Caldecott Medal winner about the Vermont farmer, born in 1865, who was infatuated with drawing and photographing snow. Bentley was the first to discover that most snowflakes have six sides or branches, and that no two snowflakes are alike.

Miss Kotcho's third graders were most taken with *Snowflake Bentley* and its striking woodcuts hand-tinted with watercolors, especially when they realized that a snow story they had just read for science class coincidentally included photos taken by none other than William Bentley. The group decided that though Bentley died of pneumonia from being out in a blizzard only two weeks after his book of snowflake photographs was published, it was somehow fitting he died from doing what he loved best—walking in the snow.

After our read-aloud session, I called on children to recall a fact that would tie in with one of the ingredients—for example, education. The response: "William Bentley's mother taught him at home. He read a whole set of encyclopedias." For the ingredient of later life, they volunteered: "Willie published a book of his snow crystal photographs when he was 66 years old."

Each child who could volunteer a pertinent fact then came up to the Cook's Table and measured out the corresponding ingredient (1 ½ cups bugles; ½ cup yellow raisins, ¼ cup sunflower seeds, etc.) into a huge bowl and stirred the contents with a large wooden spoon. I made up the amounts as we went along. This is a hard recipe to wreck. Pretty much anything goes.

By the time all ten ingredients were mixed together, the results were not only colorful, but tantalizing as well. "Are we going to taste the recipe?" the kids begged, and of course that was my intention all along. Miss Kotcho and I spooned portions into small paper cups for an all-class munch. The children heartily approved as we snacked on our crunchy, salty, sweet, and altogether satisfying trail mix, made up of all the parts of a famous person's life. I also referred the ever-ravenous class to the cookbooks in the 641.5's for more swell recipes.

Julie Kotcho, the teacher who got me re-thinking biographies, was elated. Here was a perfect new structure for her follow-up assignment. Children selected and read a biography from the library, wrote up a report using the ten ingredients as their organizing points, and prepared an oral presentation, which they made in full costume, assuming the identity of their famous person. All in all, it was a most delicious way to work collaboratively with a teacher and introduce students to people whose lives have had an impact on the world.

Recalling and Researching Biographical Facts

Use nonfiction books to reinforce prior knowledge, introduce new concepts, and stimulate curiosity. Here are some projects to consider.

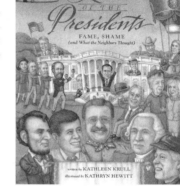

For some practice in expository writing, read aloud the biographical sketches in Kathleen Krull's Lives Of series, including *Lives of the Presidents: Fame, Shame (and What the Neighbors Thought)*, and have students write descriptive sentences about the presidents. Here are four descriptions I wrote using that book. See if you can identify each president.

1. This president—described as a paranoid, bitter workaholic, a "pale and pudgy curmudgeon," was admonished by his wife in one of her letters to "remember the ladies."
2. This president played the violin up to three hours a day, designed his own house, mumbled when speaking in public, had poor posture, bathed his feet daily in ice water to prevent colds, and died on the 4th of July, on the 50th anniversary of the Declaration of Independence.
3. This president couldn't stand the sight of animal blood, only ate meat well done, was the first president to have a woman run against him (Victoria Woodhull), had the most corrupt administration up to that time, was tone deaf, and smoked 20 cigars a day, dying at age 63 of mouth cancer.
4. This president belched loudly in public, required an oversized bed, swam nude in the White House pool, had a volcanic temper, hated dieting, had phones installed everywhere, even in the bathroom, and was an "outstanding teller of tall tales."

ANSWERS

1. John Adams, 1797–1801
2. Thomas Jefferson, 1801–1809
3. Ulysses S. Grant, 1869–1877
4. Lyndon B. Johnson, 1963–1969

So You Want to Be an Inventor?

About to launch your inventors and inventions unit? Once you read *So You Want to Be an Inventor?* by Judith St. George, your students will have a framework for their further studies. On page 95 is a worksheet I created, based on the material found in St. George's informative and engaging nonfiction picture book.

Naturally, before using this worksheet with students, you'll want to read the book aloud to them. Have them work in pairs or teams to complete the worksheet, writing the correct letter on the little line to the left of each number. See how much they retain. Or hand a copy of the

SO YOU WANT TO BE AN INVENTOR?

____ 1. two-faced clock

____ 2. windshield wipers

____ 3. submarine

____ 4. dishwasher

____ 5. assembly line

____ 6. library stepstool

____ 7. dynamite

____ 8. x-rays

____ 9. radio

____ 10. telegraph

____ 11. cotton gin

____ 12. Velcro

____ 13. helicopter

____ 14. parachute

a. Mary Anderson

b. Alexander Graham Bell

c. Clarence Birdseye

d. David Bushnell

e. Josephine Cochran

f. Georges de Mestral

g. Thomas Edison

h. Henry Ford

i. Benjamin Franklin

j. Robert Goddard

k. Charles Goodyear

l. Johannes Gutenberg

m. Thomas Jefferson

n. Leonardo da Vinci

o. Guglielmo Marconi

p. Cyrus McCormick

q. Elijah McCoy

r. Samuel F. B. Morse

s. Alfred Nobel

t. Wilhelm Roentgen

u. Igor Sikorsky

v. Nikola Tesla

w. George Washington

x. James Watt

y. Eli Whitney

z. Wright Brothers

book to each team and let them skim and scan for information to find the answers. For that expository or factual writing assignment, they can further research individual inventors, of course.

Answers can be found by reading Judith St. George's *So You Want to Be an Inventor?* and by reading this tricky key. The answer letters, written from top to bottom, spell the following phrase: "Made History Fun." So this is a paper you can check instantly, with no fuss, and know which answers students have gotten wrong. When each group has finished, ask them to read their answers, from top to bottom, for the secret message.

SCIENCE ACROSS THE CURRICULUM

Look for science books not just in the nonfiction science shelves of your library, but in fiction, picture books, poetry, biography, and even in 398.2, the folk and fairy tale section, where you can find pourquoi stories explaining natural phenomena. In *Master Man*, a West African tall tale retold by Aaron Shepard, you think you're reading a broadly humorous tale about a guy who thinks he's the strongest man in the world until he encounters two men who are vastly more powerful. It's not until you come to the very end of the story that you realize that this is a pourquoi tale, explaining how and why we have thunder. Integrate science with language arts, and ask your students to research an aspect of science—electricity, planets, volcanoes, animals, plants, or whatever is in your curriculum—and write first a factual essay describing it, and then a pourquoi tale of how it might have come to be.

Sweet Tooth

Doing a unit on the human body? Dental Health Month? Nutrition? In Margie Palatini's *Sweet Tooth*, Stuart has been having problems with his sweet tooth. It's no ordinary tooth, but a "nagging, annoying, demanding" back-of-the-mouth molar that expects a constant diet of candy bars and junk food. "I need a candy bar. Now-ow!" The Tooth announces. Its loud, bullying attitude and insatiable demands have gotten Stuart in trouble at Cousin Charlotte's wedding, on Easter morning, at the movies, and, of course, at school.

After The Tooth gets him detention again, Stuart announces his vow to go cold turkey. No more junk food. Nothing but a healthy diet. "Kid, say you don't mean it," The Tooth moans.

Looking for a fabulously funny book to talk about voice? Junk food versus healthy food? Overcoming your inner demons? Loose teeth? Bullies? Here you go. And it's not even fattening, unless the subliminal effects of talking about all that candy wears down your dieter's reserve. I liked this book the first time I read it, but only understood how brazenly funny it is when I read it to second graders. First graders loved it. But second graders got lots more of the jokes, and they went wild over it.

Teacher Lisa D'Ascensio discovered that her students have voices that speak to them from their ears, noses, eyes, and, of course, their teeth. She had them write out a cartoon-style dialogue between child and body part, and the results, which she spiral-bound into a booklet, were wildly comical.

"Aw, why can't I pick myself?" the nose asks Brandon. He replies, "No! I don't want you to bleed!"

"Aw, come on, why can't I pick myself?"
"No, no, I don't want you to bleed."

"What Our Body Is Really Trying to Say," Grade 2 class booklet, inspired by Margie Palatini's *Sweet Tooth*. Van Holten School, Bridgewater, NJ (2004).

The City of Ember

The science fiction novel *The City of Ember* by Jeanne DuPrau is a notable companion to a fourth- through sixth-grade electricity unit. In the year 241, the city of Ember is old and everything, including the power lines, needs repair. People are terrified to contemplate that someday the lights, which come on at 6 A.M. and go out at 9

THE CITY OF

ember

Jeanne DuPrau

P.M. sharp, might go off and not come back on again. When this year's two dozen 12-year-old graduating classmates are assigned their lifetime jobs, two of them—Lina Mayfleet and Doon Harrow—secretly switch their assignments. Lina becomes a messenger, delivering spoken messages for people in the city. That's how people communicate in Ember. There's no e-mail, telephones, TV, or anything else you need to plug in.

Doon becomes a pipeworks laborer, working in the tunnels that contain Ember's water and sewer pipes, down by the underground river. It's a frightening and dangerous job, but Doon, hoping to help his city, wants to learn all about the generator that powers everything. Whenever the lights go out, the city is plunged into terrifying darkness, even during the day. There is no moon or sun in Ember. Can two mere children figure out how to save Ember before the lights go out for good?

There are so many ways to pair this exciting dystopian novel with science and descriptive or expository writing. What words, inventions, and concepts would be unfamiliar to the isolated people of Ember? For starters, students will think of cars, cell phones, movies, seasons, trees, oceans, airplanes. How would you explain those things to people who had never seen them before? You'll want to bring in books on light, the sun and moon, and, of course, information on Thomas Edison, including *Inventing the Future, A Photobiography of Thomas Alva Edison* by Marie Delano.

CELEBRATING POETRY

As the inimitable children's literature expert Caroline Feller Bauer would say, "Poetry Break!" Make a sign of those two words, and when you or your students burst into a classroom, hold up the sign and shout, "Poetry Break!" Then pull out a few great poems and read them aloud. Quick and dirty, no fuss, no muss, no expense, no convoluted plans. Do it once a week, once a month, whenever you feel like it, but expose your kids to poetry on a constant and ongoing basis, even if you're scared of poetry. Especially if you're scared of poetry.

One idea I harvested from LM_NET was for writing found poetry. You know those magnetic poetry word sets you can buy to put on your refrigerator? They're boxes of little magnet strips, each with a word printed on it. You put them together and construct your own poems. There are sets made for children too.

In education, we're always looking for ways to make things ourselves, both to save money and to encourage children's creativity. What about children compiling a list of words for their own magnetic poems? You can buy magnetic sheets (look up "magnetic sheets" at Google.com and you'll find many sources) and print their list of words. Cut out the word strips, and have children use cookie sheets to arrange their poems. Or you can simply have children collect and write their own word strips on oak tag and arrange them into poems.

Poem Seeds

Mariya Rodriguez, librarian at the Oak Meadow Elementary School in San Antonio, Texas, took a slightly different approach, using poetry books as a source of wonderful words, and described the whole process in a practical post on LM_NET in November 2004:

> I teach a lesson about found poetry, using cut strips of white paper in ziploc baggies and 100 of my favorite poetry books. I tell the kids, "Today we're going to grow poems." I ask them, "If we wanted to grow apples, what would we need?" Someone always says, "Apple seeds." I pose the same questions with oranges and pumpkins. They've got the pattern down now and easily respond—orange seeds and pumpkins seeds.
>
> Then, I say, "What do I need if I want to grow poems? Some free thinker (every class has one . . . hard to believe with NCLB and standardized testing, but we haven't killed them all yet) will respond, "Poem seeds!" I ask, "What are poem seeds?"
>
> Someone will say, "Words." I remind them that poets don't just use any words; they use the right ones.

I write some strong words from poems on the overhead to model how to get good quality seeds. Next, I give each student a baggie of blank strips (about 100 strips, which is five pieces of plain white paper cut into 20 strips) and a stack of poetry books. Then they go to work. They go through the books of poetry and collect "seeds" for their own poems. They can copy one word or short phrase onto each strip, using only one side.

Every once in a while, I'll issue a challenge to the room like, "Good poets often have questions. Find a question to write on a strip." Or "Find a color word that isn't the basic box of crayons." Or "Find five strong action words (verbs)."

Once they've collected seeds from lots of different books, from poets like Shel Silverstein, Robert Frost, Jack Prelutsky, and Naomi Shihab Nye, they lay all their strips out face up and begin to find the magnetic words—the words that stick together. They write their own found poems this way, and they're always very good. The funny thing is, though, that they end up reading an awful lot of good poetry before they write their own poems.

I'll never forget the fourth grader who I overheard tell her friend, "You should use this Sandburg guy's book. He's a really good poet." It made me giggle that she thought she was discovering Sandburg's genius until I remembered that she was discovering it for herself, and in the fourth grade!

After several classes of students grew their poems from their seeds, I then did an art history lesson with them about collage and we created collage art to complement their poems. The teachers hung these up in the hallway and the principal wanted to know how the kids wrote such sophisticated poetry. The kids told my principal, "Ask Ms. Rod. She made it seem really simple. We could teach you if you want, but good poetry and good art takes time. You can't hurry. You can dig a hole in an hour, but it takes eons to create the Grand Canyon."

I just had to laugh. I didn't think they had even heard the analogy. I was wrong. The nice side benefit of this lesson however was that the circulation of my poetry section increased exponentially. So much so that one teacher asked me to limit the number of poetry books her kids could check out because that's all they wanted to do in class—read poetry. What a lovely problem to have!

Love Letters

When I told the third graders in Nancy Havran's class at Van Holten School that we were going to read a book called *Love Letters* by Arnold Adoff, they groaned. Even the word love is "embarrassing." Once they saw there would be no kissing, they settled in and loved the poems about love. After all, third graders can love lots of things: parents, siblings, friends, pets, hobbies, possessions, holidays, food. They pored over Lisa Desimini's quirky, innovative three-dimensional artwork, done in handmade paper, paint, fabric, and found objects, and they listed the things they love in their lives.

This was a four-part collaboration. I read the book aloud and we discussed it in the library. Back in the classroom, Nancy Havran asked parent volunteers to assist the children in their Writer's Workshop as they composed love letters inspired by Adoff's examples. They imitated his free-verse style, stretching out words on the page, deciding where each line break should be, and choosing lovely words to put in the mouths of their poems' narrators. One boy wrote an ode to his football, another wrote from the point of view of a pencil, admiring the paper it wrote on.

The children read aloud their works-in-progress. If you wait until students are finished with their writing, they consider it done and are reluctant to make changes. To them, it's perfect the way it comes out in the first draft. So have them read their unfinished works aloud. Hearing other people's ideas, imagery, and word choices will give them immediate ideas to make stronger their own writing.

Many children brought in found objects they wanted to incorporate in their accompanying illustrations. Art teacher Dolores Rowland worked with them to make innovative and clever collages, integrating the words of the poems with found objects, paint, and all types and textures of paper and fabric, all in one 3-D package. The collage poem reproduced here is one of the flatter ones, using paper and felt.

Poem and illustration, "Oh ice cream," inspired by Arnold Adoff's *Love Letters*, by a Grade 3 student at Van Holten School, Bridgewater, NJ (Nancy Havran's class, 1997 or 1998).

Math Curse and Science Verse

Poetry books can be ideal choices to reinforce concepts across the curriculum. Look at Jon Scieszka's *Math Curse* and its companion, *Science Verse*. Back in 1995, when *Math Curse* came out, Van Holten School third-grade teacher Carol Shields and I decided to connect the book to both her math and her science curriculum. I shared the book with her class, and we laughed like mad over the poor girl who spends her whole day solving all sorts of weird math conundrums after her teacher, Mrs. Fibonacci, announces, "You know, you can think of almost everything as a math problem." At the end of the story, when she crawls out of the hole she has gotten herself into, the girl is stunned to hear her science teacher, Mr. Newton, proclaim, "You know, you can think of everything as a science experiment."

In preparation for composing the sequel, I took the class to the library shelves to explore the many different sections of the pure sciences, the 500s, and the applied sciences, the 600s. They paired up, picked an area of science they found fascinating, checked out at least one book each on the subject, and read it for homework. In Writer's Workshop that week, they brainstormed to write and illustrate imaginative, science-based "Science Curse" stories. Incorporating facts, they were to pose a problem and a scientific solution. And they had to figure out a way to make it funny as well.

Their stories were wonderful. They wrote about Venus falling out of the sky, the electricity going out all over the school, and chemistry experiments exploding. Our favorite, however, was the simplest story of all, penned by two boys who did not consider themselves top-of-the-class writers, but who nailed the humor and attitude of author Jon Scieszka and illustrator Lane Smith perfectly. They wrote:

"One day I went to the pet shop and got a piranha. Then I went to pet it and then my hand was gone. The next day I got a hook and a new goldfish."

In Scieszka's sequel, *Science Verse*, Mr. Newton says, "If you listen closely enough, you can hear the poetry of science in everything," causing the boy narrator to "start hearing everything as a science poem." The ensuing 21 weird and frantic science-based poems are parodies of famous works, including some songs and classic poems you'll recognize, such as "I've Been Working in the Food Chain" and "Gobblegooky," which starts, "'Twas fructose and the vitamins / Did zinc and dye (red #8)." Get out your Lewis Carroll and introduce readers to Alice and "Jabberwocky."

"The outlook wasn't brilliant for my experiment that day . . ." starts another poem. The sixth graders at Joyce Kilmer School didn't recognize the format or the rhythm of the poem. Why? It turns out that none of them had ever heard or even heard of the poem "Casey at the Bat." Never heard it? Aha! A perfect opportunity to integrate science and poetry and sports, introducing the original narrative poem with Christopher Bing's fabulous Caldecott Honor-winning picture-book version.

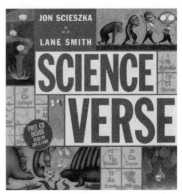

BOOKS GYM TEACHERS WILL SIT STILL FOR

When I pulled out *Lou Gehrig: The Luckiest Man*, David A. Adler's uplifting picture book biography, to share with two classes of third graders, one batch of boys averted their eyes and turned their heads as I started to read. "What are you doing?" I asked them. "Why aren't you looking at the illustrations?"

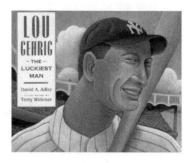

One boy explained, "Well, Miss Freeman, we're Mets fans. We hate the Yankees. So we can't look." I assured them the Mets wouldn't mind a bit, and that the Iron Horse, as Gehrig was called, could be their hero, too. "OK," they said, and settled in to enjoy the biography.

We came to the inspirational account of Gehrig's famous farewell speech at Yankee Stadium on Lou Gehrig Day, July 4, 1939—"I consider myself the luckiest man on the face of the earth," he said to the crowd, even though he was dying of amyotrophic lateral sclerosis (ALS), which we now call Lou Gehrig's Disease. The boys sniffled and wiped their eyes and breathed heavily, though too discreetly for anyone but me to notice they were crying.

Since then, I've always thought of Adler's book as "The Book That Makes Third-Grade Boys Cry," and I felt honored to witness them so emotionally engaged.

Inspired by another baseball player, Laura Carasso's fourth-grade students at Joyce Kilmer School in Milltown, New Jersey, wrote letters from the point of view of baseball greats Lou Gehrig and Babe Ruth to Jackie Mitchell. Who was Jackie Mitchell? On April 2, 1931, at an exhibition game between the New York Yankees and the Chattanooga Lookouts, something amazing happened. Jackie, the pitcher for the Tennessee team, was only 17. Babe Ruth came up to the plate and she (yes, she) struck him out. The Babe thought women were "too delicate" to play baseball. That day, Jackie proved him wrong. Then Iron Horse Lou Gehrig came up to bat. She struck him out too. The upshot of her feat? The baseball commissioner voided her contract, proclaiming he was protecting her, as baseball was "too strenuous" for a woman.

After Laura shared the excellent picture-book biography by Marissa Moss, *Mighty Jackie, the Strike-Out Queen*, students put themselves in the Yankees' shoes. How must they have felt? The boys in the class were stunned to hear of a professional girl baseball player. The girls were elated.

One student's letter to Jackie read:

> Dear Jackie,
> I was surprised when you struck me out. You played a great game; even [better] than me. You're the best pitcher I have ever seen. Not many pitchers have struck me out. I was angry when it happened, but part of me felt good for you.
>
> I see big things coming for you and me. I hope I see you in the regular season so I could bomb one of your pitches. I hope you cream the Boston Red Sox. You know that I was traded from Boston to New York. I have one more thing to say—follow your dream even when others put you down.
>
> Sincerely,
> Babe Ruth

Take your crew outside and play some ball. Boys *and* girls, of course.

Literary Field Day

In an ingenious combination of two disciplines, reading and physical education, Marjorie Pettersen, the library media specialist at East School in Torrington, Connecticut, described on LM_NET her school's upcoming field day:

> Our school is having an end of the year field day based on book titles. This activity was publicized on a PE listserv and our PE teacher decided to embrace the idea. The original idea is the brain child of Donna Carey and Laurie Foster of the Kenton Elementary School in Kenton, Colorado, so I take no credit for their wonderful idea, and I am sharing this with their permission.

This is how it works. We have selected about 15 books and linked each one to a field day activity. For example, the Harry Potter station will have a relay race with a broom, Anna Banana will be linked with a jump rope activity. At the Captain Underpants station, kids will have to dress a teammate in boxer shorts, a cape and then do a relay.

This event will also coincide with our summer reading kickoff. At the end of the day each student will receive a new book, a bookmark, the summer reading list, and directions for the summer reading program. Sounds like it will be fun.

DOING ART

Good readers use their mind's eye to see the characters they read about, especially in the case of unillustrated fiction books. When Carol Shields's fifth-grade class read *Ella Enchanted* by Gail Carson Levine, they were madly in love with the story. Carol said, "They refuse to let me stop reading this book. I've never seen them like this!" She asked them to envision their favorite episodes and they drew large, detailed illustrations with captions describing each scene. The resulting pictures of ogres and gnomes and of Ella with Prince Char were marvelous, full of imagination and emotion.

Illustration of scene from Gail Carson Levine's *Ella Enchanted*, by a Grade 5 student at Hillside School, Bridgewater, NJ (Carol Shields's class, 1997 or 1998).

Teachers in upper grades sometimes forget about the power of linking art and literature. Too often we value the writers over the artists in our classrooms. It behooves us to recognize that some of those kids who love to draw and hate to write can be drawn to the visual side of books and encouraged to illustrate what they read. You never know how this might change lives. Artist Norman Rockwell had a seventh-grade teacher who allowed him to draw illustrations of classroom events. Author/illustrator Tomie dePaola describes in his autobiographical books *The Art Lesson* (Putnam, 1989) and *26 Fairmount Avenue* how he drew on his own bedsheets as a young child.

See, also, how Nicky learns to draw from nature and finds out about his own artistic talents in Jim LaMarche's gentle, bucolic picture book for all ages, *The Raft*. And meet Korean orphan Tree Ear as he realizes his dream of becoming a potter's apprentice in Linda Sue Park's moving Newbery winner, *A Single Shard*.

As you encourage your children to read, encourage them to "Do Art" as well. Young children love to "Do Art."

On the other hand, as they get older, some children drop by the wayside, saying, "I can't draw. I'm no good at art."

Several years back, I was fortunate to sit in on a program that children's book author and illustrator Janet Stevens gave in a school in California. The small room was jammed with fifth and sixth graders. "Who loves to draw?" she asked. All hands went up, except the ones around the perimeter of the room. "It's always like this when I ask that question," she said. "The grownups never raise their hands."

Sure enough, looking around, none of us teacher types had raised our hands. I recall thinking, "Yeah, well, I'm really bad at drawing."

Janet then launched into the most wonderful speech. I'm paraphrasing, but here's her gist:

"Grownups think they're no good at art. Maybe you think that, too." (Kids nodded enthusiastically. "Yeah, I stink at art," you could almost hear them thinking.) "How many of you draw every day?" (Some hands went up.) "What makes you think you could be good at something if you never do it? Some people are good at art without trying. But for most of us, it's like playing baseball or reading or writing or doing math—if you want to be good at it, you have to *do* it. Every day. You want to be an artist? You should be doing art at least 15 minutes every day."

She's *right*. Of course she's right. Don't we tell our kids that about reading every single day?

The Dot

Have you met Vashti in Peter H. Reynolds' picture book *The Dot*? This book is for all of us who say we're no good in art and can't even draw a straight line; for all of your students who say, "I can't draw. Can you do it for me?"

Vashti is sitting glumly in art class and her teacher, peering down at her blank paper, says, "Ah! A polar bear in a snow storm."

"Very funny! I just can't draw," Vashti replies.

"Just make a mark and see where it takes you," her teacher says. So Vashti grabs a marker and jabs it at her paper. Her teacher examines the paper, then pushes it toward Vashti and says quietly, "Now sign it."

The next week, Vashti sees her signed dot framed in gold, hanging above the teacher's desk. "Hmmph! I can make a better dot than *that*!" With watercolors, she starts to paint dots. Lots of dots. Many colors of dots. Bigger and bigger dots. All kinds of dots.

At the art show a few weeks later, her dots make "quite a splash." A little boy gazes up at her, yearningly, wistfully. "You're a really great artist. I wish I could draw," he says. "I bet you can." "Me? No, not me. I can't draw a straight line with a ruler." "Show me," she says, and he does. She requests that he sign it.

And so we pass on what we learn, inspired by others. The book is dedicated to Mr. Matson, Reynolds's seventh-grade math teacher, "who dared me to 'make my mark.'"

In Milltown, New Jersey, Joyce Kilmer Middle School teachers Eileen Jung and Evie Mullane's sixth graders took to the idea of dots and talked about pointillism. Using their fine-tipped color markers, they made small, brilliantly colored pictures out of nothing but dots. They didn't know they could do that.

For a provocative discussion or writing starter, ask your kids: "What do you think you can't do that you'd be willing to give another try?" Have them analyze and assess this quote by Thomas Edison: "Genius is one percent inspiration and ninety-nine percent perspiration." Ask them, "How does this apply to you?"

The Dot is a story that can be used at any age and for every subject—math, science, reading. It is truly an allegory that encourages all of us to take risks and to try, try again. See what a good teacher does, every day?

PERFORMANCE ART:
Storytelling, Creative Drama, and Reader's Theater

WHEN WE INCORPORATE DRAMA WITH READ-ALOUDS, CHILDREN don't just *see* the story, *hear* the story, and *read* the story—they *become* the story. Take students further into the literary landscape with storytelling, where they envision, in their minds' eyes, the stories you tell to them; with creative drama, where they act out the stories you've read aloud or told; and with Reader's Theater, where you provide scripts for them to act out.

In the first volume of this series, *Books Kids Will Sit Still For*, you'll find a chapter called "Storytelling: A Crash Course." In *More Books Kids Will Sit Still For*, you'll see another called "Reader's Theater and Creative Drama." So why, then, another chapter on the same subjects? In the past decade, I've continued to incorporate the performance arts in my work with children, and thought an update would be useful.

STORYTELLING

Who tells stories? We all do. Stories change minds, change feelings, and, sometimes, change lives. If you are lucky, you've had someone like Granny Torrelli in your life, a relative who tells stories to help you figure out how to deal with your own problems.

In *Granny Torrelli Makes Soup* by Sharon Creech, 12-year-old narrator Rosie confides in her visiting grandmother the reason that she is so mad at Bailey, her best friend and neighbor. Granny Torrelli, making her lovely chicken-y soup—what she calls *zuppa*—with Rosie's help, says when you are angry with someone, you should stop and think of all the good things that person has said and done. Granny Torrelli doesn't lecture or explain, but she gets stubborn Rosie thinking about how she might have been responsible for her recent altercation with Bailey. How does Granny Torrelli get Rosie to do that? With a story. She tells Rosie a true story from long ago, from her own life back in the old country, Italy. When she was 16, right before she emigrated to America, Granny Torrelli hurt the feelings of a dear friend, a boy named Pardo, and she still hasn't forgiven herself or got over the fact that she never had the chance to make amends. After hearing that story, Rosie makes connections. She comes to understand, bit by bit, just why Bailey told her, "Rosie, get over yourself!" And why he slammed the door on her. And that she can make amends before it's too late. Her Granny Torrelli is a storyteller.

In *Gooney Bird Greene* by Lois Lowry, meet the offbeat new girl as she steps into Mrs. Pigeon's second-grade class one morning in October, wearing pajamas and cowboy boots, and holding a dictionary. The class has been learning about what makes a good story. The new girl, Gooney Bird Greene, announces: "I will tell you an absolutely true story about me." Her first story is "How

Gooney Bird Got Her Name." Each day, she spins another one of her fantastic yarns, claiming they are all "absolutely true," and they are, in their own way. She says she's from China and tells them "How Gooney Bird Came from China on a Flying Carpet." It's all true. She is from China, for instance. China, Texas. Gooney Bird might only be a second grader, but she is a storyteller. All of the other children want to be just like her.

Is storytelling too old-fashioned for today's tech-saturated children? Allen Say addresses that question in *Kamishibai Man*, a poignant picture-book trib-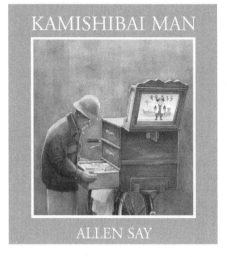
ute to the urban storytellers he heard growing up. *Kamishibai* means "paper theater" in Japanese.

After years of retirement, Jiichan, or Grandpa, has been thinking about how much he misses what he did when he was young, and decides to go on his rounds for a day. His wife, Baachan, or Grandma, makes candies for him to sell, as she used to do years before. Jiichan sets out on his bicycle for the big city, which has grown busier and more congested since he was last there. In a vacant lot across from the shops and restaurants, he opens up the wooden stage strapped to his bicycle and makes sure that his storytelling cards are in order. Then he pulls out his clappers, wooden blocks that make a loud clacking noise when he hits them together. "Come gather round me, little ones, your kamishibai man is here again," he calls.

While he waits for the children to gather, he talks aloud to himself, recalling what it was like being a kami-shibai man when he was younger—how the children loved to hear his stories and buy his sweets. While telling folktales about Japanese characters such as the Peach Boy and Little One Inch, he would display, in the frame of the wooden stage, the accompanying storytelling cards, each one illustrating a scene from the story. As he finished with each card, he would slide it out from the frame, and then slide it behind the rest of the stack.

Then television came to Japan. Suddenly, children stopped wanting to hear his stories, preferring to watch the black and white screen. "How can they like those blurry pictures better than my beautiful paintings," he asked. The day a little girl shushed him for disturbing her TV viewing, he told a final story to one little boy. "That was the last day I was a kamishibai man," he recalls wistfully.

"I was that little boy," a man's voice calls out, and the kamishibai man, startled out of his reverie, looks up to see that a crowd has gathered." We grew up with your stories," call the now-admiring office clerks and shopkeepers and other local people, who gather around the old storyteller, applauding him. You're likely to find yourself choking up when you read this part of the story, and it will take you back to the stories you heard told when you were young. We all need to connect with stories, and some of them stay with us forever.

In the past decade, I've taught courses on storytelling at Rutgers University and Pratt Institute, and I continue to see the advantages when librarians and teachers add storytelling to their teaching repertoires. All of the skills and concepts we seek to reinforce—including listening, comprehension, and higher-level thinking skills; character education and behavior issues; understanding story structure and recalling sequence and details through retelling; and making text-to-text, text-to-self, and text-to-world connections—can be introduced and reinforced with simple storytelling.

Are you worried it might be hard or too time-consuming to learn stories? I've seen my graduate students arrive the first day of class, jittery and apprehensive about telling stories in front of a group, and, without fail and without exception, they gain confidence and find personal and professional satisfaction in their new endeavor. On your way to work, instead of listening to talk radio, you could instead listen to a tape or CD you've made of yourself reading the stories you want to learn, and make it a new part of your commute.

Here are the tips I give my adult students to get them started. They also work with children, who learn stories far faster than grownups and love to tell them to other classes or groups. There are many stellar books on how to tell stories that go into far more detail. See the Professional Books Bibliography for my favorites.

HOW TO LEARN AND TELL A STORY: A REFRESHER COURSE

(Original recipe and inspiration from Laura Simms; recipe tinkered with and adapted by Alice H. Yucht and Judy Freeman, and updated and revised by Judy Freeman)

Storyteller Laura Simms says "Storytelling is like baking a cake." You gather the ingredients, mix them together in the proper order, and adjust the seasonings to make the flavor suit you. Let it bake until it's ready and then present it to your eager, hungry public.

PREPARATION

1. Choose a story you truly love, one with real staying power that you won't find boring or meaningless after spending a lot of time and energy learning it. Folk and fairy tales are a natural source, of course, but often you will find a perfect picture book that tells as well or better than it reads aloud. (See STORIES TO TELL in the Subject Index.) Photocopy the story, including the title and author of the book, for your Storytelling File. (Keep an ongoing file of stories you want to learn, and another one of stories you already know.)
2. Read the story at least three times, including at least once out loud so you can judge if it sounds as good as it looks. Talk about the story and retell the sequence of events aloud to yourself or a friend.
3. Think about what the story means to you. What is so special about it? How does it fit your own style, personality, and needs? How do you expect children to respond to it?
4. Time the story. How long does it take you to read it out loud? (As a general rule, if you're new at storytelling, don't start out with a story that takes more than 10 minutes. Keep it simple at first.)
5. Some people like to copy down the story in their own handwriting or typing (employing kinesthetic learning) and/or tape-record it.
6. Put the story away for a day. Then, after at least 24 hours, sit down and outline as much as you can remember of the story without looking at it first, to see how much you've already internalized.

PRACTICE

1. Outline the sequence of events in the story: what happens first, second, third, etc. See if you can break it down into ten or so main events in the plot.
2. Describe (or draw) the characters in the story; how they look, what they wear, how they behave, and how they think.
3. Envision the places in the story. Draw a map of the setting.
4. If there are any special phrases or sentences or refrains in the story that have to be said in a specific way, or are intrinsic to the story, or that you just plain love, memorize them so you can recite them in your sleep. Learn the beginning and ending paragraphs by heart. You usually do not need to memorize the rest of story per se; instead, internalize it and visualize it as you tell it.
5. Tell the story out loud—to a pet, a mirror, a compliant child, or a sympathetic "significant other." Keep a copy of the story with you at all times to read and reread. In the car, play your tape-recorded version and try to recite along with your own narration. Be sure to keep your eyes on the road, though!
6. Assess the sections of the story you don't know as well and focus on them. Work hardest on the parts of the story that are weakest. Continue to tell the story to yourself dozens of times and in different ways. You might sing it or chant it. Sometimes you'll even dream about it at night.
7. Keep telling it to willing listeners—it gets easier each time! As you tell it, allow your mind's eye to work so you can "see" everything you are describing, like a movie playing in your head. If you stop visualizing the story, and think, say, about chocolate, you'll lose focus and forget what comes next.

8. Be aware of pitfalls—swaying, saying "uh" or "and" too much, telling a past-tense story in the present tense, or losing your concentration. If you want to see how you look and sound, get out the video recorder and tape yourself. This can be a little scary to watch ("I can't *possibly* sound like that! And where did all those *wrinkles* come from?"), but it is an honest way to assess your presentation on all fronts.

9. Prepare the final presentation: How long does it take to tell? Are there any special gestures or voices you need to practice? How will you introduce your story? Are there any props or supporting children's books you need to have with you? What will you do when you finish to wrap up the storytelling session? You want your story to have a good, strong beginning and ending.

PERFORMANCE

You can do it—even in front of an audience. Introduce your story with its title, origin, and background. The beginning of a story is important. You're setting the stage for people to listen to you. Take charge of your audience and guide them through your story. Remember, when you tell stories to children, they are on your side. They love to hear stories of any kind and will consider you a magician for knowing how to tell them.

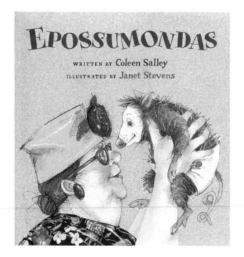

Twenty More Storyteller's Performance Tips

1. Stand or sit still. Don't fidget, rock, or sway, fiddle with keys or change in your pocket, wring your hands, or fool around with your hair, even if you feel nervous inside.

2. Make yourself the calm at the center of the story. Don't over-gesture or overact. Let the story tell itself. The story is more important than you, the teller.

3. Make eye contact. Finding friendly faces in the audience will give you reassurance, but look at everyone. Each person in your audience should feel as though you are telling the story directly to him or her.

4. Find the voices of each of your characters. Hear them and see them in your head. Concentrate, so you and your audience always know which character is speaking.

5. Speak clearly and with expression, empathy, and energy. Your audience is living the story through you. Enunciate so listeners can understand every word.

6. A loud voice can be effective when telling a story, but so can a soft one. Be sure to project so everyone can hear you clearly at all times, even if you whisper.

7. If you hear yourself overusing connecting words that make one sentence go on and on forever (such as *and*, *but*, *so*, and *well*), remind yourself to pause and take a breath instead. Don't worry that you've gone quiet for a moment—it will add space to your story.

8. Don't rush your telling, especially the ending. It's not a race. Breathe. The way you use pauses and pacing gives your story good timing, as the comedians all say. A skillfully told ending allows your audience to sit back, satisfied, and say, "Ahhh!"

9. If you lose your place or leave out something important, you don't need to stop and admit it. Don't apologize. Backtrack by saying, "And did I tell you . . ." or, "What I didn't tell you yet is that . . ." If you stay cool and focused, your audience may never know the difference. And if they do, they usually don't care. They just want to hear a good story.

10. If you mess up a large section of the story, fix it as best you can, smile, and don't let yourself get demoralized. Get on with it. Think of yourself as an Olympic ice skater. They leap, twirl, and sometimes fall on their fannies, but they always pick themselves up and try to make it look as if nothing terrible has happened. The audience members may gasp, but when they see the skater jump back into the routine, they'll cheer at the end.

11. Tell folk and fairy tales in the past tense; jokes and current stories, on the other hand, are often told in the present tense. Avoid using modern colloquialisms or slang with old tales. They feel out of place and character. Keep your stories in the "once upon a time" past. You'll want to say, simply, "The frog said, 'Princess, why are you crying?'" and not, "So the frog goes, like, you know, 'Princess, why are you crying?' and she's like, 'I, like, dropped my golden ball in the well.'"

12. Yes, you can change a story to suit your storytelling style and personality, but be careful not to rob it of its own flavor and roots.

13. Have fun. Take time to enjoy your own telling of your story. As you relax into it, you'll realize that you are having as good a time as your eager listeners.

14. If you are telling a story with a chantable refrain ("Run, run, run, as fast as you can . . . "), with animal noises, or with any possibility of audience interaction, actively encourage your listeners to join in. If they're not used to hearing stories, they might think they're being rude if they speak out loud, so you'll want to say, "Help me tell this part," or "What did the dog say?"

15. Tell your story to more than one group, and note the improvements, strengths, and weaknesses in each rendition. It takes at least three tellings before you start to feel the story becoming yours. Each time you tell it, you'll be surprised at how much heart and meaning you continue to pull from it. Even the simplest stories can reveal profound meanings. It's like peeling an endless onion, but with a far better flavor. (The tears are up to you, depending on how deep you go.)

16. Pick another irresistible tale from your folder of Stories to Learn, and start the process all over again. Pretty soon, you'll have an interesting, eclectic, and varied repertoire that you can share with your children year after year—and a reputation as a magical person who knows how to spin a good yarn.

17. Immerse yourself in stories. Read widely in the folk and fairy tale section of your library (398.2). Your library may also have professional storytelling CDs, DVDs, or videos that provide a source of new stories to tell and reveal how the experts do it.

18. Listen to other storytellers. Call your public library to see if they have a schedule of local storytelling performances in your area.

19. See if there are any storytelling groups in your area or start one with interested friends. Meet once a month and tell your new stories to each other. These groups give tellers incentive to learn and practice new stories.

20. Carry on the tradition. Teach other adults and/or children everything you have learned and keep storytelling alive in your neck of the woods.

Types of Folktales

Folklore encompasses all forms of narrative, written and oral, that have been passed down from generation to generation. These include epics, ballads, folk songs, riddles, myths, legends, fables, folktales, and tall tales, plus, of course, the well-known fairy tales. When we talk about folktales and fairy tales, the differences can be murky. I think of folktales, encompassing all of the stories in the 398.2 section of the library, as an early form of fiction, whose authors have been lost to history. Fairy tales, with their magic and royalty, are a subset of folktales. (All fairy tales are folktales, but not all folktales are fairy tales.) But don't take my word for it. Every place I have looked for a simple definition, from books to Internet sites, offers a different take on what constitutes a folktale.

Here is a breakdown of the most common types.

CUMULATIVE TALES
(Often humorous stories that incorporate repetition, chantable refrains, and a predictable sequence of events)
Examples: *The Old Woman and Her Pig, The Gingerbread Boy*

POURQUOI TALES
(How and why that stories explain a natural phenomenon and how it came to be)
Examples: *Why Mosquitoes Buzz in People's Ears* by Verna Aardema , *How Ox Star Fell from Heaven* by Lily Toy Hong

BEAST TALES
(Talking animals who act like people, with all their faults and foibles)
Examples: "The Three Little Pigs," "Brer Rabbit" stories

NOODLEHEAD, FOOL, OR NUMBSKULL STORIES
(Foolish, hapless characters, usually male, either get fooled or try to fool others; often the fool turns out to be the smartest one)
Examples: Jack (England and U.S.), Uncle Bouki (Haiti), Juan Bobo (Puerto Rico), Fools of Chelm (Jewish, from Poland), Nasreddin Hoca (Turkey)

TRICKSTER TALES
(Involving sly schemers and deliberate troublemakers; some tricksters are fools as well; tricksters often get tricked)
Examples: Coyote, Raven, Rabbit (Native American), Anansi the Spider (Africa), Iktomi (Native American), Reynard the Fox (France), Brer Rabbit (African American)

FABLES
(Short tales with a stated or easily understood moral that often involve animals in human roles)
Examples: Aesop (Greek), La Fontaine (France)

MYTHS
(All about the interactions of gods and goddesses with humans; also explain creation, or how the world came to be)
Includes: Greek, Roman, Norse

LEGENDS
(Featuring heroic people, who may or may not have lived, who achieved legendary status for their real or supposed deeds)
Examples: Johnny Appleseed, William Tell, Robin Hood, King Arthur

TALL TALES
(Exaggerated yarns with larger-than-life characters; in U.S. folklore, these include rugged, indefatigable superheros, mostly male, from the working world and the American frontier)
Examples: Paul Bunyan (logger), Pecos Bill (cowboy), John Henry (steel-driving railroad track builder)

FAIRY TALES
(Lush, detailed, and often sweepingly romantic sagas and adventures incorporating magic, enchantments, transformations, quests, tasks, and trials; plus supernatural beings such as witches, ghosts, fairies, giants, and talking animals; fairy tales represent the fulfillment of human desires—virtues of generosity, love, kindness, and truth prevail, while greed, hate, wickedness, and evil are punished)
Examples: "Snow White," "Cinderella," "Rumpelstiltskin," "Sleeping Beauty"

Using Folk and Fairy Tales: An Ideas List

Here are 20 basic ways to incorporate folk literature into your classroom or library.

1. Using a classroom world map, pinpoint tales and their places of origin. (This works well for world geography, or, more locally, with tall tales of U.S. regions.)
2. Retelling: After reading or telling a story aloud, have your listeners put the whole story back together again. Retell it, round-robin, with each child recalling a small bit, in sequence.
3. Make an outline of the story sequence. This is vital to learning a story, as it helps one recall each scene. List the ten key events of the story.
4. Maps: Each child draws a map of a story's settings, plotting the movements of all the characters and envisioning the physical details of each place.
5. Portraits: Draw detailed portraits of main characters. (Watch the mind's eye at work.) Make story character masks out of papier mâché or oak tag. Or make clay figures, puppets, flannel board figures, or dolls of main characters. Use them to retell and act out stories.
6. Compile large charts listing types of characters, settings, and/or motifs (i.e., patterns and objects common to stories such as long sleeps, the numbers 3, 7, or 12, magical objects, or magical powers) typical to the tales you are studying. (See Fairy Tale Activity below, for details.)
7. Compare variants of stories such as "Cinderella," "Rumpelstiltskin," or "Jack and the Beanstalk." As students read through fairy tale collections, have them look for other variants of stories they've heard. (See lists of some of these variants in the Subject Index, including Cinderella Stories, Little Red Hen, Little Red Riding Hood, and Rumpelstiltskin Stories.)
8. Design giant movie-style "Coming Attractions" posters or book covers advertising stories.
9. Act out stories after telling or reading them. Write Reader's Theater plays adapted from folktales. Starting in second grade, children can do this too, working in small groups. Videotape them or perform them for another class, the whole school, or just yourselves.
10. Rewrite a story as a ballad or a poem.
11. Learn folk dances and songs of countries in which your stories take place, and look up pictures of cities, national wonders, and monuments.
12. Play "20 Questions" where the object is to guess a story title. Or play the Story Character Game: Pin the name of a familiar folktale character on the back of each student's shirt. By asking each other "yes" and "no" questions, each child must ascertain his or her "identity."
13. Dress in costume as story characters. Each character tells the group a little about him- or herself and the rest try to guess each identity.
14. Compile a class book of student folklore, including jokes, riddles, tongue twisters, games, songs, autograph verse, and chants. Have children ask relatives and friends for the oral folklore they recall.
15. After hearing a wide variety of folktales and talking about the story elements, children can create their own. (Tall tales and fables work well.)

16. Rewrite well-known tales from another character's point of view as Jon Scieszka did in *The True Story of the 3 Little Pigs*, as described by Alexander T. Wolf, who claims he was framed.
17. Write fairy tale parodies à la *Falling for Rapunzel* by Leah Wilcox, or reset traditional tales in other places, as Helen Ketteman did with her *Armadilly Chili*, a Southwest version of "The Little Red Hen" with Miss Billie Armadilly in the title role. Consider updating tales to modern times as Patricia Santos Marcantonio did in *Red Ridin' in the Hood: And Other Cuentos*.
18. Put together a folktale newspaper. Students can write articles about characters and their exploits. (Possible columns: Help Wanted, Headline News, Obits, Advice to the Lovelorn.) See *The Fairytale News* by Colin and Jacqui Hawkins for inspiration.
19. Teach children your storytelling skills so they can select, practice, and tell folktales to others. For ideas on how to do this, see "Kids Tell Stories" in the chapter "Storytelling: A Crash Course" in *Books Kids Will Sit Still For*.
20. Organize a school-wide Storytelling Festival as a showcase for students' efforts.

A FAIRY TALE ACTIVITY (GRADES 2–6)

Select a variety of fairy tale picture books from the 398.2 shelves of your library. Hand out one book per pair or trio. Each group will then spend five to ten minutes looking over its story to locate and identify the following information:

1. *Beginnings* that differ from "Once upon a time."
2. *Endings* that differ from " . . . and they all lived happily ever after."
3. *Setting*, including the country of origin.
4. *Main characters*, both heroes and villains.
5. *Hero's quest or magical elements* he or she encounters on the way.

Starting with the first category, "Beginnings," ask each group to quickly identify aloud the title and author of its book, show the cover, and read aloud the beginning sentence. Then move on to "Endings," "Setting," "Characters," and "Quests."

Now break the class into five research groups and assign each group one of the categories. Each group will be responsible for making a large illustrated poster showing at least ten interesting and varied examples of their category that they've found while reading widely through the stories in the fairy tale section of the library.

1. BEGINNINGS

Example: "Once upon a time when pigs were called swine and monkeys chewed tobacco; and hens took snuff to make them tough and ducks went quack quack quack-o . . ." —Joseph Jacobs's original opening to "The Three Little Pigs"

2. ENDINGS

Example: "So snip snap snout, this tale's told out."—"The Three Billy Goats Gruff"

3. SETTINGS

Example: "Deep in the forest, in a house on chicken legs . . ."—"Baba Yaga"

4. CHARACTERS

Example: A girl with lonnnggg hair, a sorceress, and a prince—"Rapunzel"

5. QUEST OR MAGIC ELEMENTS

Example: A sister who plans to avenge her two sisters who were taken away and then declared dead by a dashing but dastardly count—"Count Silvernose"

Cumulatively, by the end of these activities, each person in the class will have hands-on experience examining fairy tale books, looking for specific details, and will have been exposed to a range of fairy tales from many countries.

Looking at Cinderella (Grades 2–6)

When you ask students to compare and contrast elements of stories, one of the most interesting fairy tales to delve into in some detail is the world's most ubiquitous: "Cinderella. Ask your listeners first to tell you the story as they know it. (This may be the Disney movie version.) Next, read or tell a standard, familiar version, followed by a version from a non-European country. Together, your class can compare and contrast characters, setting, plot, motifs, theme, and style of both stories. Finally, small groups can read other versions and make charts showing the differences and similarities. Below are some elements to consider.

COMPARE AND CONTRAST:

Characters
- Cinderella's name
- Cinderella's physical appearance
- Cinderella's personality
- "Prince Charming"
- Fairy godmother
- Other characters (father, stepmother as villain, stepsiblings, fairy godmother type, etc.)
- Relationship of main characters (names and relation to "Cinderella" character)

Setting
- Country of origin
- Cinderella's house
- Place the party or ball is held

Plot
- How Cinderella's life changes
- Cinderella's work and her place in the family; stepsisters' treatment of Cinderella
- Cinderella's assigned tasks at home before or during the ball
- How the fairy godmother helps Cinderella

Climax
- What happens to Cinderella at the ball, party, dance, or celebration
- How Cinderella is found by the prince afterward
- Endings (What happens to her and to her family)

Motifs
- Lost shoes (what they are made from: glass, gold, straw, etc.)
- Clothing (from rags to finery)
- Magical godmother (human or animal)
- Other magical objects or characters (wands, rats, pumpkins, etc.)
- Magical powers or transformations
- Beginnings and endings (Once upon a time; happily ever after, and variations)
- Use of magical numbers (3, 7, etc.)

Theme
- How does good win over evil?
- What lessons or morals are stated or implicit in the story?

Style and Format of the Retelling
- Language style and how it reflects the country of origin
- Illustrations

ADDITIONAL CINDERELLA LESSON IDEAS

GEOGRAPHY: Keep a globe handy to show the origin of versions of Cinderella from other countries and ask listeners how the story changed in each particular country.

FOOD TIE-INS: For a quick story-related snack, hand out toasted pumpkin seeds.

CREATIVE DRAMA: Conduct interviews with students posing as characters in the story. Holding a real microphone (and taping the proceedings if you like), ask each character a variety of questions, giving students the opportunity to range from yes or no answers to ones that require synthesis and analysis of a character's motives. *If the Shoe Fits: Voices from Cinderella* by Laura Whipple, told in poetry, examines the story from each character's vantage point.

POINT OF VIEW: As a warm-up to interviewing, have children get into character by repeating the following statement from a variety of points of view:

"Cinderella went to the ball."

How would each of these characters utter that sentence: the prince, the stepsisters, the fairy godmother, Cinderella, a dancer at the ball, the stepmother, an innocent bystander?

Next have the children repeat the same sentence, but using different emotional shadings. Have them say it: disgustedly, jealously, angrily, delightedly, indifferently, quizzically, sarcastically, disappointedly, pityingly, sadly, and eagerly.

WRITING ACTIVITY: Write a Cinderella story that takes place in another time and place, using research to get the supporting details right.

RESEARCH ACTIVITY: When students are researching countries of the world, have them also explore the folklore of their countries.

SOME GOOD PICTURE BOOKS OF CINDERELLA VARIANTS

Here are but a handful of the hundreds of Cinderella variants worldwide. For more information on the story and its variants, go to the SurLaLune Web site at <www.surlalunefairytales.com> and the Children's Literature Web Guide at <www.acs.ucalgary.ca/~dkbrown/cinderella.html>.

Adelita: A Mexican Cinderella Story by Tomie dePaola. Putnam, 2002 (Mexico)

Ashpet: An Appalachian Tale by Joanne Compton, illus. by Kenn Compton. Holiday House, 1994 (United States)

The Brocade Slipper and Other Vietnamese Tales by Lynnette Dyer Vuong, illus. by Vo-Dinh Mai. Addison-Wesley, 1982 (Vietnam)

Cendrillon: A Caribbean Cinderella by Robert D. San Souci, illus. by Brian Pinkney. Simon & Schuster, 1998 (Martinique)

Cinderella by K. Y. Craft. SeaStar, 2000 (France)

Cinderella by Paul Galdone. McGraw-Hill, 1978 (France)

Cinderella by Nonny Hogrogian. Greenwillow, 1981 (Germany)

Cinderella by Barbara Karlin, illus. by James Marshall. Little, Brown, 1989 (France)

Cinderella: or, The Little Glass Slipper by Marcia Brown. Scribner, 1954 (France)

The Egyptian Cinderella by Shirley Climo, illus. by Ruth Heller. HarperCollins, 1993 (Egypt)

Favorite Fairy Tales Told in Italy by Virginia Haviland. Little, Brown, 1965 ("Cenerentola"; Italy)

The Gift of the Crocodile: A Cinderella Story by Judy Sierra, illus. by Reynold Ruffins. Simon & Schuster, 2000 (Indonesia)

The Golden Sandal: A Middle Eastern Cinderella Story by Rebecca Hickox, illus. by Will Hillenbrand. Holiday House, 1998 (Iraq)

In the Land of Small Dragon by Dang Manh Kha, illus. by Tony Chen. Viking, 1979 (Vietnam)

The Irish Cinderlad by Shirley Climo, illus. by Loretta Krupinski. HarperCollins, 1996 (Ireland)

Jouanah: A Hmong Cinderella by Jewell Reinhart Coburn, illus. by Anne Sibley O'Brien. Shen's Books, 1996 (Laos)

Kong and Potgi: A Cinderella Story from Korea by Oki S. Han and Stephanie Haboush Plunkett, illus. by Oki S. Han. Dial, 1996 (Korea)

The Korean Cinderella by Shirley Climo, illus. by Ruth Heller. HarperCollins, 1993 (Korea)

Moss Gown by William H. Hooks, illus. by Donald Carrick. Clarion, 1987 (United States)

Mufaro's Beautiful Daughters by John Steptoe. Lothrop, 1987 (Africa)

Oryx Multicultural Folktale Series: Cinderella by Judy Sierra. Oryx, 1992 (Various countries)

Papa Gatto: An Italian Fairy Tale by Ruth Sanderson. Little, Brown, 1995 (Italy)

The Persian Cinderella by Shirley Climo, illus. by Robert Florczak. HarperCollins, 1999 (Iran)

Princess Furball by Charlotte Huck, illus. by Anita Lobel. Greenwillow, 1989 (United States)

The Rough-Face Girl by Rafe Martin, illus. by David Shannon. Putnam, 1992 (Native American)

Smoky Mountain Rose: An Appalachian Cinderella by Alan Schroeder, illus. by Brad Sneed. Dial, 1997 (United States)

Sootface: An Ojibwa Cinderella Story by Robert D. San Souci, illus. by Daniel San Souci. Doubleday, 1994 (Native American)

Sukey and the Mermaid by Robert D. San Souci, illus. by Brian Pinkney. Four Winds, 1992 (United States)

Tattercoats: An Old English Tale by Flora Annie Steele, illus. by Diane Goode. Bradbury, 1976 (England)

The Turkey Girl: A Zuni Cinderella Story by Penny Pollock, illus. by Ed Young. Little, Brown, 1996 (Native American)

The Way Meat Loves Salt: A Cinderella Tale from the Jewish Tradition by Nina Jaffe, illus. by Louise August. Henry Holt, 1998 (Jewish)

Wishbones: A Folk Tale from China by Barbara Ker Wilson, illus. by Meilo So. Bradbury, 1993 (China)

Yeh-Shen by Ai-Ling Louie, illus. by Ed Young. Philomel, 1982 (China)

SOME CINDERELLA PARODIES AND UPDATES

"And Then the Prince Knelt Down and Tried to Put the Glass Slipper on Cinderella's Foot" in *If I Were in Charge of the World and Other Worries* by Judith Viorst. Atheneum, 1981.

Bigfoot Cinderrrrella by Tony Johnston, illus. by James Warhola. Putnam, 1998.

Bubba the Cowboy Prince: A Fractured Texas Tale by Helen Ketteman, illus. by James Warhola. Scholastic, 1997.

Cinder Edna by Ellen Jackson, illus. by Kevin O'Malley. Lothrop, 1994.

"Cinderella" in *Roald Dahl's Revolting Rhymes*. Knopf, 2002.

Cinderella by William Wegman. Hyperion, 1993.

Cinderella Skeleton by Robert D. San Souci, illus. by David Catrow. Harcourt, 2000.

Cinder-Elly by Frances Minters, illus. by G. Brian Karas. Viking, 1993.

Cinderlily: A Floral Fairy Tale by Christine Tagg, illus. by David Ellwand. Candlewick, 2003.

Cindy Ellen: A Wild Western Cinderella by Susan Lowell. Orchard, 1997.

Dinorella: A Prehistoric Fairy Tale by Pamela Duncan Edwards, illus. by Henry Cole. Hyperion, 1997.

Ella Enchanted by Gail Carson Levine. HarperCollins, 1997.

Ella's Big Chance: A Jazz-Age Cinderella by Shirley Hughes. Simon & Schuster, 2004.

Fanny's Dream by Caralyn Buehner, illus. by Mark Buehner. Dial, 1996.

I Was a Rat by Philip Pullman, illus. by Kevin Hawkes. Knopf, 2000.

If the Shoe Fits: Voices from Cinderella by Laura Whipple; illus. by Laura Beingessner. McElderry, 2002.

Prince Cinders by Babette Cole. Putnam, 1997.

"Prinderella and the Cince," retold by Judy Freeman in *Hi Ho Librario! Songs, Chants and Stories to Keep Kids Humming*. Rock Hill Press, 1997.

Sidney Rella and the Glass Sneaker by Bernice Myers. Macmillan, 1985.

Who's Afraid of the Big Bad Book by Lauren Child. Hyperion, 2003.

PRINDERELLA AND THE CINCE

If you're doing a unit on Cinderella stories worldwide, cap it off with "Prinderella and the Cince," a wordplay version that will leave everyone tongue-tied. It's loads of fun to read aloud, and then have students try their hands at reading it to each other. (For further practice with the phonetic and frenetic aspects of the story, Shel Silverstein's *Runny Babbit* is a whole poetry book of switched-consonant poems or Spoonerisms.)

This retelling is a composite based on several versions from New Jersey folks, including Carol Phillips, head of children's services at East Brunswick Public Library; teacher Betty Butler; author and librarian consultant Alice Yucht, who originally "cranstribed" and put all three versions together; and further edited by Judy Freeman. You can hear Judy Freeman's rendition on her *Hi Ho Librario* CD (Rock Hill Press, 1997, www.rockhillworks.com).

Tonce upon a wime there lived a gritty little pearl named Prinderella. She lived in a hovely louse with her stugly sep-isters and her sticked wep-mother. All lay dong Prinderella had to do all the hork of the wousehold; wean the clindows, flub the scroor, pine the shots and shans, and do all the other wirty dirk, while her sugly isters and sticked wep-mother dept all slay on beather feds. Prinderella was treated bery vadly and had to wear roppy slags that fidn't dit. Isn't that a shirty dame?

Done way, the Quing and Keen prade a mocklimation that there would be a brand drancy-fess gall in honor of the Cince, and all the gelligible irls of the kole whingdom were invited. So the kole whingdom prepared for the brand gall. Prinderella's stugly sep-isters and sticked wep-mother made Prinderella murk all day to wake their drancy fesses.

Then poor Prinderella, in her roppy slags that fidn't dit, had to hay stome as her sugly isters and sticked wep-mother went off to the brand gall in a covely larriage. Wasn't that a shirty dame!

Prinderella dat in the soorway, crobbing and sying till her gairy fodmother, who lived in a laraway fand, heard her and came to see mat was the whatter.

"Oh! Gairy Fodmother," cried Prinderella, "I feel so serribly tad! Why can't I bo to the gall, and pree the Cince?"

"Near fot, chy mild. You *shall* bo to the gall!" said the gairy fodmother. "Now, so to the geller and bring me some pice, a mumpkin, and three rat fats."

When Prinderella brought the pice, the mumpkin, and the rat fats, the gairy fodmother fapped her sningers, touched them with her wagic mand, and changed the mumpkin into a hoach, the pice into corses, and the rat fats into moachcen.

But Prinderella still had nothing to wear but roppy slags that fidn't dit. Wasn't that a shirty dame? So the gairy fodmother quickly fapped her sningers again, winkled her tye, and there was a garkling spown of gilver and sold, all covered with pubies and rearls. It was the bost dreautiful mess in the kole whingdom! And for her feet, there was a painty dair of slass glippers.

As the gairy fodmother clelped Prinderella himb into the covely larriage, she warned her: "Don't gorfet: you must beave lefore the moke of stridnight, for the brell will be spoken when the twock clikes strelve."

Prinderella was the bost meautiful baiden at the mall. When the Cince saw her fovely lace and her dreautiful bess, all covered with pubies and rearls, he lell in fove with her. They nanced all dight, until the calace plock chegan to bime. Then, just before the last moke of stridnight, Prinderella dan out the roor to her waiting harriage and courses. But as she durried hown the stalace peps, she slopped her dripper! Now wasn't that a shirty dame?

The dext nay, the Ping issued a krocklamation that the Cince was lesperately dooking for the meautiful baiden who had slopped her dripper as she left the brand gall. The Cince hent to the wouses of all the gelligible earls of the kole whingdom in gearch of the sirl he had lallen in fove with, and now manted to warry.

When the Cince came to Prinderella's house, her stugly sep-isters all tried to tit their foes into the slass glipper, but it fidn't dit!

But whuess gat? When Prinderella flipped her soot into the slass glipper, it fid dit! So Prinderella and the Cince mere warried. She wore a gedding wown of wharkling spite, all covered with pubies and rearls. And Prinderella and the Cince hived lappily ever after. That wasn't such a shirty dame, was it?

Create an Instant Tall Tale

How do you explain the humor and exaggeration of tall tales? I have observed that younger children have literal senses of humor, and the dry, straight-faced humor of tall tales often flies over their heads.

I learned the following simple yet hilarious and instructive activity, a composite story exercise, from one of my students at Pratt Institute. I asked her if I could use it and she said, "Oh, sure. I got it from someone else, though." So I fiddled with it and made it my own. It's magical doing this activity with children to introduce or culminate a tall tales unit. You're reinforcing the Five W's—who, what, where, when, and why—in a Mad-Libs kind of way, and you're demonstrating how exaggeration works.

Third-grade teacher Nancy Havran did this with her students at Van Holten School in Bridgewater, New Jersey, and they laughed and laughed. When I came back to visit her classroom later that day, they all wanted to share their composite stories. What I didn't expect, as the children regaled me with their very silly tall tales, was that could recite them aloud from memory.

OBJECTIVE

- To reinforce the Five W's: Who, What, Where, When, Why
- To introduce the concept of absurdity in tall tales

SUPPLIES NEEDED

1 long strip of legal-sized paper, cut in half the long way (4" x 14"), for each person; a pencil for each person

PROCEDURE

1. To construct an instant absurd tall tale, each person in a group of seven writes down a response to your first writing prompt (below), folds over a flap of the paper to cover up the writing, and passes it on to the person on the right. On receiving a new paper from the person on the left, each person writes an answer for the second prompt, folds the paper over again, and passes it to the right again.
2. At the end of the exercise, each person will have written one answer to each prompt, but on seven different strips of paper. Each writer then unfolds his or her paper and reads aloud the usually hilarious composite sentence to the group or entire class.
3. Children can copy their composite tall tales onto a long piece of drawing paper—a piece of 24" x 36" paper, cut in half the long way, would work fine—and illustrate each line. This makes a very cute bulletin board, "Heard any *tall* tales lately?"

LEADER'S PROMPTS

1. **Who** (Think of a real or fictional person's name, from books, or real life, or movies, or your own mother, such as: **The Stinky Cheese Man** or **Elvis Presley**.)
2. **Did What** (Describe an activity, using an action verb, such as: **Climbed Mt. Everest** or **Baked a Cake**.)
3. **With Whom** (Think of another real or fictional person's name, and use the preposition "with": **with Cinderella** or **with George Washington**.)
4. **Where** (Think of a place or a location, and start with a preposition like "in" or "on": **On the back of a chicken** or **in Nome, Alaska**.)
5. **When** (Give a time, such as: **Last Tuesday** or **in 1776**.)
6. **Why** (Give a reason, starting with the word "because": **Because roses are red and violets are blue** or **Because I said so**.)
7. **And all the people said:** (Think of a quote, and start it with the words, "And all the people said": **And all the people said, "To be or not to be. That is the question."**)
8. Unfold your paper and let's share our new tall tales.

And here is one final, composite, cheerfully absurd, tall tale sentence, as composed by seven individual writers:

The Stinky Cheese Man
Climbed Mt. Everest
with Cinderella
On the back of a chicken
Last Tuesday
Because roses are red and violets are blue
And all the people said, "To be or not to be. That is the question."

CREATIVE DRAMA AND READER'S THEATER

Some years back, my friend and fellow teacher Carol Shields came home to find a message on her phone. "Hi, Mrs. Shields. This is Mrs. Johnson. I don't know if you remember me, but my son, Jeremy, was in your fifth-grade class about 15 years ago. You might remember that in the play you and Miss Freeman, the librarian, put on for the school, "Dumling and the Golden Goose," Jeremy played the part of Dumling."

Who could forget Jeremy Johnson, bright, cheerful, personable, a dedicated reader, and a wonderful Dumling in the Reader's Theater play the class put on, first for themselves, and then for the whole school. Dumling was the youngest brother, the fool who got stuck to the goose that laid golden eggs and ended up making the princess laugh.

Mrs. Johnson continued. "I thought you and Miss Freeman might be interested to note that Jeremy went to Northwestern, where he majored in drama, and he's acted in a couple of soap operas on TV. But he just got a part in the Broadway production of "Shakespeare's R&J," the all-male version of Romeo and Juliet, and today his picture is in the Arts & Leisure section of the Sunday *New York Times*."

Wow! It's heartening when you hear that your former students are leading interesting and productive lives. Why was Jeremy a drama major in college? And why was his photograph in the *New York Times*? And why was he in a big New York City play? I'll bet it was at least partly because, back in fifth grade, he was Dumling!

This does not mean that every child who acts in a school play will grow up to become an actor. But drama can change lives, giving shy children the opportunity to leave behind their quiet demeanors and become someone else for a little while. Think back. Can you remember being in a school play in elementary school? What was the play? Can you remember any of your lines? I'm betting that many of you remember how it felt to be in a play.

Are you an adult who dreads public speaking? I Googled "fear of public speaking" and came up with 13,600 hits. From the statistics I read, it looks as if people are more afraid of public speaking than they are of dying, which seems a wee bit extreme. What can we, as educators, do to encourage our children to face an audience and speak or sing in a loud, clear voice; to interact with other speakers; and to become more comfortable giving reports and other presentations? Like it or not, they'll be doing those things throughout their lives; if it feels natural from an early age, maybe they won't be so terrified of it when they're older. What we can do is both effective and enjoyable: we can act out stories, scenes, poems, songs, and situations using creative drama and Reader's Theater.

With creative drama, you act out a story by recalling its plot and dialogue. Creative drama is wonderful for retelling the sequence of a story, interacting with other story characters, and bringing a story to life through creativity, imagination, and improvisation. Reader's Theater incorporates elements of creative drama, but with a prescribed script to follow, and helps children develop as readers. Both are adored by children of all ages, and both foster a love and appreciation of language and literature. Let's look at some concrete examples.

Creative Drama

I read Denise Fleming's *Alphabet Under Construction* aloud for the first time to a large group of three first-grade classes at Irving School in Highland Park, New Jersey. I wanted to see if they would understand the vocabulary, bond with the story of a cheerful and energetic gray mouse zipping through the alphabet, and recall the alphabetical sequence. But as I read the book aloud, I noticed something else. The verbs in the book, one per page, all describe artistic or useful actions. They would be fun to act out.

When I finished the book, I said, "OK, everyone, you are now going to be Mouse. Find yourself a space where no one is in your way, and let's do everything Mouse did. Mouse is a small guy, so we'll need to use our whole bodies to act out his alphabet. Use your biggest motions."

What we were undertaking was a simple example of Narrative Pantomime. Usually, when you act out a story like this in unison, with all of the children playing the same character, you have them do it silently. This is partly so they'll focus on the action as you reread the story aloud, and partly to save your sanity. But *Alphabet Under Construction* is filled with noises. I told the children I also wanted them to add lots of sound to the story. They were only too eager to oblige.

"Mouse airbrushes the A, buttons the B, carves the C, dyes the D, erases the E . . ." The children busily set to work, making productive noises as they pretended to nail the N, quilt the Q, and, in our favorite, vacuum the V. When we finished the final zipping of the Z, they collapsed to the floor, exhausted.

"Now," I said, "let's see how much of Mouse's alphabet you can say." Remember, we had read the book only once and then acted it out once. And yet, they were able to recite, from memory and in sequence all 26 of the letters, including previously unfamiliar words such as "airbrushes" and "levels," which we had discussed and defined when we read the story the first time. Because they had acted out the whole alphabet, their bodies had internalized each word; as they recalled each letter, you could see them assuming appropriate poses as they came up with the related word. What fun we had.

BEARSIE BEAR

Based on my own observations, I believe children have better recall and understanding of the stories they act out. I remember the kindergarten class that acted out Bernard Waber's entire *Bearsie Bear and the Surprise Sleepover Party*, with all its many repeated refrains.

There's a knock on Bearsie Bear's door one cold snowy night. "Who is it?" calls Bearsie Bear from his warm bed.

"'It's me, Moosie Moose,' said Moosie Moose. 'Moosie Moose?' said Bearsie Bear. 'Yes, Moosie Moose,' said Moosie Moose."

Quickly, the children caught on and began joining in on the droll repeated dialogue for each knock on the door. Cowsie Cow, Piggie Pig, Foxie Fox, and Goosie Goose all come in and jump into Bearsie Bear's bed. Then Porky Porcupine knocks. "Uh-oh," say all the animals. Oblivious, Porky Porcupine jumps into bed. "Ouch!" say all the others, and run out the door.

I had already moved the library furniture so there was room on the floor for acting. I also happened to have a ridiculously long, hand-knitted scarf, and decided this could represent the blanket on Bearsie Bear's bed. It was our only prop.

"Who wants to be Bearsie Bear?" I asked.

"Me! Me!" several eager actors called out. If two or three children want to be Bearsie Bear, that's just fine. One by one, children volunteered for parts. In the story, there are six parts, and we had 21 players. No problem, if you double or even quadruple the number of actors for each part.

As we acted out the story, children recalled and replicated the structure patterns of the dialogue. Each animal jumped into bed with the three Bearsie Bears and pulled the long scarf, stretched lengthwise across the floor, up to their chins. Some children were tongue-tied or shy or didn't remember what their characters were supposed to say. The other children prompted them. We played out a glorious version of the story, with lots of laughs.

Several months later, my student teacher Beth Lommell, sitting on the Story Rug with the same class, pulled out that scarf to use with a story she had chosen to read to them. They gasped.

"That's Bearsie Bear's blanket!" they cried.

"Who's Bearsie Bear?" Beth asked.

The kindergartners launched into a spirited retelling of the story. What was amazing to me was how much of the plot and the many refrains the children recalled, all those months later. Acting out a story makes it more real.

NOVEL SCENES

Younger children love acting out stories from picture books. What about older children, in grades 3 to 6? Keep your eyes peeled for dramatic scenes and chapters from novels, such as the trial scene from Kate diCamillo's *The Tale of Despereaux*, where the mouse is brought before the Mouse Council and sentenced to death for daring to speak to a human, the Princess Pea herself.

Look for scenes with dialogue and action, such as the first two chapters of Suzanne Collins's exciting underworld fantasy, *Gregor the Overlander*.

In the laundry room of their Manhattan apartment building with his 2-year-old sister Boots, 12-year-old Gregor looks up when he hears a klunk. Boots is peering down through the opening of an air duct, through which a strange vapor is drifting. He watches in horror as Boots is somehow sucked into the opening. "No," he shouts, thrusting his head and shoulders into the hole. The next thing he knows, he, too, is falling down, down, down into the empty space.

That's just Chapter 1, Part 1: The Fall. Is it a dream? Not a chance. Thump. Somehow, he lands safely. Another thump. Boots lands beside him. He hears her squeal, "Bug! Beeg bug."

Running toward the light, Gregor sprawls over something, and when he looks up, he's looking into the face of the largest cockroach he's ever seen—standing at least 4 feet high. It speaks.

"Smells what so good, smells what?" it hisses, curious. "Be small human, be?"

"All right, okay, I'm talking to a giant cockroach," Gregor says.

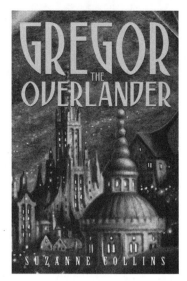

Gregor and Boots have landed in the Underland, a dark, underground world where people ride on giant bats, monstrous rats threaten Gregor's life, and there seems to be no way home. You can have children work in trios to dramatize the scenes at their own pace and then come back together in one group to discuss how they brought their scenes to life, how it felt, and what they learned about the characters.

When you're leading a class in Guided Reading or Literature Circles or Book Discussion Groups, another drama technique you can use to elicit a heightened response is the Live Interview, complete with microphone. You don't need to have the mike attached to anything. Just holding it in front of an actor's face and asking questions brings out the most wonderful responses. You may well want to tape record the exchange. At first, you, the teacher, take on the David Letterman/Jay Leno/news reporter job. You'll say, "Today, folks, we have as our guests the cast of the book *Bud, Not Buddy* by Christopher Paul Curtis. We're hoping to get to know our characters a little better. First off, is Todd in the audience? Come on up here, Toddy, and tell us about that foster child your parents took in."

Selecting a child from the class, the teacher has "Todd" come up to the Interview Chair. "Well, Todd, you and Bud certainly didn't get along the one night he spent in your house. Can you tell us your side of the story?"

And they're off and running, with bully "Todd" explaining his side of why he stuck that Ticonderoga pencil up Bud's nose while he was sleeping. You can interview major and minor characters. Even Bud's late mother can come back from the grave and tell what he was like when he was younger. This allows children to get far deeper into a character than when you ask "What kind of boy was Bud?' and wait for the six usual kids, the highly verbal ones, to raise their hands. It's the quietest children who often surprise us the most with this activity. Students can break into small interview groups, write a list of questions that they would ask each character, and then conduct interviews with a Moderator and his or her Guests.

I CAN'T PAY THE RENT!

Remember those silent movies with a villain, a damsel in distress, and an upstanding hero who saves the day? (The old Bullwinkle cartoons used to parody them with Snidely Whiplash, sweet Nell, and Dudley Do-Right of the Mounties.)

Surely you've heard or done the melodrama below, with its little problem about paying the rent. It's a humorous way to review these stock character types in literature—the poor little damsel (you may want to talk briefly about damsels not being so distressed these days, or so dependent on big strong guys to save them), the hero, and the villain—and to act them out in character.

For this short sketch, use a napkin, twisted in the center into a bow, as your all-purpose mustache, hair bow, and bow tie. If you prefer, hand out a script for children to read, but listeners will pick this up orally just as easily. Once you all know the lines, do the whole skit a final time as fast as you can, using different voices for the damsel in distress, villain, and hero. For the damsel's lines, hold the bow up by your temple; for the villain, use it as a mustache; and for the hero, hold the bow under your chin as a bow tie.

DAMSEL:	I CAN'T pay the rent!
VILLAIN:	You MUST pay the rent!
DAMSEL:	But I CAN'T pay the rent!
VILLAIN:	But you MUST pay the rent!
DAMSEL:	But I CAN'T pay the rent!
VILLAIN:	But you MUST pay the rent!
HERO:	*I'll* pay the rent!
DAMSEL:	My hero!
VILLAIN:	Curses! Foiled again!

In terms of handing out Reader's Theater scripts, use this as a template for young playwrights to extend the scene or write a new scene employing the same characters.

Using Reader's Theater

When I was a child in elementary school, my classmates and I spent a fair amount of time reading aloud from our basal readers, Round Robin-style, up and down the rows. I remember, when it was my turn, trying to read aloud with lots of expression. I could never recall any details from the passage I was assigned, focused as I was on the written text in lieu of comprehending its meaning. If I made a mistake, I felt humiliated. Kids would laugh at stumblers, stammerers, and mispronouncers, unless they were too busy nervously surveying the upcoming text for their own turns. Round Robin reading has fallen out of fashion.

So how do we help sharpen children's oral reading skills and encourage their response to literature? How do you get them to think more deeply, to go beyond the usual glib happy-sad-mad-glad-bad responses when you ask a perfectly framed question about a book like *The Trial of Cardigan Jones* by Tim Egan—"How did Cardigan Jones feel when the jury finally declared him not guilty."

If you're searching for a painless, effective way to get your children reading aloud with comprehension, expression, fluency, volume, and, most important, joy, Reader's Theater is a miracle. What is Reader's Theater? After you read a book aloud to your children, you hand out a photocopied play script of the story with a part for each child, and they simply read the script aloud and act it out. You don't need props, costumes, or scenery, unless you want them. That's it? Pretty much. And then magic happens. Children walk in a character's shoes. By participating in an activity they love, they become more proficient and self-confident as readers and as performers.

If you are looking for a way to enhance presentation and public speaking skills, to get your children working together in harmony, to enunciate when they speak, to listen to what others have to say, to get to the heart of a story, to boost self esteem, and to hone every reading skill, Reader's Theater is your free ticket to change lives and raise contented, fulfilled, and motivated children. Watch your reading scores soar while children think they're just having a great time.

In my school library, each class put on at least one Reader's Theater play each year, starting with first grade (spring is best, when their reading skills are coming along so well). Children thrive, even the quiet ones, on the thrill of being a star for a little while.

How do you get started? First off, choose a good book and read it aloud to your group. They need to hear your expressive voice in their heads and have a sense of the characters, plot, setting, and sequence. Tell them you will all be acting out the story as a Reader's Theater play. They will probably cheer.

If you're doing an all-class production, you'll most likely need to rearrange your room. In a classroom, children can push all their desks to one side. If you set up a workable procedure for doing this and practice it once or twice, it will be easy enough for them to rearrange the room in the same calm and organized way every time. In a library, you'll need to move tables, which could be trickier, but certainly not impossible. I like to arrange 24 chairs in a semicircle, with open space in the middle so actors can get up and move around for the action scenes. Set up a chair for yourself, facing the stage area, where you'll be the director, prompter, and appreciative audience.

Once the actors are sitting in their chairs, hand out the scripts. Unless you have a few parts that are particularly difficult, don't worry about who gets what part. Some of your shyest kids will shine doing this activity. I do make sure the boys get boy parts, as there's always an outcry if they don't. The girls don't usually care if they get a boy part.

About half of your group will be narrators. I put the narrators on the left side, actors on the right, and hand out the parts sequentially. Don't get fancy here. You always want to be able to figure out whose line is next.

After you hand out scripts and parts, give the cast members a few minutes to read their lines, sounding out difficult words and getting a sense of their meaning. If they can't figure out a word or phrase, they can turn to the actors on their left or right for help, or ask you.

Then it's showtime. Each time a child has a line, he or she must stand up to deliver it in a loud, clear, and expressive voice. Prompt them as needed, and laugh with them. Tell them, "This is a first reading, just like real actors do on Broadway or on TV. Nobody expects it to be perfect and nobody should care if someone misses a line or gets stuck. I'll be the prompter to help you along if that happens. If you see the person next to you has lost his place, just put your finger on his script to point out where we are."

Try to perform a Reader's Theater at least twice. The first time, the children will be struggling with words, meaning, and making sense of the play. It'll be rough, but who cares. The second reading will be much better than the first, and if you have time to do it a third time, it will seem like a revelation. Readers will be able to focus on enjoying the performance and their parts in it. You can, if you wish, carry it further, adding props, costumes, scenery; memorizing lines; or putting on the play for other groups or even the whole school. You don't have to, though. It's the process that's important here, not a finished product. I have rarely found a child who doesn't adore this activity.

Now when you ask all those lovely interpretive questions to foster higher-level thinking and reasoning skills, your children will be brilliantly prepared to discuss a story they have heard, then read, then lived.

SOURCES OF READER'S THEATER PLAYS

Where can you get plays? Look in the 812s on your library shelves for books of plays. Check out *Plays: The Drama Magazine for Young People*, <www.playsmag.com>, an indispensable magazine that comes out monthly and is filled with good, royalty-free plays for elementary through high school.

Look for scripts, instructions, and good advice in the books listed in the Reader's Theater section of the Professional Books Bibliography at the back of this book.

Authors are starting to write Reader's Theater scripts for their own books and to post them on their Web sites. See the sites of Margie Palatini <www.margiepalatini.com> and Toni Buzzeo (<www.tonibuzzeo.com>, for instance.

Another excellent online source is Rick Swallow's Readers Theater/Language Arts Home Page for Teachers at <www.surfcitydelux.com/readerstheater/index.html>, with more than 80 scripts, many from well-known children's picture books.

There are several wonderful fiction books for children that were written with Reader's Theater in mind. Paul Fleischman's *Bull Run* and *Seedfolks* both portray varying characters' points of view and are meant to be brought to life in Reader's Theater productions, according to instructions by the author. Another fine one is Sharon Creech's *Love That Dog*, a collection of free-verse poems from the pen of Jack, written in his journal as a response to the poems his perceptive teacher, Miss Stretchberry, reads aloud to the class.

At first Jack is resentful about having to write poems, which he's sure he can't do well. By the end of January, though, Jack is writing about a yellow dog he had, and he doesn't mind so much when Miss Stretchberry types up his poems. He falls hard for a poem by Mr. Walter Dean Myers and writes his own poem about that yellow dog, Sky, patterned after the poem by Mr. Walter Dean Myers. Jack is elated when Mr. Walter Dean Myers accepts Jack's invitation to visit his class for an author visit.

It'll take you very little time to read this book aloud, but keep your handkerchief ready for a surprise tear and a story that'll stay with you and give you hope. The poems Miss Stretchberry reads, by William Carlos Williams, Robert Frost, Valerie Worth, William Blake, and of course, that lovely New Jersey guy, children's book author and poet Mr. Walter Dean Myers, are appended so you can read them, too. First off, make transparencies of the poems so your listeners can read them and fully understand the context of the poems Jack writes in response. Then have them read the whole book aloud as a Reader's Theater, dividing up Jack's 47 poems, having kids practice their parts, and then performing them in sequence. You, as Miss Stretchberry, can intersperse the readings with the teacher-read poems. As Jack says, "Wow! Wow wow wow wow wow!"

WWW.AARONSHEP.COM

My favorite source of Reader's Theater scripts is the Web site of author Aaron Shepard, who has retold and published many wonderful folktales, most of which he has also written as Reader's Theater scripts. Check out his amazing site, <www.aaronshep.com>, from which you can easily download his scripts, buy his books, or ask him to visit your school to give a workshop.

In 2002, when Shepard's retelling of the West African pourquoi tale *Master Man: A Tall Tale of Nigeria*, was published, I couldn't wait to try out his script with two classes of children—a second- and a third-grade class at Van Holten School. The third grade came first, and the boy who played Shadusa, the cocksure man who considers himself the strongest man in the world, was himself a self-assured, brash kid, well-liked for his comic take on the world. He was very funny and brazen in the part. Then in came the second graders for their chance to act. I handed out the scripts in order, giving the lead part of Shadusa to one boy. His teacher pulled me aside. "Maybe he's not such a good person to play the main character," she whispered. "He's so shy, he barely talks. We haven't heard him say boo all year."

"That's OK," I told her. "It doesn't matter if he's not fabulous. The play will still be fun."

And then the miracle happened. The boy playing Shadusa got into his role. And while he wasn't as flamboyant as the third-grade boy, he was still plenty expressive and blustery, fitting the part just fine. The other children in the class looked at his new persona in amazement.

WRITING YOUR OWN READER'S THEATER SCRIPTS

You can, of course, write up your own scripts, which is far easier than you might think. Possible sources include picture books, controlled vocabulary easy-readers, scenes or chapters from fiction books, folk and fairy tales, biographies, science and history books, and narrative poems such as "Casey at the Bat." Keep your eyes peeled for dramatic possibilities.

When deciding on a book or chapter to transform into a play, I consider my **Freeman's Five Essential Ingredients**. For the elementary school audience, a story must have:

1. Peppy dialogue
2. A little action
3. Laugh-out-loud parts
4. Lively narration
5. Enough parts for all

It takes about an hour to type up a good first draft of a script adaptation of a picture book. Sometimes you'll want to turn dialogue into narration, and sometimes you'll turn narration into dialogue. You can condense scenes and sometimes leave them out entirely, especially if you're doing a long, involved chapter or scene from a fiction book. In Reader's Theater scripts, you can expand the number of parts by adding narrators, doubling up on characters, or even splitting a character's part into two or more.

The Barking Mouse by Antonio Sacre is based on an old Cuban folktale about a charming family of four mice—Mamá Ratón, Papá Ratón, and their two children, Hermana and Hermano—who go on a picnic and encounter a *gato*—a cat! "Hola, gato flaco," those two bold mouse children taunt. "Hello, skinny cat!"

So how can you put on a story with such a small cast if you have a class of, say, 22 children? There are several ways. First, you can write a script with 17 narrators. Or, you can have more than one child play each role. Five children can play the cat, and two each can play the brother and sister. Or you could divvy up the parts saying to one child, "You are Narrator 1 on pages one and two," and to the second, "And you are Narrator 1 on pages three and four."

Another way to do it is to have two casts practicing the play on opposite sides of the room. Then hold two separate readings. Everyone gets a chance to be part of both cast and audience. Another alternative is to give out two different plays, one for each cast to perform. As long as everyone gets a part, you can make it work.

Some of my favorite picture books I've adapted as Reader's Theater scripts include Helen Bannerman's *The Story of Little Babaji*, Doreen Cronin's *Click, Clack, Moo: Cows That Type*, Kate diCamillo's *Mercy Watson to the Rescue*, Tim Egan's *The Trial of Cardigan Jones*, Susan Meddaugh's *Martha Walks the Dog*, Matt Novak's *Mouse TV*, Diane Stanley's *Raising Sweetness*, and Shelley Moore Thomas's *Get Well, Good Knight*.

Here are some script tips:

1. Never photocopy a script for children on both sides of a page to save paper. They find it confusing every time they turn the page. (I learned that one the hard way.)

2. Always number the pages of your scripts.

3. Use a large font—18 point is good—and double spacing before each new character's first line. (The character's lines can be single-spaced.)

4. Put your stage directions in parenthesis and in italics, so students don't read these parts aloud. *(Like this.)*

5. Teach readers to hold their scripts down by their navels instead of over their faces. Tell them, "In Reader's Theater, you act with your face. If you can't see us, we can't see you, and we'll miss some of your best lines that way."

6. Even if you proofread and run your spellcheck, you won't catch all of the typos until you run off a script and hand it out. As for problems with the script itself, make notes as you watch your group perform their first reading. Did one character get too many lines? Not enough? Are the stage directions clear? Then go back to your computer and fix everything that wasn't perfect and run off a second draft.

Easy-Readers

When I first read the controlled vocabulary, easy-to-read chapter book *Inspector Hopper* by Doug Cushman, part of the HarperCollins I Can Read series, which we usually think of as read-alones for beginning readers and not read-alouds, light bulbs flashed and bells and whistles went off in my head. Sometimes the most unexpected book can trigger a whole blizzard of ideas.

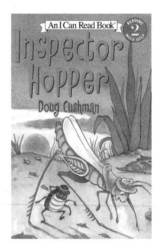

In the three chapters, dedicated detective Hopper and his faithful but always hungry sidekick McBugg find a missing ladybug (the one from the "Ladybug, Ladybug, fly away home" nursery rhyme); catch a rat stealing seeds; and solve the mystery of mosquito Skeet's missing leaf boat. (Conrad the Caterpillar ate it.) Dialogue is sparky, sprightly, and tongue-in-cheek; characters are well rounded. Each chapter is a short story in brief, with a problem, rising action, conflict, a climax, and a satisfying ending. You could break a class into three casts of three to eight readers, depending on the number of characters and possible narrators in each chapter. If you simply photocopy one chapter for each group, children can use it as a script and highlight their own parts with highlighter markers, just as real actors do. Have each group practice a few times, and then perform its skit for the others.

Most easy-readers, such as Arnold Lobel's Frog and Toad series and Cynthia Rylant's Poppleton, Mr. Putter and Tabby, and Henry and Mudge books, have the same type of short, self-contained chapters ideal for small group productions.

You can write up formal scripts, if you like, or have your students write them. Easy-readers are fine models to use for writing sequels about the characters and to teach dialogue-writing skills—and not just for first and second graders, but children in upper grades as well. Just because these stories are easy to read doesn't mean they're that easy to write.

Third through sixth graders can write new chapters for younger kids to read.

Children in grades two and up can learn to write up scripts from published books or from their own original stories. Get them started by giving them a sample play for reference and modeling how to turn dialogue in a book into play dialogue, with stage directions in italics. Consider pairing them up to write up scripts for Aesop's fables, as they're easy and short.

I taught a storytelling class for the Rutgers University School of Communication, Information, and Library Studies that included a group of crackerjack teachers from the West Windsor-Plainsboro School District, along with their fearless librarian, Connie Beadle. For one assignment, they were to select a folktale and write it up as a Reader's Theater script.

Fourth-grade resource room teacher Donna Cevoli turned to her students for help with her homework. These were kids who thought they couldn't write and couldn't read, but the assignment was awfully tempting. They took Eric Kimmel's mischievous African trickster tale *Anansi and the Moss-Covered Rock* (Holiday House, 1990) and typed it up on the computer in script format. They had a ball and felt even more all-powerful and competent when they heard that our class of grownups acted out their script and pronounced it perfect.

If you type up just one script each year, from a picture book, or a good action-packed fiction chapter, or a narrative poem, pretty soon you'll have a drawer full of scripts to use with your kids.

Singer's Theater

If you want your children to work on their fluency, or, as my mother used to put it, "Don't-read-it-one-word-at-a-time," then start singing. Every time you sing a song, hand out the words for children to follow as they sing, even if it's a song they know. They can't sing it one word at a time; keeping up with the song ensures that their eyes will move more quickly and efficiently from left to right across the printed page

The song parodies in Alan Katz's *I'm Still Here in the Bathtub: Brand New Silly Dilly Songs* make children laugh while they read and sing, which isn't so easy to do. There's "My tiny baby brother took our remote control; When I wasn't looking, he flushed it down the bowl . . ." and "Lost my parka, what'll I do?" My favorite, which my sister Sharron and I can identify with from our earlier years: "My sister fights with me / We always disagree / And it's her fault!"

You might recognize the songs on which these funny take-offs are based: "The Itsy Bitsy Spider," "Skip-to-My-Lou," and "My Country, 'Tis of Thee." Have the children read the poems aloud and try to figure out the original versions. Then warble away. Afterward, pairs or trios can write new parodies of songs they know.

Poet Jack Prelutsky has always set some of his poems to recognizable songs. "One Day in Seattle" from the book *The Frog Wore Red Suspenders* will get you singing it to the tune of "On Top of Old Smokey." When I read "The Turkey Shot Out of the Oven," from his book *Something Big Has Been Here* (Greenwillow, 1990), I found myself humming "My Bonnie Lies Over the Ocean." A perfect fit. I mentioned the poem to friend and fellow librarian Cathy Darby and she said, "But it doesn't have a chorus." So she wrote one:

Oh my, oh me, why didn't I follow the recipe?
Oh my, oh me, why didn't I follow the recipe?

Type up the words to the poem and the chorus (which makes the very funny song even more so) and hand them out for children to sing.

For a little guided imagery before you start singing, ask children to close their eyes and picture their own kitchens. Have them imagine lifting up the heavy turkey in its roasting pan and sliding it into the oven. Tell them the song is actually a mystery. As you sing it with them, have them try to figure out just how, when, and why the turkey exploded out of the oven, "completely obscuring the room."

Another thing I love about Prelutsky is his use of weighty words. In this poem alone you'll find the words demolished, ricocheted, smeared, displeasure, and chagrin, all of them easily definable in context. So children will be reading, singing, comprehending, envisioning, and making inferences, all in one poem. Oh, yes, and best of all, having a wonderful time.

Dogs Rule! by Daniel Kirk is a big book chock full of meaty poems that literally sing the praises of all dogs. It comes with an utterly hummable CD of all 22 poems, set to music by the author and sung with his band. Children will learn the tunes in no time and sing right along. When librarian Janice Steinhouse at Joyce Kilmer School in Milltown, New Jersey, showed it to several classes of fifth graders, they went bonkers, howling that they wanted that book! They followed up by writing their own pet tribute songs and poems, complete with portraits.

Let's Put On a Musical

I recently came across a terrific little company, Bad Wolf Press, <www.badwolfpress.com>, that sells musicals for children in grades K to 9 to put on in the classroom. (The catalog says it is a "*tiny* publishing company that hopes someday to grow to become a *small* company.") It was started in 1995 by lyricist John Heath and composer Ron Fink; they have written more than 30 clever, melodious, and entertaining shows for children to perform, all available at very reasonable prices. They advertise their scripts as "musical plays for musically timid teachers."

Each play comes with a spiral-bound script and practical guide for the teacher, with permission to make copies of the script for the whole class, and a CD with a recording of each song sung by Ron Fink, accompanied on piano. The second half of the CD repeats just the piano portion, so when your students have learned the songs and you stage the play, you will have instant accompaniment for your singers with no fuss. You can also purchase the sheet music, if you're planning to get fancy and put on the play for a larger audience.

I've read and listened to a batch of the literature- and folklore-based musicals, including "Jack and the Beanstalk," "Anansi and the Moss Covered Rock," and "Theseus and the Minotaur," and I loved them. Many of the plays tie in to the science and social studies curriculums. Check out the teacher-friendly Web site and give it a try. They estimate there have been 70,000 productions of their shows worldwide. I'm not surprised.

CREATIVE DRAMA ACROSS THE CURRICULUM

Creative drama can be integrated into all areas of the curriculum. The year 2003 marked the centennial of the Wright brothers' first flight, and many instructive and informative biographies were published about them. I was working with several classes of primary-grade students and went searching the library for science books that explain the concepts of flight in the simplest of terms. There wasn't much available for first graders; flight is not usually a part of the first-grade science curriculum. In *First to Fly: How Wilbur and Orville Wright Invented the Airplane*, author Peter Busby explained, in a sidebar, that there were three movements that all aircraft make: pitch, roll, and yaw. I didn't know that before. (That's why I love reading children's nonfiction books. There are always so many simply stated facts to pick up.)

Yaw was a new word to me, my fact for the day. How could I introduce those three new terms to children so they would remember them? I asked my husband, Izzy, for advice: "What did you know about airplanes when you were a boy?"

He said, "Oh, I don't know. We just used to put our arms out at our sides and fly around the house all the time, pretending to be planes."

Bingo. That's how I could introduce pitch, roll, and yaw. Through drama. We could act it all out. Integrating creative drama with nonfiction would teach the facts in a different way, without the usual memorization or paper-and-pencil activities.

When we read Robert J. Blake's picture book *Fledgling*, in which a young kestrel takes her first flight over the city, we pantomimed flying off an imaginary

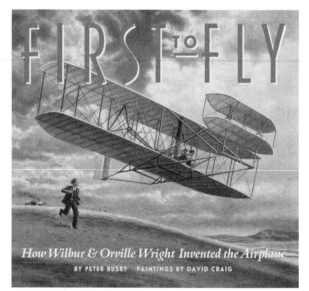

How Wilbur & Orville Wright Invented the Airplane
BY PETER BUSBY   PAINTINGS BY DAVID CRAIG

rooftop ledge. We flew soundlessly, of course, so the hawks wouldn't find us, and made it home for a safe landing.

Now we would take what we had experienced in our pretend flight, and move from pure science—birds in flight—to applied science—how airplanes imitate the flight of birds. I wrote the following as a guided science lesson in deductive reasoning and fact finding through movement.

Movement Experiments

As you guide your students through the presentation of information and questions that follow, ask them to discuss each question and use their bodies to figure out possible answers. Through movement, they will learn, kinesthetically, some basic facts of flight.

Here's your script:

How many ways can you move? Where can you bend your body?
(With the children testing out possibilities, compile a master list of all the joints they can move: fingers and toes, wrists and ankles, knees and elbows, shoulders and hips, waist and neck.)

Can you move forward? Backward? Can you sway in a circle from your waist? Can you twist from side to side? Let's experiment to see how many ways we can move.
(Ask children to demonstrate each movement along with you.)

When you ride a bicycle, how many ways can it move?
(Using their bodies as bicycles, children can demonstrate how a bike can go straight or turn to the left or right.)

What way can a car move that a bicycle cannot?
(One of your students will surely figure this out: a car can go backward.)

When the Wright brothers were figuring out how birds fly, they realized that if they wanted to make a real flying machine, they would need to include three things. What do you think they needed?
(See if children can come up with the three things Wilbur and Orville needed.

The three things were:

1. Strong wings
2. An engine to keep the machine up in the air
3. A way to steer the machine

The brothers also figured out that, unlike a bicycle moving on the ground, an airplane flying in the sky would need to make three basic movements. Their plane, the *Flyer*, was the first one that could move in all three of the following ways.)

Please stand up for a little airplane aerobics as we demonstrate the three movements all aircraft make, *pitch, roll,* and *yaw*, Y-A-W, *yaw*. First, put your arms straight out at your sides like an airplane. Try these three movements with me, and we'll say some of these words together while we fly. Ready for takeoff? Let's go!

1. First, an airplane can *pitch*. This means the nose of the plane can go up and down. **(Keep your back straight and bend up and down from your waist.)** What do we call this? That's right: *pitch*.

2. Second, an airplane can *roll*. When a plane rolls, it dips its wings up and down and moves from side to side. Another word for rolling is *"banking."* **(Keep your back straight and bend your waist sideways to the left and then to the right. When you bend or bank or roll to the left, your left arm dips down toward the ground and your right arm points toward the sky. Now *roll* or bank to the *right*.)** What do we call this? That's right: *roll*. We are *rolling*. What's the other word for it? That's right: *banking*. An airplane can *bank*.

3. Third, an airplane can *yaw* or turn sideways. The whole plane can turn from side to side, to the left and to the right, the way a car or bicycle can. **(Twist your waist to the left and then the right.)** What are we doing? Exactly. This is called *yaw*.

Since the wings on a plane can't flap up and down like a bird when it flies, the Wright brothers needed a way to steer better. They realized that a bird twists or *warps* the tips of its wings up and down to control its flight. So they figured out a way to *warp* or twist just the tip of each wing. **(Hold out your arms straight, like wings, and then flex your hands up and down at the wrists.)**

You might then want to take your group outside and practice "flying." Have them demonstrate each movement, and try a bit of flying in formation. The next time your students fly in an airplane, they'll remember how it all works because they didn't just read about airplanes, they themselves "became" airplanes and flew.

Who Killed Novella Reads?

Creative drama can take many forms. Dawn Sardes, young adult librarian at the Euclid Public Library in Euclid, Ohio, organized a library murder mystery party for her patrons. If imitation equals flattery, you may want to adapt Dawn's very well-thought-out plan for your own sleuths to solve.

Here's her description of her innovative and creative program:

> To be honest, I'd been wanting to do a mystery party and had thought and thought of how to pull it off. Then, I was in Wal-Mart and saw a kid with a Clue game and it hit me. I called our program the "Clue in the Library Mystery Dinner Party." I created a game based on the Clue board game. I came up with 10 suspects, 6 methods of murder, 10 "rooms" (areas of the library), and 8 motives. The victim was "librarian" Novella Reads.
>
> Novella is the name of our library's mannequin. Our PR person found her in a dumpster a couple of years ago. We use Novella for book displays; we might dress her in a wedding gown in June and set up wedding etiquette books, or in a dress and apron to advertise cookbooks. She's actually pretty hideous looking, and most of us at the library hate her. *Everyone* begged to be the one who killed her.

THE SET-UP

To prepare for this event, I:

1. Scoped out 10 staff members who would make good suspects. Using red card stock paper and clip art, I created and laminated a 3" x 5" game card for each suspect.
2. Identified 10 rooms or areas of the library and made a blue game card for each.
3. Came up with 6 silly methods of murder (Stapled to Death, Poisoned Lunch, A Really, Really Bad Paper Cut, Smothered by Magazines, Run Over by a Book Truck, and Hit over Head with a Dictionary) and made green game cards for each.
4. Devised 8 ridiculous motives for the killing (including: Novella steals lunches, Novella never puts books back in the right spot, Novella shushes people too much, and Novella throws teens out of the library), and created a yellow card for each.
5. Wrote scripts for each of the suspects to read and learn, providing answers for the three questions the interrogators would be allowed to ask them. The three questions were:

    - Have you heard that Novella Reads has been killed?
    - What was your opinion of Novella?
    - Where have you been for the past two hours?

    The "suspects" were to respond to any further (unsanctioned) questions by becoming affronted, saying that they were calling their attorneys, and walking away, looking as guilty as possible. In the scripts, each suspect revealed a deep-set dislike of Novella and a reason they resented her, including: She makes more money than me; She makes me do all her work; She steals my lunch every day; and She threw me out of the library.
6. Scrounged around for props for the suspects to have nearby during their interrogations. These included a pile of old magazines; a super-sized stapler, a large bottle of "poison"; and an old blonde wig from which I cut off some hair, putting one hank in the wheels of the book truck and another between the pages of the dictionary.
7. Determined, ahead of time, the room, the killer, the motive, and method, pulled the respective cards, and sealed them in an envelope.
8. Created a Detective's Notebook for each of the five teams, named after Clue characters—Plum, Scarlet, Peacock, Mustard, and Green. In each notebook was:

    a. a spreadsheet of all the variables (suspects, motives, rooms, and methods)
    b. an assortment of six of the cards
    c. instructions that said each team had to keep its cards secret. If they had a particular card, they were to strike that person or item off their list of variables.
    d. the three questions they were permitted to ask each suspect
    e. some blank pages for them to take notes of the suspects' answers and other observations

HOT ON THE TRAIL

On the day of the event, 17 children showed up, grades 6 to 9, to find the mannequin of Novella standing in the lobby as a part of a holiday display. I had put a sign on her stating that this was a memorial statue of Novella, commissioned in her image before her gruesome murder earlier that day. The children gathered in the meeting room, where they couldn't help but notice the tape outline of Novella's body on the floor. I explained that the police determined that her body was moved there after she was killed.

With three or four players assigned to each of the five teams, kids signed their names on their teams' corresponding color paper badges. Each badge had a hole punched in it and yarn threaded through the hole so the player could wear it as a necklace. Each team then selected a reporter to be the note-taker.

Getting started, handing out the Detective's Notebooks, and providing the instructions took about 20 minutes; going out into the library to find and interrogate suspects took another 20 to 30 minutes. (I used this time to set up the dinner buffet and a table of book prizes.)

So, off the kids went to find and interrogate their suspects, all of whom were in costume and wearing nametags. Remember, every suspect was happy to see Novella dead, every suspect had some sort of incriminating evidence in hand, and every suspect, in answering the questions, was in one of the suspected areas during the time of the murder.

As they interrogated their subjects, sharp-eyed investigators noted clues at hand. For example, our library secretary, Kathy, claimed she hated the deceased because Novella was always foisting her work off on Kathy and then taking all the credit. As she was being questioned, Kathy was stapling like mad with a huge stapler from tech services. (One of the methods, remember, was "Stapled to Death.") The detectives had to observe and take notes of the clues each subject provided in responses to questions, in physical appearance, and in the relevant props being used. Some of the eight possible motives were shared by more than one suspect.

Tom, the adult reference librarian, was dressed in old-time gangster attire and had the unabridged dictionary in hand, with a hank of hair hanging out of it. He hated Novella for stealing his lunches every day.

When the pizza arrived, we took a break for dinner. As the teams ate, they started making their guesses. A reporter from each team shared the responses and observations of the suspects they interrogated.

Green Team would say, "We think it was the Reference Librarian. We think he hit her over the head with the dictionary in Adult Nonfiction for being a nasty gossip."

The next team had to look through their cards until they found a card that would disprove any aspect of that guess. One sharp boy countered the Green Team's clue, explaining, "The hair in the book was blonde, but the memorial statue of Novella has black hair. Also, our team has the dictionary card." Exactly.

Then it was his team's turn to guess. Altogether, it took all of the teams nine guesses for the mystery to be solved, at which time two of our town's police officers were called to "arrest" the suspect, Tina, the circulation associate.

She was formally accused by the winning team. She broke down and admitted that she just couldn't take it anymore—that Novella was driving her nuts because she never paid her fines or returned her books on time, so she smothered her with a pile of magazines in the book-sorting room. The officers cuffed her and took her out.

At the door, she turned and warned everyone, "See, kids—if you don't return your library books on time, you may end up like Novella Reads!"

The entire program lasted almost two hours. Each member of the winning team got to choose two books from the prize table. Then the players on the other teams got to choose one each. The whole night was hysterically funny. The kids and the staff loved it. They all really got into their roles and are still talking about it.

When I spoke with Dawn about that eventful night, she told me she has been working closely these days with another live-wire librarian, a certain Madame Trebooky, the psychic librarian of Hogsmeade Public Library, who bears an uncanny resemblance to Dawn herself, though that's certainly just a coincidence. Madame Trebooky, renowned at the Euclid Public Library for providing psychic book recommendations, sports silver metallic hair, flamboyant attire, and lots of makeup, unlike Dawn, who is, well, face it, just another boring, everyday librarian like the rest of us. The library's teen patrons think Madame Trebooky is vastly more interesting than Dawn. What's a librarian to do?

THE ANNOTATED
READ-ALOUD LISTS

Rooster Can't Cock-a-Doodle-Doo

by **Karen Rostoker-Gruber** • pictures by **Paul Rátz de Tagyos**

WHAT'S IN THE BOOKLISTS

MOST OF THE NEW 1,705 CHILDREN'S BOOKS IN THE FOLLOWING BOOK-lists were published between 1995 and 2005. I have tried to provide literate and cogent descriptions of each book, a gloriously simple idea or two for a follow-up that works, a detailed list of related titles, and up to ten subject headings.

The six booklists are each arranged alphabetically by author. First is "Easy Fiction/Picture Books." This, of course, is the longest of all sections, as more picture books are published each year than any other kind of children's books. There are approximately 900 titles in this chapter; many of them for young children but you will also find picture books for older readers.

Next is the "Fiction" chapter, which includes chapter books for grades K to 6. Fiction books for grades K to 2 are listed under the heading "Fiction Books for Early Grades" in the Subject Index.

Then comes a folklore chapter—"Folk & Fairy Tales, Myths & Legends"—followed by a poetry chapter, "Poetry, Nonsense, and Language-Oriented Nonfiction," in which you will also find jokes and riddles and wordplay; a nonfiction chapter; and a biography chapter. The field of picture-book biographies has certainly mushroomed in the past decade.

Finally, to stay well-developed in your chosen field, you'll want to consult the extensive "Professional Bibliography."

AVAILABILITY OF TITLES

These days books go out of stock indefinitely or out of print so fast your head can spin. This is a perennial problem for children's book lovers. The rule of thumb is to buy new books quickly, as most of them won't be available in two years. If I had included only those titles I knew would be readily available, this would be a slim volume indeed. Many of the older titles will not be simple to obtain, but good libraries may already have them on their shelves. Persistent book hounds can track down desired copies through Amazon.com or one of the many companies on the Internet specializing in out-of-print materials.

Although many titles on my lists are available in paperback editions, they are not usually noted here, as they go in and out of print even faster than hardbacks; a quick look on Amazon.com, Follett's TitleWave.com, or your own jobber's Web site will let you know what formats are available.

A TYPICAL ENTRY

In this book, I've changed the format of the booklists to make each entry more practical, user-friendly, and comprehensive. Each recommended title has five parts. Here's what you'll find on a typical page:

670 Rostoker-Gruber, Karen. *Rooster Can't Cock-a-Doodle-Doo*. Illus. by Paul Rátz de Tagyos. Dial, 2004. 0-8037-2877-8. Unp. Gr. PreK–1

Rooster wakes with a terrible sore throat and enlists the help of the hens, cows, sheep, and pigs to figure out a way to wake up Farmer Ted without cock-a-doodle-doing. All the helpful barn animals pile atop one another to make an animal pyramid high enough to reach Farmer Ted's bedroom and then set about helping him complete his chores. Listeners will love examining the comical and expressive faces and body language of the animals as they milk the cows, shear the sheep, and pour the slop.

GERM: Looking for stories in which listeners have to brainstorm for a solution to a problem? Voilà. Puns abound in the animals' dialogue—"You look eggz-hausted," the hens tell the whispering Rooster—and all will join in on the animal noises and repeated refrains. Script this out as a Reader's Theater to perform with readers.

RELATED TITLES: Auch, Mary Jane. *Bantam of the Opera*. Holiday House, 1997. / Auch, Mary Jane. *Peeping Beauty*. Holiday House, 1993. / Bateman, Teresa. *Farm Flu*. Albert Whitman, 2001. / Cazet, Denys. *Elvis the Rooster Almost Goes to Heaven*. HarperCollins, 2003. / Cronin, Doreen. *Click, Clack, Moo: Cows That Type*. Simon & Schuster, 2000. / Dallas-Conté, Juliet. *Cock-a-Moo-Moo*. Little, Brown, 2001. / Egan, Tim. *Serious Farm*. Houghton Mifflin, 2003. / Froehlich, Margaret Walden. *That Kookoory!* Harcourt, 1995. / Krosoczka, Jarrett J. *Punk Farm*. Knopf, 2005. / Landry, Leo. *Eat Your Peas, Ivy Louise!* Houghton Mifflin, 2005. / Lobel, Arnold. *How the Rooster Saved the Day*. Greenwillow, 1977. / Meeker, Clare Hodgson. *Who Wakes Rooster?* Simon & Schuster, 1996. / Palatini, Margie. *Moo Who?* HarperCollins, 2004. / Pearson, Tracey Campbell. *Bob*. Farrar, 2002. / Schwartz, Amy. *Old MacDonald*. Scholastic, 1999. / Stevens, Janet, and Susan Stevens Crummel. *Cook-a-Doodle-Doo!* Harcourt, 1999.

SUBJECTS: ANIMAL SOUNDS. CHANTABLE REFRAIN. DOMESTIC ANIMALS. FARM LIFE. HUMOROUS FICTION. READER'S THEATER. ROOSTERS. SICK.

Format of Each Entry

The Bibliographical Data

Bibliographic information for each entry includes the author(s), complete title, illustrator(s), publisher, copyright date, ISBN (International Standard Book Number), number of pages ("unp." means unpaged, or no page numbers), and a suggested grade level range, though that is never set in stone. For instance, many picture books can and should be used through grade 6, and often beyond. (For a list, look in the Subject Index under "Picture Books for All Ages" and also under "Picture Books for Older Readers.") You should always gauge the tastes, sensibilities, maturity levels, and needs of your own children when picking titles from another person's booklist.

The authors listed in the folklore chapter are usually retellers, since often no one knows who originally composed the stories, which may be hundreds of years old. Translators' names are also included where applicable. On the poetry list, note that "comp." for compiler is written after many of the authors' names. This indicates that the author listed did not write the poems, but collected and edited them from other sources. In the subject index, check the heading "Poetry—Single Author" for a complete list of collections by one poet.

The Annotation

I strive to be meticulous not only in the books I choose to include but also in my individual description of each book. In each one- to three-sentence annotation, I try to capture, along with a synopsis of the plot or the contents, a bit of each book's heart, soul, and flavor to pique your interest and tempt you to read it to yourself and, most important, to children.

The Germ

After each book's annotation, you'll find a Germ. No, not the bad kind. My book Germs are small, pithy, practical, useful, do-able ideas to inject into your own lesson plans. They include suggestions for sharing the books with children to develop comprehension skills and creativity, and to tie into a variety of subject areas including language arts, library skills, science, social studies, math, health, art, music, and physical education. There are reading, writing, and illustrating prompts and other activities for across-the-curriculum and story hour programs, including creative drama, Reader's Theater, storytelling, group discussion, booktalks, games, crafts, research, and problem-solving.

In the Germ, I'll often highlight a related book as a particularly apt companion, follow-up, or extension on that subject or theme. You'll also find that title listed again on the Related Titles list that follows. (Most of these related books also appear as main entries in this book or, if published before

1995, in the companion volumes *Books Kids Will Sit Still For* or *More Books Kids Will Sit Still For*. Look up each of those entries for annotations that provide still more relevant activities and titles.)

Germinate each idea as you see fit, and make it better. A good Germ can inspire you to think of many other great ideas, and in no time you can grow that Germ, expand upon it, and incorporate it into a miraculous, scintillating, full-fledged lesson or unit or story hour, adding your own clever spin, personality, and know-how that you can then share with your colleagues.

RELATED TITLES LIST

Next is the Related Titles list, a careful compilation of exemplary books that will help you make book connections with old favorites and new-to-you titles alike. It pulls together books by the same author as well as those with similar themes, styles, characters, genres, or subjects. Use the Related Titles list for further read-aloud ideas and for mapping out thematic units, story hour tie-ins, and booktalks. These are often titles you can use for Guided Reading, Literature Circles, or Book Clubs, or whatever your public library or school district is calling programs in which kids read and discuss real, honest-to-goodness, spectacularly written books instead of a basal reader. And, of course, you can recommend these titles to your book hounds as wonderful follow-ups when they say, "Do you have any other books as good as that one?"

SUBJECTS LIST

Finally, you'll find up to ten subject designations listed for each title so you can consult the Subject Index at the back of the book for additional books on that topic or can simply ascertain where the book might fit thematically into your curricular or literary program.

USING THE INDEXES

The three indexes at the back of the book (Author/Illustrator, Title, and Subject) will help you in your search for the perfect read-aloud.

The extensive Subject Index contains more than 1,800 separate topics. Each entry includes author, title, and grade level, to help you make even more connections between similarly themed books. There are also numerous "see" and "see also" cross-references. Although most of the subjects use standard subject headings, I added several of my own that seemed pertinent, including:

Alliteration	Exaggeration	Pourquoi Tales
Autobiography	Fairy Tales—Satire	Self-Esteem
Biography	Fiction Books for Early Grades	Sequence Stories
Caldecott Medal	Fingerplays	Sound Effects
Call-and-Response Stories	Knock-Knock Jokes	Stories to Tell
Cause and Effect	Literary Fairy Tales	Stories with Songs
Chantable Refrain	Narrative Poetry	Superheroes
Creative Drama	Newbery Medal	Tongue Twisters
Creative Writing	Parodies	Transformations
Cumulative Stories	Picture Books for All Ages	Trickster Tales
Days of the Week	Picture Books for Older Readers	Visual Perception

If you are involved in integrating values and character education into your curriculum, these subject headings will help you locate good related materials:

Behavior	Family life	Obedience
Citizenship	Forgiveness	Patience
Compassion	Friendship	Perseverance
Conduct of life	Generosity	Problem solving
Conflict resolution	Helpfulness	Respect
Cooperation	Honesty	Responsibility
Courage	Individuality	Self-acceptance
Creativity	Kindness	Self-concept
Dedication	Leadership	Self-confidence
Determination	Love	Self-esteem
Emotions	Loyalty	Wisdom
	Neighborliness	

EASY FICTION / PICTURE BOOKS

1   **Abrams, Pam.** *Now I Eat My ABC's.* **Photos by Bruce Wolf. Scholastic, 2004. 0-439-64942-0. Unp. Gr. PreK–1**
Each page of this appetizing alphabet board book consists of two letters, each showcasing a clear color photograph of a fruit, vegetable, or food. "A is for asparagus," it says, and the A is constructed out of three asparagus spears; B is made of blueberries, M is constructed of marsh-mallows, and we visually drool our way to Z for zucchini.
GERM: Identify the mostly familiar foods and categorize them into fruits, veggies, and others. Check children's recall by having them recite the whole alphabet of foods from memory, and you'll be amazed at how many they can cite. Make your own alphabetical food concoctions and have a tasting party.
RELATED TITLES: Carle, Eric. *Today Is Monday.* Philomel, 1993. / Ehlert, Lois. *Eating the Alphabet.* Harcourt, 1989. / Ehlert, Lois. *Growing Vegetable Soup.* Harcourt, 1987. / Kalman, Maira. *What Pete Ate from A–Z.* Put-nam, 2001. / Lester, Mike. *A Is for Salad.* Putnam, 2000. / MacDonald, Margaret Read. *Pickin' Peas.* Harper-Collins, 1998. / MacDonald, Suse. *Alphabatics.* Simon & Schuster, 1986. / Mahurin, Tim. *Jeremy Kooloo.* Dutton, 1995. / Moxley, Sheila. *ABCD: An Alphabet Book of Cats and Dogs.* Little, Brown, 2001. / Pandell, Karen. *Animal Action ABC.* Dutton, 1996. / Rosenthal, Amy Krouse. *Little Pea.* Chronicle Books, 2005. / Schaefer, Lola M. *Pick, Pull, Snap! Where Once a Flower Bloomed.* HarperCollins, 2003. / Seeger, Laura Vaccaro. *The Hidden Alpha-bet.* Roaring Brook, 2003. / Yolen, Jane. *How Do Dinosaurs Eat Their Food?* Blue Sky/Scholastic, 2005.
SUBJECTS: ALPHABET BOOKS. FOOD. FRUIT. VEGETABLES.

2   **Adler, David A.** *Young Cam Jansen and the Library Mystery.* **Illus. by Susanna Natti. Viking, 2001. 0-670-89281-5. 32pp. Gr. K–2**
Introduce your mystery fans to the amazing Cam, short for "The Camera," Jansen, whose cam-era-like memory helps her see clues others never notice. At the library with her dad and her friend Eric, Cam shows off her amazing recall by reciting word-for-word passages from one of her favorite books. A stop at the supermarket gives her a reason to track down a more mun-dane collection of words: dad can't figure out where he left his shopping list.
GERM: At the end of each Young Cam Jansen book is a memory game—a list of questions to check readers' observation skills. Play another memory development game: Place 20 different objects on a tray (such as scissors, a magic marker, a stuffed animal, an apple). Bring out the tray and give children one minute to study the objects. After removing the tray, have children list as many of the items as they can recall and write them on the white board or chart, drawing a little picture in colored markers to go with each word.
RELATED TITLES: Adler, David A. *My Writing Day.* Richard C. Owen, 1999. / Adler, David A. Cam Jansen series. Putnam. / Adler, David A. Young Cam Jansen series. Putnam. / Clifford, Eth. *Flatfoot Fox and the Case of the Mising Schoolhouse.* Houghton Mifflin, 1997. (And others in the Flatfoot Fox series.) / Cushman, Doug. *Aunt Eater Loves a Mystery.* HarperCollins, 1987. (And others in the Aunt Eater mystery series.) / Cushman, Doug. *Mystery at the Club Sandwich.* Clarion, 2004. / Cushman, Doug. *The Mystery of King Karfu.* Harper-Collins, 1996. / Ernst, Lisa Campbell. *Stella Louella's Runaway Book.* Simon & Schuster, 1998. / Parish, Herman. *Amelia Bedelia, Bookworm.* Greenwillow, 2003. / Polacco, Patricia. *Aunt Chip and the Great Triple Creek Dam*

Affair. Philomel, 1996. / Sharmat, Marjorie Weinman, and Mitchell Sharmat. *Nate the Great and the Big Sniff.* Delacorte, 2001. (And others in the Nate the Great series.)

SUBJECTS: LIBRARIES. MEMORY. MYSTERY AND DETECTIVE STORIES. VISUAL DISCRIMINATION.

3   **Agee, Jon. *Milo's Hat Trick.* Illus. by the author. Hyperion, 2001. 0-7868-0902-7. Unp. Gr. K–3**
After Milo the Magnificent botches all his magic tricks and the theater manager gives him one more chance to pull a rabbit out of a hat or else, Milo meets a bear who knows how to do an even better hat trick.
GERM: Introduce aspiring magicians to the Dewey decimal number 793.8—magic books. Select four simple magic tricks from the books, photocopy them, and gather together any needed props. Hand out one trick per group. Your young Houdinis must then work together to read, figure out, practice, and perform their magic tricks for the rest of the class.
RELATED TITLES: Broekel, Ray. *Now You See It: Easy Magic for Beginners.* Little, Brown, 1979. / dePaola, Tomie. *Strega Nona's Magic Lessons.* Harcourt, 1982. / Egan, Tim. *Burnt Toast on Davenport Street.* Houghton Mifflin, 1997. / Krull, Kathleen. *Houdini: World's Greatest Mystery Man and Escape King.* Walker, 2005. / Petersen, P. J. *The Amazing Magic Show.* Simon & Schuster, 1994. / Schneider, Howie. *Uncle Lester's Hat.* Putnam, 1993. / Seeger, Pete. *Abiyoyo.* Macmillan, 1986. / Selznick, Brian. *The Houdini Box.* Knopf, 1991. / Steig, William. *Sylvester and the Magic Pebble.* Simon & Schuster, 1988.
SUBJECTS: BEARS. HATS. MAGIC. MAGICIANS.

4   **Alarcón, Karen Beaumont. *Louella Mae, She's Run Away!* Illus. by Rosanne Litzinger. Henry Holt, 1997. 0-8050-3532-X. Unp. Gr. PreK–K**
"Look in the cornfields! Look in the hay! Where, oh where, is Louella Mae?" A farm family and all of their animals search for the elusive Louella Mae, whoever she is, by the stream, in the barn, 'neath the bridge, and everywhere, until they find her in the house, nesting in the tub, with her piglets.
GERM: Before you turn each page, listeners will need to supply the upcoming rhyming word. Of course, they'll all love speculating on just where (and who) Louella Mae is. Read the story again so kids can recall each rhyming word. Write new rhyming verses about other places Louella May could be hiding.
RELATED TITLES: Dodds, Dayle Ann. *Where's Pup?* Dial, 2003. / Ehrlich, Amy. *Parents in the Pigpen, Pigs in the Tub.* Dial, 1993. / Gliori, Debi. *The Snow Lambs.* Scholastic, 1996. / Hill, Eric. *Where's Spot?* Putnam, 1980. / Lindbergh, Reeve. *The Day the Goose Got Loose.* Dial, 1990.
SUBJECTS: FARM LIFE. LOST AND FOUND POSSESSIONS. PIGS. RUNAWAYS. STORIES IN RHYME.

5   **Alborough, Jez. *My Friend Bear.* Illus. by the author. Candlewick, 1998. 0-7636-0583-2. Unp. Gr. PreK**
A boy named Eddie, taking a walk in the woods with his little teddy, comes upon a giant-sized teddy bear. Hearing a real bear approaching, Eddie hides behind the giant teddy, which belongs to the bear. When Eddie speaks, the bear is astonished, believing his big teddy can talk. Told in rhyme with soft, bear-filled watercolors, this is a story of friendship that transcends size.
GERM: Also share the first two books about Eddie and his bear pal, *It's the Bear!* and *Where's My Teddy?* Read aloud more tales to your teddies with *Three Stories You Can Read to Your Teddy Bear* by Sara Swan Miller.
RELATED TITLES: Alborough, Jez. *It's the Bear!* Candlewick, 1994. / Alborough, Jez. *Watch Out! Big Bro's Coming!* Candlewick, 1997. / Alborough, Jez. *Where's My Teddy?* Candlewick, 1992. / Freeman, Don. *Corduroy.* Viking, 1968. / McCloskey, Robert. *Blueberries for Sal.* Viking, 1948. / Miller, Sara Swan. *Three Stories You Can Read to Your Teddy Bear.* Houghton Mifflin, 2004. / Rosen, Michael. *We're Going on a Bear Hunt.* McElderry, 1989.
SUBJECTS: BEARS. FRIENDSHIP. STORIES IN RHYME. TEDDY BEARS.

6   **Alda, Arlene. *Arlene Alda's 1 2 3: What Do You See?* Photos by the author. Tricycle, 2000. 1-883672-71-6. Unp. Gr. PreK–1**
Clear, vibrant, colorful photographs display the numbers one to 10 and back again as seen in nature—the body of a swan reflected in the water looks like the number 3—and everyday objects—a split bagel with cream cheese looks like the number 8.
GERM: Number detectives can find or assemble other examples of numbers in their environment and take photos for display. Find all the letters in Alda's companion alphabet book, *Arlene Alda's A B C.*

RELATED TITLES: Alda, Arlene. *Arlene Alda's A B C.* Tricycle, 2002. / Carter, David A. *One Red Dot: A Pop-up Book for Children of All Ages.* Little Simon, 2005. / Catalanotto, Peter. *Daisy 1 2 3.* Atheneum, 2003. / Ehlert, Lois. *Fish Eyes: A Book You Can Count On.* Harcourt, 1990. / Feldman, Judy. *The Alphabet in Nature.* Children's Press, 1991. / Fleming, Denise. *Count!* Henry Holt, 1992. / Freymann, Saxton, and Joost Elffers. *One Lonely Sea Horse.* Scholastic, 2000. / MacDonald, Suse. *Look Whooo's Counting.* Scholastic, 2000. / Robert, Francois, Jean Robert, and Jane Gittings. *Find a Face.* Chronicle, 2004. / Shannon, George. *White Is for Blueberry.* Greenwillow, 2005.
SUBJECTS: COUNTING BOOKS.

7   **Alexander, Lloyd. *How the Cat Swallowed Thunder*. Illus. by Judith Byron Schachner. Dutton, 2000. 0-525-46449-2. Unp. Gr. PreK–3**
When Mother Holly leaves her rascally cat alone for the first time, with strict orders to tidy up the cottage, everything goes awry for the overwhelmed cat, who inadvertently uses the magic objects that the old woman employs for changing the seasons.
GERM: In this original pourquoi tale, we see how a stray piece of popcorn led to the cat's purr. Write new literary explanations for the singular behavior of animals, such as how dog got his bark or mouse got his squeak. Draw pictures of other magical objects Mother Holly might have in her cottage and show how they might work to produce other weather patterns, such as fog, sleet, clouds, or tornadoes. Look through a collection of Grimm's fairy tales to find the original story about the character Mother Holly, or Holle, who is responsible for the changing seasons.
RELATED TITLES: Alexander, Lloyd. *The House Gobbaleen.* Dutton, 1995. / Barrett, Judi. *Cloudy with a Chance of Meatballs.* Atheneum, 1978. / Bender, Robert. *Toads and Diamonds.* Dutton, 1995. / Cullen, Lynn. *Little Scraggly Hair: A Dog on Noah's Ark.* Holiday House, 2003. / Davol, Marguerite W. *How Snake Got His Hiss.* Orchard, 1996. / Harper, Jo. *Jalapeño Hal.* Four Winds, 1993. / Ketteman, Helen. *Heat Wave!* Walker, 1998. / Onyefulu, Obi. *Chinye: A West African Folk Tale.* Viking, 1994. / Polacco, Patricia. *Thunder Cake.* Philomel, 1990. / Sabuda, Robert. *The Blizzard's Robe.* Atheneum, 1999. / San Souci, Robert D. *The Talking Eggs.* Dial, 1989. / Schachner, Judith Byron. *The Grannyman.* Dutton, 1999. / Shepard, Aaron. *Master Man: A Tall Tale of Nigeria.* HarperCollins, 2001. / Yep, Laurence. *The Junior Thunder Lord.* BridgeWater, 1994.
SUBJECTS: BEHAVIOR. CATS. HUMOROUS FICTION. POURQUOI TALES. SEASONS. WEATHER.

8   **Aliki. *Marianthe's Story: Painted Words, Spoken Memories*. Greenwillow, 1998. 0-688-15662-2. 64pp. Gr. 1–3**
When Marianthe emigrates with her family from her poor country to America, she learns to tell her story, first in pictures and then in English, with the caring, patient support of her new teacher, Mr. Petrie.
GERM: Discuss how Marianthe told her story in two separate ways: with pictures and then, when she had acquired enough English, in words. Talk about her experience being the new person, the outsider, and the hardships her family faced before coming to America. Have listeners write and draw a message of welcome, support, and encouragement to Marianthe.
RELATED TITLES: Bartone, Elisa. *American Too.* Lothrop, 1996. / Choi, Sook Nyul. *Halmoni and the Picnic.* Houghton Mifflin, 1993. / Cohen, Barbara. *Molly's Pilgrim.* Lothrop, 1983. / Garland, Sherry. *The Lotus Seed.* Harcourt, 1993. / Kline, Suzy. *Song Lee in Room 2B.* Viking, 1993. / Maestro, Betsy. *Coming to America: The Story of Immigration.* Scholastic, 1996. / Nagda, Ann Whitehead. *Dear Whiskers.* Holiday House, 2000. / Pomeranc, Marion Hess. *The American Wei.* Albert Whitman, 1998. / Recorvits, Helen. *My Name Is Yoon.* Farrar, 2003.
SUBJECTS: IMMIGRATION AND EMIGRATION. MULTICULTURAL BOOKS. REFUGEES. SCHOOLS. STORYTELLING. TEACHERS.

9   **Allen, Susan, and Jane Lindaman. *Read Anything Good Lately?* Illus. by Vicky Enright. Millbrook, 2003. 0-7613-1889-5. Unp. Gr. K–2**
In an alliterative alphabet that champions reading, a blonde-haired bespectacled girl reads an atlas at the airport, a biography in bed, comic books around the campfire, and all the way through to the zodiac at the zoo.
GERM: The last page is a perfect writing and illustrating prompt: "And what have you read lately?" Harry Potter in the ____ (hammock? hallway?). Rev up your summer reading conversation with a freewheeling recounting of your readers' favorite books and the places they go to read them. Use the cozy, comfy, detail-filled illustrations to talk about the use of setting in stories. Have readers share their alliterative responses and then illustrate them with self-portraits, poster-style, with which you can decorate your whole room. Read also the companion book, *Written Anything Good Lately?* Introduce two fabulous librarians in *Wild About Books* by Judy Sierra and *Library Lil* by Suzanne Williams.

RELATED TITLES: Allen, Susan, and Jane Lindaman. *Written Anything Good Lately?* Millbrook, 2006. / Bertram, Debbie, and Susan Bloom. *The Best Place to Read.* Random House, 2003. / Bloom, Becky. *Wolf!* Orchard, 1999. / Bradby, Marie. *More Than Anything Else.* Orchard, 1995. / Bunting, Eve. *The Wednesday Surprise.* Clarion, 1989. / Daly, Niki. *Once Upon a Time.* Farrar, 2002. / Ernst, Lisa Campbell. *Stella Louella's Runaway Book.* Simon & Schuster, 1998. / Florczak, Robert. *Yikes!!!* Scholastic, 2003. / Hoberman, Mary Ann. *You Read to Me, I'll Read to You: Very Short Stories to Read Together.* Little, Brown, 2001. / Hopkins, Lee Bennett, comp. *Good Books, Good Times!* HarperCollins, 1990. / Lewis, J. Patrick. *Please Bury Me in the Library.* Harcourt, 2005. / McPhail, David. *Fix-It.* Dutton, 1984. / Parish, Herman. *Amelia Bedelia, Bookworm.* Greenwillow, 2003. / Polacco, Patricia. *Thank You, Mr. Falker.* Philomel, 1998. / Sierra, Judy. *Wild About Books.* Knopf, 2004. / Stanley, Diane. *Raising Sweetness.* Putnam, 1999. / Williams, Suzanne. *Library Lil.* Dial, 1997.

SUBJECTS: ALLITERATION. ALPHABET BOOKS. BOOKS AND READING. PICTURE BOOKS FOR ALL AGES.

10   **Andersen, Hans Christian. *The Ugly Duckling*. Illus. by Jerry Pinkney. Morrow, 1999. 0-688-15933-8. Unp. Gr. K–4**

Relocated to North America, this simpler version of Andersen's famous tale, brought to life with breathtaking watercolors, is a feast of a read-aloud.

GERM: Introduce children to other famous Hans Christian Andersen tales. Discussion point: What does it mean when people call someone an "ugly duckling"?

RELATED TITLES: Andersen, Hans Christian. *Fairy Tales of Hans Christian Andersen.* Illus. by Isabelle Brent. Viking, 1995. / Andersen, Hans Christian. *The Nightingale.* Retold by Stephen Mitchell. Illus. by Bagram Ibatoulline. Candlewick, 2002. / Andersen, Hans Christian. *The Nightingale.* Illus. by Jerry Pinkney. Penguin Putnam, 2002. / Andersen, Hans Christian. *The Ugly Duckling.* Illus. by Lorinda Bryan Cauley. Harcourt, 1979. / Fierstein, Harvey. *The Sissy Duckling.* Simon & Schuster, 2002.

SUBJECTS: BIRDS. DUCKS. IDENTITY. LITERARY FAIRY TALES. OUTCASTS. SELF-ACCEPTANCE. SWANS.

11   **Andreae, Giles. *K Is for Kissing a Cool Kangaroo*. Illus. by Guy Rees. Orchard, 2003. 0-439-53126-8. Unp. Gr. PreK–K**

"A is for apple that grows on the tree / b is for busy and big bumblebee." This big, bright, bouncy, rhyming, and alliterative alphabet book is full of active animals interacting and vibrant, full-bleed watercolors.

GERM: Read it first to enjoy the rhyme and ask viewers to describe what's happening on each page. Read it again to pick out all the alphabetical animals and objects on each page. Read it yet again and act it out in narrative pantomime.

RELATED TITLES: Bayer, Jane. *A My Name Is Alice.* Dial, 1984. / Bender, Robert. *The A to Z Beastly Jamboree.* Dutton, 1996. / Cherry, Lynne. *Who's Sick Today?* Dutton, 1988. / Kalman, Maira. *What Pete Ate from A–Z.* Putnam, 2001. / MacDonald, Suse. *Alphabatics.* Simon & Schuster, 1986. / Merriam, Eve. *Where Is Everybody? An Animal Alphabet.* Simon & Schuster, 1989. / Moxley, Sheila. *ABCD: An Alphabet Book of Cats and Dogs.* Little, Brown, 2001. / Rotner, Shelley. *Action Alphabet.* Atheneum, 1996. / Wegman, William. *ABC.* Little, Brown, 1994.

SUBJECTS: ALLITERATION. ALPHABET BOOKS. ANIMALS. CREATIVE DRAMA. STORIES IN RHYME.

12   **Anholt, Catherine, and Laurence Anholt. *Catherine and Laurence Anholt's Big Book of Little Children*. Illus. by the authors. Candlewick, 2003. 0-7636-2210-9. 80pp. Gr. PreK–1**

Told in rhyme, with affectionate watercolor-and-ink illustrations of a multiracial mix of children, here's the lowdown on what little ones like, love, feel, and do.

GERM: Your own little children can confirm the veracity of the opinions expressed in the text and write and draw about what they like and dislike, what makes them laugh and cry, and what makes them mad and happy.

RELATED TITLES: Ashman, Linda. *Babies on the Go.* Harcourt, 2003. / Cooke, Trish. *So Much.* Candlewick, 1994. / Curtis, Marci. *I Was So Silly! Big Kids Remember Being Little.* Dial, 2002. / Greenspun, Adele Aron, and Joanie Schwarz. *Ariel and Emily.* Dutton, 2003. / Meyers, Susan. *Everywhere Babies.* Harcourt, 2001. / Schwartz, Amy. *A Teeny Tiny Baby.* Orchard, 1994. / Willems, Mo. *Knuffle Bunny: A Cautionary Tale.* Hyperion, 2004.

SUBJECTS: BABIES. CHILDREN. MULTICULTURAL BOOKS.

13 **Anholt, Catherine, and Laurence Anholt.** *Chimp and Zee.* Illus. by the authors. Putnam, 2001. 0-8037-2671-6. Unp. Gr. PreK–1

Two naughty little chimpanzees disobey their Mumkey and get lost in Jungletown when the gray stones on which they are hiding turn out to be elephants.

GERM: Bring in bananas, of course, and recite "Five little monkeys jumping on the bed." Follow up with the sequel, *Chimp and Zee and the Big Storm*, in which the two squabbling chimpanzee siblings are blown away by a storm and their Mumkey saves the day. Then introduce the original bad boy monkey in *Curious George* by H. A. Rey.

RELATED TITLES: Anholt, Catherine, and Laurence Anholt. *Chimp and Zee and the Big Storm*. Putnam, 2002. / Christelow, Eileen. *Five Little Monkeys Jumping on the Bed*. Clarion, 1989. (And others in the Five Little Monkeys series.) / Diakité, Baba Wagué. *The Hatseller and the Monkeys*. Scholastic, 1999. / Goode, Diane. *Monkey Mo Goes to Sea*. Blue Sky/Scholastic, 2002. / Johnson, Paul Brett. *Little Bunny Foo Foo*. Scholastic, 2004. / Koller, Jackie French. *One Monkey Too Many*. Scholastic, 1999. / Martin, Bill, Jr. *Chicka Chicka Boom Boom*. Simon & Schuster, 1989. / Perkins, Al. *Hand, Hand, Fingers, Thumb*. Random House, 1969. / Rey, H. A. *Curious George*. Houghton Mifflin, 1993. (And others in the Curious George series.) / Santat, Dan. *The Guild of Geniuses*. Scholastic, 2004. / Sierra, Judy. *Counting Crocodiles*. Harcourt, 1997. / Simmons, Jane. *Come Along, Daisy*. Little, Brown, 1998. / Slobodkina, Esphyr. *Caps for Sale*. HarperCollins, 1947. / Wild, Margaret. *The Pocket Dogs*. Scholastic, 2001.

SUBJECTS: BEHAVIOR. HUMOROUS FICTION. MONKEYS.

14 **Anholt, Laurence.** *Camille and the Sunflowers: A Story About Vincent Van Gogh.* Illus. by the author. Barron's, 1994. 0-8120-6409-7. 28pp. Gr. 1–3

Camille, the postman's young son, is delighted to befriend Vincent, a painter who moves to their village in the south of France, though the other villagers jeer at the eccentric man who works hard creating his paintings but never sells any. Vincent Van Gogh really did paint Camille, as well as his postman father, his mother, his brother, and his sister. The reproductions of those paintings are integrated into the fictionalized story, along with Anholt's own Van Gogh-inspired pen-and-inks and watercolors.

GERM: Van Gogh's life story is such a sad one; this hopeful picture book will serve as an introduction to his life and work, along with *Painting the Wind* by Michelle Dionetti and *The Starry Night* by Neil Waldman.

RELATED TITLES: Björk, Christina. *Linnea in Monet's Garden*. R. & S. Books, 1987. / Dionetti, Michelle. *Painting the Wind*. Little, Brown, 1996. / Fritz, Jean. *Leonardo's Horse*. Putnam, 2001. / Garland, Michael. *Dinner at Magritte's*. Dutton, 1995. / Krull, Kathleen. *Lives of the Artists: Masterpieces, Messes (and What the Neighbors Thought)*. Harcourt, 1995. / Nichol, Barbara. *Beethoven Lives Upstairs*. Orchard, 1994. / Raczka, Bob. *Art Is . . .* Millbrook, 2003. / Rubin, Susan Goldman. *Degas and the Dance: The Painter and the Petits Rats, Perfecting Their Art*. Abrams, 2002. / Waldman, Neil. *The Starry Night*. Boyds Mills, 1999. / Weitzman, Jacqueline Preiss. *You Can't Take a Balloon into the Metropolitan Museum*. Dial, 1998.

SUBJECTS: ARTISTS. FRANCE. FRIENDSHIP. HISTORICAL FICTION. PAINTERS. VAN GOGH, VINCENT.

15 **Appelbaum, Diana.** *Cocoa Ice.* Illus. by Holly Meade. Orchard, 1997. 0-531-33040-0. Unp. Gr. 1–3

A young girl on the island of Santo Domingo describes how she helps her parents harvest, dry, roast, and pound the cocoa beans from their cacao trees, from which chocolate is made. Papa trades the beans with the sailors on the ice schooner from up north, and Mama makes cocoa ice—a cool, white drink—with ice and the pulp from a cacao pod. Meanwhile, up in Maine, another young girl explains how her Uncle Jacob, who owns that schooner, harvested blocks of the ice, cutting them from the frozen river. In illustrations of cut paper and gouache, warm island colors contrast with the cold climate reds and blues, showing summer and winter in the late 1800s when ice, ice cream, and hot cocoa were exotic luxuries.

GERM: Make hot chocolate and maybe even crank your own ice cream.

RELATED TITLES: Christiansen, Candace. *The Ice Horse*. Dial, 1993. / Greenstein, Elaine. *Ice-Cream Cones for Sale*. Scholastic, 2003. / Hopkinson, Deborah. *Fannie in the Kitchen: The Whole Story from Soup to Nuts of How Fannie Farmer Invented Recipes with Precise Measurements*. Atheneum, 2001. / Swain, Ruth Freeman. *How Sweet It Is (and Was): The History of Candy*. Holiday House, 2003.

SUBJECTS: CHOCOLATE. HISTORICAL FICTION. ICE. ISLANDS. MAINE. MULTICULTURAL BOOKS. SANTO DOMINGO. WEATHER. WINTER.

16   Appelt, Kathi. *Bubba and Beau Go Night-Night*. Illus. by Arthur Howard. Harcourt, 2003. 0-15-204593-7. Unp. Gr. PreK–K

Baby Bubba and his best friend, hound dog Beau, love to go bye-bye in Big Bubba's trusty pick-up truck, Earl. They visit the Feed and Seed, the post office, Sam's fruit and vegetable stand, and, best of all, the Freezee Deluxe, for raspberry swirl ice cream cones.

GERM: Read this in your best Texas twang. Recalling their own babyhood, big kids can retell and illustrate an episode from their distant past. You'll also fall madly in love with the first book, *Bubba and Beau, Best Friends*, and wallow in the mud with Cousin Arlene and her dog Bitsy in *Bubba and Beau Meet the Relatives*.

RELATED TITLES: Appelt, Kathi. *Bubba and Beau, Best Friends*. Harcourt, 2002. (And others in the Bubba and Beau series.) / Cook, Sally. *Good Night Pillow Fight*. HarperCollins, 2004. / Cooke, Trish. *So Much*. Candlewick, 1994. / Greenspun, Adele Aron, and Joanie Schwarz. *Ariel and Emily*. Dutton, 2003. / James, Simon. *Baby Brains*. Candlewick, 2004. / Jenkins, Emily. *That New Animal*. Farrar, 2005. / MacLachlan, Patricia, and Emily MacLachlan. *Bittle*. HarperCollins, 2004. / Markes, Julie. *Shhhhh! Everybody's Sleeping*. HarperCollins, 2005. / Meyers, Susan. *Everywhere Babies*. Harcourt, 2001. / Nye, Naomi Shihab. *Baby Radar*. Greenwillow, 2003. / Paxton, Tom. *Where's the Baby?* Morrow, 1993. / Pinkney, Andrea Davis. *Sleeping Cutie*. Harcourt, 2004. / Regan, Dian Curtis. *Chance*. Philomel, 2003. / Schwartz, Amy. *A Teeny Tiny Baby*. Orchard, 1994. / Whybrow, Ian. *The Noisy Way to Bed*. Scholastic, 2004. / Ziefert, Harriet. *Pushkin Meets the Bundle*. Atheneum, 1998.

SUBJECTS: BABIES. BEDTIME STORIES. COUNTRY LIFE. DOGS. HUMOROUS FICTION. SLEEP. TEXAS.

17   Appelt, Kathi. *Bubba and Beau Meet the Relatives*. Illus. by Arthur Howard. Harcourt, 2004. 0-15-216630-0. Unp. Gr. PreK–1

The only place baby Bubba and his dog buddy Beau can find a safe haven from the family to-do (as Mama Pearl and Big Bubba get ready for the relatives) is in the garden, in the lovely squishy squash of the mud hole. When the relatives show up, along with baby Cousin Arlene and her dog, Bitsy—"Honey, it was froufrou city"—the four youngsters head right back down to the mud hole together.

GERM: The down home Texas jargon is downright waggish. Ask your itty bitties what happens in their neck of the woods when the relatives come over. Read all the Bubba and Beau books for a bodacious view of babyhood.

RELATED TITLES: Appelt, Kathi. *Bubba and Beau, Best Friends*. Harcourt, 2002. (And others in the Bubba and Beau series.) / Ashman, Linda. *Babies on the Go*. Harcourt, 2003. / Curtis, Marci. *I Was So Silly! Big Kids Remember Being Little*. Dial, 2002. / Fleming, Candace. *Smile, Lily!* Atheneum, 2004. / Fleming, Candace. *This Is the Baby*. Farrar, 2004. / James, Simon. *Baby Brains*. Candlewick, 2004. / L'Engle, Madeleine. *The Other Dog*. SeaStar, 2001. / McMullan, Kate. *Rock-a-Baby Band*. Little, Brown, 2003. / Meyers, Susan. *Everywhere Babies*. Harcourt, 2001. / Nye, Naomi Shihab. *Baby Radar*. Greenwillow, 2003. / Rathmann, Peggy. *The Day the Babies Crawled Away*. Putnam, 2003. / Regan, Dian Curtis. *Chance*. Philomel, 2003. / Root, Phyllis. *What Baby Wants*. Candlewick, 1998. / Rylant, Cynthia. *Henry and Mudge and the Careful Cousin*. Simon & Schuster, 1994. / Schwartz, Amy. *A Teeny Tiny Baby*. Orchard, 1994. / Wells, Rosemary. *McDuff and the Baby*. Hyperion, 1997. / Willems, Mo. *Knuffle Bunny: A Cautionary Tale*. Hyperion, 2004. / Ziefert, Harriet. *Pushkin Meets the Bundle*. Atheneum, 1998.

SUBJECTS: BABIES. BATHS. DOGS. FAMILY LIFE. HUMOROUS FICTION. PARTIES. TEXAS.

18   Armstrong, Jennifer. *Magnus at the Fire*. Illus. by Owen Smith. Simon & Schuster, 2005. 0-689-83922-7. Unp. Gr. PreK–2

After ten good years as a fire horse, mighty gray Magnus is put out to pasture when Captain French brings in a "burping, belching, oil-smelling, newfangled contraption," the first motorized fire engine in the town of Hope Springs. Each time the fire bell rings, Magnus jumps the fence, follows the smell of smoke, and arrives for duty to the exasperation of the captain. On the day the motor blows on the new machine, Magnus is there to pull the heavy truck close enough to fight a hotel fire. Huge, exhilarating, full-bleed oil paintings, reminiscent of larger-than-life Depression-era murals of heroic working heroes, will have listeners cheering for the indomitable horse.

GERM: Pair this with another masterful firefighter's tale, *New York's Bravest* by Mary Pope Osborne.

RELATED TITLES: Christiansen, Candace. *The Ice Horse*. Dial, 1993. / Demarest, Chris L. *Firefighters A to Z*.

McElderry, 2000. / High, Linda Oatman. *Winter Shoes for Shadow Horse*. Boyds Mills, 2001. / Lester, Julius. *John Henry*. Dial, 1994. / Osborne, Mary Pope. *New York's Bravest*. Knopf, 2002.

SUBJECTS: FIRE. FIREFIGHTERS. HISTORICAL FICTION. HORSES.

19   **Arnold, Tedd.** *Catalina Magdalena Hoopensteiner Wallendiner Hogan Logan Bogan Was Her Name.* **Illus. by the author. Scholastic, 2004. 0-590-10994-4. Unp. Gr. K–4**

In a wacky picture-book version of the old camp song, complete with plastic googly eyes on the cover, meet a girl with a preposterous name, two hairs on her head, one eye that looks left and the other that looks right, arms that drag on the ground, and feet bigger than a bathroom mat. Illustrator Arnold has created a merry story out of the pictures, showing the exuberant girl growing up, attending school, and getting married.

GERM: Write new verses and make up long silly monikers from your own names, inspired also by Arlene Mosel's Chinese folktale, "Tikki Tikki Tembo."

RELATED TITLES: Arnold, Tedd. *Even More Parts*. Dial, 2004. / Arnold, Tedd. *More Parts*. Dial, 2001. / Arnold, Tedd. *Parts*. Dial, 1997. / Hoberman, Mary Ann. *There Once Was a Man Named Michael Finnegan*. Little, Brown, 2001. / Karas, G. Brian. *I Know an Old Lady*. Scholastic, 1984. / Mosel, Arlene. *Tikki Tikki Tembo*. Henry Holt, 1968. / Raffi. *Down by the Bay*. Crown, 1987. / Sherman, Allan, and Lou Busch. *Hello Muddah, Hello Faddah! (A Letter from Camp)*. Dutton, 2004. / Taback, Simms. *There Was an Old Lady Who Swallowed a Fly*. Viking, 1997. / Weeks, Sarah. *Mrs. McNosh Hangs Up Her Wash*. Dutton, 1998. / Westcott, Nadine Bernard. *I Know an Old Lady Who Swallowed a Fly*. Little, Brown, 1980. / Westcott, Nadine Bernard. *The Lady with the Alligator Purse*. Little, Brown, 1988.

SUBJECTS: HUMOROUS FICTION. NAMES. NONSENSE VERSES. SONGS. STORIES IN RHYME. TOY AND MOVABLE BOOKS. WEDDINGS.

20   **Arnold, Tedd.** *Even More Parts: Idioms from Head to Toe.* **Illus. by the author. Dial, 2004. 0-8037-2938-3. Unp. Gr. PreK–4**

Chip, the wacky, frantic worrier from *Parts* and *More Parts*, is back with another manic bout of human body part expressions that scare him silly, such as "I lost my head" and "I keep changing my mind." Colored pencil and watercolor wash illustrations provide off-the-wall literal renditions of each idiomatic expression, and listeners will fall down laughing every time you turn the page.

GERM: Read the additional idioms on the endpapers and then brainstorm and illustrate your own list. For more hysteria, complete the trilogy with *Parts* and *More Parts*. See how Amelia Bedelia mixes her metaphors in the series by Peggy Parish, and look at some understatement in *Just Another Ordinary Day* by Rod Clement.

RELATED TITLES: Arnold, Tedd. *Catalina Magdalena Hoopensteiner Wallendiner Hogan Logan Bogan Was Her Name*. Scholastic, 2004. / Arnold, Tedd. *More Parts*. Dial, 2001. / Arnold, Tedd. *Parts*. Dial, 1997. / Brennan-Nelson, Denise. *My Momma Likes to Say*. Sleeping Bear, 2003. / Brennan-Nelson, Denise. *My Teacher Likes to Say*. Sleeping Bear, 2004. / Clement, Rod. *Just Another Ordinary Day*. HarperCollins, 1997. / Clements, Andrew. *Double Trouble in Walla Walla*. Millbrook, 1998. / Edwards, Wallace. *Monkey Business*. Kids Can, 2004. / Ghigna, Charles. *See the Yak Yak*. Random House, 1999. / Gwynne, Fred. *A Chocolate Moose for Dinner*. Dutton, 1976. / Gwynne, Fred. *The King Who Rained*. Dutton, 1970. / Leedy, Loreen. *There's a Frog in My Throat: 440 Animal Sayings a Little Bird Told Me*. Holiday House, 2003. / Parish, Peggy. *Amelia Bedelia*. HarperCollins, 1992. (And others in the Amelia Bedelia series.) / Pulver, Robin. *Punctuation Takes a Vacation*. Holiday House, 2003. / Shields, Carol Diggory. *Food Fight!* Handprint, 2002.

SUBJECTS: BODY, HUMAN. ENGLISH LANGUAGE—IDIOMS. ENGLISH LANGUAGE—TERMS AND PHRASES. HUMOROUS FICTION. STORIES IN RHYME. WORD GAMES.

21   **Arnold, Tedd.** *No More Water in the Tub!* **Illus. by the author. Dial, 1995. 0-8037-1583-8. Unp. Gr. PreK–2**

With his little brother William in the tub, Walter turns the water on full blast, but the handle breaks off, flooding the bathroom and sending William and the tub sailing down the stairs. The wild flood picks up and carries away all of the surprised apartment dwellers, including Mable on her table and Sue and Vern, clinging to a fern.

GERM: This wet and splashy adventure is filled with comic watercolors and a rhyming cumulative refrain everyone will chant. At the end, it becomes clear that the whole escapade is just a story that Walter is telling to entertain his bathing bro. Parlay the last page—where William and the tub float out the window and down the fire escape—into a story starter for writing and telling the next installment. See what happened to Walter when he disobeyed his dad in *No Jumping on the Bed*.

RELATED TITLES: Arnold, Tedd. *No Jumping on the Bed*. Dial, 1987. / Bell, Cece. *Sock Monkey Goes to Holly-wood: A Star Is Bathed*. Candlewick, 2003. / Bond, Michael. *A Bear Called Paddington*. Houghton Mifflin, 1960. / Cole, Brock. *No More Baths*. Doubleday, 1980. / Cowan, Catherine. *My Life with the Wave*. Lothrop, 1997. / Faulkner, Matt. *The Amazing Voyage of Jackie Grace*. Scholastic, 1987. / Goodman, Joan Elizabeth. *Bernard's Bath*. Boyds Mills, 1996. / Palatini, Margie. *Tub-Boo-Boo*. Simon & Schuster, 2001. / Peck, Jan. *Way Down Deep in the Deep Blue Sea*. Simon & Schuster, 2004. / Pomerantz, Charlotte Pomerantz. *The Piggy in the Puddle*. Macmillan, 1974.

SUBJECTS: APARTMENT HOUSES. BATHS. BROTHERS. CUMULATIVE STORIES. FLOODS. HUMOROUS FICTION. IMAGINATION. STORYTELLING.

22   **Arnold, Tedd. *Parts*. Illus. by the author. Dial, 1997. 0-8037-2040-8. Unp. Gr. PreK–2**
Appalled at his body's seeming malfunctions, the 5-year-old narrator obsesses over his hair falling out, the stuffing coming out of his belly, the skin peeling from his toes, and the gray, wet chunk of brain that just fell out of his nose. And now a tooth is loose, causing him to realize, "The glue that holds our parts together isn't holding me!!!"

GERM: Wild, google-eyed illustrations of the worried boy and his manic rhyming narrative will have your more "together" listeners falling apart with laughter. Ask them to reassure the boy and explain how each body malfunction he describes is normal and nothing to worry about. Kick off your human body unit by asking them what parts they have worried about unnecessarily. Follow up with the idiom-filled sequels, *More Parts* and *Even More Parts*.

RELATED TITLES: Arnold, Tedd. *Even More Parts*. Dial, 2004. / Arnold, Tedd. *More Parts*. Dial, 2001. / Berger, Melvin. *Why I Sneeze, Shiver, Hiccup, and Yawn*. HarperCollins, 2000. / Carlson, Nancy. *There's a Big, Beautiful World Out There!* Viking, 2002. / Cole, Joanna. *The Magic School Bus Inside the Human Body*. Scholastic, 1987. / Edwards, Pamela Duncan. *The Worrywarts*. HarperCollins, 1999. / Henkes, Kevin. *Wemberly Worried*. Greenwillow, 2000. / Keller, Laurie. *Open Wide: Tooth School Inside*. Henry Holt, 2000. / Lasky, Kathryn. *Science Fair Bunnies*. Candlewick, 2000. / Lester, Helen. *Something Might Happen*. Houghton Mifflin, 2003. / Maloney, Peter, and Felicia Zekauskas. *His Mother's Nose*. Dial, 2001. / McGhee, Alison. *Mrs. Watson Wants Your Teeth*. Harcourt, 2004. / Palatini, Margie. *Sweet Tooth*. Simon & Schuster, 2004. / Seuling, Barbara. *From Head to Toe: The Amazing Human Body and How It Works*. Holiday House, 2002.

SUBJECTS: BODY, HUMAN. HUMOROUS FICTION. STORIES IN RHYME. TEETH. WORRYING.

23   **Artell, Mike. *Petite Rouge: A Cajun Red Riding Hood*. Illus. by Jim Harris. Dial, 2001. 0-8037-2514-0. Unp. Gr. 1–4**
In this rollicking narrative poem, liberally laced with Cajun patois and vocabulary, Petite Rouge Riding Hood is a resourceful and dauntless white duck who, along with her cat friend TeJean, poles her pirogue through the swamp on her way to bring her ailing Grand-mère some gumbo and boudin. Her encounters with Claude, "dat ol' gator," both in the swamp and in Grand-mère's bed, are roll-on-the-floor hilarious, with extravagant and expressive watercolors detailing that bad boy gator's chicanery and Petite Rouge's spicy retaliation.

GERM: Practice before you try reading this aloud to a group. Have your older readers exercise their use of phonics and try their hands at reading this to each other. Compare and contrast the story elements with the original folktale. See how another little Cajun girl fends off a gator in Tynia Thomassie's *Feliciana Feydra LeRoux*.

RELATED TITLES: Cox, Judy. *Rabbit Pirates: A Tale of the Spinach Main*. BridgeWater, 1998. / Cox, Judy. *The West Texas Chili Monster*. BridgeWater, 1998. / Doucet, Sharon Arms. *Why Lapin's Ears Are Long and Other Tales from the Louisiana Bayou*. Orchard, 1997. / Emberley, Michael. *Ruby*. Little, Brown, 1990. / Harper, Wilhelmina. *The Gunniwolf*. Dutton, 2003. / Hyman, Trina Schart. *Little Red Riding Hood*. Holiday House, 1983. / Lowell, Susan. *Little Red Cowboy Hat*. Henry Holt, 1997. / Marshall, James. *Red Riding Hood*. Dial, 1987. / San Souci, Robert D. *Six Foolish Fisherman*. Hyperion, 2000. / Thomassie, Tynia. *Feliciana Feydra LeRoux: A Cajun Tall Tale*. Little, Brown, 1995. / Van Laan, Nancy. *With a Whoop and a Holler*. Atheneum, 1998.

SUBJECTS: ALLIGATORS. CAJUNS. DUCKS. FAIRY TALES. HUMOROUS FICTION. LITTLE RED RIDING HOOD STORIES. LOUISIANA. PARODIES. STORIES IN RHYME.

24   **Asch, Frank. *Mr. Maxwell's Mouse*. Illus. by the author. Kids Can, 2004. 1-55337-486-X. Unp. Gr. 2-5**
Celebrating his new job promotion, Mr. Howard Maxwell, a dignified gray cat, decides to have the raw mouse as his lunch entrée at the Paw and Claw. His mouse is certainly fresh, healthy,

polite, and talkative, and though Mr. Maxwell remembers his mother's advice not to fraternize with his food, he soon finds himself drawn into a conversation, which makes the prospect of killing the mouse much more difficult.

GERM: Not for the faint at heart, this macabre and sophisticated tale, with dignified full-bleed film-noir-ish illustrations and white text on a black background, will make listeners squeal as they root for the mouse to talk his way out of being lunch. It would be satisfying to script this up as a Reader's Theater and have several small groups act out the story together. Contrast Mr. Maxwell's view of the rat race with that of Tibs in *Clever Cat* by Peter Collington.

RELATED TITLES: Collington, Peter. *Clever Cat.* Knopf, 2000. / Cox, Judy. *Rabbit Pirates: A Tale of the Spinach Main.* Harcourt, 1999. / Emberley, Michael. *Ruby.* Little, Brown, 1990. / Kelly, John, and Cathy Tincknell. *The Mystery of Eatum Hall.* Candlewick, 2004. / King-Smith, Dick. *Martin's Mice.* Crown, 1989. / King-Smith, Dick. *Three Terrible Trins.* Crown, 1994. / McKissack, Patricia C. *Flossie and the Fox.* Dial, 1986. / Meddaugh, Susan. *Hog-Eye.* Houghton Mifflin, 1995. / Scieszka, Jon. *The True Story of the 3 Little Pigs.* Viking, 1989. / Steig, William. *Doctor De Soto.* Farrar, 1982.

SUBJECTS: CATS. LETTER WRITING. MICE. READER'S THEATER. RESTAURANTS.

25   **Ashman, Linda. *Castles, Caves, and Honeycombs.* Illus. by Lauren Stringer. Harcourt, 2001. 0-15-202211-2. Unp. Gr. PreK–K**
"Many places make a home," starts a rhyming depiction of 25 animal habitats, painted in acrylics on a white background, including "A silky web. A sandy dune. A room inside a warm cocoon."

GERM: For a look at where more animals, people, and other objects reside, pair this with Mary Ann Hoberman's *A House Is a House for Me* and Elizabeth Garton Scanlon's *A Sock Is a Pocket for Your Toes.*

RELATED TITLES: Dorros, Arthur. *This Is My House.* Scholastic, 1992. / Garton, Elizabeth. *A Sock Is a Pocket for Your Toes: A Pocket Book.* HarperCollins, 2004. / Hoberman, Mary. *A House Is a House for Me.* Viking, 1978. / Lewis, J. Patrick. *Good Mousekeeping and Other Animal Home Poems.* Atheneum, 2001. / Lillegard, Dee. *Do Not Feed the Table.* Delacorte, 1993.

SUBJECTS: ANIMALS. DWELLINGS. HOUSES. STORIES IN RHYME.

26   **Ashman, Linda. *Rub-a-Dub Sub.* Illus. by Jeff Mack. Harcourt, 2003. 0-15-202658-4. Unp. Gr. PreK–1**
Sinking in his orange submarine, a little boy dives with a silky seal, darts with a dancing eel, and encounters a toothsome shark. Simple rhymes take him through the colorful underwater oceanscape until he emerges, safe in his own bathtub.

GERM: Using this as a companion to Michael Rosen's actable chant, *We're Going on a Bear Hunt*, you'll want to make up motions and undersea sound effects for each set of rhymes and vivid action verbs and act it all out. Continue the imaginative bathtime, underwater, rhyming mood with Jan Peck's *Way Down Deep in the Deep Blue Sea*, and bathe the car in Sandra and Susan Steen's *Car Wash.*

RELATED TITLES: Arnold, Tedd. *No More Water in the Tub!* Dial, 1995. / Clark, Emma Chichester. *Follow the Leader!* Simon & Schuster, 2003. / Faulkner, Matt. *The Amazing Voyage of Jackie Grace.* Scholastic, 1987. / Goodman, Joan Elizabeth. *Bernard's Bath.* Boyds Mills, 1996. / Harter, Debbie. *Walking Through the Jungle.* Orchard, 1997. / MacLean, Christine Kole. *Even Firefighters Hug Their Moms.* Dutton, 2002. / O'Connor, George. *Kapow!* Simon & Schuster, 2004. / O'Malley, Kevin. *Straight to the Pole.* Walker, 2003. / Peck, Jan. *Way Down Deep in the Deep Blue Sea.* Simon & Schuster, 2004. / Rosen, Michael. *We're Going on a Bear Hunt.* McElderry, 1989. / Steen, Sandra, and Susan Steen. *Car Wash.* Putnam, 2001. / Steig, William. *Pete's a Pizza.* HarperCollins, 1998. / Steig, William. *Toby, What Are You?* HarperCollins, 2001.

SUBJECTS: BATHS. CREATIVE DRAMA. IMAGINATION. MARINE ANIMALS. OCEAN. STORIES IN RHYME. SUBMARINES.

27   **Atkins, Jeannine. *Aani and the Tree Huggers.* Illus. by Venantius J. Pinto. Lee & Low, 1995. 1-880000-24-5. Unp. Gr. 2–5**
When men with axes come to her village in India to cut down the woods, a girl named Aani throws her arms around her favorite tree and refuses to budge. Soon all the women and children are hugging trees and, though the men offer them money to go away, the protesters are undeterred.

GERM: This book, illustrated in the style of Indian miniature painting, is based on actual events that took place in India in the 1970s and will get everyone thinking about the value of trees and the power of nonviolent protest. What happens when too many trees are cut down in a forested area? Why are trees important to you? A worthy companion read is Lynne Cherry's *The Great Kapok Tree*. For a look at a typical Indian tree, read Barbara Bash's *In the Heart of the Village: The World of the Indian Banyan Tree*.

RELATED TITLES: Bash, Barbara. *In the Heart of the Village: The World of the Indian Banyan Tree*. Sierra Club, 1996. / Brenner, Barbara. *The Earth Is Painted Green: A Garden of Poems About Our Planet*. Scholastic, 1994. / Bunting, Eve. *Someday a Tree*. Clarion, 1993. / Cherry, Lynne. *The Great Kapok Tree: A Tale of the Amazon Rain Forest*. Harcourt, 1990. / Fleming, Denise. *Where Once There Was a Wood*. Henry Holt, 1996. / George, Kristine O'Connell. *Old Elm Speaks: Tree Poems*. Clarion, 1998. / Oppenheim, Joanne. *Have You Seen Trees?* Scholastic, 1995.

SUBJECTS: CONSERVATION OF NATURAL RESOURCES. HISTORICAL FICTION. INDIA. MULTICULTURAL BOOKS. TREES. WOMEN.

28   **Auch, Mary Jane. *Bantam of the Opera*. Illus. by the author. Holiday House, 1997. 0-8234-1312-8. Unp. Gr. K–4**
Bored crowing the same old ditty every morning, rooster Luigi is awestruck when he hears opera on the farmer's radio one day. "I knew there was more to life than 'Cock-a-doodle-doo!'" he cries. The chance to see the Cosmopolitan Opera Company perform *Rigoletto* is irresistible, and Luigi flutters onto the stage, providing stiff competition for the famous and vengeful tenor, Enrico Baldini.
GERM: Play a CD of *Rigoletto* so children can hear what all the squawking is about. Children will appreciate meeting the other gifted fowl in Auch's picture books: the artist Pauline in *Eggs Mark the Spot* and ballerina Poulette in *Peeping Beauty* and *Hen Lake*. Meet another opera-lover in *Opera Cat* by Tess Weaver.
RELATED TITLES: Auch, Mary Jane. *Eggs Mark the Spot*. Holiday House, 1996. / Auch, Mary Jane. *Hen Lake*. Holiday House, 1995. / Auch, Mary Jane. *Peeping Beauty*. Holiday House, 1993. / Cazet, Denys. *Elvis the Rooster Almost Goes to Heaven*. HarperCollins, 2003. / Edwards, Pamela Duncan. *Honk! The Story of a Prima Swanerina*. Hyperion, 1998. / Ernst, Lisa Campbell. *When Bluebell Sang*. Bradbury, 1989. / Froehlich, Margaret Walden. *That Kookoory!* Harcourt, 1995. / Goss, Linda. *The Frog Who Wanted to Be a Singer*. Orchard, 1996. / Hurd, Thacher. *Art Dog*. HarperCollins, 1996. / Kinerk, Robert. *Clorinda*. Simon & Schuster, 2003. / Pearson, Tracey Campbell. *Bob*. Farrar, 2002. / Rostoker-Gruber, Karen. *Rooster Can't Cock-a-Doodle-Doo*. Dial, 2004. / Weaver, Tess. *Opera Cat*. Clarion, 2002. / West, Jim, and Marshall Izen. *The Dog Who Sang at the Opera*. Abrams, 2004.
SUBJECTS: CHICKENS. DETERMINATION. HUMOROUS FICTION. OPERA. PICTURE BOOKS FOR ALL AGES. ROOSTERS. SINGERS.

29   **Auch, Mary Jane. *Eggs Mark the Spot*. Illus. by the author. Holiday House, 1996. 0-8234-1242-3. Unp. Gr. K–2**
Mrs. Pennywort's talented hen, Pauline, studies the famous paintings at the Big City Art Gallery before hatching decorative eggs reminiscent of Modigliani, Matisse, Van Gogh, Picasso, and Klee and even foils an art thief who tries to steal a Degas.
GERM: Another art theft is foiled in *Art Dog* by Thacher Hurd. And see how Pauline got her start as an egg artist in Auch's *The Easter Egg Farm*.
RELATED TITLES: Alcorn, Johnny. *Rembrandt's Beret*. Tambourine, 1991. / Auch, Mary Jane. *The Easter Egg Farm*. Holiday House, 1992. / Browne, Anthony. *Willy the Dreamer*. Candlewick, 1998. / Hurd, Thacher. *Art Dog*. HarperCollins, 1996. / Laden, Nina. *When Pigasso Met Mootisse*. Chronicle, 1998. / Lithgow, John. *Micawber*. Simon & Schuster, 2002. / Pilkey, Dav. *When Cats Dream*. Orchard, 1992. / Raczka, Bob. *Art Is . . .* Millbrook, 2003. / Weitzman, Jacqueline Preiss. *You Can't Take a Balloon into the Metropolitan Museum*. Dial, 1998.
SUBJECTS: ART APPRECIATION. ARTISTS. CHICKENS. PAINTING. PICTURE BOOKS FOR ALL AGES. ROBBERS AND OUTLAWS.

30   **Auch, Mary Jane. *The Princess and the Pizza*. Illus. by Mary Jane Auch and Herm Auch. Holiday House, 2002. 0-8234-1683-6. Unp. Gr. K–5**
Missing her former life as a princess, Paulina heads for the castle to compete with 11 other princesses to become the royal bride to drippy Prince Drupert and, in the process, invents a winning new recipe for something she calls "pizza."
GERM: First off, this is a bit of a takeoff on the Princess and the Pea, so make sure you read or tell that story to your crew before reading this aloud. Listeners will recognize the guest appearances of several other fairy tale characters too. Paulina ends up opening a Pizza Palace in town

with 50 kinds of pizza. After reading, make little pizzas, of course, following Princess Paulina's "recipe." Or develop ads for new pizza concoctions to go on the menu at Paulina's place. Write pourquoi tales about the origin of foods you fancy, such as ice cream, chocolate, or doughnuts.

RELATED TITLES: Alexander, Lloyd. *How the Cat Swallowed Thunder*. Dutton, 2000. / Andersen, Hans Christian. *The Princess and the Pea*. Illus. by Paul Galdone. Seabury, 1978. / Bateman, Teresa. *The Princesses Have a Ball*. Albert Whitman, 2002. / Compestine, Ying Chang. *The Story of Chopsticks*. Holiday House, 2001. / Compestine, Ying Chang. *The Story of Paper*. Holiday House, 2003. / Khalsa, Dayal Kaur. *How Pizza Came to Queens*. Clarkson N. Potter, 1989. / Kovalski, Maryann. *Pizza for Breakfast*. Morrow, 1991. / Levine, Gail Carson. *The Fairy's Mistake*. HarperCollins, 1999. / Levine, Gail Carson. *The Princess Test*. HarperCollins, 1999. / Mahy, Margaret. *The Rattlebang Picnic*. Dial, 1994. / Scieszka, Jon. *The Stinky Cheese Man and Other Fairly Stupid Tales*. Viking, 1992. / Stanley, Diane. *Rumpelstiltskin's Daughter*. Morrow, 1997. / Steig, William. *Pete's a Pizza*. HarperCollins, 1998. / Sturges, Philemon. *The Little Red Hen (Makes a Pizza)*. Dutton, 1999.

SUBJECTS: CHARACTERS IN LITERATURE. COOKERY. FAIRY TALES—SATIRE. HUMOROUS FICTION. PARODIES. PIZZA. POURQUOI TALES. PRINCES AND PRINCESSES. STORIES TO TELL.

31 **Auch, Mary Jane, and Herm Auch.** *Souperchicken*. **Illus. by the authors. Holiday House, 2003. 0-8234-1704-2. Unp. Gr. K–3**

Henrietta, a farm chicken who loves to read, comes to the rescue of her aunties, who think they're being taken by truck to a lovely vacation spot, but they are really heading for the Souper Soup factory.

GERM: While Henrietta reads for pure pleasure, the message of this frantic tale, which the chicken utters while saving some misguided cows in a Happy Hamburger Company truck, is urgent: "Reading can save your lives!" Ask your readers to connect this statement to their own lives. In Dick King-Smith's fiction book, *The School Mouse*, Flora's reading skills help her to save her parents from an untimely death.

RELATED TITLES: Bloom, Becky. *Wolf!* Orchard, 1999. / Child, Lauren. *Who's Afraid of the Big Bad Book?* Hyperion, 2003. / Daugherty, James. *Andy and the Lion*. Viking, 1938. / Duvoisin, Roger. *Petunia*. Knopf, 1989. / Feldman, Thelma. *Who You Callin' Chicken?* Abrams, 2003. / King-Smith, Dick. *The School Mouse*. Hyperion, 1995. / Marshall, James. *Wings: A Tale of Two Chickens*. Viking, 1986. / Novak, Matt. *Mouse TV*. Orchard, 1994. / Numeroff, Laura Joffe. *Beatrice Doesn't Want To*. Candlewick, 2004. / Sierra, Judy. *Wild About Books*. Knopf, 2004. / Stanley, Diane. *Raising Sweetness*. Putnam, 1999.

SUBJECTS: BOOKS AND READING. CHICKENS. DOMESTIC ANIMALS. LITERACY.

32 **Avi.** *Silent Movie*. **Illus. by C. B. Mordan. Atheneum, 2003. 0-689-84145-0. Unp. Gr. 2–5**

In 1909, Papa Hans sails from Sweden to the New World. Six months later, Mama and son Gustav make the three-week voyage and pass the Statue of Liberty, but when they disembark, where's Papa? In short order, Gustav's money is stolen, Mama gets a job sewing, and Gustav is discovered by famous movie director Bartholomew Bunting, who needs a child actor for his new movie. See what a silent movie looks like in this innovative and original picture book, with white subtitles on an all-black background, done with ink on clayboard, reminiscent of Michael McCurdy's work.

GERM: Show some silent shorts so children can see what they look like. Your students can write, act out, and videotape their own silent movie, complete with title cards. Pair this historical fiction story with the picture-book biography about movie director Mack Sennett, *Mack Made Movies* by Don Brown, and with your unit on immigration.

RELATED TITLES: Bierman, Carol. *Journey to Ellis Island: How My Father Came to America*. Hyperion, 1998. / Brown, Don. *Mack Made Movies*. Roaring Brook, 2003. / Curlee, Lynn. *Liberty*. Atheneum, 2000. / Freedman, Russell. *Immigrant Kids*. Dutton, 1980. / Gish, Lillian. *An Actor's Life for Me!* Viking Kestrel, 1987. / Maestro, Betsy. *Coming to America: The Story of Immigration*. Scholastic, 1996. / Maestro, Betsy. *The Story of the Statue of Liberty*. Lothrop, 1986. / Pomeranc, Marion Hess. *The American Wei*. Albert Whitman, 1998. / Sandler, Martin W. *Immigrants*. HarperCollins, 1995. / Sorel, Edward, and Cheryl Carlesimo. *The Saturday Kid*. McElderry, 2000.

SUBJECTS: ACTORS AND ACTRESSES. IMMIGRATION AND EMIGRATION. MOTHERS AND SONS. MOTION PICTURE PRODUCERS AND DIRECTORS. MOTION PICTURES. NEW YORK CITY. SILENT FILMS. SWEDISH AMERICANS.

33 **Baker, Keith.** *Quack and Count*. **Illus. by the author. Harcourt, 2000. 0-15-292858-8. Unp. Gr. PreK–K**

In this rhyming adventure, count up to seven with seven enthusiastic ducklings as they have fun sliding, chasing, splashing, quacking, paddling, and, finally, flying. Cheerful cut-paper collages show all the ways to get to seven, such as six plus one, five plus two, and four plus three.

GERM: Pull this into your math lesson on the commutative property of addition. Then fool around with subtraction using Raffi's *Five Little Ducks*.

RELATED TITLES: Buzzeo, Toni. *Dawdle Duckling*. Dial, 2003. / Ehlert, Lois. *Fish Eyes: A Book You Can Count On*. Harcourt, 1990. / Falwell, Cathryn. *Turtle Splash! Countdown at the Pond*. Greenwillow, 2001. / Fleming, Denise. *Count!* Henry Holt, 1992. / Fleming, Denise. *In the Small, Small Pond*. Henry Holt, 1993. / MacDonald, Suse. *Look Whooo's Counting*. Scholastic, 2000. / Raffi. *Five Little Ducks*. Crown, 1988.

SUBJECTS: ADDITION. COUNTING BOOKS. DUCKS. STORIES IN RHYME.

34   **Bang, Molly. *When Sophie Gets Angry—Really, Really Angry*. Illus. by the author. Scholastic, 1999. 0-590-18979-4. Unp. Gr. PreK–2**

Follow Sophie as she starts a kicking, screaming, roaring, volcanic temper tantrum when her sister snatches her stuffed gorilla. Then watch as she calms herself down again by climbing the old beech tree and letting the wide world comfort her.

GERM: Discussion point: What do you do to cool off when you get really, really angry? What are some ways we all can try? Looking at their own faces in the mirror, children can draw self-portraits—each depicting one emotion—onto face-sized cardboard ovals. Mount them on paint sticks so they can hold the masks up to their faces.

RELATED TITLES: Everitt, Betsy. *Mean Soup*. Harcourt, 1992. / Feiffer, Jules. *I Lost My Bear*. Morrow, 1998. / Freymann, Saxton, and Joost Elffers. *How Are You Peeling? Foods with Moods*. Scholastic, 1999. / Hausman, Bonnie. *A to Z: Do You Ever Feel Like Me?* Dutton, 1999. / Henkes, Kevin. *Lilly's Purple Plastic Purse*. Greenwillow, 1996. / Shannon, David. *David Gets in Trouble*. Scholastic, 2002. / Shannon, David. *No, David!* Scholastic, 1998. / Steig, William. *Pete's a Pizza*. HarperCollins, 1998. / Vail, Rachel. *Sometimes I'm Bombaloo*. Scholastic, 2002. / Wells, Rosemary. *Noisy Nora*. Dial, 1997.

SUBJECTS: ANGER. BEHAVIOR. CONFLICT RESOLUTION. EMOTIONS.

35   **Bania, Michael. *Kumak's Fish: A Tall Tale from the Far North*. Illus. by the author. Alaska Northwest, 2004. 0-88240-583-7. Unp. Gr. PreK–3**

"Good day for fish," say Kumak, his wife, his wife's mother, his sons, and his daughters as they pull on their warm parkas, mukluks, hats, and gloves and ride their dogsled to the great frozen lake. Using his Uncle Aglu's amazing hooking stick, Kumak catches a huge fish that everyone in the family and the village tries to help pull up.

GERM: An Alaskan version of "The Enormous Turnip," this has great charm and humor for reading and will be fun to act out in a long line. Given that the people and the giant fish are competing in a huge tug of war, you might want to get out a rope to reenact the final scene. A detailed Author's Note describes Bania's real-life inspiration for the story. See what Inuit life is like at home in the companion book, *Kumak's House*.

RELATED TITLES: Andrews, Jan. *Very Last First Time*. Atheneum, 1986. / Bania, Michael. *Kumak's House: A Tale of the Far North*. Alaska Northwest, 2002. / Domanska, Janina. *The Turnip*. Macmillan, 1969. / George, Jean Craighead. *Nutik and Amoroq Play Ball*. HarperCollins, 2001. / George, Jean Craighead. *Nutik, the Wolf Pup*. HarperCollins, 2001. / Kroll, Virginia. *The Seasons and Someone*. Harcourt, 1994. / Morgan, Pierr. *The Turnip*. Philomel, 1990. / Oppel, Kenneth. *Peg and the Whale*. Simon & Schuster, 2000. / Roth, Roger. *Fishing for Methuselah*. HarperCollins, 1998. / Silverman, Erica. *Big Pumpkin*. Macmillan, 1992. / Tolstoi, Alexei. *The Great Big Enormous Turnip*. Heinemann, 1968. / Vagin, Vladimir. *The Enormous Carrot*. Scholastic, 1998.

SUBJECTS: ALASKA. ARCTIC REGIONS. COOPERATION. CREATIVE DRAMA. FISHES. FISHING. ICE FISHING. INUIT. TALL TALES.

36   **Bania, Michael. *Kumak's House: A Tale of the Far North*. Illus. by the author. Alaska Northwest, 2002. 0-88240-541-1. Unp. Gr. PreK–3**

At the edge of a great frozen river, in a too-small house, live unhappy Kumak, his unhappy wife, his wife's mother, and his four sons and daughters. Aana Lulu, the oldest and wisest elder in the village, advises Kumak to invite Rabbit to live in the house, along with Rabbit's family, but it doesn't help. In succession, Kumak is advised to bring in Fox, Caribou, Porcupine, Otter, and Bear, until there is barely room for anyone.

GERM: Discuss the pronouncements of Aana Lulu, the wise elder, when she says things like, "Unhappy is the mukluk on too big a foot." What are some of the aspects of Arctic life and culture that are gleaned from the story and its joyful pen-and-ink and watercolor illustrations? There's a detailed and fascinating Author's Note at the back that gives background on the clothing, food, and activities of Kumak and his family and explains the Arctic atmospheric phenomena of sundogs and the northern lights. For further ideas, print out the publisher's study guide at <www.gacpc.com>. And then, of course, compare and contrast this story with the many versions of the Jewish folktale on which it was based, starting with Ann McGovern's *Too Much Noise* and Margot Zemach's *It Could Always Be Worse*. In the companion book, *Kumak's Fish*, everyone tries to help Kumak catch the biggest fish ever.

RELATED TITLES: Bania, Michael. *Kumak's Fish: A Tall Tale from the Far North*. Alaska Northwest, 2004. / Cole, Joanna. *It's Too Noisy!* Crowell, 1989. / Donaldson, Julia. *A Squash and a Squeeze*. McElderry, 1993. / Dorros, Arthur. *This Is My House*. Scholastic, 1992. / Forest, Heather. *A Big Quiet House*. August House, 1996. / Fowler, Susi Gregg. *Circle of Thanks*. Scholastic, 1998. / Hirsch, Marilyn. *Could Anything Be Worse?* Holiday House, 1974. / Hoberman, Mary. *A House Is a House for Me*. Viking, 1978. / Mathews, Judith, and Fay Robinson. *Nathaniel Willy, Scared Silly*. Bradbury, 1994. / McGovern, Ann. *Too Much Noise*. Houghton Mifflin, 1967. / Murphy, Jill. *Peace at Last*. Dial, 1980. / Simms, Laura. *The Squeaky Door*. Crown, 1991. / Taback, Simms. *Joseph Had a Little Overcoat*. Viking, 1999. / Taback, Simms. *This Is the House That Jack Built*. Putnam, 2002. / Thomson, Pat. *The Squeaky, Creaky Bed*. Doubleday, 2003. / Zemach, Margot. *It Could Always Be Worse*. Farrar, 1976.

SUBJECTS: ALASKA. ANIMALS. ARCTIC REGIONS. CHANTABLE REFRAIN. CIRCULAR STORIES. HOUSES. INUIT. STORIES TO TELL.

37   **Banks, Kate. *The Cat Who Walked Across France*. Illus. by Georg Hallensleben. Farrar, 2004. 0-374-39968-9. Unp. Gr. K–3**

After the old woman who belongs to him dies, a gray-and-white cat is shipped north; however, when he arrives, he finds that there is no one there to care for him. Setting out on his own, he heads south, through Paris and the countryside, finally ending up in his own stone house by the edge of the sea. Soft smudgy Impressionist-style paintings, reminiscent of Roualt, Matisse, Cezanne, and Van Gogh, are filled with dreamy scenes of the cat in the French landscape, and a satisfying ending brings hope for a good life.

GERM: Trace the cat's route from Rouen to St.-Tropez on the map on the back cover, and show pictures of the landmarks he passes, including the Eiffel Tower, the chateau at Chambord, Mont Blanc, and the Pont du Gard. Discuss: Why and how did the cat come home? To him, home smells like the tangy smell of lemons and sounds like the crunch of dried leaves. What does your home smell, taste, look, sound, and feel like to your pet or to you? Write and draw about the elements that make your house a home.

RELATED TITLES: Graeber, Charlotte. *Nobody's Dog*. Hyperion, 1998. / McDonald, Joyce. *Homebody*. Putnam, 1991. / McFarland, Lyn Rossiter. *Widget*. Farrar, 2001. / Simont, Marc. *The Stray Dog*. HarperCollins, 2001. / Thayer, Jane. *The Puppy Who Wanted a Boy*. Morrow, 1986. / Voake, Charlotte. *Ginger Finds a Home*. Candlewick, 2003. / Wells, Rosemary. *Lucy Comes to Stay*. Dial, 1994. / Wells, Rosemary. *McDuff Moves In*. Hyperion, 1997. (And others in the McDuff series.)

SUBJECTS: CATS. FRANCE. STRAY ANIMALS. VOYAGES AND TRAVELS.

38   **Bannerman, Helen. *The Story of Little Babaji*. Illus. by Fred Marcellino. HarperCollins, 1996. 0-06-205064-8. Unp. Gr. PreK–2**

Helen Bannerman's controversial classic children's story *Little Black Sambo* has been resurrected and rescued in a delightful reworking. Illustrator Fred Marcellino reset the story in India and changed the characters' names. Little Babaji gives up his fine and colorful new clothes to five vain and growly tigers and then, through his own bravery and cleverness, outwits the tigers and reclaims his wardrobe.

GERM: This version makes a splendid Reader's Theater. Compare and contrast the illustrations, narrative, characters, and setting with Julius Lester's version, the African American-based *Sam and the Tigers*.

RELATED TITLES: Brett, Jan. *Trouble with Trolls*. Putnam, 1992. / Dowson, Nick. *Tigress*. Candlewick, 2004. / Faulkner, William J. *Brer Tiger and the Big Wind*. Morrow, 1995. / Harper, Wilhelmina. *The Gunniwolf*. Dutton, 2003. / Lester, Julius. *Sam and the Tigers*. Dial, 1996. / McCleery, William. *Wolf Story*. Linnet, 1988. / Peet, Bill. *The Spooky Tail of Prewitt Peacock*. Houghton Mifflin, 1973. / Souhami, Jessica. *No Dinner! The Story of the Old Woman and the Pumpkin*. Marshall Cavendish, 2000. / Temple, Frances. *Tiger Soup: An Anansi Story from Jamaica*. Orchard, 1994. / Wright, Kit. *Tigerella*. Scholastic, 1994.

SUBJECTS: CLOTHING AND DRESS. INDIA. MULTICULTURAL BOOKS. READER'S THEATER. TIGERS.

39   Barasch, Lynne. *Ask Albert Einstein.* **Illus. by the author. Farrar, 2005. 0-374-30435-1. Unp. Gr. 2–6**

April looks back to 1952, when she was 7 and her adored sister Annabel was 15. Her teacher has given Annabel one last chance to pass math, challenging her to solve a hard math problem in the next two weeks. "Who does she think I am, Albert Einstein?" she wails. April goes to the library to find out more about Einstein and mails a letter and the math problem to him in Princeton, New Jersey. He writes back to Annabel saying, "Do not worry about your problems with mathematics. I assure you mine are far greater." There's a drawing on the back of his letter that gives Annabel enough of a clue so she can work out the problem.

GERM: Introduce America's favorite genius, Albert Einstein, with this engaging fictional story, loosely based on a reply he sent to a 15-year-old high school girl in 1952 in answer to her letter requesting help with a math problem. A reproduction of Einstein's diagram and formula, and Annabel's solution to the problem are appended, and the endpapers contain affectionate pen-and-ink and watercolors of Einstein, with an assortment of his wonderful quotes to share and discuss. *Odd Boy Out: Young Albert Einstein* by Don Brown is a strikingly illustrated picture-book biography; *Genius: A Photobiography of Albert Einstein* by Marie Ferguson Delano goes into more depth and contains excellent photographs.

RELATED TITLES: Brown, Don. *Odd Boy Out: Young Albert Einstein.* Houghton Mifflin, 2004. / Delano, Marie Ferguson. *Genius: A Photobiography of Albert Einstein.* National Geographic, 2005. / Moore, Floyd C. *I Gave Thomas Edison My Sandwich.* Albert Whitman, 1995.

SUBJECTS: BIOGRAPHICAL FICTION. EINSTEIN, ALBERT. HISTORICAL FICTION. LETTER WRITING. MATHEMATICS. SISTERS.

40   Barrett, Judi. *Things That Are Most in the World.* **Illus. by John Nickle. Atheneum, 1998. 0-689-81333-3. 32pp. Gr. PreK–2**

"The wiggliest thing in the world is a snake ice-skating." There are 12 other ridiculous sentences incorporating whimsical superlatives, including silliest, hottest, smelliest, and stickiest.

GERM: A humorous surreal acrylic painting accompanies each statement. If you just thought, "Hmm. My kids could write and illustrate and share their own sentences using superlatives," the last page of the book is a white page that says, "The ____est thing in the world is ____." Simply photocopy that page (for which the author gives permission), and you're in business.

RELATED TITLES: Barrett, Judi. *Animals Should Definitely Not Wear Clothing.* Atheneum, 1970. / Jenkins, Steve. *Biggest, Strongest, Fastest.* Ticknor & Fields, 1995. / Jenkins, Steve. *Hottest Coldest Highest Deepest.* Houghton Mifflin, 1998. / Johnson, Lonni S. *Pickles Have Pimples and Other Silly Statements.* Atheneum, 1986. / Numeroff, Laura. *Chimps Don't Wear Glasses.* Simon & Schuster, 1995. / Numeroff, Laura. *Dogs Don't Wear Sneakers.* Simon & Schuster, 1993. / Perry, Sarah. *If . . .* J. Paul Getty Museum and Children's Library Press, 1995. / Raffi. *Down by the Bay.* Crown, 1987.

SUBJECTS: ANIMALS. IMAGINATION. SUPERLATIVES. VOCABULARY.

41   Bartoletti, Susan Campbell. *Nobody's Diggier Than a Dog.* **Illus. by Beppe Giacobbe. Hyperion, 2004. 0-7868-1824-7. Unp. Gr. PreK–2**

While the rhyming adjective-crammed narrative highlights all types of dogs—"a slurp-your-face dog, a let's-play-chase dog"—there's a side story taking place in the paintings, where a brown dog is chasing a black cat across each page.

GERM: Follow up with the author's companion book, *Nobody's Nosier Than a Cat.* Using the author's pattern, all can write and illustrate quick descriptive poems about their favorite pets. For example: Nobody's sleepier than my old cat, Sherlock—a take-a-nap cat, a snooze-on-your-lap cat.

RELATED TITLES: Bartoletti, Susan Campbell. *Nobody's Nosier Than a Cat.* Hyperion, 2003. / George, Kristine O'Connell. *Little Dog Poems.* Clarion, 1999. / Gottfried, Maya. *Good Dog.* Knopf, 2005. / Hall, Donald. *I Am the Dog, I Am the Cat.* Dial, 1994. / Johnston, Tony. *It's About Dogs.* Harcourt, 2000. / Kalman, Maira. *What Pete Ate from A–Z.* Putnam, 2001. / Kirk, Daniel. *Dogs Rule!* Hyperion, 2003. / Laden, Nina. *The Night I Followed the Dog.* Chronicle, 1994. / Lee, Chinlun. *Good Dog, Paw!* Candlewick, 2004. / McFarland, Lyn Rossiter. *Widget.* Farrar, 2001. / Meddaugh, Susan. *Martha Walks the Dog.* Houghton Mifflin, 1998. (And others in the Martha series.) / Miller, Sara Swan. *Three Stories You Can Read to Your Cat.* Houghton Mifflin, 1997. / Miller, Sara Swan. *Three Stories You Can Read to Your Dog.* Houghton Mifflin, 1995. / Simon, Seymour. *Dogs.* Harper-Collins, 2003. / Sklansky, Amy E. *From the Doghouse: Poems to Chew On.* Henry Holt, 2002.

SUBJECTS: DOGS. STORIES IN RHYME.

42 Barton, Byron. *My Car*. Illus. by the author. Greenwillow, 2001. 0-06-029625-9. Unp. Gr. PreK
In the simplest of texts, illustrated with flat, bold computer graphics, Sam describes how he keeps his car in shape and drives safely.
GERM: Act this one out, with children becoming both Sam and his car, all-in-one. Have them drive through the room and obey all the traffic signs.
RELATED TITLES: Booth, Philip. *Crossing*. Candlewick, 2001. / Hindley, Judy. *The Big Red Bus*. Candlewick, 1995. / Hort, Lenny. *The Seals on the Bus*. Henry Holt, 2000. / Kovalski, Maryann. *The Wheels on the Bus*. Little, Brown, 1987. / Mahy, Margaret. *The Rattlebang Picnic*. Dial, 1994. / Meister, Cari. *Busy Busy City Street*. Viking, 2000. / Pinkwater, Daniel. *Tooth-Gnasher Superflash*. Macmillan, 1990. / Raffi. *The Wheels on the Bus*. Crown, 1988. / Root, Phyllis. *Rattletrap Car*. Candlewick, 2001. / Roth, Carol. *The Little School Bus*. North-South, 2002. / Steen, Sandra, and Susan Steen. *Car Wash*. Putnam, 2001. / Zelinsky, Paul O. *The Wheels on the Bus*. Dutton, 1990.
SUBJECTS: AUTOMOBILES. BUSES. CREATIVE DRAMA. TRANSPORTATION. VEHICLES.

43 Bateman, Teresa. *April Foolishness*. Illus. by Nadine Bernard Westcott. Albert Whitman, 2004. 0-8075-0404-1. Unp. Gr. PreK–2
Grandpa doesn't take his two grandkids seriously when they tell him the cow got loose, the chickens are out, the pigs broke the gate, the goats are stampeding, and the sheep are gone. Why? It's April Fool's Day. Or is it?
GERM: In a rhyming romp, the tables get turned on Grandpa. Ask your listeners to explain why Grandpa doesn't believe his grandkids and how he finally gets fooled. Share your own April Fool's Day tricks and jokes.
RELATED TITLES: Babcock, Chris. *No Moon, No Milk*. Crown, 1993. / Brown, Marc. *Arthur's April Fool*. Little, Brown, 1983. / Cleveland, David. *The April Rabbits*. Coward, 1978. / Cronin, Doreen. *Click, Clack, Moo: Cows That Type*. Simon & Schuster, 2000. / Egan, Tim. *Serious Farm*. Houghton Mifflin, 2003. / Rostoker-Gruber, Karen. *Rooster Can't Cock-a-Doodle-Doo*. Dial, 2004. / Schwartz, Amy. *Old MacDonald*. Scholastic, 1999. / Speed, Toby. *Two Cool Cows*. Putnam, 1995. / Stevenson, James. *Don't Make Me Laugh*. Farrar, 1999. / Stevenson, James. *No Laughing, No Smiling, No Giggling*. Farrar, 2004. / Vail, Rachel. *Over the Moon*. Orchard, 1998. / Waddell, Martin. *Farmer Duck*. Candlewick, 1992.
SUBJECTS: APRIL FOOL'S DAY. FARM LIFE. GRANDPARENTS. STORIES IN RHYME.

44 Bateman, Teresa. *Farm Flu*. Illus. by Nadine Bernard Westcott. Albert Whitman, 2001. 0-8075-2274-0. Unp. Gr. PreK–2
Mom's out of town, so when all the farm animals start ka-choo-ing, her young son takes over and nurses them back to health just like Mom would have done.
GERM: Children can recite the rhyming refrain with you and predict what the boy will do when the animals get better. Discussion point: What do your parents do for you when you get sick? Animal ailments abound in Lynne Cherry's *Who's Sick Today?*
RELATED TITLES: Bennett, David. *One Cow Moo Moo!* Henry Holt, 1990. / Causley, Charles. *"Quack!" Said the Billy-Goat*. Lippincott, 1986. / Cherry, Lynne. *Who's Sick Today?* Dutton, 1988. / Cronin, Doreen. *Click, Clack, Moo: Cows That Type*. Simon & Schuster, 2000. / Demuth, Patricia Brennan. *The Ornery Morning*. Dutton, 1991. / Duvoisin, Roger. *Petunia*. Knopf, 1989. / Gray, Libba Moore. *Is There Room on the Feather Bed?* Orchard, 1997. / LeGuin, Ursula K. *A Visit from Dr. Katz*. Atheneum, 1988. / McPhail, David. *Pigs Aplenty, Pigs Galore*. Dutton, 1993. / Rostoker-Gruber, Karen. *Rooster Can't Cock-a-Doodle-Doo*. Dial, 2004. / Thomas, Shelley Moore. *Get Well, Good Knight*. Dutton, 2002. / Waddell, Martin. *Farmer Duck*. Candlewick, 1992. / Wells, Rosemary. *Felix Feels Better*. Candlewick, 2001. / Yolen, Jane. *How Do Dinosaurs Get Well Soon?* Blue Sky/Scholastic, 2003. / Zimmerman, Andrea. *The Cow Buzzed*. HarperCollins, 1993.
SUBJECTS: ANIMALS. CHANTABLE REFRAIN. DOMESTIC ANIMALS. FARM LIFE. HUMOROUS FICTION. SICK. STORIES IN RHYME.

45 Bateman, Teresa. *Leprechaun Gold*. Illus. by Rosanne Litzinger. Holiday House, 1998. 0-8234-1344-6. Unp. Gr. 1–4
Kindhearted Donald O'Dell, who saves a leprechaun trapped in a stream but refuses his reward of gold, falls in love with golden-haired Maureen, thanks to that same little man.
GERM: Discuss: Why didn't Donald want to accept the leprechaun's gift of gold? How and why did the leprechaun repay Donald?
RELATED TITLES: Alexander, Lloyd. *The Fortune-Tellers*. Dutton, 1992. / Balian, Lorna. *Leprechauns Never Lie*. Star Bright, 2004. / Bateman, Teresa. *The Ring of Truth*. Holiday House, 1997. / dePaola, Tomie. *Jamie O'Rourke and the Big Potato: An Irish Folktale*. Putnam, 1992. / Edwards, Pamela Duncan. *The Leprechaun's Gold*.

HarperCollins, 2004. / Grimm, Jacob. *One Gift Deserves Another*. Retold by Joanne Oppenheim. Dutton, 1992. / Haley, Gail. *Dream Peddler*. Dutton, 1993. / Hodges, Margaret. *Saint Patrick and the Peddler*. Orchard, 1993. / Kennedy, Richard. *The Leprechaun's Story*. Dutton, 1979. / Shepard, Aaron. *The Gifts of Wali Dad: A Tale of India and Pakistan*. Atheneum, 1995. / Sherrow, Victoria. *There Goes the Ghost*. HarperCollins, 1985. / Shute, Linda. *Clever Tom and the Leprechaun*. Lothrop, 1988. / Stanley, Diane. *Fortune*. Morrow, 1989. / Wojciechokski, Susan. *A Fine St. Patrick's Day*. Random House, 2004.
SUBJECTS: GIFTS. LEPRECHAUNS. LOVE.

46   **Bateman, Teresa. *The Princesses Have a Ball*. Illus. by Lynne Cravath. Albert Whitman, 2002. 0-8075-6626-8. Unp. Gr. K–4**
In a modern rhyming update on the old Grimm story "The Twelve Dancing Princesses," meet 12 multicultural sisters who confound their father, the king, who thinks they should be working on catching princes instead of wearing out their shoes nightly. It's a cobbler named Jack who figures out what those wily girls have been up to every night. Dancing? No, playing basketball.
GERM: Compare this with Jane Ray's ornate, traditional retelling of the tale. Share also the updated, rhyming, parody version of the "Sleeping Beauty" fairy tale, *Sleepless Beauty* by Frances Minters. Then go out with your royal children and shoot some hoops.
RELATED TITLES: Auch, Mary Jane. *The Princess and the Pizza*. Holiday House, 2002. / Minters, Frances. *Cinder Elly*. Viking, 1993. / Minters, Frances. *Sleepless Beauty*. Viking, 1996. / Ray, Jane. *Twelve Dancing Princesses*. Dutton, 1996. / Stanley, Diane. *Rumpelstiltskin's Daughter*. Morrow, 1997. / Wilcox, Leah. *Falling for Rapunzel*. Putnam, 2003.
SUBJECTS: BASKETBALL. FAIRY TALES—SATIRE. KINGS AND RULERS. PARODIES. PRINCES AND PRINCESSES. SPORTS. STORIES IN RHYME.

47   **Bates, Ivan. *All by Myself*. Illus. by the author. HarperCollins, 2000. 0-06-028585-0. Unp. Gr. PreK–K**
Maya may be just a little elephant, but she wants to pick her breakfast leaves from the tall trees all by herself and tries three different ways to do it. A lion, a bird, and a snake offer to fetch the leaves for her, but independent Maya refuses help until her mother lifts her up high enough so she can reach them all by herself.
GERM: Soft watercolors show the determined elephant and her patient mother on the African plain. As you begin the story, ask your audience to suggest possible solutions for Maya. Ask them: What have you figured out how to do all by yourself? What would you like to be able to do all by yourself? Have them draw themselves doing just that.
RELATED TITLES: Dunrea, Olivier. *Ollie*. Houghton, 2003. / Falwell, Cathryn. *Butterflies for Kiri*. Lee & Low, 2003. / Ford, Miela. *Little Elephant*. Greenwillow, 1994. / James, Simon. *Little One Step*. Candlewick, 2003. / Jenkins, Martin. *Grandma Elephant's in Charge*. Candlewick, 2003. / Kurtz, Jane, and Christopher Kurtz. *Water Hole Waiting*. Greenwillow, 2002. / McBratney, Sam. *Just You and Me*. Illus. by Ivan Bates. Candlewick, 1998. / Riley, Linda Capus. *Elephants Swim*. Houghton Mifflin, 1995. / Shannon, George. *Tippy-Toe Chick, Go!* Greenwillow, 2003. / Sobol, Richard. *An Elephant in the Backyard*. Dutton, 2004. / Yoshida, Toshi. *Elephant Crossing*. Philomel, 1989.
SUBJECTS: ELEPHANTS. MOTHERS AND DAUGHTERS. PERSEVERANCE. PROBLEM SOLVING. SELF-RELIANCE.

48   **Becker, Bonny. *An Ant's Day Off*. Illus. by Nina Laden. Simon & Schuster, 2003. 0-689-82274-X. Unp. Gr. PreK–2**
Tired of working underground, a sand ant named Bart, who has never seen the sky or felt the rain, sneaks out of his tunnel and takes the day off to explore and see a bit of the world.
GERM: Ask your children to write about and draw what they would do if they could play hooky from their job (attending school) just for a day. Give students some background on the lives of ants by reading them a good informational book such as Patricia Brennan Demuth's *Those Amazing Ants*. Compare fiction and nonfiction books on ants. Have your listeners figure out what the differences are between the two categories.
RELATED TITLES: Allinson, Beverly. *Effie*. Scholastic, 1991. / Demuth, Patricia Brennan. *Those Amazing Ants*. Macmillan, 1994. / Dorros, Arthur. *Ant Cities*. HarperCollins, 1987. / Hoose, Phillip M., and Hannah Hoose. *Hey, Little Ant*. Tricycle, 1998. / Laden, Nina. *Roberto the Insect Architect*. Chronicle, 2000. / Nickle, John. *The Ant Bully*. Scholastic, 1999. / Peet, Bill. *The Ant and the Elephant*. Houghton, 1972. / Pinczes, Elinor J.

One Hundred Hungry Ants. Houghton, 1993. / Van Allsburg, Chris. *Two Bad Ants*. Houghton Mifflin, 1988. / Wolkstein, Diane. *Step by Step*. Morrow, 1994.

SUBJECTS: ANTS. INSECTS. WORK.

49   Becker, Bonny. *The Christmas Crocodile*. **Illus. by David Small. Simon & Schuster, 1998. 0-689-81503-4. Unp. Gr. K–3**

Found under the family's Christmas tree, Alice Jayne's full-sized amiable crocodile doesn't mean to be bad and eat up Christmas, not really, but he gulps down all the food and everyone's presents too.

GERM: Write and illustrate cause-and-effect stories about outlandish gifts, starting, "I got a ____ for a present, and it ____." For older readers, there's lots of very funny family dialogue and plenty of parts, so script this up as a holiday Reader's Theater.

RELATED TITLES: Aliki. *Keep Your Mouth Closed, Dear*. Dial, 1966. / Burningham, John. *Harvey Slumfenberger's Christmas Present*. Candlewick, 1993. / Kellogg, Steven. *The Mysterious Tadpole*. Dial, 1977. / Kimmel, Elizabeth Cody. *My Penguin Osbert*. Candlewick, 2004. / Marcellino, Fred. *I, Crocodile*. HarperCollins, 1999. / Palatini, Margie. *Elf Help*. Hyperion, 1997. / Parish, Peggy. *No More Monsters for Me*. HarperCollins, 1981. / Small, David. *Hoover's Bride*. Crown, 1995. / Vaughan, Marcia. *Snap!* Scholastic, 1996. / Waber, Bernard. *Lyle, Lyle, Crocodile*. Houghton Mifflin, 1965. (And others in the Lyle the Crocodile series.) / Wallace, Karen. *Imagine You Are a Crocodile*. Henry Holt, 1997.

SUBJECTS: CHRISTMAS. CROCODILES. GIFTS. READER'S THEATER.

50   Bell, Cece. *Sock Monkey Goes to Hollywood: A Star Is Bathed*. **Illus. by the author. Candlewick, 2003. 0-7636-1962-0. Unp. Gr. PreK–1**

Yippee! Sock Monkey, the famous actor, has been nominated for an Oswald Award as "Best Supporting Toy in a Motion Picture." The catch? Nominees must be clean, and he is downright filthy, having never in his life taken a bath.

GERM: If you don't already have a sock monkey, you'll want to get one before you read this wacky tale of bathing. In fact, maybe this is just the push you need to give baths to all the stuffed animals in your classroom or library collection. Notice that Sock Monkey thanks his friends when he wins an award. Ask your actors: If you ever win an award for being the best in something, what will it be for and what will you say in your acceptance speech? Pull out a microphone for impromptu speeches. Teach everyone how to accept an award with the left hand and shake firmly with the right, a skill that should come in handy someday.

RELATED TITLES: Arnold, Tedd. *No More Water in the Tub!* Dial, 1995. / Bell, Cece. *Sock Monkey Boogie-Woogie: A Friend Is Made*. Candlewick, 2004. / Bond, Michael. *A Bear Called Paddington*. Houghton Mifflin, 1960. / Cole, Brock. *No More Baths*. Doubleday, 1980. / Goode, Diane. *Monkey Mo Goes to Sea*. Blue Sky/Scholastic, 2002. / Goodman, Joan Elizabeth. *Bernard's Bath*. Boyds Mills, 1996. / LaReau, Kara. *Rocko and Sparky Go to a Party*. Harcourt, 2004. / Mathers, Petra. *A Cake for Herbie*. Simon & Schuster, 2000. / Rey, H. A. *Curious George*. Houghton Mifflin, 1993. (And others in the Curious George series.) / Santat, Dan. *The Guild of Geniuses*. Scholastic, 2004.

SUBJECTS: ACTORS AND ACTRESSES. BATHS. CLEANLINESS. MONKEYS. MOTION PICTURES. STUFFED ANIMALS.

51   Berends, Polly Berrien. *I Heard Said the Bird*. **Illus. by Brad Sneed. Dial, 1995. 0-8037-1224-3. Unp. Gr. PreK–K**

A bird flies into the barnyard to tell the animals that there's a "new one" coming, and all the animals want to know who, how, when, and where. Large, soft, placid watercolors show the farm animals, large and small, from their ground-level perspective.

GERM: All will love filling in the final rhyming word of each question the animals ask— "'How?' said the ____ (cow)."—and predicting who that "new one" in the house might be.

RELATED TITLES: Appelt, Kathi. *Bubba and Beau*. Harcourt, 2002. (And others in the Bubba and Beau series.) / Cameron, Polly. *"I Can't," Said the Ant*. Coward, 1961. / Chapman, Cheryl. *Pass the Fritters, Critters*. Four Winds, 1993. / L'Engle, Madeleine. *The Other Dog*. SeaStar, 2001. / McGeorge, Constance W. *Boomer's Big Surprise*. Chronicle, 1999. / MacLachlan, Patricia, and Emily MacLachlan. *Bittle*. HarperCollins, 2004. / Rose, Deborah Lee. *Birthday Zoo*. Albert Whitman, 2002. / Stoeke, Janet Morgan. *A Friend for Minerva Louise*. Dutton, 1997.

SUBJECTS: ANIMALS. BABIES. DOMESTIC ANIMALS. STORIES IN RHYME.

52   Bertram, Debbie, and Susan Bloom. *The Best Place to Read.* **Illus. by Michael Garland. Random House, 2003. 0-375-82293-3. Unp. Gr. PreK–2**

As told in rhyme by a redheaded boy who moves from chair to chair, there's no place he can find that's comfy enough for him to read his new book until he climbs up on Mom's lap.

GERM: Be sure your listeners have a book to take home so they can try out a parent's lap to share the story. Then follow up with the companion book, *The Best Time to Read*, in which the boy wants to read to his extended family but everyone's too busy to listen just now. See where else a person can choose to read in Susan Allen and Jane Lindaman's *Read Anything Good Lately?*

RELATED TITLES: Allen, Susan, and Jane Lindaman. *Read Anything Good Lately?* Millbrook, 2003. / Bertram, Debbie, and Susan Bloom. *The Best Time to Read.* Random House, 2003. / Bloom, Becky. *Wolf!* Orchard, 1999. / Daly, Niki. *Once Upon a Time.* Farrar, 2002. / Daugherty, James. *Andy and the Lion.* Viking, 1938. / Ernst, Lisa Campbell. *Stella Louella's Runaway Book.* Simon & Schuster, 1998. / McPhail, David. *Fix-It.* Dutton, 1984. / Sierra, Judy. *Wild About Books.* Knopf, 2004.

SUBJECTS: BOOKS AND READING. CHAIRS. MOTHERS. STORIES IN RHYME.

53   Bertrand, Lynne. *Granite Baby.* **Illus. by Kevin Hawkes. Farrar, 2005. 0-374-32761-0. Unp. Gr. 1–4**

Five giant sisters from the Granite State of New Hampshire each have a special talent: Jade can twist a river in her hands, Em whittles wood, Golda is handy with string, Ruby is as strong as a bear, and Beryl is the finest stonecutter. After Beryl carves a whole new town out of a mountain, she takes a bit of pink granite and carves a real live baby whom the sisters name Lil Fella. He may fit in the palm of Beryl's hand, but he cries and caterwauls day and night, no matter how they try to appease him. It takes a backwoods little girl named Nellie to show those sisters what to do to get that baby to stop his infernal hollering. Hawkes's larger-than-life, double-page, full-bleed acrylic paintings are his grandest ever, and listeners will go wild over that teeny tiny baby confounding those gargantuan girls.

GERM: Ask your listeners to think of both tall-tale and sensible ideas to calm Lil Fella. Meet other larger-than-life females in *Swamp Angel* by Anne Isaacs, *Sally Ann Thunder Ann Whirlwind Crockett* by Steven Kellogg, and *Doña Flor* by Pat Mora.

RELATED TITLES: Andersen, Hans Christian. *Thumbelina.* Retold and illustrated by Lauren Mills. Little, Brown, 2005. / Dadey, Debbie. *Shooting Star: Annie Oakley, the Legend.* Walker, 1997. / Donaldson, Julia. *The Giants and the Joneses.* Henry Holt, 2005. / Isaacs, Anne. *Swamp Angel.* Dutton, 1994. / Kellogg, Steven. *Sally Ann Thunder Ann Whirlwind Crockett.* Morrow, 1995. / Mayer, Marianna. *The Adventures of Tom Thumb.* SeaStar, 2001. / Melmed, Laura Krauss. *Little Oh.* Lothrop, 1997. / Melmed, Laura Krauss. *The Rainbabies.* Lothrop, 1992. / Mora, Pat. *Doña Flor: A Tall Tale About a Giant Woman with a Great Big Heart.* Knopf, 2005. / Osborne, Mary Pope. *American Tall Tales.* Knopf, 1991. / San Souci, Robert D. *Larger Than Life: The Adventures of American Legendary Heroes.* Doubleday, 1991. / Schanzer, Rosalyn. *Davy Crockett Saves the World.* HarperCollins, 2001. / Walker, Paul Robert. *Big Men, Big Country: A Collection of American Tall Tales.* Harcourt, 1993. / Wood, Audrey. *The Bunyans.* Scholastic, 1996.

SUBJECTS: BABIES. EXAGGERATION. FANTASY. GIANTS. HUMOROUS FICTION. MOUNTAINS. NEW HAMPSHIRE. PICTURE BOOKS FOR ALL AGES. TALL TALES. WOMEN.

54   Best, Cari. *Shrinking Violet.* **Illus. by Giselle Potter. Farrar, 2001. 0-374-36882-1. Unp. Gr. K–2**

Though Violet is a natural actor, she hates being watched by others, which Violet's teacher Mrs. Maxwell understands when she gives her the offstage but important role of Lady Space in the class play about the solar system. Violet learns her lines, and everybody else's, and, of course, she saves the play from and for her classmate, the annoying Irwin, playing the maddest Martian on Mars.

GERM: Space fans will love reciting the mnemonic sentence, My Very Excellent Mother Just Served Us Nine Pizzas. Violet writes on the inside of her hand, "I AM ALLERGIC TO ATTENTION." For your shy kids who often bloom when cast in a play, this will be a good discussion starter. What does it mean to be shy? How does it feel? What can you do to overcome it? One solution is to put on a play, or at least a nice bit of Reader's Theater.

RELATED TITLES: Best, Cari. *Three Cheers for Catherine the Great.* DK Ink, 1999. / Fleming, Candace. *When Agnes Caws.* Atheneum, 1999. / Hoffman, Mary. *Amazing Grace.* Dial, 1991. / Lewison, Wendy Cheyette. *Shy Vi.* Simon & Schuster, 1993. / Lexau, Joan. *Benjie.* Dial, 1964. / McCully, Emily Arnold. *The Evil Spell.* HarperCollins, 1990. / McCully, Emily Arnold. *Speak Up, Blanche.* HarperCollins, 1991. / McKissack, Patricia C. *The Honest-to-Goodness Truth.* Atheneum, 2000. / Marsden, Carolyn. *The Gold-Threaded Dress.* Candlewick, 2002. /

Scott, Ann Herbert. *Brave as a Mountain Lion.* Clarion, 1996. / Stadler, Alexander. *Beverly Billingsly Takes a Bow.* Harcourt, 2003. / Waber, Bernard. *Evie and Margie.* Houghton Mifflin, 2003. / Wells, Rosemary. *Shy Charles.* Dial, 1988. / Wishinsky, Frieda. *Give Maggie a Chance.* Fitzhenry & Whiteside, 2002.

SUBJECTS: ACTING. BEHAVIOR. PLAYS. SCHOOLS. SHYNESS. STAGE FRIGHT. TEASING.

---

55   Best, Cari. *When Catherine the Great and I Were Eight!* **Illus. by Giselle Potter. Farrar, 2003. 0-374-39954-9. Unp. Gr. K–3**

Summer in the city is boiling, so Sara, her Russian grandma, Catherine the Great, plus Mama and a couple of neighbors all pile into Mr. Minsky's old blue station wagon for a meandering, bumper-to-bumper ride to the beach. They stop for ice cream, get a little carsick, play Last Letter, break down, and don't get to the beach until 6 P.M., to find they have the sand and the water—and the mosquitoes—all to themselves. When they finally make it into the ocean, you'll feel cooled off and refreshed by Giselle Potter's gorgeously transparent blue watercolors of the lot of them—even the dog—floating like flowers.

GERM: What a fine "What I did on my summer vacation" story starter—a personal narrative, told by eight-year-old Sara in a marvelously descriptive stream-of-consciousness patter. Play Last Letter, the game of going places. Start with Grandma's first word, Russia. The last letter of Russia is "a," so you need to think of a place that starts with A. Spend more quality time with Sara and her Grandma in *Three Cheers for Catherine the Great!*

RELATED TITLES: Best, Cari. *Three Cheers for Catherine the Great.* DK Ink, 1999. / Choi, Sook Nyul. *Halmoni and the Picnic.* Houghton, 1993. / Dorros, Arthur. *Abuela.* Dutton, 1991. / LaMarche, Jim. *The Raft.* HarperCollins, 2000. / Levine, Evan. *Not the Piano, Mrs. Medley.* Orchard, 1991. / Mahy, Margaret. *The Rattlebang Picnic.* Dial, 1994. / Manzano, Sonia. *No Dogs Allowed!* Atheneum, 2004. / Potter, Giselle. *Chloë's Birthday . . . and Me.* Atheneum, 2004. / Ringgold, Faith. *Tar Beach.* Crown, 1991. / Root, Phyllis. *Rattletrap Car.* Candlewick, 2001. / Schertle, Alice. *All You Need for a Beach.* Harcourt, 2004. / Skolsky, Mindy Warshaw. *Hannah and the Whistling Teakettle.* DK Ink, 2000. / Steen, Sandra, and Susan Steen. *Car Wash.* Putnam, 2001. / Stewig, John Warren. *Making Plum Jam.* Hyperion, 2002.

SUBJECTS: AUTOMOBILES. FAMILY STORIES. GRANDMOTHERS. MULTICULTURAL BOOKS. NEIGHBORLINESS. NEIGHBORS. PERSONAL NARRATIVES. RUSSIAN AMERICANS. SEASHORE. SUMMER.

---

56   Biedrzycki, David. *Ace Lacewing: Bug Detective.* **Illus. by the author. Charlesbridge, 2005. 1-57091-569-5. Unp. Gr. 1–4**

"Bad bugs are my business," states Ace Lacewing. So when Motham Mayor Buzzbee phones him with the news that Queenie Bee of the Hive Rise Honey Company has been kidnapped, Ace follows a trail of warm honey, leading to the Beetle Zoo. It's almost curtains for him when he encounters a deadly tiger beetle; lucky for Ace, his lady love, that lovely rare butterfly Doctor Xerces Blue, rescues him in time. Think Humphrey Bogart (albeit with a green head and wings) in a fedora and trench coat, skulking through the dark blue nighttime illustrations (colored in Adobe Photoshop) jammed with buggy lowlifes as he cracks the case.

GERM: Find out about the queen bee in Deborah Heiligman's informative nonfiction picture book *Honeybees.* Bring in a honeycomb for all to see and taste. Enhance the insect theme with bug poetry in Douglas Florian's *Insectlopedia*, insect humor in Katy Hall and Lisa Eisenberg's *Buggy Riddles*, and factual information about beetles in Jerry Pallotta's *The Beetle Alphabet Book*, illustrated by David Biedrzycki.

RELATED TITLES: Clifford, Eth. *Flatfoot Fox and the Case of the Mising Schoolhouse.* Houghton Mifflin, 1997. (And others in the Flatfoot Fox series.) / Cushman, Doug. *The ABC Mystery.* HarperCollins, 1993. / Cushman, Doug. *Aunt Eater Loves a Mystery.* HarperCollins, 1987. (And others in the Aunt Eater mystery series.) / Cushman, Doug. *Inspector Hopper.* HarperCollins, 2000. / Cushman, Doug. *The Mystery at the Club Sandwich.* Clarion, 2004. / Cushman, Doug. *The Mystery of King Karfu.* HarperCollins, 1996. / Florian, Douglas. *Insectlopedia: Poems and Paintings.* Harcourt, 1998. / Hall, Katy, and Lisa Eisenberg. *Buggy Riddles.* Dial, 1986. / Heiligman, Deborah. *Honeybees.* National Geographic, 2002. / Hepworth, Cathi. *Bug Off! A Swarm of Insect Words.* Putnam, 1998. / Howe, James. *Bud Barkin, Private Eye* (Tales from the House of Bunnicula series). Atheneum, 2003. / Laden, Nina. *Private I. Guana: The Case of the Missing Chameleon.* Chronicle, 1995. / Pallotta, Jerry. *The Beetle Alphabet Book.* Illus. by David Biedrzycki. Charlesbridge, 2004. / Stevenson, James. *The Mud Flat Mystery.* Greenwillow, 1997.

SUBJECTS: BEES. BEETLES. BUTTERFLIES. HONEY. INSECTS. KIDNAPPING. MYSTERY AND DETECTIVE STORIES.

57   **Blake, Robert J.** *Akiak: A Tale from the Iditarod.* **Illus. by the author. Philomel, 1997. 0-399-22798-9. Unp. Gr. 2–5**
When Akiak, the lead sled dog in the Alaskan Iditarod race, is about to be flown home because her toe pads have become impacted with ice, she escapes and takes to the trail to find her owner, Mick, and finish the thousand mile race.

GERM: This is an inspiring realistic fiction story with wonderful blue-and-white snow-clad pages, and a good introduction to units on Alaska, winter, snow, dogs, loyalty, and determination. Learn more about the original 1925 run from Anchorage to Nome in Blake's *Togo.*

RELATED TITLES: Blake, Robert. *Togo.* Philomel, 2002. / Littlefield, Bill. *Champions: Stories of Ten Remarkable Athletes.* Little, Brown, 1993. / Miller, Debbie S. *The Great Serum Race: Blazing the Iditarod Trail.* Walker, 2002. / Paulsen, Gary. *Dogteam.* Delacorte, 1993. / Seibert, Patricia. *Mush! Across Alaska in the World's Longest Sled-Dog Race.* Millbrook, 1992. / Wood, Ted. *Iditarod Dream: Dusty and His Sled Dogs Compete in Alaska's Jr. Iditarod.* Walker, 1996.

SUBJECTS: ALASKA. DETERMINATION. DOGS. IDITAROD (RACE). PICTURE BOOKS FOR ALL AGES. RACING. SLED DOG RACING.

58   **Blake, Robert J.** *Fledgling.* **Illus. by the author. Philomel, 2000. 0-399-23321-0. Unp. Gr. PreK–1**
"Today is the day we are all going to fly," declares a young kestrel as she launches herself off a city rooftop in her first flight. With a larger hawk chasing her, the now panicked kestrel soars over the city (Brooklyn), through an amusement park (Coney Island), and even into the New York City subway. Realistic pen and watercolor paintings from the kestrel's perspective allow us to soar and swoop with her, elude the hawk, and make it safely back home to the nest.

GERM: Check out the bird section of your library for photos of hawks and kestrels and other raptors. To see just how and where birds live in a big city, read *Urban Roosts* by Barbara Bash.

RELATED TITLES: Bash, Barbara. *Urban Roosts: Where Birds Nest in the City.* Little, Brown, 1990. / Blake, Robert. *Akiak: A Tale from the Iditarod.* Philomel, 1997. / Blake, Robert J. *The Perfect Spot.* Philomel, 1992. / Blake, Robert. *Togo.* Philomel, 2002. / Nicholls, Judith. *Billywise.* Bloomsbury, 2002. / Peters, Lisa Westberg. *This Way Home.* Henry Holt, 1994. / Schaefer, Lola M. *Arrowhawk.* Henry Holt, 2004. / Weller, Frances Ward. *Riptide.* Philomel, 1990. / Wells, Rosemary. *The Language of Doves.* Dial, 1996.

SUBJECTS: BIRDS. CITIES AND TOWNS. HAWKS. KESTRELS. NEW YORK CITY. POINT OF VIEW.

59   **Blake, Robert J.** *Togo.* **Illus. by the author. Philomel, 2002. 0-399-23381-4. Unp. Gr. 1–4**
Every March, mushers and their dogs run the Iditarod Trail Sled Dog Race in Alaska, commemorating the original life-and-death race from Anchorage to Nome in 1925. Fans of the Iditarod know all about the sled dog Balto, who finished that first race, but Blake's inspirational picture book commemorates Togo, another heroic dog of that run. As indefatigable lead dog in Leonhard Seppala's team, Togo raced 350 miles to relay the antitoxin serum desperately needed to fight a deadly outbreak of diphtheria in snowbound Nome. Snowy-textured oil paintings will make you shiver, but Togo never faltered through 30 below temperatures and blinding snow.

GERM: Share the epilogue and Blake's dedication to his son ("To Christian—it's the journey") and discuss Togo's role in the serum run. Does it matter that Togo did not receive the same recognition as Balto? Why or why not? Flesh out more of the details and background with Debbie S. Miller's equally exciting *The Great Serum Race: Blazing the Iditarod Trail*, which includes the names of the 20 original mushers and the distances each covered, which should give you some good ideas for writing math word problems. For up-to-date info on the Iditarod, go to <www.iditarod.com>. And don't forget Blake's thrilling modern-day picture book, *Akiak: A Tale from the Iditarod.*

RELATED TITLES: Blake, Robert. *Akiak: A Tale from the Iditarod.* Philomel, 1997. / Miller, Debbie S. *The Great Serum Race: Blazing the Iditarod Trail.* Walker, 2002. / Paulsen, Gary. *Dogteam.* Delacorte, 1993. / Seibert, Patricia. *Mush! Across Alaska in the World's Longest Sled-Dog Race.* Millbrook, 1992. / Turner, Pamela S. *Hachiko: The True Story of a Loyal Dog.* Houghton Mifflin, 2004. / Wood, Ted. *Iditarod Dream: Dusty and His Sled Dogs Compete in Alaska's Jr. Iditarod.* Walker, 1996.

SUBJECTS: ALASKA. DOGS. HISTORICAL FICTION. IDITAROD (RACE). PICTURE BOOKS FOR ALL AGES. SLED DOG RACING. VOYAGES AND TRAVELS.

60   **Bloom, Becky.** *Wolf!* **Illus. by Pascal Biet. Orchard, 1999. 0-531-33155-5. Unp. Gr. PreK–1**
A hungry wolf, lurking by a farmhouse, is vexed to find the resident pig, duck, and cow unim-

pressed by his big, dangerous presence. The irritated pig retorts, "We're trying to read. This is a farm for educated animals. Now be a good wolf and go away." His dander up, the wolf, now sporting red specs, enrolls in school and is soon at the top of his class in reading and writing. Back at the farm, he shows off his new skill, reading in a monotone, "Run, Wolf! Run! See Wolf run." Underwhelmed, the farm animals let him know he still has a way to go before he's a real reader.

GERM: With its large, goofy watercolors and the message that real reading requires style, confidence, and passion, this is just the ticket for kids who are learning to read with expression.

RELATED TITLES: Allen, Susan, and Jane Lindaman. *Read Anything Good Lately?* Millbrook, 2003. / Auch, Mary Jane, and Herm Auch. *Souperchicken.* Holiday House, 2003. / Daugherty, James. *Andy and the Lion.* Viking, 1938. / Duvoisin, Roger. *Petunia.* Knopf, 1989. / McPhail, David. *Edward and the Pirates.* Little, Brown, 1997. / McPhail, David. *Fix-It.* Dutton, 1984. / McPhail, David. *Santa's Book of Names.* Little, Brown, 1993. / Marshall, James. *Wings: A Tale of Two Chickens.* Viking, 1986. / Novak, Matt. *Mouse TV.* Orchard, 1994. / Sierra, Judy. *Wild About Books.* Knopf, 2004. / Stanley, Diane. *Raising Sweetness.* Putnam, 1999. / Williams, Suzanne. *Library Lil.* Dial, 1997. / Wishinsky, Frieda. *Give Maggie a Chance.* Fitzhenry & Whiteside, 2002.

SUBJECTS: BOOKS AND READING. DOMESTIC ANIMALS. LITERACY. PICTURE BOOKS FOR ALL AGES. WOLVES.

---

61   **Blumenthal, Deborah. *Don't Let the Peas Touch! And Other Stories.* Illus. by Timothy Basil Ering. Scholastic, 2004. 0-439-29732-X. Unp. Gr. PreK–2**

As part of the cooking class she is taking, Annie helps to prepare the meals for her parents and her picky little sister, Sophie, who declares that her omelet is stinky and screams when the peas touch the eggs on her plate. Annie is a remarkably tolerant sister, even when the impetuous, red-headed Sophie is driving her mad during quiet time. She even has the perfect solution to Sophie's need for her own pet: a seed planted in a plastic cup.

GERM: Each of the three wonderful true-to-life stories about Sophie and her big sister will get children recalling, retelling, writing, and illustrating their own quirky life stories. Discuss: What do Annie and Sophie think about each other? Which of the sisters—Annie or Sophie—is more like you and why? What special strategies do you and your siblings use to get along with each other? Tell food stories, quiet stories, and pet stories. The male counterpart to this book is Betsy Byars's *My Brother Ant.*

RELATED TITLES: Brown, Marc. *D. W. the Picky Eater.* Little, Brown, 1995. / Byars, Betsy. *My Brother, Ant.* Viking, 1996. / Cameron, Ann. *The Stories Huey Tells.* Knopf, 1995. / Child, Lauren. *I Will Never Not Ever Eat a Tomato.* Candlewick, 2000. / Cleary, Beverly. *Beezus and Ramona.* Morrow, 1955. / Demarest, Chris L. *No Peas for Nellie.* Macmillan, 1988. / Hoberman, Mary Ann. *The Seven Silly Eaters.* Harcourt, 1997. / Lasky, Kathryn. *Show and Tell Bunnies.* Candlewick, 1998. / Lerner, Harriet, and Susan Goldhor. *What's So Terrible About Swallowing an Apple Seed?* HarperCollins, 1996. / Palatini, Margie. *Zak's Lunch.* Clarion, 1998. / Rosenthal, Amy Krouse. *Little Pea.* Chronicle Books, 2005. / Seuss, Dr. *Green Eggs and Ham.* Random House, 1960. / Sharmat, Mitchell. *Gregory, the Terrible Eater.* Macmillan, 1985. / Wells, Rosemary. *Yoko.* Hyperion, 1998. / Yolen, Jane. *How Do Dinosaurs Eat Their Food?* Blue Sky/Scholastic, 2005.

SUBJECTS: FOOD. FOOD HABITS. SEEDS. SISTERS.

---

62   **Bond, Michael. *Paddington Bear.* Illus. by R. W. Alley. HarperCollins, 1998. 0-06-027854-4. Unp. Gr. PreK–3**

The story about that endearing British bear from Darkest Peru—whom the Brown family found in London's Paddington Station and brought home—has been spiffed up in a delicious picture-book version about the momentous first day he spends with the Browns and his almost disastrous first bath.

GERM: Discuss: What kind of bear is Paddington? Make a list of adjectives that describe his personality and put each in a sentence, such as, "Paddington Bear is adventurous because he survived his first bath." Use this picture book with older readers as well to introduce them to the fiction series about the resourceful, marmalade-loving bear.

RELATED TITLES: Arnold, Tedd. *No More Water in the Tub!* Dial, 1995. / Bond, Michael. *A Bear Called Paddington.* Houghton Mifflin, 1960. / Bond, Michael. *Paddington Bear and the Busy Bee Carnival.* HarperCollins, 1998. / Bond, Michael. *Paddington's Storybook.* Houghton Mifflin, 1983. / Cole, Brock. *No More Baths.* Doubleday, 1980. / Goodman, Joan Elizabeth. *Bernard's Bath.* Boyds Mills, 1996.

SUBJECTS: BATHS. BEARS. ENGLAND. HUMOROUS FICTION. LONDON (ENGLAND). LOST. PICTURE BOOKS FOR ALL AGES.

63   **Booth, Philip.** *Crossing.* **Illus. by Bagram Ibatoulline. Candlewick, 2001. 0-7636-1420-3. Unp. Gr. PreK–2**

At the Big Ear railroad crossing in town, cars, kids, grownups, and even a dog wait and watch as a freight train passes by, starting with the engine and, a hundred cars later, ending with the caboose. The rhyming recitation, naming each of the boxcars on the train—inspired by a railroad crossing in Brunswick, Maine—features ultra-realistic gouache paintings in the style of Norman Rockwell.

GERM: What a fun read-aloud to have children echo each line in rhythm. Type this up as a Reader's Theater poem, with each pair of kids reading one or two lines. Have them stand in a long, curved, train-like line as they recite the poem, one car at a time. Also share *Freight Train* by Donald Crews.

RELATED TITLES: Barton, Byron. *My Car.* Greenwillow, 2001. / Crews, Donald. *Freight Train.* Greenwillow, 1978. / Crews, Donald. *Inside Freight Train.* HarperCollins, 2001. / Hort, Lenny. *The Seals on the Bus.* Henry Holt, 2000. / Hubble, Patricia. *Trains: Steaming! Pulling! Huffing!* Marshall Cavendish, 2005. / Kirk, Daniel. *Go!* Hyperion, 2001. / Mahy, Margaret. *The Rattlebang Picnic.* Dial, 1994. / Pinkwater, Daniel. *Tooth-Gnasher Superflash.* Macmillan, 1990. / Shaw, Nancy. *Sheep in a Jeep.* Houghton Mifflin, 1986. / Shields, Carol Diggory. *Animagicals: On the Go.* Handprint, 2001. / Siebert, Diane. *Train Song.* Crowell, 1990. / Westcott, Nadine Bernard. *I've Been Working on the Railroad: An American Classic.* Hyperion, 1996. / Zelinsky, Paul O. *The Wheels on the Bus.* Dutton, 1990.

SUBJECTS: READER'S THEATER. STORIES IN RHYME. TRAINS. TRANSPORTATION.

64   **Borden, Louise.** *A. Lincoln and Me.* **Illus. by Ted Lewin. Scholastic, 1999. 0-590-45714-4. Unp. Gr. 2–4**

A brown-haired, tall, gangly boy narrator explains how not only was he born on the same day as his hero, Abe Lincoln, but they have a lot in common. When his classmates laugh at the boy's big clumsy hands and feet, his supportive teacher, Mrs. Giff, defends him, telling the children that people laughed at Lincoln too. Realistic watercolors of the boy are interspersed with pencil sketches of Lincoln.

GERM: Make a list or Venn diagram showing what the boy does and doesn't have in common with his hero and role model. Discuss: Who is your role model and why? Research other famous people born on your birthday and find out more about them to see if you have anything in common.

RELATED TITLES: Brenner, Martha. *Abe Lincoln's Hat.* Random House, 1994. / Cohn, Amy L., and Suzy Schmidt. *Abraham Lincoln.* Scholastic, 2002. / Freedman, Russell. *Lincoln: A Photobiography.* Clarion, 1987. / Harness, Cheryl. *Abe Lincoln Goes to Washington.* National Geographic, 1997. / Kunhardt, Edith. *Honest Abe.* Greenwillow, 1993. / Livingston, Myra Cohn. *Abraham Lincoln: A Man for All the People.* Holiday House, 1993. / Winnick, Karen B. *Mr. Lincoln's Whiskers.* Boyds Mills, 1996. / Winters, Kay. *Abe Lincoln: The Boy Who Loved Books.* Simon & Schuster, 2003.

SUBJECTS: BIRTHDAYS. LINCOLN, ABRAHAM. PRESIDENTS. ROLE MODELS. SELF-ESTEEM. TEACHERS.

65   **Borden, Louise.** *The A+ Custodian.* **Illus. by Adam Gustavson. McElderry, 2004. 0-689-84995-8. Unp. Gr. K–3**

John Carillo, the hardworking custodian at Dublin Elementary School, spends his days caring for the building and helping teachers and children. Third grader Gracie comes up with a plan so that the whole school can show its appreciation for everything he does.

GERM: What does the custodian do to make your building a better place? How about the secretaries, the nurse, and the cafeteria workers? Children can write thank-you letters to the support staff at your school to express their gratitude.

RELATED TITLES: Birney, Betty G. *The World According to Humphrey.* Putnam, 2004. / Borden, Louise. *Good Luck, Mrs. K.* McElderry, 1999. / Pulver, Robin. *Mrs. Toggle's Beautiful Blue Shoe.* Four Winds, 1994. / Thaler, Mike. *The Custodian from the Back Lagoon.* Scholastic, 2001.

SUBJECTS: JANITORS. SCHOOLS.

66   **Borden, Louise.** *Good Luck, Mrs. K.* **Illus. by Adam Gustavson. McElderry, 1999. 0-689-85119-7. Unp. Gr. 2–4**

Ann, the third grade narrator of this uplifting but serious story, loves the sound of her new teacher's name, Mrs. Kempczinski—KEMP-CHIN-SKI!—and is having the time of her life in her class. When Mrs. K. is out sick for a week, Mr. Rovers, the principal, tells the class that she has cancer. And though they write letters to her, they have a substitute teacher, Mrs. Dodd, for the rest of that year.

GERM: While the illness in the story is presented in an upbeat, optimistic light, this might not be not a book you'd tend to read aloud without a reason, though it is a tribute to a master teacher whose students are inspired by her. From the dedication, it's clear that it is based on an actual teacher. Ask children to make a list of things their teachers have said and done that they will never forget.

RELATED TITLES: Borden, Louise. *The A+ Custodian*. McElderry, 2004. / Hannigan, Katherine. *Ida B: And Her Plans to Maximize Fun, Avoid Disaster, and (Possibly) Save the World*. Greenwillow, 2004. / Hill, Kirkpatrick. *The Year of Miss Agnes*. McElderry, 2000. / Houston, Gloria. *My Great Aunt Arizona*. HarperCollins, 1992. / Lorbiecki, Marybeth. *Sister Anne's Hands*. Dial, 1998. / Polacco, Patricia. *Thank You, Mr. Falker*. Philomel, 1998.

SUBJECTS: CANCER. SCHOOLS. SICK. TEACHERS.

67 **Bottner, Barbara. *The Scaredy Cats*. Illus. by Victoria Chess. Simon & Schuster, 2003. 0-689-83786-0. Unp. Gr. PreK–2**

Mr. and Mrs. Scaredy Cat and Baby are afraid of bad things that might possibly ensue if they close the window, get dressed, make breakfast, drive into town, open a package, or even read a book. So they end up scared, cold, hungry, bored, mad, and disappointed, afraid to make a move, though Baby points out sagely that sometimes good things can happen too.

GERM: Talk it over: What are you afraid of? Think of a time you did something that scared you and something good came out of it. Other picture books on similar themes include *There's a Big, Beautiful World Out There!* by Nancy Carlson, *The Worry Warts* by Pamela Duncan Edwards, *Wemberly Worried* by Kevin Henkes, and *Something Might Happen* by Helen Lester.

RELATED TITLES: Allard, Harry. *The Stupids Die*. Houghton Mifflin, 1981. / Arnold, Tedd. *Parts*. Dial, 1997. / Carlson, Nancy. *There's a Big, Beautiful World Out There!* Viking, 2002. / Denim, Sue. *The Dumb Bunnies*. Scholastic, 1994. / Denim, Sue. *Make Way for Dumb Bunnies*. Scholastic, 1996. / Edwards, Pamela Duncan. *The Worrywarts*. HarperCollins, 1999. / Henkes, Kevin. *Wemberly Worried*. Greenwillow, 2000. / Lester, Helen. *Hooway for Wodney Wat*. Houghton Mifflin, 1999. / Lester, Helen. *Something Might Happen*. Houghton Mifflin, 2003.

SUBJECTS: CATS. FEAR. WORRYING.

68 **Bottner, Barbara, and Gerald Kruglik. *Wallace's Lists*. Illus. by Olof Landström. Harper-Collins, 2004. 0-06-000225-5. Unp. Gr. PreK–2**

Wallace, a bespectacled, sedentary gray mouse who makes lists for every aspect of his daily life, is dumbfounded when he meets his new neighbor Albert, a mouse who lives every day of his life as an adventure. When Albert sets out alone for far-off Glockamorra, Wallace makes his way to the airport, even though it's pouring rain outside, and faces danger and excitement on his search for his new friend.

GERM: Ask adventure seekers to make illustrated lists of things that interest or matter to them; then have them list adventures they've had or would like to have. Use these as a kickoff to some experiential or imaginative writing as your children describe real or hoped-for adventures. Write and illustrate stories of the favorite adventures you have had or would like to have.

RELATED TITLES: Brown, Laurie Krasny, and Marc Brown. *How to Be a Friend: A Guide to Making Friends and Keeping Them*. Little, Brown, 1998. / Hobbie, Holly. *Toot and Puddle*. Little, Brown, 1997. (And others in the Toot and Puddle series.) / Howe, James. *Horace and Morris But Mostly Dolores*. Atheneum, 1999. / Lobel, Arnold. *Frog and Toad Together*. HarperCollins, 1972. / Novak, Matt. *Mouse TV*. Orchard, 1994. / Raschka, Chris. *Yo! Yes?* Orchard, 1993. / Waber, Bernard. *Evie and Margie*. Houghton Mifflin, 2003. / Waddell, Martin. *Hi, Harry!* Candlewick, 2003.

SUBJECTS: AIRPORTS. FRIENDSHIP. MICE. ORDERLINESS. SPONTANEITY.

69 **Bradby, Marie. *More Than Anything Else*. Illus. by Chris K. Soentpiet. Orchard, 1995. 0-531-08764-6. Unp. Gr. 2-6**

In a poignant and inspirational slice-of-life picture book, we meet 9-year-old Booker T. Washington who works from sunup to sundown packing salt in barrels, and all the while burns with the desire to learn to read. His mother gives him an alphabet book and he learns all the letters, tracing them in the dirt without knowing their meaning. It's the newspaper man who tells him "the song—the sounds the marks make" and shows him how to write his name. Set in post-Civil War West Virginia, the nighttime watercolors lit by lantern and firelight add to the mysterious feel.

GERM: Pair this with *The Wednesday Surprise* by Eve Bunting and *The Day of Ahmed's Secret* by Florence Parry Heide and Judith Heide Gilliland, and ask your listeners to explain why reading makes a difference in their own lives.

RELATED TITLES: Bogart, Jo Ellen. *Jeremiah Learns to Read.* Orchard, 1999. / Bunting, Eve. *The Wednesday Surprise.* Clarion, 1989. / Heide, Florence Parry, and Judith Heide Gilliland. *The Day of Ahmed's Secret.* Lothrop, 1990. / Hest, Amy. *Mr. George Baker.* Candlewick, 2004. / Howard, Elizabeth Fitzgerald. *Virgie Goes to School with Us Boys.* Simon & Schuster, 2000. / Joosse, Barbara M. *Hot City.* Philomel, 2004. / Mora, Pat. *Tomás and the Library Lady.* Knopf, 1997. / Polacco, Patricia. *Aunt Chip and the Great Triple Creek Dam Affair.* Philomel, 1996. / Ransom, Candice. *Liberty Street.* Walker, 2003. / Smothers, Ethel Footman. *The Hard-Times Jar.* Farrar, 2003.

SUBJECTS: AFRICAN AMERICANS. AFRICAN AMERICANS—HISTORY. BOOKS AND READING. DETERMINATION. HISTORICAL FICTION. LITERACY. MULTICULTURAL BOOKS. PICTURE BOOKS FOR OLDER READERS. SLAVERY. WASHINGTON, BOOKER T.

70   **Braun, Trudi.** *My Goose Betsy.* **Illus. by John Bendall Brunello. Candlewick, 1999. 0-7636-0449-6. Unp. Gr. PreK–1**

As shown in large, affectionate, watercolor and colored-pencil illustrations, farmyard goose Betsy builds a nest, lays eight eggs, and sits on them all day. The goslings struggle to hatch and then off they go, following Betsy, who is now a mother.

GERM: When you're studying how an egg becomes a bird, this is the simplest explanation I've seen, perfect for preschool. A few more goose facts are appended, including how long geese live. Do you know? Thirty *years!* Whew.

RELATED TITLES: Bang, Molly. *Goose.* Scholastic, 1996. / Dunrea, Olivier. *Ollie.* Houghton, 2003. / Guiberson, Brenda Z. *The Emperor Lays an Egg.* Henry Holt, 2001. / Ryder, Joanne. *Catching the Wind.* Morrow, 1989. / Schoenherr, John. *Rebel.* Philomel, 1995. / Silverman, Erica. *Don't Fidget a Feather!* Macmillan, 1994. / Simont, Marc. *The Goose That Almost Got Cooked.* Scholastic, 1997. / Wahl, Jan. *The Singing Geese.* Dutton, 1998. / Yolen, Jane. *Honkers.* Little, Brown, 1993.

SUBJECTS: BIRTH. EGGS. GEESE.

71   **Brett, Jan.** *Daisy Comes Home.* **Illus. by the author. Putnam, 2002. 0-399-23618-X. Unp. Gr. PreK–1**

Picked on by the other hens and pushed onto the muddy floor one rainy night, Daisy leaves the henhouse to sleep in a market basket. Unaware that the river is rising, the chicken is swept downstream, away from her owner, a girl named Mei-Mei.

GERM: After reading the story of Daisy's travels down the Li River in China, children can make a Venn diagram of the setting. What is the same as, similar to, or different from life in the United States? Be sure to read Marjorie Flack's classic picture book, *The Story of Ping,* which was Jan Brett's inspiration for her tale.

RELATED TITLES: Armstrong, Jennifer. *Chin Yu Min and the Ginger Cat.* Crown, 1993. / Brett, Jan. *The First Dog.* Harcourt, 1988. / Brett, Jan. *The Hat.* Putnam, 1997. / Brett, Jan. *The Mitten.* Putnam, 1989. / Brett, Jan. *Trouble with Trolls.* Putnam, 1992. / Brett, Jan. *The Umbrella.* Putnam, 2004. / Flack, Marjorie. *The Story About Ping.* Viking, 1933. / Froehlich, Margaret Walden. *That Kookoory!* Harcourt, 1995. / Graham, Bob. *Queenie, One of the Family.* Candlewick, 1997.

SUBJECTS: CHICKENS. CHINA. RIVERS.

72   **Brett, Jan.** *The Hat.* **Illus. by the author. Putnam, 1997. 0-399-23101-3. Unp. Gr. PreK–1**

Embarrassed to have Lisa's red woolen knit sock stuck on his head, Hedgie the hedgehog tells the other animals that it's really a hat.

GERM: Pair this with Brett's *The Mitten* and act them both out. See how another animal uses a sock for a hat in Lizette's *Green Sock* by Catharina Valckx.

RELATED TITLES: Barrett, Judi. *Animals Should Definitely Not Wear Clothing.* Atheneum, 1970. / Beskow, Elsa. *Pelle's New Suit.* HarperCollins, 1929. / Brett, Jan. *The Mitten.* Putnam, 1989. / Brett, Jan. *Trouble with Trolls.* Putnam, 1992. / Brett, Jan. *The Umbrella.* Putnam, 2004. / Brett, Jan. *Who's That Knocking on Christmas Eve?* Putnam, 2002. / Hissey, Jane. *Little Bear's Trousers.* Philomel, 1987. / Klise, Kate. *Shall I Knit You a Hat?* Henry Holt, 2004. / London, Jonathan. *Froggy Gets Dressed.* Viking, 1992. / Nodset, Joan L. *Who Took the Farmer's Hat.* HarperCollins, 1963. / Slobodkina, Esphyr. *Caps for Sale.* HarperCollins, 1947. / Stoeke, Janet Morgan. *A Hat for Minerva Louise.* Dutton, 1996. / Valckx, Catharina. *Lizette's Green Sock.* Clarion, 2005.

SUBJECTS: ANIMALS. CLOTHING AND DRESS. HATS. HEDGEHOGS. WINTER.

73 **Brett, Jan.** *Honey . . . Honey . . . Lion!* **Putnam, 2005. 0-399-24463-8. Unp. Gr. PreK–2**

The day after Badger neglects to share his honeycomb with Honeyguide, she leads him on a merry chase past the great gray baobab tree (PITTER PATTER!), across the water hole (SPLISH, SPLASH!), to the top of the termite mound (SPRONG!), through a stand of papyrus (CLICK-ETY-CLICK!), and under an acacia tree. What does Badger find there? Lift the flap, and there he is: LION! Badger dashes back, reversing his journey, to the safety of his burrow. Brett came to write her sumptuously illustrated sequence story after visiting Botswana, where her guide told her facts about the honeyguide and the honey badger and the legend about honeyguides leading ungenerous ones to the lion's den.

GERM: The pattern of the story will remind you of the old call-and-response chant, "I'm Going on a Bear Hunt." Act out the journey of the honeyguide as he follows the honey badger, making up motions to go along with each of the sound effects. For more action, follow up with *Oh, Look!* by Patricia Polacco and *We're Going on a Bear Hunt* by Michael Rosen. Honeyguides also follow humans, as you'll see in *Juma and the Honey Guide* by Robin Bernard and *If You Should Meet a Honey Guide* by April Pulley Sayre.

RELATED TITLES: Bash, Barbara. *Tree of Life: The World of the African Baobab.* Sierra Club/Little, Brown, 1989. / Bernard, Robin. *Juma and the Honey Guide.* Dillon/Silver Burdett, 1996. / Cowcher, Helen. *Whistling Thorn.* Scholastic, 1993. / Heiligman, Deborah. *Honeybees.* National Geographic, 2002. / Krebs, Laurie. *The Beeman.* National Geographic, 2002. / Kurtz, Jane, and Christopher Kurtz. *Water Hole Waiting.* Greenwillow, 2002. / Martin, Francesca. *The Honey Hunters.* Candlewick, 1992. / Polacco, Patricia. *Oh, Look!* Philomel, 2004. / Rockwell, Anne. *Honey in a Hive.* HarperCollins, 2005. / Rosen, Michael. *We're Going on a Bear Hunt.* McElderry, 1989. / Sayre, April Pulley. *If You Should Meet a Honey Guide.* Houghton Mifflin, 1995. / Wallace, Nancy Elizabeth. *A Taste of Honey.* Winslow, 2001. / Yoshida, Toshi. *Young Lions.* Philomel, 1989.

SUBJECTS: AFRICA. ANIMALS. BIRDS. CALL-AND-RESPONSE STORIES. HONEY. HONEY BADGER. HONEYGUIDES. LIONS. SOUND EFFECTS. STORIES TO TELL. SYMBIOSIS.

74 **Brett, Jan.** *The Umbrella.* **Illus. by the author. Putnam, 2004. 0-399-24215-5. Unp. Gr. PreK–2**

Hoping to spy a jaguar, monkey, toucan, kinkajou, and even a shy tapir, Carlos takes his green umbrella into the cloud forest and climbs a giant fig tree for a better view. One by one, the animals climb into the upended umbrella he has left below and jockey for space.

GERM: Brett's joyful and lush look at colorful rainforest animals is a companion story to *The Mitten,* with which you can compare and contrast. This could make a great Reader's Theater script to read and act out. Each of the eight animals also utters a Spanish phrase, which children will be able to translate in context. As a first research activity, small groups can each look up one rainforest animal in a book, encyclopedia, or on the Internet to find out a bit about it.

RELATED TITLES: Brett, Jan. *The Hat.* Putnam, 1997. / Brett, Jan. *The Mitten.* Penguin, 1989. / Brett, Jan. *Trouble with Trolls.* Putnam, 1992. / Burningham, John. *Mr. Gumpy's Outing.* Henry Holt, 1971. / Cherry, Lynne. *The Great Kapok Tree: A Tale of the Amazon Rain Forest.* Harcourt, 1990. / Cherry, Lynne, and Mark J. Plotkin. *The Shaman's Apprentice: A Tale of the Amazon Rain Forest.* Harcourt, 1998. / Cowcher, Helen. *Rain Forest.* Farrar, 1988. / Cowley, Joy. *Red-Eyed Tree Frog.* Scholastic, 1999. / Crespo, George. *How Iwariwa the Cayman Learned to Share: A Yanomami Myth.* Clarion, 1995. / Jordan, Tanis. *Amazon Alphabet.* Kingfisher, 1996. / Ryder, Joanne. *Jaguar in the Rain Forest.* Morrow, 1996. / Yolen, Jane. *Welcome to the Green House.* Putnam, 1993.

SUBJECTS: ANIMALS. COSTA RICA. JUNGLE ANIMALS. MULTICULTURAL BOOKS. RAIN FORESTS. READER'S THEATER. SPANISH LANGUAGE. UMBRELLAS.

75 **Brett, Jan.** *Who's That Knocking on Christmas Eve?* **Illus. by the author. Putnam, 2002. 0-399-23873-5. Unp. Gr. K–2**

High above the Arctic Circle one Christmas Eve, a Finnish boy skiing to Oslo, accompanied by his ice bear (a placid white polar bear in harness), stops at a cozy hut along the way and knocks at the door. Kyri, preparing a Christmas feast for her father, who has gone up the mountain to chase away the trolls, welcomes the boy and his bear. When the raucous, ravenous trolls burst into the house and devour everything, one troll makes the mistake of waking the big white "kitty" sleeping under the stove.

GERM: In Brett's sumptuous trademark paintings, decorated side panels or windows on either side of the double-page paintings allow you to view characters "offstage" and predict what might happen next. This is a retelling of a comical Norwegian folktale; compare it with Tomie dePaola's version, *The Cat on the Dovrefell.* For more snowy troll mischief, also read Brett's *The*

Trouble with Trolls. After reading each of the books, have children describe how the trolls were tricked, and what the trolls' reactions were.

RELATED TITLES: Asbjørnsen, P. C., and J. E. Moe. *The Three Billy Goats Gruff.* Illus. by Marcia Brown. Harcourt, 1957. / Brett, Jan. *The Hat.* Putnam, 1997. / Brett, Jan. *Trouble with Trolls.* Putnam, 1992. / D'Aulaire, Ingri, and Edgar Parin D'Aulaire. *D'Aulaires' Trolls.* Doubleday, 1972. / dePaola, Tomie. *The Cat on the Dovrefell.* Putnam, 1979. / Galdone, Paul. *The Three Billy Goats Gruff.* Seabury, 1973. / Lunge-Larsen, Lise. *The Troll with No Heart in His Body: And Other Tales of Trolls, from Norway.* Houghton Mifflin, 1999. / Prelutsky, Jack. *Monday's Troll.* Greenwillow, 1996. / Shepard, Aaron. *Master Maid: A Tale of Norway.* Dial, 1997. / Torgersen, Don Arthur. *The Girl Who Tricked the Troll.* Children's Press, 1978. / Wolff, Patricia Rae. *The Toll-Bridge Troll.* Harcourt, 1995.

SUBJECTS: CHRISTMAS. NORWAY. TROLLS.

76   Bridges, Shirin Yim. *Ruby's Wish.* **Illus. by Sophie Blackall. Chronicle, 2002. 0-8118-3490-5. Unp. Gr. 1–6**

Among the one hundred children living in the family compound in China, one little girl, Ruby, who insisted on wearing something red every day, was better at calligraphy than all of the others. While the boys were free to play after their lessons, the girls were expected to learn about cooking and keeping house. Ruby wrote a poem: "Alas, bad luck to be born a girl; worse luck to be born into this house where only boys are cared for." When her grandfather summoned her to ask about the poem, she told him she'd much rather go to university than marry according to tradition. Dignified full-bleed gouache illustrations show Chinese life in a wealthy family before the Revolution.

GERM: On the very last page is a touching surprise that will make you want to start the book all over again—a photograph of the author's grandmother, who is the Ruby in this fictionalized but basically true story. And yes, Ruby did go to college. Talk about the value of an education and discuss why Ruby was dissatisfied with her expected role. Ask your students to go home and retell Ruby's story to their parents or grandparents or other relatives. In return, these relatives might be persuaded to relate true stories from their own childhoods that the children can write down or record and then illustrate.

RELATED TITLES: Bierman, Carol. *Journey to Ellis Island: How My Father Came to America.* Hyperion, 1998. / Houston, Gloria. *My Great Aunt Arizona.* HarperCollins, 1992. / Howard, Elizabeth Fitzgerald. *Virgie Goes to School with Us Boys.* Simon & Schuster, 2000. / Jiang, Ji Li. *Red Scarf Girl: A Memoir of the Cultural Revolution.* HarperCollins, 1997. / Lasky, Kathryn. *Marven of the North Woods.* Harcourt, 1997. / Neuberger, Anne E. *The Girl-Son.* Carolrhoda, 1995. / Say, Allen. *Tea with Milk.* Houghton Mifflin, 1999. / Schwartz, Harriet Berg. *When Artie Was Little.* Knopf, 1996. / Wells, Rosemary. *Streets of Gold.* Dial, 1999.

SUBJECTS: CHINA. CHINESE NEW YEAR. EDUCATION. FAMILY STORIES. GRANDFATHERS. HISTORICAL FICTION. PICTURE BOOKS FOR ALL AGES. SEX ROLE. WOMEN.

77   Brisson, Pat. *The Summer My Father Was Ten.* **Illus. by Andrea Shine. Boyds Mills, 1998. 1-56397-435-5. Unp. Gr. 1–4**

As the young narrator and her father plant their garden together, she retells his boyhood story of the time he and his friends unthinkingly wrecked old Mr. Bellavista's garden and how her father made up for his misbehavior.

GERM: Compare and contrast this with Patricia Polacco's *Chicken Sunday*, in which three children were wrongly accused of mischief. Children can discuss or write about something they did wrong that they will never forget, or that they now regret, or that they had to apologize for, and can describe what they did (or should have done) to make amends.

RELATED TITLES: Bunting, Eve. *A Day's Work.* Clarion, 1994. / Johnson, Dolores. *Your Dad Was Just Like You.* Macmillan, 1993. / McKissack, Patricia C. *The Honest-to-Goodness Truth.* Atheneum, 2000. / Park, Barbara. *Junie B., First Grader: Cheater Pants.* Random House, 2003. / Peters, Julie Anne. *The Stinky Sneakers Contest.* Little, Brown, 1992. / Polacco, Patricia. *Chicken Sunday.* Philomel, 1992. / Schwartz, Harriet Berg. *When Artie Was Little.* Knopf, 1996. / Wood, Audrey. *The Red Racer.* Simon & Schuster, 1996.

SUBJECTS: APOLOGIES. ELDERLY. FATHERS. GARDENING. HONESTY. PICTURE BOOKS FOR ALL AGES.

78   Brown, Marc. *Arthur Writes a Story.* **Illus. by the author. Little, Brown, 1996. 0-316-10916-9. Unp. Gr. K–2**

For homework, Mr. Ratburn asks his students to write a story with a beginning, middle, and end; to use details; and to be creative. Arthur writes about how he got his dog Pal, but when he reads his story aloud to sassy little sister D. W. and his friends and family, they each give him editorial advice.

GERM: You can use this as a springboard to discuss the differences between writing realistic stories and fantasy. Try writing one of each, based on the same theme.

RELATED TITLES: Allen, Susan, and Jane Lindaman. *Written Anything Good Lately?* Millbrook, 2006. / Brown, Marc. Arthur series. Little, Brown. / Christelow, Eileen. *What Do Authors Do?* Clarion, 1995. / Christelow, Eileen. *What Do Illustrators Do?* Clarion, 1999. / Duke, Kate. *Aunt Isabel Makes Trouble.* Dutton, 1996. / Duke, Kate. *Aunt Isabel Tells a Good One.* Dutton, 1992. / Kroll, Steven. *Patches Lost and Found.* Winslow, 2001. / Leedy, Loreen. *Look at My Book: How Kids Can Write and Illustrate Terrific Books.* Holiday House, 2004. / Lester, Helen. *Author: A True Story.* Houghton Mifflin, 1997. / Nixon, Joan Lowery. *If You Were a Writer.* Four Winds, 1988. / Schotter, Roni. *Nothing Ever Happens on 90th Street.* Orchard, 1997. / Stevens, Janet. *From Pictures to Words: A Book About Making a Book.* Holiday House, 1995.

SUBJECTS: AUTHORSHIP. BROTHERS AND SISTERS. DOGS. WRITING.

79   **Brown, Marc. *D. W. the Picky Eater*. Illus. by the author. Little, Brown, 1995. 0-316-10957-6. Unp. Gr. PreK–1**
Arthur's saucy little sister, D. W., won't eat anything with eyes, or pickles, or liver, or (worst of all) spinach, and has a tantrum in a restaurant when there's spinach in her salad. On Grandma Thora's birthday, though, before the family heads out to a fancy restaurant, D. W. promises to eat everything on her plate.

GERM: Introducing the Food Pyramid? Ask your fussy foodies what foods they love and loathe. What have they tried recently and been surprised to like? Picky eaters abound in the related titles below.

RELATED TITLES: Blumenthal, Deborah. *Don't Let the Peas Touch! And Other Stories.* Scholastic, 2004. / Child, Lauren. *I Will Never Not Ever Eat a Tomato.* Candlewick, 2000. / Demarest, Chris L. *No Peas for Nellie.* Macmillan, 1988. / Hoberman, Mary Ann. *The Seven Silly Eaters.* Harcourt, 1997. / Palatini, Margie. *Zak's Lunch.* Clarion, 1998. / Rayner, Mary. *Mrs. Pig's Bulk Buy.* Atheneum, 1981. / Rosenthal, Amy Krouse. *Little Pea.* Chronicle Books, 2005. / Seuss, Dr. *Green Eggs and Ham.* Random House, 1960. / Sharmat, Mitchell. *Gregory, the Terrible Eater.* Four Winds, 1984. / Wells, Rosemary. *Yoko.* Hyperion, 1998. / Yolen, Jane. *How Do Dinosaurs Eat Their Food?* Blue Sky/Scholastic, 2005.

SUBJECTS: AARDVARKS. FAMILY LIFE. FOOD. FOOD HABITS. GRANDMOTHERS. RESTAURANTS.

80   **Brown, Margaret Wise. *Another Important Book*. Illus. by Chris Raschka. HarperCollins, 1999. 0-06-026282-6. Unp. Gr. PreK–1**
From the author of the classic *Good Night, Moon* and *The Important Book* comes a matter-of-fact rhyming description of a child's life from ages one to six. It lists what you can do at each age and states the most important thing about it: "But the important thing about being One is that life has just begun." Raschka's expressive watercolors of children capture the essence of each year.

GERM: Discuss: What is the most important thing you have learned this year? There's a mirror on the inside back cover, so you can all have a look before drawing your own self-portraits or talking about what makes you you. *It's Hard to Be Five: Learning How to Work My Control Panel* by Jamie Lee Curtis and *When I Was Five* by Arthur Howard hone in on the kindergarten years.

RELATED TITLES: Brown, Margaret Wise. *The Important Book.* HarperCollins, 1949. / Browne, Anthony. *Willy the Dreamer.* Candlewick, 1998. / Emmett, Jonathan. *Someone Bigger.* Clarion, 2004. / Hindley, Judy. *Eyes, Nose, Fingers, and Toes: A First Book All About You.* Candlewick, 1999. / Howard, Arthur. *When I Was Five.* Harcourt, 1996. / Komaiko, Leah. *Earl's Too Cool for Me.* HarperCollins, 1988.

SUBJECTS: BIRTHDAYS. GROWTH. STORIES IN RHYME.

81   **Browne, Anthony. *My Dad*. Illus. by the author. Farrar, 2001. 0-374-35101-5. Unp. Gr. PreK–2**
"He's all right, my dad," is the refrain running through this loving tribute to a wonderful dad. As a young boy describes his father's many talents, we see his dad—clad in brown plaid bathrobe, striped pajamas, and slippers—demonstrate each one.

GERM: Ask your students to draw pictures of their dads or moms, dressed in a favorite outfit, performing a special, unique skill. "My dad can eat like a horse, and swim like a fish," says the book's narrator. Create new "My Dad" books of similes as presents for Father's Day. Give equal time with Browne's *My Mom.*

RELATED TITLES: Browne, Anthony. *Gorilla.* Knopf, 1985. / Browne, Anthony. *My Mom.* Farrar, 2005. / Browne, Anthony. *The Shape Game.* Farrar, 2003. / Browne, Anthony. *Willy the Dreamer.* Candlewick, 1998. /

Collard, Sneed B., III. *Animal Dads*. Houghton Mifflin, 1997. / Feiffer, Jules. *The Daddy Mountain*. Hyperion, 2004. / Greenspun, Adele. *Daddies*. Philomel, 1991. / High, Linda Oatman. *Winter Shoes for Shadow Horse*. Boyds Mills, 2001. / Pringle, Laurence. *Octopus Hug*. Boyds Mills, 1993. / Steptoe, Javaka. *In Daddy's Arms I Am Tall: African Americans Celebrating Fathers*. Lee & Low, 1997. / Weigel, Jeff. *Atomic Ace (He's Just My Dad)*. Albert Whitman, 2004. / Ziefert, Harriet. *33 Uses for a Dad*. Blue Apple, 2004.

SUBJECTS: FAMILY LIFE. FATHERS.

82   Browne, Anthony. *Willy the Dreamer*. Illus. by the author. Candlewick, 1998. 0-7636-0378-3. Unp. Gr. PreK–2

Willy, the gentle, amiable chimp from *Willy the Wimp, Willy the Champ, Willy and Hugh,* and *Willy the Wizard* is back, thinking about his future, in a large-format picture book that artists and banana lovers alike will find captivating. The simple text describes Willy's dreams of being a painter or an explorer, a beggar or a king, of being unable to run but able to fly. The story soars with surreal watercolor illustrations that pay witty homage to artists including Magritte, Rousseau, Tenniel, de Chirico, Dali, and Homer. Incorporated into each painting are bananas in every form: as the sail of a boat, the points of a king's crown, or the nose on a stuffed elephant.

GERM: Dreamers can record, in writing and pictures, their own reveries. Art teachers will have a ball showing pictures of the original paintings and having their students select other paintings to parody, using Dav Pilkey's *When Cats Dream* for further inspiration. Also tie this book into a lesson on careers; as a spur to encourage students to describe, write about, and draw their dreams and aspirations; and as a superb narrative pantomime text. Children can act out the story silently as you reread it aloud. Don't forget to bring in a bunch of bananas to share. *Willy's Pictures* presents reproductions of famous paintings, Willy-style, with an explanation of each one and a reproduction of the real painting at the back of the book.

RELATED TITLES: Agee, Jon. *The Incredible Painting of Felix Clousseau*. Farrar, 1988. / Alcorn, Johnny. *Rembrandt's Beret*. Tambourine, 1991. / Auch, Mary Jane. *Eggs Mark the Spot*. Holiday House, 1996. / Browne, Anthony. *The Shape Game*. Farrar, 2003. / Browne, Anthony. *Willy's Pictures*. Candlewick, 2000. (And others in the Willy series.) / dePaola, Tomie. *The Art Lesson*. Putnam, 1989. / Florczak, Robert. *Yikes!!!* Scholastic, 2003. / Garland, Michael. *Dinner at Magritte's*. Dutton, 1995. / Howard, Arthur. *When I Was Five*. Harcourt, 1996. / Hurd, Thacher. *Art Dog*. HarperCollins, 1996. / Lionni, Leo. *Matthew's Dream*. Knopf, 1991. / Lithgow, John. *Micawber*. Simon & Schuster, 2002. / MacDonald, Ross. *Another Perfect Day*. Roaring Brook, 2002. / Pilkey, Dav. *When Cats Dream*. Orchard, 1992. / Reynolds, Peter. *The Dot*. Candlewick, 2003.

SUBJECTS: CHIMPANZEES. CREATIVE DRAMA. DREAMS. IMAGINATION. OCCUPATIONS. PAINTINGS. PICTURE BOOKS FOR ALL AGES.

83   Buck, Pearl S. *Christmas Day in the Morning*. Illus. by Mark Buehner. HarperCollins, 2002. 0-688-16267-3. Unp. Gr. 3-8

Overhearing his parents talking about him, 15-year-old Rob comes to the realization that his father, a hard-working farmer, really does love him. He decides to give his father a special Christmas present, getting up at 3 A.M. on Christmas morning to do the milking and the cleaning up so his father won't have to. Dark full-bleed paintings help make this tender and memorable reminiscence even more meaningful.

GERM: Discuss: Why does Rob's father consider Rob's deed the best Christmas gift he ever had? How do Rob and his father show their love for each other? Why does Rob consider his deed "his first gift of true love"? How do you show your family that you love them? Read Mark Buehner's note at the front of the book to see how the story inspired his own daughters.

RELATED TITLES: Houston, Gloria. *The Year of the Perfect Christmas Tree*. Dial, 1988. / Medearis, Angela Shelf. *Poppa's Itchy Christmas*. Holiday House, 1998. / Paterson, Katherine. *Marvin's Best Christmas Present Ever*. HarperCollins, 1997. / Polacco, Patricia. *An Orange for Frankie*. Philomel, 2004. / Rylant, Cynthia. *Children of Christmas: Stories for the Season*. Orchard, 1987. / Rylant, Cynthia. *Silver Packages: An Appalachian Christmas Story*. Orchard, 1997.

SUBJECTS: CHRISTMAS. FARM LIFE. FATHERS AND SONS. GENEROSITY. GIFTS. LOVE.

84   Buehner, Caralyn. *Fanny's Dream*. Illus. by Mark Buehner. Dial, 1996. 0-8037-1497-1. Unp. Gr. 1–6

Sturdy Wyoming farm girl Fanny Agnes works hard on her daddy's farm but dreams of marrying a prince (or at least the tall, handsome mayor's son). As she waits in the garden for her fairy godmother to come and grant her wish, who shows up instead but farmer Heber Jensen, a really nice guy. One soft summer night, Fanny, now Heber's wife and the mother of twins, heads to the melon patch when a voice sings out, "Sorry I'm late!" It's her glittering fairy godmother, ready to grant her wish at last. "What's the matter?" she asks, impatient over Fanny's indecision. "Do you want to go to the ball or not?"

GERM: I stopped reading right there and handed out pencil and paper to a class of third graders for a Quick Write. "Think deeply about what she should do, and write down: Should she go or shouldn't she, and why or why not?" Their answers, which they read aloud, were thoughtful and heartfelt and varied. Compare and contrast this updated Cinderella tale with other reworkings, such as Ellen Jackson's *Cinder Edna*, and, of course, with the actual fairy tale.

RELATED TITLES: Calmenson, Stephanie. *The Frog Principal*. Scholastic, 2001. / Craft, K. Y. *Cinderella*. SeaStar Books, 2000. / Ehrlich, Amy. *Cinderella*. Illus. by Susan Jeffers. Dutton, 2004. / Hughes, Shirley. *Ella's Big Chance: A Jazz-Age Cinderella*. Simon & Schuster, 2004. / Jackson, Ellen. *Cinder Edna*. Lothrop, 1994. / Ketteman, Helen. *Bubba the Cowboy Prince: A Fractured Texas Tale*. Scholastic, 1997. / Kovalski, Maryann. *Pizza for Breakfast*. Morrow, 1991. / Lowell, Susan. *Cindy Ellen: A Wild Western Cinderella*. Orchard, 1997. / Minters, Frances. *Cinder Elly*. Viking, 1993. / Minters, Frances. *Sleepless Beauty*. Viking, 1996. / Myers, Bernice. *Sidney Rella and the Glass Sneaker*. Macmillan, 1985. / Pomerantz, Charlotte. *The Downtown Fairy Godmother*. Addison-Wesley, 1978. / Sanderson, Ruth. *Cinderella*. Little, Brown, 2002. / Stanley, Diane. *Rumpelstiltskin's Daughter*. Morrow, 1997. / Yolen, Jane. *Sleeping Ugly*. Coward, 1981.

SUBJECTS: CINDERELLA STORIES. FAIRIES. FARM LIFE. MARRIAGE. PARODIES. PICTURE BOOKS FOR ALL AGES.

85   **Buehner, Caralyn. *Superdog: The Heart of a Hero*. Illus. by Mark Buehner. HarperCollins, 2004. 0-06-623620-7. Unp. Gr. PreK–3**

Everything about Dexter the dachshund is little, except for his grand dreams of becoming a superhero. Deciding to follow his dreams, he puts himself through a tough exercise regimen and builds muscles. Dressed in his red-and-yellow superhero suit and green cape, he ignores the taunts of Cleevis the tomcat and sets out to do good deeds.

GERM: Talk over: Why does Cleevis belittle Dex? How does Dex handle it? How do you handle people who put you down? Why does Dexter take on Cleevis as a partner? What are the qualities of a hero? When you come to the page where Dexter is admiring his new muscles, put the book down for a minute, turn on some doggy music (such as the CD from *Dogs Rule!* by Daniel Kirk), and do some flexes with your listeners. Meet another stalwart dachshund who comes to the rescue in Dav Pilkey's *The Hallo-Wiener*.

RELATED TITLES: Calhoun, Mary. *High-Wire Henry*. Morrow, 1991. / Graham, Bob. *Benny: An Adventure Story*. Candlewick, 1999. / Grey, Mini. *Traction Man Is Here!* Knopf, 2005. / Howard, Arthur. *Cosmo Zooms*. Harcourt, 1999. / Hurd, Thacher. *Art Dog*. HarperCollins, 1996. / Kirk, Daniel. *Dogs Rule!* Hyperion, 2003. / Laden, Nina. *The Night I Followed the Dog*. Chronicle, 1994. / Meddaugh, Susan. *Martha Speaks*. Houghton Mifflin, 1992. / Meddaugh, Susan. *Perfectly Martha*. Houghton Mifflin, 2004. / O'Connor, George. *Kapow!* Simon & Schuster, 2004. / Pilkey, Dav. *The Hallo-Wiener*. Scholastic, 1995. / Pinkney, Brian. *The Adventures of Sparrowboy*. Simon & Schuster, 1997. / Rae, Jennifer. *Dog Tales*. Tricycle, 1999. / Rathmann, Peggy. *Officer Buckle and Gloria*. Putnam, 1995. / Van Draanen, Wendelin. *Shredderman: Secret Identity*. Knopf, 2004. / Weigel, Jeff. *Atomic Ace (He's Just My Dad)*. Albert Whitman, 2004. / Whayne, Susanne. *Petropolis*. Handprint, 2003.

SUBJECTS: BULLIES. CATS. DOGS. HEROES. SIZE. SUPERHEROES. TEASING.

86   **Bunting, Eve. *Dandelions*. Illus. by Greg Shed. Harcourt, 1995. 0-15-200050-X. Unp. Gr. 2–4**

Zoe describes her family's journey by covered wagon from Illinois, traveling 12 miles a day, to their claim stake in Nebraska, where their closest neighbors are three hours away by horse. Zoe's family digs a well and builds a soddie; Papa loves it there, but their pregnant Mom is understandably depressed, gazing at the never-ending grass—"Always nothing . . . Always the sameness." On a trip to town, Zoe sees dandelions growing and Papa digs them up to take home. Zoe and her sister plant them in the soddie roof as a gift to Mom, who finally seems reconciled to her new life.

GERM: *Sod Houses on the Great Plains* by Glen Rounds tells us how the prairie houses were built. Discuss what amenities we take for granted that Zoe's house would not have.

RELATED TITLES: Freedman, Russell. *Children of the Wild West*. Clarion, 1983. / Howard, Ellen. *The Log Cabin Quilt*. Holiday House, 1996. / Kinsey-Warnock, Natalie. *Wilderness Cat*. Dutton, 1992. / MacLachlan, Patricia. *Sarah, Plain and Tall*. Harper, 1985. / Rounds, Glen. *Sod Houses on the Great Plains*. Holiday House, 1995. / Russell, Marion. *Along the Santa Fe Trail: Marion Russell's Own Story*. Albert Whitman, 1993. / Turner, Ann. *Mississippi Mud: Three Prairie Journals*. HarperCollins, 1997. / Van Leeuwen, Jean. *Bound for Oregon*. Dial, 1994. / Van Leeuwen, Jean. *A Fourth of July on the Plains*. Dial, 1997. / Wilder, Laura Ingalls. *Little House on the Prairie*. Harper, 1961. / Williams, David. *Grandma Essie's Covered Wagon*. Knopf, 1993.

SUBJECTS: FAMILY LIFE. FLOWERS. FRONTIER AND PIONEER LIFE. GREAT PLAINS.
HISTORICAL FICTION. NEBRASKA. PRAIRIES.

87   **Bunting, Eve. *Gleam and Glow*. Illus. by Peter Sylvada. Harcourt, 2001. 0-15-202596-0. Unp. Gr. 2–6**

After Papa leaves the family to join the underground, Viktor, his mother, and his sister Marina must flee their house. Marina has acquired two golden fish from a man passing through their village and, before the family sets out for the border and safety, Viktor sets the fish free in a nearby pond. Inspired by a story of a villager's two fish that survived the Bosnian war in 1995, Bunting's tale, narrated by Viktor, is a solemn and hopeful tribute to every survivor of war.

GERM: Discussion point: Where and when else in the world might this story have taken place? Why was Viktor's family so happy to find the two fish still alive when they came back to their ruined house? Other important and hopeful picture books depicting lives changed forever by war include Sherry Garland's *The Lotus Seed* and Holly Keller's *Grandfather's Dream*, both set in Vietnam. Note how things haven't changed much, from Florence Parry Heide and Judith Gilliland's *Sami and the Time of the Troubles*, based in war-torn Beirut, to Jeanette Winter's *The Librarian of Basra*, set in Iraq.

RELATED TITLES: Bunting, Eve. *A Picnic in October*. Harcourt, 1999. / Bunting, Eve. *Smoky Night*. Harcourt, 1994. / Bunting, Eve. *The Wall*. Clarion, 1990. / Garland, Sherry. *The Lotus Seed*. Harcourt, 1993. / Heide, Florence Parry, and Judith Heide Gilliland. *Sami and the Time of the Troubles*. Clarion, 1992. / Stevenson, James. *Don't You Know There's a War On?* Greenwillow, 1992. / Winter, Jeanette. *The Librarian of Basra: A True Story from Iraq*. Harcourt, 2005.

SUBJECTS: FISHES. PICTURE BOOKS FOR OLDER READERS. SURVIVAL. WAR.

88   **Bunting, Eve. *My Special Day at Third Street School*. Illus. by Suzanne Bloom. Boyds Mills, 2004. 1-59078-075-2. 32pp. Gr. K–3**

In a rhyming depiction of an exciting day at school, a brown-haired boy narrator relates how Miss Amanda Drake, a real author, visits his class to talk about her books and to get the children fired up about reading and writing. Cheerful watercolors show the funkily attired author bonding with the kids and responding to the narrator's request that she write a book about them, which she does.

GERM: What an inspiring way to get your group prepped for an upcoming author visit! Have them write about their own favorite authors and illustrators, checking out information about them on their Web sites, and compile a list of questions they'd like to ask the authors. Find out more about Eve Bunting's own life as a writer in her autobiographical photoessay *Once Upon a Time*. Daniel Pinkwater's *Author's Day* will also fit, though it's wildly satirical in tone, as is Robin Pulver's *Author Day for Room 3T*.

RELATED TITLES: Barrows, Allison. *The Artist's Model*. Carolrhoda, 1996. / Bunting, Eve. *Once Upon a Time*. Richard C. Owen, 1995. / Bunting, Eve. *The Wednesday Surprise*. Clarion, 1989. / Christelow, Eileen. *What Do Authors Do?* Clarion, 1995. / Christelow, Eileen. *What Do Illustrators Do?* Clarion, 1999. / Duke, Kate. *Aunt Isabel Tells a Good One*. Dutton, 1992. / Kroll, Steven. *Patches Lost and Found*. Winslow, 2001. / Leedy, Loreen. *Look at My Book: How Kids Can Write and Illustrate Terrific Books*. Holiday House, 2004. / Lester, Helen. *Author: A True Story*. Houghton Mifflin, 1997. / Nixon, Joan Lowery. *If You Were a Writer*. Four Winds, 1988. / Pinkwater, Daniel. *Author's Day*. Atheneum, 1993. / Pulver, Robin. *Author Day for Room 3T*. Clarion, 2005. / Stevens, Janet. *From Pictures to Words: A Book About Making a Book*. Holiday House, 1995.

SUBJECTS: AUTHORS. BOOKS AND READING. MULTICULTURAL BOOKS. SCHOOLS. WRITING.

89   **Bunting, Eve. *A Picnic in October*. Illus. by Nancy Carpenter. Harcourt, 1999. 0-15-201656-2. Unp. Gr. K–3**

Tony describes how on October 28 every year, he and his family go with his Italian grandparents to Liberty Island for a chilly picnic to celebrate a very special birthday at the foot of the Statue of Liberty. The final double-page spread is a view of lower Manhattan, with the sight of the still-standing Twin Towers adding a special poignancy.

GERM: Have your group perform a choral reading of Emma Lazarus's poem "The New Colossus." Take a U.S. tour with the Statue of Liberty as she steps off her pedestal in *Liberty's Journey* by Kelly DePucchio.

RELATED TITLES: Avi. *Silent Movie*. Atheneum, 2003. / Bartone, Elisa. *American Too*. Lothrop, 1996. / Bartone, Elisa. *Peppe the Lamplighter*. Lothrop, 1993. / Bierman, Carol. *Journey to Ellis Island: How My Father Came to America*. Hyperion, 1998. / Curlee, Lynn. *Liberty*. Atheneum, 2000. / DiPucchio, Kelly. *Liberty's Journey*. Hyperion, 2004. / Drummond, Allan. *Liberty!* Farrar, 2002. / Fisher, Leonard E. *The Statue of Liberty*. Holiday House, 1985. / Freedman, Russell. *Immigrant Kids*. Dutton, 1980. / Levine, Ellen. *If Your Name Was Changed at Ellis Island*. Scholastic, 1993. / Maestro, Betsy. *Coming to America: The Story of Immigration*. Scholastic, 1996. / Maestro, Betsy. *The Story of the Statue of Liberty*. Lothrop, 1986. / Pomeranc, Marion Hess. *The American Wei*. Albert Whitman, 1998. / Stevens, Carla. *Lily and Miss Liberty*. Scholastic, 1992. / Zimelman, Nathan. *How the Second Grade Got $8,205.50 to Visit the Statue of Liberty*. Albert Whitman, 1992.

SUBJECTS: GRANDMOTHERS. IMMIGRATION AND EMIGRATION. ITALIAN AMERICANS. NEW YORK CITY. PICTURE BOOKS FOR ALL AGES. STATUE OF LIBERTY.

90 Bunting, Eve. *Riding the Tiger*. Illus. by David Frampton. Clarion, 2001. 0-395-79731-4. Unp. Gr. 2–6

An allegory about joining gangs, this provocative picture book for older readers presents a moral dilemma: new kid Danny agrees to ride a powerful tiger's back, hoping to gain respect, but soon discovers that it's dangerous up there.

GERM: Discuss: How does this story apply to real life? What is the tiger? Why does Danny get on the tiger? Why does he get off? Have you ever met the tiger? What did you do? Pair this with Bunting's picture book *Your Move*, about a boy who wants to prove himself by joining a gang.

RELATED TITLES: Bunting, Eve. *A Day's Work*. Clarion, 1994. / Bunting, Eve. *Fly Away Home*. Clarion, 1991. / Bunting, Eve. *Smoky Night*. Harcourt, 1994. / Bunting, Eve. *Summer Wheels*. Harcourt, 1992. / Bunting, Eve. *Your Move*. Harcourt, 1998. / Polacco, Patricia. *Chicken Sunday*. Philomel, 1992. / Polacco, Patricia. *Mr. Lincoln's Way*. Philomel, 2001.

SUBJECTS: ALLEGORIES. BEHAVIOR. GANGS. PICTURE BOOKS FOR OLDER READERS. TIGERS.

91 Bunting, Eve. *Train to Somewhere*. Illus. by Ronald Himler. Clarion, 1996. 0-395-71325-0. Unp. Gr. 2–5

This poignant picture book set in 1878 is based on the experiences of the children who rode the Orphan Trains. Marianne and 13 other abandoned or orphaned children are sent by train from New York to small towns in the New West, where families get the chance to adopt them. All the children are placed except for Marianne, until they reach the town of Somewhere, where an elderly couple decides to take her in even though they have been hoping for a boy.

GERM: Discuss the meaning of the quote: "Sometimes what you get turns out to be better than what you wanted in the first place." Flesh out the journey with Karen Cushman's novel *Rodzina* and with nonfiction excerpts from Andrea Warren's *Orphan Train Rider: One Boy's True Story*.

RELATED TITLES: Cushman, Karen. *Rodzina*. Clarion, 2003. / Kay, Verla. *Orphan Train*. Putnam, 2003. / Levine, Gail Carson. *Dave at Night*. HarperCollins, 1999. / Ryan, Pam Muñoz. *Riding Freedom*. Scholastic, 1998. / Snyder, Zilpha Keatley. *Gib Rides Home*. Delacorte, 1998. / Warren, Andrea. *Orphan Train Rider: One Boy's True Story*. Houghton Mifflin, 1996. / Warren, Andrea. *We Rode the Orphan Trains*. Houghton Mifflin, 2001.

SUBJECTS: HISTORICAL FICTION. ORPHAN TRAINS. ORPHANS. PICTURE BOOKS FOR OLDER READERS. WEST (U.S.)—HISTORY.

92 Bunting, Eve. *Your Move*. Illus. by James E. Ransome. Harcourt, 1998. 0-15-200181-6. Unp. Gr. 3–5

Ten-year-old James takes along his 6-year-old brother Isaac the night he decides to prove himself by joining the K-Bones, who tag buildings with spray paint, shoplift, and are planning to get a gun.

GERM: Discussion point: How do we resist peer pressure to do the right thing? Bunting's picture book *Riding the Tiger* further explores some of the same themes. Two novels that deal with gangs and the boys who sidestep them are Janet Taylor Lisle's *How I Became a Writer and Oggie Learned to Drive* and Donna Jo Napoli's *North*.

RELATED TITLES: Bunting, Eve. *Riding the Tiger*. Clarion, 2001. / Bunting, Eve. *Smoky Night*. Harcourt, 1994. / Lisle, Janet Taylor. *How I Became a Writer and Oggie Learned to Drive*. Philomel, 2002. / Napoli, Donna Jo. *North*. Greenwillow, 2004. / Polacco, Patricia. *Chicken Sunday*. Philomel, 1992. / Polacco, Patricia. *Mr. Lincoln's Way*. Philomel, 2001.

SUBJECTS: AFRICAN AMERICANS. BROTHERS. GANGS. GUNS. MULTICULTURAL BOOKS. PICTURE BOOKS FOR OLDER READERS.

93   Buzzeo, Toni. *Dawdle Duckling.* **Illus. by Margaret Spengler. Dial, 2003. 0-8037-2731-3. Unp. Gr. PreK–K**

Mama Duck's fourth little duckling dawdles and dreams, preens and plays, and says to his patient Mama, "NO! Quack! Quack! I won't catch up."

GERM: Line your little ducklings up and act this out, with you as Mama Duck, wearing your favorite straw hat. At <www.mimismotifs.com>, you'll find a set of six adorable crocheted finger puppets of the book's characters, just right for little ones to use. Groups of six children can sit in a circle and reenact the story together. Dawdle plays hide-and-seek with Mama and his three siblings in the sequel, *Ready or Not, Dawdle Duckling.* Celebrate more parent-child bonding in Buzzeo's *Little Loon and Papa.*

RELATED TITLES: Buzzeo, Toni. *Ready or Not, Dawdle Duckling.* Dial, 2005. / Buzzeo, Toni. *The Sea Chest.* Dial, 2002. / Crebbin, June. *Danny's Duck.* Candlewick, 1995. / Dunrea, Olivier. *Gossie.* Houghton Mifflin, 2002. / Dunrea, Olivier. *Ollie.* Houghton, 2003. / Hest, Amy. *In the Rain with Baby Duck.* Candlewick, 1995. / Hutchins, Pat. *Rosie's Walk.* Bradbury, 1987. / James, Simon. *Little One Step.* Candlewick, 2003. / McCloskey, Robert. *Make Way for Ducklings.* Viking, 1941. / Naylor, Phyllis Reynolds. *Ducks Disappearing.* Atheneum, 1997. / Raffi. *Five Little Ducks.* Crown, 1988. / Rankin, Joan. *Wow! It's Great Being a Duck.* McElderry, 1998. / Shannon, George. *Tippy-Toe Chick, Go!* Greenwillow, 2003. / Simmons, Jane. *Come Along, Daisy.* Little, Brown, 1998. / Simmons, Jane. *Quack, Daisy, Quack!* Little, Brown, 2002. / Waddell, Martin. *Webster J. Duck.* Candlewick, 2001. / Whippo, Walt, and Bernard Zaritzky. *Little White Duck.* Little, Brown, 2000.

SUBJECTS: ANIMALS—INFANCY. CHANTABLE REFRAIN. CREATIVE DRAMA. DUCKS. MOTHERS.

94   Buzzeo, Toni. *The Sea Chest.* **Illus. by Mary GrandPré. Dial, 2002. 0-8037-2703-8. Unp. Gr. 1–4**

Sitting with her young niece, waiting for "the stranger" to arrive, Auntie Maita relates the story of her own childhood on Sanctuary Island in Maine, where her father was lighthouse keeper of the Halley's Head Light. Surveying the beach after a terrible storm, she and her father found a sea chest containing a baby girl, and a note from the baby's parents, a ship's captain and his wife, now lost at sea. Maita named the baby Seaborne, and became her beloved sister. Sea-toned oil paintings of dark blues and violets evoke the drama and tenderness of this story-with-in-a-story.

GERM: Buzzeo has fleshed out a 19th-century legend, first turning it into a historical tale of rescue and adoption and then pulling it into the present, where Great-Aunt Maita and her little niece, Seaborne's great-granddaughter, await the arrival of the baby sister the girl's parents have adopted from overseas. The rich narrative will spark a freewheeling conversation about legends, lighthouses, storms, the ocean, rescues, sisters, family stories, storytelling, elderly relatives, and adoption.

RELATED TITLES: Cooney, Barbara. *Island Boy.* Viking, 1988. / Curtis, Jamie Lee. *Tell Me Again About the Night I Was Born.* HarperCollins, 1996. / Hopkinson, Deborah. *Birdie's Lighthouse.* Atheneum, 1997. / Lifton, Betty Jean. *Tell Me a Real Adoption Story.* Knopf, 1994. / Roop, Peter, and Connie Roop. *Keep the Lights Burning, Abbie.* Carolrhoda, 1985. / Thomas, Eliza. *The Red Blanket.* Scholastic, 2004.

SUBJECTS: ADOPTION. HISTORICAL FICTION. ISLANDS. LIGHTHOUSES. MAINE. ORPHANS. RESCUES. SISTERS.

95   Byars, Betsy. *My Brother, Ant.* **Illus. by Marc Simont. Viking, 1996. 0-670-86664-4. 32pp. Gr. 1–3**

An amiable, easy-to-read first chapter book is narrated by an unnamed older brother who tells about the unexpected glitches of life with his younger brother Anthony, who can drive him crazy sometimes. In the four vignettes, Ant is afraid of a monster under his bed, draws on his brother's perfect spelling paper, listens to his brother read him "The Three Little Figs," and wants to write a letter to Santa in July.

GERM: Readers will also delight in the sequel, *Ant Plays Bear.* Read a variety of books about siblings to examine and compare their relationships. Encourage students to write their own short chapter books with anecdotes and episodes based on their own funny sibling experiences. Chapters are just the right length for small-group Reader's Theater activities.

RELATED TITLES: Blume, Judy. *The Pain and the Great One.* Bradbury, 1984. / Blumenthal, Deborah. *Don't Let the Peas Touch! And Other Stories.* Scholastic, 2004. / Byars, Betsy. *Ant Plays Bear.* Viking, 1997. / Cameron, Ann. *The Stories Huey Tells.* Knopf, 1995. / Cameron, Ann. *The Stories Julian Tells.* Yearling, 1989. / Cutler, Jane. *Rats!* Farrar, 1996. / Johnston, Tony. *The Iguana Brothers.* Blue Sky/Scholastic, 1995. / Petersen, P. J. *The*

Amazing Magic Show. Simon & Schuster, 1994. / Steig, William. *The Toy Brother.* HarperCollins, 1996. / Stevenson, James. *Worse Than Willy.* Greenwillow, 1984.

SUBJECTS: BROTHERS. PERSONAL NARRATIVES.

96 **Cabrera, Jane. *Cat's Colors.* Illus. by the author. Dial, 1997. 0-8037-2090-4. Unp. Gr. PreK–1**
A big black and orange striped tabby cat asks and ultimately answers the question "What is my favorite color?" Ten brashly bold double-page paintings of thickly applied brush strokes, each in one basic hue, feature the smiling cat who defines each color with a cat-related statement, such as "Red is the rug where I snooze by the fire."
GERM: Make color paintings with your artists and have them label each one with their own observations about that color; ask them to indicate which color is their favorite.
RELATED TITLES: Carle, Eric. *Hello, Red Fox.* Simon & Schuster, 1998. / Carle, Eric. *The Mixed-Up Chameleon.* HarperCollins, 1984. / Frame, Jeron Ashford. *Yesterday I Had the Blues.* Tricycle, 2003. / Jonas, Ann. *Color Dance.* Greenwillow, 1989. / Lionni, Leo. *Little Blue and Little Yellow.* Morrow, 1994. / Lobel, Arnold. *The Great Blueness and Other Predicaments.* HarperCollins, 1968. / Martin, Bill, Jr. *Brown Bear, Brown Bear, What Do You See?* Henry Holt, 1983. / Micklethwait, Lucy. *Colors.* Frances Lincoln, 2005.
SUBJECTS: CATS. COLOR.

97 **Calhoun, Mary. *Blue-Ribbon Henry.* Illus. by Erick Ingraham. Morrow, 1999. 0-688-14675-9. Unp. Gr. PreK–2**
The Woman, The Man, and The Kid take Henry, their clever hind-leg-walking Siamese cat, to the country fair to enter him in the pet show. Thinking a squealing pig is fighting with his Kid, Henry unfastens his own cage and springs at the greased pig in the ring; next, he tails a lost little girl and even rides the Ferris Wheel to look for her after she disappears into the crowd. The judges award the no-nonsense cat the "Pet of the Show" award for his heroics.
GERM: Children will be full of stories about their own personable pets, though Henry is clearly a cat-in-a-million, as fans of the Henry series will most certainly attest.
RELATED TITLES: Banks, Kate. *The Cat Who Walked Across France.* Farrar, 2004. / Calhoun, Mary. *Henry the Sailor Cat.* Morrow, 1994. / Calhoun, Mary. *High-Wire Henry.* Morrow, 1991. (And others in the Henry series.) / Calhoun, Mary. *Tonio's Cat.* Morrow, 1996. / Collington, Peter. *Clever Cat.* Knopf, 2000. / Hall, Donald. *I Am the Dog, I Am the Cat.* Dial, 1994. / Meddaugh, Susan. *Martha Speaks.* Houghton Mifflin, 1992. (And others in the Martha series.) / Miller, Sara Swan. *Three Stories You Can Read to Your Cat.* Houghton Mifflin, 1997. / Pilkey, Dav. *Kat Kong.* Harcourt, 1993. / Schachner, Judith Byron. *The Grannyman.* Dutton, 1999.
SUBJECTS: CATS. FAIRS. HEROES.

98 **Calhoun, Mary. *Tonio's Cat.* Illus. by Edward Martinez. Morrow, 1996. 0-688-13315-0. Unp. Gr. 1–3**
Missing the dog he had to leave behind in Mexico when his family moved to California, Tonio feeds and watches out for a skinny orange stray cat.
GERM: Discussion point: How did Tonio and Toughy the cat help each other?
RELATED TITLES: Banks, Kate. *The Cat Who Walked Across France.* Farrar, 2004. / Dorros, Arthur. *Abuela.* Dutton, 1991. / Elya, Susan Middleton. *Home at Last.* Lee & Low, 2002. / Elya, Susan Middleton. *Say Hola to Spanish.* Lee & Low, 1996. / Joosse, Barbara M. *Nugget and Darling.* Clarion, 1997. / Pérez, Amada Irma. *My Very Own Room/Mi Proprio Cuartito.* Children's Book Press, 2000. / Schachner, Judith Byron. *The Grannyman.* Dutton, 1999. / Soto, Gary. *Chato and the Party Animals.* Putnam, 2000. / Soto, Gary. *Chato's Kitchen.* Putnam, 1995. / Soto, Gary. *Snapshots from the Wedding.* Putnam, 1997. / Soto, Gary. *Too Many Tamales.* Putnam, 1993.
SUBJECTS: CATS. HISPANIC AMERICANS. MEXICAN AMERICANS. MULTICULTURAL BOOKS. PETS. SPANISH LANGUAGE. STRAY ANIMALS.

99 **Calmenson, Stephanie. *The Frog Principal.* Illus. by Denise Brunkus. Scholastic, 2001. 0-590-37070-7. Unp. Gr. K–4**
Hard-working principal Mr. Bundy, whom we first met in Calmenson's Hans Christian Andersen parody *The Principal's New Clothes*, is back, this time as the modern-day model for the Grimm Brothers' "The Frog Prince." Inadvertently turned into a frog by an inept magician, Mr. Bundy rescues the students' softball from the pond and gets the kids to promise that he can be their principal, a promise they don't intend to keep. "Even though I'm small, green, and slimy, I can still be a good principal, can't I?" Bundy says, and he is.
GERM: Check your library for a copy of the original Grimm version of "The Frog Prince" so your listeners can compare and contrast both stories, constructing a Venn diagram or chart to

analyze how such a clever parody was constructed. Design color picture postcards that Mr. Bundy could send to his school, with an explanation of where he is and when he'll be back. What new fairy tale adventures could Mr. Bundy have next? The Principal and the Pea?

RELATED TITLES: Arnold, Tedd. *Green Wilma*. Dial, 1993. / Calmenson, Stephanie. *The Principal's New Clothes*. Scholastic, 1989. / Ernst, Lisa Campbell. *Little Red Riding Hood: A Newfangled Prairie Tale*. Simon & Schuster, 1995. / Goss, Linda. *The Frog Who Wanted to Be a Singer*. Orchard, 1996. / Griffith, Helen V. *Emily and the Enchanted Frog*. Greenwillow, 1989. / Hall, Katy, and Lisa Eisenberg. *Ribbit Riddles*. Dial, 2001. / Lewis, J. Patrick. *The Frog Princess: A Russian Tale*. Dial, 1994. / Minters, Frances. *Sleepless Beauty*. Viking, 1996. / Napoli, Donna Jo. *The Prince of the Pond*. Dutton, 1992. / Park, Barbara. *Junie B. Jones and Some Sneaky Peeky Spying*. Random House, 1994. / Scieszka, Jon. *The Frog Prince Continued*. Viking, 1991. / Scieszka, Jon. *The Stinky Cheese Man and Other Fairly Stupid Tales*. Viking, 1992. / Teague, Mark. *Frog Medicine*. Scholastic, 1991. / Wiesner, David. *Tuesday*. Clarion, 1991.

SUBJECTS: FROGS. HUMOROUS FICTION. MAGICIANS. PARODIES. PICTURE BOOKS FOR ALL AGES. PRINCIPALS. SCHOOLS. TRANSFORMATIONS.

100   Calmenson, Stephanie. *The Teeny Tiny Teacher*. Illus. by Denis Roche. Scholastic, 1998. 0-590-37123-1. Unp. Gr. PreK–1

In a whimsical school-based retelling of the "Teeny Tiny Woman," the Teeny Tiny Teacher brings a bone back to the classroom after she and her students go on an outing.

GERM: Listeners will chime in on each repetition of the words "teeny tiny" in response to the teeny tiny voice demanding the return of the teeny tiny bone the teeny tiny teacher finds on the class's teeny tiny walk. Tell the original tale. Continue thinking small with Byron Barton's *The Wee Little Woman* and Kay Winters's *The Teeny Tiny Ghost*.

RELATED TITLES: Barton, Byron. *The Wee Little Woman*. HarperCollins, 1995. / Bennett, Jill. *Teeny Tiny*. Putnam, 1986. / Brown, Ruth. *A Dark, Dark Tale*. Dial, 1981. / Galdone, Paul. *The Teeny-Tiny Woman*. Clarion, 1984. / Lillegard, Dee. *Hello School! A Classroom Full of Poems*. Knopf, 2001. / McBratney, Sam. *The Dark at the Top of the Stairs*. Candlewick, 1996. / Schwartz, Alvin. *Ghosts! Ghostly Tales from Folklore*. HarperCollins, 1991. / Schwartz, Alvin. *In a Dark, Dark Room and Other Scary Stories*. HarperCollins, 1984. / Thiesing, Lisa. *The Viper*. Dutton, 2002. / Williams, Linda. *The Little Old Lady Who Was Not Afraid of Anything*. Crowell, 1986. / Winters, Kay. *The Teeny Tiny Ghost*. HarperCollins, 1997. / Winters, Kay. *Whooo's Haunting the Teeny Tiny Ghost?* HarperCollins, 1999.

SUBJECTS: BONES. CHANTABLE REFRAIN. GHOSTS. SCHOOLS. STORIES TO TELL. TEACHERS.

101   Cannon, Janell. *Crickwing*. Illus. by the author. Harcourt, 2000. 0-15-201790-9. Unp. Gr. K–3

Angry when his sculptures built from food are destroyed by a monkey and a lizard and he is almost crushed by an ocelot, Crickwing, a cockroach with a twisted wing, takes out his frustration on some punier creatures, a colony of leaf-cutting ants. The queen of the ants orders her workers to seize him and deliver him as their annual peace offering to a ferocious army ant colony, but Crickwing offers up a feasible plan to defend the queen and all her leaf-cutters. Canon's close-up exposition of the eat-or-be-eaten insect world is articulated further in her large, square acrylics with glowing chartreuse and other green-toned backgrounds and meticulously drawn insects.

GERM: Discuss how fact and fiction are intertwined in a story like this. At the end of the book are the author's notes about the lives and behavior of cockroaches and ants. Crickwing thwarts the army ants with a strategy reminiscent of Leo Lionni's *Swimmy*. Midway through the story, have listeners predict what Crickwing's idea might be. See how the Ant Queen teaches Lucas, a human boy, to behave himself, ant-wise, in *The Ant Bully* by John Nickle.

RELATED TITLES: Allinson, Beverly. *Effie*. Scholastic, 1991. / Cannon, Janell. *Stellaluna*. Harcourt, 1993. / Cannon, Janell. *Verdi*. Harcourt, 1997. / Casanova, Mary. *The Hunter: A Chinese Folktale*. Atheneum, 2000. / Climo, Shirley. *The Little Red Ant and the Great Big Crumb: A Mexican Fable*. Clarion, 1995. / Demuth, Patricia Brennan. *Those Amazing Ants*. Macmillan, 1994. / Dorros, Arthur. *Ant Cities*. HarperCollins, 1987. / Hoose, Phillip M., and Hannah Hoose. *Hey, Little Ant*. Tricycle, 1998. / Laden, Nina. *Roberto the Insect Architect*. Chronicle, 2000. / Lionni, Leo. *Swimmy*. Pantheon, 1968. / Nickle, John. *The Ant Bully*. Scholastic, 1999. / Peet, Bill. *The Ant and the Elephant*. Houghton, 1972. / Van Allsburg, Chris. *Two Bad Ants*. Houghton Mifflin, 1988. / Wheeler, Lisa. *Old Cricket*. Atheneum, 2003. / Wolkstein, Diane. *Step by Step*. Morrow, 1994. / Young, Ed. *Night Visitors*. Philomel, 1995.

SUBJECTS: ANTS. BEHAVIOR. BULLIES. COCKROACHES. INSECTS. SCULPTORS. SIZE.

102   Cannon, Janell. *Verdi*. Illus. by the author. Harcourt, 1997. 0-15-201028-9. Unp. Gr. 1–6

Verdi, a young and vibrant yellow python with sporty stripes, declares he will never turn green like the grumbling, boring, rude, old fogey pythons who laze all day in the jungle trees and never do anything dangerous. This heartfelt story with winsome paintings will do the same for the tattered image of snakes as the author's classic *Stellaluna* did for bats.

GERM: Children will enjoy discussing why Verdi tried so hard to stem his inevitable changes and comparing his dilemma to how they feel about growing up, while we jaded adults will certainly make connections to our own mid-life crises. "I may be big and very green, but I'm still me!" Verdi proclaims. Set children to researching the lives and behavior of pythons and other fascinating snakes with books such as Sandra Markle's *Outside and Inside Snakes*.

RELATED TITLES: Ata, Te. *Baby Rattlesnake*. Children's Book Press, 1989. / Cannon, Janell. *Crickwing*. Harcourt, 2000. / Cannon, Janell. *Stellaluna*. Harcourt, 1993. / Davol, Marguerite W. *How Snake Got His Hiss*. Orchard, 1996. / Ernst, Lisa Campbell. *Bubba and Trixie*. Simon & Schuster, 1997. / Gray, Libba. *Small Green Snake*. Orchard, 1994. / Hall, Katy, and Lisa Eisenberg. *Snakey Riddles*. Dial, 1990. / Johnston, Tony. *Slither McCreep and His Brother Joe*. Harcourt, 1992. / Maestro, Betsy. *Take a Look at Snakes*. Scholastic, 1992. / Markle, Sandra. *Outside and Inside Snakes*. Macmillan, 1995. / McNulty, Faith. *A Snake in the House*. Scholastic, 1994. / Ungerer, Tomi. *Crictor*. HarperCollins, 1958.

SUBJECTS: MATURITY. PICTURE BOOKS FOR ALL AGES. SELF-ACCEPTANCE. SNAKES.

103   Carle, Eric. *From Head to Toe*. Illus. by the author. HarperCollins, 1997. 0-06-023516-0. Unp. Gr. PreK–K

Bright and expressive animals, from penguin to monkey to crocodile, ask children if they can turn their heads, wave their arms, or wiggle their hips. Each child replies, "I can do it!" and so will your listeners.

GERM: Act out each animal's motion, as instructed. Then have each child lead and verbalize a new command, saying, for example, "I am a dog and I can wag my tail. Can you do it?"

RELATED TITLES: Andreae, Giles. *K Is for Kissing a Cool Kangaroo*. Orchard, 2003. / Bayer, Jane. *A My Name Is Alice*. Dial, 1984. / Carle, Eric. *Mister Seahorse*. Philomel, 2004. / Carle, Eric. *Today Is Monday*. Philomel, 1993. / Cherry, Lynne. *Who's Sick Today?* Dutton, 1988. / Clark, Emma Chichester. *Follow the Leader*. McElderry, 2003. / Fleming, Denise. *Alphabet Under Construction*. Henry Holt, 2002. / Fox, Mem. *Boo to a Goose*. Dial, 1998. / Jarrett, Clare. *The Best Picnic Ever*. Candlewick, 2004. / Merriam, Eve. *Where Is Everybody? An Animal Alphabet*. Simon & Schuster, 1989. / Newcome, Zita. *Toddlerobics: Animal Fun*. Candlewick, 1999. / Pandell, Karen. *Animal Action ABC*. Dutton, 1996.

SUBJECTS: ANIMALS. CREATIVE DRAMA. EXERCISE. PHYSICAL FITNESS.

104   Carle, Eric. *Hello, Red Fox*. Illus. by the author. Simon & Schuster, 1998. 0-689-81775-4. Unp. Gr. PreK–1

Ostensibly, this is the story of Little Frog, who invites his friends to his birthday party. As with all Carle classics, it employs repetition and a predictable pattern. The book's color concept was inspired by the color theory of Goethe, 19th-century German poet, novelist, and philosopher. Goethe found that each color has an opposite or complimentary color. Each animal Little Frog meets is seemingly the wrong color. Red Fox appears green—that is, until we stare at him and then focus our gaze on the blank opposite page. If we concentrate—and your children will clamor to try this—his red image will appear on the blank page.

GERM: The book works both as a story and as an art or science teacher's introduction to the color wheel. Pair with *Hailstones and Halibut Bones: Adventures in Color*, Mary L. O'Neill's poetry classic, with 12 perceptive poems, one for each color. Blend more colors with Arnold Lobel's picture book *The Great Blueness and Other Predicaments* and with Leo Lionni's classic *Little Blue and Little Yellow*.

RELATED TITLES: Cabrera, Jane. *Cat's Colors*. Dial, 1997. / Carle, Eric. *The Mixed-Up Chameleon*. HarperCollins, 1984. / Ernst, Lisa Campbell. *Tangram Magician*. Blue Apple, 2005. / Frame, Jeron Ashford. *Yesterday I Had the Blues*. Tricycle, 2003. / Jonas, Ann. *Color Dance*. Greenwillow, 1989. / Lionni, Leo. *Little Blue and Little Yellow*. Morrow, 1994. / Lobel, Arnold. *The Great Blueness and Other Predicaments*. HarperCollins, 1968. / Martin, Bill, Jr. *Brown Bear, Brown Bear, What Do You See?* Henry Holt, 1983. / O'Neill, Mary. *Hailstones and Halibut Bones: Adventures in Color*. Doubleday, 1989.

SUBJECTS: ANIMALS. BIRTHDAYS. CHANTABLE REFRAIN. COLOR. FOXES. FROGS.

105   Carle, Eric. *Mister Seahorse*. Illus. by the author. Philomel, 2004. 0-399-24269-4. Unp. Gr. PreK–1

After Mrs. Seahorse lays her eggs into a pouch on Mr. Seahorse's belly, he meets up with a series of other father fishes who take care of their eggs in unusual ways, including Mr. Tilapia, who holds the eggs in his mouth until they hatch, and Mr. Kurtus, who keeps the eggs on his head. Bright neon colors electrify Carle's usual cheerful illustrative technique of painted tissue-paper collage, with the addition of painted acetate overlays that show how fish camouflage themselves in the ocean.

GERM: Be forewarned that children may find the egg scenarios hilarious, especially when you tell them that this is a story based on facts. Share a nonfiction book on seahorses. The nonfiction picture book *Animal Dads* showcases some of the atypical ways in which animal fathers look after their young.

RELATED TITLES: Carle, Eric. *A House for Hermit Crab*. Picture Book Studio, 1987. / Carle, Eric. *The Very Busy Spider*. Philomel, 1984. / Carle, Eric. *The Very Clumsy Click Beetle*. Philomel, 1999. / Carle, Eric. *The Very Hungry Caterpillar*. Putnam, 1981. / Carle, Eric. *The Very Quiet Cricket*. Philomel, 1990. / Collard, Sneed B., III. *Animal Dads*. Houghton Mifflin, 1997. / Doubilet, Anne. *Under the Sea from A to Z*. Crown, 1991. / Freymann, Saxton, and Joost Elffers. *One Lonely Sea Horse*. Scholastic, 2000. / Guiberson, Brenda Z. *The Emperor Lays an Egg*. Henry Holt, 2001. / Guiberson, Brenda Z. *Into the Sea*. Henry Holt, 1996. / Heller, Ruth. *Animals Born Alive and Well*. Grossett, 1982. / Lionni, Leo. *Swimmy*. Pantheon, 1968. / McDonald, Megan. *Is This a House for Hermit Crab?* Orchard, 1990. / MacDonald, Suse. *Sea Shapes*. Harcourt, 1994. / Rose, Deborah Lee. *Into the A, B, Sea*. Scholastic, 2000. / Swinburne, Stephen R. *Safe, Warm, and Snug*. Harcourt, 1999.

SUBJECTS: BIRTH. CAMOUFLAGE. FATHERS. FISHES. OCEAN. SEA HORSES.

106   Carle, Eric. *"Slowly, Slowly, Slowly," Said the Sloth*. Illus. by the author. Philomel, 2002. 0-399-23954-5. Unp. Gr. PreK–1

As a sloth crawls, eats, sleeps, wakes, and hangs upside down in his tree, the many animals in his lush and colorful Amazon rain forest world—a howler monkey, a caiman, an anteater, and a jaguar—ask him why he is so slow, quiet, boring, and lazy. He admits he is lackadaisical, unflappable, languid, stoic, impassive, sluggish, lethargic, placid, calm, mellow, laid-back, "and, well, slothful!" (Such wonderful adjectives and words to chew on.) He adds, "I am relaxed and tranquil, and I like to live in peace." But lazy? No, that's just how sloths do things.

GERM: As an intro to the rain forest and a meditation on our fast-paced lives, this will slow everyone down for a welcome bit, as they stop to appreciate the environment and intone the repeated "slowly, slowly, slowly" refrain in slo mo. An introduction by Jane Goodall informs us that sloths can turn their heads 270 degrees. Explain what turning 180 degrees means and ask listeners to show how far they can turn their heads. Sloths sleep 15 to 19 hours a day. (Work out the math together—how much time do they spend awake? How much time do you sleep each night?). Contrast Jane Goodall's facts with Eric Carle's commentary on the back of the book ("Why are we always in a hurry . . ."), and dig into a nonfiction book on sloths to contrast with Carle's signature brightly painted animals and tissue paper collages. Melissa Stewart's *Sloths* is particularly informative with terrific color photos. Take a one-minute sloth walk, barely moving the entire time.

RELATED TITLES: Brett, Jan. *The Umbrella*. Putnam, 2004. / Carle, Eric. *The Grouchy Ladybug*. HarperCollins, 1997. / Carle, Eric. *Mister Seahorse*. Philomel, 2004. / Carle, Eric. *The Mixed-Up Chameleon*. HarperCollins, 1984. / Carle, Eric. *The Very Clumsy Click Beetle*. Philomel, 1999. / Carle, Eric. *The Very Hungry Caterpillar*. Putnam, 1981. / Carle, Eric. *The Very Quiet Cricket*. Philomel, 1990. / Cherry, Lynne. *The Great Kapok Tree: A Tale of the Amazon Rain Forest*. Harcourt, 1990. / Cowcher, Helen. *Rain Forest*. Farrar, 1988. / Cowley, Joy. *Red-Eyed Tree Frog*. Scholastic, 1999. / Jordan, Tanis. *Amazon Alphabet*. Kingfisher, 1996. / Lester, Helen. *Score One for the Sloths*. Houghton, 2001. / Stewart, Melissa. *Sloths*. Carolrhoda, 2005. / Waddell, Martin. *Hi, Harry!* Candlewick, 2003. / Yolen, Jane. *Welcome to the Green House*. Putnam, 1993.

SUBJECTS: ANIMALS. JUNGLE ANIMALS. RAIN FORESTS. SLOTHS. SPEED.

107   Carlson, Nancy. *ABC, I Like Me!* Illus. by the author. Viking, 1997. 0-670-87458-2. Unp. Gr. PreK–1

An Awesome, Brave, and Cheerful pig describes her ebullient personality in 26 sentences that each contain an alphabetical descriptor of what she's like and what she likes to do.

GERM: Ask your little piggies: What are you like? Have them compile an alphabet of words that describe themselves and write their own self-based alphabet sentences. Find out more about the same pig in Carlson's companion book, *I Like Me*.

RELATED TITLES: Carlson, Nancy. *I Like Me*. Viking, 1988. / Carlson, Nancy. *There's a Big, Beautiful World Out There!* Viking, 2002. / Curtis, Jamie Lee. *Today I Feel Silly and Other Moods That Make My Day*. Harper-Collins, 1998. / Ernst, Lisa Campbell. *The Luckiest Kid on the Planet*. Bradbury, 1994. / Frame, Jeron Ashford. *Yesterday I Had the Blues*. Tricycle, 2003. / Hausman, Bonnie. *A to Z: Do You Ever Feel Like Me?* Dutton, 1999. / Mahurin, Tim. *Jeremy Kooloo*. Dutton, 1995.
SUBJECTS: ALPHABET BOOKS. EMOTIONS. PIGS. SELF-ESTEEM.

108   Carlson, Nancy. *There's a Big, Beautiful World Out There!* Illus. by the author. Viking, 2002. 0-670-03580-7. Unp. Gr. PreK–2
"There's a lot to be scared of, that's for sure!" begins a colorfully illustrated picture book that encourages us to confront our fears and overcome them. There are mean-looking dogs, thunderstorms, scary stories in the news, and people who look different. A brown-haired girl with braids hides under her covers in response to each of these unsettling worries, until she considers all the good things one misses when retreating from the world in trepidation. Ultimately, she rejoices in that "big, beautiful world out there just waiting for you!"
GERM: A note on the last page, showing a flag at half-staff, states: "This book was written on September 12, 2001." The rest of the reassuring, cheerful text does not mention anything that connects it directly to that time but you may decide to do so in your ensuing discussion. It's a "Get out and smell the roses" kind of book that will get kids thinking about the good things in their lives. Ask your listeners to discuss, write, and draw about: What have you been afraid of and how have you dealt with it? What advice can you give to others who share your former fears? What do you look forward to in this big, beautiful world? A good tie-in for all those shy kids who are afraid to take risks is Chris Rashka's *Yo! Yes?*, which is perfect to act out with a group.
RELATED TITLES: Cates, Karin. *The Secret Remedy Book: A Story of Comfort and Love*. Orchard, 2003. / Emberley, Ed. *Go Away, Big Green Monster!* Little, Brown, 1993. / Henkes, Kevin. *Sheila Rae, the Brave*. Greenwillow, 1987. / Henkes, Kevin. *Wemberly Worried*. Greenwillow, 2000. / King, Larry L. *Because of Lozo Brown*. Viking, 1988. / Lasky, Kathryn. *Lunch Bunnies*. Little, Brown, 1996. / Lester, Helen. *Something Might Happen*. Houghton Mifflin, 2003. / Viorst, Judith. *My Mama Says There Aren't Any Zombies, Ghosts, Vampires, Creatures, Demons, Monsters, Fiends, Goblins, or Things*. Atheneum, 1973. / Zemach, Kaethe. *The Question Song*. Little, Brown, 2003.
SUBJECTS: CONDUCT OF LIFE. FEAR.

109   Carter, David A. *One Red Dot: A Pop-up Book for Children of All Ages*. Illus. by the author. Little Simon, 2005. 0-689-87769-2. Unp. Gr. PreK–2
Here in one square book package is a wondrous pop-up masterpiece for viewers, employing alliteration, counting, shapes, and even sound. Open each of ten pop-up pop-art-like pages and up springs one perplexing puzzle box, or two twisting twirly gigs, or three burning baskets—fabulous geometric sculptures in primary colors, each sporting a small red dot waiting to be found by sharp eyes.
GERM: You may not want children to handle this book, but you can still show it for all to appreciate as an extraordinary art object and fresh look at numbers. Share Carter's many other whimsical pop-up books and try your hands at making pop-ups using his books *The Elements of Pop-Up* and *Let's Make It Pop Up*, and his noisy, fun Web site, <www.popupbooks.com>, for instruction and inspiration. Have small groups work together to construct new paper sculptures, either pop-up or freestanding, and come up with playful names for them.
RELATED TITLES: Carter, David, and James Diaz. *The Elements of Pop-Up: A Pop-Up Book for Aspiring Paper Engineers*. Little Simon, 1999. / Carter, David, and James Diaz. *Let's Make It Pop Up*. Little Simon, 2004. / Ehlert, Lois. *Color Zoo*. HarperCollins, 1989. / Irvine, Joan. *How to Make Holiday Pop-Ups*. Morrow, 1996. / Irvine, Joan. *How to Make Super Pop-Ups*. Morrow, 1992. / Sabuda, Robert. *The 12 Days of Christmas: A Pop-Up Celebration*. Simon & Schuster, 1996. / Seeger, Laura Vaccaro. *The Hidden Alphabet*. Roaring Brook, 2003. / Seeger, Laura Vaccaro. *Lemons Are Not Red*. Roaring Brook, 2004. / Steiner, Joan. *Look-Alikes: A Picture Puzzle Book*. Little, Brown, 1998. / Steiner, Joan. *Look-Alikes, Jr*. Little, Brown, 1999.
SUBJECTS: ALLITERATION. COUNTING BOOKS. PICTURE BOOKS FOR ALL AGES. SHAPES. TOY AND MOVABLE BOOKS. VISUAL PERCEPTION.

110   Casanova, Mary. *One-Dog Canoe*. Illus. by Ard Hoyt. Farrar, 2003. 0-374-35638-6. Unp. Gr. PreK–1
Setting out on the lake in her little red canoe, with her floppy-eared dog and a picnic basket, a blonde ponytailed girl is beseeched by a beaver, a loon, a wolf, a bear, and a moose to let them

come too. Much to her consternation, as each one boards, the canoe sinks lower, and when a frog jumps aboard—"Swoosh-a-bang flop!"—they all tumble into the water.

GERM: The splashing fun of this cumulative rhyming tale will make for some fine audience participation, retelling, and acting out. Compare it with John Burningham's classic, *Mr. Gumpy's Outing*.

RELATED TITLES: Brett, Jan. *The Mitten*. Penguin, 1989. / Burningham, John. *Mr. Gumpy's Outing*. Henry Holt, 1971. / Gray, Libba Moore. *Is There Room on the Featherbed?* Orchard, 1997. / Koide, Tan. *May We Sleep Here Tonight?* Atheneum, 1983. / Mathews, Judith, and Fay Robinson. *Nathaniel Willy, Scared Silly*. Bradbury, 1994. / Simms, Laura. *The Squeaky Door*. Crown, 1991. / Thomson, Pat. *The Squeaky, Creaky Bed*. Doubleday, 2003. / Waber, Bernard. *Bearsie Bear and the Surprise Sleepover Party*. Houghton Mifflin, 1997. / Wilson, Karma. *Bear Snores On*. McElderry, 2002. / Wilson, Karma. *Bear Wants More*. McElderry, 2003. / Wood, Audrey. *The Napping House*. Harcourt, 1984.

SUBJECTS: ANIMALS. CANOES AND CANOEING. CHANTABLE REFRAIN. CUMULATIVE STORIES. STORIES IN RHYME.

111   Caseley, Judith. *Bully*. Illus. by the author. Greenwillow, 2001. 0-688-17867-7. Unp. Gr. PreK–2

At school, Jack eats Mickey's lunch cookies, breaks his pencil with the dinosaur eraser, trips him, and takes his baseball cap. "You used to be a mouse," Mickey tells his former friend. "And now you've turned into a great big rat!" Taking assorted bits of advice from his parents and sister, Mickey finally figures out what makes Jack tick and becomes his friend once again.

GERM: Discuss with your listeners problems they've experienced with bullies. Make a Bully Chart, listing children's practical suggestions on what to do if a bully bothers them.

RELATED TITLES: Bottner, Barbara. *Bootsie Barker Bites*. Putnam, 1992. / Browne, Anthony. *Willy the Wimp*. Knopf, 1985. / Cole, Joanna. *Don't Call Me Names*. Random House, 1990. / Howe, James. *Pinky and Rex and the Bully*. Atheneum, 1996. / Kasza, Keiko. *The Rat and the Tiger*. Putnam, 1993. / Kelley, True. *Blabber Mouse*. Dutton, 1991. / Larson, Kirby. *Cody and Quinn, Sitting in a Tree*. Holiday House, 1996. / Lester, Helen. *Me First*. Houghton Mifflin, 1992. / Meddaugh, Susan. *Martha Walks the Dog*. Houghton Mifflin, 1998. / Naylor, Phyllis Reynolds. *King of the Playground*. Atheneum, 1991. / O'Neill, Alexis. *The Recess Queen*. Scholastic, 2002. / Wilhelm, Hans. *Tyrone the Horrible*. Scholastic, 1988.

SUBJECTS: BEHAVIOR. BULLIES. FRIENDSHIP. SCHOOLS.

112   Catalanotto, Peter. *Daisy 1 2 3*. Illus. by the author. Atheneum, 2003. 0-689-85457-9. Unp. Gr. PreK–1

Mrs. Tuttle has 20 Dalmatians in her Saturday morning obedience class, all named Daisy, but she can tell them apart, from one to 20, by their unique talents and eccentricities. For instance, "Daisy 1 has one peculiar spot. Daisy 2 wears two name tags . . ."

GERM: This is the counting companion book to *Matthew A.B.C.* Children can compile a classroom counting book incorporating the odd and endearing habits of their own pets. Take a look at 16 kittens and their colors in *Kitten Red Yellow Blue*.

RELATED TITLES: Alda, Arlene. *Arlene Alda's 1 2 3: What Do You See?* Tricycle, 2000. / Bartoletti, Susan Campbell. *Nobody's Diggier Than a Dog*. Hyperion, 2004. / Catalanotto, Peter. *Kitten Red Yellow Blue*. Atheneum, 2005. / Catalanotto, Peter. *Matthew A.B.C.* Atheneum, 2002. / Fleming, Denise. *Count!* Henry Holt, 1992. / MacDonald, Suse. *Look Whooo's Counting*. Scholastic, 2000. / Meyers, Susan. *Puppies, Puppies, Puppies*. Abrams, 2005. / Noonan, Julia. *Mouse by Mouse*. Dutton, 2003. / Reiser, Lynn. *Ten Puppies*. HarperCollins, 2003. / Walton, Rick. *So Many Bunnies: A Bedtime ABC and Counting Book*. Lothrop, 1998.

SUBJECTS: COUNTING BOOKS. DOGS.

113   Catalanotto, Peter. *Matthew A.B.C.* Illus. by the author. Atheneum, 2002. 0-689-84582-0. Unp. Gr. PreK–1

In an endearing alphabet of alliterative sentences, see how teacher Mrs. Tuttle can tell her 25 students, all named Matthew, apart, thanks to their singular behavior. Luckily, each Matthew has a last name beginning with a different letter of the alphabet, and each boy is memorable for doing something interesting, starting with the letter of his last name. Matthew A. is "extremely affectionate"; Matthew M. is moody; and Matthew N., dressed in briefs and a superhero cape, is "nearly naked." A new kid comes to school—Matthew Zee—and his clothes are filled with zippers.

GERM: Listeners will giggle and figure out which word in the sentence goes with each last name's initial letter. Children can write and illustrate their own alliterative sentences that incorporate the first letters of their last names and describe a bit of their quirky personalities. Cata-lanotto's *Daisy 1 2 3* is the counting companion book, with 20 Dalmatians, all named Daisy, in Mrs. Tuttle's Saturday morning dog obedience class. Give kittens and colors equal time with *Kitten Red Yellow Blue*.

RELATED TITLES: Bayer, Jane. *A My Name Is Alice.* Dial, 1984. / Catalanotto, Peter. *Daisy 1 2 3.* Atheneum, 2003. / Catalanotto, Peter. *Kitten Red Yellow Blue.* Atheneum, 2005. / Ernst, Lisa Campbell. *The Letters Are Lost.* Viking, 1996. / Fleming, Denise. *Alphabet Under Construction.* Henry Holt, 2002. / Grover, Max. *The Accidental Zucchini.* Harcourt, 1993. / Kalman, Maira. *What Pete Ate from A–Z.* Putnam, 2001. / Lobel, Anita. *Alison's Zinnia.* Greenwillow, 1990. / Lobel, Anita. *Away from Home.* Greenwillow, 1994. / Lobel, Arnold. *On Market Street.* Greenwillow, 1981. / McMullan, Kate. *I Stink!* HarperCollins, 2002. / Slate, Joseph. *Miss Bindergarten Gets Ready for Kindergarten.* Dutton, 1996.

SUBJECTS: ALLITERATION. ALPHABET BOOKS. BEHAVIOR. MULTICULTURAL BOOKS. SCHOOLS. TEACHERS.

114   Cates, Karin. *The Secret Remedy Book: A Story of Comfort and Love.* **Illus. by Wendy Anderson Halperin. Orchard, 2003. 0-439-35226-6. Unp. Gr. 1–3**

Visiting her aunt for a whole month, Lolly is homesick until Auntie Zep takes her to the attic to find The Secret Remedy Book. The book provides directions for seven tasks they must complete in one day before the first hoot of an owl.

GERM: Adapt the seven remedies that Lolly and Auntie Zep undertake and have your children follow them, one per day. Or have them write new remedies for situations in which they might feel worried or unsure of themselves.

RELATED TITLES: Carlson, Nancy. *There's a Big, Beautiful World Out There!* Viking, 2002. / Daly, Niki. *Once Upon a Time.* Farrar, 2003. / Houston, Gloria. *My Great Aunt Arizona.* HarperCollins, 1992. / Polacco, Patricia. *Thunder Cake.* Philomel, 1990. / Shields, Carol Diggory. *Lucky Pennies and Hot Chocolate.* Dutton, 2000.

SUBJECTS: AUNTS. BOOKS AND READING. HOMESICKNESS. OWLS.

115   Cazet, Denys. *Elvis the Rooster Almost Goes to Heaven.* **Illus. by the author. HarperCollins, 2003. 0-06-000501-7. 48pp. Gr. PreK–2**

In an easy-reader that makes an uproarious read-aloud, Elvis the rooster chokes on a bug at crowing time and when the sun still comes up without him, he faints at the shock. Distressed by his ensuing funk, his concerned fowl pals take on the job of helping him regain his pluck.

GERM: The dialogue is so jocular, it would be a shame not to write this up as a Reader's Theater so all of your readers can play around with it.

RELATED TITLES: Auch, Mary Jane. *Bantam of the Opera.* Holiday House, 1997. / Auch, Mary Jane. *Eggs Mark the Spot.* Holiday House, 1996. / Auch, Mary Jane. *Hen Lake.* Holiday House, 1995. / Auch, Mary Jane. *Peeping Beauty.* Holiday House, 1993. / Cazet, Denys. *Elvis the Rooster and the Magic Words.* HarperCollins, 2004. / Dallas-Conté, Juliet. *Cock-a-Moo-Moo.* Little, Brown, 2001. / Egan, Tim. *Serious Farm.* Houghton Mifflin, 2003. / Froehlich, Margaret Walden. *That Kookoory!* Harcourt, 1995. / Krosoczka, Jarrett J. *Punk Farm.* Knopf, 2005. / Lobel, Arnold. *How the Rooster Saved the Day.* Greenwillow, 1977. / Meeker, Clare Hodgson. *Who Wakes Rooster?* Simon & Schuster, 1996. / Pearson, Tracey Campbell. *Bob.* Farrar, 2002. / Rostoker-Gruber, Karen. *Rooster Can't Cock-a-Doodle-Doo.* Dial, 2004. / Stevens, Janet, and Susan Stevens Crummel. *Cook-a-Doodle-Doo!* Harcourt, 1999.

SUBJECTS: CHICKENS. HUMOROUS FICTION. READER'S THEATER. ROOSTERS.

116   Chen, Chih-Yuan. *Guji Guji.* **Illus. by the author. Kane/Miller, 2004. 1-929132-67-0. Unp. Gr. PreK–1**

When Mother Duck's eggs hatch, including the big one that rolled into her nest while she was busy reading, out come three little ducklings and an odd looking one who looks nothing like his siblings. Guji Guji is quicker and stronger than the others, but Mother Duck loves them all the same. When three grinning crocodiles come out of the lake and see Guji Guji, who is, as anyone can see, a fellow crocodile, they expect him to help them catch the ducks for dinner.

GERM: Whew! Now here's a moral dilemma for listeners to consider. Should Guji Guji help the crocodiles, since, as they say, ". . . we are all crocodiles and crocodiles help each other," or should he help the ducks? And, when he decides to help his family, even though he now knows he's not exactly a duck, how can he stop the crocodiles? What will happen to this crocoduck after the book ends? Have your listeners predict his future and write the sequel together as a collaborative writing project.

RELATED TITLES: Andersen, Hans Christian. *The Ugly Duckling.* Retold and illus. by Jerry Pinkney. Morrow, 1999. / Bang, Molly. *Goose*. Scholastic, 1996. / Cannon, Janell. *Stellaluna*. Harcourt, 1993. / Kasza, Keiko. *A Mother for Choco*. Putnam, 1992. / Keller, Holly. *Horace*. Greenwillow, 1991. / Paye, Won-Ldy, and Margaret H. Lippert. *Mrs. Chicken and the Hungry Crocodile*. Henry Holt, 2003.

SUBJECTS: ADOPTION. CROCODILES. DUCKS. IDENTITY. LOVE. MOTHERS. SELF-ACCEPTANCE.

117   Cheng, Andrea. *Grandfather Counts*. Illus. by Ange Zhang. Lee & Low, 2000. 1-58430-010-8. Unp. Gr. K–2

Helen's grandfather, Gong Gong, comes from China to stay with her family in America, in their house by the railroad tracks. While he speaks only Chinese and Helen only English, it isn't long before the two bond, watching and counting the cars of the passing train, in both English and Chinese.

GERM: At the front of the book are the characters and pronunciation for the numbers one to eight in Chinese, which your children can learn to write and say.

RELATED TITLES: Choi, Sook Nyul. *Halmoni and the Picnic*. Houghton, 1993. / Hall, Bruce Edward. *Henry and the Kite Dragon*. Philomel, 2004. / Levine, Ellen. *I Hate English!* Scholastic, 1989. / Lewin, Ted. *Big Jimmy's Kum Kau Chinese Take Out*. HarperCollins, 2002. / Lin, Grace. *Fortune Cookie Fortunes*. Knopf, 2004. / Mak, Kam. *My Chinatown: One Year in Poems*. HarperCollins, 2002. / Pomeranc, Marion Hess. *The American Wei*. Albert Whitman, 1998. / Rattigan, Jama Kim. *Dumpling Soup*. Little, Brown, 1993. / Recorvits, Helen. *My Name Is Yoon*. Farrar, 2003. / Sun, Chying Feng. *Mama Bear*. Houghton Mifflin, 1994. / Wong, Janet. *Apple Pie 4th of July*. Harcourt, 2002. / Yang, Belle. *Hannah Is My Name*. Candlewick, 2004. / Yee, Paul. *Roses Sing on New Snow: A Delicious Tale*. Macmillan, 1992.

SUBJECTS: ASIAN AMERICANS. CHINESE AMERICANS. CHINESE LANGUAGE. COMMUNICATION. COUNTING BOOKS. GRANDFATHERS. MULTICULTURAL BOOKS. RACIALLY MIXED PEOPLE.

118   Cherry, Lynne. *How Groundhog's Garden Grew*. Illus. by the author. Scholastic, 2003. 0-439-32371-1. Unp. Gr. K–2

Squirrel teaches Little Groundhog all about gardening, from harvesting and planting the seeds to enjoying the fruits (and vegetables) of his labor at a Thanksgiving feast with his animal friends.

GERM: The Author's Note offers gardening Web sites for children. Ask students to bring in vegetables to cut open, inspect, and taste. Collect, categorize, and identify the seeds or make vegetable soup. Take a close-up look at the growing stages of six fruits and vegetables in *Pick, Pull, Snap! Where Once a Flower Bloomed* by Lola M. Schaefer.

RELATED TITLES: Cherry, Lynne. *The Armadillo from Amarillo*. Harcourt, 1994. / Cherry, Lynne. *The Great Kapok Tree: A Tale of the Amazon Rain Forest*. Harcourt, 1990. / Cox, Judy. *Go to Sleep, Groundhog!* Holiday House, 2003. / Coy, John. *Two Old Potatoes and Me*. Knopf, 2003. / Ehlert, Lois. *Eating the Alphabet: Fruits and Vegetables from A to Z*. Harcourt, 1989. / Ehlert, Lois. *Growing Vegetable Soup*. Harcourt, 1987. / Freymann, Saxton. *Food for Thought: The Complete Book of Concepts for Growing Minds*. Scholastic, 2005. / Gibbons, Gail. *From Seed to Plant*. Holiday House, 1991. / MacDonald, Margaret Read. *Pickin' Peas*. HarperCollins, 1998. / Schaefer, Lola M. *Pick, Pull, Snap! Where Once a Flower Bloomed*. HarperCollins, 2003. / Spinelli, Eileen. *Thanksgiving at the Tappleton's*. HarperCollins, 2003. / Stevens, Janet. *Tops and Bottoms*. Harcourt, 1995.

SUBJECTS: ANIMALS. GARDENING. GROUNDHOGS. PLANTS. SQUIRRELS. THANKSGIVING. VEGETABLES.

119   Cherry, Lynne. *The Sea, the Storm, and the Mangrove Tangle*. Illus. by the author. Farrar, 2004. 0-374-36482-6. Unp. Gr. 2–6

Follow a mangrove propagule, or seed, as it is jostled from its mangrove island into the Caribbean sea by a pelican and carried by water to a faraway lagoon. There it roots, sprouts, and grows for decades until, after a century, it has become its own good-sized mangrove island, home to crabs, snails, seahorses, lizards, insects, hummingbirds, dolphins, and manatees. When a hurricane blows through, we see the cycle starting again, with a lone propagule floating away on the current. Exquisitely detailed illustrations above and below the water bring to life an ecological wonder unfamiliar to most children.

GERM: Make charts showing the life cycle of a mangrove. The Author's Note informs us of the dangers facing mangrove ecosystems from shrimp farming and overdevelopment. Research other types of trees, starting with Barbara Bash's *Desert Giant*, about the saguaro; *In the Heart of the Village*, about the banyan; and *Tree of Life*, about the baobab; plus Cherry's now-classic *The Great Kapok Tree*.

RELATED TITLES: Bash, Barbara. *Desert Giant: The World of the Saguaro Cactus.* Sierra Club, 1989. / Bash, Barbara. *In the Heart of the Village: The World of the Indian Banyan Tree.* Sierra Club, 1996. / Bash, Barbara. *Tree of Life: The World of the African Baobab.* Sierra Club/Little, Brown, 1989. / Cherry, Lynne. *The Great Kapok Tree: A Tale of the Amazon Rain Forest.* Harcourt, 1990. / Cherry, Lynne. *A River Ran Wild: An Environmental History.* Harcourt, 1992. / Gackenbach, Dick. *Mighty Tree.* Harcourt, 1992. / George, Kristine O'Connell. *Old Elm Speaks: Tree Poems.* Clarion, 1998. / Hiscock, Bruce. *The Big Tree.* Atheneum, 1991. / Kramer, Stephen. *Eye of the Storm: Chasing Storms with Warren Faidley.* Putnam, 1997.

SUBJECTS: CARIBBEAN AREA. ECOLOGY. HURRICANES. MANGROVE SWAMPS. MARINE ANIMALS.

120   **Cherry, Lynne, and Mark J. Plotkin.** *The Shaman's Apprentice: A Tale of the Amazon Rain Forest.* **Illus. by Lynne Cherry. Harcourt, 1998. 0-15-201281-8. Unp. Gr. 2–4**
Kamanya, a boy of the Amazon rain forest, can't forget how the shaman healed his sickness and saved his life using the many plants of the rain forest as his medicines, and he vows to become a healer when he grows up. Lush, full-bleed watercolor paintings capture the people and environs of the Tirio village of Kwamala, which the author and illustrator visited to create this stunning portrayal.
GERM: Based on a true story first told in Plotkin's adult book *Tales of the Shaman's Apprentice* (Penguin, 1994), the focus is on showing how traditional medicines continue to be as viable a source for healing—and maybe even more so—than modern synthetic medicine. For a study of the Amazon rain forest, continue with Cherry's conservation classic, *The Great Kapok Tree* and Jan Brett's *The Umbrella.* Also tie in some of the applicable folktales from María Cristina Brusca and Tona Wilson's *When Jaguar Ate the Moon: And Other Stories About Animals and Plants of the Americas.*
RELATED TITLES: Brett, Jan. *The Umbrella.* Putnam, 2004. / Brusca, María Cristina, and Tona Wilson. *When Jaguar Ate the Moon: And Other Stories About Animals and Plants of the Americas.* Henry Holt, 1995. / Cherry, Lynne. *The Great Kapok Tree: A Tale of the Amazon Rain Forest.* Harcourt, 1990. / Jordan, Tanis. *Amazon Alphabet.* Kingfisher, 1996. / Yolen, Jane. *Welcome to the Green House.* Putnam, 1993.
SUBJECTS: AMAZON RIVER. ENVIRONMENT. MEDICINE. RAIN FORESTS.

121   **Child, Lauren.** *Beware of the Storybook Wolves.* **Illus. by the author. Scholastic, 2001. 0-439-20500-X. Unp. Gr. PreK–2**
On the night Herb's mother forgets to take the bedtime storybook out of his bedroom, he turns on the light to discover two menacing wolves hovering over him ready to gobble him up, right down to his little pink toes. As a lead-in to exploring the world of fairy-tale characters, Herb's predicament and how he resolves it with the help of a fairy godmother will leave kids agog and laughing.
GERM: Don't assume your students all know the story of "Little Red Riding Hood" or even "Cinderella," two tales that are central to this book. Read or tell these stories, along with other folktales with bad boy wolf characters. Also make sure to counteract the negative image of wolves that children encounter in most folktales with the positive accounts found in nonfiction wolf books. Compare and contrast the wolves' story personas with their actual ones. Jump into another wild Herb adventure in *Who's Afraid of the Big Bad Book?*
RELATED TITLES: Child, Lauren. *Who's Afraid of the Big Bad Book?* Hyperion, 2003. / Christelow, Eileen. *Where's the Big Bad Wolf?* Clarion, 2002. / Ernst, Lisa Campbell. *Little Red Riding Hood: A Newfangled Prairie Tale.* Simon & Schuster, 1995. / Hoberman, Mary Ann. *You Read to Me, I'll Read to You: Very Short Fairy Tales to Read Together.* Little, Brown, 2004. / Kelly, John, and Cathy Tincknell. *The Mystery of Eatum Hall.* Candlewick, 2004. / McClements, George. *Jake Gander, Storyville Detective.* Hyperion, 2002. / Marshall, James. *The Three Little Pigs.* Dial, 1989. / Meddaugh, Susan. *Hog-Eye.* Houghton Mifflin, 1995. / Palatini, Margie. *Bad Boys.* HarperCollins, 2003. / Palatini, Margie. *Piggie Pie.* Clarion, 1995. / Scieszka, Jon. *The True Story of the 3 Little Pigs.* Viking, 1989. / Stevens, Janet, and Susan Stevens Crummel. *And the Dish Ran Away with the Spoon.* Harcourt, 2001. / Wiesner, David. *The Three Pigs.* Clarion, 2001.
SUBJECTS: CHARACTERS IN LITERATURE. HUMOROUS FICTION. LITTLE RED RIDING HOOD STORIES. PARODIES. WOLVES.

122   **Child, Lauren.** *Clarice Bean, Guess Who's Babysitting?* **Illus. by the author. Candlewick, 2001. 0-7636-1373-8. Unp. Gr. PreK–4**
Here's a wild and funny story, narrated at a gallop by Clarice Bean as she elaborates on everything that goes wrong when her firefighter Uncle Ted spends a day at her house—including a lost guinea pig and a stop at the hospital for her little brother, Minal. The frantic, antic collage

illustrations incorporate cut paper, pen-and-ink, watercolor, and photographs, with many styles and sizes of text that loop across the pages.

GERM: While you read, ask listeners to consider what might have happened if Uncle Ted babysat for two days instead of one. Have students work in groups to make a list of Clarice's zany relatives and come up with five words that describe each one. Your kids can write and illustrate one of their own family episodes with themselves as the narrators.

RELATED TITLES: Bush, Timothy. *Benjamin McFadden and the Robot Babysitter.* Crown, 1998. / Child, Lauren. *Beware of the Storybook Wolves.* Scholastic, 2001. / Child, Lauren. *Clarice Bean, That's Me.* Candlewick, 1999. / Child, Lauren. *I Will Never NOT EVER Eat a Tomato.* Candlewick, 2000. / Child, Lauren. *That Pesky Rat.* Candlewick, 2002. / Child, Lauren. *What Planet Are You From, Clarice Bean?* Candlewick, 2002. / Child, Lauren. *Who's Afraid of the Big Bad Book?* Hyperion, 2003. / Feiffer, Jules. *I Lost My Bear.* Morrow, 1998. / Harris, Robie H. *Don't Forget to Come Back!* Candlewick, 2004. / Kroll, Steven. *Patches Lost and Found.* Winslow, 2001. / Martin, Jane Read, and Patricia Marx. *Now Everybody Really Hates Me.* HarperCollins, 1993. / Martin, Jane Read, and Patricia Marx. *Now I Will Never Leave the Dinner Table.* HarperCollins, 1996. / Meade, Holly. *John Willy and Freddy McGee.* Marshall Cavendish, 1998. / Roche, Denis. *The Best Class Picture Ever.* Scholastic, 2003.

SUBJECTS: BABY-SITTERS. FAMILY LIFE. FIREFIGHTERS. GUINEA PIGS. HUMOROUS FICTION. LOST AND FOUND POSSESSIONS. PERSONAL NARRATIVES. UNCLES.

123   **Child, Lauren.** *I Am Too Absolutely Small for School.* **Illus. by the author. Candlewick, 2004. 0-7636-2403-9. Unp. Gr. PreK–2**

Little sister Lola insists she is too extremely busy doing important things at home to go to school. Her big brother, Charlie, explains that she will learn lots of useful stuff there, like counting and reading and writing and making friends, and in the end, he talks her into going, thank goodness.

GERM: Ask your now-seasoned crew to think back to their first days of school and to write and illustrate an account of what they were apprehensive about before school started. Then have them describe how it all turned out. This is an experiential writing activity that can apply to all ages. Share more sibling banter between Charlie and Lola in *I Will Never Not Ever Eat a Tomato.* Make sure to look for Lola's invisible friend, Soren Lorenson. For more invisible friend books, read *Me and Neesie* by Eloise Greenfield and *Leon and Bob* by Simon James.

RELATED TITLES: Child, Lauren. *I Will Never Not Ever Eat a Tomato.* Candlewick, 2000. / Davis, Katie. *Kindergarten Rocks.* Harcourt, 2005. / Greenfield, Eloise. *Me and Neesie.* Crowell, 1975. / Henkes, Kevin. *Chrysanthemum.* Greenwillow, 1991. / Henkes, Kevin. *Wemberly Worried.* Greenwillow, 2000. / Horse, Harry. *Little Rabbit Goes to School.* Peachtree, 2004. / James, Simon. *Leon and Bob.* Candlewick, 1997. / Lasky, Kathryn. *Lunch Bunnies.* Little, Brown, 1996. / McGhee, Alison. *Mrs. Watson Wants Your Teeth.* Harcourt, 2004. / Poydar, Nancy. *First Day, Hooray.* Holiday House, 1999. / Rohmann, Eric. *Clara and Asha.* Roaring Brook, 2005. / Schwartz, Amy. *Annabelle Swift, Kindergartner.* Orchard, 1988. / Slate, Joseph. *Miss Bindergarten Gets Ready for Kindergarten.* Dutton, 1996. / Strete, Craig. *The Rattlesnake Who Went to School.* Putnam, 2004. / Wells, Rosemary. *My Kindergarten.* Hyperion, 2004. / Wells, Rosemary. *Timothy Goes to School.* Dial, 1981. / Wells, Rosemary. *Yoko.* Hyperion, 1998.

SUBJECTS: BROTHERS AND SISTERS. FIRST DAY OF SCHOOL. IMAGINARY PLAYMATES. KINDERGARTEN. PICTURE BOOKS FOR ALL AGES. SCHOOLS. WORRYING.

124   **Child, Lauren.** *I Will Never Not Ever Eat a Tomato.* **Illus. by the author. Candlewick, 2000. 0-7636-1188-3. Unp. Gr. K–2**

Charlie's little sister, Lola, fussy about food, says that carrots are for rabbits and that peas are too small and green. Charlie tricks her into eating them by claiming the carrots are really orange twiglets from Jupiter and peas are green drops that fall from the sky in Greenland.

GERM: You'll also love the picky eaters in *Don't Let the Peas Touch! And Other Stories* by Deborah Blumenthal, *D. W. the Picky Eater* by Marc Brown, *No Peas for Nellie* by Chris L. Demarest, and *Zak's Lunch* by Margie Palatini. There's even a whole family of food-fussy kids in *The Seven Silly Eaters* by Mary Ann Hoberman. Ask your food phobics what tricks have worked on them to get them to try foods they didn't want to touch. Follow a reluctant Lola to her first day of school in *I Am Too Absolutely Small for School.*

RELATED TITLES: Blumenthal, Deborah. *Don't Let the Peas Touch! And Other Stories.* Scholastic, 2004. / Brown, Marc. *D. W. the Picky Eater.* Little, Brown, 1995. / Byars, Betsy. *My Brother, Ant.* Viking, 1996. / Child, Lauren. *Clarice Bean, Guess Who's Babysitting?* Candlewick, 2001. / Demarest, Chris L. *No Peas for Nellie.* Macmillan, 1988. / Hoberman, Mary Ann. *The Seven Silly Eaters.* Harcourt, 1997. / Lerner, Harriet, and Susan Goldhor. *What's So Terrible About Swallowing an Apple Seed?* HarperCollins, 1996. / Palatini, Margie. *Zak's*

Lunch. Clarion, 1998. / Rosenthal, Amy Krouse. *Little Pea.* Chronicle Books, 2005. / Seuss, Dr. *Green Eggs and Ham.* Random House, 1960. / Sharmat, Mitchell. *Gregory, the Terrible Eater.* Macmillan, 1985. / Wells, Rosemary. *Yoko.* Hyperion, 1998. / Yolen, Jane. *How Do Dinosaurs Eat Their Food?* Blue Sky/Scholastic, 2005.

SUBJECTS: BROTHERS AND SISTERS. FOOD. FOOD HABITS. IMAGINATION.

125 Child, Lauren. *That Pesky Rat.* **Illus. by the author. Candlewick, 2002. 0-7636-1873-X. Unp. Gr. PreK–2**

Living in Grubby Alley, a nice brown rat longs to be a pet to a nice human and enjoy some of the creature comforts of his more affluent animal friends. Mrs. Trill at the pet store says he can hang a notice in her window. In comes nearsighted old Mr. Fortesque who reads the rat's handmade sign and says, "I'll take him . . . Oh yes, I've been looking for a brown cat as nice as this one for ages." What a total riot, with Child's signature wild collage cutout illustrations and text leaping and meandering all over the page.

GERM: Ask your pet-lovers to think about the qualities they'd want in a new pet, and have them write up their own notice (with a portrait, of course) to hang in Mrs. Trill's pet store. Or they can write ads from their own pets' point of view, or personal narratives describing what their lives are like at home with their human families. For hilarious first-person animal character studies, don't miss Madeleine L'Engle's *The Other Dog*; Fred Marcellino's *I, Crocodile*; and Mark Teague's *Dear Mrs. LaRue: Letters from Obedience School.*

RELATED TITLES: Cannon, Janell. *Stellaluna.* Harcourt, 1993. / Cannon, Janell. *Verdi.* Harcourt, 1997. / Conniff, Richard. *Rats: The Good, the Bad, and the Ugly.* Crown, 2002. / Cronin, Doreen. *Diary of a Worm.* HarperCollins, 2003. / Fierstein, Harvey. *The Sissy Duckling.* Simon & Schuster, 2002. / Florczak, Robert. *Yikes!!!* Blue Sky/Scholastic, 2003. / France, Anthony. *From Me to You.* Candlewick, 2003. / French, Jackie. *Diary of a Wombat.* Clarion, 2003. / Geras, Adèle. *The Cats of Cuckoo Square: Two Stories.* Delacorte, 2001. / LaRochelle, David. *The Best Pet of All.* Dutton, 2004. / L'Engle, Madeleine. *The Other Dog.* SeaStar, 2001. / Lester, Helen. *Hooway for Wodney Wat.* Houghton Mifflin, 1999. / McMullan, Kate. *I Stink!* HarperCollins, 2002. / Marcellino, Fred. *I, Crocodile.* HarperCollins, 1999. / Teague, Mark. *Dear Mrs. LaRue: Letters from Obedience School.* Scholastic, 2002. / Waber, Bernard. *Rich Cat, Poor Cat.* Houghton Mifflin, 1963.

SUBJECTS: HUMOROUS FICTION. OUTCASTS. PERSONAL NARRATIVES. PETS. PICTURE BOOKS FOR ALL AGES. RATS.

126 Child, Lauren. *Who's Afraid of the Big Bad Book?* **Illus. by the author. Hyperion, 2003. 0-7868-0926-4. Unp. Gr. K–3**

Herb may love his storybooks, but he takes terrible care of them. One night, when he falls asleep with his head in an open book of fairy tales, he wakes to see Goldilocks standing there, shrieking, "You are not allowed in this story!" and realizes, of course, that's just where he is. When he appeals to Cinderella's fairy godmother to help him get out of the book, she's not exactly sympathetic: "What do you expect when you go about scribbling and snippering and generally causing mayhem? This is NO WAY to treat a book, you know!"

GERM: Of course you can use this wild and crazy fairy tale spoof to talk about proper book care, as Herb is one messy reader and eater. You also have a nice mixture of Goldilocks and Cinderella here to demonstrate what can happen when you put yourself in an established story as a new character. Fairy tale fans can put themselves in a story or two or write and illustrate an account of what might happen if a fairy tale character came out of a book into their own lives. For a story that comes right off the pages, also read David Wiesner's Caldecott winner, *The Three Pigs.*

RELATED TITLES: Aylesworth, Jim. *Goldilocks and the Three Bears.* Scholastic, 2003. / Child, Lauren. *Beware of the Storybook Wolves.* Scholastic, 2001. / Child, Lauren. *That Pesky Rat.* Candlewick, 2002. / Cowell, Cressida. *Little Bo Peep's Library Book.* Orchard, 1999. / Deedy, Carmen Agra. *The Library Dragon.* Peachtree, 1994. / Ernst, Lisa Campbell. *Stella Louella's Runaway Book.* Simon & Schuster, 1998. / Garland, Michael. *Miss Smith's Incredible Storybook.* Dutton, 2003. / Hawkins, Colin, and Jacqui Hawkins. *The Fairytale News.* Candlewick, 2004. / Hoberman, Mary Ann. *You Read to Me, I'll Read to You: Very Short Fairy Tales to Read Together.* Little, Brown, 2004. / McClements, George. *Jake Gander, Storyville Detective.* Hyperion, 2002. / Scieszka, Jon. *The True Story of the 3 Little Pigs.* Viking, 1989. / Sierra, Judy. *Wild About Books.* Knopf, 2004. / Stanley, Diane. *Goldie and the Three Bears.* HarperCollins, 2003. / Wiesner, David. *The Three Pigs.* Clarion, 2001.

SUBJECTS: BOOKS AND READING. CHARACTERS IN LITERATURE. CINDERELLA STORIES. FAIRY TALES—SATIRE. GOLDILOCKS. HUMOROUS FICTION. PARODIES. WOLVES.

127   Chodos-Irvine, Margaret. *Ella Sarah Gets Dressed.* **Illus. by the author. Harcourt, 2003. 0-15-216413-8. Unp. Gr. PreK–K**

Though her mother, father, and sister try to talk her out of it, Ella Sarah knows just what she wants to wear: her pink polka-dot pants, her dress with orange-and-green flowers, her purple-and-blue striped socks, her yellow shoes, and her red hat. Ella Sarah throws a wee tantrum, but she sticks to her guns and looks mighty stylish. Your fashion plates will agree.

GERM: Talk about favorite clothes and how we determine what goes together and what doesn't when we pick out the outfits we want to wear each day. Ask your fashionistas to dress up in or draw a picture of themselves wearing their favorite outfits.

RELATED TITLES: Daly, Niki. *Jamela's Dress.* Farrar, 1999. / Fox, Mem. *Shoes from Grandpa.* Orchard, 1990. / Jocelyn, Marthe. *Hannah's Dresses.* Dutton, 1998. / Jonas, Ann. *Color Dance.* Greenwillow, 1989. / London, Jonathan. *Froggy Gets Dressed.* Viking, 1992. / Peek, Merle. *Mary Wore Her Red Dress and Henry Wore His Red Sneakers.* Clarion, 1985. / Rice, Eve. *Oh, Lewis.* Macmillan, 1987. / Schwartz, Amy. *What James Likes Best.* Simon & Schuster. 2003.

SUBJECTS: CLOTHING AND DRESS. COLOR. FAMILY LIFE. INDIVIDUALITY. NONCONFORMISTS. PARTIES.

128   Choldenko, Gennifer. *Moonstruck: The True Story of the Cow Who Jumped Over the Moon.* **Illus. by Paul Yalowitz. Hyperion, 1997. 0-7868-2130-2. Unp. Gr. PreK–2**

The matter-of-fact brown horse in charge of training a team of equine Moon Jumpers relates how a dedicated catapulting Holstein gave Mother Goose her "cow jumped over the moon" reference. The entertaining and folksy horse storyteller gets us rooting for the bovine's impossible quest.

GERM: For children never exposed to Mother Goose, make sure to recite "Hey diddle diddle" before you begin. Moon-jumping cows also prevail in Chris Babcock's *No Moon, No Milk*, Paula Brown's *Moon Jump: A Countdown*, Paul Brett Johnson's *The Cow Who Wouldn't Come Down*, and Rachel Vail's *Over the Moon*.

RELATED TITLES: Babcock, Chris. *No Moon, No Milk.* Crown, 1993. / Brown, Paula. *Moon Jump: A Countdown.* Viking, 1992. / Cronin, Doreen. *Click, Clack, Moo: Cows That Type.* Simon & Schuster, 2000. / Egan, Tim. *Metropolitan Cow.* Houghton Mifflin, 1996. / Ernst, Lisa Campbell. *When Bluebell Sang.* Bradbury, 1989. / Johnson, Paul Brett. *The Cow Who Wouldn't Come Down.* Orchard, 1993. / Kinerk, Robert. *Clorinda.* Simon & Schuster, 2003. / Schertle, Alice. *How Now, Brown Cow.* Harcourt, 1994. / Speed, Toby. *Two Cool Cows.* Putnam, 1995. / Stevens, Janet, and Susan Stevens Crummel. *And the Dish Ran Away with the Spoon.* Harcourt, 2001. / Vail, Rachel. *Over the Moon.* Orchard, 1998.

SUBJECTS: CHARACTERS IN LITERATURE. COWS. HORSES. MOON. PARODIES. PERSEVERANCE. PICTURE BOOKS FOR ALL AGES.

129   Chorao, Kay. *Pig and Crow.* **Illus. by the author. Henry Holt, 2000. 0-8050-5868-X. Unp. Gr. PreK–1**

Lonely Pig bakes to raise his spirits. Though he doesn't believe in magic, when sly Crow shows him seeds that he claims can take away loneliness, Pig willingly exchanges them for his fresh-baked chocolate swirl fudge cake. Planting the seeds brings Pig pumpkins. Crow offers two more trades—pumpkin pie for a "magic" worm that hatches into a beautiful butterfly and bread pudding for a "magic" egg that hatches into a baby Canada goose.

GERM: Discussion point: Were Crow's seeds, worm, and egg magic? What did Pig learn from each of Crow's trades? This quiet story, with wistful gouache-and-ink illustrations, will get children thinking about other ways to drive away sadness and loneliness.

RELATED TITLES: Bottner, Barbara, and Gerald Kruglik. *Wallace's Lists.* HarperCollins, 2004. / Lobel, Arnold. Frog and Toad series. HarperCollins. / London, Jonathan. *What Newt Could Do for Turtle.* Candlewick, 1996. / Waddell, Martin. *Hi, Harry! The Moving Story of How One Slow Tortoise Slowly Made a Friend.* Candlewick, 2003.

SUBJECTS: BARTERING. BUTTERFLIES. CATERPILLARS. CONDUCT OF LIFE. CROWS. FRIENDSHIP. LONELINESS. PIGS.

130   Christelow, Eileen. *Five Little Monkeys with Nothing to Do.* **Illus. by the author. Clarion, 1996. 0-395-75830-0. 36pp. Gr. PreK–K**

With Grandma Bessie coming for lunch, Mama instructs her five bored little monkeys to clean their room, scrub the bathroom, beat the rugs, and pick berries for dessert. So why is the house such a disaster when Grandma gets there?

GERM: Your messy little monkeys will get a charge out of predicting what will happen when the muddy monkeys come home to their nice clean house after berry-picking down by the swamp. Get everyone reading the other playful titles in the Five Little Monkeys series.

RELATED TITLES: Anholt, Catherine, and Laurence Anholt. *Chimp and Zee*. Putnam, 2001. / Anholt, Catherine, and Laurence Anholt. *Chimp and Zee and the Big Storm*. Putnam, 2002. / Christelow, Eileen. *Five Little Monkeys Jumping on the Bed*. Clarion, 1989. (And others in the Five Little Monkeys series.) / Diakité, Baba Wagué. *The Hatseller and the Monkeys*. Scholastic, 1999. / Koller, Jackie French. *One Monkey Too Many*. Scholastic, 1999. / Perkins, Al. *Hand, Hand, Fingers, Thumb*. Random House, 1969. / Rey, H. A. *Curious George*. Houghton Mifflin, 1993. (And others in the Curious George series.) / Santat, Dan. *The Guild of Geniuses*. Scholastic, 2004. / Slobodkina, Esphyr. *Caps for Sale*. HarperCollins, 1947. / Teague, Mark. *Pigsty*. Scholastic, 1994. / Wells, Rosemary. *Max Cleans Up*. Dial, 2000.

SUBJECTS: CLEANLINESS. GRANDMOTHERS. MONKEYS. MOTHERS.

131 **Christelow, Eileen.** *The Great Pig Search*. Illus. by the author. Clarion, 2001. 0-618-04910-X. Unp. Gr. PreK–1

In the sequel to the whimsical *The Great Pig Escape*, Vermont farmers Bert and Ethel receive a mysterious postcard from Florida bearing only the word "OINK!" Obsessed with recapturing his runaway pigs, Bert buys bus tickets for a Florida vacation. Observant children will gleefully note the ubiquitous pigs driving taxis, working at the Starlight Motel, sunning at the beach, and even rescuing Bert from drowning, though Bert and Ethel remain oblivious as they search fruitlessly for their pigs.

GERM: Have pig spotters come up with a complete sentence that describes who, what, and where they see each pig on the page, such as: "The pig in the pink bathing suit, goggles, and flippers is wading in the water at the beach." See how the pigs from Old Macdonald's farm go incognito in Margie Palatini's *Piggie Pie*.

RELATED TITLES: Christelow, Eileen. *The Great Pig Escape*. Clarion, 1994. / Falconer, Ian. *Olivia*. Atheneum, 2000. / Marshall, James. *Swine Lake*. HarperCollins, 1999. / Meddaugh, Susan. *Hog-Eye*. Houghton Mifflin, 1995. / Moser, Barry. *The Three Little Pigs*. Little, Brown, 2001. / Palatini, Margie. *Piggie Pie*. Clarion, 1995. / Rayner, Mary. *Mr. and Mrs. Pig's Evening Out*. Atheneum, 1976. / Scieszka, Jon. *The True Story of the 3 Little Pigs*. Viking, 1989. / Wood, Audrey. *Piggies*. Harcourt, 1991.

SUBJECTS: FLORIDA. PIGS. SEASHORE. VISUAL DISCRIMINATION.

132 **Christelow, Eileen.** *Where's the Big Bad Wolf?* Illus. by the author. Clarion, 2002. 0-618-18194-6. Unp. Gr. PreK–2

Police Detective Phineas T. Doggedly is on the trail of that low-down, no-good, chicken-chasing, pig-poaching rascal, the Big Bad Wolf, who always promises to stay out of trouble, but is now blowing down the houses of three delectable little piggies.

GERM: Surely your students are more clever than the dog narrator of the story, and they'll figure out and point out all the clues as to where that wolf is. Make sure they've heard a traditional version of "The Three Little Pigs" before reading this spoof.

RELATED TITLES: Blundell, Tony. *Beware of Boys*. Greenwillow, 1992. / Child, Lauren. *Beware of the Storybook Wolves*. Scholastic, 2001. / Child, Lauren. *Who's Afraid of the Big Bad Book?* Hyperion, 2003. / Cowell, Cressida. *Little Bo Peep's Library Book*. Orchard, 1999. / Hawkins, Colin, and Jacqui Hawkins. *The Fairytale News*. Candlewick, 2004. / Kelly, John, and Cathy Tincknell. *The Mystery of Eatum Hall*. Candlewick, 2004. / Marshall, James. *The Three Little Pigs*. Dial, 1989. / McClements, George. *Jake Gander, Storyville Detective*. Hyperion, 2002. / Meddaugh, Susan. *Hog-Eye*. Houghton, 1995. / Offen, Hilda. *Nice Work, Little Wolf!* Dutton, 1992. / Palatini, Margie. *Bad Boys*. HarperCollins, 2003. / Scieszka, Jon. *The True Story of the 3 Little Pigs*. Viking, 1989. / Trivizas, Eugene. *The Three Little Wolves and the Big Bad Pig*. McElderry, 1993. / Vozar, David. *Yo, Hungry Wolf! A Nursery Rap*. Doubleday, 1993. / Wiesner, David. *The Three Pigs*. Clarion, 2001.

SUBJECTS: DOGS. DOMESTIC ANIMALS. MYSTERY AND DETECTIVE STORIES. PARODIES. WOLVES.

133 **Clark, Emma Chichester.** *Follow the Leader!* Illus. by the author. Simon & Schuster, 2003. 0-689-84296-1. Unp. Gr. PreK–2

A little boy in a jaunty yellow cap leads an ever-growing line of animals through the trees, up the hill, into the woods, puffing and panting, shouting and roaring, until they all encounter a menacing tiger who wants to join in their follow-the-leader game.

GERM: Ask your group how the boy tricks the tiger. Naturally, you'll want to act the whole thing out in a nice long line, as there are plenty of prepositions and joyous action verbs to bring to life.

RELATED TITLES: Appelt, Kathi. *Elephants Aloft*. Harcourt, 1993. / Ashman, Linda. *Rub-a-Dub Sub*. Harcourt, 2003. / Bodsworth, Nan. *A Nice Walk in the Jungle*. Viking, 1989. / Donaldson, Julia. *The Gruffalo*. Dial, 1999. / Dowson, Nick. *Tigress*. Candlewick, 2004. / Harter, Debbie. *Walking Through the Jungle*. Orchard, 1997. / Hoberman, Mary Ann. *It's Simple, Said Simon*. Knopf, 2001. / Jarrett, Clare. *The Best Picnic Ever*. Candlewick, 2004. / Jorgensen, Gail. *Gotcha!* Scholastic, 1997. / Livingston, Irene. *Finklehopper Frog*. Tricycle, 2003. / Mac-Donald, Margaret Read. *Mabela the Clever*. Albert Whitman, 2001. / Mitton, Tony. *Dinosaurumpus!* Scholastic, 2003. / Parker, Vic. *Bearobics*. Viking, 1997. / Polacco, Patricia. *Oh, Look!* Philomel, 2004. / Rosen, Michael. *We're Going on a Bear Hunt*. McElderry, 1989.

SUBJECTS: ANIMALS. CALL-AND-RESPONSE STORIES. CREATIVE DRAMA. ENGLISH LANGUAGE—GRAMMAR. ENGLISH LANGUAGE—PREPOSITIONS. ENGLISH LANGUAGE—VERBS. EXERCISE. GAMES. SOUND EFFECTS. TIGERS.

134   **Clark, Emma Chichester. *I Love You, Blue Kangaroo!* Illus. by the author. Doubleday, 1999. 0-385-32638-6. Unp. Gr. PreK–K**

Lily loves her stuffed animal Blue Kangaroo, but when she brings one too many other animals into the bed, he heads for the baby's crib where there's more room. To get him back, Lily trades all her other stuffed animals with her wailing baby brother, declaring, "He can have these, but nobody can have Blue Kangaroo!"

GERM: Discuss: Why does Lily decide she likes Blue Kangaroo best of all? What do you think his special qualities are? Ask children to bring in their favorite stuffed animals to introduce to the class and describe their special qualities. Follow with *It Was You, Blue Kangaroo!*, where Lily puts the blame on Blue Kangaroo every time she does something wrong.

RELATED TITLES: Clark, Emma Chichester. *It Was You, Blue Kangaroo!* Doubleday, 2002. / Clark, Emma Chichester. *Where Are You, Blue Kangaroo?* Doubleday, 2000. / Cocca-Leffler, Maryann. *Missing: One Stuffed Rabbit*. Albert Whitman, 1998. / Fitzpatrick, Marie-Louise. *Lizzy and Skunk*. DK Ink, 2000. / Freeman, Don. *Corduroy*. Viking, 1968. / Weiss, Nicki. *Hank and Oogie*. Lothrop, 1987.

SUBJECTS: JEALOUSY. LOVE. STUFFED ANIMALS. TOYS.

135   **Clark, Emma Chichester. *Where Are You, Blue Kangaroo?* Illus. by the author. Doubleday, 2000. 0-385-90003-1. Unp. Gr. PreK–K**

Every time Lily goes out—to the park, on the bus, to the zoo—she takes along her stuffed friend, Blue Kangaroo, and almost loses him. After his close brush at the zoo, Blue Kangaroo, worried about being left behind again, looks for a place where he'll be safe.

GERM: Discussion point/problem solving question: How can Emma keep from losing Blue Kangaroo again? Ask children to bring in a stuffed animal, introduce it to the other children, and tell how they lost and found it.

RELATED TITLES: Alborough, Jez. *Where's My Teddy?* Candlewick, 1992. / Clark, Emma Chichester. *I Love You, Blue Kangaroo!* Doubleday, 1999. / Cocca-Leffler, Maryann. *Missing: One Stuffed Rabbit*. Albert Whitman, 1998. / Drummond, V. H. *Phewtus the Squirrel*. Lothrop, 1987. / Falconer, Ian. *Olivia . . . and the Missing Toy*. Atheneum, 2003. / Feiffer, Jules. *I Lost My Bear*. Morrow, 1998. / Freeman, Don. *Corduroy*. Viking, 1968. / Galbraith, Kathryn O. *Laura Charlotte*. Philomel, 1990. / Hayes, Sarah. *This Is the Bear and the Scary Night*. Little, Brown, 1992. / Hughes, Shirley. *Dogger*. Lothrop, 1988. / Ichikawa, Satomi. *La La Rose*. Philomel, 2004. / Payne, Emmy. *Katy-No-Pocket*. Houghton Mifflin, 1944. / Sheldon, Dyan. *Love, Your Bear Pete*. Candlewick, 1994. / Smith, Maggie. *Paisley*. Knopf, 2004. / Willems, Mo. *Knuffle Bunny: A Cautionary Tale*. Hyperion, 2004.

SUBJECTS: KANGAROOS. LOST AND FOUND POSSESSIONS. STUFFED ANIMALS. TOYS.

136   **Clement, Rod. *Grandpa's Teeth*. Illus. by the author. HarperCollins, 1998. 0-06-027671-1. Unp. Gr. K–3**

"It'sth a distthasther!" Grandpa yells when he realizes his false teeth have been stolen. To solve the crime, the police put up missing posters and require everyone to smile all the time, but the culprit is right under Grandpa's nose.

GERM: Before revealing the ending, ask children to draw pictures of who they think the chopper bandit is and write up that character's possible motive for taking Grandpa's teeth.

RELATED TITLES: Clement, Rod. *Just Another Ordinary Day*. HarperCollins, 1997. / Clements, Andrew. *Double Trouble in Walla Walla*. Millbrook, 1998. / Davis, Katie. *Mabel the Tooth Fairy and How She Got Her Job*. Harcourt, 2003. / Joyce, William. *A Day with Wilbur Robinson*. HarperCollins, 1993. / Keller, Laurie. *Open Wide: Tooth School Inside*. Henry Holt, 2000. / Laden, Nina. *The Night I Followed the Dog*. Chronicle, 1994. /

Legge, David. *Bamboozled*. Scholastic, 1995. / Palatini, Margie. *Sweet Tooth*. Simon & Schuster, 2004. / Palatini, Margie. *The Web Files*. Hyperion, 2001. / Simms, Laura. *Rotten Teeth*. Houghton Mifflin, 1998.

SUBJECTS: DOGS. GRANDFATHERS. HUMOROUS FICTION. MYSTERY AND DETECTIVE STORIES. TEETH.

137   **Clement, Rod.** *Just Another Ordinary Day*. **Illus. by the author. HarperCollins, 1997. 0-06-027666-5. Unp. Gr. 1–3**

Amanda wakes at 6:30 A.M., gets dressed, eats an egg for breakfast, gets a lift to school with old Mrs. Ellsworth, has a pleasant day doing science experiments and listening to the librarian read a pirate story, and after dinner, curls up with a book and her big cat, Fluffy, in front of the fire. Nothing special, right? Look again. Clement's outrageous illustrations turn the text into a masterpiece of understatement. Amanda's single breakfast egg is the size of a watermelon, old Mrs. Ellsworth is a T. rex in a dress and hat, the science teacher is a giant fly, and Fluffy is a lion.

GERM: First read this aloud in a dull voice without showing the pictures or the cover, and ask children their opinion of the story. Next, show the illustrations and read it aloud with a perfectly straight face and listen to your kids howl. Illustrations and story are partners in picture books, as this story aptly demonstrates. Ask your listeners to write and illustrate new stories of their "ordinary" days, employing either understatement or hyperbole.

RELATED TITLES: Clements, Andrew. *Double Trouble in Walla Walla*. Millbrook, 1998. / Edwards, Pamela Duncan. *Muldoon*. Hyperion, 2002. / Joyce, William. *A Day with Wilbur Robinson*. HarperCollins, 1993. / Kraft, Erik. *Chocolatina*. BridgeWater, 1998. / Laden, Nina. *The Night I Followed the Dog*. Chronicle, 1994. / Legge, David. *Bamboozled*. Scholastic, 1995. / Reiss, Mike. *The Great Show-and-Tell Disaster*. Price Stern Sloan, 2001. / Shannon, David. *A Bad Case of Stripes*. Scholastic, 1998. / Simms, Laura. *Rotten Teeth*. Houghton Mifflin, 1998. / Smith, Lane. *Math Curse*. Viking, 1995. / Stevenson, James. *That Dreadful Day*. Greenwillow, 1985. / Wiesner, David. *June 29, 1999*. Clarion, 1992. / Wood, Audrey. *The Flying Dragon Room*. Scholastic, 1996.

SUBJECTS: ANIMALS. ENGLISH LANGUAGE—HYPERBOLE. HUMOROUS FICTION. PICTURE BOOKS FOR ALL AGES. SCHOOLS. UNDERSTATEMENT.

138   **Clements, Andrew.** *Double Trouble in Walla Walla*. **Illus. by Sal Murdocca. Millbrook, 1997. 0-7613-0275-1. Unp. Gr. 1–3**

On an otherwise ordinary Monday at school, every time Lulu opens her mouth her tongue goes topsy-turvy with flip-flop chit-chat, and her fancy-schmancy yak-yak proves contagious for Lulu's teacher, the principal, and the school nurse.

GERM: What a language-packed fiddle-faddle of a story this is. To clear the air and close the "knock 'em sock 'em wibble-wobble word warp," the foursome let loose with a string of silly-dilly words, which will be great fun for your group to practice reading aloud to each other as fast as they can go. Compile new lists of flapdoodle and wacky words.

RELATED TITLES: Allard, Harry. *Miss Nelson Is Missing*. Houghton Mifflin, 1977. / Calmenson, Stephanie. *The Frog Principal*. Scholastic, 2001. / Clement, Rod. *Just Another Ordinary Day*. HarperCollins, 1997. / Cox, Judy. *Don't Be Silly, Mrs. Millie!* Marshall Cavendish, 2005. / Creech, Sharon. *A Fine, Fine School*. HarperCollins, 2001. / DiPucchio, Kelly. *Mrs. McBloom, Clean Up Your Classroom*. Hyperion, 2005. / Joyce, William. *A Day with Wilbur Robinson*. HarperCollins, 1993. / Kraft, Erik. *Chocolatina*. BridgeWater, 1998. / Pulver, Robin. *Punctuation Takes a Vacation*. Holiday House, 2003. / Reiss, Mike. *The Great Show-and-Tell Disaster*. Price Stern Sloan, 2001. / Shannon, David. *A Bad Case of Stripes*. Scholastic, 1998. / Smith, Lane. *Math Curse*. Viking, 1995. / Sorel, Edward. *Johnny on the Spot*. McElderry, 1998. / Steig, William. *CDB*. Simon & Schuster, 2000. / Walton, Rick. *Once There Was a Bull. . . (Frog)*. Gibbs-Smith, 1995.

SUBJECTS: HUMOROUS FICTION. ONOMATOPOEIA. PICTURE BOOKS FOR ALL AGES. SCHOOLS. VOCABULARY. WORD GAMES.

139   **Clements, Andrew.** *Slippers at Home*. **Illus. by Janie Bynum. Dutton, 2004. 0-525-47138-3. Unp. Gr. PreK–1**

Little brown-and-white puppy Slippers loves all of the four people in the big house: Edward, the baby; Laura, the big sister; Mommy, who feeds him; and Daddy, who takes Slippers for his walk and puts him to bed every night in his little doghouse outside. Without anthropomorphizing, the story lets us see the day-to-day life of a contented and adorable puppy that listeners will love getting to know.

GERM: Discussion point: What's it like to have a pet at home? What do you think it's like for the pet? Contrast the realism of Slippers and other dog stories—such as Bob Graham's *"Let's*

Get a Pup!" Said Kate—with the fantasy elements found in *The Best Pet of All* by David LaRochelle. Draw pictures of your pets or the pets you'd like to have.

RELATED TITLES: Clements, Andrew. *Naptime for Slippers.* Dutton, 2005. / Flack, Marjorie. *Angus and the Cat.* Doubleday, 1931. / Graham, Bob. *"Let's Get a Pup!" Said Kate.* Candlewick, 2001. / Joosse, Barbara M. *Nugget and Darling.* Clarion, 1997. / Kellogg, Steven. *Pinkerton, Behave.* Dial, 1979. (And others in the Pinkerton series.) / LaRochelle, David. *The Best Pet of All.* Dutton, 2004. / McFarland, Lyn Rossiter. *Widget.* Farrar, 2001. / Miller, Sara Swan. *Three Stories You Can Read to Your Dog.* Houghton Mifflin, 1995. / Rylant, Cynthia. *The Great Gracie Chase.* Scholastic, 2001. / Simont, Marc. *The Stray Dog.* HarperCollins, 2001. / Thayer, Jane. *The Puppy Who Wanted a Boy.* Morrow, 1986. / Wells, Rosemary. *McDuff Comes Home.* Hyperion, 1997. (And others in the McDuff series.)

SUBJECTS: ANIMALS—INFANCY. DOGS. DWELLINGS. HOUSES. HUMAN-ANIMAL RELATIONSHIPS.

140   Cocca-Leffler, Maryann. *Missing: One Stuffed Rabbit.* **Illus. by the author. Albert Whitman, 1998. 0-8075-5161-9. Unp. Gr. K–2**

Ecstatic about bringing home Coco, the brown stuffed rabbit that is the class pet in Mrs. Robin's second grade, Jeanine can't wait to read to him and write journal entries about their time together. On a family trip to the mall, Coco gets lost, and Jeanine is devastated. At school, the class makes "Missing" posters to hang at the mall, where they meet someone who needs the rabbit more than they do.

GERM: You may want to introduce your own new stuffed class pet for children to read to, write about, and take home to love.

RELATED TITLES: Alborough, Jez. *Where's My Teddy?* Candlewick, 1992. / Clark, Emma Chichester. *Where Are You, Blue Kangaroo?* Doubleday, 2000. / Feiffer, Jules. *I Lost My Bear.* Morrow, 1998. / Fitzpatrick, Marie-Louise. *Lizzy and Skunk.* DK Ink, 2000. / Freeman, Don. *Corduroy.* Viking, 1968. / Galbraith, Kathryn O. *Laura Charlotte.* Philomel, 1990. / Ichikawa, Satomi. *La La Rose.* Philomel, 2004. / Sheldon, Dyan. *Love, Your Bear Pete.* Candlewick, 1994. / Smith, Maggie. *Paisley.* Knopf, 2004. / Weiss, Nicki. *Hank and Oogie.* Lothrop, 1987. / Willems, Mo. *Knuffle Bunny: A Cautionary Tale.* Hyperion, 2004.

SUBJECTS: DIARIES. LOST AND FOUND POSSESSIONS. SCHOOLS. STUFFED ANIMALS. TOYS.

141   Cocca-Leffler, Maryann. *Mr. Tanen's Tie Trouble.* **Illus. by the author. Albert Whitman, 2003. 0-8075-5305-0. Unp. Gr. K–3**

With no money left in the school budget to install a promised new playground at Lynnhurst School, principal Mr. Tanen holds a town auction to sell his comprehensive collection of 975 ties.

GERM: What does Mr. Tanen mean when he says to himself, "You have to give to get"? How does this come true? Design new ties for Mr. Tanen to fit an occasion, activity, or mood. If you're feeling ambitious, make ties with fabric and fabric paint, and children can wear theirs to school for Tie Day. Revisit the principal's office with the accompanying books, *Mr. Tanen's Ties* and *Mr. Tanen's Ties Rule.*

RELATED TITLES: Calmenson, Stephanie. *The Frog Principal.* Scholastic, 2001. / Calmenson, Stephanie. *The Principal's New Clothes.* Scholastic, 1989. / Cocca-Leffler, Maryann. *Mr. Tanen's Ties.* Albert Whitman, 1999. / Cocca-Leffler, Maryann. *Mr. Tanen's Ties Rule.* Albert Whitman, 2005. / Creech, Sharon. *A Fine, Fine School.* HarperCollins, 2001. / Polacco, Patricia. *Mr. Lincoln's Way.* Philomel, 2001. / Zimelman, Nathan. *How the Second Grade Got $8,205.50 to Visit the Statue of Liberty.* Albert Whitman, 1992.

SUBJECTS: CLOTHING AND DRESS. GENEROSITY. NECKTIES. PRINCIPALS. SCHOOLS.

142   Cohen, Peter. *Boris's Glasses.* **Illus. by Olof Landström. R&S Books, 2003. 91-29-65942-6. Unp. Gr. PreK–2**

Small brown hamster Boris finds it's not the TV that's fuzzy; it's his astigmatic eyes that need fixing. When the eye doctor gives him glasses, he is taken aback at how well he can see everything.

GERM: What a fitting story for the day the nurse checks everyone's eyes.

RELATED TITLES: Brown, Marc. *Arthur's Eyes.* Little, Brown, 1979. / Hest, Amy. *Baby Duck and the Bad Eyeglasses.* Candlewick, 1996. / Smith, Lane. *Glasses: Who Needs 'Em?* Viking, 1991.

SUBJECTS: EYEGLASSES.

143   Collington, Peter. *Clever Cat.* **Illus. by the author. Knopf, 2000. 0-375-90477-8. Unp. Gr. K–2**

Tired of waiting for his human family to feed him each day, Tibs opens up his own can of cat food and serves himself a generous portion. Amazed, Mrs. Ford gives him first his own front door key and then her cash card; pretty soon, Tibs is shopping, going to movies, and having a great time, until his unsympathetic family insists he find a job. Working as a waiter makes Tibs stop and reevaluate his life compared with all the other cats who snooze the day away.

GERM: Discussion point: How is Tibs a clever cat? Should your pets work to earn their keep? What do your pets do all day, anyway? Compare two clever hind-leg-walking cats and their families: the unappreciated Tibs and the equally clever but well-loved Henry, from the series including *Blue-Ribbon Henry* by Mary Calhoun.

RELATED TITLES: Calhoun, Mary. *Blue-Ribbon Henry.* Morrow, 1999. (And others in the Henry series.) / Ingman, Bruce. *When Martha's Away.* Houghton Mifflin, 1995. / Laden, Nina. *The Night I Followed the Dog.* Chronicle, 1994. / Meddaugh, Susan. *Martha Speaks.* Houghton Mifflin, 1992. / Miller, Sara Swan. *Three Stories You Can Read to Your Cat.* Houghton Mifflin, 1997. / Rathmann, Peggy. *Officer Buckle and Gloria.* Putnam, 1995. / Seligson, Susan, and Howie Schneider. *Amos: The Story of an Old Dog and His Couch.* Little, Brown, 1987. / Whayne, Susanne. *Petropolis.* Handprint, 2003.

SUBJECTS: CATS. WORK.

144 Collins, Suzanne. *When Charlie McButton Lost Power.* Illus. by Mike Lester. Putnam, 2005. 0-399-24000-4. Unp. Gr. K–2

Computer-obsessed Charlie is dumbfounded and devastated when lightning knocks out the electricity and he has to find something without plugs to play with. Greedily appropriating his little sister Isabel Jane's triple-A battery from her talking dolly to power up an old handheld gadget lands Charlie in the time-out chair. Feeling guilty, Charlie plays hide-and-seek with Isabel Jane, which turns out to be fun and leads to a day of actual child-like play before the lights come back on. All of this is dispatched in rambunctious and impetuous cartoons that perfectly capture the range of strong emotions Charlie hurtles through in one day.

GERM: Explore all the issues here: power failures and what you do when the lights go out, the overdependence on technology, the value of free play and imagination, and how to have fun with your siblings. Make charts of how you spend your free time to calculate the ratio between free imaginative play and sit-in-a-chair-and-stare entertainment. While lots of schools sponsor No TV weeks, it may be telling to evaluate the differences between children's physical and mental activities. Meet another computer game-crazed kid in *Power and Glory* by Emily Rodda.

RELATED TITLES: Dewan, Ted. *Crispin, the Pig Who Had It All.* Doubleday, 2000. / Feiffer, Jules. *Meanwhile . . .* HarperCollins, 1997. / Florczak, Robert. *Yikes!!!* Scholastic, 2003. / Grey, Mini. *Traction Man Is Here!* Knopf, 2005. / MacLean, Christine Kole. *Even Firefighters Hug Their Moms.* Dutton, 2002. / O'Connor, George. *Kapow!* Simon & Schuster, 2004. / Rodda, Emily. *Power and Glory.* Greenwillow, 1996. / Steig, William. *Pete's a Pizza.* HarperCollins, 1998.

SUBJECTS: BROTHERS AND SISTERS. COMPUTER GAMES. ELECTRICITY. EMOTIONS. GAMES. IMAGINATION. PLAY. POWER FAILURES. STORIES IN RHYME.

145 Compestine, Ying Chang. *The Runaway Rice Cake.* Illus. by Tungwai Chau. Simon & Schuster, 2001. 0-689-82972-8. Unp. Gr. PreK–2

"Ai yo! I don't think so!" cries the Chang family's rice cake as it pops out of the steamer, into the courtyard, and through the village. When the rice cake, or nián-gāo, collides with an old woman, Momma and Poppa offer to share it with her, even though their own three little boys are very hungry. Though the old woman eats the whole thing, the family is rewarded for its generosity both by their neighbors bearing food for the Chinese New Year celebration, and by magic bowls of food that appear on their table.

GERM: Pull in versions of "The Gingerbread Boy" to see how it was incorporated into this original folktale, and tie it in as well to your classroom Chinese New Year celebration. There's even a recipe at the back of the book for baked or steamed nián-gāo. *Moonbeams, Dumplings and Dragon Boats* by Nina Simonds and Leslie Swartz offers more background, recipes, and stories about the holiday. Note how generosity is rewarded in another Chinese village in *The Beggar's Magic* by Margaret and Raymond Chang.

RELATED TITLES: Aylesworth, Jim. *The Gingerbread Man.* Scholastic, 1998. / Chang, Margaret, and Raymond Chang. *The Beggar's Magic: A Chinese Tale.* McElderry, 1997. / Cole, Joanna. *Ms. Frizzle's Adventures: Imperial China.* Scholastic, 2005. / Compestine, Ying Chang. *The Story of Noodles.* Holiday House, 2002. / Cook, Scott. *The Gingerbread Boy.* Knopf, 1987. / Howland, Naomi. *The Matzah Man: A Passover Story.* Clarion, 2002. / Kimmel, Eric A. *The Rooster's Antlers: A Story of the Chinese Zodiac.* Holiday House, 1999. / Kimmel, Eric A. *The Runaway Tortilla.* Winslow, 2000. / Sawyer, Ruth. *The Remarkable Christmas of the Cobbler's Sons.* Viking, 1994. / Shulman, Lisa. *The Matzo Ball Boy.* Dutton, 2005. / Simonds, Nina, and Leslie Swartz. *Moonbeams, Dumplings and Dragon Boats: A Treasury of Chinese Holiday Tales, Activities and Recipes.* Harcourt, 2002. / Wallace, Ian. *Chin*

Chiang and the Dragon Dance. Atheneum, 1984. / Young, Ed. *Cat and Rat: The Legend of the Chinese Zodiac.* Henry Holt, 1995.

SUBJECTS: CHINA. CHINESE NEW YEAR. FAMILY LIFE. FOOD. GENEROSITY. GINGERBREAD BOY. RICE. STORIES TO TELL.

146   **Compestine, Ying Chang.** *The Story of Chopsticks.* **Illus. by YongSheng Xuan. Holiday House, 2001. 0-8234-1526-0. Unp. Gr. K–4**

Long ago, when people in China ate with their hands, Kùai, the youngest of three boys in the Kang family, plucked two long sticks from the kindling pile to spear his too-hot dinner, thus inventing the first chopsticks. According to the Author's Note for this charming fictional tale, illustrated with traditional Chinese-style cut paper overlaid against brightly colored backgrounds, chopsticks originated in China as early as the 11th century B.C.

GERM: The author includes Chinese rules for eating with chopsticks, instructions on how to use them, and a recipe for Sweet Eight Treasures Rice Pudding. You can buy inexpensive packets of chopsticks at your local supermarket or Chinese restaurant. If you have access to a stove, make a nice vegetable stirfry and rice so children can practice using their quick sticks. If not, use fruit cut into small pieces. Other good companion reads include *Cleversticks* by Bernard Ashley, about a preschooler who demonstrates his chopsticks expertise for his classmates, and Ina R. Friedman's *How My Parents Learned to Eat.* Discuss: What are the rules for proper eating in your family? Read Patricia Lauber's *What You Never Knew About Fingers, Forks, and Chopsticks* for a humorous but true history of food customs and manners around the world.

RELATED TITLES: Ashley, Bernard. *Cleversticks.* Random House, 1995. / Cole, Joanna. *Ms. Frizzle's Adventures: Imperial China.* Scholastic, 2005. / Compestine, Ying Chang. *The Story of Kites.* Holiday House, 2003. / Compestine, Ying Chang. *The Story of Paper.* Holiday House, 2003. / Davol, Marguerite. *The Paper Dragon.* Atheneum, 1997. / Friedman, Ina R. *How My Parents Learned to Eat.* Houghton Mifflin, 1984. / Hong, Lily Toy. *How the Ox Star Fell from Heaven.* Albert Whitman, 1991. / Lauber, Patricia. *What You Never Knew About Fingers, Forks, and Chopsticks.* Simon & Schuster, 1999. / Lin, Grace. *Fortune Cookie Fortunes.* Knopf, 2004. / Mahy, Margaret. *The Seven Chinese Brothers.* Scholastic, 1990. / Mosel, Arlene. *Tikki Tikki Tembo.* Dutton, 1972. / Rumford, James. *The Cloudmakers.* Houghton Mifflin, 1996. / Wong, Janet. *Apple Pie 4th of July.* Harcourt, 2002. / Yee, Paul. *Roses Sing on New Snow.* Macmillan, 1992.

SUBJECTS: CHINA. EMPERORS. FOOD. FOOD HABITS. INVENTIONS AND INVENTORS. MULTICULTURAL BOOKS. POURQUOI TALES. TABLEWARE.

147   **Compestine, Ying Chang.** *The Story of Paper.* **Illus. by YongSheng Xuan. Holiday House, 2003. 0-8234-1705-0. Unp. Gr. K–4**

Wanting to be able to write on something better than the ground or their hands, the three inventive Kang brothers discover a way to mash together scraps of fabric and twigs to make thin white sheets of something they name *zhi*, the Chinese word for paper. From the author's note, we learn that the oldest pieces of paper that still exist were found in a Chinese tomb dating back to the Han dynasty, 206 B.C. to 220 A.D., and that the two Chinese characters for paper combine the words for silk and cloth.

GERM: Instructions for making homemade garden paper out of roses or other flowers or plants are on the last page. After reading the other stories about the Kang brothers (*The Story of Chopsticks, The Story of Kites,* and *The Story of Noodles*), children can write new pourquoi tales about other useful items the boys might have invented. This also ties in nicely to a possible lesson about the history of books and writing and the development of libraries.

RELATED TITLES: Auch, Mary Jane. *The Princess and the Pizza.* Holiday House, 2002. / Cole, Joanna. *Ms. Frizzle's Adventures: Imperial China.* Scholastic, 2005. / Compestine, Ying Chang. *The Story of Chopsticks.* Holiday House, 2001. / Compestine, Ying Chang. *The Story of Kites.* Holiday House, 2003. / Compestine, Ying Chang. *The Story of Noodles.* Holiday House, 2002. / Davol, Marguerite. *The Paper Dragon.* Atheneum, 1997. / Leedy, Loreen. *Look at My Book: How Kids Can Write and Illustrate Terrific Books.* Holiday House, 2004. / Mahy, Margaret. *The Seven Chinese Brothers.* Scholastic, 1990. / Mosel, Arlene. *Tikki Tikki Tembo.* Dutton, 1972. / Rumford, James. *The Cloudmakers.* Houghton Mifflin, 1996. / Yee, Paul. *Roses Sing on New Snow.* Macmillan, 1992.

SUBJECTS: BEHAVIOR. BROTHERS. CHINA. EMPERORS. INVENTIONS AND INVENTORS. PAPER. POURQUOI TALES. SCHOOLS.

148   **Connor, Leslie.** *Miss Bridie Chose a Shovel.* **Illus. by Mary Azarian. Houghton Mifflin, 2004. 0-618-30564-5. Unp. Gr. 1–4**

We follow Miss Bridie, a young woman in a long dress, as she carries her practical shovel with her across the ocean in 1856 and makes a good life for herself in America with a newfound husband, children, and a farm on a hill. The rhythm of the prose makes it feel like a poem, and the sensible, homespun woodcut illustrations depict the life cycle of a family.

GERM: Discuss: What role did the shovel play in Miss Bridie's life? Sing the song "When I First Came to This Land."

RELATED TITLES: Bunting, Eve. *Dandelions*. Harcourt, 1995. / Guthrie, Woody. *This Land Is Your Land*. Little, Brown, 1998. / Hall, Donald. *Ox-Cart Man*. Viking, 1979. / Houston, Gloria. *My Great Aunt Arizona*. HarperCollins, 1992. / Johnston, Tony. *Yonder*. Dial, 1988. / Maestro, Betsy. *Coming to America: The Story of Immigration*. Scholastic, 1996. / Shannon, George. *This Is the Bird*. Houghton Mifflin, 1997. / Taback, Simms. *Joseph Had a Little Overcoat*. Viking, 1999. / Ziefert, Harriet. *When I First Came to This Land*. Putnam, 1998.

SUBJECTS: FARM LIFE. HISTORICAL FICTION. IMMIGRATION AND EMIGRATION. SHOVELS. TOOLS.

149 **Cook, Sally.** *Good Night Pillow Fight.* **Illus. by Laura Cornell. HarperCollins, 2004. 0-06-205190-3. Unp. Gr. PreK–1**

Look in the windows of one block of city apartments and spy on all those kids who don't want to go to bed and their parents desperately cajoling, yelling, and insisting. The simple rhyming text and wild watercolors depict the age-old struggle of wide-awake kids bouncing about the bedroom and parents at the end of their ropes.

GERM: Have your wide-awakers draw, write, and tell about what they do when it's bedtime. This title joins other raucous, non-sleepy bedtime stories such as Kate Lum's *What! Cried Granny: An Almost Bedtime Story*, Peggy Rathmann's *Ten Minutes Till Bedtime* and Laura Simms's *The Squeaky Door*.

RELATED TITLES: Appelt, Kathi. *Bubba and Beau Go Night-Night*. Harcourt, 2003. / Curtis, Jamie Lee. *It's Hard to Be Five: Learning How to Work My Control Panel*. HarperCollins, 2004. / Kellogg, Steven. *A-Hunting We Will Go!* Morrow, 1998. / Lum, Kate. *What! Cried Granny: An Almost Bedtime Story*. Dial, 1999. / Markes, Julie. *Shhhhh! Everybody's Sleeping*. HarperCollins, 2005. / Mathews, Judith, and Fay Robinson. *Nathaniel Willy, Scared Silly*. Bradbury, 1994. / Pinkney, Andrea Davis. *Sleeping Cutie*. Harcourt, 2004. / Rathmann, Peggy. *Good Night, Gorilla*. Putnam, 1994. / Rathmann, Peggy. *Ten Minutes Till Bedtime*. Putnam, 1998. / Rothstein, Gloria. *Sheep Asleep*. HarperCollins, 2003. / Simms, Laura. *The Squeaky Door*. Crown, 1991. / Whybrow, Ian. *The Noisy Way to Bed*. Scholastic, 2004. / Yolen, Jane. *How Do Dinosaurs Say Good Night?* Blue Sky/Scholastic, 2000.

SUBJECTS: APARTMENT HOUSES. BEDTIME STORIES. PARENT AND CHILD. STORIES IN RHYME.

150 **Cooper, Helen.** *Pumpkin Soup.* **Illus. by the author. Farrar, 1999. 0-374-36164-9. Unp. Gr. PreK–1**

Duck decides he wants to take over Squirrel's job stirring the pumpkin soup, the best you have ever tasted, and storms off in a huff when Cat and Squirrel won't allow it.

GERM: Talk it over: what are the friends' special jobs and talents? Should Duck be allowed to stir the soup? How do you make up with your friends when you have an argument? There's a recipe for pumpkin soup, if you're feeling ambitious. Everyone can stir. The threesome returns in *A Pipkin of Pepper*. Note what happens when the friends won't help with the cooking in Helen Ketteman's *Armadilly Chili* and Philemon Sturges's *The Little Red Hen (Makes a Pizza)*.

RELATED TITLES: Barton, Byron. *The Wee Little Woman*. HarperCollins, 1995. / Cooper, Helen. *A Pipkin of Pepper*. Farrar, 2005. / Everitt, Betsy. *Mean Soup*. Harcourt, 1992. / Freymann, Saxton, and Joost Elffers. *How Are You Peeling? Foods with Moods*. Scholastic, 1999. / Fuchs, Diane Marcial. *A Bear for All Seasons*. Henry Holt, 1995. / Ketteman, Helen. *Armadilly Chili*. Albert Whitman, 2004. / Rohmann, Eric. *My Friend Rabbit*. Roaring Brook, 2002. / Steig, William. *Pete's a Pizza*. HarperCollins, 1998. / Stevens, Janet, and Susan Stevens Crummel. *Cook-a-Doodle-Doo!* Harcourt, 1999. / Sturges, Philemon. *The Little Red Hen (Makes a Pizza)*. Dutton, 1999.

SUBJECTS: ARGUMENTS. CATS. CONFLICT RESOLUTION. COOKERY. DUCKS. FRIENDSHIP. PUMPKINS. RUNAWAYS. SOUP. SQUIRRELS.

151 **Coots, J. Fred, and Haven Gillespie.** *Santa Claus Is Comin' to Town.* **Illus. by Steven Kellogg. HarperCollins, 2004. 0-06-623849-8. Unp. Gr. PreK–2**

Steven Kellogg is at the top of his game in this seasonably bright, outrageously over-the-top illustrated version of the famous song. This is a gift book of the Christmas season that no Santa lover should be without.

GERM: What you may know—and I didn't until I saw the book—is that the song has an introduction, as well as several other verses. So get your music teacher to teach the kids the rest of the tune and sing along with Kellogg's glorious version of it.

RELATED TITLES: Bolam, Emily. *The Twelve Days of Christmas.* Atheneum, 1997. / Brett, Jan. *The Twelve Days of Christmas.* Putnam, 1990. / Burningham, John. *Harvey Slumfenberger's Christmas Present.* Candlewick, 1993. / Joyce, William. *Santa Calls.* HarperCollins, 1993. / Kimmel, Elizabeth Cody. *My Penguin Osbert.* Candlewick, 2004. / Krensky, Stephen. *How Santa Got His Job.* Simon & Schuster, 1998. / Krensky, Stephen. *How Santa Lost His Job.* Simon & Schuster, 2001. / McPhail, David. *Santa's Book of Names.* Little, Brown, 1993. / Palatini, Margie. *Elf Help.* Hyperion, 1997. / Pearson, Tracey Campbell. *Where Does Joe Go?* Farrar, 1999. / Primavera, Elise. *Auntie Claus.* Harcourt, 1999. / Sabuda, Robert. *The 12 Days of Christmas: A Pop-Up Celebration.* Simon & Schuster, 1996. / Van Allsburg, Chris. *The Polar Express.* Houghton Mifflin, 1985. / Wells, Rosemary. *Max's Christmas.* Dial, 1986.

SUBJECTS: CHRISTMAS. CHRISTMAS MUSIC. SANTA CLAUS. SONGS. STORIES IN RHYME.

152   **Coppinger, Tom. *Curse in Reverse.* Illus. by Dirk Zimmer. Atheneum, 2003. 0-689-83096-3. Unp. Gr. 1–4**

An old witch named Agnezza curses the folk of Hamburg for refusing her a bed for the night. Although poor childless Mr. and Mrs. Trotter do offer to share their small house and supper with her, she still gives them the Curse of the One-armed Man.

GERM: Have your listeners predict how this curse will play itself out and laugh together over the results of each of the witch's predictions. Good behavior, generosity, and kindness are also rewarded in Robert Baden's *And Sunday Makes Seven*; Joanne Oppenheim's retelling of the Brothers Grimm tale, *One Gift Deserves Another*; and Ruth Sawyer's *The Remarkable Christmas of the Cobbler's Sons*.

RELATED TITLES: Baden, Robert. *And Sunday Makes Seven.* Albert Whitman, 1990. / Grimm, Jacob. *One Gift Deserves Another.* Retold by Joanne Oppenheim. Dutton, 1992. / Melmed, Laura Krauss. *The Rainbabies.* Lothrop, 1992. / Sawyer, Ruth. *The Remarkable Christmas of the Cobbler's Sons.* Viking, 1994.

SUBJECTS: BABIES. GENEROSITY. KINDNESS. STORIES TO TELL. WITCHES.

153   **Cordsen, Carol Foskett. *The Milkman.* Illus. by Douglas B. Jones. Dutton, 2005. 0-525-47208-8. Unp. Gr. PreK–1**

Rhyming staccato couplets describe the workday of Mr. Plimpton, a milkman, as he rises before dawn, loads his milk truck at the farm, and heads off on his delivery rounds, accompanied by his orange cat. Full-bleed double-page illustrations reminiscent of Lois Lenski and cartoon art of the 1940s take us back to simpler days.

GERM: Children will be charmed to discover that milk in glass bottles was once delivered to one's door. They'll follow the secondary story in the pictures of a little lost dog who follows the milkman on his rounds. Explore how we get our milk with nonfiction books such as *Milk: From Cow to Carton* by Aliki, and sidestep into a story of a kitten who thinks the moon is a bowl of milk in *Kitten's First Full Moon* by Kevin Henkes.

RELATED TITLES: Aliki. *Milk: From Cow to Carton.* HarperCollins, 1992. / Cooper, Elisha. *Ice Cream.* Greenwillow, 2002. / Gibbons, Gail. *The Milk Makers.* Atheneum, 1985. / Henkes, Kevin. *Kitten's First Full Moon.* Greenwillow, 2004. / Pilkey, Dav. *The Paperboy.* Orchard, 1996. / Taus-Bolstad, Stacy. *From Grass to Milk.* Lerner, 2004. / Thoennes Keller, Kristin. *From Milk to Ice Cream.* Capstone, 2005. / Wolfman, Judy. *Life on a Dairy Farm.* Carolrhoda, 2004.

SUBJECTS: DAIRY PRODUCTS. DELIVERY OF GOODS. DOGS. LOST. MILK. MORNING. STORIES IN RHYME.

154   **Corey, Shana. *First Graders from Mars: Episode 1: Horus's Horrible Day.* Illus. by Mark Teague. Scholastic, 2001. 0-439-26220-8. 32pp. Gr. PreK–2**

Faced with a lot of tough schoolwork from his new teacher (the five-eyed Mrs. Vortex) and the taunts of a teasing classmate, Martian first grader Horus wishes he could go back to the good old days of martiangarten with its familiar slime table, snooze mats, and snacks.

GERM: Have your earthlings fold a piece of paper in half (like a hamburger; not lengthwise, like a hot dog). On one side, they can draw themselves at school on the first day, incorporating details from their new classroom. On the other side, they can draw themselves as Martians, adding out-of-this-world touches to their alien environment.

RELATED TITLES: Bush, Timothy. *Benjamin McFadden and the Robot Babysitter.* Crown, 1998. / Corey, Shana. *First Graders from Mars series.* Scholastic. / Cox, Judy. *The West Texas Chili Monster.* BridgeWater, 1998. / Henkes, Kevin. *Chrysanthemum.* Greenwillow, 1991. / Henkes, Kevin. *Wemberly Worried.* Greenwillow, 2000. /

London, Jonathan. *Froggy Goes to School*. Viking, 1996. / McGhee, Alison. *Countdown to Kindergarten*. Harcourt, 2002. / McNaughton, Colin. *Here Come the Aliens*. Candlewick, 1995. / Sadler, Marilyn. *Alistair in Outer Space*. Prentice-Hall, 1984. / Scieszka, Jon. *Baloney (Henry P.)*. Viking, 2001. / Shields, Carol Diggory. *Martian Rock*. Candlewick, 1999. / Van Allsburg, Chris. *Zathura*. Houghton Mifflin, 2002. / Yorinks, Arthur. *Company's Coming*. Hyperion, 2000.

SUBJECTS: EXTRATERRESTRIAL LIFE. FIRST DAY OF SCHOOL. FRIENDSHIP. MARS (PLANET). SCHOOLS. SCIENCE FICTION.

155 **Corey, Shana.** ***Players in Pigtails.*** **Illus. by Rebecca Gibbon. Scholastic, 2003. 0-439-18305-7. Unp. Gr. 1–5**

Disinterested in traditional "girl" pursuits, Katie Casey dreamed baseball. When the All-American Girls Professional Baseball League scouted for players in 1943, Katie signed up with the Kenosha Comets. Katie is a fictional character, but she is modeled on all of those baseball-mad women who played pro ball during World War II.

GERM: Simply told and illustrated with cheerful, spirited watercolors and colored pencils, this slice-of-life episode from sports history will get everyone eager to go outside and play a little ball. Did you know there are additional verses to Jack Norworth's classic 1908 baseball anthem, "Take Me Out to the Ballgame"? They start, "Katie Casey was baseball mad. Had the fever and had it bad." The words are on the endpapers; locate the music on Google.com so you can sing it together. Read aloud the Author's Note as a spur to further research into famous female or African American players of the past.

RELATED TITLES: Adler, David A. *Lou Gehrig: The Luckiest Man*. Harcourt, 1997. / Cline-Ransome, Lesa. *Satchel Paige*. Simon & Schuster, 2000. / Corey, Shana. *You Forgot Your Skirt, Amelia Bloomer!* Scholastic, 2000. / Golenbock, Peter. *Teammates*. Harcourt, 1990. / Hamm, Mia. *Winners Never Quit!* HarperCollins, 2004. / Hopkinson, Deborah. *Girl Wonder: A Baseball Story in Nine Innings*. Atheneum, 2003. / Janeczko, Paul. *That Sweet Diamond: Baseball Poems*. Atheneum, 1998. / Mochizuki, Ken. *Baseball Saved Us*. Lee & Low, 1993. / Moss, Marissa. *Mighty Jackie, the Strike-Out Queen*. Simon & Schuster, 2004. / Norworth, Jack. *Take Me Out to the Ball Game*. Four Winds, 1993. / Patrick, Jean L. S. *The Girl Who Struck Out Babe Ruth*. Carolrhoda, 2000. / Waber, Bernard. *Gina*. Houghton Mifflin, 1995.

SUBJECTS: ATHLETES. BASEBALL. HISTORICAL FICTION. SEX ROLE. SPORTS. WOMEN.

156 **Cowan, Catherine.** ***My Life with the Wave.*** **Illus. by Mark Buehner. Lothrop, 1997. 0-688-12661-8. Unp. Gr. 1–5**

A young boy brings his new seaside vacation friend, an ocean wave, back to his house, where they romp together until the wave's mood turns bleak and stormy.

GERM: Based on a story by Mexican novelist and poet Octavio Paz, this quirky and lyrical story with its sweeping waterlogged paintings will mesmerize children of all ages. Introduce the term "personification" and have children describe the wave's changing personality. Then ask them to extend the sly ending by writing and illustrating what their own experiences would be if they brought a cloud home from vacation.

RELATED TITLES: Arnold, Tedd. *No More Water in the Tub!* Dial, 1995. / Cummings, Pat. *C.L.O.U.D.S.* Lothrop, 1986. / Dayrell, Elphinstone. *Why the Sun and Moon Live in the Sky*. Houghton Mifflin, 1968. / dePaola, Tomie. *The Cloud Book*. Holiday House, 1975. / Dorros, Walter. *Follow the Water from Brook to Ocean*. HarperCollins, 1991. / Frasier, Debra. *The Incredible Water Show*. Harcourt, 2004. / Graham, Joan Bransfield. *Splish Splash*. Ticknor & Fields, 1994. / Jackson, Shelley. *The Old Woman and the Wave*. DK Ink, 1998. / Karas, G. Brian. *Atlantic*. Putnam, 2002. / Kerley, Barbara. *A Cool Drink of Water*. National Geographic, 2002. / Lewis, J. Patrick. *Earth Verses and Water Rhymes*. Atheneum, 1991. / Locker, Thomas. *Water Dance*. Harcourt, 1997. / Peters, Lisa Westberg. *Water's Way*. Little, Brown, 1991. / Wick, Walter. *A Drop of Water*. Scholastic, 1997. / Wiesner, David. *Sector 7*. Clarion, 1999.

SUBJECTS: FANTASY. FRIENDSHIP. OCEAN. PERSONIFICATION. PICTURE BOOKS FOR ALL AGES. WATER.

157 **Cowley, Joy.** ***Big Moon Tortilla.*** **Illus. by Dyanne Strongbow. Boyds Mills, 1998. 1-56397-601-3. Unp. Gr. K–2**

Out in the southwestern desert of Arizona, after her homework blows out the window and is chewed by dogs and her glasses break in two when she steps on the ear-piece, Marta Enos runs crying to her grandmother. Grandmother tells a Native American healing story that lays out four ways to deal with a problem. Should one be a tree, standing tall, and looking all ways at once; a rock, sitting still and saying nothing; a mountain lion, fierce and fighting for what's right; or an eagle, flying high and laughing at small problems far below?

GERM: Before Marta Enos seeks Grandmother's counsel, ask your listeners what Marta Enos should do about her disasters. Discuss Grandmother's four wise ways of looking at a problem. Make that text-to-life connection, thinking of times you have used each approach. Are there any other ways you handle a problem? See how Spider deals with being scared to be in the school spelling bee in *Brave as a Mountain Lion* by Ann Herbert Scott.

RELATED TITLES: Howe, James. *Pinky and Rex and the Bully.* Atheneum, 1996. / Kimmel, Eric A. *The Runaway Tortilla.* Winslow, 2000. / Schertle, Alice. *Down the Road.* Harcourt, 1995. / Scott, Ann Herbert. *Brave as a Mountain Lion.* Clarion, 1996.

SUBJECTS: ARIZONA. CRYING. DESERTS. GRANDMOTHERS. HOMEWORK. INDIANS OF NORTH AMERICA. PROBLEM SOLVING. SOUTHWEST.

158   Cowley, Joy. *Gracias, the Thanksgiving Turkey.* Illus. by Joe Cepeda. Scholastic, 1996. 0-590-46976-2. Unp. Gr. K–2

Miguel's truck-driving dad sends him a present to fatten for Thanksgiving: a large, lovable turkey that Miguel names Gracias. But as Miguel discovers, it's not easy to keep a turkey in his grandparents' New York City apartment.

GERM: There's a glossary of Spanish language words and phrases at the back, though most can be figured out in the context of the narrative. Meet more turkey rescuers in Dav Pilkey's *'Twas the Night Before Thanksgiving.* Then celebrate the continued good health of Miguel's pet turkey by singing a round of *I Know an Old Lady Who Swallowed a Pie* by Alison Jackson.

RELATED TITLES: Jackson, Alison. *I Know an Old Lady Who Swallowed a Pie.* Dutton, 1997. / Lakin, Patricia. *Fat Chance Thanksgiving.* Albert Whitman, 2001. / Pilkey, Dav. *'Twas the Night Before Thanksgiving.* Scholastic, 1990. / Spinelli, Eileen. *Thanksgiving at the Tappleton's.* HarperCollins, 2003.

SUBJECTS: HISPANIC AMERICANS. MULTICULTURAL BOOKS. NEW YORK CITY. PUERTO RICANS. SPANISH LANGUAGE. THANKSGIVING. TURKEYS.

159   Cox, Judy. *Don't Be Silly, Mrs. Millie!* Illus. by Joe Mathieu. Marshall Cavendish, 2005. 0-7614-5166-8. Unp. Gr. PreK–1

According to the kindergartners, their teacher Mrs. Millie says everything wrong and they have to correct her all the time. She says such things as "Please hang up your goats," and "Get out your paper and penguins," which lead the children to howl, "Don't be silly, Mrs. Millie! You mean our coats!" or "You mean our papers and pencils." Jolly, colorful illustrations picture the children interacting with each animal their teacher names, writing with the bills of congenial penguins, for instance.

GERM: Your listeners will join in on the title refrain and finish the sentence, "You mean . . ." The inventive wordplay will stretch children's sense of language, and you can continue to baffle and entertain them with more puns.

RELATED TITLES: Arnold, Tedd. *Even More Parts: Idioms from Head to Toe.* Dial, 2004. / Arnold, Tedd. *Parts.* Dial, 1997. / Arnold, Tedd. *More Parts.* Dial, 2001. / Brennan-Nelson, Denise. *My Momma Likes to Say.* Sleeping Bear, 2003. / Brennan-Nelson, Denise. *My Teacher Likes to Say.* Sleeping Bear, 2004. / Clement, Rod. *Just Another Ordinary Day.* HarperCollins, 1997. / Clements, Andrew. *Double Trouble in Walla Walla.* Millbrook, 1998. / Gwynne, Fred. *A Chocolate Moose for Dinner.* Dutton, 1976. / Gwynne, Fred. *The King Who Rained.* Dutton, 1970. / Parish, Peggy. *Amelia Bedelia.* HarperCollins, 1963. (And others in the Amelia Bedelia series.) / Reiss, Mike. *The Great Show-and-Tell Disaster.* Price Stern Sloan, 2001.

SUBJECTS: SCHOOLS. TEACHERS. WORD GAMES.

160   Cox, Judy. *Go to Sleep, Groundhog!* Illus. by Paul Meisel. Holiday House, 2003. 0-8234-1645-3. Unp. Gr. PreK–2

Groundhog sets his alarm for February 2, but he can't fall asleep. Half-past October, he goes out for a walk and observes things he's never seen before, including children in costumes, trick or treating. Halloween Witch flies him home on her broomstick and reads him a nice bedtime story, but he's up again for Thanksgiving and then for Christmas, encountering both Turkey and Santa Claus.

GERM: Festive seasonal acrylic-and-gouache paintings will get revelers in the winter holiday spirit, and a factual Afterword about Groundhog Day provides some interesting facts. Story starter: What would happen if Groundhog overslept until February 14?

RELATED TITLES: Cherry, Lynne. *How Groundhog's Garden Grew.* Scholastic, 2003. / Fleming, Denise. *Time to Sleep.* Henry Holt, 1997. / Fuchs, Diane Marcial. *A Bear for All Seasons.* Henry Holt, 1995. / Minarik, Else Holmelund. *It's Spring!* Greenwillow, 1989. / Peters, Lisa Westberg. *Cold Little Duck, Duck, Duck.* Greenwillow, 2000. / Swallow, Pamela Curtis. *Groundhog Gets a Say*. Putnam, 2005. / Waber, Bernard. *Bearsie Bear and the Surprise Sleepover Party*. Houghton Mifflin, 1997. / Wilson, Karma. *Bear Snores On*. McElderry, 2002. / Wilson, Karma. *Bear Stays Up for Christmas*. McElderry, 2004. / Wilson, Karma. *Bear Wants More*. McElderry, 2003.

SUBJECTS: GROUNDHOG DAY. GROUNDHOGS. HOLIDAYS. SEASONS. SLEEP. WINTER.

161 **Cox, Judy. *My Family Plays Music*. Illus. by Elbrite Brown. Holiday House, 2003. 0-8234-1591-0. Unp. Gr. K–3**

A young African American girl introduces us to each member of her musical family—including her mom, who plays fiddle in a country and western band, and her dad, who plays cello in a string quartet—and shows the percussion instruments she plays to accompany them.

GERM: Bring in the small percussion instruments from the music room—maracas, cowbells, triangles—and put on a group percussion concert. Children can each make a poster of their own family members, showing what musical instruments each plays. Or use this book to talk about common interests and have kids make posters showing each family member, and what he or she loves to do most.

RELATED TITLES: Aliki. *Ah, Music!* HarperCollins, 2003. / Curtis, Gavin. *The Bat Boy and His Violin*. Simon & Schuster, 1998. / Goss, Linda. *The Frog Who Wanted to Be a Singer*. Orchard, 1996. / Howe, James. *Horace and Morris Join the Chorus (But What About Dolores?)*. Atheneum, 2002. / Krull, Kathleen. *Lives of the Musicians: Good Times, Bad Times (And What the Neighbors Thought)*. Harcourt, 1993. / Krull, Kathleen. *M Is for Music*. Harcourt, 2003. / Millman, Isaac. *Moses Goes to a Concert*. Farrar, 1998. / Moss, Lloyd. *Music Is*. Putnam, 2003. / Ober, Hal. *How Music Came to the World*. Houghton Mifflin, 1994. / Ryan, Pam Muñoz. *When Marian Sang*. Scholastic, 2002. / Weaver, Tess. *Opera Cat*. Clarion, 2002.

SUBJECTS: FAMILY LIFE. MUSIC. MUSICAL INSTRUMENTS. MUSICIANS.

162 **Cox, Judy. *Now We Can Have a Wedding*. Illus. by DyAnne Ryan. Holiday House, 1998. 0-8234-1342-X. Unp. Gr. K–2**

A young girl describes how everyone in her apartment building is getting ready for her sister Sallie's wedding by cooking irresistible international delicacies. She helps to prepare the tantalizing multiethnic feast, whipping up dolmades with her Greek papa, tamales with the father of the groom, Jewish challah, and Italian biscotti.

GERM: Children can look up recipes and plan the menu they'd most like to serve at their own weddings or birthday parties.

RELATED TITLES: Barasch, Lynne. *The Reluctant Flower Girl*. HarperCollins, 2001. / DiSalvo-Ryan, DyAnne. *Uncle Willie and the Soup Kitchen*. Morrow, 1991. / Dooley, Norah. *Everybody Bakes Bread*. Carolrhoda, 1996. / Dooley, Norah. *Everybody Cooks Rice*. Carolrhoda, 1991. / English, Karen. *Nadia's Hands*. Boyds Mills, 1999. / Park, Barbara. *Junie B. Jones Is (Almost) a Flower Girl*. Random House, 1999. / Shelby, Anne. *Potluck*. Orchard, 1991. / Soto, Gary. *Snapshots from the Wedding*. Putnam, 1997. / Wing, Natasha. *Jalapeño Bagels*. Atheneum, 1996. / Wong, Janet. *Apple Pie 4th of July*. Harcourt, 2002.

SUBJECTS: COOKERY. FOOD. MULTICULTURAL BOOKS. SISTERS. WEDDINGS.

163 **Cox, Judy. *Rabbit Pirates: A Tale of the Spinach Main*. Illus. by Emily Arnold McCully. Harcourt, 1999. 0-15-201832-8. Unp. Gr. K–2**

Former rabbit pirates Monsieurs Lapin and Blanc are content running their small café in Provence until Monsieur Reynard, a wily fox, decides to become a patron. He says, "I look forward to eating you—I mean, eating here again, soon." Though the two rabbits have given up their old fighting ways, they come up with a delicious plan to outfox him.

GERM: Photocopy the pages with dialogue and let small groups of kids take parts, reading aloud with feeling and in character. Bring in vegetarian cookbooks and show them how to read a recipe. For a different type of writing, first have children create a vegetarian recipe for the restaurant, listing the ingredients, and writing instructions for cooking in sequence. (The younger the writers, the funnier the recipes will be.) Bring in vegetables and have them taste some. Other spicy food-based stories include Mike Artell's *Petite Rouge: A Cajun Red Riding Hood* and Judy Cox's *The West Texas Chili Monster*.

RELATED TITLES: Allard, Harry. *It's So Nice to Have a Wolf Around the House*. Houghton Mifflin, 1978. / Artell, Mike. *Petite Rouge: A Cajun Red Riding Hood*. Dial, 2001. / Cox, Judy. *The West Texas Chili Monster*. BridgeWater, 1998. / Fleming, Candace. *When Agnes Caws*. Atheneum, 1999. / Ketteman, Helen. *Armadilly Chili*. Albert Whitman, 2004. / Long, Melinda. *How I Became a Pirate*. Harcourt, 2003. / Marshall, James. *Swine Lake*. HarperCollins, 1999. / Meddaugh, Susan. *Hog-Eye*. Houghton Mifflin, 1995. / Palatini, Margie. *Zoom Broom*. Hyperion, 1998. / Rayner, Mary. *Mr. and Mrs. Pig's Evening Out*. Atheneum, 1976. / Scieszka, Jon. *The*

True Story of the 3 Little Pigs. Viking, 1989. / Stevens, Janet, and Susan Stevens Crummel. *Cook-a-Doodle-Doo!* Harcourt, 1999. / Sturges, Philemon. *The Little Red Hen (Makes a Pizza).* Dutton, 1999. / Wattenberg, Jane. *Henny-Penny.* Scholastic, 2000.

SUBJECTS: FOXES. FRIENDSHIP. HUMOROUS FICTION. PICTURE BOOKS FOR ALL AGES. RABBITS. RESTAURANTS.

164   Coy, John. *Two Old Potatoes and Me.* **Illus. by Carolyn Fisher. Knopf, 2003. 0-375-92180-X. Unp. Gr. K–3**

A young African American girl describes how, when she was staying at her dad's house last spring, she found two old sprouted potatoes in the cupboard. Dad and daughter then cut up the potatoes, with one eye per piece, and planted them outside. They watered and weeded them, picked off potato beetles, and, in August, dug up 67 glorious new spuds. The richly textured computer-generated brown- and green-toned illustrations are knockouts—with large, hand-printed text that sprawls across the page—and make you want to get out and garden.

GERM: There's even a recipe for mashed potatoes, with a sprinkle of nutmeg for good luck. Bring in different types of potatoes to examine. Boil them up and eat them. Children can invent new potato recipes. Or cut them up and make potato prints. Or play Mr. Potato Head with the real thing. For a quick and effective lesson in visual recognition, hand each child a potato to examine closely and get to know for one minute. Then put all the potatoes on a table and have the children find theirs. You'll be amazed at how well they'll do. Even if it's past gardening season, you can suspend potatoes in a container of water and grow showy foliage. Keep a batch in the back of the classroom closet to sprout in time for that spring planting unit.

RELATED TITLES: Brisson, Pat. *The Summer My Father Was Ten.* Boyds Mills, 1998. / Cherry, Lynne. *How Groundhog's Garden Grew.* Scholastic, 2003. / dePaola, Tomie. *Jamie O'Rourke and the Big Potato: An Irish Folktale.* Putnam, 1992. / Ehlert, Lois. *Eating the Alphabet: Fruits and Vegetables from A to Z.* Harcourt, 1989. / Ehlert, Lois. *Growing Vegetable Soup.* Harcourt, 1987. / Gibbons, Gail. *From Seed to Plant.* Holiday House, 1991. / Lied, Kate. *Potato: A Tale from the Great Depression.* National Geographic, 1997. / Schaefer, Lola M. *Pick, Pull, Snap! Where Once a Flower Bloomed.* HarperCollins, 2003. / Stevens, Janet. *Tops and Bottoms.* Harcourt, 1995.

SUBJECTS: AFRICAN AMERICANS. DIVORCE. FATHERS AND DAUGHTERS. GARDENING. MULTICULTURAL BOOKS. PLANTS. POTATOES. VEGETABLES.

165   Creech, Sharon. *A Fine, Fine School.* **Illus. by Harry Bliss. HarperCollins, 2001. 0-06-027736-X. Unp. Gr. K–5**

So many self-proclaimed educational pundits, politicians, and experts decry the U.S. school calendar, insisting that 210 days is the way to go instead of 180. Here's an interesting response to that mindset. Mr. Keene, the dedicated, well-meaning principal of Tillie's school, decides they should all have more school, first adding Saturdays to the schedule and then Sundays and even holidays. Finally he announces jubilantly, "Let's have school . . . all summer long . . . We can learn EVERYTHING!" Tillie undertakes to set him straight. "Not everyone is learning," she tells him, explaining how she still has things to learn on her own that school doesn't teach.

GERM: Turn this into a math lesson with graphs and charts: How many hours do you spend every day/week/month/year reading, watching TV, playing, eating, and sleeping. The answers will amaze your math whizzes. Using these statistics, set up a classroom debate on the topic or even compose a persuasive letter to the school principal explaining why we should have more, less, or the same amount of school. Talk over, write about, and draw: what do you learn about when you're not in school?

RELATED TITLES: Allard, Harry. *Miss Nelson Is Missing.* Houghton Mifflin, 1985. / Calmenson, Stephanie. *The Frog Principal.* Scholastic, 2001. / Calmenson, Stephanie. *The Principal's New Clothes.* Scholastic, 1989. / Cocca-Leffler, Maryann. *Mr. Tanen's Tie Trouble.* Albert Whitman, 2003. / DiPucchio, Kelly. *Mrs. McBloom, Clean Up Your Classroom.* Hyperion, 2005. / Finchler, Judy. *Testing Miss Malarkey.* Walker, 2000. / Henkes, Kevin. *Lilly's Purple Plastic Purse.* Greenwillow, 1996. / Marshall, James. *The Cut-Ups.* Viking, 1984. / Seuss, Dr., and Jack Prelutsky. *Hooray for Diffendoofer Day.* Knopf, 1998. / Stevenson, James. *That Dreadful Day.* Greenwillow, 1985. / Wells, Rosemary. *Timothy Goes to School.* Dial, 1981.

SUBJECTS: PICTURE BOOKS FOR ALL AGES. PRINCIPALS. SCHOOLS. TESTING.

166   Crews, Donald. *Sail Away.* **Illus. by the author. Greenwillow, 1995. 0-688-11053-3. Unp. Gr. PreK–2**

A family of four rows their dinghy out to the sailboat. They putt under the bridge, then put up the sail and WHOOSH—wind's up. The sky turns dark and the seas look angry, so they head for home and arrive in the dark. "The full-color illustrations were done with Dr. Martin's Concentrated Water Colors applied with brush and airbrush," and they're beautiful.

GERM: Like Crews's other books—*Freight Train*, *Carousel*, and *Flying*—this gives us the whole experience. Seafarers can relate their own adventures on the water.

RELATED TITLES: Bang-Campbell, Monika. *Little Rat Sets Sail*. Harcourt, 2002. / Calhoun, Mary. *Henry the Sailor Cat*. Morrow, 1994. / Crews, Donald. *Carousel*. Greenwillow, 1982. / Crews, Donald. *Flying*. Greenwillow, 1986. / Crews, Donald. *Freight Train*. Greenwillow, 1978. / Long, Melinda. *How I Became a Pirate*. Harcourt, 2003. / O'Neill, Alexis. *Loud Emily*. Simon & Schuster, 1998.

SUBJECTS: BOATS AND BOATING. SAILING.

167   Cronin, Doreen. *Click, Clack, Moo: Cows That Type*. Illus. by Betsy Lewin. Simon & Schuster, 2000. 0-689-83213-3. Unp. Gr. PreK–1

Farmer Brown can't believe his eyes when his cows find an old typewriter in the barn and post on the barn door a typed demand for electric blankets. "Cows that type? Impossible!" The farmer refuses to accede, so the cows go on strike. Their new note reads, "Sorry. We're closed. No milk today." Pretty soon the demands escalate, until the cows seek a compromise. They will exchange their typewriter for electric blankets. The black-outlined watercolor wash illustrations are as goofy and endearing as they come.

GERM: Try some persuasive letter writing in which your students pretend to be farm animals and write to Farmer Brown, trying to convince him to make improvements. This story also lends itself wonderfully to Reader's Theater. Type it up in script form and have your students read it aloud as they act it out. Write parts for cows, chickens, ducks, narrators, and, of course, the beleaguered Farmer Brown. An old computer keyboard makes a nice prop if you don't still have that old typewriter. Follow up with the Weston Woods video of *Giggle, Giggle, Quack*, the sequel, and, of course, with *Duck for President*.

RELATED TITLES: Babcock, Chris. *No Moon, No Milk*. Crown, 1993. / Choldenko, Gennifer. *Moonstruck: The True Story of the Cow Who Jumped over the Moon*. Hyperion, 1997. / Cronin, Doreen. *Duck for President*. Simon & Schuster, 2004. / Cronin, Doreen. *Giggle, Giggle, Quack*. Simon & Schuster, 2002. / Demuth, Patricia Brennan. *The Ornery Morning*. Dutton, 1991. / Doyle, Malachy. *Cow*. McElderry, 2002. / Egan, Tim. *Metropolitan Cow*. Houghton Mifflin, 1996. / Egan, Tim. *Serious Farm*. Houghton Mifflin, 2003. / Johnson, Paul Brett. *The Cow Who Wouldn't Come Down*. Orchard, 1993. / Kirby, David, and Allen Woodman. *The Cows Are Going to Paris*. Caroline House, 1991. / Krosoczka, Jarrett J. *Punk Farm*. Knopf, 2005. / Palatini, Margie. *Moo Who?* HarperCollins, 2004. / Rostoker-Gruber, Karen. *Rooster Can't Can't Cock-a-Doodle-Doo*. Dial, 2004. / Speed, Toby. *Two Cool Cows*. Putnam, 1995. / Vail, Rachel. *Over the Moon*. Orchard, 1998. / Waddell, Martin. *Farmer Duck*. Candlewick, 1992.

SUBJECTS: COWS. DOMESTIC ANIMALS. DUCKS. FARM LIFE. HUMOROUS FICTION. PICTURE BOOKS FOR ALL AGES. READER'S THEATER. TYPEWRITERS.

168   Cronin, Doreen. *Diary of a Worm*. Illus. by Harry Bliss. HarperCollins, 2003. 0-06-000151-8. Unp. Gr. K–4

Read five months' worth of unforgettable and hilarious illustrated diary entries of a lovable, personable, witty worm—at home and in school. From the endpapers (a scrapbook of captioned photos: "My first tunnel" and "The family vacation—on Compost Island") and then on to diary entries, accompanied by personable watercolors of our worm narrator in his signature red baseball cap, this is a book that generates laughter and worm empathy.

GERM: Worms are wonderfully easy to draw. Each person can pick a date and then write and illustrate a new diary entry for Worm or his friend Spider, in order to fill in more of their activities from August to March. There are lots of small, unloved, uncuddly, uncute creatures out there that the earth depends on. For Earth Day or your animal unit in science, ask your students to do some research on one of them. Then either have them do a factual report on that animal or have them write illustrated diary entries from their animal's point of view incorporating fact and fiction. Finally, ask students to share their findings with the whole group. The next time your kids have the urge to stomp on an ant or bash a spider or cut a worm in half, they'll think twice and then think better of it. See what Spider has to say in the companion book, *Diary of a Spider*. Compare and contrast Spider's and Worm's voices with that of the wombat in Jackie French's *The Diary of a Wombat*. Pick up more worm facts with Wendy Pfeffer's *Wiggling Worms at Work*.

RELATED TITLES: Cannon, Janell. *Stellaluna*. Harcourt, 1993. / Caple, Kathy. *Worm Gets a Job*. Candlewick, 2004. / Child, Lauren. *That Pesky Rat*. Candlewick, 2002. / Cronin, Doreen. *Click, Clack, Moo: Cows That Type*. Simon & Schuster, 2000. / Cronin, Doreen. *Diary of a Spider*. HarperCollins, 2005. / Cushman, Doug. *Inspector*

Hopper's Mystery Year. HarperCollins, 2003. / French, Jackie. *Diary of a Wombat.* Clarion, 2003. / McMullan, Kate. *I Stink!* HarperCollins, 2002. / Markle, Sandra. *Spiders: Biggest! Littlest!* Boyds Mills, 2004. / Pfeffer, Wendy. *Wiggling Worms at Work.* HarperCollins, 2004. / Provensen, Alice. *A Day in the Life of Murphy.* Simon & Schuster, 2003. / Teague, Mark. *Dear Mrs. LaRue: Letters from Obedience School.* Scholastic, 2002. / Tyson, Leigh Ann. *An Interview with Harry the Tarantula.* National Geographic, 2003. / Wheeler, Lisa. *Old Cricket.* Atheneum, 2003. / Wilson, Karma. *Sweet Briar Goes to School.* Dial, 2003.

SUBJECTS: DIARIES. HUMOROUS FICTION. PERSONAL NARRATIVES. PICTURE BOOKS FOR ALL AGES. POINT OF VIEW. SPIDERS. WORMS.

169　**Cronin, Doreen.** *Duck for President.* **Illus. by Betsy Lewin. Simon & Schuster, 2004. 0-689-86377-2. Unp. Gr. PreK–6**

Sick of doing his chores on Farmer Brown's farm, Duck calls an election and runs for farmer. When Farmer Brown sees the results of the election, he immediately calls for a recount, but it's too late. The voters have spoken: Duck wins. Duck quickly tires of being a farmer, and so he runs for governor, and finally, president. Once in office, however, he discovers that running a country is no fun at all.

GERM: The matter-of-fact humor and repetition in the story make this a howler to read aloud. You'll also find it a perfect discussion starter at election time, with its many wonderfully sly political asides in both the text and the watercolor illustrations. Ask your crew what the qualifications are for each job Duck covets. Bring in a sample ballot. Your group can make campaign posters and hold an election for Teacher. At the end of the book, Duck is back on the farm, working on the first line of his autobiography. Have them finish it for him. What will Duck try next? Introduce his first two tales: *Click, Clack, Moo: Cows That Type* and *Giggle, Giggle, Quack.* You'll find an activity kit for the book at the Simon & Schuster Web site, <www.simonsays.com>; to get there fast: <tinyurl.com/35z49>.

RELATED TITLES: Chandra, Deborah, and Madeline Comora. *George Washington's Teeth.* Farrar, 2003. / Christelow, Eileen. *VOTE!* Clarion, 2003. / Cronin, Doreen. *Click, Clack, Moo: Cows That Type.* Simon & Schuster, 2000. / Cronin, Doreen. *Giggle, Giggle, Quack.* Simon & Schuster, 2002. / Egan, Tim. *Serious Farm.* Houghton Mifflin, 2003. / Gutman, Dan. *The Kid Who Ran for President.* Scholastic, 1996. / Krosoczka, Jarrett. *Max for President.* Knopf, 2004. / McNamara, Margaret. *Election Day.* Simon & Schuster, 2004. / Shannon, David. *Duck on a Bike.* Scholastic, 2002. / St. George, Judith. *So You Want to Be President?* Philomel, 2000. / Stier, Catherine. *If I Were President.* Albert Whitman, 1999. / Waddell, Martin. *Farmer Duck.* Candlewick, 1992. / Willems, Mo. *Don't Let the Pigeon Drive the Bus!* Hyperion, 2003. / Winters, Kay. *My Teacher for President.* Dutton, 2004.

SUBJECTS: DUCKS. ELECTIONS. FARM LIFE. GOVERNORS. HUMOROUS FICTION. POLITICAL CAMPAIGNS. PRESIDENTS. VOTING.

170　**Crummel, Susan Stevens.** *All in One Hour.* **Illus. by Dorothy Donohue. Marshall Cavendish, 2003. 0-7614-5129-3. Unp. Gr. PreK–2**

At 6:00 A.M., a cat follows a mouse out the window and a madcap chase ensues involving a dog, a dogcatcher, a robber, a policeman, and a grocer, all described in rhyme. The text also includes the digital and analog times of each new phase of the action.

GERM: Have children divide their papers into quarters and draw and write a four-part adventure of an hour in their lives that includes the correct time for each part. This is also a fun chase story to recall in sequence and act out. Using a stopwatch, have groups time different activities: How long does it take to eat your sandwich at lunch? Get a drink of water? Tie your shoe? Sing the chorus to "This Land Is Your Land"?

RELATED TITLES: Axelrod, Amy. *Pigs on a Blanket.* Simon & Schuster, 1996. / Behrman, Carol H. *The Ding Dong Clock.* Henry Holt, 1999. / Carle, Eric. *The Grouchy Ladybug.* HarperCollins, 1997. / Emmett, Jonathan. *Someone Bigger.* Clarion, 2004. / Fenton, Edward. *The Big Yellow Balloon.* Doubleday, 1967. / Fraser, Mary Ann. *I. Q., It's Time.* Walker, 2005. / Harper, Dan. *Telling Time with Big Mama Cat.* Harcourt, 1998. / Hopkins, Lee Bennett, comp. *It's About Time.* Simon & Schuster, 1993. / Hutchins, Pat. *Clocks and More Clocks.* Macmillan, 1970. / Walton, Rick. *Bunny Day: Telling Time from Breakfast to Bedtime.* HarperCollins, 2002.

SUBJECTS: CATS. CAUSE AND EFFECT. CLOCKS AND WATCHES. CREATIVE DRAMA. MICE. NIGHT. SEQUENCE STORIES. STORIES IN RHYME. TIME.

171　**Cullen, Lynn.** *Little Scraggly Hair: A Dog on Noah's Ark.* **Illus. by Jacqueline Rogers. Holiday House, 2003. 0-8234-1772-7. Unp. Gr. K–3**

Warm-nosed mutt Little Scraggly Hair, lonely and rejected, finds a friend in Noah, a kind man building an ark in preparation for the flood God has told him is coming. When the animals come on board and the rain starts falling, there's so little space, the little dog has to stand with his nose in a knothole for 40 days.

GERM: The colloquial speech of the narration was inspired by the southern Appalachian dialect found in Richard Chase's *Grandfather Tales*, a classic collection of American folktales that are a delight to read aloud and tell. An explanation of how dogs came to have cold, wet noses, this enticing tale would pair well with Lloyd Alexander's *How the Cat Swallowed Thunder*, which tells the story of how cats got their purr.

RELATED TITLES: Alexander, Lloyd. *How the Cat Swallowed Thunder*. Dutton, 2000. / Chase, Richard. *Grandfather Tales*. Houghton Mifflin, 1948. / Dillon, Leo, and Diane Dillon. *To Everything There Is a Season*. Scholastic, 1998. / Pinkney, Jerry. *Noah's Ark*. SeaStar, 2002. / Spier, Peter. *Noah's Ark*. Bantam, 1992.

SUBJECTS: ANIMALS. BIBLE. DOGS. FLOODS. NOAH (BIBLICAL FIGURE). POURQUOI TALES. RAIN AND RAINFALL. SHIPS. WEATHER.

172   Curtis, Gavin. *The Bat Boy and His Violin*. Illus. by E. B. Lewis. Simon & Schuster, 1998. 0-689-80099-1. Unp. Gr. 1–4

Reginald's father, manager of the Dukes, the worst team in the Negro National League in 1948, is skeptical about his son's violin playing and brings him to the field as a bat boy. Listening to the soothing music, which Reginald plays when the team is up at bat, leads the players to a winning streak.

GERM: With its stellar watercolors, this is a powerful juxtaposition of baseball, music, and civil rights issues. Lisa Cline-Ransome's biography of Satchel Paige introduces us to one of the most famous Negro League players in an eye-opening look at the racism that kept African American baseball players segregated.

RELATED TITLES: Barasch, Lynne. *Knockin' on Wood: Starring Peg Leg Bates*. Lee & Low, 2004. / Cline-Ransome, Lesa. *Satchel Paige*. Simon & Schuster, 2000. / Golenbock, Peter. *Teammates*. Harcourt, 1990. / Lee, Milly. *Nim and the War Effort*. Farrar, 1997. / McKissack, Patricia C. *Goin' Someplace Special*. Atheneum, 2001. / Mitchell, Margaree King. *Granddaddy's Gift*. BridgeWater, 1997. / Mitchell, Margaree King. *Uncle Jed's Barber Shop*. Simon & Schuster, 1993. / Mochizuki, Ken. *Baseball Saved Us*. Lee & Low, 1993. / Namioka, Lensey. *Yang the Youngest and His Terrible Ear*. Little, Brown, 1992. / Nelson, Vaunda Micheaux. *Mayfield Crossing*. Putnam, 1993. / Woodson, Jacqueline. *The Other Side*. Putnam, 2001.

SUBJECTS: AFRICAN AMERICANS. BASEBALL. FATHERS AND SONS. HISTORICAL FICTION. MULTICULTURAL BOOKS. MUSICIANS. NEGRO LEAGUES. RACE RELATIONS. SEGREGATION. VIOLINS.

173   Curtis, Jamie Lee. *It's Hard to Be Five: Learning How to Work My Control Panel*. Illus. by Laura Cornell. HarperCollins, 2004. 0-06-008096-5. Unp. Gr. PreK–1

In this exuberant, rhyming tale, an irrepressible brown-haired boy explains the trials and triumphs of being 5, when his mind and fresh mouth don't always agree. He prefers to be dirty, not clean, and it takes "Superman skill" to sit still in school.

GERM: Ask your 5-year-olds what's great and not so great about being that age. Ask them: What can you do now that you couldn't do before? What do you still need to be 6 in order to do?

RELATED TITLES: Curtis, Jamie Lee. *Tell Me Again About the Night I Was Born*. HarperCollins, 1996. / Curtis, Jamie Lee. *Today I Feel Silly and Other Moods That Make My Day*. HarperCollins, 1998. / Emmett, Jonathan. *Someone Bigger*. Clarion, 2004. / Howard, Arthur. *When I Was Five*. Harcourt, 1996. / McGhee, Alison. *Countdown to Kindergarten*. Harcourt, 2002. / Shannon, David. *David Goes to School*. Scholastic, 1999. / Shannon, David. *No, David!* Scholastic, 1998. / Vail, Rachel. *Sometimes I'm Bombaloo*. Scholastic, 2002.

SUBJECTS: BEHAVIOR. GROWTH. SCHOOLS. SELF-CONTROL. STORIES IN RHYME.

174   Curtis, Jamie Lee. *Tell Me Again About the Night I Was Born*. Illus. by Laura Cornell. HarperCollins, 1996. 0-06-024529-8. Unp. Gr. PreK–2

A little girl asks her adoptive parents to tell her the riveting saga of the night she was born: how they flew on an airplane to get her after her birth mother delivered her, and how they felt after they first saw her at the hospital and brought her home. Cornell's whimsical watercolors are riotously funny and filled with adorable details of the wide-mouthed baby.

GERM: Here's a story adoptive parents and their children will treasure for opening up a dialogue on what it means to be adopted.

RELATED TITLES: Buzzeo, Toni. *The Sea Chest*. Dial, 2002. / Curtis, Jamie Lee. *It's Hard to Be Five: Learning How to Work My Control Panel*. HarperCollins, 2004. / Curtis, Jamie Lee. *Today I Feel Silly and Other Moods That*

Make My Day. HarperCollins, 1998. / Lifton, Betty Jean. *Tell Me a Real Adoption Story.* Knopf, 1994. / Little, Jean. *Emma's Yucky Brother.* HarperCollins, 2001. / London, Jonathan. *A Koala for Katie.* Albert Whitman, 1993. / Stoeke, Janet Morgan. *Waiting for May.* Dutton, 2005. / Thomas, Eliza. *The Red Blanket.* Scholastic, 2004.
SUBJECTS: ADOPTION. BABIES.

175   **Curtis, Jamie Lee.** *Today I Feel Silly and Other Moods That Make My Day.* **Illus. by Laura Cornell. HarperCollins, 1998. 0-06-024560-3. Unp. Gr. PreK–2**
An effervescent little redhead bounds across each page of exuberant watercolors, as she expounds in rhyme about her different moods, one per day, ranging from angry to joyful to confused, excited, cranky, lonely, discouraged, and great.
GERM: Try the mood wheel at the back to see all of the girl's emotions revolve. You could make your own wheels or simply fold a piece of paper in fours and have each child draw four small self-portraits of his or her most recent emotions.
RELATED TITLES: Aliki. *Feelings.* Greenwillow, 1984. / Bang, Molly. *When Sophie Gets Angry—Really, Really Angry.* Scholastic, 1999. / Curtis, Jamie Lee. *It's Hard to Be Five: Learning How to Work My Control Panel.* HarperCollins, 2004. / Curtis, Jamie Lee. *Tell Me Again About the Night I Was Born.* HarperCollins, 1996. / Frame, Jeron Ashford. *Yesterday I Had the Blues.* Tricycle, 2003. / Freymann, Saxton, and Joost Elffers. *How Are You Peeling? Foods with Moods.* Scholastic, 1999. / Harper, Jessica. *Lizzy's Ups and Downs: Not an Ordinary School Day.* HarperCollins, 2004. / Hausman, Bonnie. *A to Z: Do You Ever Feel Like Me?* Dutton, 1999. / Hopkins, Lee Bennett, comp. *Oh, No! Where Are My Pants? And Other Disasters: Poems.* HarperCollins, 2005. / Hubbard, Woodleigh. *C Is for Curious: An ABC of Feelings.* Chronicle, 1990. / Modesitt, Jeanne. *Sometimes I Feel Like a Mouse: A Book About Feelings.* Scholastic, 1992. / Vail, Rachel. *Sometimes I'm Bombaloo.* Scholastic, 2002.
SUBJECTS: EMOTIONS. STORIES IN RHYME.

176   **Cushman, Doug.** *Inspector Hopper.* **Illus. by the author. HarperCollins, 2000. 0-06-028382-3. 64pp. Gr. PreK–2**
In the three sprightly dialogue-filled chapters of this easy-reader, an astute grasshopper detective, Inspector Hopper, and his always-hungry sidekick assistant McBugg solve two mysteries and stop a crime.
GERM: Write Reader's Theater scripts for all three chapters and have small groups act them out. Continue the series with *Inspector Hopper's Mystery Year.*
RELATED TITLES: Adler, David A. Young Cam Jansen series. Putnam. / Biedrzycki, David. *Ace Lacewing: Bug Detective.* Charlesbridge, 2005. / Clifford, Eth. *Flatfoot Fox and the Case of the Mising Schoolhouse.* Houghton Mifflin, 1997. (And others in the Flatfoot Fox series.) / Cushman, Doug. *The ABC Mystery.* HarperCollins, 1993. / Cushman, Doug. *Aunt Eater Loves a Mystery.* HarperCollins, 1987. (And others in the Aunt Eater mystery series.) / Cushman, Doug. *Inspector Hopper's Mystery Year.* HarperCollins, 2003. / Cushman, Doug. *The Mystery of King Karfu.* HarperCollins, 1996. / Kellogg, Steven. *The Missing Mitten Mystery.* Dial, 2000. / Laden, Nina. *Private I. Guana: The Case of the Missing Chameleon.* Chronicle, 1995. / Stevenson, James. *The Mud Flat Mystery.* Greenwillow, 1997.
SUBJECTS: GRASSHOPPERS. INSECTS. MYSTERY AND DETECTIVE STORIES. READER'S THEATER.

177   **Cushman, Doug.** *Mystery at the Club Sandwich.* **Illus. by the author. Clarion, 2004. 0-618-41969-1. Unp. Gr. 1–3**
Rumpled raincoat- and fedora-clad elephant detective Nick Trunk investigates a case of theft when famous nightclub singer and fox Lola Gale loses her marbles. Silvery-toned watercolor washes give this hard-boiled, detective-style picture book its film noir look.
GERM: Assemble a boxful of the clues Nick examines—including an ostrich feather, a jar of peanut butter, and a fish—to pull out and display as you read the story. Before reading the conclusion, have your readers make a list of possible suspects, analyzing the clues and weighing the evidence and possible motives of each one. Ask readers to team up, discuss, and write down their predictions on who dunnit and reasons for their conclusions. If you read the story again, they will notice clues that they missed the first time. You'll also have a jolly good time checking out the casebook and decoding the secret messages of wombat Seymour Sleuth when he heads to Egypt to find a stolen chicken in Cushman's *The Mystery of King Karfu.* Other spoofs on the Humphrey Bogart-style detective genre include *Ace Lacewing: Bug Detective* by David Biedrzycki and *Bud Barkin, Private Eye* by James Howe.
RELATED TITLES: Biedrzycki, David. *Ace Lacewing: Bug Detective.* Charlesbridge, 2005. / Christelow, Eileen. *Gertrude, the Bulldog Detective.* Clarion, 1992. / Cushman, Doug. *The ABC Mystery.* HarperCollins, 1993. /

Cushman, Doug. *Aunt Eater Loves a Mystery*. HarperCollins, 1987. (And others in the Aunt Eater mystery series.) /Cushman, Doug. *Inspector Hopper*. HarperCollins, 2000. (And others in the Inspector Hopper series.) / Cushman, Doug. *The Mystery of King Karfu*. HarperCollins, 1996. / Egan, Tim. *The Trial of Cardigan Jones*. Houghton Mifflin, 2004. / Howe, James. *Bud Barkin, Private Eye* (Tales from the House of Bunnicula series). Atheneum, 2003. / Kelly, John, and Cathy Tincknell. *The Mystery of Eatum Hall*. Candlewick, 2004. / Laden, Nina. *Private I. Guana: The Case of the Missing Chameleon*. Chronicle, 1995. / McClements, George. *Jake Gander, Storyville Detective*. Hyperion, 2002. / Palatini, Margie. *The Web Files*. Hyperion, 2001. / Teague, Mark. *Detective LaRue: Letters from the Investigation*. Scholastic, 2004.

SUBJECTS: ANIMALS. ELEPHANTS. LOST AND FOUND POSSESSIONS. MYSTERY AND DETECTIVE STORIES. PEANUT BUTTER.

178   Cuyler, Margery. *Big Friends*. Illus. by Ezra Tucker. Walker, 2004. 0-8027-8887-4. Unp. Gr. PreK–2

While making porridge in his big cooking pot, lonely giant Big Hasuni spies smoke on an island nearby and heads for it, along with his pet lion and elephant, hoping to find a friend. Coming upon a campfire with nobody there, he gobbles up the lobsters he finds cooking, sits on a stool and breaks it—causing a slight tidal wave—and falls into a snory sleep in the hammock. Imagine his surprise when a giant woman wakes him.

GERM: A combination of Goldilocks and a tall tale, this funny folktale-like story has grandly proportioned realistic paintings that add to the humor. Compare and contrast the story with the original Goldilocks, of course, and make predictions as you read. Why does Big Hasuni run away from the giant woman? What will he find back at his campsite? What will he do next? For a pint-sized send-up of Goldilocks, mouse-style, read *Ruby and the Sniffs* by Michael Emberley.

RELATED TITLES: Aylesworth, Jim. *Goldilocks and the Three Bears*. Scholastic, 2003. / Brett, Jan. *Goldilocks and the Three Bears*. Putnam, 1987. / dePaola, Tomie. *Fin M'Coul, the Giant of Knockmany Hill*. Holiday House, 1981. / dePaola, Tomie. *The Mysterious Giant of Barletta*. Harcourt, 1988. / Emberley, Michael. *Ruby and the Sniffs*. Little, Brown, 2004. / Ernst, Lisa Campbell. *Goldilocks Returns*. Simon & Schuster, 2000. / Marshall, James. *Goldilocks and the Three Bears*. Dial, 1988. / Morimoto, Junko. *The Two Bullies*. Crown, 1999. / Stanley, Diane. *The Giant and the Beanstalk*. HarperCollins, 2004. / Stanley, Diane. *Goldie and the Three Bears*. HarperCollins, 2003.

SUBJECTS: FRIENDSHIP. GIANTS. GOLDILOCKS. LONELINESS. MULTICULTURAL BOOKS. PARODIES. SIZE. TALL TALES.

179   Cuyler, Margery. *100th Day Worries*. Illus. by Arthur Howard. Simon & Schuster, 2000. 0-689-82979-5. Unp. Gr. K–2

Until the very last minute, worrier Jessica can't come up with an idea for the perfect collection of 100 things to celebrate her class's 100th school day, but her loving family comes to the rescue.

GERM: Ask your counters to come up with a collection of 100 somethings for show and tell. Get them started with the 100 poems in *Counting Our Way to the One Hundredth Day* by Betsy Franco. There are an additional 300 celebration ideas on Joan Holub's 100th Day of School Web site at <users.aol.com/a100thday/ideas.html>.

RELATED TITLES: Franco, Betsy. *Counting Our Way to the 100th Day!* McElderry, 2004. / Frith, Margaret. *I'll Teach My Dog 100 Words*. Random House, 1973. / Kasza, Keiko. *The Wolf's Chicken Stew*. Putnam, 1987. / Medearis, Angela S. *The 100th Day of School*. Scholastic, 1996. / Pinczes, Elinor J. *One Hundred Hungry Ants*. Houghton Mifflin, 1993. / Rockwell, Anne. *100 School Days*. HarperCollins, 2002. / Slate, Joseph. *Miss Bindergarten Celebrates the 100th Day of Kindergarten*. Dutton, 1998. / Wells, Rosemary. *Emily's First 100 Days of School*. Hyperion, 2000.

SUBJECTS: COUNTING BOOKS. ONE HUNDREDTH DAY CELEBRATIONS. SCHOOLS.

180   Cuyler, Margery. *Skeleton Hiccups*. Illus. by S. D. Schindler. Simon & Schuster, 2002. 0-689-84770-X. Unp. Gr. K–2

Skeleton wakes up with hiccups and spends the day trying to get rid of them, holding his breath, eating sugar, and even drinking water upside down. The stark white skeleton sure stands out against each color background, and the faintly macabre visual humor will make kids scream with laughter.

GERM: Ask your listeners to propose remedies for hiccups that might work for Skeleton. Meet another skeleton with real personality in *Boogie Bones* by Elizabeth Loredo.

RELATED TITLES: Berger, Melvin. *Why I Sneeze, Shiver, Hiccup, and Yawn*. HarperCollins, 2000. / DeFelice, Cynthia C. *The Dancing Skeleton*. Macmillan, 1989. / Hubbard, Patricia. *Trick or Treat Countdown*. Holiday

House, 1999. / Johnston, Tony. *The Ghost of Nicholas Greebe*. Dial, 1996. / Leuck, Laura. *One Witch*. Walker, 2003. / Loredo, Elizabeth. *Boogie Bones*. Putnam, 1997. / San Souci, Robert D. *Cinderella Skeleton*. Harcourt, 2000. / Williams, Linda. *The Little Old Lady Who Was Not Afraid of Anything*. Crowell, 1986.

SUBJECTS: GHOSTS. HALLOWEEN. HICCUPS. PUMPKINS. SKELETONS.

181   **Dallas-Conté, Juliet. *Cock-a-Moo-Moo*. Illus. by Alison Bartlett. Little, Brown, 2001. 0-316-60505-0. Unp. Gr. PreK–K**
Poor Rooster has forgotten how to crow, shouting, "COCK-A-MOO-MOO!" when the sun comes up. "That's not right," say the cows. "Only cows go moo." Rooster quacks, oinks, and baas, only to hear a similar refrain from the other animals. When a fox sniffs and rustles and sneaks his way into the henhouse, Rooster's shouted cries wake the other animals in time to scare him off. Bright and cheerful full-bleed acrylics are winsome and sunny, even from a distance, making it an ideal story to share with large groups.
GERM: Your storytime will be filled with wonderful noises as the children act this one out with all the repeated dialogue and lots of crazy crowing. Then meet a rooster who's lost his voice entirely in *Rooster Can't Cock-a-Doodle-Doo* by Karen Rostoker-Gruber. In Tracey Campbell Pearson's *Bob*, the rooster sets out to learn to crow, but picks up other animal noises instead.
RELATED TITLES: Bateman, Teresa. *Farm Flu*. Albert Whitman, 2001. / Causley, Charles. "*Quack!*" *Said the Billy-Goat*. Lippincott, 1986. / Cazet, Denys. *Elvis the Rooster Almost Goes to Heaven*. HarperCollins, 2003. / Edwards, Pamela Duncan. *McGillycuddy Could!* HarperCollins, 2005. / Feiffer, Jules. *Bark, George*. HarperCollins, 1999. / Fox, Mem. *Hattie and the Fox*. Bradbury, 1987. / Hindley, Judy. *Do Like a Duck Does!* Candlewick, 2002. / Krosoczka, Jarrett J. *Punk Farm*. Knopf, 2005. / Most, Bernard. *Cock-a-Doodle-Moo!* Harcourt, 199. / Palatini, Margie. *Moo Who?* HarperCollins, 2004. / Pearson, Tracey Campbell. *Bob*. Farrar, 2002. / Rostoker-Gruber, Karen. *Rooster Can't Cock-a-Doodle-Doo*. Dial, 2004. / Ward, Helen. *The Rooster and the Fox*. Millbrook, 2003. / Wattenberg, Jane. *Henny-Penny*. Scholastic, 2000.
SUBJECTS: ANIMAL SOUNDS. CHANTABLE REFRAIN. CREATIVE DRAMA. DOMESTIC ANIMALS. FARM LIFE. FOXES. ROOSTERS.

182   **Daly, Niki. *Jamela's Dress*. Illus. by the author. Farrar, 1999. 0-374-33667-9. Unp. Gr. PreK–1**
Forgetting her responsibility for looking after Mama's new dress material drying on the clothesline, little Jamela drapes herself in it and parades through town.
GERM: Show South Africa, the story's setting, on a globe or map. Discussion point: Did you ever get in trouble like Jamela for disobeying your parents when you were little? Follow up with the other books about Jamela, including *What's Cooking, Jamela?* and *Where's Jamela?*
RELATED TITLES: Daly, Niki. *Not So Fast, Songololo*. Atheneum, 1986. / Daly, Niki. *What's Cooking, Jamela?* Farrar, 2001. / Daly, Niki. *Where's Jamela?* Farrar, 2004. / Mennen, Ingrid, and Niki Daly. *Somewhere in Africa*. Dutton, 1992. / Mollel, Tololwa M. *My Rows and Piles of Coins*. Clarion, 1999.
SUBJECTS: BLACKS—SOUTH AFRICA. CLOTHING AND DRESS. MULTICULTURAL BOOKS. SOUTH AFRICA.

183   **Daly, Niki. *Once Upon a Time*. Illus. by the author. Farrar, 2003. 0-374-35633-5. Unp. Gr. K–2**
In this gentle story set in South Africa, Sarie hates reading aloud in class because the other children laugh at her for stuttering and stammering over the words. But then Auntie Anna reads "Cinderella" aloud with her and makes her feel like a princess.
GERM: Discuss: How and why does Auntie Anna help Sarie to be a better reader? How can you become a better reader?
RELATED TITLES: Allen, Susan, and Jane Lindaman. *Read Anything Good Lately?* Millbrook, 2003. / Daly, Niki. *Jamela's Dress*. Farrar, 1999. / Daly, Niki. *Not So Fast, Songololo*. Atheneum, 1986. / Hest, Amy. *Mr. George Baker*. Candlewick, 2004. / Hoffman, Mary. *Amazing Grace*. Dial, 1991. / Joosse, Barbara M. *Hot City*. Philomel, 2004. / Polacco, Patricia. *Thank You, Mr. Falker*. Philomel, 1998. / Stock, Catherine. *Gugu's House*. Clarion, 2001. / Stuve-Bodeen, Stephanie. *Elizabeti's School*. Lee & Low, 2002. / Wishinsky, Frieda. *Give Maggie a Chance*. Fitzhenry & Whiteside, 2002.
SUBJECTS: AUNTS. BLACKS—SOUTH AFRICA. BOOKS AND READING. CINDERELLA STORIES. FRIENDSHIP. MULTICULTURAL BOOKS. SCHOOLS. SOUTH AFRICA.

184   **Dannenberg, Julie. *First Day Jitters*. Illus. by Judy Love. Whispering Coyote, 2000. 1-58089-054-7. Unp. Gr. K–2**
Here's a very funny one of those books in the "I don't want to go to school and you can't make me" genre, but with a twist. Sarah Jane does not want to get out of bed because she hates the

thought of starting a new school. Mr. Hartwell tries talking sense to her, and she finally drags herself out of bed, into her clothes, and into his car. "I feel sick," she says. Who is Sarah Jane Hartwell? Why, the new teacher!

GERM: Ask your students why Sarah Jane is so nervous and see if they guess the surprise ending on the last page.

RELATED TITLES: Child, Lauren. *I Am Too Absolutely Small for School.* Candlewick, 2004. / Finchler, Judy. *Miss Malarkey Won't Be in Today.* Walker, 1998. / Harris, Robie H. *I Am Not Going to School Today!* McElderry, 2003. / Henkes, Kevin. *Chrysanthemum.* Greenwillow, 1991. / Lasky, Kathryn. *Lunch Bunnies.* Little, Brown, 1996. / Lester, Helen. *Something Might Happen.* Houghton Mifflin, 2003. / London, Jonathan. *Froggy Goes to School.* Viking, 1996. / McGhee, Alison. *Countdown to Kindergarten.* Harcourt, 2002. / Poydar, Nancy. *First Day, Hooray.* Holiday House, 1999. / Schwartz, Amy. *Annabelle Swift, Kindergartner.* Orchard, 1988. / Slate, Joseph. *Miss Bindergarten Gets Ready for Kindergarten.* Dutton, 1994. / Strete, Craig. *The Rattlesnake Who Went to School.* Putnam, 2004. / Wells, Rosemary. *Emily's 100 Days of School.* Hyperion, 2000. / Wells, Rosemary. *My Kindergarten.* Hyperion, 2004. / Wells, Rosemary. *Timothy Goes to School.* Viking, 2000.

SUBJECTS: FIRST DAY OF SCHOOL. SCHOOLS. TEACHERS. WORRYING.

185 Davis, Katie. *Kindergarten Rocks.* Illus. by the author. Harcourt, 2005. 0-15-204932-0. Unp. Gr. PreK–K

Dexter is an expert on kindergarten, as he explains, because his big sister Jessie went there too one time, a long, long, long, long time ago, and she helps assuage his "what if" fears. "I was a shrimp like you," she says. Actually, according to Dexter, he's not the scared one; it's his blue stuffed dog Rufus who is nervous. Dexter has a pretty swell first day in Mrs. Sugarman's class until Rufus gets lost and Jessie has to come down from third grade to help find him. Colorful, friendly, childlike crayon drawings with cartoon-like dialogue balloons depict the amiable banter between an all-knowing sister who looks out for her brother and a jittery brother who looks up to his big sister.

GERM: Sometimes Dexter says one thing—"Kindergarten will be a piece of cake. Nooooo problem. I can't wait."—and his face tells a whole other story. Ask your school experts to describe how they think he's really feeling. Ask them how they felt about their first day. Look for some excellent advice—"Ease Kindergarten Jitters with Get-Ready-for-Kindergarten Month"—on Katie's Web site, <www.katiedavis.com>. Other first-day worrywarts include Charlie's little sister Lola in *I Am Too Absolutely Small for School* by Lauren Child, the title mouse in *Wemberly Worried* by Kevin Henkes, the little girl narrator in *Countdown to Kindergarten* by Alison McGhee, and a Native American boy in *The Rattlesnake Who Went to School.*

RELATED TITLES: Child, Lauren. *I Am Too Absolutely Small for School.* Candlewick, 2004. / Curtis, Jamie Lee. *It's Hard to Be Five: Learning How to Work My Control Panel.* HarperCollins, 2004. / Henkes, Kevin. *Wemberly Worried.* Greenwillow, 2000. / McGhee, Alison. *Countdown to Kindergarten.* Harcourt, 2002. / Slate, Joseph. *Miss Bindergarten Gets Ready for Kindergarten.* Dutton, 1996. / Strete, Craig. *The Rattlesnake Who Went to School.* Putnam, 2004. / Wells, Rosemary. *My Kindergarten.* Hyperion, 2004.

SUBJECTS: BROTHERS AND SISTERS. FIRST DAY OF SCHOOL. KINDERGARTEN. SCHOOLS. TEACHERS.

186 Davis, Katie. *Mabel the Tooth Fairy and How She Got Her Job.* Illus. by the author. Harcourt, 2003. 0-15-216307-7. Unp. Gr. K–2

Regular fairy Mabel hated brushing and flossing her teeth, so most of them fell out. Figuring she could take kids' teeth after they lost them, she started working nights and became the first-ever tooth fairy, though none of those teeth fit her just right.

GERM: Ask your loose-toothed gang to regale you with their true tooth tales. Then see how Mr. Claus started his illustrious career in *How Santa Got His Job* by Stephen Krensky.

RELATED TITLES: Beeler, Selby B. *Throw Your Tooth on the Roof: Tooth Traditions from Around the World.* Houghton Mifflin, 1998. / Birdseye, Tom. *Airmail to the Moon.* Holiday House, 1988. / Bunting, Eve. *Trouble on the T-Ball Team.* Clarion, 1995. / Keller, Laurie. *Open Wide: Tooth School Inside.* Henry Holt, 2000. / Lasky, Kathryn. *Science Fair Bunnies.* Candlewick, 2000. / MacDonald, Amy. *Cousin Ruth's Tooth.* Houghton Mifflin, 1996. / McGhee, Alison. *Mrs. Watson Wants Your Teeth.* Illus. by Harry Bliss. Harcourt, 2004. / Palatini, Margie. *Sweet Tooth.* Simon & Schuster, 2004. / Simms, Laura. *Rotten Teeth.* Houghton Mifflin, 1998. / Steig, William. *Doctor DeSoto.* Farrar, 1982.

SUBJECTS: HUMOROUS FICTION. TEETH. TOOTH FAIRY.

187   Davis, Katie. *Who Hops?* **Illus. by the author. Harcourt, 1998. 0-15-201839-5. Unp. Gr. PreK**

"Frogs hop. Rabbits hop. Kangaroos hop. Cows hop." Is there something wrong with one of those sentences? The cow part, maybe? Turn the page. "NO THEY DON'T!" it says. "Cows moo and give milk, but they don't hop!" Then find out who does and doesn't fly, slither, swim, and crawl. For each one-sentence, two-word declarative sentence, there's a day-glo colored picture of the animal, bordered in heavy black line, against an even brighter background.

GERM: The wonderfully kid-centric text and pictures will have even your littlest ones answering back and rolling on the floor in glee. Act this out, of course, and then create some new scenarios: who runs or purrs or barks or dives? Davis's companion book, *Who Hoots?*, focuses on animal noises.

RELATED TITLES: Burton, Marilee Robin. *Tails, Toes, Eyes, Ears, Nose.* HarperCollins, 1988. / Davis, Katie. *Who Hoots?* Harcourt, 2000. / Harter, Debbie. *Walking Through the Jungle.* Orchard, 1997. / Jenkins, Steve. *Big and Little.* Houghton Mifflin, 1996. / Jenkins, Steve. *Biggest, Strongest, Fastest.* Ticknor & Fields, 1995. / London, Jonathan. *Wiggle Waggle.* Harcourt, 1999. / Marzollo, Jean. *Pretend You're a Cat.* Dial, 1990. / Pandell, Karen. *Animal Action ABC.* Dutton, 1996. / Shapiro, Arnold L. *Mice Squeak, We Speak.* Putnam, 1997. / Williams, Sue. *I Went Walking.* Harcourt, 1990. / Young, Ruth. *Who Says Moo?* Viking, 1994.

SUBJECTS: ANIMAL LOCOMOTION. ANIMALS. CHANTABLE REFRAIN. CREATIVE DRAMA.

188   Davis, Patricia A. *Brian's Bird.* **Illus. by Layne Johnson. Albert Whitman, 2000. 0-8075-0881-0. Unp. Gr. K–3**

For his eighth birthday, Brian receives a green and yellow parakeet he names Scratchy, for the way the little bird feels on his finger, and tries to teach to talk. One day, when day Brian's big brother, Kevin, carelessly leaves the front door open, Scratchy flies outside. This would be a standard bird rescue story with personable and colorful illustrations of a close-knit African American family, but there's another element that makes the ordinary extraordinary: Brian is blind.

GERM: Based on a true story, this will allow young children to observe Brian as he trains his bird and deals with the usual dose of sibling rivalry he feels for his sighted big brother.

RELATED TITLES: Adler, David A. *A Picture Book of Louis Braille.* Holiday House, 1997. / Alexander, Sally Hobart. *Mom Can't See Me.* Macmillan, 1990. / Carlson, Nancy L. *Arnie and the New Kid.* Viking, 1990. / Cowen-Fletcher, Jane. *Mama Zooms.* Scholastic, 1993. / Damrell, Liz. *With the Wind.* Orchard, 1991. / Harshman, Marc. *The Storm.* Dutton, 1995. / Hermann, Spring. *Seeing Lessons: The Story of Abigail Carter and America's First School for Blind People.* Henry Holt, 1998. / Millman, Isaac. *Moses Goes to a Concert.* Farrar, 1998. / Osofsky, Audrey. *My Buddy.* Henry Holt, 1992. / Patent, Dorothy Hinshaw. *The Right Dog for the Job: Ira's Path from Service Dog to Guide Dog.* Walker, 2004. / Rodanas, Kristina. *The Blind Hunter.* Marshall Cavendish, 2003. / Whelan, Gloria. *Hannah.* Knopf, 1991.

SUBJECTS: AFRICAN AMERICANS. BIRDS. BLIND. BROTHERS. MULTICULTURAL BOOKS. PARAKEETS. PEOPLE WITH DISABILITIES. PETS. PHYSICALLY HANDICAPPED.

189   Davol, Marguerite W. *The Paper Dragon.* **Illus. by Robert Sabuda. Atheneum, 1997. 0-689-31992-4. Unp. Gr. K–3**

What is the strongest thing in the world that can be carried in paper? Humble scroll-painting artist Mi Fei must answer three difficult questions when he volunteers to face the dragon Sui Jen, newly awakened from his hundred years' sleep. Before the dragon can return to his slumber, Mi Fei must also bring fire wrapped in paper and the wind captured by paper. For the first, he fashions a lantern, and for the second, a fan. When Mi Fei paints, on paper, the people of his own village, the dragon agrees that love is truly the strongest thing in the world. The remarkable illustrations, with each double page unfolding into a three-paged spread, use the art of Chinese paper cutting, with each figure cut from multicolored painted tissue paper adhered to Japanese handmade paper.

GERM: Children will enjoy brainstorming their own answers to the dragon's questions, and you may want to start the discussion afterward by asking them to devise a fuller definition of the word "love." Stories like this one are considered literary folktales, newly composed, but in the style of oral tradition.

RELATED TITLES: Chang, Margaret, and Raymond. *The Beggar's Magic: A Chinese Tale.* McElderry, 1997. / Compestine, Ying Chang. *The Story of Paper.* Holiday House, 2003. / Davol, Marguerite W. *Batwings and the Curtain of Night.* Orchard, 1997. / Davol, Marguerite W. *How Snake Got His Hiss.* Orchard, 1996. / Hodges, Patricia. *Saint George and the Dragon.* Little, Brown, 1984. / Prelutsky, Jack. *The Dragons Are Singing Tonight.* Greenwillow, 1993. / Rumford, James. *The Cloudmakers.* Houghton Mifflin, 1996. / Tucker, Kathy. *The Seven*

Chinese Sisters. Albert Whitman, 2003. / Williams, Jay. *Everyone Knows What a Dragon Looks Like*. Four Winds, 1976. / Yep, Laurence. *The Dragon Prince*. HarperCollins, 1997. / Young, Ed. *The Sons of the Dragon King: A Chinese Legend*. Atheneum, 2004.

SUBJECTS: CHINA. DRAGONS. LOVE. MULTICULTURAL BOOKS. PAPER.

190   **Day, Nancy Raines. *Double Those Wheels*. Illus. by Steve Haskamp. Dutton, 2003. 0-525-46853-6. Unp. Gr. PreK–2**

A monkey on wheels sets out to deliver a pizza. He begins his journey riding on a unicycle, but then trades it in for a succession of wheeled vehicles, each with twice as many wheels as the one before. He moves to a bike, a car, a series of trucks, and a finally a 64-wheel train, arriving on time at a children's birthday party.

GERM: Kick off that math lesson on doubling and have children see just how big numbers can get if you keep on doubling them. Or cut up a pizza and do fractions. Or talk about wheels and transportation. Whatever your approach, all will love the noisy rhyme and the indefatigable monkey on a mission. Another good doubling story is *Minnie's Diner* by Dayle Ann Dodds.

RELATED TITLES: Demi. *One Grain of Rice*. Scholastic, 1997. / Dodds, Dayle Ann. *Minnie's Diner*. Candlewick, 2004. / Kirk, Daniel. *Go!* Hyperion, 2001. / Leedy, Loreen. *Mission: Addition*. Holiday House, 1997. / Leedy, Loreen. *2 X 2 = BOO! A Set of Spooky Multiplication Stories*. Holiday House, 1995. / Meister, Cari. *Busy Busy City Street*. Viking, 2000. / Michelson, Richard. *Ten Times Better*. Marshall Cavendish, 2000. / Pinczes, Elinor J. *One Hundred Hungry Ants*. Houghton Mifflin, 1993. / Root, Phyllis. *Rattletrap Car*. Candlewick, 2001. / Shields, Carol Diggory. *Animagicals: On the Go*. Handprint, 2001. / Sturges, Philemon. *The Little Red Hen (Makes a Pizza)*. Dutton, 1999. / Tang, Greg. *The Best of Times: Math Strategies That Multiply*. Scholastic, 2002. / Walton, Rick. *Bunnies on the Go: Getting from Place to Place*. HarperCollins, 2003.

SUBJECTS: MONKEYS. MULTIPLICATION. PIZZA. STORIES IN RHYME. TRANSPORTATION. VEHICLES.

191   **Deedy, Carmen Agra. *The Library Dragon*. Illus. by Michael P. White. Peachtree, 1994. 1-56145-091-X. Unp. Gr. K–2**

Miss Lotta Scales, the fiery new librarian at Sunrise Elementary School, is a real dragon, hired to guard the library and protect all those clean, shiny new books from the sticky fingers of children, who now dread Library Day. Not until little nearsighted Molly Brickmeyer, who has lost her glasses, wanders into the library and begins to read aloud does fierce Miss Scales understand how children are transformed by stories. She is transformed, too, from green dragon to warm, storytelling library goddess Miss Lotty.

GERM: There's a dual message here for kids, who will remember to be more careful with their library books, and for librarians and teachers, who will remember that libraries are for children and books are meant to be read. Start your school year off with this humorous cautionary tale and talk about library rules and good book care. See how Herb learns how to care for his books in *Who's Afraid of the Big Bad Book?* by Lauren Child. For more book care lessons and activities, see the related Care of Books lesson on page 56 and on page 78 of *More Books Kids Will Sit Still For*.

RELATED TITLES: Child, Lauren. *Who's Afraid of the Big Bad Book?* Hyperion, 2003. / Ernst, Lisa Campbell. *Stella Louella's Runaway Book*. Simon & Schuster, 1998. / Garland, Michael. *Miss Smith's Incredible Storybook*. Dutton, 2003. / Polacco, Patricia. *Aunt Chip and the Great Triple Creek Dam Affair*. Philomel, 1996. / Sierra, Judy. *Wild About Books*. Knopf, 2004. / Thaler, Mike. *The Librarian from the Black Lagoon*. Scholastic, 1997. / Williams, Suzanne. *Library Lil*. Dial, 1997.

SUBJECTS: BOOKS AND READING. DRAGONS. HUMOROUS FICTION. LIBRARIANS. LIBRARIES. PICTURE BOOKS FOR ALL AGES. SCHOOLS.

192   **DeFelice, Cynthia. *Old Granny and the Bean Thief*. Illus. by Cat Bowman Smith. Farrar, 2003. 0-374-35614-9. Unp. Gr. K–3**

Three nights running, a thief has snuck into Old Granny's shack and eaten up all her precious beans. On her way into town to tell the sheriff, she encounters a talking snake, pecan, cow patty, prickly pear cactus, and alligator, all of whom tell her to pick them up and put them into her sack. "In a pig's eye! My, oh, my!" she tells each one, but when she does what they ask, they help her foil that thief.

GERM: Have listeners retell this in sequence and act it out. Explore Granny's Southwest setting and how it affects the story; then soak and cook up a mess of beans for everyone to try. You'll be reminded of the Grimms' "The Bremen Town Musicians," and, if you can locate a copy, Ed Young's retelling of the Chinese folktale *The Terrible Nung Gwama*. Compare how little girl Dixie

Lee, in Marcia Vaughan's *Whistling Dixie*, also uses a snake and an alligator in tricking the nefarious creatures that come spooking around her door.

RELATED TITLES: Bang, Molly. *Wiley and the Hairy Man*. Macmillan, 1976. / Compton, Patricia A. *The Terrible Eek*. Simon & Schuster, 1991. / Ketteman, Helen. *Armadilly Chili*. Albert Whitman, 2004. / Mayer, Mercer. *Liza Lou and the Yeller Belly Swamp*. Four Winds, 1980. / Sierra, Judy. *Wiley and the Hairy Man*. Dutton, 1996. / Souhami, Jessica. *No Dinner! The Story of the Old Woman and the Pumpkin*. Marshall Cavendish, 2000. / Thomassie, Tynia. *Feliciana Feydra LeRoux: A Cajun Tall Tale*. Little, Brown, 1995. / Vaughan, Marcia. *Whistling Dixie*. HarperCollins, 1995. / Wright, Jill. *The Old Woman and the Jar of Uums*. Putnam, 1990. / Young, Ed. *The Terrible Nung Gwama: A Chinese Folktale*. Collins-World, 1978.

SUBJECTS: BEANS. COUNTRY LIFE. CREATIVE DRAMA. GRANDMOTHERS. ROBBERS AND OUTLAWS. SOUTHWEST. STORIES TO TELL.

193   **DeFelice, Cynthia. *The Real, True Dulcie Campbell*. Illus. by R. W. Alley. Farrar, 2002. 0-374-36220-3. Unp. Gr. K–2**

Mucking out the chicken coop on her family's Iowa farm one Saturday afternoon, it suddenly occurs to Dulcie that someone must have switched her from her royal crib at birth and that her real, true name is actually Princess Dulcinea. Curling up in the barn with a book of fairy tales, she soon notices that real princesses have to contend with wicked queens, hundred-year sleeping spells, and kissing frogs, all of which make her grateful to be herself.

GERM: Ask your children to fold a piece of drawing paper in half and write and illustrate two panels with one good thing about being a princess (or prince) versus one bad thing.

RELATED TITLES: Buehner, Caralyn. *Fanny's Dream*. Dial, 1996. / Craft, K. Y. *Cinderella*. SeaStar Books, 2000. / Grimm, Jacob. *The Sleeping Beauty*. Illus. by Trina Schart Hyman. Little, Brown, 1977. / Isele, Elizabeth. *The Frog Princess*. Crowell, 1984. / Karlin, Barbara. *Cinderella*. Illus. by James Marshall. Little, Brown, 1989. / Lester, Helen. *Princess Penelope's Parrot*. Houghton Mifflin, 1996. / Lewis, J. Patrick. *The Frog Princess: A Russian Tale*. Dial, 1994. / McClintock, Barbara. *Molly and the Magic Wishbone*. Farrar, 2001.

SUBJECTS: BOOKS AND READING. FAMILY LIFE. FARM LIFE. IMAGINATION. PRINCES AND PRINCESSES.

194   **Del Negro, Janice. *Lucy Dove*. Illus. by Leonid Gore. DK, 1998. 0-7894-2514-9. Unp. Gr. 4–6**

In return for a sack of gold, seamstress Lucy Dove agrees to sew a pair of trousers by the light of the full moon in the abandoned, haunted churchyard, in order to bring good fortune to a rich and superstitious laird (lord). Scratchy acrylic paintings match the shivery mood of this very spooky story, with a fearsome creature appearing from the grave, which will scare listeners to pieces but, fortunately, not brave, resourceful Lucy Dove.

GERM: Compare this original reworking of an old English folktale with Paul Galdone's version, *The Monster and the Tailor*. Meet three more feisty old dames who outwit scary creatures in Valerie Scho Carey's *Maggie Mab and the Bogey Beast*, Anita Riggio's *Beware the Brindlebeast*, and Brinton Turkle's *Do Not Open*.

RELATED TITLES: Bodkins, Odds. *The Banshee Train*. Clarion, 1995. / Carey, Valerie Scho. *Maggie Mab and the Bogey Beast*. Arcade, 1992. / Cecil, Laura, comp. *Boo! Stories to Make You Jump*. Greenwillow, 1990. / DeFelice, Cynthia C. *The Dancing Skeleton*. Macmillan, 1989. / Galdone, Joanna. *The Tailypo: A Ghost Story*. Clarion, 1977. / Galdone, Paul. *The Monster and the Tailor*. Clarion, 1982. / Hancock, Sibyl. *Esteban and the Ghost*. Dial, 1983. / Johnston, Tony. *The Ghost of Nicholas Greebe*. Dial, 1996. / Kimmel, Eric A. *Count Silvernose: A Story from Italy*. Holiday House, 1996. / Lindgren, Astrid. *The Ghost of Skinny Jack*. Viking, 1988. / Riggio, Anita. *Beware the Brindlebeast*. Boyds Mills, 1994. / San Souci, Robert D. *The Boy and the Ghost*. Simon & Schuster, 1989. / Turkle, Brinton. *Do Not Open*. Dutton, 1981. / Yep, Laurence. *The Man Who Tricked a Ghost*. BridgeWater, 1993.

SUBJECTS: MONSTERS. PICTURE BOOKS FOR OLDER READERS. SCOTLAND. STORIES TO TELL. SUSPENSE. WOMEN.

195   **Demas, Corinne. *Saying Goodbye to Lulu*. Illus. by Ard Hoyt. Little, Brown, 2004. 0-316-70278-1. Unp. Gr. PreK–2**

A freckle-faced young girl recounts the poignant last days in the life of her beloved black and white dog, Lulu. She recalls Lulu's burial in the backyard, the sorrow of being without her, and the joy of falling in love with a new puppy. This is a cycle-of-life story that will be familiar, reassuring, and healing to all of us who have lost a pet.

GERM: Read this when a child is mourning the loss of a pet to help everyone sort out their feelings and talk about life and death. The watercolor, colored pencil, and pen-and-ink illustrations are so expressive and real that children will have no trouble empathizing with the girl's many swirling emotions. Have your listeners study her face and reflect on how she must be feeling.

RELATED TITLES: Cohen, Miriam. *Jim's Dog Muffins.* Greenwillow, 1984. / Durant, Alan. *Always and Forever.* Harcourt, 2004. / Harris, Robie H. *Goodbye Mousie.* McElderry, 2001. / Heckert, Connie. *Dribbles.* Clarion, 1993. / Howard, Ellen. *Murphy and Kate.* Simon & Schuster, 1995. / James, Betsy. *Mary Ann.* Dutton, 1994. / Keller, Holly. *Goodbye, Max.* Greenwillow, 1987. / Pank, Rachel. *Under the Blackberries.* Scholastic, 1992. / Viorst, Judith. *The Tenth Good Thing About Barney.* Atheneum, 1971.

SUBJECTS: DEATH. DOGS. GRIEF.

196 **Demi.** *The Emperor's New Clothes: A Tale Set in China.* **McElderry, 2000. 0-689-83068-8. Unp. Gr. 1–3**

Sumptuously detailed gold-toned costumes and Chinese imperial architecture, plus gatefold pages and a four-page fold-out of the underwear-clad emperor's final walk past his bemused subjects mark Demi's take on the famous Hans Christian Andersen story.

GERM: Do a Quick Write and share: How does this old story apply to our lives here and now? Why do the imperial minister, the high chancellor, and the emperor himself insist they can see the invisible clothing the weaver and tailor are pretending to make? Compare the traditional setting of the story in old provincial China with the version illustrated by Angela Barrett, set stylishly in Europe in 1913. Meet the Turkish wise man and fool Nasrettin Hoca, a fellow who understands that clothes mean less than the person wearing them, in *The Hungry Coat*, also by Demi.

RELATED TITLES: Andersen, Hans Christian. *The Emperor's New Clothes.* Illus. by Angela Barrett. Candlewick, 1997. / Andersen, Hans Christian. *The Little Mermaid and Other Fairy Tales.* Illus. by Isabelle Brent. Viking, 1995. / Andersen, Hans Christian. *The Nightingale.* Retold by Stephen Mitchell. Illus. by Bagram Ibatoulline. Candlewick, 2002. / Andersen, Hans Christian. *The Nightingale.* Illus. by Jerry Pinkney. Putnam, 2002. / Andersen, Hans Christian. *The Ugly Duckling.* Illus. by Lorinda Bryan Cauley. Harcourt, 1979. / Calmenson, Stephanie. *The Principal's New Clothes.* Scholastic, 1989. / Demi. *The Empty Pot.* Henry Holt, 1990. / Demi. *The Hungry Coat: A Tale from Turkey.* McElderry, 2004. / Taback, Simms. *Joseph Had a Little Overcoat.* Viking, 1999.

SUBJECTS: CHINA. CLOTHING AND DRESS. EMPERORS. KINGS AND RULERS. LITERARY FAIRY TALES. MULTICULTURAL BOOKS.

197 **Denim, Sue.** *Make Way for Dumb Bunnies.* **Illus. by Dav Pilkey. Scholastic, 1996. 0-590-58286-0. Unp. Gr. PreK–2**

One morning when Poppa Bunny is watching the Super Bowl, Momma is watching the Orange Bowl (actually an orange bowl, filled with oranges), and Baby Bunny is watching the Toilet Bowl, it starts to pour. On such a perfect beach day, they swim, see a movie, and drive a steamroller home, flattening cars as they go. Slapstick, nonsensical, absurd, and just plain silly, this tribute to Harry Allard and James Marshall's classic series, The Stupids, will make kids fall off their chairs in hysterics.

GERM: Read one book and then set kids loose on others in the Dumb Bunnies series, along with The Stupids books, of course. Introduce the word *incongruity* and have your group point out incongruous or nonsensical behavior in both the book and in day-to-day life. Note, for your own amusement, the author's name, Sue Denim. Say it to yourself a couple of times, with the accent on the first name. Get it? Ha!

RELATED TITLES: Allard, Harry. *The Stupids Die.* Houghton Mifflin, 1981. / Allard, Harry. *The Stupids Have a Ball.* Houghton Mifflin, 1978. / Allard, Harry. *The Stupids Step Out.* Houghton Mifflin, 1974. / Allard, Harry. *The Stupids Take Off.* Houghton Mifflin, 1989. / Clement, Rod. *Grandpa's Teeth.* HarperCollins, 1998. / Clement, Rod. *Just Another Ordinary Day.* HarperCollins, 1997. / Cole, Joanna, and Philip Cole. *Big Goof and Little Goof.* Scholastic, 1989. / Denim, Sue. *The Dumb Bunnies.* Scholastic, 1994. / Denim, Sue. *The Dumb Bunnies' Easter.* Scholastic, 1995. / Denim, Sue. *The Dumb Bunnies Go to the Zoo.* Scholastic, 1997. / Edwards, Pamela Duncan. *The Worrywarts.* HarperCollins, 1999. / Egan, Tim. *Serious Farm.* Houghton Mifflin, 2003. / Legge, David. *Bamboozled.* Scholastic, 1995. / Salley, Coleen. *Epossumondas.* Harcourt, 2003.

SUBJECTS: HUMOROUS FICTION. RABBITS.

198 **dePaola, Tomie.** *Big Anthony: His Story.* **Illus. by the author. Putnam, 1998. 0-399-23189-7. Unp. Gr. K–4**

From his birth in the northern Italian hills up to the day he goes to work for Strega Nona, here is the biography of hapless klutz Big Anthony, who never pays attention, mixes up every set of instructions, and doesn't listen. Setting out to seek his fortune, Anthony is fired from every job, and even manages to straighten the Leaning Tower of Pisa.

GERM: In addition to reading the rest of the delightful stories in the Strega Nona series as part of an author study of the prolific Tomie dePaola, older students can use this entertaining character study as inspiration to invent some early childhood anecdotes of other famous children's book inhabitants, such as Peggy Parish's Amelia Bedelia or Cynthia Rylant's Mr. Putter, or the later lives of Barbara Park's Junie B. Jones or Beverly Cleary's Ramona.

RELATED TITLES: Birdseye, Tom. *Soap! Soap! Don't Forget the Soap! An Appalachian Folktale.* Holiday House, 1993. / dePaola, Tomie. *Big Anthony and the Magic Ring.* Harcourt, 1979. / dePaola, Tomie. *Strega Nona.* Simon & Schuster, 1979. / dePaola, Tomie. *Strega Nona's Magic Lessons.* Harcourt, 1982. / French, Vivian. *Lazy Jack.* Harcourt, 1996. / Montes, Marisa. *Juan Bobo Goes to Work: A Puerto Rican Folktale.* HarperCollins, 2000. / Parish, Peggy. Amelia Bedelia series. Greenwillow. / Salley, Coleen. *Epossumondas.* Harcourt, 2002. / Snyder, Dianne. *The Boy of the Three-Year Nap.* Houghton Mifflin, 1988.

SUBJECTS: BIOGRAPHICAL FICTION. FOOLS. ITALY.

199   dePaola, Tomie. *Jamie O'Rourke and the Pooka.* **Illus. by the author. Putnam, 2000. 0-399-23467-5. Unp. Gr. 2–5**

With his wife, Eileen, off to visit her sister for a week, Jamie makes a mess of the cottage, what with his friends coming over and no one washing a dish. In the middle of each night, Jamie is awakened by a donkey-like creature, a pooka, who cleans and sets everything right. Feeling sorry for the pooka, Jamie gives him his old coat, which turns out to be a big mistake.

GERM: Pair this humorous original tale about the laziest man in Ireland with dePaola's retelling of the companion folktale, *Jamie O'Rourke and the Big Potato.* Compare and contrast Jamie's encounter with the pooka with that of the shoemaker in the Grimm fairy tale *The Elves and the Shoemaker.*

RELATED TITLES: Balian, Lorna. *Leprechauns Never Lie.* Star Bright, 2004. / Bateman, Teresa. *The Ring of Truth.* Holiday House, 1997. / dePaola, Tomie. *Big Anthony and the Magic Ring.* Harcourt, 1979. / dePaola, Tomie. *Jamie O'Rourke and the Big Potato: An Irish Folktale.* Putnam, 1992. / dePaola, Tomie. *Strega Nona.* Simon & Schuster, 1979. / Edwards, Pamela Duncan. *The Leprechaun's Gold.* HarperCollins, 2004. / French, Vivian. *Lazy Jack.* Candlewick, 1995. / Grimm, Jacob. *The Elves and the Shoemaker.* Illus. by Paul Galdone. Clarion, 1984. / Lobel, Arnold. *A Treeful of Pigs.* Greenwillow, 1979. / Maitland, Anthony. *Idle Jack.* Farrar, 1979. / Shute, Linda. *Clever Tom and the Leprechaun.* Lothrop, 1988. / Snyder, Dianne. *The Boy of the Three Year Nap.* Houghton Mifflin, 1988. / Wolkstein, Diane. *Lazy Stories.* Seabury, 1976. / Zemach, Harve. *Duffy and the Devil.* Farrar, 1973.

SUBJECTS: ANIMALS, MYTHICAL. CLOTHING AND DRESS. GOBLINS. IRELAND. LAZINESS.

200   Dewan, Ted. *Crispin, the Pig Who Had It All.* **Illus. by the author. Doubleday, 2000. 0-385-32540-1. Unp. Gr. K–2**

Used to getting mega-toys for Christmas, which he ultimately breaks when they begin to bore him, Crispin Tamworth, a spoiled pig, receives a large, empty box from Santa, with a note claiming it's "the very best thing in the whole wide world." He shoves it outside, but when rabbit and raccoon kids Nick and Penny start to play Space Base in it, he's drawn into their inventive, imaginative game.

GERM: Talk about it: Why does Santa give Crispin such an odd present? Bring in a huge box for everyone to decorate and play in. Break into groups and hand each group a small box. Each group must come up with a new game that can be played using the box. Santa has a hard time delivering one simple box to the boy who lives at the top of Roly Poly Mountain in John Burningham's *Harvey Slumfenburger's Christmas Present.* Marian and a group of her playmates build their own play town out of rocks, wooden boxes, and other scraps on a cactus-strewn hill in Alice McLerran's *Roxaboxen.* And Mooch the cat gets his friend Earl the dog a present of a nice empty box in *The Gift of Nothing* by Patrick McDonnell.

RELATED TITLES: Brown, Laurie Krasny, and Marc Brown. *How to Be a Friend: A Guide to Making Friends and Keeping Them.* Little, Brown, 1998. / Burningham, John. *Harvey Slumfenburger's Christmas Present.* Candlewick, 1993. / Collins, Suzanne. *When Charlie McButton Lost Power.* Putnam, 2005. / Forward, Toby. *Ben's Christmas Carol.* Dutton, 1996. / Grey, Mini. *Traction Man Is Here!* Knopf, 2005. / Klise, Kate. *Shall I Knit You a Hat? A Christmas Yarn.* Henry Holt, 2004. / MacLean, Christine Kole. *Even Firefighters Hug Their Moms.* Dutton, 2002. / McDonnell, Patrick. *The Gift of Nothing.* Little, Brown, 2005. / McLerran, Alice. *Roxaboxen.* Lothrop, 1991. / Rylant, Cynthia. *Silver Packages: An Appalachian Christmas Story.* Orchard, 1997. / Santat, Dan. *The Guild of Geniuses.* Scholastic, 2004. / Steen, Sandra, and Susan Steen. *Car Wash.* Putnam, 2001. / Wiesner, David. *Hurricane.* Clarion, 1990.

SUBJECTS: CHRISTMAS. FRIENDSHIP. GIFTS. IMAGINATION. PIGS. PLAY.

201   Dewdney, Anna. *Llama Llama Red Pajama*. Illus. by the author. Viking, 2005. 0-670-05983-8. Unp. Gr. PreK–K

Feeling alone without his mama at bedtime, Baby Llama, in his red pajama, calls to her, but she's busy doing the dishes and talking on the phone. He boo-hoo's, stomps, pouts, shouts, and then gets scared. "What if Mama Llama's GONE?" Loudly he weeps and wails, and she comes running. The large, captivating full-bleed paintings of the two loving llamas, set against a deep indigo background, will send moms and little ones through a range of recognizable bedtime emotions.

GERM: Children and their moms can talk about how they handle bedtime. Read the title poem from Mary Ann Hoberman's collection, *The Llama Who Had No Pajama: 100 Favorite Poems*. Naturally, you'll pair this with the other favorite llama book, *Is Your Mama a Llama?* by Deborah Guarino. *Harley* by Star Livingstone presents a more pragmatic look at llama behavior, if you're looking for an all-llama story hour.

RELATED TITLES: Christelow, Eileen. *Five Little Monkeys Jumping on the Bed*. Clarion, 1989. / Cook, Sally. *Good Night Pillow Fight*. HarperCollins, 2004. / Guarino, Deborah. *Is Your Mama a Llama?* Scholastic, 1989. / Hoberman, Mary Ann. *The Llama Who Had No Pajama: 100 Favorite Poems*. Harcourt, 1998. / Livingstone, Star. *Harley*. SeaStar, 2001. / Murphy, Jill. *Peace at Last*. Dial, 1980. / Rothstein, Gloria. *Sheep Asleep*. HarperCollins, 2003. / Thomson, Pat. *The Squeaky, Creaky Bed*. Doubleday, 2003. / Walton, Rick. *So Many Bunnies: A Bedtime ABC and Counting Book*. Lothrop, 1998. / Yolen, Jane. *How Do Dinosaurs Say Good Night?* Blue Sky/Scholastic, 2000.

SUBJECTS: BEDTIME STORIES. CRYING. LLAMAS. MOTHERS AND SONS. STORIES IN RHYME.

202   DiPucchio, Kelly. *Liberty's Journey*. Illus. by Richard Egielski. Hyperion, 2004. 0-7868-1876-X. Unp. Gr. K–3

Succumbing to her wanderlust, Lady Liberty steps down from her sacred place atop the pedestal in New York Harbor and sets off across the United States in search of amber waves of grain. Recognized along the way by appreciative folks, she heads westward, sleeping in the Grand Canyon, and finally reaches the Pacific, having journeyed literally from sea to shining sea.

GERM: Children can create a list of the places that Lady Liberty might like to visit on her next trip and then write and illustrate a travelogue of her journey to those locales (be it across the country or within your home state), depicting her as a sightseer. Next, your junior tourists can start making plans for their own future travels, listing where they'd like to go and why, and can compile a No Place Like Home list, detailing what they'd miss while they were gone. Maren Vitali's second graders at Van Holten School in Bridgewater, New Jersey, compiled a travel scrapbook for the imagined trips they took with Liberty across scenic New Jersey, combining fact and fiction. Using photos and their own cut-and-pasted drawings, they also had to research one fact and then add an anecdotal sentence about their experiences with Liberty. One child wrote about a trip down the shore to Cape May: "Lady Liberty fell out of the boat. I was disappointed in her."

RELATED TITLES: Bartone, Elisa. *American Too*. Lothrop, 1996. / Borden, Louise. *America Is . . .* McElderry, 2002. / Bunting, Eve. *A Picnic in October*. Harcourt, 1999. / Curlee, Lynn. *Liberty*. Atheneum, 2000. / Drummond, Allan. *Liberty!* Farrar, 2002. / Fisher, Leonard E. *The Statue of Liberty*. Holiday House, 1985. / Guthrie, Woody. *This Land Is Your Land*. Little, Brown, 1998. / Keller, Laurie. *The Scrambled States of America*. Henry Holt, 1998. / Maestro, Betsy. *The Story of the Statue of Liberty*. Lothrop, 1986. / Melmed, Laura Krauss. *New York, New York! The Big Apple from A to Z*. HarperCollins, 2005. / Neubecker, Robert. *Wow! America!* Hyperion, 2006. / Pattison, Darcy. *The Journey of Oliver K. Woodman*. Harcourt, 2003. / Robertson, Chris. *Little Miss Liberty*. Chronicle, 2005. / Sabuda, Robert. *America the Beautiful*. Little Simon, 2004. / Stevens, Carla. *Lily and Miss Liberty*. Scholastic, 1992. / Zimelman, Nathan. *How the Second Grade Got $8,205.50 to Visit the Statue of Liberty*. Albert Whitman, 1992.

SUBJECTS: GEOGRAPHY. NEW YORK CITY. STATUE OF LIBERTY. STORIES IN RHYME. U.S.—DESCRIPTION AND TRAVEL. U.S.—GEOGRAPHY.

203   DiPucchio, Kelly. *Mrs. McBloom, Clean Up Your Classroom*. Illus. by Guy Francis. Hyperion, 2005. 0-7868-0932-9. Unp. Gr. K–3

In 50 years of teaching at Knickerbocker Elementary in the pint-sized town of Up Yonder, Mrs. McBloom has never, not once, cleaned up her classroom. It's been on her to-do list for 45 years, though, right above "Take a fancy-schmancy cruise." Now, one week before she's fixin' to retire, the room is crammed with critters, plants, books, papers, and even a full-grown Ruby Red apple tree that's growing smack dab in the middle of the room. With sweet, young Miss Bumblesprout wanting the room cleared out so she can take over in the fall, Mrs. McBloom asks her students to come up with a creative plan to clear out the mess, which they do with gusto.

GERM: A comical take on a perennial problem (and some of us can identify with it), and a warm tribute to master teachers, however messy, everywhere, this will get your students thinking about and writing descriptions of the geological and historical treasures their favorite teachers have shared with them and squirreled away. On the more serious side are two moving tributes to real teachers, *My Great Aunt Arizona* by Gloria Houston and *Thank You, Mr. Falker* by Patricia Polacco.

RELATED TITLES: Allard, Harry. *Miss Nelson Is Missing.* Houghton Mifflin, 1977. / Clements, Andrew. *Double Trouble in Walla Walla.* Millbrook, 1997. / Creech, Sharon. *A Fine, Fine School.* HarperCollins, 2001. / DiPucchio, Kelly. *Liberty's Journey.* Hyperion, 2004. / Finchler, Judy. *Miss Malarkey Doesn't Live in Room 10.* Walker, 1995. / Houston, Gloria. *My Great Aunt Arizona.* HarperCollins, 1992. / Polacco, Patricia. *Thank You, Mr. Falker.* Philomel, 1998. / Pulver, Robin. *Mrs. Toggle and the Dinosaur.* Four Winds, 1991. / Seuss, Dr. *Hooray for Diffendoofer Day.* Knopf, 1998.

SUBJECTS: CLEANLINESS. HELPFULNESS. ORDERLINESS. SCHOOLS. TEACHERS.

204   **Dodds, Dayle Ann.** *Minnie's Diner: A Multiplying Menu.* **Illus. by John Manders. Candlewick, 2004. 0-7636-1736-9. Unp. Gr. K–3**

One by one, Papa McFay's five strapping sons, each one twice the size of his next younger brother, stop doing their farmwork to run on down to Minnie's Diner, where the youngest orders the special: 1 soup, 1 salad, 1 sandwich, some fries, and one of her delicious hot cherry pies. Each brother in turn orders double what the others had. Viewers will laugh and gasp at the humorous gouache illustrations of waitress Minnie hoisting her ever-doubling tray of grub.

GERM: Relate this to the doubling sequence in Nancy Raines Day's *Double Those Wheels.* In Arlene Mosel's *The Funny Little Woman,* one grain of rice is doubled all the way up to 356. Carry the binary sequence further with Demi's folktale from India, *One Grain of Rice.*

RELATED TITLES: Appelt, Kathi. *Bats on Parade.* HarperCollins, 1999. / Day, Nancy Raines. *Double Those Wheels.* Dutton, 2003. / Demi. *One Grain of Rice.* Scholastic, 1997. / Leedy, Loreen. *2 X 2 = BOO! A Set of Spooky Multiplication Stories.* Holiday House, 1995. / Losi, Carol. *512 Ants on Sullivan Street.* Scholastic, 1997. / Michelson, Richard. *Ten Times Better.* Marshall Cavendish, 2000. / Mosel, Arlene. *The Funny Little Woman.* Dutton, 1972. / Pinczes, Elinor J. *One Hundred Hungry Ants.* Houghton Mifflin, 1993. / Pittman, Helena Clare. *A Grain of Rice.* Hastings House, 1986. / Tang, Greg. *The Best of Times: Math Strategies That Multiply.* Scholastic, 2002.

SUBJECTS: DINERS (RESTAURANTS). FARM LIFE. FATHERS AND SONS. MATHEMATICS. MULTIPLICATION. RESTAURANTS. SIZE. STORIES IN RHYME.

205   **Dodds, Dayle Ann.** *Sing, Sophie!* **Illus. by Rosanne Litzinger. Candlewick, 1997. 0-7636-0131-4. Unp. Gr. K–3**

No one in little Sophie Adams's family cares to listen when the young cowgirl strums her guitar and sings her peppy songs (yippee-ky-yee!). On the night of the big storm, when no one else can stop baby Jacob's tears, Sophie steps up to sing him a verse or two, and that works just fine.

GERM: Ask your listeners to list and describe the activities and pastimes they love best of all, the ones worth nurturing, no matter the obstacles.

RELATED TITLES: Axelrod, Alan. *Songs of the Wild West.* Simon & Schuster, 1991. / Fleming, Candace. *Smile, Lily!* Atheneum, 2004. / Frazee, Marla. *Hush, Little Baby: A Folk Song with Pictures.* Harcourt, 1999. / Goss, Linda. *The Frog Who Wanted to Be a Singer.* Orchard, 1996. / Gray, Libba Moore. *Little Lil and the Swing-Singing Sax.* Simon & Schuster, 1996. / Hoffman, Mary. *Amazing Grace.* Dial, 1991. / Howe, James. *Horace and Morris Join the Chorus (But What About Dolores?).* Atheneum, 2002. / Hurd, Thacher. *Art Dog.* HarperCollins, 1996. / Khalsa, Dayal Kaur. *Cowboy Dreams.* Crown, 1990. / Root, Phyllis. *What Baby Wants.* Candlewick, 1998.

SUBJECTS: BABIES. BROTHERS AND SISTERS. SINGING. STORMS.

206   **Dodds, Dayle Ann.** *Where's Pup?* **Illus. by Pierre Pratt. Dial, 2003. 0-8037-2744-5. Unp. Gr. PreK–1**

An emergent rhyming reader full of sly humor introduces a bespectacled little clown searching the circus grounds for his dog, asking his pals where Pup might be. Sturdy paper stock sports amiable acrylic paintings of all the circus acts: elephant, mouse leaping through a hoop, pig shot out of a cannon, trapeze artists, and, finally, acrobats. "Can't find pup? Just look up, and up, and up." Unfold the final page upwards, and there he is—at the very top.

GERM: Each time the little clown's friends suggest that he ask someone else where his dog might be—"Don't know? Go ask Jo. She's feeding Mo."—have your listeners predict what and who he will find. This would be such fun to act out as a Reader's Theater. Start off the story by asking listeners to tell you what can be seen at a circus. Afterward, see if your kids can come up with more rhyming pairs of names about which they can write and illustrate rhyming sentences, such as "Judy and Rudy are very moody."

RELATED TITLES: Alarcón, Karen Beaumont. *Louella Mae, She's Run Away!* Henry Holt, 1997. / Eastman, P. D. *Are You My Mother?* Random House, 1960. / Ehlert, Lois. *Circus.* HarperCollins, 1992. / Ernst, Lisa Campbell. *Ginger Jumps.* Bradbury, 1990. / Falconer, Ian. *Olivia Saves the Circus.* Atheneum, 2001. / Hill, Eric. *Where's Spot?* Putnam, 1980. / Rathmann, Peggy. *The Day the Babies Crawled Away.* Putnam, 2003. / Shaw, Nancy. *Sheep in a Jeep.* Houghton, 1986. / Wild, Margaret. *The Pocket Dogs.* Scholastic, 2001. / Wilson, Karma. *A Frog in the Bog.* McElderry, 2003.

SUBJECTS: CIRCUS. CLOWNS. DOGS. READER'S THEATER. STORIES IN RHYME.

207 **Donaldson, Julia. *The Gruffalo*. Illus. by Axel Scheffler. Dial, 1999. 0-8037-2386-5. Unp. Gr. PreK–1**

A mouse talks a fox, an owl, and a snake out of eating him by describing the Gruffalo, a fierce, made-up monster he is pretending to meet for lunch. When an actual Gruffalo shows up, eager to eat him, the wily mouse tells the Gruffalo that he, Mouse, is the scariest creature in the deep, dark wood, and he proves it too.

GERM: Mouse is one clever little fellow, as this charmer of a rhyming story attests. Have children discuss how he outwitted all those animals and convinced the Gruffalo to be afraid of him. All of the repetition, humor, and just a touch of danger make this story a good candidate to script up for Reader's Theater for first grade or to act out for pre-readers. Follow up with the sequel, *The Gruffalo's Child*, in which the Gruffalo's young daughter heads out in the snow to prove the existence of the Big Bad Mouse.

RELATED TITLES: Clark, Emma Chichester. *Follow the Leader.* McElderry, 2003. / Donaldson, Julia. *The Gruffalo's Child.* Dial, 1999. / Emberley, Michael. *Ruby.* Little, Brown, 1990. / Farris, Pamela J. *Young Mouse and Elephant: An East African Folktale.* Houghton Mifflin, 1996. / Kasza, Keiko. *Grandpa Toad's Secrets.* Putnam, 1995. / Kasza, Keiko. *My Lucky Day.* Putnam, 2003. / Lester, Helen. *Hooway for Wodney Wat.* Houghton Mifflin, 1999. / Lester, Helen. *Listen, Buddy.* Houghton Mifflin, 1995. / MacDonald, Margaret Read. *Mabela the Clever.* Albert Whitman, 2001. / McKissack, Patricia C. *Flossie and the Fox.* Dial, 1986. / Meddaugh, Susan. *Hog-Eye.* Houghton Mifflin, 1995. / Young, Ed. *Mouse Match: A Chinese Folktale.* Harcourt, 1997.

SUBJECTS: ANIMALS, IMAGINARY. CREATIVE DRAMA. MICE. READER'S THEATER. STORIES IN RHYME.

208 **Donaldson, Julia. *The Snail and the Whale*. Illus. by Axel Scheffler. Dial, 2004. 0-8037-2922-7. Unp. Gr. PreK–3**

A tiny itchy-footed snail who longs to sail hitches a ride around the world on the tail of a humpback whale. When the whale loses his way and is beached on the shore, the snail enlists the help of schoolchildren to save him.

GERM: The rhyming text nicely conveys an environmental message about the value of all creatures, small and large. Do some research on whales and snails and their places in the ecosystem. Transform yourself into a humpback whale in *Winter Whale* by Joanne Ryder and celebrate whales in poetry with *If You Ever Meet a Whale* by Myra Cohn Livingston.

RELATED TITLES: Berger, Gilda. *Whales.* Doubleday, 1987. / Donaldson, Julia. *The Gruffalo.* Dial, 1999. / Koch, Michelle. *World Water Watch.* Greenwillow, 1993. / Livingston, Myra Cohn, comp. *If You Ever Meet a Whale.* Holiday House, 1992. / McCloskey, Robert. *Burt Dow, Deep-Water Man.* Viking, 1963. / McMillan, Bruce. *Going on a Whale Watch.* Scholastic, 1992. / Ryder, Joanne. *The Snail's Spell.* Warne, 1982. / Ryder, Joanne. *Winter Whale.* Morrow, 1991. / Vollmer, Dennis. *Joshua Disobeys.* Landmark Editions, 1988. / Wells, Robert E. *Is a Blue Whale the Biggest Thing There Is?* Albert Whitman, 1993.

SUBJECTS: ECOLOGY. FRIENDSHIP. SIZE. SNAILS. STORIES IN RHYME. WHALES. WILDLIFE RESCUE.

209 **Dooley, Norah. *Everybody Bakes Bread*. Illus. by Peter J. Thornton. Carolrhoda, 1996. 0-87614-864-X. 40pp. Gr. K–3**

Children will yearn to taste the Barbadian, Indian, Middle Eastern, Jewish, Italian, and El Salvadorian breads Carrie samples when her mother sends her off to visit her ethnically diverse neighbors in search of a three-handled rolling pin.

GERM: Fortunately, the recipes are appended, if you are feeling ambitious. Otherwise, you can always buy an assortment of breads for all to taste, from cornbread to pita. Pair this with the first book about Carrie, *Everybody Cooks Rice*. By the way, there's no such thing as a three-handled rolling pin; it's what might be called a fool's errand.

RELATED TITLES: Baer, Edith. *This Is the Way We Eat Our Lunch: A Book About Children Around the World.* Scholastic, 1995. / Cox, Judy. *Now We Can Have a Wedding.* Holiday House, 1998. / Dooley, Norah. *Everybody Cooks Rice.* Carolrhoda, 1991. / Levenson, George. *Bread Comes to Life: A Garden of Wheat and a Loaf to Eat.* Tricycle, 2004. / Morris, Ann. *Bread Bread Bread.* Lothrop, 1989. / Priceman, Marjorie. *How to Make an Apple Pie and See the World.* Knopf, 1994. / Rattigan, Jama Kim. *Dumpling Soup.* Little, Brown, 1993. / Shelby, Anne. *Potluck.* Orchard, 1991. / Soto, Gary. *Too Many Tamales.* Putnam, 1993. / Wing, Natasha. *Jalapeño Bagels.* Atheneum, 1996. / Wong, Janet. *Apple Pie 4th of July.* Harcourt, 2002.

SUBJECTS: BAKING. BREAD. COOKERY. FOOD. MULTICULTURAL BOOKS. NEIGHBORLINESS.

210   Dorros, Arthur. *City Chicken.* Illus. by Henry Cole. HarperCollins, 2003. 0-06-028482-X. Unp. Gr. PreK–2

After hearing Lucy the cat describe cows, horses, and pigs, city chicken Henrietta (Henry for short), a chicken who happens to lay blue eggs, decides it's time to leave her little chicken coop for a trip to the farm in the country.

GERM: As the fish does in Leo Lionni's *Fish Is Fish*, Henry imagines what other animals must look like based on her own body type and Lucy the cat's less-than-thorough descriptions. Children can work in pairs to come up with one-sentence descriptions of other animals—elephants, kangaroos, whales—and draw how Henry would see them in her mind's eye. Compare Henry's city life with chicken Minerva Louise's farm life in Janet Morgan Stoeke's series.

RELATED TITLES: Cauley, Lorinda Bryan. *The Town Mouse and the Country Mouse.* Putnam, 1984. / Duvoisin, Roger. *Petunia.* Knopf, 1989. / Lionni, Leo. *Fish Is Fish.* Pantheon, 1970. / Marshall, James. *Wings: A Tale of Two Chickens.* Dutton, 1986. / Stoeke, Janet Morgan. *A Hat for Minerva Louise.* Dutton, 1996. (And others in the Minerva Louise series.)

SUBJECTS: CHICKENS. CITIES AND TOWNS. COUNTRY LIFE. IMAGINATION.

211   Dowson, Nick. *Tigress.* Illus. by Jane Chapman. Candlewick, 2004. 0-7636-2325-3. 32pp. Gr. K–3

Similes and metaphors abound in this poetic but factual depiction, along with dramatic close-up acrylics, of a tigress raising her two cubs.

GERM: Before you read this book, make a list of what children want to find out about tigers. As you read aloud to the class, ask each group of four students to listen carefully for facts about one aspect of a tiger's life, such as food, defense, habits, and raising young. Each group can add to a chart, displaying the facts they've learned. What questions did the text not address? Use the index in the back for a mini-lesson on how to use one. As a group, brainstorm for a list of subjects that should be in the index and compare their responses with what is actually there. Meet the woman who raised 27 baby tigers at the Bronx Zoo in George Ella Lyon's picture book tribute, *Mother to Tigers*.

RELATED TITLES: Arnold, Marsha Diane. *Heart of a Tiger.* Dial, 1995. / Bannerman, Helen. *The Story of Little Babaji.* HarperCollins, 1996. / Faulkner, William J. *Brer Tiger and the Big Wind.* Morrow, 1995. / Hoberman, Mary Ann. *It's Simple, Said Simon.* Knopf, 2001. / Lester, Julius. *Sam and the Tigers.* Dial, 1996. / Lyon, George Ella. *Mother to Tigers.* Atheneum, 2003. / Nagda, Ann Whitehead, and Cindy Bickel. *Tiger Math: Learning to Graph from a Baby Tiger.* Henry Holt, 2000. / Radcliffe, Theresa. *Maya, Tiger Cub.* Viking, 1999. / Temple, Frances. *Tiger Soup: An Anansi Story from Jamaica.* Orchard, 1994. / Thomson, Sarah L. *Tigers.* HarperCollins, 1994. / Winters, Kay. *Tiger Trail.* Simon & Schuster, 2000. / Wright, Kit. *Tigerella.* Scholastic, 1994.

SUBJECTS: ANIMALS—INFANCY. ENGLISH LANGUAGE—SIMILES AND METAPHORS. TIGERS.

212   Dragonwagon, Crescent. *And Then It Rained . . .* Illus. by Diane Greenseid. Atheneum, 2003. 0-689-81884-X. Unp. Gr. PreK–2

At first everybody in the city likes the rain, including a little boy and his father, but after five days folks get grouchy and wonder when it will stop. Flip the book over and read the second half of the story—*And Then the Sun Came Out*—in which everyone revels in the change from rain, until it gets hotter and hotter.

GERM: Discussion starter: Which kind of weather do you like best and why? Is it different in the city and country when it rains? As part of a weather unit, have your junior forecasters write and illustrate "And Then It Snowed," describing their snowy day experiences.

RELATED TITLES: Aardema, Verna. *Bringing the Rain to Kapiti Plain*. Dial, 1981. / Alexander, Lloyd. *How the Cat Swallowed Thunder*. Dutton, 2000. / Anholt, Catherine, and Laurence Anholt. *Chimp and Zee and the Big Storm*. Putnam, 2002. / Barrett, Judi. *Cloudy with a Chance of Meatballs*. Atheneum, 1978. / Ginsburg, Mirra. *Mushroom in the Rain*. Macmillan, 1974. / Johnson, Stephen T. *Alphabet City*. Viking, 1995. / Ketteman, Helen. *Heat Wave!* Walker, 1998. / Martin, Bill, Jr., and John Archambault. *Listen to the Rain*. Henry Holt, 1988. / Neubecker, Robert. *Wow! City!* Hyperion, 2004. / Polacco, Patricia. *Thunder Cake*. Philomel, 1990. / Schaefer, Lola M. *This Is the Rain*. HarperCollins, 2001. / Shepard, Aaron. *Master Man*. HarperCollins, 2001. / Stojic, Manya. *Rain*. Crown, 2000. / Tafuri, Nancy. *Snowy Flowy Blowy: A Twelve Months Rhyme*. Scholastic, 1999 / Yep, Laurence. *The Junior Thunder Lord*. BridgeWater, 1994.

SUBJECTS: CITIES AND TOWNS. FATHERS AND SONS. RAIN AND RAINFALL. SUN. WEATHER.

213   Drummond, Allan. *Liberty!* **Illus. by the author. Farrar, 2002. 0-374-34385-3. Unp. Gr. PreK–3**
A young boy describes how he helped give the signal to Mr. Bartholdi to unveil the face of the Statue of Liberty to all of New York on October 28, 1886.

GERM: Read and discuss this quote from the book: "Freedom is like a flame we must all hold high and give to others and keep burning bright around the world." Investigate more facts about the statue in *Liberty* by Lynn Curlee, *The Statue of Liberty* by Leonard E. Fisher, and *The Story of the Statue of Liberty* by Betsy Maestro.

RELATED TITLES: Bartone, Elisa. *Peppe the Lamplighter*. Lothrop, 1993. / Bunting, Eve. *A Picnic in October*. Harcourt, 1999. / Curlee, Lynn. *Liberty*. Atheneum, 2000. / DiPucchio, Kelly. *Liberty's Journey*. Hyperion, 2004. / Fisher, Leonard E. *The Statue of Liberty*. Holiday House, 1985. / Jakobsen, Kathy. *My New York*. Little, Brown, 2003. / Maestro, Betsy. *The Story of the Statue of Liberty*. Lothrop, 1986. / Stevens, Carla. *Lily and Miss Liberty*. Scholastic, 1992. / Zimelman, Nathan. *How the Second Grade Got $8,205.50 to Visit the Statue of Liberty*. Albert Whitman, 1992.

SUBJECTS: HISTORICAL FICTION. NEW YORK CITY. STATUE OF LIBERTY.

214   Duke, Kate. *Aunt Isabel Makes Trouble.* **Illus. by the author. Dutton, 1996. 0-525-45496-9. Unp. Gr. K–2**
Penelope the mouse helps her Aunt Isabel tell a story about Lady Penelope who, off to visit the kind and handsome Prince Augustus in his nice, safe castle, finds adventure, danger, and villains when she captures Cocky the Roach and his gang on her way. Every time Aunt Isabel's storytelling gets too predictable, Penelope says, "BUT—" and Aunt Isabel adds an episode of conflict, foreshadowing, drama, intrigue, danger, and finally, success to the saga of adventure-seeking Lady Nell's valiant efforts to make it to her true love's birthday party.

GERM: In *Aunt Isabel Tells a Good One*, the tale she spins for Penelope showcases story elements, including character, plot, and conflict. In this companion book, she demonstrates that a good plot should contain many unexpected twists and turns to "keep it full of surprises." This should prove an effective model for writers working on their own adventures.

RELATED TITLES: Brown, Marc. *Arthur Writes a Story*. Little, Brown, 1996. / Duke, Kate. *Aunt Isabel Tells a Good One*. Dutton, 1992. / Kroll, Steven. *Patches Lost and Found*. Winslow, 2001. / Leedy, Loreen. *Look at My Book: How Kids Can Write and Illustrate Terrific Books*. Holiday House, 2004. / Nixon, Joan Lowery. *If You Were a Writer*. Four Winds, 1988. / Schotter, Roni. *Nothing Ever Happens on 90th Street*. Orchard, 1997. / Zemach, Kaethe. *The Character in the Book*. HarperCollins, 1998.

SUBJECTS: AUNTS. BIRTHDAYS. MICE. STORYTELLING.

215   Dunbar, Polly. *Dog Blue.* **Illus. by the author. Candlewick, 2004. 0-7636-1736-9. Unp. Gr. PreK–1**
Bertie loves the color blue and pretends he has a blue dog. When a tiny, perfect, beautiful black and white dog turns up, all alone and looking for an owner, Bertie must figure out a way to deal with the dog's lack of blueness.

GERM: Ask your listeners to solve Bertie's dilemma. What should he do with a dog that isn't blue? Pretend you're blue dogs and run, fetch, and maybe even roll over.

RELATED TITLES: Feiffer, Jules. *Bark, George!* HarperCollins, 1999. / George, Kristine O'Connell. *Little Dog Poems*. Clarion, 1999. / Graham, Bob. *"Let's Get a Pup!" Said Kate*. Candlewick, 2001. / Jonell, Lynne. *It's My Birthday, Too!* Putnam, 1999. / Kellogg, Steven. *Pinkerton, Behave*. Dial, 1979. / McFarland, Lyn Rossiter. *Widget*. Farrar, 2001. / Rylant, Cynthia. *The Great Gracie Chase*. Scholastic, 2001. / Simont, Marc. *The Stray Dog*. HarperCollins, 2001. / Thayer, Jane. *The Puppy Who Wanted a Boy*. Morrow, 1986. / Voake, Charlotte. *Ginger*

Finds a Home. Candlewick, 2003. / Wells, Rosemary. *Lucy Comes to Stay*. Dial, 1994. / Wells, Rosemary. *McDuff Moves In*. Hyperion, 1997. (And others in the McDuff series.)
SUBJECTS: COLOR. DOGS. IMAGINATION.

216   **Dunrea, Olivier.** *Gossie*. **Illus. by the author. Houghton Mifflin, 2002. 0-618-17674-8. Unp. Gr. PreK–K**
Small yellow gosling Gossie wears her bright red boots every day to eat, sleep, and walk, until the day they go missing. Who took them? Gertie! The two little goslings then share, one boot for each. The sequel, *Gossie and Gertie*, is essential, and just as perfect, with its watercolors outlined in ink on white pages, spare but irresistible.
GERM: In this pared-down text, you'll still find wonderful story structure: a problem, rising action, climax, and boffo ending. It even fits the three Freeman S's: it Surprises, it Startles, and it Satisfies. Plus, you can use it to teach conjunctions such as over, under, above, and in. Act this one out in narrative pantomime: as you read the story, the children pretend to be Gossie walking about in her wonderful boots.
RELATED TITLES: Braun, Trudi. *My Goose Betsy*. Candlewick, 1999. / Dunrea, Olivier. *BooBoo*. Houghton, 2004. / Dunrea, Olivier. *Gossie and Gertie*. Houghton Mifflin, 2002. / Dunrea, Olivier. *Ollie*. Houghton, 2003. / Dunrea, Olivier. *Ollie the Stomper*. Houghton, 2003. / Dunrea, Olivier. *Peedie*. Houghton, 2004. / Gerstein, Mordicai. *Follow Me!* Morrow, 1983. / Hest, Amy. *In the Rain with Baby Duck*. Candlewick, 1995. / Hissey, Jane. *Little Bear's Trousers*. Philomel, 1987. / Raffi. *Five Little Ducks*. Crown, 1988. / Schoenherr, John. *Rebel*. Philomel, 1995. / Simmons, Jane. *Come Along, Daisy*. Little, Brown, 1998. / Simmons, Jane. *Quack, Daisy, Quack!* Little, Brown, 2002. / Whippo, Walt, and Bernard Zaritzky. *Little White Duck*. Little, Brown, 2000. / Wolkstein, Diane. *Step by Step*. Morrow, 1994.
SUBJECTS: BOOTS. CLOTHING AND DRESS. CREATIVE DRAMA. FRIENDSHIP. GEESE.

217   **Dunrea, Olivier.** *Ollie*. **Illus. by the author. Houghton Mifflin, 2003. 0-618-33928-0. Unp. Gr. PreK–1**
Geese friends Gossie and Gertie have been waiting for weeks for Ollie to hatch out of his egg, but he refuses to come out.
GERM: Use hard-boiled eggs for Ollie, and make popsicle stick puppets for Gossie and Gertie, so everyone can act this one out. Follow up with *Ollie the Stomper*. Find puppets of boot-clad Gossie, Gertie, and Ollie at <www.mimismotifs.com>.
RELATED TITLES: Braun, Trudi. *My Goose Betsy*. Candlewick, 1999. / Buzzeo, Toni. *Dawdle Duckling*. Dial, 2003. / Dunrea, Olivier. *Boo Boo*. Houghton Mifflin, 2004. / Dunrea, Olivier. *Gossie*. Houghton Mifflin, 2002. / Dunrea, Olivier. *Gossie and Gertie*. Houghton, 2002. / Dunrea, Olivier. *Ollie the Stomper*. Houghton, 2003. / Dunrea, Olivier. *Peedie*. Houghton, 2004. / Emmett, Jonathan. *Ruby in Her Own Time*. Scholastic, 2004. / Raffi. *Five Little Ducks*. Crown, 1988. / Rankin, Joan. *Wow! It's Great Being a Duck*. McElderry, 1998. / Schoenherr, John. *Rebel*. Philomel, 1995. / Simmons, Jane. *Quack, Daisy, Quack!* Little, Brown, 2002. / Waddell, Martin. *Webster J. Duck*. Candlewick, 2001.
SUBJECTS: CREATIVE DRAMA. EGGS. GEESE.

218   **Duquette, Keith.** *Cock-a-Doodle Moooo! A Mixed-Up Menagerie*. **Illus. by the author. Putnam, 2004. 0-399-23889-1. Unp. Gr. 1–4**
Combine two animals, such as a cow and a rooster, and what do you get? A "cooster"! Each composite creature is displayed proudly in saucy watercolor and gouache paintings, with an accompanying description in rhyme.
GERM: The author asks, "Of all the animals we could combine, what kind of creatures would you design?" At the back, an illustrated list of 12 more animal combinations introduces readers to such mythical oddities as the chimera, griffin, and kappa. *Zoodles* by Bernard Most also introduces merged animals, using a riddle format for children to guess each one.
RELATED TITLES: McMillan, Bruce, and Brett McMillan. *Puniddles*. Houghton Mifflin, 1982. / Most, Bernard. *Can You Find It?* Harcourt, 1994. / Most, Bernard. *Hippopotamus Hunt*. Harcourt, 1994. / Most, Bernard. *Zoodles*. Harcourt, 1992. / Prelutsky, Jack. *Scranimals*. Greenwillow, 2002. / Walton, Rick. *Once There Was a Bull . . . (Frog)*. Gibbs-Smith, 1995.
SUBJECTS: ANIMALS, IMAGINARY. ANIMALS, MYTHICAL. STORIES IN RHYME. WORD GAMES.

219   **Durant, Alan.** *Always and Forever*. **Illus. by Debi Gliori. Harcourt, 2004. 0-15-216636-X. Unp. Gr. K–2**
Otter, Mole, and Hare are devastated when their beloved housemate Fox falls ill and dies. They

bury him and grieve all winter, but it's not until Squirrel comes for a visit that they start reminiscing about their funny memories of Fox and start laughing again. Large, lovely pen-and-ink and watercolor illustrations take us gently through the stages of grief.

GERM: When you need to talk about the death of a loved one, use this book to bring comfort and healing.

RELATED TITLES: Cohen, Miriam. *Jim's Dog Muffins.* Greenwillow, 1984. / Demas, Corinne. *Saying Goodbye to Lulu.* Little, Brown, 2004. / Engel, Diana. *Eleanor, Arthur, and Claire.* Macmillan, 1992. / Harris, Robie H. *Goodbye Mousie.* McElderry, 2001. / Heckert, Connie. *Dribbles.* Clarion, 1993. / Howard, Ellen. *Murphy and Kate.* Simon & Schuster, 1995. / James, Betsy. *Mary Ann.* Dutton, 1994. / Keller, Holly. *Goodbye, Max.* Greenwillow, 1987. / Pank, Rachel. *Under the Blackberries.* Scholastic, 1992. / Varley, Susan. *Badger's Parting Gifts.* HarperCollins, 1984. / Viorst, Judith. *The Tenth Good Thing About Barney.* Atheneum, 1971.

SUBJECTS: ANIMALS. DEATH. FOXES. GRIEF.

220 **Edwards, Pamela Duncan.** *Barefoot: Escape on the Underground Railroad.* **Illus. by Henry Cole. HarperCollins, 1997. 0-06-027138-8. Unp. Gr. 1–4**

In a suspenseful, dramatic picture book, the animals of the woods aid the Barefoot, an escaped slave, to elude his pursuers, the Heavy Boots. Throughout the dark, night-lit paintings, as the Barefoot runs down the pathway, we see him from the animals' point of view, without catching a glimpse of his face until the final page.

GERM: Children can decide whether the frog, mouse, heron, deer, and mosquitoes aid the young man and thwart the Heavy Boots on purpose or inadvertently as the Barefoot makes his way to the house he seeks, a station on the Underground Railroad. Edwards's clear and compelling style makes this an excellent book to use when it's time to introduce younger children to the cold realities of slavery without being overly graphic.

RELATED TITLES: Adler, David A. *A Picture Book of Harriet Tubman.* Holiday House, 1992. / Hopkinson, Deborah. *Sweet Clara and the Freedom Quilt.* Knopf, 1993. / Howard, Elizabeth Fitzgerald. *Virgie Goes to School with Us Boys.* Simon & Schuster, 2000. / Johnson, Dolores. *Now Let Me Fly: The Story of a Slave Family.* Macmillan, 1993. / Nelson, Vaunda Micheaux. *Almost to Freedom.* Carolrhoda, 2003. / Ransom, Candice. *Liberty Street.* Walker, 2003. / Ringgold, Faith. *Aunt Harriet's Underground Railroad in the Sky.* Crown, 1992. / Winter, Jeannette. *Follow the Drinking Gourd.* Knopf, 1989.

SUBJECTS: ADVENTURE AND ADVENTURERS. AFRICAN AMERICANS. AFRICAN AMERICANS—HISTORY. FUGITIVE SLAVES. HISTORICAL FICTION. MULTICULTURAL BOOKS. PICTURE BOOKS FOR ALL AGES. SLAVERY. UNDERGROUND RAILROAD.

221 **Edwards, Pamela Duncan.** *Clara Caterpillar.* **Illus. by Henry Cole. HarperCollins, 2001. 0-06-028995-3. Unp. Gr. PreK–2**

Cream-colored cabbage caterpillar Clara climbs out of her cozy chrysalis and courageously confuses the crow who wants to capture crimson-colored Catisha, a catty butterfly who owes her life to Clara's courage.

GERM: Discussion points: On the last page of the story, Clara describes herself as "completely contented." Why is that? Compare and contrast her personality to Catisha's, using details from the story to help describe both of them. After sharing Edwards's other alphabet-based stories with listeners, have them write and illustrate alliterative episodes with new animals. For more caterpillar-into-butterfly tales, read Eric Carle's classic, *The Very Hungry Caterpillar*, Lois Ehlert's *Waiting for Wings*, and Lisa Campbell Ernst's *Bubba and Trixie*.

RELATED TITLES: Aylesworth, Jim. *Old Black Fly.* Henry Holt, 1992. / Bayer, Jane. *A My Name Is Alice.* Dial, 1984. / Brown, Ruth. *If at First You Do Not See.* Henry Holt, 1983. / Carle, Eric. *The Very Hungry Caterpillar.* Putnam, 1981. / Edwards, Pamela Duncan. *Dinorella: A Prehistoric Fairy Tale.* Hyperion, 1997. / Edwards, Pamela Duncan. *Four Famished Foxes and Fosdyke.* HarperCollins, 1995. / Edwards, Pamela Duncan. *Rosie's Roses.* HarperCollins, 2003. / Edwards, Pamela Duncan. *Some Smug Slug.* HarperCollins, 1996. / Edwards, Pamela. *The Wacky Wedding: A Book of Alphabet Antics.* Hyperion, 1999. / Edwards, Pamela. *The Worrywarts.* HarperCollins, 1999. / Ehlert, Lois. *Waiting for Wings.* Harcourt, 2001. / Ernst, Lisa Campbell. *Bubba and Trixie.* Simon & Schuster, 1997. / Hariton, Anca. *Butterfly Story.* Dutton, 1995. / Heiligman, Deborah. *From Caterpillar to Butterfly.* HarperCollins, 1996. / Swope, Sam. *Gotta Go! Gotta Go!* Farrar, 2000.

SUBJECTS: ALLITERATION. ALPHABET BOOKS. BUTTERFLIES. CATERPILLARS. COURAGE. CROWS. INSECTS. METAMORPHOSIS.

222   Edwards, Pamela Duncan. *Dinorella: A Prehistoric Fairy Tale.* **Illus. by Henry Cole. Hyperion, 1997. 0-7868-2249-X. Unp. Gr. K–3**

Dinosaur den-dwelling Dora and Doris are demanding of dainty and dependable stepsister Dinorella. An invitation to a dinosaur dance at dashing Duke Dudley's depresses Dinorella, who lacks decent dinosaur jewels, but the arrival of her glittering Fairydactyl soon changes all that. With her glittery glasses and petticoated pink ballgown, the long-necked dino is 1950s glamorous, and the ending is simply divine.

GERM: The course of true love can be wacky, as this alliterative Cinderella spoof demonstrates. Meet another big girl animal who comes out on top in Tony Johnston's *Bigfoot Cinderrrrella.*

RELATED TITLES: Buehner, Caralyn. *Fanny's Dream.* Dial, 1996. / Edwards, Pamela Duncan. *Clara Caterpillar.* HarperCollins, 2001. / Edwards, Pamela Duncan. *Four Famished Foxes and Fosdyke.* HarperCollins, 1995. / Edwards, Pamela Duncan. *Rosie's Roses.* HarperCollins, 2003. / Edwards, Pamela Duncan. *Some Smug Slug.* HarperCollins, 1996. / Edwards, Pamela. *The Wacky Wedding: A Book of Alphabet Antics.* Hyperion, 1999. / Edwards, Pamela. *The Worrywarts.* HarperCollins, 1999. / Hall, Katy, and Lisa Eisenberg. *Dino Riddles.* Dial, 2002. / Jackson, Ellen. *Cinder Edna.* Lothrop, 1994. / Johnston, Tony. *Bigfoot Cinderrrrella.* Putnam, 1998. / Ketteman, Helen. *Bubba the Cowboy Prince: A Fractured Texas Tale.* Scholastic, 1997. / Mitton, Tony. *Dinosaurumpus!* Scholastic, 2003. / Myers, Bernice. *Sidney Rella and the Glass Sneaker.* Macmillan, 1985. / San Souci, Robert D. *Cinderella Skeleton.* Harcourt, 2000.

SUBJECTS: ALLITERATION. CINDERELLA STORIES. DINOSAURS. PARODIES.

223   Edwards, Pamela Duncan. *Four Famished Foxes and Fosdyke.* **Illus. by Henry Cole. HarperCollins, 1995. 0-06-024926-9. Unp. Gr. K–2**

With their mom off for five days in Florida, her four feckless fox sons set off to filch fowl from the farmyard, while Fosdyke the foodie stays behind and flambées some fungi and other fabulous food.

GERM: Yes, there's all that grand alliteration, but you can also go into food mode. Each pair of feasters can pick a letter and list as many foods starting with that letter as they can gather, and then share. You'll have a whole alphabet of delicious vicarious feasting. Sing "The Fox Went Out on a Chilly Night," the old folksong about a fox's successful hunting trip, using Wendy Watson's picture-book version.

RELATED TITLES: Bayer, Jane. *A My Name Is Alice.* Dial, 1984. / Clifford, Eth. *Flatfoot Fox and the Case of the Mising Schoolhouse.* Houghton Mifflin, 1997. (And others in the Flatfoot Fox series.) / Edwards, Pamela Duncan. *Clara Caterpillar.* HarperCollins, 2001. / Edwards, Pamela Duncan. *Dinorella: A Prehistoric Fairy Tale.* Hyperion, 1997. / Edwards, Pamela Duncan. *Rosie's Roses.* HarperCollins, 2003. / Edwards, Pamela Duncan. *Some Smug Slug.* HarperCollins, 1996. / Edwards, Pamela. *The Wacky Wedding: A Book of Alphabet Antics.* Hyperion, 1999. / Edwards, Pamela. *The Worrywarts.* HarperCollins, 1999. / Kalman, Maira. *What Pete Ate from A–Z.* Putnam, 2001. / Oates, Joyce Carol. *Where Is Little Reynard?* HarperCollins, 2003. / Watson, Wendy. *Fox Went Out on a Chilly Night.* Lothrop, 1994. / Wattenberg, Jane. *Henny-Penny.* Scholastic, 2000.

SUBJECTS: ALLITERATION. FOOD. FOXES.

224   Edwards, Pamela Duncan. *Honk! The Story of a Prima Swanerina.* **Illus. by Henry Cole. Hyperion, 1998. 0-7868-2384-4. Unp. Gr. K–2**

"No birds allowed in the Opera House!" the manager cries each time he chases the ballet-obsessed Mimi the Swan out the door of the Paris Opera House where Swan Lake is being performed, but the bird finagles her way on stage and becomes a star.

GERM: Other ballet-loving animals include the chicken Poulette in *Hen Lake* by Mary Jane Auch, the dancing cow in *Clorinda* by Robert Kinerk, and the pigs of the Boarshoi Ballet in *Swine Lake* by James Marshall.

RELATED TITLES: Auch, Mary Jane. *Bantam of the Opera.* Holiday House, 1997. / Auch, Mary Jane. *Hen Lake.* Holiday House, 1995. / Auch, Mary Jane. *Peeping Beauty.* Holiday House, 1993. / Ernst, Lisa Campbell. *When Bluebell Sang.* Bradbury, 1989. / Goss, Linda. *The Frog Who Wanted to Be a Singer.* Orchard, 1996. / Hurd, Thacher. *Art Dog.* HarperCollins, 1996. / Kinerk, Robert. *Clorinda.* Simon & Schuster, 2003. / Marshall, James. *Swine Lake.* HarperCollins, 1999. / Weaver, Tess. *Opera Cat.* Clarion, 2002. / West, Jim, and Marshall Izen. *The Dog Who Sang at the Opera.* Abrams, 2004.

SUBJECTS: BALLET. BIRDS. OPERA. PARIS. SWANS.

225   Edwards, Pamela Duncan. *The Leprechaun's Gold.* **Illus. by Henry Cole. HarperCollins, 2004. 0-06-623974-5. Unp. Gr. K–3**

Humble Old Pat and Young Tom the braggart set out together to walk to the Royal Palace, where they plan to enter the king's harping contest. Young Tom surreptitiously snaps Old Pat's harp string, but when Old Pat rescues a leprechaun in need of help, he is rewarded for his self-lessness.

GERM: Have your listeners predict what the leprechauns will do after Old Pat falls asleep. Discussion point: Usually leprechauns trick their humans out of their gold. Why did they reward Old Pat? Read other leprechaun tales and make a list of things you should and should not do if you meet a leprechaun.

RELATED TITLES: Balian, Lorna. *Leprechauns Never Lie.* Star Bright, 2004. / Bateman, Teresa. *Leprechaun Gold.* Holiday House, 1998. / Bateman, Teresa. *The Ring of Truth.* Holiday House, 1997. / dePaola, Tomie. *Jamie O'Rourke and the Big Potato: An Irish Folktale.* Putnam, 1992. / Hodges, Margaret. *Saint Patrick and the Peddler.* Orchard, 1993. / Kennedy, Richard. *The Leprechaun's Story.* Dutton, 1979. / Shute, Linda. *Clever Tom and the Leprechaun.* Lothrop, 1988. / Talbott, Hudson. *O'Sullivan Stew.* Putnam, 1999. / Wojciechowski, Susan. *A Fine St. Patrick's Day.* Random House, 2004.

SUBJECTS: GREED. HARP. IRELAND. KINDNESS. KINGS AND RULERS. LEPRECHAUNS.

226   Edwards, Pamela Duncan. *Livingstone Mouse.* **Illus. by Henry Cole. HarperCollins, 1996. 0-06-025870-5. Unp. Gr. PreK–2**

Looking to build his nest in the greatest place in the world, an adventurous mouse sets off to find China. Along the way, he encounters a noisy drawer, a smelly sneaker, a picnic basket, and even a mouse trap before stumbling on his desired destination.

GERM: There's a clever play on words here, as Livingstone, in looking for China, finds an old teapot made of china. Bring in a china teapot, introduce the pottery called "china," sing that "I'm a Little Teapot" song, and then start the story. When you get to the climax, your group will laugh and laugh—they'll get the irony and humor. Act out Livingstone's dialogues and encounters with each animal at each new site. Children can imagine and illustrate other perfect mouse habitats for Livingstone's children to discover when they grow up.

RELATED TITLES: Baehr, Patricia. *Mouse in the House.* Holiday House, 1994. / Carle, Eric. *A House for Hermit Crab.* Picture Book Studio, 1987. / Donaldson, Julia. *A Squash and a Squeeze.* McElderry, 1993. / Edwards, Pamela Duncan. *The Worrywarts.* HarperCollins, 1999. / Fraser, Mary Ann. *I. Q. Goes to the Library.* Walker, 2003. / George, Lindsay Barrett. *Inside Mouse, Outside Mouse.* HarperCollins, 2004. / McBratney, Sam. *The Dark at the Top of the Stairs.* Candlewick, 1996. / McCully, Emily Arnold. *Picnic.* HarperCollins, 2003. / McDonald, Megan. *Is This a House for Hermit Crab?* Orchard, 1990. / McMillan, Bruce. *Mouse Views: What the Class Pet Saw.* Holiday House, 1993. / Peppé, Rodney. *The Mice Who Lived in a Shoe.* Lothrop, 1982. / Rand, Gloria. *Willie Takes a Hike.* Harcourt, 1996.

SUBJECTS: ANIMALS. CREATIVE DRAMA. DWELLINGS. MICE.

227   Edwards, Pamela Duncan. *McGillycuddy Could!* **Illus. by Sue Porter. HarperCollins, 2005. 0-06-029002-1. Unp. Gr. PreK–1**

Who is this strange new animal that just showed up at the farm? The animal says it's McGillycuddy, it just moved in, and what does it do? It hops. "That's all?" says the cow. "Can you make milk?" Here's the wonderful chantable refrain: "So McGillycuddy tried. But . . . McGillycuddy couldn't!" The new creature may not be able to grow wool, lay eggs, or wake up the farmer in the morning, but he CAN hop, jump, bounce, and kick the fox that comes marauding.

GERM: Lots of simple repeated refrains make this story ideal for audience participation, storytelling, flannelboard or puppet retellings, and acting out as a whole group. And what is the title animal? He's a kangaroo, of course, and a real hero.

RELATED TITLES: Fox, Mem. *Hattie and the Fox.* Bradbury, 1987. / Hindley, Judy. *Do Like a Duck Does!* Candlewick, 2002. / Payne, Emmy. *Katy-No-Pocket.* Houghton Mifflin, 1944. / Pearson, Tracey Campbell. *Bob.* Farrar, 2002. / Ward, Helen. *The Rooster and the Fox.* Millbrook, 2003. / Wattenberg, Jane. *Henny-Penny.* Scholastic, 2000.

SUBJECTS: ANIMALS. DOMESTIC ANIMALS. FARM LIFE. FOXES. KANGAROOS.

228   Edwards, Pamela Duncan. *Muldoon.* **Illus. by Henry Cole. Hyperion, 2002. 0-7868-0360-6. Unp. Gr. PreK–2**

Muldoon is an amiable brown dog who "works" for the West family, enjoying good working conditions of two square meals a day, tickles behind the ears, and lots of tummy scratches in exchange for making sure his humans thrive.

GERM: Listeners will analyze the differences between Muldoon's take on each facet of his job description and how a human might view it. Ask the kids to write a job description for their pets as a Help Wanted ad for the newspaper.

RELATED TITLES: Clement, Rod. *Just Another Ordinary Day*. HarperCollins, 1997. / Ernst, Lisa Campbell. *Ginger Jumps*. Bradbury, 1990. / Graham, Bob. *Benny: An Adventure Story*. Candlewick, 1999. / Kalman, Maira. *What Pete Ate from A–Z*. Putnam, 2001. / Kellogg, Steven. *Pinkerton, Behave*. Dial, 1979. / Laden, Nina. *The Night I Followed the Dog*. Chronicle, 1994. / Lee, Chinlun. *Good Dog, Paw!* Candlewick, 2004. / L'Engle, Madeleine. *The Other Dog*. SeaStar, 2001. / Meddaugh, Susan. *Martha Speaks*. Houghton Mifflin, 1992. / Meddaugh, Susan. *Martha Walks the Dog*. Houghton Mifflin, 1998. / Miller, Sara Swan. *Three Stories You Can Read to Your Dog*. Houghton Mifflin, 1995. / Provensen, Alice. *A Day in the Life of Murphy*. Simon & Schuster, 2003. / Rathmann, Peggy. *Officer Buckle and Gloria*. Putnam, 1995. / Rosen, Michael. *Rover*. Doubleday, 1999. / Singer, Marilyn. *Chester the Out-of-Work Dog*. Henry Holt, 1992.

SUBJECTS: DOGS. PERSONAL NARRATIVES. POINT OF VIEW. WORK.

229   Edwards, Pamela Duncan. *The Neat Line: Scribbling Through Mother Goose*. Illus. by Diana Cain Blumenthal. HarperCollins, 2005. 0-06-623970-2. Unp. Gr. PreK–2

A baby scribble, after much practice, grows up to be a Neat Line and heads off into the first page of a real book, *Mother Goose's Nursery Rhymes*. There it becomes useful, coming to the aid of Little Boy Blue by redrawing itself into the shape of a horn; of Jack and Jill by becoming a pathway; of Mary, Mary, Quite Contrary by being a big cloud; and of Little Miss Muffet by transforming itself into a big bird-scaring spider. "All in a day's work," says the Neat Line. Thick black lines outline each conflicted nursery rhyme character the Neat Line aids, and the scalloped borders of each double-page spread make it look as if you are reading an open book within a book.

GERM: Children will love the picture on the first page, of the baby scribble in its bassinet, and will recite each nursery rhyme provided along the way. For those tempted to scribble on the blank page-within-a-page last page, it's time for your Care of Books lesson (see page 56 for some ideas). Provide fresh drawing paper for all to draw new adventures, thinking up a nursery rhyme problem and a solution the Neat Line can provide. Rev up your imaginations, linewise, with Carole Lexa Schaefer's *The Squiggle* with youngest children; Peter H. Reynolds's *The Dot* for those who cry, "I don't know what to draw"; and classics Crockett Johnson's *Harold and the Purple Crayon* and Norton Juster's *The Dot and the Line* for additional inspiration.

RELATED TITLES: Crews, Nina. *The Neighborhood Mother Goose*. Greenwillow, 2004. / dePaola, Tomie. *Tomie dePaola's Mother Goose*. Putnam, 1985. / Hoberman, Mary Ann. *You Read to Me, I'll Read to You: Very Short Mother Goose Tales to Read Together*. Little, Brown, 2005. / Johnson, Crockett. *Harold and the Purple Crayon*. HarperCollins, 1955. / Juster, Norton. *The Dot and the Line: A Romance in Lower Mathematics*. SeaStar, 2000. / Lobel, Arnold. *The Random House Book of Mother Goose*. Random House, 1986. / Opie, Iona, comp. *My Very First Mother Goose*. Candlewick, 1996. / Reynolds, Peter H. *The Dot*. Candlewick, 2003. / Schaefer, Carole Lexa. *The Squiggle*. Crown, 1996. / Stevens, Janet, and Susan Stevens Crummel. *And the Dish Ran Away with the Spoon*. Harcourt, 2001. / Zalben, Jane Breskin. *Hey, Mama Goose*. Dutton, 2005. / Zelinsky, Paul O. *The Maid and the Mouse and the Odd-Shaped House*. Dutton, 1993.

SUBJECTS: CHARACTERS IN LITERATURE. COOPERATION. DRAWING. NURSERY RHYMES. PARODIES.

230   Edwards, Pamela Duncan. *Rosie's Roses*. Illus. by Henry Cole. HarperCollins, 2003. 0-06-028997-X. Unp. Gr. PreK–1

On her way with her big brother to celebrate Aunt Ruth's birthday, raccoon Rosie loses, one by one, the red roses she is bringing as a present. One is taken by a rogue of a rodent; one by a rapscallion rabbit; another by Mrs. Robin; and she gives the last one to a squirrel bride, ending up with only the rainbow ribbon she had tied around the original bouquet.

GERM: Yes, it's another of Edwards's witty and cheerful alliteration books, with the letter R appearing not just as an initial consonant, but throughout many, many words. Children can identify beginning, middle, and ending R sounds and write and illustrate new R-based sentences to share.

RELATED TITLES: Bayer, Jane. *A My Name Is Alice*. Dial, 1984. / Edwards, Pamela Duncan. *Clara Caterpillar*. HarperCollins, 2001. / Edwards, Pamela Duncan. *Dinorella: A Prehistoric Fairy Tale*. Hyperion, 1997. / Edwards, Pamela Duncan. *Four Famished Foxes and Fosdyke*. HarperCollins, 1995. / Edwards, Pamela Duncan. *Some Smug Slug*. HarperCollins, 1996. / Edwards, Pamela. *The Wacky Wedding: A Book of Alphabet Antics*. Hyperion, 1999. / Edwards, Pamela. *The Worrywarts*. HarperCollins, 1999.

SUBJECTS: ALLITERATION. AUNTS. BROTHERS AND SISTERS. FLOWERS. GIFTS. RACCOONS. ROSES.

231   **Edwards, Pamela Duncan.** *Slop Goes the Soup: A Noisy Warthog Word Book.* **Illus. by Henry Cole. Hyperion, 2001. 0-7868-0469-6. Unp. Gr. PreK–2**

In a noisy look at onomatopoeia, a sneezing warthog sets off a cacophonous chain of events when the soup goes slop, the hooves slither in the soup, the birdcage wobbles, and the picture of Uncle Fred crashes to the floor. The domestic warthog duo cleans up the mess in time to greet their animal dinner party guests, one of whom starts to A-A-A-A-CHOO! Here we go again.

GERM: A page at the back describes onomatopoeia and includes a writing prompt that you can use to get your noisy bunch writing stories incorporating "sound" words.

RELATED TITLES: Cole, Joanna. *It's Too Noisy!* Crowell, 1989. / Dodds, Dayle Ann. *Do Bunnies Talk?* HarperCollins, 1992. / Edwards, Pamela Duncan. *Rosie's Roses.* HarperCollins, 2003. / Edwards, Pamela Duncan. *Some Smug Slug.* HarperCollins, 1996. / Edwards, Pamela Duncan. *The Wacky Wedding: A Book of Alphabet Antics.* Hyperion, 1999. / Edwards, Pamela Duncan. *The Worrywarts.* HarperCollins, 1999. / Elkin, Benjamin. *The Loudest Noise in the World.* Viking, 1954. / MacDonald, Ross. *Achoo! Bang! Crash! The Noisy Alphabet.* Roaring Brook, 2003. / Spier, Peter. *Crash! Bang! Boom!* Doubleday, 1990. / Steen, Sandra, and Susan Steen. *Car Wash.* Putnam, 2001.

SUBJECTS: ANIMALS. CAUSE AND EFFECT. CLUMSINESS. ONOMATOPOEIA. SOUND EFFECTS. SOUP. WARTHOGS.

232   **Edwards, Pamela Duncan.** *Some Smug Slug.* **Illus. by Henry Cole. HarperCollins, 1996. 0-06-024792-4. Unp. Gr. K–2**

One summer Sunday, a slug senses a slope. Though sparrow and spider and other S-named animals try to stop him, up he slithers until he's atop a huge toad who swallows him. Such a shame. The illustrations are large, detailed and attractive, though kids'll probably be dismayed when the foolish slug is eaten.

GERM: Brainstorm more "S" words or write and illustrate an alliterative sequel about the toad using "T" words, or, maybe, a robin using "R" words. Share Edwards's alliterative picture books to demonstrate how one can tell a whole story by assembling many words starting with the same letter.

RELATED TITLES: Aylesworth, Jim. *Old Black Fly.* Henry Holt, 1992. / Bayer, Jane. *A My Name Is Alice.* Dial, 1984. / Brenner, Barbara. *One Small Place in a Tree.* HarperCollins, 2004. / Edwards, Pamela Duncan. *Clara Caterpillar.* HarperCollins, 2001. / Edwards, Pamela Duncan. *Dinorella: A Prehistoric Fairy Tale.* Hyperion, 1997. / Edwards, Pamela Duncan. *Four Famished Foxes and Fosdyke.* HarperCollins, 1995. / Edwards, Pamela Duncan. *Rosie's Roses.* HarperCollins, 2003. / Edwards, Pamela. *The Wacky Wedding: A Book of Alphabet Antics.* Hyperion, 1999. / Edwards, Pamela. *The Worrywarts.* HarperCollins, 1999. / Pfeffer, Wendy. *A Log's Life.* Simon & Schuster, 1997. / Van Allsburg, Chris. *Two Bad Ants.* Houghton Mifflin, 1988. / Waddell, Martin. *Hi, Harry! The Moving Story of How One Slow Tortoise Slowly Made a Friend.* Candlewick, 2003. / Wolkstein, Diane. *Step by Step.* Morrow, 1994.

SUBJECTS: ALLITERATION. SLUGS.

233   **Edwards, Pamela Duncan.** *The Wacky Wedding: A Book of Alphabet Antics.* **Illus. by Henry Cole. Hyperion, 1999. 0-7868-2248-1. Unp. Gr. K–2**

In an alphabetical adventure, an army of ants and insects attend the elegant wedding of a queen ant, dressed in white, and her tuxedoed, winged groom. Aside from the groom being hit by dropped fruit and the bride tripping into a puddle and almost drowning, it's a lovely affair. Cole's comical full-bleed acrylic paintings zoom in on the insects' point of view.

GERM: Unlike her usual alliterative picture books, Edwards tackles the whole alphabet here, relating the story by focusing on one letter per page. The letter and an object representing that letter can be found on each page. Sing about another wedding in the animal kingdom with a picture-book version of the old folksong "Froggie Went a-Courtin'," by John Langstaff, Marjorie Priceman, or Gillian Tyler.

RELATED TITLES: Andreae, Giles. *K Is for Kissing a Cool Kangaroo.* Orchard, 2003. / Aylesworth, Jim. *Old Black Fly.* Henry Holt, 1992. / Bayer, Jane. *A My Name Is Alice.* Dial, 1984. / Chess, Victoria. *Alfred's Alphabet Walk.* Greenwillow, 1979. / Edwards, Pamela Duncan. *Dinorella: A Prehistoric Fairy Tale.* Hyperion, 1997. / Edwards, Pamela Duncan. *Four Famished Foxes and Fosdyke.* HarperCollins, 1995. / Edwards, Pamela Duncan. *Rosie's Roses.* HarperCollins, 2003. / Edwards, Pamela Duncan. *Some Smug Slug.* HarperCollins, 1996. / Hepworth, Cathi. *Antics! An Alphabetical Anthology.* Putnam, 1992. / Kirk, David. *Miss Spider's ABC.* Scholastic,

1998. / Langstaff, John. *Frog Went A-Courtin'*. Illus. by Feodor Rojankovsky. Harcourt, 1955. / Priceman, Marjorie. *Froggie Went a-Courting*. Little, Brown, 2000. / Tyler, Gillian. *Froggy Went A-Courtin'*. Candlewick, 2005. / Van Allsburg, Chris. *Two Bad Ants*. Houghton Mifflin, 1988. / Wolkstein, Diane. *Step by Step*. Morrow, 1994.

SUBJECTS: ALLITERATION. ALPHABET BOOKS. ANTS. INSECTS. WEDDINGS.

234   **Egan, Tim. *Burnt Toast on Davenport Street*. Illus. by the author. Houghton Mifflin, 1997. 0-395-79618-0. Unp. Gr. K–3**

When a buzzing fly that Arthur Crandall is about to swat speaks to him, offering three wishes in exchange for sparing its life, the skeptical dog wishes foolishly. He wishes to receive a new toaster, to change the sneering crocodiles hanging out on the corner into squirrels, and to live on an exotic tropical isle filled with singing and dancing natives. Imagine his surprise when all three come true, more or less.

GERM: The broadly absurd, be-careful-what-you-wish-for story with matter-of-fact watercolors and a droll, contemporary tone will make you and your listeners laugh out loud every time you read it. Your students will be vastly tickled and will enjoy making their own three wishes and then writing about the consequences, whether the wishes go wrong or right.

RELATED TITLES: Agee, Jon. *Milo's Hat Trick*. Hyperion, 2001. / Chapman, Carol. *Barney Bipple's Magic Dandelions*. Dutton, 1988. / DiCamillo, Kate. *Mercy Watson to the Rescue*. Candlewick, 2005. / Egan, Tim. *Serious Farm*. Houghton Mifflin, 2003. / Griffith, Helen V. *Emily and the Enchanted Frog*. Greenwillow, 1989. / Kovalski, Maryanne. *Pizza for Breakfast*. Morrow, 1991. / McClintock, Barbara. *Molly and the Magic Wishbone*. Farrar, 2001. / Meddaugh, Susan. *The Witch's Walking Stick*. Houghton Mifflin, 2005. / Sadler, Marilyn. *Alistair in Outer Space*. Prentice Hall, 1984. / Steig, William. *Sylvester and the Magic Pebble*. Simon & Schuster, 1988. / Van Allsburg, Chris. *The Sweetest Fig*. Houghton Mifflin, 1993. / Yorinks, Arthur. *Hey, Al*. Farrar, 1986.

SUBJECTS: DOGS. FANTASY. FLIES. HUMOROUS FICTION. INSECTS. PICTURE BOOKS FOR ALL AGES. TRANSFORMATIONS. WISHES.

235   **Egan, Tim. *Metropolitan Cow*. Illus. by the author. Houghton Mifflin, 1996. 0-395-73096-1. Unp. Gr. K–2**

Son of noted socialites and prominent members of the herd, Bennett Gibbons is the most fortunate young cow in his neighborhood, though the only other children his age are pigs. His snooty parents believe that cows are far too dignified to play with pigs. When Webster Anderson, a pig from the country, moves into the apartment building, the two become fast friends, much to Bennett's parents' disapproval.

GERM: As an allegory, this dignified picture book with mannered watercolor and ink illustrations, can start the discussion on prejudice, preconceived notions, and stereotypes.

RELATED TITLES: Babcock, Chris. *No Moon, No Milk*. Crown, 1993. / Brown, Paula. *Moon Jump: A Countdown*. Viking, 1992. / Choldenko, Gennifer. *Moonstruck: The True Story of the Cow Who Jumped over the Moon*. Hyperion, 1997. / Cronin, Doreen. *Click, Clack, Moo: Cows That Type*. Simon & Schuster, 2000. / Doyle, Malachy. *Cow*. McElderry, 2002. / Egan, Tim. *Roasted Peanuts*. Houghton Mifflin, 2006. / Egan, Tim. *Serious Farm*. Houghton Mifflin, 2003. / Ernst, Lisa Campbell. *When Bluebell Sang*. Bradbury, 1989. / Johnson, Paul Brett. *The Cow Who Wouldn't Come Down*. Orchard, 1993. / Kinerk, Robert. *Clorinda*. Simon & Schuster, 2003. / Laden, Nina. *When Pigasso Met Mootisse*. Chronicle, 1998. / Palatini, Margie. *Moo Who?* HarperCollins, 2004. / Schertle, Alice. *How Now, Brown Cow*. Harcourt, 1994. / Speed, Toby. *Two Cool Cows*. Putnam, 1995. / Stevens, Janet, and Susan Stevens Crummel. *And the Dish Ran Away with the Spoon*. Harcourt, 2001. / Vail, Rachel. *Over the Moon*. Orchard, 1998.

SUBJECTS: COWS. FRIENDSHIP. PIGS. PREJUDICE.

236   **Egan, Tim. *Serious Farm*. Illus. by the author. Houghton Mifflin, 2003. 0-618-22694-X. Unp. Gr. K–2**

"Farmin' is serious business," Farmer Fred says. "Nothing funny about corn." The pigs, cows, horses, chickens, rabbits, and sheep are serious too, until Edna, the cow, starts the animals planning how they can make the farm more fun. Nothing makes Farmer Fred laugh, or even smile—even when the animals don mustaches, climb trees, and do tricks—until they all decide to pack up and leave the farm.

GERM: Stop reading midway. Ask: What can the animals do to make Farmer Fred smile? What makes you laugh? What's so important about having a sense of humor? This would script up beautifully as a Reader's Theater. Play the laugh game. Working in pairs, each person has 30 silent seconds to make the other laugh out loud. Then switch. Make everyone try to stop laughing with James Stevenson's *Don't Make Me Laugh* and its sequel, *No Laughing, No Smiling, No Giggling*.

RELATED TITLES: Babcock, Chris. *No Moon, No Milk.* Crown, 1993. / Bateman, Teresa. *April Foolishness.* Albert Whitman, 2004. / Cronin, Doreen. *Click, Clack, Moo: Cows That Type.* Simon & Schuster, 2000. / Egan, Tim. *Burnt Toast on Davenport Street.* Houghton Mifflin, 1997. / Egan, Tim. *Metropolitan Cow.* Houghton Mifflin, 1996. / Egan, Tim. *Roasted Peanuts.* Houghton Mifflin, 2006. / Egan, Tim. *The Trial of Cardigan Jones.* Houghton Mifflin, 2004. / Krosoczka, Jarrett J. *Punk Farm.* Knopf, 2005. / Palatini, Margie. *The Web Files.* Hyperion, 2001. / Schwartz, Amy. *Old MacDonald.* Scholastic, 1999. / Stevenson, James. *Don't Make Me Laugh.* Farrar, 1999. / Stevenson, James. *No Laughing, No Smiling, No Giggling.* Farrar, 2004.
SUBJECTS: DOMESTIC ANIMALS. FARM LIFE. HUMOROUS FICTION. LAUGHTER. READER'S THEATER.

237 **Egan, Tim.** *The Trial of Cardigan Jones.* **Illus. by the author. Houghton Mifflin, 2004. 0-618-40237-3. Unp. Gr. K–3**
Cardigan, the new moose in town, stops by Mrs. Brown's window to sniff the fresh-baked apple pie she's just put there. The next thing he knows, he's arrested and put on trial for pie theft, and the jury's convinced he's guilty!
GERM: Midway through reading the story, take a survey of your listeners' opinions regarding Cardigan's guilt or innocence, and ask them to cite evidence for their positions. Explain the components of a jury trial and then act out the trial scene, complete with judge, jury, and witnesses, and debate whether Cardigan is guilty or innocent. Children can then write their own briefs or statements for the defense or the prosecution: "I think Cardigan Jones is guilty/innocent because ____." You and your students can write this up into a Reader's Theater script to act out for other classes.
RELATED TITLES: Cushman, Doug. *Mystery at the Club Sandwich.* Clarion, 2004. / Egan, Tim. *Burnt Toast on Davenport Street.* Houghton Mifflin, 1997. / Egan, Tim. *Metropolitan Cow.* Houghton Mifflin, 1996. / Egan, Tim. *Roasted Peanuts.* Houghton Mifflin, 2006. / Egan, Tim. *Serious Farm.* Houghton Mifflin, 2003. / Kelly, John, and Cathy Tincknell. *The Mystery of Eatum Hall.* Candlewick, 2004. / McClements, George. *Jake Gander, Storyville Detective.* Hyperion, 2002. / Palatini, Margie. *Moosetache.* Hyperion, 1997. / Palatini, Margie. *The Web Files.* Hyperion, 2001. / Polacco, Patricia. *Chicken Sunday.* Philomel, 1992. / Teague, Mark. *Detective LaRue: Letters from the Investigation.* Scholastic, 2004.
SUBJECTS: ANIMALS. CREATIVE DRAMA. JUDGES. MOOSE. PICTURE BOOKS FOR ALL AGES. PIES. POLICE. READER'S THEATER. TRIALS.

238 **Ehlert, Lois.** *In My World.* **Illus. by the author. Harcourt, 2002. 0-15-216269-0. Unp. Gr. PreK–2**
"My world is made of things I like." So begins an innovative picture book, accompanied by remarkable die-cut pictures on heavy-duty pages that intersect and overlap in a riot of shapes and colors. Turn each page to reveal a visual feast of cutout images: leaping frogs, growing fruit, shining sun, and glittering stars. As you read aloud each adjective, children can look at the cutout page and identify the animal or object revealed there. "Thank you world, for everything," concludes the simple text; a free-verse rebus poem on the back cover reviews all of the objects mentioned throughout.
GERM: Try rereading the book backward, showing each object and asking listeners to recall the accompanying adjective. Ask your children to list the things they like, with an accompanying adjective for each one. Selecting one item, each child can draw an outline of it on a piece of colored oaktag and then cut it out for others to identify. This will be a natural intro to a science unit on nature and what we appreciate about it.
RELATED TITLES: Dillon, Leo, and Diane Dillon. *To Everything There Is a Season.* Scholastic, 1998. / Ehlert, Lois. *Color Zoo.* HarperCollins, 1989. / Esbensen, Barbara Juster. *Echoes for the Eye: Poems to Celebrate Patterns in Nature.* Harcourt, 2002. / Fleming, Denise. *Where Once There Was a Wood.* Henry Holt, 1996. / Marzollo, Jean. *I Love You: A Rebus Poem.* Scholastic, 1999. / Minne. *I Love . . .* Kane/Miller, 2005. / Pollock, Penny. *When the Moon Is Full: A Lunar Year.* Philomel, 1992. / Schaefer, Lola M. *What's Up, What's Down.* Greenwillow, 2002. / Shannon, George. *White Is for Blueberry.* Greenwillow, 2005. / Tafuri, Nancy. *Snowy Flowy Blowy: A Twelve Months Rhyme.* Scholastic, 1999.
SUBJECTS: EARTH. NATURE. SCIENCE.

239 **Ehlert, Lois.** *Leaf Man.* **Illus. by the author. Harcourt, 2005. 0-15-205304-2. Unp. Gr. PreK–2**
Heading east, blowing toward the marsh, over ducks and geese, past the fields of pumpkins and potatoes, and out of sight, is the Leaf Man, an ethereal guy composed of a collage of brilliantly colored fall leaves. As Ehlert says, "A Leaf Man's got to go where the wind blows." Colorful leaf-based animals are posed on bright-hued backgrounds, with each die-cut page scalloped on top, overlapping into a hilly, rolling landscape.

GERM: In this mood piece tribute to the beauty of fall leaves, viewers will point out the animals, from cows to fish to birds. For a fitting fall activity, collect colorful leaves and arrange them into pictures of leaf people and animals. Starting with the leaves identified on the endpapers, identify the trees your leaves came from. George Ella Lyon's *A B Cedar: An Alphabet of Trees* will be helpful. For props to help you present this story, go to <www.mimismotifs.com>.

RELATED TITLES: Behn, Harry. *Trees.* Henry Holt, 1992. / Ehlert, Lois. *Eating the Alphabet: Fruits and Vegetables from A to Z.* Harcourt, 1989. / Ehlert, Lois. *Growing Vegetable Soup.* Harcourt, 1987. / Ehlert, Lois. *In My World.* Harcourt, 2002. / Ehlert, Lois. *Red Leaf, Yellow Leaf.* Harcourt, 1991. / Ehlert, Lois. *Under My Nose.* Richard C. Owen, 1996. / Ehlert, Lois. *Waiting for Wings.* Harcourt, 2001. / Lyon, George Ella. *A B Cedar: An Alphabet of Trees.* Orchard, 1989. / Oppenheim, Joanne. *Have You Seen Trees?* Scholastic, 1995. / Udry, Janice May. *A Tree Is Nice.* HarperCollins, 1956.

SUBJECTS: AUTUMN. LEAVES. SEASONS. TREES. WINDS.

240   **Ehlert, Lois.** *Pie in the Sky.* **Illus. by the author. Harcourt, 2004. 0-15-216584-3. Unp. Gr. PreK–1**

Dad says the tree in the yard is a pie tree, and the unseen, unnamed narrator can't wait till summer to see if pies will grow. As summer approaches, the tree bursts into bloom, with birds abounding on each branch as cherries grow and ripen. Finally, it's time to pick the cherries and make a beautiful pie.

GERM: Ehlert's signature style of textured, mixed-media collage on gorgeous acrylic and watercolor backgrounds is filled with birds, insects, and leaves—a naturalist's dream. There's a pie on the cover with little die-cut circles on it that look like cherries, so be forewarned—you're going to have to either bake or buy a cherry pie to satisfy your listeners' and your own cravings. Then get off your duffs with *How to Make an Apple Pie and See the World* by Marjorie Priceman.

RELATED TITLES: Cherry, Lynne. *How Groundhog's Garden Grew.* Scholastic, 2003. / Coy, John. *Two Old Potatoes and Me.* Knopf, 2003. / Ehlert, Lois. *Cuckoo/Cucú: A Mexican Folktale/Un Cuento Folklórico Mexicano.* Harcourt, 1997. / Ehlert, Lois. *Eating the Alphabet: Fruits and Vegetables from A to Z.* Harcourt, 1989. / Ehlert, Lois. *Growing Vegetable Soup.* Harcourt, 1987. / Ehlert, Lois. *In My World.* Harcourt, 2002. / Ehlert, Lois. *Under My Nose.* Richard C. Owen, 1996. / Ehlert, Lois. *Waiting for Wings.* Harcourt, 2001. / Gibbons, Gail. *From Seed to Plant.* Holiday House, 1991. / Hall, Zoe. *The Apple Pie Tree.* Scholastic, 1996. / Pfeffer, Wendy. *From Seed to Pumpkin.* HarperCollins, 2004. / Priceman, Marjorie. *How to Make an Apple Pie and See the World.* Knopf, 1994. / Schaefer, Lola M. *Pick, Pull, Snap! Where Once a Flower Bloomed.* HarperCollins, 2003.

SUBJECTS: BIRDS. CHERRIES. FRUIT. PIES. TREES.

241   **Elya, Susan Middleton.** *Eight Animals Bake a Cake.* **Illus. by Lee Chapman. Putnam, 2002. 0-399-23468-3. Unp. Gr. PreK–2**

In this rhyming story interlaced with Spanish words, Ratón brings the *azúcar*, Gato brings the *mantequilla*, and the dog, bird, frog, horse, and pig provide the rest of the ingredients for the scrumptious-looking cake that they bake, and then, alas, drop on the floor. Whoops!

GERM: With Spanish words cleverly incorporated into the jaunty rhyming text and entrancing double-page-spread illustrations, children will learn new Spanish animal names, numbers, and foods effortlessly. To further celebrate the story, bring in and cut up a nice piña (pineapple) for all to enjoy. You'll find another dropped cake in *Cook-a-Doodle-Doo!* by Janet Stevens and Susan Stevens Crummel.

RELATED TITLES: Carle, Eric. *Today Is Monday.* Philomel, 1993. / Dorros, Arthur. *Abuela.* Dutton, 1991. / Elya, Susan Middleton. *Eight Animals on the Town.* Putnam, 2000. / Elya, Susan Middleton. *Say Hola to Spanish.* Lee & Low, 1996. (And others in the Say Hola to Spanish series.) / Emberley, Rebecca. *Piñata!* Little, Brown, 2004. / Guy, Ginger Foglesong. *Fiesta!* Greenwillow, 1996. / Ketteman, Helen. *Armadilly Chili.* Albert Whitman, 2004. / Kleven, Elisa. *Hooray, a Piñata!* Dutton, 1996. / Paul, Ann Whitford. *Mañana, Iguana.* Holiday House, 2004. / Reed, Lynn. *Pedro, His Perro, and the Alphabet Sombrero.* Hyperion, 1995. / Ryan, Pam Muñoz. *Mice and Beans.* Scholastic, 2001. / Soto, Gary. *Chato and the Party Animals.* Putnam, 2000. / Soto, Gary. *Chato's Kitchen.* Putnam, 1995. / Soto, Gary. *Snapshots from the Wedding.* Putnam, 1997. / Stadler, Alexander. *Beverly Billingsly Takes the Cake.* Harcourt, 2005. / Stevens, Janet, and Susan Stevens Crummel. *Cook-a-Doodle-Doo!* Harcourt, 1999.

SUBJECTS: ANIMALS. BAKING. CAKE. COOPERATION. FOOD. MULTICULTURAL BOOKS. PROBLEM SOLVING. SPANISH LANGUAGE. STORIES IN RHYME.

242   Elya, Susan Middleton. *Eight Animals on the Town.* **Illus. by Lee Chapman. Putnam, 2000. 0-399-23437-3. Unp. Gr. PreK–2**

After sitting down to a feast of the different foods they bought at the market, the mouse, the cat, the dog, the bird, the frog, the horse, the cow, and the pig set out for the *baile* (dance) where they party all night. The lively rhyming text and double-page-spread, folk art-style illustrations will help children pick up an assortment of Spanish animal names, numbers, and foods.

GERM: Put on an up-tempo recording of music and invite everyone to the *baile*. Call out each animal one at a time, so children can dance the way that animal might.

RELATED TITLES: Carle, Eric. *Today Is Monday.* Philomel, 1993. / Dorros, Arthur. *Abuela.* Dutton, 1991. / Elya, Susan Middleton. *Eight Animals Bake a Cake.* Putnam, 2002. / Elya, Susan Middleton. *Fairy Trails: A Story Told in English and Spanish.* Bloomsbury, 2005. / Elya, Susan Middleton. *Say Hola to Spanish.* Lee & Low, 1996. / Guy, Ginger Foglesong. *Fiesta!* Greenwillow, 1996. / Kleven, Elisa. *Hooray, a Piñata!* Dutton, 1996. / Marzollo, Jean. *Pretend You're a Cat.* Dial, 1990. / Mathers, Petra. *A Cake for Herbie.* Simon & Schuster, 2000. / Reed, Lynn. *Pedro, His Perro, and the Alphabet Sombrero.* Hyperion, 1995. / Ryan, Pam Muñoz. *Mice and Beans.* Scholastic, 2001. / Sacre, Antonio. *The Barking Mouse.* Albert Whitman, 2003. / Shapiro, Arnold L. *Mice Squeak, We Speak.* Putnam, 1997. / Soto, Gary. *Chato and the Party Animals.* Putnam, 2000. / Soto, Gary. *Chato's Kitchen.* Putnam, 1995. / Soto, Gary. *Snapshots from the Wedding.* Putnam, 1997.

SUBJECTS: ANIMALS. COUNTING BOOKS. MULTICULTURAL BOOKS. SPANISH LANGUAGE. STORIES IN RHYME.

243   Elya, Susan Middleton. *Eight Animals Play Ball.* **Illus. by Lee Chapman. Putnam, 2003. 0-399-23569-8. Unp. Gr. K–2**

"Eight *animales*, ready to play, head for the *parque*—the park—for the day." The animal pals decide to play a little *béisbol* (you guessed it, baseball), which leads to bickering and bad feelings until a rainstorm brings them all together again.

GERM: More than 30 Spanish-language words and phrases are effortlessly integrated into the amiable rhyming text, with a glossary and pronunciation guide that will help you all learn some new vocabulary. Play a little béisbol of your own.

RELATED TITLES: Elya, Susan Middleton. *Eight Animals Bake a Cake.* Putnam, 2002. / Elya, Susan Middleton. *Eight Animals on the Town.* Putnam, 2000. / Elya, Susan Middleton. *Say Hola to Spanish.* Lee & Low, 1996. / Mammano, Julie. *Rhinos Who Play Baseball.* Chronicle, 2003. / McCully, Emily Arnold. *Mouse Practice.* Scholastic, 1999. / Reed, Lynn. *Pedro, His Perro, and the Alphabet Sombrero.* Hyperion, 1995. / Ryan, Pam Muñoz. *Mice and Beans.* Scholastic, 2001. / Sacre, Antonio. *The Barking Mouse.* Albert Whitman, 2003. / Stadler, Alexander. *Beverly Billingsly Can't Catch.* Harcourt, 2004. / Teague, Mark. *The Field Beyond the Outfield.* Scholastic, 1992.

SUBJECTS: ANIMALS. BASEBALL. FRIENDSHIP. MULTICULTURAL BOOKS. PARKS. SPANISH LANGUAGE. SPORTS. STORIES IN RHYME.

244   Elya, Susan Middleton. *Fairy Trails: A Story Told in English and Spanish.* **Illus. by Mercedes McDonald. Bloomsbury, 2005. 1-58234-927-4. Unp. Gr. PreK–3**

Off to visit their auntie, their *tía*, for her hot quesadillas, Miguel and María take the wrong path through the woods and encounter a candy *casita* with an old *brujita*, a talking *lobo*, a girl with a glass slipper, three *osos* on a walk, and even Humpty *Huevo*. Soft, pastel-colored, full bleed illustrations of the fairy-tale forest and its inhabitants bring out the humor of the story, told in rhyme, with 34 Spanish words and phrases cleverly integrated into the text.

GERM: Ask your listeners to identify and tell a bit about the background of each fairy tale character Miguel and María encounter. There's a useful glossary and pronunciation guide at the front of the book, but you'll find that many of the Spanish words are definable in context.

RELATED TITLES: Auch, Mary Jane. *The Princess and the Pizza.* Holiday House, 2002. / Child, Lauren. *Beware of the Storybook Wolves.* Scholastic, 2001. / Child, Lauren. *Who's Afraid of the Big Bad Book?* Hyperion, 2003. / Cowell, Cressida. *Little Bo Peep's Library Book.* Orchard, 1999. / Elya, Susan Middleton. *Eight Animals Bake a Cake.* Putnam, 2002. / Elya, Susan Middleton. *Eight Animals on the Town.* Putnam, 2000. / Elya, Susan Middleton. *Eight Animals Play Ball.* Putnam, 2003. / Elya, Susan Middleton. *Home at Last.* Lee & Low, 2002. / Elya, Susan Middleton. *Oh, No, Gotta Go!* Putnam, 2003. / Elya, Susan Middleton. *Say Hola to Spanish.* Lee & Low, 1996. / Hawkins, Colin, and Jacqui Hawkins. *The Fairytale News.* Candlewick, 2004. / Ryan, Pam Muñoz. *Mice and Beans.* Scholastic, 2001. / Sacre, Antonio. *The Barking Mouse.* Albert Whitman, 2003.

SUBJECTS: CHARACTERS IN LITERATURE. FAIRY TALES—SATIRE. MULTICULTURAL BOOKS. SPANISH LANGUAGE. STORIES IN RHYME.

245   Elya, Susan Middleton. *Home at Last.* **Illus. by Felipe Davalos. Lee & Low, 2002. 1-58430-020-5. Unp. Gr. 2–5**

After moving to the United States from Mexico, 8-year-old Ana and her Papá practice their English every night, but Mamá thinks English is impossible.

GERM: Read aloud Elya's *Say Hola to Spanish* so your English speakers can see how challenging but fun a new language can be.

RELATED TITLES: Alarcón, Francisco X. *From the Bellybutton of the Moon and Other Summer Poems.* Children's Book Press, 1998. / Dorros, Arthur. *Abuela.* Dutton, 1991. / Elya, Susan Middleton. *Oh, No, Gotta Go!* Putnam, 2003. / Elya, Susan Middleton. *Say Hola to Spanish.* Lee & Low, 1996. / Levine, Ellen. *I Hate English!* Scholastic, 1989. / Lomas Garza, Carmen. *Family Pictures/Cuadros de Familia.* Children's Book Press, 1990. / Lomas Garza, Carmen. *In My Family/En Mi Familia.* Children's Book Press, 1996. / Medina, Jane. *The Dream on Blanca's Wall: Poems in English and Spanish.* Wordsong/Boyds Mills, 2004. / Mora, Pat. *Tomás and the Library Lady.* Knopf, 1997. / Pérez, Amada Irma. *My Very Own Room/Mi Proprio Cuartito.* Children's Book Press, 2000. / Pérez, L. King. *First Day in Grapes.* Lee & Low, 2002. / Sacre, Antonio. *The Barking Mouse.* Albert Whitman, 2003. / Soto, Gary. *Snapshots from the Wedding.* Putnam, 1997. / Soto, Gary. *Too Many Tamales.* Putnam, 1993.

SUBJECTS: FAMILY LIFE. FAMILY PROBLEMS. HISPANIC AMERICANS. MEXICAN AMERICANS. MOTHERS. MOVING, HOUSEHOLD. MULTICULTURAL BOOKS. SCHOOLS. SPANISH LANGUAGE.

246   Elya, Susan Middleton. *Oh, No, Gotta Go!* **Illus. by G. Brian Karas. Putnam, 2003. 0-399-23493-4. Unp. Gr. 1–4**

Out driving in the car with Mamá and Papá, the little girl in the back seat remembers the thing she forgot to do: Where is *un baño?* In a rhyming text combining English and Spanish, the girl and her parents speed frantically to a restaurant to get to the ladies' room in time.

GERM: Over the course of this story, with an urgent theme every child will recognize first hand, learn more than 50 Spanish words as you translate them using the context of the story, though there's also a glossary and punctuation guide on the last page. Accept, as soon as you finish reading, that your crew will all need to head to *el baño.*

RELATED TITLES: Dorros, Arthur. *Abuela.* Dutton, 1991. / Elya, Susan Middleton. *Eight Animals Bake a Cake.* Putnam, 2002. / Elya, Susan Middleton. *Eight Animals on the Town.* Putnam, 2000. / Elya, Susan Middleton. *Eight Animals Play Ball.* Putnam, 2003. / Elya, Susan Middleton. *Fairy Trails: A Story Told in English and Spanish.* Bloomsbury, 2005. / Elya, Susan Middleton. *Home at Last.* Lee & Low, 2002. / Elya, Susan Middleton. *Say Hola to Spanish.* Lee & Low, 1996. / Ryan, Pam Muñoz. *Mice and Beans.* Scholastic, 2001. / Sacre, Antonio. *The Barking Mouse.* Albert Whitman, 2003. / Soto, Gary. *Snapshots from the Wedding.* Putnam, 1997. / Soto, Gary. *Too Many Tamales.* Putnam, 1993.

SUBJECTS: AUTOMOBILES. FAMILY LIFE. HISPANIC AMERICANS. MULTICULTURAL BOOKS. RESTAURANTS. RESTROOMS. SPANISH LANGUAGE. STORIES IN RHYME.

247   Emberley, Ed. *The Wing on a Flea: A Book About Shapes.* **Illus. by the author. Little, Brown, 2001. 0-316-23487-7. Unp. Gr. PreK–1**

In this sparky, reillustrated version of the classic rhyming picture book, look for triangles, rectangles, and circles in everyday objects.

GERM: Observe how Emberley used three basic shapes to construct his pictures. Children can cut up circles, rectangles, and triangles and make their own shape pictures for the rest of the group to identify. To show a perfect integration of shapes and colors, read Emberley's *Go Away, Big Green Monster!*

RELATED TITLES: Adler, David A. *Shape Up! Fun with Triangles and Other Polygons.* Holiday House, 1998. / Baranski, Joan Sullivan. *Round Is a Pancake.* Dutton, 2001. / Carle, Eric. *The Secret Birthday Message.* Crowell, 1972. / Charles, N. N. *What Am I? Looking Through Shapes at Apples and Grapes.* Scholastic, 1994. / Crews, Donald. *Ten Black Dots.* Greenwillow, 1986. / Ehlert, Lois. *Color Zoo.* HarperCollins, 1989. / Emberley, Ed. *Go Away, Big Green Monster!* Little, Brown, 1993. / Ernst, Lisa Campbell. *Tangram Magician.* Blue Apple, 2005. / Falwell, Cathryn. *Clowning Around.* Orchard, 1991. / MacDonald, Suse. *Sea Shapes.* Harcourt, 1994. / Micklethwait, Lucy. *I Spy Shapes in Art.* Greenwillow, 2004. / Rogers, Paul. *The Shapes Game.* Henry Holt, 1990. / Skofield, James. *'Round and Around.* HarperCollins, 1993. / Zelinsky, Paul O. *The Maid, the Mouse, and the Odd-Shaped House.* Puffin, 1993.

SUBJECTS: MATHEMATICS. SHAPES. STORIES IN RHYME.

248   Emberley, Michael. *Ruby and the Sniffs*. Illus. by the author. Little, Brown, 2004. 0-316-23664-0. Unp. Gr. K–2

Mouse Ruby thinks she hears burglars in Mrs. Mastiff's apartment building, but really it's just the new neighbors—three enormous pigs. The confusion continues when the trio of hogs—Momma, Poppa, and Baby Sniff—think that Ruby is a gerbil. And, guess what? There is a burglar—a cat burglar—hiding in the closet.

GERM: Children will be quick to point out parts of the story that remind them of "The Three Bears." The action, vivacious dialogue, and wild humor make this a prime candidate for creating a Reader's Theater script for good readers to perform. Also read *Ruby*, the first book about the plucky mouse, as she makes her way across Boston to her grandmother's house, in a rakish update of the Red Riding Hood story.

RELATED TITLES: Aylesworth, Jim. *Goldilocks and the Three Bears*. Scholastic, 2003. / Brett, Jan. *Goldilocks and the Three Bears*. Putnam, 1987. / Cuyler, Margery. *Big Friends*. Walker, 2004. / Emberley, Michael. *Ruby*. Little, Brown, 1990. / Ernst, Lisa Campbell. *Goldilocks Returns*. Simon & Schuster, 2000. / Ernst, Lisa Campbell. *Little Red Riding Hood: A Newfangled Prairie Tale*. Simon & Schuster, 1995. / Hoberman, Mary Ann. *You Read to Me, I'll Read to You: Very Short Fairy Tales to Read Together*. Little, Brown, 2004. / Howard, Arthur. *The Hubbub Above*. Harcourt, 2005. / Marshall, James. *Goldilocks and the Three Bears*. Dial, 1988. / Meddaugh, Susan. *Hog-Eye*. Houghton Mifflin, 1995. / Scieszka, Jon. *The True Story of the 3 Little Pigs*. Viking, 1989. / Stanley, Diane. *Goldie and the Three Bears*. HarperCollins, 2003. / Wiesner, David. *The Three Pigs*. Clarion, 2001.

SUBJECTS: APARTMENT HOUSES. CATS. DOGS. GOLDILOCKS. MICE. NEIGHBORS. PARODIES. PIGS. READER'S THEATER. ROBBERS AND OUTLAWS.

249   Emberley, Rebecca. *Three Cool Kids*. Illus. by the author. Little, Brown, 1995. 0-316-23666-7. Unp. Gr. PreK–2

"Once upon a time, in a big, big city, in a small open lot, lived the Three Cool Kids: Big, Middle, and Little." Needing a change of scenery, the three set out for the vacant lot down the street, full of lovely grass and weeds, but are challenged by a potbellied, greasy-whiskered sewer rat who threatens to eat them for dinner. Emberley's city-toned cut-paper collages, made from textured paper, are just right for this sly urban update on an old favorite.

GERM: For comparisons, first make sure to read one of the picture-book versions of *The Three Billy Goats Gruff*, which include ones by Marcia Brown, Paul Galdone, and Glen Rounds. Act out the tale in creative drama using plenty of city sound effects. Give rats equal time with Lauren Child's *That Pesky Rat*.

RELATED TITLES: Brown, Marcia. *The Three Billy Goats Gruff*. Harcourt, 1957. / Child, Lauren. *That Pesky Rat*. Candlewick, 2002. / Galdone, Paul. *The Three Billy Goats Gruff*. Clarion, 1979. / Polacco, Patricia. *Oh, Look!* Philomel, 2004. / Rounds, Glen. *The Three Billy Goats Gruff*. Holiday House, 1993. / Soto, Gary. *Chato's Kitchen*. Putnam, 1995. / Souhami, Jessica. *No Dinner! The Story of the Old Woman and the Pumpkin*. Marshall Cavendish, 2000. / Wolff, Patricia Rae. *The Toll-Bridge Troll*. Harcourt, 1995.

SUBJECTS: CITIES AND TOWNS. CREATIVE DRAMA. FAIRY TALES—SATIRE. GOATS. PARODIES. RATS. READER'S THEATER. STORIES TO TELL.

250   Emmett, Jonathan. *Ruby in Her Own Time*. Illus. by Rebecca Harry. Scholastic, 2004. 0-439-57915-5. Unp. Gr. PreK–K

Ruby is the last to hatch of the five eggs Mother Duck tends. The smallest of her siblings, she is the slowest to grow and the last to learn how to eat and to swim. Even so, Mother Duck assures Father Duck that she will do all these things, in her own time.

GERM: Soft and winsomely fuzzy paintings will generate affection and identification among children who are not always first in everything. Ask them to think about what they have learned to do "in their own time," as Ruby does. The classic unhurried-child book, *Leo the Late Bloomer*, by Robert Kraus will certainly tie in well here.

RELATED TITLES: Arnosky, Jim. *All Night Near the Water*. Putnam, 1994. / Buzzeo, Toni. *Dawdle Duckling*. Dial, 2003. / Dunrea, Olivier. *Ollie*. Houghton, 2003. / Emmett, Jonathan. *Someone Bigger*. Clarion, 2004. / Freedman, Claire. *Dilly Duckling*. McElderry, 2004. / Hindley, Judy. *Do Like a Duck Does!* Candlewick, 2002. / Kraus, Robert. *Leo the Late Bloomer*. HarperCollins, 1971. / McCloskey, Robert. *Make Way for Ducklings*. Viking, 1941. / Peters, Lisa Westberg. *Cold Little Duck, Duck, Duck*. Greenwillow, 2000. / Raffi. *Five Little Ducks*. Crown, 1988. / Rankin, Joan. *Wow! It's Great Being a Duck*. McElderry, 1998. / Simmons, Jane. *Come Along, Daisy*. Little, Brown, 1998. / Stott, Dorothy. *Too Much*. Dutton, 1990. / Whippo, Walt, and Bernard Zaritzky. *Little White Duck*. Little, Brown, 2000. / Whybrow, Ian. *Quacky Quack-Quack*. Four Winds, 1991.

SUBJECTS: ANIMALS—INFANCY. DUCKS. GROWTH. INDIVIDUALITY.

251   Emmett, Jonathan. *Someone Bigger.* **Illus. by Adrian Reynolds. Clarion, 2004. 0-618-44397-5. Unp. Gr. PreK–1**

One windy day, Sam's dad won't let him fly the large, light kite they made; even when dad gets pulled aloft, he tells Sam, "No, you're too small . . . This kite needs someone bigger." Told in galloping rhyme, with lots of repetition and big, action-filled, storyhour-sized watercolors, this riotous outing—with lots of people and zoo animals dangling from the kite string—is brought to a satisfying ending with not-too-small-at-all Sam taking control of the kite and expertly guiding everyone back to the ground.

GERM: Ask the perfect prereading question: What is it you would like to try even though the grownups tell you you're not big enough to do it? How can you prove that you are? Then take the class outside to fly a kite.

RELATED TITLES: Brown, Margaret Wise. *Another Important Book.* HarperCollins, 1999. / Compestine, Ying Chang. *The Story of Kites.* Holiday House, 2003. / Crummel, Susan Stevens. *All in One Hour.* Marshall Cavendish, 2003. / Curtis, Jamie Lee. *It's Hard to Be Five: Learning How to Work My Control Panel.* Harper-Collins, 2004. / De Regniers, Beatrice Schenk. *May I Bring a Friend?* Atheneum, 1964. / Ehlert, Lois. *Color Zoo.* HarperCollins, 1989. / Emmett, Jonathan. *Ruby in Her Own Time.* Scholastic, 2004. / Fenton, Edward. *The Big Yellow Balloon.* Doubleday, 1967. / Garland, Michael. *Last Night at the Zoo.* Boyds Mills, 2001. / Gelman, Rita Golden. *I Went to the Zoo.* Scholastic, 1993. / Howard, Arthur. *When I Was Five.* Harcourt, 1996. / Paxton, Tom. *Going to the Zoo.* Morrow, 1996. / Whybrow, Ian. *Sammy and the Dinosaurs.* Orchard, 1999.

SUBJECTS: ANIMALS. CHANTABLE REFRAIN. CUMULATIVE STORIES. FATHERS AND SONS. KITES. SIZE. STORIES IN RHYME. ZOOS.

252   English, Karen. *Hot Day on Abbott Avenue.* **Illus. by Javaka Steptoe. Clarion, 2004. 0-395-98527-7. Unp. Gr. PreK–2**

On best-friend-breakup day, a day too hot to flutter a fan, best friends Kishi and Renée, are too mad at each other to speak. Renee wants Kishi to apologize for buying the last blue pop from the ice cream man when she knew that was Renee's favorite. Then they hear the irresistible sound of the other girls jumping rope down the block. Steptoe's moody cut-paper and found-object collages are so textured and detailed that readers will all want to feel the pages.

GERM: Discussion point: How can Kishi and Renee get back together again? As a writing prompt, ask your kids to recall a time they got into a fight with a friend or sibling and how they made up. See how best friends Molly and Ben end their argument in *You're Not My Best Friend Anymore* by Charlotte Pomerantz. Pull out a jump rope and ask children to recite all the jump rope and playground rhymes they can recall. Another book with a jump rope motif is *The Recess Queen* by Alexis O'Neill.

RELATED TITLES: DePaolo, Paula. *Rosie and the Yellow Ribbon.* Little, Brown, 1992. / Havill, Juanita. *Jamaica and Brianna.* Houghton Mifflin, 1993. / Hesse, Karen. *Come On, Rain.* Scholastic, 1999. / Joosse, Barbara M. *Hot City.* Philomel, 2004. / O'Neill, Alexis. *The Recess Queen.* Scholastic, 2002. / Pomerantz, Charlotte. *You're Not My Best Friend Anymore.* Dial, 1998. / Raschka, Chris. *Yo! Yes?* Orchard, 1993. / Rodman, Mary Ann. *My Best Friend.* Viking, 2005. / Schwartz, Alvin, comp. *And the Green Grass Grew All Around: Folk Poetry from Everyone.* HarperCollins, 1992. / Sierra, Judy. *Schoolyard Rhymes: Kids' Own Rhymes for Rope Skipping, Hand Clapping, Ball Bouncing, and Just Plain Fun.* Knopf, 2005. / Winthrop, Elizabeth. *Lizzie and Harold.* Lothrop, 1985.

SUBJECTS: AFRICAN AMERICANS. ARGUMENTS. BEST FRIENDS. CONFLICT RESOLUTION. EMOTIONS. FORGIVENESS. FRIENDSHIP. JUMP ROPE RHYMES. MULTICULTURAL BOOKS. SUMMER.

253   English, Karen. *Nadia's Hands.* **Illus. by Jonathan Weiner. Boyds Mills, 1999. 1-56397-667-6. Unp. Gr. 1–3**

Nadia is to be the flower girl at Aunt Laila's wedding, and she is nervous about getting *mehndi* (elaborately drawn henna designs) on her hands, which is part of the Pakistani tradition.

GERM: There's a natural and graceful juxtaposition here of the traditions of the old world with those of an Americanized child; listeners will be fascinated to compare traditional American wedding customs with Pakistani ones. Discuss: Why was Nadia worried about having the mehndi on her hands when she went back to school? What customs does your family have that are different? The concept of *sabr*, an Arabic word meaning patience or to accept waiting, is one you might find useful to use with fidgeters.

RELATED TITLES: Baraschi, Lynne. *The Reluctant Flower Girl.* HarperCollins, 2001. / Cox, Judy. *Now We Can Have a Wedding.* Holiday House, 1998. / Lorbiecki, Marybeth. *Sister Anne's Hands.* Dial, 1998. / Marsden, Carolyn. *The Gold-Threaded Dress*. Candlewick, 2002. / Park, Barbara. *Junie B. Jones Is (Almost) a Flower Girl*. Random House, 1999. / Soto, Gary. *Snapshots from the Wedding*. Putnam, 1997.

SUBJECTS: HANDS. MULTICULTURAL BOOKS. PAKISTANI AMERICANS. WEDDINGS.

254 **Ernst, Lisa Campbell.** *Bubba and Trixie*. **Illus. by the author. Simon & Schuster, 1997. 0-689-81357-0. Unp. Gr. K–2**

Meet Bubba, a nervous Nellie of a caterpillar who's afraid of becoming a butterfly, and his adventurous new ladybug pal who gets him to relax, enjoy himself, and accept his coming transformation.

GERM: Use this on two levels: to talk about insects, butterflies, and metamorphosis and to talk about fears and how to face them. Find out more about ladybugs with Rick Chrustowski's *Bright Beetle*.

RELATED TITLES: Brown, Ruth. *If at First You Do Not See*. Henry Holt, 1983. / Cannon, Janell. *Verdi*. Harcourt, 1997. / Carle, Eric. *The Grouchy Ladybug*. HarperCollins, 1997. / Carle, Eric. *The Very Hungry Caterpillar*. Putnam, 1981. / Chrustowski, Rick. *Bright Beetle*. Henry Holt, 2000. / Edwards, Pamela Duncan. *Clara Caterpillar*. HarperCollins, 2001. / Ehlert, Lois. *Waiting for Wings*. Harcourt, 2001. / Hariton, Anca. *Butterfly Story*. Dutton, 1995. / Heiligman, Deborah. *From Caterpillar to Butterfly*. HarperCollins, 1996. / Lavies, Bianca. *Monarch Butterflies: Mysterious Travelers*. Dutton, 1993. / Swope, Sam. *Gotta Go! Gotta Go!* Farrar, 2000.

SUBJECTS: BUTTERFLIES. CATERPILLARS. FEAR. FRIENDSHIP. INSECTS. LADYBUGS. METAMORPHOSIS.

255 **Ernst, Lisa Campbell.** *Goldilocks Returns*. **Illus. by the author. Simon & Schuster, 2000. 0-689-82537-4. Unp. Gr. K–2**

Fifty years after all that dreadful trouble with the bears, a now middle-aged Goldilocks, still suffering guilt over her life of crime when she was a girl, returns to the deep, dark woods to make amends with Mama, Papa, and Baby Bear. She substitutes health food bars for their porridge, redecorates the whole house, fixes the furniture, and falls asleep on Baby Bear's bed, satisfied she's made everything just right. The bears' horrified reaction when they get home from their walk? "She's back!"

GERM: Be sure your kids know the real story of Goldilocks, so they'll appreciate the humor of this update. As you read, have them predict what Goldilocks will fix up next and what the consequences will be. Another very funny Goldilocks parody is Lauren Child's *Who's Afraid of the Big Bad Book?* And, of course, you must share Ernst's other "Goldilocks and the Three Bears" book, *Stella Louella's Runaway Book*, in which a girl misplaces her overdue library book and runs all over town to track it down.

RELATED TITLES: Aylesworth, Jim. *Goldilocks and the Three Bears*. Scholastic, 2003. / Brett, Jan. *Goldilocks and the Three Bears*. Putnam, 1987. / Child, Lauren. *Beware of the Storybook Wolves*. Scholastic, 2001. / Child, Lauren. *Who's Afraid of the Big Bad Book?* Hyperion, 2003. / Emberley, Michael. *Ruby and the Sniffs*. Little, Brown, 2004. / Ernst, Lisa Campbell. *Little Red Riding Hood: A Newfangled Prairie Tale*. Simon & Schuster, 1995. / Ernst, Lisa Campbell. *Stella Louella's Runaway Book*. Simon & Schuster, 1998. / McClements, George. *Jake Gander, Storyville Detective*. Hyperion, 2002. / Marshall, James. *Goldilocks and the Three Bears*. Dial, 1988. / Scieszka, Jon. *The True Story of the 3 Little Pigs*. Viking, 1989. / Stanley, Diane. *Goldie and the Three Bears*. HarperCollins, 2003. / Stevens, Janet. *Goldilocks and the Three Bears*. Holiday House, 1986. / Wiesner, David. *The Three Pigs*. Clarion, 2001.

SUBJECTS: BEARS. CHARACTERS IN LITERATURE. GOLDILOCKS. PARODIES.

256 **Ernst, Lisa Campbell.** *The Letters Are Lost*. **Illus. by the author. Viking, 1996. 0-670-86336-X. Unp. Gr. PreK–1**

A set of 26 children's alphabet blocks have somehow become scattered all over the house. "B tumbled into the bath." Looking at each picture, observant ones will be able to predict the accompanying sentence stating where each block was found.

GERM: Each child can pick a letter and draw a new picture showing in what alliterative place that letter alphabet block got lost. Bring in alphabet blocks and have children hide each in a place starting with the same letter, putting the T in the trash can or the B by the board, for example.

RELATED TITLES: Ehlert, Lois. *Eating the Alphabet: Fruits and Vegetables from A to Z*. Harcourt, 1989. / Fleming, Denise. *Alphabet Under Construction*. Henry Holt, 2002. / Kalman, Maira. *What Pete Ate from A–Z*. Putnam, 2001. / Lester, Mike. *A Is for Salad*. Putnam, 2000. / Lobel, Arnold. *On Market Street*. Greenwillow, 1981. / MacDonald, Ross. *Achoo! Bang! Crash: The Noisy Alphabet*. Roaring Brook, 2003. / MacDonald, Suse. *Alphabatics*. Simon & Schuster, 1986. / Moxley, Sheila. *ABCD: An Alphabet Book of Cats and Dogs*. Little, Brown, 2001. / Schneider, R. M. *Add It, Dip It, Fix It: A Book of Verbs*. Houghton Mifflin, 1995. / Seeger, Laura Vaccaro. *The*

Hidden Alphabet. Roaring Brook, 2003. / Shannon, George. *Tomorrow's Alphabet*. Greenwillow, 1996. / Slate, Joseph. *Miss Bindergarten Gets Ready for Kindergarten*. Dutton, 1996. / Wood, Audrey. *Alphabet Mystery*. Blue Sky/Scholastic, 2003.

SUBJECTS: ALLITERATION. ALPHABET BOOKS. CREATIVE DRAMA. LOST AND FOUND POSSESSIONS. TOYS.

257   **Ernst, Lisa Campbell.** *Little Red Riding Hood: A Newfangled Prairie Tale*. **Illus. by the author. Simon & Schuster, 1995. 0-689-80145-9. Unp. Gr. K–3**

Riding her bike across the prairie to bring warm wheat berry muffins and cold lemonade to her grandma, Red meets up with a muffin-craving wolf. ("'Gadzooks!" he whispered. "What is that scrumptious smell?'") His plans to steal Grandma's secret prize-winning recipe are foiled by Red's savvy, tractor-riding granny, who puts him to work at her new muffin ship in town.

GERM: The muffin recipe's on the back inside cover, in case you want to cook up a batch to share. Compare the parody with the original fairy tale and with Michael Emberley's version, *Ruby*, in which a smart young city mouse and her Granny trip up a suave feline stranger.

RELATED TITLES: Artell, Mike. *Petite Rouge: A Cajun Red Riding Hood*. Dial, 2001. / Child, Lauren. *Beware of the Storybook Wolves*. Scholastic, 2001. / Child, Lauren. *Who's Afraid of the Big Bad Book?* Hyperion, 2003. / Christelow, Eileen. *Where's the Big Bad Wolf?* Clarion, 2002. / Emberley, Michael. *Ruby*. Little, Brown, 1990. / Ernst, Lisa Campbell. *Goldilocks Returns*. Simon & Schuster, 2000. / Harper, Wilhelmina. *The Gunniwolf*. Dutton, 1978. / Hartman, Bob. *The Wolf Who Cried Boy*. Putnam, 2002. / Hyman, Trina Schart. *Little Red Riding Hood*. Holiday House, 1983. / Lowell, Susan. *Little Red Cowboy Hat*. Henry Holt, 1997. / McClements, George. *Jake Gander, Storyville Detective*. Hyperion, 2002. / Marshall, James. *Red Riding Hood*. Dial, 1987. / Marshall, James. *The Three Little Pigs*. Dial, 1989. / Meddaugh, Susan. *Hog-Eye*. Houghton Mifflin, 1995. / Palatini, Margie. *Bad Boys*. HarperCollins, 2003. / Soto, Gary. *Chato's Kitchen*. Putnam, 1995.

SUBJECTS: CHARACTERS IN LITERATURE. GRANDMOTHERS. LITTLE RED RIDING HOOD STORIES. PARODIES. WOLVES.

258   **Ernst, Lisa Campbell.** *Stella Louella's Runaway Book*. **Illus. by the author. Simon & Schuster, 1998. 0-689-81883-1. Unp. Gr. PreK–2**

Book lover Stella is distraught when her now-due library book disappears on Saturday morning. She spends a frantic day rushing all over town, trying to track it down from the people who have passed it around and read it. Not to worry—wonderful librarian Mrs. Graham has Stella's book, safe and sound.

GERM: What is the title of Stella Louella's library book? By paying attention to each of the borrowers' descriptions of their favorite parts of the story, listeners will quickly deduce it's "The Three Bears." This delightful circular story with its large genial pastel illustrations will be fun to act out in Reader's Theater (if you write a script) or creative drama, or for an intro lesson on maps. Don't forget to stage a reading of "Goldilocks and the Three Bears" and have children tell you their favorite parts. In *Harry in Trouble* by Barbara Ann Porte, Harry is dismayed when he loses his third library card this year. Make sure all your students have their own public library cards!

RELATED TITLES: Allen, Susan, and Jane Lindaman. *Read Anything Good Lately?* Millbrook, 2003. / Aylesworth, Jim. *Goldilocks and the Three Bears*. Scholastic, 2003. / Brett, Jan. *Goldilocks and the Three Bears*. Putnam, 1987. / Child, Lauren. *Who's Afraid of the Big Bad Book?* Hyperion, 2003. / Deedy, Carmen Agra. *The Library Dragon*. Peachtree, 1994. / Eisen, Armand. *Goldilocks and the Three Bears*. Knopf, 1987. / Ernst, Lisa Campbell. *Goldilocks Returns*. Simon & Schuster, 2000. / Marshall, James. *Goldilocks and the Three Bears*. Dial, 1988. / Numeroff, Laura Joffe. *Beatrice Doesn't Want To*. Candlewick, 2004. / Polacco, Patricia. *Aunt Chip and the Great Triple Creek Dam Affair*. Philomel, 1996. / Porte, Barbara Ann. *Harry in Trouble*. Greenwillow, 1989. / Sierra, Judy. *Wild About Books*. Knopf, 2004. / Stanley, Diane. *Goldie and the Three Bears*. HarperCollins, 2003. / Stevens, Janet. *Goldilocks and the Three Bears*. Holiday House, 1986. / Williams, Suzanne. *Library Lil*. Dial, 1997.

SUBJECTS: BOOKS AND READING. CIRCULAR STORIES. CREATIVE DRAMA. GOLDILOCKS. LIBRARIANS. LOST AND FOUND POSSESSIONS. MAPS AND GLOBES. READER'S THEATER. RESPONSIBILITY. WORRYING.

259   **Ernst, Lisa Campbell.** *Tangram Magician*. **Illus. by the author. Blue Apple, 2005. 1-59354-106-6. Unp. Gr. PreK–3**

The story of a magician who transforms himself into objects and animals including a bird, a fish, a goat, and a teapot is secondary to the stunning geometric illustrations made out of tangrams. Spiral-bound heavy-stock pages portray the magician in his many different red tangram guises, looking like origami sculptures against a dark blue background.

GERM: The cover of this book incorporates a 3-inch-square package of the seven tangram pieces so children can finish the last page of the book, which asks, "What else can the magician become?" Make new figures and tell stories about them or use them for math. If you stare at a page for about 30 seconds and then stare at a white surface, you'll see a demonstration of Goethe's color theory. The red tangram figure will appear blue, while the blue background will appear pink. See Eric Carle's *Hello, Red Fox* for more information on color theory. Ed Emberley's *The Wing on a Flea* will be a good companion for making pictures out of shapes. Look up tangrams on <www.google.com> and you'll find a mere 75,000 hits. Try <www.tangrams.ca/> for a bit of history, directions on how to construct your own tangrams, puzzles to try, and links to other tangram sites.

RELATED TITLES: Adler, David A. *Shape Up! Fun with Triangles and Other Polygons.* Holiday House, 1998. / Carle, Eric. *Hello, Red Fox.* Simon & Schuster, 1998. / Emberley, Ed. *The Wing on a Flea: A Book About Shapes.* Little, Brown, 2001. / Ernst, Lisa Campbell. *The Letters Are Lost.* Viking, 1996. / George, Kristine O'Connell. *Fold Me a Poem.* Harcourt, 2005. / Tompert, Ann. *Grandfather Tang's Story.* Crown, 1990.

SUBJECTS: GEOMETRY. MAGICIANS. PICTURE BOOKS FOR ALL AGES. SHAPES. TANGRAMS. TRANSFORMATIONS.

260 **Falconer, Ian.** *Olivia.* Illus. by the author. Atheneum, 2000. 0-689-82953-1. Unp. Gr. PreK–2

Little pig Olivia is very good at wearing people out as she trundles through her days, building a sand Empire State Building at the beach, dancing instead of napping, and painting a spattered Jackson Pollock-style mural on the wall.

GERM: An utterly adorable creature, Olivia is an ideal heroine to use in discussing strong main characters. Have listeners come up with a list of 20 apt words that describe her and think of other activities she would enjoy. Ask your students: "What if you were an animal character in a story? What animal would you be?" Have them draw themselves as those animals, and list 20 words that define their own personalities. Next, they can do some imaginative writing, pulling in autobiographical anecdotes, to compose and illustrate a story about their daily lives, incorporating their singular talents, hobbies, and interests. This is a novel way to approach autobiographies and also to demonstrate how facts are part of all fiction writing.

RELATED TITLES: Feiffer, Jules. *Bark, George.* HarperCollins, 1999. / Hobbie, Holly. *Toot and Puddle: You Are My Sunshine.* Little, Brown, 1999. / Laden, Nina. *Roberto the Insect Architect.* Chronicle, 2000. / McPhail, David. *Pig Pig Grows Up.* Dutton, 1980. / Palatini, Margie. *Piggie Pie.* Clarion, 1995. / Pomerantz, Charlotte. *The Piggy in the Puddle.* Macmillan, 1974. / Rylant, Cynthia. *Poppleton.* Scholastic, 1997. (And others in the Poppleton series.) / Van Leeuwen, Jean. *Amanda Pig and Her Big Brother Oliver.* Dial, 1982. (And others in the Oliver and Amanda series.) / Wells, Rosemary. *Max Cleans Up.* Dial, 2000. (And others in the Max series.)

SUBJECTS: BEHAVIOR. HUMOROUS FICTION. INDIVIDUALITY. NONCONFORMISTS. PICTURE BOOKS FOR ALL AGES. PIGS.

261 **Falconer, Ian.** *Olivia . . . and the Missing Toy.* Illus. by the author. Atheneum, 2003. 0-689-85291-6. Unp. Gr. PreK–2

"Somebody took my best toy," Olivia bellows, and she looks everywhere to find her floppy stuffed animal: under the rug, under the sofa, under the cat. Practicing the piano that dark and stormy night, Olivia hears a horrible sound. Taking her lit candelabra, she creeps down the dark, dark hallway and finds . . . the culprit.

GERM: Before you reveal the whereabouts of the toy, listeners can predict what could have happened to it and draw, write, and/or tell what they think Olivia does next. For all ages, this is a fast and funny introduction to the mystery genre. Ask your mystery solvers to recall their experiences with lost treasures and how and where they've located them. Folding a paper in half, they can write "LOST" on one side, "FOUND" on the other, and complete these sentences: "I lost my . . ."; "I found it . . ."

RELATED TITLES: Adler, David A. *My Dog and the Birthday Mystery.* Holiday House, 1987. / Alborough, Jez. *Where's My Teddy?* Candlewick, 1992. / Clark, Emma Chichester. *Where Are You, Blue Kangaroo?* Doubleday, 2000. / Cushman, Doug. *Inspector Hopper.* HarperCollins, 2000. / Cushman, Doug. *Inspector Hopper's Mystery Year.* HarperCollins, 2003. / Ernst, Lisa Campbell. *Stella Louella's Runaway Book.* Simon & Schuster, 1998. / Falconer, Ian. *Olivia.* Atheneum, 2000. / Falconer, Ian. *Olivia Saves the Circus.* Atheneum, 2001. / Fitzpatrick, Marie-Louise. *Lizzy and Skunk.* DK Ink, 2000. / Ichikawa, Satomi. *La La Rose.* Philomel, 2004. / Smith, Maggie. *Paisley.* Knopf, 2004. / Willems, Mo. *Knuffle Bunny: A Cautionary Tale.* Hyperion, 2004.

SUBJECTS: LOST AND FOUND POSSESSIONS. MYSTERY AND DETECTIVE STORIES. PICTURE BOOKS FOR ALL AGES. PIGS. STUFFED ANIMALS. TOYS.

262 Falconer, Ian. *Olivia Saves the Circus.* Illus. by the author. Atheneum, 2001. 0-689-82954-X. Unp. Gr. PreK–2

"Today is Olivia's turn to tell the class about her vacation. Olivia always blossoms in front of an audience." Insouciant piglet Olivia's tale of her circus adventure—taming lions, walking the tightrope, and flying through the air as Olivia, Queen of the Trampoline—is a doozy.

GERM: A fitting tie-in to the usual "What I Did on My Summer Vacation" essay, this should enhance your kids' skills of exaggeration and inspire them to create tall tales, inflating incidents that really happened to them. You might need to explain some of Olivia's exaggerations, however, as younger listeners will accept her yarn as truth.

RELATED TITLES: Falconer, Ian. *Olivia.* Atheneum, 2000. / Falconer, Ian. *Olivia . . . and the Missing Toy.* Atheneum, 2003. / Long, Melinda. *How I Became a Pirate.* Harcourt, 2003. / Pomerantz, Charlotte. *The Piggy in the Puddle.* Macmillan, 1974. / Rylant, Cynthia. *Poppleton.* Scholastic, 1997. (And others in the Poppleton series.) / Scieszka, Jon. *Baloney (Henry P.).* Viking, 2001. / Teague, Mark. *Dear Mrs. LaRue: Letters from Obedience School.* Scholastic, 2002. / Teague, Mark. *How I Spent My Summer Vacation.* Crown, 1995. / Teague, Mark. *The Secret Shortcut.* Scholastic, 1996.

SUBJECTS: CIRCUS. EXAGGERATION. HUMOROUS FICTION. IMAGINATION. PICTURE BOOKS FOR ALL AGES. SCHOOLS. STORYTELLING.

263 Falwell, Cathryn. *Butterflies for Kiri.* Illus. by the author. Lee & Low, 2003. 1-58430-100-7. Unp. Gr. PreK–2

Kiri is frustrated, trying to fold a butterfly with the beautiful origami paper her aunt sent for her birthday; but with patience and perseverance, she is finally able to do it.

GERM: If your listeners are dexterous, try a little simple origami with them. Children who get frustrated easily when drawing a picture will take heart from the scene in which Kiri breaks down in tears over her spoiled picture, but then stops and figures out how she can make it better than ever. See how one boy spends an entire day making origami animals in the poetry book *Fold Me a Poem* by Kristine O'Connell George.

RELATED TITLES: Cohen, Miriam. *No Good in Art.* Greenwillow, 1980. / dePaola, Tomie. *The Art Lesson.* Putnam, 1989. / Falwell, Cathryn. *Feast for 10.* Clarion, 1993. / Falwell, Cathryn. *Word Wizard.* Clarion, 1998. / George, Kristine O'Connell. *Fold Me a Poem.* Harcourt, 2005. / Kleven, Elisa. *The Paper Princess.* Dutton, 1994. / McCully, Emily Arnold. *Mouse Practice.* Scholastic, 1999. / Melmed, Laura Krauss. *Little Oh.* Lothrop, 1997. / Moss, Marissa. *Regina's Big Mistake.* Houghton Mifflin, 1990. / Reynolds, Peter H. *The Dot.* Candlewick, 2003. / Reynolds, Peter H. *Ish.* Candlewick, 2004. / Wells, Rosemary. *Yoko's Paper Cranes.* Hyperion, 2001.

SUBJECTS: ASIAN AMERICANS. CREATIVITY. JAPANESE AMERICANS. MULTICULTURAL BOOKS. ORIGAMI. PAINTING. PERSEVERANCE.

264 Falwell, Cathryn. *Turtle Splash! Countdown at the Pond.* Illus. by the author. Greenwillow, 2001. 0-06-029463-9. Unp. Gr. PreK–1

One by one, each of ten eastern painted turtles is startled into sliding off their log over the pond by a bullfrog, a rabbit, a squirrel, a deer, and other benign pond dwellers. It's kind of like *Over in the Meadow,* but counts down instead of up to ten, and the collage illustrations, made from handmade paper, scraps, and small pieces of bark, will make you pine to wander in the woods. Please note: The pieces of bark that were used for the illustrations in this book were all found on the ground. As Falwell warns us, you should never take bark off a living tree.

GERM: This book provides an ideal opportunity to mix such varied topics as counting down from ten, animal and pond life studies, drama, and poetry. You can stage this as a math play, with ten turtles sitting on the log, and the various animals that come to scare them off. There's a double-page spread of life at the pond, identifying each animal and providing a paragraph of facts about it. And on the last page there are directions on how to make leaf prints, which you or your art teacher will want to try with the kids. In a fitting follow-up to the book, write your own nature stories, collect leaves, and take a closer look at the world outside.

RELATED TITLES: Berger, Melvin. *Look Out for Turtles.* HarperCollins, 1992. / Christelow, Eileen. *Five Little Monkeys Jumping on the Bed.* Clarion, 1989. / Fleming, Denise. *In the Small, Small Pond.* Henry Holt, 1993. / George, Lindsay Barrett. *Around the Pond: Who's Been Here?* Greenwillow, 1996. / Keats, Ezra Jack. *Over in the Meadow.* Viking, 1999. / MacDonald, Suse. *Look Whooo's Counting.* Scholastic, 2000. / Pollock, Penny. *When the Moon Is Full: A Lunar Year.* Little, Brown, 2001. / Raffi. *Five Little Ducks.* Crown, 1988. / Ross, Gayle. *How Tur-*

tle's Back Was Cracked: A Traditional Cherokee Tale. Dial, 1995. / Simmons, Jane. *Come Along, Daisy*. Little, Brown, 1998. / Whippo, Walt, and Bernard Zaritzky. *Little White Duck*. Little, Brown, 2000. / Wilson, Karma. *A Frog in the Bog*. McElderry, 2003. / Wise, William. *Ten Sly Piranhas: A Counting Story in Reverse*. Dial, 1993.

SUBJECTS: ANIMALS. COUNTING BOOKS. MATHEMATICS. POND LIFE. STORIES IN RHYME. TURTLES.

265   Falwell, Cathryn. *Word Wizard*. Illus. by the author. Clarion, 1998. 0-395-85580-2. Unp. Gr. K–2

Young Anna realizes that with the help of her magic spoon she can turn words around—with a simple rearrangement of letters "ocean" becomes "canoe" and "shore" turns into "horse." With her words turning into actions, she saves the day for a lost little boy.

GERM: Use this anagram story to create new anagrams and to introduce the games Scrabble Junior and Boggle. *Elvis Lives and Other Anagrams* by Jon Agee is a book of humorous, illustrated anagrams.

RELATED TITLES: Agee, Jon. *Elvis Lives and Other Anagrams*. Farrar, 2004. / Chapman, Cheryl. *Pass the Fritters, Critters*. Simon & Schuster, 1993. / Clements, Andrew. *Double Trouble in Walla Walla*. Millbrook, 1998. / Falwell, Cathryn. *Clowning Around*. Orchard, 1991. / Hepworth, Cathi. *Antics! An Alphabetical Anthology*. Putnam, 1992. / Hepworth, Cathi. *Bug Off! A Swarm of Insect Words*. Putnam, 1998. / Most, Bernard. *Can You Find It?* Harcourt, 1993. / Most, Bernard. *Hippopotamus Hunt*. Harcourt, 1993. / Pulver, Robin. *Punctuation Takes a Vacation*. Holiday House, 2003. / Raffi. *Down by the Bay*. Crown, 1987. / Slate, Joseph. *Miss Bindergarten Gets Ready for Kindergarten*. Dutton, 1996. / Steig, William. *CDB*. Simon & Schuster, 2000. / Wood, Audrey. *Silly Sally*. Harcourt, 1992.

SUBJECTS: ANAGRAMS. ENGLISH LANGUAGE—SPELLING. WORD GAMES.

266   Fearnley, Jan. *Watch Out!* Illus. by the author. Candlewick, 2004. 0-7636-2318-0. Unp. Gr. PreK–K

Every time Wilf, a rambunctious little brown mouse "full of busy," ignores his mother's warnings—"CRASH BANG WALLOP"—he falls down or makes a mess. "Oh, Wilf," says his patient mother, "I wish you'd listen to me." Wilt fixes her a beautiful surprise supper and an "I Love You" card to cheer her up, but this time, it's Mom who doesn't pay attention and knocks everything over.

GERM: Boisterous kids who don't always listen will be reassured that their vexed parents nevertheless appreciate a nice cuddle. Talk it over: How do you cheer up your parents? Make "I Love You" cards for Mother's Day or any old day.

RELATED TITLES: Brown, Margaret Wise. *The Runaway Bunny*. HarperCollins, 1972. / Lester, Helen. *Listen, Buddy*. Houghton Mifflin, 1995. / Polushkin, Maria. *Mother, Mother, I Want Another*. Crown, 1978. / Shannon, David. *No, David!* Scholastic, 1998. / Wells, Rosemary. *Noisy Nora*. Dial, 1997. / Wells, Rosemary. *Shy Charles*. Dial, 1988.

SUBJECTS: BEHAVIOR. LISTENING. MICE. MOTHERS AND SONS.

267   Feiffer, Jules. *Bark, George*. Illus. by the author. HarperCollins, 1999. 0-06-205185-7. Unp. Gr. PreK–1

George's mother says, "Bark, George," but every time the floppy brown dog tries to bark, he meows, quacks, oinks, or moos instead. The vet figures out what's wrong, pulling out a cat, duck, pig, and cow from deep, deep down inside George.

GERM: Children can act out the entire swallowing story in reverse in creative drama with lots of animal noises and a surprise ending. Use this simple story with older kids to explain story structure—beginning, rising action, climax, falling action, ending. It fulfills the mandate of a great book: it should Surprise, Startle, and Satisfy (which I call the Three Freeman S's)—and it even earns my special designation of Perfect Picture Book.

RELATED TITLES: Dallas-Conté, Juliet. *Cock-a-Moo-Moo*. Little, Brown, 2001. / DeZutter, Hank. *Who Says a Dog Goes Bow-Wow?* Doubleday, 1993. / Dodds, Dayle Ann. *Do Bunnies Talk?* HarperCollins, 1992. / Feiffer, Jules. *The Daddy Mountain*. Hyperion, 2004. / Feiffer, Jules. *I'm Not Bobby!* Hyperion, 2001. / Kellogg, Steven. *Pinkerton, Behave*. Dial, 1979. / Kopper, Lisa. *Daisy Thinks She Is a Baby*. Knopf, 1994. / Krosoczka, Jarrett J. *Punk Farm*. Knopf, 2005. / Martin, Bill, Jr. *Polar Bear, Polar Bear, What Do You Hear?* Henry Holt, 1991. / Meltzer, Maxine. *Pups Speak Up*. Bradbury, 1994. / Palatini, Margie. *Moo Who?* HarperCollins, 2004. / Rowe, John A. *Baby Crow*. North-South, 1994. / Shapiro, Arnold L. *Mice Squeak, We Speak*. Putnam, 1997. / Stenmark, Victoria. *The Singing Chick*. Henry Holt, 1999. / Waddell, Martin. *The Pig in the Pond*. Candlewick, 1992. / Walter, Virginia. *"Hi, Pizza Man!"* Orchard, 1995.

SUBJECTS: ANIMAL SOUNDS. ANIMALS. BEHAVIOR. CREATIVE DRAMA. DOGS. HUMOROUS FICTION. SWALLOWING STORIES. VETERINARIANS.

268   **Feiffer, Jules.** *The Daddy Mountain.* **Illus. by the author. Hyperion, 2004. 0-7868-0912-4. Unp. Gr. PreK–1**

A little red-haired, barefoot girl shows us how she climbs the Daddy Mountain, stepping first onto his loafers and pulling herself up a leg, to the belt, swinging up to his shoulder, until, very carefully, she's sitting on his head! Lift up the final folded page, and there she is, triumphant, with big guy Daddy saying, "No problem, she's fine," as mom covers her eyes in disbelief.

GERM: Climbers will want to try this at home, which may or may not please their dads. Ask your listeners: Do you and your parents have traditions or activities that you share?

RELATED TITLES: Browne, Anthony. *My Dad.* Farrar, 2001. / Collard, Sneed B., III. *Animal Dads.* Houghton Mifflin, 1997. / Feiffer, Jules. *Bark, George.* HarperCollins, 1999. / Feiffer, Jules. *I Lost My Bear.* Morrow, 1998. / Feiffer, Jules. *I'm Not Bobby!* Hyperion, 2001. / Greenspun, Adele. *Daddies.* Philomel, 1991. / Pringle, Laurence. *Octopus Hug.* Boyds Mills, 1993. / Tarpley, Natasha Anastasia. *Bippity Bop Barbershop.* Little, Brown, 2002. / Ziefert, Harriet. *33 Uses for a Dad.* Blue Apple, 2004.

SUBJECTS: FATHERS AND DAUGHTERS. PERSONAL NARRATIVES.

269   **Feiffer, Jules.** *I Lost My Bear.* **Illus. by the author. Morrow, 1998. 0-688-15148-5. Unp. Gr. PreK–6**

A blonde ponytailed little girl is distraught when she can't find her stuffed bear. She looks where she was playing with it last, as her mother suggests, blames her older sister, and even cries piteously, but the bear is gone. Her sister's suggestion—"If you close your eyes and throw one of your other stuffed animals, sometimes it lands in the same place"—is ingenious, though she locates all her other lost items instead. What makes this a perfect picture book for all ages and an affecting character study is the colorful watercolor-and-ink comic strip-like format that so perfectly showcases the girl's festival of emotions, from bleak despair to elation, as she searches for her bear.

GERM: Through your expressive no-holds-barred reading of the story, children will understand what it means to "always read with expression." Have them act out each scene, especially the last one when the girl finds Bearsie under her covers. Certainly they'll clamor to talk and write about the times they've lost and found treasured objects.

RELATED TITLES: Alborough, Jez. *Where's My Teddy?* Candlewick, 1992. / Child, Lauren. *I Will Never NOT EVER Eat a Tomato.* Candlewick, 2000. / Child, Lauren. *What Planet Are You From, Clarice Bean?* Candlewick, 2002. / Clark, Emma Chichester. *Where Are You, Blue Kangaroo?* Doubleday, 2000. / Falconer, Ian. *Olivia . . . and the Missing Toy.* Atheneum, 2003. / Feiffer, Jules. *The Daddy Mountain.* Hyperion, 2004. / Feiffer, Jules. *Meanwhile . . .* HarperCollins, 1997. / Hughes, Shirley. *Dogger.* Lothrop, 1988. / Miller, Sara Swan. *Three Stories You Can Read to Your Teddy Bear.* Houghton Mifflin, 2004. / Sheldon, Dyan. *Love, Your Bear Pete.* Candlewick, 1994. / Smith, Maggie. *Paisley.* Knopf, 2004. / Willems, Mo. *Knuffle Bunny: A Cautionary Tale.* Hyperion, 2004.

SUBJECTS: CREATIVE DRAMA. FAMILY LIFE. HUMOROUS FICTION. LOST AND FOUND POSSESSIONS. PICTURE BOOKS FOR ALL AGES. TEDDY BEARS.

270   **Feiffer, Jules.** *Meanwhile . . .* **Illus. by the author. HarperCollins, 1997. 0-06-205155-5. Unp. Gr. K–3**

Deeply engrossed in his comic book, Raymond muses "What if I had my own 'Meanwhile . . .,'" and writes the word in tiny letters on his wall with red marker. The next thing he knows, Raymond's on a pirate ship on the high seas, dueling with the pirate captain; on horseback, being chased by a posse out West; and then in a rocket in space, dodging Martians. Feiffer's comic strip-paneled illustrations are brash and fun; readers will love the vicarious thrill of being the hero in the midst of dangerous adventure.

GERM: What a great book for talking about characters, plot, and setting. Children can come up with more "Meanwhile . . ." situations, with themselves as the heroes, and illustrate them in storyboard fashion using dialogue balloons, à la Feiffer. They can then act out each encounter in creative drama or work in pairs to add dialogue and write their story as a Reader's Theater script, and read/perform it for the rest of the class. Next, have them do some persuasive writing: a dialogue between themselves and their pursuers, convincing their pursuers not to knock them off. They can do it in prose or script format. Pair students up to create new comic book-style escapades, using Brian Pinkney's *The Adventures of Sparrowboy* for further fun.

RELATED TITLES: Clement, Rod. *Just Another Ordinary Day.* HarperCollins, 1997. / Faulkner, Matt. *The

Amazing Voyage of Jackie Grace. Scholastic, 1987. / Florczak, Robert. *Yikes!!!* Scholastic, 2003. / Grey, Mini. *Traction Man Is Here!* Knopf, 2005. / Leverich, Kathleen. *Hilary and the Troublemakers.* Greenwillow, 1992. / Long, Melinda. *How I Became a Pirate.* Harcourt, 2003. / McPhail, David. *Edward and the Pirates.* Little, Brown, 1997. / McPhail, David. *Pig Pig and the Magic Photo Album.* Dutton, 1986. / Peterson, Beth. *Myra Never Sleeps.* Atheneum, 1995. / Pinkney, Brian. *The Adventures of Sparrowboy.* Simon & Schuster, 1997. / Rodda, Emily. *Power and Glory.* Greenwillow, 1996. / Teague, Mark. *The Field Beyond the Outfield.* Scholastic, 1992. / Van Allsburg, Chris. *Jumanji.* Houghton, 1981. / Van Allsburg, Chris. *Zathura: A Space Adventure.* Houghton, 2002. / Wood, Audrey. *The Flying Dragon Room.* Scholastic, 1996.

SUBJECTS: ADVENTURE AND ADVENTURERS. CARTOONS AND COMICS. CREATIVE DRAMA. CREATIVE WRITING. IMAGINATION. PERSUASIVE WRITING. PICTURE BOOKS FOR ALL AGES. PIRATES. READER'S THEATER.

271 **Fierstein, Harvey. *The Sissy Duckling*. Illus. by Henry Cole. Simon & Schuster, 2002. 0-689-83566-3. Unp. Gr. K–2**

None of the other boy ducklings are interested in any of the things Elmer likes, such as baking and putting on puppet shows. When Papa Duck, mortified by his son's sissy behavior, rejects him, Elmer decides to run away from home. As the rest of the ducks head south, hunters take aim. Papa is shot, and, of course, it's Elmer who drags him home and nurses him back to health over the winter.

GERM: While you are not going to sit down with your class and discuss gay vs. straight, this book gives a nice little message about celebrating what's special and different in all of us and does it without hitting us over the head. Mom explains: "Sissy is a cruel way of saying that you don't do things the way others think you should . . . You are special. And one day you will amaze us all." The other ducks consider Elmer different, but he learns to be proud of his differences. Ask your listeners to list and/or draw the things that make them unique.

RELATED TITLES: Andersen, Hans Christian. *The Ugly Duckling.* Illus. by Jerry Pinkney. Morrow, 1999. / Browne, Anthony. *Willy the Wimp.* Knopf, 1985. / Child, Lauren. *That Pesky Rat.* Candlewick, 2002. / dePaola, Tomie. *Oliver Button Is a Sissy.* Harcourt, 1979. / Fleischman, Paul. *Weslandia.* Candlewick, 1999. / Howe, James. *Horace and Morris But Mostly Dolores.* Atheneum, 1999. / Howe, James. *Pinky and Rex and the Bully.* Atheneum, 1996. / Lester, Helen. *Hooway for Wodney Wat.* Houghton Mifflin, 1999. / Pinkney, Brian. *The Adventures of Sparrowboy.* Simon & Schuster, 1997. / Yashima, Taro. *Crow Boy.* Viking, 1955.

SUBJECTS: DUCKS. FATHERS AND SONS. IDENTITY. OUTCASTS. PARODIES. SELF-ACCEPTANCE. SEX ROLE.

272 **Finchler, Judy. *Miss Malarkey Doesn't Live in Room 10*. Illus. by Kevin O'Malley. Walker, 1995. 0-8027-8387-2. Unp. Gr. K–2**

A boy is sure his teacher lives in school with all the rest of the teachers, but then she moves to his apartment house.

GERM: Have children write and draw what they think goes on at school after they leave for the day. Introduce the other titles in the Miss Malarkey series.

RELATED TITLES: Allard, Harry. *Miss Nelson Is Missing.* Houghton Mifflin, 1985. / Calmenson, Stephanie. *The Frog Principal.* Scholastic, 2001. / Calmenson, Stephanie. *The Principal's New Clothes.* Scholastic, 1989. / Clements, Andrew. *Double Trouble in Walla Walla.* Millbrook, 1998. / Creech, Sharon. *A Fine, Fine School.* HarperCollins, 2001. / Dannenberg, Julie. *First Day Jitters.* Charlesbridge, 2000. / DiPucchio, Kelly. *Mrs. McBloom, Clean Up Your Classroom.* Hyperion, 2005. / Finchler, Judy. *Miss Malarkey Won't Be in Today.* Walker, 1998. / Finchler, Judy. *Miss Malarkey's Field Trip.* Walker, 2004. / Finchler, Judy. *Testing Miss Malarkey.* Walker, 2000. / Finchler, Judy. *You're a Good Sport, Miss Malarkey.* Walker, 2002. / Gutman, Dan. *Miss Daisy Is Crazy.* HarperCollins, 2004. / Marshall, James. *The Cut-Ups.* Viking, 1984.

SUBJECTS: APARTMENT HOUSES. IMAGINATION. SCHOOLS. TEACHERS.

273 **Finchler, Judy. *Testing Miss Malarkey*. Illus. by Kevin O'Malley. Walker, 2000. 0-8027-8739-8. Unp. Gr. 2–6**

Preparing her class for the upcoming achievement test, teacher Miss Malarkey tells her students it won't affect their grades or promotion, but she's been biting her nails getting them ready for it. As the brown-haired boy narrator describes it, they've been preparing their minds and bodies for the test, eating fish as brain food for lunch, coloring in little circles in art class, and doing "yogurt" in gym with Mr. Fittanuff. At home, when his mother reads him a bedtime story, he has to complete a ditto and give her the main idea before going to sleep. Sound familiar?

GERM: This tongue-in-cheek, but not all that exaggerated, story about test anxiety and teaching-to-the-test will resonate with all teachers. Use it with your older kids to blow off a little steam and talk about how they get ready for tests and other hard activities.

RELATED TITLES: Creech, Sharon. *A Fine, Fine School.* HarperCollins, 2001. / Dannenberg, Julie. *First Day Jitters.* Charlesbridge, 2000. / Finchler, Judy. *Miss Malarkey Won't Be in Today.* Walker, 1998. / Finchler, Judy. *Miss Malarkey's Field Trip.* Walker, 2004. / Seuss, Dr., and Jack Prelutsky. *Hooray for Diffendoofer Day.* Knopf, 1998.

SUBJECTS: ACHIEVEMENT TESTS. SCHOOLS. TEACHERS.

274   **Finchler, Judy. *You're a Good Sport, Miss Malarkey.* Illus. by Kevin O'Malley. Walker, 2002. 0-8027-8815-7. Unp. Gr. K–2**

As a new soccer coach, teacher Miss Malarkey wants her novice team of children to enjoy the sport, but the cutthroat parents want them to win. At Saturday's game, when the other team scores a goal, the parents lose it. People are yelling and running onto the field, babies are crying. They have to cancel the game. Miss Malarkey takes charge: parents are no longer allowed to yell or cheer and are permitted only to clap politely. As Miss Malarkey says, it's important to remember to "HAVE FUN."

GERM: Players will recognize themselves and their parents in this story, and phys ed teachers should really appreciate it, especially right before field day. As one parent says, "If we don't play to win, what's the point?" Ask your sports fans: What is the point of playing sports? What does it mean to be a good sport? Their answers will surely vary. Then take them out for a nice, friendly game.

RELATED TITLES: Allard, Harry. *Miss Nelson Has a Field Day.* Houghton Mifflin, 1985. / Finchler, Judy. *Miss Malarkey Doesn't Live in Room 10.* Walker, 1996. / Finchler, Judy. *Miss Malarkey Won't Be in Today.* Walker, 1998. / Finchler, Judy. *Miss Malarkey's Field Trip.* Walker, 2004. / Finchler, Judy. *Testing Miss Malarkey.* Walker, 2000. / Hamm, Mia. *Winners Never Quit!* HarperCollins, 2004.

SUBJECTS: COACHING (ATHLETICS). PICTURE BOOKS FOR ALL AGES. SOCCER. SPORTS. SPORTSMANSHIP. TEACHERS. TEAMWORK.

275   **Fisher, Valerie. *Ellsworth's Extraordinary Electric Ears.* Illus. by the author. Atheneum, 2003. 0-689-85030-1. Unp. Gr. K–3**

"Alistair had an alarming appetite for acrobats," reads the first of 26 odd alliterative sentences, each illustrated with a surreal, oversized photographed collage "scene" of handmade, meticulously crafted little animals, objects, and backdrops.

GERM: Children can write and illustrate new alliterative sentences using their own or their friend's names. As a collaborative art activity, they could construct three-dimensional shoebox scenes to illustrate their sentences.

RELATED TITLES: Bayer, Jane. *A My Name Is Alice.* Dial, 1984. / Chess, Victoria. *Alfred's Alphabet Walk.* Greenwillow, 1979. / Edwards, Pamela Duncan. *Dinorella: A Prehistoric Fairy Tale.* Hyperion, 1997. / Grover, Max. *The Accidental Zucchini.* Harcourt, 1993. / Kalman, Maira. *What Pete Ate from A–Z.* Putnam, 2001. / Steiner, Joan. *Look-Alikes: A Picture Puzzle Book.* Little, Brown, 1998. / Steiner, Joan. *Look-Alikes, Jr.* Little, Brown, 1999.

SUBJECTS: ALLITERATION. ALPHABET BOOKS. VISUAL PERCEPTION.

276   **Fleischman, Paul. *Weslandia.* Illus. by Kevin Hawkes. Candlewick, 1999. 0-7636-0006-7. Unp. Gr. K–4**

Outcast Wesley spends his summer creating his own staple food crop from the mysterious, large new plant with red flowers he cultivates and names "swist," and founding his own civilization, which he calls Weslandia. He fashions new clothes from swist, adopts a base-eight counting system, devises a sport played on stilts, invents a language and an 80-letter alphabet, revels in his outdoor lifestyle, and finally finds friends.

GERM: "He's a genius," my third graders proclaimed admiringly as they pored over the inventive and detailed acrylic paintings. Read it to kick off a civilizations, inventions, or plants unit; to combat social ostracism; or to get your students trying their hands at devising a new food, game, alphabet, or language. Discussion point: Why is Wesley an outcast?

RELATED TITLES: Egan, Tim. *Burnt Toast on Davenport Street.* Houghton Mifflin, 1997. / Fierstein, Harvey. *The Sissy Duckling.* Simon & Schuster, 2002. / McLerran, Alice. *Roxaboxen.* Lothrop, 1991. / Swope, Sam. *The Araboolies of Liberty Street.* Crown, 1989. / Yashima, Taro. *Crow Boy.* Viking, 1955. / Yorinks, Arthur. *Hey, Al.* Farrar, 1986.

SUBJECTS: CIVILIZATION. FANTASY. FRIENDSHIP. GARDENING. INDIVIDUALITY. NONCONFORMISTS. OUTCASTS. PICTURE BOOKS FOR ALL AGES. PLANTS.

277   Fleming, Candace. *A Big Cheese for the White House.* **Illus. by S. D. Schindler. DK, 1999. 0-7894-2573-4. 32pp. Gr. 2–6**

In July of 1801, by pooling the milk from 932 local cows, the good people of Cheshire, Massachusetts, created the world's largest wheel of cheese—a miraculous, 1,235-pound, 4-foot cheddar. The unwieldy gift was transported to Washington, D.C., via ship and sleigh, arriving at the White House in time for President Jefferson's big New Year's Day party, where the guests pronounced it superb. While the story, accompanied by delightful, crosshatched, pen-and-watercolor illustrations, is fictionalized, the basic facts are true, as detailed in the author's Afterword.

GERM: Break out a nice wedge of cheddar to go along with your reading. Students can do a bit of digging in the library to provide more information about cheese production, Thomas Jefferson, and the White House. Also read Fleming's fictionalized tale about Ben Franklin's advice to a brooding Thomas Jefferson in *The Hatmaker's Sign.*

RELATED TITLES: Fleming, Candace. *The Hatmaker's Sign: A Story by Benjamin Franklin.* Orchard, 1998. / Harness, Cheryl. *Ghosts of the White House.* Simon & Schuster, 1998. / Harness, Cheryl. *Thomas Jefferson.* National Geographic, 2004. / Hines, Gary. *A Christmas Tree in the White House.* Henry Holt, 1998. / Karr, Kathleen. *It Happened in the White House.* Hyperion, 2000. / Krull, Kathleen. *Lives of the Presidents: Fame, Shame (and What the Neighbors Thought).* Harcourt, 1998. / Milton, Nancy. *The Giraffe That Walked to Paris.* Crown, 1992. / Ryan, Pam Muñoz. *Amelia and Eleanor Go for a Ride.* Scholastic, 1999. / St. George, Judith. *So You Want to Be President?* Philomel, 2000.

SUBJECTS: CHEESE. HISTORICAL FICTION. JEFFERSON, THOMAS. MASSACHUSETTS—HISTORY. PICTURE BOOKS FOR OLDER READERS. PRESIDENTS. WHITE HOUSE.

278   Fleming, Candace. *Boxes for Katje.* **Illus. by Stacey McQueen. Farrar, 2003. 0-374-30922-1. Unp. Gr. 1–3**

In the aftermath of World War II, Katje, a little girl who lives in the tiny Dutch town of Olst, receives a Children's Aid Society box with items she hasn't seen in years: a cake of real soap, wool socks, and even a bar of chocolate. Her subsequent correspondence with her new friend, Rosie Johnson from Indiana, is the catalyst for a flood of boxes from America, the land of plenty, when Rosie's neighbors organize a food and clothing drive to help everyone in Katje's town.

GERM: Based on a true story—the author's mother sent that first box to Katje and her family in 1945—this heartwarming tale demonstrates the concept of performing acts of kindness. When your school is holding a food drive, the story will help your students realize how their caring and involvement can help others in need and make a difference in the world. This picture book will appeal to children of all ages and can be used with older students as part of a discussion on war and its terrible effects on people.

RELATED TITLES: Garland, Sherry. *The Lotus Seed.* Harcourt, 1993. / Heide, Florence Parry, and Judith Heide Gilliland. *Sami and the Time of the Troubles.* Clarion, 1992. / Lee, Milly. *Nim and the War Effort.* Farrar, 1997. / Wetzel, JoAnne Stewart. *The Christmas Box.* Knopf, 1992. / Ziefert, Harriet. *A New Coat for Anna.* Knopf, 1986.

SUBJECTS: GENEROSITY. HISTORICAL FICTION. NETHERLANDS. PICTURE BOOKS FOR ALL AGES. WORLD WAR, 1939–1945—FICTION.

279   Fleming, Candace. *The Hatmaker's Sign: A Story by Benjamin Franklin.* **Illus. by Robert Andrew Parker. Orchard, 1998. 0-531-33075-3. Unp. Gr. 3–6**

When the Continental Congress met to hear Thomas Jefferson's draft of the Declaration of Independence, the members demanded changes in the wording, which infuriated Jefferson. They made more than 80 changes, from words to full paragraphs, and Jefferson did not appreciate anyone tampering with his text. To console him, Benjamin Franklin told him, "Tom . . . this puts me in mind of a story," and launched into a parable about a Boston hatmaker whose original shop sign was "improved upon" and edited by everyone until there was nothing left but a picture of a hat.

GERM: The large ink-and-watercolor illustrations will take listeners back to colonial times, and the lively story-within-a-story device will prove a useful lesson not just on history but on writing and editing as well. Fleming's own *Ben Franklin's Almanac* is an invaluable compendium of true stories from Ben's astonishing life. Zoom in on another president with prodigious writing talents in *Young Teddy Roosevelt* by Cheryl Harness. And discover what amazing hors d'oeuvre was served at Jefferson's White House party in Fleming's *A Big Cheese for the White House.*

RELATED TITLES: D'Aulaire, Ingri, and Edgar Parin D'Aulaire. *Benjamin Franklin.* Doubleday, 1987. / Fleming, Candace. *Ben Franklin's Almanac: Being a True Account of the Good Gentleman's Life.* Orchard, 1998. /

Fleming, Candace. *A Big Cheese for the White House.* DK Ink, 1999. / Fritz, Jean. *Shh! We're Writing the Constitution.* Putnam, 1987. / Fritz, Jean. *What's the Big Idea, Ben Franklin?* Coward, 1976. / Giblin, James Cross. *The Amazing Life of Benjamin Franklin.* Scholastic, 2000. / Harness, Cheryl. *Thomas Jefferson.* National Geographic, 2004. / Jefferson, Thomas. *The Declaration of Independence: The Words That Made America.* Illus. by Sam Fink. Scholastic, 2002. / Lawson, Robert. *Ben and Me.* Little, Brown, 1939. / McDonough, Yona Zeldis. *The Life of Benjamin Franklin: An American Original.* Henry Holt, 2006. / Maestro, Betsy, and Giulio Maestro. *A More Perfect Union: The Story of Our Constitution.* Lothrop, 1987. / Schanzer, Rosalyn. *How Ben Franklin Stole the Lightning.* HarperCollins, 2003.

SUBJECTS: FRANKLIN, BENJAMIN. HATS. HISTORICAL FICTION. JEFFERSON, THOMAS. PICTURE BOOKS FOR OLDER READERS. U.S.—DECLARATION OF INDEPENDENCE. WRITING.

280 **Fleming, Candace. *Muncha! Muncha! Muncha!* Illus. by G. Brian Karas. Simon & Schuster, 2002. 0-689-83152-8. Unp. Gr. PreK–2**
Frustrated gardener Mr. McGreely keeps building bigger and better fences to keep three, sweater-clad little bunnies from getting into his newly planted garden. Each time, they find a way in—"Tippy-tippy-tippy-pat!"; and "Spring-hurdle, Dash! Dash! Dash!"; and "Muncha muncha muncha"—and each time they contentedly chew on his crisp, growing veggies.
GERM: In Beatrix Potter's classics, *Peter Rabbit* and *Benjamin Bunny*, Mr. MacGregor was the bad guy. Compare his situation with that of Mr. McGreely. With which characters does one empathize in these books and why? Bring in some luscious vegetables in a nice big basket and have a bunny nibble party. If you are lucky enough to have a bit of land available, this story will be a great science kickoff to planting a class garden or at least a seed-planting activity.
RELATED TITLES: Bunting, Eve. *Flower Garden.* Harcourt, 1994. / Cherry, Lynne. *How Groundhog's Garden Grew.* Scholastic, 2003. / Christelow, Eileen. *The Great Pig Search.* Clarion, 2001. / Coy, John. *Two Old Potatoes and Me.* Knopf, 2003. / Cronin, Doreen. *Click, Clack, Moo: Cows That Type.* Simon & Schuster, 2000. / Ehlert, Lois. *Eating the Alphabet: Fruits and Vegetables from A to Z.* Harcourt, 1989. / Ehlert, Lois. *Growing Vegetable Soup.* Harcourt, 1987. / Gibbons, Gail. *From Seed to Plant.* Holiday House, 1991. / Kimmel, Eric A. *Anansi and the Magic Stick.* Holiday House, 2001. / MacDonald, Margaret Read. *Pickin' Peas.* HarperCollins, 1998. / Palatini, Margie. *Piggie Pie.* Clarion, 1995. / Potter, Beatrix. *The Tale of Benjamin Bunny.* Warne, 1904. / Potter, Beatrix. *The Tale of Peter Rabbit.* Warne, 1902. / Rohmann, Eric. *My Friend Rabbit.* Roaring Brook, 2002. / Stevens, Janet. *Tops and Bottoms.* Harcourt, 1995. / Waddell, Martin. *Farmer Duck.* Candlewick, 1992.
SUBJECTS: FOOD. GARDENING. GENEROSITY. HUMOROUS FICTION. PLANTS. RABBITS. STORIES TO TELL. VEGETABLES.

281 **Fleming, Candace. *Smile, Lily!* Illus. by Yumi Heo. Atheneum, 2004. 0-689-83548-5. Unp. Gr. PreK–1**
"Lily keeps on crying. Waa! Waa! Waa! . . . Oh, who knows what to do?" Mommy sings to her baby, Daddy swings her in the air, and Grandma, Grandpa, and Uncle all try to stop her crying. Only Brother knows just what to do.
GERM: Make predictions on how Brother will stop her crying. Then make text-to-life connections: What makes babies stop crying in your house? What makes you stop crying? Other siblings comfort the babies in *Sing, Sophie!* by Dayle Ann Dodds, *Hush, Little Baby* by Marla Frazee, and *Oonga Boonga* by Frieda Wishinsky.
RELATED TITLES: Appelt, Kathi. *Bubba and Beau.* Harcourt, 2002. (And others in the Bubba and Beau series.) / Berends, Polly Berrien. *I Heard Said the Bird.* Dial, 1995. / Dodds, Dayle Ann. *Sing, Sophie!* Candlewick, 1997. / Fleming, Candace. *This Is the Baby.* Farrar, 2004. / Frazee, Marla. *Hush, Little Baby.* Harcourt, 1999. / Ho, Minfong. *Hush! A Thai Lullaby.* Orchard, 1996. / James, Simon. *Baby Brains.* Candlewick, 2004. / L'Engle, Madeleine. *The Other Dog.* SeaStar, 2001. / MacLachlan, Patricia, and Emily MacLachlan. *Bittle.* HarperCollins, 2004. / McMullan, Kate. *Rock-a-Baby Band.* Little, Brown, 2003. / Meyers, Susan. *Everywhere Babies.* Harcourt, 2001. / Rathmann, Peggy. *The Day the Babies Crawled Away.* Putnam, 2003. / Regan, Dian Curtis. *Chance.* Philomel, 2003. / Root, Phyllis. *What Baby Wants.* Candlewick, 1998. / Schwartz, Amy. *A Teeny Tiny Baby.* Orchard, 1994. / Willems, Mo. *Knuffle Bunny: A Cautionary Tale.* Hyperion, 2004. / Wishinsky, Frieda. *Oonga Boonga.* Little, Brown, 1999.
SUBJECTS: BABIES. CRYING. FAMILY LIFE.

282 **Fleming, Candace. *Sunny Boy! The Life and Times of a Tortoise.* Illus. by Anne Wilsdorf. Farrar, 2005. 0-374-37297-7. Unp. Gr. 1–4**
Always longing for a quiet life, Sunny Boy, a tortoise, recounts his life saga, from almost becoming soup in New York City to being taken in by horticulturist Pelonius Pimplewhite. Since "men do not live as long as tortoises," Sunny Boy stays in the family as a companion to

nephew Cornelius, the stamp collector; then to Cornelius's nephew, Augustus, the Latin scholar; before being taken in by Augustus's nephew, Biff, a self-proclaimed "daredevil extraordinaire." Biff tries hard but fails at every one of his stunts. For the stunt of the century, Biff plans to go over Niagara Falls in a barrel, and in an odd twist of fate, Sunny Boy goes too.

GERM: Sunny Boy's droll personal narrative and endearingly expressive watercolors are fetchingly far-fetched, but you'll be stunned to find, in the notes on the final page, that indeed, a century-old tortoise named Sunny Boy did go over Niagara Falls in a barrel in 1930, survived, and then lived at the Niagara Falls Museum for another 40 years. Older students can research the daredevils listed on the endpapers who made the plunge and find out more about both tortoises and the Falls themselves. Taking an actual event from history, children can write stories behind the story. *Mirette on the High Wire* by Emily Arnold McCully involves another Niagara Falls daredevil and is loosely based on the exploits of high-wire artist Blondin. *Apples to Oregon* by Deborah Hopkinson is a tall tale based on the real-life trek of one family across the Oregon Trail. And don't forget *I, Crocodile* by Fred Marcellino, a personal narrative from the days of Napoleon.

RELATED TITLES: Fleming, Candace. *A Big Cheese for the White House.* DK Ink, 1999. / Fleming, Candace. *When Agnes Caws.* Atheneum, 1999. / Hopkinson, Deborah. *Apples to Oregon.* Atheneum, 2004. / Jacobs, Francine. *Lonesome George, the Giant Tortoise.* Walker, 2003. / McCully, Emily Arnold. *Mirette on the High Wire.* Putnam, 1992. / Marcellino, Fred. *I, Crocodile.* HarperCollins, 1999. / Mollel, Tololwa M. *The Flying Tortoise: An Igbo Tale.* Clarion, 1994. / Wells, Robert E. *What's Older Than a Giant Tortoise?* Albert Whitman, 2004.

SUBJECTS: DAREDEVILS. HISTORICAL FICTION. HUMOROUS FICTION. NIAGARA FALLS (N.Y.). PERSONAL NARRATIVES. PICTURE BOOKS FOR ALL AGES. TURTLES. WATERFALLS.

283 **Fleming, Candace. *When Agnes Caws.* Illus. by Giselle Potter. Atheneum, 1999. 0-689-81471-2. Unp. Gr. K–3**

On a bird-watching trip to Borneo with her ornithologist mother, young Agnes Peregrine discovers her greatest skill: a talent for birdcalling. Traveling to the Himalayas in search of the rare and elusive pink-headed duck, Agnes must thwart nefarious Colonel Pittsnap, who plans to steal the duck and stuff it for his collection. The delightfully melodramatic Victorian style of prose and illustration includes a satisfying ending where Agnes uses her wits and her birdcalls to thwart the dastardly fellow.

GERM: Listeners will love learning birdcalls and researching the calls of the birds in their neighborhoods. Note the labeled pictures of the various birds on the endpapers.

RELATED TITLES: Bash, Barbara. *Urban Roosts: Where Birds Nest in the City.* Little, Brown, 1990. / Cox, Judy. *Rabbit Pirates.* Harcourt, 1999. / Davies, Jacqueline. *The Boy Who Drew Birds: A Story of John James Audubon.* Houghton Mifflin, 2003. / Florian, Douglas. *On the Wing: Bird Poems and Paintings.* Harcourt, 1996. / McCloskey, Robert. *Make Way for Ducklings.* Viking, 1941. / Rankin, Joan. *Wow! It's Great Being a Duck.* McElderry, 1998. / Swinburne, Stephen R. *Unbeatable Beaks.* Henry Holt, 1999. / Yolen, Jane. *Bird Watch: A Book of Poetry.* Philomel, 1990. / Yolen, Jane. *Fine Feathered Friends: Poems for Young People.* Wordsong/Boyds Mills, 2004. / Yolen, Jane. *Wild Wings: Poems for Young People.* Wordsong/Boyds Mills, 2002.

SUBJECTS: ADVENTURE AND ADVENTURERS. BIRDS. BIRDSONGS. ORNITHOLOGISTS. PICTURE BOOKS FOR ALL AGES.

284 **Fleming, Denise. *Alphabet Under Construction.* Illus. by the author. Henry Holt, 2002. 0-8050-6848-1. Unp. Gr. PreK–1**

A hardworking but joyful gray mouse takes on the whole alphabet in this alliterative alphabet book filled with creative action verbs and cheery illustrations made by pouring colored cotton pulp through hand-cut stencils. Mouse creates oversized letters through his art: "Mouse airbrushes the A; buttons the B; carves the C; dyes the D . . ."

GERM: Mouse's arty alphabet is filled with action verbs, which are perfect for your kids to act out in narrative pantomime and then recall in alphabetical sequence. Children can each pick a letter and then write and illustrate a new alliterative activity for Mouse. Jenn Lugo's first-grade class at Irving School in Highland Park, New Jersey, created an endearing 26-page Mouse book called *Loving the Alphabet*: "Mouse is admiring the A; bringing a gift to the B; caring for the C," and so on. Check out Fleming's Web site, <www.denisefleming.com>, for activities you can do and a look at how she creates her cotton pulp illustrations.

RELATED TITLES: Bruel, Nick. *Bad Kitty.* Roaring Brook, 2005. / Ehlert, Lois. *Eating the Alphabet: Fruits and Vegetables from A to Z.* Harcourt, 1989. / Ernst, Lisa Campbell. *The Letters Are Lost.* Viking, 1996. / Fleming, Denise. *In the Small, Small Pond.* Henry Holt, 1993. / Fleming, Denise. *Lunch.* Henry Holt, 1992. / Kalman, Maira. *What Pete Ate from A–Z.* Putnam, 2001. / Lester, Mike. *A Is for Salad.* Putnam, 2000. / Lobel, Arnold. *On*

Market Street. Greenwillow, 1981. / MacDonald, Ross. *Achoo! Bang! Crash! The Noisy Alphabet*. Roaring Brook, 2003. / MacDonald, Suse. *Alphabatics*. Simon & Schuster, 1986. / Rotner, Shelley. *Action Alphabet*. Atheneum, 1996. / Schneider, R. M. *Add It, Dip It, Fix It: A Book of Verbs*. Houghton Mifflin, 1995. / Shannon, George. *Tomorrow's Alphabet*. Greenwillow, 1996. / Slate, Joseph. *Miss Bindergarten Gets Ready for Kindergarten*. Dutton, 1996. / Sobel, June. *B Is for Bulldozer: A Construction ABC*. Harcourt, 2003. / Wood, Audrey. *Alphabet Mystery*. Blue Sky/Scholastic, 2003.

SUBJECTS: ALPHABET BOOKS. CREATIVE DRAMA. ENGLISH LANGUAGE—GRAMMAR. ENGLISH LANGUAGE—VERBS. MICE.

285   **Fleming, Denise. *Mama Cat Has Three Kittens*. Illus. by the author. Henry Holt, 1998. 0-8050-5745-5. Unp. Gr. PreK–1**

Two kittens, Fluffy and Skinny, copycat Mama in everything she does—wash paws, walk the stone wall, sharpen claws, and chase leaves—while the third kitten, Boris, naps. Not until the others settle down to snooze does Boris get up to pounce on Mama Cat.

GERM: The sweet, handmade paper fiber illustrations and gentle story of nonconformity go just right with Jane Simmons's *Come Along, Daisy* about an inquisitive baby duck.

RELATED TITLES: Bauer, Marion Dane. *If You Were Born a Kitten*. Simon & Schuster, 1997. / Buzzeo, Toni. *Dawdle Duckling*. Dial, 2003. / Cauley, Lorinda Bryan. *The Three Little Kittens*. Putnam, 1982. / Fleming, Denise. *Barnyard Banter*. Henry Holt, 1994. / Fleming, Denise. *In the Small, Small Pond*. Henry Holt, 1993. / Fleming, Denise. *Time to Sleep*. Henry Holt, 1997. / Gag, Wanda. *Millions of Cats*. Coward, 1928. / Henkes, Kevin. *Kitten's First Full Moon*. Greenwillow, 2004. / Oates, Joyce Carol. *Where Is Little Reynard?* Harper-Collins, 2003. / Simmons, Jane. *Come Along, Daisy*. Little, Brown, 1998.

SUBJECTS: ANIMALS—INFANCY. CATS. CHANTABLE REFRAIN.

286   **Fleming, Denise. *Time to Sleep*. Illus. by the author. Henry Holt, 1997. 0-8050-3762-4. Unp. Gr. PreK–1**

Bear sets off to tell Snail that winter is nigh; as the other animals pass the word along, they prepare for their own hibernations.

GERM: Young children will cotton to Denise Fleming's circular animal story, with its large, expressive illustrations fashioned from handmade paper. It is also a fine story for acting out.

RELATED TITLES: Brett, Jan. *The Mitten*. Putnam, 1989. / Fuchs, Diane Marcial. *A Bear for All Seasons*. Henry Holt, 1995. / George, Lindsay Barrett. *In the Snow: Who's Been Here*. Greenwillow, 1995. / Hunter, Anne. *Possum's Harvest Moon*. Houghton Mifflin, 1996. / Koide, Tan. *May We Sleep Here Tonight?* Atheneum, 1983. / Lemieux, Michele. *What's That Noise?* Morrow, 1985. / Murphy, Jill. *Peace at Last*. Dial, 1980. / Murray, Marjorie Dennis. *Don't Wake Up the Bear!* Cavendish, 2003. / Simmons, Jane. *Little Fern's First Winter*. Little, Brown, 2001. / Waber, Bernard. *Bearsie Bear and the Surprise Sleepover Party*. Houghton Mifflin, 1997. / Waddell, Martin. *Let's Go Home, Little Bear*. Candlewick, 1993. / Wilson, Karma. *Bear Snores On*. McElderry, 2002.

SUBJECTS: ANIMALS. CIRCULAR STORIES. CREATIVE DRAMA. HIBERNATION. SEASONS. SLEEP. WINTER.

287   **Fleming, Denise. *Where Once There Was a Wood*. Illus. by the author. Henry Holt, 1996. 0-8050-3761-6. Unp. Gr. PreK–2**

In a simple but provocative rhyming picture book, we see the red fox, the woodchuck, the horned owl, the heron, the brown snake, and the raccoons that once lived in the wood, meadow, and creek and have just been displaced by a new housing development.

GERM: In the punch line on the final page, this book's pointed pro-environment message (beefed up by Fleming's earthy, rag- and cotton-pulp illustrations) conveys the rush of modern "development" that disregards nature and animals. Four info-filled pages at the back describe ways to appreciate, protect, and support the natural world, including a list of flowers that attract hummingbirds and butterflies and an explanation of the four basic needs of wild creatures: space, shelter, water, and food.

RELATED TITLES: Atkins, Jeannine. *Aani and the Tree Huggers*. Lee & Low, 1995. / Brenner, Barbara. *The Earth Is Painted Green: A Garden of Poems About Our Planet*. Holiday House, 1993. / Cherry, Lynne. *The Great Kapok Tree: A Tale of the Amazon Rain Forest*. Harcourt, 1990. / Cherry, Lynne. *A River Ran Wild: An Environmental History*. Harcourt, 1992. / Cooney, Barbara. *Miss Rumphius*. Viking, 1982. / Fleming, Denise. *Alphabet Under Construction*. Henry Holt, 2002. / Fleming, Denise. *Barnyard Banter*. Henry Holt, 1994. / Fleming, Denise. *In the Small, Small Pond*. Henry Holt, 1993. / Fleming, Denise. *Lunch*. Henry Holt, 1992. / Fleming, Denise. *Time to Sleep*. Henry Holt, 1997. / Ryder, Joanne. *Each Living Thing*. Harcourt, 2000.

SUBJECTS: ANIMALS. ECOLOGY. ENVIRONMENT. FORESTS AND FORESTRY. WILDLIFE CONSERVATION.

288 Florczak, Robert. *Yikes!!!* **Illus. by the author. Scholastic, 2003. 0-590-05043-5. Unp. Gr. K–3**

Trek through wild and dangerous places (jungle, desert, forest, and river) with a fearless explorer—an intrepid, khaki-clad child adventurer who comes face to face with a glorious assortment of fearsome creatures. The only words on each page are appropriate interjections and reactions to each huge animal—"Wow!" "Oh, no!"—and your listeners can join in on each exclamation and identify each animal, depicted in super-realistic paintings. The kick comes on the last page, where we see the child napping under a tree on the front lawn, clutching a large book entitled "Wild and Dangerous Animals of the World." The welcome message? We can travel anywhere and everywhere, vicariously, with a good book.

GERM: As you read aloud the interjection on each page, encourage your listeners to join in with expression. The final page contains a chart with a thumbnail picture of each animal and a few pithy facts about it, which is a built-in prompt for your follow-up animal reports. Ask your bookish travelers to write and draw the exotic locales and locals they've encountered in books and pair them with fitting interjections.

RELATED TITLES: Allen, Susan, and Jane Lindaman. *Read Anything Good Lately?* Millbrook, 2003. / Clement, Rod. *Just Another Ordinary Day.* HarperCollins, 1997. / Collins, Suzanne. *When Charlie McButton Lost Power.* Putnam, 2005. / Daugherty, James. *Andy and the Lion.* Viking, 1938. / Feiffer, Jules. *Meanwhile . . .* HarperCollins, 1997. / Harter, Debbie. *Walking Through the Jungle.* Orchard, 1997. / Heller, Ruth. *Fantastic! Wow! and Unreal! A Book About Interjections and Conjunctions.* Grosset, 1998. / MacDonald, Ross. *Achoo! Bang! Crash: The Noisy Alphabet.* Roaring Brook, 2003. / Moser, Madeline. *Ever Heard of an Aardwolf?* Harcourt, 1996. / Rodda, Emily. *Power and Glory.* Greenwillow, 1996. / Sierra, Judy. *Wild About Books.* Knopf, 2004. / Tyson, Leigh Ann. *An Interview with Harry the Tarantula.* National Geographic, 2003. / Van Allsburg, Chris. *Jumanji.* Houghton, 1981. / Van Allsburg, Chris. *Zathura: A Space Adventure.* Houghton, 2002. / Williams, Suzanne. *Library Lil.* Dial, 1997.

SUBJECTS: ADVENTURE AND ADVENTURERS. ANIMALS. BOOKS AND READING. ENGLISH LANGUAGE—GRAMMAR. ENGLISH LANGUAGE—INTERJECTIONS. IMAGINATION.

289 Fox, Mem. *Boo to a Goose.* **Illus. by David Miller. Dial, 1998. 0-8037-2274-5. Unp. Gr. PreK–1**

"I'd dance with a pig in a shiny green wig / But I wouldn't say 'BOO!' to a goose," begins this bouncy, rhyming book filled with 13 things a brown-haired child would do, illustrated with pop-off-the-page paper sculptures.

GERM: All the fooling around with rhyming words will have children chanting the title refrain as they make up, illustrate, and read aloud their own verses. Bill Morrison's *Squeeze a Sneeze* and Raffi's *Down by the Bay* also fool around with rhyming couplets.

RELATED TITLES: Chapman, Cheryl. *Pass the Fritters, Critters.* Simon & Schuster, 1993. / Gelman, Rita Golden. *I Went to the Zoo.* Scholastic, 1993. / Marshall, James. *Old Mother Hubbard and Her Wonderful Dog.* Farrar, 1991. / Morrison, Bill. *Squeeze a Sneeze.* Houghton Mifflin, 1977. / Nerlove, Miriam. *I Made a Mistake.* Atheneum, 1985. / Raffi. *Down by the Bay.* Crown, 1987. / Slate, Joseph. *Miss Bindergarten Gets Ready for Kindergarten.* Dutton, 1996. / Wood, Audrey. *Silly Sally.* Harcourt, 1992. / Ziefert, Harriet. *I Swapped My Dog.* Houghton Mifflin, 1998.

SUBJECTS: CHANTABLE REFRAIN. GEESE. STORIES IN RHYME.

290 Fox, Mem. *Whoever You Are.* **Illus. by Leslie Staub. Harcourt, 1997. 0-15-200787-3. Unp. Gr. PreK–2**

In this book, stylized, folk art-style oil paintings, set within heavy, gold, carved frames, are combined with a lyrical, practical text addressed directly to the reader as "little one." They bring forth the notion that "there are little ones just like you all over the world." The clear message, welcome in these fractured times, is that, in spite of differences in skin tone or houses or schooling or language, our hearts are the same the world over.

GERM: Make a list: what are the common threads that bind all people together?

RELATED TITLES: Chanko, Pamela. *Teaching with Favorite Mem Fox Books.* Scholastic Teaching Resources, 2005. / Dillon, Leo, and Diane Dillon. *To Everything There Is a Season.* Scholastic, 1998. / Hamanaka, Sheila. *All the Colors of the Earth.* Morrow, 1994. / Maddern, Eric. *The Fire Children: A West African Creation Tale.* Dial, 1993. / Ryder, Joanne. *Each Living Thing.* Harcourt, 2000. / Ryder, Joanne. *Earthdance.* Henry Holt, 1996.

SUBJECTS: ETHNICITY. INDIVIDUALITY. MULTICULTURAL BOOKS.

291   Frame, Jeron Ashford. *Yesterday I Had the Blues.* **Illus. by R. Gregory Christie. Tricycle, 2003. 1-58246-084-1. Unp. Gr. 1–4**

As a young African American boy describes it, yesterday he had "those deep down in my shoes blues, the go away, Mr. Sun, quit smilin' at me blues," but today he has the greens. Daddy's got the grays, Mama's got the reds, his sisters have the pinks and the indigos, and his whole family makes him feel golden. With moody acrylic and gouache paintings, this is a new look at colors and how they make us feel, told by a clear-sighted boy as he observes his whole family.

GERM: Written like a free-form blues poem, this is a book that gets you in the mood to feel good. Read the book aloud, accompanied by music. Track No. 9, "Blues for Marili," on T-Bone Walker's CD *T-Bone Blues* is a perfect match. Ask your kids: What color do you have today? They can write about and draw themselves feeling those colors.

RELATED TITLES: Adoff, Arnold. *Love Letters.* Scholastic, 1997. / Cox, Judy. *My Family Plays Music.* Holiday House, 2003. / Curtis, Jamie Lee. *Today I Feel Silly and Other Moods That Make My Day.* HarperCollins, 1998. / Freymann, Saxton, and Joost Elffers. *How Are You Peeling? Foods with Moods.* Scholastic, 1999. / Gray, Libba Moore. *Little Lil and the Swing-Singing Sax.* Simon & Schuster, 1996. / Greenfield, Eloise. *Honey, I Love.* HarperCollins, 2003. / Harper, Jessica. *Lizzy's Ups and Downs: Not an Ordinary School Day.* HarperCollins, 2004. / Hesse, Karen. *Come On, Rain!* Scholastic, 1999. / Hopkins, Lee Bennett, comp. *Oh, No! Where Are My Pants? And Other Disasters: Poems.* HarperCollins, 2005. / Jenkins, Jessica. *Thinking About Colors.* Dutton, 1992. / Myers, Walter Dean. *The Blues of Flats Brown.* Holiday House, 2000. / Spinelli, Eileen. *If You Want to Find Golden.* Albert Whitman, 1993.

SUBJECTS: AFRICAN AMERICANS. BLUES (MUSIC). COLOR. EMOTIONS. FAMILY LIFE. MULTICULTURAL BOOKS.

292   France, Anthony. *From Me to You.* **Illus. by Tiphanie Beeke. Candlewick, 2003. 0-7636-2255-9. Unp. Gr. PreK–2**

Suffering with a case of the Bathrobe Blues, Rat is moping around, feeling depressed, when an unsigned letter from an admirer arrives in his mailbox and brightens his day and his outlook on friendship.

GERM: Listeners can speculate about who sent the letter to Rat, but, more important, can see if they can make the connection to their own lives: how can performing simple and selfless acts of kindness and friendship change everything? Perhaps they'll want to write anonymous secret admirer notes and make someone's day. See how another life is changed by an anonymous note in Spinelli's *Somebody Loves You, Mr. Hatch.* Ask your kids: Have you ever had the Bathrobe Blues? When and why have you had them? What advice could you provide to someone trying to get over them?

RELATED TITLES: Child, Lauren. *That Pesky Rat.* Candlewick, 2002. / Raschka, Chris. *Yo! Yes?* Orchard, 1993. / Soto, Gary. *Chato and the Party Animals.* Putnam, 2000. / Spinelli, Eileen. *Somebody Loves You, Mr. Hatch.* Simon & Schuster, 1991. / Taylor, Linda. *The Lettuce Leaf Birthday Letter.* Dial, 1995. / Willems, Mo. *Leonardo the Terrible Monster.* Hyperion, 2005.

SUBJECTS: ANIMALS. FRIENDSHIP. LETTER WRITING. LONELINESS. PARTIES. RATS.

293   Frank, John. *The Toughest Cowboy, or How the Wild West Was Tamed.* **Illus. by Zachary Pullen. Simon & Schuster, 2004. 0-689-83461-6. Unp. Gr. 1–5**

Grizz Brickbottom, who drinks a quart of Tabasco sauce every day and flosses his teeth with barbed wire, might be the toughest cowboy out on the range, but he craves companionship and kisses. He wants a dog. His three cowboy pals are less than bowled over when he brings in the new cattle-herding, bobcat-chasing, companion-to-be, a miniature poodle named . . . Foofy. This Wild West spoof has deadpan, funny full-bleed oil paintings of the range and town, with graphically detailed close-up caricatures of the four big-headed cowboys and a sense of humor reminiscent of the movie *Blazing Saddles* (though without the beans).

GERM: Before introducing your audience to Foofy, ask them to make a sketch of the perfect dog for the cowboys or predict its breed and habits. Go outside and play the flying pie plate game with your own "Grizz-B." Sing cowboy songs from Alan Axelrod's *Songs of the Wild West.*

RELATED TITLES: Axelrod, Alan. *Songs of the Wild West.* Simon & Schuster, 1991. / Dadey, Debbie. *Shooting Star: Annie Oakley, the Legend.* Walker, 1997. / Freedman, Russell. *Children of the Wild West.* Clarion, 1983. / Icenoggle, Jodi. *'Til the Cows Come Home.* Boyds Mills, 2004. / Johnston, Tony. *The Cowboy and the Black-Eyed Pea.* Putnam, 1992. / Ketteman, Helen. *Bubba the Cowboy Prince: A Fractured Texas Tale.* Scholastic, 1997. / Lowell, Susan. *The Bootmaker and the Elves.* Clarion, 1996. / Lowell, Susan. *Cindy Ellen: A Wild Western Cinderella.*

Orchard, 1997. / Pinkney, Andrea D. *Bill Pickett: Rodeo-Ridin' Cowboy*. Harcourt, 1996. / Say, Allen. *El Chino*. Houghton Mifflin, 1990. / Tucker, Kathy. *Do Cowboys Ride Bikes?* Albert Whitman, 1997.

SUBJECTS: COWBOYS. DOGS. HISTORICAL FICTION. HUMOROUS FICTION. PICTURE BOOKS FOR ALL AGES. WEST (U.S.)—HISTORY—FICTION.

294 **Fraser, Mary Ann.** *I. Q. Goes to the Library*. **Illus. by the author. Walker, 2003. 0-8027-8878-5. Unp. Gr. PreK–2**

I. Q., the small brown mouse who lives in Mrs. Furber's classroom, accompanies the students to the library every day during Library Week and learns how to find the book he wants to check out and read.

GERM: Ask your library pros to compare and contrast the procedures and activities in I. Q.'s school library with those in their own. What other books would they recommend to I. Q. and why?

RELATED TITLES: Adler, David A. *Young Cam Jansen and the Library Mystery*. Viking, 2001. / Allen, Susan, and Jane Lindaman. *Read Anything Good Lately?* Millbrook, 2003. / Edwards, Pamela Duncan. *Livingstone Mouse*. HarperCollins, 1996. / Fleming, Denise. *Alphabet Under Construction*. Henry Holt, 2002. / Fraser, Mary Ann. *I. Q. Goes to School*. Walker, 2002. / Fraser, Mary Ann. *I. Q., It's Time*. Walker, 2005. / Huff, Barbara. *Once Inside the Library*. Little, Brown, 1990. / McMillan, Bruce. *Mouse Views: What the Class Pet Saw*. Holiday House, 1993. / Numeroff, Laura Joffe. *Beatrice Doesn't Want To*. Candlewick, 2004. / Numeroff, Laura. *If You Take a Mouse to School*. HarperCollins, 2003. / Parish, Herman. *Amelia Bedelia, Bookworm*. Greenwillow, 2003. / Sierra, Judy. *Wild About Books*. Knopf, 2004. / Williams, Suzanne. *Library Lil*. Dial, 1997.

SUBJECTS: BOOKS AND READING. LIBRARIES. MICE. SCHOOLS.

295 **Frasier, Debra.** *The Incredible Water Show*. **Illus. by the author. Harcourt, 2004. 0-15-216287-9. Unp. Gr. K–2**

Remember Sage in Mrs. Page's class, who flubbed a word in *Miss Alaineus: A Vocabulary Disaster*? Well, she's back with her pals to put on a fact-filled science play about that miraculous, magical, surprising, strongest, most amazing substance on earth: water. On each double-page spread, set up like a stage and illustrated with colorful Crayola markers, the six costumed student actors dramatize the properties of water and portray its nature as a perpetually recycling substance.

GERM: You will be deluged with entreaties to stage this as a Reader's Theater production to go along with that science unit on H_2O. Check out <www.debrafrasier.com> for directions on how to do just that. Who says you can't bring drama into your science curriculum?

RELATED TITLES: Cole, Joanna. *The Magic School Bus at the Waterworks*. Scholastic, 1988. / Cowan, Catherine. *My Life with the Wave*. Lothrop, 1997. / Dorros, Walter. *Follow the Water from Brook to Ocean*. HarperCollins, 1991. / Frasier, Debra. *Miss Alaineus: A Vocabulary Disaster*. Harcourt, 2000. / Graham, Joan Bransfield. *Splish Splash*. Ticknor & Fields, 1994. / Jackson, Shelley. *The Old Woman and the Wave*. DK Ink, 1998. / Hooper, Meredith. *River Story*. Candlewick, 2000. / Kerley, Barbara. *A Cool Drink of Water*. National Geographic, 2002. / Lewis, J. Patrick. *Earth Verses and Water Rhymes*. Atheneum, 1991. / Locker, Thomas. *Water Dance*. Harcourt, 1997. / Peters, Lisa Westberg. *Water's Way*. Little, Brown, 1991. / Ross, Michael Elsohn. *What's the Matter in Mr. Whisker's Room?* Candlewick, 2004. / Wick, Walter. *A Drop of Water*. Scholastic, 1997. / Wiesner, David. *Sector 7*. Clarion, 1999.

SUBJECTS: PLAYS. READER'S THEATER. SCIENCE. WATER.

296 **Frasier, Debra.** *Miss Alaineus: A Vocabulary Disaster*. **Illus. by the author. Harcourt, 2000. 0-15-202163-9. Unp. Gr. 2–5**

Mistakenly thinking "Miss Alaineus" is the correct way to write and define the word "miscellaneous," word-lover Sage is humiliated and devastated during her fifth-grade class's Vocabulary Bee. Here's a snappy, smart, definition-enhancing picture book to help all wordsmiths expand their word stock and develop their verbiage.

GERM: Children can write new alliterative vocabulary sentences just as Sage does on each page. Check Frasier's Web site <www.frasierbooks.com/missa> for many clever ideas on how to use this book with your kids. Children can also discuss and write about words they've misconceived, misspelled, misinterpreted, and misused. Learn about Mondegreens—misconstrued lyrics to songs, poems, or sayings—in "Books Across the Curriculum" on p. 70. Read some of the hilarious Mondegreens collected by Jon Carroll, *San Francisco Chronicle* columnist, at <www.sfgate.com/columnists/carroll/mondegreens>.

RELATED TITLES: Frasier, Debra. *The Incredible Water Show*. Harcourt, 2004. / Hepworth, Cathi. *Antics! An*

Alphabetical Anthology. Putnam, 1992. / Hepworth, Cathi. *Bug Off! A Swarm of Insect Words.* Putnam, 1998. / Levitt, Paul M., Douglas A. Burger, and Elissa S. Guralnick. *The Weighty Word Book.* Court Wayne, 2000. / Lowry, Lois. *Gooney Bird Greene.* Houghton Mifflin, 2002. / Lowry, Lois. *Gooney Bird and the Room Mother.* Houghton Mifflin, 2005. / Scott, Ann Herbert. *Brave as a Mountain Lion.* Clarion, 1996. / Steig, William. *CDB.* Simon & Schuster, 2000. / Viorst, Judith. *The Alphabet from Z to A: With Much Confusion on the Way.* Atheneum, 1994. / Wilbur, Richard. *The Pig in the Spigot.* Harcourt, 2000.

SUBJECTS: EMBARRASSMENT. ENGLISH LANGUAGE—SPELLING. PICTURE BOOKS FOR OLDER READERS. SCHOOLS. TEACHERS. VOCABULARY.

297   **Frazee, Marla. *Hush, Little Baby: A Folk Song with Pictures.* Illus. by the author. Harcourt, 1999. 0-15-201429-2. Unp. Gr. PreK–1**
Even when his papa and mama and big sister bring him presents, the baby keeps crying. Frazee has set the traditional American lullaby in a pioneer cabin settlement. Children will love picking out pioneer artifacts, from the large iron cooking pot in the fireplace to the candlestick and the washtubs, as well as the wool that mama's about to spin. The focus of the song, though, is that squalling baby, with big sister and parents trying desperately to placate it, seeking out a traveling peddler who supplies them with all the artifacts that the baby rejects.
GERM: Frazee's found an original way to turn the song into a story narrated with pictures, and all will love singing it as they read. Compose a new version with its own sequence, starting with the original, "Hush little baby, don't say a word . . ."
RELATED TITLES: Christelow, Eileen. *Five Little Monkeys Jumping on the Bed.* Clarion, 1989. / Dodds, Dayle Ann. *Sing, Sophie!* Candlewick, 1997. / Fleming, Candace. *Smile, Lily!* Atheneum, 2004. / Ho, Minfong. *Hush! A Thai Lullaby.* Orchard, 1996. / Kay, Verla. *Homespun Sarah.* Putnam, 2003. / Lewison, Wendy Cheyette. *Going to Sleep on the Farm.* Dial, 1992. / Paxton, Tom. *Where's the Baby?* Morrow, 1993. / Root, Phyllis. *What Baby Wants.* Candlewick, 1998. / Willems, Mo. *Knuffle Bunny: A Cautionary Tale.* Hyperion, 2004. / Williams, Vera B. *"More More More," Said the Baby.* Greenwillow, 1990. / Wishinsky, Frieda. *Oonga Boonga.* Little, Brown, 1999. / Wood, Audrey, and Don Wood. *Piggies.* Harcourt, 1991. / Zemach, Harve. *Mommy, Buy Me a China Doll.* Follett, 1966.
SUBJECTS: BABIES. BEDTIME STORIES. CIRCULAR STORIES. CRYING. FOLK SONGS. FRONTIER AND PIONEER LIFE. LULLABIES. PEDDLERS. SEQUENCE STORIES. SONGS.

298   **Frazee, Marla. *Roller Coaster.* Illus. by the author. Harcourt, 2003. 0-15-204554-6. Unp. Gr. K–2**
Take a vicarious and exhilarating roller coaster ride with a carful of folks as they zip, zoom, dip, and dive. Watch their varied reactions: some screaming with pleasure; one sweetheart couple in the back, snuggling and snogging; and two big, strong guys looking alarmingly nauseated.
GERM: Poll your group: Who has ridden on a roller coaster or other amusement park-style ride? Have them describe their own reactions to the ride. Use the book to inspire some descriptive and experiential writing and illustrating: My big adventure and how I lived to tell the tale.
RELATED TITLES: Calhoun, Mary. *Blue-Ribbon Henry.* Morrow, 1999. / Carlson, Nancy. *Harriet and the Roller Coaster.* Carolrhoda, 2003. / Crews, Donald. *Carousel.* Greenwillow, 1982. / Schotter, Roni. *Dreamland.* Orchard, 1996. / Sobel, June. *B Is for Bulldozer: A Construction ABC.* Harcourt, 2003. / Stoeke, Janet Morgan. *Minerva Louise at the Fair.* Dutton, 2000.
SUBJECTS: AMUSEMENT PARKS. FEAR. ROLLER COASTERS.

299   **Freedman, Claire. *Hushabye Lily.* Illus. by John Brunello. Orchard, 2003. 0-439-47106-0. Unp. Gr. PreK–1**
Distracted by all the farmyard noises all around her, Lily, a young rabbit, can't fall asleep until three kindly animals come to her aid: a duck, who sings her a lullaby; a cow, who tells her a story; and a hen, who makes her a nice bed of straw.
GERM: Talk it over: What are the things that best help you fall asleep? Sing some lullabies, tell some bedtime stories, and pretend to take a snooze in the straw.
RELATED TITLES: Appelt, Kathi. *Bubba and Beau Go Night-Night.* Harcourt, 2003. / Fleming, Denise. *Time to Sleep.* Henry Holt, 1997. / Hendry, Diana. *The Very Noisy Night.* Dutton, 1999. / Simmons, Jane. *Little Fern's First Winter.* Little, Brown, 2001. / Waddell, Martin. *Can't You Sleep, Little Bear?* Candlewick, 1992. / Walton, Rick. *So Many Bunnies: A Bedtime ABC and Counting Book.* Lothrop, 1998. / Wilson, Karma. *Bear Snores On.* McElderry, 2002.
SUBJECTS: ANIMALS. BEDTIME STORIES.

300   Freeman, Don. *Will's Quill, or How a Goose Saved Shakespeare.* **Illus. by the author. Viking, 2004. 0-670-03686-2. Unp. Gr. 1–4**

Are you wondering how Shakespeare became such a successful playwright? This is how it might have happened . . . In Merrie Olde England, a country goose named Willoughby Waddle set out for Londontown, looking for some way of being useful. Treated kindly by a bearded young gentleman, he followed the man to the Globe Theatre. Of course, being a goose, Willoughby understood nothing about play-acting, and so he mistakenly came to the young man's rescue during a dueling scene on stage. After that, Willoughby became a great help to the man, Will, providing him with the finest quills plucked from his own feathers so Will could finish writing his play.

GERM: First published in 1975, this reissue is a charmer, with Freeman's watercolors providing an informative glimpse of life in Elizabethan London and a rousing introduction to that fellow Will Shakespeare. Ask your group to compare and contrast the setting to city life today. Show illustrations from Aliki's *William Shakespeare and the Globe* for more details.

RELATED TITLES: Aliki. *William Shakespeare and the Globe.* HarperCollins, 1999. / Freeman, Don. *Norman the Doorman.* Viking, 1959. / King-Smith, Dick. *The Swoose.* Hyperion, 1994. / Stanley, Diane. *Bard of Avon: The Story of William Shakespeare.* Morrow, 1992.

SUBJECTS: ENGLAND. GEESE. HISTORICAL FICTION. LONDON (ENGLAND). PLAYS. SHAKESPEARE, WILLIAM.

301   French, Jackie. *Diary of a Wombat.* **Illus. by Bruce Whatley. Clarion, 2003. 0-618-38136-8. Unp. Gr. K–2**

A little brown roly-poly wombat describes a week in her life spent in the yard of a befuddled-looking human family. During her seven-day stay, she digs holes in the ground, sleeps, demands carrots, and decides that "humans are easily trained and make quite good pets." Told in diary format by the wombat, who describes herself as "a little like a bear, but smaller," this endearing picture book has affectionate and ridiculously appealing acrylic illustrations, with lots of white space, and an understated text that is very funny to read aloud.

GERM: Kids can retell the story from the humans' point of view and do some research to find out more about wombats. Animal fanciers can then research, write, and illustrate a week-long diary from the point of view of their favorite wild animal. Use this with Denise Cronin's *Diary of a Worm,* to compare and contrast writing styles and the voice of the narrators.

RELATED TITLES: Child, Lauren. *That Pesky Rat.* Candlewick, 2002. / Cronin, Doreen. *Diary of a Spider.* HarperCollins, 2005. / Cronin, Doreen. *Diary of a Worm.* HarperCollins, 2003. / Fox, Mem. *Koala Lou.* Harcourt, 1989. / Niland, Kilmeny. *A Bellbird in a Flame Tree.* Tambourine, 1991. / Provensen, Alice. *A Day in the Life of Murphy.* Simon & Schuster, 2003. / Tyson, Leigh Ann. *An Interview with Harry the Tarantula.* National Geographic, 2003. / Vaughn, Marcia K. *Wombat Stew.* Silver Burdett, 1986.

SUBJECTS: AUSTRALIA. DIARIES. HUMOROUS FICTION. PERSONAL NARRATIVES. POINT OF VIEW. WOMBATS.

302   Freymann, Saxton. *Food for Thought: The Complete Book of Concepts for Growing Minds.* **Illus. by the author. Scholastic, 2005. 0-439-11018-1. 61pp. Gr. PreK–1**

Endearing, diabolically clever portraits of fruit and vegetables, carved, posed, or assembled to look like animals and objects are photographed against solid-colored backgrounds and on heavy-stock paper. The food creatures, made from bananas, peppers, cherries, mushrooms, and more—there's a list of the more than 75 ingredients on the copyright page—exemplify a series of concepts: shapes, colors, numbers, letters, and opposites.

GERM: First of all, the expressions on the "faces" of the creatures will have everyone rolling, especially when they can identify the produce used to make them and the animals they represent. What are these "animals" thinking and saying to each other? In addition to reviewing basic concepts, you can ask your group to come up with captions or dialogue for each critter or situation, which they, or you, can write on a Post-It note and attach to the bottom of the book's page for others to read.

RELATED TITLES: Abrams, Pam. *Now I Eat My ABC's.* Scholastic, 2004. / Ehlert, Lois. *Color Zoo.* HarperCollins, 1989. / Ehlert, Lois. *Eating the Alphabet.* Harcourt, 1989. / Fleming, Denise. *Count!* Henry Holt, 1992. / Freymann, Saxton, and Joost Elffers. *Baby Food.* Scholastic, 2003. / Freymann, Saxton, and Joost Elffers. *Dog Food.* Scholastic, 2002. / Freymann, Saxton, and Joost Elffers. *How Are You Peeling? Foods with Moods.* Scholastic, 1999. / Freymann, Saxton, and Joost Elffers. *One Lonely Sea Horse.* Scholastic, 2000. / Kalan, Robert. *Moving Day.* Greenwillow, 1996. / Lobel, Arnold. *On Market Street.* Greenwillow, 1981. / MacDonald, Suse. *Look*

Whooo's Counting. Scholastic, 2000. / Schaefer, Lola M. *Pick, Pull, Snap! Where Once a Flower Bloomed.* Harper-Collins, 2003. / Seeger, Laura Vaccaro. *The Hidden Alphabet.* Roaring Brook, 2003. / Seeger, Laura Vaccaro. *Lemons Are Not Red.* Roaring Brook, 2004. / Shannon, George. *White Is for Blueberry.* Greenwillow, 2005.

SUBJECTS: ALPHABET BOOKS. COLOR. COUNTING BOOKS. ENGLISH LANGUAGE—SYNONYMS AND ANTONYMS. FRUIT. OPPOSITES. VEGETABLES.

303 **Freymann, Saxton, and Joost Elffers. *Dog Food.* Illus. by Saxton Freymann. Scholastic, 2002. 0-439-11016-5. Unp. Gr. PreK–2**

The winsome pictures found in this book, assembled from real carved fruits and vegetables and photographed against a blue background, are accompanied by 26 phrases with double meanings, all containing the word "dog" or "puppy." There's hot dog, lucky dog, puppy love, and dog bowl, which shows a red dog (fashioned out of two radishes) with a bowling ball (made from a black olive) on one arm.

GERM: Cover some of the words so children can guess the captions from the picture clues. Talk about the double meanings of some of the words, such as dog paddle and dog bowl. Then have children brainstorm a list of other expressions that employ animals—such as cool cat or quiet as a mouse—and illustrate their meanings. Pair children up and give each duo an expression to pantomime for the group to guess. If you decide to fashion new pets out of food, try soft pears, which everyone can carve with plastic spoons, adding black-eyed peas for eyeballs. Fred Gwynne's *A Chocolate Moose for Dinner*, *The King Who Rained*, and *A Little Pigeon Toad* are wonderful companions when discussing literal and figurative language.

RELATED TITLES: Chapman, Cheryl. *Pass the Fritters, Critters.* Simon & Schuster, 1993. / Downs, Mike. *Pig Giggles and Rabbit Rhymes: A Book of Animal Riddles.* Chronicle, 2002. / Freymann, Saxton, and Joost Elffers. *Baby Food.* Scholastic, 2003. / Freymann, Saxton, and Joost Effers. *Food for Thought: The Complete Book of Concepts for Growing Minds.* Scholastic, 2005. / Freymann, Saxton, and Joost Elffers. *How Are You Peeling? Foods with Moods.* Scholastic, 1999. / Gwynne, Fred. *A Chocolate Moose for Dinner.* Dutton, 1976. / Gwynne, Fred. *The King Who Rained.* Aladdin, 1980. / Gwynne, Fred. *A Little Pigeon Toad.* Aladdin, 1988. / Leedy, Loreen. *There's a Frog in My Throat: 440 Animal Sayings a Little Bird Told Me.* Holiday House, 2003. / McCall, Francis, and Patricia Keeler. *A Huge Hog Is a Big Pig: A Rhyming Word Game.* Greenwillow, 2002. / Root, Phyllis. *Meow Monday.* Candlewick, 2000. / Shields, Carol Diggory. *Food Fight!* Handprint, 2002.

SUBJECTS: DOGS. ENGLISH LANGUAGE—HOMONYMS. ENGLISH LANGUAGE—IDIOMS. ENGLISH LANGUAGE—TERMS AND PHRASES. FOOD. FRUIT. VEGETABLES. WORD GAMES.

304 **Freymann, Saxton, and Joost Elffers. *How Are You Peeling? Foods with Moods.* Illus. by the authors. Scholastic, 1999. 0-439-10431-9. 42pp. Gr. K–3**

Color photographs of real fruits and veggies with remarkably expressive faces carved into them show moods from amused to angry and accompany a rhyming text about human emotions.

GERM: Ask your crew to bring in a fruit or vegetable with attitude and describe how it is feeling. If it's not too insensitive a suggestion, once you've bonded with your anthropomorphic foods, you could make vegetable soup or fruit salad out of them.

RELATED TITLES: Curtis, Jamie Lee. *Today I Feel Silly and Other Moods That Make My Day.* HarperCollins, 1998. / Ehlert, Lois. *Eating the Alphabet: Fruits and Vegetables from A to Z.* Harcourt, 1989. / Freymann, Saxton, and Joost Elffers. *Dog Food.* Scholastic, 2002. / Freymann, Saxton, and Joost Effers. *Food for Thought: The Complete Book of Concepts for Growing Minds.* Scholastic, 2005. / Freymann, Saxton, and Joost Elffers. *One Lonely Sea Horse.* Scholastic, 2000. / Harper, Jessica. *Lizzy's Ups and Downs: Not an Ordinary School Day.* HarperCollins, 2004. / Hausman, Bonnie. *A to Z: Do You Ever Feel Like Me?* Dutton, 1999. / Modesitt, Jeanne. *Sometimes I Feel Like a Mouse: A Book About Feelings.* Scholastic, 1992. / Robert, Francois, Jean Robert, and Jane Gittings. *Find a Face.* Chronicle, 2004. / Shields, Carol Diggory. *Food Fight!* Handprint, 2002.

SUBJECTS: EMOTIONS. FRUIT. STORIES IN RHYME. VEGETABLES.

305 **Freymann, Saxton, and Joost Elffers. *One Lonely Sea Horse.* Illus. by the authors. Scholastic, 2000. 0-439-11014-9. Unp. Gr. PreK–1**

Sad and lonely seahorse Bea is reassured by two friendly crabs, three puffer fish, four lobsters, and an escalating cast of sea creatures, that she can always count on them. The appealing, soulful, underwater collage illustrations, all crafted from real fruits and vegetables, are the unifying factor in this sweet rhyming counting book.

GERM: Using the labeled vegetable photos on the endpapers, viewers can confirm that the dolphins were made out of bananas, the turtles out of pineapples, and the lobsters out of ginger.

As with the other Freymann and Elffers titles, you can make new animal sculptures using assorted produce, with black-eyed peas for the eyes.

RELATED TITLES: Carle, Eric. *Mister Seahorse*. Philomel, 2004. / Dorros, Arthur. *Ten Go Tango*. Harper-Collins, 2000. / Ehlert, Lois. *Eating the Alphabet*. Harcourt, 1989. / Ehlert, Lois. *Fish Eyes: A Book You Can Count On*. Harcourt, 1990. / Freymann, Saxton, and Joost Elffers. *Dog Food*. Scholastic, 2002. / Freymann, Saxton, and Joost Effers. *Food for Thought: The Complete Book of Concepts for Growing Minds*. Scholastic, 2005. / Freymann, Saxton, and Joost Elffers. *How Are You Peeling? Foods with Moods*. Scholastic, 1999. / Hausman, Bonnie. *A to Z: Do You Ever Feel Like Me?* Dutton, 1999. / Hubbard, Woodleigh. *C Is for Curious: An ABC of Feelings*. Chronicle, 1990. / MacDonald, Suse. *Look Whooo's Counting*. Scholastic, 2000. / MacDonald, Suse and Oakes, Bill. *Puzzlers*. Dial, 1989. / Raffi. *Five Little Ducks*. Crown, 1988. / Shields, Carol Diggory. *Food Fight!* Handprint, 2002. / Stickland, Paul. *Ten Terrible Dinosaurs*. Dutton, 1997. / Ward, Jennifer, and T. J. Marsh. *Somewhere in the Ocean*. Rising Moon, 2000. / Wood, Audrey. *Ten Little Fish*. Blue Sky/Scholastic, 2004.

SUBJECTS: COUNTING BOOKS. EMOTIONS. FRIENDSHIP. LONELINESS. MARINE ANIMALS. SEA HORSES. STORIES IN RHYME. VEGETABLES.

306   **Friedrich, Elizabeth.** *Leah's Pony.* **Illus. by Michael Garland. Boyds Mills, 1996. 1-56397-189-5. Unp. Gr. 1–3**

In a year of hard times, when grasshoppers eat the trees bare and turn the soil to dust, Leah's parents can't pay back their bank loans and must auction off their cattle, chickens, and tractor. Leah sells her precious pony so she can buy back her father's tractor.

GERM: Read aloud the Author's Note to provide background on the Great Depression and the Dust Bowl on the Great Plains. Discuss: Why did Leah sell her pony? How did her sacrifice save her family's farm? What are hard times? Sing the song and show the book of Woody Guthrie's "This Land Is Your Land," a song written during the Great Depression. Also be sure to teach your crew Guthrie's famous Dust Bowl number, "So Long, It's Been Good to Know You."

RELATED TITLES: Christensen, Bonnie. *Woody Guthrie: Poet of the People*. Knopf, 2001. / Guthrie, Woody. *This Land Is Your Land*. Little, Brown, 1998. / Lied, Kate. *Potato: A Tale from the Great Depression*. National Geographic, 1997. / Tews, Susan. *The Gingerbread Doll*. Clarion, 1993.

SUBJECTS: DEPRESSIONS—1929—U.S. FARM LIFE. HISTORICAL FICTION. HORSES. PICTURE BOOKS FOR ALL AGES. PONIES. RESPONSIBILITY. SACRIFICE.

307   **Gaffney, Timothy R.** *Wee and the Wright Brothers.* **Illus. by Bernadette Pons. Henry Holt, 2004. 0-8050-7172-5. Unp. Gr. K–2**

In 1903, while living in the bicycle shop in Dayton, Ohio, where the Wright brothers were working on their flying machines, Wee and his family published the *Mouse News* for the neighborhood mice. Unbeknownst to Wilbur and Orville, when they set out for Kitty Hawk, Wee went with them and even smuggled himself aboard the Flyer for the world's first engine-powered flight. Soft, full-bleed watercolors inject a cheerful note of mouse fantasy into the famous facts and make the Wright brothers' accomplishments accessible to younger children.

GERM: Make a chart of the factual and fantasy elements of the story. Pamela Duncan Edwards's nonfiction picture book *The Wright Brothers* is written in the style of "This Is the House That Jack Built," with a mouse that can be found in each otherwise realistic illustration. Who's to say it wasn't Wee, himself?

RELATED TITLES: Busby, Peter. *First to Fly: How Wilbur and Orville Wright Invented the Airplane*. Random House, 2003. / Collins, Mary. *Airborne: A Photobiography of Wilbur and Orville Wright*. National Geographic, 2003. / Edwards, Pamela Duncan. *The Wright Brothers*. Hyperion, 2003. / Hunter, Ryan Ann. *Into the Air: An Illustrated Timeline of Flight*. National Geographic, 2003. / Old, Wendie. *To Fly: The Story of the Wright Brothers*. Clarion, 2002. / St. George, Judith. *So You Want to Be an Inventor?* Philomel, 2002.

SUBJECTS: AERONAUTICS. AIR PILOTS. AIRPLANES. FLIGHT. HISTORICAL FICTION. INVENTIONS AND INVENTORS. MICE. WRIGHT BROTHERS.

308   **Gaiman, Neil.** *The Day I Swapped My Dad for Two Goldfish.* **Illus. by Dave McKean. Harper-Collins, 2004. 0-06-058701-6. Unp. Gr. 1–4**

In this hip and humorous book, a boy tells us about the time his sister tattled on him to his mother after he swapped his newspaper-reading dad for his friend Nathan's two goldfish. He then had to go retrieve his father, but was forced to do a lot more swapping before he could get him back.

GERM: This bizarrely absurd and funny story, with paintings that incorporate collage and scratchy pen-and-inks, will be fun to retell and act out. Siblings can chime in with accounts of the times they got in trouble and explain how they got out of it. The narrator says: "Some people have great ideas maybe once or twice in their life, and then they discover electricity or fire or outer space or something. I mean, the kind of brilliant ideas that change the whole world. Some people never have them at all. I get them two or three times a week." Ask your geniuses to write about and draw the brilliant ideas they've had lately. Meet a real genius in Don Brown's *Odd Boy Out: Young Albert Einstein*.

RELATED TITLES: Birdseye, Tom. *Soap! Soap! Don't Forget the Soap! An Appalachian Folktale*. Holiday House, 1993. / Brown, Don. *Odd Boy Out: Young Albert Einstein*. Houghton Mifflin, 2004. / Gaiman, Neil. *The Wolves in the Walls*. HarperCollins, 2003. / Medearis, Angela Shelf. *Poppa's Itchy Christmas*. Holiday House, 1998. / Polacco, Patricia. *My Ol' Man*. Philomel, 1995.

SUBJECTS: BARTERING. BROTHERS AND SISTERS. CREATIVE DRAMA. FATHERS. FISHES. GOLDFISH. HUMOROUS FICTION.

309   **Gaiman, Neil. *The Wolves in the Walls*. Illus. by Dave McKean. HarperCollins, 2003. 0-380-97827-X. Unp. Gr. 2–6**
Lucy hears sneaking, creeping, and crumpling noises all throughout the house. No one will believe her when she claims that there are wolves in the walls, but, as it turns out, there really are.

GERM: This tongue-in-cheek thriller picture book is ripe for Halloween. The first half is very scary, though it turns out to be royally funny, so consider your audience carefully. Discuss the role of the wolf as the Bad Guy in stories and literature. Contrast it with information about real wolves, as in Jim Brandenburg's *Scruffy: A Wolf Finds His Place in the Pack* or Gail Gibbons's *Wolves*.

RELATED TITLES: Brandenburg, Jim. *Scruffy: A Wolf Finds His Place in the Pack*. Walker, 1996. / Child, Lauren. *Beware of the Storybook Wolves*. Scholastic, 2001. / Gaiman, Neil. *Coraline*. HarperCollins, 2002. / Gaiman, Neil. *The Day I Swapped My Dad for Two Goldfish*. HarperCollins, 2004. / Gibbons, Gail. *Wolves*. Holiday House, 1994. / Hartman, Bob. *The Wolf Who Cried Boy*. Putnam, 2002. / McKissack, Patricia, and Onawumi Jean Moss. *Precious and the Boo Hag*. Atheneum, 2005. / Park, Barbara. *Psssst! It's Me . . . the Bogeyman*. Atheneum, 1998. / Scieszka, Jon. *The True Story of the 3 Little Pigs*. Viking, 1989. / Viorst, Judith. *My Mama Says There Aren't Any Zombies, Ghosts, Vampires, Creatures, Demons, Monsters, Fiends, Goblins, or Things*. Atheneum, 1973.

SUBJECTS: DWELLINGS. FEAR. HUMOROUS FICTION. PICTURE BOOKS FOR OLDER READERS. SUSPENSE. WOLVES.

310   **Garland, Michael. *Miss Smith's Incredible Storybook*. Illus. by the author. Dutton, 2003. 0-525-47133-2. Unp. Gr. K–2**
Convinced that this new school year will be as boring as usual, Zack is wowed by his hip new teacher, Miss Smith, who, when she reads aloud to the class, makes her storybook characters come to life. Literally.

GERM: Writing prompt: If you could have one book character come to life, who would it be and why? What would you do together? See how Herb meets up with the characters in his fairy-tale book in *Who's Afraid of the Big Bad Book?* by Lauren Child.

RELATED TITLES: Allen, Susan, and Jane Lindaman. *Read Anything Good Lately?* Millbrook, 2003. / Child, Lauren. *Who's Afraid of the Big Bad Book?* Hyperion, 2003. / Drescher, Henrik. *Simon's Book*. Lothrop, 1983. / Ernst, Lisa Campbell. *Stella Louella's Runaway Book*. Simon & Schuster, 1998. / Florczak, Robert. *Yikes!!!* Scholastic, 2003. / Hopkins, Lee Bennett. *Good Books, Good Times!* HarperCollins, 1990. / Lewis, J. Patrick. *Please Bury Me in the Library*. Harcourt, 2005. / Scieszka, Jon. *Summer Reading Is Killing Me!* Viking, 1998. / Sierra, Judy. *Wild About Books*. Knopf, 2004. / Williams, Suzanne. *Library Lil*. Dial, 1997.

SUBJECTS: BOOKS AND READING. CHARACTERS IN LITERATURE. FANTASY. LITERACY. PRINCIPALS. SCHOOLS. TEACHERS.

311   **Garton, Elizabeth. *A Sock Is a Pocket for Your Toes: A Pocket Book*. Illus. by Robin Preiss Glasser. HarperCollins, 2004. 0-06-029527-9. Unp. Gr. PreK–2**
In comfy but perceptive rhyming couplets and kid-filled pen-and-ink and watercolor illustrations, Scanlon explores every type of pocket, such as "A cave is a pocket for a bear, a breath is a pocket full of air."

GERM: Ask your students: "What kinds of pockets have you observed?" Write and draw new pocket observations and create a bulletin board with a big pocket in the middle and little pockets all around. See if the library has any old book pockets to spare. Children can tuck their pocket observations in the book pockets. Recite Beatrice Schenk de Regniers' poem, "Keep a Poem in Your Pocket," which you can easily locate at <www.google.com> or in her book *Sing a Song of Popcorn*.

RELATED TITLES: Ashman, Linda. *Castles, Caves, and Honeycombs*. Harcourt, 2001. / De Regniers, Beatrice Schenk, comp. *Sing a Song of Popcorn: Every Child's Book of Poems*. Scholastic, 1988. / Freeman, Don. *A Pocket for Corduroy*. Viking, 1978. / Hoberman, Mary Ann. *A House Is a House for Me*. Viking, 1978. / Payne, Emmy. *Katy-No-Pocket*. Houghton Mifflin, 1944.

SUBJECTS: POCKETS. STORIES IN RHYME.

312   **Gay, Marie-Louise.** *Good Morning Sam*. **Illus. by the author. Groundwood, 2003. 0-88899-528-8. Unp. Gr. PreK–1**

Stella, with her red hair flying, wakes her little brother Sam and, while helping him get ready to spend the day outside, forgets to get dressed herself.

GERM: Ask children to relate how they've helped or have been helped by their siblings. See how Stella helps Sam to overcome his nighttime fears and to find their dog, Fred, in *Good Night Sam*.

RELATED TITLES: Chodos-Irvine, Margaret. *Ella Sarah Gets Dressed*. Harcourt, 2003. / Cook, Sally. *Good Night Pillow Fight*. HarperCollins, 2004. / Gay, Marie Louise. *Good Night Sam*. Groundwood, 2003. (And others in the Sam and Stella series.) / Gay, Marie Louise. *Stella: Fairy of the Forest*. Groundwood, 2002. / Lane, Lindsey. *Snuggle Mountain*. Clarion, 2003. / London, Jonathan. *Froggy Gets Dressed*. Viking, 1992. / Rice, Eve. *Oh, Lewis*. Macmillan, 1987.

SUBJECTS: BROTHERS AND SISTERS. CLOTHING AND DRESS. MORNING.

313   **George, Jean Craighead.** *Nutik, the Wolf Pup*. **Illus. by Ted Rand. HarperCollins, 2001. 0-06-028164-2. Unp. Gr. PreK–2**

When Amoroq's sister Julie comes home from the Alaskan tundra with a wolf pup for him to tend, she warns him not to come to love the pup, Nutik, since he will be returned to the wolves when he becomes fat and healthy.

GERM: Before finishing the story, stop and ask: Should Nutik stay with Amoroq or go back to his wolf family? List the responses on a chart. Read Gail Gibbons's *Wolves* to your group to give them background information and wolf facts. Then follow up with the sequel, *Nutik and Amoroq Play Ball*.

RELATED TITLES: Bania, Michael. *Kumak's Fish: A Tall Tale from the Far North*. Alaska Northwest, 2004. / Bania, Michael. *Kumak's House: A Tale of the Far North*. Alaska Northwest, 2002. / Blake, Robert. *Akiak: A Tale from the Iditarod*. Philomel, 1997. / Brandenburg, Jim. *Scruffy: A Wolf Finds His Place in the Pack*. Walker, 1996. / Fowler, Susi Gregg. *Circle of Thanks*. Scholastic, 1998. / George, Jean Craighead. *Nutik and Amoroq Play Ball*. HarperCollins, 2001. / Gibbons, Gail. *Wolves*. Holiday House, 1994. / Kroll, Virginia. *The Seasons and Someone*. Harcourt, 1994. / London, Jonathan. *The Eyes of Gray Wolf*. Chronicle, 1993. / Winters, Kay. *Wolf Watch*. Simon & Schuster, 1997.

SUBJECTS: ALASKA. ARCTIC REGIONS. TUNDRA. WOLVES.

314   **George, Lindsay Barrett.** *Around the Pond: Who's Been Here?* **Illus. by the author. Greenwillow, 1996. 0-688-14377-6. Unp. Gr. PreK–1**

On a muggy summer afternoon, Cammy and William head off the path circling the pond to pick blueberries, but each step they take reveals traces, tracks, or clues an animal has left. Turn each page to reveal the animal, including two baby wood ducks in a tree hole, a baby raccoon, and a garter snake.

GERM: As they interpret each clue that Cammy and William discover and predict what animal could have left it, children will become more attuned to their world, taking time to observe nature more closely. Just as dramatic is *In the Snow: Who's Been Here?*, in which Cammy, William, and their dog find animal clues in the snow.

RELATED TITLES: Arnosky, Jim. *All Night Near the Water*. Putnam, 1994. / Duffy, Dee Dee. *Forest Tracks*. Boyds Mills, 1996. / Falwell, Cathryn. *Turtle Splash! Countdown at the Pond*. Greenwillow, 2001. / Fleming, Denise. *In the Small, Small Pond*. Henry Holt, 1993. / George, Lindsay Barrett. *In the Snow: Who's Been Here?* Greenwillow, 1995. / George, Lindsay Barrett. *In the Woods: Who's Been Here?* Greenwillow, 1995. / George, William T. *Box Turtle at Long Pond*. Greenwillow, 1989. / LaMarche, Jim. *The Raft*. HarperCollins, 2000.

SUBJECTS: ANIMAL TRACKS. ANIMALS. NATURE. POND LIFE. SEASONS. SUMMER.

315   George, Lindsay Barrett. *Inside Mouse, Outside Mouse.* **Illus. by the author. HarperCollins, 2004. 0-06-000466-5. Unp. Gr. PreK–1**

On the left side, the narrative begins: "Inside my house there is a mouse," and there is an oval-framed close-up view, exquisitely detailed in gouache and ink, of a gray mouse. On the facing page, it says, "Outside my house there is a mouse," and the mouse on that page is brown. Inspecting each large pair of pages, we see how the two mice are the same and different, inside and outside, as they run about.

GERM: Compare and contrast the environments of the two mice. At the end, when the mice finally see each other through the window that separates them, children can write and illustrate sentences about what the two might do together. Each page highlights a different preposition, including across, under, up, and between. This makes the story a great candidate for acting out in pairs as you read it aloud, with one child playing the inside mouse, and the other, the outside mouse.

RELATED TITLES: Baehr, Patricia. *Mouse in the House.* Holiday House, 1994. / Cauley, Lorinda Bryan. *The Town Mouse and the Country Mouse.* Putnam, 1984. / Duke, Kate. *Guinea Pigs Near and Far.* Dutton, 1984. / Edwards, Pamela Duncan. *Livingstone Mouse.* HarperCollins, 1996. / McBratney, Sam. *The Dark at the Top of the Stairs.* Candlewick, 1996. / McCully, Emily Arnold. *Picnic.* HarperCollins, 2003. / McMillan, Bruce. *Mouse Views: What the Class Pet Saw.* Holiday House, 1993. / Meade, Holly. *John Willy and Freddy McGee.* Marshall Cavendish, 1998. / Rand, Gloria. *Willie Takes a Hike.* Harcourt, 1996. / Roth, Susan L. *Cinnamon's Day Out: A Gerbil Adventure.* Dial, 1998. / Yang, James. *Joey and Jet.* Atheneum, 2004.

SUBJECTS: CREATIVE DRAMA. ENGLISH LANGUAGE—PREPOSITIONS. MICE.

316   Gliori, Debi. *The Snow Lambs.* **Illus. by the author. Scholastic, 1996. 0-590-20304-5. Unp. Gr. K–2**

With a snowstorm starting, farm boy Sam can't relax when his sheepdog Bess doesn't come home. As Sam goes though his evening routine, worrying about what the dog must be doing, we can see on each facing page that brave Bess is shepherding a lost sheep to safety.

GERM: Children will want to examine each page closely to puzzle out and describe each step of Bess's dangerous adventure. Similarly, out in the Arizona desert, see how a lost beagle named Flag survives for a month, while his owners, a father and daughter, search for him in Paul Brett Johnson and Celeste Lewis's *Lost.*

RELATED TITLES: Johnson, Paul Brett, and Celeste Lewis. *Lost.* Orchard, 1996. / Provensen, Alice. *A Day in the Life of Murphy.* Simon & Schuster, 2003. / Singer, Marilyn. *Chester the Out-of-Work Dog.* Henry Holt, 1992. / Weller, Frances Ward. *Riptide.* Philomel, 1990.

SUBJECTS: DOGS. LOST. SHEEP. SNOW. STORMS. SURVIVAL.

317   Goode, Diane. *Monkey Mo Goes to Sea.* **Illus. by the author. Blue Sky/Scholastic, 2002. 0-439-26681-5. Unp. Gr. PreK–1**

Young Bertie, a boy, and his pet monkey Mo are to meet Grandfather aboard the *Blue Star*, a snooty luxury liner. Mo decides he can indeed act like a gentleman and he apes all the actions of one of the tony chaps aboard. While Mo thinks he's behaving like a real gentleman, the comical pen-and-ink and watercolor illustrations tell a whole other story, with the well-heeled, Jazz Age passengers appalled at his cheeky behavior. When Mo's gentleman falls overboard, it's Mo to the rescue, of course.

GERM: Play a game of Monkey See, Monkey Do with your little monkeys.

RELATED TITLES: Anholt, Catherine, and Laurence Anholt. *Chimp and Zee.* Putnam, 2001. / Anholt, Catherine, and Laurence Anholt. *Chimp and Zee and the Big Storm.* Putnam, 2002. / Christelow, Eileen. *Five Little Monkeys Jumping on the Bed.* Clarion, 1989. (And others in the Five Little Monkeys series.) / Diakité, Baba Wagué. *The Hatseller and the Monkeys.* Scholastic, 1999. / Koller, Jackie French. *One Monkey Too Many.* Scholastic, 1999. / Perkins, Al. *Hand, Hand, Fingers, Thumb.* Random House, 1969. / Rey, H. A. *Curious George.* Houghton Mifflin, 1993. (And others in the Curious George series.) / Santat, Dan. *The Guild of Geniuses.* Scholastic, 2004. / Slobodkina, Esphyr. *Caps for Sale.* HarperCollins, 1947.

SUBJECTS: BEHAVIOR. CREATIVE DRAMA. GRANDFATHERS. HUMOROUS FICTION. MONKEYS. SHIPS.

318   Goodman, Joan Elizabeth. *Bernard's Bath.* **Illus. by Dominic Catalano. Boyds Mills, 1996. 1-56397-323-5. Unp. Gr. PreK–K**

"No bath," protests little elephant Bernard, but when Mama, Papa, and Grandma load the tub with toys and jump in, he changes his mind.

GERM: Ask your bathers: What do you like to take into the tub? Read aloud other stubborn-animals-who-won't-take-a-bath stories, such as *The Piggy in the Puddle* by Charlotte Pomerantz. Show pictures of how elephants in the wild take their baths, as in Miela Ford's *Little Elephant*.

RELATED TITLES: Arnold, Tedd. *No More Water in the Tub!* Dial, 1995. / Bell, Cece. *Sock Monkey Goes to Hollywood: A Star Is Bathed.* Candlewick, 2003. / Cole, Brock. *No More Baths.* Doubleday, 1980. / Ford, Miela. *Little Elephant.* Greenwillow, 1994. / Goodman, Joan Elizabeth. *Bernard's Nap.* Boyds Mills, 1999. (And others in the Bernard series.) / Pomerantz, Charlotte. *The Piggy in the Puddle.* Macmillan, 1974. / Reddix, Valerie. *Millie and the Mud Hole.* Lothrop, 1992.

SUBJECTS: BATHS. ELEPHANTS.

319 **Goss, Linda.** *The Frog Who Wanted to Be a Singer.* **Illus. by Cynthia Jabar. Orchard, 1996. 0-531-06895-1. Unp. Gr. K–3**

"Have you ever been frustrated?" That's the question the frog narrator/storyteller asks before beginning his boisterous and exuberant tale of a frog who believes in his own talent as a singer. Undaunted by the nay-saying of all the other animals, he grabs the mike at the Big Time Weekly Concert and belts it out—"in the style of what we now call Boogie-Woogie"—while the crowd grows wild, this time with delight.

GERM: The combination of Goss's jazzy, present-tense telling and Jabar's boisterous scratchboard illustrations will get the kids riled up in no time. There's music on the endpapers so you can sing Frog's boogie-woogie style of blues. Ask your listeners what hidden talents they possess or what new interests they'd like to pursue.

RELATED TITLES: Auch, Mary Jane. *Bantam of the Opera.* Holiday House, 1997. / Auch, Mary Jane. *Hen Lake.* Holiday House, 1995. / Edwards, Pamela Duncan. *Honk! The Story of a Prima Swanerina.* Hyperion, 1998. / Ernst, Lisa Campbell. *When Bluebell Sang.* Bradbury, 1989. / Gray, Libba Moore. *Little Lil and the Swing-Singing Sax.* Simon & Schuster, 1996. / Hoffman, Mary. *Amazing Grace.* Dial, 1991. / Howe, James. *Horace and Morris Join the Chorus (But What About Dolores?).* Atheneum, 2002. / Hurd, Thacher. *Art Dog.* HarperCollins, 1996. / Kinerk, Robert. *Clorinda.* Simon & Schuster, 2003. / Laden, Nina. *Roberto the Insect Architect.* Chronicle, 2000. / Pearson, Susan. *Lenore's Big Break.* Viking, 1992. / Pfeffer, Wendy. *From Tadpole to Frog.* HarperCollins, 1994. / Seeger, Pete, and Charles Seeger. *The Foolish Frog.* Macmillan, 1973. / Weaver, Tess. *Opera Cat.* Clarion, 2002. / Stevenson, James. *Clams Can't Sing.* Greenwillow, 1980.

SUBJECTS: ANIMALS. DETERMINATION. FROGS. MUSIC. PERSEVERANCE. SINGERS.

320 **Graeber, Charlotte.** *Nobody's Dog.* **Illus. by Barry Root. Hyperion, 1998. 0-7868-2093-4. Unp. Gr. K–2**

Mrs. Pepper does not want to keep the small white stray dog, but he squeezes himself into her garden and her heart.

GERM: Have children draw the pet of their dreams and list the ten attributes they would most like their pet to have.

RELATED TITLES: Banks, Kate. *The Cat Who Walked Across France.* Farrar, 2004. / Graham, Bob. *"Let's Get a Pup!" Said Kate.* Candlewick, 2001. / Joosse, Barbara M. *Nugget and Darling.* Clarion, 1997. / McFarland, Lyn Rossiter. *Widget.* Farrar, 2001. / Rylant, Cynthia. *The Great Gracie Chase.* Scholastic, 2001. / Simont, Marc. *The Stray Dog.* HarperCollins, 2001. / Thayer, Jane. *The Puppy Who Wanted a Boy.* Morrow, 1986. / Voake, Charlotte. *Ginger Finds a Home.* Candlewick, 2003. / Wells, Rosemary. *Lucy Comes to Stay.* Dial, 1994. / Wells, Rosemary. *McDuff Moves In.* Hyperion, 1997. (And others in the McDuff series.)

SUBJECTS: DOGS. ELDERLY. STRAY ANIMALS.

321 **Graham, Bob.** *Benny: An Adventure Story.* **Illus. by the author. Candlewick, 1999. 0-7636-0813-0. Unp. Gr. PreK–2**

Cast out from his job as assistant to Brillo the Magician, Benny the mutt takes to the road eager to display his own talents of juggling, harmonica playing, and tap dancing.

GERM: Children can write, illustrate, and share accounts of their pets' special talents. Meet other talented performing dogs in *Ginger Jumps* by Lisa Campbell Ernst, *The Blues of Flats Brown* by Walter Dean Myers, and *Officer Buckle and Gloria* by Peggy Rathmann.

RELATED TITLES: Auch, Mary Jane. *Bantam of the Opera.* Holiday House, 1997. / Auch, Mary Jane. *Bird Dogs Can't Fly.* Holiday House, 1993. / Auch, Mary Jane. *Eggs Mark the Spot.* Holiday House, 1996. / Auch, Mary Jane. *Peeping Beauty.* Holiday House, 1993. / Ernst, Lisa Campbell. *Ginger Jumps.* Bradbury, 1990. / Ernst, Lisa Campbell. *When Bluebell Sang.* Bradbury, 1989. / Goss, Linda. *The Frog Who Wanted to Be a Singer.* Orchard, 1996. / Graham, Bob. *"Let's Get a Pup!" Said Kate.* Candlewick, 2001. / Graham, Bob. *Max.* Candlewick, 2000. / Howard, Arthur. *Cosmo Zooms.* Harcourt, 1999. / Hurd, Thacher. *Art Dog.* HarperCollins,

1996. / McFarland, Lyn Rossiter. *Widget*. Farrar, 2001. / Meddaugh, Susan. *Martha Speaks*. Houghton Mifflin, 1992. / Myers, Walter Dean. *The Blues of Flats Brown*. Holiday House, 2000. / Rathmann, Peggy. *Officer Buckle and Gloria*. Putnam, 1995. / Simont, Marc. *The Stray Dog*. HarperCollins, 2001.

SUBJECTS: DOGS. MAGICIANS. STRAY ANIMALS.

322   **Graham, Bob.** *Jethro Byrd, Fairy Child*. **Illus. by the author. Candlewick, 2002. 0-7636-1772-5. Unp. Gr. PreK–2**

On her daily lookout for fairies, Annabelle meets Jethro Byrd, a fairy child as big as her finger, and invites his whole family, who are on their way to make ice cream at the Fairy Travelers' Picnic, to stop for tea. What a sweet story, with huge watercolor and ink illustrations.

GERM: Ask your listeners to explain why Annabelle's parents can't see the fairies. Make a fairy tea party for your kids with tiny foods—one raisin, a tiny piece of apple, a sunflower seed, a thumbnail-sized chocolate chip cookie with one chocolate chip.

RELATED TITLES: Gay, Marie-Louise. *Stella, Fairy of the Forest*. Groundwood, 2002. / Graham, Bob. *Benny: An Adventure Story*. Candlewick, 1999. / Graham, Bob. *"Let's Get a Pup!" Said Kate*. Candlewick, 2001. / Graham, Bob. *Max*. Candlewick, 2000.

SUBJECTS: FAIRIES. FANTASY. IMAGINATION.

323   **Graham, Bob.** *"Let's Get a Pup!" Said Kate*. **Illus. by the author. Candlewick, 2001. 0-7636-1452-1. Unp. Gr. PreK–2**

Missing a pet in her bed since her cat died, young Kate heads out with her parents to the Rescue Center to look for a small, cute, excited dog. There they find not one, but two dogs of their dreams: young Dave and old Rosie. Large, expressive pen-and-ink and watercolor illustrations are full of dog empathy. Beware of reading this one aloud; all of your kids will run home asking for a dog.

GERM: Before reading the story, children can make a list of all the qualities they'd like to find in their new pet and draw a portrait of it. After reading, have children list the qualities they most like about the pets they now have.

RELATED TITLES: Bartoletti, Susan Campbell. *Nobody's Diggier Than a Dog*. Hyperion, 2004. / George, Kristine O'Connell. *Little Dog Poems*. Clarion, 1999. / Graeber, Charlotte. *Nobody's Dog*. Hyperion, 1998. / Graham, Bob. *Benny: An Adventure Story*. Candlewick, 1999. / Graham, Bob. *Queenie, One of the Family*. Candlewick, 1997. / Kalman, Maira. *What Pete Ate from A– Z*. Putnam, 2001. / Kirk, Daniel. *Dogs Rule!* Hyperion, 2003. / Lee, Chinlun. *Good Dog, Paw!* Candlewick, 2004. / McFarland, Lyn Rossiter. *Widget*. Farrar, 2001. / Rylant, Cynthia. *The Great Gracie Chase*. Scholastic, 2001. / Simon, Seymour. *Dogs*. HarperCollins, 2003. / Simont, Marc. *The Stray Dog*. HarperCollins, 2001. / Voake, Charlotte. *Ginger Finds a Home*. Candlewick, 2003. / Wells, Rosemary. *Lucy Comes to Stay*. Dial, 1994. / Wells, Rosemary. *McDuff Moves In*. Hyperion, 1997. (And others in the McDuff series.) / Wolf, Jake. *Daddy, Could I Have an Elephant?* Greenwillow, 1996.

SUBJECTS: ANIMAL SHELTERS. DOGS. PETS. STRAY ANIMALS.

324   **Graham, Bob.** *Max*. **Illus. by the author. Candlewick, 2000. 0-7636-1138-7. Unp. Gr. PreK–2**

Though Max's parents—Captain Lightning and Madam Thunderbolt—and grandparents are well-known superheroes, they can't quite figure out why Max can't even fly yet. Then Max sees a baby bird about to fall from its nest and off he flies to save it.

GERM: Discussion point: As his mother says, Max is a "small hero doing quiet deeds. The world needs more of these." What are quiet deeds? What kinds of quiet deeds have you done lately? Superheroes in training can draw themselves in flight, inspired by the wonderfully expressive pen-and-ink and watercolor illustrations. This gently funny, oversized picture book will also put you in mind of an earlier classic, *Leo the Late Bloomer* by Robert Kraus. Tie in other superhero picture books such as *Superdog: The Heart of a Hero* by Caralyn Buehner, *Kapow!* by George O'Connor, *The Adventures of Sparrowboy* by Brian Pinkney, and *Atomic Ace (He's Just My Dad)* by Jeff Weigel.

RELATED TITLES: Buehner, Caralyn. *Superdog: The Heart of a Hero*. HarperCollins, 2004. / Dorros, Arthur. *Abuela*. Dutton, 1991. / Gerstein, Mordicai. *Arnold of the Ducks*. HarperCollins, 1983. / Graham, Bob. *Benny: An Adventure Story*. Candlewick, 1999. / Grey, Mini. *Traction Man Is Here!* Knopf, 2005. / Kraus, Robert. *Leo the Late Bloomer*. HarperCollins, 1971. / MacDonald, Ross. *Another Perfect Day*. Roaring Brook, 2002. / Myers, Christopher. *Wings*. Scholastic, 2000. / O'Connor, George. *Kapow!* Simon & Schuster, 2004. / Pinkney, Brian. *The Adventures of Sparrowboy*. Simon & Schuster, 1997. / Weigel, Jeff. *Atomic Ace (He's Just My Dad)*. Albert Whitman, 2004. / Woodruff, Elvira. *Show and Tell*. Holiday House, 1991. / Woodruff, Elvira. *The Wing Shop*. Holiday House, 1991.

SUBJECTS: FAMILY LIFE. FANTASY. FLIGHT. GRANDPARENTS. HEROES. SUPERHEROES.

325 Graham, Bob. *Queenie, One of the Family*. Illus. by the author. Candlewick, 1997. 0-7636-1400-9. Unp. Gr. PreK–1

When Caitlin's dad rescues a bantam hen from the middle of the lake, they bring her home and name her Queenie. They take her back to the farm where she lives, but Queenie returns to their house every day to lay a single perfect egg in their dog Bruno's basket. A fetching family story with a hen, a toddler, a dog, a new baby, and some chicks, this will be a storytime favorite.

GERM: At each juncture in the story, it says, "That might have been the end of the story . . . but it wasn't!" Have listeners predict what might happen next. And at the end, when it says, "But that's another story," speculate about future adventures Caitlin and her baby brother might have with their baby chick, looking at the last illustration for one idea.

RELATED TITLES: Brett, Jan. *Daisy Comes Home*. Putnam, 2002. / Flack, Marjorie. *The Story About Ping*. Viking, 1933. / Gibbons, Gail. *Chicks and Chickens*. Holiday House, 2003. / Graham, Bob. *Benny: An Adventure Story*. Holiday House, 2000. / Graham, Bob. *"Let's Get a Pup!" Said Kate*. Candlewick, 2001. / Graham, Bob. *Max*. Candlewick, 2000. / Sklansky, Amy E. *Where Do Chicks Come From?* HarperCollins, 2005.

SUBJECTS: CHICKENS. DOGS. FAMILY LIFE.

326 Gray, Libba Moore. *Little Lil and the Swing-Singing Sax*. Illus. by Lisa Cohen. Simon & Schuster, 1996. 0-689-80681-7. Unp. Gr. K–3

Lil's jazz-playing Uncle Sudi Man pawns his beloved sax to pay for medicine when Mama Big Lil takes sick, but generous Lil finds a way to get it back in time for Christmas.

GERM: Here's one nice quote to chew over: ". . . we didn't have much money but we had a lot of love and we laughed more than we cried."

RELATED TITLES: Cox, Judy. *My Family Plays Music*. Holiday House, 2003. / Frame, Jeron Ashford. *Yesterday I Had the Blues*. Tricycle, 2003. / Greenfield, Eloise. *Honey, I Love*. HarperCollins, 2003. / Medearis, Angela Shelf. *Poppa's Itchy Christmas*. Holiday House, 1998. / Polacco, Patricia. *An Orange for Frankie*. Philomel, 2004. / Raschka, Chris. *Charlie Parker Played Bebop*. Orchard, 1992. / Rylant, Cynthia. *Children of Christmas: Stories for the Season*. Orchard, 1987. / Rylant, Cynthia. *Silver Packages: An Appalachian Christmas Story*. Orchard, 1997. / Smothers, Ethel Footman. *The Hard-Times Jar*. Farrar, 2003.

SUBJECTS: AFRICAN AMERICANS. CHRISTMAS. FAMILY LIFE. JAZZ. MULTICULTURAL BOOKS. MUSIC. SAXOPHONE.

327 Greene, Rhonda Gowler. *The Very First Thanksgiving Day*. Illus. by Susan Gaber. Atheneum, 2002. 0-689-83301-6. Unp. Gr. PreK–2

A "This Is the House that Jack Built" rhyming format and a series of reverent acrylic paintings present a portrait of that first year in the Plymouth Colony, from the ocean voyage of 1620 to the harvest feast with the Indians who helped the Pilgrims survive.

GERM: Start the dialogue on why and how we celebrate Thanksgiving and the customs children's families observe on the holiday.

RELATED TITLES: Anderson, Laurie Halse. *Thank You, Sarah: The Woman Who Saved Thanksgiving*. Simon & Schuster, 2002. / George, Jean Craighead. *The First Thanksgiving*. Philomel, 1993. / Kay, Verla. *Tattered Sails*. Putnam, 2001. / Lakin, Patricia. *Fat Chance Thanksgiving*. Albert Whitman, 2001. / Peacock, Carol Antoinette. *Pilgrim Cat*. Albert Whitman, 2005. / Van Leeuwen, Jean. *Across the Wide Dark Sea: The Mayflower Journey*. Dial, 1996. / Waters, Kate. *Samuel Eaton's Day: A Day in the Life of a Pilgrim Boy*. Scholastic, 1993. / Waters, Kate. *Sarah Morton's Day: A Day in the Life of a Pilgrim Girl*. Scholastic, 1989.

SUBJECTS: HISTORICAL FICTION. MASSACHUSETTS—HISTORY. PILGRIMS. STORIES IN RHYME. THANKSGIVING.

328 Greenfield, Eloise. *Honey, I Love*. Illus. by Jan Spivey Gilchrist. HarperCollins, 2003. 0-06-009124-X. Unp. Gr. PreK–2

In a newly illustrated version of the classic poem, originally published in 1978, a warm and disarming African American girl lists the "whole lot of things" she loves, from the way her cousin from down South talks, to jumping in the water on a hot day, to kissing her Mama's arm, so soft and warm.

GERM: Write or tell and share the whole lot of things you all love and why. Contrast the girl's emotions in *Honey, I Love* with the boy's in *Yesterday I Had the Blues* by Jeron Ashford Frame.

RELATED TITLES: Adoff, Arnold. *Love Letters*. Scholastic, 1997. / Frame, Jeron Ashford. *Yesterday I Had the Blues*. Tricycle, 2003. / Greenfield, Eloise. *Honey, I Love, and Other Love Poems*. HarperCollins, 1978. / Grimes,

Nikki. *Meet Danitra Brown*. Lothrop, 1994. / Hesse, Karen. *Come On, Rain!* Scholastic, 1999. / Hudson, Wade. *Pass It On: African-American Poetry for Children*. Scholastic, 1993. / Minne. *I Love . . .* Kane/Miller, 2005.

SUBJECTS: AFRICAN AMERICANS—POETRY. EMOTIONS—POETRY. FAMILY LIFE—POETRY. LOVE—POETRY. MULTICULTURAL BOOKS—POETRY. STORIES IN RHYME.

329 **Greenspun, Adele Aron, and Joanie Schwarz. *Ariel and Emily*. Photos by the author. Dutton, 2003. 0-525-46861-7. Unp. Gr. PreK–1**

Through endearing hand-tinted photos, follow two babies, who are best friends, on their outing to the park, where they make noise, share a squishy banana, and play hide-and-seek.

GERM: While this is a perfect book for the "I love babies" set, and a welcome look at babyhood for all, it is also an interesting spur for all children to observe and report on the activities of the babies in their lives, or to recall their own babyhoods. They could bring in photos and caption them: "This is ____. She likes to ____." Note how baby and dog are best pals in Kathi Appelt's *Bubba and Beau Go Night-Night*.

RELATED TITLES: Appelt, Kathi. *Bubba and Beau Go Night-Night*. Harcourt, 2003. (And others in the Bubba and Beau series.) / Cooke, Trish. *So Much*. Candlewick, 1994. / Curtis, Marci. *I Was So Silly! Big Kids Remember Being Little*. Dial, 2002. / Meyers, Susan. *Everywhere Babies*. Harcourt, 2001. / Nye, Naomi Shihab. *Baby Radar*. Greenwillow, 2003. / Paxton, Tom. *Where's the Baby?* Morrow, 1993. / Regan, Dian Curtis. *Chance*. Philomel, 2003. / Schwartz, Amy. *A Teeny Tiny Baby*. Orchard, 1994. / Wild, Margaret. *Midnight Babies*. Clarion, 2001. / Willems, Mo. *Knuffle Bunny: A Cautionary Tale*. Hyperion, 2004. / Williams, Vera B. *"More More More," Said the Baby*. Greenwillow, 1990.

SUBJECTS: BABIES. FRIENDSHIP.

330 **Gregory, Nan. *How Smudge Came*. Illus. by Ron Lightburn. Orca, 1996. 0-88995-143-8. Unp. Gr. 2–4**

Cindy, a young woman with Down's syndrome, discovers a stray puppy and names him Smudge. She hides him in her room and tucks him into the big yellow apron she wears to her job cleaning at the Hospice. While the story is told by an omniscient narrator, it captures Cindy's thoughts and feelings with compassion, allowing listeners to identify with and briefly share in her universe.

GERM: This heartbreaking but uplifting picture book will make children think about what they're saying when they tease each other and call others "retards."

RELATED TITLES: Baldwin, Ann Norris. *A Little Time*. Viking, 1978. / Conly, Jane Leslie. *Crazy Lady!* HarperCollins, 1993. / Dodds, Bill. *My Sister Annie*. Boyds Mills, 1993. / Garrigue, Sheila. *Between Friends*. Bradbury, 1978. / Shyer, Marlene Fanta. *Welcome Home, Jellybean*. Macmillan, 1978.

SUBJECTS: DOGS. MENTALLY HANDICAPPED. PEOPLE WITH DISABILITIES. PICTURE BOOKS FOR OLDER READERS.

331 **Grey, Mini. *Traction Man Is Here!* Illus. by the author. Knopf, 2005. 0-375-83191-6. Unp. Gr. PreK–2**

Set up in comic book format is a derring-do adventure of a boy's action figure doll, Traction Man, and his faithful little companion and pet, Scrubbing Brush. Together they search for the Lost Wreck of the Sieve in the kitchen sink, dig up the Dollies buried in the garden by Wicked Professor Spade, and encounter the Mysterious Toes in the bath. But what's a superhero action figure to do when he's expected to wear the silly-looking, all-in-one green romper Granny has knitted just for him?

GERM: Read this aloud with great expression, drama, and a sense of high adventure. Children can draw new adventures of Traction Man and Scrubbing Brush, starting with the sequel hinted at on the final page, where they appear to be menaced by a sharp-toothed, shark-like pair of silver pinking shears. Or have them personify their own toys, describing or drawing their imagined adventures.

RELATED TITLES: Buehner, Caralyn. *Superdog: The Heart of a Hero*. HarperCollins, 2004. / Collins, Suzanne. *When Charlie McButton Lost Power*. Putnam, 2005. / Dewan, Ted. *Crispin, the Pig Who Had It All*. Doubleday, 2000. / Feiffer, Jules. *Meanwhile . . .* HarperCollins, 1997. / Graham, Bob. *Max*. Candlewick, 2000. / MacDonald, Ross. *Another Perfect Day*. Roaring Brook, 2002. / O'Connor, George. *Kapow!* Simon & Schuster, 2004. / O'Malley, Kevin. *Captain Raptor and the Moon Mystery*. Walker, 2005. / Pinkney, Brian. *The Adventures of Sparrowboy*. Simon & Schuster, 1997. / Steen, Sandra, and Susan Steen. *Car Wash*. Putnam, 2001. / Weigel, Jeff. *Atomic Ace (He's Just My Dad)*. Albert Whitman, 2004.

SUBJECTS: ACTION FIGURES (TOYS). BROOMS AND BRUSHES. CARTOONS AND COMICS.

FANTASY. HUMOROUS FICTION. IMAGINATION. PERSONIFICATION. PLAY. SUPERHEROES. TOYS.

332   **Grimes, Nikki.** *C Is for City.* **Illus. by Pat Cummings. Lothrop, 1995. 0-688-11809-7. Unp. Gr. K–2**

This A to Z alphabet of rhyming four-line poems crams in all the exhilarating sights and sounds of the city, from arcades, ads for apartments, Afghan dogs, and art shows to the zillions of churches named Zion and the zoos with their zebras. New York City is feted in the jam-packed bustling illustrations. Point out some of the sights, such as the skating rink at Rockefeller Center, the Times Square subway station, and Central Park.

GERM: Careful observers will pick out scores of additional objects on each page that correspond with the letter that's being featured, and they can also check the list at the back to see what they have missed. Ask them to tell, write, or draw what impresses them most about city life.

RELATED TITLES: Adoff, Arnold. *Street Music: City Poems.* HarperCollins, 1995. / Dorros, Arthur. *Abuela.* Dutton, 1991. / Jakobsen, Kathy. *My New York.* Little, Brown, 2003. / Johnson, Stephen T. *Alphabet City.* Viking, 1995. / Konigsburg, E. L. *Amy Elizabeth Explores Bloomingdale's.* Atheneum, 1992. / Meister, Cari. *Busy Busy City Street.* Viking, 2000. / Melmed, Laura Krauss. *New York, New York! The Big Apple from A to Z.* HarperCollins, 2005. / Neubecker, Robert. *Wow! City!* Hyperion, 2004. / Palatini, Margie. *Ding Dong Ding Dong.* Hyperion, 1999. / Priceman, Marjorie. *Froggie Went a-Courting.* Little, Brown, 2000. / Ringgold, Faith. *Tar Beach.* Crown, 1991. / Rotner, Shelley, and Ken Kreisler. *Citybook.* Orchard, 1994. / Van Laan, Nancy. *People, People, Everywhere!* Knopf, 1992. / Weitzman, Jacqueline Preiss. *You Can't Take a Balloon into the Metropolitan Museum.* Dial, 1998.

SUBJECTS: ALPHABET BOOKS. CITIES AND TOWNS. MULTICULTURAL BOOKS. NEW YORK CITY. STORIES IN RHYME.

333   **Guy, Ginger Foglesong.** *Fiesta!* **Illus. by René King Moreno. Greenwillow, 1996. 0-688-14331-8. Unp. Gr. PreK–1**

Learn to count from one to ten in both English and Spanish, aided by three children who buy little toys and candies to stuff inside their piñata for their backyard party.

GERM: Children can recite each set of English and Spanish words in *Fiesta!* and in *Siesta!*, Guy's companion book. For more party celebrations, also read Elisa Kleven's *Hooray, a Piñata!* and Pam Muñoz Ryan's *Mice and Beans.*

RELATED TITLES: Dorros, Arthur. *Abuela.* Dutton, 1991. / Elya, Susan Middleton. *Eight Animals Bake a Cake.* Putnam, 2002. / Elya, Susan Middleton. *Say Hola to Spanish.* Lee & Low, 1996. / Emberley, Rebecca. *Piñata!* Little, Brown, 2004. / Guy, Ginger Foglesong. *Siesta!* Greenwillow, 2005. / Kleven, Elisa. *Hooray, a Piñata!* Dutton, 1996. / Reed, Lynn. *Pedro, His Perro, and the Alphabet Sombrero.* Hyperion, 1995. / Ryan, Pam Muñoz. *Mice and Beans.* Scholastic, 2001. / Soto, Gary. *Chato and the Party Animals.* Putnam, 2000. / Soto, Gary. *Chato's Kitchen.* Putnam, 1995. / Soto, Gary. *Snapshots from the Wedding.* Putnam, 1997.

SUBJECTS: BIRTHDAYS. CELEBRATIONS. COUNTING BOOKS. HISPANIC AMERICANS. MULTICULTURAL BOOKS. PARTIES. PIÑATAS. SPANISH LANGUAGE.

334   **Hall, Bruce Edward.** *Henry and the Dragon Kite.* **Illus. by William Low. Philomel, 2004. 0-399-23727-5. Unp. Gr. K–4**

In New York City's Chinatown in the 1920s, 8-year-old Henry Chu's favorite thing to do is to make and fly colorful animal kites with Grandfather Chin. When Tony Guglione and his friends throw rocks and destroy the kites, the Chinese and Italian kids confront each other, fists ready to swing, until Tony reveals the understandable reason for his terrible behavior.

GERM: Stop reading at the confrontation scene and ask listeners to do a Quick Write, answering the questions: Why did Tony destroy Henry's kites? What should Henry do? What would you do? Tony's reason is a good one: he was protecting his homing pigeon. Discuss: What could Tony have done? Why did he cry? How could the children resolve their problems? Ask: Did you ever misjudge someone and find out you were wrong? Or did someone ever misjudge you? If so, what ensued? Talk about social issues: How do we treat people who are different from us? How can we respect, understand, and accept each other's cultures? What happens when two cultures clash? How can we prevent the little wars in our neighborhoods and the big wars between countries? Then, make and go fly a kite. Show how homing pigeons were used during World War I in *The Language of Doves* by Rosemary Wells.

RELATED TITLES: Bartone, Elisa. *American Too.* Lothrop, 1996. / Bartone, Elisa. *Peppe the Lamplighter.* Lothrop, 1993. / Chinn, Karen. *Sam and the Lucky Money.* Lee & Low, 1995. / Compestine, Ying Chang. *The*

Story of Kites. Holiday House, 2003. / Demi. *Kites: Magic Wishes That Fly Up to the Sky.* Crown, 1999. / Freedman, Russell. *Immigrant Kids.* Dutton, 1980. / Lee, Milly. *Nim and the War Effort.* Farrar, 1997. / Lewin, Ted. *Big Jimmy's Kum Kau Chinese Take Out.* HarperCollins, 2002. / Lin, Grace. *Fortune Cookie Fortunes.* Knopf, 2004. / Mak, Kam. *My Chinatown.* HarperCollins, 2002. / Marsden, Carolyn. *The Gold-Threaded Dress.* Candlewick, 2002. / Pomeranc, Marion Hess. *The American Wei.* Albert Whitman, 1998. / Wells, Rosemary. *The Language of Doves.* Dial, 1996. / Wong, Janet. *Apple Pie Fourth of July.* Harcourt, 2002. / Yee, Paul. *Roses Sing on New Snow.* Macmillan, 1992. / Yin. *Coolies.* Philomel, 2001. / Young, Ed. *The Sons of the Dragon King: A Chinese Legend.* Atheneum, 2004.

SUBJECTS: ASIAN AMERICANS. CHINESE AMERICANS. HISTORICAL FICTION. ITALIAN AMERICANS. KITES. MULTICULTURAL BOOKS. NEW YORK CITY. PICTURE BOOKS FOR ALL AGES. PIGEONS. PREJUDICE.

335   Hamm, Mia. *Winners Never Quit!* **Illus. by Carol Thompson. HarperCollins, 2004. 0-06-074050-7. Unp. Gr. PreK–2**

Mia loves playing soccer more than any other sport, but when she doesn't win, she quits playing and storms back home. Her friends refuse to play with quitters, however, so Mia shapes up fast, learning that playing is more important than winning.

GERM: Recalling her own experiences as a child playing soccer, Olympic Gold Medalist Mia Hamm doesn't preach, but does impart a valuable lesson to children. Don't miss the photo montage of her career, from kid to champ, at the back of the book. Do more research on her life and career. Make text-to-life connections: What do you do when you win or lose a game? How do you feel?

RELATED TITLES: Corey, Shana. *Players in Pigtails.* Scholastic, 2003. / Finchler, Judy. *You're a Good Sport, Miss Malarkey.* Walker, 2002. / Littlefield, Bill. *Champions: Stories of Ten Remarkable Athletes.* Little, Brown, 1993. / Mills, Claudia. *Ziggy's Blue-Ribbon Day.* Farrar, 2005. / Moss, Marissa. *Mighty Jackie, the Strike-Out Queen.* Simon & Schuster, 2004. / Potter, Giselle. *Chloë's Birthday . . . and Me.* Atheneum, 2004. / Stadler, Alexander. *Beverly Billingsly Can't Catch.* Harcourt, 2004.

SUBJECTS: AUTOBIOGRAPHY. BIOGRAPHICAL FICTION. HAMM, MIA. PERSEVERANCE. SOCCER. SPORTS. SPORTSMANSHIP.

336   Harper, Dan. *Telling Time with Big Mama Cat.* **Illus. by Barry Moser and Cara Moser. Harcourt, 1998. 0-15-201738-0. Unp. Gr. PreK–1**

There's a clock face with movable arms on the cover of this endearing account narrated by a large house cat, who tells us how she spends each hour of the day with her human family, starting at 6 A.M. with a big stretch. The Mosers' watercolors of this saucy, expressive tabby are priceless.

GERM: This book is terrific for learning how to tell time and can be used as an example for writing character studies. It will also be appreciated by the cat lovers in your group. Children can write and illustrate pet time tales, from the pets' points of view, explaining their schedules.

RELATED TITLES: Axelrod, Amy. *Pigs on a Blanket.* Simon & Schuster, 1996. / Behrman, Carol H. *The Ding Dong Clock.* Henry Holt, 1999. / Carle, Eric. *The Grouchy Ladybug.* HarperCollins, 1997. / Crummel, Susan Stevens. *All in One Hour.* Marshall Cavendish, 2003. / Fraser, Mary Ann. *I. Q., It's Time.* Walker, 2005. / Hopkins, Lee Bennett. *It's About Time.* Simon & Schuster, 1993. / Hutchins, Pat. *Clocks and More Clocks.* Macmillan, 1970. / Walton, Rick. *Bunny Day: Telling Time from Breakfast to Bedtime.* HarperCollins, 2002.

SUBJECTS: CATS. CLOCKS AND WATCHES. FAMILY LIFE. PERSONAL NARRATIVES. POINT OF VIEW. TIME.

337   Harper, Jessica. *Lizzy's Ups and Downs: Not an Ordinary School Day.* **Illus. by Lindsay Harper duPont. HarperCollins, 2004. 0-06-052064-7. Unp. Gr. PreK–2**

Lizzy's mom asks her to tell everything about her day, and Lizzy does just that, in detail and in rhyme. Starting with oversleeping and worrying about missing the bus, she runs through the range of emotions she experienced over the course of the entire school day.

GERM: Ask your children to describe an emotion they experienced recently and tell the story behind it. Experience an assortment of emotions with *Today I Feel Silly and Other Moods That Make My Day* by Jamie Lee Curtis, *Yesterday I Had the Blues* by Jeron Ashford Frame, and *A to Z: Do You Ever Feel Like Me?* by Bonnie Hausman. Share Lizzy's rules for her mother in Harper's companion story, *Lizzie's Do's and Don'ts.*

RELATED TITLES: Aliki. *Feelings.* Greenwillow, 1984. / Curtis, Jamie Lee. *Today I Feel Silly and Other Moods That Make My Day.* HarperCollins, 1998. / Frame, Jeron Ashford. *Yesterday I Had the Blues.* Tricycle, 2003. /

Freymann, Saxton, and Joost Elffers. *How Are You Peeling? Foods with Moods.* Scholastic, 1999. / Harper, Jessica. *Lizzie's Do's and Don'ts.* HarperCollins, 2002. / Hausman, Bonnie. *A to Z: Do You Ever Feel Like Me?* Dutton, 1999. / Hopkins, Lee Bennett, comp. *Oh, No! Where Are My Pants? And Other Disasters: Poems.* HarperCollins, 2005. / Vail, Rachel. *Sometimes I'm Bombaloo.* Scholastic, 2002.

SUBJECTS: EMOTIONS. MOTHERS AND DAUGHTERS. PERSONAL NARRATIVES. SCHOOLS. STORIES IN RHYME.

338   **Harris, Robie H. *Don't Forget to Come Back!* Illus. by Harry Bliss. Candlewick, 2004. 0-7636-1782-2. Unp. Gr. PreK–2**
Peeved when she discovers that Mommy and Daddy are going out and Sarah is coming to baby-sit, the brown-haired little girl narrator tries every type of persuasion to keep them home, including fear, guilt, sweetness, and fury, all to no avail. But then silly Sarah, the totally cool baby-sitter, comes and they end up having a wonderful time.
GERM: The narrator offers various lists of three important things. Make your own lists of important things: good advice for parents or baby-sitters.
RELATED TITLES: Bush, Timothy. *Benjamin McFadden and the Robot Babysitter.* Crown, 1998. / Child, Lauren. *Clarice Bean, Guess Who's Babysitting?* Candlewick, 2001. / Green, Phyllis. *Chucky Bellman Was So Bad.* Albert Whitman, 1991. / Gregory, Valiska. *Babysitting for Benjamin.* Little, Brown, 1993. / Harris, Robie H. *I Am Not Going to School Today!* McElderry, 2003. / McGhee, Alison. *Countdown to Kindergarten.* Illus. by Harry Bliss. Harcourt, 2002. / McGhee, Alison. *Mrs. Watson Wants Your Teeth.* Illus. by Harry Bliss. Harcourt, 2004. / Rayner, Mary. *Mr. and Mrs. Pig's Evening Out.* Atheneum, 1976. / Wells, Rosemary. *Shy Charles.* Dial, 1988.
SUBJECTS: BABY-SITTERS. PARENT AND CHILD.

339   **Harris, Robie H. *Goodbye Mousie.* Illus. by Jan Ormerod. McElderry, 2001. 0-689-83217-6. Unp. Gr. PreK–1**
A little boy can't get his pet white mouse to wake up and is sad and angry when his father gently tells him that Mousie is dead. The child describes how he prepares Mousie for burial in a shoebox, surrounded by all his favorite things, so he won't be hungry, bored, or lonely.
GERM: As a first book to use when dealing with the death of a pet, this is so gentle, on target, and realistic when examining the stages of the boy's emotions and final acceptance.
RELATED TITLES: Cohen, Miriam. *Jim's Dog Muffins.* Greenwillow, 1984. / Demas, Corinne. *Saying Goodbye to Lulu.* Little, Brown, 2004. / Durant, Alan. *Always and Forever.* Harcourt, 2004. / Heckert, Connie. *Dribbles.* Clarion, 1993. / James, Betsy. *Mary Ann.* Dutton, 1994. / Keller, Holly. *Goodbye, Max.* Greenwillow, 1987. / Pank, Rachel. *Under the Blackberries.* Scholastic, 1992. / Viorst, Judith. *The Tenth Good Thing About Barney.* Atheneum, 1971.
SUBJECTS: DEATH. EMOTIONS. GRIEF. MICE. PETS.

340   **Harshman, Marc. *The Storm.* Illus. by Mark Mohr. Dutton, 1995. 0-525-65150-0. Unp. Gr. 1–4**
Consigned to a wheelchair after his bike accident, Jonathan resents being singled out as different by his classmates. The farm boy proves his mettle to himself when he braves a tornado and single-handedly saves the family's horses.
GERM: Meet others who deal in pragmatic ways with being in wheelchairs in Nancy L. Carlson's *Arnie and the New Kid*, Jane Cowen-Fletcher's *Mama Zooms*, and Liz Damrell's *With the Wind*. Look up nonfiction books on tornadoes for dramatic pictures and supporting information.
RELATED TITLES: Adler, David A. *A Picture Book of Louis Braille.* Holiday House, 1997. / Byars, Betsy. *Tornado.* HarperCollins, 1996. / Carlson, Nancy L. *Arnie and the New Kid.* Viking, 1990. / Cowen-Fletcher, Jane. *Mama Zooms.* Scholastic, 1993. / Damrell, Liz. *With the Wind.* Orchard, 1991. / Davis, Patricia A. *Brian's Bird.* Albert Whitman, 2000. / Khan, Rukhsana. *Ruler of the Courtyard.* Viking, 2003. / Millman, Isaac. *Moses Goes to a Concert.* Farrar, 1998. / Osofsky, Audrey. *My Buddy.* Henry Holt, 1992. / Ruckman, Ivy. *Night of the Twisters.* Crowell, 1984.
SUBJECTS: COURAGE. FARM LIFE. PEOPLE WITH DISABILITIES. PHYSICALLY HANDICAPPED. STORMS. TORNADOES.

341   **Harter, Debbie. *The Animal Boogie.* Illus. by the author. Barefoot, 2000. 1-84148-094-0. Unp. Gr. PreK–1**
Down in the Indian jungle, follow the bear, monkey, elephant, vulture, leopard, cobra, and children as they shake, swing, stomp, flap, leap, slither, sway, and boogie woogie oogie through the action-filled verses and vibrant, full-bleed pen-and-ink and watercolor illustrations.
GERM: Music for the song is included in the back so you can sing and dance it with motions

and make up new verses. Pair this with Harter's book of ecosystems and animals, *Walking Through the Jungle.*

RELATED TITLES: Carle, Eric. *From Head to Toe.* HarperCollins, 1997. / Carle, Eric. *Today Is Monday.* Philomel, 1993. / Cauley, Lorinda Bryan. *Clap Your Hands.* Putnam, 1992. / Clark, Emma Chichester. *Follow the Leader!* Simon & Schuster, 2003. / Davis, Katie. *Who Hops?* Harcourt, 1998. / Halpern, Shari. *What Shall We Do When We All Go Out? A Traditional Song.* North-South, 1995. / Harter, Debbie. *Walking Through the Jungle.* Barefoot, 1997. / Hoberman, Mary Ann. *Miss Mary Mack: A Hand-Clapping Rhyme.* Little, Brown, 1998. / Jarrett, Clare. *The Best Picnic Ever.* Candlewick, 2004. / Martin, Bill, Jr. *Brown Bear, Brown Bear, What Do You See?* Henry Holt, 1983. / Paxton, Tom. *Going to the Zoo.* Morrow, 1996. / Williams, Sue. *I Went Walking.* Gulliver/Harcourt, 1990. / Williams, Sue. *Let's Go Visiting.* Harcourt, 1998. / Wilson, Karma. *Hilda Must Be Dancing.* McElderry, 2004.

SUBJECTS: ANIMALS—POETRY. DANCING. SONGS. STORIES IN RHYME. STORIES WITH SONGS.

342   Harter, Debbie. *Walking Through the Jungle.* Illus. by the author. Orchard, 1997. 0-531-30035-8. Unp. Gr. PreK–1

In this colorful and jaunty call-and-response story, a young girl is chased by a lion, a whale, a wolf, a crocodile, a snake, and a polar bear as she makes her way through jungle, ocean, mountain, river, desert, and ice.

GERM: This simple call-and-response rhyme—which you can act out and sing, if you make up a simple tune—is a great introduction to a wide variety of biomes or ecosystems. Children can come up with other animals— "I think I see a rattlesnake crawling after me"—and illustrate their habitats and the noises they make. Or collaboratively write and illustrate a new version of the story set in a city, farmyard, or lake.

RELATED TITLES: Carle, Eric. *From Head to Toe.* HarperCollins, 1997. / Clark, Emma Chichester. *Follow the Leader!* Simon & Schuster, 2003. / Davis, Katie. *Who Hops?* Harcourt, 1998. / Dodds, Dayle-Ann. *Do Bunnies Talk?* HarperCollins, 1992. / Harter, Debbie. *The Animal Boogie.* Barefoot, 2000. / Hoberman, Mary Ann. *It's Simple, Said Simon.* Knopf, 2001. / Jarrett, Clare. *The Best Picnic Ever.* Candlewick, 2004. / Jorgensen, Gail. *Gotcha!* Scholastic, 1997. / Martin, Bill, Jr. *Brown Bear, Brown Bear, What Do You See?* Henry Holt, 1983. / Park, Linda Sue. *Mung-Mung: A Folded Book of Animal Sounds.* Charlesbridge, 2004. / Polacco, Patricia. *Oh, Look!* Philomel, 2004. / Rosen, Michael. *We're Going on a Bear Hunt.* Macmillan, 1989. / Shapiro, Arnold L. *Who Says That?* Dutton, 1991. / Thomson, Pat. *The Squeaky, Creaky Bed.* Doubleday, 2003. / Walter, Virginia. *"Hi, Pizza Man!"* Orchard, 1995. / Williams, Sue. *I Went Walking.* Gulliver/Harcourt, 1990. / Williams, Sue. *Let's Go Visiting.* Harcourt, 1998.

SUBJECTS: ANIMAL SOUNDS. ANIMALS. CALL-AND-RESPONSE STORIES. CHANTABLE REFRAIN. CREATIVE DRAMA. ECOSYSTEMS. NOISE. STORIES IN RHYME.

343   Hartman, Bob. *The Wolf Who Cried Boy.* Illus. by Tim Raglin. Putnam, 2002. 0-399-23578-7. Unp. Gr. K–2

Detesting the lamburgers and Sloppy Does his mom makes for dinner, Little Wolf sets out to catch a nice boy so he can have a decent meal for once. En route, he decides to trick his parents by crying, "Boy! I've just seen a boy in the woods."

GERM: Compare this witty "Boy Who Cried Wolf" turnaround with a version of the original Aesop fable. Both would make wonderful Reader's Theaters to do with a group.

RELATED TITLES: Blundell, Tony. *Beware of Boys.* Greenwillow, 1992. / Child, Lauren. *Beware of the Storybook Wolves.* Scholastic, 2001. / Meddaugh, Susan. *Hog-Eye.* Houghton Mifflin, 1995. / Offen, Hilda. *Nice Work, Little Wolf!* Dutton, 1992. / Palatini, Margie. *Bad Boys.* HarperCollins, 2003. / Palatini, Margie. *The Web Files.* Hyperion, 2001. / Pinkney, Jerry. *Aesop's Fables.* SeaStar, 2000. / Scieszka, Jon. *The True Story of the 3 Little Pigs.* Viking, 1989. / Trivizas, Eugene. *The Three Little Wolves and the Big Bad Pig.* McElderry, 1993. / Vozar, David. *Yo, Hungry Wolf! A Nursery Rap.* Doubleday, 1993.

SUBJECTS: DIET. FOOD. HUMOROUS FICTION. PARODIES. READER'S THEATER. WOLVES.

344   Harvey, Amanda. *Dog Eared.* Illus. by the author. Doubleday, 2002. 0-385-90845-8. Unp. Gr. PreK–1

Walking home through the park with his girl, Lucy, leading him on the leash, Otis is aghast when another dog—large, brown, and sinister—pushes into him and growls, "Out of my way, Big Ears!" Otis is so demoralized, he becomes obsessed with his ears until Lucy comforts him with just the right words.

GERM: Midway through the story, ask for reactions: What does Otis do after that big dog insults him? Why did the dog say that to Otis? What should Otis do about it? At the end of the story, what made Otis stop worrying about his ears? How did he react when he ran into that bully again? How could Otis's response work for you when someone says something unkind?

RELATED TITLES: Edwards, Pamela Duncan. *Muldoon.* Hyperion, 2002. / Harvey, Amanda. *Dog Days.* Doubleday, 2003. / Harvey, Amanda. *Dog Gone.* Doubleday, 2004. / Howard, Arthur. *Cosmo Zooms.* Harcourt, 1999. / Miller, Sara Swan. *Three Stories You Can Read to Your Dog.* Houghton Mifflin, 1995. / Pilkey, Dav. *The Hallo-Wiener.* Blue Sky/Scholastic, 1995. / Provensen, Alice. *A Day in the Life of Murphy.* Simon & Schuster, 2003.

SUBJECTS: DOGS. EARS. SELF-ACCEPTANCE. SELF-ESTEEM. TEASING.

345   Hausman, Bonnie. *A to Z: Do You Ever Feel Like Me?* Photos by Sandi Fellman. Dutton, 1999. 0-525-46216-3. Unp. Gr. PreK–2

In this original and demonstrative alphabet of palpable feelings, each double-page spread contains a large color photo of an expressive child acting out one emotion and a facing paragraph describing a scenario that shows what he or she is feeling. Then listeners can supply the alphabetical word being described, from angry to zany.

GERM: Act out the body language of each emotion as you guess it. Write your own scenarios of how you are feeling and take photos of each other expressing these emotions. For a veggie-themed book with the same idea, see *How Are You Peeling? Foods with Moods* by Saxton Freymann and Joost Elffers.

RELATED TITLES: Bang, Molly. *When Sophie Gets Angry—Really, Really Angry.* Scholastic, 1999. / Carlson, Nancy. *ABC, I Like Me!* Viking, 1997. / Curtis, Jamie Lee. *Today I Feel Silly and Other Moods That Make My Day.* HarperCollins, 1998. / Frame, Jeron Ashford. *Yesterday I Had the Blues.* Tricycle, 2003. / Freymann, Saxton, and Joost Elffers. *How Are You Peeling? Foods with Moods.* Scholastic, 1999. / Harper, Jessica. *Lizzy's Ups and Downs: Not an Ordinary School Day.* HarperCollins, 2004. / Modesitt, Jeanne. *Sometimes I Feel Like a Mouse: A Book About Feelings.* Scholastic, 1992.

SUBJECTS: ALPHABET BOOKS. CREATIVE DRAMA. EMOTIONS.

346   Havill, Juanita. *Jamaica and the Substitute Teacher.* Illus. by Anne Sibley O'Brien. Houghton Mifflin, 1999. 0-395-90503-6. Unp. Gr. PreK–1

Wanting to seem perfect to her nice substitute teacher, Jamaica surreptitiously copies a word from her friend Brianna's paper during a spelling test.

GERM: This one's a good discussion starter on doing your own work and why it's wrong to copy from someone else. Discussion points: Why did Jamaica copy from Brianna's paper? How did she feel when she got 100% on her test? How did she take responsibility for what she had done?

RELATED TITLES: Havill, Juanita. *Jamaica and Brianna.* Houghton Mifflin, 1993. / Havill, Juanita. *Jamaica's Blue Marker.* Houghton Mifflin, 1995. / Henkes, Kevin. *Lilly's Purple Plastic Purse.* Greenwillow, 1996. / Park, Barbara. *Junie B., First Grader: Cheater Pants.* Random House, 2003. / Rathmann, Peggy. *Ruby the Copycat.* Scholastic, 1991. / Soto, Gary. *Too Many Tamales.* Putnam, 1993.

SUBJECTS: CHEATING. HONESTY. MULTICULTURAL BOOKS. SCHOOLS. SELF-ESTEEM. SUBSTITUTE TEACHERS. TEACHERS.

347   Havill, Juanita. *Jamaica's Blue Marker.* Illus. by Anne Sibley O'Brien. Houghton Mifflin, 1995. 0-395-72036-2. Unp. Gr. PreK–1

Reluctant to share her markers with her classmate Russell, Jamaica is outraged when he scribbles all over her drawing with a blue marker and refuses to apologize. Then she finds out why he is so angry: he's moving.

GERM: Discussion point: Why do you think Russell scribbled all over Jamaica's picture? How does Russell feel about moving? What are some of the ways you can help people feel better when they are angry or upset?

RELATED TITLES: Ballard, Robin. *Good-bye, House.* Greenwillow, 1994. / Bang, Molly. *When Sophie Gets Angry—Really, Really Angry.* Scholastic, 1999. / Caseley, Judith. *Bully.* Greenwillow, 2001. / Havill, Juanita. *Jamaica and Brianna.* Houghton Mifflin, 1993. / Havill, Juanita. *Jamaica and the Substitute Teacher.* Houghton Mifflin, 1999. / O'Donnell, Elizabeth Lee. *Maggie Doesn't Want to Move.* Four Winds, 1987. / O'Neill, Alexis. *The Recess Queen.* Scholastic, 2002. / Shannon, David. *David Goes to School.* Scholastic, 1999. / Vail, Rachel. *Sometimes I'm Bombaloo.* Scholastic, 2002.

SUBJECTS: AFRICAN AMERICANS. APOLOGIES. ASIAN AMERICANS. BEHAVIOR. FRIENDSHIP. MOVING, HOUSEHOLD. MULTICULTURAL BOOKS. SCHOOLS.

348   **Hawkins, Colin, and Jacqui Hawkins.** *The Fairytale News.* **Illus. by the authors. Candlewick, 2004. 0-7636-2166-8. Unp. Gr. PreK–3**

Old Mother Hubbard's son, Jack, gets a job delivering the *Fairytale News*, and he sets off on his route to the houses of the Three Bears, Red Riding Hood, and that giant up the beanstalk. At the back of this ebullient book is a four-page, heavy-stock, newsprint copy of the newspaper, filled with news, sports, classified ads, and advice from Mother Goose herself.

GERM: Write new fairy tale-based articles and features for a second edition of the paper.

RELATED TITLES: Ada, Alma Flor. *Dear Peter Rabbit.* Atheneum, 1994. / Ahlberg, Janet, and Allan Ahlberg. *The Jolly Postman.* Little, Brown, 1986. / Child, Lauren. *Beware of the Storybook Wolves.* Scholastic, 2001. / Child, Lauren. *Who's Afraid of the Big Bad Book?* Hyperion, 2003. / Cowell, Cressida. *Little Bo Peep's Library Book.* Orchard, 1999. / Elya, Susan Middleton. *Fairy Trails: A Story Told in English and Spanish.* Bloomsbury, 2005. / Hoberman, Mary Ann. *You Read to Me, I'll Read to You: Very Short Fairy Tales to Read Together.* Little, Brown, 2004. / McClements, George. *Jake Gander, Storyville Detective.* Hyperion, 2002. / Scieszka, Jon. *The True Story of the 3 Little Pigs.* Viking, 1989. / Stanley, Diane. *The Giant and the Beanstalk.* HarperCollins, 2004. / Stevens, Janet, and Susan Stevens Crummel. *And the Dish Ran Away with the Spoon.* Harcourt, 2001. / Wiesner, David. *The Three Pigs.* Clarion, 2001. / Zalben, Jane Breskin. *Hey, Mama Goose.* Dutton, 2005.

SUBJECTS: BEARS. CHARACTERS IN LITERATURE. FAIRY TALES—SATIRE. GIANTS. HUMOROUS FICTION. NEWSPAPERS. PARODIES. TOY AND MOVABLE BOOKS. WOLVES.

349   **Hayes, Joe.** *A Spoon for Every Bite.* **Illus. by Rebecca Leer. Orchard, 1996. 0-531-09499-5. Unp. Gr. 2–6**

A poor couple ask their wealthy neighbor to be godfather to their new baby, but in order to invite the man to dinner, they must save their pennies to afford a third spoon. The rich man, who boasts that he has so many spoons that he could use a different one every day for a year, is envious when the poor woman tells him that they have a friend who uses a different spoon for every bite he eats.

GERM: Before you reveal the ending to this tale, inspired by various versions told in the Southwest, have your listeners try to figure out how one could have so many spoons. Bring in tortillas and heat up a nice pot of beans so all can see what it's like to have a new spoon with every bite.

RELATED TITLES: Compestine, Ying Chang. *The Story of Chopsticks.* Holiday House, 2001. / Friedman, Ina R. *How My Parents Learned to Eat.* Houghton Mifflin, 1984. / Hayes, Joe. *Juan Verdades: The Man Who Couldn't Tell a Lie.* Orchard, 2001. / Lauber, Patricia. *What You Never Knew About Fingers, Forks, and Chopsticks.* Simon & Schuster, 1999.

SUBJECTS: EATING CUSTOMS. FOOD HABITS. HISPANIC AMERICANS. MULTICULTURAL BOOKS. PICTURE BOOKS FOR ALL AGES. PRIDE AND VANITY. SOUTHWEST. TABLEWARE. TORTILLAS. WEALTH.

350   **Helquist, Brett.** *Roger, the Jolly Pirate.* **HarperCollins, 2004. 0-06-623806-4. Unp. Gr. PreK–3**

Sent down below to the ship's hold every time there's serious pirating to be done, incompetent pirate Jolly Roger decides one day to do something to make the other pirates like him. While their ship is under siege, Roger sets about baking a cake, though he somehow mistakes a cannon for a big iron pot and manages to get himself blown through the deck in the middle of the battle.

GERM: Discuss how Roger's accident made him a hero and became the basis for the first pirate flag, the Jolly Roger. Present this as an example of a humorous literary pourquoi tale, made up by the author, when students are writing their own how-and-why stories. With younger children, pair this with Melinda Long's *How I Became a Pirate* for a Shiver-Me-Timbers Storyhour. Don't forget to sing "The Ballad of Jolly Roger," with words and music provided at the back of the book.

RELATED TITLES: Alexander, Lloyd. *How the Cat Swallowed Thunder.* Dutton, 2000. / Auch, Mary Jane. *The Princess and the Pizza.* Holiday House, 2002. / Compestine, Ying Chang. *The Story of Paper.* Holiday House, 2003. / Cox, Judy. *Rabbit Pirates: A Tale of the Spinach Main.* Harcourt, 1999. / Faulkner, Matt. *The Amazing Voyage of Jackie Grace.* Scholastic, 1987. / Feiffer, Jules. *Meanwhile . . .* HarperCollins, 1997. / Long, Melinda. *How I Became a Pirate.* Harcourt, 2003. / McPhail, David. *Edward and the Pirates.* Little, Brown, 1997.

SUBJECTS: HUMOROUS FICTION. PIRATES. POURQUOI TALES. STORIES WITH SONGS.

351   **Henkes, Kevin.** *Kitten's First Full Moon.* **Illus. by the author. Greenwillow, 2004. 0-06-058828-4. Unp. Gr. PreK–K**

When she sees her first full moon, Kitten thinks it's a little bowl of milk in the sky, and she wants it. She jumps at it, and chases it, and climbs a tall tree all the way to the top, but still she can't reach it, poor Kitten. This simple but enticing Caldecott winner was drawn in silvery shades of gray gouache and colored pencil with the adventurous white kitten outlined in thick black lines.

GERM: Act out the story in narrative pantomime. As you read it aloud the second time, have your children become the kitten as she tries doggedly for the moon and ends up with a nice bowl of milk back home after all.

RELATED TITLES: Asch, Frank. *Happy Birthday, Moon.* Prentice-Hall, 1982. / Asch, Frank. *Moongame.* Prentice-Hall, 1987. / Barton, Byron. *The Wee Little Woman.* HarperCollins, 1995. / Bauer, Marion Dane. *If You Were Born a Kitten.* Simon & Schuster, 1997. / Carle, Eric. *Papa, Please Get the Moon for Me.* Simon & Schuster, 1991. / Cauley, Lorinda Bryan. *The Three Little Kittens.* Putnam, 1982. / Chadwick, Tim. *Cabbage Moon.* Orchard, 1994. / Cordsen, Carol Foskett. *The Milkman.* Dutton, 2005. / Fleming, Denise. *Mama Cat Has Three Kittens.* Henry Holt, 1998. / Gag, Wanda. *Millions of Cats.* Coward, 1928. / McNulty, Faith. *If You Decide to Go to the Moon.* Scholastic, 2005. / Preston, Edna Mitchell. *Squawk to the Moon, Little Goose.* Viking, 1974. / Roth, Susan L. *Cinnamon's Day Out: A Gerbil Adventure.* Dial, 1998. / Simmons, Jane. *Little Fern's First Winter.* Little, Brown, 2001. / Waddell, Martin. *Can't You Sleep, Little Bear?* Candlewick, 1992.

SUBJECTS: ANIMALS—INFANCY. CALDECOTT MEDAL. CATS. CREATIVE DRAMA. MILK. MOON.

352   Henkes, Kevin. *Lilly's Purple Plastic Purse.* Illus. by the author. Greenwillow, 1996. 0-688-12898-X. Unp. Gr. PreK–2

Lilly, a young mouse, becomes so enraged when her adored teacher, Mr. Slinger, confiscates her new purse and sunglasses that she draws a dreadful caricature of him and slips it into his book bag. How dare that mean teacher take her show-and-tell treasures! "I do not want to be a teacher when I grow up!" Lilly proclaims. All will appreciate this honest and knowing tribute to wise and forgiving teachers who nurture their children even through tough times.

GERM: Discuss anger and negative emotions, which can lead us to say mean things when we're really mad. Then talk about how to make amends. Have you ever had to apologize for something you did wrong? How did you do it? What did you say? You'll love Mr. Slinger's *Lightbulb Lab, Where Great Ideas Are Born.* Ask your geniuses to list their own great ideas. Why does Lilly want to be a teacher when she grows up?

RELATED TITLES: Allard, Harry. *Miss Nelson Is Missing.* Houghton, 1985. / Bang, Molly. *When Sophie Gets Angry—Really, Really Angry.* Scholastic, 1999. / Brown, Marc. *Arthur's Teacher Trouble.* Little, Brown, 1987. / Carlson, Nancy. *Henry's Show and Tell.* Viking, 2004. / Greene, Stephanie. *Show and Tell.* Clarion, 1998. / Henkes, Kevin. *Chrysanthemum.* Greenwillow, 1991. / Henkes, Kevin. *Julius, the Baby of the World.* Greenwillow, 1990. / Henkes, Kevin. *Lily's Big Day.* Greenwillow, 2006. / Henkes, Kevin. *Owen.* Greenwillow, 1993. / Henkes, Kevin. *Sheila Rae the Brave.* Greenwillow, 1987. / Houston, Gloria. *My Great Aunt Arizona.* HarperCollins, 1992. / Lasky, Kathryn. *Show and Tell Bunnies.* Little, Brown, 1998. / Park, Barbara. *Junie B. Jones and Some Sneaky Peeky Spying.* Random House, 1994. / Saltzberg, Barney. *Crazy Hair Day.* Candlewick, 2003. / Shannon, David. *David Goes to School.* Scholastic, 1999. / Vail, Rachel. *Sometimes I'm Bombaloo.* Scholastic, 2002.

SUBJECTS: ANGER. APOLOGIES. CONFLICT RESOLUTION. EMOTIONS. FORGIVENESS. MICE. SCHOOLS. SHOW-AND-TELL PRESENTATIONS. TEACHERS.

353   Henkes, Kevin. *Wemberly Worried.* Illus. by the author. Greenwillow, 2000. 0-688-17027-7. Unp. Gr. PreK–1

Spotted mouse Wemberly worries about things big and small, all day and night. Her newest worry is the biggest yet: What will happen when she starts school? Wisely, her astute teacher, Miss Peachum, pairs Wemberly with another stripe-clothed, doll-clutching worrier, a mouse named Jewel, and the two become instant friends.

GERM: For your worrywarts afraid that everything is not coming up roses, this jewel of a story will help assuage their fears. Ask children to talk about (and draw a picture of) a time they worried unnecessarily, and to describe their first-day recollections. For older children, this memory enhancer will take them back to their kindergarten years, but also get them talking about how they can allay their own fears before a test or other stressful event.

RELATED TITLES: Child, Lauren. *I Am Too Absolutely Small for School.* Candlewick, 2004. / Dannenberg, Julie. *First Day Jitters.* Charlesbridge, 2000. / Davis, Katie. *Kindergarten Rocks.* Harcourt, 2005. / Harris, Robie H. *I Am Not Going to School Today!* McElderry, 2003. / Henkes, Kevin. *Chrysanthemum.* Greenwillow, 1991. / Lasky, Kathryn. *Lunch Bunnies.* Little, Brown, 1996. / Lester, Helen. *Something Might Happen.* Houghton Mifflin, 2003. / London, Jonathan. *Froggy Goes to School.* Viking, 1996. / McGhee, Alison. *Countdown to Kindergarten.* Harcourt, 2002. / Poydar, Nancy. *First Day, Hooray.* Holiday House, 1999. / Schwartz, Amy. *Annabelle Swift, Kindergartner.* Orchard, 1988. / Slate, Joseph. *Miss Bindergarten Gets Ready for Kindergarten.* Dutton, 1994.

/ Strete, Craig. *The Rattlesnake Who Went to School.* Putnam, 2004. / Wells, Rosemary. *My Kindergarten.* Hyperion, 2004. / Wells, Rosemary. *Timothy Goes to School.* Viking, 2000.

SUBJECTS: FIRST DAY OF SCHOOL. MICE. SCHOOLS. WORRYING.

354   Herold, Maggie Rugg. *A Very Important Day.* Illus. by Catherine Stock. Morrow, 1995. 0-688-13066-6. Unp. Gr. 1–5

Follow a dozen families from around the globe who are now settled in the United States, as they make their way through a snowstorm to a New York City courtroom. There we witness their swearing in, along with 200 others, as U.S. citizens.

GERM: Look at the immigrant experience a century ago, with Avi's *Silent Movie*, and in the present, with Marion Hess Pomeranc's *The American Wei.* Discuss: What does it mean to be an American citizen?

RELATED TITLES: Avi. *Silent Movie.* Atheneum, 2003. / Bartone, Elisa. *American Too.* Lothrop, 1996. / Bierman, Carol. *Journey to Ellis Island: How My Father Came to America.* Hyperion, 1998. / Bunting, Eve. *A Picnic in October.* Harcourt, 1999. / Catrow, David. *We the Kids: The Preamble to the Constitution of the United States.* Dial, 2002. / Cheney, Lynne. *America: A Patriotic Primer.* Simon & Schuster, 2002. / Freedman, Russell. *Immigrant Kids.* Dutton, 1980. / Levine, Ellen. *If Your Name Was Changed at Ellis Island.* Scholastic, 1993. / Maestro, Betsy, and Giulio Maestro. *A More Perfect Union: The Story of Our Constitution.* Lothrop, 1987. / Pomeranc, Marion Hess. *The American Wei.* Albert Whitman, 1998. / Sandler, Martin W. *Immigrants.* HarperCollins, 1995. / Yang, Belle. *Hannah Is My Name.* Candlewick, 2004.

SUBJECTS: IMMIGRATION AND EMIGRATION. MULTICULTURAL BOOKS. NATURALIZATION. NEW YORK CITY.

355   Hesse, Karen. *The Cats in Krasinski Square.* Illus. by Wendy Watson. Scholastic, 2004. 0-439-43540-4. Unp. Gr. 3–6

In a poignant, terrible, heart-wrenching picture book, loosely based on an actual incident, a young girl relates how she and her older sister Mira, who escaped the Warsaw Ghetto, take part in an effort to smuggle food to Jews still trapped there. When the Gestapo gets wind of their plan, the resistance workers gather up some of the homeless cats at the Wall of the Ghetto and set them loose at the train station to foil the Nazis and their police dogs.

GERM: As part of a Holocaust studies unit, this can open the discussion of how some people managed to fight back against the Nazi machine during World War II.

RELATED TITLES: Abels, Chana Byers. *The Children We Remember.* Greenwillow, 1986. / Adler, David A. *One Yellow Daffodil: A Hanukkah Story.* Harcourt, 1995. / Cohn, Janice. *The Christmas Menorahs: How a Town Fought Hate.* Albert Whitman, 1995. / Levine, Karen. *Hana's Suitcase.* Albert Whitman, 2003. / Lowry, Lois. *Number the Stars.* Houghton Mifflin, 1989. / McCann, Michelle R. *Luba: The Angel of Bergen-Belsen.* Tricycle, 2003. / Millman, Isaac. *Hidden Child.* Farrar, 2005. / Polacco, Patricia. *The Butterfly.* Philomel, 2000. / Propp, Vera. *When the Soldiers Were Gone.* Putnam, 1999. / Rubin, Susan Goldman. *The Flag with Fifty-Six Stars: A Gift from the Survivors of Mauthausen.* Holiday House, 2005. / Schnur, Steven. *The Tie Man's Miracle: A Chanukah Tale.* Morrow, 1995.

SUBJECTS: CATS. HEROES. HISTORICAL FICTION. HOLOCAUST, JEWISH (1939–1945). JEWS. POLAND. SISTERS. WORLD WAR, 1939–1945—FICTION.

356   Hest, Amy. *Baby Duck and the Bad Eyeglasses.* Illus. by Jill Barton. Candlewick, 1996. 1-56402-680-9. Unp. Gr. PreK–1

Afraid to hop, dance, or play in her despised new glasses, Baby Duck feels terribly sorry for herself until Grampa points out that his glasses are the same color and reassures her that she can splash and twirl without mishap.

GERM: Somehow, Grampa always knows the right words needed to make Baby Duck feel loved and secure, which the huge expressive watercolors show so perfectly in all of the books in the Baby Duck series. Ask children to draw and talk about members of their families who can always cheer them out of a slump.

RELATED TITLES: Brown, Marc. *Arthur's Eyes.* Joy Street, 1979. / Cohen, Peter. *Boris's Glasses.* R&S, 2003. / Giff, Patricia Reilly. *Watch Out, Ronald Morgan.* Viking, 1985. / Hest, Amy. *In the Rain with Baby Duck.* Candlewick, 1995. / Hest, Amy. *Off to School, Baby Duck.* Candlewick, 1999. / Hest, Amy. *You're the Boss, Baby Duck.* Candlewick, 1997. / Numeroff, Laura. *Chimps Don't Wear Glasses.* Simon & Schuster, 1995. / Smith, Lane. *Glasses: Who Needs 'Em?* Viking, 1991.

SUBJECTS: DUCKS. EYEGLASSES. GRANDFATHERS.

357   Hest, Amy. *In the Rain with Baby Duck.* **Illus. by Jill Barton. Candlewick, 1995. 1-56402-532-2. Unp. Gr. PreK–1**

Baby Duck is mad. She doesn't like walking in the rain, but it's Pancake Sunday, a Duck family tradition, and Grampa is waiting on the other side of town for her and her parents. All the way there, she grumbles about the mud and sings a pouty rain song, but Grampa understands exactly how she feels. He takes her to the attic where he finds the beautiful umbrella and matching pair of red rain boots that once belonged to her mother. Suddenly, the rainy day is perfect.

GERM: With huge pencil-and-watercolor illustrations, this is the best book ever for rainy-day story hours. The language is sublime: "They waddled. They shimmied. They hopped in all the puddles." And Grampa is an empathetic fellow who knows how to make a duckling feel special. Follow the twosome through their other books, including *You're the Boss, Baby Duck*, where she's not so happy about Hot Stuff, her new baby sister.

RELATED TITLES: Cooney, Nancy Evans. *The Umbrella Day.* Philomel, 1989. / Hest, Amy. *Baby Duck and the Bad Eyeglasses.* Candlewick, 1996. / Hest, Amy. *Guess Who, Baby Duck.* Candlewick, 2004. / Hest, Amy. *Make the Team, Baby Duck.* Candlewick, 2002. / Hest, Amy. *Off to School, Baby Duck.* Candlewick, 1999. / Hest, Amy. *You're the Boss, Baby Duck.* Candlewick, 1997. / Raffi. *Five Little Ducks.* Crown, 1988. / Stojic, Manya. *Rain.* Crown, 2000. / Stott, Dorothy. *Too Much.* Dutton, 1990. / Wood, Audrey. *The Napping House.* Harcourt, 1984.

SUBJECTS: DUCKS. GRANDFATHERS. RAIN AND RAINFALL. UMBRELLAS.

358   Hest, Amy. *Mr. George Baker.* **Illus. by Jon J Muth. Candlewick, 2004. 0-7636-1233-2. Unp. Gr. K–3**

Harry introduces us to his friend Mr. George Baker with his baggy pants and red bookbag, waiting on the stoop. He's a hundred years old, no kidding, but he's never learned how to read. Each day, young Harry and old George get on the school bus and go to their own classrooms, and both of them are learning to read. Harry thinks it's hard but, "We can do it," says George.

GERM: The warm, wise watercolors of the old African American drummer and the young white boy who dotes on him are so affecting. All will get the message: you're never too old to learn, and everyone needs to read. Discussion points: Why does Mr. George Baker want to read? Why do you want to read? When you are a hundred years old, what do you want to have done with your life? Obvious tie-ins are Eve Bunting's *The Wednesday Surprise*, about a girl who teaches her grandmother to read, and Jo Ellen Bogart's *Jeremiah Learns to Read*. Elizabeth Fitzgerald Howard's *Virgie Goes to School with Us Boys* and Marie Bradby's *More Than Anything Else*, about Booker T. Washington as a boy, both take place during Reconstruction and are true tales of two African American children who burned with the desire to read.

RELATED TITLES: Bogart, Jo Ellen. *Jeremiah Learns to Read.* Orchard, 1999. / Bunting, Eve. *The Wednesday Surprise.* Clarion, 1989. / Daly, Niki. *Once Upon a Time.* Farrar, 2002. / Heide, Florence Parry, and Judith Heide Gilliland. *The Day of Ahmed's Secret.* Lothrop, 1990. / Howard, Elizabeth Fitzgerald. *Virgie Goes to School with Us Boys.* Simon & Schuster, 2000. / Joosse, Barbara M. *Hot City.* Philomel, 2004. / Mora, Pat. *Tomás and the Library Lady.* Knopf, 1997. / Paterson, Katherine. *Marvin One Too Many.* HarperCollins, 2001. / Polacco, Patricia. *Aunt Chip and the Great Triple Creek Dam Affair.* Philomel, 1996. / Polacco, Patricia. *Thank You, Mr. Falker.* Philomel, 1998. / Stanley, Diane. *Raising Sweetness.* Putnam, 1999. / Williams, Suzanne. *Library Lil.* Dial, 1997. / Winch, John. *The Old Woman Who Loved to Read.* Holiday House, 1997. / Wishinsky, Frieda. *Give Maggie a Chance.* Fitzhenry & Whiteside, 2002.

SUBJECTS: AFRICAN AMERICANS. BOOKS AND READING. ELDERLY. FRIENDSHIP. LITERACY. MULTICULTURAL BOOKS. PICTURE BOOKS FOR ALL AGES. SCHOOLS.

359   Hest, Amy. *Off to School, Baby Duck.* **Illus. by Jill Barton. Candlewick, 1999. 0-7636-0244-2. Unp. Gr. PreK–K**

Baby Duck is nervous about starting school until Grampa interviews her new teacher, Miss Posy, asks pointed questions about how she runs her classroom ("Do you sing songs in that schoolhouse?"), and allays Baby Duck's fears.

GERM: Ask children to recall, draw, and/or write about their first recollections of school. Compare and contrast: How is Baby Duck's school the same as and different from yours?

RELATED TITLES: Harris, Robie H. *I Am Not Going to School Today!* McElderry, 2003. / Henkes, Kevin. *Chrysanthemum.* Greenwillow, 1991. / Henkes, Kevin. *Wemberly Worried.* Greenwillow, 2000. / Hest, Amy. *Baby Duck and the Bad Eyeglasses.* Candlewick, 1995. / Hest, Amy. *In the Rain with Baby Duck.* Candlewick, 1995. / Lasky, Kathryn. *Lunch Bunnies.* Little, Brown, 1996. / London, Jonathan. *Froggy Goes to School.* Viking, 1996. / McCloskey, Robert. *Make Way for Ducklings.* Viking, 1941. / Poydar, Nancy. *First Day, Hooray!* Holiday

House, 1999. / Slate, Joseph. *Miss Bindergarten Gets Ready for Kindergarten.* Dutton, 1996. / Wells, Rosemary. *Timothy Goes to School.* Dial, 1981.

SUBJECTS: DUCKS. FEAR. FIRST DAY OF SCHOOL. GRANDFATHERS.

360   **Hest, Amy.** *When Jessie Came Across the Sea.* **Illus. by P. J. Lynch. Candlewick, 1997. 0-7636-0094-6. 40pp. Gr. 2–5**

The rabbi of a small Eastern European shtetl gives his own ticket to America to Jessie, a 13-year-old orphan. Once in New York City, Jessie is expected to help the widow of the rabbi's brother with the sewing in her dress shop. Though Jessie is heartsick at leaving her grandmother, she makes the voyage, becoming friends en route with Lou, a shoemaker's son, and settles into life as a seamstress with the kind woman she calls Cousin Kay.

GERM: Sumptuous, oversized watercolor and gouache paintings provide many details about life in turn-of-the-century America. For studies of immigration and emigration, talk about why people wanted to come to America back then. The Tenement Museum in New York City has a wonderful Web site where you can take a virtual tour of a restored tenement on Orchard Street on the Lower East Side of Manhattan: <www.tenement.org>.

RELATED TITLES: Avi. *Silent Movie.* Atheneum, 2003. / Bartone, Elisa. *American Too.* Lothrop, 1996. / Bartone, Elisa. *Peppe the Lamplighter.* Lothrop, 1993. / Bierman, Carol. *Journey to Ellis Island: How My Father Came to America.* Hyperion, 1998. / Freedman, Russell. *Immigrant Kids.* Dutton, 1980. / Levine, Ellen. *If Your Name Was Changed at Ellis Island.* Scholastic, 1993. / Maestro, Betsy, and Giulio Maestro. *A More Perfect Union: The Story of Our Constitution.* Lothrop, 1987. / Pomeranc, Marion Hess. *The American Wei.* Albert Whitman, 1998. / Sandler, Martin W. *Immigrants.* HarperCollins, 1995. / Wells, Rosemary. *Streets of Gold.* Dial, 1999. / Woodruff, Elvira. *The Memory Coat.* Scholastic, 1999. / Woodruff, Elvira. *The Orphan of Ellis Island: A Time Travel Adventure.* Scholastic, 1997.

SUBJECTS: GRANDMOTHERS. HISTORICAL FICTION. IMMIGRATION AND EMIGRATION. JEWS. NEW YORK CITY. ORPHANS. PICTURE BOOKS FOR OLDER READERS. VOYAGES AND TRAVELS.

361   **Hicks, Barbara Jean.** *Jitterbug Jam.* **Illus. by Alexis Deacon. Farrar, 2005. 0-374-33685-7. Unp. Gr. PreK–3**

Bobo, a little horned monster whose big brother calls him a fraidy-cat, is indeed scared of the human boy who hides in Bobo's big old monster closet at night and sneaks under his bed in the morning. What monster wouldn't be? Then his grampa, Boo-Dad, comes to visit, and over big old monster slabs of homemade bread with jitterbug jam, he tells Bobo a scary story of the olden days, when he was young and met a girl human. He gives Bobo some good advice on the best way to deal with a boy, but when Bobo finally meets that boy under the bed, he decides instead that he'd like to be friends.

GERM: Not only is Bobo's colloquial narrative perfect for reading aloud, but Deacon's captivating full-bleed illustrations, painted on sand- and tan-colored pages, are true originals, full of the heart and soul of that monster boy. There's an open ending that will get your monsters chattering about what might happen next between that redheaded boy and Bobo. Another story about monster/human friendship is *Leonardo the Terrible Monster* by Mo Willems.

RELATED TITLES: Bunting, Eve. *Ghost's Hour, Spook's Hour.* Clarion, 1987. / Crowe, Robert L. *Clyde Monster.* Dutton, 1976. / Deacon, Alexis. *Beegu.* Farrar, 2003. / Emberley, Ed. *Go Away, Big Green Monster!* Little, Brown, 1993. / Gackenbach, Dick. *Harry and the Terrible Whatzit.* Clarion, 1977. / Mayer, Mercer. *There's a Nightmare in My Closet.* Dial, 1968. / Park, Barbara. *Psssst! It's Me . . . the Bogeyman.* Atheneum, 1998. / Viorst, Judith. *My Mama Says There Aren't Any Zombies, Ghosts, Vampires, Creatures, Demons, Monsters, Fiends, Goblins, or Things.* Atheneum, 1973. / Willems, Mo. *Leonardo the Terrible Monster.* Hyperion, 2005. / Willis, Jeanne. *The Monster Bed.* Lothrop, 1987.

SUBJECTS: BEDTIME STORIES. BROTHERS. FAMILY LIFE. FEAR. MONSTERS. PERSONAL NARRATIVES.

362   **High, Linda Oatman.** *Winter Shoes for Shadow Horse.* **Illus. by Ted Lewin. Boyds Mills, 2001. 1-56397-472-X. Unp. Gr. K–3**

A boy watches as his blacksmith father forges a set of winter shoes for a large white horse named Shadow Horse and wonders when he will be allowed to have a try. Papa replaces three of the horse's shoes, nailing and trimming them, and then turns to his son. "Your turn," he says, and under Papa's guidance, the boy does just fine. Dark nighttime watercolors, lit by the light of the forge, portray the bonding of father and son as they attend to the horse.

GERM: Discuss: What have your parents taught you to do? What difficult task have you done with their patient instruction and guidance?

RELATED TITLES: Armstrong, Jennifer. *Magnus at the Fire*. Simon & Schuster, 2005. / Christiansen, Candace. *The Ice Horse*. Dial, 1993. / Doherty, Berlie. *Snowy*. Dial, 1993. / Herriot, James. *Bonny's Big Day*. St. Martin's, 1987. / High, Linda Oatman. *Barn Savers*. Boyds Mills, 1999. / Lewin, Ted. *The Storytellers*. Lothrop, 1998. / Springer, Nancy. *Music of Their Hooves: Poems About Horses*. Boyds Mills, 1994.

SUBJECTS: FARM LIFE. FATHERS AND SONS. HORSES. PICTURE BOOKS FOR ALL AGES.

363   **Hindley, Judy.** *Do Like a Duck Does!* **Illus. by Ivan Bates. Candlewick, 2002. 0-7636-1668-0. Unp. Gr. PreK–1**

Five little ducklings are following their mother, doing everything she does, when up struts a long-tailed, furry stranger with a foxy smile. He claims he's a big, brown duck, much to the skepticism of Mama Duck.

GERM: This rhyming storytime gem is ideal for acting out. Some of the children can be the ducklings, following you, their Mama, and the others can play the fox, who has a hard time doing things just like a duck, especially when it comes to swimming in the river. Then have ducks and foxes switch parts and do it again! Play Mama Says, your own duck-like version of Simon Says.

RELATED TITLES: Arnosky, Jim. *All Night Near the Water*. Putnam, 1994. / Buzzeo, Toni. *Dawdle Duckling*. Dial, 2003. / Crebbin, June. *Danny's Duck*. Candlewick, 1995. / Edwards, Pamela Duncan. *McGillycuddy Could!* HarperCollins, 2005. / Fox, Mem. *Hattie and the Fox*. Bradbury, 1987. / Gerstein, Mordicai. *Follow Me!* Morrow, 1983. / Hutchins, Pat. *Rosie's Walk*. Bradbury, 1987. / McCloskey, Robert. *Make Way for Ducklings*. Viking, 1941. / McKissack, Patricia C. *Flossie and the Fox*. Dial, 1986. / Marshall, James. *Wings: A Tale of Two Chickens*. Dutton, 1986. / Peters, Lisa Westberg. *Cold Little Duck, Duck, Duck*. Greenwillow, 2000. / Raffi. *Five Little Ducks*. Crown, 1988. / Rankin, Joan. *Wow! It's Great Being a Duck*. McElderry, 1998. / Silverman, Erica. *Don't Fidget a Feather*. Macmillan, 1994. / Simmons, Jane. *Come Along, Daisy*. Little, Brown, 1998. / Whippo, Walt, and Bernard Zaritzky. *Little White Duck*. Little, Brown, 2000. / Whybrow, Ian. *Quacky Quack-Quack!* Four Winds, 1991.

SUBJECTS: CREATIVE DRAMA. DUCKS. FOXES. STORIES IN RHYME.

364   **Hines, Gary.** *A Christmas Tree in the White House.* **Illus. by Alexandra Wallner. Henry Holt, 1998. 0-8050-5076-0. 32pp. Gr. 1–4**

The basic elements are all true in this good-natured, fictionalized account of the year conservationist President Theodore Roosevelt decided to set a good example for all Americans by forgoing a White House Christmas tree. His two youngest boys, Quentin and Archie, smuggled a tiny tree through their bedroom window and attempted to hide it in their closet.

GERM: Read the notes about Roosevelt and his family at the back of the book and show the accompanying photograph. *Young Teddy Roosevelt* by Cheryl Harness is a splendid picture-book biography.

RELATED TITLES: Cooney, Barbara. *Eleanor*. Viking, 1996. / Coulter, Laurie. *When John and Caroline Lived in the White House*. Hyperion, 2000. / Davis, Gibbs. *Wackiest White House Pets*. Scholastic, 2004. / Fleming, Candace. *A Big Cheese for the White House*. DK Ink, 1999. / Harness, Cheryl. *Ghosts of the White House*. Simon & Schuster, 1998. / Harness, Cheryl. *Young Teddy Roosevelt*. National Geographic, 1998. / Houston, Gloria. *The Year of the Perfect Christmas Tree*. Dial, 1988. / Krull, Kathleen. *Lives of the Presidents: Fame, Shame (and What the Neighbors Thought)*. Harcourt, 1998. / Ryan, Pam Muñoz. *Amelia and Eleanor Go for a Ride*. Scholastic, 1999. / St. George, Judith. *So You Want to Be President?* Philomel, 2000. / St. George, Judith. *You're on Your Way, Teddy Roosevelt!* Philomel, 2004. / Stier, Catherine. *If I Were President*. Albert Whitman, 1999.

SUBJECTS: CHRISTMAS TREES. CONSERVATION OF NATURAL RESOURCES. PRESIDENTS. ROOSEVELT, THEODORE. TREES. WHITE HOUSE.

365   **Ho, Minfong.** *Hush! A Thai Lullaby.* **Illus. by Holly Meade. Orchard, 1996. 0-531-08850-2. Unp. Gr. PreK–1**

While her little one is sleeping in the hammock, the child's mother hushes 11 nearby animals, from mosquito to elephant, chiding them for making too much noise near her thatched home and farmyard. Gentle, eloquent, cut-paper collage illustrations give a glimpse of life in the Thai countryside.

GERM: Children can repeat the mother's refrain and try out all the Thai animal noises with you ("hoom-praa," trumpets the elephant), comparing them with the animal noises we use in North

America. Talk over: What animal noises might we hear as we fall asleep? Play peek-a-boo Thai style with Ho's companion story, *Peek!*

RELATED TITLES: Christelow, Eileen. *Five Little Monkeys Jumping on the Bed.* Clarion, 1989. / Dodds, Dayle Ann. *Sing, Sophie!* Candlewick, 1997. / Fleming, Candace. *Smile, Lily!* Atheneum, 2004. / Frazee, Marla. *Hush, Little Baby: A Folk Song with Pictures.* Harcourt, 1999. / Ho, Minfong. *Peek! A Thai Hide-and-Seek.* Candlewick, 2004. / Lewison, Wendy Cheyette. *Going to Sleep on the Farm.* Dial, 1992. / Lum, Kate. *What! Cried Granny: An Almost Bedtime Story.* Dial, 1999. / Paxton, Tom. *Where's the Baby?* Morrow, 1993. / Root, Phyllis. *What Baby Wants.* Candlewick, 1998. / Williams, Vera B. *"More More More," Said the Baby.* Greenwillow, 1990. / Wood, Audrey, and Don Wood. *Piggies.* Harcourt, 1991. / Zemach, Harve. *Mommy, Buy Me a China Doll.* Follett, 1966.

SUBJECTS: BEDTIME STORIES. LULLABIES. SLEEP. SOUND EFFECTS. STORIES IN RHYME. THAILAND.

366   **Ho, Minfong. *Peek! A Thai Hide-and-Seek.* Illus. by Holly Meade. Candlewick, 2004. 0-7636-2041-6. Unp. Gr. PreK–K**

"Jut-Ay, Baby, peek-a-boo, Want to play? Where are you," Papa calls out, seeking his little girl as she hides from him in the lush greenery outside their house in the Thai countryside. On each page of watercolor and cut-paper collages, Papa finds noisy animals, from red-tailed rooster ("Eechy-eechy egg!") to bright-striped tiger ("RA-ROAR"), though sharp-eyed viewers will spy Papa's little one peering out from the bushes nearby.

GERM: Read this aloud again and play hide-and-seek, acting out the story with children becoming the noisy animals. Along with the companion book, *Hush,* compare the Thai animal noises depicted here with the sounds we assign to them in English. Ask your group to describe the fun games they play with their parents.

RELATED TITLES: De Zutter, Hank. *Who Says a Dog Goes Bow-Wow?* Doubleday, 1993. / Feiffer, Jules. *The Daddy Mountain.* Hyperion, 2004. / Frazee, Marla. *Hush, Little Baby: A Folk Song with Pictures.* Harcourt, 1999. / Heap, Sue. *Cowboy Baby.* Candlewick, 1998. / Ho, Minfong. *Hush! A Thai Lullaby.* Orchard, 1996. / Paxton, Tom. *Where's the Baby?* Morrow, 1993. / Pringle, Laurence. *Octopus Hug.* Boyds Mills, 1993. / Robinson, Marc. *Cock-a-Doodle-Doo! What Does It Sound Like to You?* Stewart, Tabori & Chang, 1993. / Shapiro, Arnold L. *Who Says That?* Dutton, 1991. / Willems, Mo. *Knuffle Bunny: A Cautionary Tale.* Hyperion, 2004. / Wolf, Jake. *Daddy, Could I Have an Elephant?* Greenwillow, 1996.

SUBJECTS: ANIMAL SOUNDS. ANIMALS. FATHERS AND DAUGHTERS. GAMES. HIDE AND SEEK. PLAY. SOUND EFFECTS. STORIES IN RHYME. THAILAND.

367   **Hobbie, Holly. *Toot and Puddle: The New Friend.* Illus. by the author. Little, Brown, 2004. 0-316-36552-1. Unp. Gr. PreK–2**

One sunny October day, Opal brings along her talented, beautiful friend Daphne when she visits her good friends Toot and Puddle in their cozy house in the woods. Daphne is a whiz at everything—gymnastics, jumping rope, holding her breath, and playing the violin, but, as Toot notes, she's a bit of a prima donna when she doesn't get her own way.

GERM: Discussion point: Why does Toot think Daphne is a prima donna? How does Opal feel about her friend? Why does she lose her temper with her? How are Opal and Daphne different? What talents do you have that make you unique? Explore the other books in the winning Toot and Puddle series and come up with new adventures for the two pigs and their pals in Woodcock Pocket.

RELATED TITLES: Bottner, Barbara, and Gerald Kruglik. *Wallace's Lists.* HarperCollins, 2004. / Brown, Laurie Krasny, and Marc Brown. *How to Be a Friend: A Guide to Making Friends and Keeping Them.* Little, Brown, 1998. / Hobbie, Holly. *Toot and Puddle.* Little, Brown, 1997. / Hobbie, Holly. *Toot and Puddle: A Present for Toot.* Little, Brown, 1998. / Hobbie, Holly. *Toot and Puddle: Charming Opal.* Little, Brown, 2003. / Hobbie, Holly. *Toot and Puddle: I'll Be Home for Christmas.* Little, Brown, 2000. / Hobbie, Holly. *Toot and Puddle: You Are My Sunshine.* Little, Brown, 1999. / Lobel, Arnold. *The Book of Pigericks.* HarperCollins, 1983. / Waber, Bernard. *Evie and Margie.* Houghton Mifflin, 2003.

SUBJECTS: BEHAVIOR. BEST FRIENDS. FRIENDSHIP. JEALOUSY. PIGS.

368   **Hoberman, Mary Ann. *The Eensy-Weensy Spider.* Illus. by Nadine Bernard Westcott. Little, Brown, 2000. 0-316-36330-8. Unp. Gr. PreK–1**

After climbing that waterspout, the spider swims with a frog, marches in a bug parade, and even buys three pairs of fine red shoes. The tale is told in the same delightful rhythm as the original fingerplay song; music, chords, and hand-motion directions are included.

GERM: Children can decide what other adventures the spider might have and compose some new verses to sing. Compare this version with Iza Trapani's equally entertaining *The Itsy Bitsy Spider* and Lorianne Siomades's *The Itsy Bitsy Spider*.

RELATED TITLES: Cole, Joanna, and Stephanie Calmenson. *The Eentsy, Weentsy Spider: Fingerplays and Action Rhymes*. Morrow, 1991. / Hoberman, Mary Ann. *The Llama Who Had No Pajama: 100 Favorite Poems*. Harcourt, 1998. / Hoberman, Mary Ann. *Miss Mary Mack: A Hand-Clapping Rhyme*. Little, Brown, 1998. / Hoberman, Mary Ann. *Yankee Doodle*. Little, Brown, 2004. / Karas, G. Brian. *I Know an Old Lady*. Scholastic, 1984. / Kirk, David. *Miss Spider's ABC*. Scholastic, 1998. / Raffi. *Spider on the Floor*. Crown, 1993. / Rounds, Glen. *I Know an Old Lady Who Swallowed a Fly*. Holiday House, 1990. / Siomades, Lorianne. *Itsy Bitsy Spider*. Boyds Mills, 1999. / Taback, Simms. *There Was an Old Lady Who Swallowed a Fly*. Viking, 1997. / Trapani, Iza. *The Itsy Bitsy Spider*. Whispering Coyote, 1993. / Westcott, Nadine Bernard. *I Know an Old Lady Who Swallowed a Fly*. Little, Brown, 1980. / Westcott, Nadine Bernard. *Peanut Butter and Jelly: A Play Rhyme*. Dutton, 1987.

SUBJECTS: FINGERPLAYS. SONGS. SPIDERS. STORIES IN RHYME.

369   **Hoberman, Mary Ann. *It's Simple, Said Simon*. Illus. by Meilo So. Knopf, 2001. 0-375-91201-0. Unp. Gr. PreK–1**

Simon demonstrates his growl for a dog, a stretch for a cat, and a jump for a horse. "Very good," each says, and the boy replies, "It's simple." When he meets a tiger, it encourages him to growl louder, stretch longer, and jump higher, and then takes him away on its back. How will Simon get away from the tiger who looks forward to having boy for supper?

GERM: When you get to the climax, ask your children to come up with a way Simon might outwit the tiger. Animated illustrations in ink and watercolors on textured, speckled Indian rice paper and repeated actions and dialogue ensure that your listeners will get involved in the story with their whole bodies. Act it out in small groups or pairs.

RELATED TITLES: Bannerman, Helen. *The Story of Little Babaji*. HarperCollins, 1996. / Clark, Emma Chichester. *Follow the Leader*. McElderry, 2003. / Dowson, Nick. *Tigress*. Candlewick, 2004. / Feiffer, Jules. *Bark, George*. HarperCollins, 1999. / Harper, Wilhelmina. *The Gunniwolf*. Dutton, 1978. / Harter, Debbie. *Walking Through the Jungle*. Orchard, 1997. / Hindley, Judy. *Do Like a Duck Does!* Candlewick, 2002. / Hoberman, Mary Ann. *Yankee Doodle*. Little, Brown, 2004. / Kimmel, Eric A. *The Gingerbread Man*. Holiday House, 1993. / Lester, Julius. *Sam and the Tigers*. Dial, 1996. / Marzollo, Jean. *Pretend You're a Cat*. Dial, 1990. / Pandell, Karen. *Animal Action ABC*. Dutton, 1996. / So, Meilo. *Gobble, Gobble, Slip, Slop: The Tale of a Very Greedy Cat*. Knopf, 2004. / Thomson, Sarah L. *Tigers*. HarperCollins, 1994. / Whybrow, Ian. *The Noisy Way to Bed*. Scholastic, 2004.

SUBJECTS: ANIMAL SOUNDS. CHANTABLE REFRAIN. CREATIVE DRAMA. STORIES TO TELL. TIGERS.

370   **Hoberman, Mary Ann. *Miss Mary Mack: A Hand-Clapping Rhyme*. Illus. by Nadine Bernard Westcott. Little, Brown, 1998. 0-316-93118-7. Unp. Gr. PreK–1**

Your children probably already know the classic chant about Miss Mary Mack, Mack, Mack, with the silver buttons all down her back, who asked her mother for 50 cents to see the elephant jump the fence, and didn't come back till the Fourth of July. Westcott's frantic watercolors depict all that, but then poet Hoberman takes the rhyme further with ten wild new verses to read and recite and sing.

GERM: Illustrated directions are given to do the rhyme as a hand-clapping game, along with the music.

RELATED TITLES: Booth, David, comp. *Doctor Knickerbocker and Other Rhymes*. Ticknor & Fields, 1993. / Brown, Marc. *Hand Rhymes*. Dutton, 1985. / Cole, Joanna, and Stephanie Calmenson. *The Eentsy, Weentsy Spider: Fingerplays and Action Rhymes*. Morrow, 1991. / Hoberman, Mary Ann. *The Eensy-Weensy Spider*. Little, Brown, 2000. / Hoberman, Mary Ann. *Yankee Doodle*. Little, Brown, 2004. / Lass, Bonnie, and Philemon Sturges. *Who Took the Cookies from the Cookie Jar?* Little, Brown, 2000. / Raffi. *Spider on the Floor*. Crown, 1993. / Sturges, Philemon. *She'll Be Comin' 'Round the Mountain*. Little, Brown, 2004. / Taback, Simms. *There Was an Old Lady Who Swallowed a Fly*. Viking, 1997. / Trapani, Iza. *The Itsy Bitsy Spider*. Whispering Coyote, 1993. / Westcott, Nadine Bernard. *I Know an Old Lady Who Swallowed a Fly*. Little, Brown, 1980. / Westcott, Nadine Bernard. *Peanut Butter and Jelly: A Play Rhyme*. Dutton, 1987.

SUBJECTS: CHANTABLE REFRAIN. ELEPHANTS. FINGERPLAYS. NURSERY RHYMES. SONGS.

371   **Hoberman, Mary Ann. *The Seven Silly Eaters*. Illus. by Marla Frazee. Harcourt, 1997. 0-15-200096-8. Unp. Gr. K–2**

Every day, Mrs. Peters, a sweet and kind mother, prepares separate meals for each of her seven persnickety young eaters. On her birthday, her children return the favor, gathering in the kitchen to make her a special, secret (and almost disastrous) birthday breakfast in bed.

GERM: Ask listeners to recall all six ingredients of the Peters children's birthday cake. Each can then make a recipe picture of each of the ingredients that make up a favorite food they choose, with a picture of the finished dish. For instance: ICE + SUGAR + CREAM + CHOCOLATE = CHOCOLATE ICE CREAM! You can start a whole investigation of the ingredients in favorite dishes, from applesauce to pizza.

RELATED TITLES: Best, Cari. *Three Cheers for Catherine the Great.* DK Ink, 1999. / Blumenthal, Deborah. *Don't Let the Peas Touch! And Other Stories.* Scholastic, 2004. / Brown, Marc. *D. W. the Picky Eater.* Little, Brown, 1995. / Bunting, Eve. *Flower Garden.* Harcourt, 1994. / Child, Lauren. *I Will Never Not Ever Eat a Tomato.* Candlewick, 2000. / Cox, Judy. *The West Texas Chili Monster.* BridgeWater, 1998. / Elya, Susan Middleton. *Eight Animals Bake a Cake.* Putnam, 2002. / Hoberman, Mary Ann. *The Llama Who Had No Pajama: 100 Favorite Poems.* Harcourt, 1998. / Rosenthal, Amy Krouse. *Little Pea.* Chronicle Books, 2005. / Ryan, Pam Muñoz. *Mice and Beans.* Scholastic, 2001. / Wadsworth, Ginger. *Tomorrow Is Daddy's Birthday.* Boyds Mills, 1994. / Yolen, Jane. *How Do Dinosaurs Eat Their Food?* Blue Sky/Scholastic, 2005.

SUBJECTS: BIRTHDAYS. BROTHERS AND SISTERS. CAKE. FOOD. FOOD HABITS. MOTHERS. STORIES IN RHYME.

372   **Hoberman, Mary Ann.** *There Once Was a Man Named Michael Finnegan.* **Illus. by Nadine Bernard Westcott. Little, Brown, 2001. 0-316-36301-4. Unp. Gr. PreK–2**

Starting out with the old silly song about Michael Finnegan, the guy with the whiskers on his chin-igan, Hoberman has written all new verses about Michael's awful violin playing and how he finds true happiness with a dog he names Quinn-igan.

GERM: The music is on the inside front pages, so you can sing the whole thing and hand out the verses for a bit of Singer's Theater to increase children's fluency and love of ridiculous wordplay. Meet other wacky characters in singable books such as *Catalina Magdalena Hoopensteiner Wallendiner Hogan Logan Bogan Was Her Name* by Tedd Arnold and *I Know an Old Lady Who Swallowed a Fly* by Nadine Bernard Westcott.

RELATED TITLES: Arnold, Tedd. *Catalina Magdalena Hoopensteiner Wallendiner Hogan Logan Bogan Was Her Name.* Scholastic, 2004. / Hoberman, Mary Ann. *The Eensy-Weensy Spider.* Little, Brown, 2000. / Hoberman, Mary Ann. *Miss Mary Mack: A Hand-Clapping Rhyme.* Little, Brown, 1998. / Hoberman, Mary Ann. *Yankee Doodle.* Little, Brown, 2004. / Karas, G. Brian. *I Know an Old Lady.* Scholastic, 1984. / Raffi. *Down by the Bay.* Crown, 1987. / Taback, Simms. *There Was an Old Lady Who Swallowed a Fly.* Viking, 1997. / Weeks, Sarah. *Mrs. McNosh Hangs Up Her Wash.* Dutton, 1998. / Westcott, Nadine Bernard. *I Know an Old Lady Who Swallowed a Fly.* Little, Brown, 1980. / Westcott, Nadine Bernard. *The Lady with the Alligator Purse.* Little, Brown, 1988. / Zelinsky, Paul O. *Knick-Knack Paddywhack!* Dutton, 2002. / Ziefert, Harriet. *I Swapped My Dog.* Houghton Mifflin, 1998. / Ziefert, Harriet. *When I First Came to This Land.* Putnam, 1998.

SUBJECTS: FOLK SONGS. HUMOROUS POETRY. NONSENSE VERSES. SONGS. STORIES IN RHYME.

373   **Hoberman, Mary Ann.** *Yankee Doodle.* **Illus. by Nadine Bernard Westcott. Little, Brown, 2004. 0-316-14551-3. Unp. Gr. PreK–2**

In another delightful addition to their Sing-Along Stories series, Hoberman and Westcott add new wacky verses and watercolors to the traditional folksong about Yankee Doodle, who, with a girl, a poodle, a toad, and a rooster, opens up a restaurant called Yankee Doodle's Noodles.

GERM: Eat noodles and sing the song. Make macaroni necklaces.

RELATED TITLES: Compestine, Ying Chang. *The Story of Noodles.* Holiday House, 2002. / dePaola, Tomie. *Strega Nona.* Simon & Schuster, 1979. / Hoberman, Mary Ann. *The Eensy-Weensy Spider.* Little, Brown, 2000. / Hoberman, Mary Ann. *The Llama Who Had No Pajama: 100 Favorite Poems.* Harcourt, 1998. / Hoberman, Mary Ann. *Miss Mary Mack: A Hand-Clapping Rhyme.* Little, Brown, 1998. / Hoberman, Mary Ann. *The Seven Silly Eaters.* Harcourt, 1997. / Hoberman, Mary Ann. *There Once Was a Man Named Michael Finnegan.* Little, Brown, 2001. / Sturges, Philemon. *She'll Be Comin' 'Round the Mountain.* Little, Brown, 2004.

SUBJECTS: FOOD. FOURTH OF JULY. PARODIES. RESTAURANTS. SONGS. STORIES IN RHYME.

374   **Hoffman, Mary.** *Boundless Grace.* **Illus. by Caroline Binch. Dial, 1995. 0-8037-1715-6. 28pp. Gr. K–3**

Story-loving Grace lives with her mother, Nana, and Paw-Paw the cat, but she can't remember her father, who went back to Africa and now has another family. When he invites her and Nana to The Gambia for spring vacation, Grace wonders if he will love her and worries that she's "one girl too many." Binch's glowing ultra-realistic watercolors of personable Grace and her loving extended family burst with the sights and sounds of Africa.

GERM: Grace wonders, "Why aren't there any stories about families like mine, that don't live together?" Grace's situation is certainly not uncommon and will help you introduce the subject of blended families. Listeners will also be enchanted by Hoffman's earlier story of Grace at home and school, *Amazing Grace*.

RELATED TITLES: Best, Cari. *Getting Used to Harry*. Orchard, 1996. / Coy, John. *Two Old Potatoes and Me*. Knopf, 2003. / Hoffman, Mary. *Amazing Grace*. Dial, 1991. / Hoffman, Mary. *Henry's Baby*. DK, 1993. / Leach, Norman. *My Wicked Stepmother*. Macmillan, 1993.

SUBJECTS: AFRICA. BLACKS—ENGLAND. DIVORCE. GAMBIA. MULTICULTURAL BOOKS. STEPFAMILIES.

375　**Hong, Lily Toy.** *The Empress and the Silkworm*. **Illus. by the author. Albert Whitman, 1995. 0-8075-2009-8. Unp. Gr. 1–4**
Based on a Chinese legend, here is the tale of Empress Si Ling-Chi, who is credited with the discovery, around 2640 B.C., of how silk came from mulberry leaf-eating caterpillars when a cocoon fell into her cup of tea and began to unravel.

GERM: Bring in silk cloth for the children to feel and examine. Analyze other types of fabrics and yarns and explore how they are made, from knitting and crocheting to weaving. The emperor's adviser asks, "Who could imagine that something so great could come from something so small?" Discuss and write about: To what other things could this quote apply?

RELATED TITLES: Beskow, Elsa. *Pelle's New Suit*. HarperCollins, 1929. / Cole, Joanna. *Ms. Frizzle's Adventures: Imperial China*. Scholastic, 2005. / Compestine, Ying Chang. *The Story of Chopsticks*. Holiday House, 2001. / Compestine, Ying Chang. *The Story of Paper*. Holiday House, 2003. / Demi. *The Emperor's New Clothes: A Tale Set in China*. McElderry, 2000. / dePaola, Tomie. *Charlie Needs a Cloak*. Aladdin, 1982. / Hong, Lily Toy. *How the Ox Star Fell from Heaven*. Albert Whitman, 1991. / Hong, Lily Toy. *Two of Everything: A Chinese Folktale*. Albert Whitman, 1993. / Rumford, James. *The Cloudmakers*. Houghton Mifflin, 1996. / Sanders, Scott Russell. *Warm as Wool*. Bradbury, 1992.

SUBJECTS: CHINA. CLOTH. CLOTHING AND DRESS. HISTORICAL FICTION. KINGS AND RULERS. MULTICULTURAL BOOKS. SILK.

376　**Hooper, Meredith.** *Honey Cookies*. **Illus. by Alison Bartlett. Frances Lincoln, 2005. 1-84507-394-0. Unp. Gr. PreK–2**
As they bake honey cookies together, Ben's grandma describes each ingredient they need—butter, sugar, honey, egg, cinnamon, and flour—and its origins. This book was originally published by Kingfisher in 1997 and called *A Cow, a Bee, a Cookie, and Me*.

GERM: Talk about other baking ingredients and where they come from, including chocolate, salt, vanilla, and flour. Follow up with Marjorie Priceman's *How to Make an Apple Pie and See the World*. If you've an oven handy, make simple cookies with your crew.

RELATED TITLES: Carle, Eric. *Pancakes, Pancakes*. Scholastic, 1990. / Elya, Susan Middleton. *Eight Animals Bake a Cake*. Putnam, 2002. / Krebs, Laurie. *The Beeman*. National Geographic, 2002. / Lass, Bonnie, and Philemon Sturges. *Who Took the Cookies from the Cookie Jar?* Little, Brown, 2000. / Priceman, Marjorie. *How to Make an Apple Pie and See the World*. Knopf, 1994. / Robart, Rose. *The Cake That Mack Ate*. Little, Brown, 1987. / Shepard, Aaron. *The Baker's Dozen: A Saint Nicholas Tale*. Atheneum, 1995. / Wellington, Monica. *Mr. Cookie Baker*. Dutton, 1992. / Wells, Rosemary. *Bunny Cakes*. Dial, 1997.

SUBJECTS: BAKING. COOKIES. FOOD. GRANDMOTHERS.

377　**Hoose, Phillip M., and Hannah Hoose.** *Hey, Little Ant*. **Illus. by Debbie Tilley. Tricycle, 1998. 1-883672-54-6. Unp. Gr. K–3**
In a sidewalk discussion between a brown-haired, bespectacled boy and an ant, the boy announces his intention to squish the ant flat, while the ant responds with arguments buttressing his opposition to such drastic action.

GERM: Originally written as a song performed by the authors, a father and daughter, this can be performed as a Reader's (or Singer's, as the music is appended) Theater, with pairs of readers performing it. The story is open-ended, so you can discuss what the boy should do or have your children write persuasive letters to him with their advice. See how another ant hater learns his lesson in *The Ant Bully* by John Nickle. Find out more reasons to appreciate ants in eye-opening nonfiction books such as *Those Amazing Ants* by Patricia Brennan Demuth and *Ant Cities* by Arthur Dorros.

RELATED TITLES: Allinson, Beverly. *Effie*. Scholastic, 1991. / Becker, Bonny. *An Ant's Day Off*. Simon & Schuster, 2003. / Climo, Shirley. *The Little Red Ant and the Great Big Crumb: A Mexican Fable*. Clarion, 1995. / Demuth, Patricia Brennan. *Those Amazing Ants*. Macmillan, 1994. / Dorros, Arthur. *Ant Cities*. HarperCollins, 1987. / Nickle, John. *The Ant Bully*. Scholastic, 1999. / Van Allsburg, Chris. *Two Bad Ants*. Houghton Mifflin, 1988. / Wolkstein, Diane. *Step by Step*. Morrow, 1994. / Young, Ed. *Night Visitors*. Philomel, 1995.

SUBJECTS: ANTS. BULLIES. CONFLICT RESOLUTION. INSECTS. RESPONSIBILITY. SIZE. SONGS. STORIES IN RHYME.

378   **Hopkinson, Deborah.** *Apples to Oregon*. **Illus. by Nancy Carpenter. Atheneum, 2004. 0-689-84769-6. Unp. Gr. K–4**

Delicious, the girl narrator of this story and the oldest of Pa's eight children, tells a rollicking tall tale of the family's cross-country trek from Iowa to Oregon with a wagonful of fruit saplings, braving rivers, wind, drought, and frost along the way. The subtitle says plenty: "Being the (Slightly) True Narrative of How a Brave Pioneer Father Brought Apples, Peaches, Pears, Plums, Grapes, and Cherries (and Children) Across the Plains." The Author's Note explains how her tale was very loosely based on pioneer Henderson Luelling, who in 1847 undertook the journey with his wife and eight children, transporting seven hundred plants and fruit trees to Portland, where he set up "the mother of Oregon nurseries" and introduced the Bing cherry, named after a Chinese employee.

GERM: The good-natured story and expressive oil paintings present a picture of life on the Oregon Trail that you can tie into social studies units and use when you discuss personal narratives, fiction based on a true story, and tall tales and exaggeration. More simply, it can be used to provide an appreciation of apples. There's a set of apple facts on the back cover, and you can do some research—both reading and tasting—to find out more. Tie it in to Johnny Appleseed, of course. Compare and contrast Pa's family's wagon adventure out West with the stagecoach trip Ma and her five children make to the gold fields of Californ-y in *Nine for California*.

RELATED TITLES: Bertrand, Lynne. *Granite Baby*. Farrar, 2005. / Fleming, Candace. *Sunny Boy! The Life and Times of a Tortoise*. Farrar, 2005. / Glass, Andrew. *Folks Call Me Appleseed John*. Doubleday, 1995. / Hodges, Margaret. *The True Tale of Johnny Appleseed*. Holiday House, 1997. / Hopkinson, Deborah. *Fannie in the Kitchen*. Atheneum, 2001. / Howard, Ellen. *The Log Cabin Quilt*. Holiday House, 1996. / Kay, Verla. *Covered Wagon, Bumpy Trails*. Putnam, 2000. / Ketteman, Helen. *Heat Wave!* Walker, 1998. / Levitin, Sonia. *Nine for California*. Orchard, 1996. / Russell, Marion. *Along the Santa Fe Trail: Marion Russell's Own Story*. Albert Whitman, 1993. / Turner, Ann. *Mississippi Mud: Three Prairie Journals*. HarperCollins, 1997. / Van Leeuwen, Jean. *Bound for Oregon*. Dial, 1994. / Van Leeuwen, Jean. *A Fourth of July on the Plains*. Dial, 1997. / Williams, David. *Grandma Essie's Covered Wagon*. Knopf, 1993. / Wood, Audrey. *The Bunyans*. Blue Sky/Scholastic, 1996.

SUBJECTS: APPLE TREES. FRONTIER AND PIONEER LIFE. FRUIT. HISTORICAL FICTION. OVERLAND JOURNEYS TO THE PACIFIC. PERSONAL NARRATIVES. TALL TALES. WEST (U.S.)—HISTORY—FICTION.

379   **Hopkinson, Deborah.** *Fannie in the Kitchen: The Whole Story from Soup to Nuts of How Fannie Farmer Invented Recipes with Precise Measurements*. **Illus. by Nancy Carpenter. Atheneum, 2001. 0-689-81965-X. Unp. Gr. K–4**

Young Marcia Shaw isn't wild about the idea of a girl named Fannie Farmer moving in to help pregnant Mama with the cooking, but Fannie soon wins Marcia over with her delicious food and foolproof recipes (which actually evolved into *The Boston Cooking School Cookbook* in 1896). As Fannie says, "Preparing food well isn't magic. It's an art and a science that anyone can learn." The sensible, witty illustrations incorporate hand-colored 19th-century engravings into the pen-and-ink and watercolors of Fannie and Marcia cooking up a storm.

GERM: There's a very nice recipe for Fannie Farmer's Famous Griddle Cakes on the last page if you're feeling adventurous and ravenous. Bring in a copy of the *Fannie Farmer Cookbook* and incorporate the story and a few good recipes into a measurement unit. Hand out and analyze the construction of a simple recipe for children to follow at home. Next, they can compose recipes for their own favorite foods, such as spaghetti sauce, chocolate cake, or applesauce, and then compare their concoctions with actual recipes from cookbooks they find in the 641.5s in the library.

RELATED TITLES: Barrett, Judi. *Cloudy with a Chance of Meatballs*. Atheneum, 1978. / Goldstein, Bobbye S. *What's on the Menu?* Viking, 1992. / Greenstein, Elaine. *Ice-Cream Cones for Sale*. Scholastic, 2003. / Hopkinson, Deborah. *Apples to Oregon*. Atheneum, 2004. / Jones, Charlotte Foltz. *Eat Your Words: A Fascinating Look at the Language of Food*. Delacorte, 1999. / Krementz, Jill. *The Fun of Cooking*. Knopf, 1985. / Lauber, Patricia. *What You Never Knew About Fingers, Forks, and Chopsticks*. Simon & Schuster, 1999. / Priceman, Marjorie. *How to*

Make an Apple Pie and See the World. Knopf, 1994. / Stevens, Janet, and Susan Stevens Crummel. *Cook-a-Doodle-Doo!* Harcourt, 1999. / Swain, Ruth Freeman. *How Sweet It Is (and Was): The History of Candy.* Holiday House, 2003. / Westcott, Nadine Bernard. *Never Take a Pig to Lunch and Other Poems About the Fun of Eating.* Orchard, 1994. / Yee, Paul. *Roses Sing on New Snow.* Macmillan, 1992.

SUBJECTS: BIOGRAPHY. COOKERY. COOKS. FARMER, FANNIE, 1857–1915. FOOD. HISTORICAL FICTION. MEASUREMENT. WOMEN.

380   **Hopkinson, Deborah.** *Girl Wonder: A Baseball Story in Nine Innings.* **Illus. by Terry Widener. Atheneum, 2003. 0-689-83300-8. Unp. Gr. 1–4**
Inspired by the life of Alta Weiss, who in 1907 pitched for a semi-pro all-male baseball team in Ohio, this fictionalized personal narrative of Alta's remarkable foray into a men-only sport is told in the first person by the Girl Wonder herself.
GERM: Lead your students on an Internet and encyclopedia search to look for more information about Alta Weiss. See the Author's Note next to the title page for some good Web sites. At the back of the book is a list of dates— "Highlights of Women in Baseball"—noting other firsts that students can research. The author has developed a distinct voice for her subject and has written a personal narrative channeling the spirit of the courageous and determined woman who broke down barriers and loved every moment of it. Set an engrossing and challenging biography assignment for your writers: to compose a first-person account of an episode in their subject's life, told in the famous person's voice. How would Amelia Earhart tell her own story? Or irascible Thomas Edison?
RELATED TITLES: Adler, David A. *Lou Gehrig: The Luckiest Man.* Harcourt, 1997. / Cline-Ransome, Lesa. *Satchel Paige.* Simon & Schuster, 2000. / Corey, Shana. *Players in Pigtails.* Scholastic, 2003. / Golenbock, Peter. *Teammates.* Harcourt, 1990. / Hamm, Mia. *Winners Never Quit!* HarperCollins, 2004. / Janeczko, Paul. *That Sweet Diamond: Baseball Poems.* Atheneum, 1998. / Morrison, Lillian. *At the Crack of the Bat: Baseball Poems.* Hyperion, 1992. / Moss, Marissa. *Mighty Jackie, the Strike-Out Queen.* Simon & Schuster, 2004. / Nelson, Vaunda Micheaux. *Mayfield Crossing.* Putnam, 1993. / Norworth, Jack. *Take Me Out to the Ball Game.* Four Winds, 1993.
SUBJECTS: ATHLETES—BIOGRAPHY. BASEBALL. BIOGRAPHICAL FICTION. PERSONAL NARRATIVES. PREJUDICE. SEX ROLE. SPORTS—BIOGRAPHY. WOMEN.

381   **Horse, Harry.** *Little Rabbit Goes to School.* **Illus. by the author. Peachtree, 2004. 1-56145-320-X. Unp. Gr. PreK–K**
On his first day of school, Little Rabbit insists on bringing Charlie Horse, his wooden toy horse on wheels, even though Charlie Horse makes him late and gets into mischief. The understatement in the text, with irresistible pen-and-ink and watercolors that show the real cause of Charlie Horse's misbehavior—exuberant Little Rabbit himself—will not be lost on young readers.
GERM: Children can retell Charlie Horse's exploits from his point of view and recall how he gets into trouble with Miss Morag, Little Rabbit's patient teacher. Use this for talking about the first day and also to go over what to do if you get lost, just like Little Rabbit does.
RELATED TITLES: Child, Lauren. *I Am Too Absolutely Small for School.* Candlewick, 2004. / Henkes, Kevin. *Wemberly Worried.* Greenwillow, 2000. / Hest, Amy. *Off to School, Baby Duck.* Candlewick, 1999. / Horse, Harry. *Little Rabbit Lost.* Peachtree, 2002. / Lasky, Kathryn. *Lunch Bunnies.* Little, Brown, 1996. / London, Jonathan. *Froggy Goes to School.* Viking, 1996. / Moss, Miriam. *Don't Forget I Love You.* Dial, 2004. / Slate, Joseph. *Miss Bindergarten Gets Ready for Kindergarten.* Dutton, 1996. / Strete, Craig. *The Rattlesnake Who Went to School.* Putnam, 2004. / Wells, Rosemary. *Timothy Goes to School.* Dial, 1981.
SUBJECTS: BEHAVIOR. FIRST DAY OF SCHOOL. LOST. RABBITS. SCHOOLS. TEACHERS. TOYS.

382   **Hort, Lenny.** *The Seals on the Bus.* **Illus. by G. Brian Karas. Henry Holt, 2001. 0-8050-5952-0. Unp. Gr. PreK–K**
The seals go ERRP, the tigers go ROAR, the ducks go HONK, and the vipers go HISS in this riotous animal-filled rewrite of "The Wheels on the Bus."
GERM: Children can write, illustrate, and sing new verses with other animals, sounds, and motions. Contrast it with Paul Zelinsky's glorious movable and interactive version, *The Wheels on the Bus.* Then sing the Old MacDonald song with the farm animals' rock band in Jarrett Krosoczka's *Punk Farm.*
RELATED TITLES: Cauley, Lorinda Bryan. *Old MacDonald Had a Farm.* Putnam, 1989. / Christelow, Eileen. *Five Little Monkeys Jumping on the Bed.* Clarion, 1989. / Greene, Rhonda Gowler. *Barnyard Song.* Atheneum, 1997. / Jones, Carol. *This Old Man.* Houghton Mifflin, 1990. / Karas, G. Brian. *I Know an Old Lady Who Swallowed a Fly.* Scholastic, 1994. / Kovalski, Maryann. *The Wheels on the Bus.* Little, Brown, 1987. / Krosoczka, Jarrett J.

Punk Farm. Knopf, 2005. / Raffi. *Down by the Bay.* Crown, 1987. / Raffi. *The Wheels on the Bus.* Crown, 1988. / Rounds, Glen. *Old MacDonald Had a Farm.* Holiday, 1989. / Taback, Simms. *There Was an Old Lady Who Swallowed a Fly.* Viking, 1997. / Whippo, Walt, and Bernard Zaritzky. *Little White Duck.* Little, Brown, 2000. / Zane, Alexander. *The Wheels on the Race Car.* Orchard, 2005. / Zelinsky, Paul O. *The Wheels on the Bus.* Dutton, 1990.

SUBJECTS: ANIMAL SOUNDS. ANIMALS. BUSES. SONGS. SOUND EFFECTS. STORIES WITH SONGS. TRANSPORTATION. VEHICLES.

---

383   **Howard, Arthur.** *Cosmo Zooms.* **Illus. by the author. Harcourt, 1999. 0-15-201788-7. Unp. Gr. PreK–1**

Unlike all the other dogs on Pumpkin Lane, little Cosmo can't run fast, howl loudly, drool a lot, herd, or catch frisbees. He'd love to find his true talent. Flopping down under a tree for a snooze, he finds himself in motion. Cosmo's surprise trip on a skateboard takes him swooping and swerving down the lane, and boy, are the other dogs impressed at his speed.

GERM: Children can talk, draw, and write about their own pets' singular gifts and stupid pet tricks.

RELATED TITLES: Barracca, Debra, and Sal Barracca. *The Adventures of Taxi Dog.* Dial, 1990. / Best, Cari. *Montezuma's Revenge.* Orchard, 1999. / Harvey, Amanda. *Dog Eared.* Doubleday, 2002. / Howard, Arthur. *The Hubbub Above.* Harcourt, 2005. / Howard, Arthur. *When I Was Five.* Harcourt, 1996. / Ingman, Bruce. *When Martha's Away.* Houghton Mifflin, 1995. / Kirk, Daniel. *Dogs Rule!* Hyperion, 2003. / McFarland, Lyn Rossiter. *Widget.* Farrar, 2001. / Meddaugh, Susan. *Martha Speaks.* Houghton Mifflin, 1992. / Miller, Sara Swan. *Three Stories You Can Read to Your Dog.* Houghton Mifflin, 1995. / Pilkey, Dav. *The Hallo-Wiener.* Scholastic, 1995. / Rathmann, Peggy. *Officer Buckle and Gloria.* Putnam, 1995. / Rosen, Michael. *Rover.* Doubleday, 1999. / Seligson, Susan, and Howie Schneider. *Amos: The Story of an Old Dog and His Couch.* Little, Brown, 1987. / Sklansky, Amy E. *From the Doghouse: Poems to Chew On.* Henry Holt, 2002. / Whayne, Susanne. *Petropolis.* Handprint, 2003.

SUBJECTS: DOGS. INDIVIDUALITY. SKATEBOARDING.

---

384   **Howard, Arthur.** *The Hubbub Above.* **Illus. by the author. Harcourt, 2005. 0-15-204592-9. Unp. Gr. PreK–1**

Sydney loves the heavenly quiet of her apartment on the 52nd floor overlooking the city. And then the Kabooms move in upstairs. They walk and talk noisily, and have loud cha-cha parties every Saturday night. Blonde-haired Sydney, an assertive little girl, heads upstairs to complain. What do you know? Mr. Kaboom isn't just loud—he's an elephant. He's very tall, very wide, "and he looked a bit, well . . . tuskey." Mrs. Kaboom invites Sydney to join their party, and it's a blast. Watercolor cartoons contrast staid, refined, big city etiquette and ambiance with those impetuous, fun-loving elephants, who really know how to throw a party.

GERM: Close the book when you get to where Sydney rides the elevator to confront the noisy neighbors. Ask children to act out the confrontation. What will Sydney say? How will the Kabooms respond? Have pairs reenact their dialogues for the whole group. Mind you, at this point, the children will have no idea the Kabooms are, well, elephants. Ask them for some solutions of how the elephants can cut down the noise.

RELATED TITLES: Bania, Michael. *Kumak's House: A Tale of the Far North.* Alaska Northwest, 2002. / Black, Charles C. *The Royal Nap.* Viking, 1995. / Cole, Joanna. *It's Too Noisy!* Crowell, 1989. / Emberley, Michael. *Ruby and the Sniffs.* Little, Brown, 2004. / Howard, Arthur. *Cosmo Zooms.* Harcourt, 1999. / Howard, Arthur. *When I Was Five.* Harcourt, 1996. / McGovern, Ann. *Too Much Noise.* Houghton Mifflin, 1967. / Melmed, Laura Krauss. *New York, New York! The Big Apple from A to Z.* HarperCollins, 2005. / Murphy, Jill. *Peace at Last.* Dial, 1980.

SUBJECTS: APARTMENT HOUSES. CITIES AND TOWNS. CREATIVE DRAMA. ELEPHANTS. NEIGHBORLINESS. NEIGHBORS. NEW YORK CITY. NOISE. PARTIES.

---

385   **Howard, Arthur.** *When I Was Five.* **Illus. by the author. Harcourt, 1996. 0-15-200261-8. Unp. Gr. PreK–1**

Now six, Jeremy compares the things he liked last year with his newly acquired and more mature tastes in careers, cars, dinosaurs, and best friends.

GERM: Ask your children to assess their current likes and aspirations with last year's: "When I was five, I ____. Now I am six and I ____." Take another look at being five with *It's Hard to Be Five: Learning How to Work My Control Panel* by Jamie Lee Curtis. And summarize the years one to six with Margaret Wise Brown's *Another Important Book.*

RELATED TITLES: Brown, Margaret Wise. *Another Important Book.* HarperCollins, 1999. / Brown, Margaret

Wise. *The Important Book.* HarperCollins, 1949. / Curtis, Jamie Lee. *It's Hard to Be Five: Learning How to Work My Control Panel.* HarperCollins, 2004. / Emmett, Jonathan. *Someone Bigger.* Clarion, 2004. / Howard, Arthur. *Cosmo Zooms.* Harcourt, 1999. / Howard, Arthur. *The Hubbub Above.* Harcourt, 2005. / Komaiko, Leah. *Earl's Too Cool for Me.* HarperCollins, 1988. / Lester, Alison. *When Frank Was Four.* Houghton Mifflin, 1996. / Raschka, Chris. *Yo! Yes?* Orchard, 1993.

SUBJECTS: FRIENDSHIP. GROWTH. IDENTITY.

386   **Howard, Elizabeth Fitzgerald.** *Virgie Goes to School with Us Boys.* **Illus. by E. B. Lewis. Simon & Schuster, 2000. 0-689-80076-2. Unp. Gr. 1–4**

For two years, five brothers have walked seven miles to attend a school run by Quakers for former slaves, and now their little sister is determined to join them. Based on the experiences of the author's grandfather, this heartening picture book even includes a photograph of the brothers and a detailed Afterword about their lives.

GERM: Incorporate the book into discussions on the importance of education and the end of slavery. Why is Virgie so determined to go to school?

RELATED TITLES: Bogart, Jo Ellen. *Jeremiah Learns to Read.* Orchard, 1999. / Bradby, Marie. *More Than Anything Else.* Orchard, 1995. / Bunting, Eve. *The Wednesday Surprise.* Clarion, 1989. / Heide, Florence Parry, and Judith Heide Gilliland. *The Day of Ahmed's Secret.* Lothrop, 1990. / Hest, Amy. *Mr. George Baker.* Candlewick, 2004. / Houston, Gloria. *My Great Aunt Arizona.* HarperCollins, 1992. / Joosse, Barbara M. *Hot City.* Philomel, 2004. / Mitchell, Margaree King. *Granddaddy's Gift.* BridgeWater, 1997. / Mitchell, Margaree King. *Uncle Jed's Barber Shop.* Simon & Schuster, 1993. / Mora, Pat. *Tomás and the Library Lady.* Knopf, 1997. / Nelson, Vaunda Micheaux. *Almost to Freedom.* Carolrhoda, 2003. / Ransom, Candice. *Liberty Street.* Walker, 2003. / Smothers, Ethel Footman. *The Hard-Times Jar.* Farrar, 2003.

SUBJECTS: AFRICAN AMERICANS. BOOKS AND READING. EDUCATION. HISTORICAL FICTION. MULTICULTURAL BOOKS. PICTURE BOOKS FOR ALL AGES. SCHOOLS. SEX ROLE. U.S.—HISTORY—1865–1898—FICTION.

387   **Howard, Ellen.** *The Log Cabin Quilt.* **Illus. by Ronald Himler. Holiday House, 1996. 0-8234-1247-4. Unp. Gr. 1–4**

After Elviney's mam is laid to rest in the graveyard back home in Carolina, Elviney, Granny, Pap, Sis, and Bub set out in a covered wagon for the woods of Michigan, where they build a log cabin. While Pap is gone hunting, the snow begins, and with the wind blowing cold into the cabin, Elviney finds a way to chink the walls with the scraps from Granny's quilting bag.

GERM: Introduce your lesson on the pioneers with this spare, hopeful story of survival. How were Elviney's experiences moving to her new house different when compared with moving today? Good companion reads on pioneer life include *Dandelions* by Eve Bunting, *Covered Wagon, Bumpy Trails* by Verla Kay, and *Wilderness Cat* by Natalie Kinsey-Warnock. See how Jess and Caroline cope after their mother dies and their grandmother comes to stay with them on the prairie in *Dakota Spring* by D. Anne Love.

RELATED TITLES: Bunting, Eve. *Dandelions.* Harcourt, 1995. / Flournoy, Valerie. *The Patchwork Quilt.* Dial, 1985. / Hopkinson, Deborah. *Apples to Oregon.* Atheneum, 2004. / Hopkinson, Deborah. *Sweet Clara and the Freedom Quilt.* Knopf, 1993. / Kay, Verla. *Covered Wagon, Bumpy Trails.* Putnam, 2000. / Kay, Verla. *Homespun Sarah.* Putnam, 2003. / Kinsey-Warnock, Natalie. *Wilderness Cat.* Dutton, 1992. / Love, D. Anne. *Dakota Spring.* Holiday House, 1995. / Russell, Marion. *Along the Santa Fe Trail: Marion Russell's Own Story.* Albert Whitman, 1993. / Sanders, Scott Russell. *Warm as Wool.* Bradbury, 1992. / Van Leeuwen, Jean. *A Fourth of July on the Plains.* Dial, 1997. / Van Leeuwen, Jean. *Nothing Here But Trees.* Dial, 1998. / Williams, David. *Grandma Essie's Covered Wagon.* Knopf, 1993.

SUBJECTS: FAMILY LIFE. FRONTIER AND PIONEER LIFE. GRANDMOTHERS. HISTORICAL FICTION. LOG CABINS. QUILTS.

388   **Howe, James.** *Horace and Morris But Mostly Dolores.* **Illus. by Amy Walrod. Atheneum, 1999. 0-689-31874-X. Unp. Gr. PreK–2**

Three mouse best friends do everything together until the day the two boys leave Dolores behind to join the Mega-Mice, an all-boys clubhouse. Dynamic, good-natured acrylic-and-cut-paper collages are crammed with mousy details, with spunky Dolores starting her own clubhouse that everyone can join.

GERM: Read aloud on a day when the boys and girls are getting on each other's cases. Follow up with the sequel, *Horace and Morris Join the Chorus (But What About Dolores?).*

RELATED TITLES: Bottner, Barbara, and Gerald Kruglik. *Wallace's Lists.* HarperCollins, 2004. / Brown, Laurie Krasny, and Marc Brown. *How to Be a Friend: A Guide to Making Friends and Keeping Them*. Little, Brown, 1998. / DePaolo, Paula. *Rosie and the Yellow Ribbon*. Little, Brown, 1992. / Havill, Juanita. *Jamaica and Brianna*. Houghton Mifflin, 1993. / Hobbie, Holly. *Toot and Puddle: A Present for Toot*. Little, Brown, 1998. / Hoffman, Mary. *Henry's Baby*. Dorling Kindersley, 1993. / Howe, James. *Horace and Morris Join the Chorus (But What About Dolores?)*. Atheneum, 2002. / Marshall, James. *George and Martha: The Complete Stories of Two Best Friends*. Houghton Mifflin, 1997. / Pomerantz, Charlotte. *You're Not My Best Friend Anymore*. Dial, 1998. / Raschka, Chris. *Yo! Yes?* Orchard, 1993. / Waber, Bernard. *Evie and Margie*. Houghton Mifflin, 2003. / Winthrop, Elizabeth. *Lizzie and Harold*. Lothrop, 1985.

SUBJECTS: BEST FRIENDS. CLUBS. FRIENDSHIP. MICE. PICTURE BOOKS FOR ALL AGES. SEX ROLE.

389   **Howe, James. *Horace and Morris Join the Chorus (But What About Dolores?)*. Illus. by Amy Walrod. Atheneum, 2002. 0-689-83939-1. Unp. Gr. PreK–2**
Although mouse pals Horace and Morris get accepted into the school chorus, enthusiastic but tone-impaired Dolores is told by music teacher Moustro Provolone that she doesn't have an ear for music. For all those kids who have been told they can't sing, this story will be a welcome balm, as Dolores is determined to sing no matter what.

GERM: Discussion point: Dolores sticks up for herself when she feels she's been treated unfairly. Have you ever done that? What happened? Use Dolores's rhyming letter to Moustro Provolone as a kickoff to your persuasive writing lesson. Make sure your music teacher gets a copy of the book to share with music classes and the kids in the chorus.

RELATED TITLES: Cox, Judy. *My Family Plays Music*. Holiday House, 2003. / Dodds, Dayle Ann. *Sing, Sophie*. Candlewick, 1997. / Goss, Linda. *The Frog Who Wanted to Be a Singer*. Orchard, 1996. / Hoffman, Mary. *Amazing Grace*. Dial, 1991. / Howe, James. *Horace and Morris But Mostly Dolores*. Atheneum, 1999. / Hurd, Thacher. *Art Dog*. HarperCollins, 1996. / Khalsa, Dayal Kaur. *Cowboy Dreams*. Crown, 1990. / Krull, Kathleen. *M Is for Music*. Harcourt, 2003. / Stadler, Alexander. *Beverly Billingsly Takes a Bow*. Harcourt, 2003. (And others in the Beverly Billingsly series.) / Weaver, Tess. *Opera Cat*. Clarion, 2002.

SUBJECTS: AUDITIONS. DETERMINATION. MICE. MUSIC. PERSUASIVE WRITING. PICTURE BOOKS FOR ALL AGES. SCHOOLS. SINGING. TEACHERS.

390   **Howe, James. *Pinky and Rex and the Bully*. Illus. by Melissa Sweet. Atheneum, 1996. 0-689-80021-5. 48pp. Gr. 1–3**
When Kevin knocks him off his bike and taunts him for being a girl and a sissy, Pinky—who loves the color pink and has a girl for a best friend—decides he should change his name back to Billy. Pinky's wise elderly neighbor, Mrs. Morgan, whom we first met in *Pinky and Rex and the Mean Old Witch*, gives him wise counsel drawn from her own experience, including "Don't change for other people . . . Do what's right for the one person who will always be with you—yourself."

GERM: Make text-to-life connections to discuss and/or write about: How has Mrs. Morgan's advice applied to you? How are boys and girls different? Who makes the rules about what boys and girls can and can't do? Compare Pinky's reactions with Quinn's in Kirby Larson's *Cody and Quinn, Sitting in a Tree*. Send readers off in search of the other books in the series, starting with *Pinky and Rex*.

RELATED TITLES: Bottner, Barbara. *Bootsie Barker Bites*. Putnam, 1992. / Browne, Anthony. *Willy the Wimp*. Knopf, 1985. / Caseley, Judith. *Bully*. Greenwillow, 2001. / Cole, Joanna. *Don't Call Me Names*. Random House, 1990. / Greene, Stephanie. *Owen Foote, Frontiersman*. Clarion, 1999. / Howe, James. *Pinky and Rex*. Atheneum, 1990. (And others in the Pinky and Rex series.) / Krensky, Stephen. *Louise Takes Charge*. Dial, 1998. / Larson, Kirby. *Cody and Quinn, Sitting in a Tree*. Holiday House, 1996. / Meddaugh, Susan. *Martha Walks the Dog*. Houghton Mifflin, 1998. / Naylor, Phyllis Reynolds. *King of the Playground*. Atheneum, 1991. / O'Neill, Alexis. *The Recess Queen*. Scholastic, 2002. / Polacco, Patricia. *Mr. Lincoln's Way*. Philomel, 2001. / Sorel, Edward, and Cheryl Carlesimo. *The Saturday Kid*. McElderry, 2000. / Wilhelm, Hans. *Tyrone the Horrible*. Scholastic, 1988.

SUBJECTS: BEST FRIENDS. BULLIES. ELDERLY. FRIENDSHIP. IDENTITY. PROBLEM SOLVING. SELF-ACCEPTANCE. SEX ROLE.

391   **Howland, Naomi. *Latkes, Latkes, Good to Eat*. Illus. by the author. Clarion, 1999. 0-395-89903-6. Unp. Gr. K–2**
Gathering firewood on the first night of Chanukah, Sadie donates her pile to a shivering old woman, who gives her, in return, a magic frying pan. Back home, Sadie whispers the magic words and cooks up delicious latkes for her four younger brothers. When she leaves them

home alone, they disobey her instructions and try out the frying pan, but they don't know the correct words—"A great miracle happened here!"—to make it stop cooking.

GERM: There's a nice recipe for latkes at the back of the book. Tasty variants on the "Sorcerer's Apprentice" theme include Tomie dePaola's *Strega Nona* and Paul Galdone's *The Magic Porridge Pot*. Eric A. Kimmel's *The Magic Dreidels* also features magical potato pancakes for the holiday.

RELATED TITLES: dePaola, Tomie. *Jamie O'Rourke and the Big Potato: An Irish Folktale*. Putnam, 1992. / dePaola, Tomie. *Strega Nona*. Simon & Schuster, 1979. / Dewan, Ted. *The Sorcerer's Apprentice*. Doubleday, 1998. / Galdone, Paul. *The Magic Porridge Pot*. Seabury, 1976. / Hirsch, Marilyn. *Potato Pancakes All Around: A Hanukkah Tale*. Bonim, 1978. / Jaffe, Nina. *In the Month of Kislev: A Story for Hanukkah*. Viking, 1992. / Kimmel, Eric A. *Anansi and the Magic Stick*. Holiday House, 2001. / Kimmel, Eric A. *Asher and the Capmakers: A Hanukkah Story*. Holiday House, 1993. / Kimmel, Eric A. *The Chanukkah Guest*. Holiday House, 1990. / Kimmel, Eric A. *The Jar of Fools: Eight Hanukkah Stories from Chelm*. Holiday House, 2000. / Kimmel, Eric A. *The Magic Dreidels: A Hanukkah Story*. Holiday House, 1996. / Moore, Inga. *The Sorcerer's Apprentice*. Macmillan, 1989. / Newman, Lesléa. *Runaway Dreidel!* Henry Holt, 2002. / Sawyer, Ruth. *The Remarkable Christmas of the Cobbler's Sons*. Viking, 1994.

SUBJECTS: FOOD. HANUKKAH. JEWS. MAGIC.

392 **Howland, Naomi.** *The Matzah Man: A Passover Story*. **Illus. by the author. Clarion, 2002. 0-618-11750-4. Unp. Gr. PreK–2**

Taking the Passover matzah out of the oven, baker Mr. Cohen is startled when a little matzah man jumps out and runs to the door, chanting, "Hot from the oven I jumped and ran, So clever and quick, I'm the Matzah Man!" As in "The Gingerbread Man" tales upon which this delicious Passover adventure is based, the little scamp races through the village, chased by everybody. But instead of being tricked by the fox, the Matzah Man meets his end at young Mendel's house, where he is eaten during the seder.

GERM: Compare his journey with that of another Jewish morsel for Spring or Passover story-times, *The Matzo Ball Boy*, by Lisa Shulman. Bring in matzah for everyone to crunch.

RELATED TITLES: Aylesworth, Jim. *The Gingerbread Man*. Scholastic, 1998. / Compestine, Ying Chang. *The Runaway Rice Cake*. Simon & Schuster, 2001. / Cook, Scott. *The Gingerbread Boy*. Knopf, 1987. / Egielski, Richard. *The Gingerbread Boy*. HarperCollins, 1997. / Hirsch, Marilyn. *Potato Pancakes All Around; A Hanukkah Tale*. Bonim, 1978. / Howland, Naomi. *Latkes, Latkes, Good to Eat*. Clarion, 1999. / Kimmel, Eric A. *Asher and the Capmakers: A Hanukkah Story*. Holiday House, 1993. / Kimmel, Eric A. *The Chanukkah Guest*. Holiday House, 1990. / Kimmel, Eric A. *Hershel and the Hanukkah Goblins*. Holiday House, 1989. / Kimmel, Eric A. *The Runaway Tortilla*. Winslow, 2000. / Newman, Lesléa. *Runaway Dreidel!* Henry Holt, 2002. / Shulman, Lisa. *The Matzo Ball Boy*. Dutton, 2005.

SUBJECTS: CHANTABLE REFRAIN. FOOD. GINGERBREAD BOY. JEWS. PASSOVER. SEQUENCE STORIES.

393 **Hubbard, Patricia.** *Trick or Treat Countdown*. **Illus. by Michael Letzig. Holiday House, 1999. 0-8234-1367-5. Unp. Gr. PreK**

Count to ten and back again with a rhyming Halloween treat full of the usual seasonal suspects, cackling, groaning, gleaming, and screaming, and colorful night-toned illustrations that are scary, but not overly so.

GERM: Act this out, with its prowling monsters, howling werewolves, gliding bats, and creeping cats, and add sound effects for each creature. Keep counting while you cook up a witch's brew with *One Witch* by Laura Leuck.

RELATED TITLES: Bunting, Eve. *In the Haunted House*. Clarion, 1990. / Bunting, Eve. *Scary, Scary Halloween*. Clarion, 1986. / Cuyler, Margery. *Skeleton Hiccups*. Simon & Schuster, 2002. / Krosoczka, Jarrett J. *Annie Was Warned*. Knopf, 2003. / Leuck, Laura. *One Witch*. Walker, 2003. / Regan, Dian Curtis. *The Thirteen Hours of Halloween*. Albert Whitman, 1993. / Shute, Linda. *Halloween Party*. Lothrop, 1994. / Silverman, Erica. *Big Pumpkin*. Macmillan, 1992. / Sklansky, Amy E. *Skeleton Bones and Goblin Groans: Poems for Halloween*. Henry Holt, 2004. / Stutson, Caroline. *By the Light of the Halloween Moon*. Lothrop, 1993. / Williams, Linda. *The Little Old Lady Who Was Not Afraid of Anything*. Crowell, 1986.

SUBJECTS: CHANTABLE REFRAIN. COUNTING BOOKS. CREATIVE DRAMA. HALLOWEEN. STORIES IN RHYME.

394 **Hughes, Shirley.** *Ella's Big Chance: A Jazz-Age Cinderella*. **Illus. by the author. Simon & Schuster, 2004. 0-689-87399-9. Unp. Gr. K–4**

After widower Mr. Cinders, the owner of a small dress shop, marries Madame Renee, his daughter Ella has to work harder than ever sewing clothes for her stepmothers' beautiful, lazy, spiteful daughters, Ruby and Pearl. Ella's only friend is Buttons, a kind young man who works there as a doorman. When the Duchess of Arc holds a grand ball for her only son at her villa, Ella is resigned to staying home, but her Fairy Godmother arrives to send her off in style.

GERM: Set in the flapper era, this retelling features a wholesome Cinderella who finds true love, and an unexpected ending. Meet other gals who forsake their Prince Charmings for better fellows in *Fanny's Dream* by Caralyn Buehner and *Cinder Edna* by Ellen Jackson.

RELATED TITLES: Buehner, Caralyn. *Fanny's Dream*. Dial, 1996. / Craft, K. Y. *Cinderella*. SeaStar Books, 2000. / dePaola, Tomie. *Adelita: A Mexican Cinderella Story*. Putnam, 2002. / Ehrlich, Amy. *Cinderella*. Illus. by Susan Jeffers. Dutton, 2004. / Jackson, Ellen. *Cinder Edna*. Lothrop, 1994. / Ketteman, Helen. *Bubba the Cowboy Prince: A Fractured Texas Tale*. Scholastic, 1997. / Lowell, Susan. *Cindy Ellen: A Wild Western Cinderella*. Orchard, 1997. / Minters, Frances. *Cinder Elly*. Viking, 1993. / Myers, Bernice. *Sidney Rella and the Glass Sneaker*. Macmillan, 1985. / Sanderson, Ruth. *Cinderella*. Little, Brown, 2002. / Whipple, Laura. *If the Shoe Fits: Voices from Cinderella*. McElderry, 2002.

SUBJECTS: CATS. CINDERELLA STORIES. FAIRY TALES. LOVE. PARODIES. STEPMOTHERS.

395   **Huling, Jan.** *Puss in Cowboy Boots*. **Illus. by Phil Huling. Simon & Schuster, 2002. 0-689-83119-6. Unp. Gr. K–4**

When rodeo clown Clem kicks the bucket, he leaves his old cat Puss to his youngest son, Dan. Dan isn't so impressed, until Puss speaks up and asks for a pair of cowboy boots and an old burlap sack. "I got me a plan that's gonna make you gladder than a mosquito at a blood bank and will keep me in sardines and sweet cream for life!" In his red snakeskin cowboy boots, Puss sets off to impress Mr. Patoot, the most powerful oilman in the state of Texas, and his daughter, Rosie-May.

GERM: That old Puss in Boots tale from France sure does take well to Texas. Compare and contrast the lingo, plot, characters, and setting to the traditional versions by Charles Perrault, including those by Cauley, Galdone, Kirstein, and Marcellino.

RELATED TITLES: Axelrod, Alan, comp. *Songs of the Wild West*. Simon & Schuster, 1991. / Buehner, Caralyn. *Fanny's Dream*. Dial, 1996. / Cauley, Lorinda Bryan. *Puss in Boots*. Harcourt, 1986. / Frank, John. *The Toughest Cowboy*. Simon & Schuster, 2004. / Galdone, Paul. *Puss in Boots*. Clarion, 1976. / Icenoggle, Jodi. *'Til the Cows Come Home*. Boyds Mills, 2004. / Jackson, Ellen. *Cinder Edna*. Lothrop, 1994. / Johnston, Tony. *The Cowboy and the Black-Eyed Pea*. Putnam, 1992. / Ketteman, Helen. *Bubba the Cowboy Prince: A Fractured Texas Tale*. Scholastic, 1997. / Kirstein, Lincoln. *Puss in Boots*. Little, Brown, 1992. / Lowell, Susan. *The Bootmaker and the Elves*. Orchard, 1997. / Lowell, Susan. *Cindy Ellen: A Wild Western Cinderella*. Orchard, 1997. / Marcellino, Fred. *Puss in Boots*. Farrar, 1990. / Mitchell, Marianne. *Joe Cinders*. Henry Holt, 2002. / Myers, Bernice. *Sidney Rella and the Glass Sneaker*. Macmillan, 1985.

SUBJECTS: BOOTS. CATS. CHARACTERS IN LITERATURE. FAIRY TALES—SATIRE. OGRES—FOLKLORE. PARODIES. TEXAS.

396   **Hunter, Anne.** *Possum's Harvest Moon*. **Illus. by the author. Houghton Mifflin, 1996. 0-395-73575-0. Unp. Gr. PreK–2**

On an autumn evening when the moon is full and bright and yellow, Possum invites all the animals for one last dance in the moonlight—a Harvest Soiree—before the onset of winter. But the mice, crickets, raccoons, frogs, and fireflies all say they're too busy to come. Luckily, they all change their minds, and the dreamy cross-hatched illustrations of their revels will put everyone in an autumn mood.

GERM: Introduce your winter unit with this one and talk about where those animals will go, come winter. Or read animal stories that center around the seasons.

RELATED TITLES: Ehlert, Lois. *Moon Rope: Un Lazo a la Luna: A Peruvian Folktale*. Harcourt, 1992. / Fleming, Denise. *Time to Sleep*. Henry Holt, 1997. / Fuchs, Diane Marcial. *A Bear for All Seasons*. Henry Holt, 1995. / Kherdian, David. *The Cat's Midsummer Jamboree*. Philomel, 1990. / Lionni, Leo. *Frederick*. Knopf, 1967. / Minarik, Else Holmelund. *It's Spring!* Greenwillow, 1989. / Murray, Marjorie Dennis. *Don't Wake Up the Bear!* Cavendish, 2003. / Peters, Lisa Westberg. *Cold Little Duck, Duck, Duck*. Greenwillow, 2000. / Pollock, Penny. *When the Moon Is Full: A Lunar Year*. Little, Brown, 2001. / Seuling, Barbara. *Winter Lullaby*. Harcourt, 1998. / Simmons, Jane. *Little Fern's First Winter*. Little, Brown, 2001. / Waddell, Martin. *Can't You Sleep Little Bear*. Candlewick, 1992. / Yolen, Jane. *What Rhymes with Moon?* Philomel, 1993.

SUBJECTS: ANIMALS. AUTUMN. MOON. OPOSSUMS. PARTIES. SEASONS.

397 Hurd, Thacher. *Art Dog.* **Illus. by the author. HarperCollins, 1996. 0-06-024425-9. Unp. Gr. PreK–4**

Mild-mannered Dogopolis Museum of Art guard Arthur Dog dons a mask and a beret each full moon and becomes Art Dog, painter of extraordinary wall murals. Unjustly accused of stealing the "Mona Woofa," he paints his way out of jail and apprehends the real thieves. "I can smell art a mile away," he tells the grateful director, who offers him his own show.

GERM: Compare the paintings Art Dog guards, by dog artists from Pablo Poodle to Henri Muttisse, with those of their human counterparts. Listeners will revel in pointing out the styles of painters they recognize, culminating in a marvelous takeoff on Van Gogh's "Starry Night."

RELATED TITLES: Agee, Jon. *The Incredible Painting of Felix Clousseau.* Farrar, 1988. / Alcorn, Johnny. *Rembrandt's Beret.* Tambourine, 1991. / Auch, Mary Jane. *Eggs Mark the Spot.* Holiday House, 1996. / Browne, Anthony. *Willy the Dreamer.* Candlewick, 1998. / Buehner, Caralyn. *Superdog: The Heart of a Hero.* HarperCollins, 2004. / Garland, Michael. *Dinner at Magritte's.* Dutton, 1995. / Laden, Nina. *The Night I Followed the Dog.* Chronicle, 1994. / Laden, Nina. *When Pigasso Met Mootisse.* Chronicle, 1998. / LaMarche, Jim. *The Raft.* HarperCollins, 2000. / Lithgow, John. *Micawber.* Simon & Schuster, 2002. / Raczka, Bob. *Art Is . . .* Millbrook, 2003. / Rathmann, Peggy. *Officer Buckle and Gloria.* Putnam, 1995. / Reynolds, Peter H. *The Dot.* Candlewick, 2003. / Weitzman, Jacqueline Preiss. *You Can't Take a Balloon into the Metropolitan Museum.* Dial, 1998.

SUBJECTS: ARTISTS. DOGS. MUSEUMS. PICTURE BOOKS FOR ALL AGES. ROBBERS AND OUTLAWS.

398 Hurst, Carol Otis. *Rocks in His Head.* **Illus. by James Stevenson. Greenwillow, 2001. 0-06-029403-5. Unp. Gr. PreK–3**

The author relates the story of her rock-loving father, who opened up a filling station as a young man and raised a family, but continued his passion for rock-collecting, which ultimately led to a job at a science museum.

GERM: Ask students to write and illustrate an essay about interests they have that they think they'll never give up. They can interview parents to find out if they pursued an interest from an early age to now. Collect and identify local rocks as part of a geology unit.

RELATED TITLES: Barasch, Lynne. *Radio Rescue.* Farrar, 2000. / Baylor, Byrd. *Everybody Needs a Rock.* Simon & Schuster, 1974. / Christian, Peggy. *If You Find a Rock.* Harcourt, 2000. / Hooper, Meredith. *The Pebble in My Pocket: A History of Our Earth.* Viking, 1996. / Houston, Gloria. *My Great Aunt Arizona.* HarperCollins, 1992. / Lasky, Kathryn. *Marven of the North Woods.* Harcourt, 1997. / Marrin, Albert. *Secrets from the Rocks: Dinosaur Hunting with Roy Chapman Andrews.* Dutton, 2002. / Polacco, Patricia. *My Ol' Man.* Philomel, 1995.

SUBJECTS: BIOGRAPHY. FAMILY LIFE. FATHERS. PICTURE BOOKS FOR ALL AGES. ROCKS.

399 Icenoggle, Jodi. *'Til the Cows Come Home.* **Illus. by Normand Chartier. Boyds Mills, 2004. 1-56397-987-X. Unp. Gr. PreK–3**

Grateful for the fine piece of leather an old cowpuncher gives him, a young cowboy stitches it into a handsome pair of chaps, which he plans to wear "'til the cows come home." When they wear out, he makes a vest, a pair of gloves, a hatband, and finally, a button for his jeans. In the meantime, the cowboy courts and marries Sally Mae, and they have a baby daughter, to whom he tells the story of his flawless piece of leather.

GERM: This warm and affectionate version of the old Jewish folksong known as "I Had a Little Overcoat" or "The Button Story" comes with sweeping watercolor vistas of a western ranch and a glossary of western words and phrases. Have listeners retell the story in sequence and compare it with other picture-book versions, including *Something from Nothing* by Phoebe Gilman, *Bit by Bit* by Steve Sanfield, and *Joseph Had a Little Overcoat* by Simms Taback.

RELATED TITLES: Connor, Leslie. *Miss Bridie Chose a Shovel.* Houghton Mifflin, 2004. / Dragonwagon, Crescent. *Brass Button.* Atheneum, 1997. / Gilman, Phoebe. *Something from Nothing.* Scholastic, 1993. / Johnston, Tony. *The Cowboy and the Black-Eyed Pea.* Putnam, 1992. / Ketteman, Helen. *Bubba the Cowboy Prince: A Fractured Texas Tale.* Scholastic, 1997. / Lowell, Susan. *The Bootmaker and the Elves.* Orchard, 1997. / Lowell, Susan. *Cindy Ellen: A Wild Western Cinderella.* Orchard, 1997. / Mazer, Anne. *The Yellow Button.* Knopf, 1990. / Medearis, Angela Shelf. *The Zebra-Riding Cowboy: A Folk Song from the Old West.* Henry Holt, 1992. / Mitchell, Marianne. *Joe Cinders.* Henry Holt, 2002. / Sanfield, Steve. *Bit by Bit.* Philomel, 1995. / Taback, Simms. *Joseph Had a Little Overcoat.* Viking, 1999. / Ziefert, Harriet. *When I First Came to This Land.* Putnam, 1998.

SUBJECTS: BUTTONS. CHANTABLE REFRAIN. CIRCULAR STORIES. CLOTHING AND DRESS. COWBOYS. SEQUENCE STORIES. STORIES TO TELL. WEST (U.S.).

400   Ichikawa, Satomi. *La La Rose.* **Illus. by the author. Philomel, 2004. 0-399-24029-2. Unp. Gr. PreK–K**

La La Rose, a pink stuffed rabbit and the inseparable friend of her little girl, Clementine, is tragically left behind in Luxembourg Gardens when Clementine runs off to see the puppet show. Wet and dirty after a careless young man throws her in the water, La La Rose is rescued by another little girl who reunites her with a grateful Clementine.

GERM: Sweet watercolors show the helpless rabbit narrator having a not-very-good day, even if she is in Paris. Have children pair up to act out Clementine and La La Rose's reunion, discussing how each one felt and what happened during their separation.

RELATED TITLES: Alborough, Jez. *Where's My Teddy?* Candlewick, 1992. / Clark, Emma Chichester. *Where Are You, Blue Kangaroo?* Doubleday, 2000. / Falconer, Ian. *Olivia . . . and the Missing Toy.* Atheneum, 2003. / Fitzpatrick, Marie-Louise. *Lizzy and Skunk.* DK Ink, 2000. / Horse, Harry. *Little Rabbit Goes to School.* Peachtree, 2004. / Hughes, Shirley. *Dogger.* Lothrop, 1988. / Moss, Miriam. *Don't Forget I Love You.* Dial, 2004. / Rusackas, Francesca. *I Love You All Day Long.* HarperCollins, 2002. / Smith, Maggie. *Paisley.* Knopf, 2004. / Weiss, Nicki. *Hank and Oogie.* Lothrop, 1987. / Willems, Mo. *Knuffle Bunny: A Cautionary Tale.* Hyperion, 2004.

SUBJECTS: CREATIVE DRAMA. FRANCE. LOST AND FOUND POSSESSIONS. PARIS. PERSONAL NARRATIVES. POINT OF VIEW. RABBITS. STUFFED ANIMALS. TOYS.

401   Jackson, Alison. *I Know an Old Lady Who Swallowed a Pie.* **Illus. by Judith Byron Schachner. Dutton, 1997. 0-525-45645-7. Unp. Gr. PreK–2**

A ravenous and overzealous Thanksgiving guest scarfs down pie, cider, roll, squash, salad, turkey, a pot, cake, and, finally, some bread before she is sated.

GERM: Sing this at Thanksgiving time, but also compare it to the nonsense song on which it is based, using Karas's *I Know an Old Lady*, Rounds's *I Know an Old Lady Who Swallowed a Fly*, Taback's *There Was an Old Lady Who Swallowed a Fly*, or Westcott's *I Know an Old Lady Who Swallowed a Fly*. Dav Pilkey's *'Twas the Night Before Thanksgiving* is another funny Turkey Day parody.

RELATED TITLES: Karas, G. Brian. *I Know an Old Lady.* Scholastic, 1984. / Pilkey, Dav. *'Twas the Night Before Thanksgiving.* Scholastic, 1990. / Rounds, Glen. *I Know an Old Lady Who Swallowed a Fly.* Holiday House, 1990. / So, Meilo. *Gobble, Gobble, Slip, Slop: The Tale of a Very Greedy Cat.* Knopf, 2004. / Spinelli, Eileen. *Thanksgiving at the Tappleton's.* HarperCollins, 2003. / Taback, Simms. *There Was an Old Lady Who Swallowed a Fly.* Viking, 1997. / Thomson, Pat. *Drat That Fat Cat!* Scholastic, 2003. / Westcott, Nadine Bernard. *I Know an Old Lady Who Swallowed a Fly.* Little, Brown, 1980.

SUBJECTS: ELDERLY. FOOD. GREED. PARODIES. STORIES IN RHYME. STORIES WITH SONGS. SWALLOWING STORIES. THANKSGIVING.

402   James, Simon. *Baby Brains.* **Illus. by the author. Candlewick, 2004. 0-7636-2507-8. Unp. Gr. PreK–1**

The smartest baby in the whole world, Baby Brains, reads the paper, fixes the car, and works as a doctor at the hospital. But when he blasts off into space to help with the latest space mission and takes his first space walk, he wails, "I want my mommy!"

GERM: Talk about the Hurried Child syndrome! Children will be bowled over by Baby Brains's great intellect. What might Baby Brains try next? Kids can write and illustrate a new undertaking: "Baby Brains can ___." In the sequel, *Baby Brains, Superstar*, Baby Brains becomes a rock star.

RELATED TITLES: Appelt, Kathi. *Bubba and Beau.* Harcourt, 2002. (And others in the Bubba and Beau series.) / Ashman, Linda. *Babies on the Go.* Harcourt, 2003. / James, Simon. *Baby Brains, Superstar.* Candlewick, 2005. / James, Simon. *Leon and Bob.* Candlewick, 1997. / Rathmann, Peggy. *The Day the Babies Crawled Away.* Putnam, 2003. / Regan, Dian Curtis. *Chance.* Philomel, 2003. / Schwartz, Amy. *A Teeny Tiny Baby.* Orchard, 1994. / Willis, Jeanne. *Earthlets: As Explained by Professor Xargle.* Dutton, 1988.

SUBJECTS: BABIES. HUMOROUS FICTION. INTELLECT.

403   James, Simon. *Little One Step.* **Illus. by the author. Candlewick, 2003. 0-7636-2070-X. Unp. Gr. PreK–K**

Three ducklings are lost. "I want my mama," whispers the little one. "My legs feel all wobbly." His oldest brother shows him how to do One Step. Lift one foot and say "one." Then put it down in front and say "step." Wow. It works. He gets discouraged, but he keeps walking with his brothers, through the forest, across the field, through the undergrowth, and, finally, there's MAMA! Yellow watercolors lined with black ink are sweet and affectionate, and your little ones will empathize with Little One Step, trying hard to keep up.

GERM: Ask your ducklings: Have you ever had trouble keeping up with the big kids? What did you do? What other words of encouragement would you give to Little One Step? And, of course, they'll want to practice One Step walking, following you in a line around the room.

RELATED TITLES: Buzzeo, Toni. *Dawdle Duckling*. Dial, 2003. / Dunrea, Olivier. *Gossie*. Houghton Mifflin, 2002. / Dunrea, Olivier. *Gossie and Gertie*. Houghton Mifflin, 2002. / Dunrea, Olivier. *Ollie*. Houghton, 2003. / Dunrea, Olivier. *Ollie the Stomper*. Houghton, 2003. / Gerstein, Mordicai. *Follow Me!* Morrow, 1983. / Hest, Amy. *In the Rain with Baby Duck*. Candlewick, 1995. / Hutchins, Pat. *Rosie's Walk*. Bradbury, 1987. / Raffi. *Five Little Ducks*. Crown, 1988. / Shannon, George. *Tippy-Toe Chick, Go!* Greenwillow, 2003. / Simmons, Jane. *Come Along, Daisy*. Little, Brown, 1998. / Simmons, Jane. *Quack, Daisy, Quack!* Little, Brown, 2002. / Waddell, Martin. *Webster J. Duck*. Candlewick, 2001. / Whippo, Walt, and Bernard Zaritzky. *Little White Duck*. Little, Brown, 2000. / Wikler, Linda. *Alfonse, Where Are You?* Crown, 1996.

SUBJECTS: ANIMALS. BROTHERS. DUCKS. PERSEVERANCE.

404 **Jarrett, Clare.** *The Best Picnic Ever.* **Illus. by the author. Candlewick, 2004. 0-7636-2370-9. Unp. Gr. PreK–K**

On a picnic with his mom at the park, Jack wishes for someone to play with, and, lo and behold, a giraffe shows up and takes him gallopy, gallopy through the tall grass. Next, they meet an elephant who trumpets, tootley-toot; a leopard who leaps, lollopy, lollopy; and a tiger who leads them all in a dance.

GERM: Childlike, scribbly colored pencil illustrations and a vivacious story, full of motion and repeated refrains, will get your listeners dancing and acting the whole thing out.

RELATED TITLES: Carle, Eric. *From Head to Toe*. HarperCollins, 1997. / Cauley, Lorinda Bryan. *Clap Your Hands*. Putnam, 1992. / Clark, Emma Chichester. *Follow the Leader!* Simon & Schuster, 2003. / Harter, Debbie. *Walking Through the Jungle*. Orchard, 1997. / Levine, Evan. *Not the Piano, Mrs. Medley!* Orchard, 1991. / McCully, Emily Arnold. *Picnic*. HarperCollins, 2003. / Martin, Bill, Jr. *Brown Bear, Brown Bear, What Do You See?* Henry Holt, 1983. / Martin, Bill, Jr. *Polar Bear, Polar Bear, What Do You Hear?* Henry Holt, 1991. / Parker, Vic. *Bearobics*. Viking, 1997. / Root, Phyllis. *Rattletrap Car*. Candlewick, 2001. / Rosen, Michael. *We're Going on a Bear Hunt*. McElderry, 1989. / Walter, Virginia. *"Hi, Pizza Man!"* Orchard, 1995. / Williams, Sue. *I Went Walking*. Gulliver/Harcourt, 1990.

SUBJECTS: ANIMALS. CHANTABLE REFRAIN. CREATIVE DRAMA. MOTHERS AND SONS. PICNICS. PLAY.

405 **Johnson, D. B.** *Henry Hikes to Fitchburg.* **Illus. by the author. Houghton Mifflin, 2000. 0-395-96867-4. Unp. Gr. 1–4**

Heading to Fitchburg 30 miles away, bear Henry decides that walking is the fastest way to travel, while his friend plans to work for money to pay for the 90-cent train ticket there. Henry's friend chops wood, pulls weeds, and paints a fence; Henry carves a walking stick, presses flowers in a book, and walks on stone walls. Henry's friend gets there a bit ahead of Henry. "The train was faster," he says. Henry replies, "I know. I stopped for blackberries." Which way is more valuable? It depends on your outlook on the value of hard work versus the need to stop and smell the roses.

GERM: Discussion point: Which way of getting to Fitchburg appeals to you and why? This is an interesting introduction to Henry David Thoreau and his life at Walden Pond in the mid-19th century. Read aloud the About Henry page at the back of the book, including Thoreau's actual description that led to Johnson's creation of his story. Follow up with Johnson's other intriguing tales about Henry, including *Henry Builds a Cabin*, *Henry Climbs a Mountain*, and *Henry Works*. Meet Thoreau as a young man in *Louisa May and Mr. Thoreau's Flute* by Julie Dunlap and Marybeth Lorbiecki.

RELATED TITLES: Becker, Bonny. *An Ant's Day Off*. Simon & Schuster, 2003. / Dunlap, Julie, and Marybeth Lorbiecki. *Louisa May and Mr. Thoreau's Flute*. Dial, 2002. / Fleischman, Paul. *Weslandia*. Candlewick, 1999. / Johnson, D. B. *Henry Builds a Cabin*. Houghton Mifflin, 2002. / Johnson, D. B. *Henry Climbs a Mountain*. Houghton Mifflin, 2003. / Johnson, D. B. *Henry Works*. Houghton Mifflin, 2004. / Kimmel, Eric A. *Anansi and the Magic Stick*. Holiday House, 2001. / O'Neal, Deborah, and Angela Westengard. *The Trouble with Henry: A Tale of Walden Pond*. Candlewick, 2005. / Swope, Sam. *The Araboolies of Liberty Street*. Crown, 1989. / Thoreau, Henry. *Walden, or, Life in the Woods*. Knopf, 1992. / Yashima, Taro. *Crow Boy*. Viking, 1955. / Yorinks, Arthur. *Hey, Al*. Farrar, 1986.

SUBJECTS: BEARS. INDIVIDUALITY. NATURE. NONCONFORMISTS. THOREAU, HENRY DAVID. WALKING. WORK.

406   Johnson, Doug. *Never Ride Your Elephant to School.* **Illus. by Abby Carter. Henry Holt, 1995. 0-8050-2880-3. Unp. Gr. PreK–2**

Bringing an elephant to school could cause problems, so a boy describes precisely what one should and shouldn't do to keep that elephant under control during math, lunch, spelling, gym, and art.

GERM: Ask animal lovers to pick their favorite creature and make an illustrated chart, listing the pros and cons of bringing it to school. They can then flesh out their charts, writing cause-and-effect stories about their animal's school behavior. Compare and contrast the consequences of bringing an elephant and a mouse with Laura Joffe Numeroff's *If You Take a Mouse to School.*

RELATED TITLES: Barrett, Judi. *Animals Should Definitely Not Wear Clothing.* Atheneum, 1970. / Grambling, Lois G. *Can I Have a Stegosaurus, Mom? Can I? Please!?* BridgeWater, 1995. / Jenkins, Martin. *Grandma Elephant's in Charge.* Candlewick, 2003. / Kimmel, Elizabeth Cody. *My Penguin, Osbert.* Candlewick, 2004. / Numeroff, Laura. *Chimps Don't Wear Glasses.* Simon & Schuster, 1995. / Numeroff, Laura. *Dogs Don't Wear Sneakers.* Simon & Schuster, 1993. / Numeroff, Laura. *If You Give a Mouse a Cookie.* HarperCollins, 1985. / Numeroff, Laura Joffe. *If You Take a Mouse to School.* HarperCollins, 2003. / Wolf, Jake. *Daddy, Could I Have an Elephant?* Greenwillow, 1996.

SUBJECTS: BEHAVIOR. CAUSE AND EFFECT. ELEPHANTS. HUMOROUS FICTION. IMAGINATION. SCHOOLS.

407   Johnson, Paul Brett. *Little Bunny Foo Foo.* **Illus. by the author. Scholastic, 2004. 0-439-37301-8. Unp. Gr. PreK–1**

The traditional silly story-song is expanded a bit here and narrated by the Good Fairy herself, as she gives the bopping bunny three chances to behave before she turns him into a goon. (My preschoolers, with whom I loved to tell and act out this story every year, used to say, ". . . or I'll turn you into a GOOF!") The goofy bunny continues bopping field mice, woodchucks, foxes, and grizzly bears with his mud pies until the Good Fairy makes good on her threat.

GERM: At the back are the original words to the story, the music, and the moves for acting it all out. Yes, of course you'll want to explain the punny moral, "Hare today, goon tomorrow," so the kids will get it.

RELATED TITLES: Anholt, Catherine, and Laurence Anholt. *Chimp and Zee.* Putnam, 2001. / Christelow, Eileen. *Five Little Monkeys Jumping on the Bed.* Clarion, 1989. (And others in the Five Little Monkeys series.) / Harper, Wilhelmina. *The Gunniwolf.* Dutton, 2003. / Karas, G. Brian. *I Know an Old Lady.* Scholastic, 1984. / Koller, Jackie French. *One Monkey Too Many.* Harcourt, 1999. / MacDonald, Margaret Read. *Pickin' Peas.* HarperCollins, 1998. / Palatini, Margie. *Bad Boys.* HarperCollins, 2003. / Potter, Beatrix. *The Tale of Peter Rabbit.* Warne, 1902. / Rey, H. A. *Curious George.* Houghton Mifflin, 1993. (And others in the Curious George series.) / Slobodkina, Esphyr. *Caps for Sale.* HarperCollins, 1947. / So, Meilo. *Gobble, Gobble, Slip, / Slop: The Tale of a Very Greedy Cat.* Knopf, 2004. / Taback, Simms. *There Was an Old Lady Who Swallowed a Fly.* Viking, 1997.

SUBJECTS: BEHAVIOR. FAIRIES. HUMOROUS FICTION. RABBITS. STORIES WITH SONGS.

408   Johnson, Paul Brett, and Celeste Lewis. *Lost.* **Illus. by Paul Brett Johnson. Orchard, 1996. 0-531-08851-0. Unp. Gr. 1–3**

A girl and her father search for their beagle, Flag, after he chases a rabbit and gets lost in the Arizona desert. The illustrations on the right-hand page, done in sketchy, brown-toned, colored pencils, show the worried girl as she and her dad scour the canyon. On the left side, in desert-toned acrylics, we see what Flag is going through nearby as he encounters a coyote, rattlesnake, javelinas, and a mountain lion.

GERM: Amazingly, this survival story really happened to the author and her dog, Flag, though she is just speculating when she shows us Flag's side of his month-long desert sojourn. Compare Flag's desert encounters with those of sheepdog Floss as she treks through the snow in Debi Gliori's *The Snow Lambs.*

RELATED TITLES: Asch, Frank. *Cactus Poems.* Harcourt, 1998. / Carrick, Carol. *Lost in the Storm.* Clarion, 1987. / Gliori, Debi. *The Snow Lambs.* Scholastic, 1996. / Levy, Elizabeth. *Cleo and the Coyote.* HarperCollins, 1996. / Steiner, Barbara A. *Desert Trip.* Sierra Club, 1996. / Yolen, Jane. *Welcome to the Sea of Sand.* Putnam, 1996.

SUBJECTS: ARIZONA. DESERTS. DOGS. FATHERS AND DAUGHTERS. LOST AND FOUND POSSESSIONS. POINT OF VIEW.

409 Johnson, Stephen T. *Alphabet City.* Illus. by the author. Viking, 1995. 0-670-85631-2. Unp. Gr. PreK–2

In a series of photo-realistic paintings of city-based scenes, find the alphabet letters intrinsic to each picture.

GERM: Judy Feldman's *The Alphabet in Nature* uses color photography to find letters in the outdoors landscape. Children can do a new version, called Alphabet School, drawing pictures of letters they find incorporated in the classroom and around the building.

RELATED TITLES: Adoff, Arnold. *Street Music: City Poems.* HarperCollins, 1995. / Dorros, Arthur. *Abuela.* Dutton, 1991. / Dragonwagon, Crescent. *And Then It Rained . . .* Atheneum, 2003. / Feldman, Judy. *The Alphabet in Nature.* Children's Press, 1991. / Grimes, Nikki. *C Is for City.* Lothrop, 1995. / Jakobsen, Kathy. *My New York.* Little, Brown, 2003. / Konigsburg, E. L. *Amy Elizabeth Explores Bloomingdale's.* Atheneum, 1992. / Lobel, Arnold. *On Market Street.* Greenwillow, 1981. / Neubecker, Robert. *Wow! City!* Hyperion, 2004. / Priceman, Marjorie. *Froggie Went a-Courting.* Little, Brown, 2000. / Robert, Francois, Jean Robert, and Jane Gittings. *Find a Face.* Chronicle, 2004. / Rotner, Shelley, and Ken Kreisler. *Citybook.* Orchard, 1994. / Seeger, Laura Vaccaro. *The Hidden Alphabet.* Roaring Brook, 2003. / Van Laan, Nancy. *People, People, Everywhere!* Knopf, 1992. / Weitzman, Jacqueline Preiss. *You Can't Take a Balloon into the Metropolitan Museum.* Dial, 1998.

SUBJECTS: ALPHABET BOOKS. CITIES AND TOWNS. NEW YORK CITY. STORIES WITHOUT WORDS.

410 Johnston, Tony. *Bigfoot Cinderrrrrella.* Illus. by James Warhola. Putnam, 1998. 0-399-23021-1. Unp. Gr. K–3

This Cinderella spoof takes place in an old-growth California forest where a nature-loving Bigfoot prince finds the stinking beauty of his dreams—hard-working Rrrrrella—thanks to the assistance of her beary godfather.

GERM: Make a Venn diagram that includes the standards of beauty, the plot of this environmental spoof, and the real Cinderella story.

RELATED TITLES: Buehner, Caralyn. *Fanny's Dream.* Dial, 1996. / Cronin, Doreen. *Diary of a Worm.* HarperCollins, 2003. / Edwards, Pamela Duncan. *Dinorella: A Prehistoric Fairy Tale.* Hyperion, 1997. / George, Kristine O'Connell. *Old Elm Speaks: Tree Poems.* Clarion, 1998. / Jackson, Ellen. *Cinder Edna.* Lothrop, 1994. / Ketteman, Helen. *Bubba the Cowboy Prince: A Fractured Texas Tale.* Scholastic, 1997. / Myers, Bernice. *Sidney Rella and the Glass Sneaker.* Macmillan, 1985. / Oppenheim, Joanne. *Have You Seen Trees?* Scholastic, 1995. / San Souci, Robert D. *Cinderella Skeleton.* Harcourt, 2000. / Tagg, Christine. *Cinderlily: A Floral Fairy Tale.* Candlewick, 2003.

SUBJECTS: CINDERELLA STORIES. CONSERVATION OF NATURAL RESOURCES. EARTH DAY. FAIRY TALES—SATIRE. FORESTS AND FORESTRY. GIANTS. PARODIES. TREES.

411 Johnston, Tony. *Cat, What Is That?* Illus. by Wendell Minor. HarperCollins, 2001. 0-06-027742-4. Unp. Gr. 1–6

In spare rhyming verses and stately cat-filled paintings, the essence of a cat's multifaceted personality is revealed.

GERM: Photocopy the text, number the verses, then divide your class into groups of two, handing out two verses per pair. Have your students read the entire book aloud as a choral reading.

RELATED TITLES: Banks, Kate. *The Cat Who Walked Across France.* Farrar, 2004. / Bruel, Nick. *Bad Kitty.* Roaring Brook, 2005. / Calhoun, Mary. *High-Wire Henry.* Morrow, 1991. (And others in the Henry series.) / Florian, Douglas. *Bow Wow Meow Meow: It's Rhyming Cats and Dogs.* Harcourt, 2003. / Hall, Donald. *I Am the Dog, I Am the Cat.* Dial, 1994. / Harper, Dan. *Telling Time with Big Mama Cat.* Harcourt, 1998. / L'Engle, Madeleine. *The Other Dog.* SeaStar, 2001. / Martin, Ann M. *Leo the Magnificat.* Scholastic, 1996. / Miller, Sara Swan. *Three Stories You Can Read to Your Cat.* Houghton Mifflin, 1997. / Myers, Christopher. *Black Cat.* Scholastic, 1999. / Pilkey, Dav. *When Cats Dream.* Orchard, 1992. / Rosen, Michael J., ed. *Purr . . . Children's Book Illustrators Brag About Their Cats.* Harcourt, 1996. / Schachner, Judith Byron. *The Grannyman.* Dutton, 1999.

SUBJECTS: CATS. PICTURE BOOKS FOR ALL AGES. READER'S THEATER. STORIES IN RHYME.

412 Johnston, Tony. *The Ghost of Nicholas Greebe.* Illus. by S. D. Schindler. Dial, 1996. 0-8037-1649-4. Unp. Gr. 1–3

One year after Nicholas Greebe is laid to rest, a little dog digs up one of his bones in the graveyard and takes it aboard a whaling ship. Meanwhile, the man's grieving ghost haunts the farm until the bone is returned from its remarkable journey exactly 100 years later.

GERM: Make a chart showing how the bone of Nicholas Grebe comes home. Children can draw and label the 100-year cause-and-effect cycle of the bone as it is lost and found. All will love intoning the ghost's mournful chant: "From this night forth I quest, I quest, till all my bones together rest."

RELATED TITLES: Bennett, Jill. *Teeny Tiny*. Putnam, 1986. / Cecil, Laura. *Boo! Stories to Make You Jump*. Greenwillow, 1990. / Cuyler, Margery. *Skeleton Hiccups*. Simon & Schuster, 2002. / DeFelice, Cynthia C. *The Dancing Skeleton*. Macmillan, 1989. / Evans, Dilys, comp. *Monster Soup and Other Spooky Poems*. Scholastic, 1992. / Galdone, Joanna. *The Tailypo: A Ghost Story*. Clarion, 1977. / Galdone, Paul. *The Teeny-Tiny Woman*. Clarion, 1984. / Goode, Diane. *Diane Goode's Book of Scary Stories and Songs*. Dutton, 1994. / Hancock, Sibyl. *Esteban and the Ghost*. Dial, 1983. / Lindgren, Astrid. *The Ghost of Skinny Jack*. Viking, 1988. / Loredo, Elizabeth. *Boogie Bones*. Putnam, 1997. / San Souci, Robert D. *The Boy and the Ghost*. Simon & Schuster, 1989. / Williams, Linda. *The Little Old Lady Who Was Not Afraid of Anything*. Crowell, 1986. / Yep, Laurence. *The Man Who Tricked a Ghost*. BridgeWater, 1993.

SUBJECTS: BONES. CAUSE AND EFFECT. DOGS. GHOSTS. PICTURE BOOKS FOR ALL AGES.

413   **Johnston, Tony. *The Iguana Brothers*. Illus. by Mark Teague. Blue Sky/Scholastic, 1995. 0-590-47468-5. Unp. Gr. PreK–2**

In three beguiling episodes, Mexican lizard siblings Tom and Dom chew over pertinent issues in their lives. In the first vignette, Tom, sick of eating bugs, switches to flowers. Next, Tom decides that since he and Dom have scales, long, lashy tails, fearsome jaws, and can roar, they must be dinosaurs. Finally, the search for a new friend brings the realization that brothers can be perfect best friends. The two cheerful iguanas sprawl across the long, narrow pages in detailed acrylic paintings, and their lively discussions are sprinkled with Spanish words, all translated in context.

GERM: Read a comparable story about two human siblings, such as brothers Robbie and Christopher in Lynne Jonell's *It's My Birthday, Too!* and pick out differences and similarities in their relationships.

RELATED TITLES: Byars, Betsy. *My Bother, Ant*. Viking, 1996. / Johnston, Tony. *Slither McCreep and His Brother Joe*. Harcourt, 1992. / Jonell, Lynne. *It's My Birthday, Too!* Putnam, 1999. / Laden, Nina. *Private I. Guana: The Case of the Missing Chameleon*. Chronicle, 1995. / Van Leeuwen, Jean. *Amanda Pig and Her Big Brother Oliver*. Dial, 1982. (And others in the Oliver and Amanda series.)

SUBJECTS: BROTHERS. IGUANAS. LIZARDS. MULTICULTURAL BOOKS. SPANISH LANGUAGE.

414   **Jonell, Lynne. *I Need a Snake*. Illus. by Petra Mathers. Putnam, 1998. 0-399-23176-5. Unp. Gr. PreK–1**

Robby informs Mommy, "I need a snake." After looking at snakes at the pet store, Robby asks when he can get one. "When you are all grown up," says Mommy. "When you have a house of your own." "That's too long to wait," he says. "Not long enough," says Mommy. So Robby finds his own little snakes in his mother's closet, under his sister's bed, and wrapped around his father's pants. Author Jonell has two boys at home and you can tell her stories, with Petra Mathers's winsome stick-figure characters, are reality-based. Mathers dedicated her illustrations to Crictor and Madame Bodot, characters in Tomi Ungerer's classic snake story, *Crictor*.

GERM: When reading the story, bring in snake props: a shoelace, jump rope, and belt. Cut up lengths of colored yarn for snake fanciers to claim as their own. Pasting the yarn onto paper, they can draw a background incorporating it, accompanied by a sentence about their snake: "My snake, _____, is _____."

RELATED TITLES: Ata, Te. *Baby Rattlesnake*. Children's Book Press, 1989. / Gray, Libba. *Small Green Snake*. Orchard, 1996. / Hall, Katy, and Lisa Eisenberg. *Snakey Riddles*. Dial, 1990. / Johnston, Tony. *Slither McCreep and His Brother Joe*. Harcourt, 1992. / Jonell, Lynne. *It's My Birthday, Too!* Putnam, 1999. / Jonell, Lynne. *Mommy Go Away!* Putnam, 1997. / Jonell, Lynne. *When Mommy Was Mad*. Putnam, 2002. / LaRochelle, David. *The Best Pet of All*. Dutton, 2004. / McNulty, Faith. *A Snake in the House*. Scholastic, 1994. / Rohmann, Eric. *Clara and Asha*. Roaring Brook, 2005. / Schaefer, Carol Lexa. *The Squiggle*. Crown, 1996. / Shannon, David. *No, David!* Scholastic, 1998. / Ungerer, Tomi. *Crictor*. HarperCollins, 1958.

SUBJECTS: BEHAVIOR. IMAGINATION. MOTHERS AND SONS. SNAKES. SNAKES AS PETS.

415   **Jonell, Lynne. *It's My Birthday, Too!* Illus. by Petra Mathers. Putnam, 1999. 0-399-23323-7. Unp. Gr. PreK–2**

It's big brother Christopher's birthday and little brother Robbie is trying to horn in, much to superior Christopher's dismay. However, when Robbie acts like a little dog, he becomes the surprise hit of the party. Christopher asks him, "Puppy, what is on a tree?" "BARK! BARK!"

"And what is on a house?" "ROOF! ROOF!" After all is said and done, it's nice to see the two squabbling brothers then show their affection for each other.

GERM: Discuss: In the beginning of the book, why doesn't Christopher want Robbie at his party? Why does he stick up for him at the end? What do you do at your birthday parties? Kids will also have fun pretending they're puppies. Pair them up and have one give a command for the others to obey: SIT! STAY! Good dog. There's something so cute and wacky about Mathers's little stick-figure illustrations of Robbie, Christopher, and their mom, whom we met in *I Need a Snake*. These are good read-alouds, as well as read-alones, and make fine companions to other sibling books, such as the Oliver and Amanda books by Jean Van Leeuwen, the Arthur books by Lillian Hoban, and the Ant books by Betsy Byars.

RELATED TITLES: Byars, Betsy. *My Brother, Ant.* Viking, 1996. / Goldstein, Bobbye S., comp. *Birthday Rhymes, Special Times.* Doubleday, 1993. / Hamilton, Morse. *Little Sister for Sale.* Dutton, 1992. / Hoban, Lillian. Arthur series. HarperCollins. / Johnston, Tony. *The Iguana Brothers.* Scholastic, 1995. / Jonell, Lynne. *I Need a Snake.* Putnam, 1998. / Jonell, Lynne. *Mommy Go Away!* Putnam, 1997. / Jonell, Lynne. *When Mommy Was Mad.* Putnam, 2002. / Stevenson, James. *Worse Than Willy.* Greenwillow, 1984. / Van Leeuwen, Jean. Oliver and Amanda series. Dial. / Yaccarino, Dan. *Big Brother Mike.* Hyperion, 1993.

SUBJECTS: BEHAVIOR. BIRTHDAYS. BROTHERS. DOGS. IMAGINATION. PARTIES. SIBLING RIVALRY.

416   Joosse, Barbara M. *Hot City.* **Illus. by Gregory Christie. Philomel, 2004. 0-399-23640-6. Unp. Gr. PreK–2**

Mimi and her little brother Joe, sitting on the cement front steps, "hot as a fry pan, sizzlin'," spy on the blah blah ladies having tea inside with Mama, eat snow cones, and then head off to that magical coooool place, the library. In several wordless pages, painted in dreamy, hot acrylics, Mimi, lost in her princess books, rides a unicorn and Joe clings to the neck of a dinosaur, happy to be adventuring in those good places a book can take you.

GERM: This short little mood piece shows how one can get lost in a good book. Ask your library adventurers to draw one of the expeditions they've gone on, vicariously, with a book. Take them on another journey with *Yikes!!!* by Robert Florczak.

RELATED TITLES: Allen, Susan, and Jane Lindaman. *Read Anything Good Lately?* Millbrook, 2003. / Daly, Niki. *Once Upon a Time.* Farrar, 2002. / English, Karen. *Hot Day on Abbott Avenue.* Clarion, 2004. / Ernst, Lisa Campbell. *Stella Louella's Runaway Book.* Simon & Schuster, 1998. / Florczak, Robert. *Yikes!!!* Scholastic, 2003. / Hest, Amy. *Mr. George Baker.* Candlewick, 2004. / Howard, Elizabeth Fitzgerald. *Virgie Goes to School with Us Boys.* Simon & Schuster, 2000. / Huff, Barbara. *Once Inside the Library.* Little, Brown, 1990. / Lehman, Barbara. *The Red Book.* Houghton Mifflin, 2004. / McKissack, Patricia C. *Goin' Someplace Special.* Atheneum, 2001. / Mora, Pat. *Tomás and the Library Lady.* Knopf, 1997. / Numeroff, Laura Joffe. *Beatrice Doesn't Want To.* Candlewick, 2004. / Sierra, Judy. *Wild About Books.* Knopf, 2004. / Sturges, Philemon. *She'll Be Comin' 'Round the Mountain.* Little, Brown, 2004. / Williams, Suzanne. *Library Lil.* Dial, 1997.

SUBJECTS: AFRICAN AMERICANS. BOOKS AND READING. BROTHERS AND SISTERS. CITIES AND TOWNS. IMAGINATION. LIBRARIES. MULTICULTURAL BOOKS. SUMMER.

417   Joosse, Barbara M. *Nugget and Darling.* **Illus. by Sue Truesdale. Clarion, 1997. 0-395-64571-9. Unp. Gr. PreK–2**

Yellow dog Nugget has a satisfying life with Nell, his little girl companion and champion. When Nugget finds a bedraggled gray and white kitten on the lawn, he grows increasingly jealous of the attention Nell lavishes on little Darling.

GERM: Although this charmer of a story is told by an omniscient narrator, the warm pen-and-ink and watercolor illustrations speak volumes about Nugget's emotional state. Ask your listeners to verbalize how Nugget feels about the newcomer, and then have them switch to Darling's point of view. Pair this with *Widget* by Lyn Rossiter McFarland, in which the dog is the outsider among a houseful of territorial kitties.

RELATED TITLES: Calhoun, Mary. *Tonio's Cat.* Morrow, 1996. / Greene, Carol. *Where Is That Cat?* Hyperion, 1999. / Janovitz, Marilyn. *Bowl Patrol.* North-South, 1996. / L'Engle, Madeleine. *The Other Dog.* SeaStar, 2001. /MacLachlan, Patricia, and Emily MacLachlan. *Bittle.* HarperCollins, 2004. / McFarland, Lyn Rossiter. *Widget.* Farrar, 2001. / Schachner, Judith Byron. *The Grannyman.* Dutton, 1999. / Voake, Charlotte. *Ginger Finds a Home.* Candlewick, 2003. / Wells, Rosemary. *McDuff and the Baby.* Hyperion, 1997.

SUBJECTS: CATS. DOGS. JEALOUSY. STRAY ANIMALS.

418   Juster, Norton. *The Hello, Goodbye Window*. Illus. by Chris Raschka. Hyperion, 2005. 0-7868-0914-0. Unp. Gr. PreK–1

Before she goes into Nanna and Poppy's house, the little girl narrator explains how she loves to press her face against the kitchen window, the special Hello, Goodbye Window, and frighten them or make silly faces. Once inside the kitchen, Poppy plays "Oh, Susannah" on the harmonica, and they eat supper and breakfast and look out the window at the world. This stream-of-consciousness child's-eye view of an overnight with adoring grandparents includes sunny and joyful, childlike and impressionistic watercolor illustrations in cheerful primary colors that dance with happiness.

GERM: Have children tell and paint what they do with their special relatives. Look out the window together and ask Poppy's question: "Hello, world! What have you got for us today?" If the world could answer, what would it tell us?

RELATED TITLES: Caseley, Judith. *Dear Annie*. Greenwillow, 1991. / dePaola, Tomie. *Tom*. Putnam, 1993. / Gaffney, Timothy R. *Grandpa Takes Me to the Moon*. Tambourine, 1996. / Greenfield, Eloise. *Grandpa's Face*. Philomel, 1988. / Lum, Kate. *What! Cried Granny: An Almost Bedtime Story*. Dial, 1999. / Paul, Ann Whitford. *Everything to Spend the Night from A to Z*. DK Ink, 1999. / Polacco, Patricia. *Thunder Cake*. Philomel, 1990. / Shields, Carol Diggory. *Lucky Pennies and Hot Chocolate*. Dutton, 2000. / Van Leeuwen, Jean. *The Tickle Stories*. Dial, 1998.

SUBJECTS: AFRICAN AMERICANS. CALDECOTT MEDAL. GRANDPARENTS. MULTICULTURAL BOOKS. PERSONAL NARRATIVES. POINT OF VIEW. RACIALLY MIXED PEOPLE. WINDOWS.

419   Kalan, Robert. *Moving Day*. Illus. by Yossi Abolafia. Greenwillow, 1996. 0-688-13949-3. Unp. Gr. PreK–1

Having outgrown his shell, a persevering hermit crab, with a red baseball cap atop his head, totes a stick with his belongings tied in a bundle and explores the seabed. All the shells he finds are either too big, small, long, wide, light, or heavy—until he finds one that's just right. Listeners will chant the repeated rhyming-word pairs of opposites and delight in the crab's journey, expressively illustrated with watercolor washes.

GERM: Children can pick an object and a pair of opposites describing it and then illustrate each on a paper folded in half: "This ___ is too ___." "This ___ is too ___." Meet more hermit crabs in Eric Carle's *A House for Hermit Crab* and Megan McDonald's *Is This a House for Hermit Crab?*

RELATED TITLES: Carle, Eric. *A House for Hermit Crab*. Picture Book Studio, 1987. / Freymann, Saxton. *Food for Thought: The Complete Book of Concepts for Growing Minds*. Scholastic, 2005. / Freymann, Saxton, and Joost Elffers. *One Lonely Sea Horse*. Scholastic, 2000. / McDonald, Megan. *Is This a House for Hermit Crab?* Orchard, 1990. / MacDonald, Suse. *Sea Shapes*. Harcourt, 1994. / Rose, Deborah Lee. *Into the A, B, Sea*. Scholastic, 2000. / Stevenson, James. *Clams Can't Sing*. Greenwillow, 1980. / Stickland, Paul, and Henrietta Stickland. *Dinosaur Roar!* Dutton, 1994. / Ward, Jennifer, and T. J. Marsh. *Somewhere in the Ocean*. Rising Moon, 2000. / Zoehfeld, Kathleen Weidner. *What Lives in a Shell?* HarperCollins, 1994.

SUBJECTS: CRABS. DWELLINGS. ENGLISH LANGUAGE—ADJECTIVES. HERMIT CRABS. MARINE ANIMALS. MOVING, HOUSEHOLD. OPPOSITES. SHELLS. STORIES IN RHYME.

420   Kalman, Maira. *What Pete Ate from A–Z*. Illus. by the author. Putnam, 2001. 0-399-23362-8. Unp. Gr. PreK–1

Poppy Wise tells us in her chatty way that her dog Pete is a Very Good Dog. But sometimes he eats what he should not. The subtitle says it all—"Where we explore the English Alphabet (in its entirety) in which a Certain Dog DEVOURS a MYRIAD of ITEMS which he should NOT"— and the gloriously detailed gouache paintings are pretty wonderful too.

GERM: Gather together some of the things that Pete ate: a ball, a camera, a glue stick, 25 jellybeans (give to kids to munch), and, of course, Uncle Rocky's underpants! They can recall and retell the story, à la "I Unpacked My Grandmother's Trunk," as follows: I unpacked Pete's stomach and found . . . Or, you can play that memory game where you put 26 alphabetical items on a tray and give everyone two minutes to examine it. Then they have to write down as many objects as they can remember. Next, each of your pet lovers can make an original alphabet page, selecting one significant letter and showing, in words and pictures, how his or her animal relates to it in terms of food or quirky habits. Follow Pete's adventurous appetite with the sequel, *Smartypants (Pete in School)*.

RELATED TITLES: Abrams, Pam. *Now I Eat My ABC's*. Scholastic, 2004. / Bayer, Jane. *A My Name Is Alice*. Dial, 1984. / Bruel, Nick. *Bad Kitty*. Roaring Brook, 2005. / Catalanotto, Peter. *Matthew A.B.C.* Atheneum, 2002. / Fleming, Denise. *Alphabet Under Construction*. Henry Holt, 2002. / Kalman, Maira. *Smartypants (Pete in*

School). Putnam, 2003. / Kirk, Daniel. *Dogs Rule!* Hyperion, 2003. / Laden, Nina. *Bad Dog*. Walker, 2000. / Laden, Nina. *The Night I Followed the Dog*. Chronicle, 1994. / Meddaugh, Susan. *Martha Speaks*. Houghton Mifflin, 1992. / Merriam, Eve. *Where Is Everybody? An Animal Alphabet*. Simon & Schuster, 1989. / Miller, Sara Swan. *Three Stories You Can Read to Your Dog*. Houghton Mifflin, 1995. / Moxley, Sheila. *ABCD: An Alphabet Book of Cats and Dogs*. Little, Brown, 2001. / Rathmann, Peggy. *Officer Buckle and Gloria*. Putnam, 1995. / Viorst, Judith. *The Alphabet from Z to A: With Much Confusion on the Way*. Atheneum, 1994. / Wegman, William. *ABC*. Little, Brown, 1994.

SUBJECTS: ALLITERATION. ALPHABET BOOKS. DOGS. GREED. HUMOROUS FICTION.

421   Karas, G. Brian. *Atlantic*. Illus. by the author. Putnam, 2002. 0-399-23632-5. Unp. Gr. K–3
In a personal narrative by the Atlantic Ocean itself, huge blue-toned gouache, acrylic, and pencil illustrations sweep across each unbordered page. The ocean describes how the sun heats its water, turning it into clouds and storms; how the moon pulls at it so tides ebb and flood; and how fish swim in it.
GERM: Kick off your oceanography unit with some nice experiential writing, drawing on kids' personal acquaintance with an ocean. Then look up some interesting facts about the other four oceans and locate them on a map or a globe. As a mood piece for kids to appreciate their oceans, this is a dreamy and watery personal narrative suitable for talking about personification.
RELATED TITLES: Cole, Joanna. *The Magic School Bus at the Waterworks*. Scholastic, 1988. / Cole, Joanna. *The Magic School Bus on the Ocean Floor*. Scholastic, 1992. / Cowan, Catherine. *My Life with the Wave*. Lothrop, 1997. / Dorros, Walter. *Follow the Water from Brook to Ocean*. HarperCollins, 1991. / Graham, Joan Bransfield. *Splish Splash*. Ticknor & Fields, 1994. / Hathorn, Libby. *The Wonder Thing*. Houghton Mifflin, 1996. / Kerley, Barbara. *A Cool Drink of Water*. National Geographic, 2002. / Lewis, J. Patrick. *Earth Verses and Water Rhymes*. Atheneum, 1991. / Locker, Thomas. *Water Dance*. Harcourt, 1997. / Peters, Lisa Westberg. *Water's Way*. Little, Brown, 1991. / Wick, Walter. *A Drop of Water*. Scholastic, 1997. / Wolkstein, Diane. *The Day Ocean Came to Visit*. Harcourt, 2001.
SUBJECTS: OCEAN. PERSONAL NARRATIVES. PERSONIFICATION. WATER.

422   Karas, G. Brian. *I Know an Old Lady*. Illus. by the author. Scholastic, 1995. 0-590-46575-9. Unp. Gr. PreK–1
As in the Jimmy Stewart/Grace Kelly/Alfred Hitchcock movie thriller *Rear Window*, the narrator witnesses a crime from his apartment window, peering with binoculars into the window of the brick building across the way. There he sees an old woman, her hair in a tight bun and wearing a long-sleeved long black dress and stockings. She's swallowing a fly. The narrator peers in her front door and sees her chase an uncaged parrot and scarf it down, blue feathers flying. All the way into the countryside he follows her, snapping photos of her misdeeds, until her tragic death, from eating a horse, of course.
GERM: Sing and compare this version with the ones illustrated by Nadine Bernard Westcott and Glen Rounds, plus Simms Taback's *There Was an Old Lady Who Swallowed a Fly*. For more swallowing stories, read Joanna Cole's variant, *Golly Gump Swallowed a Fly*; *The Greedy Old Fat Man* by Paul Galdone; and *Gobble, Gobble, Slip, Slop* by Meilo So. Then sing Raffi's *Spider on the Floor* and Iza Trapani's *Itsy Bitsy Spider*.
RELATED TITLES: Cole, Joanna. *Golly Gump Swallowed a Fly*. Parents, 1982. / Galdone, Paul. *The Greedy Old Fat Man*. Clarion, 1983. / Ginsburg, Mirra. *Clay Boy*. Greenwillow, 1997. / Hoberman, Mary Ann. *There Once Was a Man Named Michael Finnegan*. Little, Brown, 2001. / Jackson, Alison. *I Know an Old Lady Who Swallowed a Pie*. Dutton, 1997. / Johnson, Paul Brett. *Little Bunny Foo Foo*. Scholastic, 2004. / Raffi. *Spider on the Floor*. Crown, 1993. / Rounds, Glen. *I Know an Old Lady Who Swallowed a Fly*. Holiday House, 1990. / So, Meilo. *Gobble, Gobble, Slip, Slop: The Tale of a Very Greedy Cat*. Knopf, 2004. / Taback, Simms. *There Was an Old Lady Who Swallowed a Fly*. Viking, 1997. / Thomson, Pat. *Drat That Fat Cat!* Scholastic, 2003. / Trapani, Iza. *Itsy Bitsy Spider*. Whispering Coyote, 1993. / Weeks, Sarah. *Mrs. McNosh Hangs Up Her Wash*. Dutton, 1998. / Westcott, Nadine Bernard. *I Know an Old Lady Who Swallowed a Fly*. Little, Brown, 1980. / Ziefert, Harriet. *When I First Came to This Land*. Putnam, 1998.
SUBJECTS: ANIMALS. ELDERLY. FOLK SONGS. GREED. NONSENSE VERSES. SONGS. STORIES IN RHYME. STORIES WITH SONGS. SWALLOWING STORIES.

423   Kasza, Keiko. *My Lucky Day*. Illus. by the author. Putnam, 2003. 0-399-23874-3. Unp. Gr. PreK–1
When a delicious-looking piglet comes to Fox's house, ostensibly by mistake, Fox plans a pig roast, but the pig persuades him to give him a bath, a good meal, and a massage first.
GERM: Discuss the meaning of the title: Whose lucky day was it and why? Compare and con-

trast the piglet's foray into a potentially dangerous situation with that of the pig heroine in Susan Meddaugh's *Hog-Eye*.

RELATED TITLES: Donaldson, Julia. *The Gruffalo*. Dial, 1999. / Emberley, Michael. *Ruby*. Little, Brown, 1990. / Kasza, Keiko. *Grandpa Toad's Secrets*. Putnam, 1995. / Kasza, Keiko. *The Wolf's Chicken Stew*. Putnam, 1987. / Lester, Helen. *Listen, Buddy*. Houghton Mifflin, 1995. / MacDonald, Margaret Read. *Mabela the Clever*. Albert Whitman, 2001. / McKissack, Patricia C. *Flossie and the Fox*. Dial, 1986. / Meddaugh, Susan. *Hog-Eye*. Houghton Mifflin, 1995. / Silverman, Erica. *Don't Fidget a Feather!* Macmillan, 1994.

SUBJECTS: FOXES. LUCK. PIGS. TRICKSTER TALES.

424   **Kay, Verla. *Covered Wagon, Bumpy Trails*. Illus. by S. D. Schindler. Putnam, 2000. 0-399-22928-0. Unp. Gr. K–3**

Mother, Father, and Baby John cross the country in their covered wagon, through the Rocky Mountains and on to California, where they build a cabin. Full-bleed watercolor and gouache illustrations lay out the trials and toughness of the journey, while the briefest of rhyming texts, in four-line, eight- to ten-word quatrains, inspires us to plod on with the sturdy travelers.

GERM: After listening to the story once or twice, ask your students to write a descriptive paragraph of what life was like on the overland journey.

RELATED TITLES: Freedman, Russell. *Children of the Wild West*. Clarion, 1983. / Hopkinson, Deborah. *Apples to Oregon*. Atheneum, 2004. / Howard, Ellen. *The Log Cabin Quilt*. Holiday House, 1996. / Kay, Verla. *Gold Fever*. Putnam, 1999. / Kay, Verla. *Homespun Sarah*. Putnam, 2003. / Kay, Verla. *Iron Horses*. Putnam, 1999. / Kay, Verla. *Tattered Sails*. Putnam, 2001. / Kinsey-Warnock, Natalie. *Wilderness Cat*. Dutton, 1992. / Levitin, Sonia. *Nine for California*. Orchard, 1996. / Russell, Marion. *Along the Santa Fe Trail: Marion Russell's Own Story*. Albert Whitman, 1993. / Turner, Ann. *Mississippi Mud: Three Prairie Journals*. HarperCollins, 1997. / Van Leeuwen, Jean. *A Fourth of July on the Plains*. Dial, 1997. / Van Leeuwen, Jean. *Nothing Here But Trees*. Dial, 1998. / Wilder, Laura Ingalls. *Little House on the Prairie*. Harper, 1961. / Williams, David. *Grandma Essie's Covered Wagon*. Knopf, 1993.

SUBJECTS: FRONTIER AND PIONEER LIFE. HISTORICAL FICTION. OVERLAND JOURNEYS TO THE PACIFIC. STORIES IN RHYME. WEST (U.S.)—HISTORY—FICTION.

425   **Kay, Verla. *Gold Fever*. Illus. by S. D. Schindler. Putnam, 1999. 0-399-23027-0. 32pp. Gr. 1–4**

Jasper leaves his farm and family behind to become a Forty-niner in the California Gold Rush of 1849, but quits his claim in frustration over the tough conditions. Jasper's experiences panning for gold are told in clipped rhyming verses and detailed colored pencil illustrations.

GERM: For older students, this is a fine way to introduce novels such as *The Ballad of Lucy Whipple* by Karen Cushman or the classic narrative poem from the Alaska Gold Rush, *The Cremation of Sam McGee* by Robert W. Service. Younger listeners will have fun trying to define words in context using the pictures and will enjoy sharing other trips out West, such as Deborah Hopkinson's *Apples to Oregon* and Sonia Levitin's *Nine for California*.

RELATED TITLES: Blumberg, Rhoda. *The Great American Gold Rush*. Bradbury, 1989. / Cushman, Karen. *The Ballad of Lucy Whipple*. Clarion, 1996. / Fleischman, Sid. *By the Great Horn Spoon*. Little, Brown, 1963. / Freedman, Russell. *Children of the Wild West*. Clarion, 1983. / Hopkinson, Deborah. *Apples to Oregon*. Atheneum, 2004. / Kay, Verla. *Covered Wagon, Bumpy Trails*. Putnam, 2000. / Kay, Verla. *Homespun Sarah*. Putnam, 2003. / Kay, Verla. *Iron Horses*. Putnam, 1999. / Kay, Verla. *Orphan Train*. Putnam, 2003. / Kay, Verla. *Tattered Sails*. Putnam, 2001. / Levitin, Sonia. *Nine for California*. Orchard, 1996. / Service, Robert W. *The Cremation of Sam McGee*. Greenwillow, 1987. / Siebert, Diane. *Rhyolite: The True Story of a Ghost Town*. Clarion, 2003.

SUBJECTS: ADVENTURE AND ADVENTURERS. CALIFORNIA. GOLD RUSH. HISTORICAL FICTION. PICTURE BOOKS FOR ALL AGES. STORIES IN RHYME. WEST (U.S.)—HISTORY—FICTION.

426   **Kay, Verla. *Homespun Sarah*. Illus. by Ted Rand. Putnam, 2003. 0-399-23417-9. Unp. Gr. K–3**

"Homespun Sarah, / Braided head. / Warm quilt, snuggle, / Feather bed." Through brief rhyming verses, follow the busy day of young Sarah, a colonial farm girl in 18th-century Pennsylvania, as she completes her many chores. Good-humored, full-page watercolors portray a close-knit, hard-working family taking care of their every need, including hand-stitching a spiffy new red homespun outfit for an appreciative Sarah.

GERM: Before reading, ask your students: What chores do you do at home? How do you acquire new clothes when you have outgrown the old ones? How did people get new clothes in colonial days? Have students analyze the clothes they are wearing and surmise how they were made. Bring in fabric, yarn, knitting and sewing needles, and crochet hooks and let them have a go at creating a new outfit for a class doll or stuffed animal.

RELATED TITLES: Beskow, Elsa. *Pelle's New Suit*. HarperCollins, 1929. / Corey, Shana. *You Forgot Your Skirt, Amelia Bloomer! A Very Improper Story*. Scholastic, 2000. / dePaola, Tomie. *Charlie Needs a Cloak*. Aladdin, 1982. / Frazee, Maria. *Hush, Little Baby: A Folk Song with Pictures*. Harcourt, 1999. / Kay, Verla. *Gold Fever*. Putnam, 1999. / Kay, Verla. *Iron Horses*. Putnam, 1999. / Kay, Verla. *Orphan Train*. Putnam, 2003. / Kay, Verla. *Tattered Sails*. Putnam, 2001. / Sanders, Scott Russell. *Warm as Wool*. Bradbury, 1992. / Taback, Simms. *Joseph Had a Little Overcoat*. Viking, 1999. / Ziefert, Harriet. *A New Coat for Anna*. Knopf, 1986.

SUBJECTS: CLOTH. CLOTHING AND DRESS. FAMILY LIFE. FARM LIFE. HISTORICAL FICTION. PENNSYLVANIA. STORIES IN RHYME.

427 **Kay, Verla.** *Orphan Train*. **Illus. by Ken Stark. Putnam, 2003. 0-399-23613-9. Unp. Gr. 1–4**
Written in spare but heartfelt rhyme, this 19th-century story tells the tale of three homeless orphans—Harold, David, and Lucy—who are sent out West by orphan train, where they are separated and taken in by new families.
GERM: Either discuss or have children compose and share a Quick Write: Were the three siblings better off together on the city streets or split up in the country? Give reasons.
RELATED TITLES: Bunting, Eve. *Train to Somewhere*. Clarion, 1996. / Kay, Verla. *Gold Fever*. Putnam, 1999. / Kay, Verla. *Homespun Sarah*. Putnam, 2003. / Kay, Verla. *Iron Horses*. Putnam, 1999. / Kay, Verla. *Tattered Sails*. Putnam, 2001. / Warren, Andrea. *We Rode the Orphan Trains*. Houghton Mifflin, 2001.

SUBJECTS: BROTHERS AND SISTERS. HISTORICAL FICTION. ORPHAN TRAINS. ORPHANS. STORIES IN RHYME. U.S.—HISTORY.

428 **Kay, Verla.** *Tattered Sails*. **Illus. by Dan Andreasen. Putnam, 2001. 0-399-23345-8. Unp. Gr. PreK–2**
This briefest of rhymes, set in early 17th-century England, unfolds a story of three children—Thomas, Edward, and Mary Jane—who, with their parents, leave grimy London behind for a hard journey to the New World.
GERM: Examine Verla Kay's books to explore how she so skillfully evokes a historical time, place, or journey using very few words, including *Gold Fever*, in which she describes the California Gold Rush, and *Iron Horses*, which recounts the construction of the first U.S. railroads.
RELATED TITLES: Anderson, Laurie Halse. *Thank You, Sarah: The Woman Who Saved Thanksgiving*. Simon & Schuster, 2002. / George, Jean Craighead. *The First Thanksgiving*. Philomel, 1993. / Greene, Rhonda Gowler. *The Very First Thanksgiving Day*. Atheneum, 2002. / Kay, Verla. *Gold Fever*. Putnam, 1999. / Kay, Verla. *Homespun Sarah*. Putnam, 2003. / Kay, Verla. *Iron Horses*. Putnam, 1999. / Kay, Verla. *Orphan Train*. Putnam, 2003. / Lakin, Patricia. *Fat Chance Thanksgiving*. Albert Whitman, 2001. / Peacock, Carol Antoinette. *Pilgrim Cat*. Albert Whitman, 2005. / Van Leeuwen, Jean. *Across the Wide Dark Sea: The Mayflower Journey*. Dial, 1996. / Waters, Kate. *Samuel Eaton's Day: A Day in the Life of a Pilgrim Boy*. Scholastic, 1993. / Waters, Kate. *Sarah Morton's Day: A Day in the Life of a Pilgrim Girl*. Scholastic, 1989.

SUBJECTS: HISTORICAL FICTION. MASSACHUSETTS—HISTORY. PILGRIMS. STORIES IN RHYME. U.S.—HISTORY—COLONIAL PERIOD—FICTION. VOYAGES AND TRAVELS.

429 **Keller, Holly.** *That's Mine, Horace*. **Illus. by the author. Greenwillow, 2000. 0-688-17160-5. Unp. Gr. PreK–K**
Horace, the little leopard from *Horace* and *Brave Horace*, finds a toy truck on the school playground and stuffs it in his pocket. Back in class, his tiger friend Walter sees him playing with it and says it's his, but Mrs. Pepper believes Horace when he claims it's not. "I know you would never tell a fib," his teacher tells him, and though this makes Horace feel guilty, it doesn't stop him from lying about the truck to his mother.
GERM: Horace doesn't know how to resolve his dilemma. He feels bad about what he has done, but he really likes that little truck. Ask your listeners to advise, relate, and predict: What should Horace do? What would you do? What do you think he will do? When you finish the story, ask your listeners how and why Walter helped Horace do the right thing.
RELATED TITLES: DePaolo, Paula. *Rosie and the Yellow Ribbon*. Little, Brown, 1992. / Havill, Juanita. *Jamaica and the Substitute Teacher*. Houghton Mifflin, 1999. / Keller, Holly. *Brave Horace*. Greenwillow, 1998. / Keller, Holly. *Horace*. Greenwillow, 1991. / Sharmat, Marjorie Weinman. *A Big Fat Enormous Lie*. Dutton, 1978.

SUBJECTS: ANIMALS. CONDUCT OF LIFE. FRIENDSHIP. HONESTY. LEOPARDS. SCHOOLS. TOYS.

430 **Keller, Laurie.** *Open Wide: Tooth School Inside*. **Illus. by the author. Henry Holt, 2000. 0-8050-6192-4. Unp. Gr. K–3**
Let's visit Mr. Flossman's class of personified incisors, canines, premolars, and molars as they

review everything they know about themselves. The crazy illustrations are filled with talking teeth.

GERM: Floss, brush, smile, and even fall over laughing as you relate what every dentist would love kids to know. Margie Palatini's *Sweet Tooth* will keep everyone grinning. Find out more about the 50 states with Keller's equally riotous, hilarious, and yet informative *The Scrambled States of America*.

RELATED TITLES: Beeler, Selby B. *Throw Your Tooth on the Roof: Tooth Traditions from Around the World.* Houghton Mifflin, 1998. / Birdseye, Tom. *Airmail to the Moon.* Holiday House, 1988. / Bunting, Eve. *Trouble on the T-Ball Team.* Clarion, 1995. / Chandra, Deborah, and Madeline Comora. *George Washington's Teeth.* Farrar, 2003. / Davis, Katie. *Mabel the Tooth Fairy and How She Got Her Job.* Harcourt, 2003. / Keller, Laurie. *The Scrambled States of America.* Henry Holt, 1998. / Lasky, Kathryn. *Science Fair Bunnies.* Candlewick, 2000. / MacDonald, Amy. *Cousin Ruth's Tooth.* Houghton Mifflin, 1996. / McGhee, Alison. *Mrs. Watson Wants Your Teeth.* Illus. by Harry Bliss. Harcourt, 2004. / Palatini, Margie. *Sweet Tooth.* Simon & Schuster, 2004. / Simms, Laura. *Rotten Teeth.* Houghton Mifflin, 1998. / Steig, William. *Doctor DeSoto.* Farrar, 1982. / Swain, Ruth Freeman. *How Sweet It Is (and Was): The History of Candy.* Holiday House, 2003.

SUBJECTS: DENTISTS AND DENTAL CARE. HUMOROUS FICTION. PERSONIFICATION. TEETH.

431   **Keller, Laurie.** *The Scrambled States of America.* **Illus. by the author. Henry Holt, 1998. 0-8050-5802-8. 32pp. Gr. 1–4**

When Kansas gets bored and invites all the states to the biggest party ever, they decide to switch their spots on the map. Of course, they all discover there's no place like home. Personified states sport little arms, legs, and smiles, and their little conversations are a riot.

GERM: Want your kids to be able to identify the names and locations of all 50 states? Looking for a kickoff to a research lesson using books, encyclopedias, or the Internet? Starting a states unit without this hilarious picture book is simply unthinkable. Take a cross-country jaunt with the Statue of Liberty herself in *Liberty's Journey* by Kelly DiPucchio and with an exuberant little girl named Izzy in *Wow! America!* by Robert Neubecker.

RELATED TITLES: Borden, Louise. *America Is . . .* McElderry, 2002. / Brisson, Pat. *Your Best Friend, Kate.* Bradbury, 1989. / Cherry, Lynne. *The Armadillo from Amarillo.* Harcourt, 1994. / DiPucchio, Kelly. *Liberty's Journey.* Hyperion, 2004. / Guthrie, Woody. *This Land Is Your Land.* Little, Brown, 1998. / Keenan, Sheila. *O, Say Can You See? America's Symbols, Landmarks, and Inspiring Words.* Scholastic, 2004. / Keller, Laurie. *Open Wide: Tooth School Inside.* Henry Holt, 2000. / Krupp, Robin Rector. *Let's Go Traveling.* Morrow, 1992. / Neubecker, Robert. *Wow! America!* Hyperion, 2006. / Pattison, Darcy. *The Journey of Oliver K. Woodman.* Harcourt, 2003. / Rylant, Cynthia. *Tulip Sees America.* Scholastic, 1998. / Sabuda, Robert. *America the Beautiful.* Little Simon, 2004.

SUBJECTS: GEOGRAPHY. HUMOROUS FICTION. PICTURE BOOKS FOR ALL AGES. U.S.—GEOGRAPHY.

432   **Kelley, True.** *Blabber Mouse.* **Illus. by the author. Dutton, 2001. 0-525-46742-4. Unp. Gr. PreK–2**

Blabber loves to talk, but when he gossips and blabs his friends' secrets one time too many, his classmates and teacher, Mrs. Numley, come up with a plan to change his ways.

GERM: Discussion point, midway through the story: When Blabber's friends prepare to stop him from blabbering again, predict what you think they're planning to do about it. After the story: In case Blabber Mouse's new diary is not completely effective, what techniques could you recommend that you have used to keep your own secrets?

RELATED TITLES: Caseley, Judith. *Bully.* Greenwillow, 2001. / Lester, Helen. *Hooway for Wodney Wat.* Houghton, 1999. / McKissack, Patricia C. *The Honest-to-Goodness Truth.* Atheneum, 2000. / Meddaugh, Susan. *Martha Speaks.* Houghton Mifflin, 1992. / Naylor, Phyllis Reynolds. *Keeping a Christmas Secret.* Atheneum, 1989. / Naylor, Phyllis Reynolds. *King of the Playground.* Atheneum, 1991. / Wilhelm, Hans. *Tyrone the Horrible.* Scholastic, 1988.

SUBJECTS: BEHAVIOR. MICE. SCHOOLS. SECRETS.

433   **Kellogg, Steven.** *The Missing Mitten Mystery.* **Illus. by the author. Dial, 2000. 0-8037-2566-3. Unp. Gr. PreK–1**

Annie has just lost her fifth mitten of the winter. Accompanied by her faithful dog, Oscar, she sets out to retrace her steps to search every snow-covered place she has played in all day. En route, she finds her friends' missing boots, sock, and sweater, but her mitten seems to have vanished.

GERM: Ask your listeners: "Where could that mitten could be?" Think of a real place where it could be and then use your imagination like Annie does to come up with a more outlandish explanation of how it might have got there. Where have you lost (or found) your own clothes? Cut out pairs of mittens from many colors of construction paper. Hide one of each color around the room. (If you run out of colors before you run out of kids, personalize the mittens with magic markers or stickers.) Hand out the mates, one per child, and have them search until each finds his or her missing mitten. Children can decorate their mittens with crayons or markers and then punch a hole in the ends and tie the pair together with yarn. Or use them to decorate a large branch as a mitten tree, as Annie envisions in the story.

RELATED TITLES: Bancroft, Catherine, and Hannah Coale Gruenberg. *Felix's Hat*. Four Winds, 1993. / Brett, Jan. *The Hat*. Putnam, 1997. / Brett, Jan. *The Mitten*. Putnam, 1989. / Cauley, Lorinda Bryan. *The Three Little Kittens*. Putnam, 1982. / Chapman, Cheryl. *Snow on Snow on Snow*. Dial, 1994. / Feiffer, Jules. *I Lost My Bear*. Morrow, 1998. / Hissey, Jane. *Little Bear's Trousers*. Philomel, 1987. / Keats, Ezra Jack. *The Snowy Day*. Viking, 1962. / Kellogg, Steven. *The Mystery of the Flying Orange Pumpkin*. Dial, 1992. / Kellogg, Steven. *The Mystery of the Stolen Blue Paint*. Dial, 1982. / London, Jonathan. *Froggy Gets Dressed*. Viking, 1992. / Nietzel, Shirley. *The Jacket I Wear in the Snow*. Greenwillow, 1989. / Rice, Eve. *Oh, Lewis!* Macmillan, 1974. / Rogers, Jean. *Runaway Mittens*. Greenwillow, 1988. / Teague, Mark. *The Lost and Found*. Scholastic, 1998. / Valckx, Catharina. *Lizette's Green Sock*. Clarion, 2005.

SUBJECTS: CLOTHING AND DRESS. LOST AND FOUND POSSESSIONS. MITTENS. MYSTERY AND DETECTIVE STORIES. SNOWMEN. WINTER.

434   Kellogg, Steven. *A Penguin Pup for Pinkerton*. **Illus. by the author. Dial, 2001. 0-8037-2536-1. Unp. Gr. K–3**

Emily comes home from school bursting with facts she's learned about the father emperor penguin cradling his egg on his feet for nine long weeks. Her Great Dane, Pinkerton, places an old football on his paws and waits patiently for it to hatch. The lovable dog is finally placated when Granny gives him his own stuffed penguin to care for and love.

GERM: Before finishing the story, ask children to come up with a good solution for Pinkerton's penguin problem and have them write and illustrate their ending for the story. Pair this with Brenda Z. Guiberson's *The Emperor Lays an Egg* to learn more about the real bird, and Sneed B. Collard III's nonfiction picture book, *Animal Dads*, to learn about the roles of other animal fathers. As well as using this to introduce the Pinkerton series, you can pull it into your units on emperor penguins, birds, Antarctica, baby animals, and fathers. Combine fiction and nonfiction whenever you can to let readers see that they can enjoy all kinds of books to stretch both their brains and their imaginations.

RELATED TITLES: Geraghty, Paul. *Solo*. Crown, 1996. / Guiberson, Brenda Z. *The Emperor Lays an Egg*. Henry Holt, 2001. / Jenkins, Martin. *The Emperor's Egg*. Candlewick, 1999. / Kellogg, Steven. *Pinkerton, Behave*. Dial, 1979. (And others in the Pinkerton series.) / Kopper, Lisa. *Daisy Thinks She Is a Baby*. Knopf, 1994. / L'Engle, Madeleine. *The Other Dog*. SeaStar, 2001. / Meddaugh, Susan. *Martha Speaks*. Houghton Mifflin, 1992. / Miller, Sara Swan. *Three Stories You Can Read to Your Dog*. Houghton Mifflin, 1995. / Simont, Marc. *The Stray Dog*. HarperCollins, 2001.

SUBJECTS: DOGS. HUMOROUS FICTION. PENGUINS.

435   Kelly, John, and Cathy Tincknell. *The Mystery of Eatum Hall*. **Illus. by the authors. Candlewick, 2004. 0-7636-2594-9. Unp. Gr. K–3**

Invited by the new owner of Eatum Hall for a weekend of free gourmet food, Horace Pork-Fowler and his wife, Glenda, are pleased to oblige. Upon arrival, they find a note from their host, Dr. A. Hunter, explaining that though he will be unable to join them, his house has been designed and automated to ensure their every dietary whim. The rotund pig and his large goose spouse spend the next day blissfully overindulging in wonderful nonstop repasts.

GERM: Sharp-eyed viewers will certainly notice what the two dim bulbs, Horace and Glenda, do not: a wolf is watching their every move, preparing to cook the two into a huge pie. This is a stellar example of the text telling one story and the illustrations another. Have your listeners go through the story a second time and discuss all the clues they missed in the first reading. Discuss: How does Horace's point of view add humor to the story? In what ways is this story a mystery? Who is the mysterious Dr. Hunter? What is his plan for the plump and portly duo? And how do they unwittingly foil his plans and give him his just deserts? Students can retell this story from the wolf's point of view and compare it to Jon Scieszka's *The True Story of the 3 Little Pigs*.

RELATED TITLES: Asch, Frank. *Mr. Maxwell's Mouse*. Kids Can, 2004. / Blundell, Tony. *Beware of Boys*. Greenwillow, 1992. / Child, Lauren. *Beware of the Storybook Wolves*. Scholastic, 2001. / Child, Lauren. *Who's*

Afraid of the Big Bad Book? Hyperion, 2003. / Christelow, Eileen. *Where's the Big Bad Wolf?* Clarion, 2002. / Cushman, Doug. *Mystery at the Club Sandwich.* Clarion, 2004. / Marshall, James. *The Three Little Pigs.* Dial, 1989. / McClements, George. *Jake Gander, Storyville Detective.* Hyperion, 2002. / Meddaugh, Susan. *Hog-Eye.* Houghton, 1995. / Offen, Hilda. *Nice Work, Little Wolf!* Dutton, 1992. / Palatini, Margie. *Bad Boys.* Harper-Collins, 2003. / Palatini, Margie. *Piggie Pie.* Clarion, 1995. / Scieszka, Jon. *The True Story of the 3 Little Pigs.* Viking, 1989. / Trivizas, Eugene. *The Three Little Wolves and the Big Bad Pig.* McElderry, 1993. / Vozar, David. *Yo, Hungry Wolf! A Nursery Rap.* Doubleday, 1993. / Wiesner, David. *The Three Pigs.* Clarion, 2001.

SUBJECTS: FOOD HABITS. GEESE. HUMOROUS FICTION. MYSTERY AND DETECTIVE STORIES. PICTURE BOOKS FOR ALL AGES. PIGS. POINT OF VIEW. WOLVES.

436   **Kennedy, Frances.** *The Pickle Patch Bathtub.* **Illus. by Sheila Aldridge. Tricycle, 2004. 1-58246-112-0. Unp. Gr. K–3**

"We need a real bathtub," 10-year-old Donna Delle declares after discovering that her legs are too long for the washtub in her family's farm kitchen. She and her siblings set out to earn the $10.75 needed to buy a luxurious steel bathtub in the Sears, Roebuck catalog by raising, picking, and selling thousands of pickling cucumbers.

GERM: Based on a true story from the author's mother's childhood, back in Missouri in 1925, the book includes an Author's Note with information about Donna, a photograph of her at age 10, and even her handwritten recipe for bread and butter pickles. Make bread and butter pickles, or just bring in a jar and eat them. Plant cucumber seeds as part of your plants unit. You can request a new Sears catalog from their Web site, <www.sears.com>, and use it as a source of math problems.

RELATED TITLES: Houston, Gloria. *My Great Aunt Arizona.* HarperCollins, 1992. / Johnston, Tony. *Yonder.* Dial, 1988. / Lasky, Kathryn. *Marven of the North Woods.* Harcourt, 1997. / McDonald, Megan. *The Great Pumpkin Switch.* Orchard, 1992. / Millard, Ann. *A Street Through Time.* DK, 1998. / Rector, Anne Elizabeth. *Anne Elizabeth's Diary: A Young Artist's True Story.* Little, Brown, 2004. / Schwartz, Harriet Berg. *When Artie Was Little.* Knopf, 1996. / Shannon, George. *This Is the Bird.* Houghton Mifflin, 1997. / Splear, Elsie Lee. *Growing Seasons.* Putnam, 2000. / Stewart, Sarah. *The Journey.* Farrar, 2001. / Thermes, Jennifer. *When I Was Built.* Henry Holt, 2001. / Tunnell, Michael O. *Mailing May.* Greenwillow, 1997. / Widman, Christine. *Cornfield Hide-and-Seek.* Farrar, 2003. / Yolen, Jane. *House, House.* Marshall Cavendish, 1998.

SUBJECTS: BATHS. BATHTUBS. BIOGRAPHICAL FICTION. CUCUMBERS. FAMILY STORIES. FARM LIFE. HISTORICAL FICTION. MONEYMAKING PROJECTS.

437   **Kessler, Cristina.** *Jubela.* **Illus. by JoEllen McAllister Stammen. Simon & Schuster, 2001. 0-689-81895-5. Unp. Gr. K–4**

A baby rhino's mother is killed by poachers, but Jubela manages to survive in this story from Swaziland, in southern Africa, that is based on truth.

GERM: According to the books Afterword, "Over the last 30 years, 97 percent of the world's rhino population has been lost to poachers." As a part of a unit on endangered species, investigate additional rhino facts and discuss the importance of animal rescue efforts.

RELATED TITLES: Aardema, Verna. *Bringing the Rain to Kapiti Plain.* Dial, 1981. / Cowcher, Helen. *Whistling Thorn.* Scholastic, 1993. / Geraghty, Paul. *The Hunter.* Crown, 1994. / Leigh, Nila K. *Learning to Swim in Swaziland: A Child's-Eye View of a Southern African Country.* Scholastic, 1993. / Rosen, Michael. *How the Giraffe Got Such a Long Neck . . . and Why Rhino Is So Grumpy.* Dial, 1993.

SUBJECTS: AFRICA. ANIMALS. ENDANGERED SPECIES. HUNTERS AND HUNTING.

438   **Ketteman, Helen.** *Armadilly Chili.* **Illus. by Will Terry. Albert Whitman, 2004. 0-8075-0457-2. Unp. Gr. PreK–2**

With a blue norther a-blowin', Miss Billie Armadilly asks her pals, tarantula Tex, bluebird Mackie, and horned toad Taffy to help her make a pot of hot armadilly chili, but they're all too busy to help. She makes it herself and refuses to feed them, saying, "No workin' with Billie, no sharin' the chili," but it's awfully lonesome eating alone.

GERM: You'll want to act this out, of course, with puppets (there's a great set available at <www.mimismotifs.com>), flannelboard, or just plain kids. Compare and contrast the traditional "Little Red Hen" tales with Ketteman's spicy southwestern version and with Ann Whitford Paul's *Mañana, Iguana.* How are the endings different? Meet the Little Red Hen's grandson in Janet Stevens and Susan Stevens Crummel's *Cook-a-Doodle-Doo!* and cook up another wheat-based treat in *The Little Red Hen (Makes a Pizza)* by Philemon Sturges. Dish out more heat with *The West Texas Chili Monster* by Judy Cox. For children who have never seen a real armadillo, get a load of Bianca Lavies's up-close color photos in *It's an Armadillo*. For props to help you present this story, go to <www.mimismotifs.com>.

RELATED TITLES: Cherry, Lynne. *The Armadillo from Amarillo*. Harcourt, 1994. / Cox, Judy. *The West Texas Chili Monster*. BridgeWater, 1998. / DeFelice, Cynthia. *Old Granny and the Bean Thief*. Farrar, 2003. / Downard, Barry. *The Little Red Hen*. Simon & Schuster, 2004. / Elya, Susan Middleton. *Eight Animals Bake a Cake*. Putnam, 2002. / Galdone, Paul. *The Little Red Hen*. Clarion, 1979. / Kimmel, Eric A. *Cactus Soup*. Marshall Cavendish, 2004. / Kimmel, Eric A. *The Runaway Tortilla*. Winslow, 2000. / Lavies, Bianca. *It's an Armadillo*. Dutton, 1989. / Lowell, Susan. *The Tortoise and the Jackrabbit*. Northland, 1994. / Paul, Ann Whitford. *Mañana, Iguana*. Holiday House, 2004. / Stevens, Janet. *Coyote Steals the Blanket: A Ute Tale*. Holiday House, 1993. / Stevens, Janet, and Susan Stevens Crummel. *Cook-a-Doodle-Doo! Harcourt, 1999.* / Stevens, Janet, and Susan Stevens Crummel. *The Great Fuzz Frenzy*. Harcourt, 2005. / Sturges, Philemon. *The Little Red Hen (Makes a Pizza)*. Dutton, 1999.

SUBJECTS: ARMADILLOS. CHANTABLE REFRAIN. CHILI. COOPERATION. DESERT ANIMALS. FOOD. FRIENDSHIP. LITTLE RED HEN. PARODIES. TEXAS.

439   Ketteman, Helen. *Bubba the Cowboy Prince: A Fractured Texas Tale*. Illus. by James Warhola. Scholastic, 1997. 0-590-25506-1. Unp. Gr. 2–5

In a gender-reversed Cinderella spoof, meet Bubba, the hard-working Texas ranch hand, who, with the help of a fairy godcow, wins the heart of big-haired Miz Lurleen, the purtiest and richest gal in the county.

GERM: Compare this with Susan Lowell's similarly set *Cindy Ellen: A Wild Western Cinderella*. For another Texas-sized turnaround, read Tony Johnston's *The Cowboy and the Black-Eyed Pea*.

RELATED TITLES: Axelrod, Alan, comp. *Songs of the Wild West*. Simon & Schuster, 1991. / Buehner, Caralyn. *Fanny's Dream*. Dial, 1996. / Climo, Shirley. *The Irish Cinderlad*. HarperCollins, 1996. / Craft, K. Y. *Cinderella*. SeaStar Books, 2000. / Frank, John. *The Toughest Cowboy*. Simon & Schuster, 2004. / Hughes, Shirley. *Ella's Big Chance: A Jazz-Age Cinderella*. Simon & Schuster, 2004. / Huling, Jan. *Puss in Cowboy Boots*. Simon & Schuster, 2002. / Icenoggle, Jodi. *'Til the Cows Come Home*. Boyds Mills, 2004. / Jackson, Ellen. *Cinder Edna*. Lothrop, 1994. / Johnston, Tony. *The Cowboy and the Black-Eyed Pea*. Putnam, 1992. / Lowell, Susan. *The Bootmaker and the Elves*. Orchard, 1997. / Lowell, Susan. *Cindy Ellen: A Wild Western Cinderella*. Orchard, 1997. / Minters, Frances. *Sleepless Beauty*. Viking, 1996. / Mitchell, Marianne. *Joe Cinders*. Henry Holt, 2002. / Myers, Bernice. *Sidney Rella and the Glass Sneaker*. Macmillan, 1985. / Sanderson, Ruth. *Cinderella*. Little, Brown, 2002.

SUBJECTS: CINDERELLA STORIES. COWBOYS. FAIRY TALES—SATIRE. LOVE. PARODIES. TEXAS. WEST (U.S.).

440   Ketteman, Helen. *Grandma's Cat*. Illus. by Marsha Lynn Winborn. Houghton Mifflin, 1996. 0-395-73094-5. Unp. Gr. PreK–K

A little girl figures out firsthand (and the hard way) how to get her grandmother's puffy gray cat to like her in this simplest of rhyming, emergent reader-style texts, one with real panache and winning watercolors.

GERM: Ask listeners: How do you make friends with a pet? Open the floodgates on your listeners' pet stories. They can bring in photos or draw pictures of their animal pals, labeling them, "My Friend, _____." See how Widget, a stray dog, gets the six hissing kitties at Mrs. Diggs's house to like him in Lyn Rossiter McFarland's *Widget*.

RELATED TITLES: Calhoun, Mary. *Tonio's Cat*. Morrow, 1996. / Greene, Carol. *Where Is That Cat?* Hyperion, 1999. / Janovitz, Marilyn. *Bowl Patrol*. North-South, 1996. / Joosse, Barbara M. *Nugget and Darling*. Clarion, 1997. / McFarland, Lyn Rossiter. *Widget*. Farrar, 2001. / Pilkey, Dav. *When Cats Dream*. Orchard, 1992. / Schachner, Judith Byron. *The Grannyman*. Dutton, 1999. / Simont, Marc. *The Stray Dog*. HarperCollins, 2001.

SUBJECTS: CATS. GRANDMOTHERS. STORIES IN RHYME.

441   Ketteman, Helen. *Heat Wave!* Illus. by Scott Goto. Walker, 1998. 0-8027-8645-6. Unp. Gr. 1–4

As the red baseball-hatted, overalls-clad girl narrator describes it, when the Heat Wave hit her family's Kansas farm, it popped the corn and turned the cows' milk to butter before she figured out a way to cool things down. The sassy and glossy color paintings draw out the wild humor of the straight-faced tall-tale narrative.

GERM: As you read, ask listeners to identify examples of exaggerated, figurative language. Make sure they understand the humor: Why did the hound dog turn blue when the corn popped? How did planting lettuce make the Heat Wave cool down? Make predictions: What will happen on the farm when the cold weather comes? Then have the children write and illustrate their own tall statements about how hot or cold or windy or sunny or snowy it got in their neck of the woods. Punch up that weather unit with more over-the-top forecasts, including Judi Barrett's classic, *Cloudy with a Chance of Meatballs*; Jo Harper's *Jalapeño Hal*; Deborah Hopkinson's *Apples to Oregon*; and Michael O. Tunnell's *Chinook!* And if you can find them, the books in Sid Fleischman's hilariously exaggerated McBroom series (including *McBroom Tells the Truth*) are all about an amazingly prolific one-acre farm.

RELATED TITLES: Alexander, Lloyd. *How the Cat Swallowed Thunder*. Dutton, 2000. / Barrett, Judi. *Cloudy with a Chance of Meatballs*. Atheneum, 1978. / Dadey, Debbie. *Shooting Star: Annie Oakley, the Legend*. Walker, 1997. / Fleischman, Sid. *McBroom Tells the Truth*. Little, Brown, 1966. (And others in the McBroom series.) / Harper, Jo. *Jalapeño Hal*. Four Winds, 1993. / Hopkinson, Deborah. *Apples to Oregon*. Atheneum, 2004. / Isaacs, Anne. *Swamp Angel*. Dutton, 1994. / Kellogg, Steven. *I Was Born About 10,000 Years Ago*. Morrow, 1996. / Schanzer, Rosalyn. *Davy Crockett Saves the World*. HarperCollins, 2001. / Shepard, Aaron. *Master Man: A Tall Tale of Nigeria*. HarperCollins, 2001. / Stevenson, James. *Heat Wave at Mud Flat*. Greenwillow, 1997. / Tunnell, Michael O. *Chinook!* Tambourine, 1993. / Widman, Christine. *Cornfield Hide-and-Seek*. Farrar, 2003.

SUBJECTS: EXAGGERATION. FARM LIFE. HEAT. HUMOROUS FICTION. TALL TALES. WEATHER.

442   **Khan, Rukhsana. *Ruler of the Courtyard*. Illus. by R. Gregory Christie. Viking, 2003. 0-670-03583-1. Unp. Gr. 2–6**

Saba has always been terrified of the chickens in her family's courtyard in Pakistan, but on the day she finds a deadly snake in the bathhouse, she learns a new lesson about courage. If she screams, Nani, her grandmother, will come bursting through the door. It could bite. She could die. It's all up to Saba.

GERM: Saba's unnerving story, a personal narrative about facing a fear, will catch each listener in the throat. What should she do? What would you do? For that text-to-life connection, ask children to write and illustrate a time in their lives when they or someone they know had to be brave and conquer a fear, even if it turned out to be nothing at all. Discuss: How did Saba's encounter with the snake help her deal with the chickens in the courtyard?

RELATED TITLES: Bunting, Eve. *Ghost's Hour, Spook's Hour*. Clarion, 1987. / Dewey, Jennifer Owings. *Rattlesnake Dance: True Tales, Mysteries, and Rattlesnake Ceremonies*. Boyds Mills, 1997. / English, Karen. *Nadia's Hands*. Boyds Mills, 1999. / Feldman, Thelma. *Who You Callin' Chicken?* Abrams, 2003. / Grant, Joan. *The Monster That Grew Small: An Egyptian Folktale*. Lothrop, 1987. / Hall, Bruce Edward. *Henry and the Kite Dragon*. Philomel, 2004. / Kastner, Jill. *Snake Hunt*. Four Winds, 1993. / Kipling, Rudyard. *Rikki-Tikki-Tavi*. Adapted and illus. by Jerry Pinkney. Morrow, 1997. / Marsden, Carolyn. *The Gold-Threaded Dress*. Candlewick, 2002. / McNulty, Faith. *A Snake in the House*. Scholastic, 1994.

SUBJECTS: BATHS. CHICKENS. COURAGE. FEAR. MULTICULTURAL BOOKS. PAKISTAN. PERSONAL NARRATIVES. PICTURE BOOKS FOR ALL AGES. SNAKES.

443   **Kimmel, Elizabeth Cody. *My Penguin Osbert*. Illus. by H. B. Lewis. Candlewick, 2004. 0-7636-1699-0. Unp. Gr. PreK–1**

Joe's detailed letter to Santa gets him exactly what he asked for: a real penguin from Antarctica, one foot tall, named Osbert. Osbert needs to play in the snow, bathe in cold waters, and eat cold creamed herring for breakfast; Joe sees no course but to oblige him, which causes a few problems in the house.

GERM: Compile two sets of charts: What Joe Wants to Do and What Osbert Wants to Do, and What's Good About Having a Penguin and What's Not So Good. Find out more about real penguins and their habits. What does Joe mean when he says, "But I had asked for Osbert and now I had him"? Children can pick their own perfect presents and draw the pros and cons about getting them. Predict what the outcome will be if Santa brings the helicopter Joe plans to ask for next year.

RELATED TITLES: Becker, Bonny. *The Christmas Crocodile*. Simon & Schuster, 1998. / Burningham, John. *Harvey Slumfenberger's Christmas Present*. Candlewick, 1993. / Coots, J. Fred, and Haven Gillespie. *Santa Claus Is Comin' to Town*. HarperCollins, 2004. / Geraghty, Paul. *Solo*. Crown, 1996. / Grambling, Lois G. *Can I Have a Stegosaurus, Mom? Can I? Please!?* BridgeWater, 1995. / Jenkins, Martin. *The Emperor's Egg*. Candlewick, 1999. / Johnson, Doug. *Never Ride Your Elephant to School*. Henry Holt, 1995. / Kellogg, Steven. *The Mysterious Tadpole*. Dial, 1977. / Kellogg, Steven. *A Penguin Pup for Pinkerton*. Dial, 2001. / LaRochelle, David. *The Best Pet of All*. Dutton, 2004. / McPhail, David. *Santa's Book of Names*. Little, Brown, 1993. / Palatini, Margie. *Elf Help*. Hyperion, 1997. / Primavera, Elise. *Auntie Claus*. Harcourt, 1999. / Van Allsburg, Chris. *The Polar Express*. Houghton Mifflin, 1985. / Wolf, Jake. *Daddy, Could I Have an Elephant?* Greenwillow, 1996.

SUBJECTS: CHRISTMAS. GIFTS. PENGUINS. PETS. RESPONSIBILITY. SANTA CLAUS. ZOOS.

444   Kimmel, Eric A. *The Magic Dreidels: A Hanukkah Story.* Illus. by Katya Krenina. Holiday House, 1996. 0-8234-1256-3. Unp. Gr. K–3

When Jacob loses his new brass dreidel in the well, the goblin living under the water gives him a magic dreidel that spins out latkes. Fruma Sarah, the neighborhood busybody, steals the magic dreidel, substituting an ordinary wooden one; not to worry, as she gets her comeuppance. Author Kimmel reworked the old Grimm tale, "The Table, the Donkey, and the Stick," to give it a Hanukkah flavor.

GERM: Bring in little dreidels for the children to spin, and, if you have the facilities, make potato pancakes for all to taste. Here's my family recipe: Peel and grate (or grind in the food processor) four large potatoes and one medium onion. Let drain into a sieve over a bowl for a few minutes; toss out the liquid, but save the starch in the bottom. Add the potato mixture. Mix in 2 beaten eggs, ½ teaspoon salt, and 6 tablespoons matzoh meal. In a large frying pan, heat ¼–½ cup corn oil till hot. Spoon in batter to make silver dollar-sized latkes. (Don't crowd the pan.) Fry till brown and crisp; flip and brown. Drain on brown paper bags. Serve with a sprinkling of sugar and some homemade applesauce. Yum. Compare the story elements in "Jack and the Northwest Wind" from Ray Hicks's *The Jack Tales*, in which Jack gets cheated out of a magic tablecloth, a magic egg, and a beating stick. If you can find a copy, read Paul Galdone's *The Table, the Donkey, and the Stick.*

RELATED TITLES: Diakité, Baba Wagué. *The Magic Gourd.* Scholastic, 2003. / Grimm, Jacob. *The Table, the Donkey, and the Stick.* Retold and illus. by Paul Galdone. McGraw-Hill, 1976. / Hicks, Ray. *The Jack Tales.* Callaway, 2000. / Hirsch, Marilyn. *Potato Pancakes All Around: A Hanukkah Tale.* Bonim, 1978. / Howland, Naomi. *Latkes, Latkes, Good to Eat.* Clarion, 1999. / Howland, Naomi. *The Matzah Man: A Passover Story.* Clarion, 2002. / Jaffe, Nina. *In the Month of Kislev: A Story for Hanukkah.* Viking, 1992. / Kimmel, Eric A. *Asher and the Capmakers: A Hanukkah Story.* Holiday House, 1993. / Kimmel, Eric A. *The Chanukkah Guest.* Holiday House, 1990. / Kimmel, Eric A. *Hershel and the Hanukkah Goblins.* Holiday House, 1989. / Kimmel, Eric A. *The Jar of Fools: Eight Hanukkah Stories from Chelm.* Holiday House, 2000. / Newman, Lesléa. *Runaway Dreidel!* Henry Holt, 2002. / Shulman, Lisa. *The Matzo Ball Boy.* Dutton, 2005.

SUBJECTS: DREIDEL (GAME). FOOD. GOBLINS. HANUKKAH. JEWS. SWINDLERS AND SWINDLING.

445   Kimmel, Eric A. *The Runaway Tortilla.* Illus. by Randy Cecil. Winslow, 2000. 1-890817-18-X. Unp. Gr. PreK–1

In Texas, down by the Rio Grande, one of Tía Lupe's light-as-a-cloud tortillas ups and runs away from her taquería, crying, "I'm too beautiful to eat!" Out of town and into the desert it rolls, chased by six bold buckaroos, five rattlesnakes, four jackrabbits, three donkeys, two horned toads, and Tía Lupe and her husband, Tío José. Señor Coyote is the one who stops Señorita Tortilla in her tracks. SNAP! He eats her up.

GERM: Make up a simple tune so you can sing the tortilla's teasing refrain: "Run as fast as fast can be. You won't get a bite of me. Doesn't matter what you do. I'll be far ahead of you!" Bring in tortillas to try, maybe with a little salsa or melted cheese. Compare and contrast this version with one or more retellings of the original, "The Gingerbread Man."

RELATED TITLES: Cauley, Lorinda Bryan. *The Pancake Boy: An Old Norwegian Folk Tale.* Putnam, 1988. / Compestine, Ying Chang. *The Runaway Rice Cake.* Simon & Schuster, 2001. / Cook, Scott. *The Gingerbread Boy.* Knopf, 1987. / Cox, Judy. *The West Texas Chili Monster.* BridgeWater, 1998. / Egielski, Richard. *The Gingerbread Boy.* HarperCollins, 1997. / Esterl, Arnica. *The Fine Round Cake.* Four Winds, 1991. / Ketteman, Helen. *Armadilly Chili.* Albert Whitman, 2004. / Kimmel, Eric A. *The Gingerbread Man.* Holiday House, 1993. / Lowell, Susan. *The Tortoise and the Jackrabbit.* Northland, 1994. / Sawyer, Ruth. *Journey Cake, Ho!* Puffin, 1978.

SUBJECTS: CHANTABLE REFRAIN. COYOTES. FOLKLORE. FOOD. GINGERBREAD BOY. MEXICAN AMERICANS. MULTICULTURAL BOOKS. SEQUENCE STORIES. TEXAS. TORTILLAS.

446   Kinerk, Robert. *Clorinda.* Illus. by Steven Kellogg. Simon & Schuster, 2003. 0-689-86449-3. Unp. Gr. K–3

Buoyed by the support of a farmhand friend, Clorinda the cow sets out for New York City to become a ballet dancer, but her big break as a dancer in the ballet, *Giselle,* is not as successful as she would have wished. This rhyming story, alight with Kellogg's jubilant pen-and-ink and watercolor illustrations, has that time-honored picture-book theme of an animal coveting a career in the arts.

GERM: Ask your listeners to predict what Clorinda will do as you read her inspiring tale aloud. Discussion points: Why does she go back to the farm? Is she a failure? Why or why not? Compare Clorinda's saga with other successful cow stories such as Gennifer Choldenko's *Moonstruck* and Lisa Campbell Ernst's *When Bluebell Sang* and with those of other animal performers, including Mary Jane Auch's *Peeping Beauty*, Pamela Duncan Edwards's *Honk!*, and Tess Weaver's *Opera Cat*.

RELATED TITLES: Auch, Mary Jane. *Hen Lake.* Holiday House, 1995. / Auch, Mary Jane. *Peeping Beauty.* Holiday House, 1993. / Babcock, Chris. *No Moon, No Milk.* Crown, 1993. / Choldenko, Gennifer. *Moonstruck: The True Story of the Cow Who Jumped over the Moon.* Hyperion, 1997. / Cronin, Doreen. *Click, Clack, Moo: Cows That Type.* Simon & Schuster, 2000. / Edwards, Pamela Duncan. *Honk! The Story of a Prima Swanerina.* Hyperion, 1998. / Egan, Tim. *Metropolitan Cow.* Houghton Mifflin, 1996. / Ernst, Lisa Campbell. *When Bluebell Sang.* Bradbury, 1989. / Goss, Linda. *The Frog Who Wanted to Be a Singer.* Orchard, 1996. / Graham, Bob. *Benny: An Adventure Story.* Candlewick, 1999. / Johnson, Paul Brett. *The Cow Who Wouldn't Come Down.* Orchard, 1993. / Livingston, Irene. *Finklehopper Frog.* Tricycle, 2003. / Marshall, James. *Swine Lake.* HarperCollins, 1999. / Vail, Rachel. *Over the Moon.* Orchard, 1998. / Weaver, Tess. *Opera Cat.* Clarion, 2002.

SUBJECTS: BALLET. COWS. DANCING. DOMESTIC ANIMALS. PERSEVERANCE. STORIES IN RHYME.

447   **Kinsey-Warnock, Natalie.** *Nora's Ark.* **Illus. by Emily Arnold McCully. HarperCollins, 2005. 0-06-029517-1. Unp. Gr. 1–5**

As young Wren tells it, with the rain coming down in torrents, her grandparents packed up their essentials and toted them up the hill to the as-yet-unfurnished new house Grandpa had just finished building. Grandpa headed back out to help a neighbor. By night, the house was full to bursting with displaced neighbors and their animals—23 people, three horses, five pigs, a duck, four cats, and 100 chickens, but Grandpa still wasn't back. In the morning, Wren and her grandmother, Nora, set out by rowboat, past startling scenes of destruction, to find him. Inspired by an actual event, the disastrous Vermont Flood of 1927 in which 84 people died, McCully's compassionate fictional account is paired with rain-swept watercolors.

GERM: Discuss Wren's assessment of what's important in life: ". . . family and friends and neighbors helping neighbors. Like Grandma said, everything else is just gravy." Ask your students to make a connection to their own experiences with selfless acts and hard times. *Flood* by Mary Calhoun, *River Friendly, River Wild* by Jane Kurtz, and *The Blizzard* by Betty Ren Wright also exemplify the theme of people coming together in times of natural disasters.

RELATED TITLES: Byars, Betsy. *Tornado.* HarperCollins, 1996. / Calhoun, Mary. *Flood.* Morrow, 1997. / Kurtz, Jane. *River Friendly, River Wild.* Simon & Schuster, 2000. / Pinkney, Jerry. *Noah's Ark.* SeaStar, 2002. / San Souci, Robert D. *Kate Shelley: Bound for Legend.* Dial, 1995. / Spier, Peter. *Noah's Ark.* Bantam, 1992. / Wright, Betty Ren. *The Blizzard.* Holiday House, 2003.

SUBJECTS: FARM LIFE. FLOODS. GRANDPARENTS. HISTORICAL FICTION. PICTURE BOOKS FOR ALL AGES. RESCUES. VERMONT.

448   **Kleven, Elisa.** *Hooray, a Piñata!* **Illus. by the author. Dutton, 1996. 0-525-45605-8. Unp. Gr. PreK–1**

Clara adores Lucky, the little dog piñata she picked out for her birthday party; she takes him everywhere and then can't bear the thought of filling him with candy and breaking him.

GERM: Clara has a problem, and her best friend, Simon, solves it by bringing her a monster piñata for her party. Before reading that part, ask your listeners to predict what Clara will do. Have them finish the sentence: "At my birthday party, we ____." They can illustrate their responses as well. If you're ambitious and don't mind the mess, make a monster piñata with your own kids and have a party. Rebecca Emberley's bilingual *Piñata!* includes simple instructions for constructing one.

RELATED TITLES: Dorros, Arthur. *Abuela.* Dutton, 1991. / Elya, Susan Middleton. *Eight Animals Bake a Cake.* Putnam, 2002. / Elya, Susan Middleton. *Say Hola to Spanish.* Lee & Low, 1996. / Emberley, Rebecca. *Piñata!* Little, Brown, 2004. / Guy, Ginger Foglesong. *Fiesta!* Greenwillow, 1996. / Reed, Lynn. *Pedro, His Perro, and the Alphabet Sombrero.* Hyperion, 1995. / Ryan, Pam Muñoz. *Mice and Beans.* Scholastic, 2001. / Soto, Gary. *Chato and the Party Animals.* Putnam, 2000. / Soto, Gary. *Chato's Kitchen.* Putnam, 1995. / Soto, Gary. *Snapshots from the Wedding.* Putnam, 1997.

SUBJECTS: BIRTHDAYS. DOGS. HISPANIC AMERICANS. MULTICULTURAL BOOKS. PARTIES. PIÑATAS.

449 **Klise, Kate.** *Shall I Knit You a Hat? A Christmas Yarn.* **Illus. by M. Sarah Klise. Henry Holt, 2004. 0-8050-7318-3. Unp. Gr. PreK–1**

On the eve of a Christmas blizzard, Mother Rabbit knits a special hat to keep Little Rabbit's ears warm. He is so taken with it, he proposes that he and his mother make one-of-a-kind Christmas hats for all their animal friends. Not until the snow starts piling up do the animals appreciate just how perfect their gifts are.

GERM: The theme of lovingly making and giving gifts without expecting any in return is supported by the cozy and enchanting acrylic illustrations. Children will be intrigued by the notion of making such unusual hats and may want to design and create hats for their own animals. Bring in thick yarn and big needles and show everyone how to knit, starting with a simple scarf for a stuffed animal.

RELATED TITLES: Hoban, Lillian. *Arthur's Christmas Cookies.* HarperCollins, 1972. / McDonnell, Patrick. *The Gift of Nothing.* Little, Brown, 2005. / Paterson, Katherine. *Marvin's Best Christmas Present Ever.* Harper-Collins, 1997. / Valckx, Catharina. *Lizette's Green Sock.* Clarion, 2005. / Walton, Rick. *Bunny Christmas: A Family Celebration.* HarperCollins, 2004. / Watson, Clyde. *How Brown Mouse Kept Christmas.* Farrar, 1980. / Wells, Rosemary. *Max's Christmas.* Dial, 1986.

SUBJECTS: CHRISTMAS. FRIENDSHIP. GENEROSITY. GIFTS. HATS. MOTHERS AND SONS. RABBITS. STORMS. WEATHER. WINTER.

450 **Koller, Jackie French.** *One Monkey Too Many.* **Illus. by Lynn Munsinger. Harcourt, 1999. 0-15-200006-2. Unp. Gr. PreK–1**

Though the bikeman tells the monkey that the bike is only for one, another monkey jumps on and the two crash it into a ditch. Three monkeys drive a golf cart meant for two, and four monkeys paddle a canoe meant for three, leading to disaster every time.

GERM: The rhyming text and jolly pen-and-ink and watercolor illustrations are filled with rollicking monkeys, ending with six monkeys sneaking into the author's studio and making a mess of the very book we are reading. Listeners will laugh aloud and count all the monkeys. Go in reverse with *Five Little Monkeys Jumping on the Bed* by Eileen Christelow.

RELATED TITLES: Anholt, Catherine, and Laurence Anholt. *Chimp and Zee.* Putnam, 2001. / Anholt, Catherine, and Laurence Anholt. *Chimp and Zee and the Big Storm.* Putnam, 2002. / Christelow, Eileen. *Five Little Monkeys Jumping on the Bed.* Clarion, 1989. (And others in the Five Little Monkeys series.) / Diakité, Baba Wagué. *The Hatseller and the Monkeys.* Scholastic, 1999. / Goode, Diane. *Monkey Mo Goes to Sea.* Blue Sky/Scholastic, 2002. / Johnson, Paul Brett. *Little Bunny Foo Foo.* Scholastic, 2004. / Perkins, Al. *Hand, Hand, Fingers, Thumb.* Random House, 1969. / Rey, H. A. *Curious George.* Houghton Mifflin, 1993. (And others in the Curious George series.) / Santat, Dan. *The Guild of Geniuses.* Scholastic, 2004. / Slobodkina, Esphyr. *Caps for Sale.* HarperCollins, 1947.

SUBJECTS: COUNTING BOOKS. HUMOROUS FICTION. MONKEYS. STORIES IN RHYME.

451 **Kraft, Erik.** *Chocolatina.* **Illus. by Denise Brunkus. BridgeWater, 1998. 0-8167-4544-7. Unp. Gr. K–2**

Chocolatina, a chocolate-loving girl, awakens to discover her wish has come true: she's been turned to chocolate, thus verifying her sharp-tongued health teacher's favorite adage, "You are what you eat."

GERM: Children can create portraits of themselves in the guise of their favorite foods. In *The Chocolate Touch* by Patrick Skene Catling, everything John Midas tries to eat turns to chocolate.

RELATED TITLES: Balian, Lorna. *The Sweet Touch.* Star Bright, 2005. / Catling, Patrick Skene. *The Chocolate Touch.* Morrow, 1979. / Child, Lauren. *I Will Never Not Ever Eat a Tomato.* Candlewick, 2000. / Clement, Rod. *Just Another Ordinary Day.* HarperCollins, 1997. / Cox, Judy. *The West Texas Chili Monster.* BridgeWater, 1998. / Craft, Charlotte. *King Midas and the Golden Touch.* Morrow, 1999. / Hoberman, Mary Ann. *The Seven Silly Eaters.* Harcourt, 1997. / Meddaugh, Susan. *The Witch's Walking Stick.* Houghton Mifflin, 2005. / Palatini, Margie. *Sweet Tooth.* Simon & Schuster, 2004. / Shannon, David. *A Bad Case of Stripes.* Blue Sky/Scholastic, 1998. / Smith, Robert Kimmell. *Chocolate Fever.* Putnam, 1989.

SUBJECTS: CANDY. CHOCOLATE. FANTASY. HUMOROUS FICTION. NUTRITION. SCHOOLS. TEACHERS. TRANSFORMATIONS. WISHES.

452 **Krensky, Stephen.** *How Santa Got His Job.* **Illus. by S. D. Schindler. Simon & Schuster, 1998. 0-689-80697-3. Unp. Gr. K–3**

Way back when Santa was starting out in the work world, he hated desk jobs, so he became a chimney cleaner. Next he delivered packages late at night for the post office; cooked at an all-night diner, where he put on a lot of weight; became a zookeeper and made friends with reindeer; got shot out of a cannon at the circus; and finally, hooked up with some toy-making elves. Schindler's pen-and-ink and watercolor illustrations are filled with amiable details, which listeners will point out as they trace the skills Santa acquired to help him perform his ultimate job these days.

GERM: Bring in the Help Wanted section from the newspaper and have everyone look for jobs they think they'd like. Then have them write up new Help Wanted ads for their dream jobs, listing skills, requirements, salary, and benefits. Follow up with Krensky's sequel, *How Santa Lost His Job.*

RELATED TITLES: Barracca, Debra, and Sal Barracca. *A Taxi Dog Christmas.* Dial, 1994. / Brett, Jan. *The Wild Christmas Reindeer.* Putnam, 1990. / Burningham, John. *Harvey Slumfenberger's Christmas Present.* Candlewick, 1993. / Haywood, Carolyn. *A Christmas Fantasy.* Morrow, 1992. / Joyce, William. *Santa Calls.* HarperCollins, 1993. / Kimmel, Elizabeth Cody. *My Penguin Osbert.* Candlewick, 2004. / Krensky, Stephen. *How Santa Lost His Job.* Simon & Schuster, 2001 / McPhail, David. *Santa's Book of Names.* Little, Brown, 1993. / Palatini, Margie. *Elf Help.* Hyperion, 1997. / Pearson, Tracey Campbell. *Where Does Joe Go?* Farrar, 1999. / Price, Moe. *The Reindeer Christmas.* Harcourt, 1993. / Primavera, Elise. *Auntie Claus.* Harcourt, 1999. / Van Allsburg, Chris. *The Polar Express.* Houghton Mifflin, 1985.

SUBJECTS: OCCUPATIONS. PICTURE BOOKS FOR ALL AGES. SANTA CLAUS.

453   Kroeger, Mary Kay, and Louise Borden. *Paperboy.* Illus. by Ted Lewin. Clarion, 1996. 0-395-64482-8. Unp. Gr. 1–4

After listening to the historic 1927 heavyweight boxing match between Jack Demsey and Gene Tunney, paperboy Willie Brinkman rushes back to the Times-Star building to pick up "Fight Extra" papers to sell on his Cincinnati street corner, hoping for extra money to take home to his family.

GERM: Read this along with Dav Pilkey's *The Paperboy* to compare childhood back in the 1920s with now. Investigate another big news event of that year—Charles Lindbergh's solo flight from New York City to Paris—in Robert Burleigh's *Flight: The Journey of Charles Lindbergh.*

RELATED TITLES: Bartone, Elisa. *American Too.* Illus. by Ted Lewin. Lothrop, 1996. / Bartone, Elisa. *Peppe the Lamplighter.* Illus. by Ted Lewin. Lothrop, 1993. / Brown, Don. *Kid Blink Beats the World.* Roaring Brook, 2004. / Burleigh, Robert. *Flight: The Journey of Charles Lindbergh.* Philomel, 1991. / Lasky, Kathryn. *Marven of the North Woods.* Harcourt, 1997. / Pilkey, Dav. *The Paper Boy.* Orchard, 1996. / Pinkney, Brian. *The Adventures of Sparrowboy.* Simon & Schuster, 1997.

SUBJECTS: BOXING. CHILD LABOR. HISTORICAL FICTION. LOYALTY. NEWSPAPER CARRIERS.

454   Kroll, Steven. *Patches Lost and Found.* Illus. by Barry Goff. Marshall Cavendish, 2005. 0-7614-5217-6. Unp. Gr. K–4

Stuck on a school assignment to write a story and *then* draw the pictures, Jenny finds inspiration in her own life when she comes home to find her guinea pig, Patches, missing.

GERM: For the artists in your group who can't follow Jenny's teacher's directions—"Words first, pictures second"—this story will be a godsend. Have your crew work on writing new stories, but have them think out the stories in their heads; draw the pictures first and lay them out in sequence as a storyboard, as Jenny does in the story; and then write their texts.

RELATED TITLES: Brown, Marc. *Arthur Writes a Story.* Little, Brown, 1996. / Child, Lauren. *Clarice Bean, Guess Who's Babysitting?* Candlewick, 2001. / Christelow, Eileen. *What Do Illustrators Do?* Clarion, 1999. / dePaola, Tomie. *The Art Lesson.* Putnam, 1989. / LaMarche, Jim. *The Raft.* HarperCollins, 2000. / Meade, Holly. *John Willy and Freddy McGee.* Marshall Cavendish, 1998. / Nixon, Joan Lowery. *If You Were a Writer.* Four Winds, 1988. / Reynolds, Peter H. *The Dot.* Candlewick, 2003. / Reynolds, Peter H. *Ish.* Candlewick, 2004. / Roche, Denis. *The Best Class Picture Ever.* Scholastic, 2003. / Schotter, Roni. *Nothing Ever Happens on 90th Street.* Orchard, 1997. / Stevens, Janet. *From Pictures to Words: A Book About Making a Book.* Holiday House, 1995.

SUBJECTS: ARTISTS. DRAWING. GUINEA PIGS. LOST AND FOUND POSSESSIONS. TEACHERS. WRITING.

455   Krosoczka, Jarrett J. *Annie Was Warned.* Illus. by the author. Knopf, 2003. 0-385-81567-8. Unp. Gr. K–2

On Halloween night—her birthday—Annie sneaks out to the creepy old Montgomery mansion on a dare. She claims she's not scared, but listeners will shiver.

GERM: At the climax, ask listeners if Annie should go through that door. What does the last line mean: "It was the best scare she'd ever had." Turn out the lights and read this one with a flashlight to get everyone in a Halloween mood. Find more shivers and laughs in *The Spooky Book* by Steve Patschke and *That Terrible Halloween Night* by James Stevenson.

RELATED TITLES: Bunting, Eve. *Scary, Scary Halloween.* Clarion, 1986. / Emberley, Ed. *Go Away, Big Green Monster!* Little, Brown, 1993. / Jonas, Ann. *The 13th Clue.* Greenwillow, 1992. / Leuck, Laura. *One Witch.* Walker, 2003. / McKissack, Patricia, and Onawumi Jean Moss. *Precious and the Boo Hag.* Atheneum, 2005. / Patschke, Steve. *The Spooky Book.* Walker, 1999. / Polacco, Patricia. *Some Birthday!* Simon & Schuster, 1991. / Regan, Dian Curtis. *The Thirteen Hours of Halloween.* Albert Whitman, 1993. / Shute, Linda. *Halloween Party.* Lothrop, 1994. / Silverman, Erica. *Big Pumpkin.* Macmillan, 1992. / Simms, Laura. *The Squeaky Door.* Crown, 1991. / Sklansky, Amy E. *Skeleton Bones and Goblin Groans: Poems for Halloween.* Henry Holt, 2004. / Stevenson, James. *That Terrible Halloween Night.* Greenwillow, 1980. / Stutson, Caroline. *By the Light of the Halloween Moon.* Lothrop, 1993. / Williams, Linda. *The Little Old Lady Who Was Not Afraid of Anything.* Crowell, 1986.

SUBJECTS: BIRTHDAYS. COURAGE. FEAR. HALLOWEEN. HAUNTED HOUSES. PARTIES. SUSPENSE.

456   Krosoczka, Jarrett J. *Max for President.* **Illus. by the author. Knopf, 2004. 0-375-92428-0. Unp. Gr. PreK–2**

Max and Kelly both run for class president, putting up posters, handing out campaign buttons, and making promises. When Kelly wins, she chooses Max as her vice president, and they work together to make their school a better place.

GERM: Start your discussion of the election process with this basic and appealing look at classroom civics. Talk about national elections with Eileen Christelow's *VOTE!* and introduce the role of U.S. president in terms children will understand with *If I Were President* by Catherine Stier and *My Teacher for President* by Kay Winters. Then bring on the political humor with Doreen Cronin's hilarious *Duck for President.*

RELATED TITLES: Christelow, Eileen. *VOTE!* Clarion, 2003. / Cronin, Doreen. *Duck for President.* Simon & Schuster, 2004. / McNamara, Margaret. *Election Day.* Simon & Schuster, 2004. / St. George, Judith. *So You Want to Be President?* Philomel, 2000. / Stier, Catherine. *If I Were President.* Albert Whitman, 1999. / Winters, Kay. *My Teacher for President.* Dutton, 2004.

SUBJECTS: ELECTIONS. PRESIDENTS. SCHOOLS. VOTING. WINNING AND LOSING.

457   Krosoczka, Jarrett J. *Punk Farm.* **Illus. by the author. Knopf, 2005. 0-375-82429-4. Unp. Gr. PreK–1**

After Farmer Joe heads for bed, the pig, sheep, cow, goat, and chicken set up their instruments and equipment for a final rehearsal before the evening's big rock 'n' roll concert in the barn. Onstage, their band, Punk Farm, wows the crowd with its sizzling rendition of "Old MacDonald Had a Farm."

GERM: Ask your rockers to explain to you just what rock 'n' roll is and have them sing the song the way they think it would sound as performed by Punk Farm. Bring in sunglasses, bandanas, and play a little air guitar. You can also download Punk Farm's hit single at their very cool Web site, <www.punkfarm.com>. See how other barnmates spend their down time in Doreen Cronin's *Click, Clack, Moo: Cows That Type.*

RELATED TITLES: Cauley, Lorinda Bryan. *Old MacDonald Had a Farm.* Putnam, 1989. / Cronin, Doreen. *Click, Clack, Moo: Cows That Type.* Simon & Schuster, 2000. / Dallas-Conté, Juliet. *Cock-a-Moo-Moo.* Little, Brown, 2001. / Egan, Tim. *Serious Farm.* Houghton Mifflin, 2003. / Hort, Lenny. *The Seals on the Bus.* Henry Holt, 2000. / Pearson, Tracey Campbell. *Old MacDonald Had a Farm.* Dial, 1984. / Rostoker-Gruber, Karen. *Rooster Can't Cock-a-Doodle-Doo.* Dial, 2004. / Rounds, Glen. *Old MacDonald Had a Farm.* Holiday House, 1989. / Schwartz, Amy. *Old MacDonald.* Scholastic, 1999. / Shulman, Lisa. *Old MacDonald Had a Woodshop.* Putnam, 2002.

SUBJECTS: DOMESTIC ANIMALS. FARM LIFE. MUSICIANS. ROCK MUSIC. SONGS. STORIES WITH SONGS.

458   Kuklin, Susan. *All Aboard! A True Train Story.* **Illus. by the author. Orchard, 2003. 0-439-45583-9. Unp. Gr. PreK–1**

Crisp, you-are-there, color photos take us on a vicarious ride aboard an old-style Durango & Silverton Narrow Gauge steam locomotive as it chugs through the Colorado Rocky Mountains at a top speed of 18 miles an hour.

GERM: Try out the four different train whistles described in the "Train Talk" section at the back of the book. Train enthusiasts will find more info at <www.durangotrain.com>. Sing "I've Been

Working on the Railroad" and watch other trains pass by in Philip Booth's *Crossing*, Donald Crews's *Freight Train*, and Diane Siebert's *Train Song*.

RELATED TITLES: Booth, Philip. *Crossing*. Candlewick, 2001. / Crews, Donald. *Freight Train*. Greenwillow, 1978. / Crews, Donald. *Inside Freight Train*. HarperCollins, 2001. / Kirk, Daniel. *Go!* Hyperion, 2001. / Shields, Carol Diggory. *Animagicals: On the Go*. Handprint, 2001. / Siebert, Diane. *Train Song*. Crowell, 1990. / Tunnell, Michael O. *Mailing May*. Greenwillow, 1997. / Westcott, Nadine Bernard. *I've Been Working on the Railroad: An American Classic*. Hyperion, 1996.

SUBJECTS: TRAINS. TRANSPORTATION.

459   **Kurtz, Jane. *River Friendly, River Wild*. Illus. by Neil Brennan. Simon & Schuster, 2000. 0-689-82049-6. Unp. Gr. 2–4**
In the spring of 1997, melting snow caused the Red River to overflow the dikes in Grand Forks, North Dakota, and author Jane Kurtz and her family were evacuated from their house. In this story, told in free-verse poems and based on those traumatic events, an unnamed girl narrator and her parents leave her beloved cat, Kiwi, behind in their house for two weeks when the neighborhood is flooded. Coming back to the waterlogged house, she finds no sign of her cat.
GERM: When you're studying weather and talking about various natural disasters, this story brings in the human component and shows how people deal with adversity. (And stop worrying. The cat is fine.) *Flood* by Mary Calhoun and *Nora's Ark* by Natalie Kinsey-Warnock are also powerful narratives based on actual floods.
RELATED TITLES: Byars, Betsy. *Tornado*. HarperCollins, 1996. / Calhoun, Mary. *Flood*. Morrow, 1997. / Kinsey-Warnock, Natalie. *Nora's Ark*. HarperCollins, 2005. / Roy, Ron. *Nightmare Island*. Dutton, 1981. / Ruckman, Ivy. *Night of the Twisters*. Crowell, 1984. / San Souci, Robert D. *Kate Shelley: Bound for Legend*. Dial, 1995. / Wright, Betty Ren. *The Blizzard*. Holiday House, 2003.

SUBJECTS: DISASTERS. FLOODS. NORTH DAKOTA. PERSONAL NARRATIVES. RIVERS. SURVIVAL.

460   **Kurtz, Jane, and Christopher Kurtz. *Water Hole Waiting*. Illus. by Lee Christiansen. Greenwillow, 2002. 0-06-029851-0. Unp. Gr. PreK–2**
A young vervet monkey wakes up thirsty, but his Mama must stop him from scampering down to the water hole to keep him out of danger and away from the bigger animals. One after another, the animals come to the hole to drink—herding hippopotami, sharp-hooved zebras, a crocodile lurking in the water, a lion, and a herd of elephants—before it's safe for Monkey to go.
GERM: This tale of delayed satisfaction will make everyone thirsty for a drink of water. As they drink, ask them to describe how water tastes when they are parched. For an up-close look at a water hole, Kurtz suggests visiting <www.AfriCam.com>.
RELATED TITLES: Aardema, Verna. *Bringing the Rain to Kapiti Plain*. Dial, 1981. / Bash, Barbara. *Tree of Life: The World of the African Baobab*. Sierra Club/Little, Brown, 1989. / Brett, Jan. *Honey . . . Honey . . . Lion!* Putnam, 2005. / Cowcher, Helen. *Whistling Thorn*. Scholastic, 1993. / Diakité, Baba Wagué. *The Hunterman and the Crocodile: A West African Folktale*. Scholastic, 1997. / Geraghty, Paul. *The Hunter*. Crown, 1994. / Jenkins, Martin. *Grandma Elephant's in Charge*. Candlewick, 2003. / Sayre, April Pulley. *If You Should Hear a Honey Guide*. Houghton, 1995. / Stojic, Manya. *Rain*. Crown, 2000. / Yoshida, Toshi. *Elephant Crossing*. Philomel, 1989. / Yoshida, Toshi. *Young Lions*. Philomel, 1989.

SUBJECTS: AFRICA. ANIMALS. MONKEYS. WATER.

461   **Laden, Nina. *Bad Dog*. Illus. by the author. Walker, 2000. 0-8027-8748-7. Unp. Gr. K–3**
The verbal puns of the canine narrator will make you howl with laughter as he unleashes a string of bad behavior when he gets the call of the wild and goes hunting for free-range chickens.
GERM: Identify some of the puns, wordplays, and double entendres so your listeners can "get it." Meet his behavioral opposite, saintly dachshund do-gooder Dexter, in *Superdog: The Heart of a Hero* by Caralyn Buehner and his feline counterpart in *Bad Kitty* by Nick Bruel.
RELATED TITLES: Bruel, Nick. *Bad Kitty*. Roaring Brook, 2005. / Buehner, Caralyn. *Superdog: The Heart of a Hero*. HarperCollins, 2004. / Hurd, Thacher. *Art Dog*. HarperCollins, 1996. / Kirk, Daniel. *Dogs Rule!* Hyperion, 2003. / Laden, Nina. *The Night I Followed the Dog*. Chronicle, 1994. / Lebentritt, Julia, and Richard Ploetz. *The Kooken*. Holt, 1992. / Meddaugh, Susan. *Martha Walks the Dog*. Houghton Mifflin, 1998. (And others in the Martha series.) / Meddaugh, Susan. *Perfectly Martha*. Houghton Mifflin, 2004. / Myers, Walter Dean. *The Blues of Flats Brown*. Holiday House, 2000. / Rathmann, Peggy. *Officer Buckle and Gloria*. Putnam, 1995. / Teague, Mark. *Dear Mrs. LaRue: Letters from Obedience School*. Scholastic, 2002. / Teague, Mark. *Detective LaRue: Letters from the Investigation*. Scholastic, 2004.

SUBJECTS: BEHAVIOR. CHICKENS. DOGS. HUMOROUS FICTION. PERSONAL NARRATIVES. POINT OF VIEW. POLICE. PUNS AND PUNNING. VOCABULARY.

462 Laden, Nina. *The Night I Followed the Dog*. Illus. by the author. Chronicle, 1994. 0-8118-0647-2. Unp. Gr. 1–3

When he spies his tuxedo-clad dog getting out of a limousine early one morning, a boy decides to follow him to see where he disappears to each night. Turns out the enterprising pooch sports a wild private life all his own.

GERM: Ask your writers to speculate what their pets are up to when no one's home. What would they find if they followed their pets? Laden uses wild and jazzy typefaces to illustrate key words, a format writers can incorporate into their stories. Another dog who slips out of the house and has fun is Max in Susanne Whayne's *Petropolis*. Handprint, 2003.

RELATED TITLES: Buehner, Caralyn. *Superdog: The Heart of a Hero*. HarperCollins, 2004. / Edwards, Pamela Duncan. *Muldoon*. Hyperion, 2002. / Kirk, Daniel. *Dogs Rule!* Hyperion, 2003. / Laden, Nina. *Bad Dog*. Walker, 2000. / Laden, Nina. *Roberto the Insect Architect*. Chronicle, 2000. / Laden, Nina. *When Pigasso Met Mootisse*. Chronicle, 1998. / Meddaugh, Susan. *Martha Speaks*. Houghton Mifflin, 1992. (And others in the Martha series.) / Miller, Sara Swan. *Three Stories You Can Read to Your Dog*. Houghton Mifflin, 1995. / Pilkey, Dav. *Dogzilla*. Harcourt, 1993. / Rathmann, Peggy. *Officer Buckle and Gloria*. Putnam, 1995. / Simon, Seymour. *Dogs*. HarperCollins, 2003. / Teague, Mark. *Dear Mrs. LaRue: Letters from Obedience School*. Scholastic, 2002. / Teague, Mark. *Detective LaRue: Letters from the Investigation*. Scholastic, 2004. / Whayne, Susanne. *Petropolis*. Handprint, 2003.

SUBJECTS: DOGS. FANTASY. IMAGINATION. NIGHT. NIGHTCLUBS. PICTURE BOOKS FOR ALL AGES.

463 Laden, Nina. *Private I. Guana: The Case of the Missing Chameleon*. Illus. by the author. Chronicle, 1995. 0-8118-0940-4. Unp. Gr. K–3

Drawing inspiration from 1940s-style tough-guy characters such as Philip Marlowe and Sam Spade, a trench coat-clad iguana gumshoe sets out to track down Liz the lizard's absent husband, Leon. I. Guana's shocked to find him disguised as Camille and singing with the Gila Girls, the house band at the slimy Lizard Lounge in the swamp. The tone is tongue-in-cheek, the picture book's large, dark, pastel illustrations are wonderfully brooding, and even the typewriter-like typeface with its ragged right margin puts you in the mood for mystery.

GERM: There are suggestions for possible sequels as I. Guana ponders his next case: "A frog that jumped bail . . . a turtle running a shell game . . . a poisoned snake . . ." Crime solvers can write these sequels or think up new cases for him to solve. Meet an elephant detective on a case in Doug Cushman's *Mystery at the Club Sandwich*.

RELATED TITLES: Biedrzycki, David. *Ace Lacewing: Bug Detective*. Charlesbridge, 2005. / Christelow, Eileen. *Gertrude, the Bulldog Detective*. Clarion, 1992. / Clifford, Eth. *Flatfoot Fox and the Case of the Mising Schoolhouse*. Houghton Mifflin, 1997. (And others in the Flatfoot Fox series.) / Cushman, Doug. *The ABC Mystery*. HarperCollins, 1993. / Cushman, Doug. Aunt Eater mystery series. HarperCollins. / Cushman, Doug. Inspector Hopper series. HarperCollins, 2000. / Cushman, Doug. *Mystery at the Club Sandwich*. Clarion, 2004. / Massie, Diane Redfield. *Chameleon Was a Spy*. Crowell, 1979. / Palatini, Margie. *The Web Files*. Hyperion, 2001. / Sharmat, Marjorie Weinman. Nate the Great series. Delacorte. / Teague, Mark. *Detective LaRue: Letters from the Investigation*. Scholastic, 2004.

SUBJECTS: CHAMELEONS. IGUANAS. MYSTERY AND DETECTIVE STORIES. REPTILES AND AMPHIBIANS.

464 Laden, Nina. *Roberto the Insect Architect*. Illus. by the author. Chronicle, 2000. 0-8118-2465-9. Unp. Gr. PreK–3

Too busy playing with his wood food to eat it, termite Roberto dreams of becoming a famous architect—which, after hard work and perseverance, he finally does, coming up with a plan to build an entire insect neighborhood.

GERM: Break out the blocks or Legos so aspiring architects can build, or have them create sculptures with found objects, scraps of cardboard, and fabrics.

RELATED TITLES: Auch, Mary Jane. *Eggs Mark the Spot*. Holiday House, 1996. / Auch, Mary Jane. *Hen Lake*. Holiday House, 1995. / Auch, Mary Jane. *Peeping Beauty*. Holiday House, 1993. / Cannon, Janell. *Crickwing*. Harcourt, 2000. / Ernst, Lisa Campbell. *When Bluebell Sang*. Bradbury, 1989. / Falconer, Ian. *Olivia*. Atheneum, 2000. / Florian, Douglas. *Insectlopedia: Poems and Paintings*. Harcourt, 1998. / Goss, Linda. *The Frog Who Want-*

ed to Be a Singer. Orchard, 1996. / Hurd, Thacher. *Art Dog*. HarperCollins, 1996. / Steiner, Joan. *Look-Alikes*. Little, Brown, 1998. / Steiner, Joan. *Look-Alikes, Jr.* Little, Brown, 1999.

SUBJECTS: ARCHITECTS. CREATIVITY. DETERMINATION. INDIVIDUALITY. INSECTS. TERMITES.

465   Laden, Nina. *When Pigasso Met Mootisse*. Illus. by the author. Chronicle, 1998. 0-8118-1121-2. Unp. Gr. K–6

With art-loving pigs lining up to buy Pigasso's unusual paintings, and the cattle community craving Mootisse's big, energetic, bright "Moosterpieces," the two art superstars soon weary of their relentless fans. They buy adjacent farms in the country but soon become bitter enemies, each critical of the other's work and style. Hurling invectives—"Art hog" and "Mad cow"— they angrily construct a fence between their houses. Back in their studios, the pig-headed Pigasso and the bull-headed Mootisse suddenly realize they miss each other and come up with an original artistic solution to their quarrel.

GERM: Before finishing the story, stop for a Quick Write: How can the two temperamental artists settle their differences? An Author's Note introduces the two human masters spoofed in this splashily illustrated and wittily pun-filled modern art tribute. Students can try their hands at painting using another famous artist's style.

RELATED TITLES: Alcorn, Johnny. *Rembrandt's Beret*. Tambourine, 1991. / Auch, Mary Jane. *Eggs Mark the Spot*. Holiday House, 1996. / Brown, Laurene Krasny. *Visiting the Art Museum*. Dutton, 1986. / Browne, Anthony. *The Shape Game*. Farrar, 2003. / Browne, Anthony. *Willy the Dreamer*. Candlewick, 1998. / Garland, Michael. *Dinner at Magritte's*. Dutton, 1995. / Hurd, Thacher. *Art Dog*. HarperCollins, 1996. / Lithgow, John. *Micawber*. Simon & Schuster, 2002. / Micklethwaite, Lucy. *A Child's Book of Art: Discover Great Paintings*. Delacorte, 1995. / Micklethwaite, Lucy. *A Child's Book of Play in Art: Great Pictures, Great Fun*. DK, 1996. / Pilkey, Dav. *When Cats Dream*. Orchard, 1992. / Raczka, Bob. *Art Is . . .* Millbrook, 2003. / Richardson, Joy. *Inside the Museum: A Children's Guide to the Metropolitan Museum of Art*. Abrams, 1993. / Sayre, Henry M. *Cave Paintings to Picasso: The Inside Scoop on 50 Art Masterpieces*. Chronicle Books, 2003.

SUBJECTS: ARGUMENTS. ARTISTS. BULLS. CONFLICT RESOLUTION. FRIENDSHIP. PAINTERS. PICTURE BOOKS FOR ALL AGES. PIGS.

466   Lakin, Patricia. *Fat Chance Thanksgiving*. Illus. by Stacey Schuett. Albert Whitman, 2001. 0-8075-2288-0. Unp. Gr. K–3

After a fire destroys their apartment, Carla treasures the one thing she has left: a book about Thanksgiving, which inspires her to think of herself as a Pilgrim, as she and her mother move into a tiny new place. With her new friend Julio, she organizes a communal Thanksgiving dinner in the lobby for the residents of her new building, instructing everyone to bring a dish.

GERM: Read aloud a book on the first Thanksgiving. Compare and contrast those facts with Carla's actions. How does she make the impossible happen? Meet the woman who helped make Thanksgiving a national holiday in Laurie Halse Anderson's *Thank You, Sarah: The Woman Who Saved Thanksgiving*. In Eve Bunting's Caldecott Award-winning *Smoky Night*, a boy helps bring his neighbors closer together on the night of the Los Angeles riots. Rosa is another child who copes with a house fire and perseveres in *A Chair for My Mother* by Vera B. Williams.

RELATED TITLES: Accorsi, William. *Friendship's First Thanksgiving*. Holiday House, 1992. / Anderson, Laurie Halse. *Thank You, Sarah: The Woman Who Saved Thanksgiving*. Simon & Schuster, 2002. / Bunting, Eve. *Smoky Night*. Harcourt, 1994. / Cohen, Barbara. *Molly's Pilgrim*. Lothrop, 1998. / Dooley, Norah. *Everybody Cooks Rice*. Carolrhoda, 1991. / George, Jean Craighead. *The First Thanksgiving*. Philomel, 1993. / Greene, Rhonda Gowler. *The Very First Thanksgiving Day*. Atheneum, 2002. / Kay, Verla. *Tattered Sails*. Putnam, 2001. / Pilkey, Dav. *'Twas the Night Before Thanksgiving*. Scholastic, 1990. / Prelutsky, Jack. *It's Thanksgiving*. Greenwillow, 1981. / Shelby, Anne. *Potluck*. Orchard, 1991. / Waters, Kate. *Samuel Eaton's Day: A Day in the Life of a Pilgrim Boy*. Scholastic, 1993. / Waters, Kate. *Sarah Morton's Day: A Day in the Life of a Pilgrim Girl*. Scholastic, 1989. / Williams, Vera B. *A Chair for My Mother*. Greenwillow, 1982.

SUBJECTS: APARTMENT HOUSES. FAMILY LIFE. MULTICULTURAL BOOKS. NEIGHBORS. NEW YORK CITY. THANKSGIVING.

467   LaMarche, Jim. *The Raft*. Illus. by the author. HarperCollins, 2000. 0-688-13977-9. Unp. Gr. K–2

Reluctantly spending the summer at his grandmother's riverside house, Nicky discovers a raft floating by, on which he then spends every free minute, observing and drawing the animals he sees. Children in a great hurry, with too many lessons and planned sports, will revel in Nicky's discoveries about wildlife, the woods, his talent as an artist, and his burgeoning closeness to his artist grandmother.

GERM: A quiet, unhurried, and knowing story like this, with its exquisite animal- and nature-rich watercolors, brings out the river rat and the artist in us all. We need to look closely at life if we're going to write about and draw it. Ask your artists to observe a wild animal carefully and sketch it as realistically as they can. Make a bulletin board "raft" and post people's drawings. Discussion point: Have you discovered your true talents yet?

RELATED TITLES: Best, Cari. *Three Cheers for Catherine the Great.* DK Ink, 1999. / Blake, Robert J. *The Perfect Spot.* Philomel, 1992. / dePaola, Tomie. *The Art Lesson.* Putnam, 1989. / dePaola, Tomie. *Tom.* Putnam, 1993. / Dorros, Arthur. *Abuela.* Dutton, 1991. / Erdrich, Louise. *Grandmother's Pigeon.* Hyperion, 1996. / George, Lindsay Barrett. *Around the Pond: Who's Been Here?* Greenwillow, 1996. / Levine, Evan. *Not the Piano, Mrs. Medley.* Orchard, 1991. / Lewin, Ted. *The Storytellers.* Lothrop, 1998. / McClintock, Barbara. *The Fantastic Drawings of Danielle.* Houghton Mifflin, 1996. / Mills, Claudia. *Ziggy's Blue-Ribbon Day.* Farrar, 2005. / Reynolds, Peter H. *The Dot.* Candlewick, 2003. / Reynolds, Peter H. *Ish.* Candlewick, 2004. / Schwartz, Amy. *Begin at the Beginning: A Little Artist Learns About Life.* HarperCollins, 2005. / Wallner, Alexandra. *Grandma Moses.* Holiday House, 2004.

SUBJECTS: ANIMALS. ARTISTS. CREATIVITY. DRAWING. GRANDMOTHERS. PICTURE BOOKS FOR ALL AGES. RAFTS. RIVERS. SUMMER.

468   **Lane, Lindsey.** *Snuggle Mountain.* **Illus. by Melissa Iwai. Clarion, 2003. 0-618-04328-4. Unp. Gr. PreK–1**

Today young Emma is going to climb Snuggle Mountain all by herself and wake the two-headed Giant who is caught in the Sleeping Spell, so she can get some pancakes for breakfast. As she ascends the deep purple, blue, and green hills, past a moving rock, children will be delighted to recognize her quest: she's climbing up the covers to wake her very sleepy parents.

GERM: You may want to read the first half of the book aloud so children can visualize it in their mind's eye, and then see if their mental pictures let them in on what is really happening in the story. For sure, you should read this more than once, as the descriptive language is gloriously evocative and clever. Ask the children to describe how they get their parents to wake up.

RELATED TITLES: Chodos-Irvine, Margaret. *Ella Sarah Gets Dressed.* Harcourt, 2003. / Cook, Sally. *Good Night Pillow Fight.* HarperCollins, 2004. / Gay, Marie Louise. *Good Morning Sam.* Groundwood, 2003. / Lillegard, Dee. *Wake Up House! Rooms Full of Poems.* Knopf, 2000.

SUBJECTS: BEDS. BREAKFAST. FAMILY LIFE. IMAGINATION. MORNING. PARENT AND CHILD.

469   **LaRochelle, David.** *The Best Pet of All.* **Illus. by Hanako Wakiyama. Dutton, 2004. 0-525-47129-4. Unp. Gr. PreK–1**

Though his mother tells him he can't have a dog, she says if he finds a dragon, he could keep it for a pet. The towheaded narrator finds a large one, wearing dark glasses and a hat, at the drugstore and talks the dragon into coming home with him.

GERM: Stop at that point in the story and ask listeners to predict what they think the dragon will do when he gets to the boy's home. Will he be a good pet or not? (Of course, the dragon is dreadful, making messes and dancing to loud music all night long.) Then ask the children to figure out how the boy can get the dragon to leave.

RELATED TITLES: Becker, Bonny. *The Christmas Crocodile.* Simon & Schuster, 1998. / Child, Lauren. *That Pesky Rat.* Candlewick, 2002. / Graham, Bob. *"Let's Get a Pup!" Said Kate.* Candlewick, 2001. / Grambling, Lois G. *Can I Have a Stegosaurus, Mom? Can I? Please!?* BridgeWater, 1995. / Johnson, Doug. *Never Ride Your Elephant to School.* Henry Holt, 1995. / Kellogg, Steven. *The Mysterious Tadpole.* Dial, 1977. / Kimmel, Elizabeth Cody. *My Penguin, Osbert.* Candlewick, 2004. / Reiser, Lynn. *Any Kind of Dog.* Greenwillow, 1992. / Wolf, Jake. *Daddy, Could I Have an Elephant?* Greenwillow, 1996.

SUBJECTS: DOGS. DRAGONS. HUMOROUS FICTION. MOTHERS AND SONS. PETS.

470   **Lasky, Kathryn.** *Before I Was Your Mother.* **Illus. by LeUyen Pham. Harcourt, 2003. 0-15-201464-0. Unp. Gr. PreK–2**

A mom tells her daughter what she was like as a child, before she grew up to be Katie's mother.

GERM: Have your children go home and ask their parents what they were like as children and look for photographs of them before they were parents. In addition, children can write their own narratives describing what they like to do now, and then save them as time capsules to share with their children someday. Have the children appreciate their moms and dads with Harriet Ziefert's *31 Uses for a Mom* and *33 Uses for a Dad.* One mother reminisces about her childhood in Charlotte Pomerantz's *The Chalk Doll;* another recalls the days anticipating the birth of her daughter in Marisabina Russo's *Waiting for Hannah.*

RELATED TITLES: Browne, Anthony. *My Dad*. Farrar, 2001. / Browne, Anthony. *My Mom*. Farrar, 2005. / Maloney, Peter, and Felicia Zekauskas. *His Mother's Nose*. Dial, 2001. / Pomerantz, Charlotte. *The Chalk Doll*. HarperCollins, 1989. / Pulver, Robin. *Nobody's Mother Is in Second Grade*. Dial, 1992. / Russo, Marisabina. *Trade-In Mother*. Greenwillow, 1993. / Russo, Marisabina. *Waiting for Hannah*. Greenwillow, 1989. / Shannon, George. *This Is the Bird*. Houghton Mifflin, 1997. / Thomas, Eliza. *The Red Blanket*. Scholastic, 2004. / Wells, Rosemary. *Hazel's Amazing Mother*. Dial, 1985. / Ziefert, Harriet. *31 Uses for a Mom*. Putnam, 2003. / Ziefert, Harriet. *33 Uses for a Dad*. Blue Apple, 2004.

SUBJECTS: FAMILY STORIES. MOTHERS AND DAUGHTERS. PERSONAL NARRATIVES.

471   Lasky, Kathryn. *Lunch Bunnies*. **Illus. by Marylin Hafner. Little, Brown, 1996. 0-316-51525-6. Unp. Gr. PreK–1**

Young rabbit Clyde faces his first day of school with trepidation, certain he'll never be able to manage the lunchroom routine. But, in spite of his big brother Jefferson's dire predictions, Clyde learns to face his fears. He even helps save a new friend, Rosemary, from embarrassment when she slips on spilled juice in the lunchroom.

GERM: Have children work on desired and imaginative menus for a nutrition unit. Ask for a class tour of the school lunchroom to see what goes on behind the scenes.

RELATED TITLES: Alexander, Martha. *Move Over, Twerp*. Dial, 1989. / Bottner, Barbara, and Gerald Kruglik. *Wallace's Lists*. HarperCollins, 2004. / Cooney, Nancy Evans. *Chatterbox Jamie*. Putnam, 1993. / Dannenberg, Julie. *First Day Jitters*. Charlesbridge, 2000. / Henkes, Kevin. *Chrysanthemum*. Greenwillow, 1991. / Henkes, Kevin. *Wemberly Worried*. Greenwillow, 2000. / Hest, Amy. *Off to School, Baby Duck*. Candlewick, 1999. / Lasky, Kathryn. *Science Fair Bunnies*. Little, Brown, 2000. / Lasky, Kathryn. *Show and Tell Bunnies*. Little, Brown, 1998. / Lasky, Kathryn. *Tumble Bunnies*. Little, Brown, 2005. / McGhee, Alison. *Countdown to Kindergarten*. Harcourt, 2002. / Russo, Marisabina. *I Don't Want to Go Back to School*. Greenwillow, 1994. / Schwartz, Amy. *Annabelle Swift, Kindergartner*. Orchard, 1988. / Slate, Joseph. *Miss Bindergarten Gets Ready for Kindergarten*. Dutton, 1996. / Wells, Rosemary. *Timothy Goes to School*. Dial, 1981.

SUBJECTS: BROTHERS. FEAR. FRIENDSHIP. RABBITS. SCHOOLS.

472   Lasky, Kathryn. *Marven of the North Woods*. **Illus. by Kevin Hawkes. Harcourt, 1997. 0-15-200104-2. Unp. Gr. 1–5**

In 1918, as the terrible influenza epidemic reached Duluth, the Russian Jewish immigrant parents of 11-year-old Marven sent him to a logging camp in the great north woods to keep him safe. There, among the gargantuan French Canadian loggers, he was given two jobs; as a bookkeeper, he was in charge of keeping track of the payroll, and he was also responsible for making sure that the "en retards," or late sleepers, were up. At the end of her lively and entertaining retelling, accompanied by boldly colored acrylic paintings, Lasky reveals that this story is a true one, based on the adventures of her own father, now more than 90, who still has a good head for figures.

GERM: After interviewing grandparents or parents and asking them to relate remarkable experiences they had when they were young, students can write up these biographical anecdotes as stories, accompanied by drawings or, if possible, photographs.

RELATED TITLES: Bartone, Elisa. *Peppe the Lamplighter*. Lothrop, 1993. / Brisson, Pat. *The Summer My Father Was Ten*. Boyds Mills, 1998. / Friedman, Ina R. *How My Parents Learned to Eat*. Houghton Mifflin, 1984. / Houston, Gloria. *My Great Aunt Arizona*. HarperCollins, 1992. / Howard, Elizabeth Fitzgerald. *Mac and Marie and the Train Toss Surprise*. Four Winds, 1993. / Kennedy, Frances. *The Pickle Patch Bathtub*. Tricycle, 2004. / Lied, Kate. *Potato: A Tale from the Great Depression*. National Geographic, 1997. / McDonald, Megan. *The Great Pumpkin Switch*. Orchard, 1992. / McLerran, Alice. *Roxaboxen*. Lothrop, 1991. / Paulsen, Gary. *The Cookcamp*. Orchard, 1991. / Polacco, Patricia. *My Ol' Man*. Philomel, 1995. / Schwartz, Harriet Berg. *When Artie Was Little*. Knopf, 1996. / Stewig, John Warren. *Making Plum Jam*. Hyperion, 2002. / Tunnell, Michael O. *Mailing May*. Greenwillow, 1997.

SUBJECTS: FAMILY STORIES. HISTORICAL FICTION. INFLUENZA. JEWS. LOGGERS. LUMBER CAMPS. MULTICULTURAL BOOKS. PICTURE BOOKS FOR ALL AGES. SICK.

473   Lasky, Kathryn. *Science Fair Bunnies*. **Illus. by Marylin Hafner. Candlewick, 2000. 0-7636-0729-0. Unp. Gr. K–2**

Clyde's bean plants have just keeled over and his pal Rosemary's are dead too. What can the two rabbits enter in the Science Fair next week? Clyde's loose tooth, hanging by a thread, gives him the perfect solution: what would happen to a tooth if it was steeped in tea or Jell-O or grape juice?

GERM: Photocopy the page with Clyde and Rosemary's project poster—with their list that includes object, procedure, materials, data, and conclusions—as a format to use for class science experiments or projects. Learn a bit more about living things with the companion book, *Show and Tell Bunnies*.

RELATED TITLES: Birdseye, Tom. *Airmail to the Moon*. Holiday House, 1988. / Chandra, Deborah, and Madeline Comora. *George Washington's Teeth*. Farrar, 2003. / Clement, Rod. *Grandpa's Teeth*. HarperCollins, 1998. / Davis, Katie. *Mabel the Tooth Fairy and How She Got Her Job*. Harcourt, 2003. / Keller, Laurie. *Open Wide: Tooth School Inside*. Henry Holt, 2000. / Lasky, Kathryn. *Lunch Bunnies*. Little, Brown, 1996. / Lasky, Kathryn. *Show and Tell Bunnies*. Little, Brown, 1998. / Lasky, Kathryn. *Tumble Bunnies*. Little, Brown, 2005. / McGhee, Alison. *Mrs. Watson Wants Your Teeth*. Harcourt, 2004. / Palatini, Margie. *Sweet Tooth*. Simon & Schuster, 2004. / Simms, Laura. *Rotten Teeth*. Houghton Mifflin, 1998. / Steig, William. *Doctor DeSoto*. Farrar, 1982.

SUBJECTS: FRIENDSHIP. RABBITS. SCHOOLS. SCIENCE—EXPERIMENTS. TEETH. TOOTH FAIRY.

474   **Lasky, Kathryn.** *She's Wearing a Dead Bird on Her Head!* **Illus. by David Catrow. Hyperion, 1995. 0-7868-2052-7. Unp. Gr. 2–5**

In this fictionalized but fact-based account of how dedication to an ideal can lead to change, we meet two proper Boston ladies, Harriet Hemenway and her cousin Mina Hall. Their outrage over the scandalous slaughter of countless exotic birds for the purpose of decorating ladies' hats led to their founding of the first Audubon Society in 1896 and a series of laws that were passed by Congress to protect threatened birds.

GERM: This wry and pointed picture book, with riotous, detailed watercolors, will start an open-ended debate on the ethics of using animal feathers, fur, or even meat to satisfy our human whims, fashions, or customs. See what would happen if the birds were gone in Daniel D. San Souci's cautionary tale, *The Birds of Killingworth*, based on a poem by Henry Wadsworth Longfellow.

RELATED TITLES: Armstrong, Jennifer. *Audubon: Painter of Birds in the Wild Frontier*. Abrams, 2003. / Blumberg, Rhoda. *Bloomers*. Atheneum, 1993. / Christensen, Bonnie. *The Daring Nellie Bly: America's Star Reporter*. Knopf, 2003. / Corey, Shana. *You Forgot Your Skirt, Amelia Bloomer!* Scholastic, 2000. / Davies, Jacqueline. *The Boy Who Drew Birds: A Story of John James Audubon*. Houghton Mifflin, 2003. / Facklam, Margery. *And Then There Was One: The Mysteries of Extinction*. Sierra Club/Little, Brown, 1990. / Hoose, Phillip M. *The Race to Save the Lord God Bird*. Farrar, 2004. / McCully, Emily Arnold. *The Ballot Box Battle*. Knopf, 1996. / San Souci, Daniel D. *The Birds of Killingworth*. Dial, 2002. / White, Linda Arms. *I Could Do That: Esther Morris Gets Women the Vote*. Farrar, 2005. / Wooldridge, Connie Nordhielm. *When Esther Morris Headed West: Women, Wyoming, and the Right to Vote*. Holiday House, 2001.

SUBJECTS: AUDUBON SOCIETY. BIRDS. BOSTON (MASS.). ENVIRONMENTAL PROTECTION. HISTORICAL FICTION. MASSACHUSETTS—HISTORY. WOMEN.

475   **Lasky, Kathryn.** *Show and Tell Bunnies*. **Illus. by Marylin Hafner. Candlewick, 1998. 0-7636-0396-1. Unp. Gr. PreK–1**

Two days before Show and Tell, rabbit Clyde can't come up with anything special enough to bring to school, though he searches everywhere. Looking in the basement for his grandfather's thermometer collection, he comes across just the right object. It's round, gray, and furry and feels soft and fragile. When his teacher, Mrs. McFuzz, sees it, she doesn't know what it is either. Returning to the room after lunch, the class is astonished to discover that the furry ball has hatched hundreds of tiny spiderlings.

GERM: A perfect combination of well-told story and adorable watercolor and ink illustrations, this one's a winner for the first week of school or for talking about the miracle of life. Anticipating the school lunchroom is a worry to Clyde on his first day in the companion book, *Lunch Bunnies*. Next, Clyde and his pal, Rosemary, triumph with their tooth experiments in *Science Fair Bunnies*.

RELATED TITLES: Bunting, Eve. *Trouble on the T-Ball Team*. Clarion, 1995. / Greene, Stephanie. *Show and Tell*. Clarion, 1998. / Henkes, Kevin. *Chrysanthemum*. Greenwillow, 1991. / Klein, Abby. *The King of Show-and-Tell*. Scholastic/Blue Sky, 2004. / Lasky, Kathryn. *Lunch Bunnies*. Little, Brown, 1996. / Lasky, Kathryn. *Science Fair Bunnies*. Candlewick, 2000. / Lasky, Kathryn. *Tumble Bunnies*. Little, Brown, 2005. / Lowry, Lois. *Zooman Sam*. Houghton Mifflin, 1999. / Schwartz, Amy. *Annabelle Swift, Kindergartner*. Orchard, 1988. / Simms, Laura. *Rotten Teeth*. Houghton Mifflin, 1998. / Slate, Joseph. *Miss Bindergarten Gets Ready for Kindergarten*. Dutton, 1996. / Wells, Rosemary. *Timothy Goes to School*. Dial, 1981.

SUBJECTS: BROTHERS. RABBITS. SCHOOLS. SHOW-AND-TELL PRESENTATIONS. SIBLING RIVALRY. SPIDERS. TEACHERS.

476 **Lass, Bonnie, and Philemon Sturges.** *Who Took the Cookies from the Cookie Jar?* **Illus. by Ashley Wolff. Little, Brown, 2000. 0-316-82016-4. Unp. Gr. PreK–K**

Skunk discovers that his once-full cookie jar is empty and heads out on the trail of the culprit, blaming Mouse, Raven, Squirrel, and other animals he encounters as he follows the trail of crumbs through the southwestern desert landscape.

GERM: Start by playing the classic name game, using the instructions and the song listed in the front. As you read the story and follow the trail of cookie crumbs, ask everyone to predict what creature Skunk will accuse next, based on the visual clues in the vivid watercolors. All will join in on the chantable refrain and guess the rhyming words at the end of each animal's alibi. Serve cookies as a final treat.

RELATED TITLES: Carle, Eric. *Pancakes, Pancakes.* Scholastic, 1990. / Hoberman, Mary Ann. *Miss Mary Mack: A Hand-Clapping Rhyme.* Little, Brown, 1998. / Hooper, Meredith. *Honey Cookies.* Frances Lincoln, 2005. / Priceman, Marjorie. *How to Make an Apple Pie and See the World.* Knopf, 1994. / Shepard, Aaron. *The Baker's Dozen: A Saint Nicholas Tale.* Atheneum, 1995. / Sturges, Philemon. *She'll Be Comin' 'Round the Mountain.* Little, Brown, 2004. / Wellington, Monica. *Mr. Cookie Baker.* Dutton, 1992. / Wells, Rosemary. *Bunny Cakes.* Dial, 1997. / Westcott, Nadine Bernard. *I Know an Old Lady Who Swallowed a Fly.* Little, Brown, 1980. / Westcott, Nadine Bernard. *Peanut Butter and Jelly: A Play Rhyme.* Dutton, 1987.

SUBJECTS: ANIMALS. CHANTABLE REFRAIN. COOKIES. DESERTS. FOOD. SKUNKS. SOUTHWEST. STORIES IN RHYME.

477 **Lawrence, John.** *This Little Chick.* **Illus. by the author. Candlewick, 2002. 0-7636-1716-4. Unp. Gr. PreK–K**

In this joyous rhyming romp filled with animal noises, a young chick plays with the pigs, swims with the ducks, lazes with the cows, jumps with the frogs, and skips with the lambs.

GERM: The endpapers mention this as a traditional rhyme, which I have to admit I had never heard before. If you don't know it either, it fits the tune of "Five Little Ducks," so it's lots of fun to sing. This is such a capital toddler book, with huge cheerful illustrations made from vinyl engravings, watercolor washes, and printed wood textures; lots of animal noises and acting out possibilities; and a very amiable and noisy ending. Your crew can come up with additional verses about other domestic animals.

RELATED TITLES: Baker, Keith. *Big Fat Hen.* Harcourt, 1994. / Fleming, Denise. *Barnyard Banter.* Henry Holt, 1994. / Gerstein, Mordicai. *Follow Me!* Morrow, 1983. / Hindley, Judy. *Do Like a Duck Does!* Candlewick, 2002. / Hutchins, Pat. *Rosie's Walk.* Bradbury, 1987. / Raffi. *Five Little Ducks.* Crown, 1988. / Rostoker-Gruber, Karen. *Rooster Can't Cock-a-Doodle-Doo.* Dial, 2004. / Shannon, George. *Tippy-Toe Chick, Go!* Greenwillow, 2003. / Simmons, Jane. *Quack, Daisy, Quack!* Little, Brown, 2002. / Waddell, Martin. *Webster J. Duck.* Candlewick, 2001. / Whippo, Walt, and Bernard Zaritzky. *Little White Duck.* Little, Brown, 2000. / Williams, Sue. *I Went Walking.* Gulliver/Harcourt, 1990.

SUBJECTS: ANIMAL SOUNDS. BIRDS. CHANTABLE REFRAIN. CHICKENS. DOMESTIC ANIMALS. STORIES IN RHYME.

478 **Lee, Chinlun.** *Good Dog, Paw!* **Illus. by the author. Candlewick, 2004. 0-7636-2178-1. Unp. Gr. PreK–2**

Soulful black and white dog Paw lays out his day, starting with his ten-point checkup with April, his veterinarian owner. Next they motorscooter to the clinic, where April ministers to sick animals and Paw sings soothing songs to comfort them.

GERM: Paw says the best thing April has taught him is this: "The secret of health is love." Is this true? Ask your pet lovers for personal experiences that confirm this theory, told from their pets' points of view. Look on the back flap for a photo and message from the author's own dog, Paw.

RELATED TITLES: Edwards, Pamela Duncan. *Muldoon.* Hyperion, 2002. / George, Kristine O'Connell. *Little Dog Poems.* Clarion, 1999. / Graham, Bob. *"Let's Get a Pup!" Said Kate.* Candlewick, 2001. / Harvey, Amanda. *Dog Eared.* Doubleday, 2002. / Meddaugh, Susan. *Martha Speaks.* Houghton Mifflin, 1992. / Perkins, Lynne Rae. *The Broken Cat.* Greenwillow, 2002. / Provensen, Alice. *A Day in the Life of Murphy.* Simon & Schuster, 2003. / Simon, Seymour. *Dogs.* HarperCollins, 2003.

SUBJECTS: ANIMALS. DOGS. LOVE. PERSONAL NARRATIVES. POINT OF VIEW. VETERINARIANS.

479 **Lee, Milly.** *Nim and the War Effort.* **Illus. by Yangsook Choi. Farrar, 1997. 0-374-35523-1. Unp. Gr. 2–5**

Determined to collect the most newspapers for her class paper drive during World War II, Nim competes for first place with Garland, a classmate who belittles her for being Chinese and not American, though she is proud of being both. Nim is torn between going to Chinese school, which her grandfather wants her to do, and winning the class contest.

GERM: Along with Ken Mochizuki's *Baseball Saved Us*, this is a groundbreaking picture book about what it means to be an American. There's much potential for discussion here: Did you ever do anything that your parents misunderstood but that you felt was important? Should Nim have disobeyed her grandfather? Why did Garland say Nim was not American? If your parents came from another country, are you American? Bruce Edward Hall's *Henry and the Kite Dragon* is another picture book about Chinese Americans that will get listeners talking about understanding differences and getting along.

RELATED TITLES: Bartone, Elisa. *American Too*. Lothrop, 1996. / Borden, Louise. *The Little Ships: The Heroic Rescue at Dunkirk in World War II*. McElderry, 1997. / Hall, Bruce Edward. *Henry and the Kite Dragon*. Philomel, 2004. / Levine, Ellen. *I Hate English!* Scholastic, 1989. / Maestro, Betsy. *Coming to America: The Story of Immigration*. Scholastic, 1996. / Mochizuki, Ken. *Baseball Saved Us*. Lee & Low, 1993. / Mochizuki, Ken. *Heroes*. Lee & Low, 1995. / Namioka, Lensey. *Yang the Youngest and His Terrible Ear*. Little, Brown, 1992. / Pomeranc, Marion Hess. *The American Wei*. Albert Whitman, 1998. / Stevenson, James. *Don't You Know There's a War On?* Greenwillow, 1992. / Wong, Janet. *Good Luck Gold and Other Poems*. McElderry, 1994. / Yee, Paul. *Roses Sing on New Snow*. Macmillan, 1992. / Yin. *Coolies*. Philomel, 2001.

SUBJECTS: ASIAN AMERICANS. CHINESE AMERICANS. COMPETITION. GRANDFATHERS. HISTORICAL FICTION. MULTICULTURAL BOOKS. NEWSPAPERS. PICTURE BOOKS FOR OLDER READERS. U.S.—HISTORY—20TH CENTURY—FICTION. WORLD WAR, 1939–1945—FICTION.

480   L'Engle, Madeleine. *The Other Dog*. Illus. by Christine Davenier. SeaStar, 2001. 1-58717-040-X. Unp. Gr. PreK–4

The talented poodle Touché—a dog of beauty, wit, and charm—describes her bewilderment when, without warning, her master and mistress bring another dog into their home: the tailless, practically hairless, inferior canine Jo, whom astute readers will recognize as the new baby.

GERM: Conceal the cover and don't show the illustrations until about halfway through the book so children get a picture of the Other Dog in their mind's eye. When you show the illustrations of the new baby, they will laugh. Pet owners can write a first-person account of an event that happened at their own house, with the added twist of narration by the family pet (who might have seen the entire episode from a different perspective). Just as Madeleine L'Engle explains in her Author's Note that her book was based on a true story, have your writers include their own Author's Note, as well as a tribute to a departed pet or a listing of further information on a surviving one.

RELATED TITLES: Child, Lauren. *That Pesky Rat*. Candlewick, 2002. / Feiffer, Jules. *Bark, George!* HarperCollins, 1999. / Geras, Adèle. *The Cats of Cuckoo Square: Two Stories*. Delacorte, 2001. / Hall, Donald. *I Am the Dog, I Am the Cat*. Dial, 1994. / Jenkins, Emily. *That New Animal*. Farrar, 2005. / Kellogg, Steven. *A Penguin Pup for Pinkerton*. Dial, 2001. / Laden, Nina. *The Night I Followed the Dog*. Chronicle, 1994. / MacLachlan, Patricia, and Emily MacLachlan. *Bittle*. HarperCollins, 2004. / Meddaugh, Susan. *Martha Speaks*. Houghton Mifflin, 1992. / Miller, Sara Swan. *Three Stories You Can Read to Your Dog*. Houghton Mifflin, 1995. / Rathmann, Peggy. *Officer Buckle and Gloria*. Putnam, 1995. / Schwartz, Amy. *A Teeny Tiny Baby*. Orchard, 1994. / Simont, Marc. *The Stray Dog*. HarperCollins, 2001. / Wells, Rosemary. *McDuff and the Baby*. Hyperion, 1997. / Willis, Jeanne. *Earthlets: As Explained by Professor Xargle*. Dutton, 1988. / Ziefert, Harriet. *Pushkin Meets the Bundle*. Atheneum, 1998.

SUBJECTS: BABIES. DOGS. HUMOROUS FICTION. JEALOUSY. PERSONAL NARRATIVES. PICTURE BOOKS FOR ALL AGES. POINT OF VIEW.

481   Lester, Helen. *Hooway for Wodney Wat*. Illus. by Lynn Munsinger. Houghton Mifflin, 1999. 0-395-92392-1. Unp. Gr. PreK–2

Although he is teased by all the other rodents in school because he can't pronounce his r's, hapless Rodney Rat is nevertheless the one who rids the class of the awful new bully, Camilla Capybara.

GERM: Close the book at the climax of the story and have kids brainstorm what they think Wodney will do to make Camilla go away. This is a title that empowers all those speech therapy kids who are tired of being ridiculed for their pronunciation.

RELATED TITLES: Bottner, Barbara. *Bootsie Barker Bites*. Putnam, 1992. / Browne, Anthony. *Willy the Wimp*. Knopf, 1985. / Child, Lauren. *That Pesky Rat*. Candlewick, 2002. / Cole, Joanna. *Don't Call Me Names*. Random House, 1990. / Kasza, Keiko. *The Rat and the Tiger*. Putnam, 1993. / Lester, Helen. *Hurty Feelings*. Houghton

Mifflin, 2004. / Lester, Helen. *Me First*. Houghton Mifflin, 1992. / Lester, Helen. *Something Might Happen*. Houghton Mifflin, 2003. / Meddaugh, Susan. *Martha Walks the Dog*. Houghton Mifflin, 1998. / Naylor, Phyllis Reynolds. *King of the Playground*. Atheneum, 1991. / Wilhelm, Hans. *Tyrone the Horrible*. Scholastic, 1988.

SUBJECTS: BULLIES. HUMOROUS FICTION. OUTCASTS. PICTURE BOOKS FOR ALL AGES. RATS. RODENTS. SCHOOLS. SPEECH DISORDERS.

482   Lester, Helen. *Listen, Buddy*. Illus. by Lynn Munsinger. Houghton Mifflin, 1995. 0-395-72361-2. 32pp. Gr. PreK–1

Even with his big, beautiful rabbit ears, Buddy doesn't listen to anything his parents tell him. Taking the wrong right turn to the vegetable stand, Buddy meets up with the Scruffy Varmint, a bear who plans to make bunny rabbit soup out of him.

GERM: Compare how Buddy gets away safely from the bear with the experiences of other quick-thinking animal characters such as the mouse in *The Gruffalo* by Julia Donaldson; the toad in *Grandpa Toad's Secrets* by Keiko Kasza; the pig in *My Lucky Day*, also by Kasza; and the pig in *Hog-Eye* by Susan Meddaugh.

RELATED TITLES: Blundell, Tony. *Beware of Boys*. Greenwillow, 1992. / Donaldson, Julia. *The Gruffalo*. Dial, 1999. / Kasza, Keiko. *Grandpa Toad's Secrets*. Putnam, 1995. / Kasza, Keiko. *My Lucky Day*. Putnam, 2003. / Lester, Helen. *Hooway for Wodney Wat*. Houghton Mifflin, 1999. / Lester, Helen. *Hurty Feelings*. Houghton Mifflin, 2004. / Lester, Helen. *Score One for the Sloths*. Houghton Mifflin, 2001. / Lester, Helen. *Something Might Happen*. Houghton Mifflin, 2003. / Meddaugh, Susan. *Hog-Eye*. Houghton Mifflin, 1995. / Salley, Coleen. *Epossumondas*. Harcourt, 2002.

SUBJECTS: BEARS. BEHAVIOR. HUMOROUS FICTION. LISTENING. RABBITS.

483   Lester, Helen. *Princess Penelope's Parrot*. Illus. by Lynn Munsinger. Houghton Mifflin, 1996. 0-395-78320-8. 32pp. Gr. PreK–1

"GIMME, GIMME, GIMME," says the greedy little princess on her birthday, but the new parrot she gets is no fun. No matter how she threatens him, he won't talk, until the day rich Prince Percival comes to call.

GERM: Talk about what it means to get your comeuppance. How does Princess Penelope get hers? Meet a girl who thinks she must be a princess in Cynthia DeFelice's *The Real, True Dulcie Campbell*.

RELATED TITLES: DeFelice, Cynthia. *The Real, True Dulcie Campbell*. Farrar, 2002. / Grossman, Bill. *Timothy Tunny Swallowed a Bunny*. HarperCollins, 2001. / Johnson, Paul Brett. *Little Bunny Foo Foo*. Scholastic, 2004. / Lester, Helen. *Hooway for Wodney Wat*. Houghton Mifflin, 1999. / Lester, Helen. *Me First*. Houghton Mifflin, 1992. / Lester, Helen. *Something Might Happen*. Houghton Mifflin, 2003. / Meddaugh, Susan. *Martha Walks the Dog*. Houghton Mifflin, 1998. / Thomson, Pat. *The Squeaky, Creaky Bed*. Doubleday, 2003.

SUBJECTS: BEHAVIOR. BULLIES. HUMOROUS FICTION. PARROTS. PRINCES AND PRINCESSES.

484   Lester, Helen. *Score One for the Sloths*. Illus. by Lynn Munsinger. Houghton Mifflin, 2001. 0-618-10857-2. Unp. Gr. PreK–2

In class at Sleepy Valley Sloth School, the sloths yawn, snore, roll over, and take three-hour lunches at the slotheteria, but mostly they sleep. Then Sparky comes to school, ". . . full of life and energy and vim and vigor and vitality." By mid-morning, she's driving everyone crazy, wanting to read and play music, do math, and recite poetry. Into the slothful classroom steps a wild boar, an official representative of S.O.S., the Society for Organizing Sameness, ready to close down the worst school in the Mammal District. Sparky is the only one with energy enough to save the day, which she does, of course.

GERM: Assign each group of four children to a school in the Mammal District, such as whales, mice, lions, and monkeys. Have each group design a typical school day and decide what subjects their animals should study. Each group can then put on an action-packed five-minute presentation showcasing, in character, their animal curriculum. Read Melissa Stewart's *Sloths* to compare facts and fiction.

RELATED TITLES: Carle, Eric. *"Slowly, Slowly, Slowly," Said the Sloth*. Philomel, 2002. / Kelley, True. *Blabber Mouse*. Dutton, 1991. / Lester, Helen. *Author: A True Story*. Houghton Mifflin, 1997. / Lester, Helen. *Hooway for Wodney Wat*. Houghton Mifflin, 1999. / Lester, Helen. *Hurty Feelings*. Houghton Mifflin, 2004. / Lester, Helen. *Me First*. Houghton Mifflin, 1992. / Lester, Helen. *Something Might Happen*. Houghton Mifflin, 2003. / Silverman, Erica. *Don't Fidget a Feather*. Macmillan, 1994. / Stewart, Melissa. *Sloths*. Carolrhoda, 2005.

SUBJECTS: HUMOROUS FICTION. LAZINESS. SCHOOLS. SLOTHS.

485   **Lester, Helen.** *Something Might Happen.* **Illus. by Lynn Munsinger. Houghton Mifflin, 2003. 0-618-25408-4. Unp. Gr. PreK–1**

Twitchly Fidget is afraid of almost everything, including shampoo (too bubbly), cereal (startlingly crunchy), sneakers (scarily confusing on the wrong feet), and roofs (might cave in). When Aunt Bridget Fidget drops in for a visit, she gives him a fixin' that lets him see his fears are baseless.

GERM: Discussion point: What were you afraid of doing that turned out to be just fine when you finally did it? What fears do you still need to confront? Meet other nervous types who learn to face their anxieties in *The Scaredy Cats* by Barbara Bottner, *There's a Big, Beautiful World Out There!* by Nancy Carlson, *The Worry Warts* by Pamela Duncan Edwards, *Wemberly Worried* by Kevin Henkes, and Helen Lester's own *Hooway for Wodney Wat.*

RELATED TITLES: Bottner, Barbara. *The Scaredy Cats.* Simon & Schuster, 2003. / Carlson, Nancy. *There's a Big, Beautiful World Out There!* Viking, 2002. / Edwards, Pamela Duncan. *The Worrwarts.* HarperCollins, 1999. / Henkes, Kevin. *Wemberly Worried.* Greenwillow, 2000. / Lester, Helen. *Hooway for Wodney Wat.* Houghton Mifflin, 1999. / Lester, Helen. *Hurty Feelings.* Houghton Mifflin, 2004. / Lester, Helen. *Listen, Buddy.* Houghton Mifflin, 1995. / Lester, Helen. *Score One for the Sloths.* Houghton Mifflin, 2001.

SUBJECTS: AUNTS. FEAR. LEMURS. WORRYING.

486   **Lester, Julius.** *Sam and the Tigers: A New Telling of Little Black Sambo.* **Illus. by Jerry Pinkney. Dial, 1996. 0-8037-2029-7. Unp. Gr. PreK–3**

Helen Bannerman's *The Tale of Little Black Sambo* has long been a source of contention and controversy for its racist connotations. Lester has rescued the essence of the story about a boy who outsmarts tigers and filled it with his smart, verbally nimble storyteller's voice, while Pinkney's oversized and dazzling watercolors take us to the land of Sam-sam-sa-mara, where everyone is named Sam. Meeting five tigers on his way to school, Sam appeases each with an item of his new and colorful wardrobe, all of which he gets back when the tigers get caught up in an argument among themselves.

GERM: Act out the scenes with Sam and the menacing tigers and then compare and contrast this version—set in a fantastical, turn-of-the-century America—with Fred Marcellino's retelling, *The Story of Little Babaji*, set in India. For a tiger-infused snack, whip up some butter from whipping cream or cook a batch of pancakes.

RELATED TITLES: Bannerman, Helen. *The Story of Little Babaji.* HarperCollins, 1996. / Dowson, Nick. *Tigress.* Candlewick, 2004. / Faulkner, William J. *Brer Tiger and the Big Wind.* Morrow, 1995. / Hoberman, Mary Ann. *It's Simple, Said Simon.* Knopf, 2001. / Lester, Julius. *The Knee-High Man and Other Tales.* Puffin, 1985. / Lester, Julius. *The Tales of Uncle Remus: The Adventures of Brer Rabbit.* Dial, 1987. / McCleery, William. *Wolf Story.* Linnet, 1988. / Peet, Bill. *The Spooky Tail of Prewitt Peacock.* Houghton, 1973. / Temple, Frances. *Tiger Soup: An Anansi Story from Jamaica.* Orchard, 1994. / Thomson, Sarah L. *Tigers.* HarperCollins, 1994. / Wright, Kit. *Tigerella.* Scholastic, 1994.

SUBJECTS: AFRICAN AMERICANS. CLOTHING AND DRESS. CREATIVE DRAMA. MULTICULTURAL BOOKS. TIGERS.

487   **Lester, Mike.** *A Is for Salad.* **Illus. by the author. Putnam, 2000. 0-399-23388-1. Unp. Gr. PreK–1**

"A is for salad." It is? The picture shows an Alligator eating that salad. Kids will delight in howling, "NO, A isn't for salad. A is for alligator. S is for salad!!!" They'll especially love "T is for Underpants," showing a bashful-looking tiger in his polka-dotted boxers. The endpapers have a miniature alphabet identifying each animal correctly.

GERM: Introduce the book by saying, "This is a strange alphabet book by Mike Lester. For some reason, this guy is VERY confused about the alphabet. He doesn't seem to understand it. Let's see if you do." Afterward, have kids write a new alphabet sentence with a misidentified letter and an animal wearing, eating, or doing something. They can read their sentences aloud and have the others identify the correct letter match. Also look at cause and effect with George Shannon's *Tomorrow's Alphabet: "A is for seed, tomorrow's . . . APPLE."*

RELATED TITLES: Andreae, Giles. *K Is for Kissing a Cool Kangaroo.* Orchard, 2003. / Bayer, Jane. *A My Name Is Alice.* Dial, 1984. / Bourke, Linda. *Eye Spy.* Chronicle, 1991. / Ehlert, Lois. *Eating the Alphabet.* Harcourt, 1989. / Ernst, Lisa Campbell. *The Letters Are Lost.* Viking, 1996. / Fisher, Valerie. *Ellsworth's Extraordinary Electric Ears.* Atheneum, 2003. / Fleming, Denise. *Alphabet Under Construction.* Henry Holt, 2002. / Grover, Max. *The Accidental Zucchini.* Harcourt, 1993. / Lobel, Arnold. *On Market Street.* Greenwillow, 1981. / MacDonald, Ross. *Achoo! Bang! Crash! The Noisy Alphabet.* Roaring Brook, 2003. / MacDonald, Suse. *Alphabatics.* Simon &

Schuster, 1986. / Seeger, Laura Vaccaro. *The Hidden Alphabet*. Roaring Brook, 2003. / Shannon, George. *Tomorrow's Alphabet*. Greenwillow, 1996. / Walton, Rick. *So Many Bunnies: A Bedtime ABC and Counting Book*. Lothrop, 1998. / Wood, Audrey. *Alphabet Mystery*. Scholastic, 2003.

SUBJECTS: ALPHABET BOOKS. ANIMALS.

488   **Leuck, Laura.** *One Witch.* **Illus. by S. D. Schindler. Walker, 2003. 0-8027-8861-0. Unp. Gr. PreK–1**

With ingredients donated by ten groups of her ghoulish pals, a witch cooks up a gruesome, oozing stew and sends her friends invitations to share it with her at her spooky bash.

GERM: A rhyming text and meticulously creepy ink and watercolor illustrations make this counting book just right for Halloween, along with Patricia Hubbard's *Trick or Treat Countdown* and Erica Silverman's *Big Pumpkin*, another Halloween treat illustrated by S. D. Schindler.

RELATED TITLES: Buehner, Caralyn, and Mark Buehner. *A Job for Wittilda*. Dial, 1993. / Bunting, Eve. *Scary, Scary Halloween*. Clarion, 1986. / Cuyler, Margery. *Skeleton Hiccups*. Simon & Schuster, 2002. / Hubbard, Patricia. *Trick or Treat Countdown*. Holiday House, 1999. / Krosoczka, Jarrett J. *Annie Was Warned*. Knopf, 2003. / Meddaugh, Susan. *The Witches' Supermarket*. Houghton Mifflin, 1991. / Palatini, Margie. *Broom Mates*. Hyperion, 2003. / Palatini, Margie. *Piggie Pie*. Clarion, 1995. / Regan, Dian Curtis. *The Thirteen Hours of Halloween*. Albert Whitman, 1993. / Shute, Linda. *Halloween Party*. Lothrop, 1994. / Silverman, Erica. *Big Pumpkin*. Macmillan, 1992. / Sklansky, Amy E. *Skeleton Bones and Goblin Groans: Poems for Halloween*. Henry Holt, 2004. / Stutson, Caroline. *By the Light of the Halloween Moon*. Lothrop, 1993. / Williams, Linda. *The Little Old Lady Who Was Not Afraid of Anything*. Crowell, 1986.

SUBJECTS: COUNTING BOOKS. HALLOWEEN. STORIES IN RHYME. WITCHES.

489   **Levitin, Sonia.** *Nine for California.* **Illus. by Cat Bowman Smith. Orchard, 1996. 0-531-08877-4. Unp. Gr. K–3**

Ma packs up her five children and a huge sack full of everything they will need to take a rollicking, adventure-packed, 21-day stagecoach ride to find Pa, who's been in the gold fields of Californ-y. The three other travelers aren't thrilled at having all those kids on board, but, as daughter Amanda narrates—and the action-filled watercolors attest—they do just fine. The children sing songs, play cat's cradle, name plants and presidents, sleep, meet up with peaceful Pawnee Indians, survive a buffalo stampede, and when they finally get there, reminisce about the trip.

GERM: As you read about each item Ma pulls out of her sack—sugar cubes, string, prunes, corn cakes, licorice, rope, slide whistle—you can pull the same items out of your own sack to admire and share. Listeners will enjoy reciting Amanda's refrain: "I waited and hoped for something to happen. It finally did." Share this with Verla Kay's *Gold Fever*. If you don't recall how to do cat's cradle string figures, Camilla Gryski's *Cat's Cradle, Owl's Eyes: A Book of String Games* will be a godsend.

RELATED TITLES: Cox, David. *Bossyboots*. Crown, 1987. / Freedman, Russell. *Children of the Wild West*. Clarion, 1983. / Gerrard, Roy. *Wagons West!* Farrar, 1996. / Gryski, Camilla. *Cat's Cradle, Owl's Eyes: A Book of String Games*. Morrow, 1983. / Hopkinson, Deborah. *Apples to Oregon*. Atheneum, 2004. / Kay, Verla. *Covered Wagon, Bumpy Trails*. Putnam, 2000. / Kay, Verla. *Gold Fever*. Putnam, 1999. / Patent, Dorothy Hinshaw. *West by Covered Wagon*. Walker, 1995. / Russell, Marion. *Along the Santa Fe Trail*. Albert Whitman, 1993. / Siebert, Diane. *Rhyolite: The True Story of a Ghost Town*. Clarion, 2003. / Van Leeuwen, Jean. *A Fourth of July on the Plains*. Dial, 1997. / Williams, David. *Grandma Essie's Covered Wagon*. Knopf, 1993.

SUBJECTS: FAMILY LIFE. FRONTIER AND PIONEER LIFE. GOLD RUSH. HISTORICAL FICTION. WEST (U.S.)—HISTORY—FICTION.

490   **Lewin, Ted.** *The Storytellers.* **Illus. by the author. Lothrop, 1998. 0-688-15179-5. Unp. Gr. 1–3**

In the ancient, walled city of Fez, Morocco, Abdul and his grandfather set off through the bustling cobblestoned market to get to work telling stories to the crowds. Grandfather begins his telling: "Kan ya ma kan . . . This happened, or maybe it did not." A crowd gathers and he touches their hearts with his stories. "We have the best job in the whole medina," Abdul says. Not only do we bask in the sights and sounds of a foreign place, thanks to Lewin's masterful, evocative watercolors, but we witness the age-old art of storytelling.

GERM: Introduce the 398.2 section of the library—folk and fairy tales—and tell a meaty story or two. In *The Day of Ahmed's Secret* by Florence Parry Heide and Judith Heide Gilliland, we take a walk through Cairo, Egypt, with a young Arab boy who has just learned how to write his own name. In *Ali: Child of the Desert* by Jonathan London, Ali is separated from his father during a

Saharan desert sandstorm in Morocco. *Market* by Ted Lewin is a tour of colorful outdoor markets around the world.

RELATED TITLES: Dengler, Marianna. *The Worry Stone*. Northland, 1996. / Heide, Florence Parry, and Judith Heide Gilliland. *The Day of Ahmed's Secret*. Lothrop, 1990. / Lewin, Ted. *Market!* Lothrop, 1996. / London, Jonathan. *Ali: Child of the Desert*. Lothrop, 1997. / Rumford, James. *Traveling Man: The Journey of Ibn Battuta*. Houghton Mifflin, 2001. / Say, Allen. *Kamishibai Man*. Houghton Mifflin, 2005.

SUBJECTS: ARABS. GRANDFATHERS. MARKETS. MOROCCO. MULTICULTURAL BOOKS. PICTURE BOOKS FOR ALL AGES. STORYTELLING.

491   Lied, Kate. *Potato: A Tale from the Great Depression.* **Illus. by Lisa Campbell Ernst. National Geographic, 1997. 0-7922-3521-5. Unp. Gr. K–3**

Hard times can bring out one's entrepreneurial spirit, as we learn from the author's story about her grandparents, Clarence and Agnes, and their young daughter, her Aunt Dorothy. During the Great Depression, when the bank took away their house and Clarence lost his job, the three headed out to Idaho for a job picking potatoes. At the end of two weeks, the couple had picked enough extra potatoes to fill up their car with sacks of spuds that they traded for groceries, clothes, and even a pig. The author ends her simple, matter-of-fact narrative by saying, "All this could be how I have come to like potatoes."

GERM: A careful reading of the back flap reveals a delightful surprise: The author of the book wrote this family story when she was 8 years old for a writing contest sponsored by her neighborhood bookstore; its winsome watercolors were done by popular children's book author/illustrator Ernst, who was one of the contest's judges. What better motivation could there be to hold your own contest and have children collect their own family stories for inspiration?

RELATED TITLES: Coy, John. *Two Old Potatoes and Me*. Knopf, 2003. / Friedrich, Elizabeth. *Leah's Pony*. Boyds Mills, 1996. / Lasky, Kathryn. *Marven of the Great North Woods*. Harcourt, 1997. / Perkins, Lynne Rae. *The Broken Cat*. Greenwillow, 2002. / Schwartz, Harriet Berg. *When Artie Was Little*. Knopf, 1996. / Shannon, George. *This Is the Bird*. Houghton Mifflin, 1997.

SUBJECTS: DEPRESSIONS—1929—U.S. FAMILY STORIES. MIGRANT LABOR. POTATOES.

492   Lin, Grace. *Fortune Cookie Fortunes.* **Illus. by the author. Knopf, 2004. 0-375-91521-4. Unp. Gr. K–2**

A young Chinese girl reveals the fortunes that she, her sisters, and parents get when they crack open their fortune cookies at a Chinese restaurant, and then she shows how they all come true.

GERM: Hand out fortune cookies for all to munch, so that the children can share their fortunes and discuss if and how they apply to their lives. Next, they can compose new fortunes and place them in a cookie tin so each child can draw one out and share it aloud.

RELATED TITLES: Chinn, Karen. *Sam and the Lucky Money*. Lee & Low, 1995. / Compestine, Ying Chang. *The Story of Chopsticks*. Holiday House, 2001. / Friedman, Ina R. *How My Parents Learned to Eat*. Houghton, 1984. / Hall, Bruce Edward. *Henry and the Kite Dragon*. Philomel, 2004. / Lin, Grace. *Dim Sum for Everyone*. Knopf, 2001. / Mak, Kam. *My Chinatown: One Year in Poems*. HarperCollins, 2002. / Wong, Janet. *Apple Pie Fourth of July*. Harcourt, 2002. / Yee, Paul. *Roses Sing on New Snow*. Macmillan, 1992.

SUBJECTS: ASIAN AMERICANS. CHINESE AMERICANS. COOKIES. FOOD. MULTICULTURAL BOOKS.

493   Lithgow, John. *Micawber.* **Illus. by C. F. Payne. Simon & Schuster, 2002. 0-689-83341-5. Unp. Gr. K–3**

Scampering to the skylights atop the Metropolitan Museum of Art, Central Park squirrel Micawber feasts his eyes and his heart on his favorite paintings, from Rembrandt to Miró. Down below, he sees a woman copying a Monet painting onto her own canvas, and when she leaves the museum, he stows away on the back of her bike. Borrowing her paints and canvases each night, and using his tail for a brush, Micawber becomes an artist. All of this is told in gallant rhyme, with large, full-bleed mixed-media paintings, and even a four-panel foldout of the opening of Micawber's own animal art museum.

GERM: Note the two large self-portraits on the endpapers, modeled after Rembrandt and Rockwell. Try painting your own self-portraits or pair up as painters and models. Think it's absurd for a squirrel to have artistic aspirations? Show Katya Arnold's astounding nonfiction color photoessay, *Elephants Can Paint Too!* What's in the Met? Give your aesthetes a virtual tour of the museum's collection at <www.metmuseum.org> and look at *Inside the Museum: A Children's*

Guide to the Metropolitan Museum of Art by Joy Richardson and *You Can't Take a Balloon into the Metropolitan Museum* by Jacqueline Preiss Weitzman.

RELATED TITLES: Arnold, Katya. *Elephants Can Paint Too!* Atheneum, 2005. / Auch, Mary Jane. *Eggs Mark the Spot*. Holiday House, 1996. / Browne, Anthony. *Willy the Dreamer*. Candlewick, 1998. / Hurd, Thacher. *Art Dog*. HarperCollins, 1996. / Jakobsen, Kathy. *My New York*. Little, Brown, 2003. / Laden, Nina. *When Pigasso Met Mootisse*. Chronicle, 1998. / Melmed, Laura Krauss. *New York, New York! The Big Apple from A to Z*. HarperCollins, 2005. / Palatini, Margie. *Ding Dong Ding Dong*. Hyperion, 1999. / Pilkey, Dav. *When Cats Dream*. Orchard, 1992. / Raczka, Bob. *Art Is . . .* Millbrook, 2003. / Reynolds, Peter. *The Dot*. Candlewick, 2003. / Richardson, Joy. *Inside the Museum: A Children's Guide to the Metropolitan Museum of Art*. Abrams, 1993. / Weitzman, Jacqueline Preiss. *You Can't Take a Balloon into the Metropolitan Museum*. Dial, 1998.

SUBJECTS: ARTISTS. CENTRAL PARK (NEW YORK, N.Y.). METROPOLITAN MUSEUM OF ART (NEW YORK, NY). MUSEUMS. NEW YORK CITY. PARKS. SQUIRRELS. STORIES IN RHYME.

494 Lithgow, John. *The Remarkable Farkle McBride*. Illus. by C. F. Payne. Simon & Schuster, 2000. 0-689-83340-7. Unp. Gr. 1–4

Child prodigy Farkle masters and then rejects a new instrument every year—violin, flute, trombone, percussion—until he discovers his favorite sound: musicians playing all together.

GERM: Introduce your music lovers to the orchestra and its varied instruments. Pull together as many simple instruments as you can—kazoos, triangles, bongos, or even boxes—and put on an impromptu concert.

RELATED TITLES: Curtis, Gavin. *The Bat Boy and His Violin*. Simon & Schuster, 1998. / Hayes, Ann. *Meet the Orchestra*. Harcourt, 1991. / Kuskin, Carla. *The Philharmonic Gets Dressed*. HarperCollins, 1982. / Millman, Isaac. *Moses Goes to a Concert*. Farrar, 1998. / Moss, Lloyd. *Zin! Zin! Zin! A Violin*. Simon & Schuster, 1995.

SUBJECTS: CONDUCTORS. MUSICAL INSTRUMENTS. MUSICIANS. STORIES IN RHYME.

495 Littlesugar, Amy. *Marie in Fourth Position: The Story of Degas' "The Little Dancer"*. Illus. by Ian Schoenherr. Philomel, 1996. 0-399-22794-6. Unp. Gr. 1–4

In 1881, artist Edgar Degas caused a stir when he entered his lifelike, clothed sculpture, "The Little Dancer," in an Impressionist exhibition in Paris. Littlesugar's pensive and inspirational fictionalized story explores the artistic process of both Degas and his model, young Marie, a "rat" in the Paris Opera, as they work together to create her memorable pose.

GERM: Schoenherr's insightful paintings capture the style of Degas; students can look up more about him and other Impressionists. *Degas and the Dance: The Painter and the Petits Rats, Perfecting Their Art* by Susan Goldman Rubin showcases three dozen of Degas's paintings and sketches, and details his fascination with ballet and the dancers at the Paris Opera during the last quarter of the 19th century.

RELATED TITLES: Anholt, Laurence. *Camille and the Sunflowers: A Story About Vincent Van Gogh*. Barron's, 1994. / Fritz, Jean. *Leonardo's Horse*. Putnam, 2001. / Krull, Kathleen. *Lives of the Artists: Masterpieces, Messes (and What the Neighbors Thought)*. Harcourt, 1995. / Rubin, Susan Goldman. *Degas and the Dance: The Painter and the Petits Rats, Perfecting Their Art*. Abrams, 2002. / Stadler, Alexander. *Lila Bloom*. Farrar, 2003. / Waldman, Neil. *The Starry Night*. Boyds Mills, 1999.

SUBJECTS: ARTISTS. BALLET. BIOGRAPHICAL FICTION. DANCING. DEGAS, EDGAR, 1834–1917. HISTORICAL FICTION. PAINTERS. SCULPTORS.

496 Livingston, Irene. *Finklehopper Frog*. Illus. by Brian Lies. Tricycle, 2003. 1-58246-075-2. Unp. Gr. PreK–2

Seeing everyone else outside jogging, Finklehopper buys a rockin' jogging suit and takes to the streets. Itchy Flea the dog and Yowlereen the alley cat make derisive comments about his outfit and his hopping gait, but Ruby Rabbit assures him his style suits him just fine.

GERM: This book's message, that individuality is a good thing—"there's room for everyone"—combined with the wonderfully garish acrylic illustrations, makes it just the ticket for getting those couch potatoes up and moving. Try out the stretches the frog is doing on the endpapers before you head out for a run.

RELATED TITLES: Araki, Mie. *The Perfect Tail: A Fred and Lulu Story*. Chronicle, 2004. / Clark, Emma Chichester. *Follow the Leader*. McElderry, 2003. / French, Vivian. *Growing Frogs*. Candlewick, 2000. / Kinerk, Robert. *Clorinda*. Simon & Schuster, 2003. / Livingston, Irene. *Finklehopper Frog Cheers*. Tricycle, 2005. / London, Jonathan. *Froggy Gets Dressed*. Viking, 1992. (And others in the Froggy series.) / Luby, Thia. *Children's Book of Yoga: Games and Exercises Mimic Plants and Animals and Objects*. Clear Light, 1998. / Mitton, Tony. *Dinosaurum-*

pus! Scholastic, 2003. / Parker, Vic. *Bearobics.* Viking, 1997. / Wilson, Karma. *A Frog in the Bog.* McElderry, 2003.

SUBJECTS: EXERCISE. FROGS. INDIVIDUALITY. RABBITS. RUNNING. STORIES IN RHYME.

497 Livingstone, Star. *Harley.* Illus. by Molly Bang. SeaStar, 2001. 1-58717-048-5. 64pp. Gr. K–2
Harley, a llama who can't get along with the other llamas on the ranch, is brought to a farm by a local shepherd to guard a flock of sheep and protect them from being killed and eaten by coyotes. This easy-reader, based on a true story, is just quirky and real enough that it will appeal to all animal lovers, who will fall for Harley and his stubborn but lovable persona.
GERM: Children can research more facts about llamas and their peculiar habits. If you have access to raw sheep's wool, bring it in along with some wool spun into yarn and talk about the uses of wool. For llama family stories, read *Llama Llama Red Pajama* by Anna Dewdney and *Is Your Mama a Llama?* by Deborah Guarino.
RELATED TITLES: Aardema, Verna. *Borreguita and the Coyote.* Knopf, 1991. / Alexander, Ellen. *Llama and the Great Flood.* Crowell, 1989. / Beskow, Elsa. *Pelle's New Suit.* HarperCollins, 1929. / dePaola, Tomie. *Charlie Needs a Cloak.* Aladdin, 1982. / Dewdney, Anna. *Llama Llama Red Pajama.* Viking, 2005. / Guarino, Deborah. *Is Your Mama a Llama?* Scholastic, 1989. / Haas, Jessie. *Runaway Radish.* Greenwillow, 2001. / Hale, Sarah Josepha Buell. *Mary Had a Little Lamb.* Scholastic, 1990. / Sanders, Scott Russell. *Warm as Wool.* Bradbury, 1992. / Singer, Marilyn. *Chester the Out-of-Work Dog.* Henry Holt, 1992.
SUBJECTS: FARM LIFE. LLAMAS. SHEEP.

498 Locker, Thomas. *Water Dance.* Photos by the author. Harcourt, 1997. 0-15-201284-2. Unp. Gr. K–5
Each page's brief poetic description of a different form of the water cycle—rain, stream, waterfall, lake, river, sea, mist, clouds, storm front, thunderhead, storm, and rainbow—is accompanied by a breathtaking oil painting.
GERM: At the back of the book is a more detailed description of each phase of the water cycle. Nonfiction picture books *Follow the Water from Brook to Ocean* by Walter Dorros and *Water's Way* by Lisa Westberg Peters explain different aspects of the water cycle. Sage and her classmates put on a play about water in *The Incredible Water Show* by Debra Frasier. Find out how Locker wrote this book in his photo-filled autobiography for children, *The Man Who Paints Nature.* Locker continues his look at nature with companion books, *Cloud Dance* and *Mountain Dance.*
RELATED TITLES: Cobb, Vicki. *I Get Wet.* HarperCollins, 2002. / Cole, Joanna. *The Magic School Bus at the Waterworks.* Scholastic, 1988. / Cowan, Catherine. *My Life with the Wave.* Lothrop, 1997. / Dorros, Walter. *Follow the Water from Brook to Ocean.* HarperCollins, 1991. / Graham, Joan Bransfield. *Splish Splash.* Ticknor & Fields, 1994. / Hathorn, Libby. *The Wonder Thing.* Houghton Mifflin, 1996. / Hooper, Meredith. *River Story.* Candlewick, 2000. / Jackson, Shelley. *The Old Woman and the Wave.* DK Ink, 1998. / Karas, G. Brian. *Atlantic.* Putnam, 2002. / Kerley, Barbara. *A Cool Drink of Water.* National Geographic, 2002. / Lewis, J. Patrick. *Earth Verses and Water Rhymes.* Atheneum, 1991. / Locker, Thomas. *Cloud Dance.* Harcourt, 2000. / Locker, Thomas. *The Man Who Paints Nature.* Richard C. Owen, 1999. / Locker, Thomas. *Mountain Dance.* Harcourt, 2001. / Peters, Lisa Westberg. *Water's Way.* Little, Brown, 1991. / Wick, Walter. *A Drop of Water.* Scholastic, 1997.
SUBJECTS: PERSONAL NARRATIVES. PERSONIFICATION. WATER.

499 London, Jonathan. *Froggy Goes to School.* Illus. by Frank Remkiewicz. Viking, 1996. 0-670-86726-8. Unp. Gr. PreK–1
On the first day of school, Froggy is mortified to see he is wearing only his underwear, but don't worry, it's just a dream, and his real first day turns out swell.
GERM: When Froggy's mom hears he left his lunchbox and baseball cap at school, she says, "Oh, Froggy. Will you ever learn?" "That's why I'm going to school, Mom," he says. Ask your scholars: What do YOU want to learn this year? And how can Froggy learn not to forget things? From your own experience forgetting and remembering things, what advice can you give him? Make a chart of the suggestions.
RELATED TITLES: Dannenberg, Julie. *First Day Jitters.* Charlesbridge, 2000. / Henkes, Kevin. *Chrysanthemum.* Greenwillow, 1991. / Henkes, Kevin. *Wemberly Worried.* Greenwillow, 2000. / Hest, Amy. *Off to School, Baby Duck.* Candlewick, 1999. / Lasky, Kathryn. *Lunch Bunnies.* Little, Brown, 1996. / Lobel, Arnold. *Frog and Toad series.* HarperCollins. / London, Jonathan. *Froggy Gets Dressed.* Viking, 1992. (And others in the Froggy series.) / McGhee, Alison. *Countdown to Kindergarten.* Harcourt, 2002. / Poydar, Nancy. *First Day, Hooray.* Holiday House, 1999. / Wells, Rosemary. *Timothy Goes to School.* Dial, 1981.
SUBJECTS: FIRST DAY OF SCHOOL. FROGS. HUMOROUS FICTION. SCHOOLS.

500   Long, Melinda. *How I Became a Pirate.* **Illus. by David Shannon. Harcourt, 2003. 0-15-201848- 4. Unp. Gr. PreK–2**

Building a sand castle at the beach one day, little Jeremy Jacobs encounters Brain Beard and his pirate crew and joins them as a digger when they sail off to find a safe place to bury their treasure chest of gold and jewels. Jeremy learns pirate language ("Aargh!"), pirate manners (they don't have any), and tries to teach the scurvy dogs to play soccer. He doesn't have to brush his teeth. "Maybe that's why their teeth are green," he observes cogently. But when he asks to be tucked in and read a bedtime story, they howl, "NO TUCKING!" Pirates don't tuck. Or read books. When a storm breaks, Jeremy leads them back to his own back yard where they bury the treasure.

GERM: What a perfect spur for some imaginative writing, and all will adore Shannon's expressive acrylics. You can introduce that lesson on maps too. Bury or hide some treasure around the building or in your room—gold coin chocolates will work, or even stones you've spray-painted gold (which look like mighty authentic gold nuggets to children and make inexpensive souvenirs)—and have a scavenger hunt. You can create a map or a set of maps and make up rhyming or cryptic clues for pirates to decipher. Hold a party afterward with Island Punch, tropical fruits, and coconut macaroons.

RELATED TITLES: Cox, Judy. *Rabbit Pirates: A Tale of the Spinach Main.* Harcourt, 1999. / Falconer, Ian. *Olivia Saves the Circus.* Atheneum, 2001. / Faulkner, Matt. *The Amazing Voyage of Jackie Grace.* Scholastic, 1987. / Feiffer, Jules. *Meanwhile . . .* HarperCollins, 1997. / Helquist, Brett. *Roger the Jolly Pirate.* HarperCollins, 2004. / Leedy, Loreen. *Mapping Penny's World.* Henry Holt, 2000. / McPhail, David. *Edward and the Pirates.* Little, Brown, 1997. / Scieszka, Jon. *Baloney (Henry P.).* Viking, 2001. / Shannon, David. *David Gets in Trouble.* Scholastic, 2002. / Shannon, David. *David Goes to School.* Scholastic, 1999. / Shannon, David. *No, David!* Scholastic, 1998. / Teague, Mark. *How I Spent My Summer Vacation.* Crown, 1995. / Teague, Mark. *Moog-Moog, Space Barber.* Scholastic, 1990.

SUBJECTS: ADVENTURE AND ADVENTURERS—FOLKLORE. BURIED TREASURE. HUMOROUS FICTION. IMAGINATION. OCEAN. PERSONAL NARRATIVES. PIRATES. SEASHORE. SHIPS. SOCCER. SPORTS.

501   Lorbiecki, Marybeth. *Sister Anne's Hands.* **Illus. by Wendy Popp. Dial, 1998. 0-8037-2039-4. Unp. Gr. 3–6**

Anna's new second-grade teacher, Sister Anne, makes the first day memorable with jokes, read-alouds, and counting games, but then someone sails a paper airplane with a note written on it. It says, "Roses are red, Violets are blue. Don't let Sister Anne get any black on you." The African American nun responds the next day by showing them startling and disturbing photos of black people—shot, bleeding, some hanging from trees—which she calls "the color of hatred."

GERM: Set in the civil rights era of the late 1960s, Anna's portrait of a teacher who taught her to "use her wings" will spark a discussion of race relations and tolerance. Too graphic for younger children, this is a provocative and affecting picture book to use along with *Through My Eyes* by Ruby Bridges, *Goin' Someplace Special* by Patricia McKissack, and *The Other Side* by Jacqueline Woodson. With students in grades 5 through 8, you could use it as a companion to the novel *The Watsons Go to Birmingham, 1963* by Christopher Paul Curtis.

RELATED TITLES: Adler, David A. *Dr. Martin Luther King, Jr.* Holiday House, 2001. / Adler, David A. *A Picture Book of Rosa Parks.* Holiday House, 1993. / Borden, Louise. *Good Luck, Mrs. K.* McElderry, 1999. / Bray, Rosemary L. *Martin Luther King.* Greenwillow, 1995. / Bridges, Ruby. *Through My Eyes.* Scholastic, 1999. / Coles, Robert. *The Story of Ruby Bridges.* Scholastic, 1995. / Curtis, Christopher Paul. *The Watsons Go to Birmingham, 1963.* Delacorte, 1995. / English, Karen. *Nadia's Hands.* Boyds Mills, 1999. / McKissack, Patricia C. *Goin' Someplace Special.* Atheneum, 2001. / Mitchell, Margaree King. *Uncle Jed's Barber Shop.* Simon & Schuster, 1993. / Parks, Rosa, and Jim Haskins. *I Am Rosa Parks.* Dial, 1997. / Polacco, Patricia. *Mr. Lincoln's Way.* Philomel, 2001. / Polacco, Patricia. *Pink and Say.* Philomel, 1994. / Rappaport, Doreen. *Martin's Big Words.* Hyperion, 2001. / Woodson, Jacqueline. *The Other Side.* Putnam, 2001.

SUBJECTS: AFRICAN AMERICANS. AFRICAN AMERICANS—HISTORY. CATHOLIC SCHOOLS. MULTICULTURAL BOOKS. PICTURE BOOKS FOR OLDER READERS. PREJUDICE. PRIVATE SCHOOLS. RACE RELATIONS. SCHOOLS. TEACHERS.

502   Lowell, Susan. *Cindy Ellen: A Wild Western Cinderella.* **Illus. by Jane Manning. Orchard, 1997. 0-531-33044-3. Unp. Gr. 1–4**

Cindy Ellen's pistol-totin' fairy godmother gives her some gumption and some fine cowgirl duds and sends her off to the rodeo where she turns the head of the rich rancher's son, Joe Prince.

GERM: Read "A Little Western Lore" at the back of the book, talking about cowgirls, rodeos, and Annie Oakley. Your library should have some good supporting books on those subjects with vintage photos, such as Sue Macy's *Bull's-Eye*. Compare Cindy Ellen's story with Helen Ketteman's *Bubba the Cowboy Prince*. Try on another pair of cowboy boots with Lowell's *The Bootmaker and the Elves*.

RELATED TITLES: Axelrod, Alan, comp. *Songs of the Wild West*. Simon & Schuster, 1991. / Buehner, Caralyn. *Fanny's Dream*. Dial, 1996. / Craft, K. Y. *Cinderella*. SeaStar Books, 2000. / Dadey, Debbie. *Shooting Star: Annie Oakley, the Legend*. Walker, 1997 / dePaola, Tomie. *Adelita: A Mexican Cinderella Story*. Putnam, 2002. / Jackson, Ellen. *Cinder Edna*. Lothrop, 1994. / Ketteman, Helen. *Bubba the Cowboy Prince: A Fractured Texas Tale*. Scholastic, 1997. / Lowell, Susan. *The Bootmaker and the Elves*. Orchard, 1997. / Lowell, Susan. *Dusty Locks and the Three Bears*. Henry Holt, 2001. / Lowell, Susan. *Little Red Cowboy Hat*. Henry Holt, 1997. / Lowell, Susan. *The Three Little Javelinas*. Rising Moon, 1992. / Macy, Sue. *Bull's-Eye: A Photobiography of Annie Oakley*. National Geographic, 2001. / Minters, Frances. *Cinder Elly*. Viking, 1993. / Mitchell, Marianne. *Joe Cinders*. Henry Holt, 2002. / Myers, Bernice. *Sidney Rella and the Glass Sneaker*. Macmillan, 1985.

SUBJECTS: BOOTS. CINDERELLA STORIES. CLOTHING AND DRESS. RODEOS. WEST (U.S.).

503 Lowell, Susan. *Little Red Cowboy Hat*. **Illus. by Randy Cecil. Henry Holt, 1997. 0-8050-3508-7. Unp. Gr. 1–3**

In a Wild West casting of the Riding Hood yarn, see how Little Red and her ax-wielding grandma drive off that varmint of a wolf from their ranch.

GERM: Do a reading of Susan Lowell's Wild West fairy tale parodies. Go from the ranch to a farm on the prairie with Lisa Campbell Ernst's *Little Red Riding Hood: A Newfangled Prairie Tale*.

RELATED TITLES: Artell, Mike. *Petite Rouge: A Cajun Red Riding Hood*. Dial, 2001. / Child, Lauren. *Beware of the Storybook Wolves*. Scholastic, 2001. / Ernst, Lisa Campbell. *Little Red Riding Hood: A Newfangled Prairie Tale*. Simon & Schuster, 1995. / Harper, Wilhelmina. *The Gunniwolf*. Dutton, 2003. / Hyman, Trina Schart. *Little Red Riding Hood*. Holiday House, 1983. / Ketteman, Helen. *Armadilly Chili*. Albert Whitman, 2004. / Khalsa, Dayal Kaur. *Cowboy Dreams*. Crown, 1990. / Kimmel, Eric A. *The Runaway Tortilla*. Winslow, 2000. / Lowell, Susan. *Cindy Ellen: A Wild Western Cinderella*. Orchard, 1997. / Lowell, Susan. *Dusty Locks and the Three Bears*. Henry Holt, 2001. / Lowell, Susan. *The Three Little Javelinas*. Rising Moon, 1992. / Lowell, Susan. *The Tortoise and the Jackrabbit*. Northland, 1994. / Marshall, James. *Red Riding Hood*. Dial, 1987. / Minters, Frances. *Sleepless Beauty*. Viking, 1996. / Teague, Mark. *How I Spent My Summer Vacation*. Crown, 1995.

SUBJECTS: CHARACTERS IN LITERATURE. GRANDMOTHERS. LITTLE RED RIDING HOOD STORIES. PARODIES. SOUTHWEST. WOLVES.

504 Lowell, Susan. *The Tortoise and the Jackrabbit*. **Illus. by Jim Harris. Northland, 1994. 0-87358-586-0. Unp. Gr. PreK–1**

Out in the springtime desert, patient Tortoise challenges bragging Jackrabbit to a race over the rocky hill, across the dusty flat place, under the mesquite trees, and to the water hole. You know who wins.

GERM: Before reading, examine the front cover of the book to make predictions and connections. Ask: What is the setting of this story? How can you tell? What is the old, old fable upon which this story is based? What happens in that story? After reading, bring out books of desert animals so children can see realistic drawings or photos of the actual desert plants and animals that are depicted here in Harris's genial acrylic and watercolor illustrations.

RELATED TITLES: Anaya, Rudolpho. *Roadrunner's Dance*. Hyperion, 2000. / Bash, Barbara. *Desert Giant: The World of the Saguaro Cactus*. Sierra Club, 1989. / Guiberson, Brenda. *Cactus Hotel*. Henry Holt, 1991. / Ketteman, Helen. *Bubba the Cowboy Prince: A Fractured Texas Tale*. Scholastic, 1997. / Lowell, Susan. *The Bootmaker and the Elves*. Orchard, 1997. / Lowell, Susan. *Cindy Ellen: A Wild Western Cinderella*. Orchard, 1997. / Lowell, Susan. *Dusty Locks and the Three Bears*. Henry Holt, 2001. / Lowell, Susan. *Little Red Cowboy Hat*. Henry Holt, 1997. / Lowell, Susan. *The Three Little Javelinas*. Rising Moon, 1992. / Stevens, Janet. *Coyote Steals the Blanket: A Ute Tale*. Holiday House, 1993. / Stevens, Janet. *The Tortoise and the Hare: An Aesop Fable*. Holiday House, 1984. / Yolen, Jane. *Welcome to the Sea of Sand*. Putnam, 1996.

SUBJECTS: AESOP. DESERT ANIMALS. FABLES. PARODIES. RABBITS. SOUTHWEST. TURTLES.

505 Lum, Kate. *What! Cried Granny: An Almost Bedtime Story*. **Illus. by Adrian Johnson. Dial, 1999. 0-8037-2382-2. Unp. Gr. PreK–1**

Patrick is having his first sleepover at Granny's, and at bedtime, when she tells him to go to bed, he replies, in what could be an excuse to stay up later, "But Granny . . . I don't have a bed here." "What!" she cries, in a soon-to-be repeated refrain, and rushes out to chop down a tree and make him one. In the frantic, loud, collage-style acrylics, you'll see that this is one hands-on Granny—she plucks chickens for Patrick's pillow, shears sheep to weave him a blanket, and sews him a gargantuan teddy.

GERM: Children can act out the wild story in pairs, with one half as Granny and the other half as Patrick. Collect doll-sized props—the bed, pillow, blanket, and teddy—to use when retelling the story in sequence.

RELATED TITLES: Cole, Joanna. *It's Too Noisy!* Crowell, 1989. / Cook, Sally. *Good Night Pillow Fight.* Harper-Collins, 2004. / Gray, Libba Moore. *Is There Room on the Featherbed?* Orchard, 1997. / Juster, Norton. *The Hello, Goodbye Window.* Hyperion, 2005. / Kellogg, Steven. *A-Hunting We Will Go!* Morrow, 1998. / Mathews, Judith, and Fay Robinson. *Nathaniel Willy, Scared Silly.* Bradbury, 1994. / Murphy, Jill. *Peace at Last.* Dial, 1980. / Paul, Ann Whitford. *Everything to Spend the Night from A to Z.* DK Ink, 1999. / Pinkney, Andrea Davis. *Sleeping Cutie.* Harcourt, 2004. / Rathmann, Peggy. *Ten Minutes Till Bedtime.* Putnam, 1998. / Simms, Laura. *The Squeaky Door.* Crown, 1991. / Swain, Ruth Freeman. *Bedtime!* Holiday House, 1999. / Walton, Rick. *So Many Bunnies: A Bedtime ABC and Counting Book.* Lothrop, 1998. / Whybrow, Ian. *The Noisy Way to Bed.* Scholastic, 2004.

SUBJECTS: BEDTIME STORIES. CREATIVE DRAMA. GRANDMOTHERS. HUMOROUS FICTION. SLEEP. STORIES TO TELL.

506   McBrier, Paige. *Beatrice's Goat.* **Illus. by Lori Lohstoeter. Atheneum, 2001. 0-689-82460-2. 32pp. Gr. K–4**

Growing up in the small village of Kisinga in western Uganda, Beatrice has always longed to be a schoolgirl, but her family is far too poor to pay the fees. So she spends her days helping in the fields, tending the chickens, and watching over the younger children. The life of Beatrice, her parents, and five siblings changes dramatically thanks to a goat named Mugisa, given to them by an international organization called the Heifer Project. Based on the true story of Beatrice Biira, whom the author and illustrator met in Uganda, the book is an inspirational description of the remarkable results of the Heifer Project, which has helped more than 4 million poor families in 125 countries. All these families became self-reliant after receiving their pigs, cows, sheep, or goats.

GERM: Children can compare and contrast Beatrice's life with their own by observing and discussing many of the differences apparent in the lush acrylic paintings. Children can help earn money for the Read to Feed project, where they ask adults to sponsor them and donate money for the books they read, all of which goes to the Heifer Project to purchase animals. For more information, call 800-422-0474 or check out <www.heifer.org>. Discussion point: Introduce the quote, "If you give a man a fish he will eat for a day; teach a man to fish and he will fish for a lifetime."

RELATED TITLES: Aardema, Verna. *Misoso: Once upon a Time Tales from Africa.* Knopf, 1994. / Cowen-Fletcher, Jane. *It Takes a Village.* Scholastic, 1994. / Mollel, Tololwa M. *My Rows and Piles of Coins.* Clarion, 1999. / Stock, Catherine. *Gugu's House.* Clarion, 2001. / Stuve-Bodeen, Stephanie. *Elizabeti's Doll.* Lee & Low, 1998. / Stuve-Bodeen, Stephanie. *Elizabeti's School.* Lee & Low, 2002.

SUBJECTS: AFRICA. GOATS. MULTICULTURAL BOOKS. UGANDA.

507   McCall, Francis. *A Huge Hog Is a Big Pig: A Rhyming Word Game.* **Photos by Patricia Keeler. Greenwillow, 2002. 0-06-029765-4. Unp. Gr. PreK–2**

Color photographs of children spending a day at a petting farm with a variety of farm animals accompany "hink pink" riddles that listeners can try to answer, such as: A grandmother goat is a . . . granny nanny.

GERM: Before you turn each page to reveal the photographed answer, your listeners will love trying to figure out each pair of rhyming words, which the authors call "stinky pinkies." Next, have children work in groups to make a list of animals, with each group brainstorming a list from one category, including pets, small mammals, large mammals, fish, birds, reptiles, amphibians, and insects. Come up with some hink pinks using their lists and then have each group or pair think up a new hink pink. Folding their paper in half (like a hamburger), they can write the start of the riddle on the outside and put the answer and a picture of the animal on the inside. Children can present their hink pink riddles to the rest of the group.

RELATED TITLES: Cherry, Lynne. *Who's Sick Today?* Dutton, 1988. / Cronin, Doreen. *Click, Clack, Moo: Cows That Type.* Simon & Schuster, 2000. / Downs, Mike. *Pig Giggles and Rabbit Rhymes: A Book of Animal Riddles.* Chronicle, 2002. / Lindbergh, Reeve. *The Day the Goose Got Loose.* Dial, 1990. / McMillan, Bruce. *One Sun: A*

Book of Terse Verse. Holiday House, 1990. / McMillan, Bruce. *Play Day: A Book of Terse Verse.* Holiday House, 1991. / Maestro, Giulio. *Macho Nacho and Other Rhyming Riddles.* Dutton, 1994. / Most, Bernard. *Cock-a-Doodle-Moo!* Harcourt, 1996. / Shields, Carol Diggory. *Animagicals: On the Go.* Handprint, 2001. / Shields, Carol Diggory. *Animagicals: Patterns.* Handprint, 2001. / Spires, Elizabeth. *With One White Wing: Puzzles in Poems and Pictures.* McElderry, 1995. / Young, Ruth. *Who Says Moo?* Viking, 1994.

SUBJECTS: ANIMALS. DOMESTIC ANIMALS. ENGLISH LANGUAGE—SYNONYMS AND ANTONYMS. FARM LIFE. RIDDLES. WORD GAMES.

508 McClements, George. *Jake Gander, Storyville Detective.* Illus. by the author. Hyperion, 2002. 0-7868-0662-1. Unp. Gr. PreK–2

In "The Case of the Greedy Granny," dim-bulb detective Jake Gander knows there's something strange about Red R. Hood's Granny—fur pajamas, really sharp teeth, rabbit breath—but can't put his finger on what's wrong.

GERM: An open ending will get your young flatfeet thinking about what clue Jake will find when he tackles the case of the Three Bears. Have your kids write the story of Jake's next investigation, incorporating those clues.

RELATED TITLES: Blundell, Tony. *Beware of Boys.* Greenwillow, 1992. / Child, Lauren. *Beware of the Storybook Wolves.* Scholastic, 2001. / Child, Lauren. *Who's Afraid of the Big Bad Book?* Hyperion, 2003. / Cushman, Doug. *Mystery at the Club Sandwich.* Clarion, 2004. / Hawkins, Colin, and Jacqui Hawkins. *The Fairytale News.* Candlewick, 2004. / Kelly, John, and Cathy Tincknell. *The Mystery of Eatum Hall.* Candlewick, 2004. / Marshall, James. *The Three Little Pigs.* Dial, 1989. / Offen, Hilda. *Nice Work, Little Wolf!* Dutton, 1992. / Palatini, Margie. *Bad Boys.* HarperCollins, 2003. / Palatini, Margie. *The Web Files.* Hyperion, 2001. / Scieszka, Jon. *The True Story of the 3 Little Pigs.* Viking, 1989. / Teague, Mark. *Detective LaRue: Letters from the Investigation.* Scholastic, 2004. / Trivizas, Eugene. *The Three Little Wolves and the Big Bad Pig.* McElderry, 1993. / Vozar, David. *Yo, Hungry Wolf! A Nursery Rap.* Doubleday, 1993. / Wiesner, David. *The Three Pigs.* Clarion, 2001.

SUBJECTS: CHARACTERS IN LITERATURE. HUMOROUS FICTION. MYSTERY AND DETECTIVE STORIES. PARODIES. WOLVES.

509 McClintock, Barbara. *Molly and the Magic Wishbone.* Illus. by the author. Farrar, 2001. 0-374-34999-1. Unp. Gr. K–2

At the market to buy fish for dinner, Molly, the oldest of five cat siblings, meets an old woman who claims to be her fairy godmother. She tells Molly to save the bone she will find in her fish that night, as it will be good for one wish. Molly plans to use it for a closet of silk dresses, but when her littlest sister Phylis goes missing, Molly realizes that family is more important than mere things. The delicate pen-and-ink and watercolor illustrations transport us to an elegant Dickensian city, but peopled with animals.

GERM: Ask your children what they would wish for if they had two wishes granted by their fairy godmother—one for something frivolous and one for something important. See how a dog's three wishes go awry in *Burnt Toast on Davenport Street* by Tim Egan.

RELATED TITLES: Agee, Jon. *Milo's Hat Trick.* Hyperion, 2001. / Aylesworth, Jim. *The Gingerbread Man.* Scholastic, 1998. / Chapman, Carol. *Barney Bipple's Magic Dandelions.* Dutton, 1988. / Egan, Tim. *Burnt Toast on Davenport Street.* Houghton Mifflin, 1997. / Griffith, Helen V. *Emily and the Enchanted Frog.* Greenwillow, 1989. / Kovalski, Maryanne. *Pizza for Breakfast.* Morrow, 1991. / Meddaugh, Susan. *The Witch's Walking Stick.* Houghton Mifflin, 2005. / Steig, William. *Sylvester and the Magic Pebble.* Simon & Schuster, 1988. / Yorinks, Arthur. *Hey, Al.* Farrar, 1986.

SUBJECTS: BROTHERS AND SISTERS. MAGIC. WISHES.

510 McCully, Emily Arnold. *The Ballot Box Battle.* Illus. by the author. Knopf, 1996. 0-679-97938-7. Unp. Gr. 1–4

Every day, young Cordelia goes next door to care for old Jule, the horse belonging to the elderly Elizabeth Cady Stanton. In return, Mrs. Stanton gives Cordelia riding lessons. Accompanied by Cordelia, the elderly but still feisty suffragist attempts to cast her vote on Election Day in Tenafly, New Jersey, in 1880. While Cordelia is a fictional character, the rest of the story is true, based on Stanton's memoirs.

GERM: For more background on the suffragist leader, older students will enjoy Jean Fritz's lively biography, *You Want Women to Vote, Lizzie Stanton?* Nowadays, Americans take the right to vote for granted, but in 1880, when this inspiring story-within-a-story takes place, the Nineteenth Amendment granting women the vote was still 40 years off, a fact children will find shocking. Discuss voting and its importance in our lives.

RELATED TITLES: Blumberg, Rhoda. *Bloomers!* Atheneum, 1993. / Christelow, Eileen. *VOTE!* Clarion, 2003. / Christensen, Bonnie. *The Daring Nellie Bly: America's Star Reporter.* Knopf, 2003. / Corey, Shana. *You Forgot Your Skirt, Amelia Bloomer!* Scholastic, 2000. / Fritz, Jean. *You Want Women to Vote, Lizzie Stanton?* Putnam, 1995. / Lasky, Kathryn. *She's Wearing a Dead Bird on Her Head!* Hyperion, 1995. / Maestro, Betsy. *The Voice of the People: American Democracy in Action.* Lothrop, 1996. / Mitchell, Margaree King. *Granddaddy's Gift.* Bridge-Water, 1997. / Sisulu, Elinor Batezat. *The Day Gogo Went to Vote: South Africa, April 1994.* Little, Brown, 1996. / St. George, Judith. *So You Want to Be President?* Philomel, 2000. / Stier, Catherine. *If I Were President.* Albert Whitman, 1999. / White, Linda Arms. *I Could Do That: Esther Morris Gets Women the Vote.* Farrar, 2005. / Wooldridge, Connie Nordhielm. *When Esther Morris Headed West: Women, Wyoming, and the Right to Vote.* Holiday House, 2001.

SUBJECTS: BIOGRAPHICAL FICTION. FEMINISTS. HISTORICAL FICTION. PICTURE BOOKS FOR OLDER READERS. STANTON, ELIZABETH CADY, 1815–1902. SUFFRAGISTS. VOTING. WOMEN. WOMEN'S RIGHTS.

511   McCully, Emily Arnold. *Beautiful Warrior: The Legend of the Nun's Kung Fu.* **Illus. by the author. Scholastic, 1998. 0-590-37487-7. 40pp. Gr. 2–6**

Sent to tutors to learn as if she were a son, Jingyong becomes a master at kung fu, joins the Shaolin Monastery as a Buddhist nun, and is renamed Wu Mei, meaning beautiful warrior. When Mingyi, a poor bean curd seller, is threatened by Soong Ling, a bandit who demands to marry her, she seeks out Wu Mei, who instructs her in how to use her *qi*, or vital energy. The stately picture book with impressive watercolor paintings of two nontraditional 17th-century women is based on legends that were passed down by secret societies of forbidden kung fu schools over the centuries.

GERM: Discuss with your students how women's roles have changed. Ask them to ponder what *qi* is and how their own inner strength might prevail over force.

RELATED TITLES: Nevius, Carol. *Karate Hour.* Marshall Cavendish, 2004. / San Souci, Robert D. *Fa Mulan: The Story of a Woman Warrior.* Hyperion, 1998. / Stamm, Claus. *Three Strong Women.* Viking, 1990. / Yep, Laurence. *The Dragon Prince: A Chinese Beauty and the Beast Tale.* HarperCollins, 1997. / Yep, Laurence. *The Khan's Daughter: A Mongolian Folktale.* Scholastic, 1997.

SUBJECTS: CHINA. HISTORICAL FICTION. KUNG FU. MARTIAL ARTS. MULTICULTURAL BOOKS. PICTURE BOOKS FOR OLDER READERS. SEX ROLE. WOMEN.

512   McCully, Emily Arnold. *Picnic.* **Illus. by the author. HarperCollins, 2003. 0-06-623854-4. Unp. Gr. PreK–1**

Unnoticed by the rest of the mouse family riding in the back of their little red truck, Little Bitty bounces off the back and lands in the road with her little pink stuffed mouse. The others continue on to their glorious family picnic, but when everyone gathers by the picnic blanket, where's Bitty? In 1984, McCully first published *Picnic* as a small story without words—a treasure that children could pore over and make up their own dialogue for. Now McCully has enlarged the format and added a spare text and snippets of dialogue, making reading it aloud less interactive but just as wonderful.

GERM: Hold a mouse picnic with mouse-sized food. Place a tiny bit of apple, one small grape, a chocolate chip, a tiny bit of cheese, a mini carrot, and a mini jelly sandwich on a small paper plate for each child. Wash it all down with tiny cups of pink lemonade. Make that text-to-life connection: Have you ever been lost? What happened? What did you do? Based on your own experience, what advice do you have for other children who get lost? Write and share your responses.

RELATED TITLES: Cauley, Lorinda Bryan. *The Town Mouse and the Country Mouse.* Putnam, 1984. / Edwards, Pamela Duncan. *Livingstone Mouse.* HarperCollins, 1996. / Fleming, Denise. *Alphabet Under Construction.* Henry Holt, 2002. / Fleming, Denise. *Lunch.* Henry Holt, 1992. / Jarrett, Clare. *The Best Picnic Ever.* Candlewick, 2004. / McBratney, Sam. *The Dark at the Top of the Stairs.* Candlewick, 1996. / McCully, Emily Arnold. *The Christmas Gift.* HarperCollins, 1988. / Numeroff, Laura. *If You Give a Mouse a Cookie.* HarperCollins, 1985. / Rand, Gloria. *Willie Takes a Hike.* Harcourt, 1996. / Riley, Linnea. *Mouse Mess.* Scholastic, 1997. / Wood, Audrey. *The Little Mouse, the Red Ripe Strawberry, and the Big Hungry Bear.* Child's Play, 1990.

SUBJECTS: FAMILY LIFE. LOST. MICE. PICNICS. STUFFED ANIMALS.

513   McDonald, Megan. *Insects Are My Life.* **Illus. by Paul Brett Johnson. Orchard, 1995. 0-531-08724-7. Unp. Gr. 1–3**

Amanda Frankenstein is crazy about bugs; she examines them with her magnifying glass, collects mosquito bites, and even opens her window at night to let the insects in, which doesn't sit too well with her mother. At school, classmate Victor makes fun of her passion, and no one really understands her until she hooks up with Maggie, another animal expert.

GERM: Nurture the subject specialists in your room. Each child can make a poster with his or her name on it, a self-portrait showing that one favorite thing, and an inscription, such as: "Judy Freeman: Books Are My Life!" Introduce insect lovers to the 595.7 section of the library. Follow up with Amanda and Maggie in *Reptiles Are My Life*.

RELATED TITLES: Carle, Eric. *The Very Quiet Cricket*. Philomel, 1990. / Florian, Douglas. *Insectlopedia: Poems and Paintings*. Harcourt, 1998. / Hall, Katy, and Lisa Eisenberg. *Buggy Riddles*. Dial, 1986. / Hepworth, Cathi. *Bug Off! A Swarm of Insect Words*. Putnam, 1998. / Hoose, Phillip M., and Hannah Hoose. *Hey, Little Ant*. Tricycle, 1998. / McDonald, Megan. *Reptiles Are My Life*. Orchard, 2001. / Oppenheim, Joanne. *Have You Seen Bugs?* Scholastic, 1998. / Pallotta, Jerry. *The Beetle Alphabet Book*. Charlesbridge, 2004. / Pfeffer, Wendy. *A Log's Life*. Simon & Schuster, 1997. / Rosen, Michael. *Itsy-Bitsy Beasties: Poems from Around the World*. Carolrhoda, 1992. / Sonenklar, Carol. *Bug Boy*. Henry Holt, 1997.

SUBJECTS: BROTHERS AND SISTERS. FAMILY LIFE. FRIENDSHIP. INSECTS. SCHOOLS. TEASING.

514 **MacDonald, Ross.** *Achoo! Bang! Crash! The Noisy Alphabet.* **Illus. by the author. Roaring Brook, 2003. 0-7613-2900-5. Unp. Gr. PreK–1**

"A . . . CHOO!" sneezes the man in the blue serge suit, launching himself high in the air and out of his clothes (except for his underwear, of course). Your listeners will laugh themselves silly as they talk about the cause and effect of each noisy vignette in this cacophonous alphabetical catalog of wacky sounds. Each sound is accompanied by a hilarious retro illustration of a group of befuddled kids, grownups, and animals, who create each Grrr!, Ka-Pow!, and Wham! There's a wonderful section at the back in which MacDonald explains how he used 19th-century wood type for all of the lettering and printed it on a vintage printing press.

GERM: First, the kids will want to act out and make all of these wonderful onomatopoeic noises. Then, have them compile their own class dictionary of sounds, with appropriate funny drawings. Bring in an assortment of noisemakers, such as a slide whistle, finger cymbals, and bells. Play each one and have your folks work in pairs to write down the sound it makes, using creative invented spelling. Share to compare how they spelled each sound.

RELATED TITLES: Cole, Joanna. *It's Too Noisy!* Crowell, 1989. / Edwards, Pamela Duncan. *Slop Goes the Soup: A Noisy Warthog Word Book*. Hyperion, 2001. / Elkin, Benjamin. *The Loudest Noise in the World*. Viking, 1954. / Ernst, Lisa Campbell. *The Letters Are Lost*. Viking, 1996. / Fleming, Denise. *Alphabet Under Construction*. Henry Holt, 2002. / Lester, Mike. *A Is for Salad*. Putnam, 2000. / MacDonald, Suse. *Alphabatics*. Simon & Schuster, 1986. / McGovern, Ann. *Too Much Noise*. Houghton Mifflin, 1967. / Murphy, Jill. *Peace at Last*. Dial, 1980. / Rotner, Shelley. *Action Alphabet*. Atheneum, 1996. / Showers, Paul. *The Listening Walk*. HarperCollins, 1991. / Simms, Laura. *The Squeaky Door*. Crown, 1991. / Spier, Peter. *Crash! Bang! Boom!* Doubleday, 1990. / Steen, Sandra, and Susan Steen. *Car Wash*. Putnam, 2001. / Thomson, Pat. *The Squeaky, Creaky Bed*. Doubleday, 2003.

SUBJECTS: ALPHABET BOOKS. NOISE. ONOMATOPOEIA. SOUND EFFECTS.

515 **MacDonald, Ross.** *Another Perfect Day.* **Illus. by the author. Roaring Brook, 2002. 0-7613-2659-6. Unp. Gr. PreK–2**

Superhero Jack heads for work as Chief Flavor Tester at the ice cream factory on a perfect day that turns wacky as he heads for home. Since it so happens that the entire story is young Jack's fantastical dream before he wakes up, you'll want to read this story twice so listeners can get the full effect.

GERM: Ask dreamers to describe how they wake up each morning and then have them write about and draw their most memorable dreams. In the sequel, *Bad Baby*, superhero Jack thinks his new baby sister will be someone fun to play with, but she wrecks everything. *Yikes!* by Robert Florczak and *Willie Dreams* by Anthony Browne are other eye-opening dream adventures.

RELATED TITLES: Browne, Anthony. *Willy the Dreamer*. Candlewick, 1998. / Buehner, Caralyn. *Superdog: The Heart of a Hero*. HarperCollins, 2004. / Clement, Rod. *Just Another Ordinary Day*. HarperCollins, 1997. / Dorros, Arthur. *Abuela*. Dutton, 1991. / Florczak, Robert. *Yikes!!!* Scholastic, 2003. / Graham, Bob. *Max*. Candlewick, 2000. / Grey, Mini. *Traction Man Is Here!* Knopf, 2005. / MacDonald, Ross. *Achoo! Bang! Crash: The Noisy Alphabet*. Roaring Brook, 2003. / MacDonald, Ross. *Bad Baby*. Roaring Brook, 2005. / Marx, Patricia. *Meet My Staff*. HarperCollins, 1998. / Myers, Christopher. *Wings*. Scholastic, 2000. / O'Connor, George. *Kapow!* Simon & Schuster, 2004. / Palatini, Margie. *Zak's Lunch*. Clarion, 1998. / Pilkey, Dav. *When Cats*

Dream. Orchard, 1992. / Pinkney, Brian. *The Adventures of Sparrowboy.* Simon & Schuster, 1997. / Taylor, Sean. *Boing!* Candlewick, 2004.

SUBJECTS: DREAMS. SLEEP. SUPERHEROES.

516   MacDonald, Suse. *Look Whooo's Counting.* Illus. by the author. Scholastic, 2000. 0-590-68320-9. Unp. Gr. PreK–K

Flying high through the sky from dusk to dawn, Owl learns how to count all the animals she spies down below, from one prairie dog on a hill to ten snails among the flowers. The swooping, moon-lit, cut-paper collages on the textured paintings cumulatively incorporate actual numbers into Owl's wings as she counts.

GERM: Not only are there numbers to be found in Owl's wings, but numbers appear on the other animals as well. For example, each of the nine squirrels sitting in a tree has its tail curled into the number 9. Viewers will pick up on and point out each detail. They can make new number pictures of animals using the same motif.

RELATED TITLES: Alda, Arlene. *Arlene Alda's 1 2 3: What Do You See?* Tricycle, 2000. / Baker, Keith. *Quack and Count.* Harcourt, 2000. / Catalanotto, Peter. *Daisy 1 2 3.* Atheneum, 2003. / Christelow, Eileen. *Five Little Monkeys Jumping on the Bed.* Clarion, 1989. / Ehlert, Lois. *Fish Eyes: A Book You Can Count On.* Harcourt, 1990. / Falwell, Cathryn. *Turtle Splash! Countdown at the Pond.* Greenwillow, 2001. / Fleming, Denise. *Count!* Henry Holt, 1992. / Freymann, Saxton, and Joost Elffers. *One Lonely Sea Horse.* Scholastic, 2000. / MacDonald, Suse. *Alphabatics.* Simon & Schuster, 1986. / MacDonald, Suse. *Sea Shapes.* Harcourt, 1994. / Nicholls, Judith. *Billywise.* Bloomsbury, 2002. / Noonan, Julia. *Mouse by Mouse.* Dutton, 2003. / Wood, Audrey. *Ten Little Fish.* Blue Sky/Scholastic, 2004. / Wormell, Christopher. *Teeth, Tails, and Tentacles: An Animal Counting Book.* Running Press, 2004.

SUBJECTS: ANIMALS. COUNTING BOOKS. OWLS. PICTURE PUZZLES.

517   McDonnell, Patrick. *The Gift of Nothing.* Illus. by the author. Little, Brown, 2005. 0-316-11488-X. Unp. Gr. PreK–3

Mooch the cat and Earl the dog, from the popular comic strip *Mutts*, make their picture-book debut here in a spare, sweet story about true friendship. Mooch is looking for a special gift for Earl, but what do you get a dog who has it all? Nothing! Mooch goes shopping for nothing, but all he finds is too many somethings—"the latest this, the newest that . . ." He puts nothing in a box and puts that box in a bigger box—"Now that's plenty of nothing!"—and brings it to Earl's house.

GERM: Ask children to predict Earl's response to getting nothing. They can draw their own pages, with little scratchy black line drawings of the two pet pals. On McDonnell's Web site, <muttscomics.com>, there's an archive of each daily and Sunday strip going back to 2002. If you haven't read *Mutts* before, it's a great way to catch up, and your kids will adore it too. For older children in grades three and up, read the ten short stories in *Birthday Surprises*, edited by Joanna Hurwitz, each about a child who receives a beautifully wrapped box with nothing in it. For the younger set, see how a spoiled pig comes to see the value of an empty box in *Crispin, the Pig Who Had It All* by Ted Dewan.

RELATED TITLES: Collins, Suzanne. *When Charlie McButton Lost Power.* Putnam, 2005. / Dewan, Ted. *Crispin, the Pig Who Had It All.* Doubleday, 2000. / Hurwitz, Johanna, ed. *Birthday Surprises: Ten Great Stories to Unwrap.* Morrow, 1995. / Klise, Kate. *Shall I Knit You a Hat? A Christmas Yarn.* Henry Holt, 2004. / Paterson, Katherine. *Marvin's Best Christmas Present Ever.* HarperCollins, 1997.

SUBJECTS: CATS. DOGS. FRIENDSHIP. GIFTS. PICTURE BOOKS FOR ALL AGES.

518   McFarland, Lyn Rossiter. *Widget.* Illus. by Jim McFarland. Farrar, 2001. 0-374-38428-2. Unp. Gr. PreK–K

Sad and lonely, cold and hungry, little white dog Widget pretends he's a cat to gain entrance into Mrs. Diggs's cozy little house. "Meow?" he says and matches her six cats growl for growl. When Mrs. Diggs trips on a toy and falls down, no one comes to the rescue until Widget barks for help.

GERM: Simple and winsome for preschool story hour, with endearing pen-and-ink and watercolor illustrations, this title will get kids talking about the differences between cats and dogs. Dramatize the scene when Widget acts like the cats by puffing up, hissing, and growling.

RELATED TITLES: Banks, Kate. *The Cat Who Walked Across France.* Farrar, 2004. / Bartoletti, Susan Campbell. *Nobody's Diggier Than a Dog.* Hyperion, 2004. / Feiffer, Jules. *Bark, George!* HarperCollins, 1999. / Flack, Marjorie. *Angus and the Cat.* Doubleday, 1931. / George, Kristine O'Connell. *Little Dog Poems.* Clarion, 1999. /

Graeber, Charlotte. *Nobody's Dog*. Hyperion, 1998. / Graham, Bob. *"Let's Get a Pup!" Said Kate*. Candlewick, 2001. / Joosse, Barbara M. *Nugget and Darling*. Clarion, 1997. / Ketteman, Helen. *Grandma's Cat*. Houghton Mifflin, 1996. / McFarland, Lyn Rossiter. *Widget and the Puppy*. Farrar, 2004. / Rylant, Cynthia. *The Great Gracie Chase*. Scholastic, 2001. / Simont, Marc. *The Stray Dog*. HarperCollins, 2001. / Thayer, Jane. *The Puppy Who Wanted a Boy*. Morrow, 1986. / Voake, Charlotte. *Ginger Finds a Home*. Candlewick, 2003. / Wells, Rosemary. *Lucy Comes to Stay*. Dial, 1994. / Wells, Rosemary. *McDuff Moves In*. Hyperion, 1997. (And others in the McDuff series.)

SUBJECTS: CATS. CREATIVE DRAMA. DOGS. STRAY ANIMALS.

519   McGhee, Alison. *Mrs. Watson Wants Your Teeth*. Illus. by Harry Bliss. Harcourt, 2004. 0-15-204931-2. Unp. Gr. K–2

The nervous brown-haired girl we got to know in *Countdown to Kindergarten* is back with a new problem and a secret. She starts first grade today and has it on good authority—from a savvy second grader—that her new teacher, Mrs. Watson, is actually a 300-year-old alien who steals baby teeth from her students. Our heroine's terrifying secret? She has a loose tooth.

GERM: Discussion points: So what's with that rumor-mongering second grader? Why does she tell our girl such a crazy story? What does it mean to be gullible? Tell or write about a time you were gullible. And while you're at it, how did you lose your first baby tooth? Little sister Rosie believes an apple tree is going to grow from her ears in Harriet Lerner and Susan Goldhor's *What's So Terrible About Swallowing an Apple Seed?*

RELATED TITLES: Birdseye, Tom. *Airmail to the Moon*. Holiday House, 1988. / Bunting, Eve. *Trouble on the T-Ball Team*. Clarion, 1995. / Child, Lauren. *I Am Too Absolutely Small for School*. Candlewick, 2004. / Dannenberg, Julie. *First Day Jitters*. Charlesbridge, 2000. / Harris, Robie H. *Don't Forget to Come Back*. Illus. by Harry Bliss. Candlewick, 2004. / Harris, Robie H. *I Am Not Going to School Today!* McElderry, 2003. / Henkes, Kevin. *Chrysanthemum*. Greenwillow, 1991. / Keller, Laurie. *Open Wide: Tooth School Inside*. Henry Holt, 2000. / Lasky, Kathryn. *Lunch Bunnies*. Little, Brown, 1996. / Lerner, Harriet and Susan Goldhor. *What's so Terrible About Swallowing an Apple Seed?* HarperCollins, 1996. / MacDonald, Amy. *Cousin Ruth's Tooth*. Houghton Mifflin, 1996. / McGhee, Alison. *Countdown to Kindergarten*. Harcourt, 2002. / Palatini, Margie. *Sweet Tooth*. Simon & Schuster, 2004. / Poydar, Nancy. *First Day, Hooray!* Holiday House, 1999. / Simms, Laura. *Rotten Teeth*. Houghton Mifflin, 1998. / Wells, Rosemary. *Timothy Goes to School*. Viking, 2000.

SUBJECTS: FIRST DAY OF SCHOOL. HUMOROUS FICTION. SCHOOLS. TEACHERS. TEETH. WORRYING.

520   McGeorge, Constance W. *Boomer's Big Surprise*. Illus. by Mary Whyte. Chronicle, 1999. 0-8118-1977-9. Unp. Gr. PreK–K

Big yellow dog Boomer is a bit confused, befuddled, and jealous when a little, black-nosed yellow puppy, a baby Boomer, appears in his human family's house and everyone pays attention to Baby and not him. Pretty soon, though, the two are fast friends.

GERM: You'll love the understated line, "Baby made himself right at home." The soft, full-page watercolor shows the puppy running amok through the living room, now filled with muddy paw prints, chewed upholstery, and knocked-over plants and furniture. Ask your pet lovers to recall new pet stories from their lives.

RELATED TITLES: Appelt, Kathi. *Bubba and Beau*. Harcourt, 2002. (And others in the Bubba and Beau series.) / Berends, Polly Berrien. *I Heard Said the Bird*. Dial, 1995. / Janovitz, Marilyn. *Bowl Patrol*. North-South, 1996. / Joosse, Barbara M. *Nugget and Darling*. Clarion, 1997. / McGeorge, Constance W. *Boomer Goes to School*. Chronicle, 1996. / McGeorge, Constance W. *Boomer's Big Day*. Chronicle, 1994. / Schachner, Judith Byron. *The Grannyman*. Dutton, 1999. / Simont, Marc. *The Stray Dog*. HarperCollins, 2001.

SUBJECTS: ANIMALS—INFANCY. BABIES. DOGS. JEALOUSY.

521   McGhee, Alison. *Countdown to Kindergarten*. Illus. by Harry Bliss. Harcourt, 2002. 0-15-202516-2. Unp. Gr. PreK–2

"I am in BIG trouble," obsesses a dark-eyed, brown-haired, about-to-be-kindergartner who has heard from a first grader about Rule #1: You have to know how to tie your shoes. By yourself. Without asking for help. Ever. Like Wemberly in Kevin Henkes's *Wemberly Worried*, the girl's list of What Ifs grows, but at school, she discovers that her fears were groundless.

GERM: Make sure everyone knows how to tie those shoes. Ask your students to recall what they thought the school rules would be versus what they really are. Make a list of rules for your classroom and library. Make a chart: What I CAN do. What I CAN'T do. Follow up with the first-grade sequel, *Mrs. Watson Wants Your Teeth*.

RELATED TITLES: Baer, Edith. *This Is the Way We Go to School: A Book About Children Around the World*. Scholastic, 1990. / Curtis, Jamie Lee. *It's Hard to Be Five: Learning How to Work My Control Panel*. Harper-Collins, 2004. / Dannenberg, Julie. *First Day Jitters*. Charlesbridge, 2000. / Davis, Katie. *Kindergarten Rocks*. Harcourt, 2005. / Harris, Robie H. *I Am Not Going to School Today!* McElderry, 2003. / Henkes, Kevin. *Chrysanthemum*. Greenwillow, 1991. / Henkes, Kevin. *Wemberly Worried*. Greenwillow, 2000. / Hest, Amy. *Off to School, Baby Duck*. Candlewick, 1999. / Lasky, Kathryn. *Lunch Bunnies*. Little, Brown, 1996. / London, Jonathan. *Froggy Goes to School*. Viking, 1996. / Poydar, Nancy. *First Day, Hooray*. Holiday House, 1999. / Russo, Marisabina. *I Don't Want to Go Back to School*. Greenwillow, 1994. / Slate, Joseph. *Miss Bindergarten Gets Ready for Kindergarten*. Dutton, 1996. / Wells, Rosemary. *My Kindergarten*. Hyperion, 2004.

SUBJECTS: FATHERS AND DAUGHTERS. FEAR. FIRST DAY OF SCHOOL. HUMOROUS FICTION. KINDERGARTEN. MISCONCEPTIONS. SCHOOLS. SHOES. TEACHERS.

522   **McGill, Alice. *Molly Bannaky*. Illus. by Chris K. Soentpiet. Houghton Mifflin, 1999. 0-395-72287-X. Unp. Gr. 2–5**

After seven years of bondage to a planter in Maryland, Molly Walsh stakes a claim in the wilderness, buys a slave named Bannaky to help her, and marries him, eventually becoming the grandmother to scientist and mathematician Benjamin Banneker in 1731. Glorious, glowing, oversized watercolor paintings make this true story of a little-known ancestor all the more galvanizing.

GERM: Research the life and work of Benjamin Banneker.

RELATED TITLES: Adler, David A. *A Picture Book of Harriet Tubman*. Holiday House, 1992. / Bradby, Marie. *More Than Anything Else*. Orchard, 1995. / Hopkinson, Deborah. *Sweet Clara and the Freedom Quilt*. Knopf, 1993. / Howard, Elizabeth Fitzgerald. *Virgie Goes to School with Us Boys*. Simon & Schuster, 2000. / Johnson, Dolores. *Now Let Me Fly: The Story of a Slave Family*. Macmillan, 1993. / Lasky, Kathryn. *A Voice of Her Own: The Story of Phillis Wheatley, Slave Poet*. Candlewick, 2002. / Maestro, Betsy. *Coming to America: The Story of Immigration*. Scholastic, 1996.

SUBJECTS: AFRICAN AMERICANS. BANNEKER, BENJAMIN. INDENTURED SERVANTS. MULTICULTURAL BOOKS. PICTURE BOOKS FOR OLDER READERS. SLAVERY. U.S.—HISTORY— COLONIAL PERIOD.

523   **McKissack, Patricia C. *Goin' Someplace Special*. Illus. by Jerry Pinkney. Atheneum, 2001. 0-689-81885-8. Unp. Gr. 1–6**

On her way to Someplace Special all by herself, Tricia Ann encounters Jim Crow on the bus and in the park, movie theater, and hotel before she arrives at the one desegregated place where she, an African American child of 1950s Nashville, is welcome: the public library. It's a sobering story made all the more chilling by Pinkney's glowing watercolors that depict a stately city landscape laced with intolerance. An Author's Note makes the story even more poignant: it is based on author McKissack's own childhood experiences growing up in Nashville.

GERM: Discuss the Jim Crow laws that were once supported in the United States and the changes that the civil rights movement brought about. Children can predict where they think Tricia Ann is going, and mull over her grandmother's words: "Those signs can tell us where to sit, but they can't tell us what to think." Round out the discussion of race relations with Marybeth Lorbiecki's *Sister Anne's Hands*, Ann M. Martin's novel *Belle Teal*, Patricia Polacco's *Mr. Lincoln's Way*, Deborah Wiles's *Freedom Summer*, and Jacqueline Woodson's allegorical picture book *The Other Side*. (And speaking of Nashville, next time you're downtown, drop into the gorgeous new library. The children's room is fabulous.)

RELATED TITLES: Adler, David A. *A Picture Book of Rosa Parks*. Holiday House, 1993. / Bray, Rosemary L. *Martin Luther King*. Greenwillow, 1995. / Bridges, Ruby. *Through My Eyes*. Scholastic, 1999. / Coles, Robert. *The Story of Ruby Bridges*. Scholastic, 1995. / Curtis, Gavin. *The Bat Boy and His Violin*. Simon & Schuster, 1998. / Evans, Freddi Williams. *A Bus of Our Own*. Albert Whitman, 2001. / Farris, Christine King. *My Brother Martin*. Atheneum, 2001. / Golenbock, Peter. *Teammates*. Harcourt, 1990. / Joosse, Barbara M. *Hot City*. Philomel, 2004. / Lorbiecki, Marybeth. *Sister Anne's Hands*. Dial, 1998. / Mitchell, Margaree King. *Uncle Jed's Barber Shop*. Simon & Schuster, 1993. / Nelson, Vaunda Micheaux. *Mayfield Crossing*. Putnam, 1993. / Polacco, Patricia. *Mr. Lincoln's Way*. Philomel, 2001. / Rappaport, Doreen. *Martin's Big Words*. Hyperion, 2001. / Wiles, Deborah. *Freedom Summer*. Atheneum, 2001. / Woodson, Jacqueline. *The Other Side*. Putnam, 2001.

SUBJECTS: AFRICAN AMERICANS. AFRICAN AMERICANS—HISTORY. CIVIL RIGHTS. LIBRARIES. MULTICULTURAL BOOKS. PICTURE BOOKS FOR OLDER READERS. PREJUDICE. RACE RELATIONS. SEGREGATION.

524   McKissack, Patricia C. *The Honest-to-Goodness Truth.* **Illus. by Giselle Potter. Atheneum, 2000. 0-689-82668-0. Unp. Gr. K–3**

When Libby lies to her Mama, saying she fed and watered Ol' Boss when she hadn't, "she was surprised at how easy the lie slid out of her mouth, like it was greased with warm butter." Mama punishes her by making her stay home, and Libby decides, "From now on, only the truth." There's such a thing as too much truth, though. Libby learns the hard way, from her angry classmates, the difference between telling a hurtful truth and an honest-to-goodness one.

GERM: Discussion point: Is it acceptable to lie? Have you ever had trouble telling the truth? What is the difference between truth-telling and tattle-taling?

RELATED TITLES: Brisson, Pat. *The Summer My Father Was Ten.* Boyds Mills, 1998. / Bunting, Eve. *A Day's Work.* Clarion, 1994. / Bunting, Eve. *Summer Wheels.* Harcourt, 1992. / Demi. *The Empty Pot.* Henry Holt, 1990. / DePaolo, Paula. *Rosie and the Yellow Ribbon.* Little, Brown, 1992. / Kelley, True. *Blabber Mouse.* Dutton, 2001. / Ness, Evaline. *Sam, Bangs, and Moonshine.* Henry Holt, 1996. / Park, Barbara. *Junie B., First Grader: Cheater Pants.* Random House, 2003. / Peters, Julie Anne. *The Stinky Sneakers Contest.* Little, Brown, 1992. / Polacco, Patricia. *Chicken Sunday.* Philomel, 1992. / Rothenberg, Joan. *Yettele's Feathers.* Hyperion, 1995. / Sharmat, Marjorie Weinman. *A Big Fat Enormous Lie.* Dutton, 1978. / Soto, Gary. *Too Many Tamales.* Putnam, 1993. / Turkle, Brinton. *The Adventures of Obadiah.* Viking, 1972.

SUBJECTS: AFRICAN AMERICANS. APOLOGIES. CONDUCT OF LIFE. HONESTY. MULTICULTURAL BOOKS. PICTURE BOOKS FOR ALL AGES. SCHOOLS.

525   McKissack, Patricia C., and Onawumi Jean Moss. *Precious and the Boo Hag.* **Illus. by Kyrsten Brooker. Atheneum, 2005. 0-689-85194-4. Unp. Gr. 1–4**

Up all night with a stomachache, Precious stays home alone when her Mama and big brother head to the fields to plant corn. Her Mama warns her, ". . . don't let nothing and nobody in this house," and her brother scares her silly with his description of Pruella the Boo Hag, who, he claims, is "tricky and she's scary, and she tries to make you disobey yo' mama." Pruella has no manners, hates clean water, can change her shape, and tells whoppers. Sure enough, Pruella shows up and tries hard to persuade Precious to let her in. Collage and oil paint illustrations, some in double-page full-bleed spreads and others bordered with a weathered, paint-peeling window frame, provide laughs and chills as the little African American girl fends off the bad and none-too-smart Boo Hag.

GERM: Gauge your audience carefully before reading this aloud, as some might become worried about Boo Hags coming to their houses. This is a canny cautionary tale about obeying your parents, and Precious does come through with flying colors. You can make it wickedly scary or lighthearted, depending on the voice you use for Pruella. All will sing with you on the chantable refrain Precious sings to give herself courage. Further reading for tricking creepy creatures away from or out of the house include Molly Bang and Judy Sierra's versions of *Wiley and the Hairy Man*, Dick Gackenbach's *Harry and the Terrible Whatzit*, and Sibyl Hancock's *Esteban and the Ghost.*

RELATED TITLES: Bang, Molly. *Wiley and the Hairy Man.* Macmillan, 1976. / Bunting, Eve. *Ghost's Hour, Spook's Hour.* Clarion, 1987. / Gackenbach, Dick. *Harry and the Terrible Whatzit.* Clarion, 1977. / Gaiman, Neil. *The Wolves in the Walls.* HarperCollins, 2003. / Hancock, Sibyl. *Esteban and the Ghost.* Dial, 1983. / Krosoczka, Jarrett J. *Annie Was Warned.* Knopf, 2003. / Mayer, Mercer. *Liza Lou and the Yeller Belly Swamp.* Four Winds, 1980. / Park, Barbara. *Psssst! It's Me . . . the Bogeyman.* Atheneum, 1998. / Patschke, Steve. *The Spooky Book.* Walker, 1999. / Sierra, Judy. *Wiley and the Hairy Man.* Dutton, 1996. / Vaughan, Marcia. *Whistling Dixie.* HarperCollins, 1995. / Viorst, Judith. *My Mama Says There Aren't Any Zombies, Ghosts, Vampires, Creatures, Demons, Monsters, Fiends, Goblins, or Things.* Atheneum, 1973. / Williams, Linda. *The Little Old Lady Who Was Not Afraid of Anything.* Crowell, 1986. / Yep, Laurence. *The Man Who Tricked a Ghost.* BridgeWater, 1993.

SUBJECTS: AFRICAN AMERICANS. CHANTABLE REFRAIN. COURAGE. FAMILY LIFE. MONSTERS. MULTICULTURAL BOOKS. OBEDIENCE. SICK. STORIES TO TELL. SUSPENSE.

526   MacLachlan, Patricia, and Emily MacLachlan. *Bittle.* **Illus. by Dan Yaccarino. HarperCollins, 2004. 0-06-000962-4. Unp. Gr. PreK–K**

Though they think they don't need a change in their contented lives, Nigel the cat and Julia the dog grow to love the new baby girl in the household, whom they protect and entertain as she grows, crawls, and, finally, speaks.

GERM: Ask your listeners to make inferences throughout the story and explain how they arrived at their conclusions. For instance, after reading aloud the first page, ask them to identify Nigel and Julia from their descriptions. On the next page, ask them to explain what is going on in the household when the woman brings home tiny clothes and the man paints a small room pale green. By the end of the story, have everyone predict what Bittle's first words will be. Compare and contrast the pets' reactions to the new human babies in their midst in *The Other Dog* by Madeleine L'Engle and *Pushkin Meets the Bundle* by Harriet Ziefert.

RELATED TITLES: Appelt, Kathi. *Bubba and Beau*. Harcourt, 2002. (And others in the Bubba and Beau series.) / Berends, Polly Berrien. *I Heard Said the Bird*. Dial, 1995. / Fleming, Candace. *Smile, Lily!* Atheneum, 2004. / James, Simon. *Baby Brains*. Candlewick, 2004. / Jenkins, Emily. *That New Animal*. Farrar, 2005. / L'Engle, Madeleine. *The Other Dog*. SeaStar, 2001. / Schwartz, Amy. *A Teeny Tiny Baby*. Orchard, 1994. / Wells, Rosemary. *McDuff and the Baby*. Hyperion, 1997. / Willems, Mo. *Knuffle Bunny*. Hyperion, 2004. / Ziefert, Harriet. *Pushkin Meets the Bundle*. Atheneum, 1998.

SUBJECTS: BABIES. CATS. DOGS. LOVE. PETS.

527   **MacLean, Christine Kole.** *Even Firefighters Hug Their Moms.* **Illus. by Mike Reed. Dutton, 2002. 0-525-46996-6. Unp. Gr. PreK–1**

With hats, couch cushions, chairs, and household stuff at his command, a little boy pretends to be a firefighter, police officer, EMT, construction worker, helicopter pilot, train conductor, astronaut, and garbage-truck driver, though his mom would really just like a hug.

GERM: Ask your play experts: What do you pretend and play with your brothers and sisters? What characters do you become when you play?

RELATED TITLES: Browne, Anthony. *Willy the Dreamer*. Candlewick, 1998. / Caseley, Judith. *On the Town: A Community Adventure*. Greenwillow, 2002. / Demarest, Chris L. *Firefighters A to Z*. McElderry, 2000. / McMullan, Kate. *I Stink!* HarperCollins, 2002. / Marzollo, Jean. *Pretend You're a Cat*. Dial, 1990. / Schaefer, Carol Lexa. *The Squiggle*. Crown, 1996. / Slate, Joseph. *Miss Bindergarten Takes a Field Trip with Kindergarten*. Dutton, 2001. / Steen, Sandra, and Susan Steen. *Car Wash*. Putnam, 2001. / Steig, William. *Pete's a Pizza*. HarperCollins, 1998. / Steig, William. *Toby, What Are You?* HarperCollins, 2001. / Steig, William. *Toby, Who Are You?* HarperCollins, 2004.

SUBJECTS: IMAGINATION. MOTHERS AND SONS. OCCUPATIONS. PLAY.

528   **McMullan, Kate.** *I Stink!* **Illus. by Jim McMullan. HarperCollins, 2002. 0-06-029848-0. Unp. Gr. PreK–2**

A no-nonsense, tough-talking, cheerful, grinning, sometimes scowling, New York City garbage truck explains how he scarfs down your bags of trash each night while you sleep, listing an alphabet of the smelly contents of a typical night's haul. Jim McMullan's splendid thick black-outlined watercolors evoke the eau de garbage.

GERM: Machine lovers can brainstorm a list of the machines and vehicles they admire, draw paper-bag puppets of them, and act out a first-person monologue, describing what they do. Think of it: talking airplanes, toasters, canoes—the possibilities are uproarious. Use this when you're teaching kids about recycling and talking about community helpers. Act out the pick up and roll of a garbage truck. You could play a garbage game with kids: I picked up my avocado pit and threw it in the garbage. I picked up my avocado pit and my broken balloon and threw it in the garbage. It's like "I Unpacked My Grandmother's Trunk," only smellier.

RELATED TITLES: Barracca, Debra, and Sal Barracca. *The Adventures of Taxi Dog*. Dial, 1990. / Barton, Byron. *My Car*. Greenwillow, 2001. / Burton, Virginia Lee. *Katy and the Big Snow*. Houghton Mifflin, 1943. / Burton, Virginia Lee. *Mike Mulligan and His Steam Shovel*. Houghton Mifflin, 1939. / Child, Lauren. *That Pesky Rat*. Candlewick, 2002. / Gramatky, Hardie. *Hercules*. Putnam, 1940. / Kirk, Daniel. *Go!* Hyperion, 2001. / Lyon, David. *The Biggest Truck*. Lothrop, 1988. / MacLean, Christine Kole. *Even Firefighters Hug Their Moms*. Dutton, 2002. / McMullan, Kate. *I'm Mighty!* HarperCollins, 2003. / Robbins, Ken. *Bridges*. Dial, 1991. / Shields, Carol Diggory. *Food Fight!* Handprint, 2002. / Sobel, June. *B Is for Bulldozer: A Construction ABC*. Harcourt, 2003. / Zelinsky, Paul O. *The Wheels on the Bus*. Dutton, 1990.

SUBJECTS: ALLITERATION. ALPHABET BOOKS. CREATIVE DRAMA. HUMOROUS FICTION. OCCUPATIONS. PERSONAL NARRATIVES. PERSONIFICATION. REFUSE AND REFUSE DISPOSAL. TRUCKS. VEHICLES.

529   **McMullan, Kate.** *I'm Mighty.* **Illus. by Jim McMullan. HarperCollins, 2003. 0-06-009290-4. Unp. Gr. PreK–2**

Welcome to the harbor where a saucy little tugboat describes how it tows in a tanker, a six-decker ferryboat, and even the *Queen Justine*, a super-duper cruiser.

GERM: Listeners will glory in making all the cool tugboat sound effects. Bring out the toy boats, fill up a wading pool outside, and do some small-scale floating. Bundle this with McMullan's talking garbage truck, *I Stink*.

RELATED TITLES: Burton, Virginia Lee. *Katy and the Big Snow*. Houghton Mifflin, 1943. / Burton, Virginia Lee. *Mike Mulligan and His Steam Shovel*. Houghton Mifflin, 1939. / Crews, Donald. *Sail Away*. Greenwillow, 1995. / Goode, Diane. *Monkey Mo Goes to Sea*. Scholastic, 2002. / Gramatky, Hardie. *Hercules*. Putnam, 1940. / Gramatky, Hardie. *Little Toot*. Putnam, 1967. / Kirk, Daniel. *Go!* Hyperion, 2001. / Lyon, David. *The Biggest Truck*. Lothrop, 1988. / McMullan, Kate. *I Stink!* HarperCollins, 2002. / Robbins, Ken. *Bridges*. Dial, 1991. / Sobel, June. *B Is for Bulldozer: A Construction ABC*. Harcourt, 2003. / Swift, Hildegarde Hoyt. *The Little Red Lighthouse and the Great Gray Bridge*. Harcourt, 2002. / Zelinsky, Paul O. *The Wheels on the Bus*. Dutton, 1990.

SUBJECTS: BOATS AND BOATING. PERSONAL NARRATIVES. PERSONIFICATION. SHIPS. SIZE. TRANSPORTATION. TUGBOATS. VEHICLES.

530 **McMullan, Kate. *Rock-a-Baby Band*. Illus. by Janie Bynum. Little, Brown, 2003. 0-316-60858-0. Unp. Gr. PreK–K**

Ten singing, swinging babies play kitchen percussion with pots and pans in their own band, and they shake it, baby, shake it, as they rock and roll.

GERM: Play the accompanying CD and pull out some percussion instruments for a swinging toddler story hour.

RELATED TITLES: Anholt, Catherine, and Laurence Anholt. *Catherine and Laurence Anholt's Big Book of Little Children*. Candlewick, 2003. / Appelt, Kathi. *Bubba and Beau*. Harcourt, 2002. (And others in the Bubba and Beau series.) / Ashman, Linda. *Babies on the Go*. Harcourt, 2003. / Dodds, Dayle Ann. *Sing, Sophie*. Candlewick, 1997. / Frazee, Marla. *Hush, Little Baby: A Folk Song with Pictures*. Harcourt, 1999. / Meyers, Susan. *Everywhere Babies*. Harcourt, 2001. / Nye, Naomi Shihab. *Baby Radar*. Greenwillow, 2003. / Paxton, Tom. *Where's the Baby?* Morrow, 1993. / Regan, Dian Curtis. *Chance*. Philomel, 2003. / Schwartz, Amy. *A Teeny Tiny Baby*. Orchard, 1994. / Stevenson, James. *Rolling Rose*. Greenwillow, 1992.

SUBJECTS: BABIES. MUSIC. STORIES IN RHYME.

531 **McPhail, David. *Edward and the Pirates*. Illus. by the author. Little, Brown, 1997. 0-316-56344-7. Unp. Gr. PreK–2**

When pirates visit book-loving Edward's bedroom at night, he at first refuses their demand to hand over his library book, a dusty old tome on lost pirate treasure. "It's checked out on my library card," he protests staunchly, though he relents when he realizes the pirates don't know how to read, and reads the book to them.

GERM: Introduce Edward as the boy who overcame his reading problems in *Santa's Book of Names*, and continue his adventures with *Edward in the Jungle*. Meet other book-crazed kids in James Daugherty's classic *Andy and the Lion* and Marilyn Sadler's *Alistair in Outer Space* and encounter more nonreading pirates in Melinda Long's *How I Became a Pirate*.

RELATED TITLES: Child, Lauren. *Who's Afraid of the Big Bad Book?* Hyperion, 2003. / Daugherty, James. *Andy and the Lion*. Viking, 1938. / Drescher, Henrik. *Simon's Book*. Lothrop, 1983. / Garland, Michael. *Miss Smith's Incredible Storybook*. Dutton, 2003. / Helquist, Brett. *Roger the Jolly Pirate*. HarperCollins, 2004. / Huff, Barbara. *Once Inside the Library*. Little, Brown, 1990. / Kellogg, Steven. *A-Hunting We Will Go!* Morrow, 1998. / Long, Melinda. *How I Became a Pirate*. Harcourt, 2003. / McPhail, David. *Edward in the Jungle*. Little, Brown, 2002. / McPhail, David. *Santa's Book of Names*. Little, Brown, 1993. / Marshall, James. *Wings: A Tale of Two Chickens*. Viking, 1986. / Sadler, Marilyn. *Alistair in Outer Space*. Simon & Schuster, 1984. / Sierra, Judy. *Wild About Books*. Knopf, 2004. / Teague, Mark. *Frog Medicine*. Scholastic, 1991.

SUBJECTS: BEDTIME STORIES. BOOKS AND READING. IMAGINATION. LITERACY. PIRATES.

532 **Maloney, Peter, and Felicia Zekauskas. *His Mother's Nose*. Illus. by Peter Maloney and Felicia Zekauskas. Dial, 2001. 0-8037-2545-0. Unp. Gr. PreK–2**

Percival Puddicombe becomes disgruntled with his family, all of whom see something of themselves in him, telling him he has his mother's nose, his father's eyes, his sister's mouth, and his brother's hair. Absconding with each of these features, he runs away to his grandmother's where he discovers there's a little bit of everyone in everybody.

GERM: Talk over: In what ways, physical or behavioral, are you similar to another member of your family? Children can draw self-portrait scenes that incorporate their own special talents and interests.

RELATED TITLES: Cummings, Phil. *Goodness Gracious!* Orchard, 1992. / Shannon, David. *A Bad Case of Stripes*. Blue Sky/Scholastic, 1998.

SUBJECTS: BODY, HUMAN. FAMILY LIFE. HEREDITY. IDENTITY.

533   Mammano, Julie. *Rhinos Who Play Baseball.* **Illus. by the author. Chronicle, 2003. 0-8118-3605-3. Unp. Gr. K–2**

Watch a team of determined blue- and red-uniformed rhinos, surprisingly agile, as they practice slides and throw knuckleballs, take to the field, and face their worthy alligator opponents in a mighty game of baseball. More than 40 baseball terms and slang are incorporated into the action-packed text, as the rhinos keep their eyes on the ball, steal, strike out, get out of a slump, and come through in the bottom of the ninth.

GERM: Each sport and activity has its own special vocabulary. As you read the book aloud, ask your sports fans to define each baseball term or figure out what it means from the context of the text and illustrations. At the back of the book is a glossary of terms. Mammano's rhinos are also proficient at other sports, including soccer, skateboarding, snowboarding, and surfing. Break into small groups to research other sports the rhinos might enjoy and write stories incorporating the accompanying vocabulary and alphabetical glossaries. Play a little ball and use some of your newly acquired baseball vocabulary. See how even a restaurant has its own set of words with Alexandra Day's *Frank and Ernest*, about a bear and an elephant cooking up a storm in their diner.

RELATED TITLES: Day, Alexandra. *Frank and Ernest.* Scholastic, 1988. / Egan, Tim. *Roasted Peanuts.* Houghton Mifflin, 2006. / Elya, Susan Middleton. *Eight Animals Play Ball.* Putnam, 2003. / McCully, Emily Arnold. *Mouse Practice.* Scholastic, 1999. / Mammano, Julie. *Rhinos Who Play Soccer.* Chronicle, 2001. / Mammano, Julie. *Rhinos Who Skateboard.* Chronicle, 1999. / Mammano, Julie. *Rhinos Who Snowboard.* Chronicle, 1997. / Mammano, Julie. *Rhinos Who Surf.* Chronicle, 1996. / Norworth, Jack. *Take Me Out to the Ballgame.* Four Winds, 1993. / Stadler, Alexander. *Beverly Billingsly Can't Catch.* Harcourt, 2004. / Teague, Mark. *The Field Beyond the Outfield.* Scholastic, 1992. / Welch, Willie. *Playing Right Field.* Scholastic, 1995.

SUBJECTS: BASEBALL. RHINOCEROS. SPORTS. VOCABULARY.

534   Manzano, Sonia. *No Dogs Allowed!* **Illus. by Jon J Muth. Atheneum, 2004. 0-689-83088-2. Unp. Gr. K–2**

Heading out at dawn in a caravan of cars for a picnic at Enchanted State Park, the 7-year-old narrator, Iris, and her extended family—including the dog, El Exigente—finally reach their destination after breaking down and getting lost. The sign at the lake says "No Dogs Allowed," so everyone takes turns dog-sitting in the parking lot while they try to figure out what to do.

GERM: Iris's breezy, affectionate narrative, along with the personable watercolors, introduce us to a lovable and quirky cast of family members. Children can draw their own family portraits of an outing they recall, and label each person with a moniker, as Iris does. Writing and drawing prompt: Papi the Clever says, "Only take what you really need to go on a picnic." What would you take on a picnic?

RELATED TITLES: Best, Cari. *When Catherine the Great and I Were Eight!* Farrar, 2003. / Choi, Sook Nyul. *Halmoni and the Picnic.* Houghton, 1993. / Levine, Evan. *Not the Piano, Mrs. Medley!* Orchard, 1991. / Lomas Garza, Carmen. *Family Pictures/Cuadros de Familia.* Children's Book Press, 1990. / Lomas Garza, Carmen. *In My Family/En Mi Familia.* Children's Book Press, 1996. / Medina, Jane. *The Dream on Blanca's Wall: Poems in English and Spanish.* Wordsong/Boyds Mills, 2004. / Root, Phyllis. *Rattletrap Car.* Candlewick, 2001. / Soto, Gary. *Snapshots from the Wedding.* Putnam, 1997. / Soto, Gary. *Too Many Tamales.* Putnam, 1993.

SUBJECTS: AUTOMOBILES. DOGS. FAMILY LIFE. LAKES. MULTICULTURAL BOOKS. PICNICS. PUERTO RICANS.

535   Marcellino, Fred. *I, Crocodile.* **Illus. by the author. HarperCollins, 1999. 0-06-205499-7. Unp. Gr. K–4**

The contented crocodile narrator finds his idyllic life on the Nile shattered when Napoleon has him captured and brought to Paris, where he becomes an overnight sensation. Like any novelty, Parisians and Napoleon grow tired of the attraction and plan to cook him up for supper. How the croc escapes to the sewers of Paris and gets a bit of revenge makes for a sly and hilarious ending.

GERM: Compare this fictional tale with the true account of the first giraffe in France, brought from Egypt a mere 27 years after Napoleon's conquest of 1799, as described in *The Giraffe That Walked to Paris* by Nancy Milton. Use the crocodile's narrative with older students to teach first-person monologue writing and point of view. Students can also research and describe a famous person from the fictionalized point of view of another animal character, while incorporating true details.

RELATED TITLES: Bare, Colleen. *Never Kiss an Alligator*. Dutton, 1989. / Becker, Bonny. *The Christmas Crocodile*. Simon & Schuster, 1998. / Child, Lauren. *That Pesky Rat*. Candlewick, 2002. / Dahl, Roald. *The Enormous Crocodile*. Knopf, 1978. / dePaola, Tomie. *Bill and Pete*. Putnam, 1978. / dePaola, Tomie. *Bill and Pete Go Down the Nile*. Putnam, 1987. / Diakité, Baba Wagué. *The Hunterman and the Crocodile*. Scholastic, 1997. / Fleming, Candace. *Sunny Boy! The Life and Times of a Tortoise*. Farrar, 2005. / Ho, Minfong, and Saphan Ros. *Brother Rabbit: A Cambodian Tale*. Lothrop, 1997. / Kipling, Rudyard. *The Elephant's Child*. Illus. by Lorinda Bryan Cauley. Harcourt, 1983. / Milton, Nancy. *The Giraffe That Walked to Paris*. Crown, 1992. / Thomassie, Tynia. *Feliciana Feydra LeRoux: A Cajun Tall Tale*. Little, Brown, 1995. / Waber, Bernard. Lyle the Crocodile series. Houghton Mifflin. / Wallace, Karen. *Imagine You Are a Crocodile*. Henry Holt, 1997.

SUBJECTS: CROCODILES. EGYPT. EMPERORS. HISTORICAL FICTION. HUMOROUS FICTION. NAPOLEON I, EMPEROR OF THE FRENCH, 1769–1821. PERSONAL NARRATIVES. PICTURE BOOKS FOR ALL AGES. POINT OF VIEW.

536 Markes, Julie. *Shhhhh! Everybody's Sleeping*. **Illus. by David Parkins. HarperCollins, 2005. 0-06-053-791-4. Unp. Gr. PreK–K**

On the first double-page spread of sweetly humorous full-bleed paintings is a nighttime view of all the buildings in town: the library, post office, school, zoo, bakery, police and fire departments, and hospital. Turn each page to zoom in for a look at all the grownups snuggled in their beds, with beatific smiles on their faces, clutching their stuffed animals. In the gently rhyming bedtime poem, the teacher is sleeping in bed in her classroom, of course, and the doctor is slumbering in a hospital bed, clutching a bandaged teddy. We even see the president's four-poster bed, with stars and stripes and eagles on the headboard. Who's still awake? A dark-haired child whose mother bids a loving good night.

GERM: Go back to that first page and have listeners tell you which community helper is sleeping in each building and recall what objects were in or around each bed. What might they be dreaming about? Then have listeners tell or draw what's in their own beds when they go to sleep. Take a daytime visit to all those folks with *Miss Bindergarten Takes a Field Trip with Kindergarten* by Joseph Slate.

RELATED TITLES: Appelt, Kathi. *Bubba and Beau Go Night-Night*. Harcourt, 2003. / Caseley, Judith. *On the Town*. Greenwillow, 2002. / Cook, Sally. *Good Night Pillow Fight*. HarperCollins, 2004. / Frazee, Marla. *Hush, Little Baby: A Folk Song with Pictures*. Harcourt, 1999. / Ho, Minfong. *Hush! A Thai Lullaby*. Orchard, 1996. / MacLean, Christine Kole. *Even Firefighters Hug Their Moms*. Dutton, 2002. / Slate, Joseph. *Miss Bindergarten Takes a Field Trip with Kindergarten*. Dutton, 2001. / Whybrow, Ian. *The Noisy Way to Bed*. Scholastic, 2004. / Yolen, Jane. *How Do Dinosaurs Say Good Night?* Blue Sky/Scholastic, 2000.

SUBJECTS: BEDTIME STORIES. COMMUNITIES. OCCUPATIONS. SLEEP. STORIES IN RHYME.

537 Marshall, James. *George and Martha: The Complete Stories of Two Best Friends*. **Illus. by the author. Houghton Mifflin, 1997. 0-395-85158-0. 340pp. Gr. K–2**

Introduce your readers to all of the classic stories about the unforgettable duo—lovely, lovable hippos and best friends George and Martha—collected here in one large, vibrant volume. My most treasured moments? When George pours Martha's split pea soup into his loafers. When George peeks on Martha in the bath. And, of course, that devastating chapter in which George trips while roller skating and knocks out his favorite one of his two teeth.

GERM: Ask your listeners what their best George and Martha moments are. Write and illustrate new stories about them.

RELATED TITLES: Allard, Harry. *Miss Nelson Is Missing*. Houghton Mifflin, 1977. (And others in the Miss Nelson series.) / Howe, James. *Horace and Morris But Mostly Dolores*. Atheneum, 1999. / Lobel, Arnold. *Frog and Toad Are Friends*. HarperCollins, 1970. (And others in the Frog and Toad series.) / Marshall, James. *The Cut-Ups*. Viking, 1984. (And others in the Cut-Ups series.) / Marshall, James. *Fox and His Friends*. Dial, 1982. (And others in the Fox series.) / Marshall, James. *Rats on the Roof and Other Stories*. Dial, 1991. / Marshall, James. *The Three Little Pigs*. Dial, 1989. / Martin, Bill, Jr. *The Happy Hippopotami*. Harcourt, 1991. / Rylant, Cynthia. *Poppleton*. Scholastic, 1997. (And others in the Poppleton series.) / Stevenson, James. *The Mud Flat Mystery*. Greenwillow, 1997. (And others in the Mud Flat series.) / Van Leeuwen, Jean. *Amanda Pig and Her Big Brother Oliver*. Dial, 1982. (And others in the Oliver and Amanda series.) / Waber, Bernard. *Evie and Margie*. Houghton Mifflin, 2003.

SUBJECTS: BEST FRIENDS. FRIENDSHIP. HIPPOPOTAMUS. HUMOROUS FICTION. PICTURE BOOKS FOR ALL AGES.

538   Marshall, James. *Swine Lake.* **Illus. by Maurice Sendak. HarperCollins, 1999. 0-06-205171-7. Unp. Gr. 1–4**

Finding himself in an unfamiliar part of town, a mangy wolf is drawn by the unmistakable aroma of pig to a theater where Swine Lake is being performed by the Boarshoi Ballet. Unexpectedly enraptured by the ballet, the wolf staggers out of the theater and back to his bare attic room, where he breaks into his piggy bank and spends every last penny on a seat for the evening performance. Sendak's bustling illustrations are a fitting tribute to his late friend and colleague James Marshall, whose many books, including the George and Martha series and the Cut-Ups series, remain favorites of children.

GERM: Ask your listeners if they can fathom why the wolf jumps onstage, dances with the pigs, and runs home. Introduce them to the word "stagestruck" and see if they can execute a few of their own "flashy dance steps" for the group to try.

RELATED TITLES: Allard, Harry. *It's So Nice to Have a Wolf Around the House.* Houghton Mifflin, 1978. / Auch, Mary Jane. *Hen Lake.* Holiday House, 1995. / Auch, Mary Jane. *Peeping Beauty.* Holiday House, 1993. / Edwards, Pamela Duncan. *Honk! The Story of a Prima Swanerina.* Hyperion, 1998. / Ernst, Lisa Campbell. *When Bluebell Sang.* Bradbury, 1989. / Marshall, James. *The Cut-Ups.* Viking, 1984. (And others in the Cut-Ups series.) / Marshall, James. *George and Martha: The Complete Stories of Two Best Friends.* Houghton Mifflin, 1997. / Marshall, James. *Rats on the Roof and Other Stories.* Dial, 1991. / Marshall, James. *The Three Little Pigs.* Dial, 1989. / Scieszka, Jon. *The True Story of the 3 Little Pigs.* Viking Kestrel, 1989.

SUBJECTS: BALLET. HUMOROUS FICTION. PIGS. WOLVES.

539   Martin, Ann M. *Leo the Magnificat.* **Illus. by Emily Arnold McCully. Scholastic, 1996. 0-590-48498-2. Unp. Gr. K–2**

Wandering into the churchyard, a fat and handsome black and white cat becomes a vital part of the church community, never missing a meal or a service. Based on the story of an actual church cat from Louisville, Kentucky, this heart-warming and affectionate portrayal will get children describing inspirational pets they have known.

GERM: Another amazing but true cat story is Carol Anne Timmel's *Tabitha: The Fabulous Feline,* her account of how her pet became lost in the belly of a 747 jet for 13 days. Both stories are illustrated, with a photo of the real cat at the back. This would be a good jumping-off point for an exploration of the differences between realistic fiction and fantasy. Read aloud or booktalk a variety of pet stories and discuss which are entirely true-to-life and which employ talking animals or fantastical powers.

RELATED TITLES: Perkins, Lynne Rae. *The Broken Cat.* Greenwillow, 2002. / Schachner, Judith Byron. *The Grannyman.* Dutton, 1999. / Timmel, Carol Ann. *Tabitha: The Fabulous Flying Feline.* Walker, 1996.

SUBJECTS: CATS. CHURCHES. PICTURE BOOKS FOR ALL AGES.

540   Martin, Bill, Jr. *Panda Bear, Panda Bear, What Do You See?* **Illus. by Eric Carle. Henry Holt, 2003. 0-8050-1758-5. Unp. Gr. PreK–1**

In this endangered-species companion to the now-classic *Brown Bear, Brown Bear, What Do You See* and *Polar Bear, Polar Bear, What Do You Hear?* we meet up with ten animals—including a spider monkey, a bald eagle, and a sea lion—who would like to be wild and free.

GERM: Your group will eagerly participate in the call-and-response, question-and-answer chant of the text. Note the use of strong verbs—soaring, charging, sneaking. When children write and illustrate new versions of the story, selecting other endangered animals, they can employ and share equally strong and descriptive language.

RELATED TITLES: Allen, Judy. *Panda.* Candlewick, 1993. / Cowley, Joy. *Red-Eyed Tree Frog.* Scholastic, 1999. / Johnston, Ginny, and Cutchins, Judy. *Andy Bear: A Polar Cub Grows Up at the Zoo.* Morrow, 1985. / Koch, Michelle. *World Water Watch.* Greenwillow, 1993. / Leedy, Loreen. *Tracks in the Sand.* Doubleday, 1993. / Martin, Bill, Jr. *Brown Bear, Brown Bear, What Do You See?* Henry Holt, 1983. / Martin, Bill, Jr. *Polar Bear, Polar Bear, What Do You Hear?* Henry Holt, 1991. / Rogers, Sally. *Earthsong.* Dutton, 1998. / Ryder, Joanne. *Little Panda: The World Welcomes Hua Mei at the San Diego Zoo.* Simon & Schuster, 2001. / Sobol, Richard. *An Elephant in the Backyard.* Dutton, 2004.

SUBJECTS: ANIMALS. CALL-AND-RESPONSE STORIES. ENDANGERED SPECIES. ENGLISH LANGUAGE—VERBS. STORIES IN RHYME.

541   Martin, Bill, Jr., and Steven Kellogg. *A Beasty Story.* **Illus. by Steven Kellogg. Harcourt, 1999. 0-15-201683-X. Unp. Gr. PreK–1**

Four brave mice track down a scary creature in a dark, dark wood and follow it to a dark, brown house, down a dark, red stair, and into a dark, blue cellar. Examine the endpapers, as that's where Kellogg starts the story.

GERM: You'll need to read this again so watchful viewers can figure out how mice Nick and Hank were able to scare us with their balloon trick. Other versions of the "dark, dark" chant include *A Dark, Dark Tale* by Ruth Brown and *In a Dark, Dark Wood* by David A. Carter.

RELATED TITLES: Aylesworth, Jim. *Two Terrible Frights*. Atheneum, 1987. / Brown, Ruth. *A Dark, Dark Tale*. Dial, 1981. / Calmenson, Stephanie. *The Teeny Tiny Teacher*. Scholastic, 1998. / Carter, David A. *In a Dark, Dark Wood*. Little Simon, 2002. / Edwards, Pamela Duncan. *Livingstone Mouse*. HarperCollins, 1996. / Galdone, Paul. *The Teeny-Tiny Woman*. Clarion, 1984. / Krosoczka, Jarrett J. *Annie Was Warned*. Knopf, 2003. / McBratney, Sam. *The Dark at the Top of the Stairs*. Candlewick, 1996. / Schwartz, Alvin. *Ghosts! Ghostly Tales from Folklore*. HarperCollins, 1991. / Schwartz, Alvin. *In a Dark, Dark Room and Other Scary Stories*. HarperCollins, 1984. / Thiesing, Lisa. *The Aliens Are Coming!* Dutton, 2003. / Thiesing, Lisa. *The Viper*. Dutton, 2002. / Williams, Linda. *The Little Old Lady Who Was Not Afraid of Anything*. Crowell, 1986. / Winters, Kay. *The Teeny Tiny Ghost*. HarperCollins, 1997.

SUBJECTS: COLOR. FEAR. MICE. STORIES IN RHYME. SUSPENSE.

542   **Martin, David. *Five Little Piggies*. Illus. by Susan Meddaugh. Candlewick, 1998. 1-56402-918-2. Unp. Gr. PreK–1**

Here are five short, sweet stories that explain why the piggies went to market, stayed home, had roast beef, had none, and went wee wee wee all the way home.

GERM: Don't take it for granted that all of your children have been exposed to nursery rhymes. Bring out your Mother Goose collections and welcome the excuse to introduce and review those rhymes that provide children with their first glimpse of the English language at play. For older children, use this as a simple introduction to parody. Classroom storytellers will want to search the Mother Goose books for other nursery rhymes they can flesh out more thoroughly in prose story format.

RELATED TITLES: Allen, Kathryn Madeline. *This Little Piggy's Book of Manners*. Henry Holt, 2003. / Aylesworth, Jim. *Aunt Pitty Patty's Piggy*. Scholastic, 1999. / Ernst, Lisa Campbell. *Little Red Riding Hood: A Newfangled Prairie Tale*. Simon & Schuster, 1995. / Meddaugh, Susan. *Hog-Eye*. Houghton Mifflin, 1995. / Palatini, Margie. *Piggie Pie*. Clarion, 1995. / Pomerantz, Charlotte. *The Piggy in the Puddle*. Macmillan, 1974. / Robb, Laura. *Snuffles and Snouts*. Dial, 1995. / Stevens, Janet, and Susan Stevens Crummel. *And the Dish Ran Away with the Spoon*. Harcourt, 2001. / Tollhurst, Marilyn. *Somebody and the Three Blairs*. Orchard, 1991. / Trivizas, Eugene. *The Three Little Wolves and the Big Bad Pig*. McElderry, 1993. / Wiesner, David. *The Three Pigs*. Clarion, 2001. / Wolff, Ashley. *Stella and Roy*. Dutton, 1993. / Wood, Audrey. *Piggies*. Harcourt, 1991.

SUBJECTS: CHARACTERS IN LITERATURE. NURSERY RHYMES. PARODIES. PIGS.

543   **Martin, Rafe. *The Storytelling Princess*. Illus. by Kimberly Bulcken Root. Putnam, 2001. 0-399-22924-8. Unp. Gr. 1–4**

When his father, the king, tells him about the perfect princess he has chosen for the young man's bride, the well-read prince insists he will only marry her if someone can tell him a story whose ending he does not know. Far away, across the ocean, a princess rejects her father's choice of the perfect prince, telling him she'd rather be washed overboard in a storm at sea. How the two meet and fall in love is a delightful tale of coincidences and the power of storytelling.

GERM: Have listeners make a story map and chart how the lives of both the prince and the princess come to overlap. Ask: Was it coincidence or destiny that brought them together? For another appealing literary folktale about love and a princess, follow up with *Fortune* by Diane Stanley.

RELATED TITLES: Behan, Brendan. *The King of Ireland's Son*. Orchard, 1997. / Stanley, Diane. *Fortune*. Morrow, 1989. / Sunami, Kitoba. *How the Fisherman Tricked the Genie: A Tale Within a Tale Within a Tale*. Atheneum, 2002. / Talbott, Hudson. *O'Sullivan Stew*. Putnam, 1999.

SUBJECTS: COINCIDENCE. KINGS AND RULERS. LITERARY FAIRY TALES. PRINCES AND PRINCESSES. STORYTELLING.

544   **Marx, Patricia. *Meet My Staff*. Illus. by Roz Chast. HarperCollins, 1998. 0-06-027484-0. Unp. Gr. 1–4**

Meet Walter, an average kid, who introduces us to the many helpful folks who make up his daily staff. There's Monsieur Monsieur, Walter's Personal Letter Writer; a Room Crew to fix his toys; a Homework Helper; Admiral B., who takes Walter's baths for him when he's not in the mood; and the members of the Dream Team, who sleep for him.

GERM: Ask your students to think about new staff members they wish they could bring to school. They can write a sentence or two detailing each one's job responsibilities and draw a portrait of the helper in action. Each can then present the staff members to the rest of the group. Don't forget to think of your own dream helpers: the Plan Book Writer or the Bulletin Board Changer, for example.

RELATED TITLES: Clement, Rod. *Just Another Ordinary Day.* HarperCollins, 1997. / Joyce, William. *A Day with Wilbur Robinson.* HarperCollins, 1993. / Kraft, Erik. *Chocolatina.* BridgeWater, 1998. / Legge, David. *Bamboozled.* Scholastic, 1995. / Palatini, Margie. *Zak's Lunch.* Clarion, 1998. / Reiss, Mike. *The Great Show-and-Tell Disaster.* Price Stern Sloan, 2001. / Santat, Dan. *The Guild of Geniuses.* Scholastic, 2004. / Seuss, Dr., and Jack Prelutsky. *Hooray for Diffendoofer Day.* Knopf, 1998. / Shannon, David. *A Bad Case of Stripes.* Scholastic, 1998. / Stevenson, James. *Brrr!* Greenwillow, 1991. / Weisner, David. *June 29, 1999.* Clarion, 1992. / Wood, Audrey. *The Flying Dragon Room.* Scholastic, 1996. / Yaccarino, Dan. *If I Had a Robot.* Viking, 1996.

SUBJECTS: HUMOROUS FICTION. IMAGINATION. PICTURE BOOKS FOR ALL AGES.

545   Marzollo, Jean. *I Love You: A Rebus Poem.* **Illus. by Suse MacDonald. Scholastic, 1999. 0-590-37656-X. Unp. Gr. PreK–K**

"Every bird loves a tree, every flower loves a bee, every lock loves a key, and I love you." All of the nouns in this book's simple, rhyming text are replaced with pictures and are accompanied by sunny watercolors of happy-looking critters and folks. So, as you read it aloud, even the youngest listeners will be able to read the rebus pictures and fill in all the jolly rhymes.

GERM: This one will be chanted, memorized, and—if you're handy with tunes and can think one up—sung. For starters, try "London Bridge Is Falling Down" or "Pop Goes the Weasel."

RELATED TITLES: Carter, David A. *If You're Happy and You Know It, Clap Your Hands!* Scholastic, 1997. / Ehlert, Lois. *Color Zoo.* HarperCollins, 1989. / Ehlert, Lois. *In My World.* Harcourt, 2002. / Tafuri, Nancy. *Snowy Flowy Blowy: A Twelve Months Rhyme.* Scholastic, 1999.

SUBJECTS: LOVE. REBUSES. STORIES IN RHYME.

546   Massie, Diane Redfield. *The Baby Beebee Bird.* **Illus. by Steven Kellogg. HarperCollins, 2000. 0-06-028083-2. Unp. Gr. PreK–K**

After a day of roaring, growling, hissing, and meowing, the tired zoo animals have just fallen asleep when . . . "Beebeebobbibobbi beebeebobbiboobi." What is THAT? It's the new baby beebee bird, and though the giraffe asks him to be quiet, the cheeky little chirper sings all night long, keeping everyone up.

GERM: It's a perfect story for telling, retelling, acting out, and joining in on the relentless refrain. Midway through, ask your listeners to break into small groups of animals and try to work out a plan to stop the beebee bird from chirping. Each group can then share its strategies with the rest of the class.

RELATED TITLES: Cole, Joanna. *It's Too Noisy!* Crowell, 1989. / De Regniers, Beatrice Schenk. *May I Bring a Friend?* Atheneum, 1964. / Fleming, Denise. *Time to Sleep.* Henry Holt, 1997. / Garland, Michael. *Last Night at the Zoo.* Boyds Mills, 2001. / Gelman, Rita Golden. *I Went to the Zoo.* Scholastic, 1993. / Kellogg, Steven. *A-Hunting We Will Go!* Morrow, 1998. / Murphy, Jill. *Peace at Last.* Dial, 1980. / Paxton, Tom. *Going to the Zoo.* Morrow, 1996. / Rathmann, Peggy. *Good Night, Gorilla.* Putnam, 1994. / Waber, Bernard. *Bearsie Bear and the Surprise Sleepover Party.* Houghton Mifflin, 1997.

SUBJECTS: ANIMAL SOUNDS. ANIMALS. BIRDS. CHANTABLE REFRAIN. SLEEP. STORIES TO TELL. ZOOS.

547   Mathers, Petra. *A Cake for Herbie.* **Illus. by the author. Simon & Schuster, 2000. 0-689-83017-3. Unp. Gr. PreK–2**

Herbie the duck enters a poetry contest, writing a poem about food for each letter of the alphabet, calling it "From Herbie's Kitchen, A–Z." At the contest, he starts with A: "Artie chews, Artie swallows, Artichokes." When the audience heckles him, he flees. Lucky for Herbie, he's discovered by a mouse, a cook at the Ship's Inn, who brings him into the kitchen, where they appreciate good food poetry and fete him with a cake.

GERM: The adorable watercolors will make Herbie your pal too. Have your kids recite Herbie's poems and then make up new ones about what they're planning to eat (or would like to eat) for lunch. Children can bring in and display the food inspired by their poems while they recite their short verses. Pal around with Herbie and his chicken friend, Lottie, in *Lottie's New Beach Towel* and *Lottie's New Friend.*

RELATED TITLES: Auch, Mary Jane. *Peeping Beauty.* Holiday House, 1993. / Bell, Cece. *Sock Monkey Goes to Hollywood: A Star Is Bathed.* Candlewick, 2003. / Dodds, Dayle Ann. *Sing, Sophie.* Candlewick, 1997. / Elya, Susan Middleton. *Eight Animals Bake a Cake.* Putnam, 2002. / Ernst, Lisa Campbell. *When Bluebell Sang.* Bradbury, 1989. / Goss, Linda. *The Frog Who Wanted to Be a Singer.* Orchard, 1996. / Graham, Bob. *Benny: An Adventure Story.* Candlewick, 1999. / Hurd, Thacher. *Art Dog.* HarperCollins, 1996. / Kalman, Maira. *Max Makes a Million.* Viking, 1990. / Lionni, Leo. *Frederick.* Pantheon, 1967. / Mathers, Petra. *Lottie's New Beach Towel.* Putnam, 1998. / Mathers, Petra. *Lottie's New Friend.* Putnam, 1999.

SUBJECTS: ANIMALS. CONTESTS. DUCKS. FOOD. POETRY.

548   Meade, Holly. *Inside, Inside, Inside.* **Illus. by the author. Marshall Cavendish, 2005. 0-7614-5125-0. Unp. Gr. PreK–1**

Early one morning, when Jenny finds her brother Noah's blue marble, he starts a game he calls Inside, Inside, Inside. He puts the marble in the salt shaker, which he then tucks in the cereal box, which goes in Mom's recipe box, which he puts in Jenny's hat, which goes in the waste basket, which Jenny puts in her pillowcase, and then in dad's jacket, in the hamper, and finally, they both put the hamper in the bathtub. Told entirely in dialogue between the two kids—Jenny's words are printed in green, Noah's in blue—and in appealing collage illustrations made from cut paper and watercolor, this child-centered story was inspired by the author's own children, Jenny and Noah, who played the Inside game. Compare Meade's illustrations of them with their color photo on the last page.

GERM: Listeners will be beguiled by the idea of nesting objects, like matrioshka, or nesting dolls. Using items in your room, have them work in small groups to put together their own Inside, Inside, Inside, as a way of estimating size and volume. They can unwrap their items for the group to see, or draw the objects, as Jenny and Noah do. Noah continues his drawing, showing their house inside the neighborhood, town, state, country, continent, world, and solar system. Like Lynne Cherry's *The Armadillo from Amarillo* and Anne Mazer's *The Yellow Button,* the book provides a view of small to large, starting with our homes and continuing outward to the vastness of space. To get a sense of how big the world gets, share Robert E. Wells's nonfiction picture book *Is a Blue Whale the Biggest Thing There Is?*

RELATED TITLES: Cherry, Lynne. *The Armadillo from Amarillo.* Harcourt, 1994. / Leedy, Loreen. *Mapping Penny's World.* Henry Holt, 2000. / Mazer, Anne. *The Yellow Button.* Knopf, 1990. / Meade, Holly. *John Willy and Freddy McGee.* Cavendish, 1998. / Wells, Robert E. *Is a Blue Whale the Biggest Thing There Is?* Albert Whitman, 1993.

SUBJECTS: BROTHERS AND SISTERS. EARTH. GAMES. MAPS AND GLOBES. SIZE.

549   Meade, Holly. *John Willy and Freddy McGee.* **Illus. by the author. Marshall Cavendish, 1998. 0-7614-5033-5. Unp. Gr. PreK–1**

The cat's the bad guy in this sure-to-be-a-favorite storytime adventure, tailing two adorable, poker-faced guinea pigs as they escape from their cage, scuddle across the floor, and end up scooting through the tunnel in the family pool table.

GERM: Looking for a story that uses directional words or prepositions—beneath, over, under, and through? As you read, viewers can describe where the pets are on each page (on the rug, under the table). Ask them to predict what the two guinea pigs will do when they get back to their cages.

RELATED TITLES: Bare, Colleen. *Guinea Pigs Don't Read Books.* Putnam, 1985. / Child, Lauren. *Clarice Bean, Guess Who's Babysitting?* Candlewick, 2001. / Duke, Kate. *Guinea Pigs Near and Far.* Dutton, 1984. / Duke, Kate. *One Guinea Pig Is Not Enough.* Dutton, 1998. / Edwards, Pamela Duncan. *Livingstone Mouse.* HarperCollins, 1996. / George, Lindsay Barrett. *Inside Mouse, Outside Mouse.* HarperCollins, 2004. / Kroll, Steven. *Patches Lost and Found.* Winslow, 2001. / McMillan, Bruce. *Mouse Views: What the Class Pet Saw.* Holiday House, 1993. / Meade, Holly. *Inside, Inside, Inside.* Marshall Cavendish, 2005. / Roche, Denis. *The Best Class Picture Ever.* Scholastic, 2003. / Roth, Susan L. *Cinnamon's Day Out.* Dial, 1998. / Yang, James. *Joey and Jet.* Atheneum, 2004.

SUBJECTS: ENGLISH LANGUAGE—PREPOSITIONS. GUINEA PIGS.

550   Meddaugh, Susan. *Hog-Eye.* **Illus. by the author. Houghton Mifflin, 1995. 0-395-74276-5. Unp. Gr. K–2**

A young pig regales her horrified parents and siblings with her melodramatic saga of being captured by a soup-hungry but illiterate wolf, whom she outwits with the help of a patch of poison ivy.

GERM: In Tony Blundell's *Beware of Boys*, a boy flummoxes another gluttonous wolf; in Patricia McKissack's *Flossie and the Fox*, the cunning Flossie outwits a fox. Compare with Gail Gibbons's *Wolves* for some facts.

RELATED TITLES: Blundell, Tony. *Beware of Boys.* Greenwillow, 1992. / Donaldson, Julia. *The Gruffalo.* Dial, 1999. / Emberley, Michael. *Ruby.* Little, Brown, 1990. / Gibbons, Gail. *Wolves.* Holiday House, 1994. / Lester, Helen. *Listen, Buddy.* Houghton Mifflin, 1995. / MacDonald, Margaret Read. *Mabela the Clever.* Albert Whitman, 2001. / McKissack, Patricia C. *Flossie and the Fox.* Dial, 1986. / Mayer, Mercer. *Liza Lou and the Yeller Belly Swamp.* Four Winds, 1980. / Meddaugh, Susan. *Martha Speaks.* Houghton Mifflin, 1992. (And others in the Martha series.) / Sierra, Judy. *Wiley and the Hairy Man.* Dutton, 1996. / Silverman, Erica. *Don't Fidget a Feather!* Macmillan, 1994.

SUBJECTS: BOOKS AND READING. HUMOROUS FICTION. PERSONAL NARRATIVES. PIGS. POISON IVY. STORYTELLING. WOLVES.

551   Meddaugh, Susan. *Martha Blah Blah.* **Illus. by the author. Houghton Mifflin, 1996. 0-395-79755-1. Unp. Gr. K–4**

Personable yellow dog Martha, whose daily bowl of Granny's Alphabet Soup enables her to talk, loses her ability to speak clearly when the new owner of the soup company decides to halve the amount of letters in each can.

GERM: Along with starting a discussion on corporate responsibility to consumers, have children compose and share sentences of words using just the 13 letters still available to Martha.

RELATED TITLES: Buehner, Caralyn. *Superdog: The Heart of a Hero.* HarperCollins, 2004. / Edwards, Pamela Duncan. *Muldoon.* Hyperion, 2002. / Kirk, Daniel. *Dogs Rule!* Hyperion, 2003. / Laden, Nina. *Bad Dog.* Walker, 2000. / Laden, Nina. *The Night I Followed the Dog.* Chronicle, 1994. / Lebentritt, Julia, and Richard Ploetz. *The Kooken.* Holt, 1992. / Meddaugh, Susan. *Martha Speaks.* Houghton Mifflin, 1992. (And others in the Martha series.) / Meddaugh, Susan. *The Witch's Walking Stick.* Houghton Mifflin, 2005. / Rathmann, Peggy. *Officer Buckle and Gloria.* Putnam, 1995. / Rosen, Michael. *Rover.* Doubleday, 1999. / Teague, Mark. *Detective LaRue: Letters from the Investigation.* Scholastic, 2004.

SUBJECTS: DOGS. HUMOROUS FICTION. PICTURE BOOKS FOR ALL AGES. SOUP.

552   Meddaugh, Susan. *Martha Walks the Dog.* **Illus. by the author. Houghton Mifflin, 1998. 0-395-90494-3. Unp. Gr. K–4**

Martha—that genial, alphabet soup-drinking, verbal yellow dog we've gotten to know and love from *Martha Speaks* and other tales—encounters the ferocious Bad Dog Bob, who is new to the neighborhood. When Martha confronts Bob, calling him a big bully, a ruffian, a thug, and even a meanie, the unrepentant dog comes after her, only to be stopped in his tracks by the words of a neighboring parrot. "Good dog," the parrot says, and, wonder of wonders, Bob stops growling and begins to smile.

GERM: "Words are such fun," thinks Martha, though she learns that praise and positive reinforcement work far better than disparaging words. Have listeners retell the story from Bad Dog Bob's point of view. Compile a list of words we like to hear and ones we'd rather not. Talk about that childhood saying: Sticks and stones can break my bones, but words can never hurt me. Is this true? Martha's ebullient personality shines through each book. Ask your students to draw a picture of her, captioned with what they think one of her rules of behavior might be.

RELATED TITLES: Buehner, Caralyn. *Superdog: The Heart of a Hero.* HarperCollins, 2004. / Laden, Nina. *Bad Dog.* Walker, 2000. / Laden, Nina. *The Night I Followed the Dog.* Chronicle, 1994. / L'Engle, Madeleine. *The Other Dog.* SeaStar, 2001. / Meddaugh, Susan. *Martha Blah Blah.* Houghton Mifflin, 1996. / Meddaugh, Susan. *Martha Speaks.* Houghton Mifflin, 1992. (And others in the Martha series.) / Meddaugh, Susan. *The Witch's Walking Stick.* Houghton Mifflin, 2005. / Miller, Sara Swan. *Three Stories You Can Read to Your Dog.* Houghton Mifflin, 1995. (And others in the Three Stories series.) / Pilkey, Dav. *The Hallo-Wiener.* Scholastic, 1995. / Rathmann, Peggy. *Officer Buckle and Gloria.* Putnam, 1995.

SUBJECTS: BEHAVIOR. BULLIES. DOGS. HUMOROUS FICTION. KINDNESS. PICTURE BOOKS FOR ALL AGES. SPEECH.

553   Meddaugh, Susan. *Perfectly Martha.* **Illus. by the author. Houghton Mifflin, 2004. 0-618-37857-X. Unp. Gr. K–4**

Martha the talking dog sniffs out the truth about charlatan Otis Weaselgraft, of the Perfect Pup

Institute, and his three-step training program that guarantees pet owners perfectly trained dogs in just one day.

GERM: Have your dog lovers consider: What are the qualities you want in your perfect pet? Draw and describe the pet of your dreams.

RELATED TITLES: Buehner, Caralyn. *Superdog: The Heart of a Hero.* HarperCollins, 2004. / Graham, Bob. *Max.* Candlewick, 2000. / Kellogg, Steven. *Pinkerton, Behave.* Dial, 1979. / L'Engle, Madeleine. *The Other Dog.* SeaStar, 2001. / MacDonald, Ross. *Another Perfect Day.* Roaring Brook, 2002. / Meddaugh, Susan. *Martha Walks the Dog.* Houghton Mifflin, 1998. (And others in the Martha series.) / Pinkney, Brian. *The Adventures of Sparrowboy.* Simon & Schuster, 1997. / Rathmann, Peggy. *Officer Buckle and Gloria.* Putnam, 1995. / Teague, Mark. *Dear Mrs. LaRue: Letters from Obedience School.* Scholastic, 2002. / Teague, Mark. *Detective LaRue: Letters from the Investigation.* Scholastic, 2004. / Wells, Rosemary. *McDuff Goes to School.* Hyperion, 2001. / Woodruff, Elvira. *Show and Tell.* Holiday House, 1991.

SUBJECTS: DOGS. HUMOROUS FICTION. OBEDIENCE.

554 **Meddaugh, Susan.** *The Witch's Walking Stick.* **Illus. by the author. Houghton Mifflin, 2005. 0-618-52948-9. Unp. Gr. PreK–3**

On a walk in the woods, an old witch is thinking about using her magic walking stick to turn a stray dog into a cat, when the dog grabs the stick and runs off. Meanwhile, on the other side of the forest, young Margaret is having a bad day, doing all the work for her selfish and mean big brother and sister. She runs into the forest, where she meets the witch, who promises to reward her if she can get that stick back. How Margaret and the dog meet up, make some satisfying wishes with the stick, teach Margaret's siblings a lesson or two, and thwart the witch make for a relishable tale.

GERM: Folks who already know and love Meddaugh's books about that talking dog Martha will welcome another smart dog and recall that Martha once met up with witches in *The Witches' Supermarket*. Note that Margaret's wishes were small but satisfying. Why didn't she wish for more? In terms of wishing and getting just deserts, ask your crew to write and draw the cause and effect of a wish they might make on the witch's walking stick.

RELATED TITLES: Egan, Tim. *Burnt Toast on Davenport Street.* Houghton Mifflin, 1997. / Kimmel, Eric A. *Anansi and the Magic Stick.* Holiday House, 2001. / Kraft, Erik. *Chocolatina.* BridgeWater, 1998. / McClintock, Barbara. *Molly and the Magic Wishbone.* Farrar, 2001. / Meddaugh, Susan. *Martha Speaks.* Houghton Mifflin, 1992. (And others in the Martha series.) / Meddaugh, Susan. *The Witches' Supermarket.* Houghton Mifflin, 1991.

SUBJECTS: BEHAVIOR. BROTHERS AND SISTERS. MAGIC. WISHES. WITCHES.

555 **Medearis, Angela Shelf.** *Seven Spools of Thread: A Kwanzaa Story.* **Illus. by Daniel Minter. Albert Whitman, 2000. 0-8075-7315-9. Unp. Gr. K–4**

In this pourquoi tale that reads like an African folktale but was written by the author especially for Kwanzaa, we learn how multicolored Kente cloth came to be. An old man in Ghana is disappointed in his seven quarreling sons. After he dies, the village chief tells the sons that all their father's property and possessions will be divided equally, but only if they learn how to make gold out of spools of silk thread. For the first time ever, they work together and come up with a plan, weaving the seven spools of thread together to create a special cloth of many colors.

GERM: Boldly lined and colored linoleum block prints give the story heft and authority, and the simple instructions at the back of the book for weaving a colorful belt out of yarn will be easy to follow. Discussion point: Stop midway in the story and have children write down how they think the brothers can make gold out of the spools of silk thread. Share their responses. Also ask them to explain the African proverb quoted on the first page: "Sticks in a bundle are unbreakable."

RELATED TITLES: Aardema, Verna. *Koi and the Kola Nuts.* Atheneum, 1999. / Aardema, Verna. *Misoso: Once Upon a Time Tales from Africa.* Knopf, 1994. / Chocolate, Deborah. *Kente Colors.* Walker, 1997. / Courlander, Harold. *The Cow-Tail Switch and Other West African Stories.* Henry Holt, 1988. / Day, Nancy Raines. *The Lion's Whiskers: An Ethiopian Folktale.* Scholastic, 1995. / Kurtz, Jane. *Fire on the Mountain.* Simon & Schuster, 1994. / Musgrove, Margaret. *The Spider Weaver: A Legend of Kente Cloth.* Scholastic, 2001. / Onyefulu, Obi. *Chinye: A West African Folk Tale.* Viking, 1994. / Steptoe, John. *Mufaro's Beautiful Daughters: An African Tale.* Lothrop, 1987.

SUBJECTS: BROTHERS. CLOTH. CONDUCT OF LIFE. COOPERATION. DEATH. FATHERS AND SONS. GHANA. KWANZAA. MULTICULTURAL BOOKS. STORIES TO TELL. WEAVING.

556   Melmed, Laura Krauss. *Little Oh.* **Illus. by Jim LaMarche. Lothrop, 1997. 0-688-14209-5. Unp. Gr. 1–4**

As they sit on their floor mats folding origami animals, a boy's mother tells him the story of a woman who made a little paper girl in a pink kimono, who became her beloved paper child. Delicate and soulful acrylic and colored-pencil illustrations accompany this Japanese Thumbelina-like tale, which follows the journey of resilient Little Oh, who blows away from her mother and is rescued by a crane.

GERM: Pair this with other tiny child stories, such as Hans Christian Andersen's *Thumbelina*, Barbara Brenner's Japanese folktale *Little One Inch*, and Elisa Kleven's *The Paper Princess*. Make origami figures and create stories about them.

RELATED TITLES: Andersen, Hans Christian. *Thumbelina.* Retold by Amy Ehrlich. Illus. by Susan Jeffers. Dial, 1979. / Andersen, Hans Christian. *Thumbelina.* Retold and illus. by Lauren Mills. Little, Brown, 2005. / Bertrand, Lynne. *Granite Baby.* Farrar, 2005. / Brenner, Barbara. *Little One Inch.* Coward, 1977. / Erdrich, Louise. *Grandmother's Pigeon.* Candlewick, 2003. / George, Kristine O'Connell. *Fold Me a Poem.* Harcourt, 2005. / Hughes, Monica. *Little Fingerling.* Ideals, 1992. / Kleven, Elisa. *The Paper Princess.* Dutton, 1994. / LaMarche, Jim. *The Raft.* HarperCollins, 2000. / Mayer, Marianna. *The Adventures of Tom Thumb.* SeaStar, 2001. / Melmed, Laura Krauss. *The Rainbabies.* Lothrop, 1992. / Say, Allen. *Tree of Cranes.* Houghton Mifflin, 1991. / Shute, Linda. *Momotaro the Peach Boy.* Lothrop, 1986.

SUBJECTS: BIRDS. CRANES. FAMILY LIFE. JAPAN. LOVE. MOTHERS. MULTICULTURAL BOOKS. ORIGAMI. TRANSFORMATIONS.

557   Meyers, Susan. *Everywhere Babies.* **Illus. by Marla Frazee. Harcourt, 2001. 0-15-202226-0. Unp. Gr. PreK–1**

In a rhyming tribute to the adorableness of babies, see how they are loved, dressed, fed, rocked, and carried and how they grow. Frazee's charming pen-and-ink and watercolors depict a variety of fetching babies on each double-page spread, while each verse starts the same: "Everyday, everywhere, babies . . ."

GERM: Before reading this aloud, ask your listeners to make a list of what babies do. You can read this at toddler story hours or even to first graders, who can then write and draw their earliest memories of being little. Kids can bring in baby pictures for all to identify and ask their parents to recall funny tales about when they were babies.

RELATED TITLES: Anholt, Catherine, and Laurence Anholt. *Catherine and Laurence Anholt's Big Book of Little Children.* Candlewick, 2003. / Ashman, Linda. *Babies on the Go.* Harcourt, 2003. / Cooke, Trish. *So Much.* Candlewick, 1994. / Curtis, Marci. *I Was So Silly! Big Kids Remember Being Little.* Dial, 2002. / Cutler, Jane. *Darcy and Gran Don't Like Babies.* Scholastic, 1993. / Frazee, Marla. *Hush, Little Baby: A Folk Song with Pictures.* Harcourt, 1999. / Hoffman, Mary. *Henry's Baby.* DK, 1993. / Meyers, Susan. *Puppies, Puppies, Puppies.* Abrams, 2005. / Nye, Naomi Shihab. *Baby Radar.* Greenwillow, 2003. / Paxton, Tom. *Where's the Baby?* Morrow, 1993. / Schwartz, Amy. *A Teeny Tiny Baby.* Orchard, 1994. / Wild, Margaret. *Midnight Babies.* Clarion, 2001. / Williams, Vera B. *"More More More," Said the Baby.* Greenwillow, 1990. / Wishinsky, Frieda. *Oonga Boonga.* Little, Brown, 1999. / Wood, Audrey, and Don Wood. *Piggies.* Harcourt, 1991.

SUBJECTS: BABIES. STORIES IN RHYME.

558   Meyers, Susan. *Puppies, Puppies, Puppies.* **Illus. by David Walker. Abrams, 2005. 0-8109-5856-2. Unp. Gr. PreK–1**

Take a rhyming romp with a batch of rolling, running puppies as they chase and chew, make messes, and get civilized at obedience school. Large, square, white pages are filled with amiable acrylics of every kind of joyful dog.

GERM: The repeated chantable refrain will have everyone chiming in: "Here and there and everywhere. Puppies! Puppies! Puppies!" See what's fun about little humans in the companion book, *Everywhere Babies*.

RELATED TITLES: Bartoletti, Susan Campbell. *Nobody's Diggier Than a Dog.* Hyperion, 2004. / Catalanotto, Peter. *Daisy 1 2 3.* Atheneum, 2003. / George, Kristine O'Connell. *Little Dog Poems.* Clarion, 1999. / Gottfried, Maya. *Good Dog.* Knopf, 2005. / Graham, Bob. *"Let's Get a Pup!" Said Kate.* Candlewick, 2001. / Kirk, Daniel. *Dogs Rule!* Hyperion, 2003. / Meyers, Susan. *Everywhere Babies.* Harcourt, 2001. / Miller, Sara Swan. *Three Stories You Can Read to Your Dog.* Houghton Mifflin, 1995. / Reiser, Lynn. *Ten Puppies.* HarperCollins, 2003. / Rylant, Cynthia. *The Great Gracie Chase.* Scholastic, 2001. / Simont, Marc. *The Stray Dog.* HarperCollins, 2001.

SUBJECTS: ANIMALS—INFANCY. CHANTABLE REFRAIN. DOGS. STORIES IN RHYME.

559 **Miller, Sara Swan.** *Three Stories You Can Read to Your Cat.* **Illus. by True Kelley. Houghton Mifflin, 1997. 0-395-78831-5. 48pp. Gr. PreK–3**

Here are three charming vignettes, told in the second person, about a personable black and white cat who outwaits the rain, stalks a bug, and tears up the house.

GERM: Listeners can put themselves in their cat's shoes and write new tales from their pets' points of view. Give equal time to dogs and teddy bears with the other personal narratives by Sara Swan Miller.

RELATED TITLES: Bruel, Nick. *Bad Kitty.* Roaring Brook, 2005. / Calhoun, Mary. *High-Wire Henry.* Morrow, 1991. / Florian, Douglas. *Bow Wow Meow Meow: It's Rhyming Cats and Dogs.* Harcourt, 2003. / Miller, Sara Swan. *Three More Stories You Can Read to Your Cat.* Houghton Mifflin, 2002. / Miller, Sara Swan. *Three More Stories You Can Read to Your Dog.* Houghton Mifflin, 2000. / Miller, Sara Swan. *Three Stories You Can Read to Your Dog.* Houghton Mifflin, 1995. / Miller, Sara Swan. *Three Stories You Can Read to Your Teddy Bear.* Houghton Mifflin, 2004. / Pilkey, Dav. *Kat Kong.* Harcourt, 1993. / Pilkey, Dav. *When Cats Dream.* Orchard, 1992. / Rosen, Michael. *Moving.* Viking, 1993. / Simon, Seymour. *Cats.* HarperCollins, 2003.

SUBJECTS: CATS. CREATIVE WRITING. HUMOROUS FICTION. POINT OF VIEW.

560 **Miller, Sara Swan.** *Three Stories You Can Read to Your Dog.* **Illus. by True Kelley. Houghton Mifflin, 1995. 0-395-69938-X. 48pp. Gr. PreK–3**

Now put yourselves in your dog's shoes in three endearing, easy-to-read stories, told in the second person, in which a floppy brown dog scares off what he thinks is a burglar, buries and then can't find his bone, and runs outside to be a Wild Dog.

GERM: For those who consider dogs and cats intelligent pets, ask your students to read aloud to their pets each of these three short chapters. Give equal time to *Three Stories You Can Read to Your Cat.* Listeners can write new narratives from their pets' points of view, which they can then read to their pets.

RELATED TITLES: Buehner, Caralyn. *Superdog: The Heart of a Hero.* HarperCollins, 2004. / Calhoun, Mary. *High-Wire Henry.* Morrow, 1991. / Hall, Donald. *I Am the Dog, I Am the Cat.* Dial, 1994. / Kirk, Daniel. *Dogs Rule!* Hyperion, 2003. / L'Engle, Madeleine. *The Other Dog.* SeaStar, 2001. / Meddaugh, Susan. *Martha Speaks.* Houghton Mifflin, 1992. (And others in the Martha series.) / Miller, Sara Swan. *Three Stories You Can Read to Your Cat.* Houghton Mifflin, 1997. / Miller, Sara Swan. *Three More Stories You Can Read to Your Dog.* Houghton Mifflin, 2000. / Miller, Sara Swan. *Three Stories You Can Read to Your Teddy Bear.* Houghton Mifflin, 2004. / Pilkey, Dav. *Dogzilla.* Harcourt, 1993. / Rathmann, Peggy. *Officer Buckle and Gloria.* Putnam, 1995. / Rosen, Michael. *Rover.* Doubleday, 1999. / Simon, Seymour. *Dogs.* HarperCollins, 2003.

SUBJECTS: CREATIVE WRITING. DOGS. HUMOROUS FICTION. POINT OF VIEW.

561 **Miller, Sara Swan.** *Three Stories You Can Read to Your Teddy Bear.* **Illus. by True Kelley. Houghton Mifflin, 2004. 0-618-30397-9. Unp. Gr. PreK–2**

Not only do you have stories to tell about your cat and dog (see above), but now it turns out that your teddy bear is also an active and interesting fellow when you're not watching. Notice that in all three of these droll second-person narratives, in which the teddy bear falls down the stairs, makes a mess in the kitchen preparing breakfast, and ventures outdoors, it's the same cat and dog who get blamed for all of his antics.

GERM: Bring in teddy bears and write or tell stories about what they do when their children are out of the house.

RELATED TITLES: Alborough, Jez. *Where's My Teddy?* Candlewick, 1992. / Feiffer, Jules. *I Lost My Bear.* Morrow, 1998. / Kellogg, Steven. *A-Hunting We Will Go!* Morrow, 1998. / Miller, Sara Swan. *Three More Stories You Can Read to Your Cat.* Houghton Mifflin, 2002. / Miller, Sara Swan. *Three More Stories You Can Read to Your Dog.* Houghton Mifflin, 2000. / Miller, Sara Swan. *Three Stories You Can Read to Your Cat.* Houghton Mifflin, 1997. / Miller, Sara Swan. *Three Stories You Can Read to Your Dog.* Houghton Mifflin, 1995. / Rosen, Michael. *We're Going on a Bear Hunt.* McElderry, 1989. / Sheldon, Dyan. *Love, Your Bear Pete.* Candlewick, 1994.

SUBJECTS: CATS. CREATIVE WRITING. DOGS. HUMOROUS FICTION. POINT OF VIEW. TEDDY BEARS.

562 **Millman, Isaac.** *Moses Goes to a Concert.* **Illus. by the author. Farrar, 1998. 0-374-35067-1. Unp. Gr. 1–3**

Moses and his classmates, all of whom are deaf, attend a young people's concert with their teacher, Mr. Samuels, and afterward try out the musical instruments with the inspiring Ms. Elwyn, the percussionist, who is also deaf.

GERM: Children will want to try their hand at translating the conversations that take place in this book into American Sign Language, which is incorporated into each illustration with easy-to-follow diagrams.

RELATED TITLES: Booth, Barbara D. *Mandy*. Lothrop, 1992. / Davis, Patricia A. *Brian's Bird*. Albert Whitman, 2000. / Harshman, Marc. *The Storm*. Dutton, 1995. / Hayes, Ann. *Meet the Orchestra*. Harcourt, 1991. / Hesse, Karen. *Lester's Dog*. Crown, 1993. / Holub, Joan. *My First Book of Sign Language*. Scholastic, 1996. / Millman, Isaac. *Moses Goes to a Play*. Farrar, 2004. / Millman, Isaac. *Moses Goes to School*. Farrar, 2000. / Millman, Isaac. *Moses Goes to the Circus*. Farrar, 2003. / Moss, Lloyd. *Zin! Zin! Zin! A Violin*. Simon & Schuster, 1995. / Rankin, Laura. *The Handmade Alphabet*. Dial, 1991.

SUBJECTS: CONCERTS. DEAF. MUSICIANS. PEOPLE WITH DISABILITIES. PERCUSSION. PHYSICALLY HANDICAPPED. SIGN LANGUAGE. TEACHERS.

---

563 Mills, Claudia. *Gus and Grandpa at Basketball*. Illus. by Catherine Stock. Farrar, 2001. 0-374-32818-8. 48pp. Gr. K–2

Gus is nervous at his final basketball game, playing in front of a crowd, until he takes a tip from his Grandpa. Grandpa likes to turn off his hearing aid to "hear myself think," which helps him to tune out noise and concentrate. Children who have trouble tuning out distractions will gain a valuable technique from this warm intergenerational tale, which is part of the Gus and Grandpa series of easy-readers.

GERM: Take your crew out to the blacktop or gym to shoot some baskets, using Grandpa's technique for concentrating. Have your group come up with a list of strategies they use to pay attention and focus on a task, from sports to schoolwork.

RELATED TITLES: Caseley, Judith. *Dear Annie*. Greenwillow, 1991. / Dorros, Arthur. *Abuela*. Dutton, 1991. / Greenfield, Eloise. *Grandpa's Face*. Philomel, 1988. / Mills, Claudia. *Gus and Grandpa*. Farrar, 1997. (And others in the Gus and Grandpa series.) / Rosselson, Leon. *Rosa and Her Singing Grandfather*. Philomel, 1996. / Shields, Carol Diggory. *Lucky Pennies and Hot Chocolate*. Dutton, 2000. / Van Leeuwen, Jean. *The Tickle Stories*. Dial, 1998.

SUBJECTS: BASKETBALL. GRANDFATHERS. SPORTS.

---

564 Mitchell, Margaree King. *Granddaddy's Gift*. Illus. by Larry Johnson. BridgeWater, 1997. 0-8167-4010-0. Unp. Gr. 2–5

Little Joe describes how her Granddaddy, Joe Morgan, a Mississippi farmer, became the first black man in town to register to vote after he passed the test on the state constitution in the 1960s, a time when it was dangerous to do so. Little Joe's moving and dramatic account shows how African Americans stood up to the continuing injustice of segregation in this country and effected change.

GERM: Pair this with Mitchell's *Uncle Jed's Barbershop* and other books on the Civil Rights movement of the 20th century, such as *Through My Eyes* by Ruby Bridges and *The Watsons Go to Birmingham, 1963* by Christopher Paul Curtis. Discuss why African Americans had the right to vote and yet were not permitted to do so in many places. How has this situation changed and why? Why did Little Joe's Grandaddy want her to stay in school? What difference does an education make in our lives?

RELATED TITLES: Bradby, Marie. *More Than Anything Else*. Orchard, 1995. / Bridges, Ruby. *Through My Eyes*. Scholastic, 1999. / Christelow, Eileen. *VOTE!* Clarion, 2003. / Coles, Robert. *The Story of Ruby Bridges*. Scholastic, 1995. / Curtis, Christopher Paul. *The Watsons Go to Birmingham, 1963*. Delacorte, 1995. / English, Karen. *Francie*. Farrar, 1999. / Golenbock, Peter. *Teammates*. Harcourt, 1990. / Howard, Elizabeth Fitzgerald. *Virgie Goes to School with Us Boys*. Simon & Schuster, 2000. / Lorbiecki, Marybeth. *Sister Anne's Hands*. Dial, 1998. / McCully, Emily Arnold. *The Ballot Box Battle*. Knopf, 1996. / Mitchell, Margaree King. *Uncle Jed's Barbershop*. Simon & Schuster, 1993. / Sisulu, Elinor Batezat. *The Day Gogo Went to Vote: South Africa, April 1994*. Little, Brown, 1996. / Wiles, Deborah. *Freedom Summer*. Atheneum, 2001. / Wooldridge, Connie Nordhielm. *When Esther Morris Headed West: Women, Wyoming, and the Right to Vote*. Holiday House, 2001.

SUBJECTS: AFRICAN AMERICANS. AFRICAN AMERICANS—HISTORY. CIVIL RIGHTS. DETERMINATION. GRANDFATHERS. INTEGRATION. MISSISSIPPI. MULTICULTURAL BOOKS. VOTING.

---

565 Mitton, Tony. *Dinosaurumpus!* Illus. by Guy Rees. Scholastic, 2003. 0-439-39514-3. Unp. Gr. PreK–1

Donk, bomp, twist, thwack, eeeeeek, clatter, rattle, and zoom with a swampful of amiable gargantuan dinosaurs, all done up in pen-and-ink and glowing watercolors, having a blast as they dance.

GERM: "Shake, shake, shudder near the sludgy old swamp. The dinosaurs are coming. Get ready to romp." That's the toe-tapping chantable refrain everyone will want to yell out as they dance to the beat and make lots of dino-noise in a rhyming aerobic workout. Keep them moving with *Saturday Night at the Dinosaur Stomp* by Carol Diggory Shields.

RELATED TITLES: Dodson, Peter. *An Alphabet of Dinosaurs.* Scholastic, 1995. / Hearn, Diane Dawson. *Dad's Dinosaur Day.* Macmillan, 1993. / Livingston, Irene. *Finklehopper Frog.* Tricycle, 2003. / Most, Bernard. *How Big Were the Dinosaurs?* Harcourt, 1994. / Nolan, Dennis. *Dinosaur Dreams.* Macmillan, 1990. / Rohmann, Eric. *Time Flies.* Crown, 1994. / Shields, Carol Diggory. *Saturday Night at the Dinosaur Stomp.* Candlewick, 1997. / Stickland, Paul, and Henrietta Stickland. *Dinosaur Roar!* Dutton, 1994. / Whybrow, Ian. *Sammy and the Dinosaurs.* Orchard, 1999. / Wilson, Karma. *Hilda Must Be Dancing.* McElderry, 2004. / Yolen, Jane. *How Do Dinosaurs Say Good Night?* Blue Sky/Scholastic, 2000.

SUBJECTS: DANCING. DINOSAURS. SOUND EFFECTS. STORIES IN RHYME.

566   Mollel, Tololwa M. *My Rows and Piles of Coins.* Illus. by E. B. Lewis. Clarion, 1999. 0-395-75186-1. Unp. Gr. K–3

Dreaming of his own bicycle, Saruni, a young boy in Tanzania, saves and counts the coins he earns helping his mother sell food at the open-air market. One Saturday, feeling like the richest boy in the world, Saruni shows the bicycle man his fortune—305 coins, totaling 30 shillings and 50 cents—and the man laughs at him. There's a happy ending when Saruni's father buys a *pikipiki*, or motorbike, and gives Saruni his old bike as a reward for his help. Saruni then starts thinking about the cart he'd like to buy to pull his mother's load to market. The watercolor paintings are expressive and skillful. It's satisfying to be able to give children a realistic picture of daily life in Africa and a hero they will admire and with whom they will identify.

GERM: Use this story as part of a math unit on coins. In the Author's Note, he tells us that in the 1960s, when this story takes place, ten 10-cent coins, or 100 cents, made a shilling. Eight shillings were worth about one U.S. dollar. Bikes cost 150 to 500 shillings. (Saruni's shillings are worth about $3.87. It costs $19 to $60 for a bike.) Kids can do the math to explain why the bicycle man laughed at Saruni. Go to market in Haiti with Sasifi and her mother in Karen Lynn Williams's *Tap-Tap.*

RELATED TITLES: Cowen-Fletcher, Jane. *It Takes a Village.* Scholastic, 1994. / Daly, Niki. *Not So Fast, Songololo.* Atheneum, 1986. / Lewin, Ted. *Market!* Lothrop, 1996. / McBrier, Paige. *Beatrice's Goat.* Atheneum, 2001. / Mennen, Ingrid, and Niki Daly. *Somewhere in Africa.* Dutton, 1992. / Stock, Catherine. *Gugu's House.* Clarion, 2001. / Stuve-Bodeen, Stephanie. *Elizabeti's Doll.* Lee & Low, 1998. / Stuve-Bodeen, Stephanie. *Elizabeti's School.* Lee & Low, 2002. / Williams, Karen L. *Galimoto.* Lothrop, 1990. / Williams, Karen L. *Tap-Tap.* Clarion, 1994.

SUBJECTS: AFRICA. BICYCLES. COINS. MONEY. MULTICULTURAL BOOKS. TANZANIA.

567   Montenegro, Laura Nyman. *A Bird About to Sing.* Illus. by the author. Houghton Mifflin, 2003. 0-618-18865-7. Unp. Gr. 1–3

Young Natalie is a poet, but when her poetry teacher, Monica, takes her downtown to a poetry reading full of grownup poets and it's her turn to read, she is too intimidated by all those eyes on her to say a word. On the bus ride home, everything she sees suggests a poem, and it's there that Natalie finds her own voice, ready to be heard. As she observes, "You see, poets always ride the bus." The author's gouache illustrations are soft and dreamy, expressively reminiscent of Chagall.

GERM: Quirky gouache paintings of all the poets will get kids yearning to paint portraits, and, of course, to write and recite their own poems. Start the discussion: What does it mean to be a poet? Meet another shy performer in Alexander Stadler's *Beverly Billingsly Takes a Bow.*

RELATED TITLES: Byars, Betsy. *Beans on the Roof.* Delacorte, 1988. / Daly, Niki. *Once Upon a Time.* Farrar, 2002. / Dodds, Dayle Ann. *Sing, Sophie.* Candlewick, 1997. / Hoffman, Mary. *Amazing Grace.* Dial, 1991. / Kalman, Maira. *Max Makes a Million.* Viking, 1990. / Lionni, Leo. *Frederick.* Pantheon, 1967. / Schotter, Roni. *Nothing Ever Happens on 90th Street.* Orchard, 1997. / Stadler, Alexander. *Beverly Billingsly Takes a Bow.* Harcourt, 2003. / Stadler, Alexander. *Lila Bloom.* Farrar, 2003.

SUBJECTS: POETRY. POETS. SELF-CONCEPT. SHYNESS.

568   Mora, Pat. *Doña Flor: A Tall Tale About a Giant Woman with a Great Big Heart.* Illus. by Raúl Colón. Knopf, 2005. 0-375-92337-3. Unp. Gr. PreK–3

Flor may be taller than the tallest trees, but she can speak every animal language and welcomes everyone in her pueblo to her mountain-sized *casa*, where she makes the world's biggest tortillas, which folks use as roofs and rafts. When the neighbors hide in fear from a roaring puma circling the village, it's up to Doña Flor to find it and ensure everyone's safety. Colón's bordered textured portraits of the gentle giantess (a combination of watercolor washes, etching, and colored pencils) swirl with soft blues and greens.

GERM: Other big girls include the five sisters in *Granite Baby* by Lynne Bertrand, lovely Oonagh in *Fin M'Coul, the Giant of Knockmany Hill* by Tomie dePaola, *Swamp Angel* by Anne Isaacs, and *Sally Ann Thunder Ann Whirlwind Crockett* by Steven Kellogg. Writing prompt: What might happen if these tall-tale heroines all got together for a party?

RELATED TITLES: Bertrand, Lynne. *Granite Baby.* Farrar, 2005. / Byrd, Robert. *Finn MacCoul and His Fearless Wife: A Giant of a Tale from Ireland.* Dutton, 1999. / Cuyler, Margery. *Big Friends.* Walker, 2004. / Dadey, Debbie. *Shooting Star: Annie Oakley, the Legend.* Walker, 1997 / dePaola, Tomie. *Fin M'Coul, the Giant of Knockmany Hill.* Holiday House, 1981. / DiPucchio, Kelly. *Liberty's Journey.* Hyperion, 2004. / Donaldson, Julia. *The Giants and the Joneses.* Henry Holt, 2005. / Isaacs, Anne. *Swamp Angel.* Dutton, 1994. / Kellogg, Steven. *Sally Ann Thunder Ann Whirlwind Crockett.* Morrow, 1995. / Osborne, Mary Pope. *American Tall Tales.* Knopf, 1991. / San Souci, Robert D. *Larger Than Life: The Adventures of American Legendary Heroes.* Heroes. Doubleday, 1991. / Schanzer, Rosalyn. *Davy Crockett Saves the World.* HarperCollins, 2001. / Walker, Paul Robert. *Big Men, Big Country: A Collection of American Tall Tales.* Harcourt, 1993. / Wood, Audrey. *The Bunyans.* Scholastic, 1996.

SUBJECTS: GIANTS. HISPANIC AMERICANS. MEXICAN AMERICANS. MULTICULTURAL BOOKS. PUMA. SOUTHWEST. SPANISH LANGUAGE. TALL TALES. WOMEN.

569   Mora, Pat. *Tomás and the Library Lady.* Illus. by Raúl Colón. Knopf, 1997. 0-679-90401-8. Unp. Gr. K–3

Inspired by the childhood of Tomás Rivera, a former university chancellor in California, this heartwarming story reveals how an empathetic librarian helped a migrant worker's son nurture his love for books and knowledge at the library.

GERM: Prove how the love of reading can change your life with real-life accounts like this one, Marie Bradby's *More Than Anything Else*, and Elizabeth Fitzgerald Howard's *Virgie Goes to School with Us Boys*.

RELATED TITLES: Bradby, Marie. *More Than Anything Else.* Orchard, 1995. / Bunting, Eve. *The Wednesday Surprise.* Clarion, 1989. / Hest, Amy. *Mr. George Baker.* Candlewick, 2004. / Howard, Elizabeth Fitzgerald. *Virgie Goes to School with Us Boys.* Simon & Schuster, 2000. / Joosse, Barbara M. *Hot City.* Philomel, 2004. / Pérez, Amada Irma. *My Very Own Room/Mi Proprio Cuartito.* Children's Book Press, 2000. / Pérez, L. King. *First Day in Grapes.* Lee & Low, 2002. / Polacco, Patricia. *Aunt Chip and the Great Triple Creek Dam Affair.* Philomel, 1996. / Reich, Susanna. *José! Born to Dance.* Illus. by Raúl Colón. Simon & Schuster, 2005. / Sauer, Julie L. *Mike's House.* Viking, 1954. / Smothers, Ethel Footman. *The Hard-Times Jar.* Farrar, 2003. / Williams, Suzanne. *Library Lil.* Dial, 1997.

SUBJECTS: BOOKS AND READING. DETERMINATION. LIBRARIANS. LITERACY. MEXICAN AMERICANS. MIGRANT LABOR. MULTICULTURAL BOOKS. PICTURE BOOKS FOR ALL AGES.

570   Moss, Lloyd. *Music Is.* Illus. by Philippe Roulet. Putnam, 2003. 0-399-23336-9. Unp. Gr. K–3

In this rhyming tribute to the joys of music, a boy explains just what music means to him.

GERM: Discussion point: The final verse asks, "If there never had been music, / if it never did exist, / what would life be without music? / Think of what we would have missed." Have your crew write personal essays: What kinds of music are part of my life and why I love them.

RELATED TITLES: Aliki. *Ah, Music!* HarperCollins, 2003. / Cox, Judy. *My Family Plays Music.* Holiday House, 2003. / Curtis, Gavin. *The Bat Boy and His Violin.* Simon & Schuster, 1998. / Goss, Linda. *The Frog Who Wanted to Be a Singer.* Orchard, 1996. / Howe, James. *Horace and Morris Join the Chorus (But What About Dolores?).* Atheneum, 2002. / Krull, Kathleen. *Lives of the Musicians: Good Times, Bad Times (And What the Neighbors Thought).* Harcourt, 1993. / Krull, Kathleen. *M Is for Music.* Harcourt, 2003. / Millman, Isaac. *Moses Goes to a Concert.* Farrar, 1998. / Ober, Hal. *How Music Came to the World.* Houghton Mifflin, 1994. / Ryan, Pam Muñoz. *When Marian Sang.* Scholastic, 2002. / Weaver, Tess. *Opera Cat.* Clarion, 2002.

SUBJECTS: MUSIC. STORIES IN RHYME.

571   Moss, Miriam. *Don't Forget I Love You.* Illus. by Anna Currey. Dial, 2004. 0-8037-2920-0. Unp. Gr. PreK–K

Ministering to his beloved stuffed toy bunny rabbit, Billy makes his Mama late for work, and she drops him off at school without her customary "I love you." What's just as devastating for the bear preschooler is that Rabbit gets lost too. This sweet and reassuring story with soft, warm watercolors that capture real emotions without ever being maudlin or sticky, will elicit a familiar pang from every parent and child.

GERM: All can swap stories of times they were late and what happened as a consequence. Have your children act out everything they do to get ready for school in the morning.

RELATED TITLES: Clark, Emma Chichester. *Where Are You, Blue Kangaroo?* Doubleday, 2000. / Horse, Harry. *Little Rabbit Goes to School.* Peachtree, 2004. / Ichikawa, Satomi. *La La Rose.* Philomel, 2004. / Rusackas, Francesca. *I Love You All Day Long.* HarperCollins, 2002. / Weiss, Nicki. *Hank and Oogie.* Lothrop, 1987. / Willems, Mo. *Knuffle Bunny: A Cautionary Tale.* Hyperion, 2004.

SUBJECTS: BEARS. LOST AND FOUND POSSESSIONS. LOVE. MOTHERS AND SONS. SCHOOLS. TOYS.

572 **Murphy, Stuart. *Too Many Kangaroo Things to Do!* Illus. by Kevin O'Malley. HarperCollins, 1996. 0-06-025884-5. Unp. Gr. K–2**

On his birthday, kangaroo enlists one emu, two platypuses, three koalas, and four dingoes to play with him, but they all have too many things to do. Showing simple multiplication facts up to 4 x 4, and then a bit of addition, the animals tally up 100 kangaroo things to do as they gather for kangaroo's surprise birthday party.

GERM: This is just one of many books in Murphy's cheerful and practical Mathstart series, picture-book stories that introduce math concepts to children. At the back of the book is a list of follow-up suggestions for children and adults.

RELATED TITLES: Day, Nancy Raines. *Double Those Wheels.* Dutton, 2003. / Demi. *One Grain of Rice.* Scholastic, 1997. / Dodds, Dayle Ann. *Minnie's Diner.* Candlewick, 2004. / Fox, Mem. *Koala Lou.* Harcourt, 1989. / Leedy, Loreen. *Mission: Addition.* Holiday House, 1997. / Leedy, Loreen. *2 X 2 = BOO! A Set of Spooky Multiplication Stories.* Holiday House, 1995. / Michelson, Richard. *Ten Times Better.* Marshall Cavendish, 2000. / Niland, Kilmeny. *A Bellbird in a Flame Tree.* Tambourine, 1991. / Payne, Emmy. *Katy-No-Pocket.* Houghton Mifflin, 1944. / Pinczes, Elinor J. *One Hundred Hungry Ants.* Houghton Mifflin, 1993. / Rose, Deborah Lee. *Birthday Zoo.* Albert Whitman, 2002. / Tang, Greg. *The Best of Times: Math Strategies That Multiply.* Scholastic, 2002. / Vaughn, Marcia K. *Wombat Stew.* Silver Burdett, 1986.

SUBJECTS: ADDITION. ANIMALS. AUSTRALIA. BIRTHDAYS. KANGAROOS. MATHEMATICS. MULTIPLICATION.

573 **Murray, Marjorie Dennis. *Don't Wake Up the Bear!* Illus. by Patricia Wittmann. Marshall Cavendish, 2003. 0-7614-5107-2. Unp. Gr. PreK–2**

One by one, on a cold winter's eve, a silver hare, a badger, a fox, and a squirrel snuggle against a sleeping bear to get warm, cautioning each new arrival, "Don't wake up the bear." A mouse with a cold tail settles in the bear's ear, and when she sneezes, the bear wakes up growling.

GERM: This book's large, snow-covered watercolors—filled with expressive, if sleepy, animals—complement its repeated refrain and rousing climax, making it a natural for story times and creative drama. Contrast it with another sleeping bear story, *Bear Snores On*, by Karma Wilson.

RELATED TITLES: Alborough, Jez. *It's the Bear!* Candlewick, 1994. / Burningham, John. *Mr. Gumpy's Outing.* Henry Holt, 1971. / Fleming, Denise. *Time to Sleep.* Henry Holt, 1997. / Gray, Libba Moore. *Is There Room on the Featherbed?* Orchard, 1997. / Jorgensen, Gail. *Gotcha!* Scholastic, 1997. / Koide, Tan. *May We Sleep Here Tonight?* Atheneum, 1983. / Murphy, Jill. *Peace at Last.* Dial, 1980. / Simms, Laura. *The Squeaky Door.* Crown, 1991. / Thomson, Pat. *The Squeaky, Creaky Bed.* Doubleday, 2003. / Waber, Bernard. *Bearsie Bear and the Surprise Sleepover Party.* Houghton Mifflin, 1997. / Wilson, Karma. *Bear Snores On.* McElderry, 2002. / Wilson, Karma. *Bear Wants More.* McElderry, 2003. / Wood, Audrey. *The Napping House.* Harcourt, 1984.

SUBJECTS: ANIMALS. BEARS. CHANTABLE REFRAIN. CREATIVE DRAMA. HIBERNATION. SEASONS. SLEEP. WINTER.

574 **Muth, Jon J. *Zen Shorts.* Illus. by Jon J Muth. Scholastic, 2005. 0-439-33911-1. Unp. Gr. 1–6**

Karl, Michael, and Addy meet their new neighbor Stillwater, a giant panda who speaks with a slight panda accent, when he arrives to retrieve his red umbrella from their backyard. One at a time, the siblings visit Stillwater at his house, and he tells each child a special story. The illustrations are wondrous—soft gentle watercolors of the rotund panda dressed in his white robe alternate with the pages of stark black ink and white printed against a solid pastel background that accompany the stories he tells. Each of Stillwater's stories, taken from traditional Buddhist and Taoist tales, will provoke thoughtful meditation and discussion: Uncle Ry gives his only robe to a raccoon robber; a farmer evaluates his good and bad luck; and two traveling monks assist an ungrateful young woman.

GERM: Read the whole book aloud first. Then go back and reread each of the three stories Stillwater tells and ask: Why do you think he told this story? What do you think it means? How does it apply to your own life or experiences? In the Author's Note, Muth says, "'Zen shorts' are short meditations—ideas to puzzle over—tools which hone our ability to act with intuition. They have no goal but they often challenge us to reexamine our habits, desires, concepts, and fears."

RELATED TITLES: Demi. *Buddha*. Henry Holt, 1996. / Demi. *Buddha Stories*. Henry Holt, 1997. / Demi. *The Dragon's Tale and Other Animal Fables of the Chinese Zodiac*. Henry Holt, 1996. / Demi. *The Hungry Coat: A Tale from Turkey*. McElderry, 2004. / Hodges, Margaret. *The Boy Who Drew Cats*. Holiday House, 2002.

SUBJECTS: BROTHERS AND SISTERS. BUDDHA AND BUDDHISM. COMPASSION. FOLKLORE—JAPAN. FORGIVENESS. MEDITATION. PANDAS. PICTURE BOOKS FOR ALL AGES. STORYTELLING. ZEN BUDDHISM.

575   **Myers, Christopher.** *Black Cat.* **Illus. by the author. Scholastic, 1999. 0-590-03375-1. Unp. Gr. 3–6**

A black cat meanders through the city streets to a kinetic merge of scat-style poetry and bold urban collage illustrations. The book's pictures are a combination of color photos, collage, ink, and gouache; they blare with horns, lights, and sounds of gritty but alluring city streets.

GERM: Bring in a good jazz recording to play while reading this aloud.

RELATED TITLES: Calhoun, Mary. *Cross-Country Cat*. Morrow, 1979. / Hall, Donald. *I Am the Dog, I Am the Cat*. Dial, 1994. / Igus, Toyomi. *I See the Rhythm*. Children's Book Press, 1998. / Johnston, Tony. *Cat, What Is That?* HarperCollins, 2001. / Myers, Christopher. *Harlem*. Scholastic, 1997. / Pilkey, Dav. *When Cats Dream*. Orchard, 1992. / Rosen, Michael J. *Purr . . . Children's Book Illustrators Brag About Their Cats*. Harcourt, 1996. / Steptoe, Javaka. *In Daddy's Arms I Am Tall: African Americans Celebrating Fathers*. Lee & Low, 1997. / Wagner, Jane. *J. T.* Dell, 1972.

SUBJECTS: CATS. CITIES AND TOWNS. PICTURE BOOKS FOR OLDER READERS.

576   **Myers, Tim.** *Basho and the Fox.* **Illus. by Oki Sittan. Marshall Cavendish, 2000. 0-7614-5068-8. Unp. Gr. 2–4**

In a humorous, fictional story about Basho—one of Japan's most renowned poets—who lived from 1644 to 1694, the hermit-like poet is hungry for words to describe the sweet late-summer cherries that grow on a tree near his hut. When a fox claims all the cherries for himself, he offers to give them to the poet, but only if Basho can write one good, not even great, haiku.

GERM: Introduce the life and work of Basho in Dawnine Spivak's lovely picture-book biography, *Grass Sandals: The Travels of Basho*. Analyze how Myers took the poet's life and turned it into a fictional story, replete with kimono-clad foxes who claim to be better poets than the master. Bring in cherries to sample, so your students can write cherry-based haiku as evocative and spare as Basho's. Follow up with *Basho and the River Stones*, in which the cherry-loving fox tries to trick the poet into giving the cherries back to the foxes.

RELATED TITLES: Cassedy, Sylvia, and Kunihiro Suetake, trans. *Red Dragonfly on My Shoulder*. HarperCollins, 1992. / Demi, comp. *In the Eyes of the Cat: Japanese Poetry for All Seasons*. Henry Holt, 1992. / Gollub, Matthew. *Cool Melons—Turn to Frogs! The Life and Poems of Issa*. Lee & Low, 1998. / Higginson, William J., comp. *Wind in the Long Grass: A Collection of Haiku*. Simon & Schuster, 1991. / Myers, Tim. *Basho and the River Stones*. Marshall Cavendish, 2004. / Prelutsky, Jack. *If Not for the Cat*. Greenwillow, 2004. / Spivak, Dawnine. *Grass Sandals: The Travels of Basho*. Atheneum, 1997.

SUBJECTS: BASHO (MATSUO, BASHO), 1644–1694. CHERRIES. FOXES. HAIKU. JAPAN. MULTICULTURAL BOOKS. POETRY. POETS. TREES.

577   **Myers, Walter Dean.** *The Blues of Flats Brown.* **Illus. by Nina Laden. Holiday House, 2000. 0-8234-1480-9. Unp. Gr. K–3**

Trace the career of music-loving, guitar-pickin' mutt Flats Brown—the "blues playingest dog you ever heard of"—from a Mississippi junkyard to a club in New York City.

GERM: Bring in a blues tape to play so listeners will understand the music Flats sings. All can sing "The New York City Blues"—words and music are on the inside black cover.

RELATED TITLES: Barracca, Debra, and Sal Barracca. *The Adventures of Taxi Dog*. Dial, 1990. / Frame, Jeron Ashford. *Yesterday I Had the Blues*. Tricycle, 2003. / Goss, Linda. *The Frog Who Wanted to Be a Singer*. Orchard, 1996. / Graham, Bob. *Benny: An Adventure Story*. Holiday House, 2000. / Gray, Libba Moore. *Little Lil and the Swing-Singing Sax*. Simon & Schuster, 1996. / Hurd, Thacher. *Art Dog*. HarperCollins, 1996. / Laden, Nina. *Bad Dog*. Walker, 2000. / Laden, Nina. *The Night I Followed the Dog*. Chronicle, 1994. / Lebentritt, Julia, and Richard. *Richard*. The Kooken. Henry Holt, 1992. / Rathmann, Peggy. *Officer Buckle and Gloria*. Putnam, 1995.

SUBJECTS: BLUES (MUSIC). DOGS. MUSICIANS. PICTURE BOOKS FOR ALL AGES.

578 Nash, Ogden. *The Tale of Custard the Dragon*. Illus. by Lynn Munsinger. Little, Brown, 1995. 0-316-59880-1. Unp. Gr. PreK–2

Whimsical pen-and-ink and watercolor illustrations add even more zing to Nash's classic 1936 narrative poem about Belinda, who lives with her little black kitten, gray mouse, yellow dog, red wagon, and a "reailo, trulio little pet dragon." Custard the cowardly Custard cries for a nice safe cage until the day a nasty, weapon-wielding pirate climbs in the window.

GERM: Follow up with *Custard the Dragon and the Wicked Knight*. Nash's *The Adventures of Isabel* is also a classic and funny poem-turned-picture book.

RELATED TITLES: Gag, Wanda. *The Funny Thing*. Coward, 1929. / Holabird, Katharine. *Alexander and the Dragon*. Clarkson N. Potter, 1988. / Nash, Ogden. *The Adventures of Isabel*. Little, Brown, 1991. / Nash, Ogden. *Custard and Company*. Illus. by Quentin Blake. Little, Brown, 1980. / Nash, Ogden. *Custard the Dragon and the Wicked Knight*. Illus. by Quentin Blake. Little, Brown, 1996. / Nolen, Jerdine. *Raising Dragons*. Harcourt, 1998. / Thomas, Shelley Moore. *Get Well, Good Knight*. Dutton, 2002. / Thomas, Shelley Moore. *Good Night, Good Knight*. Dutton, 2000.

SUBJECTS: COURAGE. DRAGONS. FEAR. NARRATIVE POETRY. STORIES IN RHYME.

579 Nelson, Vaunda Micheaux. *Almost to Freedom*. Illus. by Colin Bootman. Carolrhoda, 2003. 1-57505-342-X. Unp. Gr. 2–6

The harrowing tale of a slave family's life and escape on the Underground Railroad is told through the eyes of a rag doll named Sally, a beloved companion to Lindy, Miz Rachel's little girl. An Author's Note at the back explains Nelson's inspiration in writing the book: seeing a collection of black rag dolls from the 1800s at a museum and learning that some were found in hideouts of the Underground Railroad.

GERM: The story will jolt listeners with the most extraordinary details. For example, Lindy is whipped by the overseer just for asking Massa's son how to spell her name. When the white couple who shelters the family in their storeroom gives Lindy a pillow, it's something the child has heard about but never seen before. Everyone will want to start a dialogue on slavery and the effect it has had on us all. The glossary of historical words and phrases is helpful.

RELATED TITLES: Adler, David A. *A Picture Book of Harriet Tubman*. Holiday House, 1992. / Edwards, Pamela Duncan. *Barefoot: Escape on the Underground Railroad*. HarperCollins, 1997. / Hopkinson, Deborah. *Sweet Clara and the Freedom Quilt*. Knopf, 1993. / Howard, Elizabeth Fitzgerald. *Virgie Goes to School with Us Boys*. Simon & Schuster, 2000. / Johnson, Dolores. *Now Let Me Fly: The Story of a Slave Family*. Macmillan, 1993. / Lasky, Kathryn. *A Voice of Her Own: The Story of Phillis Wheatley, Slave Poet*. Candlewick, 2002. / Polacco, Patricia. *The Butterfly*. Philomel, 2000. / Ransom, Candice. *Liberty Street*. Walker, 2003. / Ringgold, Faith. *Aunt Harriet's Underground Railroad in the Sky*. Crown, 1992. / Winter, Jeannette. *Follow the Drinking Gourd*. Knopf, 1989.

SUBJECTS: AFRICAN AMERICANS. AFRICAN AMERICANS—HISTORY. DOLLS. HISTORICAL FICTION. MULTICULTURAL BOOKS. PICTURE BOOKS FOR OLDER READERS. SLAVERY. UNDERGROUND RAILROAD.

580 Neubecker, Robert. *Wow! City!* Illus. by the author. Hyperion, 2004. 0-7868-0951-5. Unp. Gr. PreK–1

Curly red-mopped little Izzy and her dad drive down their mountain and fly to New York City, where Izzy is entranced by all the sights. On each vibrant and busy page, jazzy with traffic and people and bustle, Izzy exclaims delightedly at everything she sees ("Wow! Buildings!"). Drawn with india ink and colored with Photoshop on a Mac, this vibrant and joyous panorama of New York City will make you look at the city with new appreciation.

GERM: Whether you use this an emergent reader or a read-aloud, viewers will pore over the huge pictures, looking for Izzy. Make new "Wow!" pictures in other environments, like the beach, mountains, farm, forest, or country.

RELATED TITLES: Dragonwagon, Crescent. *And Then It Rained . . .* Atheneum, 2003. / Grimes, Nikki. *C Is for City*. Lothrop, 1995. / Jakobsen, Kathy. *My New York*. Little, Brown, 1993. / Johnson, Stephen T. *Alphabet City*. Viking, 1995. / Meister, Cari. *Busy Busy City Street*. Viking, 2000. / Melmed, Laura Krauss. *New York, New York! The Big Apple from A to Z*. HarperCollins, 2005. / Neubecker, Robert. *Wow! America!* Hyperion, 2006. / Rotner, Shelley, and Ken Kreisler. *Citybook*. Orchard, 1994. / Van Laan, Nancy. *People, People, Everywhere!* Knopf, 1992. / Weitzman, Jacqueline Preiss. *You Can't Take a Balloon into the Metropolitan Museum*. Dial, 1998. / Willems, Mo. *Knuffle Bunny: A Cautionary Tale*. Hyperion, 2004.

SUBJECTS: CITIES AND TOWNS. NEW YORK CITY.

581   Neuschwander, Cindy. *Sir Cumference and the First Round Table: A Math Adventure.* **Illus. by Wayne Geehan. Charlesbridge, 1997. 1-57091-160-6. 32pp. Gr. 2–5**

Brave knight Sir Cumference, his wife, Di of Ameter, and their little son, Radius, ponder how to fix King Arthur's long rectangular table so each knight has enough room. From rectangle to square, diamond, triangle, octagon, and oval, none of the tables is suitable until they happen upon the perfect shape: a circle. Carpenter Geo of Metry builds the first giant round table from a slice of tree trunk, and all involved are honored with mathematical measurements that bear their names.

GERM: What a witty story to introduce the terms radius, diameter, circumference, and geometry in math class. Follow up with *Sir Cumference and the Dragons of Pi.*

RELATED TITLES: Lasky, Kathryn. *The Librarian Who Measured the Earth.* Little, Brown, 1994. / Myller, Rolf. *How Big Is a Foot?* Atheneum, 1969. / Neuschwander, Cindy. *Sir Cumference and the Dragons of Pi: A Math Adventure.* Charlesbridge, 1999. / Schmandt-Besserat, Denise. *The History of Counting.* Morrow, 1999. / Scieszka, Jon. *Math Curse.* Viking, 1995. / Tompert, Ann. *Grandfather Tang's Story.* Crown, 1990.

SUBJECTS: CIRCLES. GEOMETRY. KNIGHTS AND KNIGHTHOOD. MATHEMATICS. MEASUREMENT. SHAPES.

582   Newman, Lesléa. *Runaway Dreidel!* **Illus. by Kyrsten Brooker. Henry Holt, 2002. 0-8050-6237-8. Unp. Gr. PreK–2**

Borrowing the rhythm and rhyme scheme from "The Night Before Christmas" and the chase scenes of "The Gingerbread Boy," here is a city boy's sprightly tale of his dreidel's escape on the first night of Chanukah. Pursued by the boy and his relatives, the shiny new dreidel spins out of the apartment, down the street, into the countryside, and into the sky, where it shines like a star.

GERM: Pull in Tomie dePaola's illustrated version of Clement C. Moore's *The Night Before Christmas* and Richard Egielski's New York City-based version of *The Gingerbread Boy* to show the book's influences. Bring in a dreidel to spin and then read Eric A. Kimmel's Hanukkah story, *The Magic Dreidels,* which might just get you in the mood to cook up some latkes, or potato pancakes, for the holiday. (See page 285 for my own family recipe.)

RELATED TITLES: Aylesworth, Jim. *The Gingerbread Man.* Scholastic, 1998. / Cook, Scott. *The Gingerbread Boy.* Knopf, 1987. / Egielski, Richard. *The Gingerbread Boy.* HarperCollins, 1997. / Hirsch, Marilyn. *Potato Pancakes All Around; A Hanukkah Tale.* Bonim, 1978. / Howland, Naomi. *Latkes, Latkes, Good to Eat.* Clarion, 1999. / Howland, Naomi. *The Matzah Man: A Passover Story.* Clarion, 2002. / Jaffe, Nina. *In the Month of Kislev: A Story for Hanukkah.* Viking, 1992. / Kimmel, Eric A. *Asher and the Capmakers: A Hanukkah Story.* Holiday House, 1993. / Kimmel, Eric A. *The Chanukkah Guest.* Holiday House, 1990. / Kimmel, Eric A. *The Jar of Fools: Eight Hanukkah Stories from Chelm.* Holiday House, 2000. / Kimmel, Eric A. *The Magic Dreidels: A Hanukkah Story.* Holiday House, 1996. / Moore, Clement C. *The Night Before Christmas.* Illus. by Tomie dePaola. Holiday House, 1980. / Shulman, Lisa. *The Matzo Ball Boy.* Dutton, 2005.

SUBJECTS: DREIDEL (GAME). GINGERBREAD BOY. HANUKKAH. JEWS. PARODIES. SEQUENCE STORIES. STORIES IN RHYME.

583   Newman, Marjorie. *Mole and the Baby Bird.* **Illus. by Patrick Benson. Bloomsbury, 2002. 1-58234-784-0. Unp. Gr. PreK–1**

Finding a baby bird that has fallen out of its nest, Mole brings it home and cares for it, building it a cage instead of letting it fly away. Granddad leads Mole to the top of a high hill, where, feeling the wild wind trying to lift him, Mole feels like he's flying. Back home, he does the right thing. "Birds are meant to fly," he says, and he cries when the bird leaves. But seeing his bird soaring free in the forest, he's glad.

GERM: With its tender, cozy, cross-hatched pen-and-ink and watercolors, this undidactic story of self-discovery will lead to some thoughtful discussions about the difference between wild animals and pets. Discussion points: Why does Mole not want to let the bird go? What makes him change his mind? The story says, ". . . he let his bird fly away because he loved it." What does that mean?

RELATED TITLES: Ehlert, Lois. *Cuckoo/Cucú: A Mexican Folktale/Un Cuento Folklórico Mexicano.* Harcourt, 1997. / Keller, Holly. *Island Baby.* Greenwillow, 1992. / Porte, Barbara Ann. *"Leave That Cricket Be, Alan Lee."* Greenwillow, 1993.

SUBJECTS: BIRDS. GRANDFATHERS. MOLES. PETS. RESPONSIBILITY. WILDLIFE RESCUE.

584 **Nicholls, Judith.** *Billywise.* **Illus. by Jason Cockcroft. Bloomsbury, 2002. 1-58234-778-6. Unp. Gr. PreK–1**

Newborn barn owlet Billywise is afraid to glide through the midnight air, though his mother assures him that soon he will dare to fly. Dignified full-bleed paintings give an up-close look at the wood and the recalcitrant young owl as he grows and tries his wings.

GERM: Discussion point: Have you ever been afraid to try to do something and then tried it and found you could do it just fine? Is there anything you're afraid to do now? Draw a picture of yourself doing it. Observe more owls in trees with *Owl Babies* by Martin Waddell and go owling with *Owl Moon* by Jane Yolen.

RELATED TITLES: Blake, Robert J. *Fledgling.* Philomel, 2000. / Cannon, Janell. *Stellaluna.* Harcourt, 1993. / Dunrea, Olivier. *Ollie.* Houghton, 2003. / James, Simon. *Little One Step.* Candlewick, 2003. / MacDonald, Suse. *Look Whooo's Counting.* Scholastic, 2000. / Rankin, Joan. *Wow! It's Great Being a Duck.* McElderry, 1998. / Waddell, Martin. *Owl Babies.* Candlewick, 1992. / Yolen, Jane. *Owl Moon.* Philomel, 1987.

SUBJECTS: BIRDS. FEAR. FLIGHT. MOTHERS. OWLS. STORIES IN RHYME.

585 **Nickle, John.** *The Ant Bully.* **Illus. by the author. Scholastic, 1999. 0-590-39591-2. Unp. Gr. K–2**

Because Sid, the neighborhood bully is mean to him, Lucas in turn bullies the ants with his water pistol, but they take their revenge. Brought before the Ant Queen, he is diminished to ant size, brought to trial, and sentenced to hard labor with the worker ants. Surreal, colorful acrylic illustrations—including Lucas in his propeller beany, scrubbing the queen's back as she takes her bubble bath in her pink ant-shaped tub—present life from an ant's viewpoint.

GERM: Talk about bullying and how Lucas learns to be a responsible ant. What facts about ants did you learn from the story? Pull in nonfiction ant books such as *Those Amazing Ants* by Patricia Brennan Demuth and *Ant Cities* by Arthur Dorros to find out more facts and discover more reasons to be kind to ants and all living things. *Hey, Little Ant* by father and daughter team Phillip M. and Hannah Hoose tackles the same theme, while *Two Bad Ants* by Chris Van Allsburg shows life from an ant's perspective.

RELATED TITLES: Allinson, Beverly. *Effie.* Scholastic, 1991. / Becker, Bonny. *An Ant's Day Off.* Simon & Schuster, 2003. / Cannon, Janell. *Crickwing.* Harcourt, 2000. / Climo, Shirley. *The Little Red Ant and the Great Big Crumb: A Mexican Fable.* Clarion, 1995. / Demuth, Patricia Brennan. *Those Amazing Ants.* Macmillan, 1994. / Dorros, Arthur. *Ant Cities.* HarperCollins, 1987. / Hoose, Phillip M., and Hannah Hoose. *Hey, Little Ant.* Tricycle, 1998. / Van Allsburg, Chris. *Two Bad Ants.* Houghton Mifflin, 1988. / Young, Ed. *Night Visitors.* Philomel, 1995.

SUBJECTS: ANTS. BULLIES. INSECTS. SIZE. TRANSFORMATIONS.

586 **Nolen, Jerdine.** *Raising Dragons.* **Illus. by Elise Primavera. Harcourt, 1998. 0-15-201288-5. Unp. Gr. PreK–2**

Near Miller's Cave, the young narrator and her farmer Pa find a huge egg. It's love at first sight for the girl and her newly hatched fire-breathing dragon, Hank. She reads him dragon bedtime stories, rides on his back as he flies through the night skies, and tends to the crops with Hank plowing, seeding, and weeding.

GERM: The acrylic and pastel paintings will get children thinking about dragons and will inspire them to paint their own pictures of the adventures they'd have if they hatched their own dragon eggs.

RELATED TITLES: Erdrich, Louise. *Grandmother's Pigeon.* Hyperion, 1996. / Gag, Wanda. *The Funny Thing.* Coward, 1929. / Grambling, Lois G. *Can I Have a Stegosaurus, Mom? Can I? Please!?* BridgeWater, 1995. / Holabird, Katharine. *Alexander and the Dragon.* Clarkson N. Potter, 1988. / Nash, Ogden. *The Tale of Custard the Dragon.* Little, Brown, 1995. / Thomas, Shelley Moore. *Get Well, Good Knight.* Dutton, 2002. / Thomas, Shelley Moore. *Good Night, Good Knight.* Dutton, 2000.

SUBJECTS: AFRICAN AMERICANS. DRAGONS. FARM LIFE. FRIENDSHIP. MULTICULTURAL BOOKS.

587 **Noonan, Julia.** *Mouse by Mouse.* **Illus. by the author. Dutton, 2003. 0-525-46864-1. Unp. Gr. PreK–1**

Soft watercolors depict ten well-dressed mice one by one as they gather, rescue a mouse stuck in a soda bottle, and go for a swim in a bowlful of pop. With each flip of the half-page flap on the page, another mouse is introduced into the adventure, until you count all the way up to ten.

GERM: This would be fun to act out in groups of ten.

RELATED TITLES: Catalanotto, Peter. *Daisy 1 2 3*. Atheneum, 2003. / Christelow, Eileen. *Five Little Monkeys Jumping on the Bed*. Clarion, 1989. / Dorros, Arthur. *Ten Go Tango*. HarperCollins, 2000. / Ehlert, Lois. *Fish Eyes: A Book You Can Count On*. Harcourt, 1990. / Fleming, Denise. *Count!* Henry Holt, 1992. / MacDonald, Suse. *Look Whooo's Counting*. Scholastic, 2000. / Raffi. *Five Little Ducks*. Crown, 1988. / Reiser, Lynn. *Ten Puppies*. HarperCollins, 2003. / Rothstein, Gloria. *Sheep Asleep*. HarperCollins, 2003. / Walton, Rick. *So Many Bunnies: A Bedtime ABC and Counting Book*. Lothrop, 1998.

SUBJECTS: COUNTING BOOKS. CREATIVE DRAMA. MICE. STORIES IN RHYME. TOY AND MOVABLE BOOKS.

588   Novak, Matt. *Mouse TV*. Illus. by the author. Orchard, 1994. 0-531-08706-9. Unp. Gr. PreK–2

What do you watch on TV when Papa Mouse wants action, Mama longs for comedy, and the kids clamor for shows as diverse as history, mystery, science, scary stuff, music, and games? When the TV goes on the fritz, the family gets involved not just watching their favorite activities but doing them together as a family.

GERM: Write this up as a dandy Reader's Theater play and act it out for No TV Week. Charlie suffers TV and computer game withdrawal symptoms when the electricity is knocked out in *When Charlie McButton Lost Power* by Suzanne Collins.

RELATED TITLES: Allen, Susan, and Jane Lindaman. *Read Anything Good Lately?* Millbrook, 2003. / Auch, Mary Jane, and Herm Auch. *Souperchicken*. Holiday House, 2003. / Collins, Suzanne. *When Charlie McButton Lost Power*. Putnam, 2005. / McPhail, David. *Fix-It*. Dutton, 1984. / Sierra, Judy. *Wild About Books*. Knopf, 2004. / Stanley, Diane. *Raising Sweetness*. Putnam, 1999. / Williams, Suzanne. *Library Lil*. Dial, 1997. / Winch, John. *The Old Woman Who Loved to Read*. Holiday House, 1997.

SUBJECTS: BOOKS AND READING. LITERACY. MICE. PICTURE BOOKS FOR ALL AGES. READER'S THEATER. TELEVISION.

589   Numeroff, Laura Joffe. *Beatrice Doesn't Want To*. Illus. by Lynn Munsinger. Candlewick, 2004. 0-7636-1160-3. Unp. Gr. PreK–1

Brown and white dog Beatrice doesn't like books or reading, and she hates going to the library with her big brother Henry, who needs to work on his dinosaur report. "I don't want to," is her stock response, until an exasperated Henry drops her off in the children's room, just in time for an attitude-changing storytime with the librarian.

GERM: Use this as a lead-in to introduce children to the school or public library. Ask your readers to describe a book they didn't want to put down.

RELATED TITLES: Allen, Susan, and Jane Lindaman. *Read Anything Good Lately?* Millbrook, 2003. / Bertram, Debbie, and Susan Bloom. *The Best Place to Read*. Random House, 2003. / Child, Lauren. *Who's Afraid of the Big Bad Book?* Hyperion, 2003. / Daly, Niki. *Once Upon a Time*. Farrar, 2002. / English, Karen. *Hot Day on Abbott Avenue*. Clarion, 2004. / Ernst, Lisa Campbell. *Stella Louella's Runaway Book*. Simon & Schuster, 1998. / Florczak, Robert. *Yikes!!!* Scholastic, 2003. / Hoberman, Mary Ann. *You Read to Me, I'll Read to You: Very Short Stories to Read Together*. Little, Brown, 2001. / Huff, Barbara. *Once Inside the Library*. Little, Brown, 1990. / Joosse, Barbara M. *Hot City*. Philomel, 2004. / McPhail, David. *Fix-It*. Dutton, 1984. / Sierra, Judy. *Wild About Books*. Knopf, 2004. / Sturges, Philemon. *She'll Be Comin' 'Round the Mountain*. Little, Brown, 2004. / Williams, Suzanne. *Library Lil*. Dial, 1997.

SUBJECTS: BOOKS AND READING. BROTHERS AND SISTERS. LIBRARIANS. LIBRARIES.

590   Numeroff, Laura Joffe. *If You Take a Mouse to School*. Illus. by Felicia Bond. HarperCollins, 2003. 0-06-028329-7. Unp. Gr. PreK–2

In an exciting day that begins and ends in a yellow lunchbox, a pink-eared brown mouse, clad in overalls, hits the high points at his boy's school, doing a little math, conducting a fizzing volcano science experiment, writing his own book, and playing sports.

GERM: As in the other books in the If You Give a . . . series, the mouse's activities come full circle, making this a delectable story for talking about cause and effect. Draw a circle diagram of all the scenes. Lots of action makes this a good candidate for creative drama as well. You can narrate, and the kids can act out the mouse's actions.

RELATED TITLES: Fleming, Denise. *Alphabet Under Construction*. Henry Holt, 2002. / Fraser, Mary Ann. *I. Q. Goes to School*. Walker, 2002. / Fraser, Mary Ann. *I. Q. Goes to the Library*. Walker, 2003. / McMillan, Bruce. *Mouse Views: What the Class Pet Saw*. Holiday House, 1993. / Numeroff, Laura. *If You Give a Moose a Muffin*. HarperCollins, 1991. / Numeroff, Laura. *If You Give a Mouse a Cookie*. HarperCollins, 1985. / Ryan, Pam Muñoz. *Mice and Beans*. Scholastic, 2001.

SUBJECTS: CAUSE AND EFFECT. CREATIVE DRAMA. MICE. SCHOOLS.

591 Nye, Naomi Shihab. *Baby Radar.* Illus. by Nancy Carpenter. Greenwillow, 2003. 0-688-15948-6. Unp. Gr. PreK–2

In a free-form stream-of-consciousness ramble, an exuberant toddler out in the stroller with mom for a walk through town comments on all the sights as they spin past—trucks, shoes, crunchy leaves, dogs, another baby, and ducks in the water. Large pen-and-ink and watercolor illustrations show us the world from a child's down-low perspective, and listeners will enjoy puzzling out the meaning of the title.

GERM: While this reads like a book for your very youngest listeners, it has applications all through the grades. What do pre-verbal children think about as they experience the world? If you are examining point of view, have your listeners discuss the toddler's take on the sights as compared with that of his mother. Follow around a small child and record his or her reactions to everything. See how another baby views his surroundings in Amy Schwartz's *A Teeny Tiny Baby.* Then note how a dog views the world in Alice Provensen's *A Day in the Life of Murphy,* where industrious little black terrier, Murphy-Stop-That, describes his own day in a doggy stream-of-consciousness narrative. Take your crew for a walk and have them record their own observations and thoughts, creating a mighty interesting free-form group poem.

RELATED TITLES: Anholt, Catherine, and Laurence Anholt. *Catherine and Laurence Anholt's Big Book of Little Children.* Candlewick, 2003. / Appelt, Kathi. *Bubba and Beau.* Harcourt, 2002. (And others in the Bubba and Beau series.) / Ashman, Linda. *Babies on the Go.* Harcourt, 2003. / Cooke, Trish. *So Much.* Candlewick, 1994. / Curtis, Marci. *I Was So Silly! Big Kids Remember Being Little.* Dial, 2002. / Greenspun, Adele Aron, and Joanie Schwarz. *Ariel and Emily.* Dutton, 2003. / Hoffman, Mary. *Henry's Baby.* DK, 1993. / Meyers, Susan. *Everywhere Babies.* Harcourt, 2001. / Regan, Dian Curtis. *Chance.* Philomel, 2003. / Schwartz, Amy. *A Teeny Tiny Baby.* Orchard, 1994. / Segal, Lore. *Tell Me a Mitzi.* Farrar, 1970. / Wild, Margaret. *Midnight Babies.* Clarion, 2001. / Willems, Mo. *Knuffle Bunny: A Cautionary Tale.* Hyperion, 2004.

SUBJECTS: BABIES. NEIGHBORHOODS. PERSONAL NARRATIVES. PICTURE BOOKS FOR ALL AGES. POINT OF VIEW. TODDLERS.

592 Oates, Joyce Carol. *Where Is Little Reynard?* Illus. by Mark Graham. HarperCollins, 2003. 0-06-029559-7. Unp. Gr. PreK–1

Of the seven kittens in Momma Cat's litter, Lilly Smith loves the littlest one the best—the shy orange Little Reynard. When he climbs out the window to spend a joyful day playing in the snow with two little foxes, Flora and Rusty, Lilly heads out to search for him. Note that this is one of very few stories in which the foxes are not villains, but friendly playmates.

GERM: Discussion point: Why was Little Reynard so shy with his brothers and sisters? How and why did his day with the fox kits change that? What is the difference between a kitten and a fox kit?

RELATED TITLES: Edwards, Pamela Duncan. *Four Famished Foxes and Fosdyke.* HarperCollins, 1995. / Fleming, Denise. *Mama Cat Has Three Kittens.* Henry Holt, 1998. / Fox, Mem. *Hattie and the Fox.* Bradbury, 1987. / Frankenhuyzen, Robbyn Smith van. *Saving Samantha: A True Story.* Sleeping Bear, 2004. / Henkes, Kevin. *Kitten's First Full Moon.* Greenwillow, 2004. / Simmons, Jane. *Little Fern's First Winter.* Little, Brown, 2001. / Voake, Charlotte. *Ginger.* Candlewick, 1997. / Voake, Charlotte. *Ginger Finds a Home.* Candlewick, 2003.

SUBJECTS: CATS. FOXES. IDENTITY. SHYNESS. SNOW.

593 O'Connor, George. *Kapow!* Illus. by the author. Simon & Schuster, 2004. 0-689-86718-2. Unp. Gr. PreK–2

Two children pretending to be superheroes, calling themselves American Eagle and Bug Lady, barrel through the house, capturing a roaring panther (the family cat), tackling Rubber Bandit (a little brother), and KERRASH, knocking over a whole bookcase.

GERM: Have your intrepid adventurers do before and after portraits of themselves as regular kids and then as superheroes. They can caption their portraits with their regular and their superhero names and write about their habits and attributes in each role. (Here's mine: By day, Judy is a mild-mannered reader who loves chocolate, flowers, and trips to the Jersey shore. At night, she becomes COMPUTOGEEK, able to reboot a computer in a blink and find any fact in four seconds flat.)

RELATED TITLES: Buehner, Caralyn. *Superdog: The Heart of a Hero.* HarperCollins, 2004. / Collins, Suzanne. *When Charlie McButton Lost Power.* Putnam, 2005. / Graham, Bob. *Max.* Candlewick, 2000. / Grey, Mini. *Traction Man Is Here!* Knopf, 2005. / MacDonald, Ross. *Another Perfect Day.* Roaring Brook, 2002. / Myers, Christopher. *Wings.* Scholastic, 2000. / O'Connor, George. *Ker-Splash!* Simon & Schuster, 2005. / O'Malley, Kevin.

Straight to the Pole. Walker, 2003. / Steen, Sandra, and Susan Steen. *Car Wash*. Putnam, 2001. / Weigel, Jeff. *Atomic Ace (He's Just My Dad)*. Albert Whitman, 2004.

SUBJECTS: HUMOROUS FICTION. IMAGINATION. PLAY. SUPERHEROES.

594   O'Malley, Kevin. *Captain Raptor and the Moon Mystery*. **Illus. by Patrick O'Brien. Walker, 2005. 0-8027-8935-8. Unp. Gr. K–2**

High above Jurassica, a flash of light disappears on the dark side of Eon, one of the planet's moons, leading the dinosaur scientists, generals, and president to call Captain Raptor to investigate. Descending through Eon's atmosphere, the spaceship Megatooth is hit by lightning— "KA-BOOM." "Could this be the end of Captain Raptor and his brave crew?" Not a chance. The quartet of intrepid dinosaurs survives an attack of the Octocolossus and then encounters aliens from planet Earth.

GERM: Set up like a comic book, with gorgeous adventure-saturated watercolor and gouache illustrations, this will be a rousing exercise in reading aloud with excitement, energy, and voice, as you switch from captions of dialogue to narration. Your explorers and comic book mavens can work in small creative groups to plot out a storyboard for Captain Raptor's next adventure.

RELATED TITLES: Buehner, Caralyn. *Superdog: The Heart of a Hero*. HarperCollins, 2004. / Dodson, Peter. *An Alphabet of Dinosaurs*. Scholastic, 1995. / French, Vivian. *T. Rex*. Candlewick, 2004. / Grey, Mini. *Traction Man Is Here!* Knopf, 2005. / O'Malley, Kevin. *Straight to the Pole*. Walker, 2003. / Pringle, Laurence. *Dinosaurs! Strange and Wonderful*. Boyds Mills, 1995. / Sabuda, Robert. *Encyclopedia Prehistorica: Dinosaurs*. Candlewick, 2005. / Wallace, Karen. *I Am a Tyrannosaurus*. Atheneum, 2004. / Weigel, Jeff. *Atomic Ace (He's Just My Dad)*. Albert Whitman, 2004.

SUBJECTS: ADVENTURE AND ADVENTURERS. ASTRONAUTS. CARTOONS AND COMICS. DINOSAURS. HEROES. MYSTERY AND DETECTIVE STORIES. PICTURE BOOKS FOR ALL AGES. SCIENCE FICTION. SPACE FLIGHT.

595   O'Malley, Kevin. *Straight to the Pole*. **Illus. by the author. Walker, 2003. 0-8027-8866-1. Unp. Gr. PreK–2**

Here's a very funny personal narrative and a great exercise in hyperbole, melodrama, and wild exaggeration. Swathed in winter gear and a backpack, a solitary child trudges stoically through a fierce snowstorm, braving wind, ice, and even a wolf (really his dog) before he is rescued by his friends who tell him that school is closed for the day.

GERM: As a fun activity, start out by asking your children for ten ways to say, "It's cold outside." As you read, have your listeners describe what is really happening in the story and then act out the child's perceived adventure. Older kids can use this as a writing spur for overstating something that really happened to them. When they read their embellished tales aloud, others can identify what really happened.

RELATED TITLES: Ashman, Linda. *Rub-a-Dub Sub*. Harcourt, 2003. / Branley, Franklyn M. *Snow Is Falling*. HarperCollins, 2000. / Carrick, Carol. *Lost in the Storm*. Clarion, 1987. / Chapman, Cheryl. *Snow on Snow on Snow*. Dial, 1994. / Gliori, Debi. *The Snow Lambs*. Scholastic, 1996. / Keats, Ezra Jack. *The Snowy Day*. Viking, 1962. / Kellogg, Steven. *The Missing Mitten Mystery*. Dial, 2000. / Martin, Jacqueline Briggs. *Snowflake Bentley*. Houghton Mifflin, 1998. / O'Connor, George. *Kapow!* Simon & Schuster, 2004. / O'Malley, Kevin. *Captain Raptor and the Moon Mystery*. Walker, 2005. / Prelutsky, Jack. *It's Snowing! It's Snowing!* Greenwillow, 1984. / Schnur, Steven. *Winter: An Alphabet Acrostic*. Clarion, 2002. / Sherman, Allan, and Lou Busch. *Hello Muddah, Hello Faddah! (A Letter from Camp)*. Dutton, 2004. / Steen, Sandra, and Susan Steen. *Car Wash*. Putnam, 2001. / Stojic, Manya. *Snow*. Knopf, 2002. / Wright, Betty Ren. *The Blizzard*. Holiday House, 2003.

SUBJECTS: CREATIVE DRAMA. HUMOROUS FICTION. IMAGINATION. SNOW.

596   O'Neill, Alexis. *The Recess Queen*. **Illus. by Laura Beith. Scholastic, 2002. 0-439-20637-5. Unp. Gr. K–2**

Known as the Recess Queen in the school playground, Mean Jean pushed and smooshed any kid who dared to cross her, until the day a new girl—teeny tiny Katy Sue—dared to ask her to jump rope with her.

GERM: Ask your kids to tell you what bullies do and how they have dealt with them. In addition to the obvious behavior modification, values, and character ed aspects of the story, there's another wonderful thread to follow, and that's the children's poetry aspect. The sassy text and bouncy acrylic and collage illustrations will make everyone want to jump a little rope and recite their own verses. These rhymes are children's own special folklore. Have your class talk to their peers, as well as their parents and other grownups, to collect these rhymes, tape-record them, write them down, and make a class book of them, with a copy for everyone.

RELATED TITLES: Bottner, Barbara. *Bootsie Barker Bites*. Putnam, 1992. / Caseley, Judith. *Bully*. Greenwillow, 2001. / Cole, Joanna. *Don't Call Me Names*. Random House, 1990. / English, Karen. *Hot Day on Abbott Avenue*. Clarion, 2004. / Hall, Bruce Edward. *Henry and the Dragon Kite*. Philomel, 2004. / Kelley, True. *Blabber Mouse*. Dutton, 1991. / Larson, Kirby. *Cody and Quinn, Sitting in a Tree*. Holiday House, 1996. / Lester, Helen. *Me First*. Houghton Mifflin, 1992. / Meddaugh, Susan. *Martha Walks the Dog*. Houghton Mifflin, 1998. / Naylor, Phyllis Reynolds. *King of the Playground*. Atheneum, 1991. / Rodman, Mary Ann. *My Best Friend*. Viking, 2005. / Schwartz, Alvin, comp. *And the Green Grass Grew All Around: Folk Poetry from Everyone*. HarperCollins, 1992. / Sierra, Judy. *Schoolyard Rhymes: Kids' Own Rhymes for Rope Skipping, Hand Clapping, Ball Bouncing, and Just Plain Fun*. Knopf, 2005. / Wilhelm, Hans. *Tyrone the Horrible*. Scholastic, 1988.

SUBJECTS: BEHAVIOR. BULLIES. FRIENDSHIP. JUMP ROPE RHYMES. SCHOOLS.

597   Osborne, Mary Pope. *New York's Bravest*. Illus. by Steve Johnson and Lou Fancher. Knopf, 2002. 0-375-92196-6. Unp. Gr. PreK–6

Mose, New York City's mythical 19th-century firefighter, stood 8 feet tall, had hands as big as Virginia hams, and could swim the Hudson River in two strokes. "When others ran away from danger, Mose ran toward it." One night, Mose and his boys fought a hotel fire and, even though the hotel burned to the ground, Mose managed to rescue all the people inside. That night, however, Mose disappeared, although his legend still lives on as "the very spirit of New York City." Heroic paintings capture the vitality of a yesteryear New York and the firemen who defended it, led by the tall-tale hero whose character was based on an actual firefighter, Mose Humphreys.

GERM: The Dedication will elicit discussion and remembrance: "To the memory of the 343 New York City firefighters who gave their lives to save others on September 11, 2001." Also introduce your kids to the 398.22 section of your library, American tall tales of Paul Bunyan, Pecos Bill, and John Henry. Talk over: What are the qualities that make up a tall-tale hero? What kinds of heroic acts did they perform? Compare and contrast their exploits and then have children write new tall tales, either employing traditional characters such as Davy Crockett, or making up new ones that resolve modern-day problems and disasters. Construct your own group tall tales with the "Create an Instant Tall Tale" activity on page 115.

RELATED TITLES: Armstrong, Jennifer. *Magnus at the Fire*. Simon & Schuster, 2005. / Cohn, Amy L. *From Sea to Shining Sea: A Treasury of American Folklore and Folk Songs*. Scholastic, 1993. / Demarest, Chris L. *Firefighters A to Z*. McElderry, 2000. / Gerstein, Mordicai. *The Man Who Walked Between the Towers*. Roaring Brook, 2003. / Isaacs, Anne. *Swamp Angel*. Dutton, 1994. / Kalman, Maira. *Fireboat: The Heroic Adventures of the John J. Harvey*. Putnam, 2002. / Lester, Julius. *John Henry*. Dial, 1994. / Osborne, Mary Pope. *American Tall Tales*. Knopf, 1991. / Roth, Susan L. *It's Still a Dog's New York*. National Geographic, 2002. / San Souci, Robert D. *Larger Than Life: The Adventures of American Legendary Heroes*. Doubleday, 1991. / Walker, Paul Robert. *Big Men, Big Country: A Collection of American Tall Tales*. Harcourt, 1993. / Winter, Jeanette. *The Librarian of Basra*. Harcourt, 2005. / Winter, Jeanette. *September Roses*. Farrar, 2004.

SUBJECTS: CITIES AND TOWNS. FIRE. FIREFIGHTERS. NEW YORK CITY. PICTURE BOOKS FOR ALL AGES. TALL TALES.

598   Palatini, Margie. *Bad Boys*. Illus. by Henry Cole. HarperCollins, 2003. 0-06-000103-8. Unp. Gr. K–3

On the run again, Willy and Wally Wolf disguise themselves in lady sheep clothing and, calling themselves Willimina and Wallanda (AKA the Peep Sheep), set off to fleece an unsuspecting flock. You've got talking animals, fairy tale characters running amok, outlandish adventure, trickery, clever wordplay, hilarity, parody, and a comeuppance for two bad wolves in sheep's clothing who never learn their lesson. It must be a Margie Palatini book!

GERM: See if your listeners can identify the literary references in the story, such as "as close as the hair on my chinny-chin-chin," "There wasn't another huff or puff between them," "all the better to see ewes with," and "three bags full." You'll want to explain humorous plays on words, such as "go on the lam," "pull the wool over their eyes," and "fleece the flock" and talk over the meaning of "a wolf in sheep's clothing." You'll find the Reader's Theater script on the author's Web site at <www.margiepalatini.com>.

RELATED TITLES: Christelow, Eileen. *Where's the Big Bad Wolf?* Clarion, 2002. / Ernst, Lisa Campbell. *Little Red Riding Hood: A Newfangled Prairie Tale*. Simon & Schuster, 1995. / Ghigna, Charles. *See the Yak Yak*. Random House, 1999. / Hartman, Bob. *The Wolf Who Cried Boy*. Putnam, 2002. / Hawkins, Colin, and Jacqui Hawkins. *The Fairytale News*. Candlewick, 2004. / Johnson, Paul Brett. *Little Bunny Foo Foo*. Scholastic, 2004. /

McClements, George. *Jake Gander, Storyville Detective*. Hyperion, 2002. / Marshall, James. *The Three Little Pigs.* Dial, 1989. / Meddaugh, Susan. *Hog-Eye.* Houghton Mifflin, 1995. / Palatini, Margie. *Piggie Pie.* Clarion, 1995. / Palatini, Margie. *The Web Files.* Hyperion, 2001. / Scieszka, Jon. *The True Story of the 3 Little Pigs.* Viking, 1989. / Trivizas, Eugene. *The Three Little Wolves and the Big Bad Pig.* McElderry, 1993. / Vozar, David. *Yo, Hungry Wolf! A Nursery Rap.* Doubleday, 1993. / Wiesner, David. *The Three Pigs.* Clarion, 2001.

SUBJECTS: BEHAVIOR. HUMOROUS FICTION. PARODIES. READER'S THEATER. SHEEP. WOLVES.

599   **Palatini, Margie. *Bedhead*. Illus. by Jack E. Davis. Simon & Schuster, 2000. 0-689-82397-5. Unp. Gr. K–2**

Bleary-eyed Oliver wakes up fast when he gets a glimpse in the bathroom mirror of his big, bad, out-of-control hair. Mom, Dad, and sister Emily all try to help, but water, hair spray, and a brush fail to make a dent. Wearing his baseball cap to school, all is fine and dandy until his teacher insists he remove it for the class picture.

GERM: For some fun experiential narrative writing and illustrating, link this story to Palatini's *Tub-boo-boo* and to Judith Viorst's *Alexander and the Terrible, Horrible, No Good, Very Bad Day.* Ask your group to think back on a bad hair day (or bad anything day) that wasn't funny then but is now, and use humor to relate what happened.

RELATED TITLES: Palatini, Margie. *Stinky Smelly Feet: A Love Story.* Dutton, 2004. / Palatini, Margie. *Sweet Tooth.* Simon & Schuster, 2004. / Palatini, Margie. *Tub-Boo-Boo.* Simon & Schuster, 2001. / Palatini, Margie. *Zak's Lunch.* Clarion, 1998. / Roche, Denis. *The Best Class Picture Ever.* Scholastic, 2003. / Saltzberg, Barney. *Crazy Hair Day.* Candlewick, 2003. / Shannon, David. *A Bad Case of Stripes.* Blue Sky/Scholastic, 1998. / Stevenson, James. *That Dreadful Day.* Greenwillow, 1985. / Viorst, Judith. *Alexander and the Terrible, Horrible, No Good, Very Bad Day.* Atheneum, 1972.

SUBJECTS: EMBARRASSMENT. HAIR. HUMOROUS FICTION. SCHOOLS.

600   **Palatini, Margie. *Ding Dong Ding Dong*. Illus. by Howard Fine. Hyperion, 1999. 0-7868-2367-4. Unp. Gr. 1–4**

The door-to-door salesman for Ape-On Cosmetics can't get his foot in the door. "It's a jungle out there," the big ape moans, and heads for the Big Apple, where he stumbles into a job washing windows at the Empire State Building. Working his way to the top is tougher than he expects.

GERM: Aside from being an on-target parody of King Kong, filled with witty New York lingo and wordplay, the ape-filled pastel illustrations are glorious. It might be great fun to show excerpts of the original movie with Fay Wray to analyze the use of parody in *Ding Dong Ding Dong* and Dav Pilkey's *Kat Kong.* For that persuasive writing activity, kids can put themselves in the Big Guy's shoes and have him try to talk a customer into buying his Ape-On cosmetics. Be sure to bring in some cologne and cosmetics for a little realism.

RELATED TITLES: Browne, Anthony. *Willy the Dreamer.* Candlewick, 1998. / Dorros, Arthur. *Abuela.* Dutton, 1991. / Fraser, Mary Ann. *I. Q., It's Time.* Walker, 2005. / Grimes, Nikki. *C Is for City.* Lothrop, 1995. / Jakobsen, Kathy. *My New York.* Little, Brown, 2003. / Lithgow, John. *Micawber.* Simon & Schuster, 2002. / Melmed, Laura Krauss. *New York, New York! The Big Apple from A to Z.* HarperCollins, 2005. / Pilkey, Dav. *Dogzilla.* Harcourt, 1993. / Pilkey, Dav. *Kat Kong.* Harcourt, 1993. / Priceman, Marjorie. *Froggie Went a-Courting.* Little, Brown, 2000. / Rotner, Shelley, and Ken Kreisler. *Citybook.* Orchard, 1994. / Wiesner, David. *Sector 7.* Clarion, 1999.

SUBJECTS: APES. CITIES AND TOWNS. EMPIRE STATE BUILDING (NEW YORK, NY). HUMOROUS FICTION. NEW YORK CITY. PARODIES. PICTURE BOOKS FOR ALL AGES.

601   **Palatini, Margie. *Earthquack!* Illus. by Barry Moser. Simon & Schuster, 2002. 0-689-84280-5. Unp. Gr. PreK–1**

Little Chucky Ducky feels the ground rumble, goes down in a tumble, and concludes, Henny-Penny style, that the earth is crumbling. "It's a quake!" he warns Lucy Goosey, Vickie, Nickie, and Rickie Chickie, Brewster Rooster, Iggie Piggie, and the rest of the barnyard gang. A hungry weasel, disguising himself as Herman Ermine, takes advantage of the panicked pals and almost lures them to his lair.

GERM: The watercolors and wordplay are winning in this remake of the Chicken Little story, with a twist ending, Palatini-style. Read or tell the original—I'm partial to the wordplay and color photo collages in Jane Wattenberg's *Henny-Penny*—and then follow up with a Reader's Theater production. Margie's already written the script for you; download it from her gorgeous

Web site at <www.margiepalatini.com>. Variants of the Henny-Penny story include *Foolish Rabbit's Big Mistake* by Rafe Martin and *The Rumor* by Jan Thornhill.

RELATED TITLES: Fox, Mem. *Hattie and the Fox*. Bradbury, 1987. / Hindley, Judy. *Do Like a Duck Does!* Candlewick, 2002. / Martin, Rafe. *Foolish Rabbit's Big Mistake*. Putnam, 1985. / Palatini, Margie. *Moo Who?* HarperCollins, 2004. / Raffi. *Five Little Ducks*. Crown, 1988. / Rankin, Joan. *Wow! It's Great Being a Duck*. McElderry, 1998. / Shannon, George. *Tippy-Toe Chick, Go!* Greenwillow, 2003. / Thornhill, Jan. *The Rumor: A Jataka Tale from India*. Maple Tree, 2002. / Wattenberg, Jane. *Henny-Penny*. Scholastic, 2000.

SUBJECTS: ANIMALS. CHICKENS. DOMESTIC ANIMALS. FAIRY TALES—SATIRE. HUMOROUS FICTION. PARODIES. PUNS AND PUNNING. READER'S THEATER. WEASELS.

602 **Palatini, Margie.** *Elf Help.* **Illus. by Mike Reed. Hyperion, 1997. 0-7868-2304-6. Unp. Gr. K–2**

Alfred Elf, a computer whiz who works in Santa's mail room, has downloaded Santa's entire Christmas List onto one nice shiny silver disk and guarantees that his Elfcheck is totally yuleproof. But on Christmas morning, children all over the world find their Christmas wishes have been all mixed up. Johnny Chester in New York City gets a horse in his city apartment, while Connie Lester in Tucson gets ice skates.

GERM: While we're used to seeing kids writing letters to Santa asking for stuff, the kids in this story write thank you notes for the best gifts they never asked for. Add thank you notes to your letter writing lesson.

RELATED TITLES: Barracca, Debra, and Sal Barracca. *A Taxi Dog Christmas*. Dial, 1994. / Brett, Jan. *The Wild Christmas Reindeer*. Putnam, 1990. / Burningham, John. *Harvey Slumfenberger's Christmas Present*. Candlewick, 1993. / Haywood, Carolyn. *A Christmas Fantasy*. Morrow, 1992. / Joyce, William. *Santa Calls*. HarperCollins, 1993. / Katz, Alan. *Where Did They Hide My Presents? Silly Dilly Christmas Songs*. McElderry, 2005. / Kimmel, Elizabeth Cody. *My Penguin Osbert*. Candlewick, 2004. / Krensky, Stephen. *How Santa Got His Job*. Simon & Schuster, 1998. / Krensky, Stephen. *How Santa Lost His Job*. Simon & Schuster, 2001 / McPhail, David. *Santa's Book of Names*. Little, Brown, 1993. / Palatini, Margie. *Three French Hens*. Hyperion, 2005. / Pearson, Tracey Campbell. *Where Does Joe Go?* Farrar, 1999. / Price, Moe. *The Reindeer Christmas*. Harcourt, 1993. / Primavera, Elise. *Auntie Claus*. Harcourt, 1999. / Van Allsburg, Chris. *The Polar Express*. Houghton Mifflin, 1985.

SUBJECTS: CHRISTMAS. COMPUTERS. ELVES. HUMOROUS FICTION. SANTA CLAUS.

603 **Palatini, Margie.** *Moo Who?* **Illus. by Keith Graves. HarperCollins, 2004. 0-06-000105-4. Unp. Gr. PreK–1**

After being hit in the noggin by a hard and high-flying cow pie, Hilda Mae Heifer comes to not knowing who she is or how she is supposed to act. She tries honking, peeping, oinking, and mewing, while a friendly goose, chicken, pig, and cat try to set her straight on her own singular attributes. As the pig says, "You're no swine. You're bovine. You moo."

GERM: This will make an adorable Reader's Theater script. For a creative drama exercise, have your children pair up, with one playing Hilda and the other another animal. The child playing the other animal character needs to explain to Hilda why she is not, say, a cat or a rooster and to engage her in a question-and-answer session, modeled on but not necessarily the same as the dialogue in the original story.

RELATED TITLES: Causley, Charles. *"Quack!" Said the Billy-Goat*. Lippincott, 1986. / Dallas-Conté, Juliet. *Cock-a-Moo-Moo*. Little, Brown, 2001. / Egan, Tim. *Metropolitan Cow*. Houghton Mifflin, 1996. / Egan, Tim. *Serious Farm*. Houghton Mifflin, 2003. / Feiffer, Jules. *Bark, George*. HarperCollins, 1999. / Forrester, Victoria. *The Magnificent Moo*. Atheneum, 1983. / Fleming, Denise. *Barnyard Banter*. Henry Holt, 1994. / Greene, Rhonda Gowler. *Barnyard Song*. Atheneum, 1997. / Krosoczka, Jarrett J. *Punk Farm*. Knopf, 2005. / Most, Bernard. *Cock-a-Doodle-Moo!* Harcourt, 1996. / Palatini, Margie. *Earthquack!* Simon & Schuster, 2002. / Pearson, Tracey Campbell. *Bob*. Farrar, 2002. / Rostoker-Gruber, Karen. *Rooster Can't Cock-a-Doodle-Doo*. Dial, 2004. / Shapiro, Arnold L. *Mice Squeak, We Speak*. Putnam, 1997. / Vail, Rachel. *Over the Moon*. Orchard, 1998. / Zimmerman, Andrea, and David Clemensha. *The Cow Buzzed*. HarperCollins, 1993.

SUBJECTS: ANIMAL SOUNDS. COWS. CREATIVE DRAMA. HUMOROUS FICTION. READER'S THEATER.

604 **Palatini, Margie.** *Moosetache.* **Illus. by Henry Cole. Hyperion, 1997. 0-7868-2246-5. Unp. Gr. K–2**

Moose has a "horrible, hairy, prickly problem": a "big, bushy, bristly, mighty moosetache" that has grown out of control, undaunted by brushes or scissors, and is crimping his lifestyle. Each simple, easy, and perfectly perfect solution he dreams up to get the overflowing moosetache under control won't work, until the fateful day he bumps into a glamorous female moose with an outrageous bouffant, who reveals her coiffing secret.

GERM: Palatini, author of the marvelously manic *Piggie Pie*, in which Gritch the Witch is outwitted by pigs and meets her match in a wolf, will once again stimulate your reading taste buds with her lively, dancing language. Brainstorm new and creative solutions to Moose's hairy problem before finishing the story. Meet a moose with antler problems who runs afoul of the law in Tim Egan's *The Trial of Cardigan Jones*.

RELATED TITLES: Egan, Tim. *The Trial of Cardigan Jones*. Houghton Mifflin, 2004. / Numeroff, Laura. *If You Give a Moose a Muffin*. HarperCollins, 1991. / Palatini, Margie. *Bad Boys*. HarperCollins, 2003. / Palatini, Margie. *Moosekitos: A Moose Family Reunion*. Hyperion, 2004. / Palatini, Margie. *Mooseltoe*. Hyperion, 2000. / Palatini, Margie. *Piggie Pie*. Clarion, 1995. / Palatini, Margie. *Stinky Smelly Feet: A Love Story*. Dutton, 2004. / Palatini, Margie. *The Web Files*. Hyperion, 2001. / Seuss, Dr. *Thidwick, the Big-Hearted Moose*. Random House, 1948.

SUBJECTS: HAIR. HUMOROUS FICTION. LOVE. MOOSE. MUSTACHE.

605   Palatini, Margie. *Piggie Pie*. **Illus. by Howard Fine. Clarion, 1995. 0-395-71691-8. Unp. Gr. PreK–2**

Meet Gritch the Witch, whose Old Hag Cookbook provides a scrumptious secret recipe for Piggie Pie, but whose cupboards are lacking the main ingredient. Where does one find eight plump piggies in a hurry? The Yellow Pages, of course, where she looks up the number for Old MacDonald's Farm: "Call EI-EI-O; Just Over the River and Through the Woods." The piggies scatter and disguise themselves first as ducks, then as a cow, a flock of chickens, and finally as Old MacDonald himself, frustrating green-fingernailed Gritch, who is only too happy to invite a skinny, huffing and puffing wolf home for dinner.

GERM: Listeners will be eager to speculate on what might happen after the just-right open-ended finale. Find the author's Reader's Theater script for the book on her Web site, <www.margiepalatini.com>.

RELATED TITLES: Buehner, Caralyn, and Mark Buehner. *A Job for Wittilda*. Dial, 1993. / DiCamillo, Kate. *Mercy Watson to the Rescue*. Candlewick, 2005. / Meddaugh, Susan. *Hog-Eye*. Houghton, 1995. / Meddaugh, Susan. *The Witches' Supermarket*. Houghton Mifflin, 1991. / Palatini, Margie. *Bad Boys*. HarperCollins, 2003. / Palatini, Margie. *Broom Mates*. Hyperion, 2003. / Palatini, Margie. *Oink*. Simon & Schuster, 2006. / Palatini, Margie. *Sweet Tooth*. Simon & Schuster, 2004. / Palatini, Margie. *The Web Files*. Hyperion, 2001. / Palatini, Margie. *Zoom Broom*. Hyperion, 1998. / Rayner, Mary. *Mr. and Mrs. Pig's Evening Out*. Atheneum, 1976. / Scieszka, Jon. *The True Story of the 3 Little Pigs*. Viking, 1989.

SUBJECTS: DOMESTIC ANIMALS. FAIRY TALES—SATIRE. HUMOROUS FICTION. PARODIES. PICTURE BOOKS FOR ALL AGES. PIGS. READER'S THEATER. WITCHES. WOLVES.

606   Palatini, Margie. *Stinky Smelly Feet: A Love Story*. **Illus. by Ethan Long. Dutton, 2004. 0-525-47201-0. Unp. Gr. K–2**

Douglas and Dolores, two ducks smitten with each other, are spending an idyllic day picnicking in the park, but when Douglas flings off his right shoe to let the grass tickle his toes, PLUNK!—down goes Dolores. She's passed out from the stench of his stinky, smelly duck feet. In spite of bubble baths and foot powder and perfume, one whiff makes everyone keel over. ("Abandon the beach!" hollers the lifeguard at the ocean.) But true love wins out in the end.

GERM: What a hoot this'll be for Valentine's Day or beefing up that five senses unit with a bit of odiferous fun. For that problem-versus-solution lesson, have your children come up with a good solution for stinky feet. And what about Dolores? Surely she can't be perfect, either? Have them come up with a problem—an aspect of her persona that might drive Douglas crazy—and a solution for it. Compare Douglas's uncontrollable foot odor problem with Moose's uncontrollable mustache in another Palatini love story, *Moostache*. More laughs and smells abound in Dav Pilkey's *Dog Breath* and, of course, the title story in Jon Scieszka's classic, *The Stinky Cheese Man and Other Fairly Stupid Tales*.

RELATED TITLES: Palatini, Margie. *Bedhead*. Simon & Schuster, 2000. / Palatini, Margie. *Ding Dong Ding Dong*. Hyperion, 1999. / Palatini, Margie. *Moosetache*. Hyperion, 1997. / Palatini, Margie. *Sweet Tooth*. Simon & Schuster, 2004. / Palatini, Margie. *The Web Files*. Hyperion, 2001. / Pilkey, Dav. *Dog Breath: The Horrible Trouble with Hally Tosis*. Blue Sky/Scholastic, 1994. / Pulver, Robin. *Mrs. Toggle's Beautiful Blue Shoe*. Four Winds, 1994. / Scieszka, Jon. *The Stinky Cheese Man and Other Fairly Stupid Tales*. Viking, 1992.

SUBJECTS: DUCKS. FOOT. HUMOROUS FICTION. LOVE. PICNICS. SENSES AND SENSATION. SHOES. SMELL.

607   Palatini, Margie. *Sweet Tooth.* **Illus. by Jack E. Davis. Simon & Schuster, 2004. 0-689-85159-6. Unp. Gr. PreK–3**

Ordinary kid Stuart has the most "nagging, annoying, demanding" sweet tooth ever! It insists on a regular diet of candy bars with that gooey stuff in the middle and gets him in trouble with its incessant needs. When the exasperated boy announces that from now on there'll be nothing for his tooth but a healthy diet, The Tooth plans its revenge.

GERM: Looking for a fabulously funny book to talk about "voice"? Junk food versus healthy food? Overcoming your inner demons? Loose teeth? Bullies? Here you go. And it's not even fattening, unless the subliminal effects of talking about all that candy wear down your dieter's reserve. If you're talking about using voice in writing and personification, The Tooth has attitude to spare, with its blustering, bullying, self-righteous pronouncements to poor, defenseless Stuart. You can use the large shiny white generic tooth puppet from <www.mimismotifs.com> to talk up a storm. What do your other body parts have to say for themselves? Write dialogues between yourself and your ears, nose, or eyes.

RELATED TITLES: Bate, Lucy. *Little Rabbit's Loose Tooth.* Crown, 1975. / Catling, Patrick Skene. *The Chocolate Touch.* Morrow, 1979. / Chandra, Deborah, and Madeline Comora. *George Washington's Teeth.* Farrar, 2003. / Davis, Katie. *Mabel the Tooth Fairy and How She Got Her Job.* Harcourt, 2003. / Kraft, Erik. *Chocolatina.* Bridge-Water, 1998. / MacDonald, Amy. *Cousin Ruth's Tooth.* Houghton Mifflin, 1996. / McGhee, Alison. *Mrs. Watson Wants Your Teeth.* Harcourt, 2004. / Palatini, Margie. *Bedhead.* Simon & Schuster, 2000. / Palatini, Margie. *Stinky Smelly Feet: A Love Story.* Dutton, 2004. / Palatini, Margie. *Zak's Lunch.* Clarion, 1998. / Shannon, David. *A Bad Case of Stripes.* Scholastic, 1998. / Shields, Carol Diggory. *Food Fight!* Handprint, 2002. / Simms, Laura. *Rotten Teeth.* Houghton Mifflin, 1998. / Smith, Robert Kimmell. *Chocolate Fever.* Putnam, 1989. / Swain, Ruth Freeman. *How Sweet It Is (and Was): The History of Candy.* Holiday House, 2003.

SUBJECTS: BULLIES. CANDY. FOOD HABITS. HUMOROUS FICTION. PERSONIFICATION. PICTURE BOOKS FOR ALL AGES. POINT OF VIEW. SELF-ESTEEM. TEETH. TOOTH FAIRY.

608   Palatini, Margie. *Tub-Boo-Boo.* **Illus. by Glin Dibley. Simon & Schuster, 2001. 0-689-82394-0. Unp. Gr. K–3**

Lucy Hathaway gives us the inside scoop on what really happened in her house today, starting when her little brother Henry was sent upstairs to take a bath at 4:15 and tried to slow the flow of water with his big toe. Whoops. Henry's tub-boo-boo leaves him with the toe stuck in the spout, and everyone who tries to get it out gets stuck too.

GERM: "Oh, brother. What a story," Lucy concludes. You can set up TV interviews for all of the characters of this zany disaster tale, from Mom and Dad to Officer Ottley and the plumber. Ask your bathers what adventures they've had in the tub. Also lather up with an even taller tale, *No More Water in the Tub!* by Tedd Arnold.

RELATED TITLES: Arnold, Tedd. *No More Water in the Tub!* Dial, 1995. / Bond, Michael. *A Bear Called Paddington.* Houghton Mifflin, 1960. / Cole, Brock. *No More Baths.* Doubleday, 1980. / Faulkner, Matt. *The Amazing Voyage of Jackie Grace.* Scholastic, 1987. / Palatini, Margie. *Bedhead.* Simon & Schuster, 2000. / Palatini, Margie. *Sweet Tooth.* Simon & Schuster, 2004. / Palatini, Margie. *Zak's Lunch.* Clarion, 1998.

SUBJECTS: BATHS. BROTHERS AND SISTERS. HUMOROUS FICTION. PERSONAL NARRATIVES.

609   Palatini, Margie. *The Web Files.* **Illus. by Richard Egielski. Hyperion, 2001. 0-7868-0419-X. Unp. Gr. K–3**

Ducktective Web and his partner, Bill, are hot on the trail of missing about-to-be-pickled purple peppers in this deadpan barnyard takeoff on the old "Dragnet" TV show. Who's the culprit? It couldn't be . . . that Dirty Rat?

GERM: Before reading the story, brainstorm a list of terms used in mysteries. Listeners will love chiming in on the famed theme song—DUM DE DUM DUM—each time, and if you don't try the Reader's Theater script just waiting for you at <www.margiepalatini.com>, it's a crime! Working in pairs, sleuths can pick two nursery rhyme characters—a victim and a suspect—and make "Wanted" posters, with a picture of the culprit, a summary of the crime, a description of the evidence left at the scene, and the reward that's being offered upon the suspect's capture. Using their posters, flatfeet can then write up and illustrate a new mystery installment, set on the farm, for Ducktective Web to solve.

RELATED TITLES: Christelow, Eileen. *Where's the Big Bad Wolf?* Clarion, 2002. / Clifford, Eth. *Flatfoot Fox and the Case of the Mising Schoolhouse.* Houghton Mifflin, 1997. (And others in the Flatfoot Fox series.) / Cushman, Doug. *Aunt Eater Loves a Mystery.* HarperCollins, 1987. (And others in the Aunt Eater mystery series.) / Cushman, Doug. *Inspector Hopper.* HarperCollins, 2000. / Cushman, Doug. *Mystery at the Club Sandwich.* Clarion, 2004. / Cushman, Doug. *The Mystery of King Karfu*. HarperCollins, 1996. / Kelly, John, and Cathy Tinck-nell. *The Mystery of Eatum Hall*. Candlewick, 2004. / McClements, George. *Jake Gander, Storyville Detective*. Hyperion, 2002. / Palatini, Margie. *Bad Boys*. HarperCollins, 2003. / Palatini, Margie. *Piggie Pie*. Clarion, 1995. / Palatini, Margie. *Stinky Smelly Feet: A Love Story*. Dutton, 2004. / Palatini, Margie. *Sweet Tooth*. Simon & Schuster, 2004. / Scieszka, Jon. *The True Story of the 3 Little Pigs*. Viking, 1989. / Stevens, Janet, and Susan Stevens Crummel. *And the Dish Ran Away with the Spoon*. Harcourt, 2001. / Teague, Mark. *Detective LaRue: Letters from the Investigation*. Scholastic, 2004.

SUBJECTS: FARM LIFE. HUMOROUS FICTION. MYSTERY AND DETECTIVE STORIES. NURSERY RHYMES. PICTURE BOOKS FOR ALL AGES. READER'S THEATER.

610   Palatini, Margie. *Zak's Lunch*. Illus. by Howard Fine. Clarion, 1998. 0-395-81674-2. Unp. Gr. PreK–2

Instead of the yechhh-y ham and cheese sandwich his mom expects him to eat, Zak experiences the lunch of his dreams, served by diner-jargon-spouting waitress Lou at Zak's Place. There's "moo meat all the way" (cheeseburger deluxe), fried "pins" (drumsticks), and desserts to die for. When Zak comes back from his daydream to his own kitchen table, he and Great Dane George miraculously make that ham and cheese disappear.

GERM: Have children work on desired and imaginative menus for that nutrition unit. *Lunch Bunnies*, about rabbit Clyde, who's afraid he won't be able to manage the cafeteria routine when he starts school, is another one that will get listeners thinking about their next meal. Don't forget to fool around with the diner lingo in Alexandra Day's *Frank and Ernest*.

RELATED TITLES: Barrett, Judi. *Cloudy with a Chance of Meatballs*. Atheneum, 1978. / Blumenthal, Deborah. *Don't Let the Peas Touch! And Other Stories*. Scholastic, 2004. / Brown, Marc. *D. W. the Picky Eater*. Little, Brown, 1995. / Child, Lauren. *I Will Never Not Ever Eat a Tomato*. Candlewick, 2000. / Day, Alexandra. *Frank and Ernest*. Scholastic, 1988. / Demarest, Chris L. *No Peas for Nellie*. Macmillan, 1988. / Lasky, Kathryn. *Lunch Bunnies*. Little, Brown, 1996. / MacLean, Christine Kole. *Even Firefighters Hug Their Moms*. Dutton, 2002. / Palatini, Margie. *Sweet Tooth*. Simon & Schuster, 2004. / Rayner, Mary. *Mrs. Pig's Bulk Buy*. Atheneum, 1981. / Rosenthal, Amy Krouse. *Little Pea*. Chronicle Books, 2005. / Seuss, Dr. *Green Eggs and Ham*. Random House, 1960. / Sharmat, Mitchell. *Gregory, the Terrible Eater*. Four Winds, 1984. / Wells, Rosemary. *Yoko*. Hyperion, 1998. / Yaccarino, Dan. *If I Had a Robot*. Viking, 1996. / Yolen, Jane. *How Do Dinosaurs Eat Their Food?* Blue Sky/Scholastic, 2005.

SUBJECTS: DOGS. FOOD. FOOD HABITS. IMAGINATION. MOTHERS AND SONS. RESTAURANTS.

611   Palatini, Margie. *Zoom Broom*. Illus. by Howard Fine. Hyperion, 1998. 0-7868-0322-3. Unp. Gr. PreK–2

Gritch the Witch, of Piggie Pie fame, needs a zippy new form of transport, so she visits Foxy's showroom, where she faces off in hilarious repartee with the unctuous, fast-talking salesman in her search for the perfect broom.

GERM: Palatini has a ball tweaking us with her puns and clever plays on words, and you'll have a ball reading this one aloud. There's a hilarious takeoff on Abbott and Costello's "Who's on first" routine, in which Gritch asks Foxy, "Which one is the one I want?" Your actors can stage it in pairs as a Reader's Theater scene. For second graders, you'll find the original routine in Amy L. Cohn's *From Sea to Shining Sea*, which you can also read aloud in pairs, or you can play the original recording so everyone can hear the humor first-hand.

RELATED TITLES: Buehner, Caralyn, and Mark Buehner. *A Job for Wittilda*. Dial, 1993. / Cox, Judy. *Rabbit Pirates: A Tale of the Spinach Main*. Harcourt, 1999. / Meddaugh, Susan. *The Witches' Supermarket*. Houghton Mifflin, 1990. / Palatini, Margie. *Bad Boys*. HarperCollins, 2003. / Palatini, Margie. *Piggie Pie*. Clarion, 1995. / Palatini, Margie. *Sweet Tooth*. Simon & Schuster, 2004. / Palatini, Margie. *The Web Files*. Hyperion, 2001. / Van Allsburg, Chris. *The Widow's Broom*. Houghton Mifflin, 1992.

SUBJECTS: FOXES. HUMOROUS FICTION. READER'S THEATER. TRANSPORTATION. WITCHES.

612   Parish, Herman. *Amelia Bedelia, Bookworm*. Illus. by Lynn Sweat. Greenwillow, 2003. 0-06-051891-X. 64pp. Gr. K–3

When Amelia Bedelia, America's favorite housekeeper, stops by the library, she brings her own singular style of interpreting everything literally to the world of books, taking the library's bookmobile, running a story hour at a local bookstore, and making a lovely literary ruckus.

GERM: As with all of the books in this classic series, Amelia Bedelia lets us all fool around with words and their multiple meanings. Use this one as a springboard to discuss the role of the library and how we need to take care of all our books.

RELATED TITLES: Adler, David A. *Young Cam Jansen and the Library Mystery*. Viking, 2001. / Allen, Susan, and Jane Lindaman. *Read Anything Good Lately?* Millbrook, 2003. / Child, Lauren. *Who's Afraid of the Big Bad Book?* Hyperion, 2003. / Ernst, Lisa Campbell. *Stella Louella's Runaway Book*. Simon & Schuster, 1998. / Ghigna, Charles. *See the Yak Yak*. Random House, 1999. / Gwynne, Fred. *A Chocolate Moose for Dinner*. Dutton, 1976. / Gwynne, Fred. *The King Who Rained*. Dutton, 1970. / Huff, Barbara. *Once Inside the Library*. Little, Brown, 1990. / Numeroff, Laura Joffe. *Beatrice Doesn't Want To*. Candlewick, 2004. / Parish, Herman. *Amelia Bedelia 4 Mayor*. Greenwillow, 1999. (And others in the Amelia Bedelia series.) / Sierra, Judy. *Wild About Books*. Knopf, 2004. / Thaler, Mike. *The Librarian from the Black Lagoon*. Scholastic, 1997. / Williams, Suzanne. *Library Lil*. Dial, 1997.

SUBJECTS: BOOKMOBILES. BOOKS AND READING. ENGLISH LANGUAGE—HOMONYMS. ENGLISH LANGUAGE—IDIOMS. HUMOROUS FICTION. LIBRARIANS. LIBRARIES.

613   **Park, Barbara. *Psssst! It's Me . . . the Bogeyman*. Illus. by Stephen Kroninger. Atheneum, 1998. 0-689-81667-7. Unp. Gr. 1–4**

Lurking under a boy's bed is the "genuine, creepy-crawly, blood-chilling, spine-tingling . . . bogeyguy," and he's very upset. Why? A misleading, downright false headline in the *National Squealer* ("Evil Bogeyman Bellows Boo") has him all bent out of shape. So now the bogeyman wants the boy to clear his name with the truth and gives the boy the inside skinny on his true talents and professional techniques—which include scaring the socks off little whippersnappers.

GERM: What a glorious and spine-tingling tour de force to read aloud, a sterling example of voice and characterization. Delicious shivers will not stop listeners from keeping pairs of smelly socks handy so the bogeyman won't park himself under their beds. See how Harry deflects his monster in *Harry and the Terrible Whatzit* by Dick Gackenbach. Older readers will find chills and laughs in Neil Gaiman's *The Wolves in the Walls*.

RELATED TITLES: Bang, Molly. *Wiley and the Hairy Man*. Macmillan, 1976. / Bunting, Eve. *Ghost's Hour, Spook's Hour*. Clarion, 1987. / Gackenbach, Dick. *Harry and the Terrible Whatzit*. Clarion, 1977. / Gaiman, Neil. *The Wolves in the Walls*. HarperCollins, 2003. / Hancock, Sibyl. *Esteban and the Ghost*. Dial, 1983. / Mayer, Mercer. *Liza Lou and the Yeller Belly Swamp*. Four Winds, 1980. / McKissack, Patricia, and Onawumi Jean Moss. *Precious and the Boo Hag*. Atheneum, 2005. / Patschke, Steve. *The Spooky Book*. Walker, 1999. / Sierra, Judy. *Wiley and the Hairy Man*. Dutton, 1996. / Vaughan, Marcia. *Whistling Dixie*. HarperCollins, 1995. / Viorst, Judith. *My Mama Says There Aren't Any Zombies, Ghosts, Vampires, Creatures, Demons, Monsters, Fiends, Goblins, or Things*. Atheneum, 1973. / Willems, Mo. *Leonardo the Terrible Monster*. Hyperion, 2005. / Williams, Linda. *The Little Old Lady Who Was Not Afraid of Anything*. Crowell, 1986. / Yep, Laurence. *The Man Who Tricked a Ghost*. BridgeWater, 1993.

SUBJECTS: BOGEYMAN. FEAR. HUMOROUS FICTION. MONSTERS. PERSONAL NARRATIVES. PICTURE BOOKS FOR ALL AGES. SUSPENSE.

614   **Paterson, Katherine. *Marvin One Too Many*. Illus. by Jane Clark Brown. HarperCollins, 2001. 0-06-028769-1. 48pp. Gr. PreK–2**

"Books are dumb," says Marvin, when he's the only one in his first-grade class who can't read. His teacher, Mrs. Brown, wants parents to read with their children every day, but when she sends a note home with him about reading with his mother and father, he tears it up on the way to his house. When he finally reveals his problem to his dairy farmer dad, guess what? Dad was the last one to read in his class too! "Guys who take a little longer need to stick together," Dad says, promising to read with Marvin every night.

GERM: Paterson's winsome, true-to-life easy-reader makes a perfect read-aloud or read-alone for all those children who think they'll never get the hang of figuring out all those words. Have your emerging readers tell or write about their earliest reading memories: What was the first word you learned to read? What was your favorite book when you were little? How did you learn to read?

RELATED TITLES: Allen, Susan, and Jane Lindaman. *Read Anything Good Lately?* Millbrook, 2003. / Bloom, Becky. *Wolf!* Orchard, 1999. / Bunting, Eve. *The Wednesday Surprise*. Clarion, 1989. / Daly, Niki. *Once Upon a Time*. Farrar, 2003. / Heide, Florence Parry, and Judith Heide Gilliland. *The Day of Ahmed's Secret*. Lothrop, 1990. / Hest, Amy. *Mr. George Baker*. Candlewick, 2004. / Hutchins, Pat. *The Tale of Thomas Mead*. Greenwillow, 1980. / Marshall, James. *Wings: A Tale of Two Chickens*. Viking, 1986. / McPhail, David. *Fix-It*. Dutton, 1984. / McPhail, David. *Santa's Book of Names*. Little, Brown, 1993. / Paterson, Katherine. *Marvin's Best Christmas Present Ever*. HarperCollins, 1997. / Polacco, Patricia. *Thank You, Mr. Falker*. Philomel, 1998. / Williams, Suzanne. *Library Lil*. Dial, 1997. / Wishinsky, Frieda. *Give Maggie a Chance*. Fitzhenry & Whiteside, 2002.

SUBJECTS: BOOKS AND READING. FATHERS AND SONS. PERSEVERANCE. SCHOOLS.

615   Paterson, Katherine. *Marvin's Best Christmas Present Ever.* **Illus. by Jane Clark Brown. HarperCollins, 1997. 0-06-027159-0. 48pp. Gr. K–2**

Marvin hangs his huge homemade wreath on the family's trailer for Christmas, but he can't bear to take it down after the holiday is over. In spring, when his parents plan to throw out the now-brown wreath, they discover it has new occupants: a family of birds.

GERM: Follow up with another Marvin story, *Marvin One Too Many.*

RELATED TITLES: DePaolo, Paula. *Rosie and the Yellow Ribbon.* Little, Brown, 1992. / Medearis, Angela Shelf. *Poppa's Itchy Christmas.* Holiday House, 1998. / Naylor, Phyllis Reynolds. *Keeping a Christmas Secret.* Atheneum, 1989. / Paterson, Katherine. *Marvin One Too Many.* HarperCollins, 2001. / Polacco, Patricia. *An Orange for Frankie.* Philomel, 2004. / Soto, Gary. *Too Many Tamales.* Putnam, 1993. / Wetzel, JoAnne Stewart. *The Christmas Box.* Knopf, 1992.

SUBJECTS: BIRDS. CHRISTMAS. FAMILY STORIES. GIFTS.

616   Patschke, Steve. *The Spooky Book.* **Illus. by Matthew McElligott. Walker, 1999. 0-8027-8693-6. Unp. Gr. 1–4**

Alone in the house on a dark and thundery night, Andrew is reading a spooky book about a red-haired girl named Zo Zo, who is reading a spooky book about a boy who is alone in a great big haunted house. "What's there to be afraid of? . . . A book can't hurt you," says Andrew, but when the lightning crashes and shadows creep across Zo Zo's wall, she runs frightened from her house and bangs on Andrew's door. What's real and what's story, listeners will be wondering, mouths agape. Is Zo Zo real or just a character in Andrew's book or vice versa?

GERM: There are satisfying chills here, especially in the evocative, gloomy, rain-swept, full-bleed paintings, with bats and shadows on the wall setting the standard for a dark and stormy night, especially if you read it in a darkened room, in a scary voice, and with a flashlight. Listeners will have to unravel the hook of the story, which is a little like a bad weather version of Caldecott Honor winner *The Red Book* by Barbara Lehman.

RELATED TITLES: Banyai, Istvan. *Zoom.* Viking, 1995. / Bunting, Eve. *Scary, Scary Halloween.* Clarion, 1986. / Gaiman, Neil. *The Wolves in the Walls.* HarperCollins, 2003. / Garland, Michael. *Miss Smith's Incredible Storybook.* Dutton, 2003. / Lehman, Barbara. *The Red Book.* Houghton Mifflin, 2004. / McKissack, Patricia, and Onawumi Jean Moss. *Precious and the Boo Hag.* Atheneum, 2005. / Park, Barbara. *Psssst! It's Me . . . the Bogeyman.* Atheneum, 1998. / Scieszka, Jon. *The Book That Jack Wrote.* Viking, 1994. / Sklansky, Amy E. *Skeleton Bones and Goblin Groans: Poems for Halloween.* Henry Holt, 2004. / Stevenson, James. *That Terrible Halloween Night.* Greenwillow, 1980. / Stutson, Caroline. *By the Light of the Halloween Moon.* Lothrop, 1993. / Wiesner, David. *Free Fall.* Lothrop, 1988. / Williams, Linda. *The Little Old Lady Who Was Not Afraid of Anything.* Crowell, 1986.

SUBJECTS: BOOKS AND READING. FEAR. HAUNTED HOUSES.

617   Pattison, Darcy. *The Journey of Oliver K. Woodman.* **Illus. by Joe Cepeda. Harcourt, 2003. 0-15-202329-1. Unp. Gr. K–2**

Unable to spare the time to visit his niece Tameka in California, Uncle Ray in South Carolina instead constructs a full-sized wooden man and sets it out on a rock with knapsack and a sign reading "California or Bust." And sure enough, a progression of cheerful folks pick up the silent hitchhiker and drive him cross-country. His journey unfolds in a series of letters and postcards sent from his rescuers and in sprawling vistas painted in oils, with his route laid out on a U.S. map on the back endpapers.

GERM: Adventurous researchers can find out more about the places he visits and write up descriptions of them. Continue the cross-country journey with the sequel, *Searching for Oliver K. Woodman.* Pair these with *Liberty's Journey* by Kelly DiPucchio, in which the Statue of Liberty takes her own cross-country jaunt.

RELATED TITLES: Bates, Katharine Lee. *America the Beautiful.* Illus. by Chris Gall. Little, Brown, 2004. / Bates, Katharine Lee. *America the Beautiful.* Illus. by Neil Waldman. Atheneum, 1983. / Borden, Louise. *America Is . . .* McElderry, 2002. / Brisson, Pat. *Your Best Friend, Kate.* Bradbury, 1989. / Cherry, Lynne. *The Armadillo from Amarillo.* Harcourt, 1994. / DiPucchio, Kelly. *Liberty's Journey.* Hyperion, 2004. / Guthrie, Woody. *This Land Is Your Land.* Little, Brown, 1998. / Keller, Laurie. *The Scrambled States of America.* Henry Holt, 1998. / Neubecker, Robert. *Wow! America!* Hyperion, 2006. / Pattison, Darcy. *Searching for Oliver K. Woodman.* Harcourt, 2005. / Rylant, Cynthia. *Tulip Sees America.* Scholastic, 1998. / Sabuda, Robert. *America the Beautiful.* Little Simon, 2004. / Williams, Vera B. *Stringbean's Trip to the Shining Sea.* Scholastic, 2003.

SUBJECTS: AFRICAN AMERICANS. DOLLS. GEOGRAPHY. LETTER WRITING. POSTCARDS. U.S.—DESCRIPTION AND TRAVEL. U.S.—GEOGRAPHY. VOYAGES AND TRAVELS.

618   Paul, Ann Whitford. *Mañana, Iguana.* **Illus. by Ethan Long. Holiday House, 2004. 0-8234-1808-1. Unp. Gr. PreK–2**

Iguana is planning a fiesta on sábado (Saturday), and Conejo (rabbit), Tortuga (turtle), and Culebra (snake) are enthusiastic until Iguana asks for help with writing and delivering invitations, stuffing the piñata, cooking the food, and decorating. "Yo no" ("Not I"), they say each time, and each time they have the same excuses: Conejo is too fast, Tortuga is too slow, and Culebra has no arms. Bouncy watercolor and gouache illustrations bring out the humor of the Little Red Hen-style story, which sports a twist ending that redeems the three lazy ones in Iguana's and our eyes.

GERM: The Spanish glossary and pronunciation guide is helpful. This could make a very entertaining Reader's Theater, with its amusing dialogue, Spanish words, and repeated phrases. Pull in an original version of *The Little Red Hen*, and another peppy Southwest version with a new ending, *Armadilly Chili*, by Helen Ketteman, to compare and contrast. Review the days of the week in Spanish and have another party with Pam Muñoz Ryan's *Mice and Beans*.

RELATED TITLES: Downard, Barry. *The Little Red Hen.* Simon & Schuster, 2004. / Elya, Susan Middleton. *Eight Animals Bake a Cake.* Putnam, 2002. / Galdone, Paul. *The Little Red Hen.* Clarion, 1979. / Ketteman, Helen. *Armadilly Chili.* Albert Whitman, 2004. / Kimmel, Eric A. *The Runaway Tortilla.* Winslow, 2000. / Ryan, Pam Muñoz. *Mice and Beans.* Scholastic, 2001. / Stevens, Janet, and Susan Stevens Crummel. *Cook-a-Doodle-Doo!* Harcourt, 1999. / Sturges, Philemon. *The Little Red Hen (Makes a Pizza).* Dutton, 1999.

SUBJECTS: CHANTABLE REFRAIN. COOPERATION. DAYS OF THE WEEK. DESERT ANIMALS. IGUANAS. LITTLE RED HEN. MULTICULTURAL BOOKS—FOLKLORE. PARODIES. READER'S THEATER. SPANISH LANGUAGE.

619   Paxton, Tom. *Going to the Zoo.* **Illus. by Karen Lee Schmidt. Morrow, 1996. 0-688-13801-2. Unp. Gr. PreK–1**

Three kids and their parents head out on a high-spirited trip to the zoo to see the monkeys scritch, scritch, scratching and the bears huff, huff, a-puffin'. Folksinger Paxton's ebullient song is illustrated in peppy full-bleed gouache and watercolors, and the music is on the endpapers so you can sing it or read it, as you like.

GERM: Make up, illustrate, and sing new verses about other animals we can find at the zoo. Read de Regniers's classic *May I Bring a Friend?*, and see what happens when the animals break out of their cages in Michael Garland's *Last Night at the Zoo*.

RELATED TITLES: Clark, Emma Chichester. *Follow the Leader!* Simon & Schuster, 2003. / De Regniers, Beatrice Schenk. *May I Bring a Friend?* Atheneum, 1964. / Garland, Michael. *Last Night at the Zoo.* Boyds Mills, 2001. / Gelman, Rita Golden. *I Went to the Zoo.* Scholastic, 1993. / Halpern, Shari. *What Shall We Do When We All Go Out? A Traditional Song.* North-South, 1995. / Harter, Debbie. *The Animal Boogie.* Barefoot, 2000. / Harter, Debbie. *Walking Through the Jungle.* Barefoot, 1997. / Martin, Bill, Jr. *Brown Bear, Brown Bear, What Do You See?* Henry Holt, 1983. / Rathmann, Peggy. *Good Night, Gorilla.* Putnam, 1994. / Rosen, Michael. *We're Going on a Bear Hunt.* McElderry, 1989.

SUBJECTS: ANIMALS. SONGS. STORIES IN RHYME. ZOOS.

620   Pearson, Tracey Campbell. *Bob.* **Illus. by the author. Farrar, 2002. 0-374-39957-3. Unp. Gr. PreK–1**

Henrietta the cat tells Bob, a rooster who clucks, "You need to stop clucking and learn how to crow. That's what roosters do." After first learning how to meow, Bob sets out across the farm, picking up barking, ribbeting, and mooing in time to scare off a hungry fox back in the coop.

GERM: Act out the story with invented dialogue, having several actors play the parts of each animal Bob encounters. In *Cock-a-Moo-Moo* by Juliet Dallas-Conté, Rooster has forgotten how to crow and the barnyard animals try to set him straight.

RELATED TITLES: Auch, Mary Jane. *Bantam of the Opera.* Holiday House, 1997. / Bennett, David. *One Cow Moo Moo!* Henry Holt, 1990. / Causley, Charles. *"Quack!" Said the Billy-Goat.* Lippincott, 1986. / Cazet, Denys. *Elvis the Rooster Almost Goes to Heaven.* HarperCollins, 2003. / Dallas-Conté, Juliet. *Cock-a-Moo-Moo.* Little, Brown, 2001. / Fox, Mem. *Hattie and the Fox.* Bradbury, 1987. / Froehlich, Margaret Walden. *That Kookory!* Harcourt, 1995. / Hindley, Judy. *Do Like a Duck Does!* Candlewick, 2002. / Hutchins, Pat. *Rosie's Walk.* Macmillan, 1968. / Meeker, Clare Hodgson. *Who Wakes Rooster?* Simon & Schuster, 1996. / Most, Bernard. *Cock-a-Doodle-Moo!* Harcourt, 1996. / Palatini, Margie. *Moo Who?* HarperCollins, 2004. / Rostoker-Gruber, Karen. *Rooster Can't Cock-a-Doodle-Doo.* Dial, 2004. / Stevens, Janet, and Susan Stevens Crummel. *Cook-a-Doodle-Doo!* Harcourt, 1999. / Ward, Helen. *The Rooster and the Fox.* Millbrook, 2003.

SUBJECTS: ANIMAL SOUNDS. CREATIVE DRAMA. DOMESTIC ANIMALS. FOXES. ROOSTERS.

621 Pearson, Tracey Campbell. *Where Does Joe Go?* **Illus. by the author. Farrar, 1999. 0-374-38319-7. Unp. Gr. PreK–1**

Every spring, white-bearded, roly-poly Joe comes back to town to open up his popular snack bar, where young and old gather to eat hot dogs, creemees, and fries. After he leaves in the fall, folks speculate where he goes: "He's gone to the moon," cries tiny June. (Each of their guesses rhymes with their names.) Busy watercolors show Joe at the beach, on a cruise, having tea with the queen, even on a safari, but the final page shows where Joe really spends his winter: at the North Pole.

GERM: Before showing the final page, ask everyone to speculate or predict where Joe might be and what he could be doing. Read the story again and have children recall the rhyming names and then make up some speculations based on their own names. (Here's mine: "He's on jury duty," said librarian Judy.)

RELATED TITLES: Burningham, John. *Harvey Slumfenberger's Christmas Present.* Candlewick, 1993. / Joyce, William. *Santa Calls.* HarperCollins, 1993. / Kimmel, Elizabeth Cody. *My Penguin Osbert.* Candlewick, 2004. / Krensky, Stephen. *How Santa Got His Job.* Simon & Schuster, 1998. / Krensky, Stephen. *How Santa Lost His Job.* Simon & Schuster, 2001 / McPhail, David. *Santa's Book of Names.* Little, Brown, 1993. / Palatini, Margie. *Elf Help.* Hyperion, 1997. / Price, Moe. *The Reindeer Christmas.* Harcourt, 1993. / Primavera, Elise. *Auntie Claus.* Harcourt, 1999. / Van Allsburg, Chris. *The Polar Express.* Houghton Mifflin, 1985.

SUBJECTS: FAST FOOD RESTAURANTS. RESTAURANTS. SANTA CLAUS. STORIES IN RHYME.

622 Pérez, Amada Irma. *My Very Own Room/Mi Proprio Cuartito.* **Illus. by Maya Christina Gonzalez. Children's Book Press, 2000. 0-89239-164-2. Unp. Gr. K–4**

After years of sharing a room with her five little brothers in the family's small apartment, a resourceful Mexican American girl takes over a tiny storage closet for her own room—as she says, "a place where I could read the books I loved, write in my diary, and dream." Written in English and Spanish, the upbeat and inspirational tale turns out to be based on the author's own family story, which you don't discover until you turn to the final page and see the snapshots of Amada and her brothers, then and now.

GERM: When you get to the part in the story where the girl realizes the most important thing is still missing from her perfect new room, close the book and ask your children to think of or write down what she still needs. The answer? Books, of course, which she borrows from her library and shares with her brothers. Kids can also talk about a time when they worked hard to achieve a difficult-to-reach goal and succeeded.

RELATED TITLES: Hill, Elizabeth Starr. *Evan's Corner.* Henry Holt, 1967. / Lomas Garza, Carmen. *Family Pictures/Cuadros de Familia.* Children's Book Press, 1990. / Lomas Garza, Carmen. *In My Family/En Mi Familia.* Children's Book Press, 1996. / Manzano, Sonia. *No Dogs Allowed!* Atheneum, 2004. / Medina, Jane. *The Dream on Blanca's Wall: Poems in English and Spanish.* Wordsong/Boyds Mills, 2004. / Smothers, Ethel Footman. *The Hard-Times Jar.* Farrar, 2003. / Soto, Gary. *Snapshots from the Wedding.* Putnam, 1997. / Williams, Vera. *A Chair for my Mother.* Greenwillow, 1982.

SUBJECTS: BEDROOMS. FAMILY LIFE. HISPANIC AMERICANS. MEXICAN AMERICANS. MULTICULTURAL BOOKS. PICTURE BOOKS FOR ALL AGES. SPANISH LANGUAGE.

623 Pérez, L. King. *First Day in Grapes.* **Illus. by Robert Casilla. Lee & Low, 2002. 1-58430-045-0. Unp. Gr. 1–4**

On third grader Chico's first day in his new school in California, where his family has moved for grape-picking season, he stands up for himself against two fourth-grade troublemakers and even makes a new friend.

GERM: Discuss: Chico is apprehensive about his first day of school. What is he worried about and why? Before finishing the story, ask children to offer their own advice on how to be accepted in a new school and then compare their suggestions with Chico's actions. Introduce Cesar Chavez, the famed organizer who fought for migrant worker's rights, with Carmen T. Bernier-Grand's *César: ¡Sí, Se Puede! Yes, We Can!*, and Kathleen Krull's *Harvesting Hope: The Story of Cesar Chavez.*

RELATED TITLES: Alarcón, Francisco X. *From the Bellybutton of the Moon and Other Summer Poems.* Children's Book Press, 1998. / Bernier-Grand, Carmen T. *César: ¡Sí, Se Puede! Yes, We Can!* Marshall Cavendish, 2004. / Elya, Susan Middleton. *Home at Last.* Lee & Low, 2002. / Krull, Kathleen. *Harvesting Hope: The Story of Cesar Chavez.* Harcourt, 2003. / Lomas Garza, Carmen. *Family Pictures/Cuadros de Familia.* Children's Book Press, 1990. / Lomas Garza, Carmen. *In My Family/En Mi Familia.* Children's Book Press, 1996. / Medina, Jane. *The Dream on Blanca's Wall: Poems in English and Spanish.* Wordsong/Boyds Mills, 2004. / Mora, Pat. *Tomás and* *the Library Lady*. Knopf, 1997. / Pérez, Amada Irma. *My Very Own Room/Mi Proprio Cuartito*. Children's Book Press, 2000. / Smothers, Ethel Footman. *The Hard-Times Jar*. Farrar, 2003. / Soto, Gary. *Snapshots from the Wedding*. Putnam, 1997. / Soto, Gary. *Too Many Tamales*. Putnam, 1993.

SUBJECTS: CALIFORNIA. FIRST DAY OF SCHOOL. MEXICAN AMERICANS. MIGRANT LABOR. MULTICULTURAL BOOKS. SCHOOLS. SELF-CONFIDENCE.

624 **Perkins, Lynne Rae.** *The Broken Cat*. **Illus. by the author. Greenwillow, 2002. 0-06-029263-6. Unp. Gr. K–3**

Andy and his mom, his Grandma, his Aunt Cookie, and his gray tabby cat Frank are in the vet's waiting room. When Andy asks his mom to tell him (and injured Frank) the story of how she broke her arm in third grade, each person in the family has something to add to her flashbacks of the story, which is illustrated with gentle pen-and-ink and watercolors. And when the vet finally calls Frank in, they all offer her their own versions of what happened to the cat. There's a lovely compare-and-contrast page on which we watch Frank get better as we hear how Mom's arm finally healed.

GERM: There are two concurrent stories to follow here: Mom's and Frank the cat's. Both will fire up listeners to recall times they or their pets got hurt and how they got better. This might be a good opportunity to look up books on vets and what they do, and, of course, to do some experiential writing in which kids recall an interesting anecdote about one of their pets and then interpret that pet's behavior at the time. It's also a jumping-off place for writing a story from more than one point of view, perhaps by asking each person in your family to recall the same family event and then comparing their responses with your own.

RELATED TITLES: Galbraith, Kathryn O. *Laura Charlotte*. Philomel, 1990. / Lee, Chinlun. *Good Dog, Paw!* Candlewick, 2004. / LeGuin, Ursula K. *A Visit from Dr. Katz*. Atheneum, 1988. / Lied, Kate. *Potato: A Tale from the Great Depression*. National Geographic, 1997. / McDonald, Joyce. *Homebody*. Putnam, 1991. / Martin, Ann M. *Leo the Magnificat*. Scholastic, 1996. / Miller, Sara Swan. *Three More Stories You Can Read to Your Cat*. Houghton Mifflin, 2002. / Miller, Sara Swan. *Three Stories You Can Read to Your Cat*. Houghton Mifflin, 1997. / Pomerantz, Charlotte. *The Chalk Doll*. HarperCollins, 1989. / Schachner, Judith Byron. *The Grannyman*. Dutton, 1999. / Shannon, George. *This Is the Bird*. Houghton Mifflin, 1997. / Timmel, Carol Ann. *Tabitha: The Fabulous Flying Feline*. Walker, 1996.

SUBJECTS: CATS. FAMILY STORIES. HEALTH. PERSONAL NARRATIVES. POINT OF VIEW. VETERINARIANS. WOUNDS AND INJURIES.

625 **Perry, Sarah.** *If . . .* **Illus. by the author. J. Paul Getty Museum and Children's Library Press, 1995. 0-89236-321-5. Unp. Gr. 1–6**

In this imagination-provoking picture book, each of the dreamy, sometimes surreal, what-if phrases is accompanied by a sharply detailed illustration: "If cats could fly . . ."; "If ugly were beautiful . . ."; "If the moon were square . . ."

GERM: These creative writing spurs can be fleshed out into stories, and children can also dream up more strange possibilities to illustrate and present to the rest of the group.

RELATED TITLES: Barrett, Judi. *Cloudy with a Chance of Meatballs*. Atheneum, 1978. / Barrett, Judi. *Things That Are Most in the World*. Atheneum, 1998. / Van Allsburg, Chris. *The Mysteries of Harris Burdick*. Houghton Mifflin, 1984. / Wood, Audrey. *The Flying Dragon Room*. Scholastic, 1996.

SUBJECTS: IMAGINATION.

626 **Peters, Lisa Westberg.** *Cold Little Duck, Duck, Duck*. **Illus. by Sam Williams. Greenwillow, 2000. 0-688-16178-2. Unp. Gr. PreK–K**

One cold spring, a little duck shivers and shakes. As she thaws herself by thinking of warmer weather, bubbly streams, and squishy mud, a flock of geese fly by and, suddenly, spring is everywhere.

GERM: This dear tribute to ducks and warm weather, done in pencil and watercolors, is just right for those story hours when your listeners need to join in and get the wiggles out. As you reread the story, your children can all become the cold little duck.

RELATED TITLES: Alexander, Sue. *There's More . . . Much More*. Harcourt, 1987. / Arnosky, Jim. *All Night Near the Water*. Putnam, 1994. / Buzzeo, Toni. *Dawdle Duckling*. Dial, 2003. / Hest, Amy. *In the Rain with Baby Duck*. Candlewick, 1995. / Hindley, Judy. *Do Like a Duck Does!* Candlewick, 2002. / McCloskey, Robert. *Make Way for Ducklings*. Viking, 1941. / Minarik, Else Holmelund. *It's Spring!* Greenwillow, 1989. / Naylor, Phyllis Reynolds. *Ducks Disappearing*. Atheneum, 1997. / Raffi. *Five Little Ducks*. Crown, 1988. / Simmons, Jane. *Come Along, Daisy*. Little, Brown, 1998. / Stott, Dorothy. *Too Much*. Dutton, 1990. / Tafuri, Nancy. *Snowy Flowy*

Blowy: A Twelve Months Rhyme. Scholastic, 1999 / Whippo, Walt, and Bernard Zaritzky. *Little White Duck.* Little, Brown, 2000. / Whybrow, Ian. *Quacky Quack-Quack.* Four Winds, 1991.

SUBJECTS: DUCKS. SEASONS. SPRING. WINTER.

627   Pilkey, Dav. *The Hallo-Wiener.* Illus. by the author. Blue Sky/Scholastic, 1995. 0-590-41703-7. Unp. Gr. PreK–2

Dressed as a hot dog for trick-or-treat, and "looking quite frank," Oscar the dachshund endures merciless teasing until he saves his fellow dogs from a ghastly pumpkin-headed monster— actually two ornery cats in disguise.

GERM: Meet another heroic wiener dog in *Superdog: The Heart of a Hero* by Caralyn Buehner and a skunk who also has problems with teasing in *Sweet Briar Goes to School* by Karma Wilson. Compare how each character responds to teasing and draw in your students' personal experiences doing the same.

RELATED TITLES: Buehner, Caralyn. *Superdog: The Heart of a Hero.* HarperCollins, 2004. / Kirk, Daniel. *Dogs Rule!* Hyperion, 2003. / Pilkey, Dav. *Dog Breath: The Horrible Trouble with Hally Tosis.* Scholastic, 1994. / Pilkey, Dav. *Dogzilla.* Harcourt, 1993. / Pilkey, Dav. *Kat Kong.* Harcourt, 1993. / Wilson, Karma. *Sweet Briar Goes to School.* Dial, 2003.

SUBJECTS: CATS. DACHSHUNDS. DOGS. HALLOWEEN. HEROES. HUMOROUS FICTION. TEASING.

628   Pilkey, Dav. *The Paperboy.* Illus. by the author. Orchard, 1996. 0-531-08856-1. Unp. Gr. PreK–2

In the predawn hour, a young African American boy and his dog prepare for and set out on their daily paper route, after which they crawl back into bed for a final dream. Pilkey's dark-hued Chagall-like paintings and the poetic text of this quiet and thoughtful mood piece make this a nice change of pace as a read-aloud.

GERM: See how paperboys of old plied their trade way back when with Mary Kay Kroeger and Louise Borden's historical fiction picture book, *Paperboy.*

RELATED TITLES: Cordsen, Carol Foskett. *The Milkman.* Dutton, 2005. / Kroeger, Mary Kay, and Louise Borden. *Paperboy.* Clarion, 1996. / Pilkey, Dav. *Dogzilla.* Harcourt, 1993. / Pilkey, Dav. *Kat Kong.* Harcourt, 1993. / Pilkey, Dav. *When Cats Dream.* Orchard, 1992. / Pinkney, Brian. *The Adventures of Sparrowboy.* Simon & Schuster, 1997.

SUBJECTS: DOGS. MORNING. MULTICULTURAL BOOKS. NEWSPAPER CARRIERS.

629   Pinczes, Elinor J. *A Remainder of One.* Illus. by Bonnie MacKain. Houghton Mifflin, 1995. 0-395-69455-8. Unp. Gr. K–3

Two by two, the 25th squadron of bugs marches past the queen, but poor oddball tagalong bug Joe, a remainder without a partner, is told to stand aside to make the troupe even. The same thing happens when the bugs march in lines of threes and then fours, but when they divide into lines of five, Joe finally fits in perfectly.

GERM: The lighthearted rhyming story with its winsome bordered woodcuts will provide a genial introduction to your lesson on division with remainders. Pair this with the companion book, *One Hundred Hungry Ants.*

RELATED TITLES: Dodds, Dayle Ann. *Minnie's Diner.* Candlewick, 2004. / Pinczes, Elinor J. *One Hundred Hungry Ants.* Houghton Mifflin, 1993. / Tang, Greg. *The Best of Times: Math Strategies That Multiply.* Scholastic, 2002.

SUBJECTS: DIVISION. INSECTS. KINGS AND RULERS. MATHEMATICS. STORIES IN RHYME.

630   Pinkney, Andrea Davis. *Sleeping Cutie.* Illus. by Brian Pinkney. Harcourt, 2004. 0-15-202544-8. Unp. Gr. PreK–1

Adorable little Cutie LaRue is sweet as cream all day long, but when her parents try to get her to go to sleep each night, she stomps and hollers, "I'm not tired." Then they bring in Night Owl, a talking doll they find in the Trusty Trinket toy catalog. After dark, the bird brings Cutie to the Dreamland Nightclub, where she can party all night long.

GERM: Ask your little insomniacs what tricks they use to fall asleep each night. Also ask them what they would like to do at the Dreamland Nightclub.

RELATED TITLES: Appelt, Kathi. *Bubba and Beau Go Night-Night.* Harcourt, 2003. / Lum, Kate. *What! Cried Granny: An Almost Bedtime Story.* Dial, 1999. / Mathews, Judith, and Fay Robinson. *Nathaniel Willy, Scared Silly.* Bradbury, 1994. / Rathmann, Peggy. *Good Night, Gorilla.* Putnam, 1994. / Rathmann, Peggy. *Ten Minutes*

Till Bedtime. Putnam, 1998. / Rothstein, Gloria. *Sheep Asleep.* HarperCollins, 2003. / Simms, Laura. *The Squeaky Door.* Crown, 1991. / Whybrow, Ian. *The Noisy Way to Bed.* Scholastic, 2004. / Yolen, Jane. *How Do Dinosaurs Say Good Night?* Blue Sky/Scholastic, 2000.

SUBJECTS: BEDTIME STORIES. NIGHTCLUBS. OWLS. SLEEP.

631   **Pinkney, Brian.** *The Adventures of Sparrowboy.* **Illus. by the author. Simon & Schuster, 1997. 0-689-81071-7. Unp. Gr. K–4**

Paperboy Henry's almost-collision with a sparrow enables him to fly, just like his newspaper comic-strip hero, Falconman. Heroic Henry makes things better in his neighborhood—such as stopping a bully and his dog—in this action-oriented comic book-style story with detailed scratchboard illustrations.

GERM: Children might enjoy writing new adventure tales with themselves as the animal-inspired superheroes, adopting the same paneled, captioned, brightly illustrated format. They can look up facts about their animals in order to add realistic details to their fantasies.

RELATED TITLES: Buehner, Caralyn. *Superdog: The Heart of a Hero.* HarperCollins, 2004. / Dorros, Arthur. *Abuela.* Dutton, 1991. / Gerstein, Mordicai. *Arnold of the Ducks.* HarperCollins, 1983. / Grey, Mini. *Traction Man Is Here!* Knopf, 2005. / Kroeger, Mary Kay. *Paperboy.* Clarion, 1996. / Le Guin, Ursula K. *Catwings.* Orchard, 1988. / MacDonald, Ross. *Another Perfect Day.* Roaring Brook, 2002. / O'Connor, George. *Kapow!* Simon & Schuster, 2004. / Pilkey, Dav. *The Paperboy.* Orchard, 1996. / Ringgold, Faith. *Tar Beach.* Crown, 1991. / Van Draanen, Wendelin. *Shredderman: Secret Identity.* Knopf, 2004. / Weigel, Jeff. *Atomic Ace (He's Just My Dad).* Albert Whitman, 2004. / Woodruff, Elvira. *Show and Tell.* Holiday House, 1991. / Woodruff, Elvira. *The Wing Shop.* Holiday House, 1991.

SUBJECTS: BIRDS. BULLIES. CARTOONS AND COMICS. FANTASY. FLIGHT. MULTICULTURAL BOOKS. NEWSPAPER CARRIERS. SUPERHEROES. TRANSFORMATIONS.

632   **Pinkwater, Daniel.** *Irving and Muktuk: Two Bad Bears.* **Illus. by Jill Pinkwater. Houghton Mifflin, 2001. 0-618-09334-6. Unp. Gr. PreK–2**

Every winter, the little town of Yellowtooth, in the frozen north, celebrates the New Year with a Blueberry Muffin Festival. And every time, two muffin-obsessed polar bears try to disguise themselves in a desperate attempt to garner muffins. Luckily for Yellowtooth, watchful Officer Bunny always apprehends Irving and Muktuk, sending the bad bears via helicopter back to the Arctic Circle where they belong.

GERM: Bake or bring in blueberry muffins to get into the muffin mood. Compare and contrast the two fictional bears with real polar bears in nonfiction books such as Gail Gibbons's handsome *Polar Bears.* Meet another large animal who gets in trouble with the law in Tim Egan's *The Trial of Cardigan Jones.*

RELATED TITLES: Bania, Michael. *Kumak's Fish: A Tall Tale from the Far North.* Alaska Northwest, 2004. / Bania, Michael. *Kumak's House: A Tale of the Far North.* Alaska Northwest, 2002. / Egan, Tim. *The Trial of Cardigan Jones.* Houghton Mifflin, 2004. / Gibbons, Gail. *Polar Bears.* Holiday House, 2001. / Johnston, Ginny, and Cutchins, Judy. *Andy Bear: A Polar Cub Grows Up at the Zoo.* Morrow, 1985. / Pinkwater, Daniel. *Aunt Lulu.* Macmillan, 1988. / Pinkwater, Daniel. *Author's Day.* Atheneum, 1993. / Pinkwater, Daniel. *Bad Bear Detectives: An Irving and Muktuk Story.* Houghton Mifflin, 2006. / Pinkwater, Daniel. *Bad Bears and a Bunny.* Houghton Mifflin, 2005. / Pinkwater, Daniel. *Tooth-Gnasher Superflash.* Macmillan, 1990. / Pinkwater, Daniel. *Wallpaper from Space.* Atheneum, 1996. / Teague, Mark. *Detective LaRue: Letters from the Investigation.* Scholastic, 2004.

SUBJECTS: ALASKA. ARCTIC REGIONS. BEARS. HUMOROUS FICTION. POLAR BEARS. POLICE.

633   **Polacco, Patricia.** *Aunt Chip and the Great Triple Creek Dam Affair.* **Illus. by the author. Philomel, 1996. 0-399-22943-4. Unp. Gr. 1–4**

Absolutely everyone in Triple Creek loves TV except Eli's Aunt Charlotte, who took to her bed 50 years ago when the TV tower was built. "Books? How do you get a story from a book?" and "R-r-read? What's that?" asks Eli when his aunt tells him she gets stories from books. Sure enough, no one in town knows how to read anymore; this realization gets Aunt Chip out of bed to do something about it.

GERM: Make a list: What are the consequences of not reading? Why is it important not just to know how to read but to actually do it? Discussion point: How would your life be different if you couldn't read? Aunt Chip says, "Books are a treasure. All you need is the key. . . . It's called readin'." Next time your town or school starts cutting the library budget, here is the book to help set things right again.

RELATED TITLES: Bogart, Jo Ellen. *Jeremiah Learns to Read.* Orchard, 1999. / Deedy, Carmen Agra. *The*

Library Dragon. Peachtree, 1994. / Ernst, Lisa Campbell. *Stella Louella's Runaway Book.* Simon & Schuster, 1998. / Hest, Amy. *Mr. George Baker.* Candlewick, 2004. / King-Smith, Dick. *The School Mouse.* Hyperion, 1995. / Lowry, Lois. *Zooman Sam.* Houghton Mifflin, 1999. / McKissack, Patricia C. *Goin' Someplace Special.* Atheneum, 2001. / Mora, Pat. *Tomás and the Library Lady.* Knopf, 1997. / Numeroff, Laura Joffe. *Beatrice Doesn't Want To.* Candlewick, 2004. / Polacco, Patricia. *Thank You, Mr. Falker.* Philomel, 1998. / Sierra, Judy. *Wild About Books.* Knopf, 2004. / Stanley, Diane. *Raising Sweetness.* Putnam, 1999. / Williams, Suzanne. *Library Lil.* Dial, 1997. / Winch, John. *The Old Woman Who Loved to Read.* Holiday House, 1997.

SUBJECTS: BOOKS AND READING. LIBRARIANS. LIBRARIES. LITERACY. PICTURE BOOKS FOR ALL AGES. TELEVISION.

634   Polacco, Patricia. *The Butterfly.* **Illus. by the author. Philomel, 2000. 0-399-23170-6. Unp. Gr. 3–6**

Waking up in her bedroom late one night, Monique thinks the little girl she sees sitting at the end of her bed, petting the cat, Pinouff, is a ghost. The Nazi soldiers in their tall black boots have taken over her little town outside Paris, which makes it all the more terrifying when Monique sees that little girl again and learns she is a Jewish child named Sevrine, who has been hiding with her parents in the cellar. Based on the wartime experiences of the author's great-aunt and aunt, this is a chilling but accessible introduction to the Holocaust.

GERM: To give a devastating overview of what happened to children during the Holocaust, read the black-and-white photoessay, *The Children We Remember* by Chana Byers Abels. Compare Sevrine's experiences escaping the Nazis with those of Lindy, an escaped slave on the Underground Railroad, in *Almost to Freedom* by Vaunda Micheaux Nelson.

RELATED TITLES: Abels, Chana Byers. *The Children We Remember.* Greenwillow, 1986. / Bishop, Claire H. *Twenty and Ten.* Puffin, 1978. / Cohn, Janice. *The Christmas Menorahs: How a Town Fought Hate.* Whitman, 1995. / Hesse, Karen. *The Cats in Krasinski Square.* Scholastic, 2004. / Hoestlandt, Jo. *Star of Fear, Star of Hope.* Walker, 1995. / Levine, Karen. *Hana's Suitcase.* Albert Whitman, 2003. / Lowry, Lois. *Number the Stars.* Houghton, 1989. / McCann, Michelle R. *Luba: The Angel of Bergen-Belsen.* Tricycle, 2003. / McSwigan, Marie. *Snow Treasure.* Dutton, 1967. / Maguire, Gregory. *The Good Liar.* Clarion, 1999. / Millman, Isaac. *Hidden Child.* Farrar, 2005. / Nelson, Vaunda Micheaux. *Almost to Freedom.* Carolrhoda, 2003. / Polacco, Patricia. *Pink and Say.* Philomel, 1994. / Propp, Vera. *When the Soldiers Were Gone.* Putnam, 1999. / Reiss, Johanna. *The Upstairs Room.* HarperCollins, 1987. / Stevenson, James. *Don't You Know There's a War On?* Greenwillow, 1992. / Yolen, Jane. *The Devil's Arithmetic.* Viking, 1988.

SUBJECTS: BUTTERFLIES. FRANCE. FRIENDSHIP. HISTORICAL FICTION. HOLOCAUST, JEWISH (1939–1945). JEWS. PICTURE BOOKS FOR OLDER READERS. WORLD WAR, 1939–1945—FICTION.

635   Polacco, Patricia. *John Philip Duck.* **Illus. by the author. Philomel, 2004. 0-399-24262-7. Unp. Gr. K–6**

Edward, a young African American boy, takes the orphaned baby duckling he finds to work with him at the hotel, where the whole staff helps him keep it a secret from Mr. Schutt, the general manager. Edward teaches it to step in time to a John Philip Sousa march on the phonograph. Discovering the duck swimming in the hotel fountain, Mr. Schutt gives the boy one month to train other wild ducks to march in and out of the fountain on command.

GERM: This heartening tale is very loosely based on the true story of Edward Pembroke, the first Duck Master at the Peabody Hotel in Memphis, Tennessee, more than 60 years ago. Find out more about the Peabody duck tradition at: <www.arktimes.com/020201coverstoryb.html>. You'll want to play some John Philip Sousa marches for all to hear. Another true and heartwarming duck tale is *Chibi: A True Story from Japan* by Barbara Brenner and Julia Takaya.

RELATED TITLES: Brenner, Barbara, and Julia Takaya. *Chibi: A True Story from Japan.* Clarion, 1996. / Florian, Douglas. *On the Wing: Bird Poems and Paintings.* Harcourt, 1996. / McCloskey, Robert. *Make Way for Ducklings.* Viking, 1941. / Polacco, Patricia. *Chicken Sunday.* Philomel, 1992. / Polacco, Patricia. *My Ol' Man.* Philomel, 1995. / Polacco, Patricia. *Pink and Say.* Philomel, 1994. / Polacco, Patricia. *Thank You, Mr. Falker.* Philomel, 1998. / Yolen, Jane. *Bird Watch: A Book of Poetry.* Philomel, 1990. / Yolen, Jane. *Fine Feathered Friends: Poems for Young People.* Wordsong/Boyds Mills, 2004. / Yolen, Jane. *Wild Wings: Poems for Young People.* Wordsong/Boyds Mills, 2002.

SUBJECTS: AFRICAN AMERICANS. DUCKS. HISTORICAL FICTION. HOTELS, MOTELS, ETC. MULTICULTURAL BOOKS. PERSEVERANCE. TENNESSEE.

636 Polacco, Patricia. *Mr. Lincoln's Way.* Illus. by the author. Philomel, 2001. 0-399-23754-2. Unp. Gr. 2–6

Upon discovering that Eugene "Mean Gene" Esterhause, a troubled, angry, racist student, is interested in birds, African American principal Mr. Lincoln enlists the boy's help in turning the school's atrium into a bird sanctuary. The source of Eugene's prejudice is a father who disdains others who are "not our kind." Mr. Lincoln encourages the boy to treat everyone with kindness and respect, the way he instinctively treats the birds he loves.

GERM: What a stunning, insightful book to encourage that difficult discussion about race and people who are different and how even children can be intolerant. Start the dialogue, asking: What does Eugene mean when he says to Mr. Lincoln, "You showed me the way out"? Why does he want to make Mr. Lincoln proud of him? How do you think Eugene will make Mr. Lincoln proud of him? (Then show them the endpapers of the book that reveal just what Eugene did with his life.) Have you ever had a Mr. Lincoln in your life? What will you do with your life to make your teachers and parents proud of you?

RELATED TITLES: Brenner, Barbara, and Julia Takaya. *Chibi: A True Story from Japan.* Clarion, 1996. / Bunting, Eve. *Riding the Tiger.* Clarion, 2001. / Bunting, Eve. *Smoky Night.* Harcourt, 1994. / Bunting, Eve. *Summer Wheels.* Harcourt, 1992. / Hall, Bruce Edward. *Henry and the Dragon Kite.* Philomel, 2004. / Lorbiecki, Marybeth. *Sister Anne's Hands.* Dial, 1998. / McKissack, Patricia C. *Goin' Someplace Special.* Atheneum, 2001. / Polacco, Patricia. *Chicken Sunday.* Philomel, 1992. / Polacco, Patricia. *Pink and Say.* Philomel, 1994. / Polacco, Patricia. *Thank You, Mr. Falker.* Philomel, 1998. / Woodson, Jacqueline. *The Other Side.* Putnam, 2001.

SUBJECTS: AFRICAN AMERICANS. BEHAVIOR. BIRDS. MULTICULTURAL BOOKS. PICTURE BOOKS FOR OLDER READERS. PREJUDICE. PRINCIPALS. RACE RELATIONS. SCHOOLS.

637 Polacco, Patricia. *Mrs. Mack.* Illus. by the author. Philomel, 1998. 0-399-23167-6. 40pp. Gr. 2–4

The author recalls how, as a 10-year-old city girl spending the summer with her dad in Michigan, she learned to ride at a run-down stable in Dogpatch, the roughest part of town, thanks to the amazing riding instructor, Mrs. Mack, who taught her important lessons in perseverance. The chance to ride Mrs. Mack's beautiful horse Penny was the culmination of Pat's training. The life-and-death finale, in which Penny comes down with a dangerous virus, will leave listeners breathless.

GERM: Like Polacco's *Thank You, Mr. Falker,* this is an exceptional true picture book about a teacher whose love and dedication made a difference in a child's life.

RELATED TITLES: Polacco, Patricia. *Chicken Sunday.* Philomel, 1992. / Polacco, Patricia. *My Ol' Man.* Philomel, 1995. / Polacco, Patricia. *My Rotten, Redheaded, Older Brother.* Philomel, 1994. / Polacco, Patricia. *An Orange for Frankie.* Philomel, 2004. / Polacco, Patricia. *Some Birthday!* Philomel, 1991. / Polacco, Patricia. *Thank You, Mr. Falker.* Philomel, 1998. / Potter, Giselle. *Chloë's Birthday . . . and Me.* Atheneum, 2004.

SUBJECTS: AUTOBIOGRAPHY. FAMILY STORIES. HORSES. MICHIGAN. PERSEVERANCE.

638 Polacco, Patricia. *My Ol' Man.* Illus. by the author. Philomel, 1995. 0-399-22822-5. Unp. Gr. 1–4

Author/illustrator Polacco casts back to a summer in Michigan when she was a girl and her storytelling, traveling salesman dad took her and her brother Ritchie out to Potter's Pond to see a rock he claimed was magic.

GERM: There's lots to talk about after reading this heart-warming true story, a tribute to Polacco's father. Why did Da tell his kids the rock was magic? He used to say, "We may be boot-poor, but we're rich on dreams." What does this mean? Was the rock magic? What magic have you found in your life? Other autobiographical books about the author and her family include *Chicken Sunday; Mrs. Mack; My Rotten, Redheaded, Older Brother;* and *Thank You, Mr. Falker.*

RELATED TITLES: Brisson, Pat. *The Summer My Father Was Ten.* Boyds Mills, 1998. / Friedman, Ina R. *How My Parents Learned to Eat.* Houghton Mifflin, 1984. / Houston, Gloria. *My Great Aunt Arizona.* HarperCollins, 1992. / Lasky, Kathryn. *Marven of the North Woods.* Harcourt, 1997. / Polacco, Patricia. *Chicken Sunday.* Philomel, 1992. / Polacco, Patricia. *Mrs. Mack.* Philomel, 1998. / Polacco, Patricia. *My Rotten, Redheaded, Older Brother.* Philomel, 1994. / Polacco, Patricia. *An Orange for Frankie.* Philomel, 2004. / Polacco, Patricia. *Pink and Say.* Philomel, 1994. / Polacco, Patricia. *Thank You, Mr. Falker.* Philomel, 1998. / Say, Allen. *Grandfather's Journey.* Houghton Mifflin, 1993. / Say, Allen. *Tea with Milk.* Houghton Mifflin, 1999. / Say, Allen. *Tree of Cranes.* Houghton Mifflin, 1991.

SUBJECTS: BROTHERS AND SISTERS. FAMILY STORIES. FATHERS. GRANDMOTHERS. ROCKS. SINGLE-PARENT FAMILIES. STORYTELLING.

639   Polacco, Patricia. *Oh, Look!* **Illus. by the author. Philomel, 2004. 0-399-24223-6. Unp. Gr. PreK–1**

Three frisky goats go through the unlocked gate, across the bridge, up the hill, into the pond, and over to the fair, where they get scared in the Funhouse and retrace their steps home. Chasing them on their merry romp across the countryside are two young shepherd girls in colorful peasant dresses and kerchiefs.

GERM: You'll recognize the old call-and-response story "I'm Going on a Bear Hunt," joyously revamped here, and all will be eager to act out the sounds and motions, as narrated by those naughty goats. Keep up your heart rates with Jan Brett's *Honey . . . Honey . . . Lion!* and Michael Rosen's *We're Going on a Bear Hunt.*

RELATED TITLES: Brett, Jan. *Honey . . . Honey . . . Lion!* Putnam, 2005. / Clark, Emma Chichester. *Follow the Leader!* Simon & Schuster, 2003. / Emberley, Rebecca. *Three Cool Kids.* Little, Brown, 1995. / Harter, Debbie. *Walking Through the Jungle.* Orchard, 1997. / Jones, Maurice. *I'm Going on a Dragon Hunt.* Four Winds, 1987. / Polacco, Patricia. *Thunder Cake.* Philomel, 1990. / Rosen, Michael. *We're Going on a Bear Hunt.* McElderry, 1989. / Sivulich, Sandra Stroner. *I'm Going on a Bear Hunt.* Dutton, 1973.

SUBJECTS: CALL-AND-RESPONSE STORIES. CREATIVE DRAMA. FAIRS. GOATS. SOUND EFFECTS. STORIES TO TELL.

640   Polacco, Patricia. *An Orange for Frankie.* **Illus. by the author. Philomel, 2004. 0-399-24302-X. Unp. Gr. 1–6**

Here's another Polacco family story to put a lump in your throat, just in time for Christmas. It's about Frankie—Polacco's great-uncle and one of nine children—and the time he gave his best sweater to a hobo passing through town. Bad snow has delayed Pa getting home from Lansing, where he always meets the Florida train to bring home nine precious oranges for his children. After Pa finally arrives on Christmas Eve, Frankie somehow loses his orange. "Oh, Ma, I've done a terrible thing!" he confesses, but his family understands and their love and caring make it all come out right.

GERM: Discussion points: Both Frankie and his brothers and sisters do something selfless for others. What do they do and why do they do it? What selfless acts have you done or witnessed? What special holiday traditions does your family practice every year? Children can ask their parents or grandparents to describe what life was like when they grew up, and together write a story describing it or a special family memory from long ago. Why would a simple orange be such a special present?

RELATED TITLES: Buck, Pearl S. *Christmas Day in the Morning.* HarperCollins, 2002. / Gray, Libba Moore. *Little Lil and the Swing-Singing Sax.* Simon & Schuster, 1996. / Medearis, Angela Shelf. *Poppa's Itchy Christmas.* Holiday House, 1998. / Paterson, Katherine. *Marvin's Best Christmas Present Ever.* HarperCollins, 1997. / Polacco, Patricia. *Chicken Sunday.* Philomel, 1992. / Polacco, Patricia. *John Philip Duck.* Philomel, 2004. / Polacco, Patricia. *My Ol' Man.* Philomel, 1995. / Polacco, Patricia. *Pink and Say.* Philomel, 1994. / Polacco, Patricia. *Thank You, Mr. Falker.* Philomel, 1998. / Rylant, Cynthia. *Children of Christmas: Stories for the Season.* Orchard, 1987. / Rylant, Cynthia. *Silver Packages: An Appalachian Christmas Story.* Orchard, 1997. / Soto, Gary. *Too Many Tamales.* Putnam, 1993. / Tunnell, Michael O. *Mailing May.* Greenwillow, 1997.

SUBJECTS: BROTHERS AND SISTERS. CHRISTMAS. FAMILY STORIES. GENEROSITY. GIFTS. HISTORICAL FICTION. KINDNESS. MICHIGAN. ORANGES.

641   Polacco, Patricia. *Thank You, Mr. Falker.* **Illus. by the author. Philomel, 1998. 0-399-23166-8. 40pp. Gr. 2–5**

In first grade, when Trish looked at her reader, "all she saw were wiggling shapes, and when she tried to sound out the words, the other kids laughed at her." Reading was torture until fifth grade when her teacher—tall, elegant Mr. Falker, who told her that her drawings were brilliant—found out her secret and vowed to help her learn to read. On the last page, we are stunned and moved to discover that the story is a true one and that Trisha is Patricia Polacco.

GERM: This provides a wonderful opportunity to discuss topics such as the awful effects of bullying and teasing, why some people don't learn as quickly as others, the role of a great teacher, the values of perseverance and tolerance, and the sweetness of reading. Polacco's books are unforgettable examinations of her own life, making her a memorable subject for an author study. Find out more about her work in her Meet the Author series autobiography, *Firetalking.* *Chicken Sunday* is another affecting autobiographical picture book about the time she and her best friends were falsely accused of vandalism. Other tales from her past include *Mrs. Mack;* *My Ol' Man;* *My Rotten, Redheaded, Older Brother;* *Some Birthday!;* and *Thunder Cake.* In Jan Greenberg and Sandra Jordan's biography *Chuck Close Up Close*, meet another famous artist who struggled with dyslexia as a child.

RELATED TITLES: Bradby, Marie. *More Than Anything Else*. Orchard, 1995. / Greenberg, Jan, and Sandra Jordan. *Chuck Close Up Close*. Roaring Brook, 2002. / Heide, Florence Parry, and Judith Heide Gilliland. *The Day of Ahmed's Secret*. Lothrop, 1990. / Hest, Amy. *Mr. George Baker*. Candlewick, 2004. / Houston, Gloria. *My Great Aunt Arizona*. HarperCollins, 1992. / Lester, Helen. *Author: A True Story*. Houghton Mifflin, 1997. / Levy, Elizabeth. *Keep Ms. Sugarman in the Fourth Grade*. HarperCollins, 1991. / Polacco, Patricia. *Aunt Chip and the Great Triple Creek Dam Affair*. Philomel, 1996. / Polacco, Patricia. *Chicken Sunday*. Philomel, 1992. / Polacco, Patricia. *Firetalking*. Richard C. Owen, 1994. / Polacco, Patricia. *Mrs. Mack*. Philomel, 1998. / Polacco, Patricia. *My Ol' Man*. Philomel, 1995. / Polacco, Patricia. *My Rotten, Redheaded, Older Brother*. Philomel, 1994. / Polacco, Patricia. *Some Birthday!* Philomel, 1991. / Polacco, Patricia. *Thunder Cake*. Philomel, 1990.

SUBJECTS: AUTOBIOGRAPHY. BOOKS AND READING. DYSLEXIA. LEARNING DISABILITIES. LITERACY. PICTURE BOOKS FOR OLDER READERS. SCHOOLS. TEACHERS. TEASING.

642   **Pomeranc, Marion Hess.** *The American Wei*. **Illus. by DyAnne Ryan. Albert Whitman, 1998. 0-8075-0312-6. Unp. Gr. K–3**

In this modern-day immigrant story, on the day he is to become an American citizen, young Wei Fong loses his first tooth and then drops it outside the federal courthouse, right before the naturalization ceremony is to begin. Families from every country join in the search and then converge inside for the naturalization ceremony.

GERM: Talk about families. When did your family come to America and why? What does it take to be an American?

RELATED TITLES: Avi. *Silent Movie*. Atheneum, 2003. / Bartone, Elisa. *American Too*. Lothrop, 1996. / Bartone, Elisa. *Peppe the Lamplighter*. Lothrop, 1993. / Bierman, Carol. *Journey to Ellis Island: How My Father Came to America*. Hyperion, 1998. / Hall, Bruce Edward. *Henry and the Kite Dragon*. Philomel, 2004. / Levine, Ellen. *I Hate English!* Scholastic, 1989. / Levine, Ellen. *If Your Name Was Changed at Ellis Island*. Scholastic, 1993. / Maestro, Betsy. *Coming to America: The Story of Immigration*. Scholastic, 1996. / Sandler, Martin W. *Immigrants*. HarperCollins, 1995. / Wong, Janet. *Apple Pie 4th of July*. Harcourt, 2002. / Yang, Belle. *Hannah Is My Name*. Candlewick, 2004.

SUBJECTS: ASIAN AMERICANS. CHINESE AMERICANS. IMMIGRATION AND EMIGRATION. MULTICULTURAL BOOKS. NATURALIZATION. TEETH.

643   **Pomerantz, Charlotte.** *You're Not My Best Friend Anymore*. **Illus. by David Soman. Dial, 1998. 0-8037-1560-9. Unp. Gr. K–2**

Every day, best friends Molly and Ben walk to school, eat lunch, play, and do their homework together. Their birthdays are only two weeks apart in June, and this year they plan to celebrate with a joint party, deciding to pool their saved allowances to buy a tent. Molly wants a pup tent and Ben an umbrella tent, so the two begin to argue. "You're not my best friend anymore," Molly screams, and they don't speak to each other for four whole days. On the day of their party, they each find the perfect way to apologize.

GERM: Ask your listeners to describe successful ways they've made up with their friends after a fight, and brainstorm practical strategies for sustaining a friendship. Kishi and Renee are mad at each other too in *Hot Day on Abbott Avenue* by Karen English.

RELATED TITLES: Brown, Laurie Krasny, and Marc Brown. *How to Be a Friend: A Guide to Making Friends and Keeping Them*. Little, Brown, 1998. / DePaolo, Paula. *Rosie and the Yellow Ribbon*. Little, Brown, 1992. / English, Karen. *Hot Day on Abbott Avenue*. Clarion, 2004. / Havill, Juanita. *Jamaica and Brianna*. Houghton Mifflin, 1993. / Hoffman, Mary. *Henry's Baby*. Dorling Kindersley, 1993. / Raschka, Chris. *Yo! Yes?* Orchard, 1993. / Winthrop, Elizabeth. *Lizzie and Harold*. Lothrop, 1985.

SUBJECTS: APOLOGIES. ARGUMENTS. BEST FRIENDS. CONFLICT RESOLUTION. FRIENDSHIP. MULTICULTURAL BOOKS.

644   **Potter, Giselle.** *Chloë's Birthday . . . and Me*. **Illus. by the author. Atheneum, 2004. 0-689-86230-X. Unp. Gr. K–4**

Looking back on the summer her family spent in France (the same summer her little sister Chloë turned 5), author/illustrator Giselle Potter recalls—in paintings and personal narrative—her conflicting feelings of jealousy when they celebrated the birthday girl's special day at the beach.

GERM: Listeners can make inferences about how Giselle really felt about her sister getting all that attention and point out examples of her passive-aggressive behavior. Just looking at the cover should give them a good idea. Discuss: Which birthdays will you remember forever and why? Write and illustrate personal narratives of birthday stories. *The Year I Didn't Go to School* is Potter's companion book.

RELATED TITLES: Best, Cari. *Three Cheers for Catherine the Great*. Illus. by Giselle Potter. DK Ink, 1999. / Best, Cari. *When Catherine the Great and I Were Eight!* Illus. by Giselle Potter. Farrar, 2003. / dePaola, Tomie. *26 Fairmount Avenue*. Putnam, 1999. / Hamm, Mia. *Winners Never Quit!* HarperCollins, 2004. / Jonell, Lynne. *It's My Birthday, Too!* Putnam, 1999. / Polacco, Patricia. *My Rotten, Redheaded Older Brother*. Simon & Schuster, 1994. / Polacco, Patricia. *Some Birthday!* Philomel, 1991. / Potter, Giselle. *The Year I Didn't Go to School*. Atheneum, 2002.

SUBJECTS: AUTOBIOGRAPHY. BIRTHDAYS. FRANCE. GIFTS. JEALOUSY. PERSONAL NARRATIVES. SIBLING RIVALRY. SISTERS.

645   Poydar, Nancy. *First Day, Hooray!* **Illus. by the author. Holiday House, 1999. 0-8234-1437-X. Unp. Gr. PreK–1**

As Ivy Green worries about and prepares for her first day of school, her bus driver, janitor, principal, and teacher get ready too.

GERM: Draw pictures showing what you did to get ready for the first day of school. Finish off the year with Ivy and her pals and teachers with *Last Day, Hooray!*

RELATED TITLES: Baer, Edith. *This Is the Way We Go to School: A Book About Children Around the World*. Scholastic, 1990. / Child, Lauren. *I Am Too Absolutely Small for School*. Candlewick, 2004. / Dannenberg, Julie. *First Day Jitters*. Charlesbridge, 2000. / Henkes, Kevin. *Wemberly Worried*. Greenwillow, 2000. / Jackson, Ellen. *It's Back to School We Go! First Day Stories from Around the World*. Millbrook, 2003. / Lasky, Kathryn. *Lunch Bunnies*. Little, Brown, 1996. / McGhee, Alison. *Countdown to Kindergarten*. Harcourt, 2002. / Poydar, Nancy. *Last Day, Hooray*. Holiday House, 2004. / Slate, Joseph. *Miss Bindergarten Gets Ready for Kindergarten*. Dutton, 1996. / Stuve-Bodeen, Stephanie. *Elizabeti's Doll*. Lee & Low, 1998.

SUBJECTS: FIRST DAY OF SCHOOL. SCHOOLS.

646   Priceman, Marjorie. *Froggie Went a-Courting*. **Illus. by the author. Little, Brown, 2000. 0-316-71227-2. Unp. Gr. PreK–1**

Billed on the cover as "An Old Tale with a New Twist," this picture-book version of the 400-year-old Scottish folksong does turn the old one on its ear, as it's set in New York City. "Froggie went a-courting, he did ride / A taxicab to the Upper West Side." The garish cut-paper and gouache illustrations take us to all the landmarks, as Froggie and Ms. Mouse plan for their wedding at the top of the Statue of Liberty. As in the original, the festivities are interrupted by a cat, but Frog and Mouse survive to take their honeymoon in Paris.

GERM: Sing and compare this updated telling with both the original "country" version as told by John Langstaff and a more recently illustrated version by Gillian Tyler. Explore further the New York City setting in Richard Egielski's *The Gingerbread Boy* and in two books that take us on a Big Apple tour: *C Is for City* by Nikki Grimes and *My New York* by Kathy Jakobsen.

RELATED TITLES: Edwards, Pamela Duncan. *The Wacky Wedding: A Book of Alphabet Antics*. Hyperion, 1999. / Egielski, Richard. *The Gingerbread Boy*. HarperCollins, 1997. / Grimes, Nikki. *C Is for City*. Lothrop, 1995. / Jakobsen, Kathy. *My New York*. Little, Brown, 2003. / Langstaff, John. *Frog Went A-Courtin'*. Illus. by Feodor Rojankovsky. Harcourt, 1955. / Neubecker, Robert. *Wow! City!* Hyperion, 2004. / Palatini, Margie. *Ding Dong Ding Dong*. Hyperion, 1999. / Tyler, Gillian. *Froggy Went A-Courtin'*. Candlewick, 2005. / Wattenberg, Jane. *Henny-Penny*. Scholastic, 2000.

SUBJECTS: CATS. FOLK SONGS. FROGS. MICE. NEW YORK CITY. SONGS. WEDDINGS.

647   Primavera, Elise. *Auntie Claus*. **Illus. by the author. Harcourt, 1999. 0-15-201909-X. Unp. Gr. 1–3**

Even though her family lives in luxury high atop the Bing Cherry Hotel in New York City, spoiled Sophie Kringle and her little brother Joe want more, more, more. Sophie wonders about her mysterious Auntie Claus, with whom she has tea every afternoon, and who always tells her, ". . . it is far better to give than to receive." Where does Auntie Claus go after Halloween, not returning until Valentine's Day each year? Sophie stows away in a trunk and finds herself at the North Pole, where she is mistaken for an elf and put to work in the mailroom.

GERM: Ask your sweet potatoes what they've done this year to stay off Santa's Bad-Boys-and-Girls list. Check out Elise Primavera's very cute Web site, <www.auntieclaus.com>. Speaking of elves, mailrooms, and gifts, find out how an elf's computer glitch almost wrecks Christmas in *Elf Help* by Margie Palatini.

RELATED TITLES: Forward, Toby. *Ben's Christmas Carol.* Dutton, 1996. / Joyce, William. *Santa Calls.* Harper-Collins, 1993. / Katz, Alan. *Where Did They Hide My Presents? Silly Dilly Christmas Songs.* McElderry, 2005. / Kimmel, Elizabeth Cody. *My Penguin Osbert.* Candlewick, 2004. / Krensky, Stephen. *How Santa Lost His Job.* Simon & Schuster, 2001 / McPhail, David. *Santa's Book of Names.* Little, Brown, 1993. / Palatini, Margie. *Elf Help.* Hyperion, 1997. / Pearson, Tracey Campbell. *Where Does Joe Go?* Farrar, 1999. / Polacco, Patricia. *An Orange for Frankie.* Philomel, 2004. / Sabuda, Robert. *The Christmas Alphabet.* Orchard, 1994. / Sabuda, Robert. *The 12 Days of Christmas: A Pop-Up Celebration.* Simon & Schuster, 1996. / Seuss, Dr. *How the Grinch Stole Christmas.* Random House, 1957. / Van Allsburg, Chris. *The Polar Express.* Houghton Mifflin, 1985.

SUBJECTS: AUNTS. BROTHERS AND SISTERS. CHRISTMAS. GENEROSITY. GIFTS. NORTH POLE. RESPONSIBILITY. SANTA CLAUS.

648   **Provensen, Alice. *A Day in the Life of Murphy.* Illus. by the author. Simon & Schuster, 2003. 0-689-84884-6. Unp. Gr. PreK–2**

Industrious little black terrier Murphy-Stop-That patrols the farm, barks at the mouse under the sink, suffers the misery of going to the vet, scarfs up handouts at the dinner table, and barks barks barks. All his activities on a single day are described by Murphy himself in a stream-of-consciousness narrative in capital letters that follows him across the page.

GERM: Ask your human charges to act like detectives and think from a different point of view, following an animal around for an hour and writing down everything they think that cat, dog, ant, bird, or other miscellaneous critter is thinking. Contrast Murphy's reaction to his job with that of nonverbal but very expressive police dog Gloria, in Peggy Rathmann's *Officer Buckle and Gloria.*

RELATED TITLES: Child, Lauren. *That Pesky Rat.* Candlewick, 2002. / Cronin, Doreen. *Diary of a Worm.* HarperCollins, 2003. / Edwards, Pamela Duncan. *Muldoon.* Hyperion, 2002. / Feiffer, Jules. *Bark, George.* HarperCollins, 1999. / French, Jackie. *Diary of a Wombat.* Clarion, 2003. / George, Kristine O'Connell. *Little Dog Poems.* Clarion, 1999. / Harvey, Amanda. *Dog Eared.* Doubleday, 2002. / Lee, Chinlun. *Good Dog, Paw!* Candlewick, 2004. / Miller, Sara Swan. *Three Stories You Can Read to Your Dog.* Houghton Mifflin, 1995. / Rathmann, Peggy. *Officer Buckle and Gloria.* Putnam, 1995. / Simont, Marc. *The Stray Dog.* HarperCollins, 2001. / Teague, Mark. *Dear Mrs. LaRue: Letters from Obedience School.* Scholastic, 2002.

SUBJECTS: CREATIVE WRITING. DOGS. ENGLISH LANGUAGE—VERBS. FARM LIFE. PERSONAL NARRATIVES. POINT OF VIEW. VETERINARIANS.

649   **Pulver, Robin. *Author Day for Room 3T.* Illus. by Chuck Richards. Clarion, 2005. 0-618-35406-9. Unp. Gr. K–3**

For Reading Week at Lerner Elementary School, the third graders in Mr. Topple's class are eagerly anticipating the arrival of a real live writer, Mr. Harry Bookman, author of some of the library's silliest books, including *The Banana from Outer Space.* They don't believe their librarian, Mrs. Storey, when she tells them that authors are ordinary people. When their guest arrives, tapping on the library window, the students are delighted to welcome the chimpanzee, dressed in a gorgeous green plaid suit and purple bow tie, who swings from the ropes in the gym and scribbles in their books.

GERM: Listeners will love the in-jokes in both the story and the antic-filled pictures. The librarian has lost her glasses and can't see the mayhem and monkeyshines going on as the kids in Room 3T pose all of their intelligent questions about the life of a writer to the nonverbal, ebullient guy they believe is their visiting author. (You'll find an adorable chimp puppet, dressed in a suit and hat, at <www.mimismotifs.com>.) There's a list on the last page—"Harry Bookman's Tips for Hosting a Successful Author Visit"—that will be a good starting point when you host your own author visit. This is the funniest book on the subject since Daniel Pinkwater's *Author's Day.*

RELATED TITLES: Bunting, Eve. *My Special Day at Third Street School.* Boyds Mills, 2004. / Christelow, Eileen. *What Do Authors Do?* Clarion, 1995. / Howe, James. *The Day the Teacher Went Bananas.* Dutton, 1984. / Leedy, Loreen. *Look at My Book: How Kids Can Write and Illustrate Terrific Books.* Holiday House, 2004. / Lester, Helen. *Author: A True Story.* Houghton Mifflin, 1997. / Pinkwater, Daniel. *Author's Day.* Atheneum, 1993. / Pulver, Robin. *Axle Annie.* Dial, 1999. / Pulver, Robin. *Mrs. Toggle and the Dinosaur.* Four Winds, 1991. / Pulver, Robin. *Mrs. Toggle's Beautiful Blue Shoe.* Four Winds, 1994. / Pulver, Robin. *Punctuation Takes a Vacation.* Holiday House, 2003. / Stevens, Janet. *From Pictures to Words: A Book About Making a Book.* Holiday House, 1995.

SUBJECTS: AUTHORS. BOOKS AND READING. CHIMPANZEES. HUMOROUS FICTION. LIBRARIANS. SCHOOLS. TEACHERS.

650   Pulver, Robin. *Punctuation Takes a Vacation.* **Illus. by Lynn Rowe Reed. Holiday House, 2003. 0-8234-1687-9. Unp. Gr. K–6**

On the hottest, stickiest day of the year, teacher Mr. Wright decides to give punctuation a vacation and the kids a nice recess. Once the class has gone out to the playground, the periods, commas, exclamation points, and question marks, not to mention the apostrophes, decide to head out the door too for a stay at Take-a-Break Lake.

GERM: Duplicate and enlarge the vacation postcards that the different punctuation marks mail to the class and have children deduce the senders. Mr. Wright's class borrows some punctuation running wild from the class next door, and your group will love trying to edit the urgent and ridiculously punctuated letter they send in response. Children can write and design the pictures and messages on new postcards the punctuation marks might send. On the last page are Punctuation Rules that might help you decide how to proceed with your own punctuation lessons. Your kids will be inspired to write more carefully with a lot more empathy for their new friends, the punctuation marks. Get a full set of large, felt, punctuation puppets from <www.MimisMotifs.com>. Everyone can make small personal sets of puppets out of felt and popsicle sticks.

RELATED TITLES: Clement, Rod. *Just Another Ordinary Day.* HarperCollins, 1997. / Clements, Andrew. *Double Trouble in Walla Walla.* Millbrook, 1998. / Florczak, Robert. *Yikes!!!* Scholastic, 2003. / Heller, Ruth. *Fantastic! Wow! and Unreal! A Book About Interjections and Conjunctions.* Grosset, 1998. / Heller, Ruth. *Kites Sail High: A Book About Verbs.* Grosset, 1988. / Heller, Ruth. *Many Luscious Lollipops: A Book About Adjectives.* Grosset, 1989. / Heller, Ruth. *Merry-Go-Round: A Book About Nouns.* Grosset, 1990. / Heller, Ruth. *Up, Up and Away: A Book About Adverbs.* Grosset, 1991. / Leedy, Loreen. *There's a Frog in My Throat: 440 Animal Sayings a Little Bird Told Me.* Holiday House, 2003. / Pulver, Robin. *Author Day for Room 3T.* Clarion, 2005. / Pulver, Robin. *Mrs. Toggle and the Dinosaur.* Four Winds, 1991. / Pulver, Robin. *Nouns and Verbs Have a Field Day.* Holiday House, 2006. / Rose, Deborah Lee. *Birthday Zoo.* Albert Whitman, 2002. / Shields, Carol Diggory. *Brain Juice: English, Fresh Squeezed!* Handprint, 2004. / Viorst, Judith. *The Alphabet from Z to A: With Much Confusion on the Way.* Atheneum, 1994.

SUBJECTS: ENGLISH LANGUAGE—PUNCTUATION. HUMOROUS FICTION. PERSONIFICATION. SCHOOLS. TEACHERS. VACATIONS. WRITING.

651   Rankin, Joan. *Wow! It's Great Being a Duck.* **Illus. by the author. McElderry, 1998. 0-689-81756-8. Unp. Gr. PreK–1**

The smallest and skinniest little duckling in the nest, Lillee, thinks it's too dangerous to take her feet off the ground, and so she wanders into the forest, where she meets up with Mr. Furry-legs-Long-tail-Sharp-snout-Pink-tongue.

GERM: Listeners will recognize Lillee's friend as a fox long before she does. Ask them to explain why Lillee finally decides it's great being a duck. Have them draw pictures of their favorite animals in action and complete this sentence: "It's great being a ____ because I can ____." Or, they can transfer Lillee's story onto their own maturing selves: "It's great to be me because I can ____."

RELATED TITLES: Buzzeo, Toni. *Dawdle Duckling.* Dial, 2003. / Dunrea, Olivier. *Gossie.* Houghton Mifflin, 2002. / Dunrea, Olivier. *Ollie.* Houghton Mifflin, 2003. / Fox, Mem. *Hattie and the Fox.* Bradbury, 1987. / Hindley, Judy. *Do Like a Duck Does!* Candlewick, 2002. / Raffi. *Five Little Ducks.* Crown, 1988. / Shannon, George. *Tippy-Toe Chick, Go!* Greenwillow, 2003. / Silverman, Erica. *Don't Fidget a Feather.* Macmillan, 1994. / Simmons, Jane. *Come Along, Daisy.* Little, Brown, 1998. / Stenmark, Victoria. *The Singing Chick.* Henry Holt, 1999. / Whippo, Walt, and Bernard Zaritzky. *Little White Duck.* Little, Brown, 2000.

SUBJECTS: DUCKS. FOXES. HUMOROUS FICTION.

652   Ransome, Candace. *Liberty Street.* **Illus. by Eric Velasquez. Walker, 2003. 0-8027-8869-6. Unp. Gr. 2–5**

Working hard from candlelight to candlelight, day in and day out, Kezia and her mother, slaves of the widow lady Missus Grace, rejoice in sweet Sunday, their one day of liberty. After Kezia's father is sold off, her mother first arranges for Kezia to go to a secret school run by Miss Eulalie, a free black woman, and then engineers Kezia's escape to Canada on the Underground Railroad.

GERM: Somber paintings depict a loving family facing danger as they struggle to hold on to their dignity in dire times. Talk about the emotional impact slavery would have had on a child. What does Mama mean when she tells Kezia, "Inside your fear is a kernel of strength. Look deep and you'll find it." Compare Kezia's experiences to Lindy's in Vaunda Micheaux Nelson's *Almost to Freedom.*

RELATED TITLES: Adler, David A. *A Picture Book of Harriet Tubman*. Holiday House, 1992. / Bradby, Marie. *More Than Anything Else*. Orchard, 1995. / Edwards, Pamela Duncan. *Barefoot: Escape on the Underground Railroad*. HarperCollins, 1997. / Hamilton, Virginia. *The People Could Fly: The Picture Book*. Knopf, 2004. / Hopkinson, Deborah. *Sweet Clara and the Freedom Quilt*. Knopf, 1993. / Howard, Elizabeth Fitzgerald. *Virgie Goes to School with Us Boys*. Simon & Schuster, 2000. / Johnson, Dolores. *Now Let Me Fly: The Story of a Slave Family*. Macmillan, 1993. / Nelson, Vaunda Micheaux. *Almost to Freedom*. Carolrhoda, 2003. / Polacco, Patricia. *The Butterfly*. Philomel, 2000. / Ringgold, Faith. *Aunt Harriet's Underground Railroad in the Sky*. Crown, 1992. / Winter, Jeannette. *Follow the Drinking Gourd*. Knopf, 1989.

SUBJECTS: AFRICAN AMERICANS. BOOKS AND READING. DETERMINATION. HISTORICAL FICTION. LITERACY. MULTICULTURAL BOOKS. PICTURE BOOKS FOR OLDER READERS. SLAVERY. UNDERGROUND RAILROAD.

653   **Rathmann, Peggy.** *The Day the Babies Crawled Away*. **Illus. by the author. Putnam, 2003. 0-399-23196-X. 40pp. Gr. PreK–K**

In rhyme and charmingly illustrated in black silhouettes against pastel skies, Mom recalls how her brave boy saved the day when the babies all crawled away from the fair. The listeners become the vicarious heroes in this sweet, gently humorous adventure, narrated by the mother of the young protagonist.

GERM: With your adventurers, come up with new rhyming activities that the babies would've liked to have done, such as: The babies sat in a chair, combing their hair. Act out each activity and draw silhouette pictures captioned with the rhymes.

RELATED TITLES: Anholt, Catherine, and Laurence Anholt. *Catherine and Laurence Anholt's Big Book of Little Children*. Candlewick, 2003. / Appelt, Kathi. *Bubba and Beau*. Harcourt, 2002. / Ashman, Linda. *Babies on the Go*. Harcourt, 2003. / Curtis, Marci. *I Was So Silly! Big Kids Remember Being Little*. Dial, 2002. / Frazee, Marla. *Hush, Little Baby: A Folk Song with Pictures*. Harcourt, 1999. / James, Simon. *Baby Brains*. Candlewick, 2004. / Meyers, Susan. *Everywhere Babies*. Harcourt, 2001. / Paxton, Tom. *Where's the Baby?* Morrow, 1993. / Rathmann, Peggy. *Good Night, Gorilla*. Putnam, 1994. / Rathmann, Peggy. *Officer Buckle and Gloria*. Putnam, 1995. / Rathmann, Peggy. *Ten Minutes Till Bedtime*. Putnam, 1998. / Regan, Dian Curtis. *Chance*. Philomel, 2003. / Schwartz, Amy. *A Teeny Tiny Baby*. Orchard, 1994. / Sierra, Judy. *Tasty Baby Belly Buttons*. Knopf, 1999. / Stevenson, James. *Rolling Rose*. Candlewick, 1997. / Wild, Margaret. *Midnight Babies*. Clarion, 2001.

SUBJECTS: BABIES. BEDTIME STORIES. PICNICS. RESCUES. STORIES IN RHYME.

654   **Rathmann, Peggy.** *Good Night, Gorilla*. **Illus. by the author. Putnam, 1994. 0-399-22445-9. Unp. Gr. PreK–1**

After stealing the zookeeper's ring of keys, gorilla lets all the other animals out of their cages, and they follow the zookeeper home to bed. Viewers will love following the mouse that pulls the monkey's banana on a string; the black page with only eyeballs showing (when the zookeeper's wife realizes she and her husband are not alone); and the ending with monkey, mouse, and banana peel in bed with the zookeepers.

GERM: This is a hoot to act out in narrative pantomime.

RELATED TITLES: Garland, Michael. *Last Night at the Zoo*. Boyds Mills, 2001. / Lum, Kate. *What! Cried Granny: An Almost Bedtime Story*. Doubleday, 2003. / Mathews, Judith, and Fay Robinson. *Nathaniel Willy, Scared Silly*. Bradbury, 1994. / Murphy, Jill. *Peace at Last*. Dial, 1980. / Murray, Marjorie Dennis. *Don't Wake Up the Bear!* Cavendish, 2003. / Paxton, Tom. *Going to the Zoo*. Morrow, 1996. / Rathmann, Peggy. *The Day the Babies Crawled Away*. Putnam, 2003. / Rathmann, Peggy. *Officer Buckle and Gloria*. Putnam, 1995. / Rathmann, Peggy. *Ten Minutes Till Bedtime*. Putnam, 1998. / Rosen, Michael. *We're Going on a Bear Hunt*. McElderry, 1989. / Simms, Laura. *The Squeaky Door*. Crown, 1991. / Thomson, Pat. *The Squeaky, Creaky Bed*. Doubleday, 2003. / Wilson, Karma. *Bear Snores On*. McElderry, 2002. / Wood, Audrey. *The Napping House*. Harcourt, 1984. / Yolen, Jane. *How Do Dinosaurs Say Good Night?* Blue Sky/Scholastic, 2000.

SUBJECTS: BEDTIME STORIES. CREATIVE DRAMA. GORILLAS. HUMOROUS FICTION. MICE. ZOO KEEPERS. ZOOS.

655   **Rathmann, Peggy.** *Officer Buckle and Gloria*. **Illus. by the author. Putnam, 1995. 0-399-22616-8. Unp. Gr. K–2**

Well-meaning but dull Officer Buckle presents his lists of carefully collected safety tips at assemblies for the disinterested children at Napville School. "Nobody ever listened. Sometimes, there was snoring." When he brings along the department's obedient new police dog, Gloria, the children sit up and take notice. "KEEP your SHOELACES tied!" he says, unaware that, behind his back, Gloria is acting out his pronouncement. He and the endearingly dramatic Gloria are a hit and are soon in great demand. Not until a TV news team videotapes one of their performances does Officer Buckle realize the crowd's bravos are for the dog and not for him, and he is crushed.

GERM: Act out the scene in which Officer Buckle gives his rules and Gloria mimes behind his back. You can play Officer Buckle; the children can be Gloria. When you turn your back, they act out; when you whirl back to face them, they are sitting perfectly. Pat them on the head and say, "Good dog." As Gloria, they can act out each safety tip in the story and in the stars on the book's endpapers. Have your obedience specialists trace and cut out stars on white paper. Ask them to think up more safety tips, with Gloria as their subject, that they can write, illustrate, and then act out.

RELATED TITLES: Buehner, Caralyn. *Superdog: The Heart of a Hero.* HarperCollins, 2004. / Ernst, Lisa Campbell. *Ginger Jumps.* Bradbury, 1990. / Graham, Bob. *Benny: An Adventure Story.* Candlewick, 1999. / Kalman, Maira. *What Pete Ate from A–Z.* Putnam, 2001. / Kellogg, Steven. *Pinkerton, Behave.* Dial, 1979. / Laden, Nina. *The Night I Followed the Dog.* Chronicle, 1994. / Lebentritt, Julia, and Richard Ploetz. *The Kooken.* Holt, 1992. / L'Engle, Madeleine. *The Other Dog.* SeaStar, 2001. / Meddaugh, Susan. *Martha Speaks.* Houghton, 1992. / Meddaugh, Susan. *Martha Walks the Dog.* Houghton Mifflin, 1998. / Miller, Sara Swan. *Three Stories You Can Read to Your Dog.* Houghton Mifflin, 1995. / Provensen, Alice. *A Day in the Life of Murphy.* Simon & Schuster, 2003. / Weller, Frances Ward. *Riptide.* Philomel, 1990.

SUBJECTS: CALDECOTT MEDAL. CREATIVE DRAMA. DOGS. HUMOROUS FICTION. PICTURE BOOKS FOR ALL AGES. POLICE. POLICE DOGS. SAFETY. SCHOOLS.

656 Recorvits, Helen. *My Name Is Yoon.* **Illus. by Gabi Swiatkowska. Farrar, 2003. 0-374-35114-7. Unp. Gr. 1–3**

Now that she's in America, Yoon learns to write her name in English, even though she far prefers it in Korean, in which it means "Shining Wisdom." When she gets to school, she writes "cat," "bird," and even "cupcake," but shies away from writing her own name.

GERM: Discussion point: Why does Yoon write other words instead of her own name? Why does she wish she could go back to Korea? How did you feel on your first day of school? How would you help Yoon get used to her new school? Meet young Native American boy Crowboy, another nervous first-day child with a good imagination, in *The Rattlesnake Who Went to School* by Craig Strete.

RELATED TITLES: Aliki. *Marianthe's Story: Painted Words, Spoken Memories.* Greenwillow, 1998. / Choi, Sook Nyul. *Halmoni and the Picnic.* Houghton Mifflin, 1993. / Choi, Yangsook. *The Name Jar.* Knopf, 2001. / Elya, Susan Middleton. *Home at Last.* Lee & Low, 2002. / Henkes, Kevin. *Chrysanthemum.* Greenwillow, 1991. / Kline, Suzy. *Song Lee in Room 2B.* Viking, 1993. / Lasky, Kathryn. *Lunch Bunnies.* Little, Brown, 1996. / Levine, Ellen. *I Hate English!* Scholastic, 1989. / Pak, Soyung. *Sumi's First Day of School.* Viking, 2003. / Pomeranc, Marion Hess. *The American Wei.* Albert Whitman, 1998. / Strete, Craig. *The Rattlesnake Who Went to School.* Putnam, 2004. / Wong, Janet. *Apple Pie 4th of July.* Harcourt, 2002. / Yang, Belle. *Hannah Is My Name.* Candlewick, 2004.

SUBJECTS: ASIAN AMERICANS. FIRST DAY OF SCHOOL. IMMIGRATION AND EMIGRATION. KOREAN AMERICANS. MULTICULTURAL BOOKS. NAMES. SCHOOLS. TEACHERS.

657 Regan, Dian Curtis. *Chance.* **Illus. by Dee Huxley. Philomel, 2003. 0-399-23592-2. Unp. Gr. K–3**

Downright cranky with his guitar pluckin' Pa, his slobbery ol' dog, and bath-lovin' Ma, baby Chance takes his rattle and his blanket and sets off to find a more hospitable place to live. He spends fall with a bear near Moosedale, winter in the monkey house at the Hilldale Zoo, spring with the sea lions in Oceandale, and summer in a cool cave in Stonedale. But don't you worry about that bald-headed, pajama-clad baby—he writes letters or phones home each season and Mama promises him the best cake ever if he comes on home for his first birthday.

GERM: Wow, what a jaunty, action-packed personal narrative—and a perfect example of using voice in a story—told by a toddler as he rambles from place to place, finding out, of course, that it's always great to come home. Your big kids can write from Chance's point of view, describing his second year of life. For another look at how babies see the world, also read Amy Schwartz's *A Teeny Tiny Baby.*

RELATED TITLES: Appelt, Kathi. *Bubba and Beau.* Harcourt, 2002. (And others in the Bubba and Beau series.) / Cooke, Trish. *So Much.* Candlewick, 1994. / Curtis, Marci. *I Was So Silly! Big Kids Remember Being Little.* Dial, 2002. / Greenspun, Adele Aron, and Joanie Schwarz. *Ariel and Emily.* Dutton, 2003. / James, Simon. *Baby Brains.* Candlewick, 2004. / Meyers, Susan. *Everywhere Babies.* Harcourt, 2001. / Nye, Naomi Shihab.

Baby Radar. Greenwillow, 2003. / Paxton, Tom. *Where's the Baby?* Morrow, 1993. / Schwartz, Amy. *A Teeny Tiny Baby.* Orchard, 1994. / Wild, Margaret. *Midnight Babies.* Clarion, 2001. / Williams, Vera B. *"More More More," Said the Baby.* Greenwillow, 1990.

SUBJECTS: ANIMALS. BABIES. PERSONAL NARRATIVES. TALL TALES. VOYAGES AND TRAVELS.

658   Reiss, Mike. *The Great Show-and-Tell Disaster.* Illus. by Mike Cressy. Price Stern Sloan, 2001. 0-8431-7680-6. Unp. Gr. 1–4
Ned's Mix-up Ray, which he invents for show-and-tell, is an amalgam of valuable treasures he's found in the trash, all held together with duct tape and glue. He points it at a SHOE, and the shoe becomes a HOSE; his LAMP turns into a PALM, and LEMONS become MELONS. At school and on his class trip to the Museum of Art, Ned unleashes his device's full linguistic powers, even turning teacher MRS. ETON into a three-headed MONSTER. The rhyming narrative will get your wordsmiths looking at words in a whole new way.

GERM: Vigilant observers will pore over the large, genial illustrations in order to identify all the objects Ned zaps, anagram style, and figure out how rearranged letters can spell a whole new word. Pull out the Scrabble game and have children use the tiles to rearrange new words. Give them a starting list to rearrange, with words like post (stop, pots), stack (tacks), start (tarts). Put a 16-letter Boggle-like grid on the board or overhead and have the group play, looking for as many connecting words as they can list in two minutes. Then have them each come up with a word that can be rearranged. Folding construction paper in half, children can write and illustrate the first word on the outer flap and the anagram inside. For older readers, fool around with switched letters in Jon Agee's *Elvis Lives and Other Anagrams* and found words in Richard Wilbur's wordplay poetry book, *The Pig in the Spigot.*

RELATED TITLES: Agee, Jon. *Elvis Lives and Other Anagrams.* Farrar, 2004. / Clements, Andrew. *Double Trouble in Walla Walla.* Millbrook, 1998. / Cox, Judy. *Don't Be Silly, Mrs. Millie!* Marshall Cavendish, 2005. / Gackenbach, Dick. *Tiny for a Day.* Clarion, 1993. / Lasky, Kathryn. *Show and Tell Bunnies.* Candlewick, 1998. / Most, Bernard. *Hippopotamus Hunt.* Harcourt, 1994. / Nikola-Lisa, W. *Tangle Talk.* Dutton, 1997. / Smith, Janice Lee. *The Show-and-Tell War.* HarperCollins, 1988. / Smith, Lane. *Math Curse.* Viking, 1995. / Sorel, Edward. *Johnny on the Spot.* McElderry, 1998. / Steig, William. *CDB.* Simon & Schuster, 2000. / Walton, Rick. *Once There Was a Bull . . . (Frog).* Gibbs-Smith, 1995. / Wilbur, Richard. *The Pig in the Spigot.* Harcourt, 2000. / Woodruff, Elvira. *Show and Tell.* Holiday House, 1991.

SUBJECTS: ENGLISH LANGUAGE. HUMOROUS FICTION. PICTURE BOOKS FOR ALL AGES. SCHOOLS. SHOW-AND-TELL PRESENTATIONS. WORD GAMES.

659   Reynolds, Peter H. *The Dot.* Illus. by the author. Candlewick, 2003. 0-7636-1961-2. Unp. Gr. 1–6
Vashti is convinced she just can't draw until her art teacher says, "Just make a mark and see where it takes you." So Vashti jabs a piece of paper and makes a dot. When her teacher frames the dot, Vashti knows she can do better and starts painting all kinds of glorious dots.

GERM: Here's an allegory for all of those children who say, "I can't," or "I wish I could," or "I'm no good at that." This deceptively simple picture book, illustrated with ink and watercolors, may be their first step to taking a chance or trying something new and challenging. Note how Vashti then inspires another child who claims he can't draw a straight line with a ruler. Ask your kids: what do you think you can't do that you'd be willing to give another try? What does this quote by Thomas Edison mean? "Genius is one percent inspiration and ninety-nine percent perspiration." Go wild with dots: make pointillist paintings with fine tipped markers. Also read the companion story, *Ish.*

RELATED TITLES: Blake, Robert J. *The Perfect Spot.* Philomel, 1992. / Brenner, Barbara. *The Boy Who Loved to Draw: Benjamin West.* Houghton Mifflin, 1999. / Browne, Anthony. *Willy the Dreamer.* Candlewick, 1998. / Cohen, Miriam. *No Good in Art.* Greenwillow, 1980. / dePaola, Tomie. *The Art Lesson.* Putnam, 1989. / Garland, Michael. *Dinner at Magritte's.* Dutton, 1995. / Hurd, Thacher. *Art Dog.* HarperCollins, 1996. / Kroll, Steven. *Patches Lost and Found.* Winslow, 2001. / LaMarche, Jim. *The Raft.* HarperCollins, 2000. / McClintock, Barbara. *The Fantastic Drawings of Danielle.* Houghton Mifflin, 1996. / Mills, Claudia. *Ziggy's Blue-Ribbon Day.* Farrar, 2005. / Moss, Marissa. *Regina's Big Mistake.* Houghton Mifflin, 1990. / Reynolds, Peter H. *Ish.* Candlewick, 2004. / Schwartz, Amy. *Begin at the Beginning: A Little Artist Learns About Life.* HarperCollins, 2005. / Stadler, Alexander. *Lila Bloom.* Farrar, 2003. / Wallner, Alexandra. *Grandma Moses.* Holiday House, 2004. / Warhola, James. *Uncle Andy's.* Putnam, 2003.

SUBJECTS: ALLEGORIES. ARTISTS. CREATIVITY. DRAWING. PERSEVERANCE. PICTURE BOOKS FOR ALL AGES. SELF-ESTEEM. TEACHERS.

660   Reynolds, Peter H. *Ish*. Illus. by the author. Candlewick, 2004. 0-7636-2344-X. Unp. Gr. 1–6
Ramon loves to draw, but when his brother laughs at one of his drawings, he crumples it up, frustrated that he can't make it look "right." It's not until his little sister describes one of his drawings as "vase-ISH" that he is liberated to draw what he feels without worrying how it looks.
GERM: Talk about what it means to think, draw, and write "ishily" and then draw or write something ishy-ish. You'll also want to read the companion book, *The Dot*, in which Vashti thinks she can't draw until her teacher challenges her to "just make a mark."
RELATED TITLES: Blake, Robert J. *The Perfect Spot*. Philomel, 1992. / Browne, Anthony. *Willy the Dreamer*. Candlewick, 1998. / Cohen, Miriam. *No Good in Art*. Greenwillow, 1980. / dePaola, Tomie. *The Art Lesson*. Putnam, 1989. / Hurd, Thacher. *Art Dog*. HarperCollins, 1996. / Kroll, Steven. *Patches Lost and Found*. Winslow, 2001. / LaMarche, Jim. *The Raft*. HarperCollins, 2000. / Mills, Claudia. *Ziggy's Blue-Ribbon Day*. Farrar, 2005. / Moss, Marissa. *Regina's Big Mistake*. Houghton Mifflin, 1990. / Reynolds, Peter H. *The Dot*. Candlewick, 2003. / Schwartz, Amy. *Begin at the Beginning: A Little Artist Learns About Life*. HarperCollins, 2005.
SUBJECTS: ARTISTS. BROTHERS AND SISTERS. CREATIVITY. DRAWING. PICTURE BOOKS FOR ALL AGES. SELF-CONFIDENCE.

661   Riley, Linnea. *Mouse Mess*. Illus. by the author. Scholastic, 1997. 0-590-10048-3. Unp. Gr. PreK–1
Mouse climbs up on the kitchen counter, where he has a feast. The vibrant collage artwork—done with sponged watercolor on paper—along with a simple rhyming text, a pleasingly pudgy brown mouse, and some mighty fine-looking snack foods will make your kids hunger for this story.
GERM: Pair this with other mouse tales, including Denise Fleming's *Lunch* and Emily Arnold McCully's *Picnic*, for a perfect preschool story time, especially if there's a snack afterwards.
RELATED TITLES: Cauley, Lorinda Bryan. *The Town Mouse and the Country Mouse*. Putnam, 1984. / Fleming, Denise. *Alphabet Under Construction*. Henry Holt, 2002. / Fleming, Denise. *Lunch*. Henry Holt, 1992. / McCully, Emily Arnold. *Picnic*. HarperCollins, 2003. / Numeroff, Laura. *If You Give a Mouse a Cookie*. HarperCollins, 1985. / Schindel, John. *What's for Lunch?* Lothrop, 1984. / Wood, Audrey. *The Little Mouse, the Red Ripe Strawberry, and the Big Hungry Bear*. Child's Play, 1990.
SUBJECTS: FOOD. MICE. STORIES IN RHYME.

662   Roche, Denis. *The Best Class Picture Ever*. Illus. by the author. Scholastic, 2003. 0-439-26983-0. Unp. Gr. PreK–2
With the second graders of Class 202 in an uproar over their missing class guinea pig, Elvis, they troop into the auditorium to have their class picture taken by the photographer, Mr. Click, who knows just how to cheer up the whole group.
GERM: Interestingly enough, Mr. Click takes that terribly behaved class and whips them into shape by involving them and guiding them through fun and rewarding educational activities, which is a good lesson in classroom management for us all. Mr. Click is a born teacher, leading the group on a quest to make classmate Olivia smile. Just as he has the class do, have your kids make a long list of the words that make them smile and have them measure each other's smiles with rulers. Take everyone's picture. Meet two more innovative and caring male teachers in *Lily's Purple Plastic Purse* by Kevin Henkes and *Crazy Hair Day* by Barney Saltzberg.
RELATED TITLES: Allard, Harry. *Miss Nelson Is Missing*. Houghton, 1985. / Child, Lauren. *Clarice Bean, Guess Who's Babysitting?* Candlewick, 2001. / Clements, Andrew. *Double Trouble in Walla Walla*. Millbrook, 1998. / Creech, Sharon. *A Fine, Fine School*. HarperCollins, 2001. / Henkes, Kevin. *Lilly's Purple Plastic Purse*. Greenwillow, 1996. / Kroll, Steven. *Patches Lost and Found*. Winslow, 2001. / Reiss, Mike. *The Great Show-and-Tell Disaster*. Price Stern Sloan, 2001. / Saltzberg, Barney. *Crazy Hair Day*. Candlewick, 2003. / Stevenson, James. *That Dreadful Day*. Greenwillow, 1985. / Willard, Nancy. *Simple Pictures Are Best*. Harcourt, 1977.
SUBJECTS: BEHAVIOR. PHOTOGRAPHY. SCHOOLS. TEACHERS.

663   Rodanas, Kristina. *The Blind Hunter*. Illus. by the author. Marshall Cavendish, 2003. 0-7614-5132-3. Unp. Gr. 1–4
Gentle Chirobo used to be a hunter before his eyesight faded. When a young man offers to let the blind man come hunting with him, Chirobo shows that there are many ways of seeing, using his sense of hearing, smell, and touch to warn them of danger in the bush.
GERM: Based on a South African folktale, this thoughtful story will get listeners talking about fairness and wisdom as they try to figure out how the old man knew that the young hunter was

cheating him out of the duck he had trapped. Discuss: What are the other ways of seeing that Chirobo practiced? What can you "see" with your other senses? Why do people fight? How can you learn to see with your heart?

RELATED TITLES: Bash, Barbara. *Tree of Life: The World of the African Baobab.* Sierra Club/Little, Brown, 1989. / Cowcher, Helen. *Whistling Thorn.* Scholastic, 1993. / Cowen-Fletcher, Jane. *It Takes a Village.* Scholastic, 1994. / Creech, Sharon. *Granny Torrelli Makes Soup.* HarperCollins, 2003. / Dorris, Michael. *Sees Behind Trees.* Hyperion, 1996. / Freedman, Russell. *Out of Darkness: The Story of Louis Braille.* Clarion, 1997. / Grifalconi, Ann. *The Village of Round and Square Houses.* Little, Brown, 1986. / Young, Ed. *Seven Blind Mice.* Philomel, 1992.

SUBJECTS: AFRICA. BLIND. FORGIVENESS. HONESTY. HUNTERS AND HUNTING. MULTICULTURAL BOOKS. PEOPLE WITH DISABILITIES. PHYSICALLY HANDICAPPED. SENSES AND SENSATION.

664   Rodman, Mary Ann. *My Best Friend.* Illus. by E. B. Lewis. Viking, 2005. 0-670-05989-7. Unp. Gr. PreK–2

It's Wednesday playgroup day at the neighborhood pool, but when 6-year-old Lily says hi to Tamika, who's 7, Tamika ignores her and jumps into the pool with Shanice. As Lily tells it, Tamika is her best friend, but she just doesn't know it yet. Lily tries everything—getting a new bathing suit and sharing popsicles and floating noodles—but Tamika ignores her except when Shanice isn't there. Keesha is nice to Lily, though, sticking by her in spite of Tamika's unfriendliness. Shimmering watercolors make you want to go swimming and the winsome portraits of Lily capture her longing, rejection, hopefulness, and final recognition that Keesha is a real friend.

GERM: What child hasn't experienced rejection from other heedless children? This story will strike a chord. Discussion points: Why does Lily want to be best friends with Tamika? Why doesn't Tamika want the same thing? What can Lily do to solve this problem? Have you ever had a problem like this? What did you do? What are your best rules for making a new friend?

RELATED TITLES: Brown, Laurie Krasny, and Marc Brown. *How to Be a Friend: A Guide to Making Friends and Keeping Them.* Little, Brown, 1998. / DePaolo, Paula. *Rosie and the Yellow Ribbon.* Little, Brown, 1992. / English, Karen. *Hot Day on Abbott Avenue.* Clarion, 2004. / Havill, Juanita. *Jamaica and Brianna.* Houghton Mifflin, 1993. / Joosse, Barbara M. *Hot City.* Philomel, 2004. / O'Neill, Alexis. *The Recess Queen.* Scholastic, 2002. / Raschka, Chris. *Yo! Yes?* Orchard, 1993. / Winthrop, Elizabeth. *Lizzie and Harold.* Lothrop, 1985.

SUBJECTS: AFRICAN AMERICANS. BEHAVIOR. BEST FRIENDS. FRIENDSHIP. MULTICULTURAL BOOKS. SWIMMING.

665   Rohmann, Eric. *Clara and Asha.* Illus. by the author. Roaring Brook, 2005. 1-59643-031-1. Unp. Gr. PreK–1

Not sleepy, dark-haired, pony-tailed Clara waits in bed for her friend Asha, a massive blue fish who fills her window. They met in the park, where he was a water-spouting sculpture in a fountain, and now he accompanies her everywhere. Tonight they play in the indigo star-flecked sky, where they float and frolic until Clara goes back to bed and tries to sleep. The story, its understated text narrated by Clara, is told most eloquently through the heart-stirring paintings of the ebullient pair.

GERM: Don't show the last page until children have talked about or drawn who they think Clara's next nighttime visitor will be. When you do show the alligator, children can write and draw the sequel or write about their own midnight romps with imaginary friends. For another evening with the animals, read David Wiesner's Caldecott-winning *Tuesday.*

RELATED TITLES: Child, Lauren. *I Am Too Absolutely Small for School.* Candlewick, 2004. / James, Simon. *Leon and Bob.* Candlewick, 1997. / Jonell, Lynne. *I Need a Snake.* Putnam, 1998. / Paxton, Tom. *Jennifer's Rabbit.* Morrow, 1988. / Rohmann, Eric. *The Cinder-Eyed Cats.* Dragonfly, 2001. / Rohmann, Eric. *My Friend Rabbit.* Roaring Brook, 2002. / Rohmann, Eric. *Time Flies.* Crown, 1994. / Wiesner, David. *Tuesday.* Clarion, 1991.

SUBJECTS: BEDTIME STORIES. FISHES. FRIENDSHIP. IMAGINARY PLAYMATES. IMAGINATION.

666   Rohmann, Eric. *My Friend Rabbit.* Illus. by the author. Roaring Brook, 2002. 0-7613-1535-7. Unp. Gr. PreK–1

Rabbit launches Mouse into the air in his spiffy new airplane, but Mouse tumbles out. With the airplane now stuck up a tree, Rabbit directs a batch of large animals to stand on top of each other in order to try to reach it. The book's hand-colored relief prints, heavily outlined in black, are appealing and childlike, making this a good selection for preschool story hours, as well as a fun possibility for a flannelboard story.

GERM: At the end of the story, as Mouse and Rabbit are stuck in the tree in their airplane, Rabbit says, "Not to worry, Mouse, I've got an idea." Ask children to devise a clever new idea for the two to get down.

RELATED TITLES: Babcock, Chris. *No Moon, No Milk*. Crown, 1993. / Cooper, Helen. *Pumpkin Soup*. Farrar, 1999. / Cronin, Doreen. *Giggle, Giggle, Quack*. Simon & Schuster, 2002. / Duvoisin, Roger. *Petunia*. Knopf, 1989. / Riddell, Chris. *Platypus and the Lucky Day*. Harcourt, 2002. / Rohmann, Eric. *The Cinder-Eyed Cats*. Dragonfly, 2001. / Rohmann, Eric. *Clara and Asha*. Roaring Brook, 2005. / Rohmann, Eric. *Time Flies*. Crown, 1994. / Shannon, David. *Duck on a Bike*. Blue Sky/Scholastic, 2002.

SUBJECTS: AIRPLANES. BEST FRIENDS. CALDECOTT MEDAL. FRIENDSHIP. MICE. RABBITS.

667   Root, Phyllis. *Rattletrap Car*. Illus. by Jill Barton. Candlewick, 2001. 0-7636-0919-6. Unp. Gr. PreK–K

Poppa doesn't know if he and the hot hot hot kids—Junie, Jakie, and the baby—can make it all the way to the lake in his old jalopy. Just in case, Poppa packs up a thermos of fizz and some chocolate marshmallow fudge delight, Junie takes her beach ball, Jakie his surfboard, and the baby her paddle-wheel boat. The lively anticipation story with its endearing pencil and watercolor illustrations bounces along with lots of noise as each child in turn gets a chance to fix things when the floor falls off, the gas tank falls off, and the engine falls out.

GERM: Children can join in on all the jaunty chantable refrains and will love acting this out. Arrange chairs so kids feel as if they're sitting in the car. Get an old record or the lid to a large tin to use as the steering wheel, give it to the child playing Poppa, and start driving. Use your imaginations with Sandra and Susan Steen's *Car Wash* and take another bumpy car ride with Margaret Mahy's *The Rattlebang Picnic*.

RELATED TITLES: Barton, Byron. *My Car*. Greenwillow, 2001. / Day, Nancy Raines. *Double Those Wheels*. Dutton, 2003. / Hort, Lenny. *The Seals on the Bus*. Henry Holt, 2000. / Kirk, Daniel. *Go!* Hyperion, 2001. / Mahy, Margaret. *The Rattlebang Picnic*. Dial, 1994. / Pinkwater, Daniel. *Tooth-Gnasher Superflash*. Macmillan, 1990. / Rosen, Michael. *We're Going on a Bear Hunt*. McElderry, 1989. / Shaw, Nancy. *Sheep in a Jeep*. Houghton Mifflin, 1986. / Steen, Sandra, and Susan Steen. *Car Wash*. Putnam, 2001. / Zelinsky, Paul O. *The Wheels on the Bus*. Dutton, 1990.

SUBJECTS: AUTOMOBILES. CHANTABLE REFRAIN. CREATIVE DRAMA. FAMILY LIFE. LAKES. SOUND EFFECTS. TRANSPORTATION. VEHICLES.

668   Rose, Deborah Lee. *Birthday Zoo*. Illus. by Lynn Munsinger. Albert Whitman, 2002. 0-8075-0776-8. Unp. Gr. PreK–2

"'Hey, what's the big deal?' noticed the seal. 'Birthday today!' reported the ray.'" So start the joyous preparations by all 21 of the zoo animals putting together a birthday party for a redheaded little boy in a peaked birthday hat. There are presents, balloons, games, and cake for all.

GERM: Short, rhyming couplets each feature a quote from a zoo animal asking a question or making a statement, so you can demonstrate the differences between periods, exclamation points, and question marks. Action verbs abound, as do creative alternatives for the verb "said." For older children, you can explore how written dialogue works and brainstorm new animals, rhyming quotes, and alternatives for the staid "said." Don't forget to sing Happy Birthday and break out the cupcakes.

RELATED TITLES: Berends, Polly Berrien. *I Heard Said the Bird*. Dial, 1995. / Bodecker, N. M. *It's Raining Said John Twaining: Danish Nursery Rhymes*. Atheneum, 1973. / Bodecker, N. M. *Let's Marry Said the Cherry and Other Nonsense Poems*. Atheneum, 1974. / Cameron, Polly. *"I Can't," Said the Ant*. Coward, 1961. / Chapman, Cheryl. *Pass the Fritters, Critters*. Four Winds, 1993. / De Regniers, Beatrice Schenk. *May I Bring a Friend?* Atheneum, 1964. / Emberley, Barbara. *Drummer Hoff*. Simon & Schuster, 1987. / Murphy, Stuart. *Too Many Kangaroo Things to Do!* HarperCollins, 1996. / Pulver, Robin. *Punctuation Takes a Vacation*. Holiday House, 2003. / Rose, Deborah Lee. *Into the A, B, Sea*. Scholastic, 2000. / Schneider, R. M. *Add It, Dip It, Fix It: A Book of Verbs*. Houghton Mifflin, 1995. / Taylor, Linda. *The Lettuce Leaf Birthday Letter*. Dial, 1995.

SUBJECTS: ANIMALS. BIRTHDAYS. ENGLISH LANGUAGE—GRAMMAR. ENGLISH LANGUAGE—PUNCTUATION. ENGLISH LANGUAGE—VERBS. PARTIES. STORIES IN RHYME. STUFFED ANIMALS. ZOOS.

669   Rosenthal, Amy Krouse. *Little Pea*. Illus. by Jen Corace. Chronicle, 2005. 0-8118-4658-X. Unp. Gr. PreK–1

The one thing Little Pea doesn't like about his otherwise perfect life is . . . candy. That's what little peas have to eat for dinner every night, and Mama and Papa Pea insist that Little Pea eats five pieces before he can have dessert. What's for dessert? "Spinach! My favorite!" squeals Little Pea. The watercolor and ink illustrations add a whimsical touch to this funny turnaround tale.

GERM: On a white paper plate, have children draw the food groups that they need to eat each night before they get any dessert. For another point of view, there's a little girl who won't touch her peas in *No Peas* for Nellie by Chris L. Demarest.

RELATED TITLES: Abrams, Pam. *Now I Eat My ABC's*. Scholastic, 2004. / Blumenthal, Deborah. *Don't Let the Peas Touch! And Other Stories*. Scholastic, 2004. / Brown, Marc. *D. W. the Picky Eater*. Little, Brown, 1995. / Child, Lauren. *I Will Never Not Ever Eat a Tomato*. Candlewick, 2000. / Demarest, Chris L. *No Peas for Nellie*. Macmillan, 1988. / Hoberman, Mary Ann. *The Seven Silly Eaters*. Harcourt, 1997. / Palatini, Margie. *Zak's Lunch*. Clarion, 1998. / Seuss, Dr. *Green Eggs and Ham*. Random House, 1960. / Sharmat, Mitchell. *Gregory, the Terrible Eater*. Macmillan, 1985. / Wells, Rosemary. *Yoko*. Hyperion, 1998. / Yolen, Jane. *How Do Dinosaurs Eat Their Food?* Blue Sky/Scholastic, 2005.

SUBJECTS: CANDY. FOOD. FOOD HABITS. PEAS.

670   Rostoker-Gruber, Karen. *Rooster Can't Cock-a-Doodle-Doo*. Illus. by Paul Rátz de Tagyos. Dial, 2004. 0-8037-2877-8. Unp. Gr. PreK–1

Rooster wakes with a terrible sore throat and enlists the help of the hens, cows, sheep, and pigs to figure out a way to wake up Farmer Ted without cock-a-doodle-doing. All the helpful barn animals pile atop one another to make an animal pyramid high enough to reach Farmer Ted's bedroom and then set about helping him complete his chores. Listeners will love examining the comical and expressive faces and body language of the animals as they milk the cows, shear the sheep, and pour the slop.

GERM: Looking for stories in which listeners have to brainstorm for a solution to a problem? Voilà. Puns abound in the animals' dialogue—"You look eggz-hausted," the hens tell the whispering Rooster—and all will join in on the animal noises and repeated refrains. Script this out as a Reader's Theater to perform with readers.

RELATED TITLES: Auch, Mary Jane. *Bantam of the Opera*. Holiday House, 1997. / Auch, Mary Jane. *Peeping Beauty*. Holiday House, 1993. / Bateman, Teresa. *Farm Flu*. Albert Whitman, 2001. / Cazet, Denys. *Elvis the Rooster Almost Goes to Heaven*. HarperCollins, 2003. / Cronin, Doreen. *Click, Clack, Moo: Cows That Type*. Simon & Schuster, 2000. / Dallas-Conté, Juliet. *Cock-a-Moo-Moo*. Little, Brown, 2001. / Egan, Tim. *Serious Farm*. Houghton Mifflin, 2003. / Froehlich, Margaret Walden. *That Kookoory!* Harcourt, 1995. / Krosoczka, Jarrett J. *Punk Farm*. Knopf, 2005. / Landry, Leo. *Eat Your Peas, Ivy Louise!* Houghton Mifflin, 2005. / Lobel, Arnold. *How the Rooster Saved the Day*. Greenwillow, 1977. / Meeker, Clare Hodgson. *Who Wakes Rooster?* Simon & Schuster, 1996. / Palatini, Margie. *Moo Who?* HarperCollins, 2004. / Pearson, Tracey Campbell. *Bob*. Farrar, 2002. / Schwartz, Amy. *Old MacDonald*. Scholastic, 1999. / Stevens, Janet, and Susan Stevens Crummel. *Cook-a-Doodle-Doo!* Harcourt, 1999.

SUBJECTS: ANIMAL SOUNDS. CHANTABLE REFRAIN. DOMESTIC ANIMALS. FARM LIFE. HUMOROUS FICTION. READER'S THEATER. ROOSTERS. SICK.

671   Roth, Carol. *The Little School Bus*. Illus. by Pamela Paperone. North-South, 2002. 0-7358-1646-8. Unp. Gr. PreK–1

Riding on the school bus are a goat in his coat, a pig in a wig, a fox with socks, and more animals, all pulled together for a rhyming trip that you can chant or—if you can think of a tune—sing together.

GERM: Use the cloze technique as you read, so children can recall and chant the rhyming words, i.e., "a quick, quick ____" (chick). Rhymers can think of more animal rhymes and draw the animals going to the school bus.

RELATED TITLES: Chapman, Cheryl. *Pass the Fritters, Critters*. Four Winds, 1993. / Crews, Donald. *School Bus*. Greenwillow, 1984. / Hort, Lenny. *The Seals on the Bus*. Henry Holt, 2000. / Kovalski, Maryann. *The Wheels on the Bus*. Little, Brown, 1987. / Raffi. *Down by the Bay*. Crown, 1987. / Raffi. *The Wheels on the Bus*. Crown, 1988. / Zelinsky, Paul O. *The Wheels on the Bus*. Dutton, 1990.

SUBJECTS: ANIMALS. BUSES. STORIES IN RHYME. TRANSPORTATION. VEHICLES.

672   Rothstein, Gloria. *Sheep Asleep*. Illus. by Lizzie Rockwell. HarperCollins, 2003. 0-06-029105-2. Unp. Gr. PreK–K

Calling out admonitions from the bottom left side of each page, Mama advises all ten of her sheep children to stop playing and get ready for bed. One by one, they go down for the count, but the last little sheep can't fall asleep until Mama suggests counting sheep.

GERM: Soft and sweet pictures and a simple rhyming text that counts down from ten will be perfect for acting out in narrative pantomime, with you as Mama.

RELATED TITLES: Christelow, Eileen. *Five Little Monkeys Jumping on the Bed*. Clarion, 1989. / Cook, Sally. *Good Night Pillow Fight*. HarperCollins, 2004. / Dewdney, Anna. *Llama Llama Red Pajama*. Viking, 2005./ Kellogg, Steven. *A-Hunting We Will Go!* Morrow, 1998. / Raffi. *Five Little Ducks*. Crown, 1988. / Rathmann, Peggy. *Ten Minutes Till Bedtime*. Putnam, 1998. / Scotton, Rob. *Russell the Sheep*. HarperCollins, 2005. / Walton, Rick. *So Many Bunnies: A Bedtime ABC and Counting Book*. Lothrop, 1998.

SUBJECTS: BEDTIME STORIES. COUNTING BOOKS. CREATIVE DRAMA. MOTHERS. SHEEP. STORIES IN RHYME.

673   **Rumford, James.** *Dog-of-the-Sea-Waves*. **Illus. by the author. Houghton Mifflin, 2004. 0-618-35611-8. 40pp. Gr. 2–5**

In this literary folktale, written in both English and Hawaiian, we meet five brothers—the first to explore the Hawaiian Islands—and the wounded dolphin that the youngest brother, Manu, rescues and befriends. When an earthquake and erupting volcano send the brothers jumping into the sea, Dog-of-the-Sea-Waves comes to Manu's rescue.

GERM: See how the five brothers discover the Hawaiian Islands in Rumford's companion book, *The Island-Below-the-Star*. Contrast the watercolor island paintings of Hawaii back then with photos of bustling Hawaii now.

RELATED TITLES: Martin, Rafe. *The Boy Who Lived with the Seals*. Putnam, 1993. / Martin, Rafe. *The Shark God*. Scholastic, 2001. / Rumford, James. *The Cloudmakers*. Houghton Mifflin, 1996. / Rumford, James. *The Island-Below-the-Star*. Houghton Mifflin, 1998. / Rumford, James. *Sequoyah: The Man Who Gave His People Writing*. Houghton Mifflin, 2004. / Rumford, James. *Traveling Man: The Journey of Ibn Battuta*. Houghton Mifflin, 2001. / Schaefer, Carole Lexa. *The Biggest Soap*. Farrar, 2004. / Simon, Seymour. *Volcanoes*. Morrow, 1988. / Wardlaw, Lee. *Punia and the King of Sharks: A Hawaiian Folktale*. Dial, 1997.

SUBJECTS: BROTHERS. HAWAII. HISTORICAL FICTION. HUMAN-ANIMAL RELATIONSHIPS. ISLANDS. MARINE ANIMALS. MULTICULTURAL BOOKS. OCEAN. SEALS. VOYAGES AND TRAVELS.

674   **Ryan, Pam Muñoz.** *Amelia and Eleanor Go for a Ride*. **Illus. by Brian Selznick. Scholastic, 1999. 0-590-96075-X. 40pp. Gr. 2–5**

On the night of April 20, 1933, First Lady Eleanor Roosevelt entertained her friend Amelia Earhart, the aviator, at a dinner at the White House. Afterward, the two flew to Baltimore and back so they could see Washington, D.C., from the air. Eleanor returned Amelia's gift by taking her on a fast drive in her new motorcar. The parallels between the two women are detailed in glorious oversized picture-book format, illustrated in silvery colored pencils.

GERM: Based on a little-known true account, the story has been fictionalized for greater effect, but it is an inspiring story that will lead children to read more about these two remarkable role models. There's an appended recipe for Eleanor's *Pink Angel Food Cake*, an Author's Note with loads of toothsome details, and an actual photo of the two taken on that night. To illustrate the components of historical fiction, make a class chart of the fictional versus the true events described in the story. For an overview of the lives of both women, read David A. Adler's picture-book biographies, *A Picture Book of Amelia Earhart* and *A Picture Book of Eleanor Roosevelt*.

RELATED TITLES: Adler, David A. *A Picture Book of Amelia Earhart*. Holiday House, 1998. / Adler, David A. *A Picture Book of Eleanor Roosevelt*. Holiday House, 1991. / Burleigh, Robert. *Flight: The Journey of Charles Lindbergh*. Philomel, 1991. / Cooney, Barbara. *Eleanor*. Viking, 1996. / Fleming, Candace. *A Big Cheese for the White House*. DK Ink, 1999. / Harness, Cheryl. *Franklin and Eleanor*. Dutton, 2004. / Hines, Gary. *A Christmas Tree in the White House*. Henry Holt, 1998. / Kerley, Barbara. *Walt Whitman: Words for America*. Illus. by Brian Selznick. Scholastic, 2004. / Lauber, Patricia. *Lost Star: The Story of Amelia Earhart*. Scholastic, 1988. / Szabo, Corinne. *Sky Pioneer: A Photobiography of Amelia Earhart*. National Geographic, 1997.

SUBJECTS: AIRPLANES. BIOGRAPHICAL FICTION. EARHART, AMELIA. FIRST LADIES. FLIGHT. HISTORICAL FICTION. PICTURE BOOKS FOR OLDER READERS. ROOSEVELT, ELEANOR. WOMEN.

675   **Ryan, Pam Muñoz.** *Mice and Beans*. **Illus. by Joe Cepeda. Scholastic, 2001. 0-439-18303-0. Unp. Gr. PreK–2**

As Rosa María spends the week in her tiny *casita* (house) preparing a birthday party for Little Catalina, her youngest grandchild, she sets mousetraps for the mice, who are organizing their own birthday celebration.

GERM: Children will notice the mouse story within a story, as the mice secretly borrow supplies from Rosa María, but then generously figure a way to fill her birthday piñata one candy at a time. You'll have fun reviewing the days of the week and teaching your kids the Spanish words sprinkled throughout with help from the little glossary and pronunciation guide. Construct your own piñata aided by the steps listed in Rebecca Emberley's bilingual *Piñata!*

RELATED TITLES: Baehr, Patricia. *Mouse in the House.* Holiday House, 1994. / Carle, Eric. *Today Is Monday.* Philomel, 1993. / Dorros, Arthur. *Abuela.* Dutton, 1991. / Elya, Susan Middleton. *Eight Animals Bake a Cake.* Putnam, 2002. / Elya, Susan Middleton. *Say Hola to Spanish.* Lee & Low, 1996. / Emberley, Rebecca. *Piñata!* Little, Brown, 2004. / Guy, Ginger Foglesong. *Fiesta!* Greenwillow, 1996. / Kleven, Elisa. *Hooray, a Piñata!* Dutton, 1996. / Pérez, Amada Irma. *My Very Own Room/Mi Proprio Cuartito.* Children's Book Press, 2000. / Reed, Lynn. *Pedro, His Perro, and the Alphabet Sombrero.* Hyperion, 1995. / Sacre, Antonio. *The Barking Mouse.* Albert Whitman, 2003. / Soto, Gary. *Chato and the Party Animals.* Putnam, 2000. / Soto, Gary. *Chato's Kitchen.* Putnam, 1995. / Soto, Gary. *Snapshots from the Wedding.* Putnam, 1997. / Waber, Bernard. *Do You See a Mouse?* Houghton Mifflin, 1995.

SUBJECTS: BIRTHDAYS. DAYS OF THE WEEK. GRANDMOTHERS. HISPANIC AMERICANS. HUMOROUS FICTION. MICE. MULTICULTURAL BOOKS. PARTIES. SPANISH LANGUAGE.

676 **Ryder, Joanne.** *Each Living Thing.* **Illus. by Ashley Wolff. Harcourt, 2000. 0-15-201898-0. Unp. Gr. PreK–2**

This cautionary tale—dignified with gorgeous, stately gouache paintings outlined in black gesso—urges us all to watch out for all the animals that need our protection. It is a gentle but meaningful reminder to be kind, considerate, and watchful of creatures "who grace the earth," from spiders "dangling in their webs" to bears "lingering in the dusk."

GERM: Discussion point: The author's last words regarding all animals state, "Be aware of them. Take care of them. Be watchful. Let them be." Why do we need to do this? As some children think it's all right to kill spiders, ants, and other small beings, be sure to read aloud books on these animals so they will feel a responsibility toward them as well.

RELATED TITLES: Albert, Richard E. *Alejandro's Gift.* Chronicle, 1994. / Fleming, Denise. *Where Once There Was a Wood.* Henry Holt, 1996. / London, Jonathan. *Voice of the Wild.* Crown, 1993. / Martin, Jacqueline Briggs. *Washing the Willow Tree Loon.* Simon & Schuster, 1995. / Rogers, Sally. *Earthsong.* Dutton, 1998. / Ryder, Joanne. *Earthdance.* Henry Holt, 1996.

SUBJECTS: ANIMALS. ECOLOGY. ENVIRONMENT. STORIES IN RHYME.

677 **Ryder, Joanne.** *Earthdance.* **Illus. by Norman Gorbaty. Henry Holt, 1996. 0-8050-2678-9. Unp. Gr. K–3**

In this stirring free-verse poem about our own planet, we imagine ourselves as bodies larger than the moon, wrapped in a colored quilt of seas and woods and deserts, where children and animals dance as we carry them through space. Gorbaty's impressionistic, collage-like paintings with their rounded rims set the mood and start us thinking globally.

GERM: Read this aloud more than once and have your listeners act it out in narrative pantomime the second time you read it. This will also make a dramatic Reader's Theater piece, with each child or pair of children reading aloud a sentence, perfect for Earth Day or any day you want to give thanks for our planet.

RELATED TITLES: Brenner, Barbara. *The Earth Is Painted Green: A Garden of Poems About Our Planet.* Scholastic, 1994. / Dillon, Leo, and Diane Dillon. *To Everything There Is a Season.* Scholastic, 1998. / Ehlert, Lois. *In My World.* Harcourt, 2002. / Fox, Mem. *Whoever You Are.* Harcourt, 1997. / Hamanaka, Sheila. *All the Colors of the Earth.* Morrow, 1994. / Maddern, Eric. *The Fire Children: A West African Creation Tale.* Dial, 1993. / Ryder, Joanne. *Each Living Thing.* Harcourt, 2000. / Schaefer, Lola M. *What's Up, What's Down.* Greenwillow, 2002. / Scillian, Devin. *P Is for Passport: A World Alphabet.* Sleeping Bear, 2003.

SUBJECTS: CREATIVE DRAMA. EARTH—POETRY. MULTICULTURAL BOOKS. PICTURE BOOKS FOR ALL AGES. READER'S THEATER.

678 **Rylant, Cynthia.** *Mr. Putter and Tabby Feed the Fish.* **Illus. by Arthur Howard. Harcourt, 2001. 0-15-202408-5. Unp. Gr. PreK–2**

To make himself feel like a boy again, Mr. Putter buys himself three goldfish, but they make his orange cat, Tabby, get all twitchy.

GERM: In this easy-reader series, Mr. Putter is an elderly gent, but one children relate to. Have them look in the mirror and draw portraits of themselves as they might look when they are much older. Ask your kids: What are some of the things you hope you never forget about being a child when you get older?

RELATED TITLES: Juster, Norton. *The Hello, Goodbye Window*. Hyperion, 2005. / Mills, Claudia. Gus and Grandpa series. Farrar. / Parish, Peggy. Amelia Bedelia series. Greenwillow. / Porte, Barbara Ann. *Harry's Dog*. Greenwillow, 1984. (And others in the Harry series.) / Rylant, Cynthia. Henry and Mudge series. Simon & Schuster. / Rylant, Cynthia. Mr. Putter and Tabby series. Harcourt. / Rylant, Cynthia. Poppleton series. Scholastic. / Stevenson, James. *Brrr!* Greenwillow, 1991. (And others in the Grandpa series.) / Van Leeuwen, Jean. Oliver and Amanda Pig series.

SUBJECTS: CATS. ELDERLY. FISHES. GOLDFISH. PETS.

679   Rylant, Cynthia. *Mr. Putter and Tabby Write the Book*. Illus. by Arthur Howard. Harcourt, 2004. 0-15-200241-3. Unp. Gr. PreK–2

Stuck inside during a big snow, Mr. Putter decides to write a mystery novel and gets as far as the title (*The Mystery of Lighthouse Cove*), spending the rest of his time in the company of his cat, Tabby, thinking, making delicious snacks, and taking lovely naps.

GERM: Ask your own writers: Why didn't Mr. Putter write his novel? Do you ever procrastinate? Mr. Putter's deep thinking leads him to compile a list of "Good Things" in his life. Ask your writers to write and illustrate their own lists of Good Things. Lead them to the rest of the Mr. Putter and Tabby books and Rylant's other easy-readers including those about Henry and his big dog Mudge and about Poppleton the pig. Cynthia Rylant describes how she writes her books in her photo-filled autobiography, *Best Wishes*.

RELATED TITLES: Allen, Susan, and Jane Lindaman. *Written Anything Good Lately?* Millbrook, 2006. / Christelow, Eileen. *What Do Authors Do?* Clarion, 1995. / Rylant, Cynthia. *Best Wishes*. Richard C. Owen, 1992. / Rylant, Cynthia. Henry and Mudge series. Simon & Schuster. / Rylant, Cynthia. Mr. Putter and Tabby series. Harcourt. / Rylant, Cynthia. Poppleton series. Scholastic. / Stevenson, James. *Brrr!* Greenwillow, 1991. (And others in the Grandpa series.)

SUBJECTS: AUTHORSHIP. CATS. ELDERLY. SNOW. WRITING.

680   Rylant, Cynthia. *Poppleton*. Illus. by Mark Teague. Blue Sky/Scholastic, 1997. 0-590-84782-1. 48pp. Gr. PreK–2

In the great tradition of Arnold Lobel's Frog and Toad series, introduce this genial, easy-to-read chapter book about animal friends. When Poppleton the pig moves to a small town, he makes new friends with Cherry Sue, a llama; visits the library; and helps a sick pal, Fillmore the goat, take his pill.

GERM: As you read aloud "The Library," pull out of your knapsack all the things Poppleton needs for his visits there: glasses, lip balm, Kleenex, and a pocket watch. Have your readers try to position themselves the way Poppleton does, chins on the table with the book propped up in front and trotters at their sides. Encourage readers to continue the series on their own, starting with the second book, *Poppleton and Friends*.

RELATED TITLES: Huff, Barbara. *Once Inside the Library*. Little, Brown, 1990. / Lobel, Arnold. Frog and Toad series. HarperCollins. / Marshall, James. Fox series. Houghton Mifflin. / Marshall, James. *George and Martha: The Complete Stories of Two Best Friends*. Houghton Mifflin, 1997. / McPhail, David. *Pig Pig Grows Up*. Dutton, 1980. / Rylant, Cynthia. Mr. Putter and Tabby series. Harcourt. / Rylant, Cynthia. *Poppleton and Friends*. Scholastic, 1997. (And others in the Poppleton series.) / Stevenson, James. *The Mud Flat Mystery*. Greenwillow, 1997. (And others in the Mud Flat series.) / Van Leeuwen, Jean. *Amanda and Oliver Pig series*. Dial.

SUBJECTS: FRIENDSHIP. GOATS. LIBRARIES. LLAMAS. PIGS.

681   Rylant, Cynthia. *Silver Packages: An Appalachian Christmas Story*. Illus. by Chris K. Soentpiet. Orchard, 1997. 0-531-33051-6. Unp. Gr. 2–6

Frankie waits each year for the Christmas Train to appear in the Appalachian Mountains where he lives, praying that the rich man dispensing presents from the rear platform will throw him a doctor's kit. Instead, he receives warm gloves, a pair of socks, and a scarf. When he grows up, Frankie returns to his mountains, and in an ending that will bring tears to your eyes, we see he is now a doctor.

GERM: One of the six short stories from Rylant's lyric *Children of Christmas: Stories for the Season*, "Silver Packages" was made into a thoughtful and moving picture book that will get listeners thinking about the importance of repaying a debt and caring about the people around them. Ask your students to ponder the debts they would be proud to repay someday and to write about what they plan to do to make their corner of the world a better place. *Miss Rumphius* by Barbara Cooney, about an old woman who plants lupine seeds along the Maine coastline to make the world more beautiful, is a classic picture book that explores the same theme.

RELATED TITLES: Buck, Pearl S. *Christmas Day in the Morning.* HarperCollins, 2002. / Cooney, Barbara. *Miss Rumphius.* Viking, 1982. / Houston, Gloria. *The Year of the Perfect Christmas Tree.* Dial, 1988. / Kalman, Maira. *Fireboat: The Heroic Adventures of the John J. Harvey.* Putnam, 2002. / Martin, Jacqueline Briggs. *Washing the Willow Tree Loon.* Simon & Schuster, 1995. / Polacco, Patricia. *An Orange for Frankie.* Philomel, 2004. / Rylant, Cynthia. *Children of Christmas: Stories for the Season.* Orchard, 1987. / Rylant, Cynthia. *Waiting to Waltz: A Childhood.* Bradbury, 1984. / Rylant, Cynthia. *When I Was Young in the Mountains.* Dutton, 1982. / Ziefert, Harriet. *A New Coat for Anna.* Knopf, 1986.

SUBJECTS: APPALACHIAN REGION. CHRISTMAS. DOCTORS. GIFTS. PICTURE BOOKS FOR ALL AGES. TRAINS.

682 **Sabuda, Robert. *The Blizzard's Robe.* Illus. by the author. Atheneum, 1999. 0-689-31988-6. Unp. Gr. 1–4**

After Blizzard's icy robe is destroyed by fire, Teune, a robemaker for her arctic clan (the People Who Fear the Winter Night), makes him a new one, for which Blizzard repays her and honors her people with the gift of the Northern Lights. This stunning book, with its poetic language and its strikingly beautiful, swirling batik paintings, is a literary pourquoi (or "how and why") tale, meaning that a modern author—the multitalented Robert Sabuda—made it up, but wrote it in folktale style.

GERM: Explore other pourquoi tales that explain natural phenomena. Research the auroras borealis and australis, as well as the winter, the arctic, and the Inuit people, in books and on the Internet. This dramatic and chilling story does what the old folktales do—gives you a nonscientific explanation of how the Northern Lights came to be. Use it and Lloyd Alexander's more lighthearted *How the Cat Swallowed Thunder* as jumping-off points for writing literary pourquoi tales.

RELATED TITLES: Alexander, Lloyd. *How the Cat Swallowed Thunder.* Dutton, 2000. / Andrews, Jan. *Very Last First Time.* Atheneum, 1986. / Bania, Michael. *Kumak's Fish: A Tall Tale from the Far North.* Alaska Northwest, 2004. / Bernhard, Emery. *How Snowshoe Hare Rescued the Sun: A Tale from the Arctic.* Holiday House, 1993. / Blake, Robert. *Akiak: A Tale from the Iditarod.* Philomel, 1997. / Brown, Kerry Hannula. *Tupag the Dreamer.* Marshall Cavendish, 2001. / Fowler, Susi Gregg. *Circle of Thanks.* Scholastic, 1998. / Graham, Joan Bransfield. *Flicker Flash.* Houghton Mifflin, 1999. / Kroll, Virginia. *The Seasons and Someone.* Harcourt, 1994. / Larry, Charles. *Peboan and Seegwun.* Farrar, 1993. / Napoli, Donna Jo. *North.* Greenwillow, 2004. / Sloat, Teri. *The Hungry Giant of the Tundra.* Dutton, 1993. / Rogers, Jean. *Runaway Mittens.* Greenwillow, 1988. / Steltzer, Ulli. *Building an Igloo.* Henry Holt, 1995. / Van Laan, Nancy. *Shingebiss: An Ojibwe Legend.* Houghton Mifflin, 1997.

SUBJECTS: ARCTIC REGIONS. CLOTHING AND DRESS. INUIT. MULTICULTURAL BOOKS. NORTHERN LIGHTS. POURQUOI TALES. STORMS. WEATHER. WINTER.

683 **Sacre, Antonio. *The Barking Mouse.* Illus. by Alfredo Aguirre. Albert Whitman, 2003. 0-8075-0571-4. Unp. Gr. 1–4**

Mamá and Papá Ratón and their two children, Hermano and Hermana, are having a wonderful time on their picnic until they encounter a big mean *gato*, but brave Mamá thinks of just the right way to defend her mouse *familia*. At the beginning of this charmer of a story that Antonio Sacre learned from his Cuban grandmother, there's a wonderful Author's Note about Sacre's experiences speaking Spanish in an English-only culture that you'll find inspirational and sobering to read and discuss with your listeners.

GERM: There's a glossary of Spanish words on the verso of the title page, but no pronunciation guide. If you need help, consult with a Spanish-language speaker before reading this aloud, so that you don't mangle the language. Make a poster with the Spanish words on it so everyone can learn them. Ask your children what other languages their families speak at home. What a wonderful story to act out as a Reader's Theater so children better understand both the Spanish-language phrases and the humor of the ending. Talk over the final line and message: "Es muy importante hablar otra idioma! It pays to speak another language!"

RELATED TITLES: Elya, Susan Middleton. *Eight Animals Bake a Cake.* Putnam, 2002. / Elya, Susan Middleton. *Eight Animals on the Town.* Putnam, 2000. / Elya, Susan Middleton. *Eight Animals Play Ball.* Putnam, 2003. / Elya, Susan Middleton. *Fairy Trails: A Story Told in English and Spanish.* Bloomsbury, 2005. / Elya, Susan Middleton. *Home at Last.* Lee & Low, 2002. / Elya, Susan Middleton. *Oh, No, Gotta Go!* Putnam, 2003. / Elya,

Susan Middleton. *Say Hola to Spanish*. Lee & Low, 1996. / Ryan, Pam Muñoz. *Mice and Beans*. Scholastic, 2001. / Soto, Gary. *Chato and the Party Animals*. Putnam, 2000. / Soto, Gary. *Chato's Kitchen*. Putnam, 1995.

SUBJECTS: CATS. FOLKLORE—CUBA. HUMOROUS FICTION. MICE. MULTICULTURAL BOOKS—FOLKLORE. READER'S THEATER. SPANISH LANGUAGE. STORIES TO TELL.

684   Saltzberg, Barney. *Crazy Hair Day*. Illus. by the author. Candlewick, 2003. 0-7636-1954-X. Unp. Gr. K–2

Bald Eagle Elementary School is celebrating Crazy Hair Day today, and Stanley Birdbaum's newly spiked hair, dyed orange and blue for the occasion, is a work of art. Unfortunately, Stanley's made a big mistake—today is actually School Picture Day. After Stanley heads for the boys' room in embarrassment, his teacher, Mr. Winger, knows just what to do to diminish Stanley's humiliation, and the final double-page spread of the class picture is a model of class solidarity.

GERM: Ask your listeners how they have faced the music when they did something wrong or made a mistake. For another writing prompt, ask your children to think about days they will never forget, both good and bad. This story may give you good ideas for inaugurating your own all-school celebration days.

RELATED TITLES: Frasier, Debra. *Miss Alaineus: A Vocabulary Disaster*. Harcourt, 2000. / Henkes, Kevin. *Lilly's Purple Plastic Purse*. Greenwillow, 1996. / Howe, James. *Horace and Morris Join the Chorus (But What About Dolores?)*. Atheneum, 2002. / Howe, James. *Pinky and Rex and the Spelling Bee*. Atheneum, 1991. / Palatini, Margie. *Bedhead*. Simon & Schuster, 2000. / Roche, Denis. *The Best Class Picture Ever*. Scholastic, 2003. / Schertle, Alice. *Down the Road*. Harcourt, 1995. / Soto, Gary. *Too Many Tamales*. Putnam, 1993.

SUBJECTS: EMBARRASSMENT. HAIR. SCHOOLS. TEACHERS.

685   Samuels, Barbara. *Dolores on Her Toes*. Illus. by the author. Farrar, 2003. 0-374-31818-2. Unp. Gr. PreK–2

Borrowing her big sister Faye's Junior Detective Kit, the conscientious but not-so-observant Dolores sets out to track down her escaped cat Duncan, whom she had dressed in a pink tutu to help her rehearse for ballet. Dolores cracks the case by making wanted posters, sprinkling a trail of liver bits to her apartment door, and thinking like a cat.

GERM: Dolores eats from a bowl on the floor, watches the faucet drip, and chases a long piece of string. (Your listeners will point out Duncan lurking cheerfully in most of the pictures.) Ask your gumshoes to speculate: If you had to think and act like your cat or dog or brother or friend, how would you do it? Have them write or draw their responses.

RELATED TITLES: Calhoun, Mary. *High-Wire Henry*. Morrow, 1991. (And others in the Henry series.) / Feiffer, Jules. *I Lost My Bear*. Morrow, 1998. / Gauch, Patricia Lee. *Dance, Tanya*. Philomel, 1989. (And others in the Tanya series.) / Kroll, Steven. *Patches Lost and Found*. Winslow, 2001. / Miller, Sara Swan. *Three Stories You Can Read to Your Cat*. Houghton Mifflin, 1997. / Purdy, Carol. *Mrs. Merriweather's Musical Cat*. Putnam, 1994. / Samuels, Barbara. *Aloha, Dolores*. DK Ink, 2000. / Samuels, Barbara. *Duncan and Dolores*. Bradbury, 1986.

SUBJECTS: APARTMENT HOUSES. BALLET. CATS. MYSTERY AND DETECTIVE STORIES. SISTERS.

686   San Souci, Robert D. *Cinderella Skeleton*. Illus. by David Catrow. Harcourt, 2000. 0-15-202003-9. Unp. Gr. 1–5

Dwelling in Boneyard Acres, third mausoleum on the right, Cinderella Skeleton is scorned by her ghoulish stepsisters, Gristlene and Bony-Jane, and Stepmother Skreech, who won't let her go to Prince Charnel's frightfully infamous Halloween Ball. With the help of a good witch from the wood beyond, Cinderella goes, of course, looking simply skeletal, a dandelion flower atop her wisps of hair, and dances with the bony prince. But as she turns to run, pursued by the lovesick prince, her slippered foot snaps off in his hand. Whoops! This hilarious and ghoulish parody is skillfully told in the form of a narrative poem with loads of lovely wordplay and lovingly creepy and cobweb-filled, full-bleed pencil-and-watercolor illustrations.

GERM: Wonderfully icky for Halloween, for demonstrating how one can tell a story in rhyme, or for comparing and contrasting to other parodies, this is also a tale your older kids will love reading aloud as a Reader's Theater.

RELATED TITLES: Bartram, Simon. *Pumpkin Moon*. Dutton, 2001. / Cuyler, Margery. *Skeleton Hiccups*. Simon & Schuster, 2002. / DeFelice, Cynthia C. *The Dancing Skeleton*. Macmillan, 1989. / Edwards, Pamela Duncan. *Dinorella: A Prehistoric Fairy Tale*. Hyperion, 1997. / George, Kristine O'Connell. *Old Elm Speaks: Tree Poems*. Clarion, 1998. / Jackson, Ellen. *Cinder Edna*. Lothrop, 1994. / Johnston, Tony. *The Ghost of Nicholas Greebe*. Dial, 1996. / Ketteman, Helen. *Bubba the Cowboy Prince: A Fractured Texas Tale*. Scholastic, 1997. / Loredo, Elizabeth. *Boogie Bones*. Putnam, 1997. / Myers, Bernice. *Sidney Rella and the Glass Sneaker*. Macmillan, 1985. / Scieszka, Jon. *The Stinky Cheese Man and Other Fairly Stupid Tales*. Viking, 1992. / Tagg, Christine. *Cinderlily: A Floral Fairy Tale*. Candlewick, 2003.

SUBJECTS: CINDERELLA STORIES. HALLOWEEN. HUMOROUS FICTION. PARODIES. READER'S THEATER. SKELETONS. STEPMOTHERS. STORIES IN RHYME.

687   **San Souci, Robert D.** *Fa Mulan: The Story of a Woman Warrior*. **Illus. by Jean Tseng and Mou-Sien Tseng. Hyperion, 1998. 0-7868-2287-2. Unp. Gr. 2–6**

Fa Mulan, a legendary Chinese woman, disguised herself as a man and joined the Khan's army to fight against the invading Tartars more than a thousand years ago, as this inspiring and striking picture book recounts.

GERM: San Souci also wrote the screenplay for the children's movie of the same title. Meet another legendary Chinese fighter in Emily Arnold McCully's *Beautiful Warrior: The Legend of the Nun's Kung Fu*.

RELATED TITLES: Climo, Shirley. *Atalanta's Race: A Greek Myth*. Clarion, 1995. / Kimmel, Eric A. *Rimonah of the Flashing Sword: A North African Tale*. Holiday House, 1995. / Stamm, Claus. *Three Strong Women*. Viking, 1990. / Yep, Laurence. *The Dragon Prince: A Chinese Beauty and the Beast Tale*. HarperCollins, 1997. / Yep, Laurence. *The Khan's Daughter: A Mongolian Folktale*. Scholastic, 1997.

SUBJECTS: FOLKLORE—CHINA. MULTICULTURAL BOOKS—FOLKLORE. PICTURE BOOKS FOR OLDER READERS. WAR—FOLKLORE. WOMEN—FOLKLORE.

688   **Santat, Dan.** *The Guild of Geniuses*. **Illus. by the author. Scholastic, 2004. 0-439-43096-8. Unp. Gr. PreK–2**

Mr. Pip, a monkey, turns sad when he can't find the right time to give his birthday present to his busy best friend, the famous actor Frederick Lipton. Concerned about his pal, Frederick rushes the monkey to doctors, who declare him fit as a fiddle, and then to the Guild of Geniuses, four of the smartest people in the world, who spend two weeks running outlandish tests, trying to figure out what ails Pip.

GERM: The Guild of Geniuses even sends Pip to the moon to cheer him up, but nothing works. At this point in the story, break your group into several smaller groups and have them brainstorm a plan to make Pip happy and report back on their plans. Finish the story and discuss the simple solution that works.

RELATED TITLES: Anholt, Catherine, and Laurence Anholt. *Chimp and Zee*. Putnam, 2001. / Clement, Rod. *Just Another Ordinary Day*. HarperCollins, 1997. / Dewan, Ted. *Crispin, the Pig Who Had It All*. Doubleday, 2000. / Goode, Diane. *Monkey Mo Goes to Sea*. Blue Sky/Scholastic, 2002. / Joyce, William. *A Day with Wilbur Robinson*. HarperCollins, 1993. / Marx, Patricia. *Meet My Staff*. HarperCollins, 1998. / Rey, H. A. *Curious George*. Houghton Mifflin, 1993. (And others in the Curious George series.) / Weisner, David. *June 29, 1999*. Clarion, 1992. / Wood, Audrey. *The Flying Dragon Room*. Scholastic, 1996.

SUBJECTS: BEST FRIENDS. BIRTHDAYS. FRIENDSHIP. GIFTS. HUMOROUS FICTION. INVENTIONS AND INVENTORS. MONKEYS.

689   **Say, Allen.** *Kamishibai Man*. **Illus. by the author. Houghton Mifflin, 2005. 0-618-47954-6. Unp. Gr. 1–6**

It's been years since Jiichan, or Grandpa, has gone on his rounds, so his wife, Baachan, or Grandma, makes him candies, and he heads for the city on his bicycle. Once there, he sets up his small wooden stage, checks his story cards, hits two wooden blocks or clappers together, and calls out to the children to come buy his sweets and listen to his stories. The *kamishibai* man recalls how, years before, the children would cluster about him, eager to hear him tell his stories with his colorful story cards. Then television came to Japan, and the children lost interest in him.

GERM: Say's delicate watercolors and heartfelt story within a story will resonate with listeners who will recall things they loved and left behind as they grew older. Discussion point: Why did the children stop coming to hear the kamishibai man's stories? Why did the grownups applaud the kamishibai man when he came back? In these modern times, do we still need to hear stories? What are the stories you remember from your younger years? Children can write and illustrate their own kamishibai cards, using Japanese or other folktales or writing their own stories. To buy ready-made kamishibai story cards and find background and teaching ideas on the art form, go to <www.kamishibai.com>.

RELATED TITLES: Brenner, Barbara. *Little One Inch*. Coward, 1977. / Collins, Suzanne. *When Charlie McBut-*

ton Lost Power. Putnam, 2005. / Dengler, Marianna. *The Worry Stone*. Northland, 1996. / Lewin, Ted. *The Story-tellers*. Lothrop, 1998. / Say, Allen. *The Bicycle Man*. Houghton Mifflin, 1982. / Say, Allen. *Grandfather's Journey*. Houghton Mifflin, 1993. / Say, Allen. *Tea with Milk*. Houghton Mifflin, 1999. / Say, Allen. *Tree of Cranes*. Houghton Mifflin, 1991. / Say, Allen. *Under the Cherry Blossom Tree; An Old Japanese Tale*. Harper-Collins, 1974. / Shute, Linda. *Momotaro the Peach Boy*. Lothrop, 1986. / Uchida, Yoshiko. *The Dancing Kettle: And Other Japanese Tales*. Creative Arts, 1986. / Uchida, Yoshiko. *The Magic Listening Cap: More Folk Tales from Japan*. Creative Arts, 1987. / Young, Ed. *I, Doko: The Tale of a Basket*. Philomel, 2004.

SUBJECTS: ELDERLY. JAPAN. PICTURE BOOKS FOR ALL AGES. STORYTELLING. TELEVISION.

690   Say, Allen. *Tea with Milk*. Illus. by the author. Houghton Mifflin, 1999. 0-395-90495-1. 32pp. Gr. 2–5

Allen Say continues his family history with another elegant and poignant picture book that delves into his mother May's life. Raised near San Francisco, May chafes at being taken back to Japan by her homesick parents. In Japan she is called Masako and has to wear a kimono and attend high school all over again so she can learn to speak, read, and write her own language. Her skills in English lead to a job in a department store as a guide for foreign businessmen. There she meets Joseph, an orphan raised by English parents, who understands her and drinks tea with milk and sugar, the same as she does.

GERM: Students can ask their parents or grandparents how they met and married and write down or tape-record their responses. *How My Parents Learned to Eat* by Ina R. Friedman details how a girl's Japanese mother and American father met and fell in love. Discuss the limitations placed on girls and women in other cultures and at earlier times in our country and trace how times have changed.

RELATED TITLES: Brisson, Pat. *The Summer My Father Was Ten*. Boyds Mills, 1998. / Friedman, Ina R. *How My Parents Learned to Eat*. Houghton Mifflin, 1984. / Houston, Gloria. *My Great Aunt Arizona*. HarperCollins, 1992. / Lasky, Kathryn. *Marven of the Great North Woods*. Harcourt, 1997. / Lied, Kate. *Potato: A Tale from the Great Depression*. National Geographic, 1997. / Little, Mimi Otey. *Yoshiko and the Foreigner*. Farrar, 1996. / Polacco, Patricia. *My Ol' Man*. Philomel, 1995. / Say, Allen. *Grandfather's Journey*. Houghton Mifflin, 1993. / Say, Allen. *Kamishibai Man*. Houghton Mifflin, 2005. / Say, Allen. *Tree of Cranes*. Houghton Mifflin, 1991.

SUBJECTS: FAMILY STORIES. HOMESICKNESS. JAPAN. MULTICULTURAL BOOKS. PICTURE BOOKS FOR OLDER READERS.

691   Sayre, April Pulley, and Jeff Sayre. *One Is a Snail, Ten Is a Crab; A Counting by Feet Book*. Illus. by Randy Cecil. Candlewick, 2003. 0-7636-1406-8. Unp. Gr. K–3

On a day at the beach, count by feet—snails have one foot, a person has two, a person and a snail together have three, and a dog has four—all the way up to ten, and then, by tens, to one hundred in a quirkily humorous math book that combines animals and their feet. The infectiously funny oil-on-paper illustrations, with deadpan gently smiling faces on all the animals, will have everyone laughing at the absurdity of the combinations, and it's surely an ingenious look at regrouping and number combinations.

GERM: Check April Sayre's terrific Web site—<www.aprilsayre.com>—for snail and crab math sheets. Your counters can come up with their own numbers and draw the correct number of feet. Twenty-five could be an insect, a dog, a spider, two people, and three snails, for instance. Or five dogs and five snails.

RELATED TITLES: Franco, Betsy. *Counting Our Way to the 100th Day!* McElderry, 2004. / Franco, Betsy. *Mathematickles!* McElderry, 2003. / Leedy, Loreen. *Measuring Penny*. Atheneum, 1969. / Leedy, Loreen. *Mission: Addition*. Holiday House, 1997. / Michelson, Richard. *Ten Times Better*. Marshall Cavendish, 2000. / Myller, Rolf. *How Big Is a Foot?* Atheneum, 1969. / Pinczes, Elinor J. *One Hundred Hungry Ants*. Houghton Mifflin, 1993. / Schlein, Miriam. *More Than One*. Greenwillow, 1996. / Schwartz, David M. *Millions to Measure*. Harcourt, 2003. / Tang, Greg. *The Grapes of Math: Mind-Stretching Math Riddles*. Scholastic, 2001. / Tang, Greg. *Math-terpieces: The Art of Problem Solving*. Scholastic, 2003. / Wells, Robert E. *Is a Blue Whale the Biggest Thing There Is?* Albert Whitman, 1993. / Wormell, Christopher. *Teeth, Tails, and Tentacles: An Animal Counting Book*. Running Press, 2004.

SUBJECTS: ANIMALS. COUNTING BOOKS. FOOT. MATHEMATICS. SEASHORE.

692   Schachner, Judith Byron. *The Grannyman*. Illus. by the author. Dutton, 1999. 0-525-46122-1. Unp. Gr. PreK–2

Recalling his youth and feeling useless, the now blind, deaf, and toothless Siamese cat Simon is ready to breathe his last, to give up and die, when his human family surprises him with a new kitten they hope he will help raise. Caring for the kitten gives Simon new reason to live.

GERM: This is a picture book for all ages to commemorate the lives of their favorite pets. Children can draw portraits of their own pets and label them with their real names and nicknames (such as my own 18-year-old cat, Sherlock, aka Bigfoot or Mr. Bite). For a descriptive writing exercise, kids can write about their pets' personalities and what makes them fun or interesting.

RELATED TITLES: Alexander, Lloyd. *How the Cat Swallowed Thunder.* Dutton, 2000. / Calhoun, Mary. *High-Wire Henry.* Morrow, 1991. (And others in the Henry series.) / George, Carol. *Where Is That Cat?* Hyperion, 1999. / Harper, Dan. *Telling Time with Big Mama Cat.* Harcourt, 1998. / Ketteman, Helen. *Grandma's Cat.* Houghton Mifflin, 1996. / Martin, Ann M. *Leo the Magnificat.* Scholastic, 1996. / Miller, Sara Swan. *Three Stories You Can Read to Your Cat.* Houghton Mifflin, 1997. / Perkins, Lynne Rae. *The Broken Cat.* Greenwillow, 2002. / Pilkey, Dav. *When Cats Dream.* Orchard, 1992.

SUBJECTS: CATS. ELDERLY. PICTURE BOOKS FOR ALL AGES.

693 **Schaefer, Carole Lexa. *The Biggest Soap.* Illus. by Stacey McQueen. Farrar, 2004. 0-374-30690-7. Unp. Gr. PreK–2**

Kessy loves laundry day in his South Pacific island community because he gets to jump in the washing pool and listen to Mama and her cousins tell stories. When Mama sends him to the store to get the biggest bar of soap he can find, he rushes off, fast as a typhoon wind, to get back in time. On the way back, he must stop and use his soap to wash his friend's cut finger, smooth the edges on Uncle Cho's new window, and clean up his muddy big brothers. Back at the washing pool, Kessy spins an imaginative yarn about his encounters, as shown in the lush colored pencil, oil pastel, and acrylic paintings inspired by Gauguin and traditional Oceanic art.

GERM: Kessy embellishes his story like a true storyteller, and listeners can parse his account to sort the facts and the fantasy. Make a chart: What Happened to Kessy versus What Kessy Made Up. Take true personal anecdotes and, using exaggeration and a bit of story magic, turn them into fanciful fiction.

RELATED TITLES: Arnold, Tedd. *No More Water in the Tub!* Dial, 1995. / Birdseye, Tom. *Soap! Soap! Don't Forget the Soap! An Appalachian Folktale.* Holiday House, 1993. / Cole, Brock. *No More Baths.* Doubleday, 1980. / Rumford, James. *Dog-of-the-Sea-Waves.* Houghton Mifflin, 2004. / Salley, Coleen. *Epossumondas.* Harcourt, 2002. / Schaefer, Carole Lexa. *Snow Pumpkin.* Crown, 2000. / Schaefer, Carole Lexa. *Someone Says.* Viking, 2003. / Schaefer, Carole Lexa. *The Squiggle.* Crown, 1996.

SUBJECTS: EXAGGERATION. FAMILY LIFE. ISLANDS. MICRONESIA (FEDERATED STATES). MULTICULTURAL BOOKS. SOAP. STORYTELLING.

694 **Schaefer, Carole Lexa. *Someone Says.* Illus. by Pierr Morgan. Viking, 2003. 0-670-03664-1. Unp. Gr. PreK–K**

A class of nine joyful Asian children draw, imagine, and pretend they are animals, build with blocks, and make up the most wonderful onomatopoeic words as they jaunt through the preschool day. The swirling, colorful, and imaginative illustrations, rendered in Prismacolor markers and gouache on dark tan paper, are inspired by Chinese ink-brush paintings.

GERM: Have your children act out, with sound effects, what they do during a day in their classroom. Do some animal acting. Have your children pretend they are in a magical animal box. Say, "Elephants! Come out of the box," and the kids emerge, as elephants. Then, "Elephants, go back in the box!" And they jump back in. Pretend some more with Schaefer's companion book, *The Squiggle.*

RELATED TITLES: Jonell, Lynne. *I Need a Snake.* Putnam, 1998. / Marzollo, Jean. *Pretend You're a Cat.* Dial, 1990. / Peck, Jan. *Way Down Deep in the Deep Blue Sea.* Simon & Schuster, 2004. / Schaefer, Carole Lexa. *Snow Pumpkin.* Crown, 2000. / Schaefer, Carole Lexa. *The Squiggle.* Crown, 1996. / Sis, Peter. *Madlenka's Dog.* Farrar, 2002. / Slate, Joseph. *Miss Bindergarten Gets Ready for Kindergarten.* Dutton, 1996. / Steen, Sandra, and Susan Steen. *Car Wash.* Putnam, 2001. / Steig, William. *Toby, What Are You?* HarperCollins, 2001. / Steig, William. *Toby, Where Are You?* HarperCollins, 1997. / Steig, William. *Toby, Who Are You?* HarperCollins, 2004. / Wells, Rosemary. *My Kindergarten.* Hyperion, 2004.

SUBJECTS: ASIAN AMERICANS. CHINESE AMERICANS. CREATIVE DRAMA. IMAGINATION. MULTICULTURAL BOOKS. NURSERY SCHOOLS. ONOMATOPOEIA. SCHOOLS.

695 **Schaefer, Carole Lexa. *The Squiggle.* Illus. by Pierr Morgan. Crown, 1996. 0-517-70048-4. Unp. Gr. PreK–1**

Off to the park tromps a small group of Chinese preschoolers, led by their teacher. In a charming display of imagination, the young narrator finds a ribbon, which looks like a red squiggle, and pretends it's a dragon, the Great Wall of China, the path of a circus acrobat, fireworks, and a thundercloud.

GERM: Noises such as "slither slish" and "crack crickle hiss" are so satisfying to say. Given their own red ribbons, your kids can create a new scenario, complete with a noise. Also read the companion book, *Someone Says*. See how a scribble grows up to be a help to all of the nursery rhyme characters in *The Neat Line* by Pamela Duncan Edwards.

RELATED TITLES: Ashman, Linda. *Rub-a-Dub Sub.* Harcourt, 2003. / Cooney, Nancy Evans. *The Umbrella Day.* Philomel, 1989. / Edwards, Pamela Duncan. *The Neat Line: Scribbling Through Mother Goose.* Harper-Collins, 2005. / Freeman, Don. *A Rainbow of My Own.* Viking, 1966. / Jonell, Lynne. *I Need a Snake.* Putnam, 1998. / Marzollo, Jean. *Pretend You're a Cat.* Dial, 1990. / Schaefer, Carole Lexa. *The Biggest Soap.* Farrar, 2004. / Schaefer, Carole Lexa. *Snow Pumpkin.* Crown, 2000. / Schaefer, Carole Lexa. *Someone Says.* Viking, 2003. / Steen, Sandra, and Susan Steen. *Car Wash.* Putnam, 2001. / Steig, William. *Toby, What Are You?* HarperCollins, 2001. / Steig, William. *Toby, Where Are You?* HarperCollins, 1997. / Steig, William. *Toby, Who Are You?* HarperCollins, 2004.

SUBJECTS: ASIAN AMERICANS. CHINESE AMERICANS. IMAGINATION. MULTICULTURAL BOOKS. NURSERY SCHOOLS. PLAY.

696 Schaefer, Lola M. *Arrowhawk.* Illus. by Gabi Swiatkowska. Henry Holt, 2004. 0-8050-6371-4. Unp. Gr. 1–5

Based on real events, this is the dramatic and electrifying story of a red-tailed hawk that survived in the wild for eight weeks after being shot by a poacher's arrow, which remained lodged through its thigh and tail. Realistic and powerful full-bleed acrylic paintings and a descriptive text capture, without anthropomorphism, the drama and horror of Arrowhawk's ordeal.

GERM: A stellar example of descriptive factual writing, this will get bird lovers cheering when animal rescuers who capture and care for the hawk release him back into the wild. Just looking at the photo of Arrowhawk at the back of the book will inspire research on raptors, or birds of prey. Books like this help children gain respect for the natural world and take responsibility for their own part in maintaining it.

RELATED TITLES: Blake, Robert J. *Fledgling.* Philomel, 2000. / Frankenhuyzen, Robbyn Smith van. *Saving Samantha: A True Story.* Sleeping Bear, 2004. / Martin, Jacqueline Briggs. *Washing the Willow Tree Loon.* Atheneum, 1995. / Rand, Gloria. *Prince William.* Henry Holt, 1992.

SUBJECTS: BIRDS. HAWKS. POACHING. WILDLIFE RESCUE.

697 Schanzer, Rosalyn. *Davy Crockett Saves the World.* Illus. by the author. HarperCollins, 2001. 0-688-16992-9. Unp. Gr. K–3

The narrator insists, "Every single word is true, unless it is false." In this literary tall tale, Davy Crockett, Tennessee frontiersman, hunter, and scout, is enlisted by the president to pull the tail off Halley's Comet so it won't crash into the earth.

GERM: Since the story explains why Davy Crockett always wore a coonskin cap, you'll want to dig out your own hat from the attic to show. *Swamp Angel* by Anne Isaacs is another literary tall tale set in the Great Smoky Mountains. Do some research on Halley's Comet and find how close it really gets to the earth each time it comes around, every 75 years or so. Compare these fantastical exploits with a biography of the real life of Davy Crockett, who was elected to Congress and died at the Alamo. Steven Kellogg's *Sally Ann Thunder Ann Whirlwind Crockett* is a tall tale about Davy's wife.

RELATED TITLES: Dadey, Debbie. *Shooting Star: Annie Oakley, the Legend.* Walker, 1997 / Glass, Andrew. *Folks Call Me Appleseed John.* Doubleday, 1995. / Hodges, Margaret. *The True Tale of Johnny Appleseed.* Holiday House, 1997. / Isaacs, Anne. *Swamp Angel.* Dutton, 1994. / Kellogg, Steven. *I Was Born About 10,000 Years Ago.* Morrow, 1996. / Kellogg, Steven. *Paul Bunyan.* Morrow, 1992. / Kellogg, Steven. *Sally Ann Thunder Ann Whirlwind Crockett.* Morrow, 1995. / Mora, Pat. *Doña Flor: A Tall Tale About a Giant Woman with a Great Big Heart.* Knopf, 2005. / Osborne, Mary Pope. *American Tall Tales.* Knopf, 1991. / Rounds, Glen. *Ol' Paul, the Mighty Logger.* Holiday House, 1976. / San Souci, Robert D. *Larger Than Life: The Adventures of American Legendary Heroes.* Doubleday, 1991. / Walker, Paul Robert. *Big Men, Big Country: A Collection of American Tall Tales.* Harcourt, 1993. / Wood, Audrey. *The Bunyans.* Scholastic, 1996.

SUBJECTS: COMETS. CROCKETT, DAVY, 1786–1836. EXAGGERATION. FANTASY. HISTORICAL FICTION. HUMOROUS FICTION. PRESIDENTS. TALL TALES.

698   Schertle, Alice. *All You Need for a Beach*. Illus. by Barbara Lavallee. Harcourt, 2004. 0-15-216755-2. Unp. Gr. PreK–2

All you need for a beach, explains Schertle, in this rhyming picture book that follows a gaggle of children enjoying their day there, is one tiny grain of sand, and then 10 million more grains, all spread out, plus the sun, seagulls, and some water too.

GERM: Compare summer at the beach with winter in the snow, using Schertle's companion book, *All You Need for a Snowman.*

RELATED TITLES: Best, Cari. *When Catherine the Great and I Were Eight!* Farrar, 2003. / Levine, Evan. *Not the Piano, Mrs. Medley!* Orchard, 1991. / O'Donnell, Elizabeth Lee. *The Twelve Days of Summer.* Morrow, 1991. / Robbins, Ken. *Beach Days.* Viking, 1987. / Schertle, Alice. *All You Need for a Snowman.* Harcourt, 2002.

SUBJECTS: OCEAN. SEASHORE. STORIES IN RHYME.

699   Schertle, Alice. *Down the Road*. Illus. by E. B. Lewis. Harcourt, 1995. 0-15-276622-7. Unp. Gr. PreK–2

Hetty is elated when her parents finally give her permission to walk alone all the way to Mr. Birdie's Emporium and Dry Goods Store for a dozen eggs. When Hetty stops to pick apples on the way home, she accidentally tips over the eggs, all of which break on the ground. In a fine funk, she climbs up the old apple tree and hides there until her loving Papa and Mama come to find her. The two wise, caring parents climb the tree with her and know just what to say to make her feel better, as is shown in the large expressive watercolors depicting this affectionate African American family.

GERM: Bring in apples to share, as your group relates stories of how they have made mistakes and figured out how to deal with the consequences.

RELATED TITLES: Johnson, Dolores. *Your Dad Was Just Like You.* Macmillan, 1993. / McKissack, Patricia C. *Flossie and the Fox.* Dial, 1986. / Mayer, Mercer. *Liza Lou and the Yeller Belly Swamp.* Four Winds, 1980. / Powell, Consie. *Amazing Apples.* Albert Whitman, 2003. / Priceman, Marjorie. *How to Make an Apple Pie and See the World.* Knopf, 1994. / Soto, Gary. *Too Many Tamales.* Putnam, 1993.

SUBJECTS: AFRICAN AMERICANS. APPLE TREES. COUNTRY LIFE. EGGS. EMBARRASSMENT. FAMILY LIFE. MULTICULTURAL BOOKS. PARENT AND CHILD.

700   Schotter, Roni. *Nothing Ever Happens on 90th Street*. Illus. by Kyrsten Brooker. Orchard, 1997. 0-531-08886-3. Unp. Gr. 1–4

In this picture book for all ages that brings together the arts, city life, and the mysterious craft of writing, we meet young Eva, sitting on her front stoop, waiting for something unusual to happen that she can write about in her notebook. "Write about what you know," her teacher has told her, but Eva finds life-as-usual too dull. As her eccentric multicultural mix of neighbors come and go, each gives her an invaluable piece of advice: to pay attention to details, add a little action, find poetry in her writing, and ask "What if?" When an astonishing action scene unfolds in the street below, involving the pizza man, a famous actress, a stubborn cat up a tree, and true love, Eva finds more than enough to write about and even manages to suggest the perfect happy ending.

GERM: This imaginative picture book, ably illustrated with detail-filled collage paintings, is just the ticket for those creative writers who never know how to get started and for teachers who want to demonstrate all the elements that make a story sparkle. *Aunt Isabel Tells a Good One* by Kate Duke is another entertaining picture book that takes us through the creative process of setting up a successful story. Meet another young poet in Laura Nyman Montenegro's *A Bird About to Sing.*

RELATED TITLES: Allen, Susan, and Jane Lindaman. *Written Anything Good Lately?* Millbrook, 2006. / Byars, Betsy. *Beans on the Roof.* Delacorte, 1988. / Christelow, Eileen. *What Do Authors Do?* Clarion, 1995. / Conford, Ellen. *Jenny Archer, Author.* Little, Brown, 1989. / Duke, Kate. *Aunt Isabel Makes Trouble.* Dutton, 1996. / Duke, Kate. *Aunt Isabel Tells a Good One.* Dutton, 1992. / Kalman, Maira. *Max Makes a Million.* Viking, 1990. / Leedy, Loreen. *Look at My Book: How Kids Can Write and Illustrate Terrific Books.* Holiday House, 2004. / Montenegro, Laura Nyman. *A Bird About to Sing.* Houghton Mifflin, 2003. / Moss, Marissa. *Amelia's Notebook.* Tricycle, 1995. / Williams, Vera B. *Cherries and Cherry Pits.* Greenwillow, 1986.

SUBJECTS: AUTHORSHIP. CREATIVE WRITING. MULTICULTURAL BOOKS. NEIGHBORLINESS. PICTURE BOOKS FOR OLDER READERS.

701   Schwartz, Amy. *Begin at the Beginning: A Little Artist Learns About Life.* Illus. by the author.
HarperCollins, 2005. 0-06-000112-7. Unp. Gr. K–3

Picked by her teacher to do the class painting for the school art show, Sara searches for an idea
more important than just the tree outside her window. "I'm going to paint the most wonderful
painting that has ever been painted." She decides her subject will be the universe, but is frustrated to find that painting the whole world is not easy. Taking her mother's sage advice: ". . .
you can only begin at the beginning," she begins . . . with the tree outside her window.

GERM: The illustrations are in watercolors on a white background, and Sara is trying to paint
her own watercolor picture, so break out the watercolors for your artists to paint something
they consider to be important. Make a list of their ideas of what they do when they don't know
where to start, whether it's painting or writing, or completing tasks. Meet Vashti, a girl who
thinks she's no good at art until she starts painting, in *The Dot* by Peter H. Reynolds.

RELATED TITLES: Arnold, Katya. *Elephants Can Paint Too!* Atheneum, 2005. / dePaola, Tomie. *The Art Les-
son.* Putnam, 1989. / Kroll, Steven. *Patches Lost and Found.* Winslow, 2001. / LaMarche, Jim. *The Raft.* Harper-
Collins, 2000. / Mills, Claudia. *Ziggy's Blue-Ribbon Day.* Farrar, 2005. / Reynolds, Peter H. *The Dot.*
Candlewick, 2003. / Reynolds, Peter. *Ish.* Candlewick, 2004. / Stadler, Alexander. *Lila Bloom.* Farrar, 2004.

SUBJECTS: ARTISTS. CREATIVITY. PAINTING. PERSEVERANCE. PICTURE BOOKS FOR ALL AGES.

702   Scieszka, Jon. *Baloney (Henry P.).* Illus. by Lane Smith. Viking, 2001. 0-670-89248-3. 40pp. Gr.
K–4

"That's it," says Miss Bugscuffle when little green alien Henry P. comes late to school once too
often. "Permanent Lifelong Detention . . . unless you have one very good and very believable
excuse." Henry P.'s excuse is a doozy: He claims he misplaced his trusty *zimulis* and blasted off
into space on a *razzo.*

GERM: Listeners will translate the many unfamiliar words using context clues; the glossary at
the back will fill you in on the definitions and the actual language for each word. For example,
zimulis = pencil in Latvian and razzo = rocket in Italian. After I read Henry P.'s out-of-this-
world sci fi tall tale to a third-grade class, students wrote their own apology/excuse/tall-tale
letters to their teacher, explaining why their homework wasn't done. Using the Babel Fish Web
site (<www.world.altavista.com>), they then looked up a handful of nouns they'd used in their
letters and translated them into either Portuguese, Italian, French, German, or Spanish. ("My
gatto was very bad. He ate my math *heimarbeit* . . .") Finally, on the finished copies they drew little color pictures to help clarify the meanings of all the foreign words, wrote up a glossary
page, and read their letters aloud for the class to translate. It was *très magnifique!*

RELATED TITLES: Aliki. *Hello! Good-bye!* Greenwillow, 1996. / Corey, Shana. *First Graders from Mars:
Episode 1: Horus's Horrible Day.* Scholastic, 2001. / Evans, Lezlie. *Can You Count Ten Toes? Count to 10 in 10 Dif-
ferent Languages.* Houghton Mifflin, 1999. / Falconer, Ian. *Olivia Saves the Circus.* Atheneum, 2001. / Kellogg,
Steven. *I Was Born About 10,000 Years Ago.* Morrow, 1996. / Leverich, Kathleen. *Hilary and the Troublemakers.*
Greenwillow, 1992. / Sadler, Marilyn. *Alistair in Outer Space.* Prentice-Hall, 1984. / Scieszka, Jon. *Math Curse.*
Viking, 1995. / Scieszka, Jon. *The Stinky Cheese Man and Other Fairly Stupid Tales.* Viking, 1992. / Seuss, Dr.
And to Think That I Saw It on Mulberry Street. Random House, 1989. / Shannon, David. *David Goes to School.*
Scholastic, 2000. / Shields, Carol Diggory. *Martian Rock.* Candlewick, 1999. / Teague, Mark. *The Secret
Shortcut.* Scholastic, 1996. / Van Allsburg, Chris. *Zathura.* Houghton Mifflin, 2002.

SUBJECTS: EXAGGERATION. EXTRATERRESTRIAL LIFE. HUMOROUS FICTION. LANGUAGE.
LETTER WRITING. PICTURE BOOKS FOR ALL AGES. SCHOOLS. SCIENCE FICTION.
STORYTELLING. TEACHERS.

703   Scieszka, Jon. *Math Curse.* Illus. by Lane Smith. Viking, 1995. 0-670-86194-4. 32pp. Gr. 2–6

"On Monday in math class, Mrs. Fibonacci says, 'YOU KNOW, you can think of almost anything as a math problem.' On Tuesday I start having problems." In an innovative and brilliant
picture book, we follow the hapless, obsessed narrator as she worries her way through the
school day, facing daunting math problems about time, measurement, charts, lunch, distance,
money, and even the dreaded fractions.

GERM: Listeners will be eager to work out the solution to each problem as you read (the
answers are on the back cover), and, inspired by the surprise ending, they may be game to compose their own science curse experiments. Scieszka has also written a madcap, rhyming sequel,
called *Science Verse.*

RELATED TITLES: Adler, David A. *Calculator Riddles.* Holiday House, 1995. / Adler, David A. *Eaton Stanley
and the Mind Control Experiment.* Dutton, 1985 / Catling, Patrick Skene. *The Chocolate Touch.* Morrow, 1979. /

Clement, Rod. *Just Another Ordinary Day*. HarperCollins, 1997. / Cole, Joanna. Magic School Bus series. Scholastic. / Duffey, Betsy. *The Gadget War*. Viking, 1991. / Duffey, Betsy. *The Math Whiz*. Viking, 1991. / Franco, Betsy. *Mathematickles!* McElderry, 2003. / Gardiner, John. *Top Secret*. Little, Brown, 1985. / Sachar, Louis. *Wayside School Is Falling Down*. Lothrop, 1989. / Scieszka, Jon. *Baloney (Henry P.)*. Viking, 2001. / Scieszka, Jon. *Science Verse*. Viking, 2004. / Scieszka, Jon. *Seen Art?* Viking, 2005. / Scieszka, Jon. *Squids Will Be Squids: Fresh Morals, Beastly Fables*. Viking, 1998. / Scieszka, Jon. *The Stinky Cheese Man and Other Fairly Stupid Tales*. Viking, 1992.

SUBJECTS: HUMOROUS FICTION. MATHEMATICS. PICTURE BOOKS FOR OLDER READERS. SCHOOLS.

704   Scieszka, Jon. *Science Verse*. Illus. by Lane Smith. Viking, 2004. 0-670-91057-0. Unp. Gr. 2–6

In a science-based companion to *Math Curse*, a boy in Mr. Newton's class can't help turning everything he hears into a science poem. The ensuing 21 verses, all parodies of famous songs and poems, put a wildly funny scientific spin on evolution, the water cycle, black holes, the food chain, and then some.

GERM: At the back of the book is a list of the poems that inspired Scieszka. Listen to him read them aloud and joke around with artist Lane Smith on the accompanying CD. Who says poetry and science don't mix? Your poetic scientists will clamor to set their science curriculum to verse after reading these and the clever poems in *Brain Juice: Science Fresh Squeezed!* by Carol Diggory Shields. In an "Oh, no! Not again!" conclusion, art teacher Mr. Picasso says, "Your art project must be your whole life." Art attack! Your artists can then brainstorm their own impressions of what the sequel should be.

RELATED TITLES: Graham, Joan Bransfield. *Flicker Flash*. Houghton Mifflin, 1999. / Graham, Joan Bransfield. *Splish Splash*. Ticknor & Fields, 1994. / Hopkins, Lee Bennett, comp. *Spectacular Science: A Book of Poems*. Simon & Schuster, 1999. / Kos, Amy Goldman. *Where Fish Go in Winter and Other Great Mysteries*. Dial, 2002. / Lewis, J. Patrick. *Earth Verses and Water Rhymes*. Atheneum, 1991. / Lewis, J. Patrick. *Scien-trickery: Riddles in Science*. Harcourt, 2004. / Moss, Jeff. *Bone Poems*. Workman, 1997. / Peters, Lisa Westberg. *Earthshake: Poems from the Ground Up*. Greenwillow, 2003. / Scieszka, Jon. *Math Curse*. Viking, 1995. / Scieszka, Jon. *Seen Art?* Viking, 2005. / Shields, Carol Diggory. *Brain Juice: American History Fresh Squeezed!* Handprint, 2002. / Shields, Carol Diggory. *Brain Juice: Science Fresh Squeezed!* Handprint, 2003.

SUBJECTS: HUMOROUS POETRY. PICTURE BOOKS FOR OLDER READERS. SCHOOLS. SCIENCE—POETRY.

705   Scieszka, Jon. *Squids Will Be Squids: Fresh Morals, Beastly Fables*. Illus. by Lane Smith. Viking, 1998. 0-670-88135-X. 48pp. Gr. 2–6

Those two funnymen, Scieszka and Smith, have taken on Aesop with 18 hip, au courant, off-the-wall fables about "all kinds of bossy, sneaky funny, annoying dim-bulb people," transformed into animals to protect the "not-so innocent." There's Straw playing with his friend, Matches; Termite and Ant who make an unfortunate friendship with Echidna; and even Hand, Foot, and Tongue, arguing over who has the toughest job.

GERM: Each short fable is just the ticket for small groups to perform, Reader's Theater-style. Students will then clamor to write and illustrate new fables, using aphorisms from their peers and elders, and lessons that they've learned at school and at home. In order to parody Aesop, children need to go back to the literary source and read some of the originals, listed below in sterling collections that are perfect for reading aloud and acting out.

RELATED TITLES: Bader, Barbara. *Aesop and Company*. Houghton Mifflin, 1991. / Calmenson, Stephanie. *The Children's Aesop*. Doubleday, 1988. / Gatti, Anne. *Aesop's Fables*. Harcourt, 1992. / Hartman, Bob. *The Wolf Who Cried Boy*. Putnam, 2002. / Lobel, Arnold. *Fables*. HarperCollins, 1980. / Morpurgo, Michael. *The McElderry Book of Aesop's Fables*. McElderry, 2005. / Paxton, Tom. *Belling the Cat and Other Aesop's Fables: Retold in Verse*. Morrow, 1990. / Pinkney, Jerry. *Aesop's Fables*. SeaStar, 2000. / Scieszka, Jon. *Math Curse*. Viking, 1995. / Scieszka, Jon. *Science Verse*. Viking, 2004. / Scieszka, Jon. *The Stinky Cheese Man and Other Fairly Stupid Tales*. Viking, 1992. / Untermeyer, Louis. *Aesop's Fables*. Golden, 1965.

SUBJECTS: ANIMALS. FABLES. HUMOROUS FICTION. PARODIES. PICTURE BOOKS FOR OLDER READERS. READER'S THEATER.

706   Scott, Ann Herbert. *Brave as a Mountain Lion*. Illus. by Glo Coalson. Clarion, 1996. 0-395-66760-7. Unp. Gr. 1–3

Afraid to participate in the school spelling bee, Spider gets good advice from his father, who tells him to pretend he is the strongest, bravest animal; from his grandmother, who tells him he can be clever as a coyote; and from his little brother, Will, who teaches him about being silent.

GERM: Ask your listeners what advice they would give to Spider to bolster his courage and help him take on the spelling bee. For some experiential writing, ask them to think of a time they were scared or needed to be brave and tell what they did to deal with their fears.

RELATED TITLES: Best, Cari. *Shrinking Violet.* Farrar, 2001. / Cowley, Joy. *Big Moon Tortilla.* Boyds Mills, 1998. / Frasier, Debra. *Miss Alaineus: A Vocabulary Disaster.* Harcourt, 2000. / Howe, James. *Pinky and Rex and the Spelling Bee.* Atheneum, 1991. / Khan, Rukhsana. *Ruler of the Courtyard.* Viking, 2003. / Strete, Craig. *The Rattlesnake Who Went to School.* Putnam, 2004.

SUBJECTS: COURAGE. ENGLISH LANGUAGE—SPELLING. FAMILY LIFE. INDIANS OF NORTH AMERICA. MULTICULTURAL BOOKS. SCHOOLS. SHOSHONI INDIANS. STAGE FRIGHT.

707 **Sedgwick, Marcus.** *The Emperor's New Clothes.* **Illus. by Alison Jay. Chronicle, 2004. 0-8118-4569-9. Unp. Gr. PreK–4**

In this breezy, rhyming, animal-based retelling of Hans Christian Andersen's classic tale, the vain and prideful king is a lion, his advisers are a hare and a tortoise, and the fraudulent tailors are weasels. The crackle-glaze varnish over the large, attractive full-bleed paintings gives the book an antique look.

GERM: Compare this rhyming version of the story with the standard prose versions and look at the style of illustrations in the editions illustrated by Angela Barrett, Demi, and Dorothée Duntze.

RELATED TITLES: Andersen, Hans Christian. *The Emperor's New Clothes.* Illus. by Angela Barrett. Candlewick, 1997. / Andersen, Hans Christian. *The Emperor's New Clothes: A Fairy Tale.* Illus. by Dorothée Duntze. North-South Books, 1986. / Andersen, Hans Christian. *The Princess and the Pea.* Illus. by Paul Galdone. Seabury, 1978. / Calmenson, Stephanie. *The Principal's New Clothes.* Scholastic, 1989. / Demi. *The Emperor's New Clothes: A Tale Set in China.* McElderry, 2000. / Demi. *The Hungry Coat: A Tale from Turkey.* McElderry, 2004.

SUBJECTS: ANIMALS. CLOTHING AND DRESS. EMPERORS. KINGS AND RULERS. LIONS. LITERARY FAIRY TALES. STORIES IN RHYME.

708 **Seeger, Laura Vaccaro.** *The Hidden Alphabet.* **Illus. by the author. Roaring Brook, 2003. 0-7613-1941-7. Unp. Gr. PreK–1**

On each black page of this unusual alphabet book, you will find one word in white print and a textured painted representation of that word. Now lift the heavy-stock black window frame off the page to reveal, underneath, the rest of the picture, which is a painting of the letter itself. For instance, view the red and yellow balloons, then raise the black window and see how those balloons are now the center part of a large decorated "B."

GERM: Children will delight in finding the picture hidden within each letter of this stunning alphabet book. *The Hidden Alphabet* is almost the opposite of Suse MacDonald's *Alphabatics,* in which the letter transforms itself into a picture—a "D" turns into a dragon.

RELATED TITLES: Bourke, Linda. *Eye Spy.* Chronicle, 1991. / Carter, David A. *One Red Dot: A Pop-up Book for Children of All Ages.* Little Simon, 2005. / Ernst, Lisa Campbell. *The Letters Are Lost.* Viking, 1996. / Hoban, Tana. *Look! Look! Look!* Greenwillow, 1988. / Johnson, Stephen T. *Alphabet City.* Viking, 1995. / Lobel, Arnold. *On Market Street.* Greenwillow, 1981. / MacDonald, Ross. *Achoo! Bang! Crash: The Noisy Alphabet.* Roaring Brook, 2003. / MacDonald, Suse. *Alphabatics.* Simon & Schuster, 1986. / Robert, Francois, Jean Robert, and Jane Gittings. *Find a Face.* Chronicle, 2004. / Wood, Audrey. *Alphabet Mystery.* Scholastic, 2003.

SUBJECTS: ALPHABET BOOKS. TOY AND MOVABLE BOOKS. VISUAL PERCEPTION.

709 **Seeger, Laura Vaccaro.** *Lemons Are Not Red.* **Illus. by the author. Roaring Brook, 2004. 1-59643-008-7. Unp. Gr. PreK–1**

"Lemons are not RED." Such an obvious statement, but in the middle of an all-yellow page is a red lemon. Flip that page and now the die-cut lemon is yellow against a red background. "Lemons are YELLOW," it says. "Apples are RED." And there, on the facing page, is a painting of a red apple. The graphics that support each of the five color statements that follow are equally vivid and innovative.

GERM: Given enough repetition, all of your youngest children will be able to recite this emergent reader in its entirety, as they do with Bill Martin Jr.'s *Brown Bear, Brown Bear, What Do You See.* Write new three-sentence color statements and make your own three-page pictures to read aloud and show, borrowing Vaccaro's clever format. Fool around with language, concepts, and categorizing: One person says, "Lemons are vegetables." Another responds, "No lemons are not vegetables. Lemons are fruits." "Lemons are sweet." "No, lemons are not sweet. Lemons are sour." And so on.

RELATED TITLES: Cabrera, Jane. *Cat's Colors*. Dial, 1997. / Carle, Eric. *Hello, Red Fox*. Simon & Schuster, 1998. / Carle, Eric. *The Mixed-Up Chameleon*. HarperCollins, 1984. / Carter, David A. *One Red Dot: A Pop-up Book for Children of All Ages*. Little Simon, 2005. / Ehlert, Lois. *Color Zoo*. HarperCollins, 1989. / Frame, Jeron Ashford. *Yesterday I Had the Blues*. Tricycle, 2003. / Freymann, Saxton. *Food for Thought: The Complete Book of Concepts for Growing Minds*. Scholastic, 2005. / Jonas, Ann. *Color Dance*. Greenwillow, 1989. / Lionni, Leo. *Little Blue and Little Yellow*. Morrow, 1994. / Lobel, Arnold. *The Great Blueness and Other Predicaments*. Harper-Collins, 1968. / Martin, Bill, Jr. *Brown Bear, Brown Bear, What Do You See?* Henry Holt, 1983. / Micklethwait, Lucy. *Colors*. Frances Lincoln, 2005. / Seeger, Laura Vaccaro. *The Hidden Alphabet*. Roaring Brook, 2003. / Shannon, George. *White Is for Blueberry*. Greenwillow, 2005.

SUBJECTS: COLOR. TOY AND MOVABLE BOOKS.

710 Seuling, Barbara. *Winter Lullaby*. Illus. by Greg Newbold. Harcourt, 1998. 0-15-201403-9. Unp. Gr. PreK–1

From desert to farmland to forest, we see—through soft, rhyming questions and responses—where bees, snakes, mice, bats, ducks, fish, and people go in the winter.

GERM: Gather together other books about hibernation, migration, and winter and draw new pictures of where animals go when the weather turns cold.

RELATED TITLES: Fleming, Denise. *Time to Sleep*. Henry Holt, 1997. / Fuchs, Diane Marcial. *A Bear for All Seasons*. Henry Holt, 1995. / Hunter, Anne. *Possum's Harvest Moon*. Houghton Mifflin, 1996. / Lemieux, Michele. *What's That Noise?* Morrow, 1985. / Murray, Marjorie Dennis. *Don't Wake Up the Bear!* Cavendish, 2003. / Pfeffer, Wendy. *The Shortest Day: Celebrating the Winter Solstice*. Dutton, 2003. / Ryder, Joanne. *Chipmunk Song*. Dutton, 1987. / Schnur, Steven. *Winter: An Alphabet Acrostic*. Clarion, 2002. / Selsam, Millicent, and Joyce Hunt. *Keep Looking!* Macmillan, 1989. / Simmons, Jane. *Little Fern's First Winter*. Little, Brown, 2001. / Wilson, Karma. *Bear Snores On*. McElderry, 2002.

SUBJECTS: ANIMALS. HIBERNATION. SEASONS. STORIES IN RHYME. WINTER.

711 Seuss, Dr. *Hooray for Diffendoofer Day*. Illus. by Dr. Seuss and Lane Smith. Knopf, 1998. 0-679-99008-9. 60pp. Gr. K–6

Welcome to Dinkerville, where the kids love Diffendoofer School with its delightfully eccentric teachers. The narrator's teacher, Miss Bonkers, is "as bouncy as a flea," and she instructs her class on vital matters such as "how to tell a cactus from a cow." Coauthors Jack Prelutsky and Lane Smith undertook to finish the delightful narrative poem that the great Dr. Seuss had started before his death. The first half of the book is the rhyming story that describes the staff and relates how the students ace a big test in order to save themselves from being transferred to school in dreary Flobbertown.

GERM: Older students will enjoy poring over the second half of the book, composed of the 14 pages of original Seuss sketches, verses, and notes, plus an essay by Seuss's editor detailing how Prelutsky and Smith finished Seuss's story. Start with the first book by Dr. Seuss, *And to Think That I Saw It on Mulberry Street* and then show the rest of his stunning array of titles, concluding with Kathleen Krull's picture-book biography, *The Boy on Fairfield Street: How Ted Geisel Grew Up to Become Dr. Seuss*. Look at another zany school day in *Just Another Ordinary Day* by Rod Clement and decompress from your big tests with *Testing Miss Malarkey* by Judy Finchler.

RELATED TITLES: Allard, Harry. *Miss Nelson Is Missing*. Houghton Mifflin, 1985. / Clements, Andrew. *Double Trouble in Walla Walla*. Millbrook, 1998. / Creech, Sharon. *A Fine, Fine School*. HarperCollins, 2001. / Dakos, Kalli. *If You're Not Here, Please Raise Your Hand: Poems About School*. Simon & Schuster, 1990. / DiPucchio, Kelly. *Mrs. McBloom, Clean Up Your Classroom*. Hyperion, 2005. / Finchler, Judy. *Testing Miss Malarkey*. Walker, 2000. / Krull, Kathleen. *The Boy on Fairfield Street: How Ted Geisel Grew Up to Become Dr. Seuss*. Random House, 2004. / Prelutsky, Jack. *A Pizza the Size of the Sun*. Greenwillow, 1996. / Reiss, Mike. *The Great Show-and-Tell Disaster*. Price Stern Sloan, 2001. / Sachar, Louis. *Wayside School Is Falling Down*. Lothrop, 1989. / Seuss, Dr. *And to Think That I Saw It on Mulberry Street*. Random House, 1989. / Smith, Lane. *Math Curse*. Viking, 1995. / Stevenson, James. *That Dreadful Day*. Greenwillow, 1985.

SUBJECTS: ACHIEVEMENT TESTS. HUMOROUS FICTION. SCHOOLS. STORIES IN RHYME. TEACHERS.

712   Shannon, David. *A Bad Case of Stripes.* **Illus. by the author. Blue Sky/Scholastic, 1998. 0-590-92997-6. Unp. Gr. 1–5**

Here's a character study of Camilla Cream, a girl so worried about fitting in with the kids at school that she awakens to find her skin covered head to toe in wide rainbow-colored stripes, all because she was afraid to admit she liked lima beans.

GERM: As you read aloud this story, which spoofs conformity and stresses the necessity of affirming one's own identity, ask your listeners to provide medical advice on why Camilla has such a bizarre malady and what she should do to cure it.

RELATED TITLES: Benton, Jim. *The Fran That Time Forgot.* Simon & Schuster, 2005. / Catling, Patrick Skene. *The Chocolate Touch.* Morrow, 1979. / Egan, Tim. *Burnt Toast on Davenport Street.* Houghton Mifflin, 1997. / Fierstein, Harvey. *The Sissy Duckling.* Simon & Schuster, 2002. / Kraft, Erik. *Chocolatina.* BridgeWater, 1998. / Maloney, Peter, and Felicia Zekauskas. *His Mother's Nose.* Dial, 2001. / Palatini, Margie. *Sweet Tooth.* Simon & Schuster, 2004. / Swope, Sam. *The Araboolies of Liberty Street.* Crown, 1989. / Yashima, Taro. *Crow Boy.* Viking, 1955. / Yorinks, Arthur. *Hey, Al.* Farrar, 1986.

SUBJECTS: CONFORMITY. FANTASY. IDENTITY. INDIVIDUALITY. PICTURE BOOKS FOR ALL AGES. SICK. VEGETABLES.

713   Shannon, David. *David Gets in Trouble.* **Illus. by the author. Scholastic, 2002. 0-439-05022-7. Unp. Gr. PreK–1**

"I didn't mean to!" "It was an accident." These are a few of David's many excuses and explanations when he gets in trouble for over-the-top kid behavior such as skateboarding in the house or hitting a baseball that shatters a window. Simple declarative sentences culminate with David finally taking responsibility: "Yes, it was me!" he cries in the middle of the night when the guilt kicks in. Mom forgives his misdemeanors, of course, and so will you.

GERM: Children can do a little experiential writing and illustrating of true anecdotes to accompany their own favorite excuses. Introduce all of the David books for one big, sustained laugh.

RELATED TITLES: Allard, Harry. *Miss Nelson Is Missing.* Houghton Mifflin, 1985. / Curtis, Jamie Lee. *It's Hard to Be Five: Learning How to Work My Control Panel.* HarperCollins, 2004. / Feiffer, Jules. *I'm Not Bobby!* Hyperion, 2001. / Lester, Helen. *Hooway for Wodney Wat.* Houghton Mifflin, 1999. / Long, Melinda. *How I Became a Pirate.* Harcourt, 2003. / Marshall, James. *The Cut-Ups.* Viking, 1984. / Shannon, David. *David Goes to School.* Scholastic, 1999. / Shannon, David. *No, David!* Scholastic, 1998. / Vail, Rachel. *Sometimes I'm Bombaloo.* Scholastic, 2002. / Wells, Rosemary. *Noisy Nora.* Dial, 1997. / Wood, Audrey. *The Red Racer.* Simon & Schuster, 1996.

SUBJECTS: BEHAVIOR. HUMOROUS FICTION. MOTHERS AND SONS. PICTURE BOOKS FOR ALL AGES. SCHOOLS.

714   Shannon, David. *David Goes to School.* **Illus. by the author. Scholastic, 1999. 0-590-48087-1. Unp. Gr. PreK–1**

Just as David's mother reprimanded him for his boisterous indoor demeanor in *No, David!*, his teacher now gets on his case about yelling, pushing, and other riotous, typical bad-boy student behavior. Each admonition his teacher utters is written on sentence strip paper, a perfect visual accompaniment to the fresh, loud-colored gouache illustrations of David's classroom exuberance.

GERM: Children will have a grand time living vicariously by writing and illustrating sequels such as "David Goes to Camp" or David Goes on Vacation," perhaps based on times they got in and out of trouble.

RELATED TITLES: Allard, Harry. *Miss Nelson Is Missing.* Houghton Mifflin, 1985. / Curtis, Jamie Lee. *It's Hard to Be Five: Learning How to Work My Control Panel.* HarperCollins, 2004. / Lester, Helen. *Hooway for Wodney Wat.* Houghton Mifflin, 1999. / Long, Melinda. *How I Became a Pirate.* Harcourt, 2003. / Marshall, James. *The Cut-Ups.* Viking, 1984. / Shannon, David. *David Gets in Trouble.* Scholastic, 2002. / Shannon, David. *No, David!* Scholastic, 1998. / Slate, Joseph. *Miss Bindergarten Has a Wild Day in Kindergarten.* Dutton, 2005.

SUBJECTS: BEHAVIOR. HUMOROUS FICTION. PICTURE BOOKS FOR ALL AGES. SCHOOLS. TEACHERS.

715   Shannon, David. *Duck on a Bike.* **Illus. by the author. Scholastic, 2002. 0-399-23468-3 0439050235. Unp. Gr. PreK–1**

Most of the farm animals don't appear to envy Duck's riding a red bicycle around the farmyard. "That's the silliest thing I've ever seen," Cow thinks. But then a bunch of children leave their bikes in the yard, and it's too tempting for the animals to resist.

GERM: Throughout the story, we find out what each animal is thinking. When you turn to the wordless double-page spread showing all the animals looking at the bikes, have listeners verbalize what each animal is thinking and predict what the menagerie will do next. Looking at the last page, they can then forecast what Duck's next adventure might be.

RELATED TITLES: Babcock, Chris. *No Moon, No Milk*. Crown, 1993. / Bateman, Teresa. *Farm Flu*. Albert Whitman, 2001. / Cronin, Doreen. *Click, Clack, Moo: Cows That Type*. Simon & Schuster, 2000. / Cronin, Doreen. *Duck for President*. Simon & Schuster, 2004. / Duvoisin, Roger. *Petunia*. Knopf, 1989. / Hort, Lenny. *The Seals on the Bus*. Henry Holt, 2000. / Lindbergh, Reeve. *The Day the Goose Got Loose*. Dial, 1990. / Riddell, Chris. *Platypus and the Lucky Day*. Harcourt, 2002. / Rohmann, Eric. *My Friend Rabbit*. Roaring Brook, 2002. / Waddell, Martin. *Farmer Duck*. Candlewick, 1992. / Willems, Mo. *Don't Let the Pigeon Drive the Bus!* Hyperion, 2003.

SUBJECTS: BICYCLES. DOMESTIC ANIMALS. DUCKS. HUMOROUS FICTION.

716   **Shannon, David. *No, David!* Illus. by the author. Scholastic, 1998. 0-590-93002-8. Unp. Gr. PreK–1**

"Be quiet!," "That's enough, David!," and "Go to your room!" are just some of the admonitions that David's mom yells at him while he barrels around the house making mischief. "Come back here, David," she exclaims as he takes off, naked, down the street. In spite of his unruly ways, his mother assures him, "Yes, David, I love you."

GERM: Explain that David Shannon originally wrote this story when he was six, when "no" and "David" were some of the only words he could spell. Your young cut-ups can write and illustrate stories about their own recent adventures and pledge to keep their copies safe until they are old, so they can always remember what they were like when they were young.

RELATED TITLES: Bang, Molly. *When Sophie Gets Angry—Really, Really Angry*. Scholastic, 1999. / Bush, Timothy. *Benjamin McFadden and the Robot Babysitter*. Crown, 1998. / Delton, Judy. *I'm Telling You Now*. Dutton, 1983. / Fearnley, Jan. *Watch Out!* Candlewick, 2004. / Feiffer, Jules. *I'm Not Bobby!* Hyperion, 2001. / Gordon, Jeffie Ross. *Two Badd Babies*. Boyds Mills, 1992. / Hutchins, Pat. *Where's the Baby?* Greenwillow, 1988. / Jonell, Lynne. *I Need a Snake*. Putnam, 1998. / Koller, Jackie French. *One Monkey Too Many*. Harcourt, 1999. / Long, Melinda. *How I Became a Pirate*. Illus. by David Shannon. Harcourt, 2003. / Marshall, James. *The Cut-Ups*. Viking, 1984. / Shannon, David. *David Gets in Trouble*. Scholastic, 2002. / Shannon, David. *David Goes to School*. Scholastic, 1999. / Vail, Rachel. *Sometimes I'm Bombaloo*. Scholastic, 2002. / Wells, Rosemary. *Noisy Nora*. Dial, 1997.

SUBJECTS: BEHAVIOR. HUMOROUS FICTION. MOTHERS AND SONS. PICTURE BOOKS FOR ALL AGES.

717   **Shannon, George. *Tippy-Toe Chick, Go!* Illus. by Laura Dronzek. Greenwillow, 2003. 0-06-029824-3. Unp. Gr. PreK–1**

One day, when Hen takes her three chicks to the garden for their favorite treat of sweet itty-bitty beans and potato bugs, a big, grumpy, barking black-and-white dog blocks their way. Big Chick and Middle Chick try talking to the dog, to no avail, but Little Chick runs until Dog chases her and wraps his rope around the tree.

GERM: Talk over and act out the three different strategies the chicks use to get past Dog. Which one worked and why?

RELATED TITLES: Buzzeo, Toni. *Dawdle Duckling*. Dial, 2003. / Fox, Mem. *Hattie and the Fox*. Bradbury, 1987. / Gerstein, Mordicai. *Follow Me!* Morrow, 1983. / Hindley, Judy. *Do Like a Duck Does!* Candlewick, 2002. / Hutchins, Pat. *Rosie's Walk*. Bradbury, 1987. / Raffi. *Five Little Ducks*. Crown, 1988. / Simmons, Jane. *Quack, Daisy, Quack!* Little, Brown, 2002. / Stenmark, Victoria. *The Singing Chick*. Henry Holt, 1999.

SUBJECTS: CHICKENS. COURAGE. CREATIVE DRAMA. DOGS.

718   **Shannon, George. *Tomorrow's Alphabet*. Illus. by Donald Crews. Greenwillow, 1996. 0-688-13505-6. 58pp. Gr. PreK–2**

Shannon's fascinating alphabet book is a marvelous way to introduce the concept of cause and effect. Each double-sided spread presents a "before" and "after" object, illustrated in large, handsome watercolors: "A is for seed—tomorrow's APPLE." After showing the first few letters, cover up each right-hand page with a piece of cardboard so viewers can guess what the animal or object will become, using the letter as a clue.

GERM: Children can write and illustrate new puzzlers in the same format, or go backward: T is for paper—yesterday's TREE. Then they can read them aloud for all to guess. One first grader wrote, "F is for cow—tomorrow's FILET MIGNON!" In Shannon's *White Is for Blueberry*, he takes an inside-outside, then-and-now look at colors.

RELATED TITLES: Abrams, Pam. *Now I Eat My ABC's*. Scholastic, 2004. / Ehlert, Lois. *Eating the Alphabet*. Harcourt, 1989. / Fleming, Denise. *Alphabet Under Construction*. Henry Holt, 2002. / Kalman, Maira. *What Pete Ate from A–Z*. Putnam, 2001. / Lester, Mike. *A Is for Salad*. Putnam, 2000. / Lobel, Arnold. *On Market Street*. Greenwillow, 1981. / MacDonald, Ross. *Achoo! Bang! Crash: The Noisy Alphabet*. Roaring Brook, 2003. / MacDonald, Suse. *Alphabatics*. Simon & Schuster, 1986. / Schneider, R. M. *Add It, Dip It, Fix It: A Book of Verbs*. Houghton Mifflin, 1995. / Seeger, Laura Vaccaro. *The Hidden Alphabet*. Roaring Brook, 2003. / Shannon, George. *White Is for Blueberry*. Greenwillow, 2005.

SUBJECTS: ALPHABET BOOKS. CAUSE AND EFFECT.

719   Shannon, George. *White Is for Blueberry*. Illus. by Laura Dronzek. Greenwillow, 2005. 0-06-029276-8. Unp. Gr. PreK–2

Look at colors in nature that challenge our preconceived notions. "Pink is for crow . . . ," it says on the first page, though there's a black crow perched on a branch in the pink and black bordered acrylic painting in the middle of the page. Turn the page for the rest of the sentence, ". . . when it has just hatched from its egg." And there, in a full-bleed close-up picture, is a nest of hungry-looking, squawking pink baby crows.

GERM: Once children get the idea, they'll try to figure out each color statement before you turn the page and display the answer. Look at the color of a poppy, a leaf, a turnip, snow, firelight, a pine tree, a sweet potato, and the sky. On the last page is this observation: "It all depends on when we look . . . how near or far . . . outside or in." Thinking about objects in nature, children can construct new color statements. Folding a piece of construction paper in half, they can write the first half of the sentence on the front half. Next they'll open the paper to its double-page spread and add the explanation and a close-up drawing supporting it. Continue with a thoughtful look at cause and effect in Shannon's *Tomorrow's Alphabet*.

RELATED TITLES: Cabrera, Jane. *Cat's Colors*. Dial, 1997. / Carle, Eric. *Hello, Red Fox*. Simon & Schuster, 1998. / Ehlert, Lois. *Color Zoo*. HarperCollins, 1989. / Ehlert, Lois. *In My World*. Harcourt, 2002. / Feldman, Judy. *The Alphabet in Nature*. Children's Press, 1991. / Freymann, Saxton. *Food for Thought: The Complete Book of Concepts for Growing Minds*. Scholastic, 2005. / Lester, Mike. *A Is for Salad*. Putnam, 2000. / MacDonald, Suse. *Alphabatics*. Simon & Schuster, 1986. / Schaefer, Lola M. *What's Up, What's Down*. Greenwillow, 2002. / Seeger, Laura Vaccaro. *The Hidden Alphabet*. Roaring Brook, 2003. / Seeger, Laura Vaccaro. *Lemons Are Not Red*. Roaring Brook, 2004. / Shannon, George. *Tomorrow's Alphabet*. Greenwillow, 1996.

SUBJECTS: COLOR. NATURE. PERCEPTION.

720   Shapiro, Arnold L. *Mice Squeak, We Speak*. Illus. by Tomie dePaola. Putnam, 1997. 0-399-23202-8. Unp. Gr. PreK–1

"Cats purr. / Lions roar. / Owls hoot. / Bears snore." So starts Shapiro's classic poem celebrating animal language, including our own. dePaola's gentle pastel-colored bordered illustrations of each animal making its own special noise will motivate the whole class to join in.

GERM: The second time you read this aloud, ask your listeners to recall and call out each verb in the verse's sequence and mimic the animals' vocal sounds. Here's a superb and simple choral reading opportunity, for which you might also consider assigning one animal part per child and then forming a large human circle to stage an acted-out recitation.

RELATED TITLES: De Zutter, Hank. *Who Says a Dog Goes Bow-Wow?* Doubleday, 1993. / Dodds, Dayle-Ann. *Do Bunnies Talk?* HarperCollins, 1992. / Feiffer, Jules. *Bark, George*. HarperCollins, 1999. / Harter, Debbie. *Walking Through the Jungle*. Orchard, 1997. / Martin, Bill, Jr. *Polar Bear, Polar Bear, What Do You Hear?* Henry Holt, 1991. / Park, Linda Sue. *Mung-Mung: A Folded Book of Animal Sounds*. Charlesbridge, 2004. / Park, Linda Sue. *Yum! Yuck! A Foldout Book of People Sounds*. Charlesbridge, 2005. / Robinson, Marc. *Cock-a-Doodle-Doo! What Does It Sound Like to You?* Stewart, Taboori & Chang, 1993. / Shapiro, Arnold L. *Who Says That?* Dutton, 1991. / Thomson, Pat. *The Squeaky, Creaky Bed*. Doubleday, 2003. / Walter, Virginia. *"Hi, Pizza Man!"* Orchard, 1995.

SUBJECTS: ANIMAL SOUNDS. CREATIVE DRAMA. NOISE. STORIES IN RHYME.

721   Sharmat, Marjorie Weinman, and Mitchell Sharmat. *Nate the Great and the Big Sniff*. Illus. by Martha Weston. Delacorte, 2001. 0-385-32604-1. 48pp. Gr. PreK–2

In his 24th case, pancake-loving detective Nate the Great must unravel his biggest mystery ever: his faithful dog and helpmate, Sludge, is missing. Left waiting outside Weinman Brothers, Nate's favorite store, Sludge was last seen in the store, escaping an irate saleslady. This title makes a good read-aloud introduction to the two dozen books in the controlled-vocabulary easy-reader series, which trains readers to observe, look for clues, and develop an irrational craving for pancakes.

GERM: Have your class construct a large aerial map of the store, labeling the different departments and tracing Nate's investigation. Children can draw pictures of other parts of the store and caption them with a description of what might have happened to Sludge there.

RELATED TITLES: Adler, David A. Young Cam Jansen mystery series. Putnam. / Clifford, Eth. *Flatfoot Fox and the Case of the Mising Schoolhouse.* Houghton Mifflin, 1997. (And others in the Flatfoot Fox series.) / Cushman, Doug. *Aunt Eater Loves a Mystery.* HarperCollins, 1987. (And others in the Aunt Eater mystery series.) / Cushman, Doug. *The Mystery of King Karfu.* HarperCollins, 1996. / McClements, George. *Jake Gander, Storyville Detective.* Hyperion, 2002. / Palatini, Margie. *The Web Files.* Hyperion, 2001. / Sharmat, Marjorie Weinman, and Mitchell Sharmat. Nate the Great mystery series. Delacorte. / Teague, Mark. *Detective LaRue: Letters from the Investigation.* Scholastic, 2004.

SUBJECTS: DEPARTMENT STORES. DOGS. LOST. MYSTERY AND DETECTIVE STORIES.

722   Sherman, Allan, and Lou Busch. *Hello Muddah, Hello Faddah! (A Letter from Camp).* Illus. by Jack E. Davis. Dutton, 2004. 0-525-46942-7. Unp. Gr. K–3

The classic Allan Sherman novelty song has been turned into a perfectly goofy picture book. A disgruntled boy writes to his parents from Camp Granada, describing all the awful things that he's experienced and begging to come home.

GERM: To get the full effect of the rhyming verses and the farcical illustrations, you must play the original song, which is easy to find on the Internet. For another tangled experience combining letter-writing and exaggeration, read *Dear Mrs. LaRue* by Mark Teague.

RELATED TITLES: Arnold, Tedd. *Catalina Magdalena Hoopensteiner Wallendiner Hogan Logan Bogan Was Her Name.* Scholastic, 2004. / Lansky, Bruce, comp. *A Bad Case of the Giggles: Kids' Favorite Funny Poems.* Meadowbrook, 1994. / Lansky, Bruce, comp. *Kids Pick the Funniest Poems: A Collection of Poems That Will Make You Laugh.* Meadowbrook, 1991. / Lansky, Bruce, comp. *Miles of Smiles: Kids Pick the Funniest Poems, Book #3.* Meadowbrook, 1998. / O'Malley, Kevin. *Straight to the Pole.* Walker, 2003. / Raffi. *Down by the Bay.* Crown, 1987. / Teague, Mark. *Dear Mrs. LaRue: Letters from Obedience School.* Scholastic, 2002. / Teague, Mark. *How I Spent My Summer Vacation.* Crown, 1995.

SUBJECTS: CAMPS. EXAGGERATION. HUMOROUS SONGS. LETTER WRITING. SONGS. STORIES IN RHYME.

723   Shields, Carol Diggory. *Food Fight!* Illus. by Doreen Kassel. Handprint, 2002. 1-929766-29-7. Unp. Gr. K–2

In a wild rhyming rumpus late one night, the cat is the only witness when the contents of the refrigerator cut loose and have a pun-filled blast. ("'Lettuce have a party!' said the salad greens . . .") Personable three-dimensional fruit and veggie creations are constructed with colorful sculpy clay, and the wordplay is simply delectable.

GERM: Using the book's pun-filled sentences as a starting point, children can write new dialogue-filled sentences for other items that one might find in the kitchen cupboards and draw pictures to accompany them. If you have access to sculpy clay, they can make 3-D illustrations too. Teacher Maren Vitali had her second graders came up with their own food-based dialogue, which she displayed on a huge folding display board she decorated to look like the outside of a refrigerator. Inside the doors were the kids' paper foods, displayed on the shelves.

RELATED TITLES: Barrett, Judi. *Cloudy with a Chance of Meatballs.* Atheneum, 1978. / Bruel, Nick. *Bad Kitty.* Roaring Brook, 2005. / Chapman, Cheryl. *Pass the Fritters, Critters.* Simon & Schuster, 1993. / Freymann, Saxton, and Joost Effers. *Food for Thought.* Scholastic, 2005. / Freymann, Saxton, and Joost Elffers. *Dog Food.* Scholastic, 2002. / Freymann, Saxton, and Joost Elffers. *How Are You Peeling? Foods with Moods.* Scholastic, 1999. / Gerberg, Mort. *Geographunny: A Book of Global Riddles.* Clarion, 1991. / Glassman, Bruce. *The Midnight Fridge.* Blackbirch, 1998. / Keller, Charles. *Belly Laughs! Food Jokes and Riddles.* Simon & Schuster, 1990. / Laden, Nina. *The Night I Followed the Dog.* Chronicle, 1994. / McMullan, Kate. *I Stink!* HarperCollins, 2002. / Most, Bernard. *Zoodles.* Harcourt, 1992. / Palatini, Margie. *Sweet Tooth.* Simon & Schuster, 2004. / Stevens, Janet, and Susan Stevens Crummel. *Cook-a-Doodle-Doo!* Harcourt, 1999.

SUBJECTS: FOOD. STORIES IN RHYME.

724   Shields, Carol Diggory. *Lucky Pennies and Hot Chocolate.* **Illus. by Hiroe Nakata. Dutton, 2000. 0-525-46450-6. Unp. Gr. PreK–1**

A grandfather and grandson share a perfect November day together, telling knock-knock jokes, playing dominoes, driving around with the top down, sharing a good book, and playing ball.

GERM: Ask your listeners: "Who is telling this story?" You'll all be surprised when you read the last page. In fact, you'll need to read the story to them again so they can adjust their point of view. Tell knock-knock jokes. If you can find dominoes, teach your group to play. Then have everyone set them up in a line and knock them over. Hand out a lucky penny to each child. Have them read the date and help them figure out how old each coin is. Ask: If yours was a wishing penny and you could have three wishes (except for money or more wishes), what would they be? If it's a lucky penny, what kind of luck would you like it to give you?

RELATED TITLES: Caseley, Judith. *Dear Annie.* Greenwillow, 1991. / dePaola, Tomie. *Tom.* Putnam, 1993. / Gaffney, Timothy R. *Grandpa Takes Me to the Moon.* Tambourine, 1996. / Greenfield, Eloise. *Grandpa's Face.* Philomel, 1988. / Juster, Norton. *The Hello, Goodbye Window.* Hyperion, 2005. / Lum, Kate. *What! Cried Granny: An Almost Bedtime Story.* Dial, 1999. / Mills, Claudia. *Gus and Grandpa.* Farrar, 1997. (And others in the Gus and Grandpa series.) / Paul, Ann Whitford. *Everything to Spend the Night from A to Z.* DK Ink, 1999. / Polacco, Patricia. *Thunder Cake.* Philomel, 1990. / Van Leeuwen, Jean. *The Tickle Stories.* Dial, 1998. / Westcott, Nadine Bernard. *Peanut Butter and Jelly: A Play Rhyme.* Dutton, 1987.

SUBJECTS: GRANDFATHERS. KNOCK-KNOCK JOKES.

725   Shields, Carol Diggory. *Saturday Night at the Dinosaur Stomp.* **Illus. by Scott Nash. Candlewick, 1997. 1-56402-693-0. Unp. Gr. PreK–2**

Enjoy the grooving rhyme and rhythms as you dance the night away with multi-hued, rock 'n' rolling dinosaurs. Be sure to sample vicariously their Swampwater Punch and watch the fireworks show from all the erupting volcanoes.

GERM: Show the dance steps diagrammed on the endpapers and get everyone up and moving to the Triassic Twist and the Brontosaurus Bump. Keep dancing with Tony Mitton's *Dinosaurumpus!* and Paul Stickland's *Ten Terrible Dinosaurs.*

RELATED TITLES: Dodson, Peter. *An Alphabet of Dinosaurs.* Scholastic, 1995. / Hearn, Diane Dawson. *Dad's Dinosaur Day.* Macmillan, 1993. / Mitton, Tony. *Dinosaurumpus!* Scholastic, 2003. / Most, Bernard. *How Big Were the Dinosaurs?* Harcourt, 1994. / Nolan, Dennis. *Dinosaur Dreams.* Macmillan, 1990. / Rohmann, Eric. *Time Flies.* Crown, 1994. / Stickland, Paul. *Ten Terrible Dinosaurs.* Dutton, 1997. / Stickland, Paul, and Henrietta Stickland. *Dinosaur Roar!* Dutton, 1994. / Thomas, Shelley Moore. *Good Night, Good Knight.* Dutton, 2000. / Whybrow, Ian. *Sammy and the Dinosaurs.* Orchard, 1999. / Wilson, Karma. *Hilda Must Be Dancing.* McElderry, 2004. / Yolen, Jane. *How Do Dinosaurs Say Good Night?* Blue Sky/Scholastic, 2000.

SUBJECTS: DANCING. DINOSAURS. PARTIES. STORIES IN RHYME.

726   Shulman, Lisa. *The Matzo Ball Boy.* **Illus. by Rosanne Litzinger. Dutton, 2005. 0-525-47169-3. Unp. Gr. PreK–2**

On Passover morning, a lonely old *bubbe* (grandmother) makes a lovely little matzo ball boy, but he escapes from her chicken soup and runs through town. He is pursued by the old woman, a *schneider* (tailor), *yenta* (gossip), rabbi, and even a fox, but no one can catch him until he encounters a poor man who brings him home for some Passover soup.

GERM: Filled with humor and Yiddish expressions (translated in the glossary), this version is fun to compare with Naomi Howland's *The Matzah Man.* Bring in some matzo to sample.

RELATED TITLES: Aylesworth, Jim. *The Gingerbread Man.* Scholastic, 1998. / Compestine, Ying Chang. *The Runaway Rice Cake.* Simon & Schuster, 2001. / Cook, Scott. *The Gingerbread Boy.* Knopf, 1987. / Egielski, Richard. *The Gingerbread Boy.* HarperCollins, 1997. / Hirsch, Marilyn. *Potato Pancakes All Around; A Hanukkah Tale.* Bonim, 1978. / Howland, Naomi. *Latkes, Latkes, Good to Eat.* Clarion, 1999. / Howland, Naomi. *The Matzah Man: A Passover Story.* Clarion, 2002. / Kimmel, Eric A. *Asher and the Capmakers: A Hanukkah Story.* Holiday House, 1993. / Kimmel, Eric A. *The Chanukkah Guest.* Holiday House, 1990. / Kimmel, Eric A. *The Gingerbread Man.* Holiday House, 1993. / Kimmel, Eric A. *Hershel and the Hanukkah Goblins.* Holiday House, 1989. / Kimmel, Eric A. *The Runaway Tortilla.* Winslow, 2000. / Newman, Lesléa. *Runaway Dreidel!* Henry Holt, 2002.

SUBJECTS: CHANTABLE REFRAIN. FOOD. GINGERBREAD BOY. HANUKKAH. JEWS. PARODIES. PASSOVER. SEQUENCE STORIES. YIDDISH LANGUAGE.

727   Shulman, Lisa. *Old MacDonald Had a Woodshop.* **Illus. by Ashley Wolff. Putnam, 2002. 0-399-23596-5. Unp. Gr. PreK–1**

Old MacDonald, an industrious sheep, is busy with all the other animals—sawing, drilling, hammering, filing, and painting—in order to make a surprise out of wood.

GERM: You'll love the way the story, with its many woodworking tools, leads back to the original song about Old MacDonald. Bring in tools so children can act this out as they sing it.

RELATED TITLES: Cauley, Lorinda Bryan. *Old MacDonald Had a Farm.* Putnam, 1989. / Clarke, Gus. *EIEIO: The Story of Old MacDonald, Who Had a Farm.* Lothrop, 1993. / Greene, Rhonda Gowler. *Barnyard Song.* Atheneum, 1997. / Hellen, Nancy. *Old MacDonald Had a Farm.* Orchard, 1990. / Hort, Lenny. *The Seals on the Bus.* Henry Holt, 2000. / Krosoczka, Jarrett J. *Punk Farm.* Knopf, 2005. / Pearson, Tracey Campbell. *Old MacDonald Had a Farm.* Dial, 1984. / Rounds, Glen. *Old MacDonald Had a Farm.* Holiday House, 1989. / Schwartz, Amy. *Old MacDonald.* Scholastic, 1999.

SUBJECTS: BUILDING. CARPENTRY. CREATIVE DRAMA. SHEEP. SOUND EFFECTS. STORIES IN RHYME. STORIES WITH SONGS. TOOLS.

728   Sierra, Judy. *Counting Crocodiles.* **Illus. by Will Hillenbrand. Harcourt, 1997. 0-15-200192-1. Unp. Gr. PreK–1**

"On an island in the middle of the Sillabobble Sea / lived a clever little monkey in a sour lemon tree." Spying a delectable banana tree on an island across the water, Monkey connives to count the crocs that stretch across the sea, crossing their backs to reach the fruit.

GERM: Based on a Pan-Asian folktale, Sierra's retelling, with joyous, colorful, playful full-bleed paintings, will have children counting up and back, recalling rhyming phrases, and acting out the crocs' actions in narrative pantomime. In Eileen Christelow's *Five Little Monkeys Sitting in a Tree*, when the naughty monkeys tease Mr. Crocodile they disappear one by one.

RELATED TITLES: Aruego, Jose, and Ariane Dewey. *A Crocodile's Tale.* Scribner, 1972. / Baumgartner, Barbara. *Crocodile! Crocodile! Stories Told Around the World.* DK, 1994. / Christelow, Eileen. *Five Little Monkeys Sitting in a Tree.* Clarion, 1991. / Jorgensen, Gail. *Crocodile Beat.* Bradbury, 1989. / Mollel, Tololwa M. *Shadow Dance.* Clarion, 1998. / Vaughan, Marcia. *Snap!* Scholastic, 1996. / Wallace, Karen. *Imagine You Are a Crocodile.* Henry Holt, 1997.

SUBJECTS: COUNTING BOOKS. CREATIVE DRAMA. CROCODILES. MONKEYS. STORIES IN RHYME. TRICKSTER TALES.

729   Sierra, Judy. *Wild About Books.* **Illus. by Marc Brown. Knopf, 2004. 0-375-92538-4. Unp. Gr. PreK–2**

Three cheers for the Zoobrary! Springfield librarian Molly McGrew mistakenly drives her bookmobile into the zoo, where all of the animals go simply wild for all the wonderful books. The jaunty rhyming story is paired with large, amiable paintings of animals everywhere reading everything, which will get your readers all fired up to do the same.

GERM: What are the animals reading and where? Teacher Sarah Masluk's first graders at Irving School in Highland Park, New Jersey, answered that question in rhyme, coming up with their own pictures and couplets including, "In the desert I saw some snakes who liked to read books about rakes." You can take it further, matching animals with specific book titles, looking up nonfiction books about those animals, and finding out facts about them to support what they'd choose to read. See where humans do their reading in Susan Allen and Jane Lindaman's *Read Anything Good Lately?* and take an exhilaratingly dangerous safari through a good animal book with Robert Florczak's *Yikes!!!*

RELATED TITLES: Allen, Susan, and Jane Lindaman. *Read Anything Good Lately?* Millbrook, 2003. / Bertram, Debbie, and Susan Bloom. *The Best Place to Read.* Random House, 2003. / Bloom, Becky. *Wolf!* Orchard, 1999. / Child, Lauren. *Who's Afraid of the Big Bad Book?* Hyperion, 2003. / Ernst, Lisa Campbell. *Stella Louella's Runaway Book.* Simon & Schuster, 1998. / Florczak, Robert. *Yikes!!!* Scholastic, 2003. / Hopkins, Lee Bennett, comp. *Good Books, Good Times!* HarperCollins, 1990. / Huff, Barbara. *Once Inside the Library.* Little, Brown, 1990. / Krull, Kathleen. *The Boy on Fairfield Street: How Ted Geisel Grew Up to Become Dr. Seuss.* Random House, 2004. / Lewis, J. Patrick. *Please Bury Me in the Library.* Harcourt, 2005. / Numeroff, Laura Joffe. *Beatrice Doesn't Want To.* Candlewick, 2004. / Parish, Herman. *Amelia Bedelia, Bookworm.* Greenwillow, 2003. / Prelutsky, Jack. *If Not for the Cat.* Greenwillow, 2004. / Sturges, Philemon. *She'll Be Comin' 'Round the Mountain.* Little, Brown, 2004. / Williams, Suzanne. *Library Lil.* Dial, 1997.

SUBJECTS: ANIMALS. BOOKMOBILES. BOOKS AND READING. HAIKU. LIBRARIANS. LIBRARIES. PICTURE BOOKS FOR ALL AGES. STORIES IN RHYME. ZOOS.

730   Simmons, Jane. *Come Along, Daisy.* **Illus. by the author. Little, Brown, 1998. 0-316-79790-1. Unp. Gr. PreK–K**

Watching fish, chasing dragonflies, and bouncing on lily pads, Daisy strays too far from Mama Duck and is spooked by the scary rustlings of creatures above and under her.

GERM: Meet some other babies who wander too far in Toni Buzzeo's *Dawdle Duckling*, Raffi's *Five Little Ducks*, and Linda Wikler's *Alfonse, Where Are You?*

RELATED TITLES: Buzzeo, Toni. *Dawdle Duckling*. Dial, 2003. / Dunrea, Olivier. *Gossie*. Houghton Mifflin, 2002. / Dunrea, Olivier. *Gossie and Gertie*. Houghton, 2002. / Emmett, Jonathan. *Ruby in Her Own Time*. Scholastic, 2004. / Gerstein, Mordicai. *Follow Me!* Morrow, 1983. / Hest, Amy. *In the Rain with Baby Duck*. Candlewick, 1995. / McCloskey, Robert. *Make Way for Ducklings*. Viking, 1941. / Raffi. *Five Little Ducks*. Crown, 1988. / Simmons, Jane. *Daisy and the Beasty*. Little, Brown, 2000. / Simmons, Jane. *Quack, Daisy, Quack!* Little, Brown, 2002. / Waddell, Martin. *Webster J. Duck*. Candlewick, 2001. / Whippo, Walt, and Bernard Zaritzky. *Little White Duck*. Little, Brown, 2000. / Wikler, Linda. *Alfonse, Where Are You?* Crown, 1996.

SUBJECTS: DUCKS. LOST. MOTHERS.

731   Simmons, Jane. *Little Fern's First Winter.* **Illus. by the author. Little, Brown, 2001. 0-316-79667-0. Unp. Gr. PreK–1**

Two bunnies, Little Fern and her brother Bracken, play hide-and-seek outside while all the other animals prepare for the first snow of winter.

GERM: This is a lovely story to act out as part of a discussion of what animals do to get ready for winter. It's also a perfect seasonal contrast to Simmons's *Come Along, Daisy* or *Quack, Daisy, Quack*. Making a text-to-life connection, ask: What do you do to get ready for the winter? Can you remember the first time you saw snow?

RELATED TITLES: Duffy, Dee Dee. *Forest Tracks*. Boyds Mills, 1996. / Fuchs, Diane Marcial. *A Bear for All Seasons*. Henry Holt, 1995. / George, Lindsay Barrett. *Around the Pond: Who's Been Here?* Greenwillow, 1996. / George, Lindsay Barrett. *In the Snow: Who's Been Here*. Greenwillow, 1995. / Gliori, Debi. *The Snow Lambs*. Scholastic, 1996. / Gray, Libba Moore. *Is There Room on the Featherbed?* Orchard, 1997. / Henkes, Kevin. *Kitten's First Full Moon*. Greenwillow, 2004. / Hunter, Anne. *Possum's Harvest Moon*. Houghton Mifflin, 1996. / Koide, Tan. *May We Sleep Here Tonight?* Atheneum, 1983. / Peters, Lisa Westberg. *Cold Little Duck, Duck, Duck*. Greenwillow, 2000. / Simmons, Jane. *Come Along, Daisy*. Little, Brown, 1998. / Simmons, Jane. *Quack, Daisy, Quack!* Little, Brown, 2002. / Tafuri, Nancy. *Snowy Flowy Blowy: A Twelve Months Rhyme*. Scholastic, 1999. / Waber, Bernard. *Bearsie Bear and the Surprise Sleepover Party*. Houghton Mifflin, 1997.

SUBJECTS: CREATIVE DRAMA. RABBITS. SEASONS. WEATHER. WINTER.

732   Simmons, Jane. *Quack, Daisy, Quack!* **Illus. by the author. Little, Brown, 2002. 0-316-79587-9. Unp. Gr. PreK–K**

Daisy and her duckling brother Pip have a wonderful time being noisy with all the other ducks, that is, until they can't find Mama.

GERM: In this simplest of stories, Daisy and Pip go through a range of emotions from joy to anxiety, all showing clearly on their faces. Have children show you how they think ducks are feeling on each page and ask them to come up with words to describe each expression.

RELATED TITLES: Buzzeo, Toni. *Dawdle Duckling*. Dial, 2003. / Dunrea, Olivier. *Gossie*. Houghton Mifflin, 2002. / Dunrea, Olivier. *Gossie and Gertie*. Houghton Mifflin, 2002. / Emmett, Jonathan. *Ruby in Her Own Time*. Scholastic, 2004. / Gerstein, Mordicai. *Follow Me!* Morrow, 1983. / Hest, Amy. *In the Rain with Baby Duck*. Candlewick, 1995. / James, Simon. *Little One Step*. Candlewick, 2003. / McCloskey, Robert. *Make Way for Ducklings*. Viking, 1941. / Raffi. *Five Little Ducks*. Crown, 1988. / Rankin, Joan. *Wow! It's Great Being a Duck*. McElderry, 1998. / Simmons, Jane. *Come Along, Daisy*. Little, Brown, 1998. / Simmons, Jane. *Daisy and the Egg*. Little, Brown, 1998. / Simmons, Jane. *Little Fern's First Winter*. Little, Brown, 2001. / Stott, Dorothy. *Too Much*. Dutton, 1990. / Waddell, Martin. *Webster J. Duck*. Candlewick, 2001. / Whippo, Walt, and Bernard Zaritzky. *Little White Duck*. Little, Brown, 2000.

SUBJECTS: DUCKS. MOTHERS. NOISE. POND LIFE.

733   Simms, Laura. *Rotten Teeth.* **Illus. by David Catrow. Houghton Mifflin, 1998. 0-395-82850-3. Unp. Gr. K–2**

Melissa Herman, the shortest and shyest person in her first-grade class, can't think of anything special enough to bring to school for Show and Tell until her smart big brother, Nathan, helps her get down the big glass bottle of authentic pulled teeth from their dad's dentist office. Her teacher, Mrs. Swann, is not amused, but Melissa discovers her own talent for telling interesting stories.

GERM: Here's an example of a straightforward story rendered fantastical by exaggerated watercolors that show an elephant mowing the lawn and a tree growing in the house. Talk about the role of an illustrator as someone who extends the text and have children point out all the strange goings-on at Melissa's house. They can draw other rooms in the same vein. Talk it over: How did Melissa's Show and Tell change her life? What does a storyteller do? From the back flap we learn that the author, esteemed storyteller Laura Simms, based the story on her childhood experiences. Have children tell, write, and illustrate stories based on their own lives.

RELATED TITLES: Birdseye, Tom. *Airmail to the Moon*. Holiday House, 1988. / Chandra, Deborah, and Madeline Comora. *George Washington's Teeth*. Farrar, 2003. / Clement, Rod. *Just Another Ordinary Day*. HarperCollins, 1997. / Davis, Katie. *Mabel the Tooth Fairy and How She Got Her Job*. Harcourt, 2003. / Joyce, William. *A Day with Wilbur Robinson*. HarperCollins, 1993. / Keller, Laurie. *Open Wide: Tooth School Inside*. Henry Holt, 2000. / Legge, David. *Bamboozled*. Scholastic, 1995. / Lowry, Lois. *Gooney Bird Greene*. Houghton Mifflin, 2002. / MacDonald, Amy. *Cousin Ruth's Tooth*. Houghton Mifflin, 1996. / McGhee, Alison. *Mrs. Watson Wants Your Teeth*. Harcourt, 2004. / Palatini, Margie. *Sweet Tooth*. Simon & Schuster, 2004. / Reiss, Mike. *The Great Show-and-Tell Disaster*. Price Stern Sloan, 2001. / Steig, William. *Doctor DeSoto*. Farrar, 1982.

SUBJECTS: DENTISTS AND DENTAL CARE. ENGLISH LANGUAGE—HYPERBOLE. SCHOOLS. SHOW-AND-TELL PRESENTATIONS. STORYTELLING. TEETH. UNDERSTATEMENT.

734 **Simont, Marc. *The Stray Dog*. Illus. by the author. HarperCollins, 2001. 0-06-028933-3. Unp. Gr. PreK–2**

A scruffy little stray dog shows up at a family's picnic and spends a joyous day cavorting with the brother and sister, who name him Willy. Although they leave him behind, the children and their parents have Willy on their minds all week long. Saturday finds the whole family back at the picnic site, glancing furtively around. There he is! But OH NO, he's being chased by a dog warden with a net.

GERM: A Caldecott Honor winner, this is spare and easy to read, with joyful watercolors, perfect for the youngest readers or listeners. Before reading the story aloud, show just the pictures and have the children tell the story from what they see. Write down their narration and then compare it with the written text when you read it aloud, and you'll almost certainly find many similarities. Children can tell about or write and illustrate the story of how they came to acquire their pets.

RELATED TITLES: Banks, Kate. *The Cat Who Walked Across France*. Farrar, 2004. / Feiffer, Jules. *Bark, George!* HarperCollins, 1999. / George, Kristine O'Connell. *Little Dog Poems*. Clarion, 1999. / Graeber, Charlotte. *Nobody's Dog*. Hyperion, 1998. / Graham, Bob. *"Let's Get a Pup!" Said Kate*. Candlewick, 2001. / Joosse, Barbara M. *Nugget and Darling*. Clarion, 1997. / Kellogg, Steven. *Pinkerton, Behave*. Dial, 1979. / LaRochelle, David. *The Best Pet of All*. Dutton, 2004. / L'Engle, Madeleine. *The Other Dog*. SeaStar, 2001. / McFarland, Lyn Rossiter. *Widget*. Farrar, 2001. / Rylant, Cynthia. *The Great Gracie Chase*. Scholastic, 2001. / Thayer, Jane. *The Puppy Who Wanted a Boy*. Morrow, 1986. / Voake, Charlotte. *Ginger Finds a Home*. Candlewick, 2003. / Wells, Rosemary. *Lucy Comes to Stay*. Dial, 1994. / Wells, Rosemary. *McDuff Moves In*. Hyperion, 1997. (And others in the McDuff series.) / Wolf, Jake. *Daddy, Could I Have an Elephant?* Greenwillow, 1996.

SUBJECTS: DOGS. FAMILY LIFE. PICNICS. STRAY ANIMALS.

735 **Sisulu, Elinor Batezat. *The Day Gogo Went to Vote, April 1994*. Illus. by Sharon Wilson. Little, Brown, 1996. 0-316-70267-6. Unp. Gr. 2–6**

Young Thembi's caretaker—her 100-year-old great-grandmother, Gogo—insists on going to the voting booth on April 27, 1994, the day of the first elections in which black South Africans were permitted to vote. Though she has not left the house for years, Gogo is adamant about casting her ballot, in spite of facing a long bus ride and lines at the polls, asking Thembi's parents, "You want me to die not having voted?"

GERM: This picture book with dark but joyous pastel illustrations has an important implicit message of never giving up the fight for one's political rights. With older children, this can lead to a study and discussion of voting, the history of apartheid in South Africa, and the fight for civil rights in the United States. Also read Emily Arnold McCully's *The Ballot Box Battle* and Margaree King Mitchell's *Granddaddy's Gift* and talk about one's obligation to participate in elections.

RELATED TITLES: Christelow, Eileen. *VOTE!* Clarion, 2003. / Fritz, Jean. *You Want Women to Vote, Lizzie Stanton?* Putnam, 1995. / Isadora, Rachel. *At the Crossroads*. Morrow, 1994. / McCully, Emily Arnold. *The Ballot Box Battle*. Knopf, 1996. / Mitchell, Margaree King. *Granddaddy's Gift*. BridgeWater, 1997. / White, Linda Arms. *I Could Do That: Esther Morris Gets Women the Vote*. Farrar, 2005. / Wooldridge, Connie Nordhielm. *When Esther Morris Headed West: Women, Wyoming, and the Right to Vote*. Holiday House, 2001.

SUBJECTS: BLACKS—SOUTH AFRICA. GREAT-GRANDMOTHERS. MULTICULTURAL BOOKS. PICTURE BOOKS FOR OLDER READERS. SOUTH AFRICA. VOTING.

736   Slate, Joseph. *Miss Bindergarten Celebrates the 100th Day of Kindergarten.* **Illus. by Ashley Wolff. Dutton, 1998. 0-525-46000-4. Unp. Gr. PreK–1**

If your class has a 100th day of school celebration every year, this is the book you've been waiting for to help kick it off. Miss Bindergarten, the on-the-go black-and-white dog teacher we met and loved in *Miss Bindergarten Gets Ready for Kindergarten*, is now preparing for her class's 100th day. Each one in the alphabetical roster of 26 animal pupils goes home to finish assembling a collection of 100 wonderful things to bring to school.

GERM: There's the chantable title refrain, a rhyming description of inventive projects, and a visual feast of ideas incorporated into every page of the bright watercolor and gouache illustrations. Get ready to party and ask your students to assemble new collections of 100 items not already displayed in the story. Other fine titles that rally around school and the number 100 include Margery Cuyler's *100th Day Worries*, Betsy Franco's *Counting Our Way to the 100th Day!*, Angela S. Medearis's *100th Day of School*, and Rosemary Wells's *Emily's First 100 Days of School*. For a mere 300 celebration ideas, check out Joan Holub's 100th Day of School Web site at <users.aol.com/a100thday/ideas.html>.

RELATED TITLES: Cuyler, Margery. *100th Day Worries.* Simon & Schuster, 2000. / Franco, Betsy. *Counting Our Way to the 100th Day!* McElderry, 2004. / Frith, Margaret. *I'll Teach My Dog 100 Words.* Random House, 1973. / Kasza, Keiko. *The Wolf's Chicken Stew.* Putnam, 1987. / Medearis, Angela S. *The 100th Day of School.* Scholastic, 1996. / Pinczes, Elinor J. *One Hundred Hungry Ants.* Houghton Mifflin, 1993. / Rockwell, Anne. *100 School Days.* HarperCollins, 2002. / Slate, Joseph. *Miss Bindergarten Gets Ready for Kindergarten.* Dutton, 1996. / Wells, Rosemary. *Emily's First 100 Days of School.* Hyperion, 2000. / Wells, Rosemary. *My Kindergarten.* Hyperion, 2004.

SUBJECTS: ALPHABET BOOKS. ANIMALS. CELEBRATIONS. KINDERGARTEN. ONE HUNDREDTH DAY CELEBRATIONS. SCHOOLS. STORIES IN RHYME. TEACHERS.

737   Slate, Joseph. *Miss Bindergarten Gets Ready for Kindergarten.* **Illus. by Ashley Wolff. Dutton, 1996. 0-525-45446-2. Unp. Gr. PreK–1**

As the black-and-white dog teacher readies her room for her new class, the 26 animal children are getting up and at 'em for their first day at school. Told in rhyme, the alphabetically ordered students get dressed and make their way to school via bike, foot, and bus. Bright watercolor and gouache illustrations of the eager new classmates, each with an alliterative name and a matching action verb, will cheer up your human brood and make them happy to be together.

GERM: See how many alliterative rhymes your children can think up for their own names. Reminisce about how you all spent time getting ready for the first day of school.

RELATED TITLES: Baer, Edith. *This Is the Way We Go to School: A Book About Children Around the World.* Scholastic, 1990. / Child, Lauren. *I Am Too Absolutely Small for School.* Candlewick, 2004. / Dannenberg, Julie. *First Day Jitters.* Charlesbridge, 2000. / Finchler, Judy. *Miss Malarkey Doesn't Live in Room 10.* Walker, 1995. / Henkes, Kevin. *Chrysanthemum.* Greenwillow, 1991. / Hest, Amy. *Off to School, Baby Duck.* Candlewick, 1999. / Johnson, Dolores. *What Will Mommy Do When I'm at School?* Macmillan, 1990. / Lasky, Kathryn. *Lunch Bunnies.* Little, Brown, 1996. / McGhee, Alison. *Countdown to Kindergarten.* Harcourt, 2002. / Poydar, Nancy. *First Day, Hooray.* Holiday House, 1999. / Russo, Marisabina. *I Don't Want to Go Back to School.* Greenwillow, 1994. / Schwartz, Amy. *Annabelle Swift, Kindergartner.* Orchard, 1988. / Stuve-Bodeen, Stephanie. *Elizabeti's Doll.* Lee & Low, 1998. / Wells, Rosemary. *My Kindergarten.* Hyperion, 2004.

SUBJECTS: ALLITERATION. ALPHABET BOOKS. ANIMALS. FIRST DAY OF SCHOOL. KINDERGARTEN. SCHOOLS. STORIES IN RHYME. TEACHERS.

738   Slate, Joseph. *Miss Bindergarten Stays Home from Kindergarten.* **Illus. by Ashley Wolff. Dutton, 2000. 0-525-46396-8. Unp. Gr. PreK–K**

Poor Miss Bindergarten, black-and-white dog teacher to 26 animal children, has the flu, so Mr. Tusky, a gentle elephant, takes over for four days of activity-filled kindergarten subbing.

GERM: This rhyming, alliterative, animal alphabet story introduces the days of the week as each class member succumbs to illness, and is a fiitting read for when you're getting or have had a substitute. Children can draw a picture of what they did while you were gone, portraying themselves as new alliterative animals in Miss B's class. Meet the school support staff—librarian, custodian, nurse, and principal—in *Miss Bindergarten Has a Wild Day in Kindergarten*.

RELATED TITLES: Cherry, Lynne. *Who's Sick Today?* Dutton, 1988. / Havill, Juanita. *Jamaica and the Substi-*

tute Teacher. Houghton Mifflin, 1999. / LeGuin, Ursula K. *A Visit from Dr. Katz*. Atheneum, 1988. / Loomis, Christine. *One Cow Coughs*. Ticknor & Fields, 1994. / Slate, Joseph. *Miss Bindergarten Celebrates the 100th Day of Kindergarten*. Dutton, 1998. / Slate, Joseph. *Miss Bindergarten Gets Ready for Kindergarten*. Dutton, 1996. / Slate, Joseph. *Miss Bindergarten Has a Wild Day in Kindergarten*. Dutton, 2005. / Stanley, Diane. *Raising Sweetness*. Putnam, 1999. / Wells, Rosemary. *Felix Feels Better*. Candlewick, 2001. / Wells, Rosemary. *My Kindergarten*. Hyperion, 2004.

SUBJECTS: ALLITERATION. ALPHABET BOOKS. ANIMALS. KINDERGARTEN. SCHOOLS. SICK. STORIES IN RHYME. SUBSTITUTE TEACHERS. TEACHERS.

739   Slate, Joseph. *Miss Bindergarten Takes a Field Trip with Kindergarten*. **Illus. by Ashley Wolff. Dutton, 2001. 0-525-46710-6. Unp. Gr. PreK–K**

Along with her 26 alliteratively named animal students, genial Miss Bindergarten breezes through the bakery, the fire station, the post office, the public library, and the park in an entertaining and informative all-day class trip.

GERM: Finally! A fun and undidactic book about community helpers to kick off that social studies unit.

RELATED TITLES: Caseley, Judith. *On the Town*. Greenwillow, 2002. / Demarest, Chris L. *Firefighters A to Z*. McElderry, 2000. / MacLean, Christine Kole. *Even Firefighters Hug Their Moms*. Dutton, 2002. / Markes, Julie. *Shhhhh! Everybody's Sleeping*. HarperCollins, 2005. / Skurzynski, Gloria. *Here Comes the Mail*. Bradbury, 1992. / Slate, Joseph. *Miss Bindergarten Celebrates the 100th Day of Kindergarten*. Dutton, 1998. / Slate, Joseph. *Miss Bindergarten Gets Ready for Kindergarten*. Dutton, 1996. / Slate, Joseph. *Miss Bindergarten Stays Home from Kindergarten*. Dutton, 2000. / Van Laan, Nancy. *People, People, Everywhere!* Knopf, 1992. / Wellington, Monica. *Mr. Cookie Baker*. Dutton, 1992. / Wells, Rosemary. *Emily's First 100 Days of School*. Hyperion, 2000. / Wells, Rosemary. *My Kindergarten*. Hyperion, 2004. / Wells, Rosemary. *Yoko's Paper Cranes*. Hyperion, 2001. / Williams, Suzanne. *Library Lil*. Dial, 1997.

SUBJECTS: ALLITERATION. ALPHABET BOOKS. ANIMALS. COMMUNITIES. KINDERGARTEN. OCCUPATIONS. SCHOOLS. STORIES IN RHYME. TEACHERS.

740   Slate, Joseph. *Story Time for Little Porcupine*. **Illus. by Jacqueline Rogers. Marshall Cavendish, 2000. 0-7614-5073-4. Unp. Gr. PreK–1**

At bedtime, Little Porcupine wants Papa Porcupine to tell him the story of how the Big Porcupine in the Sky got his spines, and Papa tells him that pourquoi tale. Next, Papa tells about Big Porcupine's picnic, which explains why we have sunsets, and finally, "How Big Porcupine Fooled the Moon," which explains why there are stars.

GERM: Warm and tender watercolors will get everyone wanting to ask for bedtime stories told by loving parents. Have them retell the porcupine legends to their parents and ask them to share other stories that explain the hows and whys of the world. A possum's mama tells him a good story in *Why Epossumondas Has No Hair on His Tail* by Coleen Salley.

RELATED TITLES: Lester, Helen. *A Porcupine Named Fluffy*. Houghton Mifflin, 1986. / Salley, Coleen. *Why Epossumondas Has No Hair on His Tail*. Harcourt, 2004. / Slate, Joseph. *Little Porcupine's Christmas*. HarperCollins, 2001. / Waber, Bernard. *Bearsie Bear and the Surprise Sleepover Party*. Houghton Mifflin, 1997.

SUBJECTS: BEDTIME STORIES. FATHERS AND SONS. MOON. PICNICS. PORCUPINES. POURQUOI TALES. STORYTELLING. SUN.

741   Sloat, Teri. *Patty's Pumpkin Patch*. **Illus. by the author. Putnam, 1999. 0-399-23010-6. Unp. Gr. PreK–1**

In her blue overalls, specs, and a hat, Patty takes us through the alphabet as she plants, waters, weeds, and cares for her growing pumpkins, selling them at her farm stand for Halloween.

GERM: An alphabet of animals and small illustrations runs along the bottom of each page. Sharp-eyed readers will spot each animal—Ant, Beetle, Crow, Dragonfly, etc.—in the main illustration, in which Patty is working in her field. Bring in pumpkins to carve, and roast and eat the seeds.

RELATED TITLES: Cherry, Lynne. *How Groundhog's Garden Grew*. Scholastic, 2003. / Coy, John. *Two Old Potatoes and Me*. Knopf, 2003. / Gibbons, Gail. *From Seed to Plant*. Holiday House, 1991. / Hall, Zoe. *It's Pumpkin Time!* Scholastic, 1994. / Johnston, Tony. *The Vanishing Pumpkin*. Putnam, 1983. / McDonald, Megan. *The Great Pumpkin Switch*. Orchard, 1992. / Pfeffer, Wendy. *From Seed to Pumpkin*. HarperCollins, 2004. / Powell, Consie. *Amazing Apples*. Albert Whitman, 2003. / Schaefer, Lola M. *Pick, Pull, Snap! Where Once a Flower Bloomed*. HarperCollins, 2003. / Silverman, Erica. *Big Pumpkin*. Macmillan, 1992. / Williams, Linda. *The Little Old Lady Who Was Not Afraid of Anything*. Crowell, 1986.

SUBJECTS: ALPHABET BOOKS. GARDENING. HALLOWEEN. PUMPKINS. SEEDS. STORIES IN RHYME. VEGETABLES.

742   **Smith, Lane.** *The Happy Hocky Family Moves to the Country.* **Illus. by the author. Viking, 2003. 0-670-03594-7. 61pp. Gr. 1–3**

In this takeoff of old-fashioned easy-readers of Dick and Jane vintage, Mr. and Mrs. Hocky and their three kids move to a leaking country house and encounter smelly animals, poison ivy, and the country fair.

GERM: As in *The Happy Hocky Family*, the short chapters, or vignettes, are wildly funny examples of understatement, all of which would be great fun for pairs or trios of children to read and act out as simple skits.

RELATED TITLES: Clement, Rod. *Just Another Ordinary Day.* HarperCollins, 1997. / Denim, Sue. *Make Way for Dumb Bunnies.* Scholastic, 1996. / DiCamillo, Kate. *Mercy Watson to the Rescue.* Candlewick, 2005. / Legge, David. *Bamboozled.* Scholastic, 1995. / MacDonald, Ross. *Another Perfect Day.* Roaring Brook, 2002. / Pilkey, Dav. *Dog Breath: The Horrible Trouble with Hally Tosis.* Scholastic, 1994. / Pilkey, Dav. *Dogzilla.* Harcourt, 1993. / Pilkey, Dav. *Kat Kong.* Harcourt, 1993. / Smith, Lane. *The Happy Hocky Family!* Viking, 1993.

SUBJECTS: COUNTRY LIFE. FAMILY LIFE. HUMOROUS FICTION. PARODIES. PICTURE BOOKS FOR ALL AGES. READER'S THEATER. UNDERSTATEMENT.

743   **Smith, Maggie.** *Paisley.* **Illus. by the author. Knopf, 2004. 0-375-82164-3. Unp. Gr. PreK–1**

Paisley, a blue stuffed elephant on a toy store shelf, describes his arduous and perilous quest to find the Perfect Match, the Special Someone who will love him and take him home.

GERM: Note how the stuffed animal's point of view does not always match what is actually happening to him in the illustrations. How would his new little girl describe her version of the story? Match this with Don Freeman's *Corduroy* and Satomi Ichikawa's *La La Rose,* narrated by the stuffed bunny who gets left behind by her little girl.

RELATED TITLES: Alborough, Jez. *Where's My Teddy?* Candlewick, 1992. / Clark, Emma Chichester. *Where Are You, Blue Kangaroo?* Doubleday, 2000. / Cocca-Leffler, Maryann. *Missing: One Stuffed Rabbit.* Albert Whitman, 1998. / Falconer, Ian. *Olivia . . . and the Missing Toy.* Atheneum, 2003. / Feiffer, Jules. *I Lost My Bear.* Morrow, 1998. / Fitzpatrick, Marie-Louise. *Lizzy and Skunk.* DK Ink, 2000. / Freeman, Don. *Corduroy.* Viking, 1968. / Hughes, Shirley. *Dogger.* Lothrop, 1988. / Ichikawa, Satomi. *La La Rose.* Philomel, 2004. / Sheldon, Dyan. *Love, Your Bear Pete.* Candlewick, 1994. / Willems, Mo. *Knuffle Bunny: A Cautionary Tale.* Hyperion, 2004.

SUBJECTS: ELEPHANTS. LOST AND FOUND POSSESSIONS. PERSONAL NARRATIVES. POINT OF VIEW. STUFFED ANIMALS. TOYS.

744   **Smothers, Ethel Footman.** *The Hard-Times Jar.* **Illus. by John Holyfield. Farrar, 2003. 0-374-32852-8. Unp. Gr. K–3**

"No extras," says Emma's mother when Emma yearns for her own store-bought book. Emma and her family are migrant workers, following the crops, and money is scarce. Mama keeps a jar of coins for emergencies, and Emma makes her own books from brown grocery bag paper, on which she composes her stories. When her parents send her to school, she loses herself in the third-grade classroom library and sneaks two books home, even though she knows it's against the rules.

GERM: Talk over the ethics of this sobering but hopeful autobiographical tale. Why doesn't Emma own any of her own books? Why does she take two books home from her classroom? Why does her mother make her tell her teacher what she has done? Why does her mother then give her money from the hard-times jar? Then meet another girl who loves books in Amada Irma Pérez's *My Very Own Room* and Chico, whose family moves to California for grape-picking season in L. King Pérez's *First Day in Grapes.*

RELATED TITLES: Bradby, Marie. *More Than Anything Else.* Orchard, 1995. / Gray, Libba Moore. *Little Lil and the Swing-Singing Sax.* Simon & Schuster, 1996. / Howard, Elizabeth Fitzgerald. *Virgie Goes to School with Us Boys.* Simon & Schuster, 2000. / Medina, Jane. *The Dream on Blanca's Wall: Poems in English and Spanish.* Wordsong/Boyds Mills, 2004. / Pérez, Amada Irma. *My Very Own Room/Mi Proprio Cuartito.* Children's Book Press, 2000. / Pérez, L. King. *First Day in Grapes.* Lee & Low, 2002. / Williams, Vera. *A Chair for my Mother.* Greenwillow, 1982.

SUBJECTS: AFRICAN AMERICANS. BOOKS AND READING. HONESTY. MIGRANT LABOR. MULTICULTURAL BOOKS. SCHOOLS.

745   Sobel, June. *B Is for Bulldozer: A Construction ABC.* **Illus. by Melissa Iwai. Harcourt, 2003. 0-15-202250-3. Unp. Gr. PreK–1**

From the Asphalt that paves the road to the Zoom of the roller coaster, watch the men and women construction workers get the new amusement park ready for its grand opening.

GERM: Take another ride with Marla Frazee's picture book *Roller Coaster*. Look at other alphabetical ways to build with *Alphabet Under Construction* by Denise Fleming.

RELATED TITLES: Barton, Byron. *Building a House.* Greenwillow, 1981. / Burton, Virginia Lee. *Mike Mulligan and His Steam Shovel.* Houghton Mifflin, 1939. / Fleming, Denise. *Alphabet Under Construction.* Henry Holt, 2002. / Frazee, Marla. *Roller Coaster.* Harcourt, 2003. / Lyon, David. *The Biggest Truck.* Lothrop, 1988. / McMullan, Kate. *I Stink!* HarperCollins, 2002. / Schotter, Roni. *Dreamland.* Orchard, 1996.

SUBJECTS: ALPHABET BOOKS. AMUSEMENT PARKS. CONSTRUCTION EQUIPMENT. MACHINES. MULTICULTURAL BOOKS. ROLLER COASTERS. STORIES IN RHYME.

746   Sorel, Edward, and Cheryl Carlesimo. *The Saturday Kid.* **Illus. by Edward Sorel. McElderry, 2000. 0-689-82399-1. Unp. Gr. K–4**

In this affectionate tribute to New York City and the movies of the 1930s, Leo loves playing the violin and going to the movies at the Luxor Theater on Saturdays with his pals, even though Morty the Troublemaker always tries to spoil things. This satisfying and funny period piece—full of old movies and large, detailed, pen-and-ink and watercolor illustrations—shows how Leo plays violin at the Mayor's Young Musician's concert, where he shakes hands with the mayor (Fiorello LaGuardia) and shows up that smartypants, Morty.

GERM: Each time Leo thinks about that bully Morty, he fantasizes that he is in a movie getting revenge. Talk with your movie buffs about their favorite films. Have them write about and draw themselves in a memorable movie scene. You'll want to show the kids some Laurel and Hardy shorts to go along with your reading. Tomie dePaola's autobiography, *26 Fairmount Avenue*, also gives a vivid description of the same time period; there's a wonderful chapter where he goes to the movies to see *Snow White*.

RELATED TITLES: Curtis, Gavin. *The Bat Boy and His Violin.* Simon & Schuster, 1998. / dePaola, Tomie. *26 Fairmount Avenue.* Putnam, 1999. / Feiffer, Jules. *Meanwhile . . .* HarperCollins, 1997. / Jakobsen, Kathy. *My New York.* Little, Brown, 2003. / Peterson, Beth. *Myrna Never Sleeps.* Atheneum, 1995. / Sorel, Edward. *Johnny on the Spot.* McElderry, 1998.

SUBJECTS: BULLIES. CITIES AND TOWNS. HISTORICAL FICTION. MAYORS. MOTION PICTURES. NEW YORK CITY. PICTURE BOOKS FOR OLDER READERS. VIOLINS.

747   Soto, Gary. *Chato and the Party Animals.* **Illus. by Susan Guevara. Putnam, 2000. 0-399-23159-5. Unp. Gr. PreK–2**

Cool cat Chato is shocked when his best barrio buddy, stray cat Novio Boy, confesses he has never had a birthday party and doesn't even know when he was born. "*Pobrecito,*" Chato says and plans a surprise bash. Then, after the party is under way, he exclaims, "*Que tonto!*" (How dumb), when he realizes he has neglected to invite the guest of honor.

GERM: Spanish words and expressions are integrated into this hip hop, zesty sequel to *Chato's Kitchen*. Children can draw and describe the presents they'd give Novio Boy for his birthday. Try a bit of creative drama with the party games the cats play, such as Shake-Paws, Jiggle-the-Mice, Toss-the-Cat-in-the-Blanket, and, my personal favorite, Going to the Vet, where you have to scream your head off. Also read *Chato's Kitchen*, in which Chato invites the five fat, juicy, gray mice who just moved in next door for a nice dinner.

RELATED TITLES: Dorros, Arthur. *Abuela.* Dutton, 1991. / Elya, Susan Middleton. *Eight Animals Bake a Cake.* Putnam, 2002. / Elya, Susan Middleton. *Eight Animals on the Town.* Putnam, 2000. / Elya, Susan Middleton. *Fairy Trails: A Story Told in English and Spanish.* Bloomsbury, 2005. / Elya, Susan Middleton. *Say Hola to Spanish.* Lee & Low, 1996. / France, Anthony. *From Me to You.* Candlewick, 2003. / Kleven, Elisa. *Hooray, a Piñata!* Dutton, 1996. / Reed, Lynn. *Pedro, His Perro, and the Alphabet Sombrero.* Hyperion, 1995. / Ryan, Pam Muñoz. *Mice and Beans.* Scholastic, 2001. / Sacre, Antonio. *The Barking Mouse.* Whitman, 2003. / Soto, Gary. *Chato Goes Cruisin'.* Putnam, 2005. / Soto, Gary. *Chato's Kitchen.* Putnam, 1995. / Soto, Gary. *Snapshots from the Wedding.* Putnam, 1997. / Waber, Bernard. *Bearsie Bear and the Surprise Sleepover Party.* Houghton Mifflin, 1997.

SUBJECTS: BIRTHDAYS. CALIFORNIA. CATS. CREATIVE DRAMA. LOS ANGELES (CALIFORNIA). MEXICAN AMERICANS. MULTICULTURAL BOOKS. PARTIES. SPANISH LANGUAGE.

748   Soto, Gary. *Snapshots from the Wedding.* **Illus. by Stephanie Garcia. Putnam, 1997. 0-399-22808-X. Unp. Gr. 1–3**

Flower girl Maya narrates each "snapshot" scene of Rafael and Isabel's memorable Mexican American wedding, taking us down the aisle and to the reception. Children will pore over the extraordinary three-dimensional artwork—done in sculpy clay, acrylics, wood, fabric, and found objects—to figure out how each picture was put together.

GERM: Enterprising teachers will get students doing shadowbox scenes from their own lives. Children can also write about weddings they've experienced.

RELATED TITLES: Baraschi, Lynne. *The Reluctant Flower Girl.* HarperCollins, 2001. / Cox, Judy. *Now We Can Have a Wedding.* Holiday House, 1998. / English, Karen. *Nadia's Hands.* Boyds Mills, 1999. / Lomas Garza, Carmen. *Family Pictures/Cuadros de Familia.* Children's Book Press, 1990. / Lomas Garza, Carmen. *In My Family/En Mi Familia.* Children's Book Press, 1996. / Manzano, Sonia. *No Dogs Allowed!* Atheneum, 2004. / Medina, Jane. *The Dream on Blanca's Wall: Poems in English and Spanish.* Wordsong/Boyds Mills, 2004. / Park, Barbara. Junie B. Jones series. Random. / Soto, Gary. *Too Many Tamales.* Putnam, 1993.

SUBJECTS: MEXICAN AMERICANS. MULTICULTURAL BOOKS. WEDDINGS.

749   Stadler, Alexander. *Beverly Billingsly Can't Catch.* **Illus. by the author. Harcourt, 2004. 0-15-204906-1. Unp. Gr. K–2**

Oliver points out to his friend Beverly that they are always the last ones picked for softball. She stops at the library to find a book to read on how to play the game, and librarian Mrs. Del Rubio says, "That's a very interesting approach, Beverly . . . Have you ever considered practicing?" Mrs. Del Rubio agrees to coach the two friends, giving them the best advice: "The more you play, the better you become." And they do.

GERM: You'll love to see that when the two bear friends, Beverly and Oliver, aren't practicing, they're at the library, studying the rules and history of baseball. (Make the acquaintance of their spiffy librarian in *Beverly Billingsly Borrows a Book.*) Introduce your sports fans to the 796 section of the library and watch the books fly off the shelves. This is on target for both camps: the athletes who could stand to read more and the readers who could stand to play more. Get outside and play a little softball with your sluggers. LouAnn Parrino's second graders at Van Holten School in Bridgewater, New Jersey, picked their own areas of expertise and wrote expository and inspirational essays giving advice to others, starting, "If you want to be good at ____, you need to ____."

RELATED TITLES: Corey, Shana. *Players in Pigtails.* Scholastic, 2003. / Egan, Tim. *Roasted Peanuts.* Houghton Mifflin, 2006. / Elya, Susan Middleton. *Eight Animals Play Ball.* Putnam, 2003. / Finchler, Judy. *You're a Good Sport, Miss Malarkey.* Walker, 2002. / Hamm, Mia. *Winners Never Quit!* HarperCollins, 2004. / Lasky, Kathryn. *Tumble Bunnies.* Little, Brown, 2005. / McCully, Emily Arnold. *Mouse Practice.* Scholastic, 1999. / Mammano, Julie. *Rhinos Who Play Baseball.* Chronicle, 2003. / Mills, Claudia. *Ziggy's Blue-Ribbon Day.* Farrar, 2005. / Norworth, Jack. *Take Me Out to the Ballgame.* Four Winds, 1993. / Stadler, Alexander. *Beverly Billingsly Borrows a Book.* Harcourt, 2002. / Stadler, Alexander. *Beverly Billingsly Takes a Bow.* Harcourt, 2003. (And others in the Beverly Billingsly series.) / Teague, Mark. *The Field Beyond the Outfield.* Scholastic, 1992. / Waber, Bernard. *Gina.* Houghton Mifflin, 1995. / Welch, Willie. *Playing Right Field.* Scholastic, 1995.

SUBJECTS: BASEBALL. BEARS. DETERMINATION. FRIENDSHIP. LIBRARIANS. SPORTS.

750   Stadler, Alexander. *Beverly Billingsly Takes a Bow.* **Illus. by the author. Harcourt, 2003. 0-15-216816-8. Unp. Gr. K–2**

Beverly looks forward to auditioning for the school play, but when it's her turn, she freezes and is given only a small role. What's nice about this charmer of a story, with its gouache illustrations outlined in heavy black ink, is that Beverly does not star in the play, but she is nonetheless a champ, helping with every aspect of the production, which is a good object lesson for all actors.

GERM: Discussion point: What does Beverly's father mean when he quotes, "There are no small parts, only small actors"? Look at another determined performer in James Howe's *Horace and Morris Join the Chorus (But What About Dolores?).*

RELATED TITLES: Best, Cari. *Shrinking Violet.* Farrar, 2001. / Dodds, Dayle Ann. *Sing, Sophie.* Candlewick, 1997. / Goss, Linda. *The Frog Who Wanted to Be a Singer.* Orchard, 1996. / Hoffman, Mary. *Amazing Grace.* Dial, 1991. / Howe, James. *Horace and Morris Join the Chorus (But What About Dolores?).* Atheneum, 2002. / Lewison, Wendy Cheyette. *Shy Vi.* Simon & Schuster, 1993. / McCully, Emily Arnold. *Speak Up, Blanche!* HarperCollins, 1991. / Stadler, Alexander. *Beverly Billingsly Borrows a Book.* Harcourt, 2002. / Stadler, Alexander. *Beverly Billingsly Can't Catch.* Harcourt, 2004. (And others in the Beverly Billingsly series.) / Waber, Bernard. *Evie and Margie.* Houghton Mifflin, 2003.

SUBJECTS: ACTING. AUDITIONS. PLAYS. SCHOOLS. SELF-ESTEEM. STAGE FRIGHT.

751   **Stadler, Alexander.** *Lila Bloom.* **Illus. by the author. Farrar, 2004. 0-374-34474-4. Unp. Gr. 1–4**
In the midst of a miserable day, Lila Bloom announces her desire to quit ballet, which she claims she despises. Noting Lila's lackluster performance, her teacher, Madame Vera, calls her bluff, observing that she has been dancing "like an old noodle." "I'll show her," huffs infuriated Lila, and she begins to dance with utmost grace, strength, and delicacy, until "something interesting" happens to change her mind about ballet.
GERM: Discussion point: Lila intended to quit ballet, but ended up taking on an extra weekly class. Why did she want to quit? What was the "something interesting" that changed her mind and her attitude? What is your true talent or passion, the thing that you do or like best of all? What happens to you when you are doing it? Ask your kids how they find their bliss. See if the phys ed teacher can do some ballet with the group. Mention, especially to the groaning boys, that to prepare for this book, the author, a boy, took ballet lessons. Athletes do ballet too, you know.
RELATED TITLES: Curtis, Gavin. *The Bat Boy and His Violin.* Simon & Schuster, 1998. / Geras, Adèle. *Time for Ballet.* Dial, 2004. / Hoffman, Mary. *Amazing Grace.* Dial, 1991. / Isadora, Rachel. *Max.* Macmillan, 1976. / Littlesugar, Amy. *Marie in Fourth Position: The Story of Degas' "The Little Dancer."* Philomel, 1996. / Montenegro, Laura Nyman. *A Bird About to Sing.* Houghton Mifflin, 2003. / Reynolds, Peter H. *The Dot.* Candlewick, 2003. / Reynolds, Peter H. *Ish.* Candlewick, 2004. / Schwartz, Amy. *Begin at the Beginning: A Little Artist Learns About Life.* HarperCollins, 2005. / Stadler, Alexander. *Beverly Billingsly Can't Catch.* Harcourt, 2004. (And others in the Beverly Billingsly series.) / Viorst, Judith. *Alexander and the Terrible, Horrible, No Good, Very Bad Day.* Atheneum, 1972. / Waber, Bernard. *Gina.* Houghton Mifflin, 1995.
SUBJECTS: ANGER. BALLET. BEHAVIOR. DEDICATION. EMOTIONS. PICTURE BOOKS FOR ALL AGES. SELF-CONCEPT.

752   **Stanley, Diane.** *The Giant and the Beanstalk.* **Illus. by the author. HarperCollins, 2004. 0-06-000011-2. Unp. Gr. PreK–2**
Otto may be a big giant with razor-sharp teeth, beady little eyes, and enormous menacing claws, but he's embarrassingly polite and dotes on Clara, his pet hen, who lays golden eggs. When a human comes a-calling and steals Clara, Otto heads down the beanstalk to find the boy named Jack who took her. Unfortunately for Otto, there are lots of Jacks down below: one jumping over a candlestick, another rolling down a hill, and three more besides, all of whom astute nursery rhyme lovers will recognize.
GERM: Compare this sweet story of a giant you can love with the usual "Jack and the Beanstalk" tales. The nursery rhymes alluded to in the text are conveniently listed and illustrated at the back.
RELATED TITLES: Briggs, Raymond. *Jim and the Beanstalk.* Putnam, 1989. / Child, Lauren. *Beware of the Storybook Wolves.* Scholastic, 2001. / Child, Lauren. *Who's Afraid of the Big Bad Book?* Hyperion, 2003. / Compton, Paul. *Jack the Giant Chaser.* Holiday House, 1993. / Cuyler, Margery. *Big Friends.* Walker, 2004. / Garner, Alan. *Jack and the Beanstalk.* Doubleday, 1992. / Haley, Gail E. *Jack and the Bean Tree.* Crown, 1986. / Hawkins, Colin, and Jacqui Hawkins. *The Fairytale News.* Candlewick, 2004. / Hoberman, Mary Ann. *You Read to Me, I'll Read to You: Very Short Fairy Tales to Read Together.* Little, Brown, 2004. / Johnson, Paul Brett. *Fearless Jack.* McElderry, 2001. / Osborne, Mary Pope. *Kate and the Beanstalk.* Atheneum, 2000. / Stevens, Janet, and Susan Stevens Crummel. *And the Dish Ran Away with the Spoon.* Harcourt, 2001. / Still, James. *Jack and the Wonder Beans.* Putnam, 1977.
SUBJECTS: CHARACTERS IN LITERATURE. CHICKENS. COWS. GIANTS. NURSERY RHYMES. PARODIES. WOLVES.

753   **Stanley, Diane.** *Goldie and the Three Bears.* **Illus. by the author. HarperCollins, 2003. 0-06-000009-0. Unp. Gr. PreK–1**
Goldie, a little blonde girl who knows exactly what she likes, is looking for a friend she can love with all her heart. On the day she gets off the school bus at the wrong stop and wanders into a house with three sandwiches, three chairs, and three beds, she finds the perfect friend.
GERM: Naturally, your readers will see the Three Bears connection here and laugh at this clever reworking of the story. Compare it with the original tale and then, inspired by Goldie's strong opinions, make picture lists of things you like and things you don't. Ask listeners: What do you love with all your heart, and what makes it perfect for you?
RELATED TITLES: Aylesworth, Jim. *Goldilocks and the Three Bears.* Scholastic, 2003. / Brett, Jan. *Goldilocks and*

the Three Bears. Putnam, 1987. / Child, Lauren. *Beware of the Storybook Wolves*. Scholastic, 2001. / Child, Lauren. *Who's Afraid of the Big Bad Book?* Hyperion, 2003. / Emberley, Michael. *Ruby and the Sniffs*. Little, Brown, 2004. / Ernst, Lisa Campbell. *Goldilocks Returns*. Simon & Schuster, 2000. / Ernst, Lisa Campbell. *Little Red Riding Hood: A Newfangled Prairie Tale*. Simon & Schuster, 1995. / Ernst, Lisa Campbell. *Stella Louella's Runaway Book*. Simon & Schuster, 1998. / McClements, George. *Jake Gander, Storyville Detective*. Hyperion, 2002. / Marshall, James. *Goldilocks and the Three Bears*. Dial, 1988. / Scieszka, Jon. *The True Story of the 3 Little Pigs*. Viking, 1989. / Stevens, Janet. *Goldilocks and the Three Bears*. Holiday House, 1986. / Wiesner, David. *The Three Pigs*. Clarion, 2001.

SUBJECTS: BEARS. CHARACTERS IN LITERATURE. FRIENDSHIP. GOLDILOCKS. PARODIES.

754   **Stanley, Diane.** *Raising Sweetness*. **Illus. by G. Brian Karas. Putnam, 1999. 0-399-23225-7. Unp. Gr. K–3**

In this sequel to *Saving Sweetness*, the housekeeping-impaired but large-hearted sheriff, newly adoptive pa to eight orphans, receives a mysterious letter that no one can read. Sweetness, the teeniest child, volunteers to stand outside the schoolhouse, where the dreaded Mrs. Sump is substitute-teaching, so that she can learn her letters.

GERM: Have listeners write up new recipes for Pa's favorite dishes, which include tuna fish soup and pickle and banana pie. Talk over why it's so danged important to learn all of those 26 letters when you want to read something.

RELATED TITLES: Auch, Mary Jane, and Herm Auch. *Souperchicken*. Holiday House, 2003. / Hest, Amy. *Mr. George Baker*. Candlewick, 2004. / Houston, Gloria. *My Great Aunt Arizona*. HarperCollins, 1992. / Johnston, Tony. *The Cowboy and the Black-Eyed Pea*. Putnam, 1992. / Lowry, Lois. *Zooman Sam*. Houghton Mifflin, 1999. / Marshall, James. *Wings: A Tale of Two Chickens*. Viking, 1986. / Nixon, Joan Lowery. *That's the Spirit, Claude*. Viking, 1992. / Polacco, Patricia. *Aunt Chip and the Great Triple Creek Dam Affair*. Philomel, 1996. / Sierra, Judy. *Wild About Books*. Knopf, 2004. / Stanley, Diane. *Saving Sweetness*. Putnam, 1996.

SUBJECTS: BOOKS AND READING. HUMOROUS FICTION. LITERACY. ORPHANS. PERSONAL NARRATIVES. PICTURE BOOKS FOR ALL AGES. POINT OF VIEW. READER'S THEATER. SHERIFFS. TEXAS.

755   **Stanley, Diane.** *Rumpelstiltskin's Daughter*. **Illus. by the author. Morrow, 1997. 0-688-14328-8. Unp. Gr. 2–5**

You remember the fairy tale where the miller's daughter was ordered by the king to spin straw into gold, and a little man came to her rescue? Turns out the story was all wrong. According to this updated account, the girl, whose name was Meredith, never married the greedy king at all, but ran off with the other guy—Rumpelstiltskin—instead. (She had a weakness for short men.) Upon learning about Meredith's now-16-year old daughter, the king has the girl kidnapped and locked in a tower until she manages to spin straw into gold. She concocts a plan to help the starving populace and teach the gold-besotted, bewigged king a thing or two in the process.

GERM: Make sure to read or tell the original folktale of "Rumpelstiltskin" first so all can appreciate this witty sequel. The theme of the story dovetails wonderfully with Demi's *One Grain of Rice*.

RELATED TITLES: Auch, Mary Jane. *The Princess and the Pizza*. Holiday House, 2002. / Bateman, Teresa. *The Princesses Have a Ball*. Albert Whitman, 2002. / Demi. *One Grain of Rice: A Mathematical Folktale*. Scholastic, 1997. / Hamilton, Virginia. *The Girl Who Spun Gold*. Scholastic, 2000. / Minters, Frances. *Sleepless Beauty*. Viking, 1996. / Moser, Barry. *Tucker Pfeffercorn: An Old Story Retold*. Little, Brown, 1994. / Ness, Evaline. *Tom Tit Tot*. Scribner, 1965. / Pitre, Felix. *Paco and the Witch*. Lodestar, 1995. / Sage, Alison. *Rumpelstiltskin*. Dial, 1990. / San Souci, Daniel D. *The Tsar's Promise*. Philomel, 1992. / Scieszka, Jon. *The True Story of the 3 Little Pigs*. Viking, 1989. / Sierra, Judy. *Can You Guess My Name? Traditional Tales Around the World*. Clarion, 2002. / White, Carolyn. *Whuppity Stoorie: A Scottish Folktale*. Putnam, 1997. / Zelinsky, Paul O. *Rumpelstiltskin*. Dutton, 1986. / Zemach, Harve. *Duffy and the Devil*. Farrar, 1986.

SUBJECTS: CHARACTERS IN LITERATURE. FAIRY TALES—SATIRE. GREED. HUMOROUS FICTION. KINGS AND RULERS. PARODIES. PICTURE BOOKS FOR ALL AGES. RUMPELSTILTSKIN STORIES.

756   **Stanley, Diane.** *Saving Sweetness*. **Illus. by G. Brian Karas. Putnam, 1996. 0-399-22645-1. Unp. Gr. K–3**

Little Sweetness, ittiest bittiest orphan, is a scrappy heroine who runs away from her Texas orphanage, presided over by the odious Mrs. Sump, and saves the dim-witted but well-meaning sheriff from outlaw Coyote Pete.

GERM: From the point of view of the narrator—the none-too-swift-witted sheriff of Possum Trot—he is the hero who saves that little orphan. You, the reader, may get a whole different perspective on who's saving whom and retell the story from the point of view of Sweetness or of the desperado, Coyote Pete. Follow up the Texas-twanged tale with the sequel, *Raising Sweetness*, in which the sheriff has adopted all eight of those orphans.

RELATED TITLES: Appelt, Kathi. *Bubba and Beau.* Harcourt, 2002. (And others in the Bubba and Beau series.) / Gerrard, Roy. *Rosie and the Rustlers.* Farrar, 1989. / Harper, Jo. *Jalapeño Hal.* Four Winds, 1993. / Icenoggle, Jopi. *'Til the Cows Come Home.* Boyds Mills, 2004. / Johnson, Paul Brett, and Celeste Lewis. *Lost.* Orchard, 1996. / Johnston, Tony. *The Cowboy and the Black-Eyed Pea.* Putnam, 1992. / Ketteman, Helen. *Bubba the Cowboy Prince: A Fractured Texas Tale.* Scholastic, 1997. / Levitin, Sonia. *Nine for California.* Orchard, 1996. / Lowell, Susan. *Cindy Ellen: A Wild Western Cinderella.* Orchard, 1997. / Nixon, Joan Lowery. *That's the Spirit, Claude.* Viking, 1992. / Stanley, Diane. *Raising Sweetness.* Putnam, 1999.

SUBJECTS: HUMOROUS FICTION. ORPHANS. PERSONAL NARRATIVES. POINT OF VIEW. ROBBERS AND OUTLAWS. SHERIFFS. TEXAS. WEST (U.S.).

757 **Steen, Sandra, and Susan Steen.** *Car Wash.* **Illus. by G. Brian Karas. Putnam, 2001. 0-399-23369-5. Unp. Gr. PreK–2**

Sitting in the back seat of their dirty car, two giggling siblings are wide-eyed as they head into the deep dark space of the car wash, an undersea adventure where their imaginations run wild. Close hatch. Submarine. Going down. Through the foamy sea they glide, past the octopus whomping and thomping the car with its giant arms. Karas's 3-D collage illustrations—made with gouache, acrylics, pencil, and odds and ends—are just right.

GERM: Before reading, ask kids who've been in a car wash to describe the experience. As you share the simple text aloud, encourage your children to act out all the action and sound effects. Afterward, you can simulate all the components of a car wash with your group. Have each team act out a different set of motions and noises: the rolling brush, the slapping felt arms, the drying machine, while other children can be the cars driving through. Kids will all run home and beg their parents to take them to the car wash so they can write and illustrate their own reactions to all the watery mayhem.

RELATED TITLES: Ashman, Linda. *Rub-a-Dub Sub.* Harcourt, 2003. / Barton, Byron. *My Car.* Greenwillow, 2001. / Faulkner, Matt. *The Amazing Voyage of Jackie Grace.* Scholastic, 1987. / Feiffer, Jules. *I'm Not Bobby!* Hyperion, 2001. / Feiffer, Jules. *Meanwhile . . .* HarperCollins, 1997. / Gerstein, Mordicai. *Behind the Couch.* Hyperion, 1996. / Hort, Lenny. *The Seals on the Bus.* Henry Holt, 2000. / MacLean, Christine Kole. *Even Firefighters Hug Their Moms.* Dutton, 2002. / Mahy, Margaret. *The Rattlebang Picnic.* Dial, 1994. / O'Connor, George. *Kapow!* Simon & Schuster, 2004. / O'Malley, Kevin. *Straight to the Pole.* Walker, 2003. / Peck, Jan. *Way Down Deep in the Deep Blue Sea.* Simon & Schuster, 2004. / Pinkwater, Daniel. *Tooth-Gnasher Superflash.* Macmillan, 1990. / Root, Phyllis. *Rattletrap Car.* Candlewick, 2001. / Schaefer, Carol Lexa. *The Squiggle.* Crown, 1996. / Steig, William. *Pete's a Pizza.* HarperCollins, 1998. / Steig, William. *Toby, What Are You?* HarperCollins, 2001.

SUBJECTS: AUTOMOBILES. CAR WASHES. CREATIVE DRAMA. IMAGINATION.

758 **Steig, William.** *Pete's a Pizza.* **Illus. by the author. HarperCollins, 1998. 0-06-205157-1. Unp. Gr. PreK–1**

Grumpy because it's raining, Pete cheers up when his parents turn him into a pretend pizza. Based on a game Steig used to play with his daughter, this is the story of a bad mood deferred.

GERM: Act out the making of Pete into a pizza. Talk it over: What works for you when you need to get out of a bad mood? See how other kids do it in Molly Bang's *When Sophie Gets Angry—Really, Really Angry*, Betsy Everitt's *Mean Soup*, and Rachel Vail's *Sometimes I'm Bombaloo*.

RELATED TITLES: Auch, Mary Jane. *The Princess and the Pizza.* Holiday House, 2002. / Bang, Molly. *When Sophie Gets Angry—Really, Really Angry.* Scholastic, 1999. / Collins, Suzanne. *When Charlie McButton Lost Power.* Putnam, 2005. / Curtis, Jamie Lee. *Today I Feel Silly and Other Moods That Make My Day.* HarperCollins, 1998. / Everitt, Betsy. *Mean Soup.* Harcourt, 1992. / Feiffer, Jules. *I Lost My Bear.* Morrow, 1998. / Hobbie, Holly. *Toot and Puddle: You Are My Sunshine.* Little, Brown, 1999. / Kovalski, Maryanne. *Pizza for Breakfast.* Morrow, 1991. / Pringle, Laurence. *Octopus Hug.* Boyds Mills, 1993. / Steig, William. *Spinky Sulks.* Farrar, 1988. / Vail, Rachel. *Sometimes I'm Bombaloo.* Scholastic, 2002. / Wells, Rosemary. *Noisy Nora.* Dial, 1997.

SUBJECTS: ANGER. BEHAVIOR. CONFLICT RESOLUTION. CREATIVE DRAMA. EMOTIONS. IMAGINATION. PARENT AND CHILD. PIZZA. PLAY.

759 Steig, William. *Toby, What Are You?* **Illus. by Teryl Euvremer. HarperCollins, 2001. 0-06-205169-5. Unp. Gr. PreK–1**

Toby's parents have to figure out each object he pretends to be each time he says, "Guess what I am?" Young Toby, a sweet-natured, furry brown creature with a long tail, pretends to be a bridge, a sandwich, and a snow-covered mountain.

GERM: Play an acting game. Give each pair or small group of children a bag with an item inside. They must figure out how to act out that object for others to guess. Follow up with *Toby, Where Are You?* and *Toby, Who Are You?*

RELATED TITLES: De Regniers, Beatrice Schenk. *It Does Not Say Meow and Other Animal Riddle Rhymes.* Houghton Mifflin, 1983. / Hoban, Tana. *Look Again.* Macmillan, 1971. / Hoban, Tana. *Take Another Look.* Greenwillow, 1981. / MacDonald, Suse. *Acrobatics.* Bradbury, 1986. / MacLean, Christine Kole. *Even Firefighters Hug Their Moms.* Dutton, 2002. / Marzollo, Jean. *Pretend You're a Cat.* Dial, 1990. / Schaefer, Carole Lexa. *Someone Says.* Viking, 2003. / Schaefer, Carol Lexa. *The Squiggle.* Crown, 1996. / Steig, William. *Pete's a Pizza.* HarperCollins, 1998. / Steig, William. *Toby, Where Are You?* HarperCollins, 1997. / Steig, William. *Toby, Who Are You?* HarperCollins, 2004.

SUBJECTS: FAMILY LIFE. GAMES. IMAGINATION. PARENT AND CHILD. VISUAL PERCEPTION.

760 Steig, William. *The Toy Brother.* **Illus. by the author. HarperCollins, 1996. 0-06-205078-8. Unp. Gr. 1–3**

Back in the Middle Ages, Yorick works as an apprentice to his father, the famous alchemist Magnus Bede. The boy has grandiose visions of performing miracles such as turning old donkey dung into gold. When his parents leave him and his younger brother Charles alone for a week, Yorick ignores his father's admonitions to stay out of the lab, and straightaway invents a new potion that renders him fist-sized. Faithful Charles does his best to care for his now-little brother, building him a doll-sized house, preparing bite-sized meals, and working on an antidote.

GERM: As ever, Steig's picture book is a charmer, filled with wit, finely turned phrases, and a bit of magic. Read aloud his other titles, including *The Amazing Bone, Caleb and Kate, Solomon the Rusty Nail,* and *Sylvester and the Magic Pebble,* and compare their common thread of transformation. Check your science curriculum for a tie-in demonstration of actual chemical changes as opposed to alchemy.

RELATED TITLES: Bush, Timothy. *Benjamin McFadden and the Robot Babysitter.* Crown, 1998. / dePaola, Tomie. *Strega Nona.* Simon & Schuster, 1979. / Dewan, Ted. *The Sorcerer's Apprentice.* Doubleday, 1998. / Donaldson, Julia. *The Giants and the Joneses.* Henry Holt, 2005. / Gackenbach, Dick. *Tiny for a Day.* Clarion, 1993. / Galdone, Paul. *The Magic Porridge Pot.* Clarion, 1979. / Joyce, William. *George Shrinks.* HarperCollins, 1985. / Kimmel, Eric A. *Anansi and the Magic Stick.* Holiday House, 2001. / Moore, Inga. *The Sorcerer's Apprentice.* Macmillan, 1989. / Steig, William. *Sylvester and the Magic Pebble.* Simon & Schuster, 1988.

SUBJECTS: BROTHERS. MIDDLE AGES. PICTURE BOOKS FOR ALL AGES. SIZE. TRANSFORMATIONS.

761 Steiner, Barbara A. *Desert Trip.* **Illus. by Ronald Himler. Sierra Club, 1996. 0-87156-581-1. Unp. Gr. 1–3**

A young girl and her mother go backpacking in the Utah desert canyonlands, a magical place with huge rock formations, scraggly twisted trees, and quiet all around. They prepare dinner and camp under the stars at the end of an idyllic day, evoked in earth-toned watercolors.

GERM: Start off by asking what one might find in a desert. Continue the desert tour with *Cactus Poems* by Frank Asch, *Lost* by Paul Brett Johnson and Celeste Lewis, and *Welcome to the Sea of Sand* by Jane Yolen.

RELATED TITLES: Albert, Richard E. *Alejandro's Gift.* Chronicle, 1994. / Asch, Frank. *Cactus Poems.* Harcourt, 1998. / Bash, Barbara. *Desert Giant: The World of the Saguaro Cactus.* Sierra Club, 1989. / Dunphy, Madeleine. *Here Is the Southwestern Desert.* Hyperion, 1995. / Johnson, Paul Brett, and Celeste Lewis. *Lost.* Orchard, 1996. / McLerran, Alice. *Roxaboxen.* Lothrop, 1991. / Mora, Pat. *Listen to the Desert.* Clarion, 1994. / Siebert, Diane. *Mojave.* Crowell, 1988. / Yolen, Jane. *Welcome to the Sea of Sand.* Putnam, 1996.

SUBJECTS: DESERTS. MOTHERS AND DAUGHTERS.

762 Steiner, Joan. *Look-Alikes: A Picture Puzzle Book.* **Artwork by the author; photos by Thomas Lindley. Little, Brown, 1998. 0-316-81255-2. Unp. Gr. K–3**

Arriving in Look-Alike Land by train, take a stroll through town, stopping in at the general store, the park, a fair, a fancy hotel, Stanley's Sweet Shop, and even the circus. Make sure to keep your eyes peeled, though, as each photographed, realistic-looking, colorful double-page scene is actually an astonishing three-dimensional collage composed of common found objects. In the park, the sandbox is made from an upside-down tambourine. The trees are pineapple tops and broccoli.

GERM: Steiner used more than a thousand objects to construct her delightful and clever assemblages, and she challenges us, through the rhyming text, to identify each one. Lucky for us, she meticulously lists every look-alike component at the back of the book. This is one of those picture books all ages will pore over, and art teachers will find inspiration for possible look-alike projects in which children design and describe their own scenes. Follow up with *Look-Alikes, Jr.*

RELATED TITLES: Fisher, Valerie. *Ellsworth's Extraordinary Electric Ears*. Atheneum, 2003. / Handford, Martin. Where's Waldo series. / Legge, David. *Bamboozled*. Scholastic, 1995. / Marzollo, Jean. I Spy series. Scholastic. / Steiner, Joan. *Look-Alikes, Jr*. Little, Brown, 1999.

SUBJECTS: PICTURE PUZZLES. STORIES IN RHYME. VISUAL PERCEPTION.

763 **Stenmark, Victoria. *The Singing Chick*. Illus. by Randy Cecil. Henry Holt, 1999. 0-8050-5255-0. Unp. Gr. PreK–K**

After hatching, a fluffy little yellow chick is so enamored of the beautiful world that he skips through the forest singing a merry little song. "Hello, Lunch," says a fox, eating the chick in one gulp, but then he feels funny in the belly, and can't stop singing the little chick's annoying song. "Peep-peep!" he yells, and a wolf swallows him up, followed by a bear who eats the wolf, and the singing just won't stop.

GERM: With its comical oil paintings, this is a rowdy romp for story hours and acting out, with that incessant peeping refrain, for which you'll want to make up a simple tune. For another "read-it-again" swallowing story, don't miss *Bark, George* by Jules Feiffer.

RELATED TITLES: Feiffer, Jules. *Bark, George*. HarperCollins, 1999. / Hindley, Judy. *Do Like a Duck Does!* Candlewick, 2002. / Massie, Diane Redfield. *The Baby Beebee Bird*. HarperCollins, 2000. / Rankin, Joan. *Wow! It's Great Being a Duck*. McElderry, 1998. / Shannon, George. *Tippy-Toe Chick, Go!* Greenwillow, 2003. / So, Meilo. *Gobble, Gobble, Slip, Slop: The Tale of a Very Greedy Cat*. Knopf, 2004. / Taback, Simms. *There Was an Old Lady Who Swallowed a Fly*. Viking, 1997. / Thomson, Pat. *Drat That Fat Cat!* Scholastic, 2003. / Whippo, Walt, and Bernard Zaritzky. *Little White Duck*. Little, Brown, 2000.

SUBJECTS: ANIMALS. CHANTABLE REFRAIN. CHICKENS. CREATIVE DRAMA. SEQUENCE STORIES. SINGING. STORIES TO TELL. SWALLOWING STORIES.

764 **Stevens, Janet, and Susan Stevens Crummel. *And the Dish Ran Away with the Spoon*. Illus. by Janet Stevens. Harcourt, 2001. 0-15-202298-8. Unp. Gr. K–3**

After their performance of "Hey diddle diddle," Dish and Spoon don't come back. Cat, Dog, and Cow set off to find them, with help from a map the Fork in the road draws for them. Muffet's spider suggests they try Big Bad Wolf's house, and there the trail gets hot.

GERM: The huge format and the cheeky oversized watercolor and colored-pencil illustrations make this perfect for sharing with a group as a kickoff to a nursery rhyme feast. Make a bulletin board-sized map using Fork's map as a starting point and have children add sites for other rhymes and fairy tales as you read them. For a closer look at "Hey diddle diddle," also share Rachel Vail's theatrical picture-book version, *Over the Moon*, and Gennifer Choldenko's *Moonstruck*. Fiddle around with more Mother Goose characters in *The Neat Line: Scribbling Through Mother Goose* by Pamela Duncan Edwards and *The Web Files* by Margie Palatini.

RELATED TITLES: Child, Lauren. *Beware of the Storybook Wolves*. Scholastic, 2001. / Choldenko, Gennifer. *Moonstruck: The True Story of the Cow Who Jumped over the Moon*. Hyperion, 1997. / dePaola, Tomie. *Tomie dePaola's Mother Goose*. Putnam, 1985. / Edwards, Pamela Duncan. *The Neat Line: Scribbling Through Mother Goose*. HarperCollins, 2005. / Hawkins, Colin, and Jacqui Hawkins. *The Fairytale News*. Candlewick, 2004. / Hoberman, Mary Ann. *You Read to Me, I'll Read to You: Very Short Fairy Tales to Read Together*. Little, Brown, 2004. / McClements, George. *Jake Gander, Storyville Detective*. Hyperion, 2002. / Palatini, Margie. *The Web Files*. Hyperion, 2001. / Scieszka, Jon. *The Stinky Cheese Man and Other Fairly Stupid Tales*. Viking, 1992. / Stevens, Janet, and Susan Stevens Crummel. *Cook-a-Doodle-Doo!* Harcourt, 1999. / Vail, Rachel. *Over the Moon*. Orchard, 1998. / Zalben, Jane Breskin. *Hey, Mama Goose*. Dutton, 2005.

SUBJECTS: CATS. CHARACTERS IN LITERATURE. COWS. DOGS. HUMOROUS FICTION. MAPS AND GLOBES. NURSERY RHYMES. PARODIES. READER'S THEATER. TABLEWARE.

765 **Stevens, Janet, and Susan Stevens Crummel.** *Cook-a-Doodle-Doo!* **Illus. by Janet Stevens. Harcourt, 1999. 0-15-201924-3. Unp. Gr. PreK–2**

Sick of eating chicken feed, Big Brown Rooster finds the cookbook of his famous great-grand-mother, the Little Red Hen (*The Joy of Cooking Alone*), and, with the help of pals Turtle, Potbellied Pig, and Iguana, undertakes baking a strawberry shortcake. In spite of hilarious problems with literal language (when the recipe calls for flour, Iguana picks a petunia; when it says to beat one egg, Iguana grabs a baseball bat) and gluttony (Pig scarfs down their first finished cake), the four manage to produce the "most wonderful, magnificent strawberry shortcake in the whole wide world."

GERM: On the right side of each cheerful, colorful, double-page spread are directions for measuring, information about ingredients, and other useful cooking instructions, in case you want to try out the shortcake recipe printed on the final page. Explore Iguana's word misconceptions and tie them in to Fred Gwynne's look at literal language in *A Chocolate Moose for Dinner* and the Amelia Bedelia series by Peggy and Herman Parish.

RELATED TITLES: Cazet, Denys. *Elvis the Rooster Almost Goes to Heaven.* HarperCollins, 2003. / Cox, Judy. *Rabbit Pirates: A Tale of the Spinach Main.* Harcourt, 1999. / Downard, Barry. *The Little Red Hen.* Simon & Schuster, 2004. / Feldman, Thelma. *Who You Callin' Chicken?* Abrams, 2003. / Galdone, Paul. *The Little Red Hen.* Clarion, 1979. / Gwynne, Fred. *A Chocolate Moose for Dinner.* Dutton, 1976. / Ketteman, Helen. *Armadilly Chili.* Albert Whitman, 2004. / Parish, Peggy. Amelia Bedelia series. Greenwillow. / Priceman, Marjorie. *How to Make an Apple Pie and See the World.* Knopf, 1994. / Stadler, Alexander. *Beverly Billingsly Takes the Cake.* Harcourt, 2005. / Sturges, Philemon. *The Little Red Hen (Makes a Pizza).* Dutton, 1999. / Wattenberg, Jane. *Henny-Penny.* Scholastic, 2000. / Westcott, Nadine Bernard, comp. *Never Take a Pig to Lunch and Other Poems About the Fun of Eating.* Orchard, 1994.

SUBJECTS: BAKING. CAKE. COOKERY. ENGLISH LANGUAGE—HOMONYMS. FOOD. IGUANAS. LITTLE RED HEN. PIGS. ROOSTERS. WORD GAMES.

766 **Stevens, Janet, and Susan Stevens Crummel.** *The Great Fuzz Frenzy.* **Illus. by Janet Stevens. Harcourt, 2005. 0-15-204626-7. Unp. Gr. PreK–2**

When a dog drops his fuzzy green tennis ball into a prairie dog hole, the prairie dogs are entranced by the pieces of green fuzz they pull off the ball and use to adorn themselves. Once the ball is fuzzless, though, the fuzz becomes a precious commodity that the community fights over, with "friend against friend, cousin against cousin, dog against dog." It's not until Big Bark steals all the fuzz and is captured by an eagle that the community comes to its senses and works together to rescue him.

GERM: This is a pretty heavy-duty and complex theme for a children's book—how a community can become sidetracked, divided, and almost destroyed by greed, jealousy, and self-interest—but it is handled brilliantly, with humor and insight. Ask listeners to make text-to-life connections about ways jealousy or greed have affected their behavior and how they handled it. Look at the back endpaper to predict what might happen when Violet the dog drops her orange tennis ball into the hole.

RELATED TITLES: Cronin, Doreen. *Click, Clack, Moo: Cows That Type.* Simon & Schuster, 2000. / Ketteman, Helen. *Armadilly Chili.* Albert Whitman, 2004. / Stevens, Janet, and Susan Stevens Crummel. *And the Dish Ran Away with the Spoon.* Harcourt, 2001. / Stevens, Janet, and Susan Stevens Crummel. *Cook-a-Doodle-Doo!* Harcourt, 1999. / Stevens, Janet. *Tops and Bottoms.* Harcourt, 1995.

SUBJECTS: BEHAVIOR. CITIZENSHIP. COMMUNITIES. COOPERATION. DOGS. GREED. HUMOROUS FICTION. JEALOUSY. PRAIRIE DOGS. SELFISHNESS.

767 **Stevenson, James.** *Don't Make Me Laugh.* **Illus. by the author. Farrar, 1999. 0-374-31827-1. Unp. Gr. K–2**

Serious crocodile Mr. Frimdimpny, in charge of this book, lays out his rules right away. Rule 1: Do not laugh. Rule 2: Do not even smile. If you laugh or smile, he will send you back to the front of the book. The problem, of course, is that this book is very funny, what with Pierre, the excellent waiter, asking readers not to touch the X on his tuxedo (as that is his tickle spot) and Fendently, the elephant, afraid that your breathing will make him sneeze. So your listeners will most likely not be able to stop laughing. Don't say I didn't warn you.

GERM: For more practice at not laughing, read the companion book, *No Laughing, No Smiling, No Giggling.* Then pair up your students and have one try to keep a straight face while the other acts out and tries to elicit laughter. The rules? They can't touch each other and the actor may not utter a sound. Then have them switch partners. Meet a farmer with no sense of humor in Tim Egan's *Serious Farm*.

RELATED TITLES: Bateman, Teresa. *April Foolishness*. Albert Whitman, 2004. / Egan, Tim. *Serious Farm*. Houghton Mifflin, 2003. / Stevenson, James. *No Laughing, No Smiling, No Giggling*. Farrar, 2004.

SUBJECTS: ANIMALS. BEHAVIOR. CROCODILES. HUMOROUS FICTION. LAUGHTER.

768   Stewart, Sarah. *The Journey*. Illus. by David Small. Farrar, 2001. 0-374-33905-8. Unp. Gr. 1–4

Hannah considers herself "the luckiest girl on this good earth" when her Aunt Clara allows her to escape the farm and her chores for one glorious week and take a vacation with her mother in Chicago—her first trip to a big city. For each page that Hannah, a young Amish girl, writes in her diary about her Chicago trip, there's a double-page painting showing her in the city and a parallel one showing what's going on back at the farm.

GERM: Have readers describe the parallels between each pair of illustrations. Viewers will gain much information about the lives of the Amish from the pictures, and they'll make that human connection with personable Hannah and her diary. Children will need to do some research for background on the Amish. You can also pair this with *The Gardener*, also by Stewart and Small, in which Lydia Jane moves to the city during the Depression and writes letters home.

RELATED TITLES: Ammon, Richard. *Growing Up Amish*. Atheneum, 1989. / Bial, Raymond. *Portrait of a Farm Family*. Houghton Mifflin, 1995. / Polacco, Patricia. *Just Plain Fancy*. Bantam, 1990. / Stewart, Sarah. *The Gardener*. Farrar, 1997.

SUBJECTS: AMISH. CHICAGO. CITIES AND TOWNS. DIARIES. FARM LIFE. TRANSPORTATION.

769   Stewig, John Warren. *Making Plum Jam*. Illus. by Kevin O'Malley. Hyperion, 2002. 0-7868-0460-2. Unp. Gr. 1–4

Spending an idyllic August week with Aunt Jane, Aunt Lizzy, and Aunt Alice on their Minnesota farm, Jackie tags along in their old Ford coupe and helps to steal the ripe plums from Farmer Wilson's tree, much to the fury of the bachelor farmer. After Jackie and the great-aunts make plum jam, he sneaks over to Farmer Wilson's house late that night and leaves several jars in the mailbox, with a note that says, "Thank you."

GERM: A charmer of a personal narrative, this will inspire your writers to record and illustrate their own slice-of-life family stories. Bring in a jar of plum jam and crackers so everyone can have a taste of summer. Or, better yet, try out the recipe on the back flap of the dust jacket.

RELATED TITLES: Best, Cari. *When Catherine the Great and I Were Eight!* Farrar, 2003. / Houston, Gloria. *My Great Aunt Arizona*. HarperCollins, 1992. / Jones, Rebecca C. *Great Aunt Martha*. Dutton, 1995. / Kennedy, Frances. *The Pickle Patch Bathtub*. Tricycle, 2004. / Lasky, Kathryn. *Marven of the North Woods*. Harcourt, 1997. / Schwartz, Harriet Berg. *When Artie Was Little*. Knopf, 1996.

SUBJECTS: AUNTS. COOKERY. FAMILY STORIES. FARM LIFE. FRUIT. GREAT-AUNTS. JAM. PERSONAL NARRATIVES.

770   Stickland, Paul. *Ten Terrible Dinosaurs*. Illus. by the author. Dutton, 1997. 0-525-45905-7. Unp. Gr. PreK–1

Count up to ten and back again with ten dancing dinosaurs having a blast, stomping and stamping and swinging from a tree.

GERM: Act out and chant the whole story so your noisy ones can practice counting up and back while blowing off a little steam. Stay on your toes with Arthur Dorros's *Ten Go Tango*, Tony Mitton's *Dinosaurumpus!*, and Carol Diggory Shields's *Saturday Night at the Dinosaur Stomp*.

RELATED TITLES: Arnold, Tedd. *Five Ugly Monsters*. Scholastic, 1995. / Dodson, Peter. *An Alphabet of Dinosaurs*. Scholastic, 1995. / Dorros, Arthur. *Ten Go Tango*. HarperCollins, 2000. / Edwards, Pamela Duncan. *Dinorella: A Prehistoric Fairy Tale*. Hyperion, 1997. / French, Vivian. *T. Rex*. Candlewick, 2004. / Hearn, Diane Dawson. *Dad's Dinosaur Day*. Macmillan, 1993. / Mitton, Tony. *Dinosaurumpus!* Scholastic, 2003. / Most, Bernard. *How Big Were the Dinosaurs?* Harcourt, 1994. / Nolan, Dennis. *Dinosaur Dreams*. Macmillan, 1990. / Rohmann, Eric. *Time Flies*. Crown, 1994. / Shields, Carol Diggory. *Saturday Night at the Dinosaur Stomp*. Candlewick, 1997. / Stickland, Paul, and Henrietta Stickland. *Dinosaur Roar!* Dutton, 1994.

SUBJECTS: COUNTING BOOKS. CREATIVE DRAMA. DINOSAURS. STORIES IN RHYME.

771   Stier, Catherine. *If I Were President*. Illus. by DyAnne Ryan. Albert Whitman, 1999. 0-8075-3541-9. Unp. Gr. K–3

In a simple but informative picture book, children describe what their days would be like if they became president of the United States, living in the White House, giving speeches, creating laws, and working hard for the good of the country.

GERM: Your children can imagine themselves in the White House and then write about what they'd do as commander in chief. They can accompany their descriptions with illustrations of themselves in action, using Washington, D.C., as a setting.

RELATED TITLES: Catrow, David. *We the Kids: The Preamble to the Constitution of the United States.* Dial, 2002. / Cheney, Lynne. *America: A Patriotic Primer.* Simon & Schuster, 2002. / Cronin, Doreen. *Duck for President.* Simon & Schuster, 2004. / Fritz, Jean. *Shh! We're Writing the Constitution.* Putnam, 1987. / McNamara, Margaret. *Election Day.* Simon & Schuster, 2004. / Maestro, Betsy, and Giulio Maestro. *A More Perfect Union: The Story of Our Constitution.* Lothrop, 1987. / St. George, Judith. *So You Want to Be President?* Philomel, 2000. / Winters, Kay. *My Teacher for President.* Dutton, 2004.

SUBJECTS: PRESIDENTS.

772   Stock, Catherine. *Gugu's House.* **Illus. by the author. Clarion, 2001. 0-618-00389-4. Unp. Gr. K–4**

Kukamba loves visiting her grandmother, Gugu, in her rambling house in the Tanzanian countryside. She helps Gugu paint the outside of her house in loud geometric designs and sculpt the glorious colorful array of wild animals that decorate her compound. When the rainstorms come, Kukamba is dismayed to see all the colorful sculptures and paintings reduced to brown mud, but Gugu explains the blessing of the rain. An Author's Note explains that Gugu is based on an actual person, Mrs. Khosa, who rebuilds her house every year.

GERM: Compare the story Gugu tells and paints about the rabbit and the tortoise with the Aesop version. Check your library for books on African animals and animal folktales. This may be just the impetus your class needs to decorate the walls and hallways with their animal paintings.

RELATED TITLES: Bash, Barbara. *Tree of Life: The World of the African Baobab.* Sierra Club/Little, Brown, 1989. / Dorros, Arthur. *This Is My House.* Scholastic, 1992. / Grifalconi, Ann. *The Village of Round and Square Houses.* Little, Brown, 1986. / Hesse, Karen. *Come On, Rain!* Scholastic, 1999. / Mollel, Tololwa M. *My Rows and Piles of Coins.* Clarion, 1999. / Mwenye Hadithi. *Tricky Tortoise.* Little, Brown, 1988. / Pinkney, Jerry. *Aesop's Fables.* SeaStar, 2000. / Stevens, Janet. *The Tortoise and the Hare: An Aesop Fable.* Holiday House, 1984. / Stojic, Manya. *Rain.* Crown, 2000. / Stuve-Bodeen, Stephanie. *Elizabeti's Doll.* Lee & Low, 1998. / Stuve-Bodeen, Stephanie. *Elizabeti's School.* Lee & Low, 2002.

SUBJECTS: AFRICA. GRANDMOTHERS. MULTICULTURAL BOOKS. PAINTING. RAIN AND RAINFALL. STORYTELLING. TANZANIA.

773   Stojic, Manya. *Rain.* **Illus. by the author. Crown, 2000. 0-517-80085-3. Unp. Gr. PreK–1**

The animals of the African savanna—the porcupine, zebras, baboons, rhino, and lion—smell, see, hear, feel, and taste the rain coming to the hot, cracked, red-soil plain.

GERM: Children can act out the story, using all their senses. This evocative picture book with its imposing thick-brushed paintings, ties into so many possibilities. At first glance, it seems appropriate only for young children, but it can be used to introduce water, rain, weather, the five senses, animals of the African savannah, and the cycle of growth at all levels. Children can chant the repeated refrains, and the prose is ideal for demonstrating the effectiveness of strong verbs and vivid adjectives. Read it on a rainy (or non-rainy) day and make your own rain. (On p. 63 of *Books Kids Will Sit Still For*, there's a description of an onomatopoeic rain-making activity that is great fun to do.)

RELATED TITLES: Aardema, Verna. *Bringing the Rain to Kapiti Plain.* Dial, 1981. / Cowcher, Helen. *Rain Forest.* Farrar, 1988. / Dragonwagon, Crescent. *And Then It Rained . . .* Atheneum, 2003. / Ginsburg, Mirra. *Mushroom in the Rain.* Macmillan, 1974. / Hesse, Karen. *Come On, Rain!* Scholastic, 1999. / Kurtz, Jane, and Christopher Kurtz. *Water Hole Waiting.* Greenwillow, 2002. / Martin, Bill, Jr., and John Archambault. *Listen to the Rain.* Henry Holt, 1988. / Schaefer, Lola M. *This Is the Rain.* HarperCollins, 2001.

SUBJECTS: AFRICA. ANIMALS. CREATIVE DRAMA. RAIN AND RAINFALL. SENSES AND SENSATION.

774   Strete, Craig. *The Rattlesnake Who Went to School.* **Illus. by Lynne Cravath. Putnam, 2004. 0-399-23572-8. Unp. Gr. PreK–1**

Afraid of going to school, a little Native American boy named Crowboy turns himself into a mean old rattlesnake with very sharp teeth. He spends his day hissing and acting poisonous, until he is befriended by a little girl in his class.

GERM: Discussion points: How did you feel on your first day of school? How do you act when you feel nervous and how do you get yourself to feel better? What animal would you have become and why? Draw and describe yourself as that animal. Also share Te Ata's *Baby Rattlesnake*, as a story Crowboy would find appealing, or Marguerite W. Davol's *How Snake Got His Hiss*.

RELATED TITLES: Ata, Te. *Baby Rattlesnake*. Children's Book Press, 1989. / Dannenberg, Julie. *First Day Jitters*. Charlesbridge, 2000. / Davis, Katie. *Kindergarten Rocks*. Harcourt, 2005. / Davol, Marguerite W. *How Snake Got His Hiss*. Orchard, 1996. / Harris, Robie H. *I Am Not Going to School Today!* McElderry, 2003. / Henkes, Kevin. *Chrysanthemum*. Greenwillow, 1991. / Henkes, Kevin. *Wemberly Worried*. Greenwillow, 2000. / McGhee, Alison. *Countdown to Kindergarten*. Harcourt, 2002. / McGhee, Alison. *Mrs. Watson Wants Your Teeth*. Illus. by Harry Bliss. Harcourt, 2004./ Pak, Soyung. *Sumi's First Day of School*. Viking, 2003. / Recorvits, Helen. *My Name Is Yoon*. Farrar, 2003. / Scott, Ann Herbert. *Brave as a Mountain Lion*. Clarion, 1996. / Steig, William. *Toby, Who Are You?* HarperCollins, 2004. / Stuve-Bodeen, Stephanie. *Elizabeti's School*. Lee & Low, 2002. / Wells, Rosemary. *Timothy Goes to School*. Dial, 1981. / Wells, Rosemary. *Yoko*. Hyperion, 1998.

SUBJECTS: BEHAVIOR. FIRST DAY OF SCHOOL. FRIENDSHIP. INDIANS OF NORTH AMERICA. MULTICULTURAL BOOKS. RATTLESNAKES. SCHOOLS. SNAKES. TEACHERS.

775 **Sturges, Philemon.** *The Little Red Hen (Makes a Pizza).* **Illus. by Amy Walrod. Dutton, 1999. 0-525-45953-7. Unp. Gr. PreK–1**

The duck, the dog, and the cat are too busy to help the industrious hen construct her magnificent pizza, but she generously allows them to help her eat it anyway.

GERM: Compare this Little Red Hen with a version of the original folktale. Ann Whitford Paul's *Mañana, Iguana* is set in the southwestern desert, while Janet Stevens and Susan Stevens Crummel's *Cook-a-Doodle-Doo!* is another funny update on the old tale.

RELATED TITLES: Auch, Mary Jane. *The Princess and the Pizza*. Holiday House, 2002. / Cooper, Helen. *Pumpkin Soup*. Farrar, 1999. / Cox, Judy. *Rabbit Pirates: A Tale of the Spinach Main*. Harcourt, 1999. / Day, Nancy Raines. *Double Those Wheels*. Dutton, 2003. / Downard, Barry. *The Little Red Hen*. Simon & Schuster, 2004. / Galdone, Paul. *The Little Red Hen*. Clarion, 1979. / Goldstein, Bobbye S., comp. *What's on the Menu?* Viking, 1992. / Kovalski, Maryann. *Pizza for Breakfast*. Morrow, 1991. / Paul, Ann Whitford. *Mañana, Iguana*. Holiday House, 2004. / Priceman, Marjorie. *How to Make an Apple Pie and See the World*. Knopf, 1994. / Steig, William. *Pete's a Pizza*. HarperCollins, 1998. / Stevens, Janet, and Susan Stevens Crummel. *Cook-a-Doodle-Doo!* Harcourt, 1999. / Walter, Virginia. *"Hi, Pizza Man!"* Orchard, 1995. / Wattenberg, Jane. *Henny-Penny*. Scholastic, 2000. / Westcott, Nadine Bernard. *Never Take a Pig to Lunch and Other Poems About the Fun of Eating*. Orchard, 1994.

SUBJECTS: CATS. CHICKENS. COOPERATION. DOGS. DUCKS. FOOD. GENEROSITY. LITTLE RED HEN. PARODIES. PIZZA.

776 **Sturges, Philemon.** *She'll Be Comin' 'Round the Mountain.* **Illus. by Ashley Wolff. Little, Brown, 2004. 0-316-82256-6. Unp. Gr. PreK–1**

Bouncy new verses to the old folksong, sung by a banjo-pickin' lizard, describe the anticipated arrival in town by a certain special someone whom the animal folks in Reederville, a picturesque Southwest desert canyon town, can't wait to see. Who is the "she" in the "Comin' 'Round the Mountain" song? Look closely at the gouache and pastel full-bleed illustrations of the busy critters preparing for a fiesta. On every page you'll notice there are animals reading books, which may clue in sharp-eyed guessers. When she finally arrives, driving her bookmobile, "Six White Horses," book lovers will cheer for the arrival of the traveling librarian, a javelina.

GERM: Listeners will hum along and join in on the repeated refrains of "when she comes." Note that the librarian is holding a copy of another book by Sturges and Wolff, *Who Took the Cookies from the Cookie Jar?*, which you can also recite together. Go through the illustrations again and talk about the types of books the animals are reading. Ask listeners what types of books they like to borrow from their library. Meet another group of book-reading animals when a bookmobile stops at the city zoo in *Wild About Books* by Judy Sierra.

RELATED TITLES: Allen, Susan, and Jane Lindaman. *Read Anything Good Lately?* Millbrook, 2003. / Bloom, Becky. *Wolf!* Orchard, 1999. / Ernst, Lisa Campbell. *Stella Louella's Runaway Book*. Simon & Schuster, 1998. / Florczak, Robert. *Yikes!!!* Scholastic, 2003. / Hoberman, Mary Ann. *Miss Mary Mack: A Hand-Clapping Rhyme*. Little, Brown, 1998. / Hoberman, Mary Ann. *There Once Was a Man Named Michael Finnegan*. Little, Brown, 2001. / Hoberman, Mary Ann. *Yankee Doodle*. Little, Brown, 2004. / Huff, Barbara. *Once Inside the Library*. Little, Brown, 1990. / Lass, Bonnie, and Philemon Sturges. *Who Took the Cookies from the Cookie Jar?* Little, Brown, 2000. / McPhail, David. *Fix-It*. Dutton, 1984. / Numeroff, Laura Joffe. *Beatrice Doesn't Want To*. Candlewick,

2004. / Sierra, Judy. *Wild About Books.* Knopf, 2004. / Slate, Joseph. *Miss Bindergarten Gets Ready for Kindergarten.* Illus. by Ashley Wolff. Dutton, 1996. / Williams, Suzanne. *Library Lil.* Dial, 1997.

SUBJECTS: ANIMALS. BOOKMOBILES. BOOKS AND READING. DESERT ANIMALS. JAVELINAS. LIBRARIANS. SONGS. SOUTHWEST. STORIES IN RHYME.

777   **Stuve-Bodeen, Stephanie.** *Elizabeti's Doll.* **Illus. by Christy Hale. Lee & Low, 1998. 1-880000-70-9. Unp. Gr. K–2**

In their village in Tanzania, Elizabeti watches how Mama cares for her new baby brother, Obedi. Elizabeti then finds a big rock just the right size to care for as a doll and names it Eva.

GERM: Note how such a tender story makes an unfamiliar place seem universal. Children can compare the village customs—carrying water in a jug atop the head, cooking meals in the cooking hut—with their own lives and discuss what is different, and what is the same everywhere. Follow up with the subsequent books, *Mama Elizabeti* and *Elizabeti's School.*

RELATED TITLES: Cowen-Fletcher, Jane. *It Takes a Village.* Scholastic, 1994. / Grifalconi, Ann. *The Village of Round and Square Houses.* Little, Brown, 1986. / Kroll, Virginia. *Masai and I.* Aladdin, 1997. / Leigh, Nila K. *Learning to Swim in Swaziland: A Child's-Eye View of a Southern African Country.* Scholastic, 1993. / McBrier, Paige. *Beatrice's Goat.* Atheneum, 2001. / Mennen, Ingrid, and Daly, Niki. *Somewhere in Africa.* Dutton, 1992. / Mollel, Tololwa M. *My Rows and Piles of Coins.* Clarion, 1999. / Stock, Catherine. *Gugu's House.* Clarion, 2001. / Stuve-Bodeen, Stephanie. *Elizabeti's School.* Lee & Low, 2002. / Stuve-Bodeen, Stephanie. *Mama Elizabeti.* Lee & Low, 2000.

SUBJECTS: AFRICA. BABIES. DOLLS. MOTHERS. MULTICULTURAL BOOKS. ROCKS. TANZANIA.

778   **Stuve-Bodeen, Stephanie.** *Elizabeti's School.* **Illus. by Christy Hale. Lee & Low, 2002. 1-58430-043-4. Unp. Gr. K–2**

At first, Elizabeti is certain that home is the best place to be. However, in her very first day at school in her Tanzanian village, she discovers that she loves learning her letters and numbers, playing games with her friends, and working in the school's garden.

GERM: What is different and what is the same about your school and Elizabeti's? Children can describe and illustrate a typical day in their classroom, or they can fold a piece of drawing paper in half and on one side draw what they're doing in school, and show on the other side what is happening at the same time at home. Follow Elizabeti's life with *Elizabeti's Doll* and *Mama Elizabeti.*

RELATED TITLES: Cowen-Fletcher, Jane. *It Takes a Village.* Scholastic, 1994. / Grifalconi, Ann. *The Village of Round and Square Houses.* Little, Brown, 1986. / Kroll, Virginia. *Masai and I.* Aladdin, 1997. / Leigh, Nila K. *Learning to Swim in Swaziland: A Child's-Eye View of a Southern African Country.* Scholastic, 1993. / McBrier, Paige. *Beatrice's Goat.* Atheneum, 2001. / Mennen, Ingrid, and Daly, Niki. *Somewhere in Africa.* Dutton, 1992. / Mollel, Tololwa M. *My Rows and Piles of Coins.* Clarion, 1999. / Stock, Catherine. *Gugu's House.* Clarion, 2001. / Stuve-Bodeen, Stephanie. *Elizabeti's Doll.* Lee & Low, 1998. / Stuve-Bodeen, Stephanie. *Mama Elizabeti.* Lee & Low, 2000.

SUBJECTS: AFRICA. FAMILY LIFE. FIRST DAY OF SCHOOL. MULTICULTURAL BOOKS. SCHOOLS. TANZANIA.

779   **Swope, Sam.** *Gotta Go! Gotta Go!* **Illus. by Sue Riddle. Farrar, 2000. 0-374-32757-2. Unp. Gr. PreK–2**

Out of the egg comes a teeny-tiny, creepy-crawly bug, a little yellow and black caterpillar, who says, "I don't know much, but I know what I know. I gotta go! I gotta go! I gotta go to Mexico!" After eating and sleeping, she finds she's a brand-new insect with splendid orange and black wings, and off she flies to Mexico.

GERM: The life cycle of a Monarch butterfly is told as the simplest of stories, with that urgent chantable refrain that all will join in on. For some simple scientific terminology—chrysalis, molting, metamorphosis—read *From Caterpillar to Butterfly* by Deborah Heiligman. Also get hold of *Monarch Butterflies: Mysterious Travelers* by Bianca Lavies, which has wonderful color photos.

RELATED TITLES: Brown, Ruth. *If at First You Do Not See.* Henry Holt, 1983. / Carle, Eric. *The Very Hungry Caterpillar.* Putnam, 1981. / Edwards, Pamela Duncan. *Clara Caterpillar.* HarperCollins, 2001. / Ehlert, Lois. *Waiting for Wings.* Harcourt, 2001. / Ernst, Lisa Campbell. *Bubba and Trixie.* Simon & Schuster, 1997. / Hariton, Anca. *Butterfly Story.* Dutton, 1995. / Heiligman, Deborah. *From Caterpillar to Butterfly.* HarperCollins, 1996. / Lavies, Bianca. *Monarch Butterflies: Mysterious Travelers.* Dutton, 1993. / Taylor, Harriet Peck. *Coyote and the Laughing Butterflies.* Macmillan, 1995.

SUBJECTS: BUTTERFLIES. CATERPILLARS. INSECTS. MEXICO. MIGRATION. MONARCH
BUTTERFLY.

780   **Taback, Simms.** *Joseph Had a Little Overcoat.* **Illus. by the author. Viking, 1999. 0-670-87855-
3. Unp. Gr. PreK–1**
In this Caldecott Medal-winning picture book, an adaptation of an old Yiddish folksong, tailor
Joseph turns his old and worn overcoat into a succession of lesser garments. From the coat, he
makes a jacket. When that, too, becomes "old and worn," he makes a vest out of it, then a scarf,
a necktie, a handkerchief, and finally, a button. Once he loses the button, the enterprising fellow
has nothing, until he makes a book about it—which shows "you can always make something
out of nothing," a lesson those of us in education know plenty about. The sprightly, lovable
illustrations are done in watercolor, gouache, pen-and-ink, and collage, and incorporate die-cut
shapes that highlight each of Joseph's creations.
GERM: Ask the music teacher to teach everyone the song on which the story is based, which is
printed on the last page. Compare and contrast this story with variants *Something from Nothing*
by Phoebe Gilman, *Bit by Bit* by Steve Sanfield, and the out West retelling *'Til the Cows Come
Home* by Jodi Icenoggle. "Joseph" makes a great flannelboard or even cut-paper story. Cut up a
big paper shirt into its many components as you tell the story. Children can cut out and cut up
their own paper shirts along with you, ending up with a simple paper button. I bought a children's overcoat at a local thrift shop and deconstructed it into the story's components, with the
help of Velcro strips and snaps, so children can retell the story as I take the coat apart. Discussion points: Why didn't Joseph just go out and buy a new coat? What does it mean to "make
something out of nothing?" Have you ever done that?
RELATED TITLES: Connor, Leslie. *Miss Bridie Chose a Shovel.* Houghton Mifflin, 2004. / Dragonwagon, Cres-
cent. *Brass Button.* Atheneum, 1997. / Gilman, Phoebe. *Something from Nothing.* Scholastic, 1993. / Icenoggle,
Jodi. *'Til the Cows Come Home.* Boyds Mills, 2004. / Mazer, Anne. *The Yellow Button.* Knopf, 1990. / Sanfield,
Steve. *Bit by Bit.* Philomel, 1995. / Taback, Simms. *There Was an Old Lady Who Swallowed a Fly.* Viking, 1997. /
Taback, Simms. *This Is the House That Jack Built.* Putnam, 2002. / Ziefert, Harriet. *When I First Came to This
Land.* Illus. by Simms Taback. Putnam, 1998.
SUBJECTS: BUTTONS. CALDECOTT MEDAL. CHANTABLE REFRAIN. CIRCULAR STORIES.
CLOTHING AND DRESS. COATS. MULTICULTURAL BOOKS. PICTURE BOOKS FOR ALL AGES.
SEQUENCE STORIES.

781   **Taback, Simms.** *There Was an Old Lady Who Swallowed a Fly.* **Illus. by the author. Viking,
1997. 0-670-86939-2. Unp. Gr. PreK–2**
A die-cut hole in each page reveals the fly, spider, bird, and other creatures in the belly of the
ravenous old woman as she devours creature after creature.
GERM: Compare the illustrations with versions by Karas, Rounds, and Westcott; sing the song;
and make up new verses for the well-loved children's song. If you want to buy ready-made
puppets of the story, go to <www.MimisMotifs.com>.
RELATED TITLES: Ginsburg, Mirra. *Clay Boy.* Greenwillow, 1997. / Hoberman, Mary Ann. *There Once Was a
Man Named Michael Finnegan.* Little, Brown, 2001. / Jackson, Alison. *I Know an Old Lady Who Swallowed a Pie.*
Dutton, 1997. / Johnson, Paul Brett. *Little Bunny Foo Foo.* Scholastic, 2004. / Karas, G. Brian. *I Know an Old Lady.*
Scholastic, 1984. / Rounds, Glen. *I Know an Old Lady Who Swallowed a Fly.* Holiday House, 1990. / So, Meilo.
Gobble, Gobble, Slip, Slop: The Tale of a Very Greedy Cat. Knopf, 2004. / Taback, Simms. *Joseph Had a Little Over-
coat.* Viking, 1999. / Taback, Simms. *This Is the House That Jack Built.* Putnam, 2002. / Thomson, Pat. *Drat That
Fat Cat!* Scholastic, 2003. / Weeks, Sarah. *Mrs. McNosh Hangs Up Her Wash.* Dutton, 1998. / Westcott, Nadine
Bernard. *I Know an Old Lady Who Swallowed a Fly.* Little, Brown, 1980. / Zelinsky, Paul O. *Knick-Knack Paddy-
whack!* Dutton, 2002. / Ziefert, Harriet. *When I First Came to This Land.* Illus. by Simms Taback. Putnam, 1998.
SUBJECTS: ANIMALS. CHANTABLE REFRAIN. ELDERLY. FOLK SONGS. GREED. NONSENSE
VERSES. SONGS. STORIES IN RHYME. STORIES WITH SONGS. SWALLOWING STORIES.

782   **Taback, Simms.** *This Is the House That Jack Built.* **Illus. by the author. Putnam, 2002. 0-399-
23488-8. Unp. Gr. PreK–1**
Taback's signature collage illustrations are frantic and fun in this lively version of the children's
chant, first published in 1755, and there's a new verse with a mystery guest introduced at the
end.
GERM: With the traditional verses ripe for reciting, next pay attention to the riotous pictures,
and have each artist design a house, captioned, "This is the house that ____ built." Look up

information on Randolph Caldecott, the English illustrator for whom the Caldecott Medal is named.

RELATED TITLES: Bania, Michael. *Kumak's House: A Tale of the Far North*. Alaska Northwest, 2002. / Forest, Heather. *A Big Quiet House*. August House, 1996. / Rounds, Glen. *Sod Houses on the Great Plains*. Holiday House, 1995. / Stevens, Janet. *The House That Jack Built: A Mother Goose Nursery Rhyme*. Holiday House, 1985. / Taback, Simms. *Joseph Had a Little Overcoat*. Viking, 1999. / Taback, Simms. *There Was an Old Lady Who Swallowed a Fly*. Viking, 1997. / Ziefert, Harriet. *When I First Came to This Land*. Illus. by Simms Taback. Putnam, 1998.

SUBJECTS: CHANTABLE REFRAIN. HOUSES. NURSERY RHYMES. SEQUENCE STORIES.

783   **Tagg, Christine.** *Cinderlily: A Floral Fairy Tale*. **Illus. by David Ellwand. Candlewick, 2003. 0-7636-2328-8. Unp. Gr. 1–4**

Just when you think you've seen every Cinderella variation possible, here's a theatrical one told in rhyme, with real flowers as the main players. Cinderlilly is made of a white lily, the sultan is an iris, and the bad sisters have pansy heads. This may sound odd but, set against a black backdrop and staged like a ballet, the entire interpretation is original, dynamic, and visually beguiling.

GERM: Raid the flower bed for specimens children can arrange into portraits (though, of course, their artwork will wilt). While the book is not a parody, per se, it is a whole new way of looking at both the Cinderella story (to which listeners can compare and contrast it) and the ballet.

RELATED TITLES: Edwards, Pamela Duncan. *Dinorella: A Prehistoric Fairy Tale*. Hyperion, 1997. / Freymann, Saxton, and Joost Elffers. *How Are You Peeling? Foods with Moods*. Scholastic, 1999. / Izen, Marshall, and West, Jim. *Why the Willow Weeps: A Story Told with Hands*. Doubleday, 1992. / Johnston, Tony. *Bigfoot Cinderrrrrella*. Putnam, 1998. / McClintock, Barbara. *Cinderella*. Scholastic, 2005. / San Souci, Robert D. *Cinderella Skeleton*. Harcourt, 2000. / Wegman, William. *Cinderella*. Hyperion, 1993.

SUBJECTS: BALLET. CINDERELLA STORIES. FAIRY TALES. FLOWERS. PARODIES. STORIES IN RHYME.

784   **Tarpley, Natasha Anastasia.** *Bippity Bop Barbershop*. **Illus. by E. B. Lewis. Little, Brown, 2002. 0-316-52284-8. Unp. Gr. PreK–1**

An African American little boy named Miles tells about the trip he and his daddy make one Saturday morning to the neighborhood barbershop, where Miles is getting his first haircut. "Be brave, Little Man," everyone tells him, but when the barber comes close with those clippers, Miles gets scared. Daddy shows him what to do, and Miles gets brave. What kind of haircut does he get? One just like Daddy's, of course. "You sure we're not twins?" Daddy asks him. And off they go, two cool cats, side by side. E. B. Lewis's affectionate watercolors complete a perfect package.

GERM: Discussion point: What special things do you do with your mom or dad? Do you remember your first haircut? What hairstyle would you pick if you went to the barbershop or beauty parlor? Draw a picture of yourself with your best haircut.

RELATED TITLES: Browne, Anthony. *My Dad*. Farrar, 2001. / Davis, Gibbs. *Katy's First Haircut*. Houghton Mifflin, 1985. / Feiffer, Jules. *The Daddy Mountain*. Hyperion, 2004. / Freeman, Don. *Mop Top*. Viking, 1955. / Pringle, Laurence. *Octopus Hug*. Boyds Mills, 1993.

SUBJECTS: AFRICAN AMERICANS. BARBERSHOPS. FATHERS AND SONS. HAIR. HAIRCUTTING. MULTICULTURAL BOOKS.

785   **Tavares, Matt.** *Oliver's Game*. **Illus. by the author. Candlewick, 2004. 0-7636-1852-7. Unp. Gr. 1–4**

Oliver Hall loves helping out at his grandfather's baseball store, Hall's Nostalgia, and listening to Grandpa tell stories of the Chicago Cubs. When Oliver discovers an old Cubs' uniform in the store, Grandpa relates how, when he was 18 back in 1941, he had the chance to practice with the baseball team.

GERM: You'll need to pull in some World War II history here and describe what happened on that terrible day, December 7, 1941, at Pearl Harbor. Discuss the trajectory of Grandpa's short-lived baseball career and how he came to terms with it.

RELATED TITLES: Cohen, Ron. *My Dad's Baseball*. Lothrop, 1994. / Corey, Shana. *Players in Pigtails*. Scholastic, 2003. / Hall, Donald. *When Willard Met Babe Ruth*. Harcourt, 1996. / Norworth, Jack. *Take Me Out to the Ball Game*. Four Winds, 1993.

SUBJECTS: BASEBALL. GRANDFATHERS. HISTORICAL FICTION. SPORTS. WORLD WAR, 1939–1945—FICTION.

786   Taylor, Sean. *Boing!* Illus. by Bruce Ingman. Candlewick, 2004. 0-7636-2475-6. Unp. Gr. PreK–2

Practicing his quadruple headfirst flip, young Felix's dad, the Great Elastic Marvel, flips out the window, falls toward the lion house at the city zoo, and bounces skyward again. Through a series of incredible and death-defying coincidences, the Jumping Master continues bouncing all over town before landing back in his own apartment.

GERM: All will enjoy repeating the title sound effect, Boing!, and the many exclamations (including Holy Moly and Hooplah and Hup!) uttered by The Man with the Rubber Legs. In fact, perhaps listeners would like to come up with their own alternate monikers, based on their own talents.

RELATED TITLES: Clement, Rod. *Just Another Ordinary Day.* HarperCollins, 1997. / Feiffer, Jules. *Meanwhile . . .* HarperCollins, 1997. / Florczak, Robert. *Yikes!!!* Scholastic, 2003. / Heller, Ruth. *Fantastic! Wow! and Unreal! A Book About Interjections and Conjunctions.* Grosset, 1998. / Lasky, Kathryn. *Tumble Bunnies.* Little, Brown, 2005. / Van Allsburg, Chris. *Jumanji.* Houghton, 1981. / Van Allsburg, Chris. *Zathura: A Space Adventure.* Houghton, 2002.

SUBJECTS: ADVENTURE AND ADVENTURERS. CITIES AND TOWNS. ENGLISH LANGUAGE— INTERJECTIONS. FATHERS AND SONS. GYMNASTICS. HOSPITALS. JUMPING. TRAMPOLINE. WOUNDS AND INJURIES.

787   Teague, Mark. *Dear Mrs. LaRue: Letters from Obedience School.* Illus. by the author. Scholastic, 2002. 0-439-20663-4. Unp. Gr. K–3

Writing a series of letters home to his owner from the Igor Brotweiler Canine Academy, where he has been sent for a two-month term, Ike the dog—hypochondriac, serial exaggerator, and kvetcher—compares his stay there to prison and plans to run away. In the meantime, we, the readers, see two contradictory points of view in the illustrations. There's the prison Ike describes, rendered in black and white, and then, in living color, the plush and comfy accommodations at the school, where the lucky dog has his own typewriter, dog treats, and even a blender. Which one is the true picture?

GERM: Listeners will love pointing out the differences between the black-and-white pictures of the awful conditions Ike claims to be enduring and the downright country club-like atmosphere of the actual school. After you ham up your read-aloud version of Ike's mail home, photocopy the letters, hand out one per student, and let them practice this as a Reader's Theater. Talk about exaggeration and how a story can be told from conflicting points of view in both words and pictures. Pet owners can compose a letter from their pets' points of view, either explaining a transgression or stating their feeling on an issue. They can illustrate what really happened in color, and then depict their pets' version of the events in black and white.

RELATED TITLES: Bruel, Nick. *Bad Kitty.* Roaring Brook, 2005. / Buehner, Caralyn. *Superdog: The Heart of a Hero.* HarperCollins, 2004. / Clement, Rod. *Just Another Ordinary Day.* HarperCollins, 1997. / Edwards, Pamela Duncan. *Muldoon.* Hyperion, 2002. / Falconer, Ian. *Olivia Saves the Circus.* Atheneum, 2001. / Kalman, Maira. *What Pete Ate from A–Z.* Putnam, 2001. / Kellogg, Steven. *Pinkerton, Behave.* Dial, 1979. / Kirk, Daniel. *Dogs Rule!* Hyperion, 2003. / Laden, Nina. *Bad Dog.* Walker, 2000. / Laden, Nina. *The Night I Followed the Dog.* Chronicle, 1994. / Meddaugh, Susan. *Martha Speaks.* Houghton Mifflin, 1992. (And others in the Martha series.) / Miller, Sara Swan. *Three Stories You Can Read to Your Dog.* Houghton Mifflin, 1995. / Scieszka, Jon. *Baloney (Henry P.).* Viking, 2001. / Sklansky, Amy E. *From the Doghouse: Poems to Chew On.* Henry Holt, 2002. / Teague, Mark. *Detective LaRue: Letters from the Investigation.* Scholastic, 2004. / Teague, Mark. *Frog Medicine.* Scholastic, 1991. / Teague, Mark. *The Secret Shortcut.* Scholastic, 1996.

SUBJECTS: DOGS. EXAGGERATION. HUMOROUS FICTION. LETTER WRITING. OBEDIENCE. PERSONAL NARRATIVES. PETS. POINT OF VIEW. READER'S THEATER.

788   Teague, Mark. *Detective LaRue: Letters from the Investigation.* Illus. by the author. Scholastic, 2004. 0-439-45868-4. Unp. Gr. K–4

Ike LaRue, the beloved hypochondriacal black-and-white terrier from *Dear Mrs. LaRue: Letters from Obedience School,* is back to beguile us with another adventure. The police are holding Ike as a suspect in the disappearance of neighbor Mrs. Hibbins's two cats. In the text of the letters he sends to his vacationing owner, Mrs. LaRue, Ike relates his efforts to find the bad cats— whom he has linked to a string of canary burglaries all over town—and to clear his own name.

GERM: As in the first book, the two sets of acrylic illustrations on each page, one in lush color, the other in hard-boiled black and white, tell the story from two very different viewpoints. Readers will discuss and debate who is telling the whole truth—Ike or the police and the newspapers. There's lots to examine and analyze in this mystery. What did Ike have to do with those cats getting out? Why can't the police get to the bottom of the bird burglaries at local pet stores? Talk about irony, especially the final picture, captioned "Grateful cats embrace their hero." In fact, how might the two cats relate their side of the story? You could head a grand jury investigation, interviewing all those involved, from cats to cops and including Ike and Mrs. LaRue, of course. Pet lovers can recall true experiences they've had with their animals and write them up as newspaper stories incorporating the five W's, plus headlines, quotes from witnesses, and a captioned picture.

RELATED TITLES: Allard, Harry. *Miss Nelson Is Missing*. Houghton Mifflin, 1985. / Cushman, Doug. *Mystery at the Club Sandwich*. Clarion, 2004. / Cushman, Doug. *The Mystery of King Karfu*. HarperCollins, 1996. / Egan, Tim. *The Trial of Cardigan Jones*. Houghton Mifflin, 2004. / Falconer, Ian. *Olivia . . . and the Missing Toy*. Atheneum, 2003. / Hall, Donald. *I Am the Dog, I Am the Cat*. Dial, 1994. / Howe, James. *Bud Barkin, Private Eye* (Tales from the House of Bunnicula series). Atheneum, 2003. / Laden, Nina. *The Night I Followed the Dog*. Chronicle, 1994. / Meddaugh, Susan. *Martha Walks the Dog*. Houghton Mifflin, 1998. / Meddaugh, Susan. *Perfectly Martha*. Houghton Mifflin, 2004. / Miller, Sara Swan. *Three Stories You Can Read to Your Dog*. Houghton Mifflin, 1995. / Palatini, Margie. *The Web Files*. Hyperion, 2001. / Rae, Jennifer. *Dog Tales*. Tricycle, 1999. / Teague, Mark. *Dear Mrs. LaRue: Letters from Obedience School*. Scholastic, 2002.

SUBJECTS: CATS. CREATIVE DRAMA. DOGS. HUMOROUS FICTION. LETTER WRITING. MYSTERY AND DETECTIVE STORIES. NEWSPAPERS. PICTURE BOOKS FOR ALL AGES. POINT OF VIEW. POLICE.

789   **Teague, Mark. *How I Spent My Summer Vacation*. Illus. by the author. Crown, 1995. 0-517-59999-6. Unp. Gr. K–3**

When confronted with that age-old assignment to write about his summer vacation, Wallace Bleff composes a doozy of a tale, which he reads aloud to his class. Told in galloping rhyme and accompanied by large, critter-filled paintings, Wallace's narrative describes how his parents sent him West to visit Aunt Fern, so he could relax from his wild imagination for a while. Captured by cowboys, he learns instead to rope and ride and, with his new moniker, "Kid Bleff," is soon regarded as a first-rate cowhand.

GERM: In order to write fiction, one must first be a storyteller. Use this one after your winter break, and ask returning revelers to jazz up oral descriptions of their week off. Then have them write down their tall tales. Introduce two more school talesters with *Olivia Saves the Circus* by Ian Falconer and *Baloney (Henry P.)* by Jon Scieszka.

RELATED TITLES: Falconer, Ian. *Olivia Saves the Circus*. Atheneum, 2001. / Feiffer, Jules. *Meanwhile . . .* HarperCollins, 1997. / Frank, John. *The Toughest Cowboy*. Simon & Schuster, 2004. / Long, Melinda. *How I Became a Pirate*. Harcourt, 2003. / Lowry, Lois. *Gooney Bird Greene*. Houghton Mifflin, 2002. / Scieszka, Jon. *Baloney (Henry P.)*. Viking, 2001. / Sherman, Allan, and Lou Busch. *Hello Muddah, Hello Faddah! (A Letter from Camp)*. Dutton, 2004. / Teague, Mark. *The Field Beyond the Outfield*. Scholastic, 1992. / Teague, Mark. *The Lost and Found*. Scholastic, 1998. / Teague, Mark. *Moog-Moog, Space Barber*. Scholastic, 1990. / Teague, Mark. *The Secret Shortcut*. Scholastic, 1996. / Tucker, Kathy. *Do Cowboys Ride Bikes?* Albert Whitman, 1997.

SUBJECTS: COWBOYS. CREATIVE WRITING. EXAGGERATION. HUMOROUS FICTION. STORIES IN RHYME. STORYTELLING. VACATIONS. WEST (U.S.).

790   **Teague, Mark. *The Lost and Found*. Illus. by the author. Scholastic, 1998. 0-590-84619-1. Unp. Gr. K–3**

Wendell and Floyd, in trouble at the principal's office again, and Mona, the new girl, find adventure while searching for Mona's lost hat in the nether regions of the Lost and Found.

GERM: Write adventure stories for your own lost or missing articles of clothing. Accompany Wendell and Floyd on their way to school in *The Secret Shortcut*.

RELATED TITLES: Faulkner, Matt. *The Amazing Voyage of Jackie Grace*. Scholastic, 1987. / Feiffer, Jules. *Meanwhile . . .* HarperCollins, 1997. / Kellogg, Steven. *The Missing Mitten Mystery*. Dial, 2000. / Pinkney, Brian. *The Adventures of Sparrowboy*. Simon & Schuster, 1997. / Teague, Mark. *The Field Beyond the Outfield*. Scholastic, 1992. / Teague, Mark. *Moog-Moog, Space Barber*. Scholastic, 1990. / Teague, Mark. *The Secret Shortcut*. Scholastic, 1996. / Wood, Audrey. *The Flying Dragon Room*. Scholastic, 1996.

SUBJECTS: ADVENTURE AND ADVENTURERS. FANTASY. HUMOROUS FICTION. LOST AND FOUND POSSESSIONS. SCHOOLS.

791 Teague, Mark. *The Secret Shortcut.* **Illus. by the author. Scholastic, 1996. 0-590-67714-4. Unp. Gr. K–2**

Wendell and Floyd's teacher, Ms. Gernsblatt, thinks their excuses for being late to school are preposterous and absurd, so they try a new secret shortcut to get to class on time. Through jungle and swamp, across a gorge, and into the mud, they are determined to make it before the late bell rings.

GERM: Continue Wendell and Floyd's fantastical school adventures with *The Lost and Found.* Adventurers can think up new school mishaps for Wendell and Floyd. For another preposterous set of tall-tale excuses, read Jon Scieszka's *Baloney, Henry P.,* in which a space alien explains to his teacher why he was late.

RELATED TITLES: Allard, Harry. *Miss Nelson Is Missing.* Houghton Mifflin, 1985. / Clement, Rod. *Just Another Ordinary Day.* HarperCollins, 1997. / Falconer, Ian. *Olivia Saves the Circus.* Atheneum, 2001. / Faulkner, Matt. *The Amazing Voyage of Jackie Grace.* Scholastic, 1987. / Feiffer, Jules. *Meanwhile . . .* HarperCollins, 1997. / Florczak, Robert. *Yikes!!!* Scholastic, 2003. / Long, Melinda. *How I Became a Pirate.* Harcourt, 2003. / McPhail, David. *Edward and the Pirates.* Little, Brown, 1997. / Pinkney, Brian. *The Adventures of Sparrowboy.* Simon & Schuster, 1997. / Rosen, Michael. *We're Going on a Bear Hunt.* McElderry, 1989. / Seuss, Dr. *And to Think That I Saw It on Mulberry Street.* Random House, 1989. / Teague, Mark. *The Field Beyond the Outfield.* Scholastic, 1992. / Teague, Mark. *How I Spent My Summer Vacation.* Crown, 1995. / Teague, Mark. *The Lost and Found.* Scholastic, 1998. / Wood, Audrey. *The Flying Dragon Room.* Scholastic, 1996.

SUBJECTS: ADVENTURE AND ADVENTURERS. HUMOROUS FICTION. IMAGINATION. LOST. SCHOOLS.

792 Thermes, Jennifer. *When I Was Built.* **Illus. by the author. Henry Holt, 2001. 0-8050-6532-6. Unp. Gr. K–4**

An old colonial farmhouse, still standing proud, reflects on its history, comparing its situation now to its early days, when its Fairchild owners were the only people for miles. The house describes the present first, with details of its former life on the facing page.

GERM: Have your kids make butter the old-fashioned way, by whipping it with an old-fashioned egg beater or by shaking it in a jar. They can ask parents and grandparents what changes they have seen in their lifetimes. Folding a large piece of drawing paper in half, your listeners can illustrate and write about another aspect of life that has changed, such as space travel, computers, shopping, medical care, or children's games. Ask children to look forward and predict how life will change 200 years in the future. Ellen Jackson's *Turn of the Century* takes a century-by-century look at children's lives from the year 1000 to now.

RELATED TITLES: Burton, Virginia Lee. *The Little House.* Houghton Mifflin, 1978. / Dorros, Arthur. *This Is My House.* Scholastic, 1992. / Jackson, Ellen. *Turn of the Century.* Charlesbridge, 1998. / Johnston, Tony. *Yonder.* Dial, 1988. / Kennedy, Frances. *The Pickle Patch Bathtub.* Tricycle, 2004. / Levine, Ellen. *The Tree That Would Not Die.* Scholastic, 1995. / Millard, Ann. *A Street Through Time.* DK, 1998. / Shannon, George. *This Is the Bird.* Houghton Mifflin, 1997. / Yolen, Jane. *House, House.* Marshall Cavendish, 1998.

SUBJECTS: HOUSES. PERSONAL NARRATIVES. PERSONIFICATION. POINT OF VIEW.

793 Thiesing, Lisa. *The Viper.* **Illus. by the author. Dutton, 2002. 0-525-46892-7. 32pp. Gr. K–2**

When I was a kid, my best friend, Bonnie Zabell, and I used to love to tell this story to each other. Here's an easy-reader version of it, with a large amiable pig named Peggy answering the phone. Peggy gets more and more frightened each time she gets a call from "zee Viper," who says he is coming to her house in one year, month, week, and minute.

GERM: Act this one out in trios: Peggy, the Viper, and a narrator. Think of the drama and storytelling possibilities here. Bring in a phone for a prop—now you know why you never threw away those old phones and nonworking cell phones!—and have the kids retell it and act it out in pairs. Ask everyone to retell the story to a friend, parent, or sibling, and it will make kids laugh for yet another generation. What's a viper? Look it up so all will laugh and understand why Peggy is scared and why the punch line is so funny. Follow up with other "silly thrillers" about Peggy the Pig: *The Aliens Are Coming!* and *A Dark and Noisy Night.*

RELATED TITLES: Calmenson, Stephanie. *The Teeny Tiny Teacher.* Scholastic, 1998. / Galdone, Paul. *The Teeny-Tiny Woman.* Clarion, 1984. / McBratney, Sam. *The Dark at the Top of the Stairs.* Candlewick, 1996. / Schwartz, Alvin. *Ghosts! Ghostly Tales from Folklore.* HarperCollins, 1991. / Schwartz, Alvin. *In a Dark, Dark Room and Other Scary Stories.* HarperCollins, 1984. / Sherrow, Victoria. *There Goes the Ghost.* HarperCollins, 1985. / Thiesing, Lisa. *The Aliens Are Coming!* Dutton, 2003. / Thiesing, Lisa. *A Dark and Noisy Night.* Dutton,

2005. / Williams, Linda. *The Little Old Lady Who Was Not Afraid of Anything*. Crowell, 1986. / Winters, Kay. *The Teeny Tiny Ghost*. HarperCollins, 1997.

SUBJECTS: CREATIVE DRAMA. FEAR. MISCONCEPTIONS. PIGS. STORIES TO TELL. TIME.

794   Thomas, Eliza. *The Red Blanket*. Illus. by Joe Cepeda. Scholastic, 2004. 0-439-32253-7. Unp. Gr. K–4

In a tender, true account, the author relates to her daughter, PanPan, how she adopted her as a 5-month-old baby from an orphanage in China, and brought her home to Vermont.

GERM: This is a great book for parents explaining adoption or for teachers of older children discussing different types of family units. Talk it over: Why was the red blanket so important to PanPan and her mother?

RELATED TITLES: Buzzeo, Toni. *The Sea Chest*. Dial, 2002. / Curtis, Jamie Lee. *Tell Me Again About the Night I Was Born*. HarperCollins, 1996. / Friedman, Ina R. *How My Parents Learned to Eat*. Houghton, 1984. / Lasky, Kathryn. *Before I Was Your Mother*. Harcourt, 2003. / Lifton, Betty Jean. *Tell Me a Real Adoption Story*. Knopf, 1994. / Little, Jean. *Emma's Yucky Brother*. HarperCollins, 2001. / London, Jonathan. *A Koala for Katie*. Albert Whitman, 1993. / Russo, Marisabina. *Waiting for Hannah*. Greenwillow, 1989. / Say, Allen. *Tree of Cranes*. Houghton Mifflin, 1991. / Stoeke, Janet Morgan. *Waiting for May*. Dutton, 2005. / Wong, Janet. *Apple Pie Fourth of July*. Harcourt, 2002.

SUBJECTS: ADOPTION. ASIAN AMERICANS. BABIES. CHINESE AMERICANS. FAMILY STORIES. MOTHERS AND DAUGHTERS. MULTICULTURAL BOOKS. SINGLE-PARENT FAMILIES.

795   Thomas, Shelley Moore. *Get Well, Good Knight*. Illus. by Jennifer Plecas. Dutton, 2002. 0-525-46914-1. 48pp. Gr. PreK–1

After the Good Knight's three little dragon friends come down with sneezes, coughs, and fevers, he seeks a cure from the old wizard but finds that his own mother has the best soup recipe to heal them.

GERM: Make chicken soup with your kids. This easy-reader is a lively candidate for acting out or Reader's Theater.

RELATED TITLES: Bateman, Teresa. *Farm Flu*. Albert Whitman, 2001. / Cherry, Lynne. *Who's Sick Today?* Dutton, 1988. / Loomis, Christine. *One Cow Coughs: A Counting Book for the Sick and Miserable*. Ticknor & Fields, 1994. / Nolen, Jerdine. *Raising Dragons*. Harcourt, 1998. / Rylant, Cynthia. *Poppleton*. Scholastic, 1997. / Sendak, Maurice. *Chicken Soup with Rice*. HarperCollins, 1962. / Thomas, Shelley Moore. *Good Night, Good Knight*. Dutton, 2000. / Thomas, Shelley Moore. *Happy Birthday, Good Knight*. Dutton, 2006. / Wells, Rosemary. *Felix Feels Better*. Candlewick, 2001. / Yolen, Jane. *How Do Dinosaurs Get Well Soon?* Blue Sky/Scholastic, 2003.

SUBJECTS: DRAGONS. KNIGHTS AND KNIGHTHOOD. MOTHERS AND SONS. READER'S THEATER. SICK. SOUP. STORIES TO TELL.

796   Thomas, Shelley Moore. *Good Night, Good Knight*. Illus. by Jennifer Plecas. Dutton, 2000. 0-525-46326-7. 48pp. Gr. PreK–1

On his watch one night, the Good Knight helps three lonely little dragons get ready for bed in their deep, dark cave, bringing one a drink of water, telling another a bedtime story, and singing a song for the third.

GERM: Share this easy-reader when talking about getting-ready-for-bed rituals. Just right for storytelling, with its humor, simple-to-recall language, repeated refrains, and sound effects, it also makes a terrific Reader's Theater for beginning readers. Your dragon lovers can compile a list with pictures of all the things they do before they go to bed. Also read the sequel, *Get Well, Good Knight*.

RELATED TITLES: Black, Charles C. *The Royal Nap*. Viking, 1995. / Cook, Sally. *Good Night Pillow Fight*. HarperCollins, 2004. / Cushman, Doug. *Inspector Hopper*. HarperCollins, 2000. / Gag, Wanda. *The Funny Thing*. Coward, 1929. / Holabird, Katharine. *Alexander and the Dragon*. Clarkson N. Potter, 1988. / Lum, Kate. *What! Cried Granny: An Almost Bedtime Story*. Dial, 1999. / Murphy, Jill. *Peace at Last*. Dial, 1980. / Nash, Ogden. *The Tale of Custard the Dragon*. Little, Brown, 1995. / Nolen, Jerdine. *Raising Dragons*. Harcourt, 1998. / Rathmann, Peggy. *Good Night, Gorilla*. Putnam, 1994. / Rathmann, Peggy. *Ten Minutes Till Bedtime*. Putnam, 1998. / Rosen, Michael. *We're Going on a Bear Hunt*. McElderry, 1989. / Santore, Charles. *William the Curious: Knight of the Water Lillies*. Random House, 1997. / Thomas, Shelley Moore. *Happy Birthday, Good Knight*. Dutton, 2006. (And others in the Good Knight series.) / Yolen, Jane. *How Do Dinosaurs Say Good Night?* Blue Sky/Scholastic, 2000.

SUBJECTS: BEDTIME STORIES. CHANTABLE REFRAIN. DRAGONS. KNIGHTS AND KNIGHTHOOD. READER'S THEATER. SLEEP. STORIES TO TELL.

797 **Thomassie, Tynia.** *Feliciana Feydra LeRoux: A Cajun Tall Tale.* **Illus. by Cat Bowman Smith. Little, Brown, 1995. 0-316-84125-0. Unp. Gr. 1–3**

Feliciana Feydra runs off to go alligator hunting in the Louisiana bayou with all the rest of the men-children, claiming, "I can outsmart an ol' halligator any ol' day . . ." And she does just that. When her grandfather, Grampa Baby, is pulled into the murky water, the brave girl dives in and saves the day by stuffing her pecan wood baby doll upright between the gator's teeth, locking its jaws open.

GERM: This delicious read-aloud gem, with its Cajun-flavored dialect and congenial watercolors, comes complete with a glossary, pronunciation guide, and a Recipe for a Cajun Accent on the back cover. Play some zydecko music and hand out pecans as a snack. (Be aware of any nut allergies, of course, before you plan to do this.) Follow up with the sequel, *Feliciana Meets d'Loup Garou*, in which Feliciana is in a snit and befriends a swamp werewolf. Also share Thomassie's story of two Cajun brothers, Ti-Boy and Baptiste, who take their citified cousin, Remington, fishing in the bayou in *Cajun Through and Through*. For some wild Cajun dialect, *Petite Rouge: A Cajun Red Riding Hood* by Mike Artell is hysterically funny.

RELATED TITLES: Arnosky, Jim. *All About Alligators.* Scholastic, 1994. / Artell, Mike. *Petite Rouge: A Cajun Red Riding Hood.* Dial, 2001. / Bare, Colleen Stanley. *Never Kiss an Alligator.* Dutton, 1989. / Doucet, Sharon Arms. *Why Lapin's Ears Are Long and Other Tales from the Louisiana Bayou.* Orchard, 1997. / Isaacs, Anne. *Swamp Angel.* Dutton, 1994. / Kellogg, Steven. *Sally Ann Thunder Ann Whirlwind Crocket.* Morrow, 1995. / Salley, Coleen. *Epossumondas.* Harcourt, 2002. / Salley, Coleen. *Why Epossumondas Has No Hair on His Tail.* Harcourt, 2004. / San Souci, Robert D. *Six Foolish Fisherman.* Hyperion, 2000. / Thomassie, Tynia. *Cajun Through and Through.* Little, Brown, 2000. / Thomassie, Tynia. *Feliciana Meets d'Loup Garou: A Cajun Tall Tale.* Little, Brown, 1998. / Vaughan, Marcia. *Whistling Dixie.* HarperCollins, 1995.

SUBJECTS: ALLIGATORS. CAJUNS. FISHING. GRANDFATHERS. LOUISIANA. MULTICULTURAL BOOKS. TALL TALES.

798 **Thompson, Lauren.** *One Riddle, One Answer.* **Illus. by Linda S. Wingerter. Scholastic, 2001. 0-590-31335-5. Unp. Gr. 2–6**

Faced with choosing a suitable husband, the Persian sultan's youngest daughter, Aziza, who loves numbers and riddles, presents her suitors with a riddle that has only one true answer. While many hazard a guess, it is Ahmed, a young farmer, who comes up with the answer.

GERM: Before reading the end of the story, have your listeners break into groups to try and formulate an answer to the riddle: "Placed above, it makes greater things small. Placed beside, it makes small things greater. In matters that count, it always comes first. Where others increase, it keeps all things the same. What is it?" A detailed explanation at the back explains the solution to each part of Aziza's riddle. Read this attractive original folktale as a kickoff to a math lesson on the difference between Roman and Arabic numerals, and on the number one.

RELATED TITLES: Dasent, George Webbe. *East O' the Sun and West O' the Moon.* Illus. by P. J. Lynch. Candlewick, 1992. / DeFelice, Cynthia, and Mary DeMarsh. *Three Perfect Peaches: A French Folktale.* Orchard, 1995. / Demi. *One Grain of Rice: A Mathematical Folktale.* Scholastic, 1997. / Kherdian, David. *The Golden Bracelet.* Holiday House, 1998. / Kimmel, Eric A. *The Three Princes: A Tale from the Middle East.* Holiday House, 1994. / Kimmel, Eric A. *Three Sacks of Truth: A Story from France.* Holiday House, 1993. / Martin, Rafe. *The Rough-Face Girl.* Putnam, 1992. / San Souci, Robert D. *A Weave of Words: An Armenian Tale.* Orchard, 1998. / Yep, Laurence. *The Khan's Daughter: A Mongolian Folktale.* Scholastic, 1997.

SUBJECTS: IRAN. LOVE. MATHEMATICS. MULTICULTURAL BOOKS. RIDDLES.

799 **Thomson, Pat.** *Drat That Fat Cat!* **Illus. by Ailie Busby. Scholastic, 2003. 0-439-47195-8. Unp. Gr. PreK–K**

Along pads a fat, fat cat in search of food, and he eats up a rat, a duck, a dog, an old lady, and then a bee who stings his way out of the cat's belly.

GERM: The simple and joyful repetition—"But was that cat fat enough? No, he was not!"—and the noises the swallowed ones make—squeaking, quacking, woofing—make this a natural for preschool story hours. Do it up with puppets or as a flannelboard story, and act it out in sequence. Share the many versions of "I Know an Old Lady Who Swallowed a Fly," Jack Kent's *The Fat Cat*, and Meilo So's *Gobble, Gobble, Slip, Slop*, about a parrot and another hungry cat.

RELATED TITLES: Galdone, Paul. *The Greedy Old Fat Man.* Clarion, 1983. / Ginsburg, Mirra. *Clay Boy.* Greenwillow, 1997. / Karas, G. Brian. *I Know an Old Lady.* Scholastic, 1984. / Kent, Jack. *The Fat Cat.* Scholastic, 1972. / Polette, Nancy. *The Little Old Woman and the Hungry Cat.* Greenwillow, 1989. / Rounds, Glen. *I Know an Old Lady Who Swallowed a Fly.* Holiday House, 1990. / Sierra, Judy. *Nursery Tales Around the World.* Clarion,

1996. / Sloat, Teri. *Sody Sallyratus*. Dutton, 1997. / So, Meilo. *Gobble, Gobble, Slip, Slop: The Tale of a Very Greedy Cat*. Knopf, 2004. / Taback, Simms. *There Was an Old Lady Who Swallowed a Fly*. Viking, 1997. / Westcott, Nadine Bernard. *I Know an Old Lady Who Swallowed a Fly*. Little, Brown, 1980.

SUBJECTS: ANIMALS. CATS. CHANTABLE REFRAIN. CREATIVE DRAMA. GREED. SEQUENCE STORIES. STORIES TO TELL. SWALLOWING STORIES.

800   **Thomson, Pat. *The Squeaky, Creaky Bed*. Illus. by Niki Daly. Doubleday, 2003. 0-385-74630-X. Unp. Gr. PreK–1**

Every night, when the little boy's bed goes "squeak, squeak, creak!," he cries until his grandfather comes to the rescue, bringing him cumulatively a cat, a dog, a pig, and a parrot to keep him company.

GERM: Tell, retell, act out, draw, and laugh over the wonderfully humorous watercolors, noisy sound effects, predictable format, repetition, and very funny ending. Two other delightful versions of this story, which you can compare and contrast, are *Nathaniel Willy, Scared Silly* by Judith Mathews and Fay Robinson and *The Squeaky Door* by Laura Simms.

RELATED TITLES: Bania, Michael. *Kumak's House: A Tale of the Far North*. Alaska Northwest, 2002. / Casanova, Mary. *One-Dog Canoe*. Farrar, 2003. / Cole, Joanna. *It's Too Noisy!* Crowell, 1989. / Donaldson, Julia. *A Squash and a Squeeze*. McElderry, 1993. / Hirsch, Marilyn. *Could Anything Be Worse?* Holiday House, 1974. / Lester, Helen. *Princess Penelope's Parrot*. Houghton Mifflin, 1996. / Lum, Kate. *What! Cried Granny: An Almost Bedtime Story*. Doubleday, 2003. / MacDonald, Margaret Read. *The Old Woman Who Lived in a Vinegar Bottle*. August House, 1995. / McGovern, Ann. *Too Much Noise*. Houghton Mifflin, 1967. / Mathews, Judith, and Fay Robinson. *Nathaniel Willy, Scared Silly*. Bradbury, 1994. / Murphy, Jill. *Peace at Last*. Dial, 1980. / Simms, Laura. *The Squeaky Door*. Crown, 1991. / Taback, Simms. *Joseph Had a Little Overcoat*. Viking, 1999. / Taback, Simms. *This Is the House That Jack Built*. Putnam, 2002. / Zemach, Margot. *It Could Always Be Worse*. Farrar, 1976.

SUBJECTS: ANIMALS. BEDS. BEDTIME STORIES. CHANTABLE REFRAIN. CRYING. GRANDPARENTS. PARROTS. SEQUENCE STORIES. SOUND EFFECTS. STORIES TO TELL.

801   **Tucker, Kathy. *The Seven Chinese Sisters*. Illus. by Grace Lin. Albert Whitman, 2003. 0-8075-7306-4. Unp. Gr. K–4**

This is an amusing feminist reworking of the traditional tale about those identical Chinese brothers, who meet seven sisters, each with a special talent. First Sister rides her scooter as fast as the wind, while the others can do karate, count, talk to dogs, catch any ball, and cook delicious noodle soup. When the baby, Seventh Sister, is snatched away by a hungry red dragon, the six spring into action to get her back.

GERM: Children can draw story maps showing the sequence of events and describe the special action each sister takes to rescue Seventh Sister. Compare this modern version with the traditional *The Six Chinese Brothers* by Cheng Hou-Tien and *The Seven Chinese Brothers* by Margaret Mahy.

RELATED TITLES: Cheng, Hou-Tien. *The Six Chinese Brothers; An Ancient Tale*. Henry Holt, 1979. / Davol, Marguerite W. *The Paper Dragon*. Atheneum, 1997. / Grahame, Kenneth. *The Reluctant Dragon*. Illus. by Inga Moore. Candlewick, 2004. / Lin, Grace. *Dim Sum for Everyone*. Knopf, 2001. / Mahy, Margaret. *The Seven Chinese Brothers*. Scholastic, 1990. / Muth, Jon J. *Stone Soup*. Scholastic, 2003. / Rattigan, Jama Kim. *Dumpling Soup*. Little, Brown, 1993. / Sendak, Maurice. *Chicken Soup with Rice*. HarperCollins, 1962. / Williams, Jay. *Everyone Knows What a Dragon Looks Like*. Four Winds, 1976. / Young, Ed. *The Sons of the Dragon King: A Chinese Legend*. Atheneum, 2004.

SUBJECTS: CHINA. DRAGONS. SISTERS. SOUP. STORYTELLING.

802   **Tunnell, Michael O. *Mailing May*. Illus. by Ted Rand. Greenwillow, 1997. 0-688-12879-3. Unp. Gr. K–3**

With train tickets costing $1.25, there was no way Ma and Pa could afford to send young May across the mountains to visit her Grandma Mary in Lewiston, Idaho. As May herself tells it, Pa took her instead to the Grangeville, Idaho, post office and sent her on the train's mail car as parcel post. Ted Rand's watercolors of May's exciting four-hour train ride are enchanting, and it turns out that the sprightly story is based on a real occurrence back on January 1, 1913.

GERM: Children will be interested to see how a true incident can be written down and adapted as a story, which they may want to try, either with a family anecdote or a compelling human interest article in the newspaper.

RELATED TITLES: Booth, Philip. *Crossing*. Candlewick, 2001. / Crews, Donald. *Freight Train*. Greenwillow,

1978. / Howard, Elizabeth Fitzgerald. *Mac and Marie and the Train Toss Surprise.* Four Winds, 1993. / Kuklin, Susan. *All Aboard! A True Train Story.* Orchard, 2003. / Lasky, Kathryn. *Marven of the Great North Woods.* Harcourt, 1997. / Polacco, Patricia. *An Orange for Frankie.* Philomel, 2004. / Rylant, Cynthia. *Silver Packages: An Appalachian Christmas Story.* Orchard, 1997. / Siebert, Diane. *Train Song.* Crowell, 1990. / Skurzynski, Gloria. *Here Comes the Mail.* Bradbury, 1992. / Westcott, Nadine Bernard. *I've Been Working on the Railroad: An American Classic.* Hyperion, 1996.

SUBJECTS: GRANDMOTHERS. HISTORICAL FICTION. PICTURE BOOKS FOR ALL AGES. POSTAL SERVICE. TRAINS. TRANSPORTATION. VOYAGES AND TRAVELS.

803 **Turner, Ann.** *Drummer Boy.* **Illus. by Mark Hess. HarperCollins, 1999. 0-06-027697-5. Unp. Gr. 3–6**

In this sobering picture book with vivid, realistic paintings, a 13-year-old boy tells how he went to war as a drummer boy in Mr. Lincoln's army, to beat out orders to the soldiers on the battleground. He is transformed by the bloody carnage from a fresh-faced boy to a wistful battle-weary young man.

GERM: The historical note at the back says there were about 40,000 drummer boys in the Union Army alone. Share the illustrator's dedication, ". . . that one day war will only be remembered as ancient history in books," and relate the story to whatever wars are raging in the world when you read it. It will meld with the biography *Walt Whitman: Words for America* by Barbara Kerley, with the picture book *Pink and Say* by Patricia Polacco, and with the novel *Bull Run* by Paul Fleischman. For an account of the final surrender of Lee to Grant, Robin Friedman's picture book *The Silent Witness: A True Story of the Civil War* provides an interesting perspective.

RELATED TITLES: Fleischman, Paul. *Bull Run.* HarperCollins, 1993. / Friedman, Robin. *The Silent Witness: A True Story of the Civil War.* Houghton Mifflin, 2005. / Kerley, Barbara. *Walt Whitman: Words for America.* Scholastic, 2004. / Polacco, Patricia. *Pink and Say.* Philomel, 1994. / Reit, Seymour. *Behind Rebel Lines: The Incredible Story of Emma Edmonds, Civil War Spy.* Harcourt, 1988. / Winter, Jeanette. *The Librarian of Basra: A True Story from Iraq.* Harcourt, 2004.

SUBJECTS: DRUMS. HISTORICAL FICTION. U.S.—HISTORY—CIVIL WAR, 1861–1865—FICTION. WAR.

804 **Turner, Priscilla.** *The War Between the Vowels and the Consonants.* **Illus. by Whitney Turner. Farrar, 1996. 0-374-38236-0. Unp. Gr. K–3**

Writers engage in a constant battle of words as they struggle to put their ideas on paper. In this engaging picture book, it's the Vowels and Consonants who are enemies, and their distrust of each other leads to taunts, weapons, and finally, war. The fighting continues on land, sea, and air until a menacing intruder appears, a great jagged scribble of chaos that neither side can best. All letters panic except for the youngest, "Y", who gets both sides to unite to make a word: "STOP." "I can't fight that," whimpers the jumble. "Next they'll make paragraphs . . . pages . . . chapters . . ." and the intruder rolls out of town.

GERM: As a follow-up, play Boggle or have children pick 16 large letters from a hat and see how many words they can create. Have them each contribute words to the hat and then pull out a batch of words from which they can compose a sentence, a poem, or a story.

RELATED TITLES: Agee, Jon. *Elvis Lives and Other Anagrams.* Farrar, 2004. / Amato, Mary. *The Word Eater.* Holiday House, 2000. / Clements, Andrew. *Double Trouble in Walla Walla.* Millbrook, 1998. / Pulver, Robin. *Punctuation Takes a Vacation.* Holiday House, 2003. / Steig, William. *CDB.* Simon & Schuster, 2000. / Steig, William. *CDC.* Simon & Schuster, 2003. / Viorst, Judith. *The Alphabet from Z to A: With Much Confusion on the Way.* Atheneum, 1994. / Wilbur, Richard. *The Disappearing Alphabet.* Harcourt, 1998.

SUBJECTS: ALPHABET BOOKS. ENGLISH LANGUAGE—CONSONANTS. ENGLISH LANGUAGE—VOWELS. WAR.

805 **Tyson, Leigh Ann.** *An Interview with Harry the Tarantula.* **Illus. by Henrik Drescher. National Geographic, 2003. 0-7922-5122-9. Unp. Gr. 1–4**

Interviewed by Katy Did on her KBUG radio show, "Up Close and Personal," Harry Spyder, a tarantula from California, regales her with his true and horrifying account of his encounter with a human girl who scooped him up in a glass bottle. Katy asks him good meaty questions, including why he sheds his skin, what he eats, how he defends himself, and about spider reproduction—very tastefully handled, of course. At the back is a nice assortment of tarantula facts.

GERM: Use this book to introduce spiders and also to investigate the interview process. Your animal lovers can work in pairs, research a chosen creature, and then write a question-and-answer interview that provides information and a get-to-know-you attitude. Each pair can then present their interview live as a Reader's Theater. Have students interview each other, perhaps as book characters or other animals. Bring out your video camera or tape recorder, or even just a simple microphone, so children can pretend they're on the air.

RELATED TITLES: Cannon, Janell. *Stellaluna*. Harcourt, 1993. / Child, Lauren. *That Pesky Rat*. Candlewick, 2002. / Cronin, Doreen. *Diary of a Spider*. HarperCollins, 2005. / Cronin, Doreen. *Diary of a Worm*. Harper-Collins, 2003. / Florczak, Robert. *Yikes!!!* Blue Sky/Scholastic, 2003. / French, Jackie. *Diary of a Wombat*. Clarion, 2003. / Montgomery, Sy. *The Tarantula Scientist*. Houghton Mifflin, 2004. / Murawski, Darlyne A. *Spiders and Their Webs*. National Geographic, 2004. / Pallotta, Jerry. *The Beetle Alphabet Book*. Charlesbridge, 2004. / Simon, Seymour. *Spiders*. HarperCollins, 2003.

SUBJECTS: INSECTS. INTERVIEWS. PERSONAL NARRATIVES. POINT OF VIEW. RADIO. READER'S THEATER. SPIDERS. TARANTULAS.

806   Vail, Rachel. *Over the Moon*. Illus. by Scott Nash. Orchard, 1998. 0-531-33068-0. Unp. Gr. K–2

Here's a funny, tongue-in-cheek staged version of the rhyme "Hi Diddle Diddle," in which a Broadway director-like monkey, Hi, frustrated by Cow's performance, tries to convince her to jump over the moon.

GERM: Compare and contrast this parody with Gennifer Choldenko's *Moonstruck: The True Story of the Cow Who Jumped Over the Moon*. And, of course, find out what happens when two characters from that "Hey diddle diddle" rhyme don't come back in *And The Dish Ran Away with the Spoon* by Janet Stevens.

RELATED TITLES: Babcock, Chris. *No Moon, No Milk*. Crown, 1993. / Brown, Paula. *Moon Jump: A Countdown*. Viking, 1992. / Choldenko, Gennifer. *Moonstruck: The True Story of the Cow Who Jumped over the Moon*. Hyperion, 1997. / Cronin, Doreen. *Click, Clack, Moo: Cows That Type*. Simon & Schuster, 2000. / Egan, Tim. *Metropolitan Cow*. Houghton Mifflin, 1996. / Ernst, Lisa Campbell. *When Bluebell Sang*. Bradbury, 1989. / Johnson, Paul Brett. *The Cow Who Wouldn't Come Down*. Orchard, 1993. / Kinerk, Robert. *Clorinda*. Simon & Schuster, 2003. / Palatini, Margie. *Moo Who?* HarperCollins, 2004. / Schertle, Alice. *How Now, Brown Cow*. Harcourt, 1994. / Speed, Toby. *Two Cool Cows*. Putnam, 1995. / Stevens, Janet, and Susan Stevens Crummel. *And the Dish Ran Away with the Spoon*. Harcourt, 2001.

SUBJECTS: CATS. CHARACTERS IN LITERATURE. COWS. CREATIVE DRAMA. NURSERY RHYMES. PARODIES. PLAYS.

807   Vail, Rachel. *Sometimes I'm Bombaloo*. Illus. by Yumi Heo. Scholastic, 2002. 0-439-08755-4. Unp. Gr. PreK–2

Most of the time, Katie Honors is a really good kid, but when she gets mad, she becomes Bombaloo, full of angry noises and out of control. Yumi Heo's childlike paintings go from sunny yellows to angry reds and bleak blues to black and then back again. Like Molly Bang's *When Sophie Gets Angry—Really, Really Angry*, we see a normally good kid lose it and then get herself together again.

GERM: Discussion points: What does Katie mean when she says, "Sometimes I'm Bombaloo"? Who or what is Bombaloo? Katie says that it's scary being Bombaloo, and she's sorry and a little frightened. How does her mother help her? Why isn't her mother angry with her bad behavior? What advice could you give Katie to help her when she's Bombaloo? How do you get yourself back in command when you become Bombaloo? Write and draw on one side: "When I'm me, I ____"; and on the other side: "When I'm Bombaloo, I ____."

RELATED TITLES: Bang, Molly. *When Sophie Gets Angry—Really, Really Angry*. Scholastic, 1999. / Curtis, Jamie Lee. *It's Hard to Be Five: Learning How to Work My Control Panel*. HarperCollins, 2004. / Curtis, Jamie Lee. *Today I Feel Silly and Other Moods That Make My Day*. HarperCollins, 1998. / Everitt, Betsy. *Mean Soup*. Harcourt, 1992. / Feiffer, Jules. *I'm Not Bobby!* Hyperion, 2001. / Freymann, Saxton, and Joost Elffers. *How Are You Peeling? Foods with Moods*. Scholastic, 1999. / Harper, Jessica. *Lizzy's Ups and Downs: Not an Ordinary School Day*. HarperCollins, 2004. / Hausman, Bonnie. *A to Z: Do You Ever Feel Like Me?* Dutton, 1999. / Henkes, Kevin. *Lilly's Purple Plastic Purse*. Greenwillow, 1996. / Hopkins, Lee Bennett, ed. *Oh, No! Where Are My Pants? And Other Disasters: Poems*. HarperCollins, 2005. / Shannon, David. *David Gets in Trouble*. Scholastic, 2002. / Shannon, David. *No, David!* Scholastic, 1998. / Steig, William. *Pete's a Pizza*. HarperCollins, 1998. / Wells, Rosemary. *Noisy Nora*. Dial, 1997.

SUBJECTS: ANGER. BEHAVIOR. CONFLICT RESOLUTION. EMOTIONS. FAMILY LIFE. MOTHERS AND DAUGHTERS.

808 Valckx, Catharina. *Lizette's Green Sock*. Illus. by the author. Clarion, 2005. 0-618-45298-2. Unp. Gr. PreK–1

Lizette is an inquisitive, orange-beaked white bird, attired in a white- and yellow-spotted dress, with a blue kerchief tied under her chin. When she discovers a pretty green sock and puts it on her twig-like leg, cat brothers Tim and Tom make fun of her for not having the mate. What can you do with just one sock? Lizette's friend, Bert, a mouse, finds it makes a perfect cap.

GERM: Translated from the original French, this diverting little slice-of-life tale, told in present tense, will get your fashion plates talking about what they'd do with only one sock. Another creature who uses a sock as a cap is Hedgy the hedgehog in *The Hat* by Jan Brett.

RELATED TITLES: Bancroft, Catherine, and Hannah Coale Gruenberg. *Felix's Hat*. Four Winds, 1993. / Brett, Jan. *The Hat*. Putnam, 1997. / Brett, Jan. *The Mitten*. Putnam, 1989. / Cauley, Lorinda Bryan. *The Three Little Kittens*. Putnam, 1982. / Hissey, Jane. *Little Bear's Trousers*. Philomel, 1987. / Kellogg, Steven. *The Missing Mitten Mystery*. Dial, 2000. / Klise, Kate. *Shall I Knit You a Hat?* Henry Holt, 2004. / London, Jonathan. *Froggy Gets Dressed*. Viking, 1992. / Nietzel, Shirley. *The Jacket I Wear in the Snow*. Greenwillow, 1989. / Nodset, Joan L. *Who Took the Farmer's Hat*. HarperCollins, 1963. / Slobodkina, Esphyr. *Caps for Sale*. HarperCollins, 1947. / Stoeke, Janet Morgan. *A Hat for Minerva Louise*. Dutton, 1996.

SUBJECTS: BIRDS. BULLIES. CATS. CLOTHING AND DRESS. FISHES. FRIENDSHIP. LOST AND FOUND POSSESSIONS. MICE. SOCKS.

809 Van Allsburg, Chris. *Zathura*. Illus. by the author. Houghton Mifflin, 2002. 0-618-25396-3. Unp. Gr. 1–6

Remember at the end of *Jumanji*—the book, not the movie—when Judy and Peter left the game box under a tree and the Budwing brothers found the box? Well, after a mere 20 years, Van Allsburg has followed up with the sequel. (And yes, it's also been made into a movie.) In the bottom of the Jumanji box, the two battling Budwing brothers, Walter and Danny, find another more interesting board game, an outer space adventure called Zathura, which, of course, comes to life at each move and trashes their house. A meteor falls through the ceiling, Walter loses his gravity and gets stuck to the ceiling, and the boys must contend with a malfunctioning robot and a lizardy space pirate. It's not until the brothers start working together that they can finish the game successfully.

GERM: Use at all ages as an intro to the sci fi genre, along with Jon Scieszka's *Baloney (Henry P.)*. Children can design and play their own board games. You can also play a class version of a game called "Van Allsburg." First, decide what kind of adventure it should be: Ocean? Desert? City? Each player then makes up a wild move and writes it in big letters on a 12 x 12" square of paper or oak tag. To play the game, half of your group line up, holding their cards. One at a time, the players in the other half roll a die and move that many spaces. When a game piece is landed on, that person reads his or her card, and the player acts it out. For an exercise in imaginative writing, readers can also write and illustrate the next installment: what will happen to the next children who find the game box under the tree?

RELATED TITLES: Cox, Judy. *The West Texas Chili Monster*. BridgeWater, 1998. / Etra, Jonathan, and Stephanie Spinner. *Aliens for Breakfast*. Random House, 1988. / McNaughton, Colin. *Here Come the Aliens*. Candlewick, 1995. / Pinkwater, Daniel. *Fat Men from Space*. Yearling, 1980. / Pinkwater, Daniel. *Wallpaper from Space*. Atheneum, 1996. / Rodda, Emily. *Power and Glory*. Greenwillow, 1996. / Sadler, Marilyn. *Alistair in Outer Space*. Prentice Hall, 1984. / Shields, Carol Diggory. *Martian Rock*. Candlewick, 1999. / Sleator, William. *The Night the Heads Came*. Dutton, 1996. / Slote, Alfred. *My Robot Buddy*. HarperTrophy, 1986. / Van Allsburg, Chris. *The Garden of Abdul Gasazi*. Houghton Mifflin, 1979. / Van Allsburg, Chris. *Jumanji*. Houghton Mifflin, 1981. / Van Allsburg, Chris. *The Polar Express*. Houghton Mifflin, 1985. / Yorinks, Arthur. *Company's Coming*. Hyperion, 2000. / Yorinks, Arthur. *Hey, Al*. Farrar, 1986. / Wiesner, David. *June 29, 1999*. Clarion, 1992.

SUBJECTS: BROTHERS. EXTRATERRESTRIAL LIFE. FANTASY. GAMES. PLAY. SCIENCE FICTION. SIBLING RIVALRY.

810 Vaughan, Marcia. *Whistling Dixie*. Illus. by Barry Moser. HarperCollins, 1995. 0-06-021029-X. Unp. Gr. K–2

Hunting for crawdads in Hokey Pokey Swamp, young Dixie Lee brings home a little bitty gator, a snake, and a little hoot owl to keep the churn turners, bogeyman, and mist sisters at bay. All of these spooky creatures show up, of course, and kids'll love the way Dixie Lee knows just how to deal with them.

GERM: The southern flavor of the dialogue is lots of fun to read aloud, and retellers can act out or draw the cause-and-effect aspects of the plot. In the same mood are Mercer Mayer's *Liza Lou* *and the Yeller Belly Swamp,* Molly Bang's *Wiley and the Hairy Man,* and Ed Young's *The Terrible Nung Gwama.*

RELATED TITLES: Bang, Molly. *Wiley and the Hairy Man.* Macmillan, 1976. / DeFelice, Cynthia. *Old Granny and the Bean Thief.* Farrar, 2003. / Mayer, Mercer. *Liza Lou and the Yeller Belly Swamp.* Four Winds, 1980. / McKissack, Patricia, and Onawumi Jean Moss. *Precious and the Boo Hag.* Atheneum, 2005. / Park, Barbara. *Pssst! It's Me . . . the Bogeyman.* Atheneum, 1998. / Sierra, Judy. *Wiley and the Hairy Man.* Dutton, 1996. / Thomassie, Tynia. *Feliciana Feydra LeRoux: A Cajun Tall Tale.* Little, Brown, 1995. / Young, Ed. *The Terrible Nung Gwama: A Chinese Folktale.* Collins-World, 1978.

SUBJECTS: ALLIGATORS. ANIMALS. CREATIVE DRAMA. GRANDFATHERS. PETS. STORIES TO TELL. SUPERNATURAL. SWAMPS.

811   Voake, Charlotte. *Ginger Finds a Home.* Illus. by the author. Candlewick, 2003. 0-7636-1999-X. Unp. Gr. K–2

A skinny little orange stray cat, cold and hungry, comes across a plate of delicious cat food at the end of the garden each day and gradually comes to trust the little girl who has been putting it there. When the girl brings Ginger home, he's too skittish to stay there at first, and the girl is sad. But he adjusts.

GERM: Talk over: How do you make friends with a cat? Of course, if you have befriended a cat, you know there are no easy answers to this question. See how Ginger reacts when a gray kitten moves into the house in the companion book, *Ginger.*

RELATED TITLES: Banks, Kate. *The Cat Who Walked Across France.* Farrar, 2004. / Graham, Bob. *"Let's Get a Pup!" Said Kate.* Candlewick, 2001. / Greene, Carol. *Where Is That Cat?* Hyperion, 1999. / Joosse, Barbara M. *Nugget and Darling.* Clarion, 1997. / McDonald, Joyce. *Homebody.* Putnam, 1991. / McFarland, Lyn Rossiter. *Widget.* Farrar, 2001. / Oates, Joyce Carol. *Where Is Little Reynard?* HarperCollins, 2003. / Simont, Marc. *The Stray Dog.* HarperCollins, 2001. / Voake, Charlotte. *Ginger.* Candlewick, 1997. / Wells, Rosemary. *McDuff Moves In.* Hyperion, 1997. (And others in the McDuff series.)

SUBJECTS: CATS. PETS. STRAY ANIMALS.

812   Waber, Bernard. *Bearsie Bear and the Surprise Sleepover Party.* Illus. by the author. Houghton Mifflin, 1997. 0-395-86450-X. Unp. Gr. PreK–1

On a cold snowy night, as Bearsie Bear is just dozing off in his big warm bed, there's a knock on the door. It's Moosie Moose, and he wants to spend the night. In quick succession, Cowsie Cow, Piggie Pig, Foxie Fox, and Goosie Goose show up and jump into Bearsie Bear's bed, and then jump out again when Porky Porcupine shows up.

GERM: Aside from the endearing line-and-watercolor illustrations, what's so utterly adorable about Waber's gem of a tale is the use of cumulative refrains and funny asides. ("Somebody here has cold hooves.") Listeners will quickly join in on the repeated dialogue and appreciate the generosity and big heart of understated hero Bearsie Bear. You can act out the whole story, using a long scarf as your blanket. A similar story is Libba Moore Gray's *Is There Room on the Featherbed?*

RELATED TITLES: Burningham, John. *Mr. Gumpy's Outing.* Henry Holt, 1971. / Gray, Libba Moore. *Is There Room on the Featherbed?* Orchard, 1997. / Jorgensen, Gail. *Gotcha!* Scholastic, 1997. / Koide, Tan. *May We Sleep Here Tonight?* Atheneum, 1983. / Lum, Kate. *What! Cried Granny: An Almost Bedtime Story.* Doubleday, 2003. / Mathews, Judith, and Fay Robinson. *Nathaniel Willy, Scared Silly.* Bradbury, 1994. / Murphy, Jill. *Peace at Last.* Dial, 1980. / Murray, Marjorie Dennis. *Don't Wake Up the Bear!* Cavendish, 2003. / Rathmann, Peggy. *Good Night, Gorilla.* Putnam, 1994. / Simms, Laura. *The Squeaky Door.* Crown, 1991. / Slate, Joseph. *Story Time for Little Porcupine.* Marshall Cavendish, 2000. / Thomson, Pat. *The Squeaky, Creaky Bed.* Doubleday, 2003. / Wilson, Karma. *Bear Snores On.* McElderry, 2002. / Wood, Audrey. *The Napping House.* Harcourt, 1984.

SUBJECTS: ANIMALS. BEARS. BEDTIME STORIES. CHANTABLE REFRAIN. CREATIVE DRAMA. PORCUPINES. READER'S THEATER.

813   Waber, Bernard. *Do You See a Mouse?* Illus. by the author. Houghton Mifflin, 1995. 0-395-72292-6. Unp. Gr. PreK–2

Everyone at the Park Snoot Hotel insists there is no mouse there. "Do you see a mouse? I do not see a mouse," say the doorman, concierge, bellman, chef, hotel owner, and guests. Just to make sure, owner Mr. Posh engages the services of Hyde and Snide ("Elegant Pest Management, 1-800-CATCHEM") to catch the mouse. After a thorough search, everyone agrees. "No Mouse!" Including the small gray mouse who is on every page, grinning at us.

GERM: Kids will be delirious over this easy-to-read finding book with lots of repetition. After you read it to them, have them read it to you.

RELATED TITLES: Baehr, Patricia. *Mouse in the House*. Holiday House, 1994. / Cauley, Lorinda Bryan. *Treasure Hunt*. Putnam, 1994. / Greene, Carol. *Where Is That Cat?* Hyperion, 1999. / McMillan, Bruce. *Mouse Views: What the Class Pet Saw*. Holiday House, 1993. / Ryan, Pam Muñoz. *Mice and Beans*. Scholastic, 2001. / Yektai, Niki. *What's Missing*. Clarion, 1987. / Yektai, Niki. *What's Silly*. Clarion, 1989.

SUBJECTS: HOTELS, MOTELS, ETC. HUMOROUS FICTION. MICE.

814 Waber, Bernard. *Evie and Margie*. Illus. by the author. Houghton Mifflin, 2003. 0-618-34124-2. Unp. Gr. K–2

Hippo best friends Evie and Margie dream of becoming famous actors, but when they both try out for the class play, Margie, who can cry real tears on command, gets the lead of Cinderella. Evie becomes the understudy and a tree in the forest. In a hilarious yet poignant examination of how jealousy can imperil even the best friendships, the two girls each get their chance to shine.

GERM: Explore with your actors, as you plan a Reader's Theater, how they can summon up real emotions and convey them to an audience. Thespians triumph in Cari Best's *Shrinking Violet*, Mary Hoffman's *Amazing Grace*, and Alexander Stadler's *Beverly Billingsly Takes a Bow*.

RELATED TITLES: Best, Cari. *Shrinking Violet*. Farrar, 2001. / Brown, Laurie Krasny, and Marc Brown. *How to Be a Friend: A Guide to Making Friends and Keeping Them*. Little, Brown, 1998. / Greenfield, Eloise. *Grandpa's Face*. Philomel, 1988. / Hobbie, Holly. *Toot and Puddle: The New Friend*. Little, Brown, 2004. / Hoffman, Mary. *Amazing Grace*. Dial, 1991. / Howe, James. *Horace and Morris But Mostly Dolores*. Atheneum, 1999. / Marshall, James. *George and Martha: The Complete Stories of Two Best Friends*. Houghton Mifflin, 1997. / Martin, Ann. *Rachel Parker, Kindergarten Show-Off*. Holiday House, 1992. / Stadler, Alexander. *Beverly Billingsly Takes a Bow*. Harcourt, 2003. / Waber, Bernard. *Gina*. Houghton Mifflin, 1985. / Waber, Bernard. *Ira Says Goodbye*. Houghton Mifflin, 1988. / Waber, Bernard. Lyle the Crocodile series. Houghton Mifflin.

SUBJECTS: ACTING. BEST FRIENDS. CINDERELLA STORIES. FRIENDSHIP. HIPPOPOTAMUS. JEALOUSY. PLAYS.

815 Waber, Bernard. *Gina*. Illus. by the author. Houghton Mifflin, 1995. 0-395-74279-X. Unp. Gr. 1–3

Dozens of boys populate Gina's new neighborhood in Queens, but not a single girl. In Waber's amiable narrative poem, we feel Gina's frustration when the boys ignore her. But then she throws them a baseball. Wowed, they drop their guard and invite her onto the team. All summer, Gina pals around with the guys, but on the first day of school, no one recognizes her in her girl clothes until she pulls out her baseball cap.

GERM: Ask your listeners what winning qualities Gina possesses that make her "new kid" status easier to overcome. Introduce crackerjack girl baseball players from history: Alta Weiss, in *Girl Wonder* by Deborah Hopkinson, and Jackie Mitchell, in *Mighty Jackie, the Strike-Out Queen* by Marissa Moss.

RELATED TITLES: Corey, Shana. *Players in Pigtails*. Scholastic, 2003. / Hamm, Mia. *Winners Never Quit!* HarperCollins, 2004. / Hopkinson, Deborah. *Girl Wonder: A Baseball Story in Nine Innings*. Atheneum, 2003. / Moss, Marissa. *Mighty Jackie, the Strike-Out Queen*. Simon & Schuster, 2004. / Norworth, Jack. *Take Me Out to the Ballgame*. Four Winds, 1993. / Stadler, Alexander. *Beverly Billingsly Can't Catch*. Harcourt, 2004. / Welch, Willie. *Playing Right Field*. Scholastic, 1995.

SUBJECTS: ATHLETES. BASEBALL. FRIENDSHIP. MOVING, HOUSEHOLD. SPORTS. STORIES IN RHYME.

816 Waddell, Martin. *Hi, Harry!* Illus. by Barbara Firth. Candlewick, 2003. 0-7636-1802-0. Unp. Gr. PreK–K

Though none of the quick-moving animals has time to play with Harry Tortoise, Sam Snail is just Harry's speed, and the two enjoy a day of slow games together. The subtitle on the cover says it all: "The moving story of how one slow tortoise slowly made a friend."

GERM: A sweet story of the pleasures of friendship, illustrated in watercolors and ink, it will get your group trying out some of Harry and Sam's games in slow motion, as a tribute to folks who aren't always in a hurry. Discussion point: Harry Tortoise found a perfect friend. What are you looking for in the perfect friend?

RELATED TITLES: Bottner, Barbara, and Gerald Kruglik. *Wallace's Lists*. HarperCollins, 2004. / Carle, Eric. *"Slowly, Slowly, Slowly," Said the Sloth*. Philomel, 2002. / Chorao, Kay. *Pig and Crow*. Henry Holt, 2000. / Edwards, Pamela Duncan. *Some Smug Slug*. HarperCollins, 1996. / Lobel, Arnold. Frog and Toad series.

HarperCollins. / London, Jonathan. *What Newt Could Do for Turtle.* Candlewick, 1996. / Stevens, Janet. *The Tortoise and the Hare: An Aesop Fable.* Holiday House, 1984. / Wolkstein, Diane. *Step by Step.* Morrow, 1994.

SUBJECTS: ANIMALS. FRIENDSHIP. GAMES. SNAILS. SPEED. TURTLES.

817   Waddell, Martin. *Webster J. Duck.* Illus. by David Parkins. Candlewick, 2001. 0-7636-1506-4. Unp. Gr. PreK–K

After hatching out of his egg, Webster J. Duck sets off to find his mother, looking for someone who goes quack-quack like him and not bow-wow, baa-baa, or moo-moo, the way the other big ducks he meets do.

GERM: Act this out in groups of four. See how the bird finds his mom in P. D. Eastman's *Are You My Mother?*, a duckling finds his in Simon James' *Little One Step*, and a goose finds Little Bird in Linda Wikler's *Alfonse, Where Are You?*

RELATED TITLES: Buzzeo, Toni. *Dawdle Duckling.* Dial, 2003. / Dunrea, Olivier. *Ollie.* Houghton Mifflin, 2003. / Eastman, P. D. *Are You My Mother?* Random House, 1960. / Hindley, Judy. *Do Like a Duck Does!* Candlewick, 2002. / James, Simon. *Little One Step.* Candlewick, 2003. / Lawrence, John. *This Little Chick.* Candlewick, 2002. / McCloskey, Robert. *Make Way for Ducklings.* Viking, 1941. / Raffi. *Five Little Ducks.* Crown, 1988. / Simmons, Jane. *Quack, Daisy, Quack!* Little, Brown, 2002. / Whippo, Walt, and Bernard Zaritzky. *Little White Duck.* Little, Brown, 2000. / Wikler, Linda. *Alfonse, Where Are You?* Crown, 1996.

SUBJECTS: ANIMAL SOUNDS. CREATIVE DRAMA. DUCKS. LOST. MOTHERS.

818   Waldman, Neil. *The Starry Night.* Illus. by the author. Boyds Mills, 1999. 1-56397-736-2. Unp. Gr. K–6

In Central Park, young Bernard befriends Vincent, a painter, and shows him the sights of New York City, from Harlem to the Statue of Liberty, all of which the man paints in his passionate and colorful signature style.

GERM: Children familiar with Van Gogh's paintings will be eager to paint their own local landmarks, as Bernard does at the end of this haunting book. Meet Vincent through the eyes of two other children in *Camille and the Sunflowers* by Laurence Anholt and *Painting the Wind* by Michelle Dionetti.

RELATED TITLES: Anholt, Laurence. *Camille and the Sunflowers: A Story About Vincent Van Gogh.* Barron's, 1994. / Björk, Christina. *Linnea in Monet's Garden.* R. & S. Books, 1987. / Dionetti, Michelle. *Painting the Wind.* Little, Brown, 1996. / Fritz, Jean. *Leonardo's Horse.* Putnam, 2001. / Garland, Michael. *Dinner at Magritte's.* Dutton, 1995. / Jakobsen, Kathy. *My New York.* Little, Brown, 2003. / Krull, Kathleen. *Lives of the Artists: Masterpieces, Messes (and What the Neighbors Thought).* Harcourt, 1995. / Nichol, Barbara. *Beethoven Lives Upstairs.* Orchard, 1994. / Raczka, Bob. *Art Is . . .* Millbrook, 2003. / Rubin, Susan Goldman. *Degas and the Dance: The Painter and the Petits Rats, Perfecting Their Art.* Abrams, 2002. / Weitzman, Jacqueline Preiss. *You Can't Take a Balloon into the Metropolitan Museum.* Dial, 1998.

SUBJECTS: ARTISTS. NEW YORK CITY. PAINTERS. PICTURE BOOKS FOR ALL AGES. VAN GOGH, VINCENT.

819   Wallace, Nancy Elizabeth. *A Taste of Honey.* Illus. by the author. Winslow, 2001. 1-890817-51-1. Unp. Gr. PreK–2

Lily Bear asks her Poppy where honey comes from, and he says from the jar. "But . . . before that?" she asks, and step by step, he takes her backward through the process, ending up at the beginning, with the bees. Clear, attractive, cut-paper illustrations show the process of extracting and harvesting honey.

GERM: An informative page of honey facts finishes up the book. Bring in a honeycomb so all can take a taste. See the true account of how a small African bird leads a badger to honey in *Honey . . . Honey . . . Lion!* by Jan Brett and people to honey in *If You Should Meet a Honey Guide* by April Pulley Sayre.

RELATED TITLES: Bernard, Robin. *Juma and the Honey Guide.* Dillon/Silver Burdett, 1996. / Brett, Jan. *Honey . . . Honey . . . Lion!* Putnam, 2005. / Cole, Joanna. *The Magic School Bus Inside a Beehive.* Scholastic, 1996. / Heiligman, Deborah. *Honeybees.* National Geographic, 2002. / Krebs, Laurie. *The Beeman.* National Geographic, 2002. / Martin, Francesca. *The Honey Hunters.* Candlewick, 1992. / Rockwell, Anne. *Honey in a Hive.* HarperCollins, 2005. / Sayre, April Pulley. *If You Should Meet a Honey Guide.* Houghton Mifflin, 1995. / Wallace, Nancy Elizabeth. *Apples, Apples, Apples.* Winslow, 2000.

SUBJECTS: BEES. HONEY. INSECTS.

820   Walter, Virginia. *"Hi, Pizza Man!"* **Illus. by Ponder Goembel. Orchard, 1995. 0-531-08735-2. Unp. Gr. PreK–K**

While hungry Vivian waits for the pizza man to come, she and her mother envision a pizza kitty, pizza duck, and even a pizza dinosaur delivering their pie.

GERM: All will join in greeting with animal noises the various and always dignified pizza-wielding animals at the door and laughing themselves silly. Brainstorm what other creatures could show up and make the appropriate greeting noises.

RELATED TITLES: Buehner, Caralyn, and Mark Buehner. *A Job for Wittilda.* Dial, 1993. / Dodds, Dayle-Ann. *Do Bunnies Talk?* HarperCollins, 1992. / Feiffer, Jules. *Bark, George.* HarperCollins, 1999. / Harter, Debbie. *Walking Through the Jungle.* Orchard, 1997. / Martin, Bill, Jr. *Polar Bear, Polar Bear, What Do You Hear?* Henry Holt, 1991. / Park, Linda Sue. *Mung-Mung: A Folded Book of Animal Sounds.* Charlesbridge, 2004. / Shapiro, Arnold L. *Mice Squeak, We Speak.* Putnam, 1997. / Shapiro, Arnold L. *Who Says That?* Dutton, 1991. / Steig, William. *Pete's a Pizza.* HarperCollins, 1998. / Sturges, Philemon. *The Little Red Hen (Makes a Pizza).* Dutton, 1999. / Thomson, Pat. *The Squeaky, Creaky Bed.* Doubleday, 2003. / Williams, Sue. *I Went Walking.* Harcourt, 1990. / Williams, Sue. *Let's Go Visiting.* Harcourt, 1998.

SUBJECTS: ANIMALS. CHANTABLE REFRAIN. PIZZA. SOUND EFFECTS.

821   Walton, Rick. *Bunnies on the Go: Getting from Place to Place.* **Illus. by Paige Miglio. Harper-Collins, 2003. 0-06-029185-0. Unp. Gr. PreK–1**

Mom and dad take their three little bunnies on a transportation-crammed vacation via car, train, wagon, tractor, balloon, boat, bike, truck, bus, ferry, cab, and, finally, plane.

GERM: Listeners will be able to predict the next means of transport by filling in the rhyming word at the end of each page's four-line rhyming description. For more transportation fun, read the poems in Daniel Kirk's *Go!* and listen to the accompanying CD.

RELATED TITLES: Barton, Byron. *My Car.* Greenwillow, 2001. / Burningham, John. *Harvey Slumfenburger's Christmas Present.* Candlewick, 1993. / Day, Nancy Raines. *Double Those Wheels.* Dutton, 2003. / Kirk, Daniel. *Go!* Hyperion, 2001. / Raffi. *The Wheels on the Bus.* Crown, 1988. / Root, Phyllis. *Rattletrap Car.* Candlewick, 2001. / Shields, Carol Diggory. *Animagicals: On the Go.* Handprint, 2001. / Walton, Rick. *Bunny Christmas: A Family Celebration.* HarperCollins, 2004. / Walton, Rick. *Bunny Day: Telling Time from Breakfast to Bedtime.* HarperCollins, 2002. / Walton, Rick. *Bunny School: A Learning Fun-for-All.* HarperCollins, 2005. / Walton, Rick. *One More Bunny: Adding from One to Ten.* Lothrop, 2000. / Walton, Rick. *So Many Bunnies: A Bedtime ABC and Counting Book.* Lothrop, 1998.

SUBJECTS: RABBITS. STORIES IN RHYME. TRANSPORTATION. VACATIONS. VEHICLES.

822   Walton, Rick. *Once There Was a Bull . . . (Frog).* **Illus. by Greg Hally. Gibbs-Smith, 1995. 0-87905-652-5. Unp. Gr. K–2**

What a difference a syllable can make. Each time you turn the page of this deliriously silly tale of a bullfrog searching for his lost hop, you get a word surprise. "He looked under a hedge," it says, and there is a green hedge. Turn the page, and it adds, "Hog." And there is Bullfrog, standing placidly under a green-tinged hedgehog.

GERM: First, brainstorm a list of new compound words. Wordsmiths can then compose new bullfrog sentences using surprising compound words at the end. Folding a piece of drawing paper in half, write and illustrate the sentence on the front; then open up the page and write and draw the final syllable there. For example: "Bullfrog dug up a pile of earth . . . worms."

RELATED TITLES: Agee, Jon. *Elvis Lives and Other Anagrams.* Farrar, 2004. / Agee, Jon. *Go Hang a Salami! I'm a Lasagna Hog! And Other Palindromes.* Farrar, 1992. / Clement, Rod. *Just Another Ordinary Day.* HarperCollins, 1997. / Freymann, Saxton, and Joost Elffers. *Dog Food.* Scholastic, 2002. / Hepworth, Cathi. *Antics! An Alphabetical Anthology.* Putnam, 1992. / Hepworth, Cathi. *Bug Off! A Swarm of Insect Words.* Putnam, 1998. / Maestro, Betsy. *All Aboard Overnight: A Book of Compound Words.* Clarion, 1992. / Maestro, Giulio. *Macho Nacho and Other Rhyming Riddles.* Dutton, 1994. / McCall, Francis, and Patricia Keeler. *A Huge Hog Is a Big Pig: A Rhyming Word Game.* Greenwillow, 2002. / Reiss, Mike. *The Great Show-and-Tell Disaster.* Price Stern Sloan, 2001. / Root, Phyllis. *Meow Monday.* Candlewick, 2000. / Steig, William. *CDB.* Simon & Schuster, 2000.

SUBJECTS: ANIMALS. ENGLISH LANGUAGE—COMPOUND WORDS. FROGS. WORD GAMES.

823   Walton, Rick. *So Many Bunnies: A Bedtime ABC and Counting Book.* **Illus. by Paige Miglio. Lothrop, 1998. 0-688-13657-5. Unp. Gr. PreK–1**

Count Old Mother Rabbit's 26 shoe-dwelling children in alphabetical order as they prepare for bed in places that rhyme with each of their names, starting with "1 was named Abel. He slept on the table," and all the way to "26 was named Zed. He slept on the shed." Soft, sweet pen-and-ink and watercolors sure show a lot of sleepy bunnies.

GERM: As you read aloud each rabbit's name, your group can predict and anticipate the word that rhymes with it or look for the picture clue. Introduce the other bunny books in Walton's series.

RELATED TITLES: Christelow, Eileen. *Five Little Monkeys Jumping on the Bed*. Clarion, 1989. / Dewdney, Anna. *Llama Llama Red Pajama*. Viking, 2005. / Fox, Mem. *Boo to a Goose*. Dial, 1998. / Loomis, Christine. *One Cow Coughs*. Ticknor & Fields, 1994. / Loomis, Christine. *Scuba Bunnies*. Putnam, 1997. / Merriam, Eve. *Where Is Everybody? An Animal Alphabet*. Simon & Schuster, 1989. / Noonan, Julia. *Mouse by Mouse*. Dutton, 2003. / Rathmann, Peggy. *Ten Minutes Till Bedtime*. Putnam, 1998. / Rothstein, Gloria. *Sheep Asleep*. HarperCollins, 2003. / Slate, Joseph. *Miss Bindergarten Gets Ready for Kindergarten*. Dutton, 1996. / Walton, Rick. *Bunnies on the Go: Getting from Place to Place*. HarperCollins, 2003. / Walton, Rick. *Bunny Christmas: A Family Celebration*. HarperCollins, 2004. / Walton, Rick. *Bunny School: A Learning Fun-for-All*. HarperCollins, 2005. / Walton, Rick. *One More Bunny: Adding from One to Ten*. Lothrop, 2000.

SUBJECTS: ALPHABET BOOKS. BEDTIME STORIES. COUNTING BOOKS. RABBITS. STORIES IN RHYME.

824   **Ward, Helen.** *The Rooster and the Fox*. **Illus. by the author. Millbrook, 2003. 0-7613-2920-X. Unp. Gr. K–4**

Adapted from the "Nun's Priest's Tale" from Chaucer's 14th-century classic, *The Canterbury Tales*, here is strutting, vain Chanticleer the rooster, pride of the farmyard, taken in by a sweet-talking fox. When the fox carries him off, the two are pursued by all of the farmyard animals.

GERM: Like all of the Aesop and LaFontaine fables, this cautionary tale has a moral: "Beware of false flattery." Ask your listeners to talk over what this means and how it might apply to their own lives. Compare this version with Barbara Cooney's Caldecott Medal picture book, *Chanticleer and the Fox*.

RELATED TITLES: Aylesworth, Jim. *The Tale of Tricky Fox: A New England Trickster Tale*. Scholastic, 2001. / Cooney, Barbara. *Chanticleer and the Fox*. HarperCollins, 1986. / Edwards, Pamela Duncan. *McGillycuddy Could!* HarperCollins, 2005. / Frankenhuyzen, Robbyn Smith van. *Saving Samantha: A True Story*. Sleeping Bear, 2004. / Froehlich, Margaret Walden. *That Kookoory!* Harcourt, 1995. / Hastings, Selina. *Reynard the Fox*. Tambourine, 1991. / Lobel, Arnold. *How the Rooster Saved the Day*. Greenwillow, 1977. / Morpurgo, Michael. *The McElderry Book of Aesop's Fables*. McElderry, 2005. / Osborne, Mary Pope. *Favorite Medieval Tales*. Scholastic, 1998. / Pearson, Tracey Campbell. *Bob*. Farrar, 2002. / Pinkney, Jerry. *Aesop's Fables*. SeaStar, 2000. / Silverman, Erica. *Don't Fidget a Feather*. Macmillan, 1994. / Sogabe, Aki. *Aesop's Fox*. Harcourt, 1999. / Wattenberg, Jane. *Henny-Penny*. Scholastic, 2000.

SUBJECTS: DOMESTIC ANIMALS. FABLES. FLATTERY. FOXES. ROOSTERS.

825   **Weaver, Tess.** *Opera Cat*. **Illus. by Andréa Wesson. Clarion, 2002. 0-618-09635-3. Unp. Gr. K–3**

When Madame Soso gets laryngitis and can't sing a note, her talented opera-singing cat, Alma, comes to the rescue as her stand-in.

GERM: Play a bit of an opera aria for children to get in the mood for the story. Afterward, ask them to speculate what hidden talents their pets have and write a story about them. Meet a dog who thinks his singing is as good as the diva's at the Metropolitan Opera in *The Dog Who Sang at the Opera* by Jim West and Marshall Izen.

RELATED TITLES: Auch, Mary Jane. *Bantam of the Opera*. Holiday House, 1997. / Auch, Mary Jane. *Hen Lake*. Holiday House, 1995. / Auch, Mary Jane. *Peeping Beauty*. Holiday House, 1993. / Edwards, Pamela Duncan. *Honk! The Story of a Prima Swanerina*. Hyperion, 1998. / Ernst, Lisa Campbell. *When Bluebell Sang*. Bradbury, 1989. / Goss, Linda. *The Frog Who Wanted to Be a Singer*. Orchard, 1996. / Hurd, Thacher. *Art Dog*. HarperCollins, 1996. / Kinerk, Robert. *Clorinda*. Simon & Schuster, 2003. / West, Jim, and Marshall Izen. *The Dog Who Sang at the Opera*. Abrams, 2004.

SUBJECTS: CATS. ITALY. MUSIC. OPERA. SINGERS.

826   **Weeks, Sarah.** *Mrs. McNosh Hangs Up Her Wash*. **Illus. by Nadine Bernard Westcott. Harper-Festival, 1998. 0-06-000479-7. Unp. Gr. PreK–1**

In her zeal to wash everything and hang it on the clothesline to dry, jubilant Mrs. McNosh goes way overboard. "She hangs up the stockings. / She hangs up the shoes. / She wrings out the paper / and hangs up the news." She hangs up the dog, the phone, two sleepy bats, and even Grandpa McNosh's false teeth, before hanging herself up, in a comfortable chair, to dry.

GERM: Rollicking rhyme and sprightly watercolors ensure your kids will be laughing and chanting along with each verse. Hand out the words and do a round-robin choral reading. Have everyone draw pictures of other items Mrs. McNosh might hang on her line. Follow up the wordplay fun with *Oh My Gosh, Mrs. McNosh!*, in which she tries to catch her runaway dog and catches instead a trout, a wedding bouquet, a fly ball, and even a cold.

RELATED TITLES: Arnold, Tedd. *Catalina Magdalena Hoopensteiner Wallendiner Hogan Logan Bogan Was Her Name.* Scholastic, 2004. / Hoberman, Mary Ann. *There Once Was a Man Named Michael Finnegan.* Little, Brown, 2001. / Raffi. *Down by the Bay.* Crown, 1987. / Taback, Simms. *There Was an Old Lady Who Swallowed a Fly.* Viking, 1997. / Weeks, Sarah. *Oh My Gosh, Mrs. McNosh!* HarperCollins, 2002. / Westcott, Nadine Bernard. *I Know an Old Lady Who Swallowed a Fly.* Little, Brown, 1980. / Westcott, Nadine Bernard. *The Lady with the Alligator Purse.* Little, Brown, 1988. / Ziefert, Harriet. *I Swapped My Dog.* Houghton Mifflin, 1998.

SUBJECTS: HUMOROUS POETRY. NONSENSE VERSES. STORIES IN RHYME.

827   Weigel, Jeff. *Atomic Ace (He's Just My Dad).* **Illus. by the author. Albert Whitman, 2004. 0-8075-3216-9. Unp. Gr. K–4**

What's it like having a superhero for a dad? Sure he fights crime, but he's also a regular guy, cooking his son Saturday hot dog lunches (with his nuclear breath), hitting baseballs (clear into space), and missing his son's band recital (because his head has been turned into a giant bug by his ruthless nemesis, the Insect King). Illustrated in glorious glossy ink and brush illustrations—just like the comics, only on better paper—the story is related in matter-of-fact rhyming stanzas by Atomic Ace's own son, who sticks up for his famous dad even when the kids at school call him weird.

GERM: Talk about superheroes and their powers. What if your parents were superheroes? What could they do to help the world? Draw two paneled, captioned, comic book-style portraits of your superhero parents at home and on the job. Get kids writing and illustrating comics (they can work in pairs, if they like—one as the author, the other as the illustrator) to do a large-sized comic strip with balloon dialogue, narrative captions, and some action.

RELATED TITLES: Browne, Anthony. *My Dad.* Farrar, 2001. / Buehner, Caralyn. *Superdog: The Heart of a Hero.* HarperCollins, 2004. / Graham, Bob. *Max.* Candlewick, 2000. / Grey, Mini. *Traction Man Is Here!* Knopf, 2005. / O'Connor, George. *Kapow!* Simon & Schuster, 2004. / O'Malley, Kevin. *Captain Raptor and the Moon Mystery.* Walker, 2005. / Van Draanen, Wendelin. *Shredderman: Secret Identity.* Knopf, 2004. / Ziefert, Harriet. *33 Uses for a Dad.* Blue Apple, 2004.

SUBJECTS: CARTOONS AND COMICS. FATHERS AND SONS. HEROES. STORIES IN RHYME. SUPERHEROES.

828   Weitzman, Jacqueline Preiss. *You Can't Take a Balloon into the Metropolitan Museum.* **Illus. by Robin Preiss Glasser. Dial, 1998. 0-8037-2301-6. 36pp. Gr. K–3**

While a little girl and her grandmother visit the art museum, the girl's balloon takes a tour of New York City. This zany, oversized, wordless picture book parallels the themes of the museum's paintings with a look at New York's most fabulous tourist attractions. In the intricate pictures, done in black ink, watercolor washes, gouache, and colored pencils, girl and balloon are finally reunited.

GERM: Eloise may have her Plaza Hotel, but if you want to take a tour of the Metropolitan Museum of Art and see all of midtown Manhattan in the process, here's the ticket to adventure and great art. At the back is a page identifying all of the art reproductions.

RELATED TITLES: Alcorn, Johnny. *Rembrandt's Beret.* Tambourine, 1991. / Auch, Mary Jane. *Eggs Mark the Spot.* Holiday House, 1996. / Brown, Laurene Krasny. *Visiting the Art Museum.* Dutton, 1986. / Browne, Anthony. *Willy the Dreamer.* Candlewick, 1998. / Dorros, Arthur. *Abuela.* Dutton, 1991. / Grimes, Nikki. *C Is for City.* Lothrop, 1995. / Hurd, Thacher. *Art Dog.* HarperCollins, 1996. / Jakobsen, Kathy. *My New York.* Little, Brown, 2003. / Johnson, Stephen T. *Alphabet City.* Viking, 1995. / Konigsburg, E. L. *Amy Elizabeth Explores Bloomingdale's.* Atheneum, 1992. / Lithgow, John. *Micawber.* Simon & Schuster, 2002. / Melmed, Laura Krauss. *New York, New York! The Big Apple from A to Z.* HarperCollins, 2005. / Richardson, Joy. *Inside the Museum: A Children's Guide to the Metropolitan Museum of Art.* Abrams, 1993. / Ringgold, Faith. *Tar Beach.* Crown, 1991. / Scieszka, Jon. *Seen Art?* Viking, 2005. / Weitzman, Jacqueline Preiss. *You Can't Take a Balloon into the Museum of Fine Arts.* Dial, 2002.

SUBJECTS: ART APPRECIATION. BALLOONS. CITIES AND TOWNS. METROPOLITAN MUSEUM OF ART (NEW YORK, NY). MUSEUMS. NEW YORK CITY. STORIES WITHOUT WORDS.

829   Wells, Rosemary. *Bunny Cakes.* **Illus. by the author. Dial, 1997. 0-8037-2144-7. Unp. Gr. PreK–1**

For their Grandma's birthday, rabbit Max makes an earthworm birthday cake, while long-suffering sister Ruby entreats Max not to help her make an angel surprise cake with raspberry-fluff icing. "Don't touch anything, Max," says Ruby, but it's too late and somehow the eggs, milk, and flour all end up on the floor. Sent to the store for new ingredients, Max adds "Red-Hot Marshmallow Squirters" to Ruby's list, but the grocer can't read Max's scribbling.

GERM: Ask your listeners: Why can't the grocer read Max's writing? Use Max's saga with all ages to discuss the importance of writing as communication. See how toddler Trixie tries to make herself understood in *Knuffle Bunny* by Mo Willems.

RELATED TITLES: Elya, Susan Middleton. *Eight Animals Bake a Cake.* Putnam, 2002. / Hoban, Lillian. *Arthur's Christmas Cookies.* HarperCollins, 1972. / Hooper, Meredith. *Honey Cookies.* Frances Lincoln, 2005. / Robart, Rose. *The Cake That Mack Ate.* Little, Brown, 1987. / Stevens, Janet, and Susan Stevens Crummel. *Cook-a-Doodle-Doo!* Harcourt, 1999. / Wells, Rosemary. *Bunny Money.* Viking, 2000. / Wells, Rosemary. *Felix Feels Better.* Candlewick, 2001. / Wells, Rosemary. *Max's Christmas.* Dial, 1986. / Wells, Rosemary. *Max's Dragon Shirt.* Dial, 1991. / Wells, Rosemary. *Max's First Word.* Dial, 1979. / Wells, Rosemary. *Noisy Nora.* Dial, 1997. / Willems, Mo. *Knuffle Bunny.* Hyperion, 2004.

SUBJECTS: BAKING. BIRTHDAYS. BROTHERS AND SISTERS. CAKE. COOKERY. RABBITS. WRITING.

830   Wells, Rosemary. *Bunny Money.* **Illus. by the author. Dial, 1997. 0-8037-2147-1. Unp. Gr. PreK–2**

In an equally howlingly funny companion story to *Bunny Cakes*, Ruby takes spendthrift Max shopping for Grandma's birthday present. Ruby's walletful of cash dwindles quickly as Max buys a nice set of vampire teeth with oozing cherry syrup and tries them out. Next stop, the Laundromat, where Ruby washes Max's now cherry-stained overalls. After depleting all their remaining resources, Max still saves the day with his lucky quarter.

GERM: Photocopy the bunny money on the endpapers to hand out and have children find out something about the famous rabbits adorning each bill. The bunny money can also tie in to a handy math lesson; compose Max and Ruby word problems to solve. Children will also enjoy writing and illustrating a sentence or two about Max on a new buying spree. Rosemary Wells's Max and Ruby books, including *Max Cleans Up*, *Max's Christmas*, and *Max's Dragon Shirt*, are choice examples to use when you tell children, "I LOVE this book character!"

RELATED TITLES: Schertle, Alice. *Down the Road.* Harcourt, 1995. / Viorst, Judith. *Alexander Who Used to Be Rich Last Sunday.* Atheneum, 1978. / Wells, Rosemary. *Bunny Cakes.* Viking, 2000. / Wells, Rosemary. *Max Cleans Up.* Dial, 2000. / Wells, Rosemary. *Max's Chocolate Chicken.* Dial, 1989. / Wells, Rosemary. *Max's Christmas.* Dial, 1986. / Wells, Rosemary. *Max's Dragon Shirt.* Dial, 1991. / Wells, Rosemary. *Max's First Word.* Dial, 1979.

SUBJECTS: BROTHERS AND SISTERS. GRANDMOTHERS. MONEY. RABBITS. SHOPPING.

831   Wells, Rosemary. *Emily's First 100 Days of School.* **Illus. by the author. Hyperion, 2000. 0-7868-0507-2. 56pp. Gr. PreK–1**

On the first day of school, rabbit Emily's new teacher, guinea pig Miss Cribbage, hands out a number notebook, telling her charges that each morning they will write down their "new number friend," until they reach the number 100, when they'll have a party.

GERM: Count along with Emily: sing "Tea for Two" on day two, play Crazy Eights on day eight, and watch the year fly by. Number hounds will enjoy coming up with other number relationships, both well-established and personal, to record in their own number notebooks. Joan Holub's 100th Day of School Web site at <users.aol.com/a100thday/ideas.html> will give you another 300 ideas from teachers and librarians across the country. Explore the kindergarten year through the curriculum with Emily and her friends in Wells's companion book, *My Kindergarten.*

RELATED TITLES: Cuyler, Margery. *100th Day Worries.* Simon & Schuster, 2000. / Franco, Betsy. *Counting Our Way to the 100th Day!* McElderry, 2004. / Frith, Margaret. *I'll Teach My Dog 100 Words.* Random House, 1973. / Kasza, Keiko. *The Wolf's Chicken Stew.* Putnam, 1987. / Medearis, Angela S. *The 100th Day of School.* Scholastic, 1996. / Pinczes, Elinor J. *One Hundred Hungry Ants.* Houghton Mifflin, 1993. / Rockwell, Anne. *100 School Days.* HarperCollins, 2002. / Slate, Joseph. *Miss Bindergarten Celebrates the 100th Day of Kindergarten.* Dutton, 1998. / Wells, Rosemary. *My Kindergarten.* Hyperion, 2004. / Wells, Rosemary. *Yoko's World of Kindness: Golden Rules for a Happy Classroom.* Hyperion, 2005.

SUBJECTS: ANIMALS. COUNTING BOOKS. FIRST DAY OF SCHOOL. MATHEMATICS. ONE HUNDREDTH DAY CELEBRATIONS. RABBITS. SCHOOLS. TEACHERS.

832 **Wells, Rosemary.** *Felix Feels Better.* **Illus. by the author. Candlewick, 2001. 0-7636-0639-1. Unp. Gr. PreK–1**

In the morning, after staying up way too late and eating too many chocolate blimpies, little guinea pig Felix is so peaky that his mama has to take her little moonbeam to Dr. Duck for two spoonfuls of Happy Tummy before he feels perky again.

GERM: Ask your little moonbeams what their parents do for them when they don't feel well. Talk about home remedies and why it's not so good for them to eat too many chocolate blimpies. Compare get-well treatments in *Get Well, Good Knight* by Shelley Moore Thomas.

RELATED TITLES: Bateman, Teresa. *Farm Flu.* Albert Whitman, 2001. / Cherry, Lynne. *Who's Sick Today?* Dutton, 1988. / LeGuin, Ursula K. *A Visit from Dr. Katz.* Atheneum, 1988. / Loomis, Christine. *One Cow Coughs: A Counting Book for the Sick and Miserable.* Ticknor & Fields, 1994. / Slate, Joseph. *Miss Bindergarten Stays Home from Kindergarten.* Dutton, 2000. / Thomas, Shelley Moore. *Get Well, Good Knight.* Dutton, 2002. / Wells, Rosemary. *Bunny Cakes.* Viking, 1997. / Wells, Rosemary. *Bunny Money.* Viking, 2000. / Wells, Rosemary. *McDuff Moves In.* Hyperion, 1997. (And others in the McDuff series.) / Wells, Rosemary. *Noisy Nora.* Dial, 1997. / Wells, Rosemary. *Shy Charles.* Dial, 1988. / Yolen, Jane. *How Do Dinosaurs Get Well Soon?* Blue Sky/Scholastic, 2003.

SUBJECTS: DOCTORS. GUINEA PIGS. MOTHERS AND SONS. SICK.

833 **Wells, Rosemary.** *Lassie Come-Home: Erik Knight's Original 1938 Classic.* **Illus. by Susan Jeffers. Henry Holt, 1995. 0-8050-3794-2. Unp. Gr. 2–5**

Erik Knight's classic novel has been abridged into a radiant picture book that retains the essence of the heartbreaking story of Joe, a poor Yorkshire lad who must give up his beloved collie. Sold to the Duke of Rudling, Lassie escapes from his estate three times to find his beloved boy, until the Duke takes her to northern Scotland eight hundred miles away, where she manages to slip away yet again. Enduring cold, hunger, sickness, and injury, the stalwart dog perseveres for almost a year until Joe finds her, half-dead of pneumonia, waiting for him in the schoolyard.

GERM: Children who know Lassie from all those corny TV spin-offs will be moved by the sacrifice Joe must make and the honest loyalty of the dog. Be forewarned: this story with its straightforward narration and the exquisite oversized watercolor, ink, and pencil illustrations will make you and your listeners cry, but you will never forget it.

RELATED TITLES: Blake, Robert. *Togo.* Philomel, 2002. / Cullen, Lynn. *The Mightiest Heart.* Dial, 1998. / Naylor, Phyllis Reynolds. *Shiloh.* Atheneum, 1991. / Turner, Pamela S. *Hachiko: The True Story of a Loyal Dog.* Houghton Mifflin, 2004. / Waite, Michael P. *Jojofu.* Lothrop, 1996. / Wells, Rosemary. *Waiting for the Evening Star.* Dial, 1993.

SUBJECTS: DOGS. ENGLAND. LOVE. LOYALTY. PICTURE BOOKS FOR ALL AGES.

834 **Wells, Rosemary.** *McDuff Moves In.* **Illus. by Susan Jeffers. Hyperion, 1997. 0-7868-2257-0. Unp. Gr. PreK–1**

A winsome little white West Highland terrier pup leaps out of the dogcatcher's truck and spends the night searching for food and warmth, until he is taken in and loved by a kindly young married couple, Janet and Fred.

GERM: Introduce your dog lovers to the other McDuff books, in which he gets lost, becomes jealous of the new baby, meets Santa, and goes to obedience school.

RELATED TITLES: Banks, Kate. *The Cat Who Walked Across France.* Farrar, 2004. / Flack, Marjorie. *Angus and the Cat.* Doubleday, 1931. / George, Kristine O'Connell. *Little Dog Poems.* Clarion, 1999. / Graeber, Charlotte. *Nobody's Dog.* Hyperion, 1998. / Graham, Bob. *"Let's Get a Pup!" Said Kate.* Candlewick, 2001. / Kellogg, Steven. *Pinkerton, Behave.* Dial, 1979. (And others in the Pinkerton series.) / McFarland, Lyn Rossiter. *Widget.* Farrar, 2001. / Simont, Marc. *The Stray Dog.* HarperCollins, 2001. / Thayer, Jane. *The Puppy Who Wanted a Boy.* Morrow, 1986. / Voake, Charlotte. *Ginger Finds a Home.* Candlewick, 2003. / Wells, Rosemary. *Lucy Comes to Stay.* Dial, 1994. / Wells, Rosemary. *McDuff and the Baby.* Hyperion, 1997. / Wells, Rosemary. *McDuff Comes Home.* Hyperion, 1997. / Wells, Rosemary. *McDuff Goes to School.* Hyperion, 2001. / Wells, Rosemary. *McDuff's New Friend.* Hyperion, 1998.

SUBJECTS: DOGS. STRAY ANIMALS.

835 Wells, Rosemary. *Max Cleans Up.* **Illus. by the author. Viking, 2000. 0-670-89218-1. Unp. Gr. PreK–1**

While big sister Ruby is organizing the clutter in Max the rabbit's messy room, Max is busy emptying dump truck sand, Miracle Bubbles, ant farm ants, and everything else into the front pocket of his overalls.

GERM: Have your children guess what is in your pocket (such as a piece of fruit, a comb, or a stuffed animal). Assist them with their questions to show how they can narrow the possibilities instead of guessing wildly. Play this with them three or four times. Ask them to put an interesting object in their pockets from somewhere in the room and have them play the game with each other.

RELATED TITLES: McPhail, David. *Pigs Aplenty, Pigs Galore.* Dutton, 1993. / Peters, Lisa Westberg. *When the Fly Flew In.* Dial, 1994. / Pomerantz, Charlotte. *The Piggy in the Puddle.* Macmillan, 1974. / Rathmann, Peggy. *Ten Minutes Till Bedtime.* Putnam, 1998. / Teague, Mark. *Pigsty.* Scholastic, 1994. / Wells, Rosemary. *Bunny Cakes.* Dial, 1997. / Wells, Rosemary. *Bunny Money.* Dial, 1997. (And others in the Max and Ruby series.)

SUBJECTS: BEDROOMS. BROTHERS AND SISTERS. CLEANLINESS. RABBITS.

836 Wells, Rosemary. *My Kindergarten.* **Illus. by the author. Hyperion, 2004. 0-7868-0833-0. 96pp. Gr. PreK–1**

Take a glorious month-by-month tour through the kindergarten year with teacher Miss Cribbage, a guinea pig, as seen through the eyes of Emily the rabbit, one of Miss Cribbage's eight animal students. From their schoolhouse on Cranberry Island in Maine, they count, collect weeds and seeds, make maps, sing, and widen their horizons across the activity-filled curriculum. They focus on all the vital stuff, including science, reading, math, music, art, dance, weather, time, football, punctuation, measurement, money, poetry, and loving your library, of course. The gloriously detailed illustrations make this a book you'll want to share throughout your school year.

GERM: Go to the Web site <www.hyperionbooksforchildren.com>, type "My Kindergarten" in the search bar, and you'll find my (Judy Freeman's) extensive teacher's guide and her CD of 23 accompanying songs and stories, which you can print, play, and download or burn your own CD.

RELATED TITLES: Allard, Harry. *Miss Nelson Is Missing.* Houghton Mifflin, 1985. / Child, Lauren. *I Am Too Absolutely Small for School.* Candlewick, 2004. / Jackson, Ellen. *It's Back to School We Go! First Day Stories from Around the World.* Millbrook, 2003. / Lillegard, Dee. *Hello School! A Classroom Full of Poems.* Knopf, 2001. / McGhee, Alison. *Countdown to Kindergarten.* Harcourt, 2002. / Schwartz, Amy. *Annabelle Swift, Kindergartner.* Orchard, 1988. / Slate, Joseph. *Miss Bindergarten Celebrates the 100th Day of Kindergarten.* Dutton, 1998. / Slate, Joseph. *Miss Bindergarten Gets Ready for Kindergarten.* Dutton, 1996. / Strete, Craig. *The Rattlesnake Who Went to School.* Putnam, 2004. / Wells, Rosemary. *Emily's First 100 Days of School.* Hyperion, 2000. / Wells, Rosemary. *Timothy Goes to School.* Dial, 1981. / Wells, Rosemary. *Yoko.* Hyperion, 1998. / Wells, Rosemary. *Yoko's Paper Cranes.* Hyperion, 2001. / Wells, Rosemary. *Yoko's World of Kindness: Golden Rules for a Happy Classroom.* Hyperion, 2005.

SUBJECTS: FIRST DAY OF SCHOOL. KINDERGARTEN. SCHOOLS. TEACHERS.

837 Wells, Rosemary. *Noisy Nora.* **Illus. by the author. Dial, 1997. 0-8037-1836-5. Unp. Gr. PreK–K**

With Mother and Father busy taking care of all their other mouse children, Nora tries causing a commotion to get someone to pay attention to her and finally announces, "I'm leaving! And I'm never coming back!" This larger-format edition of the classic, neglected middle child story, with its all new colorful illustrations, is a prime read for groups clamoring for your attention.

GERM: Talk it over: How do you get your family to notice you?

RELATED TITLES: Bang, Molly. *When Sophie Gets Angry—Really, Really Angry.* Scholastic, 1999. / Fearnley, Jan. *Watch Out!* Candlewick, 2004. / Freymann, Saxton, and Joost Elffers. *How Are You Peeling? Foods with Moods.* Scholastic, 1999. / Shannon, David. *David Gets in Trouble.* Scholastic, 2002. / Shannon, David. *No, David!* Scholastic, 1998. / Steig, William. *Pete's a Pizza.* HarperCollins, 1998. / Vail, Rachel. *Sometimes I'm Bombaloo.* Scholastic, 2002. / Wells, Rosemary. *Bunny Cakes.* Viking, 1997. / Wells, Rosemary. *Felix Feels Better.* Candlewick, 2001. / Wells, Rosemary. *Shy Charles.* Dial, 1988. / Wells, Rosemary. *Timothy Goes to School.* Dial, 1981.

SUBJECTS: BEHAVIOR. FAMILY LIFE. MICE. SIBLING RIVALRY. STORIES IN RHYME.

838   Wells, Rosemary. *Timothy Goes to School.* **Illus. by the author. Viking, 2000. 0-670-89182-7. Unp. Gr. PreK–1**

In an irresistible reissue of a classic picture book, now larger and grander, with full-color water-colors, eager raccoon Timothy starts school, where he encounters snide, athletic, smart Claude. Luckily, Timothy meets Violet, who is also having trouble dealing with the perfect Grace, her seatmate.

GERM: Children can draw self-portraits that show something they do well. Note how Timothy proves himself a friend to an ostracized classmate in Wells's *Yoko.*

RELATED TITLES: Dannenberg, Julie. *First Day Jitters.* Charlesbridge, 2000. / Harris, Robie H. *I Am Not Going to School Today!* McElderry, 2003. / Henkes, Kevin. *Chrysanthemum.* Greenwillow, 1991. / Henkes, Kevin. *Wemberly Worried.* Greenwillow, 2000. / Hest, Amy. *Off to School, Baby Duck.* Candlewick, 1999. / Johnson, Dolores. *What Will Mommy Do When I'm at School?* Macmillan, 1990. / Lasky, Kathryn. *Lunch Bunnies.* Little, Brown, 1996. / McGhee, Alison. *Countdown to Kindergarten.* Harcourt, 2002. / Poydar, Nancy. *First Day, Hooray.* Holiday House, 1999. / Schwartz, Amy. *Annabelle Swift, Kindergartner.* Orchard, 1988. / Slate, Joseph. *Miss Bindergarten Gets Ready for Kindergarten.* Dutton, 1994. / Wells, Rosemary. *Emily's 100 Days of School.* Hyperion, 2000. / Wells, Rosemary. *My Kindergarten.* Hyperion, 2004. / Wells, Rosemary. *Read Me a Story.* Hyperion, 2002. / Wells, Rosemary. *Yoko's Paper Cranes.* Hyperion, 2001. / Wells, Rosemary. *Yoko's World of Kindness: Golden Rules for a Happy Classroom.* Hyperion, 2005.

SUBJECTS: FIRST DAY OF SCHOOL. FRIENDSHIP. RACCOONS. SCHOOLS.

839   Wells, Rosemary. *Yoko.* **Illus. by the author. Hyperion, 1998. 0-7868-2345-3. Unp. Gr. PreK–1**

When Yoko brings sushi treasures to school for her lunch, her animal classmates say, "Ick! It's green! It's seaweed!" and "YUCK-O-RAMA!" During snack time they ridicule her red bean ice cream. "Red Bean ice cream is for weirdos!" Mrs. Jenkins tries to help by organizing International Food Day in the classroom, but, though everyone loves the enchiladas, potato knishes, and mango smoothies, no one touches the sushi. Except Timothy. He's still hungry and he loves it!

GERM: Timothy and Yoko then open their own pretend restaurant in class, which might be fun to try. Using two paper plates as their palettes, children can write "My Most Favorite Food" on one and "My Least Favorite Food" on the other, and then draw these foods. Make a food-filled bulletin board of their plates. Children can then talk about and compare and share the foods they thought they would hate until they tried them.

RELATED TITLES: Alexander, Martha. *Move Over, Twerp.* Dial, 1989. / Brown, Marc. *D. W. the Picky Eater.* Little, Brown, 1995. / Child, Lauren. *I Will Never Not Ever Eat a Tomato.* Candlewick, 2000. / Demarest, Chris L. *No Peas for Nellie.* Macmillan, 1988. / Friedman, Ina R. *How My Parents Learned to Eat.* Houghton Mifflin, 1984. / Hoberman, Mary Ann. *The Seven Silly Eaters.* Harcourt, 1997. / Palatini, Margie. *Zak's Lunch.* Clarion, 1998. / Wells, Rosemary. *My Kindergarten.* Hyperion, 2004. / Wells, Rosemary. *Read Me a Story.* Hyperion, 2002. / Wells, Rosemary. *Timothy Goes to School.* Dial, 1981. / Wells, Rosemary. *Yoko's Paper Cranes.* Hyperion, 2001. / Wells, Rosemary. *Yoko's World of Kindness: Golden Rules for a Happy Classroom.* Hyperion, 2005. / Yolen, Jane. *How Do Dinosaurs Eat Their Food?* Blue Sky/Scholastic, 2005.

SUBJECTS: ANIMALS. ASIAN AMERICANS. CATS. FOOD. FOOD HABITS. JAPANESE AMERICANS. MULTICULTURAL BOOKS. SCHOOLS. SUSHI.

840   Wells, Rosemary. *Yoko's Paper Cranes.* **Illus. by the author. Hyperion, 2001. 0-7868-0737-7. Unp. Gr. PreK–1**

Having no money to buy her Obaasan, or grandmother, a birthday present, little gray cat Yoko makes her three beautiful origami paper cranes, which her Ojiisan, or grandfather, taught her to do when she was small. Yoko carefully wraps up her gift and sends it by air mail from her home in California to her grandparents' house across the ocean in Japan. Wells's jewel-like square illustrations incorporate delicate origami paper and gold leaf, so you feel as if you're holding a treasure box in your hands as you turn each page.

GERM: Children whose grandparents are far away will empathize with Yoko missing hers and will be eager to write, illustrate, and send birthday or un-birthday letters. A standard origami book will give you clear directions for teaching your children to fold paper cranes. Do an advanced search at <www.google.com> for origami and cranes, and you'll find a plethora of paper-folding ideas to try.

RELATED TITLES: Caseley, Judith. *Dear Annie.* Greenwillow, 1991. / Dorros, Arthur. *Abuela.* Dutton, 1991. / Falwell, Cathryn. *Butterflies for Kiri.* Lee & Low, 2003. / Friedman, Ina R. *How My Parents Learned to Eat.* Houghton Mifflin, 1984. / George, Kristine O'Connell. *Fold Me a Poem.* Harcourt, 2005. / Kleven, Elisa. *The*

Paper Princess. Dutton, 1994. / Melmed, Laura Krauss. *Little Oh.* Lothrop, 1997. / Say, Allen. *Grandfather's Journey.* Houghton Mifflin, 1993. / Say, Allen. *Tree of Cranes.* Houghton Mifflin, 1991. / Wells, Rosemary. *Max series.* Dial. / Wells, Rosemary. *My Kindergarten.* Hyperion, 2004. / Wells, Rosemary. *Read Me a Story.* Hyperion, 2002. / Wells, Rosemary. *Shy Charles.* Dial, 1988. / Wells, Rosemary. *Timothy Goes to School.* Dial, 1981. / Wells, Rosemary. *Yoko.* Hyperion, 1998. / Wells, Rosemary. *Yoko's World of Kindness.* Hyperion, 2005. / Wells, Ruth. *A to Zen: A Book of Japanese Culture.* Picture Book Studio, 1992.

SUBJECTS: ASIAN AMERICANS. GRANDPARENTS. JAPAN. JAPANESE AMERICANS. MULTICULTURAL BOOKS. ORIGAMI.

841   **West, Jim, and Marshall Izen.** *The Dog Who Sang at the Opera.* **Illus. by Erika Oller. Abrams, 2004. 0-8109-4928-8. Unp. Gr. 1–4**

Pasha, a regal and self-centered Russian wolfhound, is hired to appear onstage at the Metropolitan Opera House in New York City. When she arrives, she immediately looks down her nose at Sluggo, a mutt who will be appearing as a clown dog in the same opera. During opening night, when the diva begins her aria, Pasha sings along with her—"Wa-hoo, woo-hoo"—and has to be dragged offstage by her embarrassed owner, Shirley. Humiliated, the vain dog learns a bit about humility and friendship from none other than mongrel Sluggo.

GERM: This book was actually inspired by a true event, when opera star Renée Fleming was upstaged by a wolfhound named Pasha during a 1997 performance of the opera *Manon.* The appealing story concludes with a *New York Times* article about the event, a photo of the dog and the diva, and a reproduction of the letter Fleming sent to Pasha's owner. With your older students, you can talk about the way the authors took a true event and fictionalized it. Also read *Opera Cat* by Tess Weaver, in which the opera-singing cat Alma takes over for her owner, Madame Soso, when the singer comes down with laryngitis. Make sure to meet Luigi, an opera-loving rooster, who upstages a famous tenor during a production of *Rigoletto* in Mary Jane Auch's hilarious *Bantam of the Opera.*

RELATED TITLES: Auch, Mary Jane. *Bantam of the Opera.* Holiday House, 1997. / Edwards, Pamela Duncan. *Honk! The Story of a Prima Swanerina.* Hyperion, 1998. / Ernst, Lisa Campbell. *Ginger Jumps.* Bradbury, 1990. / Ernst, Lisa Campbell. *When Bluebell Sang.* Bradbury, 1989. / Goss, Linda. *The Frog Who Wanted to Be a Singer.* Orchard, 1996. / Hurd, Thacher. *Art Dog.* HarperCollins, 1996. / Kinerk, Robert. *Clorinda.* Simon & Schuster, 2003. / Marshall, James. *Swine Lake.* HarperCollins, 1999. / Ryan, Pam Muñoz. *When Marian Sang.* Scholastic, 2002. / Weaver, Tess. *Opera Cat.* Clarion, 2002.

SUBJECTS: DOGS. HUMOROUS FICTION. METROPOLITAN OPERA (NEW YORK, NY). MUSIC. NEW YORK CITY. OPERA. SINGING.

842   **Westcott, Nadine Bernard.** *I've Been Working on the Railroad: An American Classic.* **Illus. by the author. Hyperion, 1996. 0-7868-2041-1. Unp. Gr. PreK–1**

All aboard for a rousing picture-book version of the old folk song that all can read and sing.

GERM: Pull together a batch of books that are songs as well, starting with the related titles list. (You'll find more in the Subject Index under "Songs.") Hand a book to each group of three to six children, and have them sing the book together. You can either rotate titles, so each group gets to read and sing three or four separate songs, or have each group perform one specific song of their choosing.

RELATED TITLES: Booth, Philip. *Crossing.* Candlewick, 2001. / Crews, Donald. *Freight Train.* Greenwillow, 1978. / Crews, Donald. *Inside Freight Train.* HarperCollins, 2001. / Hoberman, Mary Ann. *Yankee Doodle.* Little, Brown, 2004. / Hort, Lenny. *The Seals on the Bus.* Henry Holt, 2000. / Hubble, Patricia. *Trains: Steaming! Pulling! Huffing!* Marshall Cavendish, 2005. / Kirk, Daniel. *Go!* Hyperion, 2001. / Shields, Carol Diggory. *Animagicals: On the Go.* Handprint, 2001. / Siebert, Diane. *Train Song.* Crowell, 1990. / Tunnell, Michael O. *Mailing May.* Greenwillow, 1997. / Westcott, Nadine Bernard. *I Know an Old Lady Who Swallowed a Fly.* Little, Brown, 1980. / Westcott, Nadine Bernard. *Peanut Butter and Jelly: A Play Rhyme.* Dutton, 1987. / Zelinsky, Paul O. *The Wheels on the Bus.* Dutton, 1990. / Ziefert, Harriet. *When I First Came to This Land.* Putnam, 1998.

SUBJECTS: FOLK SONGS. SONGS. TRAINS. TRANSPORTATION. VEHICLES.

843   **Whayne, Susanne.** *Petropolis.* **Illus. by Christopher Santoro. Handprint, 2003. 1-59354-001-9. Unp. Gr. PreK–2**

Mom, Dad, and Molly leave Max the puppy at home, but when he jumps through his new pet door, the pup finds himself in the bustling town of Petropolis. There pets wear clothes, play in the park, take in a good movie (*The Dogfather* is playing), and stop for kibble sundaes at the Slurp n' Burp.

GERM: Note how the watercolor illustrations move from monochrome at home to full color in Petropolis, a city that never sleeps. Ask your listeners to figure out how Max will find his way home. Other pets enjoy themselves when their owners leave in *When Martha's Away* by Bruce Ingman, *The Night I Followed the Dog* by Nina Laden, and *Amos: The Story of an Old Dog and His Couch* by Susan Seligson and Howie Schneider.

RELATED TITLES: Graham, Bob. *Benny: An Adventure Story.* Candlewick, 1999. / Howard, Arthur. *Cosmo Zooms.* Harcourt, 1999. / Ingman, Bruce. *When Martha's Away.* Houghton Mifflin, 1995. / Kirk, Daniel. *Dogs Rule!* Hyperion, 2003. / Laden, Nina. *The Night I Followed the Dog.* Chronicle, 1994. / Lee, Chinlun. *Good Dog, Paw!* Candlewick, 2004. / Meddaugh, Susan. *Martha Speaks.* Houghton Mifflin, 1992. / Miller, Sara Swan. *Three Stories You Can Read to Your Dog.* Houghton Mifflin, 1995. / Rosen, Michael. *Rover.* Doubleday, 1999. / Seligson, Susan, and Howie Schneider. *Amos: The Story of an Old Dog and His Couch.* Little, Brown, 1987.

SUBJECTS: DOGS. FANTASY. PETS. STORIES IN RHYME.

---

844 Wheeler, Lisa. *Old Cricket.* Illus. by Ponder Goembel. Atheneum, 2003. 0-689-84510-3. Unp. Gr. PreK–1

Cantankerous Old Cricket thinks up a good excuse for why he can't help his wife ready the roof for winter, but his clever plans go awry when a hungry crow comes after him, planning to eat him for lunch.

GERM: Listeners will love joining in on the many repeated sound effects as Old Cricket creaks, cricks, cracks, and hics to Doc Hopper's office. Compare Old Cricket's propensity to avoid work with the Aesop tale, "The Grasshopper and the Ant," and with Helen Ward's *The Rooster and the Fox* and talk about the morals of the stories. What happens to the liars or the lazy ones in these tales? Also compare how the weaker one gets away in both stories.

RELATED TITLES: Becker, Bonny. *An Ant's Day Off.* Simon & Schuster, 2003. / Carle, Eric. *The Very Quiet Cricket.* Philomel, 1990. / Cronin, Doreen. *Diary of a Worm.* HarperCollins, 2003. / Cushman, Doug. *Inspector Hopper.* HarperCollins, 2000. / Edwards, Pamela Duncan. *Some Smug Slug.* HarperCollins, 1996. / Florian, Douglas. *Insectlopedia: Poems and Paintings.* Harcourt, 1998. / Hall, Katy, and Lisa Eisenberg. *Buggy Riddles.* Dial, 1986. / Hepworth, Cathi. *Bug Off! A Swarm of Insect Words.* Putnam, 1998. / Lobel, Arnold. *A Treeful of Pigs.* Greenwillow, 1979. / Oppenheim, Joanne. *Have You Seen Bugs?* Scholastic, 1998. / Porte, Barbara Ann. *Leave That Cricket Be, Alan Lee.* Greenwillow, 1993. / Tyson, Leigh Ann. *An Interview with Harry the Tarantula.* National Geographic, 2003. / Van Allsburg, Chris. *Two Bad Ants.* Houghton Mifflin, 1988. / Waddell, Martin. *Farmer Duck.* Candlewick, 1992. / Ward, Helen. *The Rooster and the Fox.* Millbrook, 2003.

SUBJECTS: BEHAVIOR. BIRDS. CHANTABLE REFRAIN. CRICKETS. CROWS. HELPFULNESS. INSECTS. LAZINESS. SOUND EFFECTS.

---

845 Whippo, Walt, and Bernard Zaritzky. *Little White Duck.* Illus. by Joan Paley. Little, Brown, 2000. 0-316-03227-1. Unp. Gr. PreK–1

A guitar-playing mouse leads us in a jaunty sing-along sequence song about a little duck, a frog, a black bug, and a red snake. Mouse with his guitar sings the song, while the animals give us the sound effects: duck says quack, frog says glug, bug says buzz, and snake eats the bug, saying hiss, hiss, hiss.

GERM: Sing this one and act it out. Perfect for preschool story hours and flannelboard retellings, this picture book, based on a popular children's song written in 1950 and recorded by Danny Kaye, Burl Ives, and Raffi, is set up like a theater piece, with all of the characters appearing onstage.

RELATED TITLES: Cauley, Lorinda Bryan. *Old MacDonald Had a Farm.* Putnam, 1989. / Christelow, Eileen. *Five Little Monkeys Jumping on the Bed.* Clarion, 1989. / Greene, Rhonda Gowler. *Barnyard Song.* Atheneum, 1997. / Hort, Lenny. *The Seals on the Bus.* Henry Holt, 2000. / Karas, G. Brian. *I Know an Old Lady Who Swallowed a Fly.* Scholastic, 1994. / Raffi. *Down by the Bay.* Crown, 1987. / Raffi. *Five Little Ducks.* Crown, 1988. / Raffi. *The Wheels on the Bus.* Crown, 1988. / Simmons, Jane. *Come Along, Daisy.* Little, Brown, 1998. / Taback, Simms. *There Was an Old Lady Who Swallowed a Fly.* Viking, 1997. / Zelinsky, Paul O. *The Wheels on the Bus.* Dutton, 1990.

SUBJECTS: CREATIVE DRAMA. DUCKS. FROGS. POND LIFE. SNAKES. SONGS. STORIES IN RHYME.

---

846 Whybrow, Ian. *The Noisy Way to Bed.* Illus. by Tiphanie Beeke. Scholastic, 2004. 0-439-55689-9. Unp. Gr. PreK–1

It's almost bedtime, but each time a tired little boy starts to say, ". . . this is the way to bed," he is interrupted by sleepy animals who quack, neigh, baaa, and oink. As they follow him across the meadow and up the stairs, fuzzy, sunbright watercolor washes give way to sunset colors, and the boy and his contented animals trundle their way to bed.

GERM: Listeners will chime in on the animal noises and chant the little boy's refrain, "Hey! That's not what I meant to say. Well, you can come along." Then they can act out the whole story. Add on additional farm animals as needed.

RELATED TITLES: Appelt, Kathi. *Bubba and Beau Go Night-Night.* Harcourt, 2003. / Cook, Sally. *Good Night Pillow Fight.* HarperCollins, 2004. / Heap, Sue. *Cowboy Baby.* Candlewick, 1998. / Hoberman, Mary Ann. *It's Simple, Said Simon.* Knopf, 2001. / Lum, Kate. *What! Cried Granny: An Almost Bedtime Story.* Dial, 1999. / Markes, Julie. *Shhhhh! Everybody's Sleeping.* HarperCollins, 2005. / Murphy, Jill. *Peace at Last.* Dial, 1980. / Pinkney, Andrea Davis. *Sleeping Cutie.* Harcourt, 2004. / Rathmann, Peggy. *Good Night, Gorilla.* Putnam, 1994. / Rathmann, Peggy. *Ten Minutes Till Bedtime.* Putnam, 1998. / Rothstein, Gloria. *Sheep Asleep.* HarperCollins, 2003. / Root, Phyllis. *What Baby Wants.* Candlewick, 1998. / Simms, Laura. *The Squeaky Door.* Crown, 1991. / Walton, Rick. *So Many Bunnies: A Bedtime ABC and Counting Book.* Lothrop, 1998. / Yolen, Jane. *How Do Dinosaurs Say Good Night?* Blue Sky/Scholastic, 2000.

SUBJECTS: ANIMAL SOUNDS. BEDTIME STORIES. CHANTABLE REFRAIN. CREATIVE DRAMA. DOMESTIC ANIMALS.

847   **Widman, Christine.** *Cornfield Hide-and-Seek.* **Illus. by Pierr Morgan. Farrar, 2003. 0-374-31547-7. Unp. Gr. PreK–2**

The sun is so hot on the farm that the three kidlins and all of the animals get sun-dazzled and hide in the big green cornfield to cool off. After a while, even Mamaw and Grampy come out to join them there in the lovely, cool shade of the corn stalks.

GERM: Discussion point on a very hot or very cold day: What do you do and where do you go to cool off when you've been sun-dazzled? Since Mamaw's family ends up resting and eating peaches in the cool cornfield, bring in fresh corn to taste, popcorn to pop, or some nice ripe peaches to savor.

RELATED TITLES: Ehrlich, Amy. *Parents in the Pigpen, Pigs in the Tub.* Dial, 1993. / Harshman, Marc. *The Storm.* Dutton, 1995. / Ketteman, Helen. *Heat Wave!* Walker, 1998. / Lindbergh, Reeve. *The Day the Goose Got Loose.* Dial, 1990. / Stevenson, James. *Heat Wave at Mud Flat.* Greenwillow, 1997. / Stewart, Sarah. *The Journey.* Farrar, 2001.

SUBJECTS: CORN. FARM LIFE. HEAT. PICNICS.

848   **Wiesner, David.** *Sector 7.* **Illus. by the author. Clarion, 1999. 0-395-74656-6. Unp. Gr. PreK–2**

On a school field trip to the Empire State Building, a boy takes off from the observation deck with a friendly cloud that transports him to Sector 7, a Cloud Dispatch Center, where the boy helps design whimsical fish-shaped clouds.

GERM: Remember the end of Catherine Cowan's *My Life with the Wave,* when the boy wonders if he should bring a cloud home? Well, here's a boy who does, and it's a match made in heaven. Kids will be itching to design their own clouds after poring over the pictures and inventing dialogue to go along with the wordless story. Take a trip up the Empire State Building from the outside in the King Kong takeoff, *Ding Dong Ding Dong* by Margie Palatini.

RELATED TITLES: Barrett, Judi. *Cloudy with a Chance of Meatballs.* Atheneum, 1978. / Cowan, Catherine. *My Life with the Wave.* Lothrop, 1997. / Cummings, Pat. *C.L.O.U.D.S.* Lothrop, 1986. / dePaola, Tomie. *The Cloud Book.* Holiday House, 1975. / Dorros, Arthur. *Abuela.* Dutton, 1991. / Du Bois, William Pène. *Lion.* Penguin, 1983. / Feiffer, Jules. *Meanwhile . . .* HarperCollins, 1997. / Legge, David. *Bamboozled.* Scholastic, 1995. / Palatini, Margie. *Ding Dong Ding Dong.* Hyperion, 1999. / Pinkney, Brian. *The Adventures of Sparrowboy.* Simon & Schuster, 1997. / Rohmann, Eric. *Time Flies.* Crown, 1994. / Shaw, Charles. *It Looked Like Spilt Milk.* Harper-Collins, 1947. / Weitzman, Jacqueline Preiss. *You Can't Take a Balloon into the Metropolitan Museum.* Dial, 1998. / Wiesner, David. *Free Fall.* Lothrop, 1988. / Wiesner, David. *Tuesday.* Clarion, 1991. / Wood, Audrey. *The Flying Dragon Room.* Scholastic, 1996.

SUBJECTS: CLOUDS. EMPIRE STATE BUILDING (NEW YORK, NY). NEW YORK CITY. PICTURE BOOKS FOR ALL AGES. STORIES WITHOUT WORDS.

849   **Wiesner, David.** *The Three Pigs.* **Illus. by the author. Clarion, 2001. 0-618-00701-6. Unp. Gr. PreK–2**

Take an unexpected tour through what seems to be (on the cover and first page, at least) a traditional telling of the classic folktale. On page three, though, when the wolf blows in the house of straw, he blows the pig right off the page, out of the story, and into the page's margin. The three pigs fold a page with the wolf on it into a paper airplane, and peer out at us, the readers.

This surreal, nonlinear romp has the pigs wandering into the "Hey diddle diddle" nursery rhyme and into a page of a dragon story, where they rescue the dragon that's about to be slain by a king's eldest son.

GERM: For two open-ended writing and illustrating prompts, ask your children, "If you could step into a story, or a story character could step out of his or her story and into your life, what might happen?" If some listeners don't know the original folktale, remediate with either Barry Moser's or James Marshall's version of *The Three Little Pigs*.

RELATED TITLES: Child, Lauren. *Beware of the Storybook Wolves*. Scholastic, 2001. / Emberley, Michael. *Ruby and the Sniffs*. Little, Brown, 2004. / Ernst, Lisa Campbell. *Little Red Riding Hood: A Newfangled Prairie Tale*. Simon & Schuster, 1995. / Marshall, James. *The Three Little Pigs*. Dial, 1989. / Meddaugh, Susan. *Hog-Eye*. Houghton Mifflin, 1995. / Moser, Barry. *The Three Little Pigs*. Little, Brown, 2001. / O'Malley, Kevin. *Humpty Dumpty Egg-Splodes*. Walker, 2001. / Palatini, Margie. *Piggie Pie*. Clarion, 1995. / Scieszka, Jon. *The Stinky Cheese Man and Other Fairly Stupid Tales*. Viking, 1992. / Scieszka, Jon. *The True Story of the 3 Little Pigs*. Viking, 1989. / Stevens, Janet, and Susan Stevens Crummel. *And the Dish Ran Away with the Spoon*. Harcourt, 2001. / Trivizas, Eugene. *The Three Little Wolves and the Big Bad Pig*. McElderry, 1993. / Wiesner, David. *Free Fall*. Lothrop, 1988.

SUBJECTS: BOOKS AND READING. CALDECOTT MEDAL. FAIRY TALES—SATIRE. PARODIES. PICTURE BOOKS FOR ALL AGES. PIGS. WOLVES.

850   **Wilcox, Leah.** *Falling for Rapunzel*. **Illus. by Lydia Monks. Putnam, 2003. 0-399-23794-1. Unp. Gr. K–2**

"Once upon a bad hair day, a prince rode up Rapunzel's way." When the prince says, ". . . throw down your hair," Rapunzel, up in her tower, can't quite hear him and throws down her underwear. Instead of her "curly locks," she throws down her dirty socks. Whoops! Breezy acrylic paint, collage, and colored-pencil illustrations will keep kids laughing, especially when the prince runs off with Rapunzel's maid.

GERM: Listeners will predict her rhyming mistakes in this crazy rewrite of the old tale. Make sure to read or tell the real story first. Then compose and illustrate new rhymes of what the prince might request and what Rapunzel could throw down instead.

RELATED TITLES: Bateman, Teresa. *The Princesses Have a Ball*. Albert Whitman, 2002. / Berenzy, Alix. *Rapunzel*. Henry Holt, 1995. / Ehrlich, Amy. *Rapunzel*. Dial, 1989. / Minters, Frances. *Cinder Elly*. Viking, 1993. / Minters, Frances. *Sleepless Beauty*. Viking, 1996. / Nerlove, Miriam. *I Made a Mistake*. Atheneum, 1985. / Rogasky, Barbara. *Rapunzel*. Holiday House, 1982. / Stanley, Diane. *Petrosinella: A Neopolitan Rapunzel*. Dial, 1995. / Wood, Audrey. *Silly Sally*. Harcourt, 1992. / Zelinsky, Paul O. *Rumpelstiltskin*. Dutton, 1986.

SUBJECTS: CHARACTERS IN LITERATURE. HUMOROUS FICTION. PARODIES. STORIES IN RHYME.

851   **Wiles, Deborah.** *Freedom Summer*. **Illus. by Jerome Lagarrigue. Atheneum, 2001. 0-689-83016-5. Unp. Gr. 1–6**

Joe's best friend is John Henry Waddell, whose mama cleans and cooks for Joe's mama. Joe is white and John Henry is black and, although the two can swim together at the creek, John Henry's not allowed to swim at the town pool. The boys are elated to discover that a new law means the town pool is now desegregated. When they get there, though, they see workers, including John Henry's big brother, filling the pool with hot, spongy tar, so no one can swim.

GERM: Set at the time of the Civil Rights Act of 1964, the fiction story mirrors events in the South. Joe can walk into the General Store to buy ice pops, but his pal can't. This devastating portrayal of segregation, with powerful emotion-filled paintings, is instantly understandable to children, who will be angry at the unfairness of it all. Read the book, along with *The Other Side* by Jacqueline Woodson, and talk about how injustices can be overcome if we work together.

RELATED TITLES: Adler, David A. *Dr. Martin Luther King, Jr.* Holiday House, 2001. / Adler, David A. *A Picture Book of Rosa Parks*. Holiday House, 1993. / Bridges, Ruby. *Through My Eyes*. Scholastic, 1999. / Curtis, Gavin. *The Bat Boy and His Violin*. Simon & Schuster, 1998. / Evans, Freddi Williams. *A Bus of Our Own*. Albert Whitman, 2001. / Giovanni, Nikki. *Rosa*. Henry Holt, 2005. / Golenbock, Peter. *Teammates*. Harcourt, 1990. / Lorbiecki, Marybeth. *Sister Anne's Hands*. Dial, 1998. / McKissack, Patricia C. *Goin' Someplace Special*. Atheneum, 2001. / Mitchell, Margaree King. *Granddaddy's Gift*. BridgeWater, 1997. / Mitchell, Margaree King. *Uncle Jed's Barber Shop*. Simon & Schuster, 1993. / Nelson, Vaunda Micheaux. *Mayfield Crossing*. Putnam, 1993. / Polacco, Patricia. *Mr. Lincoln's Way*. Philomel, 2001. / Rappaport, Doreen. *Martin's Big Words*. Hyperion, 2001. / Woodson, Jacqueline. *The Other Side*. Putnam, 2001.

SUBJECTS: AFRICAN AMERICANS. AFRICAN AMERICANS—HISTORY. CIVIL RIGHTS.

FRIENDSHIP. INTEGRATION. MULTICULTURAL BOOKS. PICTURE BOOKS FOR ALL AGES.
PREJUDICE. RACE RELATIONS.

852   Willems, Mo. *Don't Let the Pigeon Drive the Bus!* **Illus. by the author. Hyperion, 2003. 0-7868-1988-X. Unp. Gr. PreK–1**

Across from the title page, the bus driver asks us to watch things until he gets back, which leads to the title of the book. Turn the page, and there's a big-eyed persistent pigeon who tries every device possible to persuade us to let it drive that bus, from whining to temper spells. What's hilarious is watching that pigeon try to talk us into something forbidden, just as your children do every day.

GERM: You know you'll be singing that "Wheels on the Bus" song forever after this one. Ask your little pigeons to reveal their strategies for nagging the grownups in their lives. Ask them, "What do you do when your parents say no?" Use this book with older children as a lighthearted way to introduce a lesson on persuasive writing. They can each write a persuasive letter to the bus driver, or the pigeon himself, with clear reasons why the pigeon should or shouldn't be allowed to drive. Go to the Web site <www.hyperionbooksforchildren.com>, look up the Pigeon books, and you'll find the teacher's guide (written by me, Judy Freeman) with lots more follow-up ideas and projects. Also check out the author's wonderful Web site at <www.mo willems.com>. There's an adorable generic pigeon puppet at <www.mimismotifs.com> that you can use as a stand-in for Pigeon.

RELATED TITLES: Cronin, Doreen. *Click, Clack, Moo: Cows That Type.* Simon & Schuster, 2000. / Cronin, Doreen. *Duck for President.* Simon & Schuster, 2004. / Cronin, Doreen. *Giggle, Giggle, Quack.* Simon & Schuster, 2002. / Hort, Lenny. *The Seals on the Bus.* Henry Holt, 2000. / Kovalski, Maryann. *The Wheels on the Bus.* Little, Brown, 1987. / Pinkwater, Daniel. *Tooth-Gnasher Superflash.* Macmillan, 1990. / Raffi. *The Wheels on the Bus.* Crown, 1988. / Rohmann, Eric. *My Friend Rabbit.* Roaring Brook, 2002. / Shannon, David. *Duck on a Bike.* Blue Sky/Scholastic, 2002. / Willems, Mo. *Don't Let the Pigeon Stay Up Late.* Hyperion, 2006. / Willems, Mo. *Knuffle Bunny: A Cautionary Tale.* Hyperion, 2004. / Willems, Mo. *Leonardo the Terrible Monster.* Hyperion, 2005. / Willems, Mo. *The Pigeon Finds a Hot Dog.* Hyperion, 2004. / Zane, Alexander. *The Wheels on the Race Car.* Orchard, 2005. / Zelinsky, Paul O. *The Wheels on the Bus.* Dutton, 1990.

SUBJECTS: BEHAVIOR. BIRDS. BUSES. HUMOROUS FICTION. PERSONAL NARRATIVES. PERSUASIVE WRITING. PICTURE BOOKS FOR ALL AGES. PIGEONS. VEHICLES.

853   Willems, Mo. *Knuffle Bunny: A Cautionary Tale.* **Illus. by the author. Hyperion, 2004. 0-7868-1870-0. Unp. Gr. PreK–1**

Leaving the Laundromat with her daddy, toddler Trixie realizes she's forgotten her beloved stuffed animal, Knuffle Bunny, but Daddy can't understand her baby talk when she tries to tell him. All children will identify with Trixie's plight in this picture book—how to make yourself clear when no one else can decode your singular "language." The book is illustrated throughout with a melding of exuberant, cartoon-like colored ink sketches that are superimposed on black-and-white photos of the author's Brooklyn neighborhood.

GERM: Former toddlers will certainly make text-to-life connections, discussing, writing, and illustrating responses to follow-up "I remember" questions: What are the first words you ever said? What is your earliest memory? What was your indispensable toy or object when you were little? What have you lost and where have you found it? All can interview parents for their memories as well. Go to the Web site <www.hyperionbooksforchildren.com>, type "Knuffle Bunny" in the search bar, and you'll find your way to the Knuffle Bunny page with a link to my (Judy Freeman's) extensive teacher's guide, which you can print out.

RELATED TITLES: Alborough, Jez. *Where's My Teddy?* Candlewick, 1992. / Clark, Emma Chichester. *Where Are You, Blue Kangaroo?* Doubleday, 2000. / Cocca-Leffler, Maryann. *Missing: One Stuffed Rabbit.* Albert Whitman, 1998. / Falconer, Ian. *Olivia . . . and the Missing Toy.* Atheneum, 2003. / Feiffer, Jules. *I Lost My Bear.* Morrow, 1998. / Fitzpatrick, Marie-Louise. *Lizzy and Skunk.* DK Ink, 2000. / Freeman, Don. *Corduroy.* Viking, 1968. / Galbraith, Kathryn O. *Laura Charlotte.* Philomel, 1990. / Hughes, Shirley. *Dogger.* Lothrop, 1988. / Ichikawa, Satomi. *La La Rose.* Philomel, 2004. / MacLachlan, Patricia, and Emily MacLachlan. *Bittle.* HarperCollins, 2004. / Moss, Miriam. *Don't Forget I Love You.* Dial, 2004. / Neubecker, Robert. *Wow! City!* Hyperion, 2004. / Smith, Maggie. *Paisley.* Knopf, 2004. / Willems, Mo. *Don't Let the Pigeon Drive the Bus.* Hyperion, 2003. / Willems, Mo. *Leonardo the Terrible Monster.* Hyperion, 2005.

SUBJECTS: CITIES AND TOWNS. CRYING. FAMILY LIFE. HUMOROUS FICTION. LANGUAGE. LOST AND FOUND POSSESSIONS. NEW YORK CITY. PICTURE BOOKS FOR ALL AGES. STUFFED ANIMALS.

854 **Willems, Mo.** *Leonardo the Terrible Monster.* **Illus. by the author. Hyperion, 2005. 0-7868-5294-1. Unp. Gr. PreK–2**

"Leonardo was a terrible monster . . . He couldn't scare anyone." Searching to find the most scaredy-cat kid in the whole world, he sneaks up on unsuspecting Sam and tries to scare the tuna salad out of him.

GERM: Act this out in pairs, with one child being the not-so-scary monster and the other, the tearful Sam. Talk it over: Other than scary monsters, what makes you cry? If you became friends with Leonardo, what would you do together? Go to the Web site <www.hyperion booksforchildren.com>, type "Leonardo the Terrible Monster" in the search bar, and you'll find a link to my (Judy Freeman's) extensive teacher's guide, which you can print out. There's another perfect pairing of monster and boy in *Jitterbug Jam* by Barbara Jean Hicks, and of two new friends in *Yo! Yes?* by Chris Raschka.

RELATED TITLES: Gackenbach, Dick. *Harry and the Terrible Whatzit.* Clarion, 1977. / Hicks, Barbara Jean. *Jitterbug Jam.* Farrar, 2005. / Komaiko, Leah. *Earl's Too Cool for Me.* HarperCollins, 1988. / Park, Barbara. *Psssst! It's Me . . . the Bogeyman.* Atheneum, 1998. / Raschka, Chris. *Yo! Yes?* Orchard, 1993. / Willems, Mo. *Don't Let the Pigeon Drive the Bus.* Hyperion, 2003. / Willems, Mo. *Knuffle Bunny: A Cautionary Tale.* Hyperion, 2004.

SUBJECTS: CONDUCT OF LIFE. CREATIVE DRAMA. CRYING. FRIENDSHIP. HUMOROUS FICTION. MONSTERS.

855 **Willems, Mo.** *The Pigeon Finds a Hot Dog.* **Illus. by the author. Hyperion, 2004. 0-7868-1869-7. Unp. Gr. PreK–2**

About to wolf down the hot dog and bun he has just found, Pigeon is interrupted by a persistent yellow duckling who says, "I've never had a hot dog before . . . What do they taste like?"

GERM: Pigeon says to Duckling, "It just tastes like a hot dog, okay!?" What exactly does a hot dog taste like? How would you describe it to someone who had never tasted one? Serve pigs in a blanket as a follow-up snack. You'll find my (Judy Freeman's) complete guide to both of the Pigeon books and a pigeon drawing lesson from Mo Willems online at <www.hyperionbooks forchildren.com>. Type in "pigeon" in the search bar, click on the title, and you'll be able to download the Teacher's Guide to all the Pigeon books.

RELATED TITLES: Cronin, Doreen. *Click, Clack, Moo: Cows That Type.* Simon & Schuster, 2000. / Stevens, Janet, and Susan Stevens Crummel. *Cook-a-Doodle-Doo!* Harcourt, 1999. / Sturges, Philemon. *The Little Red Hen (Makes a Pizza).* Dutton, 1999. / Willems, Mo. *Don't Let the Pigeon Drive the Bus.* Hyperion, 2003. / Willems, Mo. *Don't Let the Pigeon Stay Up Late.* Hyperion, 2006. / Willems, Mo. *Knuffle Bunny: A Cautionary Tale.* Hyperion, 2004. / Willems, Mo. *Leonardo the Terrible Monster.* Hyperion, 2005.

SUBJECTS: BEHAVIOR. BIRDS. DUCKS. FOOD. GENEROSITY. HUMOROUS FICTION. PERSONAL NARRATIVES. PERSUASIVE WRITING. PICTURE BOOKS FOR ALL AGES. PIGEONS.

856 **Williams, Laura Ellen.** *ABC Kids.* **Photos by the author. Philomel, 2000. 0-399-23370-9. Unp. Gr. PreK–1**

Large, entrancing color photographs of a multicultural cast of young children accompany each of 26 nouns, starting with apple and ending with zipper.

GERM: Cover each word with a Post-it note and ask your group to figure it out from the context of the photograph. Then whisk off the sticky paper and read the word together for reinforcement. Take alphabet-themed photos of your children for a new class alphabet album.

RELATED TITLES: Bayer, Jane. *A My Name Is Alice.* Dial, 1984. / Lobel, Anita. *Alison's Zinnia.* Greenwillow, 1990. / Lobel, Anita. *Away from Home.* Greenwillow, 1994. / Lobel, Arnold. *On Market Street.* Greenwillow, 1981. / Moxley, Sheila. *ABCD: An Alphabet Book of Cats and Dogs.* Little, Brown, 2001. / Rotner, Shelley. *Action Alphabet.* Atheneum, 1996.

SUBJECTS: ALPHABET BOOKS. MULTICULTURAL BOOKS.

857 **Williams, Sue.** *Let's Go Visiting.* **Illus. by Julie Vivas. Harcourt, 1998. 0-15-201823-9. Unp. Gr. PreK–K**

"Let's go visiting. What do you say? One brown foal is ready to play." A red-haired child has a glorious time playing with all the animals and getting muddy with the pigs. A simple emergent reader text will have everyone reading and chanting along in no time.

GERM: Using the pattern of the call-and-response, listeners can come up with new animals and colors, acting out each animal. Also share the companion book, *I Went Walking.*

RELATED TITLES: Carle, Eric. *From Head to Toe.* HarperCollins, 1997. / Clark, Emma Chichester. *Follow the Leader!* Simon & Schuster, 2003. / Harter, Debbie. *Walking Through the Jungle.* Orchard, 1997. / Jarrett, Clare.

The Best Picnic Ever. Candlewick, 2004. / Martin, Bill, Jr. *Brown Bear, Brown Bear, What Do You See?* Henry Holt, 1983. / Martin, Bill, Jr. *Polar Bear, Polar Bear, What Do You Hear?* Henry Holt, 1991. / Polacco, Patricia. *Oh, Look!* Philomel, 2004. / Walter, Virginia. *"Hi, Pizza Man!"* Orchard, 1995. / Williams, Sue. *I Went Walking.* Gulliver/Harcourt, 1990.

SUBJECTS: CALL-AND-RESPONSE STORIES. CHANTABLE REFRAIN. COLOR. COUNTING BOOKS. CREATIVE DRAMA. DOMESTIC ANIMALS. STORIES IN RHYME.

858   **Williams, Suzanne. *Library Lil.* Illus. by Steven Kellogg. Dial, 1997. 0-8037-1699-0. Unp. Gr. 1–3**

The townsfolk spend their spare time with the TV instead of a good book—until a big storm knocks out the power for two weeks. Lil, the public librarian, comes to the rescue by pushing the old bookmobile all over Chesterville and delivering books to the entertainment-starved locals. When Bust-'em'up Bill and his gang ride their motorcycles into the now book-loving town, he's no match for Lil, who gets the gang reading and captures the biker's heart.

GERM: Librarians everywhere will cheer at this witty, stereotype-bashing tall tale about *Library Lil,* whose first love is books. Kellogg's sunny, detail-crammed pen-and-ink and watercolor illustrations are irresistible; your listeners will want to run right to the library to check out something great to read.

RELATED TITLES: Allen, Susan, and Jane Lindaman. *Read Anything Good Lately?* Millbrook, 2003. / Collins, Suzanne. *When Charlie McButton Lost Power.* Putnam, 2005. / Dadey, Debbie. *Shooting Star: Annie Oakley, the Legend.* Walker, 1997. / Ernst, Lisa Campbell. *Stella Louella's Runaway Book.* Simon & Schuster, 1998. / Garland, Michael. *Miss Smith's Incredible Storybook.* Dutton, 2003. / Hest, Amy. *Mr. George Baker.* Candlewick, 2004. / Isaacs, Anne. *Swamp Angel.* Dutton, 1994. / Kellogg, Steven. *Sally Ann Thunder Ann Whirlwind Crockett.* Morrow, 1995. / Lewis, J. Patrick. *Please Bury Me in the Library.* Harcourt, 2005. / Mora, Pat. *Tomás and the Library Lady.* Knopf, 1997. / Numeroff, Laura Joffe. *Beatrice Doesn't Want To.* Candlewick, 2004. / Parish, Herman. *Amelia Bedelia, Bookworm.* Greenwillow, 2003. / Polacco, Patricia. *Aunt Chip and the Great Triple Creek Dam Affair.* Philomel, 1996. / Sierra, Judy. *Wild About Books.* Knopf, 2004. / Stanley, Diane. *Raising Sweetness.* Putnam, 1999. / Thaler, Mike. *The Librarian from the Black Lagoon.* Scholastic, 1997.

SUBJECTS: BOOKMOBILES. BOOKS AND READING. LIBRARIANS. LIBRARIES. LITERACY. PICTURE BOOKS FOR ALL AGES. TALL TALES.

859   **Wilson, Karma. *Bear Snores On.* Illus. by Jane Chapman. McElderry, 2002. 0-689-83187-0. Unp. Gr. PreK–1**

On a snowstormy night, mouse, hare, badger, gopher, mole, wren, and raven find their way into a sleeping bear's cave, start up a fire, pop some corn, and brew some tea until the bear awakens from his slumber, blubbering that he missed all the fun. Lush and vibrant acrylics make this one story kids will want to pore over again and again.

GERM: Pop some corn, of course, and act this one out, complete with lots of snoring and sound effects. This is that perfect preschool storyhour book, just right for chantable refrains; for dramatics and retelling with flannelboards, puppets, and kids; for predicting outcomes; and for enjoying some cozy rhymes. Go to <www.mimismotifs.com> for a complete set of puppets to go with Wilson's Bear series. Pair the book with Marjorie Dennis Murray's *Don't Wake Up the Bear!* and Bernard Waber's *Bearsie Bear and the Surprise Sleepover Party* to compare and contrast plots and characters.

RELATED TITLES: Alborough, Jez. *It's the Bear!* Candlewick, 1994. / Banks, Kate. *Close Your Eyes.* Farrar, 2002. / Fleming, Denise. *Time to Sleep.* Henry Holt, 1997. / Fuchs, Diane Marcial. *A Bear for All Seasons.* Henry Holt, 1995. / Murphy, Jill. *Peace at Last.* Dial, 1980. / Murray, Marjorie Dennis. *Don't Wake Up the Bear!* Cavendish, 2003. / Rosen, Michael. *We're Going on a Bear Hunt.* McElderry, 1989. / Simmons, Jane. *Little Fern's First Winter.* Little, Brown, 2001. / Stojic, Manya. *Snow.* Knopf, 2002. / Waber, Bernard. *Bearsie Bear and the Surprise Sleepover Party.* Houghton, 1997. / Waddell, Martin. *Can't You Sleep, Little Bear?* Candlewick, 1992. / Wilson, Karma. *Bear Stays Up for Christmas.* McElderry, 2004. / Wilson, Karma. *Bear Wants More.* McElderry, 2003. / Wilson, Karma. *A Frog in the Bog.* McElderry, 2003. / Wilson, Karma. *Sweet Briar Goes to School.* Dial, 2003. / Wood, Audrey. *The Napping House.* Harcourt, 1984.

SUBJECTS: ANIMALS. BEARS. CHANTABLE REFRAIN. CREATIVE DRAMA. SEASONS. SLEEP. STORIES IN RHYME. WINTER.

860   **Wilson, Karma. *Bear Wants More.* Illus. by Jane Chapman. McElderry, 2003. 0-689-84509-X. Unp. Gr. PreK–1**

It doesn't seem to matter how much big, friendly Bear's woodland animal friends bring him to eat—he is still ravenous. There's an irresistible little chantable refrain that accompanies each huge acrylic painting of Bear's battle with his insatiable appetite: ". . . but he still wants more!"

GERM: Share another Bear adventure in *Bear Snores On*. Bear getting wedged into the front yard of his den due to overindulgence may remind you of A. A. Milne's *Winnie-the-Pooh*, when Pooh Bear found himself in similar circumstances, so read aloud that classic chapter as well.

RELATED TITLES: Alborough, Jez. *It's the Bear!* Candlewick, 1994. / Fleming, Denise. *Lunch.* Henry Holt, 1992. / Milne, A. A. *Winnie-the-Pooh.* Dutton, 1926. / Palatini, Margie. *Zak's Lunch.* Clarion, 1998. / Rayner, Mary. *Mrs. Pig's Bulk Buy.* Atheneum, 1981. / Waber, Bernard. *Bearsie Bear and the Surprise Sleepover Party.* Houghton Mifflin, 1997. / Wilson, Karma. *Bear Snores On.* McElderry, 2002. / Wilson, Karma. *Bear Stays Up for Christmas.* McElderry, 2004. / Wilson, Karma. *A Frog in the Bog.* McElderry, 2003. / Wilson, Karma. *Sweet Briar Goes to School.* Dial, 2003. / Wood, Don, and Audrey Wood. *The Little Mouse, the Red Ripe Strawberry, and the Big Hungry Bear.* Childs Play, 1990.

SUBJECTS: ANIMALS. BEARS. CHANTABLE REFRAIN. FOOD. GREED. STORIES IN RHYME.

861 Wilson, Karma. *A Frog in the Bog.* **Illus. by Joan Rankin. McElderry, 2003. 0-689-84081-0. Unp. Gr. PreK–2**

A small, green frog on a half-sunk log in the middle of the bog swallows one tick, two fleas, three flies, four slugs, and five snails, growing a little bit bigger each time.

GERM: Children will chant along with the cumulative, rhyming, counting chant. If you print up the text, they'll have fun reading it aloud and reciting it as a buggy tongue twister. For another creature who eats more than he should, read or play the CD selection of "Hoimie the Woim" from my (Judy Freeman's) *Hi Ho Librario.*

RELATED TITLES: Christelow, Eileen. *Five Little Monkeys Jumping on the Bed.* Clarion, 1989. / Edwards, Pamela Duncan. *Some Smug Slug.* HarperCollins, 1996. / Falwell, Cathryn. *Turtle Splash! Countdown at the Pond.* Greenwillow, 2001. / Fleming, Denise. *In the Small, Small Pond.* Henry Holt, 1993. / Freeman, Judy. *Hi Ho Librario! Songs, Chants, and Stories to Keep Kids Humming.* Rock Hill, 1997. / French, Vivian. *Growing Frogs.* Candlewick, 2000. / Kalan, Robert. *Jump, Frog, Jump.* Greenwillow, 1981. / Karas, G. Brian. *I Know an Old Lady Who Swallowed a Fly.* Scholastic, 1994. / Noonan, Julia. *Mouse by Mouse.* Dutton, 2003. / Taback, Simms. *There Was an Old Lady Who Swallowed a Fly.* Viking, 1997. / Whippo, Walt, and Bernard Zaritzky. *Little White Duck.* Little, Brown, 2000. / Wiesner, David. *Tuesday.* Clarion, 1991.

SUBJECTS: COUNTING BOOKS. FROGS. INSECTS. STORIES IN RHYME.

862 Wilson, Karma. *Hilda Must Be Dancing.* **Illus. by Suzanne Watts. McElderry, 2004. 0-689-84788-2. Unp. Gr. PreK–1**

Here's a merry rhyming story about Hilda Hippo's loud and crashing love affair with dancing. Appalled by the noise, her jungle pals suggest she take up knitting or singing; though she gives those activities a try, dancing is her passion.

GERM: The full-bleed paintings are as flamboyant as can be, especially when Hilda, a full-figured gal dressed in full costume, is bouncing and bounding across the page. Your children will be eager to emulate her steps. Shake a rug with more large animals in *Ten Go Tango* by Arthur Dorros, *The Animal Boogie* by Debbie Harter, *Dinosaurumpus!* by Tony Mitton, and *Saturday Night at the Dinosaur Stomp* by Carol Diggory Shields.

RELATED TITLES: Auch, Mary Jane. *Peeping Beauty.* Holiday House, 1993. / Dorros, Arthur. *Ten Go Tango.* HarperCollins, 2000. / Edwards, Pamela Duncan. *Honk! The Story of a Prima Swanerina.* Hyperion, 1998. / Ernst, Lisa Campbell. *When Bluebell Sang.* Bradbury, 1989. / Goss, Linda. *The Frog Who Wanted to Be a Singer.* Orchard, 1996. / Harter, Debbie. *The Animal Boogie.* Barefoot, 2000. / Howe, James. *Horace and Morris Join the Chorus (But What About Dolores?).* Atheneum, 2002. / Livingston, Irene. *Finklehopper Frog.* Tricycle, 2003. / Lowery, Linda. *Twist with a Burger, Jitter with a Bug.* Houghton Mifflin, 1995. / Mitton, Tony. *Dinosaurumpus!* Scholastic, 2003. / Shields, Carol Diggory. *Saturday Night at the Dinosaur Stomp.* Candlewick, 1997.

SUBJECTS: ANIMALS. DANCING. HIPPOPOTAMUS. HUMOROUS FICTION. INDIVIDUALITY. STORIES IN RHYME.

863 Wilson, Karma. *Sweet Briar Goes to School.* **Illus. by LeUyen Pham. Dial, 2003. 0-8037-2767-4. Unp. Gr. PreK–1**

Though her adoring parents think she is the sweetest thing, Sweet Briar *is* a skunk, and smells like one too. On her first day at school, her forest animal classmates, fearful of her distinctive aroma, dive under their desks. When her worst tormentor, Wormwood Weasel, is snatched up by a lone wolf skulking nearby and her classmates panic, it's Sweet Briar to the rescue with her talented tail.

GERM: While this tale inspires empathy and celebrates a quick-thinking underdog who triumphs over the rejection of her peers, Sweet Briar is nevertheless a skunk. Ask children if they have ever smelled a skunk's singular perfume. Discuss the natural defenses that other animals employ and compose rhyming couplets about each creature's special talents.

RELATED TITLES: Harris, Robie H. *I Am Not Going to School Today!* McElderry, 2003. / Henkes, Kevin. *Chrysanthemum.* Greenwillow, 1991. / Hest, Amy. *Off to School, Baby Duck.* Candlewick, 1999. / Lasky, Kathryn. *Lunch Bunnies.* Little, Brown, 1996. / McGhee, Alison. *Countdown to Kindergarten.* Harcourt, 2002. / Peet, Bill. *The Spooky Tale of Prewitt Peacock.* Houghton Mifflin, 1973. / Pilkey, Dav. *Dog Breath: The Horrible Trouble with Hally Tosis.* Scholastic, 1994. / Pilkey, Dav. *The Hallo-Wiener.* Scholastic, 1995. / Slate, Joseph. *Miss Bindergarten Gets Ready for Kindergarten.* Dutton, 1996. / Wells, Rosemary. *Timothy Goes to School.* Dial, 1981. / Wilson, Karma. *Bear Snores On.* McElderry, 2002. / Wilson, Karma. *Bear Wants More.* McElderry, 2003. / Wilson, Karma. *Sweet Briar Goes to Camp.* Dial, 2005.

SUBJECTS: ANIMALS. FIRST DAY OF SCHOOL. SCHOOLS. SKUNKS. TEASING.

864   **Wing, Natasha.** *Jalapeño Bagels.* **Illus. by Robert Casilla. Atheneum, 1996. 0-689-80530-6. Unp. Gr. K–3**

Pablo's parents own a bakery, and when he needs to bring a treat to school to help celebrate International Day, he finds it hard to choose just the right food. His father is Jewish and his mother is Mexican, so he decides to bring his parents' special recipe—bagels with chopped jalapeños—because they are a mixture of both of their cultures, just as he is himself.

GERM: The appended recipes are from a real Mexican-Jewish-American bakery, Los Bagels Bakery and Cafe in Arcata, California. The soft, detailed watercolors will make everyone hungry for treats, so you might want to pick up a dozen bagels for all to share, and the glossary of Spanish and Yiddish words allow children to feel trilingual. Hold your own International Food Day.

RELATED TITLES: Baer, Edith. *This Is the Way We Eat Our Lunch: A Book About Children Around the World.* Scholastic, 1995. / Cox, Judy. *Now We Can Have a Wedding.* Holiday House, 1998. / Dooley, Norah. *Everybody Bakes Bread.* Carolrhoda, 1996. / Dooley, Norah. *Everybody Cooks Rice.* Carolrhoda, 1991. / Friedman, Ina R. *How My Parents Learned to Eat.* Houghton Mifflin, 1984. / Priceman, Marjorie. *How to Make an Apple Pie and See the World.* Knopf, 1994. / Rattigan, Jama Kim. *Dumpling Soup.* Little, Brown, 1993. / Ryan, Pam Muñoz. *Mice and Beans.* Scholastic, 2001. / Shelby, Anne. *Potluck.* Orchard, 1991. / Soto, Gary. *Snapshots from the Wedding.* Putnam, 1997. / Soto, Gary. *Too Many Tamales.* Putnam, 1993. / Wells, Rosemary. *Yoko.* Hyperion, 1998. / Wong, Janet. *Apple Pie 4th of July.* Harcourt, 2002.

SUBJECTS: BAGELS. BAKERS AND BAKERIES. COOKERY. FOOD. JEWS. MEXICAN AMERICANS. MULTICULTURAL BOOKS. RACIALLY MIXED PEOPLE.

865   **Winters, Kay.** *My Teacher for President.* **Illus. by Denise Brunkus. Dutton, 2004. 0-525-47186-3. Unp. Gr. PreK–3**

Oliver writes a letter to Channel 39, proposing his teacher as a candidate for the upcoming presidential election and listing the attributes that make her a great teacher and would work for her as commander in chief. The left-hand pages show Oliver's teacher working with her children, while the right-hand pages show her doing the same type of job in a presidential capacity.

GERM: Compile a presidential job description with your group and have them write up their own personal resumes. For your kids who are doing comparing and contrasting, making inferences, drawing conclusions, or working on persuasive writing, here's a perfect example of how to use logical arguments to buttress opinion with fact, and to put heart into your writing. In fact, this is a rare example of persuasive illustrating, where the pictures fill in all the rest of details for your students to put into words.

RELATED TITLES: Chandra, Deborah, and Madeline Comora. *George Washington's Teeth.* Farrar, 2003. / Christelow, Eileen. *VOTE!* Clarion, 2003. / Cronin, Doreen. *Duck for President.* Simon & Schuster, 2004. / Krosoczka, Jarrett. *Max for President.* Knopf, 2004. / McNamara, Margaret. *Election Day.* Simon & Schuster, 2004. / St. George, Judith. *So You Want to Be President?* Philomel, 2000. / Stier, Catherine. *If I Were President.* Albert Whitman, 1999. / Thimmesh, Catherine. *Madam President.* Houghton Mifflin, 2004.

SUBJECTS: ELECTIONS. LETTER WRITING. PRESIDENTS. SCHOOLS. TEACHERS.

866   **Winters, Kay.** *Whooo's Haunting the Teeny Tiny Ghost?* **Illus. by Lynn Munsinger. HarperCollins, 1999. 0-06-027359-3. Unp. Gr. PreK–K**

Coming home from Teeny Tiny School, the timid, teeny tiny ghost hears chains clinking and sees his teeny tiny chair rocking, but no one seems to be there. What's a teeny tiny ghost to do except screw up his courage and find out who is haunting and hiding in his house?

GERM: Ask your teeny tinies how and when they have been brave when they were scared. Also introduce Winters's companion books, *The Teeny Tiny Ghost* and *The Teeny Tiny Ghost and the Monster*.

RELATED TITLES: Aylesworth, Jim. *Two Terrible Frights*. Atheneum, 1987. / Brown, Ruth. *A Dark, Dark Tale*. Dial, 1981. / Calmenson, Stephanie. *The Teeny Tiny Teacher*. Scholastic, 1998. / Carter, David A. *In a Dark, Dark Wood*. Little Simon, 2002. / Galdone, Paul. *The Teeny-Tiny Woman*. Clarion, 1984. / Krosoczka, Jarrett J. *Annie Was Warned*. Knopf, 2003. / McBratney, Sam. *The Dark at the Top of the Stairs*. Candlewick, 1996. / Schwartz, Alvin. *Ghosts! Ghostly Tales from Folklore*. HarperCollins, 1991. / Schwartz, Alvin. *In a Dark, Dark Room and Other Scary Stories*. HarperCollins, 1984. / Thiesing, Lisa. *The Aliens Are Coming!* Dutton, 2003. / Thiesing, Lisa. *The Viper*. Dutton, 2002. / Williams, Linda. *The Little Old Lady Who Was Not Afraid of Anything*. Crowell, 1986. / Winters, Kay. *The Teeny Tiny Ghost and the Monster*. HarperCollins, 2004. / Winters, Kay. *Whooo's Haunting the Teeny Tiny Ghost*. HarperCollins, 1999.

SUBJECTS: COURAGE. FEAR. GHOSTS. HAUNTED HOUSES.

867   **Wishinsky, Frieda.** *Give Maggie a Chance*. **Illus. by Dean Griffiths. Fitzhenry & Whiteside, 2002. 1-55041-682-0. Unp. Gr. K–2**

Shy orange tabby cat Maggie is good at reading, but when she stands up in front of the whole class, she's too nervous to even whisper. For show-off gray and white cat Kimberly, reading is easy, and she taunts Maggie and Maggie's pal, Sam, who stutters. Defending Sam from sneering Kimberly gives Maggie the impetus to ignore her detractor and stand up for herself.

GERM: Discuss: How did Maggie work up the courage to read aloud to her class even though it was so hard for her to do? Have you ever done something you were afraid to do? How did you do it? Volunteers can act out the ending as Maggie comes up to the front of the room and reads aloud a page to the rest of the class. Compare Maggie's dilemma with Sarie's in *Once upon a Time* by Niki Daly, a heart-warming picture book about a little South African girl who hates to read aloud in class.

RELATED TITLES: Allen, Susan, and Jane Lindaman. *Read Anything Good Lately?* Millbrook, 2003. / Best, Cari. *Shrinking Violet*. Farrar, 2001. / Daly, Niki. *Once Upon a Time*. Farrar, 2002. / Hest, Amy. *Mr. George Baker*. Candlewick, 2004. / Hoffman, Mary. *Amazing Grace*. Dial, 1991. / Lewison, Wendy Cheyette. *Shy Vi*. Simon & Schuster, 1993. / Lexau, Joan. *Benjie*. Dial, 1964. / McCully, Emily Arnold. *Speak Up, Blanche*. HarperCollins, 1991. / Paterson, Katherine. *Marvin One Too Many*. HarperCollins, 2001. / Polacco, Patricia. *Thank You, Mr. Falker*. Philomel, 1998. / Stanley, Diane. *Raising Sweetness*. Putnam, 1999. / Wells, Rosemary. *Read Me a Story*. Hyperion, 2002. / Wells, Rosemary. *Shy Charles*. Dial, 1988.

SUBJECTS: BOOKS AND READING. CATS. COURAGE. FEAR. SCHOOLS. SHYNESS. TEASING.

868   **Wojciechokski, Susan.** *A Fine St. Patrick's Day*. **Illus. by Tom Curry. Random House, 2004. 0-375-92386-1. Unp. Gr. K–4**

Every year, rival towns Tralee and Tralah, hold a contest for the nicest St. Patrick's Day decorations, and, every year, Tralah wins. This year, little 6-year-old Fiona Riley has the wonderful idea to paint Tralee green. When a little man visits both towns to ask for help getting his cows out of the river mud, only the Tralee townsfolk will agree to help him, even though it means they'll lost the contest.

GERM: Make inferences: Who is that little man and why has he come? Make predictions: When the people of Tralah refuse to help, what will happen next? Make connections: What other stories have you read in which people were rewarded for being kind and helpful?

RELATED TITLES: Bateman, Teresa. *The Ring of Truth*. Holiday House, 1997. / dePaola, Tomie. *Jamie O'Rourke and the Big Potato: An Irish Folktale*. Putnam, 1992. / Haley, Gail. *Dream Peddler*. Dutton, 1993. / Hodges, Margaret. *Saint Patrick and the Peddler*. Orchard, 1993. / Kennedy, Richard. *The Leprechaun's Story*. Dutton, 1979. / Shute, Linda. *Clever Tom and the Leprechaun*. Lothrop, 1988.

SUBJECTS: COMPETITION. IRELAND. LEPRECHAUNS. ST. PATRICK'S DAY.

869   **Wolff, Patricia Rae.** *The Toll-Bridge Troll*. **Illus. by Kimberly Bulcken Root. Harcourt, 1995. 0-15-277665-6. Unp. Gr. K–2**

"Be careful of the troll," Trigg's mother warns him as he sets out for the first day of school. At the wooden bridge each day, the green-hatted troll lets Trigg pass without paying his penny toll when the little boy asks a riddle the troll can't answer.

GERM: Challenge your students to figure out the answer to each of Trigg's clever riddles, and afterward ask them to share some of their own favorite ones. Be sure to show where to find the riddle books on the library shelves.

RELATED TITLES: Brett, Jan. *Trouble with Trolls*. Putnam, 1992. / Brett, Jan. *Who's That Knocking on Christmas Eve?* Putnam, 2002. / Brown, Marcia. *The Three Billy Goats Gruff*. Harcourt, 1957. / Cole, Joanna, and Stephanie Calmenson. *Why Did the Rooster Cross the Road: And Other Riddles Old and New*. Morrow, 1994. / Emberley, Rebecca. *Three Cool Kids*. Little, Brown, 1995. / Galdone, Paul. *The Three Billy Goats Gruff*. Clarion, 1979. / Keller, Charles. *Belly Laughs: Food Jokes and Riddles*. Simon & Schuster, 1990. / Lewis, J. Patrick. *Riddle-i-cious*. Knopf, 1996. / Lewis, J. Patrick. *Riddle-Lightful: Oodles of Little Riddle Poems*. Knopf, 1998. / Marshall, Edward. *Troll Country*. Dial, 1980. / Rounds, Glen. *The Three Billy Goats Gruff*. Holiday House, 1993.
SUBJECTS: RIDDLES. TROLLS.

870   **Wong, Janet. *Apple Pie 4th of July*. Illus. by Margaret Irvine. Harcourt, 2002. 0-15-202543-X. Unp. Gr. PreK–2**
A young Chinese American girl describes how her parents cook Chinese food for their family market, even though she is sure no Americans will want to eat Chinese food on the Fourth of July. But at four o'clock, people start coming in, lining up for chow mein and sweet and sour pork. That night, she and her parents go up to the roof to watch the fireworks and eat apple pie—Americans all. The illustrations, colorful prints, are wonderfully expressive and capture the narrator's personality so effectively.
GERM: Ask your hungry crew to make a list of their favorite "American" foods from all cultures. They can write/tell/draw what they do on the Fourth—it's a holiday Americans don't usually get to celebrate in school. Maybe you should have your own classroom celebration on June 4 to make up for it.
RELATED TITLES: Compestine, Ying Chang. *The Story of Chopsticks*. Holiday House, 2001. / Cox, Judy. *Now We Can Have a Wedding*. Holiday House, 1998. / Dooley, Norah. *Everybody Bakes Bread*. Carolrhoda, 1996. / Dooley, Norah. *Everybody Cooks Rice*. Carolrhoda, 1991. / Hall, Bruce Edward. *Henry and the Kite Dragon*. Philomel, 2004. / Levine, Ellen. *I Hate English!* Scholastic, 1989. / Lewin, Ted. *Big Jimmy's Kum Kau Chinese Take Out*. HarperCollins, 2002. / Lin, Grace. *Fortune Cookie Fortunes*. Knopf, 2004. / Mak, Kam. *My Chinatown: One Year in Poems*. HarperCollins, 2002. / Pomeranc, Marion Hess. *The American Wei*. Albert Whitman, 1998. / Priceman, Marjorie. *How to Make an Apple Pie and See the World*. Knopf, 1994. / Rattigan, Jama Kim. *Dumpling Soup*. Little, Brown, 1993. / Sun, Chying Feng. *Mama Bear*. Houghton Mifflin, 1994. / Yang, Belle. *Hannah Is My Name*. Candlewick, 2004. / Yee, Paul. *Roses Sing on New Snow: A Delicious Tale*. Macmillan, 1992.
SUBJECTS: ASIAN AMERICANS. CELEBRATIONS. CHINESE AMERICANS. COOKERY. FAMILY LIFE. FOOD. FOURTH OF JULY. HOLIDAYS. MULTICULTURAL BOOKS. PIES.

871   **Wood, Audrey. *Alphabet Mystery*. Illus. by Bruce Wood. Scholastic, 2003. 0-439-44337-7. Unp. Gr. PreK–1**
When the 26 little letters from Charley's Alphabet call out their names at bedtime one night, Little X is discovered to be missing. Where could he be? One of Charley's pencils is gone as well, so the 25 remaining letters hop atop another #2 pencil and zoom over cities and towns to rescue their friend, X. Where is he? Feeling unappreciated and unused at home, X ran away.
GERM: Striking, computer-generated, 3-D illustrations of colorful, lower case letters will get everyone wanting to spell out their own secret messages with refrigerator magnet letters or other tactile letters they can arrange. There's a grand double-page spread of the 26 letters, each holding alliterative birthday gifts, which children can identify. Before showing the last page, ask them to predict how Little X might be the grand finishing touch on Mom's birthday cake. Follow up with the companion book, *Alphabet Adventure*.
RELATED TITLES: Cushman, Doug. *The ABC Mystery*. HarperCollins, 1993. / Ernst, Lisa Campbell. *The Letters Are Lost*. Viking, 1996. / Fleming, Denise. *Alphabet Under Construction*. Henry Holt, 2002. / Lester, Mike. *A Is for Salad*. Putnam, 2000. / MacDonald, Suse. *Alphabatics*. Simon & Schuster, 1986. / Martin, Bill, Jr., and John Archambault. *Chicka Chicka Boom Boom*. Simon & Schuster, 1989. / Seeger, Laura Vaccaro. *The Hidden Alphabet*. Roaring Brook, 2003. / Wood, Audrey. *Alphabet Adventure*. Blue Sky/Scholastic, 2002.
SUBJECTS: ALPHABET BOOKS. MYSTERY AND DETECTIVE STORIES.

872   **Wood, Audrey. *The Bunyans*. Illus. by David Shannon. Blue Sky/Scholastic, 1996. 0-590-48089-8. Unp. Gr. 1–4**
Make the acquaintance of an extraordinary family: tall-tale hero Paul Bunyan, his gigantic wife Carrie, and their two titanic tots, Little Jean and Teeny, whom author Audrey Wood credits with creating America's natural wonders in this deliciously deadpan original tall tale.
GERM: Have handy maps, globes, books of natural wonders, and Internet sites to look up the real stories behind the places mentioned, including Mammoth Cave, Kentucky; Niagara Falls,

New York; and Bryce Canyon, Utah. In the same vein is Anne Isaacs's *Swamp Angel*. Talk over: What is exaggeration? Have your children add exaggerated details to the sentence, "I saw a bear in my back yard." Then have them research an actual natural wonder in or out of state, and write and illustrate a new Bunyan adventure of how it came to be. Meet five larger-than-life sisters and their tiny new baby in *Granite Baby* by Lynne Bertrand.

RELATED TITLES: Bertrand, Lynne. *Granite Baby*. Farrar, 2005. / Cuyler, Margery. *Big Friends*. Walker, 2004. / DiPucchio, Kelly. *Liberty's Journey*. Hyperion, 2004. / Hopkinson, Deborah. *Apples to Oregon*. Atheneum, 2004. / Isaacs, Anne. *Swamp Angel*. Dutton, 1994. / Kellogg, Steven. *I Was Born About 10,000 Years Ago*. Morrow, 1996. / Kellogg, Steven. *Paul Bunyan*. Morrow, 1992. / Mora, Pat. *Doña Flor: A Tall Tale About a Giant Woman with a Great Big Heart*. Knopf, 2005. / Osborne, Mary Pope. *American Tall Tales*. Knopf, 1991. / Rounds, Glen. *Ol' Paul, the Mighty Logger*. Holiday House, 1976. / San Souci, Robert D. *Larger Than Life: The Adventures of American Legendary Heroes*. Doubleday, 1991. / Walker, Paul Robert. *Big Men, Big Country: A Collection of American Tall Tales*. Harcourt, 1993.

SUBJECTS: GEOGRAPHY. GIANTS. HUMOROUS FICTION. NATURAL MONUMENTS. TALL TALES. U.S.—GEOGRAPHY.

873 **Wood, Audrey. *The Flying Dragon Room*. Illus. by Mark Teague. Blue Sky/Scholastic, 1996. 0-590-48193-2. Unp. Gr. K–3**

Patrick constructs eye-popping rooms when house painter Mrs. Jenkins lends him her box of special tools. The oversized, detailed paintings give us a tour of each wondrous and kid-friendly room young Patrick builds, including the Bubble Room, Food Room, and Jumping Room.

GERM: Of course, your listeners will want to design, draw, name, and describe the room of their dreams, with livable spaces all their own. Me, I'd want the Chocolate Room, or maybe the Book Room. (Never mind—I have one of those already: the library!)

RELATED TITLES: Clement, Rod. *Just Another Ordinary Day*. HarperCollins, 1997. / Crowley, Michael. *New Kid on Spurwink Ave*. Little, Brown, 1992. / Faulkner, Matt. *The Amazing Voyage of Jackie Grace*. Scholastic, 1987. / Gerstein, Mordicai. *Behind the Couch*. Hyperion, 1996. / Joyce, William. *A Day with Wilbur Robinson*. Harper-Collins, 1993. / Legge, David. *Bamboozled*. Scholastic, 1995. / Marx, Patricia. *Meet My Staff*. HarperCollins, 1998. / McLerran, Alice. *Roxaboxen*. Lothrop, 1991. / Perry, Sarah. *If . . .* J. Paul Getty Museum and Children's Library Press, 1995. / Schotter, Roni. *Dreamland*. Orchard, 1996. / Teague, Mark. *Moog-Moog, Space Barber*. Scholastic, 1990. / Yaccarino, Dan. *If I Had a Robot*. Viking, 1996.

SUBJECTS: FANTASY. IMAGINATION. PICTURE BOOKS FOR ALL AGES.

874 **Woodruff, Elvira. *The Memory Coat*. Illus. by Michael Dooling. Scholastic, 1999. 0-590-67717-9. 32pp. Gr. 2–5**

After a two-week voyage to Ellis Island, loyal Rachel saves her cousin and best friend, Grisha, from being deported back to Russia when the doctor examining him mistakes the boy's scratched eye for a more serious problem.

GERM: Two additional, beautifully told and illustrated picture-book accounts of Jewish children who leave Russia and make the wrenching journey to America at the turn of the century are *Streets of Gold* by Rosemary Wells and *When Jessie Came Across the Sea* by Amy Hest.

RELATED TITLES: Avi. *Silent Movie*. Atheneum, 2003. / Bartone, Elisa. *American Too*. Lothrop, 1996. / Bartone, Elisa. *Peppe the Lamplighter*. Lothrop, 1993. / Bierman, Carol. *Journey to Ellis Island: How My Father Came to America*. Hyperion, 1998. / Connor, Leslie. *Miss Bridie Chose a Shovel*. Houghton Mifflin, 2004. / Freedman, Russell. *Immigrant Kids*. Dutton, 1980. / Hest, Amy. *When Jessie Came Across the Sea*. Candlewick, 1997. / Levine, Ellen. *If Your Name Was Changed at Ellis Island*. Scholastic, 1993. / Maestro, Betsy. *Coming to America: The Story of Immigration*. Scholastic, 1996. / Sandler, Martin W. *Immigrants*. HarperCollins, 1995. / Wells, Rosemary. *Streets of Gold*. Dial, 1999.

SUBJECTS: COUSINS. ELLIS ISLAND IMMIGRATION STATION (N.Y. AND N.J.). HISTORICAL FICTION. IMMIGRATION AND EMIGRATION. JEWS. ORPHANS. RUSSIA. VOYAGES AND TRAVELS.

875 **Woodson, Jacqueline. *The Other Side*. Illus. by E. B. Lewis. Putnam, 2001. 0-399-23116-1. Unp. Gr. 1–6**

Though Mama tells her not to play on the other side of the fence that stretches through their town—it's not safe, and it's the way things have always been—Clover, a young black girl, still would like to be friends with the white girl over there, on the other side. On a day when the summer rains have finally stopped and Clover is feeling brave and free, she talks to the other little girl, and the two climb up to sit on that fence together. This picture book with its heartwarming watercolors is far more than a warm story of friendship; it's a moving and innovative allegory about segregation, tolerance, and breaking down racial barriers.

GERM: As a parallel to the civil rights movement, this simple picture book can be used at all grade levels to discuss the effects of racial segregation and to explore how one courageous person can bring about change, using such examples as Rosa Parks and Ruby Bridges. Pair this with Doreen Rappaport's simply told, uplifting picture-book biography, *Martin's Big Words*, about Dr. Martin Luther King, Jr.

RELATED TITLES: Adler, David A. *Dr. Martin Luther King, Jr.* Holiday House, 2001. / Adler, David A. *A Picture Book of Rosa Parks*. Holiday House, 1993. / Bray, Rosemary L. *Martin Luther King*. Greenwillow, 1995. / Bridges, Ruby. *Through My Eyes*. Scholastic, 1999. / Coles, Robert. *The Story of Ruby Bridges*. Scholastic, 1995. / Curtis, Gavin. *The Bat Boy and His Violin*. Simon & Schuster, 1998. / Giovanni, Nikki. *Rosa*. Henry Holt, 2005. / Golenbock, Peter. *Teammates*. Harcourt, 1990. / Marzollo, Jean. *Happy Birthday, Martin Luther King*. Scholastic, 1993. / McKissack, Patricia C. *Goin' Someplace Special*. Atheneum, 2001. / Mitchell, Margaree King. *Uncle Jed's Barber Shop*. Simon & Schuster, 1993. / Nelson, Vaunda Micheaux. *Mayfield Crossing*. Putnam, 1993. / Polacco, Patricia. *Mr. Lincoln's Way*. Philomel, 2001. / Rappaport, Doreen. *Martin's Big Words*. Hyperion, 2001. / Wiles, Deborah. *Freedom Summer*. Atheneum, 2001.

SUBJECTS: AFRICAN AMERICANS. ALLEGORIES. FRIENDSHIP. INTEGRATION. MULTICULTURAL BOOKS. PICTURE BOOKS FOR ALL AGES. RACE RELATIONS.

876   **Wright, Betty Ren. *The Blizzard*. Illus. by Ronald Himler. Holiday House, 2003. 0-8234-1656-9. Unp. Gr. K–2**

With a snowstorm forecast for his December birthday, Billy is disappointed that his cousins won't be able to visit. The blizzard hits while he's at school, and his teacher and the whole class from the one-room schoolhouse trek over to Billy's nearby house to spend the night.

GERM: Share experiential stories of storms and birthday surprises.

RELATED TITLES: Branley, Franklyn M. *Snow Is Falling*. HarperCollins, 2000. / Burton, Virginia Lee. *Katy and the Big Snow*. Houghton Mifflin, 1943. / Carrick, Carol. *Lost in the Storm*. Clarion, 1987. / Gliori, Debi. *The Snow Lambs*. Scholastic, 1996. / Keats, Ezra Jack. *The Snowy Day*. Viking, 1962. / Kellogg, Steven. *The Missing Mitten Mystery*. Dial, 2000. / Martin, Jacqueline Briggs. *Snowflake Bentley*. Houghton Mifflin, 1998. / O'Malley, Kevin. *Straight to the Pole*. Walker, 2003. / Prelutsky, Jack. *It's Snowing! It's Snowing!* Greenwillow, 1984. / Schnur, Steven. *Winter: An Alphabet Acrostic*. Clarion, 2002. / Wetterer, Margaret, and Charles Wetterer. *The Snow Walker*. Carolrhoda, 1996.

SUBJECTS: BIRTHDAYS. BLIZZARDS. SCHOOLS. SNOW.

877   **Yaccarino, Dan. *Zoom! Zoom! Zoom! I'm Off to the Moon!* Illus. by the author. Scholastic, 1997. 0-590-95610-8. Unp. Gr. PreK–1**

In a rhyming rollicking ride, a boy puts on a space suit and space boots, counts down from ten, and blasts off. "There's outer space all over the place." Energetic illustrations take us along on his exhilarating journey to space and back home to bed.

GERM: Act this one out in narrative pantomime for all those kids who would love to be able to get in their personal rockets and fly. Pair it with a true nonfiction picture book of the first moon walk in 1969, Anastasia Suen's *Man on the Moon*, and with Faith McNulty's *If You Decide to Go to the Moon*.

RELATED TITLES: Brown, Don. *One Giant Leap: The Story of Neil Armstrong*. Houghton Mifflin, 1998. / Crews, Nina. *I'll Catch the Moon*. Greenwillow, 1996. / Gaffney, Timothy R. *Grandpa Takes Me to the Moon*. Tambourine, 1996. / Haddon, Mark. *The Sea of Tranquility*. Harcourt, 1996. / Krupp, E. C. *The Moon and You*. Macmillan, 1993. / McNulty, Faith. *If You Decide to Go to the Moon*. Scholastic, 2005. / Standiford, Natalie. *Astronauts Are Sleeping*. Knopf, 1996. / Suen, Anastasia. *Man on the Moon*. Viking, 1997. / Wethered, Peggy, and Ken Edgett. *Touchdown Mars! An ABC Adventure*. Putnam, 2000. / Yaccarino, Dan. *If I Had a Robot*. Viking, 1996.

SUBJECTS: ASTRONAUTS. CREATIVE DRAMA. IMAGINATION. MOON. SPACE FLIGHT TO THE MOON. STORIES IN RHYME. VOYAGES, IMAGINARY.

878   **Yin. *Coolies*. Illus. by Chris Soentpiet. Philomel, 2001. 0-399-23227-3. Unp. Gr. 1–6**

On the night of the Ching Ming festival, PawPaw tells her grandson the true story of Shek, her great-grandfather, who left China in the mid-1800s with his younger brother, Little Wong, and worked alongside thousands of other "coolies," or lowly workers, to build the Central Pacific Railroad. Inspired by actual events and illustrated with luminous, dramatic watercolors, Paw-

Paw's story of how her ancestors prevailed will get listeners thinking about their own family's part in building America.

GERM: This picture book for all ages can be tied in to discussions about having pride in one's ancestors, tracing racial discrimination in America, teaching tolerance, exploring Chinese customs and culture, and researching the building of the railroads. Hold your own Respect for Ancestors day. Students can interview family members to find out more about an ancestor, bring in photos, and share what they have learned with the rest of the group.

RELATED TITLES: Blumberg, Rhoda. *Full Steam Ahead: The Race to Build a Transcontinental Railroad.* National Geographic, 1996. / Compestine, Ying Chang. *The Story of Chopsticks.* Holiday House, 2001. / Fisher, Leonard Everett. *Tracks Across America: The Story of the American Railroad.* Holiday House, 1992. / Fraser, Mary A. *Ten Mile Day: The Building of the Transcontinental Railroad.* Henry Holt, 1993. / Hall, Bruce Edward. *Henry and the Kite Dragon.* Philomel, 2004. / Jiang, Ji Li. *Red Scarf Girl.* HarperCollins, 1997. / Kay, Verla. *Iron Horses.* Putnam, 1999. / Lee, Milly. *Nim and the War Effort.* Farrar, 1997. / Mahy, Margaret. *The Seven Chinese Brothers.* Scholastic, 1990. / Wong, Janet. *Good Luck Gold and Other Poems.* McElderry, 1994. / Yee, Paul. *Roses Sing on New Snow.* Macmillan, 1992. / Yep, Laurence. *Dragon's Gate.* Morrow, 1993. / Yep, Laurence. *The Star Fisher.* Morrow, 1991.

SUBJECTS: ASIAN AMERICANS. CHINESE AMERICANS. CIVIL RIGHTS. HISTORICAL FICTION. MULTICULTURAL BOOKS. PICTURE BOOKS FOR OLDER READERS. U.S.—HISTORY—1865–1898—FICTION.

879   **Yolen, Jane.** *How Do Dinosaurs Eat Their Food?* **Illus. by Mark Teague. Blue Sky/Scholastic, 2005. 0-439-24102-2. Unp. Gr. PreK–1**

This laugh-out-loud rhyming companion to *How Do Dinosaurs Get Well Soon?* and *How Do Dinosaurs Say Good Night?* shows ten picky-eater dinosaurs learning some manners.

GERM: Ask your noisy, fidgety, spaghetti-flipping, broccoli-hating, milk-bubbling food-osaurs what they've learned about proper eating, thanks to their proper parents. Bring in a snack of something good to eat and drink and ask them to demonstrate how to handle each component properly.

RELATED TITLES: Abrams, Pam. *Now I Eat My ABC's.* Scholastic, 2004. / Blumenthal, Deborah. *Don't Let the Peas Touch! And Other Stories.* Scholastic, 2004. / Brown, Marc. *D. W. the Picky Eater.* Little, Brown, 1995. / Brown, Marc, and Stephen Krensky. *Perfect Pigs: An Introduction to Manners.* Little, Brown, 1983. / Child, Lauren. *I Will Never Not Ever Eat a Tomato.* Candlewick, 2000. / Demarest, Chris L. *No Peas for Nellie.* Macmillan, 1988. / Hoberman, Mary Ann. *The Seven Silly Eaters.* Harcourt, 1997. / Most, Bernard. *How Big Were the Dinosaurs?* Harcourt, 1994. / Palatini, Margie. *Zak's Lunch.* Clarion, 1998. / Sharmat, Mitchell. *Gregory, the Terrible Eater.* Macmillan, 1985. / Stickland, Paul, and Henrietta Stickland. *Dinosaur Roar!* Dutton, 1994. / Wells, Rosemary. *Yoko.* Hyperion, 1998. / Yee, Wong Herbert. *Big Black Bear.* Houghton Mifflin, 1993. / Yolen, Jane. *How Do Dinosaurs Get Well Soon?* Blue Sky/Scholastic, 2003. / Yolen, Jane. *How Do Dinosaurs Say Good Night?* Blue Sky/Scholastic, 2000.

SUBJECTS: DINOSAURS. ETIQUETTE. FOOD. FOOD HABITS. HUMOROUS FICTION. PARENT AND CHILD. STORIES IN RHYME.

880   **Yolen, Jane.** *How Do Dinosaurs Get Well Soon?* **Illus. by Mark Teague. Blue Sky/Scholastic, 2003. 0-439-24100-6. Unp. Gr. PreK–1**

In an equally amusing rhyming companion book to *How Do Dinosaurs Say Good Night?* and *How Do Dinosaurs Eat Their Food?*, ten gargantuan, ailing, sniffly, flu-ish, under-the-weather, cranky dinosaurs run their human parents ragged and are dragged off to doctors who prescribe pills, juice, and lots of rest.

GERM: Make giant get-well cards for your favorite under-the-weather dinos. This is also a book to use for recognizing rhyming words, as an introduction to dinosaurs, and, of course, as a prime weapon in your health unit arsenal, where you try valiantly to get your kids to sneeze in the crook of their arms instead of on you.

RELATED TITLES: Bateman, Teresa. *Farm Flu.* Albert Whitman, 2001. / Cherry, Lynne. *Who's Sick Today?* Dutton, 1988. / Hearn, Diane Dawson. *Dad's Dinosaur Day.* Macmillan, 1993. / LeGuin, Ursula K. *A Visit from Dr. Katz.* Atheneum, 1988. / Mitton, Tony. *Dinosaurumpus!* Scholastic, 2003. / Most, Bernard. *How Big Were the Dinosaurs?* Harcourt, 1994. / Nolan, Dennis. *Dinosaur Dreams.* Macmillan, 1990. / Rohmann, Eric. *Time Flies.* Crown, 1994. / Shields, Carol Diggory. *Saturday Night at the Dinosaur Stomp.* Candlewick, 1997. / Stickland, Paul. *Ten Terrible Dinosaurs.* Dutton, 1997. / Stickland, Paul, and Henrietta Stickland. *Dinosaur Roar!* Dutton, 1994. / Thomas, Shelley Moore. *Get Well, Good Knight.* Dutton, 2002. / Wells, Rosemary. *Felix Feels Better.* Candlewick, 2001. / Yolen, Jane. *How Do Dinosaurs Eat Their Food?* Blue Sky/Scholastic, 2005. / Yolen, Jane. *How Do Dinosaurs Say Good Night?* Blue Sky/Scholastic, 2000.

SUBJECTS: DINOSAURS. DOCTORS. HUMOROUS FICTION. SICK. STORIES IN RHYME.

881 Yolen, Jane. *How Do Dinosaurs Say Good Night?* Illus. by Mark Teague. Scholastic, 2000. 0-590-31681-8. 64pp. Gr. PreK–1

Accompanied by jaunty paintings and a sprightly rhyming series of questions, ten oversized dinosaur children balk at going to bed. Each page sports a different human mom or dad as they deal with their obstreperous, sulking, crying, bedtime-phobic dinosaur children, till Mom turns out the light, tucks them in, and gives them a final hug and kiss.

GERM: Have your listeners draw themselves as dinosaur characters and show how they get ready for bed each night. Follow this up with a simple nonfiction dinosaur book featuring all types of the Triassic, Jurassic, and Cretaceous creatures, such as Peter Dodson's *Alphabet of Dinosaurs.*

RELATED TITLES: Cook, Sally. *Good Night Pillow Fight.* HarperCollins, 2004. / Dewdney, Anna. *Llama Llama Red Pajama.* Viking, 2005. / Dodson, Peter. *An Alphabet of Dinosaurs.* Scholastic, 1995. / French, Vivian. *T. Rex.* Candlewick, 2004. / Hearn, Diane Dawson. *Dad's Dinosaur Day.* Macmillan, 1993. / Mitton, Tony. *Dinosaurumpus!* Scholastic, 2003. / Most, Bernard. *How Big Were the Dinosaurs?* Harcourt, 1994. / Nolan, Dennis. *Dinosaur Dreams.* Macmillan, 1990. / Rathmann, Peggy. *Good Night, Gorilla.* Putnam, 1994. / Rohmann, Eric. *Time Flies.* Crown, 1994. / Rothstein, Gloria. *Sheep Asleep.* HarperCollins, 2003. / Shields, Carol Diggory. *Saturday Night at the Dinosaur Stomp.* Candlewick, 1997. / Stickland, Paul. *Ten Terrible Dinosaurs.* Dutton, 1997. / Stickland, Paul, and Henrietta Stickland. *Dinosaur Roar!* Dutton, 1994. / Whybrow, Ian. *Sammy and the Dinosaurs.* Orchard, 1999. / Yolen, Jane. *How Do Dinosaurs Get Well Soon?* Blue Sky/Scholastic, 2003.

SUBJECTS: BEDTIME STORIES. DINOSAURS. HUMOROUS FICTION. STORIES IN RHYME.

882 Yolen, Jane. *Merlin and the Dragons.* Illus. by Li Ming. Dutton, 1995. 0-525-65214-0. Unp. Gr. 2–6

Frightened by his disturbing dreams, the newly crowned boy King Arthur seeks solace from the magician, Merlin, who tells him the story of Emrys, a lonely boy whose dreams of dragons helped bring down the ruthless Vortigern, the self-proclaimed High King of Britain. This mystical picture book, with sweeping, heart-stopping dragon-filled paintings, extends and fictionalizes the legacy of King Arthur.

GERM: Set your readers on the trail of King Arthur with this and other picture books that introduce his story, including *Arthur and the Sword* by Robert Sabuda and *Young Arthur* by Robert D. San Souci.

RELATED TITLES: Hastings, Selena. *Sir Gawain and the Green Knight.* Lothrop, 1981. / Hastings, Selena. *Sir Gawain and the Loathly Lady.* Lothrop, 1985. / Hodges, Margaret. *Merlin and the Making of the King.* Holiday House, 2004. / Hodges, Patricia. *Saint George and the Dragon.* Little, Brown, 1984. / Mayer, Marianna. *The Adventures of Tom Thumb.* SeaStar, 2001. / Sabuda, Robert. *Arthur and the Sword.* Atheneum, 1995. / San Souci, Robert D. *Young Arthur.* Doubleday, 1997. / Shannon, Mark. *Gawain and the Green Knight.* Putnam, 1994. / Talbott, Hudson. *King Arthur and the Round Table.* Morrow, 1995. / Yolen, Jane. *Passager: The Young Merlin Trilogy, Book One.* Harcourt, 1996.

SUBJECTS: ARTHUR, KING (LEGENDARY CHARACTER). DRAGONS. FOLKLORE—ENGLAND. KINGS AND RULERS. LEGENDS. MAGICIANS. MERLIN (LEGENDARY CHARACTER).

883 Young, Ed. *Beyond the Great Mountains: A Visual Poem About China.* Illus. by the author. Chronicle, 2005. 0-8118-4343-2. Unp. Gr. 2–6

Open this book vertically and discover Young's spare, descriptive, free-verse poem about the elements of the natural world that made up the land of Middle Empire, China— mountains, rivers, grains, bamboo, plants, salt, and jade. Each line is printed on a different color of stepped or tiered pages, so you can read the whole poem at once, from top to bottom, as one would read text in Chinese. Then thumb through the book page by page and look at the poem sequentially, examining the visually ravishing collage illustrations made of textured papers. Each abstract-looking picture illustrates one line of the poem and is actually a large representative drawing of one or two ancient Chinese characters, which are reproduced in red at the bottom of the page.

GERM: Young's purpose was to show 24 Chinese characters as part of a visual poem. About the written Chinese language, which is made up of thousands of characters, Young says, "There are 214 root pictures and they are the basis of all Chinese characters . . . So in *Beyond the Great*

Mountains I am introducing ⅛ of the basis of all Chinese characters in just one picture book! And these roots become the basis of Chinese reading." Indeed, viewers will make the connections between the pictures and the labeled diagrams showing the parts that make up each character. The word "salt," for instance, is drawn as an amalgam of the symbols for "west," "bird," and "grains." On the back inside cover is a chart that compares the ancient Chinese characters, used in the book, and the modern characters, so you can see how they have evolved.

RELATED TITLES: Casanova, Mary. *The Hunter: A Chinese Folktale.* Illus. by Ed Young. Atheneum, 2000. / Cole, Joanna. *Ms. Frizzle's Adventures: Imperial China.* Scholastic, 2005. / Fisher, Leonard Everett. *The Great Wall of China.* Macmillan, 1986. / Mahy, Margaret. *The Seven Chinese Brothers.* Scholastic, 1990. / O'Connor, Jane. *The Emperor's Silent Army: Terracotta Warriors of Ancient China.* Viking, 2002. / Young, Ed. *Mouse Match: A Chinese Folktale.* Harcourt, 1997. / Young, Ed. *Night Visitors.* Philomel, 1995. / Young, Ed. *The Sons of the Dragon King: A Chinese Legend.* Atheneum, 2004.

SUBJECTS: CHINA. CHINESE LANGUAGE. MULTICULTURAL BOOKS. PICTURE BOOKS FOR OLDER READERS.

884 **Young, Ed.** *I, Doko: The Tale of a Basket.* **Illus. by the author. Philomel, 2004. 0-399-23625-2. Unp. Gr. 2–6**

Doko means "basket" in Nepalese, and in this narrative, adapted from a fable, the basket itself tell us its history. Doko's master, Yeh-yeh, and his wife, Nei-nei, use the basket to carry their baby boy to the fields, and, when the boy grows up, he carries firewood in it. When Nei-nei dies in an epidemic, Doko is used to carry her to her grave. The boy grows up, marries, and has a son, Wangal, cared for by the now elderly Yeh-yeh, who tells him wonderful stories. When the young father places Yeh-yeh in the basket to leave him on the temple steps, young Wangel advises him to bring the basket home, saying, "This way, I won't need to buy another Doko when you are old and it's time to leave you on the temple steps." Dark-toned, dignified gouache, pastel, and collage illustrations, bordered and flecked with gold, reflect the somber, contemplative tone of Doko's parable.

GERM: Discussion points: Why does Doko, the basket itself, narrate this story? What does the introductory quote mean: "What one wishes not upon oneself, one burdens not upon another." (Kung Fu Tze, aka Confucius, in the 6th century B.C.) How does this old story relate to us here and now? How are grandparents cared for in our society? In other cultures? Another moving folktale about the treatment of the elderly is *The Wise Old Woman*, a Japanese folktale retold by Yoshiko Uchida. The basket's narration provides an arresting use of personification to tell a larger story, which could spark some interesting writing from your students.

RELATED TITLES: Freedman, Russell. *Confucius: The Golden Rule.* Scholastic, 2002. / Say, Allen. *Kamishibai Man.* Houghton Mifflin, 2005. / Tompert, Ann. *Bamboo Hats and a Rice Cake: A Tale Adapted from Japanese Folklore.* Crown, 1993. / Uchida, Yoshiko. *The Magic Purse.* McElderry, 1993. / Uchida, Yoshiko. *The Wise Old Woman.* McElderry, 1994.

SUBJECTS: BASKETS. DEATH. ELDERLY. FAMILY LIFE. FOLKLORE—NEPAL. NEPAL. PERSONAL NARRATIVES. PERSONIFICATION. PICTURE BOOKS FOR OLDER READERS. RESPONSIBILITY.

885 **Zelinsky, Paul O.** *Knick-Knack Paddywhack!* **Illus. by the author. Dutton, 2002. 0-525-46908-7. Unp. Gr. PreK–1**

The still-popular one-to-ten counting song "This Old Man" is set to moving parts in a visual feast of a pop-up, pull-the-tabs, and open-the-flaps book.

GERM: As you sing, you can act out the song using simple props and hand motions. In Marissa Moss's updated version of the song, the old guy constructs a rocket ship, counts down, and then takes off to become the man in the moon. Continue with Zelinsky's other paper-engineered book, *The Wheels on the Bus*, a worthy companion.

RELATED TITLES: Cauley, Lorinda Bryan. *Old MacDonald Had a Farm.* Putnam, 1989. / Jones, Carol. *This Old Man.* Houghton Mifflin, 1990. / Karas, G. Brian. *I Know an Old Lady Who Swallowed a Fly.* Scholastic, 1994. / Kellogg, Steven. *Give the Dog a Bone.* Chronicle, 2004. / Moss, Marissa. *Knick Knack Paddywack.* Houghton Mifflin, 1992. / Pearson, Tracey Campbell. *Old MacDonald Had a Farm.* Dial, 1984. / Rounds, Glen. *Old MacDonald Had a Farm.* Holiday House, 1989. / Taback, Simms. *There Was an Old Lady Who Swallowed a Fly.* Viking, 1997. / Whippo, Walt, and Bernard Zaritzky. *Little White Duck.* Little, Brown, 2000. / Zelinsky, Paul O. *The Wheels on the Bus.* Dutton, 1990.

SUBJECTS: COUNTING BOOKS. CREATIVE DRAMA. DOGS. ELDERLY. SONGS. STORIES IN RHYME.

886   Zemach, Kaethe. *The Question Song.* **Illus. by the author. Little, Brown, 2003. 0-316-66601-7. Unp. Gr. PreK–K**

When things go wrong, a family employs "The Question Song," in which the children sing about a problem and the parents respond with a simple solution. Included are such childhood dilemmas as a broken toy train, spilled juice, and a bumped toe.

GERM: First come up with a simple, serviceable tune so you and your children can sing the story as a call-and-response. Then have them think up new problems and solutions that you can sing together.

RELATED TITLES: Carlson, Nancy. *There's a Big, Beautiful World Out There!* Viking, 2002. / Zemach, Harve. *Mommy, Buy Me a China Doll.* Follett, 1966. / Zemach, Kaethe. *The Character in the Book.* HarperCollins, 1998.

SUBJECTS: BEHAVIOR. CALL-AND-RESPONSE STORIES. CAUSE AND EFFECT. CONDUCT OF LIFE. FAMILY LIFE. PROBLEM SOLVING. SONGS. STORIES IN RHYME.

887   Ziefert, Harriet. *I Swapped My Dog.* **Illus. by Emily Bolam. Houghton Mifflin, 1998. 0-395-89159-0. Unp. Gr. PreK–1**

In rhyming couplets, easy to read and repeat, a farmer describes how he swapped his dog for a mare, his mare for a mule, his mule for a goat, and all the way, full circle, until he had his dog back again.

GERM: Children can recall the cause and effect of each animal the farmer acquires. Make puppets or flannelboard pieces with your children so they can act this out. Children can continue the pattern: "I swapped my ____ and got me a ____." Lisa Campbell Ernst's *Stella Louella's Runaway Book* and Jane Kurtz's Eritrean folktale *Trouble* also take you in a circle.

RELATED TITLES: dePaola, Tomie. *The Comic Adventures of Old Mother Hubbard and Her Dog.* Harcourt, 1981. / Ernst, Lisa Campbell. *Stella Louella's Runaway Book.* Simon & Schuster, 1998. / Fox, Mem. *Boo to a Goose.* Dial, 1998. / Greene, Rhonda Gowler. *Barnyard Song.* Atheneum, 1997. / Hoberman, Mary Ann. *There Once Was a Man Named Michael Finnegan.* Little, Brown, 2001. / Marshall, James. *Old Mother Hubbard and Her Wonderful Dog.* Farrar, 1991. / Nerlove, Miriam. *I Made a Mistake.* Atheneum, 1985. / Raffi. *Down by the Bay.* Crown, 1987. / Reeves, Mona Rabun. *I Had a Cat.* Bradbury, 1989. / Rounds, Glen. *Old MacDonald Had a Farm.* Holiday House, 1989. / Taback, Simms. *Joseph Had a Little Overcoat.* Viking, 1999. / Taback, Simms. *There Was an Old Lady Who Swallowed a Fly.* Viking, 1997. / Taback, Simms. *This Is the House That Jack Built.* Putnam, 2002. / Ziefert, Harriet. *When I First Came to This Land.* Putnam, 1998.

SUBJECTS: ANIMALS. BARTERING. CIRCULAR STORIES. CREATIVE DRAMA. SEQUENCE STORIES. STORIES IN RHYME.

888   Ziefert, Harriet. *31 Uses for a Mom.* **Illus. by Rebecca Doughty. Putnam, 2003. 0-399-23862-X. Unp. Gr. K–2**

In a numbered list of 31 of those everyday things moms do, there's one job per page (1. clock, 2. chauffeur, etc.) and wonderfully amusing, childlike, ink and paint portraits of stick figure mothers of all races and sizes interacting with their children.

GERM: Ask your children to think of more uses for moms, dads, siblings, and themselves. At Van Holten School in Bridgewater, New Jersey, Laura Curry and Lisa D'Ascenzio's second-grade classes made instant connections. "We could write 31 uses for our teachers!" And that's what they did, compiling two adorable booklets: "24 Uses for a Second Grade Teacher" and "24 Uses for a Second Grader." My favorite of their perceived jobs? "Overdoer," showing a teacher with five arms. And "detective." ("My pencil is missing, Miss Curry!" "I found it, Samantha," reads the cartoon bubble dialogue on the picture.) It was a great way to sum up their classroom interactions for the year and to recognize and appreciate all the wonderful experiences they had had with their unforgettable teachers.

RELATED TITLES: Cooper, Melrose. *I've Got a Family.* Henry Holt, 1993. / Lasky, Kathryn. *Before I Was Your Mother.* Harcourt, 2003. / Maloney, Peter, and Felicia Zekauskas. *His Mother's Nose.* Dial, 2001. / Pulver, Robin. *Nobody's Mother Is in Second Grade.* Dial, 1992. / Russo, Marisabina. *Trade-In Mother.* Greenwillow, 1993. / Wells, Rosemary. *Hazel's Amazing Mother.* Dial, 1985. / Ziefert, Harriet. *39 Uses for a Friend.* Putnam, 2001. / Ziefert, Harriet. *33 Uses for a Dad.* Blue Apple, 2004. / Ziefert, Harriet. *40 Uses for a Grandpa.* Blue Apple, 2005. / Ziefert, Harriet. *41 Uses for a Grandma.* Blue Apple, 2005. / Zemke, Deborah. *35 Uses for a Daughter.* Blue Apple, 2005.

SUBJECTS: FAMILY LIFE. MOTHERS. MULTICULTURAL BOOKS. OCCUPATIONS.

FICTION

889 **Alexander, Lloyd.** *The Arkadians.* **Dutton, 1995. 0-525-45415-2. 272pp. Gr. 5–8**
Master tale-weaver Alexander takes us to ancient Greece in an event-filled quest. When Lucian, accountant to King Bromios of Arcadia, makes the mistake of uncovering evidence of corruption in the palace storehouse, his only option is to flee. On his journey, he teams up with Fronto, a talking donkey who was a human poet before he swam in a forbidden pool, and Joy-in-the-Dance, a young pythoness oracle on her way to the mountains to see the Lady of Wild Things.
GERM: We root for the budding attraction between Lucian and Joy-in-the-Dance and for a new society based on peace, knowledge, and reconciliation of the sexes. Listeners can discuss the roles of men and women in society then and now.
RELATED TITLES: Alcock, Vivian. *Singer to the Sea God.* Delacorte, 1993. / Alexander, Lloyd. *The Book of Three.* Henry Holt, 1964. / Alexander, Lloyd. *The First Two Lives of Lucas-Kasha.* Dutton, 1978. / Bradshaw, Gillian. *Beyond the North Wind.* Greenwillow, 1993. / McCaughrean, Geraldine. *The Bronze Cauldron: Myths and Legends of the World.* McElderry, 1998. / Osborne, Mary Pope. *Favorite Greek Myths.* Scholastic, 1989. / Philip, Neil. *The Adventures of Odysseus.* Orchard, 1997. / Pratchett, Terry. *The Wee Free Men.* HarperCollins, 2003. / Sutcliffe, Rosemary. *Black Ships Before Troy! The Story of the Iliad.* Delacorte, 1993. / Sutcliffe, Rosemary. *The Wanderings of Odysseus: The Story of The Odyssey.* Delacorte, 1996. / Yolen, Jane, and Robert J. Harris. *Odysseus in the Serpent Maze.* HarperCollins, 2001.
SUBJECTS: FANTASY. GREECE, ANCIENT. MYTHOLOGY.

890 **Amato, Mary.** *The Word Eater.* **Illus. by Christopher Ryniak. Holiday House, 2000. 0-8234-1468-X. 151pp. Gr. 3–6**
Fip, an outcast worm who eats the print off the page instead of dirt, and Lerner Chase, a sixth-grade girl considered a slug (Sorry Loser Under Ground) by the popular kids in the MPOOE (Most Powerful Ones On Earth) Club, become allies in an entertaining and pointed satire about the power of words.
GERM: The story packs in many meaty issues to discuss with listeners: the use and abuse of power, the tyranny of school cliques with their leaders and followers, the triumph of social outcasts and downtrodden children, and individual accountability in perpetuating good or evil. Ask your students to make lists of words they'd consider having Fip eat, and trace the possible consequences if those words were gone for good.
RELATED TITLES: Banks, Lynne Reid. *Harry the Poisonous Centipede.* Morrow, 1997. / Clements, Andrew. *Frindle.* Simon & Schuster, 1996. / Dahl, Roald. *Matilda.* Viking, 1988. / Evans, Douglas. *Apple Island, or The Truth About Teachers.* Front Street, 1998. / Evans, Douglas. *The Classroom at the End of the Hall.* Front Street, 1996. / Evans, Douglas. *Math Rashes and Other Classroom Tales.* Front Street, 2004. / Fleischman, Paul. *Weslandia.* Candlewick, 1999. / Hornik, Laurie Miller. *The Secrets of Ms. Snickle's Class.* Clarion, 2001. / Hornik, Laurie Miller. *Zoo School.* Clarion, 2004. / MacDonald, Amy. *No More Nasty.* Farrar, 2001. / Napoli, Donna Jo. *The Prince of the Pond.* Dutton, 1992. / Pfeffer, Wendy. *Wiggling Worms at Work.* HarperCollins, 2004. / Sachar, Louis. Wayside School series. Lothrop. / Swope, Sam. *The Araboolies of Liberty Street.* Crown, 1989. / Vande Velde, Vivian. *Smart Dog.* Harcourt, 1998. / Voigt, Cynthia. *Bad Girls.* Scholastic, 1996.
SUBJECTS: BEHAVIOR. LANGUAGE. MAGIC. OUTCASTS. SCHOOLS. WORMS.

891   Andersen, Hans Christian. *The Nightingale.* **Retold and illus. by Jerry Pinkney. Putnam, 2002. 0-8037-2464-0. Unp. Gr. 2–6**

With lush watercolor and gouache paintings, Pinkney resets in Northwest Africa the classic Andersen story of the emperor who loves and then forsakes a nightingale.

GERM: Discuss: What difference does the setting make in a story? Compare and contrast the settings of this version of *The Nightingale* and Stephen Mitchell's retelling with Bagram Ibatoulline's classic Chinese illustrations, listed below.

RELATED TITLES: Andersen, Hans Christian. *The Emperor's New Clothes.* Illus. by Angela Barrett. Trans. by Naomi Lewis. Candlewick, 1997. / Andersen, Hans Christian. *Fairy Tales of Hans Christian Andersen.* Illus. by Isabelle Brent. Viking, 1995. / Andersen, Hans Christian. *The Nightingale.* Retold by Stephen Mitchell. Illus. by Bagram Ibatoulline. Candlewick, 2002. / Andersen, Hans Christian. *The Nightingale.* Illus. by Josef Pale?ek. North-South, 1990. / Andersen, Hans Christian. *The Steadfast Tin Soldier.* Retold by Tor Seidler. HarperCollins, 1992. / Andersen, Hans Christian. *The Tinderbox.* Adapted and illus. by Barry Moser. Little, Brown, 1990. / Andersen, Hans Christian. *The Ugly Duckling.* Illus. by Jerry Pinkney. Morrow, 1999. / Andersen, Hans Christian. *The Wild Swans.* Retold by Amy Ehrlich. Illus. by Susan Jeffers. Dial, 1981. / Andersen, Hans Christian. *The Wild Swans.* Retold by Deborah Hautzig. Knopf, 1992. / Demi. *The Emperor's New Clothes: A Tale Set in China.* McElderry, 2000. / San Souci, Robert D. *The Firebird.* Dial, 1992.

SUBJECTS: AFRICA. BIRDS. EMPERORS. KINGS AND RULERS. LITERARY FAIRY TALES. NIGHTINGALES.

892   Andersen, Hans Christian. *The Nightingale.* **Retold by Stephen Mitchell. Illus. by Bagram Ibatoulline. Candlewick, 2002. 0-7636-1521-8. Unp. Gr. 2–6**

Proud of his beautiful city and palace and garden, the Emperor of China is incensed to hear that travelers consider the nightingale, which he never knew existed, to be the loveliest attraction in his land, and he demands the bird be presented to sing for him.

GERM: Discussion point: Why did the emperor and his court prefer the mechanical nightingale to the real one? Which one would you prefer and why?

RELATED TITLES: Andersen, Hans Christian. *The Emperor's New Clothes.* Illus. by Angela Barrett. Trans. by Naomi Lewis. Candlewick, 1997. / Andersen, Hans Christian. *Fairy Tales of Hans Christian Andersen.* Illus. by Isabelle Brent. Viking, 1995. / Andersen, Hans Christian. *The Nightingale.* Illus. by Jerry Pinkney. Putnam, 2002. / Andersen, Hans Christian. *The Nightingale.* Illus. by Josef Pale?ek. North-South, 1990. / Andersen, Hans Christian. *The Steadfast Tin Soldier.* Retold by Tor Seidler. HarperCollins, 1992. / Andersen, Hans Christian. *The Tinderbox.* Adapted and illus. by Barry Moser. Little, Brown, 1990. / Andersen, Hans Christian. *The Ugly Duckling.* Illus. by Jerry Pinkney. Morrow, 1999. / Andersen, Hans Christian. *The Wild Swans.* Retold by Amy Ehrlich. Illus. by Susan Jeffers. Dial, 1981. / Andersen, Hans Christian. *The Wild Swans.* Retold by Deborah Hautzig. Knopf, 1992. / Demi. *The Emperor's New Clothes: A Tale Set in China.* McElderry, 2000. / San Souci, Robert D. *The Firebird.* Dial, 1992.

SUBJECTS: BIRDS. CHINA. EMPERORS. KINGS AND RULERS. LITERARY FAIRY TALES. NIGHTINGALES.

893   Anderson, M. T. *Whales on Stilts.* **Illus. by Kurt Cyrus. Harcourt, 2005. 0-15-205340-9. 186pp. Gr. 3–6**

In a postmodern farcical throwback to girl and boy heroes like Nancy Drew, the Hardy Boys, and Tom Swift, meet Lily Gefelty—a girl who considers herself too boring to ever do anything interesting—when she goes to work with her dad on Career Day. Dad is blithely oblivious to the possible incongruities of his job—he's in Sales and Marketing and works in a highly guarded, high-tech, secret scientific laboratory in an abandoned warehouse; for a company that makes stilts for whales; with a boss named Larry who appears to have blue rubbery skin, wears a grain sack to cover his head, and seems to be planning to take over the world. Lily's two best friends, Katie and Jasper, who both have book series based on their lives (the Horror Hollow series and Jasper Dash, Boy Technocrat, respectively), join her to spy on the company, Deltamax Industries, and foil Larry's dastardly "Product Launch," in which walking whales will destroy the town with their deadly laser-beam eyes.

GERM: With tongue cemented solidly in cheek, Anderson's gonzo sci fi satire takes us on a breathless, outrageous tear through product advertisements for Gargletine Breakfast Drink and Katie's latest book, Horror Hollow #215, and, of course, that anticipated vicious whale invasion. And you thought whales were our friends. Series fans can write up a new plot summary or first chapter of the supposed sequel, "Lily Gefelty and the Secret of Freytag's Pyramid." Lemony Snicket fanatics will be eager to compare and imitate the styles of writing.

RELATED TITLES: Benton, Jim. *The Fran That Time Forgot*. Simon & Schuster, 2005. (And others in the Fran-ny K. Stein, Mad Scientist series.) / Brittain, Bill. *Shape-Changer*. HarperCollins, 1994. / Conly, Jane Leslie. *The Rudest Alien on Earth*. Henry Holt, 2002. / Gaiman, Neil. *Coraline*. HarperCollins, 2002. / Gauthier, Gail. *My Life Among the Aliens*. Putnam, 1996. / Sleator, William. *Into the Dream*. Dutton, 1979. / Sleator, William. *The Night the Heads Came*. Dutton, 1996. / Snicket, Lemony. *The Bad Beginning*. HarperCollins, 1999. (And others in the A Series of Unfortunate Events series.) / Van Allsburg, Chris. *Zathura*. Houghton Mifflin, 2002.

SUBJECTS: ADVENTURE AND ADVENTURERS. BEST FRIENDS. HUMOROUS FICTION. SATIRE. SCIENCE FICTION. SCIENTISTS. WHALES.

---

894 Avi. *Crispin: The Cross of Lead*. Hyperion, 2002. 0-7868-0828-4. 261pp. Gr. 6–8

After his mother dies, Asta's Son discovers his real name is Crispin. When he is accused of crimes he didn't commit, he is pursued by the authorities as a "wolf's head" or one who is no longer considered human. The boy flees his village and takes to the woods, where he encoun-ters a juggler named Bear who becomes his new lord and protector. Together they set out for the market town of Great Wexley, where danger awaits.

GERM: This Newbery Medal winner set in 14th-century England will make a good guided read-ing/book club/literature circle book for your study of the feudal system and medieval Eng-land.

RELATED TITLES: Avi. *Beyond the Western Sea: The Escape from Home*. Orchard, 1996. / Avi. *The True Confes-sions of Charlotte Doyle*. Orchard, 1990. / Barrett, Tracy. *Anna of Byzantium*. Delacorte, 1999. / Cushman, Karen. *Catherine, Called Birdy*. Clarion, 1994. / Cushman, Karen. *Matilda Bone*. Clarion, 2000. / Cushman, Karen. *The Midwife's Apprentice*. Clarion, 1995. / McCaughrean, Geraldine. *The Kite Rider*. HarperCollins, 2002. / Osborne, Mary Pope. *Favorite Medieval Tales*. Hyperion, 2002. / Park, Linda Sue. *A Single Shard*. Clarion, 2002. / Yolen, Jane, and Robert Harris. *Girl in a Cage*. Putnam, 2002.

SUBJECTS: ENGLAND. HISTORICAL FICTION. MIDDLE AGES. NEWBERY MEDAL. ORPHANS.

---

895 Avi. *Don't You Know There's a War On?* HarperCollins, 2001. 0-380-97863-6. 200pp. Gr. 4–7

Homefront. Brooklyn, NY. Monday, March 22, 1943. Because wisecracking narrator, Howie Crispers, 11, breaks his shoelace, he's late for school and on the way learns that his teacher, the perfect Miss Rolanda Gossim, is about to be fired. Maybe it's none of Howie's beeswax, but who else can come to his teacher's rescue?

GERM: Pages of wonderfully funny, idiomatic dialogues between Howie and best friend Denny cry out to be read aloud by pairs of kids. Have your listeners keep a running list of unfamiliar slang, which they can translate into modern-day-kid lingo, and pull in nonfiction books on World War II for facts and photos.

RELATED TITLES: Borden, Louise. *The Little Ships: The Heroic Rescue at Dunkirk in World War II*. McElderry, 1997. / Bunting, Eve. *Spying on Miss Müller*. Clarion, 1995. / Colman, Penny. *Rosie the Riveter: Women Working on the Home Front in World War II*. Crown, 1995. / Giff, Patricia Reilly. *Lily's Crossing*. Delacorte, 1997. / Greene, Bette. *Summer of My German Soldier*. Bantam, 1984. / Hahn, Mary Downing. *Stepping on the Cracks*. Clarion, 1991. / Lisle, Janet Taylor. *The Art of Keeping Cool*. Atheneum, 2000. / Lowry, Lois. *Number the Stars*. Houghton Mifflin, 1989. / Mazer, Norma Fox. *Good Night, Maman*. Harcourt, 1999. / Park, Linda Sue. *When My Name Was Keoko*. Clarion, 2002. / Propp, Vera. *When the Soldiers Were Gone*. Putnam, 1999. / Stevenson, James. *Don't You Know There's a War On?* Greenwillow, 1992.

SUBJECTS: HISTORICAL FICTION. SCHOOLS. TEACHERS. U.S.—HISTORY—20TH CENTURY—FICTION. WAR. WORLD WAR, 1939–1945.

---

896 Avi. *The Good Dog*. Atheneum, 2001. 0-689-83824-7. 256pp. Gr. 4–7

McKinley, a malamute acknowledged as head dog by the other dogs in Steamboat Springs, Col-orado, finds his ideas and position challenged when he encounters a wild wolf, Lupin, who accuses McKinley of being a slave to humans.

GERM: McKinley can understand only some of what his "pup," or human boy, Jack, says to him. Each reader can observe a pet carefully for a day, taking notes on what it does and how it behaves, and write a story about the two of them from the pet's viewpoint. Pull in *Sirko and the Wolf*, Eric A. Kimmel's Ukrainian folktale of how dogs and wolves became friends.

RELATED TITLES: Brandenburg, Jim. *Scruffy: A Wolf Finds His Place in the Pack*. Walker, 1996. / Branden-burg, Jim. *To the Top of the World: Adventures with Arctic Wolves*. Walker, 1993. / Cleary, Beverly. *Ribsy*. Mor-row, 1964. / Cleary, Beverly. *Strider*. Morrow, 1991. / Franklin, Christine L. *Lone Wolf*. Candlewick, 1997. / Kimmel, Eric A. *Sirko and the Wolf: A Ukrainian Tale*. Holiday House, 1997. / Lindquist, Susan Hart. *Wander*. Delacorte, 1998. / Lowry, Lois. *Stay! Keeper's Story*. Houghton Mifflin, 1997. / Naylor, Phyllis Reynolds.

Shiloh. Atheneum, 1991. / Osborne, Mary Pope. *Adaline Falling Star*. Scholastic, 2000. / Vande Velde, Vivian. *Smart Dog*. Harcourt, 1998.

SUBJECTS: COLORADO. DOGS. FANTASY. WOLVES.

897 Avi. *Perloo the Bold*. Scholastic, 1998. 0-590-11002-0. 226pp. Gr. 4–7

Unadventurous scholar Perloo, a furry creature of the Montmer tribe, is summoned by the tribe's dying leader, Jolaine the Good, to take her place as granter. However, her own son, Berwig the Big, and his sleazy adviser, Senyous the Sly, have other plans. When Berwig declares himself granter, suspends all freedoms and liberties, and starts a war with the Felbarts, their longtime enemies, Perloo must learn quickly about politics, treachery, and the abuse of power.

GERM: Your students can create charts, maps, portraits, and illustrations of the believable physical world Avi has created, filling in details about characters and their personalities, setting, and plot. Next, they can work in small groups to come up with ideas for a new cast and plot of a fantasy of their devising. Compare our sayings with some of the popular and pithy Montmer proverbs: "A life without challenge is a life not lived"; "Of all challenges the greatest is to be yourself"; "Only the dead have no choices."

RELATED TITLES: Avi. *Poppy*. Little, Brown, 2001. / Collins, Suzanne. *Gregor the Overlander*. Scholastic, 2003. / DiCamillo, Kate. *The Tale of Despereaux*. Candlewick, 2003. / Hirsch, Odo. *Bartlett and the City of Flames*. Bloomsbury, 2003. / Jennings, Patrick. *Putnam and Pennyroyal*. Scholastic, 1999. / Lisle, Janet Taylor. *Forest*. Orchard, 1993. / Oppel, Kenneth. *Silverwing*. Simon & Schuster, 1997.

SUBJECTS: ANIMALS, IMAGINARY. FANTASY. WAR.

898 Avi. *Poppy*. Illus. by Brian Floca. Orchard, 1995. 0-531-08783-2. 147pp. Gr. 3–6

After her boyfriend, Ragweed, is killed and eaten by Mr. Ocax, the owl who rules the lives of all the forest mice in Dimwood Forest, courageous mouse Poppy sets out for New House to seek safe haven for her family. While the tyrannical Ocax claims to protect his mice from the dangerous porcupines he has taught them to fear, on her journey Poppy encounters Ereth, a tough-talking porcupine who indignantly informs her he is a vegetarian.

GERM: Children will want to do a bit of research on the habits and habitats of deer mice, owls, and porcupines. This most entertaining and suspenseful animal fantasy will start a discussion on dictators, standing up for what's right, righting wrongs, perseverance, courage in the face of fear, and the seeking of truth. And, gruesome as it sounds, this book will be a natural companion if you're doing an owl pellet dissection lesson in science. Readers will eagerly read the sequels, *Poppy and Rye* and *Ragweed*.

RELATED TITLES: Asch, Frank. *Pearl's Promise*. Delacorte, 1984. / Avi. *Poppy and Rye*. Avon, 1998. / Avi. *Ragweed*. Avon, 1999. / Cleary, Beverly. *The Mouse and the Motorcycle*. Morrow, 1965. / Heinrich, Bernd. *An Owl in the House: A Naturalist's Diary*. Joy Street/Little, Brown, 1990. / Jacques, Brian. *Redwall*. Philomel, 1987. / King-Smith, Dick. *Three Terrible Trins*. Crown, 1994. / Markle, Sandra. *Owls* (Animal Predator series). Carolrhoda, 2004. / Mowat, Farley. *Owls in the Family*. Little, Brown, 1962. / Oppel, Kenneth. *Silverwing*. Simon & Schuster, 1997. / Van Leeuwen, Jean. *The Great Christmas Kidnapping Caper*. Dial, 1975.

SUBJECTS: COURAGE. DICTATORS. FANTASY. MICE. OWLS. PORCUPINES. SURVIVAL.

899 Avi. *The Secret School*. Harcourt, 2001. 0-15-216375-1. 160pp. Gr. 3–6

When the teacher of a one-room schoolhouse in remote Elk Valley, Colorado, must resign her post to care for her ailing mother six weeks before the end of the 1925 school term, 14-year-old Ida is devastated. Without school in session, Ida won't be able to take her exams, go on to high school in the fall, and fulfill her ambition to become a teacher. Knowing that the head of the school board will never approve, Ida nevertheless decides to take over as teacher and finish the school session, a secret all seven of the other pupils plan to keep.

GERM: Make a chart with your students to compare and contrast how Ida's classroom is organized versus your own. Have your students work in small groups to list the ten most important things children need to know in your grade.

RELATED TITLES: Avi. *The Good Dog*. Atheneum, 2001. / Hill, Kirkpatrick. *The Year of Miss Agnes*. McElderry, 2000. / Houston, Gloria. *My Great Aunt Arizona*. HarperCollins, 1992. / Levine, Gail Carson. *Dave at Night*. HarperCollins, 1999. / McLachlan, Patricia. *Sarah, Plain and Tall*. HarperCollins, 1985. / Ryan, Pam Muñoz. *Riding Freedom*. Scholastic, 1998. / Snyder, Zilpha Keatley. *Gib Rides Home*. Delacorte, 1998. / Wilder, Laura Ingalls. *Farmer Boy*. HarperCollins, 1953.

SUBJECTS: COLORADO. HISTORICAL FICTION. SCHOOLS. TEACHERS. U.S.—HISTORY.

900 Banks, Lynne Reid. *Harry the Poisonous Centipede: A Story to Make You Squirm*. Illus. by Tony Ross. Morrow, 1997. 0-688-14711-9. 153pp. Gr. 2–5

Harry, an 8-inch-long shiny black 42-legged centipede who lives in the tropics with Belinda, his mother, has been warned by her never to climb up the Up-Pipe that leads to the Place of Hoo-mins. That's just where the curious centipede heads, egged on by his incorrigible friend George, and plunges into horrible escapades and narrow escapes, even crawling into the mouth of one huge, hairy sleeping Hoo-min.

GERM: Even squeamish kids will take to this funny, tongue-in-cheek chapter book with true insect empathy. Send them to the library to dig up facts about centipedes and their less-loved bug compatriots The kids can then compose two kinds of writing: a nonfiction report and a story from the bug's point of view that incorporates the facts they have discovered.

RELATED TITLES: Banks, Lynne Reid. *Harry the Poisonous Centipede's Big Adventure*. Morrow, 2000. / Dahl, Roald. *James and the Giant Peach*. Knopf, 1962. / Florian, Douglas. *Insectlopedia: Poems and Paintings*. Harcourt, 1998. / Hall, Katy, and Lisa Eisenberg. *Buggy Riddles*. Dial, 1986. / Hopkins, Lee Bennett, comp. *Flit, Flutter, Fly! Poems About Bugs and Other Crawly Creatures*. Doubleday, 1992. / James, Mary. *Shoebag*. Scholastic, 1990. / McDonald, Megan. *Insects Are My Life*. Orchard, 1995. / Rosen, Michael. *Itsy-Bitsy Beasties: Poems from Around the World*. Carolrhoda, 1992. / Selden, George. *The Cricket in Times Square*. Farrar, 1960. / Sonenklar, Carol. *Bug Boy*. Henry Holt, 1997. / Sonenklar, Carol. *Bug Girl*. Henry Holt, 1998.

SUBJECTS: ADVENTURE AND ADVENTURERS. CENTIPEDES. FANTASY. HUMOROUS FICTION. INSECTS.

901 Bath, K. P. *The Secret of Castle Cant*. Little, Brown, 2004. 0-316-10848-0. 292pp. Gr. 5–8

In the isolated, mountainous Barony of Cant, a country so small it gets lost on every map, Lucy Wickwright, maidservant to the mischievous Adored and Honorable Pauline Esmeralda Simone-Thierry von Cant, daughter of the Baron, is unable to deter her mistress from her latest madcap caper, catapulting soggy underwear toward the castle. There are nefarious plots afoot in the land, and Lucy, orphaned when her parents' carriage was forced off the road by villains unknown, is torn between spying for the revolutionary Causists and trying to keep herself and Pauline out of further trouble.

GERM: Compare Lucy's development from hapless orphan to plucky heroine with other orphan-makes-good characters. Tie the discussion in to the castle and dungeon intrigues of Kate DiCamillo's *The Tale of Despereaux*.

RELATED TITLES: Burnett, Frances Hodgson. *A Little Princess*. HarperCollins, 1992. / Creech, Sharon. *Ruby Holler*. HarperCollins, 2002. / Dahl, Roald. *The BFG*. Farrar, 1982. / Ibbotson, Eva. *Journey to the River Sea*. Dutton, 2002. / Levine, Gail Carson. *Dave at Night*. HarperCollins, 1999. / Rowling, J. K. *Harry Potter and the Sorcerer's Stone*. Scholastic, 1998. (And others in the Harry Potter series.) / Wallace, Barbara Brooks. *Peppermints in the Parlor*. Atheneum, 1980.

SUBJECTS: ADVENTURE AND ADVENTURERS. FANTASY. IDENTITY. MYSTERY AND DETECTIVE STORIES. ORPHANS.

902 Bauer, Marion Dane. *A Bear Named Trouble*. Clarion, 2005. 0-618-51738-3. 120pp. Gr. 3–5

Newly arrived in Anchorage, where his zookeeper father has just gotten a new job at the Alaska Zoo, 10-year-old Jonathan misses his schoolteacher mom and his 6-year-old sister Rhonda, still back in Duluth though they'll be moving to Alaska as soon as the school year ends. Jonathan takes solace in watching all the zoo animals, especially a snow white goose he's named Mama Goose. When he encounters a wild 3-year-old brownie in his back yard, he ignores his father's warnings, setting out food for the bear and following it to the zoo, where it digs its way in, under a fence.

GERM: There are plenty of discussable issues here: Why doesn't Jonathan's father want him to get near the bear? Why does he disobey him? After the bear kills Mother Goose, is Jonathan's reaction justified? Why does he call the television station to report on the bear's behavior? Does the bear deserve to die for its actions? Alternating chapters contrast the bear's journey to find food and companionship with Jonathan's story. Discuss how these chapters differ. An epilogue reveals that the book is based on the true story of Trouble, a bear that broke into the Alaska Zoo. Analyze the ways Bauer integrated facts with fiction.

RELATED TITLES: Bauer, Marion Dane. *On My Honor*. Clarion, 1986. / Bauer, Marion Dane. *A Question of Trust*. Scholastic, 1994. / Bauer, Marion Dane. *Runt*. Clarion, 2002. / Hill, Kirkpatrick. *Winter Camp*. McElderry, 1993. / Hill, Kirkpatrick. *The Year of Miss Agnes*. McElderry, 2000. / Hornik, Laurie Miller. *Zoo School*. Clarion, 2004. / Morey, Walt. *Gentle Ben*. Dutton, 1965.

SUBJECTS: ALASKA. BEARS. DEATH. FATHERS AND SONS. GEESE. ZOOS.

903 Benton, Jim. *The Fran That Time Forgot (Franny K. Stein, Mad Scientist; #4).* **Illus. by the author. Simon & Schuster, 2005. 0-689-86294-6. 102pp. Gr. 2–4**

Franny K. Stein, the only one in her otherwise normal family interested in mad science, comes up with a winning invention for the school science fair project: a Time Warp Dessert Plate that allows her to have her cake and eat it too. Unfortunately, at the school assembly, when the principal hands out the certificates to the winners, she announces Franny's full name—Franny Kissypie Stein—to the crowd, and Franny is infuriated when everyone laughs. But what if she could invent a Time Warper Device to take her into the past where she could change her name to something more dignified?

GERM: There's a wonderful mix here of comedy, zany inventions, a dog assistant named Igor, the notion of going back in time, and social issues as well. Franny declares, as she changes her middle name to "Kaboom," "There is nothing worse than being laughed at." Is this true? Franny visits her future as well. Your mad scientists can predict their futures as teenagers or draw and describe their own inventions, or write about past times they'd like to revisit. In the climactic scene, when Franny is battling evil Teen Franny, she gets an idea of how to defeat her older self. Stop there and ask everyone to come up with a plan, without blood or violence. What can Franny do to overcome the humiliation of being laughed at? Making that text-to-life connection, share stories of how you all have dealt with it. Also, don't forget to talk about what it means to have your cake and eat it too. Send readers off to read the other books in the series.

RELATED TITLES: Anderson, M. T. *Whales on Stilts.* Harcourt, 2005. / Benton, Jim. *The Invisible Fran.* Simon & Schuster, 2004. (And others in the Franny K. Stein, Mad Scientist series.) / Gutman, Dan. *Qwerty Stevens Back in Time: The Edison Mystery.* Simon & Schuster, 2001. / Sorel, Edward. *Johnny on the Spot.* McElderry, 1998. / St. George, Judith. *So You Want to Be an Inventor?* Philomel, 2002.

SUBJECTS: HUMOROUS FICTION. INVENTIONS AND INVENTORS. NAMES. SCIENCE FICTION. SCIENTISTS. TIME TRAVEL.

904 Billingsley, Franny. *The Folk Keeper.* **Atheneum, 1999. 0-689-82876-4. 176pp. Gr. 5–8**

Fifteen-year-old orphan Corinna, disguised as Corin so no one will know she is a girl, is sought out by the dying Lord Merton as the new Folk Keeper on his island estate at Cliffsend. There she must keep the angry, ever-ravenous underground Folk, all mouths and teeth, from destroying crops, luck, and livestock. She is befriended by Finian, the 21-year-old heir to the estate, discovers her link to the sea and the seals, and ultimately finds out the truth about her own mother. A startling original fantasy with roots in English selkie tales, Corinna's narrative, as written in her Folk Record diary, is compelling and lyrical.

GERM: Share "selkie" or seal changeling folktales, such as Sheila MacGill-Callahan's *The Seal Prince.*

RELATED TITLES: Alexander, Lloyd. *The First Two Lives of Lucas-Kasha.* Dutton, 1978. / Avi. *Bright Shadow.* Bradbury, 1985. / Billingsley, Franny. *Well Wished.* Atheneum, 1997. / Climo, Shirley. *Piskies, Spriggans, and Other Magical Beings.* Crowell, 1981. / Hesse, Karen. *The Music of Dolphins.* Scholastic, 1996. / Kindl, Patrice. *Goose Chase.* Houghton Mifflin, 2001. / Langrish, Katherine. *Troll Fell.* HarperCollins, 2004. / Levine, Gail Carson. *Ella Enchanted.* HarperCollins, 1997. / MacGill-Callahan, Sheila. *The Seal Prince.* Dial, 1995. / McGraw, Eloise. *The Moorchild.* McElderry, 1996. / McKinley, Robin. *Beauty.* HarperCollins, 1978. / Nodelman, Perry. *The Same Place But Different.* Simon & Schuster, 1995. / Pratchett, Terry. *The Wee Free Men.* HarperCollins, 2003. / Pullman, Philip. *The Golden Compass.* Knopf, 1996.

SUBJECTS: CHANGELINGS. FANTASY. FOLKLORE—ENGLAND. SEALS. TRANSFORMATIONS.

905 Birney, Betty G. *The World According to Humphrey.* **Putnam, 2004. 0-399-24198-1. 124pp. Gr. 1–5**

After wonderful Mrs. Mac leaves Room 26 of Longfellow School, hamster Humphrey is devastated, especially when the strict new teacher, Mrs. Brisbane, announces she can't stand rodents. "You can learn a lot about yourself by taking care of another species. . . . You'll teach those kids a thing or two," Mrs. Mac tells the perceptive hamster. Indeed, in each chapter of this wise and funny tale, Humphrey relates how he retrains students including shy Sayeh, loud A. J., and angry Garth; helps the lonely custodian, Mr. Morales, find a girlfriend; and even befriends the forbidding Mrs. Brisbane.

GERM: Useful tips for hamster care at the end of each chapter will start your students reading about pets in the 636 section of your library and writing stories from their pets' points of view. How have their pets helped them deal with problems in their own lives? Collaborate on additional rules to add to Humphrey's *Guide to the Care and Feeding of Humans*. "You can learn a lot about yourself by getting to know another species." That's a good quote for your children to think about and write essays on how it applies to their own lives.

RELATED TITLES: Birney, Betty G. *Friendship According to Humphrey*. Putnam, 2005. / Child, Lauren. *That Pesky Rat*. Candlewick, 2002. / Cleary, Beverly. *Ralph S. Mouse*. Morrow, 1982. / Cronin, Doreen. *Diary of a Worm*. HarperCollins, 2003. / Howe, James. *Bunnicula Strikes Again!* Atheneum, 1999. / King-Smith, Dick. *Lady Lollipop*. Candlewick, 2001. / King-Smith, Dick. *The School Mouse*. Hyperion, 1995. / L'Engle, Madeleine. *The Other Dog*. SeaStar, 2001. / Lowry, Lois. *Stay! Keeper's Story*. Houghton Mifflin, 1997. / MacDonald, Amy. *No More Nasty*. Farrar, 2001. / Teague, Mark. *Dear Mrs. LaRue: Letters from Obedience School*. Scholastic, 2002. / Van Leeuwen, Jean. *The Great Christmas Kidnapping Caper*. Dial, 1975.

SUBJECTS: FANTASY. FICTION BOOKS FOR EARLY GRADES. HAMSTERS. HUMOROUS FICTION. PERSONAL NARRATIVES. POINT OF VIEW. SCHOOLS. TEACHERS.

906 **Black, Holly, and Tony DiTerlizzi.** *The Spiderwick Chronicles, Book 1: The Field Guide.* **Illus. by Tony DiTerlizzi. Simon & Schuster, 2003. 0-689-85936-8. 108pp. Gr. 2–5**
Nine-year-old Jared, his twin, Simon, and their 13-year-old sister, Mallory, having just moved with their mother to Great-Aunt Lucinda's creepy old Victorian mansion, find a mysterious poem and an old book, a field guide to real faeries, that may help them understand all the unexplainable mischief that has been going on there.

GERM: This first book of five, so petite and enticingly old-fashioned looking—with ragged edges, covers that look like embossed leather, and satisfying pen-and-inks—will launch readers onto the others in the series, filled with mischievous and malicious boggarts, brownies, faeries, and goblins. There are several wonderful scenes that you or your readers can script out and dramatize for Reader's Theater, and lots of writing possibilities, such as the chapter where Jared is blamed by his mom for tying his sister's hair to the headboard, which of course he didn't do. Ask your kids to write about a time when they got blamed for something they didn't do, and to explain how they dealt with it.

RELATED TITLES: Banks, Lynne Reid. *The Fairy Rebel*. Doubleday, 1988. / Black, Holly, and Tony DiTerlizzi. *The Spiderwick Chronicles, Book 2: The Seeing Stone*. Simon & Schuster, 2003. (And others in the Spiderwick series.) / Climo, Shirley. *Magic and Mischief: Tales from Cornwall*. Clarion, 1999. / Climo, Shirley. *Piskies, Spriggans, and Other Magical Beings: Tales from the Droll-Teller*. Crowell, 1981. / Corbett, Sue. *12 Again*. Dutton, 2002. / Dahl, Roald. *The Witches*. Farrar, 1983. / Gaiman, Neil. *Coraline*. HarperCollins, 2002. / Gormley, Beatrice. *Fifth-Grade Magic*. Dutton, 1982. / Hahn, Mary Downing. *Time for Andrew: A Ghost Story*. Clarion, 1994. / Langrish, Katherine. *Troll Fell*. HarperCollins, 2004. / Lunge-Larson, Lise. *The Hidden Folk: Stories of Fairies, Dwarves, Selkies, and Other Secret Beings*. Houghton Mifflin, 2004. / Nodelman, Perry. *The Same Place But Different*. Simon & Schuster, 1995. / Pratchett, Terry. *The Wee Free Men*. HarperCollins, 2003. / Rupp, Rebecca. *The Dragon of Lonely Island*. Candlewick, 1998. / Snicket, Lemony. *The Bad Beginning*. HarperCollins, 1999. (And others in the A Series of Unfortunate Events series.)

SUBJECTS: BROTHERS AND SISTERS. FAIRIES. FANTASY. READER'S THEATER.

907 **Blackwood, Gary L.** *The Shakespeare Stealer.* **Dutton, 1998. 0-525-45863-8. 216pp. Gr. 5–8**
In 1587, 14-year-old orphan Widge, trained to write in "charactery," or shorthand, is brought by the mysterious Falconer to London to attend a performance of Shakespeare's new play, *Hamlet*, and copy it down line for line. Widge becomes one of Mr. Shakespeare's players, learns sword fighting, and becomes friends with two other boys, one of whom—Julian—is perhaps not who or what he seems.

GERM: Bruce Coville's done a dark and stirring prose version of the play in his picture book *William Shakespeare's Hamlet*. Introduce Shakespeare and his times with Aliki's *William Shakespeare and the Globe*, Michael Rosen's *Shakespeare: His Work and His World*, and Diane Stanley's *Bard of Avon: The Story of William Shakespeare*.

RELATED TITLES: Aliki. *William Shakespeare and the Globe*. HarperCollins, 1999. / Blackwood, Gary L. *Shakespeare's Scribe*. Dutton, 1998. / Blackwood, Gary L. *Shakespeare's Spy*. Dutton, 2003. / Broach, Elise. *Shakespeare's Secret*. Henry Holt, 2005. / Cooper, Susan. *King of Shadows*. McElderry, 1999. / Coville, Bruce. *William Shakespeare's Hamlet*. Dial, 2004. / Ganeri, Anita. *The Young Person's Guide to Shakespeare* (book and CD). Harcourt, 1999. / Garfield, Leon. *Shakespeare Stories*. Houghton Mifflin, 1995. / Graham, Harriet. *A Boy and His Bear*. McElderry, 1996. / Mannis, Celeste Davis. *The Queen's Progress: An Elizabethan Alphabet*. Viking, 2003. / Packer, Tina. *Tales from Shakespeare*. Scholastic, 2004. / Rosen, Michael. *Shakespeare: His Work and His World*. Candlewick, 2001. / Stanley, Diane. *Bard of Avon: The Story of William Shakespeare*. Morrow, 1992. / Thomas, Jane Resh. *The Princess in the Pigpen*. Clarion, 1989.

SUBJECTS: ACTORS AND ACTRESSES. ENGLAND. HISTORICAL FICTION. LONDON (ENGLAND). ORPHANS. SHAKESPEARE, WILLIAM. THEATERS.

908   Borden, Louise. *The Little Ships: The Heroic Rescue at Dunkirk in World War II.* **Illus. by Michael Foreman. McElderry, 1997. 0-689-80827-5. Unp. Gr. 3–6**

In a thrilling fictionalized picture-book account, a young girl describes how she and her fisherman father sailed the English Channel as part of a British armada of 861 small boats that helped rescue allied soldiers trapped on a French beach by German troops in the summer of 1940. Foreman's detailed watercolors capture the drama and peril of that daring rescue during World War II.

GERM: Research the rescue at Dunkirk to compare and contrast the fictionalized narrative with the facts.

RELATED TITLES: Foreman, Michael. *War Boy.* Arcade, 1990. / Foreman, Michael. *War Game.* Arcade, 1993. / Kalman, Maira. *Fireboat: The Heroic Adventures of the John J. Harvey.* Putnam, 2002. / Lee, Milly. *Nim and the War Effort.* Farrar, 1997. / Mellecker, Judith. *Randolph's Dream.* Knopf, 1991. / Mochizuki, Ken. *Heroes.* Lee & Low, 1995. / Park, Linda Sue. *When My Name Was Keoko.* Clarion, 2002. / Rabin, Staton. *Casey over There.* Harcourt, 1994. / Stevenson, James. *Don't You Know There's a War On?* Greenwillow, 1992. / Winter, Jeanette. *The Librarian of Basra: A True Story from Iraq.* Harcourt, 2005.

SUBJECTS: ADVENTURE AND ADVENTURERS. BOATS AND BOATING. HISTORICAL FICTION. SHIPS. WAR. WORLD WAR, 1939–1945—FICTION.

909   Brisson, Pat. *Hot Fudge Hero.* **Illus. by Diana Cain Blumenthal. Henry Holt, 1997. 0-8050-4551-1. 72pp. Gr. 1–3**

Three easy-to-read short stories introduce likable everyday kid Bertie, who initiates a friendship with mean neighbor Mr. Muckleberg, practices his sax, and gets a strike while bowling.

GERM: At the end of each chapter, Bertie ends up with a hot fudge sundae. Either write new hot fudge episodes or break out the ice cream and toppings for a special treat—or both. Follow up with the equally entertaining sequel, *Bertie's Picture Day*, in which Bertie loses a tooth and gets a black eye and an unexpected haircut.

RELATED TITLES: Blume, Judy. *Superfudge.* Dutton, 1980. / Blume, Judy. *Tales of a Fourth Grade Nothing.* Dutton, 1972. / Brisson, Pat. *Bertie's Picture Day.* Henry Holt, 2000. / Cameron, Ann. *More Stories Huey Tells.* Farrar, 1997. / Cameron, Ann. *More Stories Julian Tells.* Dell, 2001. / Cameron, Ann. *The Stories Huey Tells.* Knopf, 1995. / Cameron, Ann. *The Stories Julian Tells.* Yearling, 1989. / Catling, Patrick Skene. *The Chocolate Touch.* Morrow, 1979. / Danziger, Paula. *Amber Brown Is Not a Crayon.* Putnam, 1994. / Duffey, Betsy. *Hey, New Kid!* Viking, 1996. / Greene, Stephanie. *Owen Foote, Frontiersman.* Clarion, 1999. / Greene, Stephanie. *Show and Tell.* Clarion, 1998.

SUBJECTS: CHOCOLATE. FAMILY LIFE. FICTION BOOKS FOR EARLY GRADES. FRIENDSHIP. ICE CREAM. NEIGHBORLINESS.

910   Broach, Elise. *Shakespeare's Secret.* **Henry Holt, 2005. 0-8050-7387-6. 250pp. Gr. 4–7**

Hero Netherfield, named after a character in Shakespeare's *Much Ado About Nothing*, knows the kids will make fun of her name when she starts sixth grade at her new school, and she's right. "Hero?" says a girl in class, "Hey, that's my dog's name." Her kind, elderly new neighbor, Mrs. Roth, gives her the lowdown on the missing Murphy diamond, worth a million dollars, that might be hidden in Hero's house. The diamond had been part of an heirloom necklace that belonged to the late owner of the house, Eleanor Murphy, a descendant of Edward de Vere, the Earl of Oxford, whom some believe to be the actual author of Shakespeare's work. With the help of popular eighth grader Danny Cordova, Hero sets out to find the diamond, uncover more about de Vere and his Shakespeare connections, and deal with her own outcast status at school.

GERM: Brush up on Shakespeare with the nonfiction picture books, *William Shakespeare and the Globe* by Aliki and *Bard of Avon* by Diane Stanley. Give some background on the play for which Hero was named with Tina Packer's *Tales from Shakespeare*, which includes concise and clear prose retellings of ten of the major plays, both comedies and tragedies.

RELATED TITLES: Aliki. *William Shakespeare and the Globe.* HarperCollins, 1999. / Avi. *Romeo and Juliet—Together and Alive at Last.* Orchard, 1987. / Blackwood, Gary L. *The Shakespeare Stealer.* Dutton, 1998. / Cooper, Susan. *King of Shadows.* McElderry, 1999. / Coville, Bruce. *William Shakespeare's A Midsummer Night's Dream.* Dial, 1996. / Coville, Bruce. *William Shakespeare's Twelfth Night.* Dial, 1993. / Freeman, Don. *Will's Quill or, How a Goose Saved Shakespeare.* Viking, 2004. / Ganeri, Anita. *The Young Person's Guide to Shakespeare* (book and

CD). Harcourt, 1999. / Packer, Tina. *Tales from Shakespeare.* Scholastic, 2004. / Stanley, Diane. *Bard of Avon: The Story of William Shakespeare.* Morrow, 1992. / Thomas, Jane Resh. *The Princess in the Pigpen.* Clarion, 1989.

SUBJECTS: AUTHORS. ENGLAND. MARYLAND. MYSTERY AND DETECTIVE STORIES. NEIGHBORS. PLAYS. SHAKESPEARE, WILLIAM.

911 **Bruchac, Joseph.** *Sacajawea: The Story of Bird Woman and the Lewis and Clark Expedition.* **Harcourt, 2000. 0-15-202234-1. 199pp. Gr. 6–8**

Alternating viewpoints of William Clark and Sacajawea, as told to the now seven-year-old Pomp, this is the riveting fictionalized story of the Lewis and Clark expedition that set out from Missouri in 1804 and reached the Pacific Ocean more than a year later. Sacajawea's narrative connects her experiences with the telling of traditional stories and legends. Clark recounts the preparations of the Corps of Discovery (sent out by President Jefferson to explore the western part of the continent) and his own affection for Pa-ump, Sacajawea's Firstborn Son, whom Clark nicknamed Pomp. Based on original source materials—Lewis and Clark's own journals, plus their men's diaries and field notes—the novel is an expertly crafted, accurate, and important addition to the genre of historical fiction for children.

GERM: Rhoda Blumberg's handsome nonfiction account, *The Incredible Journey of Lewis and Clark,* provides wonderful paintings, maps, and reproductions. Children can trace the expedition's route using larger, more detailed, state maps and can investigate the many changes in the landscape over the intervening two centuries. For a you-are-there look, accompany your reading with the dramatic picture book, *Sacagawea,* by Lise Erdrich.

RELATED TITLES: Blumberg, Rhoda. *The Incredible Journey of Lewis and Clark.* Lothrop, 1987. / Edwards, Judith. *The Great Expedition of Lewis and Clark: By Private Reubin Field, Member of the Corps of Discovery.* Farrar, 2003. / Erdrich, Lise. *Sacagawea.* Carolrhoda, 2003. / Freedman, Russell. *Buffalo Hunt.* Holiday House, 1988. / Freedman, Russell. *Children of the Wild West.* Clarion, 1983. / Fritz, Jean. *The Double Life of Pocohontas.* Putnam, 1983. / Goldin, Barbara Diamond. *The Girl Who Lived with the Bears.* Gulliver/Harcourt, 1997. / Myers, Laurie. *Lewis and Clark and Me: A Dog's Tale.* Harcourt, 2000. / Osborne, Mary Pope. *Adaline Falling Star.* Scholastic, 2000. / Schanzer, Rosalyn. *How We Crossed the West: The Adventures of Lewis and Clark.* National Geographic Society, 1997. / Woodruff, Elvira. *Dear Levi: Letters from the Overland Trail.* Knopf, 1994.

SUBJECTS: EXPLORERS. HISTORICAL FICTION. INDIANS OF NORTH AMERICA. LEWIS AND CLARK EXPEDITION (1804–1806). MULTICULTURAL BOOKS. PERSONAL NARRATIVES. POINT OF VIEW. SACAJAWEA. U.S.—HISTORY—1783–1865—FICTION. WEST (U.S.)—HISTORY—FICTION.

912 **Bruchac, Joseph.** *The Winter People.* **Dial, 2002. 0-8037-2694-5. 176pp. Gr. 6–10**

Fourteen-year-old Abenaki Indian boy Saxso starts his narrative in 1759 in the village of St. Francis, Quebec, on the night of the talking rosebush, when the whispering voice of a Mahican Indian warns Saxso of the imminent attack of the Long Knives. Soon after, the White Devil, Major Rogers, and his British Rangers destroy the village and many are massacred. Saxso's mother and sisters are taken captive, and Saxso sets out to track them down and rescue them, a journey that takes him hundreds of miles south to Vermont.

GERM: Students will need to do some background research on the French and Indian War and the Abenaki, though you'll find much supporting information in the Author's Note. We're so used to reading history from the British point of view; this stunning, gripping, and unforgettable novel will give you a very different side.

RELATED TITLES: Bruchac, Joseph. *Sacajawea.* Harcourt, 2000. / Bruchac, Joseph, and Jonathan London. *Thirteen Moons on Turtle's Back: A Native American Year of Moons.* Philomel, 1992. / Dorris, Michael. *Sees Behind Trees.* Hyperion, 1996. / Erdrich, Louise. *The Birchbark House.* Hyperion, 1999. / Osborne, Mary Pope. *Adaline Falling Star.* Scholastic, 2000. / Pearsall, Shelley. *Crooked River.* Knopf, 2005.

SUBJECTS: CANADA. HISTORICAL FICTION. INDIANS OF NORTH AMERICA. MULTICULTURAL BOOKS. U.S.—HISTORY—FRENCH AND INDIAN WAR. WAR.

913 **Byars, Betsy.** *Dead Letter: A Herculeah Jones Mystery.* **Viking, 1996. 0-670-86860-4. 147pp. Gr. 4–7**

With her father a detective and her mother a private investigator, it's only natural that Herculeah Jones finds herself in the midst of danger and intrigue so often. This time, after buying an electric blue Russian-style secondhand coat, she finds a chilling unsigned note in the lining, apparently written by the coat's original owner in fear of her life. "If she's dead, I'm going to find the killer," Herculeah declares to her meek best friend, Meat, and she sets out to uncover more evidence.

GERM: Ask your listeners to speculate on what the note could mean and have them flesh out their own version of the mystery. Set them up with the other entertaining mysteries in the series.

RELATED TITLES: Byars, Betsy. *Cracker Jackson*. Viking, 1985. / Byars, Betsy. *The Dark Stairs: A Herculeah Jones Mystery*. Viking, 1994. / Byars, Betsy. *Tarot Says Beware: A Herculeah Jones Mystery*. Viking, 1995. / Hiaasen, Carl. *Hoot*. Knopf, 2002. / Hoobler, Dorothy and Hoobler, Thomas. *The Demon in the Teahouse*. Philomel, 2001. / Naylor, Phyllis Reynolds. *The Bodies in the Besseldorf Hotel*. Atheneum, 1986. / Roberts, Willo Davis. *The View from the Cherry Tree*. Atheneum, 1975. / Sobol, Donald J. Encyclopedia Brown series. Bantam.

SUBJECTS: MURDER. MYSTERY AND DETECTIVE STORIES. SUSPENSE.

914   **Byars, Betsy. *Tornado*. Illus. by Doron Ben-Ami. HarperCollins, 1996. 0-06-026452-7. 49pp. Gr. 2–4**

Huddled in the dark storm cellar, waiting out a twister with his brother, mother, and grandmother, the unnamed boy narrator prompts Pete, the farmhand, to tell them stories about the dog Pete had as a boy. Pete recalls the tornado that tore the roof off his house and blew a doghouse, complete with a black dog, into his yard and his life.

GERM: The spare, laconic tales Pete tells about his faithful dog, Tornado, will open up the floodgates of all pet-loving storytellers, who will be eager to relate stories about pets they have known and loved. See how other dogs came into the lives of their owners, from Ribsy, in Beverly Cleary's *Henry Huggins* to India Opal Buloni's smiling dog in *Because of Winn-Dixie* by Kate DiCamillo.

RELATED TITLES: Cleary, Beverly. *Henry Huggins*. Morrow, 1950. / DiCamillo, Kate. *Because of Winn-Dixie*. Candlewick, 2000. / Duffey, Betsy. *A Boy in the Doghouse*. Simon & Schuster, 1991. / Gardiner, John. *Stone Fox*. Crowell, 1980. / Hesse, Karen. *Sable*. Henry Holt, 1994. / Kramer, Stephen. *Eye of the Storm: Chasing Storms with Warren Faidley*. Putnam, 1997. / Love, D. Anne. *Dakota Spring*. Holiday House, 1995. / Myers, Anna. *Red-Dirt Jessie*. Walker, 1992. / Naylor, Phyllis Reynolds. *Shiloh*. Atheneum, 1991. / Rodowsky, Colby. *Dog Days*. Farrar, 1990. / Rodowsky, Colby. *Not My Dog*. Farrar, 1999. / Ruckman, Ivy. *Night of the Twisters*. Crowell, 1984.

SUBJECTS: DOGS. FARM LIFE. STORYTELLING. TORNADOES.

915   **Cameron, Ann. *Colibrí*. Farrar, 2003. 0-374-31519-1. 227pp. Gr. 5–8**

As 12-year-old Rosa tells it, her job is to be Uncle's guide when he feigns blindness and begs for money in small Guatemalan towns. Señora Celestina, the fortune-teller, helps Rosa summon the courage to run away from Uncle, a man with a dark past who kidnapped Rosa from her parents eight years ago.

GERM: Careful readers and listeners will want to examine the ways the fortune-teller's predictions come true and look for evidence of what really happened to Rosa when she came to live with Uncle.

RELATED TITLES: Alexander, Lloyd. *The First Two Lives of Lucas-Kasha*. Dutton, 1978. / Burnett, Frances Hodgson. *A Little Princess*. HarperCollins, 1992. / Cameron, Ann. *The Secret Life of Amanda K. Woods*. Farrar, 1998. / Divakaruni, Chitra Banerjee. *The Conch Bearer*. Roaring Brook, 2003. / Levine, Gail Carson. *Dave at Night*. HarperCollins, 1999. / Morpurgo, Michael. *Kensuke's Kingdom*. Scholastic, 2003.

SUBJECTS: FORTUNE-TELLING. GUATEMALA. INDIANS OF CENTRAL AMERICA. KIDNAPPING. MAYAS. MULTICULTURAL BOOKS.

916   **Cameron, Ann. *Gloria's Way*. Illus. by Lis Toft. Farrar, 2000. 0-374-32670-3. 96pp. Gr. 1–3**

With the help of her good friends Huey and his brother Julian; their father, Mr. Bates; and her own busy dad, Gloria makes a special valentine for her mom, dumps an apple pie upside down, and figures out fractions.

GERM: Gently humorous slice-of-life chapters are just right for children to recognize that their lives have generated funny stories too. Have them write experiential stories about ordinary, but amusing, things that have happened to them with family and friends. Share other titles in Cameron's Julian and Huey books.

RELATED TITLES: Cameron, Ann. *Gloria Rising*. Farrar, 2002. / Cameron, Ann. *More Stories Huey Tells*. Farrar, 1997. / Cameron, Ann. *More Stories Julian Tells*. Dell, 2001. / Cameron, Ann. *The Stories Huey Tells*. Knopf, 1995. / Cameron, Ann. *The Stories Julian Tells*. Yearling, 1989. / Caseley, Judith. *Harry and Arney*. Greenwillow, 1994. / Danziger, Paula. *Amber Brown Is Not a Crayon*. Putnam, 1994. / Greene, Stephanie. *Owen Foote, Frontiersman*. Clarion, 1999 (and others in the Owen Foote series). / Harrison, Maggie. *Angels on Roller Skates*. Candlewick, 1992. / Leverich, Kathleen. *Best Enemies*. Greenwillow, 1989. / Leverich, Kathleen. *Best Enemies Again*. Greenwillow, 1991.

SUBJECTS: AFRICAN AMERICANS. BEST FRIENDS. FAMILY LIFE. FICTION BOOKS FOR EARLY GRADES. FRIENDSHIP. MULTICULTURAL BOOKS.

917 **Cameron, Ann.** *More Stories Huey Tells.* Illus. by Lis Toft. Farrar, 1997. 0-374-35065-5. 118pp. Gr. 1–4

Huey grows sunflowers and tries to save them when they appear to be dying, figures out an inventive way to make his big brother, Julian, share their driveway basketball hoop, and tries to get his dad to quit smoking. Huey narrates each of these five short chapters about his close-knit African American family, and he makes us feel like family too.

GERM: *The Stories Huey Tells, The Stories Julian Tells,* plus *Gloria's Way,* about the brothers' good friend, are similarly irresistible. Encourage children to collect and tell family tales from their own experience, either aloud, on tape, or on paper.

RELATED TITLES: Blumenthal, Deborah. *Don't Let the Peas Touch! And Other Stories.* Scholastic, 2004. / Cameron, Ann. *Gloria's Way.* Farrar, 2000. / Cameron, Ann. *More Stories Julian Tells.* Dell, 2001. / Cameron, Ann. *The Stories Huey Tells.* Knopf, 1995. / Cameron, Ann. *The Stories Julian Tells.* Yearling, 1989. / Caseley, Judith. *Harry and Arney.* Greenwillow, 1994. / Cutler, Jane. *Rats!* Farrar, 1996. / Harrison, Maggie. *Angels on Roller Skates.* Candlewick, 1992. / Lowry, Lois. *See You Around, Sam.* Houghton Mifflin, 1996. / McDonald, Megan. *Judy Moody, M.D.: The Doctor Is In!* Candlewick, 2004 (and others in the Judy Moody series). / Willis, Meredith Sue. *Marco's Monster.* HarperCollins, 1996.

SUBJECTS: AFRICAN AMERICANS. BROTHERS. FAMILY LIFE. FICTION BOOKS FOR EARLY GRADES. HUMOROUS FICTION. MULTICULTURAL BOOKS.

918 **Child, Lauren.** *Utterly Me, Clarice Bean.* Illus. by the author. Candlewick, 2003. 0-7636-2186-2. 192pp. Gr. 2–5

Clarice Bean tells us she wasn't much of a reader until her Granny gave her a book in the Ruby Redford series about an 11-year-old girl undercover detective. Clarice has picked up so many sleuthing skills from the book that she even solves a classroom mystery when her teacher's trophy cup goes missing.

GERM: Using the excerpts of the Ruby Redford stories to get everyone thinking, discuss the different types of detectives in mystery novels. Students can put together a chart defining the novels' characteristics, types of mysteries solved, and plot devices, and draw portraits of their favorite fictional detectives labeled with a description of their singular styles.

RELATED TITLES: Child, Lauren. *Clarice Bean, Guess Who's Babysitting?* Candlewick, 2001. / Child, Lauren. *Clarice Bean Spells Trouble.* Candlewick, 2005. / Child, Lauren. *Clarice Bean, That's Me.* Candlewick, 1999. / Child, Lauren. *What Planet Are You From, Clarice Bean?* Candlewick, 2002. / Clements, Andrew. *The School Story.* Simon & Schuster, 2001. / Rocklin, Joanne. *For Your Eyes Only!* Scholastic, 1997.

SUBJECTS: BOOKS AND READING. CONTESTS. FAMILY LIFE. HUMOROUS FICTION. MYSTERY AND DETECTIVE STORIES. PERSONAL NARRATIVES. SCHOOLS.

919 **Choldenko, Gennifer.** *Al Capone Does My Shirts.* Putnam, 2004. 0-399-23861-1. 228pp. Gr. 6–8

In 1935, when Moose Flanagan's father gets a job as electrician and guard at Alcatraz prison, the family moves to the 12-acre rock island in the middle of San Francisco Bay, joining the 23 other kids who live there, not to mention the "murderers, rapists, hit men, con men, stickup men, embezzlers, connivers, burglars, [and] kidnappers" who are imprisoned there. Moose's older sister, Natalie, has an undiagnosed condition readers will recognize as severe autism, and she is to attend a new residential school. Moose is going to school in San Francisco with Piper, the warden's high-spirited troublemaking daughter, who ropes Moose into her scheme to charge their classmates 5 cents for each shirt laundered by famous Alcatraz convicts.

GERM: A glorious blend of comedy and drama, this is a book that will get kids talking about, researching, and doing some factual or expository writing on peer pressure, autism, bios of the big outlaws of those days, Alcatraz, and the Great Depression. The sixth graders in Paul Mruczinski's class at Joyce Kilmer School in Milltown, New Jersey, had a grand time visualizing the book by making poster-sized storyboards, divided into chapters, with an illustration and sentence describing the key scene or scenes in each chapter. Booktalk other books set during the same time period, such as *Bud, Not Buddy* by Christopher Paul Curtis and *Out of the Dust* by Karen Hesse.

RELATED TITLES: Avi. *Don't You Know There's a War On?* HarperCollins, 2001. / Baldwin, Ann Norris. *A Little Time.* Viking, 1978. / Choldenko, Gennifer. *Notes from a Liar and Her Dog.* Putnam, 2001. / Conly, Jane Leslie. *Crazy Lady!* HarperCollins, 1993. / Curtis, Christopher Paul. *Bud, Not Buddy.* Delacorte, 1999. / Dodds, Bill. *My Sister Annie.* Boyds Mills, 1993. / Garrigue, Sheila. *Between Friends.* Bradbury, 1978. / Hesse, Karen. *Out of the Dust.* Scholastic, 1997. / Levine, Gail Carson. *Dave at Night.* HarperCollins, 1999. / Lisle, Janet Taylor. *The Art of Keeping Cool.* Atheneum, 2000. / Lisle, Janet Taylor. *How I Became a Writer and Oggie Learned to*

Drive. Philomel, 2002. / Peck, Richard. *A Long Way from Chicago*. Dial, 1998. / Peck, Richard. *A Year Down Yonder*. Dial, 2000. / Sachar, Louis. *Holes*. Farrar, 1998. / Shyer, Marlene Fanta. *Welcome Home, Jellybean*. Macmillan, 1978. / Slepian, Jan. *Risk n' Roses*. Philomel, 1990.

SUBJECTS: AUTISM. BROTHERS AND SISTERS. CALIFORNIA. DEPRESSIONS—1929—U.S. FAMILY PROBLEMS. HISTORICAL FICTION. PEOPLE WITH DISABILITIES. PRISONS. ROBBERS AND OUTLAWS. SCHOOLS.

920   Clements, Andrew. *Frindle*. Illus. by Brian Selznick. Simon & Schuster, 1996. 0-689-80669-8. 105pp. Gr. 4–6

This year, enterprising Nick Allen has tough, sharp Mrs. Granger for fifth grade, and she is a teacher who reveres the dictionary. Nick, well known for perfecting time-wasting as an art form, asks Mrs. G. where all the dictionary's words come from. When she calls his bluff, giving him an assignment to find out, Nick plans his revenge. Inventing the word "frindle" as a substitute for the word "pen," he gets all the kids to use it and refuses to back off when Mrs. G. punishes anyone who uses the word in her class.

GERM: The enjoyable teacher/student skirmish will give you plenty of tie-in activity ideas, including looking up word origins, inventing new words, and investigating real kids' accomplishments and inventions.

RELATED TITLES: Amato, Mary. *The Word Eater*. Holiday House, 2000. / Babbitt, Natalie. *The Search for Delicious*. Farrar, 1985. / Clements, Andrew. *Lunch Money*. Simon & Schuster, 2001. / Clements, Andrew. *The School Story*. Simon & Schuster, 2001. / Clements, Andrew. *A Week in the Woods*. Simon & Schuster, 2002. / Duffey, Betsy. *Utterly Yours, Booker Jones*. Viking, 1995. / Evans, Douglas. *Apple Island, or The Truth About Teachers*. Front Street, 1998. / Fletcher, Ralph. *Flying Solo*. Clarion, 1998. / Frasier, Debra. *Miss Alaineus: A Vocabulary Disaster*. Harcourt, 2000. / Levitt, Paul M., Douglas A. Burger, and Elissa S. Guralnick. *The Weighty Word Book*. Court Wayne, 2000. / MacDonald, Amy. *No More Nasty*. Farrar, 2001. / Spinelli, Jerry. *Loser*. HarperCollins, 2002.

SUBJECTS: DICTIONARIES. ENGLISH LANGUAGE. SCHOOLS. TEACHERS. VOCABULARY.

921   Clements, Andrew. *Lunch Money*. Illus. by Brian Selznick. Simon & Schuster, 2005. 0-689-86683-6. 222pp. Gr. 4–6

Deciding that school is an excellent market for making money, sixth grader Greg Kenton starts his own one-man operation, writing, illustrating, producing, and selling his own comic books, which he calls "Chunky Comics." When his classmate and rival Maura Shaw begins selling her own "Eentsy Beentsy Book," their confrontation results in a bloody nose and a black eye for Greg and the principal's ban on selling anything in school, a ruling both kids consider unfair.

GERM: Follow Greg's instructions for making your own 16-page books out of a single sheet of paper and set your kids to writing their own comic books. Before reading the chapter in which Greg and Maura go before the School Committee to present their case for selling their comics, ask your students to write persuasive letters marshaling arguments as to why they should be allowed to do so. (The idea of opening a school store is a business plan you might find yourself considering for your school.)

RELATED TITLES: Brittain, Bill. *All the Money in the World*. HarperCollins, 1979. / Clements, Andrew. *Frindle*. Simon & Schuster, 1996. / Clements, Andrew. *The School Story*. Simon & Schuster, 2001. / Duffey, Betsy. *Utterly Yours, Booker Jones*. Viking, 1995. / Gutman, Dan. *The Get Rich Quick Club*. HarperCollins, 2004. / Herman, Charlotte. *Max Malone Makes a Million*. Henry Holt, 1991. / Leedy, Loreen. *Follow the Money*. Holiday House, 2002. / Lisle, Janet Taylor. *How I Became a Writer and Oggie Learned to Drive*. Philomel, 2002. / Schwartz, David M. *If You Made a Million*. Lothrop, 1989. / Shreve, Susan. *Jonah the Whale*. Scholastic, 1998.

SUBJECTS: CARTOONS AND COMICS. MONEYMAKING PROJECTS. PRINCIPALS. SCHOOLS. TEACHERS.

922   Clements, Andrew. *The School Story*. Illus. by Brian Selznick. Simon & Schuster, 2001. 0-689-82594-3. 160pp. Gr. 3–7

Sixth grader Natalie Nelson uses a pseudonym when she submits her first novel, a school story called "The Cheater," to her mother, the children's book editor at a publishing company.

GERM: Aspiring novelists can write a possible first chapter of "The Cheater." From this witty tale, your book hounds will find out all about the writing, editing, and publishing process, warts and all, which will get them writing their own school stories.

RELATED TITLES: Clements, Andrew. *Frindle*. Simon & Schuster, 1996. / Clements, Andrew. *A Week in the Woods*. Simon & Schuster, 2002. / Duffey, Betsy. *Utterly Yours, Booker Jones*. Viking, 1995. / Fletcher, Ralph.

Flying Solo. Clarion, 1998. / Lisle, Janet Taylor. *How I Became a Writer and Oggie Learned to Drive*. Philomel, 2002. / Rocklin, Joanne. *For Your Eyes Only!* Scholastic, 1997. / Shreve, Susan. *Jonah the Whale*. Scholastic, 1998. / Slepian, Jan. *The Broccoli Tapes*. Philomel, 1988. / Snyder, Zilpha Keatley. *Libby on Wednesday*. Delacorte, 1990.

SUBJECTS: AUTHORSHIP. BOOKS AND READING. EDITORS. MOTHERS AND DAUGHTERS. SCHOOLS. WRITING.

923 **Clements, Andrew.** *A Week in the Woods*. **Simon & Schuster, 2002. 0-689-82596-X. 190pp. Gr. 4–6**

On the fifth graders' campout, angry new kid Mark heads into the forest alone when he is accused, mistakenly, by his science teacher, Mr. Maxwell, of bringing a knife on the trip.

GERM: Discussion points: Why does Mark act like he doesn't care in school? How and why is he different at home? Have you ever been the new kid? What did you do to fit in? Talk and write about: What is a first impression? Have you ever judged someone after a first meeting, only to change your mind about that person as you got to know him? Trace how and why Mark and Mr. Maxwell misunderstood each other.

RELATED TITLES: Clements, Andrew. *Frindle*. Simon & Schuster, 1996. / Clements, Andrew. *The School Story*. Simon & Schuster, 2001. / Fletcher, Ralph. *Flying Solo*. Clarion, 1998. / Gantos, Jack. *Joey Pigza Swallowed the Key*. Farrar, 1998. / Kehret, Peg. *Earthquake Terror*. Dutton, 1996. / Paulsen, Gary. *Hatchet*. Atheneum, 1987. / Shreve, Susan. *Jonah the Whale*. Scholastic, 1998. / Slepian, Jan. *The Broccoli Tapes*. Philomel, 1988. / Snyder, Zilpha Keatley. *Libby on Wednesday*. Delacorte, 1990. / Spinelli, Jerry. *Loser*. HarperCollins, 2002.

SUBJECTS: CAMPING. SCHOOLS. SURVIVAL. TEACHERS.

924 **Clifford, Eth.** *Flatfoot Fox and the Case of the Bashful Beaver*. **Illus. by Brian Lies. Houghton Mifflin, 1995. 0-395-70560-6. 47pp. Gr. K–3**

For the smartest detective in the whole world, finding who stole Bashful Beaver's big black bag of beautiful bright blue buttons and left in its place a battered box of broken bottles is easy. What Flatfoot Fox needs to do now is prove it. This third in a series of clever, entertaining, easy-to-read chapter-book mysteries is illustrated with personable black-line drawings on each page.

GERM: Secretary Bird insists his boss is going about the case all wrong and that he must solve it the usual way: find suspects, ask questions, and look for clues. Ask your detectives whose method works best and why.

RELATED TITLES: Adler, David A. Cam Jansen series and Young Cam Jansen series. Putnam. / Biedrzycki, David. *Ace Lacewing: Bug Detective*. Charlesbridge, 2005. / Christelow, Eileen. *Gertrude, the Bulldog Detective*. Clarion, 1992. / Clifford, Eth. Flatfoot Fox series. Orchard. / Cushman, Doug. *The ABC Mystery*. HarperCollins, 1993. / Cushman, Doug. Aunt Eater mystery series. HarperCollins. / Cushman, Doug. *Inspector Hopper*. HarperCollins, 2000. / Cushman, Doug. *Mystery at the Club Sandwich*. Clarion, 2004. / Cushman, Doug. *The Mystery of King Karfu*. HarperCollins, 1996. / Laden, Nina. *Private I. Guana: The Case of the Missing Chameleon*. Chronicle, 1995. / Levy, Elizabeth. Something Queer series. Delacorte. / Palatini, Margie. *The Web Files*. Hyperion, 2001. / Sharmat, Marjorie Weinman. Nate the Great series. Delacorte. / Stevenson, James. *The Mud Flat Mystery*. Greenwillow, 1997.

SUBJECTS: ALLITERATION. ANIMALS. BEAVERS. FICTION BOOKS FOR EARLY GRADES. FOXES. MYSTERY AND DETECTIVE STORIES.

925 **Codell, Esmé Raji.** *Sahara Special*. **Hyperion, 2003. 0-796-80793-8. 175pp. Gr. 4–6**

Sahara Jones is repeating fifth grade. Her new teacher, who calls herself Madame Poitier (though the kids call her Miss Pointy), believes in Sahara when she reveals her True Ambition: she is going to be a writer. If you've read Esmé Codell's stunning book for adults, *Educating Esmé: Diary of a Teacher's First Year* (Algonquin, 2001), you'll recognize the students and the autobiographical portrayal of the quirky, fierce, and loyal teacher who flouts the rules but gets her kids passionate about learning.

GERM: Miss Pointy is such a compelling role model for us all. Appropriate her writing and teaching ideas at will. Have your students write everything they think you need to know about them, as Miss Pointy does and as Esmé did for her own students in Chicago. Use a Trouble Basket for children to load their troubles in before they come in the classroom. Tell Aesop's fables. Show slides of famous architecture. Pass out poems. Change kids' lives. Don't miss Esmé's Web site, a terrific children's lit review site at <www.planetesme.com>, which includes her complete teacher's guide for *Sahara Special* and her fabulous book for parents, *How to Get Your Child to Love Reading* (Algonquin, 2003).

RELATED TITLES: Codell, Esmé Raji. *Diary of a Fairy Godmother*. Hyperion, 2005. / Codell, Esmé Raji. *Sing a Song of Tuna Fish*. Hyperion, 2004. / Creech, Sharon. *Granny Torrelli Makes Soup*. HarperCollins, 2003. / Creech, Sharon. *Love That Dog*. HarperCollins, 2001. / Duffey, Betsy. *Utterly Yours, Booker Jones*. Viking, 1995. / Fletcher, Ralph. *Flying Solo*. Clarion, 1998. / Gantos, Jack. *Joey Pigza Swallowed the Key*. Farrar, 1998. / George, Kristine O'Connell. *Swimming Upstream: Middle School Poems*. Clarion, 2002. / Grimes, Nikki. *Meet Danitra Brown*. Lothrop, 1994. / Hannigan, Katherine. *Ida B: And Her Plans to Maximize Fun, Avoid Disaster, and (Possibly) Save the World*. Greenwillow, 2004. / Rocklin, Joanne. *For Your Eyes Only!* Scholastic, 1997. / Slepian, Jan. *The Broccoli Tapes*. Philomel, 1988. / Snyder, Zilpha Keatley. *Libby on Wednesday*. Delacorte, 1990. / Woodson, Jacqueline. *Locomotion*. Putnam, 2003.

SUBJECTS: BEHAVIOR. DIARIES. SCHOOLS. TEACHERS. WRITING.

926   Collins, Suzanne. *Gregor the Overlander*. **Scholastic, 2003. 0-439-43536-6. 311pp. Gr. 4–6**

Twelve-year-old Gregor and his 2-year-old sister Boots fall through an air duct in their New York City apartment house laundry room and land far below in the Underland, populated by pale humans, giant cockroaches, bats, and vicious, warring rats.

GERM: Take advantage of the vivid descriptions of life underground to map the Underland kingdom. Draw portraits of the main characters. Compare and contrast life underground with life in New York City, Gregor's hometown. Tie the giant bats in the novel to Kenneth Oppel's *Silverwing*, where Shade, a bat called Runt by his peers, decides to prove his courage by staying out to see the sun rise, and encounters evil giant bats bent on his destruction.

RELATED TITLES: Alexander, Lloyd. *The First Two Lives of Lucas-Kasha*. Dutton, 1978. / Collins, Suzanne. *Gregor and the Curse of the Warmbloods*. Scholastic, 2005. / Collins, Suzanne. *Gregor and the Prophecy of Bane*. Scholastic, 2003. / Divakaruni, Chitra Banerjee. *The Conch Bearer*. Roaring Brook, 2003. / DuPrau, Jeanne. *The City of Ember*. Random House, 2003. / Hirsch, Odo. *Bartlett and the City of Flames*. Bloomsbury, 2003. / L'Engle, Madeleine. *A Wrinkle in Time*. Farrar, 1962. / Lowry, Lois. *The Giver*. Houghton Mifflin, 1993. / Oppel, Kenneth. *Airborn*. HarperCollins, 2004. / Oppel, Kenneth. *Silverwing*. Simon & Schuster, 1997.

SUBJECTS: ADVENTURE AND ADVENTURERS. ANIMALS. BATS. BROTHERS AND SISTERS. COCKROACHES. FANTASY. MISSING PERSONS. NEW YORK CITY. RATS. SPIDERS.

927   Conford, Ellen. *Annabel the Actress Starring in Gorilla My Dreams*. **Illus. by Renee W. Adriani. Simon & Schuster, 1999. 0-689-81404-6. 64pp. Gr. 1–4**

Annabel's ad in the town newspaper—"Annabel the Actress: No part too big or too small"—soon yields results when she is hired to be a cake-carrying gorilla at a birthday party for a batch of 5-year-old boys. Unfortunately, she does not have a gorilla costume, but her resourceful friend Maggie fashions one out of an old raincoat lining. Annabel borrows a gorilla mask and spends the week rehearsing her part.

GERM: The way Annabel wins over her charges is hilarious and inspirational for all aspiring actors. As she puts it, "The costume doesn't make the gorilla . . . The actor makes the gorilla." Discuss: What does she mean by this? Students can pair up to read aloud the various sets of snappy dialogues between Annabel and her employer; Lowell, her arch enemy; and the birthday party boys.

RELATED TITLES: Auch, Mary Jane. *Hen Lake*. Holiday House, 1995. / Auch, Mary Jane. *Peeping Beauty*. Holiday House, 1993. / Conford, Ellen. Jenny Archer series. Little, Brown. / Edwards, Pamela Duncan. *Honk! The Story of a Prima Swanerina*. Hyperion, 1998. / Spinelli, Eileen. *Lizzie Logan, Second Banana*. Simon & Schuster, 1998. / Spinelli, Eileen. *Lizzie Logan Wears Purple Sunglasses*. Simon & Schuster, 1997.

SUBJECTS: ACTING. BIRTHDAYS. CREATIVE DRAMA. FICTION BOOKS FOR EARLY GRADES. PARTIES.

928   Conly, Jane Leslie. *The Rudest Alien on Earth*. **Henry Holt, 2002. 0-8050-6069-3. 264pp. Gr. 4–7**

Landing on Earth on a secret mission from a distant galaxy, Oluu first takes on the appearance of a border collie. Though she's been warned to tell no one about herself, she befriends Molly, a 10-year-old farm girl who is eager to teach the talking dog new words.

GERM: Discuss and analyze what Oluu needs to learn on Earth. Using the clues gleaned from the story, readers can piece together a description of Oluu's planet, its inhabitants, and how they live, and contrast it with the way of life on our planet. This is a reverse sci fi book where we see our home planet through alien eyes.

RELATED TITLES: Bechard, Margaret. *Star Hatchling*. Viking, 1995. / Brittain, Bill. *Shape-Changer*. HarperCollins, 1994. / Gauthier, Gail. *My Life Among the Aliens*. Putnam, 1996. / King-Smith, Dick. *Harriet's Hare*. Crown, 1995. / Klause, Annette. *Alien Secrets*. Delacorte, 1993. / L'Engle, Madeleine. *A Wrinkle in Time*. Farrar,

1962. / Mikaelsen, Ben. *Countdown.* Hyperion, 1996. / Service, Pamela. *Stinker from Space.* Scribner, 1988. / Sleator, William. *Into the Dream.* Dutton, 1979. / Sleator, William. *The Night the Heads Came.* Dutton, 1996. / Slote, Alfred. *My Robot Buddy.* HarperTrophy, 1986. / Slote, Alfred. *My Trip to Alpha I.* HarperTrophy, 1986.

SUBJECTS: ANIMALS. EXTRATERRESTRIAL LIFE. FRIENDSHIP. SCIENCE FICTION. TRANSFORMATIONS.

929 Corbett, Sue. *12 Again.* Dutton, 2002. 0-525-46899-4. 227pp. Gr. 5–7

When his mother, Bernadette, vanishes on Labor Day, the day before her 40th birthday, Patrick has to take care of his younger brothers and figure out a way to get her back. He has no way of knowing she has become 12 again and is now in his computer class at school. In this poignant time-travel fantasy, Bernadette's mother, an Irish woman from the old country who believed in magic and fairies, died six months ago. Falling asleep in her mother's house, Bernadette awakes to find her mother alive again, looking just as she did 28 years before in 1972.

GERM: Your students can gather information about what their parents' lives were like when they were 12 and write a story incorporating details about the times, including the politics, music, clothes, and technology. Break out some Irish fairy tales to see the source of the novel's special flavor.

RELATED TITLES: Gaiman, Neil. *Coraline.* HarperCollins, 2002. / Hahn, Mary Downing. *Time for Andrew: A Ghost Story.* Clarion, 1994. / L'Engle, Madeleine. *A Wrinkle in Time.* Farrar, 1962. / Pearce, Philippa. *Tom's Midnight Garden.* HarperCollins, 1958. / Pearson, Kit. *Awake and Dreaming.* Viking, 1997. / Peck, Richard. *The Great Interactive Dream Machine.* Dial, 1996. / Slepian, Jan. *Back to Before.* Philomel, 1993. / Tannen, Mary. *The Wizard Children of Finn.* Knopf, 1981. / Weiss, Ellen and Mel Friedman. *The Poof Point.* Knopf, 1992.

SUBJECTS: FAIRIES. FAMILY PROBLEMS. FANTASY. IRISH AMERICANS. MOTHERS AND DAUGHTERS. MOTHERS AND SONS. SCHOOLS. TIME TRAVEL.

930 Cox, Judy. *Weird Stories from the Lonesome Café.* Illus. by Diane Kidd. Harcourt, 2000. 0-15-202134-5. 72pp. Gr. 1–4

Working at his uncle's restaurant in the Nevada desert one summer, Sam meets some familiar but eccentric customers, including Bigfoot, Elvis, and Santa.

GERM: Write a new, short, funny chapter about another possible visitor to the desert café, where everyone who's anyone could show up at some point.

RELATED TITLES: Etra, Jonathan, and Stephanie Spinner. *Aliens for Breakfast.* Random House, 1988. / Hornik, Laurie Miller. *The Secrets of Ms. Snickle's Class.* Clarion, 2001. / Hornik, Laurie Miller. *Zoo School.* Clarion, 2004. / MacDonald, Amy. *No More Nice.* Orchard, 1996.

SUBJECTS: BIGFOOT. DESERTS. EXTRATERRESTRIAL LIFE. FICTION BOOKS FOR EARLY GRADES. HUMOROUS FICTION. NEVADA. RESTAURANTS. SANTA CLAUS. UNCLES.

931 Creech, Sharon. *Granny Torrelli Makes Soup.* Illus. by Chris Raschka. HarperCollins, 2003. 0-06-029291-1. 141pp. Gr. 3–6

Today, 12-year-old Rosie is furious at Bailey, her best buddy and neighbor, a boy who is better than a brother. When her wise Granny Torrelli comes over to make soup, she shares heart-rending stories about when she was a girl in Italy. Through these stories, Rosie comes to see, bit by bit, why learning Braille so she could read just like sight-impaired Bailey made him so furious at her. Both Rosie and Granny Torrelli have unmistakable, unforgettable voices you'll hear in your head for a long time.

GERM: Told in short chapters, in present tense, the dialogue is set off not in traditional quotes but in italics, which will be great for a lesson on punctuating dialogue. Discussion point: Why are Rosie and Bailey angry with each other? How do Granny Torrelli's stories of her past help them to reconcile and why? Rosie's account makes us appreciate good stories well told, and will get children talking to their parents and grandparents to ask for their stories. Talk about the wisdom of grandparents. Talk about blindness and Braille and coping with a disability. Find out more about Louis Braille and guide dogs. And you may even be inspired to make zuppa. Or pasta. Or both.

RELATED TITLES: Codell, Esmé Raji. *Sahara Special.* Hyperion, 2003. / Creech, Sharon. *Heartbeat.* HarperCollins, 2004. / Creech, Sharon. *Love That Dog.* HarperCollins, 2001. / Creech, Sharon. *Ruby Holler.* HarperCollins, 2002. / Creech, Sharon. *The Wanderer.* HarperCollins, 2000. / DiCamillo, Kate. *The Tale of Despereaux.* Candlewick, 2003. / Freedman, Russell. *Out of Darkness: The Story of Louis Braille.* Clarion, 1997. / Garfield, James. *Follow My Leader.* Viking, 1957. / Hannigan, Katherine. *Ida B.* Greenwillow, 2004. / Horvath, Polly. *Everything on a Waffle.* Farrar, 2001. / Horvath, Polly. *The Trolls.* Farrar, 1999. / Little, Jean. *Little by Little: A*

Writer's Education. Viking, 1987. / Martin, Ann M. *Belle Teal*. Scholastic, 2001. / Rocklin, Joanne. *Strudel Stories*. Delacorte, 1999. / Rodanas, Kristina. *The Blind Hunter*. Cavendish, 2003. / Woodson, Jacqueline. *Locomotion*. Putnam, 2003.

SUBJECTS: ARGUMENTS. BLIND. CONFLICT RESOLUTION. COOKERY. FRIENDSHIP. GRANDMOTHERS. ITALIAN AMERICANS. PEOPLE WITH DISABILITIES. PERSONAL NARRATIVES. SOUP.

932   Creech, Sharon. *Love That Dog*. HarperCollins, 2001. 0-06-009287-3. 103pp. Gr. 4–8

In a series of spare, free-verse journal entries, Jack reluctantly ponders the poems his teacher, Miss Stretchberry, reads aloud over the course of the year. This gorgeous little book, a novel in poems, packs a huge wallop as Jack begins to come to terms with a speeding blue car that looms so large in his memory, and to memorialize, through his poetry, the life and death of his beloved dog Sky.

GERM: Read aloud from collections of poems by the poets Miss Stretchberry introduces, including Walter Dean Myers, Valerie Worth, Arnold Adoff, and Robert Frost. Use *Love That Dog* as a kickoff to your own exploration of reading and writing poetry. Children can stage a poetry reading of favorite poets or a poetry slam of their own work. Another book where children think deeply and write about poems is Joanne Rocklin's *For Your Eyes Only!* In Jacqueline Woodson's *Locomotion*, Lonnie deals with his fallen-apart life by writing poetry. Writing prompt: Pick the poem that means the most to you and write about it.

RELATED TITLES: Adoff, Arnold. *Love Letters*. Scholastic, 1997. / Cleary, Beverly. *Strider*. Morrow, 1991. / Codell, Esmé Raji. *Sahara Special*. Hyperion, 2003. / Creech, Sharon. *The Wanderer*. HarperCollins, 2000. / George, Kristine O'Connell. *Swimming Upstream: Middle School Poems*. Clarion, 2002. / Grimes, Nikki. *My Man Blue*. Dial, 1999. / Hesse, Karen. *Sable*. Henry Holt, 1994. / Janeczko, Paul B. *How to Write Poetry*. Scholastic, 1999. / Janeczko, Paul B., comp. *Poetry from A to Z: A Guide for Young Writers*. Simon & Schuster, 1994. / Janeczko, Paul B. *Seeing the Blue Between: Advice and Inspiration for Young Poets*. Candlewick, 2002. / Kirk, Daniel. *Dogs Rule!* Hyperion, 2003. / Larrick, Nancy. *Let's Do a Poem!* Delacorte, 1991. / Lindquist, Susan Hart. *Wander*. Delacorte, 1998. / Livingston, Myra Cohn, comp. *Poem-Making: Ways to Begin Writing Poetry*. HarperCollins, 1991. / Myers, Walter Dean. *Brown Angels: An Album of Pictures and Verse*. HarperCollins, 1993. / Woodson, Jacqueline. *Locomotion*. Putnam, 2003.

SUBJECTS: DEATH. DIARIES. DOGS. POETRY. SCHOOLS. TEACHERS. WRITING.

933   Creech, Sharon. *Ruby Holler*. HarperCollins, 2002. 0-06-027732-7. 310pp. Gr. 3–6

Trouble Twins. That's what Mr. and Mrs. Trepid, who run the ramshackle Boxton Creek Home for Children, call 13-year old Dallas and his sister, Florida, and with good reason. The twins' fortunes improve when they are farmed out to new foster parents, the good-hearted Tiller and Sairy Morey, who live in idyllic Ruby Holler in a cabin with no modern conveniences.

GERM: This is a quirky, funny character study—full of danger and adventure—from an omniscient narrator who gives us insight into the personalities of all four main characters and the awful, awful Trepids. Ask your readers to write character sketches and draw portraits of Florida, Dallas, Sairy, and Tiller.

RELATED TITLES: Bath, K. P. *The Secret of Castle Cant*. Little, Brown, 2004. / Creech, Sharon. *Granny Torrelli Makes Soup*. HarperCollins, 2003. / Creech, Sharon. *The Wanderer*. HarperCollins, 2000. / Dahl, Roald. *The BFG*. Farrar, 1982. / Ibbotson, Eva. *Journey to the River Sea*. Dutton, 2002. / Levine, Gail Carson. *Dave at Night*. HarperCollins, 1999. / Paterson, Katherine. *The Great Gilly Hopkins*. HarperCollins, 1978. / Rowling, J. K. *Harry Potter and the Sorcerer's Stone*. Scholastic, 1998. (And others in the Harry Potter series.) / Sachar, Louis. *Holes*. Farrar, 1998. / Snyder, Zilpha Keatley. *Gib Rides Home*. Delacorte, 1998. / Spinelli, Jerry. *Maniac Magee*. Little, Brown, 1990. / Wallace, Barbara Brooks. *Peppermints in the Parlor*. Atheneum, 1980.

SUBJECTS: BROTHERS AND SISTERS. COUNTRY LIFE. ELDERLY. ORPHANS. VOYAGES AND TRAVELS.

934   Creech, Sharon. *The Wanderer*. Illus. by David Diaz. HarperCollins, 2000. 0-06-027730-0. 305pp. Gr. 5–7

Sophie and her cousin Cody, both 13, set sail with Cody's dad, two uncles, and cousin Brian on a 45-foot sailboat, *The Wanderer*, heading across the Atlantic to England to see Bompie, the family patriarch. Sophie, an orphan, loves the water and sailing, though she continues to have a recurring dream of a huge wave, a wall of black water breaking over her. Cody doesn't get along with his dad. Through their alternating journal entries that chronicle the tumultuous ocean voyage, Sophie and Cody confront and reveal their secrets, including what happened to Sophie's parents.

GERM: What a stunning novel to use when discussing point of view. Booktalk ocean voyage books. Juggle like Cody. Tell grandparent stories.

RELATED TITLES: Avi. *The True Confessions of Charlotte Doyle*. Orchard, 1990. / Couloumbis, Audrey. *Getting Near to Baby*. Putnam, 1999. / Creech, Sharon. *Granny Torrelli Makes Soup*. HarperCollins, 2003. / Creech, Sharon. *Walk Two Moons*. HarperCollins, 1994. / Gordon, Amy. *When JFK Was My Father*. Houghton Mifflin, 1999. / Haas, Jessie. *Unbroken*. Greenwillow, 1999. / Holm, Jennifer L. *Our Only May Amelia*. HarperCollins, 1999. / Koss, Amy Goldman. *The Ashwater Experiment*. Dial, 1999. / Mazer, Norma Fox. *Good Night, Maman*. Harcourt, 1999. / Morpurgo, Michael. *Kensuke's Kingdom*. Scholastic, 2003. / Philbrick, Rodman. *The Young Man and the Sea*. Blue Sky/Scholastic, 2004. / Slepian, Jan. *The Broccoli Tapes*. Philomel, 1988.

SUBJECTS: ADVENTURE AND ADVENTURERS. BOATS AND BOATING. COUSINS. FAMILY LIFE. OCEAN. ORPHANS. SAILING. SURVIVAL. VOYAGES AND TRAVELS.

935   Curtis, Christopher Paul. *Bud, Not Buddy*. **Delacorte, 1999. 0-385-32306-9. 245pp. Gr. 5–7**

Running away from his latest foster parents after a fight with their bullying son, 10-year-old Bud figures he'll take to the road instead of heading back to the Home where he's lived since his mother died four years before. It's 1936 and, with the Great Depression in full swing, Bud makes his way from Flint, Michigan, to Grand Rapids to find the legendary bandleader Herman E. Calloway, whom he believes to be his real father. Listeners will laugh out loud at the lively cast of characters Bud encounters and at his jaunty, wide-eyed way of looking at his predicaments, though his many encounters with racism will lead to sober discussion.

GERM: Inspired by the list Bud keeps, "Bud Caldwell's Rules and Things to Have a Funner Life and Make a Better Liar Out of Yourself," compile and illustrate your own students' book of their life lessons and rules.

RELATED TITLES: Choldenko, Gennifer. *Al Capone Does My Shirts*. Putnam, 2004. / Curtis, Christopher Paul. *The Watsons Go to Birmingham, 1963*. Delacorte, 1995. / English, Karen. *Francie*. Farrar, 1999. / Fox, Paula. *Monkey Island*. Orchard, 1991. / Hesse, Karen. *Out of the Dust*. Scholastic, 1997. / Levine, Gail Carson. *Dave at Night*. HarperCollins, 1999. / Mitchell, Margaree King. *Uncle Jed's Barbershop*. Simon & Schuster, 1993. / Peck, Richard. *A Long Way from Chicago*. Dial, 1998. / Peck, Richard. *A Year Down Yonder*. Dial, 2000. / Pinkney, Andrea Davis. *Duke Ellington: The Piano Prince and His Orchestra*. Hyperion, 1998. / Pinkney, Andrea Davis. *Ella Fitzgerald: The Tale of a Vocal Virtuosa*. Hyperion, 2002. / Recorvits, Helen. *Goodbye, Walter Malinski*. Farrar, 1999. / Sachar, Louis. *Holes*. Farrar, 1998. / Taylor, Mildred. *Roll of Thunder, Hear My Cry*. Dial, 1976.

SUBJECTS: AFRICAN AMERICANS. DEPRESSIONS—1929—U.S. HISTORICAL FICTION. JAZZ. MULTICULTURAL BOOKS. MUSIC. NEWBERY MEDAL. ORPHANS. RUNAWAYS.

936   Curtis, Christopher Paul. *The Watsons Go to Birmingham, 1963*. **Delacorte, 1995. 0-385-32175-9. 210pp. Gr. 5–8**

After Kenny's 13-year-old big brother Byron gets in trouble one time too many, his father drives the whole family in their car, the Brown Bomber, from Flint, Michigan, to Alabama, so Byron can spend the summer with strict, no-nonsense Grandma Sands, who will certainly straighten him out. Each chapter of 9-year-old Kenny's narrative is a memorable, self-contained short story, filled with uproarious comedic situations involving his parents, Byron, and little sister Joetta, whom Kenny refers to collectively as the Weird Watsons.

GERM: Woven in to the humor, however, are serious issues to discuss about the racism the Watsons face as African Americans, especially as they head down South in the tense summer of 1963. In the last part of the book, the family is caught up in the heinous church bombing in Birminghham that took the lives of four young girls. For an overview of those tumultuous times, see Diane McWhorter's *A Dream of Freedom: The Civil Rights Movement from 1954 to 1968*.

RELATED TITLES: Curtis, Christopher Paul. *Bud, Not Buddy*. Delacorte, 1999. / Giovanni, Nikki. *Rosa*. Henry Holt, 2005. / Levine, Ellen. *Freedom's Children: Young Civil Rights Activists Tell Their Own Stories*. Putnam, 1993. / McWhorter, Diane. *A Dream of Freedom: The Civil Rights Movement from 1954 to 1968*. Scholastic, 2004. / Parks, Rosa. *Rosa Parks: Mother to a Movement*. Dial, 1992. / Taylor, Mildred D. *The Friendship*. Dial, 1987. / Taylor, Mildred D. *The Gold Cadillac*. Dial, 1987. / Taylor, Mildred D. *Mississippi Bridge*. Dial, 1990. / Taylor, Mildred D. *Roll of Thunder, Hear My Cry*. Dial, 1976.

SUBJECTS: AFRICAN AMERICANS. AFRICAN AMERICANS—HISTORY. ALABAMA. BROTHERS AND SISTERS. CIVIL RIGHTS. FAMILY LIFE. HISTORICAL FICTION. MULTICULTURAL BOOKS. RACE RELATIONS. SEGREGATION.

937 **Cushman, Karen.** *The Ballad of Lucy Whipple.* **Clarion, 1996. 0-395-72806-1. 195pp. Gr. 5–8**

At the age of 12, in the summer of 1849, feisty California Morning Whipple arrives in the gold-mining settlement of Lucky Diggins, California, with her newly widowed mother and three younger brothers and sisters. Living in a tent that her mother runs as a boarding house for coarse, unshaven miners, dreamy but clever-tongued California changes her name to Lucy and yearns for the civilized life she once led with her grandparents back in Massachusetts. Now she's stuck looking after the children and helping her mother. Listeners will soon be caught up in the hard knocks-filled yarn spun by the sassy and rambunctious narrator who makes the Old West leap to life through a family saga filled with humor, tragedy, and a will to overcome adversity.

GERM: Lucy regales us with wry, matter-of-fact descriptions of inedible food and primitive living conditions that will make today's finicky children squirm. Have your group write essays comparing and contrasting their lives now with Lucy's back then.

RELATED TITLES: Cushman, Karen. *Catherine, Called Birdy.* Clarion, 1994. / Cushman, Karen. *Rodzina.* Clarion, 2003. / Fleischman, Sid. *Bandit's Moon.* Greenwillow, 1998. / Fleischman, Sid. *By the Great Horn Spoon.* Little, Brown, 1963. / Fleischman, Sid. *Jim Ugly.* Greenwillow, 1992. / Freedman, Russell. *Children of the Wild West.* Clarion, 1983. / Greer, Gery, and Bob Ruddick. *Max and Me and the Wild West.* Harcourt, 1988. / Kay, Verla. *Gold Fever.* Putnam, 1999. / Mooser, Stephen. *Orphan Jeb at the Massacree.* Knopf, 1984. / Osborne, Mary Pope. *Adaline Falling Star.* Scholastic, 2000. / Ryan, Pam Muñoz. *Riding Freedom.* Scholastic, 1998. / Schanzer, Rosalyn. *How We Crossed the West: The Adventures of Lewis and Clark.* National Geographic Society, 1997. / Siebert, Diane. *Rhyolite: The True Story of a Ghost Town.* Clarion, 2003.

SUBJECTS: CALIFORNIA. FAMILY LIFE. FRONTIER AND PIONEER LIFE. GOLD RUSH. HISTORICAL FICTION. WEST (U.S.)—HISTORY—FICTION.

938 **Cushman, Karen.** *Rodzina.* **Clarion, 2003. 0-618-13351-8. 215pp. Gr. 5–8**

Shipped out by the Little Wanderers' Refuge in Chicago like a sack of potatoes onto a westbound train in 1888, 12-year-old Polish American orphan Rodzina Brodski is expected to care for eight younger orphans also making the trip. She is sure she will die from the swaying, rattling train and the never-ending worrying and washing up of the five tough-talking, lunkhead boys and sweet, if simple, 7-year-old Lacy. As they travel farther west, the orphans are taken in one by one by farm families in Nebraska and Wyoming Territory, but Rodzina would rather die than live with strangers who don't really want her. Once again, Cushman introduces us to a feisty, independent girl, this one being tall, round, and not beautiful. All readers will root for her.

GERM: For a quick overview of what the orphan trains were all about, read Verla Kay's rhyming picture book, *Orphan Train,* and for a more thorough analysis, see Andrea Warren's *Orphan Train Rider: One Boy's True Story.* Cushman's heroines are such lively, headstrong girls. Do a Cushman author study and have readers write up profiles of her main characters and compare and contrast their lives and personalities.

RELATED TITLES: Beatty, Patricia. *That's One Ornery Orphan.* Morrow, 1980. / Bunting, Eve. *Train to Somewhere.* Clarion, 1996. / Curtis, Christopher Paul. *Bud, Not Buddy.* Delacorte, 1999. / Cushman, Karen. *The Ballad of Lucy Whipple.* Clarion, 1996. / Doherty, Berlie. *Street Child.* Orchard, 1994. / Kay, Verla. *Orphan Train.* Putnam, 2003. / Paterson, Katherine. *Jip: His Story.* Dutton, 1996. / Ryan, Pam Muñoz. *Riding Freedom.* Scholastic, 1998. / Snyder, Zilpha Keatley. *Gib Rides Home.* Delacorte, 1998. / Warren, Andrea. *Orphan Train Rider: One Boy's True Story.* Houghton Mifflin, 1996.

SUBJECTS: HISTORICAL FICTION. ORPHAN TRAINS. ORPHANS. POLISH AMERICANS. SURVIVAL. TRAINS. WEST (U.S.)—HISTORY.

939 **Cutler, Jane.** *Rats!* **Illus. by Tracey Campbell Pearson. Farrar, 1996. 0-374-36181-9. 115pp. Gr. 2–4**

In this good-natured sequel to *No Dogs Allowed,* Jason Fraser is entering fourth grade, where he has girl trouble, and he and his little brother, first grader Edward, raise two attractive rats they name Rose and Spike.

GERM: Ask your kids to recall, tell, write, and share true amusing tales about their siblings, families, and unusual pets.

RELATED TITLES: Byars, Betsy. *My Brother, Ant.* Viking, 1996. / Cameron, Ann. *More Stories Huey Tells.* Farrar, 1997. / Cameron, Ann. *The Stories Huey Tells.* Knopf, 1995. / Cameron, Ann. *The Stories Julian Tells.* Yearling, 1989. / Caseley, Judith. *Harry and Arney.* Greenwillow, 1994. / Cutler, Jane. *No Dogs Allowed.* Farrar, 1992. / Gauthier, Gail. *My Life Among the Aliens.* Putnam, 1996. / Harrison, Maggie. *Angels on Roller Skates.*

Candlewick, 1992. / Lisle, Janet Taylor. *How I Became a Writer and Oggie Learned to Drive*. Philomel, 2002. / Lowry, Lois. *See You Around, Sam*. Houghton Mifflin, 1996 (and others in the Sam series). / McDonald, Megan. *Judy Moody, M.D.: The Doctor Is In!* Candlewick, 2004 (and others in the Judy Moody series). / Petersen, P. J. *The Amazing Magic Show*. Simon & Schuster, 1994. / Willis, Meredith Sue. *Marco's Monster*. HarperCollins, 1996.

SUBJECTS: BROTHERS. FAMILY LIFE. HUMOROUS FICTION. RATS.

940 Dengler, Marianna. *The Worry Stone*. Illus. by Sibyl Graber Gerig. Northland, 1996. 0-87358-642-5. 40pp. Gr. 2–4

Sitting on a park bench, an old woman observes a lonely little boy and remembers back to her own childhood growing up alone on a Spanish hacienda, where her one true friend, Grandfather, told her wonderful stories. Finding an unusual pebble one day, she showed it to Grandfather, who identified it as a worry stone with special powers to make worries go away and told her a Chumash Indian legend of how the stones came to be. A story within a story within a story, this moving picture book with large, formal watercolors is all about the power and healing of stories.

GERM: Discussion points: How and why does the worry stone work? What stories have your grandparents told you? Why do we need stories? If you found a worry stone, what worries would you ask it to make go away?

RELATED TITLES: Hooper, Meredith. *The Pebble in My Pocket: A History of Our Earth*. Viking, 1996. / Jennings, Patrick. *Putnam and Pennyroyal*. Scholastic, 1999. / Lewin, Ted. *The Storytellers*. Lothrop, 1998. / Polacco, Patricia. *My Ol' Man*. Philomel, 1995. / Regan, Dian Curtis. *The Curse of the Trouble Dolls*. Henry Holt, 1992. / Say, Allen. *Kamishibai Man*. Houghton Mifflin, 2005. / Sunami, Kitoba. *How the Fisherman Tricked the Genie: A Tale Within a Tale Within a Tale*. Atheneum, 2002.

SUBJECTS: CHUMASH INDIANS. ELDERLY. GRANDFATHERS. INDIANS OF NORTH AMERICA—CALIFORNIA. LONELINESS. ROCKS. STORYTELLING.

941 DiCamillo, Kate. *Because of Winn-Dixie*. Candlewick, 2000. 0-7636-0776-2. 182pp. Gr. 3–5

Ten-year-old India Opal Buloni, newly moved with her preacher father to a trailer park in Naomi, Florida, goes to the supermarket and brings home a big, homely, lovable dog she names Winn-Dixie after the place she found him. She says, "It's hard not to immediately fall in love with a dog who has a good sense of humor." In the course of this sweet, picturesque book, she makes friends with a quirky group of local folk and asks her father to tell her ten things about her mama, who left her when she was a baby—one thing for each year she's been alive.

GERM: Ask listeners to recall and write about a pet they've known that changed their lives in some way. Compare dog acquisition stories, using *Henry Huggins*, in which Henry finds his dog, Ribsy, at the grocery store and brings him home on the bus in a big box.

RELATED TITLES: Byars, Betsy. *Tornado*. HarperCollins, 1996. / Byars, Betsy. *Wanted . . . Mud Blossom*. Delacorte, 1991. / Cleary, Beverly. *Henry Huggins*. Morrow, 1950. / Cleary, Beverly. *Ribsy*. Morrow, 1964. / Cleary, Beverly. *Strider*. Morrow, 1991. / DiCamillo, Kate. *The Miraculous Journey of Edward Tulane*. Candlewick, 2006. / Gardiner, John. *Stone Fox*. Crowell, 1980. / Hannigan, Katherine. *Ida B: And Her Plans to Maximize Fun, Avoid Disaster, and (Possibly) Save the World*. Greenwillow, 2004. / Hesse, Karen. *Sable*. Henry Holt, 1994. / Lindquist, Susan Hart. *Wander*. Delacorte, 1998. / Myers, Anna. *Red-Dirt Jessie*. Walker, 1992. / Naylor, Phyllis Reynolds. *Shiloh*. Atheneum, 1991. / Osborne, Mary Pope. *Adaline Falling Star*. Scholastic, 2000. / Vande Velde, Vivian. *Smart Dog*. Harcourt, 1998.

SUBJECTS: CITIES AND TOWNS. DOGS. FATHERS AND DAUGHTERS. FLORIDA.

942 DiCamillo, Kate. *Mercy Watson to the Rescue*. Illus. by Chris Van Dusen. Candlewick, 2005. 0-7636-2270-2. 73pp. Gr. K–2

On a night when Mr. and Mrs. Watson and their adored pig, Mercy, are asleep in one bed, dreaming of fast cars and hot buttered toast, the bed falls into a hole that opens in the floor, and Mercy escapes to alert the fire department. Actually, Mercy escapes to look for some of her favorite food, toast, and, not finding any, heads next door to the home of the two elderly Lincoln sisters, Baby and cranky Eugenia, in search of some sugar cookies. Looking like a 1950s-style easy-reader, with comical glossy retro-style illustrations, the book's 12 wacky slapstick chapters read like a modern-day noodlehead story.

GERM: While Mr. and Mrs. Watson laud their pig for fetching the fire department, readers will be quick to point out that the single-minded Mercy was thinking only of food, and is not such a porcine wonder after all. Talk about how Mercy inadvertently saves the day. What does it mean to do something inadvertently? On the final pages is a sneak peek at the next Mercy adventure,

Mercy Watson Goes for a Ride. Use this as a story starter for children to write and illustrate new Mercy adventures. Also at the back is a profile of author Kate DiCamillo, who describes her inspiration for the character. Make toast for all to sample and expound on its virtues.

RELATED TITLES: Egan, Tim. *Burnt Toast on Davenport Street*. Houghton Mifflin, 1997. / King-Smith, Dick. *Mr. Potter's Pet*. Little, Brown, 1996. / Palatini, Margie. *Piggie Pie*. Clarion, 1995. / Pilkey, Dav. *Dog Breath: The Horrible Trouble with Hally Tosis*. Scholastic, 1994. / Smith, Lane. *The Happy Hocky Family!* Viking, 1993. / Smith, Lane. *The Happy Hocky Family Moves to the Country*. Viking, 2003.

SUBJECTS: BREAD. FICTION BOOKS FOR EARLY GRADES. FIREFIGHTERS. HUMOROUS FICTION. NEIGHBORS. PETS. PIGS. RESCUES.

943   DiCamillo, Kate. *The Tale of Despereaux: Being the Story of a Mouse, a Princess, Some Soup, and a Spool of Thread*. Illus. by Timothy Basil Ering. Candlewick, 2003. 0-7636-1722-9. 267pp. Gr. 4–8

The only survivor of a litter, Despereaux, a ridiculously small and sickly mouse with huge ears, faints at loud noises, cannot be taught to scurry, and finds himself able to read a huge book of fairy tales in the castle library. He falls madly in love with the Princess Pea, a human girl, and breaks three of the great ancient rules of mice. He speaks to her: "My name is Despereaux. I honor you." And that, dear reader, leads to his downfall. The Mouse Council sentences him to be banished to the dungeon, where he is delivered, wearing the red thread of death, to be finished off by the rats.

GERM: Have your class draw and label portraits of each of the characters in the book, and discuss how all of them are connected. The Bloom's Taxonomy guide on page 83 provides questions and activities, if you plan to use this most magnificent Newbery Medal winner for reading aloud or book discussion groups.

RELATED TITLES: Avi. *Poppy*. Orchard, 1995. / Creech, Sharon. *Granny Torrelli Makes Soup*. HarperCollins, 2003. / DiCamillo, Kate. *Because of Winn-Dixie*. Candlewick, 2000. / DiCamillo, Kate. *The Miraculous Journey of Edward Tulane*. Candlewick, 2006. / Hoeye, Michael. *Time Stops for No Mouse*. Putnam, 2002. / Jacques, Brian. *Redwall*. Philomel, 1987. / King-Smith, Dick. *The School Mouse*. Hyperion, 1995. / King-Smith, Dick. *Three Terrible Trins*. Crown, 1994. / Oppel, Kenneth. *Silverwing*. Simon & Schuster, 1997. / Pullman, Philip. *I Was a Rat!* Knopf, 2000.

SUBJECTS: FANTASY. KINGS AND RULERS. MICE. NEWBERY MEDAL. PRINCES AND PRINCESSES. SOUP.

944   Divakaruni, Chitra Banerjee. *The Conch Bearer*. Roaring Brook, 2003. 0-7613-2793-2. 272pp. Gr. 3–6

Anand wishes that magic was real so it could help heal his sister, bring his father back home to India, and change his life as a lowly helper to the local tea merchant. Then he is sought out by a mysterious old man who claims he has come from the Brotherhood of Healers and wants Anand to join him on a dangerous journey across India.

GERM: Make a mural of the Silver Valley, the hidden valley in the Himalayas where the Brotherhood of Healers awaits the return of their magical conch. Discussion point: What magical objects from fairy tales would you like to have? How would you use them? Before Anand makes his decision whether to go with the old man or stay home to care for his mother and sister, discuss or write: Is there such a thing as magic? Should Anand take the chance? Would you? What should Anand do? Make a list of the pros and cons of each option and give him your best advice and reasons for it. Continue Anand's adventures across India, this time into the past, in the sequel, *The Mirror of Fire and Dreaming*.

RELATED TITLES: Alexander, Lloyd. *The Book of Three*. Henry Holt, 1964. / Billingsley, Franny. *The Folk Keeper*. Atheneum, 1999. / Collins, Suzanne. *Gregor the Overlander*. Scholastic, 2003. / Divakaruni, Chitra Banerjee. *The Mirror of Fire and Dreaming*. Roaring Brook, 2005. / Hirsch, Odo. *Bartlett and the City of Flames*. Bloomsbury, 2003. / Ibbotson, Eva. *The Secret of Platform 13*. Dutton, 1998. / Langrish, Katherine. *Troll Fell*. HarperCollins, 2004. / L'Engle, Madeleine. *A Wrinkle in Time*. Farrar, 1962. / Lowry, Lois. *The Giver*. Houghton Mifflin, 1993. / Pratchett, Terry. *The Wee Free Men*. HarperCollins, 2003. / Pullman, Philip. *The Golden Compass*. Knopf, 1996. / Rowling, J. K. *Harry Potter and the Sorcerer's Stone*. Scholastic, 1998. (And others in the Harry Potter series.) / Sheth, Kashmira. *Blue Jasmine*. Hyperion, 2004.

SUBJECTS: ADVENTURE AND ADVENTURERS. FANTASY. INDIA.

945 Donaldson, Julia. *The Giants and the Joneses*. Illus. by Greg Swearington. Henry Holt, 2005. 0-8050-7805-3. 215pp. Gr. 2–5

Nine-year-old giant Jambeelia loves her mij to read her that exciting bedtime story about the iggly plop who climbed up a bimplestonk into their own land of Groil. Mij says iggly plops don't exist, but Jambeelia has some bimples that she throws over the edge of Groil, and overnight, a beely bimplestonk has sprung up, waiting for her to climb down. Meanwhile, down below, Steven Jones is squabbling with his sister Colette about all the useless objects she collects, and 4-year-old sister Poppy has helped herself to a handful of Colette's feather collection. The three of them are about to be snatched up by a giant girl who brings them up the beanstalk to put in her dollhouse, and who doesn't understand a word of English.

GERM: In chapters that alternate viewpoints between the giant girl and her spiteful big brother and the three human kids trying desperately to escape, this imaginative chapter book aptly balances humor, suspense, and sibling conflict. There's even a whole new language, Groilish, which children will love to translate using context clues; turn to the back for a Groilish-English and an English-Groilish dictionary. To print out the whole dictionary of Groilish words for students to study and use, go to the author's Web site at <www.juliadonaldson.co.uk/fiction.htm>. Have them compose sentences incorporating existing Groilish vocabulary and new words that they invent, for others to translate. Writing prompt: What might happen in the sequel if Woozly came down the beanstalk to meet the Joneses?

RELATED TITLES: Beneduce, Ann Keay. *Jack and the Beanstalk*. Philomel, 1999. / Bertrand, Lynne. *Granite Baby*. Farrar, 2005. / Dahl, Roald. *The BFG*. Farrar, 1982. / Donaldson, Julia. *The Gruffalo*. Dial, 1999. / Donaldson, Julia. *The Snail and the Whale*. Dial, 2004. / Garner, Alan. *Jack and the Beanstalk*. Doubleday, 1992. / Haley, Gail E. *Jack and the Bean Tree*. Crown, 1986. / Kennedy, Richard. *Inside My Feet*. HarperCollins, 1979. / Norton, Mary. *The Borrowers*. Harcourt, 1953. / Osborne, Mary Pope. *Kate and the Beanstalk*. Atheneum, 2000. / Sleator, William. *Among the Dolls*. Dutton, 1975. / Stanley, Diane. *The Giant and the Beanstalk*. HarperCollins, 2004. / Steig, William. *The Toy Brother*. HarperCollins, 1996. / Swope, Sam. *Jack and the Seven Deadly Giants*. Farrar, 2004. / Weiss, Ellen, and Mel Friedman. *The Tiny Parents*. Knopf, 1989.

SUBJECTS: ADVENTURE AND ADVENTURERS. BROTHERS AND SISTERS. COLLECTORS AND COLLECTING. FANTASY. GIANTS. LANGUAGE. SIZE.

946 Dorris, Michael. *Sees Behind Trees*. Hyperion, 1996. 0-7868-2215-5. 104pp. Gr. 4–8

Walnut can't see well enough to hit a target with a bow and arrow, but his mother trains him in the skill of seeing with his ears. When he is able to deduce the location of a lost sewing needle, Walnut, now renamed Sees Behind Trees, is invited to accompany tribe elder Gray Fire to help find the land of water the older man visited in his youth.

GERM: Children will need to ponder, puzzle out, and discuss the layers of meaning in this quiet and introspective historical novel, set in 16th-century America. Make story maps of the journey Walnut undertakes.

RELATED TITLES: Bruchac, Joseph. *The Winter People*. Dial, 2002. / Bruchac, Joseph, and Jonathan London. *Thirteen Moons on Turtle's Back: A Native American Year of Moons*. Philomel, 1992. / Dorris, Michael. *Morning Girl*. Hyperion, 1992. / Erdrich, Louise. *The Birchbark House*. Hyperion, 1999. / Speare, Elizabeth George. *The Sign of the Beaver*. Houghton Mifflin, 1983. / Stroud, Virginia. *Doesn't Fall Off His Horse*. Dial, 1994.

SUBJECTS: BLIND. HISTORICAL FICTION. INDIANS OF NORTH AMERICA. PEOPLE WITH DISABILITIES. PHYSICALLY HANDICAPPED.

947 Duffey, Betsy. *Cody's Secret Admirer*. Illus. by Ellen Thompson. Viking, 1998. 0-670-87400-0. 90pp. Gr. 2–4

For every quandary in his life, Cody composes a "top ten" list, David Letterman style. When he receives a valentine that says, "I like you. Your Secret Admirer," he sets out to find which of the girls in his third-grade class sent it.

GERM: Ask your students: Have you ever had an embarrassing experience like Cody's, where you came to the wrong conclusion? Write or tell about it. Cody's lists ("Top Ten List of Things a Teacher Would Never Understand") will inspire your students to compile new lists that apply to their own lives. Johanna Hurwitz's *Class Clown*, Suzy Kline's *What's the Matter with Herbie Jones?*, and Paula Danziger's *Amber Brown Is Not a Crayon* are all natural follow-ups as read-alouds or read-alones when kids beg for another funny series about a third grader with troubles.

RELATED TITLES: Adoff, Arnold. *Love Letters*. Scholastic, 1997. / Duffey, Betsy. *Cody Unplugged*. Viking, 1999. / Duffey, Betsy. *Hey, New Kid!* Viking, 1996. / Duffey, Betsy. *Spotlight on Cody*. Viking, 1998. / Duffey,

Betsy. *Virtual Cody*. Viking, 1997. / Hurwitz, Johanna. *Class Clown*. Morrow, 1987. / Kline, Suzy. *What's the Matter with Herbie Jones?* Putnam, 1987. / Scribner, Virginia. *Gopher Takes Heart*. Viking, 1993.

SUBJECTS: HUMOROUS FICTION. LOVE. SCHOOLS. VALENTINE'S DAY.

948   Duffey, Betsy. *Hey, New Kid!* Illus. by Ellen Thompson. Viking, 1996. 0-670-86760-8. 89pp. Gr. 2–4

Third grader Cody figures his status as new kid will be easier to overcome if he reinvents himself. To make himself seem more interesting to his classmates, he spins a riotous web of lies and exaggerations that unravel when he attends a skating party where it becomes obvious he's not the skating champ he claimed to be. This brief, funny chapter book will strike a familiar chord with new kids everywhere.

GERM: No, Cody is not a world-class skater, he has no pet emu, and his father is not an FBI agent. Make predictions and give Cody some advice: How can he admit that he lied? What can he do to explain his behavior to his new classmates? Old- and new-timers can write about their own "first-day" experiences and how they survived.

RELATED TITLES: Danziger, Paula. *Amber Brown Is Not a Crayon*. Putnam, 1994. / Duffey, Betsy. *Cody Unplugged*. Viking, 1999. / Duffey, Betsy. *Spotlight on Cody*. Viking, 1998. / Duffey, Betsy. *Virtual Cody*. Viking, 1997. / Estes, Eleanor. *The Hundred Dresses*. Harcourt, 1944. / Giff, Patricia Reilly. *Matthew Jackson Meets the Wall*. Delacorte, 1990. / Hurwitz, Johanna. *Class Clown*. Morrow, 1987. / Joose, Barbara M. *Wild Willie and King Kyle Detectives*. Clarion, 1993. / Kline, Suzy. *Herbie Jones Moves On*. Putnam, 2003. / Kline, Suzy. *What's the Matter with Herbie Jones?* Putnam, 1987. / Marsden, Carolyn. *The Gold-Threaded Dress*. Candlewick, 2002. / Park, Barbara. *The Kid in the Red Jacket*. Knopf, 1987.

SUBJECTS: FRIENDSHIP. HUMOROUS FICTION. MOVING, HOUSEHOLD. SCHOOLS.

949   Duffey, Betsy. *Spotlight on Cody*. Illus. by Ellen Thompson. Viking, 1998. 0-670-88077-9. 74pp. Gr. 1–3

Writing poetry, telling jokes, and especially juggling eggs are not suitable talents for the third-grade talent show, so Cody Michaels racks his brain to find something original he can do.

GERM: Brainstorm a broad-based list of talents, and have your students come up with ones they're already good at and ones they'd like to work on. At the end of each chapter, we see Cody's science logbook, chronicling the transformation of caterpillar Joe into a butterfly, which will make a nice science tie-in as well as a discussion starter on how we all strive, metaphorically anyway, to unfold our wings and fly.

RELATED TITLES: Danziger, Paula. *Amber Brown Is Not a Crayon*. Putnam, 1994. / Duffey, Betsy. *Cody Unplugged*. Viking, 1999. / Duffey, Betsy. *Virtual Cody*. Viking, 1997. / Hurwitz, Johanna. *Class Clown*. Morrow, 1987. / Kline, Suzy. *What's the Matter with Herbie Jones?* Putnam, 1987. / Wojciechowski, Susan. *Don't Call Me Beanhead!* Candlewick, 1994.

SUBJECTS: BUTTERFLIES. FICTION BOOKS FOR EARLY GRADES. SCHOOLS. TALENT SHOWS.

950   Duffey, Betsy. *Utterly Yours, Booker Jones*. Viking, 1995. 0-670-86007-7. 116pp. Gr. 4–6

Now that his convalescing grandfather, Pops, has moved into his room, novelist-to-be Booker Jones has made himself at home underneath the dining room table, where he types out his novels—including *Worms from the Planet Spaghetti* and *Moon Cows*—and query letters to editors. When his best friend at Pickle Springs Middle School, Germ Germondo, volunteers Booker's help in writing a speech for a school protest rally, the usually prolific Booker suffers his first writer's block.

GERM: Duffey's descriptions of Booker's obsession with writing combine wry humor with on-target observations that should inspire listeners to think about the way they write. Have them write and present speeches.

RELATED TITLES: Byars, Betsy. *The Eighteenth Emergency*. Viking, 1973. / Byars, Betsy. *The Two-Thousand Pound Goldfish*. HarperCollins, 1982. / Clements, Andrew. *Frindle*. Simon & Schuster, 1996. / Clements, Andrew. *The School Story*. Simon & Schuster, 2001. / Codell, Esmé Raji. *Sahara Special*. Hyperion, 2003. / Creech, Sharon. *Love That Dog*. HarperCollins, 2001. / Fletcher, Ralph. *Flying Solo*. Clarion, 1998. / George, Kristine O'Connell. *Swimming Upstream: Middle School Poems*. Clarion, 2002. / Park, Barbara. *The Graduation of Jake Moon*. Atheneum, 2000. / Rocklin, Joanne. *For Your Eyes Only!* Scholastic, 1997. / Shreve, Susan. *Jonah the Whale*. Scholastic, 1998. / Slepian, Jan. *The Broccoli Tapes*. Philomel, 1988. / Snyder, Zilpha Keatley. *Libby on Wednesday*. Delacorte, 1990.

SUBJECTS: AUTHORSHIP. BROTHERS AND SISTERS. FAMILY LIFE. GRANDFATHERS. SCHOOLS. WRITING.

951 **DuPrau, Jeanne.** *The City of Ember.* **Random House, 2003. 0-375-92274-1. 270pp. Gr. 4–7**

In the city of Ember, in the year 241, the sky is always dark. There is no sun; there is no moon in Ember. The electric lights come on at 6 A.M. and go off at 9 P.M. each day. Twelve-year-olds Lina Mayfleet and Doon Harrow take it upon themselves to investigate why the lights keeps failing and to search for a way out of their doomed city.

GERM: Read this as you light into that electricity unit for science. Have your students think about words and concepts that would be unfamiliar to the isolated people of Ember. What do they depend on for survival? What aspects of our lives do we take for granted of which Lina and Doon are unaware? Readers will be eager to read the sequels, *The People of Sparks* and *The Prophet of Yonwood*.

RELATED TITLES: Collins, Suzanne. *Gregor the Overlander.* Scholastic, 2003. / Delano, Marie Ferguson. *Inventing the Future: A Photobiography of Thomas Alva Edison.* National Geographic, 2002. / DuPrau, Jeanne. *The People of Sparks.* Random House, 2004. / DuPrau, Jeanne. *The Prophet of Yonwood.* Random House, 2006. / Gutman, Dan. *Qwerty Stevens Back in Time: The Edison Mystery.* Simon & Schuster, 2001. / Hirsch, Odo. *Bartlett and the City of Flames.* Bloomsbury, 2003. / Ives, David. *Monsieur Eek.* HarperCollins, 2001. / Lowry, Lois. *The Giver.* Houghton Mifflin, 1993. / Oppel, Kenneth. *Airborn.* HarperCollins, 2004. / Schanzer, Rosalyn. *How Ben Franklin Stole the Lightning.* HarperCollins, 2003.

SUBJECTS: CITIES AND TOWNS. ELECTRICITY. FANTASY. SCIENCE FICTION.

952 **Emerson, Scott.** *The Case of the Cat with the Missing Ear.* **Illus. by Viv Mullett. Simon & Schuster, 2003. 0-689-03015-0. 237pp. Gr. 4–7**

The first volume in a ripping new mystery series—The Adventures of Samuel Blackthorne—this is set in 1887 San Francisco, where we meet Yorkshire terrier detective Samuel Blackthorne as seen through the eyes of his chronicler, friend, and fellow canine Edward R. Smithfield, a retired veterinarian. In their first thrilling case together, elegant greyhound Molly Kirkpatrick seeks their help to find out why her brother Patrick, a shy, hardworking accountant, failed to return from a neighborhood pub the night before.

GERM: In the style of Sherlock Holmes's Dr. Watson, Smithfield describes Blackthorne's "uncanny ability to see things other dogs couldn't and to smell things other dogs wouldn't" as he prowls the foggy streets of San Francisco. Blackthorne's special talent is in employing the powers of observation and deduction. After reading aloud the first chapter, in which Blackthorne explains how he has drawn so many accurate conclusions about his new friend Smithfield, ask your students to pair off and see what they can deduce about each other. For a descriptive writing activity, young authors can secretly observe another child or a teacher and compose a detailed description of that person, both physical and deductive. When they read these aloud, others can try to identify the person.

RELATED TITLES: Erickson, John R. *The Original Adventures of Hank the Cowdog.* Puffin, 1999. / Hoeye, Michael. *Time Stops for No Mouse.* Putnam, 2002. / Howe, James. *Bud Barkin, Private Eye* (Tales from the House of Bunnicula series). Atheneum, 2003. / Shipton, Paul. *Bug Muldoon: The Garden of Fear.* Viking, 2001. / Titus, Eve. *Basil of Baker Street.* McGraw-Hill, 1958. / Vande Velde, Vivian. *Smart Dog.* Harcourt, 1998. / Van Leeuwen, Jean. *The Great Christmas Kidnapping Caper.* Dial, 1975.

SUBJECTS: CALIFORNIA. CATS. DOGS. MYSTERY AND DETECTIVE STORIES. SAN FRANCISCO (CALIFORNIA). WRITING.

953 **English, Karen.** *Francie.* **Farrar, 1999. 0-374-32456-5. 199pp. Gr. 5–8**

Growing up after World War II in the tiny segregated town of Noble, Alabama, 12-year-old Frankie lives for the day she, her mother, and 10-year-old brother can leave the never-ending housework they do for the wealthier white families in town and move to Chicago where her father, a Pullman porter, has been living for a year.

GERM: Discussion point: Compare Frankie's schooling with yours. Why does Jessie Pruitt want to come to school? This unblinking look at racism and segregation will be a compelling adjunct to Ruby Bridges's autobiography, *Through My Eyes*.

RELATED TITLES: Bridges, Ruby. *Through My Eyes.* Scholastic, 1999. / Curtis, Christopher Paul. *Bud, Not Buddy.* Delacorte, 1999. / Curtis, Christopher Paul. *The Watsons Go to Birmingham, 1963.* Delacorte, 1995. / Holt, Kimberley Willis. *When Zachary Beaver Came to Town.* Henry Holt, 1999. / McKissack, Patricia C. *Run Away Home.* Scholastic, 1997. / Mitchell, Margaree King. *Uncle Jed's Barbershop.* Simon & Schuster, 1993. / Nelson, Vaunda Micheaux. *Mayfield Crossing.* Putnam, 1993. / O'Connor, Barbara. *Me and Rupert Goody.* Farrar, 1999. / Taylor, Mildred. *Roll of Thunder, Hear My Cry.* Dial, 1976.

SUBJECTS: AFRICAN AMERICANS. FRIENDSHIP. HISTORICAL FICTION. MOTHERS AND
DAUGHTERS. MULTICULTURAL BOOKS. PREJUDICE. RACE RELATIONS. SCHOOLS.

**954   Erdrich, Louise. *The Birchbark House*. Illus. by the author. Hyperion, 1999. 0-7868-2241-4.
235pp. Gr. 4–6**

In 1847, Omakayas, a 7-year-old Native American girl, spends a momentous year with her family on their island in Lake Superior, putting up with her annoying little brother Pinch, taking
care of the new baby, and taming a crow for a pet. In the winter, the smallpox comes, and she
loses her beloved baby brother to the epidemic.

GERM: Use with Native American units, reading aloud chapters where Omakayas tans hides
and scares off the crows in the field. Do some research on the Ojibwa, on smallpox, and on
maple sugaring. The sequel, *The Game of Silence*, covers another year in the life of now 9-year-
old Omakayas, starting in 1850, two years after the death of her adored baby brother Neewo.

RELATED TITLES: Brink, Carol Ryrie. *Caddie Woodlawn*. Macmillan, 1973. / Crook, Connie Brummel. *Maple
Moon*. Stoddart, 1998. / Dorris, Michael. *Morning Girl*. Hyperion, 1992. / Dorris, Michael. *Sees Behind Trees*.
Hyperion, 1996. / Erdrich, Louise. *The Game of Silence*. HarperCollins, 2005. / Esbensen, Barbara Juster. *The
Star Maiden: An Ojibway Tale*. Little, Brown, 1988. / Hill, Kirkpatrick. *Winter Camp*. McElderry, 1993. / Larry,
Charles. *Peboan and Seegwun*. Farrar, 1993. / Lunge-Larsen, Lise, and Margi Preus. *Legend of the Lady Slipper:
An Ojibwe Tale*. Houghton Mifflin, 1999. / San Souci, Robert D. *Sootface: An Ojibwa Cinderella Story*. Double-
day, 1994. / Speare, Elizabeth George. *The Sign of the Beaver*. Houghton Mifflin, 1983. / Van Laan, Nancy.
Shingebiss: An Ojibwe Legend. Houghton Mifflin, 1997. / Wilder, Laura Ingalls. *Little House in the Big Woods*.
HarperCollins, 1953.

SUBJECTS: FOLKLORE—INDIANS OF NORTH AMERICA. HISTORICAL FICTION. INDIANS OF
NORTH AMERICA. ISLANDS. MULTICULTURAL BOOKS. OJIBWA INDIANS.

**955   Erickson, John R. *The Original Adventures of Hank the Cowdog*. Illus. by Gerald L. Holmes.
Maverick Books, 1983. 0-670-88408-1. 121pp. Gr. 3–6**

In the first book of a very funny series set on a West Texas ranch, meet top dog and narrator
Hank the Cowdog, who, after quitting his post as Head of Ranch Security, runs off with the
low-down coyotes.

GERM: This first book will launch readers on to the rest of the ample series, and the interactive
Web site—<www.hankthecowdog.com>—is loads of fun. Make a chart comparing the personality differences between Hank and the coyotes.

RELATED TITLES: Emerson, Scott. *The Case of the Cat with the Missing Ear* (The Adventures of Samuel Black-
thorne, Book One). Simon & Schuster, 2003. / Hoeye, Michael. *Time Stops for No Mouse*. Putnam, 2002. /
Howe, James. *Bud Barkin, Private Eye* (Tales from the House of Bunnicula series). Atheneum, 2003. / Teague,
Mark. *Detective LaRue: Letters from the Investigation*. Scholastic, 2004.

SUBJECTS: DOGS. HUMOROUS FICTION. MYSTERY AND DETECTIVE STORIES. RANCH LIFE.
TEXAS. WEST (U.S.).

**956   Evans, Douglas. *Apple Island, or The Truth About Teachers*. Illus. by Larry Di Fiori. Front
Street, 1998. 1-886910-25-1. 144pp. Gr. 3–5**

Fourth grader Bradley used to like school, but his new teacher, the huge, menacing Mrs. Gross,
is horribly crabby and dull and seems to hate kids. On a class field trip via blimp to Apple
Island, which is inhabited solely by crabby teachers who plan to take over the world's schools,
only Bradley has the spunk to leave his compliant classmates and figure out a way to stop the
awful teachers.

GERM: Teachers will enjoy the sly satire of how the kind teachers were run out by the crabby,
crab apple-eating teachers thanks to Project Misteach. Students can discuss and write opinion
papers on what makes a great teacher. And, after hearing about how all school supplies such as
chalk, crayons, paper, pencils, and ink originated on Apple Island, children can write creative
descriptions of how other school-related items might be harvested there.

RELATED TITLES: Amato, Mary. *The Word Eater*. Holiday House, 2000. / Dahl, Roald. *Matilda*. Viking, 1988.
/ Evans, Douglas. *The Classroom at the End of the Hall*. Front Street, 1996. / Evans, Douglas. *Math Rashes and
Other Classroom Tales*. Front Street, 2004. / Gutman, Dan. *Miss Daisy Is Crazy*. HarperCollins, 2004. / Hornik,
Laurie Miller. *The Secrets of Ms. Snickle's Class*. Clarion, 2001. / Hornik, Laurie Miller. *Zoo School*. Clarion, 2004.
/ MacDonald, Amy. *No More Nasty*. Farrar, 2001. / Sachar, Louis. *Sideways Stories from Wayside School*. Mor-
row, 1985. / Sachar, Louis. *Wayside School Is Falling Down*. Lothrop, 1989. / Vande Velde, Vivian. *Smart Dog*.
Harcourt, 1998.

SUBJECTS: FANTASY. HUMOROUS FICTION. SCHOOLS. TEACHERS.

957 Evans, Douglas. *The Classroom at the End of the Hall*. Illus. by Larry Di Fiori. Front Street, 1996. 1-886910-07-3. 132pp. Gr. 2–5

In the classroom at the end of the hall, Roger, class pain-in-the-neck, gets his own genie; Emily contends with her own Messy Desk Pest lurking in the clutter; Charlie learns to draw; and Kenneth becomes a reader. In each of 11 imaginative chapters, a student contends with a problem—daydreaming, showing off, copying—and with a bit of help, overcomes it.

GERM: Write new chapters depicting other singular students and how they learned something useful. Follow up with the companion novels *Apple Island* and *Math Rashes*.

RELATED TITLES: Amato, Mary. *The Word Eater*. Holiday House, 2000. / Dahl, Roald. *Matilda*. Viking, 1988. / Evans, Douglas. *Apple Island, or The Truth About Teachers*. Front Street, 1998. / Evans, Douglas. *Math Rashes and Other Classroom Tales*. Front Street, 2004. / Gutman, Dan. *Miss Daisy Is Crazy*. HarperCollins, 2004. / Hornik, Laurie Miller. *The Secrets of Ms. Snickle's Class*. Clarion, 2001. / Hornik, Laurie Miller. *Zoo School*. Clarion, 2004. / King-Smith, Dick. *Clever Lollipop*. Candlewick, 2003. / MacDonald, Amy. *No More Nasty*. Farrar, 2001. / MacDonald, Betty. *Mrs. Piggle-Wiggle* (and others in the series). Lippincott, 1975. / Sachar, Louis. *Sideways Stories from Wayside School*. Morrow, 1985. / Sachar, Louis. *Wayside School Is Falling Down*. Lothrop, 1989. / Vande Velde, Vivian. *Smart Dog*. Harcourt, 1998.

SUBJECTS: BEHAVIOR. FANTASY. HUMOROUS FICTION. SCHOOLS. SHORT STORIES. TEACHERS.

958 Evans, Douglas. *MVP*: *Magellan Voyage Project*. Illus. by John Shelley. Front Street, 2004. 1-932425-13-6. 232pp. Gr. 3–6

Instead of heading off to summer camp, 12-year-old Adam Story sets off on an around-the-world adventure contest to be the first kid to circumnavigate the globe via land and sea in 40 days.

GERM: Trace Adam's route on a world map and have your armchair travelers research and vicariously describe the sights to see at each of his stops along the way. Inspired by Adam's favorite palindrome, Madam, I'm Adam, investigate others, starting with the ones in Jon Agee's *Go Hang a Salami! I'm a Lasagna Hog! And Other Palindromes*.

RELATED TITLES: Adler, David A. *A Picture Book of Amelia Earhart*. Holiday House, 1998. / Agee, Jon. *Go Hang a Salami! I'm a Lasagna Hog! And Other Palindromes*. Farrar, 1992. / Brown, Don. *Alice Ramsey's Grand Adventure*. Houghton Mifflin, 1997. / Brown, Don. *Ruth Law Thrills a Nation*. Ticknor & Fields, / Christensen, Bonnie. *The Daring Nellie Bly: America's Star Reporter*. Knopf, 2003. / Krensky, Stephen. *Nellie Bly: A Name to Be Reckoned With*. Aladdin, 2003.

SUBJECTS: ADVENTURE AND ADVENTURERS. CONTESTS. VOYAGES AND TRAVELS. VOYAGES AROUND THE WORLD.

959 Farmer, Nancy. *The Sea of Trolls*. Atheneum, 2004. 0-689-86744-1. 459pp. Gr. 5–8

Druid bard-in-training Jack and his little sister Lucy are kidnapped from their homeland by Olaf One-Brow and his Viking Berserker crew and taken by ship across the north seas to King Ivar the Boneless, king of the Northmen, and his half-troll wife, Queen Frith.

GERM: You may not want to read this entire book aloud, as it's long and sometimes gory, but it's so crammed full of adventure, folklore, witty dialogue, and literary allusions, including a retelling of Beowulf, that it's a goldmine for readers and booktalkers. Pair it with Eric A. Kimmel's *The Hero Beowulf*, a picture-book overview of the epic, and with Katherine Langrish's novel *Troll Fell*.

RELATED TITLES: Billingsley, Franny. *The Folk Keeper*. Atheneum, 1999. / Collins, Suzanne. *Gregor the Overlander*. Scholastic, 2003. / D'Aulaire, Ingri, and Edgar Parin D'Aulaire. *D'Aulaires' Trolls*. Doubleday, 1972. / Hirsch, Odo. *Bartlett and the City of Flames*. Bloomsbury, 2003. / Kimmel, Eric A. *The Hero Beowulf*. Farrar, 2005. / Langrish, Katherine. *Troll Fell*. HarperCollins, 2004. / L'Engle, Madeleine. *A Wrinkle in Time*. Farrar, 1962. / Lunge-Larsen, Lise. *The Troll with No Heart in His Body: And Other Tales of Trolls from Norway*. Houghton Mifflin, 1999. / Pratchett, Terry. *The Wee Free Men*. HarperCollins, 2003. / Pullman, Philip. *The Golden Compass*. Knopf, 1996. / Riordan, Rick. *The Lightning Thief* (Percy Jackson and the Olympians, Book 1). Miramax/Hyperion, 2005. / Rowling, J. K. *Harry Potter and the Sorcerer's Stone*. Scholastic, 1998. (And others in the Harry Potter series.)

SUBJECTS: ADVENTURE AND ADVENTURERS. BARDS AND BARDISM. BROTHERS AND SISTERS. FANTASY. KIDNAPPING. MYTHOLOGY. SAXONS. TROLLS. VIKINGS. VOYAGES AND TRAVELS.

960 Fine, Anne. *The Jamie and Angus Stories.* **Illus. by Penny Dale. Candlewick, 2002. 0-7636-1862-4. 110pp. Gr. PreK–1**

Jamie's constant companion is his new stuffed bull, Angus, whose silky white fur is changed forever when Granny washes him in the machine. Together, boy and his adored bull get put to bed by Uncle Edward, who teaches Angus to jump; attend Flora the babysitter's wedding; and even go to the hospital when Jamie has a terrible stomachache. This low-key but engaging chapter book for younger listeners sports perceptive pencil drawings throughout.

GERM: Children can bring in a favorite stuffed animal and relate an adventure the two have had together.

RELATED TITLES: Blumenthal, Deborah. *Don't Let the Peas Touch! And Other Stories.* Scholastic, 2004. / Cameron, Ann. *The Stories Huey Tells.* Knopf, 1995. / Cameron, Ann. *The Stories Julian Tells.* Yearling, 1989. / Greene, Stephanie. *Show and Tell.* Clarion, 1998. / Hurwitz, Johanna. *"E" Is for Elisa.* Morrow, 1991. / Hurwitz, Johanna. *Russell Sprouts.* Morrow, 1987. / Hurwitz, Johanna. *Superduper Teddy.* Morrow, 1980. / Lowry, Lois. *All About Sam.* Houghton Mifflin, 1988. / Lowry, Lois. *Zooman Sam.* Houghton Mifflin, 1999.

SUBJECTS: FAMILY LIFE. FICTION BOOKS FOR EARLY GRADES. GRANDMOTHERS. STUFFED ANIMALS. UNCLES.

961 Fleischman, Paul. *Seedfolks.* **Illus. by Judy Pedersen. HarperCollins, 1997. 0-06-027472-7. 69pp. Gr. 5–8**

As a tribute to her father who died in her native country, Vietnam, before she was born, Kim plants lima bean seeds in a vacant junk-filled lot in her Cleveland neighborhood in April, drawing the attention of elderly Ana, staring out her window three stories up. Pretty soon, the whole neighborhood is involved, cleaning up the city lot, planting plots of flowers and vegetables, making tentative contact with each other. Fleischman's slim, spare character study novel is narrated by a rainbow mix of 13 residents, all of whom get involved with the miracle of gardening and the concept of community.

GERM: As Fleischman suggested with his similarly formatted Civil War book, *Bull Run*, you can hand out a chapter per student and have them read their character's story aloud to the rest of the class, Reader's Theater style.

RELATED TITLES: Fleischman, Paul. *Bull Run.* HarperCollins, 1993. / Quattlebaum, Mary. *Jackson Jones and the Puddle of Thorns.* Delacorte, 1994.

SUBJECTS: ASIAN AMERICANS. CITIES AND TOWNS. GARDENING. MULTICULTURAL BOOKS. NEIGHBORHOODS. READER'S THEATER. VIETNAMESE AMERICANS.

962 Fleischman, Sid. *Bandit's Moon.* **Greenwillow, 1998. 0-688-15830-7. 144pp. Gr. 4–6**

Hoping to find her big brother Lank in the goldfields of California, 11-year-old orphan Annyrose Smith hooks up with notorious Mexican outlaw Joaquín, who needs her to teach him to read. Annyrose's loyalties shift from the good-hearted but fearless Joaquín to her own brother, who is part of a posse hunting him down.

GERM: As always, Fleischman throws in an amiable blend of nonstop action, humor, a feisty main character, and a bit of social history. The story line, which empathizes with the Mexicans who lost land and lives when the Yankees took over California, will appeal to the Robin Hood instincts of children and could spur a discussion on the less tidy aspects of American land grabs and treatment of its minorities.

RELATED TITLES: Blumberg, Rhoda. *The Great American Gold Rush.* Bradbury, 1989. / Cushman, Karen. *The Ballad of Lucy Whipple.* Clarion, 1996. / Fleischman, Sid. *By the Great Horn Spoon.* Little, Brown, 1963. / Freedman, Russell. *Children of the Wild West.* Clarion, 1983. / Karr, Kathleen. *The Great Turkey Walk.* Farrar, 1998. / Ryan, Pam Muñoz. *Riding Freedom.* Scholastic, 1998. / Siebert, Diane. *Rhyolite: The True Story of a Ghost Town.* Clarion, 2003.

SUBJECTS: ADVENTURE AND ADVENTURERS. CALIFORNIA. GOLD RUSH. HISTORICAL FICTION. ROBBERS AND OUTLAWS. WEST (U.S.)—HISTORY—FICTION.

963 Fletcher, Ralph. *Flying Solo.* **Clarion, 1998. 0-395-87323-1. 158pp. Gr. 4–6**

Sixth-grade teacher Mr. Fabiano is out on Friday, but the sub is sick too; a snafu in the office results in no coverage for his room, unbeknownst to the principal and staff. When the 15 kids realize they're on their own, they vote to run the class themselves. "It's wrong, it's dangerous, somebody could get hurt," says Jessica, but the others prevail. They fill the day with journal writing, a bit of fooling around, and some serious discussions about a student from their class who died early in the year. Why has classmate Rachel not spoken a word aloud since Tommy's death?

GERM: The mixture of humor and insight will lead your group into a discussion of the many implications of Mr. Fab's class's "Kids rule!" day and anaysis of the personalities and actions of each character. Ask your students to write about what the class might do if left to their own devices for the day.

RELATED TITLES: Clements, Andrew. *Frindle*. Simon & Schuster, 1996. / Clements, Andrew. *The School Story*. Simon & Schuster, 2001. / Clements, Andrew. *A Week in the Woods*. Simon & Schuster, 2002. / Duffey, Betsy. *Utterly Yours, Booker Jones*. Viking, 1995. / Gantos, Jack. *Joey Pigza Swallowed the Key*. Farrar, 1998. / Rocklin, Joanne. *For Your Eyes Only!* Scholastic, 1997. / Shreve, Susan. *Jonah the Whale*. Scholastic, 1998. / Slepian, Jan. *The Broccoli Tapes*. Philomel, 1988. / Snyder, Zilpha Keatley. *Libby on Wednesday*. Delacorte, 1990. / Spinelli, Jerry. *Loser*. HarperCollins, 2002.

SUBJECTS: DEATH. MUTISM, ELECTIVE. SCHOOLS. TEACHERS.

964 Franklin, Christine L. *Lone Wolf*. Candlewick, 1997. 1-56402-935-2. 220pp. Gr. 4–6

Living with his taciturn father in the northern Minnesota woods, Perry tries hard not to remember his little sister who died in a car accident or his mom who left their Minnesota home and whose unopened letters he saves but won't read. When Willow Pestalozzi, a girl his age, befriends him, they search the woods for the wolf Willow has sighted, play Monopoly on Saturday nights with her warm, loving family, and share Perry's secret cave. Throughout this piercingly reflective and perceptive character study, we root for Perry to finally talk to his father and for both to break free of their self-imposed isolation.

GERM: Compare and contrast this with other stories of children who come to terms with less than stellar family situations. How do the main characters help themselves in books such as Marion Dane Bauer's *A Question of Trust*, Janet Taylor Lisle's *How I Became a Writer and Oggie Learned to Drive*, and Rodman Philbrick's *The Young Man and the Sea*?

RELATED TITLES: Bauer, Marion Dane. *A Question of Trust*. Scholastic, 1994. / Byars, Betsy. *Cracker Jackson*. Viking, 1985. / Cleary, Beverly. *Strider*. Morrow, 1991. / Duffey, Betsy. *Coaster*. Viking, 1994. / Fenner, Carol. *Randall's Wall*. McElderry, 1991. / Fox, Paula. *Monkey Island*. Orchard, 1991. / Lisle, Janet Taylor. *How I Became a Writer and Oggie Learned to Drive*. Philomel, 2002. / Philbrick, Rodman. *The Young Man and the Sea*. Blue Sky/Scholastic, 2004. / Slepian, Jan. *The Broccoli Tapes*. Philomel, 1988.

SUBJECTS: DEATH. DIVORCE. FAMILY PROBLEMS. FRIENDSHIP. SELF-ESTEEM. WOLVES.

965 Gaiman, Neil. *Coraline*. Illus. by Dave McKean. HarperCollins, 2002. 0-380-97778-8. 163pp. Gr. 4–7

Coraline has just moved with her parents to a flat in a big old house. Behind the carved wooden door at the far corner of the drawing room is a wall of bricks. When the wall disappears, Coraline discovers an identical apartment and another mother, almost like Coraline's mother, only with skin as white as paper, dark-red curved fingernails, and eyes that are black, shiny buttons.

GERM: Discuss the plot elements that make this such an effective suspense story to read aloud or booktalk: foreshadowing, sinister characters, adults who don't or won't listen or help, voices in the dark, lots of rats, and an unflappable heroine.

RELATED TITLES: Anderson, M. T. *Whales on Stilts*. Harcourt, 2005. / Bellairs, John. *The House with a Clock in Its Walls*. Dial, 1973. / Corbett, Sue. *12 Again*. Dutton, 2002. / Fleischman, Paul. *The Half-a-Moon Inn*. HarperCollins, 1980. / Gaiman, Neil. *The Wolves in the Walls*. HarperCollins, 2003. / Ibbotson, Eva. *The Secret of Platform 13*. Dutton, 1998. / Kennedy, Richard. *Inside My Feet*. HarperCollins, 1979. / Rowling, J. K. *Harry Potter and the Sorcerer's Stone*. Scholastic, 1998. (And others in the Harry Potter series.) / Sleator, William. *Among the Dolls*. Dutton, 1975. / Snicket, Lemony. *The Bad Beginning*. HarperCollins, 2000. / Wallace, Barbara Brooks. *Peppermints in the Parlor*. Atheneum, 1980.

SUBJECTS: FANTASY. PARENT AND CHILD. SUPERNATURAL. SUSPENSE.

966 Gantos, Jack. *Joey Pigza Swallowed the Key*. Farrar, 1998. 0-374-33664-4. 154pp. Gr. 5–7

Joey describes his attempts to get his out-of-control life together, including his "wired" state when his meds wear off and he can't regulate his impulsive, over-the-top behavior at school and at home with Grandma. His wired dad ran off when Joey was in kindergarten; his mom ran after him. Now she's back, trying to make up for her absence. She wants the best for Joey, but love and new rules are not enough. He swallows his house key; goes berserk on a class field trip to a farm; and, in a scene that will make you scream, accidentally cuts off the tip of a girl's nose with scissors. Sent to a special ed center, Joey finally starts to learn how to control his impulsive behavior, thanks to his new teacher, Special Ed, and to new meds.

GERM: You'll gain new insight into the "wired" kids, the hyperactive kids with ADHD on

Ritalin, and see what goes on in their heads. As Special Ed says, "You gotta face the hand you're dealt with and deal with it, and make your problems be the smallest part of who you are." Ask your crew to write and discuss how that statement applies to them.

RELATED TITLES: Clements, Andrew. *A Week in the Woods*. Simon & Schuster, 2002. / Fenner, Carol. *Randall's Wall*. McElderry, 1991. / Fine, Anne. *The Tulip Touch*. Little, Brown, 1987. / Gantos, Jack. *Joey Pigza Loses Control*. Farrar, 2000. / Gantos, Jack. *What Would Joey Do?* Farrar, 2002. / Gauthier, Gail. *A Year with Butch and Spike*. Putnam, 1998. / Mazer, Harry. *The Wild Kid*. Simon & Schuster, 1998. / Quinn, Patricia O. *Putting on the Breaks: Young People's Guide to Understanding Attention Deficit Hyperactivity Disorder (ADHD)*. Magination, 1991. / Riordan, Rick. *The Lightning Thief* (Percy Jackson and the Olympians, Book 1). Miramax/Hyperion, 2005. / Shannon, David. *No, David!* Scholastic, 1998. / Spinelli, Jerry. *Loser*. HarperCollins, 2002. / Wolff, Virginia Euwer. *Probably Still Nick Swanson*. Henry Holt, 1988.

SUBJECTS: ATTENTION-DEFICIT HYPERACTIVITY DISORDER. BEHAVIOR. SCHOOLS. SINGLE-PARENT FAMILIES. TEACHERS.

967   Gauthier, Gail. *My Life Among the Aliens*. Putnam, 1996. 0-399-22945-0. 104pp. Gr. 3–5

In a very funny chapter book, Will describes his seven encounters with aliens who might look like regular kids but are not. His disbelieving mom is one reason the aliens keep coming—they can't get enough of her healthy, home-baked bran muffins with raisins, which Will wouldn't think of eating.

GERM: Will and his little brother Rob probably aren't so far-fetched when they contend that aliens are around us all the time, though only some of us can see them. Perhaps your students will recall similar run-ins with out-of-this-world folks.

RELATED TITLES: Bechard, Margaret. *Star Hatchling*. Viking, 1995. / Brittain, Bill. *Shape-Changer*. HarperCollins, 1994. / Conly, Jane Leslie. *The Rudest Alien on Earth*. Henry Holt, 2002. / Cutler, Jane. *Rats!* Farrar, 1996. / Etra, Jonathan, and Stephanie Spinner. *Aliens for Breakfast*. Random House, 1988. / King-Smith, Dick. *Harriet's Hare*. Crown, 1995. / Klause, Annette. *Alien Secrets*. Delacorte, 1993. / McNaughton, Colin. *Here Come the Aliens*. Candlewick, 1995. / Pinkwater, Daniel. *Fat Men from Space*. Dodd, Mead, 1977. / Pinkwater, Daniel. *Wallpaper from Space*. Atheneum, 1996. / Sadler, Marilyn. *Alistair in Outer Space*. Prentice Hall, 1984. / Service, Pamela. *Stinker from Space*. Scribner, 1988. / Sleator, William. *The Night the Heads Came*. Dutton, 1996. / Slote, Alfred. *My Robot Buddy*. HarperTrophy, 1986. / Slote, Alfred. *My Trip to Alpha I*. HarperCollins, 1991. / Van Allsburg, Chris. *Zathura*. Houghton Mifflin, 2002.

SUBJECTS: BROTHERS. EXTRATERRESTRIAL LIFE. HUMOROUS FICTION. MOTHERS AND SONS. SCIENCE FICTION.

968   Gauthier, Gail. *A Year with Butch and Spike*. Putnam, 1998. 0-399-23216-8. 216pp. Gr. 4–6

Perfect kid Jasper Gordon is aghast to find himself sitting between Butch and Spike Cootch, bad boy cousins who take pleasure in stirring up strict Mrs. McNulty's sixth-grade classroom.

GERM: Contrast the personalities and trouble stirred up by boys versus girls in *Bad Girls* by Cynthia Voigt.

RELATED TITLES: Byars, Betsy. *The 18th Emergency*. Viking, 1973. / Fletcher, Ralph. *Flying Solo*. Clarion, 1998. / Gantos, Jack. *Joey Pigza Swallowed the Key*. Farrar, 1998. / Getz, David. *Almost Famous*. Henry Holt, 1992. / Gorman, Carol. *Dork on the Run*. HarperCollins, 2002. / Korman, Gordon. *This Can't Be Happening at Macdonald Hall*. Scholastic, 1978. / Naylor, Phyllis Reynolds. *The Boys Start the War*. Delacorte, 1993. / Robinson, Barbara. *The Best Christmas Pageant Ever*. HarperCollins, 1972. / Robinson, Barbara. *The Best School Year Ever*. HarperCollins, 1994. / Shreve, Susan. *Jonah the Whale*. Scholastic, 1998. / Spinelli, Jerry. *Crash*. Knopf, 1996. / Spinelli, Jerry. *Wringer*. HarperCollins, 1997. / Voigt, Cynthia. *Bad Girls*. Scholastic, 1996.

SUBJECTS: BEHAVIOR. HUMOROUS FICTION. SCHOOLS. TEACHERS.

969   George, Twig C. *A Dolphin Named Bob*. Illus. by Christine Herman Merrill. HarperCollins, 1996. 0-06-025363-0. 72pp. Gr. 2–5

In a realistic fiction novel based on the real lives of several dolphins, a 10-month-old Atlantic bottlenose dolphin is washed ashore after a storm and rescued by a woman who brings her to the Maryland State Aquarium. Aster becomes one of the nine dolphins who perform daily for delighted visitors, and, years later, gives birth to an undernourished calf the staff names Bob, who not only survives but becomes the star of the aquarium.

GERM: Get some more firsthand dolphin info from Kathleen Dudzinski's *Meeting Dolphins: My Adventures in the Sea*. One of the five short stories in Michael J. Rosen's *The Heart Is Big Enough*, "The Trust of a Dolphin," is about 12-year-old Matthew, who hopes to swim with the dolphins at a Florida marine mammal research lab.

RELATED TITLES: Dudzinski, Kathleen. *Meeting Dolphins: My Adventures in the Sea*. National Geographic Society, 2000. / Hesse, Karen. *The Music of Dolphins*. Scholastic, 1996. / Rosen, Michael J. *The Heart Is Big Enough: Five Stories*. Harcourt, 1997.

SUBJECTS: DOLPHINS.

970 **Geras, Adèle.** *The Cats of Cuckoo Square: Two Stories*. **Illus. by Tony Ross. Delacorte, 2001. 0-385-72926-X. 190pp. Gr. 1–4**

Cats Blossom and Perkins, two of the four amiable cat friends who hang out in the gardens of Cuckoo Square, each narrate an episode about life with their human families. In "Blossom's Revenge," the fluffy black-and-white cat squares off against the family's 6-year-old troublemaking niece, Prissy, who comes to stay. Old, wise Perkins tells how he inadvertently became known as an artist in "Picasso Perkins."

GERM: Make a class chart outlining the two cats' personal attributes, quirks, talents, and stories. Ask your pet fanciers what amazing stories their pets would tell if they could talk. Give the dog-lovers equal time with Madeleine L'Engle's *The Other Dog*, narrated by particular poodle Touché. Learn more about the whims and fancies of pets with Donald Hall's picture book *I Am the Dog, I Am the Cat*. And, of course, you can stage a Paint Your Pet Contest for the Picassos in your group. Dick King-Smith's *Lady Lollipop* is about another spoiled young lady, Princess Penelope, who is used to getting her own way until she learns some manners from an intelligent pig.

RELATED TITLES: Child, Lauren. *That Pesky Rat*. Candlewick, 2002. / Hall, Donald. *I Am the Dog, I Am the Cat*. Dial, 1994. / King-Smith, Dick. *Lady Lollipop*. Candlewick, 2001. / King-Smith, Dick. *Martin's Mice*. Crown, 1989. / King-Smith, Dick. *The School Mouse*. Little, Brown, 1995. / L'Engle, Madeleine. *The Other Dog*. SeaStar, 2001. / LeRoy, Gen. *Taxi Cat and Huey*. HarperCollins, 1992.

SUBJECTS: CATS. PERSONAL NARRATIVES. FICTION BOOKS FOR EARLY GRADES.

971 **Gilson, Jamie.** *Stink Alley*. **HarperCollins, 2002. 0-688-17864-2. 183pp. Gr. 4–7**

After Lizzie's father dies, William Brewster, the stern, stark leader of a group of persecuted English Separatists who fled to Holland in 1608, takes her in, even though he finds her stubborn, disobedient, and full of sinful pride. When the resourceful girl gets a job as a cook's assistant in the nearby miller's house, she befriends their 8-year-old son, a mischievous boy who loves to draw.

GERM: Though Lizzie is a fictional character, this well-researched and lively historical novel fills us in on what happened in the years before the Pilgrims left for America in 1620. It gives a clear picture of what life was like for those who braved terrible hardships to come to the New World. For added background, your crew will need to do some background research on the Separatists, Holland, and the painter Rembrandt. Once the Pilgrims arrived in the New World, life was hard, as you'll see when you read *A Killing in Plymouth Colony* by Carol Otis Hurst and Rebecca Otis, a mystery loosely based on a true story from 1630.

RELATED TITLES: Blackwood, Gary L. *The Shakespeare Stealer*. Dutton, 1998. / Cushman, Karen. *The Ballad of Lucy Whipple*. Clarion, 1996. / Graham, Harriet. *A Boy and His Bear*. McElderry, 1996. / Hurst, Carol Otis, and Rebecca Otis. *A Killing in Plymouth Colony*. Houghton Mifflin, 2003. / Osborne, Mary Pope. *Adaline Falling Star*. Scholastic, 2000. / Thomas, Jane Resh. *The Princess in the Pigpen*. Clarion, 1989. / Waters, Kate. *On the Mayflower: Voyage of the Ship's Apprentice and a Passenger Girl*. Scholastic, 1996. / Waters, Kate. *Samuel Eaton's Day: A Day in the Life of a Pilgrim Boy*. Scholastic, 1993. / Waters, Kate. *Sarah Morton's Day: A Day in the Life of a Pilgrim Girl*. Scholastic, 1989.

SUBJECTS: ARTISTS. COOKS. HISTORICAL FICTION. NETHERLANDS. PURITANS. VOYAGES AND TRAVELS.

972 **Gorman, Carol.** *Dork on the Run*. **HarperCollins, 2002. 0-06-029409-4. 184pp. Gr. 3–6**

Having overcome dorkiness at his new school, Jerry Flack decides to run for sixth-grade president even though his opponent will be popular but obnoxious Gabe, who considers dirty tricks fair game. At first, Jerry responds in kind, but then he has to decide whether he is just as amoral as Gabe if he gets even. And how do you stop a guy who will stop at nothing?

GERM: Discussion points: As Jerry retaliates against Gabe's tricks, he wonders if he's just lowering himself to Gabe's level. How does he handle each of Gabe's humiliations? Have you ever come up against a bully? How did you deal with it? Write and deliver a campaign speech laying out what you'd do if you were class president.

RELATED TITLES: Amato, Mary. *The Word Eater*. Holiday House, 2000. / Fleischman, Paul. *Weslandia*. Candlewick, 1999. / Gorman, Carol. *Dork in Disguise*. HarperCollins, 1999. / Gorman, Carol. *A Midsummer Night's Dork*. HarperCollins, 2004. / Gutman, Dan. *The Kid Who Ran for President*. Scholastic, 1996. / Hurwitz, Johanna. *Class President*. Morrow, 1990. / Park, Barbara. *The Graduation of Jake Moon*. Atheneum, 2000. / Park, Barbara. *Rosie Swanson, Fourth-Grade Geek for President*. Knopf, 1991. / Spinelli, Jerry. *Crash*. Knopf, 1996. / Spinelli, Jerry. *Loser*. HarperCollins, 2002. / Spinelli, Jerry. *Maniac Magee*. Little, Brown, 1990. / Spinelli, Jerry. *Wringer*. HarperCollins, 1997.

SUBJECTS: BEHAVIOR. ELECTIONS. POPULARITY. PRACTICAL JOKES. SCHOOLS. SELF-ACCEPTANCE.

973   Graham, Harriet. *A Boy and His Bear*. McElderry, 1996. 0-689-80943-3. 196pp. Gr. 4–7

In a splendid historical novel about bear-baiting, set in Shakespeare's London at the end of the 16th century, young animal-lover Dickon must tame and teach a bear cub to dance in order to save it from sure death at the Bear Garden, a more violent place of entertainment than the nearby Globe Theater.

GERM: Students will be curious to research the time period to find out more about fairs, street performers, apprentices, and, of course, bears.

RELATED TITLES: Aliki. *William Shakespeare and the Globe*. HarperCollins, 1999. / Blackwood, Gary L. *The Shakespeare Stealer*. Dutton, 1998. / Garfield, Leon. *Shakespeare Stories*. Houghton Mifflin, 1995. / Mannis, Celeste Davis. *The Queen's Progress: An Elizabethan Alphabet*. Viking, 2003. / Morey, Walt. *Gentle Ben*. Dutton, 1965. / Stanley, Diane. *Bard of Avon: The Story of William Shakespeare*. Morrow, 1992. / Thomas, Jane Resh. *The Princess in the Pigpen*. Clarion, 1989.

SUBJECTS: APPRENTICES. BEARS. ENGLAND. FRIENDSHIP. HISTORICAL FICTION.

974   Grahame, Kenneth. *The Reluctant Dragon*. Illus. by Inga Moore. Candlewick, 2004. 0-7636-2199-4. Unp. Gr. 3–6

Kenneth Grahame's classic 1898 story of a boy and a dragon who prefers not to fight St. George, the valiant knight, has been carefully abridged and illustrated in playful, merry, colored pencil and ink illustrations, set in a bucolic English village. When the little boy, who knows about dragons because he's fond of reading, befriends the lazy, thoughtful, poetry-loving, blue-scaled dragon, he thinks up a way for the dragon and knight to stage a fight that will let them both keep their heads and save face in the village.

GERM: Pair this fetching tale with *Saint George and the Dragon*, Margaret Hodges's Caldecott Medal-winning version of the heroic English legend from Edmund Spenser's 16th-century epic poem "The Faerie Queen." Introduce Grahame's other classic, *The Wind in the Willows*.

RELATED TITLES: Domanska, Janina. *King Krakus and the Dragon*. Greenwillow, 1979. / Gannett, Ruth Stiles. *My Father's Dragon*. Random House, 1986. / Grahame, Kenneth. *The Wind in the Willows*. Scribner, 1983. / Hodges, Patricia. *Saint George and the Dragon*. Little, Brown, 1984. / Osborne, Mary Pope. *Favorite Medieval Tales*. Scholastic, 1998. / Nolen, Jerdine. *Raising Dragons*. Harcourt, 1998. / Peet, Bill. *How Droofus the Dragon Lost His Head*. Houghton Mifflin, 1971. / Prelutsky, Jack. *The Dragons Are Singing Tonight*. Greenwillow, 1993. / Rupp, Rebecca. *The Dragon of Lonely Island*. Candlewick, 1998. / Rupp, Rebecca. *The Return of the Dragon*. Candlewick, 2005. / Tucker, Kathy. *The Seven Chinese Sisters*. Albert Whitman, 2003. / Sterman, Betsy, and Samuel Sterman. *Backyard Dragon*. HarperCollins, 1993. / Van Woerkom, Dorothy. *Alexandra the Rock-Eater*. Knopf, 1978. / Wrede, Patricia. *Dealing with Dragons*. Harcourt, 1990.

SUBJECTS: DRAGONS. FANTASY. GEORGE, SAINT. KNIGHTS AND KNIGHTHOOD.

975   Greene, Stephanie. *Owen Foote, Frontiersman*. Illus. by Martha Weston. Clarion, 1999. 0-395-61578-X. 88pp. Gr. 1–3

Owen's fort is his kingdom, and when two brothers try to kick him out of it, he must come up with a "diabolical plan" to teach them a lesson. Readers will admire Owen's grit and the honest portrayal of a real kid who figures out a clever way to outsmart kids bigger and stronger than he is.

GERM: Research Owen's hero, Daniel Boone, to find out who he was and what he did. Discussion point: What can Owen do to protect his beloved fort and to deal with the bullies in a way that will not prove injurious to his health? As for that fort, all kids wish they had one, so have them design their own dream forts and decide what they'd store in there.

RELATED TITLES: Cameron, Ann. *The Stories Huey Tells*. Knopf, 1995. / Cameron, Ann. *The Stories Julian Tells*. Yearling, 1989. / Caseley, Judith. *Harry and Arney*. Greenwillow, 1994. / Danziger, Paula. *Amber Brown Is Not a Crayon*. Putnam, 1994. / Duffey, Betsy. *The Gadget War*. Viking, 1991. / Duffey, Betsy. *Hey, New Kid!* Viking, 1996. / Greene, Stephanie. Owen Foote series. Clarion. / Greene, Stephanie. *Show and Tell*. Clarion,

1998. / Kline, Suzy. *What's the Matter with Herbie Jones?* Putnam, 1987. / Larson, Kirby. *Cody and Quinn, Sitting in a Tree.* Holiday House, 1996. / Petersen, P. J. *The Sub.* Dutton, 1993. / Sachar, Louis. *Marvin Redpost: Alone in His Teacher's House.* Random House, 1994.

SUBJECTS: BULLIES. FICTION BOOKS FOR EARLY GRADES. FRIENDSHIP. MOTHERS AND SONS. OUTDOOR LIFE. TREE HOUSES.

976   Greene, Stephanie. *Show and Tell.* **Illus. by Elaine Clayton. Clarion, 1998. 0-395-88898-0. 84pp. Gr. K–2**

Woody's sure that his adored second-grade teacher, Mrs. Carver, will love his just-deceased aquarium fish, Huey, dead or alive, and he brings it to class in a little box for show-and-tell. Unfortunately, there's a new student teacher in his class. She is not the least bit empathetic about the importance of Woody's fish and tosses it in the garbage. Miss Plunkett and Woody start off on the wrong foot, and even though Woody is sure it's against the law for teachers to hate children or stay mad at them, she does seem to have it in for him.

GERM: New teachers who are still sorting out their own discipline policies will enjoy seeing both sides in this thoughtful and funny chapter book. Ask your students to think of ways for Woody to get back in Miss Plunkett's good graces.

RELATED TITLES: Danziger, Paula. *Amber Brown Is Not a Crayon.* Putnam, 1994. / Duffey, Betsy. *The Gadget War.* Viking, 1991. / Duffey, Betsy. *Hey, New Kid!* Viking, 1996. / Gutman, Dan. *Miss Daisy Is Crazy.* Harper-Collins, 2004. / Kline, Suzy. *What's the Matter with Herbie Jones?* Putnam, 1987. / Lasky, Kathryn. *Show and Tell Bunnies.* / Petersen, P. J. *The Sub.* Dutton, 1993. / Sachar, Louis. *Marvin Redpost: Alone in His Teacher's House.* Random House, 1994.

SUBJECTS: FICTION BOOKS FOR EARLY GRADES. FRIENDSHIP. SCHOOLS. SHOW-AND-TELL PRESENTATIONS. STUDENT TEACHERS. TEACHERS.

977   Gutman, Dan. *The Get Rich Quick Club.* **HarperCollins, 2004. 0-06-053441-9. 118pp. Gr. 3–5**

Gina Tumalo has always loved money and dreamed of getting rich. Along with her friends and fellow fifth graders Rob Hunnicutt and Quincy Biddle—and the annoying 8-year-old Bogle twins, Eddie and Teddy—Gina starts the GRC Club and devises a master plan to make a million dollars.

GERM: Students can dream up new money-making ventures and draw up their own Profit and Loss statements. Roni Sawin, third-grade teacher at Van Holten School in Bridgewater, New Jersey, had her students write essays and figure out the math on one of the following topics: How I Will Make a Million Dollars or How I Will Spend a Million Dollars. A clever twist ending in the book will have children discussing the difference between real and fake UFOs. And Quincy's use of Australian slang, translated into American in footnotes, makes this a book for talking about idioms, slang, and regionalisms, plus a great way to introduce those pesky footnotes.

RELATED TITLES: Adams, Barbara Johnston. *The Go-Around Dollar.* Four Winds, 1992. / Brittain, Bill. *All the Money in the World.* HarperCollins, 1979. / Clements, Andrew. *Lunch Money.* Simon & Schuster, 2005. / Conford, Ellen. *A Job for Jenny Archer.* Little, Brown, 1988. / Conford, Ellen. *What's Cooking, Jenny Archer?* Little, Brown, 1989. / Etra, Jonathan, and Stephanie Spinner. *Aliens for Breakfast.* Random House, 1988. / Herman, Charlotte. *Max Malone Makes a Million.* Henry Holt, 1991. / Leedy, Loreen. *Follow the Money.* Holiday House, 2002. / Maestro, Betsy. *The Story of Money.* Clarion, 1993. / Pfeffer, Susan Beth. *Kid Power.* Franklin Watts, 1977. / Pinkwater, Daniel Manus. *Fat Men from Space.* Dell, 1980. / Robertson, Keith. *Henry Reed's Baby-Sitting Service.* Viking, 1966. / Roy, Ron. *Million Dollar Jeans.* Dutton, 1983. / Schwartz, David M. *If You Made a Million.* Lothrop, 1989. / Service, Pamela F. *Stinker from Space.* Scribner, 1988. / Van Leeuwen, Jean. *Benjy in Business.* Dial, 1983.

SUBJECTS: CLUBS. EXTRATERRESTRIAL LIFE. HOAXES. MAINE. MONEYMAKING PROJECTS. NEWSPAPERS. VOCABULARY.

978   Gutman, Dan. *Honus and Me: A Baseball Card Adventure.* **Illus. with photos. Avon, 1997. 0-380-97350-2. 140pp. Gr. 4–6**

Joe Stoshack's parents split up two years ago, and now he helps his mom, a nurse, make ends meet by taking on odd jobs. Hired to clean out Miss Young's attic, he comes upon a mint T-206 Honus Wagner card, the most valuable baseball card in the world, and he takes it. When he holds the card, he feels a funny tingling sensation, and wishes he could meet the real Honus Wagner. Awakening in the middle of the night, who's in Joe's room, dressed in a Pittsburgh baseball uniform, but a guy who says he's Honus Wagner and thinks the year is 1909?

GERM: This entertaining time travel fantasy goes both ways, with Honus coming into the present and Joe slipping back into 1909. It's a good jumping-off point for the What-Ifs, coupled with some research: What if you could meet up with one of your sports heroes? Who would it be and what would you do together? At the back of the book, you'll find an author's note to the reader, information on the baseball card, Wagner's career stats, and even a list of baseball tips Wagner wrote in 1950. (Is the Honus Wagner card really that valuable? In 2000, a T-206 card went for over a million bucks on eBay. Have children Google the card to find out more.) Readers will want to follow up with other books in the series.

RELATED TITLES: Adler, David A. *Lou Gehrig: The Luckiest Man.* Harcourt, 1997. / Avi. *The Mayor of Central Park.* HarperCollins, 2003. / Burleigh, Robert. *Home Run: The Story of Babe Ruth.* Harcourt, 1998. / Cline-Ransome, Lesa. *Satchel Paige.* Simon & Schuster, 2000. / Cohen, Barbara. *Thank You, Jackie Robinson.* Lothrop, 1988. / Gutman, Dan. *Abner and Me.* HarperCollins, 2005. / Gutman, Dan. *Babe and Me.* Avon, 2000. / Gutman, Dan. *Jackie and Me.* Avon, 1999. / Gutman, Dan. *The Kid Who Ran for President.* Scholastic, 1996. / Gutman, Dan. *Mickie and Me.* HarperCollins, 2003. / Gutman, Dan. *Shoeless Joe and Me.* HarperCollins, 2003. / Hopkins, Lee Bennett, comp. *Extra Innings: Baseball Poems.* Harcourt, 1993. / Janeczko, Paul B. *That Sweet Diamond: Baseball Poems.* Atheneum, 1998. / Krull, Kathleen. *Lives of the Athletes: Thrills, Spills (and What the Neighbors Thought).* Harcourt, 1995. / Norworth, Jack. *Take Me Out to the Ballgame.* Four Winds, 1993.

SUBJECTS: BASEBALL. BASEBALL CARDS. BIOGRAPHICAL FICTION. FANTASY. SPORTS. TIME TRAVEL. WAGNER, HONUS, 1874–1955.

979   Gutman, Dan. *The Kid Who Ran for President.* Scholastic, 1996. 0-590-93987-4. 156pp. Gr. 3–6
Why must a candidate be 35 years old to run for U.S. president? With the help of his friend and savvy campaign manager Lane Brainard, sixth grader Judson Moon declares his candidacy for the highest office. He does it as a goof, but pretty soon the country is behind him and his Lemonade Party, and Constitutional Amendment XXVII, rescinding the age requirement, is ratified. Judson's adventure makes for witty political satire lampooning all aspects of elections, including unrealistic campaign promises ("READ MY LIPS . . . NO MORE HOMEWORK!"), campaign commercials, a live TV debate with the two regular candidates, and a scandal that rocks his campaign (Moongate). There's even a very funny rehashing of Nixon's infamous 1952 "Checkers" speech that revives Judson's chances to win.

GERM: Read this aloud as a lead-in and comparison to the real elections as you examine the pressing issues facing candidates today.

RELATED TITLES: Burns, Diane, and Clint Burns. *Hail to the Chief! Jokes About the Presidents.* Lerner, 1989. / Christelow, Eileen. *VOTE!* Clarion, 2003. / Cronin, Doreen. *Duck for President.* Simon & Schuster, 2004. / Gutman, Dan. *Honus and Me: A Baseball Card Adventure.* Avon, 1997. / Harness, Cheryl. *Ghosts of the White House.* Simon & Schuster, 1998. / Hurwitz, Johanna. *Class President.* Morrow, 1990. / Krull, Kathleen. *Lives of the Presidents: Fame, Shame (and What the Neighbors Thought).* Harcourt, 1998. / Maestro, Betsy. *The Voice of the People: American Democracy in Action.* Lothrop, 1996. / O'Connor, Jane. *If the Walls Could Talk: Family Life at the White House.* Simon & Schuster, 2004. / Park, Barbara. *Rosie Swanson, Fourth-Grade Geek for President.* Knopf, 1991. / Provensen, Alice. *The Buck Stops Here: The Presidents of the United States.* Harcourt, 2000. / St. George, Judith. *So You Want to Be President?* Philomel, 2000. / Stier, Catherine. *If I Were President.* Albert Whitman, 1999. / Winters, Kay. *My Teacher for President.* Dutton, 2004.

SUBJECTS: ELECTIONS. POLITICAL CAMPAIGNS. PRESIDENTS. SCHOOLS.

980   Gutman, Dan. *Miss Daisy Is Crazy.* Illus. by Jim Paillot. HarperCollins, 2004. 0-06-050703-9. 96pp. Gr. 1–4
A. J.'s new second-grade teacher, Miss Daisy, is crazy like a fox. She says she hates school and claims not to know how to read, spell, or do math, so the students undertake to teach her everything they know.

GERM: Take some clues from Miss Daisy and let your students show you what they know. For starters, have them each write three hard words they can spell on the board. Principal Mr. Klutz's challenge to read a million pages may start a trend in your school. Do some group math: if your school decided to read a million pages, how many pages would each person have to read? How many 32-page picture books would that be? How many 100-page fiction books? Set your readers loose with the sequels in the My Weird School series, including *Mr. Klutz Is Nuts!*, about A. J.'s accident-prone school principal, and *Mrs. Roopy Is Loopy*, about the librarian.

RELATED TITLES: Allen, Susan, and Jane Lindaman. *Read Anything Good Lately?* Millbrook, 2003. / Dahl, Roald. *Matilda.* Viking, 1988. / Evans, Douglas. *Apple Island, or The Truth About Teachers.* Front Street, 1998. / Evans, Douglas. *The Classroom at the End of the Hall.* Front Street, 1996. / Fleischman, Paul. *Weslandia.* Candlewick, 1999. / Haddix, Margaret Peterson. *Say What?* Simon & Schuster, 2004. / Gutman, Dan. *Mr. Klutz Is*

Nuts! HarperCollins, 2004. / Gutman, Dan. *Mrs. Roopy Is Loopy!* HarperCollins, 2004. / Hornik, Laurie Miller. *The Secrets of Ms. Snickle's Class.* Clarion, 2001. / Hornik, Laurie Miller. *Zoo School.* Clarion, 2004. / King-Smith, Dick. *Clever Lollipop.* Candlewick, 2003. / MacDonald, Amy. *No More Nasty.* Farrar, 2001. / Polacco, Patricia. *Thank You, Mr. Falker.* Philomel, 1998. / Sachar, Louis. *Sideways Stories from Wayside School.* Morrow, 1985. / Sachar, Louis. *Wayside School Is Falling Down.* Lothrop, 1989.

SUBJECTS: BOOKS AND READING. FICTION BOOKS FOR EARLY GRADES. HUMOROUS FICTION. PRINCIPALS. SCHOOLS. TEACHERS.

981   **Gutman, Dan. *Qwerty Stevens Back in Time: The Edison Mystery.* Simon & Schuster, 2001. 0-689-84124-8. 201pp. Gr. 3–6**

Nicknamed "Qwerty" after the six letters on the top left side of a keyboard, the 13-year-old computer-loving boy digs up a mysterious box labeled "Thomas A. Edison" in his West Orange, New Jersey, backyard and finds an unusual machine that appears to have been buried for more than 120 years. Hooking up the Anywhere Anytime Machine to his computer, Qwerty finds himself summoned via Morse code by Edison himself. Interspersed with photos of Edison and his inventions, this entertaining time-travel fantasy adventure gives a view of the eccentric inventor as he races to find a perfect filament for his new incandescent electric lamp.

GERM: Listeners can research some of Edison's 1,093 inventions and make a list of additional inventions of the past century that have affected their lives. Using their imaginations, prospective inventors can come up with a drawing and description of a useful item that the world still needs. For facts and lots of photos, consult *Inventing the Future: A Photobiography of Thomas Alva Edison* by Marie Ferguson Delano.

RELATED TITLES: Adler, David A. *Eaton Stanley and the Mind Control Experiment.* Dutton, 1985 / Delano, Marie Ferguson. *Inventing the Future: A Photobiography of Thomas Alva Edison.* National Geographic, 2002. / Gardiner, John Reynolds. *Top Secret.* Little, Brown, 1985. / Gutman, Dan. *Qwerty Stevens, Stuck in Time with Benjamin Franklin.* Simon & Schuster, 2002. / Hahn, Mary Downing. *Time for Andrew: A Ghost Story.* Clarion, 1994. / Jones, Charlotte Foltz. *Accidents May Happen: Fifty Inventions Discovered by Mistake.* Delacorte, 1996. / Moore, Floyd C. *I Gave Thomas Edison My Sandwich.* Albert Whitman, 1995. / Simon, Seymour. Einstein Anderson series. Morrow. / Woodruff, Elvira. *The Disappearing Bike Shop.* Holiday House, 1992. / Woodruff, Elvira. *George Washington's Socks.* Scholastic, 1991. / Yolen, Jane, and Robert J. Harris. *Odysseus in the Serpent Maze.* HarperCollins, 2001.

SUBJECTS: ADVENTURE AND ADVENTURERS. EDISON, THOMAS ALVA. HISTORICAL FICTION. INVENTIONS AND INVENTORS. MYSTERY AND DETECTIVE STORIES. SCIENCE. SCIENCE FICTION. TIME TRAVEL.

982   **Haas, Jessie. *Runaway Radish.* Illus. by Margot Apple. Greenwillow, 2001. 0-06-029159-1. 56pp. Gr. 1–3**

Pony Radish is smart and brave and he has a mind of his own. He teaches his first little girl, Judy, where to scratch his neck, to tie good knots, to keep her temper, and to hold on tight. Bossy Judy has a tantrum, but Radish teaches her that if she asks nicely, he will most likely do what she wants. When Judy grows too big for a pony, she takes Radish to Nina's house. Over the years, Radish teaches a succession of children about patience, responsibility, and bravery.

GERM: This is a sweet circular story—the last child Radish teaches is Judy's daughter—that is easy to read, with soft, Garth Williams-ish pencil drawings and a nice message. Children can recall all the things Radish taught his riders and the stories behind each of his lessons. Discussion point: What have your pets taught you? Readers can follow up on their own with the companion book, *Jigsaw Pony.*

RELATED TITLES: Brady, Irene. *Doodlebug.* Houghton, 1977. / Friedrich, Elizabeth. *Leah's Pony.* Boyds Mills, 1996. / Haas, Jessie. *Beware the Mare.* Greenwillow, 1996. / Haas, Jessie. *Jigsaw Pony.* Greenwillow, 2005. / High, Linda Oatman. *Winter Shoes for Shadow Horse.* Boyds Mills, 2001. / King-Smith, Dick. *Lady Lollipop.* Candlewick, 2001. / Livingstone, Star. *Harley.* SeaStar, 2001. / Polacco, Patricia. *Mrs. Mack.* Philomel, 1998.

SUBJECTS: FICTION BOOKS FOR EARLY GRADES. HORSES. PATIENCE. PETS. PONIES. RESPONSIBILITY.

983   **Haddix, Margaret Peterson. *Because of Anya.* Simon & Schuster, 2002. 0-689-83298-2. 114pp. Gr. 4–7**

When fourth grader Anya is diagnosed with alopecia areata, an autoimmune disease that causes hair loss, she decides to tell no one about the wig she must wear to hide her growing baldness. Classmates, including shy Keely and her bossy, popular friend, Stef, notice the wig and conclude that quiet Anya must be dying of cancer.

GERM: Told in alternating chapters by an omniscient narrator, this gutsy little novel takes an honest look at peer pressure, conformity, embarrassment, coming to terms with uncomfortable truths, and taking personal responsibility. There's also an author's note with facts about the disease, and an excellent Web site from the National Alopecia Areata Foundation for further information: <www.alopeciaareata.com>.

RELATED TITLES: Haddix, Margaret Peterson. *Say What?* Simon & Schuster, 2004. / Park, Barbara. *The Graduation of Jake Moon.* Atheneum, 2000. / Spinelli, Jerry. *Loser.* HarperCollins, 2002.

SUBJECTS: BALDNESS. DISEASES. EMBARRASSMENT. FRIENDSHIP. HAIR. SCHOOLS. SECRETS. SELF-ACCEPTANCE.

984   Haddix, Margaret Peterson. *Running Out of Time.* Simon & Schuster, 1995. 0-689-80084-3. 184pp. Gr. 4–6

In 1840, with more of the children falling ill in their isolated little village of Clifton, Indiana, Jessie's ma takes her into the woods to look for herbs. Ma has been acting secretive and strange, but what she now tells Jessie is incomprehensible. It seems that Clifton isn't an ordinary village; it's an authentic historical preserve and tourist site, going far beyond reenactment sites like Colonial Williamsburg. None of the children in Clifton have any idea that in the larger world, the year is 1996, and busloads of tourists come daily to view life there via the mirrors in every house and building. With many of the children dangerously ill from diphtheria, and the owner of the site seemingly unconcerned if they should die, Ma wants Jessie to escape from the compound and find the one man she thinks can help them.

GERM: Aside from the suspense of Jessie's escape into the modern world, there are good ethical issues to discuss. Why does this little community exist? Is it right that outsiders should watch the villagers live their daily lives? Why would Jessie's parents and the other adults have consented to living there? Then there are the pragmatic issues: of what other inventions and customs would Jessie be unaware? How would you explain them to her? Of course, in recent years, there have been numerous reality TV shows of families living in reconstructed houses or even communities, to see what it would be like to live in the past. *The City of Ember* by Jeanne duPrau is another interesting dystopian novel dealing with authority gone awry and children who uncover its secrets. Two good comparison novels that take place in the actual time period, the 1840s, are *The Birchbark House* by Louise Erdrich and *Adaline Falling Star* by Mary Pope Osborne.

RELATED TITLES: DuPrau, Jeanne. *The City of Ember.* Random House, 2003. / Erdrich, Louise. *The Birchbark House.* Hyperion, 1999. / Haddix, Margaret. *Among the Hidden.* Simon & Schuster, 1998. / Haddix, Margaret Peterson. *Say What?* Simon & Schuster, 2004. / L'Engle, Madeleine. *A Wrinkle in Time.* Farrar, 1962. / Lowry, Lois. *The Giver.* Houghton Mifflin, 1993. / Osborne, Mary Pope. *Adaline Falling Star.* Scholastic, 2000.

SUBJECTS: ADVENTURE AND ADVENTURERS. DIPHTHERIA. DISEASES. EUGENICS. EXPERIMENTS. HISTORICAL FICTION. INDIANA. MYSTERY AND DETECTIVE STORIES.

985   Haddix, Margaret Peterson. *Say What?* Illus. by James Bernardin. Simon & Schuster, 2004. 0-689-86255-5. 91pp. Gr. 1–5

Six-year-old Sukie and her two older brothers have an all-kid meeting to figure out why their parents are acting so weird, saying the wrong thing each time they admonish their youngsters. The children's decision—to be bad on purpose to see how Mom and Dad will react—leads to war.

GERM: Collect examples of "parentspeak," "teacherspeak," and "kidspeak" and talk over sensible, non-boring rules for behavior in your own classroom.

RELATED TITLES: Allard, Harry. *Miss Nelson Is Missing.* Houghton Mifflin, 1985. / Evans, Douglas. *Apple Island, or The Truth About Teachers.* Front Street, 1998. / Geras, Adèle. *The Cats of Cuckoo Square: Two Stories.* Delacorte, 2001. / King-Smith, Dick. *Lady Lollipop.* Candlewick, 2001. / MacDonald, Amy. *No More Nasty.* Farrar, 2001. / MacDonald, Amy. *No More Nice.* Orchard, 1996. / MacDonald, Betty. *Mrs. Piggle-Wiggle* (and others in the series). Lippincott, 1975. / Shannon, David. *David Gets in Trouble.* Scholastic, 2002. / Shannon, David. *David Goes to School.* Scholastic, 1999.

SUBJECTS: BEHAVIOR. BROTHERS AND SISTERS. ENGLISH LANGUAGE—TERMS AND PHRASES. FICTION BOOKS FOR EARLY GRADES. PARENTING.

986 Hannigan, Katherine. *Ida B: And Her Plans to Maximize Fun, Avoid Disaster, and (Possibly) Save the World.* **Greenwillow, 2004. 0-06-073025-0. 246pp. Gr. 4–6**

Since her disastrous experience with public education back in kindergarten, Ida B has been home-schooled by her parents on their farm. She's never missed school friendships, spending her free time talking to the trees she's named in the apple orchards and playing by the brook nearby. But when her mother gets cancer and they have to sell off some of their land to pay the bills, and Ida B's daddy sends her back to school, she shuts down, making her heart small and cold, and refusing to talk to anyone. Ida B's teacher, Ms. Washington, helps Ida B come out of her angry place and accept what she can't change.

GERM: Discussion points and writing prompts: Ida B talks to trees. To whom do you tell your deepest secrets and worst troubles? What kind of person is Ida B? Would you be her friend? Draw your own favorite tree. What kind of teacher is Ms. Washington? How does she help Ida B adjust to school? Describe a grown-up in your life who helped you survive tough times. Ida B has a distinct and unforgettable voice as a narrator; her observations will inspire your writers to describe their surroundings and each other more pointedly. Have them write letters to Ida B, based on their own experience, with practical advice on how she should deal with her new school. What are the things she needs to know? What should she do and shouldn't she do?

RELATED TITLES: Codell, Esmé Raji. *Sahara Special.* Hyperion, 2003. / Creech, Sharon. *Granny Torrelli Makes Soup.* HarperCollins, 2003. / Creech, Sharon. *Love That Dog.* HarperCollins, 2001. / DiCamillo, Kate. *Because of Winn-Dixie.* Candlewick, 2000. / Henkes, Kevin. *Olive's Ocean.* Greenwillow, 2003. / Slepian, Jan. *The Broccoli Tapes.* Philomel, 1988. / Snyder, Zilpha Keatley. *Libby on Wednesday.* Delacorte, 1990.

SUBJECTS: APPLE TREES. CANCER. FAMILY PROBLEMS. HOME SCHOOLING. ORCHARDS. SCHOOLS. SICK. TEACHERS. TREES. WISCONSIN.

987 Hermann, Spring. *Seeing Lessons: The Story of Abigail Carter and America's First School for Blind People.* **Illus. by Ib Ohlsson. Henry Holt, 1998. 0-8050-5706-4. 164pp. Gr. 4–6**

In 1829, 10-year-old Abigail Carter and her younger sister Sophia left their family farm for Boston, where they became the first two students at the New England Asylum for the Blind, which later became known as the Perkins Institution for the Blind. Based on letters, journals, memoirs, and articles, and told from Abigail's lively point of view, this is carefully crafted biographical fiction at its best.

GERM: Also read *Out of Darkness: The Story of Louis Braille* by Russell Freedman, a biography of the originator of the Braille system of writing and reading. Braille spent most of his life attending and then teaching at the Royal Institute for Blind Youth in Paris, the first school of its kind in the world, and the inspiration for the American counterpart. Meet Bailey, Rosie's best friend in Sharon Creech's fiction book *Granny Torrelli Makes Soup*, to see how a modern-day child deals with being blind.

RELATED TITLES: Adler, David A. *A Picture Book of Louis Braille.* Holiday House, 1997. / Alexander, Sally Hobart. *Mom Can't See Me.* Macmillan, 1990. / Creech, Sharon. *Granny Torrelli Makes Soup.* HarperCollins, 2003. / Freedman, Russell. *Out of Darkness: The Story of Louis Braille.* Clarion, 1997. / Garfield, James. *Follow My Leader.* Viking, 1957. / Hunter, Edith Fisher. *Child of the Silent Night: The Story of Laura Bridgman.* Houghton Mifflin, 1963. / Little, Jean. *Little by Little: A Writer's Education.* Viking, 1987. / Patent, Dorothy Hinshaw. *The Right Dog for the Job: Ira's Path from Service Dog to Guide Dog.* Walker, 2004. / Rodanas, Kristina. *The Blind Hunter.* Cavendish, 2003. / Whelan, Gloria. *Hannah.* Knopf, 1991.

SUBJECTS: BIOGRAPHICAL FICTION. BLIND. HISTORICAL FICTION. PEOPLE WITH DISABILITIES. PHYSICALLY HANDICAPPED. SCHOOLS.

988 Hesse, Karen. *The Music of Dolphins.* **Scholastic, 1996. 0-590-89797-7. 181pp. Gr. 5–8**

Plucked from the sea between Florida and Cuba by members of the Coast Guard, Mila is a feral child, raised by dolphins after her family's plane was lost at sea when she was small. Now she is in Boston, adjusting to being a human child, learning to talk, and read, and write on a computer. Scientist Dr. Elizabeth Beck and her assistant, Sandy, try to help Mila regain her human identity, but Mila still yearns for her dolphin family. This is an astonishing and compelling novel told by Mila, whose simple narration grows increasingly complex as she gains the language to express herself.

GERM: Students will need to search out nonfiction dolphin books to fathom what Mila's life in the sea might have been like before her rescue. In *The Wild Boy*, using a picture-book format, Mordicai Gerstein retells the true story of Victor, the wild child of Aveyron, who was captured in 1800, declared retarded, and taken in by Dr. Itard and his housekeeper.

RELATED TITLES: Billingsley, Franny. *The Folk Keeper.* Atheneum, 1999. / George, Jean Craighead. *Julie of the Wolves.* HarperCollins, 1972. / George, Twig C. *A Dolphin Named Bob.* HarperCollins, 1996. / Gerstein, Mordicai. *The Wild Boy.* Farrar, 1998. / McGraw, Eloise. *The Moorchild.* McElderry, 1996. / Morpurgo, Michael. *Kensuke's Kingdom.* Scholastic, 2003. / O'Dell, Scott. *Island of the Blue Dolphins.* Houghton Mifflin, 1960. / Philbrick, Rodman. *The Young Man and the Sea.* Blue Sky/Scholastic, 2004. / Yolen, Jane. *Passager.* Harcourt, 1996.

SUBJECTS: BOSTON (MASS.). DOLPHINS. FANTASY. FERAL CHILDREN. HUMAN-ANIMAL RELATIONSHIPS.

989   Hiaasen, Carl. *Hoot.* Knopf, 2002. 0-375-92181-8. 292pp. Gr. 6–8

Set in Florida, where—as you will know if you've read Hiaasen's adult crime novels—there's always plenty of flaky doings, this edgy, very funny environmental protest novel is a wild send-up of corruption, greed, crooked overdevelopment, lowlife-ism, and the defoliation of Florida for bucks. Seventh grader Roy Eberhardt, new kid in school, hooks up with an outlaw kid called Mullet Fingers, who is bent on stopping the construction of the latest franchise of Mother Paula's All-American Pancake House in order to save a colony of tiny burrowing owls.

GERM: Use this as a kickoff to your mystery genre booktalk or a study of endangered animals. Do some research on those little owls.

RELATED TITLES: Byars, Betsy. *Dead Letter: A Herculeah Jones Mystery.* Viking, 1996. / Byars, Betsy. *Tarot Says Beware: A Herculeah Jones Mystery.* Viking, 1995. / Hiaasen, Carl. *Flush.* Knopf, 2005. / Hoobler, Dorothy, and Thomas Hoobler. *The Demon in the Teahouse.* Philomel, 2001. / Konigsburg, E. L. *From the Mixed-Up Files of Mrs. Basil E. Frankweiler.* Atheneum, 1967. / Markle, Sandra. *Owls* (Animal Predator series). Carolrhoda, 2004. / Naylor, Phyllis Reynolds. *The Bodies in the Besseldorf Hotel.* Atheneum, 1986. / Newman, Robert. *The Case of the Baker Street Irregular.* Atheneum, 1978. / Sobol, Donald J. Encyclopedia Brown series. Bantam.

SUBJECTS: BIRDS. ENVIRONMENTAL PROTECTION. FLORIDA. HUMOROUS FICTION. MYSTERY AND DETECTIVE STORIES. OWLS.

990   Hill, Kirkpatrick. *The Year of Miss Agnes.* McElderry, 2000. 0-689-82933-7. 128pp. Gr. 3–5

In 1948, after yet another teacher has quit the one-room schoolhouse of their remote Alaskan village, 10-year-old Fred and the other dozen schoolchildren are transformed by their new teacher, the remarkable and innovative Miss Agnes Sutterfield. She wears pants, plays opera records, reads Robin Hood aloud to the class, and helps all her students take pride in learning. When she even manages to persuade Fred's skeptical mother to send 12-year-old Bokko, who is deaf, to school for the first time, the whole class joins in learning the sign language alphabet so that they can communicate with her.

GERM: Compare the lives and schooling of Miss Agnes's charges with your own. From the dedication —"In memory of Sylvia Ashton-Warner, and for all unorthodox teachers"— to the inspirational message Miss Agnes promotes—"You have to keep learning all your life"—Fred tells a treasure of a story about the transforming effect a dedicated, innovative teacher has on the lives of her children.

RELATED TITLES: Avi. *The Secret School.* Harcourt, 2001. / Clements, Andrew. *Frindle.* Simon & Schuster, 1996. / George, Jean Craighead. *Julie of the Wolves.* HarperCollins, 1972. / Hill, Kirkpatrick. *Toughboy and Sister.* McElderry, 1990. / Hill, Kirkpatrick. *Winter Camp.* McElderry, 1993. / Houston, Gloria. *My Great Aunt Arizona.* HarperCollins, 1992. / Morey, Walt. *Gentle Ben.* Dutton, 1965. / Peck, Robert Newton. *Mr. Little.* Doubleday, 1979. / Shreve, Susan. *The Gift of the Girl Who Couldn't Hear.* Morrow, 1991.

SUBJECTS: ALASKA. ATHAPASCAN INDIANS. DEAF. HISTORICAL FICTION. INDIANS OF NORTH AMERICA—ALASKA. MULTICULTURAL BOOKS. PEOPLE WITH DISABILITIES. PHYSICALLY HANDICAPPED. SCHOOLS. TEACHERS.

991   Hinton, S. E. *The Puppy Sister.* Illus. by Jacqueline Rogers. Delacorte, 1995. 0-385-32060-4. 122pp. Gr. 2–4

Nick's new puppy, Aleasha, a black-and-white Australian shepherd, recounts how she gradually turns herself into a girl person and teaches herself to talk so she can become a real member of Nick's family.

GERM: Make a chart of the good and bad things about Aleasha's becoming human from David's and Aleasha's points of view. Writing prompt: What would happen if your pet became human?

RELATED TITLES: Avi. *The Good Dog.* Atheneum, 2001. / Conly, Jane Leslie. *The Rudest Alien on Earth.* Henry Holt, 2002. / Hinton, S. E. *Big David, Little David.* Doubleday, 1995. / Howe, James. Bunnicula series.

Atheneum. / King-Smith, Dick. *George Speaks*. Roaring Brook, 2002. / Lowry, Lois. *Stay! Keeper's Story*. Houghton Mifflin, 1997. / Napoli, Donna Jo. *Jimmy, the Pickpocket of the Palace*. Dutton, 1995. / Napoli, Donna Jo. *The Prince of the Pond*. Dutton, 1992. / Vande Velde, Vivian. *Smart Dog*. Harcourt, 1998. / White, E. B. *Stuart Little*. HarperCollins, 1945.

SUBJECTS: BROTHERS AND SISTERS. DOGS. FAMILY STORIES. FANTASY. HUMAN-ANIMAL COMMUNICATION. HUMOROUS FICTION. TRANSFORMATIONS.

992 **Hirsch, Odo.** *Bartlett and the City of Flames*. **Bloomsbury, 2003. 1-58234-831-6. 201pp. Gr. 4–6**

After explorer and adventurer Bartlett and his cohorts Jacques le Grand and young Gozo emerge from the caves they have been mapping, they are taken as prisoners to the City of the Sun, where the Pasha declares Gozo his long-lost son who was kidnapped by the underground people of the City of Flames.

GERM: Do a booktalk on explorers, both real and fictional, including the first book in Hirsch's series, *Bartlett and the Ice Voyage*, in which Bartlett and Jacques set off on a quest to bring the queen an exotic melidrop, preserving that most delicate of fruits by placing it on an iceberg and towing it behind their ship.

RELATED TITLES: Alexander, Lloyd. *The First Two Lives of Lucas-Kasha*. Dutton, 1978. / Collins, Suzanne. *Gregor the Overlander*. Scholastic, 2003. / Du Bois, William Pène. *The Twenty-One Balloons*. Viking, 1947. / DuPrau, Jeanne. *The City of Ember*. Random House, 2003. / Hirsch, Odo. *Bartlett and the Forest of Plenty*. Bloomsbury, 2004. / Hirsch, Odo. *Bartlett and the Ice Voyage*. Bloomsbury, 2003. / Ives, David. *Monsieur Eek*. HarperCollins, 2001. / L'Engle, Madeleine. *A Wrinkle in Time*. Farrar, 1962.

SUBJECTS: ADVENTURE AND ADVENTURERS. CAVES. FANTASY. KIDNAPPING. KINGS AND RULERS. SUN. WAR.

993 **Hoeye, Michael.** *Time Stops for No Mouse*. **Putnam, 2002. 0-399-23878-6. 250pp. Gr. 4–8**

Mild-mannered watchmaker mouse Hermux Tantamoq becomes embroiled in mystery, intrigue, and danger when he attempts to find out why the dynamic daredevil aviatrix Linka Perflinger has not returned to pick up her broken watch. When a sinister gray rat comes to Hermux's store and demands the watch, Hermux suspects foul play and follows him.

GERM: To help your listeners gain insight into Hermux's placid but determined personality, collect a batch of broken old watches and let your students attempt to take them apart and put them back together. What's so deliciously fun about this book is the eccentric cast of small mammals and the host of small details, including descriptions of Hermux's colorful clothes, that will inspire your students to make portraits of the many memorable rodents of Pinchester. Photocopy some of the many witty dialogues and hand them out to pairs of readers to practice and perform. This will also be a popular book for discussion groups. Set your readers loose on the other books in the series, including *The Sands of Time* and *No Time Like Show Time*.

RELATED TITLES: Avi. *Poppy*. Orchard, 1995. / DiCamillo, Kate. *The Tale of Despereaux*. Candlewick, 2003. / Emerson, Scott. *The Case of the Cat with the Missing Ear* (The Adventures of Samuel Blackthorne, Book One). Simon & Schuster, 2003. / Erickson, John R. *The Original Adventures of Hank the Cowdog*. Maverick Books, 1997. / Hoeye, Michael. *No Time Like Show Time*. Putnam, 2004. / Hoeye, Michael. *The Sands of Time*. Putnam, 2002. / Jacques, Brian. *Redwall*. Philomel, 1987. / Kotzwinkle, William. *Trouble in Bugland: A Collection of Inspector Mantis Mysteries*. Godine, 1983. / O'Brien, Robert C. *Mrs. Frisby and the Rats of NIMH*. Atheneum, 1971. / Shipton, Paul. *Bug Muldoon: The Garden of Fear*. Viking, 2001. / Steig, William. *Abel's Island*. Farrar, 1976. / Titus, Eve. *Basil of Baker Street*. Pocket Books, 1989. / Van Leeuwen, Jean. *The Great Christmas Kidnapping Caper*. Dial, 1975.

SUBJECTS: ADVENTURE AND ADVENTURERS. ANIMALS. CLOCKS AND WATCHES. COURAGE. FANTASY. KIDNAPPING. MICE. MYSTERY AND DETECTIVE STORIES.

994 **Holm, Jennifer L.** *Our Only May Amelia*. **HarperCollins, 1999. 0-06-027822-6. 253pp. Gr. 4–7**

Growing up alongside the Nasel River in Washington State in 1899, the only girl in a Finnish farming family with seven older brothers, May Amelia chafes at her strict Pappa's fierce scoldings. Considering herself a "no-good girl," she causes no end of trouble for her brothers, shooting off a gun, stepping in an animal trap, and then fighting with her disapproving Grandmother Patience who comes to stay. "It's heaps more fun not being a Proper Young Lady," she reasons. When Mother's new baby girl takes sick and dies, Grandmother Patience, a most wonderfully villainous and unredeemingly venomous character, declares at the funeral, "The babe would be alive if this evil girl of yours hadn't handled her so." May Amelia runs off to her aunt's house in the city, where she can heal her shattered heart.

GERM: Narrated by May Amelia in a distinct and chatty style that uses no quotation marks to set off dialogue, this original and high-spirited novel was inspired by the diary of the author's grandaunt. English teachers bothered by the lack of punctuation can just photocopy a page, hand it out, and say, "OK, kids, put back those quotes!" Discussion and research point: How has life changed for girls since 1899? Compare May Amelia's country life with the early 20th-century New York City upbringing of Anne Elizabeth Rector in *Anne Elizabeth's Diary: A Young Artist's True Story*.

RELATED TITLES: Brink, Carol Ryrie. *Caddie Woodlawn*. Macmillan, 1973. / Couloumbis, Audrey. *Getting Near to Baby*. Putnam, 1999. / Park, Barbara. *Mick Harte Was Here*. Knopf, 1995. / Paterson, Katherine. *Preacher's Boy*. Clarion, 1999. / Peck, Richard. *The Teacher's Funeral: A Comedy in Three Parts*. Dial, 2004. / Peck, Richard. *A Year Down Yonder*. Dial, 2000. / Rector, Anne Elizabeth. *Anne Elizabeth's Diary: A Young Artist's True Story*. Little, Brown, 2004. / Van Leeuwen, Jean. *Bound for Oregon*. Dial, 1994. / Wilder, Laura Ingalls. Little House series. HarperCollins.

SUBJECTS: AUNTS. BABIES. BROTHERS AND SISTERS. DEATH. FINNISH AMERICANS. FRONTIER AND PIONEER LIFE. GRANDMOTHERS. HISTORICAL FICTION. SEX ROLE. WASHINGTON (STATE).

995 Hoobler, Dorothy, and Thomas Hoobler. *The Demon in the Teahouse.* **Philomel, 2001. 0-399-23499-3. 182pp. Gr. 5–8**

Investigating the three fires that have been set in the 18th century city of Edo, Japan, Judge Ooka suspects a geisha may be responsible. He sends his adopted son, 14-year-old Seikei, to work in a teahouse nearby and look for suspects and clues. Ooka, the shogun's official, is known for his great skill in detecting criminals through careful observation, and he discerns those same talents in Seikei.

GERM: Children will want to probe into all aspects of Japanese life to find portraits of geishas and samurai; pictures of clothing, weapons, and houses; and samples of Japanese writing and food, all of which will help them evoke the atmosphere of this suspenseful murder mystery.

RELATED TITLES: Avi. *The True Confessions of Charlotte Doyle*. Orchard, 1990. / Blumburg, Rhoda. *Shipwrecked! The True Adventures of a Japanese Boy*. HarperCollins, 2001. / Hoobler, Dorothy, and Thomas Hoobler. *The Ghost in the Tokaido Inn*. Philomel, 1999.

SUBJECTS: HISTORICAL FICTION. JAPAN. MULTICULTURAL BOOKS. MYSTERY AND DETECTIVE STORIES.

996 Hopkinson, Deborah. *A Band of Angels: A Story Inspired by the Jubilee Singers.* **Illus. by Raúl Colón. Atheneum, 1999. 0-689-81062-8. Unp. Gr. 2–5**

Aunt Beth tells her niece the true story of great-great-grandmother Ella, born into slavery, who attended Fisk School in Nashville after the Civil War and helped found the Jubilee Singers, the famous African American gospel choir.

GERM: Ask the music teacher to teach some of the songs the Jubilee Singers sang. Students can look to their own families to identify a role model about whom they can write a biography. Pair this with the inspirational picture book about opera singer Marian Anderson, *When Marian Sang* by Pam Muñoz Ryan.

RELATED TITLES: Bridges, Ruby. *Through My Eyes*. Scholastic, 1999. / Coles, Robert. *The Story of Ruby Bridges*. Scholastic, 1995. / Curtis, Gavin. *The Bat Boy and His Violin*. Simon & Schuster, 1998. / Hopkinson, Deborah. *Sweet Clara and the Freedom Quilt*. Knopf, 1993. / Howard, Elizabeth Fitzgerald. *Virgie Goes to School with Us Boys*. Simon & Schuster, 1999. / Mitchell, Margaree King. *Uncle Jed's Barbershop*. Simon & Schuster, 1993. / Pinkney, Andrea Davis. *Duke Ellington*. Hyperion, 1998. / Ringgold, Faith. *Aunt Harriet's Underground Railroad in the Sky*. Crown, 1992. / Ryan, Pam Muñoz. *When Marian Sang*. Scholastic, 2002.

SUBJECTS: AFRICAN AMERICANS. AFRICAN AMERICANS—HISTORY. HISTORICAL FICTION. JUBILEE SINGERS. MULTICULTURAL BOOKS. SINGERS.

997 Hopkinson, Deborah. *Birdie's Lighthouse.* **Illus. by Kimberly Bulcken Root. Atheneum, 1997. 0-689-81052-0. Unp. Gr. 1–4**

January 15, 1855, Birdie Holland's tenth birthday, marks the start of her new diary chronicling the year she moved with her family to Turtle Island in Maine when her father was chosen the new lighthouse keeper. On the night of a northeaster, with Papa sick in bed, Bertha braves the storm to keep the lighthouse lamps burning.

GERM: Read this short, exciting historical fiction story in diary format, inspired by true accounts of female lighthouse keepers, along with other stories of plucky heroines, including *The Sea Chest* by Toni Buzzeo and *Keep the Lights Burning, Abbie* by Peter and Connie Roop. Survive another storm in *Kate Shelley: Bound for Legend* by Robert D. San Souci, a true account of a teenage girl who braved danger to try to save a train.

RELATED TITLES: Buzzeo, Toni. *The Sea Chest.* Dial, 2002. / Cooney, Barbara. *Island Boy.* Viking, 1988. / McCloskey, Robert. *Burt Dow, Deep-Water Man.* Viking, 1963. / Roop, Peter, and Connie Roop. *Keep the Lights Burning, Abbie.* Carolrhoda, 1985. / San Souci, Robert D. *Kate Shelley: Bound for Legend.* Dial, 1995.

SUBJECTS: DIARIES. FICTION BOOKS FOR EARLY GRADES. HEROES. HISTORICAL FICTION. LIGHTHOUSES. MAINE. RESPONSIBILITY. STORMS. WEATHER.

998 **Hornik, Laurie Miller.** *The Secrets of Ms. Snickle's Class.* **Illus. by Debbie Tilley. Clarion, 2001. 0-618-03435-8. 135pp. Gr. 2–4**

Ms. Snickle has only one important rule in her unusual classroom—no telling secrets—but bossy Lacey takes it upon herself to discover all the secrets her classmates are keeping. Each student has one: Oliver sometimes wets the bed, Eva used to be a swan, Dennis's mother is also the Tooth Fairy, and Hayley is allergic to secrets. The most astonishing secret of all is that at the push of a secret button Ms. Snickle's classroom transforms into her apartment each day after school.

GERM: Children can imagine that they are students in Ms. Snickle's extraordinary class and write a chapter about their own secrets. They can also design and draw their own special rooms that change at the push of a button.

RELATED TITLES: Amato, Mary. *The Word Eater.* Holiday House, 2000. / Dahl, Roald. *Matilda.* Viking, 1988. / Evans, Douglas. *Apple Island, or The Truth About Teachers.* Front Street, 1998. / Evans, Douglas. *The Classroom at the End of the Hall.* Front Street, 1996. / Evans, Douglas. *Math Rashes and Other Classroom Tales.* Front Street, 2004. / Gutman, Dan. *Miss Daisy Is Crazy* (My Weird School series). HarperCollins, 2004. / Hornik, Laurie Miller. *Zoo School.* Clarion, 2004. / King-Smith, Dick. *Clever Lollipop.* Candlewick, 2003. / Lowry, Lois. *Gooney Bird and the Room Mother.* Houghton Mifflin, 2005. / MacDonald, Amy. *No More Nasty.* Farrar, 2001. / Sachar, Louis. *Sideways Stories from Wayside School.* Morrow, 1985. / Sachar, Louis. *Wayside School Is Falling Down.* Lothrop, 1989.

SUBJECTS: FANTASY. HUMOROUS FICTION. SCHOOLS. TEACHERS.

999 **Hornik, Laurie Miller.** *Zoo School.* **Illus. by Debbie Tilley. Clarion, 2004. 0-618-34204-4. 137pp. Gr. 2–5**

At the hands-on new Zoo School, where the motto is "Let the animals be your textbooks," the student desks are actually fish-filled tanks. "If we can take care of animals, we can take care of people," says zookeeper and new teacher Ms. Hummingfly on the first day, and so her six baffled new children learn math by counting all the animals in the adjacent zoo, and how to spell hippopotamus by meeting one up close.

GERM: Small groups can devise charts for each of the Zoo School students, headed with the character's portrait and listing words and attributes describing him or her. Have the groups trace how each character grows and changes as a pupil at the decidedly nontraditional Zoo School. Ask your students to make a text-to-world connection, incorporating real facts, and write and discuss: What have you learned from animals? As the L.I.O.N.S.—Learned Inspectors of New Schools—make their rounds of the school, they must fill in answers to dozens of ridiculous official bureaucratic questions to assess the school's effectiveness. Brainstorm questions for your own classroom as you decide what are its most important attributes that outsiders might observe. Share another extraordinary school experience with Hornik's *The Secrets of Ms. Snickle's Class.*

RELATED TITLES: Allard, Harry. *Miss Nelson Is Missing.* Houghton Mifflin, 1985. / Evans, Douglas. *Apple Island, or The Truth About Teachers.* Front Street, 1998. / Evans, Douglas. *The Classroom at the End of the Hall.* Front Street, 1996. / Evans, Douglas. *Math Rashes and Other Classroom Tales.* Front Street, 2004. / Fleischman, Paul. *Weslandia.* Candlewick, 1999. / Hornik, Laurie Miller. *The Secrets of Ms. Snickle's Class.* Clarion, 2001. / Lowry, Lois. *Gooney Bird and the Room Mother.* Houghton Mifflin, 2005. / MacDonald, Amy. *No More Nasty.* Farrar, 2001. / Sachar, Louis. *Sideways Stories from Wayside School.* Morrow, 1985. / Sachar, Louis. *Wayside School Is Falling Down.* Lothrop, 1989.

SUBJECTS: ANIMALS. BEHAVIOR. FANTASY. HUMOROUS FICTION. SCHOOLS. TEACHERS. ZOOS.

1000   Howe, James. *Bud Barkin, Private Eye.* **Illus. by Brett Helquist. Atheneum, 2003. 0-689-85632-6. 88pp. Gr. 2–5**

In his fifth book in the Tales from the House of Bunnicula series, wirehaired dachshund puppy Howie decides he'll try his hand at writing a hard-boiled detective mystery, filled with a mysterious dame, a real red herring (wrapped in newspaper), and lots of over-the-top similes. Think Dashiel Hammett, Raymond Chandler, and, of course, lots of Humphrey Bone-art . . .

GERM: Each of Howe's books in the Tales from the House of Bunnicula series explores a different genre, including sci fi, adventure, mystery, and fantasy. The writing tips in each book may be amusing, but they are also practical. Each book will inspire students to try their hands at writing stories in that genre.

RELATED TITLES: Cushman, Doug. *The Mystery at the Club Sandwich.* Clarion, 2004. / Emerson, Scott. *The Case of the Cat with the Missing Ear* (The Adventures of Samuel Blackthorne, Book One). Simon & Schuster, 2003. / Erickson, John R. *The Original Adventures of Hank the Cowdog.* Puffin, 1999. / Howe, James. Bunnicula series. Atheneum. / Howe, James. *Invasion of the Mindswappers from Asteroid 6!* Atheneum, 2002. (And others in the Tales from the House of Bunnicula series.) / Shipton, Paul. *Bug Muldoon: The Garden of Fear.* Viking, 2001. / Teague, Mark. *Detective LaRue: Letters from the Investigation.* Scholastic, 2004. / Titus, Eve. *Basil of Baker Street.* McGraw-Hill, 1958. / Vande Velde, Vivian. *Smart Dog.* Harcourt, 1998.

SUBJECTS: AUTHORSHIP. DOGS. FANTASY. HUMOROUS FICTION. MYSTERY AND DETECTIVE STORIES. PERSONAL NARRATIVES. WRITING.

1001   Howe, James. *Bunnicula Strikes Again!* **Illus. by Alan Daniel. Atheneum, 1999. 0-689-81453-1. 116pp. Gr. 3–6**

Vampire bunny Bunnicula who gets his nourishment from sucking the juices out of unsuspecting vegetables, seems to be growing weaker, possibly because Chester the cat has been drinking his carrot juice. Might Chester be trying to finish off Bunnicula once and for all? Howie, the dachshund, has been reading the countless titles in the FleshCrawlers series, scaring himself silly and driving the others crazy with his off-the-wall plot recitations. Mutt Harold, the author and narrator of the Bunnicula series, is in rare form, his narrative packed with puns and language misunderstandings and a sidesplitting plot that parallels Sherlock Holmes's deadly encounter with archvillain Moriarty.

GERM: Your students will have a fine time picking out and explaining the wordplay and will certainly want to go back and investigate the rest of the series. Photocopy a variety of the funny dialogues and monologues in the book and hand them out to kids to practice and read aloud. Howie's R. L. Stine-like plot descriptions of the horror books he's relishing can start a discussion about plot and how it drives a book.

RELATED TITLES: Emerson, Scott. *The Case of the Cat with the Missing Ear* (The Adventures of Samuel Blackthorne, Book One). Simon & Schuster, 2003. / Erickson, John R. *The Original Adventures of Hank the Cowdog.* Puffin, 1999. / Hinton, S. E. *The Puppy Sister.* Delacorte, 1995. / Hoeye, Michael. *Time Stops for No Mouse.* Putnam, 2002. / Howe, James. Bunnicula series. Atheneum. / Howe, James. Tales from the House of Bunnicula series. Atheneum. / Lowry, Lois. *Stay! Keeper's Story.* Houghton Mifflin, 1997. / Vande Velde, Vivian. *Smart Dog.* Harcourt, 1998.

SUBJECTS: CATS. DOGS. FANTASY. HUMOROUS FICTION. MYSTERY AND DETECTIVE STORIES. POINT OF VIEW. RABBITS.

1002   Howe, James. *It Came from Beneath the Bed!* **Illus. by Brett Helquist. Atheneum, 2002. 0-689-83947-2. 90pp. Gr. 2–5**

Fans of the original Bunnicula series, all narrated by Howard, the Monroe family's dog, will be eager to hear now from Howie, the Monroe's dachshund puppy, as he tries to cash in on the writing business. Relying on practical advice from Howard, Howie starts a journal filled with his writerly observations interspersed with ongoing chapters of his own fantasy novel featuring himself as the hero. Here's the plot he works out: When Pete's science potion spills under the bed, stuffed koala Pudgykins grows huge and hungry, threatening to eat Delila, Howie's doggy love.

GERM: All of Howie's books in the Tales from the House of Bunnicula series intersperse entries in Howie's writing journal with the adventure story he is working on. As you read these books aloud, compile a class chart of Howie's Writing Tips. What book might Howie publish next? Develop titles and plot statements (or even the first chapter) for Howie's next opus.

RELATED TITLES: Howe, James. Bunnicula series. Atheneum. / Howe, James. *Howie Monroe and the Doghouse of Doom.* Atheneum, 2002. (And others in the Tales from the House of Bunnicula series.) / Lester, Helen.

Author: A True Story. Houghton Mifflin, 1997. / Schotter, Roni. *Nothing Ever Happens on 90th Street.* Orchard, 1997. / Vande Velde, Vivian. *Smart Dog.* Harcourt, 1998.

SUBJECTS: AUTHORSHIP. DOGS. FANTASY. HUMOROUS FICTION. PERSONAL NARRATIVES. TOYS. TRANSFORMATIONS. WRITING.

1003 **Hunter, Sara Hoaglund.** *The Unbreakable Code.* **Illus. by Julia Miner. Rising Moon, 1996. 0-87358-638-7. Unp. Gr. 2–6**

To help his grandson, John, face the prospect of going away to a new school where no one will speak his language, Grandfather tells him how the Navajo language saved his own life in World War II. Leaving home for the first time in his life at age 17, Grandfather became one of the 200 Navajo code talkers who transmitted, in a code that Japan was never able to decipher, top-secret radio messages for the Marines fighting in the Pacific Islands.

GERM: Reproduce the alphabet in Navajo code included in the back of the book along with some of the military terms, so students can compose and send each other short messages to translate. Discuss the dichotomy the code talkers faced in their lives: resentment at having grown up forbidden to speak their language at school and pride in their role in helping America win the war.

RELATED TITLES: Borden, Louise. *The Little Ships: The Heroic Rescue at Dunkirk in World War II.* McElderry, 1997. / Coerr, Eleanor. *Sadako.* Putnam, 1993. / Foreman, Michael. *War Boy.* Arcade, 1990. / Janeczko, Paul B. *Top Secret: A Handbook of Codes, Ciphers, and Secret Writing.* Candlewick, 2004. / Mochizuki, Ken. *Baseball Saved Us.* Lee & Low, 1993. / Mochizuki, Ken. *Heroes.* Lee & Low, 1995. / Mochizuki, Ken. *Passage to Freedom: The Sugihara Story.* Lee & Low, 1997. / Morimoto, Junko. *My Hiroshima.* Viking, 1990. / Park, Linda Sue. *When My Name Was Keoko.* Clarion, 2002. / Propp, Vera W. *When the Soldiers Were Gone.* Putnam, 1999. / Rumford, James. *Sequoyah: The Man Who Gave His People Writing.* Houghton Mifflin, 2004. / Stevenson, James. *Don't You Know There's a War On?* Greenwillow, 1992.

SUBJECTS: CODES AND CIPHERS. GRANDFATHERS. HISTORICAL FICTION. INDIANS OF NORTH AMERICA. NAVAJO INDIANS. WAR. WORLD WAR, 1939–1945—FICTION.

1004 **Hurst, Carol Otis, and Rebecca Otis.** *A Killing in Plymouth Colony.* **Houghton Mifflin, 2003. 0-618-27597-5. 147pp. Gr. 5–8**

The son of Governor William Bradford of Plymouth Colony, 11-year-old John wants nothing more than the approval of his austere father, though he takes solace in his closeness with his kind stepmother and his best friend, Sam Fuller. Then Sam's little sister, Rachel, is found in the woods, immobile, unable to eat or speak. Three days later, villager John Newcomen is discovered dead in the woods—murdered. Young John Bradford does not want to believe the murderer might be John Billington, in spite of Billington's reputation as the village troublemaker. The authors have fashioned an absorbing and believable historical mystery novel, loosely based on a real murder committed in Plymouth Colony in 1630.

GERM: For your unit on the Pilgrims, this book will add human faces to the facts, and give researchers impetus to find out more about each of the characters in the story. Get a visual picture of Plymouth through Kate Waters' photoessays, *Samuel Eaton's Day, Sarah Morton's Day,* and *Tapenum's Day.*

RELATED TITLES: Gilson, Jamie. *Stink Alley.* HarperCollins, 2002. / Sewall, Marcia. *The Pilgrims of Plimoth.* Atheneum, 1986. / Waters, Kate. *Samuel Eaton's Day: A Day in the Life of a Pilgrim Boy.* Scholastic, 1993. / Waters, Kate. *Sarah Morton's Day: A Day in the Life of a Pilgrim Girl.* Scholastic, 1989. / Waters, Kate. *Tapenum's Day: A Wampanoag Indian Boy in Pilgrim Times.* Scholastic, 1996.

SUBJECTS: BRADFORD, WILLIAM, 1588–1657. FATHERS AND SONS. HISTORICAL FICTION. MASSACHUSETTS—HISTORY. MURDER. MYSTERY AND DETECTIVE STORIES. PILGRIMS. PLYMOUTH COLONY, 1620–1691. PURITANS. U.S.—HISTORY—COLONIAL PERIOD—FICTION.

1005 **Hurwitz, Johanna, comp.** *Birthday Surprises: Ten Great Stories to Unwrap.* **Morrow, 1995. 0-688-13194-8. 119pp. Gr. 3–7**

Hurwitz asked well-known children's book authors to write an original short story based on the same idea: "A child (boy or girl) receives many gifts on his or her birthday. However, on opening the presents, one beautifully wrapped package is found to be empty." The resulting chapters—including ones by Richard Peck, Ann M. Martin, Jane Yolen, David A. Adler, James Howe, Ellen Conford, and Johanna Hurwitz—are alternately funny, poignant, and startling, and always interesting.

GERM: In her introduction, Hurwitz suggests that children try their hands at writing their own empty-box stories.Also share Patrick McDonnell's delightful little picture book about his comic strip characters Mooch the cat and Earl the dog, in *The Gift of Nothing*.

RELATED TITLES: Ehrlich, Amy. *When I Was Your Age: Original Stories About Growing Up*. Candlewick, 1996. / Hurwitz, Johanna. *Class Clown*. Morrow, 1987. / Rosen, Michael J., ed. *Purr . . . Children's Book Illustrators Brag About Their Cats*. Harcourt, 1996. / McDonnell, Patrick. *The Gift of Nothing*. Little, Brown, 2005. / Rosen, Michael J., ed. *Speak! Children's Book Illustrators Brag About Their Dogs*. Harcourt, 1993. / Rylant, Cynthia. *Children of Christmas: Stories for the Season*. Orchard, 1987. / Rylant, Cynthia. *Silver Packages: An Appalachian Christmas Story*. Orchard, 1997.

SUBJECTS: BIRTHDAYS. GIFTS. SHORT STORIES.

1006 Ibbotson, Eva. *Journey to the River Sea*. **Illus. by Kevin Hawkes. Dutton, 2002. 0-525-46739-4. 298pp. Gr. 5–7**

Along with her book-loving governess, Miss Minton, orphaned Maia Fielding is sent from her posh London boarding school in 1910 to live with her aunt and uncle and twin cousins on the Amazon River, near the city of Manaus in Brazil. Upon meeting her dreadful relatives at their plantation, it becomes clear that they detest the exotic jungle climate, distrust all natives, and need Maia only for the money she will bring them. Maia becomes caught up in mystery and adventure when two bumbling English detectives come sniffing around, determined to find her new friend Bernard Taverner, the now-orphaned half-Indian son of an English naturalist, who might be living in the jungle.

GERM: Maia is entranced with life in Brazil, marveling over the flora, fauna, and, except for her odious relatives, the many people she meets. To help analyze the points of view of the numerous characters, first act as the interviewer. Ask each student to assume a different role and describe, in character, what each thinks of living in the jungle. They can then compose and perform monologues that reveal aspects of each character's personality. If you're looking to discuss the use of setting in a novel, this is an apt choice; Maia's poor-little-rich-girl saga will interest listeners in researching life on the Amazon.

RELATED TITLES: Bath, K. P. *The Secret of Castle Cant*. Little, Brown, 2004. / Burnett, Frances Hodgson. *A Little Princess*. HarperCollins, 1992. / Creech, Sharon. *Ruby Holler*. HarperCollins, 2002. / Holm, Jennifer L. *Our Only May Amelia*. HarperCollins, 1999. / Ibbotson, Eva. *The Secret of Platform 11*. Dutton, 1998. / Jordan, Tanis. *Amazon Alphabet*. Kingfisher, 1996. / Levine, Gail Carson. *Dave at Night*. HarperCollins, 1999. / Rowling, J. K. *Harry Potter and the Sorcerer's Stone*. Scholastic, 1998. (And others in the Harry Potter series.) / Snyder, Zilpha Keatley. *Gib Rides Home*. Delacorte, 1998. / Spinelli, Jerry. *Maniac Magee*. Little, Brown, 1990. / Wallace, Barbara Brooks. *Peppermints in the Parlor*. Atheneum, 1980. / Whelan, Gloria. *Listening for Lions*. HarperCollins, 2005.

SUBJECTS: ADVENTURE AND ADVENTURERS. AMAZON RIVER. HISTORICAL FICTION. MULTICULTURAL BOOKS. ORPHANS. RIVERS. SOUTH AMERICA. VOYAGES AND TRAVELS.

1007 Ibbotson, Eva. *The Secret of Platform 13*. **Illus. by Sue Porter. Dutton, 1998. 0-525-45929-4. 231pp. Gr. 4–6**

Here is another splendid English fantasy about a parallel world, dreadful substitute parents, magic in a London railway station, and a stalwart young hero unaware of his true identity. Renamed Raymond Trottle by the haughty, childless, rich woman who abducts him from his basket, the baby prince from the Island, a land hidden off the coast of England, spends nine miserable years before a motley but magical band of rescuers can set out for England to rescue him.

GERM: While it's startling and fun to note this book's many similarities to J. K. Rowling's *Harry Potter and the Sorcerer's Stone*, each book stands on its own as a rewarding introduction to the fantasy genre.

RELATED TITLES: Bath, K. P. *The Secret of Castle Cant*. Little, Brown, 2004. / Burnett, Frances Hodgson. *A Little Princess*. HarperCollins, 1992. / Divakaruni, Chitra Banerjee. *The Conch Bearer*. Roaring Brook, 2003. / Edwards, Julie. *The Last of the Really Great Whangdoodles*. HarperCollins, 1974. / Langrish, Katherine. *Troll Fell*. HarperCollins, 2004. / Levine, Gail Carson. *Dave at Night*. HarperCollins, 1999. / Rowling, J. K. *Harry Potter and the Sorcerer's Stone*. Scholastic, 1998. (And others in the Harry Potter series.) / Wallace, Barbara Brooks. *Peppermints in the Parlor*. Atheneum, 1980.

SUBJECTS: ENGLAND. FANTASY. MAGIC.

1008 Ives, David. *Monsieur Eek*. **HarperCollins, 2001. 0-06-029529-5. 179pp. Gr. 5–7**

Living in the repressed town of MacOongafoondsen, troublemakers Emmaline and her best friend Flurp, considered the town fool, rescue the sole survivor from the ghost ship that drifts up offshore, a hairy little fellow who only says "Eek."

GERM: Discussion point: The town rulers have a fear and loathing of the French. Why is this? What are they really afraid of? Children will of course recognize that Mr. Eek is in reality a monkey and not a man from France. Have them pull out descriptions and details to support their discovery.

RELATED TITLES: Amato, Mary. *The Word Eater*. Holiday House, 2000. / Avi. *Perloo the Bold*. Scholastic, 1998. / Avi. *Poppy*. Little, Brown, 2001. / James, Mary. *Shoebag*. Scholastic, 1990. / L'Engle, Madeleine. *A Wrinkle in Time*. Farrar, 1962. / Lisle, Janet Taylor. *Forest*. Orchard, 1993. / Lowry, Lois. *The Giver*. Houghton Mifflin, 1993. / Mazer, Anne. *The Oxboy*. Knopf, 1993. / McGraw, Eloise. *The Moorchild*. McElderry, 1996. / Nodelman, Perry. *The Same Place But Different*. Simon & Schuster, 1995. / Spinelli, Jerry. *Maniac Magee*. Little, Brown, 1990. / Van Allsburg, Chris. *The Widow's Broom*. Houghton Mifflin, 1992.

SUBJECTS: BEHAVIOR. MONKEYS. PREJUDICE.

1009 **Jacobson, Jennifer Richard. *Truly Winnie*. Illus. by Alissa Imre Geis. Houghton Mifflin, 2003. 0-618-28008-1. 105pp. Gr. 2–4**

Spending two weeks at summer camp for the first time, Winnie gets caught up in a web of lies; instead of telling her new friends that her mother died after Winnie was born, she tells them her mother is a famous artist.

GERM: This brief but pointed story will help you open a dialogue on why people lie and the ways we own up to our own less-than-truthful statements. Discussion points: Why does Winnie lie to her new pal Roxie? Why are her old friends Vanessa and Zoe so angry with Winnie? How does Winnie make amends with her friends? Have you ever been caught in a lie? What happened? How did you handle it? Based on your own experience with friendships, what advice would you give to Winnie?

RELATED TITLES: Brisson, Pat. *The Summer My Father Was Ten*. Boyds Mills, 1998. / Conford, Ellen. *Hail, Hail Camp Timberwood*. Little, Brown, 1978. / Demi. *The Empty Pot*. Henry Holt, 1990. / Levy, Elizabeth. *Lizzie Lies a Lot*. Delacorte, 1976. / McKissack, Patricia C. *The Honest-to-Goodness Truth*. Atheneum, 2000. / Peters, Julie Anne. *The Stinky Sneakers Contest*. Little, Brown, 1992. / Park, Barbara. *Buddies*. Avon, 1986. / Park, Barbara. *Junie B., First Grader: Cheater Pants*. Random House, 2003. / Polacco, Patricia. *Chicken Sunday*. Philomel, 1992. / Soto, Gary. *Too Many Tamales*. Putnam, 1993. / Wood, Audrey. *The Red Racer*. Simon & Schuster, 1996.

SUBJECTS: APOLOGIES. CAMPS. FATHERS AND DAUGHTERS. FRIENDSHIP. HONESTY. SINGLE-PARENT FAMILIES.

1010 **Jennings, Patrick. *Putnam and Pennyroyal*. Illus. by Jon J Muth. Scholastic, 1999. 0-439-07965-9. 163pp. Gr. 4–6**

While fishing on Coot Pond, Uncle Frank tells his 9-year-old sharp-tongued niece, Cora Lee, what he calls a true story about a pied-billed grebe (a water bird) named Putnam. After solitary, sensible Putnam becomes trapped in an underwater cave, he encounters the annoyingly nonconformist and feisty Pennyroyal, a female least grebe, whom he ultimately learns to love. Frank's absorbing and homespun bird story, filled with tidbits of bird facts and lore, draws Cora in and allows her to see parallels between Putnam's reclusive life and that of her beloved uncle.

GERM: Find books and information in the library and online about grebes, loons, and other water birds. Discussion point: How is Putnam like Uncle Frank?

RELATED TITLES: Arnosky, Jim. *Watching Water Birds*. National Geographic, 1997. / Avi. *Perloo the Bold*. Scholastic, 1998. / Avi. *Poppy*. Orchard, 1995. / Dengler, Marianna. *The Worry Stone*. Northland, 1996. / Esbensen, Barbara Juster. *Great Northern Diver: The Loon*. Little, Brown, 1990. / Florian, Douglas. *On the Wing: Bird Poems and Paintings*. Harcourt, 1996. / Hamilton, Virginia. *When Birds Could Talk and Bats Could Sing*. Blue Sky/Scholastic, 1996. / Martin, Jacqueline Briggs. *Washing the Willow Tree Loon*. Simon & Schuster, 1995. / Napoli, Donna Jo. *The Prince of the Pond*. Dutton, 1992. / Oppel, Kenneth. *Silverwing*. Simon & Schuster, 1997. / Tyrrell, Esther Quesada. *Hummingbirds: Jewels in the Sky*. Crown, 1992. / Yolen, Jane. *Bird Watch: A Book of Poetry*. Philomel, 1990.

SUBJECTS: BIRDS. GREBES. INDIVIDUALITY. NATURE. NONCONFORMISTS. STORYTELLING. UNCLES.

1011 **Joseph, Lynn. *The Color of My Words*. HarperCollins, 2000. 0-06-028233-9. 138pp. Gr. 5–8**

Growing up poor in the politically repressive Dominican Republic, 12-year-old Ana Rosa, who wants to be a writer, discovers the power and danger of words. Mami tells her, "Writers have died here. At least those brave enough to hurl words at our government." In spite of this warning, Ana Rosa writes the story of how her life changed that year, when the corrupt government tried to take over their seaside village to put up a tourist hotel, and how her adored big brother, 19-year-old Guario, led the fight to stop them.

GERM: This eloquent little novel is a read-aloud gift, a blend of poetry and narrative told by the perceptive Ana Rosa, who loves to observe everything from her perch in the gris-gris tree above the house. Students can each write a significant chapter of their own lives and compose a poem to accompany it. For an interesting pairing, Beverly Naidoo's *The Other Side of Truth* deals with two children escaping the political repression of Nigeria.

RELATED TITLES: Agard, John. *A Caribbean Dozen: Poems from Caribbean Poets.* Candlewick, 1994. / Joseph, Lynn. *A Wave in Her Pocket.* HarperCollins, 1991. / Naidoo, Beverly. *The Other Side of Truth.* HarperCollins, 2001. / Recorvits, Helen. *Goodbye, Walter Malinski.* Farrar, 1999. / Slepian, Jan. *The Broccoli Tapes.* Philomel, 1988. / Snyder, Zilpha Keatley. *Libby on Wednesday.* Delacorte, 1990. / Sturtevant, Katherine. *At the Sign of the Star.* Farrar, 2000. / Taylor, Mildred. *Roll of Thunder, Hear My Cry.* Dial, 1976. / Temple, Frances. *A Taste of Salt.* Orchard, 1992.

SUBJECTS: BROTHERS AND SISTERS. DOMINICAN REPUBLIC. FAMILY LIFE. MULTICULTURAL BOOKS. POETS. WRITING.

1012 **Karr, Kathleen.** *The Great Turkey Walk.* **Farrar, 1998. 0-374-32773-4. 199pp. Gr. 4–6**

After completing third grade for the fourth time, 15-year-old Simon Green leaves school in 1860 and sets out to walk a flock of one thousand turkeys a thousand miles from Missouri to Denver. Along the way, he accumulates a trio of traveling companions: Mr. Peece, a none-too-sober mule skinner, and his little terrier Emmett; Jabeth Ballou, a runaway slave on his way to the Kansas Territory and freedom; and Lizzie Hardwick, sole survivor of a homesteading family on the prairie, an "older woman" of 16. Trailing the trio and hoping to steal their turkeys are two villains, including Simon's own rapscallion father, Samson, a strongman in a traveling circus who deserted his family ten years before. Simon's matter-of-fact narrative, based on an actual event, is filled with humor and adventure and will get kids to consider turkeys in a whole new light.

GERM: Supplement your reading with Russell Freedman's *Children of the Wild West*, a stirring nonfiction account, laced with many captivating period photographs, that shows what it was like for settler and Indian children living and going to school out West in the second half of the 19th century.

RELATED TITLES: Cushman, Karen. *The Ballad of Lucy Whipple.* Clarion, 1996. / Fleischman, Sid. *By the Great Horn Spoon.* Little, Brown, 1963. / Fleischman, Sid. *Jim Ugly.* Greenwillow, 1992. / Freedman, Russell. *Children of the Wild West.* Clarion, 1983. / Greer, Gery, and Bob Ruddick. *Max and Me and the Wild West.* Harcourt, 1988. / Mooser, Stephen. *Orphan Jeb at the Massacree.* Knopf, 1984. / Osborne, Mary Pope. *Adaline Falling Star.* Scholastic, 2000. / Ryan, Pam Muñoz. *Riding Freedom.* Scholastic, 1998. / Schanzer, Rosalyn. *How We Crossed the West: The Adventures of Lewis and Clark.* National Geographic, 1997.

SUBJECTS: ADVENTURE AND ADVENTURERS. HISTORICAL FICTION. ROBBERS AND OUTLAWS. TURKEYS. WEST (U.S.)—HISTORY—FICTION.

1013 **Kehret, Peg.** *Earthquake Terror.* **Dutton, 1996. 0-525-65226-4. 132pp. Gr. 4–7**

A peaceful camping trip to Magpie Island in northern California with his parents, disabled younger sister Abby, and dog Moose becomes an exercise in survival for 12-year-old Jonathan when his mother fractures her ankle and leaves him in charge. Jonathan has always wondered how he'd react in an earthquake; now he finds out the hard way as the ground heaves, devastating the island and their camper. The two children and dog cope remarkably well until they realize the island is becoming flooded, and Abby can't swim.

GERM: A gripping page-turner, this novel will prove a first-rate companion to units on disasters, survival, the physically challenged, and, of course, geology and earthquakes.

RELATED TITLES: Clements, Andrew. *A Week in the Woods.* Simon & Schuster, 2002. / Cottonwood, Joe. *Quake.* Scholastic, 1995. / Dodds, Bill. *My Sister Annie.* Boyds Mills, 1993. / Roy, Ron. *Nightmare Island.* Dutton, 1981. / Ruckman, Ivy. *Night of the Twisters.* Crowell, 1984. / Shreve, Susan. *The Gift of the Girl Who Couldn't Hear.* Tambourine, 1991. / Shyer, Marlene Fanta. *Welcome Home, Jellybean.* Macmillan, 1978. / Simon, Seymour. *Earthquakes.* Morrow, 1991.

SUBJECTS: BROTHERS AND SISTERS. DISASTERS. EARTHQUAKES. PEOPLE WITH DISABILITIES. PHYSICALLY HANDICAPPED. SURVIVAL.

1014 Kennemore, Tim. *Circle of Doom*. Illus. by Tim Archibold. Farrar, 2003. 0-374-31284-2. 203pp. Gr. 4–7

After assembling a magic potion that seems to succeed in ridding them of their awful neighbors, the Potwards, 13-year-old Lizzie Sharp and her two younger brothers concoct a new potion to handle a difficult teacher. How the youngest brother, Max, gets even with nasty bullying classmate Nathan Dursley, is just one hilarious scene in a laugh-out-loud family story from England.

GERM: Though told by an omniscient narrator, the story latches on to the thoughts and emotions of each of the three Sharp children. Ask your listeners to write about the sibling they most identify with and why and to make charts describing the personalities of each of the three Sharp kids. Compare the coincidences the siblings encounter in the novel with your own true-life ones.

RELATED TITLES: Cresswell, Helen. *Ordinary Jack*. Macmillan, 1977. / Fine, Anne. *Alias Madame Doubtfire*. Bantam, 1993. / Lowry, Lois. *See You Around, Sam*. Houghton Mifflin, 1996. / McKay, Hilary. *Saffy's Angel*. McElderry, 2002. / Naylor, Phyllis Reynolds. *The Boys Start the War*. Delacorte, 1993. / Peck, Richard. *The Teacher's Funeral: A Comedy in Three Parts*. Dial, 2004. / Tolan, Stephanie. *Surviving the Applewhites*. Harper-Collins, 2002.

SUBJECTS: BROTHERS AND SISTERS. BULLIES. COINCIDENCE. ENGLAND. FAMILY LIFE. HUMOROUS FICTION. MAGIC.

1015 Kimmel, Eric A. *The Jar of Fools: Eight Hanukkah Stories from Chelm*. Illus. by Mordicai Gerstein. Holiday House, 2000. 0-8234-1463-9. Unp. Gr. 2–6

Get to know the fools of the Polish village of Chelm at Hanukkah time, where Motke Fool, voted the wisest person in town, wears his golden slippers on his ears so they won't get muddy; Silent Samson saves the town from an army of Cossacks without saying a word; and the whole village pays a stranger 1,500 zlotys for a magic latke spoon. Two of the stories are traditional Yiddish folktales, three are adaptations of stories from other cultures, and three are original tales dreamed up by Kimmel.

GERM: As Kimmel advises in his Author's Note, "Writing a good Chelm story is a challenge. You almost have to think like a Chelmer to do it." Read more Chelm stories, including ones in the collections by Isaac Bashevis Singer listed below, and give it a try. Kimmel retells the "Stone Soup" folktale as a latkes story in "The Magic Spoon." He has also transported the story to Mexico in *Cactus Soup*, to which you can compare it. Also compare Kimmel's story "Silent Samson, the Maccabee" with "The Debate" in Amy L. Cohn's *From Sea to Shining Sea*.

RELATED TITLES: Cohn, Amy L. *From Sea to Shining Sea: A Treasury of American Folklore and Folk Songs*. Scholastic, 1993. / Freedman, Florence B. *It Happened in Chelm: A Story of the Legendary Town of Fools*. Shapolsky, 1990. / Greene, Jacqueline D. *What His Father Did*. Houghton, 1992. / Kimmel, Eric A. *The Adventures of Hershel of Ostropol*. Holiday House, 1995. / Kimmel, Eric A. *Cactus Soup*. Marshall Cavendish, 2004. / Kimmel, Eric A. *Hershel and the Hanukkah Goblins*. Holiday House, 1989. / Kimmel, Eric A. *The Magic Dreidels: A Hanukkah Story*. Holiday House, 1996. / Schwartz, Amy. *Yossel Zissel and the Wisdom of Chelm*. Jewish Publication Society, 1986. / Schwartz, Howard. *Elijah's Violin and Other Jewish Fairy Tales*. HarperCollins, 1983. / Singer, Isaac Bashevis. *When Shlemiel Went to Warsaw and Other Stories*. Farrar, 1979. / Singer, Isaac Bashevis. *Zlateh the Goat and Other Stories*. HarperCollins, 1994. / Singh, Rina. *The Foolish Men of Agra and Other Tales of Mogul India*. Key Porter, 1998.

SUBJECTS: CHELM. FOOLS. HANUKKAH. JEWS. SHORT STORIES.

1016 Kindl, Patrice. *Goose Chase*. Houghton Mifflin, 2001. 0-618-03377-7. 214pp. Gr. 5–8

Shut up in a tower for the past six months, a poor orphan Goose Girl with tart tongue and boundless wit must figure out a way to avoid marriage with either the deadly King Claudio the Cruel or the handsome Prince Edmund of Dorloo, whom she considers "somewhat less intelligent than a clod of dirt." Both suitors swear they are sick with lovelonging for her, though perhaps it's because of her special "gifts": when she combs her hair, gold dust falls like rain, and when she weeps, her tears are diamonds.

GERM: Photocopy some of the Goose Girl's many caustic dialogues, including her encounters with three ravenous, human-eating ogresses, and have pairs of readers perform them aloud as Reader's Theater. Read aloud Robert Bender's retelling of the Brothers Grimm tale *Toads and Diamonds* and Hans Christian Andersen's *The Wild Swans* to analyze their connections to Kindl's novel. Gail Carson Levine's *The Fairy's Mistake* is a spoof that features another diamond-spouting princess.

RELATED TITLES: Andersen, Hans Christian. *The Wild Swans*. Retold by Deborah Hautzig. Knopf, 1992. / Bender, Robert. *Toads and Diamonds*. Dutton, 1995. / Billingsley, Franny. *The Folk Keeper*. Atheneum, 1999. / Kindl, Patrice. *Owl in Love*. Houghton, 1993. / Langrish, Katherine. *Troll Fell*. HarperCollins, 2004. / Levine, Gail Carson. *Ella Enchanted*. HarperCollins, 1997. / Levine, Gail Carson. *The Fairy's Mistake*. HarperCollins, 1999. / Levine, Gail Carson. *The Princess Test*. HarperCollins, 1999. / Matas, Carol, and Perry Nodelman. *Of Two Minds*. Simon & Schuster, 1995. / McKinley, Robin. *Beauty*. HarperCollins, 1978. / Napoli, Donna Jo. *Jimmy, the Pickpocket of the Palace*. Dutton, 1995. / Napoli, Donna Jo. *The Prince of the Pond*. Dutton, 1992. / Pullman, Philip. *I Was a Rat!* Knopf, 2000. / Vande Velde, Vivian. *Tales from the Brothers Grimm and the Sisters Weird*. Harcourt, 1995.

SUBJECTS: FAIRY TALES. FANTASY. GEESE. HUMOROUS FICTION. KINGS AND RULERS. PARODIES. READER'S THEATER. SATIRE. TRANSFORMATIONS.

1017 King-Smith, Dick. *Clever Lollipop*. Illus. by Jill Barton. Candlewick, 2003. 0-7636-2174-9. 143pp. Gr. 1–4

Under-gardener at the palace, young Johnny Skinner, who is the trainer of talented Lollipop the pig and Princess Penelope's best friend, decides he would like to learn to read. He finds the perfect teacher for Penelope, himself, and Lollipop: Collie Cobb, AKA The Conjuror. This sequel to Lady Lollipop can be read independently or in tandem with the first book, *Lady Lollipop*.

GERM: As your children learn new facts and lessons, have them recite the Conjuror's magical rhyme for remembering everything: "The facts I'm going to learn today / Will find it hard to go away. / Most will remain inside my brain. / I shan't need to be told again." Take a Reading Walk with your learners. Ask them to make a list of ten new things they'd like to learn this year, and then share.

RELATED TITLES: Dahl, Roald. *Matilda*. Viking, 1988. / Evans, Douglas. *Apple Island, or The Truth About Teachers*. Front Street, 1998. / Hornik, Laurie Miller. *The Secrets of Ms. Snickle's Class*. Clarion, 2001. / King-Smith, Dick. *Babe, the Gallant Pig*. Crown, 1985. / King-Smith, Dick. *Harriet's Hare*. Crown, 1995. / King-Smith, Dick. *Lady Lollipop*. Candlewick, 2001. / King-Smith, Dick. *Pigs Might Fly*. Viking, 1982. / King-Smith, Dick. *The School Mouse*. Little, Brown, 1995. / MacDonald, Amy. *No More Nasty*. Farrar, 2001.

SUBJECTS: FICTION BOOKS FOR EARLY GRADES. HOME SCHOOLING. MAGICIANS. PIGS. PRINCES AND PRINCESSES. TEACHERS.

1018 King-Smith, Dick. *George Speaks*. Illus. by Judy Brown. Roaring Brook, 2002. 0-7613-1544-6. 92pp. Gr. 1–4

Much to the amazement of 7-year-old Laura, her 4-week-old baby brother George, born on April 1st, speaks to her in full, complex sentences and even knows his times tables.

GERM: Pair this amiable, short chapter book with Simon James's picture book *Baby Brains*, about another smart cookie. Have children ask their parents to recall how old they were when they said their first words and what it was that they had to say. Then have them write up the event as a narrative story, incorporating the 5 Ws. Meet another verbose character, the talking African Gray parrot in King-Smith's *Harry's Mad*.

RELATED TITLES: Curtis, Marci. *I Was So Silly! Big Kids Remember Being Little*. Dial, 2002. / Hinton, S. E. *The Puppy Sister*. Delacorte, 1995. / James, Simon. *Baby Brains*. Candlewick, 2004. / King-Smith, Dick. *Harry's Mad*. Knopf, 1997. / Regan, Dian Curtis. *Chance*. Philomel, 2003. / Schwartz, Amy. *A Teeny Tiny Baby*. Orchard, 1994.

SUBJECTS: BABIES. BROTHERS AND SISTERS. FICTION BOOKS FOR EARLY GRADES. HUMOROUS FICTION. SPEECH.

1019 King-Smith, Dick. *Harriet's Hare*. Illus. by Roger Roth. Crown, 1995. 0-517-59830-2. 104pp. Gr. 2–5

Eight-year-old Harriet meets up with Wiz, an erudite talking hare newly arrived from the more advanced planet Pars. Wiz can transform himself into any shape, speak all languages, and foresee and arrange the future. Harriet and her farmer dad have been too solitary since Harriet's mother died, and Wiz employs a bit of magic to bring the two together with Jessica Lambert, a children's book writer who has a special affinity with hares.

GERM: Compare the alien Wiz with Oluu, the extraterrestrial shape-changer in Jane Leslie Conly's *The Rudest Alien on Earth*. Sci fi fans can make a chart comparing our language, customs, life forms, foods, and other out-of-the-world alien ideas and ideals with those on Pars.

RELATED TITLES: Bechard, Margaret. *Star Hatchling*. Viking, 1995. / Brittain, Bill. *Shape-Changer*. HarperCollins, 1994. / Conly, Jane Leslie. *The Rudest Alien on Earth*. Henry Holt, 2002. / Gauthier, Gail. *My Life*

Among the Aliens. Putnam, 1996. / King-Smith, Dick. *Babe, the Gallant Pig.* Crown, 1985. / King-Smith, Dick. *Pigs Might Fly.* Viking, 1982. / King-Smith, Dick. *The School Mouse.* Little, Brown, 1995. / King-Smith, Dick. *Three Terrible Trins.* Crown, 1994. / Service, Pamela. *Stinker from Space.* Scribner, 1988.

SUBJECTS: ENGLAND. EXTRATERRESTRIAL LIFE. FANTASY. FARM LIFE. FATHERS AND DAUGHTERS. HARES. SCIENCE FICTION. TRANSFORMATIONS.

1020   **King-Smith, Dick. *Lady Lollipop.* Illus. by Jill Barton. Candlewick, 2001. 0-7636-1269-3. 123pp. Gr. 2–4**

When 7-year-old Princess Penelope, spoiled rotten by her royal parents, demands a pig for her eighth birthday, her father issues a Royal Proclamation that commands every pig keeper in the kingdom to bring one pig to the palace. The only pig Penelope likes is the talented and intelligent Lollipop, who can sit and stand and even roll over on the command of her keeper, an amiable boy named Johnny Skinner, who comes to the palace to care for her. In the process, Johnny and Lollipop teach the headstrong, self-centered, sulking, shouting, selfish princess to behave herself, a lesson that might carry over to your own brood.

GERM: Dick King-Smith, former pig farmer and author of *Babe, the Gallant Pig* and dozens of beloved animal fantasies, plays it straight here, with a realistic animal story that will charm the sulks out of children, both royal and common. Discussion point: The princess wants to train her new pig, Lollipop, but the pig trains her instead. How and why does Lollipop, along with her handler, Johnny, do this? Have children make a chart showing Penelope's behavior before and after.

RELATED TITLES: Geras, Adèle. *The Cats of Cuckoo Square: Two Stories.* Delacorte, 2001. / Haddix, Margaret Peterson. *Say What?* Simon & Schuster, 2004. / King-Smith, Dick. *Babe, the Gallant Pig.* Crown, 1985. / King-Smith, Dick. *Clever Lollipop.* Candlewick, 2003. / King-Smith, Dick. *Harriet's Hare.* Crown, 1995. / King-Smith, Dick. *Pigs Might Fly.* Viking, 1982. / King-Smith, Dick. *The School Mouse.* Little, Brown, 1995. / MacDonald, Betty. *Mrs. Piggle-Wiggle* (and others in the series). Lippincott, 1975. / O'Brien, Anne Sibley. *The Princess and the Beggar: A Korean Folktale.* Scholastic, 1993. / Quindlen, Anna. *Happily Ever After.* Viking, 1997. / Robb, Laura. *Snuffles and Snouts.* Dial, 1995. / White, E. B. *Charlotte's Web.* HarperCollins, 1952.

SUBJECTS: BEHAVIOR. KINGS AND RULERS. PIGS. PRINCES AND PRINCESSES.

1021   **King-Smith, Dick. *A Mouse Called Wolf.* Illus. by Jon Goodell. Crown, 1997. 0-517-70974-0. 98pp. Gr. 1–4**

Wolfgang Amadeus Mouse, youngest and smallest of 13 mouse children, discovers his true talent: He can sing! The lady of the house, a former concert pianist named Mrs. Honeybee, soon notices the mouse with the perfect pitch and teaches Wolf a variety of melodious tunes. When Mrs. Honeybee falls and breaks her ankle, it's Wolf singing "Help!" at the top of his voice who brings a policeman to the rescue.

GERM: Play the music of Wolfgang's namesake, Mozart. Dick King-Smith, the venerable English writer, encourages the willing suspension of disbelief with his entrancing mouse fantasies, including *Martin's Mice*, *The School Mouse*, and *Three Terrible Trins*.

RELATED TITLES: Auch, Mary Jane. *Bantam of the Opera.* Holiday House, 1997. / Howe, James. *Horace and Morris Join the Chorus (But What About Dolores?).* Atheneum, 2002. / King-Smith, Dick. *Lady Lollipop.* Candlewick, 2001. / King-Smith, Dick. *Martin's Mice.* Crown, 1989. / King-Smith, Dick. *The School Mouse.* Little, Brown, 1995. / King-Smith, Dick. *Three Terrible Trins.* Crown, 1994. / Weaver, Tess. *Opera Cat.* Clarion, 2002.

SUBJECTS: FICTION BOOKS FOR EARLY GRADES. MICE. MUSIC. SINGERS.

1022   **King-Smith, Dick. *The School Mouse.* Illus. by Cynthia Fisher. Hyperion, 1995. 0-7868-0036-4. 124pp. Gr. 1–4**

Peering down at the children from her hiding place above the kindergarten teacher's desk, bright and curious mouse Flora soon learns how to decipher the little black marks found in books and becomes a reader. Because of her singular skill, when an exterminator puts down poisonous mouse pellets, she is able to read the label on the box and save her parents' lives.

GERM: Born on the first day of school, Flora's favorite word is "why?" Talk about the power of reading and knowledge. Ask your readers to make a list of what they'd like to know, questions they'd like answered, and things they're curious about. Post the lists on the walls and incorporate them into your unofficial curriculum of the year. Have everyone memorize Flora's own ABC rhyme (page 109 in the book), which begins, "ABCDEFG, Oh what clever mice are we."

RELATED TITLES: Cleary, Beverly. *Ralph S. Mouse.* Morrow, 1982. / DiCamillo, Kate. *The Tale of Despereaux.* Candlewick, 2003. / King-Smith, Dick. *Martin's Mice.* Crown, 1989. / King-Smith, Dick. *Three Terrible Trins.*

Crown, 1994. / Polacco, Patricia. *Aunt Chip and the Great Triple Creek Dam Affair*. Philomel, 1996. / Sierra, Judy. *Wild About Books*. Knopf, 2004. / Van Leeuwen, Jean. *The Great Christmas Kidnapping Caper*. Dial, 1975.

SUBJECTS: BOOKS AND READING. FANTASY. FICTION BOOKS FOR EARLY GRADES. LITERACY. MICE. SCHOOLS. TEACHERS.

1023   King-Smith, Dick. *Three Terrible Trins*. Illus. by Mark Teague. Crown, 1994. 0-517-59829-9. 105pp. Gr. 3–5

Mrs. Gray, a mouse, trains her trins, or mouse triplets, to take on the two awful cats in the Budge household of Orchard Farm. With the help of Cellermouse, Kevin, the stalwart rodents drive the two cats crazy with their bold maneuvers and organize mouse teams for a soccer-like game they call noseball, using Farmer Budge's glass eye as their ball.

GERM: "At six o'clock on the morning of her birthday, Mrs. Gray's husband was killed and eaten." That's the first sentence, which draws the reader's attention for sure. Have your group share other memorable first lines. Then ask them to write their own first lines, paragraphs, and pages, with punchy prose that will pull in any reader. Share other marvelous mouse stories by King-Smith, including *Martin's Mice, A Mouse Called Wolf,* and *The School Mouse.*

RELATED TITLES: Avi. *Poppy.* Orchard, 1995. / Cleary, Beverly. *The Mouse and the Motorcycle.* Morrow, 1965. / Cleary, Beverly. *Ralph S. Mouse.* Morrow, 1982. / DiCamillo, Kate. *The Tale of Despereaux.* Candlewick, 2003. / King-Smith, Dick. *Lady Lollipop.* Candlewick, 2001. / King-Smith, Dick. *Martin's Mice.* Crown, 1989. / King-Smith, Dick. *A Mouse Called Wolf.* Crown, 1997. / King-Smith, Dick. *The School Mouse.* Hyperion, 1995. / Van Leeuwen, Jean. *The Great Christmas Kidnapping Caper.* Dial, 1975.

SUBJECTS: CATS. FANTASY. HUMOROUS FICTION. MICE.

1024   Kipling, Rudyard. *Rikki-Tikki-Tavi*. Adapted and illus. by Jerry Pinkney. Morrow, 1997. 0-688-14321-0. 48pp. Gr. 2–6

Travel to India to introduce listeners to Kipling's classic tale of a stalwart pet mongoose, Rikki-Tikki-Tavi, who saves Teddy, the little English boy, from the deadly cobras Nag and Nagina. A mongoose's job is to fight and eat snakes; once he overhears the two cobras plotting to kill his human family, he springs into action, first killing Nag and then outwitting Nag's wife. Pinkney's grand watercolors of the chilling battle between Rikki and the vengeful snakes are worthy companions to the elegant story, which has been slightly abridged and simplified so younger children can understand it.

GERM: For the full text, read the version illustrated by Lambert Davis. Look up supporting materials on animals and customs of India.

RELATED TITLES: Cannon, Janell. *Verdi.* Harcourt, 1997. / Dewey, Jennifer Owings. *Rattlesnake Dance: True Tales, Mysteries, and Rattlesnake Ceremonies.* Boyds Mills, 1997. / Kastner, Jill. *Snake Hunt.* Four Winds, 1993. / Khan, Rukhsana. *Ruler of the Courtyard.* Viking, 2003. / Kipling, Rudyard. *Rikki-Tikki-Tavi.* Illus. by Lambert Davis. Harcourt, 1992. / Maestro, Betsy. *Take a Look at Snakes.* Scholastic, 1992. / McNulty, Faith. *A Snake in the House.* Scholastic, 1994.

SUBJECTS: COBRAS. FANTASY. INDIA. MONGOOSES. MULTICULTURAL BOOKS. SNAKES.

1025   Kipling, Rudyard. *Rudyard Kipling's Just So Stories*. Illus. by Peter Sis and others. Candlewick, 2004. 0-7636-2629-5. 127pp. Gr. 2–6

In a nicely formatted collection of eight Kipling pourquoi tales, each story has been illustrated by a different children's book illustrator, including Peter Sis, Jane Ray, and Louise Voce. Stories include "The Elephant's Child," of course, plus "How the Camel Got His Hump," "How the Rhinoceros Got His Skin," and "How the Leopard Got His Spots."

GERM: Read some of the stories without showing the illustrations and have children draw their own interpretations. Compare Kipling's literary pourquoi tales (how and why stories) with some traditional ones from folklore.

RELATED TITLES: Kipling, Rudyard. *The Beginning of the Armadillos.* Illus. by Lorinda Bryan Cauley. Harcourt, 1985. / Kipling, Rudyard. *The Elephant's Child.* Illus. by Lorinda Bryan Cauley. Harcourt, 1983. / Kipling, Rudyard. *How the Camel Got His Hump.* Illus. by Quentin Blake. Peter Bedrick, 1985. / Kipling, Rudyard. *How the Whale Got His Throat.* Illus. by Pauline Baynes. Peter Bedrick, 1983. / Kipling, Rudyard. *Just So Stories.* Illus. by Victor Ambrus. Rand, 1982. / Kipling, Rudyard. *Just So Stories.* Illus. by David Frampton. HarperCollins, 1991. / Kipling, Rudyard. *Rikki-Tikki-Tavi.* Adapted and illus. by Jerry Pinkney. Morrow, 1997. / Kipling, Rudyard. *Rikki-Tikki-Tavi.* Illus. by Lambert Davis. Harcourt, 1992.

SUBJECTS: ANIMALS. POURQUOI TALES. SHORT STORIES.

1026 **Klein, Abby.** *The King of Show-and-Tell.* **Illus. by John McKinley. Blue Sky/Scholastic, 2004. 0-439-55597-3. 96pp. Gr. K–2**

Freddy states his problem: It's his turn for show-and-tell on Monday, and he'd sure like to find something as cool as the alligator head that classmate Robbie brought for show-and-tell today. When he rescues a baby bird that has fallen from its nest, he names it Winger and sneaks the bird to school.

GERM: Do some research on how Freddy should be caring for his baby bird, Winger. At the back of the book, series author Abbie Klein asks readers to write her a letter and tell her about their special show-and-tell items. She also provides Freddy's Fun Pages, with activities and directions for making a winter bird feeder out of a pinecone. Set kids up with the other easy chapter books in this humorous series.

RELATED TITLES: Blume, Judy. *Tales of a Fourth Grade Nothing.* Dutton, 1972. / Cameron, Ann. *The Stories Huey Tells.* Knopf, 1995. / Cleary, Beverly. *Ramona the Pest.* Morrow, 1968. / Danziger, Paula. *Amber Brown Is Not a Crayon.* Putnam, 1994. / Greene, Stephanie. *Show and Tell.* Clarion, 1998. / Klein, Abby. *Tooth Trouble.* Blue Sky/Scholastic, 2004. (And others in the Ready, Freddy! series.) / Lasky, Kathryn. *Show and Tell Bunnies.* / Lowry, Lois. *Zooman Sam.* Houghton Mifflin, 1999. / McDonald, Megan. *Stink! The Incredible Shrinking Kid.* Candlewick, 2005. / Park, Barbara. *Junie B., First Grader (at Last).* Random House, 2001. (And others in the Junie B. Jones series.) / Simms, Laura. *Rotten Teeth.* Houghton Mifflin, 1998.

SUBJECTS: ANIMALS—INFANCY. BIRDS. FICTION BOOKS FOR EARLY GRADES. HUMOROUS FICTION. SCHOOLS. SHOW-AND-TELL PRESENTATIONS.

1027 **Kline, Suzy.** *Herbie Jones Moves On.* **Putnam, 2003. 0-399-23635-X. 80pp. Gr. 2–4**

Can Herbie's best buddy, Ray, really be moving to Texas with his family? Can Herbie and Ray come up with a foolproof plan to keep Ray in Miss Pinkham's fourth-grade class? Yup.

GERM: Encourage readers to trace the friendship of Herbie and Ray through the earlier books in the series. Act out some of those scenes with the scripts in Kline's *The Herbie Jones Reader's Theater: Funny Scenes to Read Aloud.*

RELATED TITLES: Danziger, Paula. *Amber Brown Is Not a Crayon.* Putnam, 1994. / Duffey, Betsy. *Hey, New Kid!* Viking, 1996. / Giff, Patricia Reilly. *Matthew Jackson Meets the Wall.* Delacorte, 1990. / Havill, Juanita. *Leona and Ike.* Crown, 1991. / Hurwitz, Johanna. *Class Clown.* Morrow, 1987. / Joose, Barbara M. *Wild Willie and King Kyle Detectives.* Clarion, 1993. / Kline, Suzy. *The Herbie Jones Reader's Theater: Funny Scenes to Read Aloud.* Putnam, 1992. / Kline, Suzy. *What's the Matter with Herbie Jones?* Putnam, 1987. (And others in the Herbie Jones series.) / Marsden, Carolyn. *The Gold-Threaded Dress.* Candlewick, 2002. / Park, Barbara. *The Kid in the Red Jacket.* Knopf, 1987. / Waber, Bernard. *Ira Says Goodbye.* Houghton Mifflin, 1988.

SUBJECTS: BEST FRIENDS. FRIENDSHIP. HUMOROUS FICTION. MOVING, HOUSEHOLD. SCHOOLS.

1028 **Krensky, Stephen.** *Louise Takes Charge.* **Illus. by Susanna Natti. Dial, 1998. 0-8037-2306-7. 80pp. Gr. 2–4**

Louise figures out a novel way to outwit and change the attitude of classmate Jasper, who has grown over the summer and is now using his size to intimidate everyone in their class. Borrowing an idea from her little brother, Lionel, about knights and their apprentices, she offers to become Jasper's apprentice, and soon everyone in class joins her, leaving him no one to bully.

GERM: Compare Louise's approach to bullies with that of Nolan Byrd who takes on one named Bubba Bixby in *Shredderman: Secret Identity*, the first of a series by Wendelin Van Draanen.

RELATED TITLES: Greene, Stephanie. *Owen Foote, Frontiersman.* Clarion, 1996. / Howe, James. *Pinky and Rex and the Bully.* Atheneum, 1996. / Krensky, Steven. *Louise Goes Wild.* Dial, 1999. / Polacco, Patricia. *Mr. Lincoln's Way.* Philomel, 2001. / Sorel, Edward, and Cheryl Carlesimo. *The Saturday Kid.* McElderry, 2000. / Van Draanen, Wendelin. *Shredderman: Secret Identity.* Knopf, 2004.

SUBJECTS: BULLIES. PROBLEM SOLVING. SCHOOLS. TEACHERS.

1029 **Langrish, Katherine.** *Troll Fell.* **HarperCollins, 2004. 0-06-058304-5. 264pp. Gr. 5–8**

After his carpenter father's funeral, Peer Ulfsson and his beloved little dog Loki are carried off by his brutish twin uncles, Grim and Baldur Grimsson, to their house and mill up on bleak Troll Fell, where Peter is worked like a slave. Luckily for Peer, he makes friends with the Nis, a house spirit, and Hilde, a girl whose father has gone to sea on the last boat Peer's father built and who helps him thwart the uncles' plan to sell him off to the trolls.

GERM: Share troll tales from Ingri and Edgar Parin D'Aulaire's classic *D'Aulaires' Trolls* and Lise Lunge-Larsen's *The Troll with No Heart in His Body.* Find books on Vikings and their ships in the 948s in your library. For a look at how mills work, examine David Macaulay's *Mill* (Houghton Mifflin, 1983).

RELATED TITLES: Billingsley, Franny. *The Folk Keeper*. Atheneum, 1999. / Black, Holly, and Tony DiTerlizzi. The Spiderwick Chronicles series. Simon & Schuster. / Collins, Suzanne. *Gregor the Overlander*. Scholastic, 2003. / D'Aulaire, Ingri, and Edgar Parin D'Aulaire. *D'Aulaires' Trolls*. Doubleday, 1972. / dePaola, Tomie. *The Cat on the Dovrefell*. Putnam, 1979. / Divakaruni, Chitra Banerjee. *The Conch Bearer*. Roaring Brook, 2003. / Farmer, Nancy. *The Sea of Trolls*. Atheneum, 2004. / Levine, Gail Carson. *Ella Enchanted*. HarperCollins, 1997. / Lunge-Larsen, Lise. *The Troll with No Heart in His Body: And Other Tales of Trolls from Norway*. Houghton Mifflin, 1999. / McGraw, Eloise. *The Moorchild*. McElderry, 1996. / Nodelman, Perry. *The Same Place But Different*. Simon & Schuster, 1995. / Pratchett, Terry. *The Wee Free Men*. HarperCollins, 2003. / Rowling, J. K. *Harry Potter and the Sorcerer's Stone*. Scholastic, 1998. (And others in the Harry Potter series.) / Shepard, Aaron. *Master Maid: A Tale of Norway*. Dial, 1997.

SUBJECTS: DOGS. FANTASY. ORPHANS. TROLLS. TWINS. UNCLES. VIKINGS.

1030 **Larson, Kirby.** *Cody and Quinn, Sitting in a Tree.* **Illus. by Nancy Poydar. Holiday House, 1996. 0-8234-1227-X. 84pp. Gr. 1–2**

Cody's best friend, Quinn, is a girl, which is just fine until class bully Royce won't stop teasing Cody about their friendship. When Royce recites that rhyme with the "k-i-s-s-i-n-g . . ." refrain, Cody loses it, screaming, "I don't love her . . . I hate her."

GERM: You'll love the class project Cody's teacher assigns: pair up, make sock puppets, and put on a puppet play of a good book. Cody and Quinn do a George and Martha story. Your puppeteers might be inspired to do the same. See how Pinky handles a similar problem of teasing in *Pinky and Rex and the Bully* by James Howe. Another good book with strategies on how to tame a bully is *The Recess Queen* by Alexis O'Neill.

RELATED TITLES: Caseley, Judith. *Bully*. Greenwillow, 2001. / Greene, Stephanie. *Owen Foote, Frontiersman*. Clarion, 1999. / Greene, Stephanie. *Show and Tell*. Clarion, 1998. / Hall, Bruce Edward. *Henry and the Dragon Kite*. Philomel, 2004. / Kline, Suzy. *What's the Matter with Herbie Jones?* Putnam, 1987. / Larson, Kirby. *Second Grade Pig-Pals*. Holiday House, 1994. / Marshall, James. *George and Martha: The Complete Stories of Two Best Friends*. Houghton Mifflin, 1997. / Naylor, Phyllis Reynolds. *King of the Playground*. Atheneum, 1991. / O'Neill, Alexis. *The Recess Queen*. Scholastic, 2002.

SUBJECTS: BEST FRIENDS. BULLIES. FICTION BOOKS FOR EARLY GRADES. FRIENDSHIP. SCHOOLS.

1031 **Levine, Gail Carson.** *Dave at Night.* **HarperCollins, 1999. 0-06-028154-5. 272pp. Gr. 4–8**

After his adored father dies falling off a roof in 1926, 11-year-old troublemaker Dave is sent to the Hebrew Home for Boys in Harlem, New York. At the HHB, nicknamed the Hellhole for Brats, Dave figures out a way to sneak out of school at night and is befriended by Solly the gonif, an elderly fortune-teller who takes Dave to a rent party in Harlem to tell fortunes. The eccentric characters—the terrifying headmaster, the art teacher who sees promise in Dave, and the partygoers of the Harlem Renaissance—make this atmospheric novel, which is loosely based on the experiences of the author's grandfather, unforgettable.

GERM: Research the icons of the Harlem Renaissance, including Paul Laurence Dunbar and Langston Hughes. Have children ask grandparents to relate stories of their school experiences. Share some of the poems from *The Dream Keeper and Other Poems* by Langston Hughes, originally published in 1932.

RELATED TITLES: Bath, K. P. *The Secret of Castle Cant*. Little, Brown, 2004. / Bierman, Carol. *Journey to Ellis Island: How My Father Came to America*. Hyperion, 1998. / Choldenko, Gennifer. *Al Capone Does My Shirts*. Putnam, 2004. / Creech, Sharon. *Ruby Holler*. HarperCollins, 2002. / Curtis, Christopher Paul. *Bud, Not Buddy*. Delacorte, 1999. / Hughes, Langston. *The Dream Keeper and Other Poems*. Knopf, 1994. / Ibbotson, Eva. *Journey to the River Sea*. Dutton, 2002. / Myers, Walter Dean. *Harlem*. Scholastic, 1997. / Propp, Vera W. *When the Soldiers Were Gone*. Putnam, 1999. / Rowling, J. K. *Harry Potter and the Sorcerer's Stone*. Scholastic, 1998. (And others in the Harry Potter series.) / Ryan, Pam Muñoz. *Riding Freedom*. Scholastic, 1998. / Sachar, Louis. *Holes*. Farrar, 1998. / Snyder, Zilpha Keatley. *Gib Rides Home*. Delacorte, 1998. / Woodruff, Elvira. *The Orphan of Ellis Island: A Time Travel Adventure*. Scholastic, 1997.

SUBJECTS: AFRICAN AMERICANS. FRIENDSHIP. HARLEM RENAISSANCE. HISTORICAL FICTION. JEWS. MULTICULTURAL BOOKS. NEW YORK CITY. ORPHANS. PRINCIPALS. SCHOOLS.

1032 **Levine, Gail Carson.** *Ella Enchanted.* **HarperCollins, 1997. 0-06-027511-1. 232pp. Gr. 4–7**

Cursed at birth by the interfering fairy Lucinda's "gift" of obedience, Ella, now 14, relates how she is shipped off to finishing school with her two cloddish and manipulating future stepsisters. Running away from that dreadful school, Ella meets up with friendly gnomes and dangerous ogres and gradually finds herself falling in love with her genial friend Prince Charmont.

GERM: You'll want to examine every available Cinderella retelling (and there are more than 500 worldwide) to compare and celebrate this superbly crafted story. Check out the alternate points of view in *I Was a Rat!* by Philip Pullman and *If the Shoe Fits: Voices from Cinderella* by Laura Whipple. Compare, contrast, and evaluate the movie of *Ella Enchanted* and the book.

RELATED TITLES: Billingsley, Franny. *The Folk Keeper*. Atheneum, 1999. / Burnett, Frances Hodgson. *A Little Princess*. HarperCollins, 1992. / Craft, K. Y. *Cinderella*. SeaStar Books, 2000. / Ehrlich, Amy. *Cinderella*. Illus. by Susan Jeffers. Dutton, 2004. / Hughes, Shirley. *Ella's Big Chance: A Jazz-Age Cinderella*. Simon & Schuster, 2004. / Jackson, Ellen. *Cinder Edna*. Lothrop, 1994 / Kindl, Patrice. *Goose Chase*. Houghton Mifflin, 2001. / Langrish, Katherine. *Troll Fell*. HarperCollins, 2004. / Levine, Gail Carson. *Dave at Night*. HarperCollins, 1999. / Levine, Gail Carson. *The Fairy's Mistake*. HarperCollins, 1999. / Levine, Gail Carson. *The Princess Test*. HarperCollins, 1999. / Matas, Carol, and Perry Nodelman. *Of Two Minds*. Simon & Schuster, 1995. / McKinley, Robin. *Beauty*. HarperCollins, 1978. / Napoli, Donna Jo. *The Prince of the Pond*. Dutton, 1992. / Pullman, Philip. *I Was a Rat!* Knopf, 2000. / Sanderson, Ruth. *Cinderella*. Little, Brown, 2002. / Vande Velde, Vivian. *Tales from the Brothers Grimm and the Sisters Weird*. Harcourt, 1995. / Whipple, Laura. *If the Shoe Fits: Voices from Cinderella*. McElderry, 2002.

SUBJECTS: CINDERELLA STORIES. FAIRIES. FANTASY. FOLKLORE. LOVE. OBEDIENCE. PARODIES. PRINCES AND PRINCESSES.

1033 Levine, Gail Carson. *The Fairy's Mistake*. Illus. by Mark Elliott. HarperCollins, 1999. 0-06-028060-3. 88pp. Gr. 4–7

Good sister Rosella, fetching water from the well, is rewarded by the fairy Ethelinda, disguised as an old lady, for offering her a drink. Every time Rosella speaks, diamonds and jewels fall from her mouth. Bad sister Myrtle, hoping to cash in on the fairy's gift, is punished instead for her rudeness. Every time she speaks, snakes and spiders fall from her mouth. In a series of ironic twists in this short, sharp-tongued novella, Rosella is exploited by a prince who pledges his love but covets her jewels to pay for castle renovations, while Myrtle uses her misfortune to extort gifts from everyone in the village.

GERM: Readers well-versed in folklore will recognize this as a reworking of Charles Perrault's French fairy tale "Toads and Diamonds." Be sure to read aloud the traditional story first so listeners understand the humor of Levine's droll parody. Good picture-book versions include those by Robert Bender and Charlotte Huck. Compare and contrast the traditional tale with the update. After reading a sampling of other old tales, students can write new fleshed-out versions.

RELATED TITLES: Bender, Robert. *Toads and Diamonds*. Dutton, 1995. / Huck, Charlotte. *Toads and Diamonds*. Greenwillow, 1996. / Jackson, Ellen. *Cinder Edna*. Lothrop, 1994 / Levine, Gail Carson. *Ella Enchanted*. HarperCollins, 1997. / Levine, Gail Carson. *The Princess Test*. HarperCollins, 1999. / McKinley, Robin. *Beauty*. HarperCollins, 1978. / Napoli, Donna Jo. *The Prince of the Pond*. Dutton, 1992. / Vande Velde, Vivian. *Tales from the Brothers Grimm and the Sisters Weird*. Harcourt, 1995.

SUBJECTS: BEHAVIOR. CHARACTERS IN LITERATURE. FAIRIES. FAIRY TALES—SATIRE. FANTASY. HUMOROUS FICTION. PARODIES. SISTERS.

1034 Levine, Gail Carson. *The Princess Test*. Illus. by Mark Elliott. HarperCollins, 1999. 0-06-028062-X. 92pp. Gr. 4–7

In the second of "The Princess Tales," illness- and accident-prone Lorelei, the blacksmith's only daughter, inadvertently foils the housekeeper trying to do away with her and captures the heart of Prince Nicholas, whose parents are searching for a real princess wife for him using the pea-under-twenty-mattresses test.

GERM: Read and contrast this funny parody with the original Hans Christian Andersen story, *The Princess and the Pea*. As a story starter, make a top ten list: How can you recognize a real princess? Mary Jane Auch's *The Princess and the Pizza* is a cute picture-book parody and pourquoi tale, while one chapter in Jon Scieszka's *The Stinky Cheese Man and Other Fairly Stupid Tales*—"The Princess and the Bowling Ball"—will have listeners rolling.

RELATED TITLES: Andersen, Hans Christian. *The Princess and the Pea*. Illus. by Paul Galdone. Seabury, 1978. / Auch, Mary Jane. *The Princess and the Pizza*. Holiday House, 2002. / Jackson, Ellen. *Cinder Edna*. Lothrop, 1994. / Levine, Gail Carson. *Ella Enchanted*. HarperCollins, 1997. / Levine, Gail Carson. *The Fairy's Mistake*. HarperCollins, 1999. / McKinley, Robin. *Beauty*. HarperCollins, 1978. / Napoli, Donna Jo. *The Prince of the*

Pond. Dutton, 1992. / Scieszka, Jon. *The Stinky Cheese Man and Other Fairly Stupid Tales*. Viking, 1992. / Vande Velde, Vivian. *Tales from the Brothers Grimm and the Sisters Weird*. Harcourt, 1995.

SUBJECTS: CHARACTERS IN LITERATURE. FAIRY TALES—SATIRE. HUMOROUS FICTION. KINGS AND RULERS. PARODIES. PRINCES AND PRINCESSES.

1035   Levitt, Paul M., Douglas A. Burger, and Elissa S. Guralnick. *The Weighty Word Book*. **Illus. by Janet Stevens. Court Wayne, 2000. 1-57098-313-5. 96pp. Gr. 4–8**
An alphabet of 26 multisyllabic words to chew on, from *abasement* to *zealot*, are fleshed out in entertaining, pun-filled stories. Janet Stevens's jovial illustrations provide unforgettable definitions of each difficult word. For instance, after the story in which you say a separate "bye" for Kate, you'll always remember that the word "bifurcate" means to split in two.

GERM: Thanks to these mnemonic stories, the definition of each word will stay in your head for a long time. Not to be dogmatic about it, but it would be expedient for your zealous writers to create and illustrate new stories incorporating weighty words.

RELATED TITLES: Agee, Jon. *Elvis Lives and Other Anagrams*. Farrar, 2004. / Amato, Mary. *The Word Eater*. Holiday House, 2000. / Babbitt, Natalie. *The Search for Delicious*. Farrar, 1985. / Clements, Andrew. *Frindle*. Simon & Schuster, 1996. / Frasier, Debra. *Miss Alaineus: A Vocabulary Disaster*. Harcourt, 2000. / Haddix, Margaret Peterson. *Say What?* Simon & Schuster, 2004. / Hepworth, Cathi. *Antics! An Alphabetical Anthology*. Putnam, 1992. / Hepworth, Cathi. *Bug Off! A Swarm of Insect Words*. Putnam, 1998. / Hirsch, Robin. *FEG: Ridiculous Poems for Intelligent Children*. Little, Brown, 2002. / MacDonald, Amy. *No More Nice*. Orchard, 1996. / Steig, William. *CDB*. Simon & Schuster, 2000. / Viorst, Judith. *The Alphabet from Z to A: With Much Confusion on the Way*. Atheneum, 1994. / Wilbur, Richard. *The Disappearing Alphabet*. Harcourt, 1998. / Wilbur, Richard. *The Pig in the Spigot*. Harcourt, 2000.

SUBJECTS: CREATIVE WRITING. ENGLISH LANGUAGE. HUMOROUS FICTION. MNEMONICS. PUNS AND PUNNING. SHORT STORIES. VOCABULARY. WORD GAMES.

1036   Lindberg, Becky Thoman. *Thomas Tuttle, Just in Time*. **Illus. by Nancy Poydar. Albert Whitman, 1994. 0-8075-7898-3. 111pp. Gr. 1–3**
Poor Thomas, a third grader in Mrs. Findlay's class, never seems to be prepared for his teacher's project assignments, and his oral reports are a disaster. Thomas buys a book, *How to Get Better Grades*, that promises that you can do well in school without even trying.

GERM: Based on their own experiences, ask your scholars to hypothesize what useful advice might have been in that book. Compile a class book of suggestions, both real and fanciful.

RELATED TITLES: Danziger, Paula. *Amber Brown Is Not a Crayon*. Putnam, 1994. / Duffey, Betsy. *Hey, New Kid!* Viking, 1996. / Hurwitz, Johanna. *Class Clown*. Morrow, 1987. / Kline, Suzy. *What's the Matter with Herbie Jones?* Putnam, 1987.

SUBJECTS: FICTION BOOKS FOR EARLY GRADES. SCHOOLS.

1037   Lindquist, Susan Hart. *Wander*. **Delacorte, 1998. 0-385-32563-0. 133pp. Gr. 4–6**
Secretly caring for a friendly stray dog is the only good thing that's happened to James and his little sister Sary since their mother died in a car accident and they moved with their grief-bound father to Aunt Lorrie's house in the country. Their father has retreated inside himself, often leaving home for days, so James has assumed responsibility for Sary, showing her how to whistle and taking her with him to the creek to look for the elusive dog they name Wander. Then ornery neighbor Wes Tiegland loses a ewe and sets out to find and shoot the very stray that has brought love back into James's and Sary's lives.

GERM: You'll want to discuss different ways a person can be hurt and healed when tragedy strikes. Have children write about a family member or pet helping them through a bad time.

RELATED TITLES: Bauer, Marion Dane. *A Question of Trust*. Scholastic, 1994. / Cleary, Beverly. *Strider*. Morrow, 1991. / Franklin, Christine L. *Lone Wolf*. Candlewick, 1997. / Hesse, Karen. *Sable*. Henry Holt, 1994. / Lindquist, Susan Hart. *Wander*. Delacorte, 1998. / Myers, Anna. *Red-Dirt Jessie*. Walker, 1992. / Naylor, Phyllis Reynolds. *Shiloh*. Atheneum, 1991. / Osborne, Mary Pope. *Adaline Falling Star*. Scholastic, 2000. / Philbrook, Rodman. *The Young Man and the Sea*. Scholastic/Blue Sky, 2004. / Slepian, Jan. *The Broccoli Tapes*. Philomel, 1988.

SUBJECTS: BROTHERS AND SISTERS. DEATH. DOGS. FATHERS. GRIEF. STRAY ANIMALS.

1038   Lisle, Janet Taylor. *The Art of Keeping Cool*. **Atheneum, 2000. 0-689-83787-9. 207pp. Gr. 5–8**
With his bomber pilot father off in England for the duration of the war, 13-year-old Robbie Saunders moves in 1942 with his mother and little sister from their Ohio farm to Sachem, Rhode Island, to live near the grandparents he's never met. Abel Hoffman, a famous painter,

disliked by the townspeople because he's German, lives as a recluse in the woods. Could he be a spy? What a gripping and tragic tale of wartime, family secrets, and community suspicions gone out of control.

GERM: Include this in a booktalk and/or study of World War II and life on the homefront.

RELATED TITLES: Avi. *Don't You Know There's a War On?* HarperCollins, 2001. / Bunting, Eve. *Spying on Miss Müller*. Clarion, 1995. / Choldenko, Gennifer. *Al Capone Does My Shirts*. Putnam, 2004. / Giff, Patricia Reilly. *Lily's Crossing*. Delacorte, 1997. / Greene, Bette. *Summer of My German Soldier*. Bantam, 1984. / Hahn, Mary Downing. *Stepping on the Cracks*. Clarion, 1991. / Howard, Ellen. *A Different Kind of Courage*. Atheneum, 1996. / Lowry, Lois. *Number the Stars*. Houghton Mifflin, 1989. / Mazer, Norma Fox. *Good Night, Maman*. Harcourt, 1999. / Stevenson, James. *Don't You Know There's a War On?* Greenwillow, 1992. / Wolitzer, Hilma. *Introducing Shirley Braverman*. Farrar, 1975.

SUBJECTS: ARTISTS. COUSINS. FAMILY PROBLEMS. GRANDPARENTS. HISTORICAL FICTION. RHODE ISLAND. U.S.—HISTORY—20TH CENTURY—FICTION. WAR. WORLD WAR, 1939–1945—FICTION.

1039 Lisle, Janet Taylor. *How I Became a Writer and Oggie Learned to Drive.* **Philomel, 2002. 0-399-23394-6. 155pp. Gr. 5–7**

After their dad moves out, 11-year-old aspiring writer Archie and his car-obsessed little brother Oggie shuttle back and forth from what they call Saturn (Dad's new apartment) and Jupiter (Mom's new apartment), while Archie tries to placate Oggie with an ongoing made-up story about the Mysterious Mole People. Oggie is still reeling from his parents' split and in mourning from having his red wallet stolen by neighborhood toughs, the Night Riders; he has the yeeks, shivers that go all over his body. It's going to be up to Archie to get that wallet back, even if he has to join the gang to do it.

GERM: Archie's descriptions of his stuffed bunny-toting but brave, determined little brother are rich in details, so funny and believable. Ask your students to observe a younger child for a week, to take notes about what they say and do, and, finally, to write a profile that brings their special quirks and personalities to light.

RELATED TITLES: Bauer, Marion Dane. *A Question of Trust*. Scholastic, 1994. / Byars, Betsy. *Cracker Jackson*. Viking, 1985. / Choldenko, Gennifer. *Al Capone Does My Shirts*. Putnam, 2004. / Cleary, Beverly. *Strider*. Morrow, 1991. / Clements, Andrew. *The School Story*. Simon & Schuster, 2001. / Franklin, Christine L. *Lone Wolf*. Candlewick, 1997. / Gauthier, Gail. *My Life Among the Aliens*. Putnam, 1996. / Lisle, Janet Taylor. *The Art of Keeping Cool*. Atheneum, 2000. / Slepian, Jan. *The Broccoli Tapes*. Philomel, 1988.

SUBJECTS: AUTHORSHIP. BROTHERS. DIVORCE. FAMILY PROBLEMS. GANGS. IMAGINATION. WRITING.

1040 Love, D. Anne. *Dakota Spring.* **Illus. by Ronald Himler. Holiday House, 1995. 0-8234-1189-3. 90pp. Gr. 2–4**

After Pa breaks his leg during a barn-raising, he asks his late wife's mother to come to the Dakota prairie from Charleston, South Carolina to help care for nine-year-old Jess and thirteen-year-old Caroline. As Caroline describes in her first person narrative, Mrs. Ravenell, as the children are instructed to call their grandmother, is cold and distant at first; as they get to know one another better, she thaws.

GERM: Discuss: How would life have been different for Mrs. Ravenell in Charleston, South Carolina and on the prairie? How does her attitude about her grandchildren change and why? What details can you list about life on the prairie in the late 1800s that are different from your life now? Meet another family of resilient motherless children in Ellen Howard's *The Log Cabin Quilt*.

RELATED TITLES: Armstrong, Jennifer. *Black-Eyed Susan*. Crown, 1995. / Bunting, Eve. *Dandelions*. Harcourt, 1995. / Byars, Betsy. *Tornado*. HarperCollins, 1996. / Freedman, Russell. *Children of the Wild West*. Clarion, 1983. / Howard, Ellen. *The Log Cabin Quilt*. Holiday House, 1996. / MacLachlan, Patricia. *Sarah, Plain and Tall*. Harper, 1985. / Osborne, Mary Pope. *Adaline Falling Star*. Scholastic, 2000. / Wilder, Laura Ingalls. *Little House on the Prairie*. Harper, 1961.

SUBJECTS: BROTHERS AND SISTERS. FRONTIER AND PIONEER LIFE. GRANDMOTHERS. GREAT PLAINS. HISTORICAL FICTION. PRAIRIES. TORNADOES.

1041 Lowry, Lois. *Gooney Bird and the Room Mother.* **Illus. by Middy Thomas. Houghton Mifflin, 2005. 0-618-53230-7. 76pp. Gr. 1–3**

Mrs. Pigeon tells her second graders, hard at work on their Thanksgiving play, that she will reward whoever can cajole a grownup into being their room mother with the lead part of

Squanto. Of course Gooney Bird, the girl who managed to get a donation of free dictionaries for all 22 children in class, is the enterprising one who comes up with a room mother, though that person wishes to remain incognito for now.

GERM: In each chapter, the iconoclastic and indefatigable Gooney Bird, a natural leader who always wants to be "right smack in the middle of everything," uses weighty words that her classmates look up in the dictionary and define. Naturally, you'll want to rescue your students from a feeling of ennui, as Gooney Bird would say, so incorporate this priceless little book into your dictionary forays. See if they can guess who Gooney Bird's secret room mother is. You'll probably want to pair this stand-alone sequel with the first book, *Gooney Bird Greene*.

RELATED TITLES: Amato, Mary. *The Word Eater*. Holiday House, 2000. / Frasier, Debra. *Miss Alaineus: A Vocabulary Disaster*. Harcourt, 2000. / Gutman, Dan. *Miss Daisy Is Crazy* (My Weird School series). Harper-Collins, 2004. / Hornik, Laurie Miller. *The Secrets of Ms. Snickle's Class*. Clarion, 2001. / Hornik, Laurie Miller. *Zoo School*. Clarion, 2004. / Lowry, Lois. *Gooney Bird Greene*. Houghton Mifflin, 2002. / Lowry, Lois. *Zooman Sam*. Houghton Mifflin, 1999. (And others in the Sam series.) / MacDonald, Amy. *No More Nasty*. Farrar, 2001. / Scieszka, Jon. *Baloney (Henry P.)*. Viking, 2001.

SUBJECTS: DICTIONARIES. FICTION BOOKS FOR EARLY GRADES. HUMOROUS FICTION. MOTHERS. PLAYS. SCHOOLS. STORYTELLING. TEACHERS. THANKSGIVING. VOCABULARY.

1042 Lowry, Lois. *Gooney Bird Greene*. **Illus. by Middy Thomas. Houghton Mifflin, 2002. 0-618-23848-4. 88pp. Gr. 1–3**

Second grader, Gooney Bird, just moved to town, tells her new class five outrageous and enthralling stories about herself, one each day for a week, and claims they are all absolutely true. There's "How Gooney Bird Got Her Name," "How Gooney Bird Came from China on a Flying Carpet," and my own personal favorite about her cat: "How Catman Is Consumed by a Cow." What a role model she is. Each of her stories has a beginning, middle, and end. She makes the class pay strict attention—"I like to have absolutely all eyes on me."—but she stops for questions and comments. She uses characters and dialogue. Her stories are full of suspense, mystery, and twists, and depend on wonderful wordplay.

GERM: Gooney Bird mesmerizes us all with her own yarns and demonstrates what makes a good story. Compile a chart of her writing tips. When her classmates clamor for more of her absolutely true stories, she tells them it's time to tell their own, and of course, that's what your own storytellers will be raring to do in an outpouring of strange but true personal narratives. For fun with the dictionary, see the sequel, *Gooney Bird and the Room Mother*.

RELATED TITLES: Falconer, Ian. *Olivia Saves the Circus*. Atheneum, 2001. / Frasier, Debra. *Miss Alaineus: A Vocabulary Disaster*. Harcourt, 2000. / Lowry, Lois. *Gooney Bird and the Room Mother*. Houghton Mifflin, 2005. / Lowry, Lois. *Zooman Sam*. Houghton Mifflin, 1999. / Rupp, Rebecca. *The Dragon of Lonely Island*. Candlewick, 1998. / Schotter, Roni. *Nothing Ever Happens on 90th Street*. Orchard, 1997. / Scieszka, Jon. *Baloney (Henry P.)*. Viking, 2001. / Teague, Mark. *How I Spent My Summer Vacation*. Crown, 1995.

SUBJECTS: FICTION BOOKS FOR EARLY GRADES. HUMOROUS FICTION. SCHOOLS. STORYTELLING. TEACHERS. VOCABULARY.

1043 Lowry, Lois. *See You Around, Sam*. **Illus. by Diane de Groat. Houghton Mifflin, 1996. 0-395-81664-5. 113pp. Gr. 2–5**

Sam Krupnick, the precocious and engaging preschooler from *All About Sam* and *Attaboy, Sam*, has decided to run away from home. His toy vampire fangs have been outlawed by his mother; Sam decides his only recourse is to move to Sleetmute, Alaska, where he'll lie around in a big pile of walruses. As Sam sets off on his journey, he stops to see various neighbors who feed him, give him traveling advice, and act as his extended family. His older sister Anastasia understands him best, and helps him see that changing his mind about running away is a very grown-up thing to do.

GERM: Lowry's endearing, humorous and empathetic character study allows children of all ages to understand the thoughts and actions of a young child. For a sure-to-be-popular writing exercise, ask children to describe their actions and feelings the last time they considered running away.

RELATED TITLES: Blume, Judy. *Tales of a Fourth Grade Nothing*. Dutton, 1972. / Cleary, Beverly. *Beezus and Ramona*. Morrow, 1955. / Cleary, Beverly. *Ramona the Pest*. Morrow, 1968. / Lowry, Lois. *All About Sam*. Houghton Mifflin, 1996. / Lowry, Lois. *Anastasia Again*. Houghton Mifflin, 1981. (And others in the Anastasia series.) / Lowry, Lois. *Attaboy, Sam*. Houghton Mifflin, 1988. / McDonald, Megan. *Judy Moody, M.D.: The Doc-*

tor Is In! Candlewick, 2004 (and others in the Judy Moody series). / Park, Barbara. *Junie B. Jones and the Stupid Smelly Bus.* Random House, 1993.

SUBJECTS: BROTHERS AND SISTERS. HUMOROUS FICTION. RUNAWAYS.

1044 Lowry, Lois. *Stay! Keeper's Story.* Illus. by True Kelley. Houghton Mifflin, 1997. 0-395-87048-8. 128pp. Gr. 4–6

"I was born in the gutter and grew up in poverty, abandoned by my parents, stealing and begging in order to survive." Thus begins the rags-to-riches saga of a sharp-witted, poetry-loving, loyal stray dog who first holes up with Jack, a down-and-out wine-loving hobo who names him Lucky. Next, he connects with a photographer who renames him Pal and catapults him into a TV phenomenon, famous for his apparent sneer.

GERM: Keeper is an erudite and endearing dog whose prodigious vocabulary will keep your listeners running to the dictionary, and whose simple couplets will start kids rhyming. Meet another talking dog in Vivian Vande Velde's *Smart Dog.*

RELATED TITLES: Avi. *The Good Dog.* Atheneum, 2001. / Conly, Jane Leslie. *The Rudest Alien on Earth.* Henry Holt, 2002. / Hinton, S. E. *The Puppy Sister.* Delacorte, 1995. / Howe, James. Bunnicula series. Atheneum. / Vande Velde, Vivian. *Smart Dog.* Harcourt, 1998.

SUBJECTS: DOGS. PERSONAL NARRATIVES. PERSONIFICATION. STRAY ANIMALS.

1045 Lowry, Lois. *Zooman Sam.* Illus. by Diane de Groat. Houghton Mifflin, 1999. 0-395-97393-7. 155pp. Gr. 2–5

Preschool genius Sam Krupnick, dressed in his homemade zookeeper's suit, brings thirty hats with animal names on them to school to share on Future Job Day. In the process of finding out about each animal, Sam teaches himself to read.

GERM: Ask your students to reminisce about learning to read. Booktalk and hand out the other titles in Lois Lowry's genial Sam series.

RELATED TITLES: Blume, Judy. *Tales of a Fourth Grade Nothing.* Dutton, 1972. / Cleary, Beverly. *Beezus and Ramona.* Morrow, 1955. / Cleary, Beverly. *Ramona the Pest.* Morrow, 1968. / Greene, Stephanie. *Show and Tell.* Clarion, 1998. / Lowry, Lois. *All About Sam.* Houghton Mifflin, 1988. (And others in the Sam series.) / McDonald, Megan. *Judy Moody, M.D.: The Doctor Is In!* Candlewick, 2004 (and others in the Judy Moody series). / Park, Barbara. *Junie B. Jones and the Stupid Smelly Bus.* Random House, 1993. / Polacco, Patricia. *Aunt Chip and the Great Triple Creek Dam Affair.* Philomel, 1996. / Stanley, Diane. *Raising Sweetness.* Putnam, 1999.

SUBJECTS: BOOKS AND READING. BROTHERS AND SISTERS. LITERACY. NURSERY SCHOOLS. OCCUPATIONS. SCHOOLS. ZOO KEEPERS.

1046 Lynch, Chris. *Gold Dust.* HarperCollins, 2000. 0-06-028175-8. 196pp. Gr. 5–8

Baseball fanatic Richard becomes friends with new classmate Napoleon Charlie Ellis, a black boy from the Caribbean island of Dominica who enrolls in St. Colmcille's, a Catholic school, at the height of the Boston school busing crisis in 1975. For children obsessed with our national pastime, here's a baseball book with wit and staying power; one that digs into a social issue that always needs airing and discussing: race.

GERM: Read aloud some of Richard's baseball descriptions and ask your kids to write essays explaining what it is about their favorite sport that makes them fanatics. Talk over important matters raised here: Does race matter in friendships? In sports?

RELATED TITLES: Bridges, Ruby. *Through My Eyes.* Scholastic, 1999. / Cline-Ransome, Lesa. *Satchel Paige.* Simon & Schuster, 2000. / Curtis, Christopher Paul. *The Watsons Go to Birmingham, 1963.* Delacorte, 1995. / Curtis, Gavin. *The Bat Boy and His Violin.* Simon & Schuster, 1998. / Golenbock, Peter. *Teammates.* Harcourt, 1990. / Gutman, Dan. *Honus and Me.* Avon, 1997. / Gutman, Dan. *Jackie and Me: A Baseball Card Adventure.* Avon, 1999. / Martin, Ann M. *Belle Teal.* Scholastic, 2001. / Mochizuki, Ken. *Baseball Saved Us.* Lee & Low, 1993. / Namioka, Lensey. *Yang the Youngest and His Terrible Ear.* Little, Brown, 1992. / Nelson, Vaunda Micheaux. *Mayfield Crossing.* Putnam, 1993. / Polacco, Patricia. *Mr. Lincoln's Way.* Philomel, 2001. / Taylor, Mildred. *Roll of Thunder, Hear My Cry.* Dial, 1976. / Thayer, Ernest Lawrence. *Casey at the Bat.* Handprint, 2000. / Wolff, Virginia Euwer. *Bat 6.* Scholastic, 1998.

SUBJECTS: AFRICAN AMERICANS. BASEBALL. BOSTON (MASS.). FRIENDSHIP. HISTORICAL FICTION. INTEGRATION. MASSACHUSETTS—HISTORY. MULTICULTURAL BOOKS. RACE RELATIONS. SCHOOLS.

1047 MacDonald, Amy. *No More Nasty.* Illus. by Cat Bowman Smith. Farrar, 2001. 0-374-35529-0. 172pp. Gr. 3–5

When Simon's favorite relative, eccentric 74-year-old Great Aunt Matilda Maxwell, becomes the new substitute teacher in his unruly fifth grade classroom, he is too embarrassed to tell anyone that they are related. Language-loving farmer, Aunt Mattie, says to the dumbfounded class, "And how does all your corporosity seem to gashiate?" Children will relish Aunt Mattie's inextinguishable spunk and how she transforms that class of bad actors.

GERM: Teachers will revel in Aunt Mattie's list of useful words which the children learn to use with aplomb, and the way she plays Dictionary with the class, having them write fake but plausible dictionary definitions for the words, and then guessing which one is the real one. Before starting the book, give each group one of the following words: muculent, pecksniffian, persiflage, proficuous, rodomontade, and whiffet. After the group looks up the real definition in the dictionary, each person in the group then makes up a new definition for that word. As each group reads its definitions aloud, including the real one, the other groups must vote on which one they think is the most plausible. You'll find Uncle Philbert's glossary of words at the back of the book. Readers will also enjoy the first book about Aunt Mattie and Simon, *No More Nice.*

RELATED TITLES: Amato, Mary. *The Word Eater.* Holiday House, 2000. / Clements, Andrew. *Frindle.* Simon & Schuster, 1996. / Duffey, Betsy. *Utterly Yours, Booker Jones.* Viking, 1995. / Evans, Douglas. *Apple Island, or The Truth About Teachers.* Front Street, 1998. / Fleischman, Paul. *Weslandia.* Candlewick, 1999. / Fletcher, Ralph. *Flying Solo.* Clarion, 1998. / Frasier, Debra. *Miss Alaineus: A Vocabulary Disaster.* Harcourt, 2000. / Gutman, Dan. *Miss Daisy Is Crazy* (My Weird School series). HarperCollins, 2004. / Haddix, Margaret Peterson. *Say What?* Simon & Schuster, 2004. / Hornik, Laurie Miller. *The Secrets of Ms. Snickle's Class.* Clarion, 2001. / Hornik, Laurie Miller. *Zoo School.* Clarion, 2004. / King-Smith, Dick. *Clever Lollipop.* Candlewick, 2003. / Levitt, Paul M., Douglas A. Burger, and Elissa S. Guralnick. *The Weighty Word Book.* Court Wayne, 2000. / Lowry, Lois. *Gooney Bird and the Room Mother.* Houghton Mifflin, 2005. / MacDonald, Amy. *No More Nice.* Orchard, 1996. / Sachar, Louis. *Sideways Stories from Wayside School.* Morrow, 1978.

SUBJECTS: AUNTS. BEHAVIOR. GREAT-AUNTS. HUMOROUS FICTION. SCHOOLS. TEACHERS. VOCABULARY. WORD GAMES.

1048 McDonald, Megan. *Judy Moody, M.D.: The Doctor Is In!* Illus. by Peter H. Reynolds. Candlewick, 2004. 0-7636-2024-6. 151pp. Gr. 1–4

In the fifth book of the series about pun-making, quick-tempered third grader, big sister to Stink, and alpha girl with an attitude, Judy Moody brings Stink's baby belly button to school for Sharing Circle; dresses as Elizabeth Blackwell, first woman doctor, and operates on a huge zucchini for Doctor Day; and spends a boring week at home with what feels like bowling ball-sized tonsils.

GERM: Your listeners who don't know Judy yet will dive for the rest of the series, with its fun wordplay, puns, and riddles, and an ear for how real third graders talk. Judy's rhyming report on Elizabeth Blackwell may inspire a whole new type of biography assignment. Do some experiential writing, reliving all the excruciating details: *What Happened When I Got Sick.* And now Stink, her little brother, has his own series, starting with *Stink: The Incredible Shrinking Kid.* Check out <www.judymoody.com> for fan club info, answers to questions, and cool activities. As Judy would say, "Rare!"

RELATED TITLES: Blume, Judy. *Superfudge.* Dutton, 1980. / Blume, Judy. *Tales of a Fourth Grade Nothing.* Dutton, 1972. / Cameron, Ann. *The Stories Huey Tells.* Knopf, 1995. (And others in the Huey series.) / Cameron, Ann. *The Stories Julian Tells.* Pantheon, 1981. (And others in the Julian series.) / Cleary, Beverly. *Beezus and Ramona.* Morrow, 1955. / Cleary, Beverly. *Ramona Quimby, Age 8.* Morrow, 1981. / Cleary, Beverly. *Ramona the Pest.* Morrow, 1968. / Cutler, Jane. *No Dogs Allowed.* Farrar, 1992. / Cutler, Jane. *Rats.* Farrar, 1996. / Greene, Stephanie. *Show and Tell.* Clarion, 1998. / Lowry, Lois. *All About Sam.* Houghton Mifflin, 1988. (And others in the Sam series.) / McDonald, Megan. Judy Moody series. Candlewick. / McDonald, Megan. *Stink: The Incredible Shrinking Kid.* Candlewick, 2005. / Petersen, P. J. *The Amazing Magic Show.* Simon & Schuster, 1994. / Polacco, Patricia. *My Rotten Redheaded Older Brother.* Simon & Schuster, 1994. / Willner-Pardo, Gina. *Daphne Eloise Slater, Who's Tall for Her Age.* Clarion, 1997.

SUBJECTS: BROTHERS AND SISTERS. DOCTORS. FICTION BOOKS FOR EARLY GRADES. FRIENDSHIP. GUINEA PIGS. MEDICAL CARE. SCHOOLS. SHOW-AND-TELL PRESENTATIONS. SICK.

1049 McDonald, Megan. *Stink: The Incredible Shrinking Kid.* **Illus. by Peter H. Reynolds. Candlewick, 2005. 0-7636-2025-4. 102pp. Gr. K–3**

Shortest in his family and the shrimpiest second grader in Class 2D, Stink is appalled when his older sister Judy measures him before bed and tells him the bad news: he's one quarter inch shorter now than he was in the morning. In other hilarious chapters, Stink is chosen to bring home the class newt, Newton, with disastrous results, and he celebrates his favorite president, the shortest one, James Madison, for Presidents' Day.

GERM: Interspersed throughout this comical easy-to-read chapter book about Judy Moody's personable little brother are Stink's own comic book pages, "The Adventures of Stink." Enlarge these on the photocopier so your group can read them together and draw their own comic adventures. Judy Moody fans will be so gratified to see a whole book about Stink, just as Beezus fans loved reading about Ramona in Beverly Cleary's classic series. Stink is short; meet a tall girl who doesn't appreciate mean comments about her height in *Daphne Eloise Slater, Who's Tall for Her Age* by Gina Willner-Pardo.

RELATED TITLES: Blume, Judy. *Superfudge.* Dutton, 1980. / Blume, Judy. *Tales of a Fourth Grade Nothing.* Dutton, 1972. / Cameron, Ann. *The Stories Huey Tells.* Knopf, 1995. (And others in the Huey series.) / Cameron, Ann. *The Stories Julian Tells.* Pantheon, 1981. (And others in the Julian series.) / Cleary, Beverly. *Beezus and Ramona.* Morrow, 1955. / Cleary, Beverly. *Ramona Quimby, Age 8.* Morrow, 1981. / Cleary, Beverly. *Ramona the Pest.* Morrow, 1968. / Cutler, Jane. *No Dogs Allowed.* Farrar, 1992. / Cutler, Jane. *Rats.* Farrar, 1996. / Greene, Stephanie. *Show and Tell.* Clarion, 1998. / Klein, Abby. *The King of Show-and-Tell.* Scholastic/Blue Sky, 2004. / Lowry, Lois. *All About Sam.* Houghton Mifflin, 1988. (And others in the Sam series.) / McDonald, Megan. *Judy Moody, M.D.: The Doctor Is In!* Candlewick, 2004 (and others in the Judy Moody series). / Willner-Pardo, Gina. *Daphne Eloise Slater, Who's Tall for Her Age.* Clarion, 1997.

SUBJECTS: BROTHERS AND SISTERS. FICTION BOOKS FOR EARLY GRADES. NEWTS. PRESIDENTS. REPTILES AND AMPHIBIANS. SCHOOLS. SIZE.

1050 McGraw, Eloise. *The Moorchild.* **McElderry, 1996. 0-689-80654-X. 241pp. Gr. 4–7**

Little Saaski, with her dark skin, pale hair, and oddly shaped eyes that seem to change color, is not an ordinary child. Unbeknownst to her, she is a changeling, half fairy folk, half human, who was left in exchange for a human child born to Anwara, wife of Yanno the blacksmith. Cast out of the Mound where the Moorfolk live, she becomes a baby again, though her new grandmother suspects the truth about her. The villagers find her frightening and threatening; the children taunt her as "freaky-odd" and "strangeling." As Saaski learns about her true self, she finds she is not accepted in either world. As the villagers' allow their fear to escalate, her parents fear for her safety.

GERM: Even McGraw's dedication: "To all children who have ever felt 'different'," will start the discussions on prejudice, belonging, and families.

RELATED TITLES: Amato, Mary. *The Word Eater.* Holiday House, 2000. / Hesse, Karen. *The Music of Dolphins.* Scholastic, 1996. / Ives, David. *Monsieur Eek.* HarperCollins, 2001. / James, Mary. *Shoebag.* Scholastic, 1990. / Lisle, Janet Taylor. *Forest.* Orchard, 1993. / Lowry, Lois. *The Giver.* Houghton Mifflin, 1993. / Mazer, Anne. *The Oxboy.* Knopf, 1993. / Nodelman, Perry. *The Same Place But Different.* Simon & Schuster, 1995. / Spinelli, Jerry. *Loser.* HarperCollins, 2002. / Swope, Sam. *The Araboolies of Liberty Street.* Crown, 1989. / Van Allsburg, Chris. *The Widow's Broom.* Houghton Mifflin, 1992.

SUBJECTS: CHANGELINGS. FAIRIES. FANTASY. IDENTITY. OUTCASTS. PREJUDICE.

1051 McKissack, Patricia C. *Run Away Home.* **Scholastic, 1997. 0-590-46751-4. 160pp. Gr. 4–6**

In Alabama in 1888, 11-year-old African American, Sarah Crossman, hides an Apache boy who has escaped from the train transporting his people to a prison camp. With the Knights of the Southern Order of Manhood intimidating and even lynching black men, and white farmers pressuring them to become sharecroppers, it is a challenge for her family to stay safe. Even so, when Sarah finds Sky in the barn and tells her parents, they nurse him back to health and encourage him to stay with them.

GERM: This is a fascinating piece of historical fiction, loosely based on the author's own ancestors and the several years the Apaches spent as prisoners of war in Alabama. You'll find it rich with issues to investigate, including race relations, early literacy tests in the South, the ideas of Booker T. Washington, and the treatment of Native Americans.

RELATED TITLES: Bradby, Marie. *More Than Anything Else.* Orchard, 1995. / Howard, Elizabeth Fitzgerald. *Virgie Goes to School with Us Boys.* Simon & Schuster, 2000. / Mitchell, Margaree King. *Granddaddy's Gift.* BridgeWater, 1997. / Mitchell, Margaree King. *Uncle Jed's Barber Shop.* Simon & Schuster, 1993. / Speare, Elizabeth George. *The Sign of the Beaver*. Houghton Mifflin, 1983. / Wood, Ted, and Wanbli Numpa Afraid of Hawk. *A Boy Becomes a Man at Wounded Knee*. Walker, 1992.

SUBJECTS: AFRICAN AMERICANS. AFRICAN AMERICANS—HISTORY. ALABAMA. APACHE INDIANS. FRIENDSHIP. HISTORICAL FICTION. INDIANS OF NORTH AMERICA. MULTICULTURAL BOOKS. PREJUDICE. RACE RELATIONS.

1052 Maguire, Gregory. *The Good Liar.* **Clarion, 1999. 0-395-90697-0. 129pp. Gr. 4–8**

Marcel looks back on 1940, an unforgettable year. His father left home, a Jewish woman and her daughter came to stay with his family, German soldiers occupied their village, and the many lies he and his two older brothers rejoiced in spinning led to a secret friendship with a young German soldier.

GERM: Read this along with Norma Fox Mazer's *Good Night, Maman* for a picture of life for Jews and non-Jews in France during World War II.

RELATED TITLES: Bishop, Claire H. *Twenty and Ten*. Puffin, 1978. / Isaacman, Clara. *Clara's Story*. Jewish Publication Society, 1984. / Levine, Karen. *Hana's Suitcase*. Albert Whitman, 2003. / Lowry, Lois. *Number the Stars*. Houghton Mifflin, 1989. / Mazer, Norma Fox. *Good Night, Maman*. Harcourt, 1999. / McSwigan, Marie. *Snow Treasure*. Dutton, 1967. / Millman, Isaac. *Hidden Child*. Farrar, 2005. / Park, Linda Sue. *When My Name Was Keoko*. Clarion, 2002. / Polacco, Patricia. *The Butterfly*. Philomel, 2000. / Propp, Vera W. *When the Soldiers Were Gone*. Putnam, 1999. / Reiss, Johanna. *The Upstairs Room*. HarperCollins, 1987. / Streatfeild, Noel. *When the Sirens Wailed*. Random House, 1976. / Verhoeven, Rian, and Ruud Van Der Rol. *Anne Frank: Beyond the Diary*. Viking, 1993.

SUBJECTS: BROTHERS AND SISTERS. FRANCE. HISTORICAL FICTION. HOLOCAUST, JEWISH (1939–1945). HONESTY. JEWS. WORLD WAR, 1939–1945—FICTION.

1053 Marcantonio, Patricia Santos. *Red Ridin' in the Hood: And Other Cuentos.* **Illus. by Renato Alarcão. Farrar, 2005. 0-374-36241-6. 186pp. Gr. 4–8**

Taking 11 traditional fairy tales, Marcantonio has reset them in the barrios of the U.S. and given them an utterly original Latino flavor, including the integration of Spanish words and contemporary plot twists. In "Jaime and Gabriela," the children of a poor adobe maker are left in the desert by their father and stepmother, and find a house made of pan dulce and tamales. Of course it's the house of a viejita, or old woman, who plans to eat them. In the title story, narrated by Roja, the girl is supposed to take the bus to see her abuelita, but decides to save the bus fare for a cool new shirt, and walks down Forest Street, where she encounters Lobo Chávez in his glossy brown low-rider Chevy. Each story sports at least three fantastical full-page half-tone pictures in shades of gray that add mood, atmosphere, and humor to each retelling.

GERM: There's a glossary of Spanish words at the back (though no pronunciation guide). These stories would be lots of fun to tell. Listeners can compare and contrast these sassy, updated tales with their European originals, and rewrite a traditional fairy tale with details from their own modern lives.

RELATED TITLES: Kindl, Patrice. *Goose Chase*. Houghton Mifflin, 2001. / Levine, Gail Carson. *Ella Enchanted*. HarperCollins, 1997. / Levine, Gail Carson. *The Fairy's Mistake*. HarperCollins, 1999. / Levine, Gail Carson. *The Princess Test*. HarperCollins, 1999. / Napoli, Donna Jo. *The Prince of the Pond*. Dutton, 1992. / Pullman, Philip. *I Was a Rat!* Knopf, 2000. / Scieszka, Jon. *The Stinky Cheese Man and Other Fairly Stupid Tales*. Viking, 1992. / Vande Velde, Vivian. *Tales from the Brothers Grimm and the Sisters Weird*. Harcourt, 1995.

SUBJECTS: CHARACTERS IN LITERATURE. FAIRY TALES—SATIRE. HISPANIC AMERICANS. LITTLE RED RIDING HOOD STORIES. MULTICULTURAL BOOKS. PARODIES. SHORT STORIES. SPANISH LANGUAGE.

1054 Marsden, Carolyn. *The Gold-Threaded Dress.* **Candlewick, 2002. 0-7636-1569-2. 73pp. Gr. 2–4**

In fourth grade at her new school, Oy doesn't know how to respond to classmate Frankie's teasing, calling her Chinese, instead of Thai, and to haughty Liliandra, who gives her an unwinnable ultimatum to join her secret clubhouse meetings. Liliandra wants Oy to bring her beautiful, pink silk traditional Thai dress to school so everyone can try it on. Tired of feeling lonely, Oy figures maybe it's worth sacrificing something precious to have friends at school. This is one thoughtful little moral dilemma story that packs a nice wallop as kids think about what it means to fit in, to conform to the group, and to keep your own identity.

GERM: Halfway through the book, stop and do a Quick Write: Oy needs your advice, based on your own experience. Should she bring the dress to school or not? Why? What would you do? What should she do? Share the responses aloud. One of the themes the story explores is what it means to be American, even though your family might have come from a different country. Research Thailand for salient facts and identify the Thai customs and traditions woven into the story. Have your students bring in a simple object to show that exemplifies their countries of origin and identify each place on the globe or pull-down map.

RELATED TITLES: Best, Cari. *Shrinking Violet.* Farrar, 2001. / Choi, Sook Nyul. *Halmoni and the Picnic.* Houghton Mifflin, 1993. / Coerr, Eleanor. *Mieko and the Fifth Treasure.* Putnam, 1993. / Cohen, Barbara. *Make a Wish, Molly.* Doubleday, 1994. / Duffey, Betsy. *Hey, New Kid!* Viking, 1996. / English, Karen. *Nadia's Hands.* Boyd's Mills, 1999. / Estes, Eleanor. *The Hundred Dresses.* Harcourt, 1944. / Hall, Bruce Edward. *Henry and the Kite Dragon.* Philomel, 2004. / Kline, Suzy. *Mary Marony and the Snake.* Putnam, 1992. / Levine, Ellen. *I Hate English!* Scholastic, 1989. / Nagda, Ann Whitehead. *Dear Whiskers.* Holiday House, 2000. / Pomeranc, Marion Hess. *The American Wei.* Albert Whitman, 1998. / Recorvits, Helen. *Goodbye, Walter Malinski.* Farrar, 1999. / Sachar, Louis. *Marvin Redpost: Alone in His Teacher's House.* / Willner-Pardo, Gina. *Daphne Eloise Slater, Who's Tall for Her Age.* Clarion, 1997.

SUBJECTS: ASIAN AMERICANS. CLOTHING AND DRESS. FRIENDSHIP. IDENTITY. MOVING, HOUSEHOLD. MULTICULTURAL BOOKS. PREJUDICE. SCHOOLS. THAI AMERICANS.

1055   Martin, Ann M. *Belle Teal.* Scholastic, 2001. 0-439-09823-8. 224pp. Gr. 4–7

It's 1962, and for the first time ever, three African American children will be attending Coker Creek Elementary School; one child, Darryl, will be in Belle Teal's fifth grade class. As her Mama says, "Hate just creates more hate," and indeed, there are parents picketing the school with hateful signs. Through narrator's Belle Teal's eyes, author Ann Martin juggles three tough subjects—racism, dementia, and child abuse—with skill and sensitivity.

GERM: Each character in the novel has a secret or a sorrow. Discuss with your students how Gran, Little Boss, Darryl, and Vanessa might have felt at key points in the story. Have them rewrite an episode from one of these character's point of view. For a true and harrowing account of school desegregation in those days, share Ruby Bridges' moving photobiography, *Through My Eyes.* Another school story about integration is *Mayfield Crossing* by Vaunda Micheaux Nelson.

RELATED TITLES: Bridges, Ruby. *Through My Eyes.* Scholastic, 1999. / Creech, Sharon. *Granny Torrelli Makes Soup.* HarperCollins, 2003. / Curtis, Christopher Paul. *The Watsons Go to Birmingham, 1963.* Delacorte, 1995. / Duncan, Alice Faye. *The National Civil Rights Museum Celebrates Everyday People.* BridgeWater Books, 1995. / English, Karen. *Francie.* Farrar, 1999. / Evans, Freddi Williams. *A Bus of Our Own.* Albert Whitman, 2001. / Joseph, Lynn. *The Color of My Words.* HarperCollins, 2000. / Lynch, Chris. *Gold Dust.* HarperCollins, 2000. / McKissack, Patricia C. *Goin' Someplace Special.* Atheneum, 2001. / Nelson, Vaunda Micheaux. *Mayfield Crossing.* Putnam, 1993. / Park, Barbara. *The Graduation of Jake Moon.* Atheneum, 2000. / Taylor, Mildred. *Roll of Thunder, Hear My Cry.* Dial, 1976. / Woodson, Jacqueline. *Locomotion.* Putnam, 2003. / Woodson, Jacqueline. *The Other Side.* Putnam, 2001.

SUBJECTS: AFRICAN AMERICANS. ALZHEIMER'S DISEASE. FRIENDSHIP. GRANDMOTHERS. HISTORICAL FICTION. INTEGRATION. MULTICULTURAL BOOKS. PREJUDICE. RACE RELATIONS. SCHOOLS.

1056   Matas, Carol, and Perry Nodelman. *Of Two Minds.* Simon & Schuster, 1995. 0-689-80138-6. 200pp. Gr. 5–8

Lately, headstrong Princess Lenora's powerful imagination has been going awry; the sending she receives, a powerful vision of a possible moment from her future, both alarms and tempts her. When her father presents clumsy, red-haired, skinny-legged Prince Coren as her husband-to-be without even asking her opinion, she escapes the wedding ceremony through another sending; somehow Coren comes too. The two find themselves in the seemingly harmonious and perfect city of Farren, where leader Hevak takes an interest in Lenora and wills Coren to disappear.

GERM: Explore and compare the concept of a perfect, ordered society in Lois Lowry's *The Giver.*

RELATED TITLES: Fleischman, Sid. *The 13th Floor.* Greenwillow, 1995. / Kindl, Patrice. *Goose Chase.* Houghton Mifflin, 2001. / Levine, Gail Carson. *Ella Enchanted.* HarperCollins, 1997. / Lowry, Lois. *The Giver.* Houghton Mifflin, 1993. / Nodelman, Perry. *The Same Place But Different.* Simon & Schuster, 1995. / Pratchett, Terry. *The Wee Free Men.* HarperCollins, 2003.

SUBJECTS: DICTATORS. FANTASY. PRINCES AND PRINCESSES.

1057   Mazer, Norma Fox. *Good Night, Maman.* Harcourt, 1999. 0-15-201468-3. 185pp. Gr. 5–8

Though Karin Levi and her older brother Marc survive the Nazi invasion of Paris and are two of the 982 grateful refugees brought on the troopship Henry Gibbins to a refugee camp in Oswego, New York in 1944, Karin longs for her beloved mother, whom they had to leave behind during their escape. While her plight is heart-wrenching, Karin's intelligent and introspective narrative, interspersed with letters she composes to her Maman, shows a resilient and thoughtful child who is drawn to her new American life of slang, cheeseburgers, school, and friends.

GERM: Explore the slang terms Karin doesn't understand when she is learning English. What are some of the words and customs we'd need to explain to children coming to America from non-English speaking backgrounds? *The Good Liar* by Gregory Maguire depicts the Nazi occupation of a small French village in 1940.

RELATED TITLES: Abels, Chana Byers. *The Children We Remember*. Greenwillow, 1986. / Gold, Alison Leslie. *Memories of Anne Frank: Reflections of a Childhood Friend*. Scholastic, 1997. / Isaacman, Clara. *Clara's Story*. Jewish Publication Society, 1984. / Jiang, Ji Li. *Red Scarf Girl: A Memoir of the Cultural Revolution*. HarperCollins, 1997. / Levine, Karen. *Hana's Suitcase*. Albert Whitman, 2003. / Lowry, Lois. *Number the Stars*. Houghton Mifflin, 1989. / McCann, Michelle R. *Luba: The Angel of Bergen-Belsen*. Tricycle, 2003. / Maguire, Gregory. *The Good Liar*. Clarion, 1999. / Millman, Isaac. *Hidden Child*. Farrar, 2005. / Polacco, Patricia. *The Butterfly*. Philomel, 2000. / Propp, Vera W. *When the Soldiers Were Gone*. Putnam, 1999. / Reiss, Johanna. *The Upstairs Room*. HarperCollins, 1987. / Verhoeven, Rian and Ruud Van Der Rol. *Anne Frank: Beyond the Diary*. Viking, 1993.

SUBJECTS: BROTHERS AND SISTERS. FRANCE. HISTORICAL FICTION. HOLOCAUST, JEWISH (1939–1945). IMMIGRATION AND EMIGRATION. JEWS. MOTHERS. REFUGEES. WORLD WAR, 1939–1945—FICTION.

1058 Mikaelsen, Ben. *Countdown.* **Hyperion, 1996. 0-7868-2207-4. 248pp. Gr. 4–8**
Chosen by lottery as the first NASA Junior Astronaut to join the crew of the space shuttle *Endeavour*, 14-year-old Elliot prepares for the mission along with alternate astronaut Mandy whom he resents for her competence and intelligence. In a powerful parallel story, Maasai cattle herder Vincent Ole Tome yearns to be able to go back to school instead of becoming a warrior as his father demands. The two boys' lives intersect when Elliot, aboard the shuttle, makes radio contact with the Kenyan boy.

GERM: Not only will readers be awed by Elliot's vigorous training exercises, but they'll learn to empathize with Victor's bewilderment at the differences between the modern world and his Maasai society, which may at first seem alien and primitive to readers. By the end of the mission, they'll be rooting for planet Earth and debating the global issues raised by the two boys during their often acrimonious radio discussions.

RELATED TITLES: Burleigh, Robert. *Flight: The Journey of Charles Lindbergh*. Philomel, 1991. / Fraser, Mary Ann. *One Giant Leap*. Henry Holt, 1993. / Hunter, Ryan Ann. *Into the Air: An Illustrated Timeline of Flight*. National Geographic, 2003. / Oppel, Kenneth. *Airborn*. HarperCollins, 2004. / Ride, Sally, and Susan Okie. *To Space and Back*. Lothrop, 1986.

SUBJECTS: AFRICA. ASTRONAUTS. FRIENDSHIP. KENYA. MASAI (AFRICAN PEOPLE). MULTICULTURAL BOOKS. SCIENCE FICTION. SPACE FLIGHT.

1059 Minne. *I Love . . .* **Illus. by Natali Fortier. Kane/Miller, 2005. 1-929132-75-1. 125pp. Gr. 1–6**
This collection of 65 careful observations is told mostly from the point of view of a young brown-haired girl who lists the day-to-day things she loves the most at school, home, outside, and on vacation. She says, "I love it when Dr. Suppo taps on my knee with his little hammer, and my leg moves all by itself." Each statement comes with an accompanying picture—small, rectangular and done in what looks like pastels, on a white background.

GERM: Listeners will say, "Oh, I love that, too!" and will share similar or new experiences, whether written and illustrated in the format of the book, or simply told. For appreciating small, everyday experiences, this book will spark memories, recognition, and connections to our own lives. Teach everyone the original French title, *J'aime*, which they can substitute for the words "I love."

RELATED TITLES: Adoff, Arnold. *Love Letters*. Scholastic, 1997. / Greenfield, Eloise. *Honey, I Love*. HarperCollins, 2003.

SUBJECTS: CREATIVE WRITING. FAMILY LIFE. FICTION BOOKS FOR EARLY GRADES. LOVE.

1060 Morpurgo, Michael. *The Butterfly Lion.* **Viking, 1997. 0-670-87461-2. 90pp. Gr. 3–6**
The unnamed narrator recalls how he ran away from his unpleasant English boarding school when he was ten, and happened upon a huge house, an old lady, and a shimmering blue lion

carved into the chalk of the hillside. The old woman enthralled him with the remarkable life story of her late husband, Bertie, who years before ran away from that same school. Bertie's beloved white lion cub pet was sold to a French circus owner when Bertie was sent away to the school. In a heartwrenching, coincidence-filled, but never cloying climax, the old woman explains how 21-year-old Bertie, recovering in France from wounds suffered in battle in the First World War, was reunited with his lion.

GERM: The story-within-a-story format is particularly effective as a read-aloud, and listeners will enjoy puzzling out the mystical conclusion. For background, check your library for a picture of an albino lion, information on World War I—*War Game* by Michael Foreman is particularly effective—and a picture of an English chalk horse.

RELATED TITLES: Day, Nancy Raines. *The Lion's Whiskers: An Ethiopian Folktale.* Scholastic, 1995. / Foreman, Michael. *War Games.* Arcade/Little, Brown, 1993. / Mellecker, Judith. *Randolph's Dream.* Knopf, 1991. / Morpurgo, Michael. *Kensuke's Kingdom.* Scholastic, 2003. / Nolan, Dennis. *Androcles and the Lion.* Harcourt, 1997. / Rabin, Staton. *Casey over There.* Harcourt, 1994. / Wells, Rosemary. *Waiting for the Evening Star.* Dial, 1993.

SUBJECTS: COINCIDENCE. ENGLAND. HISTORICAL FICTION. LIONS. WORLD WAR, 1914–1918.

1061 Morpurgo, Michael. *Kensuke's Kingdom.* **Scholastic, 2003. 0-439-38202-5. 164pp. Gr. 4–7**

Sailing around the globe with his parents on a 42-foot yacht, Michael and his dog, Stella, are swept off the deck on July 28, 1988, into the Coral Sea, north of Australia, and wash up on an island where the sole inhabitant is an old Japanese man named Kensuke. What has Kensuke been doing there for more than 40 years? (When your listeners to do the math, they'll figure it out.) This is a thrilling narrative in the time-honored tradition: think Robinson Crusoe, or even Tom Hanks in the movie, *Cast Away.*

GERM: The first page alone is enough to enthrall readers. Do a booktalk on survival stories. I loved giving a yearly booktalk to my fifth graders on Unforgettable Books to Take to a Desert Island. For the following week, I asked them to come to library dressed for an island adventure—Hawaiian shirts, sunglasses, flip flops, even grass skirts! I decorated an area of the library with a picnic blanket, seashells, and a beach umbrella. They each had to bring in their best book and tell why it was so important to them. Serve Hawaiian punch and coconut cookies or fresh coconut, and get kids talking about favorite books.

RELATED TITLES: Creech, Sharon. *The Wanderer.* HarperCollins, 2000. / Farley, Walter. *The Black Stallion.* Random House, 1941. / Hesse, Karen. *The Music of Dolphins.* Scholastic, 1996. / Hill, Kirkpatrick. *Winter Camp.* McElderry, 1993. / Morpurgo, Michael. *The Butterfly Lion.* Viking, 1997. / Morpurgo, Michael. *War Horse.* Greenwillow, 1983. / O'Dell, Scott. *Island of the Blue Dolphins.* Houghton Mifflin, 1960. / Paulsen, Gary. *The Haymeadow.* Delacorte, 1992. / Philbrick, Rodman. *The Young Man and the Sea.* Blue Sky/Scholastic, 2004. / Taylor, Theodore. *The Cay.* Delacorte, 1987.

SUBJECTS: ADVENTURE AND ADVENTURERS. CASTAWAYS. DOGS. ISLANDS. JAPANESE. SURVIVAL. VOYAGES AND TRAVELS.

1062 Moses, Will. *The Legend of Sleepy Hollow.* **Retold and illus. by Will Moses from the original story by Washington Irving. Philomel, 1995. 0-399-22687-7. Unp. Gr. 4–6**

The gangly new schoolmaster and church singing master of Sleepy Hollow, Ichabod Crane, falls for one of his singing students, the radiant Katrina Van Tassel, both for her charm and intelligence and for the prosperous farm her father owns. When her other suitor, prankster Brom Bones, learns of Ichabod's intentions, he takes advantage of the schoolmaster's superstitious nature and arranges an "encounter" with the Headless Horseman, reputed to be the ghost of a Hessian soldier. The great-grandson of folk artist Grandma Moses, Will Moses employs a similar style of primitive Americana folk art, with smaller paintings that break up each page and some double-page panoramas that give a real feel for 19th-century village life.

GERM: Moses abridged Washington Irving's classic 1820 tale of New York's Hudson Valley but kept the flavor and plenty of the rich, complex sentences, so children can get a taste for how folks wrote back then. He also did a picture book retelling of Irving's other famous tale, *Rip Van Winkle.*

RELATED TITLES: Moses, Will. *Johnny Appleseed: The Story of a Legend.* Philomel, 2001. / Moses, Will. *Rip Van Winkle.* Philomel Books, 1999. / San Souci, Robert. *The Legend of Sleepy Hollow.* Doubleday, 1986. / Wallner, Alexandra. *Grandma Moses.* Holiday House, 2004. / Wolkstein, Diane, retel. *The Legend of Sleepy Hollow.* Morrow, 1987.

SUBJECTS: GHOST STORIES. HISTORICAL FICTION. NEW YORK (STATE). PRACTICAL JOKES. PUMPKINS. TEACHERS.

1063   Myers, Anna. *The Keeping Room.* **Walker, 1997. 0-8027-8641-3. 135pp. Gr. 4–8**

After Joey's father, Colonel Joseph Kershaw, is taken prisoner by the British in 1780 and their house becomes the headquarters for Lord Cornwallis, Joey makes plans to strike back against the redcoats with a pistol which he has hidden in the woodbox.

GERM: There are no easy answers in this intelligent and carefully researched historical novel, which will be a boon to classes studying the Revolutionary War. Avi's *The Fighting Ground* and James Lincoln Collier and Christopher Collier's *My Brother Sam Is Dead* are classic novels also narrated by boys caught up in the turmoil of the war.

RELATED TITLES: Avi. *The Fighting Ground.* HarperCollins, 1987. / Collier, James Lincoln, and Christopher Collier. *My Brother Sam Is Dead.* Simon & Schuster, 1984. / Giblin, James Cross. *George Washington: A Picture Book Biography.* Scholastic, 1992. / McGovern, Ann. *The Secret Soldier: The Story of Deborah Sampson.* Four Winds, 1987. / Osborne, Mary Pope. *George Washington: Leader of a New Nation.* Dial, 1991. / Rockwell, Anne. *They Called Her Molly Pitcher.* Knopf, 2002. / Woodruff, Elvira. *George Washington's Socks.* Scholastic, 1991.

SUBJECTS: FATHERS AND SONS. HISTORICAL FICTION. U.S.—HISTORY—REVOLUTION, 1775–1783. WAR.

1064   Myers, Laurie. *Lewis and Clark and Me: A Dog's Tale.* **Illus. by Michael Dooling. Henry Holt, 2002. 0-8050-6368-4. 64pp. Gr. 3–7**

Meriwether Lewis's huge black Newfoundland dog, Seaman, narrates his version of his part in Lewis and Clark's 1804 journey west to the Pacific in a charming, dog-based adventure story. Chasing squirrels on the Ohio River, stopping a buffalo charge into camp, and almost bleeding to death after being bitten by a beaver are some of the exploits the stalwart dog describes.

GERM: Talk about the use of primary sources. Each of the nine illustrated chapters is based on a quote from Lewis's diary that involved Seaman. Examine the point of view and use of voice from Lewis's diary excerpts and compare them with the way Seaman tells each escapade. Add two more viewpoints with Joseph Bruchac's novel, Sacajawea, where William Clark and Sacajawea relate their experiences to Sacajawea's seven-year-old son, Pomp, who was born en route. Have your students write about an adventure their pets have had, first from the human perspective and then from the pets' point of view.

RELATED TITLES: Avi. *The Good Dog.* Atheneum, 2001. / Blake, Robert. *Akiak: A Tale from the Iditarod.* Philomel, 1997. / Blumberg, Rhoda. *The Incredible Journey of Lewis and Clark.* Lothrop, 1987. / Bruchac, Joseph. *Sacajawea.* Harcourt, 2000. / Edwards, Judith. *The Great Expedition of Lewis and Clark: By Private Reubin Field, Member of the Corps of Discovery.* Farrar, 2003. / Erdrich, Lise. *Sacagawea.* Carolrhoda, 2003. / Miller, Debbie S. *The Great Serum Race: Blazing the Iditarod Trail.* Walker, 2002. / Paulsen, Gary. *Dogteam.* Delacorte, 1993. / Schanzer, Rosalyn. *How We Crossed the West: The Adventures of Lewis and Clark.* National Geographic, 1997. / Seibert, Patricia. *Mush! Across Alaska in the World's Longest Sled-Dog Race.* Millbrook, 1992.

SUBJECTS: BIOGRAPHICAL FICTION. DOGS. EXPLORERS. HISTORICAL FICTION. LEWIS AND CLARK EXPEDITION (1804–1806). POINT OF VIEW. U.S.—HISTORY—1783–1865—FICTION. VOYAGES AND TRAVELS. WEST—DISCOVERY AND EXPLORATION.

1065   Nagda, Ann Whitehead. *Dear Whiskers.* **Illus. by Stephanie Roth. Holiday House, 2000. 0-8234-1495-7. 76pp. Gr. 1–3**

For her fourth-grade pen-pal project, in which they are to pretend they are mice and write short letters to second graders, Jenny draws as her partner Sameera, a new girl who speaks little English. When Sameera doesn't write back, Jenny's teacher asks her to visit with her in the classroom, where the two gradually begin to read and talk and bond.

GERM: How Jenny gets the unhappy, unresponsive Saudi Arabian girl interested and involved in her mouse project makes for a heartwarming but realistic brief chapter book that will get children thinking and talking about how it might feel to be the new kid. Don't be surprised if you find yourself baking mouse cookies and setting up your own mouse pen pal project with a neighboring class.

RELATED TITLES: Aliki. *Marianthe's Story: Painted Words, Spoken Memories.* Greenwillow, 1998. / Choi, Sook Nyul. *Halmoni and the Picnic.* Houghton Mifflin, 1993. / Cohen, Barbara. *Molly's Pilgrim.* Lothrop, 1983. / Kline, Suzy. *Song Lee in Room 2B.* Viking, 1993. / Levine, Ellen. *I Hate English!* Scholastic, 1989. / Marsden, Carolyn. *The Gold-Threaded Dress.* Candlewick, 2002. / Recorvits, Helen. *My Name Is Yoon.* Farrar, 2003.

SUBJECTS: ARAB AMERICANS. ENGLISH LANGUAGE. FICTION BOOKS FOR EARLY GRADES. FRIENDSHIP. LETTER WRITING. MULTICULTURAL BOOKS. PEN PALS. SCHOOLS.

1066 Naidoo, Beverly. *The Other Side of Truth.* **HarperCollins, 2001. 0-06-029629-1. 250pp. Gr. 6–8**

After witnessing her mother's murder by political assassins in Lagos, Nigeria, 12-year-old Sade Solaja and her younger brother, Femi, are sent to safety with their uncle in London. Once there, they find that their uncle has gone missing and they are on their own in a terrifyingly unfamiliar city.

GERM: Have your students do some research into the political situation in Nigeria, including the execution of writer Ken Saro-Wiwa, that inspired this unforgettable book. Students can compare and contrast the parallels between school and government, between democracies and dictatorships, as they weigh the relative safety of their own lives to the experiences of Sade and her family. Sade's father's credo as a journalist has always been, "The truth is the truth. How can I write what's untrue?" Consider and compare countries that have established a free press with those that haven't.

RELATED TITLES: Curtis, Christopher Paul. *Bud, Not Buddy.* Delacorte, 1999. / Joseph, Lynn. *The Color of My Words.* HarperCollins, 2000. / Mazer, Norma Fox. *Good Night, Maman.* Harcourt, 1999. / Naidoo, Beverley. *Journey to Jo'burg.* HarperCollins, 1986. / Olaleye, Isaac. *The Distant Talking Drum: Poems from Nigeria.* Boyds Mills, 1995. / Ryan, Pam Muñoz. *Esperanza Rising.* Scholastic, 2000. / Streatfeild, Noel. *When the Sirens Wailed.* Random House, 1976.

SUBJECTS: BROTHERS AND SISTERS. DEATH. LONDON (ENGLAND). MULTICULTURAL BOOKS. NIGERIA. REFUGEES.

1067 Napoli, Donna Jo. *Jimmy, the Pickpocket of the Palace.* **Illus. by Judith Byron Schachner. Dutton, 1995. 0-525-45357-1. 166pp. Gr. 4–6**

Jimmy, a frog, describes how he leaves home to save his mother and siblings from the hag who threatens to dry up their pond. In this sequel to *The Prince of the Pond*, Jimmy becomes a boy after being kissed by a princess, and meets up with his human father, a prince who once spent time as a frog.

GERM: Just as we found out what it was like to be a frog in the first book, now we see humans from a frog's perspective. Children can write point of view stories: "The Day I Became a Pet" or "The Day My Pet Became Human."

RELATED TITLES: Alexander, Lloyd. *The Cat Who Wished to Be a Man.* Dutton, 1977. / Cecil, Laura. *The Frog Princess.* Greenwillow, 1995. / Conly, Jane Leslie. *The Rudest Alien on Earth.* Henry Holt, 2002. / Coville, Bruce. *Jennifer Murdley's Toad.* Harcourt, 1992. / Hinton, S. E. *The Puppy Sister.* Delacorte, 1995. / James, Mary. *Shoebag.* Scholastic, 1990. / Kindl, Patrice. *Goose Chase.* Houghton Mifflin, 2001. / Lewis, J. Patrick. *The Frog Princess: A Russian Tale.* Dial, 1994. / MacGill-Callahan, Sheila. *The Seal Prince.* Dial, 1995. / Napoli, Donna Jo. *The Prince of the Pond.* Dutton, 1992.

SUBJECTS: FAIRY TALES—SATIRE. FANTASY. FROGS. PRINCES AND PRINCESSES. TRANSFORMATIONS. WITCHES.

1068 Napoli, Donna Jo. *North.* **Greenwillow, 2004. 0-06-057988-9. 344pp. Gr. 4–7**

Frustrated when his overprotective mother won't let him buy a mountain bike, even with his own money, or give him permission to go on the upcoming sixth grade field trip, Alvin takes his money, and buys a train ticket to Canada. Alvin's hero is Matthew Henson, the African American explorer who was part of Robert Peary's expedition to the North Pole in 1909, and his goal is to follow in Henson's footsteps as far north as Ellsmere Island, above the Arctic Circle.

GERM: Plot on a large map the route Alvin takes north. Pull in supplementary materials: a biography of Henson, books and information on the Inuit, Nunavut, the northern lights, wolves and other arctic animals, and igloos, so students can research each part of Alvin's extraordinary journey.

RELATED TITLES: Bernhard, Emery. *How Snowshoe Hare Rescued the Sun: A Tale from the Arctic.* Holiday House, 1993. / Brandenberg, Jim. *To the Top of the World: Adventures with Arctic Wolves.* Walker, 1993. / George, Jean Craighead. *Julie of the Wolves.* HarperCollins, 1972. / Hill, Kirkpatrick. *Toughboy and Sister.* McElderry, 1990. / Hill, Kirkpatrick. *Winter Camp.* McElderry, 1993. / Johnson, Dolores. *Onward: A Photobiography of African-American Polar Explorer Matthew Henson.* National Geographic, 2005. / Kroll, Virginia. *The Seasons and Someone.* Harcourt, 1994. / Norman, Howard. *The Girl Who Dreamed Only Geese and Other Tales of the Far North.* Harcourt, 1997. / Sabuda, Robert. *The Blizzard's Robe.* Atheneum, 1999. / Sloat, Teri. *The Hungry Giant of the Tundra.* Dutton, 1993. / Steltzer, Ulli. *Building an Igloo.* Henry Holt, 1995.

SUBJECTS: AFRICAN AMERICANS. CANADA. HENSON, MATTHEW. INUIT. MULTICULTURAL BOOKS. RUNAWAYS. SURVIVAL. VOYAGES AND TRAVELS.

1069 Naylor, Phyllis Reynolds. *The Great Chicken Debacle.* **Cavendish, 2001. 0-7614-5095-5. 112pp. Gr. 3–6**

Cornelia, Charles, and Mindy offer their father a deal: for one week, they'll hide the live chicken he got as their mother's birthday present and keep it secret; he, in return will take them to Starlight Park to ride the Screaming Cyclone.

GERM: For a bit of experiential writing, have your children write about their own debacles or about the time they had to keep something a secret and how they did it. They can also make a list: Ten Good Ways to Keep a Secret.

RELATED TITLES: Duffey, Betsy. *Coaster.* Viking, 1994. / Feldman, Thea. *Who You Callin' Chicken?* Abrams, 2003. / King-Smith, Dick. *Pretty Polly.* Crown, 1992. / Lowry, Lois. *Attaboy Sam!* Houghton, 1992. / Naylor, Phyllis Reynolds. *The Boys Start the War.* Delacorte, 1993. / Park, Barbara. *Operation: Dump the Chump.* Knopf, 1982. / Pinkwater, Daniel. *The Hoboken Chicken Emergency.* Simon & Schuster, 1990. / Schotter, Roni. *Dreamland.* Orchard, 1996. / Sutton, Jane. *Me and the Weirdos.* Houghton, 1981. / Wolkoff, Judie. *Wally.* Bradbury, 1977.

SUBJECTS: BIRTHDAYS. CHICKENS. FAMILY LIFE. GIFTS. HUMOROUS FICTION. SECRETS.

1070 Naylor, Phyllis Reynolds. *Shiloh Season.* **Atheneum, 1996. 0-689-80647-7. 120pp. Gr. 4–7**

In the riveting sequel to the Newbery Medal winner *Shiloh*, Marty Preston faces the uncomfortable fact that he blackmailed dog owner Judd Travers into giving him his beagle. While Marty fears for his beloved dog's safety from the vengeful and irrational Judd, he also feels responsible for causing Judd's problems in the first place.

GERM: You'll find much to debate about accepting responsibility for one's actions and behavior. Discussion Points: Can someone like Judd ever change? Why does Marty feel so responsible for Judd? Does Marty deserve to keep Shiloh? Readers will want to follow up with the third book in the trilogy, *Saving Shiloh*. All three novels deal with deep issues about Marty's love for his dog balanced against his sense of responsibility toward Judd and the meaning of honesty, trust, and friendship.

RELATED TITLES: Bauer, Marion Dane. *A Question of Trust.* Scholastic, 1994. / Byars, Betsy. *Wanted . . . Mud Blossom.* Delacorte, 1991. / Cleary, Beverly. *Strider.* Morrow, 1991. / Naylor, Phyllis Reynolds. *Saving Shiloh.* Atheneum, 1997. / Naylor, Phyllis Reynolds. *Shiloh.* Atheneum, 1991.

SUBJECTS: DOGS. HONESTY. KINDNESS. WEST VIRGINIA.

1071 Neuberger, Anne E. *The Girl-Son.* **Carolrhoda, 1995. 0-87614-846-1. 131pp. Gr. 3–8**

Born in Korea in 1896, Induk Pahk would have had no opportunity to gain an education; girls did not go to school. "Girls were expected to be quiet, obedient, gentle." Her widowed mother, realizing her daughter was bright and eager to learn, arranged to have the 7-year-old child attend school disguised as a boy. Through her mother's sacrifices and her own tenacity, Induk attended a mission high school and college in Seoul and became a teacher, only to be imprisoned for three harrowing months for participating in demonstrations against Japanese rule in Korea.

GERM: Children will be inspired by this true story, told as fictionalized autobiography, which might help them see more value in the schooling they take for granted. Set in Korea during World War II, Linda Sue Park's *When My Name Was Keoko* also deals with the Korean resistance to Japanese rule. Pam Muñoz Ryan's *Riding Freedom* is another fictionalized, but mostly true, account of a girl who disguised herself as a boy; in the mid-1800s, 12-year-old Charlotte Parkhurst ran away from her orphanage and eventually became a stagecoach driver in California.

RELATED TITLES: Choi, Sook Nyul. *The Year of Impossible Goodbyes.* Houghton Mifflin, 1991. / Park, Linda Sue. *The Kite Fighters.* Clarion, 2000. / Park, Linda Sue. *Seesaw Girl.* Clarion, 1999. / Park, Linda Sue. *A Single Shard.* Clarion, 2002. / Park, Linda Sue. *When My Name Was Keoko.* Clarion, 2002. / Ryan, Pam Muñoz. *Riding Freedom.* Scholastic, 1998. / Watkins, Yoko Kawashima. *So Far from the Bamboo Grove.* Beech Tree, 1986.

SUBJECTS: BIOGRAPHICAL FICTION. GENDER ROLE. HISTORICAL FICTION. KOREA. MULTICULTURAL BOOKS. SCHOOLS. WOMEN—BIOGRAPHY.

1072 Nodelman, Perry. *The Same Place But Different.* **Simon & Schuster, 1995. 0-671-89839-6. 131pp. Gr. 5–8**

"The hill opened and my life changed." So starts Johnny Nesbit's dangerous encounter with the fairies, or Strangers, who stole away his baby sister Andrea and replaced her with a look-alike Changeling. Liam Green, a quiet kid from school, reveals he is a Stranger and clues Johnny in on what he will need to do to get Andrea back and close the door between the two worlds.

GERM: Set in Winnipeg, Canada, Johnny's thrilling and gritty account (sometimes laced with "hells" and "damns" you may choose to edit as you read aloud) is an explosive mix of British folklore, fantasy, and the realism of a modern adolescent's view of family. Descend into another underground world in *The Wee Free Men* by Terry Pratchett.

RELATED TITLES: Ames, Mildred. *Is There Life on a Plastic Planet?* Dutton, 1975. / Bellairs, John. *The House with a Clock in Its Walls.* Dial, 1973. / Billingsley, Franny. *The Folk Keeper.* Atheneum, 1999. / Brittain, Bill. *Devil's Donkey.* Harper, 1981. / Collins, Suzanne. *Gregor the Overlander.* Scholastic, 2003. / Corbett, Sue. *12 Again.* Dutton, 2002. / Dahl, Roald. *The Witches.* Farrar, 1983. / Gaiman, Neil. *Coraline.* HarperCollins, 2002. / Ibbotson, Eva. *The Secret of Platform 13.* Dutton, 1998. / Langrish, Katherine. *Troll Fell.* HarperCollins, 2004. / Matas, Carol, and Perry Nodelman. *Of Two Minds.* Simon & Schuster, 1995. / McGraw, Eloise. *The Moorchild.* McElderry, 1996. / Nodelman, Perry. *A Completely Different Place.* Simon & Schuster, 1997. / Pratchett, Terry. *The Wee Free Men.* HarperCollins, 2003. / Smith, L. J. *The Night of the Solstice.* Macmillan, 1987.

SUBJECTS: BROTHERS AND SISTERS. CHANGELINGS. FAIRIES. FANTASY.

1073 Oppel, Kenneth. *Airborn.* HarperCollins, 2004. 0-06-053181-9. 355pp. Gr. 5–8

Aboard the airship *Aurora*, riding high above the Pacificus en route from Sydney to Lionsgate City, 15-year-old cabin boy Matt Cruse helps to rescue an unconscious man in a hot-air balloon that is about to collide with the ship. One year later, Matt meets the man's granddaughter, Kate de Vries, a headstrong and wealthy passenger just his age, who hopes to verify the "beautiful creatures" her late grandfather wrote about in his logbook.

GERM: Details of flying 400 feet in the air, encounters with pirates, a forced landing on an unknown island in the Pacificus, mysterious flying cloud cats, and the witty give-and-take between stalwart Matt and feisty Kate make this an irresistible fantasy, like the movie *Titanic* taken into the air. Readers can draw the cloud cats and write a nonfiction-like encyclopedia entry about them, describing their habitats and essential facts. The story is set in the early 20th century, though an alternate, parallel one. Readers should compile one list of clues that reveal the era (styles of dress, existing technology) and another that charts the differences between the story's fantastical reality and ours. Find out more about book and author at <www.kenneth oppel.ca and <www.airborn.ca>.

RELATED TITLES: Armstrong, Jennifer. *Shipwreck at the Bottom of the World: The Extraordinary True Story of Shackleton and the Endurance.* Crown, 1998. / Burleigh, Robert. *Earth from Above for Young Readers.* Abrams, 2002. / DuPrau, Jeanne. *The City of Ember.* Random House, 2003. / Hirsch, Odo. *Bartlett and the City of Flames.* Bloomsbury, 2003. / Hunter, Ryan Ann. *Into the Air: An Illustrated Timeline of Flight.* National Geographic, 2003. / L'Engle, Madeleine. *A Wrinkle in Time.* Farrar, 1962. / McCaughrean, Geraldine. *Gilgamesh the Hero: The Epic of Gilgamesh.* Eerdmans, 2003. / Mikaelsen, Ben. *Countdown.* Hyperion, 1996. / Oppel, Kenneth. *Silverwing.* Simon & Schuster, 1997. (And others in the Silverwing series.) / Pullman, Philip. *The Golden Compass.* Knopf, 1996.

SUBJECTS: ADVENTURE AND ADVENTURERS. AIRSHIPS. ANIMALS, IMAGINARY. FANTASY. PIRATES. VOYAGES AND TRAVELS.

1074 Oppel, Kenneth. *Silverwing.* Simon & Schuster, 1997. 0-689-81529-8. 217pp. Gr. 4–7

To prove his mettle, rebellious young bat Shade, nicknamed "Runt" by the other bats, attempts to stay up to see the sun rise, something forbidden to bats for millions of years by the owls that control their lives. Here is a breathtaking and unforgettable animal fantasy that will cause all to reevaluate their fears about bats and scramble to learn more about them.

GERM: Independent readers will want to continue the series with *Sunwing* and *Firewing*. Bats are good guys in *Gregor the Overlander* by Suzanne Collins; owls are once again the baddies in *Poppy* by Avi.

RELATED TITLES: Ackerman, Diane. *Bats: Shadows in the Night.* Crown, 1997. / Asch, Frank. *Pearl's Promise.* Delacorte, 1984. / Avi. *Poppy.* Orchard, 1995. / Collins, Suzanne. *Gregor the Overlander.* Scholastic, 2003. / DiCamillo, Kate. *The Tale of Despereaux.* Candlewick, 2003. / Jacques, Brian. *Redwall.* Philomel, 1987. / Markle, Sandra. *Owls* (Animal Predator series). Carolrhoda, 2004. / Napoli, Donna Jo. *The Prince of the Pond.* Dutton, 1992. / Oppel, Kenneth. *Airborn.* HarperCollins, 2004. / Oppel, Kenneth. *Firewing.* Simon & Schuster, 2003. / Oppel, Kenneth. *Sunwing.* Simon & Schuster, 2000. / Steig, William. *Abel's Island.* Farrar, 1976.

SUBJECTS: ADVENTURE AND ADVENTURERS. ANIMALS. BATS. FANTASY. OWLS.

1075 Osborne, Mary Pope. *Adaline Falling Star.* Scholastic, 2000. 0-439-05947-X. 170pp. Gr. 4–8

Adaline Carson, 11-year-old daughter of famous scout Kit Carson and an Arapaho mother who has recently died, is left behind at her father's cousins' home in St. Louis, where she is expected to work as a servant. The only thing she has left to love is the cornhusk doll her Pa made her. Considered a heathen savage by her cousins, Adaline, the eloquent narrator of this poignant, brief novel, becomes mute in their presence and finally escapes, disguised as a boy. Lighting out to the Mississippi River to find her Pa, she is adopted by an ugly little mongrel dog, a dog she is determined not to love.

GERM: Children can compare and contrast the lives and customs of Arapaho children with the white children in the book, which takes place in the 1840s, and research the life of Kit Carson. Another 19th-century runaway who disguised herself as a boy was Charlotte Parkhurst, seen in the biographical fiction book *Riding Freedom* by Pam Muñoz Ryan.

RELATED TITLES: Bruchac, Joseph. *Sacajawea*. Harcourt, 2000. / DiCamillo, Kate. *Because of Winn-Dixie*. Candlewick, 2000. / Freedman, Russell. *Children of the Wild West*. Clarion, 1983. / Haddix, Margaret. *Running Out of Time*. Simon & Schuster, 1995. / Karr, Kathleen. *The Great Turkey Walk*. Farrar, 1998. / Levine, Gail Carson. *Dave at Night*. HarperCollins, 1999. / Lindquist, Susan Hart. *Wander*. Delacorte, 1998. / Paterson, Katherine. *Jip: His Story*. Lodestar, 1996. / Ryan, Pam Muñoz. *Riding Freedom*. Scholastic, 1998. / Schanzer, Rosalyn. *How We Crossed the West: The Adventures of Lewis and Clark*. National Geographic Society, 1997. / Snyder, Zilpha Keatley. *Gib Rides Home*. Delacorte, 1998.

SUBJECTS: ARAPAHO INDIANS. CARSON, KIT. DOGS. HISTORICAL FICTION. INDIANS OF NORTH AMERICA. MULTICULTURAL BOOKS. RACIALLY MIXED PEOPLE. SURVIVAL.

1076 **Palatini, Margie.** *The Wonder Worm Wars.* **Hyperion, 1997. 0-7868-2295-3. 172pp. Gr. 3–5**
Elliot may be only 9 years old, but he has a 4-year-old nephew called Jonathan. With his sister about to have a baby any minute, Elliot is expected to cope with a broken arm; deal with new girl Corinne, a baseball whiz; and baby-sit irksome Jonathan, whom he learns to love in spite of himself.

GERM: Ask your listeners to write with humor and insight about a time they have had to overcome obstacles in their day-to-day lives.

RELATED TITLES: Blume, Judy. *Superfudge*. Dutton, 1980. / Blume, Judy. *Tales of a Fourth Grade Nothing*. Dutton, 1972. / Cleary, Beverly. *Beezus and Ramona*. Morrow, 1955. / Cleary, Beverly. *Ramona the Pest*. Morrow, 1968. / Greene, Stephanie. *Show and Tell*. Clarion, 1998. / Lowry, Lois. *All About Sam*. Houghton Mifflin, 1988. (And others in the Sam series.) / MacDonald, Amy. *No More Nice*. Orchard, 1996. / McDonald, Megan. *Judy Moody, M.D.: The Doctor Is In!* Candlewick, 2004 (and others in the Judy Moody series).

SUBJECTS: BABIES. BABY-SITTERS. BASEBALL. FAMILY LIFE. HUMOROUS FICTION. JEALOUSY. UNCLES.

1077 **Park, Barbara.** *The Graduation of Jake Moon.* **Atheneum, 2000. 0-689-83912-X. 116pp. Gr. 4–7**
When Jake was in third grade, his beloved grandfather, Skelly, developed Alzheimer's disease. As it worsened over the years, Jake became more and more resentful about helping to care for him. Now about to graduate from eighth grade, Jake is not a heroic kid who copes magnificently with adversity. Just when Jake thinks he can't be more miserable, Skelly wanders away from the Senior Center and disappears, forcing Jake to get his priorities straight. Don't for a minute think this is a depressing Alzheimer's treatise; Jake's first-person narrative is fresh and funny and always compelling.

GERM: Web sites listed at the back of the book offer more information about Alzheimer's, but this is also a novel about a boy afraid of peer rejection and about families. Discussion point: If you were in Jake's shoes, what would you do differently? The same? Why?

RELATED TITLES: Bahr, Mary. *The Memory Box*. Albert Whitman, 1992. / Codell, Esmé Raji. *Sahara Special*. Hyperion, 2003. / Duffey, Betsy. *Utterly Yours, Booker Jones*. Viking, 1995. / Dugan, Barbara. *Loop the Loop*. Greenwillow, 1992. / Gantos, Jack. *Joey Pigza Swallowed the Key*. Farrar, 1998. / Herman, Charlotte. *Our Snowman Had Olive Eyes*. Dutton, 1997. / Martin, Ann M. *Belle Teal*. Scholastic, 2001. / Park, Barbara. *Mick Harte Was Here*. Knopf, 1995. / Rosen, Michael J. *The Heart Is Big Enough: Five Stories*. Harcourt, 1997. / Slepian, Jan. *The Broccoli Tapes*. Philomel, 1988. / Smith, Robert Kimmel. *The War with Grandpa*. Delacorte, 1984. / Spinelli, Jerry. *Crash*. Knopf, 1996. / Woodruff, Elvira. *Dear Napoleon, I Know You're Dead, But . . .* Holiday House, 1992.

SUBJECTS: ALZHEIMER'S DISEASE. FAMILY PROBLEMS. GRANDFATHERS.

1078 **Park, Barbara.** *Junie B., First Grader: Cheater Pants.* **Illus. by Denise Brunkus. Random House, 2003. 0-375-82301-8. 86pp. Gr. 1–4**
Because the weekend zoomed by speedy quick, Junie B. didn't have time to do her homework, and she "borrows" seatmate May's perfect paper instead. Caught by her teacher, Mr. Scary, she blames others, tries to rationalize her actions, lies, does it again, and finally owns up and takes

responsibility, realizing "the word cheater makes you feel like a nasty, rotten ratty pants who can't even be trusted."

GERM: Talk it over: What's the difference between borrowing, sharing, copying, and stealing? Maybe you can nip all that Internet plagiarizing the older kids do in the bud, or at least make kids aware of that old "honesty is the best policy" maxim.

RELATED TITLES: Brisson, Pat. *The Summer My Father Was Ten*. Boyds Mills, 1998. / Cameron, Ann. *More Stories Huey Tells*. Farrar, 1997. / Cameron, Ann. *The Stories Huey Tells*. Knopf, 1995. / Cleary, Beverly. *Ramona the Pest*. Morrow, 1968. / Greene, Stephanie. *Show and Tell*. Clarion, 1998. / Havill, Juanita. *Jamaica and the Substitute Teacher*. Houghton Mifflin, 1999. / Kline, Suzy. *Mary Marony and the Chocolate Surprise*. Putnam, 1995. / Lowry, Lois. *All About Sam*. Houghton Mifflin, 1988. (And others in the Sam series.) / McKissack, Patricia C. *The Honest-to-Goodness Truth*. Atheneum, 2000. / Park, Barbara. Junie B. Jones series. Random. / Peters, Julie Anne. *The Stinky Sneakers Contest*. Little, Brown, 1992. / Polacco, Patricia. *Chicken Sunday*. Philomel, 1992. / Rathmann, Peggy. *Ruby the Copycat*. Scholastic, 1991. / Soto, Gary. *Too Many Tamales*. Putnam, 1993.

SUBJECTS: APOLOGIES. CHEATING. FICTION BOOKS FOR EARLY GRADES. HONESTY. HUMOROUS FICTION. SCHOOLS.

1079 **Park, Barbara.** *Junie B. Jones Is a Graduation Girl*. Illus. by Denise Brunkus. **Random House, 2001. 0-375-90292-9. 69pp. Gr. 1–4**

Many readers have followed Junie B.'s hilarious progress through kindergarten, and now she's about to move up, all worried about the "weirdo strangers" she'll find in first grade. Before she graduates, she manages to get sent to the principal for calling out a silly poem, tries on her "cats and gowns" with the class, and decorates her graduation gown with a purple marker. As with all of the books in this laugh-out-loud series that appeals every bit as much to fifth graders as to first graders, it's feisty Junie B.'s slightly skewed, always kid-like takes on the world that endear her to us and remind ourselves of the times we were littler.

GERM: Junie's love affair with language is filled with misunderstandings and misconceptions about what common words and phrases mean, a perfect opportunity to discuss what the real meanings are. Children can write about Junie B.'s anticipated first day of first grade or recall their own expectations when they moved up from kindergarten. Photocopy Junie B.'s dialogues and hand them out to pairs or groups of children to act out. Children in all grades enjoy getting under Junie B.'s skin and writing new chapters using her unmistakable voice.

RELATED TITLES: Cameron, Ann. *The Stories Huey Tells*. Knopf, 1995. / Cameron, Ann. *The Stories Julian Tells*. Yearling, 1989. / Cleary, Beverly. *Ramona the Pest*. Morrow, 1968. / Greene, Stephanie. *Show and Tell*. Clarion, 1998. / Lasky, Kathryn. *Lunch Bunnies*. Little, Brown, 1996. / Lowry, Lois. *All About Sam*. Houghton Mifflin, 1988. (And others in the Sam series.) / Park, Barbara. *Junie B., First Grader (at Last)*. Random House, 2001. (And others in the Junie B. Jones series.)

SUBJECTS: BEHAVIOR. FICTION BOOKS FOR EARLY GRADES. HUMOROUS FICTION. SCHOOLS.

1080 **Park, Barbara.** *Mick Harte Was Here*. **Knopf, 1995. 0-679-97088-6. 89pp. Gr. 4–7**

In a sad, funny, and affecting novel, almost too heartbreaking to read aloud, eighth grader Phoebe takes us through the days following her beloved brother's death in a bicycle accident. Mick, only ten months younger than Phoebe, was a funny kid who in sixth grade dressed for Halloween as Thomas Crapper, inventor of the modern-day flush toilet, and named a cigar Helen. ("It's a girl" the wrapper said.) The loss is traumatic for Phoebe, who wonders where he is, and for her precise, controlled chemist parents. I cried through this, even though the portrait of Mick is very funny. The climax, where Phoebe reveals at a school bike safety assembly that Mick died because he thought wearing a helmet made him look like a dork, is devastating.

GERM: This one will make kids think about life, siblings, and how every action has a consequence. They will make connections to their own lives as the story takes them through the awful, but necessary, stages of grief.

RELATED TITLES: Couloumbis, Audrey. *Getting Near to Baby*. Putnam, 1999. / Fry, Virginia Lynn. *Part of Me Died, Too: Stories of Creative Survival Among Bereaved Children and Teenagers*. Dutton, 1995. / Hermes, Patricia. *Nobody's Fault*. Harcourt, 1981. / Holm, Jennifer L. *Our Only May Amelia*. HarperCollins, 1999. / Park, Barbara. *Don't Make Me Smile*. Knopf, 1981. / Park, Barbara. *The Graduation of Jake Moon*. Atheneum, 2000. / Park, Barbara. *The Kid in the Red Jacket*. Knopf, 1987. / Park, Barbara. *Operation: Dump the Chump*. Knopf, 1982. / Park, Barbara. *Skinnybones*. Knopf, 1982. / Paterson, Katherine. *Bridge to Terabithia*. Crowell, 1977. / Recorvits, Helen. *Goodbye, Walter Malinski*. Farrar, 1999. / Slepian, Jan. *Back to Before*. Philomel, 1993. / Woodruff, Elvira. *Dear Napoleon, I Know You're Dead, But . . .* Holiday House, 1992.

SUBJECTS: BICYCLES. BROTHERS AND SISTERS. DEATH. GRIEF.

1081 Park, Linda Sue. *The Kite Fighters.* **Clarion, 2000. 0-440-41813-5. 136pp. Gr. 4–6**

In Seoul, Korea, in 1473, 11-year-old Young-sup develops his intuitive talent for flying kites, winning the admiration of the boy-king, who becomes his friend. At the royal command of the king, older brother Kee-sup designs and builds a special kite for the king to fly at the New Year kite competition.

GERM: Impeccable research on making and flying kites enriches this engrossing historical novel. Kite enthusiasts will want to try their hands at designing and flying kites. The two brothers must memorize and recite the Five Virtues of Confucius. Find out more about his life, philosophy, and wise sayings in Russell Freedman's biography, *Confucius: The Golden Rule.*

RELATED TITLES: Compestine, Ying Chang. *The Story of Kites.* Holiday House, 2003. / Freedman, Russell. *Confucius: The Golden Rule.* Scholastic, 2002. / McCaughrean, Geraldine. *The Kite Rider.* HarperCollins, 2002. / Neuberger, Anne E. *The Girl-Son.* Carolrhoda, 1995. / Park, Linda Sue. *Seesaw Girl.* Clarion, 1999. / Park, Linda Sue. *A Single Shard.* Clarion, 2002. / Park, Linda Sue. *When My Name Was Keoko.* Clarion, 2002.

SUBJECTS: BROTHERS. KINGS AND RULERS. KITES. KOREA. MULTICULTURAL BOOKS.

1082 Park, Linda Sue. *A Single Shard.* **Clarion, 2001. 0-395-97827-0. 152pp. Gr. 4–8**

In the potter's village of Ch'ulp'o in 12th-century Korea, the orphan Tree-ear, who lives under a bridge with his protector, Crane-man, yearns to become the apprentice of the gruff but gifted potter Min.

GERM: Look up Linda Sue Park's Web site <www.LindaSuePark.com> for information about and pictures of celadon pottery. This elegant and poignant Newbery winner moves at a slow, graceful pace and will make you and your listeners yearn to work with clay as you read it, which is easy enough to arrange. You'll want to have your students do some research on ancient Korea, including its dress, houses, cities, customs, and daily life. Pair your reading with another Newbery winner about an orphan in search of family, Christopher Paul Curtis's *Bud, Not Buddy.*

RELATED TITLES: Avi. *Crispin: The Cross of Lead.* Hyperion, 2002. / Curtis, Christopher Paul. *Bud, Not Buddy.* Delacorte, 1999. / Farley, Carol. *Mr. Pak Buys a Story.* Albert Whitman, 1997. / Ginsburg, Mirra. *The Chinese Mirror.* Harcourt, 1988. / Han, Oki S. *Sir Whong and the Golden Pig.* Dial, 1993. / Neuberger, Anne E. *The Girl-Son.* Carolrhoda, 1995. / Park, Linda Sue. *The Kite Fighters.* Clarion, 2000. / Park, Linda Sue. *Seesaw Girl.* Clarion, 1999. / Park, Linda Sue. *When My Name Was Keoko.* Clarion, 2002.

SUBJECTS: ARTISTS. HISTORICAL FICTION. KOREA. MULTICULTURAL BOOKS. NEWBERY MEDAL. ORPHANS. POTTERY.

1083 Park, Linda Sue. *When My Name Was Keoko.* **Clarion, 2002. 0-618-13335-6. 199pp. Gr. 5–8**

Sun-hee asks her 13-year-old brother, Tae-yul, annoying questions and listens carefully to every conversation that goes on around her. As a girl in a Korean family, she's not supposed to talk much. In wartime Korea of 1940, things are about to get much worse. First, the Japanese, who have occupied the country since 1910, decree that Koreans must forsake their Korean names for Japanese ones. Sun-hee's new name is Keoko. In alternating chapters, Sun-hee and Tae-yul describe the many changes that their village undergoes from the Japanese attack on Pearl Harbor until 1945 and the ways they and their family resist the Japanese oppressors.

GERM: Research the history, culture, food, clothing, and customs of Korea. Park's Newbery winner, *A Single Shard,* will be an essential title to compare and contrast life in medieval versus modern Korea. Another interesting comparison of life on a World War II homefront is *Don't You Know There's a War On?* by Avi.

RELATED TITLES: Avi. *Don't You Know There's a War On?* HarperCollins, 2001. / Choi, Sook Nyul. *The Year of Impossible Goodbyes.* Houghton Mifflin, 1991. / Lowry, Lois. *Number the Stars.* Houghton Mifflin, 1989. / Park, Linda Sue. *The Kite Fighters.* Clarion, 2000. / Park, Linda Sue. *Seesaw Girl.* Clarion, 1999. / Park, Linda Sue. *A Single Shard.* Clarion, 2002. / Propp, Vera W. *When the Soldiers Were Gone.* Putnam, 1999. / Watkins, Yoko Kawashima. *So Far from the Bamboo Grove.* Beech Tree, 1994.

SUBJECTS: COURAGE. FAMILY LIFE. HISTORICAL FICTION. KOREA. MULTICULTURAL BOOKS. PATRIOTISM. WORLD WAR, 1939–1945—FICTION.

1084 Paterson, Katherine. *Jip: His Story.* **Dutton, 1996. 0-525-67543-4. 181pp. Gr. 5–8**

At a Vermont town's poor farm in 1855, 11-year-old foundling Jip is put in charge of a new resident, old Put, called a lunatic for the spells of madness that overcome him. Jip befriends Put and comes to love him like a father. Jip is allowed at last to attend school, where he encounters a wondrous teacher—whom attentive readers may recognize as Lyddie from Paterson's novel of the same name— who helps him to realize that he is worthy of learning. Nothing is easy for this boy, and in a devastating series of revelations, the startling and dangerous secret of his family is uncovered when a stranger arrives in town searching him out.

GERM: Issues of slavery, freedom, madness, and poverty make this compelling story one readers will ponder over and discuss for a long time.

RELATED TITLES: Beatty, Patricia. *That's One Ornery Orphan*. Morrow, 1980. / Cushman, Karen. *Rodzina*. Clarion, 2003. / Doherty, Berlie. *Street Child*. Orchard, 1994. / Paterson, Katherine. *Lyddie*. Dutton, 1991. / Ryan, Pam Muñoz. *Riding Freedom*. Scholastic, 1998. / Wallace, Barbara Brooks. *Peppermints in the Parlor*. Atheneum, 1980.

SUBJECTS: AFRICAN AMERICANS. FUGITIVE SLAVES. HISTORICAL FICTION. IDENTITY. MENTAL ILLNESS. ORPHANS. POVERTY. SLAVERY. VERMONT.

1085 Paulsen, Gary. *Molly McGinty Has a Really Good Day*. Random House, 2004. 0-385-90911-X. 106pp. Gr. 4–6

Staid, organized sixth grader Molly can't find her indispensable multi-pocketed three-ring binder notebook; she has a black eye from crashing into her own desk; and her flamboyant grandmother, Irene, is planning her annual visit for Senior Citizen's Day at Our Lady of Mercy Middle School. What else could go wrong?

GERM: Molly's grandmother, Mrs. Irene Flynne, is a prime candidate for a lesson on strong, unforgettable characters. What does she look like? Draw pictures and write character sketches of Irene and Molly. Then have your crew write character sketches of larger-than-life adults in their own lives. Pair your reading with the classic picture book *Alexander and the Terrible, Horrible, No Good, Very Bad Day* by Judith Viorst as inspiration for writing about your own worst/best days. Hold an impromptu poetry slam.

RELATED TITLES: Creech, Sharon. *Granny Torrelli Makes Soup*. HarperCollins, 2003. / Duffey, Betsy. *Utterly Yours, Booker Jones*. Viking, 1995. / Gauthier, Gail. *A Year with Butch and Spike*. Putnam, 1998. / MacDonald, Amy. *No More Nasty*. Farrar, 2001. / Paulsen, Gary. *The Cookcamp*. Orchard, 1991. / Peck, Richard. *A Long Way from Chicago*. Dial, 1998. / Peck, Richard. *A Year Down Yonder*. Dial, 2000. / Robinson, Barbara. *The Best School Year Ever*. HarperCollins, 1994. / Viorst, Judith. *Alexander and the Terrible, Horrible, No Good, Very Bad Day*. Atheneum, 1972.

SUBJECTS: CATHOLIC SCHOOLS. GRANDMOTHERS. HUMOROUS FICTION. LOST AND FOUND POSSESSIONS. PRIVATE SCHOOLS. SCHOOLS. SELF-CONFIDENCE.

1086 Pearson, Kit. *Awake and Dreaming*. Viking, 1997. 0-670-86954-6. 228pp. Gr. 4–6

A misfit called Licehead by her fourth-grade classmates, Theo takes refuge in books where families are perfect. Her own mother, Rae, only 25, takes her into Vancouver, where Theo is expected to dance while her mother panhandles. On the ferry to Victoria, Theo meets the perfect family, the Kaldors, makes a wish on a new moon, and awakens to find herself ensconced in their house and accepted as a new family member. Is she dreaming or is it real?

GERM: This appealing and believable fantasy will make a fitting read-aloud kickoff to a research project on famous children's book classics and their authors.

RELATED TITLES: Byars, Betsy. *Cracker Jackson*. Viking, 1985. / Corbett, Sue. *12 Again*. Dutton, 2002. / Fox, Paula. *Monkey Island*. Orchard, 1991. / Gaiman, Neil. *Coraline*. HarperCollins, 2002. / Hahn, Mary Downing. *Time for Andrew: A Ghost Story*. Clarion, 1994. / Lindbergh, Anne. *Travel Far, Pay No Fare*. HarperCollins, 1992. / Slepian, Jan. *Back to Before*. Philomel, 1993.

SUBJECTS: AUTHORS. DREAMS. FAMILY LIFE. FAMILY PROBLEMS. FANTASY. GHOST STORIES.

1087 Peck, Richard. *The Great Interactive Dream Machine*. Dial, 1996. 0-8037-1989-2. 149pp. Gr. 5–7

Aaron Zimmer, the shortest, smartest kid at exclusive Huckley School in New York City, is a computer genius, as his best friend and fellow sixth grader Josh Lewis will attest. Somehow, Aaron's new computer formula begins to reorganize their cells cybernetically, causing their wishes to come true. In a series of outright hilarious encounters, interspersed with believable computer jargon, the boys find themselves at the beach, as 17-year-olds, and then in the 1940s apartment of Josh's octogenarian upstairs neighbor Miss Mather and her fearsome shih tzu Nanky-Poo.

GERM: Seeing as there's a nice bit of World War II history thrown in for good measure, everyone can do a bit of background research on the era. Project yourselves into the body of someone older and write about how you would react and what you would do. Readers will want to go back and find the first installment, *Lost in Cyberspace*.

RELATED TITLES: Alexander, Lloyd. *The Cat Who Wished to Be a Man*. Dutton, 1977. / Avi. *Bright Shadow*. Bradbury, 1985. / Avi. *Don't You Know There's a War On?* HarperCollins, 2001. / Brittain, Bill. *All the Money in the World*. HarperCollins, 1979. / Brittain, Bill. *Shape-Changer*. HarperCollins, 1994. / Brittain, Bill. *The Wish Giver*. HarperCollins, 1983. / Corbett, Sue. *12 Again*. Dutton, 2002. / Egan, Tim. *Burnt Toast on Davenport Street*. Houghton Mifflin, 1997. / Peck, Richard. *The Teacher's Funeral: A Comedy in Three Parts*. Dial, 2004. / Peck, Richard. *A Long Way from Chicago: A Novel in Stories*. Dial, 1998. / Peck, Richard. *Lost in Cyberspace*. Dial, 1994. / Peck, Richard. *A Year Down Yonder*. Dial, 2000. / Van Allsburg, Chris. *The Sweetest Fig*. Houghton, 1993.

SUBJECTS: COMPUTERS. FANTASY. FRIENDSHIP. HUMOROUS FICTION. SCHOOLS. SCIENCE FICTION. TIME TRAVEL. WISHES.

1088 Peck, Richard. *A Long Way from Chicago: A Novel in Stories*. **Dial, 1998. 0-8037-2290-7. 148pp. Gr. 5–7**

For seven years, starting in 1929 when he is 9, Joey and his kid sister Mary Alice take the train from Chicago to the small Illinois town where they spend August with their no-nonsense, whopper-spouting, tough-as-nails Grandma Dowdel. Joey's droll narrative, with one chapter for each successive summer, contains a tangible look at country life during the Great Depression and eye-popping adventures in which the unforgettable Grandma Dowdel shows her grit.

GERM: Have your students draw on their own experiences to write vivid descriptions of the personality, both physical and emotional, of a larger-than-life relative or friend. Follow up with the sequel, Newbery winner *A Year Down Yonder*.

RELATED TITLES: Choldenko, Gennifer. *Al Capone Does My Shirts*. Putnam, 2004. / Fitzgerald, John D. *The Great Brain*. Dial, 1967. / Paulsen, Gary. *The Cookcamp*. Orchard, 1991. / Peck, Richard. *Ghosts I Have Been*. Viking, 1977. / Peck, Richard. *The Great Interactive Dream Machine*. Dial, 1996. / Peck, Richard. *The Teacher's Funeral: A Comedy in Three Parts*. Dial, 2004. / Peck, Richard. *A Year Down Yonder*. Dial, 2000.

SUBJECTS: COUNTRY LIFE. DEPRESSIONS—1929—U.S. GRANDMOTHERS. HISTORICAL FICTION. HUMOROUS FICTION. ILLINOIS.

1089 Peck, Richard. *Past, Perfect, Present Tense: New and Collected Stories*. **Dial, 2004. 0-8037-2998-7. 177pp. Gr. 5–8**

Thirteen of Newbery author Richard Peck's snappy, spirited short stories—some of which are chapters from his novels, while others stand alone—form a collection that introduces characters from the past, the supernatural, and the present.

GERM: Peck's invaluable commentary on his writing, plus his chapters "How to Write a Short Story" and "Five Helpful Hints" will get readers thinking about and writing their own short stories, and lead them to Peck's other extraordinary books.

RELATED TITLES: Byars, Betsy. *The Moon and I*. Messner, 1992. / Little, Jean. *Little by Little: A Writer's Education*. Viking, 1987. / Peck, Richard. *Ghosts I Have Been*. Viking, 1977. / Peck, Richard. *A Long Way from Chicago*. Dial, 1998. / Peck, Richard. *The Teacher's Funeral: A Comedy in Three Parts*. Dial, 2004. / Peck, Richard. *A Year Down Yonder*. Dial, 2000.

SUBJECTS: AUTHORSHIP. SHORT STORIES. WRITING.

1090 Peck, Richard. *The Teacher's Funeral: A Comedy in Three Parts*. **Dial, 2004. 0-8037-2736-4. 208pp. Gr. 5–8**

After the funeral of his teacher, Miss Myrt Arbuckle, whom 15-year-old Russell Culver says "died of her own meanness," Russell is stunned to discover that his older sister Tansy will be the new teacher at their one-room country schoolhouse in the farmlands of Indiana.

GERM: Compare and contrast the differences between Russell's rural school experiences in 1904 with our own a century later. Hold a spelling bee and work on learning the names and spelling of all the state capitals, just as Tansy demands of her class of eight pupils. For another very funny look at a one-room schoolhouse, read the short story "By Far the Worst Pupil at Long Point School" in Peck's own collection, *Past, Perfect, Present Tense*.

RELATED TITLES: Avi. *The Secret School*. Harcourt, 2001. / Hill, Kirkpatrick. *The Year of Miss Agnes*. McElderry, 2000. / Houston, Gloria. *My Great Aunt Arizona*. HarperCollins, 1992. / Levine, Gail Carson. *Dave at Night*. HarperCollins, 1999. / McLachlan, Patricia. *Sarah, Plain and Tall*. HarperCollins, 1985. / Peck, Richard. *A Long Way from Chicago: A Novel in Stories*. Dial, 1998. / Peck, Richard. *Past, Perfect, Present Tense: New and Collected Stories*. Dial, 1998. / Peck, Richard. *A Year Down Yonder*. Dial, 2000. / Ryan, Pam Muñoz. *Riding Freedom*. Scholastic, 1998. / Snyder, Zilpha Keatley. *Gib Rides Home*. Delacorte, 1998. / Wilder, Laura Ingalls. *Farmer Boy*. HarperCollins, 1953.

SUBJECTS: BROTHERS AND SISTERS. COUNTRY LIFE. DEATH. HISTORICAL FICTION. HUMOROUS FICTION. INDIANA. SCHOOLS. TEACHERS.

1091 Peck, Richard. *A Year Down Yonder*. Dial, 2000. 0-8037-2518-3. 130pp. Gr. 5–8

With her dad newly unemployed because of the recession of 1937 and her big brother Joey (narrator of Newbery Honor winner, *A Long Way from Chicago*) planting trees out west in the Civilian Conservation Corps (CCC), 15-year-old Mary Alice is sent to spend the year with her fierce and indomitable Grandma Dowdel in Illinois until the family can get back on its feet. City girl Mary Alice is not looking forward to living in a hick town with no picture show, no telephone, and even an outdoor privy. You get the sights and sounds of the Depression from this laugh-out-loud collection of wry anecdotes, each featuring crafty, crusty Grandma Dowdel, who, underneath it all, really does have a heart of gold.

GERM: Conduct taped or videotaped interviews with older relatives and family friends and compile oral histories of what it was like to grow up during the Depression.

RELATED TITLES: Burch, Robert. *Ida Early Comes over the Mountain*. Viking, 1980. / Choldenko, Gennifer. *Al Capone Does My Shirts*. Putnam, 2004. / Curtis, Christopher Paul. *Bud, Not Buddy*. Delacorte, 1999. / Fitzgerald, John D. *The Great Brain*. Dial, 1967. / Haas, Jessie. *Unbroken*. Greenwillow, 1999. / Hesse, Karen. *Out of the Dust*. Scholastic, 1997. / Holm, Jennifer L. *Our Only May Amelia*. HarperCollins, 1999. / Holt, Kimberley Willis. *My Louisiana Sky*. Henry Holt, 1998. / Paulsen, Gary. *The Cookcamp*. Orchard, 1991. / Peck, Richard. *Ghosts I Have Been*. Viking, 1977. / Peck, Richard. *The Great Interactive Dream Machine*. Dial, 1996. / Peck, Richard. *A Long Way from Chicago*. Dial, 1998. / Peck, Richard. *The Teacher's Funeral: A Comedy in Three Parts*. Dial, 2004. / Recorvits, Helen. *Goodbye, Walter Malinski*. Farrar, 1999. / Taylor, Mildred. *Roll of Thunder, Hear My Cry*. Dial, 1976.

SUBJECTS: COUNTRY LIFE. DEPRESSIONS—1929—U.S. GRANDMOTHERS. HISTORICAL FICTION. HUMOROUS FICTION. ILLINOIS. NEWBERY MEDAL.

1092 Philbrick, Rodman. *The Young Man and the Sea*. Blue Sky/Scholastic, 2004. 0-439-36829-4. 192pp. Gr. 5–8

Because his fisherman dad won't help, 12-year-old Skiff Beaman asks his 94-year-old friend Mr. Woodwell for advice in raising and then repairing his sunk fishing boat, the *Mary Rose*. With Dad depressed and drinking since Mom died, Skiff fends for himself, and when he learns it will take $5,000 to fix his boat, he sets to work setting lobster traps. This is a glorious survival story, narrated by Skiff in gripping present tense, with a crackerjack first sentence: "Before I tell you about the biggest fish in the sea and how it tried to kill me and then ended up saving my life, first you got to know about the leaky boat, 'cause it all began right there."

GERM: Booktalk other survival novels and discuss how the setting is vital to each story. If you're working with an older group, make the obvious connections with Ernest Hemingway's *The Old Man and the Sea*.

RELATED TITLES: Creech, Sharon. *The Wanderer*. HarperCollins, 2000. / Franklin, Christine L. *Lone Wolf*. Candlewick, 1997. / Hemingway, Ernest. *The Old Man and the Sea*. Scribner, 1952. / Hesse, Karen. *The Music of Dolphins*. Scholastic, 1996. / Hill, Kirkpatrick. *Winter Camp*. McElderry, 1993. / Lindquist, Susan Hart. *Wander*. Delacorte, 1998. / Morpurgo, Michael. *Kensuke's Kingdom*. Scholastic, 2003. / O'Dell, Scott. *Island of the Blue Dolphins*. Houghton Mifflin, 1960. / Paulsen, Gary. *The Haymeadow*. Delacorte, 1992. / Spinelli, Jerry. *Crash*. Knopf, 1996. / Spinelli, Jerry. *Wringer*. HarperCollins, 1997. / Taylor, Theodore. *The Cay*. Delacorte, 1987.

SUBJECTS: BULLIES. FATHERS AND SONS. FISHES. FISHING. GRIEF. OCEAN.

1093 Pinkwater, Daniel. *Looking for Bobowicz*. Illus. by Jill Pinkwater. HarperCollins, 2004. 0-06-053554-7. 200pp. Gr. 3–6

In his first hour after moving with his parents to Hoboken, New Jersey, Nick's bicycle is stolen by a caped phantom, a mysterious figure who skulks around town. Nick and his new pals, Loretta and Bruno, read Classics Comics together and try to track down Arthur Bobowicz, who 25 years earlier made headlines when his pet, a 6-foot, 266-pound chicken named Henrietta, terrorized the city. Could there be a connection between Nick's missing bike and the big hen?

GERM: Read this in tandem with *The Hoboken Chicken Emergency*, which your class can first read and discuss as a Literature Circle selection. Readers can make some predictions about their own favorite fiction characters, figure out what they might be doing 10 or 25 years later when they're all grown up, and write up a summary. Will Harry Potter be having a midlife crisis in the wizard world when he's 50? And what will Junie B. Jones be like when she's 25?

RELATED TITLES: Pinkwater, Daniel. *The Artsy Smartsy Club*. Simon & Schuster, 2005. / Pinkwater, Daniel

Manus. *Fat Men from Space*. Dell Yearling, 1980. / Pinkwater, Daniel. *The Hoboken Chicken Emergency*. Simon & Schuster, 1990. / Pinkwater, Daniel Manus. *Lizard Music*. Dell Yearling, 1996. / Scieszka, Jon. *Summer Reading Is Killing Me!* Viking, 1998. / Van Draanen, Wendelin. *Shredderman: Secret Identity*. Knopf, 2004.

SUBJECTS: CHICKENS. CITIES AND TOWNS. ECCENTRICS AND ECCENTRICITIES. HUMOROUS FICTION. LIBRARIANS. LIBRARIES. MOVING, HOUSEHOLD. MYSTERY AND DETECTIVE STORIES. NEW JERSEY.

1094   Pratchett, Terry. *The Wee Free Men*. HarperCollins, 2003. 0-06-001236-6. 263pp. Gr. 6–8

There's a ripple in the walls of the world. When 9-year-old Tiffany Aching is warned away from a sharp-toothed green-headed monster by two tiny redheaded blue men in a boat, it seems that she may be the new witch of the lowlands; the Nac Mac Feegle, the most feared of all the fairy races, wouldn't make themselves known to just anybody. You see, another world is colliding with this one. All the monsters are coming back. There's no one to stop them. Except Tiffany.

GERM: This is a challenging but exhilarating read-aloud, filled with intrigue and wild humor. Make a class dictionary of the wonderful, colorful language spoken by the Wee Free Men, and practice reading their dialogue aloud in a good Scottish brogue. Projects could include compiling a portrait gallery and description of the heroes, villains, and creatures Tiffany encounters. Draw maps of the Chalk country where Tiffany lives and of Fairyland, the magic world of bad dreams, ruled by the queen.

RELATED TITLES: Alexander, Lloyd. *The Book of Three*. Henry Holt, 1964. / Billingsley, Franny. *The Folk Keeper*. Atheneum, 1999. / Black, Holly, and Tony DiTerlizzi. The Spiderwick Chronicles series. Simon & Schuster. / Climo, Shirley. *Piskies, Spriggans, and Other Magical Beings: Tales from the Droll-Teller*. Crowell, 1981. / Collins, Suzanne. *Gregor the Overlander*. Scholastic, 2003. / Dahl, Roald. *The Witches*. Farrar, 1983. / Divakaruni, Chitra Banerjee. *The Conch Bearer*. Roaring Brook, 2003. / Edwards, Julie. *Last of the Really Great Whangdoodles*. HarperCollins, 1974. / Ibbotson, Eva. *The Secret of Platform 13*. Dutton, 1998. / Kindl, Patrice. *Goose Chase*. Houghton Mifflin, 2001. / Langrish, Katherine. *Troll Fell*. HarperCollins, 2004. / L'Engle, Madeleine. *A Wrinkle in Time*. Farrar, 1962. / Nodelman, Perry. *The Same Place But Different*. Simon & Schuster, 1995. / Pratchett, Terry. *A Hat Full of Sky*. HarperCollins, 2004. / Pullman, Philip. *The Golden Compass*. Knopf, 1996.

SUBJECTS: ENGLAND. FAIRIES. FANTASY. WITCHES.

1095   Propp, Vera W. *When the Soldiers Were Gone*. Putnam, 1999. 0-399-23325-3. 102pp. Gr. 3–6

In 1945, at the end of World War II, 8-year-old Henk is retrieved from the Dutch Christian family that has raised and protected him throughout the war and taken back home by two people he sees as strangers—his real parents, who are Jewish. Based on a true story and told from a child's perspective, the book is wrenching in its simplicity. Children will readily identify with Henk/Benjamin's slow adjustment to his new life.

GERM: Discussion points: Why doesn't Henk/Benjamin remember his own parents? Why did they leave him with another family? What makes him start to remember his past? Johanna Reiss's autobiography, *The Upstairs Room*, written for children, is a similar account of her childhood years spent in hiding in a Dutch farmhouse. Both are sensitive, personal accounts that younger children in grades three and up can begin to comprehend, as is Lois Lowry's *Number the Stars*.

RELATED TITLES: Abels, Chana Byers. *The Children We Remember*. Greenwillow, 1986. / Adler, David A. *One Yellow Daffodil: A Hanukkah Story*. Harcourt, 1995. / Cohn, Janice. *The Christmas Menorahs: How a Town Fought Hate*. Whitman, 1995. / Hesse, Karen. *The Cats in Krasinski Square*. Scholastic, 2004. / Hoestlandt, Jo. *Star of Fear, Star of Hope*. Walker, 1995. / Levine, Karen. *Hana's Suitcase*. Albert Whitman, 2003. / Lowry, Lois. *Number the Stars*. Houghton, 1989. / Maguire, Gregory. *The Good Liar*. Clarion, 1999. / McCann, Michelle R. *Luba: The Angel of Bergen-Belsen*. Tricycle, 2003. / Park, Linda Sue. *When My Name Was Keoko*. Clarion, 2002. / Polacco, Patricia. *The Butterfly*. Philomel, 2000. / Schnur, Steven. *The Tie Man's Miracle: A Chanukah Tale*. Morrow, 1995. / Stevenson, James. *Don't You Know There's a War On?* Greenwillow, 1992. / Streatfeild, Noel. *When the Sirens Wailed*. Random House, 1976. / Yolen, Jane. *The Devil's Arithmetic*. Viking, 1988.

SUBJECTS: HISTORICAL FICTION. HOLOCAUST, JEWISH (1939–1945). JEWS. NETHERLANDS. PARENT AND CHILD. WORLD WAR, 1939–1945—FICTION.

1096   Pullman, Philip. *The Golden Compass*. Knopf, 1996. 0-679-87924-2. 399pp. Gr. 6–8

In a parallel world to ours, everyone has a daemon attached to them—a sort of alter ego in animal form. Young Lyra Belacqua and her daemon, Pantalaimon, thwart a murder attempt on Lyra's uncle, Lord Asriel, by one of the scholars at Oxford, where Lyra is being raised. This draws her into a spiral of danger as she tries to find out why children, including her best friend, are being kidnapped by Gobblers all over England. The glamorous and seductively dangerous Mrs. Coulter befriends Lyra and accompanies her to the far north where Lyra tries to find out more about the phenomena called Dust that appears near the Northern Lights and may be part of another parallel world. There's an armored bear, experiments on kidnapped kids to amputate their daemons, witches, and almost 400 pages of heart-stopping adventure. It's all pretty gorgeous writing too, the first in Pullman's brilliant and challenging His Dark Materials trilogy, followed by *The Subtle Knife* and *The Amber Spyglass*.

GERM: Stalwart teachers will claim this for a novel study, filled as it is with wonderful technological, but fictional, inventions and vocabulary.

RELATED TITLES: Alexander, Lloyd. *The First Two Lives of Lucas-Kasha*. Dutton, 1978. / Collins, Suzanne. *Gregor the Overlander*. Scholastic, 2003. / Divakaruni, Chitra Banerjee. *The Conch Bearer*. Roaring Brook, 2003. / DuPrau, Jeanne. *The City of Ember*. Random House, 2003. / Hirsch, Odo. *Bartlett and the City of Flames*. Bloomsbury, 2003. / L'Engle, Madeleine. *A Wrinkle in Time*. Farrar, 1962. / Lowry, Lois. *The Giver*. Houghton Mifflin, 1993. / Oppel, Kenneth. *Airborn*. HarperCollins, 2004. / Pratchett, Terry. *The Wee Free Men*. HarperCollins, 2003. / Pullman, Philip. *The Amber Spyglass*. Knopf, 2000. / Pullman, Philip. *The Subtle Knife*. Knopf, 1997. / Riordan, Rick. *The Lightning Thief* (Percy Jackson and the Olympians, Book 1). Miramax/Hyperion, 2005. / Rowling, J. K. *Harry Potter and the Sorcerer's Stone*. Scholastic, 1998. (And others in the Harry Potter series.) / Stroud, Jonathan. *The Amulet of Samarkand*. Hyperion, 2003.

SUBJECTS: ENGLAND. FANTASY. KIDNAPPING. MAGIC. WITCHES.

1097 **Pullman, Philip.** *I Was a Rat!* **Illus. by Kevin Hawkes. Knopf, 2000. 0-375-90176-0. 165pp. Gr. 4–7**

Old Bob the cobbler and his washerwoman wife, Joan, take in a disheveled little boy in a page's uniform who shows up at their doorstep and tells them, "I was a rat." Naming him Roger, they find that no one has reported the boy missing, though once the king's Philosopher Royal hears about him, he takes the boy to the palace. In the midst of everything, the Royal Wedding is coming up, as frequent articles in the newspaper, *The Daily Scourge*, remind us, and what *is* that connection between Roger and the Princess Aurelia, whom he claims to know as Mary Jane?

GERM: Listeners should look for clues to discover rat Roger's origins and figure out how they tie in to this Cinderella story. Children can rewrite or reexamine other fairy tales from a minor character's point of view. This tongue-in-cheek black comedy comes at the Cinderella tale from a new angle and will be a wonderful title for introducing other variants, from fairy tales to Gail Carson Levine's *Ella Enchanted*.

RELATED TITLES: Alexander, Lloyd. *The Cat Who Wished to Be a Man*. Dutton, 1977. / Craft, K. Y. *Cinderella*. SeaStar Books, 2000. / Ehrlich, Amy. *Cinderella*. Illus. by Susan Jeffers. Dutton, 2004. / Hinton, S. E. *The Puppy Sister*. Delacorte, 1995. / James, Mary. *Shoebag*. Scholastic, 1990. / Kindl, Patrice. *Goose Chase*. Houghton Mifflin, 2001. / Levine, Gail Carson. *Ella Enchanted*. HarperCollins, 1997. / Levine, Gail Carson. *The Princess Test*. HarperCollins, 1999. / Napoli, Donna Jo. *Jimmy, the Pickpocket of the Palace*. Dutton, 1995. / Napoli, Donna Jo. *The Prince of the Pond*. Dutton, 1992. / Pullman, Philip. *The Scarecrow and His Servant*. Knopf, 2005. / Sanderson, Ruth. *Cinderella*. Little, Brown, 2002. / Stolz, Mary. *Quentin Corn*. Godine, 1985. / Vande Velde, Vivian. *Tales from the Brothers Grimm and the Sisters Weird*. Harcourt, 1995. / Whipple, Laura. *If the Shoe Fits: Voices from Cinderella*. McElderry, 2002. / Wrede, Patricia. *Dealing with Dragons*. Harcourt, 1990.

SUBJECTS: CINDERELLA STORIES. FAIRY TALES—SATIRE. FANTASY. KINGS AND RULERS. PARODIES. RATS. TRANSFORMATIONS.

1098 **Pullman, Philip.** *The Scarecrow and His Servant*. **Illus. by Peter Bailey. Knopf, 2005. 0-375-91531-1. 229pp. Gr. 4–6**

On the night lightning strikes Mr. Pandolfo's wheat field, the scarecrow, with its big solid turnip head, a broad crack for a mouth, two stones for eyes, and nothing in the way of brains, jolts to life. A small boy named Jack, sheltering in the barn, helps it down from its stick and, having nowhere else to go, accepts the post of the Scarecrow's personal servant. Together, the impetuous, blustering, but lovable Scarecrow and the level-headed, loyal boy ramble the countryside, encountering brigands, actors, an army of soldiers, a lovely broom, and a Grand Congress of birds. Following close on their heels is a dour and relentless lawyer named Mr. Cercorelli, determined to capture the Scarecrow and bring him back to nefarious businessman and bad guy Mr. Buffaloni. As Pullman says, this satirical novel pulls together two universal human types from folklore, the silly master and the clever servant.

GERM: Make a chart of the trouble Scarecrow gets into and the ways Jack rescues him every time. Pullman's novel is a canny, insightful, and farcical satire that lampoons and skewers lawyers, businessmen, politics, power, and even war. In many ways, the adventure, drama, and the scarecrow's pure foolishness will remind you of Carlo Collodi's classic quest novel *The Adventures of Pinocchio* (and if you've only seen the movie and never made time to read it, you're in for a real treat), and L. Frank Baum's *The Wizard of Oz*.

RELATED TITLES: Alexander, Lloyd. *The Cat Who Wished to Be a Man*. Dutton, 1977. / Baum, L. Frank. *The Annotated Wizard of Oz: The Wonderful Wizard of Oz*. Norton, 2000. / Collodi, Carlo. *The Adventures of Pinocchio*. Illus. by Roberto Innocenti. Knopf, 1988. / Kindl, Patrice. *Goose Chase*. Houghton Mifflin, 2001. / Napoli, Donna Jo. *Jimmy, the Pickpocket of the Palace*. Dutton, 1995. / Napoli, Donna Jo. *The Prince of the Pond*. Dutton, 1992. / Pullman, Philip. *The Golden Compass*. Knopf, 1996. (And others in the His Dark Materials series.) / Pullman, Philip. *I Was a Rat!* Knopf, 2000. / Stolz, Mary. *Quentin Corn*. Godine, 1985.

SUBJECTS: ADVENTURE AND ADVENTURERS. FANTASY. FOOLS. HUMOROUS FICTION. LITERARY FAIRY TALES. SATIRE. SCARECROWS. SOLDIERS. TRANSFORMATIONS.

1099   Quindlen, Anna. *Happily Ever After.* **Illus. by James Stevenson. Viking, 1997. 0-670-86961-9. 43pp. Gr. 1–4**

Baseball-loving Kate, an assertive and active heroine for sure, finds her mitt is magic when she makes a wish, is transported to the time of knights and dragons, and becomes a beautiful princess.

GERM: As a story-starter, have your nonroyal charges complete the sentence they choose and then share their opinions and reasons: "I wish I could be a prince or princess because . . ."; or "I wouldn't wish to be a prince or princess because . . ."

RELATED TITLES: Auch, Mary Jane. *The Princess and the Pizza*. Holiday House, 2002. / Jackson, Ellen. *Cinder Edna*. Lothrop, 1994. / Moss, Marissa. *Mighty Jackie, the Strike-Out Queen*. Simon & Schuster, 2004. / Napoli, Donna Jo. *The Prince of the Pond*. Dutton, 1992. / Shields, Carol Diggory. *I Am Really a Princess*. Dutton, 1993. / Waber, Bernard. *Gina*. Houghton Mifflin, 1995. / Wilsdorf, Anne. *Princess*. Greenwillow, 1993. / Yolen, Jane. *Sleeping Ugly*. Coward, 1981.

SUBJECTS: BASEBALL. FANTASY. FICTION BOOKS FOR EARLY GRADES. MIDDLE AGES. PRINCES AND PRINCESSES. TIME TRAVEL.

1100   Recorvits, Helen. *Goodbye, Walter Malinski.* **Illus. by Lloyd Bloom. Farrar, 1999. 0-374-32747-5. 85pp. Gr. 3–5**

Times are bad in 1934, and Wanda hates it when her Pa, laid off from the cotton mill, fights with and belittles her 15-year-old brother Walter. She loves being in school with her wonderful fifth-grade teacher, Miss Rosalie Smith. Wanda's is a tender story, told with heart, about a family of Polish immigrants trying to make it in a new country and facing unspeakable tragedy when Walter drowns in an accident.

GERM: Use with a lesson on the Great Depression or immigration. Show photos of the life and times of the 1930s. Discussion point: Talk over the irony of how something good came out of Walter's death.

RELATED TITLES: Bartone, Elisa. *American Too*. Lothrop, 1996. / Bartone, Elisa. *Peppe the Lamplighter*. Lothrop, 1993. / Bierman, Carol. *Journey to Ellis Island: How My Father Came to America*. Hyperion, 1998. / Estes, Eleanor. *The Hundred Dresses*. Harcourt, 1944. / Freedman, Russell. *Immigrant Kids*. Dutton, 1980. / Levine, Ellen. *I Hate English!* Scholastic, 1989. / Marsden, Carolyn. *The Gold-Threaded Dress*. Candlewick, 2002. / Park, Barbara. *Mick Harte Was Here*. Knopf, 1995.

SUBJECTS: BROTHERS AND SISTERS. DEATH. DEPRESSIONS—1929—U.S. FAMILY PROBLEMS. HISTORICAL FICTION. IMMIGRATION AND EMIGRATION. MULTICULTURAL BOOKS. POLISH AMERICANS. U.S.—HISTORY—20TH CENTURY—FICTION.

1101   Riordan, Rick. *The Lightning Thief.* **Miramax/Hyperion, 2005. 0-7868-5629-7. 377pp. Gr. 5–8**

In Book 1 of a crackling new series, Percy Jackson and the Olympians, meet Percy, troubled dyslexic ADHD kid on probation at a private boarding school in upstate New York, having a bit of a problem on his sixth-grade class field trip to the Metropolitan Museum of Art in New York City. The chapter headings are most instructive and, actually, accurate, as in chapter 1: "I Accidentally Vaporize My Pre-Algebra Teacher." Well, it's true that, in the museum, Mrs. Dodds turns into a shriveled hag with bat wings, and is about to slice Percy to ribbons when his Latin teacher, Mr. Brunner, rolls his wheelchair into the gallery and tosses Percy his pen, which becomes a bronze sword. "Die, honey!" snarls Mrs. Dodds, as she lunges at him, so he swings the sword. What's going on here? It seems that Percy is about to find out about his lineage: he is a half-blood, with a mother from New York City and an unidentified father who is a Greek god. A real one.

GERM: You'll find lots of Harry Potter-like comparisons in this quest novel, but it's wonderful on its own merits as Percy first goes to a camp for half-bloods on Long Island and then must travel across the United States with a fellow half-blood, Annabelle, and his best friend, Grover, a satyr, to get back Zeus's master bolt, which has been stolen. You'll be eager to delve into the Greek myths to understand the many allusions to the gods and their rivalries. On a whole other plane, meet another ADHD kid just trying to make it through school in *Joey Pigza Swallowed the Key* by Jack Gantos.

RELATED TITLES: Alcock, Vivian. *Singer to the Sea God.* Delacorte, 1993. / Alexander, Lloyd. *The Arkadians.* Dutton, 1995. / Farmer, Nancy. *The Sea of Trolls.* Atheneum, 2004. / Fisher, Leonard Everett. *Theseus and the Minotaur.* Holiday House, 1988. / Gantos, Jack. *Joey Pigza Swallowed the Key.* Farrar, 1998. / Osborne, Mary Pope. *Favorite Greek Myths.* Scholastic, 1989. / Pratchett, Terry. *The Wee Free Men.* HarperCollins, 2003. / Spinelli, Jerry. *Loser.* HarperCollins, 2002. / Yolen, Jane, and Robert J. Harris. *Odysseus in the Serpent Maze.* HarperCollins, 2001.

SUBJECTS: ADVENTURE AND ADVENTURERS. ATTENTION-DEFICIT HYPERACTIVITY DISORDER. CAMPS. DYSLEXIA. FANTASY. GODS AND GODDESSES. MYTHOLOGY. SCHOOLS. TEACHERS. VOYAGES AND TRAVELS.

1102 **Roberts, Willo Davis.** *The Absolutely True Story . . . How I Visited Yellowstone Park with the Terrible Rupes.* **Atheneum, 1994. 0-689-31939-8. 154pp. Gr. 3–6**

Eleven-year-old Lewis thinks he and his twin sister Alison are lucky to be going to Yellowstone National Park with their new neighbors, the Rupes, who have rented a huge motor home for their three kids. Their trip from Washington State is anything but uneventful. Where did little Billy get that one-hundred-dollar bill he says he found, and why do two men in a light-blue Crown Victoria appear to be following them?

GERM: This humorous mystery and travelogue, narrated by Lewis, is filled with his incredulous observations and descriptions of the laissez-faire Rupe parents, who don't seem to care what the children eat or do, and comparisons with his own straightforward parents. Children can write up and draw character sketches and portraits of each one, and compare their own family rules with those of the Rupes. Research the natural wonders and the wildlife of Yellowstone.

RELATED TITLES: Byars, Betsy. *Dead Letter: A Herculeah Jones Mystery.* Viking, 1996. / Byars, Betsy. *Tarot Says Beware: A Herculeah Jones Mystery.* Viking, 1995. / Hiaasen, Carl. *Hoot.* Knopf, 2002. / Konigsburg, E. L. *From the Mixed-Up Files of Mrs. Basil E. Frankweiler.* Atheneum, 1967. / Roberts, Willo Davis. *The View from the Cherry Tree.* Atheneum, 1975.

SUBJECTS: BEHAVIOR. BROTHERS AND SISTERS. MYSTERY AND DETECTIVE STORIES. NATIONAL PARKS. ROBBERS AND OUTLAWS. U.S.—DESCRIPTION AND TRAVEL. VOYAGES AND TRAVELS. WEST (U.S.). YELLOWSTONE NATIONAL PARK.

1103 **Rocklin, Joanne.** *For Your Eyes Only!* **Illus. by Mark Todd. Scholastic, 1997. 0-590-67447-1. 136pp. Gr. 4–6**

Sixth-grade classmates Lucy and Andy have opposite reactions to their savvy new substitute teacher, Mr. Moffat, his assignment to keep a journal, and his weekly postings of poems on the board for students to read. We are privy to the journal entries of Lucy and Andy, one a natural writer, the other a rebellious and angry artist.

GERM: Though we only see Mr. Moffat through the eyes of two of his students, it is clear that he is a gifted and innovative teacher who encourages his students to learn more about themselves using their own writing. The interspersing of well-known poets' work is a refreshing device and should lead to further discussion and writing ideas. Other student poets include Jack in Sharon Creech's *Love That Dog* and Lonnie in Jacqueline Woodson's *Locomotion*.

RELATED TITLES: Codell, Esmé Raji. *Sahara Special.* Hyperion, 2003. / Creech, Sharon. *Love That Dog.* HarperCollins, 2003. / Duffey, Betsy. *Utterly Yours, Booker Jones.* Viking, 1995. / Fletcher, Ralph. *Flying Solo.* Clarion, 1998. / George, Kristine O'Connell. *Swimming Upstream: Middle School Poems.* Clarion, 2002. / Janeczko, Paul B. *How to Write Poetry.* Scholastic, 1999. / Janeczko, Paul B. *Poetry from A to Z: A Guide for Young Writers.* Simon & Schuster, 1994. / Janeczko, Paul B. *Seeing the Blue Between: Advice and Inspiration for Young Poets.* Candlewick, 2002. / Slepian, Jan. *The Broccoli Tapes.* Philomel, 1988. / Snyder, Zilpha Keatley. *Libby on Wednesday.* Delacorte, 1990. / Woodson, Jacqueline. *Locomotion.* Putnam, 2003.

SUBJECTS: DIARIES. POETRY—SINGLE AUTHOR. SCHOOLS. SUBSTITUTE TEACHERS.

1104 Rodowsky, Colby. *Not My Dog*. Illus. by Thomas F. Yezerski. Farrar, 1999. 0-374-35531-2. Unp. Gr. 2–4

Ellie Martin yearns for a puppy, and that does not include Preston, the "sort of square, boring brown dog with sticking-up ears" her parents take in when Great-Aunt Margaret must give him up to move into a new apartment. It takes a while for the two to bond and accept each other, as you know they will; this is a pragmatic little story, with Ellie acting understandably but disappointingly resistant, angry, and resentful to old but loyal Preston.

GERM: Discussion point or writing prompt, midway into the book: Ellie does not want her great-aunt's dog and she refuses to refer to him as her dog. Why? What do you think she should do?

RELATED TITLES: Byars, Betsy. *Tornado*. HarperCollins, 1996. / Cleary, Beverly. *Henry Huggins*. Morrow, 1950. / DiCamillo, Kate. *Because of Winn-Dixie*. Candlewick, 2000. / Duffey, Betsy. *A Boy in the Doghouse*. Simon & Schuster, 1991. / George, Kristine O'Connell. *Little Dog Poems*. Clarion, 1999. / Herzig, Alison Cragin. *The Big Deal*. Viking, 1992. / King-Smith, Dick. *The Invisible Dog*. Crown, 1993. / Rinkoff, Barbara. *Remarkable Ramsey the Talking Dog*. Scholastic, 1976. / Robinson, Nancy K. *Just Plain Cat*. Four Winds, 1983. / Rodowsky, Colby. *Dog Days*. Farrar, 1990. / Rodowsky, Colby. *The Next-Door Dogs*. Farrar, 2005. / Sachar, Louis. *Marvin K. Redpost: Alone in His Teacher's House*. Random House, 1994. / Sharmat, Marjorie Weinman. *Chasing After Annie*. HarperCollins, 1981. / Wells, Rosemary. *Lucy Comes to Stay*. Dial, 1994.

SUBJECTS: AUNTS. DOGS. GREAT-AUNTS.

1105 Rowling, J. K. *Harry Potter and the Sorcerer's Stone*. Illus. by Mary Grandpré. Scholastic, 1998. 0-590-35340-3. 309pp. Gr. 4–8

For ten miserable years, Harry has been raised by his dreadful aunt and uncle, the Dursleys, and tormented by their spoiled and cloddish son, Dudley. Magical, inexplicable things always happen to Harry; he is frequently banished to the dank cupboard under the stairs where he sleeps with the spiders. On Harry's tenth birthday, a giant named Hagrid bursts through the Dursleys' door and tells Harry the truth: Harry's parents were great wizards, killed by an evil wizard named Voldemort. And now Harry's being summoned to attend the prestigious Hogwarts School of Witchcraft and Wizardry, as he, too, has his parents' marvelous powers. Harry and his new school pals must gear up for battle with the Dark Side, in a school filled with secret passageways and doors, teachers who are ghosts or witches or wizards, and a potions professor who seems to have it in for Harry.

GERM: Listeners will thrive on the vicarious adventure and good humor of this crackling and complex high-fantasy novel, first in the series that has changed the world of reading for children and adults alike. To compare and contrast it with books on a similar theme, also read *The Secret of Platform 13* by Eva Ibbotson and *Wizard Hall* by Jane Yolen. Don't miss these spectacular Web sites: <www.jkrowling.com> and <www.scholastic.com/harrypotter>.

RELATED TITLES: Alexander, Lloyd. *The Book of Three*. Henry Holt, 1964. / Bath, K. P. *The Secret of Castle Cant*. Little, Brown, 2004. / Dahl, Roald. *The BFG*. Farrar, 1982. / Dahl, Roald. *The Witches*. Farrar, 1983. / Edwards, Julie. *The Last of the Really Great Whangdoodles*. HarperCollins, 1974. / Farmer, Nancy. *House of the Scorpion*. Simon & Schuster, 2002. / Ibbotson, Eva. *The Secret of Platform 13*. Dutton, 1998. / L'Engle, Madeleine. *A Wrinkle in Time*. Farrar, 1962. / Nodleman, Perry. *The Same Place But Different*. Simon & Schuster, 1995. / Pullman, Philip. *The Golden Compass*. Knopf, 1996. (And others in the His Dark Materials series.) / Riordan, Rick. *The Lightning Thief* (Percy Jackson and the Olympians, Book 1). Miramax/Hyperion, 2005. / Sachar, Louis. *Holes*. Farrar, 1998. / Strickland, Brad. *Dragon's Plunder*. Atheneum, 1992. / Stroud, Jonathan. *The Amulet of Samarkand*. Hyperion, 2003. / Wrede, Patricia. *Dealing with Dragons*. Harcourt, 1990. / Yolen, Jane. *Wizard's Hall*. Harcourt, 1991.

SUBJECTS: ENGLAND. FANTASY. MAGIC. SCHOOLS. WITCHES. WIZARDS.

1106 Rupp, Rebecca. *The Dragon of Lonely Island*. Candlewick, 1998. 0-7636-0408-9. 160pp. Gr. 2–5

Hannah, 12; Zachary, 10; and Sarah Emily, 8 ½, spend an enchanted summer at Great-Great-Aunt Mehitabel's house on a Maine island that is also inhabited by a three-headed storytelling dragon, Fafnyr. From the three spellbinding dragon tales Fafnyr tells them, the children each learn something new and valuable about themselves.

GERM: Have your listeners analyze each of the stories the dragon tells and discuss how it applies to and helps each child solve a problem.

RELATED TITLES: Black, Holly, and Tony DiTerlizzi. *The Spiderwick Chronicles, Book 1: The Field Guide*. Simon & Schuster, 2003. (And others in the Spiderwick series.) / Davol, Marguerite. *The Paper Dragon*. Atheneum, 1997. / Grahame, Kenneth. *The Reluctant Dragon*. Candlewick, 2004. / Hodges, Patricia. *Saint George and the Dragon*. Little, Brown, 1984. / Muth, Jon J. *Zen Shorts*. Scholastic, 2005. / Nolen, Jerdine. *Raising Dragons*.

Harcourt, 1998. / Prelutsky, Jack. *The Dragons Are Singing Tonight.* Greenwillow, 1993. / Whipple, Laura, comp. *Eric Carle's Dragons, Dragons and Other Creatures that Never Were.* Philomel, 1991. / Yolen, Jane. *Merlin and the Dragons.* Dutton, 1995.

SUBJECTS: BROTHERS AND SISTERS. DRAGONS. FANTASY. ISLANDS. STORYTELLING.

1107 Ryan, Pam Muñoz. *Esperanza Rising.* **Scholastic, 2000. 0-439-12041-1. 262pp. Gr. 5–8**

Born into a prosperous Mexican ranching family, Esperanza lived a life of privilege and plenty until the eve of her 14th birthday in 1924, when her Papa was murdered by bandits. She and her mother escaped from Mexico to California, where they found work picking crops in the San Joaquin Valley. Based on the life of the author's grandmother, this moving and involving novel deals with the overwhelming hardships faced by Mexican migrant workers, including a disastrous strike and deportation, Valley Fever, and discrimination, but also with the love and pride that helped them survive.

GERM: Pair this with another novel based on real-life relatives, Christopher Paul Curtis's *Bud, Not Buddy.* Ask students to interview parents and grandparents and record their own essential but fragile family stories before they are forgotten. Melding words and paintings, Mexican American artist Carmen Lomas Garza traces her childhood memories and family traditions in her beautifully detailed *In My Family / En Mi Familia.*

RELATED TITLES: Bernier-Grand, Carmen T. *César: ¡Sí, Se Puede! Yes, We Can!* Marshall Cavendish, 2004. / Brimner, Larry Dane. *A Migrant Family.* Lerner, 1992. / Krull, Kathleen. *Harvesting Hope: The Story of Cesar Chavez.* Harcourt, 2003. / Lomas Garza, Carmen. *In My Family/En Mi Familia.* Children's Book Press, 1996. / Mora, Pat. *Tomás and the Library Lady.* Knopf, 1997. / Pérez, Amada Irma. *My Very Own Room/Mi Proprio Cuartito.* Children's Book Press, 2000. / Pérez, L. King. *First Day in Grapes.* Lee & Low, 2002. / Soto, Gary. *Snapshots from the Wedding.* Putnam, 1997. / Soto, Gary. *Too Many Tamales.* Putnam, 1993. / Stanley, Jerry. *Children of the Dust Bowl: The True Story of the School at Weed Patch Camp.* Crown, 1992.

SUBJECTS: CALIFORNIA. FAMILY STORIES. HISTORICAL FICTION. MEXICAN AMERICANS. MIGRANT LABOR. MULTICULTURAL BOOKS.

1108 Ryan, Pam Muñoz. *Riding Freedom.* **Illus. by Brian Selznick. Scholastic, 1998. 0-590-95766-X. 138pp. Gr. 4–6**

Here is an unforgettable biographical novel based on the true and astonishing story of Charlotte Parkhurst who, orphaned at age 2 in the mid-1800s, ran away from an orphanage at 12, disguised herself as a boy, and went to work in a stable. Eventually, after wending her way to California, she became a stagecoach driver, known to all as Charley. As Charley, she was the first woman known to vote in a U.S. election, in 1869, though no one recognized it at the time.

GERM: Related in the third person, this carefully researched novel is a boon for Western Expansion studies, Women's History Month, Election Day, or just because it's a well-told story. Meet another early voter in *When Esther Morris Headed West: Women, Wyoming, and the Right to Vote* by Connie Nordhielm Wooldridge.

RELATED TITLES: Beatty, Patricia. *That's One Ornery Orphan.* Morrow, 1980. / Christensen, Bonnie. *The Daring Nellie Bly: America's Star Reporter.* Knopf, 2003. / Cushman, Karen. *The Ballad of Lucy Whipple.* Clarion, 1996. / Doherty, Berlie. *Street Child.* Orchard, 1994. / Freedman, Russell. *Children of the Wild West.* Clarion, 1983. / Fritz, Jean. *You Want Women to Vote, Lizzie Stanton?* Putnam, 1995. / McCully, Emily Arnold. *The Ballot Box Battle.* Knopf, 1996. / McGovern, Ann. *The Secret Soldier: The Story of Deborah Sampson.* Four Winds, 1987. / Osborne, Mary Pope. *Adaline Falling Star.* Scholastic, 2000. / Paterson, Katherine. *Jip: His Story.* Lodestar, 1996. / Reit, Seymour. *Behind Rebel Lines: The Incredible Story of Emma Edmonds, Civil War Spy.* Harcourt, 1988. / Snyder, Zilpha Keatley. *Gib Rides Home.* Delacorte, 1998. / Wooldridge, Connie Nordhielm. *When Esther Morris Headed West: Women, Wyoming, and the Right to Vote.* Holiday House, 2001.

SUBJECTS: CALIFORNIA. HISTORICAL FICTION. HORSES. ORPHANS. WEST (U.S.)—HISTORY—FICTION. WOMEN.

1109 Sachar, Louis. *Holes.* **Farrar, 1998. 0-374-33265-7. 240pp. Gr. 5–8**

For stealing a famous basketball player's sneakers, overweight, unlucky, but innocent Stanley Yelnats is sentenced to hot, desolate Camp Green Lake in Texas, a detention center for bad boys. Every day each of the teen inmates must dig a hole 5 feet around and 5 feet deep in the bone-dry lake bed. Zero, mocked by all because he can't read, is the best digger. He and Stanley become allies, running away together when staying at camp becomes life-threatening. Everything does tie together in unlikely but satisfying ways in this innovative and intricately plotted, all-time great and classic Newbery and National Book Award winner.

GERM: Draw portraits of the many memorable character and caption each with a written description, as part of a large mural that will help readers recall and describe the connections among the large cast of characters. Given photocopies of key scenes, children can reenact them as Reader's Theater. And, of course, discuss, compare, contrast, and evaluate the book versus the movie version. Readers will want to read the subsequent adventures of Armpit and X-Ray in the sequel, *Small Steps*.

RELATED TITLES: Choldenko, Gennifer. *Al Capone Does My Shirts*. Putnam, 2004. / Creech, Sharon. *Ruby Holler*. HarperCollins, 2002. / Farmer, Nancy. *House of the Scorpion*. Simon & Schuster, 2002. / Levine, Gail Carson. *Dave at Night*. HarperCollins, 1999. / Paterson, Katherine. *Jip: His Story*. Dutton, 1996. / Paulsen, Gary. *The Haymeadow*. Delacorte, 1992. / Rowling, J. K. *Harry Potter and the Sorcerer's Stone*. Scholastic, 1998. (And others in the Harry Potter series.) / Sachar, Louis. *Dogs Don't Tell Jokes*. Knopf, 1991. / Sachar, Louis. *Small Steps*. Delacorte, 2006. / Sachar, Louis. *There's a Boy in the Girl's Bathroom*. Knopf, 1987. / Sachar, Louis. Wayside School series. Lothrop. / Spinelli, Jerry. *Maniac Magee*. Little, Brown, 1990. / Wallace, Barbara Brooks. *Peppermints in the Parlor*. Aladdin, 1993. / Wallace, Barbara Brooks. *The Twin in the Tavern*. Atheneum, 1993.

SUBJECTS: ADVENTURE AND ADVENTURERS. BOOKS AND READING. BURIED TREASURE. FRIENDSHIP. HOMELESSNESS. JUVENILE DELINQUENCY. MULTICULTURAL BOOKS. NEWBERY MEDAL. PRISONS.

1110 Sanvoisin, Éric. *The Ink Drinker*. Illus. by Martin Matje. Delacorte, 1998. 0-385-32591-6. 48pp. Gr. 3–6

In his father's bookstore, a book-hating boy witnesses a ghostlike man suck the words out of a book with a straw, leaving all its pages blank. The man is a vampire, of course, suffering from liver problems that make ink the only food he can digest. With dazzling teeth like razor-sharp pen nibs, he descends on the boy, promising to give him his own taste for ink.

GERM: Children can write their own short stories describing how they acquired a taste for literature. Find out how reading saves lives in *The School Mouse* by Dick King-Smith. Celebrate the delights of reading with the 14 delectable poems in *Good Books, Good Times!*, compiled by Lee Bennett Hopkins.

RELATED TITLES: Child, Lauren. *Who's Afraid of the Big Bad Book?* Hyperion, 2003. / Drescher, Henrik. *Simon's Book*. Lothrop, 1983. / Garland, Michael. *Miss Smith's Incredible Storybook*. Dutton, 2003. / Hopkins, Lee Bennett, comp. *Good Books, Good Times!* HarperCollins, 1990. / King-Smith, Dick. *The School Mouse*. Hyperion, 1995. / Scieszka, Jon. *Summer Reading Is Killing Me!* Viking, 1998. / Teague, Mark. *Frog Medicine*. Scholastic, 1991. / Williams, Suzanne. *Library Lil*. Dial, 1997.

SUBJECTS: BOOKS AND READING. FANTASY. VAMPIRES.

1111 Scieszka, Jon. *Summer Reading Is Killing Me!* Illus. by Lane Smith. Viking, 1998. 0-670-88041-8. 73pp. Gr. 2–5

Fred, Sam, and narrator Joe, AKA the Time Warp Trio, time-travel via The Book to the public library in Hoboken, New Jersey, where they find the good characters from their summer reading list being held prisoner by the bad guys, including the Truchbull, the Red Queen, and Long John Silver. The big boss of the antagonists, a loony fuzzy brown teddy bear, plans to crush all the lovable characters and replace them with himself.

GERM: Teachers and kids alike will have a ball matching characters and their books, and Scieszka provides the list at the back of the book. What a great way to get kids interested in the classics. Have them compile and post a Classroom Reading List of favorites to which they can add on as the year progresses. You'll want to introduce the catalyst for the book's setting, Daniel Pinkwater's classic, *The Hoboken Chicken Emergency*, with its 266-pound runaway chicken, Henrietta; and its sequel, *Looking for Bobowicz*. In Anne Lindbergh's clever fantasy *Travel Far, Pay No Fare*, cousins Owen and Parsley use a summer reading club bookmark to venture into the stories of several children's books. Get a real taste for books with Éric Sanvoisin's *The Ink Drinker*, and top it all off by introducing the rest of the fall-on-the-floor-laughing books in the Time Warp Trio series.

RELATED TITLES: Garland, Michael. *Miss Smith's Incredible Storybook*. Dutton, 2003. / Lindbergh, Anne. *Travel Far, Pay No Fare*. HarperCollins, 1992. / Pinkwater, Daniel Manus. *Fat Men from Space*. Dell Yearling, 1980. / Pinkwater, Daniel. *The Hoboken Chicken Emergency*. Simon & Schuster, 1990. / Pinkwater, Daniel. *Looking for Bobowicz*. HarperCollins, 2004. / Sanvoisin, Eric. *The Ink Drinker*. Delacorte, 1998. / Scieszka, Jon. *Knights of the Kitchen Table*. Viking, 1991. / Scieszka, Jon. *Tut, Tut*. Viking, 1996. / Scieszka, Jon. *Your Mother Was a Neanderthal*. Viking, 1993. (And others in the Time Warp Trio series.)

SUBJECTS: BOOKS AND READING. CHARACTERS IN LITERATURE. FANTASY. HUMOROUS FICTION. LIBRARIES. MAGIC.

1112 Seidler, Tor. *Mean Margaret*. Illus. by Jon Agee. HarperCollins, 1997. 0-06-205090-7. 165pp. Gr. 3–5

A confirmed bachelor and fastidious housekeeper, woodchuck Fred marries sensible Phoebe and is horrified when she takes into their burrow a stray—a repulsive human child named Margaret, who proceeds to destroy Fred's tidy home and routine.

GERM: In a writing style reminiscent of James Stevenson and William Steig with a touch of Roald Dahl, Seidler's humorous and wry look at unconditional love will make kids think about how their parents put up with their foibles.

RELATED TITLES: Hinton, S. E. *The Puppy Sister*. Delacorte, 1995. / King-Smith, Dick. *Harriet's Hare*. Crown, 1995. / King-Smith, Dick. *The School Mouse*. Little, Brown, 1995. / Lowry, Lois. *Stay! Keeper's Story*. Houghton Mifflin, 1997.

SUBJECTS: ANIMALS. BABIES. GROUNDHOGS. WOODCHUCKS.

1113 Sheth, Kashmira. *Blue Jasmine*. Hyperion, 2004. 0-7868-1855-7. 186pp. Gr. 4–7

Twelve-year-old Seema chronicles leaving her comfortable life with her extended family—including her cousin and best friend Raju—in India and moving with her parents and little sister Mela to Iowa, where everything is different, from school to the cold winter weather.

GERM: Make charts to compare and contrast the differences between life in India and life in Iowa, at school and at home. Seema starts school in the United States with a basic knowledge of English, but has never heard expressions such as "She's pulling your leg." Make a list of some of the idioms and current slang she'd need to learn if she came to your school. What did you learn about Seema's culture that you never knew before? Research some of the Indian customs, holidays, and foods that Seema describes so eloquently. Contrast Seema's journey with Anand's fantastical one across India in Chitra Banerjee Divakaruni's fantasy *The Conch Bearer*. Gloria Whelan's *Homeless Bird* also takes place in India, where 13-year-old Koly is married off to a 16-year-old boy who dies, leaving her destitute and homeless.

RELATED TITLES: Dhami, Narinder. *Bindi Babes*. Delacorte, 2004. / Divakaruni, Chitra Banerjee. *The Conch Bearer*. Roaring Brook, 2003. / Mazer, Norma Fox. *Good Night, Maman*. Harcourt, 1999. / Naidoo, Beverly. *The Other Side of Truth*. HarperCollins, 2001. / Ness, Caroline. *The Ocean of Story: Fairy Tales from India*. Lothrop, 1996. / Shepard, Aaron. *The Gifts of Wali Dad: A Tale of India and Pakistan*. Atheneum, 1995. / Whelan, Gloria. *Homeless Bird*. HarperCollins, 2000.

SUBJECTS: FAMILY LIFE. IMMIGRATION AND EMIGRATION. INDIA. IOWA. MOVING, HOUSEHOLD. MULTICULTURAL BOOKS.

1114 Shipton, Paul. *Bug Muldoon: The Garden of Fear*. Illus. by Elwood H. Smith. Viking, 2001. 0-670-89687-X. 138pp. Gr. 3–6

The best, cheapest, and only private eye in the whole Garden, sleuth Bug Muldoon, a wise-cracking Sam Spade kind of guy, takes on the case of missing Eddie the earwig only to find there are sinister forces at work in the neighborhood. Teaming up with Velma, a hard-nosed grasshopper reporter, to track down a group of subversive ants who belong to the Individualist Club, Bug steps into danger at every turn. This is a prototype of a good, hard-boiled mystery—the world-weary detective; the smart female reporter; the patsy; the bad guys; the red herring; the eager, admiring youngster; and, of course, the wry humor.

GERM: As a homework assignment or on a class field trip, have children list and sketch all the bugs they can spot in their yards or on the playground. They can identify ones they don't know by looking them up in a good insect book from the 595.7 shelf in your library. Research the life cycles of the many intriguing insects in the story to ascertain how facts were integrated into the narrative. See how hard-boiled animal mysteries are constructed in *Bud Barkin, Private Eye* by James Howe.

RELATED TITLES: Banks, Lynne Reid. *Harry the Poisonous Centipede: A Story to Make You Squirm*. Morrow, 1997. / Biedrzycki, David. *Ace Lacewing: Bug Detective*. Charlesbridge, 2005. / Emerson, Scott. *The Case of the Cat with the Missing Ear* (The Adventures of Samuel Blackthorne, Book One). Simon & Schuster, 2003. / Erickson, John R. *The Original Adventures of Hank the Cowdog*. Puffin, 1999. / Fleischman, Paul. *Joyful Noise: Poems for Two Voices*. HarperCollins, 1988. / Florian, Douglas. *Insectlopedia: Poems and Paintings*. Harcourt, 1998. / Hall, Katy, and Lisa Eisenberg. *Buggy Riddles*. Dial, 1986. / Hepworth, Cathi. *Bug Off! A Swarm of Insect Words*. Putnam, 1998. / Hoeye, Michael. *Time Stops for No Mouse*. Putnam, 2002. / Howe, James. *Bud Barkin, Private*

Eye (Tales from the House of Bunnicula series). Atheneum, 2003. / James, Mary. *Shoebag*. Scholastic, 1990. / Sonenklar, Carol. *Bug Boy*. Henry Holt, 1997. / Titus, Eve. *Basil of Baker Street*. McGraw-Hill, 1958.

SUBJECTS: FANTASY. GRASSHOPPERS. INSECTS. MYSTERY AND DETECTIVE STORIES.

1115 Shreve, Susan. *Jonah the Whale*. **Scholastic, 1998. 0-590-37133-9. 110pp. Gr. 3–6**

Oversized 11-year-old Jonah Morrison decides to live up to his new nickname, "Jonah the Whale," at his new school. He misses Thomas Hale, his mother's former boyfriend, to whom he composes frequent letters for which he has no forwarding address. To compensate, he dreams up an idea for hosting a children's TV show that would be broadcast from a studio constructed to look like the inside of a whale, where he would interview children's heroes. With his only friend, an eccentric redheaded girl named Blister, the entrepreneurial Jonah pulls it off. Children will cheer Jonah's determination and resourcefulness in overcoming life's downturns.

GERM: Brainstorm with your students the characteristics of a hero, and compile a list of names of children and adults who fit the criteria. Working in pairs, students can put together a page of questions and conduct a taped interview of a local person they know personally and admire. Readers can follow up with the companion book, *Blister*.

RELATED TITLES: Byars, Betsy. *The Eighteenth Emergency*. Viking, 1973. / Clements, Andrew. *Frindle*. Simon & Schuster, 1996. / Clements, Andrew. *The School Story*. Simon & Schuster, 2001. / Coville, Bruce. *The Monster's Ring*. Pantheon, 1982. / Gauthier, Gail. *A Year with Butch and Spike*. Putnam, 1998. / Getz, David. *Almost Famous*. Henry Holt, 1992. / Gorman, Carol. *Dork on the Run*. HarperCollins, 2002. / Lisle, Janet Taylor. *How I Became a Writer and Oggie Learned to Drive*. Philomel, 2002. / Park, Barbara. *Maxie, Rosie, and Earl—Partners in Grime*. Knopf, 1990. / Scribner, Virginia. *Gopher Takes Heart*. Viking, 1993. / Shreve, Susan. *Blister*. Scholastic, 2001. / Shreve, Susan. *The Gift of the Girl Who Couldn't Hear*. Tambourine, 1991. / Shreve, Susan. *Joshua T. Bates Takes Charge*. Knopf, 1993. / Spinelli, Jerry. *Loser*. HarperCollins, 2002. / Wardlaw, Lee. *Seventh-Grade Weirdo*. Scholastic, 1992.

SUBJECTS: FATHERS. FRIENDSHIP. HONESTY. OUTCASTS. SCHOOLS. TELEVISION.

1116 Snicket, Lemony. *The Austere Academy*. **Illus. by Brett Helquist. HarperCollins, 2000. 0-06-028888-4. 208pp. Gr. 3–6**

In Book the Fifth of the melodramatic but hilarious and vocabulary-enhancing saga of the unremittingly unfortunate Beaudelaire siblings—A Series of Unfortunate Events—the three children are sent to Prufrock Prep, a dreadful boarding school whose cheerless motto is "Memento Mori" (Latin for "remember you will die"). The prissy narrator, who loves to explain words in context and lecture the reader, takes great pride in the plucky orphans for whom everything can only go tragically (or comically, depending on how warped your sense of humor is) wrong.

GERM: This is pre-gothic tragicomedy at its best, and you only have to read this one (or the first book in the series, *The Bad Beginning*, though your kids probably already know that one) or to mention the movie to get readers clamoring for the other witty titles about the disaster-prone Beaudelaires. Your listeners can begin defining new vocabulary words in the convoluted, long-winded Lemony Snicket-style and sharing them with each other.

RELATED TITLES: Anderson, M. T. *Whales on Stilts*. Harcourt, 2005. / Black, Holly, and Tony DiTerlizzi. *The Spiderwick Chronicles, Book 1: The Field Guide*. Simon & Schuster, 2003. (And others in the Spiderwick series.) / Curtis, Christopher Paul. *Bud, Not Buddy*. Delacorte, 1999. / Gaiman, Neil. *Coraline*. HarperCollins, 2002. / Levine, Gail Carson. *Dave at Night*. HarperCollins, 1999. / Rowling, J. K. *Harry Potter and the Sorcerer's Stone*. Scholastic, 1998. (And others in the Harry Potter series.) / Snicket, Lemony. *The Bad Beginning*. HarperCollins, 1999. (And others in the A Series of Unfortunate Events series.) / Wallace, Barbara Brooks. *Peppermints in the Parlor*. Atheneum, 1980. / Wallace, Barbara Brooks. *The Twin in the Tavern*. Atheneum, 1993.

SUBJECTS: BOARDING SCHOOLS. BROTHERS AND SISTERS. HUMOROUS FICTION. ORPHANS. SCHOOLS.

1117 Snyder, Zilpha Keatley. *Gib Rides Home*. **Delacorte, 1998. 0-385-32267-4. 248pp. Gr. 4–8**

Gib Whittaker, who remembers little of his early years, leaves the Lovell House Home for Orphaned and Abandoned Boys at age 10 to be farmed out to a family that knew his parents before they died. So why, on a fall day in 1909, more than a year after he left, does Gib return to the orphanage, toting an old roping saddle? In a long flashback, we relive Gib's years at the school, starting with his arrival there at age 5 after his mother's death.

GERM: Children revel in stories about bad schools, and they'll root for the cheerful, good-hearted Gib as he tries to learn what happened to his family. Meet other resilient orphans in historical fiction books, including Karen Cushman's *Rodzina*, Katherine Paterson's *Jip: His Story*, and Pam Muñoz Ryan's *Riding Freedom*.

RELATED TITLES: Beatty, Patricia. *That's One Ornery Orphan*. Morrow, 1980. / Curtis, Christopher Paul. *Bud, Not Buddy*. Delacorte, 1999. / Cushman, Karen. *Rodzina*. Clarion, 2003. / Doherty, Berlie. *Street Child*. Orchard, 1994. / Paterson, Katherine. *Jip: His Story*. Lodestar, 1996. / Ryan, Pam Muñoz. *Riding Freedom*. Scholastic, 1998. / Snyder, Zilpha Keatley. *Gib and the Gray Ghost*. Delacorte, 1998. / Wallace, Barbara Brooks. *Peppermints in the Parlor*. Atheneum, 1980. / Wallace, Barbara Brooks. *The Twin in the Tavern*. Atheneum, 1993.

SUBJECTS: HISTORICAL FICTION. HORSES. ORPHANS.

1118   Sorel, Edward. *Johnny on the Spot*. Illus. by the author. McElderry, 1998. 0-689-81293-0. 32pp. Gr. 2–4

Mr. Zaga, a mysterious and eccentric inventor who lives in the basement apartment, fixes Johnny's radio with a small charge of electrostatic magnetism, so it broadcasts tomorrow's news today. Now able to know a day in advance what's going to happen, Johnny is able to thwart a bank robbery and to save a girl from a burning building. Sorel's dandy sepia-toned pen-and-inks and watercolors take us back to the New York City of the 1920s or 1930s.

GERM: Mary Rodgers also dealt with this theme in her novel *A Billion for Boris*, but with a TV set. Discussion point: If you were able to predict tomorrow's news today, what would you do with the information? Reading today's local newspaper and working backwards, readers can select a news story, decide how they might have changed its outcome, and rewrite it, incorporating their own roles as part of the narrative. Take another look at New York City in the 1930s with Sorel's *The Saturday Kid*.

RELATED TITLES: Bush, Timothy. *Benjamin McFadden and the Robot Babysitter*. Crown, 1998. / Gutman, Dan. *Qwerty Stevens, Back in Time: The Edison Mystery*. Simon & Schuster, 2001. / Jakobsen, Kathy. *My New York*. Little, Brown, 2003. / Rodgers, Mary. *A Billion for Boris*. HarperTrophy, 2003. / Selznick, Brian. *The Houdini Box*. Knopf, 1991. / Sorel, Edward, and Cheryl Carlesimo. *The Saturday Kid*. McElderry, 2000. / St. George, Judith. *So You Want to Be an Inventor?* Philomel, 2002.

SUBJECTS: FANTASY. HISTORICAL FICTION. INVENTIONS AND INVENTORS. NEW YORK CITY. PICTURE BOOKS FOR OLDER READERS. RADIO. SCIENCE FICTION. SPACE AND TIME.

1119   Spinelli, Jerry. *Crash*. Knopf, 1996. 0-679-97957-3. 162pp. Gr. 5–8

When his adored grandfather has a stroke, super jock Crash Coogan learns to change the aggressive, bullying ways he deals with people, especially seventh-grade classmate Penn Webb, an affable, nonviolent Quaker with whom Crash has maintained a not-so-friendly rivalry since first grade.

GERM: Following the evolution and mellowing of Crash's overbearing personality and rigid values makes for a fascinating character study. Ask your group: How have you managed to change for the better a personality trait you didn't like?

RELATED TITLES: Alcock, Vivian. *The Trial of Anna Cotman*. Delacorte, 1990. / Gauthier, Gail. *A Year with Butch and Spike*. Putnam, 1998. / Gorman, Carol. *Dork on the Run*. HarperCollins, 2002. / Park, Barbara. *The Graduation of Jake Moon*. Atheneum, 2000. / Philbrick, Rodman. *The Young Man and the Sea*. Blue Sky/Scholastic, 2004. / Slepian, Jan. *Risk n' Roses*. Philomel, 1990. / Spinelli, Jerry. *Loser*. HarperCollins, 2002. / Spinelli, Jerry. *Maniac Magee*. Little, Brown, 1990. / Spinelli, Jerry. *There's a Girl in My Hammerlock*. Simon & Schuster, 1991. / Spinelli, Jerry. *Wringer*. HarperCollins, 1997.

SUBJECTS: BEHAVIOR. BULLIES. CONDUCT OF LIFE. FAMILY LIFE. FRIENDSHIP. GRANDFATHERS.

1120   Spinelli, Jerry. *Loser*. HarperCollins, 2002. 0-06-000193-3. 218pp. Gr. 4–8

Exuberant Donald Zinkoff smiles and laughs like crazy, even when a big kid steals his giant giraffe hat on the first day of first grade and when his second-grade teacher tells him his handwriting is atrocious. He's sloppy and he's clumsy and, because of an upside-down valve in his stomach, he even throws up a lot. Told in riveting present tense, this exquisite character study, a portrait of hapless but harmless Zinkoff, a year-by-year unfolding of his life through sixth grade, will have listeners shaking their heads in recognition, and maybe self-reproach. Zinkoff is the kid with no best friend, the one who makes his team come in dead last for fifth-grade field day, the student some teachers find annoying and all students have tagged "Loser." On the day of the big snowstorm, when a little girl goes missing, Zinkoff braves cold and sleet to search for her. Could the kid everyone has written off as a loser have heroic qualities too?

GERM: Discussion points and writing prompts: Why did Zinkoff's classmates think of him as a loser? What are Donald's good qualities? Would you be his friend? Why? Spinelli has an uncanny knack for making readers think deeply and care about all his characters and about themselves as well. Being immersed in Zinkoff's quirky and goofy and earnest persona, your students will empathize with him. They'll examine the ways they view others who are different, reevaluating the casual cruelties they inflict on each other to single out the ones who don't fit into the standard niche. Kids can write autobiographical chapters of their lives or first day of school memories, using the present tense, third person.

RELATED TITLES: Amato, Mary. *The Word Eater.* Holiday House, 2000. / Fleischman, Paul. *Weslandia.* Candlewick, 1999. / Gantos, Jack. *Joey Pigza Swallowed the Key.* Farrar, 1998. / Gorman, Carol. *Dork in Disguise.* HarperCollins, 1999. / Park, Barbara. *The Graduation of Jake Moon.* Atheneum, 2000. / Spinelli, Jerry. *Crash.* Knopf, 1996. / Spinelli, Jerry. *Maniac Magee.* Little, Brown, 1990. / Spinelli, Jerry. *Wringer.* HarperCollins, 1997.

SUBJECTS: BEHAVIOR. FAMILY LIFE. OUTCASTS. SCHOOLS. SELF-ACCEPTANCE.

1121 Spinelli, Jerry. *Wringer.* HarperCollins, 1997. 0-06-024914-5. 229pp. Gr. 4–7

Palmer dreads turning 10, when he will be expected to join in the "fun" of Pigeon Day, when five thousand pigeons are released into the air to be shot down by sharpshooters. Like his father before him, he will be a wringer, one who wrings the birds' necks to put them out of their misery. When a pigeon lands on his windowsill after a January snowstorm, Palmer names it Nipper and secretly brings it into his room at night, knowing his tough new friends will kill the bird if they discover it.

GERM: Dealing with how one maintains a moral compass in an amoral society, this novel will provoke children to make analogies to their own behavior and to issues of the day. Discussion point: What is a moral dilemma? Have you ever thought you were right even though everyone around you thought you were wrong? How did you handle it?

RELATED TITLES: Erdrich, Louise. *Grandmother's Pigeon.* Hyperion, 1996. / Hall, Bruce Edward. *Henry and the Dragon Kite.* Philomel, 2004. / Lowry, Lois. *The Giver.* Houghton Mifflin, 1993. / Mazer, Anne. *The Oxboy.* Knopf, 1993. / Naylor, Phyllis Reynolds. *Shiloh.* Simon & Schuster, 1991. / Philbrick, Rodman. *The Young Man and the Sea.* Blue Sky/Scholastic, 2004. / Spinelli, Jerry. *Maniac Magee.* Little, Brown, 1990.

SUBJECTS: BIRDS. BULLIES. COURAGE. PIGEONS. SELF-CONCEPT.

1122 Sunami, Kitoba. *How the Fisherman Tricked the Genie: A Tale Within a Tale Within a Tale.* Illus. by Amiko Hirao. Atheneum, 2002. 0-689-83399-7. Unp. Gr. 2–6

When a genie threatens to kill the poor fisherman who has rescued him from a brass bottle in the Arabian Sea, the fisherman tells him three interconnected stories to convince the genie that he should never repay a good deed with an evil one. In this literary fairy tale, your listeners will recognize many familiar story elements as each rich, foolish, and arrogant king is punished by Heaven and Fate. For example, the fisherman's final trick mirrors the end to Charles Perrault's "Puss in Boots."

GERM: Analyze and discuss: How did each of the three stories the fisherman related prove his statement that ". . . you should never repay a good deed with an evil one. For some evil will surely befall you in turn." Why does each character in turn ignore that advice, and what are the consequences? How can this apply to your own experiences?

RELATED TITLES: Andersen, Hans Christian. *The Tinderbox.* Retold and illus. by Barry Moser. Little, Brown, 1990. / Carrick, Carol. *Aladdin and the Wonderful Lamp.* Scholastic, 1989. / Dengler, Marianna. *The Worry Stone.* Northland, 1996. / Farley, Carol. *Mr. Pak Buys a Story.* Albert Whitman, 1997. / Kirstein, Lincoln. *Puss in Boots.* Little, Brown, 1992. / Marcellino, Fred. *Puss in Boots.* Farrar, 1990. / Martin, Rafe. *The Storytelling Princess.* Putnam, 2001. / Riggio, Anita. *Beware the Brindlebeast.* Boyds Mills, 1994. / Rupp, Rebecca. *The Dragon of Lonely Island.* Candlewick, 1998. / Turkle, Brinton. *Do Not Open.* Dutton, 1981.

SUBJECTS: FISHING. GENIES. KINGS AND RULERS. LITERARY FAIRY TALES. MULTICULTURAL BOOKS. REVENGE. STORYTELLING. TRANSFORMATIONS.

1123 Swope, Sam. *Jack and the Seven Deadly Giants.* Illus. by Carll Cneut. Farrar, 2004. 0-374-33670-9. 100pp. Gr. 3–5

Riding backward on a brown and white cow, young Jack sets off down the road and encounters and outwits seven giants, each of whom embodies one of the seven deadly sins, in a wild yarn inspired by Jack tales of old.

GERM: Introduce some Jack stories from English and American folklore, including "Jack and the Beanstalk," of course, but also Richard Chase's classic *The Jack Tales.* Write and illustrate new Jack Tales in which he encounters interesting new monsters to outsmart. Ask your heroes to write and illustrate a story of how they outsmarted giants. Discuss ways they've outwitted someone or been outwitted.

RELATED TITLES: Cauley, Lorinda Bryan. *Jack and the Beanstalk.* Putnam, 1983. / Chase, Richard. *The Jack Tales.* Houghton, 1943. / Compton, Kenn, and Joanne Compton. *Jack the Giant Chaser: An Appalachian Tale.* Holiday House, 1993. / Donaldson, Julia. *The Giants and the Joneses.* Henry Holt, 2005. / Galdone, Paul. *The History of Mother Twaddle and the Marvelous Achievements of Her Son, Jack.* Clarion, 1979. / Garner, Alan. *Jack and the Beanstalk.* Doubleday, 1992. / Haley, Gail E. *Jack and the Bean Tree.* Crown, 1986. / Haley, Gail E. *Mountain Jack Tales.* Dutton, 1992. / Hicks, Ray. *The Jack Tales.* Callaway, 2000. / Osborne, Mary Pope. *The Brave Little Seamstress.* Atheneum, 2002. / Osborne, Mary Pope. *Kate and the Beanstalk.* Atheneum, 2000. / Steig, Jeanne. *A Handful of Beans.* HarperCollins, 1998. / Still, James. *Jack and the Wonder Beans.* Putnam, 1977. / Thomson, Peggy. *The Brave Little Tailor.* Simon & Schuster, 1992.

SUBJECTS: FAIRY TALES. FANTASY. GIANTS. MOTHERS AND SONS. OUTCASTS.

1124 Talbott, Hudson. *O'Sullivan Stew.* Illus. by the author. Putnam, 1999. 0-399-23162-5. Unp. Gr. 2–5

Though red-haired Kate O'Sullivan tries to get help for the witch of Crookhaven, whose stallion has just been appropriated by soldiers as a tax payment to the king, the rest of the villagers declare, "She's not one of us." In a snit, the witch brings hard times on the village, so Kate makes plans to steal back the horse. Caught by the king's guards, Kate makes a bargain with the king: if she tells him a story about being in a worse spot than she is now, he will let her and her father and brothers go free. The four stories she regales him with are rife with wee folk, a sea serpent, demonic cats, wolves, and a giant.

GERM: The 48-page picture-book format makes this rollicking literary fairy tale an easy read in one or two sittings. Ask your listeners to spin and write down their own yarns about the worst spots they've ever found themselves in and how they got out of them. Meet other storytellers who tell the truth in *The Storytelling Princess* by Rafe Martin and *The Ring of Truth* by Teresa Bateman.

RELATED TITLES: Bateman, Teresa. *The Ring of Truth.* Holiday House, 1997. / Behan, Brendan. *The King of Ireland's Son.* Orchard, 1997. / Byrd, Robert. *Finn MacCoul and His Fearless Wife: A Giant of a Tale from Ireland.* Dutton, 1999. / dePaola, Tomie. *Fin M'Coul, the Giant of Knockmany Hill.* Holiday House, 1981. / Greene, Ellin. *Billy Beg and His Bull.* Holiday House, 1994. / Martin, Rafe. *The Storytelling Princess.* Putnam, 2001. / Osborne, Mary Pope. *Kate and the Beanstalk.* Atheneum, 2000. / Stanley, Diane. *Fortune.* Morrow, 1989. / Sunami, Kitoba. *How the Fisherman Tricked the Genie: A Tale Within a Tale Within a Tale.* Atheneum, 2002. / Wojciechokski, Susan. *A Fine St. Patrick's Day.* Random House, 2004.

SUBJECTS: CATS. DRAGONS. FAIRIES. GIANTS. HORSES. IRELAND. LITERARY FAIRY TALES. STORYTELLING. WITCHES. WOLVES.

1125 Tamar, Erika. *Alphabet City Ballet.* HarperCollins, 1996. 0-06-027329-1. 168pp. Gr. 5–7

Usually when faced with a book about ballet, boys will groan and turn away. This one could change their minds. Resilient New York City girl Marisol lives with her big brother Luis and her strict but loving Papi. At school, she tries out for a scholarship to the Manhattan Ballet School at Lincoln Center; she and Desirée, a shy Haitian girl who lives with her mother and little brothers in a nearby shelter, are chosen. Marisol's life becomes more complicated when her brother becomes enamored of a neighborhood drug lord and a police officer shoots and kills a young neighborhood junkie.

GERM: In spite of the serious topics, this story is also upbeat, with true-to-life dialogue, and just may get the boys interested in hearing more about Tchaikovsky's *Swan Lake.*

RELATED TITLES: Asher, Sandy. *Just Like Jenny.* Delacorte, 1982. / Griffin, Adele. *The Other Shepards.* Hyperion, 1998. / Koss, Amy Goldman. *The Ashwater Experiment.* Dial, 1999. / Perkins, Lynne Rae. *All Alone in the Universe.* Greenwillow, 1999. / Sheldon, Dyan. *Confessions of a Teenage Drama Queen.* Candlewick, 1999. / Streatfield, Noel. *Ballet Shoes.* Random House, 1991.

SUBJECTS: BALLET. BROTHERS AND SISTERS. DRUG ABUSE. FAMILY PROBLEMS. MULTICULTURAL BOOKS. NEW YORK CITY. PUERTO RICANS.

1126 Torrey, Michele. *The Case of the Gasping Garbage.* Illus. by Barbara Johansen Newman. Dutton, 2001. 0-525-46657-6. 70pp. Gr. 2–5

Science teachers take note: Meet Doyle and Fossey, science detectives, in their first lively collaboration. Fifth grader Drake Doyle, scientific genius, and his nature-loving lab partner Nell take on four vexing cases. There's the "huge-giant bloodsucking-monster" in a classmate's garbage can, a save-the-frogs campaign, a truck wedged tight under a bridge, and the problem of who is sending love notes to soft-spoken fifth grader Lilly Crump. For each case, the two observe, formulate a hypothesis, analyze their data, come up with a simple, elegant solution, and, of course, save the day.

GERM: At the back of the book is a stimulating series of enticing, easy-to-perform experiments relating to each story, including baking bread with yeast, sending an invisible message, and analyzing ink using chromatography. After selecting an area of the science curriculum that interests them, your scientists can search out related library books to read and take notes on their topics. Based on their research, they can write new Doyle and Fossey mysteries or make themselves the main characters, replete with simple experiments to perform for the class. Other books in the series include *The Case of the Graveyard Ghost* and *The Case of the Mossy Lake Monster*. Above all, have fun with science! Sing and recite your way through the poetry parodies in Jon Scieszka's *Science Verse*.

RELATED TITLES: Adler, David A. *Eaton Stanley and the Mind Control Experiment*. Dutton, 1985 / Gardiner, John Reynolds. *Top Secret*. Little, Brown, 1985. / Hopkins, Lee Bennett, comp. *Spectacular Science: A Book of Poems*. Simon & Schuster, 1999. / Kos, Amy Goldman. *Where Fish Go in Winter and Other Great Mysteries*. Dial, 2002. / Scieszka, Jon. *Science Verse*. Viking, 2004. / Shields, Carol Diggory. *Brain Juice: Science, Fresh Squeezed!* Handprint, 2003. / Simon, Seymour. Einstein Anderson series. Morrow. / Sobol, Donald J. Encyclopedia Brown series. Dutton. / Torrey, Michele. *The Case of the Graveyard Ghost*. Dutton, 2002. / Torrey, Michele. *The Case of the Mossy Lake Monster*. Dutton, 2002.

SUBJECTS: MYSTERY AND DETECTIVE STORIES. SCIENCE. SCIENCE—EXPERIMENTS.

1127   Vande Velde, Vivian. *Smart Dog.* **Harcourt, 1998. 0-15-201847-6. 146pp. Gr. 3–6**

On her way to school, fifth grader Amy Prochenko encounters an ultra-intelligent talking dog, F-32, who has escaped from the college research department lab. Not only can he read, he's even taught himself to use a computer, pressing the keys with a pencil held between his teeth. Amy renames him Sherlock and brings him to school, where, with the help of classmate Sean, she hides the dog from college students hot on his trail and gives popular but poison-tongued classmate Kaitlyn her comeuppance, all adding up to a breezily funny and perceptive school story.

GERM: Have students write about what might happen if their pets gained the power of speech. Pair this with *The Puppy Sister* by S. E. Hinton, in which Nick's new puppy, Aleasha, learns to talk and slowly develops into a human child. Another personable mutt is the poetry-spouting stray who takes charge of his life in Lois Lowry's rags-to-riches novel *Stay!: Keeper's Story*. And, of course, there's the verbal and verbose Martha in Susan Meddaugh's wonderful series of picture books starting with *Martha Speaks*.

RELATED TITLES: Amato, Mary. *The Word Eater*. Holiday House, 2000. / Avi. *The Good Dog*. Atheneum, 2001. / Conly, Jane Leslie. *The Rudest Alien on Earth*. Henry Holt, 2002. / DiCamillo, Kate. *The Tale of Despereaux*. Candlewick, 2003. / Hinton, S. E. *The Puppy Sister*. Delacorte, 1995. / King-Smith, Dick. *George Speaks*. Roaring Brook, 2002. / King-Smith, Dick. *Harriet's Hare*. Crown, 1995. / King-Smith, Dick. *The School Mouse*. Little, Brown, 1995. / Lowry, Lois. *Stay! Keeper's Story*. Houghton Mifflin, 1997. / Meddaugh, Susan. *Martha Speaks*. Houghton Mifflin, 1992. / Seidler, Tor. *Mean Margaret*. HarperCollins, 1997.

SUBJECTS: DOGS. FANTASY. HUMAN-ANIMAL COMMUNICATION. HUMOROUS FICTION. OUTCASTS. SCHOOLS. SPEECH.

1128   Vande Velde, Vivian. *Tales from the Brothers Grimm and the Sisters Weird.* **Illus. by Brad Weinman. Harcourt, 1995. 0-15-200220-0. 128pp. Gr. 5–8**

Listeners will be intrigued by the original, thoughtful, and often pointed takes on and remakes of 13 well-known fairy tales, including "Rumpelstiltskin," "The Frog Prince," "Little Red Riding Hood," "Jack and the Beanstalk," and "The Princess and the Pea."

GERM: Children accustomed to the witty parodies in Jon Scieszka's *The Stinky Cheese Man and Other Fairly Stupid Tales* and turnarounds such as Donna Jo Napoli's *The Prince of the Pond*, in which we get to know the Frog Prince in his amphibian form, will want to make comparisons. Vande Velde's instructions on the front flap, which will help children in reading and writing parodies, are as follows: "How to fracture a fairy tale: 1. Make the villain a hero. 2. Make the hero a villain. 3. Tell what really happened. 4. All of the above."

RELATED TITLES: Kindl, Patrice. *Goose Chase*. Houghton Mifflin, 2001. / Levine, Gail Carson. *Ella Enchanted*. HarperCollins, 1997. / Levine, Gail Carson. *The Fairy's Mistake*. HarperCollins, 1999. / Levine, Gail Carson. *The Princess Test*. HarperCollins, 1999. / Marcantonio, Patricia Santos. *Red Ridin' in the Hood: And*

Other Cuentos. Farrar, 2005. / Napoli, Donna Jo. *The Prince of the Pond.* Dutton, 1992. / Pullman, Philip. *I Was a Rat!* Knopf, 2000. / Scieszka, Jon. *The Stinky Cheese Man and Other Fairly Stupid Tales.* Viking, 1992. / Wrede, Patricia. *Dealing with Dragons.* Harcourt, 1990.

SUBJECTS: CHARACTERS IN LITERATURE. FAIRY TALES—SATIRE. HUMOROUS FICTION. PARODIES. SHORT STORIES.

1129   Van Draanen, Wendelin. *Shredderman: Secret Identity.* **Illus. by Brian Riggs. Knopf, 2004. 0-375-92351-9. 138pp. Gr. 2–5**

Now that he is in fifth grade, Nolan Byrd—called Nerd by his arch enemy, his lying, cheating, stealing classmate, Bubba—has just figured out a way to expose Bubba's mean ways. Assuming a cybersuperhero secret identity, he sets up a Web site, Shredderman.com, and posts photos of Bubba in action, doing wrong.

GERM: By the end of the book, Nolan realizes he can find ways to fight for truth and justice. Discuss: What can you do to change your little corner of the world? With your cyberhero students, design a Web site that emphasizes the positive vibes in your classroom or school. Find activities and fun at the Shredderman.com site: <www.randomhouse.com/kids/vandraanen/shredderman/fun.html>. Set your kids loose on the others in the series for their independent reading.

RELATED TITLES: Buehner, Caralyn. *Superdog: The Heart of a Hero.* HarperCollins, 2004. / Greene, Stephanie. *Owen Foote, Frontiersman.* Clarion, 1996. / Krensky, Stephen. *Louise Takes Charge.* Dial, 1998. / McKay, Hilary. *Indigo's Star.* McElderry, 2004. / Pinkwater, Daniel. *Looking for Bobowitz.* HarperCollins, 2004. / Sachar, Louis. *Marvin Redpost: Alone in His Teacher's House.* Random House, 1994. / Van Draanen, Wendelin. *Shredderman: Attack of the Tagger.* Knopf, 2004. / Van Draanen, Wendelin. *Shredderman: Enemy Spy.* Knopf, 2005. / Van Draanen, Wendelin. *Shredderman: Meet the Gecko.* Knopf, 2005. (And others in the Shredderman series.) / Weigel, Jeff. *Atomic Ace (He's Just My Dad).* Albert Whitman, 2004.

SUBJECTS: BEHAVIOR. BULLIES. COMPUTERS. HEROES. INTERNET. SCHOOLS. TEACHERS. TEASING.

1130   Voigt, Cynthia. *Bad Girls.* **Scholastic, 1996. 0-590-60134-2. 277pp. Gr. 5–7**

Two bad-to-the-bone fifth-grade girls, Margalo and Mikey, become classroom friends in strict Mrs. Chemsky's classroom and take great pride in all the trouble they cause.

GERM: Booktalk titles about troublemakers and their awful behavior, starting with David Shannon's hilarious picture book *No, David* and on up to Gail Gauthier comic novel *A Year with Butch and Spike.*

RELATED TITLES: Amato, Mary. *The Word Eater.* Holiday House, 2000. / Byars, Betsy. *The 18th Emergency.* Viking, 1973. / Codell, Esmé Raji. *Sahara Special.* Hyperion, 2003. / Fenner, Carol. *Randall's Wall.* McElderry, 1991. / Fitzhugh, Louise. *Harriet the Spy.* HarperCollins, 1964. / Fletcher, Ralph. *Flying Solo.* Clarion, 1998. / Gantos, Jack. *Joey Pigza Swallowed the Key.* Farrar, 1998. / Gauthier, Gail. *A Year with Butch and Spike.* Putnam, 1998. / Getz, David. *Almost Famous.* Henry Holt, 1992. / Gorman, Carol. *Dork on the Run.* HarperCollins, 2002. / Korman, Gordon. *This Can't Be Happening at Macdonald Hall.* Scholastic, 1978. / Robinson, Barbara. *The Best School Year Ever.* HarperCollins, 1994. / Rocklin, Joanne. *For Your Eyes Only!* Scholastic, 1997. / Spinelli, Jerry. *Crash.* Knopf, 1996. / Spinelli, Jerry. *Wringer.* HarperCollins, 1997. / Voigt, Cynthia. *Bad Girls.* Scholastic, 1996.

SUBJECTS: BEHAVIOR. BEST FRIENDS. FRIENDSHIP. HUMOROUS FICTION. SCHOOLS.

1131   Whelan, Gloria. *Homeless Bird.* **HarperCollins, 2000. 0-06-028454-4. 216pp. Gr. 5–8**

Married off to 16-year-old Hari, who is dying of tuberculosis, 13-year-old Koly soon becomes a widow and lives as a servant in the house of her husband's parents in a rural village in India. Her mother-in-law takes Koly to the holy city of Vrindivan, a city of widows, and abandons her there. Raji, a rickshaw driver, befriends the destitute girl and brings her to Maa Kamala, who shelters young widows and finds them jobs.

GERM: Thanks to her talent for embroidery, Koly does well, but this National Book Award winner might make American children stop to count their blessings when they whine about how bad they have it! Ask them to write an essay comparing and contrasting how Koly's life differs from theirs.

RELATED TITLES: Cushman, Karen. *Catherine, Called Birdy.* Clarion, 1994. / Divakaruni, Chitra Banerjee. *The Conch Bearer.* Roaring Brook, 2003. / Fletcher, Susan. *Shadow Spinner.* Atheneum, 1998. / Sheth, Kashmira. *Blue Jasmine.* Hyperion, 2004. / Staples, Suzanne Fisher. *Shabanu.* Knopf, 1989. / Staples, Suzanne Fisher. *Shiva's Fire.* Farrar, 2000.

SUBJECTS: CHILD LABOR. COURAGE. HOMELESSNESS. INDIA. MULTICULTURAL BOOKS.

1132   Willis, Meredith Sue. *Marco's Monster.* **HarperCollins, 1996. 0-06-027196-5. 118pp. Gr. 2–4**
Fourth grader Marco covets the part of the Main Monster in the play his class writes, "Cool Girl and the Monsters"; his teacher, Mr. Marshan, instead assigns him the role of Narrator and gives the lead to Tyrone, Marco's tough, streetwise best friend. Marco is so jealous that he provokes a fight and Tyrone accepts the blame. Quirky and funny, with unforgettable characters such as Marco's little sister Ritzi, a prodigy who likes to play Operating Room on her Barbies, this short, deftly plotted novel will hold everyone's interest from page one.

GERM: You might just end up putting on your own class play in response.

RELATED TITLES: Cameron, Ann. *More Stories Julian Tells.* Dell, 2001. / Cameron, Ann. *The Stories Julian Tells.* Yearling, 1989. / Cutler, Jane. *Rats!* Farrar, 1996. / Honeycutt, Natalie. *Juliet Fisher and the Foolproof Plan.* Bradbury, 1992. / Hurwitz, Johanna. *Class Clown.* Morrow, 1987. / Leverich, Kathleen. *Hilary and the Trouble-makers.* Greenwillow, 1992. / Lisle, Janet Taylor. *How I Became a Writer and Oggie Learned to Drive.* Philomel, 2002. / Robinson, Barbara. *The Best School Year Ever.* HarperCollins, 1994. / Spinelli, Jerry. *Fourth Grade Rats.* Scholastic, 1991. / Willis, Meredith. *The Secret Super Power of Marco.* HarperCollins, 1994.

SUBJECTS: BEHAVIOR. BEST FRIENDS. BROTHERS AND SISTERS. CITIES AND TOWNS. FRIENDSHIP. JEALOUSY. MULTICULTURAL BOOKS. PLAYS. SCHOOLS. TEACHERS.

1133   Wilson, Jacqueline. *Double Act.* **Illus. by Nick Sharrat and Sue Heap. Delacorte, 1998. 0-385-32312-3. 185pp. Gr. 4–6**
As revealed in their alternating journal entries illustrated with their humorous black-and-white sketches, identical ten-year-old twins gregarious Ruby and timid Garnet begin to stake out their own identities after a dreaded move to the English countryside, where their widowed father and his new lady friend Rose open a bookstore.

GERM: The inseparable duo have a special language of words and motions they call Twinspeak, and they take great pride in unnerving teachers and potential school friends by saying and doing the same thing at the same time. How Garnet reluctantly and painfully breaks free of her sister/best friend's domineering ways to assert her own interests makes for a perceptive and funny character study. Discuss with your students what it means to "come into your own" in the family. Have them write about true family events and interactions that reveal facets of their own personalities.

RELATED TITLES: Codell, Esmé Raji. *Sahara Special.* Hyperion, 2003. / Creech, Sharon. *Granny Torrelli Makes Soup.* HarperCollins, 2003. / Henkes, Kevin. *Olive's Ocean.* Greenwillow, 2003. / McKay, Hilary. *Saffy's Angel.* McElderry, 2002. / Moss, Marissa. *Amelia's Notebook.* Tricycle, 1995. / Park, Barbara. *Operation: Dump the Chump.* Knopf, 1982. / Rocklin, Joanne. *For Your Eyes Only!* Scholastic, 1997. / Slepian, Jan. *The Broccoli Tapes.* Philomel, 1988. / Woodson, Jacqueline. *Locomotion.* Putnam, 2003.

SUBJECTS: ENGLAND. GRANDMOTHERS. INDIVIDUALITY. SINGLE-PARENT FAMILIES. SISTERS. TWINS.

1134   Woodruff, Elvira. *The Orphan of Ellis Island: A Time Travel Adventure.* **Scholastic, 1997. 0-590-48245-9. 174pp. Gr. 4–6**
Feeling out of place on a fifth-grade class trip to Ellis Island, orphaned foster child Dominic Cantori runs from the group and hides in a broom closet. Alone all night in the museum, he manages to get himself transported back in time to 1908 Avaletto, a small Italian village where he is befriended by three orphan brothers and their goat Violetta as they make their way to Napoli to sail to America.

GERM: Classes studying the immigrant experience will live it firsthand through Woodruff's engrossing, believable, fast-paced narrative. Students can tape-record interviews with relatives who recall stories of coming to America. Take an interactive virtual tour of Ellis Island on Scholastic's excellent "Immigration" site: <teacher.scholastic.com/activities/immigration/index.htm>.

RELATED TITLES: Bartone, Elisa. *American Too.* Lothrop, 1996. / Bartone, Elisa. *Peppe the Lamplighter.* Lothrop, 1993. / Bierman, Carol. *Journey to Ellis Island: How My Father Came to America.* Hyperion, 1998. / Curtis, Christopher Paul. *Bud, Not Buddy.* Delacorte, 1999. / Doherty, Berlie. *Street Child.* Orchard, 1994. / Freedman, Russell. *Immigrant Kids.* Dutton, 1980. / Hall, Bruce Edward. *Henry and the Kite Dragon.* Philomel, 2004. / Levine, Ellen. *If Your Name Was Changed at Ellis Island.* Scholastic, 1993. / Maestro, Betsy. *Coming to America: The Story of Immigration.* Scholastic, 1996. / Pomeranc, Marion Hess. *The American Wei.* Albert Whitman, 1998. / Recorvits, Helen. *Goodbye, Walter Malinski.* Farrar, 1999. / Sandler, Martin W. *Immigrants.* HarperCollins, 1995. / Woodruff, Elvira. *George Washington's Socks.* Scholastic, 1991. / Woodruff, Elvira. *The Memory Coat.* Scholastic, 1999. / Woodruff, Elvira. *The Ravenmaster's Secret.* Scholastic, 2003.

SUBJECTS: ELLIS ISLAND IMMIGRATION STATION (N.Y. AND N.J.). FANTASY. FOSTER HOME CARE. HISTORICAL FICTION. IMMIGRATION AND EMIGRATION. ITALIAN AMERICANS. MULTICULTURAL BOOKS. ORPHANS. TIME TRAVEL.

1135 Woodruff, Elvira. *The Ravenmaster's Secret.* **Scholastic, 2003. 0-4392-8133-4. 225pp. Gr. 5–8**
The Tower of London in England in 1735 is a fearsome place, but 11-year-old Forrest Harper, whose father is a tower guard, a Yeoman Warder and Ravenmaster, has never left the prison grounds. When Maddy, the young daughter of a Scottish rebel, is brought to the Tower and condemned to death, Forrest, who is placed in charge of bringing her meals, must decide if he should help her escape.

GERM: Readers can do some research on the history of the Bloody Tower and its ravens. Supplement the historical notes at the back of the book with a look at the Tower's own Web site: <www.hrp.org.uk/webcode/tower_home.asp>.

RELATED TITLES: Blackwood, Gary L. *The Shakespeare Stealer.* Dutton, 1998. / Choldenko, Gennifer. *Al Capone Does My Shirts.* Putnam, 2004. / Graham, Harriet. *A Boy and His Bear.* McElderry, 1996. / Thomas, Jane Resh. *The Princess in the Pigpen.* Clarion, 1989. / Woodruff, Elvira. *George Washington's Socks.* Scholastic, 1991. / Woodruff, Elvira. *The Orphan of Ellis Island: A Time Travel Adventure.* Scholastic, 1997.

SUBJECTS: BIRDS. HISTORICAL FICTION. LONDON (ENGLAND). PRISONS. RAVENS. TOWER OF LONDON (LONDON, ENGLAND).

1136 Woodson, Jacqueline. *Locomotion.* **Putnam, 2003. 0-399-23115-3. 100pp. Gr. 5–8**
Lonnie's teacher, Ms. Marcus, says, "Write it down before it leaves your brain" and "Write fast, Lonnie." He does, composing a book filled with many types of free-verse poems that tell how his parents died in a fire and he came to live with Miss Edna. To create his story, he writes all types of poems, 60 in all: haiku and epistle poems, list poems, a sonnet, an occasional poem about an occasion about to happen. The poems will break your heart, but give you hope for 11-year-old Lonnie Collins Motion.

GERM: Introduce the many forms of free verse through Lonnie's poems. Of course the book goes with your poetry unit, but the way Lonnie reveals his story, bit by bit, is like unpeeling an onion. Play the old song his mother loved so much that she made it his name, <u>Lonnie Collins Motion</u>: "Come on, come on, Do the Locomotion with me." *Love That Dog* by Sharon Creech is another affecting problem novel in verse.

RELATED TITLES: Codell, Esmé Raji. *Sahara Special.* Hyperion, 2003. / Creech, Sharon. *Love That Dog.* HarperCollins, 2001. / Curtis, Christopher Paul. *Bud, Not Buddy.* Delacorte, 1999. / English, Karen. *Francie.* Farrar, 1999. / Fletcher, Ralph. *Flying Solo.* Clarion, 1998. / George, Kristine O'Connell. *Swimming Upstream: Middle School Poems.* Clarion, 2002. / Grimes, Nikki. *Meet Danitra Brown.* Lothrop, 1994. / Grimes, Nikki. *My Man Blue.* Dial, 1999. / Harley, Avis. *Fly with Poetry: An ABC of Poetry.* Boyds Mills, 2000. / Harley, Avis. *Leap into Poetry: More ABCs of Poetry.* Boyds Mills, 2001. / Hesse, Karen. *Out of the Dust.* Scholastic, 1997. / Rocklin, Joanne. *For Your Eyes Only!* Scholastic, 1997. / Slepian, Jan. *The Broccoli Tapes.* Philomel, 1988.

SUBJECTS: AFRICAN AMERICANS. BROTHERS AND SISTERS. DEATH. FOSTER HOME CARE. MULTICULTURAL BOOKS. ORPHANS. POETRY. SCHOOLS. WRITING.

1137 Yep, Laurence. *Hiroshima.* **Scholastic, 1995. 0-590-20832-2. 56pp. Gr. 5–8**
Told in the present tense by an omniscient narrator, this is a brief, terse, semi-fictionalized account of the bombing of Hiroshima and its effect on the victims. We follow 12-year-old Sachi (a composite of several Hiroshima children), burned terribly in the aftermath of the bombing, and a Hiroshima Maiden, one of the 25 who were brought to the United States in 1955 by magazine editor Norman Cousins for free surgery. Final chapters discuss expansion of A-bomb research and testing and possible outcomes of future bomb drops. To date, 125,000 people have died as a direct result of Hiroshima.

GERM: Picture books for older readers, including Eleanor Coerr's *Sadako*, Tatsuharu Kodama's *Shin's Tricycle*, Toshi Maruki's *Hiroshima No Pika*, and Junko Morimoto's *My Hiroshima* are also valuable, though chilling, assets to a discussion of those terrible times.

RELATED TITLES: Coerr, Eleanor. *Mieko and the Fifth Treasure.* Putnam, 1993. / Coerr, Eleanor. *Sadako.* Putnam, 1993. / Coerr, Eleanor. *Sadako and the Thousand Paper Cranes.* Putnam, 1977. / Kodama, Tatsuharu. *Shin's Tricycle.* Walker, 1995. / Levine, Karen. *Hana's Suitcase.* Albert Whitman, 2003. / Maruki, Toshi. *Hiroshima No Pika.* Lothrop, 1982. / Mochizuki, Ken. *Baseball Saved Us.* Lee & Low, 1993. / Mochizuki, Ken. *Passage to Freedom: The Sugihara Story.* Lee & Low, 1997. / Morimoto, Junko. *My Hiroshima.* Viking, 1990. / Park, Linda Sue. *When My Name Was Keoko.* Clarion, 2002.

SUBJECTS: HIROSHIMA. HISTORICAL FICTION. JAPAN. WAR. WORLD WAR, 1939–1945—FICTION.

1138 Yolen, Jane. *The Ballad of the Pirate Queens*. Illus. by David Shannon. Harcourt, 1995. 0-15-200710-5. Unp. Gr. 4–8

In 1720, of the 12 brave lads sailing the American coast on "Calico Jack" Rackham's pirate ship, the *Vanity*, two—Anne Bonney and Mary Reade—are actually women. While the men are playing cards below deck, the ship is captured by a man-o'-war and set afire; the pirates are jailed. Pregnant, the two women escape hanging by "pleading their bellies."

GERM: Based on a true story of courage and cowardice, Yolen has retold this as a traditional ballad, with a rousing chorus, and so pumped full of danger, emotion, and derring-do that you may find yourself borrowing or making up a tune and singing the whole thing. For another breathtaking and thrilling picture-book adventure, you'll want to read Emily Arnold McCully's biography *The Pirate Queen*, about Grania O'Malley, a 16th-century female Irish pirate.

RELATED TITLES: Longfellow, Henry Wadsworth. *The Midnight Ride of Paul Revere*. Illus. by Christopher Bing. Handprint, 2001. / Longfellow, Henry Wadsworth. *Paul Revere's Ride*. Illus. by Ted Rand. Dutton, 1990. / McCully, Emily Arnold. *The Pirate Queen*. Putnam, 1995. / Service, Robert W. *The Cremation of Sam McGee*. Illus. by Ted Harrison. Greenwillow, 1987. / Thayer, Ernest Lawrence. *Casey at the Bat*. Illus. by Gerald Fitzgerald. Atheneum, 1995. / Thayer, Ernest Lawrence. *Casey at the Bat*. Illus. by Christopher Bing. Handprint, 2000.

SUBJECTS: HISTORICAL FICTION. NARRATIVE POETRY. PICTURE BOOKS FOR OLDER READERS. PIRATES. STORIES IN RHYME. WOMEN.

1139 Yolen, Jane. *Passager: The Young Merlin Trilogy, Book One*. Harcourt, 1996. 0-15-200391-6. 76pp. Gr. 4–7

The first book in the Young Merlin Trilogy introduces us to a nameless 8-year-old boy who was abandoned by his mother in an English forest, where he survives by himself but loses the knowledge of even his own name. Taken in by Master Robin, a kind falconer, the boy regains memories of his former life. Yolen's poetic fleshing out of the Merlin legend is compelling and beautifully spare.

GERM: Children will be eager to read the sequels, *Hobby* and *Merlin*, and to explore the many legends of Merlin and King Arthur.

RELATED TITLES: Hastings, Selena. *Sir Gawain and the Green Knight*. Lothrop, 1981. / Hastings, Selena. *Sir Gawain and the Loathly Lady*. Lothrop, 1985. / Hayes, Sarah. *Robin Hood*. Henry Holt, 1989. / Hodges, Margaret. *Merlin and the Making of the King*. Holiday House, 2004. / Hodges, Patricia. *Saint George and the Dragon*. Little, Brown, 1984. / Sabuda, Robert. *Arthur and the Sword*. Atheneum, 1995. / San Souci, Robert D. *Young Arthur*. Doubleday, 1997. / Shannon, Mark. *Gawain and the Green Knight*. Putnam, 1994. / Talbott, Hudson. *King Arthur and the Round Table*. Morrow, 1995. / Winthrop, Elizabeth. *The Castle in the Attic*. Holiday House, 1985. / Yolen, Jane. *Dragon Hall*. Harcourt, 1991. / Yolen, Jane. *Hobby: The Young Merlin Trilogy, Book 2*. Harcourt, 1996. / Yolen, Jane. *Merlin and the Dragons*. Dutton, 1995. / Yolen, Jane. *Merlin: The Young Merlin Trilogy, Book 3*. Harcourt, 1997.

SUBJECTS: ENGLAND. FALCONRY. FERAL CHILDREN. HISTORICAL FICTION. LEGENDS. MAGICIANS. MERLIN (LEGENDARY CHARACTER).

1140 Yolen, Jane, and Robert J. Harris. *Odysseus in the Serpent Maze*. HarperCollins, 2001. 0-06-028734-9. 248pp. Gr. 4–7

Longing to be regarded as a hero, 13-year-old Odysseus sets out with his best friend, Mentor, to slay the deadly Boar of Parnassus, using his grandfather's prize hunting spear. The two boys encounter pirates, a satyr, and the sensible and affable Penelope, handmaiden and cousin to the devastatingly attractive and obnoxious Helen. Together, the foursome uncover the many infernal inventions of the late Daedalus, including the dreaded Labyrinth.

GERM: As an introduction to Greek myths and legends, this entertaining adventure novel fills in the thrilling childhood of hero Odysseus and Penelope, his future wife. Children will be intrigued by the descriptions of Daedalus's inventions—the mechanical bronze dog, the self-sailing ship—and other strange-looking drawings in his workshop. Not only can children draw detailed illustrations of their favorite scenes in the story, but they can draw their own prototypical plans for inventions that Daedalus might have designed. Read aloud an assortment of legends about the adult Odysseus on his 18-year journey home from the Trojan War from Neil Philip's *The Adventures of Odysseus*.

RELATED TITLES: Fisher, Leonard Everett. *Cyclops.* Holiday House, 1991. / Fisher, Leonard Everett. *Theseus and the Minotaur.* Holiday House, 1988. / Gutman, Dan. *Qwerty Stevens, Back in Time: The Edison Mystery.* Simon & Schuster, 2001. / Hutton, Warwick. *Odysseus and the Cyclops.* McElderry, 1995. / McCaughrean, Geraldine. *The Bronze Cauldron: Myths and Legends of the World.* McElderry, 1998. / Osborne, Mary Pope. *Favorite Greek Myths.* Scholastic, 1989. / Osborne, Mary Pope. *Tales from the Odyssey: The One-Eyed Giant.* Hyperion, 2003. (And others in the Tales from the Odyssey series.) / Philip, Neil. *The Adventures of Odysseus.* Orchard, 1997. / Riordan, Rick. *The Lightning Thief.* Miramax/Hyperion, 2005. / Sutcliffe, Rosemary. *Black Ships Before Troy! The Story of the Iliad.* Delacorte, 1993. / Sutcliffe, Rosemary. *The Wanderings of Odysseus: The Story of The Odyssey.* Delacorte, 1996. / Waldherr, Kris. *Persephone and the Pomegranate: A Myth from Greece.* Dial, 1993. / Yolen, Jane. *Pegasus, the Flying Horse.* Dutton, 1998. / Yolen, Jane. *Wings.* Harcourt, 1991. / Yolen, Jane, and Robert J. Harris. *Jason and the Gorgon's Blood.* HarperCollins, 2004. (And others in the Young Heroes series.)

SUBJECTS: ADVENTURE AND ADVENTURERS. FOLKLORE—GREECE. HISTORICAL FICTION. INVENTIONS AND INVENTORS. MYTHOLOGY. ODYSSEUS. SURVIVAL.

by *Meilo So*

Gobble, Gobble, Slip, Slop

A Tale of a Very Greedy Cat

FOLK & FAIRY TALES, MYTHS & LEGENDS

1141 Aardema, Verna. *Anansi Does the Impossible! An Ashanti Tale.* **Illus. by Lisa Desimini. Atheneum, 1997. 0-689-81092-X. Unp. Gr. K–3**

To buy the Sky God's stories, Anansi the Spider must complete three impossible tasks: bring the Sky God a live python, a real fairy, and 47 stinging hornets. With the sage advice of his wife, Aso, the trickster spider succeeds in all three, which, in this West African pourquoi tale, explains why people have stories today.

GERM: Compare Aardema's version with the Caldecott-winning *A Story, A Story* by Gail E. Haley, *Zomo the Rabbit* by Gerald McDermott, and *Rabbit Wishes* by Linda Shute, a rabbit trickster tale from Cuba, all of which use similar motifs.

RELATED TITLES: Aardema, Verna. *Anansi Does the Impossible! An Ashanti Tale.* Atheneum, 1997. / Aardema, Verna. *Anansi Finds a Fool.* Dial, 1992. / Cummings, Pat. *Ananse and the Lizard: A West African Tale.* Henry Holt, 2002. / Haley, Gail E. *A Story, a Story.* Atheneum, 1970. / Kimmel, Eric A. *Anansi and the Magic Stick.* Holiday House, 2001. / Kimmel, Eric A. *Anansi and the Moss-Covered Rock.* Holiday House, 1990. / Kimmel, Eric A. *Anansi and the Talking Melon.* Holiday House, 1994. / Kimmel, Eric A. *Anansi Goes Fishing.* Holiday House, 1992. / McDermott, Gerald. *Zomo the Rabbit: A Trickster Tale from West Africa.* Harcourt, 1992. / Mollel, Tololwa M. *Ananse's Feast: An Ashanti Tale.* Clarion, 1997. / Souhami, Jessica. *The Leopard's Drum: An Asante Tale from West Africa.* Little, Brown, 1996. / Temple, Frances. *Tiger Soup: An Anansi Story from Jamaica.* Orchard, 1994.

SUBJECTS: ANANSI (LEGENDARY CHARACTER). FOLKLORE—AFRICA, WEST. HUMOROUS FOLKLORE. MULTICULTURAL BOOKS—FOLKLORE. POURQUOI TALES. SPIDERS—FOLKLORE. STORYTELLING. TRICKSTER TALES.

1142 Aardema, Verna. *How the Ostrich Got Its Long Neck: A Tale from the Akamba of Kenya.* **Illus. by Marcia Brown. Scholastic, 1995. 0-590-48367-6. Unp. Gr. PreK–3**

Not all would-be tricksters are successful, as we see in an amusing pourquoi tale with good-natured watercolor and marker illustrations. A sympathetic ostrich who heeds wily crocodile's pleas to pull out a bad tooth learns the hard way not to be so trusting of dangerous creatures.

GERM: Compare crocodile encounters in *The Hunterman and the Crocodile* by Baba Wagué Diakité and in Rudyard Kipling's classic story, *The Elephant's Child.*

RELATED TITLES: Aardema, Verna. *Misoso: Once upon a Time Tales from Africa.* Knopf, 1994. / Aardema, Verna. *Why Mosquitoes Buzz in People's Ears.* Dial, 1975. / Bruchac, Joseph, and James Bruchac. *How Chipmunk Got His Stripes.* Dial, 2001. / Diakité, Baba Wagué. *The Hunterman and the Crocodile.* Scholastic, 1997. / Kipling, Rudyard. *The Elephant's Child.* Illus. by Lorinda Bryan Cauley. Harcourt, 1983. / Mollel, Tololwa M. *The Flying Tortoise.* Clarion, 1994. / Rosen, Michael. *How the Giraffe Got Such a Long Neck . . . and Why Rhino Is So Grumpy.* Dial, 1993. / Salley, Coleen. *Why Epossumondas Has No Hair on His Tail.* Harcourt, 2004.

SUBJECTS: CROCODILES—FOLKLORE. FOLKLORE—AFRICA. FOLKLORE—KENYA. HUMOROUS FOLKLORE. MULTICULTURAL BOOKS—FOLKLORE. OSTRICHES—FOLKLORE. POURQUOI TALES. TRICKSTER TALES.

1143 **Aardema, Verna.** *Koi and the Kola Nuts.* **Illus. by Joe Cepeda. Atheneum, 1999. 0-689-81760-6. Unp. Gr. K–4**

After the death of Chief Ogu Mefu, his youngest son, Koi, returns home too late to get a share of his royal possessions, and is given only a scraggly little kola tree. On his journey to see the world, Koi comes to the aid of a snake, ant, and crocodile, who in turn help him to complete three impossible tasks and parlay the kola nuts into winning the hand of another chief's beautiful daughter.

GERM: This Liberian folktale ends: "Do good and good will come back to you—in full measure and overflowing." Talk it over: How does Koi prove the truth of this saying? How has this saying applied to your life?

RELATED TITLES: Aardema, Verna. *Anansi Does the Impossible! An Ashanti Tale.* Atheneum, 1997. / Aardema, Verna. *Anansi Finds a Fool.* Dial, 1992. / Aardema, Verna. *Misoso: Once upon a Time Tales from Africa.* Knopf, 1994. / Aardema, Verna. *Tales from the Story Hat.* Putnam, 1960. / Courlander, Harold. *The Cow-Tail Switch and Other West African Stories.* Henry Holt, 1988. / Gabler, Mirko. *Tall, Wide, and Sharp-Eye.* Henry Holt, 1994. / Medearis, Angela Shelf. *Seven Spools of Thread: A Kwanzaa Story.* Albert Whitman, 2000. / Onyefulu, Obi. *Chinye: A West African Folk Tale.* Viking, 1994. / Steptoe, John. *Mufaro's Beautiful Daughters: An African Tale.* Lothrop, 1987.

SUBJECTS: ANTS—FOLKLORE. CROCODILES—FOLKLORE. FOLKLORE—AFRICA, WEST. FOLKLORE—LIBERIA. KINDNESS—FOLKLORE. KINGS AND RULERS—FOLKLORE. MULTICULTURAL BOOKS—FOLKLORE. SNAKES—FOLKLORE.

1144 **Aylesworth, Jim.** *Aunt Pitty Patty's Piggy.* **Illus. by Barbara McClintock. Scholastic, 1999. 0-590-89987-2. Unp. Gr. PreK–1**

Aunt Pitty Patty's niece enlists the help of everyone and everything she meets—dog, stick, fire, water, ox, butcher, rope, rat, cat, and farmer—in order to make that stubborn new piggy enter through her gate, but they all refuse.

GERM: The infectious rhythms of the chantable refrains—"It's gettin' late, and piggy's by the gate sayin', "No, no, no, I will not go!"—make this one stellar for storytelling and creative drama. As you read or tell the story, have children predict what animal or object the little girl will approach next. Afterward, ask them to recall the final sequence orally or by drawing the long chain of events on a long white strip of paper. Show other versions of *The Old Woman and Her Pig*, including those by Paul Galdone, Eric Kimmel, and Rosanne Litzinger, and *The Troublesome Pig* by Priscilla Lamont. Two rousing versions with a rooster instead of a pig are, from Latin America, *The Rooster Who Went to His Uncle's Wedding* by Alma Flor Ada, and from Cuba, *The Bossy Gallito* by Lucie M. Gonzalez.

RELATED TITLES: Ada, Alma Flor. *The Rooster Who Went to His Uncle's Wedding: A Latin American Folktale.* Putnam, 1993. / Aylesworth, Jim. *The Gingerbread Man.* Scholastic, 1998. / Egielski, Richard. *The Gingerbread Boy.* HarperCollins, 1997. / Galdone, Paul. *The Old Woman and Her Pig.* McGraw-Hill, 1960. / Gonzalez, Lucie M. *The Bossy Gallito: A Traditional Cuban Folktale.* Scholastic, 1994. / Hogrogian, Nonny. *One Fine Day.* Macmillan, 1971. / Kimmel, Eric A. *The Gingerbread Man.* Holiday House, 1993. / Kimmel, Eric A. *The Old Woman and Her Pig.* Holiday House, 1992. / Lamont, Priscilla. *The Troublesome Pig.* Crown, 1985. / Litzinger, Rosanne. *The Old Woman and Her Pig.* Harcourt, 1993. / Marshall, James. *The Three Little Pigs.* Dial, 1989. / Pomerantz, Charlotte. *The Piggy in the Puddle.* Macmillan, 1974. / Reddix, Valerie. *Millie and the Mud Hole.* Lothrop, 1992. / Waddell, Martin. *The Pig in the Pond.* Candlewick, 1992.

SUBJECTS: ANIMALS—FOLKLORE. CAUSE AND EFFECT. CHANTABLE REFRAIN—FOLKLORE. CIRCULAR STORIES—FOLKLORE. CREATIVE DRAMA—FOLKLORE. FOLKLORE—U.S. PIGS—FOLKLORE. SEQUENCE STORIES—FOLKLORE. STUBBORNNESS—FOLKLORE.

1145 **Aylesworth, Jim.** *The Gingerbread Man.* **Illus. by Barbara McClintock. Scholastic, 1998. 0-590-97219-7. Unp. Gr. PreK–1**

In this traditional folktale, the Gingerbread Man runs away from everyone he meets, leading them on a frantic and merry chase, until he meets up with a sneaky fox.

GERM: Compare the quaintly old-fashioned watercolor and pen-and-ink illustrations, the language, plot, chantable refrain, and the ending with the hip, contemporary, New York City version by Richard Egielski. For props to help you present this story, go to <www.mimismotifs.com>.

RELATED TITLES: Aylesworth, Jim. *Aunt Pitty Patty's Piggy.* Scholastic, 1998. / Aylesworth, Jim. *The Tale of Tricky Fox: A New England Trickster Tale.* Scholastic, 2001. / Cauley, Lorinda Bryan. *The Pancake Boy: An Old Norwegian Folk Tale.* Putnam, 1988. / Compestine, Ying Chang. *The Runaway Rice Cake.* Simon & Schuster, 2001. / Cook, Scott. *The Gingerbread Boy.* Knopf, 1987. / Egielski, Richard. *The Gingerbread Boy.* HarperCollins,

1997. / Esterl, Arnica. *The Fine Round Cake*. Four Winds, 1991. / Kimmel, Eric A. *The Gingerbread Man*. Holiday House, 1993. / Kimmel, Eric A. *The Runaway Tortilla*. Winslow, 2000. / Sawyer, Ruth. *Journey Cake, Ho!* Puffin, 1978. / Wattenberg, Jane. *Henny-Penny*. Scholastic, 2000.

SUBJECTS: CHANTABLE REFRAIN—FOLKLORE. CREATIVE DRAMA—FOLKLORE. FOLKLORE. FOOD—FOLKLORE. GINGERBREAD BOY. HUMOROUS FOLKLORE. SEQUENCE STORIES— FOLKLORE. STORIES TO TELL.

1146 **Aylesworth, Jim. *Goldilocks and the Three Bears*. Illus. by Barbara McClintock. Scholastic, 2003. 0-439-39545-3. Unp. Gr. PreK–1**

A saucy, impetuous Goldilocks disregards her mother's warnings about breaking into houses uninvited, and invades the privacy of the bear family. Old-fashioned but comical watercolor, sepia ink, and gouache illustrations portray a proper little moppet who finally learns her lesson and "never ever forgot not to do what her mother told her not to do ever, ever, ever again."

GERM: Try out the recipe for "Mama Bear's Porridge Cookies" at the back of the book. Compare and contrast this traditional retelling with the American variant, *The Gunniwolf*, by Wilhelmina Harper.

RELATED TITLES: Brett, Jan. *Goldilocks and the Three Bears*. Putnam, 1987. / Cauley, Lorinda Bryan. *Goldilocks and the Three Bears*. Putnam, 1981. / Child, Lauren. *Who's Afraid of the Big Bad Book?* Hyperion, 2003. / Eisen, Armand. *Goldilocks and the Three Bears*. Knopf, 1987. / Ernst, Lisa Campbell. *Goldilocks Returns*. Simon & Schuster, 2000. / Ernst, Lisa Campbell. *Stella Louella's Runaway Book*. Simon & Schuster, 1998. / Harper, Wilhelmina. *The Gunniwolf*. Dutton, 2003. / Hoberman, Mary Ann. *You Read to Me, I'll Read to You: Very Short Fairy Tales to Read Together*. Little, Brown, 2004. / Marshall, James. *Goldilocks and the Three Bears*. Dial, 1988. / Stanley, Diane. *Goldie and the Three Bears*. HarperCollins, 2003. / Stevens, Janet. *Goldilocks and the Three Bears*. Holiday House, 1986.

SUBJECTS: BEARS—FOLKLORE. FOLKLORE. GOLDILOCKS.

1147 **Aylesworth, Jim. *The Tale of Tricky Fox: A New England Trickster Tale*. Illus. by Barbara McClintock. Scholastic, 2001. 0-439-09543-3. Unp. Gr. PreK–2**

Tricky Fox boasts to Brother Fox that he can fool a human into putting a fat pig into his sack. He almost succeeds, thanks to all the curious matrons who can't help peering into his sack after he warns them not to. Unfortunately for Tricky Fox, the last lady he tries to outwit is a teacher, and as we all know, teachers are not so easily fooled. Instead of putting her pig into the sack, she substitutes her fierce bulldog.

GERM: Make up a jaunty tune for the refrains the fox sings so your listeners can join in. Children can pair up to act out the scenes between the fox and ladies he bamboozles. Compare and contrast this retelling of the English folktale, "The Travels of a Fox," with other picture-book versions such as Paul Galdone's *What's in Fox's Sack?* and Jennifer Westwood's *Going to Squintums*.

RELATED TITLES: Aylesworth, Jim. *Aunt Pitty Patty's Piggy*. Scholastic, 1998. / Egielski, Richard. *The Gingerbread Boy*. HarperCollins, 1997. / Galdone, Paul. *What's in Fox's Sack?* Clarion, 1982. / Hogrogian, Nonny. *One Fine Day*. Macmillan, 1971. / Kimmel, Eric A. *The Gingerbread Man*. Holiday House, 1993. / Ward, Helen. *The Rooster and the Fox*. Millbrook, 2003. / Wattenberg, Jane. *Henny-Penny*. Scholastic, 2000. / Westwood, Jennifer. *Going to Squintums: A Foxy Folktale*. Dial, 1985.

SUBJECTS: CREATIVE DRAMA—FOLKLORE. FOLKLORE—U.S. FOXES—FOLKLORE. TRICKSTER TALES.

1148 **Behan, Brendan. *The King of Ireland's Son*. Illus. by P. J. Lynch. Orchard, 1997. 0-531-09549-5. 31pp. Gr. 3–6**

In renowned Irish author Brendan Behan's rollicking story, told with grand humor and language that rolls off the tongue, the king of Ireland sends his three sons off to find the source of the heavenly music they have been hearing. The youngest son is lowered into a deep hole in the earth by his bad brothers, and there he gathers advice—first from an old man; then from an old, old man; and finally, from an old, old, old man. Next, a little white stallion takes him to the heavenly music, played on the harp by the King of Greece's daughter, who is being held captive by an old giant. With a meaty plot, flamboyant watercolors, and a glorious text that was transcribed from a tape recording of Behan, this tour de force of a read-aloud will give great pleasure to all.

GERM: See how other youngest brothers prevail in Mirko Gabler's *Tall, Wide, and Sharp-Eye*, Eric A. Kimmel's *Boots and His Brothers*, and Charles Perrault's *Puss in Boots*.

RELATED TITLES: Byrd, Robert. *Finn MacCoul and His Fearless Wife: A Giant of a Tale from Ireland*. Dutton,

1999. / Climo, Shirley. *The Irish Cinderlad*. HarperCollins, 1996. / dePaola, Tomie. *Fin M'Coul, the Giant of Knockmany Hill*. Holiday House, 1981. / Gabler, Mirko. *Tall, Wide, and Sharp-Eye*. Henry Holt, 1994. / Greene, Ellin. *Billy Beg and His Bull*. Holiday House, 1994. / Kimmel, Eric A. *Boots and His Brothers: A Norwegian Tale Retold*. Holiday House, 1992. / Kimmel, Eric A. *Seven at One Blow: A Tale from the Brothers Grimm*. Holiday House, 1998. / Kirstein, Lincoln. *Puss in Boots*. Little, Brown, 1992. / Marcellino, Fred. *Puss in Boots*. Farrar, 1990. / Martin, Claire. *Boots and the Glass Mountain*. Dial, 1992. / Souhami, Jessica. *Mrs. McCool and the Giant Cuhullin: An Irish Tale*. Henry Holt, 2002. / Talbott, Hudson. *O'Sullivan Stew*. Putnam, 1999.

SUBJECTS: BROTHERS—FOLKLORE. FATHERS—FOLKLORE. FOLKLORE—IRELAND. GIANTS—FOLKLORE. HORSES—FOLKLORE. PRINCES AND PRINCESSES—FOLKLORE.

1149   Beneduce, Ann Keay. *Jack and the Beanstalk*. Illus. by Gennady Spirin. Philomel, 1999. 0-399-23118-8. Unp. Gr. 2–6

Based on an 1881 version of this old tale, Jack sells the cow, Milky White, for ten magic beans, and, when he climbs that beanstalk, encounters a beautiful woman dressed in white who claims to be a fairy and Jack's father's guardian. It is up to Jack to avenge his father on the wicked giant who stole all his riches, which, of course, he does. Set in Tudor England, the ornate water-color and tempera paintings face a text bordered in sumptuous swirls of beans and breads.

GERM: Compare other versions of the story to show the differences in an illustrator's vision and in the styles of retelling.

RELATED TITLES: Cauley, Lorinda Bryan. *Jack and the Beanstalk*. Putnam, 1983. / Chase, Richard. *The Jack Tales*. Houghton Mifflin, 1943. / Compton, Kenn, and Joanne Compton. *Jack the Giant Chaser: An Appalachian Tale*. Holiday House, 1993. / Galdone, Paul. *The History of Mother Twaddle and the Marvelous Achievements of Her Son, Jack*. Clarion, 1979. / Garner, Alan. *Jack and the Beanstalk*. Doubleday, 1992. / Haley, Gail E. *Jack and the Bean Tree*. Crown, 1986. / Hicks, Ray. *The Jack Tales*. Callaway, 2000. / Kellogg, Steven. *Jack and the Beanstalk*. Morrow, 1991. / Osborne, Mary Pope. *Kate and the Beanstalk*. Atheneum, 2000. / Stanley, Diane. *The Giant and the Beanstalk*. HarperCollins, 2004. / Swope, Sam. *Jack and the Seven Deadly Giants*. Farrar, 2004.

SUBJECTS: FAIRIES—FOLKLORE. FAIRY TALES. FOLKLORE—ENGLAND. GIANTS—FOLKLORE.

1150   Bodkin, Odds. *The Crane Wife*. Illus. by Gennady Spirin. Harcourt, 1998. 0-15-201407-1. Unp. Gr. 2–6

In a breathtaking picture-book version of the well-known Japanese folktale, Osamu, a sail maker, nurses an injured crane back to health and then meets and marries Yukiko, a mysterious woman who weaves for him a magical sail. When he breaks his promise, and looks in on her while she is weaving, he finds out who she really is, but then loses her forever.

GERM: Ask the art teacher to treat your class to a weaving lesson. Variants of this haunting Japanese folktale include Daniel San Souci's *In the Moonlight Mist*, Robert D. San Souci's *The Snow Wife*, Diane Wolkstein's *White Wave*, and Sumiko Yagawa's *The Crane Wife*.

RELATED TITLES: Demi. *The Magic Tapestry*. Henry Holt, 1994. / Hodges, Margaret. *The Boy Who Drew Cats*. Holiday House, 2002. / San Souci, Daniel. *In the Moonlight Mist: A Korean Tale*. Boyds Mills, 1999. / San Souci, Robert D. *The Snow Wife*. Dial, 1993. / San Souci, Robert D. *A Weave of Words: An Armenian Tale*. Orchard, 1998. / Tseng, Grace. *White Tiger, Blue Serpent*. Lothrop, 1999. / Wolkstein, Diane. *White Wave: A Chinese Tale*. Crowell, 1979. / Yagawa, Sumiko. *The Crane Wife*. Morrow, 1981.

SUBJECTS: BIRDS—FOLKLORE. CRANES—FOLKLORE. FAIRY TALES. FOLKLORE—JAPAN. MULTICULTURAL BOOKS—FOLKLORE. TRANSFORMATIONS—FOLKLORE. WEAVING—FOLKLORE.

1151   Bruchac, Joseph. *The Boy Who Lived with the Bears and Other Iroquois Stories*. Illus. by Murv Jacob. HarperCollins, 1995. 0-06-021288-8. 63pp. Gr. 1–6

These six exciting and mostly humorous Native American animal tales from the Iroquois tradition are about tricksters, warriors, and friends.

GERM: Compare the humorous trickster tale "Rabbit and Fox" with the variant *Great Rabbit and the Long-Tailed Wildcat* by Andy Gregg. Contrast the experiences of the humble outcast boy in the title story with that of the chief's haughty and spoiled daughter in Barbara Goldin's *The Girl Who Lived with the Bears*, a Native American folktale of the Pacific Northwest.

RELATED TITLES: Bierhorst, John. *The Woman Who Fell from the Sky: The Iroquois Story of Creation*. Morrow, 1993. / Bruchac, Joseph. *Iroquois Stories: Heroes and Heroines, Monsters and Magic*. Crossing Press, 1985. / Bruchac, Joseph, and James Bruchac. *How Chipmunk Got His Stripes*. Dial, 2001. / Goldin, Barbara Diamond. *The Girl Who Lived with the Bears*. Harcourt, 1997. / Gregg, Andy. *Great Rabbit and the Long-Tailed Wildcat*. Albert Whitman, 1993. / Hausman, Gerald. *How Chipmunk Got Tiny Feet: Native American Animal Origin*

Stories. HarperCollins, 1995. / Martin, Rafe. *The Boy Who Lived with the Seals.* Putnam, 1993. / Mayo, Gretchen Will. *Big Trouble for Tricky Rabbit.* Walker, 1994. / Mayo, Gretchen Will. *Here Comes Tricky Rabbit.* Walker, 1994. / Ross, Gayle. *How Rabbit Tricked Otter and Other Cherokee Trickster Stories.* HarperCollins, 1994. / Van Laan, Nancy. *In a Circle Long Ago: A Treasury of Native Lore from North America.* Knopf, 1995.

SUBJECTS: ANIMALS—FOLKLORE. FOLKLORE—COLLECTIONS. FOLKLORE—INDIANS OF NORTH AMERICA. FOLKLORE—U.S. IROQUOIS INDIANS—FOLKLORE. MULTICULTURAL BOOKS—FOLKLORE. NEW YORK (STATE)—FOLKLORE. POURQUOI TALES. TRICKSTER TALES.

1152 **Bruchac, Joseph, and James Bruchac.** *How Chipmunk Got His Stripes: A Tale of Bragging and Teasing.* **Illus. by Jose Aruego and Ariane Dewey. Dial, 2001. 0-8037-2404-7. Unp. Gr. K–2**

Dramatic pen-and-ink and watercolor illustrations bring to life a lively Native American pourquoi (how and why) tale from the East Coast. Brown Squirrel asks bragging Bear if he can stop the sun from rising in the morning. Bear takes the challenge, commanding the sun not to come up; of course, much to Brown Squirrel's delight, the sun rises anyway. Foolishly, the squirrel teases Bear, and though he is able to trick Bear out of eating him, sharp-clawed Bear scratches him from the top of his head to the tip of his tail, creating the first chipmunk.

GERM: Break your group into two parts—bears and squirrels—so that they can chant or sing each animal's refrain about whether or not the sun will rise. Use this story to discuss bullying and teasing. Also read the title story in Gerald Hausman's *How Chipmunk Got Tiny Feet.*

RELATED TITLES: Bernhard, Emery. *How Snowshoe Hare Rescued the Sun: A Tale from the Arctic.* Holiday House, 1993. / Bodnár, Judit Z. *Tale of a Tail.* Lothrop, 1998. / Ehlert, Lois. *Cuckoo/Cucú: A Mexican Folktale/Un Cuento Folklórico Mexicano.* Harcourt, 1997. / Ehlert, Lois. *Moon Rope: A Peruvian Folktale.* Harcourt, 1992. / Gates, Frieda. *Owl Eyes.* Lothrop, 1994. / Hausman, Gerald. *How Chipmunk Got Tiny Feet.* HarperCollins, 1995. / Ross, Gayle. *How Turtle's Back Was Cracked: A Traditional Cherokee Tale.* Dial, 1995. / Ryder, Joanne. *Chipmunk Song.* Dutton, 1987. / Salley, Coleen. *Why Epossumondas Has No Hair on His Tail.* Harcourt, 2004. / Shannon, George. *Lizard's Home.* Greenwillow, 1999. / Shannon, George. *Lizard's Song.* Greenwillow, 1981. / Stevens, Janet. *Tops and Bottoms.* Harcourt, 1995. / Van Laan, Nancy. *In a Circle Long Ago: A Treasury of Native Lore from North America.* Knopf, 1995.

SUBJECTS: ANIMALS—FOLKLORE. BEARS—FOLKLORE. CHIPMUNKS—FOLKLORE. FOLKLORE—INDIANS OF NORTH AMERICA. FOLKLORE—U.S. MULTICULTURAL BOOKS—FOLKLORE. POURQUOI TALES. SQUIRRELS—FOLKLORE. TEASING—FOLKLORE.

1153 **Bruchac, Joseph, and James Bruchac.** *Raccoon's Last Race: A Traditional Abenaki Story.* **Illus. by Jose Aruego and Ariane Dewey. Dial, 2004. 0-8037-2977-4. Unp. Gr. PreK–2**

Long-legged Azban the Raccoon, the fastest runner of all the animals, pushes Grandfather Rock off a mountain and races it downhill. Because Azban gets careless, the rock rolls him flat, and only the smallest of creatures, the ants, will come to his aid.

GERM: Bright and cheerful illustrations and lots of good noises (Ka-boom!) make this funny Native American pourquoi tale a winner for acting out and discussing. Why wouldn't any of the other animals come to Azban's aid? Did Azban keep his promise to the ants? What were the consequences? Read about another mischievous raccoon in *Brother Wolf: A Seneca Tale* by Harriet Peck Taylor.

RELATED TITLES: Bruchac, Joseph. *The Great Ball Game: A Muskogee Story.* Dial, 1994. / Bruchac, Joseph. *Seeing the Circle.* Richard C. Owen, 1999. / Bruchac, Joseph, and James Bruchac. *How Chipmunk Got His Stripes.* Dial, 2001. / Brusca, María Cristina, and Tona Wilson. *When Jaguar Ate the Moon: And Other Stories About Animals and Plants of the Americas.* Henry Holt, 1995. / Gates, Frieda. *Owl Eyes.* Lothrop, 1994. / Goble, Paul. *Iktomi and the Boulder: A Plains Indian Story.* Orchard, 1988. / Hausman, Gerald. *How Chipmunk Got Tiny Feet: Native American Animal Origin Stories.* HarperCollins, 1995. / Ross, Gayle. *How Turtle's Back Was Cracked: A Traditional Cherokee Tale.* Dial, 1995. / Stevens, Janet. *Coyote Steals the Blanket: A Ute Tale.* Holiday House, 1993. / Taylor, Harriet Peck. *Brother Wolf: A Seneca Tale.* Farrar, 1996.

SUBJECTS: ABENAKI INDIANS—FOLKLORE. ANIMALS—FOLKLORE. CREATIVE DRAMA—FOLKLORE. FOLKLORE—INDIANS OF NORTH AMERICA. FOLKLORE—U.S. HUMOROUS FOLKLORE. MULTICULTURAL BOOKS—FOLKLORE. POURQUOI TALES. RACCOONS—FOLKLORE. ROCKS—FOLKLORE.

1154 **Bruchac, Joseph, and Gayle Ross.** *The Story of the Milky Way: A Cherokee Tale.* **Illus. by Virginia A. Stroud. Dial, 1995. 0-8037-1738-5. Unp. Gr. K–4**

A cornmeal-stealing spirit dog is chased into the sky by the wise leader known as Beloved

Woman and becomes what we now call the Milky Way, according to this Native American pourquoi tale.

GERM: Compare space facts with folklore, also reading Barbara Juster Esbensen's *The Star Maiden* and Paul Goble's *Her Seven Brothers* for other explanations of the heavens.

RELATED TITLES: Bernhard, Emery. *How Snowshoe Hare Rescued the Sun: A Tale from the Arctic.* Holiday House, 1993. / Bruchac, Joseph. *Seeing the Circle.* Richard C. Owen, 1999. / Esbensen, Barbara Juster. *The Star Maiden: An Ojibway Tale.* Little, Brown, 1988. / Gerson, Mary-Joan. *Why the Sky Is Far Away: A Nigerian Folktale.* Little, Brown, 1992. / Goble, Paul. *Her Seven Brothers.* Bradbury, 1988. / Ross, Gayle. *How Rabbit Tricked Otter and Other Cherokee Trickster Stories.* Parabola, 2003. / Rumford, James. *Sequoyah: The Man Who Gave His People Writing.* Houghton Mifflin, 2004. / Taylor, Harriet Peck. *Coyote Places the Stars.* Simon & Schuster, 1993.

SUBJECTS: ASTRONOMY—FOLKLORE. CHEROKEE INDIANS—FOLKLORE. DOGS—FOLKLORE. FOLKLORE—INDIANS OF NORTH AMERICA. FOLKLORE—U.S. FOOD—FOLKLORE. GRANDPARENTS—FOLKLORE. MULTICULTURAL BOOKS—FOLKLORE. POURQUOI TALES. STARS—FOLKLORE.

1155 Burleigh, Robert. *Pandora.* **Illus. by Raúl Colón. Harcourt, 2002. 0-15-202178-7. Unp. Gr. 2–8**

Pandora, the "all-gifted," is the first mortal woman created by the gods, and Zeus arranges for her to be married to Epimetheus, the brother of the fire-stealing Prometheus. She has been warned not to open the beautiful and mysterious jar that was bestowed unto her husband by Zeus. "The gods have commanded it," Epimetheus tells her. Burleigh's poetic retelling of the classic Greek myth is well served by the formal, framed, textured watercolor and colored pencil illustrations that match the gravity of the tale.

GERM: Discussion point: What are the evils that were released into the world? How does having hope help us to deal with them?

RELATED TITLES: Burleigh, Robert. *Hercules.* Harcourt, 1999. / Climo, Shirley. *Atalanta's Race: A Greek Myth.* Clarion, 1995. / Craft, M. Charlotte. *Cupid and Psyche.* Morrow, 1996. / Fisher, Leonard Everett. *Cyclops.* Holiday House, 1991. / Fisher, Leonard Everett. *Theseus and the Minotaur.* Holiday House, 1988. / Hutton, Warwick. *Odysseus and the Cyclops.* McElderry, 1995. / Mark, Jan. *The Midas Touch.* Candlewick, 2000. / Mayer, Marianna. *Iduna and the Magic Apples.* Macmillan, 1988. / Osborne, Mary Pope. *Favorite Greek Myths.* Scholastic, 1989. / Sutcliffe, Rosemary. *The Story of the Iliad.* Delacorte, 1993. / Sutcliffe, Rosemary. *The Wanderings of Odysseus: The Story of The Odyssey.* Delacorte, 1996. / Waldherr, Kris. *Persephone and the Pomegranate: A Myth from Greece.* Dial, 1993. / Wells, Rosemary. *Max and Ruby's First Greek Myth: Pandora's Box.* Dial, 1993. / Yolen, Jane. *Pegasus, the Flying Horse.* Dutton, 1998. / Yolen, Jane. *Wings.* Harcourt, 1991.

SUBJECTS: CURIOSITY—FOLKLORE. GODS AND GODDESSES—FOLKLORE. MYTHOLOGY. OBEDIENCE—FOLKLORE. PANDORA (GREEK MYTHOLOGY). WOMEN—FOLKLORE.

1156 Bushyhead, Robert H., and Kay Thorpe Bannon. *Yonder Mountain: A Cherokee Legend.* **Illus. by Kristina Rodanas. Marshall Cavendish, 2002. 0-7614-5113-7. Unp. Gr. K–4**

To find a worthy person to take his place as leader, elderly Chief Sky sends three young men to the top of a great nearby mountain to see what they find there. Along the way, Black Bear finds valuable stones and Gray Wolf gathers healing herbs and roots, but only Soaring Eagle follows the chief's instructions to go to the mountaintop, though he brings back nothing but a story.

GERM: According to the Foreword by Joseph Bruchac, this is a teaching story that was passed down to each generation in Reverend Robert H. Bushyhead's family. Ask your children to puzzle out what constitutes a teaching story, and what this story has taught them. Why was Soaring Eagle deemed the worthiest? Another teaching story is Bruchac's own retelling of the Abenaki tale *Gluskabe and the Four Wishes.*

RELATED TITLES: Bruchac, Joseph. *The First Strawberries: A Cherokee Story.* Dial, 1993. / Bruchac, Joseph. *Gluskabe and the Four Wishes.* Dutton, 1995. / Bruchac, Joseph, and Gayle Ross. *The Story of the Milky Way: A Cherokee Tale.* Dial, 1995. / Haley, Gail. *Two Bad Boys: A Very Old Cherokee Tale.* Dutton, 1996. / Kimmel, Eric A. *The Three Princes: A Tale from the Middle East.* Holiday House, 1994. / Roop, Peter, and Connie Roop. *Ahyoka and the Talking Leaves.* Lothrop, 1992. / Ross, Gayle. *How Rabbit Tricked Otter and Other Cherokee Trickster Stories.* HarperCollins, 1994. / Ross, Gayle. *How Turtle's Back Was Cracked: A Traditional Cherokee Tale.* Dial, 1995. / Roth, Susan L. *Kanahena: A Cherokee Story.* St. Martin's, 1988. / Rumford, James. *Sequoyah: The Man Who Gave His People Writing.* Houghton Mifflin, 2004.

SUBJECTS: CHEROKEE INDIANS. FOLKLORE—INDIANS OF NORTH AMERICA. FOLKLORE—U.S. LEADERSHIP—FOLKLORE. MOUNTAINS—FOLKLORE.

1157 Byrd, Robert. *Finn MacCoul and His Fearless Wife: A Giant of a Tale from Ireland.* **Illus. by the author. Dutton, 1999. 0-525-45971-5. Unp. Gr. 3–6**

In this full-bodied account of Finn's dealings with the brutish bully Cucullin, Finn's wife Oonagh, who has learned magic from the faeries, first asks Cucullin to turn her house around, away from the wind. Next she feeds him loaves of bread with iron pots in the middle so Cucullin breaks his teeth. With its bright, big, animated pen-and-ink and watercolor pictures based on Celtic illuminated manuscripts, this is a story for all to savor.

GERM: Compare and contrast the other versions of Finn's well-loved tale: *Fin M'Coul, the Giant of Knockmany Hill* by Tomie dePaola and *Mrs. McCool and the Giant Cuhullin* by Jessica Souhami.

RELATED TITLES: Bateman, Teresa. *The Ring of Truth.* Holiday House, 1997. / Behan, Brendan. *The King of Ireland's Son.* Orchard, 1997. / Bertrand, Lynne. *Granite Baby.* Farrar, 2005. / dePaola, Tomie. *Fin M'Coul, the Giant of Knockmany Hill.* Holiday House, 1981. / Greene, Ellin. *Billy Beg and His Bull.* Holiday House, 1994. / Morimoto, Junko. *The Two Bullies.* Crown, 1999. / Souhami, Jessica. *Mrs. McCool and the Giant Cuhullin: An Irish Tale.* Henry Holt, 2002. / Stamm, Claus. *Three Strong Women.* Viking, 1990.

SUBJECTS: FOLKLORE—IRELAND. GIANTS—FOLKLORE. HUMOROUS FOLKLORE. STRENGTH—FOLKLORE. WOMEN—FOLKLORE.

1158 Casanova, Mary. *The Hunter: A Chinese Folktale.* **Illus. by Ed Young. Atheneum, 2000. 0-689-82906-X. Unp. Gr. 2–6**

When hunter Hai Li Bu saves a little snake from a crane, the snake's father, the Dragon King of the Sea, grants Hai Li Bu the ability to understand the language of the animals so that he can be a better hunter for his village. Hearing the birds talk of an impending flood that will destroy the village, Hai Li Bu must make a terrible choice of life and death; if he reveals the source of his knowledge, he will be turned to stone by the Dragon King. Ed Young's spare pastel and gouache paintings on cinnamon-colored paper reflect perfectly the somber, reverential mood.

GERM: Ponder the "What-if" question posed here: What if you could do something to save your family and your whole town, but you would turn to stone as a result. Would you do it? The concepts of personal responsibility and the greater good are deep ones to consider. Other stories with selfless choices or unforgiving consequences include *The Dragon's Pearl* by Julie Lawson, *The Long-Haired Girl* by Doreen Rappaport, and *The Faithful Friend* by Robert D. San Souci.

RELATED TITLES: Lawson, Julie. *The Dragon's Pearl.* Clarion, 1993. / Martin, Rafe. *The Monkey Bridge.* Knopf, 1997. / Mollel, Tololwa M. *The Orphan Boy: A Maasai Story.* Clarion, 1991. / Rappaport, Doreen. *The Long-Haired Girl.* Dial, 1995. / San Souci, Robert D. *The Faithful Friend.* Simon & Schuster, 1995. / Wisniewski, David. *Rain Player.* Houghton Mifflin, 1991. / Yep, Laurence. *The Junior Thunder Lord.* BridgeWater, 1994. / Young, Ed. *Beyond the Great Mountains: A Visual Poem About China.* Chronicle, 2005. / Young, Ed. *Night Visitors.* Philomel, 1995. / Young, Ed. *The Sons of the Dragon King: A Chinese Legend.* Atheneum, 2004.

SUBJECTS: ANIMALS—FOLKLORE. FLOODS—FOLKLORE. FOLKLORE—CHINA. HUNTERS AND HUNTING—FOLKLORE. LANGUAGE—FOLKLORE. RESPONSIBILITY—FOLKLORE. SELFLESSNESS—FOLKLORE.

1159 Climo, Shirley. *Atalanta's Race: A Greek Myth.* **Illus. by Alexander Koshkin. Clarion, 1995. 0-395-67322-4. Unp. Gr. 3–5**

King Iasus orders his newborn daughter cast out on a mountain slope, where she is raised by a she-bear. Not believing in love, the now-grown Atalanta agrees to wed the man who can outrun her in a race, declaring that the penalty for defeat is death.

GERM: Compare this to other Greek myths in which a mortal heroine encounters an angry goddess, including the stories of Arachne and Pandora.

RELATED TITLES: Burleigh, Robert. *Pandora.* Harcourt, 2002. / Climo, Shirley. *Stolen Thunder: A Norse Myth.* Clarion, 1994. / Craft, M. Charlotte. *Cupid and Psyche.* Morrow, 1996. / Fisher, Leonard Everett. *Cyclops.* Holiday House, 1991. / Fisher, Leonard Everett. *Theseus and the Minotaur.* Holiday House, 1988. / Hutton, Warwick. *Odysseus and the Cyclops.* McElderry, 1995. / Kimmel, Eric A. *Rimonah of the Flashing Sword: A North African Tale.* Holiday House, 1995. / Mayer, Marianna. *Iduna and the Magic Apples.* Macmillan, 1988. / Osborne, Mary Pope. *Favorite Greek Myths.* Scholastic, 1989. / San Souci, Robert D. *Fa Mulan: The Story of a Woman Warrior.* Hyperion, 1998. / Waldherr, Kris. *Persephone and the Pomegranate: A Myth from Greece.* Dial, 1993. / Yep, Laurence. *The Khan's Daughter: A Mongolian Folktale.* Scholastic, 1997. / Yolen, Jane. *Atalanta and the Arcadian Beast.* HarperCollins, 2003.

SUBJECTS: APPLES—FOLKLORE. FOLKLORE—GREECE. FRUIT—FOLKLORE. GODS AND GODDESSES—FOLKLORE. MYTHOLOGY. RACING—FOLKLORE. WOMEN—FOLKLORE.

1160   **Climo, Shirley.** *The Irish Cinderlad.* **Illus. by Loretta Krupinski. HarperCollins, 1996. 0-06-024397-X. Unp. Gr. 2–6**

When red-haired herdboy Becan's tattling stepsisters tell his scolding stepmother about the magical speckled bull who has been feeding him, she decides to butcher it. The two escape to the forest where the bull knows he will die; he urges Becan to take his tail and use it when he needs it. With the help of the magical tail, Becan fends off a giant and rescues a princess from a dragon, but loses his big boot in the process.

GERM: Ask your listeners to figure out why this story is considered a Cinderella-like tale and compare and contrast this with other Cinderella stories. Compare Climo's softened retelling with Ellin Greene's more dramatic version, *Billy Beg and His Bull.*

RELATED TITLES: Behan, Brendan. *The King of Ireland's Son.* Orchard, 1997. / Byrd, Robert. *Finn MacCoul and His Fearless Wife: A Giant of a Tale from Ireland.* Dutton, 1999. / Climo, Shirley. *The Egyptian Cinderella.* Crowell, 1989. / Climo, Shirley. *Magic and Mischief: Tales from Cornwall.* Clarion, 1999. / Climo, Shirley. *The Persian Cinderella.* HarperCollins, 1999. / Cooper, Susan. *The Silver Cow: A Welsh Tale.* Atheneum, 1983. / dePaola, Tomie. *Fin M'Coul, the Giant of Knockmany Hill.* Holiday House, 1981. / Greene, Ellin. *Billy Beg and His Bull.* Holiday House, 1994. / Huck, Charlotte. *The Black Bull of Norroway: A Scottish Tale.* Greenwillow, 2001. / Ketteman, Helen. *Bubba the Cowboy Prince.* Scholastic, 1997. / Kimmel, Eric A. *Boots and His Brothers: A Norwegian Tale Retold.* Holiday House, 1992. / Kirstein, Lincoln. *Puss in Boots.* Little, Brown, 1992. / Marcellino, Fred. *Puss in Boots.* Farrar, 1990. / Martin, Claire. *Boots and the Glass Mountain.* Dial, 1992.

SUBJECTS: BOOTS—FOLKLORE. BULLS—FOLKLORE. CINDERELLA STORIES. COWS—FOLKLORE. DRAGONS—FOLKLORE. FAIRY TALES. FOLKLORE—IRELAND. GIANTS—FOLKLORE. PRINCES AND PRINCESSES—FOLKLORE. SHOES—FOLKLORE.

1161   **Climo, Shirley.** *The Little Red Ant and the Great Big Crumb: A Mexican Fable.* **Illus. by Francisco M. Xora. Clarion, 1995. 0-395-70732-3. 39pp. Gr. PreK–2**

A little red ant, who is smaller than her 999 cousins, comes upon a big crumb of *torta,* or cake, that is too heavy for her to lift. So she sets out to find someone strong enough to carry it for her. She asks the lizard, sun, spider, rooster, coyote, and man, and concludes that she, the ant, is truly the strongest of them all.

GERM: Spanish phrases and vocabulary are nicely integrated into the text and there's a glossary and pronunciation guide at the back. Draw story maps of the setting, characters, and action, and act out the whole thing. In the Related Titles list below are variants of this "who is the strongest" tale—from Japan, Korea, China, and Mexico—for comparing and contrasting.

RELATED TITLES: Becker, Bonny. *An Ant's Day Off.* Simon & Schuster, 2003. / Cook, Joel. *The Rat's Daughter.* Boyds Mills, 1993. / Demuth, Patricia Brennan. *Those Amazing Ants.* Macmillan, 1994. / Dorros, Arthur. *Ant Cities.* HarperCollins, 1987. / Dupré, Judith. *The Mouse Bride: A Mayan Folk Tale.* Knopf, 1993. / Farris, Pamela J. *Young Mouse and Elephant: An East African Folktale.* Houghton Mifflin, 1996. / Hoose, Phillip M., and Hannah Hoose. *Hey, Little Ant.* Tricycle, 1998. / Kimmel, Eric A. *The Greatest of All: A Japanese Folktale.* Holiday House, 1991. / Kwon, Holly H. *The Moles and the Mireuk.* Houghton Mifflin, 1993. / McDermott, Gerald. *The Stonecutter: A Japanese Folk Tale.* Puffin, 1978. / Ness, Caroline. "The Mouse-Girl" from *The Ocean of Story: Fairy Tales from India.* Lothrop, 1995. / Nickle, John. *The Ant Bully.* Scholastic, 1999. / Van Allsburg, Chris. *Two Bad Ants.* Houghton Mifflin, 1988. / Young, Ed. *Mouse Match: A Chinese Folktale.* Harcourt, 1997.

SUBJECTS: ANTS—FOLKLORE. CIRCULAR STORIES—FOLKLORE. CREATIVE DRAMA—FOLKLORE. FOLKLORE—MEXICO. INSECTS—FOLKLORE. MULTICULTURAL BOOKS—FOLKLORE. SELF-ESTEEM—FOLKLORE. STRENGTH—FOLKLORE.

1162   **Climo, Shirley.** *Magic and Mischief: Tales from Cornwall.* **Illus. by Anthony Bacon Venti. Clarion, 1999. 0-395-86968-4. 127pp. Gr. 3–6**

In a revised and reillustrated version of Climo's *Piskies, Spriggans, and Other Magical Beings,* ten sprightly folktales from Cornwall, England, introduce magical folk including giants, piskies, spriggans, knackers, fairies, changelings, witches, sea people, ghosts, and a Bucca-boo. After each story is a page of practical advice on how to deal with each creature.

GERM: Compare "The Cornish Teeny-Tiny" with *The Teeny-Tiny Woman,* a picture-book version by Paul Galdone. Read "Duffy and the Bucca" along with Harve and Margot Zemach's Caldecott Medal winner *Duffy and the Devil,* and other variants of the Rumpelstiltskin story, including Virginia Hamilton's *The Girl Who Spun Gold,* Evaline Ness's *Tom Tit Tot,* and Carolyn White's *Whuppity Stoorie.*

RELATED TITLES: Carey, Valerie Scho. *Maggie Mab and the Bogey Beast.* Arcade, 1992. / Climo, Shirley. *The Egyptian Cinderella.* Crowell, 1989. / Climo, Shirley. *The Irish Cinderlad.* HarperCollins, 1996. / Climo, Shirley. *The Korean Cinderella.* HarperCollins, 1993. / Climo, Shirley. *Piskies, Spriggans, and Other Magical Beings: Tales from the Droll-Teller.* Crowell, 1981. / Climo, Shirley. *Someone Saw a Spider: Spider Facts and Folktales.* Crowell, 1985. / Climo, Shirley. *Stolen Thunder: A Norse Myth.* Clarion, 1994. / Galdone, Paul. *The Teeny-Tiny Woman.* Clarion, 1984. / Hamilton, Virginia. *The Girl Who Spun Gold.* Scholastic, 2000. / Lunge-Larsen, Lise. *The Hidden Folk: Stories of Fairies, Dwarves, Selkies, and Other Secret Beings.* Houghton Mifflin, 2004. / Ness, Evaline. *Tom Tit Tot.* Scribner, 1965. / White, Carolyn. *Whuppity Stoorie: A Scottish Folktale.* Putnam, 1997. / Zelinsky, Paul O. *Rumpelstiltskin.* Dutton, 1986. / Zemach, Harve, and Margot Zemach. *Duffy and the Devil.* Farrar, 1986.

SUBJECTS: FAIRIES—FOLKLORE. FOLKLORE—COLLECTIONS. FOLKLORE—ENGLAND. RUMPELSTILTSKIN STORIES. SUPERNATURAL—FOLKLORE.

1163   **Climo, Shirley. *The Persian Cinderella.* Illus. by Robert Florczak. HarperCollins, 1999. 0-06-026765-8. Unp. Gr. 2–6**

Settareh, or "Star", named after the star-shaped birthmark on her cheek, is taunted by her two stepsisters who are jealous of her beauty. When all are invited by Prince Mehrdad to the Royal Palace for the celebration of No Ruz, the New Year, Settareh's father gives her money to buy cloth to make a new dress. Because she spends her coins on almonds and a compelling blue jar, and gives the rest to an old beggar woman, she will have to stay home from the festival. But, of course, that little jar is magic, supplying her with a silk gown and two diamond-studded ankle bracelets, one of which she loses at the palace.

GERM: This Cinderella variant from "The Arabian Nights" has many interesting elements for listeners to note, including the emphasis on women covering their heads so no stranger can look upon their faces; the unseen peri, or fairy, in that little blue jug; and the ways Settareh's stepsisters try to get rid of her so they can marry the prince. Compare it with another Middle Eastern Cinderella tale, *The Golden Sandal* by Rebecca Hickox, from Iraq.

RELATED TITLES: Climo, Shirley. *The Egyptian Cinderella.* Crowell, 1989. / Climo, Shirley. *A Treasury of Princesses: Princess Tales from Around the World.* HarperCollins, 1996. / Coburn, Jewell Reinhart. *Jouanah: A Hmong Cinderella.* Shen's, 1996. / Craft, K. Y. *Cinderella.* SeaStar Books, 2000. / Han, Oki S., and Stephanie Plunkett. *Kongi and Potgi: A Cinderella Story from Korea.* Dial, 1996. / Hickox, Rebecca. *The Golden Sandal: A Middle Eastern Cinderella Story.* Holiday House, 1998. / Jaffe, Nina. *The Way Meat Loves Salt: A Cinderella Story from the Jewish Tradition.* Henry Holt, 1998. / Martin, Rafe. *The Rough-Face Girl.* Putnam, 1992. / Sanderson, Ruth. *Cinderella.* Little, Brown, 2002. / Shepard, Aaron. *Forty Fortunes: A Tale of Iran.* Clarion, 1999. / Sierra, Judy. *The Gift of the Crocodile: A Cinderella Story.* Simon & Schuster, 2000. / Soifer, Margaret, and Irwin Shapiro. *Tenggren's Golden Tales from the Arabian Nights.* Golden, 2003. / Thompson, Lauren. *One Riddle, One Answer.* Scholastic, 2001. / Wilson, Barbara Ker. *Wishbones: A Folk Tale from China.* Bradbury, 1993.

SUBJECTS: ARABIAN NIGHTS. CINDERELLA STORIES. FAIRY TALES. FOLKLORE—IRAN. MULTICULTURAL BOOKS—FOLKLORE.

1164   **Coburn, Jewell Reinhart, adapt. with Tzexa Cherta Lee. *Jouanah: A Hmong Cinderella.* Illus. by Anne Sibley O'Brien. Shen's Books, 1996. 1-885008-01-5. Unp. Gr. 2–5**

In this tender Cinderella story from the Hmong people of Laos, when Jouanah's mother transforms herself into a cow so she can help her husband with their farm, he then marries another woman who works Jouanah from dawn till dark.

GERM: Compare and contrast the motifs in this variant with other Asian retellings, including Shirley Climo's *The Korean Cinderella*, Oki S. Han and Stephanie Plunkett's *Kongi and Potgi: A Cinderella Story from Korea*, Ai-Ling Louie's *Yeh-Shen: A Cinderella Story from China*, and Barbara Ker Wilson's *Wishbones: A Folk Tale from China*.

RELATED TITLES: Climo, Shirley. *The Egyptian Cinderella.* Crowell, 1989. / Climo, Shirley. *The Korean Cinderella.* HarperCollins, 1993. / Climo, Shirley. *The Persian Cinderella.* HarperCollins, 1999. / Craft, K. Y. *Cinderella.* SeaStar Books, 2000. / Han, Oki S., and Stephanie Plunkett. *Kongi and Potgi: A Cinderella Story from Korea.* Dial, 1996. / Hickox, Rebecca. *The Golden Sandal: A Middle Eastern Cinderella Story.* Dial, 1996. / Louie, Ai-Ling. *Yeh-Shen: A Cinderella Story from China.* Philomel, 1982. / Sanderson, Ruth. *Cinderella.* Little, Brown, 2002. / San Souci, Robert D. *Cendrillon: A Caribbean Cinderella.* Simon & Schuster, 1998. / Sierra, Judy. *The Gift of the Crocodile: A Cinderella Story.* Simon & Schuster, 2000. / Wilson, Barbara Ker. *Wishbones: A Folk Tale from China.* Bradbury, 1993.

SUBJECTS: CINDERELLA STORIES. FAIRY TALES. FOLKLORE—LAOS. HMONG—FOLKLORE. MULTICULTURAL BOOKS—FOLKLORE.

1165   Cohen, Barbara. *Robin Hood and Little John*. Illus. by David Ray. Philomel, 1995. 0-399-22732-6. Unp. Gr. 1–4

Off looking for adventure in Sherwood Forest, English outlaw, Robin Hood, encounters a giant of a man astride a log bridge over a stream. The two fight to knock each other into the water and prove who is the better man. In this lighthearted picture-book retelling with hearty forest green- and brown-toned illustrations, the giant John Little becomes known as Little John, Robin Hood's best friend and right-hand man.

GERM: For tellings of more of the tales, also read Margaret Early's stately picture book, *Robin Hood*, and Sarah Hayes's chapter book, *Robin Hood*.

RELATED TITLES: Early, Margaret. *Robin Hood*. Philomel, 1995. / Early, Margaret. *William Tell*. Abrams, 1991. / Fisher, Leonard Everett. *William Tell*. Farrar, 1996. / Hastings, Selina. *Sir Gawain and the Loathly Lady*. Lothrop, 1985. / Hayes, Sarah. *Robin Hood*. Henry Holt, 1989. / Osborne, Mary Pope. *Favorite Medieval Tales*. Scholastic, 1998. / San Souci, Robert D. *Young Arthur*. Doubleday, 1997. / Shannon, Mark. *Gawain and the Green Knight*. Putnam, 1994.

SUBJECTS: FOLKLORE—ENGLAND. LEGENDS. ROBBERS AND OUTLAWS—FOLKLORE. ROBIN HOOD (LEGENDARY CHARACTER).

1166   Craft, M. Charlotte. *Cupid and Psyche*. Illus. by K. Y. Craft. Morrow, 1996. 0-688-13164-6. Unp. Gr. 3–6

Cupid is sent by his mother, Venus, to deploy his arrows to make famed beauty Psyche fall in love with the most frightening creature in the world. Unfortunately, Cupid accidentally nicks himself with his own arrow and falls in love with Psyche himself.

GERM: Compare this ancient Greek myth to its more recent fairy tale variants, "Beauty and the Beast" (from France), "The Black Bull of Norroway" (from Scotland), and "East of the Sun and West of the Moon" (from Norway).

RELATED TITLES: Burleigh, Robert. *Pandora*. Harcourt, 2002. / Climo, Shirley. *Atalanta's Race: A Greek Myth*. Clarion, 1995. / Craft, Charlotte. *King Midas and the Golden Touch*. Morrow, 1999. / Dasent, George Webbe. *East O' the Sun and West O' the Moon*. Illus. by P. J. Lynch. Candlewick, 1992. / Fisher, Leonard Everett. *Cyclops*. Holiday House, 1991. / Fisher, Leonard Everett. *Theseus and the Minotaur*. Holiday House, 1988. / Hague, Kathleen. *East of the Sun and West of the Moon*. Harcourt, 1989. / Huck, Charlotte. *The Black Bull of Norroway: A Scottish Tale*. Greenwillow, 2001. / Hutton, Warwick. *Odysseus and the Cyclops*. McElderry, 1995. / Mayer, Marianna. *Baba Yaga and Vasilisa the Brave*. Morrow, 1994. / Mayer, Marianna. *Beauty and the Beast*. Four Winds, 1978. / Osborne, Mary Pope. *Favorite Greek Myths*. Scholastic, 1989. / Waldherr, Kris. *Persephone and the Pomegranate: A Myth from Greece*. Dial, 1993. / Yolen, Jane. *Pegasus, the Flying Horse*. Dutton, 1998. / Yolen, Jane. *Wings*. Harcourt, 1991.

SUBJECTS: BEAUTY—FOLKLORE. CUPID. FOLKLORE—GREECE. GODS AND GODDESSES—FOLKLORE. LOVE—FOLKLORE. MYTHOLOGY. PSYCHE.

1167   Cummings, Pat. *Ananse and the Lizard: A West African Tale*. Illus. by the author. Henry Holt, 2002. 0-8050-6476-1. Unp. Gr. PreK–3

In this comical tale from Ghana, Ananse the Spider plans to win the hand of the human chief's daughter by guessing her name. When he overhears it from the girl herself, he congratulates himself on his cleverness. Unfortunately, Ananse, the consummate trickster, gets tricked himself when he entrusts Lizard to be his messenger to the chief, and Lizard marries the girl instead. Dynamic full-bleed watercolor, gouache, and color pencil illustrations explode off the page with their up-close look at the animal kingdom.

GERM: The last page explains why lizards stretch their necks back and forth, making this trickster tale a pourquoi (how and why) tale as well. Compare and contrast other Anansi stories, including those by Verna Aardema and Eric A. Kimmel below. See what happens when another trickster, Bruh Rabbit, wants to marry the king's daughter in Alice McGill's *Sure as Sunrise*.

RELATED TITLES: Aardema, Verna. *Anansi Does the Impossible! An Ashanti Tale*. Atheneum, 1997. / Aardema, Verna. *Anansi Finds a Fool*. Dial, 1992. / dePaola, Tomie. *Strega Nona*. Simon & Schuster, 1979. / Haley, Gail E. *A Story, a Story*. Atheneum, 1970. / Kimmel, Eric A. *Anansi and the Magic Stick*. Holiday House, 2001. / Kimmel, Eric A. *Anansi and the Moss-Covered Rock*. Holiday House, 1990. / Kimmel, Eric A. *Anansi and the Talking Melon*. Holiday House, 1994. / Kimmel, Eric A. *Anansi Goes Fishing*. Holiday House, 1992. / McDermott, Gerald. *Zomo the Rabbit: A Trickster Tale from West Africa*. Harcourt, 1992. / McGill, Alice. *Sure as Sunrise: Stories of Bruh Rabbit and His Walkin' Talkin' Friends*. Houghton Mifflin, 2004. / Mollel, Tololwa M. *Ananse's Feast: An Ashanti Tale*. Clarion, 1997.

SUBJECTS: ANANSI (LEGENDARY CHARACTER). ANIMALS—FOLKLORE. FOLKLORE—AFRICA, WEST. FOLKLORE—GHANA. HUMOROUS FOLKLORE. LIZARDS—FOLKLORE. MULTICULTURAL BOOKS—FOLKLORE. POURQUOI TALES. SPIDERS—FOLKLORE. TRICKSTER TALES.

1168   **Curry, Jane Louise.** *The Wonderful Sky Boat: and Other Native American Tales of the Southeast.* **Illus. by James Watts. McElderry, 2001. 0-689-83595-7. 143pp. Gr. 3–8**
This sparkling collection comprises 27 brief but memorable tales about animals and people—including creation and pourquoi stories—that are ripe for sharing as read-alouds or for storytelling.
GERM: Source notes at the end of the book describe each of the 16 tribes represented in the stories. Pair the trickster tales about Rabbit with those in Gretchen Will Mayo's collections, *Big Trouble for Tricky Rabbit* and *Here Comes Tricky Rabbit*. Compare Gail Haley's picture book retelling of the Cherokee tale *Two Bad Boys* with both "Lodge Boy, Wild Boy, and the Monster Woman" and "Keeper of the Animals" in Curry's collection.
RELATED TITLES: Bruchac, Joseph. *The Boy Who Lived with the Bears and Other Iroquois Stories.* Harper-Collins, 1995. / Brusca, María Cristina, and Tona Wilson. *When Jaguar Ate the Moon: And Other Stories About Animals and Plants of the Americas.* Henry Holt, 1995. / Curry, Jane Louise. *Hold Up the Sky: and Other Native American Tales from Texas and the Southern Plains.* McElderry, 2003. / Curry, Jane Louise. *Turtle Island: Tales of the Algonquian Nations.* McElderry, 1999. / Haley, Gail. *Two Bad Boys: A Very Old Cherokee Tale.* Dutton, 1996. / Hausman, Gerald. *How Chipmunk Got Tiny Feet: Native American Animal Origin Stories.* HarperCollins, 1995. / Max, Jill. *Spider Spins a Story: Fourteen Legends from Native America.* Rising Moon, 1997. / Mayo, Gretchen Will. *Big Trouble for Tricky Rabbit.* Walker, 1994. / Mayo, Gretchen Will. *Here Comes Tricky Rabbit.* Walker, 1994. / Ross, Gayle. *How Rabbit Tricked Otter and Other Cherokee Trickster Stories.* HarperCollins, 1994.
SUBJECTS: ANIMALS—FOLKLORE. FOLKLORE—COLLECTIONS. FOLKLORE—INDIANS OF NORTH AMERICA. FOLKLORE—SOUTHERN STATES. FOLKLORE—U.S. POURQUOI TALES.

1169   **Demi.** *Buddha Stories.* **Illus. by the author. Henry Holt, 1997. 0-8050-4886-3. Unp. Gr. 2–6**
These 11 brief Jataka tales, or parables, taken from the 550 surviving stories told by Buddha 2,500 years ago, center around animals and people who learn about compassion, love, wisdom, and kindness. Printed on dark indigo paper with illustrations and text done in fine lines of gold, the arresting oversized format was modeled after the world's first printed book, a Buddhist *sutra*, or teaching.
GERM: Readers will find similarities to fables they know, from Aesop or La Fontaine, and can discuss each moral or teaching before you reveal the one printed at the end of the tale. "The Lion King" has been retold by Rafe Martin in *Foolish Rabbit's Big Mistake* and Jan Thornhill's *The Rumor,* and you can compare "The Monkey King" with Martin's picture-book version, *The Monkey Bridge.* Compare "The Turtle and the Geese" to the title story in *Tortoise's Flying Lesson,* an Aesop's fable retold by Margaret Mayo.
RELATED TITLES: Demi. *Buddha.* Henry Holt, 1996. / Demi. *The Dragon's Tale and Other Animal Fables of the Chinese Zodiac.* Henry Holt, 1996. / Demi. *The Hungry Coat: A Tale from Turkey.* McElderry, 2004. / Galdone, Paul. *The Monkey and the Crocodile: A Jataka Tale from India.* Clarion, 1969. / Hodges, Margaret. *The Boy Who Drew Cats.* Holiday House, 2002. / Martin, Rafe. *Foolish Rabbit's Big Mistake.* Putnam, 1985. / Martin, Rafe. *The Monkey Bridge.* Knopf, 1997. / Mayo, Margaret. *Tortoise's Flying Lesson: Animal Stories.* Harcourt, 1995. / Morpurgo, Michael. *The McElderry Book of Aesop's Fables.* McElderry, 2005. / Muth, Jon J. *Zen Shorts.* Scholastic, 2005. / Simonds, Nina, and Leslie Swartz. *Moonbeams, Dumplings and Dragon Boats: A Treasury of Chinese Holiday Tales, Activities and Recipes.* Harcourt, 2002. / Young, Ed. *Cat and Rat: The Legend of the Chinese Zodiac.* Henry Holt, 1995.
SUBJECTS: ANIMALS—FOLKLORE. BUDDHA AND BUDDHISM. FABLES. FOLKLORE—CHINA. FOLKLORE—COLLECTIONS. JATAKA STORIES.

1170   **Demi.** *The Donkey and the Rock.* **Illus. by the author. Henry Holt, 1999. 0-8050-5959-8. Unp. Gr. 1–4**
Whose fault is it when a poor Tibetan man's donkey knocks over and breaks a jar of oil that his neighbor is bringing to market? When the two men can't settle their quarrel, they go to the king for help; he arrests both the donkey and the rock upon which the jar was perched and puts them on trial. Luminous, delicate paintings done in gouache, ink, and watercolor evoke the breathtaking Tibetan setting of this gently humorous tale, which, according to the Author's Note, originated in India in 550 B.C.

GERM: Midway through the story, ask your group to brainstorm possible solutions to the men's dilemma. Afterward, ask them to discuss the judge's ruling and define "idle curiosity." How did the king make use of the spectator's idle curiosity? See how two other men settle their differences in *Yoshi's Feast* by Kimiko Kajikawa, when Sabu wants to charge Yoshi money for enjoying the aroma of Sabu's broiled eels.

RELATED TITLES: Demi. *The Empty Pot.* Henry Holt, 1990. / Demi. *The Greatest Treasure.* Scholastic, 1998. / Egan, Tim. *The Trial of Cardigan Jones.* Houghton Mifflin, 2004. / Kajikawa, Kimiko. *Yoshi's Feast.* DK Ink, 2000. / Sís, Peter. *Tibet: Through the Red Box.* Farrar, 1998.

SUBJECTS: DONKEYS—FOLKLORE. FOLKLORE—CHINA. FOLKLORE—TIBET. KINGS AND RULERS—FOLKLORE. PROBLEM SOLVING—FOLKLORE. ROCKS—FOLKLORE. TRIALS—FOLKLORE.

1171 Demi. *The Dragon's Tale and Other Animal Fables of the Chinese Zodiac.* **Illus. by the author. Henry Holt, 1996. 0-8050-3446-3. Unp. Gr. 2–6**

Twelve short fables, one for each animal in the Chinese zodiac, come with morals that all can ponder and discuss. Each fable is printed within a circular border of brilliantly colored, delicately painted scenes from the story, with an accompanying full-page circular illustration on the facing page.

GERM: Have listeners break into small groups to discuss and write down their own morals for each story, which they can then read aloud and compare with the printed one. All will marvel at Demi's note on the copyright page describing the ingredients she used in her paintings. Other Chinese zodiac tales include Eric A. Kimmel's *The Rooster's Antlers* and Ed Young's *Cat and Rat*, which explains how the zodiac came to be.

RELATED TITLES: Bader, Barbara. *Aesop and Company.* Houghton Mifflin, 1991. / Calmenson, Stephanie. *The Children's Aesop.* Doubleday, 1988. / Demi. *Buddha Stories.* Henry Holt, 1996. / Gatti, Anne. *Aesop's Fables.* Harcourt, 1992. / Kimmel, Eric A. *The Rooster's Antlers: A Story of the Chinese Zodiac.* Holiday House, 1999. / Morpurgo, Michael. *The McElderry Book of Aesop's Fables.* McElderry, 2005. / Paxton, Tom. *Belling the Cat and Other Aesop's Fables: Retold in Verse.* Morrow, 1990. / Pinkney, Jerry. *Aesop's Fables.* Illus. by Jerry Pinkney. Seastar, 2000. / Simonds, Nina, and Leslie Swartz. *Moonbeams, Dumplings and Dragon Boats: A Treasury of Chinese Holiday Tales, Activities and Recipes.* Harcourt, 2002. / Ward, Helen. *The Rooster and the Fox.* Millbrook, 2003. / Young, Ed. *Cat and Rat: The Legend of the Chinese Zodiac.* Henry Holt, 1995.

SUBJECTS: ANIMALS—FOLKLORE. CALENDARS—FOLKLORE. FABLES. FOLKLORE—CHINA. FOLKLORE—COLLECTIONS. MULTICULTURAL BOOKS—FOLKLORE. ZODIAC—FOLKLORE.

1172 Demi. *The Greatest Treasure.* **Illus. by the author. Scholastic, 1998. 0-590-31339-8. Unp. Gr. 1–5**

Too intent on counting his money to pay attention to his own five sons, Pang is also annoyed by the sounds of laughter and music that come from the house of Li, a poor but happy farmer who lives nearby with his five daughters. Figuring that Li would not have time to make so much noise playing his flute if he were rich, Pang gives the man a large bag of gold coins. Pretty soon, Li is too busy counting and worrying over his money to play his flute or enjoy his children until his wife helps him come to his senses. Demi's colorful and intricate pen-and-ink illustrations in large circular panels seem to float on a background of what looks like a pale green brocade cloth.

GERM: Before reading this cautionary folktale from China, ask your listeners what the title might refer to. Both before and after you read the story, ask them, "What is the greatest treasure in life?" Compare and contrast Pang's wife's proverb—"With money you are a dragon, without it you are a worm"—with Li's wife's proverb—"He who has heaven in his heart is never poor." What do these mean? Discuss which one speaks best to your own lives. And then talk about the meaning of this one: "Gold and silver have their price, but peace and happiness are priceless." Demi's *The Hungry Coat* explores some of the same themes.

RELATED TITLES: Chang, Margaret, and Raymond Chang. *The Beggar's Magic: A Chinese Tale.* McElderry, 1997. / Demi. *The Hungry Coat: A Tale from Turkey.* McElderry, 2004. / Demi. *The Magic Goldfish: A Russian Folktale by Aleksandr Pushkin.* Henry Holt, 1995. / Demi. *One Grain of Rice: A Mathematical Folktale.* Scholastic, 1997. / Grimm, Jacob. *The Fisherman and His Wife.* Illus. by Margot Zemach. Farrar, 1980. / Kajikawa, Kimiko. *Yoshi's Feast.* DK Ink, 2000. / Long, Jan Freeman. *The Bee and the Dream: A Japanese Tale.* Dutton, 1996. / MacDonald, Margaret Read. *The Old Woman Who Lived in a Vinegar Bottle.* August House, 1995. / Shepard, Aaron. *The Gifts of Wali Dad: A Tale of India and Pakistan.* Atheneum, 1995. / Wells, Ruth. *The Farmer and the Poor God.* Simon & Schuster, 1996.

SUBJECTS: FOLKLORE—CHINA. GREED—FOLKLORE. HAPPINESS—FOLKLORE. MONEY—FOLKLORE. WEALTH—FOLKLORE.

1173 Demi. *The Hungry Coat: A Tale from Turkey.* **Illus. by the author. McElderry, 2004. 0-689-84680-0. Unp. Gr. 1–6**

After helping to catch a wayward little goat, Nasrettin Hoca does not have time to change his worn-out, oily, smelly coat before he heads off to a banquet at the home of a rich friend. Ostracized for his appearance, he goes home, changes into a fine new silk coat, and heads back to the party, where he feeds his dinner to his coat. Demi's ornate gold-infused paintings, in the style of Turkish miniatures, bring out the humor and humanity of her wise take on an old story.

GERM: Naturally, you'll want to discuss Nasrettin's motives in feeding his dinner to his coat, and figure out what life lessons he is offering to us. As he says, "If you want to look deeply, look at the man and not at his coat. You can change the coat, but you cannot change the man." What does this final quote mean?: "He who wears heaven in his heart is always well dressed." For more tales about the Turkish wise man, the Hoca or Hodja, go to: <www.story-lovers.com/listshodjastories.html>. Of course you'll want to tie this into Demi's *The Emperor's New Clothes* and to Simms Taback's Caldecott winner, *Joseph Had a Little Overcoat*. Meet a similar character in the collection of Egyptian tales *Goha the Wise Fool* by Denys Johnson-Davies.

RELATED TITLES: Crouch, Marcus. *Ivan: Stories of Old Russia.* Oxford University, 1989. / Demi. *Buddha Stories.* Henry Holt, 1997. / Demi. *The Emperor's New Clothes: A Tale Set in China.* McElderry, 2000. / Demi. *The Empty Pot.* Henry Holt, 1990. / Demi. *The Greatest Treasure.* Scholastic, 1998. / Demi. *One Grain of Rice: A Mathematical Folktale.* Scholastic, 1997. / Gilman, Phoebe. *Something from Nothing.* Scholastic, 1993. / Johnson-Davies, Denys. *Goha the Wise Fool.* Philomel, 2005. / Price, Christine. *Sixty at a Blow.* Dutton, 1968. / Taback, Simms. *Joseph Had a Little Overcoat.* Viking, 1999. / Walker, Barbara K. *A Treasury of Turkish Folktales for Children.* Shoe String, 1988. / Walker, Barbara K. *Watermelons, Walnuts, and the Wisdom of Allah, and Other Tales of the Hoca.* Texas Tech University Press, 1991. / Yep, Laurence. *The Junior Thunder Lord.* BridgeWater, 1994.

SUBJECTS: CLOTHING AND DRESS—FOLKLORE. COATS—FOLKLORE. FOLKLORE—TURKEY. FRIENDSHIP—FOLKLORE. GOATS—FOLKLORE. HUMOROUS FOLKLORE. MULTICULTURAL BOOKS. NASREDDIN HOCA (LEGENDARY CHARACTER).

1174 Demi. *King Midas: The Golden Touch.* **Illus. by the author. McElderry, 2002. 0-689-83297-4. Unp. Gr. 2–6**

Two droll Midas tales are retold in Demi's opulent, gold-loaded version of the Greek myth, with each ravishing, richly colored illustration bordered top and bottom with handsome trim in gold and black Greek geometric patterns. First there's the account of how King Midas judges a music contest between the great god Apollo, playing heavenly music on his lyre, and the little god Pan, blowing discordant notes on his pipes. Furious at losing, Apollo gives the foolish king donkey's ears, which Midas keeps hidden from everyone except the royal barber, who can't keep his secret. Next, granted a gift from Dionysus, Midas wishes for everything he touches to turn to gold, and we all know that doesn't work out so well, either.

GERM: Compare the lighthearted tone of Demi's version with the more contemplative one of Jan Mark's *The Midas Touch*. Then make some modern-day connections with Patrick Skene Catling's fiction book, *The Chocolate Touch*, where everything that young John Midas touches to his lips turns to chocolate.

RELATED TITLES: Burleigh, Robert. *Hercules.* Harcourt, 1999. / Burleigh, Robert. *Pandora.* Harcourt, 2002. / Catling, Patrick Skene. *The Chocolate Touch.* Morrow, 1979. / Climo, Shirley. *Atalanta's Race: A Greek Myth.* Clarion, 1995. / Craft, M. Charlotte. *Cupid and Psyche.* Morrow, 1996. / Craft, Charlotte. *King Midas and the Golden Touch.* Morrow, 1999. / Fisher, Leonard Everett. *Cyclops.* Holiday House, 1991. / Fisher, Leonard Everett. *Theseus and the Minotaur.* Holiday House, 1988. / Hutton, Warwick. *Odysseus and the Cyclops.* McElderry, 1995. / Mayer, Marianna. *Iduna and the Magic Apples.* Macmillan, 1988. / Osborne, Mary Pope. *Favorite Greek Myths.* Scholastic, 1989. / Waldherr, Kris. *Persephone and the Pomegranate: A Myth from Greece.* Dial, 1993. / Yolen, Jane. *Pegasus, the Flying Horse.* Dutton, 1998. / Yolen, Jane. *Wings.* Harcourt, 1991.

SUBJECTS: CONTESTS—FOLKLORE. FOLKLORE—GREECE. GODS AND GODDESSES—FOLKLORE. GOLD—FOLKLORE. MIDAS (LEGENDARY CHARACTER). MYTHOLOGY. SECRETS—FOLKLORE. WISHES—FOLKLORE.

1175 Demi. *One Grain of Rice: A Mathematical Folktale.* **Scholastic, 1997. 0-590-93998-X. Unp. Gr. 2–6**

In a rice-farming province of India, the raja collects the farmers' rice in his royal storehouses, promising to feed everyone equitably in time of famine. During a bad year when the people are starving, the raja unthinkingly orders a feast for himself. Rani, a clever village girl, happens upon a plan to teach the greedy man a lesson and feed the people. When she is offered a reward from the raja for a good deed, Rani asks for a single grain of rice to be doubled each day for 30 days. By the 30th day, with the storehouse emptied of over a billion grains of rice, the raja promises to mend his ways.

GERM: A final page displays a grid of the result of each day's doubling, which will translate into a splendid math lesson on the binary sequence. Other variants of this story include David Birch's *The King's Chessboard*, Hugh William McKibbon's *The Token Gift*, and Helena Clare Pittman's Chinese folktale, *A Grain of Rice*. Meet another outspoken girl who teaches a king a lesson in generosity in *Rumpelstiltskin's Daughter* by Diane Stanley.

RELATED TITLES: Birch, David. *The King's Chessboard*. Dial, 1988. / Day, Nancy Raines. *Double Those Wheels*. Dutton, 2003. / Demi. *The Greatest Treasure*. Scholastic, 1998. / Demi. *The Hungry Coat: A Tale from Turkey*. McElderry, 2004. / Dodds, Dayle Ann. *Minnie's Diner*. Candlewick, 2004. / McKibbon, Hugh William. *The Token Gift*. Annick, 1996. / Pittman, Helena Clare. *A Grain of Rice*. Hastings House, 1986. / Stanley, Diane. *Rumpelstiltskin's Daughter*. Morrow, 1997.

SUBJECTS: FOLKLORE—INDIA. KINGS AND RULERS—FOLKLORE. MATHEMATICS—FOLKLORE. MULTICULTURAL BOOKS—FOLKLORE. MULTIPLICATION—FOLKLORE. RICE—FOLKLORE.

1176 dePaola, Tomie. *Adelita: A Mexican Cinderella Story.* **Illus. by the author. Putnam, 2002. 0-399-23866-2. Unp. Gr. 1–6**

After Adelita's mother dies, her father marries a widow with two daughters. When he in turn dies, those three treat Adelita harshly, even sending away her beloved Esperanza, the housekeeper who raised her.

GERM: The glossary will help with the translation and pronunciation of the many Spanish phrases. Compare and contrast the many versions of Cinderella retellings from the Americas, from Native American to Appalachian, to determine what the stories have in common.

RELATED TITLES: Compton, Joanne. *Ashpet: An Appalachian Tale*. Holiday House, 1994. / Craft, K. Y. *Cinderella*. SeaStar Books, 2000. / Ehrlich, Amy. *Cinderella*. Illus. by Susan Jeffers. Dutton, 2004. / Hooks, William H. *Moss Gown*. Clarion, 1987. / Hughes, Shirley. *Ella's Big Chance: A Jazz-Age Cinderella*. Simon & Schuster, 2004. / Lowell, Susan. *Cindy Ellen: A Wild Western Cinderella*. Orchard, 1997. / Martin, Rafe. *The Rough-Face Girl*. Putnam, 1992. / Pollock, Penny. *The Turkey Girl*. Little, Brown, 1996. / Sanderson, Ruth. *Cinderella*. Little, Brown, 2002. / San Souci, Robert D. *Cendrillon: A Caribbean Cinderella*. Simon & Schuster, 1998. / San Souci, Robert D. *The Faithful Friend*. Simon & Schuster, 1995. / San Souci, Robert D. *Sootface: An Ojibwa Cinderella Story*. Doubleday, 1994. / Schroeder, Alan. *Smoky Mountain Rose: An Appalachian Cinderella*. Dial, 1997.

SUBJECTS: CINDERELLA STORIES. FAIRY TALES. FOLKLORE—MEXICO. FOLKLORE, HISPANIC. MULTICULTURAL BOOKS—FOLKLORE. SPANISH LANGUAGE.

1177 DeSpain, Pleasant. *Thirty-three Multicultural Tales to Tell.* **Illus. by Joe Shlichta. August House, 1993. 0-87483-265-9. 126pp. Gr. K–6**

The simply told stories in this amiable round-the-world collection are full of discussable moments, people and animals who discover a thing or two about themselves and the nature of the world, and rascals and tricksters who learn their lessons.

GERM: Not only are these stories entertaining to read, they're brief and easy to learn for the storyteller, either adult or child. For more tellable tales, see *How and Why Stories* by Martha Hamilton and Mitch Weiss.

RELATED TITLES: Aardema, Verna. *Misoso: Once upon a Time Tales from Africa*. Knopf, 1994. / Baumgartner, Barbara. *Crocodile! Crocodile! Stories Told Around the World*. DK, 1994. / Brusca, María Cristina, and Tona Wilson. *When Jaguar Ate the Moon: And Other Stories About Animals and Plants of the Americas*. Henry Holt, 1995. / Cohn, Amy L. *From Sea to Shining Sea: A Treasury of American Folklore and Folk Songs*. Scholastic, 1993. / Hamilton, Martha, and Mitch Weiss. *How and Why Stories: World Tales Kids Can Read and Tell*. August House, 1999. / MacDonald, Margaret Read. *Peace Tales: World Folktales to Talk About*. Shoe String, 1992. / Medlicott, Mary. *Tales for Telling: From Around the World*. Kingfisher, 1992.

SUBJECTS: FOLKLORE—COLLECTIONS. MULTICULTURAL BOOKS—FOLKLORE. STORIES TO TELL. STORYTELLING.

1178 Diakité, Baba Wagué. *The Hatseller and the Monkeys: A West African Folktale.* **Illus. by the author. Scholastic, 1999. 0-590-96069-5. Unp. Gr. PreK–2**

Stopping under a mango tree for a nap, hat seller BaMusa is horrified when he wakes up and finds all his hats are gone, stolen by monkeys up in the tree. The fabulous and comical illustrations are painted on ceramic tile, and each page has a border of tiny painted monkey silhouettes.

GERM: Your listeners will revel in the many chantable refrains, especially "Ay manou!" which, as close as I can translate it into English, means "Oy vey!" Make and decorate cone hats and act out the story. Of course, you'll want to compare and contrast this African folktale with the perennial picture-book version, *Caps for Sale* by Esphyr Slobodkina.

RELATED TITLES: Anholt, Catherine, and Laurence Anholt. *Chimp and Zee.* Putnam, 2001. / Christelow, Eileen. *Five Little Monkeys Jumping on the Bed.* Clarion, 1989. (And others in the Five Little Monkeys series.) / Diakité, Baba Wagué. *The Hunterman and the Crocodile.* Scholastic, 1997. / Echewa, T. Obinkaram. *The Magic Tree: A Folktale from Nigeria.* Morrow, 1999. / Goode, Diane. *Monkey Mo Goes to Sea.* Blue Sky/Scholastic, 2002. / Koller, Jackie French. *One Monkey Too Many.* Scholastic, 1999. / McKissack, Patricia C., and Robert L. McKissack. *Itching and Twitching: A Nigerian Folktale.* Scholastic, 2003. / Medearis, Angela Shelf. *Too Much Talk.* Candlewick, 1995. / Perkins, Al. *Hand, Hand, Fingers, Thumb.* Random House, 1969. / Rey, H. A. *Curious George.* Houghton Mifflin, 1993. (And others in the Curious George series.) / Slobodkina, Esphyr. *Caps for Sale.* HarperCollins, 1947.

SUBJECTS: CHANTABLE REFRAIN—FOLKLORE. CREATIVE DRAMA—FOLKLORE. FOLKLORE—AFRICA, WEST. FOLKLORE—MALI. HATS—FOLKLORE. HUMOROUS FOLKLORE. MONKEYS—FOLKLORE. MULTICULTURAL BOOKS—FOLKLORE.

1179 Diakité, Baba Wagué. *The Magic Gourd.* **Illus. by the author. Scholastic, 2003. 0-439-43960-4. Unp. Gr. 1–4**

As a reward for freeing a chameleon from a thorny bush, Dogo Zan (Brother Rabbit) is given a gourd that fills itself with food and water when commanded, a gift that greedy Mansa Jugu, the king, finds irresistible.

GERM: Discuss this final lesson: "As for Rabbit and Chameleon, they have always understood that loyal friendships are the true treasures that make one rich." Read aloud the author's notes at the back of the book, where you will find interesting ideas for designing mud cloth patterns and composing a praise song, as well as finding out about the author's childhood in Mali.

RELATED TITLES: Cowley, Joy. *Chameleon, Chameleon.* Scholastic, 2005. / Diakité, Baba Wagué. *The Hatseller and the Monkeys.* Scholastic, 1999. / Diakité, Baba Wagué. *The Hunterman and the Crocodile.* Scholastic, 1997. / Duff, Maggie. *Rum Pum Pum.* Macmillan, 1978. / Galdone, Paul. *The Table, the Donkey and the Stick.* McGraw-Hill, 1976. / Ho, Minfong. *Brother Rabbit: A Cambodian Tale.* Lothrop, 1997. / Jenkins, Martin. *Chameleons Are Cool.* Candlewick, 1997. / Kimmel, Eric A. *The Valiant Red Rooster: A Story from Hungary.* Holt, 1995. / Martin, James. *Chameleons: Dragons in the Trees.* Crown, 1991. / Mwenye Hadithi. *Crafty Chameleon.* Little, Brown, 1987. / Stevens, Janet. *Tops and Bottoms.* Harcourt, 1995.

SUBJECTS: CHAMELEONS—FOLKLORE. FOLKLORE—AFRICA, WEST. FOLKLORE—MALI. KINGS AND RULERS—FOLKLORE. MULTICULTURAL BOOKS—FOLKLORE. RABBITS—FOLKLORE.

1180 Downard, Barry. *The Little Red Hen.* **Illus. by the author. Simon & Schuster, 2004. 0-689-85962-7. Unp. Gr. PreK–1**

The text may be straightforward and traditional, but Downard's hilarious photo-illustrated pictures are anything but standard, with a bespectacled, wellington boot-wearing hen, and a duck, pig, and cat who would rather play cards, shoot pool, or watch TV than give her a hand with the bread-baking.

GERM: Retell and act out this tale, and then compare and contrast it with Helen Ketteman's *Armadilly Chili*, a version set in the Southwest. Jane Wattenberg's *Henny-Penny* is also photo-illustrated and funny as all get-out.

RELATED TITLES: Cazet, Denys. *Elvis the Rooster Almost Goes to Heaven.* HarperCollins, 2003. / Feldman, Thea. *Who You Callin' Chicken?* Abrams, 2003. / Galdone, Paul. *The Little Red Hen.* Clarion, 1979. / Hobson, Sally. *Chicken Little.* Simon & Schuster, 1994. / Kellogg, Steven. *Chicken Little.* Morrow, 1985. / Ketteman, Helen. *Armadilly Chili.* Albert Whitman, 2004. / Paul, Ann Whitford. *Mañana, Iguana.* Holiday House, 2004. / Stevens, Janet, and Susan Stevens Crummel. *Cook-a-Doodle-Doo!* Harcourt, 1999. / Sturges, Philemon. *The Little Red Hen (Makes a Pizza).* Dutton, 1999. / Wattenberg, Jane. *Henny-Penny.* Scholastic, 2000.

SUBJECTS: ANIMALS—FOLKLORE. BREAD—FOLKLORE. CHANTABLE REFRAIN—FOLKLORE. CHICKENS—FOLKLORE. COOKERY—FOLKLORE. COOPERATION—FOLKLORE. CREATIVE DRAMA—FOLKLORE. FOOD—FOLKLORE. LITTLE RED HEN.

1181 Egielski, Richard. *The Gingerbread Boy.* **Illus. by the author. HarperCollins, 1997. 0-06-026030-0. Unp. Gr. PreK–1**

The talking cookie's loose in New York City! Chased by a rat, some construction workers, street musicians, and a police officer on horseback, the gingerbread guy meets his end, thanks to a sly fox, in Central Park.

GERM: Just right to act out, this contemporary urban version of the classic chasing story even includes a gingerbread cookie recipe. You can also compare how the setting affects this version and that of the Southwest-set *The Runaway Tortilla* by Eric A. Kimmel.

RELATED TITLES: Aylesworth, Jim. *Aunt Pitty Patty's Piggy.* Scholastic, 1998. / Aylesworth, Jim. *The Gingerbread Man.* Scholastic, 1998. / Aylesworth, Jim. *The Tale of Tricky Fox: A New England Trickster Tale.* Scholastic, 2001. / Cauley, Lorinda Bryan. *The Pancake Boy: An Old Norwegian Folk Tale.* Putnam, 1988. / Compestine, Ying Chang. *The Runaway Rice Cake.* Simon & Schuster, 2001. / Cook, Scott. *The Gingerbread Boy.* Knopf, 1987. / Esterl, Arnica. *The Fine Round Cake.* Four Winds, 1991. / Kimmel, Eric A. *The Gingerbread Man.* Holiday House, 1993. / Kimmel, Eric A. *The Runaway Tortilla.* Winslow, 2000. / Palatini, Margie. *Three French Hens.* Illus. by Richard Egielski. Hyperion, 2005. / Palatini, Margie. *The Web Files.* Illus. by Richard Egielski. Hyperion, 2001. / Priceman, Marjorie. *Froggie Went a-Courting.* Little, Brown, 2000. / Sawyer, Ruth. *Journey Cake, Ho!* Puffin, 1978. / Wattenberg, Jane. *Henny-Penny.* Scholastic, 2000.

SUBJECTS: CENTRAL PARK (NEW YORK, N.Y.). CHANTABLE REFRAIN—FOLKLORE. CREATIVE DRAMA—FOLKLORE. FOLKLORE. FOOD—FOLKLORE. GINGERBREAD BOY. HUMOROUS FOLKLORE. NEW YORK CITY—FOLKLORE. SEQUENCE STORIES—FOLKLORE. STORIES TO TELL.

1182 **Ehlert, Lois.** *Cuckoo / Cucú: A Mexican Folktale / Un Cuento Folklórico Mexicano.* **Illus. by the author. Harcourt, 1997. 0-15-200274-X. Unp. Gr. PreK–3**
Beautiful, lazy Cuckoo irritates the other birds with her lovely but incessant singing until the day she saves them from a fire that scorches her feathers black and turns her voice hoarse. This colorful and graphically arresting pourquoi tale of the Mayan Indians is told in English and Spanish and has stunning paper collage illustrations.

GERM: Compare Cuckoo's plight with that of another self-sacrificing bird, Tico, in Leo Lionni's *Tico and the Golden Wings.* See why owls look the way they do in *Owl Eyes,* a Mohawk Indian pourquoi tale retold by Frieda Gates.

RELATED TITLES: Bruchac, Joseph. *The Great Ball Game: A Muskogee Story.* Dial, 1994. / Carey, Valerie Scho. *Quail Song: A Pueblo Indian Tale.* Putnam, 1990. / Climo, Shirley. *King of the Birds.* HarperCollins, 1988. / Ehlert, Lois. *Moon Rope: A Peruvian Folktale.* Harcourt, 1992. / Ehlert, Lois. *Waiting for Wings.* Harcourt, 2001. / Gates, Frieda. *Owl Eyes.* Lothrop, 1994. / Lionni, Leo. *Tico and the Golden Wings.* Knopf, 1987. / McDermott, Gerald. *Raven: A Trickster Tale from the Pacific Northwest.* Harcourt, 1993. / Maddern, Eric. *Rainbow Bird: An Aboriginal Folktale from Northern Australia.* Little, Brown, 1993. / Troughton, Joanna. *How the Birds Changed Their Feathers: A South American Indian Folk Tale.* Bedrick, 1986.

SUBJECTS: BIRDS—FOLKLORE. CUCKOOS—FOLKLORE. FIRE—FOLKLORE. FOLKLORE— INDIANS OF MEXICO. FOLKLORE—MEXICO. MAYAS—FOLKLORE. MULTICULTURAL BOOKS— FOLKLORE. POURQUOI TALES.

1183 **Farley, Carol.** *Mr. Pak Buys a Story.* **Illus. by Benrei Huang. Albert Whitman, 1997. 0-8075-5178-3. Unp. Gr. 1–4**
When old Mr. and Mrs. Kim long for a good story to entertain them, their faithful servant Mr. Pak sets off to the distant city to buy a tale he can learn by heart. A cunning thief, professing to know a worthy story, relieves the simple man of his 100 gold coins, telling him an enigmatic tale that seems to make no sense. On the night the thief and his roving gang show up at the Kims' house, that same tale serves to scare off the robbers. The power of a good story can't be measured by its price, as we learn in this amusing retelling of a Korean folktale, with soft acrylic and colored pencil illustrations.

GERM: Ask your listeners to explain how the thief was tricked by his own tale. Meet another fellow who stops robbers in their tracks in a similar way in the Iranian folktale *Forty Fortunes,* by Aaron Shepard. And see how a misinterpretation led a tiger to get scared and a rabbit to lose his tail in the Korean pourquoi tale *The Rabbit's Tail,* by Suzanne Crowder Han.

RELATED TITLES: Bateman, Teresa. *The Ring of Truth.* Holiday House, 1997. / Compton, Patricia A. *The Terrible Eek.* Simon & Schuster, 1991. / Dengler, Marianna. *The Worry Stone.* Northland, 1996. / Ginsburg, Mirra. *The Chinese Mirror.* Harcourt, 1988. / Han, Oki S. *Sir Whong and the Golden Pig.* Dial, 1993. / Han, Suzanne Crowder. *The Rabbit's Tail.* Henry Holt, 1999. / Jaffe, Nina. *Older Brother, Younger Brother: A Korean Folktale.* Viking, 1995. / Lewin, Ted. *The Storytellers.* Lothrop, 1998. / Rhee, Nami. *Magic Spring: A Korean Folktale.* Putnam, 1993. / Rothenberg, Joan. *Yettele's Feathers.* Hyperion, 1995. / Shepard, Aaron. *Forty Fortunes: A Tale of Iran.* Clarion, 1999. / Sunami, Kitoba. *How the Fisherman Tricked the Genie: A Tale Within a Tale Within a Tale.* Atheneum, 2002.

SUBJECTS: FOLKLORE—KOREA. HUMOROUS FOLKLORE. MULTICULTURAL BOOKS— FOLKLORE. ROBBERS AND OUTLAWS—FOLKLORE. STORYTELLING—FOLKLORE.

1184 Foster, Joanna. *The Magpie's Nest.* **Illus. by Julie Downing. Clarion, 1995. 0-395-62155-0. Unp. Gr. K–4**

In the spring of the world, when all of the birds needed directions on building nests so they could lay their eggs in a safe place, Mother and Father Magpie showed them how. This English pourquoi tale explains how and why no two kinds of birds make the same types of nests.

GERM: Buttress the descriptions of each type of bird and bird nest with facts from Patricia Brennan Demuth's *Cradles in the Trees: The Story of Bird Nests.*

RELATED TITLES: Bash, Barbara. *Urban Roosts: Where Birds Nest in the City.* Little, Brown, 1990. / Climo, Shirley. *King of the Birds.* HarperCollins, 1988. / Demuth, Patricia Brennan. *Cradles in the Trees: The Story of Bird Nests.* Macmillan, 1994. / Florian, Douglas. *On the Wing: Bird Poems and Paintings.* Harcourt, 1996. / George, Kristine O'Connell. *Hummingbird Nest: A Journal of Poems.* Harcourt, 2004. / Hamilton, Virginia. *When Birds Could Talk and Bats Could Sing: The Adventures of Bruh Sparrow, Sis Wren and Their Friends.* Blue Sky/Scholastic, 1996. / Kajpust, Melissa. *The Peacock's Pride.* Hyperion, 1997. / Peters, Lisa Westberg. *This Way Home.* Henry Holt, 1994. / Taylor, Harriet Peck. *Brother Wolf: A Seneca Tale.* Farrar, 1996. / Yolen, Jane. *Bird Watch: A Book of Poetry.* Philomel, 1990.

SUBJECTS: BIRDS—FOLKLORE. FOLKLORE—ENGLAND. NESTS—FOLKLORE. POURQUOI TALES.

1185 Garland, Sherry. *Children of the Dragon: Selected Tales from Vietnam.* **Illus. by Trina Schart Hyman. Harcourt, 2001. 0-15-224200-7. 58pp. Gr. 3–6**

This attractive collection of six Vietnamese folktales, accompanied by magnificent full-page ink and acrylic paintings, postulates on why the tiger has stripes, why there is a man in the moon, and why the monsoon rains come to Vietnam every year. Explanatory notes provide interesting background information for each story.

GERM: Compare "The Bowman and the Sisters," about twin sisters with humps on their backs, with Robert Baden's Costa Rican folktale *And Sunday Makes Seven,* in which poor Carlos and his rich cousin Ricardo both have large brown moles on the ends of their noses. In both stories, only the kind individual gets the deformity removed. "The Old Man's Wen" from *The Goblins Giggle and Other Stories* by Molly Bang is a similar version that hails from Japan. Lynette Dyer Vuong's *The Brocaded Slipper and Other Vietnamese Tales* is another excellent collection of five tales, including variants of Cinderella and Tom Thumb. Do some research into the culture, customs, and country of Vietnam.

RELATED TITLES: Baden, Robert. *And Sunday Makes Seven.* Albert Whitman, 1990. / Bang, Molly. *The Goblins Giggle and Other Stories.* Scribner, 1973. / Huynh, Quang Nhuong. *The Land I Lost: Adventures of a Boy in Vietnam.* HarperCollins, 1986. / Kha, Dang Manh. *In the Land of Small Dragon: A Vietnamese Folktale.* Viking, 1979. / Lee, Jeanne M. *Toad Is the Uncle of Heaven.* Henry Holt, 1985. / Shea, Pegi Deitz, and Cynthia Weill. *Ten Mice for Tet.* Chronicle, 2003. / Shepard, Aaron. *The Crystal Heart: A Vietnamese Legend.* Atheneum, 1999. / Vuong, Lynette Dyer. *The Brocaded Slipper and Other Vietnamese Tales.* HarperTrophy, 1992.

SUBJECTS: FOLKLORE—COLLECTIONS. FOLKLORE—VIETNAM. POURQUOI TALES.

1186 Ginsburg, Mirra. *Clay Boy: Adapted from a Russian Folk Tale.* **Illus. by Jos. A. Smith. Greenwillow, 1997. 0-688-14410-1. Unp. Gr. PreK–1**

"More! I want more!" cries the ravenous clay boy whom lonely old Grandpa has fashioned as a new child to keep him and Grandma company. After the insatiable creature eats up all the food, he gulps down chickens, the cat, the dog, and even his new parents and heads down the road— "thump, thump, thump"—to swallow down the whole village. In this swallowing story, it's a little white goat who comes to everyone's rescue, butting the clay boy in his belly and breaking him wide open.

GERM: Listeners can make clay models of their own little clay children and then retell the story together. Another comparably greedy traveler is the cat in Meilo So's folktale from India, *Gobble, Gobble, Slip, Slop.*

RELATED TITLES: Baumgartner, Barbara. *Crocodile! Crocodile! Stories Told Around the World.* DK, 1994. / Compton, Joanne. *Sody Sallyratus.* Dutton, 1997. / Davis, Aubrey. *Sody Sallyratus.* Kids Can, 1998. / Galdone, Paul. *The Greedy Old Fat Man.* Clarion, 1983. / Karas, G. Brian. *I Know an Old Lady.* Scholastic, 1984. / Kent, Jack. *The Fat Cat.* Scholastic, 1972. / Polette, Nancy. *The Little Old Woman and the Hungry Cat.* Greenwillow, 1989. / Sloat, Teri. *Sody Sallyratus.* Dutton, 1997. / So, Meilo. *Gobble, Gobble, Slip, Slop: The Tale of a Very Greedy Cat.* Knopf, 2004. / Taback, Simms. *There Was an Old Lady Who Swallowed a Fly.* Viking, 1997. / Thomson, Pat. *Drat That Fat Cat!* Scholastic, 2003.

SUBJECTS: FOLKLORE—RUSSIA. GOATS—FOLKLORE. GREED—FOLKLORE. READER'S THEATER—FOLKLORE. SWALLOWING STORIES.

1187 Goble, Paul. *The Return of the Buffaloes: A Plains Indian Story About Famine and Renewal of the Earth.* **Illus. by the author. National Geographic, 1996. 0-7922-2714-X. Unp. Gr. 2–4**

Though spring has come to the High Plains, it is still a time of hunger, as no buffalo herds have returned. The village leaders send two young men to climb the hills, where they look to the Four Corners of the World. At the entrance to a cave, they encounter a mysterious woman who promises to send her Buffalo People to feed their village.

GERM: Make photocopies of model parfleche, the folded rawhide cases the Plains Indians used to store dried buffalo meat, and paint, cut, and assemble your own miniature versions. "The old people used to say that because birds and animals give their lives so we can eat, we give thanks for food." Discuss and assess how Paul Goble's quote does or does not, should or should not apply to our lives today. For a detailed look at how Native Americans used each buffalo carcass, Russell Freedman's *Buffalo Hunt* is an eye-opener.

RELATED TITLES: Baker, Olaf. *Where the Buffaloes Begin.* Warne, 1981. / Brusca, María Cristina, and Tona Wilson. *When Jaguar Ate the Moon: And Other Stories About Animals and Plants of the Americas.* Henry Holt, 1995. / Bushyhead, Robert H., and Kay Thorpe Bannon. *Yonder Mountain: A Cherokee Legend.* Marshall Cavendish, 2002. / Freedman, Russell. *Buffalo Hunt.* Holiday House, 1988. / Goble, Paul. *Buffalo Woman.* Bradbury, 1984. / Goble, Paul. *Crow Chief: A Plains Indian Story.* Orchard, 1992. / Goble, Paul. *Her Seven Brothers.* Bradbury, 1988. / Goble, Paul. *Iktomi and the Boulder: A Plains Indian Story.* Orchard, 1988. / Goble, Paul. *Love Flute.* Bradbury, 1992. / Haley, Gail. *Two Bad Boys: A Very Old Cherokee Tale.* Dutton, 1996. / Haviland, Virginia. *North American Legends.* Collins, 1979. / Van Laan, Nancy. *Buffalo Dance: A Blackfoot Legend.* Little, Brown, 1993. / Van Laan, Nancy. *In a Circle Long Ago: A Treasury of Native Lore from North America.* Knopf, 1995.

SUBJECTS: BUFFALOES—FOLKLORE. FAMINE—FOLKLORE. FOLKLORE—INDIANS OF NORTH AMERICA. FOLKLORE—U.S. MULTICULTURAL BOOKS—FOLKLORE. PLAINS INDIANS—FOLKLORE.

1188 González, Lucia M. *Señor Cat's Romance and Other Favorite Stories from Latin America.* **Illus. by Lulu Delacre. Scholastic, 1997. 0-590-48577-7. 48pp. Gr. K–3**

Meet a little half-chick, a cockroach, a tricky rabbit, a fool, and a cat in love in this sprightly collection of six well-told and well-known favorite folktales, or "cuentos favoritos," told throughout Latin America.

GERM: Look for other Juan Bobo stories, including *Juan Bobo and the Pig* by Felix Pitre and *Juan Bobo Goes to Work* by Marisa Montes, and other rabbit trickster tales from the Americas to share and laugh over, such as Gretchen Will Mayo's *Here Comes Tricky Rabbit.*

RELATED TITLES: Brusca, María Cristina, and Tona Wilson. *When Jaguar Ate the Moon: And Other Stories About Animals and Plants of the Americas.* Henry Holt, 1995. / dePaola, Tomie. *Adelita: A Mexican Cinderella Story.* Putnam, 2002. / Gonzalez, Lucie M. *The Bossy Gallito: A Traditional Cuban Folktale.* Scholastic, 1994. / Johnston, Tony. *The Tale of Rabbit and Coyote.* Putnam, 1994. / Mayo, Gretchen Will. *Here Comes Tricky Rabbit.* Walker, 1994. / Pitre, Felix. *Juan Bobo and the Pig: A Puerto Rican Folktale.* Lodestar, 1993. / Pitre, Felix. *Paco and the Witch: A Puerto Rican Folktale.* Dutton, 1995.

SUBJECTS: CATS—FOLKLORE. CHICKENS—FOLKLORE. FOLKLORE—COLLECTIONS. FOLKLORE—LATIN AMERICA. MULTICULTURAL BOOKS—FOLKLORE. SPANISH LANGUAGE—FOLKLORE. TRICKSTER TALES.

1189 Hamilton, Martha, and Mitch Weiss. *How and Why Stories: World Tales Kids Can Read & Tell.* **Illus. by Carol Lyon. August House, 1999. 0-87483-562-3. 96pp. Gr. 1–6**

Ever wonder how tigers got their stripes, why the sea is so salty, or why ants are found everywhere? Twenty-five brief, easy-to-learn and tell pourquoi tales from North and South America, Asia, Europe, and Africa answer these questions and then some.

GERM: The authors, known collectively as Beauty and the Beast Storytellers, include, after each story, scientific background about each question, plus practical tips to follow when telling the story to others. Children and adults looking for amusing and thought-provoking tales to share will find a rich source here, as well as in Pleasant DeSpain's *Thirty-Three Multicultural Tales to Tell.*

RELATED TITLES: Aardema, Verna. *Misoso: Once upon a Time Tales from Africa.* Knopf, 1994. / Brusca, María Cristina, and Tona Wilson. *When Jaguar Ate the Moon: And Other Stories About Animals and Plants of the Americas.* Henry Holt, 1995. / Chase, Richard. *Grandfather Tales.* Houghton Mifflin, 1948. / Chase, Richard. *The Jack Tales.* Houghton Mifflin, 1943. / Courlander, Harold, and George Herzog. *The Cow-Tail Switch and Other West African Stories.* Holt, 1947. / DeSpain, Pleasant. *Thirty-Three Multicultural Tales to Tell.* August House, 1993. / Doucet, Sharon Arms. *Lapin Plays Possum: Trickster Tales from the Louisiana Bayou.* Farrar, 2002. / Doucet, Sharon Arms. *Why Lapin's Ears Are Long and Other Tales from the Louisiana Bayou.* Orchard, 1997. / Hamilton,

Virginia. *When Birds Could Talk and Bats Could Sing*. Blue Sky/Scholastic, 1996. / Mayo, Margaret. *When the World Was Young: Creation and Pourquoi Tales*. Simon & Schuster, 1996. / Medlicott, Mary. *Tales for Telling: From Around the World*. Kingfisher, 1992.

SUBJECTS: ANIMALS—FOLKLORE. FOLKLORE—COLLECTIONS. MULTICULTURAL BOOKS—FOLKLORE. POURQUOI TALES. STORIES TO TELL. STORYTELLING.

1190 **Hamilton, Virginia. *Bruh Rabbit and the Tar Baby Girl*. Illus. by James E. Ransome. Blue Sky/Scholastic, 2003. 0-590-47376-X. Unp. Gr. PreK–4**

In this variant of the "tar baby" story from the Sea Islands of South Carolina, Bruh Wolf constructs first a scarecrow and then a Tar Baby Girl to stop Bruh Rabbit from stealing peanuts from his field. "Don't throw me in the briar bush," Bruh Rabbit begs, so, of course, that's just what Bruh Wolf does. Handsome watercolors add even more humor to a very funny African American folktale.

GERM: In pairs, act out the scenes of Bruh Rabbit's encounters with the Tar Baby Girl and Bruh Wolf. Discuss the concept of using reverse psychology. Compare and contrast other rabbit-based trickster tales, including *Why Lapin's Ears Are Long and Other Tales from the Louisiana Bayou* by Sharon Arms Doucet and *Sure as Sunrise* by Alice McGill.

RELATED TITLES: Aardema, Verna. *Rabbit Makes a Monkey Out of Lion*. Dial, 1989. / Doucet, Sharon Arms. *Lapin Plays Possum: Trickster Tales from the Louisiana Bayou*. Farrar, 2002. / Doucet, Sharon Arms. *Why Lapin's Ears Are Long and Other Tales from the Louisiana Bayou*. Orchard, 1997. / Faulkner, William J. *Brer Tiger and the Big Wind* Morrow, 1995. / Han, Suzanne Crowder. *The Rabbit's Escape*. Henry Holt, 1995. / Jacquith, Priscilla. *Bo Rabbit Smart for True*. Philomel, 1994. / Knutson, Barbara. *Love and Roast Chicken: A Trickster Tale from the Andes Mountains*. Carolrhoda, 2004. / Lester, Julius. *The Tales of Uncle Remus: The Adventures of Brer Rabbit*. Dial, 1990. / McDermott, Gerald. *Zomo the Rabbit: A Trickster Tale from West Africa*. Harcourt, 1992. / McGill, Alice. *Sure as Sunrise: Stories of Bruh Rabbit and His Walkin' Talkin' Friends*. Houghton Mifflin, 2004. / Mayo, Gretchen Will. *Here Comes Tricky Rabbit*. Walker, 1994. / Parks, Van Dyke, and Malcolm Jones. *Jump! The Adventures of Brer Rabbit*. Harcourt, 1986. / Ross, Gayle. *How Rabbit Tricked Otter and Other Cherokee Trickster Stories*. HarperCollins, 1994. / Stevens, Janet. *Tops and Bottoms*. Harcourt, 1995.

SUBJECTS: CREATIVE DRAMA—FOLKLORE. FOLKLORE—SOUTH CAROLINA. FOLKLORE—U.S. HUMOROUS FOLKLORE. MULTICULTURAL BOOKS—FOLKLORE. RABBITS—FOLKLORE. TRICKSTER TALES. WOLVES—FOLKLORE.

1191 **Hamilton, Virginia. *The Girl Who Spun Gold*. Illus. by Leo and Diane Dillon. Scholastic, 2000. 0-590-47378-6. Unp. Gr. 2–6**

Here's a breathtaking and elegant West Indian variant of the Grimm Brothers' fairy tale Rumpelstiltskin, which Virginia Hamilton adapted from a story she found in a collection of West Indian fairy tales published in 1899. Young Quashiba's mother tells Big King that her daughter can spin the finest golden thread, which, of course, is not true.

GERM: Compare components from the various retellings of Rumpelstiltskin, including the singular talents each girl is said to have, the description and name of the magical gold spinner, and the resolution when the girl discovers the name of her nemesis.

RELATED TITLES: Climo, Shirley. *Magic and Mischief: Tales from Cornwall*. Clarion, 1999. / Moser, Barry. *Tucker Pfeffercorn: An Old Story Retold*. Little, Brown, 1994. / Ness, Evaline. *Tom Tit Tot*. Scribner, 1965. / Sage, Alison. *Rumpelstiltskin*. Dial, 1990. / San Souci, Robert D. *The Faithful Friend*. Simon & Schuster, 1995. / San Souci, Daniel D. *The Tsar's Promise*. Philomel, 1992. / Sierra, Judy. *Can You Guess My Name? Traditional Tales Around the World*. Clarion, 2002. / Stanley, Diane. *Rumpelstiltskin's Daughter*. Morrow, 1997. / White, Carolyn. *Whuppity Stoorie: A Scottish Folktale*. Putnam, 1997. / Zelinsky, Paul O. *Rumpelstiltskin*. Dutton, 1986. / Zemach, Harve. *Duffy and the Devil*. Farrar, 1986.

SUBJECTS: FAIRY TALES. FOLKLORE—WEST INDIES. ISLANDS—FOLKLORE. KINGS AND RULERS—FOLKLORE. RUMPELSTILTSKIN STORIES.

1192 **Hamilton, Virginia. *The People Could Fly: The Picture Book*. Illus. by Leo and Diane Dillon. Knopf, 2004. 0-375-82405-7. Unp. Gr. 3–8**

A somber, devastating, but uplifting folktale about slavery explains how, long ago in Africa, some of the people knew magic and could fly. In the land of slavery, Sarah and her baby escape the Overseer's whip when she rises into the sky, thanks to the magic words of the old man, Toby, who helps all the slaves fly away to Free-dom.

GERM: Originally the title story of Hamilton's collection *The People Could Fly*, this picture-book version with eloquent color paintings will give you chills when you read it aloud. Discuss: Why might this story have been an important one for slaves to tell? What effect might it have had on slaves who heard it? Why does this story still exist? What does it say to us now, in the 21st century? Faith Ringgold's picture book *Aunt Harriet's Underground Railroad in the Sky*, about modern girl Cassie who flies and relives the escape of a slave, will make an interesting comparison.

RELATED TITLES: Hamilton, Virginia. *Bruh Rabbit and the Tar Baby Girl*. Scholastic, 2003. / Hamilton, Virginia. *The Girl Who Spun Gold*. Scholastic, 2000. / Hamilton, Virginia. *Her Stories: African American Folktales, Fairy Tales, and True Tales*. Scholastic, 1995. / Hamilton, Virginia. *The People Could Fly: American Black Folktales*. Knopf, 1985. / Hamilton, Virginia. *When Birds Could Talk and Bats Could Sing*. Blue Sky/Scholastic, 1996. / Hopkinson, Deborah. *Sweet Clara and the Freedom Quilt*. Knopf, 1993. / Howard, Elizabeth Fitzgerald. *Virgie Goes to School with Us Boys*. Simon & Schuster, 2000. / Johnson, Dolores. *Now Let Me Fly: The Story of a Slave Family*. Macmillan, 1993. / Nelson, Vaunda Micheaux. *Almost to Freedom*. Carolrhoda, 2003. / Ransom, Candice. *Liberty Street*. Walker, 2003. / Ringgold, Faith. *Aunt Harriet's Underground Railroad in the Sky*. Crown, 1992. / Winter, Jeannette. *Follow the Drinking Gourd*. Knopf, 1989.

SUBJECTS: FLIGHT—FOLKLORE. FOLKLORE—COLLECTIONS. FOLKLORE—U.S. FOLKLORE, AFRICAN AMERICAN. MULTICULTURAL BOOKS—FOLKLORE. SLAVERY—FOLKLORE.

1193 Hamilton, Virginia. *When Birds Could Talk and Bats Could Sing: The Adventures of Bruh Sparrow, Sis Wren and Their Friends*. Illus. by Barry Moser. Blue Sky/Scholastic, 1996. 0-590-47372-7. 64pp. Gr. 2–5

Sit yourselves down, relax, and enjoy some old tales from back in the days when Bruh Sparrow liked to cause mischief, Miss Bat still had a long tail and seven coats of multicolored feathers, and Hummer the hummingbird had a honey-sweet voice; back in the days when Bruh Blue Jay stole a bit of fire from the Firekeeper and Miss Bat could sing.

GERM: This delectable collection of eight folktales was first retold by Martha Young, Alabama's foremost folklorist in the early part of the 20th century, and rewritten again by Hamilton, who toned down the heavy dialect and made each cante fable (a tale with a verse or song and a final moral) a sheer pleasure to read aloud. Moser's large personable watercolors are a delight, and will get children fired up to find out more information about each type of bird.

RELATED TITLES: Aardema, Verna. *Misoso: Once upon a Time Tales from Africa*. Knopf, 1994. / Brusca, María Cristina, and Tona Wilson. *When Jaguar Ate the Moon: And Other Stories About Animals and Plants of the Americas*. Henry Holt, 1993. / Foster, Joanna. *The Magpie's Nest*. Clarion, 1995. / Hamilton, Virginia. *Her Stories: African American Folktales, Fairy Tales, and True Tales*. Scholastic, 1995. / Lester, Julius. *The Tales of Uncle Remus: The Adventures of Brer Rabbit*. Dial, 1987. / Mayo, Margaret. *When the World Was Young: Creation and Pourquoi Tales*. Simon & Schuster, 1996. / Parks, Van Dyke, and Malcolm Jones. *Jump! The Adventures of Brer Rabbit*. Harcourt, 1986. / Taylor, Harriet Peck. *Brother Wolf: A Seneca Tale*. Farrar, 1996.

SUBJECTS: ANIMALS—FOLKLORE. BIRDS—FOLKLORE. FOLKLORE—ALABAMA. FOLKLORE—COLLECTIONS. FOLKLORE—U.S. FOLKLORE, AFRICAN AMERICAN. HUMOROUS FOLKLORE. MULTICULTURAL BOOKS—FOLKLORE.

1194 Han, Suzanne Crowder. *The Rabbit's Tail*. Illus. by Richard Wehrman. Henry Holt, 1999. 0-8050-4580-5. Unp. Gr. K–4

"Stop crying," a mother tells her baby. "Do you want the tiger to get you?" And the hungry tiger, who has left his forest to search for food in the village, is puffed up with pride at hearing that, until the mother says, "Look! Here's a dried persimmon," whereupon the baby is quiet. The tiger concludes that a dried persimmon must be even stronger and scarier than he, so when a thief encounters him in the barn, the tiger is terrified, thinking the man must be the dreaded persimmon. This Korean folktale is a comedy of errors and misperceptions, which ends with an explanation of how rabbits came to get stumpy tails, thanks to the tiger and the thief.

GERM: If you can find one, bring in a persimmon so everyone can see exactly what the tiger believed was so frightening. Two more folktales about thieves who misinterpret their situations, leading to their undoing, are *The Terrible Eek*, a Japanese tale by Patricia A. Compton, and *Mr. Pak Buys a Story*, a Korean tale by Carol Farley. Meet the rabbit as a savvier fellow in Han's *The Rabbit's Escape* and *The Rabbit's Judgment*.

RELATED TITLES: Araki, Mie. *The Perfect Tail: A Fred and Lulu Story*. Chronicle, 2004. / Compton, Patricia A. *The Terrible Eek*. Simon & Schuster, 1991. / Dowson, Nick. *Tigress*. Candlewick, 2004. / Farley, Carol. *Mr. Pak Buys a Story*. Albert Whitman, 1997. / Han, Suzanne Crowder. *The Rabbit's Escape*. Henry Holt, 1995. / Han, Suzanne Crowder. *The Rabbit's Judgment*. Henry Holt, 1994. / Salley, Coleen. *Why Epossumondas Has No Hair on His Tail*. Harcourt, 2004.

SUBJECTS: FOLKLORE—KOREA. HUMOROUS FOLKLORE. POURQUOI TALES. RABBITS—
FOLKLORE. ROBBERS AND OUTLAWS—FOLKLORE. TAILS—FOLKLORE. TIGERS—FOLKLORE.

1195 Harper, Wilhelmina. *The Gunniwolf.* Illus. by Barbara Upton. Dutton, 2003. 0-525-46785-8.
Unp. Gr. K–3

In an American cautionary folktale with possible German and African origins, a little girl disobeys her mother and wanders off into the jungle to pick flowers, meeting up with the Gunniwolf, a wolf who makes her sing to him until he falls asleep. Unlike Little Red Riding Hood, no
one gets eaten, and the enterprising little girl manages to slip away home, having learned to listen to her mother's advice.

GERM: After reading or telling the story, with all its delectable repeating refrains, bring the
story to life. Have your children pair off; one will play the little child, while the other will be the
Gunniwolf. Have each pair act out the singing and chasing scenes, running in place, and then
switch roles and do it again. Afterward, have them retell the story and draw pictures of favorite
parts. And, of course, compare it with "Little Red Riding Hood" and its variants.

RELATED TITLES: Bannerman, Helen. *The Story of Little Babaji.* HarperCollins, 1996. / Emberley, Michael.
Ruby. Little, Brown, 1990. / Harper, Wilhelmina. *The Gunniwolf.* Illus. by William Wiesner. Dutton, 1978. /
Hoberman, Mary Ann. *It's Simple, Said Simon.* Knopf, 2001. / Hyman, Trina Schart. *Little Red Riding Hood.* Hol-
iday House, 1983. / Johnson, Paul Brett. *Little Bunny Foo Foo.* Scholastic, 2004. / Marshall, James. *Red Riding
Hood.* Dial, 1987.

SUBJECTS: CHANTABLE REFRAIN—FOLKLORE. CREATIVE DRAMA—FOLKLORE. FOLKLORE—
U.S. LITTLE RED RIDING HOOD STORIES. OBEDIENCE—FOLKLORE. STORIES WITH SONGS.
WOLVES—FOLKLORE.

1196 Hayes, Joe. *Juan Verdades: The Man Who Couldn't Tell a Lie.* Illus. by Joseph Daniel Fiedler.
Orchard, 2001. 0-439-29311-1. Unp. Gr. 2–6

Mexican American rancher don Ignacio trusts his foreman, Juan Verdades, always to tell him
the truth. Dubious that any employee would never lie to his boss, don Ignacio's fellow rancher,
don Arturo, bets his ranch that he can get Juan to tell a lie. When don Arturo's lovely daughter,
Araceli, entices Juan to pick all the apples from his employer's treasured apple tree, *el manzano
real,* it looks as if Juan will tell a lie about it. Instead, he figures out another way to reveal the
truth.

GERM: Before revealing Juan's response to his employer about the apples, break your listeners
into groups to discuss what they think he should say, what they would say, and what they
think he will say. Pair this Mexican American folktale with Hayes's story of another poor man
who tells the truth in *A Spoon for Every Bite.* Meet an Irish man full of blarney who is compelled
to tell the truth in *The Ring of Truth* by Teresa Bateman. Listeners who puzzle out Juan's riddle
will also enjoy figuring out the stories in *True Lies: 18 Tales for You to Judge* by George Shannon.

RELATED TITLES: Bateman, Teresa. *The Ring of Truth.* Holiday House, 1997. / DeFelice, Cynthia, and Mary
DeMarsh. *Three Perfect Peaches: A French Folktale.* Orchard, 1995. / Hayes, Joe. *A Spoon for Every Bite.* Orchard,
1996. / Kimmel, Eric A. *Three Sacks of Truth: A Story from France.* Holiday House, 1993. / Shannon, George.
True Lies: 18 Tales for You to Judge. Greenwillow, 1997.

SUBJECTS: APPLES—FOLKLORE. FOLKLORE—SOUTHWEST. FOLKLORE—U.S. FOLKLORE,
HISPANIC AMERICAN. FOLKLORE, MEXICAN AMERICAN. FRUIT—FOLKLORE. HONESTY—
FOLKLORE. LOVE—FOLKLORE. MULTICULTURAL BOOKS—FOLKLORE. TREES—FOLKLORE.

1197 Hickox, Rebecca. *The Golden Sandal: A Middle Eastern Cinderella Story.* Illus. by Will Hillenbrand. Holiday House, 1998. 0-8234-1331-4. Unp. Gr. 2–6

Maha begs her fisherman father to marry the kind widow who lives nearby, but when he does,
the girl soon finds herself doing all the chores. After she saves the life of a small red fish, Maha
asks him to help her attend a bride's henna party. In her haste to avoid seeing her stepmother,
Maha rushes away from the party, leaving behind her golden slipper.

GERM: Compare this Iraqi variant with other Cinderella stories with non-human fairy god-
mothers, such as the peri in *The Persian Cinderella* by Shirley Climo, the crocodile in *The Gift of
the Crocodile* by Judy Sierra, and the fish in *Wishbones* by Barbara Ker Wilson.

RELATED TITLES: Climo, Shirley. *The Egyptian Cinderella.* Crowell, 1989. / Climo, Shirley. *The Korean Cin-
derella.* HarperCollins, 1993. / Climo, Shirley. *The Persian Cinderella.* HarperCollins, 1999. / Coburn, Jewell
Reinhart. *Jouanah: A Hmong Cinderella.* Shen's, 1996. / Craft, K. Y. *Cinderella.* SeaStar Books, 2000. / Ehrlich,
Amy. *Cinderella.* Illus. by Susan Jeffers. Dutton, 2004. / Han, Oki S., and Stephanie Plunkett. *Kongi and Potgi: A*

Cinderella Story from Korea. Dial, 1996. / San Souci, Robert D. *Cendrillon: A Caribbean Cinderella*. Simon & Schuster, 1998. / Sanderson, Ruth. *Cinderella*. Little, Brown, 2002. / Sierra, Judy. *The Gift of the Crocodile: A Cinderella Story*. Simon & Schuster, 2000. / Wilson, Barbara Ker. *Wishbones: A Folk Tale from China*. Bradbury, 1993.

SUBJECTS: CINDERELLA STORIES. FAIRY TALES. FISHES—FOLKLORE. FOLKLORE—ARAB COUNTRIES. FOLKLORE—IRAQ. MULTICULTURAL BOOKS—FOLKLORE. STEPMOTHERS—FOLKLORE.

1198   **Hicks, Ray, as told to Lynn Salsi. *The Jack Tales*. Illus. by Owen Smith. Callaway, 2000. 0-9351-1258-8. 40pp. Gr. 2–5**

In an oversized volume with huge down-home illustrations and an accompanying CD, 78-year-old storyteller Ray Hicks regales us with three stories he learned from his grandfather about that trickster, Jack. Jack is sometimes a bit of a fool or a simpleton with a heart of gold, but he always wins out in the end. There's "Jack and the Northwest Wind," in which he sets out to stick his raggedy cap in the hole where the wind comes out, gets cheated out of a magic table-cloth, a magic egg, and a beating stick, but comes out okay. Next there's "Jack and the Bean Tree," and finally "Jack and the Robbers." which you can compare with the Grimm story "The Bremen Town Musicians." Huge pages and detailed country-style paintings might remind you of the movie, set in the Depression era and based on *The Odyssey*, *Oh Brother Where Art Thou* by the Coen brothers.

GERM: The CD will intrigue your listeners, who will have to listen carefully to decipher Hicks's Blue Ridge Mountain, North Carolina, dialect. If you've never read Richard Chase's *Grandfather Tales* and *The Jack Tales*, do yourself a huge favor and do so now. These stories, collected by Chase in the Appalachian Mountains, traveled here centuries ago with the early settlers from the British Isles, and have evolved into U.S. folktales. Compare them with their European ancestors, such as Grimm's "The Table, the Donkey, and the Stick" or any of the English versions of "Jack and the Beanstalk" as told by Joseph Jacobs. Start a storytelling project, "Kids Tell Stories," where everyone selects, learns, and tells a short folktale.

RELATED TITLES: Briggs, Raymond. *Jim and the Beanstalk*. Putnam, 1989. / Chase, Richard. *Grandfather Tales*. Houghton Mifflin, 1948. / Chase, Richard. *The Jack Tales*. Houghton Mifflin, 1943. / Compton, Joanne. *The Terrible Eek*. Simon & Schuster, 1991. / Compton, Paul. *Jack the Giant Chaser*. Holiday House, 1993. / Diakité, Baba Wagué. *The Magic Gourd*. Scholastic, 2003. / Galdone, Paul. *The History of Mother Twaddle and the Marvelous Achievements of Her Son, Jack*. Clarion, 1979. / Grimm, Jacob. *The Bremen Town Musicians*. Scholastic, 1992. / Grimm, Jacob. *The Table, the Donkey, and the Stick*. McGraw-Hill, 1976. / Haley, Gail E. *Jack and the Bean Tree*. Crown, 1986. / Haley, Gail E. *Jack and the Fire Dragon*. Crown, 1988. / Haley, Gail E. *Mountain Jack Tales*. Dutton, 1992. / Johnson, Paul Brett. *Fearless Jack*. McElderry, 2001. / Johnson, Paul Brett. *Jack Outwits the Giants*. McElderry, 2002. / Swope, Sam. *Jack and the Seven Deadly Giants*. Farrar, 2004.

SUBJECTS: FOLKLORE—APPALACHIAN REGION. FOLKLORE—COLLECTIONS. FOLKLORE—U.S. GIANTS—FOLKLORE. HUMOROUS FOLKLORE. SWINDLERS AND SWINDLING. TALL TALES.

1199   **Hodges, Margaret. *The Boy Who Drew Cats*. Illus. by Aki Sogabe. Holiday House, 2002. 0-8234-1594-5. Unp. Gr. 2–6**

In a country village in Japan, the youngest child of·a poor farmer is small and weak but clever, so his parents leave him with the temple priest to be educated for the priesthood. Because he has a compulsion to draw cats on the temple walls, the boy is sent away again, and seeks out the large temple in the next village, which seems to be deserted. There he paints more cats on the walls. What a caterwauling awakens him in the middle of the night! The next morning, there lies a monstrous dead rat, bigger than a cow; the mouths of the cats he has drawn on the walls are red and wet with blood.

GERM: The story was based on a legend about 15th-century Japanese artist Sesshu Toyo, whose drawings in his Zen monastery were supposedly so realistic they would sometimes come to life. Aki Sogabe's forceful collage illustrations employ black-lined watercolors, cut paper, and airbrush. Discussion point: Midway through the story, an old priest gives the boy wise words: "Avoid large places at night; keep to small." What might this mean? Why did the boy draw cats? Arthur Levine has also done a splendid version of the tale. For another absorbing look at Zen Buddhist stories, read Jon J Muth's lovely *Zen Shorts* about a storytelling panda.

RELATED TITLES: Bang, Molly Garrett. *Tye May and the Magic Brush*. Greenwillow, 1981. / Galdone, Paul. *King of the Cats*. Houghton Mifflin, 1980. / Hodges, Margaret. *Merlin and the Making of the King*. Holiday House, 2004. / Hodges, Patricia. *Saint George and the Dragon*. Little, Brown, 1984. / Hodges, Margaret. *The Wave*. Houghton Mifflin, 1964. / Kimmel, Eric A. *Three Samurai Cats: A Story from Japan*. Holiday House, 2003.

/ Levine, Arthur A. *The Boy Who Drew Cats: A Japanese Folktale*. Dial, 1994. / Muth, Jon J. *Zen Shorts*. Scholastic, 2005. / Shepard, Aaron. *King O' the Cats*. Atheneum, 2004.

SUBJECTS: ARTISTS—FOLKLORE. CATS—FOLKLORE. FOLKLORE—JAPAN. GOBLINS—FOLKLORE. RATS—FOLKLORE.

1200 **Hodges, Margaret.** *Merlin and the Making of the King*. **Illus. by Trina Schart Hyman. Holiday House, 2004. 0-8234-1647-X. 40pp. Gr. 3–6**

With exquisite, ornately-framed illustrations in the style of illuminated manuscripts, the legend of King Arthur unfurls in a much simplified version of Sir Thomas Malory's *Le Morte d'Arthur*, which was written in 1485. Composed of three of the best-known tales ("The Sword in the Stone," "Excalibur," and "The Lady of the Lake"), the retelling introduces younger readers to the basics: Arthur's crowning, marriage, and death.

GERM: Another handsome overview is Hudson Talbott's *King Arthur and the Round Table*. Also by Hodges and Hyman is the Caldecott classic, *Saint George and the Dragon*, for a further look at English legends.

RELATED TITLES: Hastings, Selena. *Sir Gawain and the Green Knight*. Lothrop, 1981. / Hastings, Selena. *Sir Gawain and the Loathly Lady*. Lothrop, 1985. / Hayes, Sarah. *Robin Hood*. Henry Holt, 1989. / Hodges, Patricia. *Saint George and the Dragon*. Little, Brown, 1984. / Mayer, Marianna. *The Adventures of Tom Thumb*. SeaStar, 2001. / Morpurgo, Michael. *Sir Gawain and the Green Knight*. Candlewick, 2004. / Osborne, Mary Pope. *Favorite Medieval Tales*. Scholastic, 1998. / Sabuda, Robert. *Arthur and the Sword*. Atheneum, 1995. / San Souci, Robert D. *Young Arthur*. Doubleday, 1997. / Shannon, Mark. *Gawain and the Green Knight*. Putnam, 1994. / Talbott, Hudson. *King Arthur and the Round Table*. Morrow, 1995. / Winthrop, Elizabeth. *The Castle in the Attic*. Holiday House, 1985. / Yolen, Jane. *Hobby: The Young Merlin Trilogy, Book 2*. Harcourt, 1996. / Yolen, Jane. *Merlin and the Dragons*. Dutton, 1995. / Yolen, Jane. *Merlin: The Young Merlin Trilogy, Book 3*. Harcourt, 1997. / Yolen, Jane. *Passager: The Young Merlin Trilogy, Book One*. Harcourt, 1996.

SUBJECTS: ARTHUR, KING (LEGENDARY CHARACTER). FOLKLORE—ENGLAND. KINGS AND RULERS—FOLKLORE. KNIGHTS AND KNIGHTHOOD—FOLKLORE. LEGENDS. MAGICIANS—FOLKLORE. MERLIN (LEGENDARY CHARACTER).

1201 **Jaffe, Nina.** *The Way Meat Loves Salt: A Cinderella Tale from the Jewish Tradition*. **Illus. by Louise August. Henry Holt, 1998. 0-8050-4384-5. Unp. Gr. 2–6**

When the rabbi's youngest daughter, Mireleh, tells him she loves him "the way meat loves salt," he misunderstands her analogy, and in his anger casts her out of the house. Helped by Elijah the Prophet, who gives her a magic stick that will grant any wish, she attends a wedding feast, dances with a young man, and loses a satin slipper—all elements of the traditional Cinderella story. At her own wedding feast, she proves to her father the truth of the words she once spoke to him.

GERM: Discuss the elements that make this a Cinderella tale. What does Mireleh's statement to her father mean? How can meat love salt? *Moss Gown* by William H. Hooks is a Southern U.S. variant of the story, which you can compare and contrast. Write new comparative statements: I love you as much as _____.

RELATED TITLES: Craft, K. Y. *Cinderella*. SeaStar Books, 2000. / Ehrlich, Amy. *Cinderella*. Illus. by Susan Jeffers. Dutton, 2004. / Han, Oki S., and Stephanie Plunkett. *Kongi and Potgi: A Cinderella Story from Korea*. Dial, 1996. / Hickox, Rebecca. *The Golden Sandal: A Middle Eastern Cinderella Story*. Holiday House, 1998. / Hooks, William H. *Moss Gown*. Clarion, 1987. / Jaffe, Nina. *In the Month of Kislev: A Story for Hanukkah*. Viking, 1992. / Martin, Rafe. *The Rough-Face Girl*. Putnam, 1992. / Pollock, Penny. *The Turkey Girl: A Zuni Cinderella Story*. Little, Brown, 1996. / Rothenberg, Joan. *Yettele's Feathers*. Hyperion, 1995. / Sanderson, Ruth. *Cinderella*. Little, Brown, 2002. / San Souci, Robert D. *Cendrillon: A Caribbean Cinderella*. Simon & Schuster, 1998. / Steptoe, John. *Mufaro's Beautiful Daughters*. Lothrop, 1987. / Wilson, Barbara Ker. *Wishbones: A Folk Tale from China*. Bradbury, 1993.

SUBJECTS: CINDERELLA STORIES. FAIRY TALES. FATHERS AND DAUGHTERS—FOLKLORE. FOLKLORE—EUROPE, EASTERN. FOLKLORE—POLAND. FOLKLORE, JEWISH.

1202 **Johnson, Paul Brett.** *Fearless Jack*. **Illus. by the author. McElderry, 2001. 0-689-83296-6. Unp. Gr. K–5**

Killing ten yellow jackets at one whack inspires country boy Jack to call himself Fearless Jack; when he wanders into town, the sheriff offers him a hundred dollars cash "ree-ward" to rid the town of some wild varmints. Through trickery and sheer good luck, Jack makes short shrift of a wild boar, a bear, and a unicorn.

GERM: Compare and contrast this Appalachian version to the assorted Jack tales listed here, and to *The Brave Little Seamstress* by Mary Pope Osborn. Also read the original Grimm tale, *Seven at One Blow*, retold by Eric A. Kimmel, and Christine Price's Turkish folktale, *Sixty at a Blow*. Follow up with Johnson's sequel, *Jack Outwits the Giants*. For more Jack tales, don't forget Richard Chase's classic American collection, *The Jack Tales*, Gail E. Haley's *Mountain Jack Tales*, and Ray Hicks's *The Jack Tales*.

RELATED TITLES: Cauley, Lorinda Bryan. *Jack and the Beanstalk*. Putnam, 1983. / Chase, Richard. *The Jack Tales*. Houghton Mifflin, 1943. / Compton, Kenn, and Joanne Compton. *Jack the Giant Chaser: An Appalachian Tale*. Holiday House, 1993. / Galdone, Paul. *The History of Mother Twaddle and the Marvelous Achievements of Her Son, Jack*. Clarion, 1979. / Garner, Alan. *Jack and the Beanstalk*. Doubleday, 1992. / Haley, Gail E. *Jack and the Bean Tree*. Crown, 1986. / Haley, Gail E. *Mountain Jack Tales*. Dutton, 1992. / Hicks, Ray. *The Jack Tales*. Callaway, 2000. / Johnson, Paul Brett. *Jack Outwits the Giants*. McElderry, 2002. / Kellogg, Steven. *Jack and the Beanstalk*. Morrow, 1991. / Osborne, Mary Pope. *The Brave Little Seamstress*. Atheneum, 2002. / Osborne, Mary Pope. *Kate and the Beanstalk*. Atheneum, 2000. / Price, Christine. *Sixty at a Blow*. Dutton, 1968. / Swope, Sam. *Jack and the Seven Deadly Giants*. Farrar, 2004. / Thomson, Peggy. *The Brave Little Tailor*. Simon & Schuster, 1992.

SUBJECTS: BEARS—FOLKLORE. FOLKLORE—APPALACHIAN REGION. FOLKLORE—U.S. HUMOROUS FOLKLORE. TALL TALES. TRICKSTER TALES. UNICORNS—FOLKLORE.

1203   Johnson, Paul Brett. *Jack Outwits the Giants*. Illus. by the author. McElderry, 2002. 0-689-83902-2. Unp. Gr. K–5

Stopping off at a farmhouse when a rainstorm catches him on the road, Jack is taken in by a two-headed giant and his one-headed wife who welcome him to spend the night in their loft. Of course, they plan to eat him for breakfast, but Jack is far too clever for that; he convinces them he can get milk out of rocks, carry the creek up to their house, and save them from the sheriff's posse.

GERM: Also share Johnson's companion tale, *Fearless Jack*. Margaret Willey's *Clever Beatrice* is a variant from Michigan with an enterprising young girl in the main role, while Dorothy Van Woerkom's *Alexandra the Rock-Eater* hails from Russia and features a dragon instead of a giant. For collections of stories about that rascal Jack, read *The Jack Tales* by Richard Chase, *Mountain Jack Tales* by Gail E. Haley, and *The Jack Tales* by Ray Hicks.

RELATED TITLES: Beneduce, Ann Keay. *Jack and the Beanstalk*. Philomel, 1999. / Chase, Richard. *The Jack Tales*. Houghton, 1943. / Compton, Kenn, and Joanne Compton. *Jack the Giant Chaser: An Appalachian Tale*. Holiday House, 1993. / Galdone, Paul. *The History of Mother Twaddle and the Marvelous Achievements of Her Son, Jack*. Clarion, 1979. / Garner, Alan. *Jack and the Beanstalk*. Doubleday, 1992. / Haley, Gail E. *Jack and the Bean Tree*. Crown, 1986. / Haley, Gail E. *Mountain Jack Tales*. Dutton, 1992. / Hicks, Ray. *The Jack Tales*. Callaway, 2000. / Johnson, Paul Brett. *The Cow Who Wouldn't Come Down*. Orchard, 1993. / Johnson, Paul Brett. *Fearless Jack*. McElderry, 2001. / Still, James. *Jack and the Wonder Beans*. Putnam, 1977. / Van Woerkom, Dorothy. *Alexandra the Rock-Eater*. Knopf, 1978. / Willey, Margaret. *Clever Beatrice: An Upper Peninsula Conte*. Atheneum, 2001.

SUBJECTS: FOLKLORE—U.S. GIANTS—FOLKLORE. HUMOROUS FOLKLORE. TALL TALES. TRICKSTER TALES.

1204   Johnson-Davies, Denys. *Goha the Wise Fool*. Illus. by Hany El Saed Ahmed from drawings by Hag Hamdy Mohamed Fattouh. Philomel, 2005. 0-399-24222-8. 40pp. Gr. 2–6

Fifteen short, droll tales introduce us to a staple of Egyptian folklore, Goha, a well-meaning fool, trickster, and sage. In each story, he either learns a lesson or he doesn't. He outwits two robbers in one tale, and is burgled in two others; he cleverly matches wits with his own wife and with three wise men, but another time he goes swimming in the river and all his clothes are stolen. Some of the stories feature green-turbaned Goha riding, counting, or buying a donkey, his main means of transportation. In some tales he offers words of wisdom, and in others he remains perplexed. All of the tales are illustrated with colorful hand-sewn tapestries, called khiyamiyas, stitched by two talented tentmakers from a covered market, or souk, in Cairo. At the back of the book is a color photograph of the two men working on their designs.

GERM: The everyman character of Goha is beloved throughout the Middle East. In Turkey, he is known as Nasreddin Hodja or Hoca; in Iran, he's called Mulla Nasrudin. Ask your children what it is about Goha that makes him such a universal figure. In what ways is he wise? In what ways is he foolish? What life lessons can you learn from him? Meet Goha's Turkish counterpart, Nasrettin, in *The Hungry Coat* by Demi.

RELATED TITLES: Courlander, Harold. *The Piece of Fire and Other Haitian Tales.* Harcourt, 1942. / Demi. *The Hungry Coat: A Tale from Turkey.* McElderry, 2004. / Singh, Rina. *The Foolish Men of Agra and Other Tales of Mogul India.* Key Porter, 1998. / Walker, Barbara K. *A Treasury of Turkish Folktales for Children.* Shoe String Press, 1988. / Walker, Barbara K. *Watermelons, Walnuts, and the Wisdom of Allah, and Other Tales of the Hoca.* Texas Tech University Press, 1991.

SUBJECTS: FOLKLORE—ARAB COUNTRIES. FOLKLORE—COLLECTIONS. FOLKLORE—EGYPT. FOOLS—FOLKLORE. NASREDDIN HOCA (LEGENDARY CHARACTER).

1205 **Kellogg, Steven.** *Sally Ann Thunder Ann Crockett.* **Illus. by the author. Morrow, 1995. 0-688-14043-2. Unp. Gr. 1–4**

As a baby, Sally Ann Thunder Ann Whirlwind can "out-talk, out-grin, out-scream, out-swim, and out-run" anyone in Kentucky, including her nine older brothers. On her eighth birthday, she heads out for the frontier and meets and defeats a great big grizzly. Rescuing a handsome young man from a couple of overzealous eagles, she falls for him, having met her match in the legendary Davy Crockett. Kellogg's zany pen-and-ink and watercolors keep the lively tall tale hopping.

GERM: Read this along with Lynne Bertrand's *Granite Baby*, Anne Isaac's *Swamp Angel*, and Pat Mora's *Doña Flor* for a story hour filled with tall-tale girl power. Find out more about Sally Ann's adventuresome husband in Rosalyn Schanzer's *Davy Crockett Saves the World*.

RELATED TITLES: Bertrand, Lynne. *Granite Baby.* Farrar, 2005. / Dadey, Debbie. *Shooting Star: Annie Oakley, the Legend.* Walker, 1997. / Hodges, Margaret. *The True Tale of Johnny Appleseed.* Holiday House, 1997. / Isaacs, Anne. *Swamp Angel.* Dutton, 1994. / Kellogg, Steven. *I Was Born About 10,000 Years Ago.* Morrow, 1996. / Kellogg, Steven. *Paul Bunyan.* Morrow, 1992. / Mora, Pat. *Doña Flor: A Tall Tale About a Giant Woman with a Great Big Heart.* Knopf, 2005. / Osborne, Mary Pope. *American Tall Tales.* Knopf, 1991. / San Souci, Robert D. *Larger Than Life: The Adventures of American Legendary Heroes.* Doubleday, 1991. / Schanzer, Rosalyn. *Davy Crockett Saves the World.* HarperCollins, 2001. / Williams, Suzanne. *Library Lil.* Dial, 1997.

SUBJECTS: EXAGGERATION—FOLKLORE. FOLKLORE—U.S. HUMOROUS FOLKLORE. TALL TALES. WOMEN—FOLKLORE.

1206 **Kimmel, Eric A.** *Anansi and the Magic Stick.* **Illus. by Janet Stevens. Holiday House, 2001. 0-8234-1443-4. Unp. Gr. PreK–2**

Anansi, that lazy, greedy, lovable trickster spider from West Africa, steals Hyena's Magic Stick so he can clean up his own ramshackle house without having to do any work. In a Sorcerer's Apprentice-like frenzy of magic, the spider gets his own property spic and span, but the stick runs amok when Anansi can't remember the magic words to stop it. Children will love the flood scene, with the comical illustration of the book's actual author and illustrator drifting downstream together.

GERM: Working in groups, children can create and illustrate new Anansi adventures, such as "Anansi Goes to School." Share and compare the other Anansi stories by Aardema, Cummings, Kimmel, and Mollel in the Related Titles below. A search in this volume's Subject Index under "Trickster Tales" will provide an extensive list of trickster tales from many cultures, with rabbits, monkeys, ravens, and coyotes as the anti-heroes. After reading a batch of them aloud, you and students will discern the many common elements of these comic tales. Have children think up their own magic spells for their own tiny sticks, coming up with starting and ending words, a description of the spell's particular powers, and an illustration onto which they can glue their twigs. Create your own spiders using black construction paper, folded in half. Each student traces his four fanned-out fingers at the fold and then cuts out the shape. Open up the paper, and voilà!—an eight-legged spider.

RELATED TITLES: Aardema, Verna. *Anansi Does the Impossible! An Ashanti Tale.* Atheneum, 1997. / Aardema, Verna. *Anansi Finds a Fool.* Dial, 1992. / Bush, Timothy. *Benjamin McFadden and the Robot Babysitter.* Crown, 1998. / Cummings, Pat. *Ananse and the Lizard: A West African Tale.* Henry Holt, 2002. / dePaola, Tomie. *Strega Nona.* Simon & Schuster, 1979. / Dewan, Ted. *The Sorcerer's Apprentice.* Doubleday, 1998. / Galdone, Paul. *The Magic Porridge Pot.* Clarion, 1979. / Howland, Naomi. *Latkes, Latkes, Good to Eat.* Clarion, 1999. / Kimmel, Eric A. *Anansi and the Moss-Covered Rock.* Holiday House, 1990. / Kimmel, Eric A. *Anansi and the Talking Melon.* Holiday House, 1994. / Kimmel, Eric A. *Anansi Goes Fishing.* Holiday House, 1992. / MacDonald, Margaret Read. *Pickin' Peas.* HarperCollins, 1998. / Mollel, Tololwa M. *Ananse's Feast: An Ashanti Tale.* Clarion, 1997. / Moore, Inga. *The Sorcerer's Apprentice.* Macmillan, 1989.

SUBJECTS: ANANSI (LEGENDARY CHARACTER). ANIMALS—FOLKLORE. FOLKLORE—AFRICA, WEST. HUMOROUS FOLKLORE. MULTICULTURAL BOOKS—FOLKLORE. SPIDERS—FOLKLORE. TRICKSTER TALES.

1207 Kimmel, Eric A. *Cactus Soup.* **Illus. by Phil Huling. Marshall Cavendish, 2004. 0-7614-5155-2. Unp. Gr. K–4**

In a lively retelling of "Stone Soup" set in Mexico in the time of the Mexican Revolution (1910–1922), a troop of soldiers arrive at a town where the mayor has urged the townsfolk to hide their food and pretend to be poor. The soldiers set about making cactus soup in the plaza out of a single cactus thorn.

GERM: Act this one out, and maybe make soup or stage your own fiesta. Compare it with other versions including Marcia Brown's classic *Stone Soup;* Jon J Muth's *Stone Soup,* set in China; and Margot Zemach's *Nail Soup.*

RELATED TITLES: Brown, Marcia. *Stone Soup.* Scribner, 1947. / Ehlert, Lois. *Growing Vegetable Soup.* Harcourt, 1987. / Ketteman, Helen. *Armadilly Chili.* Albert Whitman, 2004. / McGovern, Ann. *Stone Soup.* Scholastic, 1986. / Muth, Jon J. *Stone Soup.* Walker, 1997. / Patron, Susan. *Burgoo Stew.* Orchard, 1991. / Sendak, Maurice. *Chicken Soup with Rice.* HarperCollins, 1962. / Stewig, John Warren. *Stone Soup.* Holiday House, 1991. / Zemach, Margot. *Nail Soup.* Follett, 1964.

SUBJECTS: CACTUS—FOLKLORE. COOKERY—FOLKLORE. CREATIVE DRAMA—FOLKLORE. FOLKLORE—MEXICO. FOOD—FOLKLORE. GENEROSITY—FOLKLORE. MULTICULTURAL BOOKS. SOLDIERS—FOLKLORE. SOUP—FOLKLORE.

1208 Kimmel, Eric A. *Count Silvernose: A Story from Italy.* **Illus. by Omar Rayyan. Holiday House, 1996. 0-8234-1216-4. Unp. Gr. 3–6**

When a dashing count with a silver nose takes away two beautiful but flighty sisters to be his washerwomen and then declares to their mother that they have died, their plain but loyal sister Assunta vows to avenge them. She rescues the girls from a fiery pit behind the one door the count has warned her never to open, and then tricks him into delivering a large chest (in which both sisters are hiding) back to their mother's house. In the end, she outwits the count again, and tricks him into falling into his own fiery pit.

GERM: This Bluebeard story with watercolors inspired by a 16th-century sketchbook is riveting and dramatic and not for younger children. Great to use with a telling of Joseph Jacobs's chiller of an English folktale, "Mr. Fox," add this to the small but growing collection of folktales celebrating feisty females.

RELATED TITLES: Basile, Giambattista. *Petrosinella: A Neopolitan Rapunzel.* Warne, 1981. / Del Negro, Janice. *Lucy Dove.* DK Ink, 1998. / Lurie, Alison. *Clever Gretchen and Other Forgotten Folktales.* Crowell, 1980. / McVitty, Walter. *Ali Baba and the Forty Thieves.* Abrams, 1989. / Mayer, Marianna. *Baba Yaga and Vasilisa the Brave.* Morrow, 1994. / Minard, Rosemary. *Womenfolk and Fairy Tales.* Houghton Mifflin, 1975. / Shepard, Aaron. *Master Maid: A Tale of Norway.* Dial, 1997. / Stamm, Claus. *Three Strong Women: A Tall Tale.* Viking, 1990. / Zemach, Harve. *Duffy and the Devil.* Farrar, 1986.

SUBJECTS: FAIRY TALES. FOLKLORE—ITALY. SISTERS—FOLKLORE. SUSPENSE—FOLKLORE.

1209 Kimmel, Eric A. *The Hero Beowulf.* **Illus. by Leonard Everett Fisher. Farrar, 2005. 0-374-30671-0. Unp. Gr. 4–8**

Adapted from the oldest surviving epic poem in English literature, composed in the 8th century, this gloriously creepy tale covers the first of three parts, where hero Beowulf, after slaying five sea serpents, sails to the land of the Spear-Danes to take on Grendel, a hideous man-devouring monster. Leonard Everett Fisher's stirring, vivid paintings, especially of the green-skinned, murderous Grendel, are not for the faint of heart, though Beowulf prevails, of course.

GERM: Get yourself a copy of Seamus Heaney's *Beowulf: A New Verse Translation* (Farrar, 2000) and share a bit of it aloud so listeners can get the flavor of the original language. In Nancy Farmer's novel, *The Sea of Trolls,* Jack is apprenticed to an old bard who tells him the story of Beowulf. If your listeners are clamoring for more heroic deeds and man-eating monsters, regale them with a tale of Ulysses in Leonard Everett Fisher's also suspenseful picture book *Cyclops.*

RELATED TITLES: Farmer, Nancy. *The Sea of Trolls.* Atheneum, 2004. / Fisher, Leonard Everett. *Cyclops.* Holiday House, 1991. / Hastings, Selena. *Sir Gawain and the Green Knight.* Lothrop, 1981. / Hastings, Selena. *Sir Gawain and the Loathly Lady.* Lothrop, 1985. / Hayes, Sarah. *Robin Hood.* Henry Holt, 1989. / Hodges, Patricia. *Saint George and the Dragon.* Little, Brown, 1984. / Hutton, Warwick. *Odysseus and the Cyclops.* McElderry, 1995. / Morpurgo, Michael. *Sir Gawain and the Green Knight.* Candlewick, 2004. / Osborne, Mary Pope. *Favorite Medieval Tales.* Scholastic, 1998. / Sabuda, Robert. *Arthur and the Sword.* Atheneum, 1995. / San Souci, Robert D. *Young Arthur.* Doubleday, 1997. / Shannon, Mark. *Gawain and the Green Knight.* Putnam, 1994. / Talbott, Hudson. *King Arthur and the Round Table.* Morrow, 1995.

SUBJECTS: ADVENTURE AND ADVENTURERS—FOLKLORE. BEOWULF. FOLKLORE—ENGLAND. MONSTERS—FOLKLORE.

1210 **Kimmel, Eric A.** *Onions and Garlic: An Old Tale.* **Illus. by Katya Arnold. Holiday House, 1996. 0-8234-1222-9. Unp. Gr. 2–6**

Youngest brother Getzel the Fool is given a sack of common onions by his father to trade when he leaves home on a merchant ship, but no one is interested in buying them. Shipwrecked on an island where diamonds litter the beach, Getzel makes his fortune, for the king is only too delighted to give Getzel a sackful of diamonds in exchange for the delicious onions, which he has never tasted before. Kimmel's retelling of this humorous tale comes from the Jewish *Talmud*.

GERM: *The Tale of the Turnip* by Brian Alderson is an English variant of the story for comparing, contrasting, and laughing.

RELATED TITLES: Alderson, Brian. *The Tale of the Turnip.* Candlewick, 1999. / Bender, Robert. *Toads and Diamonds.* Dutton, 1995. / Huck, Charlotte. *Toads and Diamonds.* Greenwillow, 1996. / Jaffe, Nina. *Older Brother, Younger Brother: A Korean Folktale.* Viking, 1995. / Kimmel, Eric A. *Boots and His Brothers: A Norwegian Tale.* Holiday House, 1992. / Langton, Jane. *Salt: A Russian Folktale.* Houghton Mifflin, 1992. / Sturges, Philemon, and Anna Vojtech. *Marushka and the Month Brothers.* North-South, 1996.

SUBJECTS: BROTHERS—FOLKLORE. DIAMONDS—FOLKLORE. FOLKLORE, JEWISH. HUMOROUS FOLKLORE. KINGS AND RULERS—FOLKLORE. ONIONS—FOLKLORE. VEGETABLES— FOLKLORE. WEALTH—FOLKLORE.

1211 **Kimmel, Eric A.** *Rimonah of the Flashing Sword: A North African Tale.* **Illus. by Omar Rayyan. Holiday House, 1995. 0-8234-1093-5. Unp. Gr. 2–5**

As part of her plan to take over the kingdom, the king's new wife, a sorceress, orders a huntsman to take the king's daughter, Rimonah, to the desert and kill her; instead, he allows her to flee. Rimonah, protected by the Bedouins, becomes renowned for her prowess with dagger and sword, and is taken in by 40 thieves who pledge to drive the queen from her throne.

GERM: Compare and contrast this North African Snow White variant with the tale by the Brothers Grimm and with other fairy tales that showcase courageous young women, including Walter McVitty's *Ali Baba and the Forty Thieves*, with its opulent illustrations by Margaret Early.

RELATED TITLES: Climo, Shirley. *Atalanta's Race: A Greek Myth.* Clarion, 1995. / Grimm, Jacob. *Snow White.* Illus. by Trina Schart Hyman. Little, Brown, 1974. / Lurie, Alison. *Clever Gretchen and Other Forgotten Folktales.* Crowell, 1980. / McVitty, Walter. *Ali Baba and the Forty Thieves.* Abrams, 1989. / Minard, Rosemary. *Womenfolk and Fairy Tales.* Houghton Mifflin, 1975. / San Souci, Robert D. *Fa Mulan: The Story of a Woman Warrior.* Hyperion, 1998. / San Souci, Robert D. *The Samurai's Daughter.* Dial, 1992. / Sherman, Josepha. *Vassilisa the Wise: A Tale of Medieval Russia.* Harcourt, 1988. / Yep, Laurence. *The Khan's Daughter: A Mongolian Folktale.* Scholastic, 1997.

SUBJECTS: FAIRY TALES. FOLKLORE—ARAB COUNTRIES. FOLKLORE—EGYPT. KINGS AND RULERS—FOLKLORE. MULTICULTURAL BOOKS—FOLKLORE. ROBBERS AND OUTLAWS— FOLKLORE. WOMEN—FOLKLORE.

1212 **Kimmel, Eric A.** *The Rooster's Antlers: A Story of the Chinese Zodiac.* **Illus. by YongSheng Xuan. Holiday House, 1999. 0-8234-1385-3. Unp. Gr. K–4**

Magnificent Rooster, with his colorful feathers, bright red comb, and glorious pair of coral antlers knows he will be chosen as one of the 12 animals in the Jade Emperor's new calendar. In a generous moment, Rooster lets Centipede wheedle him into loaning his antlers to Dragon, but then Dragon refuses to return them. Furious, Rooster chases Centipede under a rock and perches on a fence, crowing to that thief, Dragon, to give back his antlers, which he does to this day.

GERM: More trickery abounds in *The Dragon's Tale and Other Animal Fables of the Chinese Zodiac* by Demi and *Cat and Rat: The Legend of the Chinese Zodiac* by Ed Young. Meet ten Chinese dragons in *The Sons of the Dragon King* by Ed Young.

RELATED TITLES: Demi. *The Dragon's Tale and Other Animal Fables of the Chinese Zodiac.* Henry Holt, 1996. / Froehlich, Margaret Walden. *That Kookoory!* Harcourt, 1995. / Ginsburg, Mirra. *The Magic Stove.* Coward, 1983. / Gonzalez, Lucie M. *The Bossy Gallito: A Traditional Cuban Folktale.* Scholastic, 1994. / Rascol, Sabina I. *The Impudent Rooster.* Dutton, 2004. / Simonds, Nina, and Leslie Swartz. *Moonbeams, Dumplings and Dragon Boats: A Treasury of Chinese Holiday Tales, Activities and Recipes.* Harcourt, 2002. / Young, Ed. *Cat and Rat: The Legend of the Chinese Zodiac.* Henry Holt, 1995. / Young, Ed. *The Sons of the Dragon King: A Chinese Legend.* Atheneum, 2004.

SUBJECTS: ANIMALS—FOLKLORE. CALENDARS—FOLKLORE. DRAGONS—FOLKLORE.

EMPERORS—FOLKLORE. FOLKLORE—CHINA. INSECTS—FOLKLORE. KINGS AND RULERS—FOLKLORE. MULTICULTURAL BOOKS—FOLKLORE. ROOSTERS—FOLKLORE. ZODIAC—FOLKLORE.

1213   Kimmel, Eric A. *Seven at One Blow: A Tale from the Brothers Grimm*. Illus. by Megan Lloyd. Holiday House, 1998. 0-8234-1383-7. Unp. Gr. 1–5

After a poor tailor kills seven flies gathered on his bread and jelly, he takes on dangerous giants and ogres, a ferocious unicorn, and a wild boar, outwitting them all and winning the king's daughter in marriage.

GERM: Compare this good-natured tale with some American versions, including Kenn and Joanne Compton's *Jack the Giant Chaser*, Paul Brett Johnson's *Fearless Jack*, and Mary Pope Osborne's *The Brave Little Seamstress*.

RELATED TITLES: Babbitt, Natalie. *Ouch! A Tale from Grimm*. HarperCollins, 1998. / Compton, Kenn, and Joanne Compton. *Jack the Giant Chaser: An Appalachian Tale*. Holiday House, 1993. / Gag, Wanda. *Tales from Grimm*. Coward, 1981. / Hogrogian, Nonny. *The Devil with the Three Golden Hairs*. Knopf, 1983. / Johnson, Paul Brett. *Fearless Jack*. McElderry, 2001. / Kirstein, Lincoln. *Puss in Boots*. Little, Brown, 1992. / Marcellino, Fred. *Puss in Boots*. Farrar, 1990. / Martin, Claire. *Boots and the Glass Mountain*. Dial, 1992. / Osborne, Mary Pope. *The Brave Little Seamstress*. Atheneum, 2002. / Price, Christine. *Sixty at a Blow*. Dutton, 1968. / Van Woerkom, Dorothy. *Alexandra the Rock-Eater*. Knopf, 1978.

SUBJECTS: COURAGE—FOLKLORE. FOLKLORE—GERMANY. GIANTS—FOLKLORE. KINGS AND RULERS—FOLKLORE. OGRES—FOLKLORE. TAILORS—FOLKLORE.

1214   Kimmel, Eric A. *Ten Suns: A Chinese Legend*. Illus. by Yongsheng Xuan. Holiday House, 1998. 0-8234-1317-9. Unp. Gr. 1–6

The emperor of the eastern sky, Di Jun, must take drastic measures when his ten sons, each of whom makes a daily walk across the sky to bring light and heat to the earth below, decide one day to undertake their routes together. He sends Hu Yi, an archer, to shoot down nine of his sons, who then become crows, and that is why there is only one sun in the sky to this day.

GERM: Pair this pourquoi tale with stories of the sun from other cultures, such as the Native American pourquoi tale *Raven* by Gerald McDermott, and—in Mary Pope Osborne's *Favorite Greek Myths*—the story "Phaethon and Helios," in which Phaethon, son of Helios, loses control of his father's sun chariot and scorches the earth. Also compare this story to a Greek myth about the seasons, *Persephone and the Pomegranate* by Chris Waldherr.

RELATED TITLES: Bernhard, Emery. *How Snowshoe Hare Rescued the Sun: A Tale from the Arctic*. Holiday House, 1993. / Choi, Yangsook. *The Sun Girl and the Moon Boy*. Knopf, 1997. / Dayrell, Elphinstone. *Why the Sun and the Moon Live in the Sky: An African Folktale*. Houghton Mifflin, 1968. / Goldin, Barbara Diamond. *Coyote and the Fire Stick: A Pacific Northwest Indian Tale*. Harcourt, 1996. / London, Jonathan. *Fire Race: A Karuk Coyote Tale About How Fire Came to the People*. Chronicle, 1993. / McDermott, Gerald. *Raven: A Trickster Tale from the Pacific Northwest*. Harcourt, 1993. / Osborne, Mary Pope. *Favorite Greek Myths*. Scholastic, 1989. / Shetterly, Susan Hand. *Raven's Light*. Atheneum, 1991. / Waldherr, Kris. *Persephone and the Pomegranate: A Myth from Greece*. Dial, 1993. / Wolkstein, Diane. *The Day Ocean Came to Visit*. Harcourt, 2001. / Young, Ed. *The Sons of the Dragon King: A Chinese Legend*. Atheneum, 2004.

SUBJECTS: BIRDS—FOLKLORE. CROWS—FOLKLORE. EMPERORS—FOLKLORE. FOLKLORE—CHINA. KINGS AND RULERS—FOLKLORE. MULTICULTURAL BOOKS—FOLKLORE. POURQUOI TALES. SUN—FOLKLORE.

1215   Kimmel, Eric A. *Three Samurai Cats: A Story from Japan*. Illus. by Mordicai Gerstein. Holiday House, 2003. 0-8234-1742-5. Unp. Gr. K–4

When the damyo, a powerful Japanese lord, is unable to rid his castle of a savage, rampaging rat, he seeks a tough, fighting samurai cat to chase him out. The first two cats try to get rid of the rat by using force, and fail. The third cat, however, is Neko Roshi, the greatest living master of the martial arts. Though he is old and decrepit, he succeeds in his task because he waits for the rat to defeat itself. Gerstein's pen, ink, and oil illustrations, inspired by 19th-century printmaster Hokusai and by Japanese anime, are full of action and humor.

GERM: As in Emily Arnold McCully's *Beautiful Warrior: The Legend of the Nun's Kung Fu*, where a big, tough bully is defeated by a mere girl, the story underscores a Zen lesson: "Draw strength from stillness. Learn to act without acting." Make both text-to-text and text-to-life connections here. Discuss or write: How and when have you seen this theory put into practice? Witness another confrontation between cats and rats in Margaret Hodges's or Arthur A. Levine's retellings of the classic Japanese tale *The Boy Who Drew Cats*.

RELATED TITLES: Hodges, Margaret. *The Boy Who Drew Cats*. Holiday House, 2002. / Levine, Arthur A. *The Boy Who Drew Cats: A Japanese Folktale*. Dial, 1994. / McCully, Emily Arnold. *Beautiful Warrior: The Legend of the Nun's Kung Fu*. Scholastic, 1998. / Mosel, Arlene. *The Funny Little Woman*. Dutton, 1972. / Sierra, Judy. *Tasty Baby Belly Buttons: A Japanese Folktale*. Houghton Mifflin, 1999. / Yep, Laurence. *The Junior Thunder Lord*. BridgeWater, 1994.

SUBJECTS: CATS—FOLKLORE. FOLKLORE—JAPAN. MULTICULTURAL BOOKS—FOLKLORE. RATS—FOLKLORE. STRENGTH—FOLKLORE.

1216   Kimmel, Eric A. *The Two Mountains: An Aztec Legend*. Illus. by Leonard Everett Fisher. Holiday House, 2000. 0-8234-1504-X. Unp. Gr. 3–6

When his father, the sun god, Tonatiuh, forbids him to go beyond the garden wall, Ixcoçauqui disobeys and there meets and falls in love with Coyalhauhqui, daughter of Mixtli, goddess of the moon. Dismayed at his son's disobedience, Tonatiuh agrees to bless their marriage only on the condition that the young couple never attempt to leave the heavens or visit earth without his permission. After they break that vow, the two must live on earth as mortals; when they die, the gods transform their bodies into two mountains in the Valley of Mexico.

GERM: One fascinating aspect of this Aztec legend is the description of the two lovers' lives after they become mortals, in which they must experience hunger, thirst, sickness, sorrow, and, finally, death. As a discussion starter, ask your students to ponder what the differences are between being mortal and immortal. The story also explains the existence of two famous volcanoes in Mexico, so be sure to read it when you're doing that unit on earthquakes and volcanoes. *Hill of Fire* by Thomas P. Lewis is based on the true story of Paricutín, a Mexican volcano that began growing in a farmer's cornfield in 1943.

RELATED TITLES: Lewis, Thomas P. *Hill of Fire*. HarperCollins, 1971. / Mathews, Sally Schofer. *The Sad Night: The Story of an Aztec Victory and a Spanish Loss*. Clarion, 1994. / McDermott, Gerald. *Musicians of the Sun*. Simon & Schuster, 1997. / Ober, Hal. *How Music Came to the World*. Houghton Mifflin, 1994. / Simon, Seymour. *Volcanoes*. Morrow, 1988. / Tanaka, Shelley. *Lost Temple of the Aztecs*. Hyperion, 1998. / Wisniewski, David. *Rain Player*. Houghton Mifflin, 1991.

SUBJECTS: AZTECS—FOLKLORE. DEATH—FOLKLORE. FOLKLORE—MEXICO. GODS AND GODDESSES—FOLKLORE. LOVE—FOLKLORE. MOUNTAINS—FOLKLORE. MULTICULTURAL BOOKS—FOLKLORE. OBEDIENCE—FOLKLORE. VOLCANOES—FOLKLORE.

1217   Knutson, Barbara. *Love and Roast Chicken: A Trickster Tale from the Andes Mountains*. Illus. by the author. Carolrhoda, 2004. 1-57505-657-7. Unp. Gr. K–3

The quick thinking of Cuy the guinea pig helps him escape from Tió Antonio, the hungry but gullible fox who believes Cuy's warnings about the sky falling and the world ending in a rain of fire. Spanish-language phrases are easily translated in context, though a glossary and pronunciation guide at the back is most helpful.

GERM: Cuy is a trickster in the time-honored tradition of such characters as Brer Rabbit, Anansi the Spider, and Coyote. Read other trickster tales, especially Virginia Hamilton's *Bruh Rabbit and the Tar Baby Girl*, to compare and contrast how tricksters talk their way out of trouble. Verna Aardema's *Borreguita and the Coyote* and "The Sky Is Falling!" in Gretchen Will Mayo's collection *That Tricky Coyote!* also have similar motifs. Discuss: How did Cuy outwit the fox three times? Have them draw and label a picture showing one of Cuy's tricks.

RELATED TITLES: Aardema, Verna. *Borreguita and the Coyote: A Tale from Ayutla, Mexico*. Knopf, 1991. / Ehlert, Lois. *Moon Rope: A Peruvian Folktale*. Harcourt, 1992. / Hamilton, Virginia. *Bruh Rabbit and the Tar Baby Girl*. Scholastic, 2003. / Mayo, Gretchen Will. *That Tricky Coyote!* Walker, 1993. / McDermott, Gerald. *Jabutí the Tortoise: A Trickster Tale from the Amazon*. Harcourt, 2001. / McGill, Alice. *Sure as Sunrise: Stories of Bruh Rabbit and His Walkin' Talkin' Friends*. Houghton Mifflin, 2004. / Meade, Holly. *John Willy and Freddy McGee*. Marshall Cavendish, 1998. / Parks, Van Dyke, and Malcolm Jones. *Jump! The Adventures of Brer Rabbit*. Harcourt, 1986.

SUBJECTS: FOLKLORE—INDIANS OF SOUTH AMERICA. FOLKLORE—PERU. FOLKLORE—SOUTH AMERICA. FOXES—FOLKLORE. GUINEA PIGS—FOLKLORE. HUMOROUS FOLKLORE. MULTICULTURAL BOOKS—FOLKLORE. SPANISH LANGUAGE. TRICKSTER TALES.

1218   Kurtz, Jane. *Trouble*. Illus. by Durga Bernhard. Harcourt, 1997. 0-15-200219-7. Unp. Gr. K–2

In a comical Eritrean folktale from the east coast of Africa, young Tekleh has a hard time keeping clear of trouble as he takes his gabeta game board and heads to the hills to graze his goats.

GERM: Talk it over: Tekleh's father says, "A gabeta board always keeps a young boy out of trouble." Is this true for Tekleh? Retell and draw the sequence of the story to see how it comes full circle in the end. If you can't find a gabeta (also called mankala) board, you can make a simple one out of an egg carton and teach your youngsters how to play. In a way, this trading story will put you in mind of Tom Birdseye's Appalachian folktale, *Soap! Soap!*

RELATED TITLES: Aardema, Verna. *Misoso: Once upon a Time Tales from Africa.* Knopf, 1994. / Birdseye, Tom. *Soap! Soap! Don't Forget the Soap! An Appalachian Folktale.* Holiday House, 1993. / Kurtz, Jane. *Fire on the Mountain.* Simon & Schuster, 1994. / Kurtz, Jane. *Pulling the Lion's Tail.* Simon & Schuster, 1995. / Mennen, Ingrid, and Nicky Daly. *Somewhere in Africa.* Dutton, 1992. / Ziefert, Harriet. *I Swapped My Dog.* Houghton Mifflin, 1998.

SUBJECTS: BARTERING—FOLKLORE. CIRCULAR STORIES—FOLKLORE. CURIOSITY—FOLKLORE. FOLKLORE—ERITREA. GOATS—FOLKLORE. HUMOROUS FOLKLORE. MULTICULTURAL BOOKS—FOLKLORE.

1219 Lunge-Larsen, Lise. *The Hidden Folk: Stories of Fairies, Dwarves, Selkies, and Other Secret Beings.* **Illus. by Beth Krommes. Houghton Mifflin, 2004. 0-618-17495-8. 72pp. Gr. 2–5**
Flower fairies, gnomes, hill folk, elves, dwarves, water horses, river sprites, and selkies are all described in eight stories from Norway and northern Europe, and brought to life with colorful scratchboard artwork done in a folk art style.

GERM: The author states, "These are the stories my mother, aunt, and grandmother told me, almost in passing, so that I would know what the world is really like and what I could find if I paid close attention." Meet more magical beings in *Magic and Mischief: Tales from Cornwall* by Shirley Climo. See which creatures turn up in the fiction fantasy series *The Spiderwick Chronicles*, by Holly Black and Tony DiTerlizzi. In *Troll Fell* by Katherine Langrish, Peer Ulfsson encounters a nisse, but has better luck than Jack in Lunge-Larsen's "The Nisse's Revenge."

RELATED TITLES: Banks, Lynne Reid. *The Fairy Rebel.* Doubleday, 1988. / Black, Holly, and Tony DiTerlizzi. *The Spiderwick Chronicles, Book 1: The Field Guide.* Simon & Schuster, 2003. (And others in the Spiderwick series.) / Climo, Shirley. *Magic and Mischief: Tales from Cornwall.* Clarion, 1999. / Corbett, Sue. *12 Again.* Dutton, 2002. / Forest, Heather. *The Woman Who Flummoxed the Fairies.* Harcourt, 1990. / Hunter, Molly. *A Furl of Fairy Wind.* HarperCollins, 1977. / Langrish, Katherine. *Troll Fell.* HarperCollins, 2004. / Lunge-Larsen, Lise, and Margi Preus. *The Legend of the Lady Slipper: An Ojibwe Tale.* Houghton Mifflin, 1999. / Lunge-Larsen, Lise. *The Troll with No Heart in His Body: And Other Tales of Trolls, from Norway.* Houghton Mifflin, 1999.

SUBJECTS: FAIRIES—FOLKLORE. FAIRY TALES. FOLKLORE—COLLECTIONS. FOLKLORE—NORWAY.

1220 Lunge-Larsen, Lise. *The Troll with No Heart in His Body: And Other Tales of Trolls, from Norway.* **Illus. by Betsy Bowen. Houghton Mifflin, 1999. 0-395-91371-3. 96pp. Gr. 2–5**
The nine troll stories in this delightful collection, some old favorites, some not so familiar, are all storyteller-worthy and illustrated with large, troll-filled woodcuts.

GERM: Students can find folktales about giants from other countries to compare. For older readers, tie in Katherine Laingrish's novel *Troll Fell.* Also introduce the classic troll collection *D'Aulaires' Trolls* by Ingri and Edgar Parin D'Aulaire. Discover other magical creatures from Norway and northern Europe in Lunge-Larsen's companion book, *The Hidden Folk.*

RELATED TITLES: Brett, Jan. *Who's That Knocking on Christmas Eve?* Putnam, 2002. / Brown, Marcia. *The Three Billy Goats Gruff.* Harcourt, 1957. / D'Aulaire, Ingri, and Edgar Parin D'Aulaire. *D'Aulaires' Trolls.* Doubleday, 1972. / dePaola, Tomie. *The Cat on the Dovrefell.* Putnam, 1979. / Langrish, Katherine. *Troll Fell.* HarperCollins, 2004. / Lunge-Larsen, Lise. *The Hidden Folk: Stories of Fairies, Dwarves, Selkies, and Other Secret Beings.* Houghton Mifflin, 2004. / Martin, Claire. *Boots and the Glass Mountain.* Dial, 1992. / Osborne, Mary Pope. *Favorite Norse Myths.* Scholastic, 1996. / Rounds, Glen. *The Three Billy Goats Gruff.* Holiday House, 1993. / Shepard, Aaron. *Master Maid: A Tale of Norway.* Dial, 1997.

SUBJECTS: FOLKLORE—COLLECTIONS. FOLKLORE—NORWAY. TROLLS—FOLKLORE.

1221 Lunge-Larsen, Lise, and Margi Preus. *The Legend of the Lady Slipper: An Ojibwe Tale.* **Illus. by Andrea Arroyo. Houghton Mifflin, 1999. 0-395-90512-5. Unp. Gr. 1–6**
When the people in her village fall ill, a courageous young girl ventures through a snowstorm to the next village to fetch *mash-ki-hi* or healing herbs. Trudging home through the deep snow, under the Northern Lights, she loses her *ma-ka-sins* and must continue on, barefoot, leaving bloody footprints in the snow. In spring, she and her brother discover new, delicate, moccasin-shaped flowers, tinged with pink, along the route she took.

GERM: Compare this pourquoi tale told by the Ojibwa people with Tomie dePaola's *The Legend of the Bluebonnet* and *The Legend of the Indian Paintbrush*. Focus on the aurora borealis with *The Blizzard's Robe*, a literary pourquoi tale of the far north by Robert Sabuda. Another winter legend of the Ojibwa is *Shingebiss* by Nancy Van Laan, about a brave merganser duck who prevails when Winter Maker tries to freeze him.

RELATED TITLES: Coatsworth, Emerson, and David Coatsworth. *The Adventures of Nanabush: Ojibway Indian Stories*. Atheneum, 1980. / dePaola, Tomie. *The Legend of the Bluebonnet: An Old Tale of Texas*. Putnam, 1983. / dePaola, Tomie. *The Legend of the Indian Paintbrush*. Putnam, 1988. / Erdrich, Louise. *The Birchbark House*. Hyperion, 1999. / Esbensen, Barbara Juster. *The Star Maiden: An Ojibway Tale*. Little, Brown, 1988. / Lunge-Larsen, Lise. *The Hidden Folk: Stories of Fairies, Dwarves, Selkies, and Other Secret Beings*. Houghton Mifflin, 2004. / Lunge-Larsen, Lise. *The Troll with No Heart in His Body: And Other Tales of Trolls, from Norway*. Houghton Mifflin, 1999. / Sabuda, Robert. *The Blizzard's Robe*. Atheneum, 1999. / San Souci, Robert D. *Sootface: An Ojibwa Cinderella Story*. Doubleday, 1994. / Van Laan, Nancy. *Shingebiss: An Ojibwe Legend*. Houghton Mifflin, 1997.

SUBJECTS: COURAGE—FOLKLORE. FLOWERS—FOLKLORE. FOLKLORE—INDIANS OF NORTH AMERICA. FOLKLORE—U.S. NORTHERN LIGHTS—FOLKLORE. OJIBWA INDIANS—FOLKLORE. PERSEVERANCE—FOLKLORE. POURQUOI TALES. SICK—FOLKLORE.

1222 **McCaughrean, Geraldine.** *Gilgamesh the Hero: The Epic of Gilgamesh*. **Illus. by David Parkins. Eerdmans, 2003. 0-8028-5262-9. 95pp. Gr. 6–8**

The mighty king Gilgamesh dreams of a friend sent to him by the gods, someone like himself, and that man is the Wild Man, Enkidu. This collection of 12 epic adventures of Gilgamesh and Enkidu is the first of all buddy stories. Based on 7th-century B.C. Assyrian clay tablets that recorded the legend of Gilgamesh, King of Uruk in Mesopotamia (now Iraq) sometime between 3200 B.C. and 2700 B.C., this collection of unforgettable adventures is retold in compelling prose. Purported to be the oldest recorded story in the world, it is also the first Flood story, ultimately told in the Bible and other ancient texts. While it can be a bit racy, that can be a good thing. Get those boys reading!

GERM: After a spurned Ishtar, goddess of love, has Enkidu killed, a grief-torn Gilgamesh seeks the secret of immortality. His journey and final acceptance of his own mortality is told so brilliantly, with such humor and insight, that it will get your students discussing the true meaning of life. Meet Ishtar in another dramatic ancient Mesopotamian myth, *Ishtar and Tammuz* by Christopher Moore. Compare and contrast the life of Gilgamesh with other legendary larger-than-life heroes, such as King Arthur and Odysseus.

RELATED TITLES: Curlee, Lynn. *Seven Wonders of the Ancient World*. Atheneum, 2002. / Fisher, Leonard Everett. *Cyclops*. Holiday House, 1991. / Fisher, Leonard Everett. *Theseus and the Minotaur*. Holiday House, 1988. / Hutton, Warwick. *Odysseus and the Cyclops*. McElderry, 1995. / McCaughrean, Geraldine. *The Bronze Cauldron: Myths and Legends of the World*. McElderry, 1998. / McCaughrean, Geraldine. *The Crystal Pool: Myths and Legends of the World*. McElderry, 1999. / McCaughrean, Geraldine. *The Golden Hoard: Myths and Legends of the World*. Simon & Schuster, 1996. / McCaughrean, Geraldine. *Roman Myths*. McElderry Books, 2001. / Moore, Christopher. *Ishtar and Tammuz: A Babylonian Myth of the Seasons*. Kingfisher, 1996. / Philip, Neil. *The Adventures of Odysseus*. Orchard, 1997. / Pinkney, Jerry. *Noah's Ark*. SeaStar, 2002. / Sabuda, Robert. *Arthur and the Sword*. Atheneum, 1995. / Sutcliffe, Rosemary. *Black Ships Before Troy! The Story of the Iliad*. Delacorte, 1993. / Sutcliffe, Rosemary. *The Wanderings of Odysseus: The Story of The Odyssey*. Delacorte, 1996.

SUBJECTS: ADVENTURE AND ADVENTURERS—FOLKLORE. ANCIENT CIVILIZATIONS—FOLKLORE. FOLKLORE—ARAB COUNTRIES. FOLKLORE—COLLECTIONS. FOLKLORE—IRAQ. GILGAMESH. HEROES—FOLKLORE. KINGS AND RULERS—FOLKLORE. LEGENDS.

1223 **McDermott, Gerald.** *Jabutí the Tortoise: A Trickster Tale from the Amazon*. **Illus. by the author. Harcourt, 2001. 0-15-200496-3. Unp. Gr. PreK–3**

Jabutí, a trickster who hails from the Amazon rain forest, once had a smooth and shiny shell, and all the birds of the air, except for jealous Vulture, loved to hear the sweet music he played on his flute. When the King of Heaven called all the birds to sing at a festival in heaven, Vulture offered to carry the tortoise up there, but once aloft, he turned upside down, and Jabutí fell to earth, cracking his shell. The illustrations, brightly colored gouache, colored pencil, and ink against a bright pink background, give the book a festive and tropical feel.

GERM: Other pourquoi tales on the same subject are *The Flying Tortoise* by Tololwa M. Mollel and *How Turtle's Back Was Cracked* by Gayle Ross. Also read the title story, an Aesop's fable, in Margaret Mayo's collection *Tortoise's Flying Lesson*.

RELATED TITLES: Fleming, Candace. *Sunny Boy! The Life and Times of a Tortoise*. Farrar, 2005. / Jacobs,

Francine. *Lonesome George, the Giant Tortoise.* Walker, 2003. / McDermott, Gerald. *Musicians of the Sun.* Simon & Schuster, 1997. / McDermott, Gerald. *Raven: A Trickster Tale from the Pacific Northwest.* Harcourt, 1993. / Mayo, Margaret. *Tortoise's Flying Lesson: Animal Stories.* Harcourt, 1995. / Mollel, Tololwa M. *The Flying Tortoise: An Igbo Tale.* Clarion, 1994. / Ross, Gayle. *How Turtle's Back Was Cracked: A Traditional Cherokee Tale.* Dial, 1995.

SUBJECTS: FOLKLORE—AMAZON RIVER REGION. FOLKLORE—INDIANS OF SOUTH AMERICA. FOLKLORE—SOUTH AMERICA. POURQUOI TALES. TURTLES—FOLKLORE. VULTURES— FOLKLORE.

1224 **MacDonald, Margaret Read.** *Mabela the Clever.* **Illus. by Tim Coffey. Albert Whitman, 2001. 0-8075-4902-9. Unp. Gr. PreK–2**

The foolish mice can't wait to join the Cat's "secret Cat Society," and heedlessly follow her into the forest, singing the song she teachers them. At the front of the line is the smallest but smartest mouse, Mabela. Just in time, she recalls her father's advice to listen, look around, pay attention, and move fast.

GERM: Your group will enjoy acting out this folktale told by the Limba people of Sierra Leone. See the Author's Note at the front of the book for instructions on playing the Mabela game and music for the Fo Feng song Mabela sings. Discuss: Mabela's father gives her four pieces of useful, life-saving advice. What advice have you received from your parents and how has it helped you? What life-saving advice do you have to offer others?

RELATED TITLES: Bodsworth, Nan. *A Nice Walk in the Jungle.* Viking, 1989. / Clark, Emma Chichester. *Follow the Leader.* McElderry, 2003. / Donaldson, Julia. *The Gruffalo.* Dial, 1999. / Emberley, Michael. *Ruby.* Little, Brown, 1990. / Farris, Pamela J. *Young Mouse and Elephant: An East African Folktale.* Houghton Mifflin, 1996. / Pilkey, Dav. *Kat Kong.* Harcourt, 1993. / Waber, Bernard. *Do You See a Mouse?* Houghton Mifflin, 1995. / Walsh, Ellen Stoll. *Mouse Count.* Harcourt, 1991. / Zelinsky, Paul O. *The Maid, the Mouse, and the Odd-Shaped House.* Puffin, 1993.

SUBJECTS: ANIMALS—FOLKLORE. CATS—FOLKLORE. FOLKLORE—AFRICA, WEST. FOLKLORE—SIERRA LEONE. MICE—FOLKLORE. MULTICULTURAL BOOKS—FOLKLORE.

1225 **MacDonald, Margaret Read.** *The Old Woman Who Lived in a Vinegar Bottle.* **Illus. by Nancy Dunaway Fowlkes. August House, 1995. 0-87483-415-5. Unp. Gr. PreK–3**

Every day, the old woman sits on the steps outside her vinegar bottle and complains that she deserves better, but when a passing fairy rewards her with a succession of bigger and better houses, she never says thank you, and she never stops complaining. You probably know people like this. MacDonald's retelling is full of repetition and humor, and it will be a fine story to learn to tell with your children.

GERM: Discuss the final sentence of the story: "After all, happiness comes from the heart, not from the house." What does this mean? How does this apply to your own life? Compare this British folktale to its German counterpart by the Brothers Grimm, *The Fisherman and His Wife.* There's a swell picture-book version illustrated by Margot Zemach, or you can find the text in any nice collection of Grimm fairy tales. Demi's *The Magic Goldfish* is a Russian variant.

RELATED TITLES: Bania, Michael. *Kumak's House: A Tale of the Far North.* Alaska Northwest, 2002. / Demi. *The Greatest Treasure.* Scholastic, 1998. / Demi. *The Magic Goldfish: A Russian Folktale by Aleksandr Pushkin.* Henry Holt, 1995. / Forest, Heather. *A Big Quiet House.* August House, 1996. / Grimm, Jacob. *The Fisherman and His Wife.* Illus. by Margot Zemach. Farrar, 1980. / Shepard, Aaron. *The Gifts of Wali Dad: A Tale of India and Pakistan.* Atheneum, 1995.

SUBJECTS: CIRCULAR STORIES—FOLKLORE. ELDERLY—FOLKLORE. FOLKLORE—GREAT BRITAIN. STORIES TO TELL. UNGRATEFULNESS—FOLKLORE. WISHES—FOLKLORE.

1226 **McGill, Alice.** *Sure as Sunrise: Stories of Bruh Rabbit & His Walkin' Talkin' Friends.* **Illus. by Don Tate. Houghton Mifflin, 2004. 0-618-21196-9. 48pp. Gr. K–5**

Retold by a master storyteller who recalls each story from her North Carolina childhood, these five crackling African American folktales about the crafty trickster Bruh Rabbit and his animal pals and rivals will get your listeners thumping their chairs with laughter. Bruh Rabbit's love of food and music get him in trouble; Bruh Possum learns a snake is always a snake; Bruh Sammy the possum plays dead; and Bruh Rabbit sets his sights on marrying the king's daughter.

GERM: The lively language and illustrations will get your kids laughin' and retellin' and comprehendin' and comparin'. Compare the first story with other variants of the briar patch story, including Virginia Hamilton's *Bruh Rabbit and the Tar Baby Girl.* Along with "Bruh Possum and the Snake," read Coleen Salley's possum folktales, *Epossumondas* and *Why Epossumondas Has No*

Hair on His Tail. In *Ananse and the Lizard* by Pat Cummings, the trickster spider also plans to win the hand of a human chief's daughter.

RELATED TITLES: Cummings, Pat. *Ananse and the Lizard: A West African Tale.* Henry Holt, 2002. / Doucet, Sharon Arms. *Why Lapin's Ears Are Long and Other Tales from the Louisiana Bayou.* Orchard, 1997. / Faulkner, William J. *Brer Tiger and the Big Wind* Morrow, 1995. / Hamilton, Virginia. *Bruh Rabbit and the Tar Baby Girl.* Scholastic, 2003. / Hamilton, Virginia. *When Birds Could Talk and Bats Could Sing.* Blue Sky/Scholastic, 1996. / Jacquith, Priscilla. *Bo Rabbit Smart for True.* Philomel, 1994. / Lester, Julius. *The Tales of Uncle Remus: The Adventures of Brer Rabbit.* Dial, 1990. / McDermott, Gerald. *Zomo the Rabbit: A Trickster Tale from West Africa.* Harcourt, 1992. / Mayo, Gretchen Will. *Here Comes Tricky Rabbit.* Walker, 1994. / Parks, Van Dyke, and Malcolm Jones. *Jump! The Adventures of Brer Rabbit.* Harcourt, 1986. / Ross, Gayle. *How Rabbit Tricked Otter and Other Cherokee Trickster Stories.* HarperCollins, 1994. / Salley, Coleen. *Epossumondas.* Harcourt, 2002. / Salley, Coleen. *Why Epossumondas Has No Hair on His Tail.* Harcourt, 2004. / Stevens, Janet. *Tops and Bottoms.* Harcourt, 1995. / Van Laan, Nancy. *With a Whoop and a Holler.* Atheneum, 1998.

SUBJECTS: ANIMALS—FOLKLORE. FOLKLORE—COLLECTIONS. FOLKLORE—U.S. FOLKLORE, AFRICAN AMERICAN. HUMOROUS FOLKLORE. MULTICULTURAL BOOKS—FOLKLORE. RABBITS—FOLKLORE. TRICKSTER TALES.

1227 **McKissack, Patricia C., and Robert L. McKissack.** *Itching and Twitching: A Nigerian Folktale.* **Illus. by Laura Freeman. Scholastic, 2003. 0-439-24224-X (paper). Unp. Gr. PreK–1**
When Rabbit and Monkey have dinner together at Monkey's house, Monkey can't stop itching and Rabbit can't stop twitching. They drive each other crazy, though each claims he can stop if he chooses to. They put it to the test, agreeing that the first to scratch or twitch must do the dishes.
GERM: Monkey and Rabbit tell each other a story that incorporates itching and twitching, which your listeners will be happy to act out. This comical easy-to-read folktale is perfect for storytelling. See how long everyone can sit without itching or twitching.
RELATED TITLES: Diakité, Baba Wagué. *The Hatseller and the Monkeys: A West African Folktale.* Scholastic, 1999. / MacDonald, Margaret Read. *Pickin' Peas.* HarperCollins, 1998. / Perkins, Al. *Hand, Hand, Fingers, Thumb.* Random House, 1969. / Rey, H. A. *Curious George.* Houghton Mifflin, 1993. (And others in the Curious George series.) / Silverman, Erica. *Don't Fidget a Feather.* Macmillan, 1994. / Slobodkina, Esphyr. *Caps for Sale.* HarperCollins, 1947.
SUBJECTS: CREATIVE DRAMA—FOLKLORE. FOLKLORE—AFRICA, WEST. FOLKLORE—NIGERIA. FRIENDSHIP—FOLKLORE. HUMOROUS FOLKLORE. MONKEYS—FOLKLORE. MULTICULTURAL BOOKS—FOLKLORE. RABBITS—FOLKLORE. STORYTELLING—FOLKLORE.

1228 **Martin, Rafe.** *The Shark God.* **Illus. by David Shannon. Scholastic, 2001. 0-590-39500-9. Unp. Gr. 2–5**
When a brother and sister can't find anyone to help them rescue a shark entangled in rope, they do it themselves. Jubilant, they race back to their village, and touch the king's drum, which is kapu—forbidden—and they are apprehended. The hardhearted king refuses to lift his sentence of death, so the children's parents visit the cave of Kauhuhu, the fearsome Shark God, to ask for help.
GERM: Based on an old Hawaiian folktale, this suspenseful shark-filled story with its powerful oil paintings will lead to discussion of unjust punishment, unforgiving rulers, the lives of sharks, and the kindness and caring of children. Another Hawaiian shark tale, a light-hearted one where the sharks are the bad guys, is *Punia and the King of Sharks* by Lee Wardlaw.
RELATED TITLES: Cerullo, Mary M. *Sharks: Challengers of the Deep.* Dutton, 1993. / Cerullo, Mary M. *The Truth About Great White Sharks.* Chronicle, 2000. / Davies, Nicola. *Surprising Sharks.* Candlewick, 2003. / Mahy, Margaret. *The Great White Man-Eating Shark.* Dial, 1990. / Martin, Rafe. *The Boy Who Lived with the Seals.* Putnam, 1993. / O'Brien, Patrick. *Megatooth.* Henry Holt, 2001. / Pringle, Laurence. *Sharks! Strange and Wonderful.* Boyds Mills, 2001. / Rumford, James. *Dog-of-the-Sea-Waves.* Houghton Mifflin, 2004. / Rumford, James. *The Island-Below-the-Star.* Houghton Mifflin, 1998. / Schaefer, Carole Lexa. *The Biggest Soap.* Farrar, 2004. / Wardlaw, Lee. *Punia and the King of Sharks: A Hawaiian Folktale.* Dial, 1997.
SUBJECTS: DRUMS—FOLKLORE. FOLKLORE—HAWAII. FOLKLORE—U.S. KINGS AND RULERS—FOLKLORE. MULTICULTURAL BOOKS—FOLKLORE. SHARKS—FOLKLORE.

1229 **Max, Jill.** *Spider Spins a Story: Fourteen Legends from Native America.* **Illus. by Robert Annesley, Benjamin Harjo, and others. Rising Moon, 1997. 0-87358-611-5. 65pp. Gr. 3–8**
Starting with creation legends about how the earth and spiders came to be, and moving onto pourquoi tales about the first loom and the first rainbow, this is a valuable source for reading

aloud and storytelling, with a full-page painting by one of five exceptional Native American artists accompanying each compellingly told story. Water Spider brought the first fire to people, according to the Cherokee, and other tales introduce Spider Woman or Grandmother Spider.

GERM: As you read the stories aloud, have groups research the 12 different tribes represented, including Kiowa, Zuni, Hopi, Lakota, Muskogee, and Navajo. Pull in factual information about spiders, too. Then see how Anansi the Spider spread the world's first stories in the African folktale—and Caldecott-winning picture book—*A Story, A Story* by Gail E. Haley.

RELATED TITLES: Berger, Melvin. *Spinning Spiders.* HarperCollins, 2003. / Bruchac, Joseph. *The Boy Who Lived with the Bears and Other Iroquois Stories.* HarperCollins, 1995. / Climo, Shirley. *Someone Saw a Spider: Spider Facts and Folktales.* Crowell, 1985. / Haley, Gail E. *A Story, a Story.* Atheneum, 1970. / Hausman, Gerald. *How Chipmunk Got Tiny Feet: Native American Animal Origin Stories.* HarperCollins, 1995. / Kimmel, Eric A. *Anansi and the Moss-Covered Rock.* Holiday House, 1990. / Montgomery, Sy. *The Tarantula Scientist.* Houghton Mifflin, 2004. / Murawski, Darlyne A. *Spiders and Their Webs.* National Geographic, 2004. / Musgrove, Margaret. *The Spider Weaver: A Legend of Kente Cloth.* Scholastic, 2001. / Ross, Gayle. *How Rabbit Tricked Otter and Other Cherokee Trickster Stories.* HarperCollins, 1994. / Simon, Seymour. *Spiders.* HarperCollins, 2003. / Van Laan, Nancy. *In a Circle Long Ago: A Treasury of Native Lore from North America.* Knopf, 1995.

SUBJECTS: FOLKLORE—COLLECTIONS. FOLKLORE—INDIANS OF NORTH AMERICA. FOLKLORE—U.S. MULTICULTURAL BOOKS—FOLKLORE. POURQUOI TALES. SPIDERS—FOLKLORE. STORYTELLING.

1230 Mayer, Marianna. *The Adventures of Tom Thumb.* **Illus. by Kinuko Y. Craft. SeaStar, 2001. 1-58717-065-5. Unp. Gr. K–3**

King Arthur's great wizard, Merlin, grants farmer Tim Tall of the Mountains and his wife Kate their fondest wish—a baby no bigger than Tim Tall's thumb, whom they name Tom Thumb. Ingested by a cow, and then carried away by a raven, Tom Thumb arrives at the castle of the dangerous giant Gembo, who wants to eat the little mite. Indeed, he tries to, but Tom outsmarts him and escapes, only to be swallowed by a fish. Craft's ornate, stunning illustrations done in oil over watercolor, were inspired by 12th-century illuminated manuscripts, and the story is based on the earliest existing printed text, dating back to 1621.

GERM: As Tom Thumb is knighted by King Arthur, pull in some of the Arthur legends, such as *Merlin and the Making of the King* by Margaret Hodges or *Arthur and the Sword* by Robert Sabuda. Provide examples of other thumb-sized heroes in classic children's stories, including Hans Christian Andersen's Thumbelina and the Japanese Issun Boshi, or Little One Inch.

RELATED TITLES: Andersen, Hans Christian. *Thumbelina.* Retold by Amy Ehrlich. Illus. by Susan Jeffers. Dial, 1979. / Andersen, Hans Christian. *Thumbelina.* Retold and illustrated by Lauren Mills. Little, Brown, 2005. / Bertrand, Lynne. *Granite Baby.* Farrar, 2005. / Brenner, Barbara. *Little One Inch.* Coward, 1977. / Hodges, Margaret. *Merlin and the Making of the King.* Holiday House, 2004. / Hughes, Monica. *Little Fingerling.* Ideals, 1992. / Kleven, Elisa. *The Paper Princess.* Dutton, 1994. / Melmed, Laura Krauss. *Little Oh.* Lothrop, 1997. / Melmed, Laura Krauss. *The Rainbabies.* Lothrop, 1992. / Shute, Linda. *Momotaro the Peach Boy.* Lothrop, 1986. / Sabuda, Robert. *Arthur and the Sword.* Atheneum, 1995. / San Souci, Robert D. *Young Arthur.* Doubleday, 1997. / Sneed, Brad. *Thumbelina.* Dial 2004.

SUBJECTS: ARTHUR, KING (LEGENDARY CHARACTER). FAIRY TALES. FOLKLORE—ENGLAND. GIANTS—FOLKLORE. KINGS AND RULERS—FOLKLORE. KNIGHTS AND KNIGHTHOOD—FOLKLORE. SIZE—FOLKLORE.

1231 Mollel, Tololwa M. *Ananse's Feast: An Ashanti Tale.* **Illus. by Andrew Glass. Clarion, 1997. 0-395-67402-6. Unp. Gr. K–3**

Before they begin eating, greedy Ananse the Spider, the West African trickster, sends his friend Akye the Turtle down to the river three times to wash his four hands; then he devours all the food himself before Akye gets back.

GERM: Ananse the Spider is well-known for his indolence and greed, his unrepentant and wily ways, and we all know that Ananse never really learns his lesson. Read other Anansi stories and talk it over: Why do we so enjoy stories about such a bad actor?

RELATED TITLES: Aardema, Verna. *Anansi Does the Impossible! An Ashanti Tale.* Atheneum, 1997. / Aardema, Verna. *Anansi Finds a Fool.* Dial, 1992. / Cummings, Pat. *Ananse and the Lizard: A West African Tale.* Henry Holt, 2002. / Kimmel, Eric A. *Anansi and the Magic Stick.* Holiday House, 2001. / Kimmel, Eric A. *Anansi and the Moss-Covered Rock.* Holiday House, 1990. / Kimmel, Eric A. *Anansi and the Talking Melon.* Holiday House, 1994. / Kimmel, Eric A. *Anansi Goes Fishing.* Holiday House, 1992. / MacDonald, Margaret Read. *Pickin' Peas.* HarperCollins, 1998. / Mollel, Tololwa M. *The Flying Tortoise: An Igbo Tale.* Clarion, 1994. / Souhami, Jessica.

The Leopard's Drum: An Asante Tale from West Africa. Little, Brown, 1996. / Stevens, Janet. Tops and Bottoms. Harcourt, 1995. / Temple, Frances. Tiger Soup: An Anansi Story from Jamaica. Orchard, 1994.

SUBJECTS: ANANSI (LEGENDARY CHARACTER). ANIMALS—FOLKLORE. FOLKLORE—AFRICA, WEST. FOOD—FOLKLORE. HUMOROUS FOLKLORE. MULTICULTURAL BOOKS—FOLKLORE. SPIDERS—FOLKLORE. TRICKSTER TALES. TURTLES—FOLKLORE.

1232 **Mollel, Tololwa M.** *Subira, Subira.* **Illus. by Linda Saport. Clarion, 2000. 0-395-91809-X. Unp. Gr. 1–6**

After Mother dies and Tatu cannot get her little brother Maulidi to obey her, she seeks out a spirit woman who instructs her to pluck three whiskers from a lion. Smudgy, deep blues and earth-colored pastels are striking from a distance.

GERM: Words and music to the song Tatu sings are appended. Compare this story set in Tanzania with two variants from Ethiopia: *The Lion's Whiskers* by Nancy Raines Day and *Pulling the Lion's Tail* by Jane Kurtz. Discussion point: How did pulling out the lion's whiskers help Tatu deal with her little brother? To stimulate some experiential writing, ask: Have you ever solved a problem with a brother or sister or friend without asking your parents or teacher or spirit woman for help? What did you do? What is your biggest problem now? What steps do you think you could take to solve it?

RELATED TITLES: Aardema, Verna. *Misoso: Once upon a Time Tales from Africa*. Knopf, 1994. / Day, Nancy Raines. *The Lion's Whiskers: An Ethiopian Folktale*. Scholastic, 1995. / Kurtz, Jane. *Fire on the Mountain*. Simon & Schuster, 1994. / Kurtz, Jane. *Pulling the Lion's Tail*. Simon & Schuster, 1995. / Kurtz, Jane. *Trouble*. Harcourt, 1997. / Mollel, Tololwa M. *My Rows and Piles of Coins*. Clarion, 1999. / Nolan, Dennis. *Androcles and the Lion*. Harcourt, 1997. / Onyefulu, Obi. *Chinye: A West African Folk Tale*. Viking, 1994. / Steptoe, John. *Mufaro's Beautiful Daughters: An African Tale*. Lothrop, 1987.

SUBJECTS: BEHAVIOR—FOLKLORE. BROTHERS AND SISTERS—FOLKLORE. DEATH— FOLKLORE. FOLKLORE—AFRICA. FOLKLORE—TANZANIA. GRIEF—FOLKLORE. LIONS— FOLKLORE. MULTICULTURAL BOOKS—FOLKLORE. PATIENCE—FOLKLORE.

1233 **Montes, Marisa.** *Juan Bobo Goes to Work: A Puerto Rican Folktale.* **Illus. by Joe Cepeda. HarperCollins, 2000. 0-688-16234-7. Unp. Gr. K–3**

In a noodlehead or fool tale from Puerto Rico, Juan Bobo obeys his mother when she sends him out to work on Don Pepe's farm, but the simple boy does everything wrong. To the dismay of his mother and the farmer, Juan Bobo shells the beans and piles them on the ground; ties the legs of the cow together so he can milk her; and loses his money when he puts his coins into his hole-filled pocket, and pours his next day's payment, a pail of fresh milk, into his burlap sack. Don't worry too much about this foolish fellow, though; he saves a rich man's beautiful daughter from dying by making her laugh and gets a nice reward.

GERM: The way Juan Bobo follows instructions literally will remind readers of the antics of Amelia Bedelia, as told by Peggy Parish, and *Epossumondas* by Coleen Salley. Meet Juan's English counterpart in *Lazy Jack* by Vivian French.

RELATED TITLES: Bernier-Grand, Carmen T. *Juan Bobo: Four Folktales from Puerto Rico*. HarperCollins, 1994. / Birdseye, Tom. *Soap! Soap! Don't Forget the Soap! An Appalachian Folktale*. Holiday House, 1993. / French, Vivian. *Lazy Jack*. Harcourt, 1996. / González, Lucia M. *Señor Cat's Romance and Other Favorite Stories from Latin America*. Scholastic, 1997. / Parish, Peggy. *Amelia Bedelia series*. Greenwillow. / Pitre, Felix. *Juan Bobo and the Pig: A Puerto Rican Folktale*. Lodestar, 1993. / Pitre, Felix. *Paco and the Witch: A Puerto Rican Folktale*. Dutton, 1995. / Salley, Coleen. *Epossumondas*. Harcourt, 2002. / Simms, Laura. *The Squeaky Door*. Crown, 1991.

SUBJECTS: FOLKLORE—PUERTO RICO. FOOLS—FOLKLORE. HUMOROUS FOLKLORE. JUAN BOBO (LEGENDARY CHARACTER). MULTICULTURAL BOOKS—FOLKLORE.

1234 **Morpurgo, Michael.** *The McElderry Book of Aesop's Fables.* **Illus. by Emma Chichester Clark. McElderry, 2005. 1-41690-290-2. 96pp. Gr. K–5**

Twenty-one fables, some familiar, along with large, full-bleed, soft, sweet watercolors, introduce the usual assortment of misbehaving and misguided rats, dogs, foxes, crows, and other animal friends and enemies, all of whom learn their lessons. The moral of each story is stated at the end, and the large print and easy-to-understand text make this good-looking collection a natural for all grades.

GERM: Act these out in small groups as skits for the rest of the class, who can determine each story's moral. Compare several retellings of the same story to see what kind of spin each author and illustrator has put on these traditional tales.

RELATED TITLES: Bader, Barbara. *Aesop and Company*. Houghton Mifflin, 1991. / Calmenson, Stephanie. *The Children's Aesop*. Doubleday, 1988. / Demi. *Buddha Stories*. Henry Holt, 1997. / Demi. *The Dragon's Tale and Other Animal Fables of the Chinese Zodiac*. Henry Holt, 1996. / Gatti, Anne. *Aesop's Fables*. Harcourt, 1992. / Lobel, Arnold. *Fables*. HarperCollins, 1980. / Paxton, Tom. *Belling the Cat and Other Aesop's Fables: Retold in Verse*. Morrow, 1990. / Pinkney, Jerry. *Aesop's Fables*. SeaStar, 2000. / Scieszka, Jon. *Squids Will Be Squids: Fresh Morals, Beastly Fables*. Viking, 1998. / Sogabe, Aki. *Aesop's Fox*. Harcourt, 1999. / Untermeyer, Louis. *Aesop's Fables*. Golden, 1965. / Ward, Helen. *The Rooster and the Fox*. Millbrook, 2003.

SUBJECTS: AESOP. ANIMALS—FOLKLORE. CREATIVE DRAMA—FOLKLORE. FABLES. FOLKLORE—COLLECTIONS. READER'S THEATER—FOLKLORE.

1235   Morpurgo, Michael. *Sir Gawain and the Green Knight*. **Illus. by Michael Foreman. Candlewick, 2004. 0-7636-2519-1. 116pp. Gr. 5–8**

At the New Year's Eve banquet, King Arthur exhorts his knights to tell him a new and stirring tale of outlandish adventure or perform an extraordinary feat of arms before they can eat their feast. Into the great hall strides a giant of a man, a massive knight dressed all in green, with green skin and hair, looking for a knight he can challenge to a fearful game. Sir Gawain accepts his terms: he will have one chance to chop off the giant's head, and in return, the fearsome knight will do the same to Gawain one year and a day hence. Morpurgo's eloquent retelling and Foreman's full-bleed watercolor and pastel illustrations flesh out this favorite King Arthur tale of loyalty and virtue into a thrilling adventure.

GERM: Selena Hastings has retold two Gawain stories as picture books—*Gawain and the Green Knight* and *Sir Gawain and the Loathly Lady*—with gorgeous illustrations by Juan Wijngaard. Compare the illustrations with those by David Shannon in Mark Shannon's version of *Gawain and the Green Knight*. For another bracing quest tale from English literature, read Eric A. Kimmel's picture-book retelling of Beowulf's encounter with the green-skinned monster Grendel in *The Hero Beowulf*.

RELATED TITLES: Hastings, Selena. *Sir Gawain and the Green Knight*. Lothrop, 1981. / Hastings, Selena. *Sir Gawain and the Loathly Lady*. Lothrop, 1985. / Hayes, Sarah. *Robin Hood*. Henry Holt, 1989. / Hodges, Margaret. *Merlin and the Making of the King*. Holiday House, 2004. / Hodges, Patricia. *Saint George and the Dragon*. Little, Brown, 1984. / Kimmel, Eric A. *The Hero Beowulf*. Farrar, 2005. / Osborne, Mary Pope. *Favorite Medieval Tales*. Scholastic, 1998. / Sabuda, Robert. *Arthur and the Sword*. Atheneum, 1995. / San Souci, Robert D. *Young Arthur*. Doubleday, 1997. / Shannon, Mark. *Gawain and the Green Knight*. Putnam, 1994. / Talbott, Hudson. *King Arthur and the Round Table*. Morrow, 1995. / Winthrop, Elizabeth. *The Castle in the Attic*. Holiday House, 1985. / Yolen, Jane. *Merlin and the Dragons*. Dutton, 1995. / Yolen, Jane. *Passager: The Young Merlin Trilogy, Book One*. Harcourt, 1996.

SUBJECTS: ARTHUR, KING (LEGENDARY CHARACTER). FOLKLORE—ENGLAND. GAWAIN (LEGENDARY CHARACTER). KINGS AND RULERS—FOLKLORE. KNIGHTS AND KNIGHTHOOD—FOLKLORE. LEGENDS.

1236   Moser, Barry. *The Three Little Pigs*. **Illus. by the author. Little, Brown, 2001. 0-316-58544-0. Unp. Gr. PreK–1**

Moser's rotund pigs, rendered in splendid watercolors, meet up with that wolf who eats the first two and gets boiled into wolf stew by the third. This is the real story, complete with the apple tree and butter churn scenes.

GERM: From other traditional versions by Paul Galdone, James Marshall, Glen Rounds, and Margot Zemach, to the Southern U.S. variant, William H. Hooks's *The Three Little Pigs and the Fox*, plus parodies like Jon Scieszka's *The True Story of the 3 Little Pigs*, and turnabouts like Eugene Trivizas's *The Three Little Wolves and the Big Bad Pig*, this is a story that speaks to us all. Be sure children know this classic tale before turning them loose with David Wiesner's Caldecott-winning fantasy, *The Three Pigs*.

RELATED TITLES: Galdone, Paul. *The Three Little Pigs*. Seabury, 1970. / Hooks, William H. *The Three Little Pigs and the Fox*. Macmillan, 1989. / Marshall, James. *The Three Little Pigs*. Dial, 1989. / Rounds, Glen. *Three Little Pigs and the Big Bad Wolf*. Holiday House, 1992. / Scieszka, Jon. *The True Story of the 3 Little Pigs*. Viking, 1989. / Souhami, Jessica. *No Dinner! The Story of the Old Woman and the Pumpkin*. Marshall Cavendish, 2000. / Trivizas, Eugene. *The Three Little Wolves and the Big Bad Pig*. McElderry, 1993. / Vozar, David. *Yo, Hungry Wolf! A Nursery Rap*. Doubleday, 1993. / Wiesner, David. *The Three Pigs*. Clarion, 2001. / Zemach, Margot. *The Three Little Pigs: An Old Story*. Farrar, 1988.

SUBJECTS: FOLKLORE. PIGS—FOLKLORE. WOLVES—FOLKLORE.

1237 Muth, Jon J. *Stone Soup.* **Illus. by Jon J Muth. Scholastic, 2003. 0-439-33909-X. Unp. Gr. K–2**
Three Chinese monks arrive in an inhospitable village and help show the people the way to happiness by making soup from a stone.
GERM: Ponder the question the youngest monk asks: "What makes one happy?" Script this as a Reader's Theater production. Compare and contrast this version with others by Marcia Brown, Eric A. Kimmel, Ann McGovern, John Warren Stewig, and Margo Zemach.
RELATED TITLES: Brown, Marcia. *Stone Soup.* Scribner, 1947. / Compestine, Ying Chang. *The Story of Chopsticks.* Holiday House, 2001. / Cooper, Helen. *Pumpkin Soup.* Farrar, 1999. / Ehlert, Lois. *Growing Vegetable Soup.* Harcourt, 1987. / Hong, Lily Toy. *How the Ox Star Fell from Heaven.* Albert Whitman, 1991. / Kimmel, Eric A. *Cactus Soup.* Marshall Cavendish, 2004. / McCully, Emily Arnold. *Beautiful Warrior: The Legend of the Nun's Kung Fu.* Scholastic, 1998. / McGovern, Ann. *Stone Soup.* Scholastic, 1986. / Mahy, Margaret. *The Seven Chinese Brothers.* Scholastic, 1990. / Muth, Jon J. *Zen Shorts.* Scholastic, 2005. / Patron, Susan. *Burgoo Stew.* Orchard, 1991. / Sendak, Maurice. *Chicken Soup with Rice.* HarperCollins, 1962. / Stamm, Claus. *Three Strong Women.* Viking, 1990. / Stewig, John Warren. *Stone Soup.* Holiday House, 1991. / Zemach, Margot. *Nail Soup.* Follett, 1964.
SUBJECTS: COOKERY. CREATIVE DRAMA—FOLKLORE. FOLKLORE—CHINA. FOOD—FOLKLORE. GENEROSITY—FOLKLORE. HAPPINESS—FOLKLORE. MULTICULTURAL BOOKS—FOLKLORE. READER'S THEATER—FOLKLORE. SOUP—FOLKLORE.

1238 Norman, Howard. *The Girl Who Dreamed Only Geese and Other Tales of the Far North.* **Illus. by Leo and Diane Dillon. Harcourt, 1997. 0-15-230979-9. 147pp. Gr. 4–6**
The ten Inuit folktales involving people and animals included in this handsome collection are amiable, personable, quirky, and sometimes downright funny. Alternating with the gorgeous full-color acrylics, the black-and-white tempera and ink scratchboard friezes were inspired by the stone-cut art of the Inuits and contain sequential elements of each story.
GERM: After sharing these tales aloud, make a chart with your listeners of what they learned about the Inuit. Look up some more facts to share. Talk about folklore and how it provides a window on a people's culture and lives.
RELATED TITLES: Bernhard, Emery. *The Girl Who Wanted to Hunt.* Holiday House, 1994. / Bierhorst, John, ed. *The Dancing Fox: Arctic Folktales.* Morrow, 1997. / George, Jean Craighead. *Julie of the Wolves.* HarperCollins, 1972. / Heinz, Brian. *Kayuktuk: An Arctic Quest.* Chronicle, 1996. / Hill, Kirkpatrick. *Winter Camp.* McElderry, 1993. / Lelooska. *Echoes of the Elders: The Stories and Paintings of Chief Lelooska.* DK Ink, 1997. / Lelooska. *Spirit of the Cedar People: More Stories and Paintings of Chief Lelooska.* DK Ink, 1998. / Napoli, Donna Jo. *North.* Greenwillow, 2004. / Simms, Laura. *The Bone Man: A Native American Modoc Tale.* Hyperion, 1997. / Sloat, Teri. *The Hungry Giant of the Tundra.* Dutton, 1993. / Steltzer, Ulli. *Building an Igloo.* Henry Holt, 1995. / Villoldo, Alberto. *Skeleton Woman.* Simon & Schuster, 1995.
SUBJECTS: FOLKLORE—ARCTIC REGIONS. FOLKLORE—COLLECTIONS. FOLKLORE, INUIT. MULTICULTURAL BOOKS—FOLKLORE.

1239 Osborne, Mary Pope. *The Brave Little Seamstress.* **Illus. by Giselle Potter. Atheneum, 2002. 0-689-84486-7. Unp. Gr. 2–6**
As she did with *Kate and the Beanstalk,* Mary Pope Osborne has turned the main character of this German tale, "The Brave Little Tailor," into a female, and hooray for it! When a little seamstress kills a swarm of flies, she proudly stitches the words "SEVEN WITH ONE BLOW" on the back of her coat. She boldly outwits first one giant, then two giants, and finally, at the king's bidding, a vicious wild unicorn and a wild boar. When the ungrateful king discovers her true identity, she outfoxes him, too. What a satisfying and amusing trickster tale for all.
GERM: Ask your listeners to explain the ways in which the seamstress used brains, not brawn, like clever Oona in *Fin M'Coul, the Giant of Knockmany Hill* by Tomie dePaola, or *Mrs. McCool and the Giant Cuhullin* by Jessica Souhami. Compare this version with the original Grimm story, *Seven at One Blow,* retold by Eric A. Kimmel, and Paul Brett Johnson's *Fearless Jack,* which is set in Appalachia. Osborne's *Kate and the Beanstalk* is a retelling of that other famous giant story, but with a girl in the title role instead of Jack.
RELATED TITLES: Cauley, Lorinda Bryan. *Jack and the Beanstalk.* Putnam, 1983. / Chase, Richard. *The Jack Tales.* Houghton, 1943. / Compton, Kenn, and Joanne Compton. *Jack the Giant Chaser: An Appalachian Tale.* Holiday House, 1993. / dePaola, Tomie. *Fin M'Coul, the Giant of Knockmany Hill.* Holiday House, 1981. / Johnson, Paul Brett. *Fearless Jack.* McElderry, 2001. / Johnson, Paul Brett. *Jack Outwits the Giants.* McElderry, 2002. / Kimmel, Eric A. *Seven at One Blow: A Tale from the Brothers Grimm.* Holiday House, 1998. / Osborne, Mary Pope. *Kate and the Beanstalk.* Atheneum, 2000. / Price, Christine. *Sixty at a Blow.* Dutton, 1968. / Souhami, Jes-

sica. *Mrs. McCool and the Giant Cuhullin: An Irish Tale.* Henry Holt, 2002. / Thomson, Peggy. *The Brave Little Tailor.* Simon & Schuster, 1992. / Van Woerkom, Dorothy. *Alexandra the Rock-Eater.* Knopf, 1978. / Willey, Margaret. *Clever Beatrice: An Upper Peninsula Conte.* Atheneum, 2001.

SUBJECTS: FOLKLORE—GERMANY. GIANTS—FOLKLORE. HUMOROUS FOLKLORE. TRICKSTER TALES. UNICORNS—FOLKLORE. WOMEN—FOLKLORE.

1240 **Osborne, Mary Pope.** *Favorite Medieval Tales.* **Illus. by Troy Howell. Scholastic, 1998. 0-590-60042-7. 86pp. Gr. 3–8**

Illustrations that look as if they come from illuminated manuscripts accompany retellings of nine classic tales that were told in England from 1000 A.D. to the mid-1400s, including "Beowulf," "The Sword in the Stone, "Robin Hood and His Merry Men," and "Chanticleer and the Fox."

GERM: At the beginning of each tale is a quote from the story in Old English or Middle English, with a modern-day translation. Have students read these quotes aloud phonetically and then ask them to try to make sense of them. Pull in other King Arthur and Robin Hood legends. Compare Osborne's version of "Gawain and the Green Knight" with the picture-book versions by Selena Hastings and Mark Shannon. Look at the story "Chanticleer and the Fox" along with Barbara Cooney's picture book of the same name and Helen Ward's *The Rooster and the Fox*, taken from Chaucer's *The Canterbury Tales*. Nancy Farmer's novel *The Sea of Trolls* incorporates a retelling of the Beowulf story, while Eric A. Kimmel's picture book *The Hero Beowulf* is a retelling of the confrontation between Beowulf and the monster Grendel.

RELATED TITLES: Cooney, Barbara. *Chanticleer and the Fox.* HarperCollins, 1986. / Farmer, Nancy. *The Sea of Trolls.* Atheneum, 2004. / Hastings, Selena. *Sir Gawain and the Green Knight.* Lothrop, 1981. / Hastings, Selena. *Sir Gawain and the Loathly Lady.* Lothrop, 1985. / Hayes, Sarah. *Robin Hood.* Henry Holt, 1989. / Hodges, Margaret. *Merlin and the Making of the King.* Holiday House, 2004. / Hodges, Patricia. *Saint George and the Dragon.* Little, Brown, 1984. / Kimmel, Eric A. *The Hero Beowulf.* Farrar, 2005. / Morpurgo, Michael. *Sir Gawain and the Green Knight.* Candlewick, 2004. / Osborne, Mary Pope. *American Tall Tales.* Knopf, 1991. / Osborne, Mary Pope. *Favorite Greek Myths.* Scholastic, 1989. / Osborne, Mary Pope. *Favorite Norse Myths.* Scholastic, 1996. / Sabuda, Robert. *Arthur and the Sword.* Atheneum, 1995. / San Souci, Robert D. *Young Arthur.* Doubleday, 1997. / Shannon, Mark. *Gawain and the Green Knight.* Putnam, 1994. / Talbott, Hudson. *King Arthur and the Round Table.* Morrow, 1995. / Ward, Helen. *The Rooster and the Fox.* Millbrook, 2003.

SUBJECTS: ARTHUR, KING (LEGENDARY CHARACTER). FOLKLORE—COLLECTIONS. FOLKLORE—ENGLAND. FOLKLORE—EUROPE. ROBIN HOOD (LEGENDARY CHARACTER).

1241 **Osborne, Mary Pope.** *Kate and the Beanstalk.* **Illus. by Giselle Potter. Atheneum, 2000. 0-689-82550-1. Unp. Gr. K–5**

Inspired by Andrew Lang's version of *Jack and the Beanstalk* published in 1890, Mary Pope Osborne has reworked the familiar tale to give us a female protagonist, the plucky Kate. Climbing up the beanstalk, she meets an old woman who tells her how the fine castle above the clouds belonged to a noble knight until a monstrous giant killed him and took it over. The knight's wife and baby were in the valley below, but now they are poor and close to starving. AHA! NOW we have justification for Kate to steal back the knight's three most precious possessions: the golden egg-laying hen, the bag of gold coins, and that talking harp. So Kate, not recognizing herself in the old woman's tale, sets out to right a few wrongs, helps out the poor mistreated giantess wife with the cooking, and robs the big boy blind.

GERM: All will love reciting the adjusted refrain: "FEE, FI, FO, FUM'UN, I SMELL THE BLOOD OF AN ENGLISHWOMAN." Giselle Potter's watercolors are loads of fun, and you can even use the book as part of that science unit where you plant bean seeds. Compare and contrast this version to others starring Jack instead of Kate, and then see how another plucky girl takes on giants in Osborne's *The Brave Little Seamstress.*

RELATED TITLES: Beneduce, Ann Keay. *Jack and the Beanstalk.* Philomel, 1999. / Briggs, Raymond. *Jim and the Beanstalk.* Putnam, 1989. / Cauley, Lorinda Bryan. *Jack and the Beanstalk.* Putnam, 1983. / Chase, Richard. *The Jack Tales.* Houghton Mifflin, 1943. / Christelow, Eileen. *What Do Illustrators Do?* Clarion, 1999. / Donaldson, Julia. *The Giants and the Joneses.* Henry Holt, 2005. / Galdone, Paul. *The History of Mother Twaddle and the Marvelous Achievements of Her Son, Jack.* Clarion, 1979. / Garner, Alan. *Jack and the Beanstalk.* Doubleday, 1992. / Gerstein, Mordicai. *Carolinda Clatter!.* Roaring Brook, 2005. / Haley, Gail E. *Jack and the Bean Tree.* Crown, 1986. / Hicks, Ray. *The Jack Tales.* Callaway, 2000. / Johnson, Paul Brett. *Fearless Jack.* McElderry, 2001. / Kellogg, Steven. *Jack and the Beanstalk.* Morrow, 1991. / Osborne, Mary Pope. *The Brave Little Seamstress.* Atheneum, 2002. / Swope, Sam. *Jack and the Seven Deadly Giants.* Farrar, 2004. / Willey, Margaret. *Clever Beatrice: An Upper Peninsula Conte.* Atheneum, 2001.

SUBJECTS: FAIRY TALES. FOLKLORE—ENGLAND. GIANTS—FOLKLORE. WOMEN—FOLKLORE.

1242 **Paye, Won-Ldy, and Margaret H. Lippert. *Head, Body, Legs: A Story from Liberia.* Illus. by Julie Paschkis. Henry Holt, 2002. 0-8050-6570-9. Unp. Gr. PreK–3**
Head, who can only eat the things he can reach on the ground, joins forces with Arms, Body, and Legs, attaching the parts together so they can work together to reach up high and pick mangoes to eat. This whimsical African pourquoi and creation tale explains how people came to be and demonstrates the importance of cooperation. Full-bleed gouache illustrations place the black body shapes against vibrant bordered backgrounds, with the effect of Matisse cut-outs.
GERM: Children can cut arms, legs, bodies and heads out of construction paper or oak tag and then act out the story, putting the parts together with brass fasteners to create little paper humans. Talk about other ways the body cooperates with itself, and ways we humans cooperate with each other to get things done.
RELATED TITLES: Cole, Joanna. *The Magic School Bus Inside the Human Body.* Scholastic, 1989. / Dee, Ruby. *Two Ways to Count to Ten: A Liberian Folktale.* Henry Holt, 1988. / Gershator, Phillis. *Zzzng! Zzzng! Zzzng! A Yoruba Tale.* Orchard, 1998. / Gerson, Mary-Joan. *Why the Sky Is Far Away: A Nigerian Folktale.* Little, Brown, 1992. / Rockwell, Lizzy. *The Busy Body Book: A Kids' Guide to Fitness.* Crown, 2004. / Seuling, Barbara. *From Head to Toe: The Amazing Human Body and How It Works.* Holiday House, 2002.
SUBJECTS: BODY, HUMAN—FOLKLORE. COOPERATION—FOLKLORE. CREATION—FOLKLORE. CREATIVE DRAMA—FOLKLORE. FOLKLORE—AFRICA, WEST. FOLKLORE—LIBERIA. FRUIT—FOLKLORE. HUMOROUS FOLKLORE. MULTICULTURAL BOOKS—FOLKLORE. POURQUOI TALES.

1243 **Paye, Won-Ldy, and Margaret H. Lippert. *Mrs. Chicken and the Hungry Crocodile.* Illus. by Julie Paschkis. Henry Holt, 2003. 0-8050-7047-8. Unp. Gr. PreK–1**
Crocodile waits in the river for her chicken dinner, but Mrs. Chicken talks Crocodile out of eating her, promising to prove that they are really sisters. Mrs. Chicken secretly switches their eggs, and when they hatch, sure enough, Crocodile's eggs look just like chicks.
GERM: Paye first heard this traditional Liberian trickster tale from his grandmother. Children can act out the scene where Mrs. Chicken uses logic to persuade Crocodile that they are alike. Look below for other folktales where gullible crocodiles are outwitted.
RELATED TITLES: Aardema, Verna. *Misoso: Once upon a Time Tales from Africa.* Knopf, 1994. / Aruego, Jose, and Ariane Aruego. *A Crocodile's Tale.* Scribner, 1972. / Baumgartner, Barbara. *Crocodile! Crocodile! Stories Told Around the World.* DK, 1994. / Diakité, Baba Wagué. *The Hunterman and the Crocodile.* Scholastic, 1997. / Feldman, Thelma. *Who You Callin' Chicken?* Abrams, 2003. / Galdone, Paul. *The Monkey and the Crocodile: A Jataka Tale from India.* Clarion, 1979. / Mollel, Tololwa M. *Shadow Dance.* Clarion, 1998. / Sierra, Judy. *Counting Crocodiles.* Harcourt, 1997.
SUBJECTS: CHICKENS—FOLKLORE. CREATIVE DRAMA—FOLKLORE. CROCODILES—FOLKLORE. FOLKLORE—AFRICA, WEST. FOLKLORE—LIBERIA. MULTICULTURAL BOOKS—FOLKLORE. TRICKSTER TALES.

1244 **Peck, Jan. *The Giant Carrot.* Illus. by Barry Root. Dial, 1998. 0-8037-1824-1. Unp. Gr. PreK–2**
Papa Joe and Mama Bess plant a carrot seed, Brother Abel waters it, but sweet Little Isabelle sings and dances around it and gets it growing. Just like the Russian folktale "The Turnip," on which the story is based, it takes some doing to pull that carrot up.
GERM: Act out the story, and compare it with other versions, from the original, *The Turnip*, to Erica Silverman's parody, *Big Pumpkin*. The recipe for sweet carrot puddin' on the last page looks mighty tasty if you're in the cooking mood.
RELATED TITLES: Bania, Michael. *Kumak's Fish: A Tall Tale from the Far North.* Alaska Northwest, 2004. / Domanska, Janina. *The Turnip.* Macmillan, 1969. / Krauss, Ruth. *The Carrot Seed.* HarperCollins, 1945. / Morgan, Pierr. *The Turnip.* Philomel, 1990. / Silverman, Erica. *Big Pumpkin.* Macmillan, 1992. / Tolstoi, Alexei. *The Great Big Enormous Turnip.* Scholastic, 1969. / Vagin, Vladimir. *The Enormous Carrot.* Scholastic, 1998.
SUBJECTS: CARROTS—FOLKLORE. CREATION—FOLKLORE. CREATIVE DRAMA—FOLKLORE. FOLKLORE—RUSSIA. FOOD—FOLKLORE.

1245 **Philip, Neil. *The Arabian Nights.* Illus. by Sheila Moxley. Orchard, 1994. 0-531-06868-4. 157pp. Gr. 4–8**
Introducing 15 well-told tales—some familiar, all exotic and compelling—is Sheherazade herself, as she spins her complex and mesmerizing narratives night after night to her woman-hating husband, King Shahryar and her sister, Dunyazad. At the beginning and end of each story, She-

herazade and the king engage in a dialogue involving questions, reactions, or lead-ins to the tales. At long last, the now-smitten king decides to let his faithful and loquacious bride keep her head.

GERM: On the back of the contents page is a wonderful plaque, adorned with gold lettering, with sage advice about stories and a definition of three types of people—the wise, the happy, and the fools. Talk over each pithy sentence, including "No story is a lie, for a tale is a bridge that leads to the truth." For further reading, explore the 11 tales in *Tenggren's Golden Tales from the Arabian Nights*, retold by Margaret Soifer and Irwin Shapiro. Mature readers grades 6 to 8 will be fascinated to follow up with a fictionalized account of Shahrazad's story in Susan Fletcher's novel *Shadow Spinner*.

RELATED TITLES: Carrick, Carol. *Aladdin and the Wonderful Lamp*. Scholastic, 1989. / Fletcher, Susan. *Shadow Spinner*. Atheneum, 1998. / Kimmel, Eric A. *The Three Princes: A Tale from the Middle East*. Holiday House, 1994. / McVitty, Walter. *Ali Baba and the Forty Thieves*. Abrams, 1989. / Mayer, Marianna. *Aladdin and the Enchanted Lamp*. Macmillan, 1985. / Philip, Neil. *The Adventures of Odysseus*. Orchard, 1997. / Soifer, Margaret, and Irwin Shapiro. *Tenggren's Golden Tales from the Arabian Nights*. Golden, 2003. / Sunami, Kitoba. *How the Fisherman Tricked the Genie: A Tale Within a Tale Within a Tale*. Atheneum, 2002. / Yeoman, John. *The Seven Voyages of Sinbad the Sailor*. McElderry, 1997.

SUBJECTS: ARABIAN NIGHTS. FAIRY TALES. FOLKLORE—ARAB COUNTRIES. FOLKLORE—COLLECTIONS. KINGS AND RULERS—FOLKLORE. PRINCES AND PRINCESSES—FOLKLORE.

1246 Philip, Neil. *Odin's Family: Myths of the Vikings*. Illus. by Maryclare Foa. Orchard, 1996. 0-531-09531-2. 124pp. Gr. 3–6

From the creation of the earth and its rulers—Odin the All-father and his brothers Vili and Ve—to the death of Balder the Beautiful and the twilight of the gods, see how the mighty Viking gods held court in Asgard. Primitive-style oil paintings and a text based on the 13th-century Icelandic Prose Edda evoke the retellings of the Viking bards.

GERM: Compare the retellings and illustrations with those in *Favorite Norse Myths* by Mary Pope Osborne. Two smashing novels that take place during the days of the Vikings and incorporate Norse folklore are Nancy Farmer's *The Sea of Trolls* and Katherine Langrish's *Troll Fell*.

RELATED TITLES: Climo, Shirley. *Stolen Thunder: A Norse Myth*. Clarion, 1994. / D'Aulaire, Ingri, and Edgar Parin D'Aulaire. *D'Aulaires' Trolls*. Doubleday, 1972.Farmer, Nancy. *The Sea of Trolls*. Atheneum, 2004. / Kimmel, Eric A. *The Hero Beowulf*. Farrar, 2005. / Langrish, Katherine. *Troll Fell*. HarperCollins, 2004. / Lunge-Larsen, Lise. *The Troll with No Heart in His Body: And Other Tales of Trolls, from Norway*. Houghton Mifflin, 1999. / McCaughrean, Geraldine. *Roman Myths*. McElderry Books, 2001. / Mayer, Marianna. *Iduna and the Magic Apples*. Macmillan, 1988. / Osborne, Mary Pope. *American Tall Tales*. Knopf, 1991. / Osborne, Mary Pope. *Favorite Greek Myths*. Scholastic, 1989. / Osborne, Mary Pope. *Favorite Medieval Tales*. Scholastic, 1998. / Osborne, Mary Pope. *Favorite Norse Myths*. Scholastic, 1996.

SUBJECTS: FOLKLORE—COLLECTIONS. FOLKLORE—NORWAY. GIANTS—FOLKLORE. GODS AND GODDESSES—FOLKLORE. MYTHOLOGY. TRICKSTER TALES.

1247 Pinkney, Jerry. *Aesop's Fables*. Retold and illus. by the author. SeaStar, 2000. 1-58717-000-0. 87pp. Gr. 2–8

Graced with Pinkney's signature lush watercolors are 60 well-told Aesop's fables, some beloved and others lesser known, all of which are natural read-alouds that lead into discussions of the morals, retelling, acting out, and writing new fables.

GERM: Children can articulate their perceived moral for each story, and/or explain the moral that is stated at the end. All of these make wonderful short skits for creative drama, Reader's Theater, puppet shows, and flannelboard stories.

RELATED TITLES: Andersen, Hans Christian. *The Nightingale*. Retold and illus. by Jerry Pinkney. Putnam, 2002. / Andersen, Hans Christian. *The Ugly Duckling*. Retold and illus. by Jerry Pinkney. Morrow, 1999. / Bader, Barbara. *Aesop and Company*. Houghton Mifflin, 1991. / Calmenson, Stephanie. *The Children's Aesop*. Doubleday, 1988. / Daugherty, James. *Andy and the Lion*. Viking, 1938. / Demi. *The Dragon's Tale and Other Animal Fables of the Chinese Zodiac*. Henry Holt, 1996. / Gatti, Anne. *Aesop's Fables*. Harcourt, 1992. / Lester, Julius. *Sam and the Tigers*. Illus. by Jerry Pinkney. Dial, 1996. / Lobel, Arnold. *Fables*. HarperCollins, 1980. / Morpurgo, Michael. *The McElderry Book of Aesop's Fables*. McElderry, 2005. / Paxton, Tom. *Belling the Cat and Other Aesop's Fables: Retold in Verse*. Morrow, 1990. / Scieszka, Jon. *Squids Will Be Squids: Fresh Morals, Beastly Fables*. Viking, 1998. / Sogabe, Aki. *Aesop's Fox*. Harcourt, 1999. / Untermeyer, Louis. *Aesop's Fables*. Golden, 1965.

SUBJECTS: AESOP. ANIMALS—FOLKLORE. CREATIVE DRAMA—FOLKLORE. FABLES. FOLKLORE—COLLECTIONS. READER'S THEATER—FOLKLORE.

1248 Rascol, Sabina I. *The Impudent Rooster.* **Illus. by Holly Berry. Dutton, 2004. 0-525-47179-0. Unp. Gr. 1–4**

A poor old man's enterprising rooster finds a purse with pennies in it, but before he can bring it home to his master, a greedy nobleman steals it from him. Though the nobleman tries hard to rid himself of the persistent rooster, having him thrown into a well to drown and an oven to burn, the rooster prevails. In swallowing water, gold, and lots of farm animals, the rooster acquires all of the greedy man's wealth to bring home to his grateful master. Folk-art paintings, done in watercolors and colored pencils, bring out the humor of this Romanian cautionary tale, with a chantable refrain listeners will crow: "Cucurigu, my great lord! Give back the pennies you stole!"

GERM: This would be fun for children to stage as a puppet show using stick or paper bag puppets. Compare two similar tales from Eastern Europe: from Russia, *The Magic Stove* by Mirra Ginsburg, and from Hungary, *The Valiant Red Rooster* by Eric A. Kimmel.

RELATED TITLES: Ada, Alma Flor. *The Rooster Who Went to His Uncle's Wedding: A Latin American Folktale.* Putnam, 1993. / Diakité, Baba Wagué. *The Magic Gourd.* Scholastic, 2003. / Duff, Maggie. *Rum Pum Pum.* Macmillan, 1978. / Froehlich, Margaret Walden. *That Kookoory!* Harcourt, 1995. / Ginsburg, Mirra. *The Magic Stove.* Coward, 1983. / Gonzalez, Lucie M. *The Bossy Gallito: A Traditional Cuban Folktale.* Scholastic, 1994. / Kimmel, Eric A. *The Valiant Red Rooster: A Story from Hungary.* Henry Holt, 1995.

SUBJECTS: CHANTABLE REFRAIN—FOLKLORE. FOLKLORE—ROMANIA. GREED—FOLKLORE. HUMOROUS FOLKLORE. MONEY—FOLKLORE. ROOSTERS—FOLKLORE. SWALLOWING STORIES.

1249 Salley, Coleen. *Epossumondas.* **Illus. by Janet Stevens. Harcourt, 2002. 0-15-216748-X. Unp. Gr. PreK–2**

Every time sweet little patootie Epossumondas visits his auntie, she gives him something to take home, and each time he carries it home the wrong way, according to his Mama. His exasperated Mama says, "Epossumondas, you don't have the sense you were born with." Storyteller Coleen Salley has refashioned the noodlehead story "Epaminondas" to reflect her New Orleans background, with an alligator, a raccoon, a nutria, and an armadillo each encountering the foolish possum as he heads on home. In a hilarious piece of casting, Janet Stevens has depicted Coleen herself, in large flowered dress, pillbox hat, and purple specs, in the parts of Mama and Auntie.

GERM: This uproarious story with huge, unforgettable watercolors will have your listeners chiming in on every refrain. It begs to be retold with props and puppets and a story apron to put them in, which you can make or buy from Mimi's Motifs at <www.mimismotifs.com>. It's also a natural to act out in creative drama or script as a Reader's Theater. Listeners can talk about what it means to take something literally. Bring in a nice pie so everyone can have a bite. Singing the kids' song, "I'm Bringing Home a Baby Bumblebee," would fit in just fine, too. Follow up with Salley's sequel, *Why Epossumondas Has No Hair on His Tail.* Marisa Montes's *Juan Bobo Goes to Work* is a Puerto Rican variant.

RELATED TITLES: Birdseye, Tom. *Soap! Soap! Don't Forget the Soap! An Appalachian Folktale.* Holiday House, 1993. / Edwards, Roberta. *Five Silly Fishermen.* Random House, 1989. / French, Vivian. *Lazy Jack.* Candlewick, 1995. / Maitland, Anthony. *Idle Jack.* Farrar, 1979. / Miranda, Anne. *To Market, to Market.* Harcourt, 1997. / Montes, Marisa. *Juan Bobo Goes to Work: A Puerto Rican Folktale.* HarperCollins, 2000. / Pitre, Felix. *Juan Bobo and the Pig: A Puerto Rican Folktale.* Lodestar, 1993. / Salley, Coleen. *Why Epossumondas Has No Hair on His Tail.* Harcourt, 2004. / Schaefer, Carole Lexa. *The Biggest Soap.* Farrar, 2004. / Snyder, Dianne. *The Boy of the Three-Year Nap.* Houghton Mifflin, 1988. / Stevens, Janet. *Tops and Bottoms.* Harcourt, 1995. / Stevens, Janet, and Susan Stevens Crummel. *And the Dish Ran Away with the Spoon.* Harcourt, 2001. / Stevens, Janet, and Susan Stevens Crummel. *Cook-a-Doodle-Doo!* Harcourt, 1999.

SUBJECTS: CHANTABLE REFRAIN—FOLKLORE. CREATIVE DRAMA—FOLKLORE. FOLKLORE—U.S. FOOLS—FOLKLORE. HUMOROUS FOLKLORE. OPOSSUMS—FOLKLORE. READER'S THEATER.

1250 Salley, Coleen. *Why Epossumondas Has No Hair on His Tail.* **Illus. by Janet Stevens. Harcourt, 2004. 0-15-204935-5. Unp. Gr. PreK–2**

When possum Epossumondas asks his loving Mama why his tail is pink and naked and funny looking, she tells him the old story about his great-great-great grandpa, Papapossum, whose love of persimmons got him in trouble with Hare and Bear.

GERM: Listeners will want to join in on Papapossum's refrain as he eats all those persimmons.

Act this one out, and also share Sally's first story, *Epossumondas*, about the lovable sweet patootie little possum. Read another version of how possum lost his tail in Gerald Hausman's collection of Native American pourquoi tales, *How Chipmunk Got Tiny Feet*, and share other pourquoi (how and why) tales to explain why animals look the way they do. Meet another possum in trouble in "Bruh Possum and the Snake" from Alice McGill's *Sure as Sunrise: Stories of Bruh Rabbit and His Walkin' Talkin' Friends*. Persimmons play a part in *The Rabbit's Tail* by Suzanne Crowder Han, a Korean folktale about a tiger, a rabbit, and a baby. For props to help you present this story, go to <www.mimismotifs.com>.

RELATED TITLES: Aardema, Verna. *How the Ostrich Got Its Long Neck: A Tale from the Akamba of Kenya'*. Scholastic, 1995. / Bodnár, Judit Z. *Tale of a Tail*. Lothrop, 1998. / Bruchac, Joseph, and James Bruchac. *How Chipmunk Got His Stripes*. Dial, 2001. / Ehlert, Lois. *Cuckoo/Cucú: A Mexican Folktale/Un Cuento Folklórico Mexicano*. Harcourt, 1997. / Gates, Frieda. *Owl Eyes*. Lothrop, 1994. / Han, Suzanne Crowder. *The Rabbit's Tail*. Henry Holt, 1999. / Hausman, Gerald. *How Chipmunk Got Tiny Feet: Native American Animal Origin Stories*. HarperCollins, 1995. / Jenkins, Steve, and Robin Page. *What Do You Do with a Tail Like This?* Houghton, 2003. / McGill, Alice. *Sure as Sunrise: Stories of Bruh Rabbit and His Walkin' Talkin' Friends*. Houghton Mifflin, 2004. / Salley, Coleen. *Epossumondas*. Harcourt, 2002. / Slate, Joseph. *Story Time for Little Porcupine*. Marshall Cavendish, 2000. / Stevens, Janet. *Tops and Bottoms*. Harcourt, 1995. / Stevens, Janet, and Susan Stevens Crummel. *Cook-a-Doodle-Doo!* Harcourt, 1999.

SUBJECTS: ANIMALS—FOLKLORE. BEARS—FOLKLORE. CHANTABLE REFRAIN—FOLKLORE. FOLKLORE—U.S. FRUIT—FOLKLORE. HARES—FOLKLORE. HUMOROUS FOLKLORE. OPOSSUMS—FOLKLORE. POURQUOI TALES. TAILS—FOLKLORE.

1251 San Souci, Daniel. *In the Moonlight Mist: A Korean Tale.* **Illus. by Eujin Kim Neilan. Boyds Mills, 1999. 1-56397-754-0. Unp. Gr. 2–6**

When a poor, goodhearted young woodcutter saves a frightened deer from a hunter, he is rewarded for his kind deed. The deer grants him his secret wish of having a loving wife and children by telling the man how to win the heart of a heavenly maiden. How he loves and loses her, due to his compassion for her and for his own aging mother, makes for a dramatic and morally interesting take on a common theme in folklore.

GERM: Compare the ending of the story with other folktales with husbands whose wives are transformed, such as Odds Bodkin's *The Crane Wife*, Robert D. San Souci's *The Snow Wife*, Diane Wolkstein's *White Wave*, and Sumiko Yagawa's *The Crane Wife*.

RELATED TITLES: Bodkin, Odds. *The Crane Wife*. Harcourt, 1998. / Climo, Shirley. *The Korean Cinderella*. HarperCollins, 1993. / Han, Oki S., and Stephanie Plunkett. *Kongi and Potgi: A Cinderella Story from Korea*. Dial, 1996. / Jaffe, Nina. *Older Brother, Younger Brother: A Korean Folktale*. Viking, 1995. / Rhee, Nami. *Magic Spring: A Korean Folktale*. Putnam, 1993. / San Souci, Robert D. *The Snow Wife*. Dial, 1993. / Wolkstein, Diane. *White Wave: A Chinese Tale*. Crowell, 1979. / Yagawa, Sumiko. *The Crane Wife*. Morrow, 1981.

SUBJECTS: DEER—FOLKLORE. FOLKLORE—KOREA. KINDNESS—FOLKLORE. LOVE— FOLKLORE. TRANSFORMATIONS—FOLKLORE.

1252 San Souci, Robert D. *Cendrillon: A Caribbean Cinderella.* **Illus. by Brian Pinkney. Simon & Schuster, 1998. 0-689-80668-X. Unp. Gr. 2–6**

On the Caribbean island of Martinique, a nannin' or godmother explains how she came to be the helpmate for Cendrillon, whose mother has died and whose stepmother works her like a serving girl. On the day of the birthday ball for elegant, prince-like Paul Thibault, the nannin' turns a breadfruit into a gilded coach, and an assortment of island animals—agoutis, field lizards, and a manicou—into the requisite horses and drivers, and attends the ball as chaperone to Cendrillon.

GERM: Pinkney's lush and darkly colorful scratchboard, gouache, and oil paintings, as well as the switch to the godmother's point of view and Cendrillon's stated desire to be loved for herself and not the magic that changed her, all give the familiar storyline a lilt and richness you'll want to compare with other, more traditional Cinderella retellings. Based on a 19th-century French Creole tale, the text includes a much welcome glossary of and pronunciation guide to the French Creole words and phrases. Start your readers on a fairy tale reading quest to familiarize them with a generous sampling of traditional stories and their many fascinating variants or other versions.

RELATED TITLES: Compton, Joanne. *Ashpet: An Appalachian Tale*. Holiday House, 1994. / Craft, K. Y. *Cinderella*. SeaStar Books, 2000. / dePaola, Tomie. *Adelita: A Mexican Cinderella Story*. Putnam, 2002. / Ehrlich, Amy. *Cinderella*. Illus. by Susan Jeffers. Dutton, 2004. / Martin, Rafe. *The Rough-Face Girl*. Putnam, 1992. / Pollock, Penny. *The Turkey Girl*. Little, Brown, 1996. /San Souci, Robert D. *The Faithful Friend*. Simon & Schuster, 1995. / Sanderson, Ruth. *Cinderella*. Little, Brown, 2002. / Steptoe, John. *Mufaro's Beautiful Daughters*. Lothrop, 1987. / Whipple, Laura. *If the Shoe Fits: Voices from Cinderella*. McElderry, 2002. / Wilson, Barbara Ker. *Wishbones: A Folk Tale from China*. Bradbury, 1993.

SUBJECTS: CINDERELLA STORIES. FAIRY TALES. FOLKLORE—CARIBBEAN AREA. FOLKLORE—MARTINIQUE. FRENCH LANGUAGE. MULTICULTURAL BOOKS—FOLKLORE. PERSONAL NARRATIVES. POINT OF VIEW. STEPMOTHERS—FOLKLORE.

1253 San Souci, Robert D. *The Faithful Friend*. Illus. by Brian Pinkney. Simon & Schuster, 1995. 0-02-786131-7. Unp. Gr. 3–6

On the Caribbean island of Martinique, Hippolyte's best friend Clement falls in love with a picture of Pauline, though she is the niece of quimboiseur, or wizard, Monsieur Zabocat. Pauline's acceptance of Clement's marriage proposal enrages her uncle, who unleashes a murderous plot of revenge to be carried out by three zombie women. Three times, Hippolyte tries to stop them, even though his interference causes him to turn to stone.

GERM: Chart how true love and friendship win out in the end of this dramatic and brooding folktale which is accompanied by huge, gorgeous, oil and scratchboard illustrations and includes a glossary and pronunciation guide to the Creole-flavored French words. While none of us particularly wishes to be turned to stone, talk and write about the special sacrifices you've made for a friend.

RELATED TITLES: Dasent, George Webbe. *East O' the Sun and West O' the Moon*. Illus. by P. J. Lynch. Candlewick, 1992. / Grimm, Jacob. *The Frog Prince: Or Iron Henry*. Trans. by Naomi Lewis. North-South, 1989. / Hamilton, Virginia. *The Girl Who Spun Gold*. Scholastic, 2000. / Huck, Charlotte. *The Black Bull of Norroway: A Scottish Tale*. Greenwillow, 2001. / Kimmel, Eric A. *The Goose Girl: A Story from the Brothers Grimm*. Holiday House, 1995. / Kimmel, Eric A. *Iron John*. Holiday House, 1994. / Rappaport, Doreen. *The Long-Haired Girl*. Dial, 1995. / San Souci, Robert D. *Cendrillon: A Caribbean Cinderella*. Simon & Schuster, 1998. / Singer, Marilyn. *The Maiden on the Moor*. Morrow, 1995. / Steptoe, John. *Mufaro's Beautiful Daughters*. Lothrop, 1987. / Yep, Laurence. *The Khan's Daughter: A Mongolian Folktale*. Scholastic, 1997. / Yolen, Jane. *Tam Lin: An Old Ballad*. Harcourt, 1990.

SUBJECTS: FOLKLORE—CARIBBEAN AREA. FOLKLORE—MARTINIQUE. FRENCH LANGUAGE. FRIENDSHIP—FOLKLORE. ISLANDS—FOLKLORE. LOVE—FOLKLORE. MULTICULTURAL BOOKS—FOLKLORE. TRANSFORMATIONS—FOLKLORE. WIZARDS—FOLKLORE.

1254 San Souci, Robert D. *The Well at the End of the World*. Illus. by Rebecca Walsh. Chronicle, 2004. 0-58717-212-7. Unp. Gr. 2–6

Plain but practical Princess Rosamond runs the kingdom for her father, the King of Colchester, but when he weds the beautiful Lady Zantippa, the new queen and her daughter, Zenobia, loot the treasury and badger the king until he falls ill. Rosamond sets off to the end of the world to find the well whose water could heal him. The well gives her jewels and coins that fall from her hair. When she returns, the queen sends her daughter to get the same riches, which most certainly does not come to pass.

GERM: You will love the role model of the practical princess who finds a prince worthy of her intellect and personality, while Zantippa gets what she deserves. You'll find the same theme in *Toads and Diamonds*, with versions by Robert Bender and Charlotte Huck, and in the African story *Chinye*, by Obi Onyefulu, and its African American counterpart, *The Talking Eggs* by Robert D. San Souci.

RELATED TITLES: Aliki. *The Twelve Months*. Greenwillow, 1978. / Bender, Robert. *Toads and Diamonds*. Dutton, 1995. / De Regniers, Beatrice Schenk. *Little Sister and the Month Brothers*. Lothrop, 1994. / Huck, Charlotte. *Toads and Diamonds*. Greenwillow, 1996. / Marshak, Samuel. *The Month Brothers: A Slavic Tale*. Morrow, 1983. / Onyefulu, Obi. *Chinye: A West African Folk Tale*. Viking, 1994. / San Souci, Robert D. *The Talking Eggs*. Dial, 1989. / Sierra, Judy. *The Gift of the Crocodile: A Cinderella Story*. Simon & Schuster, 2000. / Steptoe, John. *Mufaro's Beautiful Daughters*. Lothrop, 1987.

SUBJECTS: FAIRY TALES. FOLKLORE—ENGLAND. KINGS AND RULERS—FOLKLORE. PRINCES AND PRINCESSES—FOLKLORE. STEPMOTHERS—FOLKLORE. UNICORNS—FOLKLORE.

1255 Schroeder, Alan. *Smoky Mountain Rose: An Appalachian Cinderella*. Illus. by Brad Sneed. Dial, 1997. 0-8037-1734-2. Unp. Gr. 2–6

Written in a fun-to-read southern twang, this Cinderella retelling features a talking hog who helps poor Rose get to rich feller Seb's shindig, where she and Jeb square dance till midnight.

GERM: Look at some of the Cinderella tales reset in the Americas and talk about the setting—how it fits into each story and establishes a set place. These include *Adelita* by Tomie dePaola, *Moss Gown* by William H. Hooks, and *The Turkey Girl* by Penny Pollock. How are the European versions different?

RELATED TITLES: Climo, Shirley. *The Irish Cinderlad.* HarperCollins, 1996. / Compton, Joanne. *Ashpet: An Appalachian Tale.* Holiday House, 1994. / Craft, K. Y. *Cinderella.* SeaStar Books, 2000. / dePaola, Tomie. *Adelita: A Mexican Cinderella Story.* Putnam, 2002. / Hooks, William H. *Moss Gown.* Clarion, 1987. / Hughes, Shirley. *Ella's Big Chance: A Jazz-Age Cinderella.* Simon & Schuster, 2004. / Lowell, Susan. *Cindy Ellen: A Wild Western Cinderella.* Orchard, 1997. / San Souci, Robert D. *The Faithful Friend.* Simon & Schuster, 1995. / San Souci, Robert D. *Sootface: An Ojibwa Cinderella Story.* Doubleday, 1994. / Sierra, Judy. *The Gift of the Crocodile: A Cinderella Story.* Simon & Schuster, 2000.

SUBJECTS: CINDERELLA STORIES. FAIRY TALES. FOLKLORE—U.S.

1256 **Schroeder, Alan.** *The Tale of Willie Monroe.* **Illus. by Andrew Glass. Clarion, 1999. 0-395-69852-9. 29pp. Gr. 2–5**

Heading to North Carolina for an ". . . arm-wrestlin', log-stackin', cow-milkin', field-plowin', barn raisin' contest," which he figures he'll win, Willie Monroe, "strongest critter in all of Tennessee," encounters a little girl with a bucket balanced on her head, and he decides to tip over that bucket, just for the fun of it. Big mistake. That girl, Delilah, turns out to be stronger than she looks, and stronger by far than Willie. She totes him on home to meet her granny, who can carry a full-grown horse on her shoulders, and the two women commence to turn him into the strongest feller in Carolina. Colloquial language and comic illustrations transfer this traditional Japanese folktale into the Appalachian Mountains with side-splitting effect.

GERM: Compare the language, characters, dialogue, setting, and illustrations with the original folktale upon which this retelling was based, Claus Stamm's *Three Strong Women.* How and why are these stories considered tall tales? Children can write the sequel of Willie and Delilah's life together. What will their children be like? Meet another big gal from Tennessee, *Swamp Angel* by Anne Isaacs.

RELATED TITLES: Byrd, Robert. *Finn MacCoul and His Fearless Wife: A Giant of a Tale from Ireland.* Dutton, 1999. / dePaola, Tomie. *Fin M'Coul, the Giant of Knockmany Hill.* Holiday House, 1981. / Hicks, Ray, as told to Lynn Salsi. *The Jack Tales.* Callaway, 2000. / Isaacs, Anne. *Swamp Angel.* Dutton, 1994. / Kimmel, Eric A. *Three Samurai Cats: A Story from Japan.* Holiday House, 2003. / McCully, Emily Arnold. *Beautiful Warrior: The Legend of the Nun's Kung Fu.* Scholastic, 1998. / Kellogg, Steven. *Sally Ann Thunder Ann Whirlwind Crockett.* Morrow, 1995. / Osborne, Mary Pope. *American Tall Tales.* Knopf, 1991. / San Souci, Robert D. *Larger Than Life: The Adventures of American Legendary Heroes.* Doubleday, 1991. / Schanzer, Rosalyn. *Davy Crockett Saves the World.* HarperCollins, 2001. / Stamm, Claus. *Three Strong Women.* Viking, 1990. / Willey, Margaret. *Clever Beatrice: An Upper Peninsula Conte.* Atheneum, 2001. / Yep, Laurence. *The Dragon Prince: A Chinese Beauty and the Beast Tale.* HarperCollins, 1997.

SUBJECTS: FOLKLORE—JAPAN. FOLKLORE—U.S. HUMOROUS FOLKLORE. LOVE—FOLKLORE. STRENGTH—FOLKLORE. TALL TALES. WRESTLING—FOLKLORE.

1257 **Shannon, George.** *True Lies: 18 Tales for You to Judge.* **Illus. by John O'Brien. Greenwillow, 1997. 0-688-14483-7. 64pp. Gr. 2–6**

Challenge your children to figure out how each character in these 18 brief, amusing international folktales and jokes manages to trick or mislead others while appearing to be on the up and up. After each story, listeners must answer the questions: "Where's the truth, the whole truth? And where's the lie?" In the first story, Nate and Anna, baking cookies, are admonished by their mother to eat only one and no more so as not to spoil their appetite. At dinnertime, both are too full to eat. While it's true they ate only one apiece, adept detectives will soon come to the truth: each made and ate one huge cookie the size of the entire cookie sheet.

GERM: After reading aloud several stories so your group can exercise their problem-solving skills, hand out copies of some of the other tales to small groups to stage and act out. The rest of the class can be the jury and cross-examine the players until they ascertain what really happened. For more tales to stimulate children's deductive reasoning and thinking skills, continue with Shannon's companion book, *More True Lies,* and his Stories to Solve series.

RELATED TITLES: Bateman, Teresa. *The Ring of Truth.* Holiday House, 1997. / Egan, Tim. *The Trial of Cardigan Jones.* Houghton Mifflin, 2004. / Hayes, Joe. *Juan Verdades: The Man Who Couldn't Tell a Lie.* Orchard, 2001. / Shannon, George. *More Stories to Solve.* Greenwillow, 1991. / Shannon, George. *More True Lies: 18 Tales for You to Judge.* Greenwillow, 2001. / Shannon, George. *Still More Stories to Solve.* Greenwillow, 1994. / Shannon, George. *Stories to Solve: Folktales from Around the World.* Greenwillow, 1985.

SUBJECTS: BEHAVIOR—FOLKLORE. CONFLICT RESOLUTION. CREATIVE DRAMA—FOLKLORE. FOLKLORE—COLLECTIONS. HONESTY—FOLKLORE. PROBLEM SOLVING.

1258 Shepard, Aaron. *King o' the Cats*. Illus. by Kristin Sorra. Atheneum, 2004. 0-689-82082-8. Unp. Gr. 2–5

Father Allen is exasperated with his storytelling young sexton, Peter, who tells the priest outlandish tales about seeing cats in church crowning a big black cat, or cats riding on foxes and chasing a dog. The night Peter witnesses a cat's funeral procession, Father Allen has no choice but to believe him.

GERM: For a Reader's Theater script of the story for all to act out, go to Shepard's wonderful Web site, <www.aaronshep.com>. Paul Galdone also did a nicely spooky picture-book version of this old English folktale, if you want to compare them.

RELATED TITLES: Carlson, Natalie Savage. *King of the Cats and Other Tales*. Doubleday, 1980. / Del Negro, Janice. *Lucy Dove*. DK Ink, 1998. / Galdone, Paul. *King of the Cats*. Houghton, 1980. / Galdone, Paul. *The Monster and the Tailor*. Clarion, 1982. / Kimmel, Eric A. *Three Samurai Cats: A Story from Japan*. Holiday House, 2003. / Levine, Arthur A. *The Boy Who Drew Cats: A Japanese Folktale*. Dial, 1994. / McKissack, Patricia, and Onawumi Jean Moss. *Precious and the Boo Hag*. Atheneum, 2005. / Nimmo, Jenny. *The Witches and the Singing Mice*. Dial, 1993.

SUBJECTS: CATS—FOLKLORE. CHURCHES—FOLKLORE. CREATIVE DRAMA—FOLKLORE. FAIRY TALES. FOLKLORE—ENGLAND. READER'S THEATER—FOLKLORE. SUSPENSE—FOLKLORE.

1259 Shepard, Aaron. *Master Man: A Tall Tale of Nigeria*. Illus. by David Wisniewski. HarperCollins, 2001. 0-688-13783-0. Unp. Gr. K–5

Impressed with his own muscles, Shadusa decides to call himself Master Man, but soon finds out there are others far stronger than he in this comical West African pourquoi (how and why) story that explains, ultimately, how thunder came to be.

GERM: The comic-book-style format and eye-popping cut-paper collages painted with oil and oil pastel invite audience participation. The author has made it simple to act out his retelling of a West African pourquoi tale: he's posted his own Reader's Theater script on his Web site <www.aaronshep.com> for you to print out and act out. Use this as part of your weather unit for an unforgettable non-scientific explanation of why we have thunder.

RELATED TITLES: Alexander, Lloyd. *How the Cat Swallowed Thunder*. Dutton, 2000. / Cole, Joanna. *The Magic School Bus Inside a Hurricane*. Scholastic, 1995. / Courlander, Harold. *The Cow-Tail Switch and Other West African Stories*. Henry Holt, 1988. / Cuyler, Margery. *Big Friends*. Walker, 2004. / dePaola, Tomie. *Fin M'Coul, the Giant of Knockmany Hill*. Holiday House, 1981. / Diakité, Baba Wagué. *The Hunterman and the Crocodile*. Scholastic, 1997. / Farris, Pamela J. *Young Mouse and Elephant: An East African Folktale*. Houghton Mifflin, 1996. / Gerson, Mary-Joan. *Why the Sky Is Far Away: A Nigerian Folktale*. Little, Brown, 1992. / McDermott, Gerald. *Raven: A Trickster Tale from the Pacific Northwest*. Harcourt, 1993. / Souhami, Jessica. *The Leopard's Drum: An Asante Tale from West Africa*. Little, Brown, 1996. / Souhami, Jessica. *Mrs. McCool and the Giant Cuhullin: An Irish Tale*. Henry Holt, 2002. / Yep, Laurence. *The Junior Thunder Lord*. BridgeWater, 1994.

SUBJECTS: FOLKLORE—AFRICA, WEST. GIANTS—FOLKLORE. HUMOROUS FOLKLORE. MULTICULTURAL BOOKS—FOLKLORE. POURQUOI TALES. READER'S THEATER—FOLKLORE. WEATHER—FOLKLORE.

1260 Shepard, Aaron. *The Princess Mouse: A Tale of Finland*. Illus. by Leonid Gore. Atheneum, 2003. 0-689-82912-4. Unp. Gr. K–3

Following their father's instructions on finding a sweetheart, Mikko and his older brother each cut down a tree and follow where it points. Mikko heads into the forest where he comes to a cottage with a bright-eyed talking mouse he takes for a sweetheart. Though his older brother mocks him, it's Mikko's mouse who passes his father's test, weaving the best cloth with the help of her many mouse friends, and tucking it into a nutshell. And don't you know, when he declares his love for her, she is transformed back into the princess she really is, breaking a witch's spell.

GERM: This cheerful Finnish charmer, with dark, rich blue- and green-toned full-page pastel and acrylics, is a turnaround of Grimm's German tale, "The Frog Prince." Compare other versions, including Laura Cecil's *The Frog Princess*, from Italy, and J. Patrick Lewis's *The Frog Princess*, from Russia. Go to Shepard's Web site, <www.aaronshep.com>, for a Reader's Theater script and a recording of the song the princess mouse sings. The song is also notated on the last page of the book.

RELATED TITLES: Cecil, Laura. *The Frog Princess*. Greenwillow, 1995. / Grimm, Jacob. *The Frog Prince: Or Iron Henry*. Trans. by Naomi Lewis. North-South, 1989. / Huck, Charlotte. *The Black Bull of Norroway: A Scottish Tale*. Greenwillow, 2001. / Isele, Elizabeth. *The Frog Princess*. Crowell, 1984. / Lewis, J. Patrick. *The Frog Princess: A Russian Tale*. Dial, 1994.

SUBJECTS: FAIRY TALES. FOLKLORE—FINLAND. LOVE—FOLKLORE. MICE—FOLKLORE. PRINCES AND PRINCESSES—FOLKLORE. READER'S THEATER—FOLKLORE. TRANSFORMATIONS—FOLKLORE.

1261 Shepard, Aaron. *The Sea King's Daughter: A Russian Legend*. **Illus. by Gennady Spirin. Atheneum, 1997. 0-689-80759-7. Unp. Gr. 3–6**

Even though he makes little money and is, in truth, very lonely, Sadko loves to play his 12-string gusli at feasts in his beloved Russian city of Novgorod on the banks of the River Volkhov. When the King of the Sea invites him to play his sweet music at his underwater palace, Sadko dives into the Baltic Sea where he entertains the king and his many beautiful daughters, river maidens all. Spirin's watercolor-and-colored-pencil illustrations present a sumptuous look at palace life beneath the waves.

GERM: When Sadko is married to Princess Volkhova, he must decide whether to stay or go back to his city. Discuss what his choice should be and why. Find a Reader's Theater script and an abridged text of the story, just right for storytelling, at <www.aaronshep.com>.

RELATED TITLES: Afanasev, Nikolaevich. *Russian Folk Tales*. Trans. by Robert Chandler. Illus. by Ivan I. Bilibin. Random House, 1980. / Crouch, Marcus. *Ivan: Stories of Old Russia*. Oxford University Press, 1989. / Demi. *The Firebird*. Henry Holt, 1994. / Demi. *The Magic Gold Fish: A Russian Folktale by Aleksandr Pushkin*. Henry Holt, 1995. / Gal, Laszlo. *Prince Ivan and the Firebird*. Firefly, 1992. / Hodges, Margaret. *The Little Humpbacked Horse*. Farrar, 1980. / Lewis, J. Patrick. *The Frog Princess: A Russian Tale*. Dial, 1994. / MacGill-Callahan, Sheila. *The Seal Prince*. Dial, 1995. / San Souci, Robert D. *The Samurai's Daughter*. Dial, 1992. / San Souci, Robert D. *Sukey and the Mermaid*. Four Winds, 1992. / Winthrop, Elizabeth. *The Little Humpbacked Horse: A Russian Tale*. Clarion, 1997.

SUBJECTS: FOLKLORE—RUSSIA. KINGS AND RULERS—FOLKLORE. MUSICIANS—FOLKLORE. RIVERS—FOLKLORE.

1262 Sierra, Judy. *Can You Guess My Name? Traditional Tales Around the World*. **Illus. by Stefano Vitale. Clarion, 2002. 0-618-13328-3. 110pp. Gr. PreK–2**

A folk or fairy tale variant is a story from a different culture or country that mirrors a well-known or classic version. For each of five European folktales standards— "The Three Pigs," "The Bremen Town Musicians," "Rumpelstiltskin," "The Frog Prince," and "Hansel and Gretel"—storyteller and folklorist Judy Sierra has found and retold three compelling variants, with a total of 13 countries and five continents represented. Dramatic, handsome oil paintings on wood surfaces integrate stylistic elements from each country, including Italy, Argentina, the United States, Burma, Nigeria, Serbia, and South Africa.

GERM: Read these aloud along with the original folktales so your children can chart the differences in characters, settings, plots, story elements, and countries of origin.

RELATED TITLES: Baumgartner, Barbara. *Crocodile! Crocodile! Stories Told Around the World*. DK, 1994. / Hamilton, Virginia. *The Girl Who Spun Gold*. Scholastic, 2000. / Marshall, James. *Hansel and Gretel*. Dial, 1990. / Marshall, James. *The Three Little Pigs*. Dial, 1989. / Ness, Evaline. *Tom Tit Tot*. Scribner, 1965. / Scieszka, Jon. *The Frog Prince Continued*. Viking, 1991. / Scieszka, Jon. *The True Story of the 3 Little Pigs*. Viking, 1989. / Sierra, Judy. *Nursery Tales Around the World*. Clarion, 1996. / Stanley, Diane. *Petrosinella: A Neopolitan Rapunzel*. Dial, 1995. / Stanley, Diane. *Rumpelstiltskin's Daughter*. Morrow, 1997. / White, Carolyn. *Whuppity Stoorie: A Scottish Folktale*. Putnam, 1997. / Zelinsky, Paul O. *Rumpelstiltskin*. Dutton, 1986. / Zemach, Harve. *Duffy and the Devil*. Farrar, 1986.

SUBJECTS: FAIRY TALES. FOLKLORE—COLLECTIONS. MULTICULTURAL BOOKS—FOLKLORE. RUMPELSTILTSKIN STORIES.

1263 Sierra, Judy. *The Gift of the Crocodile: A Cinderella Story*. **Illus. by Reynold Ruffins. Simon & Schuster, 2000. 0-689-82188-3. Unp. Gr. 1–6**

In a Cinderella story from the Moluccas or Spice Islands in Indonesia, Damura is maltreated by her stepmother, but protected by Grandmother Crocodile, who repays her kindness with a silver sarong. Of course her stepsister conspires to get a nice sarong, too, but she's rude and nasty to Grandmother Crocodile and gets the sarong she deserves, full of nasty leeches. At the palace dance, Damura goes dressed in a golden sarong, losing a golden slipper to the prince.

GERM: Compare and contrast other versions of Cinderella worldwide, charting the characters, clothing, settings, and endings of each. Pull out your nonfiction crocodile books so kids can see what kind of fairy godmother they're dealing with here.

RELATED TITLES: Climo, Shirley. *The Egyptian Cinderella*. Crowell, 1989. / Coburn, Jewell Reinhart. *Jouanah: A Hmong Cinderella*. Shen's, 1996. / Craft, K. Y. *Cinderella*. SeaStar Books, 2000. / Ehrlich, Amy. *Cinderella*. Illus. by Susan Jeffers. Dutton, 2004. / Han, Oki S., and Stephanie Plunkett. *Kongi and Potgi: A Cinderella Story from Korea*. Dial, 1996. / Hickox, Rebecca. *The Golden Sandal: A Middle Eastern Cinderella Story*. Holiday House, 1998. / Hooks, William H. *Moss Gown*. Clarion, 1987. / Jaffe, Nina. *The Way Meat Loves Salt: A Cinderella Story from the Jewish Tradition*. Henry Holt, 1998. / Martin, Rafe. *The Rough-Face Girl*. Putnam, 1992. / Pollock, Penny. *The Turkey Girl: A Zuni Cinderella Story*. Little, Brown, 1996. / San Souci, Robert D. *Cendrillon: A Caribbean Cinderella*. Simon & Schuster, 1998. / Steptoe, John. *Mufaro's Beautiful Daughters*. Lothrop, 1987. / Wilson, Barbara Ker. *Wishbones: A Folk Tale from China*. Bradbury, 1993.

SUBJECTS: CINDERELLA STORIES. CROCODILES—FOLKLORE. FAIRY TALES. FOLKLORE—INDONESIA. MULTICULTURAL BOOKS—FOLKLORE. STEPMOTHERS—FOLKLORE.

1264 Sierra, Judy. *Nursery Tales Around the World*. **Illus. by Stefano Vitale. Clarion, 1996. 0-395-67894-3. 114pp. Gr. PreK–2**

In this stellar and handsome collection, compare and contrast 18 easy-to-tell stories arranged in groups of three variants on these themes: Runaway Cookies; Incredible Appetites; Victory of the Smallest; Chain Tales; Slowpokes and Speedsters; and Fooling the Big Bad Wolf.

GERM: Compare these stories with picture-book versions children will also love, such as *The Gingerbread Man* by Eric A. Kimmel and *Gobble, Gobble, Slip, Slop* by Meilo So.

RELATED TITLES: Baumgartner, Barbara. *Crocodile! Crocodile! Stories Told Around the World*. DK, 1994. / Compton, Joanne. *Sody Sallyratus*. Dutton, 1997. / Davis, Aubrey. *Sody Sallyratus*. Kids Can, 1998. / Galdone, Paul. *The Greedy Old Fat Man*. Clarion, 1983. / Ginsburg, Mirra. *Clay Boy*. Greenwillow, 1997. / Kent, Jack. *The Fat Cat*. Scholastic, 1972. / Kimmel, Eric A. *The Gingerbread Man*. Holiday House, 1993. / Polette, Nancy. *The Little Old Woman and the Hungry Cat*. Greenwillow, 1989. / Sierra, Judy. *Can You Guess My Name? Traditional Tales Around the World*. Clarion, 2002. / Sloat, Teri. *Sody Sallyratus*. Dutton, 1997. / So, Meilo. *Gobble, Gobble, Slip, Slop: The Tale of a Very Greedy Cat*. Knopf, 2004. / Stevens, Janet. *The Tortoise and the Hare: An Aesop Fable*. Holiday House, 1984. / Taback, Simms. *There Was an Old Lady Who Swallowed a Fly*. Viking, 1997.

SUBJECTS: FOLKLORE—COLLECTIONS. MULTICULTURAL BOOKS—FOLKLORE. SWALLOWING STORIES. TRICKSTER TALES—FOLKLORE.

1265 Sierra, Judy. *Tasty Baby Belly Buttons: A Japanese Folktale*. **Illus. by Meilo So. Knopf, 1999. 0-679-99369-X. Unp. Gr. K–3**

A childless old man and woman find a melon, and what should be inside but a tiny perfect baby girl they name Uriko-hime or "melon princess." When bad oni kidnap the babies of the village, bellybutton-less Uriko sets out to rescue them. In best folktale tradition, she shares her millet dumplings with her dog, a pheasant, and a monkey, all of whom sail with her to the monsters' island so she can rescue the babies and defeat the hulking bullies, of course.

GERM: Compare the oni with those in Arlene Mosel's *The Funny Little Woman*. Look for other folktales where a small, kind person prevails thanks to the help of others. This is also a good story for Reader's Theater, flannelboard or stick puppet productions, or for straight storytelling with the book as back-up.

RELATED TITLES: dePaola, Tomie. *Fin M'Coul, the Giant of Knockmany Hill*. Holiday House, 1981. / dePaola, Tomie. *The Mysterious Giant of Barletta*. Harcourt, 1988. / Hughes, Monica. *Little Fingerling*. Ideals, 1992. / Kimmel, Eric A. *Three Samurai Cats: A Story from Japan*. Holiday House, 2003. / Morimoto, Junko. *The Two Bullies*. Crown, 1999. / Mosel, Arlene. *The Funny Little Woman*. Dutton, 1972. / San Souci, Robert D. *Fa Mulan: The Story of a Woman Warrior*. Hyperion, 1998. / Shute, Linda. *Momotaro, the Peach Boy*. Lothrop, 1986. / Snyder, Dianne. *The Boy of the Three Year Nap*. Houghton Mifflin, 1988. / Stamm, Claus. *Three Strong Women*. Viking, 1990.

SUBJECTS: BABIES—FOLKLORE. FOLKLORE—JAPAN. GIANTS—FOLKLORE. MULTICULTURAL BOOKS—FOLKLORE. READER'S THEATER—FOLKLORE.

1266 Simonds, Nina, and Leslie Swartz. *Moonbeams, Dumplings and Dragon Boats: A Treasury of Chinese Holiday Tales, Activities, and Recipes*. **Illus. by Meilo So. Harcourt, 2002. 0-15-201983-9. 80pp. Gr. 2–6**

This festive celebration of five major Chinese festivals, including the one most familiar in the U.S.—Chinese New Year—is illustrated with witty and informative watercolors. Each section features a related folktale, as well as crafts, riddles, traditions, and seasonal foods.

GERM: Your group can assemble a classroom book, researching one of their chosen favorite American holidays—perhaps the Fourth of July or Earth Day—with factual information, drawings, games, poems, recipes, and stories.

RELATED TITLES: Cole, Joanna. *Ms. Frizzle's Adventures: Imperial China*. Scholastic, 2005. / Hong, Lily Toy. *How the Ox Star Fell from Heaven*. Albert Whitman, 1991. / Kimmel, Eric A. *The Rooster's Antlers: A Story of the Chinese Zodiac*. Holiday House, 1999. / Kimmel, Eric A. *Ten Suns: A Chinese Legend*. Holiday House, 1998. / Mosel, Arlene. *Tikki Tikki Tembo*. Dutton, 1972. / San Souci, Robert D. *Fa Mulan: The Story of a Woman Warrior*. Hyperion, 1998. / Yep, Laurence. *The Dragon Prince: A Chinese Beauty and the Beast Tale*. HarperCollins, 1997. / Young, Ed. *Beyond the Great Mountains: A Visual Poem About China*. Chronicle, 2005. / Young, Ed. *Cat and Rat: The Legend of the Chinese Zodiac*. Henry Holt, 1995. / Young, Ed. *Lon Po Po*. Philomel, 1989.

SUBJECTS: CHINA. FESTIVALS. FOLKLORE—CHINA. FOLKLORE—COLLECTIONS. HOLIDAYS. HOLIDAYS—FOLKLORE.

1267 **So, Meilo.** *Gobble, Gobble, Slip, Slop: The Tale of a Very Greedy Cat.* **Illus. by the author. Knopf, 2004. 0-375-82504-5. Unp. Gr. PreK–3**

In a folktale from India, a cat and a parrot decide to take turns preparing meals for each other, but when the parrot serves the cat a feast of 500 delicious little cakes—gobble, gobble, slip, slop—the cat eats them all. Then he eats the parrot, a nosy old woman, a farmer and his donkey, the sultan and his entire wedding procession, and, in what proves to be his undoing, two little sharp-clawed crabs.

GERM: This genial swallowing story, with festive ink-and-watercolor illustrations on rice paper, will be a breeze for storytelling, acting out, and joining in on the cumulative refrain. You'll find another version of the story, "The Cat and the Parrot," in Virginia Haviland's *Favorite Fairy Tales Told in India*. Go on a binge, comparing the cat's appetite with the bear's in *Sody Sallyratus* and with the title characters in Galdone's *The Greedy Old Fat Man*, Ginsburg's *Clay Boy*, Kent's *The Fat Cat*, and, of course that *Old Lady Who Swallowed a Fly*. For props to help you present this story, go to <www.mimismotifs.com>.

RELATED TITLES: Baumgartner, Barbara. *Crocodile! Crocodile! Stories Told Around the World*. DK, 1994. / Compton, Joanne. *Sody Sallyratus*. Dutton, 1997. / Davis, Aubrey. *Sody Sallyratus*. Kids Can, 1998. / Galdone, Paul. *The Greedy Old Fat Man*. Clarion, 1983. / Ginsburg, Mirra. *Clay Boy*. Greenwillow, 1997. / Haviland, Virginia. *Favorite Fairy Tales Told in India*. Little, Brown, 1973. / Hoberman, Mary Ann. *It's Simple, Said Simon*. Illus. by Meilo So. Knopf, 2001. / Karas, G. Brian. *I Know an Old Lady*. Scholastic, 1984. / Kent, Jack. *The Fat Cat*. Scholastic, 1972. / Polette, Nancy. *The Little Old Woman and the Hungry Cat*. Greenwillow, 1989. / Sloat, Teri. *Sody Sallyratus*. Dutton, 1997. / Souhami, Jessica. *No Dinner! The Story of the Old Woman and the Pumpkin*. Marshall Cavendish, 2000. / Taback, Simms. *There Was an Old Lady Who Swallowed a Fly*. Viking, 1997.

SUBJECTS: ANIMALS—FOLKLORE. CAKE—FOLKLORE. CATS—FOLKLORE. CRABS—FOLKLORE. FOLKLORE—INDIA. GREED—FOLKLORE. HUMOROUS FOLKLORE. MULTICULTURAL BOOKS. PARROTS—FOLKLORE. SWALLOWING STORIES.

1268 **Soifer, Margaret, and Irwin Shapiro.** *Tenggren's Golden Tales from the Arabian Nights.* **Illus. by Gustaf Tenggren. Golden Books, 2003. 0-375-82636-X. 114pp. Gr. 3–8**

Originally published in 1957, this lively collection of ten fairy tales, illustrated with Tenggren's exotic and colorful paintings, starts with an explanation of how Scheherazade staved off beheading by her husband, King Shahriar, by regaling him with her captivating stories for 1001 nights. You'll welcome old friends like Ali Baba, Aladdin, and Sinbad, along with some lesser knowns.

GERM: Neil Philip's *The Arabian Nights* contains longer, more complex versions of some of the same stories. Compare the universal story of dreaming about and then finding one's own treasure in "The Poor Man's Dream" with *The Greatest Treasure* by Demi, *Dream Peddler* by Gail E. Haley, *St. Patrick and the Peddler* by Margaret Hodges, *The Bee and the Dream* by Jan Freeman Long, and *The Treasure* by Uri Shulevitz.

RELATED TITLES: Carrick, Carol. *Aladdin and the Wonderful Lamp*. Scholastic, 1989. / Demi. *The Greatest Treasure*. Scholastic, 1998. / Haley, Gail. *Dream Peddler*. Dutton, 1993. / Hodges, Margaret. *Saint Patrick and the Peddler*. Orchard, 1993. / Kimmel, Eric A. *The Three Princes: A Tale from the Middle East*. Holiday House, 1994. / Long, Jan Freeman. *The Bee and the Dream: A Japanese Tale*. Dutton, 1996. / McVitty, Walter. *Ali Baba and the Forty Thieves*. Abrams, 1989. / Mayer, Marianna. *Aladdin and the Enchanted Lamp*. Macmillan, 1985. / Philip, Neil. *The Arabian Nights*. Orchard, 1994. / Shulevitz, Uri. *The Treasure*. Farrar, 1978. / Sunami, Kitoba. *How the Fisherman Tricked the Genie: A Tale Within a Tale Within a Tale*. Atheneum, 2002. / Yeoman, John. *The Seven Voyages of Sinbad the Sailor*. McElderry, 1997.

SUBJECTS: ARABIAN NIGHTS. FAIRY TALES. FOLKLORE—ARAB COUNTRIES. FOLKLORE—

COLLECTIONS. KINGS AND RULERS—FOLKLORE. PRINCES AND PRINCESSES—FOLKLORE. STORYTELLING—FOLKLORE.

1269 **Souhami, Jessica.** *The Leopard's Drum: An Asante Tale from West Africa.* **Illus. by the author. Little, Brown, 1996. 0-316-80466-5. Unp. Gr. PreK–2**

Nyame, the Sky-God, promises a reward to anyone who can bring him the drum belonging to fierce, proud, and boastful Oseba, the leopard. It's Achi-cheri, the tortoise—the "titchy little, weak little creature"—with her soft shell who succeeds, and gets, as a reward, the tough, hard shell that she still wears today.

GERM: Script this up into a nifty Reader's Theater, and create face masks for each of the animals. For other explanations of how the tortoise got her shell, read Tololwa M. Mollel's African pourquoi tale *The Flying Tortoise* and Gayle Ross's *How Turtle's Back Was Cracked: A Traditional Cherokee Tale.* Compare and contrast other tales of animals who perform impossible tasks for the Sky-God, including Verna Aardema's *Anansi Does the Impossible!*, Gail E. Haley's *A Story, a Story,* Gerald McDermott's *Zomo the Rabbit,* and Linda Shute's *Rabbit Wishes.*

RELATED TITLES: Aardema, Verna. *Anansi Does the Impossible! An Ashanti Tale.* Atheneum, 1997. / Aardema, Verna. *How the Ostrich Got Its Long Neck: A Tale from the Akamba of Kenya.* Scholastic, 1995. / Gates, Frieda. *Owl Eyes.* Lothrop, 1994. / Haley, Gail E. *A Story, a Story.* Atheneum, 1970. / Knutson, Barbara. *Sungura and Leopard: A Swahili Trickster Tale.* Little, Brown, 1993. / McDermott, Gerald. *Zomo the Rabbit: A Trickster Tale from West Africa.* Harcourt, 1992. / Mollel, Tololwa M. *The Flying Tortoise: An Igbo Tale.* Clarion, 1994. / Mollel, Tololwa M. *The King and the Tortoise.* Clarion, 1993. / Ross, Gayle. *How Turtle's Back Was Cracked: A Traditional Cherokee Tale.* Dial, 1995. / Shute, Linda. *Rabbit Wishes.* Lothrop, 1995. / Sierra, Judy. *The Mean Hyena: A Folktale from Malawi.* Dutton, 1997. / Souhami, Jessica. *No Dinner! The Story of the Old Woman and the Pumpkin.* Marshall Cavendish, 2000.

SUBJECTS: CREATIVE DRAMA—FOLKLORE. DRUMS—FOLKLORE. FOLKLORE—AFRICA, WEST. LEOPARDS—FOLKLORE. MULTICULTURAL BOOKS—FOLKLORE. POURQUOI TALES. READER'S THEATER—FOLKLORE. TURTLES—FOLKLORE.

1270 **Souhami, Jessica.** *Mrs. McCool and the Giant Cuhullin: An Irish Tale.* **Illus. by the author. Henry Holt, 2002. 0-8050-6852-X. Unp. Gr. K–4**

Irish giant Cuhullin plans to pound giant Finn McCool as flat as a pancake, but Finn's wife, Oona, has a clever plan to defeat the big bully.

GERM: Compare and contrast this longer version with Tomie dePaola's *Fin M'Coul, the Giant of Knockmany Hill* and Robert Byrd's *Finn MacCoul and His Fearless Wife.* Another enjoyable bout of mega-macho posturing can be found in the Japanese folktale *The Two Bullies* by Junko Morimoto.

RELATED TITLES: Bertrand, Lynne. *Granite Baby.* Farrar, 2005. / Byrd, Robert. *Finn MacCoul and His Fearless Wife: A Giant of a Tale from Ireland.* Dutton, 1999. / Climo, Shirley. *Stolen Thunder: A Norse Myth.* Clarion, 1994. / dePaola, Tomie. *Fin M'Coul, the Giant of Knockmany Hill.* Holiday House, 1981. / Morimoto, Junko. *The Two Bullies.* Crown, 1999. / Osborne, Mary Pope. *The Brave Little Seamstress.* Atheneum, 2002. / Osborne, Mary Pope. *Kate and the Beanstalk.* Atheneum, 2000. / Shepard, Aaron. *Master Man: A Tall Tale of Nigeria.* HarperCollins, 2001. / Sloat, Teri. *The Hungry Giant of the Tundra.* Dutton, 1993. / Souhami, Jessica. *The Leopard's Drum: An Asante Tale from West Africa.* Little, Brown, 1996. / Souhami, Jessica. *No Dinner! The Story of the Old Woman and the Pumpkin.* Marshall Cavendish, 2000. / Van Woerkom, Dorothy. *Alexandra the Rock-Eater.* Knopf, 1978.

SUBJECTS: FOLKLORE—IRELAND. GIANTS—FOLKLORE. HUMOROUS FOLKLORE. STRENGTH—FOLKLORE. WOMEN—FOLKLORE.

1271 **Souhami, Jessica.** *No Dinner! The Story of the Old Woman and the Pumpkin.* **Illus. by the author. Marshall Cavendish, 2000. 0-7614-5059-9. Unp. Gr. PreK–2**

An old woman wants to visit her granddaughter on the other side of the forests, but she's worried about meeting up with wild and dangerous animals on the way. In this Indian folktale variant of "The Three Billy Goats Gruff," with elements of "Hansel and Gretel," "The Three Little Pigs," and other well-known European folktales, the old woman tricks a wolf, tiger, and bear into not eating her.

GERM: Before reading, ask children to listen closely to see if this story resembles any others they know. Filled with humor and repeated refrains, this sly folktale is a storyteller's dream for acting out, telling and retelling, Reader's Theater, making flannelboard or puppet characters, comparing with similar stories, and predicting outcomes.

RELATED TITLES: Bannerman, Helen. *The Story of Little Babaji.* HarperCollins, 1996. / Emberley, Rebecca.

Three Cool Kids. Little, Brown, 1995. / Harper, Wilhelmina. *The Gunniwolf*. Dutton, 1978. / Hyman, Trina Schart. *Little Red Riding Hood*. Holiday House, 1983. / Kimmel, Eric A. *Anansi and the Talking Melon*. Holiday House, 1994. / Marshall, James. *Red Riding Hood*. Dial, 1987. / Marshall, James. *The Three Little Pigs*. Dial, 1989. / Pfeffer, Wendy. *From Seed to Pumpkin*. HarperCollins, 2004. / Rounds, Glen. *The Three Billy Goats Gruff*. Holiday House, 1993. / So, Meilo. *Gobble, Gobble, Slip, Slop: The Tale of a Very Greedy Cat*. Knopf, 2004. / Souhami, Jessica. *The Leopard's Drum: An Asante Tale from West Africa*. Little, Brown, 1996.

SUBJECTS: BEARS—FOLKLORE. CREATIVE DRAMA—FOLKLORE. ELDERLY—FOLKLORE. FOLKLORE—INDIA. HUMOROUS FOLKLORE. MULTICULTURAL BOOKS—FOLKLORE. PUMPKINS—FOLKLORE. READER'S THEATER—FOLKLORE. TIGERS—FOLKLORE. WOLVES— FOLKLORE.

1272   **Sutcliffe, Rosemary.** *The Wanderings of Odysseus: The Story of The Odyssey*. **Illus. by Alan Lee. Delacorte, 1993. 0-385-32205-4. 119pp. Gr. 5–8**

We read how Troy was sacked in Sutcliffe's companion volume, *Black Ships Before Troy!*, a retelling of *The Iliad*. Now she takes us on "the long sea-road back to Ithaca" as Odysseus and his men sail for home, waylaid at every step by the Cyclops; Circe, the enchantress; the Sirens; and death at sea for all on the 12 ships but Odysseus. Soft, dreamlike, yet somber watercolors add atmosphere to Odysseus's tale, especially to the last half of his journey, when he arrives home to find his wife, Penelope, holding her many suitors at bay.

GERM: Using the map of the Mediterranean at the back of the book, identify and trace the route that Odysseus took. *The Adventures of Odysseus* by Neil Philip is another handsome volume of his peripatetic voyage home. Mary Pope Osborne's *Favorite Greek Myths* will introduce you to the gods and goddesses, while *Cyclops* by Leonard Everett Fisher, is a bold picture book that describes Odysseus's first disastrous encounter on his way home from Troy. Meet Odysseus as a teen in Jane Yolen and Robert J. Harris's adventure novel *Odysseus in the Serpent Maze*.

RELATED TITLES: Fisher, Leonard Everett. *Cyclops*. Holiday House, 1991. / Fisher, Leonard Everett. *Theseus and the Minotaur*. Holiday House, 1988. / Hutton, Warwick. *Odysseus and the Cyclops*. McElderry, 1995. / McCaughrean, Geraldine. *Roman Myths*. McElderry Books, 2001. / Osborne, Mary Pope. *Favorite Greek Myths*. Scholastic, 1989. / Osborne, Mary Pope. *Tales from the Odyssey: The One-Eyed Giant*. Hyperion, 2003. (And others in the Tales from the Odyssey series.) / Philip, Neil. *The Adventures of Odysseus*. Orchard, 1997. / Sutcliffe, Rosemary. *Black Ships Before Troy! The Story of the Iliad*. Delacorte, 1993. / Yolen, Jane. *Wings*. Harcourt, 1991. / Yolen, Jane, and Robert J. Harris. *Odysseus in the Serpent Maze*. HarperCollins, 2001.

SUBJECTS: ADVENTURE AND ADVENTURERS—FOLKLORE. FOLKLORE—COLLECTIONS. FOLKLORE—GREECE. GODS AND GODDESSES—FOLKLORE. HEROES—FOLKLORE. MYTHOLOGY. ODYSSEUS. SHIPS—FOLKLORE. TROJAN WAR. VOYAGES AND TRAVELS— FOLKLORE. WAR—FOLKLORE.

1273   **Taback, Simms.** *Kibitzers and Fools: Tales My Zayda (Grandfather) Told Me*. **Illus. by the author. Viking, 2005. 0-670-05955-2. Unp. Gr. 1–4**

Do you know the difference between a shlemiel (a fool) and a shlimazel (an unlucky person)? A shlemiel will dump a plate of hot soup into the lap of a shlimazel. So says the zayda (grandfather) in this uproarious collection of 13 short tales from the Jewish tradition. Taback's busy full-bleed illustrations abound with kibitzers (know-it-alls) and a variety of fools, including nebbishes, nudniks, schmendriks, and schnooks.

GERM: Each story concludes with a saying or maxim, and there's a further list on the endpapers, which will remind you of Ben Franklin's many sayings. There's a further Franklin link in the story, "The Sign," which will remind you of Candace Fleming's nonfiction picture book, *The Hatmaker's Sign: A Story by Benjamin Franklin*. A helpful glossary of all of the Yiddish terms used in the book contains, alas, no pronunciation guide.

RELATED TITLES: Fleming, Candace. *The Hatmaker's Sign: A Story by Benjamin Franklin*. Orchard, 1998. / Freedman, Florence B. *It Happened in Chelm: A Story of the Legendary Town of Fools*. Shapolsky, 1990. / Greene, Jacqueline D. *What His Father Did*. Houghton, 1992. / Kimmel, Eric A. *The Adventures of Hershel of Ostropol*. Holiday House, 1995. / Kimmel, Eric A. *The Jar of Fools: Eight Hanukkah Stories from Chelm*. Holiday House, 2000. / Sanfield, Steve. *Bit by Bit*. Philomel, 1995. / Schwartz, Howard. *Elijah's Violin and Other Jewish Fairy Tales*. HarperCollins, 1983. / Singer, Isaac Bashevis. *When Shlemiel Went to Warsaw and Other Stories*. Farrar, 1979. / Singer, Isaac Bashevis. *Zlateh the Goat and Other Stories*. HarperCollins, 1994. / Taback, Simms. *Joseph Had a Little Overcoat*. Viking, 1999.

SUBJECTS: CHELM—FOLKLORE. FOLKLORE—COLLECTIONS. FOLKLORE—EUROPE, EASTERN.

FOLKLORE, JEWISH. FOOLS—FOLKLORE. HUMOROUS FOLKLORE. LANGUAGE. YIDDISH LANGUAGE.

1274   Thornhill, Jan. *The Rumor: A Jataka Tale from India.* **Illus. by the author. Maple Tree, 2002. 1-894379-39-X. Unp. Gr. K–2**

When a falling mango makes a loud noise, a worrywart hare is convinced the world is breaking up and she hops away, warning the other hares to run. Pretty soon, thousands of hares, boars, deer, tigers, and rhinoceri are running, too, until a wise lion stops the stampede.

GERM: This familiar Jataka tale, illustrated with elaborately bordered scenes from the animal kingdom, will lead to a discussion of herd mentality and the dangers of jumping to conclusions. Compare this telling of the ancient story with Demi's "The Lion King" in *Buddha Stories* and with Rafe Martin's variant, *Foolish Rabbit's Big Mistake.* Children will recognize the Henny Penny or Chicken Little connection, so read samples of that folktale as well in versions by Sally Hobson or Jane Wattenberg.

RELATED TITLES: Demi. *Buddha.* Henry Holt, 1996. / Demi. *Buddha Stories.* Henry Holt, 1997. / Demi. *The Dragon's Tale and Other Animal Fables of the Chinese Zodiac.* Henry Holt, 1996. / Galdone, Paul. *The Monkey and the Crocodile: A Jataka Tale from India.* Clarion, 1969. / Hobson, Sally. *Chicken Little.* Simon & Schuster, 1994. / Martin, Rafe. *Foolish Rabbit's Big Mistake.* Putnam, 1985. / Martin, Rafe. *The Monkey Bridge.* Knopf, 1997. / Mayo, Margaret. *Tortoise's Flying Lesson: Animal Stories.* Harcourt, 1995. / Palatini, Margie. *Earthquack!* Simon & Schuster, 2002. / Wattenberg, Jane. *Henny-Penny.* Scholastic, 2000.

SUBJECTS: ANIMALS—FOLKLORE. BUDDHA AND BUDDHISM. FABLES. FEAR—FOLKLORE. FOLKLORE—INDIA. FRUIT—FOLKLORE. HARES—FOLKLORE. JATAKA STORIES. LIONS—FOLKLORE.

1275   Van Laan, Nancy. *Shingebiss: An Ojibwe Legend.* **Illus. by Betsy Bowen. Houghton Mifflin, 1997. 0-395-82745-0. Unp. Gr. 2–6**

During the Spirit Moon, when Winter Maker blows his icy breath across Great Lake Superior, the little merganser duck Shingebiss shows no fear, pecking through the icy lake to catch his fish. Winter Maker tries to freeze and starve him, but the plucky duck prevails.

GERM: Joseph Bruchac and Jonathan London's *Thirteen Moons on Turtle's Back* describes the moon of each month as celebrated by Native Americans. See how the Ojibwa Indians moved from winter to spring in *Peboan and Seegwun* by Larry Charles.

RELATED TITLES: Bruchac, Joseph, and Jonathan London. *Thirteen Moons on Turtle's Back.* Philomel, 1992. / Coatsworth, Emerson, and David Coatsworth. *The Adventures of Nanabush: Ojibway Indian Stories.* Atheneum, 1980. / Esbensen, Barbara Juster. *The Star Maiden: An Ojibway Tale.* Little, Brown, 1988. / Garland, Sherry. *Why Ducks Sleep on One Leg.* Scholastic, 1993. / Larry, Charles. *Peboan and Seegwun.* Farrar, 1993. / Lunge-Larsen, Lise, and Margi Preus. *The Legend of the Lady Slipper: An Ojibwe Tale.* Houghton Mifflin, 1999. / Paterson, Katherine. *The Tale of the Mandarin Ducks.* Dutton, 1990. / San Souci, Robert D. *Sootface: An Ojibwa Cinderella Story.* Doubleday, 1994. / Taylor, Harriet Peck. *When Bear Stole the Chinook: A Siksika Tale.* Farrar, 1997.

SUBJECTS: DUCKS—FOLKLORE. FOLKLORE—INDIANS OF NORTH AMERICA. FOLKLORE—U.S. GREAT LAKES—FOLKLORE. LAKES—FOLKLORE. MULTICULTURAL BOOKS—FOLKLORE. OJIBWA INDIANS—FOLKLORE. SEASONS—FOLKLORE. WINTER—FOLKLORE.

1276   Wardlaw, Lee. *Punia and the King of Sharks: A Hawaiian Folktale.* **Illus. by Felipe Davalos. Dial, 1997. 0-8037-1683-4. Unp. Gr. K–3**

Punia, a poor, hungry, but clever young boy whose fisherman father was devoured by lobster-hoarding sharks, tricks the King of Sharks four times, stealing his sweet and tasty lobsters each time.

GERM: Pair your reading with some shark nonfiction including *Surprising Sharks* by Nicola Davies and *Sharks! Strange and Wonderful* by Laurence Pringle.

RELATED TITLES: Cerullo, Mary M. *Sharks: Challengers of the Deep.* Dutton, 1993. / Cerullo, Mary M. *The Truth About Great White Sharks.* Chronicle, 2000. / Davies, Nicola. *Surprising Sharks.* Candlewick, 2003. / Ho, Minfong, and Saphan Ros. *Brother Rabbit: A Cambodian Tale.* Lothrop, 1997. / Kesey, Ken. *Little Tricker the Squirrel Meets Big Double the Bear.* Viking, 1990. / Mahy, Margaret. *The Great White Man-Eating Shark.* Dial, 1990. / Martin, Rafe. *The Shark God.* Scholastic, 2001. / O'Brien, Patrick. *Megatooth.* Henry Holt, 2001. / Pringle, Laurence. *Sharks! Strange and Wonderful.* Boyds Mills, 2001. / Rumford, James. *Dog-of-the-Sea-Waves.* Houghton Mifflin, 2004. / Yep, Laurence. *The Man Who Tricked a Ghost.* BridgeWater, 1993.

SUBJECTS: FOLKLORE—HAWAII. FOLKLORE—U.S. HUMOROUS FOLKLORE. LOBSTERS—FOLKLORE. MULTICULTURAL BOOKS—FOLKLORE. SHARKS—FOLKLORE. TRICKSTER TALES.

1277   Washington, Donna L. *A Pride of African Tales.* **Illus. by James Ransome. HarperCollins, 2004. 0-06-024932-3. 70pp. Gr. 4–8**

In a rich collection of six thoughtful stories from West Africa, illustrated with full-bleed watercolor paintings, you'll discover an Anansi tale about laziness, a pourquoi tale of how monkeys came to be, a cautionary tale with a warning about judging people by appearance alone, a story about anger and forgiveness, a taboo story, and a fable about talking without thinking.

GERM: Each tale will generate lively discussion about its meaning or the life lesson one could draw from it. The story notes at the end provide additional information and a list of related titles for each selection. Compare the telling of "Anansi's Fishing Expedition" with Verna Aardema's *Anansi Finds a Fool,* and follow up "The Talking Skull" with *Too Much Talk* by Angela Shelf Medearis.

RELATED TITLES: Aardema, Verna. *Anansi Finds a Fool.* Dial, 1992. / Aardema, Verna. *Misoso: Once upon a Time Tales from Africa.* Knopf, 1994. / Courlander, Harold. *The Cow-Tail Switch and Other West African Stories.* Henry Holt, 1988. / Courlander, Harold. *The Hat-Shaking Dance and Other Tales from the Gold Coast.* Harcourt, 1957. / Gatti, Anne. *Tales from the African Plains.* Dutton, 1994. / Greaves, Nick. *When Lion Could Fly and Other Tales from Africa.* Barrons, 1993. / Kimmel, Eric A. *Anansi Goes Fishing.* Holiday House, 1992. / Lester, Julius. *How Many Spots Does a Leopard Have? And Other Tales.* Scholastic, 1989. / Lester, Julius. *The Knee-High Man and Other Tales.* Puffin, 1985. / Medearis, Angela Shelf. *Too Much Talk.* Candlewick, 1995. / Shepard, Aaron. *Master Man: A Tall Tale of Nigeria.* HarperCollins, 2001.

SUBJECTS: ANANSI (LEGENDARY CHARACTER). FOLKLORE—AFRICA, WEST. FOLKLORE—COLLECTIONS. MULTICULTURAL BOOKS—FOLKLORE. TRICKSTER TALES.

1278   Wattenberg, Jane. *Henny-Penny.* **Illus. by the author. Scholastic, 2000. 0-439-07817-2. Unp. Gr. PreK–2**

"CHICKABUNGA!" Henny-Penny squawks when an acorn smacks her on top of her fine red comb. "The sky is falling!" Eye-popping, color photo-based collages will knock kids out of their seats. Between the rich, crazy, rhyming, and alliterative language of this hip chick and that shifty fox, and the photos of world monuments superimposed on each illustration—the Taj Mahal, the pyramids of Egypt—that will give kids the wanderlust, here's a version of the Chicken Little story that kids will beg to hear and read and act out again and again.

GERM: As you read the book aloud the first time, listeners can chime in on all the repeated refrains, and all of Foxy's wicked little rhymes, such as "Looking JUICY, Goosey," and "You're in luck, Duck." Identify all the world landmarks. Come up with new rhyming expressions. If you've never tried creative drama with your children before, there's no better story to start you off. Cast the play, encouraging actors to paraphrase any dialogue they can't remember. They can even make nametags and draw their animal's picture on them, or construct masks or hats.

RELATED TITLES: Downard, Barry. *The Little Red Hen.* Simon & Schuster, 2004. / Feldman, Thelma. *Who You Callin' Chicken?* Abrams, 2003. / Frankenhuyzen, Robbyn Smith van. *Saving Samantha: A True Story.* Sleeping Bear, 2004. / Froehlich, Margaret Walden. *That Kookoory!* Harcourt, 1995. / Galdone, Paul. *The Little Red Hen.* Clarion, 1979. / Hobson, Sally. *Chicken Little.* Simon & Schuster, 1994. / Kellogg, Steven. *Chicken Little.* Morrow, 1985. / Martin, Rafe. *Foolish Rabbit's Big Mistake.* Putnam, 1985. / Palatini, Margie. *Earthquack!* Simon & Schuster, 2002. / Pearson, Tracey Campbell. *Bob.* Farrar, 2002. / Scieszka, Jon. *The Stinky Cheese Man and Other Fairly Stupid Tales.* Viking, 1992. / Stevens, Janet, and Susan Stevens Crummel. *Cook-a-Doodle-Doo!* Harcourt, 1999. / Sturges, Philemon. *The Little Red Hen (Makes a Pizza).* Dutton, 1999. / Thornhill, Jan. *The Rumor: A Jataka Tale from India.* Maple Tree, 2002. / Ward, Helen. *The Rooster and the Fox.* Millbrook, 2003.

SUBJECTS: ANIMALS—FOLKLORE. BIRDS—FOLKLORE. CHANTABLE REFRAIN—FOLKLORE. CHICKENS—FOLKLORE. CREATIVE DRAMA—FOLKLORE. FOLKLORE. FOXES—FOLKLORE. HUMOROUS FOLKLORE. READER'S THEATER.

1279   White, Carolyn. *Whuppity Stoorie: A Scottish Folktale.* **Illus. by S. D. Schindler. Putnam, 1997. 0-399-22903-5. Unp. Gr. K–6**

Kate of Kittlerumpit and her mother are overjoyed when their handsome but sick pig, Grumphie, helps them discover a wild fairy woman's name just in time in this charming Scottish variant of Rumpelstiltskin.

GERM: Comparing folktale variants helps children see that stories come from all corners of the world, and celebrate their diversity and their similarity. From the British Isles alone, you'll find a version in *Magic and Mischief: Tales from Cornwall* by Shirley Climo, *Tom Tit Tot* by Evaline Ness, and Caldecott Medal winner *Duffy and the Devil* by Harve Zemach.

RELATED TITLES: Climo, Shirley. *Magic and Mischief: Tales from Cornwall*. Clarion, 1999. / Hamilton, Virginia. *The Girl Who Spun Gold*. Scholastic, 2000. / Moser, Barry. *Tucker Pfeffercorn: An Old Story Retold*. Little, Brown, 1994. / Ness, Evaline. *Tom Tit Tot*. Scribner, 1965. / Pitre, Felix. *Paco and the Witch*. Lodestar, 1995. / Sage, Alison. *Rumpelstiltskin*. Dial, 1990. / San Souci, Daniel D. *The Tsar's Promise*. Philomel, 1992. / Sierra, Judy. *Can You Guess My Name? Traditional Tales Around the World*. Clarion, 2002. / Stanley, Diane. *Rumpelstiltskin's Daughter*. Morrow, 1997. / Zelinsky, Paul O. *Rumpelstiltskin*. Dutton, 1986. / Zemach, Harve. *Duffy and the Devil*. Farrar, 1986.

SUBJECTS: FAIRIES. FAIRY TALES. FOLKLORE—SCOTLAND. PIGS—FOLKLORE. RUMPELSTILTSKIN STORIES.

1280 **Willey, Margaret.** *Clever Beatrice: An Upper Peninsula Conte.* **Illus. by Heather Solomon. Atheneum, 2001. 0-689-83254-0. Unp. Gr. 1–4**

Sharp-as-a-tack little Beatrice outwits a rich giant who lives on the other side of the Michigan woods. She bets the giant ten gold coins that she can strike a blow harder than he can, carry more water from the well, and throw an iron bar farther, and while she doesn't actually do any of those things, he believes she can.

GERM: After Beatrice fools the dimwitted giant the first time, have children predict how she will outfox him the next two times. There's wonderful dialogue between Beatrice and the giant for some Reader's Theater. Photocopy those pages, hand them out to trios or quartets of kids, and let them act it out, with one or two kids reading the narrator's parts. Other female-led variants of this tale include Mary Pope Osborne's *The Brave Little Seamstress* and Dorothy Van Woerkum's *Alexandra the Rock-Eater*. An American version of this Jack tale is *Jack Outwits the Giants* by Paul Brett Johnson.

RELATED TITLES: De Regniers, Beatrice Schenk. *Little Sister and the Month Brothers*. Clarion, 1976. / Grimm, Jacob. *The Valiant Little Tailor*. Illus. by Victor Ambrus. Oxford, 1980. / Hicks, Ray. *The Jack Tales*. Callaway, 2000. / Johnson, Paul Brett. *Jack Outwits the Giants*. Simon & Schuster, 2002. / Osborne, Mary Pope. *The Brave Little Seamstress*. Atheneum, 2002. / Osborne, Mary Pope. *Kate and the Beanstalk*. Atheneum, 2000. / Stamm, Claus. *Three Strong Women*. Viking, 1990. / Swope, Sam. *Jack and the Seven Deadly Giants*. Farrar, 2004. / Thomassie, Tynia. *Feliciana Feydra LeRoux: A Cajun Tall Tale*. Little, Brown, 1995. / Van Woerkum, Dorothy. *Alexandra the Rock-Eater*. Knopf, 1978.

SUBJECTS: FOLKLORE—MICHIGAN. FOLKLORE—U.S. GIANTS—FOLKLORE. HUMOROUS FOLKLORE. READER'S THEATER. TALL TALES.

1281 **Wolkstein, Diane.** *The Day Ocean Came to Visit.* **Illus. by Steve Johnson and Lou Fancher. Harcourt, 2001. 0-15-201774-7. Unp. Gr. PreK–3**

Sun invites his new friend, Ocean, to visit him and his wife, Moon, at their large bamboo house, but, once inside, Ocean floods everything. In this pourquoi tale from Nigeria, readers will understand why Sun and Moon now live in the sky.

GERM: Read and compare creation/pourquoi tales about the sun, moon, and ocean from other cultures, including Emery Bernhard's *How Snowshoe Hare Rescued the Sun: A Tale from the Arctic*; Yangsook Choi's Korean tale *The Sun Girl and the Moon Boy*; Lois Ehlert's *Moon Rope: Un Lazo a la Luna: A Peruvian Folktale*; and Eric A. Kimmel's *Ten Suns: A Chinese Legend*. See what it would be like to bring the ocean home with Catherine Cowen's picture book *My Life with the Wave*.

RELATED TITLES: Bernhard, Emery. *How Snowshoe Hare Rescued the Sun: A Tale from the Arctic*. Holiday House, 1993. / Choi, Yangsook. *The Sun Girl and the Moon Boy*. Knopf, 1997. / Cowan, Catherine. *My Life with the Wave*. Lothrop, 1997. / Dayrell, Elphinstone. *Why the Sun and Moon Live in the Sky*. Houghton Mifflin, 1968. / Dixon, Ann. *How Raven Brought Light to People*. McElderry, 1992. / Ehlert, Lois. *Moon Rope: Un Lazo a la Luna: A Peruvian Folktale*. Harcourt, 1992. / Esbensen, Barbara Juster. *The Star Maiden: An Ojibway Tale*. Little, Brown, 1988. / Gerson, Mary-Joan. *How Night Came from the Sea: A Story from Brazil*. Little, Brown, 1994. / Goble, Paul. *Her Seven Brothers*. Bradbury, 1988. / Kimmel, Eric A. *Ten Suns: A Chinese Legend*. Holiday House, 1998. / McDermott, Gerald. *Raven: A Trickster Tale from the Pacific Northwest*. Harcourt, 1993. / Young, Ed. *Moon Mother: A Native American Creation Tale*. HarperCollins, 1993.

SUBJECTS: CREATION—FOLKLORE. FOLKLORE—AFRICA, WEST. FOLKLORE—NIGERIA. MOON—FOLKLORE. OCEAN—FOLKLORE. POURQUOI TALES. SUN—FOLKLORE.

1282 **Wooldridge, Connie Nordhielm.** *Wicked Jack.* **Illus. by Will Hillenbrand. Holiday House, 1995. 0-8234-1101-X. Unp. Gr. 2–5**

Old Jack, the blacksmith, takes such pride in his meanness that when Saint Peter offers him three wishes, Jack wishes for anyone who touches his rocker, sledgehammer, or firebush to be stuck fast to them. When the Devil comes to fetch Jack down below, Jack proves to be meaner than the Devil himself.

GERM: Have children pair up to act out the scenes where the Devil tries to get Jack to go down below with him. Find a classic version of this tale, titled "Wicked John and the Devil," in Richard Chase's *Grandfather Tales*.

RELATED TITLES: Babbitt, Natalie. *Ouch! A Tale from Grimm*. HarperCollins, 1998. / Belpré, Pura. *Oté: A Puerto Rican Folk Tale*. Random House, 1969. / Carey, Valerie Scho. *The Devil and Mother Crump*. Harper-Collins, 1987. / Chase, Richard. *Grandfather Tales*. Houghton Mifflin, 1948. / Compton, Kenn, and Joanne Compton. *Jack the Giant Chaser: An Appalachian Tale*. Holiday House, 1993. / Hogrogian, Nonny. *The Devil with the Three Golden Hairs*. Knopf, 1983. / Hooks, William H. *Mean Jake and the Devils*. Dial, 1981.

SUBJECTS: BEHAVIOR—FOLKLORE. DEVIL—FOLKLORE. FOLKLORE—U.S. HUMOROUS FOLKLORE.

1283 Yep, Laurence. *The Dragon Prince, A Chinese Beauty and the Beast Tale*. Illus. by Kam Mak. HarperCollins, 1997. 0-06-024381-3. Unp. Gr. 2–6

In a Chinese variant of "Beauty and the Beast," a farmer's youngest daughter, Seven, agrees to marry a terrifying dragon so he will spare her father's life. When she demonstrates her bravery and kindness, the creature is able to transform himself back into a handsome prince.

GERM: As many children's only exposure to the French folktale "Beauty and the Beast" comes from the greatly altered Disney movie, you'll also want to read aloud a more authentic version from any good folktale collection, or Marianna Mayer's dramatic picture book of the story. Two other versions of the "Beauty and the Beast" tale that you can use for comparison are William H. Hooks's *Snowbear Whittington*, which hails from Appalachia, and Charlotte Huck's *The Black Bull of Norroway*, which is from Scotland.

RELATED TITLES: Dasent, George Webbe. *East O' the Sun and West O' the Moon*. Illus. by P. J. Lynch. Candlewick, 1992. / Davol, Marguerite. *The Paper Dragon*. Atheneum, 1997. / Hooks, William H. *Snowbear Whittington: An Appalachian Beauty and the Beast*. Macmillan, 1994. / Huck, Charlotte. *The Black Bull of Norroway: A Scottish Tale*. Greenwillow, 2001. / Jagendorf, M. A., and Virginia Weng. *The Magic Boat and Other Chinese Folk Stories*. Vanguard, 1980. / Mayer, Marianna. *Beauty and the Beast*. Four Winds, 1978. / Prelutsky, Jack. *The Dragons Are Singing Tonight*. Greenwillow, 1993. / Simonds, Nina, and Leslie Swartz. *Moonbeams, Dumplings and Dragon Boats: A Treasury of Chinese Holiday Tales, Activities and Recipes*. Harcourt, 2002. / Whipple, Laura, comp. *Eric Carle's Dragons Dragons and Other Creatures that Never Were*. Philomel, 1991. / Yep, Laurence. *The Khan's Daughter: A Mongolian Folktale*. Scholastic, 1997.

SUBJECTS: DRAGONS—FOLKLORE. FAIRY TALES. FOLKLORE—CHINA. MULTICULTURAL BOOKS—FOLKLORE. SISTERS—FOLKLORE. TRANSFORMATIONS—FOLKLORE.

1284 Yep, Laurence. *The Khan's Daughter: A Mongolian Folktale*. Illus. by Jean Tseng and Mou-Sien Tseng. Scholastic, 1997. 0-590-48389-7. Unp. Gr. 2–6

Mongolian shepherd Möngke believes his late father's words about becoming rich someday and marrying the Khan's daughter, so he heads for the great city of domed tents where the soldiers are preparing for an enemy invasion. Through a combination of dumb luck and coincidence, Möngke succeeds at all three impossible tasks the Khan's wife assigns. He obtains the demons' treasure and drives the enemy from the land, but conquering Bagatur the Clever and Mighty (actually the Khan's clever daughter in disguise) proves more difficult.

GERM: Contrast his lesson in humility and prudence with that of the spoiled chief's daughter in *The Girl Who Lived with the Bears* by Barbara Diamond Goldin, a somber Native American folktale of the Pacific Northwest.

RELATED TITLES: Climo, Shirley. *Atalanta's Race: A Greek Myth*. Clarion, 1995. / DeFelice, Cynthia, and Mary DeMarsh. *Three Perfect Peaches: A French Folktale*. Orchard, 1995. / Goldin, Barbara Diamond. *The Girl Who Lived with the Bears*. Harcourt, 1997. / Kimmel, Eric A. *Rimonah of the Flashing Sword: A North African Tale*. Holiday House, 1995. / Kimmel, Eric A. *The Three Princes: A Tale from the Middle East*. Holiday House, 1994. / Kimmel, Eric A. *Three Sacks of Truth: A Story from France*. Holiday House, 1993. / Lewis, J. Patrick. *The Frog Princess: A Russian Tale*. Dial, 1994. / Martin, Claire. *Boots and the Glass Mountain*. Dial, 1992. / Otsuka, Zuzo. *Suho and the White Horse: A Legend of Mongolia*. Viking, 1981.

SUBJECTS: COINCIDENCE—FOLKLORE. COURAGE—FOLKLORE. FOLKLORE—MONGOLIA. HORSES—FOLKLORE. HUMOROUS FOLKLORE. MULTICULTURAL BOOKS—FOLKLORE. WOMEN—FOLKLORE.

1285 Yolen, Jane. *Mightier than the Sword: World Folktales for Strong Boys.* **Illus. by Raúl Colón. Harcourt, 2003. 0-15-216391-3. 112pp. Gr. 3–6**

In a fine collection of 14 folktales from as many countries, meet courageous, brave, pragmatic, sensitive, compassionate, smart, and wise boy heroes. Jane Yolen chose stories that reflected strength of character and brains over brawn, stating, in her open letter to her sons and grandson, "Picking up a sword doesn't make you a hero—sticking to your word does."

GERM: Some of these tales are variants of stories we know, such as "Mighty Mikko," a Norwegian variant of "Puss in Boots," with a fox instead of a cat. Others can be found in picture-book form, including "The Devil with the Three Golden Hairs," a Grimm tale to which you can compare Nonny Hogrogian's version and Natalie Babbitt's *Ouch.* Talk about the personal qualities of the heroes in these tales. Yolen's companion collection about girls is *Not One Damsel in Distress.*

RELATED TITLES: Babbitt, Natalie. *Ouch! A Tale from Grimm.* HarperCollins, 1998. / Demi. *The Magic Tapestry.* Henry Holt, 1994. / Hogrogian, Nonny. *The Devil with the Three Golden Hairs.* Knopf, 1983. / Kimmel, Eric A. *The Three Princes: A Tale from the Middle East.* Holiday House, 1994. / Kirstein, Lincoln. *Puss in Boots.* Little, Brown, 1992. / Lester, Julius. *The Knee-High Man and Other Tales.* Puffin, 1985. / Marcellino, Fred. *Puss in Boots.* Farrar, 1990. / San Souci, Robert D. *The Enchanted Tapestry.* Dial, 1987. / Tseng, Grace. *White Tiger, Blue Serpent.* Lothrop, 1999. / Yolen, Jane. *Not One Damsel in Distress: World Folktales for Strong Girls.* Harcourt, 2000.

SUBJECTS: FAIRY TALES. FOLKLORE—COLLECTIONS.

1286 Young, Ed. *Cat and Rat: The Legend of the Chinese Zodiac.* **Illus. by the author. Henry Holt, 1995. 0-8050-2977-X. Unp. Gr. K–4**

When the Emperor holds a race, offering to reward the first 12 animals across the finish line by naming a year in the Chinese calendar after them, best friends Cat and Rat plan to enter. The two ask the water buffalo to allow them a head start by riding on his back, but selfish Rat pushes Cat off into the river and comes in first. Though Cat swims as fast as she can, she comes in thirteenth, which is why the two are enemies to this day. Young's charcoal and pastel illustrations on Japanese rice paper are smudgy and mysterious and even better from a distance.

GERM: *The Rooster's Antlers* by Eric A. Kimmel is another folktale about the Chinese calendar. Hand out copies of the Chinese Zodiac so each person can correlate his or her year of birth with the animal that represents it.

RELATED TITLES: Demi. *The Dragon's Tale and Other Animal Fables of the Chinese Zodiac.* Henry Holt, 1996. / Hong, Lily Toy. *How the Ox Star Fell from Heaven.* Albert Whitman, 1991. / Kimmel, Eric A. *The Rooster's Antlers: A Story of the Chinese Zodiac.* Holiday House, 1999. / Kimmel, Eric A. *Ten Suns: A Chinese Legend.* Holiday House, 1998. / Mosel, Arlene. *Tikki Tikki Tembo.* Dutton, 1972. / Simonds, Nina, and Leslie Swartz. *Moonbeams, Dumplings and Dragon Boats: A Treasury of Chinese Holiday Tales, Activities and Recipes.* Harcourt, 2002. / Young, Ed. *Lon Po Po.* Philomel, 1989. / Young, Ed. *Mouse Match: A Chinese Folktale.* Harcourt, 1997.

SUBJECTS: ANIMALS—FOLKLORE. CALENDARS—FOLKLORE. CATS—FOLKLORE. EMPERORS—FOLKLORE. FOLKLORE—CHINA. KINGS AND RULERS—FOLKLORE. MULTICULTURAL BOOKS—FOLKLORE. POURQUOI TALES. RATS—FOLKLORE. ZODIAC—FOLKLORE.

1287 Young, Ed. *Mouse Match: A Chinese Folktale.* **Illus. by the author. Harcourt, 1997. 0-15-201453-5. Unp. Gr. 1–6**

Papa and Mama mouse would like to find the greatest and most powerful one in the world as a suitor for their wonderful daughter. They decide that the sun would be the most suitable match, and though the sun is flattered, he informs them that the cloud that blocks his rays is even more powerful. Going from cloud to wind to mountain, they ultimately realize that mice are the most powerful of all.

GERM: The story, formatted as an accordion book, or codex, that opens out into a spectacular 18-foot-long mural of brown-toned collage, pastel, and watercolor, is also written in large, striking Chinese calligraphy on the reverse side. Young says, in his Author's Note, ". . . it is a tale about looking within the uniqueness and greatness of oneself, and really seeing," a theme he also explored in *Seven Blind Mice.* Children can compare global variants, including Mexico (Judith Dupré's *The Mouse Bride*); Japan (Eric A. Kimmel's *The Greatest of All*, and Gerald McDermott's *The Stonecutter*); Korea (Holly H. Kwon's *The Moles and the Mireuk*); and India ("The Mouse Girl" from Caroline Ness's *The Ocean of Story*).

RELATED TITLES: Climo, Shirley. *The Little Red Ant and the Great Big Crumb.* Clarion, 1995. / Cook, Joel. *The Rat's Daughter.* Boyds Mills, 1993. / Demi. *Buddha Stories.* Henry Holt, 1997. / Dupré, Judith. *The Mouse Bride: A Mayan Folk Tale.* Knopf, 1993. / Farris, Pamela J. *Young Mouse and Elephant: An East African Folktale.* Houghton Mifflin, 1996. / Kimmel, Eric A. *The Greatest of All: A Japanese Folktale.* Holiday House, 1991. / Kwon,

Holly H. *The Moles and the Mireuk*. Houghton Mifflin, 1993. / McDermott, Gerald. *The Stonecutter: A Japanese Folk Tale*. Puffin, 1978. / Ness, Caroline. *The Ocean of Story: Fairy Tales from India*. Lothrop, 1995. / Olaleye, Isaac O. *In the Rainfield: Who Is the Greatest?* Scholastic, 2000. / Young, Ed. *Beyond the Great Mountains: A Visual Poem About China*. Chronicle, 2005. / Young, Ed. *Seven Blind Mice*. Philomel, 1992.

SUBJECTS: CIRCULAR STORIES—FOLKLORE. FOLKLORE—CHINA. MARRIAGE—FOLKLORE. MICE—FOLKLORE. MOUNTAINS—FOLKLORE. MULTICULTURAL BOOKS—FOLKLORE. STRENGTH—FOLKLORE. SUN—FOLKLORE.

1288 Young, Ed. *The Sons of the Dragon King: A Chinese Legend*. **Illus. by the author. Atheneum, 2004. 0-689-85184-7. Unp. Gr. 2–6**

"It is said that the Dragon King had nine sons, each one immortal, each one very different from the next." From nine separate regions of China come dire reports to the Dragon King about the unusual behaviors of his sons. Pondering their singular talents, the Dragon King finds a new job or role for which each son is best suited. To this day in China, one can see these dragons' separate images decorating various objects, such as Pu-Leo, the son who loved to make monstrous noises, whose image is still imprinted on musical instruments.

GERM: Young's whimsical ink-and-brush illustrations on textured off-white fabric are a perfect foil to this descriptive folktale that explains and displays the nine different dragon symbols still found in China. With your students' help, script out the story as a Reader's Theater production they can put on for Chinese New Year. Have them research the role of dragons in Chinese lore and contrast it with dragon tales in other countries. Your art teacher can explore Chinese brushstroke painting with your group.

RELATED TITLES: Casanova, Mary. *The Hunter: A Chinese Folktale*. Atheneum, 2000. / Davol, Marguerite. *The Paper Dragon*. Atheneum, 1997. / Grahame, Kenneth. *The Reluctant Dragon*. Candlewick, 2004. / Hall, Bruce Edward. *Henry and the Dragon Kite*. Philomel, 2004. / Kimmel, Eric A. *The Rooster's Antlers: A Story of the Chinese Zodiac*. Holiday House, 1999. / Kimmel, Eric A. *Ten Suns: A Chinese Legend*. Holiday House, 1998. / Simonds, Nina, and Leslie Swartz. *Moonbeams, Dumplings and Dragon Boats: A Treasury of Chinese Holiday Tales, Activities and Recipes*. Harcourt, 2002. / Tucker, Kathy. *The Seven Chinese Sisters*. Albert Whitman, 2003. / Yep, Laurence. *The Dragon Prince: A Chinese Beauty and the Beast Tale*. HarperCollins, 1997. / Yep, Laurence. *The Junior Thunder Lord*. BridgeWater, 1994. / Young, Ed. *Beyond the Great Mountains: A Visual Poem About China*. Chronicle, 2005. / Young, Ed. *Cat and Rat: The Legend of the Chinese Zodiac*. Henry Holt, 1995.

SUBJECTS: DRAGONS—FOLKLORE. FATHERS AND SONS—FOLKLORE. FOLKLORE—CHINA. MULTICULTURAL BOOKS. READER'S THEATER—FOLKLORE.

1289 Zelinsky, Paul O. *Rapunzel*. **Illus. by the author. Dutton, 1997. 0-525-45607-4. Unp. Gr. 3–6**

This somber, Caldecott Medal-winning version of the traditional fairy tale about the longhaired girl locked in a high tower by a jealous sorceress is visually breathtaking with its dignified Italianate paintings.

GERM: Compare various retellings of the story, noted below, and discuss the differences between the illustrator's interpretations.

RELATED TITLES: Berenzy, Alix. *Rapunzel*. Henry Holt, 1995. / Craft, Mahlon F. *Sleeping Beauty*. SeaStar, 2002. / Ehrlich, Amy. *Rapunzel*. Dial, 1989. / Isaacs, Anne. *Swamp Angel*. Dutton, 1994. / Lesser, Rika. *Hansel and Gretel*. Putnam, 1989. / Rogasky, Barbara. *Rapunzel*. Holiday House, 1982. / Stanley, Diane. *Petrosinella: A Neopolitan Rapunzel*. Dial, 1995. / Wilcox, Leah. *Falling for Rapunzel*. Putnam, 2003. / Zelinsky, Paul O. *Rumpelstiltskin*. Dutton, 1986.

SUBJECTS: CALDECOTT MEDAL. FAIRY TALES. FOLKLORE—GERMANY. PRINCES AND PRINCESSES. WITCHES—FOLKLORE.

POETRY, NONSENSE, AND LANGUAGE-ORIENTED NONFICTION

1290 **Adler, David A.** *Calculator Riddles.* **Illus. by Cynthia Fisher. Holiday House, 1995. 0-8234-1186-9. Unp. Gr. 3–6**

Find the answers to each of 45 riddles by doing the accompanying math problem on a calculator. When you turn the calculator upside down, the numbers look like letters—14 upside down looks like "hI"—and you can read the answer.

GERM: Pull out your calculators and work out the answers. To give older children practice in all four math functions, have them do the math by hand, check their work using the calculator, and then read the answer on the calculator screen. Children can also make up new riddles and come up with new math problems for others to solve in the same way.

RELATED TITLES: Adler, David A. *Easy Math Puzzles*, Holiday House, 1997. / Hopkins, Lee Bennett. *Marvelous Math: A Book of Poems*. Simon & Schuster, 1997. / Scieszka, Jon. *Math Curse*. Viking, 1995. / Tang, Greg. *The Grapes of Math: Mind-Stretching Math Riddles*. Scholastic, 2001. / Ziefert, Harriet. *Math Riddles*. Viking, 1997.

SUBJECTS: CALCULATORS. MATHEMATICS. RIDDLES.

1291 **Adoff, Arnold.** *Love Letters.* **Illus. by Lisa Desimini. Scholastic, 1997. 0-590-48478-8. 32pp. Gr. 3–6**

Each of 20 unconventional, sometimes rhyming, free-verse love notes is addressed by a child to a teacher or a parent, a friend or an unrequited love, a sibling or a pet. Accompanying full- or double-page illustrations whimsically incorporate sculpture, collage, paintings, photographs, and computer graphics. The felicitous combination makes for a memorable book that will give an eye- and earful of pleasure to all listeners.

GERM: Children will be eager to write, illustrate (making a 3-D collage of found objects), and share their own love letters to people or things they find endearing. Your art teacher will enjoy collaborating with you on this one.

RELATED TITLES: Adoff, Arnold. *Chocolate Dreams*. Lothrop, 1989. / Creech, Sharon. *Love That Dog*. HarperCollins, 2001. / Duffey, Betsy. *Cody's Secret Admirer*. Viking, 1998. / Frame, Jeron Ashford. *Yesterday I Had the Blues*. Tricycle, 2003. / Greenfield, Eloise. *Honey, I Love*. HarperCollins, 2003. / Greenfield, Eloise. *Honey, I Love, and Other Love Poems*. HarperCollins, 1978. / Minne. *I Love . . .* Kane/Miller, 2005. / Rylant, Cynthia. *Waiting to Waltz: A Childhood*. Bradbury, 1984. / Spinelli, Eileen. *Somebody Loves You, Mr. Hatch*. Simon & Schuster, 1991.

SUBJECTS: LOVE—POETRY. POETRY—SINGLE AUTHOR.

1292 **Agee, Jon.** *Elvis Lives! and Other Anagrams.* **Illus. by the author. Farrar, 2004. 0-374-32127-2. 80pp. Gr. 4–8**

A wildly creative and side-splitting selection of anagrams—made even more hilarious with small, antic, black-and-white heavy-lined drawings—transforms such phrases as "school cafeteria" into "hot cereal fiasco" and "Southern California" into "hot sun, or life in a car."

GERM: Have kids see what words they can pull out of their own full names. Since every word doesn't turn neatly into an anagram, ask them to look for meaningful words and phrases hidden within their full names, without worrying about using all of the letters. Draw and duplicate a template page with a grid of one-inch squares. Children can write their names, one letter per square, cut out the paper tiles, and have tactile letters to work with and rearrange, Scrabble-style. I used my own name: JUDITH ANN FREEMAN and came up with FINE DEAR AUNT. Other teachers and librarians found meaningful phrases: CATHERINE T. RICE = NICE TEACHER; DAWN SHIGEKO SHIBANO = I DIG BOOKS; librarian LESLIE RITA WHITMORE = THERE LIES A TALE. And the most prescient one, from the 2000 presidential election: GEORGE BUSH = HE BUGS GORE. Go to <www.puzzlemaker.com> to find more anagram and wordplay fun.

RELATED TITLES: Agee, Jon. *Go Hang a Salami! I'm a Lasagna Hog! And Other Palindromes.* Farrar, 1992. / Agee, Jon. *Palindromania!* Farrar, 2002. / Agee, Jon. *Sit on a Potato Pan, Otis! More Palindromes.* Farrar, 2000. / Agee, Jon. *So Many Dynamos! And Other Palindromes.* Farrar, 1994. / Hepworth, Cathi. *Bug Off! A Swarm of Insect Words.* Putnam, 1998. / Hirsch, Robin. *FEG: Ridiculous Poems for Intelligent Children.* Little, Brown, 2002. / Levitt, Paul M., Douglas A. Burger, and Elissa S. Guralnick. *The Weighty Word Book.* Court Wayne, 2000. / Most, Bernard. *Can You Find It?* Harcourt, 1993. / Most, Bernard. *Hippopotamus Hunt.* Harcourt, 1994. / Steig, William. *CDB.* Simon & Schuster, 2000. / Steig, William. *CDC.* Simon & Schuster, 2003. / Wilbur, Richard. *The Pig in the Spigot.* Harcourt, 2000.

SUBJECTS: ANAGRAMS. ENGLISH LANGUAGE. WORD GAMES.

1293 Agee, Jon. *Sit on a Potato Pan, Otis! More Palindromes.* **Illus. by the author. Farrar, 2000. 0-374-31808-5. 80pp. Gr. 3–8**

Dedicated to William Steig, Agee's clever batch of 62 palindromes will draw admiration from readers who will love reading forwards and backwards such wittily illustrated gems as "No way a papaya won" and "Darn ocelots stole Conrad."

GERM: Hold a day of wordplay, where punsters tell jokes, fool around with anagrams, and make up new palindromes.

RELATED TITLES: Agee, Jon. *Elvis Lives! and Other Anagrams.* Farrar, 2004. / Agee, Jon. *Go Hang a Salami! I'm a Lasagna Hog! And Other Palindromes.* Farrar, 1992. / Agee, Jon. *Palindromania!* Farrar, 2002. / Agee, Jon. *So Many Dynamos! And Other Palindromes.* Farrar, 1994. / Hepworth, Cathi. *Antics! An Alphabetical Anthology.* Putnam, 1992. / Hepworth, Cathi. *Bug Off! A Swarm of Insect Words.* Putnam, 1998. / Hirsch, Robin. *FEG: Ridiculous Poems for Intelligent Children.* Little, Brown, 2002. / Levitt, Paul M., Douglas A. Burger, and Elissa S. Guralnick. *The Weighty Word Book.* Court Wayne, 2000. / Steig, William. *CDB.* Simon & Schuster, 2000. / Steig, William. *CDC.* Simon & Schuster, 2003. / Wilbur, Richard. *The Pig in the Spigot.* Harcourt, 2000.

SUBJECTS: ENGLISH LANGUAGE. PALINDROMES. WORD GAMES.

1294 Alarcón, Francisco X. *Angels Ride Bikes and Other Fall Poems / Los Ángeles Andan en Bicicleta y Otros Poems de Otoño.* **Illus. by Maya Christina Gonzalez. Children's Book Press, 1999. 0-89239-160-X. 31pp. Gr. 2–6**

In 21 brief, astute poems, written in both English and Spanish and illustrated with upbeat, vivid paintings, a young Latino narrator observes his life in Los Angeles with a keen eye, describing his family, school, and neighborhood. Alarcón says, "These poems celebrate Los Angeles as a Promised Land where people from all over the world can make their dreams come true.

GERM: View the city at other times of the year in the author's companion books of the seasons: *Iguanas in the Snow, Laughing Tomatoes,* and *From the Bellybutton of the Moon.*

RELATED TITLES: Alarcón, Francisco X. *From the Bellybutton of the Moon and Other Summer Poems.* Children's Book Press, 1998. / Alarcón, Francisco X. *Iguanas in the Snow and Other Winter Poems.* Children's Book Press, 1991. / Alarcón, Francisco X. *Laughing Tomatoes and Other Spring Poems.* Children's Book Press, 1997. / Florian, Douglas. *Autumnblings: Poems and Paintings.* Greenwillow, 2003. / Lomas Garza, Carmen. *Family Pictures/Cuadros de Familia.* Children's Book Press, 1990. / Lomas Garza, Carmen. *In My Family/En Mi Familia.* Children's Book Press, 1996. / Medina, Jane. *The Dream on Blanca's Wall: Poems in English and Spanish.* Wordsong/Boyds Mills, 2004. / Pérez, Amada Irma. *My Very Own Room/Mi Proprio Cuartito.* Children's Book Press, 2000. / Schnur, Steven. *Autumn: An Alphabet Acrostic.* Clarion, 1997. / Soto, Gary. *Snapshots from the Wedding.* Putnam, 1997. / Updike, John. *A Child's Calendar.* Holiday House, 1999.

SUBJECTS: AUTUMN—POETRY. HISPANIC AMERICANS. LOS ANGELES (CALIFORNIA). MEXICAN AMERICANS—POETRY. MULTICULTURAL BOOKS—POETRY. POETRY—SINGLE AUTHOR. SEASONS—POETRY.

1295 Asch, Frank. *Cactus Poems.* **Photos by Ted Lewin. Harcourt, 1998. 0-15-200676-1. 48pp. Gr. 2–5**

In 18 spare, rhyming observational poems, based on the author's trips to the Southwest and paired with dozens of sharp, color photographs, Asch comments on the plants, animals, and magical ambiance of the desert.

GERM: Tying in your biome studies, ask your poets to select a photograph of a place or animal, and, studying it carefully, write a poem reacting to it. Also pull in Asch's companion book, *Sawgrass Poems*, with poems and color photos of the Florida Everglades.

RELATED TITLES: Albert, Richard E. *Alejandro's Gift*. Chronicle, 1994. / Asch, Frank. *Sawgrass Poems: A View of the Everglades*. Harcourt/Gulliver, 1996. / Bash, Barbara. *Desert Giant: The World of the Saguaro Cactus*. Sierra Club, 1989. / Dunphy, Madeleine. *Here Is the Southwestern Desert*. Hyperion, 1995. / Johnson, Paul Brett, and Celeste Lewis. *Lost*. Orchard, 1996. / McLerran, Alice. *Roxaboxen*. Lothrop, 1991. / Mora, Pat. *Listen to the Desert*. Clarion, 1994. / Siebert, Diane. *Mojave*. Crowell, 1988. / Yolen, Jane. *Welcome to the Sea of Sand*. Putnam, 1996.

SUBJECTS: CACTUS—POETRY. DESERT ANIMALS. DESERTS—POETRY. NATURE—POETRY. POETRY—SINGLE AUTHOR.

1296 Ashman, Linda. *The Essential Worldwide Monster Guide*. **Illus. by David Small. Simon & Schuster, 2003. 0-689-82640-0. Unp. Gr. 1–4**

Before setting out on your next round-the-globe jaunt, acquaint yourselves with 13 dangerous and unusual creatures—some unfamiliar but all well worth meeting—in this collection of poems and devilish watercolors that depict their gruesome habits. There's the alicanto, a gold- and silver-eating South American bird who leads fortune hunters astray; the domovik, a Russian house spirit who is easily offended; and the ravana, a demon from India with 10 heads and 20 arms.

GERM: Plot each creature on a world map, and look for more poetic descriptions in Eric Carle's *Dragons, Dragons*. Raid the folk and fairy tales of your library for more astounding, fantastical characters.

RELATED TITLES: Evans, Dilys. *Monster Soup and Other Spooky Poems*. Scholastic, 1992. / Florian, Douglas. *Monster Motel*. Harcourt, 1993. / Hopkins, Lee Bennett, comp. *Creatures*. Harcourt, 1985. / McNaughton, Colin. *Making Friends with Frankenstein: A Book of Monstrous Poems*. Candlewick, 1994. / Prelutsky, Jack. *Awful Ogre's Awful Day*. Greenwillow, 2001. / Prelutsky, Jack. *The Dragons Are Singing Tonight*. Greenwillow, 1993. / Prelutsky, Jack. *Monday's Troll*. Greenwillow, 1996. / Prelutsky, Jack. *Nightmares: Poems to Trouble Your Sleep*. Greenwillow, 1976. / Sierra, Judy. *Monster Goose*. Harcourt, 2001. / Whipple, Laura, comp. *Eric Carle's Dragons Dragons and Other Creatures That Never Were*. Philomel, 1991.

SUBJECTS: HUMOROUS POETRY. MONSTERS—POETRY. POETRY—SINGLE AUTHOR.

1297 Belle, Jennifer. *Animal Stackers*. **Illus. by David McPhail. Hyperion, 2005. 0-7868-1834-4. Unp. Gr. 1–4**

Twenty-six observant, wishful-thinking acrostic poems and gently funny watercolors take a good look at animals and the children who appreciate them. An example: "Extremely / Large is an understatement. / Empties the / Peanut butter jar. / Have to / Ask very / Nicely / To keep him." Read from top to bottom, this spells ELEPHANT. In the illustration, note the child riding atop the elephant's head, between its ears; then look down at Dad, looking up from his armchair, astonished; the headline of the newspaper he's holding reads, "Elephant Escapes."

GERM: Read the poems aloud without showing the illustrations so astute listeners can puzzle out the animal being described. For some poems, however, the illustration is essential to figuring out the animal's identity. Afterward, set everyone to work writing acrostic poems and painting pictures of favorite animals, both wild and domestic. Continue the animal theme with the haiku and illustrations in Jack Prelutsky's *If Not for the Cat*. Continue the acrostics theme with Consie Powell's *Amazing Apples* and Steven Schnur's season books: *Autumn, Winter, Spring,* and *Summer*.

RELATED TITLES: Florian, Doug. *Beast Feast*. Harcourt, 1994. / Ghigna, Charles. *Animal Tracks: Wild Poems to Read Aloud*. Abrams, 2004. / Lewis, J. Patrick. *A Hippopotamustn't and Other Animal Verses*. Dial, 1990. / Powell, Consie. *Amazing Apples*. Albert Whitman, 2003. / Prelutsky, Jack. *If Not for the Cat*. Greenwillow, 2004. / Schnur, Steven. *Autumn: An Alphabet Acrostic*. Clarion, 1997. / Schnur, Steven. *Spring: An Alphabet Acrostic*. Clarion, 1999. / Schnur, Steven. *Summer: An Alphabet Acrostic*. Clarion, 2001. / Schnur, Steven. *Winter: An Alphabet Acrostic*. Clarion, 2002. / Whipple, Laura, comp. *Eric Carle's Animals, Animals*. Philomel, 1989.

SUBJECTS: ACROSTICS. ALPHABET—POETRY. ANIMALS—POETRY. POETRY—SINGLE AUTHOR.

1298 Borden, Louise. *America Is . . .* **Illus. by Stacey Schuett. McElderry, 2002. 0-689-83900-6. Unp. Gr. K–4**

In a large-format, handsome picture book that takes us cross-country, look at what America means to its diverse people. Borden states: "We are the nation whose name means freedom to people all over the world."

GERM: Discuss: What does it mean to be an American? Do you have to be born here to be an American? Why is it a privilege to live in America? Have students write and illustrate their ending to the sentence, "America is . . ."

RELATED TITLES: Bates, Katharine Lee. *America the Beautiful.* Illus. by Chris Gall. Little, Brown, 2004. / Bates, Katharine Lee. *America the Beautiful.* Illus. by Neil Waldman. Atheneum, 1983. / Brisson, Pat. *Your Best Friend, Kate.* Bradbury, 1989. / Cheney, Lynne. *America: A Patriotic Primer.* Simon & Schuster, 2002. / Cherry, Lynne. *The Armadillo from Amarillo.* Harcourt, 1994. / DiPucchio, Kelly. *Liberty's Journey.* Hyperion, 2004. / Guthrie, Woody. *This Land Is Your Land.* Little, Brown, 1998. / Keenan, Sheila. *O, Say Can You See? America's Symbols, Landmarks, and Inspiring Words.* Scholastic, 2004. / Keller, Laurie. *The Scrambled States of America.* Henry Holt, 1998. / Pattison, Darcy. *The Journey of Oliver K. Woodman.* Harcourt, 2003. / Rylant, Cynthia. *Tulip Sees America.* Scholastic, 1998. / Sabuda, Robert. *America the Beautiful.* Little Simon, 2004.

SUBJECTS: POETRY—SINGLE AUTHOR. U.S.—POETRY.

1299 Brewer, Paul. *You Must Be Joking!* **Illus. by the author. Cricket, 2003. 0-8126-2661-3. 107pp. Gr. 3–6**

The cover of this meaty and truly funny collection of jokes and riddles sums it up nicely: "Lots of cool jokes, plus 17 ½ tips for remembering, telling, and making up your own jokes." There are jokes about school, home, and movies, and even a chapter on the Internet. One I loved: What do you get when you cross a brilliant man and a monster? Frank Einstein.

GERM: Share the tips found at the back of the book for telling and making up jokes so that you can start your jokesters on the road to comedy, storytelling, and paying attention to language and wordplay.

RELATED TITLES: Berk, Meridith, and Toni Vavrus. *Great Book of School Jokes.* Sterling, 1994. / Conford, Ellen. *Lenny Kandell, Smart Aleck.* Little, Brown, 1983. / Hartman, Victoria. *The Silliest Joke Book Ever.* Lothrop, 1993. / Hartman, Victoria. *Super-Duper Jokes.* Farrar, 1993. / Keller, Charles. *School Daze.* Prentice-Hall, 1978. / Levy, Elizabeth. *My Life as a Fifth-Grade Comedian.* HarperCollins, 1997. / Sachar, Louis. *Dogs Don't Tell Jokes.* Knopf, 1991. / Schultz, Sam. *Schoolyard Snickers: Classy Jokes That Make the Grade.* Lerner, 2003. / Terban, Marvin. *Funny You Should Ask: How to Make Up Jokes and Riddles with Wordplay.* Clarion, 1992. / Weitzman, Ilana, Eva Blank, and Roseanne Green. *Jokelopedia: The Biggest, Best, Silliest, Dumbest Joke Book Ever.* Workman, 2000.

SUBJECTS: JOKES. RIDDLES. WORD GAMES.

1300 Bunting, Eve. *Sing a Song of Piglets: A Calendar in Verse.* **Illus. by Emily Arnold McCully. Clarion, 2002. 0-618-01137-4. 32pp. Gr. PreK–1**

A blissful piggy couple ice skate, garden, fish, play softball, surf, and enjoy each other's company. The simple, sweet rhymes, singable to "Sing a Song of Sixpence," describe their activities for each month of the year, all accompanied by adorable pig-filled watercolors.

GERM: You could stage this as a Reader's Theater, either read or sung. Have your little piggies draw what they like to do most for each month of the year.

RELATED TITLES: Christelow, Eileen. *The Great Pig Search.* Clarion, 2001. / Fuchs, Diane Marcial. *A Bear for All Seasons.* Henry Holt, 1995. / Lobel, Arnold. *The Book of Pigericks.* HarperCollins, 1983. / Martin, David. *Five Little Piggies.* Candlewick, 1998. / Pollock, Penny. *When the Moon Is Full: A Lunar Year.* Little, Brown, 2001. / Rayner, Mary. *Mr. and Mrs. Pig's Evening Out.* Atheneum, 1976. / Robb, Laura. *Snuffles and Snouts.* Dial, 1995. / Roemer, Heidi B. *Come to My Party and Other Shape Poems.* Henry Holt, 2004. / Tafuri, Nancy. *Snowy Flowy Blowy: A Twelve Months Rhyme.* Scholastic, 1999. / Updike, John. *A Child's Calendar.* Holiday House, 1999.

SUBJECTS: MONTHS—POETRY. PIGS—POETRY. POETRY—SINGLE AUTHOR. READER'S THEATER—POETRY. SEASONS—POETRY.

1301 Burg, Brad. *Outside the Lines: Poetry at Play.* **Illus. by Rebecca Gibbon. Putnam, 2002. 0-399-23446-2. 32pp. Gr. 1–3**

In this energetic collection, children's games and play are the basis for 22 spry concrete poems about (mostly) outdoor activities including softball, hula hoops, playing frisbee, and jumping on the bed.

GERM: Part of the fun of reading these poems aloud is figuring out the sequence to follow, since the words can bounce all over the page. Make a color transparency of the poem "Tic-Tac-Toe (a battle plan)" and ask your children to figure out the sequence of both the poem and the game.

RELATED TITLES: Franco, Betsy. *Mathematickles!* Simon & Schuster, 2003. / Graham, Joan Bransfield. *Splish Splash.* Ticknor & Fields, 1994. / Halpern, Shari. *What Shall We Do When We All Go Out? A Traditional Song.* North-South, 1995. / Lewis, J. Patrick. *Doodle Dandies: Poems That Take Shape.* Atheneum, 1998. / Roemer, Heidi B. *Come to My Party and Other Shape Poems.* Henry Holt, 2004.

SUBJECTS: CONCRETE POETRY. PLAY—POETRY. POETRY—SINGLE AUTHOR.

1302 Burleigh, Robert. *Hoops*. Illus. by Stephen T. Johnson. Harcourt, 1997. 0-15-201450-0. Unp. Gr. 4–6

Feel the moves of the teenage boy athletes in this free-verse picture-book poem about the drama and love of playing basketball, with action-filled pastels that are so dramatic they almost smell of sweat.

GERM: Art teachers will love this for a lesson on drawing the body in motion. Gym teachers can read it aloud before setting everyone up to shoot some hoops. And writing teachers can have listeners write descriptive poems about sports or activities they love.

RELATED TITLES: Burleigh, Robert. *Home Run: The Story of Babe Ruth*. Harcourt, 1998. / Hopkins, Lee Bennett, comp. *Extra Innings: Baseball Poems*. Harcourt, 1993. / Morrison, Lillian. *At the Crack of the Bat: Baseball Poems*. Hyperion, 1992. / Morrison, Lillian. *Slam Dunk: Basketball Poems*. Hyperion, 1995. / Norworth, Jack. *Take Me Out to the Ball Game*. Four Winds, 1993. / Smith, Charles R., Jr. *Hoop Kings: Poems*. Candlewick Press, 2004. / Smith, Charles R., Jr. *Hoop Queens: Poems*. Candlewick Press, 2003. / Smith, Charles R., Jr. *Rimshots: Basketball Pix, Rolls, and Rhythms*. Dutton, 1999.

SUBJECTS: BASKETBALL—POETRY. MULTICULTURAL BOOKS—POETRY. POETRY—SINGLE AUTHOR. SPORTS—POETRY.

1303 Burns, Diane L., Connie Roop, and Peter Roop. *Backyard Beasties: Jokes to Snake You Smile*. Illus. by Brian Gable. Lerner, 2003. 1-57505-646-1. 32pp. Gr. 1–4

More than 100 pun-filled riddles and jokes about cats, snakes, bugs, and reptiles will help strengthen your listeners' sense of humor and wordplay.

GERM: Make copies of several pages of riddles. Hand a page to each pair of readers so they can practice delivering and then answering their riddles, which they can then present to the rest of the group. Refer to Marvin Terban's *Funny You Should Ask: How to Make Up Jokes and Riddles with Wordplay* for inspiration in having each twosome make up a new riddle.

RELATED TITLES: Burns, Diane L. *Animal Antics: The Beast Jokes Ever!* Lerner, 2003. (And others in the Make Me Laugh series.) / Cole, Joanna, and Stephanie Calmenson. *Why Did the Chicken Cross the Road? And Other Riddles Old and New*. Morrow, 1994. / Hall, Katy, and Lisa Eisenberg. *Buggy Riddles*. Dial, 1986. / Hall, Katy, and Lisa Eisenberg. *Snakey Riddles*. Dial, 1990. / Helmer, Marilyn. *Critter Riddles*. Kids Can, 2003. / Levine, Caroline. *Riddles to Tell Your Cat*. Albert Whitman, 1992. / Terban, Marvin. *Funny You Should Ask: How to Make Up Jokes and Riddles with Wordplay*. Clarion, 1992.

SUBJECTS: ANIMALS. JOKES. RIDDLES.

1304 Cleary, Brian P. *How Much Can a Bare Bear Bear? What Are Homonyms and Homophones?* Illus. by Brian Gable. Millbrook, 2005. 1-57505-824-3. Unp. Gr. 2–5

Three cheers for another sparkling, rhyming, instructive, and jolly addition to the Words are CATegorical series, with its cast of colorful cartoon cats and other creatures who help to demystify the world of grammar. This volume provides plenty of examples of words that sound the same but have different meanings, from be to bee and flea to flee.

GERM: Draw and label new examples of homonyms and homophones. Use them as a springboard for creating wordplay riddles with *The Dove Dove: Funny Homograph Riddles* and *Funny You Should Ask: How to Make Up Jokes and Riddles with Wordplay*, both by Marvin Terban.

RELATED TITLES: Cleary, Brian P. *Dearly, Nearly, Insincerely: What Is an Adverb?* Carolrhoda Books, 2003. / Cleary, Brian P. *Hairy, Scary, Ordinary: What Is an Adjective?* Carolrhoda, 2000. / Cleary, Brian P. *I and You and Don't Forget Who: What Is a Pronoun?* Carolrhoda, 2004. / Cleary, Brian P. *A Mink, a Fink, a Skating Rink: What Is a Noun?* Carolrhoda, 2000. / Cleary, Brian P. *Rainbow Soup: Adventures in Poetry*. Carolrhoda, 2004. / Cleary, Brian P. *To Root, to Toot, to Parachute: What Is a Verb?* Carolrhoda, 2001. / Cleary, Brian P. *Under, Over, by the Clover: What Is a Preposition?* Carolrhoda, 2002. / Gwynne, Fred. *A Chocolate Moose for Dinner*. Dutton, 1976. / Gwynne, Fred. *The King Who Rained*. Dutton, 1970. / Terban, Marvin. *The Dove Dove: Funny Homograph Riddles*. Clarion, 1992. / Terban, Marvin. *Funny You Should Ask: How to Make Up Jokes and Riddles with Wordplay*. Clarion, 1988.

SUBJECTS: ENGLISH LANGUAGE—GRAMMAR. ENGLISH LANGUAGE—HOMONYMS. HUMOROUS POETRY.

1305 Cleary, Brian P. *Rainbow Soup: Adventures in Poetry*. Illus. by Neal Layton. Carolrhoda, 2004. 1-57505-597-X. 88pp. Gr. 3–6

Along with the flippant childlike pen-and-ink illustrations goofing up each page are 83 devilishly cunning and savvy wordplay poems of all types, including concrete, haiku, limerick, palindrome, and villanelle.

GERM: Many of the pun-laced poems come with a definition, at the bottom of the page, of the poem's particular form. You'll want to use these poems as models for writing new ones. *Fly with Poetry: An ABC of Poetry* and *Leap into Poetry: More ABCs of Poetry* by Avis Harley are more systematic in their approach to poetic form, but Cleary specializes in punnery and wit, making him a poet you'll want to introduce along with Douglas Florian, Jack Prelutsky, Shel Silverstein, and Judith Viorst. Paul B. Janeczko's *A Kick in the Head* is a graphically vibrant look at poetic forms.

RELATED TITLES: Cleary, Brian P. *To Root, to Toot, to Parachute: What Is a Verb?* Carolrhoda, 2001. (And others in the Words Are CATegorical series.) / Creech, Sharon. *Love That Dog.* HarperCollins, 2001. / Driscoll, Michael, comp. *A Child's Introduction to Poetry.* Black & Leventhal, 2003. / Harley, Avis. *Fly with Poetry: An ABC of Poetry.* Boyds Mills, 2000. / Harley, Avis. *Leap into Poetry: More ABCs of Poetry.* Boyds Mills, 2001. / Janeczko, Paul B., comp. *A Kick in the Head: An Everyday Guide to Poetic Forms.* Candlewick, 2005. / Janeczko, Paul B, comp. *Poetry from A to Z: A Guide for Young Writers.* Simon & Schuster, 1994. / Janeczko, Paul B. *Seeing the Blue Between: Advice and Inspiration for Young Poets.* Candlewick, 2002. / Kennedy, X. J., comp. *Knock at a Star: A Child's Introduction to Poetry.* Little, Brown, 1982. / Prelutsky, Jack, comp. *Read a Rhyme, Write a Rhyme.* Knopf, 2005. / Woodson, Jacqueline. *Locomotion.* Putnam, 2003.

SUBJECTS: HUMOROUS POETRY. POETRY—SINGLE AUTHOR.

1306 **Cleary, Brian P. *To Root, to Toot, to Parachute: What Is a Verb?* Illus. by Jenya Prosmitsky. Carolrhoda, 2003. 1-57505-403-5. Unp. Gr. 2–4**

Part of the Words Are CATegorical series, this antic rhyming grammar primer gives scores of verb examples, each acted out on the page by a cavorting bevy of bulbous-nosed cartoonish brown cats.

GERM: Use the whole series to introduce all the parts of speech. Write and illustrate new examples and act out the verbs. Follow up with Ruth Heller's more courtly and lush rhyming intros to the world of grammar, one of which is listed below, in her World of Language series.

RELATED TITLES: Cleary, Brian P. *Dearly, Nearly, Insincerely: What Is an Adverb?* Carolrhoda Books, 2003. / Cleary, Brian P. *Hairy, Scary, Ordinary: What Is an Adjective?* Carolrhoda, 2000. / Cleary, Brian P. *I and You and Don't Forget Who: What Is a Pronoun?* Carolrhoda, 2004. / Cleary, Brian P. *A Mink, a Fink, a Skating Rink: What Is a Noun?* Carolrhoda, 2000. / Cleary, Brian P. *Rainbow Soup: Adventures in Poetry.* Carolrhoda, 2004. / Cleary, Brian P. *Under, Over, by the Clover: What Is a Preposition?* Carolrhoda, 2004. / Fleming, Denise. *Alphabet Under Construction.* Henry Holt, 2002. / Heller, Ruth. *Kites Sail High: A Book About Verbs.* Grosset, 1988. / Pulver, Robin. *Nouns and Verbs Have a Field Day.* Holiday House, 2006. / Rotner, Shelley. *Action Alphabet.* Atheneum, 1996. / Schneider, R. M. *Add It, Dip It, Fix It: A Book of Verbs.* Houghton Mifflin, 1995.

SUBJECTS: ENGLISH LANGUAGE—GRAMMAR. ENGLISH LANGUAGE—VERBS. STORIES IN RHYME.

1307 **Crews, Nina, comp. *The Neighborhood Mother Goose.* Illus. by the author. Greenwillow, 2004. 0-06-051574-0. 48pp. Gr. PreK–1**

Travel to Nina Crews's Brooklyn neighborhood where she shot the extraordinary full-page color photos of a multicultural cast of real kids acting out 41 traditional Mother Goose rhymes, about half of which will be familiar to you. Her photos are full of movement and humor, mostly realistic, but with a nice touch of magical realism when needed.

GERM: Stage your own Mother Goose photo shoot with your children, and act out the rhymes as you all recite them. Compare and contrast this book with more traditional volumes of nursery rhymes by dePaola or Lobel.

RELATED TITLES: Denton, Kady MacDonald, comp. *A Child's Treasury of Nursery Rhymes.* Kingfisher, 1998. / dePaola, Tomie, comp. *Tomie dePaola's Mother Goose.* Putnam, 1985. / Edwards, Pamela Duncan. *The Neat Line: Scribbling Through Mother Goose.* HarperCollins, 2005. / Fabian, Bobbi, comp. *Twinkle, Twinkle: An Animal Lover's Mother Goose.* Dutton, 1997. / Hoberman, Mary Ann. *You Read to Me, I'll Read to You: Very Short Mother Goose Tales to Read Together.* Little, Brown, 2005. / Lobel, Arnold, comp. *The Random House Book of Mother Goose.* Random House, 1986. / Long, Sylvia, comp. *Sylvia Long's Mother Goose.* Chronicle, 1999. / Moses, Will, comp. *Will Moses' Mother Goose.* Philomel, 2003. / Opie, Iona, comp. *Here Comes Mother Goose.* Candlewick, 1999. / Stevens, Janet, and Susan Stevens Crummel. *And the Dish Ran Away with the Spoon.* Harcourt, 2001. / Sutherland, Zena, comp. *The Orchard Book of Nursery Rhymes.* Orchard, 1990.

SUBJECTS: CITIES AND TOWNS. CREATIVE DRAMA. MOTHER GOOSE. MULTICULTURAL BOOKS—POETRY. NEW YORK CITY. NURSERY RHYMES.

1308 Dakos, Kalli. *Put Your Eyes Up Here and Other School Poems.* **Illus. by G. Brian Karas. Simon & Schuster, 2003. 0-689-81117-9. 64pp. Gr. 2–5**

Through a collection of more than 50 observational poems, a girl in eccentric Ms. Roys's class documents all the interesting events of the school year.

GERM: Children can write poems about their most memorable teachers and how they've influenced their lives. Spend more time in school with the poems in *Almost Late to School* and *Lunch Money*, both by Carol Diggory Shields. Also share Dakos's other classic school poetry book, *If You're Not Here, Please Raise Your Hand.*

RELATED TITLES: Dakos, Kalli. *Don't Read This Book, Whatever You Do! More Poems About School.* Four Winds, 1993. / Dakos, Kalli. *If You're Not Here, Please Raise Your Hand: Poems About School.* Simon & Schuster, 1990. / George, Kristine O'Connell. *Swimming Upstream: Middle School Poems.* Clarion, 2002. / Harrison, David L. *The Mouse Was Out at Recess.* Boyds Mills, 2003. / Harrison, David L. *Somebody Catch My Homework.* Boyds Mills, 1993. / Kennedy, Dorothy M. *I Thought I'd Take My Rat to School: Poems for September to June.* Little, Brown, 1993. / Shields, Carol Diggory. *Almost Late to School and More School Poems.* Dutton, 2003.

SUBJECTS: HUMOROUS POETRY. POETRY—SINGLE AUTHOR. SCHOOLS—POETRY.

1309 Denton, Kady MacDonald, comp. *A Child's Treasury of Nursery Rhymes.* **Illus. by the author. Kingfisher, 1998. 0-7534-5109-3. 96pp. Gr. PreK–1**

One hundred-plus nursery rhymes, lullabies, songs, and simple poems, some familiar, some not, are illustrated with sweet watercolors reminiscent of early Sendak and separated into four chapters: "Welcome, Little Baby," "Toddler Time," "In the Schoolyard," and "All Join In."

GERM: Read the first lines to see how many of your children can recite these by heart. Keep a chart of the verses they do know and introduce some new one as well.

RELATED TITLES: Cousins, Lucy, comp. *The Little Dog Laughed and Other Nursery Rhymes.* Dutton, 1990. / Crews, Nina, comp. *The Neighborhood Mother Goose.* Greenwillow, 2004. / dePaola, Tomie, comp. *Tomie dePaola's Mother Goose.* Putnam, 1985. / Lamont, Priscilla, comp. *Ring-a-Round-a-Rosy: Nursery Rhymes, Action Rhymes and Lullabyes.* Little, Brown, 1990. / Lobel, Arnold, comp. *The Random House Book of Mother Goose.* Random House, 1986. / Long, Sylvia, comp. *Sylvia Long's Mother Goose.* Chronicle, 1999. / Moses, Will, comp. *Will Moses Mother Goose.* Philomel, 2003. / Opie, Iona, comp. *Here Comes Mother Goose.* Candlewick, 1999. / Opie, Iona, comp. *My Very First Mother Goose.* Candlewick, 1996. / Opie, Iona, and Peter Opie, comps. *Tail Feathers from Mother Goose: The Opie Rhyme Book.* Little, Brown, 1988. / Sutherland, Zena, comp. *The Orchard Book of Nursery Rhymes.* Orchard, 1990.

SUBJECTS: NURSERY RHYMES. SONGS.

1310 Dillon, Leo, and Diane Dillon. *To Everything There Is a Season.* **Illus. by the authors. Scholastic, 1998. 0-590-47887-7. Unp. Gr. 1–6**

In 16 breathtaking single- and double-page paintings drawn from a wide variety of world cultures, the incomparable husband and wife team have set to art the well-known verses from the book of Ecclesiastes in the Bible. Detailed notes at the back of the book explain each style of art, its culture, and its time period—Egyptian tomb murals of 1000 B.C., 18th-century Japanese woodblock prints, 7th-century Mixtec Mexican picture manuscripts, plus representation from Greece, India, Germany, North America, Ethiopia, Thailand, China, Russia, Australia, the Far North, and the Middle East. Each page turn brings a visual feast amply demonstrating the shared values of people the world over, both now and back through the ages.

GERM: On the final page, with a view of Earth from space, it states, "One generation passes away, and another generation comes: but the earth abides forever." Your students will want to pore over every page and discuss the quote and its relevance to their own lives. Follow up with a class choral reading or an exercise in creative drama where you read the verses aloud while the children act them out in pantomime. Play Pete Seeger's adaptation of Ecclesiastes in his song "Turn, Turn, Turn," performed by him or by the Byrds. Research possibilities abound for older students: the styles of art, the time periods or countries depicted, or the history of each civilization.

RELATED TITLES: Collard, Sneed B., III. *1,000 Years Ago on Planet Earth.* Houghton Mifflin, 1999. / Ehlert, Lois. *In My World.* Harcourt, 2002. / Fox, Mem. *Whoever You Are.* Harcourt, 1997. / Guthrie, Woody. *This Land Is Your Land.* Little, Brown, 1998. / Hamanaka, Sheila. *All the Colors of the Earth.* Morrow, 1994. / Jackson, Ellen. *Turn of the Century.* Charlesbridge, 1998. / Maddern, Eric. *The Fire Children: A West African Creation Tale.* Dial, 1993. / Ryder, Joanne. *Each Living Thing.* Harcourt, 2000. / Ryder, Joanne. *Earthdance.* Henry Holt, 1996. / Scillian, Devin. *P Is for Passport: A World Alphabet.* Sleeping Bear, 2003.

SUBJECTS: BIBLE. CREATIVE DRAMA. EARTH. ECCLESIASTES (BIBLE). MULTICULTURAL BOOKS—POETRY. PICTURE BOOKS FOR ALL AGES. READER'S THEATER.

1311 Downs, Mike. *Pig Giggles and Rabbit Rhymes: A Book of Animal Riddles.* **Illus. by David Sheldon. Chronicle, 2002. 0-8118-3114-0. Unp. Gr. K–3**

The 21 easy-to-read "hink pink" riddles are not all so simple to figure out, but the colorful cartoon-style illustrations on each page give good clues for all to guess before you turn to the verso where the rhyming answers reside. One that stumped me: "What does an octopus like to sip? (Ink drink)"

GERM: This kind of wordplay strengthens children's rhyming abilities and encourages them to think creatively. Write and illustrate new hink pinks with them. For another animal-filled hink pink book, visit the school in Marco and Giulio Maestro's *Geese Find the Missing Piece* and the farm in Francis McCall and Patricia Keeler's *A Huge Hog Is a Big Pig.*

RELATED TITLES: Chapman, Cheryl. *Pass the Fritters, Critters.* Simon & Schuster, 1993. / Cherry, Lynne. *Who's Sick Today?* Dutton, 1988. / McCall, Francis, and Patricia Keeler. *A Huge Hog Is a Big Pig: A Rhyming Word Game.* Greenwillow, 2002. / McMillan, Bruce. *One Sun: A Book of Terse Verse.* Holiday House, 1990. / McMillan, Bruce. *Play Day: A Book of Terse Verse.* Holiday House, 1991. / Maestro, Giulio. *Macho Nacho and Other Rhyming Riddles.* Dutton, 1994. / Maestro, Marco, and Giulio Maestro. *Geese Find the Missing Piece: School Time Riddle Rhymes.* HarperCollins, 1999. / Maestro, Marco, and Giulio Maestro. *What Do You Hear When the Cows Sing? And Other Silly Riddles.* HarperCollins, 1996. / Walton, Rick. *Once There Was a Bull . . . (Frog).* Gibbs-Smith, 1995.

SUBJECTS: ANIMALS—RIDDLES. RIDDLES.

1312 Driscoll, Michael, comp. *A Child's Introduction to Poetry.* **Illus. by Meredith Hamilton. Black Dog & Leventhal, 2003. 1-57912-282-5. 96pp. Gr. 4–8**

Professor Driscoll is our guide to the world of poetry, starting with nursery rhymes and nonsense and continuing through to haiku and narrative and lyric verse, as well as the ballad, the pastoral, and the sonnet. In Part Two, he introduces us to 21 superstars of the poetry world, from Homer and Shakespeare to Octavio Paz and Maya Angelou. Accompanying each poem is an informative and lively text that explains its important aspects and provides biographical background on the poet.

GERM: The book comes with a CD that has readings of all 64 poems, but you'll be able to recite them quite well yourself, accompanied by plenty of your own power and gusto.

RELATED TITLES: Cleary, Brian P. *Rainbow Soup: Adventures in Poetry.* Carolrhoda, 2004. / Creech, Sharon. *Love That Dog.* HarperCollins, 2001. / Harley, Avis. *Fly with Poetry: An ABC of Poetry.* Boyds Mills, 2000. / Harley, Avis. *Leap into Poetry: More ABCs of Poetry.* Boyds Mills, 2001. / Janeczko, Paul B., comp. *A Kick in the Head: An Everyday Guide to Poetic Forms.* Candlewick, 2005. / Janeczko, Paul B., comp. *The Place My Words Are Looking For.* Simon & Schuster, 1990. / Janeczko, Paul B., comp. *Poetry from A to Z: A Guide for Young Writers.* Simon & Schuster, 1994. / Janeczko, Paul B., comp. *Seeing the Blue Between: Advice and Inspiration for Young Poets.* Candlewick, 2002. / Kennedy, X. J., comp. *Knock at a Star: A Child's Introduction to Poetry.* Little, Brown, 1982. / Larrick, Nancy, comp. *Let's Do a Poem!* Delacorte, 1991. / Livingston, Myra Cohn, comp. *Poem-Making: Ways to Begin Writing Poetry.* HarperCollins, 1991. / Rocklin, Joanne. *For Your Eyes Only!* Scholastic, 1997. / Woodson, Jacqueline. *Locomotion.* Putnam, 2003.

SUBJECTS: POETRY—ANTHOLOGIES.

1313 Edwards, Wallace. *Monkey Business.* **Illus. by the author. Kids Can, 2004. 1-55337-462-2. Unp. Gr. 3–6**

Twenty-six common idioms are incorporated into full sentences that caption full-page surreal paintings, each revolving around a single animal. The painting of a doleful basset hound as a sidewalk musician, playing for bones before an audience of two mice, depicts him with one ear curled around the neck of a cello and the other holding the bow. The caption? "Phil had no formal musical training, so he learned to play by ear."

GERM: For your more sophisticated children, cover up the sentence at the bottom of the page and ask them to study each painting and infer each idiom. Then read the sentence aloud and ask them to define the idiom. At the front of the book is a definition for "idiom"; at the back is an alphabetical listing and definition of each one in the book.

RELATED TITLES: Arnold, Tedd. *Even More Parts.* Dial, 2004. / Arnold, Tedd. *More Parts.* Dial, 2001. / Arnold, Tedd. *Parts.* Dial, 1997. / Base, Graeme. *Animalia.* Abrams, 1987. / Clement, Rod. *Just Another Ordinary Day.* HarperCollins, 1997. / Clements, Andrew. *Double Trouble in Walla Walla.* Millbrook, 1998. / Edwards, Wallace. *Monkey Business.* Kids Can, 2004. / Freymann, Saxton, and Joost Elffers. *Dog Food.* Scholastic, 2002. / Gwynne, Fred. *A Chocolate Moose for Dinner.* Dutton, 1976. / Gwynne, Fred. *The King Who Rained.* Dutton, 1970. / Leedy, Loreen. *There's a Frog in My Throat: 440 Animal Sayings a Little Bird Told Me.* Holiday House, 2003. / Pulver, Robin. *Punctuation Takes a Vacation.* Holiday House, 2003. / Shields, Carol Diggory.

Brain Juice: English, Fresh Squeezed! Handprint, 2004. / Viorst, Judith. *The Alphabet from Z to A: With Much Confusion on the Way.* Atheneum, 1994.

SUBJECTS: ANIMALS. ENGLISH LANGUAGE—IDIOMS.

1314   Florian, Douglas. *Bow Wow Meow Meow: It's Rhyming Cats and Dogs.* **Illus. by the author. Harcourt, 2003. 0-15-216395-6. 47pp. Gr. 1–4**

With equal time spent on cats and dogs, both domestic and wild, Florian has painted 21 full-page pictures to accompany short, remarkable observational poems that fool around with words.

GERM: Write poems about and paint paintings of your own pets, both real and longed for.

RELATED TITLES: Bartoletti, Susan Campbell. *Nobody's Diggier Than a Dog.* Hyperion, 2004. / Bartoletti, Susan Campbell. *Nobody's Nosier Than a Cat.* Hyperion, 2003. / George, Kristine O'Connell. *Little Dog Poems.* Clarion, 1999. / Gottfried, Maya. *Good Dog.* Knopf, 2005. / Hall, Donald. *I Am the Dog, I Am the Cat.* Dial, 1994. / Johnston, Tony. *It's About Dogs.* Harcourt, 2000. / Kalman, Maira. *What Pete Ate from A–Z.* Putnam, 2001. / Kirk, Daniel. *Dogs Rule!* Hyperion, 2003. / Miller, Sara Swan. Three Stories You Can Read to Your Cat series. Houghton. / Miller, Sara Swan. Three Stories You Can Read to Your Dog series. Houghton. / Singer, Marilyn. *It's Hard to Read a Map with a Beagle on Your Lap.* Henry Holt, 1993. / Sklansky, Amy E. *From the Doghouse: Poems to Chew On.* Henry Holt, 2002. / Teague, Mark. *Dear Mrs. LaRue: Letters from Obedience School.* Scholastic, 2002. / Yolen, Jane. *Raining Cats and Dogs.* Harcourt, 1993.

SUBJECTS: CATS—POETRY. DOGS—POETRY. PETS—POETRY. POETRY—SINGLE AUTHOR.

1315   Florian, Douglas. *In the Swim: Poems and Paintings.* **Illus. by the author. Harcourt, 1997. 0-15-201307-5. 48pp. Gr. 2–6**

Dive into the ocean with 21 of poet and watercolorist Florian's witty, pithy, and watery observations about piranhas, flounders, sharks, manatees, jellyfish, and other swimming creatures.

GERM: Make a chart listing each fish and compile a list of facts your students already know about each one. Have them pick a fish and then do some research on its habits and other interesting facts. Brainstorm a list of additional undersea creatures and, after researching data about them, write new observational poems incorporating those facts.

RELATED TITLES: Florian, Douglas. *Insectlopedia: Poems and Paintings.* Harcourt, 1998. / Florian, Douglas. *Lizards, Frogs, and Polliwogs: Poems and Paintings.* Harcourt, 2001. / Florian, Douglas. *Mammalabilia: Poems and Paintings.* Harcourt, 2000. / Florian, Douglas. *Omnibeasts: Animal Poems and Paintings.* Harcourt, 2004. / Florian, Douglas. *On the Wing: Bird Poems and Paintings.* Harcourt, 1996. / Lionni, Leo. *Swimmy.* Pantheon, 1968. / Wardlaw, Lee. *Punia and the King of Sharks: A Hawaiian Folktale.* Dial, 1997.

SUBJECTS: ANIMALS—POETRY. FISHES—POETRY. HUMOROUS POETRY. MARINE ANIMALS—POETRY. OCEAN—POETRY. POETRY—SINGLE AUTHOR.

1316   Florian, Douglas. *Insectlopedia: Poems and Paintings.* **Illus. by the author. Harcourt, 1998. 0-15-201306-7. 48pp. Gr. 2–6**

There are 21 amiable and insightful short, rhyming insect poems in Florian's latest foray into the animal kingdom.

GERM: Use the poems to headline insect reports or to introduce insect fiction such as *Harry the Poisonous Centipede* by Lynne Reid Banks or *Shoebag* by Mary James.

RELATED TITLES: Banks, Lynne Reid. *Harry the Poisonous Centipede.* Morrow, 1997. / Bodecker, N. M. *Water Pennies and Other Poems.* McElderry, 1991. / Fleischman, Paul. *Joyful Noise.* HarperCollins, 1988. / Florian, Douglas. *In the Swim: Poems and Paintings.* Harcourt, 1997. / Florian, Douglas. *Mammalabilia: Poems and Paintings.* Harcourt, 2000. / Florian, Douglas. *On the Wing.* Harcourt, 1996. / Hall, Katy, and Lisa Eisenberg. *Buggy Riddles.* Dial, 1986. / Hepworth, Cathi. *Bug Off! A Swarm of Insect Words.* Putnam, 1998. / Hopkins, Lee Bennett, comp. *Flit, Flutter, Fly! Poems About Bugs and Other Crawly Creatures.* Doubleday, 1992. / James, Mary. *Shoebag.* Scholastic, 1990. / McDonald, Megan. *Insects Are My Life.* Orchard, 1995. / Oppenheim, Joanne. *Have You Seen Bugs?* Scholastic, 1998. / Pallotta, Jerry. *The Beetle Alphabet Book.* Charlesbridge, 2004. / Rosen, Michael. *Itsy-Bitsy Beasties: Poems from Around the World.* Carolrhoda, 1992.

SUBJECTS: INSECTS—POETRY. POETRY—SINGLE AUTHOR.

1317   Florian, Douglas. *Laugh-eteria: Poems and Drawings.* **Illus. by the author. Harcourt, 1999. 0-15-202084-5. 158pp. Gr. 1–6**

Here's a worthy companion volume to Florian's *Bing Bang Boing!*, delivering more than 150 wacky, funny, and wordplay-filled poems calculated to make children smile. Most are short and punchy, illustrated with black, thick-lined brush-and-ink drawings. The diverse collection yields clever poems about food, school, smelly feet, dinosaurs, everyday animals, and several invented beasts, including the dreaded Dreath with its 80-odd teeth.

GERM: Children will beg to recite their favorites. Stage a Poetry Slam, a Poetry Round Table, a Poetry Fest, or a Poetry Party in your classroom. Call it what you like, but have children select, practice, and then present a favorite poem to the group. Memorizing is optional, but is always excellent brain training for future actors, brain surgeons, and everyone in-between. *Something Big Has Been Here* by Jack Prelutsky and *Falling Up* by Shel Silverstein are natural pals in the funny verse market.

RELATED TITLES: Florian, Douglas. *Bing Bang Boing!* Harcourt, 1994. / Florian, Douglas. *In the Swim: Poems and Paintings*. Harcourt, 1997. / Florian, Douglas. *Insectlopedia: Poems and Paintings*. Harcourt, 1998. / Florian, Douglas. *Omnibeasts: Animal Poems and Paintings*. Harcourt, 2004. / Florian, Douglas. *On the Wing: Poems and Paintings*. Harcourt, 1996. / Lee, Dennis. *The Ice Cream Store*. Scholastic, 1992. / Moss, Jeff. *The Butterfly Jar*. Bantam, 1989. / Prelutsky, Jack. *It's Raining Pigs and Noodles*. Greenwillow, 2000. / Prelutsky, Jack. *The New Kid on the Block*. Greenwillow, 1984. / Prelutsky, Jack. *A Pizza the Size of the Sun*. Greenwillow, 1996. / Prelutsky, Jack. *Something Big Has Been Here*. Greenwillow, 1990. / Silverstein, Shel. *Falling Up*. HarperCollins, 1996. / Silverstein, Shel. *A Light in the Attic*. HarperCollins, 1981. / Silverstein, Shel. *Where the Sidewalk Ends*. HarperCollins, 1974. / Viorst, Judith. *Sad Underwear and Other Complications: More Poems for Children and Their Parents*. Atheneum, 1995.

SUBJECTS: HUMOROUS POETRY. POETRY—SINGLE AUTHOR.

1318   Florian, Douglas. *Lizards, Frogs, and Polliwogs: Poems and Paintings*. Illus. by the author. Harcourt, 2001. 0-15-202591-X. 48pp. Gr. 2–5

Twenty-one quick, punchy poems convey the essence of all types of reptiles and amphibians.

GERM: Base your reptile and amphibian report assignments on the ones represented in Florian's collection and have students read aloud the poems to accompany their oral presentations. Pair this volume with Florian's other books about animal families: *On the Wing* (about birds), *In the Swim* (about fish), *Insectlopedia* (about bugs), and *Mammalabilia* (about mammals).

RELATED TITLES: Cowley, Joy. *Red-Eyed Tree Frog*. Scholastic, 1999. / Florian, Douglas. *In the Swim: Poems and Paintings*. Harcourt, 1997. / Florian, Douglas. *Insectlopedia: Poems and Paintings*. Harcourt, 1998. / Florian, Douglas. *Mammalabilia: Poems and Paintings*. Harcourt, 2000. / Florian, Douglas. *Omnibeasts: Animal Poems and Paintings*. Harcourt, 2004. / Florian, Douglas. *On the Wing: Bird Poems and Paintings*. Harcourt, 1996. / Prelutsky, Jack, comp. *The Beauty of the Beast: Poems from the Animal Kingdom*. Knopf, 1997. / Singer, Marilyn. *Turtle in July*. Macmillan, 1989.

SUBJECTS: ANIMALS—POETRY. HUMOROUS POETRY. POETRY—SINGLE AUTHOR. REPTILES AND AMPHIBIANS—POETRY.

1319   Florian, Douglas. *Mammalabilia: Poems and Paintings*. Illus. by the author. Harcourt, 2000. 0-15-202167-1. 46pp. Gr. 2–6

Poet Florian has picked out a winsome bunch of mammals as the subjects for his quirky, word-playing poems, with each poem faced by a large scrappy watercolor. There's the usual assortment of fox, coyote, gorilla, and bear, but also aardvarks, the ibex, a tapir, and a lemur. Florian is a master at finding tiny wordplay jokes, such as the visual stutter in "The Aardvarks": "Aardvarks aare odd. / Aardvarks aare staark. / Aardvarks look better / by faar in the daark."

GERM: After researching chosen mammals, students can use the facts they've found to write new poems about them, striving to capture the essence of each animal in their words, as Florian does so masterfully. When assigning those ever-popular animal reports for science class, have your students find a poem (and/or a fable or a folktale) about their animals, starting with Florian's books, and then using indexes of animal poetry books to find more. They can memorize their poems and draw pictures of them to present as a start to their otherwise factual oral reports.

RELATED TITLES: Florian, Douglas. *Beast Feast*. Harcourt, 1994. / Florian, Douglas. *Bing Bang Boing!* Harcourt, 1994. / Florian, Douglas. *In the Swim: Poems and Paintings*. Harcourt, 1997. / Florian, Douglas. *Insectlopedia: Poems and Paintings*. Harcourt, 1998. / Florian, Douglas. *Lizards, Frogs, and Polliwogs: Poems and Paintings*. Harcourt, 2001. / Florian, Douglas. *Omnibeasts: Animal Poems and Paintings*. Harcourt, 2004. / Florian, Douglas. *On the Wing: Bird Poems and Paintings*. Harcourt, 1996. / Prelutsky, Jack, comp. *The Beauty of the Beast: Poems from the Animal Kingdom*. Knopf, 1997. / Sierra, Judy. *There's a Zoo in Room 22*. Harcourt, 2000.

SUBJECTS: ANIMALS—POETRY. HUMOROUS POETRY. MAMMALS—POETRY. POETRY—SINGLE AUTHOR.

1320   Florian, Douglas. *Omnibeasts: Animal Poems and Paintings.* **Illus. by the author. Harcourt, 2004. 0-15-205038-8. 95pp. Gr. 1–6**

Selecting a representative sampling of poetry from all of his animal family books—*Bow Wow Meow Meow*; *In the Swim*; *Insectlopedia*; *Lizards, Frogs, and Polliwogs*; *Mammalabilia*; and *On the Wing*—Florian has compiled one big volume of all the species, illustrated with his amicable watercolors.

GERM: Find more Florian animal wordplay in *Beast Feast* and *Zoo's Who* and in each of Florian's individual books of animal poems.

RELATED TITLES: Belle, Jennifer. *Animal Stackers.* Hyperion, 2005. / Florian, Douglas. *Beast Feast.* Harcourt, 1994. / Florian, Douglas. *Bing Bang Boing!* Harcourt, 1994. / Florian, Douglas. *Bow Wow Meow Meow: It's Rhyming Cats and Dogs.* Harcourt, 2003. / Florian, Douglas. *In the Swim: Poems and Paintings.* Harcourt, 1997. / Florian, Douglas. *Insectlopedia: Poems and Paintings.* Harcourt, 1998. / Florian, Douglas. *Lizards, Frogs, and Polliwogs: Poems and Paintings.* Harcourt, 2001. / Florian, Doug. *Mammalabilia: Poems and Paintings.* Harcourt, 2000. / Florian, Douglas. *On the Wing: Bird Poems and Paintings.* Harcourt, 1996. / Florian, Douglas. *Zoo's Who: Poems and Paintings.* Harcourt, 2005. / Ghigna, Charles. *Animal Tracks: Wild Poems to Read Aloud.* Abrams, 2004. / Lewis, J. Patrick. *A Hippopotamustn't and Other Animal Verses.* Dial, 1990. / Prelutsky, Jack, comp. *The Beauty of the Beast: Poems from the Animal Kingdom.* Knopf, 1997. / Prelutsky, Jack. *The Frogs Wore Red Suspenders.* Greenwillow, 2002. / Prelutsky, Jack. *If Not for the Cat.* Greenwillow, 2004.

SUBJECTS: ANIMALS—POETRY. HUMOROUS POETRY. POETRY—SINGLE AUTHOR.

1321   Florian, Douglas. *On the Wing: Bird Poems and Paintings.* **Illus. by the author. Harcourt, 1996. 0-15-200497-1. 48pp. Gr. 2–5**

Share 21 inventive and whimsical short poems and paintings about familiar and not-so-well-known birds, from egrets to nightjars.

GERM: After reading and enjoying the playful wordplay and watercolors, ask pairs of students to select one of the birds and research factual information about it. Each pair will analyze how Florian incorporated at least one fact about that bird into the poem, and find a photograph or realistic drawing of the bird. For their oral presentation, they will read the poem aloud, show Florian's illustration and the photo, and reveal a few additional interesting facts.

RELATED TITLES: Florian, Douglas. *Bing Bang Boing!* Harcourt, 1994. / Florian, Douglas. *In the Swim: Poems and Paintings.* Harcourt, 1997. / Florian, Douglas. *Insectlopedia: Poems and Paintings.* Harcourt, 1998. / Florian, Douglas. *Omnibeasts: Animal Poems and Paintings.* Harcourt, 2004. / Foster, Joanna. *The Magpie's Nest.* Clarion, 1995. / George, Kristine O'Connell. *Hummingbird Nest: A Journal of Poems.* Harcourt, 2004. / Yolen, Jane. *Bird Watch: A Book of Poetry.* Philomel, 1990. / Yolen, Jane. *Fine Feathered Friends: Poems for Young People.* Boyds Mills, 2004. / Yolen, Jane. *Wild Wings: Poems for Young People.* Boyds Mills, 2002.

SUBJECTS: ANIMALS—POETRY. BIRDS—POETRY. HUMOROUS POETRY. POETRY—SINGLE AUTHOR.

1322   Florian, Douglas. *Summersaults: Poems & Paintings.* **Illus. by the author. Greenwillow, 2002. 0-06-029267-9. 48pp. Gr. K–5**

Along with sunlit watercolors, 28 bouncy wordplaying poems give summer's sizzle to sports, bugs, and the sea.

GERM: Follow up with Florian's other seasonal poem books, *Autumnblings* and *Winter Eyes.*

RELATED TITLES: Alarcón, Francisco X. *Angels Ride Bikes and Other Fall Poems.* Children's Book Press, 1999. / Alarcón, Francisco X. *From the Bellybutton of the Moon and Other Summer Poems.* Children's Book Press, 1998. / Alarcón, Francisco X. *Laughing Tomatoes and Other Spring Poems.* Children's Book Press, 1997. / Florian, Douglas. *Autumnblings: Poems and Paintings.* Greenwillow, 2003. / Florian, Douglas. *Winter Eyes: Poems and Paintings.* Greenwillow, 1999. / Frank, John. *Chill in the Air: Nature Poems for Fall and Winter.* Simon & Schuster, 2003. / Schnur, Steven. *Autumn: An Alphabet Acrostic.* Clarion, 1997. / Schnur, Steven. *Winter: An Alphabet Acrostic.* Clarion, 2002. / Tafuri, Nancy. *Snowy Flowy Blowy: A Twelve Months Rhyme.* Scholastic, 1999. / Updike, John. *A Child's Calendar.* Holiday House, 1999.

SUBJECTS: POETRY—SINGLE AUTHOR. SEASONS—POETRY. SUMMER—POETRY.

1323   Foreman, Michael, comp. *Michael Foreman's Playtime Rhymes.* **Illus. by the author. Candlewick, 2002. 0-7636-1812-8. 108pp. Gr. PreK–1**

This companion volume to *Michael Foreman's Mother Goose* is a collection of 74 (mostly) well-known nursery rhymes, chants, fingerplays, and songs, illustrated with good-natured, full-page, full-bleed watercolors.

GERM: At the back of the book are notes about the rhymes, showing how to use them for fingerplays, acting out, and games.

RELATED TITLES: Brown, Marc, comp. *Hand Rhymes.* Dutton, 1985. / Cole, Joanna, and Stephanie Calmenson, comp. *The Eentsy, Weentsy Spider: Fingerplays and Action Rhymes.* Morrow, 1991. / Crews, Nina, comp. *The Neighborhood Mother Goose.* Greenwillow, 2004. / dePaola, Tomie, comp. *Tomie dePaola's Mother Goose.* Putnam, 1985. / Foreman, Michael, comp. *Michael Foreman's Mother Goose.* Harcourt, 1991. / Lamont, Priscilla, comp. *Ring-a-Round-a-Rosy: Nursery Rhymes, Action Rhymes and Lullabies.* Little, Brown, 1990. / Lobel, Arnold, comp. *The Random House Book of Mother Goose.* Random House, 1986. / Long, Sylvia, comp. *Sylvia Long's Mother Goose.* Chronicle, 1999. / Opie, Iona, comp. *Here Comes Mother Goose.* Candlewick, 1999. / Sierra, Judy, comp. *Schoolyard Rhymes: Kids' Own Rhymes for Rope Skipping, Hand Clapping, Ball Bouncing, and Just Plain Fun.* Knopf, 2005. / Sutherland, Zena, comp. *The Orchard Book of Nursery Rhymes.* Orchard, 1990.

SUBJECTS: FINGERPLAYS. GAMES. MOTHER GOOSE. NURSERY RHYMES. SONGS.

1324 **Franco, Betsy.** *Counting Our Way to the 100th Day!* **Illus. by Steven Salerno. McElderry, 2004. 0-689-84793-9. 48pp. Gr. PreK–3**

One hundred clever, bouncy, good-humored poems celebrate the number 100, so you can celebrate your 100th day of school in style. The poems, two to four to a page and each accompanied by zippy, colorful little gouache illustrations, span every interest, from 100-legged centipedes to 100 kernels of popcorn to the difference between 100 degrees above and below zero.

GERM: Read a poem a day for 100 days, or ten poems a day for ten days. Make lists of all the hundreds in your lives. Write new 100-based poems. Pair this book with Rosemary Wells's *Emily's First 100 Days of School.* Go to Joan Holub's 100th Day of School Web site at <users.aol. com/a100thday/ideas.html> for a useful list of 300 ideas compiled by teachers and librarians.

RELATED TITLES: Cuyler, Margery. *100th Day Worries.* Simon & Schuster, 2000. / Franco, Betsy. *Mathematickles!* McElderry, 2003. / Frith, Margaret. *I'll Teach My Dog 100 Words.* Random House, 1973. / Hopkins, Lee Bennett, comp. *Marvelous Math: A Book of Poems.* Simon & Schuster, 1997. / Kasza, Keiko. *The Wolf's Chicken Stew.* Putnam, 1987. / Medearis, Angela S. *The 100th Day of School.* Scholastic, 1996. / Pinczes, Elinor J. *One Hundred Hungry Ants.* Houghton Mifflin, 1993. / Rockwell, Anne. *100 School Days.* HarperCollins, 2002. / Shields, Carol Diggory. *Almost Late to School and More School Poems.* Dutton, 2003. / Shields, Carol Diggory. *Lunch Money and Other Poems About School.* Dutton, 1995. / Slate, Joseph. *Miss Bindergarten Celebrates the 100th Day of Kindergarten.* Dutton, 1998. / Wells, Rosemary. *Emily's First 100 Days of School.* Hyperion, 2000. / Wells, Rosemary. *My Kindergarten.* Hyperion, 2004.

SUBJECTS: COUNTING BOOKS—POETRY. MATHEMATICS—POETRY. ONE HUNDREDTH DAY CELEBRATIONS—POETRY. POETRY—SINGLE AUTHOR. SCHOOLS—POETRY.

1325 **Franco, Betsy.** *Mathematickles!* **Illus. by Steven Salerno. Simon & Schuster, 2003. 0-689-84357-7. Unp. Gr. K–5**

Words + math + seasons = brain-tickling math. These brief, descriptive, free-verse language poems are illustrated with breezy gouache and watercolor paintings of a girl and her cat who live math all year long. An example (though you have to see the original page to get the full effect): "cold air ÷ breath = tiny cloud."

GERM: In addition to the four functions, there are equally innovative graph and fraction poems for readers to figure out, with smiles and aha's as they do. Naturally, nature and number watchers will want to try their hands at new math and poetry equations.

RELATED TITLES: Adler, David A. *Easy Math Puzzles.* Holiday House, 1997. / Demi. *One Grain of Rice: A Mathematical Folktale.* Scholastic, 1997. / Franco, Betsy. *Counting Our Way to the 100th Day!* McElderry, 2004. / Hopkins, Lee Bennett, comp. *Marvelous Math: A Book of Poems.* Simon & Schuster, 1997. / Leedy, Loreen. *Mission: Addition.* Holiday House, 1997. / Sayre, April Pulley, and Jeff Sayre. *One Is a Snail, Ten Is A Crab; A Counting by Feet Book.* Candlewick, 2003. / Schwartz, David M. *If You Hopped Like a Frog.* Scholastic, 1999. / Schwartz, David M. *Millions to Measure.* Harcourt, 2003. / Scieszka, Jon. *Math Curse.* Viking, 1995. / Tang, Greg. *The Best of Times: Math Strategies That Multiply.* Scholastic, 2002. / Tang, Greg. *The Grapes of Math: Mind-Stretching Math Riddles.* Scholastic, 2001. / Tang, Greg. *Math-terpieces: The Art of Problem Solving.* Scholastic, 2003. / Ziefert, Harriet. *Math Riddles.* Viking, 1997.

SUBJECTS: CONCRETE POETRY. MATHEMATICS—POETRY. POETRY—SINGLE AUTHOR. SEASONS—POETRY.

1326 **Frank, John.** *Chill in the Air: Nature Poems for Fall and Winter.* **Illus. by Mike Reed. Simon & Schuster, 2003. 0-689-83923-5. Unp. Gr. K–2**

Twenty-one short, good-natured, easy-to-read poems are presented from the point of view of a young boy—from fall berry-picking to the roar of winter storms to the first tentative approach of spring.

GERM: Fire up your own poets to observe the weather and the season's natural changes and write descriptive poems about what they see.

RELATED TITLES: Alarcón, Francisco X. *Angels Ride Bikes and Other Fall Poems.* Children's Book Press, 1999. / Florian, Douglas. *Autumnblings: Poems and Paintings.* Greenwillow, 2003. / Roemer, Heidi B. *Come to My Party and Other Shape Poems.* Henry Holt, 2004. / Schnur, Steven. *Autumn: An Alphabet Acrostic.* Clarion, 1997. / Schnur, Steven. *Winter: An Alphabet Acrostic.* Clarion, 2002. / Tafuri, Nancy. *Snowy Flowy Blowy: A Twelve Months Rhyme.* Scholastic, 1999. / Updike, John. *A Child's Calendar.* Holiday House, 1999.

SUBJECTS: AUTUMN—POETRY. NATURE—POETRY. POETRY—SINGLE AUTHOR. SEASONS—POETRY. WINTER—POETRY.

1327 George, Kristine O'Connell. *Fold Me a Poem.* **Illus. by Lauren Stringer. Harcourt, 2005. 0-15-202501-4. Unp. Gr. 1–4**

In a series of 31 spare, haiku-like observational poems, one per large, square page, a boy chronicles his day folding origami animals. Full-bleed acrylics burst from each page, showing the boy, accompanied by his black-and-white cat companion, as he contemplates, folds, fixes, and plays with his colorful menagerie. The package of illustrations, poetry, and paper folding is a creative tour de force.

GERM: When you get ready to start your origami and poetry unit—and you won't have much choice, for once you read the book to children, they'll be clamoring to fold and write their own—have no fear; children are usually more adept at origami than the grownups. You'll find a good bibliography at the back of the book, plus the author's and illustrator's Web sites <www.KristineGeorge.com> and <www.LaurenStringer.com>, which provide activities and links to other origami sites, a downloadable teacher's guide with directions for folding a simple dog, and a lesson on writing three different kinds of poems.

RELATED TITLES: Demi, comp. *In the Eyes of the Cat: Japanese Poetry for All Seasons.* Henry Holt, 1992. / Ernst, Lisa Campbell. *Tangram Magician.* Blue Apple, 2005. / Falwell, Cathryn. *Butterflies for Kiri.* Lee & Low, 2003. / George, Kristine O'Connell. *Hummingbird Nest: A Journal of Poems.* Harcourt, 2004. / Melmed, Laura Krauss. *Little Oh.* Lothrop, 1997. / Prelutsky, Jack. *If Not for the Cat.* Greenwillow, 2004. / Say, Allen. *Tree of Cranes.* Houghton Mifflin, 1991. / Wells, Rosemary. *Yoko's Paper Cranes.* Hyperion, 2001.

SUBJECTS: ANIMALS—POETRY. ORIGAMI. PLAY. POETRY—SINGLE AUTHOR.

1328 George, Kristine O'Connell. *Hummingbird Nest: A Journal of Poems.* **Illus. by Barry Moser. Harcourt, 2004. 0-15-202325-9. Unp. Gr. 2–6**

In 26 evocative poems, highlighted with delicate, up-close watercolors, poet George unfolds the saga of the two months she and her family observed an Anna's hummingbird build a 2-inch nest in a ficus plant on the back patio and hatch two babies.

GERM: Listeners will be mesmerized by George's attention to every detail, which could start them on an observation project, looking, writing poetry about, and drawing nearby birds or other animals. After you have read and digested the fascinating facts at the back of the book, turn to Esther Quesada Tyrrell's riveting nonfiction book *Hummingbirds: Jewels in the Sky,* for stellar photos and information. You may even wish to purchase a hummingbird feeder, if there's any way you can hang it out of your classroom window.

RELATED TITLES: Florian, Douglas. *On the Wing: Bird Poems and Paintings.* Harcourt, 1996. / George, Kristine O'Connell. *Fold Me a Poem.* Harcourt, 2005. / Peters, Lisa Westberg. *This Way Home.* Henry Holt, 1994. / Prelutsky, Jack. *If Not for the Cat.* Greenwillow, 2004. / Ryder, Joanne. *Dancers in the Garden.* Sierra Club, 1992. / Tyrrell, Esther Quesada. *Hummingbirds: Jewels in the Sky.* Crown, 1992. / Yolen, Jane. *Bird Watch: A Book of Poetry.* Philomel, 1990. / Yolen, Jane. *Fine Feathered Friends: Poems for Young People.* Boyds Mills, 2004. / Yolen, Jane. *Wild Wings: Poems for Young People.* Boyds Mills, 2002.

SUBJECTS: BIRDS—POETRY. HUMMINGBIRDS—POETRY. POETRY—SINGLE AUTHOR.

1329 George, Kristine O'Connell. *Little Dog Poems.* **Illus. by June Otani. Clarion, 1999. 0-395-82266-1. 40pp. Gr. K–2**

In 30 short, easy-to-read poems, a little girl describes her day with her adorable mop of a dog.

GERM: Have your animal lovers write free-verse poems about the pets dear to their hearts. Also read George's companion book, *Little Dog and Duncan.* Compare the poems with those in Amy E. Sklansky's *From the Doghouse,* which is narrated from the dog's point of view.

RELATED TITLES: Bartoletti, Susan Campbell. *Nobody's Diggier Than a Dog.* Hyperion, 2004. / George, Kristine O'Connell. *Little Dog and Duncan*. Clarion, 2002. / Hall, Donald. *I Am the Dog, I Am the Cat*. Dial, 1994. / Johnston, Tony. *It's About Dogs*. Harcourt, 2000. / Kirk, Daniel. *Dogs Rule!* Hyperion, 2003. / Kopper, Lisa. *Daisy Thinks She Is a Baby*. Knopf, 1994. / Laden, Nina. *The Night I Followed the Dog*. Chronicle, 1994. / Meddaugh, Susan. *Martha Speaks*. Houghton Mifflin, 1992. / Miller, Sara Swan. *Three Stories You Can Read to Your Dog*. Houghton Mifflin, 1995. / Numeroff, Laura. *Dogs Don't Wear Sneakers*. Simon & Schuster, 1993. / Rathmann, Peggy. *Officer Buckle and Gloria*. Putnam, 1995. / Rylant, Cynthia. *The Great Gracie Chase*. Scholastic, 2001. / Singer, Marilyn. *It's Hard to Read a Map with a Beagle on Your Lap*. Henry Holt, 1993. / Wells, Rosemary. *Lucy Comes to Stay*. Dial, 1994. / Wells, Rosemary. *McDuff Moves In*. Hyperion, 1997. (And others in the McDuff series.)

SUBJECTS: DOGS—POETRY. POETRY—SINGLE AUTHOR.

1330 George, Kristine O'Connell. *Old Elm Speaks: Tree Poems.* **Illus. by Kate Kiesler. Clarion, 1998. 0-395-87611-7. 48pp. Gr. 2–6**

These 30 short, perceptive poems—ranging in style from free verse to rhyme to haiku—and their accompanying oil paintings pair children and the many types of trees that inspire them to look closer.

GERM: Along with Barbara Brenner's *The Earth Is Painted Green: A Garden of Poems About Our Planet*, these nature poems are perfect for Arbor Day, Earth Day, and days when you need environmentally friendly materials that inspire listeners to appreciate the world around them.

RELATED TITLES: Atkins, Jeannine. *Aani and the Tree Huggers*. Lee & Low, 1995. / Bash, Barbara. *In the Heart of the Village: The World of the Indian Banyan Tree*. Sierra Club, 1996. / Behn, Harry. *Trees*. Henry Holt, 1992. / Brenner, Barbara, comp. *The Earth Is Painted Green: A Garden of Poems About Our Planet*. Scholastic, 1994. / Brenner, Barbara. *One Small Place in a Tree*. HarperCollins, 2004. / Bunting, Eve. *Someday a Tree*. Clarion, 1993. / Cherry, Lynne. *The Great Kapok Tree: A Tale of the Amazon Rain Forest*. Harcourt, 1990. / Gackenbach, Dick. *Mighty Tree*. Harcourt, 1992. / Hiscock, Bruce. *The Big Tree*. Atheneum, 1991. / Johnston, Tony. *Bigfoot Cinderrrrella*. Putnam, 1998. / Lyon, George Ella. *A B Cedar: An Alphabet of Trees*. Orchard, 1989. / Oppenheim, Joanne. *Have You Seen Trees?* Scholastic, 1995. / Pfeffer, Wendy. *A Log's Life*. Simon & Schuster, 1997. / Udry, Janice May. *A Tree Is Nice*. HarperCollins, 1956.

SUBJECTS: NATURE—POETRY. POETRY—SINGLE AUTHOR. TREES—POETRY.

1331 George, Kristine O'Connell. *Swimming Upstream: Middle School Poems.* **Illus. by Debbie Tilley. Clarion, 2002. 0-618-15250-4. 80pp. Gr. 5–7**

A middle-school girl narrates 75 brisk, warm, and worried poems about her first year in school, including haiku about being late and lost and cogent observations on lunch, fitting in, new friendships, pop quizzes, flute lessons, and secret crushes.

GERM: Surely, your students will identify with the narrator and write their own experiential poems about shared school goings-on, such as their first day or worst test or best memory. Take a taste of summer with George's *Toasting Marshmallows: Camping Poems*.

RELATED TITLES: Creech, Sharon. *Love That Dog*. HarperCollins, 2001. / Dakos, Kalli. *If You're Not Here, Please Raise Your Hand: Poems About School*. Simon & Schuster, 1990. / Dakos, Kalli. *Put Your Eyes Up Here and Other School Poems*. Simon & Schuster, 2002. / George, Kristine O'Connell. *Toasting Marshmallows: Camping Poems*. Clarion, 2001. / Harrison, David L. *Somebody Catch My Homework*. Boyds Mills, 1993. / Kennedy, Dorothy M. *I Thought I'd Take My Rat to School: Poems for September to June*. Little, Brown, 1993. / Shields, Carol Diggory. *Almost Late to School and More School Poems*. Dutton, 2003. / Woodson, Jacqueline. *Locomotion*. Putnam, 2003.

SUBJECTS: HUMOROUS POETRY. POETRY—SINGLE AUTHOR. SCHOOLS—POETRY.

1332 George, Kristine O'Connell. *Toasting Marshmallows: Camping Poems.* **Illus. by Kate Keisler. Clarion, 2001. 0-618-04597-X. 48pp. Gr. 2–6**

Each of these 30 free-verse poems and full-page acrylic paintings, chronicling a family camping trip, is an insightful and careful observation made by the daughter of the family as she, her parents, and her little brother explore, eat, sleep, fish, row, and experience nature outdoors.

GERM: Read this aloud around a pretend fire, built with sticks in the middle of the room, with marshmallows for listeners to eat afterward. Listeners can write their own summer mood poems to bring back the feel of that season, even when it's winter outside. For the text-to-life connection, ask your listeners to write about their own experiences with nature. Writing prompt (after sharing "The Best Paths"): Think about a path you have taken and tell/write/draw where it led you.

RELATED TITLES: Alarcón, Francisco X. *From the Bellybutton of the Moon and Other Summer Poems*. Children's Book Press, 1998. / Duffey, Betsy. *Cody Unplugged*. Viking, 1999. / Fleischman, Paul. *Weslandia*. Candlewick, 1999. / George, Kristine O'Connell. *Old Elm Speaks: Tree Poems*. Clarion, 1998. / LaMarche, Jim. *The Raft*. HarperCollins, 2000. / McCloskey, Robert. *A Time of Wonder*. Viking, 1957. / Prelutsky, Jack. *What I Did Last Summer*. Greenwillow, 1984. / Schnur, Steven. *Summer: An Alphabet Acrostic*. Clarion, 2001.

SUBJECTS: CAMPING—POETRY. POETRY—SINGLE AUTHOR.

1333 Ghigna, Charles. *Animal Tracks: Wild Poems to Read Aloud*. Illus. by John Speirs. Abrams, 2004. 0-8109-4841-9. 36pp. Gr. PreK–2

Listeners will laugh out loud at the whimsy and wordplay in these 32 sparkling animal poems and accompanying animal- and child-filled watercolors, which showcase more than 100 different kinds of animals.

GERM: There's an index of all the animals mentioned in the text, which is great to use as an example if your children are working on indexing skills. They can skim and scan the poems to locate each animal they look up in the index.

RELATED TITLES: Calmenson, Stephanie. *Never Take a Pig to Lunch: And Other Funny Poems About Animals*. Doubleday, 1982. / Florian, Douglas. *Beast Feast*. Harcourt, 1994. / Florian, Douglas. *Omnibeasts: Animal Poems and Paintings*. Harcourt, 2004. / Florian, Douglas. *Zoo's Who: Poems and Paintings*. Harcourt, 2005. / Lee, Dennis. *Dinosaur Dinner (With a Slice of Alligator Pie)*. Knopf, 1997. / Lee, Dennis. *The Ice Cream Store*. Scholastic, 1992. / Lewis, J. Patrick. *A Hippopotamustn't and Other Animal Verses*. Dial, 1990. / Prelutsky, Jack. *The Frogs Wore Red Suspenders*. Greenwillow, 2002. / Sierra, Judy. *There's a Zoo in Room 22*. Harcourt, 2000. / Singer, Marilyn. *Please Don't Squeeze Your Boa, Noah!* Henry Holt, 1995.

SUBJECTS: ANIMALS—POETRY. HUMOROUS POETRY. POETRY—SINGLE AUTHOR.

1334 Gollub, Matthew. *Cool Melons—Turn to Frogs! The Life and Poems of Issa*. Illus. by Kazuko G. Stone. Lee & Low, 1998. 1-880000-71-7. Unp. Gr. 2–6

Born in a small mountain village in Japan in 1763, Issa began writing haiku at age 7 when his schoolmaster noticed how unhappy he was, telling him, "With haiku, you can show what you are feeling inside." Gollub's inviting picture-book biography is accompanied by delicate watercolor and colored-pencil illustrations and a carefully selected sampling of 32 of Issa's more than 20,000 haiku, printed in English and in Japanese calligraphy.

GERM: Helpful notes at the back of the book will give you inspiration to get your listeners to ". . . listen and observe, and to capture one meaningful moment in time." Meet another iconic Japanese haiku master, Basho, in Dawnine Spivak's *Grass Sandals: The Travels of Basho*.

RELATED TITLES: Cassedy, Sylvia, and Kunihiro Suetake, trans. *Red Dragonfly on My Shoulder*. HarperCollins, 1992. / Demi, comp. *In the Eyes of the Cat: Japanese Poetry for All Seasons*. Henry Holt, 1992. / Higginson, William J., comp. *Wind in the Long Grass: A Collection of Haiku*. Simon & Schuster, 1991. / Kerley, Barbara. *Walt Whitman: Words for America*. Scholastic, 2004. / Myers, Tim. *Basho and the Fox*. Marshall Cavendish, 2000. / Prelutsky, Jack. *If Not for the Cat*. Greenwillow, 2004. / Spivak, Dawnine. *Grass Sandals: The Travels of Basho*. Atheneum, 1997.

SUBJECTS: BIOGRAPHY. HAIKU. ISSA (KOBATYASHI, ISSA, 1763–1827). JAPAN. MULTICULTURAL BOOKS—POETRY. POETRY—SINGLE AUTHOR. POETS.

1335 Gottfried, Maya. *Good Dog*. Illus. by Robert Rahway Zakanitch. Knopf, 2005. 0-375-83049-9. Unp. Gr. K–3

The 16 breeds of dogs featured in the right-hand, full-page oil portraits against black painted backgrounds are the narrators here. From their free-verse points of view, they address us, their beloved people, and reveal their thoughts and desires. The white Pekingese with the dark, worried face says, in his Memo to his Person, "I'm sorry about the stain on the piano bench. Accident, won't happen again." On the left-hand page, arranged around the text of each poem, are smudgy pencil sketches of that dog in different poses. As the Mutt says, "Who's a good dog? Me."

GERM: What are your pets thinking? If they could talk, what would they tell you? As a writing and drawing prompt, this should inspire children to follow their pets around and write point-of-view poems to go along with their life sketches. See your art teacher about transforming the sketches to formal painted portraits. More dog adulation abounds in the poems of Daniel Kirk's *Dogs Rule!* and Tony Johnston's *It's About Dogs*.

RELATED TITLES: Bartoletti, Susan Campbell. *Nobody's Diggier Than a Dog*. Hyperion, 2004. / Florian, Douglas. *Bow Wow Meow Meow*. Harcourt, 2003. / George, Kristine O'Connell. *Little Dog Poems*. Clarion, 1999. / Hall, Donald. *I Am the Dog, I Am the Cat*. Dial, 1994. / Johnston, Tony. *It's About Dogs*. Harcourt, 2000. / Kalman, Maira. *What Pete Ate from A– Z*. Putnam, 2001. / Kirk, Daniel. *Dogs Rule!* Hyperion, 2003. / Miller,

Sara Swan. *Three Stories You Can Read to Your Dog*. Houghton Mifflin, 1995. / Singer, Marilyn. *It's Hard to Read a Map with a Beagle on Your Lap*. Henry Holt, 1993. / Sklansky, Amy E. *From the Doghouse: Poems to Chew On*. Henry Holt, 2002. / Yolen, Jane. *Raining Cats and Dogs*. Harcourt, 1993.

SUBJECTS: DOGS—POETRY. POETRY—SINGLE AUTHOR.

1336 Graham, Joan Bransfied. *Flicker Flash*. Illus. by Nancy Davis. Houghton Mifflin, 1999. 0-395-90501-X. Unp. Gr. 2–6

Each of these 23 quirky, deceptively simple—yet inspired—concrete (or shape) poems describes the forms and properties of light (as is generated by the sun, a candle, a firefly, a flashlight) and physically incorporates words into a vibrant, graphically exciting, yellow-lit illustration.

GERM: Make transparencies of some of the poems so children can read them aloud as an introduction to either concrete poetry (which they can then write and illustrate) or light and electricity. This is a welcome companion to Graham's *Splish Splash*, with its concrete poems all about water.

RELATED TITLES: Adler, David A. *A Picture Book of Thomas Alva Edison*. Holiday House, 1996. / Burg, Brad. *Outside the Lines: Poetry at Play*. Putnam, 2002. / Delano, Marie Ferguson. *Inventing the Future: A Photobiography of Thomas Alva Edison*. National Geographic, 2002. / Graham, Joan Bransfield. *Splish Splash*. Ticknor & Fields, 1994. / Grandits, John. *Technically, It's Not My Fault: Concrete Poems*. Clarion, 2004. / Hopkins, Lee Bennett, comp. *Spectacular Science: A Book of Poems*. Simon & Schuster, 1999. / Kos, Amy Goldman. *Where Fish Go in Winter and Other Great Mysteries*. Dial, 2002. / Lewis, J. Patrick. *Doodle Dandies: Poems That Take Shape*. Atheneum, 1998. / McDermott, Gerald. *Raven: A Trickster Tale from the Pacific Northwest*. Harcourt, 1993. / Roemer, Heidi B. *Come to My Party and Other Shape Poems*. Henry Holt, 2004. / Shields, Carol Diggory. *Brain Juice: Science, Fresh Squeezed!* Handprint, 2003. / Simon, Seymour. *Lightning*. Morrow, 1997.

SUBJECTS: CONCRETE POETRY. ELECTRICITY—POETRY. LIGHT—POETRY. POETRY—SINGLE AUTHOR.

1337 Grandits, John. *Technically, It's Not My Fault: Concrete Poems*. Illus. by the author. Clarion, 2004. 0-618-42833-X. Unp. Gr. 4–7

Once you read the title poem on the cover of the book, printed in white type on a glossy black background, you'll know you are not opening just any run-of-the-mill concrete poetry book. Meet Robert, in all his hilariously snarpy moods, in a series of red-and-black-lettered poems that spin around and graphically wake you up with his humor and on-target take on school, sisters, skateboards, talking backwards, and bloodcurdling screams.

GERM: Of course your gang is going to be wild to lay out their lives in concrete poems, and maybe they can try setting them up on the computer, if you have a decent graphics program. How does one construct a poem? See the house-shaped note from the author, explaining, "Building a poem is like building a little house." For more examples of innovative concrete poetry, don't miss Paul B. Janeczko's collection *A Poke in the I*.

RELATED TITLES: Graham, Joan Bransfield. *Flicker Flash*. Houghton Mifflin, 1999. / Graham, Joan Bransfield. *Splish Splash*. Ticknor & Fields, 1994. / Janeczko, Paul B. *A Poke in the I: A Collection of Concrete Poems*. Candlewick, 2001. / Lewis, J. Patrick. *Doodle Dandies: Poems That Take Shape*. Atheneum, 1998. / Stevenson, James. *Popcorn*. Greenwillow, 1998. (And others in the Corn series.)

SUBJECTS: CONCRETE POETRY. HUMOROUS POETRY. PERSONAL NARRATIVES. POETRY—SINGLE AUTHOR. POINT OF VIEW—POETRY.

1338 Grimes, Nikki. *My Man Blue*. Illus. by Jerome Lagarrigue. Dial, 1999. 0-8037-2326-1. 32pp. Gr. 3–6

In 14 sober, introspective, casually rhymed poems, the narrator, a sensitive inner-city African American boy, describes his growing friendship with a grown man, Blue, "rugged dude," "gold-toothed guardian angel."

GERM: Make a list of words that describe Blue. In *Meet Danitra Brown*, another upbeat collection of poems by Grimes, make the acquaintance of Zuri Jackson and her best friend.

RELATED TITLES: Adoff, Arnold. *In for Winter, Out for Spring*. Harcourt, 1991. / Creech, Sharon. *Love That Dog*. HarperCollins, 2001. / Grimes, Nikki. *Danitra Brown, Class Clown*. HarperCollins, 2005. / Grimes, Nikki. *Meet Danitra Brown*. Lothrop, 1994. / Hudson, Wade, comp. *Pass It On: African-American Poetry for Children*. Scholastic, 1993. / Myers, Walter Dean. *Brown Angels: An Album of Pictures and Verse*. HarperCollins, 1993. / Woodson, Jacqueline. *Locomotion*. Putnam, 2003.

SUBJECTS: AFRICAN AMERICANS—POETRY. MULTICULTURAL BOOKS—POETRY. POETRY—SINGLE AUTHOR.

1339 Grossman, Bill. *Timothy Tunny Swallowed a Bunny.* **Illus. by Kevin Hawkes. HarperCollins, 2001. 0-06-028010-7. Unp. Gr. PreK–3**

Each of the 18 hapless subjects in these wry and wordplay-filled six-line poems has an odd countenance (such as Walter Lackwards, whose head is on backwards) or meets an unusual fate (like squeaky-clean Keith, who brushes away his own head). Weirdly whimsical portraits add to the glee.

GERM: Most of the witty verses are constructed as: AABAAB. See if your poets can write new rhymes in the same cadence and pattern, using their own names or the names of friends. The bad actors in X. J. Kennedy's slim, sly poetry book *Brats* also come to dire and dreaded ends.

RELATED TITLES: Florian, Douglas. *Bing Bang Boing!* Harcourt, 1994. / Grossman, Bill. *My Little Sister Ate One Hare.* Crown, 1996. / Kennedy, X. J. *Brats.* McElderry, 1986. / Koontz, Dean. *Paper Doorway: Funny Verse and Nothing Worse.* HarperCollins, 2001. / Livingston, Myra Cohn, comp. *Lots of Limericks.* McElderry, 1991. / McNaughton, Colin. *There's an Awful Lot of Weirdos in Our Neighborhood and Other Wickedly Funny Verse.* Candlewick, 1997. / McNaughton, Colin. *Who's Been Sleeping in My Porridge? A Book of Wacky Poems and Pictures.* Candlewick, 1998. / Marshall, James, comp. *Pocketful of Nonsense.* Artists and Writers Guild, 1993. / Prelutsky, Jack. *It's Raining Pigs and Noodles.* Greenwillow, 2001. / Silverstein, Shel. *Falling Up.* HarperCollins, 1996. / Viorst, Judith. *If I Were in Charge of the World and Other Worries.* Atheneum, 1981. / Viorst, Judith. *Sad Underwear and Other Complications: More Poems for Children and Their Parents.* Atheneum, 1995.

SUBJECTS: BEHAVIOR—POETRY. HUMOROUS POETRY. POETRY—SINGLE AUTHOR.

1340 Guthrie, Woody. *This Land Is Your Land.* **Illus. by Kathy Jakobsen. Little, Brown, 1998. 0-316-39215-4. 32pp. Gr. 1–6**

All kids know the chorus of one of America's most popular unofficial anthems. In a glowingly illustrated picture book crammed with coast-to-coast details, including quotes from Woody and his many songs, we learn the rest of the verses as we travel through the redwoods, Monument Valley, the prairies, and the cities. Written during the Dust Bowl and the Depression in the 1930s, the song reflects those hard times.

GERM: Sing the song, of course. At the back of the book, there's a final note by folksinger Pete Seeger and a biography with photos of Woody. Woody's *20 Grow Big Songs* is a charming songbook of some of Woody's classic children's songs. *America the Beautiful* by Katharine Lee Bates provides the verses to that song plus a dazzling tour of 14 fascinating U.S. monuments and natural wonders painted in pastel acrylics.

RELATED TITLES: Bates, Katharine Lee. *America the Beautiful.* Illus. by Chris Gall. Little, Brown, 2004. / Brisson, Pat. *Your Best Friend, Kate.* Bradbury, 1989. / Cherry, Lynne. *The Armadillo from Amarillo.* Harcourt, 1994. / Cheney, Lynne. *America: A Patriotic Primer.* Simon & Schuster, 2002. / Christensen, Bonnie. *Woody Guthrie: Poet of the People.* Knopf, 2001. / Coombs, Karen Mueller. *Woody Guthrie: America's Folksinger.* Carolrhoda, 2002. / DiPucchio, Kelly. *Liberty's Journey.* Hyperion, 2004. / Guthrie, Woody, and Marjorie Maza Guthrie. *Woody's 20 Grow Big Songs.* HarperCollins, 1992. / Keenan, Sheila. *O, Say Can You See? America's Symbols, Landmarks, and Inspiring Words.* Scholastic, 2004. / Keller, Laurie. *The Scrambled States of America.* Henry Holt, 1998. / Rylant, Cynthia. *Tulip Sees America.* Scholastic, 1998. / Younger, Barbara. *Purple Mountain Majesties: The Story of Katharine Lee Bates and "America the Beautiful."* Dutton, 1998.

SUBJECTS: BIOGRAPHY. FOLK SONGS. GUTHRIE, WOODY. PICTURE BOOKS FOR ALL AGES. SONGS. U.S.—GEOGRAPHY.

1341 Hall, Katy, and Lisa Eisenberg. *Mummy Riddles.* **Illus. by Nicole Rubel. Dial, 1997. 0-8037-1847-0. 48pp. Gr. 1–4**

Forty-two dead-on riddles about mummies in Egypt will wrap up your ancient civilizations units with some clever wordplay.

GERM: For your next social studies or science lesson, have students brainstorm related wordplay answers and then write riddles to go with them.

RELATED TITLES: Aliki. *Mummies Made in Egypt.* Crowell, 1987. / Bunting, Eve. *I Am the Mummy Heb-Nefert.* Harcourt, 1997. / Clements, Andrew. *Temple Cat.* Clarion, 1996. / Climo, Shirley. *The Egyptian Cinderella.* Crowell, 1989. / Cole, Joanna. *Ms. Frizzle's Adventures: Ancient Egypt.* HarperCollins, 1996. / Cushman, Doug. *The Mystery of King Karfu.* HarperCollins, 1996. / Gibbons, Gail. *Mummies, Pyramids, and Pharaohs: A Book About Ancient Egypt.* Little, Brown, 2004. / Hall, Katy, and Lisa Eisenberg. *Creepy Riddles.* Dial, 1998. / Scieszka, Jon. *Tut, Tut.* Viking, 1996. / Stolz, Mary. *Zekmet, the Stone Carver.* Harcourt, 1988.

SUBJECTS: EGYPT, ANCIENT—RIDDLES. MUMMIES—RIDDLES. RIDDLES.

1342 Hall, Katy, and Lisa Eisenberg. *Ribbit Riddles*. Illus. by Robert Bender. Dial, 2001. 0-8037-2525-6. 40pp. Gr. PreK–2

What do little frogs like to eat on a hot summer day? Hopsickles! And there are 33 more frog riddles just as good. Hall and Eisenberg are the Riddle Queens, and they've covered a multitude of animals in their easy-to-read riddle books, all of which feature a riddle and a witty and colorful illustration on each page. Set your jokesters loose with *Batty Riddles* (1993), *Buggy Riddles* (1986), *Bunny Riddles* (1997), *Chickie Riddles* (1997), *Creepy Riddles* (1998), *Fishy Riddles* (1993), *Grizzly Riddles* (1989), *Kitty Riddles* (2000), *Piggy Riddles* (2004), *Puppy Riddles* (1998), *Ribbit Riddles* (2001), *Sheepish Riddles* (1996), *Snakey Riddles* (1990), and *Spacey Riddles* (1992).

GERM: After reading aloud several of the riddles to your hoppin' crew, pair them up and hand each duo a photocopy of one riddle. Spread out on tables a copy of each answer. Pairs read their riddles and try to guess an answer, which they can write down. Then they go to the tables to find the correct answer. Finally, they read aloud the riddle for the rest of the group to answer.

RELATED TITLES: Calmenson, Stephanie. *The Frog Principal.* Scholastic, 2001. / Cushman, Doug. *Inspector Hopper.* HarperCollins, 2000. / Florian, Douglas. *Lizards, Frogs, and Polliwogs: Poems and Paintings.* Harcourt, 2001. / French, Vivian. *Growing Frogs.* Candlewick, 2000. / Hall, Katy, and Lisa Eisenberg. *Buggy Riddles.* Dial, 1986. / Hall, Katy, and Lisa Eisenberg. *Snakey Riddles.* Dial, 1990. / Lobel, Arnold. Frog and Toad series. HarperCollins. / London, Jonathan. Froggy series. Viking. / Pfeffer, Wendy. *From Tadpole to Frog.* HarperCollins, 1994. / Wiesner, David. *Tuesday.* Clarion, 1991.

SUBJECTS: FROGS. RIDDLES.

1343 Harley, Avis. *Fly with Poetry: An ABC of Poetry*. Illus. by the author. Boyds Mills, 2000. 1-56397-798-2. 48pp. Gr. 2–6

Twenty-eight observational poems compose an alphabetical dictionary of poetic forms and techniques, from an abecedarian and acrostic poem to a zoophabet. In between are samples of cinquain, haiku, sonnet, and villanelle, each of which includes a definition of the form and a soft, colored-pencil illustration.

GERM: Follow up with the companion book, *Leap into Poetry*, and get your writers to try out some poetic styles that are new to them. Meet a young poet who tries out many different forms of poetry in Jacqueline Woodson's poetic novel *Locomotion*.

RELATED TITLES: Creech, Sharon. *Love That Dog.* HarperCollins, 2001. / Harley, Avis. *Leap into Poetry: More ABCs of Poetry.* Boyds Mills, 2001. / Janeczko, Paul B. *How to Write Poetry.* Scholastic, 1999. / Janeczko, Paul B., comp. *A Kick in the Head: An Everyday Guide to Poetic Forms.* Candlewick, 2005. / Janeczko, Paul B., comp. *The Place My Words Are Looking For.* Simon & Schuster, 1990. / Janeczko, Paul B., comp. *Poetry from A to Z: A Guide for Young Writers.* Simon & Schuster, 1994. / Janeczko, Paul B., comp. *Seeing the Blue Between: Advice and Inspiration for Young Poets.* Candlewick, 2002. / Kennedy, X. J., comp. *Knock at a Star: A Child's Introduction to Poetry.* Little, Brown, 1982. / Larrick, Nancy, comp. *Let's Do a Poem!* Delacorte, 1991. / Livingston, Myra Cohn, comp. *Poem-Making: Ways to Begin Writing Poetry.* HarperCollins, 1991. / Rocklin, Joanne. *For Your Eyes Only!* Scholastic, 1997. / Woodson, Jacqueline. *Locomotion.* Putnam, 2003.

SUBJECTS: ALPHABET—POETRY. POETRY—SINGLE AUTHOR.

1344 Harrison, David L. *The Mouse Was Out at Recess*. Illus. by Eugenie Fernandes. Boyds Mills, 2003. 1-56397-550-5. Unp. Gr. 1–4

Romp through the day with two dozen jovial school poems, about everything from making noise on the bus to lunchroom troubles to mishaps on the school field trip.

GERM: Pair this with Harrison's companion book, *Somebody Catch My Homework*. Pair up and share aloud the poems for two voices. Other classic books of school-based rhymes include *If You're Not Here, Please Raise Your Hand* by Kalli Dakos and *Lunch Money* by Carol Diggory Shields.

RELATED TITLES: Dakos, Kalli. *Don't Read This Book, Whatever You Do! More Poems About School.* Four Winds, 1993. / Dakos, Kalli. *If You're Not Here, Please Raise Your Hand: Poems About School.* Simon & Schuster, 1990. / Harrison, David L. *Somebody Catch My Homework.* Boyds Mills, 1993. / Heide, Florence Parry, and Roxanne Heide Pierce. *Oh, Grow Up! Poems to Help You Survive Parents, Chores, School and Other Afflictions.* Orchard, 1996. / Kennedy, Dorothy M. *I Thought I'd Take My Rat to School: Poems for September to June.* Little, Brown, 1993. / Shields, Carol Diggory. *Almost Late to School and More School Poems.* Dutton, 2003. / Shields, Carol Diggory. *Lunch Money and Other Poems About School.* Dutton, 1995.

SUBJECTS: HUMOROUS POETRY. POETRY—SINGLE AUTHOR. READER'S THEATER. SCHOOLS—POETRY.

1345 Heard, Georgia, comp. *This Place I Know: Poems of Comfort.* **Illus. by eighteen renowned children's book artists. Candlewick, 2002. 0-7636-1924-8. 48pp. Gr. 1–6**

After 9/11, New York poetry anthologist Georgia Heard pulled together this fine collection of 18 "poems of comfort" from diverse poets including Eloise Greenfield, Gwendolyn Brooks, Walt Whitman, and Emily Dickinson. Eighteen children's book artists, including Peter Sis, Yumi Heo, Giselle Potter, and Chris Raschka, each contributed an accompanying illustration, and it's a worthy collaboration.

GERM: Poetry, read aloud, has a wonderful ability to make people feel better. After sharing these poems with your children, let them loose in the 800 section of your library, in groups of two to four, to select another "healing" poem that they can practice and then read aloud to the rest of the class.

RELATED TITLES: Gerstein, Mordicai. *The Man Who Walked Between the Towers.* Roaring Brook, 2003. / Harwayne, Shelley, ed. *Messages to Ground Zero: Children Respond to September 11, 2001.* Heinemann, 2002. / Kalman, Maira. *Fireboat: The Heroic Adventures of the John J. Harvey.* Putnam, 2002. / Levitas, Mitchell, ed. *The New York Times: A Nation Challenged: A Visual History of 9/11 and Its Aftermath, Young Reader's Edition.* Scholastic, 2002. / Osborne, Mary Pope. *New York's Bravest.* Knopf, 2002. / Winter, Jeanette. *The Librarian of Basra.* Harcourt, 2005. / Winter, Jeanette. *September Roses.* Farrar, 2004.

SUBJECTS: POETRY—ANTHOLOGIES. SEPTEMBER 11 TERRORIST ATTACKS, 2001.

1346 Heller, Ruth. *Behind the Mask: A Book About Prepositions.* **Illus. by the author. Grosset, 1995. 0-448-41123-7. 44pp. Gr. 2–6**

"Of prepositions have no fear. In phrases only they appear." In another one of her glorious grammar books in the World of Language series, Heller regales us with a wide-ranging descriptive narrative poem, accompanied by lush and vivaciously colored paintings explaining the ins and outs of one part of speech.

GERM: Heller has a gift for making the rules of grammar understandable and even memorable, giving us a crash course in collective nouns (*A Cache of Jewels*), interjections and conjunctions (*Fantastic! Wow! and Unreal!*), verbs (*Kites Sail High*), adjectives (*Many Luscious Lollipops*), nouns (*Merry-Go-Round*), pronouns (*Mine, All Mine*), and adverbs (*Up, Up and Away*). Share Heller's brief, color photo-filled autobiography, *Fine Lines*, for background on her life and work.

RELATED TITLES: Cleary, Brian P. *Hairy, Scary, Ordinary: What Is an Adjective?* Carolrhoda, 2000. / Cleary, Brian P. *Under, Over, by the Clover: What Is a Preposition?* Carolrhoda, 2002. (And others in the Words Are Categorical series.) / Heller, Ruth. *Animals Born Alive and Well.* Grossett, 1982. / Heller, Ruth. *A Cache of Jewels and Other Collective Nouns.* Grosset, 1989. / Heller, Ruth. *Fantastic! Wow! and Unreal! A Book About Interjections and Conjunctions.* Grosset, 1998. / Heller, Ruth. *Fine Lines.* Richard C. Owen, 1996. / Heller, Ruth. *Kites Sail High: A Book About Verbs.* Grosset, 1988. / Heller, Ruth. *Many Luscious Lollipops: A Book About Adjectives.* Grosset, 1989. / Heller, Ruth. *Merry-Go-Round: A Book About Nouns.* Grosset, 1990. / Heller, Ruth. *Mine, All Mine: A Book About Pronouns.* Grosset & Dunlap, 1997. / Heller, Ruth. *Up, Up and Away: A Book About Adverbs.* Grosset, 1991. / Pulver, Robin. *Punctuation Takes a Vacation.* Holiday House, 2003.

SUBJECTS: ENGLISH LANGUAGE—GRAMMAR. ENGLISH LANGUAGE—PREPOSITIONS. STORIES IN RHYME.

1347 Heller, Ruth. *Mine, All Mine: A Book About Pronouns.* **Illus. by the author. Grosset, 1997. 0-448-41606-9. Unp. Gr. 3–6**

The lively rhyming text and huge, handsome, colorful illustrations present concrete information about all types of pronouns, words that take the place of nouns, including personal, possessive, demonstrative, indefinite, interrogative, reflexive, and intensive.

GERM: Finally, there is a book that will help your grammarians sort out proper use of pronouns in a logical and useful way, getting them to recognize the problems with "Him and me are going to the store with she and I." Once they learn the rules, they'll employ them in their speaking and writing, thereby diminishing the current slide into sloppy grammar. Look for all the grammar books in Heller's World of Language series and reinforce the rules with Brian P. Cleary's Words Are Categorical books, including *I and You and Don't Forget Who: What Is a Pronoun?*

RELATED TITLES: Cleary, Brian P. *Hairy, Scary, Ordinary: What Is an Adjective?* Carolrhoda, 2000. / Cleary, Brian P. *I and You and Don't Forget Who: What Is a Pronoun?* Carolrhoda, 2004. (And others in the Words Are Categorical series.) / Heller, Ruth. *Behind the Mask: A Book About Prepositions.* Grosset, 1995. / Heller, Ruth. *A Cache of Jewels and Other Collective Nouns.* Grosset, 1989. / Heller, Ruth. *Fantastic! Wow! and Unreal! A Book About Interjections and Conjunctions.* Grosset, 1998. / Heller, Ruth. *Fine Lines.* Richard C. Owen, 1996. / Heller, Ruth. *Kites Sail High: A Book About Verbs.* Grosset, 1988. / Heller, Ruth. *Many Luscious Lollipops: A Book About*

Adjectives. Grosset, 1989. / Heller, Ruth. *Merry-Go-Round: A Book About Nouns.* Grosset, 1990. / Heller, Ruth. *Up, Up and Away: A Book About Adverbs.* Grosset, 1991.

SUBJECTS: ENGLISH LANGUAGE—GRAMMAR. ENGLISH LANGUAGE—PRONOUNS. STORIES IN RHYME.

1348 **Helmer, Marilyn.** *Critter Riddles.* **Illus. by Eric Parker. Kids Can, 2003. 1-55337-445-2. 32pp. Gr. K–3**

Thirty perky animal riddles, one per page, depend on spunky wordplay that children can also read independently and then "get" the funny parts.

GERM: After you read these puzzles aloud, have your students read them aloud again and see how many answers they can recall. Ask them to try at least one riddle on the folks at home and report their reactions.

RELATED TITLES: Burns, Diane L. *Animal Antics: The Beast Jokes Ever!* Lerner, 2003. (And others in the Make Me Laugh series.) / Cole, Joanna, and Stephanie Calmenson. *Why Did the Chicken Cross the Road? And Other Riddles Old and New.* Morrow, 1994. / Hall, Katy, and Lisa Eisenberg. *Buggy Riddles.* Dial, 1986. / Hall, Katy, and Lisa Eisenberg. *Snakey Riddles.* Dial, 1990. / Helmer, Marilyn. *Critter Riddles.* Kids Can, 2003. / Levine, Caroline. *Riddles to Tell Your Cat.* Albert Whitman, 1992. / Terban, Marvin. *Funny You Should Ask: How to Make Up Jokes and Riddles with Wordplay.* Clarion, 1992.

SUBJECTS: ANIMALS. RIDDLES.

1349 **Hepworth, Cathi.** *Bug Off! A Swarm of Insect Words.* **Illus. by the author. Putnam, 1998. 0-399-22640-0. 32pp. Gr. 2–6**

Each page of this witty vocabulary-building word book features one word—such as "frantic," "Beethoven," and "slice"—that faces a large, winning, insect-based portrait showing the meaning of the word in context. The personable insects represented are bees, moths, gnats, mites, ticks, lice, roaches, and ants.

GERM: Try covering up each of the 24 words and have children guess the word from examining the illustration. Get out your dictionaries and your students will go buggy coming up with new words to draw for the rest of the group to identify and define. The author's companion book, *Antics,* is an alphabet book of "ant" words.

RELATED TITLES: Agee, Jon. *Go Hang a Salami! I'm a Lasagna Hog! And Other Palindromes.* Farrar, 1992. / Becker, Bonny. *An Ant's Day Off.* Simon & Schuster, 2003. / Florian, Douglas. *Insectlopedia: Poems and Paintings.* Harcourt, 1998. / Hall, Katy, and Lisa Eisenberg. *Buggy Riddles.* Dial, 1986. / Hepworth, Cathi. *Antics! An Alphabetical Anthology.* Putnam, 1992. / Levitt, Paul M., Douglas A. Burger, and Elissa S. Guralnick. *The Weighty Word Book.* Court Wayne, 2000. / Most, Bernard. *Can You Find It?* Harcourt, 1993. / Most, Bernard. *Hippopotamus Hunt.* Harcourt, 1994. / Oppenheim, Joanne. *Have You Seen Bugs?* Scholastic, 1998. / Steig, William. *CDB.* Simon & Schuster, 2000. / Steig, William. *CDC.* Simon & Schuster, 2003. / Walton, Rick. *Once There Was a Bull . . . (Frog).* Gibbs-Smith, 1995. / Wilbur, Richard. *The Pig in the Spigot.* Harcourt, 2000.

SUBJECTS: INSECTS. PICTURE BOOKS FOR ALL AGES. VOCABULARY. WORD GAMES.

1350 **Hirsch, Robin.** *FEG: Ridiculous Poems for Intelligent Children.* **Illus. by Ha. Little, Brown, 2002. 0-316-36344-8. 48pp. Gr. 5–8**

Robin Hirsch and his two sons, inveterate punsters, wrote down their silly wordplay, developing it into two dozen nimble poems, employing palindromes, homonyms, spoonerisms, and many other clever games and puzzles for tenacious readers to unscramble.

GERM: After reading each poem aloud, give a copy to a group of readers and let them see if they can figure out the meaning or tricks in each one. In the introduction, Hirsch advises readers to act like detectives, armed with a dictionary, thesaurus, book of quotations, and even a dictionary of slang, to figure out the hook of each poem. There are extensive footnotes, though they give hints and not solutions. There is no answer key. Some poems may be too hard to decipher, but the challenge—say, a poem a day—should prove delectable for astute readers.

RELATED TITLES: Agee, Jon. *Elvis Lives! And Other Anagrams.* Farrar, 2004. / Agee, Jon. *Go Hang a Salami! I'm a Lasagna Hog! And Other Palindromes.* Farrar, 1992. / Amato, Mary. *The Word Eater.* Holiday House, 2000. / Levitt, Paul M., Douglas A. Burger, and Elissa S. Guralnick. *The Weighty Word Book.* Court Wayne, 2000. / Rosen, Michael, comp. *Walking the Bridge of Your Nose.* Kingfisher, 1995. / Silverstein, Shel. *Runny Babbit: A Billy Sook.* HarperCollins, 2005. / Steig, William. *CDB.* Simon & Schuster, 2000. / Steig, William. *CDC.* Simon & Schuster, 2003. / Viorst, Judith. *The Alphabet from Z to A: With Much Confusion on the Way.* Atheneum, 1994. / Wilbur, Richard. *The Disappearing Alphabet.* Harcourt, 1998. / Wilbur, Richard. *The Pig in the Spigot.* Harcourt, 2000.

SUBJECTS: ENGLISH LANGUAGE—POETRY. POETRY—SINGLE AUTHOR. PUNS AND PUNNING. VOCABULARY—POETRY. WORD GAMES.

1351   Hoberman, Mary Ann. *The Llama Who Had No Pajama: 100 Favorite Poems*. Illus. by Betty Fraser. Harcourt, 1998. 0-15-200111-5. 68pp. Gr. PreK–3

Astute wordplay and observations about childhood, animals, the natural world, and families, plus delicate, attractive watercolors mark this enjoyable compilation by a major children's poet.

GERM: Read some aloud, use some for Poetry Reader's Theater in groups, memorize some, and reillustrate some.

RELATED TITLES: Hoberman, Mary Ann. *Fathers, Mothers, Sisters, Brothers: A Collection of Family Poems*. Little, Brown, 1991. / Hoberman, Mary Ann. *One of Each*. Little, Brown, 1997. / Hoberman, Mary Ann. *The Seven Silly Eaters*. Harcourt, 1997. / Hoberman, Mary Ann. *You Read to Me, I'll Read to You: Very Short Fairy Tales to Read Together*. Little, Brown, 2004. / Hoberman, Mary Ann. *You Read to Me, I'll Read to You: Very Short Mother Goose Tales to Read Together*. Little, Brown, 2005. / Hoberman, Mary Ann. *You Read to Me, I'll Read to You: Very Short Stories to Read Together*. Little, Brown, 2001.

SUBJECTS: POETRY—SINGLE AUTHOR. READER'S THEATER—POETRY.

1352   Hoberman, Mary Ann. *You Read to Me, I'll Read to You: Very Short Fairy Tales to Read Together*. Illus. by Michael Emberley. Little, Brown, 2004. 0-316-14611-0. 32pp. Gr. K–3

The sub-subtitle reads, "In which wolves are tamed, trolls are transformed, and peas are triumphant." Eight well-known fairy tales have been adapted into witty, easy-to-read, rhyming poems for two voices, presented with a series of endearing watercolor and pastel illustrations that run down each page, accompanying each stanza.

GERM: Duplicate each story and hand out the scripts to actors who can then bring it to life, Reader's Theater style. Companion books using the same *You Read to Me, I'll Read to You* format include *Very Short Mother Goose Tales to Read Together* and *Very Short Stories to Read Together*.

RELATED TITLES: Bloom, Becky. *Wolf!* Orchard, 1999. / Ciardi, John. *You Read to Me, I'll Read to You*. HarperCollins, 1972. / Daly, Niki. *Once Upon a Time*. Farrar, 2002. / Ernst, Lisa Campbell. *Stella Louella's Runaway Book*. Simon & Schuster, 1998. / Hoberman, Mary Ann. *You Read to Me, I'll Read to You: Very Short Mother Goose Tales to Read Together*. Little, Brown, 2005. / Hoberman, Mary Ann. *You Read to Me, I'll Read to You: Very Short Stories to Read Together*. Little, Brown, 2001. / Hopkins, Lee Bennett. *Climb into My Lap: First Poems to Read Together*. Simon & Schuster, 1998. / Hopkins, Lee Bennett. *Good Books, Good Times!* HarperCollins, 1990. / Hopkins, Lee Bennett. *Good Rhymes, Good Times*. HarperCollins, 1995. / Sierra, Judy. *Wild About Books*. Knopf, 2004. / Williams, Suzanne. *Library Lil*. Dial, 1997.

SUBJECTS: BOOKS AND READING—POETRY. FAIRY TALES. FOLKLORE—POETRY. POETRY— SINGLE AUTHOR. READER'S THEATER—POETRY.

1353   Hoberman, Mary Ann. *You Read to Me, I'll Read to You: Very Short Stories to Read Together*. Illus. by Michael Emberley. Little, Brown, 2001. 0-316-36350-2. Unp. Gr. K–2

Fourteen short and utterly enchanting rhymed poem stories, with friendly pen-and-watercolor illustrations, celebrate reading in easy-to-read dialogues for two voices. Each of the two-page, two-person poems (about cats and puppies, bears and mice, snakes, telephones, snowmen, birthdays, and friendships) ends the same way—with the characters hunkering down with a good book, saying the title refrain, "You read to me, I'll read to you."

GERM: Poet Hoberman describes her poems as being "like a little play for two voices," which your children can read with each other or with a significant grownup. Pair your children as Book Buddies, or have them work in quartets, each group practicing a poem and then presenting it to the others; or team up a first- or second-grade group with older children, grades 3–6, to perform the poems aloud. Hoberman's companion books cover fairy tales and nursery rhymes.

RELATED TITLES: Bloom, Becky. *Wolf!* Orchard, 1999. / Ciardi, John. *You Read to Me, I'll Read to You*. HarperCollins, 1972. / Hoberman, Mary Ann. *You Read to Me, I'll Read to You: Very Short Fairy Tales to Read Together*. Little, Brown, 2004. / Hoberman, Mary Ann. *You Read to Me, I'll Read to You: Very Short Mother Goose Tales to Read Together*. Little, Brown, 2005. / Hopkins, Lee Bennett, comp. *Climb into My Lap: First Poems to Read Together*. Simon & Schuster, 1998. / Hopkins, Lee Bennett, comp. *Good Books, Good Times!* HarperCollins, 1990. / Hopkins, Lee Bennett. *Good Rhymes, Good Times*. HarperCollins, 1995. / McGovern, Ann. *Drop Everything, It's D.E.A.R. Time!* Scholastic, 1993. / McPhail, David. *Fix-It*. Dutton, 1984. / Paterson, Katherine. *Marvin One Too Many*. HarperCollins, 2001. / Sierra, Judy. *Wild About Books*. Knopf, 2004.

SUBJECTS: BOOKS AND READING—POETRY. POETRY—SINGLE AUTHOR. READER'S THEATER—POETRY.

1354 **Hopkins, Lee Bennett.** *Been to Yesterdays: Poems of a Life.* **Illus. by Charlene Rendeiro. Boyds Mills, 1995. 1-56397-467-3. 64pp. Gr. 4–8**

Lee Bennett Hopkins, revered for his many anthologies of children's poetry, stuns us with 28 poignant, wistful, autobiographical poems about the terrible years of his childhood when his father left home and his adored Grandma died. And yet, there's such hope and resilience there, especially on the day he announces to his class what he wants to be when he grows up—a writer—and falls "madly in love" with his teacher, Miss Ethel K. Tway, who proclaims, "Becoming a writer is a fine life-choice."

GERM: Some of the poems are so spare and yet so devastating, with an emotional resonance that lays bare tough issues: divorce, prejudice, death, loss. Talk about how Hopkins packs so many feelings and memories into so small a space. Cynthia Rylant's *Waiting to Waltz* is another heartfelt autobiography, told in free-verse poetry. Write your own autobiographical poems about defining moments in your lives.

RELATED TITLES: dePaola, Tomie. *26 Fairmount Avenue.* Putnam, 1999. / Hopkins, Lee Bennett. *Good Rhymes, Good Times.* HarperCollins, 1995. / Lomas Garza, Carmen. *In My Family/En Mi Familia.* Children's Book Press, 1996. / Rylant, Cynthia. *Waiting to Waltz: A Childhood.* Bradbury, 1984.

SUBJECTS: AUTHORS—BIOGRAPHY. AUTOBIOGRAPHY. BIOGRAPHY. DIVORCE. HOPKINS, LEE BENNETT. POETRY—SINGLE AUTHOR. POETS.

1355 **Hopkins, Lee Bennett.** *Good Rhymes, Good Times.* **Illus. by Frané Lessac. HarperCollins, 1995. 0-06-023500-4. Unp. Gr. PreK–3**

Prolific as an anthologist of other poets' work, Hopkins here offers a melange of 21 of his own succinct observational rhyming poems about friends, seasons, pets, cities, books, and bedtime, all illustrated with affable, busy, colorful paintings.

GERM: Ask your listeners to categorize the subjects of the poems in the book, looking for subjects they would like to write about and illustrate from their own experiences.

RELATED TITLES: Adoff, Arnold. *Street Music: City Poems.* HarperCollins, 1995. / Ciardi, John. *You Read to Me, I'll Read to You.* HarperCollins, 1972. / Esbensen, Barbara Juster. *Who Shrank My Grandmother's House? Poems of Discovery.* HarperCollins, 1992. / Grimes, Nikki. *C Is for City.* Lothrop, 1995. / Hopkins, Lee Bennett, comp. *April Bubbles Chocolate: An ABC of Poetry.* Simon & Schuster, 1994. / Hopkins, Lee Bennett, comp. *Good Books, Good Times!* HarperCollins, 1990. / Janeczko, Paul B., comp. *Dirty Laundry Pile: Poems in Different Voices.* HarperCollins, 2001. / Johnson, Stephen T. *Alphabet City.* Viking, 1995. / Rotner, Shelley, and Ken Kreisler. *Citybook.* Orchard, 1994. / Van Laan, Nancy. *People, People, Everywhere!* Knopf, 1992. / Yolen, Jane, comp. *Sky Scrape/City Scape: Poems of City Life.* Boyds Mills, 1996.

SUBJECTS: CITIES AND TOWNS—POETRY. POETRY—SINGLE AUTHOR.

1356 **Hopkins, Lee Bennett, comp.** *Oh, No! Where Are My Pants? And Other Disasters: Poems.* **Illus. by Wolf Erlbruch. HarperCollins, 2005. 0-688-17860-X. 32pp. Gr. 1–4**

Fourteen brief, often funny, first-person poems by a range of poets tune in to life moments of kids who are in the throes of strong emotions, including embarrassment, stage fright, homesickness, dismay, fear, and grief.

GERM: Wry full-page illustrations capture each narrator's feelings with such clarity that listeners can predict the tone of the poem before hearing it read aloud. Compose new emotions poems to illuminate telling moments in your lives. Pull together other books of emotions, including *Yesterday I Had the Blues* by Jeron Ashford Frame and *How Are You Peeling? Foods with Moods* by Saxton Freymann and Joost Elffers, with its uncanny faces on the fruits and vegetables.

RELATED TITLES: Aliki. *Feelings.* Greenwillow, 1984. / Curtis, Jamie Lee. *It's Hard to Be Five: Learning How to Work My Control Panel.* HarperCollins, 2004. / Curtis, Jamie Lee. *Today I Feel Silly and Other Moods That Make My Day.* HarperCollins, 1998. / Feiffer, Jules. *I'm Not Bobby!* Hyperion, 2001. / Frame, Jeron Ashford. *Yesterday I Had the Blues.* Tricycle, 2003. / Freymann, Saxton, and Joost Elffers. *How Are You Peeling? Foods with Moods.* Scholastic, 1999. / Harper, Jessica. *Lizzy's Ups and Downs: Not an Ordinary School Day.* HarperCollins, 2004. / Hausman, Bonnie. *A to Z: Do You Ever Feel Like Me?* Dutton, 1999. / Henkes, Kevin. *Lilly's Purple Plastic Purse.* Greenwillow, 1996. / Steig, William. *Pete's a Pizza.* HarperCollins, 1998. / Vail, Rachel. *Sometimes I'm Bombaloo.* Scholastic, 2002.

SUBJECTS: EMOTIONS—POETRY. HUMOROUS POETRY.

1357 **Hopkins, Lee Bennett, comp.** *Spectacular Science: A Book of Poems.* **Illus. by Virginia Halstead. Simon & Schuster, 1999. 0-689-81283-3. 40pp. Gr. 2–6**

In this delectable book, 15 science-themed poems ponder the wonders of such things as seeds, the microscope, magnets, dinosaur bones, rocks, and snowflakes.

GERM: What is science? Ask your scientists to brainstorm and write an answer to that question, and then read aloud the first poem, by Rebecca Kai Dotlich, which asks and answers that very question. Each poem will tuck itself nicely into a corner of your science curriculum, awaiting your discovery. David McCord's "Snowflakes" will lead you to *Snowflake Bentley* by Jacqueline Briggs Martin or *A Drop of Water* by Walter Wick. Pairs of researchers can select an area of science that intrigues them, read a related book or two to glean interesting facts, and write a new, information-based, observational poem. Other science-based poetry books include *Where Fish Go in Winter and Other Great Mysteries* by Amy Goldman Kos, *Science Verse* by Jon Scieszka, and *Brain Juice: Science, Fresh Squeezed* by Carol Diggory Shields.

RELATED TITLES: Graham, Joan Bransfield. *Flicker Flash.* Houghton Mifflin, 1999. / Graham, Joan Bransfield. *Splish Splash.* Ticknor & Fields, 1994. / Hopkins, Lee Bennett. *Marvelous Math: A Book of Poems.* Simon & Schuster, 1997. / Kos, Amy Goldman. *Where Fish Go in Winter and Other Great Mysteries.* Dial, 2002. / Lewis, J. Patrick. *Earth Verses and Water Rhymes.* Atheneum, 1991. / Lewis, J. Patrick. *Scien-trickery: Riddles in Science.* Harcourt, 2004. / Martin, Jacqueline Briggs. *Snowflake Bentley.* Houghton Mifflin, 1998. / Moss, Jeff. *Bone Poems.* Workman, 1997. / Peters, Lisa Westberg. *Earthshake: Poems from the Ground Up.* Greenwillow, 2003. / Scieszka, Jon. *Science Verse.* Viking, 2004. / Shields, Carol Diggory. *Brain Juice: Science, Fresh Squeezed!* Handprint, 2003.

SUBJECTS: SCIENCE—POETRY.

1358 **Igus, Toyomi, comp.** *I See the Rhythm.* **Illus. by Michele Wood. Children's Book Press, 1998. 0-89239-151-0. 32pp. Gr. 4–8**

Trace the roots of African American music in a poetic exploration of slave songs, blues, ragtime, jazz, gospel, soul, rock 'n' roll, funk, and hip hop.

GERM: You've got to assume a musically cool persona to do justice to this read-aloud, but you can do it! In addition to each fabulously colorful and detailed painting, there's a poem describing the artists and style of each type of music, plus, on the sides, a timeline with captions and dates of important musical milestones. If your kids understand the Chris Raschka jazz books—*Charlie Parker Played Be Bop* and *Mysterious Thelonious*—they'll dig this, too.

RELATED TITLES: Gray, Libba Moore. *Little Lil and the Swing-Singing Sax.* Simon & Schuster, 1996. / Pinkney, Andrea Davis. *Duke Ellington: The Piano Prince and His Orchestra.* Hyperion, 1998. / Pinkney, Andrea Davis. *Ella Fitzgerald: The Tale of a Vocal Virtuosa.* Hyperion, 2002. / Raschka, Chris. *Charlie Parker Played Be Bop.* Orchard, 1992. / Raschka, Chris. *Mysterious Thelonius.* Orchard, 1998.

SUBJECTS: AFRICAN AMERICANS—POETRY. MULTICULTURAL BOOKS—POETRY. MUSIC. POETRY—SINGLE AUTHOR.

1359 **Janeczko, Paul B., comp.** *Dirty Laundry Pile: Poems in Different Voices.* **Illus. by Melissa Sweet. HarperCollins, 2001. 0-688-16251-7. Unp. Gr. K–5**

Explore personification and point of view with 27 brief, perceptive poems about such objects as a kite, a tree, and a vacuum cleaner, narrated by the objects themselves.

GERM: Janeczko says, in encouraging readers to write their own poems, "In these persona or mask poems, as they are called, the poets let their imaginations fly and feel what it might be like to be a mosquito, a crayon, a kite, a turtle."

RELATED TITLES: Esbensen, Barbara Juster. *Who Shrank My Grandmother's House? Poems of Discovery.* HarperCollins, 1992. / George, Kristine O'Connell. *Old Elm Speaks: Tree Poems.* Clarion, 1998. / Hopkins, Lee Bennett, comp. *Click, Rumble, Roar: Poems About Machines.* Crowell, 1987. / Janeczko, Paul B., comp. *A Kick in the Head: An Everyday Guide to Poetic Forms.* Candlewick, 2005. / Singer, Marilyn. *Turtle in July.* Macmillan, 1989. / Stevenson, James. *Candy Corn.* Greenwillow, 1999. / Stevenson, James. *Cornflakes.* Greenwillow, 2000. / Stevenson, James. *Just Around the Corner.* Greenwillow, 2001. / Stevenson, James. *Popcorn.* Greenwillow, 1998. / Stevenson, James. *Sweet Corn.* Greenwillow, 1997. / Worth, Valerie. *All the Small Poems and Fourteen More.* Farrar, 1994. / Worth, Valerie. *Peacock and Other Poems.* Farrar, 2002.

SUBJECTS: PERSONIFICATION—POETRY. POETRY—ANTHOLOGIES. POINT OF VIEW—POETRY.

1360 Janeczko, Paul B., comp. *A Kick in the Head: An Everyday Guide to Poetic Forms.* **Illus. by Chris Raschka. Candlewick, 2005. 0-7636-0662-6. 61pp. Gr. 5–8**

In poems that exemplify 29 poetic forms, Janeczko pulls together most of his well-chosen examples from seasoned poets for children—Joan Bransfield Graham, Kristine O'Connell George, and J. Patrick Lewis, to name a few. Exploding on each page are Raschka's hip, colorful blasts of watercolor, ink, and torn-paper illustrations that pull you, elated, into each poem.

GERM: In his introduction, Janeczko advises first reading a poem and then reading the explanatory note in small print at the bottom of the page. On pages 56–59 are fuller, personalized definitions of each form, including couplet, tanka, roundel, sonnet, epitaph, and elegy. You won't run out of good ideas for poetry writing sessions; find more examples in Brian P. Cleary's *Rainbow Soup,* Avis Harley's *Fly with Poetry,* and Michael Driscoll's *A Child's Introduction to Poetry.* Janeczko and Raschka's companion book, *A Poke in the I,* has a similar mien, but focuses particularly on concrete, or shape, poems. Two exquisite poem-filled novels that are natural companions for these books are *Love That Dog* by Sharon Creech and *Locomotion* by Jacqueline Woodson.

RELATED TITLES: Cleary, Brian P. *Rainbow Soup: Adventures in Poetry.* Carolrhoda, 2004. / Creech, Sharon. *Love That Dog.* HarperCollins, 2001. / Harley, Avis. *Fly with Poetry: An ABC of Poetry.* Boyds Mills, 2000. / Harley, Avis. *Leap into Poetry: More ABCs of Poetry.* Boyds Mills, 2001. / Janeczko, Paul B. *How to Write Poetry.* Scholastic, 1999. / Janeczko, Paul B., comp. *The Place My Words Are Looking For.* Simon & Schuster, 1990. / Janeczko, Paul B., comp. *Poetry from A to Z: A Guide for Young Writers.* Simon & Schuster, 1994. / Janeczko, Paul B., comp. *A Poke in the I: A Collection of Concrete Poems.* Candlewick, 2001. / Janeczko, Paul B., comp. *Seeing the Blue Between: Advice and Inspiration for Young Poets.* Candlewick, 2002. / Kennedy, X. J., comp. *Knock at a Star: A Child's Introduction to Poetry.* Little, Brown, 1982. / Livingston, Myra Cohn, comp. *Poem-Making: Ways to Begin Writing Poetry.* HarperCollins, 1991. / Rocklin, Joanne. *For Your Eyes Only!* Scholastic, 1997. / Woodson, Jacqueline. *Locomotion.* Putnam, 2003.

SUBJECTS: POETRY. POETRY—ANTHOLOGIES.

1361 Janeczko, Paul B., comp. *A Poke in the I: A Collection of Concrete Poems.* **Illus. by Chris Raschka. Candlewick, 2001. 0-7636-0661-8. 36pp. Gr. 3–8**

Anthologist and poet Paul Janeczko has compiled a very cool set of 30 concrete (or shape) poems, with a wild and jazzy collection of collage illustrations by Chris Raschka, done in watercolor, ink, and torn paper. Some poems are only one word, still considered poems by Janeczko because of the "unusual way the type is placed on the page." They're challenging to figure out sometimes, which is why your kids will love this book.

GERM: You betcha budding poets will be itching to write and illustrate their own concrete poems or bring a word or phrase to life with illustrative flair.

RELATED TITLES: Burg, Brad. *Outside the Lines: Poetry at Play.* Putnam, 2002. / Graham, Joan Bransfield. *Flicker Flash.* Houghton Mifflin, 1999. / Graham, Joan Bransfield. *Splish Splash.* Ticknor & Fields, 1994. / Grandits, John. *Technically, It's Not My Fault: Concrete Poems.* Clarion, 2004. / Janeczko, Paul B., comp. *A Kick in the Head: An Everyday Guide to Poetic Forms.* Candlewick, 2005. / Lewis, J. Patrick. *Doodle Dandies: Poems that Take Shape.* Atheneum, 1998. / Roemer, Heidi B. *Come to My Party and Other Shape Poems.* Henry Holt, 2004. / Stevenson, James. *Popcorn.* Greenwillow, 1998. (And others in the Corn series.)

SUBJECTS: CONCRETE POETRY. POETRY—ANTHOLOGIES.

1362 Janeczko, Paul B., comp. *Seeing the Blue Between: Advice and Inspiration for Young Poets.* **Candlewick, 2002. 0-7636-0881-5. 132pp. Gr. 4–8**

Janeczko, who counsels young writers to "listen to the advice of poets who have spent years practicing their craft," has assembled essays on writing poetry and a sampling of one or two representative or instructive poems from each of 32 well-known poets.

GERM: Photocopy pages of the poets' most cogent advice, along with their poems, and assign one poet to each pair or trio of readers. Groups can read their poet's advice, look up additional poems and biographical information, and present their findings to the group.

RELATED TITLES: Cleary, Brian P. *Rainbow Soup: Adventures in Poetry.* Carolrhoda, 2004. / Creech, Sharon. *Love That Dog.* HarperCollins, 2001. / Harley, Avis. *Fly with Poetry: An ABC of Poetry.* Boyds Mills, 2000. / Harley, Avis. *Leap into Poetry: More ABCs of Poetry.* Boyds Mills, 2001. / Janeczko, Paul B. *How to Write Poetry.* Scholastic, 1999. / Janeczko, Paul B., sel. *A Kick in the Head: An Everyday Guide to Poetic Forms.* Candlewick, 2005. / Janeczko, Paul B. *The Place My Words Are Looking For.* Simon & Schuster, 1990. / Janeczko, Paul B. *Poetry from A to Z: A Guide for Young Writers.* Simon & Schuster, 1994. / Kennedy, X. J., comp. *Knock at a Star: A Child's Introduction to Poetry.* Little, Brown, 1982. / Larrick, Nancy. *Let's Do a Poem!* Delacorte, 1991. / Livingston, Myra Cohn. *Poem-Making: Ways to Begin Writing Poetry.* HarperCollins, 1991. / Rocklin, Joanne. *For Your Eyes Only!* Scholastic, 1997. / Woodson, Jacqueline. *Locomotion.* Putnam, 2003.

SUBJECTS: AUTHORSHIP. CREATIVE WRITING. POETRY. POETS.

1363 **Johnston, Tony.** *It's About Dogs.* **Illus. by Ted Rand. Harcourt, 2000. 0-15-202022-5. 48pp. Gr. 2–5**

In 43 admiring poems, Johnston celebrates puppies, guide dogs, junkyard dogs, old dogs, and even Henry VIII's dogs. She even has a tribute to Toto, Dorothy's dog in *The Wizard of Oz,* and a heartbreaker about a corgi, "Mr. Lincoln's Doctor's Dog." Ted Rand's many huge paintings capture the essence of dog.

GERM: Ask each child to consider the attributes of a favorite pet and compose a poem in tribute, accompanied by a realistic illustration. Maya Gottfried's poems in *Good Dog* are from the points of view of 16 different breeds.

RELATED TITLES: Bartoletti, Susan Campbell. *Nobody's Diggier Than a Dog.* Hyperion, 2004. / Florian, Doug. *Bow Wow Meow Meow.* Harcourt, 2003. / George, Kristine O'Connell. *Little Dog Poems.* Clarion, 1999. / Gottfried, Maya. *Good Dog.* Knopf, 2005. / Hall, Donald. *I Am the Dog, I Am the Cat.* Dial, 1994. / Hausman, Gerald, and Loretta Hausman. *Dogs of Myth: Tales from Around the World.* Simon & Schuster, 1999. / Kirk, Daniel. *Dogs Rule!* Hyperion, 2003. / Miller, Sara Swan. Three Stories You Can Read to Your Dog series. Houghton. / Simon, Seymour. *Dogs.* HarperCollins, 2003. / Singer, Marilyn. *It's Hard to Read a Map with a Beagle on Your Lap.* Henry Holt, 1993. / Sklansky, Amy E. *From the Doghouse: Poems to Chew On.* Henry Holt, 2002. / Yolen, Jane. *Raining Cats and Dogs.* Harcourt, 1993.

SUBJECTS: DOGS—POETRY. POETRY—SINGLE AUTHOR.

1364 **Katz, Alan.** *I'm Still Here in the Bathtub: Brand New Silly Dilly Songs.* **Illus. by David Catrow. Simon & Schuster, 2003. 0-689-84551-0. Unp. Gr. PreK–3**

Here is a collection of 14 seriously silly songs, each one a parody of a well-known song, that is perfect for Singers Theater; just think how everyone's fluency will advance when you hand out the words and sing up a storm.

GERM: Continue warbling with the companion book of song parodies, *Take Me Out of the Bathtub,* and the Christmas version, *Where Did They Hide My Presents?* Make a tape of these songs with your group, and then set it up at a listening/reading/singing station where individuals or small groups can sing along while following the words. Write new songs together.

RELATED TITLES: Baltuck, Naomi. *Crazy Gibberish and Other Story Hour Stretches.* Linnet, 1993. / Booth, David, comp. *Doctor Knickerbocker and Other Rhymes.* Ticknor & Fields, 1993. / Freeman, Judy. *Hi Ho Librario! Songs, Chants, and Stories to Keep Kids Humming.* Rock Hill, 1997. / Katz, Alan. *Take Me Out of the Bathtub and Other Silly Dilly Songs.* McElderry, 2001. / Katz, Alan. *Where Did They Hide My Presents? Silly Dilly Christmas Songs.* McElderry, 2005. / Koontz, Dean. *Paper Doorway: Funny Verse and Nothing Worse.* HarperCollins, 2001. / Lee, Dennis. *Dinosaur Dinner (With a Slice of Alligator Pie).* Knopf, 1997. / Prelutsky, Jack, comp. *For Laughing Out Loud: Poems to Tickle Your Funnybone.* Knopf, 1991. / Prelutsky, Jack. *The Frogs Wore Red Suspenders.* Greenwillow, 2002. / Schwartz, Alvin, comp. *And the Green Grass Grew All Around.* HarperCollins, 1992. / Sierra, Judy. *Monster Goose.* Harcourt, 2001. / Tripp, Wallace, comp. *A Great Big Ugly Man Came Up and Tied His Horse to Me.* Little, Brown, 1974.

SUBJECTS: HUMOROUS SONGS. PARODIES. POETRY—SINGLE AUTHOR. SONGS.

1365 **Kirk, Daniel.** *Dogs Rule!* **Illus. by the author. Hyperion, 2003. 0-7868-1949-9. Unp. Gr. PreK–6**

Dog lovers will have a blast with this large, personable volume of 22 dog-narrated poems, accompanied by soulful paintings of the notable pooches and a jubilant CD of poems set to music and sung by Kirk and friends. Every aspect of dogdom is covered here; titles include "In My Doghouse," "Pet Me," "Lapdog," "Chowhound," "Chasing My Tail," and my personal favorite, "Dog-Tired."

GERM: Singers Theater is a most entertaining and fabulous way to get kids reading and singing with fluency, expression, and joy. Make copies of some of the poems so children can sing along with the glorious CD of the poems set to toe-tapping music. Then they can write their own pet tribute songs or poems and draw or paint large portraits. And for you grownup dog-lovers, I hope you've seen the hilarious, unforgettable dog movie, *Best in Show.* If not, be sure to rent it— you'll laugh yourself silly.

RELATED TITLES: Florian, Douglas. *Bow Wow Meow Meow.* Harcourt, 2003. / George, Kristine O'Connell. *Little Dog Poems.* Clarion, 1999. / Gottfried, Maya. *Good Dog.* Knopf, 2005. / Hall, Donald. *I Am the Dog, I Am the Cat.* Dial, 1994. / Hausman, Gerald, and Loretta Hausman. *Dogs of Myth: Tales from Around the World.*

Simon & Schuster, 1999. / Johnston, Tony. *It's About Dogs*. Harcourt, 2000. / Kalman, Maira. *What Pete Ate from A–Z*. Putnam, 2001. / Kirk, Daniel. *Go!* Hyperion, 2001. / Laden, Nina. *Bad Dog*. Walker, 2000. / Laden, Nina. *The Night I Followed the Dog*. Chronicle, 1994. / Miller, Sara Swan. *Three Stories You Can Read to Your Dog*. Houghton, 1995. / Singer, Marilyn. *It's Hard to Read a Map with a Beagle on Your Lap*. Henry Holt, 1993. / Sklansky, Amy E. *From the Doghouse: Poems to Chew On*. Henry Holt, 2002. / Teague, Mark. *Dear Mrs. LaRue: Letters from Obedience School*. Scholastic, 2002. / Yolen, Jane. *Raining Cats and Dogs*. Harcourt, 1993.

SUBJECTS: DOGS—POETRY. POETRY—SINGLE AUTHOR. SONGS.

1366   Kirk, Daniel. *Go!* Illus. by the author. Hyperion, 2001. 0-7868-0305-3. Unp. Gr. PreK–3
What a fun book of 23 poems about all means of transportation, from pogo stick to Mama's motorcycle. If reading it aloud and looking at the huge, eye-popping, mixed-media paintings aren't enough to whet your appetite, just pop in the accompanying CD and sing along.

GERM: Duplicate the songs so children can read along and sing with the terrific CD, by Kirk himself. Kirk's other fabulous poetry book set to music in an accompanying CD is *Dogs Rule!*

RELATED TITLES: Baer, Edith. *This Is the Way We Go to School*. Scholastic, 1990. / Burningham, John. *Harvey Slumfenburger's Christmas Present*. Candlewick, 1993. / Hort, Lenny. *The Seals on the Bus*. Henry Holt, 2000. / Kirk, Daniel. *Dogs Rule!* Hyperion, 2003. / McMullan, Kate. *I Stink!* HarperCollins, 2002. / Pinkwater, Daniel. *Tooth-Gnasher Superflash*. Macmillan, 1990. / Shields, Carol Diggory. *Animagicals: On the Go*. Handprint, 2001. / Walton, Rick. *Bunnies on the Go: Getting from Place to Place*. HarperCollins, 2003. / Zane, Alexander. *The Wheels on the Race Car*. Orchard, 2005. / Zelinsky, Paul O. *The Wheels on the Bus*. Dutton, 1990.

SUBJECTS: POETRY—SINGLE AUTHOR. SONGS. TRANSPORTATION. VEHICLES.

1367   Koontz, Dean. *The Paper Doorway: Funny Verse and Nothing Worse*. Illus. by Phil Parks. HarperCollins, 2001. 0-06-029488-4. 160pp. Gr. 2–6
Well known for his scary YA and adult novels, Dean Koontz here gentles down with a handsome collection of 83 whimsical, sometimes irreverent poems that celebrate childhood. You'll enjoy lots of appealing wordplay: a poem about plurals; speculations on being a potato; and a narrative poem about a girl's trip to Snowland, where all snowmen go when they melt.

GERM: Attractive black-and-white pen-and-ink and watercolor illustrations, each containing a hidden mouse for children to find, round out a read-it-again-and-again volume to introduce with your Silversteins, Prelutskys, and Viorsts. Hand out copies of poems from the book for pairs of children to practice and share aloud for a Poetry Reading.

RELATED TITLES: Florian, Douglas. *Bing Bang Boing!* Harcourt, 1994. / Florian, Douglas. *Laugh-eteria: Poems and Drawings*. Harcourt, 1999. / McNaughton, Colin. *Who's Been Sleeping in My Porridge? A Book of Wacky Poems and Pictures*. Candlewick, 1998. / Moss, Jeff. *The Butterfly Jar*. Bantam, 1989. / Prelutsky, Jack. *It's Raining Pigs and Noodles*. Greenwillow, 2000. / Prelutsky, Jack. *The New Kid on the Block*. Greenwillow, 1984. / Prelutsky, Jack. *A Pizza the Size of the Sun*. Greenwillow, 1996. / Prelutsky, Jack. *Something Big Has Been Here*. Greenwillow, 1990. / Silverstein, Shel. *Falling Up*. HarperCollins, 1996. / Silverstein, Shel. *A Light in the Attic*. HarperCollins, 1981. / Silverstein, Shel. *Where the Sidewalk Ends*. HarperCollins, 1974. / Viorst, Judith. *If I Were in Charge of the World and Other Worries*. Atheneum, 1981. / Viorst, Judith. *Sad Underwear and Other Complications: More Poems for Children and Their Parents*. Atheneum, 1995.

SUBJECTS: HUMOROUS POETRY. POETRY—SINGLE AUTHOR.

1368   Lansky, Bruce, comp. *Miles of Smiles: Kids Pick the Funniest Poems, Book #3*. Illus. by Stephen Carpenter. Meadowbrook, 1998. 0-88166-313-1. 114pp. Gr. K–6
The third in a series of collected funny-bone-friendly poems (after *Kids Pick the Funniest Poems* and *A Bad Case of the Giggles*), here are 85 family, school, food, and nonsense poems from well-loved children's poets, guaranteed to crack up your crew.

GERM: Make a class book of favorite funny poems to recite and memorize.

RELATED TITLES: Lansky, Bruce, comp. *A Bad Case of the Giggles: Kids' Favorite Funny Poems*. Meadowbrook, 1994. / Lansky, Bruce, comp. *Kids Pick the Funniest Poems: A Collection of Poems That Will Make You Laugh*. Meadowbrook, 1991. / McNaughton, Colin. *Who's Been Sleeping in My Porridge? A Book of Wacky Poems and Pictures*. Candlewick, 1998. / Moss, Jeff. *The Butterfly Jar*. Bantam, 1989. / Prelutsky, Jack, comp. *For Laughing Out Loud: Poems to Tickle Your Funnybone*. Knopf, 1991. / Prelutsky, Jack, comp. *Poems of A. Nonny Mouse*. Knopf, 1989. / Schwartz, Alvin, comp. *And the Green Grass Grew All Around: Folk Poetry from Everyone*. HarperCollins, 1992. / Silverstein, Shel. *A Light in the Attic*. HarperCollins, 1981. / Silverstein, Shel. *Where the Sidewalk Ends*. HarperCollins, 1974. / Viorst, Judith. *Sad Underwear and Other Complications: More Poems for Children and Their Parents*. Atheneum, 1995.

SUBJECTS: HUMOROUS POETRY. POETRY—ANTHOLOGIES.

1369 Lansky, Bruce, comp. *You're Invited to Bruce Lansky's Poetry Party.* **Illus. by Stephen Carpenter. Meadowbrook, 1996. 0-88166-245-3. 83pp. Gr. K–6**

Buoyed by the success of reciting his child-centric poetry to elementary school audiences, Lansky shares 59 of his own laugh-along rhyming observations on parents, siblings, pets, school, disasters, and advice.

GERM: Stage your own poetry party, just as the author instructs.

RELATED TITLES: Booth, David, comp. *Doctor Knickerbocker and Other Rhymes.* Ticknor & Fields, 1993. / Florian, Douglas. *Bing Bang Boing.* Harcourt, 1994. / Florian, Douglas. *Laugh-eteria: Poems and Drawings.* Harcourt, 1999. / Heide, Florence Parry, and Roxanne Heide Pierce. *Oh, Grow Up! Poems to Help You Survive Parents, Chores, School and Other Afflictions.* Orchard, 1996. / Lansky, Bruce, comp. *A Bad Case of the Giggles: Kids' Favorite Funny Poems.* Meadowbrook, 1994. / Lee, Dennis. *The Ice Cream Store.* Scholastic, 1992. / McNaughton, Colin. *There's an Awful Lot of Weirdos in Our Neighborhood and Other Wickedly Funny Verse.* Candlewick, 1997. / Moss, Jeff. *The Butterfly Jar.* Bantam, 1989. / Prelutsky, Jack. *It's Raining Pigs and Noodles.* Greenwillow, 2000. / Prelutsky, Jack. *The New Kid on the Block.* Greenwillow, 1984. / Silverstein, Shel. *Falling Up.* HarperCollins, 1996. / Viorst, Judith. *Sad Underwear and Other Complications: More Poems for Children and Their Parents.* Atheneum, 1995.

SUBJECTS: HUMOROUS POETRY. POETRY—ANTHOLOGIES.

1370 Lee, Dennis. *Dinosaur Dinner (With a Slice of Alligator Pie).* **Illus. by Debbie Tilley. Knopf, 1997. 0-679-87009-1. 32pp. Gr. PreK–3**

Silly, jolly, and chantable are just a few words to describe beloved Canadian poet Dennis Lee's poems, 40 of which are gathered in this delightful collection of modern day nursery rhymes.

GERM: The cast of kids and creatures (a monster and a feisty little girl square off verbally in "I Eat Kids Yum Yum!"; babies switched at birth in "Peter Ping and Patrick Pong"; and that pre-lunch treat of "Alligator Pie") will get kids excited to try choral and dramatic readings. Sing along with "Alligator Pie," recorded on Judy Freeman's *Hi Ho, Librario* CD, and write new verses about delectable morsels such as Alligator Cake and Alligator Bread.

RELATED TITLES: Booth, David, comp. *Doctor Knickerbocker and Other Rhymes.* Ticknor & Fields, 1993. / Florian, Douglas. *Bing Bang Boing!* Harcourt, 1994. / Freeman, Judy. *Hi Ho Librario! Songs, Chants, and Stories to Keep Kids Humming.* Rock Hill, 1997. / Lee, Dennis. *The Ice Cream Store.* Scholastic, 1992. / Lee, Dennis. *Jelly Belly: Original Nursery Rhymes.* Peter Bedrick, 1985. / Prelutsky, Jack, comp. *For Laughing Out Loud: Poems to Tickle Your Funnybone.* Knopf, 1991. / Prelutsky, Jack. *The Frogs Wore Red Suspenders.* Greenwillow, 2002. / Prelutsky, Jack, comp. *Poems of A. Nonny Mouse.* Knopf, 1989. / Tripp, Wallace, comp. *A Great Big Ugly Man Came Up and Tied His Horse to Me.* Little, Brown, 1974.

SUBJECTS: HUMOROUS POETRY. POETRY—SINGLE AUTHOR.

1371 Leedy, Loreen. *There's a Frog in My Throat: 440 Animal Sayings a Little Bird Told Me.* **Illus. by the author. Holiday House, 2003. 0-8234-1774-3. 48pp. Gr. 1–6**

Doing similes, metaphors, idioms, and proverbs? This charming compendium is a linguist's dream: 440 animal sayings, sorted into species of animals, from pets and farm animals to the wild, flying, creeping, and swimming kind. Each saying has an easy-to-understand explanation and is paired with a whimsical illustration. There's an index of animals, which is helpful if you want to tie in animal sayings to a particular critter.

GERM: Photocopy a handful of pages and hand them out, one per group of two, three, or four children. Working together, the children in each group can write and illustrate an animal story incorporating the sayings from that page. Students can also make lists of animal sayings they know and then write explanations and create illustrations for them. Then the students can look them up to see if they're in the book. You'll want a classroom set of these books (which are also out in paperback), perfect for teaching the parts of a book and encouraging beginning research skills using the index and table of contents.

RELATED TITLES: Arnold, Tedd. *Even More Parts.* Dial, 2004. / Arnold, Tedd. *More Parts.* Dial, 2001. / Arnold, Tedd. *Parts.* Dial, 1997. / Clement, Rod. *Just Another Ordinary Day.* HarperCollins, 1997. / Clements, Andrew. *Double Trouble in Walla Walla.* Millbrook, 1998. / Edwards, Wallace. *Monkey Business.* Kids Can, 2004. / Freymann, Saxton, and Joost Elffers. *Dog Food.* Scholastic, 2002. / Leedy, Loreen. *Look at My Book: How Kids Can Write and Illustrate Terrific Books.* Holiday House, 2004. / Pulver, Robin. *Punctuation Takes a Vacation.* Holiday House, 2003. / Shields, Carol Diggory. *Brain Juice: English, Fresh Squeezed!* Handprint, 2004. / Viorst, Judith. *The Alphabet from Z to A: With Much Confusion on the Way.* Atheneum, 1994.

SUBJECTS: ANIMALS. ENGLISH LANGUAGE—IDIOMS. ENGLISH LANGUAGE—SIMILES AND METAPHORS. ENGLISH LANGUAGE—TERMS AND PHRASES.

1372   **Lewis, J. Patrick.** *Doodle Dandies: Poems That Take Shape.* **Illus. by Lisa Desimini. Atheneum, 1998. 0-689-81075-X. 32pp. Gr. 2–6**

In this shapely collection, 19 deft, concrete (or shape) poems about animals, nature, and even sports are imaginatively illustrated with collage paintings so that each poem is incorporated into its picture.

GERM: Children can compose and illustrate new concrete poems using subjects they're passionate about. Paul B. Janeczko's *A Poke in the I* is another collection of innovative concrete poems.

RELATED TITLES: Burg, Brad. *Outside the Lines: Poetry at Play.* Putnam, 2002. / Graham, Joan Bransfield. *Splish Splash.* Ticknor & Fields, 1994. / Grandits, John. *Technically, It's Not My Fault: Concrete Poems.* Clarion, 2004. / Janeczko, Paul B. *A Poke in the I: A Collection of Concrete Poems.* Candlewick, 2001. / Lewis, J. Patrick. *Earth Verses and Water Rhymes.* Atheneum, 1991. / Lewis, J. Patrick. *A Hippopotamustn't and Other Animal Verses.* Dial, 1990. / Lewis, J. Patrick. *Two-Legged, Four-Legged, No-Legged Rhymes.* Knopf, 1991. / Roemer, Heidi B. *Come to My Party and Other Shape Poems.* Henry Holt, 2004. / Stevenson, James. *Popcorn.* Greenwillow, 1998.

SUBJECTS: CONCRETE POETRY. POETRY—SINGLE AUTHOR.

1373   **Lewis, J. Patrick.** *Please Bury Me in the Library.* **Illus. by Kyle M. Stone. Harcourt, 2005. 0-15-216387-5. 32pp. Gr. 2–5**

Sixteen poems, illustrated with slightly surreal acrylic and mixed-media paintings, fiddle around with the subjects of books, letters, reading, and, of course, a book's best home, the library. There are three book haiku, including "Late at night, reading / Frankenstein . . . and suddenly / a pain in the neck."

GERM: The first poem, "What If Books Had Different Names?" will start your readers thinking of wacky titles to go along with Lewis's collection, which includes "Furious George" and "Green Eggs and Spam." Write new haiku, book-related acrostics, and acknowledgment poems to favorite authors. *Good Books, Good Times!* by Lee Bennett Hopkins contains another good batch of love-of-reading poems for the book-obsessed.

RELATED TITLES: Allen, Susan, and Jane Lindaman. *Read Anything Good Lately?* Millbrook, 2003. / Allen, Susan, and Jane Lindaman. *Written Anything Good Lately?* Millbrook, 2006. / Child, Lauren. *Who's Afraid of the Big Bad Book?* Hyperion, 2003. / Ernst, Lisa Campbell. *Stella Louella's Runaway Book.* Simon & Schuster, 1998. / Florczak, Robert. *Yikes!!!* Scholastic, 2003. / Garland, Michael. *Miss Smith's Incredible Storybook.* Dutton, 2003. / Goldstein, Bobbye S., comp. *Inner Chimes: Poems on Poetry.* Boyds Mills, 1992. / Hopkins, Lee Bennett, comp. *Good Books, Good Times!* HarperCollins, 1990. / Huff, Barbara. *Once Inside the Library.* Little, Brown, 1990. / Polacco, Patricia. *Aunt Chip and the Great Triple Creek Dam Affair.* Philomel, 1996. / Polacco, Patricia. *Thank You, Mr. Falker.* Philomel, 1998. / Scieszka, Jon. *Summer Reading Is Killing Me!* Viking, 1998. / Sierra, Judy. *Wild About Books.* Knopf, 2004. / Stanley, Diane. *Raising Sweetness.* Putnam, 1999. / Sturges, Philemon. *She'll Be Comin' 'Round the Mountain.* Little, Brown, 2004. / Williams, Suzanne. *Library Lil.* Dial, 1997.

SUBJECTS: BOOKS AND READING—POETRY. LIBRARIES—POETRY. POETRY—SINGLE AUTHOR.

1374   **Lewis, J. Patrick.** *Scien-Trickery: Riddles in Science.* **Illus. by Frank Remkiewicz. Harcourt, 2004. 0-15-216681-5. 32pp. Gr. 2–5**

Sixteen snappy riddle poems, each with its own kid-filled watercolor illustration, challenge thinkers to identify scientific subjects, from Albert Einstein to the number zero.

GERM: Answers can be found upside down on the page, and the notes at the back of the book explain each answer more thoroughly. Read each poem several times as viewers listen for descriptive words and look for picture clues to help them figure out the scientific object the riddle depicts. Students can research an area of interest in science and create new riddles for others to guess. Do more science in rhyme with Lee Bennett Hopkins's *Spectacular Science*, Jon Scieszka's *Science Curse*, and Carol Diggory Shields's *Brain Juice: Science, Fresh Squeezed!*

RELATED TITLES: Hopkins, Lee Bennett, comp. *Spectacular Science: A Book of Poems.* Simon & Schuster, 1999. / Kos, Amy Goldman. *Where Fish Go in Winter and Other Great Mysteries.* Dial, 2002. / Lewis, J. Patrick. *Arithme-Tickle.* Harcourt, 2002. / Lewis, J. Patrick. *Earth Verses and Water Rhymes.* Atheneum, 1991. / Lewis, J. Patrick. *A Hippopotamustn't and Other Animal Verses.* Dial, 1990. / Lewis, J. Patrick. *Riddle-i-cious.* Knopf, 1996. / Lewis, J. Patrick. *Two-Legged, Four-Legged, No-Legged Rhymes.* Knopf, 1991. / Lewis, J. Patrick. *A World of Wonders.* Dial, 2002. / Peters, Lisa Westberg. *Earthshake: Poems from the Ground Up.* Greenwillow, 2003. / Scieszka, Jon. *Science Verse.* Viking, 2004. / Shields, Carol Diggory. *Brain Juice: Science, Fresh Squeezed!* Handprint, 2003.

SUBJECTS: POETRY—SINGLE AUTHOR. RIDDLES. SCIENCE—POETRY.

1375 **Lewis, J. Patrick.** *A World of Wonders.* **Illus. by Alison Jay. Dial, 2002. 0-8037-2579-5. Unp. Gr. 2–5**

Look at the world from a geographic standpoint in a delicious collection of 25 poems about explorers, the aurora borealis, the San Andreas Fault, and the five oceans. The wordplay is ingenious and always informative, as in: "Longitudinal lines rise like porcupines." Lewis recommends "traveling by poem," and readers will certainly get the wanderlust from his collection of rhyming city riddles. A crackling varnish gives a pleasing antique look to the handsome paintings that accompany each poem. As Lewis says in his final poem, "Walk Lightly," "Make the Earth your companion. / Walk lightly on it, as other creatures do."

GERM: On a large world map, chart the places visited in each poem. In his poem "Did You Know," Lewis lists several superlatives, including the longest place name, in New Zealand. Write out this 85-letter word for all to try and sound out. For other geographic superlatives, also share Steve Jenkins's informative picture book *Hottest Coldest Highest Deepest. Earth from Above for Young Readers* by Robert Burleigh is a geographic tour of the world shown through color aerial photographs.

RELATED TITLES: Burleigh, Robert. *Earth from Above for Young Readers.* Abrams, 2002. / Gerberg, Mort. *Geographunny: A Book of Global Riddles.* Clarion, 1991. / Holub, Joan. *Geogra-fleas! Riddles All over the Map.* Albert Whitman, 2004. / Hopkins, Lee Bennett, comp. *Got Geography! Poems.* Greenwillow, 2006. / Jenkins, Steve. *Hottest Coldest Highest Deepest.* Houghton Mifflin, 1998. / Maestro, Marco, and Giulio Maestro. *Riddle City, USA! A Book of Geography Riddles.* HarperCollins, 1994. / Scillian, Devin. *P Is for Passport: A World Alphabet.* Sleeping Bear, 2003.

SUBJECTS: GEOGRAPHY—POETRY. POETRY—SINGLE AUTHOR. VOYAGES AND TRAVELS—POETRY.

1376 **Lillegard, Dee.** *Hello School! A Classroom Full of Poems.* **Illus. by Don Carter. Knopf, 2001. 0-375-81020-X. Unp. Gr. PreK–2**

Thirty-eight brief, perceptive poems point out all the objects we take for granted in school—including the daily equipment and supplies you find in the classroom and on the playground.

GERM: To introduce the book, first brainstorm a list on chart paper of all the objects children see and use at school. Then take a tour of the school and the playground so you can introduce each poem at its corresponding site, including the swings, the water fountain, and the window. For children who are already reading, these poems are short and swell for choral reading. Working in groups of two to four, kids can gather up a representative prop and recite their poem as they display it. The sturdy, three-dimensional pictures made from foam board, plaster, and acrylic paints will inspire your artists to construct a 3-D collage mural of your school, with self-portraits cut from foam or cardboard. Take a school tour from another perspective with Bruce McMillan's *Mouse Views: What the Class Pet Saw* and Janet Morgan Stoeke's *Minerva Louise at School,* about a misguided chicken who thinks the school is some sort of barn.

RELATED TITLES: Baer, Edith. *This Is the Way We Go to School: A Book About Children Around the World.* Scholastic, 1990. / Calmenson, Stephanie. *The Teeny Tiny Teacher.* Scholastic, 1998. / Dakos, Kalli. *The Bug in Teacher's Coffee and Other School Poems.* HarperCollins, 1999. / Lewis, J. Patrick. *Good Mousekeeping and Other Animal Home Poems.* Atheneum, 2001. / Lillegard, Dee. *Do Not Feed the Table.* Delacorte, 1993. / Lillegard, Dee. *Wake Up House! Rooms Full of Poems.* Knopf, 2000. / McCully, Emily Arnold. *School.* HarperCollins, 1987. / McMillan, Bruce. *Mouse Views: What the Class Pet Saw.* Holiday House, 1993. / Poydar, Nancy. *First Day, Hooray!* Holiday House, 1999. / Schwartz, Amy. *Annabelle Swift, Kindergartner.* Orchard, 1988. / Sierra, Judy. *There's a Zoo in Room 22.* Harcourt, 2000. / Slate, Joseph. *Miss Bindergarten Gets Ready for Kindergarten.* Dutton, 1996. / Stoeke, Janet Morgan. *Minerva Louise at School.* Dutton, 1996.

SUBJECTS: POETRY—SINGLE AUTHOR. SCHOOLS—POETRY.

1377 **Lillegard, Dee.** *Wake Up House! Rooms Full of Poems.* **Illus. by Don Carter. Knopf, 2000. 0-679-88351-7. Unp. Gr. PreK–3**

Take a dawn-to-sunset tour of everything in the house with these 34 descriptive, rhyming poems.

GERM: As you read these aloud, pull out of a mini dollhouse the corresponding miniature items, such as a mirror, a broom, a hanger, and a night light. *Hello School! A Classroom Full of Poems* is a companion book, as is *Do Not Feed the Table,* with 30 endearing and clever short poems about the utensils, equipment, and fixtures found in the kitchen, including the toaster, frying pan, chair, refrigerator, and faucet. Children can then look carefully around and compose their own house, schoolroom, or library poems.

RELATED TITLES: Dorros, Arthur. *This Is My House.* Scholastic, 1992. / Hoberman, Mary. *A House Is a House for Me.* Viking, 1978. / Legge, David. *Bamboozled.* Scholastic, 1995. / Lillegard, Dee. *Do Not Feed the Table.* Delacorte, 1993. / Lillegard, Dee. *Hello School! A Classroom Full of Poems.* Knopf, 2001. / Robert, Francois, Jean Robert, and Jane Gittings. *Find a Face.* Chronicle, 2004. / Wood, Audrey. *The Flying Dragon Room.* Scholastic, 1996.
SUBJECTS: DWELLINGS—POETRY. HOUSES—POETRY. POETRY—SINGLE AUTHOR.

1378 **Long, Sylvia, comp.** *Sylvia Long's Mother Goose.* **Illus. by the author. Chronicle, 1999. 0-8118-2088-2. 112pp. Gr. PreK–1**
Sylvia Long's delightful detailed watercolors bring warmth to her graceful and elegant Mother Goose collection. She describes her interpretations of some of the harsher rhymes by saying, "I didn't feel justified in changing the words, but I tried to add a gentleness to the pictures."
GERM: Each of the brightly colored pen-and-ink and watercolor illustrations has a visual element—an animal, an object, or a pattern that is connected to the rhymes on the next page—which will be fun for kids to pore over and find. Give your students a leg up on language by introducing, reintroducing, and reviewing nursery rhymes. As you no doubt know, many children start school without knowing these all-important rhymes, but it's never too late to remediate. Hold a Mother Goose recital at which pairs of children recite verses they've learned.
RELATED TITLES: Cousins, Lucy, comp. *The Little Dog Laughed and Other Nursery Rhymes.* Dutton, 1990. / dePaola, Tomie, comp. *Tomie dePaola's Mother Goose.* Putnam, 1985. / Fabian, Bobbi, comp. *Twinkle, Twinkle: An Animal Lover's Mother Goose.* Dutton, 1997. / Lamont, Priscilla, comp. *Ring-a-Round-a-Rosy: Nursery Rhymes, Action Rhymes and Lullabyes.* Little, Brown, 1990. / Lobel, Arnold, comp. *The Random House Book of Mother Goose.* Random House, 1986. / Martin, David. *Five Little Piggies.* Candlewick, 1998. / Moses, Will, comp. *Will Moses' Mother Goose.* Philomel, 2003. / Opie, Iona, comp. *Here Comes Mother Goose.* Candlewick, 1999. / Opie, Iona. *My Very First Mother Goose.* Candlewick, 1996. / Opie, Iona, and Peter Opie, comps. *Tail Feathers from Mother Goose: The Opie Rhyme Book.* Little, Brown, 1988. / Stevens, Janet, and Susan Stevens Crummel. *And the Dish Ran Away with the Spoon.* Harcourt, 2001. / Sutherland, Zena, comp. *The Orchard Book of Nursery Rhymes.* Orchard, 1990.
SUBJECTS: MOTHER GOOSE. NURSERY RHYMES.

1379 **Longfellow, Henry Wadsworth.** *The Midnight Ride of Paul Revere.* **Illus. by Christopher Bing. Handprint, 2001. 1-929766-13-0. Unp. Gr. 4–12**
Never has Longfellow's classic narrative poem been brought to life in a more magnificent and memorable style than with Christopher Bing's impeccable, heart-stopping paintings. The action-filled illustrations—pen and ink and brush on scratchboard, glazed with deep blue-toned watercolors for the nighttime scenes—aptly convey the danger and drama of Paul Revere's nighttime gallop. There is much to pore over: maps of the British plan of their secret expedition to Concord and of Paul Revere's ride that helped to thwarted that plan; appended documents on the endpapers that open up to reveal British General Thomas Gage's orders to his troops; Paul Revere's deposition for the Massachusetts Provincial Congress; and two descriptive pages of miscellany about that famous night.
GERM: Perform the poem as a dramatic choral reading, assigning each page to two or more students to practice and present aloud. Such a blending of history, poetry, and art might be your read-aloud highlight of the year. Also read Bing's equally spectacular illustrated version of *Casey at the Bat* by Ernest Thayer.
RELATED TITLES: Bober, Natalie S. *Abigail Adams: Witness to a Revolution.* Atheneum, 1995. / Cheripko, Jan. *Caesar Rodney's Ride.* Boyds Mills, 2004. / Fritz, Jean. *And Then What Happened, Paul Revere?* Coward, 1998. / Giblin, James Cross. *George Washington: A Picture Book Biography.* Scholastic, 1992. / Longfellow, Henry Wadsworth. *Paul Revere's Ride.* Illus. by Ted Rand. Dutton, 1990. / Longfellow, Henry Wadsworth. *Paul Revere's Ride: The Landlord's Tale.* Illus. by Charles Santore. HarperCollins, 2003. / Murphy, Jim. *A Young Patriot: The American Revolution as Experienced by One Boy.* Clarion, 1996. / Osborne, Mary Pope. *George Washington: Leader of a New Nation.* Dial, 1991. / Thayer, Ernest Lawrence. *Casey at the Bat.* Illus. by Christopher Bing. Handprint, 2000.
SUBJECTS: MASSACHUSETTS—HISTORY. NARRATIVE POETRY. POETRY—SINGLE AUTHOR. REVERE, PAUL. STORIES IN RHYME. U.S.—HISTORY—REVOLUTION, 1775–1783—POETRY.

1380 **Maestro, Marco, and Giulio Maestro.** *Geese Find the Missing Piece: School Time Riddle Rhymes.* **Illus. by Giulio Maestro. HarperCollins, 1999. 0-06-026221-4. 48pp. Gr. K–2**
"Where do polar bears learn their ABCs? At a cool . . . school!" In 22 easy-to-read riddles depicting genial animals at school, try to guess the second half of each rhyming answer before you turn the page.

GERM: Write some new rhyming riddles (also called "hink pinks") together. Solve more animal rhyming riddles in Mike Downs's *Pig Giggles and Rabbit Rhymes* and Francis McCall and Patricia Keeler's *A Huge Hog Is a Big Pig*, which is illustrated with lots of color photographs.

RELATED TITLES: Cherry, Lynne. *Who's Sick Today?* Dutton, 1988. / Cole, Joanna, and Stephanie Calmenson. *Why Did the Chicken Cross the Road? And Other Riddles Old and New.* Morrow, 1994. / Downs, Mike. *Pig Giggles and Rabbit Rhymes: A Book of Animal Riddles.* Chronicle, 2002. / Hills, Tad. *Knock, Knock! Who's There?* Simon & Schuster, 2000. / McCall, Francis, and Patricia Keeler. *A Huge Hog Is a Big Pig: A Rhyming Word Game.* Greenwillow, 2002. / Maestro, Giulio. *Macho Nacho and Other Rhyming Riddles.* Dutton, 1994. / Maestro, Marco, and Giulio Maestro. *What Do You Hear When the Cows Sing? And Other Silly Riddles.* HarperCollins, 1996. / Schultz, Sam. *Schoolyard Snickers: Classy Jokes That Make the Grade.* Lerner, 2003.

SUBJECTS: JOKES. RIDDLES. SCHOOLS. WORD GAMES.

1381 **Maestro, Marco, and Giulio Maestro.** *What Do You Hear When the Cows Sing? And Other Silly Riddles.* **Illus. by Giulio Maestro. HarperCollins, 1996. 0-06-024949-8. 48pp. Gr. K–3**

"What do you call a train that sneezes? Ah-choo-choo train." Here are 21 more easy-to-read riddles and silly wordplay that will be sure to get young readers and listeners giggling.

GERM: As funny as these riddles are, don't forget to make sure your punsters understand or "get" them, and then take them home to share with their families. Have the children collect riddles from family and friends and make an illustrated class book of them.

RELATED TITLES: Downs, Mike. *Pig Giggles and Rabbit Rhymes: A Book of Animal Riddles.* Chronicle, 2002. / Maestro, Giulio. *Macho Nacho and Other Rhyming Riddles.* Dutton, 1994. / Maestro, Marco, and Giulio Maestro. *Geese Find the Missing Piece: School Time Riddle Rhymes.* HarperCollins, 1999.

SUBJECTS: RIDDLES. WORD GAMES.

1382 **Medina, Jane.** *The Dream on Blanca's Wall: Poems in English and Spanish.* **Illus. by Robert Casilla. Wordsong/Boyds Mills, 2004. 1-56397-740-0. 48pp. Gr. 4–6**

Sixth grader Blanca dreams of going to college and becoming a teacher, even though her own Mamá had little schooling growing up in Mexico. Life at school isn't easy for Blanca, though—none of her teachers have brown skin like hers, her brother laughs at her ambition, and her friends mock her, calling her "schoolgirl" for trying hard. Her 26 free-verse poems, written in both English and Spanish, are accompanied by expressive pencil drawings.

GERM: In the first poem, Blanca explains how she drew her dream for her second-grade teacher: ". . . of a class full of kids / and a pretty brown teacher / who looked just like me," which is still taped to her wall, yellow tape curling at the ends. Ask your dreamers to draw their ambitions and hopes to put on their own walls as inspiration for their own futures. Discuss: What practical steps can we take to make our dreams come true? Have your students come up with a well-rounded description of Blanca's character, pulling concrete examples from the poems. There's a glossary of Spanish terms, which is helpful. See how Blanca's life now is different from another Mexican immigrant's, that of the title character in Pam Muñoz Ryan's novel *Esperanza Rising*.

RELATED TITLES: Alarcón, Francisco X. *Angels Ride Bikes and Other Fall Poems.* Children's Book Press, 1999. / Alarcón, Francisco X. *From the Bellybutton of the Moon and Other Summer Poems.* Children's Book Press, 1998. / Alarcón, Francisco X. *Laughing Tomatoes and Other Spring Poems.* Children's Book Press, 1997. / Lomas Garza, Carmen. *Family Pictures/Cuadros de Familia.* Children's Book Press, 1990. / Lomas Garza, Carmen. *In My Family/En Mi Familia.* Children's Book Press, 1996. / Medina, Jane. *My Name Is Jorge: On Both Sides of the River.* Boyds Mills, 1999. / Pérez, L. King. *First Day in Grapes.* Lee & Low, 2002. / Ryan, Pam Muñoz. *Esperanza Rising.* Scholastic, 2000.

SUBJECTS: HISPANIC AMERICANS. IMMIGRATION AND EMIGRATION—POETRY. MEXICAN AMERICANS—POETRY. MULTICULTURAL BOOKS—POETRY. POETRY—SINGLE AUTHOR. SCHOOLS—POETRY. SPANISH LANGUAGE—POETRY. TEACHERS—POETRY.

1383 **Micklos, John, Jr, comp.** *Daddy Poems.* **Illus. by Robert Casilla. Boyds Mills, 2000. 1-56397-735-4. 32pp. Gr. 2–5**

Get close to fathers in 22 warm, affectionate poems, illustrated with pleasant watercolors. The poems center around a multicultural mix of dads and their doting children and include entries by poets including Janet S. Wong and X. J. Kennedy as well as four poems by the compiler himself, John Micklos, Jr.

GERM: Find more poems about fathers in Javaka Steptoe's *In Daddy's Arms I Am Tall*. Do a

Father's Day storyhour with assorted books celebrating dads, from fiction (such as Anthony Browne's *My Dad*) to nonfiction (such as *Animal Dads* by Sneed B. Collard III).

RELATED TITLES: Brisson, Pat. *The Summer My Father Was Ten*. Boyds Mills, 1998. / Browne, Anthony. *My Dad*. Farrar, 2001. / Collard, Sneed B., III. *Animal Dads*. Houghton Mifflin, 1997. / High, Linda Oatman. *Winter Shoes for Shadow Horse*. Boyds Mills, 2001. / Polacco, Patricia. *My Ol' Man*. Philomel, 1995. / Steptoe, Javaka, comp. *In Daddy's Arms I Am Tall: African Americans Celebrating Fathers*. Lee & Low, 1997. / Strickland, Dorothy S., and Michael R. Strickland, comps. *Families: Poems Celebrating the African-American Experience*. Boyds Mills, 1994.

SUBJECTS: FATHERS—POETRY. MULTICULTURAL BOOKS—POETRY.

1384 Moses, Will, comp. *Will Moses' Mother Goose*. Illus. by the author. Philomel, 2003. 0-399-23744-5. 61pp. Gr. PreK–1

Delicate, convivial folk-art paintings in an early 19th-century New England-ish style accompany 70 mostly familiar nursery rhymes.

GERM: While each double-page spread contains five or six rhymes, each accompanied by a small illustration, turn the page and you'll discover a sweeping colorful painting that incorporates all the characters from those rhymes. Children will enjoy searching for all of the characters and reciting their rhymes. Check the illustrator's Web site for background: <www.willmoses.com>.

RELATED TITLES: Cousins, Lucy, comp. *The Little Dog Laughed and Other Nursery Rhymes*. Dutton, 1990. / Crews, Nina, comp. *The Neighborhood Mother Goose*. Greenwillow, 2004. / Denton, Kady MacDonald, comp. *A Child's Treasury of Nursery Rhymes*. Kingfisher, 1998. / dePaola, Tomie, comp. *Tomie dePaola's Mother Goose*. Putnam, 1985. / Lamont, Priscilla, comp. *Ring-a-Round-a-Rosy: Nursery Rhymes, Action Rhymes and Lullabyes*. Little, Brown, 1990. / Lobel, Arnold, comp. *The Random House Book of Mother Goose*. Random House, 1986. / Long, Sylvia, comp. *Sylvia Long's Mother Goose*. Chronicle, 1999. / Opie, Iona, comp. *Here Comes Mother Goose*. Candlewick, 1999. / Opie, Iona, comp. *My Very First Mother Goose*. Candlewick, 1996. / Opie, Iona, and Peter Opie, comps. *Tail Feathers from Mother Goose: The Opie Rhyme Book*. Little, Brown, 1988. / Sutherland, Zena, comp. *The Orchard Book of Nursery Rhymes*. Orchard, 1990.

SUBJECTS: MOTHER GOOSE. NURSERY RHYMES.

1385 Moss, Jeff. *Bone Poems*. Illus. by Tom Leigh. Workman, 1997. 0-7611-0884-X. 78pp. Gr. 3–5

Find out all sorts of info about the habits, habitats, and history of dinos and other ancient creatures through the whimsical wordplay of 43 fact-based poems.

GERM: As a companion to your science studies, analyze how the poems manage to merge wordplay and humor with real information, making these poems so perfectly child-friendly and curriculum-wise. Readers can find out a bit more data on the 30 or so dinosaurs incorporated into the rhymes. Pair this with Jack Prelutsky's *Tyrannosaurus Was a Beast*.

RELATED TITLES: Dodson, Peter. *An Alphabet of Dinosaurs*. Scholastic, 1995. / Jenkins, Steve. *Prehistoric Actual Size*. Houghton Mifflin, 2005. / Kerley, Barbara. *The Dinosaurs of Waterhouse Hawkins*. Scholastic, 2001. / Larson, Peter L. *Bones Rock! Everything You Need to Know to Be a Paleontologist*. Invisible Cities, 2004. / Moss, Jeff. *The Butterfly Jar*. Bantam, 1989. / Prelutsky, Jack. *Tyrannosaurus Was a Beast*. Greenwillow, 1988. / Sabuda, Robert. *Encyclopedia Prehistorica: Dinosaurs*. Candlewick, 2005. / Tanaka, Shelley. *New Dinos*. Atheneum, 2003.

SUBJECTS: DINOSAURS—POETRY. POETRY—SINGLE AUTHOR.

1386 Opie, Iona, comp. *Here Comes Mother Goose*. Illus. by Rosemary Wells. Candlewick, 1999. 0-7636-0683-9. 108pp. Gr. PreK–1

The watercolor and ink illustrations in this oversized Mother Goose collection of 56 lesser-known rhymes are simply smashing, as are those in Wells's first collection of the standards, *My Very First Mother Goose*.

GERM: See how many of these less-famous old rhymes you know and compare them with the better known ones.

RELATED TITLES: Cousins, Lucy, comp. *The Little Dog Laughed and Other Nursery Rhymes*. Dutton, 1990. / Denton, Kady MacDonald, comp. *A Child's Treasury of Nursery Rhymes*. Kingfisher, 1998. / dePaola, Tomie, comp. *Tomie dePaola's Mother Goose*. Putnam, 1985. / Fabian, Bobbi, comp. *Twinkle, Twinkle: An Animal Lover's Mother Goose*. Dutton, 1997. / Foreman, Michael, comp. *Michael Foreman's Playtime Rhymes*. Candlewick, 2002. / Lamont, Priscilla, comp. *Ring-a-Round-a-Rosy: Nursery Rhymes, Action Rhymes and Lullabyes*. Little, Brown, 1990. / Lobel, Arnold, comp. *The Random House Book of Mother Goose*. Random House, 1986. / Long, Sylvia, comp. *Sylvia Long's Mother Goose*. Chronicle, 1999. / Moses, Will, comp. *Will Moses' Mother Goose*. Philomel, 2003. / Opie, Iona, comp. *My Very First Mother Goose*. Candlewick, 1996. / Opie, Iona, and Peter Opie, comps.

Tail Feathers from Mother Goose: The Opie Rhyme Book. Little, Brown, 1988. / Sutherland, Zena, comp. *The Orchard Book of Nursery Rhymes.* Orchard, 1990.

SUBJECTS: MOTHER GOOSE. NURSERY RHYMES.

1387 **Opie, Iona, comp.** ***My Very First Mother Goose.*** **Illus. by Rosemary Wells. Candlewick, 1996. 1-56402-620-5. 108pp. Gr. PreK–1**

While there are loads of wonderful Mother Goose collections out there, this oversized book will quickly become a home and classroom treasure with its 68 well-chosen verses and personable entourage of typical Wells bunnies, pigs, and cats, rendered in grand and colorful watercolors.

GERM: Pair it with its companion, *Here Comes Mother Goose.* Hold a Nursery Rhyme Fest, at which children recite the rhymes they've learned and eat Mother Goose-based snacks such as Bugles (Little Boy Blue's horn), plum slices (Little Jack Horner's pie filling), and little cups of water (Jack and Jill's pails). For older students, sing: "Three myopic rodents, three myopic rodents; Observe how they perambulate, observe how they perambulate; They all circumnavigated the agriculturalist's spouse; / She excised their extremities with a carving utensil; / Did you ever observe such an occurrence in your existence / As three myopic rodents." Using dictionaries, thesauruses, and collections of Mother Goose rhymes, have students work in pairs to rewrite some of the old favorites in more erudite language and read aloud their gussied-up verses for listeners to identify.

RELATED TITLES: Crews, Nina, comp. *The Neighborhood Mother Goose.* Greenwillow, 2004. / dePaola, Tomie, comp. *Tomie dePaola's Mother Goose.* Putnam, 1985. / Edwards, Pamela Duncan. *The Neat Line: Scribbling Through Mother Goose.* HarperCollins, 2005. / Fabian, Bobbi, comp. *Twinkle, Twinkle: An Animal Lover's Mother Goose.* Dutton, 1997. / Lamont, Priscilla, comp. *Ring-a-Round-a-Rosy: Nursery Rhymes, Action Rhymes and Lullabyes.* Little, Brown, 1990. / Lobel, Arnold, comp. *The Random House Book of Mother Goose.* Random House, 1986. / Long, Sylvia, comp. *Sylvia Long's Mother Goose.* Chronicle, 1999. / Moses, Will, comp. *Will Moses' Mother Goose.* Philomel, 2003. / Opie, Iona, comp. *Here Comes Mother Goose.* Candlewick, 1999. / Opie, Iona, and Peter Opie, comps. *Tail Feathers from Mother Goose: The Opie Rhyme Book.* Little, Brown, 1988. / Stevens, Janet, and Susan Stevens Crummel. *And the Dish Ran Away with the Spoon.* Harcourt, 2001. / Sutherland, Zena, comp. *The Orchard Book of Nursery Rhymes.* Orchard, 1990.

SUBJECTS: MOTHER GOOSE. NURSERY RHYMES.

1388 **Pollock, Penny.** ***When the Moon Is Full: A Lunar Year.*** **Illus. by Mary Azarian. Little, Brown, 2001. 0-316-71317-1. Unp. Gr. PreK–4**

On each double-page spread is the traditional Native American name for one month's moon, from January, the Wolf Moon, to December, the Long Night Moon. An intensely colorful, animal-filled woodcut illustration and a brief rhyming verse open a window on the natural world. *Thirteen Months on Turtle's Back* by Joseph Bruchac and Jonathan London offers another poetic look at the moon, as described by a cross-section of Native American tribal nations.

GERM: Have children think up new names for the moon's months and draw pictures to show each month's most memorable aspects.

RELATED TITLES: Bruchac, Joseph, and Jonathan London, comp. *Thirteen Moons on Turtle's Back.* Philomel, 1992. / Ehlert, Lois. *Moon Rope; Un Lazo a la Luna.* Harcourt, 1992. / Frank, Josette. *Snow Toward Evening: A Year in a River Valley: Nature Poems.* Dial, 1990. / Johnston, Tony. *The Tale of Rabbit and Coyote.* Putnam, 1994. / Krupp, E. C. *The Moon and You.* Macmillan, 1993. / Singer, Marilyn. *Turtle in July.* Macmillan, 1989. / Tafuri, Nancy. *Snowy Flowy Blowy: A Twelve Months Rhyme.* Scholastic, 1999. / Updike, John. *A Child's Calendar.* Holiday House, 1999. / Yolen, Jane. *What Rhymes with Moon?* Philomel, 1993. / Young, Ed. *Moon Mother: A Native American Creation Tale.* HarperCollins, 1993.

SUBJECTS: ANIMALS—POETRY. INDIANS OF NORTH AMERICA—POETRY. MOON—POETRY. POETRY—SINGLE AUTHOR. SEASONS—POETRY.

1389 **Powell, Consie.** ***Amazing Apples.*** **Illus. by the author. Albert Whitman, 2003. 0-8075-0399-1. Unp. Gr. K–3**

Seventeen acrostic poems take us through a year of growing apples, incorporating words such as "orchard," "leaves," and "bees" in the spring and "pie" and "winter" at the end of the calendar. Hand-colored woodblock prints show a brother and sister interacting in the orchard and with apples all year long.

GERM: Bring in apples to share and compare, drink apple cider, read and tell apple stories, and find out more apple facts, starting with the information at the back of the book. Write and illustrate new acrostics inspired by this volume and by Jennifer Belle's *Animal Stackers* and Steven Schnur's acrostic alphabet books *Autumn* and *Spring.*

RELATED TITLES: Belle, Jennifer. *Animal Stackers*. Hyperion, 2005. / Gibbons, Gail. *Apples*. Holiday House, 2000. / Hall, Zoe. *The Apple Pie Tree*. Scholastic, 1996. / Hodges, Margaret. *The True Tale of Johnny Appleseed*. Holiday House, 1997. / Hopkinson, Deborah. *Apples to Oregon*. Atheneum, 2004. / Kellogg, Steven. *Johnny Appleseed*. Morrow, 1988. / Lerner, Harriet, and Susan Goldhor. *What's So Terrible About Swallowing an Apple Seed?* HarperCollins, 1996. / Maestro, Betsy. *How Do Apples Grow?* HarperCollins, 1992. / Polette, Nancy. *The Hole by the Apple Tree: An A–Z Discovery Tale*. Greenwillow, 1992. / Priceman, Marjorie. *How to Make an Apple Pie and See the World*. Knopf, 1994. / Robbins, Ken. *Apples*. Atheneum, 2002. / Schertle, Alice. *Down the Road*. Harcourt, 1995. / Schnur, Steven. *Autumn: An Alphabet Acrostic*. Clarion, 1997. / Schnur, Steven. *Spring: An Alphabet Acrostic*. Clarion, 1999. / Tafuri, Nancy. *Snowy Flowy Blowy: A Twelve Months Rhyme*. Scholastic, 1999.

SUBJECTS: ACROSTICS. ALPHABET—POETRY. APPLES—POETRY. FRUIT—POETRY. POETRY—SINGLE AUTHOR. SEASONS—POETRY.

1390 **Prelutsky, Jack, comp. *The Beauty of the Beast: Poems from the Animal Kingdom*. Illus. by Meilo So. Knopf, 1997. 0-679-97058-4. 101pp. Gr. 2–6**
Each double-page spread of this handsome collection of more than 200 poems is devoted to a single animal family, beginning with insects, and on to varied fish, reptiles, birds, and mammals. The poems are an eclectic mix of whimsy and insight by poets both known and less-familiar, and all are accompanied by Chinese-style nature-toned watercolors that flow across each page.

GERM: How pleasing it will be to have students begin their yearly oral animal reports with a poem recited with feeling. Pull in other collections of animal poems such as *Omnibeasts* by Douglas Florian and Eric Carle's *Animals, Animals* compiled by Laura Whipple.

RELATED TITLES: Calmenson, Stephanie, comp. *Never Take a Pig to Lunch: And Other Funny Poems About Animals*. Doubleday, 1982. / Cassedy, Sylvia, and Kunihiro Suetake, comp. *Red Dragonfly on My Shoulder*. HarperCollins, 1992. / Florian, Douglas. *Beast Feast*. Harcourt, 1994. / Florian, Douglas. *Omnibeasts: Animal Poems and Paintings*. Harcourt, 2004. / Lewis, J. Patrick. *A Hippopotamustn't and Other Animal Verses*. Dial, 1990. / Prelutsky, Jack. *The Frogs Wore Red Suspenders*. Greenwillow, 2002. / Prelutsky, Jack. *If Not for the Cat*. Greenwillow, 2004. / Prelutsky, Jack, comp. *Read a Rhyme, Write a Rhyme*. Knopf, 2005. / Prelutsky, Jack, comp. *The 20th Century Children's Poetry Treasury*. Knopf, 1999. / Sierra, Judy. *There's a Zoo in Room 22*. Harcourt, 2000. / Whipple, Laura, comp. *Eric Carle's Animals, Animals*. Philomel, 1989.

SUBJECTS: ANIMALS—POETRY. POETRY—ANTHOLOGIES.

1391 **Prelutsky, Jack. *The Frogs Wore Red Suspenders*. Illus. by Petra Mathers. Greenwillow, 2002. 0-688-16719-5. 64pp. Gr. PreK–3**
Animals rule throughout these 28 gently whimsical nursery rhyme-like poems that mention cities and towns across the United States, illustrated with enchanting watercolors that glow with sky colors.

GERM: Read the poems the second time around as a call-and-response: you read aloud two lines and your listeners recite those lines back to you. Tie them in to geography, as many of the poems mention places—Fort Worth, Tucumcari, South Dakota—that astute detectives can locate on maps and globes. Often, you'll find yourselves humming as you read; "One Day in Seattle" can be sung to "On Top of Old Smokey." Kids need to hear wonderful words, and a dose of Prelutsky each day will do wonders in creating readers and word lovers.

RELATED TITLES: Belle, Jennifer. *Animal Stackers*. Hyperion, 2005. / Florian, Doug. *Beast Feast*. Harcourt, 1994. / Ghigna, Charles. *Animal Tracks: Wild Poems to Read Aloud*. Abrams, 2004. / Lee, Dennis. *Dinosaur Dinner (With a Slice of Alligator Pie)*. Knopf, 1997. / Lewis, J. Patrick. *A Hippopotamustn't and Other Animal Verses*. Dial, 1990. / Lobel, Arnold. *The Book of Pigericks*. HarperCollins, 1983. / Prelutsky, Jack, comp. *The Beauty of the Beast: Poems from the Animal Kingdom*. Knopf, 1997. / Prelutsky, Jack, comp. *For Laughing Out Loud: Poems to Tickle Your Funnybone*. Knopf, 1991. / Prelutsky, Jack. *If Not for the Cat*. Greenwillow, 2004. / Prelutsky, Jack. *The New Kid on the Block*. Greenwillow, 1984. / Prelutsky, Jack. *A Pizza the Size of the Sun*. Greenwillow, 1996. / Prelutsky, Jack. *Something Big Has Been Here*. Greenwillow, 1990. / Sierra, Judy. *There's a Zoo in Room 22*. Harcourt, 2000. / Tripp, Wallace, comp. *A Great Big Ugly Man Came Up and Tied His Horse to Me*. Little, Brown, 1974.

SUBJECTS: ANIMALS—POETRY. GEOGRAPHY—POETRY. HUMOROUS POETRY. POETRY—SINGLE AUTHOR.

1392 **Prelutsky, Jack. *If Not for the Cat*. Illus. by Ted Rand. Greenwillow, 2004. 0-06-059678-3. 40pp. Gr. 2–6**
Ted Rand's gorgeous and soulful deep-colored paintings make glorious companions to Prelutsky's 17 slyly observant and spare animal haiku poems, one per double-page spread.

GERM: First read each haiku aloud for listeners to identify the animal being described. Then show the magnificent illustration. Animal advocates will clamor to write and illustrate their own haiku, but first have them analyze the elements that Prelutsky incorporated into the poems. Each haiku: 1) employs common haiku form—17 syllables in 3 lines that alternate between 5 syllables, 7 syllables, and 5 syllables; 2) uses rich language and imagery; 3) is told in first person, from the animal's point of view; 4) incorporates facts about the animal; and 5) is set up like a riddle. See how the insects write their own haiku in Judy Sierra's *Wild About Books*.

RELATED TITLES: Belle, Jennifer. *Animal Stackers*. Hyperion, 2005. / Demi, comp. *In the Eyes of the Cat: Japanese Poetry for All Seasons*. Henry Holt, 1992. / Florian, Douglas. *Beast Feast*. Harcourt, 1994. / George, Kristine O'Connell. *Fold Me a Poem*. Harcourt, 2005. / George, Kristine O'Connell. *Hummingbird Nest: A Journal of Poems*. Harcourt, 2004. / Gollub, Matthew. *Cool Melons—Turn to Frogs! The Life and Poems of Issa*. Lee & Low, 1998. / Higginson, William J., comp. *Wind in the Long Grass: A Collection of Haiku*. Simon & Schuster, 1991. / Myers, Tim. *Basho and the Fox*. Marshall Cavendish, 2000. / Prelutsky, Jack, comp. *The Beauty of the Beast: Poems from the Animal Kingdom*. Knopf, 1997. / Sierra, Judy. *There's a Zoo in Room 22*. Harcourt, 2000. / Sierra, Judy. *Wild About Books*. Knopf, 2004. / Spivak, Dawnine. *Grass Sandals: The Travels of Basho*. Atheneum, 1997. / Whipple, Laura, comp. *Eric Carle's Animals, Animals*. Philomel, 1989.

SUBJECTS: ANIMALS—POETRY. HAIKU. POETRY—SINGLE AUTHOR.

1393 Prelutsky, Jack. *It's Raining Pigs and Noodles*. Illus. by James Stevenson. Greenwillow, 2000. 0-06-029195-8. 160pp. Gr. K–6
As always, Prelutsky delights all our senses with more than 100 witty, wordplaying poems to recite and sing.

GERM: Photocopy a wide assortment of these ditties, as well as ones from Prelutsky's other volumes: *The New Kid on the Block, A Pizza the Size of the Sun,* and *Something Big Has Been Here*. Then hand them out to small groups to practice and perform aloud for everyone.

RELATED TITLES: Florian, Douglas. *Bing Bang Boing!* Harcourt, 1994. / Florian, Douglas. *Laugh-eteria: Poems and Drawings*. Harcourt, 1999. / Lansky, Bruce, comp. *You're Invited to Bruce Lansky's Poetry Party*. Meadowbrook, 1996. / Lee, Dennis. *The Ice Cream Store*. Scholastic, 1992. / McNaughton, Colin. *Who's Been Sleeping in My Porridge? A Book of Wacky Poems and Pictures*. Candlewick, 1998. / Moss, Jeff. *The Butterfly Jar*. Bantam, 1989. / Prelutsky, Jack. *The New Kid on the Block*. Greenwillow, 1984. / Prelutsky, Jack. *A Pizza the Size of the Sun*. Greenwillow, 1996. / Prelutsky, Jack. *Scranimals*. Greenwillow, 2002. / Prelutsky, Jack. *Something Big Has Been Here*. Greenwillow, 1990. / Silverstein, Shel. *Falling Up*. HarperCollins, 1996. / Silverstein, Shel. *A Light in the Attic*. HarperCollins, 1981. / Viorst, Judith. *If I Were in Charge of the World and Other Worries*. Atheneum, 1981. / Viorst, Judith. *Sad Underwear and Other Complications: More Poems for Children and Their Parents*. Atheneum, 1995.

SUBJECTS: HUMOROUS POETRY. POETRY—SINGLE AUTHOR.

1394 Prelutsky, Jack. *Monday's Troll*. Illus. by Peter Sís. Greenwillow, 1996. 0-688-14373-3. 40pp. Gr. 3–6
The huge oil and gouache illustrations are the standout in this collection of 17 sly poems, personal narratives by witches, trolls, ogres, wizards, and giants who describe their own peculiar and dangerous habits and idiosyncrasies.

GERM: Order this and other Prelutsky books on tape, read and sung by the author, from Listening Library. As an exercise, first let your verbivores discuss Prelutsky's use of vivid and challenging vocabulary and clever endings. Then, working in pairs, have them choose a creature from folklore and write a descriptive poem from its point of view, starting with "I'm a . . ."

RELATED TITLES: Ashman, Linda. *The Essential Worldwide Monster Guide*. Simon & Schuster, 2003. / Brett, Jan. *Who's That Knocking on Christmas Eve?* Putnam, 2002. / Evans, Dilys. *Monster Soup and Other Spooky Poems*. Scholastic, 1992. / Florian, Douglas. *Monster Motel*. Harcourt, 1993. / Hopkins, Lee Bennett, comp. *Creatures*. Harcourt, 1985. / McNaughton, Colin. *Making Friends with Frankenstein: A Book of Monstrous Poems*. Candlewick, 1994. / Prelutsky, Jack. *Awful Ogre's Awful Day*. Greenwillow, 2001. / Prelutsky, Jack. *The Dragons Are Singing Tonight*. Greenwillow, 1993. / Prelutsky, Jack. *Nightmares: Poems to Trouble Your Sleep*. Greenwillow, 1976. / Sierra, Judy. *Monster Goose*. Harcourt, 2001. / Whipple, Laura, comp. *Eric Carle's Dragons Dragons and Other Creatures That Never Were*. Philomel, 1991. / Yolen, Jane. *Best Witches: Poems for Halloween*. Putnam, 1989.

SUBJECTS: GIANTS—POETRY. HUMOROUS POETRY. MONSTERS—POETRY. OGRES—POETRY. PERSONAL NARRATIVES. POETRY—SINGLE AUTHOR. POINT OF VIEW—POETRY. SUPERNATURAL—POETRY. TROLLS—POETRY. WITCHES—POETRY.

1395 Prelutsky, Jack. *A Pizza the Size of the Sun*. Illus. by James Stevenson. Greenwillow, 1996. 0-688-13236-7. 160pp. Gr. 1–6
Prelutsky's third thick collection of 105 witty poems will bring shouts of laughter from children

who will relish meeting characters such as Dan the invisible man, the Moopies with their unorthodox manners, and Lester, who levitates for two hours each night. How can you go wrong with the indefatigable and goofy Prelutsky? Whether he's writing about eyeballs for sale or spaghetti seeds, you know you'll have some poems that set themselves to music, some interesting observations, and plenty of laughs. There's even one you'll need a mirror for; it's printed backward.

GERM: Stage a recital of everyone's favorite Prelutsky poems. Order in pizza, of course.

RELATED TITLES: Florian, Douglas. *Bing Bang Boing!* Harcourt, 1994. / Florian, Douglas. *Laugh-eteria: Poems and Drawings.* Harcourt, 1999. / Lansky, Bruce, comp. *You're Invited to Bruce Lansky's Poetry Party.* Meadowbrook, 1996. / McNaughton, Colin. *Who's Been Sleeping in My Porridge? A Book of Wacky Poems and Pictures.* Candlewick, 1998. / Moss, Jeff. *The Butterfly Jar.* Bantam, 1989. / Prelutsky, Jack. *It's Raining Pigs and Noodles.* Greenwillow, 2000. / Prelutsky, Jack. *The New Kid on the Block.* Greenwillow, 1984. / Prelutsky, Jack. *Something Big Has Been Here.* Greenwillow, 1990. / Silverstein, Shel. *Falling Up.* HarperCollins, 1996. / Viorst, Judith. *If I Were in Charge of the World and Other Worries.* Atheneum, 1981. / Viorst, Judith. *Sad Underwear and Other Complications: More Poems for Children and Their Parents.* Atheneum, 1995.

SUBJECTS: HUMOROUS POETRY. POETRY—SINGLE AUTHOR.

1396 **Prelutsky, Jack, comp.** *Read a Rhyme, Write a Rhyme.* **Illus. by Meilo So. Knopf, 2005. 0-375-82286-0. 25pp. Gr. 1–3**

If this book consisted solely of its 30 short appealing poems, harvested from well-loved children's poets, arranged thematically, three to a double-page spread, with bright, colorful watercolors all over each page, it would still be well worth having. But Prelutsky, Poetry King, takes it a few steps farther with his "poemstarts." In the upper right-hand corner of each double page, he adds the first several lines of his own poem, leaving off the last line so readers can think of their own. So on a page with three poems about dogs, you'll first read the three poems aloud, and then Prelutsky's dog poemstart: "My dog is less than one foot tall / And hasn't any tail. / She never answers when I call, / _____."

GERM: The object here is to write new last lines and share your responses. In addition to the poem, Prelutsky also provides a paragraph of ideas to think about when composing the last line. His themes are general—food, birthdays, bugs, cows, winter, rain—and your poets will continue the themes with new poems and watercolors of their own.

RELATED TITLES: Cleary, Brian P. *Rainbow Soup: Adventures in Poetry.* Carolrhoda, 2004. / Harley, Avis. *Fly with Poetry: An ABC of Poetry.* Boyds Mills, 2000. / Harley, Avis. *Leap into Poetry: More ABCs of Poetry.* Boyds Mills, 2001. / Janeczko, Paul B. *How to Write Poetry.* Scholastic, 1999. / Janeczko, Paul B., comp. *A Kick in the Head: An Everyday Guide to Poetic Forms.* Candlewick, 2005. / Janeczko, Paul B., comp. *The Place My Words Are Looking For.* Simon & Schuster, 1990. / Janeczko, Paul B., comp. *Poetry from A to Z: A Guide for Young Writers.* Simon & Schuster, 1994. / Kennedy, X. J., comp. *Knock at a Star: A Child's Introduction to Poetry.* Little, Brown, 1982. / Prelutsky, Jack, comp. *For Laughing Out Loud: Poems to Tickle Your Funnybone.* Knopf, 1991. / Prelutsky, Jack. *If Not for the Cat.* Greenwillow, 2004. / Prelutsky, Jack. *The New Kid on the Block.* Greenwillow, 1984.

SUBJECTS: AUTHORSHIP. CREATIVE WRITING. POETRY. POETRY—AUTHORSHIP.

1397 **Prelutsky, Jack.** *Scranimals.* **Illus. by Peter Sís. Greenwillow, 2002. 0-688-17820-0. 40pp. Gr. 2–6**

Accompany two adventurous children as they journey to Scranimal Island and meet the scrambled animals there, from the aromatic rhinocerose to the extinct avocadodos. In the 19 blithe poems with adventurous illustrations done in black line art and watercolor, animals and produce cross paths. You'll find detailed descriptions of the attributes of a potatoad, a hippopotomushroom, and a broccolion.

GERM: Create your own conjoined animal or animal and plant combos and draw and write descriptive poems about them.

RELATED TITLES: Duquette, Keith. *Cock-a-Doodle Moooo! A Mixed-Up Menagerie.* Putnam, 2004. / McMillan, Bruce, and Brett McMillan. *Puniddles.* Houghton Mifflin, 1982. / Most, Bernard. *Zoodles.* Harcourt, 1992. / Prelutsky, Jack. *The Dragons Are Singing Tonight.* Greenwillow, 1993. / Prelutsky, Jack. *It's Raining Pigs and Noodles.* Greenwillow, 2000. / Prelutsky, Jack. *Monday's Troll.* Greenwillow, 1996. / Wilbur, Richard. *The Pig in the Spigot.* Harcourt, 2000.

SUBJECTS: ANIMALS—POETRY. ANIMALS, IMAGINARY—POETRY. HUMOROUS POETRY. POETRY—SINGLE AUTHOR. WORD GAMES.

1398 Prelutsky, Jack, comp. *The 20th Century Children's Poetry Treasury*. Illus. by Meilo So. Knopf, 1999. 0-679-89314-8. 94pp. Gr. 1–6

More than 200 poems introduce the best children's poets from every decade of the past century, including Robert Frost and Ogden Nash. Also present are contemporary children's poets, such as Kristine O'Connell George and Valerie Worth. The poems on each page are grouped by topics—animals, flying, weather, music, for example—and paired with peppy watercolors.

GERM: As you read aloud a page of poems, have your listeners speculate on the unifying theme that made Prelutsky group them together. Investigate other collections of poetry that Prelutsky has edited, including *The Beauty of the Beast*, *For Laughing Out Loud*, and *The Random House Book of Poetry for Children*.

RELATED TITLES: Cole, Joanna, comp. *A New Treasury of Children's Poetry: Old Favorites and New Discoveries*. Doubleday, 1984. / Kennedy, Dorothy M., and X. J. Kennedy, comps. *Talking Like the Rain: A First Book of Poems*. Little, Brown, 1992. / Prelutsky, Jack, comp. *The Beauty of the Beast: Poems from the Animal Kingdom*. Knopf, 1997. / Prelutsky, Jack, comp. *For Laughing Out Loud: Poems to Tickle Your Funnybone*. Knopf, 1991. / Prelutsky, Jack, comp. *The Random House Book of Poetry for Children*. Random House, 1983. / Prelutsky, Jack, comp. *Read a Rhyme, Write a Rhyme*. Knopf, 2005. / Rosen, Michael, comp. *Poems for the Very Young*. Kingfisher, 1993.

SUBJECTS: POETRY—ANTHOLOGIES.

1399 Robb, Laura, comp. *Snuffles and Snouts*. Illus. by Steven Kellogg. Dial, 1995. 0-8037-1598-6. 40pp. Gr. 1–4

Serve up a helping of 25 jovial pig poems assembled by educational reading guru and anthologist Laura Robb and lavishly illustrated with Steven Kellogg's rambunctious swine-filled watercolors.

GERM: Do a pigtalk, with lots of pig-based titles from picture books to fiction to folklore, interspersed with these porcine poems.

RELATED TITLES: Aylesworth, Jim. *Aunt Pitty Patty's Piggy*. Scholastic, 1999. / Cole, Brock. *Nothing But a Pig*. Doubleday, 1981. / DiCamillo, Kate. *Mercy Watson to the Rescue*. Candlewick, 2005. / King-Smith, Dick. *Babe, the Gallant Pig*. Crown, 1985. / King-Smith, Dick. *Lady Lollipop*. Candlewick, 2001. / Marshall, James. *Portly McSwine*. Houghton Mifflin, 1979. / Marshall, James. *The Three Little Pigs*. Dial, 1989. / Martin, David. *Five Little Piggies*. Candlewick, 1998. / Munsch, Robert. *Pigs*. Annick, 1989. / Palatini, Margie. *Piggie Pie*. Clarion, 1995. / Phillips, Louis. *Invisible Oink: Pig Jokes*. Dial, 1992. / Pomerantz, Charlotte. *The Piggy in the Puddle*. Macmillan, 1974. / Rayner, Mary. *Mr. and Mrs. Pig's Evening Out*. Atheneum, 1976. / Rylant, Cynthia. *Poppleton*. Scholastic, 1997. / Scieszka, Jon. *The True Story of the 3 Little Pigs*. Viking Kestrel, 1989. / Teague, Mark. *Pigsty*. Scholastic, 1994. / White, E. B. *Charlotte's Web*. HarperCollins, 1952. / Wiesner, David. *The Three Pigs*. Clarion, 2001.

SUBJECTS: HUMOROUS POETRY. PIGS—POETRY.

1400 Rochelle, Belinda, comp. *Words with Wings: A Treasury of African-American Poetry and Art*. HarperCollins, 2001. 0-06-029363-2. Unp. Gr. 4–8

Pairing 20 poems with paintings and sculpture, all by African American writers and artists, makes for a stunning collection that will inspire readers to make connections with words and art. At the back is a nice meaty paragraph about each contributor, including poets Lucille Clifton, Gwendolyn Brooks, Langston Hughes, and Maya Angelou and painters including Horace Pippin and Jacob Lawrence.

GERM: Integrate art and poetry by having your kids write and illustrate a poem from their own life experience, or have them first create a picture of their lives and then write a poem to accompany it. Or you can vary it a bit: students can illustrate each other's poems or write poems to each other's pictures.

RELATED TITLES: Hudson, Wade, comp. *Pass It On: African-American Poetry for Children*. Scholastic, 1993. / Lewis, J. Patrick. *Freedom Like Sunlight: Praisesongs for Black Americans*. Creative Editions, 2000. / Myers, Walter Dean. *Brown Angels: An Album of Pictures and Verse*. HarperCollins, 1993. / Slier, Deborah, comp. *Make a Joyful Sound: Poems for Children by African-American Poets*. Scholastic, 1996. / Strickland, Dorothy S., and Michael R. Strickland, comps. *Families: Poems Celebrating the African-American Experience*. Boyds Mills, 1994.

SUBJECTS: AFRICAN AMERICANS. ARTISTS. MULTICULTURAL BOOKS—POETRY. POETRY—ANTHOLOGIES.

1401 Roemer, Heidi B. *Come to My Party and Other Shape Poems.* **Illus. by Hideko Takahashi. Henry Holt, 2004. 0-8050-6620-9. 48pp. Gr. PreK–2**

These 38 cheerful concrete (or shape) poems, wittily illustrated in acrylics, take a multicultural cast of young children through the seasons, celebrating nature, holidays, play, and weather.

GERM: Cover the title of each poem before you read it so children can look at the shape of the words and predict what it will be about. The poems are so deliciously simple, your poets and artists will want to pair up and try their hands at writing and illustrating some of their own.

RELATED TITLES: Bunting, Eve. *Sing a Song of Piglets.* Clarion, 2002. / Burg, Brad. *Outside the Lines: Poetry at Play.* Putnam, 2002. / Graham, Joan Bransfield. *Flicker Flash.* Houghton Mifflin, 1999. / Graham, Joan Bransfield. *Splish Splash.* Ticknor & Fields, 1994. / Janeczko, Paul B. *A Poke in the I: A Collection of Concrete Poems.* Candlewick, 2001. / Lewis, J. Patrick. *Doodle Dandies: Poems That Take Shape.* Atheneum, 1998. / Pollock, Penny. *When the Moon Is Full: A Lunar Year.* Little, Brown, 2001. / Schnur, Steven. *Autumn: An Alphabet Acrostic.* Clarion, 1997. / Stevenson, James. *Popcorn.* Greenwillow, 1998. (And others in the Corn series.) / Tafuri, Nancy. *Snowy Flowy Blowy: A Twelve Months Rhyme.* Scholastic, 1999. / Updike, John. *A Child's Calendar.* Holiday House, 1999.

SUBJECTS: CONCRETE POETRY. POETRY—SINGLE AUTHOR. SEASONS—POETRY.

1402 Rosen, Michael, comp. *Walking the Bridge of Your Nose.* **Illus. by Chloë Cheese. Kingfisher, 1995. 1-85697-596-7. 61pp. Gr. 1–5**

More than 90 nonsense wordplay poems fool around with language in this whimsical collection. Included are tongue twisters, nursery rhyme parodies, folk rhymes, and riddle rhymes, with lighthearted watercolors adding to the fun.

GERM: What a wonderful way to encourage curiosity about the English language. Find out how GHEAUGHTEIGHPTOUGH spells POTATO and then demonstrate the three ways to get peanut butter off the roof of your mouth. Your students will have their own wealth of riddles and rhymes, so compile a classroom or school-wide book of their best offerings. Other good sources of nonsense rhymes include *Doctor Knickerbocker and Other Rhymes* by David Booth, *Poems of A. Nonny Mouse* by Jack Prelutsky, and *And the Green Grass Grew All Around* by Alvin Schwartz.

RELATED TITLES: Booth, David, comp. *Doctor Knickerbocker and Other Rhymes.* Ticknor & Fields, 1993. / Hirsch, Robin. *FEG: Ridiculous Poems for Intelligent Children.* Little, Brown, 2002. / Prelutsky, Jack, comp. *A. Nonny Mouse Writes Again!* Knopf, 1993. / Prelutsky, Jack, comp. *Poems of A. Nonny Mouse.* Knopf, 1989. / Schwartz, Alvin, comp. *And the Green Grass Grew All Around: Folk Poetry from Everyone.* HarperCollins, 1992. / Schwartz, Alvin, comp. *I Saw You in the Bathtub and Other Folk Rhymes.* HarperCollins, 1989. / Schwartz, Alvin, comp. *Tomfoolery: Trickery and Foolery with Words.* Lippincott, 1973. / Sierra, Judy, comp. *Schoolyard Rhymes: Kids' Own Rhymes for Rope Skipping, Hand Clapping, Ball Bouncing, and Just Plain Fun.* Knopf, 2005. / Tripp, Wallace, comp. *A Great Big Ugly Man Came Up and Tied His Horse to Me; A Book of Nonsense Verse.* Little, Brown, 1973.

SUBJECTS: HUMOROUS POETRY. NONSENSE VERSES. PUNS AND PUNNING. VOCABULARY—POETRY. WORD GAMES.

1403 Sabuda, Robert. *The 12 Days of Christmas: A Pop-Up Celebration.* **Illus. by the author. Simon & Schuster, 1996. 0-689-80865-8. 24pp. Gr. PreK–5**

Open this astonishing and elegant pop-up book tour de force and out flies a snow-white partridge in a pear tree and, in the side panel, two turtledoves in a delicate paper cage.

GERM: "How does Sabuda do it?" you and your carolers will ask as you sing the verses while marveling at each intricate white paper construction rising above its pastel background. Using Joan Irvine's *How to Make Holiday Pop-Ups*, you can make your own holiday cards. Also share Sabuda's equally alluring pop-up, *The Christmas Alphabet*, with its 26 open-up panels.

RELATED TITLES: Brett, Jan. *The Twelve Days of Christmas.* Putnam, 1990. / Irvine, Joan. *How to Make Holiday Pop-Ups.* Morrow, 1996. / Irvine, Joan. *How to Make Super Pop-Ups.* Morrow, 1992. / Manushkin, Fran. *My Christmas Safari.* Dial, 1993. / Mendoza, George. *A Wart Snake in a Fig Tree.* Dial, 1968. / Moore, Clement C. *The Night Before Christmas.* Illus. by Tomie dePaola. Holiday House, 1980. / Niland, Kilmeny. *A Bellbird in a Flame Tree.* Tambourine, 1991. / Raffi, comp. *The Raffi Christmas Treasury.* Crown, 1988. / Sabuda, Robert. *America the Beautiful.* Little Simon, 2004. / Sabuda, Robert. *The Christmas Alphabet.* Orchard, 1994. / Sabuda, Robert. *Cookie Count.* Little Simon, 1997. / Sabuda, Robert. *Winter's Tale: An Original Pop-up Journey.* Little Simon, 2005. / Trivas, Irene. *Emma's Christmas.* Orchard, 1988.

SUBJECTS: CHRISTMAS. PICTURE BOOKS FOR ALL AGES. SONGS. TOY AND MOVABLE BOOKS.

1404 Schnur, Steven. *Autumn: An Alphabet Acrostic.* **Illus. by Leslie Evans. Clarion, 1997. 0-395-77043-2. Unp. Gr. 2–6**

From A to Z, here's an evocative look at autumn words, illustrated with bold, elegant, hand-colored linoleum cuts. In the 26 acrostic poems, the first letter of each line combines to form a word—read from top to bottom—that is the subject of the poem.

GERM: Brainstorm a list of season words and write, illustrate, and share new acrostic poems. See also Schnur's other season acrostic books: *Winter, Spring,* and *Summer,* plus Jennifer Belle's *Animal Stackers* and Consie Powell's *Amazing Apples.*

RELATED TITLES: Alarcón, Francisco X. *From the Bellybutton of the Moon and Other Summer Poems.* Children's Book Press, 1998. / Belle, Jennifer. *Animal Stackers.* Hyperion, 2005. / Florian, Douglas. *Autumnblings: Poems and Paintings.* Greenwillow, 2003. / Frank, Josette. *Snow Toward Evening: A Year in a River Valley: Nature Poems.* Dial, 1990. / George, Kristine O'Connell. *Toasting Marshmallows: Camping Poems.* Clarion, 2001. / Pollock, Penny. *When the Moon Is Full: A Lunar Year.* Little, Brown, 2001. / Powell, Consie. *Amazing Apples.* Albert Whitman, 2003. / Prelutsky, Jack. *What I Did Last Summer.* Greenwillow, 1984. / Schnur, Steven. *Spring: An Alphabet Acrostic.* Clarion, 1999. / Schnur, Steven. *Summer: An Alphabet Acrostic.* Clarion, 2001. / Schnur, Steven. *Winter: An Alphabet Acrostic.* Clarion, 2002. / Singer, Marilyn. *Turtle in July.* Macmillan, 1989. / Tafuri, Nancy. *Snowy Flowy Blowy: A Twelve Months Rhyme.* Scholastic, 1999. / Updike, John. *A Child's Calendar.* Holiday House, 1999.

SUBJECTS: ACROSTICS. ALPHABET—POETRY. AUTUMN—POETRY. POETRY—SINGLE AUTHOR. SEASONS—POETRY.

1405 Schultz, Sam. *Schoolyard Snickers: Classy Jokes That Make the Grade.* **Illus. by Brian Gable. Lerner, 2003. 1-57505-643-7. 32pp. Gr. 1–5**

There are almost 100 school-based jokes and dialogues in this slim, laugh-a-lot collection, two to four to a page, most of them two-part comic dialogues between irate teachers and goofy kids.

GERM: Duplicate a page or two for each pair of comedians, give them a practice session, and then it's showtime! Time to make everyone laugh. Look for more of the many funny titles in Lerner's Make Me Laugh series.

RELATED TITLES: Berk, Meridith, and Toni Vavrus. *Great Book of School Jokes.* Sterling, 1994. / Brewer, Paul. *You Must Be Joking!* Cricket, 2003. / Hartman, Victoria. *The Silliest Joke Book Ever.* Lothrop, 1993. / Hartman, Victoria. *Super-Duper Jokes.* Farrar, 1993. / Keller, Charles. *School Daze.* Prentice-Hall, 1978. / Terban, Marvin. *Funny You Should Ask: How to Make Up Jokes and Riddles with Wordplay.* Clarion, 1992.

SUBJECTS: JOKES. PUNS AND PUNNING. RIDDLES. SCHOOLS. TEACHERS.

1406 Shields, Carol Diggory. *Almost Late to School and More School Poems.* **Illus. by Paul Meisel. Dutton, 2003. 0-525-45743-7. 40pp. Gr. 1–4**

Twenty-two easy-to-read poems, along with cheery, kid-filled watercolors, take us through active days at school. An attack of the giggles, a science fair project gone awry, a bit of recess, a worn-out old blue backpack, and even a poem about having to GO—"Gotta Go"—round out a collection sure to get your kids nodding their heads in recognition.

GERM: Hand out the poems to pairs and trios to practice and put on as a bit of Poetry Reader's Theater. Have kids write new poems about their own school experiences. In "Science Fair Project" on page 10, a boy explains his science project to make his little brother disappear, perfect for introducing the language of experiments: purpose, hypotheses, materials, procedure, theorem, and conclusion. Share as well the poems in Shields's companion book, *Lunch Money and Other Poems About School.*

RELATED TITLES: Dakos, Kalli. *If You're Not Here, Please Raise Your Hand: Poems About School.* Simon & Schuster, 1990. / Dakos, Kalli. *Put Your Eyes Up Here and Other School Poems.* Simon & Schuster, 2003. / George, Kristine O'Connell. *Swimming Upstream: Middle School Poems.* Clarion, 2002. / Harrison, David L. *The Mouse Was Out at Recess.* Boyds Mills, 2003. / Harrison, David L. *Somebody Catch My Homework.* Boyds Mills, 1993. / Heide, Florence Parry, and Roxanne Heide Pierce. *Oh, Grow Up! Poems to Help You Survive Parents, Chores, School and Other Afflictions.* Orchard, 1996. / Kennedy, Dorothy M. *I Thought I'd Take My Rat to School: Poems for September to June.* Little, Brown, 1993. / Shields, Carol Diggory. *Lunch Money and Other Poems About School.* Dutton, 1995.

SUBJECTS: HUMOROUS POETRY. POETRY—SINGLE AUTHOR. READER'S THEATER—POETRY. SCHOOLS—POETRY.

1407 Shields, Carol Diggory. *Animagicals: On the Go.* Illus. by Svjetlan Junakovic. Handprint, 2001. 1-929766-14-9. Unp. Gr. PreK–2

Twelve perceptive rhyming riddles about animals and transportation have unfolding heavy-stock pages that reveal each animal answer.

GERM: When you read the poem and show the first part of the picture, have the children try to guess the animal that the book is describing. As an exercise, have each of them draw a large animal picture and hide part of it by folding the right side of the page partly over the left. Then have them show their pictures to their classmates to identify. Also read the companion books, *Animagicals: Patterns* and *Animagicals: Sports.*

RELATED TITLES: Burton, Marilee Robin. *Tails, Toes, Eyes, Ears, Nose.* HarperCollins, 1988. / De Regniers, Beatrice Schenk. *It Does Not Say Meow and Other Animal Riddle Rhymes.* Houghton Mifflin, 1983. / Goffin, Joose. *OH!* Abrams, 1991. / Guarino, Deborah. *Is Your Mama a Llama?* Scholastic, 1989. / Hoban, Tana. *Take Another Look.* Greenwillow, 1981. / Kirk, Daniel. *Go!* Hyperion, 2001. / McLoughland, Beverly. *A Hippo's a Heap: And Other Animal Poems.* Boyds Mills, 1993. / Shields, Carol Diggory. *Animagicals: Patterns.* Handprint, 2001. / Shields, Carol Diggory. *Animagicals: Sports.* Handprint, 2002. / Shields, Carol Diggory. *Martian Rock.* Candlewick, 1999. / Spires, Elizabeth. *With One White Wing: Puzzles in Poems and Pictures.* McElderry, 1995. / Walton, Rick. *Bunnies on the Go: Getting from Place to Place.* HarperCollins, 2003. / Yolen, Jane. *Alphabestiary: Animal Poems from A to Z.* Boyds Mills, 1995.

SUBJECTS: ANIMALS—POETRY. POETRY—SINGLE AUTHOR. RIDDLES. TRANSPORTATION—POETRY.

1408 Shields, Carol Diggory. *Brain Juice: American History Fresh Squeezed!* Illus. by Richard Thompson. Handprint, 2002. 1-929766-62-9. 80pp. Gr. 3–6

Billed on the cover as "41 thirst-for-knowledge-quenching poems," each of these brief, whimsical, rhyming ditties zooms in on a memorable historical moment, starting with the dinosaurs and ending with a poignant poem about September 11 and the Statue of Liberty. In between, there are droll and nimble poems, from silly to searing, in a sequential timeline covering such diverse topics as wars, explorers, politics, rock and roll, TV, and baseball, all decorated with merry, red-accented sketches.

GERM: At the top of each page runs a timeline of American historical events. Children can construct their own timelines of whatever era you're studying, running them around the perimeter of the room. Students can work in pairs to select a notable event and find out the facts, which they can use to construct a poem about it. Interspersed throughout the book is a wonderful extended romp of a poem, "Presidents on Parade," that characterizes in a nutshell each of the presidents—perfect to perform as Reader's Theater. If your actors memorize the whole poem, they'll be able to recall every president's name, from number one to forty-three. For your science units, see the companion books, *Brain Juice: English, Fresh Squeezed!* and *Brain Juice: Science, Fresh Squeezed!*

RELATED TITLES: Cleveland, Will, and Mark Alvarez. *Yo, Millard Fillmore! (And All Those Other Presidents You Don't Know).* Millbrook, 1997. / Hoose, Phillip M., *We Were There, Too! Young People in U.S. History.* Farrar, 2001. / Longfellow, Henry Wadsworth. *The Midnight Ride of Paul Revere.* Handprint, 2001. / Panzer, Nora, comp. *Celebrate America in Poetry and Art.* Hyperion, 1994. / Shields, Carol Diggory. *Brain Juice: English, Fresh Squeezed!* Handprint, 2004. / Shields, Carol Diggory. *Brain Juice: Science, Fresh Squeezed!* Handprint, 2003. / Whipple, Laura, comp. *Celebrating America: A Collection of Poems and Images of the American Spirit.* Philomel, 1994.

SUBJECTS: POETRY—SINGLE AUTHOR. READER'S THEATER—POETRY. SEPTEMBER 11 TERRORIST ATTACKS, 2001. U.S.—HISTORY—POETRY.

1409 Shields, Carol Diggory. *Brain Juice: English, Fresh Squeezed!* Illus. by Richard Thompson. Handprint, 2004. 1-59354-053-1. 80pp. Gr. 3–6

These jocular, informative, and utterly useful "40 thirst-for-knowledge-quenching poems" take you through the entire English curriculum, giving insight into grammar rules and writing tools. There are poems on punctuation, most of the parts of speech, types of poems, and even one on how to do an outline.

GERM: At the top of each page is a quote from a famous writer; get out your *Bartlett's Quotations* to locate more, and use encyclopedias, books, or the Internet to find out more about each person quoted. Also introduce the companion volumes *Brain Juice: American History, Fresh Squeezed!* and *Brain Juice: Science, Fresh Squeezed!*

RELATED TITLES: Cleary, Brian P. *Hairy, Scary, Ordinary: What Is an Adjective?* Carolrhoda, 2000. / Cleary,

Brian P. *To Root, to Toot, to Parachute: What Is a Verb?* Carolrhoda, 2001. / Heller, Ruth. *Kites Sail High: A Book About Verbs.* Grosset, 1988. / Heller, Ruth. *Many Luscious Lollipops: A Book About Adjectives.* Grosset, 1989. / Heller, Ruth. *Merry-Go-Round: A Book About Nouns.* Grosset, 1990. / Heller, Ruth. *Up, Up and Away: A Book About Adverbs.* Grosset, 1991. / Pulver, Robin. *Nouns and Verbs Have a Field Day.* Holiday House, 2006. / Pulver, Robin. *Punctuation Takes a Vacation.* Holiday House, 2003. / Shields, Carol Diggory. *Brain Juice: American History, Fresh Squeezed!* Handprint, 2002. / Shields, Carol Diggory. *Brain Juice: Science, Fresh Squeezed!* Handprint, 2003. / Viorst, Judith. *The Alphabet from Z to A: With Much Confusion on the Way.* Atheneum, 1994.

SUBJECTS: ENGLISH LANGUAGE—GRAMMAR. ENGLISH LANGUAGE—POETRY. ENGLISH LANGUAGE—SIMILES AND METAPHORS. POETRY—SINGLE AUTHOR.

1410 Shields, Carol Diggory. *Brain Juice: Science Fresh Squeezed!* Illus. by Richard Thompson. Handprint, 2003. 1-59354-005-1. 65pp. Gr. 3–6

Starting off with a heartfelt letter to her favorite science teacher, Miss Fullerton, science enthusiast and poet Shields acknowledges her inspiration for the ensuing "41 thirst-for-knowledge-quenching poems." In each of the four sections—earth and space science, life sciences, chemistry, and physics—are a riot of pithy and punchy verses that explain, observe, and take off on facts. At the top of each page is a captioned bit of info, including a useful handful of scientific mnemonic devices to introduce to your class.

GERM: Match poems to your curriculum—the water cycle, cells, matter, inertia—or read the whole book aloud to give your students a taste of the wide range of science as a subject. Selecting an area of science that intrigues them, students can read up on the facts and then compose their own poems. A natural companion read is Jon Scieszka's *Science Verse.*

RELATED TITLES: Graham, Joan Bransfield. *Flicker Flash.* Houghton Mifflin, 1999. / Graham, Joan Bransfield. *Splish Splash.* Ticknor & Fields, 1994. / Hopkins, Lee Bennett, comp. *Spectacular Science: A Book of Poems.* Simon & Schuster, 1999. / Kos, Amy Goldman. *Where Fish Go in Winter and Other Great Mysteries.* Dial, 2002. / Lewis, J. Patrick. *Earth Verses and Water Rhymes.* Atheneum, 1991. / Moss, Jeff. *Bone Poems.* Workman, 1997. / Peters, Lisa Westberg. *Earthshake: Poems from the Ground Up.* Greenwillow, 2003. / Scieszka, Jon. *Math Curse.* Viking, 1995. / Scieszka, Jon. *Science Verse.* Viking, 2004. / Shields, Carol Diggory. *Brain Juice: American History, Fresh Squeezed!* Handprint, 2002. / Shields, Carol Diggory. *Brain Juice: English, Fresh Squeezed!* Handprint, 2004.

SUBJECTS: MNEMONICS. POETRY—SINGLE AUTHOR. SCIENCE—POETRY.

1411 Sierra, Judy. *Monster Goose.* Illus. by Jack E. Davis. Harcourt, 2001. 0-15-202034-9. Unp. Gr. 2–6

Turn those Mother Goose rhymes on their beaks, and what you get are 25 Monster Goose rhymes. "Old Monster Goose, / When conditions did suit her, / Pecked out these rhymes / On her laptop computer." And indeed, you'll find the counterparts to lots of the rhymes you know well: "Mary Had a Vampire Bat," "Cannibal Horner," and "Twinkle, Twinkle, Little Slug" will make your little ghouls and boys howl for more.

GERM: As you read aloud each rhyme, ask your listeners to recite its original Mother Goose companion. Older students can try their hands at parodying and resetting other nursery rhymes into Halloween mode.

RELATED TITLES: Ashman, Linda. *The Essential Worldwide Monster Guide.* Simon & Schuster, 2003. / dePaola, Tomie, comp. *Tomie dePaola's Mother Goose.* Putnam, 1985. / Edwards, Pamela Duncan. *The Neat Line: Scribbling Through Mother Goose.* HarperCollins, 2005. / Florian, Douglas. *Monster Motel.* Harcourt, 1993. / Hoberman, Mary Ann. *You Read to Me, I'll Read to You: Very Short Mother Goose Tales to Read Together.* Little, Brown, 2005. / Hopkins, Lee Bennett, comp. *Creatures.* Harcourt, 1985. / Katz, Alan. *I'm Still Here in the Bathtub: Brand New Silly Dilly Songs.* Simon & Schuster, 2003. / Lobel, Arnold. *The Random House Book of Mother Goose.* Random House, 1986. / Long, Sylvia, comp. *Sylvia Long's Mother Goose.* Chronicle, 1999. / McNaughton, Colin. *Making Friends with Frankenstein: A Book of Monstrous Poems.* Candlewick, 1994. / Prelutsky, Jack. *Monday's Troll.* Greenwillow, 1996.

SUBJECTS: MONSTERS—POETRY. MOTHER GOOSE. NURSERY RHYMES. PARODIES. POETRY—SINGLE AUTHOR. SUPERNATURAL—POETRY.

1412 Sierra, Judy, comp. *Schoolyard Rhymes: Kids' Own Rhymes for Rope Skipping, Hand Clapping, Ball Bouncing, and Just Plain Fun.* Illus. by Melissa Sweet. Knopf, 2005. 0-375-82516-9. 31pp. Gr. 1–5

Chant along with the almost four dozen wacky children's rhymes, many of which will be familiar, spiced up with perfectly silly watercolors of kids playing. My favorite one, which I first heard from a librarian in Chicago, is in there: "Cinderella, dressed in yella, went downtown to meet her fella. On the way her girdle busted. How many people were disgusted?"

GERM: Sample your students to see which rhymes they know, which ones they know differently from the version in the book, and which ones they know that are not in the book at all. Have them write down and illustrate those for all to share. Pair this with *The Recess Queen* by Alexis O'Neill.

RELATED TITLES: Booth, David, comp. *Doctor Knickerbocker and Other Rhymes.* Ticknor & Fields, 1993. / Brown, Marc, comp. *Hand Rhymes.* Dutton, 1985. / Cole, Joanna, and Stephanie Calmenson, comp. *The Eentsy, Weentsy Spider: Fingerplays and Action Rhymes.* Morrow, 1991. / Marshall, James, comp. *Pocketful of Nonsense.* Artists and Writers Guild, 1993. / O'Neill, Alexis. *The Recess Queen.* Scholastic, 2002. / Opie, Iona, and Peter Opie, comps. *I Saw Esau: The Schoolchild's Pocket Book.* Candlewick, 1992. / Schwartz, Alvin, comp. *And the Green Grass Grew All Around: Folk Poetry from Everyone.* HarperCollins, 1992. / Schwartz, Alvin, comp. *I Saw You in the Bathtub and Other Folk Rhymes.* HarperCollins, 1989. / Tripp, Wallace, comp. *A Great Big Ugly Man Came Up and Tied His Horse to Me; A Book of Nonsense Verse.* Little, Brown, 1973.

SUBJECTS: GAMES. HUMOROUS POETRY. JUMP ROPE RHYMES. SINGING GAMES.

1413 Sierra, Judy. *There's a Zoo in Room 22.* Illus. by Barney Saltzberg. Harcourt, 2000. 0-15-202033-0. 32pp. Gr. 1–4

There are 26 marvelous pets in Miss Darling's classroom, from anaconda to zorilla, and her kids describe each one of them in jaunty rhyme.

GERM: Pet-lovers can look through animal books to select new pets that might be fun to keep in school, and write and illustrate poems about them. Meet some unusual mammals, including the zorilla, in Madeline Moser's *Ever Heard of an Aardwolf?*

RELATED TITLES: Calmenson, Stephanie, comp. *Never Take a Pig to Lunch: And Other Funny Poems About Animals.* Doubleday, 1982. / Florian, Douglas. *Beast Feast.* Harcourt, 1994. / Florian, Douglas. *Mammalabilia: Poems and Paintings.* Harcourt, 2000. / Florian, Douglas. *Omnibeasts: Animal Poems and Paintings.* Harcourt, 2004. / Ghigna, Charles. *Animal Tracks: Wild Poems to Read Aloud.* Abrams, 2004. / Lewis, J. Patrick. *A Hippopotamusn't and Other Animal Verses.* Dial, 1990. / Moser, Madeline. *Ever Heard of an Aardwolf?* Harcourt, 1996. / Prelutsky, Jack, comp. *The Beauty of the Beast: Poems from the Animal Kingdom.* Knopf, 1997. / Prelutsky, Jack. *If Not for the Cat.* Greenwillow, 2004. / Ryan, Pam Muñoz. *A Pinky Is a Baby Mouse and Other Baby Animal Names.* Hyperion, 1997. / Sierra, Judy. *Antarctic Antics: A Book of Penguin Poems.* Harcourt, 1998. / Singer, Marilyn. *Please Don't Squeeze Your Boa, Noah!* Henry Holt, 1995. / Singer, Marilyn. *Turtle in July.* Macmillan, 1989.

SUBJECTS: ANIMALS—POETRY. HUMOROUS POETRY. POETRY—SINGLE AUTHOR. SCHOOLS—POETRY.

1414 Silverstein, Shel. *Falling Up.* Illus. by the author. HarperCollins, 1996. 0-06-024802-5. 176pp. Gr. K–6

Shel Silverstein's collection of more than 100 poems and line drawings is every bit as funny, brilliant, clever, and memorable as his other classics.

GERM: Keep this on your desk for everyday read-aloud treats, along with *A Light in the Attic* and *Where the Sidewalk Ends.* When readers clamor for more, introduce them to poets Douglas Florian, Jack Prelutsky, and Judith Viorst.

RELATED TITLES: Florian, Douglas. *Bing Bang Boing!* Harcourt, 1994. / Florian, Douglas. *Laugh-eteria: Poems and Drawings.* Harcourt, 1999. / Lansky, Bruce, comp. *You're Invited to Bruce Lansky's Poetry Party.* Meadowbrook, 1996. / Lee, Dennis. *The Ice Cream Store.* Scholastic, 1992. / McNaughton, Colin. *Who's Been Sleeping in My Porridge? A Book of Wacky Poems and Pictures.* Candlewick, 1998. / Moss, Jeff. *The Butterfly Jar.* Bantam, 1989. / Prelutsky, Jack. *It's Raining Pigs and Noodles.* Greenwillow, 2000. / Prelutsky, Jack. *The New Kid on the Block.* Greenwillow, 1984. / Prelutsky, Jack. *A Pizza the Size of the Sun.* Greenwillow, 1996. / Prelutsky, Jack. *Something Big Has Been Here.* Greenwillow, 1990. / Silverstein, Shel. *A Light in the Attic.* HarperCollins, 1981. / Silverstein, Shel. *Runny Babbit: A Billy Sook.* HarperCollins, 2005. / Silverstein, Shel. *Where the Sidewalk Ends.* HarperCollins, 1974. / Viorst, Judith. *Sad Underwear and Other Complications: More Poems for Children and Their Parents.* Atheneum, 1995.

SUBJECTS: HUMOROUS POETRY. POETRY—SINGLE AUTHOR.

1415 Silverstein, Shel. *Runny Babbit: A Billy Sook.* Illus. by the author. HarperCollins, 2005. 0-06-028404-8. 89pp. Gr. 2–6

Fut a whunny bew nook! There are twenty-foo feally runny pyming rhoems about Runny Babbit and pots of his lals in this bazy crook. Didn't understand those last sentences? They are filled with spoonerisms, where consonants are switched for pairs of words. Or, as the introductory poem says, "If you say, 'Let's bead a rook' / That's billy as can se, / You're talking Runny Babbit talk / Just like mim and he." Published posthumously (Silverstein worked on these poems for more than 20 years; he died in 1999), this collection looks like his other classic volumes, with a white cover, creamy pages, and his familiar black line drawings accompanying every poem.

GERM: Your straight talkers will be flummoxed by some of these cheerful poems, so photocopy or make a transparency of one or two for your group to pore over, read aloud phonetically, and translate back into standard rhyming English. Or have pairs work on a poem to share with the group, which can then translate it. Have children try their hands at writing simple couplets and switching consonants. "Prinderella and the Cince" is a whole story written in spoonerisms, and you'll find it in my own book *Hi Ho Librario!* and recorded on the accompanying CD. You'll also find a copy in this book, on p. 114. Read it aloud after sharing Silverstein's poem, "Runny Cooks for Linderella" where Runny goes to the Boyal Rall and runs around with the slass glipper to find the princess.

RELATED TITLES: Freeman, Judy. *Hi Ho Librario! Songs, Chants, and Stories to Keep Kids Humming.* Rock Hill, 1997. / Hirsch, Robin. *FEG: Ridiculous Poems for Intelligent Children.* Little, Brown, 2002. / Silverstein, Shel. *Falling Up.* HarperCollins, 1996. / Silverstein, Shel. *A Light in the Attic.* HarperCollins, 1981. / Silverstein, Shel. *Where the Sidewalk Ends.* HarperCollins, 1974.

SUBJECTS: HUMOROUS POETRY. POETRY—SINGLE AUTHOR. PUNS AND PUNNING. WORD GAMES.

1416 **Singer, Marilyn.** *Fireflies at Midnight.* **Illus. by Ken Robbins. Atheneum, 2003. 0-689-82492-0. Unp. Gr. 1–3**

Illustrated with colorful "photographic treatments," 14 gently rhyming nature descriptions are told from animals' points of view—robin, horse, ant, bat—and take us through the course of a day outside, from dawn to dawn.

GERM: Poets can observe, compose, and illustrate new point-of-view verses from the imagined voices of animals they have observed. Also read the personified animal haiku in Jack Prelutsky's *If Not for the Cat.*

RELATED TITLES: Cassedy, Sylvia, and Kunihiro Suetake, comps. *Red Dragonfly on My Shoulder.* Harper-Collins, 1992. / Florian, Douglas. *Beast Feast.* Harcourt, 1994. / Prelutsky, Jack, comp. *The Beauty of the Beast: Poems from the Animal Kingdom.* Knopf, 1997. / Singer, Marilyn. *Please Don't Squeeze Your Boa, Noah!* Henry Holt, 1995. / Singer, Marilyn. *Turtle in July.* Macmillan, 1989. / Whipple, Laura, comp. *Eric Carle's Animals, Animals.* Philomel, 1989.

SUBJECTS: ANIMALS—POETRY. INSECTS—POETRY. POETRY—SINGLE AUTHOR. POINT OF VIEW—POETRY.

1417 **Sklansky, Amy E.** *From the Doghouse: Poems to Chew On.* **Illus. by Karla Firehammer, Karen Dismukes, Sandy Koeser and Cathy McQuitty. Henry Holt, 2002. 0-8050-6673-X. 44pp. Gr. K–2**

All told from a dog's point of view, the 25 jaunty poems about dogs' lives and loves are illustrated with colorful canvas fabric backgrounds onto which are hand-sewn thousands of beads that make up each picture.

GERM: Pet lovers can write poems from their pets' points of view, while art teachers may want to enhance those fine motor skills by undertaking a class beading project to make one large, beaded picture of the class's pets. A little girl describes her day with her dog in *Little Dog Poems* by Christine O'Connell George.

RELATED TITLES: Bartoletti, Susan Campbell. *Nobody's Diggier Than a Dog.* Hyperion, 2004. / Florian, Douglas. *Bow Wow Meow Meow.* Harcourt, 2003. / George, Kristine O'Connell. *Little Dog Poems.* Clarion, 1999. / Gottfried, Maya. *Good Dog.* Knopf, 2005. / Hall, Donald. *I Am the Dog, I Am the Cat.* Dial, 1994. / Johnston, Tony. *It's About Dogs.* Harcourt, 2000. / Kalman, Maira. *What Pete Ate from A– Z.* Putnam, 2001. / Kirk, Daniel. *Dogs Rule!* Hyperion, 2003. / Miller, Sara Swan. *Three Stories You Can Read to Your Dog.* Houghton Mifflin, 1995. / Singer, Marilyn. *It's Hard to Read a Map with a Beagle on Your Lap.* Henry Holt, 1993. / Yolen, Jane. *Raining Cats and Dogs.* Harcourt, 1993.

SUBJECTS: DOGS—POETRY. POETRY—SINGLE AUTHOR. POINT OF VIEW—POETRY.

1418 **Sklansky, Amy E.** *Skeleton Bones and Goblin Groans: Poems for Halloween.* **Illus. by Karen Dismukes. Henry Holt, 2004. 0-8050-7046-X. Unp. Gr. PreK–3**

Here are 21 spooky and wry little poems for your scarefest that will titillate even the young 'uns in your group—especially when they get a load of the very cool illustrations of all the spooksters, formed from beaded colored canvas.

GERM: Using the Halloween haiku as a model, write, illustrate, and recite some of your own poetry.

RELATED TITLES: Bennett, Jill, comp. *Spooky Poems.* Little, Brown, 1989. / Brown, Marc. *Scared Silly: A Book for the Brave.* Little, Brown, 1994. / Bunting, Eve. *In the Haunted House.* Clarion, 1990. / Bunting, Eve. *Scary, Scary Halloween.* Clarion, 1986. / Evans, Dilys. *Monster Soup and Other Spooky Poems.* Scholastic, 1992. / Florian, Douglas. *Monster Motel.* Harcourt, 1993. / Hopkins, Lee Bennett, comp. *Creatures.* Harcourt, 1985. / Hubbard, Patricia. *Trick or Treat Countdown.* Holiday House, 1999. / Krosoczka, Jarrett J. *Annie Was Warned.* Knopf, 2003. / Regan, Dian Curtis. *The Thirteen Hours of Halloween.* Albert Whitman, 1993. / Shute, Linda. *Halloween Party.* Lothrop, 1994. / Silverman, Erica. *Big Pumpkin.* Macmillan, 1992. / Stutson, Caroline. *By the Light of the Halloween Moon.* Lothrop, 1993. / Williams, Linda. *The Little Old Lady Who Was Not Afraid of Anything.* Crowell, 1986. / Yolen, Jane. *Best Witches: Poems for Halloween.* Putnam, 1989.

SUBJECTS: HALLOWEEN. HUMOROUS POETRY. POETRY—SINGLE AUTHOR. SUPERNATURAL.

1419 **Spivak, Dawnine. *Grass Sandals: The Travels of Basho*. Illus. by Demi. Atheneum, 1997. 0-689-80776-7. 32pp. Gr. 3–6**

In 17th-century Japan, master poet Basho composed haiku as he traveled the country on foot, as detailed in this haiku-filled account with meticulously detailed illustrations done with colored inks.

GERM: Meet Basho in a fictional setting in *Basho and the River Stones* and *Basho and the Fox* by Tim Myers. Also read about Issa, another haiku master, born eighty years after Basho, in *Cool Melons—Turn to Frogs!* by Matthew Gollub.

RELATED TITLES: Cassedy, Sylvia, and Kunihiro Suetake, trans. *Red Dragonfly on My Shoulder.* HarperCollins, 1992. / Demi, comp. *In the Eyes of the Cat: Japanese Poetry for All Seasons.* Henry Holt, 1992. / Gollub, Matthew. *Cool Melons—Turn to Frogs! The Life and Poems of Issa.* Lee & Low, 1998. / Higginson, William J., comp. *Wind in the Long Grass: A Collection of Haiku.* Simon & Schuster, 1991. / Kerley, Barbara. *Walt Whitman: Words for America.* Scholastic, 2004. / Myers, Tim. *Basho and the Fox.* Marshall Cavendish, 2000. / Myers, Tim. *Basho and the River Stones.* Marshall Cavendish, 2004. / Prelutsky, Jack. *If Not for the Cat.* Greenwillow, 2004.

SUBJECTS: BASHO (MATSUO, BASHO), 1644–1694. BIOGRAPHY. HAIKU. JAPAN. MULTICULTURAL BOOKS—POETRY. POETRY—SINGLE AUTHOR. POETS.

1420 **Steig, William. *CDB*. Illus. by the author. Simon & Schuster, 2000. 0-689-83160-9. 48pp. Gr. 1–6**

C D B! D B S A B-Z B. O, S N-D! Teachers are constantly on the lookout for ways to use the English language with children so they will understand how stretching and satisfying it is to fiddle with words. First published as a tiny little book in 1968, Steig's classic wordplay book has been enlarged and reprinted in full color. Each page provides a sentence written entirely in letters and numbers, along with a whimsical watercolor illustration to help you understand the context. As you read each one aloud, listeners will puzzle out the intended words. A guide at the back will help with the hardest ones. (In case you haven't figured it out yet: See the bee! The bee is a busy bee. Oh, yes indeed!)

GERM: The natural follow-up to this and the companion book, *CDC*, is to have students work in pairs to write and illustrate new *CDB* sentences to read aloud for their classmates to decode.

RELATED TITLES: Agee, Jon. *Elvis Lives! and Other Anagrams.* Farrar, 2004. / Agee, Jon. *Go Hang a Salami! I'm a Lasagna Hog! And Other Palindromes.* Farrar, 1992. / Agee, Jon. *Palindromania!* Farrar, 2002. / Agee, Jon. *Sit on a Potato Pan, Otis! More Palindromes.* Farrar, 2000. / Agee, Jon. *So Many Dynamos! And Other Palindromes.* Farrar, 1994. / Hepworth, Cathi. *Antics! An Alphabetical Anthology.* Putnam, 1992. / Hepworth, Cathi. *Bug Off! A Swarm of Insect Words.* Putnam, 1998. / Hirsch, Robin. *FEG: Ridiculous Poems for Intelligent Children.* Little, Brown, 2002. / Levitt, Paul M., Douglas A. Burger, and Elissa S. Guralnick. *The Weighty Word Book.* Court Wayne, 2000. / Most, Bernard. *Can You Find It?* Harcourt, 1993. / Most, Bernard. *Hippopotamus Hunt.* Harcourt, 1994. / Steig, William. *CDC.* Simon & Schuster, 2003. / Wilbur, Richard. *The Pig in the Spigot.* Harcourt, 2000.

SUBJECTS: ENGLISH LANGUAGE. WORD GAMES.

1421 **Steptoe, Javaka, comp. *In Daddy's Arms I Am Tall: African Americans Celebrating Fathers*. Illus. by the author. Lee & Low, 1997. 1-880000-31-8. 32pp. Gr. 2–6**

Innovative, eye-popping, cut- and torn-paper collages and paintings illuminate a collection of a dozen poems by African American poets about fathers, starting off with the Ashanti proverb "When you follow in the path of your father, you learn to walk like him." The poems range from playful to solemn and sophisticated, so pick and choose the ones your audience will most appreciate.

GERM: Along with *Love Letters* by Arnold Adoff and *Snapshots from the Wedding* by Gary Soto, you'll have a field day examining examples of innovative collages and creating new ones to illustrate favorite poems.

RELATED TITLES: Greenfield, Eloise. *Honey, I Love.* HarperCollins, 2003. / Greenfield, Eloise. *Honey, I Love, and Other Love Poems.* HarperCollins, 1978. / Grimes, Nikki. *Meet Danitra Brown.* Lothrop, 1994. / Hudson, Wade, comp. *Pass It On: African-American Poetry for Children.* Scholastic, 1993. / Micklos, John, Jr., comp. *Daddy Poems.* Boyds Mills, 2000. / Myers, Walter Dean. *Brown Angels: An Album of Pictures and Verse.* Harper-Collins, 1993. / Pringle, Laurence. *Octopus Hug.* Boyds Mills, 1993. / Slier, Deborah, comp. *Make a Joyful Sound: Poems for Children by African-American Poets.* Scholastic, 1996. / Strickland, Dorothy S., and Michael R. Strickland, comps. *Families: Poems Celebrating the African-American Experience.* Boyds Mills, 1994.

SUBJECTS: AFRICAN AMERICANS—POETRY. FATHERS—POETRY. MULTICULTURAL BOOKS—POETRY.

1422 **Stevenson, James.** *Corn Chowder.* **Illus. by the author. Greenwillow, 2003. 0-06-053059-6. 48pp. Gr. 3–7**
In this collection housing yet more poems from Stevenson's Corn series, 25 little dazzlers, (each joyfully made with delectable pen-and-ink and watercolor illustrations and a prodigious variety of typefaces) offer small, everyday observations that will make you laugh out loud in recognition and appreciation.
GERM: There are seven Stevenson "corn" books, so hand out copies to your gang and stage a reading. Bring in some nice corn products for a real celebration. Examine Stevenson's innovative use of illustration and typeface as a spur to your writers to write and illustrate their own small but perceptive poetic observations, and design the physical look of those poems as well. Valerie Worth is another poet to pair with her classic *All the Small Poems and Fourteen More.*
RELATED TITLES: Esbensen, Barbara Juster. *Who Shrank My Grandmother's House? Poems of Discovery.* HarperCollins, 1992. / Stevenson, James. *Candy Corn.* Greenwillow, 1999. / Stevenson, James. *Corn-Fed.* Greenwillow, 2002. / Stevenson, James. *Cornflakes.* Greenwillow, 2000. / Stevenson, James. *Just Around the Corner.* Greenwillow, 2001. / Stevenson, James. *Popcorn.* Greenwillow, 1998. / Stevenson, James. *Sweet Corn.* Greenwillow, 1997. / Worth, Valerie. *All the Small Poems and Fourteen More.* Farrar, 1994. / Worth, Valerie. *Peacock and Other Poems.* Farrar, 2002.
SUBJECTS: CORN—POETRY. POETRY—SINGLE AUTHOR.

1423 **Thayer, Ernest Lawrence.** *Casey at the Bat: A Ballad of the Republic Sung in the Year 1888.* **Illus. by C. F. Payne. Simon & Schuster, 2003. 0-689-85494-3. Unp. Gr. 2–Adult**
Disdainful at the first two pitches, mighty Casey waits for the third, assuming he'll save the day for the Mudville team. Stee-rike Three! C. F. Payne's illustrations of Casey in the famous baseball poem give us a big galoot of a guy with a twirled handlebar mustache, long sideburns, and a devil-may-care insouciance.
GERM: Compare this with other versions of the poem as illustrated by Christopher Bing, Gerald Fitzgerald, and Wallace Tripp. Payne's version includes, at the back, "A Note about the Poem," which describes the recitations of the poem made by comedian De Wolf Hopper, who, starting in 1888, performed the poem onstage and on the radio more than ten thousand times. *Mighty Jackie, the Strike-Out Queen* by Marissa Moss is the true story of the 17-year-old girl who struck out both Babe Ruth and Lou Gehrig in 1931.
RELATED TITLES: Gutman, Dan. *Honus and Me: A Baseball Card Adventure.* Avon, 1997. / Hopkins, Lee Bennett, comp. *Extra Innings: Baseball Poems.* Harcourt, 1993. / Janeczko, Paul. *That Sweet Diamond: Baseball Poems.* Atheneum, 1998. / Longfellow, Henry Wadsworth. *Paul Revere's Ride.* Illus. by Ted Rand. Dutton, 1990. / Morrison, Lillian, comp. *At the Crack of the Bat: Baseball Poems.* Hyperion, 1992. / Moss, Marissa. *Mighty Jackie, the Strike-Out Queen.* Simon & Schuster, 2004. / Norworth, Jack. *Take Me Out to the Ball Game.* Four Winds, 1993. / Service, Robert W. *The Cremation of Sam McGee.* Greenwillow, 1987. / Smith, Charles R., Jr. *Diamond Life: Baseball Sights, Sounds, and Swings.* Orchard, 2004. / Thayer, Ernest Lawrence. *Casey at the Bat.* Illus. by Christopher Bing. Handprint, 2000. / Thayer, Ernest Lawrence. *Casey at the Bat.* Illus. by Gerald Fitzgerald. Atheneum, 1995. / Thayer, Ernest Lawrence. *Casey at the Bat.* Illus. by Wallace Tripp. Coward, 1978.
SUBJECTS: ATHLETES. BASEBALL—POETRY. NARRATIVE POETRY. PICTURE BOOKS FOR ALL AGES. SPORTS—POETRY. STORIES IN RHYME.

1424 **Thayer, Ernest Lawrence.** *Casey at the Bat: A Ballad of the Republic Sung in the Year 1888.* **Illus. by Christopher Bing. Handprint, 2000. 1-929766-00-9. Unp. Gr. 2–Adult**
In Bing's brilliant, Caldecott Honor-winning interpretation of Thayer's classic 1888 narrative poem, we are astonished, amazed, and awestruck at the multilayered, wondrous scrapbook, set up like an old 1888 newspaper. You'll spend hours poring over the tickets, newspaper clippings, old baseball cards, a stereoscope card, and ads for Cockle's Anti Bilious Pills, all super-

imposed on the Mudville Monitor newspaper with crosshatched illustrations of the poem drawn with pen, ink, and brush on white scratchboard.

GERM: Hand out verses to pairs of kids to perform the poem as a choral reading, acting out the whole poem with props: whiffle bat, ball, hats. Set up the choral reading as a baseball diamond, with kids positioned in pairs or trios in an outfield formation, each group reading a stanza or two. Bring in Cracker Jacks, sing "Take Me Out to the Ballgame," and take the kids out to play ball. Read and compare the parody poem, "Scientific Method at the Bat" from Jon Scieszka's *Science Verse*.

RELATED TITLES: Gutman, Dan. *Honus and Me: A Baseball Card Adventure.* Avon, 1997. / Hopkins, Lee Bennett, comp. *Extra Innings: Baseball Poems.* Harcourt, 1993. / Janeczko, Paul. *That Sweet Diamond: Baseball Poems.* Atheneum, 1998. / Longfellow, Henry Wadsworth. *The Midnight Ride of Paul Revere.* Illus. by Christopher Bing. Handprint, 2001. / Longfellow, Henry Wadsworth. *Paul Revere's Ride.* Illus. by Ted Rand. Dutton, 1990. / Morrison, Lillian, comp. *At the Crack of the Bat: Baseball Poems.* Hyperion, 1992. / Norworth, Jack. *Take Me Out to the Ball Game.* Four Winds, 1993. / Scieszka, Jon. *Science Verse.* Viking, 2004. / Service, Robert W. *The Cremation of Sam McGee.* Greenwillow, 1987. / Smith, Charles R., Jr. *Diamond Life: Baseball Sights, Sounds, and Swings.* Orchard, 2004. / Thayer, Ernest Lawrence. *Casey at the Bat.* Illus. by C. F. Payne. Simon & Schuster, 2003. / Thayer, Ernest Lawrence. *Casey at the Bat.* Illus. by Gerald Fitzgerald. Atheneum, 1995. / Thayer, Ernest Lawrence. *Casey at the Bat.* Illus. by Wallace Tripp. Coward, 1978.

SUBJECTS: ATHLETES. BASEBALL—POETRY. NARRATIVE POETRY. PICTURE BOOKS FOR ALL AGES. SPORTS—POETRY. STORIES IN RHYME.

1425 Updike, John. *A Child's Calendar.* Illus. by Trina Schart Hyman. Holiday House, 1999. 0-8234-1445-0. Unp. Gr. 1–6

In this elegant collection, 12 sensible rhyming poems, one for each month, incorporate images commonly associated with the month to make for an evocative and visually stimulating experience. Detailed, thoughtful, and delicate watercolor and ink illustrations combine to take us on a visual journey of the year.

GERM: Children can write and illustrate new poems about their favorite months, placing them in settings they know intimately, and then can compile them into a classroom book, *A Year in Poetry.*

RELATED TITLES: Alarcón, Francisco X. *From the Bellybutton of the Moon and Other Summer Poems.* Children's Book Press, 1998. / Bruchac, Joseph, and Jonathan London. *Thirteen Moons on Turtle's Back.* Philomel, 1992. / Esbensen, Barbara Juster. *Swing Around the Sun.* Carolrhoda, 2003. / Florian, Douglas. *Autumnblings: Poems and Paintings.* Greenwillow, 2003. / Frank, Josette. *Snow Toward Evening: A Year in a River Valley: Nature Poems.* Dial, 1990. / Roemer, Heidi B. *Come to My Party and Other Shape Poems.* Henry Holt, 2004. / Schnur, Steven. *Autumn: An Alphabet Acrostic.* Clarion, 1997. / Schnur, Steven. *Spring: An Alphabet Acrostic.* Clarion, 1999. / Schnur, Steven. *Summer: An Alphabet Acrostic.* Clarion, 2001. / Schnur, Steven. *Winter: An Alphabet Acrostic.* Clarion, 2002. / Singer, Marilyn. *Turtle in July.* Macmillan, 1989. / Tafuri, Nancy. *Snowy Flowy Blowy: A Twelve Months Rhyme.* Scholastic, 1999.

SUBJECTS: MONTHS—POETRY. POETRY—SINGLE AUTHOR. SEASONS—POETRY.

1426 Weitzman, Ilana, Eva Blank, and Roseanne Green. *Jokelopedia: The Biggest, Best, Silliest, Dumbest Joke Book Ever.* Illus. by Mike Wright. Workman, 2000. 0-7611-1214-6. 264pp. Gr. 2–6

You won't read this whole compendium aloud, of course, but as a book to dip into for truly funny and classic jokes, riddles, practical jokes, spotlights on major comedians, and advice on becoming a comedian, it's an endless source of material.

GERM: Stage a Comedy Club in your classroom. Have your comedians memorize their favorite jokes and riddles, and work up one-minute comedy routines. Have them use a mike, just like the pros do. Wanna-be comics abound in fiction, including Ellen Conford's *Lenny Kandell, Smart Aleck*, Elizabeth Levy's *My Life as a Fifth-Grade Comedian*, and Louis Sachar's *Dogs Don't Tell Jokes*.

RELATED TITLES: Berk, Meridith, and Toni Vavrus. *Great Book of School Jokes.* Sterling, 1994. / Brewer, Paul. *You Must Be Joking!* Cricket, 2003. / Conford, Ellen. *Lenny Kandell, Smart Aleck.* Little, Brown, 1983. / Levy, Elizabeth. *My Life as a Fifth-Grade Comedian.* HarperCollins, 1997. / Sachar, Louis. *Dogs Don't Tell Jokes.* Knopf, 1991. / Terban, Marvin. *Funny You Should Ask: How to Make Up Jokes and Riddles with Wordplay.* Clarion, 1992.

SUBJECTS: COMEDIANS. JOKES. RIDDLES.

1427 Whipple, Laura. *If the Shoe Fits: Voices from Cinderella.* Illus. by Laura Beingessner. McElderry, 2002. 0-689-84070-5. 67pp. Gr. 4–8

All aspects of Cinderella's extraordinary story, accompanied by exquisite gouache illustrations, are rehashed in 33 free-verse poems narrated by Cinderella and everyone else who was there at the ball that enchanted night, including her stepmother, her fairy godmother, the prince, the rat coachman, the cat—even the glass slipper.

GERM: Find more Cinderella activities, ideas, and titles in the "Looking at Cinderella" section on page 111. And for added fun, if you have Judy Freeman's book and CD, *Hi Ho Librario,* play or read aloud "Prinderella and the Cince." Retell other fairy tales from the point of view of various characters. *I Was a Rat* by Philip Pullman and *Ella Enchanted* by Gail Carson Levine are novels with fresh takes on the old tale.

RELATED TITLES: Craft, K. Y. *Cinderella.* SeaStar Books, 2000. / Ehrlich, Amy. *Cinderella.* Illus. by Susan Jeffers. Dutton, 2004. / Hughes, Shirley. *Ella's Big Chance: A Jazz-Age Cinderella.* Simon & Schuster, 2004. / Jackson, Ellen. *Cinder Edna.* Lothrop, 1994. / Kindl, Patrice. *Goose Chase.* Houghton Mifflin, 2001. / Levine, Gail Carson. *Ella Enchanted.* HarperCollins, 1997. / Napoli, Donna Jo. *The Prince of the Pond.* Dutton, 1992. / Pullman, Philip. *I Was a Rat!* Knopf, 2000. / Sanderson, Ruth. *Cinderella.* Little, Brown, 2002. / San Souci, Robert D. *Cendrillon: A Caribbean Cinderella.* Simon & Schuster, 1998.

SUBJECTS: CHARACTERS IN LITERATURE—POETRY. CINDERELLA STORIES. POETRY—SINGLE AUTHOR. POINT OF VIEW—POETRY. STEPMOTHERS.

1428 Wilbur, Richard. *The Disappearing Alphabet.* **Illus. by David Diaz. Harcourt, 1998. 0-15-201470-5. Unp. Gr. 2–6**

What would happen if the alphabet vanished, one letter at a time? Poet and Pulitzer Prize-winner Wilbur muses on this dire scenario, with one short, droll poem for each of the 26 letters. If there were no P, for instance, a banana's peel would be a slippery eel. The wordplay is sublime, and Diaz's colorful and stylish computer-generated illustrations give each page panache.

GERM: "Be careful, then, my friends, and do not let / Anything happen to the alphabet." Listeners can disregard that advice and come up with more words, leaving out essential letters and predicting and illustrating the results. (Example: Boat would become bat without the A, and without the O, a coat would become a cat.)

RELATED TITLES: Agee, Jon. *Elvis Lives! and Other Anagrams.* Farrar, 2004. / Agee, Jon. *Go Hang a Salami! I'm a Lasagna Hog! And Other Palindromes.* Farrar, 1992. / Hepworth, Cathi. *Bug Off! A Swarm of Insect Words.* Putnam, 1998. / Hirsch, Robin. *FEG: Ridiculous Poems for Intelligent Children.* Little, Brown, 2002. / Levitt, Paul M., Douglas A. Burger, and Elissa S. Guralnick. *The Weighty Word Book.* Court Wayne, 2000. / Meddaugh, Susan. *Martha Blah Blah.* Houghton Mifflin, 1996. / Modesitt, Jeanne. *The Story of Z.* Picture Book Studio, 1990. / Steig, William. *CDB.* Simon & Schuster, 2000. / Steig, William. *CDC.* Simon & Schuster, 2003. / Turner, Priscilla. *The War Between the Vowels and the Consonants.* Farrar, 1996. / Viorst, Judith. *The Alphabet from Z to A: With Much Confusion on the Way.* Atheneum, 1994. / Wilbur, Richard. *The Pig in the Spigot.* Harcourt, 2000.

SUBJECTS: ALPHABET—POETRY. ENGLISH LANGUAGE—POETRY. POETRY—SINGLE AUTHOR. VOCABULARY—POETRY. WORD GAMES.

1429 Wilbur, Richard. *The Pig in the Spigot.* **Illus. by J. Otto Seibold. Harcourt, 2000. 0-15-202019-5. 48pp. Gr. 3–6**

In 28 wonderfully clever wordplay poems, illustrated with goofy scenes, find words within words—eat in sweater, neigh in neighborhood, ant in pantry—and see how they are related.

GERM: Brainstorm a list of words containing words and have children work in pairs to decide the words' relationships to each other. *Antics!* and *Bug Off!* by Kathi Hepworth also show words within words. Keep fooling around with words in Wilbur's *The Disappearing Alphabet.*

RELATED TITLES: Agee, Jon. *Elvis Lives! and Other Anagrams.* Farrar, 2004. / Agee, Jon. *Go Hang a Salami! I'm a Lasagna Hog! And Other Palindromes.* Farrar, 1992. / Frasier, Debra. *Miss Alaineus: A Vocabulary Disaster.* Farrar, 2000. / Hepworth, Cathi. *Antics! An Alphabetical Anthology.* Putnam, 1992. / Hepworth, Cathi. *Bug Off! A Swarm of Insect Words.* Putnam, 1998. / Hirsch, Robin. *FEG: Ridiculous Poems for Intelligent Children.* Little, Brown, 2002. / Levitt, Paul M., Douglas A. Burger, and Elissa S. Guralnick. *The Weighty Word Book.* Court Wayne, 2000. / Most, Bernard. *Can You Find It?* Harcourt, 1993. / Most, Bernard. *Hippopotamus Hunt.* Harcourt, 1994. / Prelutsky, Jack. *Scranimals.* Greenwillow, 2002. / Steig, William. *CDB.* Simon & Schuster, 2000. / Steig, William. *CDC.* Simon & Schuster, 2003. / Viorst, Judith. *The Alphabet from Z to A: With Much Confusion on the Way.* Atheneum, 1994. / Wilbur, Richard. *The Disappearing Alphabet.* Harcourt, 1998.

SUBJECTS: ANAGRAMS. ENGLISH LANGUAGE—POETRY. HUMOROUS POETRY. POETRY—SINGLE AUTHOR. VOCABULARY—POETRY. WORD GAMES.

1430 Worth, Valerie. *Peacock and Other Poems.* **Illus. by Natalie Babbitt. Farrar, 2002. 0-374-35766-8. 40pp. Gr. 2–6**

In these 26 sharp-eyed poems, we encounter everyday objects, taking a closer look at a prism, an umbrella, a pair of blue jeans, frosty icicles, and ice cream. Valerie Worth's poems magnify small objects or animals and capture their very essence in simple, spare observations.

GERM: Read the other books in Worth's Small Poems series. Some are poems you can read aloud and have listeners guess the subject. Bring in props to accompany some of the poems: an umbrella, a zinnia, a pumpkin, an acorn, or a coat hanger. Finally, children can bring in a secret object, examine it closely, and write a poem describing it, which they can then read aloud for the group to identify.

RELATED TITLES: Esbensen, Barbara Juster. *Who Shrank My Grandmother's House? Poems of Discovery.* HarperCollins, 1992. / Graham, Joan Bransfield. *Splish Splash.* Ticknor & Fields, 1994. / Lewis, J. Patrick. *Doodle Dandies: Poems That Take Shape.* Atheneum, 1998. / Stevenson, James. *Candy Corn.* Greenwillow, 1999. / Stevenson, James. *Cornflakes.* Greenwillow, 2000. / Stevenson, James. *Just Around the Corner.* Greenwillow, 2001. / Stevenson, James. *Popcorn.* Greenwillow, 1998. / Stevenson, James. *Sweet Corn.* Greenwillow, 1997. / Worth, Valerie. *All the Small Poems and Fourteen More.* Farrar, 1994.

SUBJECTS: POETRY—SINGLE AUTHOR.

1431 Yolen, Jane. *Fine Feathered Friends: Poems for Young People.* **Photos by Jason Stemple. Wordsong/Boyds Mills, 2004. 1-59078-193-7. 32pp. Gr. 2–6**

In 14 thoughtful observational poems, each about a different bird, double-page color photographs provide a courtly close-up of the bird in its habitat. A one-paragraph overview about each bird's characteristics accompanies the poems about such diverse birds as the barred owl, the pelican, the osprey, and the roadrunner.

GERM: Use these poems as report starters, with each student or duo picking a bird, looking up more information about it, taking notes, and presenting an oral report, starting with the poem that inspired their research. Douglas Florian's *On the Wing* and Yolen's companion books, *Bird Watch* and *Wild Wings*, will provide more choices.

RELATED TITLES: Bash, Barbara. *Urban Roosts: Where Birds Nest in the City.* Little, Brown, 1990. / Climo, Shirley. *King of the Birds.* HarperCollins, 1988. / Demuth, Patricia Brennan. *Cradles in the Trees: The Story of Bird Nests.* Macmillan, 1994. / Florian, Douglas. *On the Wing: Bird Poems and Paintings.* Harcourt, 1996. / George, Kristine O'Connell. *Hummingbird Nest: A Journal of Poems.* Harcourt, 2004. / Hamilton, Virginia. *When Birds Could Talk and Bats Could Sing.* Blue Sky/Scholastic, 1996. / Jennings, Patrick. *Putnam and Pennyroyal.* Scholastic, 1999. / Peters, Lisa Westberg. *This Way Home.* Henry Holt, 1994. / Yolen, Jane. *Bird Watch: A Book of Poetry.* Philomel, 1990. / Yolen, Jane. *Wild Wings: Poems for Young People.* Boyds Mills, 2002.

SUBJECTS: BIRDS—POETRY. POETRY—SINGLE AUTHOR.

1432 Yolen, Jane, comp. *Sky Scrape/City Scape: Poems of City Life.* **Illus. by Ken Condon. Boyds Mills, 1996. 1-56397-179-8. 32pp. Gr. 2–5**

This collection of 25 busy urban poems by well-loved children's poets, illustrated with chalk and oil pastels, reflects the noise and excitement of city streets.

GERM: Have children write experiential poems about their own encounters and experiences with city life, or its opposite, country life. For a deeper look, also read Arnold Adoff's *Street Music: City Poems.*

RELATED TITLES: Adoff, Arnold. *Street Music: City Poems.* HarperCollins, 1995. / Dragonwagon, Crescent. *And Then It Rained . . .* Atheneum, 2003. / Hopkins, Lee Bennett. *Good Rhymes, Good Times.* HarperCollins, 1995. / Jakobsen, Kathy. *My New York.* Little, Brown, 2003. / Johnson, Stephen T. *Alphabet City.* Viking, 1995. / Rotner, Shelley, and Ken Kreisler. *Citybook.* Orchard, 1994.

SUBJECTS: CITIES AND TOWNS—POETRY.

BIOGRAPHY

1433 Adler, David A. *America's Champion Swimmer: Gertrude Ederle.* **Illus. by Terry Widener. Harcourt, 2000. 0-15-201969-3. 32pp. Gr. 1–5**

In an enthusiastic picture-book biography, learn about Gertrude "Trudy" Ederle—the woman President Coolidge called "America's Best Girl"—who, in 1926, became the first woman to swim the English Channel.

GERM: Discussion point: As Trudy said, "I knew if it could be done, it had to be done, and I did it." What feats, both large and small, would you like to achieve in your lifetime, and how will you go about it?

RELATED TITLES: Adler, David A. *A Picture Book of Amelia Earhart.* Holiday House, 1998. / Adler, David A. *A Picture Book of Eleanor Roosevelt.* Holiday House, 1991. / Brown, Don. *Alice Ramsey's Grand Adventure.* Houghton Mifflin, 1997. / Gilliland, Judith Heide. *Steamboat: The Story of Captain Blanche Leathers.* DK Ink, 2000. / Krull, Kathleen. *Lives of the Athletes: Thrills, Spills (and What the Neighbors Thought).* Harcourt, 1995. / Krull, Kathleen. *Wilma Unlimited: How Wilma Rudolph Became the World's Fastest Woman.* Harcourt, 1996. / Littlefield, Bill. *Champions: Stories of Ten Remarkable Athletes.* Little, Brown, 1993.

SUBJECTS: ATHLETES—BIOGRAPHY. BIOGRAPHY. EDERLE, GERTRUDE, 1906–2003. SPORTS—BIOGRAPHY. SWIMMING. WOMEN—BIOGRAPHY.

1434 Adler, David A. *Dr. Martin Luther King, Jr.* **Illus. by Colin Bootman. Holiday House, 2001. 0-8234-1572-4. 48pp. Gr. K–2**

This attractively illustrated biography in easy-to-read format lays out the basic elements of King's life and beliefs, incorporating quotes and inspiration for the youngest listeners and readers.

GERM: When you share the book with your children, ask them to be thinking about these discussion questions: What is a civil rights leader? Why do we celebrate Martin Luther King's birthday every year? What did he do to change the world?

RELATED TITLES: Adler, David A. *A Picture Book of Rosa Parks.* Holiday House, 1993. / Bray, Rosemary L. *Martin Luther King.* Greenwillow, 1995. / Coles, Robert. *The Story of Ruby Bridges.* Scholastic, 1995. / Curtis, Gavin. *The Bat Boy and His Violin.* Simon & Schuster, 1998. / Farris, Christine King. *My Brother Martin: A Sister Remembers Growing Up with the Rev. Dr. Martin Luther King, Jr.* Simon & Schuster, 2003. / Golenbock, Peter. *Teammates.* Harcourt, 1990. / Greenfield, Eloise. *Rosa Parks.* HarperCollins, 1995. / King, Martin Luther. *I Have a Dream.* Scholastic, 1997. / Marzollo, Jean. *Happy Birthday, Martin Luther King.* Scholastic, 1993. / McKissack, Patricia C. *Goin' Someplace Special.* Atheneum, 2001. / Mitchell, Margaree King. *Uncle Jed's Barber Shop.* Simon & Schuster, 1993. / Parks, Rosa, and Jim Haskins. *I Am Rosa Parks.* Dial, 1997. / Rappaport, Doreen. *Martin's Big Words.* Hyperion, 2001. / Woodson, Jacqueline. *The Other Side.* Putnam, 2001.

SUBJECTS: AFRICAN AMERICANS—BIOGRAPHY. BIOGRAPHY. CIVIL RIGHTS. KING, MARTIN LUTHER, JR. MULTICULTURAL BOOKS. PREJUDICE. U.S.—HISTORY—20TH CENTURY.

1435 Adler, David A. *Lou Gehrig: The Luckiest Man.* **Illus. by Terry Widener. Harcourt, 1997. 0-15-200523-4. Unp. Gr. 2–5**

In the 14 years and 2,130 consecutive Yankee games after Lou Gehrig signed with the Yankees in 1923, he became known as the Iron Horse, the man who never missed a game. On his 36th birthday, Gehrig was diagnosed with amyotrophic lateral sclerosis, what we now call Lou Gehrig's disease; he died the next year, in 1941. This striking and poignant picture-book biography chronicles the dedication and talent of a man who considered himself lucky even when things looked bleakest. When I read this book to several classes of third graders, the boys wept.

GERM: Talk it over: Lou Gehrig called himself "the luckiest man on the face of the earth," and yet he was too weak to play baseball; and he must have known that he was dying. Why might he have felt this way? What kind of person do you think he was?

RELATED TITLES: Burleigh, Robert. *Home Run: The Story of Babe Ruth*. Harcourt, 1998. / Cline-Ransome, Lisa. *Satchel Paige*. Simon & Schuster, 2000. / Cohen, Barbara. *Thank You, Jackie Robinson*. Lothrop, 1988. / Corey, Shana. *Players in Pigtails*. Scholastic, 2003. / Golenbock, Peter. *Teammates*. Harcourt, 1990. / Gutman, Dan. *Honus and Me*. Avon, 1997. / Hall, Donald. *When Willard Met Babe Ruth*. Browndeer/Harcourt, 1996. / Hopkins, Lee Bennett, comp. *Extra Innings: Baseball Poems*. Harcourt, 1993. / Krull, Kathleen. *Lives of the Athletes: Thrills, Spills (and What the Neighbors Thought)*. Harcourt, 1995. / Morrison, Lillian, comp. *At the Crack of the Bat: Baseball Poems*. Hyperion, 1992. / Moss, Marissa. *Mighty Jackie, the Strike-Out Queen*. Simon & Schuster, 2004. / Norworth, Jack. *Take Me Out to the Ball Game*. Four Winds, 1993.

SUBJECTS: ATHLETES—BIOGRAPHY. BASEBALL—BIOGRAPHY. BIOGRAPHY. DEATH. DISEASES. GEHRIG, LOU. PERSEVERANCE. SPORTS—BIOGRAPHY.

1436   Adler, David A. *A Picture Book of Amelia Earhart*. Illus. by Jeff Fisher. Holiday House, 1998. 0-8234-1315-2. Unp. Gr. 2–4

An easy-to-digest biography provides interesting anecdotes and facts about Amelia Earhart's dedication and determination to become a flyer in her own right, and describes the groundbreaking flights of the "First Lady of the Air."

GERM: Pair this with Pam Muñoz Ryan's *Amelia and Eleanor Go for a Ride*, fictionalized but based on an actual event, and show the many wonderful photos of Earhart in Corinne Szabo's *Sky Pioneer*.

RELATED TITLES: Adler, David A. *A Picture Book of Eleanor Roosevelt*. Holiday House, 1991. / Brown, Don. *Ruth Law Thrills a Nation*. Ticknor & Fields, 1993. / Burleigh, Robert. *Flight: The Journey of Charles Lindbergh*. Philomel, 1991. / Grimes, Nikki. *Talkin' About Bessie: The Story of Aviator Elizabeth Coleman*. Orchard, 2002. / Joseph, Lynn. *Fly, Bessie, Fly*. Simon & Schuster, 1998. / Lauber, Patricia. *Lost Star: The Story of Amelia Earhart*. Scholastic, 1988. / Moss, Marissa. *Brave Harriet*. Harcourt, 2001. / Ryan, Pam Muñoz. *Amelia and Eleanor Go for a Ride*. Scholastic, 1999. / Szabo, Corinne. *Sky Pioneer: A Photobiography of Amelia Earhart*. National Geographic, 1997.

SUBJECTS: AIR PILOTS. BIOGRAPHY. EARHART, AMELIA. WOMEN—BIOGRAPHY.

1437   Adler, David A. *A Picture Book of Louis Braille*. Illus. by John Wallner and Alexandra Wallner. Holiday House, 1997. 0-8234-1291-1. Unp. Gr. 2–4

Louis Braille, blind from the age of 3, perfected a system of using raised dots in two rows of three dots each, so blind people could read. Adler's basic biography, from his excellent Picture Book Biography series, is interestingly told and illustrated with attractive watercolors, and includes a chronology and the raised Braille alphabet on the last page.

GERM: Familiarize your students with the Braille alphabet. Russell Freedman's *Out of Darkness: The Story of Louis Braille* is a longer, more detailed biography. Take advantage of the more than two dozen titles in Adler's A Picture Book Of series, covering such diverse personalities as Helen Keller, Sitting Bull, Jackie Robinson, Abraham Lincoln, and Thomas Alva Edison, to introduce the biography section of your library.

RELATED TITLES: Alexander, Sally Hobart. *Mom Can't See Me*. Macmillan, 1990. / Davis, Patricia A. *Brian's Bird*. Albert Whitman, 2000. / Freedman, Russell. *Out of Darkness: The Story of Louis Braille*. Clarion, 1997. / Garfield, James. *Follow My Leader*. Viking, 1957. / Hermann, Spring. *Seeing Lessons: The Story of Abigail Carter and America's First School for Blind People*. Henry Holt, 1998. / Hunter, Edith Fisher. *Child of the Silent Night: The Story of Laura Bridgman*. Houghton Mifflin, 1963. / Little, Jean. *Little by Little: A Writer's Education*. Viking, 1987. / Millman, Isaac. *Moses Goes to a Concert*. Farrar, 1998. / Patent, Dorothy Hinshaw. *The Right Dog for the Job: Ira's Path from Service Dog to Guide Dog*. Walker, 2004. / Whelan, Gloria. *Hannah*. Knopf, 1991.

SUBJECTS: BIOGRAPHY. BLIND. BRAILLE, LOUIS. PEOPLE WITH DISABILITIES. PHYSICALLY HANDICAPPED. TEACHERS.

1438   Adler, David A. *A Picture Book of Thomas Alva Edison*. Illus. by John Wallner and Alexandra Wallner. Holiday House, 1996. 0-8234-1246-6. 32pp. Gr. 1–4

When you mention Edison's name, children conjure up a mental picture of the light bulb, so they'll be awestruck to learn about his lifetime of experiments, resulting in 1,093 patents. "Genius is one percent inspiration and ninety-nine percent perspiration," Edison said. Adler's anecdotal, easy-to-grasp biography shows Edison first as a curious, questioning child who set up a laboratory in the cellar, and then as a driven and slightly eccentric man who nicknamed his own children "Dot" and "Dash" after the telegraph signals.

GERM: Marie Ferguson Delano's *Inventing the Future: A Photobiography of Thomas Alva Edison* is a more detailed biography, filled with large photos of the man and his work. Follow up with a slice of personal history in Floyd C. Moore's recollection of his boyhood when Edison came to his town in *I Gave Thomas Edison My Sandwich*. Then find out about another inventor who fooled around with electricity in Rosalyn Schanzer's *How Ben Franklin Stole the Lightning*.

RELATED TITLES: Brown, Don. *Odd Boy Out: Young Albert Einstein*. Houghton Mifflin, 2004. / Delano, Marie Ferguson. *Inventing the Future: A Photobiography of Thomas Alva Edison*. National Geographic, 2002. / Dooling, Michael. *Young Thomas Edison*. Holiday House, 2005. / Gutman, Dan. *Qwerty Stevens Back in Time: The Edison Mystery*. Simon & Schuster, 2001. / Moore, Floyd C. *I Gave Thomas Edison My Sandwich*. Albert Whitman, 1995. / Old, Wendie. *To Fly: The Story of the Wright Brothers*. Clarion, 2002. / Schanzer, Rosalyn. *How Ben Franklin Stole the Lightning*. HarperCollins, 2003. / St. George, Judith. *So You Want to Be an Inventor?* Philomel, 2002. / Weitzman, David. *Model T: How Henry Ford Built a Legend*. Crown, 2002.

SUBJECTS: BIOGRAPHY. EDISON, THOMAS ALVA. INVENTIONS AND INVENTORS. SCIENCE. SCIENTISTS.

1439 **Aldrin, Buzz.** *Reaching for the Moon.* **Illus. by Wendell Minor. HarperCollins, 2005. 0-06-055445-2. Unp. Gr. 2–6**

Famed astronaut Buzz Aldrin reveals how he got his first name, describes his first flight, at age 2, and relates how he become the second man to set foot on the moon in an inspirational picture-book autobiography with large, realistic paintings.

GERM: Discussion points: What are the personal and professional qualities that helped Buzz Aldrin succeed in his career? Buzz states, in his afterword, "Not everyone can explore space. But we all have our moons to reach for." What does he mean? What moons would you like to reach for in your life and how do you plan to get there? Read about the other two Apollo 11 astronauts and their mission in *The Man Who Went to the Far Side of the Moon* by Bea Uusma Schyffert and *One Giant Leap* by Don Brown.

RELATED TITLES: Brown, Don. *One Giant Leap: The Story of Neil Armstrong*. Houghton Mifflin, 1998. / Burleigh, Robert. *Earth from Above for Young Readers*. Abrams, 2002. / Krupp, E. C. *The Moon and You*. Macmillan, 1993. / McNulty, Faith. *If You Decide to Go to the Moon*. Scholastic, 2005. / Schyffert, Bea Uusma. *The Man Who Went to the Far Side of the Moon: The Story of Apollo 11 Astronaut, Michael Collins*. Chronicle, 2003. / Simon, Seymour. *The Moon*. Simon & Schuster, 2003.

SUBJECTS: ALDRIN, BUZZ. ASTRONAUTS. AUTOBIOGRAPHY. BIOGRAPHY. MOON. PROJECT APOLLO. SPACE FLIGHT TO THE MOON.

1440 **Aliki.** *William Shakespeare and the Globe.* **HarperCollins, 1999. 0-06-027821-8. 48pp. Gr. 2–8**

Accompanied by attractive, detailed watercolor paintings of Elizabethan England and portraits of Shakespeare's contemporaries, Aliki's quote-strewn, handsome, oversized picture-book biography of William Shakespeare and the history of London's Globe Theatre, past and present, is laid out like a play in five acts. The modern Globe Theatre, which opened in 1997, is a most remarkable reconstruction, with a magnificent thatched roof, "the first and only thatched roof in London since 1666," with an open hole on top so "groundlings," standing to watch the production, get wet when it rains, as they did in Shakespeare's time 400 years ago.

GERM: Start a unit on Shakespeare by investigating the many quotes sprinkled throughout the book. It's never too early to introduce the master of the English language, as evidenced by the listing of some of the 2,000 words and expressions he invented. The book is also a perfect lead-in to Diane Stanley and Peter Vennema's picture-book biography, *Bard of Avon: The Story of William Shakespeare*, not to mention the plays of the Bard himself, when your students are ready for them.

RELATED TITLES: Blackwood, Gary L. *The Shakespeare Stealer*. Dutton, 1998. / Coville, Bruce. *William Shakespeare's A Midsummer Night's Dream*. Dial, 1996. / Coville, Bruce. *William Shakespeare's Hamlet*. Dial, 2004. / Coville, Bruce. *William Shakespeare's Twelfth Night*. Dial, 1993. / Ganeri, Anita *The Young Person's Guide to Shakespeare* (book and CD). Harcourt, 1999. / Garfield, Leon. *Shakespeare Stories*. Houghton Mifflin, 1995. / Graham, Harriet. *A Boy and His Bear*. McElderry, 1996. / Kerley, Barbara. *Walt Whitman: Words for America*. Scholastic, 2004. / Mannis, Celeste Davis. *The Queen's Progress: An Elizabethan Alphabet*. Viking, 2003. / Packer,

Tina. *Tales from Shakespeare*. Scholastic, 2004. / Rosen, Michael. *Shakespeare: His Work and His World*. Candlewick, 2001. / Stanley, Diane. *Bard of Avon: The Story of William Shakespeare*. Morrow, 1992. / Thomas, Jane Resh. *The Princess in the Pigpen*. Clarion, 1989.

SUBJECTS: AUTHORS—BIOGRAPHY. BIOGRAPHY. ENGLAND. LONDON (ENGLAND). PLAYS. POETS. SHAKESPEARE, WILLIAM. THEATERS.

1441   Anderson, Laurie Halse. *Thank You, Sarah: The Woman Who Saved Thanksgiving*. Illus. by Matt Faulkner. Simon & Schuster, 2002. 0-689-84787-4. Unp. Gr. K–5

Portrayed as both superhero and dainty little lady, Sarah Hale, composer of "Mary Had a Little Lamb," spearheaded a 38-year letter-writing campaign, entreating five presidents to declare Thanksgiving a national holiday, which President Lincoln finally did in 1863.

GERM: As author Anderson says, "Pick up your pen. Change the world." Discuss: How did Sarah Hale change our world by writing letters? How can you change the world with your pen? "The pen is mightier than the sword," said writer Edward Bulwer-Lytton. What does this mean? Is it true?

RELATED TITLES: Corey, Shana. *You Forgot Your Skirt, Amelia Bloomer!* Scholastic, 2000. / Fleming, Candace. *The Hatmaker's Sign: A Story by Benjamin Franklin*. Orchard, 1998. / George, Jean Craighead. *The First Thanksgiving*. Philomel, 1993. / Greene, Rhonda Gowler. *The Very First Thanksgiving Day*. Atheneum, 2002. / Lakin, Patricia. *Fat Chance Thanksgiving*. Albert Whitman, 2001. / White, Linda Arms. *I Could Do That: Esther Morris Gets Women the Vote*I. Farrar, 2005. / Wooldridge, Connie Nordhielm. *When Esther Morris Headed West: Women, Wyoming, and the Right to Vote*. Holiday House, 2001.

SUBJECTS: BIOGRAPHY. PRESIDENTS. THANKSGIVING. U.S.—HISTORY. WOMEN—BIOGRAPHY.

1442   Anderson, M. T. *Handel, Who Knew What He Liked*. Illus. by Kevin Hawkes. Candlewick, 2001. 0-7636-1046-1. 48pp. Gr. 2–6

A high-spirited picture-book biography presents the life of George Frideric Handel from his childhood—when the stubborn boy smuggled a clavichord into the attic—through his composition of the Messiah. Kevin Hawkes's ornate acrylic paintings look splendid from a distance and capture the humor of the text and majesty of the music.

GERM: A chronology of Handel's life, a discography, and a bibliography are on the last page. Music teachers will break into song over this one. Play a recording of Handel's music as you read the book aloud.

RELATED TITLES: Aliki. *Ah, Music!* HarperCollins, 2003. / Anderson, M. T. *Strange Mr. Satie*. Viking, 2003. / Gerstein, Mordicai. *What Charlie Heard: The Story of the Composer Charles Ives*. Farrar, 2002. / Kalman, Esther. *Tchaikovsky Discovers America*. Orchard, 1995. / Krull, Kathleen. *Lives of the Musicians: Good Times, Bad Times (And What the Neighbors Thought)*. Harcourt, 1993. / Nichol, Barbara. *Beethoven Lives Upstairs*. Orchard, 1994. / Pinkney, Andrea Davis. *Duke Ellington*. Hyperion, 1998. / Ryan, Pam Muñoz. *When Marian Sang*. Scholastic, 2002. / Winter, Jeanette. *Sebastian: A Book About Bach*. Harcourt, 1999.

SUBJECTS: BIOGRAPHY. COMPOSERS. HANDEL, GEORGE FRIDERIC. MUSICIANS.

1443   Armstrong, Jennifer. *Spirit of Endurance*. Illus. by William Mauhan and with photos. Crown, 2000. 0-517-80091-8. 32pp. Gr. 4–8

An astonishing true survival story recounts how Englishman Sir Ernest Shackleton's 1914 expedition, intended to be the first to cross the Antarctic, instead became stranded when the *Endurance* was trapped in ice. Based on Armstrong's own book for older readers, *Shipwreck at the Bottom of the World*, this oversized picture-book version, alternating photos and paintings, is thrilling. The fact that not one man was lost during the harrowing two-year ordeal was miraculous, and as a study in courage and ingenuity, the voyage is certainly unforgettable.

GERM: Students can do a search at the library for other materials on polar explorers—Admiral Byrd, Robert Scott, Roald Amundsen, Douglas Mawson—and report on all aspects of Antarctica, including its wildlife.

RELATED TITLES: Armstrong, Jennifer. *Shipwreck at the Bottom of the World*. Crown, 1999. / Bredeson, Carmen. *After the Last Dog Died: The True-Life, Hair-Raising Adventure of Douglas Mawson and His 1911–1914 Antarctic Expedition*. National Geographic, 2003. / Burleigh, Robert. *Black Whiteness: Admiral Byrd Alone in the Antarctic*. Atheneum, 1997. / Fraser, Mary Ann. *On Top of the World: The Conquest of Mount Everest*. Henry Holt, 1991. / Kimmel, Elizabeth Cody. *Ice Story: Shackleton's Lost Expedition*. Clarion, 1999. / Kostyal, K. M. *Trial by Ice: A Photobiography of Sir Ernest Shackleton*. National Geographic, 1999. / McCurdy, Michael. *Trapped by the Ice: Shackleton's Amazing Antarctic Adventure*. Walker, 1997. / Swan, Robert. *Destination: Antarctica*. Scholastic, 1988. / Webb, Sophie. *My Season with Penguins: An Antarctic Journal*. Houghton Mifflin, 2000.

SUBJECTS: ADVENTURE AND ADVENTURERS. ANTARCTICA—DISCOVERY AND EXPLORATION. ARCTIC REGIONS. BIOGRAPHY. EXPLORERS. OCEAN. SHACKLETON, ERNEST HENRY, SIR. SHIPS. SURVIVAL.

1444 Atkins, Jeannine. *Mary Anning and the Sea Dragon*. Illus. by Michael Dooling. Farrar, 1999. 0-374-34840-5. Unp. Gr. 2–5

Meet Mary Anning, who in 1811, at the age of 12, dug up the first fossil of an ichthyosaur ever found from the cliffs of her seaside town of Lyme Regis, England.

GERM: If you're looking for fascinating and inspiring biographies of independent, trailblazing women, also read aloud and compare the three other outstanding picture-book accounts of Anning's life, by Anholt, Brighton, and Brown. Atkins's book has the most elegant and atmospheric paintings, with fictionalized dialogue, and is told as a story. Also introduce Benjamin Waterhouse Hawkins, the man responsible for making the first life-sized dinosaur model in the mid-1850s in Barbara Kerley's *The Dinosaurs of Waterhouse Hawkins*.

RELATED TITLES: Anholt, Laurence. *Stone Girl, Bone Girl: The Story of Mary Anning*. Orchard, 1999. / Bausum, Ann. *Dragon Bones and Dinosaur Eggs: A Photobiography of Explorer Roy Chapman Andrews*. National Geographic, 2000. / Brighton, Catherine. *The Fossil Girl: Mary Anning's Dinosaur Discovery*. Millbrook, 1999. / Brown, Don. *Rare Treasure: Mary Anning and Her Remarkable Discoveries*. Houghton Mifflin, 1999. / Kerley, Barbara. *The Dinosaurs of Waterhouse Hawkins*. Scholastic, 2001. / Larson, Peter, and Kristin Donnan. *Bones Rock! Everything You Need to Know to Be a Paleontologist*. Invisible Cities, 2004.

SUBJECTS: ANNING, MARY, 1799–1847. BIOGRAPHY. ENGLAND. FOSSILS. PALEONTOLOGY. SCIENTISTS. WOMEN—BIOGRAPHY.

1445 Barasch, Lynne. *Knockin' on Wood: Starring Peg Leg Bates*. Illus. by the author. Lee & Low, 2004. 1-58430-170-8. Unp. Gr. 1–4

A picture-book biography with full-bleed ink-and-watercolor illustrations chronicles the life of a most unusual and heroic African American dancer—Clayton "Peg Leg" Bates—who, at age 12 in 1919, lost his left leg from the knee down in a factory accident. Wearing a wooden or peg leg to match every costume, and a tap shoe on his right foot, the indefatigable Peg Leg became a vaudeville performer. Though he endured racism in his cross-country travels, he always brought the house down.

GERM: A photo of Peg Leg dancing and a page of his quotes ends an inspirational story that readers might otherwise think is fiction. Ask your listeners: What can we learn from Peg Leg Bates? What other people have overcome some type of adversity?

RELATED TITLES: Adler, David A. *A Picture Book of Louis Braille*. Holiday House, 1997. / Cline-Ransome, Lesa. *Major Taylor, Champion Cyclist*. Atheneum, 2004. / Cline-Ransome, Lisa. *Satchel Paige*. Simon & Schuster, 2000. / Duggleby, John. *Story Painter: The Life of Jacob Lawrence*. Chronicle, 1998. / Joseph, Lynn. *Fly, Bessie, Fly*. Simon & Schuster, 1998. / Krull, Kathleen. *Wilma Unlimited: How Wilma Rudolph Became the World's Fastest Woman*. Harcourt, 1996. / McKissack, Patricia C. *Goin' Someplace Special*. Atheneum, 2001. / Millman, Isaac. *Moses Goes to a Concert*. Farrar, 1998. / Pinkney, Andrea D. *Bill Pickett: Rodeo-Ridin' Cowboy*. Harcourt, 1996. / Pinkney, Andrea D. *Ella Fitzgerald: The Tale of a Vocal Virtuosa*. Hyperion, 2002. / Say, Allen. *El Chino*. Houghton Mifflin, 1990.

SUBJECTS: AFRICAN AMERICANS—BIOGRAPHY. BIOGRAPHY. DANCING. MULTICULTURAL BOOKS. PEOPLE WITH DISABILITIES. PHYSICALLY HANDICAPPED. TAP DANCING.

1446 Bartoletti, Susan Campbell. *The Flag Maker*. Illus. by Claire A. Nivola. Houghton Mifflin, 2004. 0-618-26757-3. 32pp. Gr. 2–5

It's 1812; America is at war with Britain, and flag-makers 12-year-old Caroline Pickersgill and her mother are commissioned to make a huge American flag to be flown at Fort McHenry in Baltimore, in anticipation of an attack by British ships. Delicate watercolor and gouache illustrations accompany this fictionalized account of the making of the Star Spangled Banner, the flag immortalized by Francis Scott Key after he witnessed the bombardment of Fort McHenry.

GERM: The author's note contains supporting information about the Pickersgills and some interesting facts about the flag. Hand out the words and sing the song, of course, and discuss the history behind our national anthem.

RELATED TITLES: Kroll, Steven. *By the Dawn's Early Light: The Story of the Star-Spangled Banner*. Scholastic, 1994. / Thomson, Sarah L. *Stars and Stripes: The Story of the American Flag*. HarperCollins, 2003. / Wallner, Alexandra. *Betsy Ross*. Holiday House, 1994.

SUBJECTS: BALTIMORE. BIOGRAPHY. FLAGS—U.S.—HISTORY. MARYLAND. U.S.—HISTORY—
WAR OF 1812. WAR. WOMEN—BIOGRAPHY.

1447 Bernier-Grand, Carmen T. *Cesar: ¡Sí, Se Puede! Yes, We Can!* **Illus. by David Diaz. Marshall Cavendish, 2004. 0-7614-5172-2. 48pp. Gr. 3–6**

In a moving series of 19 free-verse poems and accompanying shimmering folk art illustrations, we are inspired by the life of Mexican American migrant labor organizer César Chávez, whose nonviolent protests led to better living and working conditions for farmworkers.

GERM: At the back of the book are a glossary, biographical sketch, chronology, list of sources and Web sites, and a page of quotes by Chávez. Read this as a companion to Kathleen Krull's biography, *Harvesting Hope: The Story of Cesar Chavez,* to compare facts, writing style, illustrations, and coverage.

RELATED TITLES: Bray, Rosemary L. *Martin Luther King.* Greenwillow, 1995. / Bridges, Ruby. *Through My Eyes.* Scholastic, 1999. / Brimner, Larry Dane. *A Migrant Family.* Lerner, 1992. / Elya, Susan Middleton. *Home at Last.* Lee & Low, 2002. / Krull, Kathleen. *Harvesting Hope: The Story of Cesar Chavez.* Harcourt, 2003. / Lomas Garza, Carmen. *Family Pictures/Cuadros de Familia.* Children's Book Press, 1990. / Lomas Garza, Carmen. *In My Family/En Mi Familia.* Children's Book Press, 1996. / Mora, Pat. *Tomás and the Library Lady.* Knopf, 1997. / Pérez, Amada Irma. *My Very Own Room/Mi Proprio Cuartito.* Children's Book Press, 2000. / Pérez, L. King. *First Day in Grapes.* Lee & Low, 2002. / Rappaport, Doreen. *Martin's Big Words.* Hyperion, 2001. / Ryan, Pam Muñoz. *Esperanza Rising.* Scholastic, 2000. / Smothers, Ethel Footman. *The Hard-Times Jar.* Farrar, 2003.

SUBJECTS: BIOGRAPHY. CALIFORNIA. CHAVEZ, CESAR. HISPANIC AMERICANS. LABOR LEADERS. MEXICAN AMERICANS. MIGRANT LABOR. MULTICULTURAL BOOKS. POETRY—SINGLE AUTHOR. UNITED FARM WORKERS.

1448 *Bierman, Carol.* *Journey to Ellis Island: How My Father Came to America.* Illus. by Laurie McGaw. Hyperion, 1998. 0-7868-0377-0. 48pp. Gr. 3–6

History depends on the stories of all people, not just those who end up rich and famous. Through an attractive blend of old photos and somber, sepia-toned, oversized paintings, we accompany Rachel Weinstein and her two children, 11-year-old Yehuda and his 7-year-old sister Esther, on their voyage from Russia to New York City in the fall of 1922. Based on the author's father's recountings of his own journey, the well-told text is immediate and personal, recalling the hardships the family faced as Jews in Russia, and how Yehuda was almost sent back to Russia by the Ellis Island officials. The family settled on the Lower East Side of Manhattan where Yehuda, renamed Julius by a teacher to "Americanize" him, soon thrived in school, speaking eight languages by the time he graduated.

GERM: The color photo of Julius visiting Ellis Island in his late 80s is a touching reminder to ask our families to share their life stories with us.

RELATED TITLES: Avi. *Silent Movie.* Atheneum, 2003. / Bartone, Elisa. *American Too.* Lothrop, 1996. / Bartone, Elisa. *Peppe the Lamplighter.* Lothrop, 1993. / Bunting, Eve. *A Picnic in October.* Harcourt, 1999. / Freedman, Russell. *Immigrant Kids.* Dutton, 1980. / Hall, Bruce Edward. *Henry and the Kite Dragon.* Philomel, 2004. / Levine, Ellen. *If Your Name Was Changed at Ellis Island.* Scholastic, 1993. / Levine, Gail Carson. *Dave at Night.* HarperCollins, 1999. / Maestro, Betsy. *Coming to America: The Story of Immigration.* Scholastic, 1996. / Pomeranc, Marion Hess. *The American Wei.* Albert Whitman, 1998. / Sandler, Martin W. *Immigrants.* HarperCollins, 1995. / Wong, Janet. *Apple Pie 4th of July.* Harcourt, 2002.

SUBJECTS: BIOGRAPHY. ELLIS ISLAND IMMIGRATION STATION (N.Y. AND N.J.). FAMILY STORIES. IMMIGRATION AND EMIGRATION. JEWS. MULTICULTURAL BOOKS. RUSSIAN AMERICANS. U.S.—HISTORY—20TH CENTURY.

1449 Blumberg, Rhoda. *Shipwrecked! The True Adventures of a Japanese Boy.* **Illus. with reproductions. HarperCollins, 2001. 0-688-17484-1. 80pp. Gr. 5–8**

In January 1841, 14-year-old Manjiro Nakahama set out from Japan in a small fishing boat with four older sailors, became marooned on an island for five months, was rescued by an American whaler, and became the first Japanese person to come to the United States. On his return to Japan, he was in danger of being executed for having traveled to a foreign country, but survived and even became a samurai.

GERM: The story of Manjiro's peripatetic life is illustrated with handsome reproductions of paintings, woodblock prints, maps, and drawings by artists to whom Manjiro described what he saw, and will enrich curricular units on the Gold Rush, Japan, whaling, and biography. Manjiro commented on many of the strange customs he observed in the United States. Have your students make a list of the customs they practice that foreigners might find strange, and discuss unusual customs they've encountered in other countries or in their readings. Another sailor's survival story from the same era is *The True Adventure of Daniel Hall* by Diane Stanley.

RELATED TITLES: Avi. *The True Confessions of Charlotte Doyle*. Orchard, 1990. / Blumberg, Rhoda. *Commander Perry in the Land of the Shogun*. Lothrop, 1985. / Blumberg. Rhoda. *The Great American Gold Rush*. Bradbury, 1989. / Blumberg, Rhoda. *The Incredible Journey of Lewis and Clark*. Lothrop, 1987. / Cushman, Karen. *The Ballad of Lucy Whipple*. Clarion, 1996. / Hoobler, Dorothy, and Thomas Hoobler. *The Demon in the Teahouse*. Philomel, 2001. / Hoobler, Dorothy, and Thomas Hoobler. *The Ghost in the Tokaido Inn*. Philomel, 1999. / Murphy, Jim. *Gone a-Whaling: The Lure of the Sea and the Hunt for the Great Whale*. Clarion, 1998. / Stanley, Diane. *The True Adventure of Daniel Hall*. Dial, 1995.

SUBJECTS: BIOGRAPHY. EXPLORERS. GOLD RUSH. JAPAN. MULTICULTURAL BOOKS. U.S.—HISTORY—1783–1865. VOYAGES AND TRAVELS.

1450   **Borden, Louise.** *The Journey That Saved Curious George: The True Wartime Escape of Margaret and H. A. Rey.* **Illus. by Allan Drummond. Houghton Mifflin, 2005. 0-618-33924-2. 73pp. Gr. 3–6**

As the Nazis advanced on Paris in the spring of 1940, Hans and Margaret Rey, who were both Jewish, bought two bicycles, packed up a small pile of belongings and manuscripts of their children's books, including *The Adventures of Fifi*, and rode out of the city. Along with thousands of other fleeing refugees, the couple escaped, biking three days south to Orléans, arriving on June 14, the day the Nazis occupied Paris. The Reys made their way to Lisbon, then Rio, and finally, New York, where one year later their book was published to great acclaim, though the title was changed to *Curious George*.

GERM: This extraordinary scrapbook of the Reys' saga is formatted like a picture-book story, profusely illustrated with buoyant *Curious George*-like pen-and-ink drawings and watercolors, black and white photographs, reproductions of letters and documents, and illustrations from the Reys' books. You can tie this in to lessons on World War II and the Holocaust or focus on the couple as authors and illustrators. On the Web site <www.curiousgeorge.com> you'll find a very good teacher's guide for the book under "Educators and Librarians Activity Time." Even older children will enjoy rereading the picture book, *Curious George*, which takes on a whole new meaning when you know the history behind it.

RELATED TITLES: Borden, Louise. *The Little Ships: The Heroic Rescue at Dunkirk in World War II*. McElderry, 1997. / Engel, Dean, and Florence D. Freeman. *Ezra Jack Keats*. Silver Moon, 1995. / Foreman, Michael. *War Boy*. Arcade, 1990. / Krull, Kathleen. *The Boy on Fairfield Street: How Ted Geisel Grew Up to Become Dr. Seuss*. Random House, 2004. / Maguire, Gregory. *The Good Liar*. Clarion, 1999. / Mazer, Norma Fox. *Good Night, Maman*. Harcourt, 1999. / Millman, Isaac. *Hidden Child*. Farrar, 2005. / Peet, Bill. *Bill Peet: An Autobiography*. Houghton Mifflin, 1989. / Polacco, Patricia. *The Butterfly*. Philomel, 2000. / Rey, H. A. *Curious George*. Houghton Mifflin, 1993. (And others in the Curious George series.) / Stevenson, James. *Don't You Know There's a War On?* Greenwillow, 1992.

SUBJECTS: AUTHORS—BIOGRAPHY. BIOGRAPHY. CHARACTERS IN LITERATURE. CURIOUS GEORGE (FICTITIOUS CHARACTER). JEWS. PARIS. REFUGEES. REY, H. A. REY, MARGARET. WORLD WAR, 1939–1945.

1451   **Borden, Louise, and Mary Kay Kroeger.** *Fly High! The Story of Bessie Coleman.* **Illus. by Teresa Flavin. McElderry, 2001. 0-689-82457-2. Unp. Gr. K–4**

This attractive, easy-to-read biography, with full-color gouache paintings on beige textured paper, tells the tragic but hopeful story of Bessie Coleman's brief life. The tenth child in a poor family of 13 siblings, Bessie planned to be somebody, so she learned French, found a sponsor, and in 1920, at age 28, went to France to become the first African American pilot.

GERM: Discuss: What did women such as Bessie Coleman, Amelia Earhart, Ruth Law (in Don Brown's *Ruth Law Thrills a Nation*), and Harriet Quimby (in Marissa Moss's *Brave Harriet*) have to overcome in order to become pilots? What personal qualities did they have in common? As a writing prompt, have students write their personal reactions to Bessie's words, "You can do something, too. Keep trying! Fly high!"

RELATED TITLES: Adler, David A. *A Picture Book of Amelia Earhart*. Holiday House, 1998. / Brown, Don. *Ruth Law Thrills a Nation*. Ticknor & Fields, 1993. / Burleigh, Robert. *Flight: The Journey of Charles Lindbergh*. Philomel, 1991. / Grimes, Nikki. *Talkin' About Bessie: The Story of Aviator Elizabeth Coleman*. Orchard, 2002. / Joseph, Lynn. *Fly, Bessie, Fly*. Simon & Schuster, 1998. / Lindbergh, Reeve. *Nobody Owns the Sky: The Story of "Brave Bessie" Coleman*. Candlewick, 1996. / Moss, Marissa. *Brave Harriet*. Harcourt, 2001. / Ride, Sally, and

Susan Okie. *To Space and Back*. Lothrop, 1986. / Ryan, Pam Muñoz. *Amelia and Eleanor Go for a Ride*. Scholastic, 1999.

SUBJECTS: AFRICAN AMERICANS—BIOGRAPHY. AIR PILOTS. BIOGRAPHY. COLEMAN, BESSIE. FLIGHT. MULTICULTURAL BOOKS. WOMEN—BIOGRAPHY.

1452 Bray, Rosemary L. *Martin Luther King*. Illus. by Malcah Zeldis. Greenwillow, 1995. 0-688-13132-8. 48pp. Gr. 2–5

Bray's intelligent and thoughtful picture-book biography and Zeldis's appealing full-page gouache folk art paintings personalize King's extraordinary life and give us a realistic portrayal of a difficult but hopeful period in America's past. Growing up in Atlanta, Georgia, in the 1930s, young Martin learned early and firsthand about the ugly policies of segregation and discrimination. Starting with the Montgomery bus boycott, King's leading role in the civil rights movement encompassed civil disobedience and major demonstrations, all of which the author makes comprehensible and immediate for her audience.

GERM: Compare and contrast this with other picture-book biographies, including *My Brother Martin* by Christine King Farris and *Martin's Big Words* by Doreen Rappaport.

RELATED TITLES: Adler, David A. *Dr. Martin Luther King, Jr.* Holiday House, 2001. / Adler, David A. *A Picture Book of Rosa Parks*. Holiday House, 1993. / Bridges, Ruby. *Through My Eyes*. Scholastic, 1999. / Coles, Robert. *The Story of Ruby Bridges*. Scholastic, 1995. / Curtis, Gavin. *The Bat Boy and His Violin*. Simon & Schuster, 1998. / Farris, Christine King. *My Brother Martin*. Simon & Schuster, 2003. / Golenbock, Peter. *Teammates*. Harcourt, 1990. / Greenfield, Eloise. *Rosa Parks*. HarperCollins, 1995. / King, Martin Luther. *I Have a Dream*. Scholastic, 1997. / Marzollo, Jean. *Happy Birthday, Martin Luther King*. Scholastic, 1993. / McKissack, Patricia C. *Goin' Someplace Special*. Atheneum, 2001. / Mitchell, Margaree King. *Uncle Jed's Barber Shop*. Simon & Schuster, 1993. / Parks, Rosa, and Jim Haskins. *Rosa Parks: My Story*. Puffin, 1999. / Rappaport, Doreen. *Martin's Big Words*. Hyperion, 2001. / Woodson, Jacqueline. *The Other Side*. Putnam, 2001.

SUBJECTS: AFRICAN AMERICANS—BIOGRAPHY. BIOGRAPHY. CIVIL RIGHTS. KING, MARTIN LUTHER, JR. MULTICULTURAL BOOKS. PREJUDICE. RACE RELATIONS.

1453 Bredeson, Carmen. *After the Last Dog Died: The True-Life, Hair-Raising Adventure of Douglas Mawson and His 1911–1914 Antarctic Expedition*. Illus. with photos. National Geographic, 2003. 0-7922-6140-2. 63pp. Gr. 4–8

Shackleton fans will relish this photobiography of Douglas Mawson, Australia's greatest polar explorer, who, on an expedition in Antarctica in 1912, had to set off alone over treacherous, icy terrain after the agonizing deaths of his two fellow adventurers to make his way back to the base camp a month's journey away.

GERM: A heart-stopping and gruesome tale of survival, Mawson's story, accompanied by expedition photographer Frank Hurley's black-and-white photos, will go well with the accounts of Ernest Shackleton's voyage to Antarctica, on which Frank Hurley also was ship photographer. Do check out the appendix for a good list of print and Internet resources. Students will want to search out the other excellent biographies about explorers and adventurers, including dinosaur hunter Roy Chapman Andrews, Everest conqueror Sir Edmund Hillary, and aviator Amelia Earhart.

RELATED TITLES: Armstrong, Jennifer. *Spirit of Endurance*. Crown, 2000. / Burleigh, Robert. *Black Whiteness: Admiral Byrd Alone in the Antarctic*. Atheneum, 1997. / Fraser, Mary Ann. *On Top of the World: The Conquest of Mount Everest*. Henry Holt, 1991. / Kimmel, Elizabeth Cody. *Ice Story: Shackleton's Lost Expedition*. Clarion, 1999. / Kostyal, K. M. *Trial by Ice: A Photobiography of Sir Ernest Shackleton*. National Geographic, 1999. / Marrin, Albert. *Secrets from the Rocks: Dinosaur Hunting with Roy Chapman Andrews*. Dutton, 2002. / McCurdy, Michael. *Trapped by the Ice: Shackleton's Amazing Antarctic Adventure*. Walker, 1997. / Swan, Robert. *Destination: Antarctica*. Scholastic, 1988. / Szabo, Corinne. *Sky Pioneer: A Photobiography of Amelia Earhart*. National Geographic, 1997. / Webb, Sophie. *My Season with Penguins: An Antarctic Journal*. Houghton Mifflin, 2000.

SUBJECTS: ADVENTURE AND ADVENTURERS. ANTARCTICA—DISCOVERY AND EXPLORATION. ARCTIC REGIONS. AUSTRALIAN ANTARCTIC EXPEDITION. BIOGRAPHY. EXPLORERS. MAWSON, DOUGLAS, SIR. SURVIVAL. VOYAGES AND TRAVELS.

1454 Brenner, Barbara. *The Boy Who Loved to Draw: Benjamin West*. Illus. by Olivier Dunrea. Houghton Mifflin, 1999. 0-395-85080-0. Unp. Gr. 2–4

Often called the Father of American Art, Benjamin West, born in 1738, discovered his passion for drawing at age 7 when he used his father's goose quill pen to make a sketch of his baby cousin, Sally. In a picture-book biography with folk art-style gouache paintings, based on

West's own account of his childhood, we see how his passion for art even led him to trim the fur off the family cat to make his own hair pencils (paint brushes).

GERM: At a young age, Benjamin West already knew what he loved to do. His first formal painting, done at age 10, is reproduced at the back of the book and will astonish your students. Ask them if they have begun to discover their passions yet and what they see themselves doing when they are grownups. Talk about nature versus nurture in relation to talent, and debate which is most important and why. *The Dot* by Peter H. Reynolds supports the view that if you work hard at something, you will get better at it.

RELATED TITLES: Armstrong, Jennifer. *Audubon: Painter of Birds in the Wild Frontier*. Abrams, 2003. / Brenner, Barbara. *On the Frontier with Mr. Audubon*. Boyds Mills, 1997. / dePaola, Tomie. *The Art Lesson*. Putnam, 1989. / Duggleby, John. *Artist in Overalls: The Life of Grant Wood*. Chronicle, 1996. / Reynolds, Peter H. *The Dot*. Candlewick, 2003. / Wallner, Alexandra. *Grandma Moses*. Holiday House, 2004. / Warhola, James. *Uncle Andy's*. Putnam, 2003.

SUBJECTS: ARTISTS—BIOGRAPHY. BIOGRAPHY. DRAWING. PAINTERS. WEST, BENJAMIN.

1455 Bridges, Ruby. *Through My Eyes*. Illus. with photos. Scholastic, 1999. 0-590-18923-9. 64pp. Gr. 4–8

In 1960, first grader Ruby Bridges helped to integrate the New Orleans public schools, passing a mob of demonstrating segregationists every day on her way to class, where she was taught by a courageous white teacher, Barbara Henry. Ruby's own affecting and inspirational account is interspersed with quotes by eyewitnesses, her mother, the newspapers, and child psychiatrist Robert Coles, who worked with Ruby (and wrote about her in his book, *The Moral Life of Children*; Atlantic Monthly Press, 1986). With its haunting, sepia-toned photographs, it is an indispensable addition to literature on the civil rights movement in America and on children who made a difference.

GERM: Display a color reproduction of Norman Rockwell's painting "The Problem We All Live With" and discuss its relation to Ruby Bridges and the civil rights movement.

RELATED TITLES: Adler, David A. *Dr. Martin Luther King, Jr.* Holiday House, 2001. / Adler, David A. *A Picture Book of Rosa Parks*. Holiday House, 1993. / Bray, Rosemary L. *Martin Luther King*. Greenwillow, 1995. / Coles, Robert. *The Story of Ruby Bridges*. Scholastic, 1995. / Curtis, Gavin. *The Bat Boy and His Violin*. Simon & Schuster, 1998. / Duncan, Alice Faye. *The National Civil Rights Museum Celebrates Everyday People*. BridgeWater Books, 1995. / Golenbock, Peter. *Teammates*. Harcourt, 1990. / Greenfield, Eloise. *Rosa Parks*. HarperCollins, 1995. / Lorbiecki, Marybeth. *Sister Anne's Hands*. Dial, 1998. / Nelson, Vaunda Micheaux. *Mayfield Crossing*. Putnam, 1993. / Parks, Rosa, and Jim Haskins. *I Am Rosa Parks*. Dial, 1997. / Rappaport, Doreen. *Martin's Big Words*. Hyperion, 2001.

SUBJECTS: AFRICAN AMERICANS—BIOGRAPHY. AUTOBIOGRAPHY. BIOGRAPHY. BRIDGES, RUBY. INTEGRATION. MULTICULTURAL BOOKS. PREJUDICE. RACE RELATIONS. U.S.—HISTORY—20TH CENTURY. WOMEN.

1456 Brown, Don. *Alice Ramsey's Grand Adventure*. Illus. by the author. Houghton Mifflin, 1997. 0-395-70127-9. Unp. Gr. 1–4

A mere 50 years after the pioneers were crossing the Santa Fe and Oregon Trails by stagecoach, Alice Ramsey became the first woman to drive across the country. With three other woman, she set out from New York City in her Maxwell touring car, braving mud, mountains, and deserts on roads that were often little more than dusty dirt trails. "I'll drive every inch of the way if it kills me!" she declared. Fifty-nine days later, on August 7, 1909, the group arrived in San Francisco. Brown's watercolors enhance this energetic and exciting picture-book account.

GERM: Discuss with your students what it means to be a pioneer, a daredevil, and a trailblazer. Trace Ramsey's route on modern road maps.

RELATED TITLES: Adler, David A. *A Picture Book of Amelia Earhart*. Holiday House, 1998. / Borden, Louise, and Mary Kay Kroeger. *Fly High! The Story of Bessie Coleman*. McElderry, 2001. / Brown, Don. *Ruth Law Thrills a Nation*. Ticknor & Fields, 1993. / Christensen, Bonnie. *The Daring Nellie Bly: America's Star Reporter*. Knopf, 2003. / Corey, Shana. *You Forgot Your Skirt, Amelia Bloomer!* Scholastic, 2000. / Dooling, Michael. *The Great Horse-less Carriage Race*. Holiday House, 2002. / Gilliland, Judith Heide. *Steamboat: The Story of Captain Blanche Leathers*. DK Ink, 2000. / Hyatt, Patricia Rusch. *Coast to Coast with Alice*. Carolrhoda, 1995. / Lindbergh, Reeve. *Nobody Owns the Sky: The Story of "Brave Bessie" Coleman*. Candlewick, 1996. / Moss, Marissa. *Brave Harriet*. Harcourt, 2001. / Ryan, Pam Muñoz. *Amelia and Eleanor Go for a Ride*. Scholastic, 1999. / Weitzman, David. *Model T: How Henry Ford Built a Legend*. Crown, 2002.

SUBJECTS: ADVENTURE AND ADVENTURERS. AUTOMOBILES. BIOGRAPHY. RAMSEY, ALICE. TRANSPORTATION. VOYAGES AND TRAVELS. WOMEN—BIOGRAPHY.

1457 Brown, Don. *American Boy: The Adventures of Mark Twain.* Illus. by the author. Houghton Mifflin, 2003. 0-618-17997-6. Unp. Gr. 2–6

From this smart, language-rich picture-book biography illustrated with large, easy-going, brown-toned watercolors, one can see the origins of Mark Twain's love of a good story and how his own childhood provided inspiration for his later writings.

GERM: Discussion points: What parts of Sam Clemens's childhood influenced him as a writer when he grew up? When you are grown, what parts of your childhood will you remember and will have influenced your life? What personal qualities did Sam have that might have helped him to become a great writer? Although Twain's biography is more for younger students than for those who can read his prose independently, you can certainly share representative passages from Tom Sawyer. Check your *Bartlett's Quotations* for sayings from Twain. Note that *The Adventures of Huckleberry Finn*, considered one of America's finest novels, regularly appears on banned books lists. It would be grand to show your readers a bit of movie footage of Twain as a white-haired old gent. They'll also love the fact that he was born in 1835, when Halley's Comet was visible, and died in 1910, when the comet came back. Some research into Halley's Comet will be in order.

RELATED TITLES: Aliki. *William Shakespeare and the Globe.* HarperCollins, 1999. / Anderson, William. *River Boy: The Story of Mark Twain.* HarperCollins, 2003. / Brown, Don. *Odd Boy Out: Young Albert Einstein.* Houghton Mifflin, 2004. / dePaola, Tomie. *26 Fairmount Avenue.* Putnam, 1999. / Krull, Kathleen. *Lives of the Writers.* Harcourt, 1994. / Stanley, Diane. *Bard of Avon: The Story of William Shakespeare.* Morrow, 1992. / Stanley, Diane, and Peter Vennema. *Charles Dickens: The Man Who Had Great Expectations.* Morrow, 1993.

SUBJECTS: AUTHORS—BIOGRAPHY. BIOGRAPHY. TWAIN, MARK.

1458 Brown, Don. *Kid Blink Beats the World.* Illus. by the author. Roaring Brook, 2004. 1-59643-003-6. Unp. Gr. 2–5

In the summer of 1899, thousands of young newsies, led by New York City newspaper boy Kid Blink, went on strike to protest the penny raise in price of the papers they sold, causing sales to plummet. Brown's amiable watercolors depict the struggle and partial victory of the sassy children against the bosses, Pulitzer and Hearst, and the thugs, toughs, and even chief of police who tried to thwart them.

GERM: There are some compelling issues to think about here: Why did these children have to go on strike? Why were these children working in the first place? Read more on Kid Blink and his compatriots in *Kids on Strike* by Susan Campbell Bartoletti. For background information, see Russell Freedman's *Kids at Work: Lewis Hines and the Crusade Against Child Labor.*

RELATED TITLES: Bartoletti, Susan Campbell. *Kids on Strike.* Houghton Mifflin, 1999. / Brown, Don. *Mack Made Movies.* Roaring Brook, 2003. / Freedman, Russell. *Kids at Work: Lewis Hines and the Crusade Against Child Labor.* Clarion, 1994. / Kroeger, Mary Kay, and Louise Borden. *Paperboy.* Clarion, 1996.

SUBJECTS: CHILD LABOR. NEW YORK CITY. NEWSPAPER CARRIERS. U.S.—HISTORY—20TH CENTURY.

1459 Brown, Don. *Mack Made Movies.* Illus. by the author. Roaring Brook, 2003. 0-7613-2504-2. Unp. Gr. 1–4

From his stage debut in 1900 as a horse's rear end in a vaudeville skit in New York City to his triumph as a mogul producing silent movies more than a decade later, Mack Sennett invented slapstick comedies. He produced hundreds of hilarious films, introducing the world to the Keystone Kops and their madcap car chases, Charlie Chaplin as the Tramp, and even the first pie-in-the-face. Large and lighthearted pen-and-ink and watercolors show stage sets and pratfalls, and there are direct quotes from Mack, who dubbed himself the King of Comedy.

GERM: To give children a taste of just how funny Mack Sennett's movies were and what slapstick comedy was all about, you'll naturally want to hold a movietime, replete with popcorn and videos of the Keystone Kops and Charlie Chaplin, for starters. Read Avi's picture book, *Silent Movie*, a rags-to-riches story about an immigrant boy who makes it in film, set up like a silent movie in black-and-white with subtitle cards.

RELATED TITLES: Avi. *Silent Movie.* Atheneum, 2003. / Brown, Don. *Alice Ramsey's Grand Adventure.* Houghton Mifflin, 1997. / Brown, Don. *American Boy: The Adventures of Mark Twain.* Houghton Mifflin, 2003. / Brown, Don. *Kid Blink Beats the World.* Roaring Brook, 2004. / Brown, Don. *Rare Treasure: Mary Anning and Her Remark-*

able Discoveries. Houghton Mifflin, 1999. / Brown, Don. *Ruth Law Thrills a Nation.* Ticknor & Fields, 1993. / Gish, Lillian. *An Actor's Life for Me!* Viking Kestrel, 1987. / Kamen, Gloria. *Charlie Chaplin.* Atheneum, 1982.

SUBJECTS: ACTORS AND ACTRESSES. BIOGRAPHY. MOTION PICTURE PRODUCERS AND DIRECTORS. MOTION PICTURES. SENNETT, MACK. SILENT FILMS.

1460 Brown, Don. *Odd Boy Out: Young Albert Einstein.* **Illus. by the author. Houghton Mifflin, 2004. 0-618-49298-4. Unp. Gr. 1–4**

In an eye-opening picture-book biography, illustrated with genial pen-and-inks and watercolors, we learn that Albert Einstein valued his solitude, was an indifferent student, leading his teachers to wonder if he was dull-witted, and yet worked his own way through a geometry book at age 12, which led him to devote himself to higher mathematics.

GERM: Before reading, ask your students to factstorm and make a list of everything they know about Albert Einstein. Ask them: What kind of student do you think Einstein was in school? After reading the book aloud, discuss his behavior in school. Why did his teachers not think he was very smart? Have them write compare/contrast essays, citing examples of Einstein's personal qualities and experiences as a student and comparing them with their own. Stage a mock interview with Albert and the people who knew him. Set up a panel with three volunteers playing Albert at home, at school, and outside; and others playing his parents, teachers, and little sister. The rest of your group can ask specific panel members questions about his life, which they will answer in character, using supporting details from the biography. Ask: What makes someone a genius? Also read Lynne Barasch's picture book *Ask Albert Einstein,* loosely based on a true incident.

RELATED TITLES: Adler, David A. *A Picture Book of Thomas Alva Edison.* Holiday House, 1996. / Brown, Don. *American Boy: The Adventures of Mark Twain.* Houghton Mifflin, 2003. / Brown, Don. *Kid Blink Beats the World.* Roaring Brook, 2004. / Brown, Don. *Rare Treasure: Mary Anning and Her Remarkable Discoveries.* Houghton Mifflin, 1999. / Byrd, Robert. *Leonardo, Beautiful Dreamer.* Dutton, 2003. / Delano, Marie Ferguson. *Genius: A Photobiography of Albert Einstein.* National Geographic, 2005. / Delano, Marie Ferguson. *Inventing the Future: A Photobiography of Thomas Alva Edison.* National Geographic, 2002. / Lasky, Kathryn. *The Librarian Who Measured the Earth.* Little, Brown, 1994. / Old, Wendie. *To Fly: The Story of the Wright Brothers.* Clarion, 2002.

SUBJECTS: BIOGRAPHY. EINSTEIN, ALBERT. INTELLECT. PHYSICISTS. SCIENTISTS.

1461 Brown, Don. *One Giant Leap: The Story of Neil Armstrong.* **Illus. by the author. Houghton Mifflin, 1998. 0-395-88401-2. Unp. Gr. 1–4**

Delighted with his first airplane ride at age 6, Neil Armstrong started making airplane models and reading flying magazines, and earned his student pilot's license at 16. The second half of this engrossing picture-book biography describes his moonwalk on July 20, 1969.

GERM: As the book is illustrated with blue-toned watercolors, you'll want to compare the pictures to actual photos of Neil Armstrong. Emphasized here is the way his early passion about flying led to his illustrious career. Ask your students what they love to do and what their dreams are for the future. Have them make a list of possible strategies they can undertake to see those dreams fulfilled someday.

RELATED TITLES: Aldrin, Buzz. *Reaching for the Moon.* HarperCollins, 2005. / Fraser, Mary Ann. *One Giant Leap.* Henry Holt, 1993. / Gaffney, Timothy R. *Grandpa Takes Me to the Moon.* Tambourine, 1996. / Haddon, Mark. *The Sea of Tranquility.* Harcourt, 1996. / Schyffert, Bea Uusma. *The Man Who Went to the Far Side of the Moon: The Story of Apollo 11 Astronaut Michael Collins.* Chronicle, 2003. / Simon, Seymour. *The Moon.* Simon & Schuster, 2003. / Suen, Anastasia. *Man on the Moon.* Viking, 1997.

SUBJECTS: ARMSTRONG, NEIL. ASTRONAUTS. BIOGRAPHY. MOON. SPACE FLIGHT TO THE MOON.

1462 Brown, Don. *Rare Treasure: Mary Anning and Her Remarkable Discoveries.* **Illus. by the author. Houghton Mifflin, 1999. 0-395-92286-0. Unp. Gr. 2–5**

Celebrating the bicentennial of fossil hunter Mary Anning's birth, Brown's picture-book biography is the most chronological and fact-based of the four children's books published about her, all published in 1999, and is illustrated with watercolors.

GERM: Students can chart, analyze, and compare the other books about Anning by Anholt, Atkins, and Brighton—an undertaking that will show clearly that one picture-book biography can't tell them everything they want to know.

RELATED TITLES: Anholt, Laurence. *Stone Girl, Bone Girl: The Story of Mary Anning.* Orchard, 1999. / Atkins, Jeannine. *Mary Anning and the Sea Dragon.* Farrar, 1999. / Bausum, Ann. *Dragon Bones and Dinosaur*

Eggs: A Photobiography of Explorer Roy Chapman Andrews. National Geographic, 2000. / Brighton, Catherine. *The Fossil Girl: Mary Anning's Dinosaur Discovery.* Millbrook, 1999. / Brown, Don. *Odd Boy Out: Young Albert Einstein.* Houghton Mifflin, 2004. / Kerley, Barbara. *The Dinosaurs of Waterhouse Hawkins.* Scholastic, 2001. / Larson, Peter, and Kristin Donnan. *Bones Rock! Everything You Need to Know to Be a Paleontologist.* Invisible Cities, 2004.

SUBJECTS: ANNING, MARY, 1799–1847. BIOGRAPHY. ENGLAND. FOSSILS. PALEONTOLOGY. SCIENTISTS. WOMEN—BIOGRAPHY.

1463 Burleigh, Robert. *Black Whiteness: Admiral Byrd Alone in the Antarctic.* **Illus. by Walter Lyon Krudop. Atheneum, 1998. 0-689-81299-X. 36pp. Gr. 4–6**

For almost six months in 1934, Admiral Richard Byrd lived alone at Advance Base in Antarctica, the first inland base there, recording information from eight weather instruments and keeping a diary of his experiences. Set up in picture-book format as a prose poem told in present tense, with frequent quotes from Byrd's diaries and stark, impressionistic ice blue paintings, this true account of his survival and will to live is both riveting and terrifying.

GERM: Discover accounts of earlier 20th-century polar explorers—including Ernest Shackleton in Jennifer Armstrong's *Spirit of Endurance* and Douglas Mawson in *Carmen Bredeson's After the Last Dog Died.*

RELATED TITLES: Armstrong, Jennifer. *Shipwreck at the Bottom of the World: The Extraordinary True Story of Shackleton and the Endurance.* Crown, 1998. / Armstrong, Jennifer. *Spirit of Endurance.* Crown, 2000. / Brandenberg, Jim. *To the Top of the World: Adventures with Arctic Wolves.* Walker, 1993. / Bredeson, Carmen. *After the Last Dog Died: The True-Life, Hair-Raising Adventure of Douglas Mawson and His 1911–1914 Antarctic Expedition.* National Geographic, 2003. / Hooper, Meredith. *Tom's Rabbit: A Surprise on the Way to Antarctica.* National Geographic, 1998. / Kimmel, Elizabeth Cody. *Ice Story: Shackleton's Lost Expedition.* Clarion, 1999. / Kostyal, K. M. *Trial by Ice: A Photobiography of Sir Ernest Shackleton.* National Geographic, 1999. / McCurdy, Michael. *Trapped by the Ice: Shackleton's Amazing Antarctic Adventure.* Walker, 1997. / Swan, Robert. *Destination: Antarctica.* Scholastic, 1988. / Webb, Sophie. *My Season with Penguins.* Houghton Mifflin, 2000.

SUBJECTS: ANTARCTICA—DISCOVERY AND EXPLORATION. ARCTIC REGIONS. BIOGRAPHY. BYRD, RICHARD EVELYN, 1888–1957. EXPLORERS. SCIENTISTS. SURVIVAL. VOYAGES AND TRAVELS. WEATHER. WINTER.

1464 Burleigh, Robert. *Home Run: The Story of Babe Ruth.* **Illus. by Mike Wimmer. Harcourt, 1998. 0-15-200970-1. 32pp. Gr. 2–6**

Part poem, part tribute, and part biography, this description of Babe Ruth's home run prowess is illustrated with photo-realistic paintings that take you right onto the field with the Babe. Reproductions of period bubblegum cards—with tiny print containing quotes, stats, and anecdotes—are on each page.

GERM: Baseball fans can write and illustrate minibooks or cards about their favorite athletes from history or today, using sources including books, the sports section of the newspaper, magazines including *Sports Illustrated for Kids,* and the Internet. *Mighty Jackie, the Strike-Out Queen* by Marissa Moss is the true story of the 17-year-old girl who struck out the Babe. Read about another famous teammate in David A. Adler's heartbreaking but inspiring picture-book biography, *Lou Gehrig: The Luckiest Man.*

RELATED TITLES: Adler, David A. *Lou Gehrig: The Luckiest Man.* Harcourt, 1997. / Cline-Ransome, Lisa. *Satchel Paige.* Simon & Schuster, 2000. / Hall, Donald. *When Willard Met Babe Ruth.* Harcourt, 1996. / Hopkins, Lee Bennett, comp. *Extra Innings: Baseball Poems.* Harcourt, 1993. / Hopkinson, Deborah. *Girl Wonder: A Baseball Story in Nine Innings.* Atheneum, 2003. / Janeczko, Paul B. *That Sweet Diamond: Baseball Poems.* Atheneum, 1998. / Morrison, Lillian, comp. *At the Crack of the Bat: Baseball Poems.* Hyperion, 1992. / Moss, Marissa. *Mighty Jackie, the Strike-Out Queen.* Simon & Schuster, 2004. / Norworth, Jack. *Take Me Out to the Ballgame.* Four Winds, 1993.

SUBJECTS: ATHLETES—BIOGRAPHY. BASEBALL—BIOGRAPHY. BIOGRAPHY. RUTH, BABE. SPORTS—BIOGRAPHY.

1465 Busby, Peter. *First to Fly: How Wilbur and Orville Wright Invented the Airplane.* **Illus. by David Craig. Random House, 2003. 0-375-81287-3. 32pp. Gr. 3–6**

Along with the expertly crafted text, filled with firsthand quotes and up-close descriptions, this dazzling scrapbook contains paintings, archival photographs, and diagrams your readers will pore over. This Wright Brothers biography has it all: good looks; a meaty, quote-filled text that reads like a dream; scientific explanations your kids will inhale and understand; huge paintings; archival photos; a labeled drawing of the 1903 Wright Flyer; sidebar explanations of wing-warping; and, my personal favorite, a cogent description of the three movements all aircraft make: pitch, roll, and yaw. To round it off, there are a list of important dates, a glossary, a selected bibliography with books and Web sites, and an index. Nonfiction doesn't get any better than this!

GERM: After reading the book aloud, ask your students what made Orville and Wilbur such good inventors? Make a list of their attributes. What other qualities do they think a good inventor must have? Pair with Wendie Old's *To Fly* and then follow up with Judith St. George's *So You Want to Be an Inventor*.

RELATED TITLES: Adler, David A. *A Picture Book of Amelia Earhart*. Holiday House, 1998. / Brown, Don. *Ruth Law Thrills a Nation*. Ticknor & Fields, 1993. / Burleigh, Robert. *Flight: The Journey of Charles Lindbergh*. Philomel, 1991. / Collins, Mary. *Airborne: A Photobiography of Wilbur and Orville Wright*. National Geographic, 2003. / Freedman, Russell. *The Wright Brothers: How They Invented the Airplane*. Holiday House, 1991. / Hunter, Ryan Ann. *Into the Air: An Illustrated Timeline of Flight*. National Geographic, 2003. / Old, Wendie. *To Fly: The Story of the Wright Brothers*. Clarion, 2002. / St. George, Judith. *So You Want to Be an Inventor?* Philomel, 2002. / Szabo, Corinne. *Sky Pioneer: A Photobiography of Amelia Earhart*. National Geographic, 1997. / Weitzman, David. *Model T: How Henry Ford Built a Legend*. Crown, 2002.

SUBJECTS: AERONAUTICS. AIR PILOTS. AIRPLANES. BIOGRAPHY. FLIGHT. INVENTIONS AND INVENTORS. SCIENCE. WRIGHT BROTHERS.

1466 Byrd, Robert. *Leonardo, Beautiful Dreamer*. Illus. by the author. Dutton, 2003. 0-525-47033-6. Unp. Gr. 4–7

The amazing life of Leonardo da Vinci (1452–1519) is summed up in admiring prose and intricate pen-and-ink and watercolor illustrations in this breathtaking oversized picture book. Laced with quotes from his notebooks and descriptions of his many inventions, Leonardo's story revels in his curiosity about the world and his skill in uncovering truths about not only painting, but anatomy, architecture, mathematics, vision, flight, and much, much more.

GERM: Researchers can further investigate some of Leonardo's interests and discoveries, including kites (both the bird and the object), the city of Florence and its duomo, the story of David and Goliath, unicorns, and the eye. Ask your librarian and art teacher for books and other materials with reproductions of Leonardo's paintings for all to behold. Other essential titles include *Leonardo da Vinci* by Diane Stanley and *Leonardo's Horse* by Jean Fritz.

RELATED TITLES: Brown, Don. *Odd Boy Out: Young Albert Einstein*. Houghton Mifflin, 2004. / Fleming, Candace. *Ben Franklin's Almanac: Being a True Account of the Good Gentleman's Life*. Atheneum, 2003. / Fritz, Jean. *Leonardo's Horse*. Putnam, 2001. / Krull, Kathleen. *Lives of the Artists: Masterpieces, Messes (and What the Neighbors Thought)*. Harcourt, 1995. / Schanzer, Rosalyn. *How Ben Franklin Stole the Lightning*. HarperCollins, 2003. / Skira-Venturi, Rosabianca. *A Weekend with Leonardo da Vinci*. Rizzoli, 1993. / Stanley, Diane. *Leonardo da Vinci*. Morrow, 1996. / Stanley, Diane. *Michelangelo*. HarperCollins, 2000. / Woodruff, Elvira. *The Disappearing Bike Shop*. Holiday House, 1992.

SUBJECTS: ARTISTS—BIOGRAPHY. BIOGRAPHY. INVENTIONS AND INVENTORS. LEONARDO DA VINCI, 1452–1519. PAINTERS. SCIENTISTS.

1467 Carlson, Laurie. *Boss of the Plains: The Hat That Won the West*. Illus. by Holly Meade. DK Ink, 1998. 0-7894-2479-7. 32pp. Gr. 1–6

Digging for gold in Colorado in 1859, New Jersey hatter John Stetson found that his stylish derby hat afforded him no protection from the scorching sun and the whipping wind, so he made himself a wide-brimmed, thick, fur felt hat. His invaluable new creation, which he called "Boss of the Plains," soon became the most popular hat west of the Mississippi. Westerners said, "It gets so you can smell it across a room, but you just can't wear it out." This is a lively, humorous picture-book biography, impeccably researched, of a man who made his mark in an atypical way. The congenial collage illustrations provide a rousing portrait of life out West.

GERM: Wear your Stetson hat as you conduct a choral reading, with true cowboy emotion, of the marvelous anonymous poem printed on the back cover: "My Old Stetson Hat."

RELATED TITLES: Axelrod, Alan. *Songs of the Wild West*. Simon & Schuster, 1991. / Dadey, Debbie. *Shooting Star: Annie Oakley, the Legend*. Walker, 1997 / Freedman, Russell. *Children of the Wild West*. Clarion, 1983. / Ketteman, Helen. *Bubba the Cowboy Prince: A Fractured Texas Tale*. Scholastic, 1997. / Lowell, Susan. *The Bootmaker and the Elves*. Clarion, 1996. / Lowell, Susan. *Cindy Ellen: A Wild Western Cinderella*. Orchard, 1997. / Martin, Jacqueline Briggs. *Snowflake Bentley*. Houghton Mifflin, 1998. / Pinkney, Andrea D. *Bill Pickett: Rodeo-Ridin' Cowboy*. Harcourt, 1996. / Ryan, Pam Muñoz. *Riding Freedom*. Scholastic, 1998. / Say, Allen. *El Chino*.

Houghton Mifflin, 1990. / Schanzer, Rosalyn. *How We Crossed the West: The Adventures of Lewis and Clark.* National Geographic, 1997. / Van Leeuwen, Jean. *Bound for Oregon.* Dial, 1994. / Woodruff, Elvira. *Dear Levi: Letters from the Overland Trail.* Knopf, 1994.

SUBJECTS: BIOGRAPHY. CLOTHING AND DRESS. COWBOYS. HATS. STETSON, JOHN. U.S.—HISTORY. WEST (U.S.)—HISTORY.

1468 **Chandra, Deborah, and Madeline Comora.** *George Washington's Teeth.* **Illus. by Brock Cole. Farrar, 2003. 0-374-32534-0. Unp. Gr. 2–8**

What were George Washington's false teeth made of? Wood? Wrong. If ever anyone made a case for taking better care of one's choppers and visiting the dentist regularly, George was the guy. Told in galloping verse, the jaw-dropping life story of our first president is recounted and related to his lifelong battle with his rotting, dreadful teeth. The authors of this combination of history and poetry have taken George's lifelong tale of tooth agony and turned it into a jaunty, lively account, accompanied by frolicsome watercolors. At the back of the book is a detailed timeline with color reproductions, firsthand quotes, and startling facts.

GERM: Read the story and all the information in the timeline at the back of the book. Then read the story again so students can compare the real events in Washington's life with the retelling of it in verse. Students can then pick a famous person to research and can read a biography, draw a portrait, and incorporate facts about the person's life into a rhyming biographical sketch. Of course you'll want to link this to the inspirational Caldecott winner, *So You Want to Be President?* for background on the office and its occupants since George's time. George's dentures, by the way, were fashioned of hippopotamus, walrus, or elephant ivory, along with real human, elk, and cow teeth. Tie this in to Dental Health Month, and your students will be brushing and flossing like mad.

RELATED TITLES: Beeler, Selby B. *Throw Your Tooth on the Roof: Tooth Traditions from Around the World.* Houghton Mifflin, 1998. / Cronin, Doreen. *Duck for President.* Simon & Schuster, 2004. / Giblin, James Cross. *George Washington: A Picture Book Biography.* Scholastic, 1992. / Harness, Cheryl. *George Washington.* National Geographic, 2000. / Keller, Laurie. *Open Wide: Tooth School Inside.* Henry Holt, 2000. / Krull, Kathleen. *Lives of the Presidents: Fame, Shame (and What the Neighbors Thought).* Harcourt, 1998. / Longfellow, Henry Wadsworth. *The Midnight Ride of Paul Revere.* Illus. by Christopher Bing. Handprint, 2001. / Longfellow, Henry Wadsworth. *Paul Revere's Ride.* Illus. by Ted Rand. Dutton, 1990. / Palatini, Margie. *Sweet Tooth.* Simon & Schuster, 2004. / Schanzer, Roslyn. *George vs. George.* National Geographic, 2004. / St. George, Judith. *So You Want to Be President?* Philomel, 2000. / St. George, Judith. *Take the Lead, George Washington.* Philomel, 2005. / Stier, Catherine. *If I Were President.* Albert Whitman, 1999. / Winters, Kay. *My Teacher for President.* Dutton, 2004.

SUBJECTS: BIOGRAPHY. DENTISTS AND DENTAL CARE. PRESIDENTS. STORIES IN RHYME. TEETH. WASHINGTON, GEORGE.

1469 **Christensen, Bonnie.** *The Daring Nellie Bly: America's Star Reporter.* **Illus. by the author. Knopf, 2003. 0-375-91568-0. Unp. Gr. 2–6**

Hired as a journalist in 1885, in the days when few women had jobs except in factories and sweatshops, Elizabeth Cochran, using the pen name Nellie Bly, became famous as a stunt reporter for the *New York World.* She exposed the appalling conditions in the Women's Lunatic Asylum in New York, but is best remembered for her historic voyage around the world, which she completed on Jan. 25, 1890, in a record-breaking 72 days.

GERM: In 1890, Nellie Bly was described in the newspaper as being "the best known and most widely talked of young woman on earth today." Extrapolating details from the book, ask students to describe what a woman's role was in the United States back then and to discuss and write about how conditions changed over the next century. Bly wrote that each individual has a moral responsibility to "the whole world of mankind: good, bad and indifferent." Older students can write an editorial on their response to that quote in terms of their own experiences and observations.

RELATED TITLES: Adler, David A. *America's Champion Swimmer: Gertrude Ederle.* Harcourt, 2000. / Adler, David A. *A Picture Book of Amelia Earhart.* Holiday House, 1998. / Anholt, Laurence. *Stone Girl, Bone Girl: The Story of Mary Anning.* Orchard, 1999. / Brown, Don. *Kid Blink Beats the World.* Roaring Brook, 2004. / Brown, Don. *Ruth Law Thrills a Nation.* Ticknor & Fields, 1993. / Butcher, Nancy. *It Can't Be Done, Nellie Bly!: A Reporter's Race Around the World.* Peachtree, 2003. / Corey, Shana. *You Forgot Your Skirt, Amelia Bloomer!* Scholastic, 2000. / Evans, Douglas. *MVP*: *Magellan Voyage Project.* Front Street, 2004. / Gilliland, Judith Heide. *Steamboat: The Story of Captain Blanche Leathers.* DK Ink, 2000. / Krensky, Stephen. *Nellie Bly: A Name to Be Reckoned With.* Aladdin, 2003. / Lasky, Kathryn. *A Voice of Her Own: The Story of Phillis Wheatley, Slave Poet.* Candlewick, 2002. / Ryan, Pam Muñoz. *When Marian Sang.* Scholastic, 2002. / White, Linda Arms. *I Could Do*

That: Esther Morris Gets Women the Vote. Farrar, 2005. / Wooldridge, Connie Nordhielm. *When Esther Morris Headed West: Women, Wyoming, and the Right to Vote.* Holiday House, 2001.

SUBJECTS: BIOGRAPHY. BLY, NELLIE, 1864–1922. JOURNALISTS. NEWSPAPERS. REPORTERS. VOYAGES AND TRAVELS. VOYAGES AROUND THE WORLD. WOMEN—BIOGRAPHY.

1470 **Christensen, Bonnie.** *Woody Guthrie: Poet of the People.* **Illus. by the author. Knopf, 2001. 0-375-91113-8. Unp. Gr. 2–6**

Woodcut-style illustrations accompany a picture-book biography of songwriter and folksinger Woody Guthrie, born in Okemah, Oklahoma, in 1912 and author of the folk anthem "This Land Is Your Land."

GERM: Read in tandem with the visually dazzling picture book *This Land Is Your Land,* and sing his songs, of course.

RELATED TITLES: Coombs, Karen Mueller. *Woody Guthrie: America's Folksinger.* Carolrhoda, 2002. / Friedrich, Elizabeth. *Leah's Pony.* Boyd's Mills, 1996. / Guthrie, Woody. *This Land Is Your Land.* Little, Brown, 1998. / Guthrie, Woody, and Marjorie Mazia Guthrie. *Woody's 20 Grow Big Songs.* HarperCollins, 1992. / Hess, Karen. *Out of the Dust.* Scholastic, 1997. / Lied, Kate. *Potato: A Tale from the Great Depression.* National Geographic, 1997. / Partridge, Elizabeth. *This Land Was Made for You and Me.* Viking, 2002.

SUBJECTS: BIOGRAPHY. DEPRESSIONS—1929—U.S. FOLK SINGERS. GUTHRIE, WOODY. MUSICIANS.

1471 **Cleveland, Will, and Mark Alvarez.** *Yo, Millard Fillmore! (And All Those Other Presidents You Don't Know).* **Illus. by Tate Nation. Millbrook, 1997. 0-9632778-0-4. 112pp. Gr. 4–6**

A lighthearted review of each president includes dates and facts on the left-hand page and a cartoon-style illustration with a humorous cumulative mnemonic story to help recall each president's name and sequence on the right.

GERM: Start a discussion: Which president do you most admire and why? Make a list of the qualities of a good president. Play "Who Am I?" Each student can research interesting facts about a president, write a short paragraph describing his life, and read it aloud for others to identify. Learn the state capitals with the authors' similarly formatted *Yo, Sacramento!*

RELATED TITLES: Burns, Diane, and Clint Burns. *Hail to the Chief! Jokes About the Presidents.* Lerner, 1989. / Cleveland, Will, and Mark Alvarez. *Yo, Sacramento! (And All Those Other State Capitals You Don't Know).* Millbrook, 1997. / Davis, Gibbs. *Wackiest White House Pets.* Scholastic, 2004. / Gutman, Dan. *The Kid Who Ran for President.* Scholastic, 1996. / Harness, Cheryl. *Ghosts of the White House.* Simon & Schuster, 1998. / Jones, Rebecca C. *The President Has Been Shot: True Stories of the Attacks on Ten U.S. Presidents.* Dutton, 1996. / Krull, Kathleen. *Lives of the Presidents: Fame, Shame (and What the Neighbors Thought).* Harcourt, 1998. / Maestro, Betsy. *The Voice of the People: American Democracy in Action.* Lothrop, 1996. / O'Connor, Jane. *If the Walls Could Talk: Family Life at the White House.* Simon & Schuster, 2004. / Provensen, Alice. *The Buck Stops Here: The Presidents of the United States.* Harcourt, 2000. / St. George, Judith. *So You Want to Be President?* Philomel, 2000. / Stier, Catherine. *If I Were President.* Albert Whitman, 1999.

SUBJECTS: BIOGRAPHY. MNEMONICS. PRESIDENTS. U.S.—HISTORY.

1472 **Cline-Ransome, Lesa.** *Satchel Paige.* **Illus. by James E. Ransome. Simon & Schuster, 2000. 0-689-81151-9. 40pp. Gr. 2–5**

Leroy "Satchel" Paige became a pitcher extraordinaire for the Negro League in the 1920s, and the first African American pitcher to be drafted into the major leagues in 1948, as recounted in this energetic picture-book biography. Toting luggage for train travelers at the Mobile, Alabama station, Leroy Paige got his nickname from the satchels he carried. Expressive full-page oil paintings capture the excitement of Satchel's intense concentration and love of the game; the insightful text illustrates the devastating effects of segregation on the careers of the Negro League players.

GERM: Read this inspirational story at the start of baseball season, for Black History Month, or just to talk about indefatigable heroes. The "Vital Statistics" page will make a fine model for students doing reports on other sports greats. Take your group outside to play a little ball.

RELATED TITLES: Adler, David A. *Lou Gehrig: The Luckiest Man.* Harcourt, 1997. / Burleigh, Robert. *Home Run: The Story of Babe Ruth.* Harcourt, 1998. / Cline-Ransome, Lesa. *Major Taylor, Champion Cyclist.* Atheneum, 2004. / Cohen, Barbara. *Thank You, Jackie Robinson.* Lothrop, 1988. / Curtis, Gavin. *The Bat Boy and His Violin.* Simon & Schuster, 1998. / Golenbock, Peter. *Teammates.* Harcourt, 1990. / Gutman, Dan. *Jackie and Me: A Baseball Card Adventure.* Avon, 1999. / Krull, Kathleen. *Lives of the Athletes: Thrills, Spills (and What the Neighbors Thought).* Harcourt, 1995. / Krull, Kathleen. *Wilma Unlimited: How Wilma Rudolph Became the World's Fastest*

Woman. Harcourt, 1996. / Mochizuki, Ken. *Baseball Saved Us.* Lee & Low, 1993. / Morrison, Lillian, comp. *At the Crack of the Bat: Baseball Poems.* Hyperion, 1992. / Nelson, Vaunda Micheaux. *Mayfield Crossing.* Putnam, 1993. / Norworth, Jack. *Take Me Out to the Ballgame.* Four Winds, 1993.

SUBJECTS: AFRICAN AMERICANS—BIOGRAPHY. ATHLETES—BIOGRAPHY. BASEBALL—BIOGRAPHY. BIOGRAPHY. MULTICULTURAL BOOKS. NEGRO LEAGUES. PAIGE, LEROY "SATCHEL". PREJUDICE. SPORTS—BIOGRAPHY.

1473 Cohn, Amy L., and Suzy Schmidt. *Abraham Lincoln.* Illus. by David A. Johnson. Scholastic, 2002. 0-590-93566-6. Unp. Gr. 2–5

Along with a gentle, folksy retelling of Lincoln's life, soft, full-page ink-and-watercolor wash illustrations give an up-close and personal look at a giant of a man.

GERM: Compare the illustrations in the book with the photos in Russell Freedman's *Lincoln: A Photobiography.* Discuss: What do they reveal to us about Lincoln?

RELATED TITLES: Borden, Louise. *A. Lincoln and Me.* Scholastic, 1999. / Brenner, Martha. *Abe Lincoln's Hat.* Random House, 1994. / Freedman, Russell. *Lincoln: A Photobiography.* Clarion, 1987. / Harness, Cheryl. *Abe Lincoln Goes to Washington.* National Geographic, 1997. / Kunhardt, Edith. *Honest Abe.* Greenwillow, 1993. / Lincoln, Abraham. *The Gettysburg Address.* Houghton Mifflin, 1995. / Livingston, Myra Cohn. *Abraham Lincoln: A Man for All the People.* Holiday House, 1993. / Winnick, Karen B. *Mr. Lincoln's Whiskers.* Boyds Mills, 1996. / Winters, Kay. *Abe Lincoln: The Boy Who Loved Books.* Simon & Schuster, 2003.

SUBJECTS: BIOGRAPHY. LINCOLN, ABRAHAM. PRESIDENTS.

1474 Cooney, Barbara. *Eleanor.* Illus. by the author. Viking, 1996. 0-670-86159-6. 40pp. Gr. 2–4

"From the beginning the baby was a disappointment to her mother," begins Cooney's visually graceful but somber picture-book biography about the stark and difficult childhood of one of our most admired heroines, Eleanor Roosevelt. A solemn, shy, plain child, Eleanor lost both her parents by the time she was 9, and was sent to the loveless house of her grandmother. What's so compelling about this "poor-little-rich-girl" story is the way Eleanor prevailed, attending Allenswood, an English boarding school where an inspirational headmistress imbued her with a sense of worth and challenged her to think for herself.

GERM: Children need to know it is possible to triumph over terrible odds. Fast forward to Roosevelt's life in the White House with *Amelia and Eleanor Go for a Ride* by Pam Muñoz Ryan.

RELATED TITLES: Adler, David A. *A Picture Book of Eleanor Roosevelt.* Holiday House, 1991. / Freedman, Russell. *Eleanor Roosevelt.* Clarion, 1995. / Harness, Cheryl. *Franklin and Eleanor.* Dutton, 2004. / Krull, Kathleen. *Lives of Extraordinary Women: Rulers, Rebels (and What the Neighbors Thought).* Harcourt, 2000. / Ryan, Pam Muñoz. *Amelia and Eleanor Go for a Ride.* Scholastic, 1999.

SUBJECTS: BIOGRAPHY. FIRST LADIES. ORPHANS. ROOSEVELT, ELEANOR. WOMEN—BIOGRAPHY.

1475 Corey, Shana. *You Forgot Your Skirt, Amelia Bloomer! A Very Improper Story.* Illus. by Chesley McLaren. Scholastic, 2000. 0-439-07819-9. 32pp. Gr. 2–4

"Amelia Bloomer was NOT a proper lady." So begins a delightful, breezy picture book about the suffragist who started her own women's newspaper, *The Lily,* in Seneca Falls, New York, in 1851, and changed the fashion world with her revolutionary, scandalous "Bloomers," as the pantaloons came to be called.

GERM: Cheerful, colorful watercolors accompany the high-spirited text, which will encourage listeners to think about how clothing influences and is influenced by the customs and standards of each era, and to take a closer look at what is now in vogue. Children can interview parents and grandparents to find out which of the styles they wore shocked their parents, and perhaps bring in some outfits from the past or draw fashion sketches of them.

RELATED TITLES: Blumberg, Rhoda. *Bloomers.* Atheneum, 1993. / Brown, Don. *Ruth Law Thrills a Nation.* Ticknor & Fields, 1993. / Christensen, Bonnie. *The Daring Nellie Bly: America's Star Reporter.* Knopf, 2003. / Corey, Shana. *Players in Pigtails.* Scholastic, 2003. / Fritz, Jean. *You Want Women to Vote, Lizzie Stanton?* Putnam, 1995. / Gilliland, Judith Heide. *Steamboat: The Story of Captain Blanche Leathers.* DK Ink, 2000. / Krull, Kathleen. *Lives of Extraordinary Women: Rulers, Rebels (and What the Neighbors Thought).* Harcourt, 2000. / Krull, Kathleen. *A Woman for President: The Story of Victoria Woodhull.* Walker, 2004. / McCully, Emily Arnold. *The Ballot Box Battle.* Knopf, 1996. / Moss, Marissa. *Mighty Jackie, the Strike-Out Queen.* Simon & Schuster, 2004. / White, Linda Arms. *I Could Do That: Esther Morris Gets Women the Vote.* Farrar, 2005. / Wooldridge, Connie Nordhielm. *When Esther Morris Headed West: Women, Wyoming, and the Right to Vote.* Holiday House, 2001.

SUBJECTS: BIOGRAPHY. BLOOMER, AMELIA, 1818–1894. CLOTHING AND DRESS. FEMINISTS. SUFFRAGISTS. U.S.—HISTORY. WOMEN—BIOGRAPHY. WOMEN'S RIGHTS.

1476 Cummings, Pat, comp. *Talking with Artists*, Vol. 3. Clarion, 1999. 0-395-89132-9. 96pp. Gr. 2–5
Thirteen noted children's book illustrators provide their responses to editor Cummings's probing interview questions. Photos—of the artists as children and adults, as well as of their pets—plus reproductions of their past and present artwork and autobiographical descriptions round out each entry.
GERM: Using all three volumes of this insightful series, researchers can each pick an illustrator, read his or her books, and work up a presentation combining biographical facts and art.
RELATED TITLES: *The Art of Reading: Forty Illustrators Celebrate RIF's 40th Anniversary.* Dutton, 2005. / Christelow, Eileen. *What Do Illustrators Do?* Clarion, 1999. / Cummings, Pat, ed. *Talking with Artists.* Bradbury, 1992. / Cummings, Pat, ed. *Talking with Artists*, Volume Two. Simon & Schuster, 1995. / Ehrlich, Amy, ed. *When I Was Your Age: Original Stories About Growing Up.* Candlewick, 1996. / Engel, Dean, and Florence D. Freedman. *Ezra Jack Keats: A Biography with Illustrations.* Silver Moon, 1995. / Marcus, Leonard S., ed. *Author Talk.* Simon & Schuster, 2000. / McPhail, David. *In Flight with David McPhail.* Heinemann, 1996. / Peet, Bill. *Bill Peet: An Autobiography.* Houghton Mifflin, 1989. / Polacco, Patricia. *Firetalking.* Richard C. Owen, 1994. (And others in the Meet the Author series.) / Rosen, Michael J., ed. *Purr . . . Children's Book Illustrators Brag About Their Cats.* Harcourt, 1996. / Rosen, Michael J., ed. *Speak! Children's Book Illustrators Brag About Their Dogs.* Harcourt, 1993. / *Wings of an Artist: Children's Book Illustrators Talk About Their Art.* Abrams, 1999.
SUBJECTS: ARTISTS—BIOGRAPHY. AUTOBIOGRAPHY. BIOGRAPHY. ILLUSTRATORS.

1477 Davies, Jacqueline. *The Boy Who Drew Birds: A Story of John James Audubon.* Illus. by Melissa Sweet. Houghton Mifflin, 2003. 0-618-24343-7. Unp. Gr. 1–5
Living on a Pennsylvania farm in 1804, where his father had sent him from his home in France to learn English and to avoid fighting in Napoleon's war, 18-year-old John James Audubon was obsessed with birds. He kept in his room what he called a musée (museum) of nests, eggs, stuffed birds, and his own drawings and paintings. Observing the small pewee flycatchers from spring to fall, Audubon tied a thread around the leg of each baby bird in one nest before they disappeared for the winter. In the spring, the birds returned, and Audubon, the first person in America to band a bird, proved that many birds return to the same nests each spring, a behavior called homing.
GERM: Meticulous soft watercolor and mixed media illustrations add depth to a story of observation and discovery that will inspire children to look more closely and draw the birds around them. Your library should have a book of Audubon's bird paintings to share. *Audubon: Painter of Birds in the Wild Frontier* by Jennifer Armstrong depicts him at a later age, while *Capturing Nature: The Writings and Art of John James Audubon* is filled with anecdotes from his personal journals and some of his glorious paintings.
RELATED TITLES: Armstrong, Jennifer. *Audubon: Painter of Birds in the Wild Frontier.* Abrams, 2003. / Audubon, John James. *Capturing Nature: The Writings and Art of John James Audubon.* Ed. by Peter Roop and Connie Roop. Walker, 1993. / Brenner, Barbara. *The Boy Who Loved to Draw: Benjamin West.* Houghton Mifflin, 1999. / Brenner, Barbara. *On the Frontier with Mr. Audubon.* Boyds Mills, 1997. / Burleigh, Robert. *Into the Woods: John James Audubon Lives His Dream.* Atheneum, 2003. / DeFelice, Cynthia. *Lostman's River.* Macmillan, 1994. / Fleming, Candace. *When Agnes Caws.* Atheneum, 1999. / Florian, Douglas. *On the Wing: Bird Poems and Paintings.* Harcourt, 1996. / Kerley, Barbara. *The Dinosaurs of Waterhouse Hawkins.* Scholastic, 2001. / Ray, Deborah Kogan. *The Flower Hunter: William Bartram, America's First Naturalist.* Farrar, 2004. / Swinburne, Stephen R. *Unbeatable Beaks.* Henry Holt, 1999. / Yolen, Jane. *Bird Watch: A Book of Poetry.* Philomel, 1990.
SUBJECTS: ARTISTS—BIOGRAPHY. AUDUBON, JOHN JAMES. BIOGRAPHY. BIRDS. NATURALISTS. ORNITHOLOGISTS. PAINTERS. SCIENTISTS.

1478 Delano, Marie Ferguson. *Inventing the Future: A Photobiography of Thomas Alva Edison.* Illus. with photos. National Geographic, 2002. 0-7922-6721-4. 64pp. Gr. 4–8
"What seems impossible today, may not be tomorrow." These prophetic words came from Thomas Edison, responsible for more than 1,000 inventions. Huge full- and double-page black-and-white photos of Edison and his inventions, firsthand quotes from the "old man," as his workers called him, and an overview of his life and work, told in clear, compelling prose, make this an unforgettable biography.
GERM: Compile a list with your group: What still needs to be invented? Which of Edison's inventions affect our lives the most? Get to know the irascible Edison in Dan Gutman's delight-

ful time-travel adventure novel, *Qwerty Stevens Back in Time: The Edison Mystery*, in which 13-year-old Qwerty helps Edison with his new invention: the light bulb.

RELATED TITLES: Brown, Don. *Odd Boy Out: Young Albert Einstein*. Houghton Mifflin, 2004. / Delano, Marie Ferguson. *Genius: A Photobiography of Albert Einstein*. National Geographic, 2005. / DuPrau, Jeanne. *The City of Ember*. Random House, 2003. / Gutman, Dan. *Qwerty Stevens Back in Time: The Edison Mystery*. Simon & Schuster, 2001. / Moore, Floyd C. *I Gave Thomas Edison My Sandwich*. Albert Whitman, 1995. / Old, Wendie. *To Fly: The Story of the Wright Brothers*. Clarion, 2002. / St. George, Judith. *So You Want to Be an Inventor?* Philomel, 2002.

SUBJECTS: BIOGRAPHY. EDISON, THOMAS ALVA. INVENTIONS AND INVENTORS. SCIENCE. SCIENTISTS.

1479   **dePaola, Tomie. *26 Fairmount Avenue*. Illus. by the author. Putnam, 1999. 0-399-23246-X. 58pp. Gr. 1–4**

Tomie dePaola, beloved author and illustrator of the Strega Nona stories and charming autobiographical picture books about his Irish and Italian family, now details in easy-to-read chapter-book format his own kindergarten year, in 1938, when his family built a new house.

GERM: As readable as fiction, with short, funny, child-centered chapters laced with small black-and-white illustrations, this first book in the series will inspire children to start keeping track of their own childhood memories in words and pictures. Use the Snow White chapter—in which an indignant young Tomie yells at the movie screen because Mr. Walt Disney has changed the plot of the classic fairy tale—as a lead-in to an assignment on comparing a book with its movie. Children can continue reading the subsequent autobiographies in the series on their own.

RELATED TITLES: dePaola, Tomie. *The Art Lesson*. Putnam, 1989. / dePaola, Tomie. *Here We All Are*. Putnam, 2000. / dePaola, Tomie. *Nana Upstairs and Nana Downstairs*. Putnam, 1998. / dePaola, Tomie. *On My Way*. Putnam, 2001. / dePaola, Tomie. *Stagestruck, 2005*. Putnam, 2005. / dePaola, Tomie. *Things Will Never Be the Same*. Putnam, 2003. / dePaola, Tomie. *Tom*. Putnam, 1993. / dePaola, Tomie. *What a Year*. Putnam, 2002. / Elleman, Barbara. *Tomie dePaola: His Art and His Stories*. Putnam, 2000. / Engel, Dean, and Florence D. Freeman. *Ezra Jack Keats: A Biography with Illustrations*. Silver Moon, 1995. / Krull, Kathleen. *The Boy on Fairfield Street: How Ted Geisel Grew Up to Become Dr. Seuss*. Random House, 2004. / Lester, Helen. *Author: A True Story*. Houghton Mifflin, 1997. / Polacco, Patricia. *Chicken Sunday*. Philomel, 1992. / Polacco, Patricia. *Thank You, Mr. Falker*. Philomel, 1998. / Potter, Giselle. *Chloë's Birthday . . . and Me*. Atheneum, 2004. / Stevenson, James. *Don't You Know There's a War On?* Greenwillow, 1992.

SUBJECTS: ARTISTS—BIOGRAPHY. AUTHORS—BIOGRAPHY. AUTOBIOGRAPHY. BIOGRAPHY. DEPAOLA, TOMIE. DRAWING. ILLUSTRATORS. MOTION PICTURES.

1480   **Duggleby, John. *Artist in Overalls: The Life of Grant Wood*. Paintings by Grant Wood. Chronicle, 1996. 0-8118-1242-1. 56pp. Gr. 4–8**

Illustrated with full-page color reproductions of his work, this is a splendid and accessible anecdote-filled biography of unassuming Iowa farm boy Grant Wood, born in 1891, who achieved fame for developing his own American heartland style of painting, which we call Regionalism.

GERM: Listeners will relish the accounts of Wood's unconventional methods as a junior high school art teacher, and will appreciate the art lesson at the back of the book showing how he drew a chicken. Students will also want to study the photograph of the artist's sister standing with a local dentist, and then compare it with Wood's most famous painting, "American Gothic."

RELATED TITLES: Duggleby, John. *Story Painter: The Life of Jacob Lawrence*. Chronicle, 1998. / Gardner, Jane Mylum. *Henry Moore: From Bones and Stones to Sketches and Sculptures*. Four Winds, 1993. / Greenberg, Jan, and Sandra Jordan. *Action Jackson*. Roaring Brook, 2002. / Greenberg, Jan, and Sandra Jordan. *Chuck Close Up Close*. Roaring Brook, 2002. / Krull, Kathleen. *Lives of the Artists: Masterpieces, Messes (and What the Neighbors Thought)*. Harcourt, 1995. / Wallner, Alexandra. *Grandma Moses*. Holiday House, 2004. / Warhola, James. *Uncle Andy's*. Putnam, 2003.

SUBJECTS: ARTISTS—BIOGRAPHY. BIOGRAPHY. PAINTERS. WOOD, GRANT.

1481   **Duggleby, John. *Story Painter: The Life of Jacob Lawrence*. Illus. by Jacob Lawrence. Chronicle, 1998. 0-8118-2082-3. 57pp. Gr. 4–8**

Illustrated with electric full-page color reproductions of his work, this is a splendid and eye-opening biography of Jacob Lawrence, the African American painter whose life and art paralleled many of the vital issues, both racial and social, of the 20th century.

GERM: Discuss the content of Lawrence's paintings, which reflect the lives of African Americans in the 19th century (his Harriet Tubman paintings) and 20th century (the Migration of the Negro series and his Harlem paintings). Note Lawrence's own technique of painting one color at a time. Break out the tempera paints and give that a try.

RELATED TITLES: Barasch, Lynne. *Knockin' on Wood: Starring Peg Leg Bates*. Lee & Low, 2004. / Duggleby, John. *Artist in Overalls: The Life of Grant Wood*. Chronicle, 1996. / Freedman, Russell. *The Voice That Challenged a Nation: Marian Anderson and the Struggle for Equal Rights*. Clarion, 2004. / Greenberg, Jan. *Romare Bearden: Collage of Memories*. Abrams, 2003. / Greenberg, Jan, and Sandra Jordan. *Action Jackson*. Roaring Brook, 2002. / Greenberg, Jan, and Sandra Jordan. *Chuck Close Up Close*. Roaring Brook, 2002. / Krull, Kathleen. *Lives of the Artists: Masterpieces, Messes (and What the Neighbors Thought)*. Harcourt, 1995. / Lawrence, Jacob. *Harriet and the Promised Land*. Simon & Schuster, 1993. / Lyons, Mary E. *Starting Home: The Story of Horace Pippin, Painter*. Scribner, 1993. / Pinkney, Andrea Davis. *Ella Fitzgerald: The Tale of a Vocal Virtuosa*. Hyperion, 2002. / Sayre, Henry M. *Cave Paintings to Picasso: The Inside Scoop on 50 Art Masterpieces*. Chronicle Books, 2003. / Warhola, James. *Uncle Andy's*. Putnam, 2003.

SUBJECTS: AFRICAN AMERICANS—BIOGRAPHY. ARTISTS—BIOGRAPHY. BIOGRAPHY. LAWRENCE, JACOB. MULTICULTURAL BOOKS. PAINTERS.

1482 Ehlert, Lois. *Under My Nose*. Photos by Carlo Ontol. Richard C. Owen, 1996. 1-57274-027-2. 32pp. Gr. 1–4

See how Lois Ehlert came to be a children's book illustrator and then an author of her own stories in this photoessay from the Meet the Author series.

GERM: Make transparencies of the two pages of thumbnail sketches Ehlert did for her book *Feathers for Lunch*. Compare and contrast her rough story ideas with the finished book. Ask children to share their own tips on what to do when their story ideas won't come. What does Ehlert mean when she says, "I believe ideas need fresh air, too." Read over the list of fishy words she used when writing *Fish Eyes*. In preparation for writing an animal story, ask each writer to first compile and then share a list of descriptive words about a chosen animal.

RELATED TITLES: Ehlert, Lois. *Color Zoo*. HarperCollins, 1989. / Ehlert, Lois. *Cuckoo/Cucú: A Mexican Folktale/Un Cuento Folklórico Mexicano*. Harcourt, 1997. / Ehlert, Lois. *Eating the Alphabet: Fruits and Vegetables from A to Z*. Harcourt, 1989. / Ehlert, Lois. *Feathers for Lunch*. Harcourt, 1990. / Ehlert, Lois. *Fish Eyes: A Book You Can Count On*. Harcourt, 1990. / Ehlert, Lois. *In My World*. Harcourt, 2002. / Ehlert, Lois. *Leaf Man*. Harcourt, 2005. / Ehlert, Lois. *Moon Rope: A Peruvian Folktale*. Harcourt, 1992. / Ehlert, Lois. *Waiting for Wings*. Harcourt, 2001. / Martin, Bill, Jr., and John Archambault. *Chicka Chicka Boom Boom*. Simon & Schuster, 1989.

SUBJECTS: AUTHORS—BIOGRAPHY. AUTOBIOGRAPHY. BIOGRAPHY. EHLERT, LOIS. ILLUSTRATORS.

1483 Engel, Dean, and Florence D. Freeman. *Ezra Jack Keats: A Biography with Illustrations*. Illus. by Ezra Jack Keats. Silver Moon, 1995. 1-881889-65-3. 81pp. Gr. 3–6

Based on conversations the authors had with Ezra Jack Keats and on Keats's own autobiographical essays, this biography of the beloved author and illustrator of such picture-book classics as *The Snowy Day* and *Whistle for Willie* takes us back to Brooklyn, New York, where Keats was born in 1916, and follows his development into an artist, much to the disapproval of his father.

GERM: The first chapter describes the night young Ezra was left home alone and drew all over the kitchen table with pen and ink. Compare his childhood with that of Tomie dePaola, as described in his autobiographical picture book, *The Art Lesson*, and his autobiography, *26 Fairmount Avenue*.

RELATED TITLES: Christelow, Eileen. *What Do Illustrators Do?* Clarion, 1999. / Cummings, Pat, comp. and ed. Talking with Artists series. Clarion. / Keats, Ezra Jack. *The Snowy Day*. Viking, 1962. / Keats, Ezra Jack. *Whistle for Willie*. Viking, 1964. / Krull, Kathleen. *The Boy on Fairfield Street: How Ted Geisel Grew Up to Become Dr. Seuss*. Random House, 2004. / McPhail, David. *In Flight with David McPhail*. Heinemann, 1996. / Peet, Bill. *Bill Peet: An Autobiography*. Houghton Mifflin, 1989. / Polacco, Patricia. *Firetalking*. Richard C. Owen, 1994. (And others in the Meet the Author series.)

SUBJECTS: ARTISTS—BIOGRAPHY. AUTHORS—BIOGRAPHY. BIOGRAPHY. JEWS. KEATS, EZRA JACK.

1484 Erdrich, Lise. *Sacagawea*. Illus. by Julie Buffalohead. Carolrhoda, 2003. 0-87614-646-9. Unp. Gr. 3–6

Kidnapped by Hidatsa warriors when she was 11 or so, the Shoshone girl was given the name Sacagawea, or "Bird Woman," and then given in marriage, at age 16, to a French Canadian fur trapper 20 years her senior. In 1804, the pregnant young woman, accompanied by her husband, became the interpreter for Lewis and Clark's Corps of Discovery on their journey to the Pacific Ocean. Large, solemn paintings and a picture-book format enhance her extraordinary life story.

GERM: As you read about the expedition, ask your listeners to listen for ways in which Sacagawea helped the otherwise all-male group. Why is she remembered today? Why don't we know for sure what became of her? Joseph Bruchac's novel *Sacajawea* describes the journey from her point of view and from that of William Clark.

RELATED TITLES: Adler, David A. *A Picture Book of Sacagawea*. Holiday House, 2000. / Blumberg, Rhoda. *The Incredible Journey of Lewis and Clark*. Lothrop, 1987. / Bruchac, Joseph. *Sacajawea*. Harcourt, 2000. / Edwards, Judith. *The Great Expedition of Lewis and Clark: By Private Reubin Field, Member of the Corps of Discovery*. Farrar, 2003. / Goldin, Barbara Diamond. *The Girl Who Lived with the Bears*. Gulliver/Harcourt, 1997. / Myers, Laurie. *Lewis and Clark and Me: A Dog's Tale*. Henry Holt, 2002. / Osborne, Mary Pope. *Adaline Falling Star*. Scholastic, 2000. / Schanzer, Rosalyn. *How We Crossed the West: The Adventures of Lewis and Clark*. National Geographic, 1997.

SUBJECTS: BIOGRAPHY. EXPLORERS. INDIANS OF NORTH AMERICA—BIOGRAPHY. LEWIS AND CLARK EXPEDITION (1804–1806). MULTICULTURAL BOOKS. SACAGAWEA. SHOSHONI INDIANS—BIOGRAPHY. U.S.—HISTORY—1783–1865. WEST—DISCOVERY AND EXPLORATION. WOMEN—BIOGRAPHY.

1485   Farris, Christine King. *My Brother Martin: A Sister Remembers Growing Up with the Rev. Dr. Martin Luther King, Jr.* Illus. by Chris Soentpiet. Simon & Schuster, 2003. 0-689-84387-9. Unp. Gr. K–6

In an affectionate personal memoir, Martin Luther King, Jr.'s older sister, Christine, recalls growing up with Martin and their baby brother, A.D., describing their pranks and games they played together as well as the prejudice they experienced growing up in Atlanta, Georgia. "Mother Dear, one day I'm going to turn this world upside down," Martin said, when their mother explained the grim facts of segregation to them. In a fascinating illustrator's note, Chris Soentpiet explains how King's own family and friends posed as models for the huge, realistic watercolors that depict Martin's childhood experiences.

GERM: Before reading Farris's book aloud, try some factstorming with your students. First, have them work in small groups and write down everything they know about Martin Luther King, Jr. Coming together, the class can share their lists and construct a chart of all their collected facts. From this, you can ascertain what they know, and what they think they know. Discuss the differences between a famous figure's personal, professional, and public life. Discussion point: What happened to Martin as a child that influenced his life as an adult? Doreen Rappaport's picture-book tribute, *Martin's Big Words*, is a natural companion read to compare points of view.

RELATED TITLES: Adler, David A. *A Picture Book of Rosa Parks*. Holiday House, 1993. / Bray, Rosemary L. *Martin Luther King*. Greenwillow, 1995. / King, Martin Luther. *I Have a Dream*. Scholastic, 1997. / Livingston, Myra Cohn. *Let Freedom Ring: A Ballad of Martin Luther King, Jr.* Holiday House, 1992. / Marzollo, Jean. *Happy Birthday, Martin Luther King*. Scholastic, 1993. / Rappaport, Doreen. *Martin's Big Words*. Hyperion, 2001. / Woodson, Jacqueline. *The Other Side*. Putnam, 2001.

SUBJECTS: AFRICAN AMERICANS—BIOGRAPHY. BIOGRAPHY. CIVIL RIGHTS. KING, MARTIN LUTHER, JR. MULTICULTURAL BOOKS. PREJUDICE. RACE RELATIONS.

1486   Fleming, Candace. *Ben Franklin's Almanac: Being a True Account of the Good Gentleman's Life*. Illus. with paintings and reproductions. Atheneum, 2003. 0-689-83549-3. 120pp. Gr. 5–Adult

What the author describes as a scrapbook is a handsome and mesmerizing collection of biographical and often humorous anecdotes—"bits and pieces" arranged within a broader subject, starting with "Boyhood Memories," and covering all aspects of Franklin's life and career, from scientist to statesman. Copiously illustrated with portraits, cartoons, paintings, and reproductions, this browsing volume is a rich source of information about Franklin and his times.

GERM: Read aloud and analyze aspects of Franklin's life and spirited opinions on such diverse subjects as being a vegetarian (page 11), naming the bald eagle as an American symbol (page 90), traveling by his wits (page 42), and even his own epitaph (page 104). For math, try out his most complex magic square (page 47). The author became interested in Franklin as a fourth grader when she read the classic novel *Ben and Me*, by Robert Lawson. Read the two books in tandem to see how Lawson incorporated facts about Franklin into his biographical tale, narrated by Ben's good mouse, Amos.

RELATED TITLES: Adler, David A. B. *Franklin, Pronter*. Holiday House, 2001. / Byrd, Robert. *Leonardo, Beautiful Dreamer*. Dutton, 2003. / D'Aulaire, Ingri, and Edgar Parin D'Aulaire. *Benjamin Franklin*. Doubleday, 1987. / Delano, Marie Ferguson. *Inventing the Future: A Photobiography of Thomas Alva Edison*. National Geographic, 2002. / Fleming, Candace. *The Hatmaker's Sign: A Story by Benjamin Franklin*. Orchard, 1998. / Fleming, Candace. *Our Eleanor*. Atheneum, 2005. / Fritz, Jean. *What's the Big Idea, Ben Franklin?* Coward, 1976. / Giblin, James Cross. *The Amazing Life of Benjamin Franklin*. Scholastic, 2000. / Gutman, Dan. *Qwerty Stevens, Stuck in Time with Benjamin Franklin*. Simon & Schuster, 2002. / Lawson, Robert. *Ben and Me*. Little, Brown, 1939. / Schanzer, Rosalyn. *How Ben Franklin Stole the Lightning*. HarperCollins, 2003. / St. George, Judith. *So You Want to Be an Inventor?* Philomel, 2002.

SUBJECTS: BIOGRAPHY. ELECTRICITY. FRANKLIN, BENJAMIN. INVENTIONS AND INVENTORS. SCIENTISTS. STATESMEN. U.S.—HISTORY—REVOLUTION, 1775–1783.

1487 **Freedman, Russell.** *Out of Darkness: The Story of Louis Braille.* **Illus. by Kate Kiesler. Clarion, 1997. 0-395-77516-7. 81pp. Gr. 4–6**
Blinded because of an accident at the age of 3 in 1812, Louis Braille, known to us as the originator of the Braille system of writing, spent his formative years at the Royal Institute for Blind Youth in Paris. Freedman's graceful prose reads effortlessly, like fiction.

GERM: Use David A. Adler's *A Picture Book of Louis Braille*, meant for younger readers, to compare similarities and differences in content, format, illustration, and writing style. Inspired by the French school, the New England Asylum for the Blind, which later became the Perkins Institution for the Blind, was established for children in the United States in the early 19th century, as described in Spring Hermann's *Seeing Lessons*, a novel based on the life of Abigail Carter. Readers can compare and contrast the two schools and the methods they used to teach their students. Give your group the opportunity to learn and read Braille.

RELATED TITLES: Adler, David A. *A Picture Book of Louis Braille*. Holiday House, 1997. / Alexander, Sally Hobart. *Mom Can't See Me*. Macmillan, 1990. / Creech, Sharon. *Granny Torrelli Makes Soup*. HarperCollins, 2003. / Garfield, James. *Follow My Leader*. Viking, 1957. / Hermann, Spring. *Seeing Lessons: The Story of Abigail Carter and America's First School for Blind People*. Henry Holt, 1998. / Hunter, Edith Fisher. *Child of the Silent Night: The Story of Laura Bridgman*. Houghton Mifflin, 1963. / Little, Jean. *Little by Little: A Writer's Education*. Viking, 1987. / Patent, Dorothy Hinshaw. *The Right Dog for the Job: Ira's Path from Service Dog to Guide Dog*. Walker, 2004. / Rodanas, Kristina. *The Blind Hunter*. Cavendish, 2003. / Whelan, Gloria. *Hannah*. Knopf, 1991.

SUBJECTS: BIOGRAPHY. BLIND. BRAILLE, LOUIS. PEOPLE WITH DISABILITIES. PHYSICALLY HANDICAPPED. TEACHERS.

1488 **Freedman, Russell.** *The Voice That Challenged a Nation: Marian Anderson and the Struggle for Equal Rights.* **Illus. with photos. Clarion, 2004. 0-618-15976-2. 128pp. Gr. 5–12**
From her childhood in Philadelphia, where she joined her church's junior choir at age 6, to fame as a concert singer and opera star, Marian Anderson loved to sing. The most dramatic and moving part of this stately photobiography, of course, is the description of her famed concert on the steps of the Lincoln Memorial in Washington, D.C., on Easter Sunday, 1939.

GERM: Compare and contrast Freedman's longer and more detailed treatment with Pam Muñoz Ryan's stunning picture-book biography, *When Marian Sang*.

RELATED TITLES: Barasch, Lynne. *Knockin' on Wood: Starring Peg Leg Bates*. Lee & Low, 2004. / Bridges, Ruby. *Through My Eyes*. Scholastic, 1999. / Duggleby, John. *Story Painter: The Life of Jacob Lawrence*. Chronicle, 1998. / Freedman, Russell. *Eleanor Roosevelt*. Clarion, 1995. / Krull, Kathleen. *Lives of the Musicians: Good Times, Bad Times (And What the Neighbors Thought)*. Harcourt, 1993. / McWhorter, Diane. *A Dream of Freedom: The Civil Rights Movement from 1954 to 1968*. Scholastic, 2004. / Pinkney, Andrea Davis. *Ella Fitzgerald: The Tale of a Vocal Virtuosa*. Hyperion, 2002. / Ryan, Pam Muñoz. *When Marian Sang*. Scholastic, 2002.

SUBJECTS: AFRICAN AMERICANS—BIOGRAPHY. AFRICAN AMERICANS—HISTORY. ANDERSON, MARIAN, 1897–1993. BIOGRAPHY. CIVIL RIGHTS. MULTICULTURAL BOOKS. MUSICIANS. RACE RELATIONS. SINGERS. WOMEN—BIOGRAPHY.

1489 **Fritz, Jean.** *Leonardo's Horse.* **Illus. by Hudson Talbott. Putnam, 2001. 0-399-23576-0. Unp. Gr. 4–8**
In an intriguing discussion of Leonardo's life and work, Fritz describes his unsuccessful efforts to make a 24-foot-high bronze horse as a gift for the duke of Milan, and how 500 years later, a commemorative project was undertaken by an American art-lover, Charlie Dent, who died in

1994 before his horse could be cast in bronze. Nina Akamu, an American sculptor, took over the project, and the finished horse was unveiled in its new home in Milan in 1999, 500 years to the day of the destruction of Leonardo's clay horse.

GERM: Fritz's carefully researched story is given a fitting home, with elegant illustrations in watercolors, pen-and-ink, and colored pencil, and collage inserts of da Vinci's own drawings. In a most unusual format, the top third of the book has been die-cut into a rounded arch that frames each handsome page. For additional background, also read Diane Stanley's *Leonardo da Vinci* and Robert Byrd's *Leonardo, Beautiful Dreamer*. To see photos of the horse, go to the splendid Web site <www.leonardoshorse.org>. Bring out the modeling clay and have your sculptors construct models of horses and animals they admire, using photographs in books for reference.

RELATED TITLES: Aliki. *William Shakespeare and the Globe*. HarperCollins, 1999. / Byrd, Robert. *Leonardo, Beautiful Dreamer*. Dutton, 2003. / Krull, Kathleen. *Lives of the Artists: Masterpieces, Messes (and What the Neighbors Thought)*. Harcourt, 1995. / Skira-Venturi, Rosabianca. *A Weekend with Leonardo da Vinci*. Rizzoli, 1993. / Stanley, Diane. *Leonardo da Vinci*. Morrow, 1996. / Stanley, Diane. *Michelangelo*. HarperCollins, 2000. / Woodruff, Elvira. *The Disappearing Bike Shop*. Holiday House, 1992.

SUBJECTS: ARTISTS—BIOGRAPHY. BIOGRAPHY. HORSES. ITALY. LEONARDO DA VINCI, 1452–1519. SCULPTORS.

1490 Fritz, Jean. *You Want Women to Vote, Lizzie Stanton?* **Illus. by DyAnne DiSalvo-Ryan. Putnam, 1995. 0-399-22786-5. 88pp. Gr. 5–8**

Jean Fritz, who has written so many delightful biographies humanizing such august historical figures as Paul Revere, Ben Franklin, and Christopher Columbus, dazzles us anew with her portrait of suffragist Elizabeth Cady Stanton. Children will be shocked when they learn that women were not permitted to vote in the United States until 1920. Suffragist Elizabeth Cady Stanton, born in 1815, helped start the fight that ultimately led to the Nineteenth Amendment. In 1848, along with Quaker abolitionist Lucretia Mott, she organized the first "Women's Rights Convention" in Seneca Falls, New York, and spent ten years crisscrossing the country on the lecture circuit to promote issues of women's rights.

GERM: Pair this with Emily Arnold McCully's *The Ballot Box Battle*, a fictionalized picture book about the elderly Stanton's attempt to cast her vote on Election Day in Tenafly, New Jersey, in 1880, and Shana Corey's *You Forgot Your Skirt, Amelia Bloomer!* As an interesting aside, Kathryn Lasky's wry and pointed picture book *She's Wearing a Dead Bird on Her Head!* shows how dedication to an ideal led to change.

RELATED TITLES: Blumberg, Rhoda. *Bloomers*. Atheneum, 1993. / Christensen, Bonnie. *The Daring Nellie Bly: America's Star Reporter*. Knopf, 2003. / Krull, Kathleen. *Lives of Extraordinary Women: Rulers, Rebels (and What the Neighbors Thought)*. Harcourt, 2000. / Krull, Kathleen. *A Woman for President: The Story of Victoria Woodhull*. Walker, 2004. / Lasky, Kathryn. *She's Wearing a Dead Bird on Her Head!* Hyperion, 1995. / McCully, Emily Arnold. *The Ballot Box Battle*. Knopf, 1996. / White, Linda Arms. *I Could Do That: Esther Morris Gets Women the Vote*.I Farrar, 2005. / Wooldridge, Connie Nordhielm. *When Esther Morris Headed West: Women, Wyoming, and the Right to Vote*. Holiday House, 2001.

SUBJECTS: BIOGRAPHY. FEMINISTS. STANTON, ELIZABETH CADY, 1815–1902. SUFFRAGISTS. U.S.—HISTORY. WOMEN—BIOGRAPHY. WOMEN'S RIGHTS.

1491 Gerstein, Mordicai. *The Man Who Walked Between the Towers.* **Illus. by the author. Roaring Brook, 2003. 0-7613-2868-8. Unp. Gr. K–6**

French aerialist Philippe Petit planned and carried out a daring walk on a cable seven-eighths of an inch thick, stretched 140 feet between the tops of the just-completed twin towers of the World Trade Center, a quarter of a mile high, in New York in 1974. Gerstein's detailed paintings of the towers from Petit's perspective up high and from astonished spectators in the streets below are masterful and breathtaking, with two fold-out three-panel views that will give you vertigo. A love story to the Twin Towers, this true, bittersweet, life-affirming tribute will inspire gasps of disbelief from your listeners.

GERM: Place a long rope on floor for children to walk across, trying to keep their balance, to get an idea of how hard it is to do, even on the ground. Read this in conjunction with *Fireboat: The Heroic Adventures of the John J. Harvey*, Maira Kalman's true picture-book account of September 11, 2001, and Emily Arnold McCully's *Mirette on the High Wire*.

RELATED TITLES: Harwayne, Shelley, ed. *Messages to Ground Zero: Children Respond to September 11, 2001*. Heinemann, 2002. / Heard, Georgia, sel. *This Place I Know: Poems of Comfort*. Candlewick, 2002. / Jakobsen, Kathy. *My New York*. Little, Brown, 2003. / Kalman, Maira. *Fireboat: The Heroic Adventures of the John J. Harvey*.

Putnam, 2002. / Levitas, Mitchell, ed. *The New York Times: A Nation Challenged: A Visual History of 9/11 and Its Aftermath, Young Reader's Edition*. Scholastic, 2002. / McCully, Emily Arnold. *Mirette on the High Wire*. Putnam, 1992. / McCully, Emily Arnold. *Starring Mirette and Bellini*. Putnam, 1977. / Osborne, Mary Pope. *New York's Bravest*. Knopf, 2002. / Roth, Susan L. *It's Still a Dog's New York*. National Geographic, 2002. / Winter, Jeanette. *The Librarian of Basra: A True Story from Iraq*. Harcourt, 2005. / Winter, Jeanette. *September Roses*. Farrar, 2004.

SUBJECTS: AERIALISTS. BIOGRAPHY. CALDECOTT MEDAL. DAREDEVILS. NEW YORK CITY. PETIT, PHILIPPE. SEPTEMBER 11 TERRORIST ATTACKS, 2001. TIGHTROPE WALKING. U.S.—HISTORY—20TH CENTURY. WORLD TRADE CENTER (NEW YORK, NY).

1492 Gerstein, Mordicai. *What Charlie Heard: The Story of the Composer Charles Ives*. Illus. by the author. Farrar, 2002. 0-374-38292-1. Unp. Gr. 2–6

American composer Charles Ives (1874–1954) is profiled in an affectionate, noise-infused picture-book biography of his sound-filled life and music.

GERM: The sun-bright pen-and-ink and watercolor illustrations of word- and sound-filled pages will inspire kids to do a little listening of their own to the sounds and music around them. Play a CD of Ives's Fourth Symphony, said to be his masterpiece.

RELATED TITLES: Aliki. *Ah, Music!* HarperCollins, 2003. / Anderson, M. T. *Handel, Who Knew What He Liked*. Candlewick, 2001. / Anderson, M. T. *Strange Mr. Satie*. Viking, 2003. / Kalman, Esther. *Tchaikovsky Discovers America*. Orchard, 1995. / Krull, Kathleen. *Lives of the Musicians: Good Times, Bad Times (And What the Neighbors Thought)*. Harcourt, 1993. / Nichol, Barbara. *Beethoven Lives Upstairs*. Orchard, 1994. / Winter, Jeanette. *Sebastian: A Book About Bach*. Harcourt, 1999.

SUBJECTS: BIOGRAPHY. COMPOSERS. IVES, CHARLES. MUSICIANS. NOISE.

1493 Gerstein, Mordicai. *The Wild Boy*. Illus. by the author. Farrar, 1998. 0-374-38431-2. Unp. Gr. 2–6

Using a picture-book format, Gerstein retells the true story of Victor, the wild child of Aveyron, who was captured in southern France in 1800 and then brought to Paris to be studied by experts at the Institute for Deaf-Mutes. When they declared him to be hopelessly retarded, the boy was taken in by a young doctor, Jean-Marc Itard, and his housekeeper, Madame Guérin, who taught him to dress himself, to read and write a bit, and to play, though they were never able to teach him to speak. In the author's note, we learn that Victor died in 1828 at about the age of 40. "His origins are still a mystery."

GERM: Use this intriguing account to discuss handicaps, language, and the uses of reading, writing, and speaking. Have your students try to communicate without words. Discussion point: Why couldn't Victor speak? How did you learn to speak? What does it mean to be human? Karen Hesse's novel *The Music of Dolphins* tackles the same themes for older readers.

RELATED TITLES: Gerstein, Mordicai. *The Man Who Walked Between the Towers*. Roaring Brook, 2003. / Gerstein, Mordicai. *What Charlie Heard: The Story of the Composer Charles Ives*. Farrar, 2002. / Hesse, Karen. *The Music of Dolphins*. Scholastic, 1996. / Mayer, Marianna. *The Boy Who Ran with the Gazelles*. Dial, 2005. / Yolen, Jane. *Passager*. Harcourt, 1996.

SUBJECTS: BIOGRAPHY. FERAL CHILDREN. FRANCE.

1494 Giovanni, Nikki. *Rosa*. Illus. by Bryan Collier. Henry Holt, 2005. 0-8050-7106-7. Unp. Gr. 3–6

Told as a story, Giovanni's eloquent picture-book biography introduces a pivotal hero in the civil rights movement, Rosa Parks. On a normal Thursday, December 1, 1955, after working all day, seamstress Rosa was looking forward to going home and cooking a meatloaf for her husband. What she did instead changed the course of American history. Refusing to get up from her seat in the "neutral section" of that Montgomery, Alabama, bus, she said to the bus driver, "Why do you pick on us?" and waited for the police to arrest her. As he did in his Caldecott Honor-winning *Martin's Big Words* by Doreen Rappaport, Collier combines watercolors and cut paper collage to great effect, assembling worshipful and dignified portraits, ending with a four-page gatefold of African Americans walking for justice.

GERM: Combine this inspirational book with Parks's own autobiography, written for children, *Rosa Parks: My Story*, and with *Martin's Big Words* by Doreen Rappaport and *Through My Eyes*, Ruby Bridges's autobiography.

RELATED TITLES: Adler, David A. *Dr. Martin Luther King, Jr.* Holiday House, 2001. / Adler, David A. *A Picture Book of Rosa Parks*. Holiday House, 1993. / Bray, Rosemary L. *Martin Luther King*. Greenwillow, 1995. / Coles, Robert. *The Story of Ruby Bridges*. Scholastic, 1995. / Golenbock, Peter. *Teammates*. Harcourt, 1990. /

Greenfield, Eloise. *Rosa Parks*. HarperCollins, 1995. / Livingston, Myra Cohn. *Let Freedom Ring: A Ballad of Martin Luther King, Jr*. Holiday House, 1992. / McKissack, Patricia C. *Goin' Someplace Special*. Atheneum, 2001. / Marzollo, Jean. *Happy Birthday, Martin Luther King*. Scholastic, 1993. / Mitchell, Margaree King. *Uncle Jed's Barber Shop*. Simon & Schuster, 1993. / Parks, Rosa, and Jim Haskins. *Rosa Parks: My Story*. Puffin, 1999. / Rappaport, Doreen. *Martin's Big Words*. Hyperion, 2001. / Woodson, Jacqueline. *The Other Side*. Putnam, 2001.
SUBJECTS: AFRICAN AMERICANS—BIOGRAPHY. BIOGRAPHY. CIVIL RIGHTS. MULTICULTURAL BOOKS. PARKS, ROSA. PREJUDICE. RACE RELATIONS. SEGREGATION.

1495 **Gold, Alison Leslie.** *Memories of Anne Frank: Reflections of a Childhood Friend*. **Illus. with photos. Scholastic, 1997. 0-590-90722-0. 176pp. Gr. 5–8**
Children familiar with Anne Frank's diary and its mentions of her childhood friend "Hannelie" or "Lies" will be drawn to this extraordinary biography of Hannah Goslar, based on interviews the author conducted with her in Israel. Friends from the age of 4, Anne and Hannah were separated at 13 when the Franks went into hiding and the Goslars were sent first to a transit camp and then to the German concentration camp of Bergen-Belsen. In February of 1944, Hannah discovered that Anne was being held nearby, and somehow managed to throw socks and some scraps of food over the wire fence to her. It was their last encounter, for Anne died soon after, and the rest of the camp was evacuated. The dramatic and wrenching tale will leave readers wondering how they would endure such horrific events.
GERM: *Anne Frank: Beyond the Diary* by Rian Verhoeven and Ruud Van Der Rol, which contains many period photographs, is an excellent source of biographical and historical background. Other books based on true stories of Jewish children who went into hiding during the war include *Hidden Child* by Isaac Millman, *When the Soldiers Were Gone* by Vera W. Propp, and *The Upstairs Room*, Johanna Reiss's autobiography.
RELATED TITLES: Abels, Chana Byers. *The Children We Remember*. Greenwillow, 1986. / Isaacman, Clara. *Clara's Story*. Jewish Publication Society, 1984. / Jiang, Ji Li. *Red Scarf Girl: A Memoir of the Cultural Revolution*. HarperCollins, 1997. / Levine, Karen. *Hana's Suitcase*. Albert Whitman, 2003. / Lowry, Lois. *Number the Stars*. Houghton Mifflin, 1989. / McCann, Michelle R. *Luba: The Angel of Bergen-Belsen*. Tricycle, 2003. / Mazer, Norma Fox. *Good Night, Maman*. Harcourt, 1999. / Millman, Isaac. *Hidden Child*. Farrar, 2005. / Poole, Jospehine. *Anne Frank*. Knopf, 2005. / Propp, Vera W. *When the Soldiers Were Gone*. Putnam, 1999. / Reiss, Johanna. *The Upstairs Room*. HarperCollins, 1987. / Verhoeven, Rian, and Ruud Van Der Rol. *Anne Frank: Beyond the Diary*. Viking, 1993.
SUBJECTS: AMSTERDAM (NETHERLANDS). BIOGRAPHY. FRANK, ANNE, 1929–1945. HOLOCAUST, JEWISH (1939–1945). JEWS. WOMEN—BIOGRAPHY.

1496 **Greenberg, Jan, and Sandra Jordan.** *Action Jackson*. **Illus. by Robert Andrew Parker. Roaring Brook, 2002. 0-7613-2770-3. 32pp. Gr. 2–8**
In a picture-book format, moody and expansive double-page watercolors and a present-tense text describe how Jackson Pollock painted "Lavender Mist" in his barn studio in 1950, using house paints and what he called "energy and motion made visible." Not a standard biography per se, this is a summer in Pollock's life, based on firsthand reports, that lets us see how he painted.
GERM: Show other, larger reproductions of Pollock's work, as the ones in the book are too tiny to see. This is a text to life to art connection that will let kids in on the creative process, and make them want to try a little drip painting themselves, if you or your art teacher can figure out how to do it without trashing the room.
RELATED TITLES: Duggleby, John. *Artist in Overalls: The Life of Grant Wood*. Chronicle, 1996. / Duggleby, John. *Story Painter: The Life of Jacob Lawrence*. Chronicle, 1998. / Greenberg, Jan, and Sandra Jordan. *Chuck Close Up Close*. Roaring Brook, 2002. / Krull, Kathleen. *Lives of the Artists: Masterpieces, Messes (and What the Neighbors Thought)*. Harcourt, 1995. / Rubin, Susan Goldman. *Degas and the Dance: The Painter and the Petits Rats, Perfecting Their Art*. Abrams, 2002. / Sayre, Henry M. *Cave Paintings to Picasso: The Inside Scoop on 50 Art Masterpieces*. Chronicle, 2003. / Waldman, Neil. *The Starry Night*. Boyds Mills, 1999. / Wallner, Alexandra. *Grandma Moses*. Holiday House, 2004. / Warhola, James. *Uncle Andy's*. Putnam, 2003.
SUBJECTS: ARTISTS—BIOGRAPHY. BIOGRAPHY. PAINTING. POLLOCK, JACKSON.

1497 **Greenberg, Jan, and Sandra Jordan.** *Chuck Close Up Close*. **Illus. with photos and reproductions. Roaring Brook, 2002. 0-7894-2486-X. 48pp. Gr. 4–8**
How Chuck Close, labeled "dumb," "a shirker," and "lazy" in school, back in the 1940s before dyslexia was recognized, grew up to become an acclaimed artist makes for a compelling art- and photo-filled biography. Laced with full-page color reproductions of Close's 20-foot portraits, composed of thousands of small multicolored ovals and squares, this combination biog-

raphy/art book will be especially appreciated by students who are working hard to overcome learning disabilities.

GERM: Close says, "When every kid on the block wanted to become a policeman or fireman, I wanted to be an artist. It was the first thing that I was good at, the first thing that really made me feel special. I had skills the other kids didn't have. Art saved my life." Have your students talk and write about this question: What is your life-saving talent or interest?

RELATED TITLES: Duggleby, John. *Artist in Overalls: The Life of Grant Wood.* Chronicle, 1996. / Duggleby, John. *Story Painter: The Life of Jacob Lawrence.* Chronicle, 1998. / Gardner, Jane Mylum. *Henry Moore: From Bones and Stones to Sketches and Sculptures.* Four Winds, 1993. / Greenberg, Jan and Sandra Jordan. *Action Jackson.* Roaring Brook, 2002. / Krull, Kathleen. *Lives of the Artists: Masterpieces, Messes (and What the Neighbors Thought).* Harcourt, 1995. / Wallner, Alexandra. *Grandma Moses.* Holiday House, 2004. / Warhola, James. *Uncle Andy's.* Putnam, 2003.

SUBJECTS: ARTISTS—BIOGRAPHY. BIOGRAPHY. CLOSE, CHUCK. DYSLEXIA. LEARNING DISABILITIES. PAINTERS. PEOPLE WITH DISABILITIES. PHYSICALLY HANDICAPPED.

1498 **Grimes, Nikki.** *Talkin' About Bessie: The Story of Aviator Elizabeth Coleman.* **Illus. by E. B. Lewis. Orchard, 2002. 0-439-35243-6. 48pp. Gr. 3–6**

The life of the first African American woman pilot—from her birth in 1892 to her untimely death in a plane accident during a test flight in 1926 at the age of 34—is described in free-verse poems through the eyes of 21 observers—family, friends, sponsors, and admirers. This Coretta Scott King Illustrator Award Winner and Author Award Honor Book is illustrated with wistful brown-toned watercolors.

GERM: Your class can easily stage a Reader's Theater reading of the whole book.

RELATED TITLES: Adler, David A. *A Picture Book of Amelia Earhart.* Holiday House, 1998. / Borden, Louise, and Mary Kay Kroeger. *Fly High! The Story of Bessie Coleman.* McElderry, 2001. / Brown, Don. *Ruth Law Thrills a Nation.* Ticknor & Fields, 1993. / Burleigh, Robert. *Flight: The Journey of Charles Lindbergh.* Philomel, 1991. / Joseph, Lynn. *Fly, Bessie, Fly.* Simon & Schuster, 1998. / Lindbergh, Reeve. *Nobody Owns the Sky: The Story of "Brave Bessie" Coleman.* Candlewick, 1996. / Moss, Marissa. *Brave Harriet.* Harcourt, 2001. / Ride, Sally, and Susan Okie. *To Space and Back.* Lothrop, 1986. / Ryan, Pam Muñoz. *Amelia and Eleanor Go for a Ride.* Scholastic, 1999.

SUBJECTS: AFRICAN AMERICANS—BIOGRAPHY. AIR PILOTS. BIOGRAPHY. COLEMAN, BESSIE. FLIGHT. MULTICULTURAL BOOKS. POINT OF VIEW. READER'S THEATER. WOMEN— BIOGRAPHY.

1499 **Harness, Cheryl.** *Ghosts of the White House.* **Illus. by the author. Simon & Schuster, 1998. 0-689-80872-0. 48pp. Gr. 3–6**

On a class field trip to the White House, Sara, the blonde, bespectacled child narrator, immerses us in a fantastical tour. First, the portrait of George Washington in the East Room comes to life as her tour guide. In each room, she meets a series of presidents who regale her with spirited anecdotes of their experiences there. The gimmick of using dialogue balloons and side panels that offer snippets of info about each of the 42 presidents may seem cluttered and confusing to adults (similar in style to the Magic School Bus books), but kids will find it fun and invigorating to identify each one. Harness's realistic watercolor and colored pencil illustrations are grand, with several fabulous double-page group portraits, including the endpapers, and a final page of still-living presidents.

GERM: What a kickoff to kids' presidents reports, made even more interesting if students emulate the first-person dialogue style when they give their oral reports and include a timeline.

RELATED TITLES: Burns, Diane, and Clint Burns. *Hail to the Chief! Jokes About the Presidents.* Lerner, 1989. / Cleveland, Will, and Mark Alvarez. *Yo, Millard Fillmore! (And All Those Other Presidents You Don't Know).* Millbrook, 1997. / Cronin, Doreen. *Duck for President.* Simon & Schuster, 2004. / Davis, Gibbs. *Wackiest White House Pets.* Scholastic, 2004. / Hines, Gary. *A Christmas Tree in the White House.* Henry Holt, 1998. / Krull, Kathleen. *Lives of the Presidents: Fame, Shame (and What the Neighbors Thought).* Harcourt, 1998. / O'Connor, Jane. *If the Walls Could Talk: Family Life at the White House.* Simon & Schuster, 2004. / Provensen, Alice. *The Buck Stops Here: The Presidents of the United States.* Harcourt, 2000. / Ryan, Pam Muñoz. *Amelia and Eleanor Go for a Ride.* Scholastic, 1999. / St. George, Judith. *So You Want to Be President?* Philomel, 2000. / Stier, Catherine. *If I Were President.* Albert Whitman, 1999. / Thimmesh, Catherine. *Madam President: The Extraordinary, True (and Evolving) Story of Women in Politics.* Houghton Mifflin, 2004. / Winters, Kay. *My Teacher for President.* Dutton, 2004.

SUBJECTS: BIOGRAPHY. PRESIDENTS. U.S.—HISTORY. WASHINGTON, D.C. WHITE HOUSE.

1500 Harness, Cheryl. *Young Teddy Roosevelt.* **Illus. by the author. National Geographic, 1998. 0-7922-7094-0. 40pp. Gr. 2–6**

In this picture-book biography with handsome, colorful, people-packed watercolors, we follow Teddy from birth through asthmatic childhood to cowboy and Rough Rider to election as the 26th president after McKinley's assassination in 1901.

GERM: Read Teddy's own childhood journal describing his family's year abroad in *My Tour of Europe: By Teddy Roosevelt, Age 10* and then note the fun his children had when he was president in *A Christmas Tree in the White House* by Gary Hines.

RELATED TITLES: Cooney, Barbara. *Eleanor.* Viking, 1996. / Hines, Gary. *A Christmas Tree in the White House.* Henry Holt, 1998. / Jones, Rebecca C. *The President Has Been Shot: True Stories of the Attacks on Ten U.S. Presidents.* Dutton, 1996. / Krull, Kathleen. *Lives of the Presidents: Fame, Shame (and What the Neighbors Thought).* Harcourt, 1998. / Roosevelt, Theodore. *My Tour of Europe: By Teddy Roosevelt, Age 10.* Millbrook Press, 2003. / St. George, Judith. *You're on Your Way, Teddy Roosevelt!* Philomel, 2004.

SUBJECTS: BIOGRAPHY. PRESIDENTS. ROOSEVELT, THEODORE.

1501 Hoose, Phillip M. *We Were There, Too! Young People in U.S. History.* **Illus. with photos and reproductions. Farrar, 2001. 0-374-38252-2. 265pp. Gr. 5–12**

If you are tired of history texts that describe the accomplishments of and wars fought mainly by DWM (dead white males), Hoose's riveting look at American history through the eyes of its activist youth is a revelation. Two- to eight-page profiles—based on primary sources, diaries, and interviews, along with reproductions of prints, paintings, and portraits—acquaint the reader with a diverse examination of 68 courageous children and teenagers who participated in ground-breaking events. Starting with 12-year-old Diego Bermúdez who sailed with Columbus in 1492, the text is divided into nine time periods, with the final chapters introducing modern-day heroes who encountered segregation, war, sexual discrimination, AIDS, and environmental pollution. All of the profiles are written in a conversational but dramatic narrative style that personalizes each young person, followed by a description of what happened to each of them later in life.

GERM: Read aloud a chapter a day to broaden your children's interests and knowledge of historical eras. They can write about their own lives in the context of what is going on in the world around them. In the picture book *Miss Rumphius* by Barbara Cooney, the title character's grandfather tells her she must do something to make the world "more beautiful." Ask your young citizens to write an essay on what they plan to do to make a difference in their lives and the lives of others.

RELATED TITLES: Cooney, Barbara. *Miss Rumphius.* Viking, 1982. / Freedman, Russell. *Children of the Wild West.* Clarion, 1983. / Harness, Cheryl. *Remember the Ladies: 100 Great American Women.* HarperCollins, 2001. / Hoose, Phillip M. *It's Our World, Too! Stories of Young People Who Are Making a Difference.* Little, Brown, 1993. / Murphy, Jim. *A Young Patriot: The American Revolution as Experienced by One Boy.* Clarion, 1996. / Shields, Carol Diggory. *Brain Juice: History, Fresh Squeezed!* Handprint, 2002.

SUBJECTS: BIOGRAPHY. CHILDREN—BIOGRAPHY. MULTICULTURAL BOOKS. U.S.—HISTORY.

1502 Jiang, Ji-li. *Red Scarf Girl: A Memoir of the Cultural Revolution.* **HarperCollins, 1997. 0-06-027585-5. 240pp. Gr. 5–8**

Ji-li grew up in Shanghai where, in 1966, when she was 12, Chairman Mao's Cultural Revolution caused her "bourgeois" family to become outcasts. To build a strong socialist country, people were told to eradicate the "Four Olds": old ideas, culture, customs, and habits; and to denounce the so-called revisionist teachers, the educational system, and local "class enemies." Over the next three years, Ji-li's family was denounced, her actor father was declared a rightist, and their house was ransacked by Red Guards.

GERM: Jiang's compelling memoir covers unfamiliar territory for American students, and proves unsettling, disturbing, but always fascinating reading. You will want to bone up on recent Chinese history to be able to answer your students' questions about how and why such things could happen. Paired with Alison Leslie Gold's biography *Memories of Anne Frank*, and Lois Lowry's dystopian *The Giver*, you'll be able to start a dialogue on the value of personal and political freedoms.

RELATED TITLES: Bridges, Ruby. *Through My Eyes.* Scholastic, 1999. / Gold, Alison Leslie. *Memories of Anne Frank: Reflections of a Childhood Friend.* Scholastic, 1997. / Lee, Milly. *Nim and the War Effort.* Farrar, 1997. / Levine, Karen. *Hana's Suitcase.* Albert Whitman, 2003. / Lowry, Lois. *The Giver.* Houghton Mifflin, 1993. / Reiss, Johanna. *The Upstairs Room.* HarperCollins, 1987. / Verhoeven, Rian, and Ruud Van Der Rol. *Anne*

Frank: Beyond the Diary. Viking, 1993. / Yep, Laurence. *The Star Fisher.* Morrow, 1991. / Yin. *Coolies.* Philomel, 2001.

SUBJECTS: AUTOBIOGRAPHY. BIOGRAPHY. CHINA—HISTORY. MULTICULTURAL BOOKS. OUTCASTS. PERSONAL NARRATIVES.

1503 **Joseph, Lynn.** *Fly, Bessie, Fly.* **Illus. by Yvonne Buchanan. Simon & Schuster, 1998. 0-689-81339-2. 32pp. Gr. 1–4**

It was not until her two brothers returned from World War I with stories of women fighter pilots that Bessie Coleman decided what she wanted to do with her life. No one in the United States would teach a black woman to fly a plane, so in 1920, she moved to France. She became the first black woman in the world to earn a pilot's license, and returned home eager to make enough money as a barnstormer at air shows around the country to start a flying school for other African American men and women. Before she could fulfill that dream, she was killed during a test flight in 1926 at the age of 34. This fictionalized biography is told in the present tense, with detailed, full-page watercolor and pen-and-ink illustrations.

GERM: Ask your students to think about what they dream of doing to make a difference in the world, and what hurdles they will need to overcome.

RELATED TITLES: Adler, David A. *A Picture Book of Amelia Earhart.* Holiday House, 1998. / Borden, Louise, and Mary Kay Kroeger. *Fly High! The Story of Bessie Coleman.* McElderry, 2001. / Brown, Don. *Ruth Law Thrills a Nation.* Ticknor & Fields, 1993. / Burleigh, Robert. *Flight: The Journey of Charles Lindbergh.* Philomel, 1991. / Grimes, Nikki. *Talkin' About Bessie: The Story of Aviator Elizabeth Coleman.* Orchard, 2002. / Lindbergh, Reeve. *Nobody Owns the Sky: The Story of "Brave Bessie" Coleman.* Candlewick, 1996. / Moss, Marissa. *Brave Harriet.* Harcourt, 2001. / Ride, Sally, and Susan Okie. *To Space and Back.* Lothrop, 1986. / Ryan, Pam Muñoz. *Amelia and Eleanor Go for a Ride.* Scholastic, 1999.

SUBJECTS: AFRICAN AMERICANS—BIOGRAPHY. AIR PILOTS. BIOGRAPHY. COLEMAN, BESSIE. FLIGHT. MULTICULTURAL BOOKS. WOMEN—BIOGRAPHY.

1504 **Kerley, Barbara.** *The Dinosaurs of Waterhouse Hawkins.* **Illus. by Brian Selznick. Scholastic, 2001. 0-439-11494-2. Unp. Gr. 2–6**

Until Waterhouse Hawkins began sculpting his life-sized cement-cast models of an iguanadon, megalosaurus, and other extinct creatures in England in 1853, most people had no idea what a dinosaur looked like. This grand and flamboyant picture-book biography is summarized on the title page: "A true dinosaur story in three ages: From a childhood love of art, to the monumental dinosaur sculptures at the Crystal Palace in England, to the thwarted work in New York's Central Park . . . It's all here!" Extensive, fascinating author and illustrator notes at the back of the book clarify additional details.

GERM: Dinosaur aficionados will relive the excitement generated by Hawkins's massive models, and explore the latest dinosaur discoveries that have changed our notions of how they looked and acted. Children looking at Selznick's wonderful Caldecott Honor-winning paintings, modeled after original sketches made by Hawkins and on the dinosaur models themselves, will be quick to point out the inaccuracies in his dinosaurs. You can use this as an example of how information changes rapidly with each new scientific discovery. Dinosaur expert Peter Larson and journalist Kristin Donnan put together a remarkable color photo-illustrated handbook, *Bones Rock! Everything You Need to Know to Be a Paleontologist,* for all seriously dinosaur-obsessed kids.

RELATED TITLES: Anholt, Laurence. *Stone Girl, Bone Girl: The Story of Mary Anning.* Orchard, 1999. / Atkins, Jeannine. *Mary Anning and the Sea Dragon.* Farrar, 1999. / Bausum, Ann. *Dragon Bones and Dinosaur Eggs: A Photobiography of Explorer Roy Chapman Andrews.* National Geographic, 2000. / Brown, Don. *Rare Treasure: Mary Anning and Her Remarkable Discoveries.* Houghton Mifflin, 1999. / Dixon, Dougal. *Amazing Dinosaurs: The Fiercest, the Tallest, the Toughest, the Smallest.* Boyds Mills, 2000. / Dodson, Peter. *An Alphabet of Dinosaurs.* Scholastic, 1995. / Kerley, Barbara. *Walt Whitman: Words for America.* Illus. by Brian Selznick. Scholastic, 2004. / Larson, Peter, and Kristin Donnan. *Bones Rock! Everything You Need to Know to Be a Paleontologist.* Invisible Cities, 2004. / Marrin, Albert. *Secrets from the Rocks: Dinosaur Hunting with Roy Chapman Andrews.* Dutton, 2002. / Moss, Jeff. *Bone Poems.* Workman, 1997. / Tanaka, Shelley. *Graveyards of the Dinosaurs.* Hyperion, 1998. / Zoehfeld, Kathleen. *Dinosaur Parents, Dinosaur Young: Uncovering the Mystery of Dinosaur Families.* Clarion, 2001.

SUBJECTS: ANIMALS, EXTINCT. BIOGRAPHY. DINOSAURS. HAWKINS, BENJAMIN WATERHOUSE, 1807–1889. SCIENTISTS.

1505 Kerley, Barbara. *Walt Whitman: Words for America*. Illus. by Brian Selznick. Scholastic, 2004. 0-439-35791-8. Unp. Gr. 4–8

"Walt Whitman loved words." So begins a dignified yet personal picture-book biography of America's best-known poet. Selznick's ravishing portraits provide an intimate view of the poet as an ink-spotted 12-year-old setting type as a printer's apprentice, and as a war-weary older man with his familiar white beard, tending wounded soldiers in a Washington, D.C., hospital during the Civil War.

GERM: The Author's and Illustrator's Notes at the back are filled with information, poems, and the photo of Whitman that inspired the book. You'll want to pull this moving and unforgettable book into both Civil War and literature studies.

RELATED TITLES: Aliki. *William Shakespeare and the Globe*. HarperCollins, 1999. / Gollub, Matthew. *Cool Melons—Turn to Frogs! The Life and Poems of Issa*. Lee & Low, 1998. / Kerley, Barbara. *The Dinosaurs of Waterhouse Hawkins*. Illus. by Brian Selznick. Scholastic, 2001. / Lasky, Kathryn. *A Voice of Her Own: The Story of Phyllis Wheatley, Slave Poet*. Candlewick, 2002. / Polacco, Patricia. *Pink and Say*. Philomel, 1994. / Ryan, Pam Muñoz. *When Marian Sang*. Illus. by Brian Selznick. Scholastic, 2002. / Spivak, Dawnine. *Grass Sandals: The Travels of Basho*. Atheneum, 1997. / Stanley, Diane. *Bard of Avon: The Story of William Shakespeare*. Morrow, 1992. / Turner, Ann. *Drummer Boy: Marching to the Civil War*. HarperCollins, 1998. / Whitman, Walt. *When I Heard the Learn'd Astronomer*. Simon & Schuster, 2004.

SUBJECTS: AUTHORS—BIOGRAPHY. BIOGRAPHY. NURSES. POETS. U.S.—HISTORY—CIVIL WAR, 1861–1865. WHITMAN, WALT, 1819–1892.

1506 Kostyal, Kim. *Trial by Ice: A Photobiography of Sir Ernest Shackleton*. Illus. with photos. National Geographic, 1999. 0-7922-7393-1. 64pp. Gr. 5–8

Born in Ireland in 1874, Ernest R. Shackleton grew up in a London suburb, where he loved to read adventure stories, and went to sea at age 16. In 1901, he set out on his first polar trek, joining Robert Scott's expedition to the South Pole. This heart-pounding biography of Shackleton, whose own 1914 expedition has thrilled generations, is packed with black-and-white photographs of the explorers in the Antarctic landscape and, by the end, will have you reaching for a sweater.

GERM: Discussion point: What are the qualities that make a person a leader? Write definitions for "leader" and then make a list of great leaders from history, stating their accomplishments. The Afterword of the book provides an apt summation of Shackleton's legacy. Before reading it aloud, ask your students why we still remember Shackleton today, even though his expedition was not successful in the traditional sense.

RELATED TITLES: Armstrong, Jennifer. *Shipwreck at the Bottom of the World: The Extraordinary True Story of Shackleton and the Endurance*. Crown, 1998. / Armstrong, Jennifer. *Spirit of Endurance*. Crown, 2000. / Brandenberg, Jim. *To the Top of the World: Adventures with Arctic Wolves*. Walker, 1993. / Burleigh, Robert. *Black Whiteness: Admiral Byrd Alone in the Antarctic*. Atheneum, 1997. / Hooper, Meredith. *Tom's Rabbit: A Surprise on the Way to Antarctica*. National Geographic, 1998. / Kimmel, Elizabeth Cody. *Ice Story: Shackleton's Lost Expedition*. Clarion, 1999. / McCurdy, Michael. *Trapped by the Ice: Shackleton's Amazing Antarctic Adventure*. Walker, 1997. / Swan, Robert. *Destination: Antarctica*. Scholastic, 1988. / Webb, Sophie. *My Season with Penguins: An Antarctic Journal*. Houghton Mifflin, 2000.

SUBJECTS: ADVENTURE AND ADVENTURERS. ANTARCTICA—DISCOVERY AND EXPLORATION. ARCTIC REGIONS. BIOGRAPHY. EXPLORERS. OCEAN. SHACKLETON, ERNEST HENRY, SIR. SHIPS. SURVIVAL. VOYAGES AND TRAVELS.

1507 Krensky, Stephen. *Shooting for the Moon: The Amazing Life and Times of Annie Oakley*. Illus. by Bernie Fuchs. Farrar, 2001. 0-374-36843-0. Unp. Gr. 1–4

Filled with dark, somber, full-bleed oil paintings, this picture-book biography of famed sharpshooter Annie Oakley hits the highlights of her life, from her tough childhood in a two room, dirt-floored cabin in Ohio to her father's death in 1865 to her rise to fame as a performer in Buffalo Bill Cody's Wild West Show.

GERM: For more information and many photographs of the famed sharpshooter, pair this with Sue Macy's *Bull's-Eye: A Photobiography of Annie Oakley*. Debbie Dadey's *Shooting Star: Annie Oakley, the Legend* provides some facts while also presenting Annie as a tall tale heroine.

RELATED TITLES: Dadey, Debbie. *Shooting Star: Annie Oakley, the Legend*. Walker, 1997. / Macy, Sue. *Bull's-Eye: A Photobiography of Annie Oakley*. National Geographic, 2001. / Pinkney, Andrea D. *Bill Pickett: Rodeo-Ridin' Cowboy*. Harcourt, 1996. / Ryan, Pam Muñoz. *Riding Freedom*. Scholastic, 1998.

SUBJECTS: BIOGRAPHY. OAKLEY, ANNIE, 1860–1926. SHARPSHOOTERS. WEST (U.S.). WOMEN—
BIOGRAPHY.

1508 **Krull, Kathleen.** *The Boy on Fairfield Street: How Ted Geisel Grew Up to Become Dr. Seuss.*
Illus. by Steve Johnson and Lou Fancher. Random House, 2004. 0-375-92298-9. 43pp. Gr. K–4
Born in Springfield, Massachusetts, in 1904, Ted Geisel, whose father ran the city zoo, loved to
draw animals and funny, exaggerated creatures, which led one high school art teacher to warn
him he would never be successful at art. Ted, of course, became our own beloved Dr. Seuss,
and this poignant picture-book biography takes him up to the start of his career at age 22 in
New York City's Greenwich Village. The final pages give an overview of the rest of his life,
highlighting the stories behind his most famous books.
GERM: Discuss: Trace the influences on Ted's life that led him to become one of the most successful children's author and illustrator in history. Why did he always avoid being in public?
Talk about his humiliating experience as a cub scout when he met Theodore Roosevelt, and
how his Dartmouth classmates voted him "Least Likely to Succeed." This should give fans a
whole new perspective on his books and get them thinking about what it means to overcome
the odds. Ask them to recall their own defining moments, both good and bad, or to write an
essay on why they think Ted persevered.
RELATED TITLES: Christelow, Eileen. *What Do Authors Do?* Clarion, 1995. / Christelow, Eileen. *What Do
Illustrators Do?* Clarion, 1999. / dePaola, Tomie. *26 Fairmount Avenue.* Putnam, 1999. / Engel, Dean, and Flo-
rence D. Freeman. *Ezra Jack Keats.* Silver Moon, 1995. / Leedy, Loreen. *Look at My Book: How Kids Can Write and
Illustrate Terrific Books.* Holiday House, 2004. / Lester, Helen. *Author: A True Story.* Houghton Mifflin, 1997. /
Seuss, Dr. *And to Think That I Saw It on Mulberry Street.* Random House, 1989. / Sierra, Judy. *Wild About Books.*
Knopf, 2004. / Stevens, Janet. *From Pictures to Words: A Book About Making a Book.* Holiday House, 1995.
SUBJECTS: AUTHORS—BIOGRAPHY. AUTHORSHIP. BIOGRAPHY. ILLUSTRATORS. SEUSS, DR.

1509 **Krull, Kathleen.** *Harvesting Hope: The Story of Cesar Chavez.* **Illus. by Yuyi Morales. Harcourt, 2003. 0-15-201437-3. Unp. Gr. 3–6**
Growing up as a Mexican American migrant worker in the Southwest, César Chávez dropped
out of school in the eighth grade, but went on to found the National Farm Workers Association,
a nonviolent union that fought for the rights and dignity of farmworkers in the United States.
Sweeping full-page paintings dramatize the life and times of the civil rights leader.
GERM: Read this in tandem with Doreen Rappaport's Martin's *Big Words.* Write expository
essays comparing and contrasting the lives and accomplishments of Chávez and Martin Luther
King, Jr.
RELATED TITLES: Bernier-Grand, Carmen T. *César: ¡Sí, Se Puede! Yes, We Can!* Marshall Cavendish, 2004. /
Elya, Susan Middleton. *Home at Last.* Lee & Low, 2002. / Lomas Garza, Carmen. *Family Pictures/Cuadros de
Familia.* Children's Book Press, 1990. / Lomas Garza, Carmen. *In My Family/En Mi Familia.* Children's Book
Press, 1996. / Pérez, L. *King. First Day in Grapes.* Lee & Low, 2002. / Rappaport, Doreen. *Martin's Big Words.*
Hyperion, 2001. / Ryan, Pam Muñoz. *Esperanza Rising.* Scholastic, 2000. / Smothers, Ethel Footman. *The Hard-
Times Jar.* Farrar, 2003.
SUBJECTS: BIOGRAPHY. CALIFORNIA. CHAVEZ, CESAR. HISPANIC AMERICANS. LABOR
LEADERS. MEXICAN AMERICANS. MIGRANT LABOR. MULTICULTURAL BOOKS. UNITED FARM
WORKERS.

1510 **Krull, Kathleen.** *Houdini: World's Greatest Mystery Man and Escape King.* **Illus. by Eric
Velasquez. Walker, 2005. 0-8027-8953-6. Unp. Gr. 2–5**
Starting with the milk-can escape, five of Harry Houdini's greatest tricks are illustrated in a
series of framed, color, snapshot-like oil paintings set onstage, like a grand vaudeville act, and
proclaimed by a mustachioed gent in white gloves, tails, and spats, standing in front of the curtain. Interspersed is a boldly illustrated biography of Erik Weiss, who was born, perhaps in
1874, the son of a poor Hungarian rabbi and who changed his name in honor of the French
founder of modern magic, Robert-Houdin. Realizing he would never get rich doing just magic
tricks, Houdini made his mark as an escape artist, jumping, chained and handcuffed, off
bridges, and being suspended, straitjacketed, from tall buildings.
GERM: Listed in the bibliography are several Web sites, including <lcweb2.loc.gov/ammem/
vshtml/vshchrn.html>, which is the Library of Congress site of Houdini's Biographical
Chronology, as they call it, filled with links to pictures and fascinating additional information.
Brian Selznick's first book, *The Houdini Box,* is an enigmatic fictional tale of a boy who meets

Harry Houdini right before the magician's untimely death. Introduce your awed children to 793.8, the magic section of the library, and have them work on their sleight of hand.

RELATED TITLES: Agee, Jon. *Milo's Hat Trick*. Hyperion, 2001. / Broekel, Ray. *Now You See It: Easy Magic for Beginners*. Little, Brown, 1979. / Cobb, Vicki. *Harry Houdini: A Photographic Story of a Life*. DK, 2005. / Kraske, Robert. *Magicians Do Amazing Things*. Random House, 1979. / MacLeod, Elizabeth. *Harry Houdini: A Magical Life*. Kids Can, 2005. / Petersen, P. J. *The Amazing Magic Show*. Simon & Schuster, 1994. / Selznick, Brian. *The Houdini Box*. Knopf, 1991. / White, Florence. *Escape! The Life of Harry Houdini*. Julian Messner, 1979.

SUBJECTS: BIOGRAPHY. DAREDEVILS. ESCAPE ARTISTS. HOUDINI, HARRY, 1874–1926. JEWS. MAGICIANS.

1511 **Krull, Kathleen. *Lives of Extraordinary Women: Rulers, Rebels (and What the Neighbors Thought)*. Illus. by Kathryn Hewitt. Harcourt, 2000. 0-15-200807-1. 95pp. Gr. 4–12**

In a groundbreaking compilation of the stories of 20 powerful women through history, meet "queens, warriors, prime ministers, revolutionary leaders, Indian chiefs, first ladies or other government officials." Krull's skillful use of anecdotes makes her subjects' lives and personal quirks seem sometimes endearing, sometimes shocking, but always real. The accompanying watercolor-and-colored-pencil caricatures are masterfully done.

GERM: What's so wonderful about this book of role models—"the good, the bad, and some who were both"—(and all others in the Lives Of series), is how much fun it is to read as an appetite-whetter for longer biographies. Have children study the wonderfully expressive eyes in each portrait. Students can brainstorm a list of other interesting women and men who attempted to overcome prejudice and oppression, research their lives, and write similarly structured biographies with illustrations. In presenting their findings to the class, they can dress as their heroes or heroines and tell their life stories in the first person.

RELATED TITLES: Christensen, Bonnie. *The Daring Nellie Bly: America's Star Reporter*. Knopf, 2003. / Fritz, Jean. *You Want Women to Vote, Lizzie Stanton?* Putnam, 1995. / Glaser, Isabel Joshlin, sel. *Dreams of Glory: Poems Starring Girls*. Atheneum, 1995. / Krull, Kathleen. *Lives of the Presidents: Fame, Shame (and What the Neighbors Thought)*. Harcourt, 1998. / Krull, Kathleen. *A Woman for President: The Story of Victoria Woodhull*. Walker, 2004. / McCully, Emily Arnold. *The Ballot Box Battle*. Knopf, 1996. / McDonough, Yona Zeldis. *Sisters in Strength: American Women Who Made a Difference*. Henry Holt, 2000. / Rappaport, Doreen. *Living Dangerously: American Women Who Risked Their Lives for Adventure*. HarperCollins, 1991. / Ryan, Pam Muñoz. *Amelia and Eleanor Go for a Ride*. Scholastic, 1999. / Thimmesh, Catherine. *Madame President: The Extraordinary True (and Evolving) Story of Women in Politics*. Houghton Mifflin, 2004. / White, Linda Arms. *I Could Do That: Esther Morris Gets Women the Vote.* I Farrar, 2005. / Wooldridge, Connie Nordhielm. *When Esther Morris Headed West: Women, Wyoming, and the Right to Vote*. Holiday House, 2001.

SUBJECTS: BIOGRAPHY. KINGS AND RULERS. MULTICULTURAL BOOKS. WOMEN— BIOGRAPHY.

1512 **Krull, Kathleen. *Lives of the Artists: Masterpieces, Messes (and What the Neighbors Thought)*. Illus. by Kathryn Hewitt. Harcourt, 1995. 0-15-200103-4. 96pp. Gr. 4–8**

Compelling tidbits, anecdotes, and sometimes eyebrow-raising stories about artists' lives and how they created their work can be found here in profiles, arranged chronologically, of the foibles and talents of 19 mostly well-known painters and sculptors, starting with Leonardo da Vinci and ending with 20th century Pop artist Andy Warhol.

GERM: Flesh out each entertaining biographical chapter with samples of the artists' work from books, encyclopedias, or the Internet. You'll find single volume biographies of several of the artists—da Vinci, Michelangelo, Van Gogh, and Warhol, for example—including *Uncle Andy*, a picture book memoir by James Warhola, children's book illustrator and Warhol's nephew. For a look at the music world, read Krull's equally fascinating *Lives of the Musicians*.

RELATED TITLES: Brenner, Barbara. *The Boy Who Loved to Draw: Benjamin West*. Houghton Mifflin, 1999. / Duggleby, John. *Artist in Overalls: The Life of Grant Wood*. Chronicle, 1996. / Duggleby, John. *Story Painter: The Life of Jacob Lawrence*. Chronicle, 1998. / Greenberg, Jan. *Romare Bearden: Collage of Memories*. Abrams, 2003. / Greenberg, Jan, and Sandra Jordan. *Action Jackson*. Roaring Brook, 2002. / Greenberg, Jan, and Sandra Jordan. *Chuck Close Up Close*. Roaring Brook, 2002. / Krull, Kathleen. *Lives of the Musicians: Good Times, Bad Times (And What the Neighbors Thought)*. Harcourt, 1993. / LaMarche, Jim. *The Raft*. HarperCollins, 2000. / Raczka, Bob. *Art Is . . .* Millbrook, 2003. / Reynolds, Peter H. *The Dot*. Candlewick, 2003. / Stanley, Diane. *Leonardo da Vinci*. Morrow, 1996. / Stanley, Diane. *Michelangelo*. HarperCollins, 2000. / Wallner, Alexandra. *Grandma Moses*. Holiday House, 2004. / Warhola, James. *Uncle Andy's*. Putnam, 2003.

SUBJECTS: ARTISTS—BIOGRAPHY. BIOGRAPHY.

1513 Krull, Kathleen. *Lives of the Athletes: Thrills, Spills (and What the Neighbors Thought).* **Illus. by Kathryn Hewitt. Harcourt, 1997. 0-15-200806-3. 96pp. Gr. 4–12**

Twenty athletes, in a wide-ranging multicultural mix of legends and lesser knowns, both men and women, are profiled in short, fascinating biographical sketches, each accompanied by a full-page, detailed watercolor caricature.

GERM: Finally! A meaty volume that phys ed teachers will have a ball sharing with their classes, reading aloud a chapter a week. Krull's three- to five-page write-ups are jammed with intriguing facts, anecdotes, and eye-opening details that make each personality resonate. Using the same format, children can research and retell the salient features of additional athletes' lives.

RELATED TITLES: Adler, David A. *America's Champion Swimmer: Gertrude Ederle.* Harcourt, 2000. / Adler, David A. *Lou Gehrig: The Luckiest Man.* Harcourt, 1997. / Cline-Ransome, Lisa. *Satchel Paige.* Simon & Schuster, 2000. / Krull, Kathleen. *Lives of the Artists: Masterpieces, Messes (and What the Neighbors Thought).* Harcourt, 1995. (And others in the Lives Of series.) / Krull, Kathleen. *Wilma Unlimited: How Wilma Rudolph Became the World's Fastest Woman.* Harcourt, 1996. / Littlefield, Bill. *Champions: Stories of Ten Remarkable Athletes.* Little, Brown, 1993. / Macy, Sue. *Winning Ways: A Photohistory of American Women in Sports.* Henry Holt, 1996. / Moss, Marissa. *Mighty Jackie, the Strike-Out Queen.* Simon & Schuster, 2004.

SUBJECTS: ATHLETES—BIOGRAPHY. BIOGRAPHY. MULTICULTURAL BOOKS. SPORTS—BIOGRAPHY.

1514 Krull, Kathleen. *Lives of the Presidents: Fame, Shame (and What the Neighbors Thought).* **Illus. by Kathryn Hewitt. Harcourt, 1998. 0-15-200808-X. 96pp. Gr. 4–12**

Intriguing and entertaining details about each of the presidents, plus a color caricature painting make this a must-have collective biography that will spur history lovers to find out more.

GERM: Have each student choose a president and read the entry about him. The student then can write up a fact-laden question and challenge the rest of the group to identify its subject. Here's an example, distilled from the facts in one entry: This president couldn't stand the sight of animal blood, only ate meat well done, was the first president to have a woman run against him (Victoria Woodhull), had the most corrupt administration up to that time, was tone deaf, and smoked 20 cigars a day, dying at age 63 of mouth cancer (Ulysses S. Grant, 1869–1877).

RELATED TITLES: Burns, Diane, and Clint Burns. *Hail to the Chief! Jokes About the Presidents.* Lerner, 1989. / Cleveland, Will, and Mark Alvarez. *Yo, Millard Fillmore! (And All Those Other Presidents You Don't Know).* Millbrook, 1997. / Davis, Gibbs. *Wackiest White House Pets.* Scholastic, 2004. / Gutman, Dan. *The Kid Who Ran for President.* Scholastic, 1996. / Harness, Cheryl. *Ghosts of the White House.* Simon & Schuster, 1998. / Jones, Rebecca C. *The President Has Been Shot: True Stories of the Attacks on Ten U.S. Presidents.* Dutton, 1996. / Maestro, Betsy. *The Voice of the People: American Democracy in Action.* Lothrop, 1996. / O'Connor, Jane. *If the Walls Could Talk: Family Life at the White House.* Simon & Schuster, 2004. / Provensen, Alice. *The Buck Stops Here: The Presidents of the United States.* Harcourt, 2000. / St. George, Judith. *So You Want to Be President?* Philomel, 2000. / Stier, Catherine. *If I Were President.* Albert Whitman, 1999. / Thimmesh, Catherine. *Madam President: The Extraordinary True (and Evolving) Story of Women in Politics.* Houghton Mifflin, 2004.

SUBJECTS: BIOGRAPHY. PRESIDENTS. U.S.—HISTORY.

1515 Krull, Kathleen. *Wilma Unlimited: How Wilma Rudolph Became the World's Fastest Woman.* **Illus. by David Diaz. Harcourt, 1996. 0-15-201267-2. 40pp. Gr. 2–5**

Born in 1940 in Tennessee, the youngest of 20 children, Wilma Rudolph contracted polio at age 5 and was told she'd never walk again. How she fought against her illness and the rejection of other children and, at the 1960 Rome Olympics, became the first American woman to win three gold medals, makes for a gripping and inspiring picture-book biography of this African American heroine and role model.

GERM: Introduce other athletes who defied the odds, including Jackie Mitchell, in *Mighty Jackie, the Strike Out Queen* by Marissa Moss and *The Girl Who Struck Out Babe Ruth* by Jean L. S. Patrick.

RELATED TITLES: Adler, David A. *America's Champion Swimmer: Gertrude Ederle.* Harcourt, 2000. / Adler, David A. *Lou Gehrig: The Luckiest Man.* Harcourt, 1997. / Barasch, Lynne. *Knockin' on Wood: Starring Peg Leg Bates.* Lee & Low, 2004. / Cline-Ransome, Lisa. *Satchel Paige.* Simon & Schuster, 2000. / Glaser, Isabel Joshlin, sel. *Dreams of Glory: Poems Starring Girls.* Atheneum, 1995. / Krull, Kathleen. *Lives of the Athletes: Thrills, Spills (and What the Neighbors Thought).* Harcourt, 1995. / Littlefield, Bill. *Champions: Stories of Ten Remarkable Athletes.* Little, Brown, 1993. / Macy, Sue. *Winning Ways: A Photohistory of American Women in Sports.* Henry

Holt, 1996. / Moss, Marissa. *Mighty Jackie, the Strike-Out Queen*. Simon & Schuster, 2004. / Patrick, Jean L. S. *The Girl Who Struck Out Babe Ruth*. Carolrhoda, 2000.

SUBJECTS: AFRICAN AMERICANS—BIOGRAPHY. ATHLETES—BIOGRAPHY. BIOGRAPHY. MULTICULTURAL BOOKS. OLYMPIC GAMES. RUDOLPH, WILMA, 1940–1994. SPORTS— BIOGRAPHY. TRACK AND FIELD ATHLETES. WOMEN—BIOGRAPHY.

1516 Krull, Kathleen. *A Woman for President: The Story of Victoria Woodhull*. **Illus. by Jane Dyer. Walker, 2004. 0-8027-8909-9. Unp. Gr. 3–6**

As described in this handsome picture-book biography, the scandalous and daring business-woman and suffragist Victoria Woodhull fought to prove women's equality by announcing herself the first woman candidate for president, the choice of the Equal Rights Party in the 1872 election.

GERM: Investigate the paths other women have taken in politics in Catherine Thimmesh's *Madam President*.

RELATED TITLES: Adler, David A. *A Picture Book of Eleanor Roosevelt*. Holiday House, 1991. / Blumberg, Rhoda. *Bloomers*. Atheneum, 1993. / Christensen, Bonnie. *The Daring Nellie Bly: America's Star Reporter*. Knopf, 2003. / Fritz, Jean. *You Want Women to Vote, Lizzie Stanton?* Putnam, 1995. / Krull, Kathleen. *Lives of Extraordinary Women: Rulers, Rebels (and What the Neighbors Thought)*. Harcourt, 2000. / McCully, Emily Arnold. *The Ballot Box Battle*. Knopf, 1996. / McDonough, Yona Zeldis. *Sisters in Strength: American Women Who Made a Difference*. Henry Holt, 2000. / St. George, Judith. *So You Want to Be President?* Philomel, 2000. / Thimmesh, Catherine. *Madam President*. Houghton Mifflin, 2004. / White, Linda Arms. *I Could Do That: Esther Morris Gets Women the Vote.*I Farrar, 2005. / Winters, Kay. *My Teacher for President*. Dutton, 2004. / Wooldridge, Connie Nordhielm. *When Esther Morris Headed West: Women, Wyoming, and the Right to Vote*. Holiday House, 2001.

SUBJECTS: BIOGRAPHY. FEMINISTS. PRESIDENTIAL CANDIDATES. SUFFRAGISTS. WOMEN— BIOGRAPHY. WOODHULL, VICTORIA, 1838–1927.

1517 Lasky, Kathryn. *The Man Who Made Time Travel*. **Illus. by Kevin Hawkes. Farrar, 2003. 0-374-34788-3. Unp. Gr. 4–8**

In 1714, John Harrison, a 22-year-old small-town carpenter with a passion for clock making, began his 50-year endeavor to perfect a series of timepieces that could accurately measure a ship's longitude. His tireless quest is captured in an engrossing, provocative, and visually spellbinding picture book for older readers. Children will root for and be inspired by Harrison who, without any formal education but with an unquenchable commitment to discovery, solved the age-old problem of determining longitude.

GERM: *Sea Clocks* by Louise Borden is another splendid picture-book biography of Harrison. For an understanding of how clocks work, have a take-apart day when students dismantle and examine discarded old clocks and watches.

RELATED TITLES: Borden, Louise. *Sea Clocks: The Story of Longitude*. McElderry, 2003. / Delano, Marie Ferguson. *Inventing the Future: A Photobiography of Thomas Alva Edison*. National Geographic, 2002. / Kerley, Barbara. *The Dinosaurs of Waterhouse Hawkins*. Scholastic, 2001. / Lasky, Kathryn. *The Librarian Who Measured the Earth*. Little, Brown, 1994. / Martin, Jacqueline Briggs. *Snowflake Bentley*. Houghton Mifflin, 1998. / Old, Wendie. *To Fly: The Story of the Wright Brothers*. Clarion, 2002. / St. George, Judith. *So You Want to Be an Inventor?* Philomel, 2002. / Wells, Robert E. *How Do You Know What Time It Is?* Albert Whitman, 2002. / Wetterer, Margaret. *Clyde Tombaugh and the Search for Planet X*. Carolrhoda, 1996.

SUBJECTS: BIOGRAPHY. CHRONOMETERS. CLOCKS AND WATCHES. INVENTIONS AND INVENTORS. LONGITUDE—MEASUREMENT. SCIENTISTS.

1518 Lasky, Kathryn. *A Voice of Her Own: The Story of Phillis Wheatley, Slave Poet*. **Illus. by Paul Lee. Candlewick, 2002. 0-7636-0252-3. Unp. Gr. 3–6**

Phillis Wheatley, abducted from Africa to Boston on a slave ship in 1761 as a young child, grew up to become a renowned poet in Boston during the Revolutionary War, publishing her first book of poems in 1774.

GERM: Throughout her life, Phillis encountered injustice and tyranny in many forms and wrote about violence and issues of freedom facing colonists from a unique perspective. Discuss the many instances of oppression she faced and how she tried to overcome them, and also how, as the first black woman poet, she used her advantages and voice to make a difference. Lasky's eloquent picture-book biography will start a discussion about the effect an education can have on a person's life.

RELATED TITLES: Hamilton, Virginia. *Her Stories: African American Folktales, Fairy Tales, and True Tales.*

Scholastic, 1995. / Hoose, Phillip M. *We Were There, Too! Young People in U.S. History*. Farrar, 2001. / Howard, Elizabeth Fitzgerald. *Virgie Goes to School with Us Boys*. Simon & Schuster, 2000. / Hughes, Langston. *The Dream Keeper and Other Poems*. Knopf, 1994. / Hudson, Wade. *Pass It On: African-American Poetry for Children*. Scholastic, 1993. / Kerley, Barbara. *Walt Whitman: Words for America*. Scholastic, 2004. / McGill, Alice. *Molly Bannaky*. Houghton Mifflin, 1999. / Nelson, Vaunda Micheaux. *Almost to Freedom*. Carolrhoda, 2003. / Slier, Deborah. *Make a Joyful Sound: Poems for Children by African-American Poets*. Scholastic, 1996. / Strickland, Dorothy S., and Michael R. Strickland. *Families: Poems Celebrating the African-American Experience*. Wordsong: Boyds Mills, 1994.

SUBJECTS: AFRICAN AMERICANS—BIOGRAPHY. AFRICAN AMERICANS—HISTORY. BIOGRAPHY. MASSACHUSETTS—HISTORY. MULTICULTURAL BOOKS. POETS. SLAVERY. U.S.— HISTORY—REVOLUTION, 1775–1783. WHEATLEY, PHILLIS, 1753–1784. WOMEN—BIOGRAPHY.

1519 **Lester, Helen.** *Author: A True Story*. **Illus. by the author. Houghton Mifflin, 1997. 0-395-82744-2. Unp. Gr. K–4**

Helen Lester's upbeat picture-book account of how she became a real children's book writer, starting with indecipherable scribbled grocery lists at age 3, gets us excited about writing. After ten years as a second-grade teacher, Lester began submitting her own stories to publishers. When her seventh title was finally accepted, she was elated. "I was the first author I had ever met."

GERM: Lester's colorful cartoon-like illustrations will start your students thinking about what authors do and will likely inspire them to write and illustrate their own autobiographies in picture-book format. She keeps a box full of "fizzled thoughts and half-finished books" that she calls her Fizzle Box to which she refers when she needs an idea. Ask your writers to start their own Fizzle Boxes, and to brainstorm and compile a list of good advice for other writers. Post their resulting chart for all to contemplate when preparing to write. Watch how author Bramwell Wink-Porter holds up during an all-day school visit in Daniel Pinkwater's hilarious picture book *Author's Day*.

RELATED TITLES: Bunting, Eve. *My Special Day at Third Street School*. Boyds Mills, 2004. / Christelow, Eileen. *What Do Authors Do?* Clarion, 1995. / dePaola, Tomie. *The Art Lesson*. Putnam, 1989. / Krull, Kathleen. *The Boy on Fairfield Street: How Ted Geisel Grew Up to Become Dr. Seuss*. Random House, 2004. / Leedy, Loreen. *Look at My Book: How Kids Can Write and Illustrate Terrific Books*. Holiday House, 2004. / Lester, Helen. *Hooway for Wodney Wat*. Houghton Mifflin, 1999. / Lester, Helen. *Score One for the Sloths*. Houghton Mifflin, 2001. / McPhail, David. *In Flight with David McPhail*. Heinemann, 1996. / Nixon, Joan Lowery. *If You Were a Writer*. Four Winds, 1988. / Pinkwater, Daniel. *Author's Day*. Atheneum, 1993. / Polacco, Patricia. *Firetalking*. Richard C. Owen, 1994. / Pulver, Robin. *Author Day for Room 3T*. Clarion, 2005. / Rylant, Cynthia. *Best Wishes*. Richard C. Owen, 1992. / Stevens, Janet. *From Pictures to Words: A Book About Making a Book*. Holiday House, 1995.

SUBJECTS: AUTHORS—BIOGRAPHY. AUTOBIOGRAPHY. BIOGRAPHY. LEARNING DISABILITIES. LESTER, HELEN. WOMEN—BIOGRAPHY.

1520 **Levine, Karen.** *Hana's Suitcase*. **Illus. with photos. Albert Whitman, 2003. 0-8075-3148-0. 111pp. Gr. 3–8**

When Fumiko Ishioka, Director of the Tokyo Holocaust Center, acquired the suitcase of Hana Brady, a Jewish child who was at Auschwitz, she set out to discover what happened to the child who owned it. In alternating chapters, we learn about her research, and the fate of the young girl from a small town in Czechoslovakia, whose family was wrenched apart.

GERM: The photos of Hana and her family provide moving testimony of her life before the war. This book, read aloud, is more accessible to younger children than the books on Anne Frank and certainly as moving. Another unforgettable true story is Michelle R. McCann's *Luba: The Angel of Bergen-Belsen*.

RELATED TITLES: Abels, Chana Byers. *The Children We Remember*. Greenwillow, 1986. / Adler, David A. *One Yellow Daffodil: A Hanukkah Story*. Harcourt, 1995. / Coerr, Eleanor. *Sadako*. Putnam, 1993. / Cohn, Janice. *The Christmas Menorahs: How a Town Fought Hate*. Whitman, 1995. / Gold, Alison Leslie. *Memories of Anne Frank: Reflections of a Childhood Friend*. Scholastic, 1997. / Hoestlandt, Jo. *Star of Fear, Star of Hope*. Walker, 1995. / Lowry, Lois. *Number the Stars*. Houghton, 1989. / Mazer, Norma Fox. *Good Night, Maman*. Harcourt, 1999. / McCann, Michelle R. *Luba: The Angel of Bergen-Belsen*. Tricycle, 2003. / Morimoto, Junko. *My Hiroshima*. Viking, 1990. / Poole, Josephine. *Anne Frank*. Knopf, 2005. / Propp, Vera. *When the Soldiers Were Gone*. Putnam, 1999. / Schnur, Steven. *The Tie Man's Miracle: A Chanukah Tale*. Morrow, 1995. / Schroeder, Peter W., and Dagmar Schroeder-Hildebrand. *Six Million Paper Clips: The Making of a Children's Holocaust Memorial*. Kar-Ben, 2004.

SUBJECTS: BIOGRAPHY. CONCENTRATION CAMPS. CZECH REPUBLIC. HOLOCAUST, JEWISH (1939–1945). JAPAN. JEWS. WORLD WAR, 1939–1945.

1521 Lindbergh, Reeve. *Nobody Owns the Sky: The Story of "Brave Bessie" Coleman.* **Illus. by Pamela Paperone. Candlewick, 1996. 1-56402-533-0. Unp. Gr. 2–4**

In a moving tribute, told in rhyme, to a female role model, meet the daredevil stunt flyer Bessie Coleman, who in 1921 became the world's first licensed African American aviator.

GERM: Compare and contrast all four terrific children's books about Bessie: Louise Borden and Mary Kay Kroeger's *Fly High!*, Nikki Grimes's *Talkin' About Bessie*, and Lynn Joseph's *Fly, Bessie, Fly.*

RELATED TITLES: Adler, David A. *A Picture Book of Amelia Earhart.* Holiday House, 1998. / Borden, Louise, and Mary Kay Kroeger. *Fly High! The Story of Bessie Coleman.* McElderry, 2001. / Brown, Don. *Ruth Law Thrills a Nation.* Ticknor & Fields, 1993. / Burleigh, Robert. *Flight: The Journey of Charles Lindbergh.* Philomel, 1991. / Grimes, Nikki. *Talkin' About Bessie: The Story of Aviator Elizabeth Coleman.* Orchard, 2002. / Joseph, Lynn. *Fly, Bessie, Fly.* Simon & Schuster, 1998. / Moss, Marissa. *Brave Harriet.* Harcourt, 2001. / Ride, Sally, and Susan Okie. *To Space and Back.* Lothrop, 1986. / Ryan, Pam Muñoz. *Amelia and Eleanor Go for a Ride.* Scholastic, 1999.

SUBJECTS: AFRICAN AMERICANS—BIOGRAPHY. AIR PILOTS. BIOGRAPHY. COLEMAN, BESSIE. FLIGHT. MULTICULTURAL BOOKS—POETRY. PICTURE BOOKS FOR ALL AGES. STORIES IN RHYME. WOMEN—BIOGRAPHY.

1522 Lomas Garza, Carmen. *In My Family/En Mi Familia.* **Illus. by the author. Children's Book Press, 1996. 0-89239-138-3. 32pp. Gr. 3–6**

In this companion to her *Family Pictures/Cuadros de Familia*, Mexican American artist Carmen Lomas Garza offers an engrossing series of paintings with descriptions in English and Spanish of her memories growing up in Kingsville, Texas, near the Mexican border. Beautifully detailed scenes of making empanadas, her mother's unusual earache treatment, and a Saturday night dance at a local restaurant give readers an entrée into her close-knit extended family.

GERM: Children can draw or paint scenes from their own family traditions and describe them in writing.

RELATED TITLES: Alarcón, Francisco X. *Angels Ride Bikes and Other Fall Poems.* Children's Book Press, 1999. / Bernier-Grand, Carmen T. *César: ¡Sí, Se Puede! Yes, We Can!* Marshall Cavendish, 2004. / Elya, Susan Middleton. *Home at Last.* Lee & Low, 2002. / Lomas Garza, Carmen. *Family Pictures/Cuadros de Familia.* Children's Book Press, 1990. / Manzano, Sonia. *No Dogs Allowed!* Atheneum, 2004. / Medina, Jane. *The Dream on Blanca's Wall: Poems in English and Spanish.* Wordsong/Boyds Mills, 2004. / Medina, Jane. *My Name Is Jorge: On Both Sides of the River.* Wordsong/Boyds Mills, 1999. / Nye, Naomi Shihab. *The Tree Is Older Than You Are: A Bilingual Gathering of Poems and Stories from Mexico.* / Pérez, Amada Irma. *My Very Own Room/Mi Proprio Cuartito.* Children's Book Press, 2000. / Ryan, Pam Muñoz. *Esperanza Rising.* Scholastic, 2000. / Soto, Gary. *Snapshots from the Wedding.* Putnam, 1997. / Soto, Gary. *Too Many Tamales.* Putnam, 1993.

SUBJECTS: AUTOBIOGRAPHY. BIOGRAPHY. FAMILY STORIES. HISPANIC AMERICANS. MULTICULTURAL BOOKS. PERSONAL NARRATIVES. SPANISH LANGUAGE.

1523 Lyon, George Ella. *Mother to Tigers.* **Illus. by Peter Catalanotto. Atheneum, 2003. 0-689-84221-X. Unp. Gr. K–3**

When Helen Martini's zookeeper husband brought home MacArthur, an ailing tiger cub, she did not expect it to be the first of 27 tigers she would raise, and the first tiger born at the Bronx Zoo to survive. As told in this spare, engrossing picture book illustrated in watercolor, charcoal, and torn paper, Martini started her animal nursery in 1944, and became the Bronx Zoo's first woman keeper, saving and nurturing baby gorillas, marmosets, and lemurs, as well as lots of tigers and other big cats.

GERM: Check your library, encyclopedia, and Internet to find out more about what zookeepers do. Go to <www.bronxzoo.com> to see the types of programs they run nowadays, including extensive information on their terrific new Tiger Mountain exhibit.

RELATED TITLES: Dowson, Nick. *Tigress.* Candlewick, 2004. / Johnston, Ginny, and Judy Cutchins. *Andy Bear: A Polar Cub Grows Up at the Zoo.* Morrow, 1985. / Nagda, Ann Whitehead, and Cindy Bickel. *Tiger Math: Learning to Graph from a Baby Tiger.* Henry Holt, 2000. / Patterson, Francine. *Koko's Story.* Scholastic, 1987. / Pfeffer, Wendy. *Popcorn Park Zoo: A Haven with a Heart.* Messner, 1992. / Thomson, Sarah L. *Tigers.* HarperCollins, 1994.

SUBJECTS: ANIMALS—INFANCY. BIOGRAPHY. TIGERS. WOMEN—BIOGRAPHY. ZOO KEEPERS.

1524 McCann, Michelle R. (As told to Michelle R. McCann by Luba Tryszynska-Frederick.) *Luba: The Angel of Bergen-Belsen.* **Illus. by Ann Marshall. Tricycle, 2003. 1-58246-098-1. Unp. Gr. 3–6**

On her first night at Bergen-Belsen concentration camp, Luba heard children crying outside her barracks and brought them inside, risking her life to shelter and care for the 54 orphaned Dutch children over the next four months until the camp was liberated by British soldiers in 1944. Based on the experiences of Luba Tryszynska-Frederick, the sober but uplifting picture-book account concludes with an epilogue of what happened to Luba and her children after the war.

GERM: Certainly one question you will want to pose to start your discussion is this: Why did Luba, whose own son was taken from her at Auschwitz two years before, risk her life to care for these children?

RELATED TITLES: Abels, Chana Byers. *The Children We Remember.* Greenwillow, 1986. / Adler, David A. *One Yellow Daffodil: A Hanukkah Story.* Harcourt, 1995. / Cohn, Janice. *The Christmas Menorahs: How a Town Fought Hate.* Whitman, 1995. / Gold, Alison Leslie. *Memories of Anne Frank: Reflections of a Childhood Friend.* Scholastic, 1997. / Hesse, Karen. *The Cats in Krasinski Square.* Scholastic, 2004. / Hoestlandt, Jo. *Star of Fear, Star of Hope.* Walker, 1995. / Levine, Karen. *Hana's Suitcase.* Albert Whitman, 2003. / Lowry, Lois. *Number the Stars.* Houghton, 1989. / Park, Linda Sue. *When My Name Was Keoko.* Clarion, 2002. / Polacco, Patricia. *The Butterfly.* Philomel, 2000. / Poole, Josephine. *Anne Frank.* Knopf, 2005. / Propp, Vera. *When the Soldiers Were Gone.* Putnam, 1999. / Rubin, Susan Goldman. *The Flag with Fifty-Six Stars: A Gift from the Survivors of Mauthausen.* Holiday House, 2005. / Schnur, Steven. *The Tie Man's Miracle: A Chanukah Tale.* Morrow, 1995.

SUBJECTS: BIOGRAPHY. CONCENTRATION CAMPS. HEROES. HOLOCAUST, JEWISH (1939–1945). JEWS. WOMEN—BIOGRAPHY. WORLD WAR, 1939–1945.

1525 Marrin, Albert. *Secrets from the Rocks: Dinosaur Hunting with Roy Chapman Andrews.* Illus. with photos. Dutton, 2002. 0-525-46743-2. 64pp. Gr. 4–8

"I was born to be an explorer," scientist, adventurer, and expedition leader Roy Chapman Andrews said about himself. Starting in 1922, he led five expeditions to the Gobi Desert in Mongolia, encountering sandstorms, bandits, pit vipers, and, finally, dinosaur fossils. He discovered the first known dinosaur eggs and several new dinosaur species, including oviraptor, iguanadon, and protoceratops. Marrin's engrossing biography includes many striking full-page black-and-white photos of Andrews and his crew.

GERM: Have your paleontology-minded students research and report on what has been discovered about each of the ten creatures—shown on the chart at the back of the book—since Andrews's group dug them up. To help place dinosaurs in perspective with the rest of the world's history, read aloud Steve Jenkins's clearly explained and exquisitely illustrated *Life on Earth: The Story of Evolution.*

RELATED TITLES: Brown, Don. *Rare Treasure: Mary Anning and Her Remarkable Discoveries.* Houghton Mifflin, 1999. / Floca, Brian. *Dinosaurs at the Ends of the Earth: The Story of the Central Asiatic Expeditions.* DK Ink, 2000. / Hurst, Carol Otis. *Rocks in His Head.* Greenwillow, 2001. / Jenkins, Steve. *Life on Earth: The Story of Evolution.* Houghton Mifflin, 2002. / Kerley, Barbara. *The Dinosaurs of Waterhouse Hawkins.* Scholastic, 2001. / Larson, Peter, and Kristin Donnan. *Bones Rock! Everything You Need to Know to Be a Paleontologist.* Invisible Cities, 2004. / Relf, Pat. *The Dinosaur Named Sue: The Story of the Colossal Fossil: The World's Most Complete T. Rex.* Scholastic, 2000. / Tanaka, Shelley. *Graveyards of the Dinosaurs.* Hyperion, 1998. / Tanaka, Shelley. *New Dinos.* Atheneum, 2003.

SUBJECTS: ANDREWS, ROY CHAPMAN. ANIMALS, EXTINCT. ANIMALS, PREHISTORIC. BIOGRAPHY. DINOSAURS. FOSSILS. MONGOLIA. NATURALISTS. PALEONTOLOGY. SCIENTISTS.

1526 Martin, Jacqueline Briggs. *Snowflake Bentley.* Illus. by Mary Azarian. Houghton Mifflin, 1998. 0-395-86162-4. 32pp. Gr. 1–4

In this outstanding Caldecott Medal biography, meet Vermont native Wilson Bentley, born in 1865, who spent 50 years of his life photographing snowflakes, discovered that no two snowflakes are alike, and was known as the world's expert on snow. Azarian's hand-tinted woodcuts are sensible and compelling; the book's design is perfect, with sidebars to be read along with the regular text, and a final photo of Bentley and his snowflakes.

GERM: Try the delicious and fact-filled Biography Hash lesson (page 92) in which my students and I actually created a trail mix to correspond to the ten ingredients in a good biography and then ate Snowflake Bentley. Compare Bentley's black-and-white snow photographs with the color photograph of snow in Walter Wick's *A Drop of Water.* The Bentley Snow Crystal Collection of the Buffalo Museum of Science at <www.informatics.buffalo.edu/faculty/abbas/bms/index.htm> is a wonderful online resource.

RELATED TITLES: Branley, Franklyn M. *Snow Is Falling.* HarperCollins, 2000. / Carlson, Laurie. *Boss of the Plains: The Hat That Won the West.* DK Ink, 1998. / Kinsey-Warnock. *From Dawn till Dusk.* Houghton Mifflin, 2002. / Lasky, Kathryn. *The Librarian Who Measured the Earth.* Little, Brown, 1994. / Prelutsky, Jack. *It's Snow-*

ing! It's Snowing! Greenwillow, 1984. / Schnur, Steven. *Winter: An Alphabet Acrostic.* Clarion, 2002. / Wetterer, Margaret. *Clyde Tombaugh and the Search for Planet X.* Carolrhoda, 1996. / Wick, Walter. *A Drop of Water: A Book of Science and Wonder.* Scholastic, 1997. / Wright, Betty Ren. *The Blizzard.* Holiday House, 2003.

SUBJECTS: BENTLEY, WILSON. BIOGRAPHY. CALDECOTT MEDAL. FARM LIFE. NATURE. PHOTOGRAPHY. SCIENTISTS. SNOW.

1527 Millman, Isaac. *Hidden Child.* Illus. by the author. Farrar, 2005. 0-374-33071-9. 74pp. Gr. 4–8

Children's book author/illustrator Isaac Millman was a happy little boy growing up with his parents in Paris until the German army invaded France in 1940, when he was 7. As the restrictions on Jews in Paris worsened, Isaac's father was sent to an internment camp, and Isaac and his mother attempted to escape to the free French zone, only to be captured by a German soldier and jailed. After his mother bribed a guard, Isaac was taken to a hospital and then to the home of his mother's friend, who wouldn't take him in. Sitting, crying, on the sidewalk, he met Héna, a Polish Jew like him, who arranged to have him looked after by a series of caretakers until the war ended. Millman's astonishing, harrowing, and heartbreaking memoir is illustrated with his own black-and-white photos and double-page illustrations—detailed, heartfelt color montages based on his photos and memories.

GERM: This will be an important book for your Holocaust curriculum, as it provides a firsthand account of what happened to ordinary people, including children, during the war. Of Millman's whole family, only he, an uncle, and one cousin survived. Millman came to the United States in 1948, when he was 15, was adopted by a family, went to college, married, and had two children. Students will be intrigued to compare his own story with the picture books he has written and illustrated, including *Moses Goes to a Concert.* Another book, about writers H. A. and Margaret Ray, *The Journey That Saved Curious George* by Louise Borden, details their fortunate escape from Paris to America during the same time period.

RELATED TITLES: Abels, Chana Byers. *The Children We Remember.* Greenwillow, 1986. / Borden, Louise. *The Journey That Saved Curious George: The True Wartime Escape of Margaret and H. A. Rey.* Houghton Mifflin, 2005. / Gold, Alison Leslie. *Memories of Anne Frank: Reflections of a Childhood Friend.* Scholastic, 1997. / Hoestlandt, Jo. *Star of Fear, Star of Hope.* Walker, 1995. / Isaacman, Clara. *Clara's Story.* Jewish Publication Society, 1984. / Levine, Karen. *Hana's Suitcase.* Albert Whitman, 2003. / Lowry, Lois. *Number the Stars.* Houghton, 1989. / Maguire, Gregory. *The Good Liar.* Clarion, 1999. / Mazer, Norma Fox. *Good Night, Maman.* Harcourt, 1999. / Millman, Isaac. *Moses Goes to a Concert.* Farrar, 1998. / Polacco, Patricia. *The Butterfly.* Philomel, 2000. / Poole, Josephine. *Anne Frank.* Knopf, 2005. / Propp, Vera. *When the Soldiers Were Gone.* Putnam, 1999. / Reiss, Johanna. *The Upstairs Room.* HarperCollins, 1987. / Rubin, Susan Goldman. *The Flag with Fifty-Six Stars: A Gift from the Survivors of Mauthausen.* Holiday House, 2005.

SUBJECTS: AUTHORS—BIOGRAPHY. AUTOBIOGRAPHY. BIOGRAPHY. FRANCE. HOLOCAUST, JEWISH (1939–1945). JEWS. WORLD WAR, 1939–1945.

1528 Mochizuki, Ken. *Passage to Freedom: The Sugihara Story.* Illus. by Dom Lee. Lee & Low, 1997. 1-880000-49-0. 32pp. Gr. 3–6

In 1940, when Hiroki Sugihara was a boy, his father, a Japanese diplomat working in a small town in Lithuania, disobeyed his own government and issued thousands of visas to Jews who were desperate to escape the Nazis. This somber and intense picture book, with haunting sepia-toned illustrations, recounts Hiroki's story of how his father handwrote 300 visas every day for a month, working from early morning until late at night, watering down the ink to make it last. An Afterword by Hiroki states that although his father saved thousands of lives, he and his family were imprisoned for 18 months in a Soviet internment camp, and he was asked to resign from the diplomatic service. In 1985 Sugihara became the first and only Asian honored by Israel for his acts of courage.

GERM: Ask your students to discuss and write their explanations of the Jewish and Japanese proverbs quoted in the book: "If you save the life of one person, it is as if you saved the world entire" and "Even a hunter cannot kill a bird that comes to him for refuge."

RELATED TITLES: Abels, Chana Byers. *The Children We Remember.* Greenwillow, 1986. / Coerr, Eleanor. *Sadako.* Putnam, 1993. / Hoestlandt, Jo. *Star of Fear, Star of Hope.* Walker, 1995. / Lee, Milly. *Nim and the War Effort.* Farrar, 1997. / Levine, Karen. *Hana's Suitcase.* Albert Whitman, 2003. / Mochizuki, Ken. *Baseball Saved Us.* Lee & Low, 1993. / Mochizuki, Ken. *Heroes.* Lee & Low, 1995. / Morimoto, Junko. *My Hiroshima.* Viking, 1990. / Polacco, Patricia. *The Butterfly.* Philomel, 2000. / Propp, Vera. *When the Soldiers Were Gone.* Putnam, 1999. / Schnur, Steven. *The Tie Man's Miracle: A Chanukah Tale.* Morrow, 1995. / Stevenson, James. *Don't You Know There's a War On?* Greenwillow, 1992.

SUBJECTS: BIOGRAPHY. HEROES. HOLOCAUST, JEWISH (1939–1945). JAPANESE. JEWS. MULTICULTURAL BOOKS. WAR. WORLD WAR, 1939–1945.

1529 **Montgomery, Sy.** *The Tarantula Scientist.* **Photos by Nic Bishop. Houghton Mifflin, 2004. 0-618-14799-3. 80pp. Gr. 4–8**

Meet arachnologist Sam Marshall as he explores the floor of the rainforest of French Guiana, studying the habits and habitat of the Goliath birdeater tarantula. This addition to the exemplary Scientists in the Field series highlights an enthusiastic and articulate expert in his field and abounds with life-sized color photographs that show the majesty of the world's largest spiders.

GERM: For some spectacular color photos of many types of tarantulas, go to the American Tarantula Society Web site at <atshq.org/gallery>.

RELATED TITLES: Berger, Melvin. *Spinning Spiders.* HarperCollins, 2003. / Climo, Shirley. *Someone Saw a Spider: Spider Facts and Folktales.* Crowell, 1985. / Kramer, Stephen. *Hidden Worlds: Looking Through a Scientist's Microscope.* Houghton, 2001. / Markle, Sandra. *Spiders: Biggest! Littlest!* Boyds Mills, 2004. / Max, Jill. *Spider Spins a Story: Fourteen Legends from Native America.* Rising Moon, 1997. / Montgomery, Sy. *The Snake Scientist.* Houghton Mifflin, 1999. / Murawski, Darlyne A. *Spiders and Their Webs.* National Geographic, 2004. / Tyson, Leigh Ann. *An Interview with Harry the Tarantula.* National Geographic, 2003. / White, E. B. *Charlotte's Web.* HarperCollins, 1952.

SUBJECTS: BIOGRAPHY. SCIENTISTS. SPIDERS. TARANTULAS.

1530 **Moses, Will.** *Johnny Appleseed: The Story of a Legend.* **Illus. by the author. Philomel, 2001. 0-399-23153-6. Unp. Gr. 2–5**

A folksy account of the real life of John Chapman (1774–1845)—more commonly remembered as tall-tale frontiersman Johnny Appleseed—this lengthy picture-book biography sports nostalgic primitive folk art paintings by Will Moses, the grandson of Grandma Moses.

GERM: Investigate some of the ways described for enjoying apples: ". . . you could make dried apples, apple butter, applesauce, apple pie, apple cider, apple brandy, applejack, apple vinegar and best of all, apples just tasted so good!" See how Rosemary and Stephen Vincent Benét distilled Chapman's life into verse in the picture-book version of their short, classic, narrative poem *Johnny Appleseed.* Tie in the tall-tale versions by Andrew Glass and Steven Kellogg, and another simpler picture-book biography, *The True Tale of Johnny Appleseed* by Margaret Hodges.

RELATED TITLES: Benét, Rosemary, and Stephen Vincent Benét. *Johnny Appleseed.* McElderry, 2001. / Cohn, Amy L. *From Sea to Shining Sea: A Treasury of American Folklore and Folk Songs.* Scholastic, 1993. / Glass, Andrew. *Folks Call Me Appleseed John.* Doubleday, 1995. / Hodges, Margaret. *The True Tale of Johnny Appleseed.* Holiday House, 1997. / Hopkinson, Deborah. *Apples to Oregon.* Atheneum, 2004. / Kellogg, Steven. *Johnny Appleseed.* Morrow, 1988. / Moses, Will. *The Legend of Sleepy Hollow.* Philomel, 1995. / Oppenheim, Joanne. *Have You Seen Trees?* Scholastic, 1995. / Osborne, Mary Pope. *American Tall Tales.* Knopf, 1991. / Osborne, Mary Pope. *New York's Bravest.* Knopf, 2002. / Powell, Consie. *Amazing Apples.* Albert Whitman, 2003. / San Souci, Robert D. *Larger than Life: The Adventures of American Legendary Heroes.* Doubleday, 1991. / Walker, Paul Robert. *Big Men, Big Country: A Collection of American Tall Tales.* Harcourt, 1993.

SUBJECTS: APPLE TREES. APPLESEED, JOHNNY. BIOGRAPHY. CHAPMAN, JOHN. FRONTIER AND PIONEER LIFE. FRUIT. TREES.

1531 **Moss, Marissa.** *Brave Harriet.* **Illus. by C. F. Payne. Harcourt, 2001. 0-15-202380-1. Unp. Gr. 2–6**

Harriet Quimby, who was the first woman to receive a pilot's license, narrates this fact-based but fictionalized picture book of another "first" for her sex: a solo flight across the English Channel in 1920 in a wooden open-air aeroplane.

GERM: Compare Harriet's feat with those of other flyers such as Bessie Coleman, Amelia Earhart, Ruth Law, and Charles Lindbergh.

RELATED TITLES: Adler, David A. *A Picture Book of Amelia Earhart.* Holiday House, 1998. / Borden, Louise, and Mary Kay Kroeger. *Fly High! The Story of Bessie Coleman.* McElderry, 2001. / Brown, Don. *Ruth Law Thrills a Nation.* Ticknor & Fields, 1993. / Burleigh, Robert. *Flight: The Journey of Charles Lindbergh.* Philomel, 1991. / Joseph, Lynn. *Fly, Bessie, Fly.* Simon & Schuster, 1998. / Lindbergh, Reeve. *Nobody Owns the Sky: The Story of "Brave Bessie" Coleman.* Candlewick, 1996. / Moss, Marissa. *Mighty Jackie, the Strike-Out Queen.* Simon & Schuster, 2004. / Ride, Sally, and Susan Okie. *To Space and Back.* Lothrop, 1986. / Ryan, Pam Muñoz. *Amelia and Eleanor Go for a Ride.* Scholastic, 1999.

SUBJECTS: AIR PILOTS. BIOGRAPHY. FLIGHT. HISTORICAL FICTION. QUIMBY, HARRIET, 1875–1912. TRANSPORTATION. WOMEN—BIOGRAPHY.

1532 Moss, Marissa. *Mighty Jackie, the Strike-Out Queen.* **Illus. by C. F. Payne. Simon & Schuster, 2004. 0-689-86329-2. Unp. Gr. 2–5**

On April 2, 1931, in Tennessee, in a game between the Chattanooga Lookouts and the legendary New York Yankees, 17-year-old Jackie Mitchell struck out both Babe Ruth and Lou Gehrig. Baseball was, and still is, considered a man's game, but, as this inspiring picture book makes clear, girls can play, too, as Jackie so skillfully demonstrated.

GERM: The Author's Note explains how, after the game, Jackie's contract with the team was voided, on the grounds that baseball was "too strenuous" for a woman. Discuss and debate: What other unfair rules and laws in this country have changed in the last century? Should women be allowed to play baseball? To vote? To own property? Why or why not? Students can write opinion pieces to back up their arguments. Meet other women who played the sport in Shana Corey's *Players in Pigtails*, about the All-American Girls Professional Baseball League that formed in 1943 during World War II, and Deborah Hopkinson's *Girl Wonder: A Baseball Story in Nine Innings*, about Alta Weiss, who in 1907 pitched for a semi-pro all-male baseball team in Ohio. Jean L. S. Patrick's *The Girl Who Struck Out Babe Ruth* is another account of Jackie Mitchell's amazing game.

RELATED TITLES: Adler, David A. *America's Champion Swimmer: Gertrude Ederle*. Harcourt, 2000. / Adler, David A. *Lou Gehrig: The Luckiest Man*. Harcourt, 1997. / Adler, David A. *A Picture Book of Amelia Earhart*. Holiday House, 1998. / Corey, Shana. *Players in Pigtails*. Scholastic, 2003. / Corey, Shana. *You Forgot Your Skirt, Amelia Bloomer!* Scholastic, 2000. / Hall, Donald. *When Willard Met Babe Ruth*. Harcourt, 1996. / Hopkinson, Deborah. *Girl Wonder: A Baseball Story in Nine Innings*. Atheneum, 2003. / Krull, Kathleen. *Lives of Extraordinary Women: Rulers, Rebels (and What the Neighbors Thought)*. Harcourt, 2000. / Morrison, Lillian, comp. *At the Crack of the Bat: Baseball Poems*. Hyperion, 1992. / Moss, Marissa. *Brave Harriet*. Harcourt, 2001. / Norworth, Jack. *Take Me Out to the Ballgame*. Four Winds, 1993. / Patrick, Jean L. S. *The Girl Who Struck Out Babe Ruth*. Carolrhoda, 2000. / Waber, Bernard. *Gina*. Houghton Mifflin, 1995.

SUBJECTS: ATHLETES—BIOGRAPHY. BASEBALL—BIOGRAPHY. BIOGRAPHY. GEHRIG, LOU. MITCHELL, JACKIE. RUTH, BABE. SEX ROLE. SPORTS. WOMEN—BIOGRAPHY.

1533 Old, Wendie. *To Fly: The Story of the Wright Brothers.* **Illus. by Robert Andrew Parker. Clarion, 2002. 0-618-13347-X. 48pp. Gr. 3–8**

When Orville Wright was in second grade, his teacher caught him playing with pieces of wood instead of doing his work. Even then, he was thinking about flying, trying to make a large model helicopter using wood and a rubber band. Old's stellar science-based biography of the two brothers—who never graduated from high school and who ran a print shop and then a bicycle store before getting back to their first love, flight—is a thrilling adventure and lesson in determination. The large format, with quirky full-page watercolors, allows the reader to fly vicariously with the brothers' glider experiments in 1899 and their first successful self-propelled flying machine on December 17, 1903.

GERM: Visit the Wright Brothers Aeroplane Company and Museum of Pioneer Aviation, a virtual museum with lots of photographs and fascinating information at <www.wrightbrothers.org>. Also delve into the photo-filled *First to Fly: How Wilbur and Orville Wright Invented the Airplane* by Peter Busby.

RELATED TITLES: Busby, Peter. *First to Fly: How Wilbur and Orville Wright Invented the Airplane*. Random House, 2003. / Collins, Mary. *Airborne: A Photobiography of Wilbur and Orville Wright*. National Geographic, 2003. / Delano, Marie Ferguson. *Inventing the Future: A Photobiography of Thomas Alva Edison*. National Geographic, 2002. / Freedman, Russell. *The Wright Brothers: How They Invented the Airplane*. Holiday House, 1991. / Hunter, Ryan Ann. *Into the Air: An Illustrated Timeline of Flight*. National Geographic, 2003. / St. George, Judith. *So You Want to Be an Inventor?* Philomel, 2002. / Szabo, Corinne. *Sky Pioneer: A Photobiography of Amelia Earhart*. National Geographic, 1997. / Weitzman, David. *Model T: How Henry Ford Built a Legend*. Crown, 2002.

SUBJECTS: AERONAUTICS. AIR PILOTS. AIRPLANES. BIOGRAPHY. FLIGHT. INVENTIONS AND INVENTORS. SCIENCE. WRIGHT BROTHERS.

1534 Parks, Rosa, and Jim Haskins. *I Am Rosa Parks.* **Illus. by Wil Clay. Dial, 1997. 0-8037-1207-3. 48pp. Gr. 1–3**

It's not often that famous people write autobiographies for very young audiences. In her inspirational, easy-to-read text, African American civil rights icon Rosa Parks describes how her arrest in Montgomery, Alabama, in 1955 led to the bus boycott that sparked the civil rights movement.

GERM: Parks's inspirational message and her hope that today's children of all colors will grow up without hate and learn to respect each other are important for all children to discuss.

RELATED TITLES: Adler, David A. *Dr. Martin Luther King, Jr.* Holiday House, 2001. / Adler, David A. *A Picture Book of Rosa Parks.* Holiday House, 1993. / Bray, Rosemary L. *Martin Luther King.* Greenwillow, 1995. / Coles, Robert. *The Story of Ruby Bridges.* Scholastic, 1995. / Curtis, Gavin. *The Bat Boy and His Violin.* Simon & Schuster, 1998. / Golenbock, Peter. *Teammates.* Harcourt, 1990. / Greenfield, Eloise. *Rosa Parks.* HarperCollins, 1995. / Livingston, Myra Cohn. *Let Freedom Ring: A Ballad of Martin Luther King, Jr.* Holiday House, 1992. / Marzollo, Jean. *Happy Birthday, Martin Luther King.* Scholastic, 1993. / Mitchell, Margaree King. *Uncle Jed's Barber Shop.* Simon & Schuster, 1993. / Rappaport, Doreen. *Martin's Big Words.* Hyperion, 2001. / Woodson, Jacqueline. *The Other Side.* Putnam, 2001.

SUBJECTS: AFRICAN AMERICANS—BIOGRAPHY. AUTOBIOGRAPHY. BIOGRAPHY. CIVIL RIGHTS. MULTICULTURAL BOOKS. PARKS, ROSA. PREJUDICE. RACE RELATIONS.

1535 Pinkney, Andrea Davis. *Bill Pickett: Rodeo-Ridin' Cowboy.* **Illus. by Brian Pinkney. Harcourt, 1996. 0-15-200100-X. 32pp. Gr. 1–4**

A mind-boggling but true picture-book biography surveys the life of African American rodeo stuntman Bill Pickett. Born in Texas to ex-slaves after the Civil War, Pickett invented "bulldog-ging," the art of bringing down a rodeo bull by biting on its lower lip. Performing at rodeos throughout the West, Bill endured racism, but, known as the "Dusky Demon," still became a star attraction throughout the United States, Mexico, Canada, South America, and England. Pinkney's trademark scratchboard and oil paint illustrations are full of motion and verve, and the lengthy note at the end about black cowboys and the bibliography are welcome additions.

GERM: Children who have no knowledge of rodeos will want to do some research to find out more about them. Go to <www.billpickettrodeo.com> to find out all about the annual Bill Pick-ett Invitational Rodeo.

RELATED TITLES: Axelrod, Alan, comp. *Songs of the Wild West.* Simon & Schuster, 1991. / Barasch, Lynne. *Knockin' on Wood: Starring Peg Leg Bates.* Lee & Low, 2004. / Carlson, Laurie. *Boss of the Plains: The Hat That Won the West.* DK Ink, 1998. / Dadey, Debbie. *Shooting Star: Annie Oakley, the Legend.* Walker, 1997 / Freed-man, Russell. *Children of the Wild West.* Clarion, 1983. / Johnston, Tony. *The Cowboy and the Black-Eyed Pea.* Put-nam, 1992. / Krensky, Stephen. *Shooting for the Moon: The Amazing Life and Times of Annie Oakley.* Farrar, 2001. / Medearis, Angela Shelf. *The Zebra-Riding Cowboy: A Folk Song from the Old West.* Henry Holt, 1992. / Pinkney, Andrea Davis. *Duke Ellington: The Piano Prince and His Orchestra.* Hyperion, 1998. / Ryan, Pam Muñoz. *Riding Freedom.* Scholastic, 1998. / Say, Allen. *El Chino.* Houghton Mifflin, 1990.

SUBJECTS: AFRICAN AMERICANS—BIOGRAPHY. BIOGRAPHY. COWBOYS. MULTICULTURAL BOOKS. PICKETT, BILL. RODEOS. WEST (U.S.)—HISTORY.

1536 Pinkney, Andrea Davis. *Duke Ellington: The Piano Prince and His Orchestra.* **Illus. by Brian Pinkney. Hyperion, 1998. 0-7868-2150-7. 32pp. Gr. 2–6**

"You ever hear of the jazz-playing man, the man with the cats who could swing with his band?" So begins a jazzy picture-book biography of Duke Ellington, the King of the Keys, the Piano Prince, the Duke, born in 1888, who started out playing ragtime piano and soon devel-oped his own sound and his own orchestra. Pinkney's signature colorful scratchboard illustra-tions have sparkle and snap, while the language envelops the swing and the sizzle of the music Ellington played, culminating in his famous Carnegie Hall performance in New York City in 1943.

GERM: You'll want to visit your library or music store to obtain a tape or CD of Ellington's music so children can dance to "Take the 'A' Train" and others of his more than 1,000 musical compositions.

RELATED TITLES: Anderson, M. T. *Handel, Who Knew What He Liked.* Candlewick, 2001. / Anderson, M. T. *Strange Mr. Satie.* Viking, 2003. / Curtis, Christopher Paul. *Bud, Not Buddy.* Delacorte, 1999. / Freedman, Rus-sell. *The Voice That Challenged a Nation: Marian Anderson and the Struggle for Equal Rights.* Clarion, 2004. / Ger-stein, Mordicai. *What Charlie Heard: The Story of the Composer Charles Ives.* Farrar, 2002. / Gray, Libba Moore. *Little Lil and the Swing-Singing Sax.* Simon & Schuster, 1996. / Igus, Toyomi. *I See the Rhythm.* Children's Book Press, 1998. / Krull, Kathleen. *Lives of the Musicians: Good Times, Bad Times (And What the Neighbors Thought).* Harcourt, 1993. / Pinkney, Andrea D. *Bill Pickett: Rodeo-Ridin' Cowboy.* Harcourt, 1996. / Pinkney, Andrea Davis. *Ella Fitzgerald: The Tale of a Vocal Virtuosa.* Hyperion, 2002. / Raschka, Chris. *Charlie Parker Played Bebop.* Orchard, 1992. / Raschka, Chris. *Mysterious Thelonius.* Orchard, 1998.

SUBJECTS: AFRICAN AMERICANS—BIOGRAPHY. BIOGRAPHY. COMPOSERS. ELLINGTON, DUKE, 1899–1974. JAZZ. MULTICULTURAL BOOKS. MUSICIANS.

1537 **Pinkney, Andrea Davis.** *Ella Fitzgerald: The Tale of a Vocal Virtuosa.* **Illus. by Brian Pinkney. Hyperion, 2002. 0-7868-2483-X. Unp. Gr. 2–6**

Nattily dressed, hip alley cat narrator Scat Cat Monroe recalls the story of Ella Fitzgerald's rise to fame as a singer who wowed fans for more than a half-century. Ella's career was launched in 1934, when the then 17-year-old won a singing contest at the Apollo Theater in Harlem—she was too scared to dance and sang instead. This biography is set up like a record album (and, of course, you'll have to show kids what those look like!) with four tracks from her life. Scat Cat addresses the reader in a colloquial style that bops like jazz as it mimics the improvisation and playful language of scat singing. And the scratchboard Art Deco-inspired paintings soar.

GERM: To research the history of jazz or to find out more facts about Ella Fitzgerald, the following Web sites will prove helpful: PBS—Jazz (a thorough site accompanying Ken Burns's film *Jazz*): <www.pbs.org/jazz>; and PBS—Jazz Kids: <www.pbs.org/jazz/kids>. Buy or borrow a CD of her greatest hits mentioned in the text so your listeners can hear the voice behind the story. You'll also want to introduce the Pinkneys' Caldecott Honor-winning biography of another jazz legend, *Duke Ellington: The Piano Prince and His Orchestra.* Both would be great companion reads along with Newbery winner *Bud Not Buddy* by Christopher Paul Curtis.

RELATED TITLES: Barasch, Lynne. *Knockin' on Wood: Starring Peg Leg Bates.* Lee & Low, 2004. / Duggleby, John. *Story Painter: The Life of Jacob Lawrence.* Chronicle, 1998. / Freedman, Russell. *The Voice That Challenged a Nation: Marian Anderson and the Struggle for Equal Rights.* Clarion, 2004. / Igus, Toyomi. *I See the Rhythm.* Children's Book Press, 1998. / Krull, Kathleen. *Lives of the Musicians: Good Times, Bad Times (And What the Neighbors Thought).* Harcourt, 1993. / Pinkney, Andrea Davis. *Duke Ellington: The Piano Prince and His Orchestra.* Hyperion, 1998. / Raschka, Chris. *Charlie Parker Played Bebop.* Orchard, 1992. / Ryan, Pam Muñoz. *When Marian Sang.* Scholastic, 2002.

SUBJECTS: AFRICAN AMERICANS—BIOGRAPHY. BIOGRAPHY. FITZGERALD, ELLA. MULTICULTURAL BOOKS. MUSICIANS. SINGERS. WOMEN—BIOGRAPHY.

1538 **Rappaport, Doreen.** *Martin's Big Words.* **Illus. by Bryan Collier. Hyperion, 2001. 0-7868-2591-X. Unp. Gr. K–6**

A huge portrait of Martin Luther King, Jr. on the front cover, which otherwise sports no identifying title or author, and the stained glass endpapers prepare you for the reverence combined with warmth that this Caldecott Honor book projects. The simple-to-read but not simplistic biography employs direct quotes from King's writings and speeches and large, stately watercolor and cut-paper collage illustrations. It is a perfect vehicle for introducing King to young children, but it is also a stepping-off point for older kids who can research different aspects of King's life and times.

GERM: Use the many quotations, such as "Sooner or later, all the people of the world will have to discover a way to live together," as discussion starters. Ask children: How will you help to do that? Explore how the illustrator used windows and light to tell King's story in the pictures. Incorporate the book into your values and character ed curriculums, as it easily fits into the following categories and values: citizenship, dedication, determination, dignity, fairness, justice, leadership, and morality. To do some research on the Web, go to <www.thekingcenter.com>, which is the King Center in Georgia.

RELATED TITLES: Adler, David A. *Dr. Martin Luther King, Jr.* Holiday House, 2001. / Bray, Rosemary L. *Martin Luther King.* Greenwillow, 1995. / Farris, Christine King. *My Brother Martin.* Simon & Schuster, 2003. / King, Martin Luther. *I Have a Dream.* Scholastic, 1997. / Livingston, Myra Cohn. *Let Freedom Ring: A Ballad of Martin Luther King, Jr.* Holiday House, 1992. / Marzollo, Jean. *Happy Birthday, Martin Luther King.* Scholastic, 1993. / McKissack, Patricia C. *Goin' Someplace Special.* Atheneum, 2001. / Mitchell, Margaree King. *Granddaddy's Gift.* BridgeWater, 1997. / Mitchell, Margaree King. *Uncle Jed's Barber Shop.* Simon & Schuster, 1993. / Parks, Rosa, and Jim Haskins. *Rosa Parks: My Story.* Puffin, 1999. / Woodson, Jacqueline. *The Other Side.* Putnam, 2001.

SUBJECTS: AFRICAN AMERICANS—BIOGRAPHY. BIOGRAPHY. CIVIL RIGHTS. KING, MARTIN LUTHER, JR. MULTICULTURAL BOOKS. PREJUDICE. RACE RELATIONS.

1539 **Rector, Anne Elizabeth.** *Anne Elizabeth's Diary: A Young Artist's True Story.* **Additional text by Kathleen Krull. Illus. by the author. Little, Brown, 2004. 0-316-07204-4. 64pp. Gr. 3–6**

In 1912, at age 12, Anne Elizabeth Rector, an aspiring artist who lived in New York City, kept a diary that she filled with tiny, delicately colored pen-and-ink drawings of her day. This diary has been beautifully reproduced with added sidebars by Kathleen Krull about varied aspects of New York life a century ago, sepia-toned photographs of Anne Elizabeth and her family, and a follow-up description of how she spent the rest of her life.

GERM: Share Krull's final chapter, "Some Tips on Keeping a Diary," as inspiration for your students to start writing and illustrating one of their own. Have them write an essay on the differences between life a century ago and their lives now. How has life changed for children, especially girls, since 1912? What kind of person was Anne Elizabeth? How would her life be different if she grew up in New York City today? See what life was like at the turn of centuries past, from the year 1000 to now in Ellen Jackson's *Turn of the Century*.

RELATED TITLES: Audubon, John James. *Capturing Nature: The Writings and Art of John James Audubon*. Ed. by Peter Roop and Connie Roop. Walker, 1993. / Holm, Jennifer L. *Our Only May Amelia*. HarperCollins, 1999. / Jackson, Ellen. *Turn of the Century*. Charlesbridge, 1998. / Krull, Kathleen. *The Boy on Fairfield Street: How Ted Geisel Grew Up to Become Dr. Seuss*. Random House, 2004. / Roosevelt, Theodore. *My Tour of Europe: by Teddy Roosevelt, Age 10*. Millbrook, 2003. / Spear, Elsie Lee. *Growing Seasons*. Putnam, 2000. / Whiteley, Opal. *Only Opal: The Diary of a Young Girl*. Philomel, 1994.

SUBJECTS: ARTISTS—BIOGRAPHY. AUTOBIOGRAPHY. BIOGRAPHY. CHILDREN—BIOGRAPHY. DIARIES. DRAWING. NEW YORK CITY. PERSONAL NARRATIVES. WOMEN—BIOGRAPHY.

1540 **Reich, Susanna. *José! Born to Dance*. Illus. by Raúl Colón. Simon & Schuster, 2005. 0-689-86576-7. Unp. Gr. 1–3**
Born in Mexico in 1908, famed dancer and choreographer José Limón loved to watch the dancers at the theater where his father worked as a musician. When civil war broke out in Mexico, José's family moved north, settling in Tucson, Arizona, where children laughed at José's poor English. He loved drawing and playing the piano, and when he finished high school, he headed for New York to become an artist but immersed himself in learning to dance instead. Reich's stirring and poetic picture-book biography is laced with Spanish phrases and sounds; Colón's textured watercolor and colored-pencil illustrations glow with light. The words and pictures together reflect the passion and determination of an icon, or, as he was named by the Dance Heritage Coalition, one of "America's Irreplaceable Dance Treasures."

GERM: The Limón Dance Company has a brief video of José dancing at <www.limon.org>. Discussion point: What hurdles did José Limón overcome in his life? What kind of person do you think he was? Other picture book biographies of artists of the same era include *Duke Ellington: The Piano Prince and His Orchestra* by Andrea Davis Pinkney; *Ella Fitzgerald: The Tale of a Vocal Virtuosa*, also by Pinkney; and *When Marian Sang* by Pam Muñoz Ryan, about African American opera diva Marian Anderson.

RELATED TITLES: Bernier-Grand, Carmen T. *César: ¡Sí, Se Puede! Yes, We Can!* Marshall Cavendish, 2004. / Hopkinson, Deborah. *A Band of Angels: A Story Inspired by the Jubilee Singers*. Illus. by Raúl Colón. Atheneum, 1999. / Lomas Garza, Carmen. *Family Pictures/Cuadros de Familia*. Children's Book Press, 1990. / Medina, Jane. *The Dream on Blanca's Wall: Poems in English and Spanish*. Wordsong/Boyds Mills, 2004. / Mora, Pat. *Tomás and the Library Lady*. Illus. by Raúl Colón. Knopf, 1997. / Pinkney, Andrea Davis. *Duke Ellington: The Piano Prince and His Orchestra*. Hyperion, 1998. / Pinkney, Andrea Davis. *Ella Fitzgerald: The Tale of a Vocal Virtuosa*. Hyperion, 2002. / Ryan, Pam Muñoz. *When Marian Sang*. Scholastic, 2002.

SUBJECTS: BIOGRAPHY. CHOREOGRAPHERS. DANCERS. HISPANIC AMERICANS. LIMÓN, JOSÉ. MEXICAN AMERICANS. MULTICULTURAL BOOKS.

1541 **Rockwell, Anne. *They Called Her Molly Pitcher*. Illus. by Cynthia von Buhler. Knopf, 2002. 0-679-89187-0. Unp. Gr. 3–6**
On a scorching June day in 1777, at the Battle of Monmouth, New Jersey, Molly Hays earned her place in American history by bringing water in her pewter pitcher to the American soldiers fighting the British. When her husband was injured, Molly helped fire his cannon, for which General Washington rewarded her with the rank of sergeant. Dramatic oil paintings aptly convey the action, danger, and grit of this thrilling battle tale.

GERM: Students can research and write descriptive expository passages about other heroes of the Revolutionary War.

RELATED TITLES: Ammon, Richard. *Valley Forge*. Holiday House, 2004. / Avi. *The Fighting Ground*. HarperCollins, 1987. / Brady, Esther Wood. *Tolliver's Secret*. Random House, 1976. / Brown, Drollene P. *Sybil Rides for Independence*. Albert Whitman, 1985. / Cheripko, Jan. *Caesar Rodney's Ride*. Boyds Mills, 2004. / Fritz, Jean. *And Then What Happened, Paul Revere?* Putnam, 1973. / Gauch, Patricia Lee. *This Time, Tempe Wick?* Coward, 1974. / Giblin, James Cross. *George Washington: A Picture Book Biography*. Scholastic, 1992. / Lasky, Kathryn. *A Voice of Her Own: The Story of Phillis Wheatley, Slave Poet*. Candlewick, 2002. / McGovern, Ann. *The Secret Soldier: The Story of Deborah Sampson*. Scholastic, 1975. / Osborne, Mary Pope. *George Washington: Leader of a New Nation*. Dial, 1991. / Rappaport, Doreen. *Living Dangerously: American Women Who Risked Their Lives for Adventure*. HarperCollins, 1991. / Woodruff, Elvira. *George Washington's Socks*. Scholastic, 1991.

SUBJECTS: BIOGRAPHY. NEW JERSEY. PITCHER, MOLLY, 1754–1832. U.S.—HISTORY—REVOLUTION, 1775–1783. WAR. WOMEN—BIOGRAPHY.

1542 Rumford, James. *Sequoyah: The Man Who Gave His People Writing.* **Illus. by the author. Houghton Mifflin, 2004. 0-618-36947-3. Unp. Gr. 1–6**

Where did the name of the huge California redwood tree, the Giant Sequoia, come from? In a dignified picture-book biography, with the text in both English and Cherokee, we are introduced to the tree's namesake, Sequoyah, son of a Cherokee mother and white father, born in Tennessee in the 1760s, who invented a syllabary of 84 signs, one for each syllable of the Cherokee language.

GERM: After people burned down Sequoya's cabin to make him stop writing, which they feared was evil, the author notes, "Sometimes disaster happens for a reason. Sometimes it says, "Follow a different path."" What does this mean? What different path did Sequoyah follow? Why were his neighbors opposed to what he was doing? Why did they change their minds? Do some follow-up reading on Cherokee history, such as the Trail of Tears, alluded to but not discussed in the text, and on the Giant Sequoia. Reproduce a copy of the syllabary so readers can see and pronounce each syllable. Peter and Connie Roop's *Ahyoka and the Talking Leaves* is a fictionalized telling of the Sequoya story, about his daughter, also spelled Ayoka. *Books and Libraries* by Jack Knowlton gives an interesting history of writing, which will help in putting Sequoyah's important contribution in context.

RELATED TITLES: Bruchac, Joseph. *The First Strawberries: A Cherokee Story.* Dial, 1993. / Bruchac, Joseph, and Gayle Ross. *The Story of the Milky Way: A Cherokee Tale.* Dial, 1995. / Bushyhead, Robert H., and Kay Thorpe Bannon. *Yonder Mountain: A Cherokee Legend.* Cavendish, 2002. / Fisher, Leonard Everett. *Alphabet Art: Thirteen ABCs from Around the World.* Four Winds, 1978. / Hunter, Sara Hoaglund. *The Unbreakable Code.* Rising Moon, 1996. / Knowlton, Jack. *Books and Libraries.* HarperCollins, 1991. / Roop, Peter, and Connie Roop. *Ahyoka and the Talking Leaves.* Lothrop, 1992. / Roth, Susan L. *Kanahena: A Cherokee Story.* St. Martin's, 1988. / Rumford, James. *The Cloudmakers.* Houghton Mifflin, 1996. / Rumford, James. *Dog-of-the-Sea-Waves.* Houghton Mifflin, 2004. / Rumford, James. *Traveling Man: The Journey of Ibn Battuta.* Houghton Mifflin, 2001.

SUBJECTS: ALPHABET. BIOGRAPHY. CHEROKEE INDIANS. DETERMINATION. INDIANS OF NORTH AMERICA—BIOGRAPHY. MULTICULTURAL BOOKS. SEQUOYAH, 1770?–1843. WRITING.

1543 Rumford, James. *Traveling Man: The Journey of Ibn Battuta.* **Illus. by the author. Houghton Mifflin, 2001. 0-618-08366-9. Unp. Gr. 3–6**

In 1325, 21-year-old Ibn Battuta set out from his home in Morocco and traveled the world for almost 30 years by camel, by boat, and on foot—75,000 miles in all—as this remarkable picture book documents. Based on his own account, written in 1355, this intriguing volume uses his own words, plus quotes in Arabic calligraphy that are translated at the back of the book, to give us all a bit of wanderlust. Battuta was hit by a rebel's arrow in India, escaped the plague, and was almost eaten by a crocodile. Through North Africa, Turkey, Mongolia, Arabia, Iran, India, and on up to Beijing, this guy knew how to get around. A map of his travels and a glossary round out the voyage.

GERM: This is a book to pore over. Plot out each page on a map as you read it aloud, and have listeners look up info on the many cities he visited. Ibn Battuta said, "Traveling—it offers you a hundred roads to adventure, and gives your heart wings!" and "Traveling—it leaves you speechless, then turns you into a storyteller." Have your sightseers relate these quotes to their own travels.

RELATED TITLES: Armstrong, Jennifer. *Spirit of Endurance.* Crown, 2000. / Burleigh, Robert. *Earth from Above for Young Readers.* Abrams, 2002. / Columbus, Christopher. Ed. by Steve Lowe. *Log of Christopher Columbus.* Illus. by Robert Sabuda. Philomel, 1992. / Fritz, Jean. *Around the World in a Hundred Years: From Henry the Navigator to Magellan.* Putnam, 1994. / Goodman, Joan Elizabeth. *A Long and Uncertain Journey: The 27,000-Mile Voyage of Vasco da Gama.* Mikaya, 2001. / Jenkins, Steve. *Hottest Coldest Highest Deepest.* Houghton Mifflin, 1998. / Maestro, Betsy. *The Discovery of the Americas.* Lothrop, 1991. / Rumford, James. *The Cloudmakers.* Houghton Mifflin, 1996. / Rumford, James. *Dog-of-the-Sea-Waves.* Houghton Mifflin, 2004. / Rumford, James. *Sequoyah: The Man Who Gave His People Writing.* Houghton Mifflin, 2004. / Schanzer, Rosalyn. *How We Crossed the West: The Adventures of Lewis and Clark.* National Geographic, 1997.

SUBJECTS: ARABS. AUTOBIOGRAPHY. BIOGRAPHY. EXPLORERS. MULTICULTURAL BOOKS. VOYAGES AND TRAVELS.

1544 Ryan, Pam Muñoz. *When Marian Sang*. Illus. by Brian Selznick. Scholastic, 2002. 0-439-26967-9. Unp. Gr. 2–6

In a stately and moving picture-book biography, learn how African American opera sensation Marian Anderson battled segregation and became one of the leading voices of the 20th century. In 1939, when the Daughters of the American Revolution refused to allow her to give a concert at Constitution Hall in Washington, D.C., she sang outside instead, on the steps of the Lincoln Memorial on Easter Sunday for an enraptured audience of 75,000. Selznick's huge, soulful, brown-toned acrylics are the perfect companion to Ryan's stirring text, which integrates the words of the spirituals she loved to sing.

GERM: Ask the music teacher to teach your singers the spirituals quoted throughout the book, all of which you can find on the CD *Marian Anderson: Spirituals* (BMG Entertainment, 1999). The appended extensive notes, dates, and bibliography are most appreciated. Discuss how Marian dealt with segregation: "No matter what humiliations she endured, Marian sang her heart with dignity." The text states, "Her voice left audiences weeping or in hushed awe as they strained to hold on to the memory of every opulent note." Have each child bring in a CD of a favorite singer and discuss what makes a great voice. Get to know Marian's friend Eleanor Roosevelt better with Muñoz and Selznick's *Amelia and Eleanor Go for a Ride*. Share Jacqueline Woodson's allegorical picture book *The Other Side*, about a young girl who longs to meet the girl on the other side of the fence that stretches through town.

RELATED TITLES: Adler, David A. *A Picture Book of Eleanor Roosevelt*. Holiday House, 1991. / Barasch, Lynne. *Knockin' on Wood: Starring Peg Leg Bates*. Lee & Low, 2004. / Bridges, Ruby. *Through My Eyes*. Scholastic, 1999. / Christensen, Bonnie. *The Daring Nellie Bly: America's Star Reporter*. Knopf, 2003. / Cooney, Barbara. *Eleanor*. Viking, 1996. / Duggleby, John. *Story Painter: The Life of Jacob Lawrence*. Chronicle, 1998. / Freedman, Russell. *The Voice That Challenged a Nation: Marian Anderson and the Struggle for Equal Rights*. Clarion, 2004. / Harness, Cheryl. *Franklin and Eleanor*. Dutton, 2004. / Hopkinson, Deborah. *A Band of Angels: A Story Inspired by the Jubilee Singers*. Atheneum, 1999. / Igus, Toyomi. *I See the Rhythm*. Children's Book Press, 1998. / Kerley, Barbara. *Walt Whitman: Words for America*. Scholastic, 2004. / Krull, Kathleen. *Lives of the Musicians: Good Times, Bad Times (And What the Neighbors Thought)*. Harcourt, 1993. / Pinkney, Andrea Davis. *Ella Fitzgerald: The Tale of a Vocal Virtuosa*. Hyperion, 2002. / Ryan, Pam Muñoz. *Amelia and Eleanor Go for a Ride*. Scholastic, 1999. / Woodson, Jacqueline. *The Other Side*. Putnam, 2001.

SUBJECTS: AFRICAN AMERICANS—BIOGRAPHY. AFRICAN AMERICANS—HISTORY. ANDERSON, MARIAN, 1897–1993. BIOGRAPHY. CIVIL RIGHTS. MULTICULTURAL BOOKS. MUSICIANS. SINGERS. U.S.—HISTORY—20TH CENTURY. WOMEN—BIOGRAPHY.

1545 St. George, Judith. *So You Want to Be an Inventor?* Illus. by David Small. Philomel, 2002. 0-399-23593-0. 48pp. Gr. 3–8

The attributes and achievements of 40 intrepid, indefatigable inventors are described and illustrated with informative, whimsical watercolors. From this fact-filled nonfiction picture book, we learn that even children can be inventors (12-year-old Ben Franklin's first inventions were swim and kick paddles for the hands and feet). It helps to keep your eyes open, be a dreamer, be stubborn as a bulldog, and ignore it if people laugh at you. "Being an inventor means pushing the limits of what human beings can do." The ink, watercolor, and pastel chalk illustrations are as inspirational and enjoyably quirky as the anecdote-laden text.

GERM: What a splendid catalyst for your inventors and inventions unit. Researching in the library and on the Internet, students can flesh out the biographical sketches of the men and women introduced in the book. Pair it with St. George and Small's Caldecott-winning companion, *So You Want to Be President*.

RELATED TITLES: Benton, Jim. *The Fran That Time Forgot*. Simon & Schuster, 2005. / Busby, Peter. *First to Fly: How Wilbur and Orville Wright Invented the Airplane*. Random House, 2003. / Byrd, Robert. *Leonardo, Beautiful Dreamer*. Dutton, 2003. / Delano, Marie Ferguson. *Inventing the Future: A Photobiography of Thomas Alva Edison*. National Geographic, 2002. / Jones, Charlotte Foltz. *Accidents May Happen: Fifty Inventions Discovered by Mistake*. Delacorte, 1996. / Jones, Charlotte Foltz. *Mistakes That Worked*. Doubleday, 1991. / Murphy, Jim. *Weird and Wacky Inventions*. Random House, 1978. / Schanzer, Rosalyn. *How Ben Franklin Stole the Lightning*. HarperCollins, 2003. / St. George, Judith. *So You Want to Be an Explorer?* Philomel, 2005. / St. George, Judith. *So You Want to Be President?* Philomel, 2000. / Thimmesh, Catherine. *Girls Think of Everything: Stories of Ingenious Inventions by Women*. Houghton Mifflin, 2000. / Wulffson, Don. *The Kid Who Invented the Popsicle: And Other Surprising Stories About Inventions*. Dutton, 1997.

SUBJECTS: BIOGRAPHY. INVENTIONS AND INVENTORS. MACHINES. SCIENCE. SCIENTISTS.

1546 St. George, Judith. *So You Want to Be President?* Illus. by David Small. Philomel, 2000. 0-399-23407-1. 53pp. Gr. 3–6

"There are good things about being president and there are bad things about being president." Thus starts a riotously funny, anecdote-loaded picture-book tribute to the number one job, illustrated with grandly humorous but affectionate watercolor caricatures of our presidents in action. There's Nixon bowling, Taft bathing, and Andrew Jackson brawling. Throughout, we learn about what made the presidents tick, their sizes, ages, personalities, quirks, talents, interests, looks, and political accomplishments.

GERM: Certainly, your students will be fired up to learn more about the presidents who fascinate them, and, in election years, to analyze candidates, comparing their foibles and fancies. Students can create a Presidents Gallery: a bulletin board or wall dedicated to portraits and biographical sketches of each president, listing such facts as birth and death dates, home town, education, marriages, children, interests and talents, and, of course, political achievements. As future presidential material, your students can then draw up a list of their own qualifications for the office, formulate a platform of ideas and causes, and make their own presidential posters. Consider holding a mock debate and election, inspired by Dan Gutman's witty satire, *The Kid Who Ran for President*, where a sixth grader runs for the national office and wins, or by Doreen Cronin's hilarious picture book *Duck for President*.

RELATED TITLES: Burns, Diane, and Clint Burns. *Hail to the Chief! Jokes About the Presidents*. Lerner, 1989. / Cleveland, Will, and Mark Alvarez. *Yo, Millard Fillmore! (And All Those Other Presidents You Don't Know)*. Millbrook, 1997. / Cronin, Doreen. *Duck for President*. Simon & Schuster, 2004. / Gutman, Dan. *The Kid Who Ran for President*. Scholastic, 1996. / Harness, Cheryl. *Ghosts of the White House*. Simon & Schuster, 1998. / Jones, Rebecca C. *The President Has Been Shot: True Stories of the Attacks on Ten U.S. Presidents*. Dutton, 1996. / Karr, Kathleen. *It Happened in the White House*. Hyperion, 2000. / Krull, Kathleen. *Lives of the Presidents: Fame, Shame (and What the Neighbors Thought)*. Harcourt, 1998. / O'Connor, Jane. *If the Walls Could Talk: Family Life at the White House*. Simon & Schuster, 2004. / Provensen, Alice. *The Buck Stops Here: The Presidents of the United States*. Harcourt, 2000. / St. George, Judith. *So You Want to Be an Inventor?* Philomel, 2002. / Stier, Catherine. *If I Were President*. Albert Whitman, 1999. / Thimmesh, Catherine. *Madam President: The Extraordinary, True (and Evolving) Story of Women in Politics*. Houghton Mifflin, 2004. / Winters, Kay. *My Teacher for President*. Dutton, 2004.

SUBJECTS: BIOGRAPHY. CALDECOTT MEDAL. PRESIDENTS. U.S.—HISTORY.

1547 St. George, Judith. *You're on Your Way, Teddy Roosevelt!* Illus. by Matt Faulkner. Philomel, 2004. 0-399-23888-3. Unp. Gr. 2–5

A sickly child who suffered with asthma, stomachaches, headaches, and nightmares, young Teedie Roosevelt's passion was collecting animals for his bedroom museum in his family's New York City brownstone, which he missed terribly when his family traveled to Europe the year he was ten. After his father inspired him to build up his frail body, the future president joined the gym, went camping in the Adirondacks, got glasses, and took charge of his own health.

GERM: First in a series of picture-book biographies that highlight "turning points" in the youths of American presidents, the narrative allows readers to empathize and identify with Teedie (as his family called him) and compare their lives with his. Writing prompt: What obstacles have you overcome or are you facing in your life? How did or will you overcome them? *My Tour of Europe: By Teddy Roosevelt, Age 10* is a picture book based on the diary he kept during the year his family spent abroad. To introduce TR as a president, read aloud Chapter 12, "A Household of Children," from Betsy Harvey Kraft's biography, *Theodore Roosevelt: Champion of the American Spirit*, to show what life was like in the White House for his five children. For more about him, check the Theodore Roosevelt Association's Web site: <www.theodoreroosevelt.org>.

RELATED TITLES: Chandra, Deborah, and Madeline Comora. *George Washington's Teeth*. Farrar, 2003. / Harness, Cheryl. *Young Teddy Roosevelt*. National Geographic, 1998. / Hines, Gary. *A Christmas Tree in the White House*. Henry Holt, 1998. / Kraft, Betsy Harvey. *Theodore Roosevelt: Champion of the American Spirit*. Clarion, 2003. / Krull, Kathleen. *Lives of the Presidents: Fame, Shame (and What the Neighbors Thought)*. Harcourt, 1998. / Provensen, Alice. *The Buck Stops Here: The Presidents of the United States*. Harcourt, 2000. / Roosevelt, Theodore. *My Tour of Europe: By Teddy Roosevelt, Age 10*. Millbrook, 2003. / St. George, Judith. *So You Want to Be President?* Philomel, 2000.

SUBJECTS: BIOGRAPHY. PRESIDENTS. ROOSEVELT, THEODORE.

1548 San Souci, Robert D. *Kate Shelley: Bound for Legend*. Illus. by Max Ginsburg. Dial, 1995. 0-8037-1290-1. 32pp. Gr. 3–6

When a storm hit Iowa on July 6, 1881, the waters of Honey Creek rose to record levels, causing a deadly train wreck. Fifteen-year-old Kate Shelley set out on foot for the Moingona Station to warn the stationmaster to stop the midnight train. With time running out, Kate climbed the 50 feet to the Des Moines River Bridge and, after the wind extinguished her lantern, crawled across the 700-foot open grid of railroad ties over the river raging below. If this true picture-book adventure with its dark, rain-slicked oil paintings doesn't get your listeners panting with excitement and anxiety, nothing will.

GERM: Ask them: What does it mean to be a hero? Since it turned out the midnight train wasn't in danger, why is Kate Shelley still remembered as a hero? Meet other child heroes in T. A. Barron's *A Hero's Trail: A Guide for a Heroic Life*.

RELATED TITLES: Barron, T. A. *A Hero's Trail: A Guide for a Heroic Life*. Philomel, 2002. / Calhoun, Mary. *Flood*. Morrow, 1997. / Kalman, Maira. *Fireboat: The Heroic Adventures of the John J. Harvey*. Putnam, 2002. / Rappaport, Doreen. *Living Dangerously: American Women Who Risked Their Lives for Adventure*. HarperCollins, 1991. / Williams, Gurney. *True Escape and Survival Stories*. Watts, 1977. / Winter, Jeanette. *The Librarian of Basra: A True Story from Iraq*. Harcourt, 2005.

SUBJECTS: ACCIDENTS. BIOGRAPHY. DISASTERS. FLOODS. HEROES. RESCUES. STORMS. SURVIVAL. TRAINS. WOMEN—BIOGRAPHY.

1549 Schanzer, Rosalyn. *How Ben Franklin Stole the Lightning*. **Illus. by the author. HarperCollins, 2003. 0-688-16994-5. 32pp. Gr. 1–6**

A jaunty white-haired Ben Franklin romps through the cheery watercolors that accompany a refreshingly peppy picture-book biography of Ben's scientific achievements, inventions, discoveries, and firsts. These included swim paddles and fins, invented at age 11; the first clock with a second hand; the saying "an apple a day keeps the doctor away;" and, of course, his marvelous kite experiment that proved that lightning was pure electricity. Franklin's most celebrated and lifesaving invention? The lightning rod.

GERM: For further anecdotes, send Franklin fans to Candace Fleming's compendium, *Ben Franklin's Almanac*. Read how, one century later, another memorable scientist's further experiments with electricity revolutionized society in Marie Ferguson Delano's splendid photo-filled *Inventing the Future: A Photobiography of Thomas Alva Edison*. Children can write essays about and discuss which of Franklin's and Edison's inventions affect our lives the most and why. Make a list with your group. What still needs to be invented?

RELATED TITLES: Adler, David A. *A Picture Book of Thomas Alva Edison*. Holiday House, 1996. / Borden, Louise. *Sea Clocks: The Story of Longitude*. McElderry, 2004. / Brown, Don. *Odd Boy Out: Young Albert Einstein*. Houghton Mifflin, 2004. / D'Aulaire, Ingri, and Edgar Parin D'Aulaire. *Benjamin Franklin*. Doubleday, 1987. / Delano, Marie Ferguson. *Inventing the Future: A Photobiography of Thomas Alva Edison*. National Geographic, 2002. / Fleming, Candace. *Ben Franklin's Almanac: Being a True Account of the Good Gentleman's Life*. Orchard, 1998. / Fleming, Candace. *The Hatmaker's Sign: A Story by Benjamin Franklin*. Orchard, 1998. / Fritz, Jean. *What's the Big Idea, Ben Franklin?* Coward, 1976. / Giblin, James Cross. *The Amazing Life of Benjamin Franklin*. Scholastic, 2000. / Lawson, Robert. *Ben and Me*. Little, Brown, 1939. / McDonough, Yona Zeldis. *The Life of Benjamin Franklin: An American Original*. Henry Holt, 2006. / St. George, Judith. *So You Want to Be an Inventor?* Philomel, 2002.

SUBJECTS: BIOGRAPHY. ELECTRICITY. FRANKLIN, BENJAMIN. INVENTIONS AND INVENTORS. KITES. LIGHTNING. SCIENCE. SCIENTISTS.

1550 Schyffert, Bea Uusma. *The Man Who Went to the Far Side of the Moon: The Story of Apollo 11 Astronaut Michael Collins*. **Illus. with photos. Chronicle, 2003. 0-8118-4007-7. 77pp. Gr. 3–8**

On July 16, 1969, Michael Collins, Neil Armstrong, and Buzz Aldrin set off for the moon. Armstrong and Aldrin became household names as the first to set foot on the moon. Collins stayed on board the spacecraft Columbia, orbiting the moon 14 times waiting for the two to finish their day on the lunar surface. Set up like a scrapbook, this overview of their voyage includes reproduced excerpts of Collins's notes written on board, plus photos, diagrams, and detailed charts. Read aloud, the text gives a fascinating overview of the men and their mission, with an interesting slant on the one who didn't get to walk on the moon.

GERM: Photocopy the biographical charts about each astronaut. Have students compare and contrast the information given on the men's backgrounds, interests, personal belongings brought on board, and subsequent lives. Ask children to make inferences about the personal and professional qualifications the three men brought to the mission. *The Moon* by Seymour Simon provides spectacular huge photographs and additional information about the first moon walk. Read Buzz Aldrin's firsthand account in his picture-book autobiography, *Reaching for the Moon*.

RELATED TITLES: Aldrin, Buzz. *Reaching for the Moon*. HarperCollins, 2005. / Burleigh, Robert. *Earth from*

Above for Young Readers. Abrams, 2002. / Lasky, Kathryn. *The Librarian Who Measured the Earth.* Little, Brown, 1994. / McNulty, Faith. *If You Decide to Go to the Moon.* Scholastic, 2005. / Simon, Seymour. *The Moon.* Simon & Schuster, 2003.

SUBJECTS: ASTRONAUTS. BIOGRAPHY. MOON. PROJECT APOLLO. SPACE FLIGHT TO THE MOON.

1551 **Slaymaker, Melissa Eskridge.** *Bottle Houses: The Creative World of Grandma Prisbrey.* **Illus. by Julie Paschkis. Henry Holt, 2004. 0-8050-7131-8. Unp. Gr. 2–5**

Looking for a place to settle down when she wasn't traveling, and room to display the thousands of pencils she'd collected, Grandma Prisbrey decided to build a house out of bottles she picked up at the dump. When you start to read this remarkable picture book, you'll think it's an interesting story about an eccentric old woman until you realize, with much amazement, that it's true. Starting in 1956, Grandma Prisbrey constructed a series of 13 one-room buildings and 22 sculptures on her California property, incorporating countless glass bottles, shells, rocks, and car headlights.

GERM: Glowing gouache paintings capture the vibrant constructions and the pragmatic woman who created them. At the back of the book are photos of the Bottle Village and one of Tressa "Grandma" Prisbrey, who said of herself, "They call me an artist even though I can't draw a car that looks like one. But I guess there are different kinds of art." Art teachers will surely want to incorporate this book into their teaching. Visit the Preserve Bottle Village Committee's Web site at <echomatic.home.mindspring.com/bv>. Introduce your young artists to another older artist in Alexandra Wallner's picture-book biography *Grandma Moses.*

RELATED TITLES: Brenner, Barbara. *The Boy Who Loved to Draw: Benjamin West.* Houghton Mifflin, 1999. / Cooney, Barbara. *Miss Rumphius.* Viking, 1982. / Duggleby, John. *Artist in Overalls: The Life of Grant Wood.* Chronicle, 1996. / Duggleby, John. *Story Painter: The Life of Jacob Lawrence.* Chronicle, 1998. / Greenberg, Jan, and Sandra Jordan. *Action Jackson.* Roaring Brook, 2002. / Greenberg, Jan, and Sandra Jordan. *Chuck Close Up Close.* Roaring Brook, 2002. / Krull, Kathleen. *Lives of the Artists: Masterpieces, Messes (and What the Neighbors Thought).* Harcourt, 1995. / LaMarche, Jim. *The Raft.* HarperCollins, 2000. / Reynolds, Peter H. *The Dot.* Candlewick, 2003. / Wallner, Alexandra. *Grandma Moses.* Holiday House, 2004. / Warhola, James. *Uncle Andy's.* Putnam, 2003.

SUBJECTS: ARTISTS—BIOGRAPHY. BIOGRAPHY. CALIFORNIA. PRISBREY, TRESSA. WOMEN—BIOGRAPHY.

1552 **Splear, Elsie Lee.** *Growing Seasons.* **Illus. by Ken Stark. Putnam, 2000. 0-399-33460-8. Unp. Gr. 3–6**

In an autobiographical look at one year on her family's Illinois farm in the early 1900s, Elsie Lee Splear describes all aspects of her childhood, including baths by the kitchen stove, planting seed potatoes, wash day, summer storms, milking, and Christmas. Each page of text is faced by a handsome, full-page painting of one aspect of life on the farm.

GERM: Compare Elsie Lee's childhood with your own now, a century later. At about the same time as Elsie was growing up in New York City, 12-year-old Anne Elizabeth Rector was writing her own journal about her life, which has been published as *Anne Elizabeth's Diary: A Young Artist's True Story.* Compare and contrast Elsie Lee's country upbringing with aspects of Anne Elizabeth's life in the big city. Back in Missouri in 1925, see how another farm family saved up for a real bathtub in Frances Kennedy's *The Pickle Patch Bathtub.*

RELATED TITLES: Bierman, Carol. *Journey to Ellis Island: How My Father Came to America.* Hyperion, 1998. / Jackson, Ellen. *Turn of the Century.* Charlesbridge, 1998. / Johnston, Tony. *Yonder.* Dial, 1988. / Kennedy, Frances. *The Pickle Patch Bathtub.* Tricycle, 2004. / Krull, Kathleen. *The Boy on Fairfield Street: How Ted Geisel Grew Up to Become Dr. Seuss.* Random House, 2004. / Lomas Garza, Carmen. *Family Pictures/Cuadros de Familia.* Children's Book Press, 1990. / Rector, Anne Elizabeth. *Anne Elizabeth's Diary: A Young Artist's True Story.* Little, Brown, 2004. / Roosevelt, Theodore. *My Tour of Europe: by Teddy Roosevelt, Age 10.* Millbrook, 2003. / Stewart, Sarah. *The Journey.* Farrar, 2001. / Whiteley, Opal. *Only Opal: The Diary of a Young Girl.* Philomel, 1994. / Widman, Christine. *Cornfield Hide-and-Seek.* Farrar, 2003.

SUBJECTS: AUTOBIOGRAPHY. BIOGRAPHY. FARM LIFE. ILLINOIS. U.S.—HISTORY—20TH CENTURY. WOMEN—BIOGRAPHY.

1553 **Stanley, Diane.** *Leonardo da Vinci.* **Illus. by the author. Morrow, 1996. 0-688-10437-1. 48pp. Gr. 4–7**

Children may know of Leonardo as an artist, but as this intriguing and comely picture-book biography makes clear, he was far more interested in his discoveries as an inventor, military engineer, and scientist. Born in 1452, Leonardo was an illegitimate child who received little formal schooling, yet the descriptions of his many talents and intellectual pursuits will leave you breathless.

GERM: The combination of Stanley's meticulously detailed paintings of Renaissance life and reproductions of da Vinci's paintings and sketches from his notebooks will make readers eager to draw and invent. Also grand, and grandly illustrated, are Robert Byrd's *Leonardo, Beautiful Dreamer* and Jean Fritz's *Leonardo's Horse*. Meet up with Leonardo again in the guise of an elderly bike shop owner who helps out two modern-day boys, Tyler and Freckle, in Elvira Woodruff's fantasy novel, *The Disappearing Bike Shop*.

RELATED TITLES: Byrd, Robert. *Leonardo, Beautiful Dreamer*. Dutton, 2003. / Fleming, Candace. *Ben Franklin's Almanac: Being a True Account of the Good Gentleman's Life*. Atheneum, 2003. / Fritz, Jean. *Leonardo's Horse*. Putnam, 2001. / Isaacson, Philip M. *A Short Walk Around the Pyramids and Through the World of Art*. Knopf, 1993. / Krull, Kathleen. *Lives of the Artists: Masterpieces, Messes (and What the Neighbors Thought)*. Harcourt, 1995. / Morrison, Taylor. *Antonio's Apprenticeship: Painting a Fresco in Renaissance Italy*. Holiday House, 1996. / Skira-Venturi, Rosabianca. *A Weekend with Leonardo da Vinci*. Rizzoli, 1993. / Stanley, Diane. *Michelangelo*. HarperCollins, 2000. / Woodruff, Elvira. *The Disappearing Bike Shop*. Holiday House, 1992.

SUBJECTS: ARTISTS—BIOGRAPHY. BIOGRAPHY. INVENTIONS AND INVENTORS. LEONARDO DA VINCI, 1452–1519. PAINTERS.

1554 **Stanley, Diane.** *Michelangelo*. **Illus. by the author. HarperCollins, 2000. 0-688-15085-3. Unp. Gr. 4–8**

In a lavish picture-book biography covering Michelangelo's many achievements—including the Pieta, David, and the Sistine Chapel—Stanley has incorporated his masterpieces of painting and sculpture into her own stately watercolors.

GERM: Contrast the lives and work of rivals da Vinci and Michelangelo, starting with Stanley's biographies about each. While students obviously will not be able to try their hands at marble sculpture, bring out clay and have them work on making realistic heads or torsos.

RELATED TITLES: Aliki. *William Shakespeare and the Globe*. HarperCollins, 1999. / Gardner, Jane Mylum. *Henry Moore: From Bones and Stones to Sketches and Sculptures*. Four Winds, 1993. / Greenberg, Jan, and Sandra Jordan. *Chuck Close Up Close*. Roaring Brook, 2002. / Krull, Kathleen. *Lives of the Artists: Masterpieces, Messes (and What the Neighbors Thought)*. Harcourt, 1995. / Skira-Venturi, Rosabianca. *A Weekend with Leonardo da Vinci*. Rizzoli, 1993. / Stanley, Diane. *Bard of Avon: The Story of William Shakespeare*. Morrow, 1992. / Stanley, Diane. *Charles Dickens: The Man Who Had Great Expectations*. Morrow, 1993. / Stanley, Diane. *Leonardo da Vinci*. Morrow, 1996.

SUBJECTS: ARTISTS—BIOGRAPHY. BIOGRAPHY. MICHELANGELO BUONARROTI, 1475–1564. PAINTERS. SCULPTORS.

1555 **Suen, Anastasia.** *Man on the Moon*. **Illus. by Benrei Huang. Viking, 1997. 0-670-87393-4. Unp. Gr. K–2**

This simplest of nonfiction picture books describes the 1969 moon flight and Neil Armstrong's historic walk on the moon.

GERM: People said it couldn't be done, that no one would ever walk on the moon. Discuss other events and inventions that have changed history such as the personal computer, the automobile, the telephone, and the electric light. For a first-hand account of the Apollo mission, read Buzz Aldrin's picture-book autobiography, *Reaching for the Moon*. See what it would be like to take a moon trip in Faith McNulty's travelogue *If You Decide to Go to the Moon*.

RELATED TITLES: Aldrin, Buzz. *Reaching for the Moon*. HarperCollins, 2005. / Brown, Don. *One Giant Leap: The Story of Neil Armstrong*. Houghton Mifflin, 1998. / Crews, Nina. *I'll Catch the Moon*. Greenwillow, 1996. / Gaffney, Timothy R. *Grandpa Takes Me to the Moon*. HarperCollins, 1996. / Haddon, Mark. *The Sea of Tranquility*. Harcourt, 1996. / Krupp, E. C. *The Moon and You*. Macmillan, 1993. / McNulty, Faith. *If You Decide to Go to the Moon*. Scholastic, 2005. / Schyffert, Bea Uusma. *The Man Who Went to the Far Side of the Moon: The Story of Apollo 11 Astronaut, Michael Collins*. Chronicle, 2003. / Simon, Seymour. *The Moon*. Simon & Schuster, 2003. / Standiford, Natalie. *Astronauts Are Sleeping*. Knopf, 1996. / Yaccarino, Dan. *Zoom! Zoom! Zoom! I'm Off to the Moon!* Scholastic, 1997.

SUBJECTS: ARMSTRONG, NEIL. ASTRONAUTS. BIOGRAPHY. MOON. PROJECT APOLLO. SPACE FLIGHT TO THE MOON.

1556 Szabo, Corinne. *Sky Pioneer: A Photobiography of Amelia Earhart*. Illus. with photos. National Geographic, 1997. 0-7922-3737-4. 63pp. Gr. 3–6

This handsome photobiography incorporates large black-and-white photographs on every page, which makes Szabo's fascinating depiction of the life of groundbreaking flyer Amelia Earhart all the more personal and affecting.

GERM: With your older students, compare and contrast the content, visuals, and scope of Szabo's biography with David Adler's simpler account, *A Picture Book of Amelia Earhart*. Get a feel for Earhart's personality and passion for flying in Pam Muñoz Ryan's picture book *Amelia and Eleanor Go for a Ride*, based on a true event about Earhart and her friend, Eleanor Roosevelt.

RELATED TITLES: Adler, David A. *A Picture Book of Amelia Earhart*. Holiday House, 1998. / Borden, Louise, and Mary Kay Kroeger. *Fly High! The Story of Bessie Coleman*. McElderry, 2001. / Brown, Don. *Ruth Law Thrills a Nation*. Ticknor & Fields, 1993. / Burleigh, Robert. *Flight: The Journey of Charles Lindbergh*. Philomel, 1991. / Collins, Mary. *Airborne: A Photobiography of Wilbur and Orville Wright*. National Geographic, 2003. / Grimes, Nikki. *Talkin' About Bessie: The Story of Aviator Elizabeth Coleman*. Orchard, 2002. / Lauber, Patricia. *Lost Star: The Story of Amelia Earhart*. Scholastic, 1988. / Moss, Marissa. *Brave Harriet*. Harcourt, 2001. / Ride, Sally, and Susan Okie. *To Space and Back*. Lothrop, 1986. / Ryan, Pam Muñoz. *Amelia and Eleanor Go for a Ride*. Scholastic, 1999.

SUBJECTS: AIR PILOTS. BIOGRAPHY. EARHART, AMELIA. FLIGHT. WOMEN—BIOGRAPHY.

1557 Thimmesh, Catherine. *Madam President: The Extraordinary, True (and Evolving) Story of Women in Politics*. Illus. by Douglas B. Jones. Houghton Mifflin, 2004. 0-618-39666-7. 80pp. Gr. 4–8

You'll find the contents of this book either heartening or heart-rending. Marching across the first three pages are a variety of children, stating what they want to be when they grow up. One feisty girl in bell-bottoms and braids declares, "When I grow up, I'm going to be the president of the United States." "You . . .?" scoffs a boy, pointing incredulously, "a . . . GIRL?" "Well," says another girl, "maybe you could marry a president . . ." Next are six biographical sketches, with full-page illustrations, of influential First Ladies from Abigail Adams to Hillary Rodham Clinton. There are also profiles of women's rights advocates, congresswomen, women appointed to posts by presidents, and women presidents from other countries. Checking the Constitution, our young feminist heroine discovers that there is no real reason a woman can't be president.

GERM: A timeline at the back includes each of the 23 women profiled. Although each generation has marked progress for women and minorities in government, no one has cracked the all-male, white, Christian bastion. Maybe, after reading books like this one and Thimmesh's others, your students will be inspired to change the world when they grow up. *So You Want to Be President?* by Judith St. George lays some of the ground rules. Introduce the first American woman to be elected to public office, in 1869, in Connie Nordhielm Wooldridge's *When Esther Morris Headed West*.

RELATED TITLES: Adler, David A. *A Picture Book of Eleanor Roosevelt*. Holiday House, 1991. / Blumberg, Rhoda. *Bloomers*. Atheneum, 1993. / Fritz, Jean. *You Want Women to Vote, Lizzie Stanton?* Putnam, 1995. / Krull, Kathleen. *Lives of Extraordinary Women: Rulers, Rebels (and What the Neighbors Thought)*. Harcourt, 2000. / McDonough, Yona Zeldis. *Sisters in Strength: American Women Who Made a Difference*. Henry Holt, 2000. / St. George, Judith. *So You Want to Be President?* Philomel, 2000. / Thimmesh, Catherine. *Girls Think of Everything: Stories of Ingenious Inventions by Women*. Houghton Mifflin, 2000. / Thimmesh, Catherine. *The Sky's the Limit: Stories of Discovery by Women and Girls*. Houghton Mifflin, 2002. / Winters, Kay. *My Teacher for President*. Dutton, 2004. / Wooldridge, Connie Nordhielm. *When Esther Morris Headed West: Women, Wyoming, and the Right to Vote*. Holiday House, 2001.

SUBJECTS: PRESIDENTS. U.S.—HISTORY. WHITE HOUSE. WOMEN—BIOGRAPHY.

1558 Wallner, Alexandra. *Grandma Moses*. Illus. by the author. Holiday House, 2004. 0-8234-1538-4. Unp. Gr. 2–5

Born on a farm in New York State in 1860, Anna Mary Robertson married farmer Thomas Moses in 1887, bore nine children, and didn't start painting until after her husband's death in 1927. Wallner's sensible and attractive picture-book biography integrates quotes by Anna Mary, who was "discovered" as a painter at age 80 and died in 1961 at 101.

GERM: Show reproductions of Grandma Moses' paintings. How do they reflect her early life? How are the scenes they depict the same or different from life now? Grandma Moses once said, ". . . life is what we make it, always has been, always will be." How did that philosophy apply to her own life? How does it apply to your life? Meet another American primitive artist who started later in life in Melissa Eskridge Slaymaker's *Bottle Houses: The Creative World of Grandma Prisbrey*.

RELATED TITLES: Brenner, Barbara. *The Boy Who Loved to Draw: Benjamin West*. Houghton Mifflin, 1999. / Duggleby, John. *Artist in Overalls: The Life of Grant Wood*. Chronicle, 1996. / Duggleby, John. *Story Painter: The Life of Jacob Lawrence*. Chronicle, 1998. / Greenberg, Jan, and Sandra Jordan. *Action Jackson*. Roaring Brook, 2002. / Greenberg, Jan, and Sandra Jordan. *Chuck Close Up Close*. Roaring Brook, 2002. / Krull, Kathleen. *Lives of the Artists: Masterpieces, Messes (and What the Neighbors Thought)*. Harcourt, 1995. / LaMarche, Jim. *The Raft*. Harper-Collins, 2000. / Reynolds, Peter H. *The Dot*. Candlewick, 2003. / Slaymaker, Melissa Eskridge. *Bottle Houses: The Creative World of Grandma Prisbrey*. Henry Holt, 2004. / Warhola, James. *Uncle Andy's*. Putnam, 2003.

SUBJECTS: ARTISTS—BIOGRAPHY. BIOGRAPHY. MOSES, GRANDMA. WOMEN—BIOGRAPHY.

1559 Warhola, James. *Uncle Andy's*. Illus. by the author. Putnam, 2003. 0-399-23869-7. Unp. Gr. 2–6

Author/artist James Warhola casts his eye and palette back to 1962, when he was a boy in the western Pennsylvania countryside and his family took a trip to New York City to pay a surprise visit to his uncle, Pop Art icon Andy Warhol. From this entertaining look inside the artist's home, we see how James became serious about his own art.

GERM: Elicit responses to the author's statement of what he learned from his uncle: ". . . art is something that is all around us all the time." Show a variety of Andy Warhol's art and various books illustrated by Warhola, such as *Bubba the Cowboy Prince* by Helen Ketteman. Compare and contrast their styles. This is a terrific example not only of descriptive narrative writing, but also of illustrating. Ask kids to write about and illustrate a time they were influenced by an interesting family member.

RELATED TITLES: Christelow, Eileen. *What Do Illustrators Do?* Clarion, 1999. / Cummings, Pat, ed. *Talking with Artists*, Volume Three. Clarion, 1999. / dePaola, Tomie. *The Art Lesson*. Putnam, 1989. / Garland, Michael. *Dinner at Magritte's*. Dutton, 1995. / Greenberg, Jan, and Sandra Jordan. *Action Jackson*. Roaring Brook, 2002. / Greenberg, Jan, and Sandra Jordan. *Chuck Close Up Close*. Roaring Brook, 2002. / Ketteman, Helen. *Bubba the Cowboy Prince*. Illus. by James Warhola. Scholastic, 1997. / Krull, Kathleen. *The Boy on Fairfield Street: How Ted Geisel Grew Up to Become Dr. Seuss*. Random House, 2004. / Krull, Kathleen. *Lives of the Artists: Masterpieces, Messes (and What the Neighbors Thought)*. Harcourt, 1995. / Raczka, Bob. *Art Is . . .* Millbrook, 2003. / Reynolds, Peter. *The Dot*. Candlewick, 2003. / Sayre, Henry M. *Cave Paintings to Picasso: The Inside Scoop on 50 Art Masterpieces*. Chronicle, 2003. / Schwartz, David M. *If You Hopped Like a Frog*. Illus. by James Warhola. Scholastic, 1999.

SUBJECTS: ARTISTS—BIOGRAPHY. AUTOBIOGRAPHY. BIOGRAPHY. FAMILY STORIES. ILLUSTRATORS. WARHOL, ANDY. WARHOLA, JAMES.

1560 Wells, Rosemary. *Streets of Gold*. Illus. by Dan Andreasen. Dial, 1999. 0-8037-2149-8. Unp. Gr. 2–5

Twelve-year-old Mary Antin arrived in Boston from Russia with her family in 1894. Using excerpts from Antin's own autobiographical book, *The Promised Land*, author Rosemary Wells retells Antin's heartfelt account of her early life in a shtetl or small village, where Jewish girls were not permitted to attend school, through her first year in America. In a Boston tenement, on a street paved "not with bricks of gold" but "piled high with garbage people threw out of windows," Masha changed her name to Mary, quickly learned English, and was promoted from first grade to fifth within six months. In an uplifting climax, the poem about George Washington that she wrote for a school assignment was printed in the *Boston Herald*, all 35 verses of it.

GERM: The beautifully told and illustrated picture book elucidates the immigrant experience, sensitizes children to the hardships all newcomers face, and affirms the life-changing advantages of a good education.

RELATED TITLES: Avi. *Silent Movie*. Atheneum, 2003. / Bartone, Elisa. *American Too*. Lothrop, 1996. / Bartone, Elisa. *Peppe the Lamplighter*. Lothrop, 1993. / Bierman, Carol. *Journey to Ellis Island: How My Father Came to America*. Hyperion, 1998. / Freedman, Russell. *Immigrant Kids*. Dutton, 1980. / Hest, Amy. *When Jessie Came Across the Sea*. Candlewick, 1997. / Levine, Ellen. *If Your Name Was Changed at Ellis Island*. Scholastic, 1993. / Maestro, Betsy. *Coming to America: The Story of Immigration*. Scholastic, 1996. / Sandler, Martin W. *Immigrants*. HarperCollins, 1995. / Woodruff, Elvira. *The Memory Coat*. Scholastic, 1999. / Woodruff, Elvira. *The Orphan of Ellis Island: A Time Travel Adventure*. Scholastic, 1997.

SUBJECTS: ANTIN, MARY, 1881–1949. BIOGRAPHY. BOSTON (MASS.). IMMIGRATION AND EMIGRATION. JEWS. MASSACHUSETTS—HISTORY. VOYAGES AND TRAVELS. WOMEN—BIOGRAPHY.

1561 **Wetterer, Margaret, and Charles Wetterer.** *The Snow Walker.* **Illus. by Mary O'Keefe Young. Carolrhoda, 1996. 0-87614-891-7. 48pp. Gr. 1–3**

In a true account, meet an enterprising good Samaritan, Milton Daub, who, as a 12-year-old boy, constructed his own snowshoes and then braved the New York blizzard of 1888 to deliver food and medicine to his snowbound neighbors in the Bronx.

GERM: Pair this with some info on snow from the Caldecott Medal biography *Snowflake Bentley,* by Jacqueline Briggs Martin. As a spur to writing descriptively and experientially, ask everyone to compose a detailed description of a memorable experience in snow or rain.

RELATED TITLES: Branley, Franklyn M. *Snow Is Falling.* HarperCollins, 2000. / Carrick, Carol. *Lost in the Storm.* Clarion, 1987. / Martin, Jacqueline Briggs. *Snowflake Bentley.* Houghton Mifflin, 1998. / Moskin, Marietta D. *The Day of the Blizzard.* Coward, 1978. / O'Malley, Kevin. *Straight to the Pole.* Walker, 2003. / Pfeffer, Wendy. *The Shortest Day: Celebrating the Winter Solstice.* Dutton, 2003. / Prelutsky, Jack. *It's Snowing! It's Snowing!* Greenwillow, 1984. / San Souci, Robert D. *Kate Shelley: Bound for Legend.* Dial, 1995. / Wright, Betty Ren. *The Blizzard.* Holiday House, 2003.

SUBJECTS: BIOGRAPHY. BLIZZARDS. NEW YORK CITY. SELFLESSNESS. SNOW. U.S.—HISTORY—1865–1898.

1562 **White, Linda Arms.** *I Could Do That: Esther Morris Gets Women the Vote.* **Illus. by Nancy Carpenter. Farrar, 2005. 0-374-33527-3. Unp. Gr. 2–6**

Born in 1814, independent-minded Esther McQuigg opened up her own hat shop in Owego, New York, at 19. In 1869, at age 55, she moved with her husband, John Morris, to the Wyoming Territory, a place where men outnumbered women six to one. That year, John opened a saloon and Esther started another hat shop, but she also began to lobby for a bill in the legislature to allow women the vote, which became law on December 10, 1869. In this high-spirited and inspirational picture-book biography, see how Morris helped jump-start the women's suffrage movement in 1870 when she became the first woman in the country to hold public office.

GERM: Read the Author's Note, which includes a fact that will startle your listeners: Esther Morris never got to vote for president because women were not granted the vote in the United States until 1920, 18 years after her death. Compare the writing style, illustrations, and information presented in another marvelous picture-book biography of her life, *When Esther Morris Headed West: Women, Wyoming, and the Right to Vote* by Connie Nordhielm Wooldridge. Kathleen Krull's *A Woman for President: The Story of Victoria Woodhull* is a picture-book biography of the suffragist who ran for president in 1872.

RELATED TITLES: Blumberg, Rhoda. *Bloomers.* Atheneum, 1993. / Christelow, Eileen. *VOTE!* Clarion, 2003. / Christensen, Bonnie. *The Daring Nellie Bly: America's Star Reporter.* Knopf, 2003. / Corey, Shana. *You Forgot Your Skirt, Amelia Bloomer!* Scholastic, 2000. / Fritz, Jean. *You Want Women to Vote, Lizzie Stanton?* Putnam, 1995. / Harness, Cheryl. *Remember the Ladies: 100 Great American Women.* HarperCollins, 2001. / Krull, Kathleen. *A Woman for President: The Story of Victoria Woodhull.* Walker, 2004. / Lasky, Kathryn. *She's Wearing a Dead Bird on Her Head!* Hyperion, 1995. / McCully, Emily Arnold. *The Ballot Box Battle.* Knopf, 1996. / Mitchell, Margaree King. *Granddaddy's Gift.* BridgeWater, 1997. / Ryan, Pam Muñoz. *Riding Freedom.* Scholastic, 1998. / Sisulu, Elinor Batezat. *The Day Gogo Went to Vote: South Africa, April 1994.* Little, Brown, 1996. / Thimmesh, Catherine. *Madam President: The Extraordinary, True (and Evolving) Story of Women in Politics.* Houghton Mifflin, 2004. / Wooldridge, Connie Nordhielm. *When Esther Morris Headed West: Women, Wyoming, and the Right to Vote.* Holiday House, 2001.

SUBJECTS: BIOGRAPHY. ELECTIONS. SUFFRAGISTS. U.S.—HISTORY. VOTING. WOMEN—BIOGRAPHY. WYOMING.

1563 **Winter, Jeanette.** *The Librarian of Basra: A True Story from Iraq.* **Illus. by the author. Harcourt, 2004. 0-15-205445-6. Unp. Gr. 2–6**

With the invasion of Basra, Iraq, imminent on April 6, 2003, the chief librarian of Basra's Central Library, Alia Muhammad Baker, rescued 70 percent of the library's priceless collection, hiding 30,000 books in her house and a neighboring restaurant. This moving and chilling picture book puts a human face on the war in Iraq through the inspiring story of one woman who was determined to save the books, even as the city was firebombed and the library burned to the ground.

GERM: Winter began work on the book after reading an article about Alia in the *New York Times* ("Books Spirited to Safety Before Iraq Library Fire," July, 27, 2003). If you can get a copy of the article, then use it to demonstrate how an author can turn an idea or an event into prose. Analyze how she created such a poignant and perceptive story, through which children can understand that war involves real people on both sides of the conflict. Discussion points: Why did Alia save the books? Why did they matter to her? What's so important about having a library? How can one person make a difference in the world? Read aloud *Miss Rumphius* by Barbara Cooney and ask listeners what they will do to make the world more beautiful.

RELATED TITLES: Borden, Louise. *The Little Ships: The Heroic Rescue at Dunkirk in World War II*. McElderry, 1997. / Bunting, Eve. *Gleam and Glow*. Harcourt, 2001. / Cooney, Barbara. *Miss Rumphius*. Viking, 1982. / Cutler, Jane. *The Cello of Mr. O*. Dutton, 1999. / Garland, Sherry. *The Lotus Seed*. Harcourt, 1993. / Gerstein, Mordicai. *The Man Who Walked Between the Towers*. Roaring Brook, 2003. / Heide, Florence Parry, and Judith Heide Gilliland. *Sami and the Time of the Troubles*. Clarion, 1992. / Kalman, Maira. *Fireboat: The Heroic Adventures of the John J. Harvey*. Putnam, 2002. / Lee, Milly. *Nim and the War Effort*. Farrar, 1997. / Mochizuki, Ken. *Passage to Freedom: The Sugihara Story*. Lee & Low, 1997.

SUBJECTS: BIOGRAPHY. HEROES. IRAQ. IRAQ WAR. LIBRARIANS. LIBRARIES. WAR. WOMEN—BIOGRAPHY.

1564 **Wood, Ted.** *Iditarod Dream: Dusty and His Sled Dogs Compete in Alaska's Jr. Iditarod*. **Photos by the author. Walker, 1996. 0-8027-8407-0. 48pp. Gr. 4–6**

In a color photoessay, meet 15-year-old Dusty Whittemore from Cantwell, Alaska, a gifted musher who trained his sled dogs for, ran, and won the 158-mile Jr. Iditarod, for ages 14 to 17, in 1994.

GERM: Make a list: What are the qualities a person would need to win a race like this? Debbie S. Miller's *The Great Serum Race: Blazing the Iditarod Trail* recounts the story behind the original race to save the town of Nome, Alaska, from a diphtheria epidemic in 1925. For more about the Jr. Iditarod, including photos and bios of each year's racers, check out the race's Web site at <www.jriditarod.com>.

RELATED TITLES: Blake, Robert. *Akiak: A Tale from the Iditarod*. Philomel, 1997. / Blake, Robert. *Togo*. Philomel, 2002. / Miller, Debbie S. *The Great Serum Race: Blazing the Iditarod Trail*. Walker, 2002. / Paulsen, Gary. *Dogteam*. Delacorte, 1993. / Paulsen, Gary. *Woodsong*. Simon & Schuster, 1990. / Seibert, Patricia. *Mush! Across Alaska in the World's Longest Sled-Dog Race*. Millbrook, 1992.

SUBJECTS: ALASKA. BIOGRAPHY. DOGS. IDITAROD (RACE). SLED DOG RACING.

1565 **Wooldridge, Connie Nordhielm.** *When Esther Morris Headed West: Women, Wyoming, and the Right to Vote*. **Illus. by Jacqueline Rogers. Holiday House, 2001. 0-8234-1597-X. Unp. Gr. 2–6**

In 1869, 55-year-old Esther Morris, a determined woman with the revolutionary idea that women should be able to vote and hold office, became not just a judge in the Wyoming Territory, but the first woman in the United States to hold public office. In this nonfiction picture book with large, good-humored watercolors you will discover an inspiring and important true story.

GERM: For more information and even a photograph of Esther Morris, go to <www.wow museum.org/gallery/suffrage/justice_full.html>. To see a statue of her at the Capitol Building in Washington, D.C., visit <www.aoc.gov/cc/art/nsh/morris.htm>. Searching "Esther Morris" and "Wyoming" together at <www.google.com> yields more than 200 Web sites. Discussion point: Wyoming's nickname is "The Equality State." What does that mean? Why is it essential for every citizen to vote? Another picture-book biography about her life is *I Could Do That: Esther Morris Gets Women the Vote* by Linda Arms White. Also read Emily Arnold McCully's *The Ballot Box Battle* to see how Elizabeth Cady Stanton attempted to cast her vote in 1880, in Tenafly, New Jersey.

RELATED TITLES: Blumberg, Rhoda. *Bloomers*. Atheneum, 1993. / Christelow, Eileen. *VOTE!* Clarion, 2003. / Christensen, Bonnie. *The Daring Nellie Bly: America's Star Reporter*. Knopf, 2003. / Corey, Shana. *You Forgot Your Skirt, Amelia Bloomer!* Scholastic, 2000. / Fritz, Jean. *You Want Women to Vote, Lizzie Stanton?* Putnam, 1995. / Harness, Cheryl. *Remember the Ladies: 100 Great American Women*. HarperCollins, 2001. / Krull, Kathleen. *A Woman for President: The Story of Victoria Woodhull*. Walker, 2004. / Lasky, Kathryn. *She's Wearing a Dead Bird on Her Head!* Hyperion, 1995. / McCully, Emily Arnold. *The Ballot Box Battle*. Knopf, 1996. / Mitchell, Margaree King. *Granddaddy's Gift*. BridgeWater, 1997. / Ryan, Pam Muñoz. *Riding Freedom*. Scholastic, 1998. / Sisulu, Elinor Batezat. *The Day Gogo Went to Vote: South Africa, April 1994*. Little, Brown, 1996. / Thimmesh, Catherine. *Madam President: The Extraordinary, True (and Evolving) Story of Women in Politics*. Houghton Mifflin, 2004. / White, Linda Arms. *I Could Do That: Esther Morris Gets Women the Vote*. Farrar, 2005.

SUBJECTS: BIOGRAPHY. ELECTIONS. SUFFRAGISTS. U.S.—HISTORY. VOTING. WOMEN—BIOGRAPHY. WYOMING.

1566   Yolen, Jane. *The Perfect Wizard: Hans Christian Andersen.* **Illus. by Dennis Nolan. Dutton, 2004. 0-525-46955-9. Unp. Gr. 1–5**
Yolen's exquisitely told picture-book biography of the renowned Danish fairy tale author does not stint on the sorrows, anguish, and sheer strangeness of his life, no "beautiful fairy tale . . . rich and happy," as he wrote in his autobiography. Born in Odense, Denmark, in 1805, to a poor shoemaker and a washerwoman, Hans was a homely, superstitious, imaginative child who loved to hear, read, tell, and, finally, write stories. He considered himself a *digter*, Danish for "poet" or "author," and was sure he was destined to be an actor and a great man, telling his mother, "First you go through terrible suffering and then you become famous." Of the courtly, pensive, exquisite pastel paintings in muted colors, the full-sized ones mirror actual events from Anderson's life and the small oval-shaped ones each depict an accompanying and relevant quote from one of his stories.
GERM: Discuss and analyze the beautifully chosen quotes, many from Andersen's lesser-known stories, to determine each one's connection to his life. Kick off your April 2 celebrations for International Children's Book Day, Hans Christian Andersen's birthday, with a pairing of his life story and one of his fairy tales. In the Related Titles list below, I've included only a few of the many outstanding versions of Andersen's tales, both picture books and collections. For a more thorough look, see "Andersen, Hans Christian" in the author index.
RELATED TITLES: Andersen, Hans Christian. *The Emperor's New Clothes.* Illus. by Angela Barrett. Candlewick, 1997. / Andersen, Hans Christian. *Fairy Tales of Hans Christian Andersen.* Illus. by Isabelle Brent. Viking, 1995. / Andersen, Hans Christian. *The Little Mermaid and Other Fairy Tales.* Illus. by Isabelle Brent. Viking, 1995. / Andersen, Hans Christian. *The Nightingale.* Retold by Stephen Mitchell. Illus. by Bagram Ibatoulline. Candlewick, 2002. / Andersen, Hans Christian. *The Nightingale.* Illus. by Jerry Pinkney. Putnam, 2002. / Andersen, Hans Christian. *The Princess and the Pea.* Illus. by Paul Galdone. Seabury, 1978. / Andersen, Hans Christian. *Tales of Hans Christian Andersen.* Trans. by Naomi Lewis. Candlewick, 2004. / Andersen, Hans Christian. *The Ugly Duckling.* Illus. by Jerry Pinkney. Morrow, 1999. / Brust, Beth Wagner. *The Amazing Paper Cuttings of Hans Christian Andersen.* Ticknor & Fields, 1994. / Hesse, Karen. *The Young Hans Christian Andersen.* Scholastic, 2005.
SUBJECTS: ANDERSEN, HANS CHRISTIAN. AUTHORS. BIOGRAPHY.

1567   Younger, Barbara. *Purple Mountain Majesties: The Story of Katharine Lee Bates and "America the Beautiful."* **Illus. by Stacey Schuett. Dutton, 1998. 0-525-45653-8. 32pp. Gr. 2–6**
In 1893, when Wellesley College English professor Katharine Lee Bates was invited to lecture in Colorado Springs, she traveled cross-country, seeing Niagara Falls and the World's Fair in Chicago en route. After an expedition by wagon to the top of Pike's Peak, she composed the poem that became the song "America the Beautiful."
GERM: This attractively illustrated picture-book travelogue and biography will get everyone tracing Lee's cross-country route. Sing the song, with the help of two picture-book versions of it, as illustrated by Chris Gall and Neil Waldman.
RELATED TITLES: Bates, Katharine Lee. *America the Beautiful.* Illus. by Chris Gall. Little, Brown, 2004. / Bates, Katharine Lee. *America the Beautiful.* Illus. by Neil Waldman. Atheneum, 1983. / Borden, Louise. *America Is . . .* McElderry, 2002. / Cheney, Lynne. *America: A Patriotic Primer.* Simon & Schuster, 2002. / Christensen, Bonnie. *Woody Guthrie: Poet of the People.* Knopf, 2001. / DiPucchio, Kelly. *Liberty's Journey.* Hyperion, 2004. / Guthrie, Woody. *This Land Is Your Land.* Little, Brown, 1998. / Keenan, Sheila. *O, Say Can You See? America's Symbols, Landmarks, and Inspiring Words.* Scholastic, 2004. / Keller, Laurie. *The Scrambled States of America.* Henry Holt, 1998. / Rylant, Cynthia. *Tulip Sees America.* Scholastic, 1998. / Williams, Vera B. *Stringbean's Trip to the Shining Sea.* Scholastic, 2003.
SUBJECTS: AUTHORS—BIOGRAPHY. BATES, KATHARINE LEE, 1859–1929. BIOGRAPHY. NATURAL MONUMENTS. POETS. SONGS. U.S.—POETRY. WOMEN—BIOGRAPHY.

NONFICTION

1568 Aliki. *Ah, Music!* **Illus. by the author. HarperCollins, 2003. 0-06-028719-5. 48pp. Gr. 2–5**
Using delicate, sometimes boxed, watercolors and pen-and-ink illustrations, as well as an insightful, child-centered text, Aliki explores all aspects of music as experienced by a joyous crew of multiracial children who look at sound, rhythm, composition, style, vocal music, orchestras, and music throughout history.
GERM: Ask your music lovers to define what music means to them. Older students can explore further by researching a favorite composer, musician, or musical form.
RELATED TITLES: Anderson, M. T. *Handel, Who Knew What He Liked.* Candlewick, 2001. / Auch, Mary Jane. *Bantam of the Opera.* Holiday House, 1997. / Cox, Judy. *My Family Plays Music.* Holiday House, 2003. / Curtis, Gavin. *The Bat Boy and His Violin.* Simon & Schuster, 1998. / Goss, Linda. *The Frog Who Wanted to Be a Singer.* Orchard, 1996. / Krull, Kathleen. *Lives of the Musicians: Good Times, Bad Times (And What the Neighbors Thought).* Harcourt, 1993. / Krull, Kathleen. *M Is for Music.* Harcourt, 2003. / Millman, Isaac. *Moses Goes to a Concert.* Farrar, 1998. / Moss, Lloyd. *Music Is.* Putnam, 2003. / Ober, Hal. *How Music Came to the World.* Houghton Mifflin, 1994. / Ryan, Pam Muñoz. *When Marian Sang.* Scholastic, 2002. / Weaver, Tess. *Opera Cat.* Clarion, 2002.
SUBJECTS: MULTICULTURAL BOOKS. MUSIC.

1569 Aliki. *Hello! Good-bye!* **Illus. by the author. Greenwillow, 1996. 0-688-14334-2. Unp. Gr. K–2**
In delicate bordered illustrations—each a child-filled scene rendered in colored pencil, watercolor, and black pen—Aliki explores aspects of what the words "hello" and "good-bye" can mean and how and when we use them.
GERM: Look at other ways we communicate with Aliki's companion books, *Communication* and *Feelings.* For salutations in 42 other languages, see Manya Stojic's *Hello World.*
RELATED TITLES: Aliki. *Communication.* Greenwillow, 1993. / Aliki. *Feelings.* Greenwillow, 1984. / Ets, Marie Hall. *Talking Without Words.* Viking, 1968. / Leventhal, Debra. *What Is Your Language?* Dutton, 1994. / Park, Linda Sue. *Yum! Yuck! A Foldout Book of People Sounds.* Charlesbridge, 2005. / Raschka, Chris. *Yo! Yes?* Orchard, 1993. / Stojic, Manya. *Hello World! Greetings in 42 Languages Across the Globe.* Scholastic, 2002.
SUBJECTS: COMMUNICATION. ENGLISH LANGUAGE. MULTICULTURAL BOOKS. SALUTATIONS.

1570 Arnold, Katya. *Elephants Can Paint Too!* **Photos by the author. Atheneum, 2005. 0-689-86985-1. Unp. Gr. K–4**
Children's book artist and writer Katya Arnold teaches art to young children at a school in Brooklyn, New York, and to young elephants in Asia. On some of the left-hand pages of this remarkable photoessay are full-page color photographs of her human students as they paint in art class. On the right, and in many double-page spreads, are photographs of the elephants she has taught to manipulate paintbrushes and paint actual pictures. Children interested in art and animals will be astonished at the photos and the brief text that explains how the elephants learn and enjoy the activity.
GERM: Find out more about Asian elephants in Thailand and how they perform for tourists in another eye-opening photoessay, *An Elephant in the Backyard* by Richard Sobol.

RELATED TITLES: Bateman, Robert, and Rick Archbold. *Safari*. Little, Brown, 1998. / Ford, Miela. *Little Elephant*. Greenwillow, 1994. / Ho, Minfong. *Peek! A Thai Hide-and-Seek*. Candlewick, 2004. / Jenkins, Martin. *Never Ride Your Elephant to School*. Candlewick, 2003. / Leslie-Melville, Betty. *Elephant Have the Right of Way: Life with the Wild Animals of Africa*. Doubleday, 1993. / Schwartz, Amy. *Begin at the Beginning: A Little Artist Learns About Life*. HarperCollins, 2005. / Sobol, Richard. *An Elephant in the Backyard*. Dutton, 2004. / Yoshida, Toshi. *Elephant Crossing*. Philomel, 1989.

SUBJECTS: ARTISTS. ELEPHANTS. MULTICULTURAL BOOKS. PAINTING. THAILAND.

1571 Ashman, Linda. *Babies on the Go.* **Illus. by Jane Dyer. Harcourt, 2003. 0-15-201894-8. Unp. Gr. PreK–1**

In soft, gentle, but detailed watercolors and a simple rhyming text, we find out how all kinds of babies, both human and animal, are transported from one place to another.

GERM: For each animal, ask children to name both the animal and its family (insect, fish, bird, reptile, amphibian, mammal). While there are several less common animals included, such as sloth and snow monkey, there is a picture chart with each of the 20 animals labeled.

RELATED TITLES: Bauer, Marion Dane. *If You Were Born a Kitten*. Simon & Schuster, 1997. / Browne, Philippa-Alys. *Kangaroos Have Joeys*. Atheneum, 1996. / Collard, Sneed B., III. *Animal Dads*. Houghton Mifflin, 1997. / Jenkins, Steve. *Big and Little*. Houghton Mifflin, 1996. / Jenkins, Steve. *Biggest, Strongest, Fastest*. Ticknor & Fields, 1995. / Lyon, George Ella. *Mother to Tigers*. Atheneum, 2003. / Meyers, Susan. *Everywhere Babies*. Harcourt, 2001. / Ryan, Pam Muñoz. *A Pinky Is a Baby Mouse and Other Baby Animal Names*. Dial, 1998. / Swinburne, Stephen R. *Safe, Warm, and Snug*. Harcourt, 1999. / Waddell, Martin. *Owl Babies*. Candlewick, 1992.

SUBJECTS: ANIMAL LOCOMOTION. ANIMALS—INFANCY. BABIES.

1572 Bang, Molly. *My Light.* **Illus. by the author. Blue Sky/Scholastic, 2004. 0-439-48961-X. Unp. Gr. 1–5**

The sun, Earth's golden star, narrates this exciting scientific look at the many types of energy generated by the sun's light, including water, wind, coal, and solar cells, all of which can be turned into electric power.

GERM: Teaching personification? Here's one that will tie in to science and language arts. For more information on the author and her research for this visually stunning nonfiction picture book, go to <www.mollybang.com>. Follow up with sun and light experiments. Make scientists out of your students with a book that will work at a wide range of grade levels.

RELATED TITLES: Delano, Marie Ferguson. *Inventing the Future: A Photobiography of Thomas Alva Edison*. National Geographic, 2002. / DuPrau, Jeanne. *The City of Ember*. Random House, 2003. / Graham, Joan Bransfield. *Flicker Flash*. Houghton Mifflin, 1999. / Simon, Seymour. *The Sun*. Morrow, 1996.

SUBJECTS: ELECTRICITY. ENERGY. LIGHT. SCIENCE. SUN.

1573 Barron, T. A. *The Hero's Trail: A Guide for a Heroic Life.* **Illus. with photos. Philomel, 2002. 0-399-23860-3. 131pp. Gr. 4–8**

Children's book author Barron has compiled a series of inspirational anecdotes about five types of heroic people: the hero on the spot, the survivor hero, the hero within, the hero to others, and the hero for all time. He defines a hero as "someone who, faced with a tough challenge, reaches down inside and finds the courage, strength, and wisdom to triumph." Acting as a guiding narrator, he takes us on an exhilarating, symbolic hike, introducing us to memorable people who exhibited courage, perseverance, and wisdom, including Ruby Bridges, the first black child to desegregate the all-white public schools of New Orleans in 1960; scientist Stephen Hawking; and baseball legend Lou Gehrig.

GERM: What does it take to be a hero? Students can make a class list of character traits and then write an essay describing a hero they admire, from a special family member to someone they've read about. Compare and contrast being a hero with being a celebrity, which the author defines as "someone who has won our attention" instead of accomplishing something really important. Students can also do more research on some of the lives described, using the bibliography as a starting point.

RELATED TITLES: Bridges, Ruby. *Through My Eyes*. Scholastic, 1999. / Kalman, Maira. *Fireboat: The Heroic Adventures of the John J. Harvey*. Putnam, 2002. / McCann, Michelle R. *Luba: The Angel of Bergen-Belsen*. Tricycle, 2003. / Mochizuki, Ken. *Passage to Freedom: The Sugihara Story*. Lee & Low, 1997. / Rappaport, Doreen. *Living Dangerously: American Women Who Risked Their Lives for Adventure*. HarperCollins, 1991. / San Souci, Robert D. *Kate Shelley: Bound for Legend*. Dial, 1995. / Williams, Gurney. *True Escape and Survival Stories*. Watts, 1977. / Winter, Jeanette. *The Librarian of Basra: A True Story from Iraq*. Harcourt, 2005.

SUBJECTS: CONDUCT OF LIFE. HEROES.

1574 **Bash, Barbara.** *In the Heart of the Village: The World of the Indian Banyan Tree.* **Illus. by the author. Sierra Club, 1996. 0-87156-575-7. 32pp. Gr. 2–5**

This lyrical and visually elegant nonfiction picture book examines the life that thrives in and around a sacred banyan tree in a small village in India, from the villagers who set up a market underneath its roomy, cool canopy to the nesting egrets, spotted owls, langur monkeys, and flying foxes that live there.

GERM: The ornate and glowing watercolors and hand-lettered calligraphy are welcome features of Bash's fascinating Tree Tales series, which includes *Tree of Life: The World of the African Baobab* and *Desert Giant: The World of the Saguaro Cactus.*

RELATED TITLES: Atkins, Jeannine. *Aani and the Tree Huggers.* Lee & Low, 1995. / Bash, Barbara. *Desert Giant: The World of the Saguaro Cactus.* Sierra Club, 1989. / Bash, Barbara. *Tree of Life: The World of the African Baobab.* Sierra Club/Little, Brown, 1989. / Behn, Harry. *Trees.* Henry Holt, 1992. / Brenner, Barbara. *The Earth Is Painted Green: A Garden of Poems About Our Planet.* Scholastic, 1994. / Bunting, Eve. *Someday a Tree.* Clarion, 1993. / Cherry, Lynne. *The Great Kapok Tree: A Tale of the Amazon Rain Forest.* Harcourt, 1990. / Cherry, Lynne. *The Sea, the Storm, and the Mangrove Tangle.* Farrar, 2004. / Cowcher, Helen. *Whistling Thorn.* Scholastic, 1993. / Gackenbach, Dick. *Mighty Tree.* Harcourt, 1992. / George, Kristine O'Connell. *Old Elm Speaks: Tree Poems.* Clarion, 1998. / Guiberson, Brenda. *Cactus Hotel.* Henry Holt, 1991. / Hiscock, Bruce. *The Big Tree.* Atheneum, 1991. / Oppenheim, Joanne. *Have You Seen Trees?* Scholastic, 1995.

SUBJECTS: ANIMALS. BANYAN TREES. INDIA. MULTICULTURAL BOOKS. TREES.

1575 **Berger, Melvin.** *Spinning Spiders.* **Illus. by S. D. Schindler. HarperCollins, 2003. 0-06-028697-0. 32pp. Gr. K–3**

Basic and fascinating spider facts and attractive, realistic paintings are combined into a first look at a few of the 30,000 types of spiders and how they construct their webs.

GERM: If you have access to greenery, go on a spiderweb search. At the back of the book are directions for mounting a real spiderweb onto construction paper.

RELATED TITLES: Carle, Eric. *The Very Busy Spider.* Philomel, 1984. / Cronin, Doreen. *Diary of a Spider.* HarperCollins, 2005. / Hoberman, Mary Ann. *The Eensy-Weensy Spider.* Little, Brown, 2000. / Markle, Sandra. *Spiders: Biggest! Littlest!* Boyds Mills, 2004. / Montgomery, Sy. *The Tarantula Scientist.* Houghton Mifflin, 2004. / Murawski, Darlyne A. *Spiders and Their Webs.* National Geographic, 2004. / Raffi. *Spider on the Floor.* Crown, 1993. / Simon, Seymour. *Spiders.* HarperCollins, 2003. / Trapani, Iza. *The Itsy Bitsy Spider.* Whispering Coyote, 1993. / Tyson, Leigh Ann. *An Interview with Harry the Tarantula.* National Geographic, 2003.

SUBJECTS: SPIDERS.

1576 **Berger, Melvin.** *Why I Sneeze, Shiver, Hiccup, and Yawn.* **Illus. by Paul Meisel. HarperCollins, 2000. 0-06-028143-X. 32pp. Gr. K–2**

Ah-choo! In a reassuring entry in the superior Let's-Read-and-Find-Out Science series, learn how nerves and the nervous system control our reflexes.

GERM: The suggested activities throughout and at the back of the book will help reinforce the interesting facts presented. Ask the school nurse to check out everyone's reflexes with that little rubber hammer.

RELATED TITLES: Arnold, Tedd. *Parts.* Dial, 1997. / Berger, Melvin. *You Can't Make a Move Without Your Muscles.* HarperCollins, 1982. / Cole, Joanna. *The Magic School Bus Inside the Human Body.* Scholastic, 1987. / Rockwell, Lizzy. *The Busy Body Book: A Kids' Guide to Fitness.* Crown, 2004. / Seuling, Barbara. *From Head to Toe: The Amazing Human Body and How It Works.* Holiday House, 2002. / Seuling, Barbara. *You Can't Sneeze with Your Eyes Open and Other Freaky Facts About the Human Body.* Dutton, 1986.

SUBJECTS: BODY, HUMAN. HEALTH. REFLEXES.

1577 **Branley, Franklyn M.** *What Makes a Magnet?* **Illus. by True Kelley. HarperCollins, 1996. 0-06-026442-X. 32pp. Gr. 1–3**

Not only does this easy-to-read entry in the stellar Let's-Read-and-Find-Out Science series explain magnetism and how magnets work, but it also provides simple hands-on experiments anyone can do.

GERM: Follow the lead of the mouse in the humorous watercolors and construct your own magnet and compass out of a magnet, a sewing needle, a bowl of water, and a bit of cork.

RELATED TITLES: Hopkins, Lee Bennett, comp. *Spectacular Science: A Book of Poems.* Simon & Schuster, 1999.

/ Kos, Amy Goldman. *Where Fish Go in Winter and Other Great Mysteries*. Dial, 2002. / Pfeffer, Wendy. *Marta's Magnets*. Silver Press, 1995.

SUBJECTS: MAGNETS. SCIENCE. SCIENCE—EXPERIMENTS.

1578 Brenner, Barbara, and Julia Takaya. *Chibi: A True Story from Japan.* **Illus. by June Otani. Clarion, 1996. 0-395-69623-2. 64pp. Gr. 1–4**

See how the whole city of Tokyo became enamored with a family of wild ducks that settled in the decorative pool of a downtown office park, much the way the mallard family did in Robert McCloskey's fictional *Make Way for Ducklings*.

GERM: Get to know ducks through nonfiction, folklore, picture books, and poetry. True accounts like these help make children more aware of the importance and value of nature in our increasingly materialistic lives. *John Philip Duck* by Patricia Polacco is loosely based on the true story of the ducks at the Peabody Hotel in Memphis, Tennessee.

RELATED TITLES: Florian, Douglas. *On the Wing: Bird Poems and Paintings*. Harcourt, 1996. / McCloskey, Robert. *Make Way for Ducklings*. Viking, 1941. / Naylor, Phyllis Reynolds. *Ducks Disappearing*. Atheneum, 1997. / Newman, Leslea. *Hachiko Waits*. Henry Holt, 2004. / Polacco, Patricia. *John Philip Duck*. Philomel, 2004. / Turner, Pamela S. *Hachiko: The True Story of a Loyal Dog*. Houghton Mifflin, 2004.

SUBJECTS: DUCKS. JAPAN. MULTICULTURAL BOOKS.

1579 Brown, Laurie Krasny, and Marc Brown. *How to Be a Friend: A Guide to Making Friends and Keeping Them.* **Illus. by Marc Brown. Little, Brown, 1998. 0-316-10913-4. 32pp. Gr. K–2**

Marc Brown uses his genial pen-and-ink and watercolor illustrations of a cast of friendly green dinosaur kids to show us a variety of helpful ways to overcome shyness, join in, deal with bosses and bullies, and talk instead of arguing.

GERM: Children can have fun and learn a bit about friendship by pairing up to role-play different situations for the rest of the class to watch and critique.

RELATED TITLES: Bottner, Barbara, and Gerald Kruglik. *Wallace's Lists*. HarperCollins, 2004. / DePaolo, Paula. *Rosie and the Yellow Ribbon*. Little, Brown, 1992. / Henkes, Kevin. *Chrysanthemum*. Greenwillow, 1991. / Hobbie, Holly. *Toot and Puddle*. Little, Brown, 1997. (And others in the Toot and Puddle series.) / Howe, James. *Horace and Morris But Mostly Dolores*. Atheneum, 1999. / Lobel, Arnold. *Frog and Toad Together*. Haper-Collins, 1972. / O'Neill, Alexis. *The Recess Queen*. Scholastic, 2002. / Raschka, Chris. *Yo! Yes?* Orchard, 1993. / Rodman, Mary Ann. *My Best Friend*. Viking, 2005. / Waber, Bernard. *Evie and Margie*. Houghton Mifflin, 2003. / Waddell, Martin. *Hi, Harry!* Candlewick, 2003. / Winthrop, Elizabeth. *Lizzie and Harold*. Lothrop, 1985.

SUBJECTS: FRIENDSHIP.

1580 Browne, Anthony. *The Shape Game.* **Illus. by the author. Farrar, 2003. 0-374-36764-7. Unp. Gr. 2–5**

In an autobiographical story filled with art from the Tate Britain gallery in London, author/illustrator Anthony Browne recalls a life-changing visit to an art museum with his parents and brother George on his mother's birthday. In clever visual renderings, he incorporates his dad and family into his own parallel versions of the paintings, asking us to spot the differences. With a blank drawing book and two pens they buy in the museum gift shop, Mom then shows her sons the drawing game she used to play with her own father, where one person draws a shape and the other person changes it into a picture of something interesting.

GERM: There's a lot to think about in this visually appealing and intriguing picture book that will get your kids looking closely and drawing. Note how a chance experience can change your life ("And in a way I've been playing the shape game ever since.") and how Browne is still drawing his family in many of his books, including *My Dad*. Pair up and play the shape game, of course.

RELATED TITLES: Blake, Quentin. *Tell Me a Picture*. Millbrook, 2003. / Brown, Laurene Krasny. *Visiting the Art Museum*. Dutton, 1986. / Browne, Anthony. *My Dad*. Farrar, 2001. / Browne, Anthony. *My Mom*. Farrar, 2005. / Browne, Anthony. *Willy the Dreamer*. Candlewick, 1998. / dePaola, Tomie. *The Art Lesson*. Putnam, 1989. / Garland, Michael. *Dinner at Magritte's*. Dutton, 1995. / Hurd, Thacher. *Art Dog*. HarperCollins, 1996. / Kroll, Steven. *Patches Lost and Found*. Winslow, 2001. / LaMarche, Jim. *The Raft*. HarperCollins, 2000. / Raczka, Bob. *Art Is . . .* Millbrook, 2003. / Reynolds, Peter H. *The Dot*. Candlewick, 2003. / Reynolds, Peter H. *Ish*. Candlewick, 2004. / Richardson, Joy. *Inside the Museum: A Children's Guide to the Metropolitan Museum of Art*. Abrams, 1993. / Sayre, Henry M. *Cave Paintings to Picasso: The Inside Scoop on 50 Art Masterpieces*. Chronicle Books, 2003. / Scieszka, Jon. *Seen Art?* Viking, 2005. / Warhola, James. *Uncle Andy's*. Putnam, 2003.

SUBJECTS: ART APPRECIATION. ARTISTS. AUTHORS. AUTOBIOGRAPHY. BROWNE, ANTHONY. DRAWING. ILLUSTRATORS. MUSEUMS. PICTURE BOOKS FOR OLDER READERS.

1581 Burleigh, Robert. *Earth from Above for Young Readers*. Photos by Yann Bertrand. Abrams, 2002. 0-8109-3486-8. 77pp. Gr. 1–6

For this hefty, round-the-world photo album, renowned photographer Yann Arthus-Bertrand toured dozens of countries by helicopter, shooting spectacular color aerial photographs that will bedazzle and enthrall readers as they try to identify each landscape.

GERM: Assign pairs of students a country to investigate further, to research essential facts and present these to the rest of the group.

RELATED TITLES: Gerberg, Mort. *Geographunny: A Book of Global Riddles*. Clarion, 1991. / Holub, Joan. *Geogra-fleas! Riddles All Over the Map*. Albert Whitman, 2004. / Hopkins, Lee Bennett, comp. *Got Geography! Poems*. Greenwillow, 2006. / Jenkins, Steve. *Hottest Coldest Highest Deepest*. Houghton Mifflin, 1998. / Lewis, J. Patrick. *A World of Wonders*. Dial, 2002. / Maestro, Marco, and Giulio Maestro. *Riddle City, USA! A Book of Geography Riddles*. HarperCollins, 1994. / Scillian, Devin. *P Is for Passport: A World Alphabet*. Sleeping Bear, 2003. / Smith, David J. *If the World Were a Village: A Book About the World's People*. Kids Can, 2002.

SUBJECTS: EARTH. GEOGRAPHY. PHOTOGRAPHY. SCIENCE.

1582 Cheney, Lynne. *America: A Patriotic Primer*. Illus. by Robin Preiss Glasser. Simon & Schuster, 2002. 0-689-85192-8. Unp. Gr. K–4

Glasser's ornate and cheerful oversized pen-and-ink and watercolors provide a memorable backdrop to an alphabetical description of the heroes, history, and ideals that bring us together.

GERM: Your class can compose and illustrate an Alphabet of America project, with a new word for each letter. If you have each child select a letter and decorate a paper square, you can make an eye-opening quilt to cover a large bulletin board. If you're handy, they can decorate actual fabric squares and sew a real American quilt.

RELATED TITLES: Bates, Katharine Lee. *America the Beautiful*. Illus. by Chris Gall. Little, Brown, 2004. / Bates, Katharine Lee. *America the Beautiful*. Illus. by Neil Waldman. Atheneum, 1983. / Borden, Louise. *America Is . . .* McElderry, 2002. / Brisson, Pat. *Your Best Friend, Kate*. Bradbury, 1989. / Catrow, David. *We the Kids: The Preamble to the Constitution of the United States*. Dial, 2002. / Fritz, Jean. *Shh! We're Writing the Constitution*. Putnam, 1987. / Guthrie, Woody. *This Land Is Your Land*. Little, Brown, 1998. / Jefferson, Thomas. *The Declaration of Independence: The Words That Made America*. Illus. by Sam Fink. Scholastic, 2002. / Keenan, Sheila. *O, Say Can You See? America's Symbols, Landmarks, and Inspiring Words*. Scholastic, 2004. / Keller, Laurie. *The Scrambled States of America*. Henry Holt, 1998. / Maestro, Betsy, and Giulio Maestro. *A More Perfect Union: The Story of Our Constitution*. Lothrop, 1987.

SUBJECTS: ALPHABET BOOKS. PATRIOTISM. U.S.—HISTORY.

1583 Christelow, Eileen. *VOTE!* Illus. by the author. Clarion, 2003. 0-618-24754-8. 47pp. Gr. 2–6

Follow the fictional campaign of Chris Smith, an African American woman running for mayor of her town, bolstered by her supportive daughter, husband, and even her helpful dogs. Chris's family dogs provide much of the commentary in this peppy picture book, which reminds us that, originally, only white men who owned property could vote in this country, and provides us with info on how campaigns are run. It's fast and funny, with lots of balloon-filled dialogue and entertaining, kid-friendly pen-and-ink and watercolor illustrations. The book includes a glossary, a timeline of voting rights, and a batch of good Web sites. This one will get your vote!

GERM: Christelow got the idea for this inspired and informative exploration of the voting process on a school visit in Hastings, Minnesota. They start voter education early in that state, and kids are encouraged to go with their parents to the polls. They can even register their votes in a special kids' section and they get an "I Voted!" button when they do. Bring in the ballot for your local elections, research and discuss the candidates and issues coming up for a vote, and maybe even hold your own school elections.

RELATED TITLES: Gutman, Dan. *The Kid Who Ran for President*. Scholastic, 1996. / McCully, Emily Arnold. *The Ballot Box Battle*. Knopf, 1996. / Maestro, Betsy. *The Voice of the People: American Democracy in Action*. Lothrop, 1996. / Mitchell, Margaree King. *Granddaddy's Gift*. BridgeWater, 1997. / Sisulu, Elinor Batezat. *The Day Gogo Went to Vote: South Africa, April 1994*. Little, Brown, 1996. / St. George, Judith. *So You Want to Be President?* Philomel, 2000. / Stier, Catherine. *If I Were President*. Albert Whitman, 1999. / White, Linda Arms. *I Could Do That: Esther Morris Gets Women the Vote*. Farrar, 2005. / Wooldridge, Connie Nordhielm. *When Esther Morris Headed West: Women, Wyoming, and the Right to Vote*. Holiday House, 2001.

SUBJECTS: AFRICAN AMERICANS. ELECTIONS. MAYORS. MULTICULTURAL BOOKS. POLITICAL CAMPAIGNS. VOTING.

1584 Christelow, Eileen. *What Do Authors Do?* Illus. by the author. Clarion, 1995. 0-395-71124-X. 32pp. Gr. 1–4

Follow two writers and next-door neighbors as each creates a manuscript and publishes a new book, both based on the same idea. Watching Max the dog chase Rufus the cat, Rufus's owner decides to write a chapter book about the two pets, and Max's owner starts work on a picture book. Step by step we see how the two writers have separate but related problems as they research their subjects and struggle to find the right words to describe them. Publishers accept their stories; now come the rewrites, the design and illustrations, and the printing process.

GERM: You'll love the ending, when both neighbors look out their windows at the snow, getting new ideas for writing stories about a blizzard. Perhaps your writers can put pen to paper and write their own snow tales. Take a closer look at the writing and illustrating process with Christelow's companion book, *What Do Illustrators Do?*, Loreen Leedy's *Look at My Book: How Kids Can Write and Illustrate Terrific Books*, and Janet Stevens's *From Pictures to Words: A Book About Making a Book*.

RELATED TITLES: Barrows, Allison. *The Artist's Model.* Carolrhoda, 1996. / Christelow, Eileen. *What Do Illustrators Do?* Clarion, 1999. / Duke, Kate. *Aunt Isabel Tells a Good One.* Dutton, 1992. / Leedy, Loreen. *Look at My Book: How Kids Can Write and Illustrate Terrific Books.* Holiday House, 2004. / Marcus, Leonard S., ed. *Author Talk.* Simon & Schuster, 2000. / Nixon, Joan Lowery. *If You Were a Writer.* Four Winds, 1988. / Pulver, Robin. *Author Day for Room 3T.* Clarion, 2005. / Schotter, Roni. *Nothing Ever Happens on 90th Street.* Orchard, 1997. / Stevens, Janet. *From Pictures to Words: A Book About Making a Book.* Holiday House, 1995.

SUBJECTS: AUTHORSHIP. BOOKS AND READING. CREATIVE WRITING. ILLUSTRATORS. WRITING.

1585 Christelow, Eileen. *What Do Illustrators Do?* Illus. by the author. Clarion, 1999. 0-395-90230-4. 40pp. Gr. 1–4

In a companion book to *What Do Authors Do?*, meet two illustrators, both of whom get the idea to illustrate "Jack and the Beanstalk." Though their styles of drawing and approaches to the story differ, the process they undergo is similar: making a plan, creating a dummy, sketching and re-sketching, designing each page, and submitting the finished books to an editor and a designer. Thanks to the woman artist's dog, Scooter, and the male artist's cat, Leonard, we are privy to a wealth of behind-the-scenes info that the two friendly, talking pets impart. From rough sketches to finished book, the pets keep an eye on their owners' works-in-progress, all laid out in cartoon-style paneled watercolor illustrations, replete with dialogue balloons and an entertaining but informative text.

GERM: Showing the creative process from two perspectives will be a valuable teaching tool for children working on their own writing and illustrating. Hand out the text of a well-known folktale (a "Baba Yaga" story like Joanna Cole's *Bony Legs* would work well, as would "Rapunzel" or "Rumpelstiltskin") for the class to read together. Children can work alone or in small groups to illustrate the story's main plot events, incorporating the setting and the main characters. Compare and discuss their different interpretations.

RELATED TITLES: Barrows, Allison. *The Artist's Model.* Carolrhoda, 1996. / Christelow, Eileen. *What Do Authors Do?* Clarion, 1995. / Cole, Joanna. *Bony Legs.* Simon & Schuster, 1984. / Drescher, Henrik. *Simon's Book.* Lothrop, 1983. / Heller, Ruth. *Color.* Putnam, 1995. / Krull, Kathleen. *The Boy on Fairfield Street: How Ted Geisel Grew Up to Become Dr. Seuss.* Random House, 2004. / Leedy, Loreen. *Look at My Book: How Kids Can Write and Illustrate Terrific Books.* Holiday House, 2004. / Nixon, Joan Lowery. *If You Were a Writer.* Four Winds, 1988. / Schotter, Roni. *Nothing Ever Happens on 90th Street.* Orchard, 1997. / Seuss, Dr., and Jack Prelutsky. *Hooray for Diffendoofer Day.* Knopf, 1998. / Stevens, Janet. *From Pictures to Words: A Book About Making a Book.* Holiday House, 1995. / *Wings of an Artist: Children's Book Illustrators Talk About Their Art.* Abrams, 1999.

SUBJECTS: ARTISTS. BOOKS AND READING. CREATIVE WRITING. ILLUSTRATORS. WRITING.

1586 Christian, Peggy. *If You Find a Rock.* Photos by Barbara Hirsch Lember. Harcourt, 2000. 0-15-239339-0. Unp. Gr. PreK–3

In a thoughtful hand-colored photoessay, we discover various ways rocks can be used— for wishing, splashing, worrying, hiding, walking, and remembering.

GERM: Children can collect their own special rocks to identify and describe, figuring out their best functions. Use with Byrd Baylor's classic, *Everybody Needs a Rock*.

RELATED TITLES: Baylor, Byrd. *Everybody Needs a Rock.* Scribner, 1974. / Hiscock, Bruce. *The Big Rock.* Atheneum, 1988. / Hooper, Meredith. *The Pebble in My Pocket: A History of Our Earth.* Viking, 1996. / Hurst,

Carol Otis. *Rocks in His Head*. Greenwillow, 2001. / Kimmel, Eric A. *Anansi and the Moss-Covered Rock*. Holiday House, 1990. / Polacco, Patricia. *My Ol' Man*. Philomel, 1995. / Steig, William. *Sylvester and the Magic Pebble*. Simon & Schuster, 1988.
SUBJECTS: GEOLOGY. ROCKS.

1587 **Chrustowski, Rick. *Bright Beetle*. Illus. by the author. Henry Holt, 2000. 0-8050-6058-8. Unp. Gr. 1–3**

In a meadow at the end of summer, a ladybug lays nine yellow eggs on the leaf of a Black-eyed Susan. We follow one of them as the larva emerges, hunts aphids, sheds her skin several times, becomes a pupa, and finally emerges a red and black ladybug. The beetle's life cycle is illustrated in full-page colored pencil drawings that provide a close-up look at the insect's habitat and the dangers she faces.

GERM: Identify other beetles in *The Beetle Alphabet Book* by Jerry Pallotta. Compare fact with fiction using Eric Carle's *The Grouchy Ladybug*.

RELATED TITLES: Carle, Eric. *The Grouchy Ladybug*. HarperCollins, 1997. / Carle, Eric. *The Very Hungry Caterpillar*. Putnam, 1981. / Chrustowski, Rick. *Turtle Crossing*. Henry Holt, 2006. / Ehlert, Lois. *Waiting for Wings*. Harcourt, 2001. / Fischer-Nagel, Heiderose, and Andreas Fischer-Nagle. *Life of the Ladybug*. Carolrhoda, 1981. / Hariton, Anca. *Butterfly Story*. Dutton, 1995. / Heiligman, Deborah. *From Caterpillar to Butterfly*. HarperCollins, 1996. / Johnson, Sylvia. *Ladybug*. Lerner, 1983. / Pallotta, Jerry. *The Beetle Alphabet Book*. Charlesbridge, 2004. / Pfeffer, Wendy. *A Log's Life*. Simon & Schuster, 1997. / Swope, Sam. *Gotta Go! Gotta Go!* Farrar, 2000.
SUBJECTS: BEETLES. INSECTS. LADYBUGS.

1588 **Cobb, Vicki. *I Face the Wind*. Illus. by Julia Gorton. HarperCollins, 2003. 0-689-17841-3. Unp. Gr. PreK–1**

A young girl demonstrates the properties of wind through observation and several simple, easy-to-read-and-perform activities that teach science through experience. Not only are the experiments right on target in this simple to follow but intellectually challenging book for the youngest scientist, but the appealing collage illustrations of a young girl experiencing all aspects of wind and an involving question-filled text will get your students thinking, testing, and drawing scientific conclusions.

GERM: As you read the book aloud, stop to discuss the questions the text poses and try out the different experiments. Children can draw and label wind pictures showing different ways they have experienced the wind first hand. This is one in a dynamic series of veteran science writer Cobb's Science Play books, which includes *I Get Wet* (about water), *I See Myself* (about mirrors), and *I Fall Down* (about gravity). Books like these create scientists out of kids.

RELATED TITLES: Bauer, Marion Dane. *Wind*. Simon & Schuster, 2003. / Climo, Shirley. *The Match Between the Winds*. Macmillan, 1991. / Cobb, Vicki. *I Fall Down*. HarperCollins, 2004. / Cobb, Vicki. *I Get Wet*. HarperCollins, 2002. / Cobb, Vicki. *I See Myself*. HarperCollins, 2002. / Littledale, Freya. *Peter and the North Wind*. Scholastic, 1988. / Martin, Bill, Jr. *Old Devil Wind*. Harcourt, 1993. / McKissack, Patricia C. *Mirandy and Brother Wind*. Knopf, 1988. / Simon, Seymour, and Nicole Fauteux. *Let's Try It Out in the Air: Hands-On Early-Learning Science Activities*. Simon & Schuster, 2001.
SUBJECTS: SCIENCE. SCIENCE—EXPERIMENTS. WIND. WIND—EXPERIMENTS.

1589 **Cobb, Vicki. *I Get Wet*. Illus. by Julia Gorton. HarperCollins, 2002. 0-688-17839-1. Unp. Gr. PreK–1**

In the simplest of explanations and experiments, find out what shape water is, how drops stick together, and, of course, why we get wet.

GERM: Try out each experiment as you read the book to your budding scientists. Follow with others in the Science Play series, including *I Face the Wind*, *I Fall Down*, and *I See Myself*.

RELATED TITLES: Cobb, Vicki. *I Face the Wind*. HarperCollins, 2003. / Cobb, Vicki. *I Fall Down*. HarperCollins, 2004. / Cobb, Vicki. *I See Myself*. HarperCollins, 2002. / Dorros, Arthur. *Follow the Water from Brook to Ocean*. HarperCollins, 1991. / Hathorn, Libby. *The Wonder Thing*. Houghton Mifflin, 1996. / Kerley, Barbara. *A Cool Drink of Water*. National Geographic, 2002. / Peters, Lisa Westberg. *Water's Way*. Little, Brown, 1991.
SUBJECTS: SCIENCE. SCIENCE—EXPERIMENTS. WATER—EXPERIMENTS.

1590 **Cohn, Janice. *The Christmas Menorahs: How a Town Fought Hate*. Illus. by Bill Farnsworth. Albert Whitman, 1995. 0-8075-1152-8. 40pp. Gr. 2–5**

Based on the occurrence of racist and anti-Semitic incidents that shook Billings, Montana, in

1993, this is the inspiring true story of a town that fought back. On the third night of Hanukkah, a rock was thrown through the window of young Isaac Schnitzer's bedroom. In response, Police Chief Inman called a community meeting during which people decided to put menorahs in all of their windows to show their support for the Jewish families in town.

GERM: Use this powerful discussion starter to defuse misconceptions your students harbor about people of other races or beliefs. As Isaac's mother said, ". . . hate can make a lot of noise. Love and courage are usually quieter. But in the end, they're the strongest." The Southern Poverty Law Center publishes an excellent magazine for teachers, *Teaching Tolerance*, and a community response guide called "Ten Ways to Fight Hate." Check out their Web site at <www.tolerance.org>.

RELATED TITLES: Abels, Chana Byers. *The Children We Remember*. Greenwillow, 1986. / Adler, David A. *One Yellow Daffodil: A Hanukkah Story*. Harcourt, 1995. / Bridges, Ruby. *Through My Eyes*. Scholastic, 1999. / Bunting, Eve. *Smoky Night*. Harcourt, 1994. / *Lowry, Lois*. Number the Stars. Houghton Mifflin, 1989. / McCann, Michelle R. Luba: The Angel of Bergen-Belsen. *Tricycle, 2003*. / Polacco, Patricia. Chicken Sunday. *Philomel, 1992*. / Polacco, Patricia. Mr. Lincoln's Way. *Philomel, 2001*. / Propp, Vera. When the Soldiers Were Gone. *Putnam, 1999*. / Schnur, Steven. The Tie Man's Miracle: A Chanukah Tale. *Morrow, 1995*. / Woodson, Jacqueline. The Other Side. *Putnam, 2001*.

SUBJECTS: CHRISTMAS. HANUKKAH. JEWS. MONTANA. PREJUDICE. RESPONSIBILITY.

1591 Cole, Joanna. *The Magic School Bus Inside a Hurricane*. Illus. by Bruce Degen. Scholastic, 1995. 0-590-44686-X. Unp. Gr. 1–4
On their way to visit the weather station, Ms. Frizzle and her class take a brief detour, thousands of miles away, to experience a hurricane first-hand.

GERM: This is a must for your weather unit. Read how thunder came to be in Aaron Shepard's pourquoi tale *Master Man: A Tall Tale of Nigeria*. See some hair-raising weather photos in Stephen Kramer's *Eye of the Storm: Chasing Storms with Warren Faidley*.

RELATED TITLES: Cole, Joanna. The Magic School Bus series. Scholastic. / Cole, Joanna. *Ms. Frizzle's Adventures: Ancient Egypt*. Scholastic, 2001. / Ketteman, Helen. *Heat Wave!* Walker, 1998. / Kramer, Stephen. *Eye of the Storm: Chasing Storms with Warren Faidley*. Putnam, 1997. / Ruckman, Ivy. *Night of the Twisters*. Crowell, 1984. / Shepard, Aaron. *Master Man: A Tall Tale of Nigeria*. HarperCollins, 2001. / Simon, Seymour. *Lightning*. Morrow, 1997. / Simon, Seymour. *Storms*. Morrow, 1989. / Wiesner, David. *Hurricane*. Clarion, 1990. / Yep, Laurence. *The Junior Thunder Lord*. BridgeWater, 1994.

SUBJECTS: HURRICANES. STORMS. TEACHERS. WEATHER.

1592 Cole, Joanna. *Ms. Frizzle's Adventures: Ancient Egypt*. Illus. by Bruce Degen. Scholastic, 2001. 0-590-44680-0. Unp. Gr. K–5
Ms. Frizzle, the eclectic, creatively clad teacher all readers have until now connected solely with science and the Magic School Bus, sets out on her school vacation as part of a group tour to Egypt. "I knew my teaching experience would come in handy on this trip," she says, and that's no understatement. Taking over from droning tour leader Herb, "the Friz" supplies the others in the group with parachutes and they head out of the plane, straight to ancient Egypt. This first book in the delightfully informative and witty history time-travel series, narrated by the red-haired teacher, sports colorful, detail-laden illustrations, which are studded with tongue-in-cheek dialogue balloons and informative sidebars. Ms. Frizzle takes her wise-cracking group to a marketplace and a school for scribes. They swim down the Nile, work construction on a pyramid, and even attend a mummification and funeral for the late pharaoh.

GERM: As the tourists trek through ancient times, at the bottom of each page we see the bullhorn-toting guide Herb continuing his tour in modern Egypt, enabling us to compare the past with the present. Children can draw self portraits, Egyptian-style, combining front and side views of their bodies and faces. Appetites whetted, head to the library to investigate and revel in more books on ancient Egypt. Use a book about hieroglyphics to have students invent hieroglyphs for their own names, which they can inscribe on their own handmade scrolls or wooden boards.

RELATED TITLES: Aliki. *Mummies Made in Egypt*. Crowell, 1987. / Bower, Tamara. *How the Amazon Queen Fought the Prince of Egypt*. Atheneum, 2005. / Bunting, Eve. *I Am the Mummy Heb-Nefert*. Harcourt, 1997. / Clements, Andrew. *Temple Cat*. Clarion, 1996. / Climo, Shirley. *The Egyptian Cinderella*. Crowell, 1989. / Cole, Joanna. Magic School Bus series. Scholastic. / Cole, Joanna. *Ms. Frizzle's Adventures: Imperial China*. Scholastic, 2005. / Cole, Joanna. *Ms. Frizzle's Adventures: Medieval Castle*. Scholastic, 2003. / Cushman, Doug. *The Mystery of King Karfu*. HarperCollins, 1996. / Gibbons, Gail. *Mummies, Pyramids, and Pharaohs: A Book About Ancient Egypt*. Little, Brown, 2004. / Hall, Katy, and Lisa Eisenberg. *Mummy Riddles*. Dial, 1997. / Heide, Florence

Parry, and Judith Heide Gilliland. *The Day of Ahmed's Secret*. Lothrop, 1990. / Krupp, Robin Rector. *Let's Go Traveling*. Morrow, 1992. / McDermott, Gerald. *The Voyage of Osiris: A Myth of Ancient Egypt*. Dutton, 1977. / Price, Leontyne. *Aïda*. Harcourt, 1990. / Scieszka, Jon. *Tut, Tut*. Viking, 1996. / Stolz, Mary. *Zehmet, the Stone Carver*. Harcourt, 1988.

SUBJECTS: ANCIENT CIVILIZATIONS. EGYPT, ANCIENT. TEACHERS. TIME TRAVEL.

1593 **Cole, Joanna. *Ms. Frizzle's Adventures: Imperial China*. Illus. by Bruce Degen. Scholastic, 2005. 0-590-10822-0. 40pp. Gr. K–5**
On her way to have a Chinese New Year's dinner with her student Wanda's family, Ms. Frizzle—with Wanda, her brother Henry, and the ever-recalcitrant Arnold—takes a detour back in time to a Chinese village a thousand years in the past. En route to see the emperor to complain about the farmers' high taxes, the band of sightseers ride down the Yangtze River on a barge, work in a silk factory, and meet up with invaders at the Great Wall.
GERM: You'll learn how to use chopsticks and about how rice is grown, so cook up some rice for everyone to eat with chopsticks. Bottom panels provide bits of information about Chinese inventions (the compass, paper, silk, tea, porcelain, gunpowder), and even how to bow or kowtow, which all can try. Use Ms. Frizzle as your inspiration and template for researching and writing reports about other cultures and times in history.
RELATED TITLES: Compestine, Ying Chang. *The Runaway Rice Cake*. Simon & Schuster, 2001. / Compestine, Ying Chang. *The Story of Chopsticks*. Holiday House, 2001. / Compestine, Ying Chang. *The Story of Kites*. Holiday House, 2003. / Compestine, Ying Chang. *The Story of Paper*. Holiday House, 2003. / Davol, Marguerite. *The Paper Dragon*. Atheneum, 1997. / Fisher, Leonard Everett. *The Great Wall of China*. Macmillan, 1986. / Hong, Lily Toy. *The Empress and the Silkworm*. Albert Whitman, 1995. / Mahy, Margaret. *The Seven Chinese Brothers*. Scholastic, 1990. / O'Connor, Jane. *The Emperor's Silent Army: Terracotta Warriors of Ancient China*. Viking, 2002. / Simonds, Nina, and Leslie Swartz. *Moonbeams, Dumplings and Dragon Boats: A Treasury of Chinese Holiday Tales, Activities and Recipes*. Harcourt, 2002. / Young, Ed. *Beyond the Great Mountains: A Visual Poem About China*. Chronicle, 2005. / Young, Ed. *Cat and Rat: The Legend of the Chinese Zodiac*. Henry Holt, 1995.
SUBJECTS: ANCIENT CIVILIZATIONS. CHINA. CHINESE NEW YEAR. EMPERORS. KINGS AND RULERS. TEACHERS. TIME TRAVEL.

1594 **Collard, Sneed B., III. *Animal Dads*. Illus. by Steve Jenkins. Houghton Mifflin, 1997. 0-395-83621-2. Unp. Gr. K–2**
Each page features a male animal in an appealing full-page illustration of cut-paper collage, accompanied by a simple statement about fathers in general and a brief descriptive paragraph relating how these particular fathers assist their offspring. "They keep us snug and warm," it says on the page depicting the emperor penguin, and then describes how the father holds the newly laid egg on his feet until the mother gets back from searching for food.
GERM: Readers can categorize each animal into its broader family—birds, fish, reptiles and amphibians, mammals—and then go off searching for some new animal facts to share. Use this for science, sure, but also for Father's Day when children assess the good things their dads do for them.
RELATED TITLES: Browne, Anthony. *My Dad*. Farrar, 2001. / Carle, Eric. *Mister Seahorse*. Philomel, 2004. / Heller, Ruth. *Animals Born Alive and Well*. Grossett, 1982. / Jenkins, Steve. *Actual Size*. Houghton Mifflin, 2004. / Jenkins, Steve. *Big and Little*. Houghton Mifflin, 1996. / Jenkins, Steve. *Biggest, Strongest, Fastest*. Ticknor & Fields, 1995. / Jenkins, Steve, and Robin Page. *What Do You Do with a Tail Like This?* Houghton Mifflin, 2003. / Simon, Seymour. *Animal Fact, Animal Fable*. Crown, 1987. / Swinburne, Stephen R. *Safe, Warm, and Snug*. Harcourt, 1999. / Ziefert, Harriet. *33 Uses for a Dad*. Blue Apple, 2004.
SUBJECTS: ANIMALS. FATHERS.

1595 **Cowley, Joy. *Chameleon, Chameleon*. Photos by Nic Bishop. Scholastic, 2005. 0-439-66663-8. Unp. Gr. PreK–2**
With up-close color photographs of a pebbly-green, jewel-toned panther chameleon from Madagascar that looks almost too beautiful to be real, and an elemental text that reads like an intelligent emergent reader, delve into a look at the life and challenges of this most photogenic of creatures. While searching for food, the male chameleon encounters a gecko, frog, and scorpion in his quest to find a suitable new tree with a ready supply of food, and then meets up with a female chameleon.
GERM: The "Did You Know" pages at the back of the book provide additional facts. All nonfiction for young children should be this good. Look up panther chameleons on <www.google.com>, and you'll find many sites that describe the care and feeding of these little reptiles as

pets. Do some research on other creatures that can be found in the tropical rain forests of Madagascar. Also share Cowley's eye-catching rain forest book of South America, *Red-Eyed Tree Frog*.

RELATED TITLES: Cowley, Joy. *Red-Eyed Tree Frog*. Scholastic, 1999. / Diakité, Baba Wagué. *The Magic Gourd*. Scholastic, 2003. / Jenkins, Martin. *Chameleons Are Cool*. Candlewick, 1997. / Kessler, Cristina. *Konte Chameleon Fine, Fine, Fine! A West African Folk Tale*. Boyds Mills, 1997. / Martin, James. *Chameleons: Dragons in the Trees*. Crown, 1991. / Mwenye Hadithi. *Crafty Chameleon*. Little, Brown, 1987.

SUBJECTS: CHAMELEONS. MADAGASCAR. RAIN FORESTS. REPTILES AND AMPHIBIANS.

1596 Cowley, Joy. *Red-Eyed Tree Frog*. **Photos by Nic Bishop. Scholastic, 1999. 0-590-87175-7. 32pp. Gr. PreK–2**

Prepare to be wowed by this compelling, simple-to-read color photoessay on the red-eyed tree frog as it searches for food and avoids being eaten in a South American rain forest.

GERM: The dramatic color close-ups of the 2-inch, green-backed, cream-bellied frog are breathtaking in their clarity and detail and the final "Did You Know?" page of additional facts will have newfound frog-lovers hanging on every word. Use this for all ages as a kickoff to that yearly study unit on animals or the rain forest. From the Madagascar rain forest, meet the panther chameleon in Cowley's *Chameleon, Chameleon*.

RELATED TITLES: Brett, Jan. *The Umbrella*. Putnam, 2004. / Carle, Eric. *"Slowly, Slowly, Slowly," Said the Sloth*. Philomel, 2002. / Cherry, Lynne. *The Great Kapok Tree: A Tale of the Amazon Rain Forest*. Harcourt, 1990. / Cowcher, Helen. *Rain Forest*. Farrar, 1988. / Cowley, Joy. *Chameleon, Chameleon*. Scholastic, 2005. / Florian, Douglas. *Lizards, Frogs, and Polliwogs: Poems and Paintings*. Harcourt, 2001. / French, Vivian. *Growing Frogs*. Candlewick, 2000. / Jordan, Tanis. *Amazon Alphabet*. Kingfisher, 1996. / Kalan, Robert. *Jump, Frog, Jump*. Greenwillow, 1981. / Pfeffer, Wendy. *From Tadpole to Frog*. HarperCollins, 1994. / Ryder, Joanne. *Jaguar in the Rain Forest*. Morrow, 1996. / Wiesner, David. *Tuesday*. Clarion, 1991. / Yolen, Jane. *Welcome to the Green House*. Putnam, 1993.

SUBJECTS: ANIMALS. FROGS. JUNGLE ANIMALS. RAIN FORESTS.

1597 Curlee, Lynn. *Seven Wonders of the Ancient World*. **Illus. by the author. Atheneum, 2002. 0-689-83182-X. 40pp. Gr. 3–6**

Dignified full-page acrylic paintings illuminate the fascinating descriptions of and anecdotes about such legendary ancient monuments as the Great Pyramid at Giza (the only one of the Seven Wonders still standing), the Hanging Gardens of Babylon, and the Colossus of Rhodes.

GERM: Children can research and report on some of the other ancient wonders mentioned in the text.

RELATED TITLES: Cole, Joanna. *Ms. Frizzle's Adventures: Ancient Egypt*. HarperCollins, 1996. / Cole, Joanna. *Ms. Frizzle's Adventures: Imperial China*. Scholastic, 2005. / Curlee, Lynn. *Brooklyn Bridge*. Atheneum, 2001. / Curlee, Lynn. *Liberty*. Atheneum, 2000. / Curlee, Lynn. *Parthenon*. Atheneum, 2004. / Fisher, Leonard Everett. *The Great Wall of China*. Macmillan, 1986. / Krupp, Robin Rector. *Let's Go Traveling*. Morrow, 1992. / Moore, Christopher. *Ishtar and Tammuz: A Babylonian Myth of the Seasons*. Kingfisher, 1996. / O'Connor, Jane. *The Emperor's Silent Army: Terracotta Warriors of Ancient China*. Viking, 2002.

SUBJECTS: ANCIENT CIVILIZATIONS. ARCHAEOLOGY. BUILDINGS. SCULPTURE. SEVEN WONDERS OF THE WORLD.

1598 Davies, Nicola. *Surprising Sharks*. **Illus. by James Croft. Candlewick, 2003. 0-7636-2185-4. 29pp. Gr. PreK–3**

Learn about sharks and their way of life, thanks to a punchy text, easily accessible to all, waterlogged acrylic and pastel illustrations, and cool facts—"Sand tiger sharks give birth to just two live young— which is all that's left after those two have eaten the other six babies in their mother's belly." OK, it's not really the mother's belly, but a 28-page picture book for young kids doesn't need to get into a shark sex ed discussion.

GERM: The ending is clever and sobering: "Every year, people kill 100 million sharks. If you were a shark swimming in the lovely blue sea, the last word you'd want to hear would be . . . human!" This could make a good kick-off to a research lesson in which students find out more about some of the shark species mentioned in the text.

RELATED TITLES: Cerullo, Mary M. *Sharks: Challengers of the Deep*. Dutton, 1993. / Cerullo, Mary M. *The Truth About Great White Sharks*. Chronicle, 2000. / Maestro, Betsy. *A Sea Full of Sharks*. Scholastic, 1990. / Mahy, Margaret. *The Great White Man-Eating Shark*. Dial, 1990. / O'Brien, Patrick. *Megatooth*. Henry Holt, 2001.

/ Pringle, Laurence. *Sharks! Strange and Wonderful*. Boyds Mills, 2001. / Wardlaw, Lee. *Punia and the King of Sharks: A Hawaiian Folktale*. Dial, 1997.

SUBJECTS: FISHES. OCEAN. SHARKS.

1599   Dewey, Jennifer Owings. *Rattlesnake Dance: True Tales, Mysteries, and Rattlesnake Ceremonies.* **Illus. by the author. Boyds Mills, 1997. 1-56397-247-6. 48pp. Gr. 3–6**

In three fascinating chapters, illustrated with detailed drawings and snake facts, the author recalls being bitten by a rattler as a child, witnessing a Hopi snake ceremony, and watching two rattlers battle for dominance.

GERM: Introduce your researchers to the snake section of your library (597.96) and the Hopi and Native American books (throughout the 970s, though you'll find interesting materials in folklore and other sections too). As an example of personal narrative interspersed with facts, this would be a grand model for asking writers to describe and illustrate a life-changing experience and to research additional facts to buttress their stories.

RELATED TITLES: Byars, Betsy. *The Moon and I.* Messner, 1992. / Khan, Rukhsana. *Ruler of the Courtyard.* Viking, 2003. / Kipling, Rudyard. *Rikki-Tikki-Tavi.* Adapted and illus. by Jerry Pinkney. Morrow, 1997. / Maestro, Betsy. *Take a Look at Snakes.* Scholastic, 1992.

SUBJECTS: HOPI INDIANS. INDIANS OF NORTH AMERICA. PERSONAL NARRATIVES. RATTLESNAKES. SNAKES.

1600   Dooling, Michael. *The Great Horse-less Carriage Race.* **Illus. by the author. Holiday House, 2002. 0-8234-1640-2. Unp. Gr. 2–6**

On November 28, 1895, a Chicago newspaper sponsored a 52-mile horseless carriage race through the city to show the superiority of the newfangled machines to the horse and buggy. The winner, after a mere 11 hours, averaging a heart-stopping seven miles per hour, was Frank Duryea, driving his own "buggyaut," the only American-made machine in the race. Dooling's snow-infused oil paintings superbly capture the fervor and humor of this true story.

GERM: With your students, write up the action-packed story into a Reader's Theater script for them to act out. For the actors who play the three carriage-driving contenders, jerry-rig steering levers by attaching a bicycle bugle horn to a yardstick. After reading David Weitzman's *Model T: How Henry Ford Built a Legend*, they can also act out the assembly-line process that Henry Ford devised.

RELATED TITLES: Brown, Don. *Alice Ramsey's Grand Adventure.* Houghton Mifflin, 1997. / Hyatt, Patricia Rusch. *Coast to Coast with Alice.* Carolrhoda, 1995. / Weitzman, David. *Model T: How Henry Ford Built a Legend.* Crown, 2002.

SUBJECTS: AUTOMOBILE RACING. AUTOMOBILES. READER'S THEATER. U.S.—HISTORY—1865–1898.

1601   DuQuette, Keith. *They Call Me Woolly: What Animal Names Can Tell Us.* **Illus. by the author. Putnam, 2002. 0-399-23445-4. 32pp. Gr. PreK–2**

An animal's name can give you information on where it's from (African elephant), its habitat (polar bear), how it moves (roadrunner), the sounds it makes (hummingbird), or its unique features (hammerhead shark). Each of three dozen animals is grouped by the features of its name and pictured in detailed watercolor, gouache, and colored pencil illustrations. At the back are interesting facts about each animal, and an additional page of 16 animals with revealing names.

GERM: Students can research more facts about the animals portrayed here and present them in an oral report. Make a graph of the different categories of names identified in the book, and brainstorm a list of other animals whose names describe their functions.

RELATED TITLES: Collard, Sneed B., III. *Animal Dads.* Houghton Mifflin, 1997. / Heller, Ruth. *Animals Born Alive and Well.* Grossett, 1982. / Hooper, Patricia. *A Bundle of Beasts.* Houghton Mifflin, 1987. / Jenkins, Steve. *Actual Size.* Houghton Mifflin, 2004. / Jenkins, Steve. *Big and Little.* Houghton Mifflin, 1996. / Jenkins, Steve. *Biggest, Strongest, Fastest.* Ticknor & Fields, 1995. / Jenkins, Steve. *What Do You Do When Something Wants to Eat You?* Houghton Mifflin, 1997. / Jenkins, Steve, and Robin Page. *What Do You Do With a Tail Like This?* Houghton Mifflin, 2003. / MacCarthy, Patricia. *Herds of Words.* Dial, 1991. / Moser, Madeline. *Ever Heard of an Aardwolf?* Harcourt, 1996. / Ryan, Pam Muñoz. *A Pinky Is a Baby Mouse and Other Baby Animal Names.* Dial, 1998. / Simon, Seymour. *Animal Fact, Animal Fable.* Crown, 1987. / Singer, Marilyn. *A Wasp Is Not a Bee.* Henry Holt, 1995.

SUBJECTS: ANIMAL NAMES. ANIMALS. VOCABULARY.

1602 Edwards, Judith. *The Great Expedition of Lewis and Clark: By Private Reubin Field, Member of the Corps of Discovery.* **Illus. by Sally Wern Comport. Farrar, 2003. 0-374-38039-2. Unp. Gr. 2–5**

As Reubin Field recalls it, in this lively fictionalized but fact-based nonfiction picture book, the grand 863-day adventure through the western wilderness to the Pacific Ocean from 1804 to 1806 was filled with marvels. His folksy storytelling captures the highlights encountered by the 31 men, one woman, and her baby: fending off snakes, mosquitoes, and grizzly bears; encountering both helpful and hostile Native American tribes; hunting buffalo; and paddling and portaging their six canoes and two pirogues a mere 4,162 miles.

GERM: Illustrated with genial, action-filled watercolors, this approach to personal narrative can lead to researching and writing historical fiction from supporting witnesses' points of view. Students can also seek information about the many Indian tribes the Corps met along their journey, including the Oto, Missouri, Sioux, Mandan, Shoshone, Nez Perce, Clatsop, Chinook, Walla Walla, and Blackfoot. For other points of view, read Laurie Myers's *Lewis and Clark and Me: A Dog's Tale* and Rosalyn Schanzer's *How We Crossed the West: The Adventures of Lewis and Clark.*

RELATED TITLES: Blumberg, Rhoda. *The Incredible Journey of Lewis and Clark.* Lothrop, 1987. / Bruchac, Joseph. *Sacajawea.* Harcourt, 2000. / Erdrich, Lise. *Sacagawea.* Carolrhoda, 2003. / Myers, Laurie. *Lewis and Clark and Me: A Dog's Tale.* Henry Holt, 2002. / Schanzer, Rosalyn. *How We Crossed the West: The Adventures of Lewis and Clark.* National Geographic, 1997. / St. George, Judith. *So You Want to Be an Explorer?* Philomel, 2005.

SUBJECTS: EXPLORERS. INDIANS OF NORTH AMERICA. LEWIS AND CLARK EXPEDITION (1804–1806). PERSONAL NARRATIVES. U.S.—HISTORY—1783–1865. VOYAGES AND TRAVELS. WEST—DISCOVERY AND EXPLORATION.

1603 Ehlert, Lois. *Waiting for Wings.* **Illus. by the author. Harcourt, 2001. 0-15-202608-8. Unp. Gr. PreK–1**

Large garden-bright handmade paper collages on overlaid cut pages present the life cycles of monarchs, painted ladies, tiger swallowtails, and buckeyes in a rhyming flight through fields of flowers. On half- and full-sized pages, every turn of the page brings a surprise; the butterflies and their accompanying flowers seem to burst forth in a riot of color.

GERM: If you're feeling ambitious, bring in a monarch caterpillar on a milkweed stem so children can observe, write about, and draw its stages as the caterpillar changes and emerges as a butterfly. Instructions for creating your own butterfly garden are at the back of the book.

RELATED TITLES: Brown, Ruth. *If at First You Do Not See.* Henry Holt, 1983. / Carle, Eric. *The Very Hungry Caterpillar.* Putnam, 1981. / Edwards, Pamela Duncan. *Clara Caterpillar.* HarperCollins, 2001. / Ernst, Lisa Campbell. *Bubba and Trixie.* Simon & Schuster, 1997. / Hariton, Anca. *Butterfly Story.* Dutton, 1995. / Heiligman, Deborah. *From Caterpillar to Butterfly.* HarperCollins, 1996. / Lavies, Bianca. *Monarch Butterflies: Mysterious Travelers.* Dutton, 1993. / Swope, Sam. *Gotta Go! Gotta Go!* Farrar, 2000. / Taylor, Harriet Peck. *Coyote and the Laughing Butterflies.* Macmillan, 1995.

SUBJECTS: BUTTERFLIES. CATERPILLARS. FLOWERS. INSECTS. METAMORPHOSIS. STORIES IN RHYME.

1604 Elya, Susan Middleton. *Say Hola to Spanish.* **Illus. by Loretta Lopez. Lee & Low, 1996. 1-880000-29-6. 32pp. Gr. K–4**

"Spanish is fun, so give it a try. Hola is hello, adiós is good-bye." In this sprightly rhyming language lesson, you will learn more than 70 common Spanish words. The bright, cheerful gouache and colored pencil illustrations are a great help for understanding each word in context, and the glossary at the back includes the pronunciation and English meaning of each Spanish word, from "accidente" to "un zapatero."

GERM: Your students will effortlessly acquire a vocabulary of more than 70 Spanish words after reading this jazzy and entertaining picture book, a rhyming language lesson where each new word is defined in context.

RELATED TITLES: Dorros, Arthur. *Abuela.* Dutton, 1991. / Elya, Susan Middleton. *Eight Animals Bake a Cake.* Putnam, 2002. / Elya, Susan Middleton. *Eight Animals on the Town.* Putnam, 2000. / Elya, Susan Middleton. *Eight Animals Play Ball.* Putnam, 2003. / Elya, Susan Middleton. *Fairy Trails: A Story Told in English and Spanish.* Bloomsbury, 2005. / Elya, Susan Middleton. *Home at Last.* Lee & Low, 2002. / Elya, Susan Middleton. *Oh, No, Gotta Go!* Putnam, 2003. / Elya, Susan Middleton. *Say Hola to Spanish at the Circus.* Lee & Low Books, 2000. / Elya, Susan Middleton. *Say Hola to Spanish.* Lee & Low, 1996. / Reed, Lynn. *Pedro, His Perro, and the Alphabet Sombrero.* Hyperion, 1995. / Ryan, Pam Muñoz. *Mice and Beans.* Scholastic, 2001. / Sacre, Antonio.

The Barking Mouse. Whitman, 2003. / Soto, Gary. *Chato's Kitchen*. Putnam, 1995. / Soto, Gary. *Snapshots from the Wedding*. Putnam, 1997. / Soto, Gary. *Too Many Tamales*. Putnam, 1993.

SUBJECTS: MULTICULTURAL BOOKS. SPANISH LANGUAGE. STORIES IN RHYME.

1605 Evans, Lezlie. *Can You Count Ten Toes? Count to Ten in Ten Different Languages*. **Illus. by Denis Roche. Houghton Mifflin Mifflin, 1999. 0-395-90499-4. Unp. Gr. K–3**

There are ten objects one can count on each friendly page, with a wide sampling of world languages from Chinese to Zulu, and phonetic spellings beside each word so children can sound it out easily.

GERM: The map at the back will help children locate where in the world each language is spoken. Plot each country's place on the globe as you count to ten in that language.

RELATED TITLES: Aliki. *Hello! Good-bye!* Greenwillow, 1996. / Leventhal, Debra. *What Is Your Language?* Dutton, 1994. / Park, Linda Sue. *Yum! Yuck! A Foldout Book of People Sounds*. Charlesbridge, 2005. / Scieszka, Jon. *Baloney (Henry P.)*. Viking, 2001. / Stojic, Manya. *Hello World! Greetings in 42 Languages Across the Globe*. Scholastic, 2002. / Weiss, Nicki. *The World Turns Round and Round*. Greenwillow, 2000.

SUBJECTS: COUNTING BOOKS. LANGUAGE. MULTICULTURAL BOOKS.

1606 Frankenhuyzen, Robbyn Smith van. *Saving Samantha: A True Story*. **Illus. by Gijsbert van Frankenhuyzen. Sleeping Bear, 2004. 1-58536-220-4. Unp. Gr. 1–4**

While walking with her dog to the farthest corner of her 40-acre family farm, the author found a young fox pup caught in a rusty trap. She freed it, took it home, set its broken front leg in a plaster cast, and named it Samantha. A combination of third-person narrative, the author's own diary entries, and warm, stately oil paintings by her husband, Gijsbert, make this account of Samantha's two-month recovery and reintroduction into the wild compelling and inspiring.

GERM: Read aloud the fox facts at the back of the book, and have listeners refer to the narrative to match the facts with Samantha's behavior. Discuss: How does the treatment of foxes in folklore and fiction dovetail or diverge from the lives of real foxes?

RELATED TITLES: Bunting, Eve. *Red Fox Running*. Clarion, 1993. / Hastings, Selina. *Reynard the Fox*. Tambourine, 1991. / Oates, Joyce Carol. *Where Is Little Reynard?* HarperCollins, 2003. / Schaefer, Lola M. *Arrowhawk*. Henry Holt, 2004. / Spier, Peter. *The Fox Went Out on a Chilly Night*. Doubleday, 1993. / Ward, Helen. *The Rooster and the Fox*. Millbrook, 2003. / Watson, Wendy. *Fox Went Out on a Chilly Night*. Lothrop, 1994. / Wattenberg, Jane. *Henny-Penny*. Scholastic, 2000.

SUBJECTS: DIARIES. FOXES. RED FOX. WILDLIFE RESCUE.

1607 French, Vivian. *T. Rex*. **Illus. by Alison Bartlett. Candlewick, 2004. 0-7636-2184-6. 29pp. Gr. PreK–1**

In a museum, a boy and his grandfather stop at the dinosaur exhibit, where the boy asks his granddad question after question about the giant animals. His grandfather tells him everything he knows about Tyrannosaurus Rex, but, to the boy's frustration—"Don't you know? Why don't you know?"—Grandfather can't answer every question—"It was millions and millions of years ago." Though he does give the boy impetus to do some reading and maybe even become a paleontologist someday.

GERM: Make a list with your dino-fans. What do we know? What do we still want to find out about T. Rex? Show how scientists are always learning new facts and discarding old theories with Kathleen V. Kudlinski's *Boy, Were We Wrong About Dinosaurs!*

RELATED TITLES: Dodson, Peter. *An Alphabet of Dinosaurs*. Scholastic, 1995. / Kudlinski, Kathleen V. *Boy, Were We Wrong About Dinosaurs!* Dutton, 2005. / Most, Bernard. *How Big Were the Dinosaurs?* Harcourt, 1994. / Nolan, Dennis. *Dinosaur Dreams*. Macmillan, 1990. / Prelutsky, Jack. *Tyrannosaurus Was a Beast*. Greenwillow, 1988. / Sabuda, Robert. *Encyclopedia Prehistorica: Dinosaurs*. Candlewick, 2005. / Stickland, Paul. *Ten Terrible Dinosaurs*. Dutton, 1997. / Stickland, Paul, and Henrietta Stickland. *Dinosaur Roar!* Dutton, 1994. / Wallace, Karen. *I Am a Tyrannosaurus*. Atheneum, 2004. / Yolen, Jane. *How Do Dinosaurs Say Good Night?* Blue Sky/Scholastic, 2000.

SUBJECTS: DINOSAURS. GRANDFATHERS. MUSEUMS.

1608 Friedman, Robin. *The Silent Witness: A True Story of the Civil War*. **Illus. by Claire A. Nivola. Houghton Mifflin, 2005. 0-618-44230-8. Unp. Gr. 3–6**

In 1861, when Lulu McLean was 4, General Beauregard took over Lulu's family's plantation in Manassas, Virginia, as his headquarters for the Confederate Army. After the Battle of Bull Run was fought nearby, Lulu's father moved the family to a house in the small village of Appomattox

Court House, where four years later, Robert E. Lee surrendered to Ulysses S. Grant. Lulu had left her rag doll in the parlor where the surrender was signed, and soldiers dubbed the doll "the silent witness." This true story, with its delicate, somber watercolor and gouache paintings framed against stark white pages, looks at the civilian side of war, interspersed with descriptions of Lincoln's Gettysburg Address, General Sherman's march through the South, and the surrender.

GERM: An Author's Note provides more details of Lulu and her doll, which was taken by a Union officer as a "war trophy" and is now on display in Appomattox Court House National Historic Park. Pair this with two fictional but realistic picture books about the war: Patricia Polacco's *Pink and Say*, about a black soldier who rescues a wounded white soldier, and Ann Turner's *Drummer Boy*, a first-person account of a 13-year-old boy's experiences in battle.

RELATED TITLES: Bartoletti, Susan Campbell. *The Flag Maker*. Illus. by Claire A. Nivola. Houghton Mifflin, 2004. / Fleischman, Paul. *Bull Run*. HarperCollins, 1993. / Kerley, Barbara. *Walt Whitman: Words for America*. Scholastic, 2004. / Polacco, Patricia. *Pink and Say*. Philomel, 1994. / Reit, Seymour. *Behind Rebel Lines: The Incredible Story of Emma Edmonds, Civil War Spy*. Harcourt, 1988. / Turner, Ann. *Drummer Boy*. HarperCollins, 1999.

SUBJECTS: DOLLS. U.S.—HISTORY—CIVIL WAR, 1861–1865. VIRGINIA. WAR.

1609 George, Jean Craighead. *The Tarantula in My Purse, and 172 Other Wild Pets*. Illus. by the author. HarperCollins, 1996. 0-06-023637-2. 134pp. Gr. 4–6

Jean Craighead George, author of more than 60 books, but best known for her Newbery-winning *Julie of the Wolves*, has been a naturalist since childhood, when she raised her first pet, a baby turkey vulture that her entomologist father rescued and brought home to her. The mother of three children (including Twig, who wrote *A Dolphin Named Bob*), Jean encouraged her kids to rescue wild animals that then became part of the household, including Yammer, a screech owl who loved to watch TV; Crowbar, a scrappy little crow they taught to say "Hiya, Babe;" and two white mice that quickly multiplied to 50.

GERM: Each short chapter is a funny and affectionate tribute to a memorable member of their animal menagerie, and the book as a whole is likely to make naturalists of your children, who can then write their own animal memoirs. Also read Farley Mowat's comical childhood memoir, *Owls in the Family*.

RELATED TITLES: Davies, Jacqueline. *The Boy Who Drew Birds: A Story of John James Audubon*. Houghton Mifflin, 2003. / George, Jean Craighead. *Julie of the Wolves*. HarperCollins, 1972. / George, Twig. *A Dolphin Named Bob*. HarperCollins, 1996. / Leslie-Melville, Betty. *Elephant Have the Right of Way: Life with the Wild Animals of Africa*. Doubleday, 1993. / Montgomery, Sy. *The Tarantula Scientist*. Houghton Mifflin, 2004. / Mowat, Farley. *Owls in the Family*. Little, Brown, 1962. / Sobol, Richard. *An Elephant in the Backyard*. Dutton, 2004.

SUBJECTS: NATURALISTS. PETS. WILD ANIMALS AS PETS. WOMEN—BIOGRAPHY.

1610 Gifford, Scott. *Piece=Part=Portion: Fractions=Decimals=Percents*. Illus. by Shmuel Thaler. Tricycle, 2003. 1-58246-102-3. Unp. Gr. 2–4

Fourteen big, clear color photos of children portray situations involving fractions and show different ways to write fractions including decimals and percentages. For example, on the left of one double-page spread, it says "$\frac{1}{10}$ of your toes" and ".10" and "10%." On the right side is a photograph of two kid-sized feet encased in purple socks, with one big toe sticking out.

GERM: This is a simple, clear, and easy-to-visualize way to introduce your fractions lesson. Using an inexpensive disposable or a digital camera, students can assemble and photograph other fraction examples.

RELATED TITLES: Adler, David A. *Fraction Fun*. Holiday House, 1996. / Franco, Betsy. *Counting Our Way to the 100th Day!* McElderry, 2004. / Leedy, Loreen. *Fraction Action*. Holiday House, 1994. / McMillan, Bruce. *Eating Fractions*. Scholastic, 1991. / Nagda, Ann Whitehead, and Cindy Bickel. *Polar Bear Math: Learning About Fractions from Klondike and Snow*. Henry Holt, 2004. / Pinczes, Elinor J. *One Hundred Hungry Ants*. Houghton Mifflin, 1993.

SUBJECTS: DECIMAL FRACTIONS. FRACTIONS. MATHEMATICS. PERCENTAGE.

1611 Greenstein, Elaine. *Ice-Cream Cones for Sale*. Illus. by the author. Scholastic, 2003. 0-439-32728-8. Unp. Gr. 2–4

The question of who created the first ice cream cone, which made a big splash at the World's Fair in St. Louis, Missouri, in 1904, is not an easy one to unravel, since seven different people claimed to have been responsible for its invention. The author of this nonfiction picture book combines facts and speculation to come up with her own conclusions, based on careful research. Monoprints overpainted with gouache give the large illustrations an old-timey feel that meshes well with the light-hearted writing style.

GERM: What a novel way to introduce fiction, nonfiction, and the research process. Have children discuss which statements in the story are facts, conjecture, and rumor. Why are all the facts not known about this simple invention? Compile a list of all the places they think a good researcher could look for information on a given topic. An Author's Note supplies additional information Greenstein discovered in her quest, and a bibliography of the sources she used is included. As a spur to research, send kids on the hunt to discover who invented other popular items, such as the safety pin, the zipper, and Velcro. What other useful things still need to be invented?

RELATED TITLES: Appelbaum, Diana. *Cocoa Ice*. Orchard, 1997. / Cooper, Elisha. *Ice Cream*. Greenwillow, 2002. / Fleischman, Paul. *Weslandia*. Candlewick, 1999. / Hopkinson, Deborah. *Fannie in the Kitchen: The Whole Story from Soup to Nuts of How Fannie Farmer Invented Recipes with Precise Measurements*. Atheneum, 2001. / Jones, Charlotte Foltz. *Accidents May Happen: Fifty Inventions Discovered by Mistake*. Delacorte, 1996. / Jones, Charlotte Foltz. *Eat Your Words: A Fascinating Look at the Language of Food*. Delacorte, 1999. / Lauber, Patricia. *What You Never Knew About Fingers, Forks, and Chopsticks*. Simon & Schuster, 1999. / Murphy, Jim. *Weird and Wacky Inventions*. Random House, 1978. / Priceman, Marjorie. *How to Make an Apple Pie and See the World*. Knopf, 1994. / St. George, Judith. *So You Want to Be an Inventor?* Philomel, 2002. / Swain, Ruth Freeman. *How Sweet It Is (and Was); The History of Candy*. Holiday House, 2003.

SUBJECTS: FAIRS. FOOD. ICE CREAM. INVENTIONS AND INVENTORS.

1612 Guiberson, Brenda Z. *The Emperor Lays an Egg*. Illus. by Joan Daley. Henry Holt, 2001. 0-8050-6204-1. Unp. Gr. PreK–3

Read the strange and true story of how emperor penguins care for their eggs. After the mother penguin lays her egg in May, she transfers it onto the feet of the father, who takes full care of it for 65 days while the mother is off in search of food. Simple hand-painted paper collage illustrations bring a depth of feeling to this most eye-opening picture book, which you can use for units on animals, birds, eggs, continents, Antarctica, winter, and weather. It also models good expository writing (the nonfiction, factual kind), and incorporates fascinating details, a lively writing style, and a narrative that is readable and entertaining while being informative and accurate.

GERM: Find something for kids to balance on top of their feet—a bean bag or even a white index card cut in an oval—and have them try shuffling in a circle to appreciate how the father penguin manages his egg. See how other animal fathers care for their offspring in Sneed B. Collard III's *Animal Dads*.

RELATED TITLES: Collard, Sneed B., III. *Animal Dads*. Houghton Mifflin, 1997. / Esbensen, Barbara Juster. *Great Northern Diver: The Loon*. Little, Brown, 1990. / Geraghty, Paul. *Solo*. Crown, 1996. / Heller, Ruth. *Animals Born Alive and Well*. Grossett, 1982. / Jenkins, Martin. *The Emperor's Egg*. Candlewick, 1999. / Kellogg, Steven. *A Penguin Pup for Pinkerton*. Dial, 2001. / Lewin, Betsy. *Booby Hatch*. Clarion, 1995. / Markle, Sandra. *A Mother's Journey*. Charlesbridge, 2005. / Sayre, April Pulley. *If You Should Meet a Honey Guide*. Houghton Mifflin, 1995. / Webb, Sophie. *My Season with Penguins: An Antarctic Journal*. Houghton Mifflin, 2000.

SUBJECTS: ANIMALS. ANTARCTICA. ARCTIC REGIONS. BIRDS. FATHERS. PENGUINS.

1613 Guiberson, Brenda Z. *Into the Sea*. Illus. by Alix Berenzy. Henry Holt, 1996. 0-8050-2263-5. Unp. Gr. 1–3

It's the sweeping, violet-tinted color pencil and gouache illustrations that will draw you to this nonfiction picture book. From a sea turtle's hatching until her return to land 20 years later to lay her own eggs, we experience the dangers and the daily life of the turtle, first in the tropical sea and then out in the ocean.

GERM: For your oceanography unit, children can search for supplemental information on the other animals the sea turtle encounters, including crabs, jellyfish, barracudas, starfish, plankton, seahorses, sharks, and humpback whales.

RELATED TITLES: Berger, Melvin. *Look Out for Turtles*. HarperCollins, 1992. / Carle, Eric. *Mister Seahorse*. Philomel, 2004. / Cole, Joanna. *The Magic School Bus on the Ocean Floor*. Scholastic, 1992. / Doubilet, Anne. *Under the Sea from A to Z*. Crown, 1991. / Gibbons, Gail. *Sea Turtles*. Holiday, 1995. / Leedy, Loreen. *Tracks in the Sand*. Doubleday, 1993. / Shaw, Alison. *Until I Saw the Sea: A Collection of Seashore Poems*. Henry Holt, 1995.

SUBJECTS: MARINE ANIMALS. OCEAN. SEA TURTLES. TURTLES.

1614 Hall, Zoe. *The Apple Pie Tree*. Illus. by Shari Halpern. Scholastic, 1996. 0-590-62382-6. Unp. Gr. PreK–1

As depicted in soft, appealing collage illustrations, two children watch their apple tree through the year: it blossoms in the spring, the apples grow in the summer, and finally in the fall, they pick the apples and make a delicious pie.

GERM: If you're feeling ambitious, you and your students can make the apple pie recipe that's at the back of the book. Or simply bring in apples for all to enjoy.

RELATED TITLES: Carle, Eric. *Pancakes, Pancakes!* Scholastic, 1990. / Ehlert, Lois. *Pie in the Sky.* Harcourt, 2004. / Elya, Susan Middleton. *Eight Animals Bake a Cake.* Putnam, 2002. / Lerner, Harriet, and Susan Goldhor. *What's So Terrible Sbout Swallowing an Apple Seed?* HarperCollins, 1996. / Polette, Nancy. *The Hole by the Apple Tree: An A–Z Discovery Tale.* Greenwillow, 1992. / Powell, Consie. *Amazing Apples.* Albert Whitman, 2003. / Priceman, Marjorie. *How to Make an Apple Pie and See the World.* Knopf, 1994. / Schertle, Alice. *Down the Road.* Harcourt, 1995. / Sturges, Philemon. *The Little Red Hen (Makes a Pizza).* Dutton, 1999.

SUBJECTS: APPLE TREES. COOKERY. FRUIT. PIES. TREES.

1615 Heiligman, Deborah. *From Caterpillar to Butterfly.* Illus. by Bari Weissman. HarperCollins, 1996. 0-06-024268-X. 32pp. Gr. K–2

In an elementary school classroom, the children observe metamorphosis as the caterpillar in a big glass jar grows, molts, and finally hatches from its chrysalis to become a Painted Lady butterfly, which they release outside the window.

GERM: The pleasant watercolors and informative but personal text of this Let's-Read-and-Find-Out Science series book will be an excellent introduction for your own butterfly unit. Find out how monarch butterflies migrate in Sam Swope's *Gotta Go! Gotta Go!*

RELATED TITLES: Brown, Ruth. *If at First You Do Not See.* Henry Holt, 1983. / Carle, Eric. *The Very Hungry Caterpillar.* Putnam, 1981. / Edwards, Pamela Duncan. *Clara Caterpillar.* HarperCollins, 2001. / Ehlert, Lois. *Waiting for Wings.* Harcourt, 2001. / Ernst, Lisa Campbell. *Bubba and Trixie.* Simon & Schuster, 1997. / Hariton, Anca. *Butterfly Story.* Dutton, 1995. / Lavies, Bianca. *Monarch Butterflies: Mysterious Travelers.* Dutton, 1993. / Swope, Sam. *Gotta Go! Gotta Go!* Farrar, 2000. / Taylor, Harriet Peck. *Coyote and the Laughing Butterflies.* Macmillan, 1995.

SUBJECTS: BUTTERFLIES. CATERPILLARS. INSECTS.

1616 Heller, Ruth. *Color.* Illus. by the author. Putnam, 1995. 0-399-22815-2. 46pp. Gr. 2–6

Explore how artwork goes from the artist's paper onto the printed page in this spirited and lavishly illustrated demonstration of how the three primary colors and black are mixed in glorious combinations through printing technology.

GERM: Students will start to examine the books they are reading with a more practiced and critical eye. Tie this in to a study of how books are made. Look at the color wheel in Eric Carle's picture book *Hello, Red Fox.* Find out more about illustrator Ruth Heller and her work in her autobiography for children, *Fine Lines.*

RELATED TITLES: Barrows, Allison. *The Artist's Model.* Carolrhoda, 1996. / Carle, Eric. *Hello, Red Fox.* Simon & Schuster, 1998. / Christelow, Eileen. *What Do Illustrators Do?* Clarion, 1999. / Heller, Ruth. *Fine Lines.* Richard C. Owen, 1996. / Leedy, Loreen. *Look at My Book: How Kids Can Write and Illustrate Terrific Books.* Holiday House, 2004. / Stevens, Janet. *From Pictures to Words: A Book About Making a Book.* Holiday House, 1995.

SUBJECTS: ARTISTS. BOOKS AND READING. COLOR. ILLUSTRATORS.

1617 Henderson, Douglas. *Asteroid Impact.* Illus. by the author. Dial, 2000. 0-8037-2500-0. 40pp. Gr. 3–8

What happened 65 million years ago to bring the late Cretaceous Period to an abrupt end? Scientists have evidence that an asteroid, 6 miles wide and traveling 18 miles per second, hit Earth. Good-bye Cretaceous Period, and all the dinosaurs. This reads like a horror novel, with lots of juicy scientific explanations; and an adventure story, with scary but masterful paintings. Plus, the dramatic, evocative prose will suck kids in and leave them gasping.

GERM: Read this aloud to wind up your dinosaur unit with a real bang.

RELATED TITLES: Facklam, Margery. *And Then There Was One: The Mysteries of Extinction.* Little, Brown, 1990. / Gillette, J. Lynett. *Dinosaur Ghosts: The Mystery of Coelophysis.* Dial, 1997. / Goodman, Susan E. *On This Spot: An Expedition Back Through Time.* Greenwillow, 2004. / Hooper, Meredith. *The Pebble in My Pocket: A History of Our Earth.* Viking, 1996. / Jenkins, Steve. *Life on Earth: The Story of Evolution.* Houghton Mifflin, 2002. / Larson, Peter L. *Bones Rock! Everything You Need to Know to Be a Paleontologist.* Invisible Cities, 2004. / Marrin, Albert. *Secrets from the Rocks: Dinosaur Hunting with Roy Chapman Andrews.* Dutton, 2002. / Moss, Jeff. *Bone Poems.* Workman, 1997. / Simon, Seymour. *Earth: Our Planet in Space.* Simon & Schuster, 2003.

SUBJECTS: ANIMALS, EXTINCT. ASTEROIDS. ASTRONOMY. DINOSAURS. EXTINCTION (BIOLOGY). SCIENCE.

1618 Hooper, Meredith. *The Pebble in My Pocket: A History of Our Earth.* **Illus. by Chris Coady. Viking, 1996. 0-670-86259-2. Unp. Gr. 3–6**

"Pick up a pebble and you are holding a little piece of history of our planet." In an engrossing and fact-laden nonfiction picture book, we are treated to a trip back in geological time to trace the pebble's origin in a volcanic eruption 480 million years ago and its subsequent development.

GERM: The expansive and lush paintings are a visual feast, and the intriguing text will send children to the great outdoors to find a pebble to ponder and research in rock books. Construct a timeline across a wall to help children grasp the concept of the book's time frame. Note the ten rules for finding a perfect rock in Byrd Baylor's classic picture book *Everybody Needs a Rock,* and see what other rules your collectors can develop.

RELATED TITLES: Baylor, Byrd. *Everybody Needs a Rock.* Simon & Schuster, 1974. / Christian, Peggy. *If You Find a Rock.* Harcourt, 2000. / Dengler, Marianna. *The Worry Stone.* Northland, 1996. / Goodman, Susan E. *On This Spot: An Expedition Back Through Time.* Greenwillow, 2004. / Hiscock, Bruce. *The Big Rock.* Atheneum, 1988. / Hurst, Carol Otis. *Rocks in His Head.* Greenwillow, 2001. / Jenkins, Steve. *Life on Earth: The Story of Evolution.* Houghton Mifflin, 2002. / Kimmel, Eric A. *Anansi and the Moss-Covered Rock.* Holiday House, 1990. / Marrin, Albert. *Secrets from the Rocks: Dinosaur Hunting with Roy Chapman Andrews.* Dutton, 2002. / Moss, Jeff. *Bone Poems.* Workman, 1997. / Polacco, Patricia. *My Ol' Man.* Philomel, 1995. / Steig, William. *Sylvester and the Magic Pebble.* Simon & Schuster, 1988.

SUBJECTS: EARTH. GEOLOGY. ROCKS. SCIENCE.

1619 Hunter, Ryan Ann. *Into the Air: An Illustrated Timeline of Flight.* **Illus. by Yan Nascimbene. National Geographic, 2003. 0-7922-5120-2. Unp. Gr. 3–6**

From the first giant dragonflies 325 million years ago to famous firsts in aviation, the history of flight is laid out sequentially in a handsome picture book.

GERM: Each of the boxed illustrations and accompanying one-sentence facts about persevering flyers, both animal and mechanical, provides a topic for report writers to research more thoroughly.

RELATED TITLES: Adler, David A. *A Picture Book of Amelia Earhart.* Holiday House, 1998. / Brown, Don. *Ruth Law Thrills a Nation.* Ticknor & Fields, 1993. / Burleigh, Robert. *Flight: The Journey of Charles Lindbergh.* Philomel, 1991. / Busby, Peter. *First to Fly: How Wilbur and Orville Wright Invented the Airplane.* Random House, 2003. / Collins, Mary. *Airborne: A Photobiography of Wilbur and Orville Wright.* National Geographic, 2003. / Freedman, Russell. *The Wright Brothers: How They Invented the Airplane.* Holiday House, 1991. / Old, Wendie. *To Fly: The Story of the Wright Brothers.* Clarion, 2002. / Szabo, Corinne. *Sky Pioneer: A Photobiography of Amelia Earhart.* National Geographic, 1997. / Weitzman, David. *Model T: How Henry Ford Built a Legend.* Crown, 2002.

SUBJECTS: AERONAUTICS. AIR PILOTS. AIRPLANES. FLIGHT. SCIENCE.

1620 Jackson, Ellen. *It's Back to School We Go! First Day Stories from Around the World.* **Illus. by Jan Davey Ellis. Millbrook, 2003. 0-7613-2562-X. 32pp. Gr. K–3**

Eleven children, ages 6 to 9, from six continents, describe what they wore for the first day of school and what they did when they arrived there. Each facing page provides more background on what life is like for children in that country.

GERM: Put together charts and graphs comparing foods, interests, sports, dress, and customs for each country. Go back in time with Jackson's similarly formatted *Turn of the Century,* which profiles one child per century, from the year 1000 all the way up to 2000.

RELATED TITLES: Baer, Edith. *This Is the Way We Go to School: A Book About Children Around the World.* Scholastic, 1990. / Dannenberg, Julie. *First Day Jitters.* Charlesbridge, 2000. / Dorros, Arthur. *This Is My House.* Scholastic, 1992. / Jackson, Ellen. *Turn of the Century.* Charlesbridge, 1998. / Lankford, Mary. *Birthdays Around the World.* HarperCollins, 2002. / Lankford, Mary. *Hopscotch Around the World.* Morrow, 1992. / Lankford, Mary. *Jacks Around the World.* Morrow, 1996. / Lasky, Kathryn. *Lunch Bunnies.* Little, Brown, 1996. / Lewin, Ted. *Market!* Lothrop, 1996. / Lobel, Anita. *Away from Home.* Greenwillow, 1994. / Poydar, Nancy. *First Day, Hooray!* Holiday House, 1999. / Slate, Joseph. *Miss Bindergarten Gets Ready for Kindergarten.* Dutton, 1996. / Stuve-Bodeen, Stephanie. *Elizabeti's School.* Lee & Low, 2002. / Weiss, Nicki. *The World Turns Round and Round.* Greenwillow, 2000.

SUBJECTS: EDUCATION. FIRST DAY OF SCHOOL. MULTICULTURAL BOOKS. SCHOOLS.

1621 Jackson, Ellen. *Turn of the Century.* **Illus. by Jan Davey Ellis. Charlesbridge, 1998. 0-88106-369-X. Unp. Gr. 2–6**

In a cheerful nonfiction picture book, peer into the lives of 11 children, ages 7 to 10, on New

Year's Day of each new century, starting with the year 1000. In England, we meet first a peasant boy, and then a wealthy "lady," a page, a merchant's son, a chambermaid, a ship's boy, and an earl's daughter, all of whom tell us about their day. The final three centuries showcase children from four different states in the United States. The highly detailed watercolor and colored pencil illustrations show a cross-section of the children's homes, their clothing, and customs. An additional list of facts for each century sums up advancements, games, food, sanitation, and general customs, all of which conspire to make us grateful to be living now and not then.

GERM: Children will be keen to investigate other time periods by reading historical fiction or doing research. Start a Millennium Project in which children work in groups to write about their lives and accouterments, and draw themselves in a 21st-century setting. Next they can extend their knowledge back a century by interviewing elderly family members and parents, or project what they think their great-grandchildren's lives will be like in 2100.

RELATED TITLES: Collard, Sneed B., III. *1,000 Years Ago on Planet Earth*. Houghton Mifflin, 1999. / Dillon, Leo, and Diane Dillon. *To Everything There Is a Season*. Scholastic, 1998. / Jackson, Ellen. *It's Back to School We Go! First Day Stories from Around the World*. Millbrook, 2003. / McGovern, Ann. *If You Lived in Colonial Times*. Scholastic, 1969. / Millard, Ann. *A Street Through Time*. DK, 1998. / Shannon, George. *This Is the Bird*. Houghton Mifflin, 1997. / Smith, David J. *If the World Were a Village: A Book About the World's People*. Kids Can, 2002. / Thermes, Jennifer. *When I Was Built*. Henry Holt, 2001. / Waters, Kate. *Samuel Eaton's Day: A Day in the Life of a Pilgrim Boy*. Scholastic, 1993. / Waters, Kate. *Sarah Morton's Day: A Day in the Life of a Pilgrim Girl*. Scholastic, 1989. / Yolen, Jane. *House, House*. Marshall Cavendish, 1998.

SUBJECTS: CHILDREN. GREAT BRITAIN—HISTORY. U.S.—HISTORY. U.S.—SOCIAL LIFE AND CUSTOMS.

1622 Jacobs, Francine. *Lonesome George, the Giant Tortoise*. Illus. by Jean Cassels. Walker, 2003. 0-8027-8865-3. Unp. Gr. 2–6

George, the last surviving saddleback tortoise on Pinta Island in the Galápagos, was found in 1972. Wardens from Galápagos National Park took him to the Charles Darwin Research Station, where he lives today. Realistic gouache paintings depict George's life and habitat.

GERM: Have listeners recall and pull in supporting details from the text as they discuss why George is the last saddleback tortoise. For more information, check out <www.darwin foundation.org> and <www.galapagos.org>. Read aloud, this will provide a nice intro to your endangered animals unit. There's a chapter on Lonesome George in Margery Facklam's *And Then There Was One: The Mysteries of Extinction*.

RELATED TITLES: Facklam, Margery. *And Then There Was One: The Mysteries of Extinction*. Sierra Club/Little, Brown, 1990. / Fleming, Candace. *Sunny Boy! The Life and Times of a Tortoise*. Farrar, 2005. / Leedy, Loreen. *Tracks in the Sand*. Doubleday, 1993. / Lewin, Betsy. *Booby Hatch*. Clarion, 1995. / McDermott, Gerald. *Jabutí the Tortoise: A Trickster Tale from the Amazon*. Harcourt, 2001. / Wells, Robert E. *What's Older Than a Giant Tortoise?* Albert Whitman, 2004.

SUBJECTS: ENDANGERED SPECIES. GALAPAGOS ISLANDS. TURTLES.

1623 Jefferson, Thomas. *The Declaration of Independence: The Words That Made America*. Illus. by Sam Fink. Scholastic, 2002. 0-439-40700-1. 160pp. Gr. 4–12

Realizing how much he had enjoyed reading the text of Jefferson's Declaration of Independence inspired artist Sam Fink to write down the words in his own hand and to illustrate each phrase of the document. "When in the course of human events," starts the Declaration, written in June 1776 and adopted by the Second Continental Congress on July 4. Fink's accompanying cross-hatched pen-and-ink and watercolors in the style of political cartoons not only help to explain each phrase, but add a comic air of celebration. About his simple, large, black and yellow hand-lettered text on each facing page, Fink says, "Thomas Jefferson's words are powerful and need no further embellishment from me."

GERM: Prepare a choral reading of the Declaration, with each pair of readers declaiming two or three of the 36 sentences. The full text is included in the back, along with a chronology of events leading to the Declaration, a glossary, a bibliography including print material and Web sites, and an index. In the same vein, *We the Kids: The Preamble to the Constitution of the United States* by David Catrow explains the big ideas of that 52-word one-sentence statement through riotously humorous kid- and dog-infused illustrations.

RELATED TITLES: Catrow, David. *We the Kids: The Preamble to the Constitution of the United States*. Dial, 2002. / Cheney, Lynne. *America: A Patriotic Primer*. Simon & Schuster, 2002. / Fritz, Jean. *Shh! We're Writing the Constitution*. Putnam, 1987. / Harness, Cheryl. *George Washington*. National Geographic, 2000. / Keenan, Sheila.

O, Say Can You See? America's Symbols, Landmarks, and Inspiring Words. Scholastic, 2004. / Maestro, Betsy, and Giulio Maestro. *A More Perfect Union: The Story of Our Constitution*. Lothrop, 1987.

SUBJECTS: JEFFERSON, THOMAS. PRESIDENTS. U.S.—DECLARATION OF INDEPENDENCE. U.S.—HISTORY—REVOLUTION, 1775–1783.

1624 Jenkins, Steve. *Actual Size.* **Illus. by the author. Houghton Mifflin, 2004. 0-618-37594-5. Unp. Gr. PreK–6**

The eighteen animals in this spectacular science picture book, illustrated with eye-popping collages of cut and torn paper, are shown actual size. Children can compare and contrast the smallest fish (dwarf goby, length: ⅓ inch) with the 12-inch eye of the giant squid. They can examine the biggest spider (the 12-inch Goliath birdeater tarantula) and open out a three-page spread showing the head of the world's largest reptile (the man-eating saltwater crocodile).

GERM: The final pages provide a paragraph of facts about each of the animals. Children can measure an animal (such as an ant, a beetle, or a cat), draw it actual size, and then find out a few fascinating facts about it. Use this as an introduction to a measuring unit in which children measure and draw something actual size, taking care to make it as realistic as possible. Art teachers can tie in a lesson on collage and papermaking, using Jenkins's illustrations for inspiration and technique. Also show the companion book, *Prehistoric Actual Size.*

RELATED TITLES: Collard, Sneed B., III. *Animal Dads.* Houghton Mifflin, 1997. / DuQuette, Keith. *They Call Me Woolly: What Animal Names Can Tell Us.* Putnam, 2002. / Jenkins, Steve. *Big and Little.* Houghton Mifflin, 1996. / Jenkins, Steve. *Biggest, Strongest, Fastest.* Ticknor & Fields, 1995. / Jenkins, Steve. *Hottest Coldest Highest Deepest.* Houghton Mifflin, 1998. / Jenkins, Steve. *Life on Earth: The Story of Evolution.* Houghton Mifflin, 2002. / Jenkins, Steve. *Prehistoric Actual Size.* Houghton Mifflin, 2005. / Jenkins, Steve. *What Do You Do When Something Wants to Eat You?* Houghton Mifflin, 1997. / Jenkins, Steve, and Robin Page. *What Do You Do With a Tail Like This?* Houghton Mifflin, 2003. / Moser, Madeline. *Ever Heard of an Aardwolf?* Harcourt, 1996. / Prelutsky, Jack. *If Not For the Cat.* Greenwillow, 2004. / Singer, Marilyn. *A Wasp Is Not a Bee.* Henry Holt, 1995. / Wells, Robert E. *Is a Blue Whale the Biggest Thing There Is?* Albert Whitman, 1993.

SUBJECTS: ANIMALS. BODY SIZE. MEASUREMENT. SIZE. SUPERLATIVES.

1625 Jenkins, Steve. *Big and Little.* **Illus. by the author. Houghton Mifflin, 1996. 0-398-72664-6. Unp. Gr. K–3**

Eleven pairs of related animals are displayed in scale to show their relative sizes, big and small. A one-sentence description and textured cut-paper collage pairs tiger and Siamese cat, ostrich and ruby-throated hummingbird, and African rock python and coral snake.

GERM: Integrate science and math by measuring the actual size of each animal. First, measure each animal on the page and then multiply by eight (one inch equals eight inches) for its true dimensions. Notes at the back of the book provide interesting facts about each creature. For more measuring, also read Jenkins's *Actual Size.*

RELATED TITLES: Collard, Sneed B., III. *Animal Dads.* Houghton Mifflin, 1997. / Jenkins, Steve. *Actual Size.* Houghton Mifflin, 2004. / Jenkins, Steve. *Biggest, Strongest, Fastest.* Ticknor & Fields, 1995. / Jenkins, Steve. *What Do You Do When Something Wants to Eat You?* Houghton Mifflin, 1997. / Jenkins, Steve, and Robin Page. *What Do You Do With a Tail Like This?* Houghton Mifflin, 2003. / Moser, Madeline. *Ever Heard of an Aardwolf?* Harcourt, 1996.

SUBJECTS: ANIMALS. SIZE. SUPERLATIVES.

1626 Jenkins, Steve. *Biggest, Strongest, Fastest.* **Illus. by the author. Ticknor & Fields, 1995. 0-395-69701-8. Unp. Gr. K–3**

In a visually appealing nonfiction animal record book filled with fabulous facts and illustrated with cut-paper collages, see how much your students know about animal record-breakers, including the African elephant (the largest land animal), the ant (the strongest animal for its size), the cheetah (the fastest runner), and the blue whale (the biggest animal on Earth). Each double-page spread contains one fact, a large illustration of the animal, a smaller silhouette of the animal next to a human to show relative size, and a few extra salient facts.

GERM: The last page gives a chart of facts that you can use to kick off animal-based research projects and to find other superlatives.

RELATED TITLES: Barrett, Judi. *Things That Are Most in the World.* Atheneum, 1998. / Feldman, Judy. *The Alphabet in Nature.* Children's Press, 1991. / Jenkins, Steve. *Actual Size.* Houghton Mifflin, 2004. / Jenkins, Steve. *Big and Little.* Houghton Mifflin, 1996. / Jenkins, Steve. *Hottest Coldest Highest Deepest.* Houghton Mifflin, 1998. / Jenkins, Steve. *What Do You Do When Something Wants to Eat You?* Houghton Mifflin, 1997. / Jenkins, Steve, and Robin Page. *What Do You Do With a Tail Like This?* Houghton Mifflin, 2003. / Moser, Madeline. *Ever Heard of an Aardwolf?* Harcourt, 1996. / Most, Bernard. *Zoodles.* Harcourt, 1992. / Simon, Seymour. *Animal Fact, Animal Fable.* Crown, 1992. / Wells, Robert E. *Is a Blue Whale the Biggest Thing There Is?* Albert Whitman, 1993. / Wells, Robert E. *What's Faster Than a Speeding Cheetah?* Albert Whitman, 1997.

SUBJECTS: ANIMALS. SIZE. SUPERLATIVES.

1627 Jenkins, Steve. *Hottest Coldest Highest Deepest.* Illus. by the author. Houghton Mifflin, 1998. 0-395-89999-0. Unp. Gr. K–3

Tour Earth's natural wonders and discover the longest river (the Nile: 4,145 miles), highest mountain (Mount Everest: 29,028 feet), and coldest place (Vostok, Antarctica, at 129° below zero). Each double-page spread of visually stunning paper collage illustrations depicts a geographical record-holder and includes a small inset map and an additional paragraph of fascinating supporting facts.

GERM: Not only will you travel the world vicariously, but the mathematical comparisons encompass measurements in miles, feet, inches, and temperature, making this an across-the-curriculum star for math, science, and geography. Children can search out supporting information about each of the 14 sites in books, encyclopedias, and on the Internet, and can find more facts in Steve Jenkins's animal record books: *Actual Size*; *Big and Little*; and *Biggest, Strongest, Fastest.* As part of a language lesson on superlatives, also tie in Judi Barrett's imaginative picture book *Things That Are Most in the World.*

RELATED TITLES: Barrett, Judi. *Things That Are Most in the World.* Atheneum, 1998. / Burleigh, Robert. *Earth from Above for Young Readers.* Abrams, 2002. / Collard, Sneed B., III. *Animal Dads.* Houghton Mifflin, 1997. / Jenkins, Steve. *Actual Size.* Houghton Mifflin, 2004. / Jenkins, Steve. *Big and Little.* Houghton Mifflin, 1996. / Jenkins, Steve. *Biggest, Strongest, Fastest.* Ticknor & Fields, 1995. / Jenkins, Steve. *What Do You Do When Something Wants to Eat You?* Houghton Mifflin, 1997. / Scillian, Devin. *P Is for Passport: A World Alphabet.* Sleeping Bear, 2003.

SUBJECTS: GEOGRAPHY. SIZE. SUPERLATIVES.

1628 Jenkins, Steve. *Life on Earth: The Story of Evolution.* Illus. by the author. Houghton Mifflin, 2002. 0-618-16476-6. 40pp. Gr. 3–6

To help put human beings in perspective with the rest of the natural world's history, this nonfiction picture book illustrated with exquisite cut- and torn-paper collage animals, describes how life evolved and how Charles Darwin developed his theories of evolution, including natural selection, variation and mutation, and extinction.

GERM: Using the 24-hour timeline at the back of the book, measure out the events listed using a long hallway, with students standing at the markers for different life forms appearing on Earth. Consult Jenkins's *Prehistoric Actual Size* to see what some of the ancient animals looked like.

RELATED TITLES: Anholt, Laurence. *Stone Girl, Bone Girl: The Story of Mary Anning.* Orchard, 1999. / Facklam, Margery. *And Then There Was One: The Mysteries of Extinction.* Little, Brown, 1990. / Goodman, Susan E. *On This Spot: An Expedition Back Through Time.* Greenwillow, 2004. / Jenkins, Steve. *Biggest, Strongest, Fastest.* Ticknor & Fields, 1995. / Jenkins, Steve. *Prehistoric Actual Size.* Houghton Mifflin, 2005. / Jenkins, Steve. *What Do You Do When Something Wants to Eat You?* Houghton Mifflin, 1997. / Kerley, Barbara. *The Dinosaurs of Waterhouse Hawkins.* Scholastic, 2001. / Marrin, Albert. *Secrets from the Rocks: Dinosaur Hunting with Roy Chapman Andrews.* Dutton, 2002. / Moss, Jeff. *Bone Poems.* Workman, 1997. / Strauss, Rochelle. *Tree of Life: The Incredible Biodiversity of Life on Earth.* Kids Can, 2004.

SUBJECTS: ANIMALS. ANIMALS, EXTINCT. EVOLUTION (BIOLOGY). SCIENCE.

1629 Jenkins, Steve. *What Do You Do When Something Wants to Eat You?* Illus. by the author. Houghton Mifflin, 1997. 0-395-82514-8. 32pp. Gr. K–2

This startling and engrossing text, made even more exciting by the artist's extraordinary collages, informs us about ways animals defend themselves against predators, from the octopus who squirts black ink to the pangolin who rolls into an armor-plated ball.

GERM: Before turning each page to reveal the answer, ask your animal lovers to predict, recall, or infer what each animal's singular defense strategy is. Make a chart of the different defenses, and list other animals that use each one. Brainstorm a list of other animal defenses, from hissing cats to quill-laden porcupines.

RELATED TITLES: Heller, Ruth. *Animals Born Alive and Well.* Grossett, 1982. / Jenkins, Steve. *Actual Size.* Houghton Mifflin, 2004. / Jenkins, Steve. *Big and Little.* Houghton Mifflin, 1996. / Jenkins, Steve. *Biggest,*

Strongest, Fastest. Ticknor & Fields, 1995. / Jenkins, Steve, and Robin Page. *What Do You Do With a Tail Like This?* Houghton Mifflin, 2003. / Simon, Seymour. *Animal Fact, Animal Fable*. Crown, 1987.

SUBJECTS: ANIMAL DEFENSES. ANIMALS.

1630 Jenkins, Steve, and Robin Page. ***What Do You Do With a Tail Like This?*** **Illus. by the authors. Houghton Mifflin, 2003. 0-618-25628-8. Unp. Gr. PreK–3**

Take a jaunt through the animal kingdom to identify the noses, ears, tails, eyes, mouths, and feet of a variety of familiar (mole, alligator) and not so familiar (water strider, archerfish, blue-footed booby, giant anteater) creatures, 30 in all.

GERM: After reading the text, ask your children to act out each animal's use of senses and body parts in creative drama. Children will pore over each of Jenkins's large, appealing, detailed cut- and torn-paper collage animals, and identify the family of each: insect, reptile and amphibian, fish, bird, or mammal. At the back of the book is an additional paragraph and small reproduction of each animal illustration. Working in pairs or small groups, students can select an animal and, using books, encyclopedias, or the Internet, read about and write a report about its other remarkable qualities.

RELATED TITLES: Collard, Sneed B., III. *Animal Dads*. Houghton Mifflin, 1997. / DuQuette, Keith. *They Call Me Woolly: What Animal Names Can Tell Us*. Putnam, 2002. / Jenkins, Steve. *Actual Size*. Houghton Mifflin, 2004. / Jenkins, Steve. *Big and Little*. Houghton Mifflin, 1996. / Jenkins, Steve. *Biggest, Strongest, Fastest*. Ticknor & Fields, 1995. / Jenkins, Steve. *What Do You Do When Something Wants to Eat You?* Houghton Mifflin, 1997. / Jolivet, Joëlle. *Zoo-ology*. Roaring Brook, 2003. / Moser, Madeline. *Ever Heard of an Aardwolf?* Harcourt, 1996. / Stojic, Manya. *Rain*. Crown, 2000.

SUBJECTS: ANIMALS. CREATIVE DRAMA. EARS. EYES. FOOT. MOUTHS. NOSES. SENSES AND SENSATION. TAILS.

1631 Jones, Charlotte Foltz. ***Accidents May Happen: Fifty Inventions Discovered by Mistake.*** **Illus. by John O'Brien. Delacorte, 1996. 0-385-32162-7. 86pp. Gr. 4–8**

Find out how common objects—raisins, rayon, dynamite—were developed or came about by accident. As the author notes, "It takes intelligence, creativity, and often a fresh approach to make something out of an accident."

GERM: As your junior scientists work on their own inventions and discoveries, also read them Jones's *Mistakes That Worked: 40 Familiar Inventions and How They Came to Be* and Judith St. George's *So You Want to Be an Inventor*.

RELATED TITLES: Delano, Marie Ferguson. *Inventing the Future: A Photobiography of Thomas Alva Edison*. National Geographic, 2002. / Fleischman, Paul. *Weslandia*. Candlewick, 1999. / Gardiner, John Reynolds. *Top Secret*. Little, Brown, 1985. / Greenstein, Elaine. *Ice-Cream Cones for Sale*. Scholastic, 2003. / Jones, Charlotte Foltz. *Eat Your Words: A Fascinating Look at the Language of Food*. Delacorte, 1999. / Jones, Charlotte Foltz. *Mistakes That Worked*. Doubleday, 1991. / Murphy, Jim. *Weird and Wacky Inventions*. Random House, 1978. / Old, Wendie. *To Fly: The Story of the Wright Brothers*. Clarion, 2002. / St. George, Judith. *So You Want to Be an Inventor?* Philomel, 2002. / Wulffson, Don. *The Kid Who Invented the Popsicle: And Other Surprising Stories About Inventions*. Dutton, 1997. / Wulffson, Don. *Toys: Amazing Stories Behind Some Great Inventions*. Henry Holt, 2000.

SUBJECTS: INVENTIONS AND INVENTORS. SCIENCE. SCIENTISTS.

1632 Kalman, Maira. ***Fireboat: The Heroic Adventures of the John J. Harvey.*** **Illus. by the author. Putnam, 2002. 0-399-23953-7. Unp. Gr. 1–8**

For more than 50 years, until it was sidelined in 1995, the *John J. Harvey* fought fires along New York City's piers. A group of friends bought the boat and restored it. "But then on September 11, 2001, something so huge and horrible happened that the whole world shook." Maira Kalman's usual quirky, detailed gouache paintings and portraits in this astonishing and groundbreaking true picture book about 9/11 range from friendly and intimate to huge and catastrophic. Though she shows the Twin Towers exploding in smoke and flames, she brings us back to the people, the heroes of that awful day, including the crew of the *John J. Harvey* who rushed to the scene, where they helped to fight the fires and pumped water to the fire trucks for four days and nights.

GERM: Our world has changed since 9/11, and we're still struggling with the fallout. How do we handle political trauma with our kids? As the saying goes, think globally, act locally. Ask your students to recall large or small acts of kindness, compassion, and selflessness they have participated in or witnessed in their lives and how they have been affected or changed. What can we do to make the world a better place?

RELATED TITLES: Borden, Louise. *The Little Ships: The Heroic Rescue at Dunkirk in World War II.* McElderry, 1997. / Bunting, Eve. *A Picnic in October.* Harcourt, 1999. / Cooney, Barbara. *Miss Rumphius.* Viking, 1982. / Demarest, Chris L. *Firefighters A to Z.* McElderry, 2000. / Gerstein, Mordicai. *The Man Who Walked Between the Towers.* Roaring Brook, 2003. / Heard, Georgia, comp. *This Place I Know: Poems of Comfort.* Candlewick, 2002. / Jakobsen, Kathy. *My New York.* Little, Brown, 2003. / Osborne, Mary Pope. *New York's Bravest.* Knopf, 2002. / Roth, Susan L. *It's Still a Dog's New York.* National Geographic, 2002. / Weitzman, Jacqueline Preiss. *You Can't Take a Balloon into the Metropolitan Museum.* Dial, 1998. / Winter, Jeanette. *The Librarian of Basra: A True Story from Iraq.* Harcourt, 2005. / Winter, Jeanette. *September Roses.* Farrar, 2004.

SUBJECTS: BOATS AND BOATING. DISASTERS. FIRE. FIREFIGHTERS. NEW YORK CITY. RIVERS. SEPTEMBER 11 TERRORIST ATTACKS, 2001. TERRORISM. WORLD TRADE CENTER (NEW YORK, NY).

1633 Kerley, Barbara. *A Cool Drink of Water.* Illus. with photos. National Geographic, 2002. 0-7922-6723-0. Unp. Gr. PreK–2

"Somewhere, right now, someone is drinking water . . ." Full-page color photos give a global glimpse of people drinking water from a river, a well, a fountain, and a pump; and collecting it in buckets, brass pots, a tin cup, and even a burlap bag. A world map plus captioned thumbnail photos at the back of the book identify the countries where each photo was taken and provide additional facts about water.

GERM: A two-page note on water conservation by the National Geographic Society's president, John M. Fahey, Jr., urges all of us to protect Earth's water by reducing our personal water consumption and describes several simple ways to do it, such as turning off the tap water when we brush our teeth. Brainstorm and make a chart of other ways we can conserve Earth's resources. Children can take photos of different types of water and how they use it in their lives. Make a bulletin board of their photos, for which they can write descriptive and fact-filled captions.

RELATED TITLES: Cobb, Vicki. *I Get Wet.* HarperCollins, 2002. / Cole, Joanna. *The Magic School Bus at the Waterworks.* Scholastic, 1988. / Cowan, Catherine. *My Life with the Wave.* Lothrop, 1997. / Dorros, Walter. *Follow the Water from Brook to Ocean.* HarperCollins, 1991. / Frasier, Debra. *The Incredible Water Show.* Harcourt, 2004. / Graham, Joan Bransfield. *Splish Splash.* Ticknor & Fields, 1994. / Hooper, Meredith. *River Story.* Candlewick, 2000. / Lewis, J. Patrick. *Earth Verses and Water Rhymes.* Atheneum, 1991. / Locker, Thomas. *Water Dance.* Harcourt, 1997. / Peters, Lisa Westberg. *Water's Way.* Little, Brown, 1991. / Wick, Walter. *A Drop of Water.* Scholastic, 1997. / Wiesner, David. *Sector 7.* Clarion, 1999.

SUBJECTS: WATER.

1634 Kos, Amy Goldman. *Where Fish Go in Winter and Other Great Mysteries.* Illus. by Laura J. Bryant. Dial, 2002. 0-8037-2704-6. 32pp. Gr. K–3

Fourteen bouncy poems answer common science questions: Why does popcorn pop? How do birds fly? Do islands float? With detailed watercolors, this easy-reader provides scientific information in an appealing and genial package that stimulates curiosity about the natural world.

GERM: Ask your young scientists to make lists of the questions they have about the world around them. For a paired or buddy reading activity that links science, research, and writing, have older students research answers to the younger children's questions and perhaps even try explaining their findings in simple rhyme.

RELATED TITLES: Hopkins, Lee Bennett, comp. *Spectacular Science: A Book of Poems.* Simon & Schuster, 1999. / Jenkins, Steve. *Biggest, Strongest, Fastest.* Ticknor & Fields, 1995. / Lewis, J. Patrick. *Earth Verses and Water Rhymes.* Atheneum, 1991. / Simon, Seymour. *Animal Fact, Animal Fable.* Crown, 1987.

SUBJECTS: ANIMALS. POETRY—SINGLE AUTHOR. QUESTIONS AND ANSWERS. SCIENCE—POETRY.

1635 Krull, Kathleen. *M Is for Music.* Illus. by Stacy Innerst. Harcourt, 2003. 0-15-201438-1. Unp. Gr. K–6

From classical to pop to jazz, scores of music-related words are introduced in alphabet book format, with each letter accompanied by moody, slyly humorous paintings. "A is for anthem and accordion." Examine the "A" page and read the other "A" words there: aria, a cappella, alto, and allegro, along with a portrait of Louis Armstrong playing his horn.

GERM: All of this is starter dough for music teachers. Music-minded children can make "Music Is" alphabet pages, reflecting their own musical preferences. Or they can each pick a letter and research the words on that page—write a definition, sing an example, or bring in CDs for the Beatles, Beethoven, Brahms, Bach, bluegrass, or Broadway. They could then research and create a whole new alphabet on a topic they are passionate about or a curricular tie-in to sports, history, or science.

RELATED TITLES: Aliki. *Ah, Music!* HarperCollins, 2003. / Cox, Judy. *My Family Plays Music.* Holiday House, 2003. / Curtis, Gavin. *The Bat Boy and His Violin.* Simon & Schuster, 1998. / Goss, Linda. *The Frog Who Wanted to Be a Singer.* Orchard, 1996. / Howe, James. *Horace and Morris Join the Chorus (But What About Dolores?).* Atheneum, 2002. / Krull, Kathleen. *I Hear America Singing! Folk Songs for American Families.* Knopf, 2003. / Krull, Kathleen. *Lives of the Musicians: Good Times, Bad Times (And What the Neighbors Thought).* Harcourt, 1993. / Lowery, Linda. *Twist with a Burger, Jitter with a Bug.* Houghton Mifflin, 1995. / Millman, Isaac. *Moses Goes to a Concert.* Farrar, 1998. / Moss, Lloyd. *Music Is.* Putnam, 2003. / Ober, Hal. *How Music Came to the World.* Houghton Mifflin, 1994. / Raschka, Chris. *Charlie Parker Played Bebop.* Orchard, 1992. / Ryan, Pam Muñoz. *When Marian Sang.* Scholastic, 2002. / Wargin, Kathy-jo. *M Is for Melody: A Music Alphabet.* Sleeping Bear, 2004. / Weaver, Tess. *Opera Cat.* Clarion, 2002.

SUBJECTS: ALPHABET BOOKS. MUSIC.

1636 Kudlinski, Kathleen V. *Boy, Were We Wrong About Dinosaurs!* Illus. by S. D. Schindler. Dutton, 2005. 0-525-46978-8. Unp. Gr. K–4

From ancient to recent times, Kudlinski describes in straightforward, logical, easy-to-absorb prose what people once believed about dinosaurs, correcting each misconception and inaccuracy with updated information on what we have learned about dinosaur legs, tails, skin, color, eggs, and extinction. Colorful, detailed, full-bleed pen-and-ink and watercolor illustrations are both handsome and informative for younger children infatuated with dinosaurs.

GERM: For young scientists, it can be an eye-opener to realize that experts in their fields can be wrong and that new discoveries help us update, revise, and discard inaccurate information we once accepted as fact. As a case in point, read Barbara Kerley's extraordinary biography, for which Brian Selznick's illustrations won a Caldecott Honor, *The Dinosaurs of Waterhouse Hawkins*, about the man who constructed the first life-sized dinosaur models, back in 1853. Look at dinosaurs in all their 3-D glory in Robert Sabuda's spectacular pop-up book, *Encyclopedia Prehistorica Dinosaurs.*

RELATED TITLES: French, Vivian. *T. Rex.* Candlewick, 2004. / Gibbons, Gail. *Dinosaur Discoveries.* Holiday House, 2005. / Jenkins, Steve. *Prehistoric Actual Size.* Houghton Mifflin, 2005. / Kerley, Barbara. *The Dinosaurs of Waterhouse Hawkins.* Scholastic, 2001. / Nolan, Dennis. *Dinosaur Dreams.* Macmillan, 1990. / Prelutsky, Jack. *Tyrannosaurus Was a Beast.* Greenwillow, 1988. / Pringle, Laurence. *Dinosaurs! Strange and Wonderful.* Boyds Mills, 1995. / Sabuda, Robert. *Encyclopedia Prehistorica: Dinosaurs.* Candlewick, 2005. / Wallace, Karen. *I Am a Tyrannosaurus.* Atheneum, 2004.

SUBJECTS: DINOSAURS. SCIENCE.

1637 Lauber, Patricia. *What You Never Knew About Fingers, Forks, and Chopsticks.* Illus. by John Manders. Simon & Schuster, 1999. 0-689-80479-2. 32pp. Gr. 2–5

Starting with the Stone Age, the informative text and numerous comical illustrations take us through a history of cooking, eating utensils, and the food habits of mostly the well-to-do, who had time to fuss over such notions as good manners.

GERM: Children can come up with two charts, one listing good manners and the other, bad manners. Compare forks and chopsticks in Ina R. Friedman's charmer of a picture book, *How My Parents Learned to Eat.*

RELATED TITLES: Chandra, Deborah, and Madeline Comora. *George Washington's Teeth.* Farrar, 2003. / Compestine, Ying Chang. *The Story of Chopsticks.* Holiday House, 2001. / Friedman, Ina R. *How My Parents Learned to Eat.* Houghton Mifflin, 1984. / Goldstein, Bobbye S., comp. *What's on the Menu? Food Poems.* Viking, 1992. / Greenstein, Elaine. *Ice-Cream Cones for Sale.* Scholastic, 2003. / Hayes, Joe. *A Spoon for Every Bite.* Orchard, 1996. / Hopkinson, Deborah. *Fannie in the Kitchen.* Atheneum, 2001. / Jackson, Ellen. *Turn of the Century.* Charlesbridge, 1998. / Jones, Charlotte Foltz. *Eat Your Words: A Fascinating Look at the Language of Food.* Delacorte, 1999. / Keller, Charles. *Belly Laughs! Food Jokes and Riddles.* Simon & Schuster, 1990. / Swain, Ruth Freeman. *How Sweet It Is (and Was): The History of Candy.* Holiday House, 2003.

SUBJECTS: EATING CUSTOMS. FOOD HABITS. MULTICULTURAL BOOKS. TABLEWARE.

1638 Leedy, Loreen. *Follow the Money.* Illus. by the author. Holiday House, 2002. 0-8345-1587-2. 32pp. Gr. K–4

A loquacious quarter describes how, after being stamped out at the U.S. Mint, it finds itself being spent all over town—at a grocery store cash register, a soda machine, a parking meter, and a yard sale—before ending up back in the bank. Along the way, lots of money-wise math problems are integrated into the text; use the book as a stepping-off point to an exploration of moolah. In the back are money facts and Web sites, and a glossary of Money Words. You'll love the page numbers, which are tiny pictures of coins or bills adding up to the relevant number.

GERM: Have children bring in their own quarters and write about how the coins came to be in their possession or write stories or math problems from the coin's point of view. Check out Loreen Leedy's Web site to find out more about her books: <www.loreenleedybooks.com>. Look up the word *money* in a thesaurus and read aloud its many synonyms.

RELATED TITLES: Adams, Barbara Johnston. *The Go-Around Dollar.* Four Winds, 1992. / Axelrod, Amy. *Pigs Will Be Pigs.* Simon & Schuster, 1994. / Gill, Shelley, and Deborah Tobola. *The Big Buck Adventure.* Charlesbridge, 2000. / Kennedy, Frances. *The Pickle Patch Bathtub.* Tricycle, 2004. / Leedy, Loreen. *The Great Graph Contest.* Holiday House, 2005. / Leedy, Loreen. *Mapping Penny's World.* Henry Holt, 2000. / Leedy, Loreen. *Measuring Penny.* Atheneum, 1969. / Maestro, Betsy. *The Story of Money.* Clarion, 1993. / Schwartz, David M. *How Much Is a Million?* Lothrop, 1985. / Schwartz, David M. *If You Made a Million.* Lothrop, 1989. / Viorst, Judith. *Alexander Who Used to Be Rich Last Sunday.* Atheneum, 1978. / Williams, Vera B. *A Chair for My Mother.* Greenwillow, 1982. / Zimelman, Nathan. *How the Second Grade Got $8,205.50 to Visit the Statue of Liberty.* Albert Whitman, 1992.

SUBJECTS: COINS. MATHEMATICS. MONEY. PERSONAL NARRATIVES. PERSONIFICATION.

1639 **Leedy, Loreen.** *Look at My Book: How Kids Can Write and Illustrate Terrific Books.* **Illus. by the author. Holiday House, 2004. 0-8234-1590-2. 32pp. Gr. K–5**

A girl, a boy, and a dog think, discuss, draw, and write their way through an idea-packed, child-friendly, and practical instruction manual that lays out each step of the book-writing process. They show us how they brainstorm for story ideas, conduct research, develop characters and setting, make a rough draft and sketches, revise, edit, design a layout, create the art, and, finally, bind the finished books.

GERM: Make your own books, of course. Or put together a classroom or school literary magazine. Other excellent books in the same vein are Eileen Christelow's *What Do Authors Do?* and *What Do Illustrators Do?* and Janet Stevens's *From Pictures to Words: A Book About Making a Book.*

RELATED TITLES: Barrows, Allison. *The Artist's Model.* Carolrhoda, 1996. / Christelow, Eileen. *What Do Authors Do?* Clarion, 1995. / Christelow, Eileen. *What Do Illustrators Do?* Clarion, 1999. / Drescher, Henrik. *Simon's Book.* Lothrop, 1983. / Duke, Kate. *Aunt Isabel Tells a Good One.* Dutton, 1992. / Heller, Ruth. *Color.* Putnam, 1995. / Krull, Kathleen. *The Boy on Fairfield Street: How Ted Geisel Grew Up to Become Dr. Seuss.* Random House, 2004. / Leedy, Loreen. *Follow the Money.* Holiday House, 2002. / Leedy, Loreen. *The Furry News.* Holiday House, 1990. / Leedy, Loreen. *Messages in the Mailbox.* Holiday House, 1991. / Nixon, Joan Lowery. *If You Were a Writer.* Four Winds, 1988. / Pulver, Robin. *Author Day for Room 3T.* Clarion, 2005. / Schotter, Roni. *Nothing Ever Happens on 90th Street.* Orchard, 1997. / Sierra, Judy. *Wild About Books.* Knopf, 2004. / Stevens, Janet. *From Pictures to Words: A Book About Making a Book.* Holiday House, 1995.

SUBJECTS: ARTISTS. AUTHORSHIP. BOOKS AND READING. CREATIVE WRITING. ILLUSTRATORS. WRITING.

1640 **Leedy, Loreen.** *Mapping Penny's World.* **Illus. by the author. Henry Holt, 2000. 0-8050-6178-9. Unp. Gr. 1–3**

Lisa's teacher, Mr. Jayson, gives one of his interactive assignments: he wants his students to make maps of anyplace—a room, a yard, or a neighborhood. He wants them to include: title, key, symbols, scale, compass rose, and labels. Lisa decides to map all of the places her amiable Boston terrier, Penny, hangs out, including the bedroom, the yard, and their hike and bike trails.

GERM: Map skill lessons will be immeasurably pepped up by Lisa's approach to mapping and by a glimpse at Boston terrier Penny's daily routine. Children working on map skills and discovering the beauty and fun of the World Atlas will be itching to map out their pets' best places in response. Get to know Lisa's dog in *Measuring Penny.*

RELATED TITLES: Brisson, Pat. *Your Best Friend, Kate.* Bradbury, 1989. / Cherry, Lynne. *The Armadillo from Amarillo.* Harcourt, 1994. / Guthrie, Woody. *This Land Is Your Land.* Little, Brown, 1998. / Keller, Laurie. *The Scrambled States of America.* Henry Holt, 1998. / Leedy, Loreen. *Follow the Money.* Holiday House, 2002. / Leedy, Loreen. *The Great Graph Contest.* Holiday House, 2005. / Leedy, Loreen. *Measuring Penny.* Henry Holt, 1998. / Long, Melinda. *How I Became a Pirate.* Harcourt, 2003. / McMillan, Bruce. *Mouse Views: What the Class Pet Saw.* Holiday House, 1993. / Meade, Holly. *Inside, Inside, Inside.* Marshall Cavendish, 2005. / Sheldon, Dyan. *Love, Your Bear Pete.* Candlewick, 1994. / Singer, Marilyn. *It's Hard to Read a Map with a Beagle on Your Lap.* Henry Holt, 1993. / Thiesing, Lisa. *The Aliens Are Coming!* Dutton, 2003.

SUBJECTS: DOGS. MAPS AND GLOBES.

1641 Leedy, Loreen. *Measuring Penny.* **Illus. by the author. Henry Holt, 1998. 0-8050-5360-3. 32pp. Gr. 1–3**

Lisa's homework assignment for her teacher, Mr. Jayson, is to measure something using standard units (inches, feet, teaspoons, cups, pounds, minutes, etc.) and nonstandard ones (paper clips, bricks, frogs, etc.). Lisa's Boston terrier, Penny, is her choice of subject; she measures Penny's nose (one inch long), ears (one cotton swab high), paws (3 centimeters wide), weight, temperature, speed (she can run from her bed to her food dish in 6 seconds), and then some.

GERM: Visually appealing acrylics and a nonthreatening approach to math will get your kids raring to measure everything in sight. Pull out the yardstick with Rolf Myller's classic *How Big Is a Foot?*, about a king who commissions for his queen a bed 3 feet wide and 6 feet long, back in the days before a standard foot measurement was established. Also share Leedy's companion book, *Mapping Penny's World.*

RELATED TITLES: Lasky, Kathryn. *The Librarian Who Measured the Earth.* Little, Brown, 1994. / Leedy, Loreen. *Follow the Money.* Holiday House, 2002. / Leedy, Loreen. *Fraction Action.* Holiday House, 1994. / Leedy, Loreen. *The Great Graph Contest.* Holiday House, 2005. / Leedy, Loreen. *Mapping Penny's World.* Henry Holt, 2000. / Leedy, Loreen. *Mission: Addition.* Holiday House, 1997. / Leedy, Loreen. *2 X 2 = BOO! A Set of Spooky Multiplication Stories.* Holiday House, 1995. / Myller, Rolf. *How Big Is a Foot?* Atheneum, 1969. / Schwartz, David M. *How Much Is a Million?* Lothrop, 1985. / Schwartz, David M. *If You Hopped Like a Frog.* Scholastic, 1999. / Wells, Robert E. *Is a Blue Whale the Biggest Thing There Is?* Albert Whitman, 1993. / Wells, Robert E. *What's Smaller Than a Pygmy Shrew?* Albert Whitman, 1995.

SUBJECTS: DOGS. MATHEMATICS. MEASUREMENT.

1642 Lewin, Ted. *Market!* **Illus. by the author. Lothrop, 1996. 0-688-12162-4. Unp. Gr. PreK–3**

Lewin's spectacular watercolors transport us to markets around the world, showing vendors selling potatoes and woolens in Ecuador, thatch and flutes in Nepal, horses in Ireland, fish at the Fulton Fish Market in New York City, and more. You'll salivate at the sight of all the fresh food and almost swear you can hear the sounds of market day.

GERM: Get out your globe and locate each country. Books like these give children wonderful subliminal messages to travel and see everything firsthand when they grow up. You can also use this as a kick-off to a study of countries and cultures. Eve Bunting's *Market Day*, about two girls who spend market day engrossed in the sights, smells, and sounds of their small Irish village, will tie in well here.

RELATED TITLES: Baer, Edith. *This Is the Way We Eat Our Lunch: A Book About Children Around the World.* Scholastic, 1995. / Baer, Edith. *This Is the Way We Go to School: A Book About Children Around the World.* Scholastic, 1990. / Bunting, Eve. *Market Day.* HarperCollins, 1996. / Dorros, Arthur. *This Is My House.* Scholastic, 1992. / Leventhal, Debra. *What Is Your Language?* Dutton, 1994. / Mollel, Tololwa M. *My Rows and Piles of Coins.* Clarion, 1999. / Williams, Karen L. *Tap-Tap.* Clarion, 1994.

SUBJECTS: MARKETS. MULTICULTURAL BOOKS.

1643 Linz, Kathi. *Chickens May Not Cross the Road and Other Crazy (But True) Laws.* **Illus. by Tony Griego. Houghton Mifflin, 2002. 0-618-11257-X. Unp. Gr. 2–6**

Lighthearted full-page pen-and-ink and watercolors illustrate silly laws—all on the record books—such as this one from Lexington, Kentucky: "It is against the law to carry an ice cream cone in a pocket." Interspersed are pages with information about how and why laws are made.

GERM: Use this as a comic way to introduce, list, or compile the laws or rules you have in your own classroom or library. More crazy laws are laid out in *You Can't Eat Peanuts in Church* by Barbara Seuling.

RELATED TITLES: Cheney, Lynne. *America: A Patriotic Primer.* Simon & Schuster, 2002. / Seuling, Barbara. *You Can't Eat Peanuts in Church and Other Little-Known Laws.* Doubleday, 1975. / Stier, Catherine. *If I Were President.* Albert Whitman, 1999.

SUBJECTS: GOVERNMENT. LAW.

1644 McMillan, Bruce. *Nights of the Pufflings.* **Photos by the author. Houghton Mifflin, 1995. 0-395-70810-9. 32pp. Gr. 1–4**

Every April on Heimaey Island, Iceland, millions of North Atlantic puffins return from their winter at sea to lay eggs and raise their chicks. It's the only time they come ashore. Shown from the eyes of a young girl, Halla, and through McMillan's extraordinary color photos, we see these "clowns of the sea" or "sea parrots" flying overhead, carrying translucent fish in their beaks to feed their young. The most amazing thing is that many of the baby pufflings crash-land in the village, where the children stay up late for two weeks to collect them in boxes and then toss them back out to sea.

GERM: With this nifty title, you'll want to talk about bird behavior with books like *Great Northern Diver: The Loon* by Barbara Juster Esbensen or *If You Should Meet a Honey Guide* by April Pulley Sayre.

RELATED TITLES: Demuth, Patricia Brennan. *Cradles in the Trees: The Story of Bird Nests.* Macmillan, 1994. / Esbensen, Barbara Juster. *Great Northern Diver: The Loon.* Little, Brown, 1990. / Peters, Lisa Westberg. *This Way Home.* Henry Holt, 1994. / Sayre, April Pulley. *If You Should Meet a Honey Guide.* Houghton Mifflin, 1995. / Schoenherr, John. *Rebel.* Philomel, 1995. / Yolen, Jane. *Bird Watch: A Book of Poetry.* Philomel, 1990.

SUBJECTS: BIRDS. ICELAND. PUFFINS.

1645   McNulty, Faith. *If You Decide to Go to the Moon.* **Illus. by Steven Kellogg. Scholastic, 2005. 0-590-48359-5. Unp. Gr. K–3**

"If you decide to go to the moon in your own rocket ship, read this book before you start." So begins a resplendent you-are-there nonfiction picture book with sensational full-bleed paintings by the great Steven Kellogg. Follow an eager blonde-haired boy as he blasts off and rockets solo to the moon, takes a moon walk, and looks out over the gray sand and stone into the blackness of space. On his way back to Earth, the clouds and continents and seas appear, a swirling ball of color in the black void. A four-page foldout in technicolor displays a majestic sweep of biomes; animals of land, sea, and air; people and buildings through history; and a multicultural mix of children leaping into a lake.

GERM: Yes, this is a book that supplies facts about the moon, but the real message, implicit in the illustrations, is repeated in the last page: ". . . you promise you will always do your best to protect all life on our beautiful Earth." Brainstorm ways you can do just that. Get familiar with Earth's geology in McNulty's companion classic, *How to Dig a Hole to the Other Side of the World.* Look at ravishing color photos of Earth's regions, taken from a helicopter, in *Earth from Above for Young Readers* by Robert Burleigh.

RELATED TITLES: Aldrin, Buzz. *Reaching for the Moon.* HarperCollins, 2005. / Brown, Don. *One Giant Leap: The Story of Neil Armstrong.* Houghton Mifflin, 1998. / Burleigh, Robert. *Earth from Above for Young Readers.* Abrams, 2002. / Cole, Joanna. *The Magic School Bus Lost in the Solar System.* Scholastic, 1990. / Crews, Nina. *I'll Catch the Moon.* Greenwillow, 1996. / Gaffney, Timothy R. *Grandpa Takes Me to the Moon.* Tambourine, 1996. / Haddon, Mark. *The Sea of Tranquility.* Harcourt, 1996. / Krupp, E. C. *The Moon and You.* Macmillan, 1993. / Leedy, Loreen. *Postcards from Pluto: A Tour of the Solar System.* Holiday House, 1993. / McNulty, Faith. *How to Dig a Hole to the Other Side of the World.* HarperCollins, 1979. / Schyffert, Bea Uusma. *The Man Who Went to the Far Side of the Moon: The Story of Apollo 11 Astronaut, Michael Collins.* Chronicle, 2003. / Simon, Seymour. *The Moon.* Simon & Schuster, 2003. / Suen, Anastasia. *Man on the Moon.* Viking, 1997. / Wethered, Peggy, and Ken Edgett. *Touchdown Mars! An ABC Adventure.* Putnam, 2000. / Yaccarino, Dan. *Zoom! Zoom! Zoom! I'm Off to the Moon!* Scholastic, 1997.

SUBJECTS: ASTRONAUTS. MOON. SPACE FLIGHT TO THE MOON. VOYAGES, IMAGINARY.

1646   Maestro, Betsy. *Coming to America: The Story of Immigration.* **Illus. by Susannah Ryan. Scholastic, 1996. 0-590-44151-5. Unp. Gr. 2–4**

Starting with the earliest Native Americans who crossed a land bridge from Asia to what is now Alaska, Maestro describes how America has been settled by people from around the globe in search of a better life. This attractive multicultural nonfiction picture book begins "America is a nation of immigrants" and although the tone is optimistic and upbeat, serious issues are introduced: mistreatment of Indians, African slavery, the ordeal of Ellis Island, the plight of refugees, and the difficulties of starting a new life in an unfamiliar place.

GERM: Do some digging for roots. Have students do an oral history, interviewing relatives to find out when their families came to America and why.

RELATED TITLES: Bartone, Elisa. *American Too.* Lothrop, 1996. / Bartone, Elisa. *Peppe the Lamplighter.* Lothrop, 1993. / Bierman, Carol. *Journey to Ellis Island: How My Father Came to America.* Hyperion, 1998. / Connor, Leslie. *Miss Bridie Chose a Shovel.* Houghton Mifflin, 2004. / Freedman, Russell. *Immigrant Kids.* Dutton, 1980. / Levine, Ellen. *I Hate English!* Scholastic, 1989. / Levine, Ellen. *If Your Name Was Changed at Ellis Island.* Scholastic, 1993. / Maestro, Betsy. *Coming to America: The Story of Immigration.* Scholastic, 1996. / Pomeranc, Marion Hess. *The American Wei.* Albert Whitman, 1998.

SUBJECTS: ELLIS ISLAND IMMIGRATION STATION (N.Y. AND N.J.). IMMIGRATION AND EMIGRATION. MULTICULTURAL BOOKS. U.S.—HISTORY.

1647 Melmed, Laura Krauss. *New York, New York! The Big Apple from A to Z.* Illus. by Frané Lessac. HarperCollins, 2005. 0-06-054876-2. Unp. Gr. 1–6

Teeming with details, 26 vibrant full-bleed paintings, each representing a famous New York City scene or place to visit, are labeled in tiny print with additional facts and are accompanied by descriptive rhyming poems. From A—American Museum of Natural History—to Z—The Bronx Zoo—armchair travelers get a fast-paced tour of the many-faceted aspects of the New York experience, including the Brooklyn Bridge, Central Park, the Empire State Building, Fifth Avenue, Harlem, Jones Beach, the Metropolitan Museum of Art, and Yankee Stadium.

GERM: Inspired by the amount of information that one mere picture, poem, and set of sidebars can provide, students can research, paint, write, and put together another alphabet book highlighting their own city or state. Show the wordless picture book *You Can't Take a Balloon into the Metropolitan Museum* by Jacqueline Preiss Weitzman to see how many of the New York sites everyone can identify. Climb the Empire State Building with the big ape in *Ding Dong Ding Dong* by Margie Palatini and fly over the city with *Abuela* by Arthur Dorros and with *Tar Beach* by Faith Ringgold.

RELATED TITLES: Adoff, Arnold. *Street Music: City Poems.* HarperCollins, 1995. / Dorros, Arthur. *Abuela.* Dutton, 1991. / Jakobsen, Kathy. *My New York.* Little, Brown, 2003. / Johnson, Stephen T. *Alphabet City.* Viking, 1995. / Konigsburg, E. L. *Amy Elizabeth Explores Bloomingdale's.* Atheneum, 1992. / Neubecker, Robert. *Wow! City!* Hyperion, 2004. / Palatini, Margie. *Ding Dong Ding Dong.* Hyperion, 1999. / Priceman, Marjorie. *Froggie Went a-Courting.* Little, Brown, 2000. / Ringgold, Faith. *Tar Beach.* Crown, 1991. / Rotner, Shelley, and Ken Kreisler. *Citybook.* Orchard, 1994. / Weitzman, Jacqueline Preiss. *You Can't Take a Balloon into the Metropolitan Museum.* Dial, 1998.

SUBJECTS: ALPHABET BOOKS. CITIES AND TOWNS. NEW YORK CITY. PICTURE BOOKS FOR ALL AGES. STORIES IN RHYME.

1648 Michelson, Richard. *Ten Times Better.* Illus. by Leonard Baskin. Marshall Cavendish, 2000. 0-7614-5070-X. 40pp. Gr. 1–3

On each page of this collection of numerically based poems, two animals tout their most striking features: the bactrian camel boasts about its two humps and the sage male grouse brags about having ten times that many—i.e., twenty—feathers in his tail.

GERM: What a harmonious blending of counting, multiplication, animal facts, appealing watercolors, and poetry told from each animal's point of view. Pull in *If Not for the Cat* by Jack Prelutsky for the poetry and the point of view, and Steve Jenkins's *Actual Size* for the measurement and the animal facts.

RELATED TITLES: Day, Nancy Raines. *Double Those Wheels.* Dutton, 2003. / Dodds, Dayle Ann. *Minnie's Diner.* Candlewick, 2004. / Jenkins, Steve. *Actual Size.* Houghton Mifflin, 2004. / Leedy, Loreen. *2 X 2 = BOO! A Set of Spooky Multiplication Stories.* Holiday House, 1995. / Murphy, Stuart. *Too Many Kangaroo Things to Do!* HarperCollins, 1996. / Pinczes, Elinor J. *One Hundred Hungry Ants.* Houghton Mifflin, 1993. / Prelutsky, Jack. *If Not for the Cat.* Greenwillow, 2004. / Tang, Greg. *The Best of Times: Math Strategies That Multiply.* Scholastic, 2002. / Wormell, Christopher. *Teeth, Tails, and Tentacles: An Animal Counting Book.* Running Press, 2004.

SUBJECTS: ANIMALS. COUNTING BOOKS. MULTIPLICATION. POETRY—SINGLE AUTHOR. STORIES IN RHYME.

1649 Miller, Debbie S. *The Great Serum Race: Blazing the Iditarod Trail.* Illus. by Jon Van Zyle. Walker, 2002. 0-8027-8811-4. Unp. Gr. 3–6

In 1925, when Nome, Alaska, was stricken with a diphtheria outbreak and the nearest serum was 1,000 miles away in Anchorage, a relay of sled dogs made the trip immortalized today in the yearly Iditarod Race. In a gripping picture-book account, meet the heroic mushers and faithful dogs who saved the town.

GERM: The list of names of the 20 mushers and the distances each covered should give you some good ideas for writing math word problems. For up-to-date info on the Iditarod, go to <www.iditarod.com>.

RELATED TITLES: Blake, Robert. *Akiak: A Tale from the Iditarod.* Philomel, 1997. / Blake, Robert. *Togo.* Philomel, 2002. / Paulsen, Gary. *Dogteam.* Delacorte, 1993. / Paulsen, Gary. *Woodsong.* Simon & Schuster, 1990. / Seibert, Patricia. *Mush! Across Alaska in the World's Longest Sled-Dog Race.* Millbrook, 1992. / Wood, Ted. *Iditarod Dream: Dusty and His Sled Dogs Compete in Alaska's Jr. Iditarod.* Walker, 1996.

SUBJECTS: ALASKA. DOGS. IDITAROD (RACE). SLED DOG RACING. U.S.—HISTORY—20TH CENTURY. VOYAGES AND TRAVELS.

1650 Moser, Madeline. *Ever Heard of an Aardwolf?* Illus. by Barry Moser. Harcourt, 1996. 0-15-200474-2. Unp. Gr. 1–4

Twenty unusual mammals, including the pangolin, platypus, and zorilla, are profiled here, with handsome portraits of each done in dark-toned wood engravings and a paragraph of facts about their appearance, habits, and habitats.

GERM: Make a list of other lesser known animals for children to research in books, encyclopedias, or on the Internet, and draw realistic portraits. Introduce the 590 section of the library: animals.

RELATED TITLES: Browne, Philippa-Alys. *A Gaggle of Geese: The Collective Names of the Animal Kingdom.* Atheneum, 1996. / DuQuette, Keith. *They Call Me Woolly: What Animal Names Can Tell Us.* Putnam, 2002. / Johnson, Jinny. *National Geographic Animal Encyclopedia.* National Geographic Society, 2001. / *National Geographic Book of Mammals.* National Geographic Society, 1981. / Prelutsky, Jack, comp. *The Beauty of the Beast: Poems from the Animal Kingdom.* Knopf, 1997. / Ryan, Pam Muñoz. *A Pinky Is a Baby Mouse and Other Baby Animal Names.* Dial, 1998. / Sierra, Judy. *There's a Zoo in Room 22.* Harcourt, 2000. / Singer, Marilyn. *A Wasp Is Not a Bee.* Henry Holt, 1995.

SUBJECTS: ANIMALS.

1651 Nagda, Ann Whitehead, and Cindy Bickel. *Tiger Math: Learning to Graph from a Baby Tiger.* Illus. with photos. Henry Holt, 2000. 0-8050-6248-3. 29pp. Gr. 2–4

On the right-hand page is a color photoessay about T. J., a baby Siberian tiger that was raised by the animal hospital staff at the Denver Zoo after his mother died; on each left-hand page is a bar, line, or circle graph charting his growth over four years.

GERM: Math teachers will welcome sharing such a clear description of the graphing process tied in to animal studies. The authors continue their innovative approach to math and science with *Polar Bear Math*, about fractions, and *Chimp Math*, about time.

RELATED TITLES: Dowson, Nick. *Tigress.* Candlewick, 2004. / Hopcraft, Carol Cawthra. *How It Was with Dooms.* McElderry, 1997. / Johnston, Ginny, and Cutchins, Judy. *Andy Bear: A Polar Cub Grows Up at the Zoo.* Morrow, 1985. / Leedy, Loreen. *The Great Graph Contest.* Holiday House, 2005. / Leslie-Melville, Betty. *Daisy Rothschild: The Giraffe That Lives with Me.* Doubleday, 1987. / Nagda, Ann Whitehead, and Cindy Bickel. *Chimp Math: Learning About Time from a Baby Chimpanzee.* Henry Holt, 2002. / Nagda, Ann Whitehead, and Cindy Bickel. *Panda Math: Learning About Substraction from Hua Mei and Mei Sheng.* Henry Holt, 2005. / Nagda, Ann Whitehead, and Cindy Bickel. *Polar Bear Math: Learning About Fractions from Klondike and Snow.* Henry Holt, 2004. / Patterson, Francine. *Koko's Story.* Scholastic, 1987. / Winters, Kay. *Tiger Trail.* Simon & Schuster, 2000.

SUBJECTS: ANIMALS—INFANCY. GRAPHS AND GRAPHING. MATHEMATICS. TIGERS. ZOOS.

1652 O'Connor, Jane. *The Emperor's Silent Army: Terracotta Warriors of Ancient China.* Illus. with photos. Viking, 2002. 0-670-03512-2. 48pp. Gr. 4–8

After being buried underground in northern China for 2,200 years, thousands of life-sized terracotta soldiers were excavated near the tomb of Qin, China's first emperor, as described here and shown in thrilling color photographs. This is nonfiction bookmaking at its best, starting with the three farmers who, while digging a well in 1974, uncovered a pottery man and called in the archaeologists. The book then goes back in time to 221 B.C., when Emperor Qin Shihuang was buried with the 7,500 statues, and concludes by describing the current excavations going on today.

GERM: Spark your studies of ancient civilizations with this exploration of the Qin empire and the emperor who built the Great Wall. The book states, "Along with the Great Pyramids in Egypt, the buried army is now considered one of the true wonders of the ancient world." Someday, some of your students will travel to China to see this sight, and all because of a good book that piqued their interest.

RELATED TITLES: Cole, Joanna. *Ms. Frizzle's Adventures: Imperial China.* Scholastic, 2005. / Curlee, Lynn. *Seven Wonders of the Ancient World.* Atheneum, 2002. / Fisher, Leonard Everett. *The Great Wall of China.* Macmillan, 1986. / Freedman, Russell. *Confucius: The Golden Rule.* Scholastic, 2002. / Hong, Lily Toy. *The Empress and the Silkworm.* Albert Whitman, 1995. / Krupp, Robin Rector. *Let's Go Traveling.* Morrow, 1992. / Mahy, Margaret. *The Seven Chinese Brothers.* Scholastic, 1990. / Young, Ed. *Beyond the Great Mountains: A Visual Poem About China.* Chronicle, 2005. / .

SUBJECTS: ANCIENT CIVILIZATIONS. ARCHAEOLOGY. CHINA—HISTORY. EMPERORS. KINGS AND RULERS. SCULPTURE.

1653 O'Connor, Jane. *If the Walls Could Talk: Family Life at the White House*. Illus. by Gary Hovland. Simon & Schuster, 2004. 0-689-86863-4. Unp. Gr. 2–6

This light-hearted history, illustrated with witty pen-and-ink and watercolor cartoons, provides quotes and anecdotes about each of the White House's famous inhabitants—starting with George Washington, who chose the design of the White House and the location of the new capital (which he wanted to call "Federal City")—and describes the construction, destruction, rebuilding, and remodeling of this most famous of buildings.

GERM: This will push readers to find out more about each president, and is a natural companion to Judith St. George's *So You Want to Be President*. At the back of the book is a question-and-answer segment called "Ask the Presidents." Use the questions to get your scholars to do research in books, encyclopedias, or online, and then compare their answers with those in the book. For more info about the White House, read *It Happened in the White House* by Kathleen Karr, and then do some Internet research at <www.whitehouse.gov>.

RELATED TITLES: Coulter, Laurie. *When John and Caroline Lived in the White House*. Hyperion, 2000. / Davis, Gibbs. *Wackiest White House Pets*. Scholastic, 2004. / Fleming, Candace. *A Big Cheese for the White House*. DK Ink, 1999. / Harness, Cheryl. *Ghosts of the White House*. Simon & Schuster, 1998. / Karr, Kathleen. *It Happened in the White House: Extraordinary Tales from America's Most Famous House*. Hyperion, 2000. / Krull, Kathleen. *Lives of the Presidents: Fame, Shame (and What the Neighbors Thought)*. Harcourt, 1998. / Provensen, Alice. *The Buck Stops Here: The Presidents of the United States*. Harcourt, 2000. / Ryan, Pam Muñoz. *Amelia and Eleanor Go for a Ride*. Scholastic, 1999. / St. George, Judith. *So You Want to Be President?* Philomel, 2000. / Stier, Catherine. *If I Were President*. Albert Whitman, 1999.

SUBJECTS: PRESIDENTS. U.S.—HISTORY. WHITE HOUSE.

1654 Pallotta, Jerry. *The Beetle Alphabet Book*. Illus. by David Biedrzycki. Charlesbridge, 2004. 1-57091-551-2. Unp. Gr. K–3

Jerry Pallotta, king of the alphabet book, has created a sassy, fact-packed guide to beetles, with huge, gaudy, human-hand-sized beetles on each alphabetical page. The details are astounding and the variety of beetles is impressive.

GERM: Pallotta's many alphabet books inspire readers of all ages to research, write, and illustrate their own alphabet books on subjects that fuel their passions. Beetle lovers can follow up with insect poems, stories, and tales of personal encounters. Amanda Frankenstein, the heroine in Megan McDonald's picture book *Insects Are My Life*, would love this book.

RELATED TITLES: Banks, Lynne Reid. *Harry the Poisonous Centipede: A Story to Make You Squirm*. Morrow, 1997. / Chrustowski, Rick. *Bright Beetle*. Henry Holt, 2000. / Florian, Douglas. *Insectlopedia: Poems and Paintings*. Harcourt, 1998. / Hopkins, Lee Bennett, comp. *Flit, Flutter, Fly! Poems About Bugs and Other Crawly Creatures*. Doubleday, 1992. / McDonald, Megan. *Insects Are My Life*. Orchard, 1995. / Oppenheim, Joanne. *Have You Seen Bugs?* Scholastic, 1998. / Sonenklar, Carol. *Bug Boy*. Henry Holt, 1997. / Tyson, Leigh Ann. *An Interview with Harry the Tarantula*. National Geographic, 2003.

SUBJECTS: ALPHABET BOOKS. BEETLES. INSECTS.

1655 Pandell, Karen. *Animal Action ABC*. Photos by Art Wolfe and Nancy Sheehan. Dutton, 1996. 0-525-45486-1. 40pp. Gr. PreK–2

In this action-verb-filled, innovative, oversized, animal ABC book, each of the huge, colorful photos of wild animals is accompanied by a brief rhyming description and corresponding color photos of energetic children mimicking each animal's behavior. A board book version, published in 2003, is available from Handprint.

GERM: Your animal fanciers can act out each action verb, portraying each animal's style and behavior, and then think up new verbs and animals to draw and impersonate.

RELATED TITLES: Abrams, Pam. *Now I Eat My ABC's*. Scholastic, 2004. / Bender, Robert. *The A to Z Beastly Jamboree*. Dutton, 1996. / Burton, Marilee Robin. *Tails, Toes, Eyes, Ears, Nose*. HarperCollins, 1988. / Davis, Katie. *Who Hops?* Harcourt, 1998. / Harter, Debbie. *Walking Through the Jungle*. Orchard, 1997. / Hoberman, Mary Ann. *It's Simple, Said Simon*. Knopf, 2001. / Jenkins, Steve. *Big and Little*. Houghton Mifflin, 1996. / Jenkins, Steve. *Biggest, Strongest, Fastest*. Ticknor & Fields, 1995. / Jenkins, Steve, and Robin Page. *What Do You Do With a Tail Like This?* Houghton Mifflin, 2003. / Marzollo, Jean. *Pretend You're a Cat*. Dial, 1990. / Rotner, Shelley. *Action Alphabet*. Atheneum, 1996. / Shapiro, Arnold L. *Mice Squeak, We Speak*. Putnam, 1997. / Shields, Carol Diggory. *Animagicals: Patterns*. Handprint, 2001.

SUBJECTS: ALPHABET BOOKS. ANIMALS. CREATIVE DRAMA. ENGLISH LANGUAGE—GRAMMAR. ENGLISH LANGUAGE—VERBS. STORIES IN RHYME.

1656 Pfeffer, Wendy. *From Seed to Pumpkin.* **Illus. by James Graham Hale. HarperCollins, 2004. 0-06-028038-7. 32pp. Gr. PreK–2**

See how a farmer plants his pumpkin seeds, leading to pumpkin vines and, of course, lots of pumpkins.

GERM: This easy-to-follow entry in the Let's-Read-and-Find-Out Science series, attractively illustrated with watercolors, provides just enough explanation if you're planning a gardening unit or need a nonfiction tie-in for Halloween or Thanksgiving stories. At the back of the book is a recipe for roasted pumpkin seeds and an experiment to demonstrate how plants with tubes draw up water from the ground.

RELATED TITLES: Cherry, Lynne. *How Groundhog's Garden Grew.* Scholastic, 2003. / Coy, John. *Two Old Potatoes and Me.* Knopf, 2003. / Ehlert, Lois. *Eating the Alphabet.* Harcourt, 1989. / Ehlert, Lois. *Growing Vegetable Soup.* Harcourt, 1987. / Gibbons, Gail. *From Seed to Plant.* Holiday House, 1991. / Hall, Zoe. *It's Pumpkin Time!* Scholastic, 1994. / Jackson, Alison. *I Know an Old Lady Who Swallowed a Pie.* Dutton, 1997. / Johnston, Tony. *The Vanishing Pumpkin.* Putnam, 1983. / Kimmel, Eric A. *Anansi and the Talking Melon.* Holiday House, 1994. / McDonald, Megan. *The Great Pumpkin Switch.* Orchard, 1992. / Schaefer, Lola M. *Pick, Pull, Snap! Where Once a Flower Bloomed.* HarperCollins, 2003. / Silverman, Erica. *Big Pumpkin.* Macmillan, 1992. / Sloat, Teri. *Patty's Pumpkin Patch.* Putnam, 1999. / Stevens, Janet. *Tops and Bottoms.* Harcourt, 1995. / Williams, Linda. *The Little Old Lady Who Was Not Afraid of Anything.* Crowell, 1986.

SUBJECTS: GARDENING. PLANTS. PUMPKINS. SEEDS.

1657 Pfeffer, Wendy. *A Log's Life.* **Illus. by Robin Brickman. Simon & Schuster, 1997. 0-689-80636-1. 32pp. Gr. K–2**

Observe how little-appreciated crawlers such as wood-boring beetles, termites, and slugs speed the decomposition of a fallen log from an oak tree.

GERM: The eloquent text and the realistic paper collage paintings will inspire kids to go outside for some firsthand research.

RELATED TITLES: Behn, Harry. *Trees.* Henry Holt, 1992. / Brenner, Barbara. *One Small Place in a Tree.* HarperCollins, 2004. / Bunting, Eve. *Someday a Tree.* Clarion, 1993. / Edwards, Pamela Duncan. *Some Smug Slug.* HarperCollins, 1996. / Ehlert, Lois. *Leaf Man.* Harcourt, 2005. / Florian, Douglas. *Insectlopedia: Poems and Paintings.* Harcourt, 1998. / Gackenbach, Dick. *Mighty Tree.* Harcourt, 1992. / Hiscock, Bruce. *The Big Tree.* Atheneum, 1991. / Lyon, George Ella. *ABCedar: An Alphabet of Trees.* Orchard, 1989. / McDonald, Megan. *Insects Are My Life.* Orchard, 1995. / Oppenheim, Joanne. *Have You Seen Bugs?* Scholastic, 1998. / Oppenheim, Joanne. *Have You Seen Trees?* Scholastic, 1995. / Pallotta, Jerry. *The Beetle Alphabet Book.* Charlesbridge, 2004. / Rosen, Michael. *Itsy-Bitsy Beasties: Poems from Around the World.* Carolrhoda, 1992. / Udry, Janice May. *A Tree Is Nice.* HarperCollins, 1956.

SUBJECTS: ANIMALS. ECOLOGY. FORESTS AND FORESTRY. INSECTS. TREES.

1658 Pfeffer, Wendy. *The Shortest Day: Celebrating the Winter Solstice.* **Illus. by Jesse Reisch. Dutton, 2003. 0-525-46968-0. 40pp. Gr. 1–4**

Instructive but easy to understand, this engaging nonfiction picture book describing the winter solstice and how and why it occurs looks back 5,000 years to see how ancient peoples came to identify the first day of winter.

GERM: At the back of the book, a series of thoughtful and easy-to-perform experiments includes making a winter sunrise/sunset chart, measuring shadows on the shortest day, finding the sun's northernmost and southernmost points, demonstrating how the earth's tilt makes the seasons, and throwing a winter solstice party for the birds. A bibliography and Web sites for further research are listed. Incorporate a fast look at the four seasons through poetry in *Snowy Flowy Blowy: A Twelve Months Rhyme* by Nancy Tafuri.

RELATED TITLES: Andrews, Jan. *Very Last First Time.* Atheneum, 1986. / Bernhard, Emery. *How Snowshoe Hare Rescued the Sun: A Tale from the Arctic.* Holiday House, 1993. / Branley, Franklyn M. *Snow Is Falling.* HarperCollins, 2000. / De Regniers, Beatrice Schenk. *Little Sister and the Month Brothers.* Lothrop, 1994. / Emberley, Michael. *Welcome Back Sun.* Little, Brown, 1993. / Larry, Charles. *Peboan and Seegwun.* Farrar, 1993. / Sabuda, Robert. *The Blizzard's Robe.* Atheneum, 1999. / Schnur, Steven. *Winter: An Alphabet Acrostic.* Clarion, 2002. / Seuling, Barbara. *Winter Lullaby.* Harcourt, 1998. / Tafuri, Nancy. *Snowy Flowy Blowy: A Twelve Months Rhyme.* Scholastic, 1999. / Updike, John. *A Child's Calendar.* Holiday House, 1999. / Van Laan, Nancy. *When Winter Comes.* Simon & Schuster, 2000. / Wells, Robert E. *How Do You Know What Time It Is?* Albert Whitman, 2002. / Wright, Betty Ren. *The Blizzard.* Holiday House, 2003.

SUBJECTS: CELEBRATIONS. SEASONS. SOLSTICE. WINTER.

1659 Pfeffer, Wendy. *Wiggling Worms at Work.* **Illus. by Steve Jenkins. HarperCollins, 2004. 0-06-028449-8. 32pp. Gr. PreK–3**

Another stellar addition to the Let's-Read-and-Find-Out series, this is an eloquently phrased tribute to the thousands of worms tunneling beneath our feet, portraying the creatures' movement, feeding habits, and mating.

GERM: At the back of the book are several worm projects, including examining a real earthworm (if you are not the squeamish type), finding a worm's tunnel by looking for its castings, and a soil experiment. Of course, you'll want to personify worms and make them your new friends by reading Doreen Cronin's companionable picture book, *Diary of a Worm.*

RELATED TITLES: Amato, Mary. *The Word Eater.* Holiday House, 2000. / Caple, Kathy. *Worm Gets a Job.* Candlewick, 2004. / Cronin, Doreen. *Diary of a Worm.* HarperCollins, 2003.

SUBJECTS: ANIMALS. WORMS.

1660 Pringle, Laurence. *Bats! Strange and Wonderful.* **Illus. by Meryl Henderson. Boyds Mills, 2000. 1-56397-327-8. 32pp. Gr. 1–4**

An easy-to-understand text and glamorous watercolors promote the charms of some of the world's almost 1,000 kinds of bats.

GERM: When we want kids to read nonfiction cover to cover, it's books like this one that pull them in and keep them turning the pages. Get more bat info from the Web site of Bat Conservation International <www.batcon.org/catalog> or call for a printed catalog at 1-800-538-BATS (2287).

RELATED TITLES: Ackerman, Diane. *Bats: Shadows in the Night.* Crown, 1997. / Bash, Barbara. *Shadows of Night: The Hidden World of the Little Brown Bat.* Sierra Club, 1993. / Cannon, Annie. *The Bat in the Boot.* Orchard, 1996. / Cannon, Janell. *Stellaluna.* Harcourt, 1993. / Dragonwagon, Crescent. *Bat in the Dining Room.* Marshall Cavendish, 1997. / Hall, Katy, and Lisa Eisenberg. *Batty Riddles.* Dial, 1993. / Hamilton, Virginia. *When Birds Could Talk and Bats Could Sing.* Blue Sky/Scholastic, 1996. / Maestro, Betsy. *Bats.* Scholastic, 1994. / Markle, Sandra. *Outside and Inside Bats.* Atheneum, 1997. / Mollel, Tololwa M. *A Promise to the Sun.* Little, Brown, 1992. / Pringle, Laurence. *Batman: Exploring the World of Bats.* Simon & Schuster, 1991. / Pringle, Laurence. *Sharks! Strange and Wonderful.* Boyds Mills, 2001.

SUBJECTS: BATS.

1661 Raczka, Bob. *Art Is . . .* **Illus. with reproductions. Millbrook, 2003. 0-7613-2874-2. 32pp. Gr. 1–6**

This book enchants us with crisp color reproductions of paintings, sculptures, famous art, folk art, tapestries, and many other art forms, as well as providing clear-eyed descriptions and definitions in rhyme of what art is.

GERM: Collaborating with the art teacher, ask children to write their own one-sentence definitions of art, starting with "Art is . . .", and then have them create their own best examples. Turned into a Powerpoint computer presentation or exhibit, this might provide you with excellent ammunition the next time your school board tries to cut art funding in your district. Pair it with Raczka's *No One Saw: Ordinary Things Through the Eyes of an Artist* and *Unlikely Pairs: Fun with Famous Works of Art.*

RELATED TITLES: Brown, Laurene Krasny. *Visiting the Art Museum.* Dutton, 1986. / Hurd, Thacher. *Art Dog.* HarperCollins, 1996. / Koch, Kenneth, and Kate Farrell, comps. *Talking to the Sun: An Illustrated Anthology of Poems for Young People.* Henry Holt, 1985. / Micklethwaite, Lucy. *A Child's Book of Art: Discover Great Paintings.* DK, 1999. / Raczka, Bob. *No One Saw: Ordinary Things Through the Eyes of an Artist.* Millbrook, 2002. / Raczka, Bob. *Unlikely Pairs: Fun with Famous Works of Art.* Millbrook, 2005. / Richardson, Joy. *Inside the Museum: A Children's Guide to the Metropolitan Museum of Art.* Abrams, 1993. / Sayre, Henry M. *Cave Paintings to Picasso: The Inside Scoop on 50 Art Masterpieces.* Chronicle Books, 2003. / Scieszka, Jon. *Seen Art?* Viking, 2005. / Weitzman, Jacqueline Preiss. *You Can't Take a Balloon into the Metropolitan Museum.* Dial, 1998. / Wyse, Lois. *How to Take Your Grandmother to the Museum.* Workman, 1998.

SUBJECTS: ART APPRECIATION. STORIES IN RHYME.

1662 Raczka, Bob. *Unlikely Pairs: Fun with Famous Works of Art.* **Illus. with reproductions. Millbrook, 2005. 0-7613-2936-6. 32pp. Gr. K–6**

Art enthusiast Bob Raczka has taken 26 famous works of art, both paintings and sculptures, ranging from the 16th century to the present, and paired them together on facing pages. On the left of one are graffiti artist Keith Haring's day-glo-colored dancers grooving to the music. On the right is Jan Vermeer's 1672 painting "The Guitar Player"; the way the guitarist's head is tilted, it looks as if she's smiling at those dancers as she strums her instrument.

GERM: Show each double-page spread for children to examine. Read the title of each painting, as sometimes it helps to clarify what you're seeing, such as Claes Oldenburg's 1962 soft sculpture entitled "Floor Burger," paired with Jean Dubuffet's 1954 painting, "The Cow with the Subtle Nose." What viewers need to do is figure out the cause-and-effect connections between the two works of art and discuss their thought processes in linking them. As Raczka says in his genial introduction, "Each pair seems to tell a funny story, and it's up to you to figure out what that story is . . . Who knows? It might inspire you to create some unlikely pairs of your own." At the back of the book are small reproductions of each work and a bit of background on the artist.

RELATED TITLES: Fox, Dan, comp. *Go In and Out the Window: An Illustrated Songbook for Young People.* Henry Holt, 1987. / Koch, Kenneth, and Kate Farrell, comps. *Talking to the Sun: An Illustrated Anthology of Poems for Young People.* Henry Holt, 1985. / Micklethwaite, Lucy. *A Child's Book of Art: Discover Great Paintings.* DK, 1999. / Micklethwaite, Lucy. *A Child's Book of Play in Art: Great Pictures, Great Fun.* DK, 1996. / Raczka, Bob. *Art Is . . .* Millbrook, 2003. / Raczka, Bob. *No One Saw: Ordinary Things Through the Eyes of an Artist.* Millbrook, 2002. / Richardson, Joy. *Inside the Museum: A Children's Guide to the Metropolitan Museum of Art.* Abrams, 1993. / Sayre, Henry M. *Cave Paintings to Picasso: The Inside Scoop on 50 Art Masterpieces.* Chronicle Books, 2003. / Scieszka, Jon. *Seen Art?* Viking, 2005. / Weitzman, Jacqueline Preiss. *You Can't Take a Balloon into the Metropolitan Museum.* Dial, 1998. / Wyse, Lois. *How to Take Your Grandmother to the Museum.* Workman, 1998.

SUBJECTS: ART APPRECIATION. CAUSE AND EFFECT. PAINTINGS.

1663 **Raschka, Chris. *Charlie Parker Played Bebop.* Illus. by the author. Orchard, 1992. 0-531-05999-5. Unp. Gr. 1–6**

In a funky picture book of moody quirky watercolors, Charlie Parker plays saxophone to a rhyming, bebop text that conveys the moods of his music.

GERM: Play a Charlie Parker tune on your CD player while you read this aloud, and then ask your listeners to explain why there were such whimsical words in the text and what bebop now means to them.

RELATED TITLES: Aliki. *Ah, Music!* HarperCollins, 2003. / Gray, Libba Moore. *Little Lil and the Swing-Singing Sax.* Simon & Schuster, 1996. / Krull, Kathleen. *M Is for Music.* Harcourt, 2003. / Pinkney, Andrea Davis. *Duke Ellington: The Piano Prince and His Orchestra.* Hyperion, 1998. / Pinkney, Andrea Davis. *Ella Fitzgerald: The Tale of a Vocal Virtuosa.* Hyperion, 2002. / Raschka, Chris. *Mysterious Thelonius.* Orchard, 1998.

SUBJECTS: JAZZ. MULTICULTURAL BOOKS. MUSIC. MUSICIANS. PARKER, CHARLIE. PICTURE BOOKS FOR ALL AGES. SAXOPHONE.

1664 **Riley, Linda Capus. *Elephants Swim.* Illus. by Steve Jenkins. Houghton Mifflin, 1995. 0-395-73654-4. Unp. Gr. PreK–1**

Languid cut-paper collages and a brief rhyming text showcase animals that don't mind getting wet, from armadillos walking underwater to whales singing. An Author's Note at the back supplies a bit more information on each animal.

GERM: Act this one out in narrative pantomime. Find out more about water itself with Libby Hathorn's *The Wonder Thing* and Barbara Kerley's *A Cool Drink of Water.*

RELATED TITLES: Collard, Sneed B., III. *Animal Dads.* Houghton Mifflin, 1997. / Dorros, Walter. *Follow the Water from Brook to Ocean.* HarperCollins, 1991. / Falwell, Cathryn. *Turtle Splash! Countdown at the Pond.* Greenwillow, 2001. / Graham, Joan Bransfield. *Splish Splash.* Ticknor & Fields, 1994. / Hathorn, Libby. *The Wonder Thing.* Houghton Mifflin, 1996. / Jenkins, Steve. *Big and Little.* Houghton Mifflin, 1996. / Jenkins, Steve. *Biggest, Strongest, Fastest.* Ticknor & Fields, 1995. / Jenkins, Steve, and Robin Page. *What Do You Do With a Tail Like This?* Houghton Mifflin, 2003. / Jolivet, Joëlle. *Zoo-ology.* Roaring Brook, 2003. / Kerley, Barbara. *A Cool Drink of Water.* National Geographic, 2002. / Pandell, Karen. *Animal Action ABC.* Dutton, 1996. / Peters, Lisa Westberg. *Water's Way.* Little, Brown, 1991. / Rose, Deborah Lee. *Into the A, B, Sea.* Scholastic, 2000.

SUBJECTS: ANIMALS. CREATIVE DRAMA. STORIES IN RHYME. SWIMMING. WATER.

1665 **Robert, Francois, Jean Robert, and Jane Gittings. *Find a Face.* Photos by the authors. Chronicle, 2004. 0-8118-4338-6. Unp. Gr. PreK–2**

Each page features a crisp, clear color photograph of a common object that, if you study it carefully, looks as if it has a face. A rhyming text accompanies the faces in the side of a grater, the heel of a shoe, and an upside-down pair of headphones, with each object identified in tiny, upside-down print ("I am a radio dial!").

GERM: First ask your viewers to identify each of the faces in the photos and then start looking for faces in the objects around you. Seek out letters and numbers in the clever photographs found in Arlene Alda's picture books *A B C* and *1 2 3*. Then explore all 26 letters in the photorealistic paintings of Stephen T. Johnson's *Alphabet City* and in *The Alphabet in Nature* by Judy Feldman. Identify larger objects from a partial glimpse in *Look! Look! Look!* by Tana Hoban. See how Saxton Freymann finds faces in fruits and vegetables in *Food for Thought*.

RELATED TITLES: Alda, Arlene. *Arlene Alda's A B C.* Tricycle, 2002. / Alda, Arlene. *Arlene Alda's 1 2 3: What Do You See?* Tricycle, 2000. / Emberley, Ed. *The Wing on a Flea: A Book About Shapes.* Little, Brown, 2001. / Feldman, Judy. *The Alphabet in Nature.* Children's Press, 1991. / Freymann, Saxton. *Food for Thought: The Complete Book of Concepts for Growing Minds.* Scholastic, 2005. / Freymann, Saxton, and Joost Elffers. *How Are You Peeling? Foods with Moods.* Scholastic, 1999. / Freymann, Saxton, and Joost Elffers. *One Lonely Sea Horse.* Scholastic, 2000. / Hoban, Tana. *Look! Look! Look!* Greenwillow, 1988. / Johnson, Stephen T. *Alphabet City.* Viking, 1995. / Lillegard, Dee. *Do Not Feed the Table.* Delacorte, 1993. / Lillegard, Dee. *Wake Up House! Rooms Full of Poems.* Knopf, 2000. / MacDonald, Suse. *Alphabatics.* Simon & Schuster, 1986. / MacDonald, Suse. *Look Whooo's Counting.* Scholastic, 2000. / MacDonald, Suse. *Sea Shapes.* Harcourt, 1994.

SUBJECTS: FACES. PHOTOGRAPHY. VISUAL PERCEPTION.

1666   Rose, Deborah Lee. *Into the A, B, Sea: An Ocean Alphabet.* **Illus. by Steve Jenkins. Scholastic, 2000. 0-439-09697-9. Unp. Gr. PreK–2**
Steve Jenkins's lifelike textured handmade cut-paper collages bring you underwater "where Anemones sting, and Barnacles cling" and all the way through the alphabet.
GERM: Each animal is highlighted in the glossary, for possible further research. The rich and rhyming action verbs make this a story to act out in narrative pantomime the second time you read it aloud. Also read the companion counting book, *One Nighttime Sea.*
RELATED TITLES: Carle, Eric. *A House for Hermit Crab.* Picture Book Studio, 1987. / Falwell, Cathryn. *Turtle Splash! Countdown at the Pond.* Greenwillow, 2001. / Freymann, Saxton, and Joost Elffers. *One Lonely Sea Horse.* Scholastic, 2000. / McDonald, Megan. *Is This a House for Hermit Crab?* Orchard, 1990. / MacDonald, Suse. *Sea Shapes.* Harcourt, 1994. / Pandell, Karen. *Animal Action ABC.* Dutton, 1996. / Rose, Deborah Lee. *One Nighttime Sea.* Scholastic, 2003. / Stevenson, James. *Clams Can't Sing.* Greenwillow, 1980. / Ward, Jennifer, and T. J. Marsh. *Somewhere in the Ocean.* Rising Moon, 2000. / Zoehfeld, Kathleen Weidner. *What Lives in a Shell?* HarperCollins, 1994.

SUBJECTS: ALPHABET BOOKS. CREATIVE DRAMA. ENGLISH LANGUAGE—VERBS. MARINE ANIMALS. OCEAN. STORIES IN RHYME.

1667   Ross, Michael Elsohn. *What's the Matter in Mr. Whisker's Room?* **Illus. by Paul Meisel. Candlewick, 2004. 0-7636-1349-5. 45pp. Gr. 1–4**
Blonde-haired, bearded, enthusiastic Mr. Whiskers sets up seven science stations to encourage his eight curious, ethnically diverse young students through a hands-on study of matter—solids, liquids, and gases. Using a method of open-ended discovery that includes investigation, observation, exploration, experiments, and play, they make gloop and oobleck, turn ice into water, weigh rocks, and make mud, all before coming together to share everything they've learned.
GERM: Mr. Whiskers's style and technique will be inspiring to teachers and students alike. At the back of the book are recipes for gloop and oobleck, plus ideas for implementing each of the science stations. (You'll want to do a reading, of course, of Dr. Seuss's *Bartholomew and the Oobleck.*) This wow of a science book is appealingly illustrated with pen-and-inks and watercolors, and will provide inspiration for you, the teacher or librarian, when working on your lesson plans, not to mention your kids, who will be bursting to try out the many easy-to-follow experiments and explorations. Learn more about water with the kids in Mrs. Page's class in *The Incredible Water Show* by Debra Frasier.
RELATED TITLES: Cobb, Vicki. *I Get Wet.* HarperCollins, 2002. / Cole, Joanna. Magic School Bus series. Scholastic. / Cowan, Catherine. *My Life with the Wave.* Lothrop, 1997. / Dorros, Walter. *Follow the Water from Brook to Ocean.* HarperCollins, 1991. / Frasier, Debra. *The Incredible Water Show.* Harcourt, 2004. / Graham, Joan Bransfield. *Splish Splash.* Ticknor & Fields, 1994. / Kerley, Barbara. *A Cool Drink of Water.* National Geographic, 2002. / Lewis, J. Patrick. *Earth Verses and Water Rhymes.* Atheneum, 1991. / Lewis, J. Patrick. *Scientrickery: Riddles in Science.* Harcourt, 2004. / Locker, Thomas. *Water Dance.* Harcourt, 1997. / Peters, Lisa Westberg. *Water's Way.* Little, Brown, 1991. / Wick, Walter. *A Drop of Water.* Scholastic, 1997. / Wiesner, David. *Sector 7.* Clarion, 1999. / Zoehfeld, Kathleen Weidner. *What Is the World Made Of? All About Solids, Liquids, and Gases.* HarperCollins, 1998.

SUBJECTS: MATTER. SCIENCE. SCIENCE—EXPERIMENTS. TEACHERS.

1668 Rubin, Susan Goldman. *The Flag with Fifty-Six Stars: A Gift from the Survivors of Mau-thausen.* **Illus. by Bill Farnsworth. Holiday House, 2005. 0-8234-1653-4. 40pp. Gr. 4–8**

As the Nazis began to lose the war in 1944, and 1945, they transported tens of thousands of prisoners from other camps to Mauthausen, one of the worst of the 60 concentration camps. Simon Wiesenthal, who had been there for four years, wrote, "The hunger was almost unbearable . . . I had virtually given up all hope of staying alive." In the spring of 1945, with the Allied forces approaching, most of the SS guards bolted. To welcome the U.S. Army, one American prisoner, Lieutenant Jack H. Taylor, taught the camp's band to play "The Star-Spangled Banner." Other prisoners began work on a secret project: they constructed and sewed a large American flag. Himmler planned to seal all of the prisoners in a tunnel and blow them up, but he was foiled by a platoon of American soldiers. This devastating and yet ultimately uplifting picture book, with grave, intense, full-page oil paintings and a photograph of the actual flag, provides an unflinching window on the Holocaust that will stun you and your listeners.

GERM: An Afterword provides an update on Simon Wiesenthal and on the flag, with its extra row of stars—56 instead of 48—which is on display at the Simon Wiesenthal Center's Museum of Tolerance in Los Angeles. You'll find an outstanding teacher's guide for the book at <www.holidayhouse.com> (click on Free Materials) and at the Museum of Tolerance Web site, <www.museumoftolerance.com>, which provides a variety of teacher lesson plans on the Holocaust, though mostly for grades 7 and up.

RELATED TITLES: Abels, Chana Byers. *The Children We Remember.* Greenwillow, 1986. / Gold, Alison Leslie. *Memories of Anne Frank: Reflections of a Childhood Friend.* Scholastic, 1997. / Levine, Karen. *Hana's Suitcase.* Albert Whitman, 2003. / McCann, Michelle R. *Luba: The Angel of Bergen-Belsen.* Tricycle, 2003. / Poole, Josephine. *Anne Frank.* Knopf, 2005. / Rubin, Susan Goldman. *Fireflies in the Dark: The Story of Friedl Dicker-Brandeis and the Children of Terezin.* Holiday House, 2000. / Schroeder, Peter W., and Dagmar Schroeder-Hildebrand. *Six Million Paper Clips: The Making of a Children's Holocaust Memorial.* Kar-Ben, 2004.

SUBJECTS: AUSTRIA. CONCENTRATION CAMPS. FLAGS. HOLOCAUST, JEWISH (1939–1945). JEWS. MAUTHAUSEN (CONCENTRATION CAMP). WORLD WAR, 1939–1945.

1669 Ryder, Joanne. *Little Panda: The World Welcomes Hua Mei at the San Diego Zoo.* **Photos by the World Famous San Diego Zoo. Simon & Schuster, 2001. 0-689-84310-0. Unp. Gr. PreK–4**

Observe baby panda Hua Mei (the first giant panda cub to survive in captivity in the Western Hemisphere), in a captivating color photoessay chronicling her life from birth to age one.

GERM: Use other books on pandas, the encyclopedia, and the Internet to research additional facts about pandas and other endangered animals. Ann Whitehead Nagda and Cindy Bickel introduce the same panda and integrate math concepts along the way in *Panda Math: Learning About Subtraction from Hua Mei and Mei Sheng.*

RELATED TITLES: Allen, Judy. *Panda.* Candlewick, 1993. / Cowley, Joy. *Red-Eyed Tree Frog.* Scholastic, 1999. / Johnston, Ginny, and Judy Cutchins. *Andy Bear: A Polar Cub Grows Up at the Zoo.* Morrow, 1985. / Nagda, Ann Whitehead, and Cindy Bickel. *Panda Math: Learning About Substraction from Hua Mei and Mei Sheng.* Henry Holt, 2005. / Nagda, Ann Whitehead, and Cindy Bickel. *Tiger Math: Learning to Graph from a Baby Tiger.* Henry Holt, 2000. / Patterson, Francine. *Koko's Story.* Scholastic, 1987.

SUBJECTS: ANIMALS. ENDANGERED SPECIES. PANDAS.

1670 Sabuda, Robert. *America the Beautiful.* **Illus. by the author. Little Simon, 2004. 0-689-84744-0. Unp. Gr. All Ages**

In another wow of a pop-up masterpiece from paper engineering genius, Sabuda, each unfolding page illustrates a line of "America the Beautiful" and an important monument or symbol of the United States. What a thrill to open up the white 3-D replicas of the Golden Gate Bridge; Mount Rushmore; Mesa Verde; the Capitol; and the Statue of Liberty, with a background of the Empire State Building and the Chrysler Building.

GERM: A final pop-up mini-book on the last page provides all of the verses in Katharine Lee Bates's 1895 song. Use the book as a lead-in to stories about U.S. geography, including *Liberty's Journey* by Kelly DiPucchio, which employs phrases from the song. Find out how Bates came to write the song in *Purple Mountain Majesties: The Story of Katharine Lee Bates and "America the Beautiful"* by Barbara Younger. Pull out other Sabuda pop-up books to savor and marvel over.

RELATED TITLES: Bates, Katharine Lee. *America the Beautiful.* Illus. by Chris Gall. Little, Brown, 2004. / Bates, Katharine Lee. *America the Beautiful.* Illus. by Neil Waldman. Atheneum, 1983. / Borden, Louise. *America Is . . .* McElderry, 2002. / Cheney, Lynne. *America: A Patriotic Primer.* Simon & Schuster, 2002. / DiPucchio, Kelly. *Liberty's Journey.* Hyperion, 2004. / Guthrie, Woody. *This Land Is Your Land.* Little, Brown, 1998. /

Keller, Laurie. *The Scrambled States of America.* Henry Holt, 1998. / Pattison, Darcy. *The Journey of Oliver K. Woodman.* Harcourt, 2003. / Sabuda, Robert. *Encyclopedia Prehistorica: Dinosaurs.* Candlewick Press, 2005. / Sabuda, Robert. *The 12 Days of Christmas: A Pop-Up Celebration.* Simon & Schuster, 1996. / Younger, Barbara. *Purple Mountain Majesties: The Story of Katharine Lee Bates and "America the Beautiful."* Dutton, 1998.

SUBJECTS: SONGS. TOY AND MOVABLE BOOKS. U.S.—DESCRIPTION AND TRAVEL. U.S.—GEOGRAPHY. U.S.—POETRY.

1671 Sayre, April Pulley. *If You Should Hear a Honey Guide.* Illus. by S. D. Schindler. Houghton Mifflin, 1995. 0-395-71545-8. 32pp. Gr. K–3

In this story, told to us in the second person, we become active participants in the remarkable true adventure of a small brown and white bird as she traverses the wild bush lands of Kenya. Follow the honey guide as she leads you past elephants, zebras, a snake, a sleeping lion, and a hungry crocodile, all of which are en route to her destination: a bee's nest. When you arrive at the nest, she expects you to reward her with a piece of the honeycomb, which you take from the hive.

GERM: Schindler's exquisitely detailed paintings depict the animals in their natural habitats and will motivate readers to search out other books about them. Act out the text, with children playing the different animals, and the honey guides leading the way, calling, "Weet-err." Compare the nonfiction versus realistic fiction approach to presenting the same basic information, using *Juma and the Honey Guide* by Robin Bernard, a story about a father and son who follow the bird. Then read Jan Brett's *Honey . . . Honey . . . Lion!*, a picture book about the honey guide and a thoughtless honey badger.

RELATED TITLES: Bash, Barbara. *Tree of Life: The World of the African Baobab.* Sierra Club/Little, Brown, 1989. / Bernard, Robin. *Juma and the Honey Guide.* Dillon/Silver Burdett, 1996. / Brett, Jan. *Honey . . . Honey . . . Lion!* Putnam, 2005. / Cowcher, Helen. *Whistling Thorn.* Scholastic, 1993. / Demuth, Patricia Brennan. *Cradles in the Trees: The Story of Bird Nests.* Macmillan, 1994. / Florian, Douglas. *On the Wing: Bird Poems and Paintings.* Harcourt, 1996. / George, Kristine O'Connell. *Hummingbird Nest: A Journal of Poems.* Harcourt, 2004. / Heiligman, Deborah. *Honeybees.* National Geographic, 2002. / Krebs, Laurie. *The Beeman.* National Geographic, 2002. / Martin, Francesca. *The Honey Hunters.* Candlewick, 1992. / Peters, Lisa Westberg. *This Way Home.* Henry Holt, 1994. / Rockwell, Anne. *Honey in a Hive.* HarperCollins, 2005. / Wallace, Nancy Elizabeth. *A Taste of Honey.* Winslow, 2001.

SUBJECTS: AFRICA. BEES. BIRDS. CREATIVE DRAMA. HONEY. HONEYGUIDES. HUMAN-ANIMAL RELATIONSHIPS. KENYA.

1672 Schaefer, Lola M. *Pick, Pull, Snap! Where Once a Flower Bloomed.* Illus. by Lindsay Barrett George. HarperCollins, 2003. 0-688-17834-0. 32pp. Gr. PreK–2

In garden, berry patch, field, and orchard, a group of children observe the plant growing process, starting with the flower and ending with the ripe fruit or vegetable. Large, dignified watercolors open up into three-page panels that show a child harvesting the fruit from the mature plant.

GERM: Bring in samples of fresh peas, raspberries, corn, peaches, peanuts, and pumpkins for children to peel, examine, and taste. Then, wherever possible, harvest seeds for spring planting. Plant pea seeds in two planters on the windowsill; one with enough seeds so everyone can pull one up to examine at different stages of growth, and the other to let grow undisturbed.

RELATED TITLES: Cherry, Lynne. *How Groundhog's Garden Grew.* Scholastic, 2003. / Coy, John. *Two Old Potatoes and Me.* Knopf, 2003. / Ehlert, Lois. *Eating the Alphabet: Fruits and Vegetables from A to Z.* Harcourt, 1989. / Ehlert, Lois. *Growing Vegetable Soup.* Harcourt, 1987. / Gibbons, Gail. *From Seed to Plant.* Holiday House, 1991. / Pfeffer, Wendy. *From Seed to Pumpkin.* HarperCollins, 2004. / Freymann, Saxton. *Food for Thought: The Complete Book of Concepts for Growing Minds.* Scholastic, 2005. / Sloat, Teri. *Patty's Pumpkin Patch.* Putnam, 1999. / Stevens, Janet. *Tops and Bottoms.* Harcourt, 1995.

SUBJECTS: FLOWERS. FRUIT. GARDENING. PLANTS. SEEDS. VEGETABLES.

1673 Schaefer, Lola M. *What's Up, What's Down.* Illus. by Barbara Bash. Greenwillow, 2002. 0-06-029758-1. Unp. Gr. PreK–2

In a uniquely formatted picture book that illustrates the physical makeup of the world, you turn the book sideways, and read from the bottom of each page up to the top. What's up if you're a mole? Roots and rich soil are up, and then the grass, and flowers, and trees, and the birds, which fly "rushing here and there on invisible highways," and finally, high above it all, the moon. Now you turn the book around, and it asks, "What's down if you're the moon?" Turning each page and reading from top to bottom, you plunge through the clouds and travel all the way down to the ocean floor.

GERM: Your group can work together to make perspective drawings on very tall paper—floor to ceiling—of the different vantage points presented in the story, from ground to sky and sky to sea bottom. Children can observe an aspect of nature by lying on the ground and looking up, drawing and describing everything they see, and looking down at the ground, perhaps using binoculars or a magnifying glass to get a closer look.

RELATED TITLES: Brenner, Barbara. *The Earth Is Painted Green: A Garden of Poems About Our Planet.* Scholastic, 1994. / Dorros, Arthur. *Abuela.* Dutton, 1991. / Ehlert, Lois. *In My World.* Harcourt, 2002. / Hamanaka, Sheila. *All the Colors of the Earth.* Morrow, 1994. / Pollock, Penny. *When the Moon Is Full: A Lunar Year.* Philomel, 1992. / Ryder, Joanne. *Each Living Thing.* Harcourt, 2000. / Ryder, Joanne. *Earthdance.* Henry Holt, 1996. / Shannon, George. *White Is for Blueberry.* Greenwillow, 2005.

SUBJECTS: NATURE. SCIENCE.

1674 Schanzer, Rosalyn. *How We Crossed the West: The Adventures of Lewis and Clark.* Illus. by the author. National Geographic, 1997. 0-7922-3738-2. 40pp. Gr. 3–6

In 1804, Lewis and Clark journeyed with their band of men and one woman—Shoshoni guide Sacajawea—from the Midwest to the Pacific Ocean. This riveting picture book for older students uses primary sources—in this case the journals of the Corps of Discovery—to describe the dangers and excitement of the explorers' successful expedition.

GERM: Books like these whet children's appetites for more complex and varied accounts such as Rhoda Blumberg's *The Incredible Journey of Lewis and Clark,* and Joseph Bruchac's historical novel, *Sacajawea. The Great Expedition of Lewis and Clark: By Private Reubin Field, Member of the Corps of Discovery* is a fictionalized but fact-based nonfiction picture book told from the point of view of one of the men. For a whole different slant, introduce the Newfoundland dog Seaman, who narrates his own version in *Lewis and Clark and Me* by Laurie Myers.

RELATED TITLES: Blumberg, Rhoda. *The Incredible Journey of Lewis and Clark.* Lothrop, 1987. / Bruchac, Joseph. *Sacajawea: The Story of Bird Woman and the Lewis and Clark Expedition.* Harcourt, 2000. / Edwards, Judith. *The Great Expedition of Lewis and Clark: By Private Reubin Field, Member of the Corps of Discovery.* Farrar, 2003. / Erdrich, Lise. *Sacagawea.* Carolrhoda, 2003. / Freedman, Russell. *Buffalo Hunt.* Holiday House, 1988. / Freedman, Russell. *Children of the Wild West.* Clarion, 1983. / Myers, Laurie. *Lewis and Clark and Me: A Dog's Tale.* Harcourt, 2000. / Osborne, Mary Pope. *Adaline Falling Star.* Scholastic, 2000. / St. George, Judith. *So You Want to Be an Explorer?* Philomel, 2005.

SUBJECTS: EXPLORERS. INDIANS OF NORTH AMERICA. LEWIS AND CLARK EXPEDITION (1804–1806). U.S.—HISTORY—1783–1865. VOYAGES AND TRAVELS. WEST (U.S.)—HISTORY.

1675 Schwartz, David M. *If You Hopped Like a Frog.* Illus. by James Warhola. Scholastic, 1999. 0-590-09857-8. 32pp. Gr. K–6

"If you hopped like a frog . . . you could jump from home plate to first base in one mighty leap." In a delightful math picture book that can be used by all ages, find out how to use ratio and proportion in relating animal behavior to human behavior.

GERM: After working out the math problems at the back of the book, children can research and write new math questions about animals for other children to solve. Follow up with Schwartz's related book on relative size, *If Dogs Were Dinosaurs,* which includes this startling example: "If the Milky Way filled the U.S.A. . . . the solar system could fit in the palm of your hand." Find out how big animals are in *Actual Size* by Steve Jenkins.

RELATED TITLES: Lasky, Kathryn. *The Librarian Who Measured the Earth.* Little, Brown, 1994. / Leedy, Loreen. *Measuring Penny.* Atheneum, 1969. / Myller, Rolf. *How Big Is a Foot?* Atheneum, 1969. / Schwartz, David M. *G Is for Googol.* Tricycle, 1998. / Schwartz, David M. *How Much Is a Million?* Lothrop, 1985. / Schwartz, David M. *If Dogs Were Dinosaurs.* Scholastic, 2005. / Schwartz, David M. *Millions to Measure.* HarperCollins, 2003. / Scieszka, Jon. *Math Curse.* Viking, 1995. / Wells, Robert E. *Is a Blue Whale the Biggest Thing There Is?* Albert Whitman, 1993. / Wells, Robert E. *What's Older Than a Giant Tortoise?* Albert Whitman, 2004. / Wells, Robert E. *What's Smaller Than a Pygmy Shrew?* Albert Whitman, 1995.

SUBJECTS: ANATOMY, COMPARATIVE. ANIMALS. MATHEMATICS. RATIO AND PROPORTION. SIZE.

1676 Schwartz, David M. *Millions to Measure.* Illus. by Steven Kellogg. HarperCollins, 2003. 0-06-623784-X. Unp. Gr. 1–5

In his hot air balloon, Marvelosissimo the Mathmagical Magician takes four children and a dog back in time to see how people measured things long ago and developed standardized systems of measurement. Steven Kellogg's signature pen-and-ink and watercolor illustrations are a perfect match for the humorous but informative text that shows how measuring distance using feet, weight using stones, or volume using containers became standardized. The magician then explains the metric system, developed by a French priest in the 1700s. Fold out the two center pages and there is a colorful four-page spread of an affable-looking one-meter-long snake.

GERM: With your students, measure out a 100-meter lane, which Olympic runners can do in ten seconds, and try a timed race. Afterward, pour out water from liter bottles into cups so your thirsty crew can drink a liter or two. Next they can measure their height in centimeters. In helping us become familiar with measuring like a scientist, Schwartz advises readers to start by checking household foods and products to find containers labeled in metric units. The author's Afterword gives ample ideas for further study of the more logical and scientific metric system. Take flight with Marvelosissimo again in *How Much Is a Million?*, *If You Made a Million*, and *On Beyond a Million*. *The Librarian Who Measured the Earth* by Kathryn Lasky is the picture-book biography of astronomer, geographer, and librarian Eratosthenes, who, in the 3rd century B.C., figured out a way to measure the circumference of the earth. Take more animal measurements in *Actual Size* by Steve Jenkins.

RELATED TITLES: Jenkins, Steve. *Actual Size*. Houghton Mifflin, 2004. / Lasky, Kathryn. *The Librarian Who Measured the Earth*. Little, Brown, 1994. / Leedy, Loreen. *Measuring Penny*. Atheneum, 1998. / Myller, Rolf. *How Big Is a Foot?* Atheneum, 1969. / Schmandt-Besserat, Denise. *The History of Counting*. Morrow, 1999. / Schwartz, David M. *G Is for Googol*. Tricycle, 1998. / Schwartz, David M. *How Much Is a Million?* Lothrop, 1985. / Schwartz, David M. *If You Hopped Like a Frog*. Scholastic, 1999. / Schwartz, David M. *If You Made a Million*. Lothrop, 1989. / Schwartz, David M. *On Beyond a Million: An Amazing Math Journey*. Doubleday, 1999. / Scieszka, Jon. *Math Curse*. Viking, 1995. / Wells, Robert E. *Can You Count to a Googol?* Albert Whitman, 2000. / Wells, Robert E. *Is a Blue Whale the Biggest Thing There Is?* Albert Whitman, 1993. / Wells, Robert E. *What's Smaller Than a Pygmy Shrew?* Albert Whitman, 1995.

SUBJECTS: BALLOONS. MATHEMATICS. MEASUREMENT. METRIC SYSTEM. WEIGHTS AND MEASURES.

1677 Scillian, Devin. *P Is for Passport: A World Alphabet*. Illus. by a collection of nationally acclaimed artists. Sleeping Bear, 2003. 1-58536-157-7. Unp. Gr. 2–6

In this attractive, meaty, rhyming travelogue, an ABC of Earth's notable places and attributes, each large, double-page spread includes a descriptive verse, a detailed painting showcasing the featured word, and a sidebar of additional facts. You get an overview of the planet with entries on Animals, Bread, Currency, and Deserts, all the way up to Z for time Zones.

GERM: Teams of researchers can investigate one topic more systematically or elaborate on other essential words that the book didn't cover.

RELATED TITLES: Burleigh, Robert. *Earth from Above for Young Readers*. Abrams, 2002. / Gerberg, Mort. *Geographunny: A Book of Global Riddles*. Clarion, 1991. / Holub, Joan. *Geogra-fleas! Riddles All over the Map*. Albert Whitman, 2004. / Hopkins, Lee Bennett, comp. *Got Geography! Poems*. Greenwillow, 2006. / Jenkins, Steve. *Hottest Coldest Highest Deepest*. Houghton Mifflin, 1998. / Lewis, J. Patrick. *A World of Wonders*. Dial, 2002. / Maestro, Marco, and Giulio Maestro. *Riddle City, USA! A Book of Geography Riddles*. HarperCollins, 1994. / Paladino, Catherine, comp. *Land, Sea, and Sky: Poems to Celebrate the Earth*. Little, Brown, 1993. / Simon, Seymour. *Earth: Our Planet in Space*. Simon & Schuster, 2003. / Smith, David J. *If the World Were a Village: A Book About the World's People*. Kids Can, 2002.

SUBJECTS: ALPHABET BOOKS. EARTH. GEOGRAPHY. MULTICULTURAL BOOKS. STORIES IN RHYME. VOYAGES AND TRAVELS.

1678 Seuling, Barbara. *From Head to Toe: The Amazing Human Body and How It Works*. Illus. by Edward Miller. Holiday House, 2002. 0-8234-1699-2. 32pp. Gr. 2–5

Filled with easy-to-perform experiments, this spirited examination of all the systems and parts of the human body—bones, joints, muscles, brain and nervous system, organs, and skin—is crammed with fabulous facts that will give listeners newfound respect for their bodies.

GERM: "The human body is a well-run machine," declares Seuling, and indeed, as you read each chapter aloud, children will be twisting and flexing and thinking and breathing in response. Find interactive activities and reproducible sheets to go along with the book on illustrator Ed Miller's Web site: <www.edmiller.com>. Have children trace each other's bodies on kraft paper and draw in each system as they learn about it.

RELATED TITLES: Arnold, Tedd. *Parts*. Dial, 1997. / Berger, Melvin. *Why I Sneeze, Shiver, Hiccup, and Yawn*. HarperCollins, 2000. / Berger, Melvin. *You Can't Make a Move Without Your Muscles*. HarperCollins, 1982. / Cole, Joanna. *The Magic School Bus Inside the Human Body*. Scholastic, 1987. / Paye, Won-Ldy, and Margaret H.

Lippert. *Head, Body, Legs: A Story from Liberia*. Henry Holt, 2002. / Rockwell, Lizzy. *The Busy Body Book: A Kids' Guide to Fitness*. Crown, 2004. / Seuling, Barbara. *You Can't Sneeze with Your Eyes Open and Other Freaky Facts About the Human Body*. Dutton, 1986.

SUBJECTS: BODY, HUMAN. HEALTH. SCIENCE—EXPERIMENTS.

1679   **Shea, Pegi Deitz, and Cynthia Weill.** *Ten Mice for Tet*. **Illus. by To Ngoc Trang; embroidery by Pham Viet Dinh. Chronicle, 2003. 0-8118-3496-4. Unp. Gr. PreK–2**

Counting up to ten, joyful mice prepare for Tet, the four-day Vietnamese New Year celebration that takes place at the end of January. They prepare a feast, dance, make music, and watch fireworks, all of which is presented in a visual display of brightly colored, hand-embroidered pictures.

GERM: An Afterword, "About Tet," provides ample details about each aspect of the holiday. Make a chart comparing Tet with Chinese and American New Year's customs.

RELATED TITLES: Kimmel, Eric A. *The Rooster's Antlers: A Story of the Chinese Zodiac*. Holiday House, 1999. / Young, Ed. *Cat and Rat: The Legend of the Chinese Zodiac*. Henry Holt, 1995.

SUBJECTS: CELEBRATIONS. COUNTING BOOKS. HOLIDAYS. MULTICULTURAL BOOKS. NEW YEAR. VIETNAM. VIETNAMESE NEW YEAR.

1680   **Showers, Paul.** *A Drop of Blood*. **Illus. by Edward Miller. HarperCollins, 2004. 0-06-009108-8. 26pp. Gr. K–4**

In a pragmatic and fact-filled Let's-Read-and-Find-Out Science series addition, a black-caped Dracula, aided by his little green Igor-like assistant, takes us through a tutorial on the composition and function of blood in the human body. Along with the witty and ghoulish illustrations are electron microscope pictures of actual blood cells, and information on red and white blood cells, plasma, platelets, and a description of how blood circulates food and oxygen.

GERM: There are nicely gory blood facts at the back of the book to enhance the many facts in the text, and even a poem about blood that children can recite. Travel through the circulation system with Ms. Frizzle in Joanna Cole's *The Magic School Bus Inside the Human Body*. Barbara Seuling's *From Head to Toe: The Amazing Human Body and How It Works* give a mighty interesting overview as well.

RELATED TITLES: Berger, Melvin. *Why I Sneeze, Shiver, Hiccup, and Yawn*. HarperCollins, 2000. / Berger, Melvin. *You Can't Make a Move Without Your Muscles*. HarperCollins, 1982. / Cole, Joanna. *The Magic School Bus Inside the Human Body*. Scholastic, 1987. / Seuling, Barbara. *From Head to Toe: The Amazing Human Body and How It Works*. Holiday House, 2002. / Seuling, Barbara. *You Can't Sneeze with Your Eyes Open and Other Freaky Facts About the Human Body*. Dutton, 1986.

SUBJECTS: BLOOD. BODY, HUMAN. HEALTH. SCIENCE.

1681   **Siebert, Diane.** *Rhyolite: The True Story of a Ghost Town*. **Illus. by David Frampton. Clarion, 2003. 0-018-09073-0. Unp. Gr. 3–6**

Siebert tells a fascinating true tale of the boom and bust of Rhyolite, a prosperous Nevada gold rush and mining town that sprang from the desert in 1904, grew to 10,000 people, and went bust six years later after a financial panic. Illustrated with handsome old-timey woodcuts, the entire history is related as a rhyming narrative poem.

GERM: There's a wonderful, rhyming refrain that anchors the story and provides foreshadowing: "The coyotes heard what coyotes hear." When you read the book aloud, ask your listeners to pay attention to the facts of the story, assembling an outline of the sequence of events, and then write it up as a more traditional news story. Discuss: Why might the author have decided to tell this story in rhyme? There's an extensive Author's Note that provides more information. Do some research on other ghost towns and why they were abandoned. Pair your reading with Robert W. Service's classic narrative poem, written in 1907, about the Alaska gold rush, *The Cremation of Sam McGee*.

RELATED TITLES: Asch, Frank. *Cactus Poems*. Harcourt, 1998. / Blumberg, Rhoda. *The Great American Gold Rush*. Bradbury, 1989. / Cushman, Karen. *The Ballad of Lucy Whipple*. Clarion, 1996. / Dunphy, Madeleine. *Here Is the Southwestern Desert*. Hyperion, 1995. / Fleischman, Sid. *By the Great Horn Spoon*. Little, Brown, 1963. / McLerran, Alice. *Roxaboxen*. Lothrop, 1991. / Mora, Pat. *Listen to the Desert*. Clarion, 1994. / Service, Robert W. *The Cremation of Sam McGee*. Greenwillow, 1987. / Siebert, Diane. *Mojave*. Crowell, 1988. / Yolen, Jane. *Welcome to the Sea of Sand*. Putnam, 1996.

SUBJECTS: COYOTES. DESERTS—POETRY. GHOST TOWNS. NARRATIVE POETRY. NEVADA. STORIES IN RHYME. U.S.—HISTORY—20TH CENTURY—POETRY. WEST—POETRY.

1682 Simon, Seymour. *Earth: Our Planet in Space.* **Illus. with photos. Simon & Schuster, 2003. 0-689-83562-0. Unp. Gr. 2–6**

Take a look at Earth from above through bold, colorful, full-page NASA photographs and an easy-to-digest text overview about Earth's seasons, atmosphere, surface, and relation to the sun and planets.

GERM: Read this as a kickoff to your life on Earth or Earth in space science unit. Look for Simon's other titles on the planets, the sun, and the moon. Use Simon's writing as your standard for what clear, accurate, and riveting expository writing can and should be. Take a closer look at Earth's landmarks in the color photoessay *Earth from Above for Young Readers* by Robert Burleigh.

RELATED TITLES: Burleigh, Robert. *Earth from Above for Young Readers.* Abrams, 2002. / Henderson, Douglas. *Asteroid Impact.* Dial, 2000. / Jenkins, Steve. *Hottest Coldest Highest Deepest.* Houghton Mifflin, 1998. / Jenkins, Steve. *Life on Earth: The Story of Evolution.* Houghton Mifflin, 2002. / Lasky, Kathryn. *The Librarian Who Measured the Earth.* Little, Brown, 1994. / Lewis, J. Patrick. *A World of Wonders.* Dial, 2002. / Paladino, Catherine, comp. *Land, Sea, and Sky: Poems to Celebrate the Earth.* Little, Brown, 1993. / Simon, Seymour. *From Paper Airplanes to Outer Space.* Richard C. Owen, 2000. / Simon, Seymour. *The Moon.* Simon & Schuster, 2003. / Smith, David J. *If the World Were a Village: A Book About the World's People.* Kids Can, 2002. / Strauss, Rochelle. *Tree of Life: The Incredible Biodiversity of Life on Earth.* Kids Can, 2004.

SUBJECTS: ASTRONOMY. EARTH. PLANETS. SCIENCE.

1683 Smith, David J. *If the World Were a Village: A Book About the World's People.* **Illus. by Shelagh Armstrong. Kids Can, 2002. 1-55074-779-7. 32pp. Gr. 2–6**

The author takes us on a walk through the global village, looking at its nationalities, languages, ages, religions, food, environment, schooling, and money. Each resident of this village of 100 inhabitants represents 62 million people, for a global total of 6.2 billion. Black-outlined Roualt-style acrylics depict each aspect of the village, while the text breaks down statistics to ponder. On the Languages page, we find that, of the 100 in the village, 22 people would speak Chinese, 9 would speak English, 8 Hindi, 7 Spanish, 4 Arabic, 4 Bengali, 3 Portuguese, and 3 Russian, altogether representing 60 percent of the world. The author's aim is to "foster world-mindedness in children." He says, "Knowing who our neighbors are, where they live and how they live, will help us live in peace."

GERM: At the back are practical guidelines and activities about using maps, naming world capitals, looking at Web sites, and encouraging children to become passionate about their world. Note how our world has changed or stayed the same with *Turn of the Century*, Ellen Jackson's look at children in England and America at the start of each century from 1000 A.D. to now.

RELATED TITLES: Baer, Edith. *This Is the Way We Go to School: A Book About Children Around the World.* Scholastic, 1990. / Burleigh, Robert. *Earth from Above for Young Readers.* Abrams, 2002. / Collard, Sneed B., III. *1,000 Years Ago on Planet Earth.* Houghton Mifflin, 1999. / Dorros, Arthur. *This Is My House.* Scholastic, 1992. / Hamanaka, Sheila. *All the Colors of the Earth.* Morrow, 1994. / Jackson, Ellen. *It's Back to School We Go! First Day Stories from Around the World.* Millbrook, 2003. / Jackson, Ellen. *Turn of the Century.* Charlesbridge, 1998. / Lewis, J. Patrick. *A World of Wonders.* Dial, 2002. / Maddern, Eric. *The Fire Children: A West African Creation Tale.* Dial, 1993. / Ryder, Joanne. *Each Living Thing.* Harcourt, 2000. / Ryder, Joanne. *Earthdance.* Henry Holt, 1996. / Scillian, Devin. *P Is for Passport: A World Alphabet.* Sleeping Bear, 2003. / Simon, Seymour. *Earth: Our Planet.* Simon & Schuster, 2003. / Spier, Peter. *People.* Bantam, 1980.

SUBJECTS: EARTH. HUMAN GEOGRAPHY. MULTICULTURAL BOOKS. POPULATION.

1684 Sobol, Richard. *An Elephant in the Backyard.* **Photos by the author. Dutton, 2004. 0-525-47288-6. Unp. Gr. K–4**

Tha Klang, a small village in Thailand, is known as the home of 80 of the country's strongest, smartest, and largest elephants. The villagers train the elephants, including the one featured in this fascinating color photoessay—4-year-old Wan Pen—to perform for tourists.

GERM: Make a chart of the facts you have learned about Asian elephants from reading about Wan Pen. Compare the Thai elephants with the African ones in Betty Leslie-Melville's *Elephant Have the Right of Way: Life with the Wild Animals of Africa.* Also marvel over the Asian elephants of Thailand and Southeast Asia that have learned how to paint on huge canvases as described in Katya Arnold's color photoessay, *Elephants Can Paint Too!*

RELATED TITLES: Arnold, Katya. *Elephants Can Paint Too!* Atheneum, 2005. / Bateman, Robert, and Rick Archbold. *Safari.* Little, Brown, 1998. / Ford, Miela. *Little Elephant.* Greenwillow, 1994. / Ho, Minfong. *Peek! A Thai Hide-and-Seek.* Candlewick, 2004. / Jenkins, Martin. *Never Ride Your Elephant to School.* Candlewick, 2003. / Leslie-Melville, Betty. *Daisy Rothschild: The Giraffe That Lives with Me.* Doubleday, 1987. / Leslie-Melville,

Betty. *Elephant Have the Right of Way: Life with the Wild Animals of Africa*. Doubleday, 1993. / Yoshida, Toshi. *Elephant Crossing*. Philomel, 1989.

SUBJECTS: ELEPHANTS. ENDANGERED SPECIES. MULTICULTURAL BOOKS. THAILAND.

1685 **Steltzer, Ulli.** *Building an Igloo*. **Photos by the author. Henry Holt, 1995. 0-8050-3753-5. Unp. Gr. 2–6**

In a stark and crisp black-and-white photoessay, Tookillkee Kiguktak and his grown son Jopee demonstrate step by step how to build an igloo for shelter, cutting 20-pound blocks of snow and arranging them into a spiral.

GERM: If you are in a snowy place, you could take the children out to build doll-sized or—if you're feeling ambitious—full-sized igloos. If not, building with sugar cubes will have the same effect, though lacking the atmosphere and the shivering.

RELATED TITLES: Andrews, Jan. *Very Last First Time*. Atheneum, 1986. / Fowler, Susi Gregg. *Circle of Thanks*. Scholastic, 1998. / Grifalconi, Ann. *The Village of Round and Square Houses*. Little, Brown, 1986. / Hill, Kirkpatrick. *Winter Camp*. McElderry, 1993. / Kroll, Virginia. *The Seasons and Someone*. Harcourt, 1994. / Napoli, Donna Jo. *North*. Greenwillow, 2004. / Norman, Howard. *The Girl Who Dreamed Only Geese and Other Tales of the Far North*. Harcourt, 1997. / Sabuda, Robert. *The Blizzard's Robe*. Atheneum, 1999. / Sloat, Teri. *The Hungry Giant of the Tundra*. Dutton, 1993.

SUBJECTS: ARCTIC REGIONS. DWELLINGS. IGLOOS. INUIT. MULTICULTURAL BOOKS. SNOW.

1686 **Sturges, Philemon.** *Bridges Are to Cross*. **Illus. by Giles Laroche. Putnam, 1998. 0-399-23174-9. 32pp. Gr. 1–4**

Visit bridges around the world, from San Francisco to Japan. Each double-page spread features a precise, strikingly beautiful, paper-cut collage-style illustration of one type of bridge, including a covered bridge, Tower Bridge in London, a Roman aqueduct, a rope suspension bridge in the Andes of Peru, and the Rialto in Venice.

GERM: Very brief descriptive sentences give a bit of information, but children can certainly find out more in encyclopedias (there not being an overabundance of books on famous bridges for elementary school). It's an appetite-whetter for geography and engineering fans, and could inspire readers to go visit some of these someday—I've crossed 6 of the 15 actual bridges listed!—or to design and construct a new bridge. *The Great Bridge-Building Contest* by Bo Zaunders is the true story of a bridge built in West Virginia in 1852.

RELATED TITLES: Burleigh, Robert. *Earth from Above for Young Readers*. Abrams, 2002. / Curlee, Lynn. *Brooklyn Bridge*. Atheneum, 2001. / Jenkins, Steve. *Hottest Coldest Highest Deepest*. Houghton Mifflin, 1998. / Krupp, Robin Rector. *Let's Go Traveling*. Morrow, 1992. / Lewis, J. Patrick. *A World of Wonders*. Dial, 2002. / Robbins, Ken. *Bridges*. Dial, 1991. / Sturges, Philemon. *Bridges Are to Cross*. Putnam, 2005. / Zaunders, Bo. *The Great Bridge-Building Contest*. Abrams, 2004.

SUBJECTS: BRIDGES. GEOGRAPHY.

1687 **Sturges, Philemon.** *I Love Trucks*. **Illus. by Shari Halpern. HarperCollins, 1999. 0-06-027819-6. Unp. Gr. PreK–1**

A brown-haired child explains in rhyme what trucks do; the big, blocky, primary-colored truck pictures will make truck-lovers joyful.

GERM: As simple as it gets, this one goes perfectly with personified truck stories such as *I Stink!* by Kate McMullan, featuring a garbage truck, and *Isaac the Ice Cream Truck* by Scott Santoro.

RELATED TITLES: Barton, Byron. *My Car*. Greenwillow, 2001. / Burton, Virginia Lee. *Katy and the Big Snow*. Houghton Mifflin, 1943. / Burton, Virginia Lee. *Mike Mulligan and His Steam Shovel*. Houghton Mifflin, 1939. / Gramatky, Hardie. *Hercules*. Putnam, 1940. / Kirk, Daniel. *Go!* Hyperion, 2001. / Lyon, David. *The Biggest Truck*. Lothrop, 1988. / McMullan, Kate. *I Stink!* HarperCollins, 2002. / McMullan, Kate. *I'm Mighty!* Harper-Collins, 2003. / Santoro, Scott. *Isaac the Ice Cream Truck*. Henry Holt, 1999. / Sobel, June. *B Is for Bulldozer: A Construction ABC*. Harcourt, 2003. / Zelinsky, Paul O. *The Wheels on the Bus*. Dutton, 1990.

SUBJECTS: STORIES IN RHYME. TRANSPORTATION. TRUCKS. VEHICLES.

1688 **Swain, Ruth Freeman.** *Bedtime!* **Illus. by Cat Bowman Smith. Holiday House, 1999. 0-8234-1444-2. Unp. Gr. 1–4**

During ancient times, the Egyptians used headrests and mosquito nets, the Chinese slept on heated platforms called kíangs, and natives of Central and South America swung in hammocks. In this breezy yet informative picture book with good-humored watercolors, learn about sleeping habits and customs around the globe from ancient times to now.

GERM: Make those text-to-life connections: how do you sleep now? Children can draw and write about their own quirky nighttime habits. Throw a pajama party.

RELATED TITLES: Baer, Edith. *This Is the Way We Eat Our Lunch: A Book About Children Around the World.* Scholastic, 1995. / Baer, Edith. *This Is the Way We Go to School: A Book About Children Around the World.* Scholastic, 1990. / Cook, Sally. *Good Night Pillow Fight.* HarperCollins, 2004. / Dorros, Arthur. *This Is My House.* Scholastic, 1992. / Lauber, Patricia. *What You Never Knew About Fingers, Forks, and Chopsticks.* Simon & Schuster, 1999. / Swain, Ruth Freeman. *How Sweet It Is (and Was): The History of Candy.* Holiday House, 2003.

SUBJECTS: BEDS. BEDTIME. MULTICULTURAL BOOKS. SLEEP.

1689 **Swain, Ruth Freeman.** *How Sweet It Is (and Was): The History of Candy.* **Illus. by John O'Brien. Holiday House, 2003. 0-8234-1712-3. Unp. Gr. 2–6**

Greedy sweet-eaters will be sated by this lighthearted but factual look at candy through the ages, from the origin of the word "candy" in India to facts about candy today.

GERM: Sweet-toothed children can work in pairs, pick a favorite candy, and research its origin, using the "All About Candy" button on the Web site <www.candyusa.org> to find out when it was first made and where. Jaunty pen-and-ink and watercolor illustrations might make you crave a bit of sugar, as will the Candy Time Line that starts with Columbus and the recipes for 16th-century sugar paste and Vassar Fudge, which you could concoct. To stave off cavities, tie this in to your dental health unit, which should also include *George Washington's Teeth,* a biography told in rhyme by Deborah Chandra and Madeline Comora, and *Sweet Tooth* by Margie Palatini.

RELATED TITLES: Appelbaum, Diana. *Cocoa Ice.* Orchard, 1997. / Chandra, Deborah, and Madeline Comora. *George Washington's Teeth.* Farrar, 2003. / Greenstein, Elaine. *Ice-Cream Cones for Sale.* Scholastic, 2003. / Hopkinson, Deborah. *Fannie in the Kitchen: The Whole Story from Soup to Nuts of How Fannie Farmer Invented Recipes with Precise Measurements.* Atheneum, 2001. / Jones, Charlotte Foltz. *Eat Your Words: A Fascinating Look at the Language of Food.* Delacorte, 1999. / Jones, Charlotte Foltz. *Mistakes That Worked.* Doubleday, 1991. / Keller, Laurie. *Open Wide: Tooth School Inside.* Henry Holt, 2000. / Lauber, Patricia. *What You Never Knew About Fingers, Forks, and Chopsticks.* Simon & Schuster, 1999. / Palatini, Margie. *Sweet Tooth.* Simon & Schuster, 2004. / Priceman, Marjorie. *How to Make an Apple Pie and See the World.* Knopf, 1994. / Swain, Ruth Freeman. *Bedtime!* Holiday House, 1999.

SUBJECTS: CANDY. FOOD.

1690 **Swinburne, Stephen R.** *Safe, Warm, and Snug.* **Illus. by Jose Aruego and Ariane Dewey. Harcourt, 1999. 0-15-201734-8. Unp. Gr. PreK–2**

How do animals protect their young from predators? The informative, rhyming text, with large, colorful, affectionate illustrations, showcases the efforts of 11 animal parents to ensure the safely of their babies.

GERM: The final pages give additional information about the animals, which include the kangaroo, killdeer, Surinam toad, seahorse, and tumble bug. Search out more facts about each animal, using books, encyclopedias, or the Internet. Meet more babies and their fathers in *Animal Dads* by Sneed B. Collard, III.

RELATED TITLES: Ashman, Linda. *Babies on the Go.* Harcourt, 2003. / Bauer, Marion Dane. *If You Were Born a Kitten.* Simon & Schuster, 1997. / Browne, Philippa-Alys. *Kangaroos Have Joeys.* Atheneum, 1996. / Collard, Sneed B., III. *Animal Dads.* Houghton Mifflin, 1997. / Jenkins, Steve. *Big and Little.* Houghton Mifflin, 1996. / Jenkins, Steve. *Biggest, Strongest, Fastest.* Ticknor & Fields, 1995. / Meyers, Susan. *Everywhere Babies.* Harcourt, 2001. / Ryan, Pam Muñoz. *A Pinky Is a Baby Mouse and Other Baby Animal Names.* Dial, 1998. / Waddell, Martin. *Owl Babies.* Candlewick, 1992.

SUBJECTS: ANIMALS—HABITS AND BEHAVIOR. ANIMALS—INFANCY. STORIES IN RHYME.

1691 **Tang, Greg.** *The Best of Times: Math Strategies that Multiply.* **Illus. by Harry Briggs. Scholastic, 2002. 0-439-21033-X. Unp. Gr. 2–5**

To help children develop a more intuitive understanding of multiplication concepts and shortcuts, here are poems and pictures to puzzle over that illustrate techniques and strategies for multiplying each number from 0 to 10.

GERM: Solve the first few visual math problems with your students, reading aloud the answers at the back of the book, and then let them try to work out the other answers by themselves. Photocopy sets of problems and their pictures for pairs or trios to figure out, and then have them report back to the whole group before you read the author's solutions aloud.

RELATED TITLES: Adler, David A. *Easy Math Puzzles.* Holiday House, 1997. / Demi. *A Grain of Rice.*

Scholastic, 1997. / Franco, Betsy. *Counting Our Way to the 100th Day!* McElderry, 2004. / Franco, Betsy. *Mathematickles!* McElderry, 2003. / Leedy, Loreen. *Mission: Addition.* Holiday House, 1997. / Leedy, Loreen. *2 X 2 = BOO! A Set of Spooky Multiplication Stories.* Holiday House, 1995. / Michelson, Richard. *Ten Times Better.* Marshall Cavendish, 2000. / Murphy, Stuart. *Too Many Kangaroo Things to Do!* HarperCollins, 1996. / Pinczes, Elinor J. *One Hundred Hungry Ants.* Houghton Mifflin, 1993. / Scieszka, Jon. *Math Curse.* Viking, 1995. / Tang, Greg. *The Grapes of Math: Mind-Stretching Math Riddles.* Scholastic, 2001. / Tang, Greg. *Math Appeal: Mind-Stretching Math Riddles.* Scholastic, 2003. / Tang, Greg. *Math for All Seasons: Mind-Stretching Math Riddles.* Scholastic, 2001. / Tang, Greg. *Math Potatoes: Mind-Stretching Brain Food.* Scholastic, 2005.
SUBJECTS: MATHEMATICS. MULTIPLICATION. RIDDLES. STORIES IN RHYME.

1692 Tang, Greg. *The Grapes of Math: Mind-Stretching Math Riddles.* **Illus. by Harry Briggs. Scholastic, 2001. 0-439-21033-X. Unp. Gr. 2–5**
Sixteen engagingly illustrated, rhyming math problems test children's problem solving and creative thinking skills as they look for patterns and symmetries and learn an alternative way to add using visual tricks.
GERM: Once you've read and solved the 16 math problems, with the help of the answers at the back, have your math crew write up new addition problems in verse and compose mathematics-based pictures to go along.
RELATED TITLES: Adler, David A. *Easy Math Puzzles.* Holiday House, 1997. / Demi. *A Grain of Rice.* Scholastic, 1997. / Franco, Betsy. *Mathematickles!* McElderry, 2003. / Leedy, Loreen. *Mission: Addition.* Holiday House, 1997. / Leedy, Loreen. *2 X 2 = BOO! A Set of Spooky Multiplication Stories.* Holiday House, 1995. / Murphy, Stuart. *Too Many Kangaroo Things to Do!* HarperCollins, 1996. / Pinczes, Elinor J. *One Hundred Hungry Ants.* Houghton Mifflin, 1993. / Schwartz, David M. *How Much Is a Million?* Lothrop, 1985. / Scieszka, Jon. *Math Curse.* Viking, 1995. / Tang, Greg. *The Best of Times: Math Strategies That Multiply.* Scholastic, 2002. / Tang, Greg. *Math Appeal: Mind-Stretching Math Riddles.* Scholastic, 2003. / Tang, Greg. *Math for All Seasons: Mind-Stretching Math Riddles.* Scholastic, 2001. / Tang, Greg. *Math Potatoes: Mind-Stretching Brain Food.* Scholastic, 2005. / Tang, Greg. *Math-terpieces: The Art of Problem Solving.* Scholastic, 2003.
SUBJECTS: ADDITION. MATHEMATICS. RIDDLES. STORIES IN RHYME.

1693 Tang, Greg. *Math-terpieces: The Art of Problem Solving.* **Illus. by Greg Paprocki. Scholastic, 2003. 0-439-44388-1. 31pp. Gr. K–2**
Tang takes a fresh approach to math, asking children to look at a famous painting (there are 12 in all) and read the rhyming addition problem below it. He then has them solve the problem using the groups of related objects from the painting reproduced on the facing page.
GERM: An original look at set theory, Tang's merging of art and addition nicely integrates art and math. Solutions at the back of the book will help students develop strategies for grouping objects and numbers. As a quick intro to famous painters, the brief, rhyming descriptions of the artists' work can be jumping-off points for older children to use in research projects, report writing, and presentations. Greg Tang's other math picture books, including *The Grapes of Math* and *Math Appeal*, also encourage children to use problem-solving strategies in adding, multiplying, and counting.
RELATED TITLES: Brown, Laurene Krasny. *Visiting the Art Museum.* Dutton, 1986. / Franco, Betsy. *Mathematickles!* McElderry, 2003. / Hopkins, Lee Bennett, comp. *Marvelous Math: A Book of Poems.* Simon & Schuster, 1997. / Leedy, Loreen. *Mission: Addition.* Holiday House, 1997. / Pilkey, Dav. *When Cats Dream.* Orchard, 1992. / Pinczes, Elinor J. *One Hundred Hungry Ants.* Houghton Mifflin, 1993. / Raczka, Bob. *Art Is . . .* Millbrook, 2003. / Reynolds, Peter. *The Dot.* Candlewick, 2003. / Schwartz, David M. *How Much Is a Million?* Lothrop, 1985. / Tang, Greg. *The Grapes of Math.* Scholastic, 2001. / Tang, Greg. *Math Appeal: Mind-Stretching Math Riddles.* Scholastic, 2003. / Tang, Greg. *Math Fables.* Scholastic, 2004. / Tang, Greg. *Math for All Seasons: Mind-Stretching Math Riddles.* Scholastic, 2001.
SUBJECTS: ADDITION. ART APPRECIATION. ARTISTS. COUNTING BOOKS. MATHEMATICS. PAINTINGS. PICTURE BOOKS FOR ALL AGES. SET THEORY.

1694 Turner, Pamela S. *Hachiko: The True Story of a Loyal Dog.* **Illus. by Yan Nascimbene. Houghton Mifflin, 2004. 0-618-14094-8. Unp. Gr. 1–4**
The fictional narrator, Kentaro, recalls his childhood encounter with the admirable Hachiko, a dog that waited patiently at the Shibuya Train Station in Tokyo each day for the train carrying his beloved master, Dr. Ueno. When Dr. Ueno died suddenly in 1925, the dog continued his daily vigil at the station until his own death in 1935. Spare, somber watercolors, inspired by Japanese woodblock prints, frame the true story of a dog whose love and devotion inspired a statue in his honor.

GERM: Discussion point: Why do people in Japan still celebrate Hachiko's life? What loyal dogs have you known? For another fictional version of the dog's life, see *Hachiko Waits* by Leslea Newman.

RELATED TITLES: Blake, Robert. *Togo*. Philomel, 2002. / Brenner, Barbara, and Julia Takaya. *Chibi: A True Story from Japan*. Clarion, 1996. / Cullen, Lynn. *The Mightiest Heart*. Dial, 1998. / Miller, Debbie S. *The Great Serum Race: Blazing the Iditarod Trail*. Walker, 2002. / Newman, Leslea. *Hachiko Waits*. Henry Holt, 2004. / Paulsen, Gary. *Dogteam*. Delacorte, 1993. / Seibert, Patricia. *Mush! Across Alaska in the World's Longest Sled-Dog Race*. Millbrook, 1992. / Waite, Michael P. *Jojofu*. Lothrop, 1996.

SUBJECTS: DOGS. JAPAN. LOYALTY. TOKYO.

1695 **Waters, Kate.** *On the Mayflower: Voyage of the Ship's Apprentice and a Passenger Girl*. **Photos by Russ Kendall. Scholastic, 1996. 0-590-67308-4. 40pp. Gr. 2–5**

Follow Will Small, 8-year-old ship's apprentice, as the *Mayflower* sets sail for the New World. This color photo-filled reenactment was staged aboard the *Mayflower II*, which is a replica of the original ship.

GERM: Other personal narratives in the series by Kate Waters that brings to life American history in the time of Plymouth Colony include *Samuel Eaton's Day*, *Sarah Morton's Day*, and *Tapenum's Day*.

RELATED TITLES: Aliki. *Marianthe's Story: Painted Words, Spoken Memories*. Greenwillow, 1998. / Anderson, Laurie Halse. *Thank You, Sarah: The Woman Who Saved Thanksgiving*. Simon & Schuster, 2002. / Cohen, Barbara. *Molly's Pilgrim*. Lothrop, 1998. / Garland, Sherry. *The Lotus Seed*. Harcourt, 1993. / George, Jean Craighead. *The First Thanksgiving*. Philomel, 1993. / Harness, Cheryl. *Three Young Pilgrims*. Bradbury, 1992. / Kay, Verla. *Tattered Sails*. Putnam, 2001. / Van Leeuwen, Jean. *Across the Wide Dark Sea: The Mayflower Journey*. Dial, 1996. / Waters, Kate. *Samuel Eaton's Day: A Day in the Life of a Pilgrim Boy*. Scholastic, 1993. / Waters, Kate. *Sarah Morton's Day: A Day in the Life of a Pilgrim Girl*. Scholastic, 1989. / Waters, Kate. *Tapenum's Day: A Wampanoag Indian Boy in Pilgrim Times*. Scholastic, 1996.

SUBJECTS: MASSACHUSETTS—HISTORY. MAYFLOWER (SHIP). PILGRIMS. PLYMOUTH COLONY, 1620–1691. SHIPS. U.S.—HISTORY—COLONIAL PERIOD.

1696 **Wells, Robert E.** *Can You Count to a Googol?* **Illus. by the author. Albert Whitman, 2000. 0-8075-1060-2. Unp. Gr. 1–4**

"Put a zero after the number 1 and it becomes 10." So begins a genial but factual look at how big numbers get as you add a zero to the end of each one, all the way up to a googol, with 100 zeroes. Pen-and-acrylic illustrations follow a boy and girl as they interact with 100 penguins eating 1,000 scoops of ice cream or pack 1 million dollar bills in a crate.

GERM: Show everyone how big a number a googol is. I used 34 attached sheets of accordion-folded dot matrix computer paper, laid out in the hallway, and had students draw a 10 and a comma on the first page, and then three large zeroes followed by a comma on each of the following pages.

RELATED TITLES: Lasky, Kathryn. *The Librarian Who Measured the Earth*. Little, Brown, 1994. / Schmandt-Besserat, Denise. *The History of Counting*. Morrow, 1999. / Schwartz, David M. *G Is for Googol*. Tricycle, 1998. / Schwartz, David M. *How Much Is a Million?* Lothrop, 1985. / Schwartz, David M. *On Beyond a Million: An Amazing Math Journey*. Doubleday, 1999. / Wells, Robert E. *How Do You Know What Time It Is?* Albert Whitman, 2002. / Wells, Robert E. *Is a Blue Whale the Biggest Thing There Is?* Albert Whitman, 1993. / Wells, Robert E. *What's Faster Than a Speeding Cheetah?* Albert Whitman, 1997. / Wells, Robert E. *What's Older Than a Giant Tortoise?* Albert Whitman, 2004. / Wells, Robert E. *What's Smaller Than a Pygmy Shrew?* Albert Whitman, 1995.

SUBJECTS: DECIMAL SYSTEM. MATHEMATICS. MEASUREMENT. MULTIPLICATION. NUMBERS.

1697 **Wells, Robert E.** *How Do You Know What Time It Is?* **Illus. by the author. Albert Whitman, 2002. 0-8075-7939-4. Unp. Gr. 2–4**

Travel back in history to see how our ancestors measured time, from Egyptian shadow stick clocks and sundials all the way to modern-day atomic clocks, which now keep Earth's official time. This picture book crams lots of facts into the hand-lettered text and cheerful pen-and-acrylic illustrations. Along with a boy, a girl, and a dog, we learn all about the moon's orbit and lunar calendars, the sun's orbit and solar calendars, and our 24 time zones.

GERM: Do a bit of digging into time zones and figure out what time it is in cities around the world. *Is Anybody Up?* by Ellen Kandoian and *Nine O'Clock Lullaby* by Marilyn Singer are picture-book stories that take us around the world to various time zones.

RELATED TITLES: Borden, Louise. *Sea Clocks: The Story of Longitude*. McElderry, 2003. / Hopkins, Lee Bennett, comp. *It's About Time*. Simon & Schuster, 1993. / Kandoian, Ellen. *Is Anybody Up?* Putnam, 1989. / Lasky, Kathryn. *The Librarian Who Measured the Earth*. Little, Brown, 1994. / Lasky, Kathryn. *The Man Who Made Time Travel*. Farrar, 2003. / Singer, Marilyn. *Nine O'Clock Lullaby*. HarperCollins, 1991. / Wells, Robert E. *Can You Count to a Googol?* Albert Whitman, 2000. / Wells, Robert E. *Is a Blue Whale the Biggest Thing There Is?* Albert Whitman, 1993. / Wells, Robert E. *What's Faster Than a Speeding Cheetah?* Albert Whitman, 1997. / Wells, Robert E. *What's Older Than a Giant Tortoise?* Albert Whitman, 2004. / Wells, Robert E. *What's Smaller Than a Pygmy Shrew?* Albert Whitman, 1995.

SUBJECTS: CALENDARS. CLOCKS AND WATCHES. SEASONS. TIME.

1698   Wells, Robert E. *What's Faster Than a Speeding Cheetah?* Illus. by the author. Albert Whitman, 1997. 0-8075-2281-3. Unp. Gr. 1–4

At a top speed of 15 miles an hour, we humans are bested by the fastest two-legged runner, the ostrich; as well as by a cheetah; a swooping peregrine falcon; an airplane; a rocket ship; a meteor; and the fastest thing of all: the speed of light. Wells takes us from fast to fastest with his amiable, hand-lettered pen-and-acrylic illustrations and his facts about very fast things.

GERM: Bring in a flashlight and start your study of the properties of light using this book. There's an interesting chart at the back showing how long it would take each speedy thing to get to the moon, about 239,000 miles away.

RELATED TITLES: Jenkins, Steve. *Actual Size*. Houghton Mifflin, 2004. / Jenkins, Steve. *Big and Little*. Houghton Mifflin, 1996. / Wells, Robert E. *Can You Count to a Googol?* Albert Whitman, 2000. / Wells, Robert E. *Is a Blue Whale the Biggest Thing There Is?* Albert Whitman, 1993. / Wells, Robert E. *What's Older Than a Giant Tortoise?* Albert Whitman, 2004. / Wells, Robert E. *What's Smaller Than a Pygmy Shrew?* Albert Whitman, 1995.

SUBJECTS: LIGHT. SCIENCE. SOUND. SPEED.

1699   Wells, Robert E. *What's Older Than a Giant Tortoise?* Illus. by the author. Albert Whitman, 2004. 0-8075-8831-8. Unp. Gr. 1–4

"Some giant tortoises live more than 150 years—longer than any other known land animal." Wells introduces us to a succession of things older than the giant tortoise, ending with the oldest thing of all, our universe, believed to be a mere 13.7 billion years old. His humorous pen-and-acrylic illustrations and easy-to-digest hand-lettered text make for an appealing picture-book format you can use with fact-lovers of all ages.

GERM: Reading this (and all of Wells's books) aloud to curious learners will send them scrambling to find out more. After finishing this book, they can conduct research of their own, looking up information and doing expository or factual writing about sequoias, pyramids, meteors, fossils, mammoths, Mount Everest, T. rex, the earth, the moon, and the universe.

RELATED TITLES: Collard, Sneed B., III. *1,000 Years Ago on Planet Earth*. Houghton Mifflin, 1999. / Fleming, Candace. *Sunny Boy! The Life and Times of a Tortoise*. Farrar, 2005. / Goodman, Susan E. *On This Spot: An Expedition Back Through Time*. Greenwillow, 2004. / Hooper, Meredith. *The Pebble in My Pocket: A History of Our Earth*. Viking, 1996. / Jenkins, Steve. *Biggest, Strongest, Fastest*. Ticknor & Fields, 1995. / Jenkins, Steve. *Hottest Coldest Highest Deepest*. Houghton Mifflin, 1998. / Jenkins, Steve. *Life on Earth: The Story of Evolution*. Houghton Mifflin, 2002. / Wells, Robert E. *Is a Blue Whale the Biggest Thing There Is?* Albert Whitman, 1993. / Wells, Robert E. *What's Faster Than a Speeding Cheetah?* Albert Whitman, 1997. / Wells, Robert E. *What's Smaller Than a Pygmy Shrew?* Albert Whitman, 1995.

SUBJECTS: AGE. EARTH. GEOLOGY. SCIENCE.

1700   Wells, Robert E. *What's Smaller Than a Pygmy Shrew?* Illus. by the author. Albert Whitman, 1995. 0-8075-8837-7. Unp. Gr. 2–5

In a simple explanation of the world's smallest particles, work your way down in size from small animals to cells, bacteria, and finally, atoms, made up of electrons, protons, neutrons, and quarks.

GERM: Go from smallest to largest with Wells's *Is a Blue Whale the Biggest Thing There Is?*

RELATED TITLES: Jenkins, Steve. *Actual Size*. Houghton Mifflin, 2004. / Jenkins, Steve. *Big and Little*. Houghton Mifflin, 1996. / Wells, Robert E. *Is a Blue Whale the Biggest Thing There Is?* Albert Whitman, 1993. / Wells, Robert E. *What's Faster Than a Speeding Cheetah?* Albert Whitman, 1997. / Wells, Robert E. *What's Older Than a Giant Tortoise?* Albert Whitman, 2004.

SUBJECTS: ATOMS. SCIENCE. SIZE.

1701   Wethered, Peggy, and Ken Edgett. *Touchdown Mars! An ABC Adventure*. Illus. by Michael Chesworth. Putnam, 2000. 0-399-23214-1. Unp. Gr. 1–3

"You are an astronaut! These are your crewmates. You are going to Mars!" Join up with a group of eight space-suited, ethnically diverse kids and a pet cat as they board their spacecraft and set off for a three-year mission to Mars. Watercolor and ink illustrations and an alphabet book-style text take us on a weightless journey inside the spacecraft and then for a hike on the Red Planet itself, with its canyons and volcanoes and a temperature that ranges from 200° below zero at the north pole to a cozy 70° by its equator.

GERM: The "Mars A-B-Cyclopedia" at the back of the book provides more alphabetical facts about the planet, and the endpapers trace our route there and back. Move from the imaginative text of *I'll Catch the Moon* by Nina Crews to more fact-based (though also fictional) space adventures such as *The Magic School Bus Lost in the Solar System* by Joanna Cole, Loreen Leedy's *Postcards from Pluto*, and Faith McNulty's *If You Decide to Go to the Moon*.

RELATED TITLES: Burleigh, Robert. *Earth from Above for Young Readers*. Abrams, 2002. / Cole, Joanna. *The Magic School Bus Lost in the Solar System*. Scholastic, 1990. / Crews, Nina. *I'll Catch the Moon*. Greenwillow, 1996. / Fraser, Mary Ann. *One Giant Leap*. Henry Holt, 1993. / Haddon, Mark. *The Sea of Tranquility*. Harcourt, 1996. / Hopkins, Lee Bennett, comp. *Blast Off! Poems About Space*. HarperCollins, 1995. / Krupp, E. C. *The Moon and You*. Macmillan, 1993. / Leedy, Loreen. *Postcards from Pluto: A Tour of the Solar System*. Holiday House, 1993. / McNulty, Faith. *If You Decide to Go to the Moon*. Scholastic, 2005. / Ride, Sally. *To Space and Back*. Lothrop, 1986. / Shields, Carol Diggory. *Martian Rock*. Candlewick, 1999. / Simon, Seymour. *Earth: Our Planet in Space*. Simon & Schuster, 2003. / Simon, Seymour. *Planets Around the Sun*. SeaStar, 2002. / Suen, Anastasia. *Man on the Moon*. Viking, 1997. / Wetterer, Margaret. *Clyde Tombaugh and the Search for Planet X*. Carolrhoda, 1996.

SUBJECTS: ALPHABET BOOKS. MARS (PLANET). PLANETS. SCIENCE. SPACE FLIGHT. VOYAGES, IMAGINARY.

1702 **Wick, Walter.** *A Drop of Water: A Book of Science and Wonder*. **Photos by the author. Scholastic, 1997. 0-590-22197-3. 40pp. Gr. 3–6**
Wick's crystal-clear color close-up photos and equally compelling text lead us to discover the many interesting and unusual properties of water. Each photograph—of such subjects as surface tension, soap bubbles, ice, water vapor, and condensation—is accompanied by a thoughtful description that children can use as the basis for an easy-to-perform experiment.

GERM: Break your group into pairs or trios and have each work on a different experiment that they can then demonstrate to the others. Enhance your water or matter unit with *Water Dance* by Thomas Locker, with its sweeping paintings and poetic tribute to all forms of water. *Splish Splash* by Joan Bransfield Graham is a flamboyant collection of 21 graphically exciting, concrete poems about water. In the picture book *My Life with the Wave* by Catherine Cowan, a boy brings home from the seaside an ebullient wave that romps through the house with him until its mood turns bleak and stormy. And meet a science teacher who gets his children finding out all about solids, liquids, and gasses through play, observation, and simple science experiments in *What's the Matter in Mr. Whisker's Room?* by Michael Elsohn Ross.

RELATED TITLES: Cole, Joanna. *The Magic School Bus at the Waterworks*. Scholastic, 1988. / Cowan, Catherine. *My Life with the Wave*. Lothrop, 1997. / Dorros, Walter. *Follow the Water from Brook to Ocean*. HarperCollins, 1991. / Frasier, Debra. *The Incredible Water Show*. Harcourt, 2004. / Graham, Joan Bransfield. *Splish Splash*. Ticknor & Fields, 1994. / Hathorn, Libby. *The Wonder Thing*. Houghton Mifflin, 1996. / Kerley, Barbara. *A Cool Drink of Water*. National Geographic, 2002. / Levy, Constance. *Splash! Poems of Our Watery World*. Orchard, 2002. / Lewis, J. Patrick. *Earth Verses and Water Rhymes*. Atheneum, 1991. / Locker, Thomas. *Water Dance*. Harcourt, 1997. / Peters, Lisa Westberg. *Water's Way*. Little, Brown, 1991. / Ross, Michael Elsohn. *What's the Matter in Mr. Whisker's Room?* Candlewick, 2004. / Wiesner, David. *Sector 7*. Clarion, 1999.

SUBJECTS: SCIENCE—EXPERIMENTS. WATER.

1703 **Wormell, Christopher.** *Teeth, Tails, and Tentacles: An Animal Counting Book*. **Illus. by the author. Running Press, 2004. 0-7624-2100-2. Unp. Gr. PreK–2**
From 1 to 20, count the physical characteristics of 20 animals, including the 2 humps on a camel, the 8 tentacles on an octopus, and the 12 antler points on a stag. Each double-page spread includes the number and name of the body part on the left-hand page, and a large, dignified, and assertive animal portrait (a lino-cut print bordered in black) on the right.

GERM: As you count up to 20, this handsome volume is also an appetite-whetter for identifying the characteristics of each animal. Notes at the back provide more facts about the animals that Wormell profiles. Children can find separate books on each creature or draw new animal counting pages for other interesting species, emulating Wormell's style of dark, black-bordered portraits. Use this with *Actual Size* by Steve Jenkins to produce contented aahhh's from all of those animal-lovers.

RELATED TITLES: Ehlert, Lois. *Fish Eyes: A Book You Can Count On.* Harcourt, 1990. / Freymann, Saxton. *Food for Thought: The Complete Book of Concepts for Growing Minds.* Scholastic, 2005. / Freymann, Saxton, and Joost Elffers. *One Lonely Sea Horse.* Scholastic, 2000. / Harshman, Marc. *Only One.* Dutton, 1993. / Jenkins, Steve. *Actual Size.* Houghton Mifflin, 2004. / Jenkins, Steve, and Robin Page. *What Do You Do with a Tail Like This?* Houghton Mifflin, 2003. / Jolivet, Joëlle. *Zoo-ology.* Roaring Brook, 2003. / MacDonald, Suse. *Look Whooo's Counting.* Scholastic, 2000. / Michelson, Richard. *Ten Times Better.* Marshall Cavendish, 2000. / Sayre, April Pulley, and Jeff Sayre. *One Is a Snail, Ten Is a Crab; A Counting by Feet Book.* Candlewick, 2003. / Wormell, Christopher. *The New Alphabet of Animals.* Running Press, 2004.
SUBJECTS: ANIMALS. COUNTING BOOKS.

1704 **Zaunders, Bo.** *The Great Bridge-Building Contest.* **Illus. by Roxie Munro. Abrams, 2004. 0-8109-4929-6. Unp. Gr. 3–6**
In 1850, Virginia cabinetmaker Lemuel Chenoweth submitted to the Board of Public Works his model for a covered bridge to be built over a river in western Virginia (now West Virginia). Competing against experienced professional engineers, Lemuel demonstrated the sturdiness of his model by walking across the top of it, won the commission, and constructed a bridge that is still used today.
GERM: The back of the book includes a biography of Chenoweth, who was illustrator Roxie Munro's great-great-grandfather, and a description of 18 existing covered bridges, each depicted in Munro's meticulous pen-and-inks and watercolors. Highlight other self-taught folks who followed their passions, such as 17th-century clockmaker John Harrison, featured in *The Man Who Made Time Travel* by Kathryn Lasky; snowflake photographer Willie Bentley, using *Snowflake Bentley* by Jacqueline Briggs Martin; and Clyde Tombaugh, the man who discovered Pluto, in *Clyde Tombaugh and the Search for Planet X* by Margaret Wetterer.
RELATED TITLES: Curlee, Lynn. *Brooklyn Bridge.* Atheneum, 2001. / Lasky, Kathryn. *The Man Who Made Time Travel.* Farrar, 2003. / Martin, Jacqueline Briggs. *Snowflake Bentley.* Houghton Mifflin, 1998. / Robbins, Ken. *Bridges.* Dial, 1991. / Sturges, Philemon. *Bridges Are to Cross.* Putnam, 1998. / Wetterer, Margaret. *Clyde Tombaugh and the Search for Planet X.* Carolrhoda, 1996.
SUBJECTS: ARCHITECTS. BIOGRAPHY. BRIDGES. CIVIL ENGINEERS. CONTESTS. WEST VIRGINIA.

1705 **Zoehfeld, Kathleen Weidner.** *What Is the World Made Of? All About Solids, Liquids, and Gases.* **Illus. by Paul Meisel. HarperCollins, 1998. 0-06-027144-2. 32pp. Gr. K–3**
In this practical, concrete, and easy-to-follow science picture book from the Let's-Read-and-Find-Out Science series, children observe, experiment, and learn about the three forms of matter.
GERM: Try out the varied science experiments, including turning water into a solid and a gas, and smelling perfume from an unstopped bottle. Make charts of the three states of matter, using examples from your students' experiences. Also about the subject of matter are *What's the Matter in Mr. Whisker's Room?* by Michael Elsohn Ross and *A Drop of Water* by Walter Wick.
RELATED TITLES: Cobb, Vicki. *I Face the Wind.* HarperCollins, 2003. / Cobb, Vicki. *I Get Wet.* HarperCollins, 2002. / Cobb, Vicki. *I See Myself.* HarperCollins, 2002. / Cowan, Catherine. *My Life with the Wave.* Lothrop, 1997. / Dorros, Arthur. *Follow the Water from Brook to Ocean.* HarperCollins, 1991. / Frasier, Debra. *The Incredible Water Show.* Harcourt, 2004. / Graham, Joan Bransfield. *Splish Splash.* Ticknor & Fields, 1994. / Kerley, Barbara. *A Cool Drink of Water.* National Geographic, 2002. / Peters, Lisa Westberg. *Water's Way.* Little, Brown, 1991. / Ross, Michael Elsohn. *What's the Matter in Mr. Whisker's Room?* Candlewick, 2004. / Wick, Walter. *A Drop of Water.* Scholastic, 1997.
SUBJECTS: MATTER. SCIENCE. SCIENCE—EXPERIMENTS. WATER.

BIBLIOGRAPHY AND INDEXES

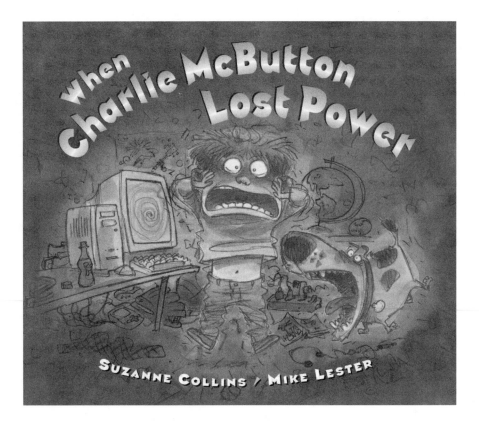

PROFESSIONAL BIBLIOGRAPHY

AN OVERVIEW OF CHILDREN'S LITERATURE: TEXTBOOKS

Barton, James. *Teaching With Children's Literature.* Christopher-Gordon, 2001. ISBN 1-929024-21-5.

Edwards, Margaret A. *The Fair Garden and the Swarm of Beasts: The Library and the Young Adult.* American Library Association, 2002. ISBN 0-8389-3533-8.

Galda, Lee, and Bernice Cullinan. *Literature and the Child.* 3rd ed. Wadsworth, 2006. ISBN 0-534-55544-6.

Huck, Charlotte, and Barbara Z. Kiefer, with Susan Hepler and Janet Hickman. *Children's Literature in the Elementary School.* 8th ed. McGraw-Hill, 2002. ISBN 0-07-287841-X.

Lukens, Rebecca J. *A Critical Handbook of Children's Literature.* 7th ed. Allyn & Bacon, 2002. ISBN 0-205-36013-0.

Norton, Donna E., and Saundra E. Norton. *Through the Eyes of a Child: An Introduction to Children's Literature.* 5th ed. Prentice-Hall, 1998. ISBN 0-13-667973-0.

Sloan, Glenna Davis. *The Child as Critic: Teaching Literature in the Elementary School.* 4th ed. Teachers College Press, 2003. ISBN 0-8077-4340-2.

Sutherland, Zena. *Children and Books.* 9th ed. Longman, 1997. ISBN 0-673-99733-2.

CHILDREN'S LITERATURE: ANNOTATED BIBLIOGRAPHIES

Bamford, Rosemary A., and Janice V. Kristo. *Checking Out Nonfiction K–8: Good Choices for Best Learning.* Christopher-Gordon, 2000. ISBN 1-929024-02-9.

Barr, Catherine. *From Biography to History: Best Books for Children's Entertainment and Education.* R. R. Bowker, 1998. ISBN 0-8352-4012-6.

Barr, Catherine, and John T. Gillespie. *Best Books for Children: Preschool Through Grade 6.* 8th ed. Libraries Unlimited, 2005. ISBN 1-59158-085-4.

Barstow, Barbara, and Judith Riggle. *Beyond Picture Books: A Guide to First Readers.* 2nd ed. R. R. Bowker, 1995. ISBN 0-8352-3519-X.

Baxter, Kathleen A., and Marcia Agness Kochel. *Gotcha! Nonfiction Booktalks to Get Kids Excited About Reading.* Libraries Unlimited, 1999. ISBN 1-56308-683-2.

Baxter, Kathleen A., and Marcia Agness Kochel. *Gotcha Again! More Nonfiction Booktalks to Get Kids Excited About Reading.* Libraries Unlimited, 2002. ISBN 1-56308-940-8.

Baxter, Kathleen A., and Michael Dahl. *Gotcha Covered! More Nonfiction Booktalks to Get Kids Excited About Reading.* Libraries Unlimited, 2005. ISBN 1-59158-225-3.

Beck, Peggy. *GlobaLinks: Resources for Asian Studies, Grades K–8.* Linworth, 2002. ISBN 1-58683-009-0.

Beck, Peggy. *GlobaLinks: Resources for World Studies, Grades K–8.* Linworth, 2002. ISBN 1-58683-040-6.

Cianciolo, Patricia. *Informational Picture Books for Children.* American Library Association, 2000. ISBN 0-8389-0774-1.

Cianciolo, Patricia. *Picture Books for Children.* 4th ed. American Library Association, 1997. ISBN 0-8389-0701-6.

Freeman, Judy. *Books Kids Will Sit Still For: The Complete Read-Aloud Guide.* Libraries Unlimited, 1990. ISBN 0-8352-3010-4.

Freeman, Judy. *More Books Kids Will Sit Still For: A Read-Aloud Guide.* Libraries Unlimited, 1995. ISBN 0-8352-3520-3.

Gillespie, John T. *The Children's and Young Adult Literature Handbook: A Research and Reference Guide.* Libraries Unlimited, 2005. ISBN 1-56308-949-1.

Gillespie, John T., and Corinne J. Naden. *The Newbery/Printz Companion: Booktalk and Related Materials for Award Winners and Honor Books.* Libraries Unlimited, 2006. ISBN 1-59158-313-6.

Hearne, Betsy, with Deborah Stevenson. *Choosing Books for Children: A Commonsense Guide.* Rev. ed. University of Illinois Press, 2000. ISBN 0-252-06928-5.

Lima, Carolyn W., and John A. Lima. *A to Zoo: Subject Access to Children's Picture Books.* 7th ed. Libraries Unlimited, 2005. ISBN 1-59158-232-6.

Lipson, Eden Ross. *The New York Times Parent's Guide to the Best Books for Children.* 3rd ed. Three Rivers Press, 2000. ISBN 0-8129-3018-5.

Silvey, Anita. *100 Best Books for Children.* Houghton Mifflin, 2004. ISBN 0-618-27889-3.

Thomas, Rebecca L., and Catherine Barr. *Popular Series Fiction for K–6 Readers: A Reading and Selection Guide.* Libraries Unlimited, 2004. ISBN 1-59158-203-2.

Reading, Writing and Children's Literature: Ideas and Annotations

Bamford, Rosemary A., and Janice V. Kristo, eds. *Making Facts Come Alive: Choosing Quality Nonfiction Literature K–8.* Christopher-Gordon, 1998. ISBN 0-926842-67-6.

Barchers, Suzanne I., and Patricia C. Marden. *Cooking Up U.S. History: Recipes and Research to Share with Children.* 2nd ed. Libraries Unlimited, 1999. ISBN 1-56308-682-4.

Bauer, Caroline Feller. *Read for the Fun of It: Active Programming with Books for Children.* Illus. by Lynn Gates Bredeson. H. W. Wilson, 1992. ISBN 0-8242-0824-2.

Bauer, Caroline Feller. *This Way to Books.* Illus. by Lynn Gates. H. W. Wilson, 1985. ISBN 0-8242-0678-9.

Benedict, Susan. *Beyond Words: Picture Books for Older Readers and Writers.* Heinemann, 1992. ISBN 0-435-08710-X.

Bradbury, Judy. *Children's Book Corner: A Read-Aloud Resource with Tips, Techniques, and Plans for Teachers, Librarians and Parents, Level Pre-K–K*. Libraries Unlimited, 2003. ISBN 1-59158-048-X.

Bradbury, Judy. *Children's Book Corner: A Read-Aloud Resource with Tips, Techniques, and Plans for Teachers, Librarians, and Parents, Grades 1 and 2*. Libraries Unlimited, 2004. ISBN 1-59158-047-1

Bradbury, Judy. *Children's Book Corner: A Read-Aloud Resource with Tips, Techniques, and Plans for Teachers, Librarians and Parents, Grades 3 and 4*. Libraries Unlimited, 2005. ISBN 1-59158-046-3.

Braddon, Kathryn L., Nancy J. Hall, and Dale Taylor. *Math Through Children's Literature: Making the NCTM Standards Come Alive*. Teacher Ideas Press, 1993. ISBN 0-87287-932-1.

Brown, Jean E., and Elaine C. Stephens. *Exploring Diversity: Literature Themes and Activities for Grades 4-8*. Teacher Ideas Press, 1996. ISBN 1-56308-322-1.

Butzow, Carol M., and John W. Butzow. *Science Through Children's Literature: An Integrated Approach*. 2nd ed. Teacher Ideas Press, 2000. ISBN 1-56308-651-4.

Buzzeo, Toni. *Collaborating to Meet Standards: Teacher/Librarian Partnerships for K–6*. Linworth, 2002. ISBN 1-58683-023-6.

Codell, Esmé Raji. *How to Get Your Child to Love Reading: For Ravenous and Reluctant Readers Alike*. Algonquin, 2003. ISBN 1-56512-308-5.

Cullinan, Bernice E. *Read to Me: Raising Kids Who Love to Read*. Rev. ed. Scholastic, 2000. ISBN 0-439-08721-X.

Forgan, James W. *Teaching Problem Solving Through Children's Literature*. Teacher Ideas Press, 2003. ISBN 1-56308-981-5.

Fox, Mem. *Reading Magic: Why Reading Aloud to Our Children Will Change Their Lives Forever*. Illus. by Judy Horacek. Harcourt, 2001. ISBN 0-15-100624-5.

Fredericks, Anthony D. *The Integrated Curriculum: Books for Reluctant Readers, Grades 2–5*. 2nd ed. Illus. by Anthony Allan Stoner. Teacher Ideas Press, 1998. ISBN 1-56308-604-2.

Fredericks, Anthony D. *More Social Studies Through Children's Literature: An Integrated Approach*. Teacher Ideas Press, 2000. ISBN 1-56308-761-8. Also see *Social Studies Through Children's Literature: An Integrated Approach* (1991).

Glandon, Shan. *Caldecott Connections to Language Arts*. Libraries Unlimited, 2000. ISBN 1-56308-846-0.

Hall, Susan. *Using Picture Storybooks to Teach Character Education*. Oryx, 2000. ISBN 1-57356-349-8.

Hall, Susan. *Using Picture Storybooks to Teach Literary Devices: Recommended Books for Children and Young Adults, Volume 3*. Oryx, 2002. ISBN 1-57356-350-1. Also see *Using Picture Storybooks to Teach Literary Devices, Volume 1* (1990) and *Using Picture Storybooks to Teach Literary Devices, Volume 2* (1994).

Harris, Violet J. *Using Multiethnic Literature in the K–8 Classroom*. Christopher-Gordon, 1997. ISBN 0-926842-60-9.

Irving, Jan. *Stories NeverEnding: A Program Guide for Schools and Libraries*. Libraries Unlimited, 2004. ISBN 1-56308-997-1.

Kaye, Peggy. *Games with Books: 28 of the Best Children's Books and How to Use Them to Help Your Child Learn—From Preschool to Third Grade.* Farrar, 2002. ISBN 0-374-52815-2.

Keane, Nancy J. *Booktalking Across the Curriculum: The Middle Years.* Libraries Unlimited, 2002. ISBN 1-56308-937-8.

Knowles, Elizabeth, and Martha Smith. *Talk About Books: A Guide for Book Clubs, Literature Circles, and Discussion Groups, Grades 4–8.* Libraries Unlimited, 2003. ISBN 1-59158-023-4.

Kuta, Katherine Wiesolek, and Susan Zernial. *Novel Ideas for Young Readers! Projects and Activities.* Teacher Ideas Press, 2000. ISBN 1-56308-791-X.

Langemack, Chapple. *The Booktalker's Bible: How to Talk About the Books You Love to Any Audience.* Libraries Unlimited, 2003. ISBN 1-56308-944-0.

Levene, Donna B. *Music Through Children's Literature: Theme and Variations.* Illus. by Susan Kochenberger Stroeher. Teacher Ideas Press, 1993. ISBN 1-56308-021-4.

McElmeel, Sharron L. *Character Education: A Book Guide for Teachers, Librarians, and Parents.* Libraries Unlimited, 2002. ISBN 1-56308-884-3.

Maddigan, Beth, and Stefanie Drennan. *The Big Book of Reading, Rhyming and Resources: Programs for Children, Ages 4–8.* Illus. by Roberta Thompson. Libraries Unlimited, 2005. ISBN 1-59158-220-2.

Maddigan, Beth, and Stefanie Drennan. *The Big Book of Stories, Songs, and Sing-Alongs: Programs for Babies, Toddlers, and Families.* Illus. by Roberta Thompson. Libraries Unlimited, 2003. ISBN 1-56308-975-0–

Marantz, Sylvia S. *Picture Books for Looking and Learning: Awakening Visual Perceptions Through the Art of Children's Books.* Oryx, 1992. ISBN 0-89774-716-X.

Miller, Pat. *Stretchy Library Lessons: Seasons & Celebrations.* Upstart Books, 2004. ISBN 1-932146-08-3. Other books in the series, all by Pat Miller, include: *Library Skills* (2003), *More Library Skills* (2005), *Multicultural Activities* (2003), *Reading Activities* (2003), and *Research Skills* (2003.)

Montgomery, Paula Kay. *Approaches to Literature Through Literary Form.* Oryx, 1995. ISBN 0-89774-775-5.

Odean, Kathleen. *Books for Boys: More than 600 Books for Boys 2 to 14.* Ballantine, 1998. ISBN 0-345-42083-7.

Odean, Kathleen. *Great Books About Things Kids Love: More Than 750 Recommended Books for Children 3 to 14.* Ballantine, 2001. ISBN 0-345-44131-1.

Odean, Kathleen. *Great Books for Babies and Toddlers: More Than 500 Recommended Books for Your Child's First Three Years.* Ballantine, 2003. ISBN 0-345-45254-2.

Odean, Kathleen. *Great Books for Girls: More Than 600 Books to Inspire Today's Girls and Tomorrow's Women.* Rev. ed. Ballantine, 2002. ISBN 0-345-45021-3.

Perez-Stable, Maria A., and Mary Hurlbut Cordier. *Understanding American History Through Children's Literature: Instructional Units and Activities for Grades K–8.* Oryx, 1994. ISBN 0-89774-795-X.

Polette, Nancy J. *Gifted Books, Gifted Readers: Literature Activities to Excite Young Minds.* Libraries Unlimited, 2000. ISBN 1-56308-822-3.

Polette, Nancy J. *Teaching Thinking Skills with Fairy Tales and Fantasy.* Teacher Ideas Press, 2005. ISBN 1-59158-320-9.

Reid, Rob. *Something Funny Happened at the Library: How to Create Humorous Programs for Children and Young Adults.* American Library Association, 2003. ISBN 0-8389-0836-5.

Soltan, Rita. *Reading Raps: A Book Club Guide for Librarians, Kids, and Families.* Libraries Unlimited, 2005. ISBN 1-59158-234-2.

Steiner, Stanley F. *Promoting a Global Community Through Multicultural Children's Literature.* Illus. by Peggy Hokom. Libraries Unlimited, 2001. ISBN 1-56308-705-7.

Stephens, Claire Gatrell. *Picture This! Using Picture Story Books for Character Education in the Classroom.* Libraries Unlimited, 2003. ISBN 1-59158-001-3.

Stripling, Barbara K., and Sandra Hughes-Hassell. *Curriculum Connections Through the Library.* Libraries Unlimited, 2003. ISBN 1-56308-973-4.

Tiedt, Iris McLellan. *Teaching With Picture Books in the Middle School.* International Reading Association, 2000. ISBN 0-87207-273-8.

Trelease, Jim. *The Read-Aloud Handbook.* 5th ed. Penguin, 2001. ISBN 0-8446-6172-4.

Wadham, Tim, and Rachel L. Wadham. *Bringing Fantasy Alive for Children and Young Adults.* Linworth, 1999. ISBN 0-938865-80-3.

Watt, Letty S., and Terri Parker Street. *Developing Learning Skills Through Children's Literature: An Idea Book for K–5 Classrooms and Libraries, Volume 2.* Oryx, 1994. ISBN 0-89774-746-1.

Webber, Desiree, Dee Ann Corn, Elaine Harrod, Donna Norvell, and Sandy Shropshire. *Travel the Globe: Multicultural Story Times.* Libraries Unlimited, 1998. ISBN 1-56308-501-1.

CHILDREN'S LITERATURE-BASED WEB PAGES

Aaron Shepard's Home Page (Check out author Aaron Shepard's amazing Web site, download one of his many fine Reader's Theater scripts, or book him for a workshop at your school): www.aaronshep.com

Advanced Book Exchange (ABE is the "world's largest online marketplace for books" new, used, rare, or out-of-print, including children's books): www.abebooks.com

Amazon (Offers full-text reviews from professional journals plus readers' own submissions): www.amazon.com and www.amazon.co.uk

American Library Association: www.ala.org

American Association of School Librarians: www.ala.org/aasl

Association for Library Service to Children: www.ala.org/alsc

Caldecott Medal: www.ala.org/alsc/caldecott.html

Newbery Medal: www.ala.org/alsc/newbery.html

Young Adult Library Services Association: www.ala.org/yalsa

The Book Hive (Short book reviews categorized by age level): www.bookhive.org

Carol Hurst's Children's Literature Site (Includes reviews of great children's books, author pages, classroom activities, lesson plans, and professional topics): www.carolhurst.com

Children's Book Council (Features information about new children's books, info on getting published, hundreds of links to authors' Web sites, and lots of great literacy materials to buy for Children's Book Week and Young People's Poetry Week): www.cbcbooks.org

Children's Writing Resource Center (Useful info for children's writers of all levels; this Best of the Net-nominated site is presented by the editors of the Children's Book Insider newsletter): www.write4kids.com

Cynthia Leitich Smith's Children's Literature Resources (Named one of the Top 10 Writers' Sites by Writer's Digest and selected as one of the "Great Web Sites for Kids" by ALA/ALSC, this site contains info on books, stories, articles, teacher/reader guides, and links to multicultural booklists and articles for concerned educators): www.cynthialeitichsmith.com

GUYSREAD (Jon Scieszka's push for getting boys to read): www.guysread.com

Jim Trelease (America's Reading Guru includes thoughtful commentary on reading, censorshop, AR, and getting children to read): www.trelease-on-reading.com

Kay E. Vandergrift's Special Interest Page (From well-known Rutgers professor Kay Vandergrift, a rich resource for students of children's literature who are interested in theory and research as they relate to teaching practice): www.scils.rutgers.edu/~kvander

Meet Authors and Illustrators (A vendor site with alphabetical-by-author listing of links): www.childrenslit.com/f_mai.htm

Mimi's Motifs (Fabulous source for storytelling dolls and puppets that can be tied into a variety of children's books): www.mimismotifs.com

Mona Kerby's Author Corner (Links to Web sites of Mid-Atlantic authors and illustrators): ccpl.carr.org/authco

Mona Kerby's Reading Corner (For Kids) (Short book reviews written for readers in grades 2 to 8): ccpl.carr.org/read

Nancy Keane's Booktalks (Booktalks, quick and simple. Includes indexes by author, title, subject, and interest level as well as general booktalking tips and student-written talks): nancykeane.com/booktalks

Nancy Polette (Ideas for using the best of the best picture books, fiction and nonfiction. Features a monthly sample literature guide): www.nancypolette.com

Planet Esme (Book reviews and ideas by Esmé Raji Codell, effervescent author of *Educating Esmé*): www.planetesme.com

Purple Crayon (Well-known children's editor Harold Underdown shares his knowledge about writing, illustrating, and publishing children's books): www.underdown.org

Society of Children's Book Writers & Illustrators (SCBWI) (For professional and aspiring writers and illustrators of children's books): www.scbwi.org

On the Teaching of Reading and Writing in the Classroom

Allington, Richard L. *What Really Matters for Struggling Readers: Designing Research-Based Programs*. 2nd ed. Allyn & Bacon, 2005. ISBN 0-205-44324-9.

Au, Kathryn H., Jacquelin H. Carroll, and Judith A. Scheu. *Balanced Literacy Instruction: A Teacher's Resource Book*. Christopher-Gordon, 2001. ISBN 1-929024-26-6.

Avery, Carol. . . . *And with a Light Touch: Learning About Reading, Writing, and Teaching with First Graders*. Heinemann, 2002. ISBN 0-325-00066-2.

Calkins, Lucy McCormick. *The Art of Teaching Writing*. New ed. Heinemann, 1994. ISBN 0-435-08817-3.

Calkins, Lucy McCormick, with Shelley Harwayne. *Living Between the Lines*. Heinemann, 1990. ISBN 0-435-08538-7.

Carr, Eileen, Loviah Aldinger, and Judythe Patberg. *Teaching Comprehension: A Systematic and Practical Framework with Lessons and Strategies*. Scholastic, 2004. ISBN 0-439-53135-7.

Casey, Jean M. *Early Literacy: The Empowerment of Technology*. Rev. ed. Libraries Unlimited, 2000. ISBN 1-56308-865-7.

Codell, Esmé Raji. *Educating Esmé: Diary of a Teacher's First Year.* Algonquin, 2001. ISBN 1-56512-225-9.

Cole, Ardith Davis. *Knee to Knee, Eye to Eye: Circling in on Comprehension.* Heinemann, 2003. ISBN 0-325-00494-3.

Culham, Ruth. *6 + 1 Traits of Writing: The Complete Guide for the Primary Grades.* Scholastic, 2005. ISBN 0-439-57412-9.

Culham, Ruth. *6 + 1 Traits of Writing: The Complete Guide, Grades 3 and Up.* Scholastic, 2003. ISBN 0-439-28038-9.

Daniels, Harvey. *Literature Circles: Voice and Choice in Book Clubs and Reading Groups.* 2nd ed. Stenhouse, 2002. ISBN 1-57110-333-3.

Daniels, Harvey, and Nancy Steineke. *Mini-Lessons for Literature Circles.* Heinemann, 2004. ISBN 0-325-00702-0.

Fisher, Bobbi. *Joyful Learning in Kindergarten.* Heinemann, 1998. ISBN 0-325-00038-7.

Fletcher, Ralph, and Joann Portalupi. *Craft Lessons: Teaching Writing K–8.* Stenhouse, 1998. ISBN 1-57110-073-3.

Fountas, Irene C., and Gay Su Pinnell. *Guiding Readers and Writers Grades 3–6: Teaching Comprehension, Genre, and Content Literacy.* Heinemann, 2001. ISBN 0-325-00310-6.

Graves, Donald. *Writing: Teachers & Children at Work.* 20th anniversary ed. Heinemann, 2003. ISBN 0-325-00525-7.

Graves, Michael, and Bonnie Graves. *Scaffolding Reading Experiences: Designs for Student Success.* 2nd ed. Christopher-Gordon, 2003. ISBN 1-929024-48-7.

Graves, Michael, Connie Juel, and Bonnie B. Graves. *Teaching Reading in the 21st Century.* 3rd ed. (with Assessment and Instruction Booklet). Christopher-Gordon, 2003. ISBN 0-205-40737-4.

Harvey, Stephanie. *Nonfiction Matters: Reading, Writing, and Research in Grades 3–8.* Stenhouse, 1998. ISBN 1-57110-072-5.

Harvey, Stephanie, and Anne Goudvis. *Strategies That Work: Teaching Comprehension to Enhance Understanding.* Stenhouse, 2000. ISBN 1-57110-310-4.

Hill, Bonnie Campbell, Nancy J. Johnson, and Katherine L. Schlick Noe. *Literature Circles and Response.* Christopher-Gordon, 1995. ISBN 0-926842-48-X.

Hoyt, Linda. *Revisit, Reflect, Retell: Strategies for Improving Reading Comprehension.* Heinemann, 1999. ISBN 0-325-00071-9.

Hoyt, Linda. *Spotlight on Comprehension: Building a Literacy of Thoughtfulness.* Heinemann, 2005. ISBN 0-325-00719-5.

Jonson, Kathleen Feeney. *60 Strategies for Improving Reading Comprehension in Grades K–8.* Corwin Press, 2006. ISBN 0-7619-8837-8.

Jurenka, Nancy Allen. *Teaching Phonemic Awareness Through Children's Literature and Experiences.* Teacher Ideas Press, 2005. ISBN 1-59469-000-6.

Kaye, Peggy. *Games for Writing: Playful Ways to Help Your Child Learn to Write.* Farrar, 1995. ISBN 0-374-52472-0.

Keene, Ellin Oliver, and Susan Zimmermann. *Mosaic of Thought: Teaching Comprehension in a Reader's Workshop.* Heinemann, 1997. ISBN 0-435-07237-4.

Knowles, Elizabeth, and Martha Smith. *Boys and Literacy: Practical Strategies for Librarians, Teachers, and Parents.* Libraries Unlimited, 2005. ISBN 1-59158-212-1.

Krashen, Stephen D. *The Power of Reading: Insights from the Research.* 2nd ed. Libraries Unlimited, 2004. ISBN 1-59158-169-9.

Kristo, Janice V., and Rosemary A. Bamford. *Nonfiction in Focus: A Comprehensive Framework for Helping Students Become Independent Readers and Writers of Nonfiction, K–6.* Scholastic, 2004. ISBN 0-439-36598-8.

Lane, Barry. *After the End: Teaching and Learning Creative Revision.* Heinemann, 1993. ISBN 0-435-08714-2.

Meyer, Anita Meinbach, Anthony Fredericks, and Liz Rothlein. *The Complete Guide to Thematic Units: Creating the Integrated Curriculum.* 2nd ed. Christopher-Gordon, 2000. ISBN 1-929024-10-X.

Miller, Debbie. *Reading with Meaning: Teaching Comprehension in the Primary Grades.* Stenhouse, 2002. ISBN 1-57110-307-4.

Neamen, Mimi, and Mary Strong. *More Literature Circles: Cooperative Learning for Grades 3–8.* Libraries Unlimited, 2001. ISBN 1-56308-895-9. Also see *Literature Circles: Cooperative Learning for Grades 3–8* (Teacher Ideas Press, 1992).

Noe, Katherine L. Schlick, and Nancy J. Johnson. *Getting Started with Literature Circles.* Christopher-Gordon, 2004. ISBN 0-926842-97-8.

Owocki, Gretchen. *Comprehension: Strategic Instruction for K–3 Students.* Heinemann, 2003. ISBN 0-325-00576-1.

Payne, Carleen daCruz. *Shared Reading for Today's Classroom: Lessons and Strategies for Explicit Instruction in Comprehension, Fluency, Word Study, and Genre.* Scholastic, 2005. ISBN 0-439-36595-3.

Pinnell, Gay Su, and Irene C. Fountas. *Word Matters: Teaching Phonics and Spelling in the Reading/Writing Classroom.* Heinemann, 1998. ISBN 0-325-00051-4.

Pinnell, Gay Su, and Patricia L. Scharar. *Teaching for Comprehension in Reading, Grades K–2.* Scholastic, 2003. ISBN 0-439-54258-8.

Portalupi, Joann, and Ralph Fletcher. *Nonfiction Craft Lessons: Teaching Information Writing K–8.* Stenhouse, 2001. ISBN 1-57110-329-5.

Ray, Katie Wood. *Wondrous Words: Writers and Writing in the Elementary Classroom.* National Council of Teachers of English, 1999. ISBN 0-8141-5816-1.

Rhodes, Lynn K., and Curt Dudley-Marling. *Readers and Writers with a Difference: A Holistic Approach to Teaching Struggling Readers and Writers.* 2nd ed. Heinemann, 1996. ISBN 0-435-07215-3.

Robb, Laura. *Nonfiction Writing from the Inside Out: Writing Lessons Inspired by Conversations with Leading Authors.* Scholastic, 2004. ISBN 0-439-51368-5.

Routman, Regie. *Conversations: Strategies for Teaching, Learning and Evaluating.* Heinemann, 2000. ISBN 0-325-00109-X.

Routman, Regie. *Reading Essentials: The Specifics You Need to Teach Reading Well.* Heinemann, 2003. ISBN 0-325-00492-7.

Ruzzo, Karen, and Mary Anne Sacco. *Significant Studies for Second Grade: Reading and Writing Investigations for Children.* Heinemann, 2004. ISBN 0-325-00512-5.

Sauerteig, Judy. *Teaching Emergent Readers: Collaborative Library Lesson Plans.* Libraries Unlimited, 2005. ISBN 1-59158-251-2.

Serafini, Frank, and Cyndi Giorgis. *Reading Aloud and Beyond: Fostering the Intellectual Life with Older Readers.* Heinemann, 2003. ISBN 0-325-00522-2.

Shaw, Darla. *Retelling Strategies to Improve Comprehension: Effective Hands-on Strategies for Fiction and Nonfiction That Help Students Remember and Understand What They Read.* Scholastic, 2005. ISBN 0-439-56035-7.

Sloan, Megan S. *Trait-Based Mini-Lessons for Teaching Writing in Grades 2–4.* Scholastic, 2001. ISBN 0-439-22247-8.

Spiegel, Dixie Lee. *Classroom Discussion: Strategies for Engaging All Students, Building Higher-Level Thinking Skills, and Strengthening Reading and Writing Across the Curriculum.* Scholastic, 2005. ISBN 0-439-56757-2.

Stephens, Elaine C., and Jean E. Brown. *A Handbook of Content Literacy Strategies: 125 Practical Reading and Writing Ideas.* Christopher-Gordon, 2005. ISBN 1-929024-81-9.

Storytelling and Folklore, Creative Drama, and Reader's Theater

Bauer, Caroline Feller. *Handbook for Storytellers.* American Library Association, 1977. ISBN 0-8389-0293-6.

Bauer, Caroline Feller. *New Handbook for Storytellers: With Stories, Poems, Magic, and More.* Illus. by Lynn Gates Bredeson. American Library Association, 1993. ISBN 0-8389-0613-3.

Bauer, Caroline Feller. *Presenting Readers Theater: Plays and Poems to Read Aloud.* Illus. by Lynn Gates Bredeson. H. W. Wilson, 1987. ISBN 0-8242-0748-3.

Bettelheim, Bruno. *The Uses of Enchantment: The Meaning and Importance of Fairy Tales.* Vintage Books, 1989. ISBN 0-679-72393-5.

Brady, Martha, and Patsy T. Gleason. *Artstarts: Drama, Music, Movement, Puppetry, and Storytelling Activities.* Teacher Ideas Press, 1994. ISBN 1-56308-148-2.

Bruchac, Joseph. *Tell Me a Tale: A Book About Storytelling.* Harcourt, 1997. ISBN 0-15-201221-4.

Champlin, Connie, and Nancy Renfro. *Storytelling with Puppets.* 2nd ed. American Library Association, 1998. ISBN 0-8389-0709-1.

Dailey, Sheila. *Putting the World in a Nutshell: The Art of the Formula Tale.* H. W. Wilson, 1994. ISBN 0-8242-0860-9.

De Vos, Gail. *Storytelling for Young Adults: A Guide to Tales for Teens.* 2nd ed. Libraries Unlimited, 2003. ISBN 1-56308-903-3.

Freeman, Judy. *Hi Ho Librario: Songs, Chants, and Stories to Keep Kids Humming* (Book and accompanying CD). Rock Hill, 1997. ISBN 1-890604-00-3.

Fujita, Hiroko. *Stories to Play With: Kids' Tales Told with Puppets, Paper, Toys, and Imagination.* August House, 1999. ISBN 0-87483-553-4.

Geisler, Harlynne. *Storytelling Professionally: The Nuts and Bolts of a Working Performer.* Libraries Unlimited, 1997. ISBN 1-56308-370-1.

Greene, Ellin. *Storytelling: Art and Technique.* 3rd ed. Libraries Unlimited, 1996. ISBN 0-8352-3458-4.

Hamilton, Martha, and Mitch Weiss. *Children Tell Stories: Teaching and Using Storytelling in the Classroom.* 2nd ed. Richard C. Owen, 2005. ISBN 1-57274-663-7.

Haven, Kendall. *Super Simple Storytelling: A Can-Do Guide for Every Classroom, Every Day.* Teacher Ideas Press, 2000. ISBN 1-56308-681-6.

Heinig, Ruth Beall. *Improvisation with Favorite Tales: Integrating Drama into the Reading/Writing Classroom.* Heinemann, 1992. ISBN 0-435-08609-X.

Holt, David, and Bill Mooney, eds. *More Ready-to-Tell Tales from Around the World.* August House, 2000. ISBN 0-87483-592-5.

Holt, David, and Bill Mooney, eds. *Ready-to-Tell Tales: Sure-fire Stories from America's Favorite Storytellers.* August House, 1994. ISBN 0-87483-380-9.

Irving, Jan. *Stories, Time and Again: A Program Guide for Schools and Libraries.* Illus. by Joni Giarratano. Libraries Unlimited, 2006. ISBN 1-56308-998-X.

Kelner, Lenore Blank. *The Creative Classroom: A Guide for Using Creative Drama in the Classroom, PreK–6.* Heinemann, 1993. ISBN 0-435-08628-6.

Kraus, Anne Marie. *Folktale Themes and Activities for Children, Volume 1: Pourquoi Tales.* Illus. by Susan K. Bins. Teacher Ideas Press, 1998. ISBN 1-56308-521-6.

Kraus, Anne Marie. *Folktale Themes and Activities for Children, Volume 2: Trickster and Transformation Tales.* Illus. by Susan K. Bins. Teacher Ideas Press, 1999. ISBN 1-56308-608-5.

Lehrman, Betty, ed. *Telling Stories to Children: A National Storytelling Guide.* National Storytelling Press, 2005. ISBN 1-879991-34-9.

Lipman, Doug. *Improving Your Storytelling: Beyond the Basics for All Who Tell Stories in Work or Play.* August House, 1999. ISBN 0-87483-530-5.

Lipman, Doug. *Storytelling Games: Creative Activities for Language, Communication, and Composition Across the Curriculum.* Oryx, 1994. ISBN 0-89774-848-4.

Livo, Norma J. *Bringing Out Their Best: Values Education and Character Development Through Traditional Tales.* Libraries Unlimited, 2003. ISBN 1-56308-934-3.

Livo, Norma J., and Sandra A. Rietz. *Storytelling Folklore Sourcebook.* Libraries Unlimited, 2001. ISBN 0-87287-601-2.

MacDonald, Margaret Read. *Celebrate the World: Twenty Tellable Folktales for Multicultural Festivals.* Illus. by Roxane Murphy Smith. H. W. Wilson, 1994. ISBN 0-8242-0862-5.

MacDonald, Margaret Read. *Look Back and See: Twenty Lively Tales for Gentle Tellers.* Illus. by Roxane Murphy. H. W. Wilson, 1991. ISBN 0-8242-0810-2.

MacDonald, Margaret Read. *A Parent's Guide to Storytelling: How to Make Up New Stories and Retell Old Favorites.* HarperCollins, 1995. ISBN 0-06-446180-7.

MacDonald, Margaret Read. *Shake-It-Up Tales! Stories to Sing, Dance, Drum, and Act Out.* August House, 2000. ISBN 0-87483-590-9.

MacDonald, Margaret Read. *The Storyteller's Start-Up Book: Finding, Learning, Performing and Using Folktales.* August House, 1993. ISBN 0-87483-305-1.

MacDonald, Margaret Read. *Three-Minute Tales: Stories from Around the World to Tell or Read When Time Is Short.* August House, 2004. ISBN 0-87483-728-6.

MacDonald, Margaret Read. *Twenty Tellable Tales: Audience Participation Folktales for the Beginning Storyteller.* Illus. by Roxane Murphy. H. W. Wilson, 1986. ISBN 0-8242-0719-X.

MacDonald, Margaret Read. *When the Lights Go Out: Twenty Scary Stories to Tell.* Illus. by Roxane Murphy. H. W. Wilson, 1988. ISBN 0-8242-0770-X.

MacDonald, Margaret Read, and Brian W. Sturm. *The Storyteller's Sourcebook: A Subject, Title, and Motif Index to Folklore Collections for Children, 1983–1999.* Gale, 2001. ISBN 0-8103-5485-3.

Mooney, Bill, and David Holt. *The Storyteller's Guide: Storytellers Share Advice for the Classroom, Boardroom, Showroom, Podium, Pulpit, and Center Stage.* August House, 1996. ISBN 0-87483-482-1.

Pellowski, Anne. *Drawing Stories from Around the World and a Sampling of European Handkerchief Stories.* Libraries Unlimited, 2005. ISBN 1-59158-222-9.

Pellowski, Anne. *The Family Storytelling Handbook: How to Use Stories, Anecdotes, Rhymes, Handkerchiefs, Paper and Other Objects to Enrich Your Family Traditions.* Illus. by Lynn Sweat. Macmillan, 1987. ISBN 0-02-770610-9.

Pellowski, Anne. *The Storytelling Handbook: A Young People's Collection of Unusual Tales and Helpful Hints on How to Tell Them.* Illus. by Martha Soberock. Simon & Schuster, 1995. ISBN 0-689-80311-7.

Pellowski, Anne. *The Storytelling Vine: A Source Book of Unusual and Easy-to-Tell Stories from Around the World.* Illus. by Lynn Sweat. Macmillan, 1984. ISBN 0-02-770590-0.

Rydell, Katy, ed. *A Beginner's Guide to Storytelling.* National Storytelling Press, 2003. ISBN 1-879991-32-2.

Shepard, Aaron. *Folktales on Stage: Children's Plays for Reader's Theater (or Readers Theatre), with 16 Scripts from World Folk and Fairy Tales and Legends, Including Asian, African, Middle Eastern, European, and Native American.* Shepard, 2004. ISBN 0-938497-20-0.

Shepard, Aaron. *Readers on Stage: Resources for Reader's Theater (or Readers Theatre), With Tips, Play Scripts, and Worksheets, or How to Do Children's Plays Anywhere, Anytime, Without Scenery, Costumes, or Memorizing.* Shepard, 2004. ISBN 0-938497-21-9.

Shepard, Aaron. *Stories on Stage: Children's Plays for Reader's Theater (or Readers Theatre), With 15 Play Scripts From 15 Authors, Including Roald Dahl's The Twits and Louis Sachar's Sideways Stories from Wayside School.* 2nd ed. Shepard, 2005. ISBN 0-938497-22-7.

Sierra, Judy. *Fantastic Theater: Puppets and Plays for Young Performers and Young Audiences.* H. W. Wilson, 1991. ISBN 0-8242-0809-9.

Sierra, Judy, and Robert Kaminski. *Twice Upon a Time: Stories to Tell, Retell, Act Out, and Write About.* H. W. Wilson, 1989. ISBN 0-8242-0775-0.

Sima, Judy, and Kevin Cordi. *Raising Voices: Creating Youth Storytelling Groups and Troupes.* Libraries Unlimited, 2003. ISBN 1-56308-919-X.

Sloyer, Shirlee. *From the Page to the Stage: The Educator's Complete Guide to Readers Theatre.* Teacher Ideas Press, 2003. ISBN 1-56308-897-5.

Weir, Beth. *Introducing Children to Folk Tales.* Christopher-Gordon, 2000. ISBN 1-929024-16-9.

Wisniewski, David, and Donna Wisniewski. *Worlds of Shadow: Teaching with Shadow Puppetry.* Teacher Idea Press, 1997. ISBN 1-56308-450-3.

Wolf, Joan M. *The Beanstalk and Beyond: Developing Critical Thinking Through Fairy Tales.* Teacher Ideas Press, 1997. ISBN 1-56308-482-1.

Worthy, Jo. *Readers Theater for Building Fluency: Strategies and Scripts for Making the Most of This Highly Effective, Motivating, and Research-Based Approach to Oral Reading.* Scholastic, 2005. ISBN 0-439-52223-4.

Yolen, Jane. *Touch Magic: Fantasy, Faerie and Folklore in the Literature of Childhood.* August House, 2000. ISBN 0-87483-591-7.

Ziskind, Sylvia. *Telling Stories to Children.* H. W. Wilson, 1976. ISBN 0-8242-0588-X.

FOLKLORE AND STORYTELLING SITES

Aesop's Fables (Contains all 655 Aesop's fables—indexed in table format—with morals listed, illustrations, lesson plan links, and Real Audio narrations): www.aesopfables.com

International Storytelling Center (Web site of the International Storytelling Center in Jonesboro, Tennessee, "dedicated to building a better world through the power of storytelling," and a sponsor of the National Storytelling Festival in Jonesboro every October): www.storytellingfoundation.net

Legends (A comprehensive site providing "guided access to primary source material and up-to-date scholarship; personal essays and extended reviews"; includes texts of King Arthur, Robin Hood, and Andrew Lang's Fairy Books series): www.legends.dm.net

Storyarts (Useful site from Heather Forest, the well-known storyteller and writer, with loads of stories to download, as well as telling techniques, ideas, lesson plans, and activities): www.storyarts.org

STORYNET (Web site of the National Storytelling Association; provides a U.S. calendar of events and links to resources for storytelling): www.storynet.org

STORYTELL (A forum for discussion about storytelling sponsored by the School of Library and Information Studies at Texas Woman's University in Denton, Texas; home page contains all info on how to subscribe): www.twu.edu/cope/slis/storytell.htm

Storytelling Arts of Indiana (Teaching guides, games, activities, and resources): www.storytellingarts.org

Surlalune Fairy Tale Pages (Annotated texts of 35 well-known fairy tales, with detailed analysis of illustrations, history, variants, and modern interpretations of each): www.surlalunefairytales.com

Tales of Wonder (An archive of more than 100 folktales from Africa, Asia, and Europe, plus a selection of Native American stories): www.darsie.net/talesofwonder

Turner Learning Network (An "Educator's Guide to Learning Through Storytelling" includes resources, a how-to list for beginners, and practical lesson plans for teaching children how to be storytellers): www.turnerlearning.com/turnersouth/storytelling/index.html

Poetry

Armor, Maureen W. *Poetry, the Magic Language: Children Learn to Read and Write It.* Teacher Ideas Press, 1994. ISBN 1-56308-033-8.

Bauer, Caroline Feller. *The Poetry Break: An Annotated Anthology with Ideas for Introducing Children to Poetry.* Illus. by Edith Bingham. H. W. Wilson, 1995. ISBN 0-8242-0852-8.

Denman, Gregory. *When You've Made It Your Own: Teaching Poetry to Young People.* Heinemann, 1988. ISBN 0-435-08462-3.

Florian, Douglas, and Joan Novelli. *Teaching with the Rib-Tickling Poetry of Douglas Florian.* Scholastic, 2003. ISBN 0-439-19940-9.

Hopkins, Lee Bennett. *Pass the Poetry, Please!* 3rd ed. HarperCollins, 1998. ISBN 0-06-446199-8.

Janeczko, Paul B. *How to Write Poetry.* Scholastic, 1999. ISBN 0-590-10077-7.

Perfect, Kathy A. *Poetry Lessons: Everything You Need.* Scholastic, 2005. ISBN 0-439-49157-6.

POETRY SITES

Gigglepoetry.com (Poetry site for kids with funny poems, poetry contests, teaching ideas, and more): www.gigglepoetry.com/index.cfm

Poetry for Kids by Kenn Nesbitt (Funny poems by Kenn Nesbitt, as well as games, contests, lessons, and a rhyming dictionary): www.poetry4kids.com

Poetry Zone (For children and teenagers to publish their own poetry and reviews online): www.poetryzone.ndirect.co.uk/index2.htm

Writer's Workshop with Jack Prelutsky (In an online tutorial, beloved children's poet Prelutsky takes children through the steps of writing their own poems; this site will also lead you to Writer's Workshop with Karla Kuskin and Writing I Spy Riddles with Jean Marzollo): teacher.scholastic.com/writewit/poetry/jack_home.htm

About Authors and Illustrators of Children's Books

Buzzeo, Toni. *Terrific Connections with Authors, Illustrators, and Storytellers: Real Space and Virtual Links.* Libraries Unlimited, 1999. ISBN 1-56308-744-8.

Buzzeo, Toni. *Toni Buzzeo and You.* (Meet the Author series) Libraries Unlimited, 2005. ISBN 1-59158-211-3.

Day, Frances Ann. *Multicultural Voices in Contemporary Literature: A Resource for Teachers.* Rev. ed. Heinemann, 1999. ISBN 0-325-00130-8.

Elleman, Barbara. *Tomie dePaola: His Art and His Stories.* Illus. by Tomie dePaola. Putnam, 1999. ISBN 0-399-23129-3.

McElmeel, Sharron L. *100 Most Popular Picture Book Authors and Illustrators: Biographical Sketches and Bibliographies.* Libraries Unlimited, 2000. ISBN 0-87287-722-1.

McElmeel, Sharron, and Deborah L. McElmeel. *Authors in the Kitchen: Recipes, Stories, and More.* Libraries Unlimited, 2005. ISBN 1-59158-238-5. See also *Authors in the Pantry: Recipes, Stories, and More* (2006).

Melton, David. *How to Capture Live Authors and Bring Them to Your Schools: Practical and Innovative Ways to Schedule Authors for Author-in-Residence Programs, Children's Literature Festivals, and Young Authors' Days.* Landmark Editions, 1986. ISBN 0-933849-03-6.

Rockman, Connie C., ed. *Ninth Book of Junior Authors and Illustrators.* H. W. Wilson, 2004. ISBN 0-8242-1043-3.

Scott, Jon C. *Gerald McDermott and You.* (Meet the Author series) Illus. by Gerald McDermott. Libraries Unlimited, 2004. ISBN 1-59158-175-3.

Silvey, Anita, ed. *Essential Guide to Children's Books and Their Creators: From Alphabet Books to Young Adult Novels, Alice in Wonderland to Harry Potter—An Indispensable Guide to the Best Books for Children.* Houghton Mifflin, 2002. ISBN 0-618-19082-1.

Waltz, Josephine M. *Write Out of the Oven! Letters and Recipes from Children's Authors.* Teacher Ideas Press, 2005. ISBN 1-59469-008-1.

Wildberger, Mary Elizabeth. *Approaches to Literature Through Authors.* Oryx, 1993. ISBN 0-89774-776-3.

AUTHOR, ILLUSTRATOR, AND BOOK CHARACTER WEB SITES

As the site names for so many authors' and illustrators' Web sites use their own names, such as <www.kevinhenkes.com>, it's usually easier to type in that Web address first. If that doesn't work, look up the person on a search engine such as Google. I type in the search bar the author's name, enclosed in quotation marks, plus additional key words as follows: ("Eric Carle" author website children's books). If the author has his or her own site, you will often find it at or near the top of the listings, as in <www.Eric-Carle.com>.

Where else can you find the Web sites of authors and illustrators? Among the many sites offering scores of links are:

Children's Book Council: Author & Illustrator Sites: www.cbcbooks.org/contacts

Internet Public Library: www.ipl.org/kidspace/browse/rzn0000

Internet School Library Media Center: Index to Internet Sites: Children's and Young Adults' Authors and Illustrators: falcon.jmu.edu/~ramseyil/biochildhome.htm

Once Upon A Time . . . : A Children's Literature Web Site: Authors' and Illustrators' Pages: www.bsu.edu/classes/vancamp/aaip.html

Of the hundreds of author and illustrator Web sites I have visited in the past few years, there are some that stand out. When it comes to innovative design, the illustrators have the edge, of course, as they can beautify their sites with their own gorgeous artwork. Some folks have obviously spent a fortune on their sites, with sound, color, graphics, interactive home pages, games, and video clips. Others are much more print-based. A good author or illustrator site will include a biography, a personal message, photographs, descriptions and pictures of published books, teacher's guides, activities for children, working links to other good sites, and contact information.

When compiling my list of exemplary sites I was looking for ones that went beyond the everyday and provided surprises and some heart. That doesn't necessarily mean visual hoopla, although that is certainly welcome. Some sites included a series of questions from children and the author's thoughtful, personal responses. Others included revealing essays; a series of well-thought-out teacher's guides for each of an author's books, or Reader's Theater scripts; an illustrator's description of how he or she created the art; or useful ways to bring children and adults to reading. When we finish wending our way through one of these sites, we should feel as if we've got to know that author or illustrator a bit as a person. I love a Web site with personality and passion.

Children are using author Web sites to do research into authors' and illustrators' lives, find out information about their books, and get motivated to read them. Teachers and librarians use them to plan author visits to schools and libraries and to find teaching guides to books they plan to read aloud or use with students.

The possibilities are growing as authors and illustrators grapple with just how much they want to reveal on the now ubiquitous sites. Can they afford to be left behind?

58 Exemplary Author and Illustrator Web Sites

Adler, David A.	www.davidaadler.com
Armstrong, Jennifer	www.jennifer-armstrong.com
Arnold, Tedd	www.teddarnold.com
Arnosky, Jim	www.jimarnosky.com
Asch, Frank	www.frankasch.com
Blume, Judy	www.judyblume.com
Brett, Jan	www.janbrett.com
Buzzeo, Toni	www.tonibuzzeo.com

Carle, Eric	www.eric-carle.com
Carlson, Nancy	www.nancycarlson.com
Choldenko, Gennifer	www.choldenko.com
Christelow, Eileen	www.christelow.com
Cleary, Beverly	www.beverlycleary.com
Cobb, Vicki	www.vickicobb.com
Coville, Bruce	www.brucecoville.com
Creech, Sharon	www.sharoncreech.com
Curtis, Christopher Paul	www.ChristopherPaulCurtis.com
Davis, Katie	www.katiedavis.com
dePaola, Tomie	www.tomie.com
DiPucchio, Kelly	www.kellydipucchio.com
DiTerlizzi, Tony	www.diterlizzi.com
Fleming, Denise	www.denisefleming.com
Fox, Mem	www.memfox.net
Frasier, Debra	www.debrafrasier.com
George, Kristine O'Connell	www.kristinegeorge.com
Grimes, Nikki	www.nikkigrimes.com
Gutman, Dan	www.dangutman.com
Henkes, Kevin	www.kevinhenkes.com
Jacques, Brian	www.redwall.org
Krull, Kathleen	www.kathleenkrull.com
Leedy, Loreen	www.loreenleedybooks.com
McDonald, Megan	www.meganmcdonald.net
MacDonald, Suse	www.susemacdonald.com
McMillan, Bruce	www.brucemcmillan.com
Martin, Jacqueline Briggs	www.jacquelinebriggsmartin.com
Martin, Rafe	www.rafemartin.com
Munsch, Robert	www.robertmunsch.com
Numeroff, Laura	www.lauranumeroff.com
Palatini, Margie	www.margiepalatini.com
Park, Barbara	www.randomhouse.com/kids/junieb
Pilkey, Dav	www.pilkey.com
Pulver, Robin	www.robinpulver.com
Reynolds, Peter H.	www.peterhreynolds.com
Riordan, Rick	www.rickriordan.com
Rowling, J. K.	www.jkrowling.com
	www.scholastic.com/harrypotter
Sabuda, Robert	www.robertsabuda.com
Sayre, April Pulley	www.aprilsayre.com
Shepard, Aaron	www.aaronshep.com
Silverstein, Shel	www.shelsilverstein.com
Smith, Cynthia Leitich	www.cynthialeitichsmith.com
Snicket, Lemony	www.lemonysnicket.com
Spinelli, Jerry	www.jerryspinelli.com
Stevens, Janet	www.janetstevens.com
Willems, Mo	www.mowillems.com
Wood, Audrey	www.audreywood.com
Woodson, Jacqueline	www.jacquelinewoodson.com
Yolen, Jane	www.janeyolen.com

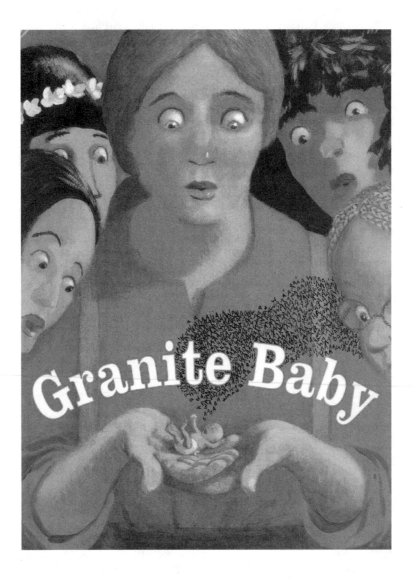

AUTHOR/ILLUSTRATOR INDEX

Authors and illustrators are arranged alphabetically by last name, followed by book titles that are main entries in the Annotated Booklists. Illustrators, indicated by (illus.), are listed only when the illustrator is not the author. All references are to entry numbers, not page numbers.

TITLE INDEX

This index refers to titles that are main entries in the Annotated Booklists. All references are to entry numbers, not page numbers.

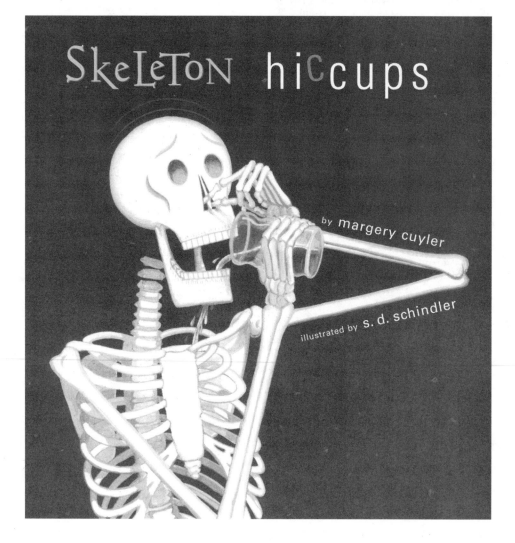

SUBJECT INDEX

Recommended grade levels appear in brackets, following the titles. All references are to entry numbers in the Annotated Booklists, not page numbers.

Kalman, Maira. *What Pete Ate from A–Z* [PreK–1], 420

McMullan, Kate. *I Stink!* [PreK–2], 528

Slate, Joseph. *Miss Bindergarten Gets Ready for Kindergarten* [PreK–1], 737

Miss Bindergarten Stays Home from Kindergarten [PreK–K], 738

Miss Bindergarten Takes a Field Trip with Kindergarten [PreK–K], 739

ALPHABET

Rumford, James. *Sequoyah* [1–6], 1542

ALPHABET—POETRY

Belle, Jennifer. *Animal Stackers* [1–4], 1297

Harley, Avis. *Fly with Poetry* [2–6], 1343

Powell, Consie. *Amazing Apples* [K–3], 1389

Schnur, Steven. *Autumn* [2–6], 1404

Wilbur, Richard. *The Disappearing Alphabet* [2–6], 1428

ALPHABET BOOKS

Abrams, Pam. *Now I Eat My ABC's* [PreK–1], 1

Allen, Susan, and Jane Lindaman. *Read Anything Good Lately?* [K–2], 9

Andreae, Giles. *K Is for Kissing a Cool Kangaroo* [PreK–K], 11

Carlson, Nancy. *ABC, I Like Me!* [PreK–1], 107

Catalanotto, Peter. *Matthew A.B.C.* [PreK–1], 113

Cheney, Lynne. *America* [K–4], 1582

Edwards, Pamela Duncan. *Clara Caterpillar* [PreK–2], 221

The Wacky Wedding [K–2], 233

Ernst, Lisa Campbell. *The Letters Are Lost* [PreK–1], 256

Fisher, Valerie. *Ellsworth's Extraordinary Electric Ears* [K–3], 275

Fleming, Denise. *Alphabet Under Construction* [PreK–1], 284

Freymann, Saxton. *Food for Thought* [PreK–1], 302

Grimes, Nikki. *C Is for City* [K–2], 332

Hausman, Bonnie. *A to Z* [PreK–2], 345

Johnson, Stephen T. *Alphabet City* [PreK–2], 409

Kalman, Maira. *What Pete Ate from A–Z* [PreK–1], 420

Krull, Kathleen. *M Is for Music* [K–6], 1635

Lester, Mike. *A Is for Salad* [PreK–1], 487

MacDonald, Ross. *Achoo! Bang! Crash!* [PreK–1], 514

McMullan, Kate. *I Stink!* [PreK–2], 528

Melmed, Laura Krauss. *New York, New York!* [1–6], 1647

Pallotta, Jerry. *The Beetle Alphabet Book* [K–3], 1654

Pandell, Karen. *Animal Action ABC* [PreK–2], 1655

Rose, Deborah Lee. *Into the A, B, Sea* [PreK–2], 1666

Scillian, Devin. *P Is for Passport* [2–6], 1677

Seeger, Laura Vaccaro. *The Hidden Alphabet* [PreK–1], 708

Shannon, George. *Tomorrow's Alphabet* [PreK–2], 718

Slate, Joseph. *Miss Bindergarten Celebrates the 100th Day of Kindergarten* [PreK–1], 736

Miss Bindergarten Gets Ready for Kindergarten [PreK–1], 737

Miss Bindergarten Stays Home from Kindergarten [PreK–K], 738

Miss Bindergarten Takes a Field Trip with Kindergarten [PreK–K], 739

Sloat, Teri. *Patty's Pumpkin Patch* [PreK–1], 741

Sobel, June. *B Is for Bulldozer* [PreK–1], 745

Turner, Priscilla. *The War Between the Vowels and the Consonants* [K–3], 804

Walton, Rick. *So Many Bunnies* [PreK–1], 823

Wethered, Peggy, and Ken Edgett. *Touchdown Mars!* [1–3], 1701

Williams, Laura Ellen. *ABC Kids* [PreK–1], 856

Wood, Audrey. *Alphabet Mystery* [PreK–1], 871

ALZHEIMER'S DISEASE

Martin, Ann M. *Belle Teal* [4–7], 1055

Park, Barbara. *The Graduation of Jake Moon* [4–7], 1077

AMAZON RIVER

Cherry, Lynne, and Mark J. Plotkin. *The Shaman's Apprentice* [2–4], 120

Ibbotson, Eva. *Journey to the River Sea* [5–7], 1006

AMERICA

SEE U.S.

AMERICAN REVOLUTION

SEE U.S.—History—Revolution, 1775–1783

AMISH

Stewart, Sarah. *The Journey* [1–4], 768

AMPHIBIANS

SEE Reptiles and amphibians

AMSTERDAM (NETHERLANDS)

Gold, Alison Leslie. *Memories of Anne Frank* [5–8], 1495

AMUSEMENT PARKS

Frazee, Marla. *Roller Coaster* [K–2], 298

Sobel, June. *B Is for Bulldozer* [PreK–1], 745

ANAGRAMS

Agee, Jon. *Elvis Lives!* [4–8], 1292

Falwell, Cathryn. *Word Wizard* [K–2], 265

Wilbur, Richard. *The Pig in the Spigot* [3–6], 1429

ANANSI (LEGENDARY CHARACTER)

Aardema, Verna. *Anansi Does the Impossible!* [K–3], 1141

Cummings, Pat. *Ananse and the Lizard* [PreK–3], 1167

Kimmel, Eric A. *Anansi and the Magic Stick* [PreK–2], 1206

Mollel, Tololwa M. *Ananse's Feast* [K–3], 1231

Washington, Donna L. *A Pride of African Tales* [4–8], 1277

ANATOMY, COMPARATIVE

Schwartz, David M. *If You Hopped Like a Frog* [K–6], 1675

ANCIENT CIVILIZATIONS

Cole, Joanna. *Ms. Frizzle's Adventures: Ancient Egypt* [K–5], 1592

Ms. Frizzle's Adventures: Imperial China [K–5], 1593

Curlee, Lynn. *Seven Wonders of the Ancient World* [3–6], 1597

O'Connor, Jane. *The Emperor's Silent Army* [4–8], 1652

ANCIENT CIVILIZATIONS— FOLKLORE

McCaughrean, Geraldine. *Gilgamesh the Hero* [6–8], 1222

ANDERSEN, HANS CHRISTIAN

Yolen, Jane. *The Perfect Wizard* [1–5], 1566

ANIMALS—FOLKLORE

BABIES

Anholt, Catherine, and Laurence Anholt. *Catherine and Laurence Anholt's Big Book of Little Children* [PreK–1], 12

Appelt, Kathi. *Bubba and Beau Go Night-Night* [PreK–K], 16

Bubba and Beau Meet the Relatives [PreK–1], 17

Ashman, Linda. *Babies on the Go* [PreK–1], 1571

Berends, Polly Berrien. *I Heard Said the Bird* [PreK–K], 51

Bertrand, Lynne. *Granite Baby* [1–4], 53

Coppinger, Tom. *Curse in Reverse* [1–4], 152

Curtis, Jamie Lee. *Tell Me Again About the Night I Was Born* [PreK–2], 174

Dodds, Dayle Ann. *Sing, Sophie!* [K–3], 205

Fleming, Candace. *Smile, Lily!* [PreK–1], 281

Frazee, Marla. *Hush, Little Baby* [PreK–1], 297

Greenspun, Adele Aron, and Joanie Schwarz. *Ariel and Emily* [PreK–1], 329

Holm, Jennifer L. *Our Only May Amelia* [4–7], 994

James, Simon. *Baby Brains* [PreK–1], 402

King-Smith, Dick. *George Speaks* [1–4], 1018

L'Engle, Madeleine. *The Other Dog* [PreK–4], 480

McGeorge, Constance W. *Boomer's Big Surprise* [PreK–K], 520

MacLachlan, Patricia, and Emily MacLachlan. *Bittle* [PreK–K], 526

McMullan, Kate. *Rock-a-Baby Band* [PreK–K], 530

Meyers, Susan. *Everywhere Babies* [PreK–1], 557

Nye, Naomi Shihab. *Baby Radar* [PreK–2], 591

Palatini, Margie. *The Wonder Worm Wars* [3–5], 1076

Rathmann, Peggy. *The Day the Babies Crawled Away* [PreK–K], 653

Regan, Dian Curtis. *Chance* [K–3], 657

Seidler, Tor. *Mean Margaret* [3–5], 1112

Stuve-Bodeen, Stephanie. *Elizabeti's Doll* [K–2], 777

Thomas, Eliza. *The Red Blanket* [K–4], 794

BABIES—FOLKLORE

Sierra, Judy. *Tasty Baby Belly Buttons* [K–3], 1265

BABY ANIMALS

SEE Animals—Infancy

BABY-SITTERS

Child, Lauren. *Clarice Bean, Guess Who's Babysitting?* [PreK–4], 122

Harris, Robie H. *Don't Forget to Come Back!* [PreK–2], 338

Palatini, Margie. *The Wonder Worm Wars* [3–5], 1076

BAGELS

SEE ALSO Baking; Bread

Wing, Natasha. *Jalapeño Bagels:* [K–3], 864

BAKERS AND BAKERIES

Wing, Natasha. *Jalapeño Bagels:* [K–3], 864

BAKING

SEE ALSO Cake; Cookery; Cookies; Food

Dooley, Norah. *Everybody Bakes Bread* [K–3], 209

Elya, Susan Middleton. *Eight Animals Bake a Cake* [PreK–2], 241

Hooper, Meredith. *Honey Cookies* [PreK–2], 376

Stevens, Janet, and Susan Stevens Crummel. *Cook-a-Doodle-Doo!* [PreK–2], 765

Wells, Rosemary. *Bunny Cakes* [PreK–1], 829

BALDNESS

Haddix, Margaret Peterson. *Because of Anya* [4–7], 983

BALLET

SEE ALSO Dancing

Edwards, Pamela Duncan. *Honk!* [K–2], 224

Kinerk, Robert. *Clorinda* [K–3], 446

Littlesugar, Amy. *Marie in Fourth Position* [1–4], 495

Marshall, James. *Swine Lake* [1–4], 538

Samuels, Barbara. *Dolores on Her Toes* [PreK–2], 685

Stadler, Alexander. *Lila Bloom* [1–4], 751

Tagg, Christine. *Cinderlily* [1–4], 783

Tamar, Erika. *Alphabet City Ballet* [5–7], 1125

BALLOONS

Schwartz, David M. *Millions to Measure* [1–5], 1676

Weitzman, Jacqueline Preiss. *You Can't Take a Balloon into the Metropolitan Museum* [K–3], 828

BALTIMORE

Bartoletti, Susan Campbell. *The Flag Maker* [2–5], 1446

BANNEKER, BENJAMIN

McGill, Alice. *Molly Bannaky* [2–5], 522

BANYAN TREES

Bash, Barbara. *In the Heart of the Village* [2–5], 1574

BARBERSHOPS

Tarpley, Natasha Anastasia. *Bippity Bop Barbershop* [PreK–1], 784

BARDS AND BARDISM

Farmer, Nancy. *The Sea of Trolls* [5–8], 959

BARTERING

Chorao, Kay. *Pig and Crow* [PreK–1], 129

Gaiman, Neil. *The Day I Swapped My Dad for Two Goldfish* [1–4], 308

Ziefert, Harriet. *I Swapped My Dog* [PreK–1], 887

BARTERING—FOLKLORE

Kurtz, Jane. *Trouble* [K–2], 1218

BASEBALL

SEE ALSO Athletes; Basketball; Soccer; Sports; Sportsmanship

Corey, Shana. *Players in Pigtails* [1–5], 155

Curtis, Gavin. *The Bat Boy and His Violin* [1–4], 172

Elya, Susan Middleton. *Eight Animals Play Ball* [K–2], 243

Gutman, Dan. *Honus and Me* [4–6], 978

Hopkinson, Deborah. *Girl Wonder* [1–4], 380

Lynch, Chris. *Gold Dust* [5–8], 1046

Mammano, Julie. *Rhinos Who Play Baseball* [K–2], 533

Palatini, Margie. *The Wonder Worm Wars* [3–5], 1076

Quindlen, Anna. *Happily Ever After* [1–4], 1099

Stadler, Alexander. *Beverly Billingsly Can't Catch* [K–2], 749

Tavares, Matt. *Oliver's Game* [1–4], 785

Waber, Bernard. *Gina* [1–3], 815

BASEBALL—BIOGRAPHY

Adler, David A. *Lou Gehrig* [2–5], 1435

Burleigh, Robert. *Home Run* [2–6], 1464

Cline-Ransome, Lesa. *Satchel Paige* [2–5], 1472

Moss, Marissa. *Mighty Jackie, the Strike-Out Queen* [2–5], 1532

BIRDS

CHANUKKAH
SEE Hanukkah

CHAPMAN, JOHN

CHARACTER EDUCATION
SEE Behavior; Citizenship; Compassion; Conduct of life; Conflict resolution; Cooperation; Courage; Creativity; Dedication; Determination; Forgiveness; Friendship; Generosity; Helpfulness; Honesty; Kindness; Leadership; Love, Loyalty; Neighborliness; Obedience; Patience; Perseverance; Problem solving; Respect; Responsibility, Self-acceptance; Self concept; Self-confidence; Self-control; Self-esteem; Self-reliance; Teamwork; Wisdom

CHARACTERS IN LITERATURE

CHARACTERS IN LITERATURE—POETRY

CHAVEZ, CESAR

CHEATING

CHEESE

CHELM

CHELM—FOLKLORE

CHEROKEE INDIANS

Brett, Jan. *Who's That Knocking on Christmas Eve?* [K–2], 75

Buck, Pearl S. *Christmas Day in the Morning* [3–8], 83

Cohn, Janice. *The Christmas Menorahs* [2–5], 1590

Coots, J. Fred, and Haven Gillespie. *Santa Claus Is Comin' to Town* [PreK–2], 151

Dewan, Ted. *Crispin, the Pig Who Had It All* [K–2], 200

Gray, Libba Moore. *Little Lil and the Swing-Singing Sax* [K–3], 326

Kimmel, Elizabeth Cody. *My Penguin Osbert* [PreK–1], 443

Klise, Kate. *Shall I Knit You a Hat?* [PreK–1], 449

Palatini, Margie. *Elf Help* [K–2], 602

Paterson, Katherine. *Marvin's Best Christmas Present Ever* [K–2], 615

Polacco, Patricia. *An Orange for Frankie* [1–6], 640

Primavera, Elise. *Auntie Claus* [1–3], 647

Rylant, Cynthia. *Silver Packages* [2–6], 681

Sabuda, Robert. *The 12 Days of Christmas* [PreK–5], 1403

CHRISTMAS MUSIC

Coots, J. Fred, and Haven Gillespie. *Santa Claus Is Comin' to Town* [PreK–2], 151

CHRISTMAS TREES

Hines, Gary. *A Christmas Tree in the White House* [1–4], 364

CHRONOMETERS

Lasky, Kathryn. *The Man Who Made Time Travel* [4–8], 1517

CHUMASH INDIANS

Dengler, Marianna. *The Worry Stone* [2–4], 940

CHURCHES

Martin, Ann M. *Leo the Magnificat* [K–2], 539

CHURCHES—FOLKLORE

Shepard, Aaron. *King o' the Cats* [2–5], 1258

CINDERELLA STORIES

Buehner, Caralyn. *Fanny's Dream* [1–6], 84

Child, Lauren. *Who's Afraid of the Big Bad Book?* [K–3], 126

Climo, Shirley. *The Irish Cinderlad* [2–6], 1160

The Persian Cinderella [2–6], 1163

Coburn, Jewell Reinhart, adapt.

with Tzexa Cherta Lee. *Jouanah* [2–5], 1164

Daly, Niki. *Once Upon a Time* [K–2], 183

dePaola, Tomie. *Adelita* [1–6], 1176

Edwards, Pamela Duncan. *Dinorella* [K–3], 222

Hickox, Rebecca. *The Golden Sandal* [2–6], 1197

Hughes, Shirley. *Ella's Big Chance* [K–4], 394

Jaffe, Nina. *The Way Meat Loves Salt* [2–6], 1201

Johnston, Tony. *Bigfoot Cinderrrrella* [K–3], 410

Ketteman, Helen. *Bubba the Cowboy Prince* [2–5], 439

Levine, Gail Carson. *Ella Enchanted* [4–7], 1032

Lowell, Susan. *Cindy Ellen* [1–4], 502

Pullman, Philip. *I Was a Rat!* [4–7], 1097

San Souci, Robert D. *Cendrillon* [2–6], 1252

Cinderella Skeleton [1–5], 686

Schroeder, Alan. *Smoky Mountain Rose* [2–6], 1255

Sierra, Judy. *The Gift of the Crocodile* [1–6], 1263

Tagg, Christine. *Cinderlily* [1–4], 783

Waber, Bernard. *Evie and Margie* [K–2], 814

Whipple, Laura. *If the Shoe Fits* [4–8], 1427

CIPHERS

SEE Codes and ciphers

CIRCLES

SEE ALSO Shapes

Neuschwander, Cindy. *Sir Cumference and the First Round Table* [2–5], 581

CIRCULAR STORIES

SEE ALSO Cumulative stories; Sequence stories; Swallowing stories

Bania, Michael. *Kumak's House* [PreK–3], 36

Ernst, Lisa Campbell. *Stella Louella's Runaway Book* [PreK–2], 258

Fleming, Denise. *Time to Sleep* [PreK–1], 286

Frazee, Marla. *Hush, Little Baby* [PreK–1], 297

Icenoggle, Jodi. *'Til the Cows Come Home* [PreK–3], 399

Taback, Simms. *Joseph Had a Little Overcoat* [PreK–1], 780

Ziefert, Harriet. *I Swapped My Dog* [PreK–1], 887

CIRCULAR STORIES—FOLKLORE

Aylesworth, Jim. *Aunt Pitty Patty's Piggy* [PreK–1], 1144

Climo, Shirley. *The Little Red Ant and the Great Big Crumb* [PreK–2], 1161

Kurtz, Jane. *Trouble* [K–2], 1218

MacDonald, Margaret Read. *The Old Woman Who Lived in a Vinegar Bottle* [PreK–3], 1225

Young, Ed. *Mouse Match* [1–6], 1287

CIRCUS

Dodds, Dayle Ann. *Where's Pup?* [PreK–1], 206

Falconer, Ian. *Olivia Saves the Circus* [PreK–2], 262

CITIES AND TOWNS

SEE ALSO Country life; Farm Life

Blake, Robert J. *Fledgling* [PreK–1], 58

Crews, Nina, comp. *The Neighborhood Mother Goose* [PreK–1], 1307

DiCamillo, Kate. *Because of Winn-Dixie* [3–5], 941

Dorros, Arthur. *City Chicken* [PreK–2], 210

Dragonwagon, Crescent. *And Then It Rained . . .* [PreK–2], 212

DuPrau, Jeanne. *The City of Ember* [4–7], 951

Emberley, Rebecca. *Three Cool Kids* [PreK–2], 249

Fleischman, Paul. *Seedfolks* [5–8], 961

Grimes, Nikki. *C Is for City* [K–2], 332

Howard, Arthur. *The Hubbub Above* [PreK–1], 384

Johnson, Stephen T. *Alphabet City* [PreK–2], 409

Joosse, Barbara M. *Hot City* [PreK–2], 416

Melmed, Laura Krauss. *New York, New York!* [1–6], 1647

Myers, Christopher. *Black Cat* [3–6], 575

Neubecker, Robert. *Wow! City!* [PreK–1], 580

Osborne, Mary Pope. *New York's Bravest* [PreK–6], 597

Palatini, Margie. *Ding Dong Ding Dong* [1–4], 600

Pinkwater, Daniel. *Looking for Bobowicz* [3–6], 1093

Sorel, Edward, and Cheryl Carlesimo. *The Saturday Kid* [K–4], 746

Stewart, Sarah. *The Journey* [1–4], 768

Taylor, Sean. *Boing!* [PreK–2], 786

Weitzman, Jacqueline Preiss. *You*

CREATIVE DRAMA— FOLKLORE

HISTORY—U.S.

HMONG—FOLKLORE

HOAXES

HOLIDAYS

HOLIDAYS—FOLKLORE

HOLOCAUST, JEWISH (1939–1945)

HOME SCHOOLING

HOMELESSNESS

HOMESICKNESS

HOMEWORK

HOMONYMS

HONESTY

HUMOROUS FOLKLORE

Shepard, Aaron. *Master Man* [K–5], 1259

So, Meilo. *Gobble, Gobble, Slip, Slop* [PreK–3], 1267

Souhami, Jessica. *Mrs. McCool and the Giant Cuhullin* [K–4], 1270

No Dinner! [PreK–2], 1271

Taback, Simms. *Kibitzers and Fools* [1–4], 1273

Wardlaw, Lee. *Punia and the King of Sharks* [K–3], 1276

Wattenberg, Jane. *Henny-Penny* [PreK–2], 1278

Willey, Margaret. *Clever Beatrice* [1–4], 1280

Wooldridge, Connie Nordhielm. *Wicked Jack* [2–5], 1282

Yep, Laurence. *The Khan's Daughter* [2–6], 1284

HUMOROUS POETRY

Ashman, Linda. *The Essential Worldwide Monster Guide* [1–4], 1296

Cleary, Brian P. *How Much Can a Bare Bear Bear?* [2–5], 1304

Rainbow Soup [3–6], 1305

Dakos, Kalli. *Put Your Eyes Up Here and Other School Poems* [2–5], 1308

Florian, Douglas. *In the Swim* [2–6], 1315

Laugh-eteria [1–6], 1317

Lizards, Frogs, and Polliwogs [2–5], 1318

Mammalabilia [2–6], 1319

Omnibeasts [1–6], 1320

On the Wing [2–5], 1321

George, Kristine O'Connell. *Swimming Upstream* [5–7], 1331

Ghigna, Charles. *Animal Tracks* [PreK–2], 1333

Grandits, John. *Technically, It's Not My Fault* [4–7], 1337

Grossman, Bill. *Timothy Tunny Swallowed a Bunny* [PreK–3], 1339

Harrison, David L. *The Mouse Was Out at Recess* [1–4], 1344

Hoberman, Mary Ann. *There Once Was a Man Named Michael Finnegan* [PreK–2], 372

Hopkins, Lee Bennett, comp. *Oh, No! Where Are My Pants? And Other Disasters* [1–4], 1356

Koontz, Dean. *The Paper Doorway* [2–6], 1367

Lansky, Bruce, comp. *Miles of Smiles* [K–6], 1368

You're Invited to Bruce Lansky's Poetry Party [K–6], 1369

Lee, Dennis. *Dinosaur Dinner (With a Slice of Alligator Pie)* [PreK–3], 1370

Prelutsky, Jack. *The Frogs Wore Red Suspenders* [PreK–3], 1391

It's Raining Pigs and Noodles [K–6], 1393

Monday's Troll [3–6], 1394

A Pizza the Size of the Sun [1–6], 1395

Scranimals [2–6], 1397

Robb, Laura, comp. *Snuffles and Snouts* [1–4], 1399

Rosen, Michael, comp. *Walking the Bridge of Your Nose* [1–5], 1402

Scieszka, Jon. *Science Verse* [2–6], 704

Shields, Carol Diggory. *Almost Late to School and More School Poems* [1–4], 1406

Sierra, Judy, comp. *Schoolyard Rhymes* [1–5], 1412

Sierra, Judy. *There's a Zoo in Room 22* [1–4], 1413

Silverstein, Shel. *Falling Up* [K–6], 1414

Runny Babbit [2–6], 1415

Sklansky, Amy E. *Skeleton Bones and Goblin Groans* [PreK–3], 1418

Weeks, Sarah. *Mrs. McNosh Hangs Up Her Wash* [PreK–1], 826

Wilbur, Richard. *The Pig in the Spigot* [3–6], 1429

HUMOROUS SONGS

Katz, Alan. *I'm Still Here in the Bathtub* [PreK–3], 1364

Sherman, Allan, and Lou Busch. *Hello Muddah, Hello Faddah!* [K–3], 722

HUMOROUS STORIES

SEE Humorous fiction; Humorous folklore; Humorous poetry; Humorous songs

HUNTERS AND HUNTING

Kessler, Cristina. *Jubela* [K–4], 437

Rodanas, Kristina. *The Blind Hunter* [1–4], 663

HUNTERS AND HUNTING—FOLKLORE

Casanova, Mary. *The Hunter* [2–6], 1158

HURRICANES

SEE ALSO Blizzards; Clouds; Rain; Storms; Water; Weather

Cherry, Lynne. *The Sea, the Storm, and the Mangrove Tangle* [2–6], 119

Cole, Joanna. *The Magic School Bus Inside a Hurricane* [1–4], 1591

HYGIENE

SEE Cleanliness

HYPERBOLE

SEE English Language—Hyperbole

ICE

Appelbaum, Diana. *Cocoa Ice* [1–3], 15

ICE CREAM

Brisson, Pat. *Hot Fudge Hero* [1–3], 909

Greenstein, Elaine. *Ice-Cream Cones for Sale* [2–4], 1611

ICE FISHING

Bania, Michael. *Kumak's Fish* [PreK–3], 35

ICELAND

McMillan, Bruce. *Nights of the Pufflings* [1–4], 1644

IDENTITY

Andersen, Hans Christian. *The Ugly Duckling* [K–4], 10

Bath, K. P. *The Secret of Castle Cant* [5–8], 901

Chen, Chih-Yuan. *Guji Guji* [PreK–1], 116

Fierstein, Harvey. *The Sissy Duckling* [K–2], 271

Howard, Arthur. *When I Was Five* [PreK–1], 385

Howe, James. *Pinky and Rex and the Bully* [1–3], 390

McGraw, Eloise. *The Moorchild* [4–7], 1050

Maloney, Peter, and Felicia Zekauskas. *His Mother's Nose* [PreK–2], 532

Marsden, Carolyn. *The Gold-Threaded Dress* [2–4], 1054

Oates, Joyce Carol. *Where Is Little Reynard?* [PreK–1], 592

Paterson, Katherine. *Jip* [5–8], 1084

Shannon, David. *A Bad Case of Stripes* [1–5], 712

IDIOMS

SEE English Language—Idioms

IDITAROD (RACE)

Blake, Robert J. *Akiak* [2–5], 57

Togo [1–4], 59

Miller, Debbie S. *The Great Serum Race* [3–6], 1649

Wood, Ted. *Iditarod Dream* [4–6], 1564

IGLOOS

Steltzer, Ulli. *Building an Igloo* [2–6], 1685

IGUANAS

Johnston, Tony. *The Iguana Brothers* [PreK–2], 413

Sayre, April Pulley. *If You Should Hear a Honey Guide* [K–3], 1671

KESTRELS

Blake, Robert J. *Fledgling* [PreK–1], 58

KIDNAPPING

Biedrzycki, David. *Ace Lacewing* [1–4], 56

Cameron, Ann. *Colibrí* [5–8], 915

Farmer, Nancy. *The Sea of Trolls* [5–8], 959

Hirsch, Odo. *Bartlett and the City of Flames* [4–6], 992

Hoeye, Michael. *Time Stops for No Mouse* [4–8], 993

Pullman, Philip. *The Golden Compass* [6–8], 1096

KINDERGARTEN

SEE ALSO Nursery schools; Schools

Child, Lauren. *I Am Too Absolutely Small for School* [PreK–2], 123

Davis, Katie. *Kindergarten Rocks* [PreK–K], 185

McGhee, Alison. *Countdown to Kindergarten* [PreK–2], 521

Slate, Joseph. *Miss Bindergarten Celebrates the 100th Day of Kindergarten* [PreK–1], 736

Miss Bindergarten Gets Ready for Kindergarten [PreK–1], 737

Miss Bindergarten Stays Home from Kindergarten [PreK–K], 738

Miss Bindergarten Takes a Field Trip with Kindergarten [PreK–K], 739

Wells, Rosemary. *My Kindergarten* [PreK–1], 836

KINDNESS

Coppinger, Tom. *Curse in Reverse* [1–4], 152

Edwards, Pamela Duncan. *The Leprechaun's Gold* [K–3], 225

Meddaugh, Susan. *Martha Walks the Dog* [K–4], 552

Naylor, Phyllis Reynolds. *Shiloh Season* [4–7], 1070

Polacco, Patricia. *An Orange for Frankie* [1–6], 640

KINDNESS—FOLKLORE

Aardema, Verna. *Koi and the Kola Nuts* [K–4], 1143

San Souci, Daniel. *In the Moonlight Mist* [2–6], 1251

KING, MARTIN LUTHER, JR

Adler, David A. *Dr. Martin Luther King, Jr.* [K–2], 1434

Bray, Rosemary L. *Martin Luther King* [2–5], 1452

Farris, Christine King. *My Brother Martin* [K–6], 1485

Rappaport, Doreen. *Martin's Big Words* [K–6], 1538

KING ARTHUR

SEE Arthur, King (Legendary character); Legends

KINGS AND RULERS

SEE ALSO Emperors

Andersen, Hans Christian. *The Nightingale:* [2–6], 891

The Nightingale: [2–6], 892

Bateman, Teresa. *The Princesses Have a Ball* [K–4], 46

Cole, Joanna. *Ms. Frizzle's Adventures* [K–5], 1593

Demi. *The Emperor's New Clothes* [1–3], 196

DiCamillo, Kate. *The Tale of Despereaux* [4–8], 943

Edwards, Pamela Duncan. *The Leprechaun's Gold* [K–3], 225

Hirsch, Odo. *Bartlett and the City of Flames* [4–6], 992

Hong, Lily Toy. *The Empress and the Silkworm* [1–4], 375

Kindl, Patrice. *Goose Chase* [5–8], 1016

King-Smith, Dick. *Lady Lollipop* [2–4], 1020

Krull, Kathleen. *Lives of Extraordinary Women* [4–12], 1511

Levine, Gail Carson. *The Princess Test* [4–7], 1034

Martin, Rafe. *The Storytelling Princess* [1–4], 543

O'Connor, Jane. *The Emperor's Silent Army* [4–8], 1652

Park, Linda Sue. *The Kite Fighters* [4–6], 1081

Pinczes, Elinor J. *A Remainder of One* [K–3], 629

Pullman, Philip. *I Was a Rat!* [4–7], 1097

Sedgwick, Marcus. *The Emperor's New Clothes* [PreK–4], 707

Stanley, Diane. *Rumpelstiltskin's Daughter* [2–5], 755

Sunami, Kitoba. *How the Fisherman Tricked the Genie* [2–6], 1122

Yolen, Jane. *Merlin and the Dragons* [2–6], 882

KINGS AND RULERS—FOLKLORE

Aardema, Verna. *Koi and the Kola Nuts* [K–4], 1143

Demi. *The Donkey and the Rock* [1–4], 1170

One Grain of Rice [2–6], 1175

Diakité, Baba Wagué. *The Magic Gourd* [1–4], 1179

Hamilton, Virginia. *The Girl Who Spun Gold* [2–6], 1191

Hodges, Margaret. *Merlin and the Making of the King* [3–6], 1200

Kimmel, Eric A. *Onions and Garlic* [2–6], 1210

Rimonah of the Flashing Sword [2–5], 1211

The Rooster's Antlers [K–4], 1212

Seven at One Blow [1–5], 1213

Ten Suns [1–6], 1214

McCaughrean, Geraldine. *Gilgamesh the Hero* [6–8], 1222

Martin, Rafe. *The Shark God* [2–5], 1228

Mayer, Marianna. *The Adventures of Tom Thumb* [K–3], 1230

Morpurgo, Michael. *Sir Gawain and the Green Knight* [5–8], 1235

Philip, Neil. *The Arabian Nights* [4–8], 1245

San Souci, Robert D. *The Well at the End of the World* [2–6], 1254

Shepard, Aaron. *The Sea King's Daughter* [3–6], 1261

Soifer, Margaret, and Irwin Shapiro. *Tenggren's Golden Tales from the Arabian Nights* [3–8], 1268

Young, Ed. *Cat and Rat* [K–4], 1286

KITES

Emmett, Jonathan. *Someone Bigger* [PreK–1], 251

Hall, Bruce Edward. *Henry and the Dragon Kite* [K–4], 334

Park, Linda Sue. *The Kite Fighters* [4–6], 1081

Schanzer, Rosalyn. *How Ben Franklin Stole the Lightning* [1–6], 1549

KNIGHTS AND KNIGHTHOOD

Grahame, Kenneth. *The Reluctant Dragon* [3–6], 974

Neuschwander, Cindy. *Sir Cumference and the First Round Table* [2–5], 581

Thomas, Shelley Moore. *Get Well, Good Knight* [PreK–1], 795

Good Night, Good Knight [PreK–1], 796

KNIGHTS AND KNIGHTHOOD—FOLKLORE

Hodges, Margaret. *Merlin and the Making of the King* [3–6], 1200

Mayer, Marianna. *The Adventures of Tom Thumb* [K–3], 1230

Morpurgo, Michael. *Sir Gawain and the Green Knight* [5–8], 1235

KNOCK-KNOCK JOKES

SEE ALSO Puns and punning;

Practical jokes; Riddles; Word games

Shields, Carol Diggory. *Lucky Pennies and Hot Chocolate* [PreK–1], 724

KOREA
SEE ALSO Folklore—Korea

Neuberger, Anne E. *The Girl-Son* [3–8], 1071

Park, Linda Sue. *The Kite Fighters* [4–6], 1081

A Single Shard [4–8], 1082

When My Name Was Keoko [5–8], 1083

KOREAN AMERICANS
SEE ALSO Asian Americans

Recorvits, Helen. *My Name Is Yoon* [1–3], 656

KUNG FU
McCully, Emily Arnold. *Beautiful Warrior* [2–6], 511

KWANZAA
Medearis, Angela Shelf. *Seven Spools of Thread* [K–4], 555

LABOR LEADERS
Bernier-Grand, Carmen T. *Cesar* [3–6], 1447

Krull, Kathleen. *Harvesting Hope* [3–6], 1509

LADYBUGS
Chrustowski, Rick. *Bright Beetle* [1–3], 1587

Ernst, Lisa Campbell. *Bubba and Trixie* [K–2], 254

LAKES
SEE ALSO Pond life

Manzano, Sonia. *No Dogs Allowed!* [K–2], 534

Root, Phyllis. *Rattletrap Car* [PreK–K], 667

LAKES—FOLKLORE
Van Laan, Nancy. *Shingebiss* [2–6], 1275

LANGUAGE
SEE ALSO Chinese language; English language; French language; Spanish language; Sign language; Vocabulary; Word games; Yiddish language

Amato, Mary. *The Word Eater* [3–6], 890

Donaldson, Julia. *The Giants and the Joneses* [2–5], 945

Evans, Lezlie. *Can You Count Ten Toes?* [K–3], 1605

Scieszka, Jon. *Baloney (Henry P.)* [K–4], 702

Taback, Simms. *Kibitzers and Fools* [1–4], 1273

Willems, Mo. *Knuffle Bunny* [PreK–1], 853

LANGUAGE—FOLKLORE
Casanova, Mary. *The Hunter* [2–6], 1158

LAUGHTER
Egan, Tim. *Serious Farm* [K–2], 236

Stevenson, James. *Don't Make Me Laugh* [K–2], 767

LAW
Linz, Kathi. *Chickens May Not Cross the Road and Other Crazy (But True) Laws* [2–6], 1643

LAWRENCE, JACOB
Duggleby, John. *Story Painter* [4–8], 1481

LAZINESS
dePaola, Tomie. *Jamie O'Rourke and the Pooka* [2–5], 199

Lester, Helen. *Score One for the Sloths* [PreK–2], 484

Wheeler, Lisa. *Old Cricket* [PreK–1], 844

LEADERSHIP—FOLKLORE
Bushyhead, Robert H., and Kay Thorpe Bannon. *Yonder Mountain* [K–4], 1156

LEARNING DISABILITIES
Greenberg, Jan, and Sandra Jordan. *Chuck Close Up Close* [4–8], 1497

Lester, Helen. *Author* [K–4], 1519

Polacco, Patricia. *Thank You, Mr. Falker* [2–5], 641

LEAVES
Ehlert, Lois. *Leaf Man* [PreK–2], 239

LEGENDS
Cohen, Barbara. *Robin Hood and Little John* [1–4], 1165

Hodges, Margaret. *Merlin and the Making of the King* [3–6], 1200

McCaughrean, Geraldine. *Gilgamesh the Hero* [6–8], 1222

Morpurgo, Michael. *Sir Gawain and the Green Knight* [5–8], 1235

Yolen, Jane. *Merlin and the Dragons* [2–6], 882

Passager [4–7], 1139

LEMURS
Lester, Helen. *Something Might Happen* [PreK–1], 485

LEONARDO DA VINCI, 1452–1519
Byrd, Robert. *Leonardo, Beautiful Dreamer* [4–7], 1466

Fritz, Jean. *Leonardo's Horse* [4–8], 1489

Stanley, Diane. *Leonardo da Vinci* [4–7], 1553

LEOPARDS
Keller, Holly. *That's Mine, Horace* [PreK–K], 429

LEOPARDS—FOLKLORE
Souhami, Jessica. *The Leopard's Drum* [PreK–2], 1269

LEPRECHAUNS
SEE ALSO Elves; Fairies; Genies; Giants; Goblins; Ireland; Monsters; Ogres; St. Patrick's Day; Trolls

Bateman, Teresa. *Leprechaun Gold* [1–4], 45

Edwards, Pamela Duncan. *The Leprechaun's Gold* [K–3], 225

Wojciechokski, Susan. *A Fine St. Patrick's Day* [K–4], 868

LESTER, HELEN
Lester, Helen. *Author* [K–4], 1519

LETTER WRITING
SEE ALSO Postal service

Asch, Frank. *Mr. Maxwell's Mouse* [2-5], 24

Barasch, Lynne. *Ask Albert Einstein* [2–6], 39

France, Anthony. *From Me to You* [PreK–2], 292

Nagda, Ann Whitehead. *Dear Whiskers* [1–3], 1065

Pattison, Darcy. *The Journey of Oliver K. Woodman* [K–2], 617

Scieszka, Jon. *Baloney (Henry P.)* [K–4], 702

Sherman, Allan, and Lou Busch. *Hello Muddah, Hello Faddah!* [K–3], 722

Teague, Mark. *Dear Mrs. LaRue* [K–3], 787

Detective LaRue [K–4], 788

Winters, Kay. *My Teacher for President* [PreK–3], 865

LEWIS AND CLARK EXPEDITION, 1804–1806
Bruchac, Joseph. *Sacajawea* [6–8], 911

Edwards, Judith. *The Great Expedition of Lewis and Clark* [2–5], 1602

Erdrich, Lise. *Sacagawea* [3–6], 1484

Myers, Laurie. *Lewis and Clark and Me* [3–7], 1064

MISSISSIPPI

Mitchell, Margaree King. *Grand-daddy's Gift* [2–5], 564

MITCHELL, JACKIE

Moss, Marissa. *Mighty Jackie, the Strike-Out Queen* [2–5], 1532

MITTENS

SEE ALSO Clothing and dress

Kellogg, Steven. *The Missing Mitten Mystery* [PreK–1], 433

MNEMONICS

Cleveland, Will, and Mark Alvarez. *Yo, Millard Fillmore!* [4–6], 1471

Levitt, Paul M., Douglas A. Burger, and Elissa S. Guralnick. *The Weighty Word Book* [4–8], 1035

Shields, Carol Diggory. *Brain Juice* [3–6], 1410

MOLES

Newman, Marjorie. *Mole and the Baby Bird* [PreK–1], 583

MONARCH BUTTERFLY

Swope, Sam. *Gotta Go! Gotta Go!* [PreK–2], 779

MONEY

Leedy, Loreen. *Follow the Money* [K–4], 1638

Mollel, Tololwa M. *My Rows and Piles of Coins* [K–3], 566

Wells, Rosemary. *Bunny Money* [PreK–2], 830

MONEY—FOLKLORE

Demi. *The Greatest Treasure* [1–5], 1172

Rascol, Sabina I. *The Impudent Rooster* [1–4], 1248

MONEYMAKING PROJECTS

Clements, Andrew. *Lunch Money* [4–6], 921

Gutman, Dan. *The Get Rich Quick Club* [3–5], 977

Kennedy, Frances. *The Pickle Patch Bathtub* [K–3], 436

MONGOLIA

Marrin, Albert. *Secrets from the Rocks* [4–8], 1525

MONGOLIA—FOLKLORE

SEE Folklore—Mongolia

MONGOOSES

Kipling, Rudyard. *Rikki-Tikki-Tavi* [2–6], 1024

MONKEYS

SEE ALSO Chimpanzees; Gorillas

Anholt, Catherine, and Laurence Anholt. *Chimp and Zee* [PreK–1], 13

Bell, Cece. *Sock Monkey Goes to Hollywood* [PreK–1], 50

Christelow, Eileen. *Five Little Monkeys with Nothing to Do* [PreK–K], 130

Day, Nancy Raines. *Double Those Wheels* [PreK–2], 190

Goode, Diane. *Monkey Mo Goes to Sea* [PreK–1], 317

Ives, David. *Monsieur Eek* [5–7], 1008

Koller, Jackie French. *One Monkey Too Many* [PreK–1], 450

Kurtz, Jane, and Christopher Kurtz. *Water Hole Waiting* [PreK–2], 460

Santat, Dan. *The Guild of Geniuses* [PreK–2], 688

Sierra, Judy. *Counting Crocodiles* [PreK–1], 728

MONKEYS—FOLKLORE

Diakité, Baba Wagué. *The Hatseller and the Monkeys* [PreK–2], 1178

McKissack, Patricia C., and Robert L. McKissack. *Itching and Twitching* [PreK–1], 1227

MONSTERS

SEE ALSO Bogeyman; Fairies; Ghosts; Giants; Goblins; Halloween; Haunted houses; Leprechauns; Ogres; Skeletons; Supernatural; Trolls; Vampires; Witches

Del Negro, Janice. *Lucy Dove* [4–6], 194

Hicks, Barbara Jean. *Jitterbug Jam* [PreK–3], 361

McKissack, Patricia C., and Onawumi Jean Moss. *Precious and the Boo Hag* [1–4], 525

Park, Barbara. *Psssst! It's Me . . . the Bogeyman* [1–4], 613

Willems, Mo. *Leonardo the Terrible Monster* [PreK–2], 854

MONSTERS—FOLKLORE

Kimmel, Eric A. *The Hero Beowulf* [4–8], 1209

MONSTERS—POETRY

Ashman, Linda. *The Essential Worldwide Monster Guide* [1–4], 1296

Prelutsky, Jack. *Monday's Troll* [3–6], 1394

Sierra, Judy. *Monster Goose* [2–6], 1411

MONTANA

Cohn, Janice. *The Christmas Menorahs* [2–5], 1590

MONTHS

SEE Seasons

MONTHS—POETRY

Bunting, Eve. *Sing a Song of Piglets* [PreK–1], 1300

Updike, John. *A Child's Calendar* [1–6], 1425

MOON

SEE ALSO Astronomy; Earth; Planets; Space flight to the Moon; Sun

Aldrin, Buzz. *Reaching for the Moon* [2–6], 1439

Brown, Don. *One Giant Leap* [1–4], 1461

Choldenko, Gennifer. *Moonstruck* [PreK–2], 128

Henkes, Kevin. *Kitten's First Full Moon* [PreK–K], 351

Hunter, Anne. *Possum's Harvest Moon* [PreK–2], 396

McNulty, Faith. *If You Decide to Go to the Moon* [K–3], 1645

Schyffert, Bea Uusma. *The Man Who Went to the Far Side of the Moon* [3–8], 1550

Slate, Joseph. *Story Time for Little Porcupine* [PreK–1], 740

Suen, Anastasia. *Man on the Moon* [K–2], 1555

Yaccarino, Dan. *Zoom! Zoom! Zoom! I'm Off to the Moon!* [PreK–1], 877

MOON—FOLKLORE

Wolkstein, Diane. *The Day Ocean Came to Visit* [PreK–3], 1281

MOON—POETRY

Pollock, Penny. *When the Moon Is Full* [PreK–4], 1388

MOOSE

Egan, Tim. *The Trial of Cardigan Jones* [K–3], 237

Palatini, Margie. *Moosetache* [K–2], 604

MORNING

Cordsen, Carol Foskett. *The Milkman* [PreK–1], 153

Gay, Marie-Louise. *Good Morning Sam* [PreK–1], 312

Lane, Lindsey. *Snuggle Mountain* [PreK–1], 468

Pilkey, Dav. *The Paperboy* [PreK–2], 628

MOROCCO

Lewin, Ted. *The Storytellers* [1–3], 490

MOSES, GRANDMA

Wallner, Alexandra. *Grandma Moses* [2–5], 1558

Mother Goose; Nursery rhymes;
Stories in rhyme

Arnold, Tedd. *Catalina Magdalena
Hoopensteiner Wallendiner
Hogan Logan Bogan Was Her
Name* [K–4], 19

Hoberman, Mary Ann. *There Once
Was a Man Named Michael
Finnegan* [PreK–2], 372

Karas, G. Brian. *I Know an Old
Lady* [PreK–1], 422

Rosen, Michael, comp. *Walking the
Bridge of Your Nose* [1–5], 1402

Taback, Simms. *There Was an Old
Lady Who Swallowed a Fly*
[PreK–2], 781

Weeks, Sarah. *Mrs. McNosh Hangs
Up Her Wash* [PreK–1], 826

NORSE MYTHOLOGY

SEE Folklore—Norway;
Mythology

NORTH DAKOTA

Kurtz, Jane. *River Friendly, River
Wild* [2–4], 459

NORTH POLE

Primavera, Elise. *Auntie Claus*
[1–3], 647

NORTHERN LIGHTS

Sabuda, Robert. *The Blizzard's Robe*
[1–4], 682

NORTHERN LIGHTS—
FOLKLORE

Lunge-Larsen, Lise, and Margi
Preus. *The Legend of the Lady
Slipper* [1–6], 1221

NORWAY

SEE ALSO Folklore—Norway

Brett, Jan. *Who's That Knocking on
Christmas Eve?* [K–2], 75

NOSES

Jenkins, Steve, and Robin Page.
*What Do You Do With a Tail Like
This?* [PreK–3], 1630

NUMBERS

SEE ALSO Counting books;
Mathematics; Measurement

Wells, Robert E. *Can You Count to a
Googol?* [1–4], 1696

NURSERY RHYMES

SEE ALSO Humorous poetry;
Mother Goose; Nonsense verses

Crews, Nina, comp. *The Neighborhood Mother Goose* [PreK–1],
1307

Denton, Kady MacDonald, comp.
*A Child's Treasury of Nursery
Rhymes* [PreK–1], 1309

Edwards, Pamela Duncan. *The
Neat Line* [PreK–2], 229

Foreman, Michael, comp. *Michael
Foreman's Playtime Rhymes*
[PreK–1], 1323

Hoberman, Mary Ann. *Miss Mary
Mack* [PreK–1], 370

Long, Sylvia, comp. *Sylvia Long's
Mother Goose* [PreK–1], 1378

Martin, David. *Five Little Piggies*
[PreK–1], 542

Moses, Will, comp. *Will Moses'
Mother Goose* [PreK–1], 1384

Opie, Iona, comp. *Here Comes
Mother Goose* [PreK–1], 1386

My Very First Mother Goose
[PreK–1], 1387

Palatini, Margie. *The Web Files*
[K–3], 609

Sierra, Judy. *Monster Goose* [2–6],
1411

Stanley, Diane. *The Giant and the
Beanstalk* [PreK–2], 752

Stevens, Janet, and Susan Stevens
Crummel. *And the Dish Ran
Away with the Spoon* [K–3], 764

Taback, Simms. *This Is the House
That Jack Built* [PreK–1], 782

Vail, Rachel. *Over the Moon* [K–2],
806

NURSERY SCHOOLS

SEE ALSO Kindergarten; Schools

Lowry, Lois. *Zooman Sam* [2–5],
1045

Schaefer, Carole Lexa. *Someone
Says* [PreK–K], 694

The Squiggle [PreK–1], 695

NURSES

Kerley, Barbara. *Walt Whitman*
[4–8], 1505

NUTRITION

Kraft, Erik. *Chocolatina* [K–2], 451

OAKLEY, ANNIE, 1860–1926

Krensky, Stephen. *Shooting for the
Moon* [1–4], 1507

OBEDIENCE

Levine, Gail Carson. *Ella Enchanted*
[4–7], 1032

McKissack, Patricia C., and
Onawumi Jean Moss. *Precious
and the Boo Hag* [1–4], 525

Meddaugh, Susan. *Perfectly Martha*
[K–4], 553

Teague, Mark. *Dear Mrs. LaRue*
[K–3], 787

OBEDIENCE—FOLKLORE

Burleigh, Robert. *Pandora* [2–8],
1155

Harper, Wilhelmina. *The Gunniwolf* [K–3], 1195

Kimmel, Eric A. *The Two Mountains* [3–6], 1216

OCCUPATIONS

Browne, Anthony. *Willy the
Dreamer* [PreK–2], 82

Krensky, Stephen. *How Santa Got
His Job* [K–3], 452

Lowry, Lois. *Zooman Sam* [2–5],
1045

MacLean, Christine Kole. *Even
Firefighters Hug Their Moms*
[PreK–1], 527

McMullan, Kate. *I Stink!* [PreK–2],
528

Markes, Julie. *Shhhhh! Everybody's
Sleeping* [PreK–K], 536

Slate, Joseph. *Miss Bindergarten
Takes a Field Trip with Kindergarten* [PreK–K], 739

Ziefert, Harriet. *31 Uses for a Mom*
[K–2], 888

OCEAN

SEE ALSO Animals; Dolphins;
Fishes; Marine animals; Sea
turtles; Seals; Seashore; Whales

Armstrong, Jennifer. *Spirit of
Endurance* [4–8], 1443

Ashman, Linda. *Rub-a-Dub Sub*
[PreK–1], 26

Carle, Eric. *Mister Seahorse*
[PreK–1], 105

Cowan, Catherine. *My Life with the
Wave* [1–5], 156

Creech, Sharon. *The Wanderer*
[5–7], 934

Davies, Nicola. *Surprising Sharks*
[PreK–3], 1598

Guiberson, Brenda Z. *Into the Sea*
[1–3], 1613

Karas, G. Brian. *Atlantic* [K–3], 421

Kostyal, Kim. *Trial by Ice* [5–8],
1506

Long, Melinda. *How I Became a
Pirate* [PreK–2], 500

Philbrick, Rodman. *The Young
Man and the Sea* [5–8], 1092

Rose, Deborah Lee. *Into the A, B,
Sea* [PreK–2], 1666

Rumford, James. *Dog-of-the-Sea-
Waves* [2–5], 673

Schertle, Alice. *All You Need for a
Beach* [PreK–2], 698

OCEAN—FOLKLORE

Wolkstein, Diane. *The Day Ocean
Came to Visit* [PreK–3], 1281

OCEAN—POETRY

Florian, Douglas. *In the Swim*
[2–6], 1315

ODYSSEUS

Sutcliffe, Rosemary. *The Wanderings of Odysseus* [5–8], 1272

Yolen, Jane, and Robert J. Harris.
Odysseus in the Serpent Maze
[4–7], 1140

PARROTS

PARROTS—FOLKLORE

PARTIES

PARTS OF SPEECH

PASSOVER

PATIENCE

PATIENCE—FOLKLORE

PATRIOTISM

PEANUT BUTTER

PEAS

PEDDLERS

PEN PALS

PENGUINS

Howard, Elizabeth Fitzgerald. *Virgie Goes to School with Us Boys* [1–4], 386

Howe, James. *Horace and Morris But Mostly Dolores* [PreK–2], 388

Pinky and Rex and the Bully [1–3], 390

McCully, Emily Arnold. *Beautiful Warrior* [2–6], 511

Moss, Marissa. *Mighty Jackie, the Strike-Out Queen* [2–5], 1532

SHACKLETON, ERNEST HENRY, SIR

Armstrong, Jennifer. *Spirit of Endurance* [4–8], 1443

Kostyal, Kim. *Trial by Ice* [5–8], 1506

SHAKESPEARE, WILLIAM

Aliki. *William Shakespeare and the Globe* [2–8], 1440

Blackwood, Gary L. *The Shakespeare Stealer* [5–8], 907

Broach, Elise. *Shakespeare's Secret* [4–7], 910

Freeman, Don. *Will's Quill, or How a Goose Saved Shakespeare* [1–4], 300

SHAPES

SEE ALSO Geometry; Mathematics

Carter, David A. *One Red Dot* [PreK–2], 109

Emberley, Ed. *The Wing on a Flea* [PreK–1], 247

Ernst, Lisa Campbell. *Tangram Magician* [PreK–3], 259

Neuschwander, Cindy. *Sir Cumference and the First Round Table* [2–5], 581

SHARING

SEE Generosity; Selfishness

SHARKS

Davies, Nicola. *Surprising Sharks* [PreK–3], 1598

SHARKS—FOLKLORE

Martin, Rafe. *The Shark God* [2–5], 1228

Wardlaw, Lee. *Punia and the King of Sharks* [K–3], 1276

SHARPSHOOTERS

Krensky, Stephen. *Shooting for the Moon* [1–4], 1507

SHEEP

Gliori, Debi. *The Snow Lambs* [K–2], 316

Livingstone, Star. *Harley* [K–2], 497

Palatini, Margie. *Bad Boys* [K–3], 598

Rothstein, Gloria. *Sheep Asleep* [PreK–K], 672

Shulman, Lisa. *Old MacDonald Had a Woodshop* [PreK–1], 727

SHELLS

Kalan, Robert. *Moving Day* [PreK–1], 419

SHERIFFS

Stanley, Diane. *Raising Sweetness* [K–3], 754

Saving Sweetness [K–3], 756

SHIPS

SEE ALSO Boats and boating

Armstrong, Jennifer. *Spirit of Endurance* [4–8], 1443

Borden, Louise. *The Little Ships* [3–6], 908

Cullen, Lynn. *Little Scraggly Hair* [K–3], 171

Goode, Diane. *Monkey Mo Goes to Sea* [PreK–1], 317

Kostyal, Kim. *Trial by Ice* [5–8], 1506

Long, Melinda. *How I Became a Pirate* [PreK–2], 500

McMullan, Kate. *I'm Mighty* [PreK–2], 529

Waters, Kate. *On the Mayflower* [2–5], 1695

SHIPS—FOLKLORE

Sutcliffe, Rosemary. *The Wanderings of Odysseus* [5–8], 1272

SHOES

SEE ALSO Boots; Clothing and dress

McGhee, Alison. *Countdown to Kindergarten* [PreK–2], 521

Palatini, Margie. *Stinky Smelly Feet* [K–2], 606

SHOES—FOLKLORE

Climo, Shirley. *The Irish Cinderlad* [2–6], 1160

SHOPPING

SEE ALSO Department stores

Wells, Rosemary. *Bunny Money* [PreK–2], 830

SHORT STORIES

Evans, Douglas. *The Classroom at the End of the Hall* [2–5], 957

Hurwitz, Johanna, comp. *Birthday Surprises* [3–7], 1005

Kimmel, Eric A. *The Jar of Fools* [2–6], 1015

Kipling, Rudyard. *Rudyard Kipling's Just So Stories* [2–6], 1025

Levitt, Paul M., Douglas A. Burger, and Elissa S. Guralnick. *The Weighty Word Book* [4–8], 1035

Marcantonio, Patricia Santos. *Red Ridin' in the Hood* [4–8], 1053

Peck, Richard. *Past, Perfect, Present Tense* [5–8], 1089

Vande Velde, Vivian. *Tales from the Brothers Grimm and the Sisters Weird* [5–8], 1128

SHOSHONI INDIANS

Scott, Ann Herbert. *Brave as a Mountain Lion* [1–3], 706

SHOSHONI INDIANS— BIOGRAPHY

Erdrich, Lise. *Sacagawea* [3–6], 1484

SHOVELS

Connor, Leslie. *Miss Bridie Chose a Shovel* [1–4], 148

SHOW-AND-TELL PRESENTATIONS

Greene, Stephanie. *Show and Tell* [K–2], 976

Henkes, Kevin. *Lilly's Purple Plastic Purse* [PreK–2], 352

Klein, Abby. *The King of Show-and-Tell* [K–2], 1026

Lasky, Kathryn. *Show and Tell Bunnies* [PreK–1], 475

McDonald, Megan. *Judy Moody, M.D.* [1–4], 1048

Reiss, Mike. *The Great Show-and-Tell Disaster* [1–4], 658

Simms, Laura. *Rotten Teeth* [K–2], 733

SHYNESS

Best, Cari. *Shrinking Violet* [K–2], 54

Montenegro, Laura Nyman. *A Bird About to Sing* [1–3], 567

Oates, Joyce Carol. *Where Is Little Reynard?* [PreK–1], 592

Wishinsky, Frieda. *Give Maggie a Chance* [K–2], 867

SIBLING RIVALRY

Jonell, Lynne. *It's My Birthday, Too!* [PreK–2], 415

Lasky, Kathryn. *Show and Tell Bunnies* [PreK–1], 475

Potter, Giselle. *Chloë's Birthday . . . and Me* [K–4], 644

Van Allsburg, Chris. *Zathura* [1–6], 809

Wells, Rosemary. *Noisy Nora* [PreK–K], 837

SICK

Bateman, Teresa. *Farm Flu* [PreK–2], 44

Borden, Louise. *Good Luck, Mrs. K.* [2–4], 66

Hannigan, Katherine. *Ida B* [4–6], 986

Edwards, Pamela Duncan. *Barefoot* [1–4], 220

Lasky, Kathryn. *A Voice of Her Own* [3–6], 1518

McGill, Alice. *Molly Bannaky* [2–5], 522

Nelson, Vaunda Micheaux. *Almost to Freedom* [2–6], 579

Paterson, Katherine. *Jip* [5–8], 1084

Ransome, Candace. *Liberty Street* [2–5], 652

SLAVERY—FOLKLORE

Hamilton, Virginia. *The People Could Fly* [3–8], 1192

SLED DOG RACING

Blake, Robert J. *Akiak* [2–5], 57
Togo [1–4], 59

Miller, Debbie S. *The Great Serum Race* [3–6], 1649

Wood, Ted. *Iditarod Dream* [4–6], 1564

SLEEP

SEE ALSO Bedtime stories

Appelt, Kathi. *Bubba and Beau Go Night-Night* [PreK–K], 16

Cox, Judy. *Go to Sleep, Groundhog!* [PreK–2], 160

Fleming, Denise. *Time to Sleep* [PreK–1], 286

Ho, Minfong. *Hush! A Thai Lullaby* [PreK–1], 365

Lum, Kate. *What! Cried Granny* [PreK–1], 505

MacDonald, Ross. *Another Perfect Day* [PreK–2], 515

Markes, Julie. *Shhhhh! Everybody's Sleeping* [PreK–K], 536

Massie, Diane Redfield. *The Baby Beebee Bird* [PreK–K], 546

Murray, Marjorie Dennis. *Don't Wake Up the Bear!* [PreK–2], 573

Pinkney, Andrea Davis. *Sleeping Cutie* [PreK–1], 630

Swain, Ruth Freeman. *Bedtime!* [1–4], 1688

Thomas, Shelley Moore. *Good Night, Good Knight* [PreK–1], 796

Wilson, Karma. *Bear Snores On* [PreK–1], 859

SLOTHS

Carle, Eric. *"Slowly, Slowly, Slowly," Said the Sloth* [PreK–1], 106

Lester, Helen. *Score One for the Sloths* [PreK–2], 484

SLUGS

Edwards, Pamela Duncan. *Some Smug Slug* [K–2], 232

SMELL

Palatini, Margie. *Stinky Smelly Feet* [K–2], 606

SNAILS

Donaldson, Julia. *The Snail and the Whale* [PreK–3], 208

Waddell, Martin. *Hi, Harry!* [PreK–K], 816

SNAKES

SEE ALSO Reptiles and amphibians

Cannon, Janell. *Verdi* [1–6], 102

Dewey, Jennifer Owings. *Rattlesnake Dance* [3–6], 1599

Jonell, Lynne. *I Need a Snake* [PreK–1], 414

Khan, Rukhsana. *Ruler of the Courtyard* [2–6], 442

Kipling, Rudyard. *Rikki-Tikki-Tavi* [2–6], 1024

Strete, Craig. *The Rattlesnake Who Went to School* [PreK–1], 774

Whippo, Walt, and Bernard Zaritzky. *Little White Duck* [PreK–1], 845

SNAKES—FOLKLORE

Aardema, Verna. *Koi and the Kola Nuts* [K–4], 1143

SNAKES AS PETS

Jonell, Lynne. *I Need a Snake* [PreK–1], 414

SNOW

SEE ALSO Blizzards; Rain and rainfall; Storms; Water; Weather; Winter

Gliori, Debi. *The Snow Lambs* [K–2], 316

Martin, Jacqueline Briggs. *Snowflake Bentley* [1–4], 1526

Oates, Joyce Carol. *Where Is Little Reynard?* [PreK–1], 592

O'Malley, Kevin. *Straight to the Pole* [PreK–2], 595

Rylant, Cynthia. *Mr. Putter and Tabby Write the Book* [PreK–2], 679

Steltzer, Ulli. *Building an Igloo* [2–6], 1685

Wetterer, Margaret, and Charles Wetterer. *The Snow Walker* [1–3], 1561

Wright, Betty Ren. *The Blizzard* [K–2], 876

SNOWMEN

Kellogg, Steven. *The Missing Mitten Mystery* [PreK–1], 433

SOAP

Schaefer, Carole Lexa. *The Biggest Soap* [PreK–2], 693

SOCCER

SEE ALSO Athletes; Sports; Sportsmanship

Finchler, Judy. *You're a Good Sport, Miss Malarkey* [K–2], 274

Hamm, Mia. *Winners Never Quit!* [PreK–2], 335

Long, Melinda. *How I Became a Pirate* [PreK–2], 500

SOCKS

Valckx, Catharina. *Lizette's Green Sock* [PreK–1], 808

SOLAR SYSTEM

SEE Astronomy; Moon; Planets; Stars; Sun

SOLDIERS

Pullman, Philip. *The Scarecrow and His Servant* [4–6], 1098

SOLDIERS—FOLKLORE

Kimmel, Eric A. *Cactus Soup* [K–4], 1207

SOLSTICE

Pfeffer, Wendy. *The Shortest Day* [1–4], 1658

SONGS

SEE ALSO Folk songs; Music; Stories with songs

Arnold, Tedd. *Catalina Magdalena Hoopensteiner Wallendiner Hogan Logan Bogan Was Her Name* [K–4], 19

Coots, J. Fred, and Haven Gillespie. *Santa Claus Is Comin' to Town* [PreK–2], 151

Denton, Kady MacDonald, comp. *A Child's Treasury of Nursery Rhymes* [PreK–1], 1309

Foreman, Michael, comp. *Michael Foreman's Playtime Rhymes* [PreK–1], 1323

Frazee, Marla. *Hush, Little Baby* [PreK–1], 297

Guthrie, Woody. *This Land Is Your Land* [1–6], 1340

Harter, Debbie. *The Animal Boogie* [PreK–1], 341

Hoberman, Mary Ann. *The Eensy-Weensy Spider* [PreK–1], 368
Miss Mary Mack [PreK–1], 370
There Once Was a Man Named Michael Finnegan [PreK–2], 372
Yankee Doodle [PreK–2], 373

Hoose, Phillip M., and Hannah Hoose. *Hey, Little Ant* [K–3], 377

Hort, Lenny. *The Seals on the Bus* [PreK–K], 382

Karas, G. Brian. *I Know an Old Lady* [PreK–1], 422

Katz, Alan. *I'm Still Here in the Bathtub* [PreK–3], 1364

STORIES TO TELL

San Souci, Robert D. *Kate Shelley* [3–6], 1548

Yolen, Jane, and Robert J. Harris. *Odysseus in the Serpent Maze* [4–7], 1140

SUSHI

Wells, Rosemary. *Yoko* [PreK–1], 839

SUSPENSE

Byars, Betsy. *Dead Letter* [4–7], 913

Del Negro, Janice. *Lucy Dove* [4–6], 194

Gaiman, Neil. *Coraline* [4–7], 965
The Wolves in the Walls [2–6], 309

Krosoczka, Jarrett J. *Annie Was Warned* [K–2], 455

McKissack, Patricia C., and Onawumi Jean Moss. *Precious and the Boo Hag* [1–4], 525

Martin, Bill, Jr., and Steven Kellogg. *A Beasty Story* [PreK–1], 541

Park, Barbara. *Psssst! It's Me . . . the Bogeyman* [1–4], 613

SUSPENSE—FOLKLORE

Kimmel, Eric A. *Count Silvernose* [3–6], 1208

Shepard, Aaron. *King o' the Cats* [2–5], 1258

SWALLOWING STORIES

SEE ALSO Circular stories; Cumulative stories; Sequence stories

Feiffer, Jules. *Bark, George* [PreK–1], 267

Ginsburg, Mirra. *Clay Boy* [PreK–1], 1186

Jackson, Alison. *I Know an Old Lady Who Swallowed a Pie* [PreK–2], 401

Karas, G. Brian. *I Know an Old Lady* [PreK–1], 422

Rascol, Sabina I. *The Impudent Rooster* [1–4], 1248

Sierra, Judy. *Nursery Tales Around the World* [PreK–2], 1264

So, Meilo. *Gobble, Gobble, Slip, Slop* [PreK–3], 1267

Stenmark, Victoria. *The Singing Chick* [PreK–K], 763

Taback, Simms. *There Was an Old Lady Who Swallowed a Fly* [PreK–2], 781

Thomson, Pat. *Drat That Fat Cat!* [PreK–K], 799

SWAMPS

Vaughan, Marcia. *Whistling Dixie* [K–2], 810

SWANS

Andersen, Hans Christian. *The Ugly Duckling* [K–4], 10

Edwards, Pamela Duncan. *Honk!* [K–2], 224

SWEDISH AMERICANS

Avi. *Silent Movie* [2–5], 32

SWIMMING

Adler, David A. *America's Champion Swimmer* [1–5], 1433

Riley, Linda Capus. *Elephants Swim* [PreK–1], 1664

Rodman, Mary Ann. *My Best Friend* [PreK–2], 664

SWINDLERS AND SWINDLING

Hicks, Ray, as told to Lynn Salsi. *The Jack Tales* [2–5], 1198

Kimmel, Eric A. *The Magic Dreidels* [K–3], 444

SYMBIOSIS

Brett, Jan. *Honey . . . Honey . . . Lion!* [PreK–2], 73

SYNONYMS

SEE English Language—Synonyms

TABLEWARE

Compestine, Ying Chang. *The Story of Chopsticks* [K–4], 146

Hayes, Joe. *A Spoon for Every Bite* [2–6], 349

Lauber, Patricia. *What You Never Knew About Fingers, Forks, and Chopsticks* [2–5], 1637

Stevens, Janet, and Susan Stevens Crummel. *And the Dish Ran Away with the Spoon* [K–3], 764

TAILORS—FOLKLORE

Kimmel, Eric A. *Seven at One Blow* [1–5], 1213

TAILS

Jenkins, Steve, and Robin Page. *What Do You Do With a Tail Like This?* [PreK–3], 1630

TAILS—FOLKLORE

Han, Suzanne Crowder. *The Rabbit's Tail* [K–4], 1194

Salley, Coleen. *Why Epossumondas Has No Hair on His Tail* [PreK–2], 1250

TALENT SHOWS

Duffey, Betsy. *Spotlight on Cody* [1–3], 949

TALL TALES

SEE ALSO Exaggeration

Bania, Michael. *Kumak's Fish* [PreK–3], 35

Bertrand, Lynne. *Granite Baby* [1–4], 53

Cuyler, Margery. *Big Friends* [PreK–2], 178

Hicks, Ray, as told to Lynn Salsi. *The Jack Tales* [2–5], 1198

Hopkinson, Deborah. *Apples to Oregon* [K–4], 378

Johnson, Paul Brett. *Fearless Jack* [K–5], 1202
Jack Outwits the Giants [K–5], 1203

Kellogg, Steven. *Sally Ann Thunder Ann Crockett* [1–4], 1205

Ketteman, Helen. *Heat Wave!* [1–4], 441

Mora, Pat. *Doña Flor* [PreK–3], 568

Osborne, Mary Pope. *New York's Bravest* [PreK–6], 597

Regan, Dian Curtis. *Chance* [K–3], 657

Schanzer, Rosalyn. *Davy Crockett Saves the World* [K–3], 697

Schroeder, Alan. *The Tale of Willie Monroe* [2–5], 1256

Thomassie, Tynia. *Feliciana Feydra LeRoux* [1–3], 797

Willey, Margaret. *Clever Beatrice* [1–4], 1280

Williams, Suzanne. *Library Lil* [1–3], 858

Wood, Audrey. *The Bunyans* [1–4], 872

TANGRAMS

Ernst, Lisa Campbell. *Tangram Magician* [PreK–3], 259

TANZANIA

Mollel, Tololwa M. *My Rows and Piles of Coins* [K–3], 566

Stock, Catherine. *Gugu's House* [K–4], 772

Stuve-Bodeen, Stephanie. *Elizabeti's Doll* [K–2], 777
Elizabeti's School [K–2], 778

TAP DANCING

Barasch, Lynne. *Knockin' on Wood* [1–4], 1445

TARANTULAS

Montgomery, Sy. *The Tarantula Scientist* [4–8], 1529

Tyson, Leigh Ann. *An Interview with Harry the Tarantula* [1–4], 805

TEACHERS

SEE ALSO Principals; Schools

Adler, David A. *A Picture Book of Louis Braille* [2–4], 1437

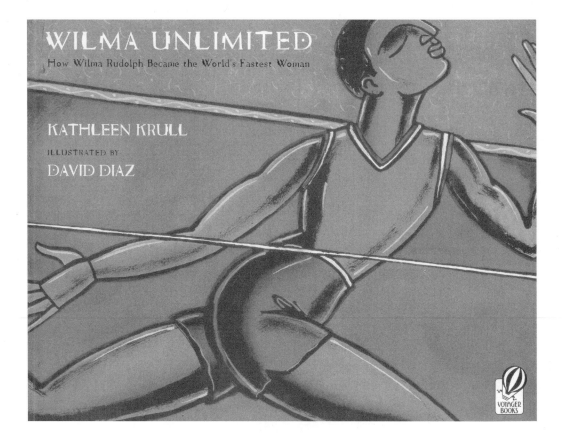

WILMA UNLIMITED

How Wilma Rudolph Became the World's Fastest Woman

KATHLEEN KRULL

ILLUSTRATED BY

DAVID DIAZ

VOYAGER
BOOKS

ABOUT THE AUTHOR

JUDY FREEMAN (www.JudyReadsBooks.com) IS A WELL-KNOWN CON-sultant, writer, and international speaker on all aspects of children's literature, storytelling, booktalking, and librarianship. She is a visiting lecturer in the School of Information and Library Science at Pratt Institute in New York City, where she teaches graduate courses on children's literature and storytelling. A former school librarian, she also gives seminars, workshops, speeches, and performances on children's literature throughout the world for teachers, librarians, parents, and children and is a national presenter for BER (Bureau of Education & Research). Judy served as a member of the committee to select the Newbery Medal book for the year 2000.

Judy's popular companion books, *Books Kids Will Sit Still For: The Complete Read-Aloud Guide* (Libraries Unlimited, 1990) and *More Books Kids Will Sit Still For* (Libraries Unlimited, 1995) are indispensable resources for literature-based classrooms. Her *Hi Ho Librario! Songs, Chants, and Stories to Keep Kids Humming* (Rock Hill Press, 1997) is a book and CD full of her book-related songs and stories. Judy also writes about children's literature for periodicals including *School Library Media Activities Monthly* and *Instructor*.

At home with her husband, Izzy Feldman, in Highland Park, New Jersey, she plays tennis, gardens, reads too many books, and keeps track of her geriatric six-toed cat.